ROGER WILLIAMS.

From a Photograph of the

MONUMENT AT PROVIDENCE, R.I.

Simmons, Sculptor. — S. Sartain, Eng.

THE
BAPTIST ENCYCLOPÆDIA.

A DICTIONARY

OF

THE DOCTRINES, ORDINANCES, USAGES, CONFESSIONS OF FAITH, SUFFERINGS, LABORS, AND SUCCESSES, AND OF THE GENERAL HISTORY OF THE

BAPTIST DENOMINATION IN ALL LANDS.

WITH

NUMEROUS BIOGRAPHICAL SKETCHES OF DISTINGUISHED AMERICAN AND FOREIGN BAPTISTS, AND A SUPPLEMENT.

EDITED BY

WILLIAM CATHCART, D.D.,

AUTHOR OF "THE PAPAL SYSTEM," "THE BAPTISTS AND THE AMERICAN REVOLUTION," AND "THE BAPTISM OF THE AGES."

WITH MANY ILLUSTRATIONS.

PHILADELPHIA:
LOUIS H. EVERTS.
1881.

Copyright, 1880, by LOUIS H. EVERTS.

PREFACE.

The preparation of such a work as this imposes a vast responsibility and an immense amount of labor. Years of study devoted to the subjects embraced in it, and the assistance of brethren of distinguished ability, encouraged the Editor to undertake its compilation.

The Baptists are the parents of absolute religious liberty wherever it exists in Christian nations. They founded the first great Protestant Missionary Society of modern times. Through the counsels of a Baptist the British and Foreign Bible Society was established, and in it every Bible Society in the world. Baptists have been the warmest friends of civil liberty in all great struggles for freedom. Their fifty colleges and theological seminaries, and their numerous and splendid academies, show their deep interest in education. The religious press is sending forth through their ninety-five periodicals an unsurpassed amount of sanctified literature. Governors, judges, generals, educators, philanthropists, authors, ministers, and benefactors of great distinction and in large numbers have been identified with our denomination. Baptist missionaries in the East have gathered glorious harvests for Jesus; and in our own land they have toiled everywhere with heaven-given enthusiasm. In this country there are 26,060 Baptist churches, and 2,296,327 members; and in all lands there are 30,699 churches of our faith, with 2,769,389 members. There are not less than eight millions of persons belonging to the Baptist denomination. And besides these, our principles are extensively held by members of other communities.

Dr. Chalmers, at the close of a very able sermon on infant baptism, pays this tribute to our British brethren: "Let it never be forgotten of the Particular Baptists of England that they form the denomination of Fuller, and Carey, and Ryland, and Hall, and Foster; that they have originated among the greatest of all missionary enterprises; that they have enriched the Christian literature of our country with authorship of the most exalted piety, as well as of the first talent and the first eloquence; that they have waged a very noble and successful war with the hydra of Antinomianism; that perhaps there is not a more intellectual community of ministers in our island, or who have put forth to their number a greater amount of mental power and mental activity in the defense and illustration of our common faith; and, what is better than all the triumphs of genius and understanding, who, by their zeal and fidelity, and pastoral labor among the congregations which they have reared, have done more to swell the lists of genuine discipleship in the walks of private society,—and thus both to uphold and to extend the living Christianity of our nation." (Lectures on Romans, Lecture XIV., p. 76. New York, 1863.) This is a just tribute to our British brethren, coming gracefully from the greatest of Scotch preachers, and with equal appropriateness every word of it might be applied to the Baptists of America.

The Baptists began their denominational life under the ministry of the Saviour. They flourished at various periods in the gloomy ages between the first great apostasy and the Reformation of the sixteenth century. And in the coming conquests of truth they are destined to spread over the world, and unfurl their banner of truth over every home and heart of Adam's family, upon which the finger of inspiration has inscribed the words, "One Lord, one faith, one baptism."

The Editor has aimed to give sketches of distinguished Baptists everywhere, living and dead; of the important events of Baptist history; of ancient Baptist Confessions of Faith; of the scattered and persecuted communities that held Baptist principles in the bleak centuries of triumphant Romanism; and of all doctrines, practices, and usages peculiar to Baptists. He has designed to place before the reader a grand "conspectus" of the Baptists, their principles, institutions, monuments, labors, achievements, and sufferings throughout the world and throughout the Christian ages.

Biography is used extensively in this work. From the earliest times it has been employed to impart historical information. Plutarch's "Lives" have traveled down the ages for eighteen hundred years with unfailing interest, giving invaluable sketches of the greatest events and of the mightiest men of the far-distant past. Macaulay's biographies, in his "Essays" and in his great "History," describe occurrences and men in a form that impresses and fascinates. But while biography is a conspicuous feature of the "Encyclopædia," it has also an immense number of purely historical and doctrinal articles.

If the learned Thomas Wilson Haynes had completed his "Baptist Cyclopædia," the first volume of which was issued in Charleston, S. C., in 1848, the editor would have been relieved of a portion of his labor, and Baptist churches would have been blessed by a work of great value; but unfortunately "the first volume of Part I." was the last that came from the press.

Among the able brethren who have rendered assistance to the Editor he would name President H. G. Weston, D.D., Pennsylvania; Thomas Armitage, D.D., New York; J. L. M. Curry, D.D., LL.D., Virginia; J. M. Pendleton, D.D., Pennsylvania; George W. Samson, D.D., New York; William T. Brantly, D.D., Maryland; H. A. Tupper, D.D., Virginia; J. C. Long, D.D., LL.D., Pennsylvania; T. J. Conant, D.D., New York; M. Hillsman, D.D., Tennessee; J. A. Edgren, D.D., Illinois; J. V. Scofield, D.D., Missouri; Rev. R. S. Duncan, Missouri; Rev. T. A. Gill, U.S.N., Pennsylvania; C. C. Bitting, D.D., Maryland; Franklin Wilson, D.D., Maryland; Professor S. M. Shute, D.D., District of Columbia; Professor A. H. Newman, New York; C. E. Barrows, D.D., Rhode Island; Rev. Frederick Denison, Rhode Island; J. C. Stockbridge, D.D., Rhode Island; Rev. R. G. Moses, New Jersey; H. F. Smith, D.D., New Jersey; H. L. Wayland, D.D., Pennsylvania; Rev. J. G. Walker, Pennsylvania; George M. Spratt, D.D., Pennsylvania; A. J. Rowland, D.D., Pennsylvania; Col. C. H. Banes,

Pennsylvania; B. F. Dennison, Esq., Pennsylvania; James Butterworth, Esq., Pennsylvania; Rev. J. P. Hetric, Pennsylvania; Rev. B. D. Thomas, Pennsylvania; W. Fred. Snyder, Esq., Pennsylvania; Rev. J. W. Willmarth, Pennsylvania; Rev. James Waters, Tennessee; Joseph H. Borum, D.D., Tennessee; Rev. Isaac Willmarth, Pennsylvania; Justin A. Smith, D.D., Illinois; President Kendall Brooks, D.D., Michigan; Rev. D. E. Halteman, Wisconsin; J. R. Murphy, D.D., Iowa; President W. T. Stott, D.D., Indiana; Rev. S. Boykin, Georgia; President T. H. Pritchard, D.D., North Carolina; W. B. Carson, D.D., South Carolina; W. Pope Yeaman, D.D., Missouri; J. H. Spencer, D.D., Kentucky; Rev. R. B. Cook, Delaware; Rev. M. Bibb, West Virginia; Rev. J. S. Gubelmann, Pennsylvania; President W. Carey Crane, D.D., LL.D., Texas; J. J. D. Renfroe, D.D., Alabama; Rev. William Wilder, Iowa; H. J. Eddy, D.D., New York; Rev. W. N. Chaudoin, Florida; Rev. W. E. Paxton, Arkansas; C. A. Buckbee, D.D., California; Rev. O. A. Williams, Nebraska; Rev. George Armstrong, Nova Scotia; Francis Jennings, Esq., Pennsylvania; Hon. H. G. Jones, Pennsylvania; William M. Lawrence, D.D., Illinois; O. N. Worden, Esq., Pennsylvania; S. Haskell, D.D., Michigan; Rev. J. D. King, Toronto.

That the work may be a blessing to Baptists, and to all who love the triumphs of grace, and that it may be useful to students of history generally, is the earnest wish of

WILLIAM CATHCART.

PHILADELPHIA, October, 1881.

LIST OF ILLUSTRATIONS.

	PAGE
Adams, S. W	12
Albany, Emmanuel Baptist Church	19
Alexander, John	1289
Allen, Alanson	22
Anderson, Galusha	31
Anderson, Geo. W	32
Anderson, M. B	33
Anderson, Thos. D	36
Andrews, Reddin, Jr	36
Armitage, Thos	40
Arnold, Albert N	41
Arnold, Samuel G	42
Atlanta Theological Seminary	47
Backus, Isaac	52
Bacon, Joel Smith	54
Bailey, C. T	57
Bailey, Silas	59
Bailey, Thomas M	60
Bainbridge, W. F	60
Baldwin, Geo. C	62
Baldwin, Thomas	63
Baltimore, Eutaw Place Baptist Church	66
Banes, Chas. H	67
Banvard, Joseph	67
Baptistery of Milan	73
Barlow, F. N	79
Barney, Eliam E	81
Barratt, J	82
Barrows, C. E	843
Bateman, Calvin A	84
Battle, Archibald J	86
Baylor, R. E. B	89
Baylor University	90
Beebee, Alex. M	93
Benedict, David	94
Benedict Institute	95
Benedict, Stephen	96
Berry, Joel H	97
Bethel College	98
Bishop, Nathan	102
Bitting, C. C	103
Bixby, Moses H	103
Bliss, Geo. Ripley	106
Blitch, Jos. Luke	107
Boardman, Geo. Dana	108
Boise, James Robinson	110
Borum, Joseph Henry	115
Bostick, Jos. M	116
Bosworth, Geo. Wm	118
Bouic, Wm. Veirs	119
Boutelle, Timothy	120
Boyce, James Pettigru	121
Boyd, Willard W	123
Boykin, Samuel	124
Boykin, Thomas Cooper	125
Branham, Isham R	127
Brantly, John J	127
Brantly, Wm. T., Jr	128
Brayman, Mason	129
Brayton, Geo. Arnold	131
Bridgman, C. D. W	132
Briggs, George Nixon	133
Broadus, John Albert	139

	PAGE
Brooks, Kendall	142
Brotherton, Marshall	143
Brown, Joseph E	146
Brown, Nicholas	150
Brown University	153
Buchanan, James	156
Buck, William Calmes	156
Buckbee, Charles Alvah	157
Buckner, Robert C	158
Bunyan in Bedford Jail	160
Burchett, G. J	163
Burleson, Rufus C	164
Burlingham, Aaron H	165
Burlington Collegiate Institute	165
Burney, Thomas J	167
Bush, Alva	171
Cade, Baylus	174
Caldwell, Samuel L	175
Carey, Geo. M. W	181
Carey, William	182
Carroll, B. H	186
Carter, John W	189
Castle, John Harvard	190
Caswell, Alexis	191
Cathcart, William	196
Champlin, James Tift	200
Chaplin, Charles Crawford	203
Chase, Irah	205
Chaudoin, W. N	207
Chicago Baptist Union Theological Seminary	212
Chicago, First Baptist Church of	210
Chicago, University of	215
Chowan Female Institute	219
Chown, J. P	221
Christian, Joseph	221
Church, Pharcellus	224
Clovis, Baptism of	235
Coburn, Abner	238
Cocke, Charles Lewis	239
Colby Academy	240
Colby, Anthony	241
Colby, Gardner	242
Colby University	243
Cole, Addison L	245
Cole, Isaac	245
Cole, Nathan	246
Coleman, James Smith	247
Colgate Academy	248
Colgate, William	250
Conant, John	260
Conant, Thomas J	261
Cone, Spencer Houghton	263
Cook Academy	271
Cook, Richard Briscoe	272
Cooper, James	274
Cooper, Mark A	275
Corcoran, William Wilson	278
Corey, Charles Henry	279
Cotton, John H	281
Courtney, Franklin	283
Cramp, John M	286
Crane, Cephas B	287
Crane, James C	287
Crane, William	288

	PAGE
Crane, William Carey	289
Crawley, Edmund Albern	292
Creath, Joseph W. D	293
Crosby, Moreau S	296
Crozer, John Price	298
Crozer Theological Seminary	299
Cummings, E. E	300
Curry, J. L. M	301
Cuthbert, James H	304
Dargan, J. O. B	308
Davidson, Thomas Leslie	309
Davies, Daniel	310
Davis, Geo. F	311
Davis, John	313
Dawson, John Edmonds	1298
Day, Henry	318
Deane, Richard	322
Denison, Frederic	327
Denison University	328
Denovan, Joshua	1299
De Votie, J. H	331
Dickerson, James Stokes	332
Dickinson, A. E	333
Dillard, Ryland Thompson	334
Dockery, Alfred	338
Dodge, Daniel	339
Dodge, Ebenezer	340
Duncan, James Henry	347
Durfee, Thomas	352
Earle, T. J	355
Eaton, Geo. W	357
Eddy, Daniel C	359
Elder, Joseph F	363
Elliott, Victor A	366
England, House in which the Baptist Missionary Society was formed	370
Espy, T. B	379
Estes, Hiram Cushman	380
Evans, Benjamin	381
Evans, Christmas	382
Everts, William W	385
Ewart, Thomas W	386
Ferguson, William	807
Field, James G	392
Field, S. W	393
Fish, Henry Clay	394
Fisher, Thomas Jefferson	397
Fleischmann, Konrad A	399
Foljambe, S. W	403
Ford, Samuel Howard	405
Foster, John	407
Fox, Norman	410
Franklin College	413
French, George R	1302
French, James	418
Fristoe, Edward T	419
Fuller, Andrew	421
Fuller, Richard	423
Furman, J. C	426
Furman, Richard, Sr	426
Furman University	427
Fyfe, Robert A	428

6

LIST OF ILLUSTRATIONS.

	PAGE
Gale, Amory	430
Gano, John	434
Gardner, Geo. W.	436
Garrett, O. H. P.	438
Germany, Hamburg Mission Chapel	449
Gill, John	453
Gillette, A. D.	455
Gilmore, Joseph A.	455
Gove, Elijah	462
Graves, J. R.	466
Graves, Samuel	468
Greene, Roger Sherman	471
Greene, Samuel Stillman	472
Gregory, Uriah	474
Griffith, Benjamin	476
Gubelmann, J. S.	479
Hackett, H. B.	483
Haldeman, Isaac Massey	486
Halteman, David Emory	490
Hanna, William Brantly	493
Hanna, T. A. T.	494
Hardin, Charles Henry	495
Hardin College	496
Harkness, Albert	497
Harris, Henry Herbert	498
Harris, Ira	499
Harrison, James E.	501
Hart, John, signature of	505
Hascall, Daniel	508
Haskell, Samuel	508
Havelock, Sir Henry	510
Hawthorne, J. B.	512
Haycraft, Samuel	513
Henson, P. S.	519
Hill, David J.	523
Hill, Stephen P.	524
Hillsman, Matthew	525
Hobbs, Smith M.	530
Hodge, Marvin Grow	530
Holmes, Willet	539
Hooper, William	542
Hornberger, Lewis P.	543
Hoskinson, Thomas J	544
Houston, Sam	546
Hovey, Alvah	547
Howard, John	548
Hoyt, James M	552
Hoyt, Wayland	553
Hubbard, Richard Bennett	553
Hufham, J. D.	555
Humphrey, Friend	558
Huntington, Adoniram J.	560
Hutchinson, John	563
Hutchinson, Mrs. Lucy	565
Ide, Geo. B.	568
Ireland, Jos. Alexander	585
Ives, Dwight	587
Ivimey, Joseph	588
Jackson, Henry	589
James, J. H.	593
Jameson, Ephraim H. E.	595
Jeffrey, Reuben	597
Jessey, Henry	600
Jeter, Jeremiah Bell	601
Johnson, Joseph	605
Johnson, Okey	607
Johnson, W. B.	609
Jones, David	610
Jones, J. William	617
Jones, Samuel	619
Jones, T. G.	620
Jones, Washington	621
Jones, William P	623
Judson, Adoniram	626
Judson, Mrs. Ann Hasseltine	628
Kalamazoo College	633
Keach, Benjamin	637

	PAGE
Keen, Joseph	640
Keen, William Williams	641
Keith, Geo. H.	643
Kendall, Amos	645
Kendrick, Adin A.	646
Kendrick, Nathaniel	648
Kennard, Joseph Hugg	649
Kerr, John	653
Kiffin, William	654
Kilpatrick, J. H. T.	656
Kinney, Robert Crouch	661
Knollys, Hanserd	664
La Grange College	668
Landrum, Sylvanus	670
Lasher, Geo. William	671
Lathrop, Edward	672
Lawler, Levi W.	673
Lawrence, William Mangam	674
Learning, First Baptist Seminary of, in America	677
Lee, Franklin	681
Leland, John	682
Leland University	683
Leslie, Preston H	685
Levering, Charles	688
Levering, Eugene	688
Levy, John P.	690
Lewis, Henry Clay	691
Lewisburg University	693
Lincoln, Heman	703
Link, J. B.	705
Lofton, Geo. Augustus	713
Loomis, Justin R.	716
Lorimer, George C.	718
Louisville, Ky., Walnut Street Baptist Church	721
Lowry, M. P.	720
Lucas, Elijah	723
Lumpkin, Wilson	724
Lush, Sir Robert	727
Luther, John Hill	727
Mabie, H. C.	1308
Macarthur, Robert Stewart	730
Mackenzie, Alexander	731
Maclay, Archibald	732
Madison University	735
Magoon, Elias Lyman	739
Malcom, Howard	740
Mallary, Charles Dutton	742
Manly, Basil	744
Manning, James	745
Marcy, William Learned	748
Mason, Sumner R.	758
Mather, Asher E.	759
Maxey, Samuel Bell	762
McCune, Henry E.	768
McDaniel, James	768
McDonald, Charles J.	769
McIntosh, W. H.	770
McMaster, William	773
McPherson, William	774
Mell, Patrick Hughes	777
Mercer, Jesse	779
Mercer University	783
Miles, Samuel	792
Milton, John	796
Montague, Robert L	810
Morgan, Abel	815
Morgan, T. J	815
Mount Pleasant College	821
Mulford, Horatio J	822
Murdock, John Nelson	824
Nashville, First Colored Baptist Church of	828
Nashville Institute	829
Neale, Rollin Heber	830
Newman, Albert Henry	839
Newman, Thomas W	839
Newton Theological Seminary	845

	PAGE
New York, First Baptist Church	849
Nisbet, Ebenezer	851
Noel, Baptist W	852
Northrup, G. W	857
Norton, E. H	858
Nott, Abner Kingman	858
Nugent, George	864
Olney, Edward	868
Oncken, John Gerhard	869
O'Neall, John Belton	870
Owen, Alfred	877
Palmer, Albert Gallatin	880
Palmer, Ethan B	880
Palmer, Lyman	881
Parmly, Wheelock H.	885
Pattison, Robert E.	887
Pattison, T. Harwood	888
Patton, Alfred S.	888
Paxton, William Edwards	890
Peddie Institute	894
Peddie, John	895
Peddie, Thomas B.	896
Pepper, G. D. B.	905
Peto, Samuel Morton	910
Phelps, Sylvanus Dryden	916
Philadelphia, Baptist Home of	917
Philadelphia, Fifth Baptist Church	911
Philadelphia, Memorial Baptist Church	915
Philadelphia, Second Baptist Church of	919
Pingry, William M.	922
Pitman, John	923
Posey, Humphrey	928
Post, Albert L.	928
Potter, Walter McD	930
Pritchard, T. H.	940
Providence, First Baptist Church of	946
Puryear, Bennet	951
Quincy, Josiah	952
Rand, Theodore Harding	955
Randolph, Warren	957
Rauschenbusch, Augustus	959
Rawdon College	960
Ray, D. B.	960
Rees, George Evans	965
Regent's Park College	967
Renfroe, J. J. D	969
Rhodes, Elisha Hunt	978
Richmond College	983
Richmond, First Baptist Church of	985
Robins, Henry E.	995
Robinson, Ezekiel Gilman	996
Robinson, Robert	997
Rochester Theological Seminary	1000
Rochester, University of	1002
Rochester University (Sibley Hall)	1003
Rothwell, Andrew	1011
Rowland, A. Judson	1013
Royall, William	1014
Runyon, Peter P.	1015
Sage, Adoniram Judson	1021
Salter, Melville Judson	1023
Samson, Geo. Whitefield	1024
San Francisco, First Baptist Church of	1028
Sawyer, Artemus W	1031
Schofield, J. V.	1034
Searcy, James B	1037
Sears, Barnas	1038
Semple, Robert B.	1040
Shailer, William H.	1044
Shallenberger, Wm. S.	1046

LIST OF ILLUSTRATIONS.

Name	PAGE
Sharp, Daniel	1047
Shaver, David	1048
Sherwood, Adiel	1053
Shorter, John Gill	1055
Shute, Samuel M	1058
Smith, James Wheaton	1067
Smith, John Lawrence	1068
Smith, Justin A	1070
Smith, Samuel Francis	1072
Smith, William E	1073
South Jersey Institute	1076
Spalding, Albert Theodore	1088
Speight, Joseph Warren	1090
Spratt, Geo. M	1092
Spratt, Geo. S	1092
Spurgeon, Charles Haddon	1093
Spurgeon's Tabernacle	1094
Staughton, William	1309
Stevens, John	1104
Stillman, Samuel	1107
St. Louis, Mo., Second Baptist Church	1110
Stockbridge, John Calvin	1109
Stow, Baron	1115
Strong, Augustus H	1119
Suffield Literary Institution	1297
Sunday-School, First Infant	1122
Swan, Jabez Smith	1125
Thomas, B. D	1147
Thomas, Jesse B	1149
Thresher, Ebenezer	1151
Ticknor, William D	1153
Toronto, Canada, Jarvis Street Baptist Church of	1160
Tremont Temple, Boston	1163
Tucker, Henry Holcombe	1171
Tupper, Henry Allen	1174
Tupper, James	1175
Turner, Thomas	1176
Tustin, Francis Wayland	1178
Van Husan, Caleb	1187
Vassar College	1190
Vaughan, William	1191
Vawter, John	1193
Vince, Charles	1194
Waco University	1197
Wake Forest College	1199
Walker, Jacob Garrett	1202
Walter, Thomas U	1207
Ward, Milan L	1209
Warren, E. W	1212
Watts, Thomas Hill	1218
Wayland, President Francis	1220
Wayland, Francis	1222
Wayland Seminary	1223
Welch, Bartholomew T	1226
Weston, Henry G	1233
Wharton, Morton Bryan	1235
Wiberg, Andreas	1240
Wilder, William	1243
William Jewell College	1246
Williams, J. W. M	1248
Williams, Roger	*Frontispiece*
Exile, fac-simile of Order of	1325
Letter, fac-simile of	1326
Williams, William R	1255
Wilson, Adam	1257
Wilson, Franklin	1258
Wingate, W. M	1261
Winkler, Edwin Theodore	1261
Womack, B. R	1268
Woodburn, B. F	1272
Woods, Alva	1273
Worcester Academy	1277
Wright, Lyman	1279
Wynn, Isaac Caldwell	1282
Yates, M. T	1283
Yeaman, W. Pope	1283
Young, George Whitefield	1285
Young, Robert F	1286

THE BAPTIST ENCYCLOPÆDIA.

A.

Aaron, Rev. Samuel, was born in New Britain, Pa., Oct. 19, 1800. In 1826 the Saviour found him and washed him in his blood. In 1829 he was ordained as pastor of the New Britain church. Subsequently he took charge of the Burlington, N. J., High School, and of the Baptist church in that place. In 1841 he removed to Norristown, Pa., founded the Tremont Seminary there, and served the Baptist church as pastor. Afterwards he accepted the call of the church in Mount Holly, N. J., where he ended his earthly labors, and entered upon the eternal rest, in the sixty-fifth year of his age.

Mr. Aaron was a fine scholar and a man of extraordinary ability. His logic was irresistible. He was the natural leader of his associates. He was not afraid to differ from a whole community, nor could the penalties inflicted upon independent thinking move him. He uttered his convictions with a manly boldness, and he sustained them with great power. Few cared to encounter him in debate, and large numbers admired his great intellect and his Christian deportment. He lived an earnest Christian life, and he died in the Saviour's peace.

Abbe, Prof. Cleveland, was born in the city of New York, Dec. 3, 1838, and graduated from the New York City Free College in 1857. He united with a Baptist church in that city in 1853, and has been actively engaged in Sunday-school work. He is at present a member of the Calvary Baptist church, Washington, D. C. During 1859–60 he was instructor of Mathematics and Engineering in the University of Michigan, and for a short time in the Agricultural College of that State. From 1860 to 1864 he was engaged in the United States Coast Survey under Dr. B. A. Gould, at Cambridge, Mass. In 1865–66 he visited the European observatories. During 1867–68 he was an assistant at the Naval Observatory, Washington, D. C. From 1868 to 1870 he was director of the Cincinnati Observatory, where, among other labors, he established and carried on a system of daily telegraphic weather reports and predictions, and issued a "Daily Weather Bulletin" for the Cincinnati Chamber of Commerce, which began in 1869, and which rapidly developed into the present national system of weather "probabilities." In January, 1871, he was called to the responsible position of meteorologist of the Weather Bureau of the Army Signal-Office, where he compiled the published weather probabilities, the storm-signals, monthly reviews, and international bulletin, and where he still officiates. Prof. Abbe has made numerous valuable contributions to scientific journals, especially the *American Journal of Science*, *Monthly Notices*, *Royal Astronomical Society*, Army Signal-Office Reports, *Astromische Nachrichten*, Smithsonian Annual Reports, Baird's "Annual Record," Appleton's and Johnson's Encyclopædias, etc.

Abbot, Hon. Charles F., was born in Boston, Mass., April 5, 1821. In early life he went to Richmond, Va., where he was baptized by Rev. E. L. Magoon, D.D. He subsequently removed to Philadelphia and united with the church at the Falls of Schuylkill, where for many years he has remained a faithful member and an honored office-bearer. As a trustee of the university at Lewisburg, and a manager of the American Baptist Publication Society, he has been actively engaged in promoting the educational and missionary work of the denomination. He is a man of strong intellect, clear judgment, broad views, and sterling piety. In secular life he has repeatedly been elected to aid in the management of important trusts. At one time he represented his fellow-citizens in the Pennsylvania Legislature, and he is at present a member of the Board of Public Education in the city of Philadelphia.

Abbott, Granville S., D.D., son of Ebenezer Tilden and Ruth Hewes, was born at North Reading, Mass., Feb. 27, 1837; baptized at the age of fifteen by Rev. Asa C. Bronson; licensed by the North Reading church in 1859; was ordained by the South Boston church in 1863, of which he was pastor for six years, during which period an elegant house of worship was erected. He spent ten years in study for his life-work, graduating with honor from Pierce Academy in 1856, from Brown University in 1860, and from Newton Theological Institution in 1863. After his South Boston pastorate he was pastor at Watertown, Mass., from Oct. 1, 1869, to Jan. 1, 1877. One year later he became pastor of the First Baptist church, San Francisco, Cal., and resigned Jan. 1, 1879. April 1, 1879, he became pastor of the First church, Oakland, where, in connection with his pastoral work, he accepted the editorship of the *Herald of Truth*, a monthly Baptist paper, established Jan. 1, 1880. His work for the denomination and the cause of religion has been varied and constant. For four years he edited the Sunday-school department of *The Watchman*, of Boston. For five years he was editor of the American Baptist Publication Society's "Question Books" and of its "Lesson Leaves," whose monthly circulation was 250,000. While in New England he was a member of various boards of benevolence,—the American Baptist Missionary Union, New England Educational Society, Massachusetts State Convention, president of New England Ministerial Institute, and secretary of the Massachusetts Ministerial Institute. In May, 1880, California College conferred upon him the degree of D.D. The church at Oakland, of which he is pastor, in 1880, is one of the largest in California, and is distinguished for its foreign mission zeal, in which it is an example for all the churches.

Abbott, Rev. Henry.—"To this man," Burkitt, the historian, says, "we are indebted for some of our religious rites." He was born in London, and was the son of the Rev. John Abbott, canon of St. Paul. He came to this country without the knowledge of his father, and first appeared in Camden Co., N. C., as a school-teacher. He soon joined a Baptist church and began to preach. He was a member of the Legislature, and was also a member of the Provincial Congress when the State and Federal constitutions were adopted. He died May, 1791.

Abbott, Rev. L. A.—Rev. L. A. Abbott, now pastor of the Baptist church in Alton, Ill., was born in Beverly, Mass., in 1824, and was baptized at the age of fourteen by the now venerable Rev. Benjamin Knight, uniting with the Second Baptist church in Beverly. In his early life he was a sailor. Deciding to prepare for the ministry, he studied at Worcester Academy, but his health failing midway in the course, he again went to sea, and made several voyages as mate and master. Leaving the sea, he returned to his native town and spent some years in teaching, meantime representing the district two years in the Massachusetts Legislature. In 1855 he was ordained pastor of the Central Baptist church, Metford, Mass., but in consequence of lung difficulty was compelled to resign in 1858. Partially recovering, he accepted the pastorate of the Weymouth church, and was again chosen by that town to represent it in the Legislature. In 1863 he became pastor of the Central Baptist church of Middleborough, the seat of Pierce Academy, then flourishing under the principalship of Prof. J. W. P. Jenks. Here he was once chosen to the Legislature, in which body, in this as in former terms, he served upon important committees. In 1868, removing to Minnesota for the benefit of his health, he was four years a pastor at Rochester, then at La Crosse, Wis., where he remained seven years. In 1879 he became pastor, at Alton, of the church which he still efficiently serves.

Acworth, James, LL.D., late president of Rawdon College, England (formerly known as Horton College), from 1836 to 1863. Studied for the ministry at the Bristol Baptist College, whence he proceeded to Glasgow University and graduated. On May 29, 1823, he was ordained co-pastor of the South Parade church, Leeds, his colleague being the venerable Thomas Langdon, then in the forty-first year of his ministry. In 1836 he entered upon the duties of president of Horton College, and distinguished himself by many important services to the denomination in that capacity. Since his retirement, in 1863, he has resided at Scarborough, Yorkshire. Both as a pastor and theological professor Dr. Acworth will long be gratefully remembered.

Adams, George F., D.D., was born in Dorchester, Mass., Oct. 3, 1802, and died in Baltimore, Md., April 16, 1877. His father, Seth Adams, removed to Ohio in 1805, and settled first in Marietta, and afterwards in Zanesville. Mr. Adams was baptized in 1812, by the Rev. George C. Sedwick. He was licensed to preach in 1822. In 1824 he entered the preparatory school of the Columbian College, graduated from the college in 1829, and was principal of the school during the year 1829–30. While still pursuing his collegiate course he was elected pastor of the Central Baptist church, Washington, at that time worshiping in the city hall, which, however, was soon after merged into the E Street church. During his college course he also spent several of his vacations with the Rev. Dr. Ryland as missionary in Eastern Virginia. He was ordained at the Navy-Yard Baptist church, Washington, April 22, 1827. In 1830 he settled in Falmouth, Va., as principal of a female school, and as the assistant of the Rev. R. B. Semple, pastor of the church in Fredericksburg, of which he soon became himself the pastor, continuing such until December of 1835, supplying at the same time the pulpit at Falmouth, and also of one other church. In January, 1836, he became pastor of the Calvert Street Baptist church, Baltimore, where he was useful and successful. In 1842 he became general missionary for the State of Maryland, visiting and stimulating all the churches. In 1843 he preached to the Hereford, Gunpowder, and Forest churches. In 1848 he accepted the pastorate of the Second Baptist church, Baltimore, where, during thirteen years, he labored with great success. In 1860, Mr. Adams became pastor of the Hampton Baptist church, but the war occurring, he served for a short time as chaplain in the Confederate army. He was arrested and imprisoned for a while at the Rip-raps. In 1862 he returned to Baltimore, and was appointed State missionary, serving in that capacity until 1865, when he took charge of the Atlantic Female College at Onancock, Va. In 1867 he was called a second time to the pastorate of the church in Hampton, where he remained for nine years, until, his voice failing, he resigned, and removed to Baltimore, where he was appointed a city missionary, laboring as such with great fidelity until nearly the day of his death, which was caused by a cancerous affection of the throat. As a preacher Mr. Adams was instructive and stimulating. His style was clear, simple, and forcible, and his sermons were rich in Christian experience. During a ministry of more than fifty years he had labored faithfully for the advancement of every good cause, baptizing hundreds of converts, and giving much of his time to the cause of missions, Sunday-schools, temperance, and the distribution of religious publications. One who knew him well has said, "He was one of the four ministers who, in 1836, laid the foundation of the Maryland Baptist Union Association, and to him more than to any other man are we indebted under God for the origin and present glorious success of that body, numbering then only 345, now over 10,000." Mr. Adams also wrote and published numerous articles of interest in our religious periodicals, and was for one year the editor of the *True Union*, published in Baltimore. He had also in preparation a "History of the Maryland Baptist Churches,"—a work for which he was specially fitted from his intimate acquaintance with the churches, and which he undertook at the request of the M. B. U. A. He left it unfinished at his death, but it will be completed by the Rev. John Pollard, D.D., of Baltimore. Dr. Adams received the degree of D.D. from the Columbian College.

Adams, Rev. Henry, a distinguished colored minister, was born in Franklin Co., Ga., Dec. 17, 1802. He was converted at the age of eighteen years, and the same year licensed to preach within the bounds of his church. In 1823 his license was extended without limits, and in 1825 he was ordained. After preaching a few years in South Carolina and Georgia, he emigrated to Kentucky, and was settled as pastor of the First Colored Baptist church in Louisville in 1829. Here he spent the remainder of a long and eminently useful life. The church was very small when he took charge of it, and was the only colored Baptist church in the city. At his death it numbered over 1000 members, and was the parent of six other churches, with a total membership of 4000. Mr. Adams was a fair scholar, having a good knowledge of several of the ancient languages. After the emancipation of the colored people he expressed constant anxiety for the establishment of schools and the improvement of the condition of his race. He was especially solicitous for the formation of a school in Louisville for the training of colored ministers. He died in Louisville, Nov. 3, 1872.

Adams, Rev. John Quincy, was born in Philadelphia, Pa., Feb. 25, 1825: was liberally educated; ordained pastor of Bloomfield church, N. J., Jan. 31, 1849. He has had charge of the Keyport church, N. J., and of the North, Antioch, and Cannon Street churches in New York City. He has published a number of religious works. Eleven years ago he had baptized 540 persons, nine of whom became ordained ministers. Mr. Adams is full of zeal for the salvation of the perishing, and for the triumph of what he regards as the truth of God.

Adams, Seymour Webster, D.D., was born in Vernon, Oneida Co., N. Y., Aug. 1, 1815; converted at the age of seventeen; received his literary education at Hamilton College, N. Y., and his theological training at Hamilton Theological Seminary; was ordained in February, 1843, and after supplying the churches at Durhamville and Johnstown, N. Y., became pastor of the church at Vernon, his native place, where he remained two years. In 1846 he accepted the call of the First Baptist church, Cleveland, O., and continued its pastor until his death, Sept. 27, 1864. During these eighteen years he had the affection of a devoted people, and exercised great influence in the city and State. In 1859 he wrote a memoir of his father-in-law, Dr. Nathaniel Kendrick. His death was hastened by his services at the seat of war as a volunteer in the Christian Commission. His

S. W. ADAMS, D.D.

memoir was published under the editorship of J. P. Bishop in 1866. His character was greatly admired and his early death lamented by all.

Adams, Rev. Spencer Gavitt, the pastor of the Baptist church in Walworth, Wis., was born in Marion Co., O., Sept. 7, 1844. His parents were Methodists, and he received his early religious training under the influence of that denomination. He obtained hope in Christ when thirteen years of age, and united with the M. E. Church. His attention having been called to the views held by Baptists, after careful and prayerful examination of the subject he united with the Baptist Church. He was educated at Denison University, O., and at the Morgan Park Baptist Theological Seminary, Ill. He was ordained in June, 1875. While a student in the theological seminary he supplied regularly for two years the Baptist church in Thompsonville, Racine Co. He has been four years pastor of the Walworth Baptist church.

Adams, Rev. Thomas, a prominent minister of the Mississippi River Baptist Association, was born in South Carolina in 1804, and began to preach in 1830. He was a graduate of Furman Theological Institute. After laboring many years in his native State, he removed to East Feliciana Parish, La., in 1853, where he labored efficiently until his death, July 20, 1859.

Adkins, E., D.D., was born in Greenfield, Saratoga Co., N. Y., Dec. 17, 1805. His parents moving to what was then the wilderness of Western New York, he was deprived of the advantages of an early education, but impelled by his thirst for knowledge, at the age of twenty-seven he entered an academy at Rochester, N. Y., graduating finally from Marietta College, O., in 1839. For three years after his graduation he was tutor at Marietta, where he also studied law. Having taught in Tennessee and Peoria, Ill. (where he was baptized), he accepted in 1847 the chair of Belles-Lettres in Shurtleff College, Ill., remaining in the faculty nine years at great personal sacrifice, and giving himself to the interests of the college with unwearied devotion. The latter part of his time at Shurtleff, Prof. Adkins had the chair of Languages. Having become profoundly interested in Bible revision, he resigned at Shurtleff and removed to New York, where he devoted his entire time to this work. After a year's service he was, however, obliged to desist on account of failure of sight. In 1857 he took a position in Marietta College, resigning this in 1859 to accept the Professorship of Greek in Richmond College, Va., a post which he held but a short time on account of the war. Returning, he accepted a pastorate at Brimfield, Ill., where he was ordained. In 1863 he again entered the faculty of Marietta College, where he remained until partial blindness compelled him to retire. Of late years he has been living with his son at Elyria, O.

Dr. Adkins has been an industrious writer. In his early life he published "What is Baptism?" and in his later years "Ecclesia; The Church: Its Polity and Fellowship," and "The Ages to Come, or the Future States." He has also written largely for newspapers and magazines.

Adkins, Frank, A.M., son of the preceding, was born at Marietta, O., Nov. 21, 1841. Converted at the age of ten, during revival meetings held at Upper Alton, Ill.; baptized two years later. After preparatory studies at Shurtleff and Pierce Academies, and collegiate studies at Marietta, O., graduated at Madison University in 1861. After graduation engaged in teaching, but feeling called to preach took a course of theological study at Madison and Rochester, graduating at the latter place in 1866. Same year settled as pastor at Akron, O., where he remained two and a half years. After a short period of missionary work became, in 1870, pastor of the First church, Iowa City, Iowa, where he remained five and a half years, when ill health compelled him to resign. For two years after this was Professor of Greek in Central University, Pella, Iowa. In December, 1878, he became pastor at Elyria, O., where he still remains. Mr. Adkins is a scholarly and cultured man, and ranks very high on account of his attainments and the excellencies of his character.

Adlam, Rev. Samuel, was born in Bristol, England, February, 1798. He was ordained at West Dedham, Mass., Nov. 3, 1824. Having been in the ministry several years, he felt the need of a more extended course of study than he had been able to secure, and went to Newton, where he remained for four years, from 1834 to 1838. His pastorates have been in West Dedham, Marblehead, and Gloucester, Mass.; Hallowell, Dover, and Foxcroft, Me.; and Newport, R. I. He resigned his pastorate of the First church in the latter place some years since.

Admission of Members into the Church.—When a man desires admission into an orderly Baptist church, he is carefully examined by the pastor or some other judicious brother in reference to his repentance for sin, and utter helplessness without the Saviour's grace; in reference to his faith in Jesus as his substitute and sacrifice on the cross, without whose blood his sins would cling to him forever; and in reference to his knowledge of the teachings of God's word. He is instructed in the great doctrines of the trinity, election, the offices of the three sacred persons, depravity, regeneration, atonement, justification, providence, final perseverance, and believing prayer. Satisfied that the man is washed by faith in the blood of the Lamb and saved, the pastor brings him to the deacons, who hear from him an account of God's dealings with his soul. Having convinced them that he is a child of God, he repeats his experience at a weeknight service, at the close of which a special church-meeting is held, and a resolution is passed authorizing his baptism and reception into the church. After baptism he is formally received into the church by the right hand of fellowship. In a few churches the pastor, just before giving the hand of fellowship, places his hands upon the candidate's head, and tenderly prays for him.

Africa, Mission to.—In his admirable "History of American Baptist Missions" Prof. Gammell says, "No one of the missions planted by the Managers of the General Convention has had such serious obstacles to encounter, or has been so often paralyzed by their influence, as that on the western coast of Africa. Its history conducts us to a portion of the earth pervaded by a pestilential climate, and perpetually ravaged by the cupidity of civilized man; to a race degraded by the barbarism and wrongs of ages, and, by common consent, long doomed to slavery and oppression among almost every people of Christendom. No relics of a departed civilization, no scenes of storied events, attract attention to this gloomy region. No hoary superstitions, blending with the rude traditions of an elder age, lend a philosophic interest to the people who inhabit it. It presents only a blank and dreary waste of barbarism, occupied by the lowest and most abject forms of humanity." Since these words were written, more than a quarter of a century ago, a new interest has been thrown over this dark country by the discoveries of modern travelers, and we may cherish the hope that, with the advance of the years, Africa will become as much the scene of missionary activity as Asia has been during the past fifty years.

The operations of American Baptists in Africa have been confined to Liberia, on the west coast of the continent, and to the Bassa tribe living in the territory. Colonists from America laid the foundations of Monrovia, now the capital of the republic of Liberia, in 1821. Lott Carey and Collin Teague, two colored men who had been ordained at Richmond, Va., in January, 1821, commenced their missionary labors in Monrovia in 1822. A church was formed, of which Mr. Carey was appointed pastor. His decided superiority in intellectual ability over the colonists gave him great influence in the new settlement, and he was able, in many ways, to promote the interests of the people. He was appointed vice-agent in 1826, and in 1828 governor, during the temporary absence of Mr. Ashmun to the United States. The death of Mr. Carey was a sad blow to the interests of the colony and the church. Two white missionaries, Rev. Calvin Holton, appointed Jan. 24, 1826, and Rev. Benjamin R. Skinner, appointed Jan. 11, 1830, both died of the "coast fever," the one in 1826 and the other in 1831. The board was so discouraged by what seemed a fatality to white men, in the character of the climate of the west coast of Africa, that they gave up the hope of carrying on the mission through any other agency than that of colored preachers of the gospel. Five years elapsed before another white missionary was sent out to Africa. Two brethren offered to go, Rev. W. G. Crocker and Rev. W. Mylne, and they were appointed early in 1835, and reached the field of their labors. They were instructed to preach among the native tribes, and it was decided to establish a mission at Bassa Cove, with the hope that, from this point as headquarters, they might more effectually teach the natives. Schools were at once commenced at Bassa Cove, Edina, and other places. A house of worship was dedicated at Bassa Cove in 1836, where Mr. Mylne preached until a pastor was settled in the following year. It was not long before the insidious malaria of West Africa so affected the physical system of Mr. Mylne that he was obliged to give up his work, and, a broken-down man, he returned to this country in 1838. Mr. Crocker had a better constitution, and was able to go on with his work. He directed his attention to the work of translation, in which he was especially successful. Rev. Ivory Clarke and his wife arrived at Edina early in 1838, and having passed safely through an attack of the fever, entered upon their missionary labors with zeal. In 1840, Messrs. Constantine and Fielding, with their wives, offered themselves to the board, and were appointed to labor among the tribes living farther back from the coast, with the hope that the climate would prove more favorable to their health than the climate of the coast. The hope was not realized. Mr. and Mrs. Fielding both died within six weeks after their arrival. Mr. and Mrs. Constantine were so completely broken down in health that they returned to this country in June, 1842. Mr. Crocker left his work in Africa a year preceding the return of Mr. Constantine, and came to the United States. After two years' residence here he returned to the scene of his former labors. On the Sabbath after his arrival in Monrovia he was seized with a sudden illness, and in two days he died. His wife, after a year or two of experience of missionary life on this treacherous coast, returned to her native land. Mr. Clarke, in his turn, fell a victim to disease, dying at sea, April 4, 1848, on his passage to America.

Ainslie, Rev. Thomas, was born in 1769; converted and baptized at Sussex, New Brunswick, in 1802. He soon commenced preaching, and traveled as an evangelist for about four years. He was ordained in 1806, in the United States, and resumed his work in New Brunswick. In 1810 he became pastor of the Baptist church at Upper Granville, Nova Scotia, and so continued to the end; evangelized, however, very extensively in Eastern Nova Scotia; was, in 1828, the means of a powerful revival at Aylesford. He died at St. Andrew's, New Brunswick, Dec. 7, 1831, in the zenith of his power and usefulness as a minister of Christ, especially owned and blessed of heaven.

Aitchison, John Young, D.D., the pastor of the Baptist church in Eau Claire, Wis. He was born in Berwickshire, Scotland, July 5, 1824. He was educated in Glasgow University, and he was ordained at Paisley, Scotland, in 1849. He began his work in the ministry at Glasgow the same year. He has had successful pastorates in Brooklyn, N. Y., Waukesha, Wis., Cedar Rapids and Clinton, Iowa; and he has been twice settled at Eau Claire, Wis., his present field of labor. He received the honorary degree of D.D., from the Central University of Iowa, in 1878. His literary attainments are of a high order. He occasionally speaks from the platform as a lecturer, with great acceptance.

ALABAMA BAPTISTS.

Alabama,—"*Here we rest,*" the Indian signification of the word. It is reasonably assumed that this region was visited by Ferdinand de Soto in 1539. It was originally part of what is known in the history of our country as Mississippi Territory. Some settlements were made in that portion of the territory now embraced in the State of Mississippi before the American Revolution; but Alabama continued the undisturbed hunting-ground of savage aborigines until a much later period. At the end of the struggle for American independence Georgia claimed this vast region, and exercised jurisdiction over it as her "Western Territory." In 1800 it was erected into a territorial government. In 1802 Georgia ceded to the United States all her western territory for $1,250,000. In 1817 the territory was divided, and the western portion was authorized by Congress to form a constitution, and it became the State of Mississippi. The eastern portion was then formed into a Territory, and received the name Alabama. In July, 1819, a convention of delegates assembled in Huntsville and adopted a State constitution, which being approved by Congress the December following, the State of Alabama was admitted as a member of the National Union, thenceforth to stand, alphabetically, at the head of the sacred roll of the United States. As the vast domain of the united and independent States, protected by our national banner, is the land of the free and the home of the oppressed, where the weary of every land come and find civil and ecclesiastical "*rest,*" so Alabama, whether by accident or by Providence, was the right name to be placed at the head of this "more perfect union."

Alabama Baptists, History of.—That part of this State which lies north of the Tennessee River, generally known as "North Alabama," a beautiful and fertile country, was settled many years before any other considerable section of the State. Madison County of that region was the first to receive the civilization of thrifty settlements, and in the first settling of that county there were some Baptists. John Canterbery and Zadock Baker were the first Baptist ministers who labored in this wilderness, and Elder John Nicholson was the first pastor of the first church in the State, or, rather, in the Territory,—the old Flint River church, a few miles northeast of Huntsville, in Madison County, which was organized at the house of James Deaton, on the 2d of October, 1808, by twelve persons. The beauty of the country, the fertility of the soil, the excellent springs of water, the ease with which partial land-titles were procured, combined with many other influences, soon drew a large population into this region, and in the course of a few years a number of Baptist churches were formed. Worldly inducements brought ministers, as other men, into this inviting country, some of whom held elevated positions in the estimation of the people, and here they lived and labored until they finished their course. Of these early North Alabama ministers, Elders R. Shackleford, W. Eddins, and Bennet Wood seem to have been the most distinguished. About the same time Elders Jeremiah Tucker, George Tucker, John Smith, J. C. Latta, and J. Thompson labored in the same region. As early as the 26th September, 1814, the first Association of Alabama Baptists was organized,—the Flint River Association. At first some of its churches were from Tennessee.

About the year 1808 some Baptists were found in the southern part of the Territory, near the Tombigbee River, in Clarke and Washington Counties. William Cochran, a licensed preacher from Georgia, is said to have been the first in Clarke County, and one Mr. Gorham the first in Washington County. Elder J. Courtney organized the first church in that part of the State in 1810,— the Bassett's Creek church, the second in the Territory. It has for many years been connected with the Bethel Association. Elder Joseph McGee settled in the same region shortly after the planting of this church, and was much esteemed as a minister of Christ. About the year 1815 the tide of emigration began to flow into South and West Alabama from almost every State in the Union. With this flood of emigrants a number of able, zealous, and indefatigable preachers came. There is an account of one family from South Carolina who furnished to Alabama and Mississippi in those early times eight or ten ministers of our faith. Many of the preachers for the first forty years of the history of Alabama often made extended evangelistic tours, pushing the outposts of the Redeemer's kingdom farther and farther; and in these pioneering labors churches were planted in most of the new settlements, and existing churches were confirmed in the faith. It has been common from the first for one minister to serve at the same time several churches. This is still the case. As a result pastoral work has been very imperfectly performed. The early ministers of Alabama generally received little support from the churches,— in many cases nothing; and though frequently they were in straitened circumstances, they were rich in faith, and many of them mighty in the Scriptures, and rapid and enlarged success followed their labors. They are to be held in everlasting remembrance.

In 1820 there were about 50 Baptist churches in Alabama. At the close of the year 1821 there were 70, and 2500 members. In 1825 there were 6 Associations, 128 churches, 70 ministers, and about 5000 members. In 1833 there were 130 ministers, 250 churches, 11,408 members. In 1836 there were 333 churches, 188 ministers, 15,630 members. In 1840 there were 30 Associations, 500 churches, 300 ministers, and 25,000 members, 4000 of whom were baptized the previous year. Mr. Holcombe, the historian, says, "This increase is without a parallel in the United States, and perhaps in the known world, especially in modern times." In the years 1838-39 extensive revivals were experienced. The churches in many counties of the State, embracing all Middle Alabama, received the power of the Holy Ghost, great numbers were led to Christ, and many new churches were planted. Houses for the worship of God were for years scarce and rude. Large congregations often assembled in shady groves and anxiously heard the gospel from the lips of the men of God, and many churches were organized in such bowers and in private residences, and under busharbors. About the year 1830 the churches began to build better houses of worship than those which had before existed in the State, and many of them were an honor to the religion of a new country.

Between the years 1835 and 1840 the Baptists of Alabama had their greatest troubles with the anti-missionaries,—a strong party who arrayed themselves against all missionary and benevolent enterprises, and against ministerial education. The contest was fierce and evil-spirited. One by one the Associations and churches divided until division occurred in most of them. Five Associations split asunder in 1839. The enemies of missions declared non-fellowship, and were the seceding parties. The missionary churches have been blessed with prosperity. Retrogression has constantly marked the movements of the opponents of missions.

Total number of members in the Baptist churches of the State, 165,000.

Alabama Baptist Convention.—The Convention was formed in October, 1823, at Salem church, near Greensborough, chiefly through the instrumentality of the Rev. J. A. Ranaldson, who came into the State from Louisiana, and afterwards returned to that State. At the organization of the Convention messengers were present from seven missionary societies,—then and for some years the only class of bodies that sought representation; subsequently and at present it was and is composed of messengers from churches, Associations, and missionary societies. At the first session fifteen ministers were appointed from different parts of the State to spend all the time practicable as domestic missionaries. For ten years the Convention devoted its energies to the cause of missionary work within the State, with occasional contributions of money to other objects. State missions and ministerial education were the first objects of this Convention. For the first fifteen years it was not very successful, and had to contend against the most serious hindrances that an extensive and fierce anti-missionary spirit could engender; a number of the strongest of our early ministers taking that side of the great effort questions then in controversy, they hindered the cause very much; the great majority of the ministers who claimed to be missionary Baptists were entirely neutral on these matters. But there were some giants in those days,—noble spirits who were every way worthy of their high calling; men who confronted the enemies of missions and every other enemy, and laid the foundations of our State enterprises deep down on the solid rock. Such were Hosea Holcombe, Alexander Travis, J. McLemore, D. Winbourne, S. Blythe, C. Crow, A. G. McCrow, J. Ryan, and a number of others who might be gratefully mentioned here. It is worthy of remark that in those early times in Alabama, both in our Associations and in the Convention, decided union and sympathy of feeling were manifested toward "the Baptist General Convention of the United States," and handsome sums were contributed for foreign missions, and especially for Dr. Judson's Burmese Bible. The benevolent operations of the Convention were then largely carried forward by efficient agents who were appointed by the body. It was at the tenth session, in 1833, at Grant's Creek church, in Tuskaloosa County, when there were only four delegates present except those from the immediate vicinity, that the Convention took steps to start an educational institution,—the Manual Labor Seminary,—which, after absorbing almost the entire attention of the Convention, was abandoned in about five years. From this time onward for many years Revs. B. Manly, J. Hartwell, D. P. Bestor, and J. H. De Votee were the great preachers who constantly attended the Convention, and their superiors have never been banded together in any Southern Baptist Convention; and in their day a number of others, scarcely a whit behind them, lived in Alabama, and regularly met in the counsels of the Convention. And besides these, many wealthy planters, intelligent merchants, and distinguished lawyers gave the meetings of the Convention their presence, their counsels, and their money. This happy state of things continued until it was estopped by the coming in of the late war between the North and South. After the failure of the Manual Labor School, the Convention returned for some years with increased purpose and energy to the work of State evangelization, and to assisting young men to obtain an education in any school that they might enter to make preparation for the ministry. It was about the year 1842 that the Convention entered on the incipient work which finally resulted in the establishment of Howard College and the Judson Female Institute. After the organization of the Southern Baptist Convention, and the location of its Domestic Board at Marion, Ala., the Convention discontinued the work of State evangelization, except that it supported the work as carried on by the General Board at Marion. Thenceforth it was an important part of the State Convention's business to foster the Boards of the Southern Convention. This, with the absorbing attention which it gave to its own institutions of learning, and to the Southern Theological Seminary, comprised its business for the second twenty years of its existence. Howard College and Judson Institute are the property of the Convention, and have from their beginning occupied very much of its deliberations and liberality. In 1871 the Convention formed a Sabbath-school Board as a sort of compromise with those who were contending for a system of State Missions. In 1875 this Board was changed into a State Mission Board. In these directions it has done a vast work, which is joyously recognized by the brotherhood of the State. Through this provisional period the Board was located in Talladega, with Rev. J. J. D. Renfroe, D.D., as President, and Rev. T. C. Boykin as Sabbath-school Evangelist for the first eighteen months; after which the Rev. T. M. Bailey became Evangelist and Corresponding Secretary, a position which he still holds (1880), and in which he has maintained first-class efficiency. At the session of this year the location of the Board was changed to Selma, because a more central place, and Rev. W. C. Cleveland, D.D., became its president. This Board now has in charge the entire mission work of Alabama Baptists as auxiliary to the General Boards, with an effort among the colored people, the work of colportage, and raising funds for ministerial education; all this in addition to its immediate work of State evangelization. Its work has taken a strong hold on the hearts of Alabama Baptists. During the year 1879–80 it had in the field constantly about twenty able and efficient evangelists. The Convention of Alabama has again become a very able body of Christian men; with a powerful ministry, it has present every year a number of the leading merchants and farmers, and some of the most distinguished lawyers and civilians of the State, and never fails to make a first-class impression on the community at large. So far as can now be ascertained the following have been the presidents of the Convention: Rev. Charles Crow, at its organization; Rev. Daniel Brown, Rev. Lee Compere, Rev. J. Ryan, Rev. Hosea Holcombe, for six sessions; Rev. Jesse Hartwell, for five sessions; Rev. Thomas Chilton, for five sessions; Chief-Justice W. P. Chilton, Rev. H. Talbird, D.D., for five sessions; Rev. A. G. McCrow, for five sessions: Rev. W. H. McIntosh, D.D., Hon. J. L. M. Curry, LL.D., for five sessions; Rev. S. Henderson, D.D., for six sessions; and the Hon. Jon. Haralson, for seven sessions,—the present incumbent.

ALABAMA BAPTIST NEWSPAPERS.

Alabama Baptist.—In the year 1841, Rev. M. P. Jewett and Rev. J. H. De Votee established the old *Alabama Baptist* in Marion, under the editorial management of Mr. Jewett. He was succeeded as editor by Rev. J. M. Breaker and Rev. A. W. Chambliss. Dr. Chambliss filled this position for several years with rare ability, and changed the name of the paper to that of *Southwestern Baptist*.

In 1852 it was placed under the editorship of Rev. S. Henderson, and published in Montgomery one year, when it was moved to Tuskegee, where Dr. Henderson was pastor, and issued from that place until the close of the late war, when Dr. Henderson, by Federal authority, was placed under a twenty-thousand-dollar bond not to publish it again, —it had been a strong secession organ. This bond led to its consolidation with the *Christian Index*, of Atlanta, Ga. From time to time Dr. Henderson had the editorial assistance of Rev. Albert Williams, Rev. J. M. Watt, Rev. J. E. Dawson, D.D., and Rev. H. E. Taliaferro, the latter for seven years. It was a paper of great ability, reached under Dr. Henderson an extensive circulation, and wielded a leading influence. After it was merged into the *Christian Index* that paper was for eight years recognized as the organ of Alabama Baptists. But it could not be made to subserve the wants of the denomination in the State.

Alabama Baptist.—In 1873-74 the Convention of Alabama, by its Board of Directors, started the present *Alabama Baptist* at Marion, with Drs. E. T. Winkler, J. J. D. Renfroe, E. B. Teague, and D. W. Gwin as editors. It was edited gratuitously for four years. In 1878 the Convention transferred the paper to Dr. Winkler and Rev. J. L. West. Mr. West has since become sole proprietor, with Drs. Winkler and Renfroe as editors. The paper gives universal satisfaction to the brotherhood, and is contributing efficiently to the development and unification of the Baptists in all their enterprises. It now issues from Selma.

Baptist Correspondent.—For a few years prior to the war the late venerable Dr. W. C. Buck and his son, the Rev. C. W. Buck, published in Marion the above-named paper, which was an earnest and vigorous controversial paper.

Baptist Pioneer.—A spirited paper now published in Selma for colored Baptists, with Rev. W. H. McAlpine as editor.

Christian Herald.—Published soon after the war, and for several years at Tuskumbia, with Rev. Joseph Shackelford, D.D., as editor. A paper of much merit; had it been published south of the mountains it must have succeeded. It was removed to Nashville, Tenn., and afterwards merged into the *Christian Index*.

Southwestern Baptist Pioneer.—In 1834 the Rev. William Wood, M.D., started a paper of the above name in Jacksonville. It was the first Baptist paper in the State. Published only a year or two. In 1838 the Rev. George F. Heard published a Baptist paper in Mobile for a short time.

Alabama Central Female College.—This institution is located in the city of Tuscaloosa, and occupies the buildings of the former State Capitol, which are singularly well adapted to their present use, and are worth at least $150,000. The Baptists hold a lease of ninety-nine years on this property, with no other obligation than to keep it in order and maintain a female school in it. The college has now existed more than twenty-five years, and has reached a high reputation, and is destined to still greater prosperity. Prof. A. K. Yancey, the present president of the college, is giving entire satisfaction and increasing its fame.

Alabama, Several Educational Enterprises of.—THE TALLADEGA BAPTIST MALE HIGH SCHOOL, erected thirty years ago by the Coosa River Baptist Association at a cost of $30,000. Lost by indebtedness. Now a Congregational school for colored people.

MOULTON COLLEGE, at Moulton, Ala., a flourishing school before the war. It is not prosperous now.

THE BAPTIST HIGH SCHOOL, at Lafayette, is an old and good institution.

SOUTH ALABAMA FEMALE INSTITUTE, at Greenville, is in a flourishing condition, with Prof. J. M. Thigpen for president.

MALE HIGH SCHOOL, at the same place, is also in prosperity, with Prof. G. W. Thigpen for principal.

THE SOUTHEAST ALABAMA HIGH SCHOOL for some years did well under the control of the late General Association of that part of the State, but has been discontinued.

Alabama Colored Baptists.—Before their liberation from slavery the great body of colored Baptists in this State held church membership in the same churches with the whites, having the same pastor and worshiping in the same house. Nearly all houses of worship had an apartment for the colored people, which was uniformly well filled. Where they were numerous they had a separate service in the afternoon of the Sabbath, when the pastor preached to them. In such cases they were virtually a separate church. This state of things continued for a short time after they became free. They soon began to show a disposition to get away into organizations of their own, and this was encouraged by the whites. Most of their churches were formed and their officers ordained by white pastors, and the whites assisted them to erect houses of worship. The colored people have ever had a strong tendency to Baptist sentiments.

Convention.—Their State Convention was organized Dec. 17, 1868. There were 32 churches represented and 60 delegates present. Churches had then been constituted in all the leading towns and cities in the State; there were then about 50 colored churches in Alabama, but there had as yet been no Association formed. Steps were taken by the Convention to influence the organization of the churches into Associations, and by the session in 1875 there were about 20 Associations. Churches were then forming in all parts of the State where they had sufficient numbers. There are now 50 Associations, 600 churches, and 700 ordained preachers, with a great many licentiates, and about 90,000 members. They own $250,000 worth of church property, and school property in Selma which they estimate at $15,000. They have a "normal and theological school" in that city in a flourishing condition, with Rev. Mr. Woodsmall as president. In locating this institution they purchased and paid for the Selma Fair-Ground with its buildings, at a cost of $3000. It is valuable property and could not be better located. It is owned and managed by their State Convention. They also have an educational association, which meets in connection with the Convention.

Albany, Emmanuel Baptist Church of.—The noble edifice of the Emmanuel church of Albany, N. Y., was dedicated to the worship of Almighty God in February, 1871. The church proper is 110 feet deep and 81 feet wide. The church and chapel together are 157 feet deep. The chapel is 110 feet deep and 47 feet wide. The spire is 234 feet high. The church seats 1400 persons. The house and lot cost $203,686, and no debt rests upon the structure or its site.

Albigenses, The, received this name from the town of Albi, in France, in and around which many of them lived. The Albigenses were called Cathari, Paterines, Publicans, Paulicians, Good Men, Bogomiles, and they were known by other names. They were not Waldenses. They were Paulicians, either directly from the East, or converted through the instrumentality of those who came from the earlier homes of that people.

The Paulicians were summoned into existence by the Spirit of God about A.D. 660. Their founder was named Constantine. The reading of a New Testament, left him by a stranger, brought him to the Saviour. He soon gathered a church, and his converts speedily collected others. Armenia was the scene of his labors. They were denounced as Manicheans, though they justly denied the charge. They increased rapidly, and in process of time persecution scattered them. In the ninth century many of them were in Thrace, Bulgaria, and Bosnia; and, later still, they became very numerous in these new fields, especially in Bosnia.* Indeed, such a host had they become that in 1238 Coloman, the brother of the king of Hungary, entered Bosnia to destroy the heretics. Gregory IX. congratulated him upon his success, but lived to learn that the Bogomiles were still a multitude. A second crusade led to further butchery, but the blood of martyrs was still the seed of the church, and they continued a powerful body until the conquest of their country by the Turks, in 1463. There was direct communication between these Bogomiles and the Albigenses in France. Matthew Paris† tells us that the heretic Albigenses in the provinces of Bulgaria, Crotia, and Dalmatia elected Bartholomew as their pope, that Albigenses came to him from all quarters for information on doubtful matters, and that he had a vicar who was born in Carcassone, and who lived near Thoulouse.

At an early period the Paulicians entered Italy and established powerful communities, especially in Milan. They spread over France, Germany, and other countries. In the eleventh century they were to be found in almost every quarter of Europe. St. Bernard, in the twelfth century, says of them: "If you interrogate them about their faith nothing can be more Christian, if you examine into their conversation nothing can be more blameless, and what they say they confirm by their deeds. As for what regards life and manners, they attack no one, they circumvent no one, they defraud no one." Reinerius Saccho belonged to the Cathari (not the Waldenses, he was never a member of that community) for seventeen years. He was afterwards a Romish inquisitor, and he describes his old friends and the Waldenses, in 1254, in these words: "Heretics are distinguished by their manners and their words, for they are sedate and modest in their manners. They have no pride in clothes, for they wear such as are neither costly nor mean. They do not carry on business in order to avoid falsehoods, oaths, and frauds, but only live by labor as workmen. Their teachers also are shoemakers and weavers. They do not multiply riches, but are content with what is necessary, and they are chaste, especially the Leonists. They are also temperate in meat and drink. They do not go to taverns, dances, or other vanities." The Leonists were the followers of Peter Waldo, of Lyons, the Waldenses, as distinguished from his own old sect, the Albigenses. Reinerius then proceeds to charge these men who shun business to avoid falsehoods with hypocrisy. No body of men could receive a better character than St. Bernard and the inquisitor give these enemies of the Church of Rome, and no community could be more wickedly abused by the same men than these identical heretics. For some centuries the Albigenses figure universally in history as externally the purest and best of men, and secretly as guilty of horrible crimes, such as the pagans charged upon the early Christians.

Reinerius mentions several causes for the spread of heresy. His second is that all the men and women, small and great, day and night, do not cease to learn, and they are continually engaged in teaching what they have acquired themselves. His third

---

* Evans's Bosnia, pp. 36, 37, 42. London, 1876.

† Matthew Paris, at A.D. 1223.

EMMANUEL BAPTIST CHURCH, ALBANY, N. Y.

cause for the existence and spread of heresy is the translation and circulation of the Old and New Testaments into the vulgar tongue. These they learned themselves and taught to others. Reinerius[*] was acquainted with a rustic layman who repeated the whole book of Job, and with many who knew perfectly the entire New Testament. He gives an account of many schools of the heretics, the existence of which he learned in the trials of the Inquisition. Assuredly these friends of light and of a Bible circulated everywhere were worthy of the curses and tortures of men like Reinerius and lordly bigots like St. Bernard. In a council held at Thoulouse in 1229 the Scriptures in the language of the people were first prohibited. The Albigenses surviving the horrid massacre of the Pope's murderous crusaders were forbidden to have the " books of the Old or New Testament, unless a Psalter, a *Breviary*, and a *Rosary*, and they forbade the translation in the vulgar tongue." No doubt many of the members of the council supposed that the Breviary and Rosary were inspired as well as the Psalter.

Reinerius gives a catalogue of the doctrines of the Cathari, which corresponds with the list of heresies charged against them for two hundred years before he wrote by popes, bishops, and ecclesiastical gatherings, the substance of which has no claim upon our credulity, though some of the forms of expression may have been used by certain of these venerable worthies.

Reinerius[†] says that the Cathari had 16 churches, the church of the Albanenses, or of Sansano, of Contorezo, of Bagnolenses, or of Bagnolo, of Vincenza, or of the Marquisate, of Florence, of the Valley of Spoleto, of France, of Thoulouse, of Cahors, of Albi, of Sclavonia, of the Latins at Constantinople, of the Greeks in the same city, of Philadelphia, of Bulgaria, and of Dugranicia. He says, " They all derive their origin from the two last." That is, they are all Paulicians, originally from Armenia. He says that " the churches number 4000 Cathari, of both sexes, in all the world, but believers innumerable." By churches we are to understand communities of the Perfect devoted to ministerial and missionary labor. The Believers in the time of Reinerius were counted by millions.

Upon *infant baptism* the Albigenses had very decided opinions. A council[‡] held in Thoulouse in 1119, undoubtedly referring to them, condemns and expels from the church of God those who put on the appearance of religion and condemned the sacrament of the body and the blood of the Lord and the *baptism of children*.

At a meeting of " archbishops, bishops, and other pious men" at Thoulouse, in 1176, the Albigenses were condemned on various pretexts. Roger De Hoveden,[§] a learned Englishman, who commenced to write his " Annals" in 1189, gives a lengthy account of this meeting. He says that Gilbert, bishop of Lyons, by command of the bishop of Albi and his assessors, condemned these persons as heretics; and the third reason, according to Hoveden, given by Gilbert for his sentence was that they would not save children by baptism. He also preserves a " Letter of Peter, titular of St. Chrysogonus, Cardinal, Priest, and Legate of the Apostolic See," written in 1178, in which, speaking of the Albigenses, he says, " Others stoutly maintained to their faces that they had heard from them that baptism was of no use to infants." Collier[||] gives the meaning of Hoveden correctly when he represents him as stating, in reference to the Albigenses, " These heretics refused to own infant baptism." Evervinus, in a letter to St. Bernard, speaking evidently of Albigenses, in Cologne, in 1147, and consequently before the conversion of Peter Waldo, says, " They do not believe infant baptism, alleging that place of the gospel, 'Whosoever shall believe and be baptized shall be saved.'" Eckbert, in 1160, in his work against the Cathari, written in thirteen discourses, says in the first, " They say that baptism profits nothing to children who are baptized, for they cannot seek baptism by themselves, because they can make no profession of faith."

The Paulicians received their name because they were specially the disciples of the Apostle Paul. They were established as a denomination by a gift of the Scriptures to their founder, through which he received Christ, became a mighty teacher, and gathered not converts simply, but churches.

At the great trial in Thoulouse in 1176 they would not accept anything as an authority but the New Testament. Throughout their wide-spread fields of toil from Armenia to Britain, and from one end of Europe to the other, and throughout the nine hundred years of their heroic sufferings and astonishing successes, they have always shown supreme regard for the Word of God. If these men, coming from the original cradle of our race, journeying through Thrace, Bulgaria, Bosnia, Italy, France, and Germany, and visiting even Britain, were not Baptists, they were very like them.

If all the wicked slanders about them were discarded it would most probably be found that some of them had little in common with us, but that the majority, while redundant and deficient in some things as measured by Baptist doctrines, were substantially on our platform. This position about

---

[*] Bibliotheca Patrum, tom. iv. p. ii., Coll. 746.
[†] Du Pin's Eccles. Hist., ii. 456. Dublin.
[‡] Du Pin, ii. 392.
[§] Annals of Roger De Hoveden, i. 427, 480. London, 1853.
[||] Collier's Eccles. Hist., ii. 358. London, 1840.

the Paulicians of the East is ably defended by Dr. L. P. Brockett in "The Bogomils."

Albritton, Rev. J. T., was born in Greene Co., N. C., Jan. 26, 1836; baptized by Rev. J. D. Coulling; ordained in 1856. Is an able and useful minister; was, and is now, pastor of Selma and other churches.

Alden, Rev. John, was born in Ashfield, Mass., Jan. 10, 1806, and was a graduate of Amherst College, in the class of 1831. He took a course of theological study at Newton, which he completed in 1833, and was ordained the same year at Shelburne Falls, Mass., where he remained for seven years,—from 1833 to 1840. His next settlement was at North Adams, Mass. He was the pastor of the church in this place for five years, and of the church at Fayville two years. In 1848 he removed to Westfield, Mass., and was pastor of the church there five years. Subsequently he removed to Windsor, Vt. For several years he was an agent of the American Baptist Missionary Union, and of the American and Foreign Bible Society. Mr. Alden retired from active service some years since, and now resides in Providence, R. I.

Alden, Rev. Noah, was born in Middleborough, Mass., May 30, 1725. On his father's side he was a lineal descendant from John Alden, famous in the early annals of the Pilgrims of Plymouth. Both himself and wife became members of the Congregational church in Stafford, Conn., whither they had removed. He changed his sentiments on the mode and subjects of Christian baptism in 1753, and became a member of a Baptist church. Feeling it his duty to preach the gospel, he was ordained at Stafford on the 5th of June, 1755, and was pastor of the Baptist church in that place for ten years. In 1766 he was installed as pastor of the church in Bellingham, Mass., where his ministry was attended with the Divine blessing.

Mr. Alden was active, not only in his special vocation as a minister of the gospel, but as a delegate from Bellingham to the State Convention; he did good service in drafting a constitution for the State of Massachusetts, pleading especially the cause of religious liberty. He performed also other acceptable service as a public man. As a wise counselor he was often called to adjust difficulties in churches, and to assist in the examination and ordination of candidates for the Christian ministry. Mr. Alden died May 5, 1797. "He was," says Dr. A. Fisher, "for many years one of our most distinguished and honored ministers, and his name deserves to be held in grateful remembrance."

Alden, William H., D.D., was born in Middleborough, Mass. He graduated at Brown University in the class of 1849, and at the Newton Theological Institute in the class of 1852. He was ordained pastor of the church in North Attleborough, Mass., where he remained from 1852 to 1857. He was then called to the pastorate of the First Baptist church in Lowell, officiating there from 1857 to 1864. For four years he was pastor of the Tabernacle church in Albany. He removed to Portsmouth, N. H., in 1868, and has been the pastor of the Baptist church in that city down to the present time.

The degree of Doctor of Divinity was conferred on Dr. Alden by Colby University in 1873.

Alderson, Rev. John, was born in New Jersey, March 5, 1738, and was the first Baptist minister that visited the southern part of West Virginia. As early as 1777 he settled on Greenbrier River, in Greenbrier County, near the present site of the town of Alderson. Owing to the hostility of the Indians, he and his neighbors were compelled, at times, to take shelter in a fort on Wolf Creek, and much of the time he followed the plow with his rifle swinging by his side. He commenced preaching in the forts, and in the houses of the settlers. In 1781 the Greenbrier church was organized with 12 members, and as this was the fourth church in what is now the State of West Virginia, its field included a large portion of the State. Mr. Alderson labored as a minister for seven years without seeing another Baptist preacher. Though he lived at this early day, and comparatively isolated in his home, he was an enthusiastic missionary; doing much personal work, and urging his brethren to spread the gospel over the State. He was mighty in the Scriptures, a good preacher, a wise counselor, and an untiring worker. He died March 5, 1821, at the advanced age of eighty-three years, in great peace, and his body now sleeps in the cemetery adjoining the Greenbrier church. His influence lives among his descendants and others to-day.

Aldis, John, one of the most eminent English preachers of the present time, but now retired from stated ministerial service, studied at Horton College, Bradford, and commenced his ministry at Manchester in 1829. During his first pastorate he established his reputation as a pulpit orator of rare gifts, and attracted a large circle of cultivated hearers. After seven years' pastoral service at Manchester, he was invited to take the oversight of the church at Maze Pond, London, one of the oldest and most influential Baptist churches of the metropolis. Here Mr. Aldis labored with distinguished ability and success seventeen years, and then removed to Reading. At the close of fifteen years' ministry at Reading, he accepted a call to the church at Plymouth, where he labored for nearly eight years, closing an active life of upwards of forty-seven years of uninterrupted public service in May, 1877. During this long period Mr. Aldis enjoyed almost unbroken health, and was abundant in labors. His chastened and vigorous eloquence, his high culture, and generous public spirit early placed him in the first rank of the leaders of the denomination. He was president of the Baptist Union in 1866. Three of his sons have distinguished themselves at Cambridge University, the eldest, Mr. William Steadman Aldis, being senior wrangler in 1861. This was the first time in the history of the university that a non-conformist student had won the honor. Mr. W. S. Aldis's success, and his subsequent steadfast adhesion to Baptist principles (which involved the forfeiture of the valuable prizes bestowed upon a senior wrangler), largely contributed to the abolition of religious tests in the universities, and the opening of the college fellowships and other lucrative honors to non-conformists as well as to the members of the Established Church.

Aldrich, Rev. Byron L., born in Thompson, Conn., in 1849, received a thorough education, became a fine linguist, a master of seven languages, graduated at Chicago University in 1873, entered the ministry, and located in California, where he became pastor of the Fifth church, San Francisco, the Napa, and Nevada City churches. He is a preacher of much ability, but his thorough classical training fitted him for the duties of instructor. He held for some time an important position in one of the San Francisco high schools, and was two years Professor of Modern Languages in California College. He is now pastor at Nevada City.

Aldrich, Rev. Jonathan, was born at St. Johnsbury, Vt., Sept. 2, 1799. He pursued his preparatory studies at Peacham, Vt., and with his uncle, Rev. Dr. Abial Fisher, then residing in Bellingham, Mass. So far was he advanced in his studies that he was able to enter the Sophomore class in Brown University in 1823. He graduated in 1826, and having spent a year in theological study at Newton, he was ordained pastor of the Baptist church in West Dedham, in January, 1828. Subsequently, he had short pastorates in East Cambridge, Mass., Worcester, Mass., Newburyport, Mass., Philadelphia, Pa., Baltimore, Md., and Middleborough, Mass. In 1853 he was appointed an agent by the Missionary Union to collect funds for foreign missions. He continued in the employ of the society until his death, a period of about nine years. He was a settled pastor for twenty-five years, and was highly esteemed as an active, zealous worker in the cause of his Master. His death occurred on Jan. 19, 1862.

Allen, Hon. Alanson, was born in Bristol, Vt., Aug. 22, 1800. He lived twenty years after cherishing a hope in Christ before he made a public profession of his faith in the Redeemer. After residing some years in Bristol, he removed to Hartford, N. Y., where he remained eight years engaged in mercantile business. In 1836 he went to Fair Haven, Vt., which was his home through the rest of his life. Commencing business in a somewhat humble way, he went on year after year enlarging

HON. ALANSON ALLEN.

his operations, making a specialty of quarrying the slate of the region in which he lived, which, under the different forms of roofing and school slate, found its way into the markets of the country. He then went into the marble business, and developed the famous quarries of West Rutland, Vt. After some years he retired from the marble business and again resumed his old occupation of slate-quarrying.

Mr. Allen, from intelligent conviction, was a decided Baptist, and took the liveliest interest in all matters pertaining to the prosperity of his denomination. He was frequently a member of the Board of the State Convention, and everywhere recognized in Vermont as a firm and liberal Baptist. As might be supposed, he was a friend to all good causes. The prosperity of the town in which he lived was largely due to his enterprise. He was a public-spirited citizen, ready to second any plan devised for its welfare. Twice he was a member of the State Senate, two years each time. He was also assistant judge for a time, and one of the State's Presidential electors for President Grant's second term. His death occurred Sept. 5, 1878.

Allen, Rev. Hogan, missionary of the General Association of Southeast Arkansas, was born in North Carolina in 1829; came to Arkansas in 1851; united with the Methodists, and was a preacher in that connection from 1858 to 1861. He then united with the Baptists, and was at once licensed, and ordained the following year. His labors have been chiefly confined to Ashley and Drew Counties, Ark., and he has served the following churches: Flat Creek, seven years; Mount Olive, fourteen years; Promised Land, seven years; Fellowship, ten years; Mount Zion, six years; and Beulah, New Prospect, Poplar Bluff, Egypt, Gilgal, and other churches a part of the time.

Allen, Rev. Marvin, whose name was once familiar to all Michigan Baptists, was born in Fabius, N. Y., Nov. 1, 1800. He graduated from Hamilton in one of the earlier classes, and labored ten years in Williamson and Canandaigua. He was called to Adrian in 1837, and in 1844 became pastor of the church in Ann Arbor. Failing health interfered with his ministerial labors, but his ardent zeal for the cause of Christ, not allowing him to rest, urged him on to the work of the denomination at large. He became general agent of the Convention, and as such was very useful in organizing its different departments of work and in systematizing the contributions of the churches and stimulating them to further efforts. From 1848 until his death, in 1861, he was the publisher of the *Michigan Christian Herald*. He was an untiring worker throughout the entire State, and became an almost indispensable part of all denominational gatherings. As a man of business his character was untarnished, and he fulfilled all the trusts committed to his care without leaving a stain upon his name.

Allen, Rev. Orsemus, was born at Westfield, Mass., in 1804. At the age of sixteen was baptized into the fellowship of the Westfield Baptist church. After graduating from Hamilton Literary and Theological Institution, was ordained pastor of the church at Seneca Falls, N. Y., where he remained four years. After a short interval took charge of the church at Bristol, Conn., where he continued many years. Forced by ill health from the ministry, he removed about 1845 to Ohio, where he engaged in business. For twenty-two years was treasurer of the Ohio Baptist State Convention, and in this position won the confidence and affection of his brethren throughout the entire State. Died in Columbus, O., May 19, 1870.

Allen, Rev. William B., for twenty-seven years moderator of the Eastern Louisiana Association, was born in South Carolina in 1809, and began to preach at the age of twenty. Shortly after he removed to Eastern Louisiana and settled in Livingston Parish, where he has successfully labored until the present time, having served one church more than forty years.

Alexander, Charles, M.D., a prominent physician of Eau Claire, Wis., was born at Pittston, Me., April 28, 1824. He was deprived of his father and mother in his childhood, and at the age of five years he was placed in the family of Rufus Allen, of Farmington, Me., which became his home until seventeen years of age. Being thrown entirely upon his own resources he had a sharp struggle in the school of adversity; and yet, overcoming all obstacles, he completed courses of study in the academies at Yarmouth and Farmington, Me., and fitted himself for the Sophomore class in Bowdoin College. In 1845 he began the study of medicine with Dr. W. H. Allen, of Orono, Penobscot Co. He attended lectures at the Medical Department of Harvard University, Jefferson Medical College, Philadelphia, and the Medical Department of the University of New York, from which he received his diploma March 8, 1850. Dr. Alexander began the practice of his profession at Orono, where he remained eight years. He entered the army as surgeon of the 16th Regiment Maine Volunteers, and remained in the service until the close of the war. At Gettysburg he was wounded and taken prisoner. He was twice promoted for distinguished services. In September, 1866, he removed from his native State to Wisconsin, and settled at Eau Claire, which has since been his home. He has an extensive practice.

For many years he has been a member of the Baptist Church. He is the senior deacon in the Baptist church of Eau Claire, and superintendent of the Sunday-school. He is a popular lecturer on geology and chemistry, of which sciences he has a thorough knowledge. He is often heard with great favor on the subject of temperance, always bringing to its treatment his knowledge of its relation to science.

Alexander, Rev. Lewis D., was born in Wilkes Co., N. C., Sept. 17, 1799. He emigrated with his parents to Scott Co., Ky., in 1803; was converted and baptized into the fellowship of Stamping-Ground church by James Suggett in 1823. After exercising profitably his gift as an exhorter two or three years, he settled in Owen Co., Ky., in 1835; was ordained at New Liberty church in March, 1836, and became its pastor in 1838. His preaching gifts were extraordinary, and no minister in Concord Association, of which he was a member, ever exercised a stronger or more beneficial influence. He baptized about 2000 persons, and was moderator of Concord Association twenty-two years. He died Dec. 20, 1862.

Allison, Rev. Burgiss, D.D., was born in Bordentown, N. J., Aug. 17, 1753. He was converted young, and became a member of the Upper Freehold church, in his native State. From sixteen years of age he had a strong desire to preach the gospel, and he carried out this call of God in Bordentown for several years on Sunday evenings. He studied for the ministry under Dr. Samuel Jones, of Lower Dublin, Pa., and in Rhode Island College. He was ordained pastor of the church of Bordentown, over which he presided for many years, and in which he always cherished a fatherly interest.

Dr. Allison possessed an intellect of a high order, and a culture seldom enjoyed in his day. Senator Horatio Gates Jones says, "He occupied a high position among the most scientific men of his day; he was devoted to such pursuits and to philosophical inquiries; he became deeply interested in the proposed propulsion of boats by steam." The celebrated Morgan Edwards says of him, "He is as remarkable a mechanic as he is an artist and philosopher; the lathe, the plane, the hammer, the chisel, the graver, etc., have displayed his skill in the use of tools. His accomplishments have made him a member of our [the American] Philosophical Society."

Dr. Allison was acquainted with the French, Spanish, and Portuguese, as well as with the dead languages. He was skilled in music, drawing, and painting, and in praying, preaching Jesus, and walking humbly with his God.

He was a chaplain to Congress for a time, and afterwards at the navy-yard in Washington, where he died Feb. 20, 1827.

Almira College.—This excellent school, merely founded with a view to the promotion of both education and general culture in Southern Illinois, was the result of a visit made to Greenville, Ill., in 1854, by Prof. John B. White, then of Wake Forest College, in North Carolina. It was founded as a college for young ladies. The gift of $6000 towards its endowment by Mrs. Morse, wife of Prof. Morse, an old friend and college associate of Prof. White, and visiting in Greenville, led to the naming of the college for this generous lady. Hence its name,—Almira College. The citizens of Greenville and Bond County entered with much zeal into the enterprise, and a handsome and commodious building was soon erected upon a beautiful site near the town. The cost of the building was $20,000. It is three stories in height, 146 feet long and 46 wide. Prof. White was made president of the new college, and has remained so during its entire history, with the exception of an interval spent as chaplain in the army during the war. Like all Western schools, Almira College has had to contend with many financial embarrassments, but has during its entire history maintained a very high rank as a school of instruction for young women.

Alston, Rev. John, was born a slave in the State of South Carolina, and was emancipated by the results of the late war after his removal to Florida. He resides at Fernandina, where he has built up a large, well-disciplined church, over which he presides as a much-respected bishop. The church has several mission stations, which are under his special supervision, and they have built and nearly finished a large and beautiful house of worship in the Gothic style. The work has been done under the pastor's direction, and some of it by his own hands.

Mr. Alston went to New York and solicited aid to build the house. For some time he was assisted by the Home Mission Society while the church was weak. He is a prominent man in his Association and in the State. As a speaker he is dignified and calm, and he uses very good language. He reads much, and his memory is retentive.

Mr. Alston is a thorough and an intelligent Baptist, and is remarkably well informed in the "faith and order" of his denomination. He is quick to discern any innovations among his colored brethren, to whom his counsels are of great value.

Ambler, Rev. I. V., was born in Saratoga Co., N. Y., in 1814. He graduated at Madison University; was ordained pastor of the Baptist church of Lanesborough, Mass., in which he labored for eight years during his first settlement, and to which he returned after a two years' absence for a second period of nine years. After serving the American and Foreign Bible Society and the American Baptist Home Mission Society as "agent," he became district secretary of the American Baptist Missionary Union for Pennsylvania, Delaware, New Jersey, and the District of Columbia. He discharged the duties of this laborious office with great fidelity, wisdom, and courtesy for eleven years, knitting the hearts of the pastors and church members to himself to an extent never surpassed, and seldom equaled, by the brethren who hold such difficult positions. The writer became acquainted with Mr. Ambler twenty-four years before his death, was never under any obligation to him, knew him intimately, and was constrained to regard him as one of the best Christian men and most efficient secretaries he has ever known. He had accepted a call to the church at Media, Pa., and was in Pittsfield, Mass., preparing for removal to his new field, when he was called to the skies. He was sixty-four years of age. His death occasioned wide-spread grief.

Ambrose, Rev. J. E., one of the pioneer Baptist ministers of Illinois, was born in Sutton, N. H., July 5, 1810, and born again at Rochester, N. Y., in 1826, and baptized there in May of that year into the fellowship of the First Baptist church. By that church he was licensed to preach at twenty years of age. In 1834, under appointment of the Home Mission Society, he removed to Illinois, and began labor in the northern part of that State. He was the first pastor of the churches of Hadley, Plainfield, Batavia, and St. Charles. In 1838 he was called to Elgin; and in all these places he was a laborious and successful missionary. In 1838 he became connected with the *Northwestern Baptist,* a semi-monthly, and subsequently with the *Western Christian*, published at Elgin, issuing the latter paper, as its publisher, some five years. This was the beginning of journalism in Northern Illinois. Mr. Ambrose has been a resident of Illinois nearly forty years. His home is now in California.

American and Foreign Bible Society.—This society was organized in 1837 with Rev. Dr. Spencer H. Cone, President; Charles G. Sommers, Corresponding Secretary; William Colgate, Treasurer; John West, Recording Secretary; and with thirty-one Vice-Presidents. The occasion of its organization was the refusal of the American Bible Society to appropriate funds for the printing and circulation of the translations made by the Baptist missionaries in India, in which the words relating to baptism were rendered by those equivalent to immersion. Its first annual meeting was held in Oliver Street Baptist church. There were delegates from fifteen States, and much enthusiasm prevailed. The treasurer reported contributions amounting to $38,714.14. Ninety-eight auxiliaries were added to it during the year. In its first report it recorded the names of 92 life-directors and 420 life-members, the former obtained by the payment of $100, the latter by $30 each. Appropriations were made to aid in printing and circulating the Scriptures in various languages and dialects of the East.

The society made rapid progress, as with few exceptions all the Baptists of America united in its support. At the annual meeting in May, 1850, a majority of the Board of Managers recommended the society to engage in the revision of the English Scriptures. The recommendation of the Board was rejected, and the action resulted in the organization of the American Bible Union, and the withdrawal of many of the supporters of the society. Up to this time it had received and disbursed upwards of $411,000.

In 1852 the project of building a Bible House in Nassau Street, New York, was started by friends of the society, and in 1858 the work was accomplished, and a large marble building was presented to the society, for which $80,000 had been paid. A considerable indebtedness remained, but it was expected that the rents for rooms not needed by the society would speedily extinguish it. The expectation was not realized, and eventually the Bible House passed into other hands.

The entire amount of money raised by the society and disbursed for the distribution of the Scriptures in home and foreign countries up to the date of this writing is $1,294,898.27.

Amsbury, Deacon Jabez, son of Mowry and Betsey Whipple (Clark) Amsbury, was born Oct. 13, 1825, in Newton, Mass. He removed to Killingly, Conn., in 1826. He was educated at Wesleyan and Leicester Academies, Mass. In 1842 he moved to Norwich, Conn., and in February, 1846, was converted and baptized into the fellowship of the Central Baptist church, under the ministry of Rev. M. G. Clark. In 1852 he became teller in Quinebaug Bank. In 1855 he was chosen cashier of Danbury Bank, and removed to that place, where he still (1880) fills the office. He was superintendent of a Sunday-school in Norwich three years, and of that of the Second Baptist church in Danbury in 1854–55, and from 1870 to the present time; trustee of the Second Baptist Society for fifteen years; deacon since 1862; one of the principal officers of the borough of Danbury since 1862; been constantly in Sunday-school work since 1845; for past eleven years deputy collector of United States Internal Revenue; clerk of board of education of Danbury, and chairman of Centre District. A pure, earnest, energetic, executive man.

ANABAPTISTS.

The name "Anabaptist" was originally a reproachful epithet applied to those Christians in the time of the Reformation who, from rigid adherence to the Scriptures as the infallible and all-sufficient standard of faith and practice, and from the evident incompatibility of infant baptism with regenerate church membership, rejected infant baptism and inaugurated churches of their own on the basis of believers' baptism. While reproached by their enemies with *rebaptizing* those that had been already baptized in the established churches, they maintained that the baptism of believers, such as was administered by themselves, was the only Christian baptism, the baptism of infants being unworthy of the name.

Anabaptists, The German and Swiss.—The Anabaptist Reformation was nothing more than a consistent carrying out of the principles at first laid down by the Reformers, Luther and Zwingle, who both proposed, at the outset, to make the Bible the only standard of faith and practice. Many men of great religious earnestness, filled with this idea, could not bear to see the godly and the ungodly living together in the church, the latter as well as the former partaking of the Lord's Supper. The necessity of a separation of Christians from the ungodly was, therefore, the most fundamental thing with the Anabaptists of the sixteenth century, as it is with Baptists to-day. If only the regenerate are to be members of this body, it follows, necessarily, that those baptized in unconscious infancy, or later in life without faith, are not truly baptized. They understood the Scripture to make faith a prerequisite to baptism; and they found in Scripture no precept nor example for infant baptism. They rejected infant baptism as a matter of course and baptized anew all that came to them. Hence the name of reproach—"Anabaptist." Luther was as uncompromising as Baptists in making personal faith prerequisite to valid baptism. He reproached the Waldenses for baptizing infants, and yet denying that such infants have faith, thus taking the name of the Lord in vain. Not baptism, Luther held, but personal faith, justifies. If the infant has not personal faith, parents lie when they say for it "I believe." But Luther maintained that through the prayers of the church the infant does have faith, and he defied his adversaries to prove the contrary. This was more than the average man could believe. Hence he would be likely to accept the principle and to reject the application. Luther attached great importance to baptism: Zwingle very little. Hübmaier and Grebel both asserted that, in private conversation with them, Zwingle had expressed himself against infant baptism. His earlier writings show that for a time he doubted the scripturalness of infant baptism, and preferred to postpone baptism until the subject should be able to profess his faith. We have indisputable evidence that almost every other leader in the Reformation, Melancthon, Œcolampadius, Capito, etc., had a struggle over the question of baptism. It seems equally certain that they were deterred from rejecting infant baptism by the manifest consequences of the Baptist position. It appeared to them impossible that any movement should succeed which should lose the support of the civil powers, and should withdraw the true Christians from the mass of the people. Endless divisions, the triumph of the papists, and the entire overthrow of the Reformation, seemed to them inevitable. Hence their defense of infant baptism, and their zeal in the suppression of the Anabaptists. Those that rejected infant baptism believed that Zwingle thought as they did, but held back from unworthy motives. We may divide the Anabaptists into three classes: (1) *The fanatical Anabaptists*. (2) *The Baptist Anabaptists*. (3) *The mystical Anabaptists*. Great injustice has been done to many that fall under the name Anabaptist by failing to make this distinction. Was a certain party fanatical? The stigma is attached to all. Were a few mystics Anabaptists? All classes are blamed for it.

Anabaptists, The Fanatical.—These were for the most part a result of Luther's earlier writings. It is remarkable that fanatical developments occurred in connection with Lutheranism, and not in connection with Zwinglianism.

Thomas Münzer and the Zwickau Prophets.—Thomas Münzer was never really an Anabaptist. Though he rejected infant baptism in theory, he held to it in practice, and never submitted to rebaptism himself nor rebaptized others. Yet he is usually regarded as the forerunner of the movement, and he certainly was influential in that direction. Having studied previously at Halle, he came to Wittenberg, where he came under Luther's influence, and where he received his Doctor's degree. Like Luther, Münzer was a great reader of the German Mystics, and when Luther came forward as a Reformer, Münzer became one of his most decided and faithful supporters. On Luther's recommendation he came to Zwickau in 1520 as parish priest. Here he entered into controversy with the Erasmic rationalistic Egranus. The common people, especially the weavers, took sides with Münzer. Chief among these was Nicholas Storch, a Silesian, probably a Waldensian. Münzer was naturally inclined to fanaticism, and this controversy, together with the zealous support he received from the common people, did much to bring it out. He regarded Luther's movement as a half-way affair, and demanded the establishment of a pure church. He denounced Luther as an incapable man, who allowed the people to continue in their old sins, taught them the uselessness of works, and preached a dead faith more contradictory to the gospel than the teachings of the papists. While he held to the inspiration of the Scriptures, Münzer maintained that the letter of Scripture is of no value without the enlightenment of the Spirit, and that to believers God communicates truth directly alike in connection with and apart from the Scriptures. The excitement among the common people became intense, and Storch and others began to prophesy, to demand the abolition of all papal forms, and objects, and to speak against infant baptism. Münzer had gone to Bohemia to preach in 1521. Here he published an enthusiastic address to the people in German, Bohemian, and Latin, denouncing the priests, and declaring that a new era was at hand, and that if the people should not accept the gospel they would fall a prey to the Turks. Meanwhile, Storch's party attempted to carry out their ideas by force, and proclaimed that they had a mission to establish the kingdom of Christ on earth. They were suppressed by the authorities, and some of them thrown into prison; but Storch, Stubner, and Cellarius escaped and fled to Wittenberg. Stubner, a former student of the university, was entertained by Melancthon, who for a time was profoundly impressed by the prophets. Carlstadt especially was brought under their influence. Storch traveled widely in Germany and Silesia, disseminating his views mostly among the peasants. He seems to have been a man of deep piety, great knowledge of Scripture, and uncommon zeal and activity in propagating his views. In Silesia, he is said to have labored for some time in connection with Lutheranism, which had just been planted there, withholding his peculiar views until he had gained a sufficient influence to preach them effectively. Then he brought large numbers to his views. Here also the attempt to "set up the kingdom of God on earth" was accompanied with tumult, and Storch was driven from Glogau. Driven from place to place, he established Anabaptist communities in various places, in the villages, and among the peasants. From Silesia Storch went to Bavaria, where he fell sick and died. But he left behind him many disciples, and two strong men who became leaders: Jacob Hutter and Gabriel Scherding. From Silesia and Bavaria many Anabaptists fled into Moravia and Poland, where they became very numerous, and although they were afterwards persecuted severely they continued to exist for a long time. The followers of Storch practiced in many instances community of goods, and under persecution manifested some fanaticism. But we do Storch some injustice in classing him among the fanatics. Inasmuch, however, as he was closely connected with Münzer at the beginning, and inasmuch as our information about him is not definite, we class him here with the expression of a probability that he repudiated much of Münzer's proceedings, and was in most respects a true preacher of the gospel. In 1523, Münzer became pastor at Alstedt. Here he married a nun, set aside the Latin Liturgy and prepared a German one. In this he retained infant baptism. About the beginning of 1524 he published two tracts against Luther's doctrines with regard to faith and baptism. He had become convinced of the unscripturalness of infant baptism, yet continued to administer it, telling the people that true baptism was baptism of the Spirit. Münzer's ministry in Alstedt was brought to a close by the iconoclastic zeal of his followers. His preaching all along was of a democratical tendency, for he longed to see all men free and in the enjoyment of their rights. During this year he went to Switzerland, where he attempted to persuade Œcolampadius and others of the right of the people to revolt against oppression. Here also he probably met the men who soon became leaders of the Swiss Anabaptists: Grebel, Manz, Hübmaier, etc. His main object in this tour seems to have been to secure co-operation in the impending struggle for liberty. Returning to Muhlhausen he became chief pastor and member of the Council. The whole region was soon under his influence. Luther visited the principal towns and attempted to dissuade the people from revolution. He also attempted to induce the rulers to accord to the peasants their rights. But in neither respect did he succeed. When the peasants revolted, Luther, although he knew that they had cause for dissatisfaction, turned against them and counseled the most unmerciful proceedings. Münzer showed no military capacity. The peasants had no military discipline, and were deceived by Münzer into reliance upon miraculous divine assistance. The result was that they were massacred in large numbers. Münzer was taken prisoner and afterwards beheaded.

Melchior Hoffman, born in Sweden, accepted Luther's doctrine about 1523, preached with great zeal in Denmark and Sweden, laboring with his hands for his support. In the same year he came under the influence of Storch and Münzer. Like these, he believed that the last day was at hand, and with great earnestness warned men to turn from their sins. His interpretation of Scripture, especially the prophetical parts, which he freely applied to his own time, and his constant effort to arouse men to flee from the wrath to come, led to his being hunted from place to place by Lutherans as well as by papists.

In 1526, King Frederick of Denmark came to his aid and gave him a comfortable stipend and freedom to preach the gospel throughout Holstein. Here Hoffman remained about two years, and might have remained longer had he not declared in favor of the Carlstadt-Zwinglian view of the Lord's Supper. This led to controversy, which caused his expulsion and the confiscation of his goods. In company with Carlstadt he took refuge in Switzerland, and in 1529 went to Strassburg. Here he was joyfully received by the Zwinglians, but his preaching soon disgusted them, the difficulty here, as elsewhere, being that he claimed a special inspiration of God to interpret Scripture, and did this in a manner that tended to produce an unwholesome popular excitement. Hoffman now came to see that there was a wide breach between him and the other evangelical preachers. Their apprehension of Scripture, he thought, was an apprehension of the letter, his, of the spirit. Their religion was of the understanding, his, of the heart. Their religion admitted of pride and pomp, his, only of humility. The Anabaptists had by this time become numerous in Southern Germany. When Hoffman came to know them it is not strange that he should have been led to unite with them. In 1530 he declared his acceptance of their views on baptism, justification, free-will, church discipline, etc.; and as most of the Anabaptist leaders had either suffered martyrdom or died of the pest, Hoffman became a leader among them, and led many to his own fanatical and false views. Under Hoffman's influence the opinions of the Anabaptists, which had been in great part sound and biblical, underwent many changes. Hoffman believed that Christ did not receive his body from the virgin. This view was perpetuated by the Mennonites (a sort of Manichean view). His Millenarian views also became common among the Anabaptists. Through him the Anabaptist movement spread over all the Netherlands, and he came to be regarded as a great prophet. At Embden, in Friesland, the Anabaptists became so strong that they were able to baptize openly in the churches and on the streets. The most influential leader in the Netherlands (after Hoffman) was Matthiesen. In 1532 Hoffman was thrown into prison in Strassburg. Here he became more and more fanatical. Several men and women began to have visions and to interpret them with reference to current events. Hoffman they called Elias; Schwenkfeldt was Enoch, etc. The enthusiasm spread, and the Anabaptist movement made rapid conquests. Persecution was probably the cause, and certainly a means of promoting the fanaticism. Hoffman died in prison, January, 1543, after more than ten years' confinement.

The Münster Uproar.—The episode in the history of the Reformation that did most to make the Anabaptists abominable in the eyes of the world, and from the effects of which Baptists long suffered in England and America, and even now suffer in Germany, was the Münster kingdom. Doubtless the preaching of Hoffman, and still more that of his followers, had something to do with this event. Yet the idea that this preaching constitutes the chief factor is utterly unfounded. In 1524-25, Münster shared in the communistic movement (Peasants' War), but the magistrates and clergy had been strong enough to crush out the communism and Lutheranism together. After this the Reformation gained scarcely any visible ground there until 1529. About this time, Bernard Rothmann, an educated and eloquent young man, as chaplain in the collegiate church at St. Mauritz, near Münster, began to preach Protestant sermons. Despite the determined opposition of magistrates and clergy, the Münster people forsook the parish churches and flocked to St. Mauritz. In 1533 the Protestants obtained in Münster the right to the free exercise of their religion, and six parish churches came into their hands. Soon they obtained the supremacy in the Council, and began to carry out their principles of reform. The bishop and Romish clergy were driven away, and an army was equipped for the protection of Lutheranism. Thousands of insurrectionary spirits assembled from the surrounding regions, and among them many of the Hoffmanite Anabaptists. It was natural that, when these latter saw the papal party crushed, they should have supposed that the kingdom of Christ was about to be set up at Münster. In 1532, Rothmann, the recognized leader of the Lutheran party at Münster, became an Anabaptist. As a Lutheran, Rothmann is said to have been dissolute. When he became an Anabaptist he adopted an almost ascetical mode of life. He exhorted the people to the practice of charity and humility, and warned them against yielding to the senses and passions. He also declared that the millennium had come, and that the end of the world would come a thousand years later. The Anabaptists gained the ascendancy just as the Lutherans had done before them. Once in full power, their fanaticism increased until a king was set up, polygamy was introduced in accordance with pretended revelations of the Spirit, and many other abominations were practiced. After a few months the Münster kingdom was overthrown and the leaders executed. This affair has commonly been looked upon as a natural culmination of Anabaptism. The fact is, that Lutheranism was responsible for it far more than Anabaptism, and that the rigor with which evangelical Christianity was suppressed in Münster until 1531 was the most potent cause of all.

It may be remarked that while none of the Anabaptists were free from what we regard as errors, the great body of the Swiss Anabaptists made a very close approach to our position; and if we take into consideration the circumstances under which they were placed, we shall not be inclined to judge them harshly in the things wherein they seem to have gone astray. Fundamentally they were Baptists, but it required time for them to reach a complete development. Röubli, when expelled from Basle, came to Wyticon, near Zürich, and under his influence the parishioners almost all refused to have their children baptized, as early as 1524. Röubli did not yet insist on rebaptism, but simply set forth the unscripturalness of infant baptism. In 1524, Grebel, Manz, and others began to manifest their dissatisfaction with the state of ecclesiastical affairs at Zürich. They pressed upon Zwingle the necessity of a further reformation of the churches, and reproved him for tardiness and coldness in the matter. Zwingle urged that the unregenerate had been retained in the churches, on the ground that "he that is not against us is for us;" and that in the parable it is commanded to let the tares grow with the wheat. They objected also to the dependence of religion on the civil magistracy. They were answered that the magistracy, while not free from human elements, was not merely not opposed to the Word of God, but gave protection to the preaching of the same. They soon began to accuse Zwingle of sacrificing willfully the truth in order to maintain the favor of the civil rulers. They now began to absent themselves from the churches, to hold secret meetings, in which they discussed freely the desirableness of setting up pure churches. During this year the writings of Carlstadt and Münzer became known to them, and they instituted a correspondence with these men. How far the Zürich Anabaptists were influenced by Münzer it is not possible to ascertain. It is certain that they read his writings against Luther and admired them, before September, 1524. It is equally certain that they were not first led to their views of thorough reform by these writings, but were only strengthened and encouraged thereby in their already progressing work. The letter of Grebel, Manz, and others to Münzer, Sept. 5, 1524, shows that they had already advanced far beyond Münzer in their true views of reform, and that they felt themselves competent to pronounce judgment upon Münzer's inconsistencies and upon his revolutionary utterances. They expostulate with him for having translated the mass instead of abolishing it. They claim that there is no precept or example in the New Testament for the chanting of church services. They insist that what is not expressly taught by word or example is the same as if it were forbidden. No ceremonies are allowable in connection with the Lord's Supper, except the reading of the Scriptures bearing upon this ordinance. Common bread and common wine, without any idolatrous ceremonies, are to be employed in the Supper. The ordinance is declared to be an act of communion, expressive of the fact that communicants are truly one body. Inasmuch as the ordinance is a communion, no one is to partake of it alone on a sick-bed. It should not be celebrated in temples, on account of superstitious associations. It should be celebrated frequently. They exhort Münzer to abandon all non-scriptural usages, insisting that it is better that a few should believe and act in accordance with the Word of God than that many should believe in a doctrine mingled with falsehood. They are pleased with his theoretical rejection of infant baptism, but grieved that he should continue to practice what he has shown to be unwarranted. Moreover, they have heard that he has been preaching against the magistracy, and maintaining the right of Christians to resist abuses with the sword. They set forth their conviction that neither are we to protect the gospel nor ourselves with the sword. Thus the Swiss Anabaptists were from the outset free from fanaticism, and they appear even in 1524 not as disciples, but as teachers of Münzer. The opposition to the established church had by this time become so formidable, that the Council appointed a public disputation for Jan. 17, 1525; but there was no intention on the part of the Council or of Zwingle to decide the matter fairly in accordance with the weight of the arguments, and the decision of the Council was, therefore, against the Anabaptists; and a mandate was at once issued requiring the baptism within eight days of every unbaptized child, on pain of the banishment of the responsible parties. This action was soon followed by a prohibition of the assemblies of the radicals. Grebel and Manz were exhorted to leave off their disputing against infant baptism and in favor of regenerate church membership. In order to insure quiet, Röubli, Hätzer, and others, foreigners, were warned to leave the canton within eight days. This only led to greater boldness on the part of the Anabaptists, and soon George Blaurock, having first been baptized by Grebel, baptized a number of others. From this time the cause of the Anabaptists, notwithstanding the severe persecution to which they were subjected, made rapid progress. The breaking out of the Peasants' War in 1525 tended to increase the apprehensions of the Swiss authorities, and the rigor towards Anabaptists now became greater. Many, both men and women, were thrown into prison, and released only on the payment of heavy fines and the promise to desist from their heresy, or, in some cases, to leave the canton. The penalty of returning from banishment was drowning. Grebel, Manz, Hübmaier, and Blaurock were imprisoned and banished. Manz was finally drowned. Though continually harassed, these noble witnesses for Christ were very active, traveling from place to place, preaching at night in private houses to the people, who were anxious to hear. Some preachers baptized hundreds, if not thousands, of persons. From Zürich they spread throughout Switzerland, Southern Germany, the Netherlands, Moravia, etc.

Doctrines of the Swiss Anabaptists.—Although most of the leaders held some views peculiar to themselves, they may be said to have been agreed on the following points, as exhibited in the Confession of 1527, which also forms the basis of Zwingle's "Refutation" of 1527. (1) Baptism of believers. (The form of baptism never came up for discussion, and was, in some instances, immersion, but in most instances affusion.) (2) Discipline and exclusion of unworthy members. (3) Communion of baptized believers. (4) Separation from the impure churches and the world. This involved a refusal to have any social intercourse with evil-doers, to attend church services with unbelievers and those in error, to enter into marriage relations with them, etc. This absolute separatism gave them as much trouble, perhaps, as any other single doctrine. (5) They condemned the support of pastors by taxation of the people. The pastors, when they required support, were rather to be supported by voluntary offerings of the members. (6) As to magistracy, they maintained that true Christians, as being entirely subject to the laws of Christ, have no need of magistracy. Yet they did not deny that magistracy is necessary in the ungodly world; neither did they refuse obedience to magistracy in whatever did not come athwart their religious convictions. (7) They rejected oaths on the ground of Christ's command, "Swear not at all." They distinguished, however, between *swearing* as a promise with an oath to do or be something in the future, and *testifying* with regard to things past or present. The latter they did not condemn. Some of these Anabaptists held, in addition to these views, to community of goods, on the ground of the example of the Apostolic Church. But most of them insisted only on great liberality in relieving the wants of their needy brethren.

The Mystical and Speculative Anabaptists.—Here may be classed a large number of able and learned men, some who allied themselves with the Anabaptists and were active in evangelical work, as Denk and Haetzer; others who contented themselves with the theoretical rejection of infant baptism, but who either cared so little for ordinances in general as to be unwilling to make rejection of infant baptism a prominent feature of their creed, as Schwenkfeldt, Sebastian, Frank, etc., or else were so occupied with graver doctrinal controversies that their Anabaptist views attracted comparatively little attention, as Michael Servetus, Faustus Socinus, etc. Almost all the Antitrinitarians were rejecters of infant baptism, and several who diverged very widely from accepted views with regard to the person of Christ were especially noted as Anabaptists. With many the unspeakable love and mercy of God came to be a favorite theme. Such being the case, the propitiatory character of Christ's death came to be viewed by some as unnecessary and contrary to God's character. There being thus no need of an infinite sacrifice, many came to deny the absolute eternity of the Son and his absolute equality with the Father. On the other hand, it was perfectly natural that those who went so far as to call in question the great doctrinal formulæ should call in question such practices as infant baptism, for which there is no New Testament authority whatever. We are to make a clear distinction between men who were led into error by excessive Mysticism, as Denk, Haetzer, etc., and those who were professed rationalists, as Laelius and Faustus Socinus. (See DENK and HAETZER.)

Anabaptists, The Dutch.—We give separate consideration to the early Dutch Anabaptists, on account of their relation to the Mennonites, who still constitute an important party. We shall have space only for the following remarks. 1. A considerable number of moderate Swiss Anabaptists when persecuted at home took refuge in the Netherlands and made many converts before the time of Hoffman and Matthiesen. 2. Most of these were absorbed by the much more vigorous movement in which Hoffman's influence preponderated (1529–34). 3. A small number of Dutch Anabaptists maintained their moderation even in the time of the Münster uproar. 4. A still larger number were restored to their senses after the suppression of the Münster kingdom. 5. Menno Simon, a Roman Catholic priest, was led through a profound religious experience, gradually and almost independently of Anabaptist influence, to the rejection of infant baptism and the restoration of believer's baptism. After the Münster uproar, the better element of the Anabaptists in the Netherlands repudiated all connection with the Münster men; and with Menno Simon as their leader (1536 onward), soon became an exceedingly strong party. They suffered persecution under the Inquisition, and thousands died at the stake, but they finally secured toleration, and have maintained themselves to the present day. Their doctrines are, in the main, the same as those held by earlier Anabaptists. They reject infant baptism, oaths, magistracy, the sword, marriage with unbelievers, communion with the unregenerate. They adopted Hoffman's view as to Christ's body.

Anderson, Christopher, was born in Edinburgh in 1782. In the midst of youthful gayety and worldliness, he was attracted to the Circus chapel by the preaching of the celebrated Haldane brothers, then at the zenith of their remarkably useful career. The earnest appeals of James Haldane were the means of his conversion, and he joined the church at the Circus in 1799. This church was then a Pedobaptist body. The visit of some English Baptist students to the university led to a change in his opinions respecting baptism, and on being baptized he was summarily excommunicated from the Circus. In conjunction with his English student friends and others he endeavored to establish a Baptist church, and took a leading part in conducting the meetings of the little assembly. Andrew Fuller's first missionary tour in Scotland in 1799, and his subsequent visit in 1802, awakened in young Anderson a fervent interest in missions to the heathen. He sought an interview with Mr. Fuller, and was encouraged to offer himself for the Indian work. In 1805 he proceeded to the seminary at Olney, presided over by the revered Joseph Sutcliff, where missionary candidates attended a preparatory course of study. Anderson's constitution proving unfitted for the tropics, he was transferred to Bristol College, but his academical course was brief. His acceptable preaching procured him pressing invitations to settle as pastor in England, and the church at Prescott Street, London, which had lately lost its venerable and eminent pastor, Abraham Booth, urged him repeatedly to accept its charge. But his heart was set on raising a church in his native city. The Scotch Baptist churches of that period were not organized after his mind, and he thought them deficient in evangelistic zeal. He commenced labor in Edinburgh in 1806. After the erection of the spacious and handsome edifice known as Charlotte chapel, his ministry was well attended and the membership considerably increased. By his exertions the "Itinerant Society" was formed, now merged into the "Scottish Baptist Home Missionary Society," and also the Edinburgh branch of the British and Foreign Bible Society. Whilst abundant in home missionary labor, he never lost his first love for the foreign work which Andrew Fuller's preaching had inspired. Fuller, indeed, designated him as his successor in the secretaryship of the Baptist Missionary Society. Notwithstanding the pressure of his pulpit and philanthropic labors, he found time for a literary work involving great research and study. His zeal for the circulation of the Scriptures in the vernacular had kindled in him an enthusiastic admiration of the history of the English version, and some investigations which he prosecuted on the occasion of its third centenary celebration in 1835 led him to devote his energies to a work in which the "Annals of the English Bible" should be accurately and completely set forth. The results of his persevering toil appeared in two volumes, 8vo, 1845, under the above title. This work possesses the cardinal excellencies such a book should have. It is accurate and trustworthy in statement of facts, and casts light on many obscure and misunderstood matters. The noble character and services of Tyndale, Frith, and others are vividly presented, with the record of the singular providential circumstances of the origin and circulation of the English Bible. Some years before the preparation of the Annals he wrote a volume on "The Domestic Constitution, or the Family Circle the Source and Test of National Stability," which had a wide circulation, not only in Great Britain but also in this country. Several editions of it were published at Boston, New York, and elsewhere. In 1847 he revised and improved the book, and issued a new edition, with a preface which expressed forcibly the author's solicitude for the cause of civil and religious liberty, as exposed on the one hand to the machinations of the Romish priesthood, and on the other to the godless fervors of socialism. With this publication his literary labors ended, and retirement from public life became obviously necessary. On the 18th of February, 1852, he peacefully fell asleep in Jesus, aged seventy years. His numerous public labors secured him the respect of a wide circle of the worthiest of his countrymen as well as of his own denomination. His "Life and Letters," by his nephew, Hugh Anderson, is a valuable biography, especially rich in interesting correspondence.

Anderson, Rev. David, was born in Nelson Co., Ky., in 1806. He was converted and baptized at the age of twenty-seven years. He was ordained in 1850. He labored in Northwest Missouri for twenty years. At his death he was pastor of the Missouri City church. He was sound in doctrine and exemplary in life.

Anderson, Rev. Galusha, D.D., president of the University of Chicago, was born in Bergen, Genesee Co., N. Y., March 7, 1832. His father, though born in this country, is of pure Scottish descent, and was reared in the strict forms of the Scotch Presbyterians. In his own family government he was always kind, but very firm. In all weathers the whole family were required to attend church. Morning and evening prayer was never

REV. GALUSHA ANDERSON, D.D.

omitted. In this thoroughly religious method of family life his wife sustained him, while the children, as they advanced in years, fully realized the advantages of early fidelity to principle and to law. Dr. Anderson's father and mother are at this date (1880) both living, the former at the age of eighty, the latter of seventy-six.

Until the age of seventeen Galusha was engaged upon his father's farm, with such intervals of study as the district school of the place allowed. At that time he was determined to be a lawyer, made political speeches and delivered temperance lectures to cows and trees on the farm; being in politics a warm partisan of Henry Clay and a protective tariff on the one hand, and a staunch advocate of total abstinence on the other. He was also an active participant in the exercises of a debating society at the district school-house, reciting pieces at exhibitions given by the society, when everybody in the neighborhood came to hear.

At thirteen years of age he was converted, and was baptized by Rev. Martin Coleman in the town of Sweden, Monroe Co., N. Y., in the spring of 1844. At seventeen, after a severe struggle, he yielded to convictions of duty upon the subject of becoming a minister, and entered Alfred Academy, in Alleghany County, to prepare for college. In 1851 he entered the Sophomore class of the University of Rochester. His course at the university was an unusually successful one. He took the prize in Sophomore debate, the first prize in Sophomore declamation, had the place of honor at the Junior exhibition, and on behalf of the students of the university delivered the address to Dr. A. C. Kendrick upon his return from Greece. It may be also mentioned in this connection that Dr. Anderson was the first Rochester alumnus to receive the degree of Doctor of Divinity from that university. Graduating in 1854, he entered the Theological Seminary, and from it graduated in 1856. In the autumn of that year he was ordained as pastor of the Baptist church in Janesville, Wis.

At Janesville Dr. Anderson remained two years, a pastorate which he regards as the most successful work of his life. At the earnest solicitation of brethren both in St. Louis and in the East, he accepted, in the fall of 1858, the pastorate of the Second Baptist church in St. Louis. Here he remained until 1866, holding his post during all the agitations of the war, and keeping his church strongly loyal. In St. Louis he organized a society for church extension, through whose means three churches were helped into a self-supporting condition. In the autumn of 1866 he was called to the chair of Homiletics, Church Polity, and Pastoral Duties in the Newton Theological Institution. Here he remained seven years, but was drawn back to the pastorate by his love for that work in 1873, at the Strong Place church, Brooklyn, and in June, 1876, at the Second Baptist church, Chicago. In February, 1878, he was elected president of the University of Chicago, and, resigning his pastorate, entered at once upon the duties of that office.

The university at this time stood in need of the qualities of character, intellect, and moral force which Dr. Anderson brought to its service. The good effect of his firm, intelligent, manly course began at once to appear. New friends rallied to the support of the institution, old friends took heart anew, and as we now write there are reasons to believe that this work, to which, in the prime of his powers, Dr. Anderson is now giving himself, is to crown a distinguished and successful career with a service to which few men would be found equal.

Anderson, Rev. George W., D.D., was born in Philadelphia, Pa., May 15, 1816. He was baptized March 20, 1836, by Rev. J. J. Woolsey, and received into the fellowship of the Central church, Philadelphia. He graduated from Madison University, N. Y., in 1844, and from Hamilton Theological Seminary in 1846. Received the degree of Doctor of Divinity from Lewisburg University.

In 1846 efforts were made to establish the university at Lewisburg, Pa., and as one means for facilitating these efforts it was thought wise to publish a Baptist paper. The *Christian Chronicle* was the outgrowth of this enterprise, and Dr. Anderson was invited to the editorship. From this date a new and better era began for the Baptists of Pennsylvania.

REV. GEORGE W. ANDERSON, D.D.

In 1849 he was elected to the chair of the Latin Language and Literature in the university at Lewisburg. In 1854 he was ordained pastor of the Northeast church, Dutchess Co., N. Y. Although he had preached previously, yet up to this time he had refused ordination because he was not engaged in pastoral work. In August, 1858, he became pastor of the Lower Merion church, Montgomery Co., Pa. In 1864 he was made book editor of the American Baptist Publication Society, in which position he still continues to render valuable service to our denominational literature. On the boards of the Publication Society, and of the trustees of the Crozer Theological Seminary, he has also contributed largely to the success of missionary and educational work. He is a clear thinker and a forcible writer.

He was married April, 1847, to Miss Maria Frances, daughter of Thomas F. Hill, Esq., of Exeter, England.

Anderson, Rev. J. D., pastor at Byhalia, Miss., is a native of that State, born in 1852. He began to preach in 1868. Spent two years at Mississippi College, and two at the Southern Baptist Theological Seminary. He taught Latin and Greek in Blue Mountain College five years, and supplied country churches. After one year at Longtown he accepted his present pastorate.

Anderson, Rev. J. Richard, pastor of the Second African Baptist church in St. Louis, was born in Shawneetown, Ill. His parents were slaves in Virginia. He came with the sister of Attorney-General Bates to Missouri. His education began in the Sabbath-school of the First Colored church in St. Louis, organized by Dr. J. M. Peck. He was converted under Rev. Jerry Meachum's preaching, and he was baptized in the First African church of St. Louis. In 1847 he became associate pastor with Rev. Richard Snethen of the Second African Baptist church in St. Louis; and in 1849 he took sole charge of the church, which he retained till his death, four years after. His son is now his successor in this pastorate.

Mr. Anderson built a house of worship, which, with the lot, cost $12,000. He gave his whole salary one year to the edifice fund, and he solicited the rest of the money. He was a wise pastor. He had a revival every year in his church. He was acquainted with Greek and Latin, and expounded the Scriptures systematically on Sabbath mornings. Dr. Galusha Anderson, in his memorial sermon of him, says "his sermons were clear and pointed." He was loved in his home and church, and respected in the community. One hundred and seventy-five carriages were in the procession that followed him to his grave.

Anderson, Martin Brewer, LL.D., president of the University of Rochester, N. Y., was born in Brunswick, Me., Feb. 12, 1815. He inherited from his father, who was of Scotch-Irish descent, an unusual degree of physical and intellectual vigor, strong emotional impulses, and a sympathetic nature. His mother, who was of English origin, was a woman of marked intellectual qualities, possessing quick powers of discernment, a cautious but firm judgment, combined with intensity of moral conviction.

At the age of sixteen he devoted all his leisure to the acquisition of general knowledge. A well-organized debating club, composed of men of mature age and experience, furnished a motive for independent study and an arena for intellectual discipline. With this as an incentive, he pursued a course of reading which extended over a wide range of subjects, including history, politics, and general literature. The passion for learning thus developed, accompanied by an awakened interest in religion, led him to look towards a professional career. He completed his preparatory course of study, and in 1836 entered Waterville College (now Colby University). His college training gave a severer discipline to his already vigorous mind, and reduced to a more scientific form the knowledge he had previously acquired. While in college he was specially devoted to mathematics, the natural sciences, and intellectual philosophy. He graduated in 1840, holding a very high position in his class. During the following year he pursued a course of study in the theological seminary at Newton, Mass.

M. B. ANDERSON, LL.D.

In 1841 he was appointed tutor of Latin, Greek, and Mathematics in Waterville College, which position he held for two years. During the winter vacation of 1842-43 he supplied the pulpit of the E Street Baptist church in Washington, D. C. He there delivered a sermon in the House of Representatives which brought him into the favorable notice of a number of public men, among whom was John Quincy Adams. Unfortunately, at this time, on account of the loss of his voice, he was compelled to discontinue public speaking. In the fall of 1843 he was promoted to the professorship of Rhetoric in Waterville College. Besides his regular instruction in rhetoric and literary criticism, he taught classes in Latin, delivered a course of lectures upon modern history, and pursued a special investigation upon the origin and growth of the English language. This position not only afforded a means of giving greater breadth and thoroughness to his general scholarship, but also, on account of his special duties, opened a sphere for the development of the administrative capacity for which he has since become distinguished.

In 1850 he resigned his professorship and removed to New York City, where he became proprietor and editor-in-chief of the *New York Recorder*, a weekly Baptist journal. As a journalist he was marked by great energy and perseverance, by the learning and discrimination of his literary criticisms, and by the vigor and incisiveness of his editorials, which, from the necessities of his position at that time, were frequently of a controversial character. Through the independent position which he assumed as an editor, and the intellectual capacity which he displayed, he obtained a wide influence in the denomination, and was brought prominently before the public at large.

In 1853 he was unanimously elected the first president of the University of Rochester. This position he has since retained, notwithstanding the many inducements held out to him to change his field of labor. By his unswerving devotion to the cause of education, and by a career of uninterrupted success, he has attained a position among the foremost educators of the present day. His success as an educator during this period has depended largely upon his extensive and varied acquirements as a scholar, his high conception of the functions of the teacher, and his unusual capacity for administration.

His scholarship has been of the most comprehensive and liberal type. It has been developed not so much by the exclusive study of any special science as by the application of a general *method* to many branches of thought. This method, combining the comparative and historical modes of investigation, has been a constant incentive to push his inquiries beyond the limits of any single science or any special group of sciences. Gifted by nature with an untiring industry and a versatile mind, with a capacity for rapid acquisition and a genius for perceiving the broadest relations among the facts of nature and mind, he has pursued his investigations into an unusual number of the departments of human knowledge. The results of many of these lines of investigation have been organized into courses of study and presented to the students under his charge.

These courses are illustrative of the direction and range of his scholarship, and the most important of them may be briefly referred to. The first completed course of lectures, made after his accession to the presidency, was upon Intellectual Philosophy. This was prefaced by a discussion of scientific method, illustrating the fundamental principles involved in the genesis and organization of the various sciences, and also the possibility of subjecting mental facts to scientific analysis and interpretation. As a prominent feature of his philosophical teaching, he enforced the reality of perception as a fact of consciousness as opposed to idealism on the one hand and sensationalism on the other. He also expounded the history of the doctrine of perception from the time of Plato to the present, and showed the relation of the various forms of the doctrine to the theory accepted as the true one. While recognizing elements of truth in opposing systems of philosophy, he combated the tendencies alike of idealistic pantheism and of modern materialistic evolution. This course, which has been continued in its essential plan to the present time, was supplemented by lectures on Moral Philosophy, in which he enforced the reality of moral distinctions as opposed to associations and utilitarian theories. He also organized a new course of lectures on History, comprising such subjects as the Decline of the Roman Empire, the Feudal System, Mohammedanism, the Crusades, the Canon Law, the history of Labor, Transportation, and the series of agencies which developed the States System of Europe. An extended course of lectures was subsequently developed upon Political Economy, which comprehended not only the general principles of production, exchange, and consumption as usually treated, but special and exhaustive discussions upon the Scientific Theories of Money, the Banking System, Taxation, International Commerce, and the Effects of Free Trade and Protection upon National Prosperity, these lectures being frequently illustrated by examples taken from ancient and modern history. He has also delivered lectures upon Constitutional Law, drawing comparative illustrations from the Constitutions of the United States and Great Britain, upon the Relation of Ethics to Jurisprudence, which course was originally presented at Cincinnati in 1876, and also upon Art Criticism, and the History of the Fine Arts, including Architecture, Sculpture, Painting, and Engraving. Besides the investigations necessary for the organization of these definite courses of study, he has preserved a scholarly interest in the other departments of a collegiate course, especially Mathematics, the Natural Sciences, Philology, and General Literature.

His broad scholarship has yet been made tributary and conducive to his work as a teacher and general administrator. He has acquired knowledge in order to impart it, and to make it the instrument of power and the means of moulding character. As an administrative officer he holds a pre-eminent position among educators. This is due, in great part, to the magnetic inspiration which he gives to young men, the personal supervision and interest which he manifests in all the departments of instruction, and the common organic spirit which he impresses upon all the educational agencies placed under his control.

While his attention and energies have been devoted principally to the cause of education and the interests of the institution with which he is connected, he has also taken an important part in religious and denominational affairs. He has delivered sermons in various parts of the country, and has rendered valuable assistance in organizing and extending the work connected with American and foreign missions. He has been president of the Home Mission Society, and for three years was president of the Foreign Mission Society. He has, besides, been actively engaged in matters of social and political importance, in which he has exhibited the practical capacity of the man of affairs.

During the war of the Rebellion he was earnestly devoted to the national cause. He wrote many editorials and delivered stirring speeches in favor of the Union, and rendered efficient service on committees for the raising of soldiers. In 1868 he was appointed on the New York State Board of Charities as member from the seventh judicial district. As member of this board he has served on committees of investigation, and has written valuable reports to the Legislature upon economical subjects. As a kind of recognition of his position as a public man might be mentioned his election in 1872 as an honorary member of the Cobden Club in England.

The writings of President Anderson have been considerable, although never published in a collected form. They have accompanied and grown out of the work and special lines of inquiry in which he has been engaged. They are comprised for the most part in newspaper editorials, in articles for reviews, in discourses and essays on education, religious addresses, papers on social science, official reports, and articles for encyclopædias. Many of his editorials possess a permanent literary value from their scholarly treatment of subjects relating to religion, politics, and education. He published, some years ago, a series of articles in the *Christian Review*, the most important of which are the following: "The Origin and Political Life of the English Race" (1850), "Language as a Means of Classifying Man" (1859), "Sir William Hamilton's Lectures" (1860), "Berkeley and His Works" (1861), "Growth and Relation of the Sciences" (1862), and "The Arabian Philosophy" (1862). His discourses upon education comprise among others his inaugural address on "The Ends and Means of a Liberal Education," delivered July 11, 1854; a paper on the "Study of the Fine Arts," published in the Report of the Commissioner of Education; a paper on the "University of the Nineteenth Century," read before the National Baptist Educational Convention; a paper on "Voluntaryism in Education," read before the University Convocation of the State of New York. Among his published religious addresses may be mentioned an address delivered in Brooklyn in 1874, on the "Laymen of the Baptist Church," a speech at the Evangelical Alliance on the "Doctrine of Evolution," a paper before the same body on the "Right Use of Wealth." The most important of his official reports are those which he has made as member of the New York State Board of Charities, upon "Out-Door Relief," and upon "Alien Paupers," published in the Eighth Annual Report (1875), and also a report on the condition of the Institution for the Blind at Batavia, N. Y. As a further illustration of his economical opinions may be noticed a paper read before the Social Science Congress at Saratoga, on the "Means of Relief from the Burden of Foreign Paupers" (1875), as well as a speech delivered at the Adam Smith centennial, held in New York (1876). As associate editor of Johnson's Cyclopædia, he has contributed articles to that work on ethnology, philosophy, æsthetics, and Baptist Church history. All these writings are characterized by rhetorical vigor and directness, and by the appropriation of a wide range of knowledge for the purpose of clearly illustrating and of giving weight and significance to the special subjects treated.

The most important part of the life and labors of President Anderson has been devoted to the general cause of education, and to the special interests of the University of Rochester. His educational labors have scarcely been interrupted by any cause whatever since his connection with this institution. A severe illness in 1877, during which his life was despaired of, compelled a temporary discontinuance of his duties. But his complete recovery has enabled him to resume his former position, which he now fills with unabated vigor.

Anderson, Rev. Robert T., was the son of John Anderson, an influential citizen and a zealous Baptist. He was born in Caroline Co., Va., April 9, 1782, and was educated in the private school of Rev. Mr. Nelson. At the age of twenty-three he married Patsy Lowry, an accomplished Christian woman, and in 1818 he moved to Green Co., Ky. Here he found peace in Jesus, and was baptized by William Warder in 1821. He was set apart to the gospel ministry about the year 1829, in Mount Gilead church. The year following he moved to Logan Co., Ky. In 1832 he took charge of Hopewell church, in Tennessee. At different periods he was pastor of Keysburg, Hopkinsville, West Union, and some other churches. He was an able and laborious minister, and through grace accomplished much for the Master. Mr. Anderson was a distinguished educator, and was probably the first man in the West who attempted to teach letters to deaf-mutes. In this he succeeded so well that he taught some of his pupils to articulate distinctly. He died June 8, 1854.

Anderson, Thomas D., D.D., was born in Philadelphia, Pa., June 30, 1819. In his early years his parents removed to Washington, D. C., where the son received his academic training. He graduated at the University of Pennsylvania in 1838, and at Newton Theological Seminary in 1841. He was ordained and settled in 1842 as pastor of the First Baptist church of Salem, Mass. Settled with this old church at the age of twenty-two years, he soon won his way into the hearts of the entire community. Many useful lives have borne witness to the good accomplished during the six years of that pastorate.

THOMAS D. ANDERSON, D.D.

In June, 1848, he settled with the First Baptist church in Roxbury, Mass., remaining nearly fourteen years, during which the congregation largely increased, the church erected one of the most beautiful edifices in the country, and he was instrumental in bringing many to Christ. Constrained by his convictions of duty, but sorrowing greatly to leave his charge, Dr. Anderson accepted, in January, 1862, the call extended to him to become the pastor of the First Baptist church of New York City. In a few years they built the beautiful edifice on the corner of Thirty-ninth Street and Park Avenue, which was dedicated Oct. 1, 1871. The following extract from the letter of a member of the New York bar expresses the writer's opinion of the pastor of the First church, N. Y.: "Dr. Anderson is tall and commanding in appearance, has a mild and pleasant expression of face, and his presence, whether in or out of the pulpit, is attractive and impressive. He is a man of marked purity of character and sincerity and earnestness of purpose, an accurate thinker, and strong and zealous in his convictions. . . . As a preacher he probably has few superiors. He has no difficulty in securing the attention of his hearers." Dr. Anderson's illustrations are vivid pictures, which, having once been seen, are never effaced from the memory. Dr. Anderson has been connected during nearly the whole of his ministry with the American Baptist Missionary Union, the American Baptist Home Mission Society, and all our denominational institutions. He has been a trustee of Newton Theological Institute and of Madison University. He has also, in addition to his pastorate, for four years administered the presidency of Rutgers Female College, in the city of New York.

A morbid reluctance to appear in print has prevented Dr. Anderson from submitting his writings for publication, hence only occasional sermons and addresses have been published. Among these are "A Funeral Oration on President Zachary Taylor" before the city government of Roxbury, and "The Election Sermon" before the executive and legislative departments of the government of Massachusetts. His degree of D.D. was bestowed by Brown University in 1859.

Dr. Anderson resigned his charge in New York in the autumn of 1878, and accepted a call to Boston. A more devoted Christian or an abler pastor does not labor in our denomination.

Andrews, Rev. Reddin, Jr., A.M., was born in Fayette Co., Texas, Jan. 18, 1848. In July, 1863,

REV. REDDIN ANDREWS, JR., A.M.

in his fifteenth year, he joined the Confederate army, and remained in it two years. In July, 1865, he was baptized in the Colorado River by Elder P. B. Chandler. He was licensed to preach by Shiloh church in January, 1867. He entered Baylor University Feb. 4, 1867, and remained there, with some interruptions, till June, 1871, when he graduated with distinction. In September, 1871, he entered the Southern Baptist Theological Seminary, Greenville, S. C., where he remained till May, 1873. He entered upon the pastorate with bright prospects, and discharged its duties with signal success. In 1875 he became a professor in Baylor University. At present he is the beloved pastor of Culvert church.

No man in Texas of his age stands higher for scholarship, doctrinal soundness, firmness of purpose, and entire consecration to the gospel ministry.

Andrews, Newton Lloyd, Ph.D., Professor of the Greek Language and Literature in Madison University, was born in Fabius, N. Y., in 1841. He prepared for college at the public high school in Newark, N. J., where his parents then resided. In 1858 he became a member of the First Baptist church in that city, and the same year entered the Freshman class of Madison University. He graduated from the university in 1862, and from the Hamilton Theological Seminary in 1864. Immediately after he was appointed principal of the Grammar School, then connected with the university. From 1866 to 1868 he was Professor of Latin, but in 1868 he was elected to the Greek professorship, which department of instruction he has since held. Hamilton College (Clinton, N. Y.) conferred on him the degree of Ph.D. in 1878.

Angell, Rev. George, was born in Smithfield, R. I., March 24, 1786. In early life he was brought in contact with skeptical companions, and at the age of twenty-one was a confirmed infidel. It pleased God, however, to show him his error, and lead him through the deep waters of conviction for sin out into "the liberty wherewith Christ maketh free." He was baptized, and joined the First Baptist church in Providence in May, 1809. Impressed that it was his duty to preach the gospel, he applied for a license from the church of which he was a member, and received their approbation March 7, 1812, and was ordained as pastor of the Second Baptist church in Woodstock, Conn., Aug. 28, 1813. In June, 1816, he removed to Smithbridge, Mass., and became pastor of a church which was gathered by his efforts and constituted in February, 1817. In this relation he was blessed, the church growing from year to year in spiritual strength and numbers. Mr. Angell died Feb. 14, 1827. He had a warm place in the hearts of his own people and of his ministering brethren.

Angus, Joseph, D.D., LL.D., was born in Northumberland, England, Jan. 16, 1816. His family had been long connected with the Baptist congregation in Newcastle, and when quite a youth he became a member of the church and gave promise of gifts for the ministry. After several years' study at the Newcastle grammar school he was sent to King's College, London, and thence proceeded to Edinburgh University. In 1834 he entered Stepney College, London. Subsequently he returned to Edinburgh, and took his degree of A.M., obtaining the first prize in mathematics, in Greek, in logic, and in belles-lettres, and the gold medal in ethics and political philosophy. He was also the successful competitor for the students' prize essay of fifty guineas "on the influence of the writings of Lord Bacon," open to the whole university. When he was scarcely twenty-one years of age he received a call to the pastorate of the New Park Street church, London (now the Metropolitan Tabernacle), to succeed the venerable Dr. Rippen. Dr. Angus held the pastorate two years, and in 1840 accepted the appointment of co-secretary of the Baptist Missionary Society with the Rev. W. Dyer, on whose death, in 1842, he became sole secretary. While he held the secretaryship the income of the society was largely increased and steadily maintained in its upward tendency. Missions were begun in Africa, in the West Indies, and on the European continent. He also visited the societies stationed in the West Indies to complete the arrangements looking towards the independence of the Jamaica churches. In 1850 he was offered the presidency of Stepney College, and retired from the secretaryship of the Missionary Society. From that time to the present Dr. Angus has been the distinguished head of that institution, now known as Regent's Park College, and is one of the most eminent public men of the Baptist faith in the United Kingdom. His literary labors have been abundant. After Dr. Chalmers's visit to London in 1838 to deliver a course of lectures in defense of church establishments, a prize of one hundred guineas was offered for the best essay in answer to Dr. Chalmers. The essay of the youthful pastor of New Park Street obtained the prize, and was immediately published under the title of "The Voluntary System." Some years later he delivered a series of four lectures on "The Advantages of a Classical Education as an Auxiliary to a Commercial Education." Dr. Angus has been singularly successful in writing prize essays and lectures. Seldom has he entered the lists without obtaining a prize. In 1862 his essay entitled "Christian Churches: the noblest form of social life; the representatives of Christ on earth; the dwelling-place of the Holy Spirit," obtained the first award out of a large number of competitors for the prizes offered by the Congregational Union to celebrate the bi-centenary of non-conformity in England. At a later period a gentleman in the service of the government in India invited the publication of a small volume on the life of Christ, adapted to missionary purposes, and suitable for translation into the languages of India. Dr. Angus's book, "Christ our Life, in its Origin, Law, and End," obtained the prize out of sixty-four essays sent in to the adjudicators. He has been a frequent contributor to the periodical literature of the day, and several valuable educational works have proceeded from his ready pen. Among these may be named "The Bible Hand-book," published in 1854; "The Hand-book of the English Tongue," for students unacquainted with the history of the language and its principles of grammar, etc.; "The Hand-book of English Literature," written with a similar aim, and carrying the student farther on this valuable line of study; "Specimens of English Literature," illustrating the principles of criticism laid down in the previous volumes; also an edition of Bishop Butler's Analogy and Sermons. Besides these works, which are included in the Religious Tract Society's publications, Dr. Angus has edited Wayland's "Moral Science" and "Life of Judson." When the revision of the Scriptures was undertaken Dr. Angus was invited to become a member of the New Testament Company, and in this great public service he has continuously labored to the present time. On the passing of the education act Dr. Angus was elected on the London school board, and was re-elected in 1877. He has also held for several years the office of examiner in English literature and history in the London University. The degree of D.D. was conferred upon him by Brown University in 1852. From his brethren in England he received in 1865 the highest honor they have to confer in being chosen president of the Baptist Union, when he delivered two addresses which had a wide circulation. He enunciated the distinctive principles of the body in a clear and striking manner, and effectively aided the movement towards united and aggressive denominational activity. In 1871 he preached one of the annual sermons before the Missionary Society, and by a cogent array of statistics demonstrated the practicability of the speedy evangelization of the world, so far at least as to secure the publication of the gospel to all the nations. For his devout spirit, varied accomplishments, and incessant activity Dr. Angus commands the esteem and confidence of Christians of all communions in the mother-country.

Appelegate, James L., was born Sept. 3, 1836, in Charleston Co., Mo. He was converted May 10, 1853, and baptized by Elder James H. Tuttle. He first joined the Keytesville Baptist church, and after five years' membership united with the church at Brunswick, Mo. In 1875 he transferred his membership to the Third Baptist church of St. Louis, where he now resides. He is a member of the board of William Jewell College, and of the General Association of Missouri. He is a man of intelligence and piety, a great friend of religious work. He loves his church and denomination, and is a generous contributor to every good cause.

Appleton, Prof. John Howard, was born in Portland, Me., Feb. 3, 1844. He was fitted for college in the Providence High School, and graduated at Brown University in the class of 1863. In 1864 he was appointed assistant in the Chemical Laboratory of Brown University, and in 1868 the "Newport-Rogers Professor of Chemistry." Prof. Appleton has published several books on chemistry, viz.: "The Young Chemist," "The Class-book of Modern Chemistry," "The Book of Chemical Reactions," "A Short Course in Qualitative Analysis," and "An Introduction to Quantitative Analysis."

Ardis, Rev. Henry Z., a prominent minister residing near Homer, La.; born in South Carolina in 1811. After preaching some time in his native State he removed to Florida, where he labored efficiently for twenty-five years. He then went to Louisiana in 1871, in which State he has filled several prominent pastorates.

Arkadelphia High School, located at Arkadelphia, Ark., was established by Rev. J. F. Shaw in 1875. It is under the patronage of the Liberty Baptist Association, and is in a flourishing condition. During the term which closed June, 1880, about 175 pupils were in attendance.

Arkansas.—One of the States of the American Union, lying west of the Mississippi River. Pop. 484,500. Baptists (estimated), whites, about 45,000; colored, about 20,000. The sentiments of the Baptists were first propagated towards the close of the last century in the northeastern portion of Arkansas, which was then a part of the territory of Louisiana. A few zealous Baptist preachers followed the tide of population that flowed into this territory from the settlements along the Mississippi River in the southeastern part of Missouri. Of their labors it must be confessed too little notice has been taken, and few records have been preserved. Dr. Benedict, in his history, says, "Rev. David Orr appears to have been the instrument in planting a considerable number of the first churches of which I have gained any information. Cotemporary with Mr. Orr, or perhaps a short time before him on this ground, were Benjamin Clark, Jesse James, and J. P. Edwards. The first church of our order organized in the territory of Arkansas was at Fonche à Thomas, in Lawrence County, towards the close of the last century."

At the end of twenty years a sufficient number of churches had been gathered in the northeastern part of the State to organize the White River Association, and a few years later two other Associations appear in this region.

The southern part of the State was settled somewhat later. About 1830, Rev. E. B. Carter was operating in Saline County, where he had probably been living several years. By his instrumentality some of the first churches were organized. Soon afterwards Isaac C. Perkins settled in Hempstead County, and gathered a number of churches in this and the surrounding counties. In 1836 the churches in South Arkansas were organized into an Association called Saline, from the county of the same name in which most of the churches were located. Soon after these early preachers were joined by others, the most distinguished of whom was Dr. John Meek, who settled in Union County near the Ouachita River. In 1841 the anti-mission troubles resulted in the withdrawal of a number of churches and ministers, and the formation of an Association of the anti-mission order. During the next decade many distinguished ministers arose in this region. Among those ordained here may be named H. H. Coleman, Aaron Yates, J. V. McColloch, W. H. Wyatt, R. J. Coleman, Dr. John T. Craig, and R. M. Thrasher, all of whom have exercised a wide influence in the State. In 1845, Dr. F. Courtney settled at Eldorado, and the year following W. H. Bayless became pastor at Tulip, and Judge Rutherford began to preach at Camden. In 1847, A. E. Clemmons settled at Lewisville, and in 1848, Rev. Jesse Hartwell, D.D., located at Camden. These were all men of great ability, and gave character to the denomination in this part of the State.

Previous to 1844 there was no Baptist church in all the region between the Ouachita and Mississippi River south of what is now Dallas County. There were a few Anti-Mission Baptists who about this time gathered a small church. About the same time Young R. Royal, a missionary Baptist preacher, settled in Drew County, and Uriah H. Parker, Joel Tomme, and Robert Pully in Bradley. By their labors, assisted at a later day by B. C. Hyatt, Solomon Gardner, and others, the first churches in this region were planted.

Subsequently, but chiefly since the war, churches have been planted in that part of the State lying between the Arkansas and Mississippi Rivers, and in the northwestern part of the State, but our space does not allow of details. The following is a list of Associations, with the date of their origin, as far as we have been able to ascertain: White River, 1820; Spring River, 1829; Saline, 1836; Washington, 1837; Rocky Bayou, 1840; Salem, 1840; Liberty, 1845; St. Francis, 1845; Red River, 1848; Bartholomew, 1848; Columbia, 1852; Judson, 1854; Pleasant Hill, 1854; Friendship; Pine Bluff; Caroline; Little Red River; Baptist; Bartonville; Bethel; Caddo River; Cadron; Cane Creek; Clear Creek; Concord; Crooked Creek; Dardanelles; Fayetteville; Independence; Mount Vernon; Spring Town; Mount Zion; Ouachita Sixth Missionary; Springfield; State Corner; Union; Grand Prairie; Antioch District; First Missionary; Ouachita. Many of the last mentioned are formed by churches composed of colored Baptists.

Arkansas Baptist Banner is published at Judsonia, the seat of Judson University. After the suspension of the *Western Baptist* in 1879 Mr. Joshua Hill started a Baptist paper at Beebe, in White County, called *The Arkansas Baptist*. In a little while Mr. Hill sold out to Rev. J. H. Ruberson, who changed the name to *Arkansas Baptist Banner*, and removed it to Judsonia. Mr. Ruberson subsequently sold to James P. Green, by whom the paper is still published.

Arkansas Baptist Convention was organized in 1848. Its officers elected in 1879 were Rev. J. M. Hart, Eldorado, President; Rev. J. R. G. Adams, Dardanelles, Recording Secretary; Rev. Benjamin Thomas, D.D., Little Rock, Corresponding Secretary.

Arkansas Baptist Index is a paper the publication of which was begun at Texarkana, Ark., in 1880, by Rev. J. F. Shaw, in connection with Mrs. Viola Jackson, a lady of literary distinction in the South. It is a small but ably-conducted sheet, and circulates chiefly in the three States upon the borders of which the city of Texarkana is situated.

Arkansas Baptist, The, a religious newspaper devoted to the interests of the Baptist denomination in Arkansas, was started at Little Rock, Jan. 15, 1859. It was edited by Rev. P. S. G. Watson, and under his able direction it took rank among the first religious journals in the South. It had secured a good subscription list and was on the way to prosperity at the breaking out of the war, when it was compelled to suspend. This took place in May, 1861. At the close of the war an ineffectual effort was made to revive it by Rev. N. P. More, but after a few issues it was found that the unsettled state of the country was very unfavorable to the publication of a religious paper, the enterprise was abandoned, and the State Convention adopted as its organ the *Memphis Baptist*, with an Arkansas department, which supplied the means of communication.

Arkansas, Northwestern General Association of, was organized a few years since, and is accomplishing a good work.

Arkansas, Southeastern General Association of, was organized in 1874. The officers elected in 1880 were Rev. John T. Craig, Edinburg, Moderator; Rev. J. D. Searcy, Anover, Recording Secretary.

Armitage, Rev. Thomas, D.D., was born in Yorkshire, England, in 1819. He is descended from the old and honored family of the Armitages of that section of Yorkshire, one of whom, Sir John Armitage, of Barnsley, was created a baronet by Charles I. in 1640. He lost his father a few years since, and his mother when five years old. She was the granddaughter of the Rev. Thomas Barrat, a Wesleyan Methodist minister. She had great faith in Jesus, and prayed often and confidently for the salvation of her oldest son, Thomas. At her death she gave him her Bible, her chief treasure, which she received as a reward from her teacher in the Sunday-school. Her last prayer for him was that he might be converted and become a good minister of the Saviour.

REV. THOMAS ARMITAGE, D.D.

The religious influence of his godly mother never forsook him. While listening to a sermon on the text, "Is it well with thee?" his sins and danger filled him with grief and alarm, and before he left the sanctuary his heart was filled with the love of Christ.

In his sixteenth year he preached his first sermon. His text was, "Come unto me all ye that labor and are heavy laden, and I will give you rest." The truth was blessed to the conversion of three persons. He declined pressing calls to enter the regular ministry of the English Methodist Church, but used his gifts as a local preacher for several years.

Like many Englishmen he imbibed republican doctrines, and these brought him in 1838 to New York. He received deacon's orders from Bishop Waugh, and those of an elder from Bishop Morris. He filled many important appointments in the M. E. Church in New York, and when he united with the Baptists he was pastor of the Washington Street church in Albany, one of its most important churches, where the Lord had given him a precious revival and eighty converts. At this period his influence in the M. E. Church was great, and its highest honors were before him. When he was first examined for Methodist ordination he expressed doubts about the church government of the Methodist body, and about sinless perfection, falling from grace, and their views of the ordinances; but he was the great-grandson of a Methodist minister, his mother was of that communion, and he himself had been a preacher in it for years, and his misgivings were regarded as of no moment. In 1839 he witnessed a baptism in Brooklyn by the Rev. S. Ilsley, which made him almost a Baptist, and what remained to be done to effect that end was accomplished by another baptism in Albany, administered by the Rev. Jabez Swan, of Connecticut. An extensive examination of the baptismal question confirmed his faith, and placed him without a misgiving upon the Baptist platform in everything. Dr. Welsh baptized him into the fellowship of the Pearl Street church, Albany. Soon after a council was called to give him scriptural ordination. Dr. Welsh was moderator; Friend Humphrey, mayor of Albany, and Judge Ira Harris were among its members. A letter of honorable dismissal from the M. E. Church, bearing flattering testimony to his talents and usefulness, was read before the council, and after the usual examination he was set apart to the Christian ministry in the winter of 1848. He was requested to preach in the Norfolk Street church, New York, in the following June. The people were charmed with the stranger, and so was the sickly pastor, the Rev. George Benedict. He was called to succeed their honored minister, who said to Mr. Armitage, "If you refuse this call it will be the most painful act of your life." Mr. Benedict never was in the earthly sanctuary again. Mr. Armitage accepted the invitation, in his twenty-ninth year, July 1, 1848. In 1853–54 140 persons were baptized, and in 1857 152, while other years had great blessings.

The first year of his ministry in Norfolk Street the meeting-house was burned, and another erected. Since that time the church reared a house for God in a more attractive part of the city, which they named the "Fifth Avenue Baptist church." The property is worth at least $150,000, and it is free from debt. The membership of the church is over 700. In 1853, Mr. Armitage was made a Doctor of Divinity by Georgetown College, Ky. He was then in his thirty-fourth year.

At a meeting held in New York, May 27, 1850, by friends of the Bible, Dr. Armitage offered resolutions which were adopted, and upon which the Bible Union was organized two weeks later, with Dr. S. H. Cone as its president, and W. H. Wyckoff, LL.D., as its secretary. In May, 1856, Dr. Armitage became the president of the society. In this extremely difficult position he earned the reputation of being one of the ablest presiding officers in our country. The Bible Union reached its greatest prosperity while he presided over its affairs.

Dr. Armitage is a scholarly man, full of information, with a powerful intellect; one of the greatest preachers in the United States; regarded by many as the foremost man in the American pulpit. We do not wonder that he is so frequently invited to deliver sermons at ordinations, dedications, installations, missionary anniversaries, and to college students. As a great teacher in Israel, the people love to hear him, and their teachers are delighted with the themes and with the herald.

Seventeen years ago a gentleman wrote of Dr. Armitage, "The expression of his face is one of mingled intelligence and kindness. As he converses it is with animation, and his eyes sparkle. His manners are easy, graceful, and cordial. He fascinates strangers and delights friends. He appears before you a polished gentleman, who wins his way to your esteem and affection by his exalted worth." The description has been confirmed by time.

Armstrong, Andrew, was born near Dublin, in Ireland, and studied at Hamilton. He married the daughter of Judge Swaim, of Pemberton, N. J. He has been pastor at Upper Freehold, Lambertville, Kingwood, Frenchtown, and New Brooklyn, where he now ministers. While his preaching is edifying to the spiritual body, he has also been particularly blessed in leading congregations to build meeting-houses and pay for them. He has also acted as agent for the State Convention and Education Society.

Armstrong, Rev. George, M.A., was born in Ireland, Dec. 5, 1814; brought when an infant by his parents to St. John's, Newfoundland, where they continued till his sixteenth year; then removed with them to Sydney, Cape Breton, where, three years after, he was converted, and was in the following year baptized by Rev. Dr. Crawley. Studied at Horton Academy in 1836–38, and graduated from Acadia College June, 1844; ordained at Port Medway, Nova Scotia, in 1848; was subsequently pastor at Chester; became in 1854 pastor of the Baptist church, Bridgetown, Nova Scotia, and so continued for twenty years; then was pastor at Sydney, Cape Breton, for two years; was editor of the *Christian Visitor*, St. John's, New Brunswick, from January, 1876, for three years; evangelized in Newfoundland in the summer of 1879; and he is now pastor of the Baptist church, Kentville, Nova Scotia.

Armstrong, Rev. John.—Mr. Armstrong was born in Philadelphia, Pa., November, 1798. He graduated at Columbian College, D. C., in 1825. Some time after he moved to North Carolina, and was for five years pastor of the Newberne Baptist church. He became a professor in Wake Forest College in 1835, and for a time acted as agent of the college. He went to Europe in 1837, and spent two years in France and Italy, preparing himself the better to discharge his duties as teacher. He had as his companions in his voyage Dr. E. G. Robinson, the distinguished president of Brown University, and J. J. Audubon, the great naturalist. In 1841, Mr. Armstrong accepted the pastorate of the Baptist church in Columbus, Miss., where he married a lady of fortune. He died in 1844. He is said to have been a fine scholar, a blameless Christian gentleman, and an able and eloquent preacher.

Arnold, Albert Nicholas, D.D., was born in Cranston, R. I., Feb. 12, 1814. While engaged in mercantile pursuits in Providence his mind became

ALBERT NICHOLAS ARNOLD, D.D.

interested on the subject of preaching the gospel. Having decided to enter the ministry, he took the full courses of study in Brown University and the Newton Theological Institution, graduating from the one in 1838, and from the other in 1841. He was ordained pastor of the Baptist church in Newburyport, Mass., Sept. 14, 1841, and in 1844 received an appointment as a missionary to Greece, where he remained ten years. Returning to his native land, he was made Professor of Church History at Newton, holding the office for three years. For the next six years he was pastor of the Baptist church in Westborough, Mass., for five years Professor of Biblical Interpretation and Pastoral Theology in the Hamilton Theological Institution, and for four years Professor of New Testament Greek in the Theological Institution in Chicago. He resigned in 1878, and for the last few years has had a home near Providence, where he has been engaged in such literary and other work as the state of his health allows him to perform. Dr. Arnold is one of the most accomplished scholars in the denomination. Probably no man in the country is better acquainted with modern Greek than he.

Arnold, Richard James, was born in Providence, R. I., Oct. 5, 1796. He came from an illustrious ancestry on the side of both father and mother. Having graduated at Brown University, in the class of 1814, he studied law for a short time in the office of the celebrated Hon. Tristam Burgess. Not finding the study of this profession congenial to his tastes, he became a merchant, in connection with an elder brother, and was especially interested in the China trade. In 1823, having married a lady living in the South, he made a home on his plantation in Georgia, in Bryan County, near Savannah, spending his winters there, and his summers in Rhode Island. Mr. Arnold took a deep interest in the First Baptist church in his native city, where he always worshiped when he was at his Providence home. He was a trustee of Brown University for nearly forty-seven years. His death occurred March 10, 1873.

Arnold, Hon. Samuel Greene, was born in Providence, R. I., April 12, 1821, and was a graduate of Brown University in the class of 1841. He studied law at the Harvard School, where he received the degree of Bachelor of Laws in 1845. Soon after he went abroad, and spent several years in study and travel, visiting first the different countries of Europe, and thence passing to Egypt and the Holy Land. In 1847 he crossed from Europe to South America, where he spent a year, chiefly in Chili. He returned to his home in 1848. He now gave himself to a work which he had long meditated, the writing of a history of his native State. The first volume of this work appeared in 1859, and was followed by the second in 1860. These two volumes comprise the annals of the State of Rhode Island from the settlement in 1636 to the adoption of the Federal Constitution in 1790. This history, the result of careful study and research, and thoroughly imbued with the true Rhode Island spirit, at once placed its author in the front rank of American historians. Without doubt it will always be a standard authority for the period which it covers.

Mr. Arnold took a deep interest in all matters affecting the prosperity of the First Baptist church in Providence. For twenty-five years he was moderator of the society. In 1864 he projected a permanent fund of $20,000, the interest of which was to be appropriated to pay for the support of public worship. He headed the subscription list with a contribution of $5000. On the 25th of May, 1875, he delivered a discourse commemorative of the one

HON. SAMUEL GREENE ARNOLD.

hundredth anniversary of the dedication of the meeting-house for public worship. In 1852, Mr. Arnold was elected lieutenant-governor of the State, and again in 1861, and a third time in 1862. After his last election he was chosen to fill the unexpired term of Hon. James F. Simmons in the Senate of the United States, and held office from December, 1862, to March 3, 1863. Governor Arnold died in Providence, Feb. 13, 1880. He will be long honored as the Christian scholar, patriot, historian, and statesman.

Arnold, Rev. T. J., born in Hendricks Co., Ind., in 1835, moved to Iowa with his parents, Stephen and Nancy Arnold; baptized at Fairview in 1853; was licensed to preach in 1854. He was educated at Mount Vernon Methodist Academy and Pella University. While studying he entered the ministry as an evangelist, preaching at various places. He was ordained while preaching for the Iola and Coleridge churches. At Martinsburg was married to Miss J. Smith, in 1860, who proved herself a faithful and devoted Christian wife. In 1875 he moved to California; was pastor one year at Santa Clara, two years at Reno and Virginia City, Nev., and in 1879 he returned to California, and preached as evangelist or pastor at Vallejo and Yountville, precious revivals attending his labors in almost every place. He has baptized about 400, and led many others to Christ, who have been baptized by the pastors whom he has assisted in revival meetings.

Arracan, Mission to.—Arracan is a division of British Burmah. It is bounded on the north by the Bengal district of Chittagong, on the east by the Yumadoung Mountains, which separate it from independent Burmah and the British district of Pegu, and on the south and west by the Bay of Bengal. The population in 1871 was near half a million, made up of Buddhists, Mohammedans, Hindoos, and a few Christians. Its principal town is Akyab. In the province there are four districts, Akyab, Ramree, Sandoway, and Aeng. The attention of the Missionary Union was turned towards Arracan as far back as 1835, when Mr. and Mrs. Comstock were appointed by the board to begin a mission at some suitable place on the coast of Arracan. The station selected by Mr. Comstock was in the Ramree district, at the north point of Ramree Island. Its name was Kyouk Phyoo, and the place contained about 2000 natives, besides English residents, troops, etc. Mr. Comstock commenced his work in this village early in March, 1835. Three months' labor began to show some fruit, and a spirit of inquiry was awakened among the people about the new religion. The next year Mr. and Mrs. Ingalls joined Mr. Comstock, and new energy was given to the enterprise. During one of the excursions of Mr. Comstock in the mountainous districts he met with the Kyens, a branch of the Karens, who seemed ready to welcome the good tidings of salvation which were brought to them. In the spring of 1837 another reinforcement was made to the mission by the arrival of Mr. and Mrs. Hall. Their connection with the mission was of but brief duration, both of them dying within a few months of the commencement of their work. The station at Kyouk Phyoo was abandoned in November of this year on account of its insalubrity, and a new station at Ramree was occupied by Messrs. Comstock and Stilson in the spring of 1838. The town in which they had made their residence contained a population of 10,000 inhabitants. A church was formed the 29th of May, and a school commenced by Mrs. Comstock.

Messrs. Kincaid and Abbott began another Arracanese station at Akyab in the spring of 1840. It was not long before interesting inquirers appeared, and in May three persons were baptized. The following August, 30 persons professed their faith in Christ. The report was that "the prospects of the mission were good; a mission house and premises had been purchased, and Mr. Kincaid, though his heart was still turned to Ava, was content to abide in Arracan, according as the spirit of God might be." In 1841 there was an additional station commenced at Sandoway, under the charge of Mr. Abbott, who reported 193 baptisms for the year, and in the three stations there were 4 missionaries, 4 female assistants, and 27 native helpers.

One hundred and fifty miles south of Akyab there lives a tribe called the Kemees. From the chief of this tribe, Chetea, there came early in May, 1841, a message to the mission, entreating that the missionaries would teach them about the true God, and give them his holy book. In the following December a similar message was sent, and Mr. Kincaid, accompanied by Mr. Stilson, decided to visit the Kemees. The visit was made, and good seed was sown. Various changes took place in the Arracan stations during the next two or three years. Mrs. Comstock died April 28, 1843, and Mr. Comstock, April 25, 1844. The Karen department, under the special charge of Mr. Abbott, was greatly prospered. During the year 1844, 2039 Karens were brought by baptism into connection with the churches of the Arracan missions. Mr. and Mrs. Ingalls arrived at Akyab in the spring of 1846. At the close of this year there were 29 out-stations, and 3240 members in the churches in Akyab and these out-stations. Mr. Abbott, worn down with disease and care, returned to his native land in the fall of 1845. He remained in the United States a little over two years, and then returned to Sadoway, to have the supervision of the Karen department. Mr. Moore became connected with the Ramree stations in the spring of 1848. Mr. Beecher and Mr. Van Meter were apppointed to the Sandoway station. In the churches in this station and its out-stations there was reported at the close of 1848 a membership of 4500, and 5124 *unbaptized* Christians, "who have maintained as religious a life in all respects as the members of the churches, only they were not baptized." The Karen department of the Sandoway mission was removed to Bassan, and its connection with the Arracan mission ceased. The station at Kyouk Phyoo was resumed in November, 1850. Mr. Rose joined the mission at Akyab in 1853. The deputation to the East, Rev. Drs. Peck and Granger, visited early in the year 1853 the stations in Arracan, reported that the mission showed signs of prosperity, and the Convention which met at Maulmain recommended that, at once, these men be sent to reinforce the mission. For a few years, however, there was but little apparent success in Arracan. The missionaries were removed by death, or by assignment to other fields of labor. Mr. Satterlee arrived in Arracan in September, 1855, and died the following July. The executive committee, in their annual report in 1857, say, "In view not only of the unhealthiness of the Arracan climate, but also of the demand for labor in Burmah proper and elsewhere, and of the diminished supply, we respectfully suggest that the mission be brought to a close." The suggestion was carried out, and a mission which at one time was so hopeful, and for which so many valuable lives had been sacrificed, ceased to exist.

Arrowsmith, Col. George, was born in Middletown, N. J., in 1839. He graduated at Madison University at the age of twenty, and became tutor in the Grammar School. In 1861 he went to the war as captain of a company. He rose to be lieutenant-colonel in 157th Regiment, N. Y. Vols., and was killed on the Gettysburg battle-field, July 1, 1863. He was a brave man, and gave promise of excelling in his profession.

Arvine, Rev. Kazlitt, was born in Western New York in 1820. He was a graduate of the Wesleyan University at Middletown, Conn., and of the Newton Theological Institution. In 1845 he was ordained pastor of the church in Woonsocket, R. I., where he remained two years, and then removed to New York to take charge of what was known as the "Providence" church. His connection with this church continued but a few months, on account of failing health. Respite from ministerial labor so far restored him that he accepted a call to become pastor of the church in West Boylston, Mass. Here he continued until his removal to Worcester, to avail himself of medical treatment for the disease which finally caused his death. This event took place at Worcester, July 15, 1851. Mr. Arvine is best known as the compiler of the "Cyclopædia of Moral and Religious Anecdotes," a work which has obtained a flattering circulation. A volume of his poetical productions was also published, which was well received. He was a man of refined and scholarly parts, and his comparatively short life was not spent in vain.

Ash, John, LL.D., was a native of Dorsetshire, England. Early in life he was drawn to the Saviour, after which he united by baptism with the church at Loughwood, near Lyme. He was educated at Bristol College, in which he made remarkable progress in learning. In 1751 he became pastor of the church at Pershore. In his youth he was distinguished for his mathematical attainments, for which he was commended in the periodicals of the day. Ivimey says that "his philological works, his elaborate grammar, and dictionary are universally known and highly prized." The learning which marked his writings secured for him in 1774 the degree of Doctor of Laws. His religious opinions were Paul's, without any human additions. He lived honored for his great abilities and learning, and he died in the full enjoyment of the peace of God in 1779.

Asher, Rev. Jeremiah, was born in North Branford, Conn., Oct. 13, 1812. Ruel Asher, his father, was born in the same place. Gad Asher, his grandfather, was a native of Africa, from which he was stolen when about four years of age, and brought to East Guilford, now Madison, Conn., and there sold to Linus Bishop, who gave him his biblical name.

Mr. Asher was licensed to preach by the First Baptist church of Hartford, Conn., and he became pastor of a church in Providence, R. I., soon after, where he labored with much acceptance. Subsequently he became pastor of the Shiloh Baptist church of Philadelphia. In this field his talents and labors were highly appreciated, and he speedily secured the respect of a numerous circle of friends. Finding that his church was heavily burdened with debt, he sailed for England to secure funds for its extinction. He carried credentials with him from leading Baptist ministers of the city of Brotherly Love, attested by the mayor, and he was received with kind greetings and considerable gifts by the British churches.

After his return he entered upon his pastoral labors with renewed vigor, and he had the happiness of seeing the Shiloh church increasing its numbers and growing in the grace of our Lord Jesus Christ. For a time he was a chaplain to a colored regiment in the army. He died in the enjoyment of a blessed hope.

Mr. Asher was a clear thinker, an able gospel preacher, a Christian of undoubted piety, and a minister widely known and highly respected by Baptists and by other Christians of both races.

Ashley, Rev. William W., was born in Hillsborough, N. C., in 1793. His early studies were interrupted in consequence of his entering into military service in 1814. He was in Mobile when the battle of New Orleans was fought. He became a subject of converting grace in the fall of 1815, and united with a Free-Will Baptist church. He was set apart to the work of the ministry in 1817, and for some time itinerated as an evangelist in the Southern and Southwestern States. He was in Nova Scotia in 1821, laboring with great zeal and energy. He was settled as a Free-Will Baptist minister in several places, but in the later years of his life, his views becoming Calvinistic, he connected himself with the regular Baptists, and was pastor of churches in Barnstable and Harwich, Mass. Mr. Ashley was a warm advocate of temperance. In the provinces of New Brunswick and Nova Scotia he established or assisted in organizing over 300 temperance societies. At the time of his death two of his brothers and five of his sons were in the Baptist ministry. He died at South Gardiner, Mass., June 6, 1860.

Ashmore, William, D.D., was born in Putnam, O., Dec. 25, 1821. He was a graduate of Granville College, and of the Covington Theological Institution. In 1848 he was ordained pastor of the Baptist church at Hamilton, O. The following year he received an appointment as a missionary to the foreign field, and sailed from New York Aug. 17, 1850, for China, arriving at Hong-Kong Jan. 4, 1851, and at Bangkok, April 14, 1851. He applied himself with conscientious diligence to the acquisition of the Chinese language, and was soon able to come into closer contact with the people. Excursions were made to the adjacent villages and out-stations selected for occupancy. Mr. Ashmore labored from house to house, conversing with the inmates, distributing tracts, and in such ways as his wisdom dictated sought to bring home the truth to the hearts and consciences of the people. In this kind of work, quiet and unostentatious, the faithful missionary labored on for several years. The health of Mrs. Ashmore made it necessary that her husband and herself should leave Bangkok for a season. The hope that the change would benefit her was doomed to be disappointed. She died at sea, off the Cape of Good Hope, May 19, 1858. A lady of rare qualities of mind and heart, her death was a sad loss to her bereaved husband. The January previous to her death Dr. Ashmore had been transferred to Hong-Kong, which, for some time, continued to be the scene of his missionary toils. It was his purpose to have gone to Swatow, to labor among the Chinese in the Tie Chiu district, but his health was so poor that he was compelled to abandon his purpose and return to his native land, which he reached in the summer of 1860. In the month of July, 1864, he returned to China, accompanied by his second wife, the youngest daughter of Judge Dunlevy, of Lebanon, O. Another locality having been better suited to missionary purposes than Swatow, Dr. Ashmore and the other missionaries removed to Kak-Chie, not far from their former residence. Several out-stations were under his charge, and the work progressed successfully, taking into consideration all the circumstances under which it was done. The number of church members under the watch-care of Dr. Ashmore in 1870 was 142. He reports for the next year 40 persons baptized, and for the next, 42. In 1875, Dr. and Mrs. Ashmore returned to the United States on account of the poor health of Mrs. Ashmore. On their return-trip they reached Swatow about the 1st of December, 1877, " very much to the relief and gratification of the other missionary." Under date of April, 1878, Dr. Ashmore writes a hopeful letter, as he sums up what has been accomplished within the past dozen years, and adds, " We have had some 20 applicants for baptism. 12 of these were baptized." The latest intelligence from him was under date of July 15, when at the monthly church-meeting there were 15 or 16 candidates for baptism. That the life of so valuable a missionary as Dr. Ashmore may be spared we may earnestly pray.

Ashton, Rev. William E., was born in Philadelphia, Pa., May 18, 1793. At the age of ten he first became interested in the salvation of his soul. At sixteen he was baptized into the fellowship of the Second Baptist church of his native city. He studied under Dr. Staughton, and in his twenty-second year he was ordained pastor of the Baptist church of Hopewell, N. J. He afterwards served the church of Blockley, Philadelphia, as pastor, and then the Third church, Philadelphia, in which he labored till his death. Mr. Ashton was a ripe scholar, and possessed that polished ease and culture which made him welcome in any social circle. His talents otherwise were respectable, and his piety was felt and seen by all who knew him. He was a useful minister of the Lord Jesus, whom his denominational brethren delighted to honor, and other Christians highly esteemed. Princeton College in 1830 gave him the degree of Master of Arts.

Assam, Mission to.—On the northwestern frontier of Burmah lies the country of Assam, stretching across the plains of the Brahmaputra, from 70 to 100 miles in breadth, and extending on the northeast to the very borders of China. Many races inhabit this large territory. The inhabitants are known by the general name of Shans, which word by changes of the language has become Assam. Since 1826 the country has been under British rule. The conclusion to commence a mission in Assam was reached in 1835, and Messrs. Brown and Cutter were sent to Sodiya, in the northeastern part of the country. Messrs. Thomas and Bronson joined them July 17, 1836. The missionaries entered upon their work with great zeal. The language was learned and reduced to printing, Roman letters being used; tracts were prepared, and portions of the New Testament published and freely circulated. There are now several stations in Assam, of which we give a brief sketch.

1. Gowahati. A church was formed in this place in February, 1845. Rev. Mr. Danforth arrived there in May, 1848, and having acquired the language began at once a career of great usefulness. Schools were established, buildings were erected, hopeful conversions took place, and the church was enlarged. Mr. Danforth made extensive tours into the adjacent regions, and by means of tracts and religious books, as well as with the living voice, he reached large numbers of the people, and much good seed was sown. The liberality of the English residents in Gowahati furnished the means for the erection of a pleasant chapel, 65 feet by 25, which was dedicated the first Sabbath in February, 1853. For many years the mission at Gowahati was in a very depressed condition. Under the labors of Mr. Comfort and his assistants there has been steady progress from year to year. Mr. Comfort's efforts among the Garos have been especially blessed. His health failing, Dr. Bronson removed to Gowahati in 1874. The work seemed to receive a new impulse, and in the report of the executive committee for

1875 we find 28 baptisms recorded, and 102 church members; and the next year 111 baptisms, and the following year 148. At this time, 1880, the number of baptisms last reported was 118, and the church membership 378.

2. Gowalapara is the English civil and military station for the district in which the Garos live; it is situated on the south bank of the Brahmaputra. From this Assamese station the missionaries go forth to preach the gospel to the Garos, who live among the hills on the south of the river. In the spring of 1867, Dr. Bronson visited this interesting people and baptized 26 of them, and formed them into a church. Mr. Stoddard and his family were stationed at Gowalapara in the fall of 1867. In the spring of 1868 he and Dr. Bronson made a five weeks' tour among the Garos, preaching, baptizing, establishing schools, etc. They returned to Gowalapara greatly encouraged by what they had seen of the good work of the Lord among the Garos. So much interested were the English authorities in the success of the missionaries that they cheerfully granted them pecuniary aid in carrying on the schools. The increasing labors of the missionaries called for reinforcements, and the appeal was responded to. Others have gone to this most promising field, and have been greatly encouraged in their work. From the last report we learn that there are nine churches in the district of which Gowalapara is the centre, and in these churches there are 704 members.

3. Nowgong. This place was made a station in 1841. Dr. Bronson established an orphan institution in 1843 in Nowgong, which accomplished great good, not only in promoting the temporal welfare of the children gathered within its walls, but in the conversion of many of them. In 1856 this institution took on somewhat the character of a preparatory and normal school. In consequence of the smallness of the appropriations for its support and the fewness of its pupils it was thought best to suspend it in 1857. Various circumstances transpired to weaken and almost destroy the station at Nowgong. For several years but little progress was made. The efforts of the missionaries among the Mikirs were fruitful for good. Dr. Bronson after laboring faithfully for many years returned to the United States in 1869, and the station was placed in the charge of Rev. E. P. Scott and his wife. Mr. Scott died in May, 1870. Dr. Bronson returned to Nowgong early in 1871, and with invigorated health resumed his work, employing himself in the Assamese department, and Rev. Mr. Neighbor, who had joined him, in the Mikir department. Dr. Bronson removed to Gowahati in 1875. At present there is one church with 106 members.

4. Sibsagor. The Sibsagor station was commenced in 1841. It has been the headquarters from which excursions have been made to the Naga hills, where successful evangelical work has been done. The lamented Dr. Ward and his wife deserve honorable mention in connection with this station. There was reported in May last one church with 126 members.

The mission in Assam has on the whole been a successful one, especially in its connection with the Garos. We may confidently look for large results in the future in this mission.

Associations, Baptist.—According to Dr. Underhill an association or general assembly of the churches in Somersetshire and the adjacent counties, in England, was formed about 1653, several meetings of which were held during succeeding years at Wells, Tiverton, and Bridgewater. Others are under the impression that regular Associations were instituted at a later period, and that they sprung from the inconvenience of meeting in larger bodies than those gathered in Somersetshire. The first general assembly, representing the nation, met in London in September, 1689; it was composed of delegates from more than a hundred churches scattered over England and Wales; it gave its sanction to the celebrated creed now known with additions as the Philadelphia Confession of Faith. This convention disclaimed all "power to prescribe or impose anything upon the faith or practice of any of the churches of Christ," even though they were represented in the assembly; and they further resolved "that whatever is determined by us in any case shall not be binding upon any one church till the consent of that church be first had." In it every motion about "counsel or advice had to be proved out of the Word of God, and the Scriptures given with the fraternal counsels." The messengers composing the assembly brought letters from the churches commending them to it. Its "breviats" or minutes were "transcribed," and a copy sent to every church. The assembly, at a time when traveling was expensive and dangerous, was found to be inconvenient, and Associations, with exactly the same aims and powers, took the place of the larger body. This is Crosby's account. Ivimey states that one Association of west of England Baptist Churches met in Bristol and another in Frome in 1692. These were probably the first regular Baptist Associations of modern times.

The Philadelphia Association was formally established in 1707, and it has lived and flourished ever since. Dr. Samuel Jones, in his "Century Sermon," published in the volume of "Minutes from 1707 to 1807," informs us that this body originated in what were "called general and sometimes yearly meetings." These meetings were commenced in 1688, and in many of their features they appear to have been Associations. But in 1707 they had regular delegates from Lower Dublin, Middletown, Cohansie, Piscataqua, and Welsh Tract, the five churches composing the Association; and their meetings instead of being almost exclusively devotional, became assemblies for worship and for the transaction of considerable business for their churches. We have now 1005 Associations in the United States.

Associations, The Oldest American Baptist.—The Philadelphia Association, 1707.

The Charleston Association, South Carolina, 1751.

The Sandy Creek Association, North Carolina, 1758.

The Kehukee Association, North Carolina, 1765.
The Ketocton Association. Virginia, 1766.
The Warren Association, Rhode Island, 1767.
The Stonington Association, Connecticut, 1772.
The Red Stone Association, Pennsylvania, 1776.
The New Hampshire Association, New Hampshire, 1776.
The Shaftesbury Association, Vermont, 1781.
The Woodstock Association, Vermont, 1783.
The Georgia Association, Georgia, 1784.
The Holston Association, Tennessee, 1786.
The Bowdoinham Association, Maine, 1787.
The Vermont Association, Vermont, 1787.

Atkinson, Rev. Wm. D., was born in Greene Co., S. C., Nov. 17, 1818. He died Oct. 17, 1879. His paternal grandfather was a North Carolinian, who fought in the Revolutionary war, and at its close moved to Georgia and settled in Greene County. Wm. D. Atkinson, after four years of academical preparation, entered Mercer University in 1844 and graduated in 1848. He had been converted and baptized in the fall of 1839, was licensed by Shiloh church soon after graduation, and was ordained in Monticello, Ga., in September, 1848. For thirty years he served various churches in Monroe, Jasper, Harris, Greene, Glynn, Pierce, and Tatnall Counties. He was an industrious, energetic, and sympathizing pastor, and an earnest, forcible, and sensible speaker, wielding great influence over his audiences. His piety was most sincere, and in labors he was truly abundant. He taught school frequently, and was a successful instructor, and as an advocate of the temperance cause he was earnest and uncompromising. That he baptized more than a thousand persons proves his success as a pastor. He turned many to righteousness. In erecting houses of worship, in building up weak churches, and in enlisting the pious endeavors of church members he proved himself a master-workman. Above medium size, he was also large in heart and soul. His death produced a profound sensation in Southern Georgia, where he was laboring at the time, and all classes and persuasions united in performing the last sad duties to his remains, exclaiming, "His place can never be filled!"

ATLANTA THEOLOGICAL SEMINARY.

Atlanta Theological Seminary.—This seminary, for the education of colored Baptist ministers in Georgia, is sustained chiefly by the American Baptist Home Mission Society, whose headquarters are in New York. The building is very neat and appropriate. This seminary has been in existence eight years. It was located for a time in Augusta, under the name of the "Augusta Institute." It has given instruction to 296 students, of whom 187 were ministers, or candidates for the ministry. It contains now 100 students, 60 of whom are preparing for the pulpit.

Atonement, The.—The atonement is *a transfer of our guilt to Jesus*. This doctrine is strikingly foreshadowed by the Jewish scapegoat. Of it Moses says, "And Aaron shall lay both his hands upon the head of the live goat, and confess over him all the iniquities of the children of Israel, and all their transgressions in all their sins, putting them upon the head of the goat, and shall send him away by the hand of a fit man into the wilderness; and the goat shall bear upon him all their iniquities unto a land not inhabited; and he shall let go the goat in the wilderness." Lev. xvi. 21, 22. The blood of the goat was not spilled, no blow was inflicted upon it; but the sins of the children of Israel were typically placed upon it to prefigure the transfer of our sins to the Son of God. In the case of the scapegoat the transfer was figurative, in the Saviour's it was literal. "He was numbered with the transgressors, and he bare the sin of many." Isa. liii. 12. "The Lord hath laid on him the iniquity of us all." Isa. liii. 6. "For he hath made him to be sin for us, who knew no sin; that we might be made the righteousness of God in him." 2 Cor. v. 21. Paul shows that he means the actual transfer of our guilt to Christ by saying, "Who knew no sin,"—that is, of his own; he was made sin, he says, by reckoning our sins to him, not by any sins which he committed. The word translated sin cannot mean a sin-offering in this text, for it is contrasted with righteousness. If the one is a sin-offering the other must be a righteousness-offering; but the word translated righteousness has no such meaning. And sin, not a sin-offering, must be the sense of the word in this connection. This is the common use of the word elsewhere. Men may put forth as many philosophical pleas as their ingenuity can furnish, but according to Paul the sins of the whole saved family were reckoned to—transferred to Jesus.

The atonement is *a transfer of our pains to Jesus*. The entire sufferings demanded by our sins were inflicted upon the Saviour. Isaiah liii. 5, says, "He was wounded for our transgressions, he was bruised for our iniquities; the chastisement of our peace was upon him; and with his stripes we are healed." Here he suffers the innocent for the guilty; he takes our wounds, our bruises, and the chastisement of our peace; and his stripes give perfect healing to the soul; "the blood of Jesus Christ, God's Son, shed by the transferred pains of the believing family, cleanses us from all sin." Christ lived and died as the proper substitute of his people; so that his acts were theirs, and all his pains. This doctrine is foreshadowed by the death of the paschal lamb, and all the sacrifices of the law of Moses; and it is presented in all its fullness by the dread scenes of Calvary. As Peter says in his First Epistle, iii. 18, "For Christ also hath once suffered for sins, the just for the unjust, that he might bring us to God." The believer has lost his sins and pains eternally in the death of his loving Lord.

The *design of the atonement was to satisfy* the mercy of God. The heart of God is a fountain of love continually overflowing, and nothing can keep in its bursting streams. To gratify this irresistible affection of Jehovah Jesus became a man and endured our pains, and our death; and now "God is in Christ reconciling the world unto himself not imputing their trespasses unto them." He is busy by his Spirit removing the blind hatred to himself of human hearts, that his love in the crucified Lamb might bring multitudes to trust and love him.

The atonement was also intended *to meet the demands of God's law*. It complies with these perfectly. In the obedience and death of Christ the precepts of the law have been fulfilled and its penalties have been endured, and he is "the end of the law for righteousness to every one that believeth." Rom. x. 4. That is, he is its *completion*, its *fulfillment*; and when a soul trusts the Saviour the law justifies him and gives him the righteousness which Christ acquired when he obeyed its precepts and suffered its penalties. "Even the righteousness of God which is by faith of Jesus Christ unto all and upon all them that believe." Rom. iii. 22. Moreover, the law demanded for God supreme love from men, and a holy life. And when the Spirit changes a human heart, and gives the faith which secures the forgiveness of God in the soul, the happy recipient is melted in adoring gratitude before the Redeemer, and his heart looks up to God while it says, "Whom have I in heaven but thee? And there is none upon earth that I desire besides thee." And the spirit of grace leads him into the holy dispositions and practices enjoined by the pure law of Jehovah.

The atonement transfers our sins and pains to Christ our substitute, and by faith in Jesus it opens up to the soul a channel through which God's pardoning love may reach and rejoice it, and by which the Spirit's sanctifying grace may purify the heart, and fit it for the everlasting rest.

Atwell, Rev. George Benjamin, son of Rev. George and Esther (Rogers) Atwell; born in Lyme,

Conn., July 9, 1793; his mother was a sister of Rev. Peter Rogers, of Revolutionary fame; his father a worthy preacher of his time; converted when nine years old; licensed to preach by the Second Baptist church in Colchester, Conn., in 1820; ordained in Longmeadow, Mass., in 1822, the first Baptist minister in the place; pastor in West Woodstock, Conn., ten years; in Cromwell one year; in Meriden two years; in Canton ten years; in Pleasant Valley twelve years; was distinguished for his originality of expression, purity of life, nobleness of character, and fidelity to his calling; died in Pleasant Valley, April 23, 1879, in his eighty-sixth year. A record of his worthy life has been given to the public in a volume of "Memorial Sketches," by his daughter, Harriet G. Atwell.

Augusta, Ga., First Baptist Church of.—The First Baptist church in Augusta originated thus, to quote from the earliest church record: "In the year 1817, Jesse D. Green, a layman, was active in gathering together the few scattered Baptists in Augusta, and, after holding one or more preliminary meetings, the brethren and sisters, to the number of eighteen, had drawn up and adopted a covenant, to which they affixed their names." This was styled "The Baptist Praying Society." On the fourth Saturday and Sunday in May, 1817, the society assembled in the court-house, and were regularly constituted, by the advice and assistance of brethren Abraham Marshall, Matthews, Carson, and Antony. Brother Matthews preached from Matt. xvi. 18. At the various meetings of 1818, and during the early part of 1819, Rev. Abraham Marshall acted as pastor. Subsequently, by his advice, Rev. Jesse Mercer was elected pastor, but declined to accept. In 1820, Rev. Wm. T. Brantly was chosen to the pastoral office, and consented to serve without any pecuniary consideration for his services, and, by permission of the trustees, services were held twice every Lord's day in the chapel of the academy, of which Dr. Brantly was rector. Through his exertions a lot was secured, and a brick house which cost $20,000 was built and dedicated May 6, 1821. A large congregation was soon collected. Dr. Brantly's labors were greatly blessed, many conversions followed, and members were added, embracing in some instances men and women of prominence and wealth; and when Dr. Brantly resigned, in 1826, the church was able to give his successor a comfortable support. Perhaps the church owes more to Dr. Wm. T. Brantly, Sr., than to any other man. Since his time it has gone steadily forward, increasing in strength and usefulness, sending out four colonies, and aiding all the grand enterprises sustained by the denomination. The list of pastors embraces the following: Rev. James Shannon, from 1826 to 1829, a distinguished scholar, under whose labors the church was prospered; Rev. C. D. Mallory, from 1829 to 1835. Earnest in godliness, he was a great blessing to the church. Rev. W. J. Hard succeeded, and labored faithfully until 1839. In the autumn of 1840, Rev. Wm. T. Brantly, the younger, took charge, and continued in office eight years. During his term of office several precious revivals occurred, and much good fruit resulted to bless the church. It was found necessary to enlarge the house in 1846 to accommodate the congregation. The belfry then erected contains the bell, a present from Wm. H. Turpin, for more than forty years a devoted friend and member of the church. Brief pastorates then ensued of Rev. N. G. Foster and Rev. C. B. Jannett. Dr. J. G. Binney was pastor from 1852 to 1855, when he resumed missionary work in Burmah. During his ministry twenty feet more were added to the rear of the building. Rev. J. E. Ryerson, a most eloquent man, followed, serving until 1860. Dr. A. J. Huntington then became pastor, and continued in charge until the summer of 1865. Rev. J. H. Cuthbert was his successor, under whose earnest ministry the church was revived, and some valuable additions made to the membership. The next pastor was Rev. James Dixon, who served until 1874; then Dr. M. B. Wharton took charge and labored one year very successfully. By his advice, and under his superintendence, a chapel or lecture-room, which is without a superior in the State, was added to the building. Dr. Wharton was succeeded by Rev. W. W. Landrum, who has been in charge since Feb. 18, 1876. This church is perhaps the second Baptist church in the State as regards the influence, wealth, and the social position of its members, coming next after the Second Baptist church of Atlanta. Its building, in which the Southern Baptist Convention was organized in 1845, though not architecturally beautiful and commanding, is capacious and comfortable. With one exception it is the largest Protestant audience-room in the city. Its location is central, and now, as when first selected, on one of the most eligible lots in the city.

Austin, Rev. Richard H., born in Uniontown, Pa., Oct. 19, 1831, was converted in early life, and united with the Methodist Church; graduated in the Law Department of Madison College, Pa., and afterwards practiced in the courts of Fayette Co., Pa. In 1856 he was baptized at Uniontown, by Rev. I. D. King; was ordained in 1857, and settled as pastor of the church at Brownsville, Pa.; was subsequently pastor at Pottsville, Meadville, and Franklin, Pa. Failing health obliged him to withdraw from the pastorate, and he entered upon a business life. His labors soon became abundantly remunerated, and in recognition of God's claim upon his accumulating wealth he scattered and still increased. Many needy churches and pastors became the recipients of his benefactions, and he delighted to honor God with his substance. In 1879 he was elected president of the Pennsylvania Baptist General Association. This position he still holds, and, having retired from active business pursuits, he labors with zeal and liberality to advance the interests of State mission work. He is also a member of the board of curators of the university at Lewisburg. He is an earnest preacher, and has a warm heart and ready hand for every good word and work.

Australian Baptists.—The earliest mention in official reports of the churches founded by the Baptists in Australia is in the appendix to the account of the session of the Baptist Union of Great Britain and Ireland, held in London, April 19–24, 1844. It is there stated that the following churches had been established: Sydney, 3; Port Jackson, 1; Port Philip, 1; Van Diemen's Land, 2; South Australia, 2; in all, *nine* churches. The number of members does not appear, and probably was very small, the colonies being then in their infancy. During the next twenty years the population of the several colonies greatly increased, and the steady stream of immigration from the mother-country strengthened the existing churches and promoted the formation of others. In 1865 the official report of the Baptist Union stated that there were 26 churches in Australia and 2 in New Zealand, nearly all of them having pastors. The 2 churches in Melbourne reported an aggregate membership of 727, but most of the others were small, only 1 besides having more than 100 members. During the next few years some efforts were made in England to secure for the Australian field the services of ministers of superior training and ability, and the principal cities were supplied with pastors whose presence and efforts gave an impetus to denominational growth. In 1874 there were 22 churches in New South Wales, 10 in Queensland, 41 in South Australia, 51 in Victoria, 14 in New Zealand, 3 in Tasmania, or Van Diemen's Land. The population of Victoria was 731,538, and the aggregate Baptist membership about 1700. From the Baptist Union report for the present year (1880) it appears that much has been done in later years to consolidate and unify the denomination. Scarcely any of the Australian churches are unassociated, and societies for promoting missions in foreign countries, for succoring weak churches, and for educating students for the ministry are in regular working order. The Victorian Association reports 34 churches, with a membership of 2636, and 19 branch schools and stations, 367 Sunday-school teachers, and 3880 scholars. Besides a home mission, this Association supports several native missionaries in India. The South Australian Association has 38 churches and 5 preaching stations, 21 preachers engaged in ministerial work, and 2311 members. The New South Wales Baptist Union reports 14 churches and 4 stations, 716 members, 1035 Sunday-school scholars, 118 teachers, and it circulates a denominational paper. The Queensland Association has 21 churches and stations, 729 members, 10 pastors, not including 6 German Baptist churches, with a membership of about 300. In New Zealand there is 1 Association in the south of the island, with 7 churches, and there are about twice as many unassociated. The aggregate membership is 1450, with 15 ministers. No progress appears to have been made in Tasmania, the report showing the existence of only 3 churches, but giving no statistics. The total number of Baptist churches in Australasia may be given approximately as 127, with 87 ministers and 7700 members. In the leading cities the church edifices are large and elegant, that in Collins Street, Melbourne, accommodating 1050 persons. The largest membership is reported by the Hinders Street church, Adelaide, namely, 474. Two of the Melbourne churches report more than 400 members in each.

Avery, Angus Clark, was born Jan. 26, 1836, in Henry Co., Mo. The Averys first settled in Groton, Conn. Nine of them were killed in the war of the Revolution. Five were wounded at Groton Heights in 1781, and four were commissioned officers in the struggle for independence. His mother's ancestors settled in Virginia, and were active in the war for independence. His great-grandfather was killed in the battle of Blue Lick. Mr. Avery studied two years in Burrett College, and a year in the State University of Missouri, and graduated from Burrett College with valedictory honors in 1858. He studied law, and was admitted to the bar in 1860, and he practiced law in Clinton, Mo., till the war suspended business. He then turned his attention to real estate, and is now the largest land-holder in the county, and he has done more than any other man for the surrounding country. Through great difficulties he built portions of the Missouri, Kansas and Texas Railroad, and he secured the completion of this great highway. He established the first National Bank of Clinton. He is a member and a deacon of the Baptist church of Clinton, and superintendent of its Sabbath-school, and he contributed $10,000 to build its house of worship. He is a trustee of William Jewell College, Mo., and a large contributor to its endowment. Few men are more favorably known than Mr. Avery. He is a man of large means and of great humility, and he is an untiring worker for Jesus. He holds many important offices, and he is growing in usefulness as a citizen and as a Christian.

Ayer, Gen. L. M., was born in Barnwell Co., S. C., in 1830, of wealthy parents. He is a graduate of the South Carolina College; studied law, but gave his attention chiefly to politics; served several terms in the Legislature, was a general of militia, and was elected to the United States Congress, but the beginning of the war prevented him from taking his seat. He was afterwards in the Confederate Congress. About ten years ago he became a Baptist, and was ordained to the ministry. He is remarkable for kindness and hospitality, and is an able speaker. He has recently published a work on infant salvation, which has elicited high commendation.

B.

Babcock, Gen. Joshua, born in Westerly, R. I., in 1707; graduated at Yale College; studied medicine and surgery in Boston and in England; settled in his native town; was an accomplished scholar; much in public business; became chief justice of the Supreme Court of Rhode Island; intimate with Benjamin Franklin; first postmaster in Westerly in 1776; had an elegant mansion, still standing; enrolled a Baptist; one of the first corporators of Brown University in 1764, and one of the board of fellows in 1770; a major-general of militia in 1776; very active in the Revolution; had two half-brothers and three sons that graduated at Yale College. His son, Col. Henry, became distinguished, and was a Baptist, having united with the First Baptist church in Boston, Mass. Dr. Joshua died in Westerly, April 1, 1783, aged seventy-six.

Babcock, Rev. Oliver W., the pastor of the Baptist church in Omro, Wis., is a native of Swanton, Franklin Co., Vt., where he was born in 1818, and where he passed his childhood and youth. He began his ministry in his native State with the Baptist church at Enosburg Falls, where he was ordained Sept. 24, 1849. He was pastor at East Enosburg, North Fairfax, North and South Fairfield, and Fletcher, in Vermont. In New York he served the Baptist church at Stockholm two years, Malone five years, Madrid one year, and Gouverneur seven years. In 1867, under appointment of the American Baptist Home Missionary Society, he went to Wisconsin, and became pastor at Manasha and Neenah, where he labored six years. He subsequently became pastor for a brief period at Appleton, and he is now pastor of the Baptist church at Omro, where he has labored with much acceptance for six years.

Babcock, Rev. Rufus, son of Elias Babcock, was born in North Stonington, Conn., April 22, 1758. His father, a Separatist and then a Baptist, moved with his parents, about 1775, to North Canaan, Conn.; was two or three times called out as a soldier in the Revolution; served with the company of Capt. Timothy Morse, whose daughter he married; in 1783 was baptized by Rev. Joshua Morse; united with the Baptist church in Landisfield, Mass., by which, afterwards, he was licensed to preach; gathered a church in Colebrook, Conn., where he was ordained in 1794; the first minister of any denomination settled in that town; began his preaching in a barn in mid-winter; preached also widely in the towns adjacent with large success; served the Colebrook church as pastor till he was seventy-three years old; received above 500 members; educated his two younger sons, Cyrus Giles, and Rufus, Jr., at Brown University,—the former graduated in 1816, and died soon after,—the latter graduated in 1821 and became the widely-known Baptist preacher, Dr. Rufus Babcock; he had a vigorous mind, was an effective preacher, widely known and greatly honored. He died in November, 1842, aged eighty-four years.

Babcock, Rufus, D.D., was born in Colebrook, Conn., Sept. 18, 1798. His father was the pastor of the Baptist church in that place. He entered Brown University in 1817, and passed through the full course of study, graduating in 1821. Among his classmates were President Eliphaz Fay, of Waterville College; Hon. Levi Haile, judge of the Supreme Court of Rhode Island; and the well-known Dr. Samuel G. Howe, of Boston. Not long after leaving college he was appointed tutor in Columbian College, now Columbian University, which, under Rev. Dr. Staughton, had recently been established in Washington, D. C. During his connection with the college he pursued his theological studies under the direction of its gifted president, having already received a license to preach from the church of which he was a member. He was ordained in 1823 by the Hudson River Association at Poughkeepsie, N. Y., and shortly after his ordination became pastor of the Baptist church in that place. Here he remained until invited to Salem, Mass. There he had a most happy and successful ministry from 1826 to 1833. He was then invited to take the presidency of Waterville College (now Colby University), which office he held for nearly four years. Retiring from it, he took charge successively of the Spruce Street church in Philadelphia, the First Baptist church in New Bedford, Mass., then again of the church in Poughkeepsie where he commenced his ministry. His last pastorate was in Paterson, N. J. In the work of religious organizations which were concerned in giving the gospel to the destitute he took great interest. He was president of the American Baptist Publication Society, the corresponding secretary of the American and Foreign Bible Society, to promote whose interests he wrote and traveled extensively. At different times he acted also as an agent of the American Sunday-School Union. For these places of trust and useful labor he possessed rare qualifications, and did good service in the cause of his Master. Dr. Babcock had a ready pen, and always maintained an intimate connection with the religious press. From 1841 to 1845 he was the editor of the *Baptist Memorial*. He wrote and published during his life several volumes. His correspondence with the *Watchman*, as it is now called, extended over almost the entire period of its existence. He devoted himself with ceaseless diligence to the work to which he consecrated the dew of his youth and the energies of his riper years. His death created a void which has never in all respects been filled. When he left the world it could truly be said, "Blessed are the dead which die in the Lord from henceforth. Yea, saith the Spirit, that they may rest from their labors; and their works do follow them."

Dr. Babcock died at Salem, Mass., where he had gone to visit among his old parishioners. The event occurred May 4, 1875.

Babcock, Rev. Stephen, born in Westerly, R. I., Oct. 12, 1706, was a constituent member of the Presbyterian church in Westerly in 1742, and was chosen a deacon; became a Separatist; organized the Baptist church (Hill church) in Westerly, April 5, 1750, and was ordained the pastor on the same day; acted a conspicuous and effective part in the great "New Light" movement; aided in organizing many new churches; joined in calling the famous council of May 29, 1753, held in North Stonington, Conn., and the council in Exeter, R. I., in September, 1854; bold, faithful standard-bearer in troublous times; died full of historic honor Dec. 22, 1775. He was succeeded by his son, Rev. Oliver Babcock; ordained Sept. 18, 1776; good and faithful; died Feb. 13, 1784, in his forty-sixth year.

Backus, Elizabeth, wife of Samuel Backus, of Norwich, Conn., and mother of Rev. Isaac Backus, the Baptist historian, was a descendant of the Plymouth Winslows, and a talented, heroic Christian woman; was converted in 1721; lost her husband in 1740; became a Separatist with her son in 1745; was suspended from communion of the Congregational church, with her son and seven others, Oct. 17, 1745; was imprisoned for refusing to pay rates for the standing order in October, 1752, when she wrote her son the letter that has become historic; and died Jan. 26, 1769. Though she did not unite with the Baptists, as there was then no Baptist church in that region, yet she evidently held firmly and suffered bravely for some of their distinguishing principles.

Backus, Rev. Isaac, was born at Norwich, Conn., Jan. 9, 1724, of parents who were actively

REV. ISAAC BACKUS.

identified with the "pure" Congregationalism as opposed to the Saybrook platform, and his early religious training influenced greatly his future life. He was converted in 1741 during the Great New England Awakening, but did not join himself to the church until ten months later, and then with much hesitation, owing to the laxity of church discipline and its low state of religious feeling. From this church—the First Congregational of Norwich —he and others soon separated themselves, and began to hold meetings on the Sabbath for mutual edification. Feeling himself called by God to the work of his ministry, he shortly after began to exhort and preach, although there were at that time penal enactments against public preaching by any except settled pastors, unless with their consent and at their express desire. He was, however, unmolested, and addressed himself earnestly to the work of a pastor and evangelist, his first pastorate being that of a Separate church at Middleborough, to which he was ordained in 1748. In the following year he married Susannah Mason, of Rehoboth, with whom he lived fifty-one years, and of whom he wrote near the close of his life that he considered her the greatest earthly blessing God had given him.

The subject of baptism was agitating the church of which Mr. Backus took charge, and it was only after a long and bitter struggle with himself that two years later he was enabled to put aside all doubts and perplexities on the subject and come out unreservedly for baptism through a profession of faith. His stand on this subject and his baptism by Elder Peirce, of Rhode Island, soon led to his exclusion from the church, although he did not consider himself a Baptist, nor did he desire to connect himself with that denomination. He continued his labors as an evangelist until 1756, when, with six baptized believers, a Baptist church was formed in Middleborough, and Mr. Backus was ordained its pastor. In 1765 he was elected a trustee of Brown University, which position he held for thirty-four years.

At this time the Baptists were subject to much oppression and persecution by the civil powers of Massachusetts. They were taxed for the maintenance of the state churches, and upon refusal of payment of rates their lands and goods were distressed, and themselves put in prison. In 1774, Mr. Backus was chosen agent of the Baptist churches of Massachusetts, and to his faithful and untiring labors we owe much of our present civil liberty. For ten years he labored and struggled and wrote for exemption from the burdens laid upon the Baptists; but although not entirely unsuccessful he did not live to see the fruit of his work, the entire severance of church and state in Massachusetts not taking place until 1833.

In 1774, Mr. Backus was sent as the agent of the Baptist churches of the Warren Association to Philadelphia to endeavor to enlist in their behalf the Continental Congress, which met there at that time. He with agents from other Associations conferred with the Massachusetts delegation and others, and President Manning, of Brown University, read a memorial setting forth the grievances and oppressions under which the Baptists labored, and praying for relief therefrom. The result of this effort on the part of the New England Baptists to obtain religious freedom was hurtful rather than advantageous. After the adjournment of the Continental Congress most unjust and untruthful reports were circulated in regard to the proceedings of the conference. The Baptists were accused of presenting false charges of oppression in order to prevent the colonies uniting in defense of their liberties. To counteract if possible these injurious reports Mr. Backus met the Committee of Grievances at Boston, and they drew up an address affirming their loyalty to the colonies and defending their action at Philadelphia, and it was presented to the Congress of Massachusetts then in session. In 1775, when the General Court met at Watertown, Mr. Backus sent in a memorial, setting forth with great plainness the policy of the State towards those who were not of the Standing Order, and demanding religious liberty as the inherent right of every man. This memorial was twice read in the Assembly, and permission was given Dr. Fletcher to bring in a bill for the redress of the grievances "he apprehended the Baptists labored under." The bill was brought in but never acted upon by the House. Under the direction of the Association, which met that year at Warren, Mr. Backus then drew up a letter to all the Baptist societies asking for a general meeting of their delegates for devising the best means for attaining their religious freedom. In 1777 he read an address before the Warren Association "To the People of New England" on the subject of religious freedom, and the same year his first volume of the "History of New England" was issued. In the following year he read before the Warren Association another paper on religious liberty, which was published at their unanimous request. In 1779 he published in the *Independent Chronicle*, of Boston, a reply to the statement made at the drafting of the proposed new State constitution, that the Baptists had never been persecuted, and they had sent their agent to Philadelphia in 1774 with a false memorial of their grievances in order to prevent the union of the colonies. This false assertion was made in order to obtain votes necessary to carry Article III. in the Bill of Rights, which gave to civil rulers powers in religious matters. In 1780 the Baptist Convention published an appeal to the people against this article, which led to a newspaper controversy, in which the Baptists were defended by Mr. Backus. A protest was then issued by the Association, but the General Court nevertheless adopted the objectionable article, and the Warren Association through their agent again addressed the Baptists of the State. Under the new constitution the Baptists, "if they gave in certificates to the ruling sect that they belonged to a Baptist society, and desired their money to go to the minister thereof, he (the minister) could sue the money out of the hands of those who took it." Mr. Backus met the Committee of Grievances in 1785 to consult with them in relation to their course of action under such ruling. They concluded to accept the compromise despite the earnest objections of Mr. Backus. Had they been willing to resist, even to the loss of their property, the giving in of certificates, and had they demanded the entire separation of church and state, the desired end would no doubt have been attained many years before it was.

In 1789, Mr. Backus visited Virginia and North Carolina, at the request of the brethren, for the purpose of strengthening and building up their churches. He spent six months in this work, and was the means of accomplishing much good. The distance he traveled while there—some 3000 miles—and the number of sermons preached—126—show the marvelous energy of the man, and the immense amount of work he must have accomplished during his ministerial life.

Mr. Backus continued in the active duties of a pastor and evangelist until within a short time of his death, which occurred Nov. 20, 1806. In appearance he was tall and commanding, and in later years inclined towards portliness. He possessed an iron constitution, and was capable of great physical endurance.

The historical works of Mr. Backus are of great value on account of the deep research he made in the collection of his material, and his impartiality in presenting the facts. The Baptists owe much to him for the discovery and preservation of many interesting and important events concerning their history during colonial times.

Backus, Jay S., D.D., a Baptist clergyman, was born in Washington Co., N. Y., Feb. 17, 1810, and died in Groton, N. Y., 1879. He studied at Madison University, but by reason of serious illness, which crippled him for life, he did not finish his course. Nevertheless the degrees of Master of Arts and Doctor of Divinity were conferred on him by that university. He was ordained as pastor of the Baptist church of Groton, N. Y., which he served with marked success. During this pastorate he labored as an evangelist, assisting other ministers in special revival meetings. In this work he was known as a preacher of great power. He also served as pastor of the First Baptist church of Auburn, N. Y., the McDougal Street and the South Baptist churches of the city of New York, and the First Baptist church of Syracuse, whose house of worship had been burned while uninsured. By undaunted effort, perseverance, and financial tact he secured a new and better house, and dedicated it free from debt.

For a few years he was associate editor of the *New York Chronicle* with Dr. Pharcellus Church. In 1862 he was elected secretary of the American Baptist Home Mission Society, a position of great responsibility and high honor. The energy, the zeal, the sanctified ambition, so characteristic of the man, made him one of the most successful managers of that great enterprise.

Bacon, Joel Smith, D.D., was born in Cayuga Co., N. Y., Sept. 3, 1802. In 1821 he entered Homer Academy, and after two years' study he was admitted to the Sophomore class at Hamilton College, Clinton, N. Y., where, in 1826, he graduated with honors. While at college he was distinguished for scholarship and readiness in debate. Among his classmates were Dr. Hague, Judge Bosworth, Dr. Carmichael, and others eminent in church

JOEL SMITH BACON, D.D.

and state. For one year after his graduation Dr. Bacon taught school in Amelia Co., Va. The year following he took charge of a classical school in Princeton, N. J., and while there associated intimately with members of the faculties of the college and the seminary, and was highly esteemed by them. In 1829 he accepted the presidency of Georgetown College, and held it for ten years, with the universal respect of the students, of the trustees, and of the community. In 1831 he was ordained to the ministry. In 1833 he resigned the presidency of Georgetown College and accepted the position of Professor of Mathematics and Natural Philosophy, at Hamilton, N. Y. Shortly after entering upon his duties, at his request, he was transferred to the chair of Moral and Mental Philosophy, a department of study usually conducted by presidents of colleges. The death of his father-in-law, Capt. Porter, led Prof. Bacon, in 1837, to resign his professorship, and removing to Salem, he became pastor of the First Baptist church in Lynn, Mass. He remained for nearly three years, greatly esteemed by the church and all who knew him. In December, 1839, Dr. Bacon resigned his pastorate. In 1843, two years after the resignation of Dr. Chapin, Dr. Bacon was elected president of the Columbian College, Washington, D. C. His connection with the college was a successful one, and, as in all the positions which he occupied, he showed himself well adapted to the responsible and arduous duties of the station. After serving as president for eleven years he resigned, and devoted his energies to female education in Georgia, Louisiana, Virginia, and Alabama. He accepted an appointment in 1866 from the American and Foreign Bible Society to distribute Bibles among the colored people, and the amount of good he accomplished by way of counsel, instruction, and encouragement among the freedmen the records of eternity only will reveal. It was a lowly work for one who for so many years had been a leader among the most intellectual of the land, but a work which, nevertheless, he enjoyed with his whole heart. In this work of two or three years Dr. Bacon ' finished his course." On Sunday, Oct. 31, 1869, Dr. Bacon had the pleasure of baptizing two of his daughters, then pupils at Edgewood, a school at Fluvanna, Va., in the Rivanna River, one of them relating her experience on the bank in the presence of a large and weeping circle of spectators. He reached his home in Richmond November 3; in two days after he was attacked by pleurisy and pneumonia, and on the following Wednesday fell asleep in Christ. Dr. Bacon's mind was versatile and practical, and he was fond of studying men and things as well as books. He was an acute inquirer; he was an interesting and practical preacher, always commanding attention and awakening and stimulating thought. As a man, he was of pure and lofty sentiments, with broad and generous sympathies, and with kindly affections.

The honorary degree of D.D. was conferred upon Dr. Bacon in 1845.

Bacon, Prof. Milton E., a distinguished educator in Mississippi, was born in 1818 in the State of Georgia. He graduated at the University of Georgia in 1838, and soon after engaged in teaching. In 1843 he founded the "Southern Female College" at Lagrange, Ga., where he labored about fourteen years. He then removed to Aberdeen, Miss., and established the Aberdeen Female College, where he taught nine years. He was very much loved by his pupils, and often received the highest testimonials of their esteem. In 1879, by invitation of the alumni of Lagrange College, there was a reunion of Prof. Bacon with his old pupils at Atlanta, Ga. This interesting meeting was attended by hundreds of ladies from a number of the surrounding States. Prof. Bacon has long been an active and zealous Baptist.

Bacon, Rev. William, M.D., was born at Greenwich, N. J., June 30, 1802. Early in life he united with the Presbyterian Church. Soon afterwards his thoughts were turned towards the ministry, and, encouraged by his friends, he entered upon a course of collegiate study at the University of Pennsylvania, where he graduated at the age of twenty. About this time, having begun to question the reality of his conversion, and consequently his call to the ministry, he studied medicine, and commenced practice at Allowaystown, Salem Co., N. J. Here he was brought under the ministry of Rev. Joseph Sheppard, the loved and revered pastor of the church at Salem, through whose intelligent and faithful counsels he was brought into the liberty of the children of God, and by whom he was baptized. The desire to preach the gospel was now kindled anew in his heart. Ordained as an evangelist, he went everywhere preaching the Word, the Lord working with him and crowning his labors with great success. In 1830 he became pastor of the church at Pittsgrove, in 1833 of the church at Woodstown, and in 1838 of the church at Dividing Creek. In all these churches he served faithfully and well his Lord and the souls of the people. His pastorate at the latter place lasted eleven years, and appears to have been one of unusual prosperity. Weighed down by these years of toil, and hindered by domestic cares and afflictions from giving himself wholly to the work of the ministry, he retired from pastoral duties and resumed the practice of medicine, in which he continued till his death. He was held in much esteem by the public, and at the earnest request of the people of the district in which he lived he served them two successive terms in the Legislature of the State, commanding, by his intelligence, integrity, and moral worth, the respect of every member of the House. At the age of sixty-six, after a brief sickness, he fell asleep in Jesus, at Newport, N. J.

Bacon, Winchell D., of Waukesha, Wis., was born at Stillwater, Saratoga Co., N. Y. His father was a farmer. His mother's maiden name was Lydia Barber Daisley. He remained on his father's farm until nineteen years of age, and then went to Troy, N. Y., and served as a clerk in a store for two years. In 1837 he accompanied his father's family to Butternuts, Otsego Co., N. Y., where his father had purchased land, and here he again engaged in farming. In September, 1841, he started with his wife for the West, and settled in Prairieville, now Waukesha. Here he bought a farm, and engaged in the occupation for which he was trained. In connection with his farming he entered extensively into business pursuits in Waukesha, in which he was pre-eminently successful. In 1863, Mr. Bacon was appointed paymaster in the army, and served in that capacity for some time. In 1865 he, with other citizens, organized the Farmers' National Bank of Waukesha, and he was elected president. In 1853 he was a member of the Legislature. He has been a member of the board of trustees of the Hospital for the Insane, of the Deaf and Dumb Institute, and of the University of Chicago.

In early life Mr. Bacon made a profession of religion and united with the Baptist Church. He is decided in his religious convictions and denominational preferences. Mr. Bacon in some communities would be called a radical man. He certainly has the courage of his convictions, and is outspoken on all subjects that relate to the reformation of society and the State. He is the fearless enemy of all oppression and wrong. He has a wife and three children living. Joshua, his only son, is one of the rising physicians of the county and State.

Bagby, Rev. Alfred, was born June 15, 1828, at Stevensville, King and Queen Co., Va., and is a son of John Bagby, who is still living, and in his eighty-seventh year. Two brothers also entered the ministry, Rev. Prof. G. F. Bagby, of Bethel College, Ky., and Rev. R. H. Bagby, D.D., who died in 1870. He was educated mainly at Stevensville Academy and at the Columbian College, where he graduated in 1847. In 1850 he entered Princeton Theological Seminary, N. J., but owing to the failure of his health he was obliged to leave in 1851. He spent two years in teaching in New Kent Co., Va., and was principal of the Stevensville Academy from 1856 to 1859. Mr. Bagby has been pastor of churches at Hicksford and at Mount Olivet, Va. In 1855 he took charge of the church at Mattapony, where he has been the honored and successful pastor for twenty-three years. He also started an interest at West Point, Va., where he is now laboring in conjunction with Mattapony. The latter church has been greatly blessed under Mr. Bagby's ministry in the development of the gifts of its members, among whom it has sent forth Rev. R. H. Bagby, D.D., pastor of Bruington church, Va.; Rev. John Pollard, D.D., pastor of Lee Street church, Baltimore; Rev. W. B. Todd, Virginia; and Rev. W. T. Hundley, Edgefield, S. C. The meeting-house at Mattapony was built in colonial times by the government for the Established Church. The adjacent grounds are crowded by graves and monuments of the dead, not a few of which antedate the Revolution for years. The remains of George Braxton, the father of one of the signers of the Declaration of Independence, repose here under a plain marble slab.

Bagby, Richard Hugh, D.D., the son of John and Elizabeth Bagby, was born at Stevensville, Va., June 16, 1820. He was converted while a student at the Virginia Baptist Seminary, now Richmond College, and became a member of the Bruington Baptist church in his native county of King and Queen. Of his conversion he writes, " I entered the seminary at Richmond, and nothing important happened, except that from my entrance my religious impressions increased, and my views of the pardon of sin through Christ grew brighter and clearer, until my distress on account of my sins was so great that I gave up all as lost. But one morning while at worship in the chapel, and in the act of praying, I determined to give myself to God, to work for him while life lasted, and to trust my salvation in his hands through the riches of his grace in Christ Jesus. I at once felt relief." He graduated at the Columbian College in 1839, after which he studied law. Having determined, however, to devote himself to the ministry, he relinquished the practice of his profession; was licensed to preach in 1841 by the Mattapony church, and in 1842 ordained. He was immediately called to the pastorate of the Bruington church, into whose fellowship he had been baptized eight years before. In this field he remained twenty-eight years, a laborious and eminently successful pastor, baptizing large numbers, and encouraging the membership in every good work. After this long and fruitful pastorate with the Bruington church, he accepted, in 1870, the appointment of associate secretary of State Missions in Virginia. He was for several consecutive sessions president of the Baptist General Association of the State, and served with great efficiency. He received the honorary degree of D.D. from the Columbian College in 1869. He died Oct. 29, 1870, from the effects of an illness brought on by exhausting labors in assisting in protracted meetings. He sleeps in the burial-ground of the church at Bruington, which he loved so earnestly and served so well, and the people of his charge have erected over his remains a neat marble monument. Dr. Bagby stood among the foremost of the Virginia ministry of his day. Some surpassed him in learning and in the graces of style; but for clearness and force, for directness, earnestness, and effectiveness of thought and manner, he was rarely excelled. As a pastor he had but few peers. His labors were largely and equally blessed in turning souls to God and in training them for usefulness in the service of truth and holiness.

Bailey, Rev. Alvin, one of the pioneers of the Baptist denomination in Illinois, was born at Westminster, Vt., Dec. 9, 1802. At the age of fourteen he united with the Baptist church in Coventry. He studied for the ministry at Hamilton, graduating in 1831. In the same year, in company with his classmate, Gardner Bartlett, afterwards associated with him in Western labor, he was ordained at Coventry, Vt. Removing soon after to Illinois with his wife, a sister of Dr. George B. Ide, he opened a school at Upper Alton, which may perhaps be regarded as a first step towards the foundation of the college now there. He at the same time served the church in Alton City as its pastor. Removing in due time to Carrollton, he became pastor of the church there. Here his wife died, and he married the widow of Rev. Allen

B. Freeman, of whose early death in Chicago mention is made elsewhere. Besides at Carrollton, he was pastor at Winchester and Jacksonville, publishing at the latter place the *Voice of Truth*, and afterwards the *Western Star*. In 1847 he returned to New York, and until 1853 served churches at East Lansing and Belfast in that State. In the last-named year he accepted a recall to Carrollton, Ill., but in 1855 returned to New York, and after a six-years' pastorate at McGrawville and one at Dryden, he died of typhoid pneumonia, at Etna, Tompkins Co., May 9, 1867. "Alvin Bailey," says Dr. J. D. Cole, "was one of the best ministers that ever labored in the Prairie State."

Bailey, Rev. C. T., the editor of the *Biblical Recorder*, the organ of the Baptists of North Carolina,

REV. C. T. BAILEY.

was born in Williamsburg, Va., Oct. 24, 1835. He was the last candidate ever baptized by Scervant Jones; was educated at William and Mary College, and at Richmond College; was ordained in 1858, Revs. W. M. Young, William Martin, and W. A. Crandall forming the presbytery, at Williamsburg; went into the army as a private in 1861, but did not remain in the service long; preached to several country churches in Surrey Co., Va.; came to North Carolina in October, 1865, and became master of the Reynoldson Academy in Gates County; removed to Edenton in 1868, where he remained as pastor till 1871, when he became pastor of the Warrenton church. In 1875 he became proprietor of the *Biblical Recorder*, which he has since conducted with distinguished ability and success.

Bailey, Gilbert Stephen, D.D., son of George A. Bailey, was born in Abington, Pa., Oct. 17, 1822. While a student in Oberlin College he became a disciple of Christ, and was baptized in Abington, Oct. 16, 1842. Leaving college on account of illness, he taught for a while, and preached occasionally. He was ordained May 20, 1845, at Abington, and immediately became pastor in Canterbury, Orange Co., N. Y. The next year he was sent by the American Baptist Home Mission Society to Springfield, Ill., and accepted the pastorate of the church there. In 1849 he removed to Tremont, Tazewell Co., Ill., and labored there and at Pekin, in the same county, six years. In December, 1855, he became pastor at Metamora, Woodford Co., Ill., and continued in that relation till May, 1861. He labored at Morris, Ill., from May, 1861, till December, 1863, when he became superintendent of missions for the Baptist General Association of Illinois. His work in this office was of great value, and was, to say the least, contemporaneous with a remarkable growth of Baptist churches in Illinois. From October, 1867, to July, 1875, he was secretary of the Baptist Theological Union, which was formed to establish and endow the theological seminary now located at Morgan Park. For these years his work was laborious and self-sacrificing, but eminently successful. From Aug. 1, 1875, to April 1, 1878, he ministered to the church at Pittston, Pa., and since the latter date has been pastor at Niles, Mich., where a new house of worship has meanwhile been built. He is the author of the following works, viz.: "History of the Illinois River Baptist Association," "The Caverns of Kentucky," "Manual of Baptism," "The Trials and Victories of Religious Liberty in America," and five tracts. Dr. Bailey first proposed and inaugurated a ministers' institute in 1864, and his suggestion has been widely accepted.

Bailey, Rev. John, a distinguished pioneer preacher of Kentucky, and one of the first pulpit orators of the West in his day, was born in Northumberland Co., Va., 1748. He united with a Baptist church in his youth, and began to exhort at the age of eighteen years. He was ordained to the ministry in early manhood. He moved from his birthplace to Pittsylvania, where he gained considerable reputation as a pulpit orator. In 1784 he moved to Kentucky, and settled in what is now Lincoln County. Here he gathered Rush Branch church, and became its pastor in 1785. In the course of a few years he gathered McCormack's and Green River churches. He was a member of the convention that formed the first constitution of Kentucky, in 1792. He was also a delegate from Logan County to the convention which formed the second constitution of that State, in 1799. About

5

this period he adopted the doctrine of "Universal Restoration," and was excluded from his church. This resulted in a division of South District Association. A majority of the churches followed the eloquent Bailey without adopting his theory. This faction were known by the name of "South Kentucky Association of Separate Baptists." It has since become three Associations, all of which are now weak and in a perishing condition. Mr. Bailey labored with much zeal and diligence among the churches of this sect to a good old age. He maintained a spotless moral character, and was very successful in building up these churches. He was regarded by all who knew him as a good and great man. He died at his home in Lincoln Co., Ky., July 3, 1816.

Bailey, Rev. Joseph Albert, born in Middletown, Conn., Aug. 17, 1823; baptized in 1837 by Rev. J. Cookson, and united with the Baptist church in Middletown; felt a call to the ministry; preached first sermon in 1847; graduated from Wesleyan University in 1849; studied theology at Newton, Mass., and Rochester, N. Y., graduating from the latter seminary in 1851; ordained pastor of the Baptist church in Essex, Conn., Oct. 22, 1851, the sermon by Rev. R. Turnbull, D.D.; labored in Essex four years with great favor; settled with the Baptist church in Waterbury, Conn., in September, 1855, where with remarkable success he preached for about eighteen years, and until his health failed; was for years secretary of the Connecticut Baptist State Convention; was school visitor for Waterbury, and engaged in temperance and other good causes. In March, 1873, for the recovery of his health he sailed for Europe; went to Carlsbad, in Baden, for his health; there died May 11, 1873, in his fiftieth year. In him were blended force and sweetness; clear, strong, fervid preacher; wise, faithful pastor; hearty friend; beloved by all.

Bailey, Hon. Joseph Mead, LL.D.—Among the laymen of the Baptist denomination in this country Judge Bailey deservedly holds a conspicuous place. While eminently successful in his chosen profession, having achieved as a jurist a foremost position, he is known in all circles as a man of fine culture, an intelligent, earnest Christian, always willing to be known as such, and as a steadfast Baptist. He was born in Middlebury, Wyoming Co., N. Y., June 22, 1833, and united with the Baptist church in that place in 1847. He prepared for college at the Wyoming Academy, entering the University of Rochester as Sophomore in 1851, and graduating in 1854. As a student he was known rather for his quiet diligence than for brilliance in the various college exercises, ranking, however, as a scholar with the best. He studied law at Rochester, and in 1856 entered upon the practice of his profession at Freeport, Ill. His success was immediate and marked. In 1867 he was elected a member of the Illinois Legislature, and re-elected in 1869. In 1876 he was one of the Presidential electors for the State of Illinois. In 1877 he was chosen judge of the Thirteenth Judicial Circuit; in 1878 judge of the First District of the Illinois Appellate Court, and in 1879 chief justice of the same court. His official duties are discharged at Chicago, though his residence remains at Freeport. His known interest in the cause of higher education led to his election in 1878 as trustee of the University of Chicago, in which board he now also holds the office of vice-president. In 1879 he received from the universities of Rochester and Chicago the degree of LL.D. In his own place of residence, as well as throughout the State, Judge Bailey is held in great respect, and in the church of his membership is a valued counselor and co-laborer, while always ready with liberal donations.

Bailey, Rev. Napoleon A., was born in Lawrence Co., Ala., Sept. 5, 1833. His mother was from Maryland, and his father was a native of Virginia. In July, 1850, he was baptized and united with the Liberty Baptist church, in his native county. In 1853 he was licensed, and in September, 1854, he entered Union University, Murfreesborough, Tenn., where, for three years, he diligently pursued his studies, graduating in July, 1869. He was regularly set apart to the gospel ministry by ordination in November, 1857. On the 1st of January, 1858, he took charge of Liberty church, into whose fellowship he was baptized, and soon after moved to Florida, on account of a severe cough which he contracted while preaching in a revival meeting. His health being restored by the balmy climate of Florida, he removed to Georgia, where for a number of years he preached to several churches while acting as president of the Houston Female College. He served afterwards the churches at Milledgeville and Dalton, and then went to California, where he remained a year and a half. He then returned to his native State, and subsequently removed to Georgia, in which State he now resides, at Quitman. For six years Mr. Bailey has filled the position of assistant secretary of the Georgia Baptist Convention. He is a faithful and zealous pastor, an able preacher, clinging tenaciously to the cardinal principles of the denomination. His conscientious piety and hearty co-operation in all the leading enterprises of the denomination are universally recognized, and it has been said of him that he is one of those few "to whom giving seems to be a real luxury." Candor, sincerity, and a firm adherence to his convictions of right are prominent traits in his character, while gentleness and self-sacrifice are in him happily blended with fortitude and courage.

Bailey, Rosa Adams, second wife of Dr. Silas Bailey, was born in Shelbyville, Ind., May 3, 1843. Her father was related to the family of John Quincy Adams. She showed an earnest love for study. She entered the Indianapolis Baptist Female Institute. While a student there she was converted and joined the First Baptist church. After graduation she became a teacher in the institute, and was one of the most efficient. Mrs. Ingalls came with a call for help in Burmah. Mrs. Bailey went with her as a missionary to Henthada. After several years of labor, failing health obliged her to come home. While at home she was married to Dr. Bailey, but still longed to return to Burmah. In 1873 they sailed for France. After the doctor's death she came back to this country, preparatory to a return to Burmah. She resumed her work there with great zeal, but was attacked with cholera, and died at Zeegong, July 26, 1878.

Mrs. Bailey was a lady of rare talents, of winning graces, of great piety, and of extensive usefulness. She was in Philadelphia for a short time prior to her last departure for Burmah, and gained the affections of hundreds of ladies for herself and her distant mission.

Bailey, Silas, D.D., LL.D., was born in Sterling, Worcester Co., Mass., June 12, 1809. In 1828 he went to Amherst, Mass., to pursue a course of study to fit him for college. Having finished his preparations, he heard an address of Dr. Francis Wayland that led him to enter Brown University. He was always an admirer of President Wayland, and the president has often expressed his regard for the ability of his pupil.

During a great revival in the university he was born again. In the language of Dr. J. G. Warren, his college-mate, "The work of regeneration was done throughout his whole being; done for all time and for all eternity." In 1834 he became principal of the Worcester Academy, Mass., and was very successful in conducting its operations. In 1839 he became pastor of the church at Thompson, Conn. In 1842 he was appointed agent for the Missionary Union for the State of New York. In 1845 he settled as pastor of the church at Westborough, Mass., and in 1847 was called to the presidency of Granville College, O. He labored here several years, cheerfully and effectively. He left his impress upon many a young man by the labors of both class-room and pulpit; for during a considerable part of the time he was both president of the college and pastor of the church. Not to speak of others, it is sufficient to mention President Talbot, a prince in thought and manhood, a graduate under Dr. Bailey during his presidency at Granville.

In 1852 he was called to the presidency of Franklin College, Ind., and he was soon recognized as a leader by the Baptists of the State. His failing health compelled him to resign in 1862. In 1863 he was called to the pastorate of the La Fayette (Indiana) church. In 1866 he was invited to the chair of Theology in Kalamazoo Theological Seminary, Mich. He labored here in both the seminary and college till debility compelled him to resign in

SILAS BAILEY, D.D., LL.D.

1869. He then returned to La Fayette. Here, in 1873, within two weeks, his adopted daughter, Mrs. Moore, and his wife died. After several months he conceived the idea of visiting the Old World. He was married to Miss Rosa Adams, a lady of great worth, a returned missionary, and they took passage for France. He died, after a short illness, in Paris on the 30th of June, 1874. He left his library and a part of his estate to Franklin College. He was, in 1860, president of the Board of the Baptist Missionary Union. Several of his sermons have been published.

A memorial volume of Dr. Bailey was published by J. W. T. Booth, D.D., of La Fayette, Ind., in 1876.

Bailey, Rev. Thomas M., was born in Gracehill, County Antrim, Ireland, Dec. 27, 1829; attended a Moravian school up to his fifteenth year, then went into business, in which he remained seven years, three of the seven in the city of Dublin; felt a strong desire of heart to preach the gospel in his sixteenth year. In his twenty-first year he was appointed by the Foreign Mission Board of the Moravian Church to foreign missionary work in the island of St. Thomas, Danish West

Indies. After a few months' service there he was prostrated with yellow fever; becoming convalescent, his physician ordered him to St. Croix for a change, and there his labors as a missionary were expended; in the foreign field nearly four years;

REV. THOMAS M. BAILEY.

came to the United States in December, 1855; was baptized into the fellowship of the Gilgal Baptist church, in South Carolina, by Rev. E. F. Whatley, in the spring of 1856; remained in South Carolina two years, and then moved to Alabama; has been a very useful pastor of various country and village churches until the year 1874, when he became State evangelist and corresponding secretary of the Alabama Baptist State Mission Board,—a position which he still holds with great distinction and with rare ability and efficiency. He is a man of all work, a good preacher, a fine speaker, with the most pleasant social qualities, and withal a most useful man. He has contributed largely to the development and efficiency of the Baptists of Alabama.

Bainbridge, Rev. W. F., was born in Stockbridge, N. Y., Jan. 15, 1843. He was baptized by his father, Rev. S. M. Bainbridge, at Wheatland, N. Y., March 27, 1853, at the early age of ten years. He entered Rochester University in the class which graduated in 1862. He then took the course of study in the Rochester Theological Institution, and was ordained in May, 1865, as pastor of the First Baptist church in Erie, Pa. During the three and a half years of his connection with the church in Erie he baptized 237 persons. During nine months of this pastorate Mr. Bainbridge made an extended foreign tour, embracing parts of Europe, Egypt, and Palestine. He decided to accept a call to the Central Baptist church in Providence, where the pulpit had been made vacant by the removal of Rev. Heman Lincoln, D.D., to the Newton Theological Institution. His ministry in Providence commenced Jan. 1, 1869. During ten years of service Mr. Bainbridge's ministry has been a successful one. He has received 460 new members, 233 of whom he has baptized. It is his purpose to devote the coming two or three years to travel,

REV. W. F. BAINBRIDGE.

having in view especially a visit to the missionary stations of the different Christian denominations in various parts of the world.

Baker, Rev. A. F., was born in Owen Co., Ky., April 16, 1835. He joined the Dallasburg Baptist church in his native county in 1854, was ordained at Hodgenville, Ky., December, 1859, and called to the pastoral care of the Baptist church at Bardstown, Ky. While here he established the Bardstown Baptist Female Seminary, now one of the most flourishing schools in the State. He has since been pastor of several prominent churches in Kentucky. He was for a time co-editor of the *Prophetic Key*, a monthly magazine. He has labored much as an evangelist, and has conducted protracted meetings in which several hundred persons have been approved for baptism. He is a strong preacher, a good pastor, and a man of tireless energy. He is at present (1880) pastor of the church at Owenton, Ky.

Baker, Rev. Elijah, was born in the county of Lunenburg, Va., in 1742, and born again and baptized in 1769. In 1773, in conjunction with one or two others, he organized the Boar Swamp church in Henrico County; he was the chief agent in forming churches in James City, Charles City, and York; he established a church in Gloucester, at a place called Guinea; and on the Eastern Shore of Virginia, and in Maryland, he planted the first ten churches of our faith that worshiped God in those parts. He died Nov. 6, 1798. Mr. Baker was a good man, full of the Holy Spirit, and attended by extraordinary usefulness. He was imprisoned in Accomac jail for a considerable period. He was put on board a vessel as a *disturber of the peace* to be carried beyond the seas, and he was to pay for his passage by performing the duties of a seaman, but the Lord opened the captain's eyes to see his character, and he sent him ashore. He died full of hope.

Baker, Rev. J. C., is pastor of the Baptist church at Salem, the capital of Oregon. In 1875, having been for years a faithful pastor, and for some time a very efficient general missionary of the American Baptist Publication Society in the Northwest, he was appointed to take charge of its Pacific Coast Depository, located at San Francisco. He traveled extensively, visiting most of the churches in California, Oregon, and Washington Territory; moved to Salem, Oregon, in 1877; became pastor there; continued his work on behalf of the Publication Society; established *The Beacon*, the Baptist paper of Oregon; and during all his residence on the Pacific coast has been active in organizing Sunday-schools; is an admirable Sunday-school worker, a good preacher; earnest in mission work, effective in revivals, and influential in the councils, Associations, and conventions of the denomination.

Baker, Rev. John H., son of Elisha and Henrietta (Miner) Baker, born in Stonington, Conn., Sept. 26, 1805; a student and lover of books; converted Sept. 26, 1822; united with the Baptist church in Stonington borough; taught school; entered Hamilton Seminary; became an evangelist; labored with marked success in Eastern Connecticut and Western Rhode Island; strong against intemperance; blessed with many revivals; founded in 1839 the church in Charlestown, R. I.; strengthened many churches by his evangelistic efforts; struck down by paralysis while carrying on a great work on Block Island, after he had baptized 98; died in East Greenwich, R. I., Jan. 16, 1869, in his sixty-fourth year.

Baker, Dr. Joseph S., was born in Liberty Co., Ga., in 1798, of Presbyterian parents, and died at Quitman Co., Ga., in 1877. He was educated at Yale and at Hampden Sidney College, Va., where he graduated in 1823.

On leaving college he returned to Liberty Co., Ga., and engaged in farming and merchandising, having inherited considerable property. He was then, at the age of twenty-five, a member of the Presbyterian church near Riceborough, and placed himself under the care of the Presbytery with a view to entering the ministry at a session held with the Midway church in the fall of 1823. The Presbytery assigned him, as the subject of his first thesis, "Was John's Baptism Christian Baptism?" The investigation of the subject by him led to his adoption of Baptist views a few years later. He removed to Virginia in 1825, having sold all his property in Georgia. He graduated in the medical department of Columbian College, D. C., in 1828, and practiced medicine in Nottaway Co., Va., until 1831, when he moved to Petersburg. There he united with the Baptists, was licensed and ordained. He preached in Virginia at Petersburg, Norfolk, and other places, part of the time as a missionary, until 1839 or 1840, when he moved to Georgia and settled in Columbus. In 1843 he became editor of the *Christian Index*, and moved to Penfield, where the paper was then published. For six years he occupied the editorial chair with an ability so distinguished, and with a pen so trenchant and powerful, evidencing at the same time so much of genuine piety and such a thorough acquaintance with Baptist doctrines and practices, that he acquired a denominational influence that expired only with his life.

He resided for a while with a son who was a lawyer at Jacksonville, Fla., and mayor of the town. He then served the churches at Albany and Palmyra, Ga., and Jacksonville, Fla., until the war. During that struggle he preached to the soldiers as an evangelist. After the war he moved to Quitman, Ga., where he resided until his death, in 1877, ripening more and more to the last for the skies. Dr. Baker was a man of great natural abilities. He was a deep thinker, a perspicuous writer, and he did much to assist denominational progress in Georgia. He was a most decided Baptist. He had read much, was a fine scholar, and he was deeply versed in the polity and principles of all denominations. An excellent preacher, he was a man of strong faith in divine providence, and bore the severe sufferings of his last days with great Christian fortitude and resignation. For years he exerted a strong and healthy influence among the Georgia Baptists, and it was always employed in favor of sound doctrine and practical godliness.

Baker, Samuel, D.D., distinguished for critical learning and extensive reading, was born in the county of Sussex, England, Oct. 2, 1812. He received an academic education, and engaged in mercantile business in his native country. In 1834 he emigrated to the United States and settled in Upper

Alton, Ill. Here he was licensed to preach, and immediately entered Shurtliff College as a student in both the literary and theological departments, and remained three years. In 1837 he was ordained at Alton, and soon afterwards took charge of Cape Girardeau church, Mo. He was pastor of the church at Shelbyville, Ky., from 1839 to 1841; at Russellville, Ky., from 1841 to 1846; at Hopkinsville, Ky., from 1846 to 1850; at the first church in Nashville, Tenn., from 1850 to 1853. From this time until 1865 he was pastor of the First Baptist church in Williamsburg, N. Y. The next three years he was at the Wabash Avenue church in Chicago, Ill.; next year he took charge of the church at Evansville, Ind. He then became pastor of the Herkimer Street Baptist church of Brooklyn, N. Y. In 1872 he again located with the church at Russellville, Ky., where he still remains. Dr. Baker is a close student, has a splendid library, and but for an embarrassing defect in his enunciation would be one of the leading orators in the Kentucky pulpit. He is well versed in ecclesiastical history, and excels as a writer on that subject.

Baldwin, Rev. Charles Jacob, son of George C. Baldwin, D.D., and Cynthia M. Baldwin, was born at Charleston, N. Y., Aug. 10, 1841. At the age of fourteen he was converted, and joined the First church, Troy, N. Y., of which his father was pastor. He entered Madison University, N. Y., in 1859, but left during the Junior year to enter the army, in which he served as adjutant of the 157th Regiment N. Y. Vols., and on the staff of Brig.-Gen. Potter until the close of the war. While in the service he received the rank of major from the governor of the State of New York.

In 1868 he was graduated at Rochester Theological Seminary. He was ordained at Chelsea, Mass., as pastor of the First Baptist church, which he served from 1868 to 1872, when he resigned and visited Europe. On his return he became pastor of the First Baptist church of Rochester, where he now is. Mr. Baldwin is a good preacher and writer, and proves himself fully equal to the important post he fills as pastor of one of the most cultivated congregations in the country.

Baldwin, George C., D.D., was born in Pompton, N. J., Oct. 21, 1817. His early life was spent in the country until his parents removed to Paterson. Here he was converted under the ministry of Rev. Z. Grenell, and united with the Baptist church of which he was pastor. Almost immediately he felt a call to preach the gospel, and so urgent was it that he left his business and entered upon a course of study at Hamilton, N. Y., to fit himself for his sacred vocation, where he graduated in 1844. In the same year he accepted the call of the First Baptist church of Troy, where he still labors.

He has been almost equally devoted to the pulpit and to pastoral duties. As a preacher he follows the textual method of sermonizing. His discourses are clear and cogent. His emotional nature is ardent, his judgment deliberate, and his practical

GEORGE C. BALDWIN, D.D.

sense supreme. His ministry has been very effective in winning and in edifying souls.

He has a preference for extended courses of lectures, which give room for variety and continuous treatment. Some of these series have been published, under the titles "Representative Women," "Representative Men," and "The Model Prayer." These have reached a large circulation. His habits of study are regular and unyielding, except to the pressure of an irresistible necessity, so that his preparations are always invested with freshness.

He has seen the largest Baptist church in the State except one grow up under his care, and nearly an entire generation come and go under his ministry. It is his delight to be at every meeting of the church, minor or more important. A remarkable flexibility characterizes his methods: changes are as frequent as fluctuating circumstances demand. Nothing is permitted to grow obsolete. The young people are organized and active. The prayer-meetings are conducted with fresh and varied methods.

His son, Charles J., after being pastor of the First church of Chelsea, Mass., has been settled over the First church of Rochester, N. Y., since 1874.

Dr. Baldwin has a large heart, a blameless life, and a ministerial record seldom equaled, and only at distant intervals, if ever, surpassed.

Baldwin, Rev. Moses, was born in Richmond Co., N. C., Dec. 4, 1825; was baptized in October, 1845; graduated at Wake Forest College in 1856; was ordained the same year, Rev. Drs. Harper, Wingate, McDowell, Walters, Skinner, and Brooks constituting the presbytery. Mr. Baldwin has served the churches of Hillsborough, Oxford, Mocksville, and a number of country churches, and has taught thirteen years and aided several young ministers in securing an education. He now resides in Salem.

Baldwin, Rev. Norman B., A.M., was born in New Milford, Litchfield Co., Conn., Aug. 23, 1824. His father, Rev. Daniel Baldwin, was an esteemed and highly useful Baptist minister. He was educated at Hamilton Literary and Theological Institution (now Madison University), from which he graduated in 1846. In October, 1846, he became pastor of the Baptist church at Monticello, Sullivan Co., N. Y. After a most prosperous settlement he accepted the unanimous call of the Bethesda Baptist church, New York City, June 1, 1849, in which God greatly blessed him; but disease compelled him to leave New York, and he accepted the call of the Second Southwark (now Calvary) Baptist church, Philadelphia, and entered on his labors Feb. 1, 1854. From this body he went out with a colony of 220 members and organized the Olivet Baptist church, Oct. 7, 1856. They built the fine edifice at the southeast corner of Sixth and Federal Streets. Extensive revivals, in which hundreds were converted and immersed, together with the other labors of his office, so impaired his health that in September, 1864, he closed his eleven years' pastorate in Philadelphia and retired to his farm, near Colmar, Montgomery Co., Pa. As his health soon began to improve he gave short periods of service to New Britain Baptist church, Bucks Co., Bristol church, and the Gwynedd Baptist church. In November, 1869, he entered upon his labors as pastor of the Montgomery church. For eleven years God's blessing has attended this union. He has baptized 500 persons during his ministry.

Baldwin, Thomas, D.D., was born Dec. 23, 1753, in Bozrah, Conn. As in many similar cases, it seems to have been the mother who left the impress of a fine moral and intellectual character on her son. Early in life he developed a taste for books. It is an indication of the regard in which he was held by his fellow-townsmen that when comparatively a young man he was chosen to represent the village of Canaan, N. H., to which he had removed, in the Legislature of the State. It was his purpose to fit himself for the legal profession, and he commenced his studies to prepare to practice law. But the Master had another work for him to do. In 1780 he was brought to see his condition as a sinner, and to accept Christ as his personal Lord and Redeemer. He felt it his duty to leave the church in which he had been brought up and avow himself a Baptist. This he did at the sacrifice of personal feeling and the sundering of many a tie which bound him to old friends. The

THOMAS BALDWIN, D.D.

step which he thus took was soon followed by another. He decided to spend his life in the work of winning souls to Christ, and building up the cause of him who had by his grace brought him to the saving knowledge of the truth. In due time he was set apart to the work of the ministry by ordination as an evangelist, and for seven years performed the duties of pastor of the Baptist church in Canaan.

The Second Baptist church in Boston, known for so many years by the honored name of the "Baldwin Place church," now the "Warren Avenue church," was destitute of a pastor. Such was the reputation of the laborious country minister of New Hampshire that he was sent for to preach to them. The result of this invitation was a call to become their minister, which was accepted. In the year 1791 not far from 70 were added to the church, and in 1803 commenced another revival, the fruit of which was an addition to the church of 212 persons.

The labors of Dr. Baldwin were not confined to the ministry. In 1803 he took the editorial charge of the *Massachusetts Baptist Magazine*, and for fourteen years conducted that journal with an ability which made it an efficient aid in promoting the interests of the denomination. Until the time of his death he was its senior editor, receiving help when the pressure of other duties forced him to cease from its full management.

Amid all the demands made on him in the various directions to which we have referred, Dr. Baldwin found time to write and publish several controversial works, in which with great ability he vindicated the peculiar views of his denomination. Perhaps his ablest work of this character is one which he published in 1810, "A Series of Letters," in which the distinguishing sentiments of the Baptists are explained and vindicated, in answer to a late publication by the Rev. Samuel Worcester, A.M., addressed to the author, entitled "Serious and Candid Letters." The work took so high a stand that Andrew Fuller declared it to be the ablest discussion of the matters in controversy that he had ever read.

Dr. Baldwin went to Waterville in 1826. He spent the afternoon of the 29th of August in looking over the college premises, and informing himself respecting the internal workings of the institution. During the succeeding night he uttered one deep groan and entered into rest. It was for the good man almost a translation. From such a "sudden death" we have no occasion to pray "Good Lord deliver us."

It is not necessary to enumerate the honors that were conferred on Dr. Baldwin, or name the offices of trust and responsibility to which he was called. It is sufficient to say that the honors were as numerous as those which any other minister of the denomination has ever had conferred upon him, while the offices were of the highest respectability, and such as have been filled by our ablest and worthiest men.

His publications were numerous. His controversial works have already been alluded to, some of which were acknowledged to be of the very ablest character. Dr. Wayland says of him, "He retained to the last the entire confidence of men of most conflicting opinions, and even came off from the arena of theological controversy rich in the esteem of those whom his argument failed to convince. He was in the very front ranks of the distinguished ministers who have adorned their profession in connection with the denomination which he so faithfully and for so many years served." He uniformly, towards the close of life, left upon every one the impression of old age in its loveliest and most interesting aspect, and Christianity in its mildest and most attractive exhibition.

Balen, Deacon Peter, was born in Hackensack, N. J., in 1804. He was often in straitened circumstances in early life; but there, in his own home, he knelt and consecrated himself to God. He resolved that the Lord should have a portion of his earnings while yet he was making a poor living. On a certain occasion when he was sorely tempted by Satan to withdraw a subscription made to a benevolent object, he fought and overcame. He prospered in business, and has done an extensive wholesale trade. Churches in New York City and the benevolent societies have received large sums from him. Years ago he removed to Plainfield, where he is exerting a wide Christian influence. He has always been a Sunday-school man, and as superintendent or teacher has led many to Christ. He is a studious searcher of the Scriptures, and has read the Bible through many times.

Ball, Rev. Eli, was born in Marlborough, Vt., Nov. 2, 1786. Having removed to the city of Boston, Mass., when about nineteen, he was baptized there in the latter part of the year 1805. He preached his first sermon in that city in December, 1807, and was licensed in the following July. While pursuing his studies under the Revs. Daniel Stanford and Caleb Blood, he preached for the church in Malden, a few miles from Boston, for more than a year. Until the year 1823 he supplied successively the Baptist churches in Harwich, Mass.; Wilmington and Lansingburg, N. Y.; and Middletown, Conn. In June, 1823, he visited Virginia, and in July became pastor of the church in Lynchburg. At the end of two years he removed to Henrico County, where for seven or eight years he labored with much success, preaching day and night, conducting Bible-classes, and instituting prayer-meetings, so that many were hopefully converted and added to the churches through his instrumentality. Besides his regular pastoral labors, a large amount of pulpit labor was bestowed upon other churches of the State at protracted meetings, ordinations, etc. As an agent, too, Mr. Ball was greatly successful, in which capacity he served the Bible Society of Virginia, the Baptist General Association, and especially the Foreign Mission Board of the Southern Baptist Convention, in the State of Georgia. For a short time he was also a professor in the Baptist seminary (Richmond College), and also editor of the *Religious Herald*. He served as agent for the Columbian College, and during two visits to South Carolina and Georgia secured $5000. His labors in behalf of temperance were also remarkably successful. His deep interest in the foreign mission cause led him in 1828 to make a visit to the coast of Africa, to examine the condition of the Liberian Mission, during which visit he gathered a mass of information with respect to the work there, which was of great service to the board. After prosecuting his agency for a year after his return, he was preparing to visit Africa a second time, when he was attacked by disease, and died in Richmond, July 21, 1853. Few men have been more diligent and active in Christian labors than Mr. Ball. These were crowned with abundant success; up to 1849 he had baptized 914 persons, and had been the means, doubtless, of the conversion of very many more. His loss was keenly mourned and deeply felt. "Doubtless," says his biographer, "Eli Ball will long be remembered by Virginia Baptists as one of their soundest, best, and most useful proclaimers of the glorious gospel."

Ball, Rev. Lewis, an active and efficient minister in Northwestern Mississippi, was born in South Carolina in 1820, came to Mississippi and began to preach in 1844. His abundant labors have greatly advanced the cause of truth. By his labors the Sunflower Association was established. He was a colonel in the Confederate army.

Ball, Rev. Martin, an early Baptist preacher in North Mississippi, was born in South Carolina in 1809. He came to Mississippi as a preacher in 1845, and until the time of his death, 1859, exerted a wide influence in the northern part of the State. He was successful as an evangelist, as a presiding officer, and especially as a peace-maker.

Baltimore, Eutaw Place Baptist Church of. — The edifice of this church was completed early in 1871. The material is white marble. It is 75 feet wide and 100 feet deep. The spire is 190 feet high. The house and lot, counting the cash value of the site, which was donated, cost $122,000. The structure was reared for a colony brought by the late Dr. Richard Fuller from the Seventh Baptist church, of which he was pastor till his death. The church is one of the most beautiful and commodious in Baltimore.

Bampfield, Rev. Francis, M.A. — Francis Bampfield descended from a distinguished family in Devonshire, England. He was born in 1615. In his sixteenth year he became a student of Wadham College, Oxford. He was at the university about seven years, and left it with talents and culture of a high order. He was ordained deacon and presbyter by Bishops Hall and Skinner. His first settlement was in a parish in Dorsetshire, where he spent his entire income from the church in Bibles and religious books for the poor, and in providing work for them, and in giving alms to those who could not labor. He removed to Sherborne, in the same county, to become the parish minister, after a short stay with his first charge, and he remained at Sherborne till ejected, in 1662, by the act of uniformity. Before he removed to Sherborne he became a Puritan, and he grew in knowledge till he became a Baptist. For some time after he became an advocate of an extensive reformation in the church; he still continued, to the great astonishment of all his religious friends, an earnest advocate of the cause of Charles I. and a decided enemy of the Parliament; he even hesitated for a time to pay taxes levied by the legislature. In process of time his opinions changed, for we find him among the Triers appointed by Cromwell to secure pious ministers for the church and the removal of unworthy men from it. His family, too, seem to have changed their political course, for his brother, Thomas Bampfield, Esq., was the speaker of one of Oliver Cromwell's Parliaments.

Francis Bampfield was, above all things, a living servant of Jesus; the frowns and smiles of men were vainly used to turn him from his Master. Worldly losses and bodily sufferings appeared to him as trifles compared to the supreme felicity of a conscience void of offense before God.

After he resigned his living he began preaching in his own house at Sherborne, and not quite a month after the Act of Uniformity went into operation, while he was holding a religious service, he and twenty-six others of those who were present were carried to prison, where they were kept in one room with but a single bed. They were, however, soon released on bail. Not long after he was again put in jail in Dorchester, and kept there for nine years. In this prison he preached almost daily, and was enabled to gather a church within its walls.

He founded a church in Pinner's Hall, in London, on the 5th of March, 1675, to which he preached as often as he was out of jail during seasons of worship till he died. He departed for the eternal rest from the prison of Newgate, Feb. 16, 1683. He died at last from the injury inflicted on his health by his prolonged imprisonments.

Mr. Bampfield was a scholarly man, and "one of the most celebrated preachers in the west of England." He was a giant in defense of the truth, and a devout man full of the Holy Spirit. He belonged to the Seventh-Day Baptists.

Bancroft, Rev. Samuel, was born in 1789 in Annapolis Co., Nova Scotia. He was converted when young, and baptized by Rev. Thomas Ainslie. He was ordained in 1828, at Westport, Nova Scotia, and removed to New Brunswick in 1831, where his pastoral and missionary labors were very successful. His life was a ministry of goodness. He died Jan. 1, 1876.

Banes, Col. Charles H., was born in Philadelphia, Pa., Oct. 24, 1831. His education was liberal, and his thirst for knowledge has led to the acquisition of a valuable library, and of an extensive amount of information upon all questions that interest Christians and men of culture. He was engaged in mercantile pursuits until the commencement of the late war, when he gave up the prospects of financial success for the perils of the battle-field and the protection of our national flag. He entered the service as a captain of infantry in August, 1861. At Fredericksburg, in December, 1862, he was promoted to be assistant adjutant-general.

EUTAW PLACE BAPTIST CHURCH, BALTIMORE.

He was brevetted major, July, 1863, "for gallant and meritorious services" at Gettysburg. In May, 1864, he was brevetted lieutenant-colonel for the same reasons. At Cold Harbor, in June, 1864, he received a painful and dangerous wound, which

COL. CHARLES H. BANES.

confined him to a couch of helplessness and suffering for months, and from the effects of which he can never recover. His last battle compelled his retirement from the army, in which his skill and bravery had been so conspicuously exhibited.

As soon as returning strength permitted he entered business once more; and now the firm of which he is a prominent and active member owns one of the most extensive and prosperous manufacturing establishments in their branch of industry in the United States.

Col. Banes wrote a history of the Philadelphia Brigade, for which his scholarly tastes, exact information, and personal experiences gave him eminent qualifications. The work has been deservedly and highly commended, and has taken a creditable place in the literature of our Great Struggle.

Col. Banes is an untiring worker in various scientific, benevolent, and religious organizations, and though the last man to seek prominence in anything, his friends will push him forward as trustee of the Franklin Institute, president of the Baptist Social Union, of the Baptist City Mission, and of other kindred enterprises. At the last Congressional election in his district his political and other friends placed him before the people as a candidate for the House of Representatives, and his popular name secured some twelve hundred more votes than his predecessor in a similar struggle obtained two years before.

The generous gifts of Col. Banes have already removed heavy church debts and gladdened laborers in other benevolent fields.

Courteous, cultured, and Christian, his brethren love him, and wish that his spirit might seize every Baptist in America.

Banvard, Joseph, D.D., was born in the city of New York, May 9, 1810. On his father's side he was descended from the French Huguenots, and on his mother's from the early settlers of New England. His parents being members of the Moravian Church he was brought up under its influence. He was converted through the instrumentality of the late Rev. Dr. Charles G. Sommers, and united with the church of which he was the pastor in New York. He received his preparatory education at the South Reading Academy, and then pursued the full course of study at the Newton Theological Institution. He graduated from Newton in the class of 1835, and a few days after was ordained

JOSEPH BANVARD, D.D.

pastor of the Second, now the Central Baptist, church in Salem, Mass. While conscientiously performing his ministerial duties Dr. Banvard has found time to gratify his love for history and the natural sciences. He has been honored on account of his attainments in the departments referred to by having been chosen an honorary member of the Boston Society of Natural History, and of the Historical Society of Wisconsin. He was at one time vice-president of the Worcester Co., Mass., Natural

History Society, and president of the Historical Society of Passaic Co., N. J.

The pastorates of Dr. Banvard have been as follows. He remained in Salem eleven years, 1835–46, and then accepted a call to the Harvard Street church in Boston, where he continued five years, 1846–51. He then became pastor of the church in West Cambridge, where, during his ministry, a new and attractive house of worship was built. He was pastor of this church two years, 1851–53, and then took up his residence in New York as pastor of the Cannon Street church. Here he remained three years, 1853–56, and then returned to New England to take charge of the First Baptist church in Pawtucket, R. I. This position he held for five years, 1856–61, and then went to Worcester, Mass., where he was pastor of the Main Street church five years, 1861–66. He was then chosen president of the National Theological Institute, District of Columbia, for the education of colored teachers and preachers. When this work was assumed by the American Baptist Home Mission Society he resigned, and accepted a call to the pastorate of the First Baptist church in Paterson, N. J., where he remained ten years, 1866–76. Resigning his pastorate in Paterson he returned once more to New England, and became pastor of the church in Neponset, Mass. Dr. Banvard received the honorary degree of A.M. from Columbian College, Washington, D. C., and the degree of Doctor of Divinity from Shurtleff College, Upper Alton, Ill. Among the productions of his pen are several series of Sunday-school question books, a series of eight volumes on natural history, five volumes on American history, "Priscilla, or Trials for the Truth," and two hymn-books. The present residence (1878) of Dr. Banvard is Neponset, Mass.

Baptism a Breach of the Sixth and Seventh Commandments.—Few men have done more than Richard Baxter to serve the Redeemer's kingdom. In his own day his name was a tower of strength. Against our brethren he wielded all his immense influence with untiring energy, and with the grossest misrepresentations. He says,—

"That which is a plain breach of the sixth commandment, '*Thou shalt not kill*,' is no ordinance of God, but a most heinous sin; but the ordinary practice of baptizing by dipping over head in cold water, as necessary, is a plain breach of the sixth commandment; therefore it is no ordinance of God, *but an heinous sin*. And as Mr. Craddock, in his book of 'Gospel Liberty,' shows, the magistrate ought to restrain it, to save the lives of his subjects; even on their principles, that will yet allow the magistrate no power directly in matters of worship. That this is flat murder, and no better, being ordinarily and generally used, is undesirable to any understanding man. For that which directly tendeth to overthrow men's lives, being wilfully used, is plain murder." He then proceeds to prove that our fathers violated the seventh commandment, "*Thou shalt not commit adultery*." "My seventh argument is also against another wickedness in their manner of baptizing, which is their dipping persons naked, as is very usual with many of them: or next to naked,* as is usual with the modestest, that I have heard of." There is not a solitary case on record among the English Baptists of baptism in a state of nudity. Nor is there a single instance in the history of the Christian Church, even during the first twelve centuries, when immersion was universal, of injury to any one by baptismal dipping.

The misrepresentations of men like Mr. Baxter had so much weight in England that the Rev. Samuel Oates was tried on the charge of murder at Chelmsford, in 1646, the victim of his supposed crime being Anne Martin, whom he baptized some time before her death. But Mr. Oates[†] had an intelligent jury, and he was acquitted. Against the slanders of hosts of men, many of them persons of great piety and of extensive reputation, our honored fathers had to contend; and they have lived and even triumphed in the furnace filled with such unholy flames.

Baptism of Ten Thousand English.—England received its name from the Angles, who, with the Saxons, came to that country in the middle of the fifth century; the country previous to their conquest was called Britain. Its ancient inhabitants were Christians from the end of the second century. The Anglo-Saxons were savage pagans, who destroyed the Britons, or drove them into Wales and Cornwall, and removed every trace of Christianity. In 596 a mission came to convert the idolatrous English, from Rome, led by Augustine, a monk, and in 597, 10,000 of them were baptized in one day in the Swale; this stream is not the Yorkshire River of the same name; it flows between the Isle of Sheppy, in Kent, and the mainland, and its two extremities are now called East and West Swale. It extends for 12 miles, and is navigable for vessels of 200 tons burden. The East Swale is 9 miles from Canterbury, the seat of Augustine's mission, and on that account, ever since, the see of the chief prelate of the English Church. (Cathcart's "Baptism of the Ages," pp. 22. Publication Society, Philadelphia.)

Gocelin, a monk of Canterbury, in the eleventh century, with the ancient "Chronicles of Kent" before him, two of which were collated by him in his "Life of St. Augustine," says,—

"More than 10,000 of the English were born again in the laver of holy baptism, with an infinite

---

* Baxter's "Plain Scripture Proof," pp. 134–36.
† Crosby's "History of the English Baptists." Preface, 34–36.

number of women and children, in a river which the English call Sirarios, the Swale, as if at one birth of the church, and from one womb. These persons, at the command of the teacher, as if he were an angel from heaven calling upon them, *all entered the dangerous depth of the river* (*minacem fluminis profunditatem*) two and two together, as if it had been a solid plain ; and in the true faith, confessing the exalted Trinity, they were baptized one by the other in turns, the apostolic leader blessing the water. So great a progeny for heaven *born out of a deep whirlpool*" (*de profundo gurgite nasceretur*). (Vita Sanct. August. Patrol. Lat., vol. lxxx. pp. 79, 80, migne Parisiis.) This was the first baptism among the people, whose new country, after a portion of them, was called England ; the mode of the baptism in the Swale was clearly immersion.

Baptism, The Scriptural Mode of.—The form of a ceremony is essential to its existence. A ceremony teaches truth, not by direct statements, but by material symbols; and if the figures are changed you alter their teaching. Bread was used by the Saviour to represent his body, because it is the chief part of the food of all nations, and, probably, because the grain of which it is made was " peeled by the flail, heated intensely by the kiln, ground by the millstones, and baked in the oven." This figure teaches that through intense sufferings Jesus becomes the soul food of all believers. The cup of the Lord's Supper contains wine made by the crushing of grapes. These two symbols teach most powerfully that a bruised and wounded Saviour is the bread of life to all believers. Substitute fish and vegetables for bread and wine and the teaching of the ordinance is gone ; or take away either the bread or the cup and you destroy the most sacred of ceremonial institutions. The ceremony of hand-shaking loses all its symbolical teaching by a change in its form. When you extend your open hand to an acquaintance, if he were to place his closed fist in it there would be no friendly grasp there, and while two hands met the ceremony would look more like fighting on the part of one than familiar greeting. A ceremonial ordinance teaches by form, and if you change the form you mar or destroy the instruction. In the Scriptures baptism is immersion in water. The mode is fixed for all time. No authority out of heaven can change it. One Lord, one faith, and one baptism. Any change in this ceremonial institution destroys it.

Baptism is intended to show that we are dead and buried with Christ, and that we have risen to a regenerated life: " Therefore we are *buried* with him *by baptism* into death: that like as Christ was raised up from the dead by the glory of the Father, even so we also should walk in newness of life."—Rom. vi. 4. " *Buried* with him *in baptism*, wherein also ye are risen with him through the faith of the operation of God."—Col. ii. 12. In immersion a man is covered over as if he were in his grave ; there can be no breathing, except for a second, as if the man were dead ; he rises up out of the water as if he were ascending from the grave. Immersion shows all this. Do sprinkling and pouring cover over a man as if he were buried? or stop his breathing as if he were dead ? or raise him up as if he were coming out of a grave? Our Pedobaptist brethren sometimes playfully tell us that our differences about baptism simply relate to the quantity of water, we want more and they desire less. This statement is a serious mistake. Novatian, in the third century, when he supposed he was dying, thinking that he could not bear to be dipped, had water " poured around" him until he was saturated with it. He was probably as wet as if he had been dipped three times in water, according to the custom of that day, but he was not *buried by baptism*, his breath was not stopped for a moment under the water as if he were dead, he did not rise out of the water as if he were rising out of a grave. Novatian had not Christian baptism, as Eusebius* gravely hints. He gives us the first *living* example of pouring in baptism, which had, perhaps, not fifty imitators for six centuries afterwards. It is not the quantity of water used in baptism that makes it scriptural or the reverse. If a stream of water had been poured on Novatian which ran away and formed a river, he would not have been *buried* or covered over by baptism, nor would his baptism have resembled death and the resurrection. The Roman Catholic cardinal Pullus, in the middle of the twelfth century, thus beautifully and truly describes baptism : " Whilst the candidate for baptism in water is immersed the death of Christ is suggested ; whilst immersed, and covered with water, the burial of Christ is shown forth ; whilst he is raised from the waters, the resurrection of Christ is proclaimed."† Anything assuming to be baptism which does not cover the baptized with water, and lift him out of the water, as if raising him from the dead, is a fraudulent ceremony destitute of any divine sanction ; immersion was the baptismal burial of Paul, and the custom of all Christian countries during the first twelve centuries of our era.

Jesus was baptized in the river Jordan, " out of the water of which he went up straightway" (Matt. iii. 16) when the Spirit of God descended upon him like a dove. Of John the Baptist it is said, " Then went out to him Jerusalem, and all Judea, and all the region round about Jordan, and were *baptized of him in Jordan*, confessing their sins."

---

* Eccles. Hist., vi. 43.
† Patrol. Lat., vol. 150, p. 315, migne Parisiis.

—Matt. iii. 5. These baptisms in Jordan were immersions. If we read that twenty persons were baptized in the James River at Lynchburg, no one in the full use of his mental faculties would doubt their immersion. When it is said, "John also was baptizing in Enon, near to Salim, because there was much water there,"—John iii. 23,—the inference cannot be resisted that they were immersed.

The Saviour speaking of his sufferings says, "I have a baptism to be baptized with; and how am I straitened till it be accomplished!"—Luke xii. 50. This was not his baptism in water, that had taken place some time ago; nor yet his baptism of the Spirit, that he already enjoyed. This verse refers to his dreadful sufferings. He was to be plunged in agonies and covered completely by them. This is the most fitting figure ever employed to describe them. The Saviour's brow in his atoning sorrows was not sprinkled with pains, his face had not a few drops of anguish poured upon it, his whole soul and body were *completely* covered with the sufferings of atonement. He was immersed in woe, as the believer is in the waters of baptism.

When Paul was converted to God Ananias was sent by Jehovah to him, and he said, "And now why tarriest thou? Arise and be baptized, and wash away thy sins, calling on the name of the Lord Jesus." Baptism according to Ananias, fresh from God, is a figure of the washing away of sins. This washing is not applied to the face or the brow of the spirit, the whole soul is washed, and its sins are all removed. As the washing of the soul from its guilt leaves not a speck of it uncleansed, the figure of this washing must be a complete submersion of the whole body in water.

Luther[*] says, "Baptism is a Greek word; in Latin it can be translated *immersion, as when we plunge something into water that it may be completely covered with water.*" Calvin, after declaring that the mode of baptism is indifferent, says, "The very word baptize, however, *signifies to immerse;* and it is certain *that immersion was observed by the ancient church.*"[†] In the first liturgy made for the Episcopal Church in the reign of Edward VI., 1549, the priest is enjoined, after naming the child, to "*dip it in the water thrice. First dipping the right side; second, the left side; the third time dipping the face toward the font;* so it be discreetly and warily done."[‡] Then weak children are permitted the use of pouring. John Wesley writes in his Journal, while he was on a visit to Georgia, in 1736: "Saturday, Feb. 21st.—Mary Welsh, aged eleven days, was baptized *according to the custom of the first church, and the rule of the Church of England, by immersion.*"[§] By the testimony of the modern scholarship of the world the Greek word translated baptize means to immerse. This is its use in the New Testament. This was the practice of Christendom for twelve centuries after Christ.[||] And when immersion is not conferred in baptism the candidate for the rite is not baptized.

Baptism, the Scriptural Subjects of.—It is common for nations to confer favors upon their own subjects, and upon their friends. It would be a singular and very unwise procedure for any great state to bestow special privileges upon those who are not its friends, and who without a radical change of heart never can be. Baptism is an exalted honor; infants are not the friends of Christ's kingdom, and they never will be unless they are born of the Spirit of God. Baptism has no tendency to produce a new heart, and its bestowal upon unconscious infants is a senseless and unwise abuse of a blessed ordinance intended only for the Saviour's friends.

The Scriptures know nothing of any baptism for unconscious infants. The commission of Jesus to preach and baptize is given in Matt. xxviii. 19: "Go ye therefore and teach all nations, baptizing them in the name of the Father, and of the Son, and of the Holy Spirit." The lessons to be given the nations are on the love of God in giving Jesus, his atoning merits and mercies, his precious promises, solemn warnings, and final judgment, and on the power of faith in Jesus to appropriate him and all his spiritual wealth. Infants cannot receive such lessons; they were not intended for unconscious babes. It would be an outrage on common sense to try to teach the multiplication table to a babe of a week or a month old, and a far greater absurdity to command the profound teachings of Calvary to be imparted to little ones who do not understand one word of any language. The commission is a command to instruct those in all nations who are capable of understanding it, and to baptize them when taught. The verb "teach" is "make disciples," the pronoun "them" is instead of the noun "disciples,"—to baptize *them* is to immerse *disciples.* And this is further confirmed by what the Saviour adds, "Teaching them to observe all things whatsoever I have commanded you." The persons to be baptized are first to be made disciples by repentance and faith; then they are to receive immersion, and immediately after they are to have full instruction in all the inspired words of Jesus. The commission commands the baptism not of unconscious infants, but of believers only.

On the day of Pentecost 3000 persons were bap-

---

[*] Opera Lutheri, De Sacram. Bapt., i., p. 319, 1564.
[†] Instit. Christ. Relig., lib. iv., cap. 15, sec. 19, p. 644, London, 1576.
[‡] The Two Liturgies, p. 111-12, Parker Society.
[§] Wesley's Works, i., 130, Phila., 1826.
[||] Cathcart's Baptism of the Ages, Baptist Pub. Society, Phila.

tized, of whom it is written, "Then they that gladly received his word were baptized, and the same day there were added unto them about three thousand souls."—Acts ii. 41. No unconscious babe received "the word gladly." These persons were believers. When the evangelist, Philip, told the story of the cross in Samaria, "They believed Philip preaching the things concerning the kingdom of God and the name of Jesus Christ, and they were baptized both men and women."—Acts viii. 12. Philip's converts were all professed believers, and these only were baptized. The eunuch claimed to be a disciple before he was baptized. Paul was a believer before Ananias immersed him. —Acts xxii. 16. Of Cornelius and his household it is said that he was "a devout man, and one that feared God *with all his house.*" "Then answered Peter, 'Can any man forbid water, that these should not be baptized, *who have received the Holy Spirit* as well as we?' And he commanded them to be baptized in the name of the Lord."—Acts x. 2, 24, 47, 48. This devout household that had received the Holy Spirit and baptism was a believing family, and the "kinsmen and near friends of Cornelius," who shared in his privileges, were believers. Of Lydia it is said that "the Lord opened her heart, that she attended unto the things which were spoken of Paul," and she was "baptized, and her household."—Acts xvi. 14, 15. Nothing is said about the persons composing her household. But if her heart was opened by the Lord her family needed the same blessing; as for her family being baptized on her faith, the writer of the Acts gives no hint of it; he does not say she had children or a husband, or that husband and children and servants were baptized on her faith. She was a visitor on business at Philippi, apparently without husband or children, and there is no evidence that any infant received baptism in her household. Of the jailer at Philippi, it is said that Paul and Silas "spake unto him the word of the Lord, and *to all that were in his house*," and that "he was baptized, he and all his, straightway," and that "he rejoiced, believing in God with all his house."—Acts xvi. 32, 33, 34. Among these hearers of the Word who were rejoicing believers there was no unconscious infant. If the household of Crispus was baptized, it is said that "he believed on the Lord with all his house," and in this supposed baptism the subjects were believers. Of the twelve men who had only John's baptism, whom Paul met at Ephesus, and whom he is *supposed* to have rebaptized,—Acts xix. 2,—it cannot be said that there was an unconscious infant among them. Nor could there be in the household of Stephanas, baptized by Paul, and of whom he says, that "they *addicted themselves to the ministry of the saints.*"—1 Cor. xvi. 15. John's baptism was precisely the same as Christ's, as Calvin (Institutes, lib. iv., cap. 15, sec. 7) and others teach, and of it Mark says, "John did baptize in the wilderness, and preach the baptism of repentance for the remission of sins. And there went out unto him all the land of Judea, and they of Jerusalem, and were all *baptized* of him *in the river Jordan, confessing their sins.*"—Mark i. 4, 5. No unconscious infant confessed its sins in these Jordan immersions. The apostle John gives the Saviour's exact idea of the qualifications for baptism when he says, "When therefore the Lord knew how the Pharisees had heard that Jesus *made and baptized* more disciples than John."—John iv. 1. This is the Saviour's law of baptism,—*make disciples*, then baptize them : "Go ye and teach all nations (make disciples of all nations), baptizing them in the name," etc. This was the uniform practice of the apostles, to which there are no exceptions. There is not an instance of infant baptism in the New Testament, nor is there any command enjoining it. It has no more Scriptural foundation than the infallibility of the Pope, or the inspiration of the "Book of Mormon." Neander writes with authority when he says, "Baptism, at first, was administered only to adults, as men were accustomed to conceive *baptism and faith as strictly connected. We have all reason for not deriving infant baptism from apostolic institution.*" There is but one New Testament scripture which can be used to *countenance* infant baptism : "Submit yourself to *every ordinance of man* for the Lord's sake,"—1 Peter ii. 13,—but unfortunately the same scripture requires *submission* to every enormity instituted by earthly governments.

Baptist, Rev. Edward, Sr., D.D., 1790-1863, was born in Mecklenburg Co., Va., May 12, 1790; becoming a Christian at the age of eighteen, he united with the Presbyterian Church, of which his mother was a member, his father being an Episcopalian. He graduated in Hampden Sidney College with a view to the practice of medicine. He became dissatisfied with his ecclesiastical relations, and on a thorough investigation of the subject of baptism, united with the Baptists, and was baptized by the Rev. Richard Dobbs. Realizing that God had called him to the gospel ministry, he returned to Hampden Sidney, and graduated in the course of theology under the celebrated Dr. Hoge; and in 1815, at the age of twenty-five, he was set apart by ordination to his high calling, and settled in Powhatan County; was married to Miss Eliza J. C. Eggleston, who survived him; built up several strong churches in Virginia; held an influence among the Baptists of that State second to no man in his day; was the prime mover in the origination of the General Association in 1822, and drafted its constitution. He was also the originator of the Baptist Educational Society and Seminary of that State, and by appointment instructed a number of young men who were studying for the ministry. Being a preacher of great ability, piety, and eloquence, a revival began under his ministry which extended over a large part of the State, and joyously affected the churches in the city of Richmond. After a brilliant ministry of twenty years in Virginia, he moved to Alabama in 1835, settling in Marengo County, where he remained to his death. In his new field he again planted and established several strong churches, among a wealthy and liberal people. One of them was at Uniontown, where he was many years pastor. He took an active part in the Baptist Convention of this State, and in all our denominational schools and enterprises. He received several calls to large city churches, which he declined, believing that a country pastorate suited his frail health better. He wrote extensively for the *Religious Herald* and other Christian papers; held honorable contests in the public prints with Alexander Campbell and Dr. John L. Rice. A series of thirty letters published in the *Religious Herald* was subsequently put in book-form. A volume of his sermons was in the hands of the Southern Baptist Publication Society at Charleston for publication, but with much other valuable Baptist literature it was destroyed in the late war. Dr. Baptist died at his residence in Marengo Co., Ala., March 31, 1863, having lived in that State twenty-eight years. He was always in comfortable worldly circumstances; reared a charming family. His son, Rev. Edward Baptist, Jr., is now a distinguished minister in Virginia. Dr. Baptist was a devout, zealous, happy, Christian gentleman.

Baptist General Convention for Missionary Purposes. See TRIENNIAL CONVENTION.

Baptist Pioneers in Religious Enterprise.—Through Roger Williams they founded the first government on earth where absolute religious liberty was established. Through the protracted labors of the Rev. John Canne they placed marginal references in the English Bible. (Neal's "History of the Puritans," ii. 50. Dublin, 1755.) Through Dr. William Carey they gave modern missions to the pious regards and efforts of Christians in all lands. Through the Rev. Joseph Hughes, of London, on May 4, 1804, they established the British and Foreign Bible Society, and in it every kindred institution on earth. (Ivimey's "History of the English Baptists," ii. 93.) For their numbers Baptists have shown an extraordinary measure of holy enterprise.

Baptist Weekly, The, is a quarto journal, devoted, as its name indicates, to the promotion of Christianity as held by the Baptists. The *Christian Contributor* and the *Western Christian* were purchased by the American Baptist Free Mission Society, and they were united, and received the name of the *American Baptist*, Rev. Warham Walker, editor. The paper, with the headquarters of the society, was located at Utica, N. Y., until 1857, when it was removed to the city of New York. Mr. Walker was assisted for a year by the well-known Rev. Nathan Brown, D.D., a returned missionary from Assam, after which Dr. Brown was appointed editor, assisted by Rev. John Duer, of Massachusetts, and he remained in the position till 1872, when he resigned to accept an appointment from the American Baptist Missionary Union as missionary to Japan. The paper under Dr. Brown was opposed to slavery, all secret societies, and the honorary titles of clergymen.

In May, 1872, A. L. Patton, D.D., purchased the paper, changed it from a folio to a quarto, enlarged it, and improved it in many respects. Its specialties were dropped, and it entered on a vigorous advocacy of all the great interests of the Baptist denomination. It earnestly maintains the distinctive principles and practices of the Baptists. It is eminently conservative, patient with those who differ from it, conciliatory to those who strike out on "new departures" in matters not essential to purity of life or evangelical teaching. It is eminently a peace-maker in Zion. Dr. Patton and Dr. Middleditch make an admirable paper, whose weekly visits are welcomed by a large number of subscribers.

Baptistery, an Ancient Roman and a Modern.—The Rev. Dr. A. J. Rowland, of Philadelphia, gives the following account of a celebrated baptistery in Rome:

"I visited it on Sunday afternoon, Sept. 24, 1876; the building is octagonal in form, and stands a little distance from the fine old church of St. John de Lateran, which gives it its name (and for the use of which it was appropriated). One is struck with the antiquity of its appearance, and is not surprised to learn from the guide that it dates back to the time of Constantine. The building is about 50 feet in diameter. The pool of the baptistery is of green basalt; and it is about *twenty feet long by fifteen wide*, the form being that of an ellipse. There seemed to be a false wooden floor in the bottom, but the depth, *even with this, was something over three feet*. I asked the guide, who seemed to belong to one of the lower orders of the clergy, the use of this large font, so unlike those in modern churches, and he replied 'that its size was due to the fact that *anciently people were immersed*.' I inquired if it was ever used for immersion now. 'Yes,' he said; 'on Easter-eve, *Jews and pagans who accept the faith of the church are baptized here in that way*.' This fact I subsequently found also in Baedeker's celebrated guide-book. On the right and left of the baptistery building doors open into two small apartments, now known as chapels; on the ceiling of one of them is an old mosaic, dating back to the fifth century, representing John the Baptist *performing the rite of immersion*. It appeared to me that these two apartments may have been originally dressing-rooms for baptismal occasions. Between the pool and the outer walls of the building there is space enough, I think, for four or five hundred spectators to witness a baptism." (Cathcart's "Baptism of the Ages," pp. 152–53.)

A thousand years ago, at Easter, immersion was the customary mode of baptism in this church, and the pope himself was occasionally the administrator, wearing a "pair of waxed drawers," which, of course, were water-proof. ("History of Baptism," by Robinson, p. 106. Nashville, 1860.) There are still many ancient baptisteries in Italy.

A modern baptistery is generally in the church edifice; that of the Second Baptist church, Philadelphia, rests on, not in, the pulpit platform. It is 8 feet long, about 6 feet wide, and 4 feet 6 inches deep. It is octagonal in form. It is built of white statuary marble, lined with zinc. It is filled by one opening in the bottom, and emptied by another. It is entered by two sets of iron stairs coated with zinc, each of which is protected from sight by a walnut curtain, of about 7 feet in height from the pulpit platform. Six inches from the top of the baptistery there is an opening to prevent an overflow of the platform. Under each set of steps is the end of a bent pipe, rising a few inches from the bottom of the pool, the bend of the pipe being in a furnace in the cellar; when the water is in the font and a fire in the furnace, this water will reach a comfortable temperature in half an hour. Back of the baptistery, on the same floor, are two preparing-rooms for the accommodation of candidates. The pool is one of the most beautiful of modern fonts, but it is a poor vessel compared with many ancient fonts still to be seen in Italy.

Baptistery in an Episcopal Church.—Ivimey says that "in the parish church of Cranbrook, Kent, England, there is at present (1814) a baptistery built for the purpose of immersion. It is a brick cistern placed against the wall within the church above the floor. There are steps both outside and inside, for the convenience of the person baptized, while the administrator stands by the side of the baptistery to immerse the person. It is supposed that the baptistery was built by the vicar, a Mr. Johnson, in the beginning of the last century." ("History of the English Baptists," ii., 227. London, 1814.) Probably there are several other baptisteries in Episcopal churches in England just now. The law of that church *requires* dipping unless it is certified to the priest "that the *child is weak.*" And as many adults in England, of Baptist training, have not been baptized, if any one of them united with the Episcopal Church, he would most likely insist on immersion. The writer of this article saw a beautiful baptistery in 1848 in the vestibule of the parish church, Bradford, York, England.

Baptistery of Milan, The.—Three friends at different times searched Milan for photographs of its ancient baptistery at the request of the writer. The first two failed to secure any picture, because no photograph of it was ever taken. The last obtained, with some difficulty, and perhaps by using a golden argument, a lithograph sketch of the font

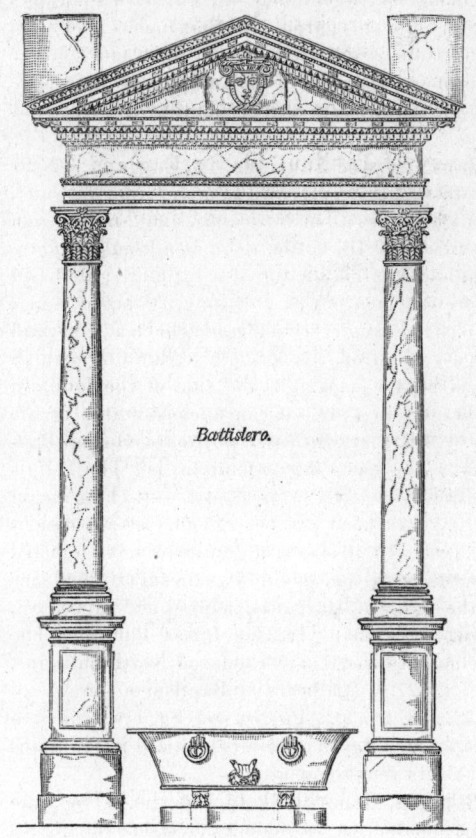

BAPTISTERY OF MILAN.

from a sacristan. It is an ancient sarcophagus, said to have contained the ashes of an early saint; its material is porphyry. According to the measurement of our friend it is 6 feet 8 inches long and 24 inches deep. Until a very recent period full immersion was the baptism always administered in this Catholic font. Dean Stanley utters the testimony of Christendom about immersion in the church of St. Ambrose when he says, "With the two exceptions of the Cathedral of Milan and the sect of the Baptists, a few drops of water are now the Western substitute for the threefold plunge into the rushing rivers, or the wide baptisteries of the

East." In 1830 the late Dr. Howard Malcom witnessed an immersion in the sarcophagus font, a full account of which is in "The Baptism of the Ages," pp. 150, 151.

The friend already alluded to says, "On Sunday, Aug. 25, 1878, I witnessed a baptism in the Cathedral of Milan. After anointing the ears of the child, it was placed on the arms of the officiating priest, his left arm being under its neck; then, by movements from the left to the right, the back part of its head was passed three times through the water."

How much later than 1830 the font has been used for immersion we cannot tell, but it was always employed for this purpose till that time. And more than 40 other baptisteries now in Italy, much larger than the sarcophagus of Milan, have given immersion for centuries to the people that lived around them.

Baptistery of Paulinus, in England.—Near the Cheviot Hills, dividing England from Scotland, about 30 miles from Newcastle, and 2 miles from the village of Harbottle, there is a beautiful fountain, issuing from the top of a little hill; its basin at present is about 34 feet long, 20 broad, and 2 deep. This cavity could easily be made several feet deeper; from the spring a stream flows which forms a little creek. At the side of the fountain the writer, in 1869, saw an ancient statue of life size called the "Bishop," no doubt Bishop Paulinus. The name of the fountain is "The Lady's Well," evidently "Our Lady,"—"The Virgin Mary." At hand are the remains of an ancient nunnery. In it stands a granite crucifix erected about thirty years ago, under the superintendence of the vicar of Harbottle, a graduate of Oxford, on which is cut: "In This Place, Paulinus, The Bishop, Baptized Three Thousand Northumbrians, Easter, 627." (Cathcart's "Baptism of the Ages," pp. 27, 28, 29, 30. Publication Society, Philadelphia.) Our English ancestors baptized in fountains and rivers very frequently.

Baptists, General Sketch of the.—The Baptist denomination was founded by Jesus during his earthly ministry. Next to the Teacher of Nazareth, our great leaders were the apostles, and the elders, bishops, and evangelists, who preached Christ in their times. The instructions of our Founder are contained in the four Gospels, the heaven-given teachings of our earliest ministers are in the inspired Epistles. The first Baptist missionary journal was the Acts of the Apostles. For the first two centuries all the congregations of the Church Universal (Catholic) were Baptist communities. During the two succeeding centuries the baptism of unconscious babes had such a limited existence that it is scarcely worthy of notice. During the fifth and sixth centuries the baptism of catechumens, that is, of catechized persons instructed beforehand for the sacred rite, was still common throughout Christendom. Though the candidates were constantly becoming younger, they always professed their own faith. Nor was the baptism of catechumens laid aside entirely in Rome itself in the ninth century. From the beginning of the fifth century infants commonly were baptized when very ill to take away Adam's guilt, lest they might die and be lost. And though there were a few cases of infant baptism before this period, it was about this time it began to spread, but it required a good many centuries to gain the complete mastery of the Church Universal (Catholic); and before it succeeded, heretics, so called, flourished outside of the great corrupted Church Universal (Catholic). And even infant baptism itself, when it sprang up, had to take the apostolic idea that faith was a prerequisite to baptism, and borrow faith from the sponsors or parents of the child, or from the whole church, to make good its claim to the initiatory rite of the Christian Church. And it follows this course still.

The first great error among Christians was that water baptism in some way removed the sins of *penitents*. This heresy was common in the third century. About the same time the Lord's Supper began to be regarded by some as possessing soul-healing efficacy for him who partook of it, and a magical power to protect the dwelling, or a ship at sea, if a portion of the bread was in the one or the other. These two follies led Christians to magnify the minister enormously, who could impart the soul-cleansing immersion, and consecrate the heart-healing, and house- and ship-protecting, sacramental supper. These heresies, with their priestly reverence, fostered sacerdotal ambition, and led to the creation of gradations of rank among the clergy, until in process of time the Universal Church had little to show but a pyramid of priests, with the inferior ministry as its broad base, and the pope at its head, and two sacred ceremonies, the one giving imaginary salvation through baptismal water, and the other the supposed body and blood of the Lord, through real bread and wine. And as evils grow at a rapid rate, these perversions of baptism and the Lord's Supper generated the whole brood of Romish ceremonies and superstitions.

When this conviction about the power of baptism to take away the sins of believers became common in the third century, then for the first time the baptism of unconscious babes was thought of; but in that century there is only one case of the kind, and not many more in the fourth; but in the fifth, Augustine of Hippo began to frighten the Christian world with the falsehood that infants would perish through Adam's sin without baptism. At the same time bits of the bread of the Lord's Supper were forced upon the unconscious child, or a little of the wine, to give double salvation from two redeeming sacraments. As we have said, for long ages after this hosts in the Church Universal fought this wicked rite, which usurped the place of Christ's holy sacrament, and induced the Saviour's servants to trust saving water, instead of the blood of atonement and the arm of omnipotence.

When these superstitions gained extensive sway in the Church Universal (Catholic), communities of Christians sprang up in various quarters, some of which held the old truths of our mighty Founder whom John baptized in the river Jordan when he had reached the age of full manhood. The Paulicians, originating in the seventh century in Armenia, were Baptists. This community, brought into life by reading the Word of God, flourished for a time in its native place, then it sent missionaries into Thrace, Bulgaria, Bosnia, Servia, Italy, France, Germany, and other countries, and gathered millions of adherents, and terrified popes, and drew kings with crusading armies of vast strength to kill its members. Between five hundred thousand and a million of them were put to death in France in the thirteenth century.

This people was most commonly known in Europe as Albigenses, but they bore many names and malignant reproaches; and the worst doctrines and practices were falsely imputed to them. The Paulician, Bogomilian, Albigenses existed in strength in Bosnia till 1463, and were found there till a later day.

From the twelfth century till the Reformation the Waldenses occupied a conspicuous place in the hatred of Catholic Europe, and in the violence of fierce persecutions. And some of these illustrious sufferers were Baptists.

In the same century which gave birth to the Waldenses the Henricians and Petrobrusians commenced their existence as gospel communities, and held forth the lamp of life to the perishing, so that large numbers were saved. These so-called heretics were Baptists.

During that mighty upheaval in the days of Luther which shook the papacy to its lowest foundations, men with Anabaptist principles appeared in every direction with a suddenness that startled the world, and they were welcomed immediately with cruel greetings to foul dungeons and barbarous deaths. Their blood flowed in torrents upon the continent of Europe; and even in England it was wickedly shed.

It is not improbable that the ancient Britons were opponents of infant baptism when the Romish missionary Augustine met them in 603. But the evidence furnished by Bede, Eccles. Hist., lib. ii., cap. 2, is not sufficient to establish this. In the early period of the Reformation Anabaptists became quite numerous in England, and they excited the indignation of King Henry VIII. and the clergy, and they are often alluded to in denunciatory language in public documents. A little further on they were subjected to cruel persecutions. In the time of Edward VI., Joan of Kent, who carried Bibles into the palace of Henry VIII. for distribution, concealed under her apron, when the penalty for the act was death, was given to the flames by King Edward by the over-persuasion of Archbishop Cranmer. Others shared her harsh fate, but Baptist doctrines spread, to the dismay of the clergy, and found a place in hearts opened of God in all parts of the kingdom. And even in Scotland mighty John Knox found it necessary to write a book against them. Queen Elizabeth and James I. treated them with royal barbarity, and Charles I. would have imitated their example had not the rising spirit of Anglo-Saxon liberty put a bit in his mouth, and finally cut off the tyrant's head. For some years preceding and following 1649, the date of this event, the Baptists enjoyed extraordinary prosperity; they filled the English army in Ireland with officers, and they had a large number over the troops located in Scotland and England, and even in Cromwell's own regiment. So sturdy was their republicanism that many of them could see no difference between Charles I. reigning without a Parliament and Oliver Cromwell governing without a Legislature. The Protector distrusted them, and procured a letter from the celebrated London Baptist minister, William Kiffin, which others signed, exhorting their brethren in Ireland to submission. (Hansred Knollys Society's Confessions of Faith, p. 322.) Cromwell was so concerned about the opposition of some members of this now powerful body that he had spies to watch their movements and report their supposed conspiracies. Thurloe gives the letter of one of these spies describing the proceedings of a Baptist Association in England, and mentioning its prayers, letters, sermons, and speakers just as the proceedings of such a body might be described to-day. Generals Harrison, Lilburn, Overton, and Ludlow, and others in the army; Admiral-General Richard Deane, of both the army and the navy, Admiral Sir John Lawson, and a large number of other distinguished officers of the navy, reflected a glory upon themselves and their Baptist brethren which created fear or joy throughout their island home. It was said that alarm lest the Baptists should seize the government after Cromwell's death actually led the Presbyterians to unite with the Episcopalians in bringing from Holland to the English throne Charles II., the greatest profligate that ever dishonored the family relation. In the reign of Charles, and his brother James, the most wicked persecutions were applied to Dissenters, and while the English Presbyterians from them and from subsequent heresy were annihilated, the Baptists received blows the effects of which they feel in England to-day.

They are now divided into General and Particular Baptists, the former being the smaller body. The word "General" was put in their name to describe their doctrine of the atonement; they hold Arminian views of it and of all the doctrines of grace; the word "Particular" was originally assumed to show that this section of the English Baptists held a limited atonement, and Calvinistical views of the doctrines of grace. These British Baptists have been enterprising, and have had many distinguished men, but they have been sadly hindered by persecutions and by the social tyranny of a powerful and intolerant state church. There are in England, Wales, Scotland, and Ireland 2620 Baptist churches, with a membership of 269,836.

Roger Williams, a Welshman by birth, an Episcopalian by training, a Congregationalist by choice, and a graduate of the University of Cambridge, England, came to New England in 1631. Two or three years afterwards he was appointed assistant minister to the Congregational church of Salem, Mass. While there he denied the right of the magistrates to punish offenses of a purely religious character, and "in one year's time he filled the place with principles of rigid separation (from the Church of England) and tending to Anabaptism." For these "high crimes and misdemeanors" he was finally ordered to leave the colony; and failing to render obedience to the lordly Puritans of that day, and learning that he was about to be sent home by force, he fled in the depth of winter to the Narragansett Indians, and established the city of Providence in 1636, and the first Baptist church in America in that city in 1639. The community which gathered around him adopted from him the old Baptist doctrine of absolute freedom of conscience, and incorporated it in their laws; and when Joshua Verin, a little time after the settlement of Providence, restrained his wife from attending some religious meetings, he was disfranchised as a punishment for his offense.

The church founded by Mr. Williams is still in existence, and it is regarded with veneration as the first Baptist church in the New World. It worships in a noble building erected one hundred and five years ago.

In Massachusetts cruel persecutions were inflicted on Baptists and Quakers for a long period. In Virginia the hand of legal violence was frequently raised with wicked force against our saintly fathers, but in Rhode Island, long under the control of the Baptists, whose governor at this time worships in a Baptist church, no man ever suffered any penalty for his religious convictions.

Bancroft, the historian, says of Roger Williams: "He was the first person in modern Christendom to assert in its plenitude the doctrine of the liberty of conscience, the equality of opinions before the law; and in its defense he was the harbinger of Milton (a Baptist), the precursor and the superior of Jeremy Taylor. . . . Williams would permit persecution of no opinion, of no religion, leaving heresy unharmed by law, and orthodoxy unprotected by the terrors of penal laws." Vol. i., 375. "Freedom of conscience, unlimited freedom of mind, was from the first the trophy of the Baptists." ii., 67. This is justly said of Roger Williams, and it is all true except the statement that he was "the first person in modern Christendom" to assert this doctrine. Leonard Busher, an English Baptist, published in London in 1614 "Religious Peace," in which Williams's doctrine is repeatedly asserted. This was more than twenty years before Mr. Williams broached it, and Busher had many predecessors in announcing his inspired principles. This little work is in the Hanserd Knollys volume of "Traits on Liberty of Conscience," London, 1846. The blessed truth Mr. Williams unfolded on this continent his Baptist brethren everywhere preached, and they have given it sovereign sway in all this land.

The Baptists of this country hold that the Word of God is the only authority in religion, that its teachings are to be sacredly observed, and that to religious doctrines and observances there can be no additions except from it; they hold that a man should repent and be saved through faith in the meritorious Redeemer before he is baptized; that immersion alone is Scripture baptism; that only by it can the candidate represent his death to the world, burial with Christ, and resurrection to newness of life; that baptism is a prerequisite to the Lord's Supper; they hold the doctrines of the Trinity, of eternal and personal election, total depravity, regeneration by the Holy Spirit, justification by the imputed righteousness of Christ, progressive sanctification, final perseverance a special providence, immediate and eternal glory for the righteous after death, and instant and unending misery for the ungodly. They hold the doctrinal articles of the Presbyterian Church, and they only differ from that honored Calvinistical community in the mode and subjects of baptism, and in their congregational church government. They hold that all regenerated believers are saved, whether they are immersed or sprinkled, or lack both ceremonies; and they insist on the immersion of believers because Christ was immersed, and because he enjoins immersion upon all believers.

In this country we have 38 colleges and theological seminaries, and many superior academies. We have in North America 63 religious periodicals.

The Baptist motto ever has been, "Let there be light, secular, sacred, and redeeming, till it covers the earth and bathes humanity in its shining waves!"

In the United States we have 24,794 churches, 15,401 ministers, and 2,200,000 members, which, with adherents, young and old, give us more than 5,000,000 of persons who hold our principles. In the various provinces of Canada, and in the British West India Islands, there are 849 churches, with 89,938 members. Baptist missions in Germany, France, Sweden, and other sections of Europe, and in Asia and Africa, will be noticed under the names of the countries in which they are located. In the world there are 29,400 Baptist churches, with a membership of 2,663,172, which, with other adherents in Sunday-schools and congregations, would probably give us between 7,000,000 and 8,000,000 of Baptists. This does not include denominations in the United States that hold believer's immersion, which are not Regular Baptists, such as the Old-School Baptists, Winebrennarians or Church of God, Seventh-Day Baptists, Six-Principle Baptists, Tunkers, Disciples, Adventists, and Free-Will Baptists. These communities have 6951 churches and 615,541 members.

The origin and growth of the denomination in each of the United States will be found in sketches under the names of the States in this work.

The Baptists have a firm confidence in the truth, and in the ultimate triumph of their principles; and while they will not sacrifice a jot of inspired teaching to gain the good will of the whole Christian family, they love all true believers of every name, from Pascal, the Catholic, to Joseph John Gurney, the Friend.

See the following articles: THE BAPTISM OF CATECHUMENI, THE ALBIGENSES, THE HENRICIANS, THE PETROBRUSIANS, THE WALDENSES, THE ANABAPTISTS.

Baptists, Primitive, or Old School. — The Primitive Baptists are often called "Old School," or "Anti-Mission," or "Anti-Effort," and, in derision, "hardshell" Baptists. They usually, if not invariably, adopt the Philadelphia Confession of Faith, founded upon that approved by over a hundred leading men in London, in 1689. They do not materially differ from the Regular Baptists as to Scripture doctrine, agreeing with them as to the necessity of regeneration, the mode and subjects of baptism, baptism preceding the Supper, and congregational church government. Some style themselves "Predestinarians," and are charged with pushing the "doctrines of grace," called "Calvinistic," into "hyper-Calvinism," or *fatalism*, denying any responsibility in man for his own conduct or condition. Baptists generally dwell upon the lessons given by John, the Forerunner, the adorable Redeemer, and his apostles and disciples, as to the necessity of seeking repentance and forgiveness; for how can immortal beings believe in Him of whom they have not heard? and how can they hear without a preacher? and how can preachers go forth unless others aid them? They urge "that it pleased God by the foolishness of preaching to save them who believe." But many of the Old-School brethren, while they comfort saints, do not feel it a duty to warn sinners, and few conversions occur under their ministrations. They allege that God carries on his own work, "without the least instrumentality whatever," and that "all the preaching from John the Baptist until now, if made to bear on one unregenerate sinner, could no more quicken his poor dead soul than so much chattering of a crane or of a swallow." (*Circular of Warwick Association, 1840, copied by Chemung soon afterwards.*) And it would not but for God's accompanying Spirit.

This system is not entirely new, but has prevailed at times elsewhere. It is claimed that it humbles the pride of man; but it is charged, also, that it pampers ease, lulls to sleep, and shrivels benevolence. The decline of some Baptist churches in Great Britain is attributed by many to this contracted view of man's duty and privilege.

The Great Awakening under Edwards, Whitefield, and Wesley, over a century since, aroused many in the Baptist and other denominations to the fact of each person's own accountability as a laborer in the Lord's great harvest-field, leaving to him the issues, in grace as in nature. William Carey's entrance upon his mission work in India was a result of this reformation.

In America the same divergence of views among Baptists resulted in alienations and divisions, while opposing parties yet remained in the same body.

At length, in September, 1835, the Chemung Association (New York and Pennsylvania), at a meeting with Sullivan church, Charleston, Tioga Co., Pa., passed the following:

"*Whereas*, a number of the Associations with whom we have held correspondence have departed from the simplicity of the doctrine and practice of the gospel of Christ, and have followed cunningly devised fables (the inventions of men), uniting themselves with the world in what are falsely called benevolent societies, founded upon a moneyed basis, with a profession to spread the gospel, which is another gospel differing from the gospel of Christ. *Resolved*, therefore, that we discontinue our correspondence with the Philadelphia, Abington, Bridgewater, Franklin, Steuben, Madison, and all other Associations which are supporting the popular institutions of the day; and most affectionately invite all those churches, or members of churches, among them who cannot fellowship them to come out from among them and leave them."

In May following (1836) the Baltimore Association met at Black Rock, Baltimore Co., Md., and passed the same in substance. It is generally known as "the Black Rock declaration."

The minority members of these bodies at once founded others on the platform of aiding missionary, temperance, Sunday-school, and such other organizations as they deemed in harmony with Bible teachings.

Similar divisions ran through other churches and Associations, mostly in the South and West. In 1844 the *Baptist Almanac* attempted to distinguish between the Regular or Mission Baptists and those who opposed missionary work in formal organizations for that purpose. The record of 1844 reported 184 Old-School Associations, 1622 churches, 900 ordained ministers, 2374 baptized in the year preceding, and 61,162 members. The *Year Book* for 1880 returns 900 Old-School churches, 400 ordained ministers, and 40,000 members,—a loss of one-third in thirty-six years. The Old-School brethren have declined in numbers almost every year since they made the division. They have some periodicals, but no seminaries of learning and no national organizations.

Many of the Old-School brethren in the ministry possess decided ability as expounders of Scripture, the members of their churches are commonly persons of deep piety, and of extensive Biblical knowledge. The creed which they generally hold is the Confession most venerated by all the Regular Baptists of America, from whom they originally withdrew, and with whom they decline to hold any ecclesiastical relations.

Barebone, Rev. Praise-God, had the misfortune to bear a singular name, which subjected him to considerable ridicule in his own age, when absurd names were very common, and to a great deal more in every generation since. In 1640 he became pastor of a Baptist church in London which separated from the community over which the Rev. Henry Jessey presided. Like many ministers of that day, he was compelled to support himself either wholly or partly by a worldly calling. Mr. Barebone sold leather. He was a man of intellect, widely known and esteemed by the friends of liberty throughout England.

When Oliver Cromwell summoned men to form a Parliament he called upon Mr. Barebone to take a seat in the legislature. This fact showed that he was a well-known patriot, whose zeal against despotism in the state and tyrannical ritualism in the church had reached the great Protector himself. In the Parliament his ability was speedily recognized, and he exerted such a controlling influence over its decisions that it was called "Barebone's Parliament." When General Monk was in London, in 1660, preparing the way for Charles II., Mr. Barebone, at the head of a "crowd of sectaries" (a multitude of Congregationalists and Baptists), says Clarendon, presented a petition to Parliament demanding, among other things, "that no person whatsoever might be admitted to the exercise of any office in the state, or in the church, no, not so much as to teach a school, who did not first take the oath of abjuration of the king, and of all his family; and that he would never submit to the government of any one single person whatsoever; and that whosoever should presume so much as to propose, or mention the restoration of the king in Parliament, or any other place, should be adjudged guilty of, and condemned for high treason." The man to head the petitioners was this Baptist minister. He was not afraid to defy Monk, the betrayer of his country's liberties, and his whole army, ready as it was and at hand to execute their general's wishes. And this petition shows that Mr. Barebone was a republican of our Thomas Jefferson's order. Clarendon, speaking of a part of Cromwell's Parliament of 1653, of which Mr. Barebone was a member, says, "In which number, that there may be a better judgment made of the rest, it will not be amiss to name one, from whom that Parliament itself was afterwards denominated, Praise-God Barebone, a leather-seller in Fleet Street, from whom, he being an *eminent* speaker in it, it was afterwards called Praise-God Barebone's Parliament."* Neal says of the members of the same Parliament, "It was much wondered at, says Whitlocke, that these gentlemen, many of whom were persons of fortune and estate, should accept the supreme authority of the nation upon such a summons and from such hands (Cromwell's). Most of them were men of piety, but no great politicians, and were therefore in contempt sometimes called the Little Parliament, and by others Barebone's Parliament, from a leather-seller of that name, who was one of *the most active* members."† Rapin says, "Amongst these members was one Barebone, a leather-seller, who, in his neighborhood, passed for *a notable speaker* because he used to entertain them with long harangues upon the times. From this man the people in derision called them Barebone's Parliament."‡ A foot-note in Rapin says, "His name was Praise-God Barebone, from whom, *he being a great speaker* in it, the Parliament was called as above." These witnesses all show that our worthy brother was really the master-spirit of the legislature that bore his name. And whatever it may have lacked in the technicalities of legislation, it wanted nothing of the spirit of freedom. It passed

---

* Clarendon's "History of the Rebellion," iii. 482, 714. Oxford, 1706.
† Neal's "History of the Puritans," iv. 55, 67. Dublin, 1755.
‡ Rapin's "History of England," ii. 590. London, 1733.

a law, according to Neal, to repeal enactments that hindered the progress of the gospel, and to give liberty to all that feared God to worship him without molestation. Mr. Barebone undoubtedly gave effective assistance in the passage of this law.

Mr. Barebone was unquestionably a godly and a great man; and he wielded such a powerful influence that when he presented the petition to the Parliament, to which reference has been made, Walter Wilson* states that "Monk, who knew the popularity of Barebone, was obliged to make a general muster of the army, and write a letter to the Parliament, expostulating with them for giving too much countenance to that furious zealot and his adherents."

The names of Mr. Barebone had a tendency to make him ridiculous. But he triumphed over these and other disadvantages.

Barker, Rev. Cyrus, was born at Portsmouth, R. I., March 27, 1807. He pursued his studies at the Hamilton Literary and Theological Institution, and was ordained in Newport, R. I., September, 1839, having previously received an appointment as a missionary to the foreign field. He sailed from Boston, Oct. 22, 1839. After his arrival in Calcutta he went to Jaipur, one of the principal posts of the East India Company in Assam, remaining there a little over a year, and, May 18, 1841, going to Sibsager, another flourishing post of the East India Company, three days' journey below Jaipur. He labored for several years in this city. He was subsequently stationed at Gowahati. While here his health failed, and he left the foreign field hoping to gain new strength for his work. He died at sea, and was buried in the Mozambique Channel, Jan. 31, 1850.

Barker, Prof. Isaac Bowen, was born in Hanson, Mass., Nov. 25, 1839. He was fitted for college at the Middleborough Academy, then under the charge of Prof. J. W. P. Jenks, now of Brown University, where his pupil graduated with the highest honors of his class in 1861. Shortly after his graduation he received the appointment of Assistant Professor of Ethics and English Literature at the U. S. Naval Academy, then at Newport, but since removed to Annapolis, Md. Prof. Barker resigned his office on the transfer of the institution to Maryland, and went abroad for two years. When he came back, for one year he filled the chair of Rhetoric and English Literature in Brown University, which had been made vacant by the death of the lamented Prof. Dunn. On completing his term of service he was called to the University of East Tennessee, at Knoxville. Here, for five years, he performed the duties of his office. In September, 1874, he was appointed instructor in the German language in Harvard College. For six months only was he able to attend to his duties. An attack of pneumonia so prostrated him that in a few days he was forced to yield to the disease, and died March 22, 1875, in the prime of his life and usefulness. Prof. Barker was a consistent member of a Baptist church, a ripe scholar, whose untimely death brought sorrow to many hearts.

Barlow, Rev. F. N., late pastor of the Baptist church at Stockton, Cal., was born at Kent, Conn.

REV. F. N. BARLOW.

His mother died when he was four years old. At sixteen he began the world for himself,—worked hard, and studied until he was able to teach. He began the study of law in Western New York, but was turned from that profession to educational and pastoral work, in which his wife, Miss Harriet T. Healey, of Connecticut, has been a true helper. In 1849 he began preaching in Fairfield Co., Conn.; was ordained in 1850; organized a church in Danbury in 1851, and was its pastor four years. His other pastorates were at Franklindale, Cold Spring, and Cornwall, Saratoga Co., and Middletown, N. Y.; Alpina, Mich., where he organized a church, and built a meeting-house; Monroe, Mich.; and Chatham, Canada. In 1877 he went to California; was pastor eight months at Santa Clara, and at Stockton from Jan. 1, 1878, till prostrated by illness, beloved by all, he was compelled to resign, intending to return to his Eastern home. In all his pastorates he has been blessed with gracious revivals. He is a finished scholar, a spirited and eloquent preacher,

---

* Wilson's "History and Antiquities of Dissenting Churches," i. 47, 49. London, 1808.

and a model pastor. In 1862 he joined the Union army as lieutenant of the 115th Regiment, N. Y. Vols.; was taken prisoner, released, and returned to the service, till broken health compelled him to resign. His church received him joyfully as its pastor. A sickness in early youth impaired his constitution, so that twice during his ministry he had to give up preaching for a time. He is one of the few men in the Baptist ministry of the Pacific coast whose counsel and business character give him a place of pre-eminence among his brethren.

Barlow, Rev. Joseph Lorenzo, was born at Kent, Litchfield Co., Conn., Oct. 27, 1818; ordained in 1853 at Seymour, Conn., where he was settled as pastor of the Baptist church one year. He subsequently held pastorates at Sandisfield, Mass.; Greenfield Center, Stillwater, Broadalbin, and Lansingburg, N. Y.; Ridgetown, Conn.; Dundee and Bloomingdale, Ill.; and he is now the pastor of the church in Menomonee, Wis. Mr. Barlow baptized about 400 converts in connection with these pastorates. His labors have been extensively sought by pastors in seasons of special religious interest. During the war he was the chaplain of the 125th Regiment of N. Y. Vols. He was captured by the Confederates at Harper's Ferry, in 1862, when two weeks out, and resigned his commission the following February, owing to broken health. He is still, at the age of sixty-two years, in active service and doing an excellent work for the church to which he ministers.

Barnaby, Rev. James, was born at Freetown, Mass., June 25, 1787. He was a student at Bristol Academy, Taunton, Mass., during his preparatory course, and graduated at Brown University in the class of 1809. He intended to study law, but the Master whom he served for so many years had other work for him to do. While a member of college he had made a public profession of his faith in Christ, and was received into the First Baptist church in Providence. He soon after decided to enter the Christian ministry, and was ordained in July, 1811, and at once accepted a call to the pastorate of the Baptist church in Harwick, Mass. He continued in this relation for eight years, when he took charge of the church in New Bedford, Mass. For four years he was the pastor of this church, and in 1823 removed to Amesbury, Mass. Having completed his term of service here, he was pastor of several churches until 1849, when he accepted an appointment from the Baptist Sunday-School Union, for which society he labored three years. He became pastor again of the first church he had served, that of Harwick, in 1852, and remained seven years. Having a third time resigned, he had the charge of two or three churches for that period of time, and in 1862 came back once more to his old church in Harwick, and there he remained the rest of his life,—fifteen years. For sixty-seven years he was a minister of the gospel, thirty-nine of which were spent with the Harwick church. Twenty-eight hundred persons received the ordinance of baptism at his hands. He was a man of remarkable physical endurance. It was a remark of his which we know not by whom it could truthfully be uttered except by himself, that "he did not fail to preach the gospel on a Sunday for more than forty years." He died at Harwick, Dec. 10, 1877, aged ninety years and nearly six months.

Barnes, Rev. Daniel H., was born in Canaan, Columbia Co., N. Y., April 25, 1785. He graduated from Union College in 1809. He studied Hebrew under one of the most eminent teachers of that sacred tongue. In 1811 he united with the Baptist church of Poughkeepsie, and in 1813 he received a license to preach. In 1819 he accepted the "Professorship of Languages" in a theological seminary in New York, which was subsequently transferred to Hamilton. After this change he opened an English and classical school in New York, and in 1827 he was elected president of Columbian College, Washington, D. C., but he declined the appointment. Mr. Barnes preached frequently and acceptably; but he was a teacher, and an instructor of noble pupils; among them were Francis Wayland, William R. Williams, Bishop Potter, of Pennsylvania, and other great men. He rendered service in the preparation of Webster's Dictionary, and his contributions to Silliman's Journal showed that he was a learned student of geological science. He died October 27, 1828.

Barnes, Rev. James Edward, was born near Carrsville, Ky., June 16, 1828. Was converted and baptized in 1847. In 1851 he was elected to a public office, and while in the line of political promotion, in 1860, he removed to California. His zeal and ready address led many to urge him to enter the ministry. On arriving at the gold mines he established an altar of prayer, and his cabin was often filled with attentive listeners. Here he heard the call, "Go work in my vineyard," and obeyed, preaching first at Gold Hill, in 1865, on Sundays, and digging for gold during the week. In two years he had gathered large congregations, where churches were subsequently organized. He was ordained by the Uniontown church, Feb. 8, 1867. In 1872 he spent a year at Greenville, S. C., in studying theology. His native eloquence and zeal have enabled him to win many souls for Christ. He has been pastor of 11 churches, has baptized about 700 converts, and is now engaged in evangelistic labors with different churches in California.

Barnett, Rev. Joseph, a zealous and efficient pioneer both in Virginia and Kentucky, was probably a native of Virginia. He was active in forming the churches of which the Ketocton Association, Va., was composed. He was among the early settlers of the Western wilderness, and in connection with John Whitaker and John Gerrard founded the first two churches in Kentucky,—Severns Valley, constituted June 18, 1781, and Cedar Creek, constituted July 4, 1781. Of the latter Mr. Barnett was the first pastor. He was also the first moderator of Salem Association, constituted of four churches, at Cox's Creek, Nelson Co., Ky., Oct. 29, 1785.

Barnett, Rev. William Paddox, was born in Jefferson Co., Ky., in 1803. In early life he became a member of the Cumberland Presbyterian church, but afterwards united with the Baptist church at Fisherville, Ky., and was ordained to the ministry. He was pastor of several churches at different periods, but his principal pastorate was that of King's church, in Bullitt Co., Ky., to which he ministered with great success for a period of forty-three years. In 1850 he was elected moderator of Long Run Association, and on two occasions preached the introductory sermon before that body. Died Sept. 18, 1876.

Barney, Eliam E., educator and manufacturer, was born in Adams, Jefferson Co., N. Y., Oct. 14, 1807. Both parents were earnest Christians. Their son was converted and baptized at Henderson, N. Y., at the age of eleven. Having received his academic education at Lowville and Union Academies, he entered Union College, N. Y., and graduated in 1831. For two years after his graduation he was principal of Lowville Academy. In 1833 he removed to Ohio, and taught for six months in Granville College. In the spring of 1834 he became principal of the Dayton Academy, Dayton, O., and continued teaching for several years. His health failing, he engaged in business. In 1845 he was called to take charge of the Cooper Female Academy of Dayton, in which position he remained with great success until 1851. In the summer of 1850, with a partner, he established the Dayton Car-Works. After various changes in the firm, a joint-stock company was formed in 1867, under the name of the Barney & Smith Manufacturing Company, with a capital stock of $750,000, Mr. Barney being elected president. This establishment is now the largest of its kind in this country. The buildings occupy eighteen acres, and about one thousand men are employed in them. The great success of the enterprise is largely due to Mr. Barney.

Mr. Barney has never been an aspirant for public office. He is president of the Dayton Hydraulic Company, and of the Second National Bank.

As a Christian, Mr. Barney has always taken a firm and prominent stand. He was instrumental in rescuing the First Baptist church of Dayton from extinction when, in 1835, the majority of its members followed the pastor into the Disciple or Campbellite body, and the courts gave the seceders the church property. For several years he was the

ELIAM E. BARNEY.

superintendent of the Sunday-school, and has been a deacon since 1843. He has also been largely interested in the various educational and missionary enterprises of the denomination. For many years he has been a trustee of Denison University, and has given to that institution more than $35,000.

Barnhurst, Rev. Washington, was born in Philadelphia, Dec. 30, 1830. He was converted at the Broad Street church, and baptized by J. Lansing Burrows, D.D., March 8, 1846. He entered the junior class of Lewisburg University, and graduated in 1851. He pursued his theological studies at the Rochester Seminary. He was an excellent exegetical scholar. He was ordained at Chestnut Hill, Pa., Sept. 8, 1853. He was greatly blessed with revivals in 1853–54. He was called to Burlington, N. J., and there he baptized many. In 1856 he took charge of the Third Baptist church of St. Louis. In 1858 he had a glorious revival. His health failed from overwork for years, and in 1860 he removed to a farm in Miller Co., Mo. On April 29, 1862, he called his wife and sister, and told them he was dying, spoke of Jesus, and, waving his hand, said, "Higher, higher!" and passed into glory. His was a brief, earnest, and blessed ministry. He was a blameless Christian man.

Barrass, Edward, was born at Nailstone,

County of Leicester, England, Oct. 7, 1790; emigrated to this country in 1830; was licensed to preach by the Flemington Baptist church, March 31, 1833; died at Montana, Warren Co., Sept. 16, 1869, after a brief illness. He served the churches of Delaware, Oxford, and Mansfield, in Warren Co., N. J., and afterwards two churches in Pennsylvania, with which he labored until he was called from his earthly toils. In all these churches his work and worth are held in grateful remembrance.

Barrass, Rev. Thomas, was born in Leicestershire, England, July 22, 1793. He was baptized and united with the Baptist Church in his native land in the year 1817; came to this country in 1828, and united with the Baptist church in Flemington; was licensed to preach by that church Jan. 10, 1830, and ordained at Flemington, April 14, 1831. He itinerated in the upper part of Hunterdon, and through a considerable part of Warren County, as a missionary; was instrumental in gathering a constituency for the following churches: Oxford, Delaware, Bethlehem, and Mansfield. He served as pastor at Oxford, Bethlehem, and Kingwood, all of which churches were strengthened and enlarged, and bear uniform testimony to his earnest, faithful, and devoted labors. He died Sept. 27, 1869, eleven days after his brother Edward.

Barratt, Rev. J., of North Topeka, Kansas, is a faithful and successful minister, and a successful

REV. J. BARRATT.

bank director and merchant. The church of North Topeka which he gathered, and of which he is pastor, is a model church. Composed at first of less than a score of mechanics and farmers, it has increased till it numbers over 200. The church edifice has cost them about $12,000, and they have paid for it themselves as they proceeded. The house arose as the church and congregation and Sabbath-school grew. They have 6 missions within a radius of some fifteen miles, which are all likely to become self-sustaining and efficient churches. The whole community is permeated with Baptist sentiment. A church so occupied with Christian work is of course eminently peaceful, as well as aggressive. He did not *seek* an inviting field, but *made* one. Being an excellent organizer, his services have been sought repeatedly for a wider sphere. But his people will not let him go.

Barre, W. L., author and editor, was born in Warren Co., Ky., July 18, 1830. He was educated at Franklin College, Tennessee. In early life he became a Baptist, and was licensed as a preacher, although he seldom occupied the pulpit, preferring literary work to pastoral labors. He has been connected, as principal or associate editor, with the *Louisville Journal*, *Louisville Courier*, *Cincinnati Times*, *Cincinnati Gazette*, *Nashville Union and Dispatch*, the *Memphis Daily Dispatch*, and the *St. Joseph* (Mo.) *Daily Commercial*. In 1857 he removed to Cincinnati, where he remained nearly three years, and during this period wrote and published "Lives of Illustrious Men of America," a book of 1000 octavo pages, which passed through 11 editions. He wrote (in 1856) the "Life and Public Services of Millard Fillmore," and edited the "Speeches and Writings of Hon. Thomas F. Marshall," which passed through ten editions. During the civil war he was army correspondent of the *New York Times* and other leading journals. After the war he was engaged on various newspapers in several different States until 1873, when he became editor of the *Green River Pantagraph*.

Barrell, Rev. Noah, was born in Hartford, Washington Co., N. Y., May 5, 1794; died at Geneva, Wis., April 16, 1875, aged eighty-one years. During an active ministry of fifty-three years he served as pastor 15 churches in New York, Ohio, Wisconsin, and baptized about 1200 converts. He was a man of good natural endowments, of most winning and gentle spirit. He excelled in his work as pastor. His end was great peace.

Barrett, Hon. James M., a native of Mason, N. H. He spent his early years in Livingston Co., N. Y., and was educated at Nunda Academy, N. Y. He came to Wisconsin twenty-four years ago, and settled at Trempeleau, Trempeleau Co., where he now resides. He has filled many positions of public trust. Among them he has been a member of the Legislature, president of the County Agricultural Society, president of the Board of Education for twenty-three years. He is an active member of the Baptist church, and has been superintendent of its Sunday-school over twenty years. He is a member of the Board of State Missions, in whose work he takes a deep interest.

Barrett, Rev. T. W., was born in 1835, in Wood Co., West Va. United with the Baptist church at Marietta, O., in 1856; moved to Missouri the same year; was educated at William Jewell College; ordained Oct. 28, 1860, and entered immediately upon his work as missionary of North Liberty Association; in 1861 became pastor of the church at Weston; in 1862 was called to the care of the Tabernacle Baptist church at Leavenworth, Kansas; in 1864 became pastor of the First Baptist church, St. Joseph, Mo.; failing health compelled him to resign after a fifteen months' pastorate, and for a year he had no charge; in 1866 he was financial agent of the Sunday-school Board of the Southern Baptist Convention for North Missouri; was general missionary and agent for the General Association for a part of 1866 and 1867; was recalled to Weston in 1867, where through his efforts a beautiful and substantial church edifice was erected and dedicated free of debt; in 1869 was called to Hannibal, where an elegant house of worship was built and paid for during his pastorate, and large accessions made to the church; in 1873 he took charge of the church at Jefferson City, where he still labors; he has removed a heavy debt from the church, and he is building up a strong and vigorous body of believers; in 1872 he received the degree of A.M. from William Jewell College, and for a number of years has been an active member of the Executive Board of the General Association, and also of the State Sunday-school Convention. He is a laborious and successful worker in the Master's vineyard.

Barrett, Rev. W. C., was born in Wood Co., W. Va., July 8, 1810; united with Mount Zion Baptist church 1835; ordained Aug. 16, 1845; called to Mount Zion, Mount Vernon, and Stillwell churches; was missionary of the General Association of Virginia seven years; organized and built up many churches in the counties of Wood, Wirt, Jackson, and Pleasant; was moderator of the Parkersburg Association in 1854 and 1855; moved to Missouri in 1856; settled in Clay County; appointed agent and missionary of the General Association in the same year; organized and built up most of the churches in Clinton County; built houses of worship at Crooked River, Haynesville, Plattsburg, and Lawson; was eleven years pastor at Crooked River, seven at Plattsburg, two at Richmond, Ray Co., two at Liberty, Clay Co., three at Cameron and Missouri City, besides several country churches; was seven years moderator of North Liberty Association. Has been one of the most laborious and successful of all the old ministers who have laid the foundations upon which the younger generation are now building.

Barron, Rev. James, an aged and decrepit, but zealous and useful minister of Bowdon, Ga., was born in Washington County, Dec. 25, 1801. He connected himself with the church at Antioch, Upson Co., April 3, 1827, and soon began to preach. He settled in Carroll County in 1842, and was ordained at Carrollton church in 1850. For the next twelve years of his life he labored as a missionary of the Domestic Board of the Southern Baptist Convention, in Western Georgia and Eastern Alabama, and then, for the five succeeding years, he was an associational missionary. Since that time rheumatism has laid its hands heavily upon him, disabling him from all active work, and he has simply preached wherever an opportunity has been afforded. His controlling desire is to win souls to Jesus, and to accomplish this he is instant in season and out of season. His has been a life of faithful service in the face of many disadvantages and discouragements.

Barrow, Rev. David, was an eminent pioneer preacher among the Baptists of Virginia and Kentucky, and a man of great ability, both as a preacher and a writer. He was born in Brunswick Co., Va., Oct. 30, 1753; was baptized in his seventeenth year, and in his eighteenth began to preach the gospel. In 1774 he was ordained, and became pastor of Mill Swamp, Black Creek, and South Quay churches, in Virginia. He also traveled and preached in Virginia and North Carolina, in consequence of which he suffered much persecution. In 1778 he was seized at one of his meetings by a gang of twenty men, dragged a half-mile, and forcibly dipped under water twice, with many jeers and mockeries. "A short time afterwards three or four of these men died in a distracted manner, one of them wishing he had been in hell before he joined the mob." Mr. Barrow was a soldier in the war of independence. In 1798 he removed to Montgomery Co., Ky., and took charge of the church at Mount Sterling. Here he became a zealous advocate for the abolition of African slavery. This led to a division of his church, a majority adhering to their pastor. In 1807 an association of emancipators was formed in Kentucky, of which Mr. Barrow became the principal leader. He published a book against slavery, which was regarded as a very able work. He also published a treatise in defense of the Trinity, which was much esteemed. He died Nov. 14, 1819.

Barrows, Rev. Comfort Edwin, son of Comfort and Mela (Blake) Barrows, was born in Attleborough, Mass., Dec. 11, 1831, and was a graduate of Brown University in the class of 1858, and of the Newton Theological Institution in the class of 1861. He was ordained Dec. 25, 1861, as pastor of the Baptist church in South Danvers (now Peabody), Mass., where he remained three years and three months, and then accepted a call to the pastorate of the First Baptist church in Newport, with which he began his ministerial labors March 12, 1865, which position he now (1880) holds. Among his published writings are a memorial sermon commemorating the life and services of the Rev. Erastus Willard, for twenty-one years missionary in France; an historical discourse upon "The Development of Baptist Principles in Rhode Island," preached May 12, 1875, the semi-centennial anniversary of the Rhode Island Baptist State Convention. This discourse was first published by the Convention, and subsequently, with slight additions, it was issued by the American Baptist Publication Society as one of its series of short historical and denominational works. Mr. Barrows published also a discourse delivered on Thanksgiving-day, Nov. 30, 1876, on the history of the First Baptist church in Newport, R. I., and a discourse commemorative of Benjamin B. Howland, for fifty years clerk of the town and city of Newport. He has also contributed articles for reviews and papers. Mr. Barrows is one of the ablest men in the Baptist denomination. His historical works should be read by his brethren everywhere. He is a manly Baptist who courageously asserts the truth, and always presents it in a loving spirit.

Barss, John W., was born in 1812, at Liverpool, Nova Scotia; converted and baptized at Wolfville, July, 1833; commenced business at Halifax, 1836; and returned to Wolfville in 1850. Mr. Barss is a successful ship-owner and a liberal supporter of the denominational enterprises. He contributed $2000 to build the North church, Halifax, and $4000 towards the erection of the Baptist church at Wolfville. He donated 9 acres of land to that town for a public cemetery, and has contributed $11,000 to Acadia College.

Batchelder, Rev. William, was born in Boston, March 25, 1768. Early in life he gave promise of what he afterwards became, a man of rare intellectual ability. He lost both his parents in the thirteenth year of his age. His early religious experience was quite remarkable. After he thought he had passed through "the great change," his mind became tinctured with infidel sentiments. But he was led by the Spirit of God to see his error, and at length he became a Christian, and was baptized at Deerfield, N. H., in June, 1792. Being impressed with his duty to preach the gospel, after due preparation he was ordained as pastor of the Baptist church in Berwick, Me., Nov. 29, 1796. His labors were singularly blessed. In a revival which continued for two years 150 persons were hopefully converted. He baptized in the adjoining town of York 70 persons, also fruits of the same work of grace. In November, 1805, he received an invitation to become the pastor of the First Baptist church in Haverhill, and was publicly recognized December 4. His ministry, connected with which there were most abundant fruits, continued nearly thirteen years. He died April 8, 1818, in the fifty-first year of his age and the twenty-seventh of his ministry.

All the traditions which have come down to us with regard to the character and the ministerial life of Mr. Batchelder show that he was one of the ablest men intellectually, and one of the best preachers of the times in which he lived. He took a warm interest in the cause of education as affecting his own denomination, and was one of the prime movers in the enterprise which led to the founding of the Maine Literary and Theological Seminary, afterwards Waterville College, now Colby University. Brown University, in 1809, conferred on him the honorary degree of Master of Arts.

Bateman, Rev. Calvin A., was born at Groveland, N. Y., April 18, 1833; is of Scotch descent;

REV. CALVIN A. BATEMAN.

grandson of Deacon Zadoc Bateman, a soldier of distinction in the war for American independence; son of Rev. Calvin Bateman, an eminent Baptist minister, who, while preaching in New York, had his skull fractured by a stone hurled by a drunken man through the church window, resulting in insanity until his death. His mother, daughter of Rev. Benjamin Barber, was a lovely Christian, and prominent in her zeal for foreign missions; her eldest son was dedicated to the work in Burmah, but died just as he was nearly ready for his mission. His death and the father's insanity left the family largely dependent upon young Calvin, then only ten years old. At the age of fifteen he was converted and baptized by Rev. Edgar Smith at Milan. Soon after the family moved to Mount Vernon, Mich., where young Bateman was urged by his brethren to preach. He rebelled, feeling unfit for the work, until 1859, when he yielded to his convictions, began to preach, was licensed in 1860 by the Iowa Point church, and in 1863 was ordained at Atchison, Kansas. His life has been given largely to pioneer mission work in Missouri, Kansas, Nebraska, Dakota, Colorado, Cherokee Nation, Nevada, and California. He has aided in organizing over 60 new churches, conducted hundreds of revivals, baptized over 1900 converts, and witnessed the baptism of other hundreds converted under his labors. For three years he was U. S. superintendent of the Indians of Nevada. In 1875 he settled permanently in California as general State missionary. In this field he has traveled 25,000 miles, preached more than 1300 sermons, and baptized nearly 400 converts. His son, Rev. Cephus Bateman, entered the ministry in 1878, and is a successful pastor at Santa Cruz, Cal.

Bates, Rev. John, was born in Bugbrook, Northamptonshire, England, Jan. 26, 1805. He was baptized Dec. 25, 1829, and became a member of the Eagle Street church, where Rev. Joseph Irving labored. Encouraged by his pastor and brethren, he turned his thoughts towards the Christian ministry, intending to go out as a missionary among the colored people of the West Indies. This purpose was not put into execution. He decided to enter the service of the Baptist Irish Society, in order to work among the Roman Catholics of Ireland, and accepted an appointment from that body in January, 1833. While in Ireland he labored at Ballina and Sligo, and in other localities, and again took up his abode in Ballina, where he continued for nine years, during which time he baptized 60 persons, the fruits of missionary toil. The next five years were devoted to similar work in other places in Ireland, making the whole period of his service in the employ of the Baptist Irish Society seventeen years.

Mr. Bates came to America in the spring of 1850, and established himself in Cascade, Iowa, becoming the pastor of the Baptist church. In the State of Iowa he came to be recognized as a power, and his counsels in the Association and Convention were carefully weighed. He went to Canada in 1864, and became pastor of the church in Dundas. In April, 1867, he took charge of the church in Woodstock, and identified himself with the interests of the Canadian Literary Institute. While living here he consecrated two of his daughters, Mrs. A. V. Timpany and Mrs. John McLaurin, to the foreign mission work.

The labors of Mr. Bates were so onerous that he felt obliged to resign his pastorate at the end of June, 1873. He has received into the fellowship of the church during his six years' ministry in Woodstock by baptism and letter 211 persons. For nearly a year he remained without a regular pastoral charge. He died May 8, 1875.

A memoir of Mr. Bates, with selections from his sermons, essays, and addresses, compiled by Rev. Dr. J. A. Smith, of Chicago, a large volume of nearly 500 pages, was published in Toronto in 1877. Mr. Bates was a man of great power and of ardent piety.

Bates, Samuel P., LL.D., was born in Mendon, Mass., and educated at Brown University, graduating in 1851. He was baptized into the fellowship of the First church, in Providence, R. I., by the Rev. James M. Granger in 1849. In 1852 he transferred his membership to the Meadville Baptist church, where it still remains. Although never licensed, he has occasionally delivered discourses from the pulpit as a supply, and this labor of love has been well received by his brethren.

As an author he has acquired not only a local, but even a national reputation of a high order. Various works have been issued, and they have received the popular favor. Several editions of his "Lectures on Mental and Moral Culture" have been published by Messrs. A. S. Barnes & Co., of New York. This work forms one of the volumes of their Teachers' Library. The same house published, in 1861, a small volume entitled "Methods of Conducting Teachers' Institutes," and this also met with equal success. "The History of the Battle of Gettysburg" has received the hearty indorsement of the English press, as also of prominent Union and Confederate generals, and French and English military critics. In 1866, Governor Curtin, of Pennsylvania, appointed him State historian, in which service he was engaged seven years, producing five large volumes, thus preserving the annals of the military organizations which were gathered from the State in its conflict with the Rebellion. This monument cost the State nearly half a million of dollars, and was worthily expended. "The Lives of the Governors of Pennsylvania" is another work on which he was employed after the completion of the State History. The "Martial Deeds of Pennsylvania" is still another large octavo volume, illustrated with numerous portraits of officers and others who were brought to the front during the war.

In 1857, Mr. Bates was elected superintendent of public schools in Crawford Co., Pa. At the expiration of his first term of three years he was again honored by re-election, but resigned to accept the still wider work of deputy State superintendent, and this position he held for six years.

In 1862 he was employed by the State as agent to visit and report upon the condition of the colleges of Pennsylvania. These reports were published from time to time in the *Journals*. Other duties have crowded out the desire to issue them in book-form.

In 1865 the degree of LL.D. was conferred upon him.

In 1877 he made a tour through Scotland, England, France, Italy, Switzerland, and the cities of the Rhine. This visit laid the foundations for four lectures, which have been favorably received wherever delivered.

Bath, Rev. Levi, was born in Unadilla, N. Y.; died at Columbus, Wis., March 4, 1876, aged fifty-seven years. He was educated at Poultney, Vt., and at Union College, New York. He held pastorates in Grass Lake, Danville, and other places in Michigan. In 1861 he came to Columbus, Wis., and became pastor of the Baptist church there. Owing to ill heath he was obliged to retire from the active work of the ministry. During the latter part of his life he filled a number of town and county offices, and was highly esteemed by a large circle of personal friends.

Battle, Rev. Archibald J., D.D., president of Mercer University, Macon, Ga., was born at Powelton, Hancock Co., Ga., Sept. 10, 1826. When ten years of age he moved to Alabama with his father, Dr. Cullen Battle, where he was baptized in 1839, and where he graduated at the University of Alabama in 1846, under the administration of Dr. Basil Manly, Sr. In 1847 he was appointed tutor of Ancient Languages in the University of Alabama. He entered on a professorship in East Alabama Female College in the year 1852, and the following year he was ordained to the ministry by the Tuskegee Baptist church, continuing still to occupy his chair in the Female College. In 1855 he assumed the pastorate of the Tuscaloosa Baptist church; subsequently he became Professor of Greek in the University of Alabama, president of the Alabama Central Female College, and president of the Judson Female Institute at Marion, Ala., which position he retained until 1872, when he accepted the presidency of Mercer University, at Macon, Ga.

Dr. Battle grew up amid the best social and religious influences, and he comes from one of the first families of Georgia. He is a highly cultivated Christian gentleman, of refined manners, and superior social qualities, and with a character that commands universal esteem. His pastorates have been signally blessed by revivals, which brought large and valuable accessions to the church. One of the results of a revival in the Tuscaloosa church, when he was its pastor, was the establishment of the Alabama Central Female College, an institution of learning which reflects the highest honor upon its founders, the first conception of which is due to Dr. Battle. He is a cultivated and polished preacher, and a favorite with all denominations, owing to his excellent spirit and sound evangelical views. While his sermons, which are usually written, are models of composition, they are elevated in thought, earnest in spirit, and chaste in expression. Had his life been devoted to the pastorate, he would have attained a success rarely granted to ministers; for while his preaching is pointed, clear, evangelical in doctrine, and practical in teaching, his pervasive piety, affectionate and sympathetic nature and refined delicacy, indicate the existence in him of the highest and best attributes of a pastor. He is a scholar worthy to stand at the head of a noble institution of learning; and he possesses administrative ability which fits him admirably for the position. To great courtesy of manner he unites firmness of purpose, excellence of judgment, and aptness for teaching and governing young men. In person he is six feet high. In 1869, during the interim between the call of Dr. Warren and the retirement of Dr. Skinner, he was invited to the pastorate of the Macon church, and filled the position most acceptably and successfully. The degree of Doctor of Divinity was conferred on him by three institutions,—by Howard College, Ala., and Columbian College, Washington City, in 1872, and by the University of Georgia in 1873. He is the author of a work on the human will, which has elicited distinguished commendation, as manifest-

REV. ARCHIBALD J. BATTLE, D.D.

ing, in a high degree, the attributes of an acute metaphysician; while, as a belles-lettres scholar, he has long been recognized as ranking among the foremost.

Battle, Cullen, M.D.—Dr. Battle was born in North Carolina in 1785, where he spent his early manhood in the successful practice of his profession. In 1818 he removed to Powelton, Ga., where he retired from the practice of medicine to attend to his increasing planting interests. The cause of education, and every public interest, found in him an ardent advocate and a liberal benefactor. He was baptized in 1827 by Dr. Jesse Mercer, between whom and Dr. Battle there subsisted a warm and lifelong friendship. In 1836 he removed to Eufaula, Ala. Here he was prominent in civilizing and Christianizing the new country, and in every public work, and fostered the Baptist Church with a wise and tender care. In Tuskegee, where he resided several years, he rendered signal service to the church, to education, and to every good cause. Always a man of active mind, positive character, unfaltering energy, sound piety, and broad intelligence, he exercised great influence among his brethren and in society generally. The hospitality of his home was famous. Of great wealth and liberality, his contributions to secular and religious enterprises were many and munificent. Mercer University, of which his son, Dr. A. J. Battle, is now president, received from him the largest sum for its endowment ever bestowed on it by any man, save from its founder, Dr. Mercer. He also was a large contributor to Howard College and the East Alabama Female College. He always exhibited an active zeal for the welfare of the negro race. Dr. Battle was the father of A. J. Battle, D.D., Gen. C. A. Battle, of the Confederate army, and of Mrs. M. J. Shorter, wife of Gov. Shorter; and was himself descended from a highly honorable Christian ancestry. He died in Eufaula, Ala., in 1878.

Battle, Elisha.—The ancestor of the large and influential family of Battles in North Carolina, Tennessee, Alabama, and Georgia, was born in Nansemond Co., Va., Jan. 9, 1723. In 1748 he removed to Tar River, Edgecombe Co., N. C.; joined the Baptist church, known as Falls of Tar River, in 1764, of which he was a deacon for twenty-eight years. He was often moderator of the Kehukee Association; was a member of the General Assembly for twenty years; a member of the convention which formed the State constitution; and was chairman of the convention when the Federal Constitution and Bill of Rights were considered in a committee of the whole. He died in 1799, and Revs. Gilbert and Burkitt attended his funeral services, both preaching.

Battle, Rev. Henry W., the gifted young pastor at Columbus, Miss., belongs to a distinguished family in the South, being a son of Maj.-Gen. Cullen A. Battle, and a nephew of A. J. Battle, D.D., president of Mercer University. He was born in Tuskegee, Ala., in 1855, and admitted to the practice of law at the age of nineteen; but abandoning the most flattering worldly prospects, he entered the Southern Baptist Theological Seminary at Louisville, Ky., where he remained some time, and then accepted the pastorate of the First Baptist church at Columbus, Miss., where the success of his labors gives promise of great future usefulness.

Battle, Reuben T., was born Sept. 10, 1784, and died Dec. 6, 1849, in the sixty-fifth year of his age. For thirty years he was a deacon, and a prominent, useful, and benevolent man; his whole character illustrated the truths of Christianity, the beauty of true piety, and the loveliness of charity. His large wealth enabled him, by his benefactions, to aid greatly the cause of religion and to promote that of education. He was a most useful and enlightened citizen, a kind and self-sacrificing father and husband, and a staunch supporter of the interests of his denomination.

His ancestors were Baptists, who fled from England before our Revolution to avoid persecution, and his father, as well as the men of his mother's family, took an active part in the Revolutionary war. His father and mother were Jesse Battle and Susanna Fawcette, who resided in North Carolina when Reuben T. Battle was born. Two years after that event they moved to Georgia and settled in Hancock County, where Reuben grew up, inheriting the homestead. In January, 1805, he married Bethiah Alexander, by whom he had three daughters, afterwards Mrs. Judge E. A. Nisbet, Mrs. C. M. Irwin, and Mrs. W. J. Harley.

He was converted at an early age; was baptized by Jesse Mercer, and united with the Powelton church, of which he remained an active and influential member until his death, co-operating heartily with Dr. Jesse Mercer, John Veazy, Gov. Rahm, Judge Thomas Stock, and Thomas Cooper, all men of great piety and religious zeal. To Reuben T. Battle was Powelton mostly indebted for its excellent schools, both male and female, which rendered the village famous as a seat of learning. His piety was of a high order, and both the church and the community felt its influence. His hospitality was unbounded, and his large means enabled him to exercise it to the fullest extent. To the orphan and widow, to the sick and sorrowing, he was most attentive, and his relations to his numerous servants were paternal, about whose temporal and spiritual interests he was always solicitous. He filled the office of deacon well, having labored in it for thirty years, in conjunction with John Veazy, at whose funeral he was taken ill, and he survived six days only. Co-laborers in the Lord's vineyard, they often together visited the sick and the afflicted, often mingled their prayers and tears, and often took sweet counsel together about the honor of God and the good of man. Useful in life, mourned at death, their memory is yet fragrant in the church they served faithfully for so long a period.

Baumes, John R., D.D., was born at Carlisle, N. Y., Dec. 28, 1833; graduated with honor from Madison University in 1857, and shortly after began legal studies in New York City. Being convinced, however, of his duty to preach, he gave up the law, and in the spring of 1858 returned to Hamilton to take a theological course. Immediately after completing his theological studies, in 1859, accepted the call of the Baptist church at Westfield, Mass., where he was ordained and remained ten years. In 1861, after a short period spent in the chaplaincy of a New York regiment, became pastor of the First church, New London, Conn., where he remained until 1863, when the health of his wife having become impaired, he removed to Springfield, O., and assumed the charge of the First church of that city. Here, in a few weeks, Mrs. Baumes died. A second church being formed in Springfield, Dr. Baumes became its pastor, and labored with great success until 1872.

In 1872, Dr. Baumes became editor and proprietor of the *Journal and Messenger*, of Cincinnati, O., then in a declining state and embarrassed with debt. In a few years he succeeded in extinguishing this debt and in greatly extending the field and influence of the paper. In 1876 he sold his interest to Dr. G. W. Lasher, and, after a year or two of rest, began the publication of the *Baptist Review*, a quarterly which has already secured a paying list of subscribers. Dr. Baumes resides near Cincinnati, O.

"Baxter Baptized in Blood."—About 1673 Baptists in England had everything to bear that could pain the heart and make life wretched. In that year, according to Ivimey, whose veracity and information are worthy of all credit, a pamphlet was issued bearing the heading at the top of this article, and of which he gives the following sketch:

"This work, which we have perused, gives an account of a barbarous murder committed by four Anabaptists at Boston, New England, upon the body of a godly minister named Josiah Baxter, for no other reason than that he had worsted them in disputation, which was set forth with all the circumstances and formalities of names, speeches, actions, times, and place, to make it look the more authentic; orderly and most pathetically describing the most execrable murder that ever was known, viz., of first stripping and cruelly whipping, then disemboweling and flaying alive a sound and godly minister in his own house, in the midst of the howlings, groans, and shriekings of his dear relations lying bound before him. And the better to create belief, this sad story is pretended to be published by the mournful brother of the said murdered minister, named Benjamin Baxter, living in Fenchurch Street, London. This infamous libel concludes in the following manner: 'I have penned and published this narrative *in perpetuam rei memoriam*, that the world may see the spirit of these men, and that it may stand as an eternal memorial of *their cruelty and hatred to all orthodox ministers*.' Multitudes were thirsting for the blood of our Baptist brethren at this time, and this pamphlet, written by some classical scholar, was the very thing to enrage the whole nation against them; and it had that for its object. After the murder should have taken place some twenty days, a vessel sailed from Boston for London; and the master of this ship and three other persons took an affidavit before the Lord Mayor that they never heard of Mr. Josiah Baxter, that there was no such murder reported in America, and that they believed the story to be a very great falsehood. It was a murderous fabrication. But so dangerous a forgery was it that Mr. Kiffin, a man of great wisdom, and of much influence with Lord Clarendon, felt compelled to bring it before the King's Council; and so fitted to shed innocent blood by mob violence was it regarded that the Council, though without any love for Baptists, issued an order through the *Gazette*, which, after describing the story, declared 'the whole matter to be altogether false and fictitious.'"

Bayliss, Rev. William H., was born near Augusta, Ga., in 1806; educated at the University of Georgia, Athens; practiced law many years in Georgia and Mississippi; was converted at Hernando, Miss., and immediately commenced preaching; was pastor of First Baptist church, Nashville, Tenn., the churches at Marshall and Waco, Texas, the church at Shreveport, La., and Coliseum Place church, New Orleans; in all served twelve churches. He was president of the Bible Board, Southern Baptist Convention at Nashville, and also of Louisiana Baptist Convention. He was a man of noble presence, and possessed oratorical gifts of the highest order. His labors in Mississippi, Tennessee, Louisiana, and Texas were productive of great good in bringing souls to Christ.

Baylor Female College, Independence, Washington Co., Texas. Until 1866 this institution constituted "The Female Department of Baylor University." It is located about three-fourths of a mile from it. It has educated a large number of the most prominent women of Texas, and sustains the reputation of a first-class female college. Its buildings, apparatus, and library are superior. For nineteen years Horace Clark, LL.D., was its president. His successors have been B. S. Fitzgerald, A.M., Rev. Henry L. Graves, A.M., Col. W. W. Fontaine, A.M., and Rev. William Royall, D.D. In 1878, Rev. J. H. Luther, D.D., was elected president. It sustains a relation to the Texas Baptist State Convention similar to that of Baylor University. It had 90 pupils for the year 1877-78.

Baylor, Hon. R. E. B., was born in Bourbon Co., Ky., May 10, 1791; studied law in Kentucky;

HON. R. E. B. BAYLOR.

was deeply impressed by the preaching of Jeremiah Vardeman, whom he considered a pulpit orator of the first grade. He removed to Alabama, and practiced law at Cahaba and Tuscaloosa. Was a member of the U. S. Congress from the Tuscaloosa district for two terms. He was converted in Talladega County in 1839, and was licensed to preach. Shortly afterwards he removed to Texas. Participated in the struggles against Mexicans and Indians in 1842-44. Served in the Texan Congress, and for twenty-five years was a judge of the Circuit Court, embracing Washington, Fayette, and other leading counties of the State. For a short time he was on the Supreme Court bench. Wherever he held courts he there also preached, often deciding cases on the bench during the day and holding a protracted meeting at night. He was a man of commanding presence, fine oratorical powers, genial disposition, and attractive manners. His religious character aided him no little in his judicial career, at a time and among a people accustomed to violence, lawlessness, and misrule. He thoroughly identified himself with the people of God wherever he went. He served as moderator of the Union Association, president of the State Convention, and president of the board of trustees of Baylor University at different times. Baylor University was named after him. He and William M. Tryon drew up and procured the enactment of its charter, and he gave to the institution its first $1000 at a time when money was exceedingly scarce in the young republic. The last ten years of his life were spent chiefly in attending religious meetings. He died Dec. 30, 1873, and his remains are buried a short distance in the rear of the first edifice erected for the institution named after him. His memory is precious among all classes of people in the State of Texas.

Baylor University, Independence, Washington Co., Texas, was chartered by the republic of Texas in 1845. Its location is unsurpassed in Texas for society, salubrity, and scenery. It has educated in whole or in part over 3000 persons. Many of the most prominent ministers of the gospel, lawyers, physicians, merchants, and planters in Texas were trained in this institution. It had in 1878 a corps of 6 instructors, 2 professorships, endowed in part, 94 students, and a valuable library. The society and officers' libraries contain about 3000 volumes. The value of its grounds, buildings, etc., is estimated at $35,000. The amount proposed to be raised for endowment is $200,000, and for other buildings $25,000. Its presidents have been Rev. Henry L. Graves, A.M., Rev. R. C. Burleson, D.D., Rev. George W. Baines, A.M. The present incumbent, Rev. William Carey Crane, D.D., LL.D., has been president since July, 1863. The standard of education is equal to that of the principal American institutions, and a special course is promised for young men studying for the gospel ministry. Annual tuition is from $30 to $60. The average age of students is higher than any other Texas college, being near nineteen years. The Texas Baptist State Convention appoints five of its trustees annually, and receives its yearly report.

Baynham, Rev. William A., M.D., was born in Essex Co., Va., Oct. 19, 1813. His father was Dr. William Baynham, F.R.S.L., also a native of Virginia. Young Baynham received a thorough early training in several of the best schools in the neighborhood, and in 1828 entered the University of Virginia, although under the age required by the regulations of that institution, continuing three years in the literary schools, and the remainder of the time, up to 1834, attending lectures in the medical schools, and taking his degree in medicine in that year. In the fall of 1834 he went to Philadelphia, and attended medical lectures there until 1836. In 1834 he professed a hope in Christ, and in 1835 became a member of the Episcopal Church; but on a change of views respecting baptism and

BAYLOR UNIVERSITY, INDEPENDENCE, TEXAS.

other doctrines, was baptized by the Rev. A. D. Gillette, D.D., into the fellowship of the Sansom Street Baptist church, Philadelphia, in February, 1836. In the same year he returned to Virginia, and united with the Enon Baptist church, Essex County. He practiced medicine for one year only; was then ordained to the ministry, and in 1842 was invited to the pastorate of the Enon church, which he accepted, and which he has faithfully served to the present time. In 1854, Dr. Baynham also took charge of the Upper Zion church, Carolina County, where he still preaches, and in addition to which he has supplied two other fields of labor. He occasionally contributes to the *Religious Herald;* has been for some years a trustee of Richmond College, and at different times connected with one or more of the denominational boards.

Beall, Hon. R. L. T., was born in Westmoreland Co., Va., May 22, 1819, and after pursuing his studies in the neighboring schools, entered Dickinson College, Pa., where he remained about a year and a half. He then pursued the study of law at home for about eighteen months; entered the law school of the University of Virginia, where he graduated in 1838, and began the practice of his profession in 1839. Although averse to politics, being the only Democratic lawyer in the two counties when he practiced law, he was obliged to answer all Whig orators who chanced to speak in that district. He was elected a member of Congress in 1847, but declined a re-election. In 1850 he was elected a delegate to the convention to reform the State constitution of Virginia; and in 1859 was elected to the Senate of the same State, in which he served two sessions and then resigned. In 1861, on the breaking out of the war, Mr. Beall joined, as a private, a cavalry company, and was soon elected first lieutenant. He received in 1861 commissions of captain and then major from the State; in 1862 commissions of lieutenant-colonel and colonel from the Confederate States; and in 1865 that of brigadier-general. He was a most efficient officer and was wounded several times. At the close of the war he returned to his practice, and in 1878 was nominated for Congress. Mr. Beall was baptized by his eldest son, the Rev. Geo. W. Beall, into the fellowship of the Machedoc church, Va., in 1873. He is deeply interested in all denominational movements, and takes an active part in the proceedings of district and State Associations. He holds the position of vice-president of the General Association of Virginia, and also of the Historical Society. Mr. Beall was a contributor to that excellent magazine, the *Southern Literary Messenger*, and has written occasionally for the press, both secular and religious. He was united in marriage to Miss Lucy M. Brown, of Westmoreland Co., Va., May 28, 1840.

Beaver Dam.—The seat of Wayland Academy, on the Milwaukee and St. Paul Railroad, 61 miles northwest of Milwaukee, the commercial centre of one of the richest portions of Wisconsin. To the Baptists of Wisconsin the place is associated with the early struggles of the denomination in founding and establishing its institution of learning,—Wayland Academy.

Beck, Rev. Andrew J., a trustee of Mercer University, was born in Hancock Co., Ga., in 1850. A regular graduate of Mercer University; soon after graduation he edited an agricultural paper in Atlanta for some time, but feeling himself called to preach, he was ordained to the ministry. He was prevailed upon, however, to accept the position of principal of the Perry High School, which he held for several years, but declining health compelled him to abandon the school-room and engage in the more active labors of a secular life until sufficiently restored to perform pastoral labor. After serving the Marietta church for some years, he became connected with the editorial corps of the *Christian Index;* afterwards moving to Milledgeville, the old capital of the State, he took charge of the Baptist church,—a responsible position, the duties of which he still discharges. Mr. Beck is a fine thinker, a good preacher and pastor, and one of the rising ministers of Georgia.

Beck, Hon. Joseph Marcus, one of the judges of the Supreme Court of Iowa, was born in Clermont Co., O., near the village of Bethel, April 21, 1823. His family removed to Jefferson Co., Ind., in October, 1834. He was educated at Hanover College, Ind., read law in Madison, in the office of Judge Miles C. Eggleston, and was admitted to the bar in 1846. May 1, 1847, he became a resident of Iowa, and soon after settled in Montrose. In 1850 he removed to Fort Madison, of which he is still a citizen. He was actively engaged in the practice of the law until 1867, when he was elected judge of the Supreme Court of the State, and has been continued in the position by two subsequent elections. He was chosen to the bench of the Supreme Court from the bar, having previously held no judicial or other public offices, except those of mayor of Fort Madison and prosecuting attorney of Lee County. The parents and grandparents of Judge Beck were Baptists. His mother's father, Isaac Morris, was born in Wales, and was a Baptist minister of prominence in Harrison Co., Va. he was the father of Thomas Morris, a U. S. Senator of Ohio. Judge Beck was baptized in 1842, becoming a member of the church in Madison, Ind., and he was the superintendent of its Sunday-school while he was a law student. He was one of the constituent members of the Fort Madison church. He has been, for more than eleven years, the superintendent of the Sunday-school connected with the Iowa State Penitentiary at Fort Madison, and for twenty years he has been president of the board of trustees of the Burlington Collegiate Institute.

Beck, Rev. Levi G., was born in Philadelphia, Aug. 20, 1810; baptized into the fellowship of the Fourth Baptist church of that city in September, 1830; licensed to preach Aug. 5, 1833; ordained in January, 1835; labored two years as a missionary in Montgomery Co., Pa., during which the Mount Pleasant Baptist church was organized and their meeting-house erected. In 1836 he became pastor of the church at Milestown, Pa. In 1839 he took charge of the church at Upper Freehold, Monmouth Co., N. J. In February, 1844, he settled as pastor of the First Baptist church in Trenton, N. J., and in 1849 he took charge of the church in Flemington, N. J. In 1851 he removed to Philadelphia and took the oversight of the North Baptist church, and superintended the erection of their church edifice. He removed to New Britain, Bucks Co., Pa., and succeeded in remodeling and enlarging their house of worship. In 1859 he was called to the church in Pemberton, N. J., and he had the pleasure of seeing their present commodious house of worship erected and paid for. In 1864 he removed to Chester, Pa., the First church then numbering but 28 members; and in about two years a handsome house of worship, 46 by 80 feet, was erected, paid for, and occupied by a good congregation. In 1866 he became secretary of the Pennsylvania Baptist General Association, and held the office for fourteen years, to the great advantage of the cause of Christ in Pennsylvania. Mr. Beck succeeded in every place where he labored, and he is one of the purest and most devoted men known to the writer.

Beck, Rev. Thomas J., Sr., was born in Buncombe Co., N. C., Dec. 2, 1805, of pious parents. On reaching his majority he moved to Wilkes Co., Ga., where he was converted and baptized in 1833, joining the Rehoboth church. He was ordained at New Providence church, in Warren County, in 1835, and, during a ministerial career of twenty-seven years, preached to various churches in Warren, McDuffie, Columbia, Taliaferro, Greene, and Wilkes Counties. At his death he had charge of four churches. He died in Warren Co., Ga., Sept. 2, 1862, at the age of fifty-six.

The chief features of his character were firmness, boldness, humility, modesty, sincerity, and kindness. Utterly free from envy, he praised the worthy deeds and superior talents of others. He was honest in the scriptural sense of the term, and there was nothing mean or selfish in his nature. He was very successful in winning souls to Jesus and in building up and strengthening the churches he served, and, according to his talents and education, few have done more for the denomination in Georgia than he. He was a true Baptist, and in hearty sympathy with the great principles and doctrines which are peculiar to our denomination. He was a diligent student of the Bible and a very effective speaker, delivering what he had to say in an earnest, hearty, straightforward manner. As a pastor he had few superiors. Not many ministers were more successful than he in building up churches and in establishing and utilizing their membership. He always left his churches in a better condition than they were when he took charge of them. He was greatly beloved and esteemed as a pastor, as a Christian, as a neighbor, and as a man, and in every relation which he sustained his life was a blessing. In his family his Christian life shone most brightly, and his walk with God appeared most intimate. He looked carefully after the salvation of his children, and before his death had the pleasure of baptizing all but one, who, then only ten years old, was afterwards baptized at fourteen. In his life we have a striking exemplification of the truth that in obedience to and in close communion with God lie the true secret of success and usefulness in the service of Christ. Mr. Beck always appeared before his people as if he had just come out from the presence of God, and his hearers received his messages gladly, and many of them were converted.

Beckwith, Mayhew, was a governor of Acadia College, a member of the Nova Scotia House of Assembly, the treasurer of the Baptist Home Missionary Board, and a warm friend of the Baptist denomination. He died at Cornwallis in 1871, aged seventy-two years.

Beddome, Rev. Benjamin, was born at Henley, England, Jan. 23, 1717. He was baptized in London in 1739. He was educated at Bristol College and at the Independent College, Milend, London. He was ordained to the Baptist ministry at Bourton-on-the-Water, Sept. 23, 1743. He continued pastor of this church till Sept. 3, 1797, when he rested from his labors and entered the church in glory.

Mr. Beddome was accustomed to prepare a hymn to be sung every Lord's day after his morning sermon. These compositions were collected when he died and published in a volume, and since that time they have been placed in most selections of hymns in the English language. For the last eight years of his life he gave away in charitable contributions the entire money he received as salary for his services.

"In his preaching he laid Christ at the foundation of religion as the support of it; he placed him at the top of it as its glory; and he made him the centre of it, to unite all its parts, and to add beauty and vigor to the whole." "His inventive faculty was extraordinary, and threw an endless variety into his public services. Nature, providence, and grace had formed him for eminence in the church of Christ." He was loved and honored by the whole Baptist denomination in England and America in his day. Rhode Island College, now known as Brown University, gave him the honorary degree of A.M. Three volumes of his sermons were published after his death.

Beebee, Alexander M., D.D., son of Alexander M. Beebee, LL.D., of the New York *Baptist Register*, was born in Utica, Feb. 6, 1820; graduated at Madison University in 1847, and Hamilton Theological Seminary in 1849; pastor in Jordan, N. Y., 1849-50; 1850, Professor of Logic and English Literature in Madison University; Lecturer on Sacred Rhetoric, 1857-61; at present Professor of Homiletics in Hamilton Theological Seminary, and Professor of Logic in Madison University.

Beebee, Alexander M., LL.D., was born in Newark, N.J., Sept. 29, 1783. He graduated with

ALEXANDER M. BEEBEE, LL.D.

honor at Columbia College, N. Y., in the class of 1802. After leaving college Mr. Beebee studied law with Ogden Hoffman, Sr., having Washington Irving and James K. Paulding as fellow-students. With Mr. Irving he formed a friendship which only death ended. He practiced law in New York till 1807, when he transferred his business to Skaneateles. There he followed his profession for fifteen years, and became a leading member of the bar of Onondaga County.

While living in Skaneateles he lost his first child, and his distressed heart found no rest till Jesus inspired in it the hope of heaven. He joined a Baptist church seven miles from his residence, the nearest one to his house. Now the legal profession had lost its attractions. In 1824 there was no Baptist newspaper in the State of New York, and only three or four in the United States. In 1825, Mr. Beebee accepted the editorship of a very small sheet called the *Baptist Register*, and soon the paper increased in size and in subscribers, and it became a great blessing to the rapidly-growing Baptist denomination in Central New York. Mr. Beebee conducted the *Register* until a short period before his death, in November, 1856. "Mr. Beebee was one of the noblest and gentlest of men, a burning and a shining light in our Zion. He belonged by birth and social position to the aristocracy of intellect and wealth in the metropolis. He was a man of broad intellect, generous culture," childlike faith, and boundless charity, and of such loyalty to Christ that he would sacrifice nothing which he taught for the gift of a globe or the smiles of all humanity. In 1852 Madison University conferred the degree of LL.D. upon Mr. Beebee.

Beech, Rev. Henry Hudson.—The subject of this sketch is the pastor of the Baptist church in Sheboygan Falls, Wis. He is a native of Eaton, Madison Co., N. Y., where he was born in 1843. He spent his childhood and youth in Eaton and Hamilton, N. Y., and when older, on a farm, in Augusta, Oneida Co., N. Y. Having decided the question of his call to the work of the ministry, he began a course of study when yet under twenty years of age with that end in view. He was graduated from Shurtleff College, Ill., in the class of 1866, and from Newton Theological Seminary, Newton Centre, Mass., in the class of 1869. In January, 1870, he was ordained by the Market Street Baptist church in Zanesville, O., where he began the active work of his ministry as the stated supply of that church. His first pastorate was with the Sycamore Street Baptist church (now Grand Avenue), Milwaukee. Leaving Milwaukee, he had two pastorates in Minnesota,—at Owatonna and Lake City. Returning in 1877 to Wisconsin, he settled as the pastor of the Baptist church in Sheboygan Falls, his present field of labor. During the war he enlisted as a private in the 133d Regiment, Illinois Volunteers, in which he served 100 days.

Mr. Beech is an earnest and faithful minister of the gospel and a good pastor. His preaching is pointed, vigorous, and searching. He abounds in evangelical fervor and earnestness. He has a clear conception of the distinctive doctrines of the church of which he is a minister. He has a hearty style of writing and speaking that arrests attention and wins favor. He is the popular and valuable secretary of the Wisconsin Baptist State Convention, in whose work he takes a deep interest.

Belcher, Joseph, D.D., was born in Birmingham, England, April 5, 1794. In 1814 he put his trust in Jesus as his Saviour, and in 1819 he was ordained as pastor of the church at Somersham. He was pastor of several churches in England, and he founded one. In 1844 he crossed the Atlantic and visited the United States. He became pastor that year of a Baptist church in Halifax, Nova Scotia; three years later he took charge of the Mount Tabor church, Philadelphia.

He edited the complete works of Andrew Fuller, and was the author of the following: "The Religious Denominations of the United States," Lives of Carey, Whitefield, the Haldanes, and Robert Raikes, and also of "The Tri-Jubilee Sermon of the Philadelphia Association."

"His store of facts, anecdotes, and illustrations was inexhaustible, he abounded in useful suggestions, his conversation was full of instruction and wisdom."

His death was eminently peaceful. When a dear one inquired, "Is Jesus precious to you now?" he replied with energy, "Yes, ten thousand times more precious than ever."

Belden, Rev. Clarendon Dwight, A.M., son of Deacon Stanton and Antoinette P. (Manchester) Belden, was born in North Providence, R. I., May 3, 1848; graduated at Brown University in 1869; studied theology at Crozer Theological Seminary; was ordained to the Baptist ministry in Philadelphia; now settled as pastor in Austin, Minn., where he has been greatly prospered.

Belden, Deacon Stanton, A.M., son of Martin and Prudence (Shales) Belden, was born in Sandisfield, Mass., Jan. 15, 1808; united with the Baptist church in Colebrook, Conn., under Rev. Rufus Babcock, in 1822; graduated at Yale College in 1833; founded the Fruit Hill Classical Institute, in North Providence, R. I., in 1835, and, with the exception of four years, remained the honored and successful principal till 1861, receiving students from all parts of the world except Asia; was ordained deacon of the Fruit Hill Baptist church.

Bell, A. K., D.D., was born Dec. 9, 1815, in Blair Co., Pa. He was renewed by divine grace when he was seventeen years of age, and baptized into the fellowship of the Logan's Valley Baptist church. He graduated at Washington College, Pa., in 1842. He was ordained the same year in Pittsburgh. His first pastorate was in Hollidaysburg, and the second in Logan's Valley. In 1854 he accepted the office of treasurer and general agent of the university at Lewisburg. In 1859 he became pastor of the Sandusky Street church, Alleghany City, one of the strongest churches in the State. In 1865 he received the title of Doctor of Divinity from Lewisburg. In 1870 failing health compelled him to resign his pastorate. In 1871 he visited Europe, and on his return spent several years in Hollidaysburg, preaching, and part of the time being pastor in Altoona. In 1878 he resumed his old position as treasurer of the Pennsylvania Baptist University.

Dr. Bell belongs to a family full of generous impulses and deeds, and he bears the stamp of his near kindred. He is an able preacher, a devout Christian, a blameless man, and a successful pastor.

Benedict, David, D.D., the Baptist historian, was born in Norwalk, Conn., Oct. 10, 1779. His

DAVID BENEDICT, D.D.

love for historical reading and investigation developed itself in early life. At twenty he made a profession of his faith in Christ. Religion did for him what it has done for so many thousands of others,—quickened his intellectual nature, and made him aspire after something elevating. He entered Brown University, where he graduated in 1806. Soon after he was ordained as pastor of the Baptist church in Pawtucket, R. I., where he remained twenty-five years. During all this time he had been busy in gathering, from every part of the country, the materials out of which to form a comprehensive history of the Baptist denomination, and had sent to press several volumes relating to the subject of his investigations. After retiring from his pastorate, he gave himself with great diligence to the work of completing the task he had undertaken. He felt it to be his special vocation to do this work, and he made everything bend to its accomplishment. Among his published writings are the following: "History of the Baptists," 1813;

"Abridgment of Robinson's History of Baptism," 1817; "Abridgment of History of the Baptists," 1820; "History of all Religions," 1824; "History of the Baptists Continued," 1848; "Fifty Years among the Baptists," 1860. He wrote also a history of the Donatists, which was completed just before he was ninety-five years of age, and which, since his death, has been printed. All through his life he was in the habit of writing much for the public press. He took a leading part in the founding of various religious organizations in his denomination, in promoting the cause of education, in the formation of new churches, etc. He carried the habits of hard work, which he had formed in the maturity of his years, down to the close of life. He was remarkably favored with good eyesight, and his vision was unimpaired to the last. At the time of his death he had been the senior member of the board of trustees of Brown University for sixteen years, and had been in the corporation for fifty-six years. Dr. Benedict died at Pawtucket, Dec. 5, 1874, having reached the great age of ninety-five years one month and twenty-five days.

Benedict, Rev. George, a Baptist clergyman, was born in Southeast, Dutchess Co., N. Y., April 15, 1795, and died Oct. 28, 1848. His youthful days were spent with his parents in Danbury, Conn. He united with the Baptist church in that place in the twenty-second year of his age. He was licensed to preach May 12, 1822, and in 1823 was settled and ordained as pastor of the church. He served the church in Danbury eight years, when he accepted the charge of the Stanton Street Baptist church, of New York, a new interest of only about 200 members. After ten years the church had grown so large, that he went out with a colony and founded a church in Norfolk Street. His labors were blessed with great prosperity, but in the height of his power and usefulness, and in the prime of life, he passed away, lamented by all who knew him. He was a natural orator, devoted to his work, social in manner, fervid, zealous, and persuasive. His place was always thronged, and conversions and baptisms were continuous during the seventeen years of his labor in the last-named churches.

Benedict Institute, The, is located at Columbia, S. C. The house is 65 feet wide and the same depth. It is two stories high; it has a wide veranda. It is located in a beautiful park of 80 acres, full of fine trees; it has numerous out-buildings. It is chiefly the generous gift of Deacon Benedict,

THE BENEDICT INSTITUTE, COLUMBIA, S. C.

of Rhode Island, and his noble wife, for the Christian education of colored ministers.

Benedict, Deacon Stephen, son of Thomas and Zelota (Sprague) Benedict, was born in Milton, Saratoga Co., N. Y., Jan. 15, 1801; removed to Pawtucket, R. I., and became a manufacturer of cotton goods; for thirty-seven years a partner with Hon. Joseph Wood; afterwards conducted the business alone; industrious, careful, and successful; united early with the First Baptist church in Pawtucket, under his half-brother, Rev. David Benedict, D.D.; a deacon of the church about twenty-five years; president of two banks; a man of superior judgment, and highly esteemed; died Dec. 25, 1868, nearly sixty-eight years of age; left in his will, among other worthy legacies, $2000 to the American Baptist Home Mission Society, to which his devoted and excellent widow has added, at different times, sums now amounting to about $30,000, with which has been purchased, and largely sustained, the widely-known Benedict Institute in Columbia, S. C., for the education of the freedmen; and donations

DEACON STEPHEN BENEDICT.

by this widow of about $1000 a year are still continued. Really, the Benedict Institute is her work, and should be counted in history as a monument to her largeness of heart and her Christian benevolence.

Benjamin, Rev. Judson, was born in Rodman, N. Y., Feb. 2, 1819. He graduated at Brown University, in the class of 1846. He took a partial course of study at the Newton Theological Institution; was ordained at Providence, R. I., Oct. 13, 1848. Having received an appointment as a missionary, he sailed from Boston, Oct. 21, 1848, and arrived at Tavoy, in Burmah, April 9, 1849. In March, 1850, he removed to Mergui, where he devoted himself specially to the work of the conversion of the Talaings. Mergui was given up as a station in 1853, and Mr. Benjamin was transferred to Maulmain. He returned to his native country in 1854, and died at Boston, Feb. 20, 1855.

Bennett, Rev. Alfred, was born in Mansfield, Conn., Sept. 26, 1780. In his eighteenth year, in a powerful revival of religion with which Mansfield was blessed, he was drawn to Jesus by the Spirit of God. He was baptized in February, 1800, and united with the Baptist church in Hampton. In February, 1803, he became a resident of Homer, Courtland Co., N. Y. He was ordained pastor of the little church of Homer, June 18, 1807. He was visited with great revivals of religion, the result of no imported human agency, but of the special power of the divine Spirit upon the prayers and labors of pastor and people. This required a larger edifice in 1812; and in 1827 it rendered necessary the sending forth of two colonies as churches, one locating at Cortland and the other at McGrawville.

He rendered much service as a missionary in the "Holland Purchase," and in Tioga, Steuben, and Allegany Counties. He was one of the most indefatigable and successful workers that ever toiled for Jesus in the Empire State. There was no benevolent or Christian cause that appealed to his heart or purse in vain. In 1832 he resigned his pastorate to accept an agency from the Executive Board of Foreign Missions, to plead the cause of the perishing heathen in the churches. To this cause he devoted all his energies and the rest of his days; and the Lord greatly blessed his public and private appeals. He died May 10, 1851, in possession of perfect peace.

Mr. Bennett was a man of great benevolence; he had superior mental powers; he was an effective speaker; he was a holy man; the Crucified was everything in his heart and in his ministry; he was the best-known minister in several counties, and the love with which he was regarded was intense enough to hand down his memory with reverence to several succeeding generations.

Bentley, Rev. William, son of Thomas and Abigail Bentley; born in Newport, R. I., March 3, 1775; on the capture of the city by the British in 1777 removed with his parents to Providence, R. I.; at the age of fourteen went to Boston; joined the First Baptist church, under Dr. Samuel Stillman, June 5, 1791; transferred his membership to the Second Baptist church, under Dr. Thomas Baldwin; was induced to give himself to the ministry; commenced preaching in 1806; ordained at Salem, Mass., Oct. 9, 1807; settled as pastor of the Baptist church in Tiverton, R. I.; in 1812 removed to Worcester, Mass., and became pastor of a church which he had instrumentally established; in 1815 settled as pastor in Wethersfield, Conn., and labored with great success for six years; afterwards labored with marked efficiency and power as an itinerant and missionary in different parts of Connecticut: was distinguished for tenderness, devotion, purity, boldness, energy, and faithfulness; died Dec. 24, 1855, greatly beloved and lamented.

Bently, Rev. Samuel N., was born in 1822, in Stewiack, Nova Scotia, and joined the Baptist church there when quite young. He studied at Acadia College and at Newton Theological Seminary. He was ordained at Liverpool, Nova Scotia, Nov. 23, 1851, and became pastor of North church, Halifax, in 1856. He was secretary of the Baptist Home Missionary Board. He died Nov. 28, 1859.

Bernard, James C.—Mr. Bernard was born in Logan Co., Ky., in 1807. He was converted in 1833, and baptized by Rev. Robert Anderson. The next year he removed with his family to Quincy, Ill. At that time there was no Baptist church in Quincy. In 1835 he removed to the then new settlement of Payson, and united with the little Baptist church which had recently been organized there. He returned to Quincy in 1843, and united with the First Baptist church in that city. Soon after that he was elected to the office of county clerk for Adams County, and at the expiration of his term was re-elected. He served the First church for a number of years as deacon, and also as superintendent of the Sabbath-school. When the Vermont Street church was organized, he with his family went into the new organization, and his time, energy, and means were bestowed without stint in sustaining that new interest. Here also he was chosen deacon and superintendent, in both of which offices he continued to labor efficiently until his removal to Chillicothe, Mo., in 1865. In 1871 he returned to Quincy in failing health, and at the prayer-meeting, just at the close of a few remarks, he was stricken with paralysis, and fell into the arms of some of the brethren who happened to be near him. He lingered for two years, a helpless invalid, before the release of death came. For a number of years in succession he had been either moderator or corresponding secretary of the Quincy Association, and was, until his health so completely failed, active and useful in various conspicuous positions.

Berry, Hon. Joel H., an eminent Baptist deacon, who died at Baldwyn, Miss., in 1874, was born in South Carolina in 1808; served four years in the Legislature of his native State; removed to Tippah Co., Miss., in 1843; was four years in the Mississippi Legislature and eight years in the State Senate. As a Christian he was abundant in every good word and work, giving a consistent example and active personal labors, and contributing largely but unostentatiously of his ample means to the cause of God.

Bethel College is located at Russellville, Ky., on the Louisville and Memphis Railroad, 143 miles southwest from Louisville. It was projected by Bethel Baptist Association in 1849. The main college building was erected, and a high school was opened in it, under the management of B. T. Blewett, A.M., Jan. 3, 1854. In 1856 a new charter was secured, and the institution entered upon its career as a college, under the presidency of Mr. Blewett, in the fall of 1856. The institution was prosperous until the breaking out of the civil war. In 1861–62 the buildings were used for a hospital. In 1863 the college was reopened under the presidency of Rev. George Hunt. On the resignation of Mr. Hunt, in 1864, J. W. Rust, A.M., was elected president. Under his management the institution continued to gain strength, until he was compelled by impaired health to resign, in February, 1868. He was succeeded by Noah K. Davis, LL.D. In 1872 the

HON. JOEL H. BERRY.

president's house was built, at a cost of $7000. In 1873, Dr. Davis resigned to take the chair of Moral Philosophy in the University of Virginia, and the discipline of the college was committed to Prof. Leslie Waggener, as chairman of the faculty. In 1876–77 the northern long hall was built, at a cost of $20,000, "to furnish board to students at reduced rates." In 1877, Prof. Leslie Waggener was elected president, and is still in that office.

Since the war Bethel College has steadily prospered, and is now one of the most flourishing institutions of learning in the West. The faculty numbers 5 professors and 2 tutors, and the catalogue of 1876–77 shows the attendance of 127 students. The college has an endowment in stocks, bonds, and real estate estimated at $100,000, besides the college ground and buildings.

Bethel Female College is located in Hopkinsville, Ky. It was erected under the auspices of Bethel Baptist Association for the higher education of women, and was chartered in 1854. The buildings cost about $30,000. Prof. J. W. Rust is and has been for several years past the president of this flourishing institution.

The average number of students is about 100. The management and discipline of the college are excellent, and few schools in the country offer better facilities for the education of young ladies.

Bibb, Rev. Martin, was born in Amherst Co., Va., Aug. 19, 1824, and in 1829 his father, with his family, located at what is now Sewell Depot, on the Chesapeake and Ohio Railroad, in West Virginia. He united with the church in his twentieth year, and very soon began to speak in prayer-meetings and to superintend a Sunday-school; was licensed to preach in 1849. Acted as colporteur of the American Tract Society until 1852, when he was ordained and took charge of churches. He was pastor of churches in Fayette, Nicholas, and Kanawha Counties until 1861, when he removed to Giles Co., Va. In 1865 he returned to his home and resumed his work with his churches, but after a brief period moved to Monroe County, remaining five years. He now resides in Hinton, on the Chesapeake and Ohio Railroad, and devotes all his time to the Hinton church. He has acted as clerk of Associations for about twenty years, and has frequently written for the press. During his ministry he has baptized about 1000 persons and has preached a large number of sermons. Many of his positions have required hard work and self-denial, and he has had gracious evidences of the divine blessing.

Bible Union, The American, was formed in New York, June 10, 1850, by a number of individuals, chiefly Baptists, who had co-operated with the American and Foreign Bible Society, until it decided that it was not its duty to revise the common English Bible, nor to procure such a revision from others; and so would confine its circulation in that tongue to that version. The Baptists of America had withdrawn from the American Bible Society because it refused aid to the Bengalee and Burmese translations, made by Baptist missionaries, in which the Greek term βαπτίζω and its cognates had been rendered by words signifying "immerse," "immersion," etc. The English translation had been made the standard to which all other translations should conform and not the inspired originals, and the founders of the Union felt compelled by consistency to demand that on the principle of fidelity translations in all languages should be conformed to the Hebrew and Greek texts. Hence the constitution of the Union defines its purpose thus: "To procure and circulate the most faithful versions of the Sacred Scriptures in all languages throughout the world." Under this broad provision it selected ripe scholars from nine different Christian denominations in Europe and America, to whom it committed the revision of the English Bible. This was the first organized attempt ever made to apply the accumulated fruits of Biblical scholarship, since 1611, to a revision of the English Bible for the benefit of the unlearned reader, and it met with the most determined resistance. But in an unswerving adherence to a divine principle the attempt was pushed, believing that both ignorance and prejudice must yield at last to the demands of true scholarship. No expense was spared to secure the oldest translations of the Bible, copies of the ancient manuscripts, and other aids for making the revisions and translations as perfect as possible. Nor were the scholars employed restricted as to time and free conference. The New Testament passed through three thorough revisions, the first covering a period of eight years, the second four, and the third more than two.

The following are the rules for the government of the scholars employed by the Union in revising the English New Testament, namely:

"The received Greek text, critically edited, with known errors corrected, must be followed.

BETHEL COLLEGE, RUSSELLVILLE, KY.

"The common English version must be the basis of revision, and only such alterations must be made as the exact meaning of the text and the existing state of the language may require.

"The exact meaning of the inspired text, as that text expressed it to those who understood the original Scriptures at the time they were first written, must be given in corresponding words and phrases, so far as they can be found in the English language, with the least possible obscurity or indefiniteness."

Under the operation of these rules not only the English, but the Spanish and Italian New Testaments have been revised. And the same general principles have been applied in revising the English Old Testament, that is, the books of Genesis, Exodus, Joshua, Ruth, 1 and 2 Samuel, 1 and 2 Kings, 1 and 2 Chronicles, Job, Psalms, Proverbs, etc., and also in the new translations of the New Testament into the Chinese character and the Ningpo colloquial. In these forms the Union has circulated over a million copies of the Scriptures, and although at present its work has been largely suspended for want of necessary funds, it has created such a demand for a corrected English Bible as now takes hold of the public mind, and cannot be relaxed till this aim is accomplished in harmony with the real wants of the age.

Bickel, Rev. Dr. P. W., was born in Weinheim, grand duchy of Baden, Germany, Sept. 7, 1829. In his youth he received a thorough training in the dead languages in the Bender Classical Institute of his native place, where he studied for six years. An enthusiastic adherent of liberal political views, he became involved in the struggle in Baden in 1848. The revolution being overthrown, Mr. Bickel left his native land and came to America, spending the first years of his sojourn as a printer, and engaging also to some extent in literary efforts and teaching. At that time he was a confirmed infidel. But it pleased God to give him the light of heavenly truth. He was converted and baptized into the membership of the Baptist church of Waukegaw, Wis. Feeling impelled to preach the faith which he had formerly attacked, Mr. Bickel repaired to Rochester, N. Y., where he graduated from the Rochester Theological Seminary in 1855. Even while he was a theological student his ability as a talented writer manifested itself. His first field of labor was Cincinnati, O., where, among a German population of formalists and avowed skeptics, he succeeded in gathering a warm, loving German church. He labored as German city missionary in Cincinnati, O., from 1855 to 1857; was ordained pastor of the German church formed through his labors in September, 1857, and continued his pastorate with increasing success from 1857 to 1865. During a large portion of his pastorate he was editor of the monthly periodical of the Western German Baptist Conference, and of a Sunday-school paper, superintending at the same time the publication work of that Conference. In 1865 the German Baptists in America uniting in a Triennial Conference appointed Mr. Bickel secretary of the newly-formed German Publication Society, and editor of its weekly periodicals. This position he filled ably, wielding a facile pen and showing great practical talent in furthering the publication work. As a recognition of his various and eminent services the degree of Doctor of Divinity was conferred upon him by Granville College, Ohio. In 1878, Dr. Bickel was selected by the American Baptist Publication Society, and by the Baptists in Germany, to establish and superintend a Baptist publication work in Germany. Dr. Bickel is now performing these duties in Hamburg, and editing at the same time the new weekly Baptist paper issued in Germany. The work is in a very prosperous condition. Dr. Bickel is an excellent writer, a good poet, a man of high culture, gifted with great practical talent, one of the most useful of the German Baptist ministers, a man whose life and work will prove a lasting blessing to German Baptists in Europe and America.

Biddle, Rev. William P., was born in Princess Anne Co., Va., Jan. 8, 1787. Mr. Biddle began to preach early in life, and coming to North Carolina, married, in February, 1810, Mary N., the daughter of Gen. Samuel Simpson. He was present at the formation of the Baptist State Convention in 1830, as was also his son, Col. H. S. Biddle, and was until his death, which occurred in Newberne, Aug. 8, 1853, thoroughly identified with all the enterprises of the denomination. Being a man of large wealth he preached gratuitously, and thus, as he drew near the close of his life, did a serious injury to the churches to which he ministered. He was eminent for a devout spirit, a godly walk, and a large measure of usefulness in his day.

Biggs, Rev. David, was born in Camden Co., N. C., in 1763. He commenced preaching when thirty years of age. He removed to Virginia in 1792, and was pastor eighteen years of the Baptist church at Portsmouth. In 1810 he removed to Kentucky, and took charge of Georgetown, Bethlehem, and Silas churches, in Bourbon County. In 1820 he came to Missouri, and settled in Pike County, and preached to Mount Pleasant, Ramsey Creek, and Bethlehem churches, and organized the Noix Creek church. He labored with marked success for fifty years, and the prosperity of the denomination in Northeast Missouri is largely due to his ministry. He died Aug. 1, 1845, in his eighty-third year.

Biggs, Deacon Noah, is one of the most liberal and useful laymen of North Carolina, a merchant of Scotland Neck, a trustee of Wake Forest College, and a lover of all good men and good works. He was born in Martin Co., N. C., in 1842, and was baptized in 1876.

Bigotry, Baptist.—The Baptists regard every man as a Christian who truly repents and who puts his entire trust in the atoning merits of Jesus for the salvation of his soul. They believe that such a regenerated man will enter heaven from the membership of any church, evangelical or heterodox, or even from the great world outside of all churches. They think that such children of God should show their love to Jesus by keeping his commandments; but whether they are immersed or not, it is the firm conviction of all Baptists that the entire earthly regenerated family of Jesus, of all names, will be saved in glory. They love all the true followers of Jesus wherever they find them, from Pascal, the Catholic, to William Penn, the Quaker. This love is a great reality; and it is quite as strong as the love of a Methodist for a Presbyterian, or of a Presbyterian for an Evangelical Episcopalian, or of a Dutch for a German Reformed. Nay, we think it quite as potent as the affection which a Reformed (Covenanter) Presbyterian bears to the great Presbyterian body of this country, or which a follower of Dr. Henry A. Boardman, or of Albert Barnes, bears to the religious descendants of the grand men who framed and adopted the "Solomon League and Covenant." The writer has extensive knowledge of the charity of Pedobaptists for Baptists, and he gives it as his deliberate conviction that Baptist charity for godly persons who are not in their own fold is very largely in excess of the love which our Pedobaptist brethren cherish for us. If there was a standard by which charity could be measured, we should, without hesitation or delay, submit Baptist and Pedobaptist love for each other to its decision without any doubt about the result. And if it be objected that we do not admit unimmersed Pedobaptists to the Lord's table, we reply that the exclusion springs from no want of charity, for we do not bring our own unbaptized converts to the Lord's table, whom we love with the warmest affection. Baptism, as Baptists and nearly all Pedobaptists view it, is a prerequisite to the Lord's Supper, and heaven-revealed charity does not require or permit the sacrifice of heaven-revealed truth. No charity requires a Calvinist to give up his inspired creed to please an Arminian; no charity demands from a Democratic Republican the surrender of his just political principles to gratify a monarchist; and if charity requires a Baptist not only to give his love to an unbaptized Christian, but to surrender his Bible baptism to please the prejudices of his believing Pedobaptist brother, it is not in harmony with his teachings who says, "Buy the truth and sell it not," "Hold fast the form of sound words which thou hast heard of me in faith and love, which is in Christ Jesus." Our motto about charity is, " Love for Christians and all mankind, and supreme love for God and his truth." This is Baptist bigotry.

Bill, Hon. Caleb R., brother of Rev. Ingram E. Bill, and a member of Billtown Baptist church, Nova Scotia; became wealthy by careful attention to business. He was a member of the Nova Scotia Parliament for several years, and at confederation became a member of the Senate of Canada, and so continued till his death, in 1872. Senator Bill left a handsome bequest to the Foreign Missionary Board of the Maritime Provinces.

Bill, Rev. Ingram E., was born in Cornwallis, Nova Scotia, where he was converted, and joined the Cornwallis Baptist church; ordained at Nictaux, March 3, 1829; became pastor of the Baptist church at Fredericton, New Brunswick, in 1841. In 1842 he resumed the pastorate at Nictaux. In 1852 he became pastor of Germain Street Baptist church, St. Johns, New Brunswick. Subsequently he became editor of the *Christian Visitor*, and so continued for over twenty years. Mr. Bill is now the useful pastor of the Baptist church, St. Martins, New Brunswick.

Bingham, Rev. Abel.—In 1828, this brother having been a preacher among the Tonawanda Indians, was sent from Western New York to establish a mission among the Indians at Sault Ste. Marie. At this post he labored steadily for twenty-five years, being useful with the soldiers there stationed, as well as in his own work. Amid many discouragements his patient continuance stood him in good stead. When the scattering of the tribes made it necessary to abandon the mission, he retired to the society of his children at Grand Rapids, and, through a serene and loved old age, passed to his rest in 1865.

Binney, Joseph Getchell, D.D., was born in Boston, Mass., Dec. 1, 1807, and was educated at Yale College and Newton Theological Seminary. He was ordained at West Boylston, Mass., in 1832, and settled at Savannah, Ga., where his ministry was remarkably successful. His congregation was large and intelligent, and grew rapidly in number and efficiency. Their interest in foreign missions was especially marked, and large contributions were regularly given to the cause. In 1843 the acting board of the Triennial Convention urged him to engage in the foreign missionary work, and also "to establish and conduct a school for the training of a native ministry among the Karens." He was also requested to unite with his missionary associates in inaugurating a system of general education for the Karens, then but recently known, but who had received the gospel with great alacrity. A school was opened by Dr. Binney in Maulmain, May, 1845, with 13 adult pupils, all converts from heathenism, and who had already been quite useful in making known to their countrymen, as best they could, the gospel truth. At first instruction in the Bible only was given, but afterwards in arithmetic, geography, and astronomy. The school increased each year in numbers and efficiency, and quite an advance was made in the grade of the studies. At the end of five most encouraging years, the health of Mrs. Binney, who had taken an active part in teaching, failed, and Dr. Binney and she were obliged to return to America. The school became almost extinct during the three ensuing years, as but little time could be devoted to it by the brethren who were actively engaged in missionary work. After Dr. Binney's return to this country, in 1853, he was engaged for a while as pastor at Elmira, N. Y., and subsequently at Augusta, Ga. In 1855 he was invited to accept the presidency of the Columbian College, which he did, remaining in that position only three years, yet long enough to give an influence to its methods of instruction and discipline which it still feels. An urgent call from his missionary associates in Burmah, and importunate solicitation on the part of prominent brethren in this country upon Dr. Binney to return and resume his labors of instruction in the Karen Seminary, induced him, in 1858, to resign the presidency of the college and to enter again on the work for which he was so admirably fitted, and which lay so near his heart. He sailed for Burmah in 1859, at which time the seminary was removed from Maulmain to Rangoon, the new capital of British Burmah. The seminary opened with 80 pupils, and for a while the whole labor of conducting it, with much additional work of preaching, translating, and publishing, fell upon Dr. Binney, assisted by his faithful wife. From this time until 1876 the seminary was blessed with an uninterrupted career of prosperity and usefulness. A literary department was added to it, buildings erected, text-books printed, treatises on anatomy, physiology, and hygiene, a manual of theology, and manuscript works on mental and moral science prepared. His onerous labors during this protracted period greatly impaired the health of Dr. Binney, and in November, 1875, being entirely prostrated in health, he was obliged to leave the seminary in the care of the Rev. Sau Tay and return to America. After a brief sojourn in this country, with health somewhat improved, he sailed again for Burmah in the fall of 1877, being accompanied by Mrs. Binney, but he died upon the voyage, November 26, and was buried in the Indian Ocean. His work in Asia will be his enduring monument. More than 300 Karen ministers were educated by him, and they have accomplished an amount of good among their countrymen which no man can measure. As a thinker, Dr. Binney had a clear, incisive, analytic, and unusually logical mind. As a preacher, he was impressive, dignified, and instructive. As a teacher, he stimulated the dullest into quickness and accuracy of thought; while, as a man, there was a humility, sincerity, trust, and oneness of purpose in all his acts that stamped him as one of the very best of the good ministers of Christ.

Birt, Caleb Evans, son of the Rev. Isaiah Birt, was born at Devonport, England, on March 11, 1795. In his seventeenth year he entered Cambridge University with a view of studying for the bar. His conscience was aroused and agitated by the prospective necessity of signing the articles of the Church of England. The conflict of mind ended in his abandonment of the plan of life he had cherished, and he determined to devote himself to the ministry of the gospel among his own people, the Baptists. He was baptized by his brother, the Rev. John Birt, then pastor of the Baptist church at Hull, and made his first pulpit efforts in that neighborhood. Soon after he was entered at Bristol College as a ministerial student, whence he proceeded to Edinburgh University. At the close of his studies, in 1816, he was invited to become pastor of a church in Derby, and was ordained in the following year. After ten years' labor in Derby he removed to Portsea, where he labored until 1837, when he was invited to Broadmead church, Bristol. In 1844 he removed to Wantage, and held the pastoral charge of the church there until his death, Dec. 13, 1854, aged sixty years. His high character and fervent piety, together with the advantages of a liberal education, qualified him for eminent usefulness. In Portsea particularly his ministry was remarkably successful, and his memory is affectionately cherished throughout the community.

Bishop, Miss Harriet E., the third daughter of Putnam and Miranda Bishop, was born in Panton, Addison Co., Vt., Jan. 1, 1818. At thirteen she was converted and baptized by Rev. John A. Dodge in Lake Champlain, and for several years was the youngest member of the church in her native town. She remained a member of that church until the organization of the First Baptist church of St. Paul, Minn. The reading of the memoirs of Harriet Newell and Ann H. Judson awoke a missionary spirit which never slept. Where she should labor was a subject of serious consideration whilst the preparatory work of securing an education was going on. In 1840 the Board of National Popular Education called for its first class of female Christian teachers for destitute portions of the West. She entered this open door, and at once commenced her life-work.

July 13, 1847, the teacher arrived at a government Indian trading town having the unclassic name of "Pig's Eye." A few rude homes stood on the bluff, but there was not a Christian man or woman in one of them. Here the queenly city of St. Paul now flourishes. There was no meeting- or school-house within 500 miles. About two weeks after Miss Bishop arrived she organized a Sunday-school which is a mighty power; at present the school of the First Baptist church. For several months she labored without a Christian helper in the school. At the close of the year a part of her school formed the nucleus of one organized by the Methodists, and another portion for one organized by the Presbyterians; the larger number of scholars, however, remained in the original school. Meanwhile, the log-cabin school had grown into a pioneer seminary. Though the only Baptist at the Indian trading-post for one year, she ever remained true to her convictions of Bible truth. Feeble churches have been strengthened by her wise counsels. Missions, both home and foreign, have ever been cherished and efficiently aided by her labors. Nobly has she advocated the temperance reformation, visiting prisons and the homes of drunkards to rescue them from hopeless ruin. Though now in the evening of life, heart and hands are ever busy in gospel work.

Bishop, Hon. Jesse P., was born in New Haven, Vt., June 1, 1815. After a childhood and youth of many vicissitudes and much toil, he removed in 1836 to Cleveland, O. In 1837 he entered the Senior class of Western Reserve College, graduating the following year. In 1839, having completed his law studies, he began legal practice as a member of the firm of Card & Bishop. In 1856 he was elected to the Common Pleas judgeship of his county, and served to the end of the term with great satisfaction, both to the members of the profession and to the public. At the end of the term he declined re-election, and resumed the practice of law. In this he still continues, having associated with him his son L. J. P. Bishop, and Seymour F. Adams.

Judge Bishop has led a very busy and earnest life. As a judge he was accurate and discriminating; as a lawyer, he is considered one of the most reliable and well informed in the city of Cleveland. He has a fine memory and a comprehensive mind, and is seldom mistaken in his decision. For forty-five years he has been an honored and trusted member of the First church of Cleveland. His uniform courtesy, his tried integrity, his sincere and unselfish friendship, his liberality, and his blameless life, have attracted to him universal respect and esteem.

Bishop, Nathan, LL.D., was born at Vernon, Oneida Co., N. Y., in 1808. He graduated at Brown University, where he also served for some time as tutor. For years he was a member of the board of his *alma mater*, and afterwards he was one of the Fellows. He was a superintendent of

NATHAN BISHOP, LL.D.

schools in Providence, and subsequently for some years in the city of Boston; while in the latter position Harvard University showed its appreciation of his great abilities by conferring on him the degree of Doctor of Laws.

After removing to New York City he was appointed by the governor a member of the State Board of Charities, and by President Grant a member of the United States Indian Commission. He has served for years on the Board of the American Baptist Home Mission Society and in many similar positions. He was chairman of the Finance Committee of the American Committee of Bible Revision. He served for two years as corresponding secretary of the Baptist Home Missionary Society without compensation, and when he retired from the office, in 1876, he paid its entire indebtedness, amounting to $30,000.

About twenty-five years ago he married the widow of Garrett N. Bleecker, a daughter of Deacon Ebenezer Cauldwell, of New York City. Dr. and Mrs. Bishop for many years have given princely contributions to all the great benevolent enterprises of the Baptist denomination.

For the last fifteen years he was a member, deacon, and trustee of the Calvary Baptist church of New York. He was specially interested in the education of the freedmen, and gave liberally for that object. He died at Saratoga Springs, Aug. 7, 1880.

He was a man of rare talents, benevolence, and integrity. He was unostentatious, earnest, and humble. The world seldom has the death of such a man as Nathan Bishop to lament.

Bitting, C. C., D.D., was born in Philadelphia, Pa., March, 1830; was graduated from the Central

C. C. BITTING, D.D.

High School in 1850; baptized at the age of seventeen by the Rev. J. L. Burrows, D.D., and united with the Broad Street Baptist church. After having prosecuted his studies at Lewisburg and Madison Universities, he was engaged in teaching in the Tennessee Baptist Female College at Nashville, and after its removal, at Murfreesborough, Tenn. Having been ordained to the work of the ministry while here, he was invited to the pastorate of the Mount Olivet and Hopeful Baptist churches, in Hanover Co., Va., at that time two of the most prominent county churches in the State; he accepted the position, and after a period of the most successful labor in this field, he was chosen, in 1859, the pastor of the Baptist church in Alexandria, Va. In 1866, Dr. Bitting was urged to accept the secretaryship of the Sunday-School Board of the Southern Baptist Convention, located in Greenville, S. C., which he did; but on the removal of the board to Memphis, Tenn., he became pastor of the Baptist church in Lynchburg, Va., and removed there in May, 1868. His labors here were eminently successful. More than 300 united with the church in that place during his pastorate of four years, and thus it became one of the strongest and most effective societies in the State. In 1872 he was chosen district secretary for the Southern States of the American Baptist Publication Society, with headquarters at Richmond, Va., but in the following year he became pastor of the Second Baptist church in that city. While in Richmond, Dr. Bitting's labors were manifold, for while pressed with the cares of a large congregation he was also acting as statistical secretary of the Virginia Baptist General Association and chairman of the Memorial Committee of the Virginia Centennial to secure an endowment for Richmond College. In September, 1876, he became pastor of the Franklin Square Baptist church, Baltimore, Md., where he still labors with marked success. Dr. Bitting is one of the most popular preachers in his State. He is studious in his pulpit preparations, and earnest and eloquent in his preaching. He has also made valuable additions to the literature of the denomination. In 1874, Dr. Bitting visited Europe, Palestine, and Egypt. Furman University conferred upon him the honorary degree of Doctor of Divinity.

Bixby, Moses H., D.D., was born in Warren, Grafton Co., N. H., Aug. 20, 1827. He became a

MOSES H. BIXBY, D.D.

hopeful Christian at the early age of twelve, and when quite young had his thoughts turned to the Christian ministry. After ten years devoted to study, the latter part of the period being spent at a college in Montreal, he was ordained in Vermont in 1849. During the next three years—1849–52—he preached in Vermont, where his labors were greatly blessed. In 1852 he was appointed by the Missionary Union to the Burman field, and continued in service for about four years,—1852-56,—at the end of which period he returned to this country, on account of what proved to be the fatal illness of his wife, and for three years was pastor of a church in Providence, intending, when the providence of God should open the way, to return to Burmah. In 1860 he once more entered upon his missionary work, devoting himself especially to the Shans, for whose spiritual welfare he labored for eight successive years,—1861-69. Worn down by his excessive and protracted work, he again returned to his native land, and once more established himself in Providence, R. I. Commencing his ministerial labors in a destitute but growing part of the city, he gathered a new Baptist church, which was organized in October, 1870, and is known as the "Cranston Street church." This church and the Sunday-school connected with it have had a remarkable growth, and in point of numbers rank with the largest churches and Sunday-schools in the city. Dartmouth College, in 1868, conferred on him the honorary degree of Master of Arts, and the Central University of Iowa, in 1875, that of Doctor of Divinity.

Black, Col. J. C. C.—An eminent lawyer of Augusta, Ga., a deacon in the First Baptist church in that city, and a trustee of Mercer University,—a man of unquestionable ability, integrity, and devotion to principle, and a refined, social, Christian gentleman. He was born in Scott Co., Ky., May 9, 1842; completed his college course at Georgetown College, Ky., in 1862; entered the Confederate army as a common soldier, under Gen. Morgan, and was promoted to be colonel of his regiment. In 1865 he moved to Augusta, Ga., entered upon the study of law, and was admitted to the bar in 1866, and to-day he is one of the best thinkers and most eloquent pleaders in the State.

Mr. Black has been a Sunday-school superintendent, a representative in the Legislature of the State, president of the Young Men's Christian Association, and in every way an able, earnest, zealous Christian worker. Of a charitable disposition, he is pleasant in conversation, popular in his manners, stern in his principles, and thoroughly identified with the Baptist cause. Honored for his abilities and beloved for his generous qualities, he wields great moral influence in the community where he dwells.

Blackall, Christopher R., M.D.—Dr. Blackall is known chiefly for his long and efficient service in connection with the American Baptist Publication Society.

He was born in Albany, N. Y., in 1830. He graduated from Rush Medical College, of Chicago, and early in the history of the civil war was commissioned a surgeon of the 33d Infantry Regiment, of Wisconsin. After efficient service in that capacity, he resigned and was honorably discharged, and he settled in Chicago, Ill.

In May, 1866, he accepted an appointment as general superintendent of the Chicago Sunday-School Union, and a year later was appointed district secretary of the American Baptist Publication Society for the Northwest. His great success in managing the business department of the society committed to him, and of promoting the Sunday school work on that extensive field, is well known.

In 1879, by appointment of the society, he was transferred to New York, and assumed the management of its branch house in that city.

Dr. Blackall is the author of the well-known charming cantatas "Belshazzar" and "Ruth." He has also largely contributed to our Sunday-school literature. Among his works may be mentioned "Lessons on the Lord's Prayer," "Our Sunday-School Work, and How to do it," "Nellie's Work for Jesus," "Gems for Little Ones." For eight years he edited *Our Little Ones*, also the "Bible Lessons." His industry, fidelity, tact, social nature, and Christian devotion fit him for the eminent position he has so long filled.

Blackman, Rev. James F., a prominent preacher of the Ouachita region, Louisiana, a native of the State, was born in 1828, and brought up to the occupation of a printer and publisher. He was active and successful in the ministry. He died Dec. 11, 1874.

Blackwood, Rev. A. D., was born in Orange Co., N. C., June 10, 1820; baptized November, 1838; ordained in Alabama in December, 1846; has preached 3600 times, and baptized 1000 persons; was much blessed in pioneer and revival work, and was moderator of Raleigh Association for eight years. He is now pastor at Corey, N. C.

Blackwood, Rev. Christopher, was born in 1606, and graduated at the University of Cambridge. He was rector of a parish in Kent at the beginning of the Parliamentary war.

In 1644 the Rev. Francis Cornwell, in preaching a sermon at Cranbrook, in Kent, before a number of ministers and others, stated that infant baptism was an anti-Christian innovation, a human tradition, and a practice for which there was neither precept, example, nor true deduction from the Word of God. On hearing this several of the ministers were greatly startled and seriously offended, and after service they agreed to examine the subject and to report the result of their investigations at their conference within a fortnight. Mr. Blackwood studied the subject thoroughly, and felt compelled to renounce infant baptism forever. He presented his views on paper to the brethren, which none of them pretended to answer; and he subsequently published them. He did not continue long in the national church after this; for he disapproved of an established church as much as he disliked infant baptism. The Presbyterians wrote against him not only because of his rejection of infant baptism, but because of his advocacy of liberty of conscience.

He gathered a Baptist church at Spilshill, near Staplehurst, in connection with Richard Kingsworth, and labored in that field until the opposition of his co-pastor to the doctrine of personal election led him to retire from the church. Mr. Blackwood received the whole counsel of God, and he would neither hide the truth nor promote discord.

He entered the army as a chaplain and went to Ireland, probably with Gen. Fleetwood and Lieut.-Gen. Ludlow. He formed a Baptist church in Dublin, which grievously offended the Pedobaptists of that city; and of this church he was the pastor for several years. The Baptists at this period in Ireland were quite numerous, and they held important positions in the English army. Mr. Harrison, a Pedobaptist, writing to Thurloe, Cromwell's chief secretary, says of Mr. Blackwood, "He is the oracle of the Anabaptists in Ireland." He was regarded as "a very learned man," better acquainted with the early Christian fathers than most men in his day. He was the author of several valuable works, which were very popular, and which rendered effective service to the cause of truth.

Blain, Rev. John, was born in Fishkill, N. Y., Feb. 14, 1795; converted at the age of fifteen; united with the First Baptist church in Albany, under Rev. Joshua Bradley; studied for the ministry, and began preaching in 1819; served various churches, and labored as an evangelist in New York, Connecticut, Rhode Island, and Massachusetts; was blessed with powerful revivals; a leader in the temperance movement; baptized about 3000 persons; preached more than 9500 sermons; assisted in nearly 100 revivals; married about 2000 couples; spoke in about 1000 different places; gave, while living, to home and foreign missions more than $19,000, and left his property to missions; had three brothers, who were also preachers. He died in Mansfield, Dec. 26, 1879, in his eighty-fifth year; a man of great spiritual might.

Blake, E. Nelson.—Mr. Blake, at present the leading partner in the Dake Bakery, an extensive and prosperous establishment in Chicago, was born in 1831, at West Cambridge, now Arlington, Mass. Changes in the family, caused by his father's death, interfered with his studies at an early age, and threw upon him unusual responsibilities. His proficiency at school, nevertheless, was such that opportunities to begin life as a teacher were opened to him. Declining these, he chose a business life, removing to California with this view in 1850. Some brilliant openings for acquiring a large fortune were offered him, but a pledge to his family that he would not make California a permanent home compelled him to decline all such, and he returned East in 1853. Engaging in business in Boston, he made such progress that in 1869 he was able, in company with others, to purchase the Dake Bakery in Chicago, which has since grown to the dimensions of the largest establishment of the kind in this country. To remarkable business capacity Mr. Blake unites perfect integrity, and at the same time a spirit of Christian liberality which prompts him to use his large means in enterprises of Christian usefulness. He was converted at the age of nineteen, and uniting with a Baptist church, began a career of Christian activity in various departments of church work, in which he still finds great delight. His membership is now with the Second church in Chicago. As a trustee of the university and of the theological seminary, he has rendered important service, helping both institutions in their pecuniary straits with a free and open hand. His donations to the seminary, in particular, are believed to aggregate more than that of any other man.

Blakewood, Rev. B. W., LL.D., an active and zealous worker in the Louisiana Association, was born in South Carolina, and is about fifty years of age. After a literary course he studied medicine in Philadelphia and New York, and was offered the chair of Surgery in Oglethorpe Medical College. Subsequently he graduated in law at Harvard University. He came to Louisiana about the year 1850 as a Baptist, having been immersed in Georgia in 1849. He settled on Bayou de Glaise, and became an active promoter of the cause of the Baptists. He has filled many important positions, —moderator of Louisiana Association, vice-president of the Baptist State Convention, president of the State Sunday-School Convention, and a member of the Legislature. A few years ago Dr. Blackwood was ordained to the ministry, and is zealously devoting himself to the work.

Blanton, Rev. William C., was born in Franklin Co., Ky., Feb. 3, 1803. He was baptized into the fellowship of the Forks of Elkhorn church in 1827, and ordained to the ministry in 1833. After preaching one year as a licentiate, he accepted a call to the pastoral care of Lebanon and North Benson churches. With these churches he labored until near the time of his death. At different periods he preached as supply for Pigeon Fork, Mount Pleasant, Providence, and Buffalo Lick churches. His great zeal, unaffected piety, and the "sweet simplicity" of his preaching won the hearts of the multitudes, and by him many were led to the Saviour. He died at his home in his native county, Aug. 21, 1845.

Bleakney, Rev. James, was born in New

Brunswick, and ordained in 1833. He was pastor at Norton, Upham, Little River, and Gondolon Point churches. His labors as missionary in the northern counties and other parts of New Brunswick were highly useful. He baptized over a thousand converts. He died Dec. 14, 1861. Three of his sons—W. A. J. Bleakney, James E. Bleakney, and J. C. Bleakney—are useful pastors in Nova Scotia.

Bledsoe, Hon. Thomas W., was born in Green Co., Ga., April 11, 1811; was for several years presiding judge of the Inferior Court of Tolbert Co., Ga. He settled as a planter in Louisiana in 1845; was four years moderator of Red River Association, and eight years president of the Louisiana Baptist Convention. He died in 1871.

Bleecker, Garrat Noel, an eminent iron merchant of New York City, was born in New York in 1815, and died May 28, 1853. His father, by the same name, was also a prominent citizen, and was at one time comptroller of New York. Father and son were members of the Oliver Street Baptist church, and from the commencement to the close of their religious life the personal consecration of each seemed complete. The son joined the church at twenty-one, but from fifteen had been a zealous teacher in the Sunday-school, and was apparently from his childhood a devout Christian.

Habits of prayer, taught him in his infancy, and never intermitted through life, but increased to three times a day, morning, noon, and night, as he came to years of discernment, were the foundation of the saintly character for which he was distinguished. He was as active in labors in the church and Sunday-school and missionary work as he was devoted in spirit. He was successful in business, and generous in dispensing its profits, which he regarded as truly the Lord's.

He withdrew from his first partnership because it involved the necessity of profiting by the sale of intoxicating liquors. He, with a friend, then entered into the iron business. Success came rapidly, and the application of his rule, to make wealth useful, conferred upon many a needy cause a timely benefit. He made his pastor, Rev. Elisha Tucker, D.D., the almoner of many charitable gifts to the poor, for whom he felt the tenderest sympathies, because he was so constant a laborer among them in evangelistic work. About the time of his death the educational interests of New York Baptists were in a condition to make endowments necessary, and he gave $3000 to the theological seminary at Hamilton. Had his life been spared, no doubt large donations would have followed. In his will he bequeathed $12,000 more to that institution, which was promptly paid by his executors, being the first large donation to its funds.

Besides $8000 to the American Baptist Home Mission Society, he left liberal bequests to our other denominational societies.

Blewett, Prof. B. T., was born in 1820 in Bowling Green, Ky. He entered Georgetown College in 1841, and graduated in 1846, and taught in that institution till 1853. Mr. Blewett left Georgetown, and for some time was Professor of Moral and Intellectual Philosophy at Bethel College, Russellville, Ky. In 1860 he became connected with Augusta College, Ky.; in 1871 he removed to St. Louis Co., Mo. He is now president of the St. Louis Female Seminary. He made a profession of religion in 1840, and was baptized in Kentucky. He was licensed to preach the same year. Prof. Blewett is a cultured Christian gentleman, enjoying the confidence of all who know him.

Bliss, George Ripley, D.D., LL.D., was born in Sherburne, N. Y., June 20, 1816; entered Madi-

GEORGE RIPLEY BLISS, D.D., LL.D.

son University in 1837, and graduated in 1838; graduated from Hamilton Theological Seminary in 1840; was tutor in Madison University for three years. In December, 1843, he became pastor of the church at New Brunswick, N. J., and remained until May, 1849, when he accepted the Greek professorship in the university at Lewisburg. He was also for two years president of the theological department. Thus his connection with the university dates almost from its beginning, and its subsequent growth was largely due to the influence of his profound scholarship and self-sacrificing labors. In 1874 he was called to the chair of Biblical Exegesis in the Crozer Theological Seminary, which position he now holds. He has also been prominently identified with the work of Bible revision. He received the degree of D.D. in 1860 from Madison University, and that of LL.D. in 1878 from the university at Lewisburg.

Dr. Bliss is a noble specimen of intellectual and spiritual manhood. His scholarly attainments are widely known and recognized, notwithstanding the hindrances to publicity that are imposed by his quiet and unobtrusive manners. His sermons and writings display a rich fund of sublime thought, elegant diction, and convincing argument.

Blitch, Joseph Luke, D.D., was born March 3, 1839, in Duval Co., Fla.; is the son of Rev. Benj. Blitch, an eminent Baptist preacher. He

JOSEPH LUKE BLITCH, D.D.

was converted at fifteen, but "boy conversions" being then unpopular, he was baptized two years later. He began talking for Jesus as soon as converted, and the Sunday after his baptism he went fifty miles to hear a great preacher. Crowds had gathered at Ready Creek; the preacher failed, and young Brother Blitch took charge of the meeting, and almost unconsciously began preaching from the words, "Behold the Lamb of God!" From that day till now he has preached every Sunday save one from one to four sermons. He graduated at Mercer University in 1863, the only graduate that year, preaching to three churches while in college, having been ordained by the Macedonia church in 1860. He was pastor at Aberlare, near Augusta, several years. At one time he immersed 99 converts before leaving the water. He next served Shiloh, Macedonia, and Lafayette churches; thence to Macon, Ga., where he established the Second church, and at the close of a two years' pastorate left it with a good house and over one hundred members. He was pastor one year at Little Rock, Ark.; two years at Marshall, Texas; Boenville, one year; Lee Summit, Mo., three years. In 1873 he went to California; was pastor at Dixon six years, taking an active part, officially, in education and mission interests. In 1879 he located at Walla Walla, Washington Territory, and has already organized a vigorous church. About 2000 have been converted under his ministry, of whom he has baptized 1636. La Grange University, Mo., conferred upon him the degree of D.D. Several of his sermons have been published, one of which, "Thy kingdom come," so delighted Spurgeon, of London, that he said of it, "Every sentence carries the sound of a glorious victory. I love it."

Blodgett, Rev. John, was born in Randolph, Vt., Nov. 20, 1792; born again in 1817, when he united with the Baptist church in Denmark, N.Y.; licensed to preach in 1818; he became in subsequent years pastor at Champion, Lowville, and Broad Street, Utica, N.Y. After a year in Tennessee, he became pastor of the church at Lebanon, O. From Lebanon he went to Centreville, and thence to Casstown, O., where he remained two years. In 1854 he left Ohio for a two years' sojourn in Indiana, but returned to settle at Franklin, O., where he continued until disease and old age terminated his active work. He died July 24, 1876.

Father Blodgett was a man of wide popularity. He was familiarly called in Ohio "John, the Beloved." Kind and conciliatory in his manner, and full of earnest love for men, he endeared himself to all. Probably no one is more affectionately remembered by those who knew him and had the pleasure of hearing him preach.

Blood, Rev. Caleb, was born in Charlton, Mass., Aug. 18, 1754. His conversion took place when he was twenty-one, "his first serious impressions having been received amidst the gayeties of the ball-room." He commenced to preach a year and a half after joining the church, and was ordained as an evangelist in the fall of 1777. He became pastor of the church in Weston, Mass., and remained such for seven years, and then removed to Shaftsbury, Vt., early in 1788. Here a large blessing was vouchsafed to him. In one revival—that of the winter of 1798–99—175 persons were added to the church. Besides looking after the spiritual interests of his own flock, he performed the work of an itinerant, visiting in his preaching tours the northwest parts of New York and the neighboring province of Canada. The fame of his excellence and success as a minister reached the metropolis of New England, and when the Third

Baptist church, then recently formed, were looking out for a pastor, their attention was turned to him. For three years he acted as the pastor of this infant church, and then removed to Portland, Me., where he became the pastor of the First Baptist church. Here he continued until removed by death, March 6, 1814. Mr. Blood was strongly Calvinistic in his doctrinal views, and was a good type of a large class of some of the most worthy and successful ministers of his denomination in the times in which he lived. He was always strongly in favor of "law and order." His preaching was attended with powerful revivals, but he always discouraged an excess of mere animal feeling, and knew well the difference between the genuine operations of the Holy Spirit and mere human excitement. We are told that "in the earlier part of his ministry, attending a meeting marked with excitement and zeal, but, as he thought, 'not according to knowledge,' a good woman, at the close, came to him, with uplifted hands, exclaiming, 'Oh, Mr. Blood, did you ever see such a meeting before?' 'No,' he promptly replied, 'and I hope I never shall again.'" The reply was the true index of the man, and of the principles by which he was governed through his ministerial life.

Blue Mountain College, located at Blue Mountain, Miss., is the leading female college in North Mississippi; Rev. M. P. Lowery, D.D., Principal.

Boardman, George Dana, D.D., son of the Rev. George Dana Boardman, and step-son of Rev. Adoniram Judson, was born in Tavoy, Burmah, Aug. 18, 1828. At six years of age he embarked for America, and journeyed the entire distance alone. During the voyage, which lasted nine months, he was subjected to severe hardship and ill treatment, and was nearly captured by Malay pirates when in a small boat off Singapore. But the young and enfeebled life was graciously spared for a career of remarkable vigor and usefulness; he was baptized, while yet a lad, by Dr. William Lamson, at Thomaston, Me.; entered Brown University in 1846; became disheartened during his Sophomore year, and spent two years in Indiana, Illinois, and Missouri, reading law and engaging in mercantile pursuits. He subsequently re-entered Brown University, and graduated in 1852; graduated from Newton Theological Institution in 1855. In consequence of pulmonary troubles he settled at Barnwell Court-House, S. C., where he was ordained, December, 1855. After a five months' pastorate he returned to the North, and became pastor of the Second church at Rochester, N. Y., where he remained until May, 1864. He then entered upon the pastorate of the First church at Philadelphia, where he still remains, esteemed, honored, and beloved.

To his wife he lovingly dedicated one of his choicest publications, speaking of her as one "whose poetic insight into the meaning of nature has been my inspiration."

During his pastorate in Philadelphia he has traveled extensively in Europe, Asia, and Africa;

GEORGE DANA BOARDMAN, D.D.

and in his journeys abroad, as well as in his studies at home, he has, with careful intensity, sought to understand the truths of divine revelation. With a soul full of devout inquiry, and with an intellectual vigor that sometimes threatened the prostration of his physical powers, he has diligently endeavored to know and preach the gospel of Christ; and those who attend upon his ministry are enriched by his devout and scholarly expositions. At the Wednesday evening services of the church he has delivered 184 lectures on the Life of our Lord, 55 on the Acts of the Apostles, 14 on the Epistles to the Thessalonians, 16 on the Epistle to the Galatians, 39 on the Epistles to the Corinthians, 39 on the Epistle to the Romans, 11 on the Epistle to the Ephesians, 8 on the Epistle to the Colossians, 12 on the Epistle to the Philippians, 14 on the Epistles to Timothy, 3 on the Epistles to Titus, and 1 on the Epistle to Philemon, making 396 weekly expository lectures. These are to be continued through the entire New Testament. He has also published numerous sermons, pamphlets, and review articles, etc.

During 1878 he delivered 14 lectures on "The Creative Week" to immense audiences gathered at mid-day on successive Tuesdays in the hall of the Young Men's Christian Association. These lectures have since been published in book-form. He has also published "Studies in the Model Prayer" and "Epiphanies of the Risen Lord."

His varied and cultured abilities have received repeated and well-merited recognition. The missionary and educational boards of the denomination have been honored by his membership; and at the Saratoga meetings in 1880 he was unanimously chosen president of the American Baptist Missionary Union. He is also a trustee of the University of Pennsylvania and a member of the American Philosophical Society. Such honors justly belong to one who is widely known and esteemed as a courteous and scholarly Christian gentleman.

Boardman, Rev. George Dana, Sr., was born in Livermore, Me., Feb. 8, 1801. His father, Rev. Sylvanus Boardman, at the time of his birth was the pastor of the Baptist church in that place. Mr. Boardman was a member of the first class that was formed in Waterville College; he graduated in 1822. He was ordained at North Yarmouth, Me., Feb. 16, 1825, and, with his wife, sailed in the 16th of July for Calcutta, arriving there early in the following December. They took up their residence at Chitpore, near Calcutta. Here they remained until March 20, 1827, when they embarked for Amherst, in Burmah. From Amherst Mr. Boardman proceeded at once to Maulmain. In April, 1828, Mr. and Mrs. Boardman removed to Tavoy, and commenced missionary work in that town. It was a place of upwards of 9000 inhabitants. It was, moreover, one of the principal strongholds of the religion of Gaudama, filled with temples and shrines dedicated to heathen worship. Within the limits of the town there were nearly a thousand pagodas. As soon as his zayat was built Mr. Boardman began his work with apostolic zeal, and with a firm trust in God that this work would not be in vain. Two converts soon rewarded his labors, and a wide-spread interest in the new religion began very soon to show itself in Tavoy.

In the family of Mr. Boardman there lived a man in middle life, once a slave, but now free through the kindness of the missionaries, who had bought his freedom. This man was a Karen, Ko Thah-byu by name. He belonged to a race among whom Mr. Boardman was to gain a multitude of converts to the Christian religion. This people are found in the forests and mountains of Burmah and Siam, and in some sections of China. The name by which they are known is Kanairs or Karens, which means *wild men.* They seem to have been singularly prepared to receive the gospel. It was to this interesting race that Mr. Boardman, assisted by his faithful co-laborer, Ko Thah-byu, directed his principal attention in the prosecution of his missionary work.

The constitution of Mr. Boardman, never very strong, began to give way under the severe labors of his missionary life. He had been entreated once more to visit the Karens in their villages, and administer to the new converts the sacred rite of Christian baptism. In spite of his feeble health he determined to yield to their request. Lying on a cot borne on the shoulders of the Karens, and accompanied by Mrs. Boardman, and Mr. and Mrs. Mason, who had lately arrived at Tavoy, he set out on his journey. Three days they toiled slowly on through the valleys and over the hills of Burmah, and reached at length the zayat which the faithful disciples had built for them. "It stood," says Prof. Gammell, "on the margin of a beautiful stream, at the foot of a range of mountains, whose sloping sides were lined with the villages of the strange people whom they had come to visit. More than a hundred were already assembled at the zayat, nearly half of whom were candidates for baptism. At the close of the day, just as the sun was sinking behind the mountains, his cot was placed at the river-side, in the midst of the solemn company that was gathered to witness the first baptism which that ancient mountain-stream had ever beheld. As he gazed in silent gratitude upon the scene, he felt that his work was finished, his last promise to these scattered disciples was now fulfilled, and he was ready to depart in peace." The next day the missionaries started to return to Tavoy, hoping to reach the home of Mr. Boardman, so that he might die beneath his own roof, but it was ordered otherwise. Before the close of the second day's journey the end had come, and the weary spirit passed to its home in the skies. The event took place Feb. 11, 1831. The remains were taken to Tavoy and laid in a tomb, in what was at one time a Buddhist grave. How much had been crowded into that brief thirty years' life! What trains of holy influence were set in motion within the few short years of that missionary career! We may, as a denomination, be truly grateful to God that he gave us so pure, so holy, so thoroughly consecrated a pioneer in the early missions among the Burmese and the Karens.

Boardman, Rev. Sylvanus, father of the honored missionary, George Dana Boardman, and grandfather of Rev. G. D. Boardman, D.D., of Philadelphia, was born in Chilmark, Mass., Sept. 15, 1757. In early life his religious connection was with the Congregationalists, but in 1793 he changed his sentiments and became a Baptist. In February, 1802, he was ordained pastor of the church with which he originally united, the First Baptist church in Livermore, Me. Here he remained not far from eight years,—1802-10,—when he was called to the pastoral charge of the church in North Yarmouth, Me. With this church he continued until 1816, and then accepted a call to New Sharon, Me. Of the church in this place he was pastor about twenty-seven years, when he was compelled, on account of feeble heath and the infirmities of age, to resign. He lived to a good old age, and died in New Sharon, March 16, 1845.

Bodenbender, Rev. Conrad.—The subject of this sketch was born July 10, 1823, in Heskem, Hesse-Cassel, Germany. He was brought up in the Lutheran faith, and confirmed when he was fourteen years old. In the twenty-second year of his age he met with Baptists, and was converted. On the 16th of June, at midnight, he was baptized upon profession of his faith. Baptism could not at that time be administered in daylight on account of fierce persecution. Emigrating to America in 1849, Mr. Bodenbender remained for two years in Buffalo, N. Y., working as a cabinet-maker. At the expiration of that time, feeling called to preach, he entered the German Department of Rochester Theological Seminary, pursuing his studies from 1854 to 1858. His first charge was in Newark, N. J., where he was ordained pastor of the German Baptist church in September, 1856. Since leaving Newark he has been pastor successively over the German churches of Tavistock and Berlin, Ontario, and Chicago, Ill. Since 1873 Mr. Bodenbender has been the honored pastor of the First German church in Buffalo, N. Y. Calm and thoughtful, scriptural in his method of sermonizing, genial in social intercourse, unblamable in character, Mr. Bodenbender is widely known and highly esteemed in the German churches.

Boise, James Robinson, Ph.D., D.D., LL.D. —Dr. Boise was born in Blandford, Hampshire Co., Mass., Jan. 27, 1815. He was descended from a French family, which took refuge from persecution, with many of the Huguenots, in the north of Ireland, and afterwards emigrated to New England. His grandfather was the second white child born in his native town. His father, Enos Boise, was for many years the only Baptist in Blandford, and was in intimate relations with Gurdon Robins and Elisha Cushman, prominent Baptists of Connecticut, and founders of the *Christian Secretary.* On the side of his mother, Alice Robinson, he was related to Edward Robinson, the eminent Biblical scholar. At the age of sixteen he was baptized, and not long afterwards repaired to Hamilton Seminary, now Madison University, to begin a course of classical studies. After about three years spent in Hamilton he entered Brown University, where he graduated in 1840. He was then elected tutor, and three years later assistant Professor of Ancient Languages. In 1850 he resigned his position in Brown University, and spent a year in Germany and six months in Greece and Italy. On his return home he again took a position in Brown University, but six months later accepted an invitation to the University of Michigan as Professor of the Greek Language and Literature. Here he remained till Jan. 1, 1868, when he accepted the Professorship of Greek in the University of Chicago. In 1877 he was called to the chair of New Testament Interpretation in the Baptist Union Theological Seminary, which he still occupies.

JAMES ROBINSON BOISE, PH.D., D.D., LL.D.

In 1868, Professor Boise received the degree of Doctor of Philosophy from the University of Tübingen, in Germany. In the same year the degree of Doctor of Laws was conferred by the University of Michigan, and in 1879 that of Doctor of Divinity by Brown University.

The reputation of Dr. Boise rests chiefly upon his success as a teacher, and as editor of Greek classical authors. He is best known as editor of portions of Homer, Herodotus, Thucydides, Xenophon, Plato, and Demosthenes, and also as author of "Exercises in Greek Composition." His attention is now turned towards similar labors in connection with the New Testament. His editions of classical works are valued for their critical accuracy and their scholarly finish, alike in versions of the text and in annotations. As a teacher, Dr. Boise is stimulating, skillful, and exact,—a born educator. In the wide circle of his personal friends he is valued for qualities of sterling excellence as a Christian and as a man.

Bolles, Augustus, son of Rev. David and Susannah (Moore) Bolles, was born in Ashford, Conn., Dec. 28, 1776; inherited superior powers; received a good education; commenced preaching in February, 1810; ordained pastor of the Baptist church in Tolland, Conn., in May, 1814; in May,

1818, settled with the church in Bloomfield, and remained till 1825, when impaired health from severe labor induced his removal to Hartford; preached for several years to destitute churches; for about four years ably conducted the denominational paper of the State, the *Christian Secretary;* in 1837 removed to Indiana and organized a Baptist church at La Porte; returned to Connecticut, and in 1839 began to preach at Colchester; supplied the church for some years, but refused settlement. He was a rare scholar and preacher; died in Colchester.

Bolles, David, son of Enoch and grandson of John Bolles, was born in New London, Conn., Jan. 14, 1743; married, Jan. 10, 1765, Susannah Moore, of New London, and moved to Ashford (now Eastford), Conn.; in October, 1797, in his fiftieth year, was ordained an evangelist at the annual meeting of the Stonington Union Association; preached the gospel to destitute churches in the vicinity of Ashford; in June, 1801, settled with the First Baptist church in Hartford, and remained two years; chose to labor with country churches that were destitute; left four sons,— Judge David Bolles and three Baptist preachers.

Bolles, Hon. James G., son of Rev. Matthew, was born in Eastford (then Ashford), Conn., Jan. 17, 1802; when fifteen, entered a printing-office in Bridgeport, Conn., and remained till twenty; went to Boston, Mass., and was partner in the firm that published the *Christian Watchman;* in 1825 settled in Hartford, Conn., for a time as clerk; became secretary of the Hartford Fire Insurance Company; then president of the North American Insurance Company; under President Lincoln was collector of internal revenue in first Connecticut district; converted in 1840; baptized Jan. 24, 1841; united with First Baptist church in Hartford; chosen deacon Feb. 4, 1845; was noted for benevolence, purity, courtesy, and consistent piety; in Dr. R. Trumbull's writings he is sketched as the "Christian gentleman"; discriminating reader of books; greatly beloved; was successful in business; acquired wealth; gave largely; made legacies to benevolent objects; died March 27, 1871, aged sixty-nine years.

Bolles, John, son of Thomas Bolles, was born in New London, Conn., in 1678; dissatisfied with the views of the standing order, he adopted those of the Baptists, and was baptized by John Rogers, the founder of the "Rogerene sect"; engaged with tongue and pen in theological discussions; he was of vigorous mind and great earnestness; published several books and tracts devoted to the cause of religious liberty; was the grandfather of the evangelist, David Bolles; died in 1767, in his ninetieth year; was a pioneer in bringing into Connecticut freedom of conscience.

Bolles, Hon. John Augustus, LL.D., son of Rev. Matthew Bolles, a Baptist minister, was born in Ashford, now Eastford, Conn., April 16, 1809. He entered Amherst College in 1825, where he spent two years, and then became a student in Brown University, where he was graduated with high honor in the class of 1829. For a short time after leaving college he was principal of the preparatory department of the Columbian College, Washington. He studied law in the office of Hon. Richard Fletcher, in Boston, and was admitted to the bar of Suffolk in 1833, and soon acquired distinction both as a lawyer and a man of letters. For several years he was a member of the Massachusetts Board of Education. When the Boston *Daily Journal* was commenced, in 1833, he was one of its original editors. In 1834 he wrote the prize essay for the American Peace Society; the same year he was appointed Secretary of State for Massachusetts. He continued in the practice of his profession in Boston and occupied in literary pursuits until the breaking out of the civil war, when he received an appointment on the military staff of Gen. John A. Dix. While serving in this capacity he was appointed judge-advocate of the Seventh Army Corps, and provost-judge, with the rank of major. Subsequently his rank was raised to that of lieutenant-colonel, and he received the appointment of solicitor of the navy and naval judge-advocate-general, and was stationed at Washington, where he died, May 25, 1878.

"At all periods of his life," says Prof. Gammell, "Mr. Bolles was exceedingly fond of literary studies. His published writings, besides those which were official, are numerous, and are scattered through many of the leading magazines and journals of the day, the most considerable of which are the *North American Review,* the *Christian Review,* and the *Atlantic Monthly.* He was also the author of an essay on "Usury and Usury Laws," which was published by the Boston Chamber of Commerce, and led to important modifications of the laws on this subject then existing in Massachusetts. He received from Brown University, in 1866, the honorary degree of Doctor of Laws.

Bolles, Lucius, D.D., was born in Ashford, Conn., Sept. 25, 1799, of godly parents, who spared no pains in his early religious education. He became a member of Brown University in 1797, and graduated under President Maxcy in 1801. His conversion took place in one of the vacations of his college course, and he decided to turn his attention to the gospel ministry. For nearly three years he pursued his theological studies under Dr. Stillman, at the same time making himself familiar with the practical duties of the profession to which he meant to devote his future life. Having completed his term of study, he accepted an invitation to become the pastor of the recently-formed First

Baptist church in Salem, Mass., and was ordained on the 9th of January, 1805. The result of such a course of procedure was most happy. The new society greatly prospered, and in a year from the time of their pastor's ordination entered a new, and for the times elegant, edifice, which, remodeled and improved from time to time, is now the beautiful house of worship of the First church in Salem. The ministry of Dr. Bolles continued for twenty-two years, and was a singularly happy one. In very many respects it was a model pastorate, regarded as such by the church he so long and so faithfully served, even down to the present day. There were 512 added to the church during the first twenty years of his ministry. The little church of 24 members had grown to be two bands, a flourishing colony having gone out to constitute a second Baptist church in Salem.

In the earlier stages of that grand movement which took its origin from the appeals of Judson and Rice to the Baptist churches to enter with heartier zeal into the work of foreign missions, Dr. Bolles took the warmest interest. At his suggestion, as far back as 1812, a society had been formed for the purpose of aiding in the translation of the Holy Scriptures into the Eastern languages, under the supervision of Dr. Carey. This society was called the "Salem Bible Translation and Foreign Missionary Society," and was among the earliest organizations in the denomination having for its object the conversion of the world to Christ. And when, at length, the rising tide of sentiment and thorough-conviction of the duty of the church to carry out the last commission of her ascending Lord, assumed more definite shape and outline in the formation of a foreign missionary society, it was not surprising that the eyes of his brethren were turned to Dr. Bolles as a most suitable person to be its corresponding secretary. He received his appointment to that office in 1826, and discharged its onerous and often delicate duties for more than sixteen years with a devotion which seemed never to tire, and a zeal which no discouragement could dampen. How much the cause of foreign missions owes to his prudence and discretion and good common sense the records of eternity alone will disclose.

Having most faithfully served his generation by the will of God, the good man fell asleep in Jesus. His death occurred Jan. 5, 1844.

Bolles, Rev. Matthew, son of Rev. David and Susannah (Moore) Bolles, was born in Ashford, Conn., April 21, 1769; had a good education; in early and middle life engaged in secular business; in 1812 began to preach in Pleasant Valley, Lyme, Conn., where he was ordained and settled in June, 1813, remaining till 1816, his labors being greatly blessed; from 1817 to 1838 was successively pastor of churches in Fairfield, Conn., Milford, N. H., Marblehead and West Bridgewater, Mass.; an eloquent, effective preacher, mighty in prayer; died in Hartford, of typhus fever, Sept. 26, 1838, in his seventieth year.

Bond, Prof. Emmons Paley, son of Joseph and Esther (Ford) Bond, was born in Canterbury, Conn., Sept. 6, 1824; in 1840 taught a school in Tolland, where he was converted; baptized in November, 1840, by Rev. Sylvester Barrows, and united with the Tolland Baptist church; fitted for college in the Connecticut Literary Institution; entered Brown University in 1846, and graduated in 1851, meanwhile having been an assistant teacher in the Worcester Academy from February, 1849, to August, 1850; studied for the ministry at the Hamilton Theological Seminary, N. Y.; in October, 1852, settled with the Baptist church in New Britain, Conn.; ordained Dec. 2, 1852, and remained till August, 1865; during this pastorate, from November, 1864, to May, 1865, was chaplain of the 14th Conn. Vols. in the Army of the Potomac; became principal of the Connecticut Literary Institution at Suffield, and filled that chair five years; in October, 1870, settled with the Baptist church in Agawam, Mass., and remained about three years; in 1873 was chosen Professor of Latin, Greek, Intellectual and Moral Philosophy in Peddie Institute, N. J., and after three years became acting principal; in May, 1879, settled with the Baptist church in Wethersfield, Conn., where he now (1880) labors; wrote the Sunday-school Expositions for the *Christian Era*, of Boston, from January, 1873, to December, 1875; a man of universal talent and strength.

Bond, Rev. William P., son of Lewis Bond, was born in Bertie Co., N. C., Oct. 16, 1813. He professed religion at Chapel Hill, in 1831, and was baptized by Dr. Hooper; united with Mount Carmel church in 1832; moved to Tennessee in 1837, and settled in Brownsville, and engaged in the legal profession; was elected judge of the Circuit Court in 1865, which office he held until 1871; January, 1871, was ordained to the gospel ministry; Presbytery, Revs. G. W. Young, Mat. Hillsman, I. R. Branham, and J. F. B. Mays; and he became pastor of the Brownsville Baptist church, which position he held for three years. Brother Bond as a judge wore the *ermine* with great dignity. As a speaker he is fluent and impressive. His moral character is unsurpassed. His attainments are of the first order, and yet he is very modest and unpretending. He was at one time the president of the West Tennessee Baptist Convention, and he was elected the president of the Tennessee Baptist Convention at its organization.

Boomer, Rev. Job Borden, was born in Fall River, Mass., Sept. 8, 1793, his father being the pastor of the Baptist church in Charlton, Mass., for thirty years. He was ordained in Sutton, Mass., June 9, 1819, and like his father had a long and useful pastorate in one church, his connection with it continuing twenty-four years. At the end of this period he resigned, and subsequently sustained the pastoral relation to two other churches, the one in East Brookfield, Mass., and the other in Uxbridge, Mass. He spent his last days in Worcester, where he died Aug. 16, 1864. In that part of his native State in which he passed his ministerial life his name is held in high esteem, and his saintly virtues will long be cherished by the many to whom he broke the bread of life.

Boone, Col. Daniel, the celebrated hunter and explorer, though a Baptist in principle, was never in communion with any church. He was a man of great integrity, enlarged charity to his race, and profound reverence to God. His bravery was undaunted, and he was almost womanly in the gentleness and amiability of his manners. His love of the beauties of nature, rather than his fondness for adventure, led him to spend most of his life in the great forests of the West. He explored Kentucky in 1769–71, moved to the Territory in 1775. About 1795 he went to Missouri, where he died Sept. 26, 1820, in the eighty-sixth year of his age. His remains and those of his wife were removed to Kentucky and interred in the State cemetery at Frankfort in 1845.

Boone, Rev. J. B., was born in Northampton Co., N. C., Oct. 1, 1836; baptized at thirteen; went to Wake Forest College in 1860; served in the army during the war; was ordained in 1867; spent two years at the theological seminary at Greenville, S. C.; was pastor in Charlotte; was the first principal of a graded school in North Carolina; has been for several years pastor at Statesville and Salisbury; is moderator of the South Yadkin Association; a man of solid worth, strong faith, and unflagging perseverance. Mr. Boone is a trustee of Wake Forest College.

Boone, Hon. Levi D., M.D.—Since 1836 Dr. Boone has been a resident of Chicago; at present, therefore, one of its oldest, as he is one of its most respected citizens. He was a native of Kentucky, and grand-nephew of the famous Daniel Boone. He was born Dec. 8, 1808. His father died while the son was still but a boy, his death being the ultimate effect of a wound received at the battle of Horseshoe Bend, in Kentucky. In 1829, Dr. Boone removed to Illinois, his home being first at Edwardsville, where he entered the office of Dr. B. F. Edwards, subsequently at Hillsborough. Upon the breaking out of the Black Hawk war, Dr. Boone at once offered his services, the first man in his county to do so, and in command of a company of cavalry served till the close of the war. In 1836, as mentioned above, he made his home at Chicago, where he has since resided.

Dr. Boone as a physician was successful and beloved. During the three cholera years, 1848, 1849, and 1850, he served as city physician, filling that position of exposure and exhausting labor to eminent acceptance. He was, however, early called to positions of public service apart from his profession: for three terms, a period of six years, as alderman of the city, and in 1855 as mayor. It was during his mayoralty that the improvements of various kinds which so much changed the character of Chicago as a place of residence were either commenced or so organized as to secure their rapid prosecution; the high school and reform school were also established, while in the same period that growth in population began which made Chicago the marvel of American cities. In all posts of public service, and in his relation to public questions of every kind, Dr. Boone has commanded universal respect as a patriotic citizen and an able administrator. During the war, notwithstanding his Southern birth, he took his position upon the right side, and was conspicuous by his activity in behalf of the government. Dr. Boone has associated with his medical practice extensive business relations, and of late years these latter have chiefly occupied him. In all such he has ever been respected for his sagacity and integrity, and even amidst the reverses consequent upon disasters that have befallen the city, has borne himself resolutely and with fidelity to every manner of trust.

Dr. Boone was one of the earliest members of the First Baptist church in Chicago, and during many years was a deacon in that church,—one of the most liberal, active, and valued of the entire body. For some years past he has been a member of the Michigan Avenue church. In all the enterprises of the denomination centring at Chicago he has influentially shared, giving largely of his means and holding a foremost place in all denominational councils. He was one of the incorporators of the university at Chicago, and during nearly the entire history of that institution has been perhaps the most influential man upon its board of trustees, contributing generously to its funds. Among the Baptist laymen of Illinois Dr. Boone's name should stand with those which it is almost a denominational duty and privilege to hold in lasting remembrance.

Boone, Rev. Squire, a celebrated explorer of Kentucky, son of Squire Boone, and brother of the famous hunter, Col. Daniel Boone, was born in Berks Co., Pa., in 1737. Soon after his birth his parents removed to North Carolina, and settled on the Yadkin, eight miles from Wilkesborough. Here he remained until 1770. It is not known at what period he united with the church or when he began to preach, but it was previous to his removing to the West. The first day of May, 1769, Daniel Boone and five other men set out from the Yadkin "to explore the wilderness of America in quest of the country called Kentucky." On the 7th of June they first saw from an eminence "the beautiful level" of Kentucky. They spent the summer and fall in hunting. The other members of the company having returned home, Boone and Steward were captured by the Indians, December 22. After seven days they escaped and returned to camp on Red River. "About this time," says Boone, in his autobiography, "my brother, Squire Boone, with another adventurer, who came to explore the country shortly after us, . . . accidentally found our camp." "Our meeting, fortunately in the wilderness, gave us the most sensible satisfaction. Soon after this John Steward was killed by the savages, and the man that came with my brother returned home." The two brothers, now left alone, built "a cottage," and spent the winter in hunting. On the 1st of May, 1770, Squire Boone, unaccompanied, returned to his home for horses and ammunition, and rejoined his brother on the 27th of July. The two brothers explored the country together as far west as the Cumberland River, giving names to the different rivers. In March, 1771, the brothers returned to North Carolina. In the summer of 1775 they again moved to Kentucky, and settled in a fort on the south bank of the Kentucky River, in what is now Madison County. The first marriage of white people in Kentucky was that of Samuel Henderson to Betsy Calloway, and was celebrated by Squire Boone, Aug. 7, 1776. Squire Boone remained in the fort at Boonesborough until 1779, when he built a fort in what is now Shelby Co., Ky. He was prominent in the political affairs of Kentucky, a member of the Transylvania Convention, and a delegate from the Territory of Kentucky to the Virginia Legislature. He moved from Shelby County to Louisville, and a short time before his death, which occurred in 1815, he moved across the Ohio into Indiana Territory. His son, Squire Boone, and his grandson, Thomas Boone, were valuable Baptist ministers in Kentucky.

Booth, Rev. Abraham, was born in Blackwell, Derbyshire, England, May 20, 1734. At ten years of age he was first made to feel a deep concern for his salvation. At twenty-one he was baptized among the General or Arminian Baptists. They encouraged him to preach among them. While engaged in ministering to a church at Kirbywood House he at first was a bitter enemy of "personal election and particular redemption," and he printed a poem "in reproach" of these doctrines. When it pleased God to open his eyes to see the whole truth he began to plan a work that would commend the doctrines of grace, and when he was about thirty-three years old he published his "Reign of Grace." Speaking of his Arminian poem, he says, "As a poem, if considered in a critical light, it is despicable; if in a theological view, detestable; as it is an impotent attack on the honor of divine grace, in respect to its glorious freeness, and bold opposition to the sovereignty of God, and as such I renounce it."

His "Reign of Grace" was published through the persuasions of Mr. Venn, a distinguished Episcopal clergyman, who took copies sufficient to enable the author to pay the printer. The publication of this work was the cause of Mr. Booth's removal to London. He was ordained pastor of the Prescott Street church in that city Feb. 16, 1769. In this field of labor Mr. Booth was eminently useful, and obtained a celebrity which will never perish.

He was a man of vast reading in his own language and in Latin, and he was justly reputed one of the most learned men of his day. His friend Dr. Newman says, "As a divine he was a star of the first magnitude, and one of the brightest ornaments of the Baptist denomination to which he belonged. Firm in his attachment to his religious principles, he despised the popular cant about charity, and cultivated genuine candor, which is alike remote from the laxity of latitudinarians and the censoriousness of bigots." His "Reign of Grace," and indeed all his works, will continue to instruct and delight the Christian world till the end of time.

He was instrumental in founding Stepney College, which has been such a blessing to the British Baptist churches.

Mr. Booth was a man of strict integrity, of great devoutness, and of a large knowledge of the divine Word. Few men have served the cause of God by their writings, sermons, counsels, and example more effectively than Abraham Booth. He died Jan. 27, 1806, in his seventy-third year, after a pastorate of thirty-seven years in London. He was the author of eight works, besides a number of printed sermons; some of these works have passed through many editions.

Booth, Rev. A. H., a leading minister in Mississippi, was born in Virginia in 1822, and began to preach in Tennessee in 1845. For many years he has exerted a wide influence in Mississippi in building up and strengthening the churches.

Booth, Rev. C. O.—About thirty-eight years of age, reared under favorable circumstances, liberally educated, first studied and practiced medicine, then pastor at Citronville, then at Talladega, now in Montgomery. Has labored some among the colored people of the State as a missionary; a graceful speaker, a gifted preacher, apt in the selection of language, and though a man of feeble health, his services have been of distinguished value in organizing the interests of colored Baptists in Alabama.

Borum, Joseph Henry, D.D., son of Deacon James and Martha (Tucker) Borum, was born in

JOSEPH HENRY BORUM, D.D.

Prince Edward Co., Va., July 20, 1816. His parents were highly respectable. Both were members of the Baptist church of Christ. His father and family moved from Virginia to Tennessee, December, 1828, Joseph being then twelve years old, and settled in Wilson County, eight miles east of Lebanon, where he remained three years; and in December, 1831, he removed to Tipton County, where he resided up to the time of his death, which occurred March 29, 1843.

After devoting a number of years to mercantile pursuits, Mr. Borum, on Sept. 20, 1836, made a public profession of religion among the Methodists. There being no Baptist church nearer than fifteen miles, he was over-persuaded by his Methodist friends to unite with them, having the promise of the preacher in charge to immerse him, with which, however, he never complied. The next Conference sent another preacher, to whom he communicated the fact that he had joined the Methodists with the express understanding that he was to be immersed. The preacher now in charge put it off from time to time. A sermon against immersion by the presiding elder taught Mr. Borum his duty, and a few days after he heard it he presented himself to Beaver Creek church, Fayette Co., Tenn., for membership, where he was cordially received, but at the time it had no pastor. He was referred to Rev. Peter S. Gayle, then living near Brownsville, Tenn., to baptize him, who, on Aug. 17, 1837, near Covington, Tenn., buried him with Christ in baptism. The Beaver Creek church being without a pastor, and having no regular meetings, he could not be licensed to preach. Impressed with the duty of calling sinners to repentance, he conferred with several brethren on the subject, who urged him to go forward and preach the gospel. So, on the third Lord's day in September, one month after his baptism, he preached his first sermon at Liberty meeting-house, Tipton Co., Tenn., forty years ago.

On March 24, 1839, a church was organized at Covington, Tenn., of which he was a constituent member. He was chosen clerk at its organization, and soon after he was elected deacon. He was ordained to the gospel ministry by the Covington church on the 21st day of September, 1845. Not long after this he removed to Durhamville, Lauderdale Co., Tenn., and united with the Elon church, and became associated with Rev. Geo. W. Young, the pastor of said church, worshiping in Haywood County. Durhamville was then the only Regular Baptist church in Lauderdale County. Mr. Young and he rode and preached together (mainly in Lauderdale County) for about three years, when they had to separate to take charge of churches which they had constituted. There are now twenty Baptist churches, white and colored, in the same county. Mr. Borum and Mr. Young never engaged in union meetings, nor did they invite Pedobaptist ministers into their pulpits to preach, regarding this practice as inconsistent with Bible teachings and injurious to the truth. By pursuing this straightforward and consistent course the Lord abundantly blessed their labors. Mr. Borum has served the following churches: Elon, Grace, Ripley, Covington, Dyersburg, Newbern, Stanton, Mount Olive, Harmony, Society Hill, Salem, and Poplar Grove, in Tennessee, and also Osceola, Ark. He had charge of the Elon church for about twenty-eight years, first and last. He served the Covington church about fifteen years, and the Dyersburg church ten years. He and Rev. G. W. Young assisted in the organization of Elon, Salem, Hermon, Grace (Pleasant Plains, in conjunction with Rev. M. G. Turner), and Ripley, in Lauderdale County, Dyersburg, in Dyer County. Rev. J. H. Borum has acted as agent for the Brownsville Female College, and the West Tennessee Baptist Convention and the Southern Baptist Publication Society, Memphis, Tenn. He has been clerk of Big Hatchie Association for twenty-eight years, and moderator for two years; and he has acted as secretary of the West Tennessee Baptist Convention and the Tennessee Baptist Convention for thirty years. He is now engaged in writing the history of the Baptist ministers of Tennessee (living and dead) by the request of his brethren of the State. He is a "*Land-marker*," deeming their practice as most consistent, and most agreeable to the teachings of God's Word. He has removed to Dyersburg, Dyer Co., Tenn., where he expects to finish his course. He is now (1880) the pastor of Dyersburg, Elon, Newbern, and Poplar Grove churches.

Bostick, Rev. Joseph M., a native of Beaufort, now Hampton Co., S. C. He grew up surrounded

REV. JOSEPH M. BOSTICK.

by every luxury and advantage that wealth could afford, yet remarkably free from the vices too often incident to his station in life. He graduated at Furman University, Greenville, S. C., and at Princeton Theological Seminary. He was for several years pastor at Cheraw, S. C. He now ministers to the church at Barnwell, S. C., where he is greatly beloved.

Naturally an utter stranger to fear, it is well for him and others that he was converted in early life. His vehemence was at once turned into a new channel. His piety is more like that of Paul and John than the cold and respectable type now so common. Generosity is, perhaps, even a fault in him. His talents, superior literary attainments, and his devoted piety fit him eminently for usefulness in a far higher position than he has ever occupied. His modesty has kept him in the background, while others without a tithe of his qualifications have occupied more conspicuous positions.

Bostick, Rev. W. M., was born in Richmond Co., N. C.; attended an academy in Carthage at eighteen; was baptized by Rev. A. D. Blackwood in August, 1853; read theology for two years with the Rev. Archibald McQueen, a Presbyterian minister; was ordained by a Presbytery, consisting of Revs. Enoch Crutchfield, John Mercer, Nath. Richardson, and F. M. Jordan, and has been, since 1871, the moderator of the Pee Dee Association.

Boston, First Baptist Church.—On the 7th of June, 1865, the First church in Boston celebrated its two hundredth anniversary.

On "the 28th of the third month, 1665, in Charlestown, Mass., the church of Christ, commonly, though falsely, called Anabaptists, were gathered together, and entered into fellowship and communion with each other; engaging to walk together in all the appointments of their Lord and Master, the Lord Jesus Christ, as far as he should be pleased to make known his mind and will unto them, by his Word and Spirit, and then were baptized." Here follows the names of sundry persons who, with others from Old England of like faith, formed themselves into a Baptist church. Such is the first record on the books of the First Baptist church in Boston. The "third month" here alluded to dates from the 1st of March, according to the old reckoning, and taking into the account the change from the "old style" to the "new style," we are brought to the 7th of June, as corresponding to "the 28th of the third month."

The little band of disciples of Christ began at once to feel the rigor of ecclesiastical persecution. Having erected what we doubt not was a plain, unpretending house of worship, they were, by legal enactment, forbidden to use it for religious purposes. Orders were issued to the marshal to see to it that its doors were not opened, and in the faithful performance of his duty he caused to be nailed up on the door this interesting order:

"All persons are to take notice, that by order of the court the doors of this house are shut up, and that they are inhibited to hold any meeting therein, or to open the doors thereof, without license from authority, till the court take further order, as they will answer the contrary at their peril.

"EDWARD RAWSON, Secretary."

In vain they protested against such treatment, and pointed out the inconsistency of those who had fled from persecution in the Old World resorting to it in the New. A public disputation was appointed by the governor, with the hope that the obstinate Baptists might be convinced of their error, and come into the more respectable and the more orderly fold of the "standing order." The time set apart to hold this important discussion was nine o'clock in the morning of April 14, 1668. "The Baptists," says Dr. Neale, "were on hand promptly at the appointed hour, each with his New Testament, ready marked, and the leaves turned down. Nothing pleased them better than an opportunity for free speech and Scripture quotations. They came from all quarters. Three brethren were sent from the church in Newport to assist their brethren in Boston, it was said, though the Boston Baptists then, as now, felt abundantly competent to manage their own affairs. Providence, no doubt, was ably represented. The followers of Roger Williams were always courageous, and like the sons of Rhode Island in the late conflict, were never known to flee or flinch in the presence of an enemy." And yet after all "the flourish of arms," the poor Baptists were regarded as miserable heretics, whom learned divines might lecture, but to whom they were not permitted to reply. Their cause was already prejudged before the appointed hearing commenced.

As the years rolled by, and a more liberal spirit began to spread through the community, the severity of persecution was mitigated. The first pastor of the church was Thomas Gould. He was followed by Isaac Hull, both of them being assisted in their work by John Russell. Pastors and associate "elders" seem to have been the order of things for several years. We come down to the time of the ordination of Elisha Callender, a young man of much promise, who had graduated from Harvard College in the class of 1810, and was set apart to the work of the gospel ministry May 21, 1718. Mr. Callender was the greatly beloved pastor of the church for twenty years, and died March 31, 1738. His last words were, "I shall sleep in Jesus."

The next pastor was Rev. Jeremiah Lundy, who held the office for twenty-five years. He was followed by Samuel Stillman, D.D., of whose pastorate the reader will find a full account in the biographical sketch of him in this volume. Dr. Neale says of him, "No pastor before or since was ever more beloved by his church. His popularity was uninterrupted, and greater, if possible, in his old age than in his youth. A few individuals who sat under his ministry, and who were quite young when he was an old man, still survive. They never weary of talking about him, and even now speak of this as Dr. Stillman's church. They looked at the venerable pastor not only with the profoundest respect, but with the observant eye of childhood. They noticed and remembered everything in his external appearance, his wig and gown and bands, his horse and carriage, and negro man Jephtha,— how he walked, how he talked, how he baptized, the peculiar manner in which he began his prayers, 'O thou Father of mercies and God of all grace.'

"Dr. Stillman," continues Dr. Neale, "was probably the most popular orator of his day. The most distinguished men in the Commonwealth were often present at his public services. The elder President Adams was a delighted listener to his sermons. Governor Hancock became, in the latter part of his life, a regular member of his congregation. Persons who cared nothing for his theology were attracted by his fame as a public speaker. A strange gentleman of this class was one day present at church, and seemed restless and uneasy under the strong doctrines of human depravity, divine sovereignty, and future retribution that were often on the preacher's lips. On the present occasion his denunciations of sin had been unusually pointed and scathing. 'Really,' the gentleman remarked, as he went out of the sanctuary, 'the doctor makes us all out a set of rascals, but he does it so gracefully and eloquently that I am not disposed to find fault.'" Dr. Stillman died on the 12th of March, 1807.

The Rev. Joseph Clay, of Georgia, who had been called to be a colleague with Dr. Stillman, entered upon his duties as sole pastor of the church, and was installed as such in the August succeeding the death of his predecessor. He preached to the church, however, only a year, and then his health giving way, he resigned and returned to his native South. James Manning Winchell was the successor of Mr. Clay. Notice of his ministry will be found in the sketch under his name. The same may be said of the ministry of his successor, Francis Wayland. Rev. Cyrus P. Grosvenor was the next pastor, continuing in office for nearly four years. He was followed by Rev. William Hague, who was installed Feb. 5, 1831, and resigned at the end of six years to go to the First Church, in Providence, R. I. His successor was Rollin Heber Neale, D.D., who was installed Sept. 27, 1837, and continued sole pastor of the church, which has been remarkably blessed under his long ministry, until its union with the Shawmut Avenue church, in 1877, at the time of the writing of this sketch. Rev. Dr. Crane, for many years pastor of the Second Baptist church, in Hartford, Conn., is the pastor of the united churches, which retained the old and honored name, "The First Baptist church of Boston."

Boston, Rev. S. C., was born near Rehoboth, Somerset Co., Md., Aug. 23, 1820. For three years he pursued his studies at the Baptist Seminary (Richmond College), Va., and then entered the Columbian College, where he graduated in 1845. He entered at once on the work of the ministry, and for several years labored as missionary under the board of the Maryland Union Association, in the lower part of the Eastern Shore of Maryland. Mr. Boston was instrumental in building several church edifices in the State, and in repairing and beautifying others. From 1857 to 1859 he was pastor of the Second Baptist church in Petersburg, Va.; from 1860 to 1867, pastor of the church in Farmville, Va.; from 1867 to 1869, pastor of the Lee Street church, Baltimore; from 1870 to 1872, pastor of the church at Frenchtown, N. J.; and from 1872 to 1877, pastor of the Bruington church,

Va. In 1877 he entered on the pastorate of the Onancock church, Accomac Co., Va., where he still labors. Mr. Boston has been greatly blessed in his labors, having baptized nearly 300 persons, and having trained his churches to the performance of all good works. He has been an occasional contributor to the religious papers and periodicals, and is deeply interested in all the educational movements of the denomination. Mr. Boston is the father of the Rev. F. R. Boston, a successful young minister, now settled at Hampton, Va.

Bosworth, Hon. Alfred, was born in Warren, R. I., Jan. 28, 1812. He graduated at Brown University, in the class of 1835. He studied law in the office of Judge Haile, and was admitted to the bar in 1838, and, after a brief residence in another place, returned to Warren, where he practiced his profession until the year 1854, when, on the death of Judge Haile, he was appointed his successor as a justice of the Supreme Court of Rhode Island. While in the practice of his profession he conducted many important cases, not only in the courts of his own State, but in the Supreme Court of the United States, being associated with some of the most distinguished lawyers in the country. He was elected a member of the corporation of Brown University on the Baptist foundation in 1854, and for eight years was faithful in the discharge of his duties as a trustee of the college. Although not a member of the Baptist church in Warren, he was an attendant upon its worship, and interested in all that concerned its prosperity. Judge Bosworth died at Warren, May 10, 1862, aged fifty years and four months.

Bosworth, Geo. Wm., D.D., was born in Bellingham, Norfolk Co., Mass., Sept. 30, 1818. His parents were members of the Baptist church. At the age of thirteen he became deeply interested in religion and united with the church, being baptized by Rev. Calvin Newton, then the pastor, by whose encouragement he soon began to speak and pray in religious meetings.

In 1831, Mr. Newton became a professor in Waterville College, and the year following took young Bosworth into his family and fitted him for college, which he entered in the class of 1837. His collegiate course was interrupted by ill health, but he was awarded graduation rank by the board of trustees, also the degree of A.M. in 1854, and that of D.D. in 1862. He took the regular course in Newton Theological Institution, graduating in 1841.

In September, 1841, he was ordained as pastor of the Baptist church in Medford, near Boston, the church being publicly "recognized" on the same occasion. After a successful ministry of nearly five years in Medford, he became the pastor of the South Baptist church in Boston, his installation occurring March 29, 1846. Here he remained for nine years, during which the church enjoyed prosperity. He then removed to Portland, Me., and became pastor of the Free Street Baptist church, February, 1855, which connection was sustained till Sept. 3, 1865.

GEO. WM. BOSWORTH, D.D.

During this period Dr. Bosworth took a very active part in the service which secured the endowment of Waterville College, now Colby University.

To obtain a partial relief from exhausting labors he severed his union with the Free Street church, against their urgent remonstrances, and became pastor of the First Baptist church in Lawrence, Mass., Aug. 10, 1865, and remained there till the close of January, 1869, when he became pastor of the First Baptist church in Haverhill, commencing his labors Feb. 7, 1869.

From his ordination till now he has not been out of the pastoral connection for a single Sabbath. Aside from the ministerial service he has been much engaged in denominational activities,—secretary of the Massachusetts Convention from 1852 to 1855; secretary of the board of trustees of Newton Theological Institution from 1865 till this time; secretary and treasurer of the Maine Baptist Education Society from 1856 till he left the State, in 1865; corresponding secretary of the Northern Baptist Education Society from 1865 till the present time. And he has been elected to fill the place of secretary and superintendent of the Massachusetts Baptist Convention, and has accepted the appointment, having announced to the church in Haverhill his purpose to close his pastoral labors at the termination of ten years of service.

Botsford, Rev. Edmund, came to Charleston, S. C., in 1766. November 1 of the same year he was converted under the ministry of Oliver Hart, "a day," says Mr. Botsford, "of light, a day of joy and peace." Having expressed a wish to enter the ministry, he was placed under the instruction of Mr. Williams, a learned and pious member of the church. Mr. Hart directed his theological studies. He was licensed in February, 1771, and ordained March, 1772. The fathers of those days regarded, more than we do, the injunction, "Lay hands suddenly on no man." Dr. Manly, Sr., says, "The young men were not ordained until they had visited some of the churches and preached before the Association and obtained their approbation."

He labored with great acceptance in Charleston for a time, and then traveled and preached extensively and with eminent success in several States. He finally settled in Georgetown, S. C., where he was the beloved and honored pastor for twenty-three years. There he rested on the 25th of December, 1819, in the seventy-fifth year of his age.

Mr. Botsford had a strong faith in the Saviour's abiding presence, and he enjoyed much of the Spirit's power in his heart. His labors in Georgia were eminently blessed, and he is revered as one of the illustrious and heaven-honored founders of the Baptist denomination in that State, and he has the same distinguished position in the Baptist history of South Carolina.

Boucher, Joan, was a lady of Kent, England, whose position in society was so exalted that she had access to the court of Henry VIII., and for a time held an honorable position in it. This lady was accustomed to take Bibles into the palace for distribution, concealed under her apparel. She visited the persecuted in prison, and contributed to their support and encouragement. She loved Christ, and she received such courageous grace from him that she feared nothing human and nothing painful. She would defy a dozen bishops, or as many executioners, if they attempted to compel her to deny her faith. Her talents made her a serious opponent in any discussion, even though Cranmer or Ridley took the other side.

Joan was a firm Baptist, and she held a peculiar opinion about the origin of the Saviour's body. "You believe," said Cranmer to her, "that the Word was made flesh in the virgin, but that Christ took flesh of the virgin you believe not, because the flesh of the virgin being the outward man [was] sinfully gotten, and born in sin, but the Word, by the consent of the inward man of the virgin, was made flesh." This conceit held by Joan did not impugn the divinity or humanity of Christ, or the maternal relations of Mary to Jesus, and Cranmer might have safely passed it by. But she was an Anabaptist, and she must recant or be burned. She defended her doctrine of Christ's purity of nature with great power and perseverance, and the protracted efforts of two of the ablest prelates in the Church of England failed to make any impression upon her. She was then delivered up to the secular power for punishment. Cranmer had much trouble in persuading the youthful king Edward VI. to sign her death-warrant. He told him with tears in his eyes that if he did wrong, since it was in submission to his authority, the archbishop should answer for it before God. "This struck him with much horror, so that he was very unwilling to have the sentence executed." But other attempts to make Joan renounce her opinions were made with provoking results; and this distinguished Baptist was burned to ashes almost exclusively through the efforts of Archbishop Cranmer. She passed through the flames to paradise May 2, 1550, in Smithfield, London. Her death was marked by perfect fearlessness and by the full peace of God. In Mary's time poor Cranmer had to drink the cup he forced on Joan Boucher, and the lady's courage far surpassed the archbishop's when the time of trial first approached.

Bouic, Hon. William Veirs, was born near Edward's Ferry, Montgomery Co., Md., May 11,

HON. WILLIAM VEIRS BOUIC.

1818. His father's family were for many generations the honored residents of Acqueville, France, some of whom were distinguished among the clergy of the Roman Catholic Church of that country, and especially Louis Domince, who was a canon of the Cathedral church of Rouen. Judge Bouic's father was Peter Anable Tranquelle Bouic, who died in Maryland in 1823. Mr. Bouic received his early education at a school in the neighborhood, and at the age of twelve removing to Rockville, Md., he attended the academy there for several years, and finally graduated in the full course. Upon leaving school he entered the law-office of John Brewer, Esq., Rockville, and at the termination of his course he was admitted to the bar. Having practiced for a while at Warrenton, Mo., he returned to Rockville to prosecute his profession. Judge Bouic rendered valuable services to his country during the war by restraining violence and mitigating its terrible evils wherever he had the power. He is interested in all educational enterprises; a firm friend of the academy in his town, and one of the overseers of the Columbian University, at which a son of his, a promising young lawyer, graduated with honors. Although Judge Bouic's father was a Catholic and his mother an Episcopalian, he, at his conversion, united with the Baptist church in Rockville when he was eighteen years of age, and still is an active member of that body. He was appointed in 1849, by the attorney-general of the State of Maryland, deputy attorney-general for Montgomery County, and that office having been abolished, he was elected in 1851 to the office of State attorney for the same county for the period of four years, which office he continued to hold and adorn by successive elections until 1867. In that year he was elected an associate judge of the Circuit Court for the Sixth Judicial Circuit of the State for the term of fifteen years. Judge Bouic is ever awake to the interests of his fellow-townsmen, and has done much by his personal efforts to make Rockville one of the most beautiful towns in the State.

Boulware, Rev. Theodorick, was born in Virginia, November 13, 1780. He was converted at the age of ten years. He was ordained in 1810. He spent seventeen years preaching in Kentucky. He removed to Missouri in 1827, and lived in Callaway County. He was a man of a high order of talent, well educated, energetic, and an impressive preacher, and he stood in the front rank as a defender of the faith. He took a bold stand against the organization of the General Association because of his anti-mission principles, and lived and died connected with the Old-School Baptists. He died Sept. 21, 1867.

Boutette, Hon. Timothy, was born at Leominster, Mass., Nov. 10, 1777. The labors of the farm, on which he passed his early days, making too severe a draft on a naturally delicate constitution, his father was induced to give him an education. In this decision he was greatly encouraged by observing in his son evidences of mental vigor and an aptness for study, which gave promise of success in whatever profession he might select as the business of his life. He graduated at Harvard College in the class of 1800. Among his classmates were

HON. TIMOTHY BOUTETTE.

Washington Allston, the celebrated painter, the Rev. J. S. Buckminster, the eloquent pastor of the Brattle Square church in Boston, and the late Chief-Justice Shaw, of Massachusetts, who was his roommate. In a class thus distinguished for ability, Mr. Boutette graduated with high reputation as a scholar. For one year after he was an assistant teacher at the Leicester Academy. In 1801 he entered the law-office of Hon. Abijah Bigelow, of Leominster, with whom he remained three years. Having been admitted to the bar in 1804, he removed to Waterville, Me., and commenced the practice of his profession. He soon rose to eminence as a lawyer, and had in some respects the best practice in his county. "He uniformly had the respect and confidence of the court as a sound and able lawyer, and was influential with the jury, because he presented his views with clearness and force, and appeared before them with the moral power of an honest man." For a number of years he represented his town in both branches of the Legislature, where he was during his whole term of service on the important Judiciary Committee, and frequently its chairman. It was while he was in the Senate that mainly through his influence a charter was obtained, in 1820, for Waterville College, now Colby University. For many years he was a trustee of the college, and its treasurer, and received from the institution, in 1839, the honorary degree of Doctor of Laws.

Mr. Boutette was an habitual worshiper at the First Baptist church in Waterville. The writer of this sketch recalls with pleasure the constancy of his attendance upon the public services of the Sabbath, and the devoutness of his demeanor in the house of God. It was no small encouragement to him that he had in his congregation one who cast the full weight of his great influence on the side of good order and religion. His was a life of great activity, honorably and well spent. He died Nov. 12, 1855, at the ripe age of seventy-eight years.

Bowers, Charles M., D.D., was born in Boston, Jan. 10, 1817. He graduated at Brown University in the class of 1838. Having spent one year in the Newton Theological Institution, he was ordained pastor of the church in Lexington, Mass., Sept. 9, 1841. The relation continued for four years,—1841-45,—when he decided to accept a call to the church in Clinton, Mass., where he has been the pastor ever since. He was a member of the Massachusetts Legislature one year,—the session of 1865-66. For twelve years he has been the efficient secretary of the Massachusetts Baptist State Convention.

Dr. Bowers received his degree from Brown University in 1870.

Bowers, Marmion H., was born at Moore's Hill, Dearborn Co., Ind.; educated at Farmer's College, O.; studied law at the State University, Bloomington, Ind.; practiced law at Aurora, Ind., and edited a newspaper; removed to Texas in 1852; resumed practice of law at Austin, 1853; raised a company for Confederate service in 1861; elected captain of Company C, 16th Regt. Texas Volunteer Infantry (Flournoy's); loss of health caused his early resignation; elected, while absent from Austin, a member of 10th Legislature from Travis County; made his reputation by urging legislative enactments against irregular impressments of property by Confederate States agents and others; edited *Southern Intelligencer* a few months after the war; in 1869 elected State Senator from Travis district; took a commanding part in all important measures of the several sessions of that Legislature, resisting the arbitrary school, militia, and police bills. His speech on martial law in time of peace is regarded as exhaustive and conclusive. He reached a high position at the Austin bar. He was a consistent and earnest member of the Baptist church at Austin from 1854 to the time of his death, March 3, 1872.

Bowker, S. D., M.D., was born in Courtland Co., N. Y., Feb. 10, 1830. He graduated at Fairmount Theological Seminary, and was a successful minister at several important points. He had baptized over 800 persons when fifty years of age. Several church edifices stand as monuments of his untiring labors. The last one built under his superintendence was the one at Leadville, Col. Without his self-sacrificing labor it would not have been erected. Having graduated in medicine as well as in theology, he practiced the healing art. He ranks among the most skillful physicians of Leadville, and is much respected for his good deeds of sympathy and benevolence as well as for his abilities.

Bowles, Rev. Ralph H., son of Ralph H. and Rebecca Bowles, was born in Hartford, Conn.; fitted for college in Connecticut Literary Institution; graduated at Trinity College in 1848; received the degree of A.M. in 1851; was ordained as pastor of the Baptist church in Tariffville, Conn., in 1850; settlements afterward were in Branford, Conn.; Lee, Brighton, West Newton, Lee (second time), Mass.; Greenbush, N. Y.; Jewett City, New Hartford, and Canton, Conn.; a devout, earnest, and indefatigable worker.

Boyce, James Pettigru, D.D., LL.D., Professor of Systematic Theology, Church Government, and

JAMES PETTIGRU BOYCE, D.D., LL.D.

Pastoral Duties in the Southern Baptist Theological Seminary, and chairman of its faculty, was born of Scotch-Irish parents at Charleston, S. C., Jan. 11, 1827. After spending two years at Charleston College, he entered Brown University, where he graduated in 1847. He was baptized by

Rev. Richard Fuller, D.D., and united with the First Baptist church at Charleston in 1846. He was licensed to preach in 1847, and for six months of the following year he edited the *Southern Baptist*. In 1849 he entered Princeton Theological Seminary, where he remained two years. In 1851 he was ordained pastor of the Baptist church in Columbia, S. C., where he preached until 1855, when he accepted a professorship of Theology in Furman University. His inaugural address was delivered during the succeeding commencement, in July, 1856. Its subject was, "Three Changes in Theological Education." The address did much in strengthening the cause of theological education in the South, leading many to favor it who had hitherto opposed it, and laying the foundation of the peculiar system of teaching afterwards adopted in the Southern Baptist Theological Seminary. In 1858 and 1859, Dr. Boyce was elected professor in this institution, with the privilege of selecting his chair, and was also made chairman of its faculty. To these offices have since been added those of treasurer and general agent, which positions he still holds.

He was elected to a seat in the South Carolina Legislature in 1862, and re-elected in 1864. He took a prominent part in the business of that body. Two of his speeches, advocating the indorsement of a definite amount of Confederate bonds by the State, were published. He also published a pamphlet on that subject.

His principal publications are, "A Brief Catechism on Bible Doctrines"; "The Doctrine and Uses of the Sanctuary," a sermon at the dedication of Columbia Baptist Church; "Death and Life the Christian's Portion," occasioned by the death of Rev. B. Manly, Sr., D.D.; and "The Suffering Christ," published in the *Baptist Quarterly* of October, 1870. He has a great intellect, tireless energy, and extraordinary executive ability, and to him, more than to all others, the Southern Baptist Theological Seminary owes its existence. His private library comprises over 13,000 volumes.

Boyd, Robert, D.D. — This widely known minister of Christ was born in Girvin, Ayrshire, Scotland, Aug. 24, 1816, and died at his home in Waukesha, Wis., Aug. 1, 1879, aged sixty-three years. His parents were devoted members of the Presbyterian Church, and he was indebted to them for an early Christian education. Converted at the age of fifteen, impressed almost simultaneously that it was his duty to preach, he began at once to address public assemblies with great acceptance. His attention having been called to the question of baptism, he gave the subject prayerful and unprejudiced examination, which resulted in his becoming a Baptist. In 1843, Dr. Boyd came to America, and settled as pastor at Brockville, Canada. Subsequently he served the churches at London and Hamilton, Canada, with great efficiency. Owing to failure of health he came in 1854 to Waterville, Wis., and settled on a farm. His health having been restored, he accepted the pastorate of the Baptist church in Waukesha, and afterwards he took charge of the Edina Place Baptist church, Chicago, Ill. In 1863, owing to an attack of paralysis so impairing his health as to unfit him for the duties of his city pastorate, he came again to Waukesha. The same year Shurtleff College conferred upon him the degree of D.D. Although paralyzed to such an extent that he had to be carried into the pulpit in his chair, and to preach sitting, he proclaimed the good news with great power for four years to the Baptist church in Waukesha. In 1867 he was finally prostrated to such an extent as to be confined thereafter to his house until death summoned him up higher. Although he resigned his pastorate, the church declined to accept it. For about twelve years he was helpless on his bed. His intellect, however, remained unimpaired, and during these years the best work of his life was accomplished. He employed his time in the production of the books which he left as a precious legacy to the church of Christ. As the result of his labor he prepared for the press "Glad Tidings," "None but Christ," "Grace and Truth," "The Good Shepherd," "The World's Hope," "Wee Willie," "My Enquiry Meeting," "Lectures to Young Converts," "Words of Comfort to the Afflicted," and an autobiography in manuscript. Dr. Boyd was gifted with a mind of a high order, and every power he possessed was brought into service for Christ. He had a profound reverence for the sacred Scriptures, and he unfolded their themes with a variety and richness of illustration hardly ever surpassed. His delight was to preach the gospel, and he easily found Christ crucified in every theme. The great salvation always absorbed his soul, and the atonement was to him the radiating centre of saving knowledge. As a pastor he lived in the hearts of his people. In this relation, if more remarkable in one thing than another, it was in the confidence which he inspired. His people gave up their minds and hearts to him without suspicion or reserve. In the midst of great suffering he evinced remarkable fortitude and submission to the will of God. He was a noble specimen of a man and a Christian minister. He has bequeathed to his family and the church of God the memory of a life without reproach, devoted to the cause of truth without reserve.

Boyd, Willard W., D.D., was born Nov. 22, 1843, in Chemung Co., N. Y. His parents moved to Saco, Me., when he was two years old.

He was prepared for college at fourteen years of age. He was converted at the age of twelve years. His father died when he was eighteen years of age, and Willard succeeded him in superintending a

WILLARD W. BOYD, D.D.

factory at Springville, Me. In this place there was but one church, a Baptist, whose members were few in number. Dr. Boyd read Spurgeon's sermons to them, and soon began to speak in his own language; a revival followed, and the converts asked for baptism. He being a Congregationalist, studied the question of baptism, and soon, with those who had lately found Jesus, he was baptized. In 1866 his mother died, and the following year he entered Harvard University, where he graduated with honor in 1871. After spending a year at a German university he was appointed tutor in Harvard College, and held the position till, in 1873, he accepted the pastorate of the First Baptist church in Charlestown,—a part of Boston, Mass. With this church he remained four years, and received about 400 members into its fellowship. In June, 1877, he was installed as pastor of the Second Baptist church of St. Louis, Mo. In June, 1878, he received the honorary degree of Doctor of Divinity from Shurtleff College, Ill. In Dr. Boyd are combined scholarship, executive ability, and pulpit eloquence. He possesses great energy and piety. Many have been added to his church in St. Louis since his settlement, and the house of worship has been twice built, owing to fire. He occupies one of the most responsible positions in the Baptist denomination in the Mississippi Valley, and preaches to very large congregations.

Boyden, Rev. Jabez S., was born in Essex Co., N. Y., in 1831; brought to Michigan while still an infant; baptized in Mooreville, in June, 1850, and educated for the ministry at Kalamazoo College, from which he graduated in 1856. He settled at once as pastor in Novi, and was ordained in November of the same year. His successive pastorates were, in Flint, four years; in Novi, again three years; in Howell, four years; in Franklin, Ind., one year; in Ypsilanti, seven years. During all this time he was continuously in the pastorate without the intermission of a single day. At Novi he baptized 117; in Flint, 63; in Howell, 163; and during the time of the Franklin and Ypsilanti pastorates, 163. While pastor at Flint he was one year chaplain of the 10th Regiment of Mich. Vols., Infantry.

In August, 1879, he became financial secretary of Kalamazoo College, and is at present residing in Kalamazoo, engaged most vigorously in the work of securing an adequate endowment for the college, and the means for defraying its current expenses.

Boykin, James, a deacon of the Baptist church at Columbus, Ga., was born in 1792, near Camden, in South Carolina. With his father, Francis Boykin, he moved to Georgia, and settled on a large plantation in Washington County, ten miles south of Milledgeville; in 1829 he sold his home and planting interests to his brother, Dr. Samuel Boykin, and moved to Columbus, and settled on another plantation in Stewart County, twenty miles from Columbus. He united with the Columbus church, and was ordained a deacon, which office he filled worthily until his death, in 1846. He was at that time quite wealthy, and gave liberally of his means to sustain the gospel and to establish Mercer University. He was an exceedingly kind man. To his children he was the most tender and affectionate of parents; to his wife the most devoted of husbands; he was a Christian without reproach. A security debt swept away nearly $100,000 of his property, yet he never murmured, or spoke an unkind word of the man who caused his financial ruin, but preserved his cheerfulness and gentle serenity until called "up higher" at the age of fifty-four.

He did much in founding and sustaining the church at Columbus, and was a most useful, zealous, and liberal Christian, whose memory is even yet fragrant among those who knew him.

Boykin, Rev. Samuel, was born in Milledgeville, Baldwin Co., Ga., Nov. 24, 1829. His mother's maiden name was Narcissa Cooper, daughter of Thomas Cooper, whose ancestors came from England. His paternal ancestor, Edward Boykin, came from Caernarvonshire, Wales, and settled in Isle of Wight Co., Va., in 1685. William Boykin, the grandson of Edward Boykin, emigrated to Kershaw Co., S. C., in 1755 or 1756, and settled six miles south of Camden. His third son, Francis Boykin, participated in most of the battles of the State during the Revolutionary war, and rose to be a major of infantry in the

REV. SAMUEL BOYKIN.

army, having taken part in the battle of Fort Moultrie.

About the year 1800 Mr. Boykin moved to Georgia, and settled near Milledgeville, where he died in 1821. Three of his children grew to maturity,—Eliza, Samuel, and James. Samuel, born in 1786, died in 1848, was the father of the subject of this sketch. He graduated at the State University of Georgia and at a medical college in Philadelphia, and practiced medicine in Georgia for twenty-five or thirty years. He was also a large planter. He removed to Columbus, Ga., where he spent the last years of his life. He engaged in planting and in banking, and was very prosperous. He was fond of books, and a lover of science; and at his hospitable home distinguished literary and scientific men of the New and Old World were pleased to visit, and ever found in Dr. Boykin a congenial spirit.

Samuel Boykin, his son, spent his earliest years in Columbus. He was sent to Pennsylvania and Connecticut for education, but came back to Georgia and took a full course at the State University, where he graduated in 1851. He then spent nearly a year in foreign travel. While prosecuting his studies at the State University he made a profession of religion and joined the Baptist church. He was licensed to preach in 1852, and ordained Sept. 16, 1861. In 1859 he became the editor of the *Christian Index*, then published in Macon, Ga., and owned by the Baptist Convention of the State. In 1861 he became the sole proprietor of the *Index*. He continued successfully its publication until 1865, when the disasters of the war between the States stopped it. His editorial management was characterized by decided ability. He subsequently sold the *Index* to J. J. Toon, of Atlanta, by whom it was revived. For several years he also published and edited the *Child's Index*, which he resumed after the war. This child's paper was merged into *Kind Words* in 1872, a paper owned by the Southern Baptist Convention, and published at Memphis, Tenn. In 1873, Mr. Boykin was elected editor of *Kind Words*, which position he has held ever since. Under his management the paper has reached a very large circulation, is now well established, and it is a paper of great value. Mr. Boykin was pastor for one year of the Second Baptist church of Macon, but having been called to Memphis to edit *Kind Words* in 1873, he resigned that charge.

When the Sunday-School Board was abolished in 1874, the paper was removed to Macon, and there published. Mr. Boykin then returned to Georgia. Editing has been his chief employment, for which he is peculiarly fitted. He has been identified with Baptist interests in Georgia for many years. In the cause of missions and Sunday-schools he has been very useful, wielding a large influence over the young of the denomination as editor and expositor of the "Sunday-School Lessons." He is now in the prime of life, with an active mind and untiring industry. The Baptist denomination may still expect large results from his labors and his commanding talents.

Boykin, Rev. Thomas Cooper, State school evangelist for the Georgia Baptist Convention, brother of the foregoing, was born in Baldwin County, ten miles from Milledgeville, Jan. 1, 1836. His parents moved to Columbus soon after his birth, and he was reared in that city. Converted under the ministry of John E. Dawson, he joined the Columbus church in 1851, and was educated at Penfield, in Mercer University, and at Columbia, S. C., in the South Carolina College, from which he was graduated with distinction in 1856. In 1858 he began a planter's life in Russell Co., Ala., near Columbus, transferring his membership to the Mount Lebanon church in 1863. That church licensed him in 1864, and by it he was called to ordination in 1865. It was while acting as pastor for this church that he developed a strong passion for the Sunday-school work, and the brethren of the Alabama Convention, recognizing his zeal and ability, placed him at the head of their State Sunday-school efforts in 1872. But his native State called him to her service on the 1st of September, 1874, and he removed to Georgia, settled in Atlanta,

REV. THOMAS COOPER BOYKIN.

and, under an appointment of the State Baptist Convention, began a work in the Sunday-school cause which he has continued to prosecute most vigorously and prosperously until the present time (1880). Through his exertions the Sunday-school work in the State has been pretty thoroughly organized; 26 Sunday-school conventions have been put in operation, and 500 schools have been established, while all over the State a healthy and enthusiastic Sunday-school spirit has been aroused in the denomination.

Mr. Boykin is a preacher of ability, and in his style is exceedingly pointed and practical. During a pastorate of three years he baptized 70 persons into the Mount Lebanon,—a country church. He has the happy faculty of making himself interesting and instructive to all, especially to the young. He is an indefatigable laborer, and he is thoroughly conversant with every phase of the Sunday-school work.

Boynton, Hon. Nehemiah, was born in what is now Rockport, but then a section of Gloucester, Mass., Dec. 2, 1804. When he was twenty-one years of age he commenced business at St. George, Me., where he remained nine years, and then removed to West Thomaston, Me. Here he carried on business for eleven years. At the end of this period he removed to Boston, and embarked in the business which he prosecuted with energy and success for the remainder of his life. Mr. Boynton's residence was in Chelsea, where, as a member and an officer in the First Baptist church, he gave himself with great devotion to the service of his Lord and Master. For two years he was a senator from his district in the Massachusetts Senate, and for three years, 1862, 1864, and 1865, a period of great responsibility, he was a member of Gov. Andrew's Executive Council for the county of Suffolk.

If Mr. Boynton was a successful merchant and an honorable councillor, he filled also another post, which to him was one of higher honor and more sacred trust than either of the other two. A vacancy having occurred in the Executive Committee of the Missionary Union in 1853, he was appointed to fill it. At once his business capacities pointed him out as the proper person to be selected as chairman of the Committee on Finance. In 1855 he was chosen treasurer of the Union, and held the office for nine years in succession. In the hands of no better man could the great trust have been placed. He entered upon the duties of his office when the society was burdened with a heavy debt. He lived to see the debt wiped out and the credit of the Union, in all parts of the world where it transacted its business, placed upon the soundest basis, so that its drafts were as promptly honored as those of any banking or mercantile house then or since known.

"The prominent personal qualities of Mr. Boynton," says one who knew him well, "were fittingly symbolized by his commanding personal presence. Weight and symmetry of character were his in an eminent degree. No man was ever less influenced by personal fears or preferences. His action was based on public and solid reasons. No member of the committee ever commanded greater influence for his opinions. The answer to the question, 'What does Deacon Boynton think of it?' was almost enough to conclude any matter of weight. To the high personal qualities which contributed to this beautiful wholeness he added a faith in God, and in the loyalty of his redeemed people, that made him confident, where to human sense there seemed more ground for despondency." With the record of such a life as he lived before all men, there was no need of a dying testimony. Deacon Boynton died Nov. 22, 1868.

Bradford, Rev. C. G., is quite young, probably not more than thirty, but a man of unusual promise. His delivery is quiet but exceedingly impressive, and he is one of the few whose sermons would lose nothing by being read instead of heard. They are brief and elegantly finished. He has tried again and again to leave the Beech Island church, in Aiken Co., S. C., having been reared in that vicinity, and thinking he might be more useful elsewhere, but the church still retains him.

Bradford, Rev. Shadrach S., was born at Plympton, Mass., May 24, 1813. He took a part of his college course at Waterville, Me., graduating at Columbian College, Washington, D. C., in the class of 1837. His theological studies were pursued at Newton, where he graduated in 1840. He was ordained pastor of the church at Pawtucket, R. I., June 8, 1841, and remained in this position for ten years, resigning in 1851. Such was the state of his health that he was obliged to abandon the ministry. For several years he was in active business in Providence. Mr. Bradford was elected a trustee of Brown University in 1863, and a Fellow in 1865.

Bradford, Rev. Zabdiel, was born in Plympton, Mass., on the 13th of August, 1809. On the side of both parents he was of genuine Puritan stock, his paternal ancestor being Gov. William Bradford, and his maternal ancestor the renowned Capt. Miles Standish. Of such an ancestry any man might justly be proud. Before he reached his eighteenth year he became a subject of God's converting grace. The state of his health being such as to settle the question of his physical inability to enter into active business, it was decided that he should obtain a liberal education. In the year 1830 he became a member of Waterville College, with the intention of fitting himself for the Christian ministry. After his graduation he prosecuted his theological studies for nearly three years, and then accepted a call to the Baptist church in what is now Yarmouth, Cumberland Co., Me. The ministry of Mr. Bradford, extending over a period of eight years, was one of great spiritual prosperity. He had the happiness of witnessing more than one powerful revival. As the result of one of these outpourings of the Spirit he baptized nearly 100 persons.

The long winters and uncongenial springs of the sea-coast of Maine were too trying to the constitution of Mr. Bradford, and, with a severe pang, he felt compelled to sever the ties which united him to a most affectionate people. He accepted a call from what was then the Pine Street, now Central Baptist church, in Providence, and was recognized as pastor in November, 1844, and labored with his customary fidelity and success for more than four years. He died May 16, 1849, at the comparatively early age of forty years.

Mr. Bradford was a man of much more than ordinary ability. He possessed a singularly vivid imagination, and sometimes the play of his fancy in his discourses was most striking, and arrested the attention of the most careless and thoughtless. He concentrated all his faculties to the cause of his Master, and in his closing hours was sustained by that grace the riches of which he had proclaimed so earnestly from the sacred desk. "That plan," he said, "that capital plan! I have looked it through and through this winter, and it is all I want." Who can doubt that when he came into the presence of his God and Saviour he did find it was all he wanted?

Bramlette, Gov. Thomas E., was born in Cumberland Co., Ky., Jan. 3, 1817. In early life he joined a Baptist church, and was active in the councils of his denomination. He was admitted to the practice of law in 1837. In 1841 he was elected to the State Legislature; here his splendid abilities speedily attracted public attention. In 1849 he was appointed Commonwealth's attorney. In 1852 he moved from Burksville to Columbia, Ky., and was elected circuit judge, and filled the position during six years. At the breaking out of the Rebellion he accepted a colonel's commission, raised a regiment of volunteers, and entered the Federal army. In 1862 he resigned to accept the appointment of U. S. attorney for Kentucky. In 1863 he was commissioned major-general. While organizing his division he was nominated candidate for governor. Again he resigned his position in the army, and was elected governor of the Commonwealth, in which capacity he served four years. He now became weary of the burdens of public office, and settled in Louisville, where he enjoyed an extensive and lucrative practice of law until his death, Jan. 12, 1875.

Branham, Joel R., D.D., was born in Eatonton, Putnam Co., Ga., Dec. 23, 1825. His parents were Dr. Joel Branham and Emily, daughter of Thomas Cooper, the devoted Baptist deacon of Eatonton. He went to Penfield to school in the year 1838, while quite young, and remained three years. He was a pupil there when Mercer Institute was organized as a college, and was a member of the first Freshman class. After leaving Penfield he attended the Eatonton school until about his eighteenth year. In 1845 he entered Emory College, at which he was graduated in 1847. He was converted and joined the Baptist church at Penfield in 1838. He was ordained in 1866, in Madison, Ga. He was called to ordination by the Madison Baptist church, and immediately after to the charge of that church, in which he continued two and a half years. While residing in Tennessee he incidentally served the churches at Brownsville, Humboldt, and Stanton. Compelled by ill health to return to Georgia in 1874, he was called to the pastorate of the church in Marietta, at the same time preaching once a month to the church at Noonday. He is at present pastor of the Baptist church at Eatonton, Ga., and preaches once a month to the church at Harmony, Putnam Co., and also to the church at Monticello, Jasper Co., Ga. He was a member of the faculty of the Georgia Female College in its early organization; was president of the same institution after the war. From 1868 to 1874 was president of Brownsville Baptist Female College, the leading Baptist institution of West Tennessee at that period. He was for a time trustee of Mercer University.

Dr. Branham is one of the best educated and most highly cultivated of the living Georgia Baptist ministers, and to pulpit ability of high rank he unites fine oratorical powers and an exceeding amiability of disposition. He is remarkably clear in all his statements, because of a keen mental vision and a strong intellectual grasp. His talents are of a high order, and his sermons are surpassed by few, if by any, of the State ministry.

Many of the years of his life have been spent in imparting instruction, generally as the president of a college for young ladies, and he is a teacher of rare ability.

Brantly, John J., D.D., Professor of Belles-Lettres and Modern Languages in Mercer University, Macon, Ga., and son of Dr. Wm. T. Brantly, Sr., and half-brother of Dr. Wm. T. Brantly, Jr., was born in Augusta, Ga., Dec. 29, 1821. The first twelve years of his life were spent in Philadelphia, when his father was pastor of the First Baptist church of that city. He then went with his father to Charleston, S. C., where he entered the Sophomore class of Charleston College, of which his father was president. While a student in the Charleston College he paid a summer visit during vacation to relatives at Scottsborough, a few miles from Milledgeville, Ga., and during a protracted meeting in the Milledgeville church, of which Dr. S. G. Hillyer was then pastor, he made a profession of religion, and was baptized by his father in the Oconee River, near Milledgeville.

JOEL R. BRANHAM, D.D.

JOHN J. BRANTLY, D.D.

Graduating in 1840, he went to Chatham Co., N. C.,—his father's old home,—and afterwards to Pittsborough, in both of which places he engaged in teaching. As he was debating in his mind whether to study law or medicine, he went in the fall of 1844, to Charleston, on a visit to his father, who had been stricken with paralysis. During that visit his thoughts were turned to the ministry, and he decided that his duty lay in that direction. He was licensed by the First church of Charleston, his father signing the license, the last official act he performed. Mr. Brantly was ordained at Fayetteville, N. C., in 1845, having accepted a call to the pastoral charge of the church in that place. In a year or two he resigned to take charge of the high school there; but in the spring of 1850 he accepted the pastoral charge of the church at Newbury Court-House, S. C., where he remained until elected to his present position, in 1867. During the interval between the resignation of Dr. Warren and the settlement of Dr. Skinner he served the Macon church as temporary pastor. Dr. J. J. Brantly is a thorough scholar. He is well read in the ancient classics, both Greek and Latin, and he is the master of several modern languages. With the writings of "the fathers" he is familiar. He is also a perfect master of English composition. His extreme modesty only has prevented him from being widely known as one of the most finished scholars and able preachers of our denomination in the United States.

Brantly, William T., Jr., D.D., son of the Dr. W. T. Brantly of sainted memory, was born in Beaufort, S. C. He removed with his father, at the age

WILLIAM T. BRANTLY, JR., D.D.

of nine years, to Philadelphia, where, in 1826, the father became the pastor of the First Baptist church. Under a careful home culture, supplemented by the training of the best schools, young Brantly was prepared to enter college at an early age. While thus preparing, in 1834, he was baptized into the fellowship of the First church of Philadelphia, the baptism being in the Delaware River; and in 1838 he was licensed by the same church to preach. Having entered Brown University, he graduated with distinction in 1840. The same year he was invited to the pastorate of the First Baptist church of Augusta, Ga., which position he accepted and held with marked success for eight years, during which time the membership was doubled, and the house enlarged to accommodate the increasing congregation. Dr. Brantly's varied culture and polished scholarship attracted to his ministrations an unusual number of the more intelligent of the community, and soon the authorities of the University of Georgia were anxious to secure his services as one of its faculty of instruction. Accordingly, in 1848 he was elected Professor of Belles-Lettres and Evidences of Christianity and History in that institution, a position which he filled with distinguished ability until 1856. In 1853 he was elected pastor of the First Baptist church, Philadelphia, but declined the invitation.

In 1856 he was invited to the pastorate of the Tabernacle church in the same city, and anxious to be engaged again in the active and, to him, congenial duties of pastoral life, he accepted the position. He continued to serve the Tabernacle church for five years, during which time he had the pleasure of seeing the membership greatly increase in number and efficiency. In 1861, Dr. Brantly was invited to take charge of the Second Baptist church at Atlanta, Ga., where he remained, with the exception of an interruption arising from the troubles of the war, until 1871, in which year he became the pastor of the Seventh Baptist church, Baltimore, Md., succeeding the honored Dr. R. Fuller, when he and a large number of the members of that church withdrew to constitute the present Eutaw Place church. Dr. Brantly still remains pastor of the Seventh church, and is eminently successful in his ministrations. As a preacher, he is earnest, graceful, and instructive; as a pastor, genial, loving, and companionable, and ever a welcome guest in the homes of his people. No one feels a warmer interest in all the denominational movements of the day than he; while for educational institutions and their instructors he cherishes that ardent and unwavering attachment which stamps him, as by nature, one of the *guild*. He is an overseer of the Columbian University, and no one is more heartily welcomed to its meetings for business and its commencement exercises than himself. The University of Georgia in 1854 conferred on him the honorary degree of D.D.

Brantly, William T., Sr., D.D., was born in Chatham Co., N. C., Jan. 23, 1787. He was converted to God in his fifteenth year. He was educated at South Carolina College, Columbia, S. C., of which Jonathan Maxcy, D.D., was president. He graduated with distinction in 1808, inspiring hopes in those who became acquainted with his talents of a bright future for the young minister. In 1811 he became a pastor, though he had preached regularly for years before, and he took the oversight of the church of Beaufort, S. C., where he spent eight years in toil and triumphs. The church was increased in numbers, knowledge, and spiritual strength, and the pastor was regarded as one of the most eloquent preachers in the South. In 1819 he became rector a second time of Richmond Academy, Augusta, Ga., an institution endowed by that State; and immediately he began to preach every Sunday in the chapel of the academy, for there was no Baptist church in Augusta. His talents soon drew throngs, a church was organized, and in two years a meeting-house was built and paid for, at a cost of $20,000, the equal of any similar structure in the State. His services as preacher and pastor, like many of the earlier Baptist ministers in the South, he, unwisely for the people, but generously, gave for nothing. His usefulness was felt throughout every part of Georgia.

Dr. Holcombe, pastor of the First Baptist church of Philadelphia, on his death-bed, recommended Dr. Brantly as his successor. After a second invitation had been extended to him by the First church, he removed to Philadelphia in the spring of 1826. In that city his success was remarkable,—in eleven years he baptized 600 persons into the fellowship of the First church, and he was instrumental in founding the Norristown church. Declining health compelled him to turn southward again, and in 1837 he accepted the pastorate of the First church, Charleston, S. C. Shortly after he came to that city he was appointed president of the College of Charleston, the duties of which he discharged till disease forbade him. He died in March, 1845.

Dr. Brantly was a man of fine talents; his learning was profound, his classical scholarship was of the highest order, his voice had unusual compass and melody, and his heart went with his eloquent utterances, so that his oratory was overwhelming; the whole audience would be alternately bathed in tears or carried up to the third heaven in jubilant delight. Christ was everything in his heart and in his sermons, and his ministry was a blessing to the North and to the South of untold value.

Bray, Rev. Nathan H., the apostle of the Sabine region, Louisiana, was born in Petersborough, England, April 29, 1809; emigrated to the United States in 1840, and landed at New Orleans. He began to preach in 1847, and under his labors churches were planted in all that portion of Louisiana bordering on the Sabine River. He was indefatigable, and 50 or 60 churches and 3 Associations sprang up as the fruit, more or less direct, of his efforts. He was over twenty years moderator of Sabine Association, and for many years an officer in the Grand Lodge of Louisiana, and for the last three years parish judge. He died Feb. 18, 1875.

Brayman, Mason, was born in Buffalo, N. Y., May 23, 1813. His parents, Daniel and Anna Brayman, were among the pioneers of Western New York, and settled in the town of Hamburgh, Erie Co., in 1811. At the beginning of the war of 1812–15 they removed to Buffalo, not knowing what course the Seneca Indians, whose reservation lay between the two towns, might take in the contest. On the restoration of peace they returned to their farm in Hamburgh, accompanied by the subject of this sketch, where he remained until he was between seventeen and eighteen years old, when he went to Buffalo, and entered the office of the *Journal* as an apprentice to the printing business. While serving his time he began the study of the law, which he continued while subsequently editing the *Republican* and *Bulletin*. He was admitted to the bar in 1836. He removed to Monroe, Mich., in the summer of 1837, where he pursued his favorite professions of law and journalism. He remained here until 1839, and after a brief sojourn at Wooster,

MAJ.-GEN. MASON BRAYMAN.

O., we next find him at Louisville, Ky., as editor of the *Daily Advertiser*. After a successful career of about three years as editor, Mr. Brayman made another westward move, and pitched his tent in Springfield, Ill., in 1842, where he again entered upon the practice of law in partnership with the Hon. Jesse B. Thomas. Not forgetting his propensity for editorial life, he wrote much for the *State Register*, and also acted as assistant State treasurer for several years. He was appointed by Gov. Ford to revise and codify the laws of the State, and the result of his labors, which the legal profession facetiously called the "Braminical Code," was authority in all Illinois courts for many years. He was also commissioned by Gov. Ford special State's attorney to prosecute the offenses which grew out of the "Mormon war" at Nauvoo.

After the transfer of the Congressional land grant by the State to the Illinois Central Railroad Company, Mr. Brayman became the attorney of the corporation, which necessitated his removal to Chicago, where, in 1853, he opened an office, and engaged in securing the right of way and the transaction of the general business of that company. His connection with the company having terminated, he was appointed land agent of the Cairo and Fulton Railroad Company of Missouri and Arkansas, and subsequently became general superintendent for the construction of the road.

The opening of the civil war found him again in Springfield. He enlisted in the 29th Illinois Volunteers, of which he was soon commissioned as major by Gov. Yates, and was also appointed adjutant on the staff of Gen. McClernand. The first battle in which he was under fire was the short but bloody one of Belmont, in Missouri. Then followed Forts Henry and Donelson, where Major Brayman is credited with having done brave and efficient service. At the great battle of Pittsburgh Landing he commanded a brigade, and for meritorious conduct on the field was promoted to be a brigadier-general. He followed the fortunes of the victorious army, and was assigned to separate commands. His health having become impaired by a partial sun-stroke, Gen. Brayman left the active duties of the field, and was subsequently in command of Camp Denison, at Columbus, O., the district of Cairo, in Illinois and Kentucky, and of Natchez, in Mississippi, and towards the conclusion of the war was appointed president of a commission or court to adjudicate upon the important cotton cases which had been accumulating at New Orleans. So well satisfied were the President and Secretary of War with his varied and important services that he was brevetted major-general.

The war being over, Gen. Brayman returned to Springfield. Having become part proprietor of the Quincy *Whig* and its editor, he removed to that city, but subsequently returned to Springfield, as editor and co-proprietor of the *Daily Journal*. But his health having been much impaired by the hard services of the war, he was impelled to remove to Green Lake, Wis., which is his present home. In 1876, Gen. Grant, his old commander, tendered him the governorship of Idaho, which he accepted, and is still at his post when this sketch is written, though his term of office has nearly expired.

Gen. Brayman was a member of the Baptist church when he came to Illinois, having been baptized by Rev. Charles Morton at Wooster, O., in 1839. He immediately identified himself actively with the local and general work of the denomination in this State, and has ever been an efficient and liberal helper. In 1855 he was elected president of the American Baptist Publication Society, and has been several times president of the General Association of the State. He also has ever taken an active interest in educational movements. He has been trustee and one of the regents of the University of Chicago, and trustee of the Illinois State Industrial University, and was one of the founders and first members of the Chicago Historical Society. While in command at Natchez he established schools for the colored people; while in Little Rock, Ark., on railroad business, he gave positive aid in school matters, and since his residence in Wisconsin has been connected with the management of Wayland Institute, at Beaver Dam.

Brayton, Rev. Durlin L., was born in Hubbardston, Vt., Oct. 27, 1808. Having decided to enter the Christian ministry, he pursued his collegiate studies at Brown University, and his theological studies at Newton, where he graduated in 1837. He was ordained at Providence, Oct. 15, 1837, having received his appointment as a missionary the June previous. He sailed from Boston Oct. 28, 1857, and reaching Maulmain, Feb. 19, 1858, became connected with the Karen department of the Maulmain mission, from which he was transferred to Mergui the April following, where he devoted himself to labors among the Pwo Karens. Near the close of this year Mr. and Mrs. Brayton returned to this country, on account of the illness of Mrs. Brayton. He remained but a few months, and then resumed his work at Mergui. For several years he was occupied with his missionary labors, making Mergui his headquarters, and visiting the adjacent regions to preach the gospel as opportunity presented. In March, 1854, he removed to Donabew for the purpose of reaching a numerous Pwo Karen population in that vicinity. He remained here until May, 1855, when he established himself at Kemmendine. His relation with the Union was dissolved by a letter of resignation bearing date July 28, 1856, and was resumed in October, 1861. With the exception of the time spent in a second visit to his native land, Mr. Brayton has devoted himself to missionary labors among the Pwo Karens in the Rangoon Karen department, where, at the last report, there were 13 churches, with 398 members. Mr. Brayton's forty years of service as a missionary have been accompanied with the richest blessings from heaven.

Brayton, Hon. George Arnold, LL.D., son of Charles and Rebecca (Havens) Brayton, was born in Warwick, R. I., Aug. 4, 1803. He was prepared for college at Kent Academy, in East Greenwich, R. I., and was graduated with high rank at Brown University, in the class of 1824. Among his classmates were the eminent Prof. George W. Keely, of Waterville College; Hon. Ezra Wilkinson, justice of the Supreme Court of Massachusetts; and Rev. William Leverett, of Newport, R. I. He was admitted to the bar in 1827, and at once opened an office in his native town. He was called during a succession of years to fill various offices of honor and trust in the gift of his fellow-citizens of his native town. In 1843 he was chosen by the General Assembly associate justice of the Supreme Court of Rhode Island. He held this office until 1868, when he was elected chief justice, remaining in office until 1874, when ill health obliged him to resign, after a judicial service of thirty-one years, the longest in the history of Rhode Island. So highly was he appreciated that his salary was continued until his death. He spent the last years of his life in the retirement of his home in East Greenwich. He contemplated the close of life with Christian calmness and composure. Although

CHIEF JUSTICE GEORGE ARNOLD BRAYTON.

Judge Brayton never made a public profession of religion, his sympathies were with the Baptists, and, had his health not given way, it was his purpose to have been baptized on a profession of his personal faith in Christ. His death occurred April 21, 1880. He received from Brown University, in 1870, the honorary degree of Doctor of Laws. In 1831 he married Celia Greene Clarke, a descendant of Joseph Clarke, of Newport, R. I., a brother of Dr. John Clarke, a name distinguished in the annals of Baptist history in Rhode Island.

Brayton, Rev. Jonathan, son of Lodowick and Betsey (Knight) Brayton, was born in Cranston, R. I., June 12, 1811. The first eighteen years of his life were spent on his father's farm. He then worked at the trade of a carpenter four years. At the end of this period he came very near losing his life in consequence of a fall of sixty feet from the steeple of a church upon which he was at work in Providence. Previous to this his thoughts had been directed to his personal spiritual state, and after his conversion, to the work of the ministry. In the event which laid him aside from his trade he seemed to hear the call of God to prepare himself to become a minister of the gospel. Although he was now twenty-two years of age, he entered upon a course of preparatory study, and in the fall of 1839 entered the Hamilton Theological Institution, where he remained two years, completing his course of study in 1841. Peculiar circumstances led him to decide to be ordained at Hamilton, and he was publicly set apart to the work of the Christian ministry by the faculty of the institution performing the services of his ordination. At once he returned to Rhode Island, and commenced his ministry at Phenix, where a powerful revival followed his labors and a prosperous church was established. The other settlements of Mr. Brayton have all been in his native State, in two villages in Warwick, in one village in Coventry, and in Pawtucket. Such has been the state of his health that he has been unable always to perform the duties of a pastor, but in all matters affecting the welfare and prosperity of his denomination he has ever taken the most substantial interest. He has held many important local offices, and his name has been mentioned in connection with the governorship of Rhode Island.

Brayton, Hon. William Daniel, son of Hon. Charles and Rebecca (Havens) Brayton, was born in Warwick, R. I., Nov. 6, 1815; studied at Kingston Academy and Brown University; engaged in the lumber trade; was representative in the General Assembly in 1841 and 1842; a major during the "Dorr war"; became town clerk of Warwick; president of the town council; in 1848, State senator; in 1851 was again in the General Assembly; in 1855 was again State senator; in 1856, Presidential elector; in 1857, elected representative to Congress, and re-elected in 1859; served on a war committee during the Rebellion; in 1862 was appointed collector of internal revenue; in 1872, delegate to National Republican Convention; a steadfast Baptist and earnest patriot; and has had charge of the money-orders of the Providence post-office.

Breaker, Rev. J. M. C., was born near Camden, Kershaw District, S. C., July 25, 1824; graduated from Furman Literary and Theological Institution, Fairfield, S. C., June, 1846; ordained to the ministry July 3, 1846; has been pastor of Greenville, Grahamville, Beaufort, Columbia, Spartansburg, S. C.; Newbern, N. C.; Park Avenue, St. Louis, Liberty and First church, St. Joseph, Mo.; and has been pastor at Houston, Texas, since April, 1877, where he is excelled by no other city minister in ability and influence; for several years was secretary of the South Carolina Baptist State Convention; founded and edited at Columbia, S. C., during the war, a weekly paper called *The Confederate Baptist;* received the degree of D.D. from Lagrange College,. Mo.; is a life-member of the American Baptist Missionary Union, American Baptist Publication Society, and the American Bible Society; has baptized 1520 persons; is author of a prize essay on "Communion," published in

1859, and has contributed a number of articles to the *Christian Review* and other periodicals.

Breedlove, Charles R., was born in Danville, Va., April 3, 1831; educated at Baylor University, Texas; graduated both from the collegiate department and the law school; served three years in Col. L. M. Martin's Confederate regiment; has been a member of the Baptist Church twenty-one years; since 1865 has practiced law at Brenham, Texas, with distinguished success and profit. He has been president of the Texas Baptist Sunday-School Convention, and is connected with all the prominent benevolent enterprises of the denomination, working earnestly and contributing freely. He is in the front rank as a lawyer, and he holds a high place among the earnest working Christians of the United States.

Breland, Rev. O. F., was a leading minister in Southeast Mississippi. He was born in Copiah Co., Miss., in 1825; began to preach in 1859; ordained in 1866; supplied a number of churches in Neshoba, Newton, and Leake Counties, from two to twelve years; baptized 300; assisted in organizing seven churches and in the ordination of three ministers; wrote the history of Mount Sinai church, and has preserved much historical material. His residence is at Dixon, Neshoba Co., Miss.

Brewer, Rev. George E., was born in Covington, Ga., Oct. 13, 1832; came with his father to Alabama at fifteen years of age; began life for himself as a teacher in 1851. In 1852 was with his father, Rev. A. G. Brewer (one of the founders of the Methodist Protestant Church), engaged in the publication of the *Christian Telegraph*, a weekly paper for that denomination. Returning to Alabama, was in 1856 elected superintendent of public schools for Coosa County. In 1857 he was elected representative from that county to the State Legislature. In 1859 he was chosen to the State Senate for a term of four years. In 1862 he entered the Confederate army as captain of a company. His field-officers being prisoners from the 16th of May, 1863, to the close of the war, he commanded the 46th Regiment of Alabama soldiers, and surrendered the regiment at Salisbury, N. C. In 1866, Gov. Patton appointed him inspector-general of Alabama. This office was resigned that he might enter upon the work of an evangelist, under appointment of the Domestic Mission Board. The religious side of his history is as follows: Baptized at Rockford, Ala., in 1854, by Rev. Madison Butler. Ordained in 1859 to take charge of the church in the city of Wetempka, a connection which continued until he entered the army. As an evangelist after the war, through privation, and yet "with great spiritual joy," he continued this work for several years, part of the time without the patronage of any board, and, on foot, reaching all his appointments, giving satisfaction to the churches and receiving satisfactory support. Since 1870 he has devoted himself to pastoral work, having charge for some years of Talassee and other churches; then for some years at Opelika. Mr. Brewer is one of our most clear-headed and warm-hearted men. A bold, gifted, able preacher, with a high order of consecration.

Bridgman, C. D. W., D.D.—Dr. Bridgman was born in Saugerties, N. Y., Jan. 1, 1835. He

C. D. W. BRIDGMAN, D.D.

was baptized by Rev. Josiah Hatt into the fellowship of the Baptist church of Hoboken, N. J. His first pastorate was at Morristown, N. J., then at Jamaica, Mass., and in 1862 he took charge of Emmanuel Baptist church of Albany, N. Y. During his labors the church erected one of the largest and finest edifices for public worship in our denomination in the State. Supported by such well-known men as Gov. Marcy, Hon. Ira Harris, Hon. Friend Humphrey, Hon. Geo. Dawson, and others of wealth and high social influence, the church became a power for good in the capital of the State, and throughout the country. During that pastorate several of his sermons were printed and published by his people; among them may be noted a discourse delivered before the Pearl Street Baptist church, Aug. 28, 1870, on the occasion of leaving their old house of worship; also a sermon entitled "The Nation's Exodus," a review of the civil war, and a thanksgiving for peace. A discourse at the funeral of Col. Lewis Benedict, who fell in battle fighting for the Union. A memorial discourse on the life and service of Rev. Bartholomew T. Welsh,

D.D., was so highly prized that the Hudson River North Association published it in its annual report. Perhaps his published discourse on the death of Hon. Ira Harris produced the deepest impression on the public mind. The subject of the memorial was an officer of his church, and had a national reputation for probity, learning, wisdom, and piety, giving the preacher a theme well suited to his ability.

Dr. Bridgman is a scholarly preacher, of orthodox views, faultless rhetoric, and fervid zeal for the Master.

In 1878 he accepted a call from the Madison Avenue Baptist church, New York, a field well adapted to his style of work, and he has had marked success in building up a congregation which had been greatly reduced.

Brierly, Rev. Benjamin, was one of the most distinguished, eloquent, and influential of the early preachers in California. Born in York, England, Nov. 24, 1811, he came with his parents to America in 1821, and during the great revival in Massachusetts in 1831, he was baptized at Cunningham. He believed that he was converted in his early childhood. As soon as he was baptized he gave great promise of usefulness by his fervent prayers and exhortations, and devoted himself to the ministry. His four years of study at Newton and New Hampton were years of diligence, and he graduated with high honor. He was ordained in 1835 at Dover, N. H., and during the next fourteen years was a popular pastor at Dover, Great Falls, Springfield, Middlebury, Vt.; Manchester, N. H.; and Salem, Mass. For the benefit of his health he took a sea voyage *via* Cape Horn to California, arriving there in August, 1849. He was chaplain of the first Legislature held in that State, preached at San José, and was pastor at Sacramento. After a short visit to the East he returned with his family to California in 1852; was pastor of the First church, San Francisco, six years; at San José two years; and three years at Nevada City, where he died July 21, 1863. He was a man of great power in the discussion of special religious themes. His address in 1847 before the American Baptist Home Mission Society, giving his reasons for becoming a Baptist, was published by vote of the society, and had a wide circulation.

Briggs, Hon. George Nixon.—"Governor" Briggs, for by this title he was best known, was born in Adams, Mass., April 12, 1796. His father was a man of generous impulses and patriotic spirit. In the war of the Revolution he fought with Stark and Allen, and rejoiced in the victories of the American army. He removed to Manchester, Vt., when George was seven years of age, and then to White Creek, Washington Co., N. Y. For five years he devoted himself to the study of law, and at the age of twenty-one was admitted to the bar. One or two cases which he carried successfully through the courts won for him a reputation, and led to his being chosen to fill several important posts of honor and responsibility.

GOV. GEORGE NIXON BRIGGS.

In 1830 he was chosen to represent his section of the State of Massachusetts in the House of Representatives at Washington. In this relation he was always the consistent Christian, the warm advocate of temperance, as well as the accomplished statesman. For twelve years he served his district in the councils of the nation, leaving behind him a name in Congress of unsullied honor.

In 1843 his fellow-citizens, appreciating the excellencies of his character, elected him governor of the State. "He was a candidate," says his son, "without caucus or convention or nomination, save by the voice of the people." When he was chosen representative to Congress, so warm a place did he come to have in the hearts of the people while he filled the office of governor, that he justified the course pursued by his constituents in sending him to Washington and keeping him there so many years. For nine years he held the office of governor, and administered the affairs of the State in a way which secured him the respect and affection of his fellow-citizens.

Having retired from his office, he was appointed one of the judges of the Court of Common Pleas, until some change was made in the courts, when his services were no longer in demand. During this long period of civil service Gov. Briggs received some of the highest honors that his own denomination could confer on him. He was president of the Missionary Union, and those who witnessed the dignity and urbanity and tact with which he presided over its annual meetings, will not be unwilling to concede that he was a model presiding officer. He was also president of the American Tract Society at Boston, and the American Temperance Union. Positions of honor and trust were offered him, which he declined, among these was that of chancellor of Madison University.

The death of Gov. Briggs was caused by a serious accident. His last words were, "I am at the lowest point of animal existence. I don't see. God and Christ are my all. I love you. Do what you think best. Leave all to God, God, God." He died Sept. 12, 1861.

No warmer or more sincere eulogies were ever passed on the characters of any of Massachusetts' distinguished statesmen—and no State can boast of a larger or more honored number—than were passed on Gov. Briggs. He was firm and unwavering in his religious convictions, and true to the principles of the denomination with which he connected himself when he was but twelve years of age. It was understood that he was a conscientious Baptist, and that did not make him the less a conscientious Christian. But the warmth of his attachment to his own church in his Pittsfield home it is not easy to measure. Its public and its private worship were exceedingly dear to him. Very touching were the questions which his pastor, Dr. Porter, asked at his funeral: "Can it be, dear brethren, that he will walk these aisles no more? Can it be that his noble form, and mild blue eye, and benevolent face will not be seen again in the sanctuary?"

We, as Baptists, count it a great honor that we can point to the name of the pure-minded governor of Massachusetts, upon whose fair reputation no stain rests, and whose moral integrity was never challenged by even the most violent partisan animosity.

Briggs, Hon. Henry C., was born in West Haven, Vt., June 29, 1831. In his infancy his father removed to Allegan Co., Mich. He was educated partly in Kalamazoo College and partly in the University of Michigan. He was admitted to the bar in 1861, having previously been chosen State senator from Allegan County. He was prosecuting attorney for Kalamazoo County four years, and judge of probate eight years. Soon after entering on the practice of his profession he was baptized by Rev. Samuel Haskell, and has ever since been specially interested in whatever pertains to the kingdom of Christ. As superintendent of the Sunday-school, as trustee of Kalamazoo College, as a steadfast friend of temperance, he has won a good name. Every Baptist in the State knows him as a Christian lawyer desirous of honoring Christ.

Briggs, Rev. Joel, was born in Norton, Mass., April 15, 1757; hopefully converted in January, 1770; fitted for college with Rev. William Nelson and Rev. William Williams; went to Brown University; was ordained as pastor of the Baptist church in Randolph, Mass., Dec. 5, 1787, and remained with this church until the time of his death, which occurred Jan. 18, 1828. The pastorate of Mr. Briggs was one of unusual length, and was fruitful for good. He witnessed four or five special revivals among his people, in one of which his church received an accession of between 70 and 80 members. From his church there were formed two others, viz., the church in Canton and the North church in Randolph.

Briggs, W. A., of Blue Rapids, Kansas, is a native of Western Massachusetts, and a nephew of the late Gov. Briggs. The church at Blue Rapids was organized and their house of worship erected under his efficient labors. His business qualifications being of a high order, he has been induced to accept the office of mayor of the city, which position he has held several years, to the great satisfaction of the people.

Bright, Rev. Thomas, was born in Walton, England, in 1808. He was baptized in Utica, N. Y., and soon after entered the ministry. He labored as pastor of the churches in Richland, Pulaski, and Adams, N. Y., and in Elkhorn, Walworth, Spring Prairie, Geneva, Fox Lake, Waupaca, and Madison, Wis. He came to Wisconsin in 1852. He was a widely-known and greatly-beloved minister of Christ, a clear and strong preacher of the gospel. He clung tenaciously to its doctrines, and delighted in a full exposition of the plan of salvation. And while he was a great expounder of divine truth, he was at the same time richly experimental in his preaching. His doctrines were personal experiences coming from his heart to the hearts of his hearers. He was a safe and judicious counselor, a wise man. His presence in the church, the council, the Association, the convention, was always sought by his brethren. He had no enemies.

He fell with the harness on. While preaching in his pulpit in Madison, Wis., on Sabbath evening, Sept. 10, 1876, he sank back on the sofa in death. In his decease the Baptists of Wisconsin lost one of the best of ministers,—a man whose well-balanced mind, large heart, and clear and experimental knowledge of God's Word raised him far above many.

Brine, Rev. John, was born at Kettering, England, about 1703. When very young the Saviour found him and revealed his love in him, and he united by baptism with the immersed church of Kettering, by which he was called to the ministry.

After preaching for a short time in the country, he went to London in 1730 to enter upon the pastorate of the church in St. Paul's Alley, Cripplegate. He remained in this position thirty-five years, and left it for his heavenly reward Feb. 21, 1765.

Mr. Brine was a great man measured by his intellect, his usefulness, and his influence. He was a man of deep piety; he was intimately acquainted with the Holy Scriptures. He had an enthusiastic love for the doctrines of grace, and next to Dr. Gill, whose early ministrations brought him to Jesus, he was for years the most influential leader in the Baptist denomination. His doctrinal sentiments were in exact harmony with those of Dr. Gill. The doctor preached his funeral sermon, and in it said, "I might take notice of his natural and acquired abilities, his great understanding, clear light, and sound judgment in the doctrines of the gospel, and the great deep things of God, and of his zeal, skill, and courage in vindicating important truths published by him to the world, and by which he being dead yet speaketh."

Mr. Brine was the author of 24 sermons, published separately at various times during his ministry, and of 14 pamphlets and larger works.

Brinson, Rev. James, a pioneer in the region between Ouachita and Red River, was born in Tennessee. By his labors some of the earliest churches in this region were gathered. He died in 1831.

Brisbane, Dr. Wm. H., was born near Charleston, S. C. His ancestors were of aristocratic English and Irish families, and he was the heir of large wealth. His early education was intrusted to Bishop England, of the Roman Catholic Church, and subsequently to Rev. Wm. T. Brantly, then president of Beaufort College. At the age of fifteen he was sent North, to the military school at Middletown, Conn., from which he was graduated with honor at the age of nineteen. Soon after this he was converted, and at once felt it to be his duty to preach the gospel. His fine culture and attainments, and his consecration to the work, placed him very early in the front ranks of the Baptist ministry of the South. He had among his personal friends such men as Fuller, Howell, Jeter, and Brantly; and among well-known public men he enjoyed the friendship of Jackson, Calhoun, Clay, Webster, and Benton. He was thoroughly familiar with public affairs and current political matters, and his splendid culture and large wealth gave him access to the best society of the country. He spent much time at the State and National capitals, where he became deeply interested in questions then agitating both State and nation, among them the question of American slavery. This subject had early in life taken a deep and absorbing hold upon his mind, he himself being a large slave-holder. After an honest and prayerful consideration of the question, extending through several years, he became convinced that the system was wrong; and he resolved to give freedom to his slaves. He bought back the servants he had sold, and having purchased land in Ohio, he came with his former slaves and settled them in new homes, abundantly supplying the means for their immediate support. And Dr. Brisbane himself became a resident of Cincinnati, O. Here he labored with renewed consecration in the work of the ministry. He became a radical and uncompromising leader in the cause of human emancipation.

For twenty-five years Wisconsin was honored in having this good man among her citizens. He was widely known as the friend and champion of every good cause. He preached the gospel in his declining years with great power at Madison, Mazomanie, Spring Green, and other places. He was greatly admired for his undoubted conscientiousness, his deep humility, his great services to the cause of truth and sound reform. He died at his home at Arena, Wis., on the 5th of April, 1878, aged seventy-five years.

Bristol Baptist College, England, is the oldest of the theological seminaries of the denomination. Many of the eminent men who founded the early Baptist churches in England and Wales had been educated at the universities of Oxford and Cambridge, and when the doors of these great national institutions were closed against Nonconformists by law, after the restoration of Charles II., they felt themselves compelled to provide for the continuance of an educated ministry. In 1675 the Baptist ministers in London invited their brethren throughout the country to meet in the following May in the metropolis with a view to form "a plan for providing an orderly standing ministry who might give themselves to reading and study, and so become able ministers of the New Testament." Four years after this meeting, in 1679, an excellent deacon of the Broadmead church, Bristol, Mr. Edward Terrill, executed a deed leaving a considerable part of his property to the pastor of the Broadmead church for the time being, "provided he be a holy man, well skilled in the Greek and Hebrew tongues, and devote three half-days a week to the instruction of any number of young students, not exceeding twelve, who may be recommended by the churches." In 1689 what was called a General Assembly was convened in London, in which more than one hundred churches were represented, and it was resolved to raise a fund, one object of which should be to assist "members of churches who had promising gifts, were sound in fundamentals, and inclined to study, in attaining to the knowledge of Latin, Greek, and Hebrew." Progress, however, was slow for various reasons. Mr. Terrill's fund did not become available until the death of his widow, but there is evidence showing that Mr. Caleb Jope was chosen as one of the ministers of the Broadmead church, Bristol, for the purpose of teaching, and that he received support from Terrill's fund from 1714 to 1719. With the acceptance of the pastorate at Broadmead by Mr. Bernard Foskett, in 1720, the Bristol Academy became a recognized institution among the churches. The Particular Baptist Fund, which had been established in 1717, included ministerial education among its objects, and from this quarter the work at Bristol received considerable aid. Sixty-five students were taught by Mr. Foskett, of whom the most noteworthy were Benjamin Beddome, John Ryland, Sr., Benjamin Francis, Hugh Evans, Morgan Edwards (afterwards of Philadelphia), Dr. Ash, and Dr. Llewellyn. Hugh Evans succeeded Mr. Foskett, and was succeeded by his son, Dr. Caleb Evans. Under their direction the interests of the college flourished, and in 1770 the Bristol Education Society was formed "for the enlargement of the number of students in this seminary, and its more effectual and permanent support." Among the students admitted to the college during Dr. Evans's presidency were John Rippon, John Sutcliff, Robert Hall, Samuel Pearce, Joseph Hughes, the founder of the British and Foreign Bible Society, William Steadman, Joseph Kinghorn, John Foster, and William Staughton, afterwards of Philadelphia. In 1785, Robert Hall became one of the tutors in the institution, and as assistant minister at Broadmead gave brilliant promise of the oratorical fame which in subsequent years he attained. On Dr. Evans's death, Dr. John Ryland, of Northampton, accepted the presidency, and continued his official service thirty-two years, until his death, in 1825. The present edifice in Stokes Croft, Bristol, was built in 1811. Dr. Ryland was succeeded by the Rev. T. S. Crisp, who for several years had filled the classical professorship and served the Broadmead church as assistant minister. Mr. Crisp held the office until his death, in 1868, when he was succeeded by the present distinguished president, Dr. F. W. Gotch, who had been Mr. Crisp's colleague since 1846, and also a former student of the institution. Under Dr. Gotch Bristol College maintains its ancient reputation, and enjoys the confidence of the churches. During its continuous history from 1720 to the present time about 600 students have been registered on its roll, several of whom have become presidents and professors in Baptist colleges. Between forty and fifty missionaries of the Baptist Missionary Society received their education at Bristol, among whom were Dr. Marshman, Dr. Yates, John Mack, Thomas Burchell, and C. B. Lewis. Bristol College possesses a remarkably valuable library, and a choice collection of rare and antique articles of various kinds, the munificent bequest of Dr. Andrew Gifford. The library contains a manuscript copy of Wycliff's translation of the Epistles, the Acts, and the Apocalypse, and another of a Wycliffite version of Matthew and the Acts, which belonged to the celebrated Lord Cobham, the Lollard leader; the copy of the great charter of Edward I. which Blackstone used in preparing his Commentaries; a copy of the first edition of "Paradise Lost," supposed to have been Milton's own copy; a Concordance published in 1673, with the autograph of John Bunyan. In English Bibles and Testaments the library is very rich, the most valuable book in the collection being a copy of the first edition of Tyndale's New Testament, of which no other complete copy is known to exist. It is literally the FIRST English Testament, and as such it is justly styled the most interesting book in the language. There are no less than thirty-five different editions of English Bibles and Testaments published during the reigns of Henry VIII. and Edward VI., including the rare and valuable first and second editions of Coverdale's folio Bible. Of early printed books, there are three from Caxton's press in 1481-82, the first books printed in England; the second, third, and fifth editions of Erasmus's Greek Testament; the " Nuremberg Chronicle," 1493; and a book called " Roberti Sermones," printed in 1475. The walls of the library and museum are adorned with a large collection of portraits, both paintings and prints, of notable persons, for the most part identified with the denomination. An exquisitely finished miniature of Cromwell, one of the few authentic likenesses of the great hero, is the chief treasure in the museum, which is crowded with objects of varied interest from all lands. A bust of the Rev. Dr. Gifford, with an appropriate Latin inscription, is placed over the entrance to the museum.

Brittain, Rev. Jabez Mercer, of Georgia, youngest child of Henry and Louisa Brittain, was born May 4, 1842, near Lexington, Oglethorpe County. His grandparents came into Georgia from Virginia in 1797, and settled in Oglethorpe County. His father was a soldier under Gen. Floyd in the Indian war of 1814, and was clerk of the Court of Ordinary for Oglethorpe County for many years. His mother was a meek and pious woman, who devoted herself assiduously to the training of her children. Mr. Brittain was prepared for college by Prof. T. B. Moss, a distinguished educator in Lexington, Ga., and entered Franklin College, now the University of Georgia, in January, 1859, graduating in 1861. He enlisted in the Confederate army in September, 1861, and became attached to Lawton's brigade in Stonewall Jackson's division. After taking part in several engagements, he was appointed chaplain to the 38th

Georgia Regiment in the summer of 1863. He took an active part in the great revival which occurred in the Army of Northern Virginia, and baptized many converts. In August, 1864, he resigned his commission on account of a severe family affliction, and was exempted from further military duty. He returned home and engaged in farming for three years, after which he taught in the institutions of learning at Dalton, Acworth, and Conyers, and he is now principal of the Connington Male Institute. He has also continuously engaged in pastoral work for Baptist churches in Whitfield, Gordon, Bartow, Rockdale, and Newton Counties, and he has filled acceptably the position of moderator of the Stone Mountain Association.

Mr. Brittain was converted in 1857, and the same year was baptized by Dr. P. H. Mell and joined the Antioch church, Oglethorpe County. He was ordained in the fall of 1863.

The frequent descent of genuine revivals in the churches of his charge proves his faithfulness and excellence as a minister; while the constant unanimity with which he has been called by his churches, and the various and numerous tokens of affection he has received from their members, show the appreciation in which his services are held. Though he is a well-educated man and a thorough Christian gentleman, his greatest ambition is to excel in winning and training souls for the service of Christ.

Broaddus Female College.—This institution was established in Winchester, Va., September, 1871, as Winchester Female Institute, Rev. S. F. Chapman, Principal. After a brief service Mr. Chapman was succeeded by Rev. E. J. Willis. The school became prosperous, and the list of students increased until in the third year the number reached 72.

The fourth session was opened under the name of Broaddus Female College, in honor of Rev. Wm. F. Broaddus, D.D. Two other denominational schools were opened in the town, and the money crisis occurring at the same time, the interests of the school were so affected that, in 1876, it was moved to Clarksburg, W. Va., and is in a flourishing condition. The Baptists of the State have adopted the school and pledged to it their support. Rev. E. J. Willis continues as principal, and is assisted by seven well-qualified teachers. The course of instruction is extensive, furnishing opportunities equal to those of any school for young ladies in the middle Southern States. Nearly all its sessions have been characterized by special religious interest among the students, many of whom have professed faith in Christ.

Broaddus, Wm. F., D.D., was born in Culpeper Co., Va., April 30, 1801. His mind developed rapidly, and he soon secured and held a prominent position among his associates. He married at the early age of eighteen, and was converted at the age of twenty. In April, 1824, he was ordained to the work of the gospel ministry. He settled in Middleburg, Loudoun Co., Va., where he conducted with great success a large school for young ladies, serving at the same time as pastor, Mount Salem, "F. T." Bethel, Upperville, Long Branch, and Middlebury churches. In this field he labored most successfully for sixteen years, serving the churches in some cases without compensation, and in others for merely a nominal salary. Antinomianism at that period held sway over this entire region, and its advocates exerted themselves to the utmost to render futile his plain gospel teachings and faithful labors. But the truth gradually won its way, until a complete revolution was made in the views, feelings, and actions of individuals and churches, so that no more exemplary and fruitful churches can be found than those in the region where Dr. Broaddus began his ministerial career. The denomination at large knows but little of what they really owe to him for having been the means of driving out a "dead orthodoxy," and planting in its stead a vital, active Christian life. In 1840 he removed to Lexington, Ky., where he engaged in teaching and preaching, serving, besides other churches, those at Versailles and Shelbyville. About the year 1851 he returned to Virginia and accepted an agency for the Columbian College, Washington, D. C., to raise an endowment fund for that institution. In this he was quite successful. In 1835 he accepted an invitation to become pastor of the church in Fredericksburg, Va., where he was soon instrumental in building a handsome church edifice, and in gathering a large and efficient congregation. Still retaining his strong predilection for teaching, he opened here a school of a high grade for young ladies, which was conducted successfully for several years. In 1859 he undertook an agency for raising money in Virginia towards the endowment of the Southern Baptist Theological Seminary. Returning to Fredericksburg on the successful accomplishment of this agency, he resumed his pastoral labors, and continued them until 1863, when the city was occupied by U. S. troops and the inhabitants scattered over the State. Dr. Broaddus was held for a while by the U. S. authorities as prisoner in the "Old Capitol" at Washington, and by his gentlemanly bearing, genial humor, fund of anecdote, and straightforward, manly conduct he won the kindest regards of all who came in contact with him. Many a lonely hour did he lighten up in the old prison-house as he narrated, in his peculiarly interesting way, to friends grouped around him, various adventures that he had met with in the diversified course of his eventful life. Dr. Broaddus, soon after his release, removed to

Charlotteville, Va., and became pastor of the church in that place, which position he held until 1868, when he resigned and returned to Fredericksburg to prosecute an agency under the appointment of the General Association for the education of the children of deceased and disabled Confederate soldiers. This labor he carried on with great success until 1872, when the further prosecution of the work became unnecessary. Dr. Broaddus was enabled by his persevering efforts to keep at school for several years some thousands of poor children with the money raised for that purpose. For a brief period subsequent to this he devoted himself to the work of a voluntary and independent evangelist, preaching wherever invited, until blindness and increasing bodily infirmities prevented the further prosecution of these congenial labors. He died in Fredericksburg, Sept. 8, 1876, in the seventy-sixth year of his age. The degree of D.D. was conferred upon Mr. Broaddus by the Columbian College in 1854. As a man, Dr. Broaddus was genial, gentle, and courteous. His constant and varied intercourse with all classes of men gave him a shrewd insight into the more recondite workings of human nature. His companionship was as attractive to the young as it was to the middle-aged and the old. His home was open to all, and troops of friends have rested beneath his hospitable roof. As a peace-maker he was pre-eminent, and the blessings of many a household rested upon him for his judicious and kindly counsel. To every good work he gave his voice and his money, and frequently his personal labor, so that many now rise up to call him blessed. As a preacher, he was earnest, persuasive, practical. Obliged for years to combat the erroneous views of those who abused the doctrine of God's sovereignty, and necessarily polemic in many of his earlier discourses, he nevertheless held tenaciously to the fundamental doctrines of grace, while he urged men everywhere to prove their new spiritual life by new spiritual works. A very large number, many hundreds perhaps, were converted through his instrumentality; and as a consequence no name in the long list of faithful Virginia ministers is more earnestly loved and tenderly revered than that of William F. Broaddus.

Broaddus, Rev. Andrew, was born in Carolina Co., Va., Nov. 4, 1770. His love of letters and his studiousness were such that he became one of the most thorough Biblical scholars of his times. About the age of eighteen he experienced a change of heart, and, although strenuously opposed by his father, who was a rigid adherent of the Episcopal Church, he was baptized May 28, 1789, and became a member of the Baptist church of Upper King and Queen, then under the care of the Rev. Theodoric Noel. The duty of preparing himself to preach the gospel at once pressed itself upon his attention, and having been convinced that it was his duty to do so, he preached his first sermon at the house of Mrs. Lowrie, where, upon this, the first occasion, Rev. R. B. Semple also preached. From the very beginning Mr. Broadus was popular as a preacher. He was ordained Oct. 16, 1791, in the church in which he was baptized. Among the first churches he served were Burrus's and Bethel, in the county of Carolina, and also the church in Fredericksburg. While supplying these churches he also taught a school, and applied himself closely to study. Subsequently he became pastor of Upper Zion, Beulah, Mangohic, Salem, and Upper King and Queen, with the last two of which he continued to labor until the close of his life. Although Mr. Broadus was known but to few personally beyond the limits of his own State, yet, when in the prime of life, he received invitations to become the pastor of numerous churches in distant cities: from the First church in Boston, in 1811; from the First church in Philadelphia, in 1811; from the First church in Baltimore, in 1819; from the New Market Street church, Philadelphia, in 1819; from the Sansom Street church, Philadelphia, in 1824; and from the First church, New York, in 1832. An ineradicable constitutional timidity, which sometimes made him almost powerless in speech when in the presence of strangers, and a deeply-rooted attachment to old friends and old scenes, prevented his acceptance of all such tempting offers. He made the trial once in removing to Richmond to take charge of the First Baptist church in that city, but his stay there was short, and he soon returned to labor again with his country congregations. As a preacher, Mr. Broadus was the foremost man of his generation. "In clearness of conception, beauty of imagery, aptness of illustration, and tenderness of soul he was pre-eminent. With a well-proportioned form, graceful manner, natural gesticulation, benignant countenance, and musical voice, he held, as by a pleasing spell, his enraptured hearers. All hung upon his lips, unwilling to lose a word, while with softly insinuating power he found access to the innermost depths of the soul, causing all its fountains of emotions to gush forth." His chief excellence consisted in the exposition of the Scriptures, and especially those passages suited to edify and comfort the people of God. Contrary to what many suppose to have been the case, his most effective sermons were not preached on great occasions. His love of quiet, and inveterate dislike of large and promiscuous assemblies, generally kept him away from Associations and conventions; and when present and persuaded to preach, there was no certainty that he would be able to fulfill his appointment. It is recorded of him that having been appointed to preach at a meeting of the Dover Association in Matthews Co., Va., he went through the preliminary services in his usual felicitous manner, and when the large audience had settled themselves to enjoy a spiritual feast, he came to a sudden pause and said, "The circumstances of the case—*I mean my case*—make it necessary to excuse myself from proceeding with the discussion." His biographer adds, "The thought had probably seized him that the expectations of the people could not be met; or he had recognized in the congregation some one whose criticism he dreaded; or the wind and roar of the ocean had disturbed his nervous system; whatever it was, a serious surprise and regret were felt by all." This painful dread of a crowd was, however, in a measure overcome towards the latter part of his life. Mr. Broadus's literary labors were also of a high order. He wrote a small volume, of some 70 pages, entitled "The Age of Reason and Revelation," which was a reply to Paine's celebrated attack on Christianity. This little work was published in 1795, while he was still quite young, and gives evidence of a well-stored mind and vigorous logical powers. In 1816 he published "A Bible History, with Occasional Notes, to Explain and Illustrate Difficult Passages." These "notes" are, indeed, valuable for the clear and satisfactory views they open up of many of the dark passages of the Word of God. The Dover Association requested him, at one of their sessions, to prepare a commentary upon the Scriptures, which, however, he did not undertake. He prepared an admirable little "Catechism for Children," which was issued by the American Baptist Publication Society. He also prepared a manual of church polity and discipline. He did much for the hymnology of the churches. As early as 1790 he prepared and published a collection of "Sacred Ballads," most of which were in popular use at that time. About 1828 he prepared the "Dover Selection," and afterwards the "Virginia Selection," several of whose hymns were of his own composition, and all of which were very extensively used by the churches. Only a few of Mr. Broadus's sermons have been published, for, although he prepared his sermons with the greatest care, making more or less extended notes, he rarely wrote out his discourses. Mr. Broadus was also a frequent contributor to the *Religious Herald*, for which he wrote a valuable series of essays on Campbellism and its errors. The Columbian College conferred the degree of D.D. upon Mr. Broadus, but he respectfully declined to accept the honor.

"The Baptists of Virginia will long cherish the fond memory of the excellence of his character, the superior mental and oratorical powers with which he was endowed, and the genial, useful influence he exercised on the churches and the world."

Broadus, John Albert, D.D., LL.D., Professor of Homiletics and Interpretation of the New Tes-

JOHN ALBERT BROADUS, D.D., LL.D.

tament in the Southern Baptist Theological Seminary, was born in Culpeper Co., Va., Jan. 24, 1827. His family is of Welsh extraction, and the name was formerly spelt Broadhurst. His father was a prominent member of the Virginia Legislature a number of years. Dr. Broadus was educated at the University of Virginia, where he took the degree of A.M. in 1850. In 1851 he was elected Assistant Professor of Latin and Greek in that institution, and filled the place two years. He was pastor of the Baptist church at Charlottesville during the same period and till 1855, when he was elected chaplain of the university, and served two years. He then returned to his former pastorate. In 1859 he was elected to his present professorship. In 1863 he preached as missionary in Gen. R. E. Lee's army. From this period till 1865 he was corresponding secretary of the Sunday-School board of the Southern Baptist Convention. During this period he published various small works, which were circulated in such of the Southern States as were accessible at that time. In 1870 he published a book on the "Preparation and Delivery of Sermons," which was republished in England, and has been adopted as a text-book in various theological seminaries of different denominations in Europe and America. Besides various review articles, sermons, and numberless newspaper articles, he published in 1867–69, in the *Religious Herald*, of

Richmond, Va., a series of papers criticising the American Bible Union's version of the New Testament, and in 1872-73 another series entitled "Reflections of Travel," in which he gave an account of a tour he made through Europe, Egypt, and Palestine in 1870-71. In 1876 he published a series of lectures on the history of preaching. Dr. Broadus ranks with the ablest preachers of his generation.

Brock, William, D.D., was born Feb. 14, 1807, at Honiton, in Devonshire, England. On his father's side he was descended from certain Dutch refugees of the same name who had settled in the neighborhood some time in the sixteenth century. William Brock was only four years old when his father died. As the only free scholar in the endowed grammar school of the town he had a rough schooling, and but for the native vigor of body and mind the hardships of this early period of his life would have crushed him. He was apprenticed at the age of thirteen to a watchmaker at Sidmouth, and served an apprenticeship of seven years. He obtained a situation in Hertford, and during a two years' residence there he professed Christ in baptism, and began to exhort sinners to repent and believe the gospel. He was admitted a member of the Baptist church at Highgate, London, of which his kinsman, the Rev. Mr. Lewis, was pastor, on Jan. 10, 1830, and in the following month, having given satisfactory proofs of a divine call to become a preacher of the Word, he was recommended to the committee of Stepney College as a student for the ministry. His energy and diligence in study were conspicuous, but his oratorical powers were so evident and exceptional that his services were too frequently in request to permit of his giving undivided attention to his studies. Before the second year of his college course was ended he had received more than one invitation to the pastorate, and in the course of the third year the pressure from two different churches became so strong that the college authorities finally agreed to release him from the remainder of the four years' course of study. He had by this time been led to accept the invitation of the church meeting in St. Mary's chapel, in the old city of Norwich. Dr. Brock began his ministry in Norwich, May 10, 1833. The congregation were soon increased by the attraction of the pulpit. The young pastor of twenty-five years of age threw his whole soul into his work and gave full proof of his ministry. Enlargements of the edifice took place again and again. But in 1848 his friend, Sir Morton Peto, proposed that Mr. Brock should become the minister of the new church to be gathered in the edifice he was then building in London, to be called Bloomsbury chapel. After long and anxious deliberation the Norwich church received their pastor's resignation, and in December he commenced his London ministry. It was a great venture, but it was a great success from the first. The munificent liberality of the builder of the edifice and the courageous ability of the minister were well matched. A crowded congregation was immediately gathered; conversions and accessions from various quarters continually augmented the membership; and the whole neighborhood felt the influence of the new church, which poured forth help for all manner of benevolent and educational work. Bloomsbury chapel became the centre of a Christian evangelization and philanthropy the like of which could not then be easily found in London. But notwithstanding the cost of these home enterprises, foreign missions and all good works received effective support. During the twenty-five years of Dr. Brock's ministry at Bloomsbury, as previously in Norwich, he took a prominent part in the religious movements of the time, and contributed to establish some of the modes of evangelism now common, such as special services in theatres and public halls. In denominational work he was a trusted counselor and leader. When the London Baptist Association was reorganized, in 1866, he was unanimously chosen president; and in 1869 he was cordially invited to the chair of the Baptist Union of England and Wales. His services to the Missionary Society were exceedingly valuable, and he ever held himself ready to obey its call. He was one of the founders of the Society for augmenting Pastors' Incomes, promoting it himself with zealous liberality, and in the recent movement towards a compacter organization of the denomination his influence was very effective. His literary labors were considerable for a man so full of public work. His biography of Gen. Sir Henry Havelock had a very extensive sale, and some of his occasional sermons and lectures on denominational and general topics have a permanent interest and value. He received the degree of D.D. from Harvard University, and although he was reluctant to assume it, his friends and the public carried the point against him. Finding his strength failing, he resigned his charge in 1872, and thenceforward gave himself to the service of the churches. With commendable liberality the church at Bloomsbury made provision for his remaining days, but they were destined to be few. His death occurred somewhat suddenly on Nov. 13, 1875.

Brockett, Linus Pierpont, A.M., M.D., a son of Rev. Pierpont Brockett, for fifty years a Baptist minister in New England, was born in Canton, Conn., Oct. 16, 1820; fitted for college at Hill's Academy, Essex, Conn., and Connecticut Literary Institution, Suffield, Conn.; entered Brown University in 1837, but owing to ill health did not graduate; attended medical lectures at New Haven,

Conn., Washington, D. C., and New York City; graduated M.D. in 1843; practiced medicine in New England and in Georgetown, Ky. Since 1846 he has devoted most of his time to literary pursuits. He received the honorary degree of A.M. from Amherst College in 1857. He has published "Geographical History of New York," 1847; "Memoir of James Edward Meystre," 1855; "The Pioneer Preacher," 1857; several reports and essays on idiot education, 1855–57; "History of Education," 1859; "History of the Civil War," 1865; "Life of Abraham Lincoln," 1865; "Our Great Captains," 1865; "Philanthropic Results of the War," 1865; "Camp, Battle-Field, and Hospital," 1866; "Woman's Work in the Civil War," 1867; "Men of Our Day," 1868, and a new and enlarged edition in 1872; "Woman, her Rights, Wrongs, Privileges, and Responsibilities," 1869; "The Year of Battles, a History of the Franco-German War," 1871, and German edition, 1872; "The Silk Industry in America," 1876; "The Cross and the Crescent," 1877, etc. He has also edited numerous religious works, and was, from 1856 to 1862, on the editorial staff of the New American Cyclopædia, and from 1861 to 1875, one of the editors of the Annual Cyclopædia, and from 1872 to 1877, one of the editors of Johnson's Universal Cyclopædia. He has also been a frequent contributor to religious quarterlies, magazines, and weekly periodicals. He is the author of "The Bogomils," the early Baptists of the East, who form, as he believes, the missing link between the Baptists of the fifth and those of the fourteenth and fifteenth centuries, and has other religious works in the course of preparation. His residence is in Brooklyn, N. Y.

Bronson, Rev. Asa Clarke, son of Rev. Asa and Marinda (Jennings) Bronson, was born in Stratfield, Conn., Aug. 7, 1822; united with First Baptist church in Fall River, Mass., in 1835; licensed to preach in 1848 by Wakefield church, R. I.; ordained, December, 1849, in South Hanson, Mass., his father and brothers, S. J. and B. F. Bronson, assisting; prospered in his settlement; in May, 1851, settled with North Reading church, and had an extensive revival; in December, 1854, became pastor at Leominster; in June, 1857, took charge of Third Baptist church in Groton, Conn., and remained twelve years, greatly prospered in revivals, and in uniting Second and Third churches, even joining together the meeting-houses; became pastor of Wallingford church in January, 1870, erected a superb edifice, and baptized 80 persons; in July, 1876, settled in Paterson, N. J., and remained three and a half years; in November, 1879, took the oversight of churches in Lebanon, Conn. Calm, wise, energetic, prudent, persevering; sound in the faith like his honored father.

Bronson, Benjamin Franklin, D.D., son of Rev. Asa and Marinda (Jennings) Bronson, was born in North Salem, N. Y., April 21, 1821; converted and baptized in Fall River, Mass., in 1836; graduated from Madison University in 1844, and Theological Department in 1846; ordained in Ashland, Mass., 1846; pastor in Methuen, 1850; in Woburn, 1858; in Boston Highlands (Ruggles Street church), 1862; in Southbridge, 1867; in Putnam, Conn., 1872, where he is still laboring (1880); has been much engaged in directing common and high schools; was one of the editors of "First Half Century of Madison University"; for several years secretary of "Freedman's Aid Commission"; for two years secretary of Massachusetts Baptist Convention; received degree of D.D. from Madison University in 1869.

Bronson, Miles, D.D., was born in Norway, N. Y., July 20, 1812; having passed through the course of study at the Hamilton Literary and Theological Institution, he was ordained at Whitesborough, N. Y., and received his appointment as a missionary April 29, 1836. He sailed for the field of his labor the October following, and reached Sadiya, Assam, July 17, 1837, where he remained until his removal to Jaipur, May 13, 1838. His interest having become awakened in the Nagas, a tribe of people occupying the high ranges of mountains southeast of Jaipur, he visited some of them in January, 1839, and in 1840 repeated his visit. In March of this year a station was established among the Naga Hills, which was placed under his charge for a short time, when it was deemed desirable that he should remove to Nowgong. Dr. Bronson occupied this position for several years, one of the most important works accomplished being the founding and supervision of the Nowgong Orphan Institution, of which a fuller account may be found in the article on Assam. In 1849, Mr. Bronson returned to the United States, and remained here for more than a year, reaching his field of labor early in 1851. He continued to look after the interests of the Orphan Institution, and, in his missionary tour, to care for the spiritual interests of the natives. His labors were owned and blest of God. In the fall of 1857 he once more visited his native land, and earnestly appealed to his brethren to cultivate more thoroughly the missionary spirit, and give the men and the means to carry on the work abroad. Returning again to Assam in 1860, Dr. Bronson resumed his work at Nowgong, and carried it on for some nine years, when he made another short visit to this country. In July, 1874, he removed to Gowahati to take the charge of that important station. Although suffering from poor health for the past few years, he has been able to accomplish much in his station. Forty-one years of his life have been devoted to the cause of his Master and Lord as a missionary of the cross.

Bronson, Rev. Samuel Jennings, son of Rev. Asa Bronson, was born in Danbury, Conn., in 1819; converted at the age of ten; baptized in Fall River, Mass., at eighteen; graduated from Madison University in 1844, and Theological Department in 1846; ordained in Millbury, Mass., Dec. 16, 1846; in 1854 settled at Hyannis, Mass., and remained thirteen years; in 1867 settled in Winchester, Mass.; in 1870 returned to Millbury; through failure of health, resigned and traveled; in 1874 settled in West Woodstock, Conn.; died in West Woodstock, Conn., Jan. 10, 1879, and was buried at Fall River, Mass. A thoughtful, edifying, preacher; says his classmate, Dr. Graves, "one of the best, purest, and most genial men."

Brooks, Rev. Durin Pinkney, a pioneer Baptist and preacher of Oregon, was born Oct. 8, 1832, in St. Joseph Co., Mich.; moved to Iowa in 1838; thence to Oregon in 1850. Baptized in 1853; he was for years an active layman: and in 1868 he entered the ministry, serving the Hepner, Meadows, and Pleasant Valley churches; he assisted in organizing all these bodies. He is a self-denying, devout, and earnest preacher, and frequently travels 40 or 50 miles to preach to the scattered members of these feeble churches in Oregon.

Brooks, Rev. Ivison L., was born in North Carolina, Nov. 2, 1793. He graduated with distinction at the University of North Carolina. Here he was contemporary with Thos. H. Benton and Jas. K. Polk. With the latter he kept up a correspondence during life. He was a lieutenant in the war of 1812. He was baptized after retiring from the army, and at once began to preach. His first pastorate was in Georgetown, S. C.

He finally settled in Edgefield Co., S. C. He devoted himself to preaching to several country churches and to the instruction of his servants. Rev. J. C. Butler, one of our most useful and respected colored ministers, gratefully remembers the instructions of his former master.

He ceased from his labors on the 14th of March, 1865, at the age of seventy-two.

Brooks, Kendall, D.D., son of Deacon Kendall Brooks, was born in Roxbury (now Boston), Mass., Sept. 3, 1821. He became a member, by baptism, of the Dudley Street church, Aug. 28, 1836. Having fitted for college at the public Latin school of Roxbury, he entered Brown University in 1837, and graduated in 1841. For the next two years he was tutor in the Columbian College, D. C., and during most of that time preached to the E Street church, Washington. He finished the prescribed course of study in the Newton Theological Institution in 1845, and having previously accepted a call to the pastorate of the Baptist church in Eastport, Me., was ordained in Roxbury, Aug. 31, 1845. He remained in the pastoral work in Eastport seven years, and after a few months of service as associate secretary of the American Baptist Publication

KENDALL BROOKS, D.D.

Society, he became Professor of Mathematics and Natural Philosophy in Waterville College. During his three years of service in Waterville he was stated supply for the church in Bloomfield. In October, 1855, he became pastor in Fitchburg, Mass., where he remained till May, 1865. In both Eastport and Fitchburg he was officially connected with the public schools, holding the office of member of the Board of Education of the State of Maine for two terms. From May, 1865, till October, 1868, he was editor of the *National Baptist*. Oct. 1, 1868, he became president of Kalamazoo College, and still holds that office.

In 1866 Brown University made him a Doctor of Divinity. From 1877 to 1879 he was president of the Baptist State Convention of Michigan, having previously served the Convention as treasurer seven years. In 1852, President M. B. Anderson, then editor of the New York *Recorder*, said of him, "No man among us is better acquainted with Baptist history and statistics in the United States."

Brooks, Samuel, D.D., son of Deacon Kendall Brooks, was born in Roxbury (now Boston), Aug. 30, 1831. Having fitted for college at the Roxbury Latin school, he graduated at Brown University in the class of 1852. He had received baptism at the hands of Rev. Dr. T. D. Anderson during his Sophomore year. The first year after graduating he spent as assistant in the college library, and subsequently one year as instructor in Greek. He finished the course of theological study at Newton in 1857, and immediately became pastor of the Second church in Beverly, Mass., being ordained Oct. 22, 1857. In September, 1860, he was appointed for one year instructor in Hebrew in the Newton Theological Institution. After the expiration of the year he was acting pastor of the church in South Framingham, Mass., for three years. But his health, which had been seriously impaired while he was a student, compelled him to take a protracted rest from pastoral work. It was not till the autumn of 1866 that he was well enough to resume his duties, and then he took charge of the church in West Medway, Mass. Three years later he was chosen Professor of Latin in Kalamazoo College, and he began the work of that office on the 1st of January, 1870. This chair he still fills to the entire satisfaction of every one connected with the college. In his method of work he is quiet and persistent. His influence is greatest in his own field of labor and in the church to which he belongs.

Brooks, Walter R., D.D., was born Aug. 3, 1821; entered the class of 1843, Madison University; ordained at Ashville, Chatauqua Co., N. Y., July 5, 1842; pastor in Media, Perry, and Hamilton; in this last place for fifteen years. Here his ministry was greatly blessed. Large accessions were made to the church. His congregations were composed not only of residents of the village, but also of the professors and students of the university and other educational institutions in the place; to all of whom he endeared himself by his faithful and sympathetic presentation of gospel truths.

In 1859 was made secretary of the Education Board of New York; in 1863 received the degree of D.D. from Madison University; in 1868 visited Europe, Egypt, and Palestine with his family; in 1875 appointed Lecturer in Natural History in Madison, which position he still retains.

Brooks, W. T., D.D., was born in Chatham Co., N. C., Dec. 6, 1809; professed faith in Christ in 1832; was ordained at the session of the Convention held with Rives chapel church in 1836, Dr. Wait and Rev. Thomas Crocker constituting the Presbytery; graduated at Wake Forest College in 1839, and for many years was tutor and professor in that institution. Dr. Brooks was pastor of Mount Vernon Baptist church for thirty-two years; of the Henderson church for twenty years; and has served churches at Forestville, Selma, Brossfields, and other points. For many years Dr. Brooks was chairman of the board of trustees of Wake Forest College, and presided over the State Convention during several sessions. He was honored with the title of D.D. by Wake Forest College in 1874.

Broome, Gov. J. E., was elected governor of the State of Florida, and served one term. Prior to his being elected governor he resided at Fernandina, and was an active member of the Baptist church there, and one of its most liberal supporters. He was also one of its deacons.

Gov. Broome is a native of South Carolina, and for a few years past has lived in the State of New York. He is now about seventy-two years old, and vigorous for one of his years. The first effort to organize a Baptist church and build a house of worship at Tallahassee, the capital, was during the administration of Mr. Broome as governor.

He is prepossessing in appearance and dignified in bearing. Though a man of decided convictions and fixed principles, for which he would make any sacrifice, like all true Baptists, he has a liberal spirit towards men of every persuasion, and he gives generously to benevolent objects.

Brotherton, Hon. Marshall, was born in Erie, Pa., Feb. 11, 1811, and was brought to Missouri

HON. MARSHALL BROTHERTON.

when quite young. He held the highest offices in the city of St. Louis, and in the county. In 1845 he made a profession of religion; afterwards he united with the Second Baptist church of St. Louis. Mr. Brotherton was a man of benevolence, integrity, and modesty, "his heart was an asylum for the sorrowing, his purse a treasury for the needy," and the man and all he possessed, a sacrifice for Christ. His reputation never bore a stain, he enjoyed unusual popularity, and he deserved the love of his fellow-citizens, and especially of the friends of Christ. He died in 1871.

Brouner, Rev. Jacob H., was born in the city of New York, Jan. 1, 1791. In the fifteenth year of his age he was baptized into the fellowship of the First Baptist church by the pastor, Rev. William Parkinson. It was evident to the members of the church that the lad possessed promising gifts for the work of the ministry. He received from the church, while yet quite young, an informal license to preach. He labored with his friend, Rev. C. G. Sommers, for some time as a missionary among the destitute. He was ordained in the Tabernacle church by Rev. Archibald Maclay, D.D., and others, in 1812. His first pastorate was at Sing Sing, N. Y., which lasted fourteen years. In 1828 he accepted the pastorate of the North Baptist church, New York, which terminated only with his death, after twenty years of successful labor. During the time a commodious house of worship was built, and 330 converts were baptized. His son for the last twelve years has filled the same post with marked success.

Brouner, Rev. John J., is a son of the well-known Jacob H. Brouner, so long the pastor of the North Baptist church of New York. He was born in New York, Sept. 2, 1839. He was baptized by Rev. John Quincy Adams, educated at Madison University, and in 1864 was ordained in the old North church, and settled as pastor of Mariner's Harbor church, on Staten Island. During his stay of four years the church was greatly enlarged and strengthened. In 1869 he was called to his father's old field,—the North church,—and he has succeeded so well that the church has resolved to build a more commodious house of worship in a very desirable location on West Eleventh street.

Brown, Rev. E. T., was born March 22, 1818, in Lancaster, Pa. His father died when he was young. He was apprenticed at an early age in Greensburg, Pa.; there he was converted, and joined the only church in the place, the Methodist, but he would not be immersed by one who had not been himself immersed. He was baptized by a Baptist minister. Brother Brown joined a Baptist church in Virginia. He soon after entered Recton College, and studied till ill health compelled him to cease. While at this school he was licensed to preach, and in 1842 he was ordained. Brother Brown was pastor at Mount Vernon, Wooster, and Warren, O. Hundreds were baptized by him in these places. He was appointed chaplain in 1863 in the 2d Ohio Cavalry. After the war he moved to Sedalia, Mo., and was a missionary of the Home Mission Society. He built a good house of worship in Sedalia, and one of the best west of the Mississippi River in Clinton, Mo., and another substantial edifice for railroad men in Sedalia, and when he had installed a pastor over the last church of his care in Sedalia he fell dead with paralysis, June 9, 1879.

The memory of Mr. Brown is precious to large numbers, and his works will bless him for generations.

Brown, Rev. Esek, was born in Warren, R. I., Sept. 17, 1787; baptized by Rev. Ebenezer Burt in Hardwick, Mass., in 1809; licensed by the Baptist church in Sutton, Mass., Feb. 20, 1814; ordained pastor of the church in Dudley, Mass., June 15, 1815; commenced his labors in Lebanon, Conn., Sept. 13, 1818; here remained till his death; preached with power before the Connecticut Baptist State Convention in 1827; often preached with acceptance before Associations; was a man of remarkable readiness; modest in deportment, untiring in zeal, "devoted to the salvation of the world, few ministers have gone down to the grave carrying with them a greater amount of the unalloyed affections of a bereaved people;" died at Lebanon, after a pastorate of fifteen years, Sept. 11, 1833.

Brown, Rev. Freeman G., was born in Cambridge, Mass., January, 1813, and graduated at Columbian College, Washington, D. C., in the class of 1835. He entered Newton Theological Institution one year afterwards, and graduated in 1839. He was ordained pastor of the Baptist church in Portsmouth, N. H., Feb. 5, 1840, and remained there for three years. His subsequent pastorates were at North Dorchester and West Townsend, Mass. He was the agent of the American and Foreign Bible Society from 1853 to 1856. He was pastor in Hamilton, Canada West, from 1861 to 1863. He now resides in Cambridge, having no pastoral charge.

Brown, Rev. Gustavus, a colored Baptist preacher, was born in Fauquier Co., Va., in 1815. In 1828 he was brought to Kentucky. He experienced religion in 1832, at seventeen years of age, and was baptized in Cheautau's Pond, St. Louis, by Elder Jerry Meachum, the first colored pastor in Missouri. Brother Brown was licensed to preach in 1839, and ordained by Rev. J. M. Peck, D.D., and Dr. S. Lynd, in 1846. He was called to the pastorate of the Nineteenth Street Baptist church in Washington, D. C., in 1849; labored six years in that church, and four in the Second church of Washington. Came again to St. Louis in 1859, and still preaches there; is a useful and good man.

Brown, Rev. Henry A., was born in Rockingham Co., N. C., Sept. 28, 1846; baptized in June, 1866; graduated at Wake Forest College in 1871; was ordained at Yanceyville, August, 1871, the Presbytery consisting of Revs. W. S. Fontain, L. G. Mason, F. H. Jones, and F. M. Judan. Mr. Brown has served the church in Fayetteville for three years, and has been the pastor of the Winston church for nearly three years. A good pastor and preacher.

Brown, Rev. Hugh Stowell, pastor of the Myrtle Street Baptist church, Liverpool, England, is the son of a clergyman of the Church of England, and was born at Douglas, in the Isle of Man, on Aug. 10, 1823. When about seventeen years old he was placed in the engine-works of the Northwestern Railway at Wolverton, and remained there some three years, becoming during that time practically acquainted with the manufacture and driving of locomotives. In his working hours, as well as in his leisure, he diligently carried on his studies of languages, mathematics, and philosophy. Returning home when about twenty years of age, he entered King William College as a student, with a view to the ministry of the Established Church, and attracted favorable notice by his ardor and diligence. At this time the principles involved in the church and state controversy deeply exercised his mind, and in his perplexity he hesitated to seek ordination. His home training had made him familiar with religious truth, but a succession of severe family bereavements, including the death of his excellent father, had a powerful and chastening influence upon his mind. Ultimately he determined to join the Baptist denomination, and he was baptized at Stoney Stratford, near Wolverton, by the Rev. E. L. Forster, the pastor of the Baptist church there, with whom he had previously become intimately acquainted. Very soon after his baptism he accepted an engagement in town mission work at Liverpool, and whilst in this service he attracted the attention of the Myrtle Street church, whose venerable pastor, the Rev. James Lister, needed an assistant. About the close of 1847 he received an invitation to the pastorate of the church, being then in his twenty-fifth year. His predecessor was a man of much ability and strength of character, and had ministered to the church upwards of forty years. It was, therefore, no easy task to fill his place, but from the first Mr. Brown's ministry was successful. In 1847 the Myrtle Street church reported 317 members and 554 Sunday-school scholars. In 1877 the membership was 900, the Sunday-school scholars 1850, and there were seven mission stations connected with the church. Mr. Brown's Sunday afternoon lectures to workingmen, in a public hall, won for him the ears and hearts of thousands. In this field he has the honor of leading the way. Stirred by his signal success, many other ministers in different parts of the country, especially in the large cities, gave themselves to the work, and the work has gone on ever since with gratifying results. These lectures are widely known, large editions of them having been printed in England and America. For plain, downright speech on prevalent social evils and common sins Mr. Brown can hardly be surpassed. On the lecture platform, as well as in the pulpit, he is equally popular, and in both spheres of effort he has rendered most valuable public services. In Liverpool, where he has ministered for more than thirty years, he occupies a leading position among public men. By the Baptists of the United Kingdom he is regarded with affectionate esteem as a tower of strength. He was elected to the chair of the Baptist Union in 1878 by unanimous consent, and has frequently been called to prominent service in the interests of the body. As a preacher he excels in exposition, and his utterances have a singular freshness and point, with an unconventionality of phraseology which is very striking. The Myrtle Street church under his leadership has done much for the promotion of denominational principles in Liverpool and the neighborhood, besides raising large sums of money annually for foreign missions and other evangelistic enterprises. Mr. Brown visited the United States and Canada in 1872, and was cordially welcomed everywhere. He has taken a lively interest in the recent movements looking towards a unification of the churches in denominational work. His preaching is richly evangelical, and has been attended with marked spiritual power.

Brown, James F., D.D., was born at Scotch Plains, N. J., July 4, 1819. He graduated from the University of Pennsylvania in 1841, and studied theology with Rev. Dr. Dagg. He was ordained pastor of Gainesville Baptist church, Ala., and in 1846 took charge of the Great Valley church, Pa., in which he remained eight years, and was then called to his native place in 1854, where he ministered six years. The First church of Bridgeton had his valuable services for about eight years, and the old church at Piscataway then was under his charge for ten years and a half, when failing health compelled him to resign in 1878. A man of scholarly attainments, gentle spirit, sound theological views, large sympathies, and blessed in his past ministry, it is hoped that he may have sufficient health to resume the pastorate. The university at Lewisburg, Pa., of whose board of curators he is a member, and of which he was chancellor for several years, conferred upon him the Doctorate of Divinity in 1863.

Brown, Jere.—It is regretted that the writer failed to obtain matter out of which to make a sketch of the late Deacon Jere Brown, of Sumter County, Ala.; a man of great wealth before the war, a princely planter, an intelligent and cultivated gentleman of vast influence, and liberal with his money. At one time, some twenty-five years ago, he gave $25,000 to the endowment of a theological chair in Howard College, and a beneficiary fund, which was blessed to the assistance of many young ministers in securing an education. Another Deacon Brown, a near relative of Jere Brown, in the same community, though not so wealthy (yet quite wealthy), was a man of equal worth and influence.

Brown, J. Newton, D.D., was born in New London, Conn., in June, 1803; was baptized in Hudson, N. Y., in 1817; graduated from Hamilton, N. Y., in 1823; ordained in Buffalo in 1824; pastor in Malden, Mass., in 1827; in 1829 pastor of a church in Exeter, N. H.; in 1838 Professor of Theology and Pastoral Relations in the New Hampton Institution, N. H.; in 1845 pastor of the church of Lexington, Va.; in 1849 editorial secretary of the Baptist Publication Society. He was the author of the little creed so commonly adopted in newly organized Baptist churches, and known as "The New Hampshire Confession." Like the mild Dr. Brown, it is gently Calvinistical. He edited the "Encyclopædia of Religious Knowledge," one of the valuable works of modern times.

Dr. Brown had poor health most of his life, but it was the only poor thing about him; he had great faith; he was never angry; he loved every one; he was the meekest man the writer ever knew; he walked very closely with God. He fell asleep in Jesus May 14, 1868, in Germantown, Pa.

Brown, Rev. Joseph, was born in Wickford, R. I. His early life was spent on the farm and in one of the woolen-mills belonging to his father. By private study he fitted himself for the Freshman class at Yale. He completed the course, graduating with special honor in a class of ninety. In 1844 he returned to Yale and took his second degree. A few years later he taught in the Pittsburgh Female Seminary. Under the auspices of the Ohio Baptist State Convention he organized a church at Gallipolis and was then ordained. He spent ten years as pastor of the First Baptist church of Springfield, O., and during the time completed a theological course in Wittenberg College of the same city. In 1860 he became pastor of the Baptist church in Terre Haute, Ind. In 1870 he moved to Indianapolis, and soon entered upon the duties of corresponding secretary for the Indiana Baptist State Convention, and served for five years, when failing health obliged him to resign. He was a truly modest man, a preacher of decided ability, and a faithful servant of his Master. His illness was protracted. He expressed a wish that he might die on Sunday. The Lord called him Sunday, Aug. 11, 1878. He left $1000 to the Indiana Baptist State Convention.

Brown, Hon. Joseph Emerson, United States Senator and ex-governor of Georgia, and one of the most remarkable and distinguished men of the day, was born in Pickens District, S. C., April 15, 1821. His ancestors emigrated from Ireland in 1745 and settled in Virginia, afterwards they moved to South Carolina, and from it to Georgia. During his minority, down to his nineteenth year, Jos. E. Brown

GOV. JOSEPH E. BROWN.

lived upon a farm. In 1840 he entered Calhoun Academy, in Anderson District, S. C., where he remained three years. He then engaged in teaching at Canton, Ga., reading law at night, till he was admitted to the bar, in August, 1845. Afterwards he spent a year in the law school of Yale College, and in the fall of 1846 he entered regularly upon the legal profession at Canton, Ga. He was elected to the State Senate in 1849, serving two years, and in 1855 he was elected judge of the Superior Court of the Blue Ridge Circuit. He was elected governor in 1857. In 1859 he was unanimously renominated for governor, and was re-elected. In 1861 he was again renominated for governor, and again re-elected, and in 1864 the people for the fourth time in succession called him to the gubernatorial chair. As governor of the State he espoused the cause of secession, and sent not less than 120,000 men to the field from Georgia.

Subsequently to the war Gov. Brown "accepted the situation," acquiesced in the reconstruction measures of Congress as a necessity resulting from the war, and published a letter advising his friends to follow the same course.

In 1868 he was appointed chief justice of the Supreme Court of Georgia by Gov. Bullock for twelve years, which was confirmed by the State Senate; but he resigned in 1870, and became one of the lessees for twenty years of the Western and

Atlantic Railroad, belonging to the State of Georgia. He was chosen president of the company, which office he still retains, and under his excellent management the road pays into the State treasury $300,000 per annum, besides benefiting the company. Gov. Brown is also president of the Southern Railway and Steamship Association, which embraces nearly all the railroad corporations east of the Mississippi, and from the Potomac to the Ohio River. For twenty years he has been a trustee of the State University; has been president of the Board of Education of Atlanta ever since its organization; has had much to do with shaping the public school system of that city; and during the present year (1880) he made the handsome donation of $50,000 to the Southern Baptist Theological Seminary at Louisville, Ky. In the summer of 1880 he was appointed by Gov. Colquitt to fill the unexpired term of Senator Gordon in the U. S. Senate, where, as in every other position held by him, he did himself credit, and gave evidence of that large mental capacity which has always characterized him. Gov. Brown has ever been a faithful and active Baptist since uniting with the church when he was a young man. For years he has been chairman of the finance committee of the Second Baptist church of Atlanta, the financial management devolving mainly upon him. As a financier he is probably unsurpassed, and he is now very wealthy.

He frequently attends the public convocations of his brethren, and he is always received with the highest respect. A man of wonderful firmness, sagacity, power of will, and excellence of judgment, he has always succeeded in his undertakings. Almost every honor a State can bestow upon a favored citizen has been conferred upon him, and he exerts an influence in Georgia wielded by no other man.

Brown, Rev. Joseph Prentice, son of Henry and Lucy (Prentice) Brown, was born in Waterford, Conn., Oct. 27, 1820; a cousin of Rev. J. Newton Brown, D.D.; converted at the age of seventeen; united with First Baptist church of Waterford, Conn., at the age of twenty; educated at East Greenwich Academy, R. I., and New Hampton Theological Institution, N. H.; ordained in Charlestown, R. I., January, 1847; remained two years, blessed in toil; in March, 1849, settled with the Union Baptist church in Plainfield, Conn., and labored with signal success for twenty-two years; in 1871 settled with the Second Baptist church in New London, and served about six years; a man of native strength and sound judgment; spiritual and earnest in his work; both pastor and evangelist; baptized above 300 persons; a member of the State Legislature, in 1865, from Plainfield; served on Boards of Education; more than twenty years on the Board of the Connecticut Baptist State Convention, and once its president; always wise in council.

Brown, Nathan, D.D., was born in New Ipswich, N. H., June 22, 1807. He graduated at Williams College, Mass., in 1827, and at the Newton Theological Institution in 1830. He was ordained at Rutland, Vt., April 15, 1831. Having been appointed as a missionary, he sailed from this country Dec. 22, 1832, and reached Calcutta, May 5, 1833, and proceeded at once to take charge of a mission to the Shans. He commenced his work March, 1836, in Sadiya, at the northeast extremity of Assam. He removed, in 1839, to Jaipur, and to Sibsagor in 1841. While here, Dr. Brown directed his special attention to the work of translation. The whole New Testament in Assaman was printed in 1848. Year after year new and revised editions were issued from the press, and Dr. Brown had the satisfaction of knowing that he had been an instrument in the hands of God of giving the knowledge of the truth "as it is in Jesus" to millions of the human race. In 1855, Dr. Brown, after twenty years of faithful service, returned to his native land. Differences of opinion as to matters of missionary policy having come between Dr. Brown and the Executive Committee, his connection with the Missionary Union was dissolved July 26, 1859. For several years Dr. Brown was engaged in editorial work in this country, and in advocating the claims of the Free Mission Society. In 1872 the Union unanimously voted to take charge of the Japan mission of the American Baptist Free Mission Society, and Dr. Brown's connection with the Union was restored, and he was sent to Japan. He reached Yokohama in February, 1873, and entered upon his missionary work. During a part of the five years past he has given his special attention to the work of the translation of the Bible into the Japanese language. In the report of 1878 we find that, within the last three years, over 1,000,000 pages of Scripture, including the first three gospels and portions of the Old Testament, have been printed. When the whole Bible, faithfully translated, shall have been given to the 33,000,000 that inhabit Japan, Dr. Brown may well thank God for the part which he has been permitted to take in so blessed an undertaking.

Brown, Obadiah B., D.D., was born in Newark, N. J., July 20, 1779. He was educated a Presbyterian, but in early life espoused the views of Baptists. He was engaged in teaching for several years, and about the age of twenty-four was baptized. Wishing to devote himself to the ministry, he studied theology under the care of the Rev. W. Van Horn, of Scotch Plains. After his ordination he preached for a short time at Salem, N. J., and removing thence to Washington, D. C., in 1807, he became pastor of the First Baptist church in that city, in which relation he continued for upwards of forty years (1850), until growing physical infirmities prevented his officiating longer. He was chosen repeatedly chaplain to Congress. Dr. Brown took a deep interest in education, and was for a long time a most efficient member of the board of trustees of the Columbian College. He was greatly interested also in missions, and in connection with Rice and others promoted the organization of the Baptist General Convention for missionary purposes. His pulpit efforts were marked by an unusual vigor of mind, and sometimes by great power and effectiveness. He died May 2, 1852.

Brown, Gen. P. P., was born in Madison Co., N. Y., Oct. 8, 1823. He was converted at eight years of age. After teaching in various places he removed to Alton, Ill., and became principal of the Preparatory Department of Shurtleff College. In 1862 he organized the 157th Regiment of N. Y. Vols. He was soon promoted to be a brigadier-general for gallant service; he was commended for his bravery at the battle of Chancellorsville. At the battle of Gettysburg he guarded a battery in a very hazardous position. With honor he closed his military career.

Gen. Brown has since the war resided in St. Louis, and is a faithful member of the Second Baptist church of that city.

Brown, Rev. Simeon, was born in North Stonington, Conn., Jan. 31, 1722; a man of native talents; belonged to the standing order; was converted under Whitefield's preaching about 1745; joined the New Lights; united with Rev. Stephen Babcock in forming the Baptist church in Westerly in 1750, and was deacon; opened his house in North Stonington to the famous Council of May 29, 1754; was baptized by Rev. Wait Palmer in 1764; in March, 1765, organized the Second Baptist church in North Stonington, and was ordained pastor; was associated in the ministry with brethren Babcock, Morse, Palmer, Darrow, Lee, Wightman, Silas Burrows, Backus, West, and Asa Wilcox; remained pastor of the church fifty years; was assisted by Rev. Ashur Miner; a strong, pure, earnest man; died Nov. 24, 1815, in his ninety-fourth year, leaving a shining record.

Brown, T. Edwin, D.D., was born in Washington, D. C., Sept. 26, 1841, and was educated in the schools of his native city, graduating at Columbian College in 1861 with the highest honors of his class. He was immediately appointed tutor of Greek and Latin in the college, which position he filled with great acceptance for two years. But feeling moved to enter the ministry, he accepted a call to the Tabernacle Baptist church in Brooklyn, where he was ordained pastor in November, 1862. This relation continued for seven years, during which time he greatly endeared himself to his people by his arduous labors, his excellent spirit, and his superior talents as a preacher. He also steadily gained in reputation and influence in New York and Brooklyn. His scholarly habits and polished manners qualified him for any circle of society, and it was with deep regret the people of Brooklyn parted with him when, in November, 1869, he accepted the call of the Second church of Rochester. During his pastorate at Rochester Mr. Brown has developed rare powers as a preacher and student. He is a young man, and yet ministers acceptably to one of the most cultivated congregations in the State of New York. The University of Rochester conferred upon him the degree of Doctor of Divinity in the year 1875.

Brown, Rev. Thomas, was born in Newark, N. J., Nov. 1, 1779. He was converted at sixteen. Shortly after reaching twenty-one he left the Presbyterian for the Baptist denomination. He was educated in the academy of Dr. Samuel Jones, of Lower Dublin, Pa. In 1806 he was ordained as pastor of Salem Baptist church, N. J. In 1808 he took charge of the Scotch Plains church, over which he presided for twenty years, and in which the richest blessings of heaven rested upon his efforts. He removed to the Great Valley church, Pa., in 1828, where the Lord was pleased to smile upon his labors. The church was greatly prospered, and the pastor was tenderly loved. He died Jan. 17, 1831. He was a good man, a faithful minister, and a happy Christian.

Brown, Rev. William L., was born in Providence, R. I., January, 1813, and graduated at Brown University in the class of 1836. He pursued a two years' course of theological study at Newton. He was ordained Feb. 14, 1839. His pastorates have been with the churches at Ann Arbor, Mich.; Bristol, R. I.; West Springfield, Westborough, and Watertown, Mass.; at Mount Pleasant and Ottumwa, Iowa; and North Reading, Mass., where he is at the present time (1880) in active service.

Brown, Rev. William Martin, a prominent Baptist minister, was born in Halifax Co., Va., Aug. 18, 1794. He came to Mercer Co., Ky., in 1813, and two years afterwards settled in Hart County of that State. He united with Bacon Creek church in 1821, and five years afterwards became its pastor, and served in that capacity thirty-two years. He was also pastor of Knox's Creek and South Fork churches. Under his ministry two of these churches became the largest in Lynn Association. Mr. Brown traveled and preached extensively in that region of the State, and formed several churches. He died June 3, 1861. Two of his sons, James H. and D. J., became useful Baptist preachers.

BROWN, OF PROVIDENCE, THE FAMILY OF.

Brown, Rev. Chad, the ancestor of the distinguished Brown family of Rhode Island, was born in England about 1610. He is said to have been " one of that little company who fled with Roger Williams from the persecution of the then colony of Massachusetts." The lot which was assigned to him in the division of lands which was made in Providence included within it what is now the college grounds of Brown University. He seems to have been a man of importance in those early times, having been chosen, with four other citizens, to draw up a plan of agreement for the peace and government of the colony, which for several years constituted the only acknowledged government of the town. Mr. Brown may be regarded as the first "elder," or regular minister of the First Baptist church in Providence, the church founded by Roger Williams. While Mr. Brown was the minister of the First church in Providence there arose a great controversy, which agitated not only the town, but the whole colony. It was with reference to the "laying on of hands," alluded to in Heb. vi. 1, 2, and Mr. Brown was earnest in maintaining the obligatoriness of the rite, as being one of divine authority. He died about the year 1665. "His death," says Dr. Guild, "was regarded by the colonists as a public calamity, for he had been the successful arbitrator of many differences, and had won the not unenviable reputation of being a peace-maker." Roger Williams spoke of him, after his death, " as that wise and godly soul, now with God." He was the worthy head of honored descendants.

Brown, John, the oldest son of Rev. Chad Brown, was born in England in 1630. According to Dr. Guild, " he appears to have been a man of influence in the colony, and to have inherited the character and spirit of his father; he appears to have taken an active part in the affairs of the colony, and to have occupied positions of trust and honor."

Brown, Rev. James, the second son of John, was born in Providence in 1665. He was associated for a time with the Rev. Pardon Tillinghast as one of the pastors of the First Baptist church of Providence. He is spoken of as an example of piety and meekness worthy of admiration.

Brown, James, the second son of the Rev. James Brown, was born March 22, 1698; he devoted himself to mercantile pursuits, and his efforts were successful. His wife was a lady of great wisdom, and gave a home training to four sons which made them the most distinguished men in the colony. The names of the celebrated " four brothers" were Nicholas, Joseph, John, and Moses.

Brown, Nicholas, the first of the " four brothers," was born in Providence, July 28, 1729. He was called at an early age to assume grave responsibilities in consequence of the death of his father. With a decided taste for a business life, he entered upon his career as a merchant, and was eminently successful. Engrossed in business, he devoted himself to his chosen calling with great diligence, and reaped abundantly the reward of his fidelity. Like so many others who bore his name, he was a friend to the college and the church which have done so much for the Baptist cause. He died May 29, 1791. His religious character is thus described by Dr. Stillman: " Religion was his favorite subject. To Christianity in general as founded on a fullness of evidence, and to its peculiar doctrines, he was firmly attached: and from his uniform temper, his love for the gospel and for pious men, together with his many and generous exertions to promote the cause of Christ, we may safely conclude that he had tasted that the Lord is gracious. ' Therefore we sorrow not as those who have no hope.' He was a Baptist from principle. Blessed with opulence, he was ready to distribute to public and to private uses. In his death the college of this place, this church and society, the town of Providence, and the general interests of religion, learning, and liberality, have lost a friend indeed."

Brown, Joseph, was born Dec. 3, 1733; he was the second of the " four brothers"; he was engaged in mercantile pursuits. He had scholarly tastes, and in the department of natural sciences he was justly regarded as occupying a high place. He sustained an intimate connection with the college; in 1784 he was appointed Professor of Natural Philosophy, and he performed the duties of this office without financial compensation. For many years he was a member of the First Baptist church, and contributed largely towards the erection of its elegant edifice. He died Dec. 3, 1785. By the decease of the late Mrs. Eliza B. Rogers, the daughter of Mary Brown, who married Dr. Stephen Gano, this branch of the Brown family became extinct.

Brown, John, the third of the distinguished " four brothers Brown," of Providence, and a lineal descendant of Rev. Chad Brown, the first minister of the venerable First Baptist church, Providence, R. I., was born in that town Jan. 27, 1736. He early developed a decided aptness for business, and was the first merchant in Providence who carried trade to China and the East Indies. The interests of the church, with which so many of his ancestors had been connected, were especially fostered by him. To his generous aid and his far-seeing wisdom is largely due the erection of the splendid house of worship which for more than a century has been the place of meeting for the church. Under the pastoral care of President Manning, of Brown University, the congregation grew so large that the old meeting-house erected in 1726 was entirely inadequate to meet its wants.

The following resolution was passed Feb. 11, 1774: "*Resolved*, That we will all heartily unite as one man, in all lawful ways and means, to promote the good of this society, and particularly attend to the affair of building a meeting-house for the public worship of Almighty God, and also for holding commencements in." At a meeting of the society, April 25, 1774, the following resolution was passed: "That Mr. John Brown be the committee-man for carrying on the building of the new meeting-house for said society." It shows how much confidence was felt in Mr. Brown that upon him should be placed the chief responsibility of carrying out the wishes of the society. The meeting-house so justly admired exhibited the marks of his good taste. The steeple is similar to that of St. Martin's in the Fields in London, a church of faultless proportions, in the neighborhood of Trafalgar Square.

Mr. Brown was a warm patriot. By his special orders the captains of his ships returning to this country in 1775 were directed to bring munitions of war, especially gunpowder, as freight, and he was able to render great assistance to Gen. Washington's army in Boston. He had already made himself obnoxious to the enemy for causing the destruction, in 1772, of the British armed schooner "Gaspee." He escaped, however, all the perils of the war, and was able to serve his country in the councils of the nation as he had in the arena of public strife. He was sent as delegate to Congress in 1784 and 1785. In 1799 he was elected a member, and served two years. He died Sept. 20, 1803.

Brown, Moses, was the youngest of the "four brothers." He was born Sept. 23, 1738. By his marriage he obtained a competent fortune, which, added to what he had made in business, in partnership with his three brothers, enabled him to retire to the more quiet life which suited his tastes. Although brought up a Baptist, at the age of thirty-five he joined the Society of Friends, and became one of the most liberal supporters of all the institutions of that body of Christians. He lived to the great age of nearly ninety-eight years, his death taking place at Providence, Sept. 6, 1836. An excellent portrait of Mr. Brown is in the portrait-gallery of Brown University.

Brown, Hon. Nicholas, the munificent friend of the university which bears his honored name, was born in Providence, R. I., April 4, 1769. We trace his ancestry "on this side of the water" back to Mr. Chad Brown, the friend and sharer of the sacrifices of Roger Williams in his new home. In the sixth generation from Chad Brown we find the family name borne by four brothers, each of them distinguished in the annals of the city. The name of the third of these brothers was Nicholas, and this name was given to his son, the subject of this sketch. Young Brown, at the early age of fourteen, became a member of Rhode Island College, in the foundation of which his father and uncle had taken the deepest interest. He graduated in 1786.

Having completed his college course of study, Mr. Brown at once entered the counting-room of his father to prepare himself to carry on the business of the mercantile house which he represented. When he reached the age of twenty-two his father was removed by death, and he found himself possessed of what in those days was a large patrimony. Taking to himself as a partner Mr. Thomas P. Ives, whose tastes were congenial with his own, he entered upon that long career of prosperity which made the firm of Brown & Ives so well known and so highly respected in almost every quarter of the world.

HON. NICHOLAS BROWN.

But it is not simply as a merchant laying broad and far-sighted plans for amassing wealth that we are to view the subject of this sketch. He lived in times when society had passed and was passing through radical changes. As an intelligent, high-minded man, he could be no other than a sincere patriot, seeking the welfare of the country, which was now taking its place as an independent nation among the nations of the earth. He took a lively interest in the politics of his day, and for fourteen years was for most of the time a member of either the lower or the upper house of the General Assembly of his native State.

In such a sketch as this our special concern with Mr. Brown is in the character of a man of simple piety and a large-hearted benevolence. Although, from some peculiar views which he cherished on the subject of making a public profession of his faith in Christ, he never became a member of the church, no one who was intimate with him could have any doubt that he was a sincere Christian. Few persons read more devoutly and more habitually the Word of God. He believed in the public institutions of religion, and by his own example and generous contributions sustained them. Especially attached was he to the faith of his fathers, and the church where for so many generations they had worshiped. He gave to it what in those days was regarded as an organ of great value, and in his last will he left to it the sum of $3000. Other churches, not only in Providence, but elsewhere, shared in his bounty. The great religious organizations of the day found in him a liberal supporter.

His benefactions to the university which bears his name deserve special mention. They commenced four years after his graduation, and continued until his death. His first generous gift was a valuable collection of law books. A few years after he gave $5000 to Rhode Island College towards the foundation of a professorship of Rhetoric and Oratory. In consequence of the interest shown by Mr. Brown in the college its name was changed to Brown University. At his own charges, he caused to be erected the second dormitory of the university, known as "Hope College," which cost not far from $20,000. By this gift he transmitted to posterity the name of his only sister, Mrs. Hope Ives. In May, 1826, he gave to the university lands the estimated value of which was $20,000. A few years after, in connection with his brother-in-law, Thomas P. Ives, Esq., a valuable philosophical apparatus. He started, in 1832, the library fund of $25,000 with a subscription of $10,000. He paid all the bills incurred in the erection of Manning Hall, amounting to $18,500. The building was dedicated February 4, 1835, President Wayland delivering on the occasion a discourse on the "Dependence of Science on Religion." In 1839 he gave $10,000 to the corporation, $7000 of the sum to be appropriated towards the erection of the president's house, and $3000 towards the erection of a third college building, to be used for the accommodation of the departments of Natural Philosophy, Chemistry, Mineralogy, and Natural History. He also furnished three valuable lots as sites of these buildings. "The entire sum of his recorded benefactions," says Dr. Guild, "amounts to $160,000, assigning to the donations of lands and buildings the valuation which was put upon them at the time they were made." A part of this sum was realized after his decease, when the corporation of the university came into possession of certain lots of land valued at $42,500, and a bequest out of which has come the Nicholas Brown scholarships, eleven in number, and valued at $12,000. The large amount thus contributed to the university made him, at the time of his death, the most generous donor to the cause of education the country had produced. If he has been outstripped in the number and the value of his gifts by lovers of good learning in more modern times, it may be doubted, considering how changed is the standard of giving, whether he does not still occupy the rank which he has held among the warmest friends of liberal culture and advanced education.

As a Baptist, Mr. Brown did not confine his bounty to the university within whose walls he received his education. He gave to Columbian College, to the Newton Theological Institution, and to Waterville College, all designed to promote the better training of young men in the Baptist denomination. By his will, also, he left something to the Northern Baptist Education, and to the American and Foreign Bible Society.

Mr. Brown took an active part in founding the Providence "Athenæum," giving to it the valuable lot on which the library building stands, $6000 towards the erection of this building, and $4000 to the library fund. In his will, moreover, he gave $30,000 towards the erection of a lunatic hospital, now known as the "Butler Hospital for the Insane," taking its name from Cyrus Butler, Esq., whose gift of $40,000 was added to that of Mr. Brown.

Dr. Guild, as has already been stated, places the amount of his "recorded benefactions at $160,000." Other sums, given in other directions besides those which have been indicated, swell the amount, according to the estimate of Professor Gammell, to the large sum of $211,500. Thus did this "steward of the Lord" scatter in every direction the possessions which a kind Providence gave to him. He earned money not to hoard it, not to expend it on personal gratification, but to do good with it. He "sowed bountifully," and God enabled him to "reap bountifully." No finite mind can measure the blessed influences which a man of such large and generous heart sets in motion. For generation after generation they widen and extend in a thousand directions to the glory of God and the benefit of mankind. May the number of successful Baptist merchants like Nicholas Brown be increased an hundredfold!

Brown, Hon. John Carter, the second son of Nicholas Brown, the benefactor of the university which bears his name, was born in Providence, Aug. 28, 1797. He graduated at Brown University in the class of 1816. Inheriting the tastes of his ancestors for mercantile pursuits, he entered the counting-room of Brown & Ives, his father and uncle, and in due time became a member of the firm. He took the responsibilities which his honored father had so long borne in connection with the university when death removed that father to his reward. As a member of its corporation, in both branches, he performed excellent service for his *alma mater.* In his gifts to the university he has been surpassed by no one but his father. The value of these gifts was not far from $155,000.

Mr. Brown was a great lover of books, and in one department it is believed that no library in this or any other country has a more valuable collection. We refer to the department of American history. It was his aim to secure every publication relating to either North or South America between the year 1492 and the year 1800. "This design," says Prof. Gammell, "has been accomplished, not indeed with absolute completeness, but to an extent which must awaken the admiration of all who are acquainted with the vast treasures of his collection. It contains the materials for illustrating the discovery of the New World, and the entire history of its development and progress in all its divisions to the close of the eighteenth century." It shows the kindness of Mr. Brown's heart that he placed this most rare and magnificent collection at the service of any scholar who might wish to avail himself of its treasures, and to that pleasant library where the writer of this sketch has spent so many happy hours many a literary pilgrim has come and met a most hearty welcome.

Although possessed of large wealth, Mr. Brown, like his father, was simple in his tastes, and shunned notoriety in every form. He lived to see the fruits of his benevolence as shown to the university and some of the leading charitable institutions of his native city. He died in Providence, R. I., June 10, 1874. Mr. Brown closes our sketches of the Brown family of Providence.

Brown University.—This institution, like so many other colleges in this country, owes its origin to the deep-seated conviction that religion and learning should unite their forces to elevate and save the race. The Baptist denomination needed an institution, first of all, for the fitting of young men to enter the Christian ministry, and also to prepare others to engage in scientific and literary pursuits honorably for themselves and beneficially for the community in which they were to live. The Philadelphia Baptist Association was formed in 1707, and at once took a decided stand in favor of an educated ministry. Many years elapsed, however, before a definite plan was formed to establish a college suited to the wants of the denomination. The founding of such an institution in Rhode Island was the project of Rev. Morgan Edwards, the pastor of the First Baptist church in Philadelphia. Rev. (afterwards President) James Manning was sent to Newport to see what interest could be awakened among the Baptists of that flourishing town in carrying out the proposed plan. Meeting with sufficient encouragement to commence operations, Mr. Manning took up his residence in Warren, R. I., became pastor of the Baptist church in that place, and in September, 1765, was elected president of the infant college, to which was given the name " Rhode Island College." The first commencement was celebrated at Warren, Sept. 7, 1769, at which time seven young men took the degree of Bachelor of Arts. On the 7th of February, 1770, the corporation voted that the college should be removed to Providence, this town having offered a subscription of £4280 as an inducement for the institution permanently to locate itself there. At the time of its establishment there were but four denominations of Christians in the colony. With a liberal spirit, which shows the generous character of the founders of the college, it was decided that each of these denominations should be represented in the corporation. There were incorporated 36 trustees, 22 of whom, by the charter, are to be forever Baptists, 5 to be of the denomination called Friends or Quakers, 4 Congregationalists, and 5 Episcopalians. There is incorporated also another branch in the corporation, known as " the Fellows." This branch of the government consists of 12 members, including the president, " 8 of whom are to be Baptists, and the rest indefinitely of any or all denominations." It is required that the president shall be a Baptist. The other members of the faculty may be of other denominations. The charter contains the following noteworthy provision : " Into this liberal and catholic institution shall never be admitted any religious tests. But, on the contrary, all the members hereof shall forever enjoy full, free, absolute, and uninterrupted liberty of conscience ; and that the places of professors, tutors, and all other officers, the president alone excepted, shall be free and open for all denominations of Protestants [Brown University is a Baptist institution, and all its instructors should be Baptists.— EDITOR] ; and that youth of all religious denominations shall and may be admitted to the equal advantages, emoluments, and honors of the college or university ; and that the public teaching shall, in general, respect the sciences ; and that the sectarian differences shall not make any part of the public and classical instruction." The name of " Rhode Island College" was changed to " Brown University" in honor of its generous benefactor, Hon. Nicholas Brown, the change having been made by an act of the corporation passed Sept. 6, 1804. The university has had seven presidents. Its first was the founder of the college, Rev. James Manning, D.D., of Nassau Hall College, Princeton, who entered upon the duties of his office September, 1765, and continued in the same until his death, July 29, 1791. His successor was Rev. Jonathan Maxcy, D.D., of the class of 1787, elected in 1797, and resigned in 1802. Subsequently he was president of Union College, and afterwards of South Carolina

BROWN UNIVERSITY.

College, and died in 1820. The president at that time was Rev. Asa Messer, D.D., LL.D., of the class of 1790, who was elected in 1804, and resigned in 1826. He died in 1836. He was succeeded by Rev. Francis Wayland, D.D., LL.D., a graduate of Union College of the class of 1813; elected, 1827; resigned, 1855; died, 1865. The next president was Rev. Barnas Sears, D.D., LL.D., of the class of 1825, who was elected 1825, and resigned 1867. He died July 6, 1880. He was succeeded by Rev. Alexis Caswell, D.D., LL.D., of the class of 1822, who was elected 1868, and resigned 1872. He died in 1877. The present incumbent of the office, Rev. Ezekiel Gilman Robinson, D.D., LL.D., of the class of 1838, was elected in 1872. According to the recently published general catalogue (1880) the whole number of graduates of the college, including those who have received honorary degrees, is 3494, of which number 1758 are living. The whole number of alumni is 2932, of whom 1614 are now living. The whole number of ministers who have been educated at Brown University is 733, of whom 388 are now living; 562 persons have received honorary degrees from the university, of whom 144 are now living. The whole amount of the funds of the university, not including the grounds and the older college buildings, is $825,445.93. The average number of students is about 275.

Brownfield, Rev. William, was born in 1773, and in early life was converted and called into the ministry. He was pastor of the churches at Smithfield and Uniontown, Pa., where his labors were chiefly expended, and was instrumental in organizing a church in Stewartstown. Following the apostolic example of many of our fathers in the ministry, he traveled extensively, and preached wherever he went. Several counties of Pennsylvania, and parts of West Virginia and Ohio, heard from him the blessed gospel. He was a sound divine, an able preacher, and a fearless advocate of the truth. His efforts were extensively blessed. He died Jan. 18, 1859, after being a preacher sixty-five years.

Browning, Francis P.—As early as 1826, when as yet there had been no Baptist meetings in Detroit, Mr. Browning, from England, a young merchant in the city, had, as a faithful church member, connected himself with the Baptists at Pontiac. The next year he entered into the organization of the church in Detroit, and became its leading spirit until his death from cholera, in 1834. He was of superior intelligence and great Christian enterprise. He made the wants of Detroit known throughout the country. He led the social meetings and the Sabbath worship; secured, largely at his own cost, the erection of the first small chapel, and the second commodious brick edifice; superintended the Sunday-school; performed deacon's duties, and made them include all pastoral work; and led the little society in its Christian career. He fell under the stroke of the pestilence as he was hastening to and fro through the wasted and frightened city ministering to others. Noble first standard-bearer of our cause in the metropolis of the State.

Broyles, Rev. Moses, was born about 1826, on the Eastern Shore of Maryland. After some changes in his situation he became the property of a planter named Broyles, who, in 1831, moved from Tennessee to Kentucky. When a lad he was so faithful and kind that the children of his master were often left in his care. Gradually, also, he began to be intrusted with the affairs of the farm. When he was about fourteen years old his master told him that if he would continue a good boy he should have his freedom in 1854. In 1851 he proposed to buy the rest of his time, and the bargain was made. After a few months he bought a horse and then a dray, and so made money more rapidly, and soon paid the price of his freedom. He had cultivated a decided taste for history, having learned to read. He read the Old Testament through twice, and the New five times; he then turned his attention to such works as the History of the United States, the Lives of Washington and Marion, A. Campbell's writings, Barnes's "Notes," Benedict's "History of the Baptists," etc. Having learned of the institution at College Hill, Jefferson County, he came there in 1854. He remained in it nearly three years. He gave his principal attention to science, Latin, and Greek. "That school, even if it had done nothing more, justified its claim to recognition by the successful education of Rev. Moses Broyles, the leader of the colored Baptists of Indiana." He was converted in his seventeenth year. At that time there was active agitation in Kentucky upon "mission" and "anti-mission" questions, and also about the doctrines set forth by Alexander Campbell. Mr. Broyles joined Mr. Campbell's sect. When he went to Paducah he united with the Baptists, and helped to build the first colored Baptist meeting-house in that place. There was a great effort made to persuade him to remain with the Campbellists, but he had canvassed the whole matter, and he must be a Baptist.

In 1857 he went to Indianapolis and began teaching school. He soon commenced to preach for the Second church. He was ordained Nov. 21, 1857. The church rapidly increased in numbers. The church has a house and lot which cost $25,000; it is the mother of six colored churches organized since 1866. Since 1857 it has sent 21 men into the ministry. When Mr. Broyles came to Indianapolis there was no Association of the colored Baptists of the State. Chiefly through his energy and foresight and fidelity the Indiana Association has now (statistics of 1877) 53 churches and 3482 members.

The church of which Mr. Broyles is pastor has 645 members.

Bryan, Rev. Andrew, colored, the first pastor of the First colored church of Savannah. The church was organized by Rev. Abraham Marshall, of Kiokee, in 1788, and Andrew Bryan continued its pastor until his death, in October, 1812. He stood exceedingly high in public estimation, and brought great numbers into his church. When he was young he was persecuted for preaching; but when he died the Sunbury Association adopted a complimentary resolution of regret concerning him, and the white Baptist and Presbyterian ministers of Savannah delivered addresses in his honor.

Bryan, Hon. Nathan, a man of reputation, piety, and wealth, was born in Jones Co., N. C.; was baptized when eighteen by Rev. Mr. McDaniel, and represented his county in the General Assembly. In 1794 he was elected to Congress from the Newbern district. He died in 1798, and was buried in the yard of a Baptist church, probably old Sansom Street, in Philadelphia.

Bryant, Rev. Daniel, one of the pioneers among Ohio Baptists, was born in New Jersey in the year 1800. At the age of twenty-one he was converted, and united with the Baptist church at Lyons, N. Y. In the year 1824, having removed to Ohio, he was ordained by the Mill Creek church. For more than fifty years he devoted himself to the building up of the cause of Christ in Southern Ohio. In the face of great opposition he was the friend of missions and ministerial education. When in 1836 the old Miami Association excluded the churches of Cincinnati, Middletown, Lebanon, and Dayton for sympathy with missions, Father Bryant went cheerfully with the minority. He was liberal in giving, steadfast in his convictions, simple in his life. His labors were abundant, and often attended with hardship. He died in the year 1875, with the harness on, having been stricken down in the pulpit while preaching, only a few hours before he passed away. He was a favorite with both old and young, and will be long remembered as one of the sainted few who laid the foundations of Baptist churches in Ohio, and for many years preached in faithful simplicity the Word of life.

Bryce, Rev. John, was born of Scotch parents in Goochland Co., Va., May 31, 1784. His parents were strict churchmen, and he was confirmed in the Episcopal Church. Under the preaching of the celebrated Andrew Broadus, at the age of twenty-one, he was convicted of sin, was converted, and united with a small Baptist church in his native county. About the same period he was admitted to the bar. He soon began to exhort sinners to repent, and in the course of two or three years was ordained. For a considerable period he practiced law and preached the gospel in Richmond and Lynchburg. He was master in chancery some years under Chief Justice Marshall. In 1810 he was chosen assistant pastor of the First Baptist church in Richmond, the aged and infirm Rev. John Courtney being the nominal pastor. He remained in this position (except during a brief period in which Rev. Andrew Broadus filled it) until 1822. He was one year chaplain in the U. S. army, during the war of 1812-15. In 1822 he accepted a call to the pastorate of the church at Fredericksburg, Va. After preaching there two years he became pastor of a church in Alexandria, Va., where he remained one year, and then returned to Fredericksburg.

Mr. Bryce was one of the principal movers in the erection of Columbian College. He was also an active member of the American Colonization Society, and at one time liberated about 40 of his own slaves and sent them to Liberia. In 1827 he moved to Georgetown, Ky., where he established himself in the practice of law, and took a prominent part in the political affairs of the State, as well as in the establishment of Georgetown College. In 1832 he located in Crawfordsville, Ind. Here he remained ten years, preaching and practicing law, and representing his county in the State Legislature at least one term. In 1844 he was appointed surveyor of Shreveport, La. This was pending the annexation of Texas to the United States, and Mr. Bryce is supposed to have been President Tyler's confidential agent in that important affair. After his term of office expired he was elected mayor of Shreveport. While here he performed the most important work of his life in the ministry. When he arrived at Shreveport, in 1844, he supposed there was not a Baptist church or another Baptist preacher within 200 miles of him; when he left there in 1851 there were about 20 churches and two Associations in that region. He was instrumental in accomplishing this great work while the ground was contested by Bishop Polk. In 1851, Mr. Bryce returned to Kentucky, and the next year took charge of the Baptist church in Henderson, in that State. Here he spent the evening of a long and eventful life. He died July 26, 1864.

Buchanan, James, was born at Ringoes, N. J., June 17, 1839; studied at the Clinton Academy; entered the law-office of John T. Bird, Esq., in 1860; attended the law school at Albany, and was admitted to the bar in the fall of 1864. He was reading clerk in the Assembly in 1866, and was appointed law judge of Mercer County in 1874. The university in Lewisburg conferred upon him the honorary degree of A.M. in 1875.

He and his brother Joseph joined the Cherryville Baptist church on the same day in March, 1865. Judge Buchanan has identified himself fully with the cause of God, and stands in the fore front of pastors' helpers in Trenton, where he resides. On the death of Hon. D. M. Wilson, in 1873, Judge Buchanan was heartily chosen to the presidency of the New Jersey Baptist State Convention, and has been annually re-elected. In associational, benevolent, and educational interests he is frequently called upon, and is always ready with his voice and influence.

Buchanan, Joseph C., was born at Ringoes, N. J., March 27, 1841. He entered the Sophomore class of Madison University in October, 1863, and graduated in 1866, taking the degree of A.M. in course three years later. Was ordained pastor of the church at Scotch Plains, N. J., Oct. 1, 1867. He labored there until Sept. 1, 1878. During his ministry there a fine meeting-house was built, at a cost of $34,000. In September, 1878, Mr. Buchanan became pastor of the church at Pemberton. He is a good theologian, a thoughtful preacher, and has been prospered in winning souls.

Buck, Rev. William Calmes, son of Charles Buck and Mary Richardson, was born Aug. 23, 1790, in Shenandoah (now Warren) Co., Va. His father was a farmer in good circumstances, and gave him such advantages as were common in those days, which did not satisfy his desires for a thorough education. He told his father that he would relinquish all claim on his estate if he would send him off to a good school for one year, but his father was not willing to make any distinction as to education among his children. While a boy he read all the volumes of the "British Encyclopædia," and some of them, more than once, by fire-light, besides such histories and scientific works as he could procure from a public library of which his father was a share-holder. His thirst for knowledge was so great that he continued to improve himself, until in middle age he acquired such an acquaintance with the Greek and Hebrew languages as enabled him to read the Scriptures in those languages with pleasure. For some years he was occupied in farming, which he relinquished to give himself entirely to the Christian ministry, and joined the Water Lick Baptist church, Va., in his seventeenth year. Commenced public speaking soon after, but was not ordained till 1812. He then became pastor of the church of which he was a member. Was a lieutenant in the U. S. army during the war of 1812. Moved to Union Co., Ky., in 1820, where he had the care of several churches, and resided for a short time in Woodford County. During all these years his time was filled with most laborious missionary work. Moved to Louisville in 1836 and assumed the pastorate of the First church; he soon resigned the care of it, and, with a few others, formed the East church, to which he furnished a house and preached until it was able to sustain itself. Was editor of the *Baptist Banner* and *Western Pioneer* during most of his residence in Louisville. Was elected secretary of the Bible Board of the Southern Baptist Convention at Nashville, Tenn., May, 1851, in which position he continued until called to the pastorate of the Baptist church, Columbus, Miss., March, 1854; continued in this position till May, 1857, when he accepted a call to the Greenborough church, Ala. The next year, 1858, he served the church at Selma, Ala. In the fall of 1859, having moved to Marion, Ala., he commenced the publication of *The Baptist Correspondent*, but after two years it was suspended by the events of the war, and he went to the Confederate army as a missionary, laboring wherever he thought he could be most useful. In 1864 he located at Lauderdale Springs, Miss., as superintendent of the Orphans' Home, and also had the care of the Sharon church, Noxubee Co., Miss., till he removed to Texas, in 1866. He had not the care of any church in Texas, but continued to labor for the Master by word and pen so long as his health permitted. Died at Waco, Texas, May 18, 1872. He was an earnest worker in all enterprises of the denomination. Gifted by nature with a ringing, powerful voice, fluent speech, and a retentive memory, he was unsurpassed as a platform speaker. He was often elected a vice-president of the Southern Baptist Convention. He prepared and published "The Baptist Hymn-Book," "The Philosophy of Religion," and "The Science of Life."

CHARLES ALVAH BUCKBEE, D.D.

Buckbee, Charles Alvah, D.D., was born in Penn Yan, N. Y., April 3, 1824. In 1835 his parents moved to New York City. He was converted in 1837, and joined a Methodist class. In 1839 he united with the Tabernacle Baptist church, and soon after devoted himself to the ministry, entering Madison University in May, 1840, and graduating in August, 1848. Settled as pastor at Conway, Mass., Oct. 6, 1848; was blessed with two revivals and baptized many converts. In March, 1851, he resigned; moved to New York; was associate editor of the New York *Chronicle*, and in June, 1852, entered the service of the American Bible Union, in which he remained as an officer and manager seventeen years. He was one of the editors of the first volumes of its "Documentary History," the *Bible Union Monthly*, and the *Quarterly*. In 1867 he visited the Pacific coast as a special delegate of the Union, and held two public debates on revision of the English Scriptures. The debates were published and widely circulated. During his connection with the Union he established the Baptist church in West Hoboken, N. J.; was its pastor nearly ten years, and immersed nearly 150 converts into its fellowship. In June, 1869, he settled permanently in San Francisco, Cal.; was nearly three years pastor of the Fifth church, which he organized, and into whose membership he baptized nearly 100 converts. He edited, for five years, *The Evangel*, and continues in the conduct of its Sunday-school department. In all Baptist organizations he has been active, as secretary of the State Convention, president one year of the Board of California College, and member of the Missionary Board of California. In 1879 he received from California College the degree of D.D. In 1870 he accepted a position in the U. S. Mint, which he still holds, and though not a pastor preaches to feeble churches nearly every Lord's day. During his ministry he has helped pastors in many revivals and baptized about 400 converts. He is one of the most laborious men in the Baptist ministry of the Pacific coast.

Buckner College is a new institution located at Wicherville, in the northeastern part of Arkansas, in charge of Rev. E. L. Compere. It is under the patronage of the Baptist General Association of Northwestern Arkansas. The collegiate department was opened in September, 1880.

Buckner, Rev. Xerxes Xavier, A.M.—This excellent minister of Christ was born in Spencer Co., Ky., Feb. 20, 1828. He was converted at the age of nineteen years, and united with the Plumb Creek Baptist church in his native county. He graduated at Georgetown College, Ky., and was ordained in the church where he was converted, and labored with great acceptance for years at Taylorsville and Fisherville. In 1855 he removed to Missouri, and was pastor of the Baptist church in that educational centre, and aided in establishing the school now known as Stephen College. In 1860 he located as pastor in Boonville, Mo. From over-exertion in church and school work his health failed, and he removed to Kansas City, Mo., where he engaged as pastor at West Port, and performed evangelistic work for one year; then he removed to Liberty, Mo., and became pastor of the Baptist church and president of the Female Seminary.

The second year he resigned the pastorate but retained the school, and at the end of the third year he returned to Kansas City, where he lived till June 19, 1872, when he died. For years he was trustee of William Jewell College and president of the Board of Ministerial Education. He was presiding officer at the last General Association he attended. He was elected a member of the Board of Public Schools in Kansas City, and the presidency of the Kansas City National Bank was literally forced upon him. As a minister of Christ, a peace-maker in our last war, a public-spirited citizen, an humble Christian, Brother Buckner has few equals; and no spot dims his bright character.

Buckner, Rev. Robert C., was born in Madisonville, Tenn., Jan. 3, 1837; educated in Georgetown College, Ky.; professed religion October,

REV. ROBERT C. BUCKNER.

1844, and commenced his ministry at Somerset, Ky., in 1852; was pastor at Albany, Owensborough, Salvisa, Ky., and Paris, Texas, twenty-seven years in all. He was the first agent in Kentucky of the Home Mission Board of the Southern Baptist Convention; was twelve years moderator of Red River Association, Texas; is now general superintendent of Orphan Home work in Texas, president of the Sunday-School Convention of Northern Texas, and corresponding secretary of the Texas Baptist General Association. He is editor and proprietor, at this time, of the *Texas Baptist*, published at Dallas. He is also proprietor of the Texas Baptist Publishing House, which is in a flourishing condition.

Buel, Rev. Abel P., was born in Wallingford, Conn., Nov. 29, 1820; converted and baptized at New Haven, Conn., in April, 1836; studied at Connecticut Literary Institution; entered Yale College in 1843, and remained till 1846; received the degree of A.M. from Rochester University; ordained at Peekskill, N. Y., 1846, and served about three years; pastor of Baptist church in Tarrytown, N. Y., about nine years; afterwards settled in New London and Southington, Conn.; was blessed with revivals in his pastorates; fervent in spirit, earnest in work, eloquent in speech; an easy and graceful writer; withal a poet whose productions have merit; now in Cleveland, O.

Buist, Rev. James F., was born Sept. 29, 1839, in Charleston, S. C. His parents died when he was eight years of age, but his uncle, E. T. Buist, D.D., took him in charge. He was educated at Furman University. He was baptized in 1859, and ordained in 1860.

During the war he was a chaplain in the army, and since its termination he has been pastor of the Philadelphia and Saltkehatchie churches. He has been moderator of the Barnwell Association for several years.

His father and uncle were distinguished Presbyterian ministers, one of his brothers is a pastor in the same denomination, while another and himself are in the oldest church in Christendom, to whose members Christ preached when he was on earth.

The long pastorates of James, and the frequency of his election as moderator of the Association, show the esteem of his brethren for him.

Bulkley, Justin, D.D.—Dr. Bulkley, Professor of Church History and Church Polity at Shurtleff College, was born at Leicester, Livingston Co., N. Y., July 23, 1819. His father, an industrious farmer, and a man of high character, removed subsequently to Illinois, and died at Barry, July 24, 1859, his wife surviving him only a few years. The son was seventeen years of age at the date of this removal to Illinois. At the age of twenty-three he entered the preparatory department of Shurtleff College, his education until that time being such as the imperfect school system in Central Illinois then afforded. He graduated in 1847. His first post of service was that of principal of the preparatory department in his college, to which he was chosen immediately upon his graduation. Two years later, in February, 1849, he was ordained pastor of the Baptist church in Jerseyville. After four years of unusually successful service in this pastorate, he was elected Professor of Mathematics in Shurtleff College, resigning that position in 1855, and becoming pastor of the church in Carrollton. After nine years at Carrollton he returned to Upper Alton, the seat of Shurtleff College, and at the end of a year accepted the post in the college which he now fills.

Dr. Bulkley's service in the several positions he has held has been one of marked usefulness. As a preacher, he has a peculiar power over the sympathies as well as the convictions of his hearers. As a pastor, his excellent judgment, his kind spirit, his sympathetic nature, make him the trusted friend no less than the honored leader and teacher. As a professor, he has always gained in a peculiar degree the confidence and affection of his pupils, while his teaching has been thorough, critical, and exact. The estimation in which he is held by the denomination in the State is shown by his election during successive years as moderator of the General Association, and in the fact that since the year 1851 the often delicate and important service of chairman of the Committee on Elections in the General Association has, year by year, been committed to him.

Bullen, George, D.D., was born in New Sharon, Me. He graduated at Waterville College in the class of 1855, and at the Newton Theological Institution in the class of 1858. He was ordained as pastor of the church in Skowhegan, Me., June 13, 1860, where he remained until, in 1863, he accepted an appointment as chaplain in a regiment of U. S. volunteers. He ministered to the Wakefield Baptist church, 1864-67, and entered upon his duties as pastor of the church in Pawtucket, R. I., in 1868, and continues in this relation at this time. Colby University has just conferred on him the degree of Doctor of Divinity.

Bunn, Rev. Henry, was born in Nash Co., N. C., Dec. 18, 1795. He was left an orphan at an early age. He moved in 1817 to Twiggs Co., Ga., where he spent the remainder of his life. By steady industry and prudent management he accumulated a handsome estate, which he shared liberally with benevolent institutions and good and wise schemes for the benefit of his fellow-men. He for years acted as justice of the peace and judge of the County Court, and between 1825 and 1831 he represented his county in several sessions of the State General Assembly. He made a public profession of religion in 1837, and thenceforth scrupulously practiced all his religious duties. His church called him to the gospel ministry in 1851, and on the 7th of December in that year he was ordained. For several years he was pastor of the Richland church; for many sessions he was moderator of the Ebenezer Association, and, also, a trustee of Mercer University and a member of the Executive Committee of the Georgia Baptist Convention. He was eminently a pacificator by his influence and prudent counsels; he settled or prevented many troubles among neighbors and in churches; he was scrupulously honest, fair, and liberal in all transactions; many widows and orphans found in him a friend and a wise counselor.

In all the relations of life, as husband, father, citizen, church member, and minister, he illustrated the characteristics of a genuine Christian, no blot ever stained his fair fame; yet, looking heavenward, he felt the power and ruin of sin, and for salvation trusted in the merits of Jesus only. He passed away peacefully on the morning of Sept. 23, 1878, in the sixty-first year of his residence in Twiggs County, and in the eighty-third year of his age.

Bunyan, Rev. John, was born at Elstow, England, about a mile from Bedford, in 1628. His father was a man of more intelligence than those who generally followed his calling, and he had John taught to read and write. When the little boy was ten years of age he first became conscious that he was very sinful. He speedily shook off these fears.

He was "drawn out" in 1645, with others, at the siege of Leicester to perform sentinel's duty before the city, when another member of his company expressed a desire to take his place; the request was granted, and that night Bunyan's substitute was shot in the head and died. This deliverance produced a powerful impression upon Bunyan.

Soon after he left the army he married, and his wife and he were so poor that they had neither a "dish nor a spoon."

His first permanent conviction of sin was produced by a sermon denouncing the violation of the Lord's day by labor, sports, or otherwise. This came home to Bunyan with peculiar force, for his greatest enjoyment came from sports on the Lord's day.

A long while after this, Bunyan, in passing through the streets of Bedford, heard "three or four poor women," sitting at a door, "talking about the new birth, the work of God in their hearts, and the way by which they were convinced of their miserable state by nature. They told how God had visited their souls with his love in Christ Jesus, and with what words and promises they had been refreshed, comforted, and supported against the temptations of the devil; moreover, they reasoned of the suggestions and temptations of Satan in particular." From these women Bunyan learned to loathe sin and to hunger for the Saviour. He sought their company again and again, and he was strengthened to go to Jesus. One day, as he was passing into the fields, he says, "This sentence fell upon my soul, 'Thy righteousness is in heaven.' I also saw that it was not my good frame of heart that made my righteousness better, nor yet my bad frame that made my righteousness worse, for my righteousness was Jesus Christ himself, the same yesterday, to-day, and forever." Then, as he says, "his chains fell off," and he went home rejoicing. In 1655, Mr. Bunyan was immersed by the Rev. John Gifford, of

JOHN BUNYAN IN BEDFORD JAIL, 1667. HIS BLIND CHILD LEAVING HIM FOR THE NIGHT.

Bedford. The same year he was called to preach the gospel.

Bunyan was arrested Nov. 12, 1660, and he was in jail more than twelve years. His imprisonment was peculiarly trying. "The parting with my wife and poor children," says Bunyan, "hath often been to me, in this place (the prison), like pulling the flesh from my bones." And of his blind daughter he adds, "Poor child, what sorrow thou art like to have for thy portion in this world! Thou must be beaten, must beg, suffer hunger, cold, nakedness, and a thousand calamities, though I cannot now endure the wind should blow upon thee." "The Pilgrim's Progress" was written in Bedford jail.

During Bunyan's lifetime there were 100,000 copies of that book circulated in the British islands, besides which there were several editions in North America. And in the ten years which Bunyan lived, after his wonderful book was first issued, it was translated into French, Flemish, Dutch, Welsh, Gaelic, and Irish. Since Bunyan's death it has been translated into Hebrew for Christian Jews in Jerusalem, and into Spanish, Portuguese, Italian, Danish, German, Armenian, Burmese, Singhalese, Orissa, Hindostanee, Bengalee, Tamil, Maratthi, Canarese, Gujaratti, Malay, Arabic, Samoan, Tahitian, Pihuana, Bechuana, Malagasy, New Zealand, and Latin. This list of translations ends with 1847. Since that time it has been rendered into several additional tongues of our race. Nor will "The Pilgrim's Progress" stop in its travels until it visits every land occupied by human beings, and tells its blessed story in the language of all nations.

There is a French Roman Catholic version of "The Pilgrim's Progress," greatly abridged, with the head of the Virgin on the title-page. It leaves out giant Pope and the statement that Peter was afraid of a sorry girl. An English ritualistic clergyman has tried to adapt it to the sacramental jugglery of his system. Of Bunyan's "Holy War" Lord Macaulay says, "If 'The Pilgrim's Progress' did not exist it would be the best allegory that ever was written;" and he proclaims "John Bunyan the most popular religious writer in the English language."

The pardon which secured Bunyan's release from prison was ordered by the Privy Council, presided over by the king, May 17, 1672. After his liberation he became the most popular preacher in England; 3000 persons gathered to hear him in London before breakfast. Men of all ranks and of all grades of intelligence listened to his burning words, and heralded the fame of his eloquence to the king. The learned Dr. John Owen told Charles II. that he would relinquish all his learning for the tinker's preaching abilities.

While Bunyan was journeying upon an errand of mercy he was exposed to a heavy rain, which brought on a violent fever, from the effect of which he died in ten days, in London, Aug. 12, 1688. His last hours were full of peace. He was buried in Bunhill Fields Cemetery, where his monument is still seen.

Bunyan's church, now of the Congregational denomination, is still in Bedford. His chair is in the meeting-house, and some other relics of the immortal dreamer. A few years since the Duke of Bedford erected a handsome monument to Bunyan in Bedford, on which a statue of the great dreamer stands.

John Bunyan was one of the few men of our race who possessed genius of the highest order.

Burbank, Gideon Webster, was born at Deerfield, N. H., May 24, 1803, and died at Rochester, N. Y., March 4, 1873. His father, when Gideon was eighteen years of age, removed to New York City, and gave him a business education. Here the son remained for several years as a clerk in a dry goods house. The father went to North Carolina, and became a successful merchant. Upon his death the son went for a time to that State to settle his father's affairs. On his return to New York he decided to go into business for himself, and in 1824 fixed upon Kendall, Orleans Co., as his future home. The region was then just emerging from a wilderness, but he foresaw the opportunity opening there for a man of nerve and enterprise, and embracing it, he prospered with the growth of the country. At length he found a better field for his capacities in Rochester, the rising city of Western New York, and in 1839 he removed there to manufacture flour, for which that city is so celebrated. Here, honored by all men, he lived, illustrating the virtues of a Christian character to the age of threescore and ten. He was a member of the First Baptist church of that city.

His interest in education was shown by the gift of $20,000 towards the endowment of the professorship of Intellectual and Moral Philosophy which bears his name in the University of Rochester. This gift was supplemented by one from his son-in-law, Mr. Lewis Roberts, a member of the board of trustees of the university, and a liberal donor to its later funds. This donation to the young institution did more probably than any sum of double the amount since to create confidence in the permanent success of the enterprise. He will always have a distinguished place among the founders of the university, and the citizens of Rochester, among whom his memory is warmly cherished.

Burbank, Rev. John F., was born in Standish, Me., in 1812, but spent most of his youth in Portland. Immediately on his conversion he decided to enter the Christian ministry. He spent three years in Waterville College, and graduated at Columbian College, Washington, D. C. He took the full three years' course at Newton, and was ordained pastor of the church in Taunton, Mass., where he continued for a year, and then settled at Webster, Mass. He found that his health would not permit him to exercise his calling, and, having purchased a farm near Worcester, he retired to it to recruit his failing strength. Here he resided, preaching as he felt able, and trying to make his life a useful one in the cause of his Master. He was much respected by his fellow-citizens, filling several offices of honor and trust, and among them at one time that of president of the Common Council of the city of Worcester. He died Nov. 15, 1853.

Burchard, Hon. Charles A., late of Beaver Dam, Wis., was born in Leyden, Lewis Co., N. Y. In his early years he engaged in agricultural pursuits in his native State. When quite young he obtained a hope in Christ and united with the Baptist church. He took a deep interest in the establishment of the Literary and Theological Institution at Hamilton, and made a canvass of the Baptist churches in New York and Vermont to raise funds for its support. In 1845 he removed with his family to Waukesha, Wis. Here he cultivated a farm. In 1855, Mr. Burchard moved with his family to Beaver Dam, which has since been the family home. He was in the first Territorial Convention, which met in 1846 to form a State constitution. He has served his district for several sessions in the State Legislature. During the civil war he was a government commissioner, having the oversight of the raising and forwarding of troops. In 1847 he was elected president of the Wisconsin Baptist State Convention, to which position he was re-elected for five successive years. He was for many years a useful member of the board of Wayland Academy. In all the early history of the Baptists in the State he was a prominent actor. He was a man of strong convictions, a decided Baptist, a warm friend of ministers of the gospel, the uncompromising enemy of all wrong and fraud. He died in 1879, in the trust and triumph of the gospel of Christ.

Burchard, Hon. Seneca B., was born at Granby, Mass., Oct. 7, 1790. At seventeen he was converted, and united with the Baptist church of that place. He came to Hamilton, N. Y., in 1825, where he united with the Baptist church, and identified himself with the institutions of learning in that place.

In 1826 he became a member of the executive committee, also treasurer, steward, and agent. In 1834 he was the building agent for the erection of East College. He continued treasurer for twelve years, a member of the Education Board for thirty-nine years, president of said board seven years, and twenty-five years vice-president.

In 1846, the date of the charter of Madison University, he was made by the Legislature one of the original corporators, and was elected vice-president. He died at Hamilton, February, 1861, at about seventy-one years of age, his mind still strong and vigorous, and his faith in God and the educational enterprise at Hamilton unyielding. He was one of those stalwart men whom, in those early times, Dr. N. Kendrick drew around him when he was the energizing spirit at Hamilton.

Deacon Burchard was no ordinary man. He was massive and solid in every direction. He could endure great physical exertion as well as mental strain. Not easily discouraged or thwarted in his plans, slow in deliberation, wise in counsel, prompt in execution, when he had received an appointment he did not rest till he was sure of its accomplishment. As a member of the State Legislature, as a citizen, as a church member and deacon, as treasurer, executive officer, counselor on the board, he was highly respected, honored, and trusted till the end of his life.

To the close of his life he was a remarkably diligent student of the Scriptures. He either taught a Bible-class or was a member of one till near the eternal rest, and he used to tell how the Bible, as he re-read it, kept opening its truths to his heart.

Burchard, Theodore.—Mr. Theodore Burchard, who died at Lacon, Ill., Dec. 9, 1868, at the age of seventy-four, was a native of Granby, Mass. In early life he removed to Oneida County, in the State of New York, and from that place, later, to Hamilton, where he resided some twenty years, an active member of the church, and, like his two brothers, also residents of Hamilton, interested in all denominational enterprises. In 1854 he removed to Quincy, Ill., where he became a member of the Vermont Street Baptist church. During the last four years of his life he resided mostly at Lacon, where he died. His remains were taken to Hamilton for burial, where his wife and his two brothers also lie. "Father Burchard," writes one who knew him well, "was manly and noble in his bearing, tall, standing considerably over six feet, and every inch a Baptist. Strong in his convictions of truth and duty, strong in faith, there was no compromise of error in his nature."

Burchett, Rev. G. J., president of McMinnville College, Oregon, was born in Lee Co., Va., Nov. 15, 1847. In 1867, at Austin, Mo., he was converted and baptized. Impressed with the duty of preaching, he studied, and graduated at William Jewell College in 1874; was ordained; spent two years at Chicago, taking a course of lectures in theology; supplied some small churches, and held revival meetings during vacations. In 1876 he went to California, organized the Reeds church; preached a few months at Reeds, Wheatland, and Marysville.

In 1877 moved to Astoria, Oregon, built a house of worship for the church there, and in 1878 was elected president of McMinnville. His energy,

REV. G. J. BURCHETT.

enthusiasm, and ability have inspired the Baptists of Oregon to united and vigorous efforts on behalf of the college. He is a fine speaker and scholar, and a magnetic teacher.

Burdette, Robert J., was born at Greensborough, Pa., July 30, 1844. In 1852 he removed with his parents to Peoria, Ill. In 1862 he enlisted in the 47th Regiment of Ill. Vols. He served through the war, taking part in the battle of Corinth, the siege of Vicksburg, and the Red River Expedition. In 1870 he became editor of the Peoria *Transcript*, and subsequently of the Peoria *Review*. In 1874 he took charge of the Burlington (Iowa) *Hawkeye*, with which his name has ever since been associated, and to which he has imparted a world-wide reputation. He has attained a high position as a humorist, as an editor, and as a lecturer. His humor is always of the purest morality, and is subservient to the best and loftiest purposes. He is a member of the Burlington Baptist church, and he is an efficient, acceptable, and valued teacher in the Bible school.

Burk, Rev. B. J., pastor in Mobile for sixteen years over a large church, a man of positive character, a sterling Baptist, holding his church to "old land-mark" principles; liberally educated, a good preacher, he wields a powerful influence among colored Baptists.

Burkitt, Rev. Lemuel, the historian of the Kehukee Association, was baptized by Rev. Henry Abbot into the fellowship of Yeopim Baptist church in July, 1771. A good and useful man, and worthy to be held in perpetual remembrance.

Burleigh, Rev. Lucian, son of Deacon Rinalde and Lydia (B.) Burleigh, was born in Plainfield, Conn., Dec. 3, 1817; brought up a Congregationalist; educated in the public school, the Plainfield Academy, and the Connecticut Literary Institution at Suffield; chose the profession of teaching; was converted at the age of twenty; baptized by Rev. Smith Lyon; united with the Baptist church in North Oxford, Mass., where he was then teaching; removed to Packersville, Conn., where he was ordained as an evangelist; taught and preached in South and North Killingly, and North Granby, where he was principal of Green Academy; soon after 1840 began his large and effective labors in the Temperance Reform, which he advocated widely throughout the country; he wrote with a masterly pen; in 1849 he was agent of the American Association for the Suppression of Gambling; made a temperance campaign in Wisconsin, filling 70 appointments in 36 days; did the like in the State of New York; preached in the mean time; by request returned, and became principal of the Plainfield Academy, and served five years; supplied also destitute churches; taught the high school in Central Village; settled as pastor of the South Centre Baptist church in Ashford, Conn. (now Warrenville); then served for thirteen years as agent of the Connecticut Temperance Union; his discourses and poems have won an extensive reputation; is now preaching and lecturing.

Burleson, Richard Byrd, LL.D., son of Jonathan Burleson, was born near Decatur, Ala., and died at Waco, Dec. 21, 1879. In 1839 he was converted, and three days after was baptized by Rev. William H. Holcombe. In 1840 he entered Nashville University, and remained three years. During the pastorate of Dr. R. B. C. Howell he was licensed to preach by the First Baptist church of Nashville in 1841. He was called to ordination by the church at Athens, Ala., November, 1842, and was the pastor of that church for two years. In 1845 he accepted the call of the Baptist church in Tuscumbia, and remained their pastor four years.

In 1849 he was made president of Moulton Female Institute, and held that position about six years. In December, 1855, he removed to Texas, and became, in 1856, pastor of the Austin church, conducting at the same time a female school. In 1857 he was chosen Professor of Natural Science in Baylor University. In 1861 he was elected vice-president of Waco University, and Professor of Natural Science in that institution. As a student in theology, geology, botany, and astronomy he had no superior, and probably no equal, in Texas. Governor Richard Coke, knowing his eminence, gave him an appointment for the geological survey of Texas; but he resigned this position after one year's service, as it conflicted with his life work of founding a great Baptist university for Texas. As a teacher, thousands can testify that his zeal and ability were never surpassed. Neither private interest nor bodily pains ever detained him from the post of duty for twenty-three years. He contributed largely to the great success of Baylor and Waco Universities; to the latter of which he gave eighteen years of toil and sacrifice, and intense anxiety for its firm establishment.

He was a preacher of distinguished ability, and a teacher eminently qualified for his work. His piety was ardent, his life was holy, and his death was blessed. The hymn which was sung several times at his request, at his expiring couch, showed the character of his dying exercises:

"How firm a foundation, ye saints of the Lord,
Is laid for your faith in his excellent Word!"

A procession of carriages a mile in length followed his remains to their last resting-place, and sorrow filled thousands of hearts for the loss that had fallen upon the university, the churches, and the whole State.

Burleson, Rufus C., D.D., the son of Jonathan Burleson, was born near Decatur, Ala., Aug. 7, 1823. He was converted on the 21st of April, 1839, and baptized the following Sabbath by Rev. William H. Holcombe.

While a student in Nashville University in 1840 he abandoned his aspirations for legal eminence, and from deep convictions of duty devoted his life to the ministry. He was licensed to preach Dec. 12, 1840, by the First Baptist church of Nashville, under the pastoral care of Dr. R. B. C. Howell. He commenced preaching immediately, though only seventeen years old, but did not relax any of his devotion to study. He was ordained "with prayer and fasting" June 8, 1845. He graduated in the Western Baptist Literary and Theological Institute, Covington, Ky., June 10, 1847. During all these seven years of laborious preparation for the ministry he preached almost every Sunday, and scores were converted under his preaching.

A few months after graduating he was elected pastor of the First Baptist church at Houston, Texas, to succeed that great and good man, William M. Tryon, who had died of yellow fever. During the three and a half years of his pastorate the church became self-sustaining, paid off a heavy mortgage, became the largest in the city, and the most liberal in the State. His zeal, learning, piety, and eloquence placed him in the front rank, and for more than thirty years he has acted a conspicuous part in every great social, religious, and educational enterprise in Texas. Though attacked by yellow fever he stood firmly at his post.

He was elected, June, 1851, president of Baylor University, to succeed Dr. H. L. Groves. Though ardently devoted to his church at Houston and peculiarly fitted for the pulpit, he felt the glory of Texas and the success of his denomination demanded a great Baptist university, hence he consecrated himself to the work. Though he had the hearty co-operation of such eminent men as Gen. Houston, Gov. Horton, Judges Lipscomb, Wheeler, and Baylor, he knew it was a herculean task that would require a long lifetime. At once Baylor University became one of the leading institutions of the South, and continues so till now.

While pastor at Houston he baptized Mrs. Dickenson, the heroine of the Alamo, and while pastor at Independence he baptized Gen. Houston, the hero of San Jacinto.

In 1861 he, with his brother, Dr. Richard Burleson, and the entire faculty associated with him in Baylor University, desiring a central and accessible location in the wheat region, removed to the city of Waco and inaugurated Waco University. This

RUFUS C. BURLESON, D.D.

institution at once rose to distinction. Dr. Burleson is a firm believer in co-education, and is the pioneer in the great movement in the Southwest. He has instructed over 2800 young men and ladies.

Dr. Burleson's characteristics are fixedness of purpose, amiability of manners, generosity, and courage. From these characteristics it is not strange that every church of which he has been pastor, and every college over which he has presided, has prospered. His advice and co-operation are frequently sought on educational questions in Texas.

Burlingham, Aaron H., D.D.—Dr. Burlingham was born Feb. 18, 1822, in Castile, N. Y. He was graduated from Madison University in 1848, and from the Theological Seminary of Hamilton in 1850, and in the same year he was ordained as pastor over the Grant Street Baptist church of Pittsburgh, Pa. After one year he accepted the pastorate of the Baptist church of Owego, N. Y. Two years afterwards he took charge of the Harvard Street Baptist church, Boston, Mass. In 1853 he was chosen chaplain of the State Senate.

In 1856 he moved to New York, and became pastor of the South Baptist church. This settlement continued nine years, but the labor was so arduous that he resigned and went to Europe. For several months he filled the pulpit of the celebrated American chapel in Paris. After a year's residence abroad visiting various places of historical interest he returned, and accepted a call from the Second

AARON H. BURLINGHAM, D.D.

Baptist church of St. Louis, Mo. This commanding position he held for several years, with credit to himself and the continual growth of the church.

As a lecturer he drew large and delighted audiences. His course of lectures on the "Women of the Bible," delivered in St. Louis, attracted great attention, and was highly spoken of by the secular press.

From St. Louis he went to Brooklyn, N. Y., and took the pastoral charge of the Willowby Avenue Baptist church, and in 1879 he was chosen district secretary of the American Baptist Missionary Union for New York.

Burlington Collegiate Institute, at Burling-

BURLINGTON COLLEGIATE INSTITUTE.

ton, Iowa, was located by the vote of an Educational Convention of the Baptists of Iowa, held at Iowa City in 1852, and incorporated under the name of Burlington University. It is situated on a beautiful slope on the west of the city. The building is 65 by 45 feet, with a wing in the rear 30 by 30 feet, all three stories high, of brick, and trimmed with stone. The campus contains several acres covered with a fine growth of native shade-trees. The city has so extended its limits and increased its population that the school is now about the centre, and occupies a very commanding position. It is now in first-class condition, with a good telescope, chemical laboratory, and philosophical apparatus, and a well-selected library. The buildings and grounds are worth $40,000, and the institution has a small endowment, and it has no encumbrance of any kind.

The present officers of the board of trustees are Hon. J. M. Beck, President; Rev. E. C. Spinney, Vice-President; Hon. T. W. Newman, Secretary; F. T. Parsons, Treasurer; and E. F. Stearns, A.M., Principal of the Institute.

Burmah.—The Burman Mission, being the first established by the Baptists in America, will always occupy a peculiar place in their regards. Burmah is that part of India beyond the Ganges which lies between Hindostan on the west and China on the east. The population is probably not far from 10,000,000, a third of this number speaking the Burmese language. The government is a despotic monarchy, and the religion Buddhism, "one of the most ancient and wide-spread superstitions existing on the earth, and one which, in its various branches, holds beneath its gloomy sway the minds of a third of the human race." The mission to Burmah was commenced by Mr. and Mrs. Judson in 1813, at Rangoon, the principal seaport of the empire. The formal appointment of Mr. Judson as a missionary of the Baptist Triennial Convention was made in May, 1814. The first work of the new missionary was the preparation of a tract on the nature of the Christian religion, with a brief abstract of its leading doctrines. On the 15th of October, 1816, Rev. Mr. Hough and wife joined Mr. and Mrs. Judson at Rangoon. Mr. Hough was a practical printer, and he addressed himself at once to the printing of portions of the Scriptures and short religious treatises to be placed in the hands of the natives, whose curiosity was awakened to see the sacred books of the new religion. Four years passed before the first sincere inquirer came to Mr. Judson to ask after the way of salvation. He found the Saviour, and was baptized at Rangoon, June 27, 1819. From that time the missionaries had persecution, discouragement, and progress marking their experiences; but viewing all the facts in their history, the mission in Burmah has enjoyed much prosperity.

The *Karen* Mission is bound up with the mission to the Burmese by geographical ties.

The word Karen means *wild man*, and applies to a rude people who are scattered over the mountains and forests of Burmah, Siam, and the adjacent countries. They are divided into several tribes, the chief of which are the S'gau and Pwo. They have been the subjects of cruel oppression, especially by the Burmese, who have compelled them, for a long time, to act about as if they were their slaves, exacting from them the hardest tasks, and forcing from them large tributes of money. Their life, in consequence of the cruelties inflicted upon them, has been a nomadic one, and they hide themselves away in jungles and mountainous retreats to escape from the persecutions of their enemies. In many respects, even before they were reached by the civilizing influences of Christianity, they were said to be superior to the Burmese, who, in a special manner, were their foes. Whence these people originated is not definitely known. By some they are supposed to have been the aborigines of the country, while others regard them as immigrants from India.

At the time the Karens came into special notice by the contact of American missionaries they did not seem to have any well-defined form of religious belief, nor any distinct priesthood. There were among them some remarkable traditions, which strikingly corresponded with the teachings of the Bible, as the account of the creation of man, the temptation in the garden of Eden, the deluge, etc.

They had also some prophecies which pointed on to happier times when they should no longer be degraded, but should be lifted up out of the condition in which for so long a time they had groaned. Among such a people, apparently so well prepared to receive the gospel, the missionaries were welcomed most heartily.

The first Karen converted and baptized was Ko-Tha-byu; this occurred in 1828. He was a man of middle age, once a slave, whose freedom had been purchased by the missionaries; his conversion commenced the Karen Mission, so greatly honored of God. In 1831, Mr. Boardman visited the jungle homes of the Karens, after conversing with many of them at his own residence, and preached Jesus to them.

Without any further reference to the race distinction between Karens and Burmese, we will state that

The Rangoon Mission was established in 1813, and in 1880 it had 25 missionaries, 71 native preachers, 98 churches, and 4031 members.

The Maulmain Mission was established in 1827, and at that station there are 19 missionaries, 23 native preachers, 18 churches, and 1240 members.

The Tavoy Mission, founded in 1828, has 3 missionaries, 20 native preachers, 21 churches, and 1038 members.

The Bassein Mission, commenced in 1840, has 12 missionaries, 142 native preachers, 90 churches, and 7808 members.

The Henthada Mission, instituted in 1853, has 1 missionary, 45 native preachers, 58 churches, and 1998 members.

The Swaygyeen Mission, begun in 1853, has 4 missionaries, 24 native preachers, 23 churches, and 867 members.

The Toungoo Mission, started in 1853, has 14 missionaries, 98 native preachers, 117 churches, and 3910 members.

The Thongzai Mission, the foundations of which were laid in 1855, has 2 missionaries, 10 native preachers, 3 churches, and 297 members.

The Prome Mission was commenced in 1854, and has 3 missionaries, 7 native preachers, 3 churches, and 225 members.

The Zeegong Mission, established in 1876, has 1 missionary, 2 native preachers, 2 churches, and 110 members.

The Bhamo Mission, founded in 1877, has 4 missionaries, 6 native preachers, and 10 members.

The missions among the Burmese and Karens have 88 missionaries, 448 native preachers, 433 churches, and 21,594 members. This is just about half our missionary strength in the East, in laborers and baptized converts, and we have our garnered harvests in Sweden, Germany, and France besides.

The translation of the whole Bible into the Burmese language was completed Jan. 31, 1834. A Karen newspaper, *The Morning Star*, was established at Tavoy in September, 1841. The whole New Testament was issued in Karen, Nov. 1, 1843, and the entire Bible in January, 1851. In 1857 all the Karen churches concluded to support themselves, and the mission churches in Burmah are among the most liberal contributors to send the gospel to the heathen. Books for schools and a Christian literature have been created by the missionaries in Burmah, and the unprejudiced observer of their labors cannot fail to regard them as the benefactors of the races for whose welfare they have toiled and sacrificed so much. Schools of various grades have been established for the education of the people, in which large numbers receive instruction from accomplished and godly teachers; and a theological seminary was established in Maulmain in 1844, which was subsequently removed to Rangoon, which has trained a large number of native ministers and teachers for the Karens. A sketch of this institution will be found in the article "Rangoon College." Nowhere in the whole range of modern missionary toil have Christian labors among the heathen been more signally blessed than in Burmah.

Burn, Rev. W. G., was born in Guilford Co., N. C., April 4, 1820; baptized by Barton Roby, Sept. 20, 1840; ordained in 1843; has been pastor of Flat Rock church for twenty-seven years; has baptized 1200 souls, constituted 5 churches, and aided in the ordination of 25 ministers; was moderator of the Yadkin Association for several years, and has three sons in the ministry.

Burnett, Robert H., long president of the Louisiana Baptist Convention, was born in South Carolina in 1812, and in 1837 united in the constitution of Mount Lebanon church, the first church organized in Northeastern Louisiana; was also for many years moderator of Red River Baptist Association.

Burney, Thomas J., greatly distinguished and honored among Georgia Baptists for his able and successful management of the finances of the Georgia Baptist Convention for a long series of years, during which he acted as treasurer of that body, was born in Greene Co., April 29, 1801. He died June 22, 1876, most of his life having been spent in Madison, Ga. When young he had fair educational advantages; was for a time a student at the famous law school of St. George Tucker, Winchester, Va., and for a brief period he engaged in the practice of law. Although he served in the United States land-office at Cahawba, Ala., for some time, and was all his life a man of business, yet Mr. Burney was distinguished more for his deep religious convictions and for his usefulness in church and educational matters than for eminence in any other respect. He was baptized by Dr. Adiel Sherwood in November, 1834, and for forty years was an active, useful, and faithful member of the Madison church, of which he was for many years deacon and treasurer. He was secretary and treasurer of the Georgia Female College, a member of the board of trustees for that institution and also of Mercer University, and was the treasurer of the university and a member of the Executive and Prudential Committees of the Georgia Baptist Convention for many years. So skillfully did he manage the vast

THOMAS J. BURNEY.

interests intrusted to his hands as treasurer of the Georgia Baptist Convention and of Mercer University that his brethren gave him unlimited authority over all the funds. He was a man of firm purpose, dauntless resolution, and unswerving integrity, all his other duties yielding to his religious obligations. He was calm, self-possessed, temperate, and thoughtful. He was not known as a speaker in the conventional meetings, but his few and pointed words ever received respectful attention. His house was the preacher's home, and from its altar the incense of morning and evening sacrifice ascended each day. His death was calm, peaceful, and happy.

Burnham, Prof. S., A.M., graduated from Bowdoin College, Brunswick, Me., in 1862, and from the theological seminary at Newton, Mass., in 1873. Pastor at Amherst, Mass., 1873–74; teacher in Worcester Academy, Worcester, Mass., in 1874; elected Professor of Hebrew and Old Testament Exegesis in Hamilton Theological Seminary in 1875, which position he still retains.

Burns, Dawson, M.A., son of Jabez Burns, D.D., was born in London in 1828. He studied at the General Baptist Theological Seminary at Leicester, and commenced his ministry in 1850. For several years Mr. Burns was occupied in public work in connection with the temperance movement. In 1874 he was elected co-pastor with his father, after whose death he succeeded to the sole charge. Mr. Burns is widely known as one of the leaders of the United Kingdom Alliance for the suppression of the traffic in intoxicating drinks, a society which attracts a large body of supporters of various religious and political opinions, and wields a potent influence in Parliamentary elections in the large cities and towns.

Burns, Jabez, D.D., for many years an eminent minister of the English General Baptists, was born in Oldham, Lancashire, Dec. 18, 1805. In his youth he connected himself with the Methodists, but some years later he was baptized, and became associated with the General Baptists. He was engaged for some years in lecturing and preaching in Scotland, mainly in connection with the temperance movement, of which throughout life he was an able and conspicuous leader. In June, 1835, he was called to the pastorate of the church in London. Here for upwards of forty years he labored with distinguished success. He also wrote and published largely, his best-known works being "Helps to Students and Lay Preachers" and "Manuals for Devotional Use and Family Worship." He visited this country in 1847 as a delegate from the General Baptist Association to the Free-Will Baptist Triennial Conference, and also in 1872. His "Retrospect of a Forty Years' Ministry," published in 1875, gives an interesting description of the modern progress of religion, temperance, and philanthropic enterprises. In recognition of his merits as a religious writer, and particularly of the character of his "Pulpit Cyclopædia," the Wesleyan University of Connecticut conferred upon him the degree of D.D. in 1846, and in 1872 Bates College, Me., added the degree of LL.D. He was very efficient to the end of his life, and as a preacher and public speaker he was highly esteemed. He died Jan. 31, 1876, aged seventy.

Burr, Normand, was born in Hartford, Conn., Oct. 5, 1802; his business was printing and publishing; converted in 1838, and united with the South Baptist church, being baptized by Rev. Robert Turnbull, D.D.; was editor and publisher of the *Christian Secretary*, with others, from 1840 to his death, Dec. 5, 1861. He had two children, a son and a daughter. Mrs. Sigourney, the poetess, wrote of him, and wrote truly,—

> "We knew him as a man of sterling worth,
> Whose good example is a legacy
> Better than gold for those he leaves behind.
> His inborn piety flowed forth in streams
> Of social kindness and domestic love."

Burrage, Rev. Henry S., was born in Fitchburg, Mass., and graduated at Brown University in the class of 1861. He was connected with the Newton Theological Institution six years,—1861–67. For three years during the late war he was in the military service of the United States. His ordination took place in December, 1869, and he was pastor of the church in Waterville, Me., 1870–73. He became in 1873 the proprietor and editor of *Zion's Advocate*, a weekly religious paper published in Portland, Me., and still holds this position.

Mr. Burrage is the compiler of a volume entitled "Brown University in the War," containing sketches of the graduates and students of the university who were in the service of the United States in the late civil war, and he is the author of a learned work entitled "The Act of Baptism."

Burroughs, J. C., D.D., LL.D.—Dr. Burroughs is a native of Western New York, and was born in the year 1819. His literary education he received at Yale College, and his theological at Hamilton. His first settlement as pastor was at Waterford, N. Y., and his second at West Troy, in the same State. He soon became well known in New York as an efficient pastor and a highly acceptable preacher, and while yet in the early part of his ministerial career he was called upon for special service on important occasions, and his counsel sought in connection with the management of denominational affairs. In the year 1852, after a pastorate of some ten years in the East, he was called to the First Baptist church of Chicago. In the same month, October, 1852, that Mr. Burroughs began his labors with this church the house of worship, built in 1843, was burned. Immediate measures were taken for the erection of a new edifice upon the same ground, the church meanwhile worshiping in a small building near by. The corner-stone was laid July, 1853, and the new house dedicated in the November following, a commodious and tasteful structure, costing $30,000. In connection with the labors of his pastorate, in these circumstances unusually exacting, Mr. Burroughs established, in association with brethren Weston and Joslyn, the weekly Baptist paper in Chicago, the *Christian Times*, now the *Standard*, having purchased, as preliminary to this, the subscription list of the paper previously issued by Rev. Luther Stout, *The Watchman of the Prairies*. About the year 1855, the presidency of Shurtleff College having become vacant, Mr. Burroughs was strongly solicited to accept that post. This he declined, but an opening occurring, providentially, for the founding of a university in Chicago, he felt it to be his duty to give himself to this, and with that view resigned his pastorate in 1856. The deed of gift from Senator Douglas for the university site of ten acres was procured by Mr. Burroughs. To these two men, and to the latter certainly not less than the former, the Baptist denomination is chiefly indebted for the university at Chicago. Dr. Burroughs was the first president of the university, holding this office until the creation of that of chancellor, in the year 1876, to which he was elected, Dr. Lemuel Moss taking the presidency. He held the chancellorship until 1878, when he resigned this office also. During the early years of the university he consecrated himself to its interest with absolute self-devotion. Large amounts were obtained by him in subscriptions and pledges,— much of it lost subsequently through the financial disasters which made collection impossible, but none the less a fruit of earnest and well-directed labor on his own part. In the whole work of university organization he of course largely shared, while in the department of instruction the quality of his teaching is witnessed by the strong affection cherished for him by his pupils in their after-life. Dr. Burroughs still has his residence at Chicago, although his official connection with the university has ceased.

Burroughs, Rev. Joseph, was born in London, England, Jan. 1, 1685. He was converted and called to the ministry in early life, and for the proper discharge of a pastor's duties he received a liberal education at a private academy in London and at the University of Leyden. He was ordained May 1, 1717, as pastor of the church in Paul's Alley, Barbican, London. Here he labored with great success and untiring faithfulness for more than forty years. He was a great admirer of the Word of God, upon the exposition of which he expended his unusual abilities and his extensive learning. He had a special desire to promote the practical duties of the Saviour's religion, and to secure as far as possible a church wholly consecrated to God. He was a warm friend to the cause of Christ in general, but to the Baptist churches specially, among which he was one of the most popular men of his day. Though a Christian of the largest charity he believed that baptism was a prerequisite to the Lord's Supper, and his faith and practice walked together in scriptural harmony. Towards the close of life he manifested a spirit of extraordinary humility, charging himself with many defects and relying for salvation wholly upon the mercy of God. He passed from earth without a struggle on the 23d of November, 1761, in his seventy-seventh year. Mr. Burroughs was a General Baptist.

Burrows, John Lansing, D.D., son of Samuel Burrows, a naval officer of the war of 1812, was born in New York in 1814. His father died of yellow fever at Mobile in 1822, after which he became the ward of his grandfather, Nathaniel Burrows, of Bucks Co., Pa., who educated him with much care. He finished his education at Andover, Mass. In 1835 he was ordained to the ministry in Poughkeepsie, and became assistant pastor of a church in New York City. In 1836 he removed to Kentucky, and engaged in teaching at Shelbyville, and subsequently at Elizabethtown. In 1839 he took charge of the church at Owensborough, and also organized and took charge of the church at Henderson. In 1840 he became pastor of Sansom Street church in Philadelphia. In 1844 he founded the Broad Street church, same city, and was its successful pastor for ten years. In 1854 he accepted the pastorate of the First Baptist church in Richmond, Va., a relation which he sustained for twenty years. He returned to Kentucky in 1874, and became pastor of the Broadway Baptist church in Louisville, where he still ministers (1880).

Dr. Burrows has a national fame as a graceful and eloquent pulpit orator, an easy, elegant writer, and a man of varied learning and extensive reading, and, best of all, Dr. Burrows has been one of the most useful men in the ministry of our denomination.

Burrows, Rev. Silas, son of Amos and Mary (Rathbone) Burrows, was born in Groton, Conn., in 1741. His father, educated in the standing order, became a speaker among the Liberalists, or New Lights. His brother Amos became a licensed Baptist preacher. Silas was converted when about twenty-three years of age, under the preaching of Rev. Mr. Reynolds, a Baptist from Norwich, and was one of the first members of the Second Baptist church in Groton, which chose him as their leader. He was ordained about 1765, and held the pastoral office of the church for fifty-three years. Amid the agitations resulting from the great awakening, the Revolutionary war, and the inroads of infidelity, he stood firmly by the truth and the cause of liberty. He had two brothers captured in Fort Griswold. During the powerful revival of 1782–83 several of his children were converted, among them Daniel and Roswell, who afterwards became preachers. His ministry was crowned by another mighty reformation, beginning in January, 1809, and extending through eighteen months, during which he baptized 130 persons. He married first, Mary Smith, and second, Mrs. Phebe (Denison) Smith. Of sound native talents, ardent piety, eminently prayerful spirit, plainness of speech, and firmness of purpose, he made strong and permanent impressions upon the people. He was a wise builder. He fell asleep in 1818, aged seventy-seven years, and was buried in his own church-yard.

Burrows, Rev. Roswell, son of Rev. Silas Burrows, was born in Groton, Sept. 2, 1768. He was converted while a merchant's clerk at Guilford, Conn., when home on a visit. Though he became a successful merchant in Hopkinton, R. I., he finally returned to the home of his father in Groton, where he yielded to his convictions and the persuasions of his brethren, and received ordination in August, 1806, as associate pastor of the Second Baptist church in Groton, with his honored and aged father, whose place he filled after 1818, when his father died. After his ordination, by appointment from the Groton Union Conference, he spent several months in a missionary tour, riding more than 1300 miles, and preaching once or twice daily, giving a great impulse to the cause of missions in the churches. He was always active and efficient in the Groton Union Conference, and in the Stonington Union Association. Through his instrumentality a church was organized in Preston, Conn., in 1812. He also labored somewhat at Greenport, L. I., and in Western New York, on missionary tours. In his later years he was aided in his own pulpit by Revs. Erastus Dennison and Ira R. Steward. His ministry at home was attended with seven special revivals, and he baptized 635 persons, and preached 2886 times. At the age of twenty-one he married Jerusha Avery, and was the father of seven children, one of whom became a member of Congress. He died May 28, 1837, in his sixty-ninth year. His funeral sermon was preached by Rev. Daniel Wildman, of New London. He was buried in the church-yard by the side of his father.

Burrows, Roswell S., a prominent layman of Albion, N. Y., was born in Groton, Conn., Feb. 22, 1798. He was the grandson of Rev. Silas Burrows and son of Rev. Roswell Burrows, one pastor for fifty-three years and the other for thirty-five years of the Second Baptist church in Groton. He entered the Sophomore class of Yale College at the age of twenty-one. He was compelled to leave college in the middle of the junior year by reason of continued ill health. In 1867 the college conferred on him the honorary degree of A.M. In 1824 he established himself in Albion, N. Y., where he still lives, having been for the last ten years the oldest resident of the place.

He is distinguished chiefly for remarkable business talents, having been connected with numerous large public and private enterprises, which have yielded him an ample fortune. He has been identified with the university and seminary at Rochester through all their history, and gave the latter institution "The Neander Library," now valued at $20,000. He has been a member of the United States House of Representatives.

Burton, Rev. John, was born in 1760 in England. He came to Halifax, Nova Scotia, in 1792. He visited the United States, embraced Baptist principles, and was baptized here. He returned to Halifax, June 17, 1793, and administered the first baptism witnessed there the following August 24. He organized a Baptist church in that city in 1795, the second one organized in the provinces. Mr. Burton continued as its pastor until his death, which occurred Feb. 6, 1838. He was a Christian gentleman, useful in the community in which he labored, and enjoying the respect and love of those around him.

Burton, Nathan Smith, D.D., was born at Manlius, N. Y., Feb. 5, 1821; baptized by Rev. I. Hall, at Akron, O., 1843; graduated from Western Reserve College in 1846; spent one year at Western Reserve College in theological study; the second year at Newton, and then returned as classical tutor to Western Reserve, where he graduated in theology in 1850; ordained Nov. 6, 1850, as pastor at Elyria, O., where he remained until 1853. After a short pastorate in Cleveland became pastor at Granville, O., where he remained until 1862. While pastor here, in 1859, established the Young Ladies' Institute. In 1862 took charge of the church at Akron, O.; in 1866, of the church at Ann Arbor, Mich.; in 1871, of the church at Davenport, Iowa. In 1876 he accepted the professorship of Philosophy in Kalamazoo College, but on account of the failure of the endowment resigned the following year and returned to Akron, O., where, as pastor of the church, he still remains.

The honorary degree of D.D. was conferred upon him by Denison University, in 1863. He is universally regarded as standing in the front of Ohio Baptists, and he is profoundly interested in all that pertains to the interests of the kingdom of Christ.

Burton, Rev. William, was born in Margaree, Cape Breton; baptized by Rev. Joseph Dimock in 1826; ordained July 20, 1828; was co-pastor of Yarmouth church with the venerable Harris Harding from 1830 to 1853; then pastor at Portland, St. John, New Brunswick, and at Hantsport, Nova Scotia, where he died in 1867. An earnest, useful minister.

Bush, Rev. Alexander, was born in Lowville, Lewis Co., N. Y., Feb. 1, 1810. He was hopefully converted at the age of seventeen, and baptized in July, 1827. He devoted some time to the work of teaching, and feeling that it was his duty to preach, he entered Hamilton Theological Institution in 1835. In 1838 he received a call from the Tyringham and Lee church, Mass., and on the 17th of October of this year he was ordained as the pastor of the church. He labored diligently and faithfully, and God permitted him to see the rich fruits of his ministerial toil. His ministry was a short one. In the spring of 1842 he was forced partially to suspend his work. He preached his last sermon July 30 of this year. For a year or two he lingered, a great and constant sufferer. He died June 17, 1844.

Bush, Rev. Alva, LL.D., was born in Busti, Chautauqua Co., N. Y., Jan. 25, 1830. He was the second son of Seldin F. Bush and Florina Blackman. He was converted and joined the Baptist church in Busti in 1840, under the pastorate of Rev. E. R. Swain. He completed his education in Burlington University. He was licensed to preach by the church at Strawberry Point in 1858, and ordained at the same place in 1859. He supplied the church one year during an interim in the pastorate of Rev. George Scott. He was pastor of the church at Fayette in 1860, imparting instruc-

REV. ALVA BUSH, LL.D.

tion part of the time in the Upper Iowa University, during which Rev. J. E. Clough and Hattie Sunderland, afterwards Mrs. Clough, were students in that institution, and part of the time members of Mr. Bush's family.

He was settled in Osage, and opened the school which was to be the Cedar Valley Seminary, January, 1863. During the eighteen years of his connection with the seminary he served the Baptist church of Osage as pastor something over ten years, and preached regularly at out-stations during the remainder of the time.

Bussy, Rev. B. W., was born and brought up in Columbus, Ga., but preached for years in Huntsville and Mobile, Ala. He is now the able pastor of the Americus Baptist church, having returned to his native State. A man of more than ordinary ability, he is a fine pastor and preacher, and an efficient Sunday-school worker.

Bussy, Hon. James, a prominent lawyer at Bastrop, La., was born in Georgia in 1830. Judge Bussy is a striking example of what may be accomplished under almost insurmountable difficulties. In early life an incurable paralysis made him a helpless dependent. By perseverance he developed strength in his arms, and acquired the power of balancing himself on crutches. By dint of application he made himself an intelligent lawyer, and has risen to distinction in church and state. He has made it a rule of life to devote one-tenth of his gross income to the Lord. Under the blessing of God he has prospered, and is now a man of wealth. He has presided as moderator of Bayou Macon Association and as president of the State Convention.

Butler, Rev. David E., who has deservedly been greatly honored by the Baptists of Georgia with places of trust, was born in Wilkes County. When a young man and a practicing lawyer, in Washington, Wilkes County, he was the personal friend of Jesse Mercer, whose will he wrote, and whose executor he was. Mr. Butler is a graduate of Mercer. It was not until after his marriage that he felt constrained to enter the ministry; while living on his farm in the country he was unable to restrain his inclinations to point sinners to the Lamb slain for us; he gradually became convinced that it was his duty to preach, and he submitted to ordination, and entered upon the ministry. He has been an eloquent pleader for Jesus and a good preacher. He has had charge of various churches, while his home has generally been at Madison. Before the war he was a wealthy planter, and never sought remuneration for pulpit services. Since the return of peace he has maintained his farming interests, not being dependent on the ministry. In the Central Association he has been a ruling spirit, and frequently has been its moderator, by election. For five years, from 1872 to 1876, inclusive, he was president of the Georgia Baptist Convention; for many years he has been the president of the board of trustees of Mercer University; and for several years he was the efficient editor of the *Christian Index*. Since the war his influence in the denomination has been great and beneficial, and he has almost been the central figure around which Georgia Baptist interests have gravitated. Mr. Butler is an eloquent speaker and an exceedingly ready man, possessing a fine command of language. He is universally held in the highest esteem, and amid many diversified employments has never ceased eloquently to proclaim the gospel. As the friend of education and missions, the friend and supporter of Mercer and the Convention, he stands out in bold relief in the denomination. He is exceedingly popular all over the State, among all classes and denominations; his name has been freely spoken of in connection with the gubernatorial office of Georgia.

Butler, Gov. Ezra, was born in Lancaster, Mass., in September, 1763. He lived for some years with Dr. Stearns, of Claremont, N. H., where he had the management of a large farm. In his twenty-second year he removed to Waterbury, Vt., where he commenced farming. He was almost literally in a wilderness, there being but one other family in the whole place. Indeed, the whole section was but little better than a dense forest for miles in every direction. When he was twenty-seven years of age he became a hopeful Christian. His conversion was a remarkable one, and plainly the work of the Holy Spirit. He was baptized by " Elder" Call in his wilderness home. In due time Waterbury attracted to itself inhabitants, and towards the end of the year 1800 there were a sufficient number of persons holding Baptist sentiments to lead to the formation of a Baptist church, and Mr. Butler was chosen and ordained its pastor, which office he held over thirty years.

Being a person of superior education he was called to fill various civil offices, as town clerk, justice of the peace, and representative for several terms to the General Assembly of Vermont. For a number of years he was chief justice for Washington County. From 1813 to 1815 he was a member of Congress, and for two years he was governor of the State. "His administration as governor was distinguished chiefly by a vigorous and successful effort for the suppression of lotteries, and by some essential improvement in the system of common school education." In 1836 he officiated as one of the electors of the President of the United States. Amidst all the responsibilities connected with the civil trusts committed to his hands he never lost sight of the higher office which he held as an ambassador of Christ. While he was governor of the State an extensive revival was in progress in his own town, in which he took the deepest interest, his heart being greatly gladdened by the circumstance that several members of his own family were among its fruits. Gov. Butler died July 12, 1838, in the seventy-fifth year of his age.

In the report of the travels of Messrs. Cox and Hoby—a deputation from the Baptist churches in England to the Baptist churches in this country—we find the following extract taken from Dr. Sprague's "Annals." The language is Mr. Hoby's:

"At Waterbury I paid a visit to Gov. Butler, who, you remember, though a pastor in our denomination, had once the honor of being governor of the State of Vermont. His eye is not so dimmed with age but that you may clearly discern that it was once expressive of the intelligence and energy equal to the responsibilities of such an office, however undesirable it may be to blend it with pastoral engagements. Forever let his name be honored among those who steadfastly determined and labored with untiring zeal to disencumber the State of the burden of a religious establishment, and religion of the manifold evils of State patronage. As he walked towards the town he told me that fifty years ago he cleared the first spot in this cultivated district, which was then all wilderness. Now his children's children are growing up around him, to inherit the land and the liberties they owe so literally to their fathers."

Butterfield, Rev. Isaac, was born in Andover, Vt., Oct. 16, 1812; removed to New Ipswich, N. H., at the age of twenty-one years; was baptized by Rev. Asaph Merriam in May, 1835, and studied for a short time in Appleton Academy, New Ipswich, after his conversion. He was licensed to preach in the spring of 1836, and was ordained in January, 1837, as pastor of the church in Cicero, N. Y. He remained ten years in the Onondaga Association, five of which were spent in Elbridge. Then followed nearly ten years of service in Oswego, part as pastor of the First church, and then he went out with a colony which formed the West church. He was for seven years pastor in Davenport, Iowa, also served for brief terms in Watertown, N. Y.; Adrian, Mich.; Hightstown, N. J.; Monroe, Mich.; and Grand Rapids. Then for six years he was again at the West church in Oswego. In 1875 he yielded to an urgent appeal from the First church in Jackson to come to them in a time of special exigency, and for five years he gave his service with great self-devotion. The last of the five years Rev. C. E. Harris was his colleague. Mr. Butterfield now resides in Grand Rapids. He has been a laborious worker in the Lord's vineyard, and has counted it a pleasure to serve in fields from which others would shrink. His influence has been that of a peace-maker, and his churches have been greatly attached to him. He was married Sept. 14, 1838, to Miss Sarah A. Templeton, of Northfield, Mass.

Buys, Rev. James, M.D., was long an efficient minister in North Louisiana. He was born in Georgia in 1800; removed to Louisiana in 1848, and died in Winn Pas, La., Oct. 26, 1867.

Byron, Deacon Wm. Henry, a native of New York City, where he was born June 21, 1808. His father died when he was a child. His mother, a lady of fine mental and Christian culture, devoted herself to his early training. His religious education was her special care. His mental culture she intrusted to the best schools of the city. When of a suitable age he was placed in a large mercantile establishment, and he became a member of the family of one of the partners, who belonged to St. George's church, New York. His Christian influence over the youth was of a most marked character, and had much to do with his subsequent conversion. At eighteen years of age he obtained a hope in Christ, and was baptized by Rev. Dr. Cone into the fellowship of the Oliver Street Baptist church, of which his mother had long been a member. He afterwards connected himself with the Amity Street Baptist church, under the pastoral care of Dr. Wm. R. Williams. In March, 1835, he removed to Painesville, O., where he engaged in business until 1843, when he removed to Milwaukee, Wis. Here he founded a mercantile establishment, which for many years was one of the most extensive in the city. He continued this business until a painful disease compelled him to retire from active pursuits.

But it is chiefly as a Christian worker that Deacon Byron is best known. Nature had given him pre-eminent qualifications for usefulness in the Sunday-school, and to this field he devoted himself with a consecration and zeal rarely surpassed. Even while at the head of a large and extensive business, taxing all his resources, he found time to labor in the work he loved so well. Deacon Byron's active Sunday-school career began before his conversion. As early as 1822 he was a teacher in a mission school in New York. It was in it that James Brainard Taylor was converted, and in it, Deacon Wm. H. Byron was taught his sinfulness and led to Christ.

It was through Deacon Byron's influence, chiefly, that the Wisconsin State Sunday-School Association was formed in 1846, and he became its first president, which office he held until 1853. In 1860 the Wisconsin Sunday-School Union was formed, and Deacon Byron was elected its president. One year later he was appointed its general agent and superintendent of its work in the State. From the spring of 1861, until the summer of 1864, he was actively engaged in its service, and although almost entirely without the use of his limbs, he traveled thousands of miles and held hundreds of Conventions, in which he made addresses. Even when his disease assumed the most painful and alarming forms he continued in the field. Indeed, so great was his love for the work and so consuming his zeal in it, that it was clear that he could not remain out of it, and that he should die with the harness on. After he could no longer walk, he was borne in the arms of friends to institutes and Conventions and Sunday-schools.

He died at Sparta, Wis., Sept. 12, 1875, to which place he had been removed from his home in Milwaukee. He was a man of fine endowments, all of which from the hour of conversion he consecrated to Christ. He was singularly fortunate in having as his early Christian instructors such men as Spencer H. Cone, D.D., and Wm. R. Williams, D.D. He had a profound acquaintance with the Word of God. He devoted to the Scriptures the most earnest and prayerful study throughout his life. He lived for Christ and Christ lived in him. He died in great peace, aged sixty-seven years.

C.

Cade, Rev. Baylus, one of the most distinguished preachers of West Virginia, was born Sept. 3, 1844, in Barbour County, now a part of West Virginia. He made a profession of faith and was

REV. BAYLUS CADE.

baptized Dec. 9, 1864. In October, 1866, he entered Richmond College as a student, remaining there until June 30, 1869. He was ordained in 1869 and began his work as a minister, and he is now (1880) filling one of the most important positions in the State, as pastor of Greenbrier church at Alderson, to which work he is devoting all his time and energy. Mr. Cade took a very active part in establishing Shelton College, giving liberally to its support, and inducing others to follow his example. His work in connection with this institution has been very laborious, but he has the satisfaction of enjoying the success of his labors. His extensive reading and retentive memory, united with great native ability, place him in the front ranks as an organizer and leader in our denominational movements, and in his ministerial calling.

Cain, Rev. Moses Powel, was born in Jefferson Co., Ga., Aug. 7, 1836. His father, James Cain, was a South Carolinian and a distinguished deacon. His mother was a woman of great piety, and thus it happened that he was reared in the fear of God. In 1856 he graduated at Penfield, having been converted during his college course. For several years after graduating Mr. Cain taught school; he was ordained in 1859, and from that time to the present he has been engaged in teaching, preaching, and farming. At present he resides on the old homestead, preaching to neighboring churches. He is a man of talent and of deep piety.

Calahan, Rev. Charles W., pastor of Hope, Ark., was born in Alabama in 1851; graduated at Union University, Tenn.; ordained in 1873; after preaching some time in his native State he became pastor at Monticello, Ark., in 1877; spent one year at Longtown, Miss., returned to Monticello, and in 1879 accepted his present pastorate.

Caldicott, T. F., D.D., was born in the village of Long Buckley, Northamptonshire, England, in March, 1803. His father was a deacon in the Baptist church in Long Buckley, and occasionally officiated as a preacher. In 1824, Dr. Caldicott came to Canada as the tutor to the children of some military officers, and for some time made his home in Quebec. He taught subsequently in Toronto and Kingston, where his services commanded the patronage of some of the best citizens of these places. In 1831 he became connected with Madison University as a student, and in 1834 was ordained as pastor of the Baptist church in Lockport, where he remained for four years, when he was called to the pastorate of what is now the Dudley Street church, Boston Highlands, then Roxbury, and continued in this relation for seven or eight years. Upon resigning his pastorate in Roxbury, he acted for some time as the secretary of the Northern Baptist Education Society, devoting himself with great zeal to the cause of ministerial education. Subsequently he was pastor of the church in Charlestown, and of Baldwin Place church in Boston, and then removed to Williamsburg, N. Y., from which place he removed to Toronto, to become the pastor of the Bond Street Baptist church. It was in Toronto that he died, the event taking place July 9, 1869. Dr. Caldicott had the pleasing art of making warm friends. He was eminently of a happy, social disposition, and his very presence was a benediction. Wherever he was settled he was an earnest, laborious minister of the gospel, and was the means of introducing a large number of persons into the churches to which he ministered. It is pleasant to pay this tribute of affection to his memory.

Caldwell, Hon. Robert P., of Trenton, Tenn., was born in Adair Co., Ky., Dec. 16, 1821; had a public school education; studied and practiced law; was in the lower branch of the General Assembly of Tennessee in 1847–48, and was in the upper branch in 1855–56, and was elected attorney-general in the sixteenth judicial circuit of Tennessee in 1858; was major in the 12th Tenn. Infantry of the Confederate service; had his disabilities removed by act of Congress; and was elected to the 42d Congress, receiving 8227 votes, against 1848 votes for his opponent.

Hon. Mr. Caldwell professed religion, and was baptized by Rev. Dr. Hillsman into the fellowship of the Trenton Baptist church, October, 1863, and has continued a reputable and useful member up to this writing, 1880.

Mr. Caldwell is a gentleman of fine intellect, and stands high as a lawyer and as a Christian.

Caldwell, Samuel L., D.D., president of Vassar College, was born in Newburyport, Mass., Nov. 13,

SAMUEL L. CALDWELL, D.D.

1820. His ancestors were early settlers on that coast. He was prepared for college in the grammar school of his native town. After a four years' course he was graduated from Waterville College, Me., in 1839. On leaving college he took charge of the Academy at Hampton Falls, N. H. Soon after that he was head-master of the West Grammar School, of Newburyport, for three years. After teaching three years he entered the theological seminary at Newton, Mass., where he was graduated in 1845. During the subsequent winter he preached for the Baptist church in Alexandria, Va. In the spring of 1846, he took charge of the First Baptist church of Bangor, Mich., and was ordained as its pastor. The union continued twelve years, and the church was greatly strengthened. In 1856 he accepted the pastoral charge of the First Baptist church of Providence, R. I., whose pulpit had been vacated by the death of James N. Granger, D.D. After a ministry of over fifteen years, he resigned to accept the professorship of Church History in Newton Theological Institution. He ably filled this post five years, and on the death of John H. Raymond, LL.D., the president of Vassar College, Dr. Caldwell was elected his successor, and entered upon the duties of the position in September, 1858. His ability and special fitness for the high office are admitted by all, and that noble educational institution will, it is believed, rise to still grander proportions under his administration.

Caldwell, William B., M.D., was born in Columbia, Ky., April 3, 1818. After finishing his literary education he studied medicine at Lexington, Ky., for a time, graduated in that science at the University of Pennsylvania, and located in his native town in 1841. In 1846 he removed to Louisville, where he rapidly acquired one of the most extensive and lucrative practices in the city. This he retained until failing health compelled his retirement. He confined himself strictly to his profession, and thereby acquired a large fortune. In 1869 he consented to fill a seat in the Legislature of his State. He united with the Baptist church in Columbia in 1837, and continues a faithful and efficient member. He has been prominent in the Executive Board of the General Association of Baptists in Kentucky since 1846. In 1837 he married Miss Ann Augusta, daughter of Hon. James Guthrie, who was also a Baptist, a woman of intelligence, culture, and piety, and whose large estate was liberally used for the cause of Christ.

Calhoun, Hon. J. R., is a member of the Baptist church, Summerside, Prince Edward's Island, and a merchant remarkable for his excellent abilities and large contributions in support of denominational objects; is also a member of the Prince Edward's Island House of Assembly, and is strong in support of right and religion.

California.—One of the largest of the United States, bordering on the Pacific Ocean, 600 miles long and nearly 200 broad; noted for its immense productions of gold since 1849, its abundant harvests of wheat, and all the fruits of the tropics and temperate zones. All Baptist and other Protestant, as well as Catholic churches, are laying foundations for the future. Population of the State is about 1,000,000. Baptists began their work in California in 1849. They now have 121 churches, with nearly 7000 members, 1 college, 3 academical institutions, 6 Associations, 1 weekly paper, *The Evangel*, and 1 monthly, *The Herald of Truth*, a State Convention, College and Mission Boards, a Woman's Home Mission and a Woman's Foreign Mission Society, a State Ministers' Institute, and about 120 ordained ministers. The churches are most of them widely scattered and not wealthy. (See article SAN FRANCISCO.)

California College, Cal.—In 1870, it was announced at the meeting of the Pacific Association, held at Santa Rosa, that the property of the Pacific Methodist College at Vacaville was for sale. A committee appointed to make inquiries reported favorably at a conference in Napa. The purchase was made, a Baptist Convention was called, which organized a college board, obtained a charter, and elected Prof. Mark Bailey president. The institution was opened Jan. 4, 1871, with 14 students. A productive endowment fund of $20,000 has since been raised. The sacrifices incident to establishing a college in a new State have endeared the institution to the hearts of its friends. In the spring of 1873, Dr. A. S. Worrell succeeded Prof. Bailey as president; in November, 1875, he resigned, and was succeeded by the lamented T. W. Greene, whose death occurred in 1877. His successor was Rev. S. A. Taft, D.D.; and his resignation occurring in 1878, Rev. U. Gregory, D.D., entered upon the presidency in January, 1879. Since its organization, 956 students have been in attendance; 38 have graduated; and in 1880 the number of students was 81. The college is beautifully situated, centrally for the State,—at Vacaville, Solano County, midway between San Francisco and Sacramento. The locality is one of the healthiest in California.

Callaghan, George, Esq., was born in Scotland, Jan. 29, 1827. His parents emigrated to this country in 1829. He was baptized at West Chester, Pa., by Rev. Alfred Taylor, March 5, 1845, and was subsequently a member of the churches at Upland, First West Philadelphia, and Angora, Philadelphia. He is extensively engaged in the manufacture of cotton goods at the last place, and he has for many years been connected with various educational and missionary boards. The church at Angora was organized and has been sustained chiefly through the labors and benefactions of himself and his brother, Robert J. Callaghan, both of whom were among its constituent members. These brothers are noted for being among that class of wealthy Baptists who prefer acting as their own executors of the riches intrusted to their stewardship; hence their gifts to denominational and other religious enterprises have been frequent and generous. They live in the enjoyment of visible and blessed results.

Callaway, Rev. Enoch, a distinguished and very useful minister of Georgia, was born in Wilkes County, Sept. 14, 1792. He was converted and baptized in December, 1808, uniting with Sardis church, at which he was ordained Nov. 7, 1823. He became the pastor of the following churches: Sardis, Rehoboth, County Line, Beaver Dam, in Wilkes County, and of Bairdstown and Milltown churches, in Oglethorpe County, serving some of them as much as twenty-five or thirty years. He died Sept. 12, 1859, at the age of sixty-seven, of an affliction which continued four years. He was never heard to murmur, so wonderful was his patience. Death was not dreaded, but was welcomed by him. He made the Bible his text-book, and made its study his daily occupation. As a pastor he was faithful, and as a minister he was humble and unostentatious, but highly useful, from his great earnestness and sincerity. His preaching was usually extemporaneous, combining the doctrinal, practical, and experimental, but he excelled in exhortation.

In building up and establishing the cause of Christ in his field of labor few have accomplished more. Decidedly missionary in principle and practice, and a thorough Baptist in doctrine, he left his impress in these respects wherever he labored. Of his numerous offspring, numbering now about 300, who are living, it is said that, without exception, they are all professed Christians and Baptists.

Callaway, Rev. Joshua S., was born in Wilkes Co., Ga., May 30, 1789. He was the son of Joshua and Isabella Callaway. He was converted when a boy, and was baptized by Jesse Mercer, Sept. 23, 1809. When in his twentieth year he moved to Jones County, in 1818, and joined the Sardis church, by which he was called to ordination in 1820. He preached ten years in Jones County with great success, and then removed to Henry County. When the division in the denomination took place he sustained mission views strongly, and under his leadership the Flint River Association took decided missionary grounds. He was moderator of that Association for about fifteen years, after representing it in the State Convention, by which body he was highly respected. Mr. Callaway was a pleasant and persuasive speaker, with a winning address. He was strongly Calvinistic in faith, and very clear and scriptural in his preaching. He baptized many hundreds of converts during his ministry. He possessed a strong will, indomitable perseverance, and unflinching integrity, and to the day of his death maintained an unblemished reputation. He died at Jonesborough in the year 1854.

Callaway, Rev. Pitt Milner, son of Rev. Joshua S. Callaway, was born in Wilkes Co., Ga., Oct. 10, 1812. Settled in Macon Co., Ala., in 1838. On a visit to Georgia in 1844 he united with the church of which his father was pastor. For some years after this he resided in the city of Eufaula, where he faithfully served as deacon, he and Gov. John Gill Horter having been ordained at the same time and serving together. He was ordained to the ministry at Mount Zion church in Macon County in 1857, Revs. S. Henderson, E. Y. Von Hoose, and F. M. Moss forming the Presbytery. He has delivered on an average two sermons a week, and baptized many hundreds. He has been pastor of a number of the most influential churches in Southeast Alabama. Was the prime mover in the origination and history of the late General Association of that part of the State. For eighteen years now he has resided at Newton, Dale County.

Callaway, Rev. Wm. A., was born in Wilkes Co., Ga., about 1804, of pious Baptist parents. He grew up to manhood and married before his conversion. He was ordained in 1833 at McDonough, and soon made his influence felt in all the region around by his zeal. He would engage in protracted meetings day and night for weeks and months in succession, seeming to feel no weariness; in truth, he was, both by gifts and temperament, admirably suited for a revival preacher. He assisted in organizing the Central Association, and in the great revivals that occurred in his day he was the modest yet able coadjutor of such men as Sherwood, Dawson, and Campbell. Tall and rather slender in person, he had a benign expression, an easy and natural elocution, and he was a sweet singer. In protracted meetings he often became the soul of the meeting, enchaining attention and going right home to the consciences of the impenitent by the simplicity, fervency, and tenderness of his address. His pulpit abilities were good; his manner ordinarily was grave and decorous. He died in June, 1865, and left two able sons in the ministry.—J. M. Callaway and S. P. Callaway.

Callender, Rev. Elisha, son of Ellis Callender, who for about thirty years was the principal speaker in the First Baptist church in Boston, was born in Boston in 1680. He was a graduate of Harvard College in the class of 1710, and became a member of the church Aug. 10, 1713. About five years later, May 21, 1718, he was ordained, and became the pastor of the church with which his honored father had so long been connected. Although not very vigorous in health Mr. Callender performed a large amount of ministerial labor, preaching in different sections of the Commonwealth where his services were in demand. Spiritual prosperity attended his ministry with his own church, scarcely a month passing without some additions being made to it. While in the midst of his great usefulness he was cut down by death, the event occurring March 31, 1738, in the twentieth year of his ministry. He was the first native Baptist minister in this country who had received a collegiate education. He published a "Century Sermon" in the year 1720, commemorative of the landing of the Pilgrim Fathers.

Callender, Rev. John, was born in Boston in 1706, and was the nephew of Rev. Elisha Callender. In early youth he evinced unusual intellectual ability, and it was deemed best by his friends that he should have a liberal education. His preparatory studies having been completed he entered Harvard College, where he availed himself for his pecuniary support of the Hollis foundation. He was graduated in the class of 1723. A few years after his graduation he was ordained as co-pastor, in Newport, R. I., with Rev. William Peckham, succeeding in this relation that gifted young preacher, Rev. John Comer. His ordination took place Oct. 13, 1731. Few Baptist ministers of his times were better educated than Mr. Callender. He was held in high respect in the community in which he lived, which at that time was among the most cultivated in New England. His best-known work as an author is a "Historical Discourse on the Civil and Religious Affairs of the Colony of Rhode Island and Providence Plantation from the First Settlement in 1638 to the End of the First Century." An edition of this valuable discourse was prepared with great care by Rev. Romeo Elton, D.D., and forms one of the volumes of the Rhode Island Historical Society's collections. It is regarded as standard authority in the matters of which it treats. Mr. Callender collected also many papers, which Rev. Mr. Backus found to be of great service to him in the preparation of his history of the Baptists. Mr. Callender died Jan. 26, 1748.

Campbell, Rev. Abner B., eldest son of Rev. J. H. Campbell, and a native of Georgia, is a man of great ability, sincere piety, and exceeding prudence. As a preacher he ranks high; a graduate of Mercer University; he has had charge of several churches in different parts of the State, and now in the prime of life he is the beloved pastor of the Columbus church. He is a trustee of Mercer University.

Campbell, Rev. Charles D., son of Rev. J. H. Campbell, the able pastor of the Baptist church at Athens, Ga., was educated at Mercer University. He is a preacher of more than ordinary power, and a man of decided intellectual ability. He has been engaged in the ministry in Florida and Southern Georgia for quite a number of years, and was called from the charge of the church at Quitman to his present field of labor.

Campbell, Duncan R., LL.D., was born in Perthshire, Scotland, Aug. 14, 1814. He was educated for the Presbyterian ministry, and in this relation entered the pastorate at Nottingham, England, and subsequently became a missionary in London. He emigrated to the United States in May, 1842, and soon after his arrival at Richmond, Va., sought membership in the First Baptist church of that city, and was baptized by Rev. Dr. Jeter. In the fall of 1842 he accepted the pastorate of Leigh Street church in Richmond, and in 1845, being in poor health, he removed to Kentucky, and accepted the pastorate of the church at Georgetown, where he labored with great success four years. He was then elected Professor of Hebrew and Biblical Literature in the theological seminary at Covington, Ky. In 1852 he was elected president of Georgetown College, filling the position with great ability until his death at Covington, Ky., Aug. 16, 1865.

Campbell, Rev. E. A., an efficient minister, who long labored in the Red River Valley, La., was born in North Carolina in 1818, and was brought up in East Baton Rouge Parish, La. He settled west of Red River in 1845, and labored efficiently in this part of the State until his death, in 1857.

Campbell, Rev. Israel S., is about fifty years of age; was born in Kentucky during the days of slavery; is nearly white in complexion, and presents the appearance of a well-bred gentleman. His style of speech is so generally correct that, were you not looking at him, you would suppose that a well-educated white man was speaking. By hard work he has been enabled to obtain an education sufficient to make him very useful among the colored people. He was licensed to preach in the State of Tennessee, and ordained in British North America in 1858. He has ministered successfully to the following churches: Friendship, Franklin Co., Tenn.; Sandwich, Little River, Buckstone, Chatham, Windsor, all of Ontario; Sandusky, Cleveland, O.: Baton Rouge, Gros Tête, La.; Houston, Hearne, Columbus, and Galveston, Texas. He has been pastor of the Galveston church thirteen years. He has been moderator of Associations in Michigan, Louisiana, and Texas, and in the latter State of one Association for twelve years. He was president of the Freedman's Baptist State Convention two years. He has acted as a general missionary for Texas while pastor at Galveston. He has baptized as many as 90 at one time, and 1100 persons in all.

Israel S. Campbell stands well among all classes of citizens in Galveston, and he has been occasionally spoken of as a candidate for Congress, when any one of his race has been considered as suitable for a representative. He has fortunately escaped from the entanglements of political life.

Campbell, J. H., D.D., was born in McIntosh Co., Ga., on the 10th of February, 1807. His father, of the same name, could trace his lineage in a direct line to the Scottish clan of Campbell. His mother's name was Denham, and her parents, John Denham and Sarah Clancy, came to this country as emigrants in the same ship with Gen. Oglethorpe, in 1733. He was educated in early life at Sunbury, Liberty County, under the tuition of Rev. James Shannon, a teacher of distinguished excellence. Entering the State University at Athens, he spent part of a year there, being recalled home by the death of his father to take charge of the estate and protect his two orphan sisters. Converted in his sixteenth year, he was baptized, joined the church, and soon began to preach. He immediately exhibited remarkable powers as a preacher, and was designated the "boy preacher." In his twenty-second year, after the marriage of his sisters, he repaired to Eatonton, Ga., and remained for two years in the theological school taught by Rev. Adiel Sherwood, pastor of the Eatonton Baptist church. He was ordained in 1830, by a Presbytery consisting of C. O. Screven, S. S. Law, J. H. Dunham, and Luther Rice. His first pastorate was at Macon, Ga., in 1831; then he served at various times during a long, laborious, and very useful life the churches at Clinton, McDonough, Richland, Twiggs County, Lumpkin, Griffin, and Perry, among others. All through life he devoted himself entirely to the duties of his sacred calling, never turning aside to engage in any secular occupation, and through his instrumentality thousands have been brought into the kingdom of Jesus. For five years he was the very successful agent for foreign missions in Georgia, after which he entered upon the work of an evangelist for the State at large, in which he was also eminently successful. While thus engaged the late war commenced, when he became a voluntary missionary in the army, in which useful work he persevered until the conflict ended. His labors were sanctified to the salvation of hundreds, if not of thousands.

Mr. Campbell has been a willing and active fellow-laborer with the most prominent Baptists of Georgia for the last half-century, participating actively in all their educational and benevolent schemes and enterprises. For more than thirty years he acted upon the board of trustees for Mercer University; was instrumental in founding colleges for young ladies at Lumpkin and Cuthbert, and in establishing the Georgia Deaf and Dumb Institution at Cave Spring.

Perhaps no man of modern times has been more devoted to the work of preaching Christ and him crucified, and few have been more successful in building up his kingdom. As a revival preacher he is very powerful, his style being ardent, earnest, pathetic, and eloquent. He is a man of great firmness of will, never abandoning an object when convinced of its propriety and importance. His chief literary work is "Georgia Baptists—Historical and Biographical," an exceedingly valuable book, in which is gathered much information which otherwise would have been lost. Two of his sons are now ministers of the gospel, occupying prominent pastorates in the State.

Mr. Campbell's life has been no failure. Side by side with the wisest and best of the denomination he has labored faithfully and efficiently to build up the Baptist interests of Georgia and promote the honor of Jesus.

Campbell, Hon. John Price, Jr., son of John Price Campbell, was born in Christian Co., Ky., Dec. 8, 1820. He was educated for the law, and practiced the profession for nine years at Lexington, Mo., serving two terms in the Legislature of that State; removing to his native State, was elected to Congress in 1855. At the close of his term he declined re-election and retired to private life on his farm in Christian County, where he has since remained.

Campbell, Rev. William J., was born in 1812, and was, until he reached manhood, the servant of Mr. Paulding. As the body-servant of his master he traveled extensively, and gathered general information, which was valuable to him as a preacher and pastor. He was baptized by Andrew Marshall, and became a member of the First Colored Baptist church in Savannah; was elected a deacon, and in a few years after this was licensed to preach. Andrew Marshall took a great interest in him, and when he left home on a collecting mission in the North, Wm. J. Campbell was placed in charge of the church. Andrew Marshall never returned, having died in Virginia. Wm. J. Campbell became pastor about the year 1856. He entered with energy upon the work of completing the brick building on Franklin Square. He secured means for this purpose at home and abroad. It was finished and opened for worship during the war, and the dedication sermon was delivered by Rev. S. Landrum. It is a very neat and large church edifice. Mr. Campbell regarded its dedication to God as sacred. At the close of the war, when other colored churches were opened for political purposes, this was kept closed against all such assemblies. The church became very large. A few years ago a difficulty arose, which resulted in the pastor and deacons, with 700 members, retiring from the building, but claiming still to be the church. After this Mr. Campbell and his friends worshiped in a hall of the Beech Institute.

Mr. Campbell was fully African, quite black, about five feet eight inches high. He died on the 10th of October, 1880, aged sixty-eight. He left a wife, but no children. His funeral was attended by twelve or fifteen hundred people from the First Bryan Baptist church, Rev. U. L. Houston pastor.

He had the respect of the people of Savannah, and especially of the white population. The pastorates of Andrew Bryan, Andrew Marshall, and Wm. J. Campbell over the same church, virtually, extended from 1775 to 1880, a period of 105 years.

Canadian Literary Institute.—A few friends of ministerial education in Canada, not wholly discouraged by the failure to establish a permanent institution at Montreal (see article MONTREAL COLLEGE), resolved, in the autumn of 1856, to make another experiment, which, while having special reference to the training of young men for the ministry, should also look to the general education of the young of either sex. Liberal offers were made by three places—Fonthill, Brantford, and Woodstock—to induce the friends of the enterprise to locate the institute in these towns. Woodstock was selected, responsible parties having pledged $16,000 to be given to the institute. In due time Rev. Dr. R. A. Fyfe was called to take charge of the institution, and the school was opened July 4, 1860, and its prospects looked hopeful. These prospects were apparently blighted by a fire, which, on the 8th of January, consumed the institute building. A large number of students had just come to Woodstock, after a vacation, to commence work in their respective classes, and, in spite of the great misfortune which had befallen the school, it was decided to go on. A deep interest was awakened among the Canadian Baptists in consequence of the disaster referred to, and what at first seemed a great calamity turned out to be a rich blessing. In a few weeks $21,000 were pledged towards the erection of a new building, larger and better than the one that had been burned. But there are other and more pressing wants of a young struggling seat of learning besides proper buildings. One by one these have been met, and successful work done in both the literary and the theological departments. The statistics which we are able to give of what the institute has accomplished since it was opened in 1860 show that hundreds have been the recipients of its advantages, many of whom have entered the ministry; 61 have graduated from the theological department; 40 have settled as pastors who were unable to take a full course of study. A large number of persons, both male and female, who have enjoyed the benefits of the courses of study which the institute has furnished, are in the different professions and callings of life, owing to it a debt of gratitude which they cannot easily repay. The school has now reached a period to which all similar seminaries of learning sooner or later come, when its future usefulness, and existence even, depend on the solution of the question of endowment. The late lamented president, Dr. Fyfe, asked that at least $120,000 should be raised for such an endowment. The question of the removal of the theological department to Toronto has been discussed. Should the funds necessary to place both the literary and the theological departments on a firm foundation be secured, the proposed plan may be carried out. Since the above was written it has been decided that a theological seminary shall be erected near Toronto, the site and buildings of which will cost $75,000, and a generous member of the Jarvis Street church of Toronto, whose liberality is known throughout Canada, has agreed to defray the entire expense of the ground and structure.

Candee, John Dutton, editor of the Bridgeport *Republican Standard*, Conn., son of Benjamin and Almira C. (Dutton) Candee, was born in Pompey, N. Y., June 12, 1819. His ancestors were among the earliest settlers of New England; his parents were natives of Oxford, Conn.; the Candees were of Huguenot blood and the Duttons of English extraction. At the age of nine, soon after the death of his father, he became a farm-boy; afterwards serving in a printing-office; was fitted for college in Hamilton, N. Y.; passed two years at Madison University; entered Yale College, and graduated in 1847. He studied law, and practiced the legal profession for about twelve years; in 1863 he began his career as an editor, and has continued as such until the present time (1880); was baptized in May, 1835, by Rev. Rollin H. Neale, D.D., in New Haven, Conn.; always interested in Sunday-schools; has been prominently connected with the religious interests of Connecticut; was clerk of the State Legislature; served for years as prosecuting officer of New Haven, two years as city attorney, and one year as city councilman; three years as common councilman of Bridgeport, Conn. He is known by his graceful pen, decided views, strong principles, and purity of life. His able conduct of the daily and weekly *Standard*, of Bridgeport, Conn., as editor and publisher, has given him a worthy historical niche.

Canne, Rev. John.—Mr. Canne was a native of England. He was born about 1590. For some time he ministered to a church in the Episcopal establishment of his native country, and for many years he was pastor of "The Ancient English Church" of Amsterdam, in Holland. In Amsterdam he carried on the business of a printer and bookseller, though it is certain that he could have given little, if any, personal attention to these pursuits, when we consider his zeal and journeys to preach the gospel and found churches, and his very numerous writings.

In 1634 he published in Amsterdam "The Necessity of Separation," a work which was widely circulated in England, and which produced very important results. The object of the book was to show the Puritans in the English Church that they were bound to forsake her ceremonies, her bishops, and her comfortable livings and found pure churches of their own. The Boston Puritans were angry with Roger Williams for holding the same doctrine. One of the most successful efforts of Mr. Canne's life resulted from a visit he paid to Bristol in 1641. At that time there was a clergyman in Bristol named Hazzard, rector of one of the city churches, a Puritan. Mrs. Dorothy Hazzard, his wife, was a lady of great faith and of firm resolution. When Bristol was besieged, as the rumor spread that some of the enemy had penetrated within the lines of its defenders, "she and other women, with the help of some men, stopped up Froome gate with woolsacks and earth to keep the enemy from entering the city; and when the women had done this they went to the gunners and told them that if they would stand out and fight they would stand by them, and they should not want for provisions." Mrs. Hazzard, Goodman Atkins, Goodman Cole, Richard Moone, and Mr. Bacon had formed a separate meeting in 1640, in Mrs. Hazzard's house, to worship the Lord according to the requirements of his Holy Word. The meeting, however, was not intended to be a church, and in all probability would have perished, like thousands of similar unions for social worship, had not John Canne visited Bristol in 1641. "This *baptized* man," as he is called, or Baptist, "was very eminent in his day for godliness and for reformation in religion, having great understanding in the way of the Lord." Mrs. Hazzard having heard of his arrival, brought him from the hotel to her residence, and he instructed the little meeting in the way of the Lord more perfectly, and constituted them into a church of Christ, and he showed them the difference between a true and a false church, and when he left them he gave them books to confirm and establish them in church order and gospel purity. Broadmead church, Bristol, thus ushered into life, is a flourishing community at this day, and its record for usefulness is behind few churches of any denomination in the Old World.

Edward Terrill, baptized seventeen years after John Canne formed the church, at his death, left a valuable bequest to educate young men for the Baptist ministry. His enlightened liberality led to the establishment of Bristol College, and indirectly of our other British colleges.

The greatest work of John Canne's laborious and useful life was his marginal references to the Bible. It was published at Amsterdam about 1637. It was the first English Bible that had marginal references throughout. This effort of Canne has been a blessing of the greatest magnitude to the readers of the English Bible ever since, and, like the "Pilgrim's Progress," it justly purchased for Mr. Canne an immortality of fame. The labor expended upon it was immense. Before the writer lies a copy of the Edinburgh edition of 1747, with Canne's preface, in which he states: "It is said of Jacob that he served seven years for Rachel, and it seemed but a few days for the love he had for her. I can truly speak it; I have served the Lord in this work more than thrice seven years, and the time hath not seemed long, neither hath the work been any way a burden to me for the love I have had for it."

One reason which he gives for the preparation of his work is, "Some people will be more willing and forward to read and search the Scriptures, having by them a guide and help, as when they meet with any place that is dark, and they understand it not, than by direction to some other text of Scripture immediately to be informed and satisfied, without looking into commentaries, which it may be they have not. A Scripture interpreter will encourage men to exercise themselves in the meditation and study of the Scriptures, as when a man hath a light carried before him he goeth more cheerfully than if he were in the dark and groped for his way. By this means not only the knowledge of God and his truth will grow and increase, but the Scriptures will be unto people more familiar and more their own (as I may say) than they were before." His leading principle is that "the Scripture is the best interpreter of the Scripture." Mr. Canne was governed by the Baptist maxim that the Bible is everything in religion, and as a result of this that the Scripture should be studied by every human being. To his eighteen published works, Canne intended to add "an edition of the Bible in a large and fair character, with large annotations," a work upon which he had spent many years, a commentary; but he did not live to see it completed.

He was frequently persecuted, very much loved, and widely useful. He died in 1667.

Caperton, Alexander Cotton, D.D., was born in Jackson Co., Ala., Feb. 4, 1831. His early childhood was spent on a farm in Mississippi, whither his parents had removed. He received the rudiments of an education in the common schools of his neighborhood, and afterwards taught school to procure the means for entering Mississippi College, where he graduated in 1856. He then went to Rochester, N. Y., and in 1858 graduated in the theological seminary at that place. He returned home and accepted a professorship in Mississippi College. During the civil war he engaged in farming as a means of support for his family, but did not desist from preaching. At the close of the war he was chosen pastor of a church in Memphis, and was subsequently stationed at Mayfield, Ky., and Evansville, Ind. In 1871 he became co-editor, and soon after sole editor and proprietor of the *Western Recorder*, a leading Baptist weekly paper, published at Louisville, Ky. He is also editor and proprietor of the *American Baptist*, a paper published at Louisville for the colored people, and has established a book and publishing house in Louisville. In addition to these labors, Dr. Caperton preached several hundred times a year, and is an active member of the missionary and Sunday-school boards of his denomination in Kentucky.

Capwell, Albert B., Esq., a well-known lawyer and prominent Baptist layman of Brooklyn, N. Y., was born in Middlebury, N. Y., in 1818, and died in Brooklyn, Aug. 23, 1880. He was graduated from Yale College in 1842. He studied law at the Harvard Law School, and commenced practice in New York in 1845. He devoted himself to civil cases, especially to those involving life insurance and real estate titles. He was a prominent member of Strong Place Baptist church, and one of its founders; served as a deacon for many years, and was an active worker in the Sunday-school. He was president of the board of trustees of the Baptist Home for the Aged in Brooklyn, and also of the Baptist Social Union. He has been elected on several occasions moderator of the Long Island Baptist Association. He was also president of the board of trustees of the Rochester Theological Seminary. He was identified with many of the great benevolent enterprises of the Baptists, and philanthropic institutions of the country.

Carey, Rev. George Montgomery W., A.M., was born in Belfast, Ireland, March 10, 1829, and trained at the Moravian School, Grace Hill, near

REV. GEORGE MONTGOMERY W. CAREY, A.M.

Belfast; converted in Glengarry County, Canada, and baptized at Breadalbane, in the same county, July, 1847; graduated from Rochester University

July, 1856; ordained at St. Catharines, Ontario, soon after; graduated from Rochester Theological Seminary, 1858, and continued at St. Catherines; became in 1865 pastor of German Street Baptist church, St. John, New Brunswick, and still continues in the office with great acceptance and usefulness. Mr. Carey is very popular in the pulpit and on the platform.

Carey, William, D.D., was born in Purey, Northamptonshire, England, Aug. 17, 1761. In his boyhood he was an extreme Episcopalian, regarding dissenters with sovereign contempt. His father and grandfather officiated as clerks in the Episcopal Church, and young Carey from childhood loved the house in which they held this humble position.

WILLIAM CAREY, D.D.

Mr. Carey was baptized by Dr. Ryland, Oct. 5, 1783, in the river Nen, just above Dr. Doddridge's church, Northampton. For three years and a half he preached to a little community in Boston, walking six miles each way to render the service.

He was ordained pastor of the church of Moulton Aug. 1, 1787; the sermon on the occasion was preached by the Rev. Andrew Fuller. His salary at Moulton was just $75 a year, and when he entered upon his labors in that field he had a wife and two children to support.

Mr. Carey had probably the greatest facility for acquiring foreign languages ever possessed by any human being. At any rate, no one ever possessed a larger measure of this extraordinary talent. In seven years he learned Latin, Greek, Hebrew, French, and Dutch, and in acquiring these languages he had scarcely any assistance.

In reading the voyages of the celebrated Captain Cook he first had his attention directed to the heathen world, and especially to its doomed condition; the topic soon filled his mind and engrossed his heart. And though the subject was beset by innumerable and apparently insurmountable difficulties, and though the work was novel to him and to every one of his friends, yet he felt impelled by an unseen power to go and preach the gospel to the heathen. His first selected field of labor was Tahiti.

He issued a pamphlet entitled "An Inquiry into the Obligation of Christians to Use Means for the Conversion of the Heathen." This publication made a deep impression upon Mr. Carey's friends, and it had an extensive influence in turning their minds and hearts to the idolaters of distant lands. Mr. Carey became pastor of the church in Leicester in 1789, and there he labored with untiring faithfulness among his flock, and formed plans with unquenchable zeal for the salvation of the heathen. From this church he went forth to India to give God's Word to its vast population.

At the meeting of his Association, which was held at Nottingham, May 30, 1792, he preached on Isaiah liv. 2, 3, announcing the two memorable divisions of his discourse: "Expect great things from God; attempt great things for God." The sermon stirred up the hearts of his hearers as they had never been before; every one felt the guilt of keeping the gospel from perishing myriads, and the need of making an effort to win his ignorant enemies to their Master. At Kettering, the church of Andrew Fuller, the Baptist Missionary Society was organized Oct. 2, 1792. The society was formally instituted in the house of the widow of Deacon Beeby Wallis. The little parlor which witnessed the birth of this society was the most honored room in the British Islands, or in any part of Christendom; in it was formed the first society of modern times for spreading the gospel among the heathen, the parent of all the great Protestant missionary societies in existence.

The British East India Company had the government of India at this period. No white man could settle in that country without their permission, nor remain in it longer than they pleased. No ship could trade with it except one of their vessels. The Company was intensely hostile to missionaries, and to please the people of India they were ready to show the greatest respect for their gods. In 1801 a deputation from the government went in procession to the Kalee ghaut, the most opulent and popular shrine of the metropolis, and presented 5000 rupees to the idol in the name of the Company for the success which had attended the British arms.

A Baptist surgeon in India, named Thomas, had preached Christ occasionally to the natives, and in 1793 he was in England to secure some fellow-worker to go back with him to that dark land. Carey and he were appointed missionaries by the new society. They engaged passage on the "Earl of Oxford" to sail for the East, and they went on board to leave their native land; but Mr. Carey had no license to go to India from the Company, and both the missionaries were put ashore; Carey was greatly distressed by this unexpected blow, and felt as if his hopes were permanently crushed, but soon the Danish East Indiaman, the "Kron Princessa Maria," was found, and in her they sailed June 13, 1793. The voyage was a prosperous one, and the missionaries landed in health. For a few years Mr. Carey had charge of an indigo-factory, from which he received £240 per annum; and at the same time he labored unobtrusively as a missionary. He could not stay in British India as an avowed missionary, and when, on their landing in Calcutta, Marshman and Ward were ordered back to England, because the captain of their vessel returned them to the authorities as missionaries, Carey determined to make his abode at Serampore for the future, and to take Marshman and Ward with him, where they could stay in defiance of the British East India Company. Serampore was a Danish settlement on the river Hoogly, 15 miles from Calcutta. The kings of Denmark had sent out missionaries to convert the natives, and their government was in hearty sympathy with missions. Col. Bie, the representative of the Danish sovereign at Serampore, received Carey and his brethren with generous hospitality, and he protected them for years against the powerful governors of British India. The providence of God evidently kept this little spot under the rule of Denmark as a refuge for the missionaries until the pious people of Great Britain should abolish the heathenish law which excluded missionaries from India. Even the king of Denmark himself, as he learned from the governor of Serampore the character and worth of the missionaries, became their firm friend. In 1821, Frederick VI., king of Denmark, sent the missionaries a gold medal, as an expression of his appreciation of their labors, and endowed the college which they had founded with the rent of a house worth about $5000. And when in 1845 the successor of Frederick ceded the Serampore settlement to the British government, he had an article inserted in the treaty confirming the Danish charter of the Serampore Baptist College.

At Serampore the missionaries set up printing-presses and a large boarding-school, and in process of time founded a college. They preached incessantly, and Carey particularly studied the languages of the country with a measure of success never equaled before or since by any other settler in India. He soon became the most learned man in the country. When Lord Wellesley founded the College of Fort William, in Calcutta, in 1801, to teach the language of Bengal to young Englishmen in the civil service of the Company in India, Dr. Carey was the only man in the East or in Great Britain qualified to teach that language correctly, and he received and accepted the appointment of professor in Fort William. In December, 1829, an act, for which he had long labored, was passed by the Council in India, abolishing the practice of burning widows with the bodies of their dead husbands. It was determined to publish the English and Bengali copies of the act simultaneously, and Dr. Carey was selected to make the version for the people of Bengal. Every day cost the lives of two widows, and instead of going into the pulpit on the morning of the Lord's day, when he received the order from Henry Shakespear, the secretary of the government, he commenced his translation, and completed it before night, and that glorious act of Lord William Bentinck, so dear to William Carey's heart, went forth to the nations of India in the polished Bengali of the great Baptist missionary.

Carey was the author of a Mahratta grammar, and of a Sanscrit grammar, extending over more than a thousand quarto pages, a Punjabi grammar, a Telinga grammar, and of a Mahratta dictionary, a Bengali dictionary, a Bhotanta dictionary, and a Sanscrit dictionary, the manuscript of which was burned before it was printed. He was also the author of several other secular works.

"The versions of the Sacred Scriptures, in the preparation of which he took an active and laborious part, include the Sanscrit, Hindu, Brijbbhassa, Mahratta, Bengali, Oriya, Telinga, Karnata, Maldivian, Gurajattee, Bulooshe, Pushtoo, Punjabi, Kashmeer, Assam, Burman, Pali, or Magudha, Tamul, Cingalese, Armenian, Malay, Hindostani, and Persian. In six of these tongues the whole Scriptures have been translated and circulated; the New Testament has appeared in 23 languages, besides various dialects in which smaller portions of the sacred text have been printed. In thirty years Carey and his brethren rendered the Word of God accessible to one-third of the world." And even this is not all: before Carey's death 212,000 copies of the Scriptures were issued from Serampore in 40 different languages, the tongues of 330,000,000 of the human family. Dr. Carey was the greatest tool-maker for missionaries that ever labored for God. His versions are used to-day by all denominations of Christians throughout India.

Most of his income was given away in Bible distribution. The missionaries at Serampore placed their gains in a common fund, from which they drew a scanty support; Marshman's successful school and Carey's professorship furnished a large surplus for the printing and circulation of the Scriptures. Carey, Marshman, and Ward gave during their stay in India nearly $400,000 to the spread of revealed light in that country cursed by miserable gods.

The first Hindoo convert baptized by Dr. Carey in India was the celebrated Krishna Pal. Dr. Carey founded churches and mission stations in many parts of India, and planted seed from which he gathered precious harvests, and from which his successors have reaped abundantly.

A visitor in 1821 describes Dr. Carey as short in stature, with white hair, and a countenance equally bland and benevolent in feature and expression.

He had three wives, one of whom reluctantly accompanied him from his native land, and the second and third he married in India.

The last sickness of Dr. Carey found him with perfect peace of mind; he was ready and anxious to go to his blessed Saviour. Lady Bentinck, the wife of the governor, frequently visited him, and Bishop Wilson, of Calcutta, came and besought his blessing. He died June 9, 1834, in his seventy-third year.

Dr. Carey had great decision of character. After he had thoroughly weighed a subject his resolution about it was taken, and nothing could make him change the purpose he had formed. His perseverance to accomplish a proper end knew no bounds; he would labor through discouragements for twenty years or more to carry out a Christian purpose. When he had a clear conviction of duty he could not disobey his conscience; to keep it without offense was one of the great aims of his life. He never doubted the help of God in his own time to aid him in carrying out the plan of love which he had formed. He carefully husbanded every moment, and in that way he was able to perform more labor than any man in Europe or Asia in his day. He had as unselfish a heart as ever beat with love to Jesus.

In denouncing contemptuous sneers poured on Carey, Marshman, and Ward, the celebrated Dr. Southey says, "These low-born, low-bred mechanics have done more to spread the knowledge of the Scriptures among the heathen than has been accomplished, or even attempted, by all the world beside." In the British House of Commons the celebrated William Wilberforce said of Dr. Carey, "He had the genius as well as the benevolence to devise the plan of a society for communicating the blessings of Christian light to the natives of India. To qualify himself for this truly noble enterprise he had resolutely applied himself to the study of the learned languages; and after making considerable proficiency in them, applied himself to several of the Oriental tongues, and more especially to the Sanscrit, in which his proficiency is acknowledged to be greater than that of Sir William Jones, or any other European." At his death resolutions expressive of admiration for the great benevolence and vast learning of Dr. Carey were passed by many societies in Europe and Asia. Nor is there any doubt that had Carey been a Catholic he would have been canonized immediately after death, and held up as worthy of more exalted veneration than St. Francis Xavier himself. The Protestant world, however, unites in honoring him as the father of modern missions.

Carnahan, Rev. David Franklin, was born in White Hall, Montour Co., Pa., Sept. 16, 1825. He graduated at Lewisburg University, Aug. 18, 1852, and the same year, September 28, he was ordained as pastor of the Bridgeport church, Montgomery Co., Pa. In 1856 he was settled as pastor of the Calvary Baptist church in Philadelphia. In 1859 he was called to the pastorate of the First Baptist church in Zanesville, O. He was subsequently pastor at Dayton, O.; Burlington, Iowa; Aurora (First church), Springfield, Urbana, Dixon, and Streator, Ill. He is now pastor of the Baptist church in Appleton, Wis. He was corresponding secretary and superintendent of missions of the Ohio Baptist State Convention from 1856 to 1861. He was superintendent of missions of the General Association of Illinois in 1867–68, and agent of the American and Foreign Bible Society in 1863. He acted as financial agent of the Wayland Academy for a brief period in 1878–79. During the war he was major of the 78th Regiment Ohio Vol. Infantry in 1861–62, and was present with his regiment at Fort Donelson, Pittsburg Landing, Corinth, and Iuka. He served the Philadelphia Association as clerk in 1855–56, and was recording secretary of the Baptist State Convention of Pennsylvania in 1856. Mr. Carnahan has been and is still one of the most useful ministers in the Baptist Church in the Northwest, and has never done a more successful work in his fruitful ministry than he is now doing in Appleton, Wis.

Carpenter, Rev. C. H., was born in 1835, and was a graduate of Harvard University and the Newton Theological Institution. He received his appointment July 1, 1862, and sailed the following October for Burmah. On reaching Rangoon the following May, Mr. and Mrs. Carpenter found a home in the family of Dr. Binney, whose assistant he was to be in the management of the theological seminary. At once his warmest sympathies were enlisted for the Karens, of whom he says, "If there is a people anywhere eager to learn, it is the Karens. They come down to Kemendine sometimes hundreds of miles, on foot, not to make money, but to study. I wish you could see Dr. Binney's 62 bare-footed, bare-legged students of theology." Dr. Binney, under date of Oct. 24, 1863, wrote, "Mr. Carpenter has commenced to give some instruction in arithmetic, and I think he is doing well. The main object of this early effort is to get, as soon as possible, into communication with the pupils, and then to feel his way along. It is hard work, but it is to be hoped it will pay well." A year from this date, he speaks in warm terms of the success of his assistant and wife, and of the progress he had made in learning the language. Dr. Binney having retired from the institution in 1865, Mr. Carpenter and Mr. Smith had the supervision of its affairs. After the return of Dr. Binney, near the close of 1866, Mr. Carpenter continued his connection with him, Mr. Smith removing to Henthada. Mr. Carpenter remained in the department of instruction in the theological seminary until his transfer to Bassein, in December, 1868, to fill the place made vacant by the death of Mr. Thomas. His labors at this station were eminently successful, until his failing health obliged him for a time to be absent from his field. He left for the United States early in 1872. At the request of the Burmah Baptist Association, Mr. Carpenter on leaving Bassein visited Siam, on a missionary exploring expedition. He crossed the boundary between British Burmah and Siam, at a point known as "Three Pagodas," and made his way to the residence of the Pwo Karen, governor of the district of Phra-thoo-wan. He was accompanied in this journey by several native assistants. Together they visited 43 villages. The households, which were in the valley of one of the rivers which they passed through, were believed to be more than 1000 in number, or about 5000 persons. The estimate of the whole number of Karens in the country which was traversed made it not far from 50,000.

After remaining in this country for some time, Mr. Carpenter returned to Burmah, under appointment as president of the Rangoon Baptist College. He was convinced that it would be better to remove the college to Bassein, but his wishes in this respect were overruled, and he was transferred to the Bassein station, to resume the work which had previously occupied his thoughts and energies. The report of the first twelve months' work presents many things to inspire hope and encouragement. The number baptized was 282. In like manner, the next twelve months were crowded with hard work, and attended with some peculiar trials. He reports in the stations and out-stations under his special charge 85 churches and 114 native preachers, the number of church members being 6366. The work at Bassein has gone forward under the direction of Mr. Carpenter with healthful progress. The report of the Executive Committee, presented in May last, speaks encouragingly of his labors. If the life and health of Mr. Carpenter are spared, his usefulness will increase from year to year, and the Bassein, S'gau, and Karen missions will be among the most prosperous in Asia.

Carpenter, Rev. John M., was born Sept. 30, 1804, at Mechanicstown, Orange Co., N. Y. He was converted and baptized when about twenty; he was licensed to preach in 1836, and was immediately appointed by the board of the New Jersey Baptist State Convention to labor at Schooley's Mountain. He was ordained in 1837. Mr. Carpenter was pastor for thirteen years at Jacobstown, N. J., and has filled other important pastorates. As secretary of the Convention for seventeen years, and in other services for the board, he has been very useful. His thorough knowledge of the denominational statistics, and his memory of Baptist history in New Jersey, make him the source of information for all who wish to obtain facts and figures on those topics. Mr. Carpenter's library is rich in associational minutes, pamphlets, and works pertaining to the Baptists. He is a logical thinker and sermonizer, and an energetic preacher. He may be aptly called "The living Baptist Cyclopædia of New Jersey."

Carpenter, Rev. Mark, was born at Guildford, Vt., Sept. 23, 1802. He pursued his studies at Amherst College, and at Union College, where he graduated in the class of 1829. He studied theology at Newton, graduating in 1833. He was ordained at Milford, N. H., Feb. 12, 1834, where he remained for six years. His next settlement was at Keene, N. H. He was the pastor of the Baptist church in this place for five years, and then removed to New London, N. H., remaining there four years, and to Holyoke, Mass., where he was pastor ten years. From Holyoke he went to Brattleborough, Vt., in 1861, resigning his charge there in 1867. His next settlements were in West Dummerston, Vt., and South Windham, from which place he removed to Townshend, Vt.

Carpenter, Prof. Stephen Hopkins, was born Aug. 7, 1831, at Little Falls, Herkimer Co., N. Y. He died at Geneva, N. Y.

Prof. Carpenter graduated from Rochester University in 1852. In 1855 he received the degree of A.M., and in 1872 that of LL.D. He was appointed tutor in the Wisconsin State University in 1852. He was elected in 1860 to the professorship of Ancient Languages in St. Paul College at Palmyra, Mo. In 1866 he was tendered the chair of Rhetoric in the Wisconsin State University, which he filled with great ability until his death. He occupied for a time the position of Superintendent of Public Instruction of Wisconsin. He was a diligent student, and his attainments were very extensive. He wrote largely on educational and religious subjects, and delivered frequent addresses on science and literature. Ten or twelve of his addresses are published, and many articles of an educational and religious character were printed in the periodicals of the denomination with which he was connected. Although not an ordained minister, he preached frequently for the church of which he was a member, with great ability. His sermons on the inspiration of the Scriptures are considered as among the ablest ever published on that subject. Although occupying a conspicuous place among the educators of the State, and eminent in his attainments in science and literature, he will be longest remembered as the sincere Christian and loyal disciple of the Lord Jesus Christ.

Carroll, Rev. B. H., pastor of the First Baptist church, Waco, Texas, and associate editor of the

REV. B. H. CARROLL.

Texas Baptist, was born December, 1843, in Carroll Co., Miss.; has been in Texas about twenty years; served four years in the Confederate States army; was wounded in the battle of Mansfield, La., 1864; was converted in the summer of 1865, and ordained in 1866. He was educated at Baylor University. Besides many published sermons and addresses, he is the author of two pamphlets, "Communion from a Bible Standpoint," and "The Modern Social Dance," which have attained a wide circulation both in and out of Texas. He has been for years vice-president of the Baptist General Association of Texas, and is the vice-president from Texas on the Domestic Mission Board of the Southern Baptist Convention.

He is one of the first preachers of his age in the Baptist ministry of the Southern States.

Carroll, Rev. John Lemuel, was born in Duplin Co., N. C., Dec. 21, 1836. He made a profession of religion at the early age of nine, and became a member of the Beaver Dam church; he was licensed to preach by the same church, January, 1858; was educated at Wake Forest College and at the University of North Carolina, graduating at the latter institution with distinction in 1863. He was ordained in the college chapel May 12, 1862, and was the pastor of several churches in his native State. Mr. Carroll was also an instructor in Oxford Female College, and afterwards pastor of the Oxford church. In 1869 he became agent for St. John's College, Oxford, in which he was very successful, after which he resided at Wake Forest College, being at the time a trustee of the institution and secretary of the board, and being also the pastor of several churches. In March of 1871 he was invited to the pastorate of the church in Warrenton, Va., in which field he is still laboring. Few men excel Mr. Carroll in apt and vigorous extemporaneous speaking in denominational meetings.

Carson, Alex., LL.D., of Tubbermore, County Londonderry, Ireland, was born not far from Cookstown, County Tyrone, Ireland, in 1776. The family is of Scotch origin, and probably came to the north of Ireland in the time of James I., when the people who have built Belfast and Derry, and who now make linen for the world, first accepted an Irish for their Scottish home. The region around his birthplace has been desolated many times since the Scotch settlement of Ulster by Irish rebellions and massacres, and by popish treachery and cruelty. Opposition to Rome burns more fiercely over that locality than perhaps in any other section of Europe.

Alexander Carson in early life was called into sacred relations with the Redeemer, and from that hour he became a decided Christian. At the University of Glasgow he was proverbial for his diligence, and for the thoroughness with which he pursued his studies. And though in his class there were young men of brilliant talents, who attained distinguished positions in subsequent life in Scotland, Mr. Carson graduated with the first honor.

He was settled when a very young man as minister of the Presbyterian church of Tubbermore. The place had a population of perhaps 500, and it was surrounded by a large population of Scotch-Irish farmers. Very early in his ministry Mr. Carson was led to see that the Congregational was the Scripture form of church government, and that believers' immersion was the baptism of the New Testament. When this change of conviction occurred Mr. Carson was placed in a situation of great embarrassment. He was receiving £100 per annum from the British government, under the name of *Regium Donum*, in common with all other

Presbyterian ministers of that day. His church gave him probably about £40 a year. This *Regium Donum* had demoralized the benevolent efforts of the Ulster Presbyterians so completely that if Mr. Carson's entire congregation had become Baptists he could not expect even a moderate support from their unaided liberality. And he well knew that his people were stern men, with all the steady attachment to principle which marked their Scottish fathers in times of fierce persecution. There was no Baptist missionary society for Ireland at that period, and the young minister had absolutely nothing to trust for his support except the naked providence of God; but he was wholly Christ's, and he came out from a community dear to him by the tenderest associations and cast his burden on the Lord. His favorite hymn at this time was:

"And must I part with all I have,
My dearest Lord, for thee?
It is but right, since thou hast done
Much more than that for me.

"Yes, let it go, one look from thee
Will more than make amends
For all the losses I sustain
Of wealth, of credit, friends."

He placed himself upon our Baptist foundation, and gathered a community around him who received the Saviour's teachings as he proclaimed them, and he lived to see a church waiting upon his ministrations, of 500 members, with a congregation very much larger, the descendants of the grand old Presbyterians who in Scotland and Ireland often faced death rather than desert their principles, many of whom walked from seven to ten miles to meet with the church at Tubbermore.

In a few years his fame spread throughout England and Scotland. Robert and James Haldune, of Edinburgh, so well known for their great gifts to Christ's cause, their distinguished position in society, and their burning zeal as Baptist ministers, were his admiring and lasting friends. He was frequently invited to visit England to preach at mission anniversaries, or to aid in other great denominational undertakings; and in process of time he was recognized as the leading man in the Baptist denomination.

Mr. Carson read extensively. He made the Greek language a special study, and it is not too much to say that he was among the first Greek scholars that have lived for centuries. It is well known that if he would sign the "Standards" of the Church of Scotland he could have had the professorship of Greek in the University of Glasgow, a position requiring fine scholarship and promising a large income, the indirect offer of which to the pastor of a little company of Baptists in an obscure Scotch-Irish village was a strong testimonial to Mr. Carson's profound knowledge of the Greek tongue.

Mr. Carson was one of the clearest reasoners of his day. He had an intellect so piercing that it could see through any sophistry in a moment. He was a logician with whom it was not wise to come in collision, unless one wished to know the confusion and mortification of being mercilessly beaten. He was a philosopher of no ordinary grade, as his works clearly exhibit, and we are not surprised that his former Presbyterian friends, years after his connection with them, described him as "the Jonathan Edwards of the nineteenth century."

He preached the word of God in expository lectures, pouring out its rich treasures and the wealth of his own sacred learning upon the throngs that united with him in the worship of God. Few ever heard him take a little text and suspend some weighty subject upon it by a slender connecting link.

He practiced weekly communion, and his church follows the same custom still. He was in the habit of beginning the service by saying, "According to the apostolic example, let us salute one another with an holy kiss." He then kissed one of the deacons, and the injunction was observed around. This command of Paul in reference to a local custom is not now observed in Tubbermore. After the sermon was over on the Lord's day the brethren arose and enforced it, or some other Christian theme, by appropriate exhortations. Nor did they feel backward to stand up, nor abashed to express their views in the presence of one of the greatest thinkers of the age, whose fatherly kindness was as familiar to them all as a household word.

Space will not permit us to give a list of Dr. Carson's works, for they were very numerous. His octavo volume on baptism is a masterpiece of learning and logic; it overthrows quibbles about the Abrahamic covenant, giving authority to baptize children, as old as Augustine of Hippo, and as wide-spread as Pedobaptist Christendom, and allegations that baptism might mean sprinkling or pouring, with as much ease as a horse, unaccustomed to a rider, hurls to the ground the little boy who has ventured to mount him. A number of men in the Baptist ministry to-day, and very many in the membership of our churches, were drawn, or perhaps driven, to the Baptist fold by "Carson on Baptism." It was first published in London. It has been republished by the Baptist Publication Society in Philadelphia. His works should be in every Christian's library.

His style to some seems a little dogmatical. He saw things clearly himself; he was wholly for truth and entirely against error, and his distinct perception and whole-heartedness made him impatient with the dull, and with those who tried to make the worse appear the better side, with full knowledge of its weakness. Anyhow, truth coming forth like a defiant giant is more attractive than when it appears making simpering apologies for venturing to show its face, and to disturb the equanimity of error and wrong, though sturdy truth, carrying a sharp and needful sword in a sheath of love, pleases us most.

Dr. Carson received the degree of LL.D. from Bacon College, Ky., an honor which no living man better deserved than he.

In returning from England in 1844, where he had been delivering addresses in various places for the Baptist Missionary Society, he fell into the dock at Liverpool, where the water was twenty-five feet deep; he was immediately rescued, and he sailed for Belfast. During the night he became alarmingly ill, and died the next day after landing, Aug. 24, 1844. He was nearly fifty years in the ministry. His death caused universal grief, and it left a vacancy in the ranks of scholarly Baptists which few men of any community on earth have the learned qualifications to fill. Since James Usher, archbishop of Armagh, was laid in his grave, no native of Ireland of Anglo-Irish or Scotch-Irish origin fully equaled Alexander Carson in learning and logic, and the aboriginal natives of Ireland are out of the question since the days of John Scotus Erigena, the friend of Charles the Bald.

Carson, W. B., D.D., was born in Pickens Co., S. C., Dec. 14, 1821. Mr. Carson took an unusually extensive course in the academical institution in Wetumpka, Ala. He joined the Presbyterian Church, the denomination of his ancestors, at eighteen. In 1849 he entered the theological seminary in Columbia, S. C., but after a very thorough investigation of the subject of baptism, he was baptized by James P. Boyce, D.D., LL.D. After he graduated he spent six years as pastor in Gillisonville, Beaufort District, now Hampton Co., S. C., where the society combined high culture, integrity, and piety in an uncommon degree. In 1859 he became editor of the *Southern Baptist*, in Charleston, S. C., which position he occupied until the war caused the suspension of the paper. During this period its circulation greatly increased.

Although opposed to secession, he went with his native State. He volunteered as a private, but was soon after made a chaplain. He, however, always went into the ranks in battle. After the war he was for two years principal of the State Academy at Reidville, Spartanburg Co., S. C., and for the same period of the Gowensville Seminary in Greenville County. In 1873 the Furman University conferred upon him the title of D.D. He is at present pastor of the old Kirkland, now Smyrna, church, in Barnwell Co., S. C. He has written somewhat extensively for papers and reviews.

Carswell, Rev. Eginardus Ruthven, M.D., was born in Burke Co., Ga., Oct. 22, 1822. His parents were both native Georgians. His ancestors came from Ireland, his grandfather being a captain in the Revolutionary war. He was educated chiefly at Penfield, attending both Mercer Institute and Mercer University. He graduated in medicine at the Medical College of Georgia, Augusta, in March, 1844, and practiced medicine for ten years in Burke County. He experienced regenerating grace at the young men's twilight meeting at Penfield in the spring of 1840, and was baptized by Dr. Adiel Sherwood. Impressed early that it was his duty to preach, he became a licentiate, and frequently engaged in proclaiming the gospel, meanwhile studying theology irregularly during the ten years of his medical practice. He was ordained at Bushy Creek church, Dec. 12, 1852. His first pastorate was that of Way's church in Jefferson County. Afterwards he served Du Hart's, Louisville, Piney Grove, Big Buckhead, Bark Camp, and Sardis churches, in the Hephzibah Association, besides others in both Georgia and South Carolina. Mr. Carswell has been a strenuous advocate of temperance, of the Sunday-school cause, of missions, and of the distinctive peculiarities of Baptists. He has always been in full sympathy with the work of his Association and of the Georgia Baptist and Southern Baptist Conventions, and he was, perhaps, the youngest delegate present at the formation of the Southern Baptist Convention at Augusta in 1845. Utterly fearless in his support of what he deems the truth, Mr. Carswell possesses great natural eloquence. He is noted for the power and pungency of his appeals, for logical force, and for rhetorical and figurative illustrations. Mr. Carswell married Miss L. A. Pior, Nov. 2, 1847, and they have raised six children, all of whom are members of Baptist churches, and two of whom are promising young ministers. Often made the moderator of the Hephzibah Association, he has been honored by his brethren in various other ways in evidence of their confidence and high esteem. In 1872 he was selected to preach the first centennial sermon delivered in Georgia,—that of the Bottsford Baptist church in Burke County.

Carter, Rev. E. J. G., a promising young man of Union Association, Ark., was born in Mississippi in 1846; he removed to Arkansas in 1852; began to preach about 1870; ordained 1876. He labored extensively with churches in Washita and Nevada Counties. He died in 1879.

Carter, Rev. James, was one of the most earnest-minded, zealous, pious, and useful of all the ministers who have aided in building up the Baptist cause in Georgia. He was born near Powelton, Hancock County, in 1797, and, after a laborious life, died at Indian Springs, Butts County, Aug. 25,

1859. His parents were Virginians, who emigrated to Georgia, and he was the youngest child. Hopefully converted at an early age, he was baptized by Jesse Mercer; was licensed at twenty years of age, and began to preach in Butts County, where he had settled about 1823. He was instrumental, soon after being licensed, in constituting Macedonia church in Butts County, of which he continued pastor thirty years, residing all the while upon a farm which belonged to him. Besides Macedonia, Mr. Carter was the pastor of the churches at Holly Grove, Indian Springs, and other places; but, while his labors were confined mostly to Butts and contiguous counties, he frequently made extensive preaching tours to other parts of the State, and, owing to his strong constitution and vigorous health, performed an immense amount of labor.

Dr. J. H. Campbell, in his "Georgia Baptists," says, "It is doubtful whether any of our ministers ever preached more, or did more good by preaching, than James Carter." During his long pastorate of the Macedonia church he received into it, by baptism at his own hands, 1000 members; and he baptized, in addition, not less than 1000 others, according to his own statement. His zeal was as ardent as that of Paul, and his doctrinal sentiments were as strongly Calvinistic as those of Paul himself. He was a powerful preacher, and some of his appeals to sinners were exceedingly impressive and convincing. Among his brethren he was regarded as a pious, devout, sound, and zealous preacher of a high order, whose successful labors won for him universal respect. For years he was moderator of the Flint River Association, which, at its session following his death, listened to a funeral discourse in his honor by Rev. J. H. Campbell.

It was at the house of James Carter that Jesse Mercer died. They were old and attached friends, and when Jesse Mercer was at Indian Springs for his health in 1841, he visited Mr. Carter, and was taken worse and expired, amid the most careful and loving attentions.

Carter, Rev. Joseph E., was born in Murfreesborough, N. C., Feb. 6, 1836; was baptized in 1852; read law, and began to practice in 1857; graduated from Union University in 1861; was ordained at Murfreesborough, N. C., June 30, 1861, Dr. A. M. Poindexter preaching the sermon; served churches in Tennessee, Kentucky, and Alabama as pastor and evangelist, and accepted a call to Wilson, N. C., in March, 1880; a zealous, gifted, and useful man.

Carter, Rev. John W., was born in Albemarle Co., Va., Dec. 31, 1836. When he was seven years of age his parents removed to Upshur Co., W. Va., where he grew up to manhood. He was a diligent student in private, and an industrious pupil at Alleghany College, and now he is one of the most scholarly ministers in the State. He was converted and baptized in 1858, and ordained in 1860. He labored for some years in country churches in Lewis and Upshur Counties, and in 1864 took charge of the church in Parkersburg, where he still sus-

REV. JOHN W. CARTER.

tains the pastoral relation. The church has built a fine edifice since Mr. Carter became its pastor, and has prospered in other ways. Mr. Carter is a preacher of acknowledged ability, and a minister of great piety and worth.

Carter, Prof. Paschal, was born in Benson, Vt., Sept. 17, 1807. His father was Josiah Carter, a Revolutionary soldier and sea-captain, and his mother, Charlotte De Angelis, was of Italian descent. After persistent toil he entered Middlebury College, Vt., in 1825, and graduated with honor in 1829. On leaving college he became tutor in Columbian College, Washington, D. C., and was subsequently principal of the Keysville Academy, N. Y., agent of the Philadelphia Baptist Tract Society, and principal of the Academy of South Reading, Mass., one of the largest and most flourishing schools of that day. In 1832 he became Professor of Mathematics and Natural Philosophy in Granville College, O., and remained in this position over twenty-two years. During part of this time he taught the ancient languages and other branches, and most of the time he was the college treasurer,—a difficult and responsible position. In 1854 he resigned his chair at Granville, and accepted a similar position in Georgetown College, Ky. After an interim of two years spent in business life he became, in 1858, president of Central Collegiate Institute, Ala., where he remained until 1861. Since 1861 he has been living at Centralia, Ill., engaged in mercantile pursuits.

Cartwright, Rev. Immanuel, was born in Tennessee. He removed to St. Louis in 1854, and became pastor of the First African church, a position which he held efficiently for twenty years. Large additions were made to the membership, till it numbered over a thousand. He is awaiting the appointed time for the Master's call to his eternal home.

Cary, Rev. Lott, was born a slave about 1780, in Virginia. In 1804 he was brought to Richmond, where for a time he led a depraved life; the Spirit of God, however, changed his heart and gave him faith in Jesus. He was baptized in 1807 into the fellowship of the First Baptist church in Richmond, by which he was subsequently licensed to preach. He taught himself, with some little aid, to read; he bought his freedom and the liberty of his two children. In 1815 he became deeply interested in African missions, and at last he resolved to carry the gospel there himself. In 1821 he was ordained to the missionary work, and appointed to labor in Africa by the board of the Baptist General Convention. In 1822 he settled in Liberia. He ministered faithfully to the church originally formed in Richmond, then located in Monrovia. He spent much time in instructing the Africans who had been rescued from slave-ships; he labored successfully to establish schools. In 1824 he was appointed physician to the settlers, a position the duties of which his studies of the diseases of the country enabled him to discharge; in 1828 he became acting governor of Liberia. He perished by an accident, Nov. 8, 1828. He was beloved by all his people, and greatly blessed of God.

Case, Rev. Isaac.—"Father Case" was born at Rehoboth, Mass., Feb. 25, 1761. At the age of eighteen he became a subject of God's converting grace. He was ordained in 1783, and went to Maine. He was, in the best sense of the word, an evangelist, and when converts to Christ were made, he formed them into churches, some of which afterwards became able and most useful organizations. "Of the number of converts to whom he administered the ordinance of baptism, he kept no account, but he supposed them to have been more than a thousand." Mr. Case lived to an advanced age, and died at Readfield, Me., Nov. 3, 1852. Without remarkable talents, by his earnest piety and good common sense he became one of the most useful ministers of his day.

Castle, John Harvard, D.D., was born in Milestown, Philadelphia, Pa., in 1830; baptized in 1846; graduated from the Central High School, of Philadelphia, 1847. In the same year he entered the university at Lewisburg, Pa., where he graduated with first honors in 1851, and from that institution he received the degree of Doctor of Divinity in 1866. He completed his studies at Rochester Theological Seminary, N. Y., in 1853, and was licensed to preach by the Broad Street Baptist church, Philadelphia. He was ordained at Pottsville, Pa., where he labored for two years and a half, after which he settled with the church at Newburgh, N. Y. In 1859 he returned to his native city, and entered upon the pastorate of the First Baptist church, West Philadelphia. Here he re-

JOHN HARVARD CASTLE, D.D.

mained for fourteen years, universally beloved by the church and community. Here also he gave much time and labor to missionary and educational interests, serving on the boards of the Publication and Education Societies, the General Association, the trustees of the university at Lewisburg, and of Crozer Theological Seminary. He served as moderator of the Philadelphia Baptist Association, and was also elected president of the Ministerial Conference. In the spring of 1871 he traveled extensively in Europe.

In 1872 he was urgently invited to take charge of the Bond Street church of Toronto, Canada, which invitation he accepted, and commenced his pastorate there Feb. 1, 1873. In this field of labor he still remains, in close and affectionate relations with his people. A secular journal in Toronto, under date of Oct. 5, 1877, thus speaks of him:

"Into the work of the denomination and in all Christian movements he has thrown himself with all his heart, and has become a leading spirit therein. His congregation has increased rapidly and erected a handsome church building, which is now one of the recognized sights of the city. He is a strong temperance advocate, and a consistent enemy to frivolity of all descriptions. His oratorical powers are of a high order, his enunciation being singularly distinct, and his manner graceful and effective. Though an earnest upholder of the doctrines of his denomination, he seldom gives utterance to any remarks which members of other communions cannot listen to without impatience. Never slow to do battle when controversies arise, he proves an adept in polemics; but is ever ready to recognize and admire all that is Christ-like beyond his own ecclesiastical boundaries."

Castle, Prof. Orlando L., for some twenty-seven years Professor of Rhetoric and Belles-Lettres in Shurtleff College, was born at Jericho, Chittenden Co., Vt., July 20, 1822. When he was about ten years of age the family removed to Ohio, and at Granville College, in that State, he received his education, graduating in 1846. His first service in education was as superintendent of public schools in Zanesville, O. In 1853 he was invited to the professorship at Alton, which he still holds. The length of time during which he has occupied this chair bears witness to the value of his service, a testimony confirmed by that of the many students who have enjoyed his instruction. He is a member of the Baptist church in Upper Alton, a genial and cultured Christian gentleman, a trained scholar in the classics and in mathematics, as well as in his special department, and he is a superior teacher.

Caswell, Alexis, D.D., LL.D., one of the most eminent educators and most widely-known ministers in the denomination, was born in Taunton, Mass., Jan. 29, 1799. He was a twin brother of Alvaris Caswell, of Norton, Mass. His ancestors were among the earliest settlers of his native town, and devoted themselves to agricultural pursuits. The subject of this sketch spent his boyhood days on the paternal farm. The bent of his mind towards a larger and better culture than he could expect to obtain if he devoted himself to the calling of his father early showed itself, and nothing but a full collegiate course of study would satisfy him. At the age of nineteen he became a member of the Freshman class in Brown University, where he was graduated with the highest honors of his class in 1822. It was during his college course that he became a decided, and what he ever continued to be, a most cheerful and consistent Christian. In July, 1820, he was received into the membership of the First Baptist church in Providence, and his connection with that venerable church was never dissolved until the tie was severed by death.

Soon after closing his college studies he became a tutor in what was then Columbian College, at Washington, D. C., being one of the earliest instructors in the institution. His connection with the college continued for five years. In 1825 he was raised from the rank of tutor to that of Professor of the Ancient Languages. But it was not his purpose to devote himself to the profession of teaching. His strong desire was to become a preacher of the gospel. The eloquent Dr. William Staughton was the president of the college, and under his guidance Prof. Caswell read theology and prepared sermons, enjoying also the instructions of Dr. Irah Chace in the Hebrew. Having thus prepared himself for what no doubt he considered would be his life-work, he was directed by a somewhat remarkable providence of God to Halifax, Nova Scotia, where he was ordained as a Christian minister, and agreed, temporarily at least, to act as pastor of the recently organized Baptist church in that city. "It was a ministry," says

ALEXIS CASWELL, D.D., LL.D.

Prof. Lincoln, "fruitful of good to himself and his people. It was one which laid under contribution all the resources he could command, both intellectual and spiritual; for though the church was not large, yet it united, especially in the persons of its leaders, intelligence, culture, and social consideration with a simple and sincere piety, and an earnest desire for growth in Christian knowledge and experience, and in Christian service." We are told that "he was a popular and attractive preacher, and that his discourses, which were written, but preached without the use of notes, attracted full and overflowing houses."

It might seem as if such evident adaptedness to the active labors of the ministry, and marked success in that work, plainly pointed out what were the sure indications of Divine Providence as to his future career. His reputation as a preacher and pastor led the church of which he was a member—the First church in Providence—to think of him as a most suitable person to fill the place made vacant by the resignation of their venerable minister, the Rev. Dr. Gano. But before any action could be taken on the subject he was called to the chair of Mathematics and Natural Philosophy in Brown University, and assumed the duties of his professorship at the commencement of the fall term of 1828. He at once and most heartily entered into the plans of the new president, Dr. Wayland, and faithfully stood by him, as he endeavored, with what success is well known, to raise the standard of education in the college of which he was the honored head. The fortunes of the university were at this time at a low ebb, and only by generous sacrifice and heroic, persistent effort was the tide in its affairs made to rise. Prof. Caswell threw himself into the work he had undertaken with his characteristic zeal,—a zeal coupled with good sense and sound judgment. He labored for the interests of his beloved *alma mater* not only in his special department of instruction, but outside of college walls he enlisted the sympathy and secured the substantial aid of its friends in promoting in many ways its prosperity. But amid the most engrossing labors of the profession to which he consecrated his best energies, Prof. Caswell never lost sight of that higher calling, in the discharge of the duties of which he had expected to spend his days. If he was the college instructor, he was also the Christian minister. As Prof. Lincoln has so well said, "To his habitual conception, religion and education were indissolubly united, and the Christian religion was the soul and the sacred presiding genius of a place of education. To his view a college was a fountain not merely of a liberal education, but of a Christian liberal education; not Christian, however, in the sense of giving theological instruction, or only training men to be of service as pastors and preachers, though he never forgot that leading design of the fathers of this college and other colleges of New England, but Christian in the more catholic sense of educating and rearing up Christian men for Christian service in whatsoever vocation and business of life."

Dr. Caswell went abroad in 1860, and spent a year making himself familiar with the scenes and the social life of the Old World. Among scientific men, whose special attention had been devoted to the study of astronomy, which was his favorite branch of instruction, he met with a cordial welcome. His genial and affable manners, his inquiring spirit, and warm enthusiasm in the direction of research into the wonderful mysteries of the heavens, won for him a warm place in the hearts of those whose pursuits were kindred to his own, and he formed friendships which remained unbroken until death. When he came back to his home he resumed at once the duties of his profession, and continued his official relations with Brown University until the fall of 1863, when he resigned his professorship, after having so ably filled the chair he had occupied for thirty-five years.

A few years of varied service were spent in the community in which he was so well known and so highly respected and loved. The resignation of Dr. Sears as president of Brown University to enter upon that career of usefulness to which for so many years he has devoted himself, was followed in a few months by the election of Dr. Caswell to the office thus vacated. Although sixty-nine years of age when thus called to this responsible position, no one on terms of familiar intimacy with him ever thought of the new president as being an old man. He was in vigorous health. The pressure of so many years even, as he had lived, had not bowed that manly, erect form. He was the model of Christian refinement and gentlemanly courtesy, and had a rare gift for commanding the respect and winning the affection of young men. The expectations of his friends in calling him to the presidency of the university were not disappointed, and his administration of its affairs proved to be a success. For nearly five years he discharged the duties which devolved on him as the head of an institution with which he had so long been connected. His resignation took place in September, 1872, and he once more retired to comparatively private life. For thirty-nine years and a half he had filled an important place in the department of instruction in Brown University, and for nearly the rest of his life he watched over its interests as a member of its corporation, first as a trustee and then as a Fellow. No one person has been so long and so closely identified with all that concerned its prosperity as Dr. Caswell.

Space does not permit to enumerate all the positions of trust and honor to which, during his long and useful life, Dr. Caswell was called. He was warmly attached to the denomination with which in his early manhood he connected himself. In everything that had to do with its elevation he took the liveliest interest. The cause of sound theological learning always found in him a warm friend. Through his whole life he took an active part in promoting the prosperity of the Newton Theological Institution, succeeding to the presidency of its board of trustees on the death of Dr. Sharp, and retaining to the close of life his place on that board. The cause of foreign missions had no more earnest advocate and friend than he. He was chosen president of the Missionary Union in 1867, and re-elected in 1868. Like his early pupil and lifelong friend, Baron Stow, both pen and voice were employed in doing what he could to hasten the coming of the day when the knowledge of the Lord shall be the common heritage of the nations of the earth. The Baptist denomination may justly be proud of having had in its ranks an educator of so large and worthy a reputation, and a minister of Jesus who rendered such efficient aid in advancing its best interests in so many directions.

Cate, Rev. George W., was born in Sanbornton, N. H., in 1815. He became a hopeful Christian while residing in Amesbury, Mass. He pursued his preparatory studies for the Christian ministry at New Hampton and Hampton Falls, and graduated at Brown University in 1841, and at Newton in 1844. In September of 1844 he was ordained as pastor of the church in Barre, Mass. His ministry with this church continued for four years. He was then obliged to give up preaching on account of his health. For a few months he lingered, and then passed away. His death took place May 13, 1849. After much long and thorough preparation for his work, it seemed mysterious that this servant of Christ should have been removed so early in his public ministry, but the Master whom he tried to serve knew best what disposition to make of him.

Catechumeni, or Catechumens, Baptism of.—Believers who received the Word gladly were the subjects of baptism in the Saviour's day and during the ministry of his apostles. About A.D. 150, the same class of persons received baptism. Justin Martyr, one of the most talented and reliable of the early Christian writers, says, "In what manner we dedicate ourselves to God, after being renewed by Christ, we will now explain, lest by omitting we should seem to dissemble in our statement; as many as are persuaded and believe that the things which we teach and declare are true, and promise that they are determined to live accordingly, are taught to pray to God, and to beseech him with fasting to grant them remission for their past sins, while we also pray and fast with them. We then lead them to a place where there is water, and then they are regenerated (baptized) in the same manner as we also were, for they receive a washing in water ('εν τῷ ὕδατι) in the name of God, the Father and Lord of the universe, and of our Saviour, Jesus Christ."[1] The "Apology," from which this is taken, was addressed to the emperor Antoninus Pius, and there is no doubt about its authenticity. According to Justin, the only persons baptized in his day were believers, resolved to live for God. Later than his time, but still in the second century, before men were baptized they were instructed for some time and catechized, and then baptized. This catechumenical system preceded baptism for centuries in the Christian church. The most celebrated school for catechumeni in the Christian world was at Alexandria, in Egypt, and Origen was its most distinguished instructor, as he had been its most illustrious pupil under Cluneus Alexandrinus.[2] Catechists, to conduct the instruction of the catechumeni, in process of time were appointed all over the Christian world; and twice a year the scholars went forth to baptism, at Easter and Whitsuntide in the West, and at Easter and Whitsuntide, or at the Epiphany, in the East. No catechised candidate for baptism employed another to profess his faith, he attended to that duty himself.

The learned Bingham says, "The πιστὸι, or *believers, being such as were baptized*, and thereby made complete and perfect Christians, were upon that account dignified with several titles of honor and marks of distinction above the catechumens;" after mentioning their titles, he describes their privileges: "It was their sole prerogative to partake of the Lord's Supper," "another of their prerogatives above the catechumens was to stay and join with the minister in all the prayers of the church, which the catechumens were not allowed to do, the use of the Lord's prayer was the sole prerogative of the πιστὸι (believers); the catechumens were not allowed to say 'Our Father' till they had first made themselves sons by regeneration in the waters of baptism. They were admitted to hear all discourses made in the church, even those that treated of the most abstruse and profound mysteries of the Christian religion, which the catechumens were strictly prohibited from hearing." Bingham speaks of four classes of catechumeni, those who were instructed privately, the hearers, the kneelers, and the competentes and electi, that is, those who petitioned for baptism, and were chosen to observe that sacred ordinance. They were strictly examined, according to Bingham, in the Christian instructions imparted to them by the catechist before they were elected to receive baptism.

As the same erudite writer informs us, the catechumeni were placed with their faces to the west, the region of darkness, and there they renounced the devil and his works, and the world with its luxury and pleasures. And they struck their hands together as if they were ready for conflict with Satan. They afterwards faced the east, the region of light, where the rising sun first appears, that before the sun of righteousness they might record their sacred profession as Christians. They made a solemn vow of obedience to God, and "there was also exacted *a profession of faith of every person to be baptized*. And this was always to be made in the same words of the creed that every church used for the baptism of her catechumens."[3] They were solemnly questioned publicly in the church on the several parts of the Christian faith, and after some ceremonial observances without warrant of Scripture they were led into the baptismal waters and immersed. Ambrose of Milan gives us an illustration of believer's baptism in catechumenical times when he says, "Thou wast asked, Dost thou believe in God the omnipotent Father? and thou saidst, I believe; and thou wast immersed, that is, thou wast buried. Again thou wast asked, Dost thou believe in our Lord Jesus Christ and in his cross? and thou saidst, I believe; and thou wast immersed, and therefore thou wast buried with Christ, for he who is buried with Christ shall rise with Christ; a third time thou wast asked, Dost thou believe in the Holy Spirit? and a third time thou wast immersed, . . . for when thou dost immerse (mergis) thou dost form a likeness of death and burial."[4] The baptism of the catechumeni, the baptism of the Church Universal (Catholic) was the immersion of professed *believers*.

According to the forty-second canon of the Council Eliberis, or Elvira, held about A.D. 305, the regular period of probation for the catechumeni was two years. In special cases it might be shortened, but this was the ordinary time. It reads, "Those who give in their names to be entered into the church shall be baptized two years after, if they lead a regular life, unless they are obliged to relieve them sooner upon account of any dangerous sickness, or that it is judged convenient to grant them this grace because of the fervor of their prayers."[5] The two years' probation, the fervent prayers, and the catechetical instruction unite in showing that candidates for baptism were not babes, but enlightened persons.

It is pretended that catechumenical instruction was only for converts from heathenism. This statement is entirely unsupported by evidence. The catechumenical preparation was a prerequisite to baptism for all classes of persons for ages, except in the case of a babe threatened with death, after superstition created and gave a little encouragement to infant baptism.

For various reasons infant baptism made slow progress against the baptism of catechised persons. It was thought that baptism washed out all sin, and parents regarded it as an unwise waste of so great a treasure to apply it to babes who had only Adam's guilt, when they would need its cleansing power so much more as they grew older. Hence, even in Africa, the dark birthplace of infant immersion, and in the days of Augustine, the grand patron of the unscriptural rite, we find that it was necessary to use the curses of an episcopal council to help infant baptism in its efforts to spread. The Council of Carthage, held A.D. 418, in its second canon "pronounces an anathema against such as deny that children ought to be baptized as soon as they are born."[6] The bishops of Africa had hearers who needed maledictions, and a good many of them, to give up the baptism of believers. No curses are needed now in Pedobaptist clerical assemblies to assist the infant rite into extensive popularity. At least, none have been needed for centuries, until within the last fifty years, when our principles have invaded the strongholds of Pedobaptism and injured it in the sanctuaries of its friends.

The great Basil was born of pious parents, and baptized, after being a catechumenus, in his twenty-eighth year.[7] The same thing is true of Gregory Nazianzen, Ambrose, Jerome, and Augustine, the distinguished churchmen of the fourth century, and in the case of Augustine, of the fourth and a part of the fifth. Gibbon, speaking of this period, says, "The discretion of parents often suspended the baptism of their children till they could understand the obligations they contracted; the sacrament of baptism was supposed to contain a full and absolute expiation of sin, the soul was instantly restored to its original purity, and entitled to the promise of eternal salvation."[8] Archbishop Cranmer says, "St. Gregory Nazianzen, as great a clerk (clergyman) as ever was in Christ's church, and master to St. Hierome, counseled that children should not be baptized until they came to three years of age, or thereabout, except they were in danger of life."[9] Cranmer's testimony about Gregory's advice is correct, but he might have added that even this famous archbishop of Constantinople was heeded by few about the early reception of baptism; that the reigning emperor, Theodosius, "who, according to Socrates, had been instructed in Christian principles by his pious ancestors," only submitted to baptism when dangerously ill at Thessalonica;[10] and that baptisms at three years old were rare occurrences. The celebrated Bishop Jewel says, "Likewise in old times they that were called catechumeni were warned aforehand to prepare their hearts that they might worthily receive baptism."[11] After making the statement he proceeds to quote Clement and Augustine in support of it. Mosheim, speaking of the third century, says, "Baptism was publicly administered twice a year to candidates who had gone through a long preparation and trial."[12] Neander declares the same thing, speaking of the early churches. "Many pious but mistaken parents . . . wished rather to reserve baptismal grace (for their children) against the more decided and mature age of manhood, as a refuge from the temptations and storms of an uncertain life."[13] The baptism of catechised persons, after the apostolic age and the times of the primitive fathers, spread everywhere, and it existed for centuries after it is commonly supposed that infant baptism had banished it from the world. We have this statement confirmed by the administration of baptism only twice a year, on two important church feasts, down at least in many cases to the tenth century. In the West, the great baptisms at Easter and Whitsuntide were in their full glory in the ninth century. They were universal for adults in the fourth century. And there is every reason for believing that in many cases the children baptized in the ninth century were in some degree instructed, though no doubt it was but to a limited extent. One hundred years ago every child in Europe and America of Pedobaptist parentage was baptized within a month after birth. In the ninth century, and afterwards, only sick children were baptized, except at Easter and Pentecost. The abandonment of the two great baptisms in the year shows an unquestionable change in the subjects of the rite. Milman says, "At Easter and Pentecost, and in some places at the Epiphany, baptism was administered publicly, that is, in the presence of the faithful, to all the converts of the year."[14] The Council of Gerunda, held in A.D. 517, in its fourth and fifth canons, decrees, "Baptism shall be administered only at Easter and Whitsuntide; at the other festivals only the sick shall be baptized. Children shall be baptized whenever they are presented *if they be sick or cannot nurse the breast*."[15] This baptism is clearly for the old candidates, and only sick infants are to receive the rite at other times. Pope Nicholas I., in his 69th letter, written A.D. 858, testifies that "the solemn times of administering baptism are the feasts of Easter and Whitsuntide, but that it is not necessary to observe this (rule) in regard to people newly converted, or in reference to those in danger of death."[16] In 868, the Council of Worms, in its first canon, decreed "that baptism should be solemnly administered only at Easter and Whitsuntide."[17] In 895, the Council of Tribur, in its twelfth canon, ordained that "the sacrament of baptism should not be administered out of the solemn times—at Easter and Whitsuntide."[18] Whitsuntide, it has been justly observed, "was one of the stated times for baptism in the ancient church, when those who were baptized put on white garments as types of that spiritual purity they receive in baptism,"[19] hence the name, Whitsunday, Whitmonday. This is a season of rejoicing in several European countries now, though the grand baptisms have ceased long since. In the ninth century they still had the two great annual baptisms, and the customs that obtained when all the candidates for baptism were instructed beforehand. Of course, if the present practice of infant baptism had prevailed, and each child had been baptized a few days after birth, the Easter and Pentecost baptisms would never have existed. But the probabilities are that in many places in Europe, as late as the ninth century, or later, the persons baptized were two or three years old, or more, so that they could answer all the usual questions themselves. As soon as the baptism of unconscious babes in a few days or weeks after birth became universal, then the great baptisms of Easter and Pentecost ended.

From Alcuin, the distinguished Englishman, who rendered such important literary and religious services to Charlemagne in the eighth century, we learn that there were catechumeni in his day; commenting on the Gospel of John, ii. 23, 24, he says, "Ecclesiastical custom does not give the communion of the body and blood of Christ to the catechumeni, because they are not born of water (baptized) and of the Spirit."[20] There were certainly catechumeni at this time. He states in another place, "We say that no catechumenus (an instructed candidate for baptism), although dying in good works, has eternal life, unless he becomes a martyr, by which all the mysteries of baptism are perfected; for by blood, fire, and other pains the confessors were baptized."[21] He speaks of a catechumenus as one of the existing characters of his day. So that instruction was still demanded in some parts of Christendom outside the ranks of the Anabaptists as a qualification for baptism.

Robinson[22] describes a baptism which took place in the Lateran baptistery in Rome, in which three children, representing John and Peter and Mary, after being catechised by a priest and instructed for the occasion, were solemnly immersed by the pope himself. He wore waxed drawers, the ceremony took place on the Saturday before Easter, and the children were the recipients of some religious knowledge. The account is taken from ancient Roman ordinals collected by Father Mabillon, and it is undoubtedly reliable. The baptism may be attributed to any period from the ninth to the twelfth century.

Muratori, conservator of the public archives of Modena in the beginning of the eighteenth century, of whom it is recorded that "literary societies vied with each other in sending him diplomas, and authors who had attained eminence in different departments of literature paid him the homage of enscribing to him their works," himself a learned Roman Catholic, in view of a mass of ancient documents treating of the baptismal history of his church, from the tenth to the fourteenth century, says, "From monuments thus far produced, we may learn how many ages the custom among Christians of *not baptizing infants immediately at birth*, as we now do, *continued*. Unless sickness or danger threatened life, a reception of the sacrament (of baptism) was delayed by most persons till the Saturday before Easter Sunday and Whitsunday, on which days the church celebrated the solemn baptism."[23]

Baptism was conferred by the apostles on a confession of faith. In the third century there was a period of instruction imposed before the rite was conferred, and this catechumenical course continued, the candidates for baptism growing younger every century, for a considerable period after the ninth century. The baptism of unconscious babes to reach universal empire in the great church and drive believer's baptism to the shelter of the little sects, had to fight the Word of God, the old creeds and customs of Christendom, the prejudices of all Christian countries, and the fierce opposition of Baptists under various denominational names, and it succeeded at last, after the ninth century. But the profession of faith of the sponsors for the child still shows the old divine demand for faith in the candidates of baptism.

[1] Just. Philos. et Mart., Apol. i. Patrol. Græca, tom. vi. p. 140. Migne. Parisiis. [2] Euseb. Eccles. Hist., lib. vi. 46. [3] Bingham's Antiquities, book i. 4, x. 2, xi. 7. [4] De Sacramentis, lib. iv. 7, vol. xvi. p. 448. Patrol. Lat. Migne. [5] Du Pin's Eccles. Hist., i. 593. Dublin. [6] Idem., i. 635. [7] Robinson's Hist. of Baptism, pp. 91–95. Nashville. [8] Decline and Fall, i. 450. Magowan, London. [9] Miscellaneous Writings, p. 175. Parker Society. [10] Eccles. Hist., lib. v. cap. 6. [11] Jewel's Works, p. 119. Parker Society. [12] Eccles. Hist., p. 106. London, 1848. [13] Church History, ii. 319. Boston. [14] History of Christianity, p. 466. New York, 1841. [15] Du Pin, i. 688. [16] Idem., ii. 143. [17] Idem., ii. 115. [18] Idem., ii. 118. [19] Buck's Theological Dictionary, p. 450. [20] Patrol. Lat., tom. c. p. 777. Migne. [21] Idem., tom. ci. p. 1074. [22] Robinson's History of Baptism, p. 102. [23] Antiquitates Italicæ Medii Ævi, tom. iv. diss. 57. De Ritibus, Mel., 1738.

Cathcart, William, D.D., was born in the County of Londonderry, in the north of Ireland, Nov. 8, 1826; his parents, James Cathcart and Elizabeth Cously, were of Scotch origin, the stock known as Scotch-Irish in the United States. He was brought up in the Presbyterian Church, of which, for some years, he was a member. The Saviour called him into his kingdom in early life, and taught him that he should preach the gospel. He was baptized by Rev. R. H. Carson, of Tubbermore, in January, 1846. He studied Latin and Greek in a classical school near the residence of his father. He received his literary and theological education in the University of Glasgow, Scotland, and in Horton, now Rawdon College, Yorkshire, England. He was ordained pastor of the Baptist church of Barnsley, near Sheffield, England, early in 1850. From political and anti-state church considerations he determined to come to the United States in 1853, and on the 18th of November in that year he arrived in New York. In the latter part of the following month he became pastor of the Third Baptist church of Groton, in Mystic River, Conn. In April, 1857, he took charge of the Second Baptist church of Philadelphia, Pa., where he has since labored.

In 1873, the University of Lewisburg conferred on Mr. Cathcart the degree of Doctor of Divinity. In 1876, on the retirement of Dr. Malcom from the presidency of the American Baptist Historical Society, Dr. Cathcart was elected president, and has been re-elected at each annual meeting since. In

WILLIAM CATHCART, D.D.

1875, in view of the Centennial year of our national independence, the Baptist Ministerial Union, of Pennsylvania, appointed Dr. Cathcart to prepare a paper, to be read at their meeting in Meadville in 1876, on "The Baptists in the Revolution." This paper, by enlargement, became a duodecimo volume, entitled "The Baptists and the American Revolution." Dr. Cathcart has also published a large octavo, called "The Papal System," and "The Baptism of the Ages and of the Nations," a 16mo.

Catlin, Rev. S. T., was born in Montville, Me., and died May 1, 1878, aged fifty-nine years; ordained to the work of the ministry in 1839. After serving several churches in his native State, he came to Hudson, Wis., in 1851. He was appointed Indian missionary by the American Baptist Missionary Union in 1854. He subsequently preached at Osceola, St. Croix Falls, and Taylor Falls. He was a faithful and successful pioneer preacher, a man of good ability, highly esteemed by the churches that knew him.

Cauldwell, Ebenezer, a prominent Baptist layman of New York, was born in England in 1791, and died in New York in 1875. He came with his father in early life to New York, and engaged with him in merchandising; and securing the entire business of the firm on the death of his father, he built up a commercial house without a superior in his line. When a lad he was converted, and joined the Oliver Street church, and became one of its most efficient members. He was chosen a deacon of his church, and a member of the board of the American Baptist Home Mission Society, and its treasurer. He gave liberally to its funds, as he did to all other enterprises of the Baptist denomination. He was one of the founders of the Hope Chapel Baptist church, which, about 1850, built a house on Broadway. A few years later the church erected a large edifice on Twenty-third Street, and changed its name to the Calvary church. With this community he held the office of deacon while he lived. He was a Christian without blemish, dear to all his Master's servants who knew him.

Causler, Rev. A. G., a leading member of Columbia Association, in the southern part of Arkansas, was born in the State of South Carolina in 1825. He began to preach in 1852. He labored efficiently in his native State until 1867, when he removed to the northern part of Arkansas, and after a few years there came to Columbia Association, and engaged in the active duties of his calling. He died in 1872.

Cedar Valley Seminary, Osage, Iowa, had its origin in a proposition from the citizens of Osage to the Cedar Valley Baptist Association, September, 1862, that they would furnish appropriate buildings if the Association would establish and maintain an institution of learning suited to the wants of the community. After careful deliberation, the Association

"*Resolved*, That we fully approve of the acceptance of said buildings, and pledge our hearty co-operation in the execution of the enterprise."

After fully canvassing the subject, and after a conference with the parties concerned, Rev. Alva Bush, who had just concluded his engagement as Professor of Mathematics in the Upper Iowa University, moved his family to Osage, and on Jan. 10, 1863, commenced a school in the court-house, to which was given the name of Cedar Valley Seminary. In September, 1864, the Association assumed the control of the school and appointed a board of trustees. In December, 1867, a legal organization was completed. In 1867, property was purchased, and a fine seminary building was erected during the following two years by the citizens of Osage, according to their original proposal. In September, 1869, this property was formally tendered to the Association on condition that they raise $20,000 and maintain a good school. The offer, with its conditions, was accepted, and the raising of the endowment undertaken. But owing to the great severity of the times the sum was not raised till 1876. The title was transferred to the board of trustees in May, 1876, who now have the ownership and absolute control. At each recurring meeting of the Association, trustees are appointed to fill vacancies in the board, and renewed evidence of sympathy and interest in the institution throughout the bounds of the Association is manifested from year to year. Prof. Alva Bush, LL.D., has been continued at the head of the institution since 1863. In 1871, the seminary sent out its first graduating class.

Centennial Institute, located at Warren, Bradley Co., Ark., under the patronage of the General Association of Southeastern Arkansas, was opened in 1875. It is at present under the direction of Rev. W. E. Paxton, A.M., with three other teachers. A plan for the endowment of the school has been put on foot, and an agent is at work in this field. It is located in the midst of the most fertile portion of the State, on the line of the Mississippi, Ouachita and Red River Railroad. The spring term of 1880 closed with 100 matriculates.

Central Female College is located at Clinton, Hinds Co., Miss. The want of suitable facilities in the State for the education of the daughters of Baptists was long felt. At length the venerable Dr. Phillips made a movement in this direction in the Central Baptist Association, which resulted in the establishment of this school. In 1856, Dr. Walter Hillman and his accomplished lady were called to this institution, and for twenty-four years under their management it has prospered, and her daughters are filling the highest social positions in the State. The spring term of 1880 closed with 104 students and 6 teachers. The buildings are the private property of Dr. Hillman and his wife.

Central University, Pella, Iowa, was established by a Convention representing the Baptists of the State, which located the institution at Pella, Marion County, and named it Central University. They appointed a board of 30 trustees, divided into 3 classes of 10 each, and an executive committee of 7. They determined to open the academical department of the school at once, of which, on their appointment, E. H. Scarff, A.M., took charge and commenced the school. During the first two years it steadily advanced in numbers and in the grade of scholarship, and the board were encouraged in June, 1858, to open a regular collegiate course. They elected Rev. E. Gunn president. In the same year Mrs. D. C. A. Stoddard was chosen principal of the ladies' department. From 1857 to 1861, the prospects of the institution were very flattering, and classes were formed as high as the Junior class. The aggregate number of students for the year 1861 was 377. At the opening of the war, in 1861, many of the students responded to the call for soldiers, and at the close of the summer term, 1862, there was not an able-bodied man of sufficient age to bear arms, in the college. Rev. E. Gunn resigned the presidency and Prof. Currier enlisted in the army. Of the 114 students who went to the war, 26 were commissioned officers, 17 non-commissioned officers, and 21 fell on the field. In 1865, Prof. Currier returned from the army to his place in the university. At the annual meeting in June, 1870, it was resolved to raise $10,000 as the nucleus of endowment. The effort was successful. The board, in June, 1871, resolved to prosecute the work of endowment, and elected Rev. L. A. Dunn, D.D., of Fairfax, Vt., president. At the opening of the winter term he delivered his inaugural address and entered upon his labors, and he has earnestly pressed forward the work of the university. Among those educated at the institution there are 7 editors, 7 doctors, 31 ministers, 42 lawyers, and hundreds of school-teachers, and a large number of others in various walks of life. The university has a full college course; the Senior class numbers 7, the Junior 8, the Sophomore 12, the Freshman 19, the Sub-Freshman 36. It also has an academical department and a musical class, in all some 200 students. The president of the university is assisted in his work by a full corps of able instructors.

Chace, Prof. George Ide, LL.D., was born in Lancaster, Mass., Feb. 19, 1808. He fitted for college at the academy in his native town, and was a graduate of Brown University in the class of 1830. Soon after leaving college he took charge of the Preparatory Classical School in Waterville, Me., where he remained through the academic year of 1830–31, and then accepted an appointment as tutor of Mathematics and Natural Philosophy in Brown University, and was shortly made adjunct professor with the late Dr. Caswell. His connection with the university covered a period of forty-one years. For fifteen years he occupied the chair of Chemistry, Physiology, and Geology, and for five years, 1867–72, the chair of Moral Philosophy and Metaphysics. On the resignation of Rev. Dr. Sears to enter upon his duties as superintendent of the Peabody Educational Fund, Prof. Chace held the office of president of the university one year, when he was succeeded by Dr. Robinson. He closed his connection with the university in 1872, and went abroad, spending a year and a half in foreign travel, extending his trip as far as Egypt. For the few years past Prof. Chace has occupied prominent and useful positions in the city of Providence, as a member of the municipal government, and as the president of the State Board of Charities and of Rhode Island Hospital. In 1853, he received the degree of Ph.D. from Lewisburg University, and that of LL.D. from Brown University. He is a prominent member of the venerable First Baptist church, and takes a deep interest in its prosperity.

Challis, Rev. James M., was born in Philadelphia, Pa., Jan. 4, 1779. At an early age he lost his father, and went with his mother to reside at Salem, N. J. There he grew up under the ministry of Rev. Mr. Sheppard, by whom he was baptized and encouraged to turn his attention to the ministry. He was licensed by the church, and after spending a short time in preparatory study with Dr. Holcomb, pastor of the First Baptist church, Philadelphia, he accepted a call to the pastorate of the church at Upper Freehold, N.J., where, in 1822, he was ordained. He removed to Lower Dublin, Pa., in 1838. With this ancient church he remained seven years, when he returned to New Jersey and became pastor of the churches at Moorestown and Marlton, and in 1842 of the Cohansey church. Here he labored eight years, when, owing to advancing age, he resigned his charge and ended all pastoral labors. Removing to Bridgeton, he united with the First Baptist church. Here he resided till his death, in April, 1868, preaching, however, at different points, as opportunity offered, and sometimes supplying vacant churches for months in succession. His whole ministry covered a period of more than forty years, during which he was instrumental in bringing many to Christ, some of whom now occupy positions of prominence and usefulness in our churches. During his last illness, which was short but exceedingly painful, he experienced great peace of mind, and a sweet assurance through grace of entering into the everlasting rest.

Chambers, Rev. K., was born about six miles from Milledgeville, April 7, 1814. He became the subject of religious impressions when young, and in 1832, he was baptized into the fellowship of Mount Olive church by Elder T. D. Oxford. He was ordained in 1839 by J. P. Leverett, J. J. Salmon, and Wiley M. Pope. From that time till he left the State he was pastor of four churches, and one year served the Washington Association as missionary and colporteur. He removed to Florida in 1854, and settled in Columbia County, where he yet resides. Here, as in Georgia, his services were in demand, and the first year he lived in the State he preached to three churches.

At his suggestion, and through his influence in part, the Santa Fé River Association was organized, and he served it two years as missionary, and in one year built up eight churches. He was several times elected moderator of the Association, and presided once or twice over the State Convention, and he was State evangelist for two or three years. More than 500 persons have been baptized by him in Florida. It is questionable whether any minister has been more largely instrumental in building up the denomination in the State to its present condition, than Kinsey Chambers.

He is strong in the gospel, and a thorough Baptist. He makes no compromises. He abounds in charity, but it is the charity that "rejoices in the truth." Though somewhat controversial in his ministry, and a man of decided convictions, he is generally beloved, and commands the respect of those who differ from him. He held a controversy with a Pedobaptist minister in 1860, and afterwards had the pleasure of immersing some who had been immersed by him. He is a conservative, however, in reference to disputed questions in religion. He is a good and useful man, "whose foot has never slipped," and who preaches by his example. Not a spot can be found upon his character. He has proved his devotion to the cause of Christ by his labors and sacrifices. Blessed with a good constitution, he has worked hard as a preacher of the gospel he loves so much.

Chambliss, J. A., D.D., the able and popular pastor of the Citadel Square church, Charleston, S. C., was born at Athens, Ga., Aug. 30, 1840, his father, A. W. Chambliss, D.D., being at that time pastor of the Baptist church at Athens, and teacher of the University Grammar School. The subject of this sketch studied in the preparatory department of Howard College, Marion, Ala., to which place his father had moved, until 1855, when he entered Georgetown College, Ky., and remained two years, returning to Marion, where, in 1858, he entered Howard College, graduating with the first honor in 1859. In the fall of the same year he entered the Southern Baptist Theological Seminary at Greenville, and was graduated alone—*the first graduate*—in May, 1861. He professed conversion at eleven years of age, and was baptized at Marion, Ala., by Rev. J. H. DeVotie. His convictions in regard to preaching became settled and permanent when at Howard College, and God raised up friends to enable him to complete his education there and at the seminary,—first, in Jeremiah Brown, and then in ex-Gov. John Gill Shorter, two of God's noblemen; both are now gone to their reward. Graduating at the seminary in his twenty-first year, he immediately settled as pastor of the church at Sumter, S. C.; but the war coming on and bringing years full of anxiety and interruptions, by calls to labor among the soldiers, he accepted a chaplaincy in the army and resigned his charge of the church, severing ties of the tenderest and most loving character. In 1866 he settled for a brief period as pastor of the Aiken, S. C., church, removing in 1867 to Richmond, Va., at the call of the Second Baptist church of that city. This pastorate continued four years, until the expression, by the pastor, of opinions on the communion question not in unison with those of the church, led to his resignation. That the Christian love and confidence of the church were retained by him is evidenced by the present to him from the church, at parting, of a purse containing nearly $1000. For one year Mr. Chambliss taught a large classical and English school in Richmond, preaching constantly in the city and vicinity. In the summer of 1872 it became known that his views were substantially in harmony with those of the denomination at large, and he received several calls from different churches. In October, 1872, he accepted the call of the Citadel Square church, Charleston, where he still remains. Nothing but eminent abilities and an unimpeachable character, added to untiring exertions, could have given Mr. Chambliss the success in life he has met, and obtained for him the love and confidence he has ever received. Should he live he will undoubtedly take rank among the highest in the denomination, and accomplish results that will make his name honorable in the annals of Christian labor. Mr. Chambliss is gentle in manners, and is universally popular. His churches have always been enthusiastically attracted to him, and he seems to possess in the highest degree the magnetic power of winning the affections of all who come in contact with him. As a preacher, he is simple, earnest, forcible, and pre-eminently evangelical. There are few more effective preachers of the simple, soul-saving truths of the gospel.

Champlin, James Tift, D.D., was born in Colchester, Conn., June 9, 1811. He entered Brown University in 1830, and graduated with the highest honors of his class in 1834. Among his classmates were Rev. Dr. Silas Bailey and Hon. J. R. Bullock, afterwards governor of Rhode Island. From 1835 to March, 1838, he was a tutor in the university, at the end of which period he was invited to the pastorate of the First Baptist church in Portland, Me. Here he remained until the fall of 1841, when he was called to the chair of Ancient Languages in Colby University, then Waterville College. He remained in this position sixteen years, when he was invited to assume the office of president of the college. He entered upon his duties in this capacity in 1857, and continued in the presidential chair until 1872, thus making his connection with the college extend over a period of thirty-one years. The administration of Dr. Champlin was successful in adding greatly to the resources of the college, and increasing its facilities for giving a thorough training to young men seeking an education. He knew how to influence men of wealth, and awaken in them an interest in the cause of good learning. It was while he was president that the name which was given to the college in its original charter was changed to Colby University, in honor of Gardner Colby, Esq., of Boston, a large-hearted benefactor of the college.

While acting as professor and president of the college, Dr. Champlin published several text-books to be used in the departments of instruction which came under his special supervision. Among these were an edition of "Demosthenes on the Crown," "Demosthenes' Select Orations," "Æschines on the Crown," "A Text-Book on Intellectual Philosophy," "First Principles of Ethics," "A Text-

JAMES TIFT CHAMPLIN, D.D.

Book of Political Economy." He has written also for the periodical press. Soon after his resignation he removed to Portland, where he now (1878) resides.

Chandler, Rev. Asa, a very prominent member of the Sarepta Association, Georgia, and a man who, for years, stood in the front rank of Baptist ministers of his section as a pious, able, and influential preacher. He was a strong supporter of missions and education; was often moderator of his Association, and died after a long life of great usefulness, in which he had the loving confidence and respect of every one in the community. He possessed a fine person, an open, intelligent face, with an amiable and pleasant expression.

Chandler, George Clinton, D.D., was born March 19, 1807, at Chester, Vt.; baptized in 1825, and licensed to preach in 1831; graduated at Madison University in 1835, and in 1838, after a three years' course, at Newton; Sept. 5, 1838, was ordained, and soon after went to Indiana as a home missionary, and preached one year at Terre Haute. In 1839, he became pastor at Indianapolis, and in 1843 was appointed president of Franklin College. After seven years of great success as an educator, he was urged to go to Oregon as president of the young Baptist college there. He crossed the plains in 1851, and was for many years at the head of the institution, but subsequently gave himself to pastoral and missionary work, preaching and traveling over nearly all parts of the State. In 1874 he was summoned to the vacant pulpit at Dalles, Oregon, and promptly heeded the call. In November, 1874, after preaching from the words, "I can do all things through Christ," he was listening to the Sunday-school song, "Shall we meet beyond the River?" when the book fell from his hands; he sat motionless, having been struck by paralysis. From that attack he has never recovered. In his home, at Forest Grove, he sits speechless still, apparently unconscious of all that is passing around him, or of the great work he has done in his long and useful life. His family is one of the most devotedly pious in Oregon. His oldest son, Rev. E. K. Chandler, is a successful pastor at Rockfield, Ill.

Chandler, Rev. P. B., was born in Oglethorpe Co., Ga., Jan. 27, 1816; joined the church in August, 1838. Having decided that he was called to preach, he also determined to prepare for the work, consequently he sold out his home and farm and went, with his wife and three children, to Mercer University, Penfield, Ga., and spent three years. Taught two years in Georgia, and in November, 1846, migrated to Texas, where he labored for two years as a missionary of the Home Mission Board of the Southern Baptist Convention. For twenty-eight years he resided in Fayette Co., Texas, preaching to churches in Fayette, Washington, and Savaca Counties, serving three or four at one time. Since 1874 he has resided near Gatesville, Coryell County, and preached to several churches. Has been for some years moderator of Colorado Association, and is moderator of Leon River Association. He has brought up four sons and eight daughters, all of whom are consistent members of Baptist churches. As a preacher, moderator of Associations, vice-president of the State Convention, trustee of Baylor University, and in other relations of life, he has impressed the population among whom he has resided as few men have ever done in Texas.

Chaney, Rev. Bailey E., a pioneer Baptist preacher of Mississippi, removed from South Carolina about 1790 and settled near Natchez. During the persecution against Curtis and his companions, Chaney concealed himself. When the territory was transferred to the United States the people assembled in large numbers, a brush arbor was constructed, and Bailey E. Chaney was sent for, and while the flag of the United States floated over him he preached the gospel of Christ unawed by the minions of Rome. In 1798 he visited an American settlement near Baton Rouge, in Louisiana, and preached; but being arrested, he obtained release by promising to preach no more. After this he returned to Mississippi and labored there until his death, which occurred about 1816.

Chanler, Rev. Isaac, was born in 1701 in Bristol, England, and removed to South Carolina when he was about thirty-two years of age. He settled near Charleston, and was chosen pastor of the church in that city. He filled the office with great acceptance and success till his death, which occurred Nov. 30, 1749. He was distinguished for his talents and for his devoted piety. He published a work called "The Doctrines of Glorious Grace Unfolded, Defended, and Practically Improved," which was very highly esteemed. He also issued "A Treatise on Original Sin" and some minor publications.

Chapell, Rev. Frederick Leonard, the pastor of the First Baptist church at Janesville, Wis., was born in Waterford Township, adjoining the city of New London, Conn., Nov. 9, 1836. His parents were Baptists, and members of the church in Waterford of which Elder Darrow was for so many years pastor. But his mother dying in his infancy, he was adopted by an uncle and aunt who were Congregationalists. He was brought up under the religious influence of that denomination, attending the ministry of the venerable Dr. Abel McEwen, fifty-four years pastor of the First Congregational church of New London. He was a member of the "Gilead" Sunday-school, Waterford, of which Hon. Gilbert P. Haven was the founder, and for forty years the superintendent. Here, in this school, he laid the foundation of what has since grown up into a solid structure of Christian character. His religious exercises began early in his childhood, but he did not obtain a hope in Christ until he was in his sixteenth year. Now began a struggle. His foster-parents and numerous friends desired that his public profession of Christ should be made in connection with the Congregational church. His convictions, after mature and prayerful study, would not allow him to be anything but a Baptist. Having settled the question of duty, his friends cordially concurring in his decision, he was baptized in October, 1853, into the Huntington Street church of New London by the pastor, Elder Jabez Swan. Immediately upon his conversion, having clear convictions that he was called to the work of the ministry, "not consulting with flesh and blood," he began at once a course of preparation for that work. He entered Yale College in 1856 and graduated in 1860, and entered Rochester Theological Seminary in 1861, graduating in the class of 1864. He was licensed to preach the gospel by the Wooster Place church of New Haven, of which Prof. W. C. Wilkinson was then pastor. Upon graduating in 1864, he accepted a call to the pastorate of the Baptist church in Middletown, O., and was ordained in September of that year. Dr. Henry Harvey was the moderator of the Council and preached the ordination sermon.

During his first pastorate he grew in strength as a minister, and rapidly built up the church in Christian usefulness and power. The church edifice was enlarged, improved, and refurnished at a cost of $12,000. In the summer of 1871 he accepted the urgent call of the Baptist church in Evanston, Ill., the principal suburban town of Chicago, and entered at once upon his work in this new field. During his pastorate here the church rapidly grew in all the elements of healthy church life. Many families of wealth and influence were added to the congregation. A new church site was secured and a new house of worship erected, costing, with furnishing, $35,000. During Mr. Chapell's pastorate at Evanston he took an active part in all the denominational matters in the city of Chicago, being a member of the boards of the university and theological seminary, and secretary of the Northwestern Theological Union. He was a leading spirit in the ministers' meetings of the city. In July, 1878, he became pastor of the Baptist church in Janesville, Wis. During the sixteen years of his ministry he has preached 1501 times and conducted 1328 social meetings. He has served as moderator of each of the Associations with which he has been connected. Mr. Chapell has on several occasions been selected as one of the lecturers before the students of the Chicago Baptist Theological Seminary. He has contributed valuable historical and philosophical articles to the periodical literature of the day, and a series of sermons on revivals, published by him several years since in the *Standard*, created much attention. He has a logical mind, and a special fondness for historical and philological investigation. He is a clear and able expounder of the Word of God in the pulpit, and among his people a wise and faithful shepherd of the flock of God.

Chapin, Rev. Nelson Elisha, is a native of Granville, Washington Co., N. Y., where he was born March 10, 1815, and where he passed his early childhood and youth. His impressions that Christ called him to preach the gospel were clear and convincing, and early in life he gave himself to preparation for the work of the ministry. He pursued a course of study at Granville Academy, N. Y., and was also a student at Meriden Academy, N. H. He was under the instruction of Prof. Hascall, one of the founders of Madison University, N. Y. He was ordained in 1839 at Smithport, McKean Co., Pa., and immediately settled as pastor of the Baptist church in Bradford, same county. After serving several churches in New York and Pennsylvania, he received, in 1845, a commission from the Genesee Baptist Association, N. Y., to operate as its missionary in the lead-mine district of Wisconsin. He immediately set out on his journey to his field of labor, with his wife and two children, traveling the entire distance, about 1000 miles, in his own wagon, subjecting himself and family to great exposure and hardship in accomplishing it. He began his ministry in Grant Co., Wis. His field, however, covered several entire counties, and to reach the dozen or more little churches of which he was the missionary pastor, and most of which he had gathered, he had to travel over a circuit of 200 miles every two weeks. He was of the heroic order of men and of great physical endurance, or he could not have sustained the vast strain that came upon him in these pioneer labors. He has been pastor at Lancaster, Beaver Dam, Darlington, Aztelan, Merton, and is now pastor at Lodi. His ministry in Wisconsin covers a period of forty years, and he is connected with the history and growth of the Baptist denomination in the State. For a brief period Mr. Chapin served the American Baptist Publication Society as agent, and the Baptist Theological Seminary at Chicago. The results of his ministry can be seen all over the State in the churches he gathered, the meeting-houses he built, and the hundreds of converts to whom he administered the ordinance of baptism. Mr. Chapin is known as a humble and devoted minister of Christ, a plain and scriptural preacher of the gospel. These qualities, combined with his fervent piety and sterling common sense, have made him an efficient and able missionary pioneer.

Chapin, Stephen, D.D., son of Stephen and Rachel Chapin, was born in Milford, Mass., Nov. 4, 1778. In 1798 he began to prepare for college, under the instruction of the Rev. Caleb Alexander, of Meriden, and made such rapid progress that he entered Cambridge University, Mass., in July, 1799, graduating in 1804. He studied theology with the Rev. Nathaniel Emmons, Franklin, Mass., and was licensed to preach Oct. 10, 1804. He was ordained in Hillsborough, N. H., in June, 1805, but severed his connection with the church there in 1808 on account of difficulties respecting the so-called "Half-way Covenant," and in November, 1809, was installed as pastor of the church in Mount Vernon, N. H. It is a fact worthy of mention that Dr. Chapin was present as a deeply-interested friend at the sailing of the first American missionaries from Boston in 1811. In 1818 he was dismissed from his connection with the church on account of his change of views on the mode and subjects of baptism, having been until that time a Congregational Pedobaptist. In 1819 he was ordained pastor of the Baptist church in North Yarmouth, Me. In 1822 he left this field of labor to accept the professorship of Theology in Waterville College, Me.; was inaugurated in August, 1823, and held the same until September, 1828, when he was called to the presidency of the Columbian College, Washington, D. C. This position he resigned in 1841 in consequence of declining health, and died Oct. 1, 1845, in the sixty-seventh year of his age.

Dr. Chapin was an intelligent and interested participant in all the denominational movements of his day. When the Triennial Baptist Convention was threatened with disruption, in consequence of the antagonistic views of its members on the question of slavery, he did all in his power to prevent the division which soon followed, and when the Southern Baptist Convention was formed he was made a delegate, although he did not attend its sessions. When Dr. Chapin entered upon the presidency of the Columbian College a crushing debt of upwards of $100,000 was hanging over it and crippling its energies. He sacrificed his ease and his health to remove this debt, and by frequent visits to the South to collect funds, and by the contribution of three years of his own salary, he finally succeeded in the onerous effort. Dr. Chapin had a very wide circle of most intimate friends. He was personally intimate with most of the great statesmen of his day, many of whom, like Jackson, Clay, Calhoun, Webster, Woodbury, McDuffie, Preston, Van Buren, Choate, Marshall, Taney, McLean, Mangum, were often seen at his hospitable board, and many of whose sons were under his personal instruction in the college. In the ministry his compeers and friends were Sharp, Wayland, Chaplin, Stow, Rice, Judson, Mercer, Brantly, Dagg, Semple, Broaddus, Ryland, Brown, and hosts of others, whom he frequently met at his own fireside. His whole life was marked by those traits of character which inevitably win the warm regard and most tender love of men. But little of Dr. Chapin's literary labors are left us except a few sermons and tracts and essays, but they show us the superior culture of his mind. Among them are "Letters on the Mode and Subjects of Baptism," a valuable discussion of the question. "The Messiah's Victory," a discourse at the ordination of the Rev. Samuel Cook, Effingham, N. H.; on the "Conversion of Mariners," "The Duty of Living for the Good of Posterity," a discourse delivered in commemoration of the second centennial of the landing of the forefathers of New England; "The Superior Glory of Gospel Worship," "Moral Education," "The Proclamation of Christ Crucified the Delight of God," "An Inaugural Address," delivered as president of the Columbian College; "The Spirit of the Age," "The Design of God in Afflicting Ministers of the Gospel," "On the Death of Luther Rice," and an interesting letter to President Van Buren "On the Proper Disposition of the Smithsonian Bequest."

Chaplains in the U. S. Navy.—The corps of chaplains in the U. S. navy is limited by law to twenty-four. Any clergyman of unexceptionable character is eligible to the position, provided his age does not exceed thirty-five years, and his piety, culture, and general fitness commend him to the President of the United States as one suitably qualified for the position, and to the Senate, by whose action the choice of the President is confirmed. Chaplains are designated as "staff-officers," the same as those of the medical and engineer corps, in distinction from "officers of the line," and rank according to seniority of service as captains, commanders, lieutenant-commanders, and lieutenants. In pursuance of the law governing the retirement of commissioned officers, they are retired from active service on reaching the age of sixty-two years, or from disability contracted in the service. Their duties are various, in connection with navy-yards, hospitals, receiving- and training-ships, and the flag-ships of the several squadrons. The Naval Academy at Annapolis and the Naval Asylum at Philadelphia furnish important fields for the work of the chaplain. The recent introduction of "school- or training-ships" as an organized system for training boys in order to constantly recruit the naval service with competent and intelligent seamen, likewise offers a sphere of peculiar usefulness to chaplains. In addition to his functions as a preacher, where men or boys are in need of instruction he is to select competent teachers for this purpose, and he is held responsible for the faithful discharge of their duties. There are at present five Baptist chaplains in the navy.

Chaplin, Charles Crawford, D.D., son of Hon. W. R. Chaplin, was born in Danville, Va., Sept. 22, 1831. He is the descendant of an old English family, one of whom emigrated from England in the latter part of the last century. He is related to the Chaplins of New England, many of whom are Baptist preachers. He was educated at Richmond College, Va., the honors of which he was prevented from taking because of ill health; was converted in 1853; entered college in 1854; retired from college in the spring of 1856, and was ordained in Sandy Creek meeting-house, Va., December, 1856; took charge of the Danville church immediately after his ordination, and retained it until June, 1870; took charge of Owensborough church, Ky., in 1870; resigned and became pastor, April, 1873, of the First Baptist church, Paducah, Ky., of which he was pastor till Jan. 1, 1877, when he settled with the First Baptist church of Austin, Texas; has held meetings, during which between 4000 and 5000 have been converted, 2500 of whom have joined Baptist churches. He has written ably for denominational periodicals. He has frequently presided over deliberative bodies of which he was a member, discharging his duties with skill and ability. The honorary degree of D.D. was conferred on him in 1878 by Baylor and Waco Universities. As a preacher, he ranks among the foremost for point, impressiveness, and forcible delivery. He has written some poetry, which has been well received both by the secular and religious press. He was present on the field during seven pitched battles in the war between the States, and ministered to many wounded and dying Federal and Confederate soldiers. During his pastorate at

CHARLES CRAWFORD CHAPLIN, D.D.

Danville he was instrumental in building a parsonage, a meeting-house, and a college edifice; at Owensborough, a parsonage; at Paducah, in remodeling the church edifice; and at Austin is likely soon to see the church edifice remodeled and a parsonage built. The present governor and family (1878), and many other prominent people at the capital of Texas, are regular attendants upon his ministry.

Chaplin, Jeremiah, D.D., was born in Rowley, Mass., Jan. 2, 1776. The name of his birthplace has been changed to Georgetown. When but ten years of age he became a Christian, and was received by baptism into the church. Like so many eminent men in the denomination, he spent his youth upon his father's farm, strengthening his physical system by forming habits of inestimable value for after-life. At the age of nineteen he entered Brown University, and was graduated as the first scholar in his class in 1799. For one year he was tutor in the university, and then pursued his theological studies under Rev. Dr. Baldwin, of Boston. In the summer of 1802 he became the pastor of the Baptist church in Danvers, Mass. Besides performing with strict fidelity his work as a minister, he gave instruction to young men looking forward to the Christian ministry. His ministry in Danvers continued for fourteen years.

The reputation of Dr. Chaplin as a profound theologian and a devout Christian grew every year of his pastorate, and when, in 1807, it was proposed to open in Waterville, Me., a school for theological instruction with a view to meet the wants of the rising ministry in the district of Maine, the attention of the friends of the enterprise was turned to the Danvers pastor as a most suitable person to take charge of the institution. Three years' experiment led the trustees to decide to enlarge the sphere of its operations, and in 1820 a charter was secured, and Waterville College, now Colby University, commenced its existence, with Dr. Chaplin as its first president, which relation he sustained for thirteen years. It was a period of great toil and self-sacrifice, and a man of less heroic courage and persistency would have sunk under the heavy burdens which he bore through all these arduous years. The college was his idol, if he had any, and with unceasing effort he labored for its welfare. "Under his wise and efficient administration of its affairs," says Prof. Conant, "the college was provided with the necessary buildings, library, philosophical and chemical apparatus, and the foundation laid of permanent prosperity in the confidence and attachment of its numerous friends."

Dr. Chaplin resigned the presidency of the college in 1833. Freed now from the weighty cares and responsibilities which had pressed so heavily upon him for thirteen years, he entered once more upon the work he so much loved, that of preacher and pastor of a church of Christ. This service he performed in Rowley, Mass., and at Willington, Conn., for several years. He died at Hamilton, N. Y., May 7, 1841.

No one could be brought in contact with Dr. Chaplin without feeling that he was worthy of the universal respect which he inspired as a scholar, and especially as a profound theologian. The Hon. James Brooks, who was a student under him, says of him,—

"His discourses were as clear, as cogent, as irresistibly convincing as problems in Euclid. He indulged in little or no ornament, but pursued one train of thought without deviation to the end. I attribute to him more than to any one else the fixture in my own mind of religious truths which no subsequent reading has ever been able to shake, and which have principally influenced my pen in treating of all political, legal, or moral subjects, the basis of which was in the principles of the Bible." This is high praise from the accomplished editor of the New York *Evening Express*.

In an appreciative notice of his venerated teacher, Dr. Lamson thus speaks of him as a preacher:

"There were none of the graces of oratory about him. Nature had not formed him to exhibit them, and he was far enough from aiming to do it. The tones of his voice were so peculiar that the ear that once heard them would recognize them if heard the next time years afterwards and in the most distant land. His gestures were few and by no means varied. And yet, though it has been my privilege to listen to some of the most able and some of the most popular preachers in my own denomination and in others, I have seldom heard the man who could more closely confine my attention. I never heard a sermon from him which did not interest me. There was the greatest evidence of sincerity; the skeptics could not for a moment doubt that he was uttering the honest convictions of his own heart. There was nothing like dullness in his pulpit services. Though his voice was so little varied as to be monotonous, and the gestures were so few and so much alike, yet there was somehow imparted to the whole service an air of animation. The style was chaste, simple, suited to the subject, and remarkable, I should think, for its purity. His discourses were often enlivened by striking illustrations drawn most frequently from the commonest relations of life, and yet so presented as to fully sustain the dignity of the place and the subject. It is striking as showing the importance of this power of illustration in the preacher, that now, at this distance of time, I can recall some illustrations used by him, while every other portion of the sermons of which they are a part is irrevocably lost."

Chaplin, Jeremiah, Jr., D.D., was born in Danvers, Mass., March 22, 1813, and was a graduate of Waterville College in the class of 1833. He was settled in Bangor, Me., as pastor of the First Baptist church, his service there commencing in December, 1841. His subsequent settlements were in Norwalk, Conn., and Dedham and Newton, Mass. For quite a number of years he has devoted himself to authorship, and has written "Memorial Hour," "Life of President Dunster," "Life of Charles Sumner," "Life of Benjamin Franklin." He has also compiled "Riches of Bunyan," and has now in preparation a "Life of Galen." He has also written for the *Christian Review* and *Baptist Quarterly*, and for the leading Baptist papers of the North.

Dr. Chaplin received the degree of Doctor of Divinity from Colby University, of which he was a trustee from 1843 to 1849, in 1857. His present residence is in Boston.

Chaplin, John O'Brien, was born in Danvers, Mass., March 31, 1807. He was the eldest son of President Chaplin. He pursued his preparatory studies under the direction of students of Waterville College, where he graduated in 1825. He had charge of the Latin Preparatory School connected with the college not far from two years, when he was chosen tutor, and subsequently Professor of the Latin and English Languages and Literature, which office he held for one year. Upon the resignation of his father as president of the college, Prof. Chaplin also left Waterville, and accepted an appointment as Professor of Greek and Latin in Columbian College, D. C. His connection with the college continued for ten years, from 1833 to 1843, when ill health compelled him to resign. For several years he continued his residence in Washington, giving occasional instruction, as his strength permitted, in the college, with which he had been connected so many years. He came North about 1850, and made his home with his brother, Rev. A. J. Chaplin, and his brothers-in-law, Drs. B. F. Bronson and T. J. Conant. He was an invalid for several years, and was incapable of assuming much responsibility or performing much labor. Prof. Chaplin was a ripe, accomplished scholar. We are told that "a memory remarkably retentive to the last" made him ready master of his rich and varied learning. He is said to have been a most able and skillful critic of style; and his friends have deeply regretted that he did not leave to the world, as an essayist, some fruits of his remarkable knowledge and critical acumen. But, diffident in temperament, fastidious in taste, possessed by lofty ideals, abstracted in mind and enfeebled in body, his class-room instructions, his conversation, and private letters gave only to his personal friends and pupils evidence of his real intellectual capacity and power. And a life blameless, devout, and tenderly religious was clouded by a mental gloom which he inherited from his distinguished father, and which was greatly aggravated by disease. Prof. Chaplin died at Conway, Mass., Dec. 22, 1872.

Charlton, Rev. Frederick, was born in Connecticut in 1822; converted at the age of sixteen, and baptized at eighteen; he consecrated himself to the ministry; graduated at Madison University; was pastor three years at Webster, Mass., five years at Wilmington, Del., and then entered the service of the American Baptist Publication Society, in which he continued two years. In 1860 he removed to Sacramento, Cal., and was pastor of the church in that city until the time of his death, Aug. 9, 1871. He was a man of stern principle, courteous, generous, scholarly, and eloquent. His sermons were always thoroughly studied, and delivered without notes. His pastorates were all blessed with large revivals; and in his pastoral work he reaped the fruit by educating the converts to active church work. The church at Sacramento was one of the largest and most influential in California.

Chase, Irah, D.D., was born in Stratton, Vt., Oct. 5, 1793. His early years were spent on his father's farm, but he had no tastes for agricultural pursuits, and was, indeed, entirely unfitted for them, on account of the delicacy of his health. His love for learning early developed itself, and led to his preparation to enter upon a liberal course of study. In 1811 he became a member of the Sophomore class in Middlebury College, Vt. Among his classmates were the well-known missionaries of the American Board of Commissioners for Foreign Missions, Pliny Fisk and Levi Parsons, and the scholarly translator of Hengstenberg's "Christology." During his Junior year he gave his heart to Christ, and henceforth devoted himself to the advancement of his kingdom. Soon after leaving college he went to Andover, there being no theological seminary among the Baptists in which to pursue his studies. He was the only representative of his denomination in the institution, but he was always treated courteously. "My experience," he says, "was an exemplification of the possibility of much Christian communion, without communion in baptism and the Lord's Supper."

IRAH CHASE, D.D.

Having been ordained as an evangelist, he devoted some time to missionary work in Western Virginia. While thus occupied he was solicited by the Rev. Dr. Staughton to unite with him in opening a theological school in Philadelphia. When a transfer of this school was made to Washington, he went with it, and was connected with it for seven years. At the end of this period there seemed to be a call in Providence for him to remove to some other locality, and the cloud which, as he thought, led his footsteps, at last rested over Newton. Here he began his work Nov. 28, 1825. It was "the day of small things," and the foundations of what has come to be so noble and so useful an institution were laid with many prayers, and a faith which was "the substance of things hoped for, the evidence of things not seen." In those early days, however, there were a few friends, like Nathaniel R. Cobb and Levi Farwell, who pledged themselves, out of love to Christ and his cause, to stand by its fortunes so long as it was in their power to help forward its interests. The strong, long-cherished desire of Prof. Chase was to be a teacher of strictly Biblical theology,—to pursue a strictly Baconian method of ascertaining exactly what the Holy Scriptures teach, and from the knowledge thus obtained to construct his system of theology. Twenty years of his life were spent at Newton. How he toiled, what sacrifices he made, with what enthusiasm he engaged in his work; how careful and painstaking he was in learning the precise meaning of the Scriptures by the diligent study of the languages in which they were written; how he encouraged desponding students, and by his cheering words poured new life into many a depressed spirit; how his prayers and his benedictions followed the young men as they went forth from under the training of his careful hand to become the teachers of religion and the guides of the church,—these are things which only the revelations of eternity will disclose. The denomination owes to him a debt which it can never pay. He believed in a properly-educated ministry. It was his conviction that no denomination of Christians had a right to think it could get a strong hold on any intelligent community and retain that hold until it had in its ranks cultivated men, "apt to teach," and train up the disciples of Christ in knowledge and holy living. He did his part in securing for the Baptist churches such an order of men, and if we should mention the names of some of those who came under his instructions we should find them among the bright lights of the denomination.

On ending his relation with the Newton Theological Institution, Prof. Chase removed to Boston, and became a member of Dr. Sharp's church. It was here that the writer of this sketch was brought into intimate relations with him as his pastor. Often did he speak the word of encouragement to him when weighed down by the cares and burdens of a city minister's life.

Prof. Chase, by personal observation, made himself acquainted with the gifted men in the Old World whose lines of thought and study were in the direction of his own. He spent several months of the year 1823 at Halle and Leipsic. He also heard the lectures of distinguished professors at Göttingen. He studied out the history and the church polity of the Mennonites, by going directly to the sources of knowledge respecting that interesting class of Christians, and subsequently gave the results of his investigations in a published article on that subject. Whether working at home or abroad in his favorite profession, he spared no pains in obtaining information, and none in giving to the world fairly and truthfully the knowledge he had obtained. It would be a wonder indeed to find him making a loose and unreliable statement of any doctrine, or opinion, or fact which he had made a matter of special investigation. If Prof. Chase had not the magnetic power of Moses Stuart, who seemed to arouse and electrify his classes as if with the wand of a magician, and when thus excited would quite boldly assert as truth what afterwards he was compelled to modify, he had what, as a Biblical teacher, was better worth possessing, the will to investigate patiently, and the honesty to state exactly what he had discovered. In many respects he was a model teacher of theology, to a class of inquiring minds who were desirous of knowing with precision, what they were to communicate as teachers of God's Word from the sacred desk.

Prof. Chase's useful life closed amid the scenes he so much loved at Newton, Nov. 1, 1864. His remains were laid away in the beautiful cemetery of his village home.

Chase, Rev. Supply, was born in Guilford, Vt., Sept. 30, 1800. His parents removed soon after to Tully, Onondaga Co., N. Y., and here their son grew to manhood, eagerly desiring a better education than seemed within his reach, but studying as best he could. He taught school for several years, and had a special fondness for military life. At the age of thirty-one he was colonel of the 62d Regiment of New York State troops. He became a disciple of Christ in 1831, and was baptized July 3, in Tully. Immediately after joining the church he was summoned by its great Head to work in the gospel ministry, but he disregarded the call for several years. He preached for the first time March 1, 1835, and was ordained Nov. 10, 1835. In February following he was commissioned by the American Baptist Home Mission Society to preach in Pontiac, Mich., but reaching that place in May he found another man engaged as pastor, and therefore he turned to Mount Clemens. He was pastor successively in Mount Clemens, Mount Pleasant, Washington, Stony Creek, Romeo, Northville, and in the Second church, Detroit. Between the two pastorates last named he served the American Baptist Publication Society three years, and engaged in work as an evangelist three years. Since reaching the age of seventy-three years he has not been a pastor, but has been supplying destitute churches and laboring in protracted meetings. His residence is Detroit. During his ministry he has enjoyed many seasons of revival. He was one of the original members of the Baptist Convention of the State of Michigan.

Chaudoin, Rev. W. N.—William Nowell Chaudoin is of French descent on his father's side, being great-grandson of Francis Chaudoin, a Huguenot, who brought the name to this continent. His father and grandfather, and some of his more remote relatives, were Baptist ministers. Mr. Chaudoin was born in Robertson Co., Tenn., Aug. 10, 1829; was converted in his sixteenth year, and baptized by Rev. William F. Luck, in Davidson Co., Tenn. Two years after he commenced to preach, and was ordained by W. S. Baldry, W. D. Baldwin, and William Brumberlow, in Davidson

REV. W. N. CHAUDOIN.

County. While laboring in Nashville, Tenn., he contracted a cough that has baffled all efforts to cure. This led to his removal to the State of Georgia, in 1857, and also to his leaving the pastorate, in 1869, and entering as missionary agent, the service of the Home Mission Board, then called the Domestic Mission Board of the Southern Baptist Convention. In that capacity he has labored partly in Florida each year since 1872, and now his labors are nearly all in that State, as a missionary and as editor of the Florida department of the *Christian Index*, of Georgia.

Cheever, Daniel.—Sept. 1, 1858, Daniel Cheever died at Delavan, Ill., in the eighty-ninth year of his age. He was born at Wrentham, Mass., Dec. 20, 1769. Though educated a Congregationalist, he was led, upon his conversion at the age of nineteen, by personal study of the Scriptures to adopt Baptist views, and presenting himself to the North Attleborough Baptist church, he was received and baptized. He removed to Illinois in 1857, uniting with the Delavan Baptist church in Tazewell County, of which he remained a member until his death. For sixty-nine years he had walked with God as a faithful member of a Christian church.

Cheney, David Batchelder, D.D.—Since entering fully upon the active duties of the ministry in 1843, a period of thirty-seven years, Dr. Cheney has had a career of signal activity and usefulness. We regret that, as in other cases, only a brief outline of it can be given here. He was born in Southbridge, Mass., June 8, 1820, and spent his childhood and early youth upon his father's farm. He was baptized May 20, 1836, by the late Dr. J. G. Binney, to whom also in his earlier Christian life he was greatly indebted. Simultaneously with his conversion came the conviction that he must preach the gospel, and with this view he began a course of study, in prosecuting which he was dependent entirely upon such resources as he could command by efforts of his own. Under the strain his health began to suffer. After six years spent in the Worcester and Shelburne Falls Academies, and in Amherst College, he decided to prosecute what remained of needful study in connection with his ministerial work. He began preaching when only nineteen or twenty years of age, but was ordained at the age of about twenty-three, October, 1843, at Mansfield, Conn. His mind was already turned towards the West, so that he hardly considered himself a pastor at Mansfield, though he spent two fruitful years with that people: the house of worship was rebuilt, the congregation greatly increased, while the benevolent contributions of the church were enlarged some twentyfold. Near the close of the second year he was called to two open fields, but as his thoughts were still towards the West he hesitated to accept either. At length he decided for Greenville, a part of Norwich, Conn., where a church was to be organized and a house of worship built. A church was accordingly soon formed, with 100 members, and the new house built. A precious revival began before the house was complete, and upon the dedication of the new sanctuary the congregation so increased that very soon the house was filled from pulpit to door. Between 30 and 40 were baptized as the fruit of the revival.

The interest in Western work, however, remained unabated, and correspondence with the board in New York, and a visit to Columbus, O., resulting in a call from the church in the last-named city, with aid towards his support from the Home Mission treasury, he removed to Columbus in April, 1847. The pastorate here was a remarkable one.

The church as he found it numbered some 200 members, but was poor and heavily in debt. At the end of five and a half years the church had become one of the largest and most efficient in the State, its available financial strength having increased fifteen-fold. Three years of the period named were cholera years. Mr. Cheney remained at his post while, especially in the first of the three years, every other Protestant pastor left the city. His labors among the sick and the dying and in attendance upon funerals were constant. The first year was passed by himself and family in safety, but in the second his wife died of the terrible disease, and himself and two children were attacked and barely escaped with life. The result was broken health, and the assurance on the part of his physicians that a change of residence had become imperative. A second attack of cholera left no alternative, and accepting one of the various calls which he had before him, he removed to Philadelphia and became pastor of the Eleventh Baptist church in that city, entering upon his duties there Nov. 15, 1852. Here he remained until 1859. Three of the seven years were blessed by an almost constant revival of religion. While here, also, the marked executive ability which he was known to possess led to the offer successively of the secretaryship of the Missionary Union, the American and Foreign Bible Society, the Home Mission Society, and the Publication Society. The last was offered him in the year 1856, the post having fallen vacant in the middle of the year; he served for the latter half of the year, writing the Annual Report, but, declining further service, surrendered the place to the present able secretary, whom he had the pleasure of introducing to the office he has filled so long and so successfully. While in Philadelphia, also, he took a leading part in the work of ministerial education, being made secretary of the Pennsylvania Education Society soon after his residence in the State began, and continuing in that office till his removal to San Francisco, in July, 1859.

In San Francisco Mr. Cheney remained eight years. He then returned East, accepting the pastorate of the Central Square church in Boston. His pastorate here had a duration of three years and a half. He found a church of 267 members, and left it with one of 484, 233 of the additions having been by baptism. The house of worship, which had been destroyed by fire, was also in the mean time rebuilt. During the last two years of his stay in Boston Mr. Cheney served on the Executive Committee of the Missionary Union. In April, 1874, he removed to Chicago, as pastor of the Fourth church, formed by the union of the Ashland Avenue and Union Park churches. This union, consummated as the result of his coming, restored strength where there had been feebleness, and inaugurated a pastorate of great value not only to the church but to the denomination. After some four years of service here he accepted the call of the First Baptist church in Elgin, Ill., where he is still the useful and valued pastor.

Mr. Cheney has served upon boards of trustees, missionary and educational, during many years. While in Ohio he was one of the trustees of Granville University; in California, of the State University, the presidency of which was also offered him. In Illinois, almost from the time of his arrival in the State, he has been called to similar service on the boards of the theological seminary and the university at Chicago. The boards of home and foreign missions, and others, have also had his service. In these positions he never fails to take a leading part, and to command for his opinions and measures the confidence of his associates.

Chessman, Rev. Daniel, was born in Boston, July 15, 1787, and was baptized by Rev. Dr. Baldwin, Oct. 30, 1803. Believing himself called of God to preach the gospel, he entered Brown University in 1807 to prepare himself for his future work. While pursuing his studies he was not idle in his Master's cause. In connection with two or three other students he laid the foundations of what, until recently, was the Third Baptist church in Providence, now a constituent part of the Union church. He graduated in 1811. For a short time he was inclined to study law, but prayerful consideration brought him to the conclusion that in the ministry he could best glorify God and benefit the souls of his fellow-men. He was licensed by his church July 5, 1812, and not long after was ordained and settled as pastor of the church in Warren, R. I., where he remained two years, and then accepted a call to Hallowell, Me. Here he was pastor for nine years. From Hallowell he went to Lynn, Mass., where he spent four years, and then became pastor of the church in Barnstable, Mass., where he died May 21, 1839.

Mr. Chessman was a much more than ordinary preacher. Easy and graceful in his manner, with a ready utterance, and sincere interest in his work, he commanded and secured the love and respect of the churches and congregations to which he ministered.

Chicago, Baptist Churches in.—Near the end of May, in the year 1867, at the annual meeting for that year of the Home Mission Society of the Baptist denomination of the United States, held in Chicago, the president of the society, Hon. J. M. Hoyt, of Cleveland, in his opening address, said, "In September, 1833, the Pottawattomies, 7000 strong, were assembled here where we are now convened. Here they deliberated, and finally, through the agency of their chiefs, formally ceded the territory of Illinois and the site of the city of Chicago to the United States government. Having done this they passed on to the Mississippi. Immediately the American Baptist Home Mission Society detailed a *Freeman* (Rev. Allen B. Freeman) to stand as sentinel at this post."

The attention of the secretary of the society, Dr. Jonathan Going, had been called to this point in a letter to Rev. C. G. Sommers, of New York, by Dr. John T. Temple, then a resident here, and a member of the Baptist denomination. "We have no servant of the Lord Jesus Christ," writes Dr. Temple, "to proclaim the glad tidings of salvation. I write to beg you will see Dr. Going, and ask that a young man of first-rate talent, whose whole heart is in the cause of Christ, may be sent out immediately, before the ground shall be occupied by some other organization. I will myself become responsible for $200 per annum for such a missionary." This passage in Dr. Temple's letter was sent by Dr. Going to Allen B. Freeman, a young man who was then just finishing his studies at what is now Madison University, in Hamilton, N. Y. Mr. Freeman was the son of Rev. Rufus B. Freeman, an esteemed Baptist minister of Central New York, described to Dr. Temple by Dr. Going as "a talented, pious, and efficient man." Such he proved himself to be even in the brief period of the ministry performed by him as a missionary of the society at Chicago. He arrived at Chicago in August, 1833, finding a home with Dr. Temple, and entering at once upon earnest and diligent labor, not only in preaching, but "from house to house." Measures were almost immediately taken for the erection of a house of worship. "It was," says Cyrus Bentley, Esq., in his "History of the First Baptist Church," "an humble edifice, designed both as a place of religious worship and as a school-house, and cost when completed the sum of $600, $150 of which was in arrears, and remained as a debt upon the property."

Oct. 19, 1833, a church of 15 members was organized,—the First Baptist church of Chicago and the first Baptist church in the whole northwestern region north of Peoria, save one, the church at Plainfield having come into existence a few months earlier.

Mr. Freeman continued in service only one year and a half. In December, 1834, while upon one of his itinerating tours, having administered the rite of baptism at Bristol, in the Fox River, as he was returning homeward his horse gave out, and much of the journey had to be made on foot, amidst inclement weather and great exposure. The consequence was a fever, of which he died Dec. 15, 1834. His last words were, "Tell my revered father that I die at my post and in my Master's work."

These were the beginnings of Baptist history in Chicago. Subsequent events must be noticed less in detail. Mr. Freeman was succeeded, in 1835, by Rev. I. T. Hinton. After him came Rev. C. B. Smith, in 1842. In 1843, Rev. E. H. Hamlin became pastor, and in October, 1845, Rev. Miles Sanford. After some two years of service he also resigned, and for fourteen months following Rev. Luther Stone, editor of the *Watchman of the Prairies*, served as acting pastor. In September, 1848, Rev. Elisha Tucker, D.D., became pastor, continuing in service until 1851, when he resigned, the pulpit remaining vacant until October, 1852, when Rev. John C. Burroughs became pastor. Almost immediately upon the commencement of his labors the house of worship, which had been built in 1843, under the pastorate of Rev. E. H. Hamlin, was burned. Measures were taken at once for the rebuilding; the corner-stone was laid July 4, 1853, and the house dedicated November 12 following. In 1856, Mr. Burroughs resigned, and Dr. W. G. Howard, of Rochester, was called to the pastorate. He was succeeded, in 1859, by Dr. W. W. Everts; and he, in 1879, by Dr. Geo. C. Lorimer, the present pastor.

The second Baptist church in order of time in Chicago was the Tabernacle church, composed of 32 members of the First church, who left that body in 1842, and organized upon the west side of the river. This church was served by successive pastors, among others Rev. Lewis Raymond, Rev. Archibald Kenyon, Rev. J. E. Kenney, and Rev. Nathaniel Calver, D.D., until the year 1864, when an important change took place, affecting favorably the situation of all the Baptist churches in the city. In that year the First church sold its property at the corner of La Salle and Washington Streets to the Chamber of Commerce, receiving for it the sum of $65,000. Of this sum such a use was made as should be helpful to the other churches of the city. The house, built, as we have said, in 1853, was given to such members of the church as should unite with the Tabernacle church upon the west side of the river, with a location more favorable, the resulting organization to be called the Second Baptist church of Chicago. It was accordingly taken down, removed to the west side, and there re-erected at the corner of Morgan and Monroe Streets. In the union of the Tabernacle church with members of the First church living on the west side of the river a strong, efficient church was formed. The removal and rebuilding of the house cost some $20,000. Rev. E. J. Goodspeed, of Janesville, was called to the pastorate, and years of signal Christian activity, growth, and prosperity followed. Dr. Goodspeed, in the later years of his

FIRST BAPTIST CHURCH, CHICAGO.

pastorate, was assisted by his brother, Rev. T. W. Goodspeed. Upon the termination of their joint pastorate, occasioned by the failing health of the senior pastor, Dr. Galusha Anderson, of Brooklyn, was called. He was succeeded by Dr. John Peddie, of Philadelphia. Dr. Peddie having accepted a call to the pastorate of the First Baptist church in New York City, was succeeded by the Rev. W. M. Lawrence, of Philadelphia.

The third Baptist church in order of time in Chicago was the Edina Place, organized by members of the First church, by whom a house of worship was built at the corner of Edina Place and Harrison Street. Rev. Robert Boyd was called as the first pastor. Under his remarkable ministry the church enjoyed great prosperity. A better location was found for it in due time at the corner of Wabash Avenue and Eighteenth Street; subsequently it removed to Michigan Avenue and Twenty-third Street, erecting there a fine house of worship and changing its name to the Michigan Avenue Baptist church. The successive pastors have been Robert Boyd, D.D., E. G. Taylor, D.D., Samuel Baker, D.D., Jesse B. Thomas, D.D., Rev. F. M. Ellis, J. W. Custis, D.D., and Rev. James Patterson. Rev. K. B. Tupper is the acting pastor at present.

Union Park Baptist church was the fourth in order of date organized in Chicago. This took place in September, 1856, the location chosen being near Union Park. Rev. A. J. Joslyn was the first pastor. After him came Rev. J. S. Mahan, E. G. Taylor, D.D., Rev. Florence McCarthy, D. B. Cheney, D.D., and E. B. Hulbert, D.D., the last named being still in service. The house of worship now occupied—the second built by the church in the course of its history—stands at the corner of West Washington and Paulina Streets. The name of the church has been changed to the Fourth Baptist church of Chicago.

In November, 1857, the North Baptist church was organized, under the ministry of Rev. J. A. Smith, of the *Standard*. The place of meeting was at first the lecture-room of Rush Medical College, on the north side of the river. In the following spring and summer a house of worship was built at the corner of Ohio and Dearborn Streets. The church having become sufficiently strong to sustain a pastor, Mr. Smith resigned, and Dr. S. W. Lynd was called. He was succeeded by Rev. A. H. Strong, now president of the Rochester Theological Seminary, and he by Rev. A. A. Kendrick, now president of Shurtleff College. Mr. Kendrick was succeeded by Reuben Jeffrey, D.D., and he by Rev. O. T. Walker. In the great fire of 1871 the house of worship of the church—a new edifice upon Chicago Avenue, purchased from a Unitarian church—was destroyed, and the organization broken up. The ground it had held remained mostly unoccupied until the organization of the Central church by Rev. E. O. Taylor in 1877. This prosperous society may be regarded as the successor of the North church, and as continuing its history.

The North Star Baptist church is also upon the north side of the river, at the corner of Division and Sedgwick Streets. It began as a mission of the First church, established in 1860. A property was there acquired at a cost of some $30,000, consisting of a chapel and parsonage. These were destroyed by the fire of 1871, but rebuilt, through the efforts of Dr. Everts. The mission became a church in 1870, Rev. Geo. L. Wrenn being its first pastor. After a service of five years he was succeeded by Rev. E. R. Pierce. After him came Rev. J. M. Whitehead, who was succeeded by Rev. R. P. Allison, and he by Rev. Joseph Rowley, the present pastor.

The Indiana Avenue Baptist church, at the corner of Indiana Avenue and Thirtieth Street, in the south part of the city, was organized in 1864. It grew out of a mission founded there by the First church in 1863, a neat house of worship being erected in that year upon lots donated for the purpose. The organization of a church occurred in the year following. J. A. Smith, D.D., served as pastor five years. He was followed by M. S. Riddle, D.D., to whom succeeded Rev. F. D. Rickerson, followed by Rev. W. W. Everts, Jr. Upon the removal of the First church to the corner of South Park Avenue and Thirty-first Street, in 1875, the Indiana Avenue church was dissolved, and its members united with the First church.

Near the close of 1868 the University Place church was organized in the chapel of the university, being composed of members of the Indiana Avenue and First churches living in that vicinity. J. A. Smith, D.D., served as the first pastor, being followed by Wm. Hague, D.D., who was succeeded as acting pastor by J. B. Jackson, D.D., and he by Rev. A. J. Frost, now of California. A. Owen, D.D., came next, who was succeeded by Rev. J. T. Burhoe, the present pastor. The house of worship built by the church stands on Thirty-fifth Street near Rhodes Avenue.

The Western Avenue church, on the west side of the river, was organized in 1869. Its first pastor, Rev. John Gordon, was signally successful in building up the church to a strong and independent position. The present pastor, Rev. C. Perrin, is also much prospered in his work. Other churches in the vicinity are the Centennial, organized in 1875; Coventry Street, 1870; South church, 1867; Central, 1877; Olivet (colored), 1853; Providence (colored), 1871; Dearborn Street, 1875; Twenty-fifth Street; with a Danish, a Swedish, and a German. Mention should also be made of the Tabernacle, conducted by Mr. B. F. Jacobs, and various missions in different parts of the city, sustained by the several churches.

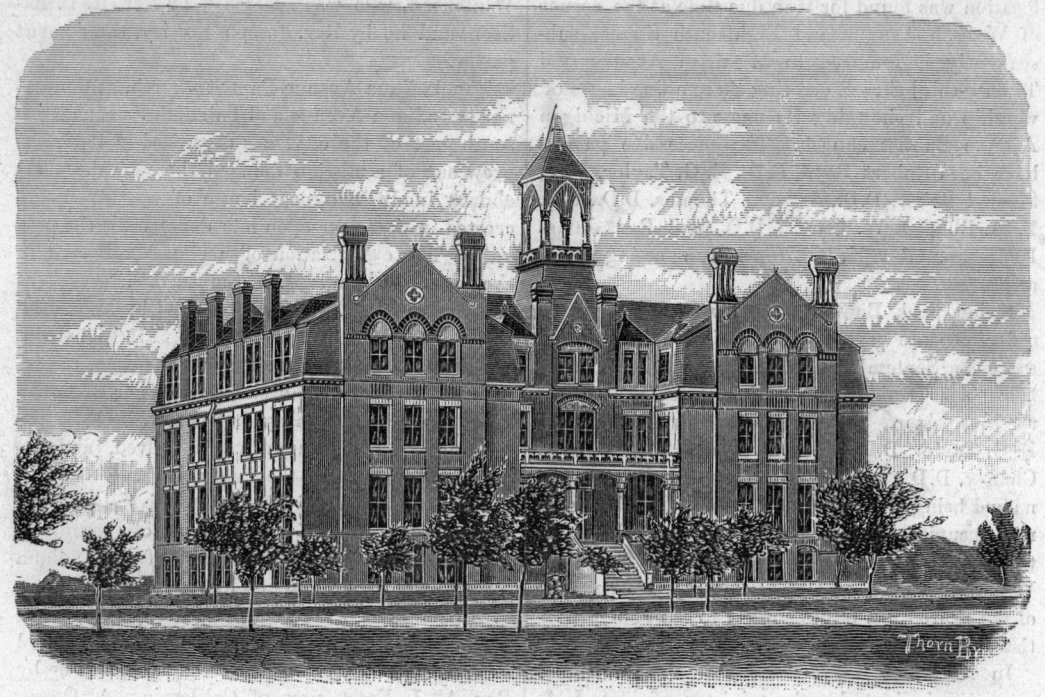

Chicago, Baptist Union Theological Seminary at.—About the year 1860 a conviction had become quite general in various parts of the Northwestern States that provision should be made at some suitable point west of the lakes for distinctively theological education. The University of Chicago had been recently established, and was already giving promise of permanent growth and power. Colleges of considerably older date existed in other parts of the West, and were acquiring financial independence and literary reputation. For theological education, however, the West was wholly dependent upon the East. It was felt that an institution more easily accessible, and in which the Western ministry could have a Western theological training, was becoming indispensable. In the year 1859 a convention of delegates representing the denomination in several Northwestern States was held at Chicago for the consideration of this subject. No result was reached, further than to make it clear that while a conviction of the need referred to was unanimous, there were decided, and possibly irreconcilable differences of opinion as to the point at which to locate the proposed theological seminary, should one be decided upon.

In view of these facts, a few brethren in Chicago decided to take the responsibility of an initiative; influenced by the persuasion that the true theological centre for the Northwest, as also its commercial and literary centre, is at Chicago, and also that if they were right in this, they must be equally justified in their confidence that, planted thus at the true centre, the institution would make its own way. Accordingly a meeting was called by the three brethren who decided to assume this responsibility, viz., W. W. Everts, J. B. Olcott, and J. A. Smith, to be held at the First Baptist church in Chicago. This took place in the year 1860. But few were present, yet it was decided there to organize the Baptist Theological Union for the Northwest, which was accordingly done. Officers were chosen, and a committee appointed to report a constitution at a meeting to be held in the following year. At the meeting in 1861 other members were received, and further preliminary steps taken. The organization, however, was not perfected until the meeting held Aug. 13, 1863. A constitution was then adopted and officers chosen; Hon. Richard S. Thomas being made President, Rev. Luther Stone, Secretary, and Edward Goodman, Esq., Treasurer. The charter of incorporation was given, by act of the Illinois Legislature, Feb. 16, 1865.

As appears by this recital, the steps of progress were slow. Care was exercised that no measure should be premature; that the enterprise should rest, for its growth, upon an increasing conviction of its necessity in the denomination to which it must look for the means of success. Strenuous effort was made, also, at this time in behalf of the

CHICAGO BAPTIST UNION THEOLOGICAL SEMINARY.

university endowment, and it was judged unwise to bring forward another claimant to the liberality of our people in a way that might embarrass both undertakings. No more, accordingly, was attempted than simply to hold the enterprise in such a state of forwardness as would facilitate more direct and energetic effort when the time for it should come. In the mean time theological instruction was commenced, under a temporary arrangement, first by Dr. Nathaniel Colver, as Professor of Doctrinal Theology, and in 1866 by Dr. Colver and Prof. J. C. C. Clarke, who organized at the university theological classes, numbering in all about a dozen students. The expenses of this service were met chiefly by personal friends of Dr. Colver at the East,—W. W. Cook, Esq., of Whitehall, N. Y., and Messrs. Barnes and Davis, of Burlington, Vt.

In the autumn of 1866 a faculty was organized by the election of Rev. G. W. Northrup, D.D., then Professor of Ecclesiastical History in the Rochester Theological Seminary, as president, and Professor of Christian Theology, and of Rev. J. B. Jackson, pastor of the Baptist church in Albion, N. Y., as Professor of Ecclesiastical History. Dr. Colver became president of the Freedmen's Institute at Richmond, Va., and Prof. Clarke entered the pastorate. More direct effort was now made for the raising of funds. Generous friends in Chicago and elsewhere came forward with donations in sums ranging from $1000 to $5000, and the enterprise was vigorously pressed. In September, 1867, Rev. G. W. Warren, A.M., of Boston, was elected Professor of Hebrew and Exegesis, and on October 2 of that year the work of instruction under the new organization began. In the year 1867–68, 20 students were in attendance, 2 in the middle class, 18 in the Junior. Rev. G. S. Bailey, D.D., at the time of the organization of the new faculty, was chosen corresponding and financial secretary, and, aided by Rev. Thos. Allen and Rev. Wm. M. Haigh, prosecuted with energy and success the work of raising funds. In 1868, lots of land having been secured near the university, the erection of a building was commenced, and the edifice was completed and dedicated July 1, 1869. It was built of brick, 214 feet in length, 48 feet wide, and 4 stories high. The cost was $60,000. Of this sum $30,000 remained as a debt, in bonds secured upon the property. The number of students had now increased to 25, three of whom graduated that year. The assets of the seminary at this point in its history were reported at $144,000; its liabilities, including bonds and indebtedness for the ground on which the buildings stood, and otherwise, at $54,266. Of these assets, $80,000 were in buildings and grounds, $11,250 in other real estate, and the remainder in notes and subscriptions.

At the date last given, July 1, 1869, the connection of Prof. Warren with the seminary was terminated, and Prof. A. N. Arnold, D.D., of the Theological Seminary at Hamilton, N. Y., was made Professor of Biblical Literature and Exegesis, and Rev. Wm. Hague, D.D., Professor of Homiletics and Pastoral Duties. For the year 1869–70 the number of students had increased to 40. In this year, also, the library of Dr. Hengstenberg, of Berlin, Prussia, consisting of 13,000 volumes, was purchased through the liberality of friends of the seminary and university. It is a remarkably rich collection, especially in patristic and mediæval literature, and in works by foreign authors of later date. In September, 1870, Prof. Jackson resigned, and soon after, Dr. Hague, being obliged by his wife's state of health to return East, also resigned. Prof. E. C. Mitchell, D.D., of Shurtleff College, was elected Professor of Hebrew and Old Testament Literature, and R. E. Pattison, D.D., Professor of Biblical Interpretation and History of Doctrines.

The Scandinavian department in the seminary was organized in 1873 under the instruction of Prof. J. A. Edgren. It has from year to year more and more proved itself an important feature of the institution. As the only department of the kind in this country, and as providing an educated ministry for a large and increasing Scandinavian population in the Northwestern States, it is entitled to special consideration.

In 1874, Rev. T. J. Morgan, president of the State Normal School of Nebraska, was elected Professor of Homiletics, continuing in that chair until 1879, when he was transferred to that of Church History. In the same year, 1874, W. W. Everts, Jr., was elected Assistant Professor of Church History, but left at the end of the year to enter the pastorate. Dr. Pattison's connection with the faculty terminated at his death, Nov. 21, 1874. In 1875, Dr. Bailey resigned his secretaryship, and in 1876, Rev. T. W. Goodspeed was chosen to the same office, which he still holds. In 1877, Prof. J. R. Boise, Ph.D., LL.D., of the university, was elected to fill the place of Dr. Arnold, who had been compelled by failure of health to resign.

Dr. Mitchell also retired from the service of the seminary, his place in the chair of Hebrew being filled for one year by Prof. B. Maimon. Prof. W. R. Harper was then chosen to the chair, which he now occupies.

The faculty now stands: G. W. Northrup, D.D., President and Professor of Systematic Theology; J. R. Boise, Ph.D., D.D., LL.D., Professor of New Testament Exegesis and Literature; T. J. Morgan, D.D., Professor of Church History; W. R. Harper, Ph.D., Professor of Hebrew and Old Testament Literature; J. A. Edgren, D.D., Professor in the

Scandinavian department; Galusha Anderson, D.D., Special Lecturer on Homiletics and Pastoral Duties; J. A. Smith, D.D., Special Lecturer on Modern Church History, Origin of Religions, and Philosophy.

The removal of the seminary to Morgan Park in 1877 was a measure of great importance. It secures by this means a valuable site and building, with other real estate adjoining, mostly by donation, and at the same time it is sufficiently near the city to answer all the most needful ends of a city location. It graduated 26 in the class of 1880, raising its whole number of graduates during the history of the seminary to 338.

Chicago, University of.—About the year 1856 it was ascertained that Senator Stephen A. Douglas had made proposals to donate the site for a university upon lands owned by him in Cottage Grove, a little south of what was then the southern limit of the city. Learning this fact, and having reason to believe that Mr. Douglas would prefer that the proposed university should be founded under denominational auspices, as also that out of regard for the memory of his deceased wife, who was a Baptist, his choice among the denominations would be that to which she had belonged, Rev. J. C. Burroughs, at that time pastor of the First Baptist church, decided to visit Mr. Douglas and secure the proposed site for a university to be under Baptist control. He found the views of Mr. Douglas to be as had been represented. After a full consultation upon the subject, with especial reference to the character that should be given to the university, and the relations to it of the Baptist denomination, the desired arrangement was effected. Mr. Douglas gave to Mr. Burroughs, in trust for the purpose named, a deed of gift of ten acres of land in Cottage Grove, located near the lake, and fronting upon Cottage Grove Avenue. The terms of the deed provided that upon this ground a building to cost not less than $100,000 should be erected within a specified time, upon the completion of which a deed of the property should be given to the board of trustees, for the creation of which provision was made in the deed of gift; that the property as so deeded should be forever secured to the Baptist denomination for the uses of a university, and not to be alienated for any purpose whatever; that while denominational in the sense of being under the general care of the Baptist denomination, the university should be for purposes of general education only, while, save that the president and a majority of the trustees must always be Baptists, its board and faculty should be open to representation on the part of all denominations, as well as to those of none; and that no sectarian tests of any kind should ever be introduced.

The deed of gift thus conditioned was accepted by Mr. Burroughs, who immediately proceeded to secure the necessary organization and charter. This was speedily effected, and the university regularly incorporated by act of the Legislature under the name of the University of Chicago. Mr. Douglas was himself the first president of the board. Resigning his pastorate, Mr. Burroughs now applied himself to the work of raising necessary funds. Calling to his aid Rev. J. B. Olcott, an experienced agent, he, with his aid, prosecuted the effort with so much energy that by Oct. 1, 1856, he could report that the sum of $100,000 had been secured in the city of Chicago alone in subscriptions and pledges, while in the country the enterprise was viewed with similar favor. When, in September, 1858, the grammar school of the university was opened and the work of instruction begun, the pledges had amounted to above $200,000 in city and country. In the mean time, steps had been taken for the erection of a building suited to the present needs of the university. As it was found impracticable while providing for other needs of the enterprise to expend so large a sum as $100,000 upon the building at once, Mr. Douglas consented to waive this condition in his grant of the site, and gave to the trustees a deed to the property. The corner-stone of the building, which in the general plan of the edifice is in the south wing, was laid July 4, 1857, addresses on the occasion being made by Mr. Douglas, Hon. I. N. Arnold, Rev. Robert Boyd, Rev. A. J. Joslyn, Rev. W. G. Howard, D.D., and others. The grammar school, pending the completion of this building, occupied a room in St. Paul's Universalist church, on Wabash Avenue. The principal was Prof. L. R. Satterlee, of Rochester, who was also Professor of the English Language and Literature. Prof. A. H. Mixer, also of Rochester, was Professor of Modern Languages. For the time, however, these gentlemen gave instruction in all the studies of a college preparatory course.

From the beginning it was the wish of the trustees that Mr. Burroughs should be the president of the new university. His own preference was that the office should be given to some one with a reputation already national as an educator. He endeavored to secure, with this view, Dr. Francis Wayland and others, but failing in this effort, he finally accepted the presidency, which the board meantime had not ceased to urge upon him. He held the office for some fifteen years, from 1858 to 1873. They were years of vicissitude, not only in the affairs of the university but in those of the city and the whole country. In about two years after the opening of the university came the war of the Rebellion. Following upon this were financial reverses, the disasters of two great fires in the city, with other similar causes seriously affecting all in-choate enterprises, in the West especially. The university was a sufferer to such an extent that only a small percentage of the large subscription noticed above, with others additional procured later, could be collected. Meantime, as the university grew expenses enlarged; additions to the building, making it what it now is, became necessary; an increased faculty was indispensable. The result was loans and arrearages eventuating in a cumbersome and threatening debt. The oversight of finances in these circumstances seemed in Dr. Burroughs's view to fall to himself as a duty, while the association of such growing complications with the usual cares and labors of a college presidency, made his task one of extreme difficulty. He had associated with him, however, able men and enthusiastic teachers: in the Greek department, first Prof. A. H. Mixer, afterwards Prof. J. R. Boise; in Latin, Prof. J. W. Stearns, subsequently Prof. J. C. Freeman; in Mathematics, Prof. A. J. Sawyer, till succeeded by Prof. A. J. Howe; in Astronomy, Prof. Safford; in Natural Sciences, Prof. McChesney, and subsequently Profs. Dexter and Wheeler. The university under his administration and the instruction of this faculty, achieved a highly creditable literary reputation, and even when most oppressed with financial embarrassment ranked in the real value of its work with the best colleges. In this connection should be mentioned the highly important service rendered to the university by Dr. W. W. Everts, especially in procuring, jointly with Prof. Mixer, the endowment of the Greek chair, amounting to nearly $25,000; which, however, we are sorry to say, was in the subsequent difficulties of the university absorbed.

The limits necessarily assigned to this sketch compel the omission of many details. In 1873 it was thought best to make some changes in the administration of the university. With this view an act of the Legislature was procured empowering the board to create the office of chancellor. Dr. Burroughs, resigning the presidency, was elected to this office, and Rev. Lemuel Moss, D.D., to that of president. This arrangement, however, continued only for one year, Dr. Moss then becoming president of the Indiana State University. After the interval of a year, Hon. Alonzo Abernethy, Superintendent of Public Instruction in the State of Iowa, and who had been educated at the university, was chosen president. After some two years President Abernethy resigned, and Dr. Galusha Anderson was elected to the office, which he still holds.

The faculty of the university at present is Dr. Galusha Anderson, President; Edward Olson, Professor of the Greek Language and Literature; D. A. Stuart, Professor of the Latin Language and Literature; J. H. Sanford, Professor of Rhetoric and Belles-Lettres; A. J. Howe, Professor of Mathematics; E. S. Bastin, Professor of Botany; Ransom Dexter, Professor of Zoology, Physiology, and Anatomy; C. Gilbert Wheeler, Professor of Chemistry.

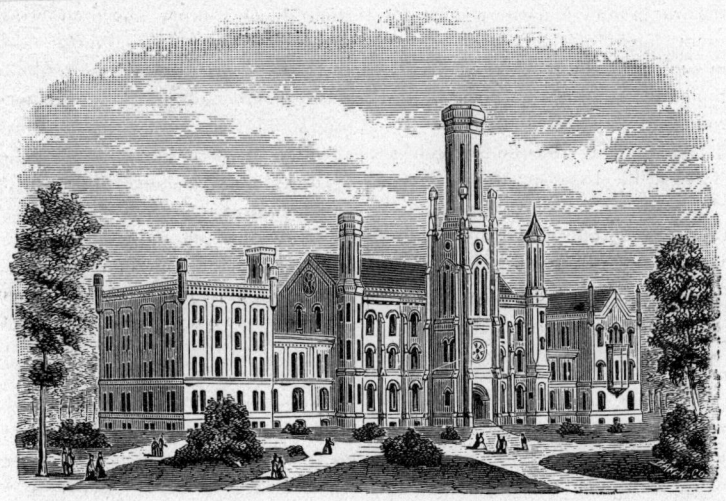

Child, William Chauncy, D.D., was born in Johnstown, N. Y., in August, 1817, and was a graduate of Union College in the class of 1840, and of the Newton Theological Institution in the class of 1844. He was ordained at Charlestown, Mass., Oct. 30, 1844, and was pastor of the First Baptist church in that city six years,—1844–50,—and subsequently pastor of the church in Framingham, Mass., eight years,—1851–59. In 1861 he was chosen district secretary of the American Tract Society, of Boston, which position he held for eight years,—

1861–69. Soon after retiring from this office he was elected district secretary of the American Baptist Publication Society, and was in office until 1873. He occupied during the latter years of his life a responsible position on the editorial staff of *The Watchman and Reflector*. He died suddenly at Boston, Jan. 14, 1876.

Chilton, Hon. Thomas, was born in Garrard Co., Ky., July 30, 1798; educated at Paris, Ky.; studied and practiced law at Owingsville, Bath County; elected to the Legislature of Kentucky in 1819, and served several sessions; was a member of Congress from Kentucky during the Presidency of Gen. Jackson four terms; removed to Alabama, where he practiced law with signal success. He was converted, and commenced preaching before he left Kentucky; was pastor of Hopkinsville church. In 1841 he was elected president of the Alabama Baptist State Convention, and shortly afterwards abandoned the practice of law; became general agent of the Alabama Convention, and then succeeded Dr. W. Carey Crane as pastor of Montgomery church in 1842; was pastor also of Greenborough and Newbern churches. Removed to Texas, served the Houston church as pastor, and died Aug. 15, 1854, at Montgomery, Texas.

He was a man of strong reasoning powers, fine delivery, and commanding influence. He was no ordinary thinker. His descendants hold prominent places in Texas society.

Chilton, Rev. Thomas John, a pioneer preacher among the Separate Baptists of Kentucky, was born about the year 1769, most probably in Virginia. He was taken to Kentucky in his childhood. At the age of about twenty years he professed conversion, and united with a Separate Baptist church in Lincoln County, and soon afterwards was set apart to the ministry. In 1801 he wrote the "Terms of General Union," upon which all the Baptists of Kentucky were united under the name of *United Baptists*. In 1803 he adhered to a faction drawn off from the General Union by John Bailey. Of this faction, which assumed the name of South Kentucky Association of Separate Baptists, Mr. Chilton was the principal leader until No-Lynn Association was formed, when he moved from Lincoln to Hardin County, in 1822, and became the principal preacher in that body of Separate Baptists. In 1835 he published a small volume in vindication of his Association and its peculiar tenets. Soon after this he moved to Christian County, and joined the United Baptists. He died an able and honored minister of Christ in 1840.

Chilton, Hon. William P., was born in Kentucky. In 1834, when quite a young man, he emigrated to Talladega, Ala., prior to the removal of the Creek Indians west of the Mississippi, and began the practice of law. At that time, among a frontier population, in a nascent condition, strong will, wise intellect, and steady principles were required for leadership. Chilton had the needed qualifications,—tall and commanding in person, graceful and courteous in manners, fluent in speech, unswerving in integrity, he exerted an educatory influence on a population heterogeneous in character and origin, eager in the pursuit of wealth, and unembarrassed by the restraints of a stable civilization. A county distinguished since for intelligence, patriotism, and a large number of able men contributed to the bar and to politics, owes much to what Chilton did in that formative period.

An active politician and an effective popular speaker, he was, in 1839, elected to the Legislature, and took rank at once as an able debater, discreet in counsel, and never negligent of the details of business. In 1859 he was elected to the senate from Macon County, and his rare abilities and ripe experience made him a most valuable legislator. During the brief life of the Confederate States he was a member of the Congress, serving on important committees, and enjoying the confidence and affection of his fellow-members.

In 1848 he was elected to the Supreme Court, and served as justice, or chief justice, for ten years, showing untiring industry, hatred of wrong, and marked love for the true and the right.

On Jan. 20, 1871, he died. Unusual honors were paid to his memory by the governor, the Legislature, the bar, and the Masonic fraternity, of which he was grand master and high-priest.

Judge Chilton was converted and baptized at an early age, and as a successful lawyer, bold politician, and an honored judge kept his garments unspotted; generous to a fault, he was also a consistent church member, a faithful deacon, a diligent student of the Bible, and a help to his various pastors.

China, Mission to.—In the report of the board of the Triennial Convention for the year ending April, 1834, we find the following: "In regard to China, the board are deeply desirous to fix upon the best method of reaching and benefitting its vast population, and they have accordingly instructed Mr. Jones to make the requisite investigations and communicate his views without delay. It is confidently believed that the time is come when God will bless with success a judicious, persevering attempt to give to the crowded millions of that great empire the glorious gospel." Acting on these instructions, Mr. Jones on reaching Bangkok, in Siam, sought out such Chinese as he could find in that city, and preached to them the gospel. The next step in this movement to reach the Chinese was the appointment of Rev. W. Dean, who has now become a veteran in the service, as the first special missionary in Bangkok to do what he could for the evangelization of the multitudes of the Chinese who had taken up their abode in that city. Macao, which Rev. J. L. Shuck occupied in 1836, was the second point selected for the missionary purposes which were contemplated. Following the chronological order of the establishment of the missions among the Chinese we speak:

1. Of the mission among the Chinese residing either temporarily or permanently in Siam, particularly in Bangkok. For eight years Messrs. Dean and Shuck remained at their respective stations. Mr. Dean labored in Bangkok, with special reference to the spiritual wants of the Chinese. He preached to them, and prepared religious reading for them, performing that sort of preparatory work which must be done at the commencement of a new mission. Mr. Goddard joined Mr. Dean at the close of 1840. In 1842, by the treaty between China and England, Hong-Kong was ceded to England, and Mr. Dean repaired to this island, and, in connection with Mr. Shuck, established a station in the principal city of Hong-Kong, Victoria by name. Up to this time, the whole number of Chinese baptized in Bangkok had been 18. The departure of Mr. Dean did not suspend all efforts for the spiritual good of those for whom he had labored for so many years. In 1846, more than 40,000 pages of religious reading were printed for their use. In 1850, Dr. Jones was chosen pastor of the Chinese church, which numbered 35. Not much visible progress was made for several years. In 1860, we find that 20 Chinese were baptized. In 1861, the Siamese and China departments, which for some time had been united, were separated, and in 1865 Dr. Dean returned to his former field of labor, and a new impulse was given to the work. During the year 1867, 40 persons were baptized in Bangkok and the outlying stations. Under the administration of Dr. Dean, the history of the Bangkok Chinese mission has been one of continued success. The last report gives us 6 churches with 425 members.

2. The mission in Eastern China. Dr. D. J. Macgowan, in the autumn of 1843, went to Ningpo, one of the five ports opened to the English, and established a mission hospital, which was in operation for three months, and reopened the next spring. Rev. E. C. Lord arrived in Ningpo, June 20, 1847, to engage in special missionary work among the Chinese. Dr. Macgowan acted as his interpreter while preaching until he was able to use the language himself. Mr. Goddard joined Mr. Lord in 1848. For several years affairs at Ningpo went on with a good degree of prosperity. A convenient chapel was opened for religious worship Sept. 26, 1852. The work of preaching, translation, printing, and teaching was carried on hopefully, and much good seed was sown. Rev. M. J. Knowlton reached Ningpo early in June, 1854. How well and how faithfully he did his work may be seen in the sketch of his life. The memory of Mr. Goddard in connection with this mission is most precious. His service of fifteen years is recorded on high. The mantle of the father fell on his son, Rev. Josiah R. Goddard, who joined the mission in June, 1868. The most recent intelligence we have from this station is that there are in Ningpo and its out-stations, 7 churches with 263 members, and that the work in every department has been pushed with vigor and success.

3. The Southern Chinese Mission. The headquarters of this mission is Swatow, about 150 miles east of Hong-Kong. The mission was established in 1860, and was designed to reach in its operations the Chinese who spoke the Tie-Chin dialect. These people inhabit the most densely-populated region in China. It embraces nine walled cities, and towns and villages in such close contiguity that one or more is ever in sight. It is said that there are more people in this district than the entire population of Burmah, including the Karens and other subjugated tribes. The field of labor in many respects was most discouraging, owing to the exceedingly debased character of the people, "but," says the report which speaks of the opening of the mission, "out of the materials here now so unpromising, to human view so hopeless, can grace raise up and fit polished stones for the spiritual temple." The mission at Hong-Kong was given up and the missionaries transferred to Swatow. Rev. Mr. Sawtelle joined the mission in 1861. His health failing he was forced to retire from the field in a few months, and Mr. Johnson was left in charge of the station for some time, until Rev. W. Ashmore joined him in the autumn of 1863. During the year from Oct. 1, 1864, to Oct. 1, 1865, 24 were received into the church by baptism. Year after year new out-stations were established in the neighborhood of Swatow, which, from time to time, have been reinforced by the addition of workers, both male and female, to the laborers in a field from which so much good fruit has been gathered. In the last report from the Southern Chinese mission we find that with Swatow as the principal station there are 17 out-stations, 109 were baptized during the year, and the number of church members is 687. (See article on SOUTHERN BAPTIST CONVENTION.)

Chinese Missions in America.—The discovery of gold in California in 1849, attracted large numbers of men from China. In 1856 there were many thousands. They continued in the worship of idols, their temples standing near to Christian sanctuaries. Baptists became interested in their salvation. In 1856, the first Chinese church edifice in America was built for the Chinese Baptist church in Sacramento, Cal., under the pastoral care of Rev.

J. Lewis Shuck. It was a handsome and commodious building, and was one of the attractions of that city for many years, and was given a place in an early volume of illustrations of Sacramento. The church flourished while Mr. Shuck remained in California. A mission was opened in San Francisco about the year 1869 under the supervision of Rev. John Francis, who was associated with Rev. Z. L. Simmons, Rev. Mr. Graves, and finally succeeded by Rev. Dr. J. B. Hartwell. Several converts were baptized and became members of the First church, San Francisco. Other churches held mission schools, and were rewarded by the conversion and baptism of numbers. About 50 have become consistent Christians. The first Chinese convert baptized by Dr. Francis in 1865 was Dong Gong. He became the successful Baptist minister at the head of a Chinese mission in Portland, Oregon, which was begun about the year 1874. The first Chinaman to receive Christian burial in America was Fang Saung Nam. He died as a missionary of the American Baptist Home Mission Society in San Francisco. A marble slab in the Masonic Cemetery records the fact, "Here rests the first Christian Chinaman buried in America."

Chipman, Prof. Isaac, was born in Cornwallis, Nova Scotia, and was a graduate of Waterville College, now Colby University, in the class of 1839. He was an enthusiastic student, and maintained a high rank as a scholar. In January, 1840, he was appointed Professor of Mathematics and Natural Philosophy in Acadia College. In his "Centenary of the Baptists of Nova Scotia," 1860, Dr. Cramp says, "Among the men of our time Prof. Chipman holds the first place." On the 7th of June, 1852, in company with some friends, he was returning in a boat from Cape Blomidon, when a gale overtook them, the boat was swamped, and all on board were drowned, except one boatman. His untimely death produced a great shock in the community. Dr. Cramp alludes to it as "the greatest calamity that ever befell Nova Scotia Baptists."

Chipman, Rev. Thomas Handley, one of the founders and fathers of the Baptist denomination in Nova Scotia, was born Jan. 17, 1756. His first religious impressions were received under the ministry of the celebrated Henry Alline; was baptized at Horton, 1779, by Rev. Nicholas Pierson, and soon commenced preaching; was ordained in 1782. The churches to which he ministered were *mixed*,— composed of Baptists and Pedobaptists. Mr. Chipman, however, subsequently became clear and fixed in his views of the church of Christ and its ordinances, and his ministry proved a great blessing in Annapolis, Yarmouth, and Queen's Counties. He took part in forming the Baptist Association, June 23, 1800. In 1809, Mr. Chipman removed from Bridgetown to Nictaux, and became pastor of the Baptist church formed there, June 10, 1810, and continued his labors with much usefulness till his death, Oct. 11, 1830. Many of the early churches in Nova Scotia were open in their communion, but they gave up the practice as inexpedient and unscriptural.

Chipman, Rev. William, was born in Cornwallis, Nova Scotia, Nov. 29, 1781. He was converted and baptized when a youth, and ordained as pastor of the Second Cornwallis Baptist church in 1829. He died July 14, 1865. Mr. Chipman was clerk of the Baptist Association from 1838 to 1850. He was also secretary of the Educational Society. He was remarkable for his sound theological views, and for his piety and fidelity in the performance of his duty.

Chipman, Hon. William Allen, treasurer of the Nova Scotia Baptist Home Missionary Board, was born Nov. 8, 1756; was a merchant, large landowner, and justice of the peace in Cornwallis, Nova Scotia; was a member of the House of Assembly for over twenty years, from 1799. Died 1845.

Chisholm, Henry, one of the most enterprising and successful business men of Cleveland, O., is of Scotch origin, having been born in Lochgelly, Fifeshire, April 27, 1822. When he was ten years old his father died. At the age of twelve he was apprenticed to a carpenter, and served five years in learning the trade, after which he went as a journeyman to Glasgow.

In 1842, Mr. Chisholm came to America, settling in Montreal, Canada. He soon began to undertake work on his own account, and in 1850, in partnership with a friend, took a contract for building at Cleveland, O., a breakwater for the Cleveland & Pittsburgh Railroad, a task which was successfully accomplished in three years. This was succeeded by other contracts, which employed his time and energies until he turned his attention to the iron business. For several years he has been president of the Cleveland Rolling Mill, which has large and important branches in Indiana and Illinois, a company which it is said supports more people than there were in the entire city of Cleveland, when, as an unknown stranger, he came to it years ago.

Mr. Chisholm is a valued member of the Euclid Avenue Baptist church of Cleveland, and is in full sympathy with the educational and religious enterprises of the day. As a Christian business man he stands in the very front rank.

Chowan Female Institute.—The oldest school for girls in North Carolina, next to the Moravian school at Salem, is the Chowan Institute, at Murfreesborough. It was founded in 1848, by the Chowan Baptist Association. The next year a contiguous Association in Virginia, the Portsmouth, united with the Chowan, and up to the late war a joint board of trustees from the two bodies managed the affairs of the seminary. The war, which suspended collections and destroyed property of all kinds, did not pay debts or even suspend interest, and thus it happened that at its close the institute was hopelessly involved. In this emergency a joint-stock company was formed, the institute was bought for $3000, its debts, to the amount of $24,000, were assumed, and honorably liquidated, and for ten years the company successfully conducted the school, and added several thousand dollars' worth of improvements to the establishment. Two years ago the stockholders donated the property to the denomination at large, and it is now one of the few female schools of the country belonging exclusively to the Baptists. This act of generosity was so remarkable that the names of the parties involved are regarded as worthy to be preserved,

and are as follows: W. W. Mitchell, $4000; Mark Gregory, $1000; John Mitchell, $1000; J. W. Mitchell, $500; Mary Mitchell, $500; Miss N. S. Askew, $500; A. McDowell, $500; L. D. Spiers, $250; and J. N. Barnes, $250; which sum of $8500, bearing interest for ten years at eight per cent., makes a donation to the cause of education of over $15,000.

A. McDowell, D.D., then just out of college, was its first president. In 1849, Rev. M. R. Ferry, of New York, took charge, and presided over the institute till 1854, when he was succeeded by Dr. Wm. Hooper. In 1855, Dr. McDowell again became connected with the school as co-principal with Dr. Hooper, and since Dr. Hooper's withdrawal, in 1862, has been the sole principal of the institute. Thousands of young ladies have attended this excellent school, and it is earnestly to be hoped that as it has been the cherished school of the Baptists in Eastern North Carolina for so many years, they will heartily sustain the movement, recently projected, for its adequate endowment.

Chowles, John Overton, D.D., was born in Bristol, England, Feb. 5, 1801, of parents who were Wesleyans. He was deprived of their tender care when he was but twelve years of age, and came under the guardianship of his uncle, Henry Overton Wells, Esq., a wealthy merchant of Bristol. When a little more than eighteen years of age he became a subject of renewing grace, and was baptized by Rev. Dr. Ryland, and received into the Broadmead Baptist church. In order to carry on his education he was placed with Rev. William Anderson, under whose instructions he made rapid progress. In 1822, he entered Bristol College, under the charge of Dr. Ryland, to pursue his theological studies. He came to New York in 1824, and for a year or two was occupied in teaching an academy at Red Hook, N. Y., until called to the pastorate of the Second Baptist church in Newport, R. I. He was ordained Sept. 27, 1827. Immediate success followed his labors. Fifty persons were baptized during the year which succeeded his ordination. For six years he was the popular pastor of the Newport church. During this time he prepared for the press two or three books, among them his "History of Missions," in two quarto volumes, a work commenced by Rev. Thomas Smith, of England, who died in 1830.

Mr. Chowles resigned his pastorate in Newport to accept a call to the First Baptist church in New Bedford, where he remained for three years, and then went to Buffalo, N. Y. His connection with this church continued four years, when he was invited to take charge of the Sixth Street Baptist church in New York. It was not an inviting field of labor, and the hope of success not very flattering. Amid many discouragements he toiled on for a year or two, but no human power could save the enterprise, and it was ultimately abandoned. In 1843, he was called to the church of Jamaica Plain, near Boston, where he found a most congenial and happy home. While acting as pastor of this church he found time to prepare for the press his edition of "Neal's History of the Puritans," which took a high place in the literature which treated of the character and the work of those heroic men, who in an age of great dissoluteness and irreligion, wrought such a moral and religious change in England.

The connection of Dr. Chowles with the Jamaica church closed, in 1847, in consequence of an urgent call to return to his former charge in Newport. During his second residence in that city his busy pen prepared for the press several volumes, and was constantly employed in writing for the periodicals of the day. He was also a popular lecturer, and addressed large audiences in different sections of the country on themes both interesting and instructive. He lived a life of constant activity. Indeed, with his buoyancy of spirit and his strong vital energies, and social tendencies, he could not well have lived any other life. The last sermon he preached was from Eph. v. 14: "Awake thou that sleepest, and arise from the dead, and Christ shall give thee light." He left his home in Newport for New York, intending to be absent but a few days. He was seized with a sudden illness after arriving in New York. When the assurance came to him that without doubt the time for his departure was near, he said to his weeping friends, "I had not looked for this; if it had been the Lord's will I would have liked another month to have looked over the road more clearly; but it does not matter after all: 'twould have been the same thing, only simple faith in Christ. I have been hurried away through life by a tide of the most impulsive, impetuous nature, perhaps, that ever man had to contend with." Soon after he said, "I have loved Christ; I have preached Christ and him alone; I have loved to preach Christ and him crucified." These were among his last words. They indicate that he well knew himself, what in him there was that was frail and imperfect, and that he knew also what an almighty compassionate Redeemer he had. To that Redeemer, he committed himself with the simple trust of a little child, and we doubt not his faith was honored and he entered into rest. Dr. Chowles died Jan. 5, 1856.

Chown, Rev. J. P., the widely-known pastor of Bloomsbury chapel, London, England, began his ministry in the neighborhood of Northampton, England, about 1844. In 1846, he resigned the pastorate of the village church, to which he had been ordained, and entered Horton College. Two years after, the retirement of the Rev. T. Pottenger left

Sion chapel, Bradford, without a pastor, the gifts and high promise of Mr. Chown led to his being engaged to occupy the pulpit, while still a student, and eventually to his becoming pastor, in June, 1848. His

REV. J. P. CHOWN.

ministry was conspicuously successful from the first, and the membership was largely increased. In 1863, the church erected a new building, known as Hallfield chapel, and dismissed 120 members to form a new church there. Mr. Chown remained in his old field, and in 1873 a new edifice, called Sion Jubilee chapel, was erected for the accommodation of the church and its institutions, as a thank-offering for the labors and successes of fifty years. Mr. Chown's public work on behalf of benevolent and educational institutions in Bradford received emphatic acknowledgment repeatedly, one of the most interesting and valuable tokens of public appreciation being the gift of his residence, which was presented to him on his return from a visit to this country. He has been a leader of the temperance movement for many years. In 1875, he obeyed what seemed to him an imperative providential call, and accepted the pastorate at Bloomsbury chapel, London, where his ministry is eminently successful. Mr. Chown is endowed with a fine presence and a magnificent voice, and his platform speeches, as well as pulpit services, attract large audiences. For his earnestness and noble simplicity of character, as well as for his great abilities, he is held in the highest esteem by the churches.

Christian, Judge Joseph, LL.D., eldest son of Dr. R. A. Christian, was born at Hewick, Middlesex Co., Va., July 10, 1828. While still a boy he gave promise of distinction. He pursued his academic studies for a while in Richmond, but chiefly at the Columbian College, where he graduated with honor in 1847. In 1853, he received the degree of A.M. Having studied law in his father's neighborhood, with the late John D. McGill, Esq., and afterwards in Staunton, Va., he established himself in practice, immediately after his admission to the bar, in his native county of Middlesex, and soon became one of the leading lawyers and advocates in that part of the State. He was also, both before and after the breaking out of the war, sent to the senate of Virginia, from the counties of Matthews and Middlesex, and in this body he gained the reputation of one of its very best debaters. Soon after the close of the war he was made judge of the sixth judicial district of Virginia, which responsible office he filled for years with such distinguished ability that he was appointed a judge of the Supreme Court of Appeals, a position which he has held for some nine years, with like honor to himself and to the judicial department of the State government. In the last election for a U. S. senator for Virginia, he was, at no solicitation of his own, one of the prominent candidates for that position; and we understand that his name was also conspicuous on the list of those Southern jurists who were strongly recommended to the President for the lately vacant seat on the bench of the Supreme Court of the United States. No man, perhaps, of his years, in Virginia,

JUDGE JOSEPH CHRISTIAN, LL.D.

has a higher judicial reputation. The deliberative assembly, however, on account of his rare gifts as an orator, would, perhaps, exhibit his talents in a more striking light. As a gentleman, he is distinguished for his urbanity and fine social qualities. Judge Christian was baptized by his father soon after he entered upon the practice of the law, and united with one of his churches. He is now connected with the Second Baptist church of Richmond, of which the Rev. Dr. McDonald is pastor. The Columbian College conferred upon him, in 1872, the degree of LL.D.

Christian, Rev. J. T., a prominent young minister of Columbus Association, Miss., was born in Kentucky in 1854; began to preach in 1874; graduated at Bethel College, Ky., in 1876; became pastor at Tupelo, Miss., in 1877, and supplied Verona at the same time; after two years he removed to West Point and engaged in his present work. At the last commencement at Bethel College he received the degree of A.M.

Christian Review and Home Monthly, a religious periodical published at Texarkana, Ark., by J. F. Shaw & Sons, and edited by Rev. J. F. Shaw and Mrs. Viola Jackson. It takes the place of the *Baptist Index*, published at the same place, which is discontinued. Mr. Shaw is fast gaining reputation as a vigorous writer, and Mrs. Jackson is well known in the South, having been connected with Mayfield's *Happy Home* and Ford's *Christian Repository*. The first number was issued August, 1880, and is well filled with excellent original and selected matter. It meets a want in the Baptist literature of the Southwest.

Christian, Rev. Richard Allen, M.D., was born in Charles City Co., Va., July 27, 1798. At the age of about twenty-one years he graduated as Doctor of Medicine at the University of Pennsylvania, and immediately began the practice of his profession at Urbana, Middlesex Co., Va. In 1838, he made a public profession of faith in Christ, became a member of the Baptist church at Clark's Neck, and soon afterwards was ordained to the ministry. Still continuing in the practice of medicine, he did not for some years assume any pastoral charge, although he preached regularly on the Sabbath in the neighboring churches. At a later period he became pastor of Clark's Neck and Hamilton churches (and for a time, also, Zoar and Glebe Landing churches), and he held this relation until his failing health compelled him, two or three years before his death, to relinquish it. After repeated strokes of paralysis, he died May 8, 1862. Dr. Christian was deservedly one of the most influential and popular men, not only of the county, but also of the region in which he lived. His mind was strong and active, his person large and imposing, and his manners polished and winning. As a neighbor, he was kind and charitable in the highest degree, and ever sought the things that make for peace. As a citizen, he was characterized by the strictest integrity, and by a decided talent for the management of public business. As a physician, he was eminently skillful, attentive, and tenderhearted, and by these qualities he secured and retained the largest practice in his county, which, however, after the period of middle life, he gradually relinquished for the purpose of devoting his energies to the Christian ministry. Although Dr. Christian was some forty years of age before he entered the ministry, and although for several years after his ordination he was laboriously engaged in the practice of medicine, yet he became an able and instructive preacher. His sermons were well arranged, abounded in apt illustrations, were filled with the very spirit of the gospel, and were uniformly earnest, and sometimes powerful. His ministry, although comparatively brief, resulted in the edification of the churches which he served, and in numerous conversions. His talents were held in high estimation, and for a long time to come no name in the district of Virginia to which his labors were confined, will be pronounced with greater reverence than that of Dr. Richard A. Christian.

Christian, William Steptoe, M.D., second son of Dr. R. A. Christian, was born at Hewick, Middlesex Co., Va., Dec. 26, 1830. He prepared for college at the schools in the neighborhood, and entered the Columbian College, where he graduated with the degree of A.B. in 1848. Having studied medicine with his father, and afterwards at the Jefferson Medical College of Philadelphia, he graduated there in 1851, and immediately entered upon the labors of his profession in his native county, where he still resides, occupied with the duties of a very extensive practice. At the beginning of the war he entered the Confederate service as a captain of infantry, was soon made colonel, was captured in the retreat from Gettysburg, was for many months prisoner (during most of the time at Johnson's Island), and was several times severely wounded in battle. He was a gallant and exceedingly popular officer. Dr. Christian is held in the highest respect by all who know him for the various qualities that most adorn the man, the neighbor, and the citizen. He is a physician of rare intelligence and skill. For several years past he has been a leading member of the temperance organization known as the Good Templars, and has repeatedly been elected grand worthy chief, the highest officer of the order in the State. As a speaker he is impressive and eloquent. At the age of about sixteen years he was baptized by his father, and united with the Clark's Neck Baptist church, of which he is still a most active and useful member, having served for many years most efficiently as teacher or superintendent of the Sabbath-school.

Church, A True Gospel.—The fabric in which

the worship of God is celebrated is not a church; the clergy are not the church. The Baptist Confession of 1611, in Articles X. and XIII., says,—

"The church of Christ is a company of faithful people, separated from the world by the word and Spirit of God, being knit unto the Lord, and one to another by baptism, upon their own confession of the faith and sins." "Every church is to receive in all their members by baptism, upon the confession of their faith and sins, wrought by the preaching of the gospel, according to the primitive institution and practice." The Confession of 1646 says, "The church is a company of visible saints, called and separated from the world by the word and Spirit of God to the visible profession of the faith of the gospel, being baptized into that faith and joined to the Lord, and each to other by mutual agreement in the practical enjoyment of the ordinances commanded by Christ, their head and king."—Article XXXIII. The Philadelphia Confession of Faith says, "The members of these churches are saints by calling, visibly manifesting and evidencing, in and by their profession and walking, their obedience unto that call of Christ, and do willingly consent to walk together according to the appointment of Christ, giving up themselves to the Lord and one to another, by the will of God, in professed subjection to the ordinances of the gospel."—Article XXVII.

Church, Rev. Leroy, was born in Western New York, Jan. 8, 1813. He was baptized in Lake Ontario in 1832. His studies preparatory to the ministry were pursued at Hamilton, where he entered in the fall of 1834, graduating in 1839 from the college, and from the seminary in 1841. His first pastorate was at Schenectady, N. Y., where he entered upon service in September of 1841, being ordained in November of the same year. On the first Sabbath of the December following he baptized his first convert, a young man led to Christ by a few words addressed to him in the shop where he was at work. During the three years of this pastorate at Schenectady about 100 were added to the church by baptism. Mr. Church became pastor of the church at Hudson, N. Y., in the fall of 1845, holding this important position until the fall of 1853, when he removed to Chicago, having purchased the *Christian Times*, now the *Standard*, with which paper he remained connected as senior proprietor and associate editor until 1875, when he disposed of his interest to Dr. J. S. Dickerson. This period of twenty-two years in Baptist journalism brought him into active and influential relations with a variety of Western interests, and his service in that connection was active, judicious, and effective. He wrote largely and well for the columns of the paper, while in connection with its financial administration, and in representing it in various parts of its wide field, his good judgment and tact and knowledge of men were elements of high efficiency.

The Church family, to whom belong also Dr. Pharcellus Church and Rev. Volney Church, came from England in 1630 and settled at Plymouth, Mass. A deed is preserved in the museum at Plymouth conveying a tract of land to Benjamin Church in the precinct now known as Marshfield, where Daniel Webster had his home. A branch of the family subsequently settled in Rhode Island. Capt. Church, belonging to this branch, has a marked record in the early Indian wars as the antagonist of King Philip. The father of Rev. Leroy Church was a soldier of the Revolution.

Church Meetings are composed exclusively of members, and are convened to receive additions by letter, to grant letters of dismission, to try fallen brethren, to order letters to Associations and other bodies, to elect pastors, and to perform other church work.

The pastor presides almost universally, and this position is generally accorded to him in virtue of his office, but in a few instances it is given to him by election at each meeting. There is a clerk at every church meeting, who keeps a correct record of all its proceedings. The church meeting is governed by parliamentary law.

In the great majority of our churches each member has a vote, irrespective of age, sex, or the length or brevity of membership. The writer has, however, known one or two cases where there was an age qualification to prevent the very young from controlling the church. In the church meeting the pastor has the right of voting, and he has an influence according to the measure of his wisdom and piety. Beyond these he has no other privileges, and he ought to have none.

In large cities church meetings are generally held once a month, or once in three months, and they are summoned for a week-night. Special meetings are called by the pastor, or by a paper signed by a few brethren, five or seven, and read from the desk.

Church of God.—This community, sometimes called Winebrennarians, claims precedence of all religious bodies in its origin. Jesus Christ is claimed as founder. The name, it is declared, is the only one justified by divine authority. Gal. i. 13; 1 Tim. iii. 15. This denomination started into life in connection with extensive revivals of religion enjoyed in and around Harrisburg soon after the settlement of the Rev. John Winebrenner in that city, in 1820. These revivals were renewed and far more widely extended in 1825; out of the converts churches were organized, and converts were called into the ministry. In October, 1830, the representatives of these churches met in Harrisburg, and formally set up the denomination called the "Church of God," the original representative of which was established by the Saviour.

The doctrines of the Church of God differ from Regular Baptists only in the following points: free will is accepted, election is denounced, feet-washing is practiced, the Lord's Supper is observed always in the evening. It is likely that the "final perseverance of the saints" is rejected by this community, though in their doctrinal articles this is not stated. In other respects the *creed* of the Church of God is a Baptist Confession of Faith.

The government of this community is not Baptistical: the preacher in charge of a church and a competent number of elders and deacons constitute the church council, which admits and excludes members. The Annual Eldership is very much like a Methodist Annual Conference, with laymen among its members. Every three years a General Eldership convened for the first twenty years, after which it was to assemble every five years. This body is composed of delegates from the Annual Elderships, and it has powers very like those of a General Conference of the M. E. Church.

Every minister in the Church of God in good standing must have a license, and this license must be renewed *annually* by his Eldership. No minister is allowed to remain longer than three years in one station, and generally not more than one or two. The doctrinal articles, with the exceptions named, agree with the opinions of Baptists; the church polity resembles the Methodist.

The writer was unable to obtain exact statistics of the Church of God, but he procured something near the figures. They have about 500 ministers, 1200 churches, and 20,000 members.

The members of the Church of God live chiefly in Pennsylvania, Ohio, Indiana, Illinois, Michigan, and Iowa.

Church, Pharcellus, D.D., was born Sept. 11, 1801, near Geneva, N. Y. He spent the most of his first ten years of life at what is now called Hopewell Centre, five miles from Canandaigua. At eleven years of age his home was changed to the shores of Lake Ontario, at that time without religious privileges. His Sabbaths were spent in the rough sort of life peculiar to the wilderness of a new country. In the midst of his rude sports a respect for religion, instilled in his mind early in life by a tender, loving mother, asserted itself, and led him to follow her counsel and study the Divine Word. While thus engaged as a matter of filial duty, and obeying the outward forms of religion, he was deeply affected by portions of the Gospel of John. These impressions led to his conversion at thirteen and a half years of age. He attended no church and heard no domestic or sanctuary worship, and yet enjoyed communion with God, which was greatly increased by an open confession to his pious mother. Soon after this event, a Baptist church was formed in the vicinity, and in June, 1816, he was immersed upon profession of his faith. He became immediately more or less active in social meetings, and at the age of seventeen he felt called to the Christian ministry.

Through the influence of friends he devoted himself to study, and finally took a classical and theological course at Hamilton, N. Y. He was first settled as pastor at Poultney, Vt., where he was ordained in June, 1825, and where he remained until 1828. In the latter year he was married to Miss Conant, daughter of Deacon John Conant, of Brandon, and in the fall of that year became pastor of what is now the Central Baptist church of Providence, R. I. He spent the winter of 1834–35 in New Orleans, and while there wrote "Philosophy of Benevolence," published in New York in 1836. Upon his return to the North he located with the church at Rochester. From thence he removed, in 1848, to accept the pastorate of Bowdoin Square Baptist church, Boston. This position he left on account of sickness. In 1855 he became editor of the New York *Chronicle*, in which service he remained ten years. Since 1865 he has spent the time partly in Europe, making the original Scriptures a principal study, preaching occasionally, and writing for the press. His home has been at Tarrytown for the last eight years.

PHARCELLUS CHURCH, D.D.

An offer of a premium for a work on religious discussions being made in the summer of 1836, he wrote a book on that subject of 400 or 500 12mo pages, which was published in 1837. The revival interest among his people in Rochester turned his attention to the subject of spiritual power, and he published in 1842 a work entitled "Antioch, or the Increase of Moral Power in the Church," which contained an able introduction by Dr. Stow, of Boston. Another publication of a like character, in 1843, entitled "Pentecost," being the substance of a sermon preached at Albany before the Foreign Mission Board in the spring of that year, was printed by request. In Boston, he compiled "Memoirs of Mrs. Theodosia Dean," which was published in that city about 1851, and is now included in the American Baptist Publication Society's lists. While in Canada he wrote "Mapleton, or more Work for the Maine Law," a temperance tale; and while in Bonn, on the Rhine, he wrote "Sad Truths," a work embodying a good deal of thought on Bible subjects, which was published in Edinburgh and in New York. Dr. Church has written largely for reviews and other periodicals, and is still engaged in the same service.

Dr. Church is a grand old man, with a noble intellect, a great heart, splendid culture, an unsullied record, and a saintly piety, one of those men whom we would keep forever in the church on earth, and whom we would endow with undying vigor, if his state and place were in our charge.

Churches, English Baptist.—According to Orchard there were in England in 1771, 251 Baptist churches; in 1794, 379; in 1811, 537; and in 1820 there were 620. Bogue and Bennet give a list of 708 Baptist churches in England and Wales in 1808. In 1880, there were 2620 churches, 3354 meeting-houses, 269,836 members, and 372,242 Sunday-school scholars belonging to our denomination in the British Islands. How many persons there were in 1880, with Baptist principles, not a few of whom were actually immersed, in the membership of Pedobaptist churches in Great Britain, we have no means of finding out. Their number, however, may be regarded as very large. By the unscriptural teachings of "open communion" they have been foolishly led to suppose that baptism was of too little importance to disturb their ecclesiastical relations. The principal effect of open communion is not to bring Pedobaptists to the Lord's table in Baptist churches, but to keep men holding Baptist principles in Pedobaptist communities.

Churches, One Minister Pastor of many.—In reading the sketches of ministers in this volume it will appear as if some of them were given to many changes in their pastoral relations. There are two considerations to be kept in view in reflecting upon such cases. The first is, that in large sections of our country, especially in the South, one minister is frequently pastor of four or more churches at the same time. If he changes his field of labor four times in his life, he has been pastor of sixteen churches, while in one of our cities the same man would only have ministered to four. The second is, that a small number of our ministers are of an impulsive, and of a revival order, as many commonly use the word revival; and after a brief settlement, and considerable success, they are anxious for the special harvests which they commonly reap in new fields; and their removals are frequent for this reason. Generally our ministers have comparatively long settlements; and this practice is growing rapidly among us.

Citations.—When a member of a Baptist church has sinned grievously against his Master, and when the remonstrances of his brethren fail to bring him to repentance, our last resort is excommunication. Previous to this sorrowful act a notification, or citation, as it is called, is sent to the offender inviting him to attend the church meeting to be held at a time and place mentioned, to show cause why he should not be excluded from the rights and privileges of the church of which he is a member. If he accepts the invitation he has every opportunity to defend himself, or to confess his sin and sorrow, and thereby avert the impending expulsion.

To send a citation is the uniform law of all Baptist churches when the residence of the accused can be found, except in a small number of cases, such as sexual crimes or murders, when no amount of repentance would justify retention in church membership, and the testimony against the accused is overwhelming.

Clark, Rev. Albion B., was born in New Sharon, Me., March 24, 1826. He prepared for college at the Farmington and Waterville Academies, and graduated at Waterville College in 1854. For three years he was the principal of the academy at Shelbourne Falls, Mass., and in 1854 he entered the Newton Theological Institution, where he took the full three years' course of study. He was ordained Sept. 12, 1855, and was pastor of the church in Skowhegan, Me., for three years,—1855-58. He became an agent of the American Baptist Publication Society, and continued in the employ of the society for four years,—1859-63. He died at Skowhegan, Sept. 9, 1865.

Clark, Rev. Andrew, of Bishop Creek, Cal., a self-denying and faithful pastor, is the only Baptist preacher east of the Sierra range, his preaching stations extending nearly 100 miles north and south. He was born in Alleghany Co., Pa., July 14, 1832; baptized in 1852 at Marshall, Iowa; married at twenty-two to Miss Rachel L. Sehern, a Presbyterian, who with all her family became Baptists. He served in the U. S. army; was induced by his father to go to California just after his ordination at Red Oak, Iowa, in 1867; located at Bishop Creek, where he has built a house of worship, and is doing a good work for Christ. Twice he has traveled 1500 miles (once with his wife) over the mountains to attend the Association.

Clark, Rev. Edward W., was born in the town of North-East, Dutchess Co., N. Y., Feb. 25, 1830. He was converted and called to the ministry in early life. He graduated from Brown University in 1857, and from Rochester Theological Seminary in 1859. He was pastor in Logansport, Ind., from 1859 to 1861. He was editor and publisher of the *Witness*, Indianapolis, from 1861 to 1867. He was appointed missionary to Sibsagor, and sailed in October, 1868. He took charge of missionary printing, and assisted in other missionary work for five years, when he became deeply interested in the people of the Naga Hills. He made a visit to one of the tribes, and was afterwards appointed missionary to the Nagas. His wife, Mrs. Mary M. Clark, helps him in his missionary work. She returned to this country in 1873, and stayed three years. She spent much of the time in forming missionary circles among Baptist women.

Clark, George Whitfield, D.D., was born at South Orange, N. J., Feb. 15, 1831. He was converted and baptized when twelve years old into the fellowship of the Northfield Baptist church. He graduated at Amherst College in 1853, and completed his theological course at Rochester in 1855. He was ordained pastor of the church at New Market, Oct. 3, 1855. In June, 1859, he became pastor of the First Baptist church in Elizabeth, and continued there until 1868, when he went to the church at Ballston, N. Y., from which he removed to Somerville, N. J., Sept. 1, 1873. In 1872 Rochester University conferred upon him the degree of D.D. Dr. Clark has been a close and thorough student. His notes on the gospels and "New Harmony of the Gospels" are thorough, sound, and popular. They have been extensively used. Close and continuous study brought on a failure in health that induced a resignation of his prosperous pastorate in Somerville in 1877. He is so far restored that further work on the New Testament is contemplated. He has contributed a number of articles to the quarterlies.

Clark, Rev. Henry, was born Nov. 12, 1810, at Canterbury, Windham Co., Conn.; was educated at Hamilton Literary and Theological Institution; ordained June 13, 1834, at Seekonk, Mass., where he had his first pastorate. Subsequently served as pastor at Taunton two and a half years, Canton two years, Randolph five years, Cheshire six years. These pastorates were all in Massachusetts. Mr. Clark came to Wisconsin in 1869, where he has since resided. He was pastor at Kenosha five years, Pewaukee two years, and he has been settled over the Second Baptist church in Oshkosh, where he now resides, about one year. Mr. Clark is a Baptist preacher of the old-fashioned New England type, sound in the faith, plain and direct in his style, always bringing to the cause of the church and of Christ an undivided devotion, able and ready to speak at all times, and to fight (if needful) in defense of the old Baptist faith, rather than abandon a hair's breadth of the principles of the church of which he is a member and minister. His spirit has been made meek and gentle in the furnace of affliction. All his family except his wife—two sons and five daughters—have preceded him to the land of rest. He is passing the evening of his life in preaching Christ in one of the most beautiful cities of Wisconsin.

Clark, Ichabod, D.D., was born in Franklin Co., Mass., Oct. 30, 1802, and died at Lockport, Ill., April 14, 1869, after an active and useful ministry of forty-seven years. His conversion took place when he was about fourteen years of age. At the age of eighteen he was licensed to preach by the Baptist church of Truxton, N. Y.; ordained at Scipio, N. Y., in 1823. His pastorates in New York were at Lockport, Lagrange, Batavia, Le Roy, Brockport, and Nunda. In 1848 he accepted an appointment from the New York State Convention as missionary at Galena, Ill. He thus became identified with the denomination in that State, and for the most part remained so until his death. His next pastorate after that at Galena was at Rockford, where he labored several years with signal success. Midway in this pastorate he engaged for a year as superintendent of missions of the General Association of the State, the church giving him leave of absence for this purpose, and supplying the pulpit meanwhile. At the end of the year he resumed his work at Rockford, and continued it until 1860. During his labors there 453 were added to the church, 211 by baptism. Five years in a pastorate at Le Roy, N. Y., one year in renewed service as superintendent of missions in Illinois, a brief service at Lockport as pastor, and his active, wise, and efficient ministry was finished.

Clark, Rev. James A., Professor of the Latin Language in Kalamazoo College, Mich., was born in Pittsfield, Mass., in 1827, and died in Kalamazoo in August, 1869. He was in early life converted and began preparation for the work of the ministry. He graduated from Williams College in 1853, and after teaching a year studied at Newton, where he finished the usual course in 1857. Soon after he became pastor at Adrian, Mich., and subsequently at Fairfield. From the latter place he was called to the professorship in Kalamazoo College, but during his residence there he served the college as financial agent, and as editor of the Michigan *Christian Herald*, and he was treasurer of the State Convention for three years preceding his death. He was a man of large practical sagacity, and self-sacrificing devotion to the church. His death at the age of forty-two was sincerely and deeply lamented.

Clark, Rev. John.—This pioneer preacher was born in Scotland, Nov. 29, 1758. At seven he began to study Latin and Greek. In 1778 he went to sea on a British ship, which he deserted at Charleston, S. C. He went to Georgia and taught school. He was converted in 1785, and became a Methodist preacher. He was ordained by Bishop Asbury in 1795. He visited Scotland, and found that his father and mother were dead. He returned to America, preached in Georgia, and taught school. In 1796 he walked from Georgia to Kentucky, and taught and preached in the Crab Orchard country. He exchanged the rod in school for firmness and love. He came to Missouri in 1798. He preached in St. Louis County when the Catholic foreign commander threatened him with imprisonment. He became a Baptist, and another Methodist, named Talbot, adopted the same opinions, and they immersed each other. The Lemmons, early Illinois ministers, studied under Clark, and acknowledged their obligations to him for their instruction in languages and theology. He went in a canoe in 1808 and 1810 down the Mississippi to Baton Rouge, and preached and taught school, and walked back. He was easy of address, social, pious, intelligent, and useful. He wrote in a beautiful hand many family records in the Bible by request. In 1820 he visited the Boones in Lick County, and he was the first to go so far west. He belonged to the Coldwater Baptist church in St. Louis County. He died at William Patterson's, Oct. 11, 1833, at seventy-five years of age. He had performed great labor. Multitudes attended his funeral. The Lemmons, by his request, preached his funeral sermon.

Clark, Rev. John Henry, was born in Loudon Co., Va., Dec. 12, 1812. He was converted at sixteen years of age, and baptized by Dr. W. F. Broadus. He moved to Missouri in 1839, and united with the church at Cape Girardeau. He was licensed in 1842, and ordained in 1844 to the pastorate of the church at the Cape. He had a talent for languages and acquired them. He gave much time to teaching, and was successful in it, and he was effective as a preacher. Brother Clark was for years moderator of Cape Girardeau Association. He died April 4, 1869. He was honored and beloved as a good minister of Jesus.

Clark, J. W. B., D.D., was born in Rushford, N. Y., May 8, 1831; graduated from Alleghany College in 1855. For two years after he was principal of Randolph Academy, now Chamberlain Institute, N. Y. The next six years he devoted to preaching. In 1863 he entered Rochester Theological Seminary, from which he was graduated in 1866. The next four years he was pastor in Portsmouth, O. In May, 1870, he removed to Albion, N. Y., where he still remains, and where he is doing a noble work in one of the strongest and most efficient churches of Western New York. Rochester University conferred upon him the degree of Doctor of Divinity in 1877. His parents were from Southampton, Mass. His father's name was Elam Clark. Dr. Clark is a man of strong constitution and character. His solid frame and manly face fitly represent his vigorous intellect. As a preacher he ranks among the best in the State, and his fine judgment and earnest, patient, hopeful spirit eminently qualify him for leadership in the great concerns of the denomination. He has written sermons for the *Examiner and Chronicle*, and occasional newspaper articles, in all of which he shows a masterly hand.

Clark, Deacon Thomas, father of Rev. Andrew Clark, of Bishop Creek, Cal., assisted in organizing the McKeesport church, Pa.; was a pioneer Baptist in Iowa, where his house was the meeting-place of an infant church; and a pioneer Baptist in Eastern California, settling at Bishop Creek in 1864, where he opened his house for public worship, a Sunday-school, and for the meetings of the First Baptist church, which was organized in 1869, and of which he was deacon until his death, Nov. 4, 1878, aged seventy-eight years.

Clarke, Prof. Benjamin F., son of Thomas and Martha Clarke, was born in Newport, Me., July 14, 1831. He took the course of study in the Bridgewater, Mass., State Normal School, graduating in 1855, purposing to make teaching his profession. For some time he taught in district schools, in a grammar school in the city of Salem, Mass., and in the Normal School in Bridgewater. Working to prepare himself for more extended usefulness, he commenced a course of study to qualify himself for entering college. He was for some time under the tuition of ex-President Thomas Hill, D.D., formerly of Harvard University, and at the time pastor of the Unitarian church in Waltham, Mass. While residing in Waltham he made a public profession of his faith in Christ, and was baptized by Rev. M. L. Bickford in 1857. Having completed his preparatory course of study, he entered Brown University, and was graduated in the class of 1863, and soon after was appointed instructor in Mathematics, which office he held until 1868, when he was appointed Professor of Mathematics and Civil Engineering, which position he now (1880) holds.

Clarke, John, M.D., one of the most eminent men of his time, and a leading spirit among the founders of Rhode Island, was, according to the best authorities, born in Suffolk, England, Oct. 8, 1609. His father's name was Thomas, to whom belonged a family Bible which is still in existence and contains a family record. His mother, Rose Herrige, was of an ancient Suffolk family. The tradition that he was a native of Bedfordshire may have had its rise from the fact that there he married his first wife, Elizabeth, daughter of John Hayes, Esq. To receive a legacy given her by her father out of the manor of Wreslingworth, Bedfordshire, he signed a power of attorney, March 12, 1656, styling himself John Clarke, physician, of London. During his youth he received a careful training, and shared in the intellectual quickening of the period, though at what university he was graduated is not known. His religious and political convictions closely identified him with that large and growing body of men who bravely sought to limit kingly prerogative, and to throw around the personal liberty of subjects the protection of constitutional safeguards. He was indeed a Puritan of the Puritans. All efforts to reform abuses in either church or state proving abortive, he directed his footsteps toward the New World, arriving at Boston in the month of November, 1637.

A bitter disappointment, however, awaited him. The Antinomian controversy had just culminated, and one of the parties was being proscribed. Differences of opinion he expected to find on these Western shores, but he was surprised to find, as he tells us, that men "were not able to bear each with other in their different understandings and consciences as in these utmost parts of the world to live peaceably together." Since the government at Boston was as repressive and intolerant as that from which he had just fled, he proposed to a number of the citizens, for the sake of peace, to withdraw and establish themselves elsewhere, and consented to seek out a place. He had boldly resolved to plant a new colony, and upon a new basis; to incorporate into its foundation principles hitherto deemed impracticable, and even subversive of government, and indeed of all order.

The choice company he had gathered signed, March 7, 1638, the following compact: "We, whose names are underwritten, do here solemnly, in the presence of Jehovah, incorporate ourselves into a Body Politic, and as he shall help, will submit our persons, lives, and estates unto our Lord Jesus Christ, the King of Kings and Lord of Lords, and to all those perfect and most absolute laws of his given us in his Holy Word of truth, to be guided and judged thereby." They found in the Word of God warrant for their civil government, and claimed for it divine authority. It was, nevertheless, "a democracy or popular government," and no one was "to be accounted a delinquent for doctrine." Liberty of conscience was most sacredly guarded. The magistrate was to punish only "breaches of the law of God that tend to civil disturbance." The largest personal freedom consistent with stability of government was provided for. There are good reasons for believing that to the hand of Mr. Clarke this initial form of government must be traced.

The place selected for the colony was an island in the Narragansett Bay, known by the Indians as Aquidneck, but subsequently named Rhode Island, which, Neal says, "is deservedly called the paradise of New England." The lands were obtained by purchase of the aborigines, the deed bearing date 24th March, 1638, the settlers "having bought them off to their full satisfaction." At first established at the north end of the island, the government was, the following April, transferred to the south end, which received the name of Newport. When in 1647 the island was united, under the charter of 1643, in a confederacy with the other towns included in what afterwards became the State of Rhode Island, the government of the united towns was framed by some one on the island. It is generally supposed, and for good reasons, that Mr. Clarke was the author of the government framed, both of the code of laws and of the means of enforcing it. "From the islanders," says Gov. Arnold in his history, "had emanated the code of laws, and to them it was intrusted to perfect the means of enforcing that code." The code, which has received from most competent judges the highest praise, concludes with these words: "And otherwise than thus what is herein forbidden, all men may walk as their consciences persuade them, every one in the name of his God. And let the saints of the Most High walk in this colony without molestation, in the name of Jehovah, their God, for ever and ever."

While constantly busy with the affairs of state, Mr. Clarke did not neglect the higher claims of religion. He is spoken of by early writers as the religious teacher of the people, and as such from the beginning. A church was gathered in 1638, probably early in the year, of which Mr. Clarke became pastor or teaching elder. He is mentioned (in 1638) as "preacher to those of the island," as "their minister," as "elder of the church there." Mr. Lechford writes in 1640, after having made a tour through New England, that "at the island . . . there is a church where one Master Clarke is pastor." On his return to England, he adds, when revising his manuscript for the press, that he heard that this church is dissolved. A report had doubtless reached him of the controversy which had arisen on the island respecting the authority of the Bible and the existence upon earth of a visible church, when some became Seekers and afterwards Quakers. Missionary tours were made in various directions, and numbers were added to the church from sections quite remote, as from Rehoboth, Kingham, Weymouth. Some of them continued to live at a distance. One of these was William Witter, whose home was in Lynn. Becoming infirm he was visited by his pastor, Mr. Clarke, in 1651, who reached his house the 19th of July, accompanied by Obadiah Holmes and John Crandall, elders in the church. The three visitors were summarily arrested, and without there being produced " either accuser, witness, jury, law of God, or man," were sentenced. They were each to pay a fine, " or else to be well whipped." Some one unknown to him paid, it is said, Mr. Clarke's fine of twenty pounds. At any rate he was, after a detention reaching into the middle of August, set free as summarily as he had been apprehended. He had hoped for the sake of the truth that there might be a public disputation, his last communication on the subject to the governor and his advisers being dated from prison, 14th August. Though disappointed in this hope, the results of the visit were far-reaching and most gratifying. Many eyes were opened to the truth, and "divers were put upon a way of inquiry."

Meanwhile the colony was in peril, its government in jeopardy, and its very life threatened. On his return from Lynn he was importuned to go to England and represent the infant colony at the English court, and, complying with the request, set sail in November, 1651. The following year, 1652, his famous work in defense of liberty of conscience, entitled " Ill News from New England," etc., was published in London. The immediate object of his visit—the revocation of Gov. Coddington's commission—having been attained, he continued to reside abroad to watch over the imperiled interests of the unique State, and succeeded not only in parrying the attacks of enemies, but in gaining for it a substantial advantage over its older and more powerful rivals. The boundaries of the State were even enlarged. The charter obtained in 1663 guaranteed to the people privileges unparalleled in the history of the world. It is an evidence of his skill in diplomacy that he could obtain from King Charles, against the earnest prayers of the older colonies, a charter that declared " that no person within the said colony, at any time hereafter, shall be anywise molested, punished, disquieted, or called in question for any differences of opinion or matters of religion." In the second of two addresses presented to the king he said respecting his colony, that it desires " to be permitted to hold forth in a lively experiment that a flourishing civil state may stand, yea, and best be maintained, and that among English spirits, with a full liberty of religious concernments." To these labors in England his colony was deeply indebted, owed indeed its existence. Yet they have never been duly appreciated, nor have the difficulties environing his way been sufficiently considered. The consummate fruit of his toils—the securing of the great charter—has even been ascribed to another, as indeed have also the results of others of his labors. The charter was received by the colony with public demonstrations of great joy.

His return home in July, 1664, after an absence of more than twelve years, was hailed with delight. He was immediately elected to the General Assembly, and re-elected year by year until 1669, when he became deputy-governor, and again in 1671. During these years he performed much important public service; was in 1664 the chief commissioner for determining the western boundary of the State, and the same year chairman of a committee to codify the laws; two years later he was appointed alone " to compose all the laws into a good method and order, leaving out what may be superfluous, and adding what may appear unto him necessary." Although he retired from public life in 1672, his counsels were still sought in emergencies. Only six days before his death he was summoned to attend a meeting of the General Assembly, which desired " to have the advice and concurrence of the most judicious inhabitants in the troublous times and straits into which the colony has been brought." He died suddenly, April 20, 1676, leaving most of his property in the hands of trustees for religious and educational purposes. His last act was in harmony with one of the first on the colony's records, which was to establish a free school, said to have been the first in America, if not in the world.

He was a man of commanding ability, and from first to last planned wisely and well for his colony. His endowments of both mind and heart were of a very high order. He was " an advanced student of Hebrew and Greek." Arnold says, " He was a ripe scholar, learned in the practice of two professions, besides having had large experience in diplomatic and political life. . . . With all his public pursuits, he continued the practice of his original profession as a physician, and also retained the pastoral charge of his church. He left a confession of his faith, from which it appears that he was strongly Calvinistic in doctrine." His views of Christian doctrine have been pronounced " so clear and Scriptural that they might stand as the confession of faith of Baptists to-day, after more than two centuries of experience and investigation." He has, and perhaps not inaptly, been called the " Father of American Baptists." And his, it has been claimed, " is the glory of first showing in an actual government that the best safeguards of personal rights is Christian law." Allen (Biog. Dict.) says, " He possessed the singular honor of contributing much towards establishing the first government upon the earth which gave equal liberty, civil and religious, to all men living under it." Backus: " He was a principal procurer of Rhode Island for sufferers and exiles." Bancroft: " Never did a young commonwealth possess a more faithful friend." Palfrey, although ungenerous and unjust in his judgments upon Rhode Island affairs and Rhode Island men, and especially toward Mr. Clarke, is constrained to admit that he "had some claim to be called the father of Rhode Island;" and that "for many years before his death he had been the most important citizen of his colony." Arnold says he was "one of the ablest men of the seventeenth century." "His character and talents appear more exalted the more closely they are examined."

See, for fuller details, besides general histories, especially Backus's "History of the Baptists," second edition, a sketch of his life and character by Rev. C. E. Barrows, in the *Baptist Quarterly* for 1872 (vol. vi. pp. 481–502); for a vigorous discussion of his place in history, articles in the same periodical for 1876 (vol. x. pp. 181–204, 257–281), by Prof. J. C. C. Clarke, under the title of "The Pioneer Baptist Statesman"; for a thorough review of the visit to Lynn and the adverse criticisms thereon, a pamphlet of 39 pages, by H. M. King, D.D., published in 1880. A full memoir of Mr. Clarke's life and times is still a desideratum.

Clarke, Prof. John C. C., of Shurtleff College, was born at Providence, R. I., Feb. 27, 1833, being descended from Joseph Clarke, a brother of Dr. John Clarke, one of the founders of Newport. He graduated at the public school in Providence, and showed then his predilections as a student by taking up independently such languages as French and Spanish, acquiring in private study a free use of them. At the age of seventeen he went to New York City as clerk in the importing house of Booth & Edgar, remaining there some four years. In 1853 he was converted and baptized in the fellowship of the Strong Place church, Brooklyn. Deciding to prepare for the ministry, he entered the University of Rochester in 1855, and graduated in 1859, having taken the second prize in the Sophomore class for Latin, and the first junior prize for Greek. He graduated from the seminary in 1861, and in September of that year was called to Yonkers, N. Y., where he remained four years, the church having meanwhile a large growth. Removing then to Chicago, he served one year as Professor of Greek in the university, Prof. Misen being engaged in the general service of the institution. In 1866, in connection with the supply of the North Baptist church, Chicago, he was associated with Dr. Colver in giving theological instruction at the university. Dr. Colver removing to Richmond, Prof. Clarke entered the pastorate at Madison, Wis., remaining there until the winter of 1870–71, the church in the mean time paying off an old debt and improving its house of worship, while about fifty were added by baptism. In 1871 he became pastor of the Mount Auburn church, Cincinnati, teaching metaphysics and moral philosophy at the Young Ladies' Institute there. In 1873 he accepted a call to the Beaumont Street church, St. Louis, and in 1875 to the professorship in Shurtleff College, which he now fills. Among Prof. Clarke's writings may be mentioned essays in different reviews upon "Platonism and Early Christianity," "History in Alphabet," "The Pioneer Statesmen," "John Clarke of Newport," besides various contributions to the weekly press. He is an exact scholar, an inspiring teacher, a man of refined tastes, and highly esteemed in all relations.

Clarke, Judge John T., the son of James Clarke and Permelia T. Willborn, a native of Georgia, was born Jan. 12, 1834. He was educated in Mercer University and in Columbian College, D. C., graduating in the former institution in July, 1853, and sharing the first honor with Henry T. Wimberly and J. H. Kilpatrick. He was admitted to the bar in 1854, and entered into partnership with his uncle, Judge M. J. Wellborn, in Columbus. In 1858 he abandoned the law for the ministry, while practising at Lumpkin, and accepted the charge of the Second Baptist church in Atlanta, in January, 1859, having been ordained in 1858. Throat disease terminated his pastorate at the end of two years, when he retired to the country and rusticated until January, 1863, preaching only occasionally. Gov. Jos. E. Brown appointed him judge of the Superior Courts of the Pataula circuit in January, 1863, to which position he was elected in March, 1867, receiving a new commission for four years. During the time when Gen. Meade was placed in charge of the military district, of which Georgia was a part, some general orders were issued by him which Judge Clarke felt conscientiously bound to ignore; and, when another order was given threatening trial by a military commission, and punishment by fine and imprisonment for all judges who disregarded the military orders of Gen. Meade, Judge Clarke adjourned the courts of Early and Miller Counties, on the ground that the "illegal, unconstitutional, oppressive, and dangerous" orders of Gen. Meade deprived the court of freedom of action. For this he was removed from office by Gen. Meade. In 1868 he returned to the practice of law, in which he is still engaged; but he has always preached, even when holding courts, if an opportunity permitted. Judge Clarke has represented his district in the State senate with honor to himself. He is a member of the board of trustees for Mercer University, and is mainly to be credited with the passage, at the Convention, of that resolution which resulted in the removal of Mercer University from Penfield to Macon.

Judge Clarke has always been an active church member, and for years has been an efficient Sunday-school superintendent. He is a fine speaker, a good Latin, Greek, and French scholar, and has some knowledge of German, Hebrew, and Italian. He is well read in polite literature, is a graceful and strong writer, possesses a quick, discriminating, logical, and resolute mind, and, as a business man, is well known for his energy, accuracy, and integrity.

Clarke, Rev. Miner G.—After some forty years of remarkably efficient service, Mr. Clarke is now spending the evening of life at Sandwich, Ill., unable, through infirmity of health, to share as formerly in the work, but still deeply interested in all that concerns the prosperity of Christ's cause. He was born Dec. 9, 1809, at Woodstock, Conn., and is descended from the same family stock as the Rev. John Clarke, who, in the seventeenth century, gathered the First Baptist church of Newport, R. I. Mr. Clarke was converted when but a youth, and was baptized by Rev. J. B. Atwell. He studied at Newton, graduating there in 1837. Thrown upon his own resources during this five years' course of study, his health was injured by overwork, and the consequences have continued to be felt during his whole life since. He was ordained in the autumn of 1837 as pastor of the Baptist church in Suffield, Conn.; his health failing, he was obliged to resign his pastorate after a brief service. Rest having in some degree restored him, he accepted a call to Grafton, Mass. Here he gathered a Baptist church, and, in the course of an eighteen months' pastorate, saw a flourishing Sunday-school established and a neat and tasteful house of worship built. Health again failed, so that a suspension of labor became necessary. After his strength had been in some measure re-established, he was called to the work of gathering a church in the centre of Norwich City, Conn. The result was the organization of the Central Baptist church of that city, in whose forty years of blessed history he is now permitted to rejoice. The first six years of that history, under his own pastorate, during which time hundreds were baptized, old dissensions healed, and two flourishing Baptist churches made to stand where before were only the *débris* of past mistakes and failures, must be regarded as having largely determined the direction and the character of that which has since followed. After six years in that pastorate, a like service called him to Springfield, Mass. Accepting the care of the First church in that city, by a change of location and methods of work, and the erection of a fine new house of worship, with large additions to the church, a new face was put upon the Baptist cause there. Failure of health again compelled a suspension of labor, but rest having in a measure restored him, after supplying for a time the pulpit of the First church, Williamsburgh, made vacant by the lamented death of Rev. M. J. Rhees, and after some months' service for the Bible Society, as its financial secretary, he accepted the call of the Tabernacle church, Philadelphia, and removed to that city in 1851. A five-years' prosperous pastorate followed. Constant additions to the church rewarded the devoted joint labor of pastor and people, the present beautiful and convenient house was built, and congregations gathered which filled its pews. With the labors of this pastorate was associated service upon the board of the Publication Society, and in other spheres of important public duty. In 1856 the state of his health made another change necessary. Removing to Indianapolis, he established there the *Witness*, a Baptist weekly, and conducted it during six years with admirable skill and with most excellent effect, as regards denominational interests in Indiana and the West. After six years, believing that a residence near the lakes would benefit his health, he sold the *Witness* to Rev. E. W. Clark, and removed to Chicago, entering into business in that city with his sons, and associating with this, important service as financial secretary of the university. With this, a brief pastorate at Evanston, near Chicago, and four years' service as financial secretary of the Home Mission Society for New York, his active labors reached a close. An injury received in New York City, followed by nervous prostration, left him no alternative, and retiring from public service, he made his home at Sandwich, Ill. Remembered with admiration and affection by his associates in many spheres of service, he now (1880) awaits the higher call.

Clarke, Rev. N. L., pastor at Decatur, Miss., for the past thirty-three years, was born in North Carolina in 1812; settled in Mississippi in 1840, and the year following was ordained. His labors have been chiefly confined to the counties of Kemper, Neshoba, Leake, Scott, Newton, Lauderdale, Clarke, Jasper, Jones, Covington, Simpson, Smith, and Rankin, and the adjoining parts of Alabama. He has baptized over one thousand persons; aided in constituting between forty-five and fifty churches; about forty of which were gathered by his own labors; has presided as moderator of Mount Pisgah Association twenty-four years, and of the General Association of Mississippi from its organization; he has also been associate editor of the *Southern Baptist*.

Clay, Judge Joseph.—This distinguished minister of the gospel was born in Savannah, Aug. 16, 1764. His father was a Revolutionary soldier; he was also an eminent lawyer and an esteemed judge. The subject of this sketch graduated at Princeton, with the highest honors of his class, in 1784. After admission to the bar he soon became one of the ablest and most popular lawyers in Georgia, and his reputation reached the most distant parts of his country. In 1796 he was appointed United States judge for the district of Georgia, by President George Washington. He held this position for about five years, the duties of which he discharged with such wisdom and uprightness as secured for him the respect of all good citizens.

In 1803 the Spirit of God led him to see his sinfulness, and to trust the precious Saviour for salvation; and though brought up under Pedobaptist influence, like many other men of culture, he united with the Baptists, and soon after he was ordained to the ministry, and became assistant pastor of the First Baptist church of Savannah. In 1806 he visited New England and preached in many of the principal centres of population, to the great spiritual enjoyment of the large congregations that heard his blessed teachings. He was for a time associate pastor with Dr. Samuel Stillman in the First Baptist church of Boston, and in August, 1807, he became his successor. His health permitted him only for a short period to discharge the duties of his office; but during that time throngs of the intelligent and refined waited on his ministrations, and Christians of all conditions heard him gladly. His residence in Boston was a great blessing to the Baptists and to the whole city.

He had a commanding appearance, an eye of singular beauty, a heart overflowing with tenderness, and an eloquence that moved the congregations which he addressed to tears or ecstasies at his pleasure. He had a spirit of deep humility, and as he believed that the love of Christ had purchased and applied his salvation, and would certainly render it triumphant, he was ready to give up all the errors of his Episcopalian education and unite with the first denomination of Christians that ever followed Jesus; and he was fully prepared to renounce the honors and emoluments of a distinguished lawyer, who had occupied the position of a United States judge, that he might preach Jesus to the perishing.

Clay, Rev. Porter, was the brother of Henry Clay, and the fifth son of the Rev. John Clay, a Baptist minister of Hanover Co., Va. He was born in Virginia, March, 1779, and removed to Kentucky in early life with his mother and her husband, and reached manhood in that State, where so many Virginia Baptists found homes. He studied the legal profession, and received the appointment of Auditor of Public Accounts from Governor Slaughter, a distinguished Baptist. The position was highly respectable, and financially one of the best in the State. His second wife was Mrs. Elizabeth Hardin, the widow of Hon. M. D. Hardin, formerly a Senator of the United States, who brought him the occupancy of "one of the best farms in Kentucky."

He was converted and baptized in 1815, and soon after gave himself to the ministry of the Word. He was a popular preacher, greatly esteemed by the churches which he served. After he had lost all his property, his brother Henry offered him "a residence and the means of support at Ashland, but he declined it, saying, 'he owed his service to God, and he would take care of him.' Nor was he disappointed." He died in 1850, in the full enjoyment of the Christian's hope.—*From a sketch written by Henry Clay.*

Clemmons, A. E., D.D., was born in Shelbyville, Tenn., Sept. 14, 1822; educated at Shelbyville Academy; professed religion when seventeen years old; commenced preaching in his twentieth year; ordained at New Bethel church, Noxubee Co., Miss., in 1844; ministered to New Bethel church, Miss.; Lewisville church, Ark.; Mount Lebanon and Meriden churches, La.; performed hard and useful service as a missionary in Mississippi and Arkansas, and as agent for the endowment of Mount Lebanon University, La.; served Marshall church, Texas, from 1855 to 1861, and 1865–69; was chaplain of the 3d Texas Regiment during the war; was pastor of Shreveport church, La., from 1869 to 1874; has been pastor of Longview church, Texas, since 1874. Although in charge of this church and others during his residence in Texas, he has lived at Marshall twenty-one years. Received the degree of D.D. from Waco University. He is moderator of Loda Lake Association, was president of the General Association of Texas a number of years, and is now president of East Texas Convention. He has served various Baptist bodies as agent, and aided in the establishment of several Baptist schools. He has been a prominent, popular, laborious, and able preacher from his ordination up to the present time, and exercises a commanding influence in Eastern Texas.

Cleveland, W. C., M.D., D.D., a native of Dallas Co., Ala., was born June 22, 1835. His father, Deacon Carter W. Cleveland (deceased), was one of the most prominent citizens of that county, and one of the most influential laymen in the State; he was wealthy, intelligent, wise, and upright. Dr. Cleveland graduated when a youth in the University of Alabama, and in medicine in the city of New York, and arose to distinction as a physician. He abandoned that profession and entered the ministry in 1869; was called immediately to Carlowville; soon after and for several years his time as pastor was divided between that place, Snow Hill, and Pleasant Hill,—three village churches in refined and intelligent communities,—where most gratifying results attended his ministrations. Some four years since he was called to the church in the city of Selma, where he labors with distinguished ability and success in charge of a church which has become second to none in the State. The title of D.D. was conferred on him by Howard College in 1875. Dr. Cleveland is an accomplished Christian gentleman, of courtly bearing, of eminent consecration and piety, a laborious and wise pastor, standing in the front rank of the Southern Baptist pulpit. Regarded in Alabama as among the very best preachers and safest counselors, taking hold of all our denominational interests with zeal and determination, he exerts the highest influence. None is more trusted, none more able, none from whom more is expected.

Clift, Hon. Amos, son of Capt. Amos and Thankful (Denison) Clift, was born in Groton, Aug. 7, 1805; became a distinguished masterbuilder; in military life rose to be colonel of 8th Regiment of Connecticut militia; filled, first and last, nearly every town office; was representative in the General Assembly of the State; became judge of the Probate Court; greatly interested in educational and religious affairs; converted and baptized at the age of sixteen; first a member of Second Baptist church in Groton, afterwards of Third church; died at his residence in Groton, Aug. 18, 1878, aged seventy-three years; a man of honor and of wide influence.

Clinch, Charles F., Esq., is a member of the Baptist church at Musquash, St. John Co., New Brunswick; was president of the Baptist Convention of the Maritime Provinces for the year ending August, 1880; is a liberal supporter of home missions and all other benevolent operations of the Baptist denomination.

Clinic Baptism.—This baptism received its name from the Greek word κλίνη, a bed, because the sick persons who received it were generally unable to move from their beds. It was regarded as a defective baptism. Eusebius says, "It was not lawful to promote one baptized by pouring on his sick-bed to any order of the clergy." (Eccles. Hist., lib. vi. 43, p. 244. Parisiis, 1659.) And in the same chapter he declares his approbation of the opinion of Cornelius, bishop of Rome, in which he expresses doubts about the validity of the famous clinic baptism of Novatian, when he was poured around (περιχὲω) in a time of sickness, and he adds, "If indeed it be proper to say that one like him did receive baptism."

Some greeted these persons on recovery with contempt and ridicule, and called them *Clinics* instead of *Christians.* Cyprian denounces such treatment. "As to the nickname," says he, "which some have thought fit to fix upon those who have thus (by baptism on their beds) obtained the grace of Christ through his saving water and through faith in him, and their calling such persons *Clinics* instead of *Christians,* I am at a loss to find the original of this appellation," etc. (Ep. 76, ad Magnum, pp. 121, 122. Coloniæ, 1607.) Clinic baptism appears more frequently in modern controversy than the extent of its use justified. It was regarded as a doubtful, defective, and cowardly baptism, subjecting the recipient to the sneers of his acquaintances if he recovered, and as a consequence it was very little practised. Novatian's case is by far the most prominent; the other allusions to the abortive rite are so rare among the ancients who performed it that it is scarcely worthy of notice. But while it existed it was abundant proof that the baptism of unconscious infants was either unknown or but little used. If almost every child, as in France or Italy now, was baptized in infancy, there could be no room for baptizing terrified dying adults, as they had the rite already, and it was not lawful to repeat it.

Clopton, Rev. Abner W., was born in Pittsylvania Co., Va., March 24, 1784. Until the age of sixteen he attended school and made remarkably rapid progress. For five years he was engaged as clerk in a store in the neighborhood of his home. At the age of nineteen he married,—a most unfortunate event, as it afterwards proved, tingeing with gloom his whole after-life. He resolved to enter one of the learned professions; prosecuted a classical course at several schools; engaged himself as teacher in South Carolina, and entered, about 1808, the Junior class at Chapel Hill, N. C., where he graduated, receiving the degree of A.B., and afterwards that of A.M. Having decided to enter the medical profession, he went to Philadelphia in 1811 to attend the courses of lectures there. A severe illness brought him to reflection upon his lost condition, and was the means of his conversion. He returned to Virginia, was baptized in August, 1812, and joined the Shockoe church. Soon after he was engaged as tutor at Chapel Hill, and began the practice of medicine under very favorable auspices. Another severe illness brought him to the decision to consecrate himself wholly to the work of his Master, which, however, was not carried into effect until about 1823, when, receiving an invitation to become the pastor of several churches in Charlotte Co., Va., he settled there. Here he was eminently successful in his labors, many being converted and baptized, and the churches purified and greatly strengthened. Shortly after his settlement in Virginia he became deeply interested in the promotion of the tract cause. More than 100 societies auxiliary to the Baptist General Tract Society were formed by him during his journeyings in Virginia. He was also instrumental in bringing many excellent books into circulation among the churches, and especially Scott's Commentary. He was deeply interested also in the temperance movement. With several other pastors he formed the Virginia Society for the Promotion of Temperance, a few months only after the organization of the American Temperance Society. He traveled everywhere throughout the State, and had the pleasure of seeing a most marked improvement in the social habits of the people. In 1831 he accepted a temporary agency in behalf of the Columbian College, and, though death soon removed him from the scene of his labors, he was quite successful. Besides performing the duties of agent gratuitously, he contributed himself the sum of $3000 towards its funds. He was also specially active in the erection of new and more commodious buildings for public worship, and in providing ample room and accommodations for the colored members of his congregations. As a preacher, he was greatly successful. His sermons were marked by simplicity, pathos, and a pointed practical bearing, and, as a result, many were brought, through his ministrations, to a knowledge of the truth. On his death-bed, racked with keen agony, he wrote a most touching letter to his aged parents, in which occur these words, showing his love of his Lord and the submissiveness with which he yielded himself to his fatherly chastisements: "On other occasions of distress and affliction my mind has been distracted with fear and anxiety; but in this, I feel neither murmurs nor repinings. I would not have died without this affliction, or something resembling it, on any consideration, believing it to be as necessary in the scheme of my salvation as the atonement of Christ."

Again, after having carefully reviewed his life, useful as it had been made to multitudes, and comparing it with the holy law of God, he writes, "My heart and life again passed in review before me, and I appeared to myself more vile than I suppose it is possible for you to conceive. I felt, however, and I still feel, that if God should lock me up in hell, I would attempt to praise him there for his great goodness towards me." Of this faithful laborer in the Master's vineyard Dr. Jeter says, "He was one of the most devotedly pious men he had ever known."

Clough, Rev. John E., the Teloogoo missionary, whose labors in the East have produced the most extensive harvests gathered in any heathen field in modern times, was born July 16, 1836, near Frewsbury, Chautauqua Co., N. Y. When a mere child he was taken to Illinois, and soon after to Iowa. He was in the employment of the United States government with a party of surveyors in Minnesota for four years, and during this period he became thoroughly acquainted with their business. As he left the wilderness he resolved to perfect his education as his next great duty, and to devote himself to the legal profession as his life-work. For this purpose he entered Burlington Collegiate Institute in Iowa in 1857, and commenced the study of law in 1858. In the college "his attention was arrested by the difference between the character and bearing of the persons whom he had just left and those with whom he was now brought into hourly contact. Immediately upon this came the unbidden query, 'Why this difference?' What is it that makes everything here so gentle, kind, and pure as compared with the scenes and persons recently left? These people read the Bible and pray to God. Does this fact point to the source of the contrast which I see and feel, and must confess? So his thoughts ran. His anxiety at length drove him to the Bible, the Bible drew him to the throne of grace, and to the life and love of a bleeding Redeemer, and that Redeemer gave him peace in believing." He was baptized by Dr. G. J. Johnson into the fellowship of the Burlington church, whose ministry was greatly blessed to Mr. Clough in leading him to Christ, and in counseling him when he found Jesus.

After his conversion he felt that God had called him to be a minister, and to proclaim Jesus to the most benighted people under heaven. He graduated at Upper Iowa University in 1862, and was appointed a missionary to India in August, 1864. He arrived in that country in March, 1865, and labored more than a year among the Teloogoos at Nellore. In September, 1866, he removed to Ongole, and on the 1st of January, 1867, organized a church with 8 members; that community at the end of 1879 had 13,106 members, probably the largest church in the world. It has 46 native preachers, and 30 helpers or lay preachers. Of this throng of converts, 3262 were baptized at Ongole on three successive days. From June 16 to July 31, 1878, 8691 persons were immersed in the name of the Trinity. In this mighty work there was no excitement, and no efforts to press the people into the church. Owing to special aid which Mr. Clough was enabled to render the inhabitants in a dreadful famine, he delayed his great baptisms for a considerable period, and sought help from his missionary brethren to make a careful and protracted examination of the candidates. A mighty outpouring of the Spirit of God brought this multitude to Jesus, and the same Spirit is keeping them in the narrow and blessed way. Mr. Clough was the chief human instrument in this marvelous work. And he still toils in the field where grace has wrought such wonders.

He has a clear intellect, a powerful will, an orderly mind, and a heart full of love to Jesus and perishing souls. With the strictest truth he might say, "To me to live is Christ," and with equal veracity we may declare, that Christ has given eternal life through his ministry to the greatest number of converts ever brought into his fold, in so brief a space by the labors of one man.

Peint par J. Rigo.

BAPTÊME DE CLOVIS À NOTRE DAME DE REIMS, 25 DÉCEMBRE, 496.

Gravé par Jazet.

Clovis, The Baptism of.—Clovis I. was born about A.D. 456. He was the enterprising and daring chief of a small tribe of the Franks of Tournai. In a projected war against the Alemanni, in 496, the Frankish tribes elected him general-in-chief, during hostilities, according to their custom. The Alemanni were attacked at Zülpich, near Cologne. The battle was very desperate, and Clovis fearing defeat, and distrusting his idols, prayed to the God of his Christian wife, Clotilda, for the victory. He routed the enemy, and, according to a vow made on the field of battle, he was baptized at Rheims, with a large number of his soldiers and others. Hincmar, archbishop of Rheims, in the middle of the ninth century, a successor of Remigius who baptized Clovis, a writer of great talents, with all needful information, thus describes the most important event in the early history of France:

"The way leading to the baptistery was put in order; on both sides it was hung with painted canvas and curtains; overhead there was a protecting shade; the streets were leveled; the baptistery of the church was prepared for the occasion, and sprinkled with balsam and other perfumes. Moreover, the Lord bestowed favor on the people that they might think that they were refreshed with the sweet odors of Paradise.

"The holy pontiff Remigius, holding the hand of the king, went forth from the royal residence to the baptistery, followed by the queen and the people; the holy gospels preceded them, with all hymns and spiritual songs and litanies, and the names of the saints were loudly invoked. . . . The blessed Remigius officiated on the solemn occasion. . . . Clovis having entered the life-giving fountain, . . . after confessing the orthodox faith in answer to questions put by the holy pontiff, *was baptized by trine immersion according to ecclesiastical usage* (*secundum ecclesiasticam morem, baptizatus est trina mersione*), in the name of the holy and undivided Trinity, Father, Son, and Holy Spirit. . . . Moreover, from his *army three thousand men were baptized, without counting women and children*. His sisters, also, Albofledis and Landeheldis, were baptized." (Vita Sanct. Remig. Patrol. Lat., vol. cxxv. pp. 1160–61, Migne. Parisiis.)

The name Clovis is the same as Louis, and, no doubt, the candidate baptized by Remigius gave his name to seventeen subsequent monarchs of France, and a host of other Frenchmen and Germans. Clovis was the first king of the Franks, and his baptism is commemorated in French paintings, and represented in pictures in French books, and distributed throughout the nation in handsome engravings. The fine steel engraving from which the picture of the baptism of Clovis was taken was purchased for the writer in Paris. In primary French histories for the use of schools it is common in France to use a woodcut representing Clovis in a baptistery nearly full of water. We have one of these pictures. By the engraving accompanying this article, artistic, historic France testifies that immersion was the early mode of baptism.

Clowes, Francis, was born at Heacham, Norfolk, England, Jan. 10, 1805, of Baptist parentage. He entered Bristol College to prepare for the ministry, having been commended by the church in his native place, and at the conclusion of the regular course of study he proceeded to Aberdeen University. He returned to Bristol in 1831 to become pastor of the Thrinell Street church, and labored there until, in 1836, he was appointed classical tutor of Horton College, now Rawdon. He occupied this post until 1851, when he retired in failing health. The promotion of Baptist periodical literature engaged his hearty sympathy. He took a leading part in establishing and maintaining *The Church* and *The Appeal*, monthly magazines, and after his retirement from collegiate work he became one of the editors of *The Freeman*. With this weekly paper he was connected for several years, and rendered efficient service in his editorial capacity to the various interests of the denomination. He was ardent and impassioned in his attachment to Baptist principles. He died suddenly, May 7, 1873.

Coats, Rev. A. J., is an eloquent, laborious, and successful pastor, located at Portland, Oregon, where he was ordained in September, 1877. The church under his ministry has grown very rapidly in power and numbers, and is foremost in educational and mission work for the city, the State, and the world. He was born at Schuyler Lake, N. Y., Sept. 1, 1847, and converted in 1861. He graduated at Hamilton College, Clinton, N. Y., in 1874, and from Rochester Theological Seminary in 1877.

Cobb, Gov. Howell, one of the most distinguished of all the great men whom Georgia has produced, was born in Jefferson County, Sept. 7, 1815. His father, Col. John A. Cobb, was a native of North Carolina.

Gov. Cobb graduated at the State University of Georgia in the year 1834, taking the third honor. In 1836 he was admitted to the bar, and gave such evidence of ability and legal attainments that he was elected by the Legislature solicitor-general of the Western Circuit in the year following. He held the office for three years, and was elected to Congress in October, 1842, taking his seat December, 1843. He was chosen Speaker of the House in 1849, and was successively re-elected three times. In Congress he gained great celebrity by the delivery of speeches on various subjects; and his election to the speakership was a flattering tribute to his ability and integrity. In 1851 he was elected governor of Georgia by the largest majority ever given in the State up to that period. He was re-elected to Congress in 1855, and when Mr. Buchanan became President, in 1857, Mr. Cobb entered the Cabinet as Secretary of the Treasury. This position he resigned Dec. 6, 1860, and returned to Georgia.

After secession, when the Provisional Congress convened at Montgomery, Ala., Feb. 4, 1861, to form a government and frame a constitution, he was elected president. When the war began Gov. Cobb became an active participant, and rose from the rank of colonel to that of major-general. After the return of peace he resumed the practice of his profession, and at once occupied a position in the front rank of the legal brotherhood. He died suddenly at the Fifth Avenue Hotel, New York, while on a visit to that city on the 9th of October, 1868, aged fifty-three years, one month and two days. No man ever died in Georgia more lamented by the lowly, more honored by the great. In the domestic circle, as a citizen, at the bar, and in the loftiest walks of political life, he was always the amiable, patriotic, able, eloquent, generous, and benevolent man. No public man in the State has ever been more loved than he; none upon whom the affections of so many were concentrated. Whether viewed as a statesman, orator, lawyer, or public man, he was undoubtedly great,—his abilities soared almost beyond the reach of emulation; yet, as a private citizen, a friend, and the head of a family, he was still greater, and far more admirable. But to all his other beauties and excellencies of character Gov. Cobb added that of being a Christian. During his whole life he had been a perfect model of all that is noble and generous, high-minded, and charitable; perhaps no higher type of the gentleman, the friend, the master, the father, the husband, existed; but it was only late in life that he professed faith in Jesus and became a Christian. In reply to a question asked him by his Baptist pastor, he said, " I accept Jesus Christ as divine, as the anointed Saviour of man. My doubts on this subject are all gone."

"General," was the rejoinder, "do you trust him as your Saviour?"

"I do, sir," he replied. Gen. Cobb attended the services of a Baptist church, and was identified with that denomination all his life.

Cobb, Col. John A., son of John Cobb, was born in Virginia, but brought up in North Carolina, by his maternal grandfather, Howell Lewis, of Granville. He married Miss Sarah R. Rootes, of Fredericksburg, Va., and emigrated to Georgia, where he spent the remainder of his life, occupying a high social position, and bringing up a family most eminent for ability and the highest mental and moral excellence. He was born July 5, 1783, and died at the age of seventy-four, at Athens, Clarke Co., Ga. He was a member of the Baptist church in that city.

He was a man distinguished for integrity, generosity, and kindness of heart. The strictest morality and uprightness of character marked his whole life. A maxim of his still revered by his descendants is, "If you can say nothing in praise of a person, hold your tongue." While on his death-bed he calmly gave directions in regard to his burial to his youngest son, Maj. John B. Cobb; then calling his children and grandchildren around his bedside, the dying patriarch placed his emaciated hands upon their heads and blessed them in the name of the Father, Son, and Holy Ghost.

His oldest son was Gen. Howell Cobb, who had been Speaker of the House of Representatives, governor of Georgia, and Secretary of the Treasury under President Buchanan. His second son was Gen. T. R. R. Cobb, who was killed at Fredericksburg, a man of exalted worth and abilities. These, with his loving wife and daughters, were present at the death-scene.

The dying patriarch requested his son, Gen. T. R. R. Cobb, to lead in worship, as he wished to go to sleep. After a tearful prayer, amid the weeping of all present, he gently fell asleep,—the sleep that knew no awakening till the resurrection morning.

His memory is held in the highest veneration by one of the largest and most distinguished family connections in the State of Georgia.

Cobb, Rev. N. B., was born in Wayne Co., N. C., Feb. 1, 1836; graduated at Chapel Hall, at eighteen, in 1854; taught school in Cabarrus County and Goldsborough till 1857, when he read law with Chief Justice Pearson, and practised in Pitt, Wayne, and Green Counties till October, 1859, when he left the Episcopal Church, in which he had been a vestryman for several years, and was baptized by Rev. H. Petty, and ordained in Wilson in 1860, the Presbytery consisting of Revs. Levi Thorne, I. B. Solomon, H. Petty, G. W. Keene, W. C. Lacy, and J. G. Barclay. Mr. Cobb was chaplain of the 4th N. C. Regiment for a time, and rendered distinguished service to the cause of religion as superintendent of army colportage from 1862 till the close of the war. After the war ended Mr. Cobb, in connection with Dr. J. D. Hufham, edited the *Daily Record* of Raleigh for six months; he then became corresponding secretary of the Sunday-School Board, and has since served as pastor of the churches of Elizabeth City; Second church of Portsmouth, Va.; Shelby, N. C.; Tilesville, Rockingham, and Fayetteville, and has taught much in connection with preaching. Mr. Cobb is the Baptist statistician of North Carolina, and at present the president of the Baptist State Convention.

Cobb, Nathaniel R., was born in Falmouth,

Me., near the city of Portland, Nov. 3, 1798. His father dying when he was very young, he removed with his mother to Plymouth, Mass. In the sixteenth year of his age he became a clerk in the store of Ripley & Freeman, enterprising merchants in Boston, and at the age of twenty-one established himself in business as one of the partners of the house of Freeman & Cobb. He had already become a hopeful Christian, and joined the Charles Street Baptist church, under the ministry of Rev. Dr. Sharp. The spirit of consecration of himself, his talents, and his possessions took strong hold on Mr. Cobb's mind, and he drew up the following resolutions, subscribing them with his own hand, in November, 1821:

"By the grace of God, I will never be worth over $50,000.

"By the grace of God, I will give one-fourth of the net profits of my business to charitable and religious uses.

"If I am ever worth $20,000, I will give one-half of my net profits, and if I am ever worth $30,000 I will give three-fourths, and the whole after $50,000.

"So help me God, or give to a more faithful steward and set me aside.

"N. R. COBB."

These resolutions Mr. Cobb, by "the grace of God," was enabled to keep to the letter. It was not long before he reached, in spite of some heavy losses, the outside limit of $50,000, which he had assigned as the sum with which he would be content. Nine years after he was established in business he offered a surplus of $7500, which had accumulated in his hands, to found a professorship at Newton. To the theological institution, then in its infancy, he gave at different times some $15,000. "Although there is a group of other names associated with that now celebrated institution, yet eminent among the few whom we honor as founders that were benefactors for many years is the name of the young merchant of Boston, Nathaniel R. Cobb."

Mr. Cobb's example, we cannot doubt, stimulated other men in the business walks of life to imitate his course of action, and did its part in bringing forth those generous sums which, by our Christian merchants, have been given to help on so many noble causes. He lived long enough to see some of the rich and ripe fruits of his benevolence, and to thank God that he had put it into his heart to render to the cause of Christ a service so acceptable. His death occurred May 24, 1834.

Cobb, Gov. R. W., was born in St. Clair Co., Ala., the 25th of February, 1829. He is a lawyer of distinguished ability, an ex-officer of the Confederate army, and the owner of a large interest in one of the iron companies at Helena, Ala., where he resides. He was elected to the State senate from the counties of Shelby and Bibb in 1872; re-elected to the senate from the counties of Shelby, Jefferson, and Walker in 1876, and he was elected president of the senate the succeeding session of the General Assembly. In these positions he gained great distinction and popularity, and he was elected governor of the State in 1878, and re-elected to that position in 1880, by the largest vote ever polled in Alabama for any candidate. He is a popular chief executive, meeting all the demands of that responsible station. His church membership is with the little church of Helena, after the welfare of which he watches with a deep and active interest. Gov. Cobb is a genial, social, pleasant-spirited man: plain and unpretending, he has the power of drawing men around him in confidence and affection. He has been twice married, and has a most interesting family.

Coburn, Gov. Abner, was born in that part of Skowhegan which was formerly Bloomfield, Me., March 22, 1803. His father, Eleazar Coburn, moved from Dracut, Mass., in 1792, at the age of fifteen,

GOV. ABNER COBURN.

and was one of the early settlers in the upper Kennebec valley. He was a farmer and land surveyor. Soon after arriving at age, Abner, with a younger brother, Philander, assisted his father in surveying, exploring, and appraising the million acres known as the "Bingham Kennebec Purchase" for the Bingham heirs. They, soon after, formed a co-partnership, under the firm-name of E. Coburn & Sons, which continued until the death of one of his sons in 1845. The two brothers still carried on the business under the firm-name of A. & P. Coburn, till the death of Philander, in 1876. Their principal business was lumbering, including the purchase and sale of land, and the cutting, driving, and selling of logs. The company owns about 450,000 acres in Maine, and about 100,000 in the West.

Gov. Coburn has always taken a decided interest in politics, but has been too much engaged in business to be much in public life. He was a member of the Legislature in 1838, 1840, and 1844, a member of the governor's council in 1855 and 1857, and governor in 1863. His largest public charities have been $50,000 to his native county to build a court-house, and about $75,000 to Colby University, formerly Waterville College, of which $50,000 were for the endowment of Waterville Classical Institute. Gov. Coburn is characterized by a remarkable memory of facts, practical sagacity, and scrupulous integrity and good faith in business. He is a constant worshiper at the Baptist church, taking a deep interest, although not a member, in all matters that affect its prosperity.

Coburn, Samuel Weston, was born in Bloomfield, Me., July 14, 1815. He was a graduate of Waterville College, now Colby University, of the class of 1841. He belonged to a family of great energy of character, his father, Eleazar Coburn, Esq., being one of the wealthiest and most influential citizens of the section of the State in which he lived. After graduating, Mr. Coburn was engaged in business as a merchant and manufacturer for twelve years, and spent the remainder of his life on his farm. He was a consistent member of the Baptist church, and took a deep interest in educational matters in his native town for many years. He died July 30, 1873.

Four brothers out of the Coburn family were graduates of Waterville College: Stephen (class of 1839), Alonzo and Samuel W. (class of 1841), and Charles (class of 1844). They were brothers of Gov. Abner Coburn.

Cocke, Prof. Charles Lewis, was born Feb. 21, 1820, in King William Co., Va. He was trained in the schools of the neighborhood under Maj. Thomas Dabney and Thomas H. Fox. At the age of ten he entered the Virginia Baptist Seminary (Richmond College), where he remained more than two years, holding the position of superintendent of the grounds, the school at that time being conducted on the manual labor system. At eighteen he entered the Columbian College, and after two years' study graduated in 1840. While at college was hopefully converted, and baptized by Dr. O. B. Brown into the fellowship of the First church of Washington, in 1839, and took at once a most active part in all its services. Mr. Cocke, before his graduation, was called to a tutorship of mathematics in the Virginia Baptist Seminary, which he held until 1846, filling at the same time the position of steward of the college. In 1846 he took charge of the Hollins Institute, at Botetourt Springs, Va., and by his untiring energy and tact he made it one of the best educational institutions for girls in the entire South. (See article HOLLINS INSTITUTE.) Female education is with him a sacred duty. He is striving to give to daughters as liberal an education as is so freely offered to sons, and he has the happiness to know that some of the most accomplished and useful of the women of the South received their education under his

PROF. CHARLES LEWIS COCKE.

stimulating and judicious guidance. No man in the country perhaps has written so many valuable practical articles for publication in behalf of higher female education as Prof. Cocke, and they have been instrumental in stimulating others in different parts of the country to aid in the organization of similar institutions. He has been an indefatigable laborer too in all church work, acting as deacon, superintendent of Sunday-schools, leader in prayer-meetings and meetings for church business, introducing new ministers into destitute regions beyond the Ridge, and encouraging all the benevolent organizations of the denomination. He is a valuable counselor in all associational meetings, and has repeatedly served as moderator of those bodies. For years previous to the war, and during its continuance, he took an active part in the religious training of the colored people, and they greatly honor him for his labors in their behalf.

Cohoon, Rev. Alwood, was born in 1843 at Port Medway, Nova Scotia. He was converted in 1863 and baptized the following year. In 1871 he graduated from Acadia College, and in 1872 was ordained as pastor at Paradise, Nova Scotia. At the present time he has charge of a church at Hebron, Nova Scotia, and is corresponding secretary of the Board of Baptist Home Missions in the Maritime Provinces. He is a good organizer, pastor, and preacher.

Coit, Rev. Albert, was born Oct. 1, 1837, in the town of Hastings, Oswego Co., N. Y. He worked on his father's farm until nineteen years of age, receiving his early education in the district schools. At nineteen he began his academic studies at Mexico, Oswego County; completed them at Valley Seminary in the same county. In 1862 he entered Genesee College, Lima, N. Y., and two years later the Junior class of the University of Rochester, from which he graduated in 1866, and from the theological seminary in 1869. His parents were Presbyterians, but he early in life became convinced that the Baptists were nearer the truth, and united with the Baptist church in Central Square, his native village.

While at college at Lima, he was licensed to preach, and while at the theological seminary was ordained assistant pastor of the First Baptist church in Rochester, to take charge of its Lake Avenue mission, now Lake Avenue church. In June, 1870, he assumed the pastorate of the Wellsville Baptist church, where he still remains. During the second seminary year Mr. Coit was employed by the Congregational church of Brighton, Monroe County, to supply their pulpit, and the following vacation by the Rhinebeck church on the Hudson. It was during his period of service for this church that Hon. William Kelly made a public profession of faith and joined the church, being baptized by Rev. William R. Williams, D.D.

Mr. Coit is an able preacher, of decided convictions, a thorough Baptist because of the severe discipline which led him to become one. Still a young man, he commands the respect of the brotherhood throughout a wide section of the State, and is a recognized leader in his Association. His publications are mainly through the newspaper press.

Colby Academy.—This institution is located in New London, N. H. Prof. E. J. McEwan, A.M., is at its head; it has four gentlemen and three ladies engaged in imparting instruction. Last year it had 93 students. It has property worth $175,000. Its endowment amounts to $94,000. Colby Academy has been a great blessing to its numerous pupils, and to the families and communities brought under their influence. Its prospects for continued and increased usefulness are very bright.

Colby, Hon. Anthony, was born in New London, N. H., Nov. 13, 1792. His father, Joseph Colby, established himself in that place in his early man-

COLBY ACADEMY.

hood, having removed from his home in Massachusetts from motives of enterprise and independence, which always characterized him.

Anthony was his second son. From childhood he evinced great fitness for practical life. His nature was eminently sympathetic,—inheriting from his mother a keen discernment of character, he knew men by intuition.

Having been trained in a strictly orthodox, Christian household, and growing up amidst most impressive natural scenery, he was strong, honest, cheerful, and heroic.

He married early in life Mary Everett, a lady of gentleness and delicacy, whose religious character always influenced him.

GOV. ANTHONY COLBY.

He dated his conversion at an early age, but did not make a Christian profession until after his second marriage, to Mrs. Eliza Richardson, of Boston, who was baptized with him by Rev. Reuben Sawyer, in 1843, when they both joined the Baptist church of his native town, of which he had been for many years a faithful supporter. At this time his father, Joseph Colby, died, having been for more than fifty years a pillar in the church and denomination.

Anthony succeeded him in religious responsibilities, and entertaining the same strong doctrinal views, did much towards consolidating the interests of the Baptist denomination in the State.

Naturally intrepid, he originated and carried on a variety of business operations much in advance of his times, and fearlessly assumed the responsibilities of a leader. Identified with the militia, railroads, manufactures, legislative, educational, and religious interests of his native State, he held places of trust in connection with them all. He was major-general of the militia, president of a railroad, an owner of factories, an organizer of Conventions, a trustee of Dartmouth College, and in 1846 governor of the State.

He was as active and successful in politics as in business. He was a personal friend of Daniel Webster, as his father had been with Mr. Webster's father before him. He was adjutant-general of the militia of the State during the war, both at home and in the field.

He was a man of extraordinary kindness and bravery. His wit and brilliancy made him socially a favorite, while he was always faithful in his friendships, honorable and noble in every sentiment of his heart.

The last work of his life was an effort to establish upon a substantial basis the educational institution of his native town, to which the trustees have given his name.

He died peacefully July 13, 1873, at the age of eighty years, in the home of his father, in which he always lived, and he was buried in the cemetery by the side of his parents.

Colby, Hon. Charles L., a son of Gardner and Mary L. R. Colby, was born in 1839 at Boston Highlands, formerly Roxbury, Mass. He was educated at Brown University, and graduated in the class of 1858; married in 1864 to Anna S. Knowlton, of Brooklyn, N. Y. Mr. Colby has been six years a resident of Milwaukee, Wis. He is the president of the Wisconsin Central Railroad Company. He was a member of the Wisconsin Legislature in the winter of 1880, and is a trustee of Brown University. Although occupying high and responsible public and commercial positions requiring much time and labor, Mr. Colby is widely known as an active and earnest Christian worker. He is a member of the First Baptist church in Milwaukee, and the superintendent of its Sunday-school. His Christian and benevolent labors are not confined to his own church and denomination, but are extended to almost every Christian work of the city and State in which he resides.

Colby, Gardner, was born in Bowdoinham, Me., Sept. 3, 1810. The death of his father, whose fortune was lost in consequence of the war with England in 1812-15, devolved upon his mother, a woman of great energy of character, the care of three sons. To meet the wants of her growing family she removed to Charlestown, Mass., and undertook a business which in her skillful hands proved successful. Having secured for himself the rudiments of a good education, young Colby, after an experience of a year's application to the grocery business, opened a retail dry-goods store in Boston when he was but twenty years of age. His energy and prudence were rewarded, and after the lapse of a few years he established himself as a jobber in the city, with whose business interests he was identified for the remainder of his life. Not confining his attention wholly to his regular business, he embarked in enterprises which his mercantile sagacity assured him would be successful. He was largely interested at one time in navigation, and was extensively engaged in the China trade. He made profitable investments in "South Cove" lands in Boston. The manufacture of woolen goods in his hands became very profitable, and during the late war he was one of the largest contractors for the supply of clothing for the soldiers of the Union army. In 1870 he received the appointment of president of the Wisconsin Central

GARDNER COLBY.

Railroad, and gave to the great work of building a road, some 340 miles in length, and much of it through primeval forests, the best thought of his ever active, fertile brain.

But, as has been well said, "Mr. Colby has been known chiefly by his benevolence. His gifts have been large and uniform and cheerful. In early manhood he was associated with those noble laymen, Cobb and Farwell, and Freeman and Kendall, and the Lincolns, Ensign and Heman. He caught their spirit, and set a blessed example by the largeness of his gifts. He began to give freely as clerk with a small salary, and gave liberally from that time to the day of his death. He gave on principle, and no worthy claimant was turned from his door. His courage and hopefulness did much to save Newton and Waterville in dark hours, and his large donations stimulated others to create the endowments which assured the future prosperity of these institutions. His benefactions were liberal to Brown University and other institutions, and flowed in a perennial stream to the Missionary Union and other agencies for Christian work at home and abroad." His gift of $50,000 to what was Waterville College led to the change which took place in the name of that institution, causing it thenceforth to be known as Colby University. Mr. Colby was chosen a trustee of Brown University in 1855, and held that office up to the time of his death. For many years he was the treasurer of the Newton Theological Institution, and he contributed most liberally to its endowment. As an honored and benevolent layman of the Baptist denomination his name will go down to posterity, and his memory be long cherished as the wise counselor and the generous benefactor, who lived and planned for the glory of his Lord and the highest spiritual interests of those whom he sought to bless. Mr. Colby died at his residence in Newton Centre, Mass., April 2, 1879, aged sixty-eight years and seven months.

Colby, Rev. Henry F., A.M., son of Hon. Gardner and Mrs. Mary L. R. Colby, was born at Roxbury (now Boston Highlands), Mass., Nov. 25, 1842, and spent his childhood and youth at Newton Centre, Mass. In 1862 he graduated with the honor of the Latin salutatory of Brown University. After nearly a year spent abroad, he went through a course of study with the class of 1867 at Newton Theological Seminary; was ordained to the work of the ministry as pastor of the First church at Dayton, O., January, 1868, where he still remains.

Mr. Colby has published a class poem, a poem before a convention of the Alpha Delta Phi Fraternity, a discussion on restricted communion, a memoir of his father, Gardner Colby, and occasional sermons. He is closely identified with educational and denominational work in the State of Ohio, and is much esteemed both as a preacher and pastor.

Colby University.—The institution which now bears this name, began its existence as the majority of our Baptist seats of learning commenced life, in a very humble way. An act was passed by the Legislature of Massachusetts, Feb. 27, 1813, establishing a corporation under the title of "The President and Trustees of the Maine Literary and Theological Institution," and endowing it with a township of land, a few miles above the city of Bangor. It was a very good timber section, but a most unsuitable place in which to commence a literary and theological seminary. There is some reason to suspect, as President Champlin has suggested, that "it was a cunning device to defeat the whole project, or at least, to secure in this case, as formerly,

COLBY UNIVERSITY.

that if the voice of John the Baptist must be heard at all, it should be heard only ' crying in the wilderness!'" Not thinking it worth while to attempt to commence an enterprise in a location where sure disaster and defeat would be the consequence, the corporation obtained the consent of the Legislature to start the new institution in any town in Somerset or Kennebec Counties. Waterville, now one of the most attractive villages on the banks of the Kennebec River, was the site selected. Rev. Jeremiah Chaplin, of Danvers, Mass., was chosen Professor of Theology, and Rev. Irah Chase, of Westford, Vt., Professor of Languages, and the 1st of May, 1818, was the day appointed to commence instruction in the institution. Prof. Chaplin accepted his appointment, but Prof. Chase declining his, Rev. Avery Briggs was chosen Professor of Languages, and commenced his duties October, 1819. The Professor of Theology brought several pupils with him, who were already in training for the ministerial office.

In 1820 the Legislature of Maine, now an independent State, granted to the institution a charter, by virtue of which it was invested with collegiate powers, and took the name of Waterville College. The first elected president was Rev. Daniel H. Barnes, of New York, a gentleman of fine culture, and possessing rare qualifications for the position to which he was invited. Mr. Barnes declined the call which had been extended to him. The corporation then elected Prof. Chaplin to the presidential chair, and added to the faculty Rev. Stephen Chapin as Professor of Theology. The first class which graduated was in 1820, and consisted of two persons, one of whom was Rev. George Dana Boardman, the story of whose missionary life is invested with so thrilling an interest. Mr. Boardman, immediately on graduating, was appointed tutor.

The new institution was now fairly started on its career of usefulness. An academy was commenced, with the design to make it what it has so generously proved to be, a feeder of the college. A mechanic's shop also was erected, to furnish such students as wished to earn something by their personal labor an opportunity to do so. The academy lived and ripened into the vigorous, healthy institution now known as the "Waterville Classical Institute." The mechanic's shop, after a twelve years' experiment, was adjudged on the whole to be a failure. Meanwhile, the needed college buildings were, one after another, erected. The usual experience of most institutions starting into life as this had done was the experience of Waterville College. There was self-denial on the part of teachers, an appeal in all directions for funds to carry on the enterprise; struggles, sometimes, for very life; alternations of hope and despondency on the part of its friends; but yet gradual increase of strength, growing ability to carry the burden of responsibility which had been assumed, and a deeper conviction that a favoring Providence would grant enlarged success in due time. To its first president, Rev. Dr. Chaplin, it owes a debt of gratitude and respect, of which it never should lose sight.

President Chaplin resigned after thirteen years of toil and sacrifice endured for the college, and was succeeded by Rev. Rufus Babcock, D.D., who remained in office from 1833 to 1836. The next president, Rev. Robert E. Pattison, D.D., was also three years in office, from 1836 to 1839. His successor was Eliphaz Fay, who was in office from 1841 to 1843, and was succeeded by Rev. David N. Sheldon, D.D., who was president nine years, from 1843 to 1852. Upon the resignation of President Sheldon, Dr. Pattison was recalled, and continued in office another three years, from 1854 to 1857. His successor was Rev. James T. Champlin, D.D., who had filled the chair of Professor of the Greek and Latin Languages from 1841. His term of service commenced in 1857, and closed in 1873. The present incumbent is Rev. H. E. Robins, D.D., who was elected in 1873.

Colby University takes its name from Gardner Colby, Esq., of Boston, whose generous gifts to the college place him among the munificent patrons of our seats of learning. Its endowment is sufficiently large to meet its present necessities, but will need additions to it with the increasing wants of the institution. It may reasonably congratulate itself on the general excellence of its buildings, which are Chaplin Hall, South College, Champlin Hall, Coburn Hall, and Memorial Hall. The first two of these are dormitories of the students, the third contains the pleasant recitation-rooms, the fourth is used for the department of Chemistry and Natural History, and the last named, built to honor the memory of the alumni who fell in their country's service during the late civil war, has in its eastern wing the university library, with its 15,000 volumes and 7500 pamphlets, and in its western wing the college chapel, a room 40 by 38 feet in dimensions. The university has also an observatory and a gymnasium. Three institutions in the State have been brought into close connection with the university,—the Waterville Classical Institute, the Hebron Academy, and the Houlton Academy,—all these are "feeders" of the university. There are at present 62 scholarships, founded by churches or individuals, yielding from $36 to $60 a year. The regular expenses which the student incurs are placed as low as they can reasonably be put, and no really deserving young man will be suffered to dissolve his connection with the university if he is in earnest to prosecute his studies with diligence and fidelity.

Cole, Rev. Addison Lewis, was born in Culpepper Co., Va., Feb. 9, 1831. The family moved to Cass Co., Ill., in 1833, where he lived on a farm until 1858. He was converted and baptized at the

REV. ADDISON L. COLE.

age of seventeen. In 1858 he entered Shurtleff College, Ill., graduating with honor in 1862. He was then ordained, and afterwards studied theology at Shurtleff, graduating in 1866. He was pastor at Owatonna, Minn.; Milwaukee, Wis.; and Minneapolis, Minn. Constant revivals characterized these pastorates. The churches grew rapidly in numbers, strength, and permanent influence. He was two years chaplain to the Minnesota senate. Health failing, he was unable to preach from 1871 to 1877. From 1874 to 1877, in order to gain and retain health, he studied hygienic medicine at a celebrated institute in New York. In 1877 he began preaching again at St. Cloud, Minn., with his usual success, and in 1878 he moved to California, in response to a call from the First Baptist church, Sacramento, which he served one year, and in 1879 he assumed charge of the church at Dixon. Mr. Cole is secretary of the board of California College; an independent thinker, a strong and vigorous writer, a sound theologian, an industrious, conscientious student, a magnetic, eloquent speaker, and a man of marked influence among the Baptists of California.

Cole, George, was born at Sterling, Conn., June 22, 1808; graduated at Brown University in 1834; was Professor of Mathematics in Granville College, O., 1834-37; became editor of the *Cross and Journal* (now *Journal and Messenger*), Cincinnati, O., in 1838, and continued in that position nine years.

From 1847 to 1856 engaged in business, being part of the time one of the editors of the Cincinnati *Gazette;* again took charge of the *Journal and Messenger* in 1856, and continued as its editor until 1864, when failing health compelled him to resign; died in Dayton, Ky., July 14, 1868.

Cole, Rev. Isaac, M.D., was born in Baltimore Co., Md., Sept. 13, 1806. He was educated for the medical profession, and graduated at the University of Maryland in 1827, after which he entered upon its practice in the city of Baltimore. In 1830 he became a member of the Methodist Episcopal Church, serving as a local preacher for about fifteen years, and was then ordained an elder. Having changed his views with regard to baptism and certain doctrinal points, he withdrew from the Methodist Church by certificate, and was baptized by the Rev. Dr. Fuller, on Sept. 28, 1851, and was ordained Oct. 5, 1851. In 1852, Dr. Cole relinquished the practice of medicine and became pastor of the Second Baptist church, Washington, D. C. During his first year here a new house of worship was erected, and during his pastorate 96 persons were baptized. In 1855, Dr. Cole became pastor of the North Baptist church, Philadelphia, and during his stay with them, which was a little more than three years, the membership increased from 140 to 400. In 1858 he became pastor of the Thirteenth Street Baptist church, Washington, and continued to act as such until the union of the Thirteenth Street

REV. ISAAC COLE, M.D.

and the First Baptist church took place, Sept. 25, 1859. In 1860 he became pastor of the Lee Street Baptist church, Baltimore, and while there he built for them a new house of worship, and baptized a large number into the fellowship of the church. Being urgently invited a second time to become pastor of the North church, Philadelphia, Dr. Cole accepted, and during the four years he was with this church upwards of a hundred persons were baptized. After leaving the North church he filled the pulpit of the Eleventh church for a time. From Philadelphia he went to Westminster, Md., and there built another house of worship for the denomination. Feb. 1, 1878, he became pastor of Second Baptist church of Washington, D. C. (the Navy-Yard church), where he has been very successful in his labors, baptizing quite a large number, and greatly improving and beautifying their house of worship.

Cole, Jirah D., D.D., was born in Catskill, N. Y., Jan. 14, 1802. His father, though educated a Presbyterian, was a decided Baptist in conviction. The son was a subject of various impressions from childhood, but was finally awakened under a sermon by Rev. Howard Malcom, then a young pastor in Hudson, and speedily found peace in believing. On Sabbath, 4th March, 1821, he was baptized at Catskill, in company with his father and others. Aug. 23, 1822, having decided to prepare for the ministry, he entered the Literary and Theological Institution at Hamilton, then under the care of Prof. Daniel Hascall. Jonathan Wade and Eugenio Kincaid had just graduated in the first class sent out. A lively missionary spirit had been aroused, and a missionary society formed, of which Mr. Cole was chosen corresponding secretary. At that time it was ascertained that there were only two such societies in the country, one at Andover, the other at Auburn. He graduated in 1826, and almost immediately his active ministry began with the church in Greenville, N. Y. His ordination, however, took place at Ogden, Sept. 12, 1827, of which church he became pastor, and so remained until Nov. 21, 1831, having in the mean time baptized 57. His subsequent labors in New York were three years at Fredonia, several months as supply of the Second Baptist church of Rochester, where he baptized between 40 and 50, another supply of some months at Parma Corners, and two and a half years at Fabius. He then entered the service of the Missionary Union as agent, upon the earnest and repeated solicitations of Elder Alfred Bennett, the first year being spent in New York, and the second in Ohio, Indiana, Illinois, and Missouri. Resigning this agency in 1841, he served as pastor two years at Ithaca, N. Y., accepting then an agency for the Home Mission Society in Maine, New Hampshire, and Vermont. In 1843 he became pastor of the church in Whitesborough, N. Y., and remained there some five years, serving meanwhile also as corresponding secretary of the State Convention.

Thence to Nunda in 1848. In 1850 he was offered the Northwestern agency for foreign missions, his location to be at Chicago. This he accepted, continuing in the service seven and a half years. He then became pastor of the church in Delavan; in 1860, of the church in Barry, Ill., subsequent pastorates being at Valparaiso, Ind.; Galva, Cordova, Atlanta, Lockport, and Rozetta, Ill., where he is now laboring with vigor and success, in spite of his advancing years and infirmity of health.

Dr. Cole has rendered important service with his pen, not only as secretary, but as author and compiler of different works. He was one of the editorial committee in preparing the memorial volume of the first half-century of Madison University, performing a large amount of valuable work. He had previously prepared a "History of the Rock Island Association." Having been appointed historian of the Baptists for the State of Illinois, he has, with great labor and fidelity, prepared a work which, although it remains in manuscript, is one of great value. Dr. Cole's ministry of over fifty years has been one of signal activity and usefulness.

Cole, Hon. Nathan, M.C., was born July 26, 1821. His father came to St. Louis in 1821, from

HON. NATHAN COLE, M.C.

Seneca Co., N. Y. In 1842 he professed religion at Alton, and he has been a member of the Second Baptist church of St. Louis since 1852. He is a diligent student of God's Word now, and he loves to expound it in Sunday-schools. In 1869 he was chosen mayor of St. Louis, and he filled the office to the great satisfaction of his fellow-citizens. In

1876 he was elected president of the Merchants' Exchange. In the autumn of the same year he was sent to Congress to represent the second district of Missouri. He is vice-president of the St. Louis National Bank of Commerce. In 1863 he took an active part in building the first grain-elevator in St. Louis. Nathan Cole is a friend to the poor, to education, and to religion. He has given large amounts to sustain and advance the cause of Jesus, and to further public interests. He is a firm Baptist, with a large scriptural charity. Mr. Cole has been sought by offices, but he aspires to no public position. He is one of the most enlightened, unselfish, and blameless men that ever occupied a seat in Congress.

Coleman, James Smith, D.D., was the only child of pious German parents, and was born in

JAMES SMITH COLEMAN, D.D.

Ohio Co., Ky., Feb. 23, 1827. In early childhood he displayed a great fondness for books, and being taught by his parents to read, he eagerly sought instruction. At the age of eleven he was converted, and soon after was baptized by Alfred Taylor into the fellowship of Beaver Dam Baptist church. In obtaining his education he labored under the disadvantages incidental to frontier life, and at the age of seventeen commenced teaching school and attending a seminary alternately. In his fifteenth year he communicated to his mother the fact of his being powerfully impressed with a call to preach the gospel. This he resisted, and commenced the study of medicine. Abandoning this pursuit, he applied himself to the study of law. He was elected sheriff of his county, then commissioned brigadier-general of the militia, but yielded to the irresistible convictions of duty to preach the gospel. He was ordained in October, 1854, and became the pastor of four churches, preaching much among the destitute with remarkable success. He rapidly increased in popularity and influence. In 1857 he was elected moderator of Gasper River Association, and in 1859 was chosen moderator of the General Association of Kentucky Baptists, holding the position until 1873. He also served the General Association as State evangelist several years. He was called to the pastorate of the First church in Owensborough, Ky., in 1878, and served one year, during which 250 members were added to the church. He resigned on account of impaired health. He is now (1880) pastor of Walnut Street church in Owensborough. During his ministry he has baptized over 3000 persons, about 700 of whom were from other denominations,—principally Methodists. Among the latter may be mentioned Rev. W. P. Yeaman, D.D., now of Glasgow, Mo.

Coleman, Prof. Lewis Minor, was born in Hanover Co., Va., Feb. 3, 1827. He was the son of Thomas B. Coleman, an honored citizen of Carolina County, and for several years its representative in the Virginia Assembly. Until the age of twelve young Coleman received an excellent training under his mother, a pious and highly-accomplished lady. At that period he entered Col. Fontain's school, and in 1841, Concord Academy, an institution of high grade under the charge of his distinguished uncle, F. W. Coleman, afterwards Virginia State senator. His progress here was so rapid and thorough that, in 1844, when only seventeen, he entered the University of Virginia, and graduating in all its schools with distinguished honor, he took the degree of Master of Arts in two years. Immediately after graduation he professed a hope in Christ, and in November, 1846, was baptized into the fellowship of the First Baptist church, Richmond, by the Rev. Dr. Jeter. Soon after Mr. Coleman became an assistant teacher in the academy of his uncle, Mr. F. W. Coleman, and a few years later established, himself, the Hanover Academy, which soon became one of the very best schools of its kind in the State. On the death of that distinguished scholar, Dr. Gessner Harrison, Professor of the Latin Language and Literature in the University of Virginia, Mr. Coleman, in 1859, was chosen to fill that arduous and honorable position, and he adorned the chair which had been, for so many previous years, crowned with distinction. When the war broke out, he left the pleasant surroundings of professional life and the quiet of his loved home for the battle-field. He raised an artillery company and became its captain, and in 1862 was appointed major of artillery. At the battle of Fredericksburg, amid the terrible havoc and slaughter which accompanied it, Prof. Coleman received a wound near the knee, which ultimately proved fatal. For ninety-eight weary days he suffered the most intense physical agony, and at last, under the ministrations of a host of relatives and friends, he triumphantly fell asleep in the Saviour whom he loved. Prof. Coleman was no ordinary person. As a man, he was rigidly conscientious, unaffectedly pious, and very liberal in his benefactions. As a scholar, his knowledge was varied and remarkably accurate. As a teacher, he won the regard of all, and moulded the rudest into symmetrical characters. As a father, a son, a brother, he was almost faultless; while as a Christian worker, the Bible-classes for students, and the Sunday-school for colored children, were his noble monuments.

was ordained in 1845 at North Esk; his last pastorate was at Sackville. During his ministry Mr. Coleman baptized over 1000 converts. He died March 7, 1877.

Colgate Academy was opened in 1832 as a preparatory school at Hamilton, N. Y., and in 1853 it was duly chartered as the grammar school of Madison University. It has not only a thorough classical course of three years preparatory to college, but a general academic course in English, mathematics, and natural science. It has graduated about 1000, and at present numbers 103 students. It has a principal and 6 associate teachers. A beautiful and commodious academic building was erected in 1873 at the cost, including grounds, of $60,000, by James B. Colgate, of New York, in memory of whose parents it is named. It is 100 by 60 feet, 3 stories high, and surmounted by a mansard-roof.

While the academy has its own faculty apart in government and discipline from that of the university proper, it is under the control of the corporation of Madison University, and is a part of the general system of education maintained by that board. At the time of the opening it was partially endowed by Messrs. James B. Colgate and John B. Trevor by a gift of $30,000, since increased by a donation of $25,000 from Mr. James B. Colgate. (See, also, MADISON UNIVERSITY article.)

COLGATE ACADEMY.

Coleman, Rev. R. J., an early preacher in Arkansas, was born in Virginia in 1817; removed to Clark Co., Ark., in 1843; began to preach in 1852. He supplied a number of churches near his home until 1858, when he settled near Pine Bluff, and continued to supply churches in Jefferson and Saline Counties until 1865, when he removed to Austin, where he still resides. He has served many of the most prominent churches of his region with great success.

Coleman, Rev. William, was born in New Brunswick, and he was baptized into the fellowship of the Baptist church, Portland, St. John. He

Colgate, James B., son of William and Mary Colgate, was born in the city of New York, March 4, 1818, and educated in the higher schools of New York, and in academies in Connecticut. After a clerkship of seven years he was for nine years in the wholesale dry-goods trade. In 1852, he became partner with Mr. John B. Trevor, in Wall Street; this firm continued until 1872, when, on the retirement of Mr. Trevor, Mr. Robert Colby became his partner, under the firm-name of James B. Colgate & Co. Mr. Colgate became a member of the Tabernacle Baptist church in the city of New York in his youth, having been baptized by Rev. Beniah Hoe. His residence now is in Yonkers, where the Warburton Avenue Baptist church, one of the best church edifices in the country, stands a monument of his and Mr. Trevor's liberality. The greater part of the expense of building this house was borne by these two brethren. Mr. Colgate has been the chief benefactor of Madison University, and in her darkest days she has ever found in him not only a wise counselor, but a warm friend and supporter. Mr. Colgate has also given liberally to the University of Rochester and its theological seminary, to the academy at New London, N. H., to Peddie Institute, N. J., and to Columbian University, at Washington, D. C. With all his liberality towards institutions of learning, it hardly surpasses that with which he cherishes needy churches, missionary fields, and denominational societies. Mr. Colgate is a man of vigorous constitution and large frame. He is an outspoken Baptist, of decided convictions, and he is always ready to defend them in private or public. In business circles his house is regarded as one of the most reliable and substantial in Wall Street, and in the dark days of the late civil war, the government found in it a power of which it might have been afraid, but for the incorruptible integrity and loyalty with which its business was uniformly conducted.

Colgate, Mrs. Mary Gilbert, wife of William Colgate, was born in London, England, Dec. 25, 1788. She came to this country in 1796. She had the advantages of an excellent education and was a woman of many accomplishments. Her marriage with Mr. Colgate took place April 23, 1811. A devout Christian, a generous and self-sacrificing friend, as wife and mother most tender, wise, and faithful, she adorned every relation. She sought out and relieved the poor; she dispensed with a real enjoyment the liberal hospitalities of her home. The education of the rising ministry was one of the chief interests of her practical life; not a vague and general care, but definite and personal, manifesting itself in concern for particular students, many of whom she made welcome guests at her house. In all the generous efforts for the church and for humanity in which her husband had so extensive a share, she proved herself a helper worthy of him. She died October, 1854.

The surviving sons of William and Mary Colgate are Robert, James B., and Samuel.

Colgate, Samuel, a son of William Colgate of precious memory, was born in the city of New York, March 22, 1822. He was baptized and became a member of the Tabernacle Baptist church in 1839. From that early age he has been an earnest worker in the cause of Christ. He succeeded to his father's business, greatly enlarging it, and to his father's benevolence and interest in the great enterprises of the Baptists. He is a member of the board of Madison University, and a liberal patron of that institution. It is well known that Samuel and James B. Colgate erected the Colgate Academy edifice at Hamilton, an important adjunct to the university, at an expense only a little short of $60,000. Mr. Colgate has been for several years a member of the board of the American Tract Society. He is president of the board of the New York Education Society; he is also president of that famous association of New York, "The Society for the Suppression of Vice."

Colgate, William, was born in the parish of Hollingbourn, County of Kent, England, on the 25th of January, 1783. He was the son of Robert and Mary (Bowles) Colgate.

Robert Colgate was a farmer by occupation, and a man of superior intelligence. He warmly sympathized with the American colonies in their struggle with the mother-country before and during the war of the Revolution. Hating despotism in every form, he hailed the triumph of the French revolutionists in their struggles to throw off the regal yoke. Political considerations constrained him to leave England for this country in March, 1798. The family settled on a farm in Hartford Co., Md.

William Colgate came to New York City in 1804. He there obtained employment as an apprentice to a soap-boiler, and learned the business. Young as he was, he showed even then that quickness of observation which distinguished him in after-life. He closely watched the methods practised by his employer, noting what seemed to him to be mismanagement, and learned useful lessons for his own guidance. At the close of his apprenticeship he was enabled, by correspondence with dealers in other cities, to establish himself in the business with some assurance of success. He followed it through life, and became one of the most prosperous men in the city of New York. This circumstance, together with his great wisdom in counsel, and his readiness to aid in all useful and practicable enterprises, gave him a wide influence in the community, and especially in the denomination of which he was from early life an active and honored member.

Of the occurrence which led to his connection with that denomination he gave the following account to the writer of this sketch. For some time after coming to New York, he attended worship with the congregation of the Rev. Dr. Mason, then one of the most eminent preachers of the Presbyterian Church. Writing to his father, an Arian Baptist, of his purpose to make a public profession of his Christian faith in connection with the Presbyterian Church, he stated the chief points of his religious belief, quoting a "thus saith the Lord" for each. He received a kind reply cordially approving of that course, and asking for a "thus saith the Lord" in proof of sprinkling as Christian baptism, and

WILLIAM COLGATE.

of the baptism of infants as an ordinance of Christ. Happening to read the letter in an evening company of Christian friends, members of the church he attended, he remarked on leaving them that he must go home and answer his father's questions. "Poor young man," exclaimed an intelligent Christian lady when he was gone, "he little knows what he is undertaking!" He found it so. And he found it equally hard to be convinced, by Dr. Mason's reasoning, that something else than a "thus saith the Lord" would do just as well.

He was baptized in February, 1808, by the Rev. William Parkinson, pastor of the First Baptist church in New York. In 1811 he transferred his membership to the church in Oliver Street. In 1838 he became a member of the church worshiping in the Tabernacle, to the erection of which he had himself largely contributed.

He annually subscribed money to assist in defraying the current expenses of Hamilton Literary and Theological Institution, afterward Madison University and Theological Seminary; and he was among the most strenuous opposers of their removal to the city of Rochester. He was a regular contributor to the funds of the Baptist Missionary Union, and took upon himself the entire support of a foreign missionary. His other benefactions were numerous, but not such as admit of specification.

Our acquaintance with Deacon Colgate commenced in 1837, when he was about to resign his place on the Board of Managers of the American Bible Society. That board, following the example of the British and Foreign Bible Society, had refused to aid in printing translations of the Holy Scriptures by Baptist missionaries. He desired the writer to put in proper form his reasons for withdrawing from the board. In compliance with his request we prepared a full statement of the case, from the printed documents on both sides. The ground was taken that grievous injustice was done to Baptists by the refusal to aid in printing the translations of their missionaries; Baptists having freely contributed to the funds of the society, and given it their moral support as managers and life-directors, without any dictation to missionaries employed in translating by other organizations represented in the society. The charge of denominational favoritism was fully proved against the society; and the Baptist members of the Board of Managers withdrew from it.

Baptists, finding that they could not expect fair treatment from this professedly undenominational body, retired from it, and formed the American and Foreign Bible Society, for the circulation of the Bible in our own and in foreign lands. Deacon Colgate served it as its treasurer. He was one of thirteen ministers and laymen who organized the American Bible Union in 1850, and was treasurer of that society till his death.

In 1811 he married Miss Mary Gilbert, daughter of Edward Gilbert; a happy union with a partner of congenial spirit.

In all domestic relations he was without fault. He made generous provision for his aged parents, for whom he purchased a pleasant home on a farm in a neighboring county, and ministered to their wants while they lived. His own home was made happy by his personal influence. Of a cheerful habit of mind, tempered by serious earnestness, he shared the playful jest and the good-humored retort, and innocent gayety felt no restraint in his presence. He aimed to make home pleasant, and the family circle the chief attraction for its members.

If he made any life-long mistake, it was in the endeavor to keep an even balance between the two elements of power, knowledge and wealth. He resisted the permanent endowment of the Literary and Theological Institution at Hamilton, while willingly aiding in its support by annual contributions, and thus insuring mutual dependence. It was the error of his time; and his sons have since nobly retrieved it.

Collier, Rev. William, was born in Scituate, Mass., Oct. 11, 1771. Having removed to Boston in his youth, he attended upon the ministry of Stillman and Baldwin, whose preaching led to his hopeful conversion. He became a member of Dr. Baldwin's church, and under the genial influence of his newly-formed love for his Saviour desired to become a preacher of the gospel. To fit himself for this work he entered Brown University, and graduated in the class of 1797. He pursued his theological studies under Dr. Maxey, and was licensed to preach June 3, 1798. His ordination took place in Boston, July 11, 1799. After brief pastorates in Newport, R. I., and in New York City, he became pastor of the First Baptist church in Charlestown, Mass., and remained there for sixteen years, acting for a part of the time as chaplain of the State prison in that city. On account of impaired health he was obliged to resign his pastorate in 1820. He was appointed "minister at large" in Boston, where he proved himself "a workman indeed," performing a vast amount of ministerial labor, his term of service reaching beyond the seventieth year of his life. He secured for himself the sincere affection and respect of the community in which, for so long a time and so faithfully, he wrought for his Master. The messenger of death came to him in the midst of his work, and he was allowed but a brief respite from his labors. Suddenly smitten down, he lingered a few weeks and then died, March 19, 1843.

A hymn-book, which was used somewhat extensively in Baptist churches, was compiled by Mr. Collier. He edited also the *Baptist Preacher*. He prepared for the press an edition of Saurin's sermons, the "Gospel Treasury," an edition of Andrew Fuller's works, and some other productions. Dr. Stow says of him, "The memory of Mr. Collier is fragrant in this community. The sphere that he filled was not large, but he filled it well. He walked with God."

Collis, Rev. S. M., was born in Burke Co., N. C., Jan. 30, 1818; baptized by Rev. S. Mugan in August, 1838; ordained in June, 1844, Revs. S. Mugan, R. Patterson, and Peter Miller forming the Presbytery; has served many churches as pastor, one of them for thirty years; was for nine years clerk of the Roon Mountain Association, and fourteen years moderator of the same body; a strong temperance man, and a great advocate of missions.

Colman, Rev. James, was born in Boston, Mass., Feb. 19, 1794. Having completed his studies, he was ordained in Boston, Sept. 10, 1817; was appointed a missionary to Burmah the previous May. He sailed from Boston, Nov. 16, 1817, with Rev. E. W. Wheelock, and arrived in Calcutta April 15, 1818, and in Rangoon the following September. He was associated with Dr. Judson in missionary labor, and was his companion in the visit to Ava to see what could be done to secure the favor of the king, and toleration for the religion which they were trying to preach to his subjects. The story of this excursion is related in the first volume of Dr. Wayland's "Memoir of Dr. Judson," and the whole transaction is invested with an air of Oriental romance which makes it full of interest. The errand was a fruitless one, and the missionaries returned to the field of their labors, feeling that in God alone could they put their trust. It seemed desirable that a mission station should be established on the borders of Burmah, to which, in case of severe persecution, the missionaries might flee. Chittagong was chosen, and Mr. and Mrs. Colman proceeded to the place thus selected. After a brief residence here Mr. Colman decided to remove to Cox's Bazaar, that he might be brought into more immediate contact with the class of people whom he wished especially to influence. It was an unhealthy village in which he had made his home. After a few months of unremitting labor he took the jungle fever, and died July 4, 1822.

Colman, Jeremiah James, member of Parliament for the city of Norwich, England, belongs to an old Baptist family well known for many years in that district. He became in early life a member of the church in St. Mary's chapel, Norwich, during the pastorate of Dr. Brock, and has served with fidelity and honor in the deacon's office for a long period. The firm with which he is connected gives employment to about 2000 persons, and does business with all parts of the world. He was first chosen a member of Parliament for Norwich in 1871, and again at every succeeding election at the head of the poll. His generous interest in popular education was demonstrated by the erection, at his own cost, of an elegant and substantial school for the children of families employed at his works. Few large employers have succeeded in winning the respect and esteem of their people to a greater extent than the Colmans of Norwich. Mr. Colman has for many years rendered substantial aid to every good work in his neighborhood, without regard to party or sect, but he is equally well known for his attachment to liberal and non-conformist principles.

Columbian University, Washington, D. C., was, in its origin, a direct outgrowth of the missionary spirit. When Judson, who had graduated at Brown University and then at Andover Theological Seminary, and Rice, who was his associate in study, had, on their voyage as the first American missionaries to India, become Baptists, there was but one college—Brown University, organized in 1764—under the control of the Baptist denomination. For fifty years from that time, down to the organization of the Baptist Triennial Convention, and the return of Rice to awaken the Baptists to the need of sustaining Judson in the work of foreign missions, no second college and no theological seminary had been originated. In about ten years from that time, however, no less than five institutions of learning, which have grown into colleges and theological seminaries, were founded, at Hamilton, N. Y., in 1819; Waterville, Me., in 1820; Washington, D. C., in 1822; Georgetown, Ky., in 1824; and at Newton, Mass., in 1825; while, during the next ten years, five other centres caught the same impulse, resulting in the founding of the Richmond College, Va.; Wake Forest, N. C.; Furman University, S. C.; Mercer University, Ga.; and New Hampton Institute, N. H. There must have been some new and controlling sentiment that caused this simultaneous and wide-spread movement, and the history of the Columbian College reveals that sentiment most clearly, as it was for a time the centre of the new interest. Luther Rice, in traveling through the country as a recent convert to Baptist views of Scripture truth, and having as his first and great object the awakening of an interest in foreign missions, was struck with the deep hold which the views he had been led to receive had taken on the popular mind; while at the same time he found no institution whose special mission it was to train young men to defend those views at home and abroad. A thorough knowledge of the Hebrew and Greek languages of the original Old and New Testament Scriptures was, of course, indispensable for those who were to become foreign missionaries, and who would be called upon to translate the Scriptures into tongues whose vocabulary was but ill-fitted to have incorporated into it the great truths of the gospel. That knowledge, also, was of prime importance for all those who, as heralds of that truth at home, must be able to defend the faith as first given. Furthermore, it seemed a necessary part of the individual duty of those who regarded the Bible as the only rule of faith that they should, above all others, seek its meaning in the words used by the inspired writers. The conviction of Rice that the Baptists should have new centres of learning, and should found at least one central theological seminary, soon became common. In locating this central institution two ideas prevailed with Rice: first, that from his intimate personal acquaintance with the Baptists of the entire country the theological seminary should be located at the geographical and national centre; and, second, that the city of Washington was the most suitable place, since, from the origin of the government, that place had been regarded by the leading statesmen of the nation as a centre where promising youth from every section of the country could best gather for a common education. President Washington, in his message addressed to Congress, Jan. 8, 1790, had urged the adoption of such a course, and when for seven years these recommendations had been neglected, he, in his last message, used these emphatic words: "Such an institution would secure the assimilation of the principles, opinions, and manners of our countrymen by the common education of a portion of our youth from every quarter. . . . The more homogeneous our citizens can be made in these particulars the greater will be the prospect of permanent union. . . . Its desirableness has so constantly increased with every new view I have taken of the subject, that I cannot omit the opportunity of once for all recalling your attention to it." Presidents Jefferson and Monroe made similar recommendations at different times. During the administration of President Monroe the Columbian College was founded, and he, together with many other able statesmen of the time, among them John Quincy Adams, gave it their aid by written recommendations and by donations; and, until the war in 1861, the Presidents and their Cabinets, without exception, attended the annual commencements, thus justifying the conviction of its founders in the propriety of its location.

In 1817, at the second meeting of the Baptist General Convention, the plan was approved. By the efforts of Luther Rice, who was appointed agent, grounds north of the city, extending between Fourteenth and Fifteenth Streets, were purchased, and a college building, with two houses for professors, was erected. In 1821, the charter was obtained from Congress, and the Baptist Convention, which met that year in Washington, approved the measures thus taken. The college opened in 1822, and among its first officers were Dr. Stoughton, President; Irah Chase and Alvah Woods, Theological Professors; Thomas Sewall and Jas. M. Staughton, Medical Professors; William Cranch and Wm. T. Carroll, Law Professors; Rufus Babcock, J. D. Knowles, Thomas J. Conant, and Robt. E. Pattison, Tutors; also Wm. Ruggles and Alexis Caswell were afterwards appointed professors. Among its earliest graduates were Hon. Thos. D. Eliot, Robt. W. Cushman, Baron Stow, Rolin R. Neale, and others since eminent in three professions. At its first commencement all branches of the government, with Lafayette as visitor, were present.

The special claims of the college proper led to the early withdrawal of the theological professors, and to the founding, in 1825, of the Newton Theological Institution by Dr. Chase. Financial embarrassments soon troubled the college, and led to the suspension of all its departments in 1827, when, for a year, Wm. Ruggles, then Professor of Mathematics and Natural Philosophy, alone of all its officers remained at his post. The Rev. Dr. Staughton, one of the most brilliant and popular of American preachers, and attractive and inspiring as a teacher, after efforts to relieve and sustain the college which fatally impaired his health, while on his way to accept the presidency of the new college organized at Georgetown, Ky., was arrested by sickness at Washington, D. C., and died at the residence of his son, who had been one of the medical faculty. During the business troubles of this period Dr. Alvah Woods acted as financial agent, aiding Luther Rice in 1822-23, and Rev. Elon Galusha, in 1826-27. In 1827, Rev. Robt. B. Semple, of Virginia, became president of the board of trustees, and financial agent, in which self-denying service he was engaged till 1833. In 1835, the Rev. Luther Rice died in Edgefield District, S. C. For more than twenty years he denied himself the comforts of home and family; rode night and day; preached almost constantly; received contributions for missions and for the college; would take no salary; and leaving at his death only a horse and worn-out sulky, his last message, when asked what should be done with his scanty effects, showed the ruling principle of his life still dominant, as he replied, "*Send them to the college!*"

In 1828, Dr. Stephen Chapin was elected president, and the college was reopened. His administration continued thirteen years,—from 1828 to 1841. Dr. Chapin was pre-eminent for those calm and solid qualities of mind and heart, which made him so instructive a preacher and teacher, and so patient a worker both within and without the college, and which secured for it a gradual increase of students, and a final recovery from indebtedness.

During Dr. Chapin's administration the medical department was sustained with Dr. Thomas Sewall as its head; and the college was favored with the instructions of Prof. J. O'B. Chaplin and Dr. Adiel Sherwood, the latter, after the death of Luther Rice, acting as financial agent from 1836 to 1840. On the resignation of Dr. Chapin, the college was presided over for nearly two years, by Prof. William Ruggles, when, in 1843, Dr. Joel S. Bacon became president, at which time it was free from debt, but without endowment. Dr. Bacon brought to his work a genial and winning address, and a well-stored and inventive mind, and the patronage of the college was soon increased. Under his administration the medical department had the eminent services of Drs. Harvey Lindsly, Thomas Miller, John F. May, L. F. Gale, Grafton Tyler, Joshua Riley, and William P. Johnston. The college faculty secured, first as tutor, in 1843, and then as professor, in 1846, the services of Prof. A. J. Huntington, D.D., in Greek, whose connection, though interrupted by several years spent at two different periods in the charge of churches, has added greatly to the efficiency of the college instruction. Prof. R. P. Latham was also an efficient officer from 1852 to 1854. From 1847 to 1849 the Rev. A. M. Poindexter, D.D., acted as a successful agent in securing the first funded endowment. In 1851-52 the Rev. W. F. Broaddus, D.D., obtained subscriptions to the amount of $20,000, thus securing a conditional promise of John Withers, of Alexandria, Va., for a similar amount. During this and two succeeding administrations of the college Col. James L. Edwards was the efficient president of the board of trustees. After a presidency of eleven years, Dr. Bacon resigned in 1854, and the college for another year was presided over by Prof. William Ruggles. In 1855, the Rev. Joseph G. Binney, who, after many years as president of the Karen Theological Seminary in Burmah, had become pastor in Augusta, Ga., was elected president. Dr. Binney brought to his office a mind of unusual analytical power and special educational skill; and the system of instruction and the discipline of the college were made eminently efficient. The patronage of the college was extended, and had not Dr. Binney felt it to be his duty to return to Burmah, his administration would have proved still more beneficial to the institution. Dr. Binney was aided in the college faculty by the services of Drs. L. H. Steiner, John S. Newberry, and Nathan Smith Lincoln, in Chemistry and Natural History; of Prof. William E. Jillson, in Rhetoric; and of Prof. E. T. Fristoe, LL.D., in Mathematics and Natural Philosophy. The medical department had added to its efficient faculty during this period Drs. J. A. Waring, E. W. Hilgard, and N. S. Lincoln. After a presidency of three years Dr. Binney, in 1858, resigned, to return to his work in Burmah. During 1858-59 the college was presided over by Prof. William Ruggles, LL.D.

In 1859, the Rev. G. W. Samson, D.D., who had been elected a year previously, became president. The administration of Dr. Binney, as the result showed, had awakened a public confidence in the future of the college which led to three simultaneous bequests made in the year 1857,—that of John Withers, of Alexandria, Va., giving one-fifth of his estate; that of Prof. Romeo Elton, D.D., then of Bath, England, giving one-half of his estate after other bequests; and that of James McCutchen, of Georgetown, D. C.; these bequests being founded on the expectation that the fourth president would retain his office, though the first two were given in the name of the fifth president, who for about fifteen years had been an efficient trustee. At this juncture Prof. S. M. Shute, D.D., Prof. G. C. Schaeffer, M.D., and Edwin Cull were added to the faculty, the last of whom, after one year as tutor and a second year as adjunct professor, closed his career of the brightest promise as a classical scholar, while pursuing his studies in Germany. Dr. Wm. Ruggles still acted as professor, his department being changed to that of Political Philosophy, in which his instructions, given amid the excitements preceding the war, left an impression on the minds of the youth of both sections of the country never to be forgotten. The number of students at this time was larger than at any other period in the history of the college, but the war soon scattered them. The president, with Profs. Shute and Ruggles, determined, with the aid of tutors, to maintain college instruction during the progress of the war. The rental of the college buildings by the U. S. government met the expense, and also canceled a debt of $9000 incurred under the previous administration in maintaining an able faculty. The classes were small but the instruction was thorough, and some of the most successful of our younger lawyers and clergymen graduated during that trying period. The close of the war demanded a thorough readjustment of all the departments. At the death of Col. Edwards the Hon. Amos Kendall became president of the board of trustees. A building was given by W. W. Corcoran, LL.D., to the medical department; another was secured for a law department, in which a large and most efficiently conducted school was gathered, and the building paid for out of its proceeds. The college grounds were graded and improved; a building for the preparatory school was erected; the three legacies before mentioned matured and were in part paid; and during a period of six years $150,000 was added, in various ways, to the property of the college. Much of the efficiency that marked the recuperation after the war was due to the able co-operation of the board of trustees residing in Washington, among whom were J. C. Welling, LL.D., now president of the college; Prof. Joseph Henry, LL.D., of the Smithsonian Institution; W. W. Corcoran, LL.D., Dr. Chr. H. Nichols, and others. In 1871, after twelve years' service, Dr. Samson resigned and accepted the presidency of Rutgers Female College, N. Y. Recently the name of the college was changed to the Columbian University; and under the talented leadership of President Welling bright hopes are entertained of its future usefulness.

Colver, Nathaniel, D.D.—Although most of Dr. Colver's life was spent elsewhere than in Illinois, yet his connection with important work at Chicago in his later years, and his death and burial there, render it fitting that his memorial should appear in this connection. Nathaniel Colver was born at Orwell, Vt., May 10, 1794. His father, Nathaniel Colver, Sr., as also *his* father, was a Baptist minister, for many years active in pioneer service in Vermont and Northern New York. While Nathaniel was still a child the family removed to Champlain, in the northern portion of the last-named State,—and that continued to be their home until he had reached the age of fifteen. It was at West Stockbridge, Mass., to which the family then removed, that he was converted, and that he decided to enter the ministry. He served as pastor at Clarendon, Vt.; at Fort Covington, N. Y.; as also, later, in various places farther south in the same State,—Kingsbury, Fort Ann, and Union Village. In 1839 he was called to Boston, and, in association with Timothy Gilbert and others like-minded, organized the church which then and since became famous as the Tremont Temple church. His ministry here was a remarkable one, unique in the history of the Boston pulpit, and scarcely equaled anywhere in this country at any time for boldness, energy, the mastery of formidable difficulties, and its hold upon popular interest. In the higher results of spiritual effectiveness it was no less notable. In 1852, Mr. Colver left Boston for South Abington, a village in the vicinity, where he remained as pastor until his call to Detroit in 1853. Here he remained until 1856 as pastor of the First Baptist church. At the date just named he became pastor of the First church in Cincinnati. While here the degree of Doctor of Divinity was given to him by the college at Granville. Leaving Cincinnati in 1861, he came to Chicago as pastor of the Tabernacle, now Second church. It was at Cincinnati that he first became personally enlisted in the education of young men for the ministry; a class meeting him there, steadily, in his study. At Chicago this work was resumed, and when the preliminary steps towards the organization of a theological seminary were taken, he was invited to become the professor of doctrinal theology. During the years 1867-70, Dr. Colver was at Richmond, Va., as president of the Freedmen's Institute there. His health failing him, in the last-named year he returned to Chicago, where he died on Sabbath morning, Dec. 25, 1870.

With what was so marked and signal in Dr. Colver's career as a preacher must be associated his active share in various public movements. As a zealous advocate of the principles of anti-Masonry, as a thorough-going temperance man, as one of the foremost in the anti-slavery ranks, he was during much of his life identified with radical reformers, and one of their most conspicuous champions. As a preacher, he was doctrinal, fervid, and often exceedingly eloquent. His commanding figure, his speaking face, his melodious voice, his sparkling, resolute eye were physical helps in oratory of no mean kind. While the racy, often quaint forms of speech, with a certain beautiful homeliness in them, made him popular with the masses, cultivated people as well found in its simple strength an element often lacking in what is more finished. In his last days he often reviewed the incidents of his eventful career, and while recognizing the personal Christian excellence of many with whom he had differed, declared his unshaken confidence in the principles he had advocated.

Comer, Rev. John, was born in Boston, Aug. 1, 1704. He was the eldest son of John and Mary Comer. While on a voyage to England to visit his relatives his father died, leaving his child, then less than two years of age, to the care of his widowed mother and his grandfather, who bore the same name with himself. When he reached the age of fourteen he was placed as an apprentice with a glover to learn that trade. His heart, however, was not in his work. He longed to obtain an education. Through the intercession of Dr. Increase Mather arrangements were made to release him from his apprenticeship when he was in the seventeenth year of his age. He commenced at once a course of preparatory study, and entered Harvard College, and subsequently became a student in Yale College. While a member of Harvard College he became a Christian, and united with the Congregational church of which Rev. Nathaniel Appleton was the pastor. He afterwards became a Baptist, and was baptized by his uncle, Rev. Elisha Callender, Jan. 31, 1725, and united with the First Baptist church in Boston. Soon after he connected himself with the church in Boston he began to preach, first as a supply of the venerable church in Swanzey, Mass., where he remained a short time, and then went to Newport, R. I., where he was ordained as a colleague with Rev. William Peckham, of the First Baptist church, in 1726. He remained with this church not far from three years, and then resigned in consequence of his attempt to have the practice of laying on of hands uniformly observed by the church in the admission of new members. The next two years Mr. Comer acted as a supply of the Second Baptist church in Newport, and then became the pastor of a church in the southern part of old Rehoboth, Mass., near to Swanzey. This church maintained his peculiar views on the subject of the laying on of hands. His connection with this church continued about two years, and was terminated by his death, which occurred May 23, 1734, in his thirtieth year.

Rev. Dr. Henry Jackson says of Mr. Comer, "He was a gentleman of education, piety, and great success in his profession. During his brief life he collected a large body of facts, intending at some future period to write the history of the American Baptist churches. His manuscripts he never printed, nor did he, as I learn, ever prepare them for publication. He was even unable to revise them, and they were, of course, left in their original condition. Nevertheless, he made an able and most valuable contribution to Rhode Island history. His papers were probably written about 1729–31." From all the accounts which we have of Mr. Comer he gave promise of great usefulness. Mr. Comer was the most remarkable young man in the Baptist history of New England, and his early death was a calamity to the churches in that section of our country, suffering at the time so severely from Puritan persecutions, and needing so much his unusual talents and splendid acquirements for the marvelous prosperity, the bright day of which was so soon to break upon our struggling and hopeful communities.

Communion, Close, or Restricted.—That the ordinances of the Lord's house are for his own children admits of no discussion; so that in any case there must be some restriction. And when we examine the Word of God we find believer's baptism always preceding every other Christian duty and privilege. When the Saviour gives his commission he orders his apostles " to teach (*make disciples of*) all nations, baptizing them in the name of the Father, and of the Son, and of the Holy Spirit; teaching them to observe all things whatsoever he commanded them."—Matt. xxviii. 10, 20. After faith comes baptism, then other duties and privileges. Baptism precedes all Christian exercises, after faith, according to Jesus. Under the dispensation of the Spirit the same instruction is imparted. When he descended on the day of Pentecost in great power, many gladly received the Word and " were baptized, and the same day there were added unto them about three thousand souls; and they continued steadfastly in the apostles' doctrine and fellowship, and in breaking of bread, and in prayers."—Acts ii. 41, 42. These three thousand are not brought to the Lord's table first after receiving the Word gladly; after believing, the rite of baptism is immediately administered; then they are formally added to the church, and continue steadfastly in the apostles' doctrine (teaching) and fellowship, and in breaking of bread, and in prayers. The breaking of bread, or participation in the Lord's Supper, comes after baptism and teaching. This is the law of Christ, and the practice of the Spirit, his earthly representative after his ascension. In the book of Acts throughout, baptism follows professed faith *immediately and invariably*. And as the cases are very numerous, and as the administrators of the baptism were generally inspired men, they prove that immersion should precede the Supper and all other Christian duties and privileges. The jailer's case significantly shows this. He and his household believe rejoicing in God, at "midnight;" "and he took them (Paul and Silas) *the same hour of the night* and washed their stripes, and was baptized, he and all his, straightway."— Acts xvi. 25–33. Paul does not spread the Lord's table for them first, but they are "straightway" baptized. This is the uniform record of such conversions in the Scriptures. In no instance in the Holy Word is it said, or even hinted, that an unbaptized man came to the communion. Even Robert Hall, the apostle of open communion, "admits, without hesitation, that subsequently to our Lord's resurrection the converts to the Christian faith submitted to that ordinance (baptism) *prior to their reception into the Christian church*. As little," says he, "are we disposed to deny that it is at present the duty of the sincere believer to follow their example, and that supposing him to be convinced of the nature and import of baptism, *he would be guilty of a criminal irregularity who neglected to attend to it, previous to his entering into Christian fellowship. On the obligation of both the positive rites enjoined in the New Testament, and the prior claim of baptism to the attention of such as are properly enlightened on the subject, we have no dispute.*"* Then, according to the brilliant preacher of Cambridge, Leicester, and Bristol, believers should be baptized before coming to the Supper, if "they are properly enlightened;" that is, God gives baptism the precedence; for no amount of enlightenment or ignorance in men could give baptism a "prior claim to the attention of such as are properly enlightened on the subject," unless God had bestowed the precedence upon it. And according to the Book of Books, *open communion rests upon a foundation outside the boundaries of Revelation.*

Whatever may be the opinion of individuals, all Christian communities, recognizing baptism and the Supper to be binding rites, except Open Communion Baptists, require baptism before admission to the communion. This declaration is true of the entire history of Christianity. Speaking of the early Christians, the learned Lord Chancellor King, in his "Primitive Church," says, "The persons communicating were not indifferently all that professed the Christian faith, as Origen writes, 'It doth not belong to every one to eat of this bread, and to drink of this cup.' But they were only such as were in the number of the faithful, 'such as were baptized and received both the credentials and practicals of Christianity.' . . . Baptism always preceded the Lord's Supper, as Justin Martyr says, 'It is not lawful for any one to partake of the sacramental food except he be baptized.'"† Dr. Dwight, a Congregationalist, and a former president of Yale College, says, "It is an indispensable qualification for this ordinance that the candidate for communion be a member of the visible church of Christ, in full standing. By this I intend that he should be a man of piety; that he should have made a public profession of religion, and that he should have been baptized."‡

The author of a Methodist work on baptism, a minister of some repute among his own people, writes, "Before entering upon the argument before us, it is but just to remark that in one principle the Baptist and Pedobaptist Churches agree. They both agree in rejecting from communion at the table of the Lord, and in denying the rights of church fellowship to all who have not been baptized. . . . Their (Baptists) views of baptism force them upon the ground of strict communion, and herein they act upon the same principles as other churches,— *i.e.*, they admit only those whom they deem baptized persons to the communion table."§ Other denominations might be cited to give the same testimony, but it is needless. That baptism is a prerequisite to the Lord's Supper is the law of Christendom. *Open communion rests on a foundation outside the pale of revelation, where the unscriptural structure of Romanism stands, and it lives outside the limits of Christian creeds and denominational standards*, with the unimportant exception already mentioned.

Baptism is immersion in water, as Baptists view it; and as there is but one Lord, one faith, and one baptism, those who have had only pouring and sprinkling for baptism are not baptized; and as baptism is a prerequisite to the Lord's Supper, with both Baptists and Pedobaptists, we cannot invite the unbaptized to the table which Jesus has placed in our charge, with believer's immersion as the way to it.

This is not a question of charity, or want of charity. In the edifice in which the writer ministers, besides the church, there is the *congregation*, —the unbaptized hearers. Many of these are converted persons, generous benefactors of the community, believers of lovely character, dear to the hearts of the pastor and the church. Unbaptized though they are, they have a warmer place in the affections of their pastor than any similar number of regularly baptized members of any one of our most orderly churches. They are cherished personal friends, for whom we would make any proper sacrifice. Yet we never think of inviting them to the Lord's Supper; they feel no slight

---

* Hall on Terms of Communion, pp. 39, 40. London, 1851.
† King's Primitive Church, pp. 231–32. London, 1839.
‡ System of Theology. Sermon, 160.
§ F. G. Hibbard's Christian Baptism, p. 174.

from such omission. They are the only persons on earth who have any reason to take offense. They have contributed largely for church purposes; they love and are loved with Christian affection; and they know that the cause of their not being invited to come to the Supper is not a lack of love on the part of the church, but their own want of obedience. If we do not invite them to the table of the Lord, and this course shows no unkindness, there can be nothing uncharitable in giving no invitation to the communion to unbaptized strangers, though they may be members of honored but sprinkled religious communities.

We love the Lord Jesus Christ, and we love his servants of every name; and if we do not invite his unbaptized children in Pedobaptist churches to the memorial Supper, it is because we reverence the Lord, who has made believer's baptism the door into the visible kingdom, and they have removed it. With our venerable brother, Dr. Cone, we conclude, " Nor can this course of conduct be righteously construed into a breach of brotherly love and Christian forbearance, until it can be proved that we ought to love men more than we love God, and that the charity which rejoiceth not in iniquity, but rejoiceth in the truth, requires us to disregard the commandments of God, and dispense with the ordinances of our Lord and Saviour, Jesus Christ." "Finally, brethren, farewell! Adhere steadfastly to the doctrines and ordinances of Christ, as he has delivered them to us; and as there is *one body and one spirit, even as ye are called in one hope of your calling; one Lord, one faith, one baptism, so we beseech you that ye walk worthy of the vocation wherewith ye are called, with all lowliness and meekness, with long suffering, forbearing one another in love; endeavoring to keep the unity of the Spirit in the bond of peace.*"* (See articles on OPEN COMMUNION, and THE LORD'S SUPPER.)

Communion, Open.—This practice is of comparatively modern origin, and its history presents little to recommend it. It seems to have been a natural outgrowth of persecuting times, when the people of God were few in number and were compelled to worship in secret places; and when the preservation of the fundamentals of divine truth made men blind to grave errors that were regarded as not soul destroying. In the first half of the seventeenth century it made its appearance in England. John Bunyan was its ablest defender, and the church of which he was the honored pastor illustrates the natural tendencies of the system by its progress backward, in adopting infant sprinkling and the Congregational denomination.

Open communion refers to fellowship at the Lord's table, and it has three forms,—a mixed membership; occasional communion by the unbaptized in a church whose entire membership is immersed; and two churches in the same building, meeting *together* for ordinary worship, but celebrating the Lord's Supper at separate times. The first was Bunyan's, the second is followed by Spurgeon, the third was the plan adopted by Robert Hall in Leicester. The community in Hall's chapel, which he called "The Open Communion Church," was composed of "The Congregation" as distinct from the church and such members of the church as might unite with them. On his retirement from his pastorate in Leicester, he sent two resignations to the people of his charge in that city,—one to "The Church of Christ meeting in Harvey Lane," and another to "The Open Communion Church meeting in Harvey Lane."†

In this country the mixed membership form of open communion had a very extensive trial, not in regular Baptist churches nor in regular Baptist Associations. At quite an early period in our history there were communities practising immersion and *tolerating* infant sprinkling, or placing both upon an equal footing. No one of our original Associations held open communion. The annual or other gathering among Open Communists similar to an Association was called "A Conference,"‡ "A General Meeting," or "A Yearly Meeting." John Asplund, in giving an account of the Associations and other meetings of the communities that practised immersion, says, "*The Groton Conference* was begun 1785. . . . Their sentiments are general provision (the Arminian view of the atonement) and open or large communion. *Keep no correspondence.*" That is, they were not recognized by the Warren or any New England Baptist Association. He speaks of a "*General Meeting*" in Maine, and he states that it was "gathered about 1786. They hold to the Bible without any other confession of faith. *Keep no correspondence.* Very strict in the practical part of religion. Their sentiments are universal provision and final falling from grace."§ These people were Arminians, and were not in fraternal relations with Baptists.

In the New Light revivals in New England, where the converted people left the Congregational and formed "Separate Churches," the membership was often equally divided between Baptists and Pedobaptists. They loved one another; they were hated by the state religious establishment; they made special efforts and sometimes solemn pledges that they would not slight each other's opinions. Open communion never had a fairer field, and yet it was a complete failure. Instead of promoting charity it broke up the peace of churches, and it

---

* Circular Letter of Hudson River Association, 1824, pp. 15, 16.

† Hall's Works, vol. i. 125–26. London, 1851.
‡ Backus's History of the Baptists, ii. 44. Newton.
§ Annual Register, pp. 48, 49. 1790.

was finally renounced by pretty nearly all its original friends. Isaac Backus, the historian, while pastor of an open communion church at Titicut, was actually compelled by the malice stirred up by open communion to form a new organization, that he and his people might have peace. Hovey says, "If any member of the church desired to have his children baptized, he had permission to call in a minister from abroad to perform the act; and if any member who had been sprinkled in infancy wished to be baptized, full permission was granted Mr. Backus to administer the rite. Moreover, it was agreed that no one should introduce any conversation which would lead to remarks on the subjects or the mode of baptism. . . . These persistent endeavors to live in peace were unavailing. For when infants were sprinkled the Baptists showed their dissatisfaction without leaving the house, and when Mr. Backus baptized certain members of his own church, the Congregationalists would not go to witness the immersion, but called it rebaptizing and taking the name of the Trinity in vain. And when the members of the church met for conference they were afraid to speak their minds freely, lest offense might be given, and this fear led to an unbrotherly shyness."* For the sake of peace Backus was driven, Jan. 16, 1756, to have a Baptist church formed. And the same cause, aided by increasing light from the Word of God, destroyed this pernicious feature in nearly all the open communion bodies in New England.

In Nova Scotia mixed communion was the custom of the churches in which Baptists held their membership. In 1798, when the Nova Scotia Association was formed, its churches were all on this platform, and some of the ministers were Pedobaptists. About 1774, when one of the churches was destitute of a pastor, Mr. Allen had two ruling elders ordained, one a Baptist and the other a Congregationalist, with power to administer the ordinances "each in his own way, agreeably to the sentiments of his brethren; but this was a short-lived church." In 1809, the Association passed a resolution that no church should be a member of it that permitted open communion.† And long since the churches of that province discarded the unscriptural practice altogether. The pioneer Baptist ministers of Ontario and Quebec were open communionists, and their little churches caught their spirit; but to-day the Baptists of these provinces are men whose orthodoxy their brethren everywhere may regard with admiration. Open communion in England is a splendid worldly door for a Baptist to pass through when he wishes to exchange the plain Dissenting chapel for the gorgeous State church, but it has no attraction for the Pedobaptist, unless a Spurgeon for a brief season may excite his curiosity.

Nearly twenty years ago an open communion church was established in San Francisco, known as the Union Square Baptist church. The members were godly, the pastor was able, earnest, and devoted. No similar experiment was ever tried under more favorable circumstances. But after testing the project for many years the discovery forced itself upon the pious leaders of the enterprise that there was a defect in the scriptural basis of their church, and the pastor withdrew and subsequently united with the Regular Baptists. The church, at a meeting held April 28, 1880, by a vote almost unanimous, placed itself in harmony with the great Baptist denomination of the United States.

Our doctrine of restricted communion is more generally and intensely cherished among us at this time than at any previous period in our history. Open communion is regarded as a departure from scriptural requirement, as an attack upon the convictions of nearly all Christendom, and as a source of faction and discord. (See articles on CLOSE COMMUNION and THE LORD'S SUPPER.)

Compere, Rev. Lee, a distinguished preacher in Mississippi, was born in England in 1789; went as a missionary to Jamaica in 1816, but after one year his health compelled him to give up an interesting work. He then came to the United States and labored some time in South Carolina. He was six years at the head of the Baptist mission to the Creek Indians, until it was broken up by the removal of the Indians west of the Mississippi. He then followed the tide of emigration first into Alabama, and thence into Mississippi, and settled in Yazoo County. In this State he labored in various localities with distinguished ability until the late civil war, when he removed to Arkansas, and thence to Texas, where he died in 1871.

Comstock, Rev. Elkanah, was the first Baptist minister ordained to labor in Michigan. Under appointment of the Baptist Convention of New York he settled at Pontiac in 1824. He was born in New London, Conn., and there early became a member of the church. As a young man he shared in the seafaring life of that noted port, among whose ship captains the name of Comstock is an honored one. He commenced preaching in 1800; was located first in Albany Co., N. Y., afterwards in Cayuga County, from whence he was appointed to Michigan Territory. His qualifications as an organizer and leader on the frontier were excellent. Of active mind, good education, high moral and Christian worth, rare practical wisdom, soundness in the faith, and fearless fidelity in advocating it, he was

---

* Hovey's Life and Times of Isaac Backus, 115–18.
† Benedict's History of the Baptist Denomination, pp. 521, 523, 539. New York, 1848.

a workman that needed not to be ashamed. He was prized as a citizen, and his home was a model of well-ordered Christian life. After ten years of devoted labor, broken in health, he visited his native place, only to finish there a laborious and useful life at the age of sixty-three years.

Comstock, Hon. Oliver C., was born in Warwick, R. I., March 1, 1781. His father's family removed to Schenectady, N. Y., while he was yet a child. He studied medicine and practised it for a time near Cayuga Bridge. He was a member of Congress from New York six years, and while in this office was baptized by Rev. O. B. Brown, of Washington City. He was ordained as a Christian minister in the same city, Feb. 27, 1819. A few years after he practised medicine in Trumansburg, N. Y. From 1825 to 1834 he was pastor of the First Baptist church in Rochester. Later in life he removed to Michigan. For four years he was Superintendent of Public Instruction. He died in Marshall in 1859. Rev. Grover S. Comstock, missionary to Arracan, was his son.

Conant, Alban Jasper, was born in Vermont Sept. 24, 1821. He was prepared for college when he was fifteen years of age, and he taught school for some time. He took an eclectic course of study in the university. He visited a distinguished artist in New York City, and received lessons in painting from him. He lived in Troy twelve years. In 1857 he came to St. Louis. He took at once position as an artist, and he secured the establishment of an art-gallery. He visited Washington, and painted the portrait of Attorney-General Bates and his family, and of Hon. E. M. Stanton, Secretary of War. His best portraits are one of President Lincoln and some in possession of James B. Eads. Mr. Conant has resided in St. Louis since the close of the war. Many homes there have been made attractive by the features of dear ones on canvas which he has placed within them. Prof. Conant occupies a high social position. His learning and genial disposition make him many friends. He is the author of the "Foot-Prints of Vanished Races in the Mississippi Valley," a work highly commended for originality and research. He is a curator in the University of Missouri, and he has lectured in it and before literary societies with great acceptance. He is a member of the Second Baptist church of St. Louis. He was baptized by Dr. Baldwin, of Troy, N. Y.

While he is charmed by art he is devoted to Christ, the fountain of all beauty, goodness, and mercy.

Conant, Ebenezer, Jr., one of the founders and a deacon of the Baptist church in Ashburnham and Ashby, Mass.,* was born in 1743, and died in 1783.

He was a lineal descendant, in the fifth generation, from Roger Conant,† founder of Salem and governor of Cape Ann Colony. He was a patriot soldier of the Revolution, holding an adjutant's commission from the Council of Massachusetts Bay in the Continental army during the first four years of the war. His commission, signed by James Bowdoin, president of the Council, and afterwards governor of Massachusetts, is dated the 20th day of June, 1776. He withdrew from the service in 1780, with a shattered constitution, and a malady that proved fatal after a lingering illness of two years. He returned to his home wrecked in fortune as in health, having lost his pay by the depreciation of the Continental currency, large sheets of which he brought home, and of which a hundred dollars would not buy him a breakfast.

He married Lydia Oakes, of Stow, Mass., a woman of great strength of character, and, after her conversion and union with the Baptist church, a devoted Christian in the church and the household. While her husband was absent in the army, and after his decease, she maintained family worship, and opened her house for meetings of the church and for ministers of the gospel on their missionary travels.

On the birth of their first child, some years before, not being members of the Congregational Church, they owned the covenant (half-way covenant) that the infant might receive baptism. In the great religious awakening which followed the preaching of Whitefield, his parents, who were members of the Congregational Church, became converts and disciples, or "new lights," as then derisively called. He himself and his wife became dissatisfied with their half-way relation to the church, and convinced that they had no true religion. About that time they heard the preaching of a faithful Baptist minister by the name of Fletcher,‡ who visited Ashburnham. His preaching was blessed to their salvation. They were baptized with others, among them his aged father, and a small Baptist church was formed. The "covenant made between the Baptist brethren in Ashburnham and Ashby at their first coming into church order" is dated 1778, and is preserved in a manuscript volume containing his views of Christian doctrine and experience, a profession of faith, and other religious writings. The little church, having no stated preaching and no place of worship, met for religious services at his house; where during his long illness, as his nephew, the late Rev. Dr. Dodge, of Philadelphia, informed the writer of this article, he was accustomed to address them with words of

---

* Backus, History of the Baptists, 3d ed., vol. ii. p. 464.

† A brother of Dr. John Conant, of Exeter College, one of the Westminster Assembly of Divines. The family were Huguenot refugees.

‡ Backus, History of the Baptists, 3d ed., vol. ii. p. 535.

instruction and encouragement from the door of his sick-room.

What the little band suffered from the oppression of the "standing order" is told by Backus (History, vol. ii. 464, foot-note). The "grain" there referred to, as seized under authority of law for the parish minister's use, was Ebenezer Conant's. But though poor and oppressed, they were enriched with spiritual blessings.

His funeral sermon was preached by Father Case, the home missionary, long after known and honored in the churches of Maine.

Conant, John, son of the preceding, was born in Ashburnham, Mass., in 1773; died in Brandon, Vt., in 1856. At a very early age he was the subject of deep religious impressions, which matured and strengthened with the growth of years, and were the inspiring and controlling influence of his long and active life.

These early impressions were made by the conversation and prayers of Mr. Fletcher, the Baptist minister referred to in the preceding article.

JOHN CONANT.

"When he came to the town," says the subject of this sketch, in his manuscript diary, "he was mocked and hooted at by the populace. Some out of curiosity went to hear him preach. My father and mother went, and were pricked in the heart." He was invited to their house, and became their guest, with permission to preach there to all who desired to hear. "His conversation," says the diary, "attracted my attention. I loved him, and ate his words as sweet morsels, and they were blessed of God for the salvation of my young soul. I think now that if ever I loved religion, and enjoyed its sweets, it was then." He was eight or nine years of age.

In 1786 occurred the great revival under the preaching of another Baptist minister, the Rev. Joel Butler. "He came to our house," says the diary, "the place where meetings were held, and with him a godly man by the name of Smith. A meeting was notified, and the house was filled. The text was Genesis xix. 14: 'Up, get you out of this place,' etc. The sermon was powerful, searching out all the hiding-places of professors and non-professors. Mr. Smith then rose and requested parents to allow him to address their children. His earnest and pathetic appeals were felt by all. The place seemed to be shaken, and overshadowed by the Holy Spirit. A powerful revival followed, and many were born into the kingdom." The following entry in his diary is instructive, as characteristic of the spirit of the time: "On the 30th day of July, 1786, the church obtained a faint hope for me, and I had but a faint one for myself. I was that day, with thirteen others, baptized and received into the Baptist Church, enjoying greatly that ordinance. I have ever since been favored, though unworthy, with a name and a place in the church of God." He was then in the fourteenth year of his age.

His father had died after a lingering sickness of two years, during which his slender means were exhausted, leaving a wife and seven children, the oldest but ten years of age. A week before his death, the anxious mother pressed him to intrust some of them to dear friends who would care for them. "My dear wife," said he, looking up into her face with a smiling, joyful countenance, "I have already done that. I have given away all your children to the dearest Friend in the world." This prayerful consecration of them to God, says the diary, I believe was blest to the salvation of all his children.

The support of the family devolved mainly on his mother and himself, as the oldest son, from the time he was eight years of age, while his father was absent in the army. He records in his diary that he was then accustomed to go into the woods with a yoke of oxen, cut down a young tree and draw it to the house. "My father," he says, "having left a chest of carpenter's tools, I soon became a proficient in carpenter and joiner work; and when seventeen years of age I built a saw-mill for my mother, mostly with my own hands." So early were habits of self-reliance formed. At the age of eighteen he could compete with the good workmen of the town; and at twenty he was promoted to be master of the interior work of the new church at Bolton, Mass. Finding the parish priest of the "standing order" a very dull preacher, he walked five miles every Sunday to hear a Baptist minister.

At the age of twenty-one, having assumed the responsibility of providing a home for his aged mother and her surviving parent, he found it necessary to seek a more productive field of enterprise. On a visit to his relatives in Brandon, Vt., his attention was attracted to a waterfall, which he purchased. Having removed to Brandon in 1797, he constructed a dam and mills on the waterfall. " I soon united," says the diary, " with the Baptist church here ; with which I have always felt a sweet union, and, as I humbly hope, have tried to aid both in its religious and pecuniary interests." The feeble band met for a time in his rough tenement of sawn timber. In 1800 he united with eleven others in building a plain house of worship of moderate dimensions, doing the principal part of the work. In 1802 he built a house for himself. "In 1832," says the diary, " I wished to see a better house of worship for my Baptist brethren. I thought it my duty to go forward in the work, and build such a house as would be respectable, that others might be induced to come and see and hear for themselves. With much toil, and infirmity of body, I went through this undertaking, strengthened all along by the belief that I was doing that which it was my duty to do, and for which no one had a like mind. I have lived to see the house finished, and to see the church abundantly blessed in it." He afterwards erected a large seminary building for a high school, under the direction of Baptists. For his personal use he put up numerous buildings, mills, stores, dwelling-houses, an iron-foundry, etc. ; his diary recognizing the good hand of God in all his labors and successes.

Through life he was active in the public affairs of the town and of the State. In 1801 he was appointed a justice of the peace, and held the office forty years. In 1809 he represented the town in the State Legislature, and, with a brief interval, continued to do so till 1822. During the war with England, 1812–15, he was appointed by the national government to assess the township for a direct tax. He was a member of the convention for revising the constitution of the State, and was one of the electoral college that cast the vote of the State for Harrison. For many years he served the town as one of the selectmen, and of the listers of ratable estate, and was postmaster of the town fifteen years.

In 1806 he was chosen clerk of the church, and served it in that office thirty-seven years. In 1818 he was elected a deacon of the church. The responsibilities of that office weighed heavily upon his mind. He could not persuade himself that he had the spiritual qualifications of one who serves at the Lord's table, and is an example to believers.

At length he yielded to the voice of his brethren, and till his death, eight-and-thirty years, was a devoted servant in the house of his Lord. " This office," he says in his diary, " I have considered the most responsible and honorable ever conferred on me by man. I have always felt myself unworthy to hold it, seeing as I do so much unfitness in myself."

In 1794 he married Miss Charity Broughton, a daughter of Wait Broughton, of Pepperell, Mass.; " A happy union" (says his diary), " with a faithful partner in all the joys and sorrows of life."

When the Board of Foreign Missions was formed in Boston for the support of Mr. Judson, then in the missionary field, they sent him a copy of their first printed circular. He wrote on it his name and subscription and placed it on the front of the pulpit, and was ever after a regular contributor to the funds of the mission.

His characteristics are well summed up by the Rev. Dr. Collyer in his life of the nephew of the subject of this sketch.*

Conant, Thomas J., D.D., was born Dec. 13, 1802, at Brandon, Vt. He graduated at Middle-

THOMAS J. CONANT, D.D.

bury College in 1823, and for two years afterwards pursued philosophical studies under the personal

---

* A Man in Earnest; Life of A. H. Conant. By Robert Collyer, 1872. " We can see that John Conant held and nursed a sweet and well-toned religious spirit. . . . The man was a noble specimen of that sturdy, capable, self-contained nature only found in its perfection in New England ; determined always to get along in the world, to gather property and influence, but with a solemn religious element woven through and through the business faculty. The sort of man most faithful, wherever he is found, in the support of schools, churches, and public libraries."

supervision of Prof. R. B. Patton. After teaching a short time in Columbian College, he accepted the professorship of Languages in Waterville College, Me. He was deeply interested in Oriental philology, and having resigned his chair at Waterville, he repaired to the vicinity of Boston that he might have the assistance of the learned men of Newton, Cambridge, and Andover, with the libraries of these centres of education, as aids in the study of the Hebrew, Chaldee, Syriac, and Arabic languages. In 1835, he was made Professor of Biblical Literature and Criticism in the Theological Seminary at Hamilton, N. Y., and in 1850, he filled a similar chair in Rochester Seminary. While professor at Hamilton he spent two years abroad perfecting his scholarship in the German universities. For some years he has concentrated his labors on the revision of the commonly received English version of the Scriptures, chiefly in the employ of the American Bible Union. His first elaborate production was a paper on the laws of translation, and the subject has been a specialty with him ever since. In 1839 he prepared a translation of Gesenius's Hebrew grammar, which he has since enlarged and improved, and it is still the standard Hebrew grammar of the schools in America and Europe. His first published work on the Bible was the revision of the Book of Job, with notes. It opens that wonderful poem to the pious reader in a way that the old version could not, so that he may see and admire its beauties and truths. Since that he has brought out many of the books of the Bible, not as perfect translations, but as specimens of work to be submitted to the criticisms of scholars. He has thrown great light on many obscure texts of the common version. It is now admitted that he stands in the front rank of Oriental scholars.

It is in place here to notice that Mrs. Conant, daughter of Rev. Dr. Chaplin, first president of Waterville College, has been a fitting helpmeet to her husband in his literary work. For years she edited the *Mother's Journal*. She translated "Lea, or the Baptism in Jordan," by Strauss, the court preacher of Berlin. In 1850–52 she translated Neander's practical commentaries on the epistles of John and James, and on Philippians. She then published a biographical sketch of Dr. Judson, entitled "The Earnest Man," a "History of English Bible Translations," "New England Theocracy," and a "History of the English Bible." With such a wife to aid him in his studies it is not strange that Dr. Conant has accomplished so much in his specific field of labor.

Conard, Rev. William H., was born at Montgomery Square, Pa., Oct. 8, 1832; was baptized by Rev. George Higgins, Jan. 1, 1855; graduated from the university at Lewisburg in 1862; was ordained September, 1862, and settled as pastor of the church at Davisville, Pa., where he remained fourteen years. Removed to Bristol, Pa., September, 1876, where he remained until the summer of 1880, when he was called to the secretaryship of the Pennsylvania Baptist General Association. For the administration of this office he possesses marked adaptation, and he is giving to the work such an energy of purpose and devotion as will doubtless be productive of large and beneficent results. He is a member of the board of curators of the university at Lewisburg, and is actively engaged in denominational work. He is a sound and forceful preacher, and has been a faithful and successful pastor. Under his ministry a capacious and beautiful church edifice was built at Davisville and paid for.

Concord Institute, located at Shiloh, Union Parish, La., was organized in 1876, under the patronage of the Concord Baptist Association, with a capital of $14,000, obtained in a few months by the labors of Rev. S. C. Lee, who was appointed by the Association to raise this amount. It is conducted upon the plan of the co-education of the sexes, and has proved very successful. From 100 to 150 pupils receive instruction annually. The course of instruction is thorough and extensive. Rev. C. B. Freeman is principal, aided by a corps of competent teachers.

Concrete College, Concrete, De Witt Co., Texas, was organized in 1862 and chartered in 1873. It is a private institution, but controlled and managed by Baptists. It has done a good work in educating both sexes. Its president, J. E. V. Corey, D.D., and Prof. W. Thomas, A.M., are its owners, and have succeeded well in their enterprise. Its buildings and grounds are worth $17,000.

Cone, Spencer Houghton, D.D., was born in Princeton, N. J., April 30, 1785. His parents were persons of intellectual and moral worth. His father was a native of East Haddam, Conn., where for several generations the family had lived, and his mother was the daughter of Joab Houghton, of New Jersey, who was very active in the Revolution. She was a woman of more than ordinary excellence of character, being noted as a person of great prayer.

At the age of eight, and while spending a little time with his grandfather, Spencer Cone was deeply convicted of sin. It was while they were in attendance upon the annual meeting at the Hopewell church; but the feeling was only transient, though revived some two years afterwards, when he was taken by his mother to hear a sermon delivered by the Rev. Ashbel Green in Philadelphia. His efforts, however, were merely legal in nature, and he soon relapsed into his ordinary way of life.

His health in his boyhood was not robust, and so it was considered wise to permit him to pass some time on the farm of his grandfather. The consequence was that he outgrew his former weakness and acquired a vigorous constitution. His early life was marked also by an intellectual development almost precocious. At twelve he entered the Freshman class of Princeton, and at once gained the highest esteem of faculty and students, the president prophesying for him a brilliant future as an orator. Without doubt, had young Cone been permitted to graduate, he would have left the college bearing away its highest honors. But such was not to be his lot. His father became the subject of a serious and protracted disease, and in this emergency Spencer was the sole hope of the family.

SPENCER HOUGHTON CONE, D.D.

With true manliness he resigned his studies at the age of fourteen. His first effort was unsuccessful. His weary journey on foot to obtain the position of assistant teacher was rewarded only by the knowledge that the place was filled. His second met with better results, and on a small salary sufficient only to keep them from absolute want, he labored for some months as teacher of Latin in the Princeton Academy, which position he resigned for that of master in the school of Burlington. Though not sixteen, he bore himself with such propriety as to secure for himself the permanent esteem of all with whom he came in contact.

This position was relinquished that he might accept another with Dr. Abercombie, who had formed for Mr. Cone the highest regard. To fulfill his duties he moved his family to Philadelphia. But he found that an increase of salary does not mean an addition to comforts, for the expenses became enlarged and he was obliged to do something to supplement his insufficient salary. He resolved to study law, and as soon as school duties were completed he was found reading law till far into the night, much to the injury of his health.

Beyond doubt it was the question of living that led him to adopt the stage. His mother's wishes and his own taste were against it, but his magnificent native endowment led him to foresee a speedy way out of his pecuniary difficulties, and so he appeared on the stage, July, 1805, as Achmet, in the tragedy of "Mahomet." He subsequently acted in Philadelphia, Baltimore, and Alexandria, meeting with great success. His own views are expressed in a letter written in 1810, wherein he says, "My profession, adopted from necessity, is becoming more disgusting to me. I pray heaven that I may speedily exchange it for something better in itself and more congenial to my feelings. What can be more degrading than to be stuck upon a stage for fools and clowns to gape at or criticise?" To prepare the way out Mr. Cone endeavored to open a school in Baltimore, but the proprietors of the theatre would not allow him to be absent from morning rehearsals, nor did public sentiment encourage teaching by an actor. This was in 1812. The same year he joined the Baltimore Union Artillery with the intention of enlisting in the war, but domestic considerations restrained him, and in the same year he entered the office of the Baltimore *American* as treasurer and book-keeper. Soon after he and his brother-in-law purchased and published the Baltimore *Whig*. He at once quitted the stage, and by his vigorous articles did much to strengthen the administration of Mr. Madison in the war.

In the year 1810, an attachment had begun between himself and Miss Sally Wallace, of Philadelphia, which resulted in their marriage in 1813. In November of the same year he was converted to God. Noticing that a book sale was advertised, he called in to examine the works. The book which he first took up was one of John Newton's; he had read it while at Princeton, to his mother. Solemn reflections were awakened by the incident, and he seemed to hear a voice saying, "This is your last time!" His past life came before him. The day wore away. He sat down to the study of the Bible. Weeks passed in darkness, which was finally dispelled by reading John xiii. On Feb. 4, 1814, he was baptized by Mr. Richards. His wife afterwards was led to trust the great Saviour.

He procured a position under the government, and he took his family to Washington, and transferred his membership to the church under the care of Rev. Obadiah B. Brown.

It was at this time that Mr. Cone began preaching, being desired to lead the prayer-meeting of the little Baptist church at the navy-yard, then pastorless. Crowds at once waited upon his ministrations.

It was evident that God had intended him for the pulpit, and he procured a license.

His popularity was at once recognized by the House of Representatives, who appointed him their chaplain in 1815-16. Soon after he was invited to take charge of the feeble interest at Alexandria, where he labored for seven years with great success, and from which he came to Oliver Street, New York. This connection, attended with wonderful prosperity, was severed after eighteen years, and one was formed with the First Baptist church of New York, which ended only with his death.

For many years Dr. Cone was the most active Baptist minister in the United States, and the most popular clergyman in America. He was known and venerated everywhere all over this broad land. In his own denomination he held every position of honor which his brethren could give him, and outside of it men loved to recognize his worth. He had quick perceptions, a ready address, a silvery voice, impassioned eloquence, and deep-toned piety; throngs attended his church, and multitudes lamented his death. He entered the heavenly rest Aug. 28, 1855.

Confession, The London, of 1689.—See THE PHILADELPHIA CONFESSION OF FAITH.

Confession of Faith, The Philadelphia.—The London Confession of 1689 was the basis of our great American Articles of Faith, and its composition and history are worthy of our careful consideration.

It was adopted "by the ministers and messengers of upwards of one hundred *baptized* congregations in England and Wales, denying Arminianism." Thirty-seven ministers signed it on behalf of the represented churches.

The sessions of the Assembly which framed it were held from the 3d to the 12th of September, 1689.

The Confession of the Westminster Assembly—the creed of all British and American Presbyterians—was published in 1647; the Savoy Confession, containing the faith of English Congregationalists, was issued in 1658. The Baptist Assembly gave their religious beliefs to the world in 1689. This was not the first Baptist deliverance on the most momentous questions.

It was styled by its authors, "A Confession of Faith put forth by the Elders and Brethren of Many Congregations of Christians *Baptized upon Profession of their Faith*, in London and the Country, with an Appendix concerning Baptism." The authors of the Confession say that in the numerous instances in which they were agreed with the Westminster Confession, they used the same language to describe their religious principles.

The Appendix to the London Confession occupies 16 octavo pages, and the Articles 52. The former is a vigorous attack on infant baptism, apparently designed to give help to the brethren in defending the clause of Article XXIX., which defines the subjects of baptism as believers. Dr. Rippon gives the Minutes of the London Assembly which adopted the Confession. These include the topics discussed, the residences of the signatory ministers, and the Articles, but not the Appendix.* In addition to his "Narrative of the Proceedings of the General Assembly," as the London Convention was called, Rippon issued a pamphlet edition of the Articles without the Appendix, with an advertisement of his *Register* on the cover. Crosby does not give it in his Confession of 1689. No one ever questioned the right of either to drop the Appendix. It was not one of the Articles, but chiefly a mere argument in favor of one of them.

The Appendix has this statement: "The known principle and state of the consciences of divers of us that have agreed in this Confession is such that *we cannot hold church communion with any other than baptized believers, and churches constituted of such;* yet some others of us have a greater liberty and freedom in our spirits that way." This refers to the admission of unbaptized persons to the Lord's Table by some churches, and their rejection by others.

Within a few years, an effort has been made in this country to prove that our Baptist fathers of the Philadelphia, and other early Associations, practised "open communion" because of this item in the Appendix of the London Confession. The learned "strict communion" author of "Historical Vindications"† has contributed to this error, by making the grave mistake that the Appendix was Article XXXIII. of *The Philadelphia Confession of Faith.* And he gives as his authorities for this extraordinary statement the Hanserd Knollys Society's copy of the Confession of 1689, and the Pittsburgh edition of *The Philadelphia Confession of Faith.* In the former, it is not placed as an *Article,* but as an *Appendix.* In the latter, it *is not to be found in any form.* It *never appeared in any edition of The Philadelphia Confession of Faith,* from Benjamin Franklin's first issue down to the last copy sent forth from the press. And this could have been easily learned from the title-page. In the end of the title in the Hanserd Knollys Society's copy of the Confession of 1689 are the words, "*With an Appendix concerning Baptism.*" The portion of the title covering the Appendix, and the Appendix itself, cannot be found in any copy of our oldest American Baptist creed. That the honored writer acted in good faith in this part of his valuable work, I have no doubt; but that he was led astray himself, and that he has

---

* Appendix to volume i. of Rippon's Annual Register.
† Historical Vindications, p. 105.

drawn others into a grave mistake, I am absolutely certain.

The Appendix admits that "open communion" existed among the English Baptists. It does not assert the truth of it; the "strict communion" members of the body which adopted the Confession would tolerate nothing of that nature. And as *no such practice existed in the Philadelphia Association when its Confession was adopted, or at any other period in its history*, such an admission would have been destitute of a fragment of truth. The Cohansie church, in 1740, sent a query to the Philadelphia Association, asking if a pious Pedobaptist, who declined to have his children baptized, might come to the Lord's Table without being baptized; and they wished also to know from the Association if the refusal of such a request would not betray a want of charity. The Association unanimously decided that the man should be refused a place at the Lord's Table in the Cohansie church, and that such action showed no lack of charity. Their action, and their reasons for it, read: "Given to vote, and passed, *all in the negative. Nemine contradicente*. Reasons annexed. First. It is not for want of charity that we thus answer. Our practice shows the contrary; for we baptize none but such as, in the judgment of charity, have grace, being baptized; but it is because we find, in the Commission, that no unbaptized persons are to be admitted to church communion. Matt. xxviii. 19, 20; Mark xvi. 16. Compare Acts ii. 41; 1 Cor. xii. 13. Second. Because it is the church's duty to maintain the ordinances as they are delivered to us in the Scripture. 2 Thess. ii. 15; 1 Cor. xi. 2; Isa. viii. 20. Third. Because we cannot see it agreeable, in any respect, for the procuring that unity, unfeigned love, and undisturbed peace, which are required, and ought to be in and among Christian communities.* 1 Cor. i. 10; Eph. iv. 3." This wise decision, supported by solid reasons, shows, that two years before *the formal adoption* of the Confession of 1689, as the greater portion of the Philadelphia Confession of Faith, the Philadelphia Association was unanimously opposed to an "open communion" proposition. Thirty-three years after the Association was formed, and while the Confession of 1689 was "owned" as a Baptist creed, without the *special adoption* which it afterwards received, one of the oldest churches in the Association would not admit a pious Pedobaptist to the Lord's Supper without consulting the Association. And that body voted as a unit against the practice.

The declaration of the orthodox London brethren, in reference to themselves, could have been used by the Philadelphia Association about *all* its churches, *at any period in its past history:* "The known principle and state of the consciences of us all is such that we cannot hold church communion with any other than baptized believers, and churches constituted of such." And hence the truth required the exclusion of the Appendix from the Confession of the Philadelphia Association.

The London Confession of 1689, in Article XXVI., section 6, says, "The members of these churches are saints by calling, . . . and do willingly consent to walk together according to the appointment of Christ, giving up themselves to the Lord and one to another, by the will of God, in *professed subjection to the ordinances of the gospel.*" And in Article XXVIII., section 1, it says, "*Baptism and the Lord's Supper are ordinances of positive and sovereign institution*, appointed by the Lord Jesus, the only Law-giver, to be continued in his church to the end of the world." And in Article XXIX., section 2, it says, "Those who do actually profess repentance towards God, faith in and obedience to our Lord Jesus, are the only proper subjects of this ordinance;" and in section 4, "Immersion, or dipping the person in water, is necessary to the due administration of this ordinance."

In Article XXX., "On the Lord's Supper,"† there is no clause giving the unbaptized authority to come to the Lord's Table. Their existence in connection with this institution is not noticed by a single word. And as the Articles declare that the members of the churches which adopted them lived in "professed subjection to the *ordinances of the gospel;*" that *baptism* and *the Lord's Supper* were "*ordinances appointed by the Lord Jesus*, to be continued in his church to the end of the world;" and that repentance, faith, and immersion are necessary to baptism, the Articles describe orderly believers only, who lived in professed subjection to the ordinances of the gospel. There is not a word in them which the strictest Baptist on earth might not heartily receive. The men who avow that "The known principle and state of the consciences of divers of us, that have agreed in this Confession, is such, that we cannot hold church communion with any other than baptized believers, and churches constituted of such"—men like Hanserd Knollys and William Kiffin—were the last men to sign a Confession favoring "open communion." The Philadelphia Association, while avowing the most stringent "close communion" doctrines in 1740, owned, *in a general way*, the Confession of 1689. The Charleston Association, S. C., adopted the London Articles, and imported two hundred copies of them; and yet was restricted in its com-

---

* Minutes of Philadelphia Association for 1740.

† Hanserd Knollys Society's volume of "Confessions," etc., pp. 221, 225, 226, 244.

munion. In 1802, in answer to a question in reference to the consistency of Baptists inviting pious Pedobaptists to the Lord's Table, that body replied, "We cannot but say *it does not appear to be consistent with gospel order.*"* In England and America, churches, individuals, and Associations, with clear minds, with hearts full of love for the truth, and with a tenacious attachment to "restricted communion," have held with veneration the Articles of 1689. The Article, "*On the Lord's Supper,*" needs safeguards, and the *Philadelphia Confession of Faith* furnishes them.

THE PHILADELPHIA CONFESSION OF FAITH IS NOT THE LONDON CREED OF 1689.

Almost every writer on this question falls into the mistake of supposing that it is, and he proceeds to prophesy evils, if he is a scriptural communionist, or he begins forthwith to whip us with the supposed *liberal* scourge of our fathers, if he is a free communionist. The London Creed has thirty-two Articles, and an Appendix; the Philadelphia has thirty-four, and, instead of an Appendix, it has "*A Treatise of Discipline,*" which was held in as great regard as the Confession for many years. Thirty-two of the thirty-four Articles in the Philadelphia Confession are taken from the English fathers of 1689. One of the two new Articles is on Singing in the Worship of God,—a practice which it commends as a divine ordinance. This Article would have entirely changed the character of the Confession of 1689 to some of the churches that adopted it; for they looked with horror upon such a custom. But in Article XXXI. in the new Confession, "*On Laying on of Hands,*" the Lord's Supper receives its appropriate safeguards. In section 1 we read, "We believe that laying on of hands, with prayer, *upon baptized believers, as such,* is an ordinance of Christ, and ought to be submitted unto *by all such persons that are admitted to the Lord's Supper.*"

According to the compilers of this Article, no man should come to the Lord's Table without baptism and the imposition of hands. It has been declared, with an air of victory, that the Philadelphia Confession of Faith requires no ceremonial qualification before approaching the Lord's Table. This jubilant spirit is the result of carelessness in examining the venerable Confession: "All *such persons that are admitted to partake of the Lord's Supper*" should *be baptized believers, who have received the imposition of hands, with prayer.* So that *two ceremonial prerequisites to the Lord's Supper—baptism and the laying on of hands—are demanded by the Philadelphia Confession of Faith.*

THE PHILADELPHIA CONFESSION OF FAITH, AND NOT THE ENGLISH CONFESSION OF 1689, WAS THE BASIS ON WHICH NEARLY ALL THE ORIGINAL ASSOCIATIONS OF THIS COUNTRY WERE FOUNDED.

In 1742, the Philadelphia Association adopted the Confession which bears its name. Some deny that the Association ever formally adopted it; or if it did they assert that we know nothing of the time when such action took place. This statement is based upon a certain amount of recognition which the London Articles undoubtedly received in the Philadelphia Association before 1742; and also upon the fact that the Association simply voted to "*reprint*" the London Confession. When a publishing house resolves to reprint an English work now it *adopts it; it makes the work its own.* The Confession of 1689, in 1742 had never been printed in America; the Philadelphia Association voted to reprint it, that is, to adopt its Articles; and they also added two Articles to it, and *A Treatise on Discipline.* And every copy printed since Benjamin Franklin's first edition appeared in 1743, bears on its title-page, "Adopted by the Philadelphia Association, Sept. 25th, 1742." This statement on the title-page would have been canceled at the next meeting of the Association after its appearance if it had not been true. The Warren Association makes the same record about the date of its adoption;† Morgan Edwards gives 1742 as the date of its adoption, on page 5 of his "Materials towards the History of the Baptists, etc.," published in Philadelphia, 1770, and the act cannot be reasonably doubted, nor the date called in question.

The Kehukee Association, founded in 1765, adopted the Philadelphia Confession.‡ The Ketockton Association of Virginia, founded 1766, adopted the Philadelphia Confession.§ The Warren Association of Rhode Island, organized 1767, adopted the same Confession.‖ The General Association of Virginia received the Philadelphia Confession in 1783 with explanations, none of which favored "open communion."¶ The Elkhorn Association of Kentucky, formed in 1785, adopted the Philadelphia Confession.** The Holston Association of Tennessee, established in 1788, accepted the Philadelphia Confession.†† The Charleston Association of South Carolina was established by Oliver Hart in 1751, fresh from the Philadelphia Association, and full of admiration for its principles and its usefulness. It adopted the Articles of 1689, and a Treatise on Discipline, prepared by Oliver Hart, and Brethren Pelot, Morgan Edwards, and David Williams. This Association, though not adopting

---

* History of Charleston Association, p. 43.

† Historical Vindications, p. 91.
‡ Semple's History of the Baptists in Virginia, p. 338.
§ Semple, p. 302.
‖ Manning and Brown University, p. 80.
¶ Semple, p. 68.
** Benedict's General History of the Baptist Denomination, p. 82.
†† Semple, p. 275.

the Philadelphia Confession, followed its spirit and plan, and it practised "restricted communion."

There was not one of the original Baptist Associations of this country that invited the unbaptized to the Lord's Table. Once we have seen the statement rashly made, and Asplund given as its authority, that there was one early Baptist Association that held "open communion,"—evidently referring to the Groton Conference, Connecticut. But the writer omitted to state that Asplund gave an account, in the same list of Associations, of Six Principle Baptists, Free-Will Baptists, and Seventh-Day Baptists. The "open communion" body of which he speaks was not composed of Regular Baptists, nor were the Seventh-Day brethren named by Asplund as members of our denomination. They did not assume the name of an Association,—they called themselves the Groton Conference. And Asplund says that "*they keep no correspondence*,"*—that is, they were not recognized as Regular Baptists. They neither enjoyed, nor were they entitled to, such recognition.

Asplund mentions several other early Baptist Associations that adopted THE Confession of Faith, —that is, the Philadelphia. But further reference to this question is needless. Nearly all the original Associations of America adopted the Philadelphia Confession of Faith; and not one of these bodies held "open communion." There were "open communionists" outside of our organizations, when our early Associations sprang into life,—especially in New England,—whose erring judgments soon learned the way of the Lord more perfectly, and they united with Regular Baptist communities.

If the Philadelphia Confession of Faith had been accepted in England, as the legitimate successor of the Confession of 1689, the Strict Baptists of Norwich would never, by a just legal decision, have been deprived of their church edifice for the advantage of "open communionists."

The Philadelphia Association never had an "open communion" church in its fellowship; and it has repeatedly declared the practice to be unscriptural. Its Confession of Faith as adopted in 1742 *never was repealed or modified in any of its parts. The latest edition is an exact reprint of the first*, and "open communion" cannot even find a shelter in it. (See Appendix.)

Confessions of Faith.—In 1611 a church of English Baptists, residing in Holland, adopted a Confession of Faith, prepared most probably by Thomas Helwys, their pastor. Not many months after the Confession was published they returned to their native country and settled in London. The Confession has twenty-six articles, and though most of them are thoroughly sound, others are Arminian, and show clearly that those who framed them were troubled by a defective knowledge of New Testament teachings.

The Confession of Faith of 1644, was adopted by seven London churches. It is the first Calvinistical creed published by our English brethren. It has fifty articles. The first name which appears on the Confession is that of the illustrious William Kiffin. The twenty-first article reads, "Jesus Christ did purchase salvation for the elect that God gave unto him. These only have interest in him, and fellowship with him, for whom he makes intercession to his Father, and to them alone doth God by his Spirit apply this redemption; also the free gift of eternal life is given to them and none else." The thirty-ninth article is, "Baptism is an ordinance of the New Testament, given by Christ, to be dispensed upon persons professing faith, or that are made disciples, who, upon profession of faith, *ought to be baptized, and after to partake of the Lord's Supper*."

An "Appendix" to this Confession of Faith, written by Benjamin Cox, and printed in 1646, has twenty-two articles, a part of the twentieth of which reads, "The apostles first baptized disciples, and then admitted them to the use of the Supper; we, therefore, do not admit any to the use of the Supper, *nor communicate with any in the use of this ordinance but disciples baptized*, lest we should have fellowship with them in their doing contrary to order."

The "Confession of Faith of Several Churches of Christ in the County of Somerset," and of some churches in adjacent counties, in England, was issued in 1656. It was signed by the representatives of sixteen churches, and it was probably written by Thomas Collier, who was ordained in 1655 to the "office of general superintendent and messenger to all the associated churches." The Confession has forty-six articles; it is Calvinistic, Baptistic, and, consequently, thoroughly Scriptural.

The London Confession of Faith was signed in the English metropolis in 1660. It was prepared by members of the General (Arminian) Baptist churches. On some disputed questions it is nearer the truth than the Confession of 1611, but this statement does not apply to its representation of the doctrine of final perseverance. It has twenty-five articles. This Confession was "owned and approved by more than twenty thousand persons."

"An Orthodox Creed," published in London in 1678, gives another view of the doctrines of the General Baptists. It has fifty articles, and it is remarkable for its Calvinistic tone, though it came from a body professedly Arminian. Its mode of describing election, providence, free will, and final perseverance is in the main scriptural. The extent of the atonement is the only question about which

---

* Asplund's Annual Register for 1790, p. 49.

it differed from the opinions of our orthodox brethren of that day.

The Confession of 1689 was "put forth by the elders and brethren of many congregations of Christians, baptized (immersed) upon profession of their faith, in London and the country." It has thirty-two articles, and "an appendix concerning baptism." It is in many respects the best compilation of Christian belief ever published. After dropping its lengthy appendix, and *inserting* two new articles, it became, in 1742, " The Philadelphia Confession of Faith," and it was adopted by most of the early Baptist Associations of this country. (See article on THE PHILADELPHIA CONFESSION OF FAITH.)

The New Hampshire Confession of Faith was written by the late Dr. J. Newton Brown while laboring in the State whose name it bears. It was prepared with a view "to pending controversies with the Free-Will Baptists, who are numerous there." Dr. Cutting says, " It has been sometimes criticised as aiming at the difficult task of preserving the stern orthodoxy of the fathers of the denomination, while at the same time it softens the terms in which that orthodoxy is expressed, in order to remove the objections of neighboring opponents." (Historical Vindications, p. 105.) We have unlimited faith in the goodness and sanctity of the late Dr. Brown, but we very much prefer the Philadelphia Confession of Faith, so dear to our fathers, to the New Hampshire Creed. (For Confessions of Faith, see the Appendix.)

Conger, Rev. O. T., was born in Indiana, and brought up chiefly in Illinois. At the age of twenty-one he was converted in Iowa, during an extensive revival. He was called to preach soon after the Lord had found and saved him.

He studied for the ministry at Burlington University, and in due time was ordained as pastor of Edgington, Ill. He labored afterwards at Winterset and Malvern, Iowa, and at Lincoln and Omaha, Neb. He has been chaplain of the Legislature of Nebraska, and twice moderator of the Nebraska State Convention. He represented the University of Des Moines in the Centennial movement of 1876. Recently he has taken charge of the church at Osage, Iowa. Mr. Conger is a frequent contributor to the Chicago *Standard*, and other papers. He has published two books, one of which, " The Autobiography of a Pioneer," has passed through three editions.

Mr. Conger is a diligent student, an industrious pastor, a strong Baptist, and a growing and successful minister.

Connally, Rev. John Kerr, a grandson of the eloquent Rev. John Kerr. Col. Connally was born in Madison Co., Tenn., Sept. 3, 1839 ; was educated at the U. S. Naval Academy, Annapolis, Md. ; was wounded when colonel of the 55th North Carolina Regiment at Gettysburg, losing an arm ; practised law in Galveston, Texas, several years after the war ; settled in Richmond, Va., in 1867 ; was chosen senator for four years ; was brought to Christ by being caught in the timbers of the falling capitol, and remaining for hours in suffering and peril ; resigned as senator, and spent some time at theological seminary, Greenville, S. C., and was ordained at Ashville, November, 1875 ; Col. Connally is missionary of the Eastern Baptist Convention.

Connecticut, The Baptists of.—Connecticut began her career with the Puritan doctrine of church and state. The standing order was Presbyterian,—now Congregational,—and held the ground by law until the opening of the present century. The new constitution, giving full freedom of conscience, was adopted in 1818, and the article on religious liberty was drawn by Rev. Asahel Morse, a Baptist minister from Suffield. The leaven of liberty was early introduced into the colony by the Baptists from Rhode Island, and gradually wrought the transformation of the State.

The first New Testament baptisms were solemnized in Waterford in 1674, the persons uniting with a church in Rhode Island. A great excitement followed, and the Legislature was invoked to suppress the innovation. The first Baptist church was organized in Groton, in 1705, by Rev. Valentine Weightman, a man of liberal education for his time. The second was formed in Waterford in 1710. A third was gathered in Wallingford in 1735. Three more were planted in 1743,—one in North Stonington, one in Lyme, and one in Colchester. A seventh was formed in Saybrook in 1744. In the latter place " fourteen persons were arrested for holding a Baptist meeting, . . . tried, fined, and driven on foot through a deep mud (in February) to New London, a distance of twenty-five miles, and thrust into prison, without fire, food, or beds, where they remained, enduring dreadful sufferings, for several weeks." In this State, however, Baptist principles began to spread more rapidly on account of the Great Awakening, which gave birth to evangelical sentiments and to a strong party in the standing order, known as Separatists and New Lights, who appealed to the New Testament. Yale College took ground against the reformation and expelled some who favored it. The colony was in a ferment from 1740 to 1760. About forty separate churches were formed. The Separatists " generally turned Baptists." Among some in this transition period, and for a time after, there was a mixture of ecclesiastical views and some experimental affiliations. Baptist principles, however, eventually triumphed, and the standing order was greatly modified and mollified, and the Baptists stood forth in all their proper distinctness and independence.

The Stonington Union Association was formed in 1772. In the Revolution the Baptists were ardent patriots. In 1789 they counted about 30 churches and 20 ordained ministers. The Groton Union Conference, a mixed association of Baptists and Separatists, had but a temporary existence. The Hartford Association was organized in 1789. In 1795 the State contained about 60 churches, 40 ministers, and 3500 members. The New London Association was formed in 1817, the Ashford Association in 1824, the New Haven Association in 1825, the Fairfield Association in 1837. In 1848 the State counted over 100 churches, and more than 16,000 members. The Connecticut Baptist Education Society was organized in 1819, the State Convention was formed in 1823, the *Christian Secretary* was started in 1822, the Connecticut Literary Institution was founded in 1833, the Connecticut Baptist Social Union was formed in 1871, and the State Sunday-school Convention was organized in 1877.

Evangelization and education were early pursued by the denomination, and efforts have been constant and systematic for domestic, home, and foreign missions, and for Sunday-schools and a denominational literature. Yale College to-day gladly admits the Baptists to its halls and privileges. Truth has conquered its way to an open field. The present Baptist statistics of the State are as follows (given in 1879): 6 Associations, 119 churches, 20,767 members, 1 institution of learning, 1 periodical, 1 education society, 2 Conventions, 1 social union, various missionary societies.

Connecticut Literary Institution was founded by the Connecticut Baptist Education Society in Suffield, Conn., in June, 1833; opened at first in the old town hall; the south building entered in 1834; the institution incorporated in 1835. Principals: Harvey Ball, assisted by Reuben Granger, 1833–35; N. H. Shailer, 1835–37; Julius L. Shailer, 1837–40; C. C. Burnett, 1840–48; W. W. Woodbury, 1848–56; H. A. Pratt, 1856–61; F. B. Gammell, 1861–65; E. P. Bond, 1865–70; E. Benjamin Andrews, 1870–72; J. A. Shores, 1872–80; Martin H. Smith, 1880. During the first ten years only males were admitted; in 1843 females admitted; in 1845 ladies' building erected; this was burned in 1871; a larger edifice was erected; well equipped with library, chemical and philosophical apparatus; ample corps of instructors; young men fitted for colleges; young ladies fitted for Vassar or Wellesley; it has a noble history.

Conner, Champ C., D.D., the son of John Conner, was born in Culpepper Co., Va., March 13, 1811, and was baptized by Rev. Cumberland George into the fellowship of the Broad Run Baptist church, Fauquier Co., Va., Sept. 14, 1828, and very soon after commenced preaching the gospel, being in his eighteenth year. He married Ann Eliza Slaughter, Dec. 23, 1833, and moved to West Tennessee, November, 1835; he died at Indian Mound, Lauderdale Co., Feb. 14, 1875. He was an able presiding officer, and when present at the Big Hatchie Association and West Tennessee Baptist Convention, he was nearly always chosen to fill the chair; he presided with dignity and precision. He possessed rare talent as a minister of the gospel; he was of almost unequaled eloquence; he could hold his audience spell-bound for hours, and was an able defender of Baptist doctrine and practice, contending always "most earnestly for the faith once delivered to the saints." He was a "land-marker" both in faith and practice, yet, while he was bold and fearless in the advocacy of the doctrines he held, he was always courteous and respectful to those who differed from him. He was not only gifted as a preacher, but he was a man of extensive information about medicine and jurisprudence, and also about matters pertaining to State and National governments. At the time of his decease he was the pastor of four churches,—Grace, Society Hill, Woodlawn, and Zion. He died in the field assigned by the Master, with the harness on. He died at his post, and left a vacancy in the denomination which cannot be easily filled. He left us in his sixty-fourth year, after a few days of suffering, to join the company of the redeemed.

"Servant of God, well done;
Rest from thy loved employ;
The battle fought, the victory won,
Enter thy Master's joy."

The following resolutions were adopted at a meeting of brethren, representing Elim, Grace, Ripley, Society Hill, and Woodlawn churches, held in the town of Ripley, Feb. 20, 1875:

"*Resolved*, That in the death of Champ C. Conner, D.D., the church of Christ has lost a great and good man, and the community a valued citizen.

"*Resolved*, That we bow with submission to this bereavement of Providence, and deeply sympathize with the dear afflicted family in the irreparable loss which they have sustained, a loss which we feel assured has conferred upon our brother eternal and glorious gain."

Dr. Conner had attractive social qualities, a happy disposition, and a clear and logical mind. His piety increased with his years. There was more humility, meekness, submission, patience, and diligence in the Master's service as he advanced in life. He would frequently say that his work was almost done. His opposition to pulpit affiliations with teachers of error grew and strengthened up to the day of his death. He was a great friend of missions and Sabbath-schools. Being one of the pioneer preachers of West Tennessee, he had to meet and combat Antinomianism in all its varied forms; but he lived to see it almost extinct. Dr. Conner was called to preside for a term of years over the Baptist Female College at Hernando, Miss. He was also pastor of Hernando church during the same period. He served as pastor of the Brownsville church for some time. He was a minister of brilliant parts. But the orator is gone! We shall hear no more his earnest voice, or see the tearful eye; his tongue is silent in the grave.

Conrad, Rev. P.—One of the earliest pioneer missionaries in Wisconsin. He was a native of Wyoming Co., N. Y. Converted when a boy, he heard early in life the call of God to preach the gospel. He entered Hamilton Literary and Theological Institution at sixteen years of age, and graduated with honor from both departments. He came to Wisconsin in 1842, with a commission from the American Baptist Home Mission Society as missionary for Wisconsin. He was pastor at Milwaukee, Geneva, Prairie-du-Sac, Baraboo, Delton, Killbourne, Berlin, and East Troy. His great work, however, was accomplished as itinerant missionary under the direction of the State Convention or American Baptist Home Mission Society. There is hardly a town of any note in the State in which he did not sow the gospel seed. He was for many years the "missionary apostle" of Wisconsin, since he preached the gospel "throughout all this region." He served the American Bible Union as its financial agent in the State for a short term. It was while on his missionary tours, preaching the gospel to the destitute, gathering the scattered sheep into churches, that he was most happy. He was a sound preacher, a good student of the Bible, exemplary in his life. He died Nov. 1, 1875, at Santa Barbara, Cal., where he had gone to seek health. It is befitting that one whose life-work was done in Wisconsin should have a place among the annals of its ministers.

Conventicle Act, The.—This act condemns all persons, refusing peremptorily to come to church, after conviction, to banishment; and in case of return, to death without benefit of the clergy. It also enacts, "That if any person above the age of sixteen, after July 1, 1664, shall be present at any meeting, under color or pretense of any exercise of religion, in any other manner than is allowed by the liturgy or practice of the Church of England, where there shall be five or more persons than the household, shall, for the first offense, suffer three months' imprisonment, upon record made upon oath under the hand and seal of a justice of the peace, or pay a sum not exceeding five pounds; for the second offense six months' imprisonment or ten pounds; and for the third offense the offender to be banished to some of the American plantations for seven years or pay one hundred pounds, excepting New England and Virginia; and in case they return or make their escape, such persons are to be adjudged felons, and *suffer death without benefit of clergy.* Sheriffs, or justices of the peace, or others commissioned by them, are empowered to dissolve, dissipate, and break up all unlawful conventicles, and to take into custody such of their number as they think fit. They who suffer such conventicles in their houses or barns are liable to the same forfeitures as other offenders. The prosecution is to be within three months. Married women taken at conventicles are to be imprisoned for twelve months, unless their husbands pay forty shillings for their redemption." No scourge could create a greater panic among Dissenters in England than the Conventicle Act, and the havoc it made among them was dreadful. Informers abounded, and the prisons groaned with persecuted Baptists and others. Some conformed occasionally to Episcopal worship; but the Baptists were enthusiastic and resolute, and suffered the loss of goods and of liberty, and many of them died in prison. But no acts of Parliament could suppress the truth of God, and the sufferings of saints planted seed in new hearts.

Conveyances of Real Estate for Church Uses.—Conveyances, according to an old British statute called the "Statute of Frauds," in some form are in force universally in this country. Every transfer of land must be made in writing and signed by the grantor. A gift of land for church purposes must therefore be in writing, and legally signed and witnessed, or it is not binding. There are also statutes in many of the States of the Union requiring all gifts for charities (and all religious uses are charities) to be made within a certain time, varying from one to six months, before the death of the giver, and this applies whether the gift be made by deed or will. Such gifts must also be signed in presence of two or more subscribing witnesses. The pious intentions of persons who wished to dedicate a portion of their wealth to the service of God have been frustrated and disappointed by a failure to attend to these formalities. In conveying property to a church just formed, great care should be exercised and competent legal advice taken, when practicable, to have the deed made and executed in legal form. Where the property is bought before the church is organized and chartered, the conveyance may be made to certain persons chosen as trustees to hold it until a charter can be procured; but if afterwards the society changes the trustees the title does not, as a general rule, follow the change, but remains in the old trustees. Such a trust, however, will always be enforced by the courts, and the trustees compelled to hold and convey the property so as to carry out fully the trust. Where a church owns property it should procure a charter without delay, and have the title legally conveyed to the corporation or trustees of the church. The general rule of law is that an unincorporated society cannot take and hold property in its own name; but in many of the States great indulgence is shown to religious societies as charitable institutions, and conveyances and devises to them are sustained on that ground, which would not otherwise be valid. In the States bordering on the Atlantic coast many unincorporated churches and religious societies received and used property acquired by them for their proper purposes in early times before the laws with regard to incorporations became generally known, and the usage thus established has become the foundation of the law on this subject in those States and in many others.

the same year the board of trustees organized under the charter by the appointment of the following officers, viz.: President, Elbert W. Cook; Secretary, Rev. Joel Hendrick; Treasurer, Elbert P. Cook, Esq. These officers have held their respective positions to the present time.

The purpose of Col. Cook is expressed in the following words: "I would found a purely classical, literary, and scientific institution, and place it on a firm basis and under Christian influences. I desire a school of the first class, but I do not desire a godless school. I would establish in connection with the institution a thorough classical course, so that young gentlemen, and young ladies also, can prepare themselves for entering college in the most complete and thorough manner. I am desirous that this department shall take the highest rank in the preparation of students for college. I would

COOK ACADEMY, HAVANA, SCHUYLER CO., N. Y.

Cook Academy, N. Y.—This institution is located in the village of Havana, Schuyler Co., N. Y., and had its origin in a proposition of Col. E. W. Cook to the New York Baptist State Convention in 1870. He tendered to the Convention the magnificent property previously known as the People's College, valued at $123,000, on condition that it should be thoroughly equipped and well supported.

The property was purchased by Col. Cook, transferred to the persons named as trustees, and the charter obtained in August, 1872. In October of

have also a thorough literary and scientific course, in which young gentlemen and ladies not intending to advance to higher institutions may obtain a thorough education, second only to a collegiate one. I am greatly desirous that the academy shall always be accessible to students of limited means."

In full sympathy with this expressed purpose the school was opened in September, 1873, having a faculty of eight teachers, with Charles Fairman, LL.D., late of Shurtleff College, Ill., as principal. The average number of pupils the first year was

101; second year, 139; third year, 154; fourth year, 163; fifth year, 170. A healthful religious atmosphere has prevailed in the school from the beginning. About 40 conversions occurred among the students the first year, and about 120 during the first four years.

As a literary institution it now ranks among the best of its kind in the State, but the trustees desire to increase its facilities by endowments, and by additions to its library and apparatus.

Cook, Hon. C. M., was born in Franklin County in 1844. He was educated at Wake Forest College. He was adjutant of the 55th N. C. Regiment in the late war, and was severely wounded in the last battles around Richmond. He began the practice of law in 1868. He has repeatedly represented his district in the Legislature, and he was president of the Baptist State Convention during the session of 1876. Mr. Cook is a good Sunday-school worker and a devout Christian.

Cook, J. F., LL.D., was born in Shelby Co., Ky., in 1837. He made a profession of religion when twelve years of age. Prepared for college at the Fayette High School in Howard Co., Mo. He entered Georgetown College in 1855, and graduated in 1858, and was ordained to the ministry in the same year.

He took the presidency of the La Grange College in 1866. During his administration the institution has constantly gained in finances and character. He is a fine scholar and an excellent teacher, and while he rules his school he has the love of all his students, and he is highly esteemed by all who know him. He is gentle and yet firm, modest and yet dignified. He exerts a happy influence over all that enjoy his society. He is making numerous pillars to support our great republic with wisdom and honor in coming days.

Cook, Rev. Richard Briscoe, was born in Baltimore, Md., Nov. 11, 1838. After receiving an elementary education in the public schools and in the academy of the Newton University of his native city, he entered mercantile life, and spent five years in the counting-room and store. At his conversion he was baptized by the Rev. Dr. Fuller, April 12, 1857, and received into the fellowship of the Seventh Baptist church, Baltimore, of which he became an active member. At the earnest solicitation of Dr. Fuller he gave up his position in the mercantile house, and in 1859 entered the Columbian College, to prepare himself for the work of the ministry. In the Junior year of his course he received the Davis prize medal for elocution, and in 1863 graduated with the degree of A.B., sharing with one other the highest honors of the class. After his graduation he was chosen tutor in Greek in the college, in which position he served during 1863–64. The degree of A.M. in course was conferred upon him in 1866. He took a private course in theology, mainly under the supervision of the Rev. Dr. Samson; was licensed to preach by the Seventh Baptist church, Baltimore, and was ordained by a council called by the same church in October, 1864, Rev. Drs. Fuller, Samson, Wilson, and others officiating. Immediately after, he was

REV. RICHARD BRISCOE COOK.

engaged to supply the pulpit of the Baptist church at Holmesburg, Philadelphia, and eventually became its pastor. On the 2d of April following, the meeting-house, which was a rude-looking building, was destroyed by fire, and there was erected in its stead a handsome brownstone edifice, costing upwards of $22,000, which, in 1867, within two years and a half after the fire, was dedicated, free of debt. The church had prospered so much in the mean time, that a few years afterwards a neat chapel was also erected in Byberry for mission purposes, costing nearly $4000. Mr. Cook remained with the church at Holmesburg eleven years, during which time twice as much money was raised for benevolent purposes as had been contributed during the thirty-two previous years; the pastor's salary was tripled; the home Sunday-school was greatly enlarged, and a mission school established. In December, 1875, he became pastor of the Second Baptist church in Wilmington, Del., at which place there were, during his first year as pastor, 147 baptisms, the membership being increased by 155 additions, and the number of the Sunday-school doubled, as well as a very large adult Bible-class formed. In 1869 he served as moderator of the Central Union Association, in all the deliberations of which he was accustomed to take an active part. For one year, also, he acted as president of the Philadelphia Baptist Ministerial Conference, after having previously served as vice-president. Mr. Cook has in preparation, and almost ready for publication, a popular "History of the Baptists," designed more especially for Sunday-schools and for the young, which will add to his reputation as a scholar and a writer, and he has a valuable history of the Baptists of Delaware now passing through the press. No minister in Pennsylvania or Delaware enjoys a larger measure of the confidence of his brethren than Mr. Cook. He is an able minister of the Saviour.

Cook, Rev. Samuel, was born in Eastham, Mass., in 1791. Early in his life his parents removed to the State of Maine, and there he resided for many years. At the age of twenty-four he became a hopeful Christian, and united with the Baptist church in Clinton, Me. He studied at Waterville, under the direction of Rev. Dr. Chapin. After leaving the institution he was called to the Baptist church of Effingham, N. H., where he was ordained, Dr. Chapin preaching the sermon, which was published. On leaving Effingham he served in succession the churches in Brentwood, N. H., Hampton Falls, Hopkinton, Meredith Village, and Dunbarton. For some time he was the agent of the New Hampshire State Convention, and labored among the feeble churches. His last regular ministerial service was in Concord, N. H., where for eight years he acted as chaplain of the State prison. His life was a laborious one as a minister of Christ, and God blessed his labors abundantly. Mr. Cook died at Concord, N. H., Feb. 15, 1872.

Cooke, Rev. Nathaniel B., was born at Cambridgeport, Mass., in 1816; was converted at the age of eleven and baptized by Rev. Howard Malcom in 1834. He prepared for college at the Phillips Academy, and graduated at Brown University in the class of 1840. It was his strong desire at this period of his life to become a minister of the gospel, but circumstances temporarily prevented, and he devoted himself to teaching for a time in Bristol, R. I. Subsequently he studied medicine at Yale, and practised his profession for a period at Leicester, Mass., and then returned to Bristol, R. I., where he was the principal of the high school for nine years. The way now being opened for him to carry out his long cherished wishes to preach, he was ordained at Greenville, Mass., where for six years he was a faithful minister of Christ. He then removed to Lonsdale, R. I., where he died May 14, 1871. He won the sincere respect and affection of the communities in which he lived and labored.

Cooley, Darwin H., D.D., was born in Clarendon, Orleans Co., N. Y., Feb. 5, 1830, and united with the Baptist church in Sweden, N. Y., in March, 1841. He fitted for college at the Brockport Collegiate Institute, entering the Sophomore class of the University of Rochester in 1852, and graduating in 1855, and from the theological seminary at Rochester in 1857. He was ordained at Clyde, N. Y., July 16, 1857. Removing West the following year, under appointment of the Home Mission Society, he settled at Stevens Point, Wis., June 1, 1858, being the first pastor of the church there. Here he remained until June 1, 1861, during which time a good house of worship was built and paid for. At the date last given he removed to Appleton, Wis., laboring there as pastor six years and three months. He then, in 1867, settled at Cedar Rapids, Iowa, remaining there three years. Under his ministry there was a large ingathering at this point, and a fine house was built. In the beginning of 1871, Mr. Cooley became pastor of the church in Canton, Ill., where he remained eight years. From Canton he removed to Freeport, settling there Nov. 14, 1879. At Freeport, during the pastorate which he still holds, the beautiful house has been finished and all the expenses of its erection met, while here as elsewhere, he has commended himself as an able and "good minister of Jesus Christ." Dr. Cooley received his degree of D.D. from the theological seminary at Morgan Park in 1878.

Coon, Rev. James McCowen, the pastor of the Baptist church in Beaver Dam, Wis., is a native of Frankfort, Clinton Co., Ind., where he was born July 19, 1844. His father is Rev. R. R. Coon, for many years a well-known Baptist minister in Illinois. The subject of this sketch spent his boyhood in Peoria and Alton, Ill. He was educated at the University of Chicago, graduating in the class of 1869. Having the profession of law in view, immediately upon graduating from the university he entered the Union Law School of Chicago, and graduated from that institution in 1870. Subsequently yielding to long-continued convictions that God called him to the work of the Christian ministry, he entered the Baptist Theological Seminary of Chicago, and completing the full course graduated in 1874. Having received a call to the pastorate of the Baptist church in Galva, Ill., he was ordained by that church in August, 1874.

Mr. Coon's pastorate at Galva continued four years. Having received a call to the pastorate of the Baptist church in Beaver Dam, Wis., he resigned his position at Galva, in 1879, to accept the invitation at Beaver Dam, which has since been his home. For two years past he has ably conducted a department of the International Sunday-School Lessons published in the *Standard*. His expositions have been scholarly and his practical deductions pointed and clear. He is a young minister of culture and character.

Cooper, Deacon Dan Smith, son of Samuel and Emily L. (Linsley) Cooper, was born Oct. 4, 1819, in North Haven, Conn.; nephew to Rev. James H. Linsley; moved to New Haven at the age of fourteen; converted at the age of eighteen, while a clerk, and united with the First Baptist church in New Haven; in 1840 began as a merchant on State Street, and has continued till the present (1880); honored by all the people of the city; in 1858 he was chosen deacon under the pastorate of S. D. Phelps, D.D., and remains in office; known and beloved by all the Baptists in the State; a representative citizen and a warm-hearted Christian.

Cooper, Rev. David, M.D., a distinguished pioneer Baptist in Southwest Mississippi, who combined the calling of minister and physician. He came to the State in 1802, and from this time until his death, in 1830, he was assiduous in his labors in Southwestern Mississippi and Eastern Louisiana, and perhaps did more than any other man to give character to these early Baptists. Himself a man of learning, he was a vigorous advocate of ministerial education. He was also an active promoter of missions. He was long moderator of the Mississippi Association, which he assisted in organizing, and wrote many valuable papers which appear as circular letters in the minutes of the Association.

Cooper, Rev. George, was born in Edinburgh, Scotland, Dec. 10, 1840; was baptized by his father, Rev. James Cooper, D.D., at Woodstock, Ontario, Dec. 27, 1857; was educated at the University of Toronto, Canada, and at Hamilton Theological Seminary, N. Y., graduating from the latter institution in 1866; was ordained June 1, 1866, and settled as pastor at North Attleborough, Mass., and remained until December, 1869, when he removed to Gloversville, N. Y. In May, 1873, he entered upon his present field of labor with the First church, West Philadelphia. He is a member of the Board of Managers of the American Baptist Publication Society, and of the curators of the university at Lewisburg, and is prominently identified with the management of educational and missionary work in the State. He is a man of scholarly attainments and of a sprightly and social disposition. As a preacher, he unfolds Bible truths with marked clearness of enunciation, and as a pastor he is diligent, constant, and successful. Mr. Cooper is one of the ablest men in the Baptist ministry in Pennsylvania.

Cooper, James, D.D., was born in the southern part of Scotland, Dec. 27, 1812. His parents being Presbyterians, he was brought up in that faith, and he married a lady who held the same sentiments. On the birth of their first child, now Rev. George Cooper, of Philadelphia, their attention was called to the subject of infant baptism. As a result they both became Baptists, and were baptized in Edinburgh by Rev. Christopher Anderson, author of the "Annals of the English Bible." Though trained for secular business, a call to the ministry now prevailed. He studied at Bradford, England, and at the University of Edinburgh, in the latter attending the lectures of Sir W. Hamilton. He left Scotland in 1843, and became pastor of the church at Perth, Canada. He was afterwards pastor of the churches at Kemptville and Brockville. He also did much missionary work in the country adjoining. In 1853 he took charge of the church at Woodstock. A new house of

JAMES COOPER, D.D.

worship was at once built. He gathered around him some young men from other churches who desired to study for the ministry, and aided them in their instruction. He entered heartily into the plans of the denomination for the theological training of its young men, out of which grew the Canadian Literary Institute. He did much toward the planting of the school at Woodstock, and ever bore helpful relations to it. In 1865 he became pastor of the church at London, where for fourteen years he enjoyed great success. As a result a second church was formed in the city. In August, 1879, he left the province and his work to live in Kelso, Scotland, and spend life's evening in rest. Being a most exact and careful Biblical student, his has been a teaching ministry as well as an evangelistic. The churches to which he ministered were well trained in the Word, and so the gains of many spiritual awakenings were permanent. In 1869

Madison University conferred on him the degree of D.D.

Cooper, James, D.D., was born in Boston, Mass., Jan. 2, 1826; removed to Cincinnati in 1832; joined the Ninth Street church in that city, by baptism, early in 1840, and the same year went to Woodward College. At the end of two years, ill health compelled him to suspend study and enter into active business. In 1847 he resumed study in the preparatory department of the Western Theological Institute, at Covington, Ky. In 1848 he went to Granville College (now Denison University), where he graduated in 1850. The next three years he spent in the Newton Theological Institution, and finished the usual course of study. After spending fifteen months in mission work in Cincinnati, he was ordained in December, 1854. His successive pastorates have been as follows: Madison, Wis., one year; Waukesha, Wis., three years; Melrose, Mass., three years; the Berean church, West Philadelphia, Pa., six years; Rondout, N. Y., eight years; Flint, Mich., three years. He resigned his charge in Flint, at the call of the American Baptist Home Mission Society, to become its district secretary for Ohio, Indiana, and Michigan. His present residence is Detroit. His ministry has been attended with large ingatherings to the churches he has served. In 1880 he was made a Doctor of Divinity by Denison University.

Cooper, Hon. Mark A., a distinguished Georgian, and for a number of years a member of Congress, was born in Hancock County, April 20, 1800. His parents on both sides were Virginians, his ancestors having emigrated from England and Holland. He was educated in youth by Nathan S. Beman, at Mount Zion Academy, and by Ira Ingram, at Powelton Academy. At seventeen he entered Franklin College, at Athens, but left the institution on the death of Dr. Finley, and entered the South Carolina College, at Columbia, where he graduated in 1819. Choosing law for his profession, he studied under Judge Strong, was admitted to the bar in 1821, and settled in Eatonton, Ga., where he began to practise. During the same year he was converted and joined the Eatonton Baptist church. In 1825, when Gov. Geo. M. Troup called for volunteers to protect our Florida border from the Seminole Indians, Mark A. Cooper tendered his services, joining a regiment formed by Col. Edward Hamilton, and served through the war, being appointed paymaster, and paying off the soldiers at its close. He was then elected solicitor of the Ocmulgee circuit by the Legislature, and, afterwards, becoming prominent in politics, was elected to Congress, where he served two terms in the House of Representatives. His position before the entire country became so prominent that he was prevailed upon by his friends to accept the nomination for governor of Georgia, in opposition to George W. Crawford, in 1843; but he was defeated, and Mr. Crawford was elected.

In 1836 he again responded to the call of the

HON. MARK A. COOPER.

United States for volunteers to subdue the Seminole Indians, who were waging war in Florida. His was one of five companies formed into a battalion in Middle Georgia, of which he was elected major. He accepted the command, marched to Florida, and served through Gen. Winfield Scott's campaign in that State. Major Cooper was one of the very first Georgians to advocate the building of railroads in the State; and, in connection with Chas. P. Gordon, called the first railroad meeting in the State, and made the first railroad speech; and afterwards, as a member of the Legislature, assisted in securing the charter of the Georgia Railroad. Nor did he cease his efforts until that road was built from Augusta to Atlanta, and extended by the State from Atlanta to Chattanooga.

No man in Georgia has done more to build up her manufacturing interests than Mr. Cooper. He helped to organize one of the first cotton-mills in the State, at Eatonton. He established, and for years maintained an extensive iron and flour manufacturing company, at Etowah, Cass Co. (now Bartow), which was completely destroyed by the Federal army. He was for several years the president of a successful bank in Columbus; and was the first to open the coal mines in Dade County, and on the Tennessee River, for the shipment of coal to Georgia for manufacturing purposes. He founded the State Agricultural Society, which is still in vigorous existence, drew up the constitution himself, and for a series of years presided over its affairs successfully. For a while he was a trustee of Mercer University, and assisted in its location; and for nearly fifty years has been a trustee of the State university.

In all his life he has been a man of mark. Of very commanding appearance, with a splendid intellect, fine oratorical powers, and with exceptional abilities in every respect. Even as late as 1877 he was sent by the people of his district to represent them in the State senate, and in 1878 he was a member of the State Constitutional Convention. Now in his eightieth year, he enjoys good health, so remarkable are his physical powers.

Mr. Cooper has always been a firm Baptist, and a strong supporter of all our denominational projects. He built a Baptist house of worship at Etowah, and for years was its Sunday-school superintendent and main supporter. He lost two sons in the war, both most promising young men, and each of whom took the first honor in the State university.

Cooper, Thomas, a layman and deacon of remarkable piety and extended influence and usefulness, was born in Henry Co., Va., in 1767, and died at Eatonton, Ga., in 1842. His ancestors on the maternal side, Antony by name, came from Holland; on the paternal side from England, and both settled in Virginia. Thomas Cooper, Sr., a member of the House of Burgesses, in Virginia, married Sallie Antony, and they were the parents of eleven children. Thomas Cooper, Jr., the third son, moved from Virginia to Hancock Co., Ga., where, in 1797, he married Judith Harvey, by whom he had five children,—Clinton, who died in infancy; Mark Antony Cooper, for years a member of Congress and still living at the age of eighty-one; Mrs. Harriet Nisbit, Mrs. Narcissa Boykin, and Mrs. Emily Branham, all of whom are dead. In 1822, Thomas Cooper moved from Hancock County to Eatonton, Putnam Co., where he lived until his death. He was a man of large property, one of the first planters in Georgia who raised cotton to sell, and was the inventor of a roller cotton-gin. He was a well-informed man, a great reader and a deep thinker, and was very fond of the study of natural philosophy and astronomy. He was a diligent student of the Bible, and made himself familiar with such theological works as those of Andrew Fuller and Dr. John Gill, whose Commentary was his favorite work of reference.

His religious convictions began in 1810, soon after the death of his wife Judith. He was baptized by Jesse Mercer, and joined the Baptist church at Powelton about 1811, transferring his membership eleven years afterwards to Eatonton, where for years, as a deacon, he continued an active and zealous church member, using his office well and purchasing to himself a good degree and great boldness in the faith. He was distinguished for godliness; he was an earnest and liberal supporter of schools and colleges, and an ardent and generous friend of missions and Sunday-schools. He was not only a worthy church member, who was referred to by all who knew him as a standard of Christian character and excellence, but he was a thorough Baptist, who was very active in building up the denomination in Georgia. He was regular in the exercise of family prayer, in which he was always impressive and frequently eloquent. His son, Mark A. Cooper, received his first religious convictions while at family devotions when twelve years of age,—convictions so deep as to be apparent to all, and so lasting that they have never faded away.

Mr. Cooper was among the number of those who were instrumental in founding Mercer University, and delighted to aid worthy young men who were studying for the ministry. He was a devoted friend of the temperance cause, seldom indulged in anecdote, and never in light table-talk, always preferring to converse on grave subjects. In demeanor he was austere and decisive, unwavering in his family administration, yet always kind and considerate in his domestic relations. He was the friend, companion, and co-laborer of Jesse Mercer, B. M. Sanders, Reuben Battle, Adiel Sherwood, C. D. Mallary, John E. Dawson, and many others of like character.

"As a member he was scarcely less distinguished than Jesse Mercer as a minister. In him were joined to a native intellect remarkably clear, discriminating, and vigorous, the most excellent qualities of heart, all sanctified by fervent and exalted piety. Three times a day would he retire to commune with God. For the last twelve or fifteen years of his life this wise and venerable man was a humble pupil in a Bible-class. His faithfulness in encouraging, counseling, and, if necessary, reproving his brethren was worthy of all praise; and, as a judicious, watchful, conscientious, punctual, painstaking deacon, a brighter model has never appeared in our churches. His pecuniary bounties were scattered over a broad field with a liberal hand. For many years before he died his entire income beyond his necessary expenses was consecrated to pious purposes. For a long time, to the writer's knowledge, he contributed annually $100 to each of some half-dozen religious objects, whilst his extra contributions of sums varying from $100 to $1000, unknown, indeed, to many, were not infrequent. In his will the claims of Zion were as sacredly remembered as his children. Long will it be before we shall see in our midst such a *minister* as Jesse Mercer, and, perhaps, as long before we shall see such a *deacon* as Thomas Cooper." (C. D. Mallary in his "Memoirs of Jesse Mercer.")

In person he was six feet high and very erect, of quick, elastic step, strong and muscular frame, but by no means corpulent, weighing 150 or 160 pounds. He had very expressive blue eyes, overshadowed by marked eyebrows, with light chestnut-colored hair, which in the latter part of his life became slightly intermixed with gray.

Ministers of all denominations were always welcome at his large mansion, which was, peculiarly, the home of the preachers and members of the Baptist denomination when traveling in his vicinity.

Cooper, Rev. T. B., A.M., B.D., of Ogeechee, Ga., was born Dec. 26, 1824, in Montgomery Co., Ga., and was in youth educated by Dr. P. H. Mell and Milton E. Bacon. He professed conversion in 1845, graduated regularly in the literary department of Mercer University in 1849, and was ordained at Savannah, Feb. 9, 1852. He has served as pastor the churches at Waynesville, Brunswick, Wades, and Little Ogeechee. He has held the positions of Professor of Belles-Lettres in the Georgia Female College, of president of the Marietta Female College, and of agent in Georgia for the Foreign Mission Board of the Southern Baptist Convention.

He has been a useful preacher and instructor, a successful agent, and a talented contributor to the denominational papers.

Cooper, Rev. W. B., a minister of culture who labored successfully to build up our denomination in Florida. He was born in Abbeville District, S. C., in 1807. His father, Joseph Cooper, of Virginia, was a man of rare culture and intellect, and the early education of the son was under his father's training till 1828, when he attended an academy near his home, which was then in Laurens District.

While at the institution he was converted, under the preaching of Daniel Mangram, of Newberry District, and was baptized by him at Mount Pleasant church.

On leaving the academy he went to a theological school at a place called High Hills, in Sumter District, the commencement of the Southern Baptist Theological Seminary now at Louisville, Ky., where he remained two years, and in the spring of 1835 he entered Columbian College, in the District of Columbia, where he graduated in 1837.

After his graduation he went to Augusta, Ga., where he was ordained, probably in 1838. He removed to Florida as early as 1839 or 1840, and located at Madison Court-House, and from that time till his death, in 1878, he labored mainly in what is called "Middle Florida," occasionally crossing the line into Georgia.

For meekness, prudence, and humility he was hardly ever excelled and not often equaled.

He was a very earnest minister, and the people loved to hear him. His style of preaching was very instructive. He was a *leader* in all moral, religious, and denominational works, and he frequently presided over Associations and Conventions. In Hamilton, Columbia, Madison, Jefferson, and other counties he did a grand work for Jesus and for his beloved denomination. The Florida Association, with which he was chiefly identified, is going to erect a monument over his grave.

Cooper, Rev. W. H., of Fort Gaines, Ga., though a young man, is one of the most useful and hard-working Baptist ministers in the State. His father came from England in 1835, and after various removals settled in Lee Co., Ga., in 1840, where his son was born, Jan. 15, 1842. Mr. Cooper was educated at Penfield, in both the literary and theological departments of Mercer University. He united with the Palmyra church in his seventeenth year, was ordained in his twenty-third year, and began a succession of very prosperous pastorates in Southwestern Georgia. Moving to Fort Gaines in 1878, he has since that time served the churches in that place and at Cuthbert.

He has engaged much in teaching; was for three years school commissioner of Dougherty County, and has for years been president of the Bethel Sunday-School Association, and an ardent worker in the Sunday-school. Perhaps no white man in Georgia is more highly esteemed by the colored people, or has a more healthy influence among them. At the earnest request of the ministers and laymen of the Fowl Town (colored) Association, he has for years acted as their clerk, giving them the benefit of his services and experience.

Mr. Cooper is an amiable and well-informed gentleman and a good preacher. He is a zealous, pious worker, and stands high in the estimation of his denomination. Notwithstanding the constant pain and inconvenience he endures from the stump of an arm, lost during the war, he has made an enviable record for himself.

Corbley, Rev. John, was born in England in 1733, and emigrating to this country, became a minister in Virginia. The violence of persecution drove him from the "Old Dominion" in 1768 into the southwestern portion of Pennsylvania, then a mere wilderness. Here he assisted in planting churches. John Sutton, a native of New Jersey, faithfully co-operated with him. In 1775 he became pastor of the Goshen church on Big Whitely Creek, Greene Co. Richly endowed both by nature and grace, his ministry was one of great success. But in the midst of his joys he was called to drink the cup of sorrow in the loss of his wife and five children, all of whom were killed by the Indians on a Sabbath morning while on their way to the house of God. No name is more venerated in the south-western portion of the State than the name of this brother. A numerous progeny has sprung from the only surviving daughter, who, though scalped by the Indians and left for dead, was mercifully brought back to life. Brother Corbley lived to attain the age of seventy, dying, greatly lamented, in 1803. "The memory of the just is blessed."

Corcoran, William Wilson, LL.D., was born in Georgetown, D. C., Dec. 27, 1798. His father

WILLIAM WILSON CORCORAN, LL.D.

was Thomas Corcoran, a native of Ireland, who settled in Baltimore, Md., and engaged in business there. In 1787 he removed to Georgetown, where he resided until his death, in 1830, holding the office of mayor of the town for many years, and highly esteemed by the entire community. One of his two daughters married the Rev. Dr. S. P. Hill, of Washington, D. C. Mr. W. W. Corcoran first engaged in the dry-goods business, and afterwards in the commission business. From 1828 to 1836 he was in charge of the real estate of the Bank of Columbia, and of the branch of the United States Bank at Washington. From 1836 to 1854 he was in the exchange business. Subsequently to 1840, Mr. Corcoran, in connection with Mr. G. W. Riggs, became one of the most successful financial men of the country, and negotiated all the large loans of the government during the Mexican war. These great burdens were carried with such ability as not only to relieve the government from all embarrassment, but also to insure to the negotiator the remuneration to which his financial skill so justly entitled him. In 1835, Mr. Corcoran married the accomplished daughter of Commodore Morris, who lived, however, only five years after their marriage, dying, in 1840, of a pulmonary affection, and leaving an only child, Louise. In 1859, Miss Louise Corcoran was united in marriage to the Hon. George Eustis, a member of Congress from Louisiana; but the daughter, like the mother, survived her marriage only a few years, dying in Cannes, France, in 1867, of the same disease. These sad bereavements in his home, instead of turning the genial nature of Mr. Corcoran into a gloomy and isolating moroseness, only opened more widely the many channels through which his beneficence had before been bestowed upon the needy. Of his private benefactions this is not the place to write, even if we were sufficiently familiar with them; but many an aching heart and many a saddened home have been made glad by the unexpected sunshine which has streamed in upon them from his generous gifts. It is as a public benefactor that we now speak of him.

In 1847, Mr. Corcoran purchased in Georgetown the land that is now known as Oak Hill Cemetery, a beautiful spot commanding a view of the city and the surrounding country, and having expended upon it about $120,000 in architectural and floral decorations, he presented it to his native town. In 1857 he began the erection of a beautiful Temple of Art, situated near the President's House, on which he lavished about $300,000; in addition to which he added a fund of over $880,000, an endowment yielding an annual income of $60,000. This building was used by the government during the war as a depot for military stores, and at the close of the contest it was completed at a cost of $40,000, and conveyed to trustees for the benefit of the city and nation. To this rich gift he added his entire gallery of paintings, statuary, and other works of art, a collection which for years had drawn a constant stream of visitors to his private residence. One of the choicest of his gifts is the Louise Home, a beautiful tribute to the memory of his wife and daughter. An imposing building, with beautiful surroundings, and internal conveniences such as the wealthiest could scarcely enjoy, he has erected it as a home for aged ladies of education and refinement who, by the reverses of fortune, have been reduced from affluence to poverty. The value of the lot and the cost of erecting the building were about $200,000, added to which is an endowment of $280,000, producing an annual income of $18,000. He has also given valuable land, amounting to at least $50,000, to the Washington Orphan Asylum, as well as smaller sums to six or seven similar institutions in the South.

Mr. Corcoran has also made large contributions to churches and colleges. To the theological seminary of the Diocese of Virginia he has given

$10,000; to the Diocese of Mississippi, 11,000 acres of land; and to the church of the Ascension in Washington City, of which he is a member, $80,000, one-half of the entire cost of the handsome church edifice just erected. To the Washington and Lee University of Virginia he presented the "Howard Library," containing about 4000 volumes, the most valuable classical library in the State of Virginia, in collecting which Mr. Howard, a gentleman of eminent scholastic attainments, spent more than forty years. In addition to this Mr. Corcoran made the same university a donation of $30,000. He has given to the University of Virginia $5000 for its library, and $100,000 to endow two professorships in the same institution. Mr. Corcoran, although a staunch Episcopalian, has been remarkably generous to the Baptist denomination. Soon after the close of the war he presented to the Columbian College the handsome building now used by the National Medical College (the medical school of the Columbian University); and within the past four or five years he has also given to the Columbian University a large tract of land adjacent to the city of Washington, and known as "Trinidad," valued at $150,000, the proceeds of which are to be devoted to the founding of a scientific school of the highest grade. Large as these benefactions are, they are only a part of what Mr. Corcoran has done for asylums, churches, and educational institutions. He has long been personally interested in the prosperity of the Columbian University, of which his father was an original trustee, and of whose board he is himself the president, aiding not only by his contributions, but also by his judicious counsel, the various plans devised by the governing body for the enlargement and more assured success of the institution.

Mr. Corcoran's private life is as pure and unostentatious as his public benefactions have been large and far-reaching,—a life truly honorable and without a stain.

Corey, Rev. Charles Henry, was born Dec. 12, 1834, at New Canaan, New Brunswick, Canada. He was baptized Feb. 15, 1852, at Petitcodiac, New Brunswick. After a short academic course at the Baptist Seminary in Fredericton, New Brunswick, he entered Acadia College, at Wolfville, Nova Scotia, in 1854, and in 1858 graduated with the highest honors of his class. Acadia College conferred upon him, in 1861, the degree of A.M. After completing his collegiate course he entered the Newton Theological Institution, and graduated in 1861. In September of this year he was ordained pastor of the First Baptist church, Seabrook, N. H., where he remained until Jan. 1, 1864, at which time he resigned and entered the service of the U. S. Christian Commission. He remained in the field until the close of the war. Upon the invitation of the American Baptist Home Mission Society, Mr. Corey went to South Carolina as a missionary to the freedmen, and during his residence there of two years he organized a number of churches and se-

REV. CHARLES HENRY COREY.

cured for them ministers of their own race. In the fall of 1867 he was appointed principal of the Augusta Institute, Augusta, Ga., and in 1868 was selected to succeed N. Colver, D.D., as president of the institution for training colored preachers and teachers at Richmond, Va., over which most successful school he still presides. Mr. Corey has been a frequent contributor to the religious and secular press, and during the war wrote a very interesting series of letters for the *Christian Visitor*, of St. John, New Brunswick. His work in Richmond has been carried on with great skill and success, and is resulting in incalculable good both to the colored men and the cause of Christ.

Corley, William, Esq., an active, influential, and generous member of the Vermont Street Baptist church in Quincy, and one of its deacons, was born in New York City, Dec. 27, 1821; he became a resident of Quincy in 1853. During the years 1857-61 he lived in St. Louis, where he experienced religion and united with the Second Baptist church, Dr. Galusha Anderson, pastor. In 1861 he returned to Quincy and united with the Vermont Street church, by which, also, he was elected deacon in 1867, serving in that capacity until his death, Feb. 25, 1875. He was a zealous worker, a ready giver, and an eminently spiritual man.

Cornelius, Samuel, D.D., was born in Devonport, England, in 1794. His parents removed to

Philadelphia and died while he was a child. He became a member of the church under Dr. William Staughton early in life. Encouraged and instructed by this eminent man he commenced preaching, and was settled as pastor in Norfolk, Va., from 1817 to 1824, when he succeeded Dr. Cone as pastor in Alexandria. During this fruitful pastorate of thirteen years, he was, with Noah Davis, the originator of what is now the American Baptist Publication Society. He was also an official and hearty helper in the early building of the Columbian College. Afterwards he spent eleven years in pastoral work in Mount Holly, N. J., and in agency service for the Colonization Society. In 1848 he came to Michigan, preaching as supply at Adrian, as pastor at Troy, and in a missionary capacity at Bay City and elsewhere while living in Detroit. At different times he performed much self-sacrificing and successful agency work for the educational interests of the Convention, and became endeared to the churches and ministry. His work closed with a useful pastorate at Ann Arbor. His preaching was rich in Scripture truth, felicitous in diction, and abounding in proofs of culture and in the Spirit's power. He died in 1870.

Cornell, Rev. Alfred, was born in Madison Co., N. Y., July 7, 1813, and was educated at Madison University. In April, 1844, he was ordained at Macedon, Wayne Co., N. Y. Two years later he removed to Ionia, Mich., and served the church in that place as its pastor till 1862. After four years in Norwalk, O., he was recalled to Ionia. From 1866 to 1870 he was pastor in Smyrna, from 1870 to 1877 in Portland. Since 1877 he has been chaplain of the State prison in Ionia. In 1848 and in 1849 he was chaplain in the State House of Representatives. He is known among his brethren as a prudent and faithful minister of the gospel.

Cornwell, Francis, A.M., was educated at Emmanuel College, Cambridge, England. During the tyranny of Archbishop Laud over the English Church he was torn from his home in Marden, Kent, and lodged in Maidstone jail. He offended Laud because he objected to the surplice, kneeling at the Lord's Supper, and making the sign of the cross in baptism. While Mr. Cornwell was in prison a lady visited those in confinement, and in conversation spoke of her doubts about infant baptism being in the Scriptures. Mr. Cornwell tried to remove her misgivings by the Word of God, but failed to satisfy either her or himself. Mr. Wilson, a fellow-prisoner, who had listened to the conversation, informed Mr. Cornwell that he always understood that infant baptism was not in the Scriptures, that it was a tradition handed down from early times. Mr. Cornwell recognized no religious institution as possessing any right to live unless it was found in the Bible, and he immediately began to search the Scriptures thoroughly for infant baptism, the result of which was that he became a Baptist, and was immersed by the Rev. Wm. Jeffery.

In 1644, soon after his adoption of Baptist doctrines, and before his opinions were known to have been changed, he preached his celebrated sermon before the clergy at the Cranbrook "Visitation," in which he avowed his sentiments so boldly that some were startled, and most were indignant; the Rev. Christopher Blackwood went away to examine the Scriptures, and Mr. Jeffery in a little time baptized him too.

He published a work at this time in defense of his new principles, called "The Vindication of the Royal Commission of King Jesus." In this treatise he proved that christening children is a popish tradition and an anti-Christian custom, contrary to the commission given by the Saviour. He dedicated it to the Parliament, and had it distributed at the door of the House of Commons to the members. It created much excitement and some wrath.

He believed that a true church consisted only of those who had really repented, and, after putting their trust in the Saviour, had been baptized. This led him to leave the state church and gather a community of saved persons in the neighborhood of his old fold, to whom he ministered with great faithfulness as long as he lived.

Mr. Cornwell was a man of extensive erudition. Neal speaks of him as "one of the most learned divines that espoused the cause of the Baptists." This was the opinion entertained of his scholarship wherever he was known. He feared no mortal; his life was pure, his end was peace. He was the author of four works.

Corporation and Test Acts.—The Corporation Act says, "In order to perpetuate the succession in corporations in the hands of persons well affected to the government, it is ordained that every mayor, alderman, common councilman, or any other officer in a corporation, should be obliged, besides the common oath of allegiance and supremacy, and a particular declaration against the Solemn League and Covenant, to take an oath declaring that it was not lawful, upon any pretense whatsoever, to take arms against the king; and that he did abhor that traitorous position of taking arms by his authority against his person or against those commissioned by him." This act became a law in 1661.

No dissenter could take this oath conscientiously. So that Baptists and all other dissenters were excluded from every corporation in England.

The Test Act required that "All persons enjoying any office or place of trust and profit should take the oaths of allegiance and supremacy in public and open court, and should also receive the sacrament in some parish church, immediately after divine service; and deliver certificates signed by the ministers and church wardens, attested by the oaths of two credible witnesses and put upon record." It also required an express denial of transubstantiation in the bread and wine of the Lord's Supper after consecration.

The act received the king's approval March 29, 1673. All Baptists, and all other conscientious nonconformists, and all true Catholics were excluded from every corporation in England; and from every office of "trust and profit" under the government, by the Corporation and Test Acts.

But these acts only secured the orthodoxy or hypocrisy of a person on entering upon the duties and privileges of his office. It had no penalties for him if he became a Baptist or a member of some other nonconformist community afterwards. To remedy this defect, in 1711 the Schism Bill became the law of the land. This infamous act commanded, "That if any persons in office, who by the laws are obliged to qualify themselves by receiving the sacrament or test, shall ever resort to a conventicle or meeting of dissenters for religious worship, during the time of their continuance in such office, they shall forfeit twenty pounds for every such offense, and be disqualified for any office for the future till they have made oath that they have entirely conformed to the church, and have not been at any conventicle for the space of a whole year." The entire officials of the government must be Episcopalians on their appointment, and continue faithful to that church under heavy penalties. In every way our Baptist brethren in England were crippled; they were branded with infamy, fined, imprisoned, transported, and threatened with death. The Schism Bill was repealed in 1718. But the Corporation and Test Acts disgraced the statute book of England till 1828.

Corson, Hon. William, was born in Frederick Co., Va., May 14, 1798. He removed to Missouri in 1819. He was register of lands under appointment from President Monroe. He removed from Ralls County to Palmyra, where he lived till his death. He was teller in the bank, commissioner of lands for the Hannibal and St. Joseph Railroad, U. S. mail agent, director in the board of public schools, and for many years a member of the lower and upper house of the Missouri Legislature. He was for years moderator of Bethel Association, and helped to organize the Central Association in 1834, now the General Association of Missouri. He was a member of the Convention to locate William Jewell College, and drew up its charter and petitioned the Legislature for an act of incorporation. He was a quartermaster in the army, from 1862 to 1864. In all public positions he discharged his duties with honor to himself. No stain rests upon his character. He gave light in his home and in the church. His energy overcame all obstacles and his faith made him submissive to all providences. The Bible was his daily study. The ministers found in his family a welcome home. He was baptized in August, 1819, in Virginia. In 1820 he joined the Peno church in Pike Co., Mo., then the Bethel church in Marion County, then the church in Palmyra. He organized the Sabbath-school in Palmyra in 1825. He died Nov. 3, 1873, aged seventy-five years, five months, and nineteen days. Many followed him to the grave. He lived a long, useful, and honored life.

Cotton, Hon. John H., of Puritan descent, was born in Middletown, Conn., Aug. 20, 1778. He

HON. JOHN H. COTTON.

received a good English education. He was married May 30, 1802, and early engaged in mercantile business; after residing several years in Catskill and Kortright, State of New York, he removed to Bradford, Orange Co., Vt., about the year 1807. He made a public profession of religion Nov. 11, 1814, and united with the Congregational church in that place. He was often elected to offices of honor and trust, having represented the town in the State Legislature five years, from 1814 to 1818, and was town clerk from 1816 to 1820; was at one time a member of the governor's council, and was chosen Presidential elector. While residing in Bradford he was appointed associate judge of the County Court.

In 1820, having been elected by the Legislature superintendent of the Vermont State prison, located at Windsor, he, with his family, in December, removed to that place; to this office he was re-elected sixteen consecutive years. Having become, from thorough conviction, a believer in the doctrines and ordinances held by the Baptist denomination, he was baptized by the Rev. Leland Howard, May 5, 1822, and united with the Baptist church in Windsor. Within a few years he was elected a deacon of that church, and after the death of Abner Forbes, in 1828, he became the senior deacon, which position he held until his death, which occurred May 1, 1850. He held the honorable office of vice-president of the American Baptist Home Mission Society from 1834 to 1843. He was a very decided Christian, and ever exerted a strong religious influence, not only on his own family, but with the public at large.

The Rev. Dr. S. S. Cutting, who knew him well, writes as follows: "The Hon. John H. Cotton brought with him to Windsor a very high reputation for intelligence and moral worth, and this reputation he maintained for the long period of his later life. From the time he came into the Baptist church in 1822, a high position was accorded to him by a spontaneous recognition of his fitness to sustain it. In him, and in his compeer, Gen. Forbes, the church had deacons who seemed born to the office, so complete were their qualifications for its dignities and its duties. They were never absent from their places on the Sabbath, and meetings for conference and prayer without them would have seemed unnatural and unsatisfactory. In such meetings Judge Cotton uniformly took part, always listened to with attention in talking of the Scriptures, or of the experience of Christian life. He was recognized as a leading citizen of the town, at a time when it was distinguished by the number of its men of ability and standing. His honor was unsullied. He was a man of dignified bearing, whose presence rebuked trifling, and, though never austere, his manner was always that of a man whose life was given to serious purposes, under a high responsibility. He lived among men as one who fulfilled his daily duties by serving well his God and his generation."

Coulston, Rev. Thomas P., was born in Philadelphia, Nov. 30, 1833; was baptized by Rev. Benjamin Griffith, D.D., into the fellowship of the New Market Street (Fourth) church, Philadelphia, in 1853; graduated with first honors from the university at Lewisburg in 1859, and subsequently pursued theological studies at Lewisburg and Hamilton, N. Y.; was ordained by the Fourth church, Philadelphia, in 1862, and settled with the Frankford church, Philadelphia, where he has continued in faithful service to the present time.

Mr. Coulston is a man of quiet and unassuming manners, of fervent piety, and possessed of an innate fondness for metaphysical research. His sermons and writings are masterly and striking specimens of intellectual vigor and devout loyalty to the truth as it is in Jesus.

Council, An Ecclesiastical.—This body claims no authority over any church, or an individual member of any church. It is in every case *advisory*, and only *advisory*. It is commonly composed of the pastor and two laymen from a certain number of churches. In large cities it is not unusual to invite all the churches to send delegates to a council, even though there may be fifty churches represented. But in such great centres of Baptist strength frequently not more than ten or twelve churches are called to a council. There is no law fixing the number of churches necessary to form such advisory bodies. We have occupied a seat in a council in which only three churches had messengers. It was a perfectly orderly body, but its decisions could not command the respect which would have been freely accorded if its membership had been ten times larger. A council is commonly called by a church, but it may be summoned by individuals, or by one person. Attendance is, of course, voluntary.

When there is a difficulty among the members of a church, a *mutual* council is generally invited to give its advice. Such a body is composed of brethren, an equal number of whom is selected by each party to the controversy. And this wise course is often followed after the minority has been excluded, under the conviction that a just cause loses nothing by a careful examination from a fair jury.

An *ex-parte* council, chosen by one portion of the disputants, as the name intimates, ought never to be called unless it is impossible to secure a *mutual* body. Such a meeting of brethren must form a judgment under many disadvantages; and yet, when wisely selected, *ex-parte* councils are useful.

A council may be summoned from a distance, or from the neighborhood where its advice is desired. In a bitter strife it is occasionally wise to secure the opinions of brethren who have no local prejudices to fetter their judgments.

The action of a council is necessary in the ordination of a minister among American Baptists. A church calls it for this purpose and delegates to it this service. Where a church is formed, a council is always called to recognize it. Councils are often convened to give advice about church and individual troubles. English Baptists have no councils.

Courtney, Rev. Ezra, a pioneer preacher in Louisiana, was born in Pennsylvania in 1771. Living in Mississippi, he preached as early as 1804 in Eastern Louisiana, then West Florida, and under Spanish rule; he settled in East Feliciana Parish in 1814. He was an efficient and popular preacher, often elected moderator of the Mississippi Association and other bodies of which he was a member; and he continued his labors until disabled by age. He died in 1855.

Courtney, Rev. Franklin, M.D., was born in Virginia in 1812. After receiving a classical education he began the study of medicine, and was graduated by the University of Pennsylvania in 1833. Shortly afterwards he settled in Alabama to pursue his profession. He began to preach in 1845, about which time he went to Arkansas, and became pastor at Eldorado. In 1853 he removed to Mount Lebanon, La., engaged in the practice of medicine there, and accepted the pastorate of the church. He has often been elected moderator of Red River Association, and vice-president of the State Convention; filled the chair of Theology for a time in Mount Lebanon University; was long the editor of the *Louisiana Baptist*, and editorial contributor to the *Memphis Baptist*; a forcible speaker, a pungent writer, an active Sunday-school worker and promoter of missions.

REV. FRANKLIN COURTNEY, M.D.

Covenant, A Church.—All our older churches have "covenants," and most of those of later origin have followed the example of their fathers, though some have neither Articles of Faith nor church covenants. The covenant is a solemn obligation taken by each member of a church to perform certain religious duties, as the following will show:

CHURCH COVENANT.

First. We believe that the Holy Scriptures were given by inspiration of God, and that they are the only certain rule of faith and practice.

Second. Whereas various interpretations of the Sacred Word have been given by different denominations of professed Christians, we hereby declare that the foregoing Articles of Faith (the covenant follows the articles) express our views of the meaning of the Word of God, which Holy Word we promise to search diligently and to make the man of our counsel.

Third. We agree to contribute towards the support of the worship of God in our own church, and to spread the knowledge of Jesus in our own country and throughout the world according to our ability.

Fourth. We hereby covenant and agree to walk in love and to live in peace, to sympathize with each other under all conditions and circumstances in life, to pray with and for one another, and to exhort and stir up each other unto every good word and work.

Fifth. We solemnly promise, by the assistance of the Holy Spirit, to watch over each other with all kindness and Christian affection; not suffering sin to rest upon a brother, but as far as God in his providence shall make it known to us, we will, in all cases of offense, take our Lord's direction in the 18th chapter of Matthew, which says, "Moreover, if thy brother shall trespass against thee, go and tell him his fault between thee and him alone; if he shall hear thee, thou hast gained thy brother. But if he will not hear thee, then take with thee one or two more, that in the mouth of two or three witnesses every word may be established. And if he shall neglect to hear them, tell it unto the church: but if he neglect to hear the church, let him be unto thee as an heathen man and a publican." And we will urge our utmost endeavors to maintain a scriptural discipline in the church.

Sixth. Moreover, we covenant to meet on the first day of the week for public worship, and to fill up our places at all the appointed meetings of the church, as God shall give us health and opportunity. All and each of these duties we freely and most solemnly promise (by the assistance of the great Head of the church) to observe, until we are planted in the glorious church above.—AMEN.

Covenant Meetings.—Before the monthly celebration of the Lord's Supper, in many parts of our country, a meeting is held for the members of the church, where they relate briefly their religious experience and renew their covenant with God and with each other. After the devotional exercises at the commencement of the service are over, the pastor relates such of God's dealings with his soul as in his judgment it is proper to communicate, then others follow, commonly in the order in which they are seated, beginning at the right or left of the pastor, and continuing until the end of the opposite side is reached. In these meetings the sisters speak as well as the brethren. No one is obliged to utter a word. In some sections of our country covenant meetings are unknown. Where they are held they are regarded as eminently profitable. They are generally observed on the Saturday before the Lord's Supper is celebrated.

Covey, J. N., D.D., was born in Madison Co., N. Y., Feb. 11, 1821; educated at Madison University, N. Y., receiving his A.B., A.M., and D.D. from his *alma mater;* ordained at Lebanon, Tenn., 1847, R. B. C. Howell preaching the ordination sermon; raised the funds for the building of the female college at Brownsville, Tenn.; president of Campbell Academy, Lexington, Tenn., and Masonic College, Palestine, Texas; founded Concrete College, De Witt Co., Texas; has been its president, and pastor of the church, at its location, for fourteen years.

Cox, Francis Augustus, D.D., LL.D., was born at Leighton Buzzard, Bedfordshire, England, in 1793. He was an only son, and inherited a considerable property. His family had for a long time been connected with the Baptist church of his native town, and he therefore grew up under favorable religious influences, which led him in early life to devote himself to the ministry. When about eighteen years old he was admitted to Bristol College, then under the direction of Dr. Ryland. On the completion of his studies he went to Edinburgh University, and at the expiration of the regular course took his degree. On the 4th of April, 1804, he was ordained pastor of the church at Clipstone, Northamptonshire, a service in which Andrew Fuller, Joseph Sutcliffe, and Robert Hall participated. His ministry was very successful for several years. On the failure of Mr. Hall's health, he was invited to supply the pulpit of the church at Cambridge, and arranged to do so for twelve months. No permanent engagement resulted, and Mr. Cox returned to Clipstone. Soon afterwards he resigned his charge, and at length accepted an invitation to settle at Hackney, London, in October, 1811. The congregation being large, a new meeting-house was erected in Mare Street, and opened in the following year. With this charge he continued the remainder of his life, a period of nearly forty-two years. During the last six years of his ministry the Rev. Daniel Katterns, the present pastor, was happily associated with him as co-pastor. Throughout the greater part of this long career he took a leading place among the English Baptists, especially identifying himself with public movements and philanthropic enterprises, general and denominational. He took a lively interest in the foreign mission; promoted the formation of the Baptist Irish Society; for three years he was the secretary to the General Body of Dissenting Ministers of the three denominations in London; and he assisted at the formation of the Anti-State-Church Association, now known as the Liberation Society. His literary labors were considerable. He aided in the starting and direction of the *Baptist Magazine;* was one of the founders of University College, London, and its librarian for some time. A variety of works, including the well-known "History of the Baptist Missionary Society," "Female Scripture Biography," and the "Life and Times of Melancthon," proceeded from his ever-ready pen. In 1824 he took part in a controversy concerning Scripture baptism with Drs. Dwight, Ewing, and Wardlaw, and ably maintained his denominational principles. At the request of the Baptist Union he visited this country with Dr. Hoby, as a deputation from the English Baptists, in 1835, and wrote subsequently a narrative of the visit. He received degrees from Waterville and from Glasgow University, and was held in high esteem by a very large circle of his contemporaries, as well without as within his own denomination. He died Sept. 5, 1853, aged seventy years. His genial manners, graceful courtesy, and practical wisdom gave him a wide influence, which was ever consecrated to the service of his brethren and the promotion of the gospel in the world.

Coxe, Benjamin, M.A., was educated at either Oxford or Cambridge. After he graduated he received episcopal ordination, and for a considerable period he was a follower of the Romish Arminianism of Archbishop Laud. By the grace of God his heart was changed and his mind enlightened, and he became a strong Baptist. He was the son of an English lord bishop; and he was a man of profound learning. His influence in favor of Baptists was very great all over his country. He came to Coventry once to encourage the Baptist church; Richard Baxter was then chaplain of the garrison of that town, and a "dispute first by word of mouth, then by writing, about infant baptism," took place between them. Mr. Baxter evidently had not the best part in the controversy; for when the champion of the Baptists came again to Coventry he was arrested, and Mr. Baxter was charged with using this conclusive argument to quiet Mr. Coxe. The Kidderminster bishop, while denying the charge, felt the accusation so keenly that he took steps to secure his release. He was an old man in 1644, but the time of his death is unknown.

Craig, Rev. Elijah, an eminent pioneer preacher of Virginia and Kentucky, and brother of the famous Lewis Craig, was born in Orange Co., Va., about the year 1743. He was awakened to a knowledge of his lost estate under the preaching of the renowned David Thomas, in 1764. Next year he was encouraged by Samuel Harris to hold meetings among his neighbors. This he did, using his tobacco-barn for a meeting-house. Many were converted. In 1766, Mr. Craig went to North Carolina, to get James Read to come and baptize him and others. He was ordained in May, 1771, at which time he became pastor of Blue Run church. Some time after this he was imprisoned for preaching the gospel. In jail he lived on rye bread and water, and preached to the people through the prison bars. He remained in Culpepper jail one month. After this "he was honored with a term in Orange jail." He became one of the most useful and popular preachers in Virginia. He was several times sent as a delegate from the General Association to the Virginia Legislature, to aid in securing religious liberty. In 1786 he removed to Scott Co., Ky. After this he labored but little in the ministry. Being a good business man, he soon amassed a fortune, and was of great value to the new country. He established the first school in which the classics were taught, built the first rope-walk, the first fulling-mill, and the first paper-mill that existed in Kentucky. He died in 1808.

Craig, Hugh K., D.D., was born Jan. 30, 1830, near Claysville, Washington Co., Pa. In July, 1851, he was baptized into the fellowship of Pleasant Grove church. He was ordained in October, 1854. For some time he devoted himself chiefly to mission work until 1858, when he became pastor of the Beulah Baptist church, Greene Co., Pa. In 1868 he took pastoral charge of Waynesburgh and Bethlehem churches, Greene County. During this pastorate he was elected to the professorship of Greek and Hebrew in Waynesburgh College. In 1875 he was appointed president of the Monongahela College, Jefferson, Pa.; and at the same time he was chosen pastor of the Jefferson Baptist church. In June, 1880, the university at Lewisburg conferred its doctorate of divinity upon him. The president of Monongahela College is a brother of scholarly attainments, a fine educator, a successful pastor, and a man of extensive influence for the truth.

Craig, Rev. John T., was born in Alabama in 1816; studied medicine in 1836 and 1837, and settled in Dallas Co., Ark., 1838. He began to preach in 1846, and labored efficiently in Dallas and the surrounding counties, building up several strong churches. After the war he settled at his present place of residence, New Edinburgh, Ark., where he gathered a church.

Craig, Rev. Lewis, a distinguished pioneer Baptist preacher of Virginia and Kentucky, was born in Orange Co., Va., about the year 1737. He was first awakened by the preaching of Samuel Harris, about the year 1765. A great pressure of guilt induced him to follow the preacher from one meeting to another, and after the sermon he would rise in tears and assert that he was a justly condemned sinner, and unless he was born again he could not be saved. His ministry thus began before he had hope of conversion, and after conversion he continued preaching a considerable time before being baptized; many were led to Christ under his labors. Soon after his conversion and before his baptism (there being no ordained minister near to baptize him) he was indicted "for preaching the gospel contrary to law." The celebrated John Waller was one of the jurors in the case. The pious and prudent deportment of Mr. Craig during the trial was blessed to the conviction and conversion of Mr. Waller. The exact period of Mr. Craig's baptism is not known. He continued preaching with great zeal until the 4th of June, 1768, when being engaged in public worship, he and John Waller and James Childs were seized by the sheriff and brought before three magistrates in the meeting-house yard, who held them to bail in the sum of £1000 to appear before the court next day. They were required by the court to give security not to preach in the county within twelve months. This they refused to do, and were committed to jail. As they passed through the streets of Fredericksburg, from the court-house to the jail, they sang the hymn beginning,

"Broad is the road that leads to death."

During his confinement Mr. Craig preached through the prison bars to large crowds. He remained in jail a month and was then released. He immediately hastened to Williamsburg, and soon secured the liberation of his companions. Their imprisonment seemed only to inflame their zeal, and they went everywhere preaching the Word. Mr. Craig was ordained and became pastor of Upper Spottsylvania church in November, 1770. But this did not prevent his preaching in the surrounding counties. In 1771 he was again arrested and imprisoned for three months in Caroline County. He continued preaching with great zeal and success until 1781, when he and a majority of his church moved to Kentucky. He located on Gilbert Creek, in what is now Garrard County, early in December. The next year he gathered Forks of Dix River church in the same county. In 1783 he and most of Gilbert's Creek church moved to the north side of Kentucky River and organized South Elkhorn church, in Fayette County. Here he remained about nine years, laboring zealously in all the surrounding country. A number of churches were founded, and Elkhorn Association was formed Oct. 1, 1785. About 1792 he moved to Bracken Co., Ky. Here he formed several churches, and "became in a manner the father of Bracken Association." About the year 1828 "he died suddenly, of which he was forewarned, saying, 'I am going to such a house to die,' and with solemn joy went on to the place, and with little pain left the world."

Cramb, Rev. A. B., was born in Weare, N. H., Jan. 2, 1827. At the age of thirteen the family removed to Illinois, settling in Woodford County, near Metamora. At sixteen he experienced religion, and the year following entered Shurtleff College. He was licensed to preach in 1848, and entered upon service at once. Oct. 13, 1849, he was ordained at Richland. His principal pastorates were Metamora, Ill., and St. Cloud, Minn. His health, however, began to fail early in his ministry, and all efforts to re-establish it being in vain, he died at Metamora, Feb. 19, 1857, at the age of thirty. He was a young man of uncommon promise. His contributions to the denominational press were highly valued, while as a preacher he had excited expectations of high usefulness. His death thus early in his career was an occasion of widely-felt sorrow.

Cramp, John M., D.D., was born in England, July 25, 1796; baptized by his father Sept. 13,

JOHN M. CRAMP, D.D.

1812; ordained pastor of the Baptist church, Dean Street, London, May 7, 1818; was from 1827 to 1840 associated with his father in the care of the Baptist church at St. Peter's, Isle of Thanet: became in 1840 pastor of the Baptist church of Hastings, Sussex; took charge in 1844 of the Baptist college, Montreal, Canada; became president of Acadia College, Nova Scotia, in 1851, and retired in 1869 from that position. Dr. Cramp has published "A Text-Book of Popery;" also a Baptist history and "Paul and Christ." Dr. Cramp's theology is sound, his labors have been abundant, and his influence and usefulness have been very great in the maritime provinces. He is also widely and favorably known in the United States, in which his works have been extensively circulated.

Crandall, Rev. David, the son of Rev. Joseph Crandall, was born in 1798 in New Brunswick, Canada, where he was converted and baptized. He was ordained January, 1831; shared largely in the missionary spirit of his venerable father, and, though a pastor, did much work as an evangelist in his native province; his labors have resulted in much spiritual good. He resides at Springfield, New Brunswick.

Crandall, Rev. Joseph, one of the founders and fathers of the Baptist denomination in the maritime provinces of Canada, was born in Nova Scotia, and converted under a sermon by Rev. Joseph Dimock at Harris Harding's ordination, Sept. 16, 1794, at Onslow, Nova Scotia; Oct. 8, 1799, he was ordained pastor of the Baptist church just formed at Sackville, New Brunswick. His evangelistic labors at Sackville, Salisbury, and other portions of Westmoreland, Albert, and King's Counties, up the river St. John, and in the northern counties of New Brunswick, were abundant, and attended with the blessing of God. In 1825 he evangelized in Prince Edward's Island. Mr. Crandall was deep in Christian experience, a sound theologian, an eloquent and a useful preacher of the gospel. His ministry exerted a powerful influence in building up the Baptist denomination, especially in New Brunswick. He died Feb. 20, 1858, aged eighty-six years.

Crandall, Rev. Peter, brother of Rev. Joseph Crandall, entered the ministry in 1800; became pastor of Digby Neck church, Nova Scotia, in 1809; visited Briar Island in 1819, preaching there with great success and baptizing. Preached for nearly thirty years on Digby Neck, Briar Island, and Long Island. He was earnest in the ministry of the gospel and mighty in prayer. Died April 2, 1838, in the sixty-ninth year of his age.

Crane, Cephas B., D.D., son of Rev. W. J. Crane, was born in Marion, Wayne Co., N. Y., March 28, 1833. He graduated at the University of Rochester in the class of 1858, and at the Rochester Theological Seminary in 1860. In October, 1860, he was ordained pastor of the South Baptist church, Hartford, Conn., and remained there nearly eighteen years. In April, 1878, he accepted a call to the pastorate of the First Baptist church in Boston, where he is now laboring. Rochester University conferred upon him the degree of Doctor of Divinity in 1868.

Crane, James C., was born in Newark, N. J., Sept. 7, 1803. He was the youngest brother of William Crane, and from his boyhood to his death was associated with him in business, and one with him in all the great and noble enterprises which occupied the hand and heart of the older brother. His early education was limited, and yet, like his brother, he became a man of very varied and accurate information. He was a leader in every religious and philanthropic enterprise. As a business man neither Richmond nor Baltimore ever saw his superior in accuracy, dispatch, or integrity. He was an excellent vocalist, and had natural gifts as a speaker. He filled successfully, and for a long series of years, the offices either of clerk, secretary, treasurer, or moderator of the Dover Association and the General Association of Virginia. He was a model Sunday-school superintendent. He was a Christian merchant and made money to do good with it. His pastors, D. Roper, J. B. Taylor, J. B. Jeter, B. Manly, Jr., and J. L. Burrows regarded him as no ordinary deacon, and when he died Dr. Burrows took for the text of his funeral discourse, "And he will be missed, for his seat will be empty." One son survives him. He died March 31, 1856, in Richmond, Va., where he had lived about forty years. A brief and interesting memoir of him was prepared and published by Dr. J. L. Burrows.

Crane, Rev. Origen, was born in Mansfield, Conn., July 26, 1804. He connected himself with the Newton Theological Institution, and graduated in the class of 1826. Immediately on graduation he accepted a call to the Second Baptist church in Newton, located at Newton Upper Falls. He was the pastor of this church three years, and in 1839 he accepted a call to the church in Weston, Mass., where he remained thirteen years. For two or three years he was the agent of the American and Foreign Bible Society. The last years of his life were spent in trying to help the feeble churches by such labors as his health allowed him to perform. He died April 20, 1860, at New England Village, Mass.

Crane, William, was born in Newark, N. J., May 6, 1790. His great-great-grandfather, Jasper Crane, was one of the original settlers of Newark, and its first magistrate. His great-grandfather, Azariah Crane, married Mary Treat, daughter of Gov. Robert Treat, who withstood Sir Edmund Andross in his demand for that charter of the colony which was hidden in "the Charter Oak." His father, Rufus Crane, was a soldier of the Revolutionary war. His mother was Charity Campbell, a descendant of Benjamin Baldwin, who, with Jasper Crane, was also one of the original settlers of Newark. His father lost his property by the Revolutionary war, and he was compelled at eleven years of age to leave the paternal roof and rely on himself, and thereafter was never dependent on any human being for assistance in the affairs of life. He learned a trade and pursued it till twenty-one years of age. In 1811 he migrated to Richmond, Va., and was an eye-witness of the burning of the Richmond theatre, which destroyed the governor of Virginia and many others. He married Miss Lydia Dorset, July 9, 1812, and after her decease, Sept. 26, 1830, married Miss Jean N. Daniel, July 30, 1831. With varying success and severe reverses he prosecuted his mercantile business in Richmond till November, 1834, never failing to meet every financial obligation. From 1834 to 1866 he carried on his business in Baltimore, Md., associated with his brother, James C. Crane, for a large portion of the time in both cities, and with his sons Andrew Fuller, John Daniel, and James Conway the latter part of his life. He was in all

WILLIAM CRANE.

respects a Christian merchant, doing business for the honor of God and with an eye to his glory. He was converted under the preaching of Daniel Sharp and Edmund Dorr Griffin in Newark, N. J. For a while he was a member of Dr. Archibald Maclay's church in New York City. But his life's work was in Richmond and Baltimore. He was one of the original members of the Second Baptist church, Richmond, Va., and for many years its leading supporter. He was the founder of the Richmond African Baptist Missionary Society, from which Lott Cary was induced to go to Liberia. He taught, with David Roper, the first African school ever started in Richmond. He conceived the design, initiated the plan, accepted the first draft of $677 for outfit of the *Religious Herald*, and for three years advanced the sums needed to secure it the patronage necessary to give the paper a living support. These sums afterwards were refunded by William Sands to his firm when success attended the enterprise. He was one of the originators of Richmond College (then Virginia Baptist Seminary), and with Archibald Thomas purchased Spring Farm, each giving $1000, and taking subscriptions from others, in the name of Virginia Baptist Education Society, for the balance. He originated the idea of organizing Calvert Street church, Baltimore, purchased the house, and saw a flourishing and prosperous church grow from ten members (six of whom were of his own family), and then divided, a part to become High Street church, and another part, with himself and family, to amalgamate with the Seventh church, under the pastorship of Richard Fuller, under whose ministry he lived for the last twenty-one years of his life. He labored zealously to establish Saratoga Street African Baptist church, and through all his life employed tongue, pen, and purse to benefit the African race. In missions and general benevolence he was worthy of being the associate of William Colgate, of New York, Friend Humphrey, of Albany, and Heman Lincoln, of Boston. He enjoyed the confidence of, and was co-laborer in all good enterprises in Virginia with, Robert B. Semple, James B. Taylor, Robert Ryland, Jeremiah B. Jeter, and Abner W. Clopton, and in all Northern organizations was the trusted counselor and co-worker with Spencer H. Cone, Francis Wayland, Nathaniel Kendrick, and Daniel Sharp. He was a Sunday-school teacher for nearly fifty years, and annually read the Bible through for the same time. He was a trustee of, and liberal contributor to, Columbian College, D. C. His sagacity in matters of church and state was so rare that results generally happened as he predicted. He died in Baltimore, Sept. 28, 1866, having given away large sums of money for Christ's cause, having led many to Christ by his conversation, and having exerted all his powers for God's glory. Of his children four are known to the religious, literary, or political world. A notice of his son, William Carey, appears on another page. His second son, Adoniram Judson Crane, was born Nov. 2, 1817; educated at Richmond College, Va.; Mount Pleasant Classical Institution, Amherst, Mass.; Columbian College, D. C.; Madison University, N. Y.; and graduated from Union College, Schenectady, N. Y.; was a member of Second church, Richmond, Va., for many years; married a great-granddaughter of John Adams, second President of the United States; practised law at the Richmond bar twenty-eight years; edited political and literary journals; served in the Legislature of Virginia as representative of Richmond, and as U. S. District Attorney under Abraham Lincoln. He wrote some small poems which are gems, and delivered many lectures, such as the "Toils and Rewards of Literature," "Mechanism of Faces," and others worthy of a place in standard English literature. As a lawyer, politician, orator, literary man, man of genius, no one ranked him at the Richmond bar, when his untimely decease occurred, Jan. 2, 1867. Andrew Fuller Crane, the third son, born Feb. 17, 1820, was educated in the Richmond schools and Oneida Institute, Whitesborough, N. Y.; was associated with his father in Baltimore in business nearly all his life; distinguished as a worker in all noble Christian enterprises, remarkable as a Sunday-school superintendent, gifted as a speaker and as a vocalist of superior musical powers, genial as a friend, and attractive as a conversationalist; a leader in the city and State organizations of Maryland for charities, reform, and education; often an officer of the representative bodies of Baptists in Maryland, and the Southern Baptist Convention. He has been ever a warm supporter of Richard Fuller and William T. Brantly, Jr.

Crane, Wm. Carey, D.D., LL.D., was born in Richmond, Va., March 17, 1816; educated in the

WM. CAREY CRANE, D.D., LL.D.

best schools of the city of Richmond; also in Richmond College, Va.; Mount Pleasant Classical Institution, Amherst, Mass.; Columbian College, D. C.; and Madison University, N. Y. His A.B. and A.M. are from Columbian College, D. C.; his D.D. from Howard College, Ala.; and his LL.D. from Baylor University, Texas. His opportunities have enabled him to become a profound scholar, and he now ranks among the most useful, laborious, and able Baptists in the Southern States. His early life was passed in Virginia. He was converted through the agency of a conversation with Robert Ryland, first president of Richmond College, and he was baptized by James B. Taylor, D.D., July 27, 1832. He is the oldest son of William Crane,—sketched in another article,—late of Baltimore, Md. He was licensed to preach by Second church, Richmond, Va., and ordained Sept. 23, 1838, in Baltimore, Md., by request of Calvert Street church. When twenty-one years of age he was elected a professor in the Baptist Seminary, now Richmond College, Va., but declined, and spent from November, 1837, to February, 1839, teaching and preaching in Georgia. From February, 1839, to January, 1851, he was pastor at Montgomery, Ala., Columbus, Vicksburg, and Yazoo City, Miss. He has been called to the presidency of five colleges for males, and six for females, which he declined. He has been president of Yazoo Classical Hall, Miss.; Mississippi Female College, Hernando, Miss.; Semple Broaddus College, Centre Hill, Miss.; Mount Lebanon University, La. He was elected president of Baylor University, Independence, Texas, in July, 1863, and has held that position ever since, and J. W. D. Creath expresses the sentiments of Texas in saying that no one in or out of Texas could have done better than he has done in its administration, under all the surrounding difficulties during that time. He has sacrificed $40,000 of salary, spent over $5000 of his own means, and contributed nearly $2000 from his own purse for various objects connected with its interests. He has been either a contributor to or editor of news journals, periodicals, magazines, and reviews since his seventeenth year; has preached in all sorts of places, from a stump in the forest to the elegantly-furnished audience-room in New York, Louisville, Richmond, and Baltimore; has published a large number of sermons and literary addresses; has addressed large convocations of Masons, Odd-Fellows, and Friends of Temperance, and held the most honorable State offices in these orders; is a member of numerous national and State literary and scientific organizations; has by invitation of the Legislature delivered addresses from the Speaker's stand at Jackson, Miss., and Austin, Texas; was selected by his county in 1870 to deliver the memorial address of Robert E. Lee, and in 1876 was chosen to deliver the Centennial oration; has published the "Memoir of Mrs. A. F. Crane," "Literary Discourses," and a "Collection of Arguments and Opinions on Baptism;" and he is now publishing in lessons a "Baptist Catechism." A collection of his writings would fill half a dozen volumes. He was first married to Miss Alceta Flora Galusha, of Rochester, N. Y., whose grandfather, grand-uncle, and great-grandfather were twenty-nine years governors of Vermont. She lived ten years. He was next married to Miss Jane S. Wright, at Rome, N. Y., who lived about sixteen months. His last marriage was April 26, 1845, to Miss Kate Jane Shepherd, Mobile, Ala.

The Rev. Z. N. Morrell, in his "Flowers and Fruits from the Wilderness, or Thirty-six Years in Texas," says, "As a scholar, he has but few equals, and his superiors are very scarce. His conversation, his literary addresses, and his sermons all show that he is not only a profound scholar, but that he has always been a student, and he is a student still. His mental discipline is of the most rigid character. In person he is of medium height, with compact form, inclined to corpulency." For twelve years he was secretary of the Southern Baptist Convention, and in 1870, 1874, 1877, and 1878 he was a vice-president of that body. In fact, during a long life, and ever since his seventeenth year, he has been an officer of religious bodies in the States of Virginia, Alabama, Mississippi, Louisiana, and Texas. He was president of the Mississippi State Convention for two years; of the Louisiana State Convention for three years; and he has been president of the Texas Baptist State Convention since 1871, and he now discharges the duties of this office, with three other offices, as well as the presidency of Baylor University, and the pastorate of Independence church. He is now occupied on works for the press, among them the "Life of Sam Houston." Though engaged most of his life as an educator, with happy success, he has always had charge of churches in such important places as Montgomery, Ala.; Columbus, Vicksburg, Yazoo City, Hernando, Miss.; Memphis, Tenn.; Mount Lebanon, La.; and Independence, Texas. He is a member of the "American Philological Association," and various college societies. He has preached a large number of sermons. It is supposed about 2500 persons have been converted through his instrumentality. He has exercised no little influence in the denomination, and stands among the first as a scholar, a speaker, a theologian, a parliamentarian, and a sound, thoroughgoing Baptist, one who has performed a large share of that hard work which has given tone and character to the Baptist denomination South, and elevated it to its present position of power and usefulness.

Crawford, Charles E., a prominent teacher and Sunday-school worker in Northwestern Louisiana, was born in Alabama in 1838; graduated at Mississippi College in 1858; at the time of his death, in 1877, he was principal of Keachi Male Academy.

Crawford, N. M., D.D., for years the ablest Baptist scholar in Georgia, and one of the best preachers in the State, was born near Lexington, in Oglethorpe County, March 22, 1811. His father was Hon. Wm. H. Crawford, U. S. Senator, and Secretary of War under President Taylor. The boyhood of N. M. Crawford was spent in Washington City; but in his fifteenth year he entered the University of Georgia, graduating at eighteen with the first honor. At twenty-five he became a professor in Oglethorpe College, near Milledgeville. At that time he was a Presbyterian.

When twenty-nine years of age he married, and it was while seeking Scripture authority for infant baptism, after the birth of his first child, that he became convinced of the correctness of Baptist views. Soon afterwards he was baptized, and leaving Oglethorpe College, he became pastor of the Baptist church at Washington, Ga., where he resided a year. He was then transferred to a larger field, succeeding Dr. Wm. T. Brantly, the elder, in the pastorate of the First Baptist church at Charleston, S. C. His ministry there continued for two years only, as he accepted the chair of Theology in Mercer University in 1846, which he filled with great ability for ten years, preaching constantly in the neighboring churches. He then succeeded Dr. Dagg in the presidency of Mercer University, but soon retired from the position and accepted the professorship of Moral Philosophy in the University of Mississippi, at Oxford. In the fall of 1857 he became Professor of Theology in Georgetown, Ky., but in the following summer he was recalled to his native State, and installed, for the second time, as president of Mercer University, and he remained at the head of that institution seven successive years. In 1865, after the war, the great monetary depression caused a suspension of the exercises of Mercer University, and Dr. Crawford accepted the presidency of Georgetown College, Ky., and continued in that position until failing health, in 1871, caused his resignation. He expired at the residence of his son, in Walker Co., Ga., Oct. 27, 1871.

Dr. Crawford was a man of surpassing talents and wonderful acquirements. He was in the true sense of the term a genius. In the entire circle of science he was thoroughly versed, and his acquaintance with the whole range of knowledge was astonishing. As a linguist, besides his native tongue, he knew thoroughly French, Latin, Greek, and Hebrew. As a mathematician his knowledge extended through the calculus. He was familiar with the great problems of astronomy and with the teachings of natural philosophy. He had a very respectable knowledge of natural science, including chemistry, mineralogy, geology, and botany. In metaphysics he was well-read, and before his conversion he made himself perfectly familiar with law as a science. Few men were his equals in knowledge of English literature, while he had carefully studied the history of the world, from Adam down to the present time. And in theology he was conversant with the thoughts of all our best writers. Take him all in all, Dr. Crawford was perhaps the most learned man the State of Georgia has ever produced. While a college president he could take the post of any professor who might be temporarily absent, with equal facility hearing a recitation in the higher branches of mathematics, or in chemistry, natural philosophy, Latin, Greek, logic, theology, or in secular or ecclesiastical history. Accepting the New Testament as his only teacher, he brought all his learning to the feet of Jesus, and a "thus saith the Lord" was for him decisive of every question of faith or duty. Hence he was a thorough Baptist. In the pulpit he was an exceedingly instructive preacher: his method was clear, his style was transparent, and his argument was conclusive. In preaching he relied chiefly for his good effects upon his appeals to the understanding, for in pathos, in appeals to the feelings, and in the power of persuasion he was not equal to many who were his inferiors in learning. But he more than made up for his deficiency in these respects by the power of his facts and the conclusiveness of his reasoning; yet there were times when he spoke with melting pathos and the most commanding eloquence. His heart was tender and sympathetic, and large-souled generosity and benevolence were natural to him. He was a man of remarkable frankness, uttering his sentiments always with most outspoken candor. Though far removed from levity, his conversation abounded with humor, and he seemed to have an inexhaustible fund of anecdotes, with which to entertain a friend or illustrate a truth. One phase of his character should not be overlooked: he had in a high degree the qualities of a statesman; had he chosen politics for his profession, he would have been among the foremost of our great national leaders, whose fame would have lived as long as our glorious republic.

His mind was brilliant, his fancy luxuriant, and his oratorical powers of the first order. A man of the highest moral excellence, his Christian spirit shone with distinguished lustre in all the relations of life; and his Christian character was not only without a blemish, but was in a most eminent degree exalted. Throughout his life of untiring industry and persevering study, of profound humility and childlike simplicity, of wide-spread benevolence, adorned by a genial flow of pleasant humor, a genuine and thorough consecration to Jesus reigned. With genius and capacity that would have made him shine brightly in any sphere of life, and which would have reached not only distinction, but fame, in any pursuit, he preferred to give himself to the service of him whose kingdom is not of this world. In that service he rose to exalted eminence among his brethren, accomplished an amount of good rarely allotted to one man, and exerted an influence beneficial in the highest degree for religion and for his own denomination.

Crawford, Rev. Peter, was born in Virginia in 1809; professed religion in 1831, and soon after became a minister; received a liberal education in what is now known as Richmond College, Virginia. Having a rare faculty for teaching, his life was principally devoted to educating the young, although engaged regularly in preaching. In 1835 he removed to Marion, Ala., and founded the now justly famed Judson Female Institute. After teaching some time in Central Female College, Miss., in 1866 he became president of Keachi Female College, at Keachi, La., where he ended his labors, April 25, 1873.

Crawford, Rev. Wm. B., pastor of the Baptist church at Madison, Ga., is the son of the distinguished Wm. H. Crawford, and younger brother of Dr. N. M. Crawford, for years president of Mercer University. He was born on the 14th of September, 1821, at Washington City, and was educated at Oglethorpe University, Ga., and at Lexington, Ky., where he studied medicine. He received the degree of M.D. from the medical college at Augusta, Ga., and for thirty-three years practised his profession with great success, except when president of a female college at Cedar Town, Ga., in 1854 and 1855, and, also, for the brief period during which he occupied the chair of Natural Science at Mercer University, in 1846.

He united with the Madison church in 1848, and was licensed to preach the following year. The church called him to its pastorate and to ordination in 1874, and he has sustained the pastoral relation to the present time, rendering valuable and acceptable service. He belongs to the expository class of preachers, his discourses being marked with great plainness and simplicity. He is a man of high mental cultivation, of comprehensive learning, of great independence of character, and a clear and accurate thinker. For some years he was a Presbyterian, but a careful study of the New Testament led him to change his ecclesiastical relations and unite with the Baptists. Had he entered the ministry in early life, he would have achieved high reputation as a preacher. Unaffected modesty and self-distrust have kept him in the background somewhat, but he is a most faithful preacher of the gospel, and the purity and integrity of his private life, united with his constant endeavors exactly to obey the Word of God, give him an exalted Christian character. In social intercourse he is pleasant, humorous, and instructive, though not inclined readily to cultivate the acquaintance of others.

Crawford, Rev. William Jackson, is editor of *The Beacon,* the Baptist paper of Oregon, secretary of the Baptist Convention of the North Pacific Coast, and pastor of the Baptist church at Albany, Oregon. As pastor of one of the important churches, and editor, by election of the Convention, of which he is secretary, he occupies positions of great prominence and responsibility for one so young. Albany is his first pastorate, which he assumed Dec. 11, 1878. His work has been blessed, 42 converts having been baptized. He was born in Macoupin Co., Ill., Dec. 12, 1849; was converted and baptized at seventeen; studied at Blackburn

(Presbyterian) College for a time, and five years at Shurtleff College, graduating at the close of a full classical and theological course in 1878. He was ordained Dec. 21, 1875, by Mount Pleasant church, Ill. While in college supplied several churches.

Crawford, Rev. Wm. L., a minister of Georgetown, Ga., was born Feb. 22, 1802, and was baptized into the fellowship of the Benevolence church, in Randolph County, in July, 1842, after reaching the age of forty. In April, 1846, he was ordained. He was truly a man of God. He began to preach about three years after his baptism, and soon became a strong and zealous minister. He served many churches, and was universally popular, although a high-toned Calvinist in sentiment, and to the day of his death an old landmark Baptist. He possessed a firm mind, a retentive memory, and an intellect of towering capacity. One of the most sociable of men, he was truly a peace-maker; through modesty and meekness rarely speaking at Conventions and Associations. He was made moderator of the Bethel Association for fourteen years in succession, and within the bounds of that able body no man stood higher. In person he was large and portly, his mind and body seeming to be admirably apportioned. He had charge of various churches in Southwestern Georgia during a ministerial career of about thirty years, and he was a successful preacher and pastor. When he died, in 1878, the Bethel Association adopted in his honor a report very complimentary to his character and abilities.

Crawford, Rev. W. W., a prominent minister at Dardanelles, Ark., was born in Pennsylvania in 1816; was baptized at Mount Lebanon, La., in 1845; began to preach in 1853, and was ordained at Meriden, La., in 1856, and supplied the church at Fillmore, La. In 1859 he removed to Avoyelles Parish, and became joint pastor of Evergreen and Big Cane churches. Both these churches prospered under his ministry. Here he continued nine years, sharing with them all the hardships incident to a country where hostile armies were constantly marching and countermarching. He was pastor one year at Gilmer, Texas, after which he accepted a call from Dardanelles, Ark. Under his ministry a new church was built, and the membership grew from 25 to 84 members.

Crawley, Rev. Arthur R. R., was born in Cape Breton in 1831. He graduated at Acadia College in 1849, and pursued his theological studies at Newton, where he graduated in 1853. He sailed from this country the following December, under appointment as a missionary to Burmah. In October, 1854, he went to Henthada, a town having a population of from 20,000 to 30,000 inhabitants, and situated 120 miles above Rangoon, on the river Irrawaddy. Here he labored for several years with marked ability and success. At the end of one year the Henthada Mission included 8 churches and 150 members, and at the time of Mr. Crawley's death, twenty-three years after he commenced his labors there, the number of churches, Burman and Karen, was 54, with a membership of 1930 persons. The Executive Board testifies that Mr. Crawley "was one of the most unsparing and effective workers that ever labored among the heathen. And he was as judicious as he was enterprising. It is seldom that a Christian laborer has built more wisely; and no man who has labored among the Burmans has attained a more marked success in winning souls. After more than twenty-one years spent in the field, while in the harness, and producing larger numerical results than any other man devoted to Burman evangelization, he laid down his work with his life on the 9th of October, 1876, at the early age of forty-five years. He has left a name worthy to be enrolled among the heroes of the heroic age of Christian missions."

Crawley, Edmund Albern, D.D., was born in England, Jan. 20, 1799; brought up in Sydney,

EDMUND ALBERN CRAWLEY, D.D.

Cape Breton; graduated from King's College, Nova Scotia, 1819; converted in Granville, and baptized at Halifax, Nova Scotia, in 1827; abandoned the law, and studied Biblical interpretation under Prof. Moses Stuart, at Andover; was ordained at Providence, R. I., in 1830; from 1832 was pastor of Granville Street church, Halifax, Nova Scotia, for thirteen years; became professor in Acadia College at its inception, January, 1839. Brown University honored him in 1846 with D.D. Became president of Acadia College in 1854; subsequently spent some years in the United States; and in 1867 resumed professorship in Acadia, and is now principal of the theological department in that college. Dr. Crawley was very prominent in originating the educational movement among the Baptists in Nova Scotia, and also in carrying forward the work. He possesses a philosophic mind and splendid talents; is highly cultured. He is a sound theologian and a magnificent preacher.

Creath, Rev. Joseph W. D., was born in Mecklenburg Co., Va., Feb. 3, 1809. His father,

REV. JOSEPH W. D. CREATH.

Wm. Creath, was a Baptist minister between thirty and forty years. He was educated at the Virginia Baptist Seminary (now Richmond College), and graduated December, 1837; served churches in Virginia as pastor till 1846, then he removed to Texas under appointment as a missionary from the Domestic Mission Board of the Southern Baptist Convention. From that time to this period, whether as pastor at Huntsville or Cold Springs, chaplain of the penitentiary, or as agent for Bible revision, the San Antonio church, or the State Convention, no man has been in labors more abundant, untiring, and self-sacrificing. He raised more money for missions and the erection of houses of worship, and he constituted more churches, than any man in the Southwest. Ever busy doing good in all attainable ways, singing, praying, writing, preaching. J. W. D. Creath is the most apostolic man in Texas, and never received over $500 as an annual salary. He has been moderator of Union Association, president of the State Convention, president of the trustees of Baylor University, and vice-president of the Southern Baptist Convention. As a financier, a sound theologian, a thorough Baptist, and a bold, effective, evangelical preacher, he stands very high.

Credentials, or Certificate of Ordination.—This document is given by the Council or Presbytery that ordains a brother to the ministry, and the following form has been used:

"To all people to whom these presents shall come the subscribers send greeting: Convened at Blanktown on the 1st day of May, 1818, by the Baptist church of that city, for the purpose of setting apart the bearer to the work of the Christian ministry by solemn ordination, we made a careful examination of the candidate in reference to his conversion, call to the ministry, and views of Bible doctrine, and being fully satisfied about his piety, divine call, knowledge of the Word, and gifts for the ministry, we did, therefore, in the presence of said church, and at its request, solemnly ordain to the sacred office of the ministry, by prayer and the imposition of hands, our worthy brother, the Rev. —— ——, whom we recommend to the confidence and respect of the churches.

"—— ——, *Clerk.*

"—— ——, *Moderator.*"

Creeds, Advantageous.—Every thinking man has a creed about politics, religion, and the best manner of conducting the business with which he is most familiar. It may not be printed, it may not be communicated in words except in special cases, but it surely exists in all intelligent minds. And if the reader can remember a denomination without an avowed Confession of Faith he will find that in that community there is an understood creed just as real, and as well known by those familiar with its people and its teachings, as if every one of its members carried a printed copy of it in his hand.

Baptists have always gloried that the Bible was their creed, and at the same time for centuries they have had published Confessions of Faith. In our denomination these articles of belief have always occupied a subordinate position; they are never placed on a level with the Scriptures, much less above them. They are used to protect our unity, to preserve our peace, and to instruct our members. In the church to which the writer ministers a copy of its "Articles of Faith" and "Church Covenant" is given to each person intending to unite with it by baptism or letter. That the universal adoption of this practice would be attended by the happiest results we have no doubt.

We have been present at many councils to recognize new churches for the last twenty-seven years, and in every instance the community gave either a well-known Confession of Faith as their creed, or they submitted a series of Articles of Faith compiled for their own use in harmony with our acknowledged doctrines. We do not think it possible for any body of professed Christians to be "acknowledged" by a council of our denomination as a regular Baptist church, without Articles of Faith.

No candidate for the ministry would be ordained by a church unless the council called to give it advice on the question had received from the young man a confession of faith which embraced the teachings of our revered fathers,—views of doctrine resting wholly on the Word of God.

Our demand for many hundreds of years, that nothing shall exist among us in faith or practice without an inspired warrant, has made the authors of our creeds extremely careful in their preparation, and the common use of such Articles of Faith among Baptists has trained them to a uniformity in orthodox sentiment which occasionally excites surprise in other communities. We have no section of our denomination denouncing the creeds of their brethren as unworthy of the progress of this advanced age. It is an extraordinary occurrence when an intelligent Baptist strays into the crooked paths of so-called rationalism, or into any of the misnamed "liberal" Christian communities.

The extensive use of a creed in Baptist churches should be encouraged by earnest Christians who love our Scriptural principles. We are not surprised to see that the greatest of living Baptist preachers writes, "The arch-enemy of truth has invited us to level our walls and take away our fenced cities. He has cajoled some true-hearted but weak-headed believers to advocate this crafty policy; and, from the best of motives, some foolish brethren are almost prepared to execute the cunning design. 'Away with creeds and bodies of divinity!' This is the cry of the day. Ostensibly, it is reverence for the Bible and attachment to charity which dictates the clamorous denunciation; but at the bottom it is hatred of definite truth, and especially of the doctrines of grace, which has suggested the absurd outcry. As Philip of Macedon hated the Grecian orators because they were the watch-dogs of the flock, so there are wolves who desire the destruction of our doctrinal formularies, that they may make havoc of the souls of men by their pestilent heresies. . . . Were there no other argument in favor of articles and creeds, the detestation of Neologians might go far to establish them in Christian estimation. Weapons which are offensive to our enemies should never be allowed to rust. . . . The pretense that articles of faith fetter the mind, is annihilated by the fact that the boldest thinkers are to be found among men who are not foolhardy to forsake the old landmarks. He who finds his creed a fetter has none at all, for to the true believer a plain statement of his faith is no more a chain than a sword-belt to the soldier, or a girdle to the pilgrim. If there were any fear that Scripture would be displaced by handbooks of theology, we should be the first to denounce them; but there is not the shadow of a reason for such a dream, since the most Bible-reading of all nations is that in which the Assembly's (Westminster) Catechism is learned by almost every mother's son." (Spurgeon's "Prefatory Recommendation" to Stock's "Handbook of Theology," pp. 7, 8, 9. London, 1862.)

We strongly urge the enlarged use of Confessions of Faith among church members; and with them, for the young, we could not too earnestly advise parents to employ the Catechism in their own homes. This neglected custom of the past should be revived in every Baptist family in the world, and all our Lord's-day schools should place the same little work in their regular system of religious training. Keach's Catechism, with all the soundness of its distinguished author, two hundred years old, and others of later date, can be had for a trifle from the Baptist Publication Society. We, ourselves, derived incalculable benefits from a thorough drilling in the Westminster Catechism in childhood, and we commend to all our brethren a Baptist Catechism and Confession for children and adults.

Cressey, Rev. George Angell, pastor of the Baptist church in Kenosha, Wis., is a native of Cincinnati, O., where he was born Nov. 8, 1843. He is a son of Rev. T. R. Cressey, a well-known and dearly-beloved pioneer missionary of the Northwest, who died in 1870. His mother was Josephine Going Cressey. His father was pastor in Indianapolis, Ind., and here the subject of this sketch spent his early youth. At the age of ten years his father removed to St. Paul, Minn., which became the family home for several years. In 1862, George enlisted, and served three years in the ranks. While in the army, in 1864, he obtained a hope in Christ, having been deeply convicted of his sinful condition by the death of an irreligious comrade. In 1867 he was baptized by Rev. Dr. Buckley into the fellowship of the Baptist church in Upper Alton, Ill. He was educated at Shurtleff College and at the Baptist Union Theological Seminary at Chicago, Ill. Having received an invitation to the Baptist church in McLean, Ill., he was ordained by this church in March, 1869. He was subsequently pastor of the Grand Avenue Baptist church in Milwaukee two years, of the Baptist church in Elkhorn five years, and of his present church in Kenosha, Wis., one year.

Mr. Cressey is a successful pastor and an excellent preacher. His ministry has been blessed with many tokens of the divine favor.

Cressey, Rev. Timothy R., was born at Pomfret, Conn., Sept. 18, 1800; died at Des Moines,

Iowa, Aug. 30, 1870; converted to Christ when twenty years of age, and soon after answered affirmatively what seemed to be God's call to preach the gospel. He graduated from Amherst College in 1828, and from Newton Theological Seminary in 1830.

His first settlement was at Hingham, Mass., in March, 1831, where he remained three and a half years, and then went to the South church, Boston. While in college he solemnly dedicated himself to the work of home missions, and in June, 1835, he most gladly improved his first opportunity of going to the West and becoming pastor of the church at Columbus, O. Here he remained seven years, building the church edifice still in use, and leaving a broad and deep mark for Christ on the church and in the community at large. Here also he lost his first wife, Mary Peck, and married his second, Josephine Going, daughter of the late Rev. Jonathan Going, D.D., then president of Granville College, who still survives her husband, living at Des Moines. A two-years' pastorate of the First church, Cincinnati, was succeeded by an equal length of time spent as an agent of the Bible Society for Ohio, Kentucky, and Indiana.

In July, 1846, he became pastor of the church at Indianapolis, Ind., remaining six years. During these years he secured the erection of a new meeting-house seating 400 persons, with rooms for Sabbath-school and other purposes. In addition to pastoral duties more than sufficient for the strength of an ordinary man, there was added, immediately on his entering the State, the labor of corresponding secretary of the Convention. It was also his duty to make a careful examination of all applications for home mission aid, while as trustee of Franklin College he attended all the meetings of the board, though they were held twenty miles away by carriage-drive. He also gave much attention to general education, preparing by request of a State Convention, in 1847, an address on common schools, which is believed by many to have proved a great turning-point in that work.

In May, 1852, he became pastor at St. Paul, Minn., being the third Baptist minister to enter the Territory. After two years thus spent, home missionary work began in real earnest. Though fifty-four years old, he spent the summer and autumn journeying on foot through the southern part of the Territory, and sometimes was compelled to walk a dozen or more miles without seeing a human being. Seven years were mainly employed in such work, preaching the first sermon ever heard in many places, and having much to do with the organization of not a few churches. He frequently rode on horseback sixty miles in the depth of a Minnesota winter to preach in a log cabin. All appointments were sacredly kept. In Minnesota, as elsewhere, he took a deep interest in educational matters, drawing up in 1854 the charter of a Baptist college, the enacting of which by the Legislature was due mainly to his individual efforts.

In August, 1861, he became chaplain of the 2d Minnesota Regiment of Volunteers, and gave to his country two years of unfaltering devotion. He was pastor two years at Kendallville, Ind., and one each at Plainfield and Olney, Ill., after which, in 1868, he removed to Indianola, Iowa, where he spent two years abounding in labor and success.

In May, 1870, he removed to Des Moines, and, after six weeks' rest, he accepted an appointment as railroad missionary, to begin labor the 1st of September; but on the 31st of August sudden and severe sickness quickly removed his spirit to the enjoyment of heavenly freedom. His last words were, "My work is done; I am going home."

Obstacles furnished him the inspiration of success and not the discouragement of defeat. He seemed to seek the most difficult fields of service. He recognized the simple, earnest preaching of the gospel as God's instrument to secure man's salvation. In his discourses he loved especially to dwell on the doctrines and character of Christ. He was a Christian of great spirituality of mind. Our denominational history in Ohio, Indiana, and Minnesota could not be written without making mention of his work and worth. He left three sons in the ministry.

Crisp, Thomas S., was born in 1788, at Beccles, Suffolk, England, and died June 16, 1868, aged eighty years. His family were members of the Congregational body, and in his early manhood he was ordained to the ministry of that denomination. In 1818 he embraced Baptist principles, and soon after his baptism received an invitation to the classical tutorship of Bristol College. He was also elected assistant minister of Broadmead chapel. On the death of Dr. Ryland, in 1825, Mr. Crisp was chosen president of the college, and for nearly forty years he discharged the duties of this office. During the latter years of his presidency he enjoyed the valuable co-operation of the Rev. Dr. Gotch, the present head of the institution. Mr. Crisp was distinguished as an accurate scholar and a prudent administrator, but he is specially remembered for the rare excellence of his character and life.

Crist, Hon. Henry, a distinguished Indian-fighter and legislator of Kentucky, was born in Berkeley Co., Va., in 1764. His father having removed to Pennsylvania, Henry, with other daring youths, visited Kentucky in 1779, and soon afterwards took up his abode in the wilderness. In 1788 he was wounded by the Indians near Shepherdsville, Ky., and lay helpless in the woods many days, when upon the point of starvation he was accidentally discovered and rescued. After engaging in the manufacture of salt some years, he settled on a farm in Bullitt County. Here he became a member of Cox's Creek Baptist church. After serving several terms in the Kentucky Legislature, he was elected to a seat in the U. S. Congress in 1808. At the expiration of his term he retired from public life to his farm, where he died Sept. 26, 1844.

Crittenden, Rev. Orrin, an eloquent preacher, was born in Berkshire Co., Mass., Feb. 13, 1814; converted at the age of fourteen, he joined the Union Baptist church, Jersey Co., Ill., in 1848; was licensed in 1849, and ordained at the meeting of Apple Creek Association, in 1850. He preached and held revival meetings in various places, and in 1854 crossed the plains to California. He has preached with great success at Mountain View, Santa Cruz, South Clara, Salinas, and elsewhere. He helped to organize the Mountain View, San Juan, Napa, and other churches, as the result of revival labors, and he has baptized many converts. Excessive labor impaired his health; but in his advanced years he is still a preacher of great force, and is honored as one of the "fathers" in the Baptist ministry of California. His home is at Mountain View, near San Francisco, Cal.

Crocker, Rev. Thomas.—For more than thirty years Thomas Crocker was a faithful and successful preacher of the gospel, and hundreds of persons in the counties of Wake, Warren, Granville, and Franklin, N. C., were brought to Christ by his labors. He was born in 1786, and died Dec. 8, 1848, aged sixty-two years.

Crosby, Rev. David, pastor of the Baptist church in Ripon, Wis., was born in Bath, Steuben Co., N. Y., in 1839. Having early in life obtained a hope in Christ, he determined to fit himself for whatever position the Lord and his church might assign to him. He prepared for college at Ann Arbor, Mich. He entered the University of Rochester at Rochester, N. Y., in 1864, and graduated in the class of 1868. Immediately upon graduating he entered the Rochester Theological Seminary, and graduated in the class of 1871. Having received a call to the Baptist church of Mount Morris, N. Y., he was ordained by that church in September, 1871. Having received an invitation to the pastorate of the First Baptist church in Lansing, Mich., he resigned his pastorate at Mount Morris to go to Lansing. Here he continued five years, the church growing rapidly in numbers and influence under his able ministrations. In 1877, Mr. Crosby came to Wisconsin to accept the pastorate of the Baptist church at Ripon, which has since been his home. He is a scholar of ripe acquirements and a good preacher. In the pulpit he is clear and logical, and as a pastor, he bestows the most laborious care on all the work of his parish. During the civil war Mr. Crosby served as a private in one of the regiments of his native State.

Crosby, Hon. Moreau S., of Grand Rapids, was born in Manchester, Ontario Co., N. Y., Dec

HON. MOREAU S. CROSBY.

2, 1839. He joined the Second Baptist church in Rochester in June, 1857, being baptized by Rev. G. D. Boardman. He graduated from the University of Rochester in 1863, and has since resided in Grand Rapids. He was associated with his father in the insurance business until the death of the latter, in 1875, and he has since continued in it. In 1872 he was chosen a member of the State senate, and he became at once an active and influential member of that body. He has been for five years a member of the State Board of Charities, and for six years a trustee of Kalamazoo College. He was the first president of the Grand Rapids Young Men's Christian Association, and has been president of the State Association. For several years he has been superintendent of the Sunday-school.

He has just been elected lieutenant-governor of Michigan.

Crosby, Thomas, was a London Baptist of great influence in our denomination. He was married to a daughter of the celebrated Benjamin Keach. He taught an advanced school for young gentlemen. He was a Baptist deacon for many years, and he was selected to make the usual statement on behalf of the church when Dr. Gill was ordained the pastor of the church of which Mr. Crosby was a member.

Mr. Stinton, the brother-in-law of Thomas Crosby, and the predecessor of Dr. Gill, had collected materials for a work on Baptist history, which was never published. These materials were given to Crosby. And he says, "That if the ingenious collector of the materials had lived to digest them into proper order, according to his design, they would have appeared to much greater advantage" (than in his book). When the Rev. Daniel Neal, a Congregationalist, was preparing his well-known "History of the Puritans," Mr. Crosby sent Mr. Stinton's materials to Neal, thinking that the history of the Baptists in England would necessarily be a part of the history of the Puritans. After keeping the manuscripts for several years, less than five pages of his third volume contained all that he said about the Baptists. This circumstance, and the unkind reflections upon the few Baptist ministers whose names he condescended to notice, furnished the reasons why Mr. Crosby wrote his "History of the Baptists." Bunyan, Kiffin, Keach, and Stenneet failed, by their great positions, to persuade Neal to give them a place in his work, though all England knew them.

Mr. Crosby's "History of the English Baptists," published in London in 1738, 1739, and 1740, is worth its weight in gold many times over. Like Ivimey's "History of the English Baptists," it is very scarce, and a copy of it brings a high price.

Cross, Edmund B., D.D., was born in Georgetown, N. Y., June 11, 1814, and was a graduate of the Hamilton Literary and Theological Institution. He was ordained at Georgetown, Sept. 2, 1841, and received his appointment as a missionary to the foreign field Nov. 28, 1842. He did not leave the country until Oct. 30, 1844, arriving at Maulmain Feb. 24, 1845, and commencing his missionary work at Tavoy March 25. A school for native preachers was opened on the 1st of May, 1846, under his charge, teaching in which and preaching as occasion presented fully occupied his time. These labors in and about Tavoy were followed with success. The impaired health of Mrs. Cross made it necessary for him to return to the United States, which was reached Jan. 2, 1853. Mr. Cross remained here two years, and then returned to resume his work at Tavoy, where he remained until he was removed to Toungoo, in the early part of 1860, and, as in Tavoy, he was connected with a school for the training of preachers as an associate with Dr. Mason, which relation continued until Dr. Mason left the service of the Missionary Union, in 1864, when Mr. Cross was put in full charge of the interests of the Tavoy station. A few years of quiet, persistent work resulted in giving prosperity to the Toungoo station and its out-stations. In December, 1869, Mr. and Mrs. Cross, who had again spent some time in this country, returned once more to Tavoy. The mission has had its severe trials during the past years, especially in connection with the terrible famine which has brought such desolation to the country. There has been a gradual recovery from the consequences of the fearful scourge. At the last report the number of churches connected with the department of which Dr. Cross has the charge was 61, with a membership of nearly 2000 persons.

Cross, Rev. Henry, was born in Nottinghamshire, England, Dec. 12, 1840. His parents were Baptists, and he was early brought to the Saviour. He was baptized in 1854. While very young he commenced to exercise his gifts publicly. He was licensed to preach when only seventeen years of age. He entered the Baptist College of Nottingham in 1859, and graduated in 1863. During the same year he was ordained as pastor of the Baptist church in Coventry, England. Revivals followed, and the church rose from one of the smallest among the Dissenters to the largest in the city. He came to America in 1874, and settled as pastor of the First Baptist church in St. Paul, Minn. During his pastorate there of five years the magnificent edifice of that church was completed and dedicated. He accepted a call from the Pilgrim church in New York in 1879, and the Lord has blessed his labors in his new field. Mr. Cross is a man of ability and piety, and if his life is spared he has a bright future before him.

Crow, Rev. Charles.—For many years one of the most prominent men among the early Baptists of Alabama; pastor at Ocmulgee and other leading churches. No man in the State in those days was considered to be his superior as an influential and strong preacher, giving earnest co-operation to every work. He was the first president of the State Convention. His memory is still fragrant in Alabama.

Crozer, John Price, Esq., was born in the former home of the celebrated painter, Benjamin West, at Springfield, Delaware Co., Pa., Jan. 13, 1793. He became the subject of religious convictions in very early life, and was baptized by Dr. William Staughton into the fellowship of the First church, Philadelphia, April, 1807. After several unsuccessful business ventures, he engaged in the manufacture of cotton goods, and by his tireless industry, undaunted perseverance, and unimpeachable integrity he achieved great and well-deserved success. His riches were held as a trust received from God, and he coveted only a faithful stewardship. Upon removing to Upland, Pa., in 1847, he erected a building for Sunday-school purposes and for public worship. In 1852 he built a neat church edifice, which he also enlarged in 1861. In 1858 he erected a building at a cost of $45,000, designed to be used in furnishing at a reduced cost a comprehensive and thorough education for business, teaching, or any literary pursuit. This building was generously offered and used as a hospital for sick and wounded soldiers during the war of 1861-65, and it was subsequently consecrated as a "school of the prophets." He was a man of generous sympathies, and contributed largely to missionary, educational,

JOHN PRICE CROZER, ESQ.

and humanitarian enterprises. In 1855 he was elected president of the Pennsylvania Baptist Education Society, which position he retained until his death, and during this period he endowed seven scholarships of $1500 each. He was also officially connected with the American Baptist Publication Society, and while in this connection endowed a Sunday-school Library Fund of $10,000, and a Ministers' Library Fund of $5000. The University of Lewisburg also shared largely in his frequent and munificent benefactions. Nor were his princely gifts confined to the enterprises of his own denomination. The Pennsylvania Training School for Feeble-Minded Children received a generous measure of his attention and aid. He was also one of the founders of the U. S. Christian Commission, and a working member of its executive committee. He was married March 12, 1825, to Miss Sallie M. Knowles. He died March 11, 1866. His widow still lives, full of years and good works, and of his children, Samuel A., J. Lewis, George K., Robert H., Mrs. Lizzie, wife of Dr. Benjamin Griffith, and Mrs. Emma Knowles still continue in the faith and labors of their sainted father. Another daughter, Mrs. Maggie, wife of Mr. William Bucknell, has since entered into rest, after a life abundant in the blessed results of Christian toil. Soon after the death of Mr. Crozer, the widow and surviving children established a Missionary Memorial Fund of $50,000, to be used by the American Baptist Publication Society in mission work among the freedmen in the South. On Nov. 2, 1866, they also jointly endowed the Crozer Theological Seminary with contributions amounting to $275,000. Thus the life of the father survives in the children, recalling the memory of one who will ever be known as the benefactor of the poor, the friend of the feeble-minded, the patron of learning, and the steadfast supporter of religion. The oldest son, Mr. Samuel A. Crozer, is president of the trustees of Crozer Seminary. The library building, "Pearl Hall," perpetuates the name of the deceased daughter, Mrs. Maggie Bucknell.

Crozer Theological Seminary is situated in the borough of Upland, Pa., just outside the limits of the city of Chester, 14 miles south of Philadelphia, on the railroad which connects Philadelphia and New York with Baltimore, Washington, and the South. Its principal building commands, from a gentle elevation, a fine view of the two adjacent towns, and of a long stretch of the Delaware River. It is accordingly visible to the multitude who pass to and fro between North and South, between the land and the ocean, on the great thoroughfares of travel just mentioned. Here are combined the advantages of rural seclusion with those of close proximity to city, manufacturing, and commercial life.

The origin of the seminary was connected with a prior agency for promoting the same objects at the university at Lewisburg, Pa. A theological department of instruction for candidates for the ministry had been there sustained for some years under the patronage of Baptist churches. Of that institution Mr. J. P. Crozer, founder of the borough of Upland, had long been a prominent and most liberal supporter. He had also erected on the present site of the Crozer Theological Seminary a building for a school of more general design, with ample grounds about it for all needful uses. After his death, in the year 1866, the members of his family, in particular his oldest son, Mr. Samuel A. Crozer, were moved to establish on this site the present institution. The edifice already existing was modified and adapted to its new destination; other buildings were added, and especially separate houses, ample and commodious, were provided for the residence of the needed professors. All this, with an endowment fund in money, adequate to the keeping up of the property and the maintenance of the professors, so that instruction to all pupils should be free, was made over to a board of trustees, incorporated by the Legislature April 4, 1867.

In due time professors were appointed, and the school went into operation, under the presidency of Rev. Henry G. Western, D.D., in September, 1868. The first class graduated in 1870, since which the seminary, by the successive classes, has contributed annually its quota to the ranks of men usefully engaged in the Master's service, in other lands, as well as throughout the wide extent of our own. From its fortunate geographical position, the school has been conveniently resorted to by young men from both the northern and the southern sections of our country; and the liberality has not been wanting to insure that all who had *proved themselves worthy* of aid should be enabled to accomplish their course of study.

This course extends regularly over a period of three years, and presupposes on the part of students a collegiate education, or what is equivalent, for the full enjoyment of its advantages. It includes constituting a partial course, occupying two years, is provided.

The need of a library for such an institution was met by the donation of nearly $30,000 by Wm. Bucknell, Esq., of Philadelphia, for the purchase of books. His generous interest in the cause of ministerial education went much further, and provided, on the seminary ground, a beautiful and convenient stone building, fire-proof, for the safe-keeping of the books. This is large enough to accommodate easily 40,000 or 50,000 volumes, and capable of extension as future needs may require.

A fund of $10,000 has also been given by Mr. Samuel A. Crozer to sustain an annual or less frequent course of lectures to the seminary, by men who may be selected of eminent qualifications to

CROZER THEOLOGICAL SEMINARY, CHESTER, PA.

study and training in the knowledge of the Bible, in all the historical relations of the book, and in the interpretation of its contents; of the history of the church, as the record of the life, struggles, and progress of Christianity; the scientific discussion and orderly arrangement of the doctrines of Christianity in a system of theology; and, finally, in the theory of the church, and of the ministerial functions of preaching and the pastoral care. In all this teaching and training it has constantly been a prominent aim to cultivate at once a scientific understanding and a devout and consecrated spirit, with tact and practical adaptation to the work of the ministry.

For those whose age, lack of previous education, or other impediments have hindered from pursuing the full course, a selection of important studies, give valuable instruction on subjects outside of the regular course.

Crudup, Rev. Josiah, was born in Wake Co., N. C., Jan. 5, 1791. He lived for some time in the family of Mr. Babbitt, master of the Lewisburg Academy, a ripe scholar, a devoted Christian, and a good teacher. He was ordained in August, 1813, Revs. John Purefoy, William Lancaster, and Robert T. Daniel forming the Presbytery. Having been elected by his county to the State Legislature, and being refused a seat in that body because he was a pastor, his friends ran him for Congress, and he served in that body in the session of 1821–23. He was beaten in the next campaign by Hon. W. P. Mangum by a very small majority. Mr. Crudup served as pastor of Hepzibah, Perry's Chapel, and other churches, preaching the gospel for fifty years.

He was a cultivated Christian gentleman, and in his prime was a preacher of surpassing eloquence. He died May 20, 1872.

Culpeper, Hon. John, was born in Anson Co., N. C., in 1761. He was baptized by Silas Mercer in Georgia and at once began to preach. Returning to North Carolina while still young, his ministry was blessed with many gracious revivals. His great popularity induced his friends to nominate him for Congress in order to defeat an unpopular incumbent. He was for many years a useful member of our National House of Representatives; he was twice agent for the Baptist State Convention of North Carolina. He died in the seventy-sixth year of his age at the residence of his son, Rev. John Culpeper, South Carolina.

Culver, Rev. S. W., was born in Groton, Conn., in 1825. At the age of eighteen he was baptized into the fellowship of the First Baptist church of his native place. His early studies and education were intended as preparatory to a course in medical science, but at this period of life he was impressed with the call of God to the ministry, and he entered heartily into the study of theology. This had to be temporarily abandoned on account of alarming sickness. Upon his recovery at the age of twenty-six, Mr. Culver was ordained to the ministry. His pastorates have been Ontario Centre, Rhinebeck, Vernon, Oneida Co.; Holland Patent, Lowville, Lewis Co.; Mumford, Monroe Co.; West Henrietta and Geneseo, all in New York State. His life has been one of great activity in the pastorate and in the field of literature. As a preacher he was loyal to truth, seeking the presentation of correct principles rather than popular approval, logical rather than emotional, with a good command of language, and with a style of much elegance and force. He has been a frequent contributor to the denominational papers; he is the author of a volume entitled "Crowned and Discrowned," and he has in course of publication two new works.

Cummings, E. E., D.D., was born in Claremont, N. H., Nov. 9, 1800. His early education he obtained in the district school of his native place. He joined the Baptist church in Claremont in 1821. His college course was pursued at Waterville, Me., where he graduated in the class of 1828. He was ordained pastor of the Baptist church in Salisbury, Sept. 17, 1828. Here he remained until called to the pastorate of the First Baptist church in Concord, N. H., where he commenced his labors March 2, 1832, and continued them until Jan. 11, 1854, when he became pastor of the Pleasant Street church in Concord, and remained in that position for ten years. For thirty-two years he served in the Baptist ministry in Concord. Dr. Cummings has published several sermons, and has now in manuscript "The Baptist Ministry of New Hampshire for the First Century of our History." It is after the plan of Dr. Sprague's "Annals." He received the degree of Doctor of Divinity from Dartmouth College in 1855. In the educational

E. E. CUMMINGS, D.D.

institutions of the Baptists of New Hampshire he has had a personal interest. He has been president of the board of trustees of the New London Institution from its beginning, and is a trustee of Colby University. He still resides in Concord, N. H.

Cunningham, Rev. Richard, was born in Halifax, Nova Scotia, in 1812; was converted and baptized in Horton by Rev. T. S. Harding; commenced preaching in 1828; was ordained pastor of Wilmot Mountain church March 25, 1829, where he labored usefully for about twenty years; subsequently he was pastor of the Baptist church of Digby, Nova Scotia. He died Jan. 15, 1858. He had a keen mind; he was a good theologian and an effective preacher.

Cunningham, Rev. V. G., the gifted young Baptist pastor in the old French town of Natchitoches, in Louisiana, was born in Caddo Parish, La., in 1844. He received his classical education in Homer Male Academy and Mount Lebanon University. He began to preach in 1867, and was ordained as pastor at Caldwell, Texas, in 1868. Subsequently he entered Waco University, where he graduated in 1871. In 1878 he returned to Louisiana, and began to preach at Natchitoches, where he found a few unorganized Baptists. These he gathered into a church and began to hold regular services. Others have been added, and the little body now numbers 35, with a Sunday-school and weekly prayer-meeting, with a neat house of worship in course of construction. Mr. Cunningham is partly sustained in his work by the State Convention.

Currey, Hon. Samuel, was born near Fredericton, Nova Scotia, Oct. 12, 1806. He pursued his preparatory studies at South Reading, and joined the Sophomore class in Brown University in 1832. He graduated in 1835. Having studied law, he was admitted to the bar April 21, 1837, and opened an office in Providence, which was his residence during his professional life. He had a large practice, no small part of it in the higher courts, not only of several States, but in the Supreme Court of the United States. For a number of years he served either as a representative or senator in the General Assembly of Rhode Island. Mr. Currey was for many years a member of the First Baptist church in Providence. He died Feb. 28, 1878.

Curry, Prof. J. L. M., D.D., LL.D., was born in Lincoln Co., Ga., and at the age of thirteen removed to Alabama. Upon his father's estate he

PROF. J. L. M. CURRY, D.D., LL.D.

grew up to manhood, when he became the owner of a cotton plantation, which he managed with success. In 1843 he graduated at the University of Georgia, and in 1845 completed his legal course at the Harvard Law School, having as classmates President Hayes, of Ohio, Anson Burlingame, and others distinguished in the councils of the nation. In 1846 he served in the Mexican war with Hays's Texan Rangers. Returning from Mexico, he represented Talladega County for several years in the Alabama Legislature. He also represented his district in the 35th and 36th Congress, in which were such men as Lamar, Stephens, Cox, Conkling, Adams, and Sherman. Mr. Curry's first speech in Congress, delivered Feb. 23, 1858, in favor of the admission of Kansas under the Lecompton constitution, established his reputation as an orator. During his terms of service in Congress he made several forcible speeches on current national questions, and always held the earnest attention of the House. On the secession of Alabama, he was appointed in 1861, by the convention of that State, a deputy to the Southern Convention, which met in Montgomery in February of that year. In August, 1861, Mr. Curry was elected a delegate to the first regular Congress of the Confederate States from the fourth Congressional district of Alabama. He was chairman of the Committee on Commerce, and at one time Speaker *pro tempore*. The address to the people of the Confederate States, signed by every member of Congress, was the production of his pen. Upon the adjournment of Congress, he joined the army of Gen. J. E. Johnston, then in Georgia, and served in various capacities until the close of the war. In 1865 he was elected president of Howard College, Ala., and in 1868, Professor of English in Richmond College, Va., which position he still holds. In addition to the school of English, Prof. Curry holds that of Philosophy, teaching Logic, and Mental and Moral Science. For several years he also gave lectures in the Law School on Constitutional and International Law. He is an earnest advocate of public schools and of higher education, and has made more addresses in behalf of education than, perhaps, any other man in Virginia. In the recent effort to endow Richmond College, he traveled over a great part of the entire State, and aroused an enthusiasm in behalf of that institution the like of which has never been enlisted in behalf of any other college in the country. Nor should his masterly address before the Evangelical Alliance be forgotten, in which he urged the complete separation of church and state, and which was reprinted and distributed in England by the disestablishment party. Prof. Curry, although a clergyman, has never felt it to be his duty to become a permanent pastor of any church. He preaches, however, whenever and wherever occasion calls for his services, and the large congregations which assemble when he officiates attest his high excellence and deserved reputation as a pulpit orator. Dr. Curry is closely identified with all denominational enterprises. He served as clerk and afterwards as moderator of the Coosa Association, of Alabama; was president of the Alabama State Convention; president of the National Baptist Sunday-School Convention, of Cincinnati, and is now president of the General Association of Virginia, and a trustee of the Southern Baptist Theological Seminary. He is a frequent contributor to our religious papers, and is at present writing an interesting series of articles on Government, in course of publication in the *Religious Herald*. In 1867 Mercer University, Ga., conferred on him the honorary degree of LL.D., and in 1871 Rochester University the degree of D.D. Dr. Curry's present wife was Miss May W. Thomas, daughter of James Thomas, Jr., of Richmond. She is the very successful teacher of the infant class of the First Baptist church of that city. It numbers from 180 to 225 pupils, and is said to be by the *Sunday-School Times* the best conducted infant class its editor has ever seen.

Curry, Rev. W. G., son of Allen H. Curry, was born in Monroe Co., Ala., Sept. 11, 1843; was baptized in 1858, at fourteen years of age; removed to Louisiana the same year, and was there licensed to preach at the age of sixteen, and spent some time at school in that State; returned to Alabama in 1860, and entered school at the Newtown Academy, and obtained a liberal education; in 1861 entered the Confederate army as a volunteer, and served as a private soldier two years, when, "in consideration of a faithful discharge of duty," he was made chaplain of the 5th Alabama Regiment, in which capacity he served to the close of the war. He was ordained to the ministry while in the army, at Orange Court-House, Va., by order of the Pineville church in Alabama, of which he was a member, Drs. Quarles, J. W. Jones, W. F. Broadus, and Rev. Mr. Marshall acting as the Presbytery. On returning home he became pastor of Monroeville, Bellville, Pineville, and Bethany churches, a relation which he sustained with eminent success until he undertook the work of evangelist, in 1877, under appointment of the Alabama State Mission Board, in which position he rendered most successful service for two years. After this he returned to the pastorate at Snow Hill, Ala. Mr. Curry is a fluent speaker and a gifted preacher. He is one of our most trusted pastors, and he is still growing in all the elements of ministerial power.

Curtis, Rev. David, was born in Stoughton, Mass., Feb. 17, 1782. He prepared for college under Rev. William Williams, of Wrentham, Mass., and graduated at Brown University in the class of 1808. For thirteen years he was pastor of the Coventry and Warwick churches in Rhode Island. Subsequently he was the pastor of several other churches in Massachusetts and Rhode Island. For sixty years he was a preacher of the gospel, and served his Master faithfully in his vocation.

Curtis, Rev. Henry, was born in Illston, Leicestershire, England, Oct. 11, 1800. In 1812 his parents emigrated to this country and settled in Otsego Co., N. Y. In the same year both his parents died, and at the age of sixteen he went to the city of New York, and there, under the labors of Rev. John Williams, he was led to Christ, and was baptized into the fellowship of the Oliver Street Baptist church. He was licensed March 10, 1824, by this church, then under the joint pastorates of the venerable Williams and the Rev. S. H. Cone. On the 13th of March he was married to Miss Eliza Banning. He was ordained at Harpersville in the same year. In 1832 he became pastor of the church in Bethany and Canaan, now called the Clinton church, whose interests as pastor he served fourteen years. Here he preached his first sermon in this State, and in its fellowship he remained until his death. For thirty-five years he labored in Wayne County, and thirteen churches were during this period built up under his pastoral care, while a vast amount of missionary labor fell to his lot. His baptisms exceeded 1000. No condition of weather or of roads prevented him from meeting his engagements, however distant.

Brother Curtis possessed more than ordinary ability. His mind was active and clear, his conclusions formed with marked care, and his convictions firm and immovable. Courteous and gentlemanly in his manners, he became a wise counselor and an able preacher. It may here be noted that his earliest religious impressions sprung from the closet prayer of a mother, "Oh, shadow us under the wings of a precious Jesus." His experience in life was the cry, "Oh, my rock;" "I know whom I have I desire to depart and be with Christ I wish to greet in heaven is Jesus, the is my mother, for she led me to him." Four sons and two daughters were baptized by this revered father, and these all continue active members of the denomination, honoring the various spheres of life to which God has called them.

Curtis, Rev. Richard, the younger of two of the same name who led a Baptist colony into Southwest Mississippi, was born either in Virginia or South Carolina about 1750. With his company of Baptists he settled on Cole's Creek, near Natchez, in 1780, and shortly after constituted Salem church. He was then a licensed preacher. The country in 1783 passed for a time under the government of Spain, and he soon incurred the displeasure of the authorities and was compelled to fly from persecution. He went back to South Carolina, where he remained nearly three years, during which he was ordained. He then returned to Mississippi and renewed his labors. He was joined by a number of young ministers, by whom several churches were gathered, and which were organized into an Association in 1806. He died Oct. 28, 1811, shortly after attending the meeting of the Association.

Curtis, Thomas, D.D.—This distinguished divine was a native of England. He came to this country about 1845, being then over fifty years of age. Having preached with great acceptance for some time in Charleston, S. C., he and his son, Wm. Curtis, D.D., purchased Limestone Spring, which had been fitted up for a watering-place, and established a school for young ladies, which, for extent and thoroughness of instruction, has probably never been surpassed and seldom equaled in the South. The number of pupils ranged from 150 to 200. He was a man of sound learning. He lost his life on a steamer that was burnt on the Potomac in 1858.

Curtiss, Rev. Emory, was born in Middlebury, Genesee Co., N. Y., March 26, 1812; was baptized by Rev. Joseph Elliott in September, 1830. He was urged almost immediately after his conversion to prepare for the ministry, but not recognizing the call as from God he engaged in teaching for several years. In 1834, however, the way seemed plain before him, and he began to study theology with his pastor and to preach as opportunity offered. In January, 1836, he was ordained at Morganville, N. Y., and immediately found evidence of God's approval in a precious revival. In April, 1837, he was appointed a missionary by the New York State Convention to labor in Erie County. He filled this appointment for four years, and then went to Michigan, where, with a brief exception, his ministry has since been exercised. In Redford for ten years, in Ypsilanti for three years, in Niles for eight years, in Greenville for six years, with shorter terms of service in Coldwater, Hastings, and Sturgis, he has enjoyed large success as a winner of souls, and has been eminent among his brethren for the harmony of his pastoral relations.

From 1862 till 1866, he was not engaged as a pastor, having removed to Kalamazoo with reference to the education of his son, and being also connected with the Michigan *Christian Herald* as proprietor and publisher. The son, his last surviving child, died in 1864, and the father sought at once to become a pastor again, but the paper held him longer than he intended, and it was not till 1866 that he resumed pastoral service.

In March, 1871, Mr. Curtiss yielded to the repeated solicitation of the American Baptist Home Mission Society to perform service in Oregon and Washington Territory as a general missionary. After less than two years' work the failure of his voice compelled him to withdraw from it, but he had labored with zeal and success, had aided in the organization of sixteen churches, and the erection and dedication of eight houses of worship. His health did not allow him to resume full duty till July, 1874. He is now pastor in Lapeer.

Cushman, Rev. Elisha, son of Elisha and Lydia (Fuller) Cushman, was born in Kingston, Mass., May 2, 1788; he was a descendant of Robert Cushman, a Pilgrim father; was converted in 1808 and united with the Baptist church in Kingston, under Rev. Samuel Grover; studied for the ministry; preached in Grafton, Mass., and in Providence, R. I.; ordained pastor of the First Baptist church in Hartford, Conn., June 10, 1813, and remained till 1825; was prominent in all public affairs; assisted in establishing, in 1814, the Baptist Missionary Society, and was corresponding secretary till 1822, when it was reorganized under the name of the Baptist Convention, of which he became a trustee, and, finally, president from 1830 to 1834; in 1822, when Mr. Philemon Canfield started the *Christian Secretary*, the first Baptist paper in Connecticut, he became editor; in 1824 received the honorary degree of A.M. from Yale College; a member of the corporation of Trinity College; in 1825 settled with the New Market Street Baptist church in Philadelphia; in 1829 returned to Connecticut and settled in Stratfield till 1831, when he became pastor of the Baptist church in New Haven; in 1835 removed to Plymouth, Mass., but from failing health returned in 1838 to Hartford, Conn., to resume the editorship of the *Christian Secretary;* published numerous addresses and sermons; a noble, effective man. Died in Hartford, Oct. 26, 1838, aged fifty years.

Cushman, Rev. Elisha, Jr., son of Rev. Elisha, was born in Hartford, Conn., July 4, 1813; learned the printer's art, and entered the office of the *Christian Secretary* under Deacon P. Canfield, and worked from 1831 to 1836; in 1836, with Isaac Bolles, began the publication of the *Northern Courier* (finally called the *Hartford Courier*), a paper of talent and racy wit. On the death of his father, in 1838, he published the *Christian Secretary*. He was converted in 1839 and baptized by Rev. G. S. Eaton; united with First Baptist church in Hartford; was licensed to preach, and ordained in 1840 as pastor of the Baptist church in Willington, Conn.; ill health induced his resignation in 1845; returned to Hartford and supplied the Baptist church in New Britain; in 1847 settled with the church at Deep River, Conn., and remained there twelve years; in 1859 he became pastor of a new church in West Hartford, and remained till 1862, when he took charge of the *Christian Secretary*, and retained it till his death, acting as occasional supply also to needy churches. For many years he was the able secretary of the Connecticut Baptist State Convention; a ready speaker and equally ready writer; an extensive reader, with a retentive memory; a man of the sweetest spirit, yet firm in opinion and utterance. He died in Hartford, Jan. 4, 1876, aged sixty-two years.

Cushman, Robert W., D.D., was born in Woolwich, Me., April 10, 1800. His parents died when he was a child. He became a Christian when he was sixteen years of age, and decided to enter the ministry. He pursued his studies at Columbian College, Washington, graduating in the class of 1825. He was ordained as pastor of the Baptist church in Poughkeepsie, N. Y., in August, 1826. After three years of labor there, desiring a milder climate, he removed to Philadelphia, where he opened a school for the education of young ladies, which was called the "Cushman Collegiate Institute." He remained in charge of it until 1841, when he received a call from the Bowdoin Square church in Boston. He continued in this position for six years, and then removed to Washington, D. C., and started an institution similar in character to the one of which he was the originator in Philadelphia. A few years having been devoted to this work, he returned to Boston, and for some time was at the head of the "Mount Vernon Ladies' School," supplying meanwhile the pulpit of the First Baptist church in Charlestown, Mass. His last years were passed at a rural home which he had purchased in what is now Wakefield, Mass., where he died April 7, 1868.

It was justly said of Dr. Cushman at the time of his death, "Thus has fallen, in ripeness of years and Christian character, one of the most widely known, intelligent, and faithful in the ranks of our ministry. He was throughout a consistent Baptist, firm and unwavering in fidelity to every principle, an able defender of his denominational polity. If 'blessings brighten as they take their flight,' his friends may be happy in the assurance that his merits will hereafter be appreciated and acknowledged, and he will be reckoned a star in the firmament of our Zion."

Custis, J. W., D.D., is a descendant of the well-known Custis family of Accomac Co., Va., and was born in Washington, D. C. In 1855, at the early age of twelve years, he was converted and baptized into the fellowship of the Second Baptist church of that city. His parents being members of the E Street church, his membership was afterwards removed thither. From the time of his conversion he attracted the attention of his pastor, Rev. Isaac Cole, by his youthful zeal, and was encouraged to look forward to the work of the ministry. In changing his church relations he had the happiness of receiving the pastoral care of Rev. G. W. Samson, D.D., an ardent friend of the young, who took a deep interest in the welfare of Mr. Custis. In 1856 he entered the preparatory department of Columbian College, and pursued the regular course, having in view the profession of law. Gradually, and after some years, he was led to turn his attention to the ministry. He spent two years in the university at Lewisburg, Pa., and then returned to Columbian College, and graduated June, 1865. In the same month he was ordained in the Broad Street church, Philadelphia, to which his membership had been removed two years previously. After spending nearly a year laboring with the church in Hudson City, N. J., he accepted a call to Bordentown in the same State. His pastorate of nearly four years was very successful. He then removed to Philadelphia, becoming pastor of the Spruce Street Baptist church, where like success attended his ministry. In 1875, against the wishes of the church, he resigned and went to Chicago, accepting a call to the Michigan Avenue church. In 1877 the University of Chicago conferred upon him the honorary degree of Doctor of Divinity. The rigor of the climate soon broke down his health, and, under the advice of his physician, he returned East and became pastor of the Tabernacle church, Utica, N. Y. Dr. Custis is a close student and an able preacher.

Cuthbert, James H., D.D., was born Dec. 13, 1823, in Beaufort, S. C., being the eldest son of

JAMES H. CUTHBERT, D.D.

Lucius and Charlotte Fuller Cuthbert. His earliest school days were spent at Beaufort College, where he remained until 1839. He then entered the Sophomore class of Columbia College, S. C., at that time under the presidency of the highly gifted Robert W. Barnwell. In 1841 he went to Princeton College, N. J., entering the Junior class, and remaining until his graduation in 1843, on which occasion he was selected as one of the class orators. From Princeton he returned home with the intention of studying law, but being converted under the preaching of his uncle, Dr. Richard Fuller, in the spring of 1844, he determined to devote his life to the ministry of the gospel. After three years' study with Dr. Fuller he was ordained at Charleston in 1847, and became at once the assistant pastor of the Wentworth Street Baptist church in that city, then under the pastorate of Dr. Fuller. On Dr. Fuller's being called to Baltimore to take charge of the Seventh Baptist church of that city, Mr. Cuthbert was chosen pastor, and continued in that relation until 1855. While pastor here he was married to Miss Julia Elizabeth Turpin, of Augusta, Ga. In 1855 he accepted a call to the First Baptist church of Philadelphia, then located in Lagrange Place, which soon afterwards removed to its present location at Broad and Arch Streets. In 1861 he removed to Augusta, Ga., being without any pastoral charge for about a year. In 1862 he became pastor of Kollock Street church, with which he remained until 1865, when he accepted the pastorate of the Green Street Baptist church of that city, and ministered to it for four years. In 1869 he was invited to the pastorate of the First Baptist church, Washington, D. C., where he still labors. The degree of Doctor of Divinity was conferred upon him by Wake Forest College, N. C.

Dr. Cuthbert has made several valuable contributions to Baptist literature. He has written occasionally for the *Baptist Quarterly*, and published in 1878 a very interesting biography of his distinguished relative, Dr. Fuller. His style is easy and graceful, and the book is prepared with excellent taste. As a preacher, Dr. Cuthbert is earnest and impressive, reminding one frequently by his appearance and the tones of his voice of Dr. Fuller. As a man, Dr. Cuthbert is among the few who are without stain or reproach.

Cuthbert, Rev. Lucius, is a native of Beaufort, S. C., a brother of Dr. J. H. Cuthbert, of Washington, D. C., and a nephew of the late Dr. Richard Fuller, of Baltimore. He was for some time pastor of the Citadel Square Baptist church of Charleston, S. C., but failing health compelled his retreat to Aiken, S. C., where he has spent nearly thirty years in the Master's service. The churches of which he is pastor regard him with admiration and love, his brethren in the ministry cherish him in their hearts, and the providence and Spirit of God have bestowed their blessings liberally upon his home, heart, and ministry.

Cutting, Sewell S., D.D., was born at Windsor, Vt., Jan. 19, 1813. At the age of fourteen he became a member of the Baptist church of Westport, N. Y. When a child he commenced the study of Latin, and purposed to enter the legal profession. Before he was sixteen he became a student of law, but at seventeen he concluded to enter the ministry. He completed his preparation for college at South Reading, Mass., and when eighteen years of age he entered Waterville College. After studying two years in that institution he went to the University of Vermont. In it he had the instruction of able educators, and he was graduated with the highest honors. From it he received all his degrees. Ill health forced him to leave college before the day for graduation, and to relinquish his design to pursue a regular theological course, and on March 31, 1836, he was ordained pastor of the Baptist church in West Boylston, Mass. Soon after he accepted a call to Southbridge, Mass., as successor to Dr. Binney, the distinguished missionary, where he remained eight years. In 1845 he was called to edit *The Baptist Advocate* in New York, which position he accepted and changed its name to *The New York Recorder*. He found the paper in a depressed condition, and organized a new departure not only in name but in everything that goes to make a successful religious journal. He succeeded, bought the paper, and immediately sold it to Rev. Lewis Colby, a publisher, who sold a share of it to Rev. Joseph Ballard. The subscriptions increased rapidly, and the paper began to exert a great power in promoting the interests of the Baptist denomination. In 1850 it was sold to Martin B. Anderson, LL.D., and J. S. Dickerson, D.D., and Dr. Cutting retired. This occurred just at the crisis of the revision controversy and the formation of the American Bible Union. He was elected corresponding secretary of the American and Foreign Bible Society, accepted it provisionally, and took a prominent part in the discussions between the two societies. In 1851 he accepted an editorial position on the *Watchman and Reflector*, of Boston. In 1849 he became the editor of *The Christian Review*, which he conducted until 1852. In 1853, Dr. Anderson was called to the presidency of Rochester University, and Dr. Cutting was summoned back to edit the *Recorder*. In 1855, Dr. Cutting and Dr. Edward Bright bought the New York *Baptist Register*, consolidated it with the *Recorder*, and founded *The Examiner*. He then accepted the professorship of Rhetoric and of History in the University of Rochester, which chair he filled till 1868, when he resigned to accept the secretaryship of the American Baptist Educational Commission. In 1879, he was elected secretary of the American Baptist Home Mission Society, and after a year's service he went to Europe to find needed rest. His "Struggles and Triumphs of Religious Liberty," and his "Historical Vindications," with notes and appendices, have been widely read. He compiled a hymn-book for the vestry and fireside. Many of his discourses and some of his poems have been published. Dr. Cutting is a clear thinker, a scholarly writer, and one of the ablest men in the American ministry.

D.

Dabbs, Rev. Richard, was born in Charlotte Co., Va., date unknown. He became pious in early life, but did not enter the ministry until several years after his conversion. His first pastorate was with the Ash Camp church, Charlotte County. He delighted to visit Associational and other large meetings of his brethren. His excursions were very numerous and extensive. He was in the habit of visiting those parts of the country where Baptist churches had not been constituted, or where they were feeble and declining. Among the happy results of these efforts may be mentioned the origin of the Baptist church in Petersburg, Va. It was chiefly through his influence that the few Baptists in that place were induced to unite under a regular constitution and to make exertions for the erection of a house of worship. In 1820 he spent one-fourth of his time, a portion of the year, in assisting to supply with preaching the church in Lynchburg, Va. His ministry there was very popular. Closing his labors in Lynchburg, he came to Nashville, Tenn., and took charge of the First Baptist church in that city, where he was very successful in building up the Baptist cause. Here he closed a useful life. His manner in the pulpit was very attractive. With a musical voice and a happy faculty of illustration, he rarely, if ever, addressed a small congregation. He died on the 21st day of May, 1825, in full assurance of a blessed immortality, honored and respected by all.

Dagg, John L., D.D.—Among the most distinguished men of the Baptist denomination in the United States, Dr. Dagg of right holds a place. He was born at Middleburg, Loudon Co., Va., Feb. 13, 1794. He was early the subject of religious impressions, and he said to the writer, "I obtained a joyful sense of acceptance with God on my birthday in 1809." He was baptized in 1813; began to preach in 1816; was ordained in 1817; preached to several churches in Virginia, and in 1825 accepted a call to the pastorate of the Fifth Baptist church in the city of Philadelphia; in 1833 he retired from the pastorate with diseased throat, and in the following spring his voice so failed that he was unable to preach, and for a considerable time could not speak above a whisper, and it has been so weak ever since that he has never been able to return to regular service as a minister. Eminent as had been his ministry, the Lord had other ways for him to serve with still greater usefulness. In 1836 he removed to Tuscaloosa, and took charge of the "Alabama Female Atheneum," and in 1844 to Penfield, Ga., as president of Mercer University, where he also gave instruction in theology. Many of the best ministers in Georgia and other States cherish the most grateful recollections of his great worth to them while in that position. The twelve years of his presidency comprised perhaps the brightest period of the brilliant history of grand old Mercer University. In 1856 he retired from that institution with the purpose, while bearing the pressure of infirmities and advancing age, of serving the cause of Christ by the use of his gifted pen, and thousands can rise up and call him blessed in testimony of the happy way in which he has carried out that purpose.

His "Manual of Theology" appeared in 1857, "Treatise on Church Order" in 1858, "Elements of Moral Science" in 1859, "Evidences of Christianity" in 1868. These are his great works, and they will bear comparison with any other American books on the same subjects. In addition to these, a discussion on baptism with the Rev. David Jones, which appeared in letters in the *Christian Index*, was put in book-form by the Baptist General Tract Society.

His pamphlets are "The More Excellent Way," "An Interpretation of John iii. 5," "An Essay in Defense of Strict Communion," "A Decisive Argument against Infant Baptism, furnished by one of its own Proof-texts."

He has for many years been regarded as one of our wisest, most profound, most critical, and safest newspaper writers. Our venerable and learned brethren have watched the productions of his pen with marks of the highest regard.

Dr. Dagg, in great age and with many infirmities, still lives (1880), under the tender and affectionate care of his accomplished daughter, at Hayneville, Ala., and all who visit him return feeling that it has been an honor and a Christian feast to hold converse with this man of God.

Dallas Male and Female College, Dallas, Texas, was organized in 1875, and commanded a respectable patronage for one collegiate year. It is under the control of stockholders, who appoint a majority of the trustees. Rev. Geo. W. Rogers, D.D., is now president. The college, after a two years' suspension, was reorganized and opened September, 1878.

Daniel, Rev. Robert T.—In a letter to Dr. R. B. C. Howell, Mr. Daniel wrote, "During the thirty years of my ministry I have traveled about 60,000 miles, preached about 5000 sermons, and baptized more than 1500 people. Of that number many now are ministers, twelve of whom are men of distinguished talents and usefulness."

Mr. Daniel was born in Middlesex Co., Va., June 10, 1773. His parents emigrating to North Carolina, he grew to man's estate in Chatham County. He was baptized into the fellowship of Holly Springs church, Wake County, by Rev. Isaac Hicks, in July, 1802. He was ordained in 1803, Isaac Hicks and Nathan Gully forming the Presbytery. He was an able preacher and a great evangelist. He was one of the first, if not the first, missionary of the North Carolina Baptist Benevolent Society, and while thus engaged organized the First Baptist church of Raleigh in 1812, of which he was twice pastor. "His was a missionary heart, a missionary tongue, and a missionary hand," and after brief pastorates and arduous revival labors in North Carolina, Virginia, Mississippi, and Tennessee, this prince among the tribes of Israel fell asleep in Jesus, in Paris, Tenn., Sept. 14, 1840.

D'Anvers, Gov. Henry, is supposed to have been a very near relative of the Earl of Danby, who died in 1643. He was a soldier, who distinguished himself in wars in Holland, France, and Ireland. Henry D'Anvers was a colonel in the Parliamentary army. He was for a time governor of Stafford. He had such a reputation for integrity among the people over whom he exercised authority, that he was noted as one who would not take bribes. While governor of Stafford he adopted the sentiments of the Baptists, and notwithstanding his position, and the prejudices his baptism would stir up against him, he was immersed by Henry Hagger, the minister at Stafford at that time. After the return of Charles II. his situation was very critical; he was a man of prominence by his family connections, by the respectable estate which he owned, and by his military services. A proclamation was issued offering £100 for his arrest; he was seized at length and sent a prisoner to the Tower of London; but his wife had great influence in the court of King Charles, and he was released on bail.

He was one of the ministers of a Baptist church near Aldgate, London. In this position he maintained a character so spotless that he greatly commended the truth which he proclaimed.

Mr. D'Anvers was the author of a work which he called "Theopolis, or City of God," treating of the coming and personal reign of Christ in his millennial glory and triumphs. He also wrote a work on baptism, which was the ablest on the subject published by any Baptist till that time. It stirred up Richard Baxter most uncomfortably; and many others most slanderously. David Russen abused Mr. D'Anvers and his book with a vehemence which shows how powerfully he had been moved by it. He says that Mr. D'Anvers's book "is calculated for the meridian of Ignorance; that it is full of plagiary, prevarication, impertinencies, and manifold falsehoods; that no man of learning, but one who designedly (for an evil design) carries on a cause, will ever defile his fingers with such pitch; and that he should be ashamed to produce a book of that nature in a matter of controversy." But poor Mr. Russen defiled his own fingers with the work, and shows by his angry and slanderous words that Mr. D'Anvers had given him and other Pedobaptist sacramental warriors very heavy blows. The book, even in our own times, has been so highly esteemed that the Hanserd Knollys Society, a body representing the intelligence and learning of our English Baptist brethren, had resolved to publish it; and the Rev. William Henry Black was performing editorial labor upon it for that end, and only lack of funds hindered the publication. The same misfortune stopped the entire labors of the society.

Mr. D'Anvers believed that it would be a blessing if James II. was relieved of the royalty of England. There could not be a worse king in a country where the monarch was limited in powers. He was a tyrannical Catholic, bent on overthrowing the Protestant religion of England; he was a mean tyrant, determined to destroy her liberties; he had ungracious manners, an unattractive appearance, a fountain of selfishness in his heart, and an abundance of cowardice. A son of Lucy Walters and Charles II., the Duke of Monmouth, a Protestant, a brave, generous young man, was encouraged to rebel against his uncle. His troops were routed at Sedgemore. Two days later he was captured, and soon after executed. Mr. D'Anvers was concerned in some meetings held to help the unfortunate duke. After the fight at Sedgemore he fled to Holland, where he died in 1686.

Dargan, Rev. Jeremiah.—Miss Anna More, of Bertie Co., N. C., wishing to be baptized, went into South Carolina in search of a Baptist preacher. She there met Mr. Dargan, who, having baptized her, also married her, and with her returned to North Carolina. He was the founder of Coslin and Wiccacon churches, and died in 1786.

Dargan, J. O. B., D.D.—Mr. Dargan's ancestors were conspicuous in both church and state during the Revolutionary war. His grandfather, Rev. Timothy Dargan, and Dr. Richard Furman were co-laborers in religious and political fields, and the intimate friendship formed between them has descended unbroken through several generations.

Dr. Dargan was born in Darlington Co., S. C., on the 9th of August, 1813. His early advantages

J. O. B. DARGAN, D.D.

for education were good, and he "remembered his Creator in the days of his youth." He was baptized in his seventeenth year, and at once became an active worker in the Master's vineyard. Having been licensed to preach, he entered Furman Institution in 1833, and spent two years in preparing for his life-work.

His first pastorate was with the Cheraw church. In 1836 he became pastor of the Black Creek church, and he still sustains this relation.

A very gratifying part of his labors has been among the colored people. During the war he baptized 97 in one day.

He has always been an active friend of missions, Sunday-schools, and of every good work. He is one of the oldest and most respected ministers in the State. He has never changed his residence in the forty-four years of his married life. Few ministers indeed have maintained themselves so long in one community.

Of his wife, it is enough to say she is a granddaughter of Rev. Evan Pugh, and she is in all respects worthy of her grandfather.

Darrow, Rev. Zadoc, only son of Ebenezer Darrow, was born Dec. 25 (O. S.), 1728. His mother was a Rogers, and a descendant of the martyr John. He was educated as an Episcopalian, but was converted under the preaching of Rev. Joshua Morse, a New Light, and afterwards a Baptist. He was ordained as pastor of the Baptist church in Waterford, Conn., in 1769, and continued in that relation, with large and happy success, till his death, in 1827, at the age of ninety-nine, closing a ministry of nearly sixty years. A large portion of Eastern Connecticut felt the deep impress of his thoughts and character. His grandson, Rev. Francis Darrow, was associated with him in 1809, and continued to serve the church till his death, in 1851, at the age of seventy-one, in the forty-first year of his ministry. His success was like that of his grandfather.

Davidson, Rev. George, was born Feb. 14, 1825, at Pruntytown, Taylor Co., W. Va. He married in 1851, and was baptized by Rev. Cleon Keys, March, 1854; was licensed to preach March, 1857, and ordained as pastor of the Pruntytown church March 14, 1858. He continued as pastor of the Pruntytown and other churches for nine years, and is now and has been for the last fifteen years pastor of the Baptist church at Grafton. He has attained a good degree of eminence and success in his work; has been president of the General Association of the State; is a fine preacher, and a model pastor; and his church is efficient in benevolent enterprises and in Christian influence.

Davidson, Thomas Leslie, D.D., was born in Edinburgh, Scotland, Sept. 6, 1825. When a lad of eight years of age he left his native country and came to Canada. He was baptized in 1841, and was educated at the Baptist college in Montreal, where he spent four years (1843–47). In the month of August, 1847, he was ordained pastor in Pickering, Ontario, where he remained until December, 1850, and then accepted a call to the church in the city of Brantford, with which he remained a little more than nine years, resigning in April, 1860. He was greatly prospered in his ministry while at Brantford, having baptized 308 persons and built two churches. In 1854 he became editor of the *Christian Messenger*, now the *Canadian Baptist*, of Toronto. He was elected secretary of the Baptist Missionary Convention of Ontario in 1857, and held the office fifteen years successively. He was re-elected in 1876 and served two years. His pastorates after leaving Brantford were in St. George (1860–66), Elgin (1866–73), and in Guelph (1873–77). For one year (1877–78) he was general financial and traveling secretary of the Ontario Baptist Convention. In December, 1878, he became pastor of the church in Chatham, where he now (1880) resides. Rochester University, in 1855, conferred on him the degree of A.M., and in 1863 that of D.D. He published, in 1858, a work on baptism and communion.

Up to the time of writing this sketch Dr. Davidson has secured the building of six Baptist churches, has baptized over 1000 persons, preached at the dedication of over fifty Baptist meeting-houses in the province of Ontario, and taken part in the ordination of about sixty pastors. As the result of his ministerial labors a number of Baptist churches have been gathered in the province.

THOMAS LESLIE DAVIDSON, D.D.

Davies, Benjamin, Ph.D., LL.D., was born Feb. 26, 1814, in Carmarthenshire, Wales. In early life he gave evidence of fervent piety, and began to preach before he was sixteen years old. He was received as a ministerial student at Bristol College in 1830, where he made marked progress in those studies by which in after-life he was so distinguished. On the conclusion of his course at Bristol he proceeded to the Universities of Dublin and Glasgow, and finally to Germany, where he formed life-long friendships with Tholuck, Ewald, Rodiger, and other eminent scholars in Hebrew and Oriental literature. He left Germany in 1838 with the degree of Ph.D. from Leipsic University, and took charge of the Baptist Theological Institution at Montreal, Canada. Here he resided for six years, and married Miss Eliza Try, of Portland, Me. In 1844 he went to England to take the presidency of Stepney College, which position he held until 1847, when he returned to Canada as professor in McGill College, Montreal. He spent ten years at this post, and pursued with ardor his favorite Oriental studies. He finally returned to England in 1857, and became classical and Oriental tutor at Stepney College, just then removed to Regent's Park, under the presidency of Dr. Angus. Here for eighteen years he labored, attracting the almost filial attachment of his students and the high respect of distinguished Biblical scholars of all denominations. Trinity College, Dublin, honored him with the degree of LL.D. He engaged largely in literary work, writing or editing the notes to portions of the Annotated Paragraph Bible, published by the Religious Tract Society; assisting Dr. Payne Smith, the Dean of Canterbury, in the preparation of his "Syriac Lexicon"; and in preparing successive editions of his own well-known "Student's Grammar" and "Student's Lexicon of the Hebrew Language." He was an active member of the Philological Society, and when the work of revising the Authorized Version of the Holy Scriptures was undertaken by a committee of the Convocation of the Established Church, the name of Dr. Davies was one of the first which it was resolved to include as representing Biblical scholarship among the Non-conformists. He became a member of the Old Testament Company of Revisers, he and his old friend and fellow-student, Dr. Gotch, being the Baptist members of the company. In this great and honorable work he took the deepest interest. His health began to fail in the spring of 1876, and he died July 19, in his sixty-second year.

Davies, Daniel, D.D., was born in Carmarthenshire, Wales, Dec. 15, 1797. His parents removed to Dowlais, Glamorganshire, when he was quite young. At the age of seven he had an attack of smallpox, which left him sightless. In his sixteenth year he was admitted into the college for the blind at Liverpool. He united in his boyhood with the Welsh Presbyterians, and commenced preaching in connection with that body. His ability was such as to command attention. He continued laboring with growing acceptance in the church of his parents until a book written by Abraham Booth on the "Kingdom of Christ" was read to him. This had the effect of revolutionizing his mind on several questions bearing on the polity of the New Testament church. Having declared himself a convert to Baptist principles, he was baptized on a profession of his faith by David Saunders, a man of eminence in his day. He was at this time twenty-three years of age. Having spent five years with the Welsh church in London, he was invited to succeed the Rev. Joseph Harries (Gomer), one of the most gifted men of his age, at Bethesda, Swansea. Here he labored with distinguished success for a period of thirty years, having under his care one of the largest and most intellectual churches in the Principality. In 1855 he left Swansea for Cardigan, another stronghold of Baptist influence. His later years were spent in Glamorganshire, under the genial roof of his son-in-law, the Rev. John Rowlands.

For at least forty years the Rev. Daniel Davies was one of the most conspicuous figures in the

Baptist pulpit of the Principality. His reputation was as far-reaching as the language in which he preached. No Associational gathering was considered complete without his presence, and however

DANIEL DAVIES, D.D.

highly wrought the expectations of the multitude, they were never disappointed in the "blind man."

His mind was richly stored with every variety of useful knowledge. Although deprived of sight, he had an acquaintance with books which impressed with wonder those who casually associated with him. He could converse freely and intelligently upon almost any subject that would be likely to interest the thoughtful. He kept some one ever at his side whose business it was to unfold the treasures of the wise and learned, while he assorted, arranged, and labeled them for their appropriate places in his well-ordered mind.

He was intellectually fitted to feel at home in the discussion of great truths and principles. It was a rich treat to hear him on an important occasion. He was like one of those transatlantic steamers that must be seen in deep waters and a heavy sea to be appreciated. He never appeared to better advantage than when out in mid-ocean, with sails full set and filled with an impassioned gale of feeling, when the steam-power of conviction and the sail-power of inspirational enthusiasm united to propel him through the deep and turbulent waters of some great discussion.

He was a delightful ministerial companion. Even to old age he retained his youthfulness and vivacity. Though dead, he still lives in the affections and spiritually-quickened lives of thousands of his countrymen, among whom is the writer of this sketch.

Davies, George, of Charlottetown, Prince Edward Island, is of Welsh extraction, a wealthy merchant, and prominent member of the Baptist church in that town; is very benevolent, and has made magnificent contributions to the various enterprises sustained by the Baptist denomination in the maritime provinces.

Davies, Rev. John, son of William and Mary (Jones) Davies, was born in Birmingham, England, April 11, 1837; spent his early years in Shrewsbury; was educated at Rawden College, Yorkshire; at the age of twenty-five was ordained, in Birmingham, pastor of the Bond Street Baptist church, where he successively labored for more than five years; came to the United States in 1867; preached first in Danbury, Conn., then accepted a call to the Baptist church in South Norwalk, where his ministry was blessed, for more than four years; in April, 1872, he became pastor of the Central Baptist church in Norwich, one of the principal churches in the State; his assiduous toil was largely prospered; easy and eloquent as a speaker; withal a poet and writer for periodicals; thoroughly interested in every good cause,—missions, education, and temperance; served the city on the School Board; was active in the Baptist State Convention; beloved by all who knew him in England and in this country; married, November, 1863, Emily White, of Birmingham, England, a lady of rare talents, attainments, and character; had three sons and two daughters. On Sunday, Dec. 28, 1879, while delivering an annual memorial discourse, he fell in the pulpit, and was unconscious for a time; went to England, seeking rest and recuperation. Died April 19, 1880, aged forty-three years, and was buried in Birmingham, where he expired.

Davies, Thomas, D.D., president of the Baptist College, Haverford-West, Wales, was born near Saint Mellon's, Monmouthshire, in 1812. He was baptized when about eighteen years of age by the Rev. Evan Jones Caesbach, a minister of considerable distinction in his day. He began to exercise his gifts as a preacher in 1831. He was educated at the Baptist College, Bristol, and spent the years of his early ministry in Merthyr-Tydvil, Glamorganshire.

In the year 1855 the presidency of the college at Haverford-West became vacant through the death of the venerated David Davies, who had occupied the position with signal ability and acceptance from its incipiency. In the effort of the denomination to secure a man to carry forward a work which had been so well begun, the unanimous choice fell upon the Rev. Thomas Davies, of Merthyr. He brought to his new and arduous position a cultivated mind and ripe scholarship. Under his administration the institution has grown in importance and influence, giving to the churches some of their most efficient leaders.

During all the years of Dr. Davies's presidency he has sustained, either jointly or alone, the pastorate of one of the largest churches in the county. To hear him preach twenty years ago was an inspiration. He was a model of eloquence, which for purity and pungency could scarcely be surpassed. It is generally admitted by those who were under his preceptorship in those earlier years, that his efforts in the pulpit left a deeper impress on their character, both as men and as ministers, than his efforts in the class.

He is now in his sixty-ninth year, prosecuting his work both in the college and in the church with recognized efficiency.

Davis, Rev. Elnathan, was born in Maryland in 1739; his parents were Seventh-Day Baptists, but he was wild and reckless.

"He heard that one John Steward was to be baptized on a certain day by Mr. Stevens; the candidate was a very large man, and the minister small of stature, and he concluded that there would be some diversion, if not drowning, and so he gathered eight or ten of his companions in wickedness and went to the spot. When Mr. Stevens commenced his sermon Elnathan drew near to hear him, while his companions stood at a distance. He was no sooner in the throng than he perceived that some of the people trembled as if in an ague fit. He ran to his companions, but the charm of Stevens's voice drew him to the listening multitude again. He, with many others, sank to the ground; when he came to himself he found nothing in himself but dread and anxiety. He obtained relief by putting his trust in Jesus."

He was baptized on a profession of his faith, and he began at once to preach Jesus. He moved to North Carolina in 1757, and was ordained in 1764 by the celebrated Samuel Harriss, of Virginia. He remained in North Carolina till 1798, when he settled in South Carolina, in the bounds of the Saluda Association, and he labored in that region till his death. Mr. Davis was a miracle of mercy, and a useful minister of Jesus.

Davis, Judge Ezekiel W., settled at Grand Rapids in 1834. He commenced his Christian life in another denomination. His first child was the devoted and efficient Mrs. Jewett, our missionary among the Teloogoos. The question of her baptism as an infant led him to investigations which made him a Baptist. He united with the Indian mission church at Grand Rapids, until another was formed in the city, after which he ever bore an interested and leading part in this church. He was always ready to do the work of an evangelist among the destitute and afflicted, preaching to them as Providence called, though not bearing or seeking the ministerial name. His death was in 1874, on the verge of fourscore years, half of which he had spent at Grand Rapids. He was born in Elizabeth, N. J., but grew to manhood in the vicinity of Utica, N. Y., where he was baptized by Rev. Elon Galusha.

Davis, Rev. George Edwin, of Welsh parents, was born in London, England, March 7, 1824; emigrated with his parents to the United States in 1828; was educated in New York; was first officer of a ship sailing to California in 1849; converted and baptized the same year; began to preach and talk of Jesus at once, in San Francisco, especially among seamen; licensed in 1855, ordained in 1856, and became pastor of the Mariners' church; has done much mission work in California; organized the San Pablo and other churches; was pastor at San Pablo and Redwood City; is now pastor of the South San Francisco Mission church. He has much Welsh fire and magnetism in preaching. Excessive labor has impaired his vocal organs, but in missionary zeal the ardor of youth is unabated.

Davis, Hon. George F., was born in Brighton, Mass., Feb. 16, 1820. His father, Samuel Davis,

HON. GEORGE F. DAVIS.

originally a Unitarian, became a Baptist, and on his removal to Quincy, Ill., in 1835, was instrumental in forming the First Baptist church of that city. At the first baptism after the organization of this church, George F. confessed Christ. In 1838 he left his father's home in Quincy and removed to Cincinnati, O., where he engaged in business, and where he still lives.

Mr. Davis has been an active and successful business man, and has been much in public life. He was president of the first board of aldermen in the city of Cincinnati, and has been several times president of the Chamber of Commerce. He is a very effective public speaker, and has represented his city and denomination on many important public occasions. He has also frequently been called to preside over conventions in Sunday-school and church work, and has been on almost all the official boards of our national organizations. All his life he has been engaged in the Sunday-school. He was one of the constituent members of the Mount Auburn Baptist church, and also one of the projectors and owners of the Mount Auburn Institute, a school of high grade for young ladies. He is one of the most valued trustees of Denison University.

Mr. Davis is a pronounced Baptist, and has the confidence of the entire community. He was married in 1841 to Miss N. W. Wilson, who is still living. He has five sons, all located in Cincinnati.

Davis, Gustavus Fellowes, D.D., son of Isaac Davis, was born in Boston, Mass., March 17, 1797; at his father's death, in 1803, moved to Roxbury; studied in Dedham, under Rev. Mr. White, and in Roxbury under Dr. Prentiss: in 1813 went to Worcester to learn a trade, and was converted under the preaching of Rev. William Bentley, and joined the Baptist church; was devoted to the study of the Bible and of books; began preaching at the age of seventeen, in Hampton, Conn.; in March, 1815, moved to Preston, Conn., where he was ordained June 13, 1816; the first person baptized by him was but nine years old, and a great impression was made; in 1818 settled with the Baptist church in South Reading, Mass., and remained eleven years; studied Greek and Latin, walking to Boston to recite to Mr. Winchell and Dr. Francis Wayland; in 1829 removed to Hartford, Conn., first to assist Rev. W. Bentley, but finally settled as pastor of the Baptist church; in 1835 received the honorary degree of D.D. from Wesleyan University, Middletown; married Jan. 5, 1817, Abigail Leonard, of Preston, Conn.; had three sons and three daughters; wrote and published numerous addresses and sermons; at South Reading compiled a hymn-book for conference meetings; was a chief agent in establishing the Connecticut Literary Institution in Suffield; a studious, executive, devout, noble, efficient man; died Sept. 17, 1836, in his fortieth year.

Davis, Gustavus Fellowes, Esq., a banker of Hartford, Conn., son of Rev. Gustavus F. Davis, D.D., was born in North Stonington, Conn., Jan. 4, 1818; was educated at the Hartford Grammar School, and in the academy at Westfield, Mass.; was prevented from pursuing his collegiate course by weak eyes; entered business circles; has now (1880) been engaged in the banking business for forty-six years; is president of the City National Bank, of Hartford, and of the State Savings Bank; vice-president of the Travelers' Insurance Company; director in the Ætna Insurance Company; trustee in Connecticut Mutual Safe Deposit Company; treasurer of the South School District of Hartford; trustee of the Connecticut Literary Institution at Suffield, and of the Baptist Education Society; was elected during the past year a representative from Hartford to the State Legislature; has maintained through life an active interest in educational affairs; is a prominent member of the Baptist denomination, and deeply interested in its prosperity; a worthy son of a worthy father.

Davis, Isaac, LL.D., was born in Northborough, Mass., June 2, 1799. He graduated at Brown University in the class of 1822. Among his classmates were Rev. Dr. Caswell, Rev. Dr. B. C. Cutler, Prof. J. W. Farnum, and Hon. Solomon Lincoln. Mr. Davis studied law, and having been admitted to the bar, commenced the practice of his profession in Worcester, Mass., in which he achieved great success. He has always been a decided Baptist, identifying himself in many ways with the interests of the denomination, and by his counsels and benefactions, helping forward every good cause represented by the different religious organizations which were brought into existence by the zeal and benevolence of leading Baptists. His love for the college where he received his education has never flagged, but amid all its fortunes he has proved himself its staunch and constant friend. He was chosen a member of its board of trustees in 1838, and a Fellow in 1851. For forty years he was president of the board of trustees of the Worcester Academy, which has done so much in fitting young men for Brown University. Mr. Davis has also taken an active part in all plans designed to promote the welfare of the city which for so many years has been his home. He was its mayor for three years. In the politics of the State he has also been interested. For eleven years he was in the State senate. He has been one of the governor's council. For a number of years he was a member of the Massachusetts Board of Education, and rendered efficient service in elevating the tone of public sentiment with reference to popular education, thus making the schools of Massachusetts the glory of the old Bay State. In some respects Mr. Davis may be regarded as among the most influential Baptists in New England. He has loved the cause in which at an early day he embarked, when the Baptists occupied a position in society far below what they have now reached. To him, and to such as he, the denomination are greatly indebted, under God, for what has been done during the past fifty years, to give it the rank which it now holds among the other Christian denominations.

Davis, Rev. James, was born in Hopkinton, N. H., Nov. 6, 1772; converted about 1791; graduated at Dartmouth College in 1798; ordained in Vermont by the Congregationalists in 1804; in 1816 became a Baptist, and was baptized Oct. 12, 1816, by Rev. Asa Wilcox; by his own request was reordained in Lyme, Conn., Nov. 14, 1816; labored successfully as an evangelist; was of great service in founding the Connecticut Literary Institution, at Suffield, Conn.; was the instrument of adding 800 members to Baptist churches; died in Abington, Mass., May 28, 1821; a noble toiler in Connecticut.

Davis, Rev. James, one of the most useful ministers that ever lived in the western part of Georgia, including Coweta, Troup, Heard, Meriwether, and the adjacent counties, was born in Wilkes County, Jan. 22, 1805. He married, and joined the church when quite a young man, and never afterwards could relate his Christian experience without manifesting deep emotion. He moved from Elbert to Jasper County in 1826, where he was both licensed and ordained. Returning to Elbert County in 1828, he preached there for several years, with increasing power and success. About 1830 he moved to the western part of the State, where he spent the remaining portion of his life, acting as a pioneer Baptist, and proclaiming those Baptist principles which, to-day, flourish so extensively in that section. Strong in native intellect, robust in constitution, untiring in energy, and impelled by the sole desire to "preach Christ crucified," Mr. Davis left his impress on the entire section of country in which he lived. He assisted in the constitution of the Baptist church at La Grange, and, indeed, of most of the Baptist churches in the counties where he labored. A friend of education, strongly missionary in spirit, an earnest, devout, gifted, and eloquent preacher, he struggled nobly to disseminate the great truths of Christianity, as maintained by our denomination; and he did as much to give moral tone to the community in which he lived as any man.

Good and useful while here, he died as he lived, in the faith of Jesus. He passed away in September, 1859, at his home in Heard County. To his only absent son, Rev. Wm. H. Davis, then residing at Hephzibah, Ga., he sent this simple message: "Strive, my son, to be a good minister of the gospel, and meet me in glory." We know that one injunction has been fulfilled, and we have every reason to believe that both have been.

Davis, Rev. John, was born at Pennepek, Pa., Sept. 10, 1721. He was ordained in 1756, and, removing to Maryland, he became pastor of the Baptist church at Winter Run, Hartford Co., Md., which became the mother-church of Baptists in that State. He continued to serve this church with great success for fifty-three years. The First Baptist church in Baltimore, as well as several others still vigorous, owe their origin to his efforts. He was a man of untiring energy and zeal, and of deep piety. He traveled much and preached constantly, meeting with much opposition at the hands of those who despised and persecuted the Baptists, but through it all was greatly blessed.

Davis, Gen. John, Bucks Co., Pa.—The father of Gen. Davis was born in October, 1760. Before he was sixteen years of age he entered the Revolutionary army, in which he served till the war was over. He fought at Brandywine, Germantown, Monmouth, Stony Point, and at Cowpens. From

GEN. JOHN DAVIS.

Trenton to Yorktown he was at his country's service to fight or die. He was an ensign in Lafayette's light infantry, and assisted in carrying that general from the field when he was wounded at Brandywine. He was very obnoxious to the Tories, and on one occasion when at home on leave of absence he was only saved from capture in his own house by an ingenious effort at concealment when it was searched.

Gen. John Davis was the second of the seven children of John Davis, Sr., and of Ann Simpson, his wife. He was born Aug. 7, 1788, and died April 1, 1878, in his ninetieth year. He was about six feet high, with a commanding and courteous presence; with a face beaming with intelligence, and an ample forehead. In any company the appearance of Gen. Davis would have proclaimed him a natural leader of men, not only where the stern authority of the commander was needed, but where large mental resources were required.

The educational advantages possessed by the general in early life were supplemented by extensive reading, and by the retentiveness of a memory that seemed to forget nothing, and when he entered upon the active duties of manhood he had the culture and attainments of one far in advance of his young neighbors. In March, 1813, he married Miss Amy Hart, and settled in the neighborhood where Davisville now stands, a village to which the community gave the name of the general, and in that beautiful region he spent the last sixty-five years of his life.

Soon after he was married the blood of his brave father was stirred up within him by the wrongs his country suffered from the hostile efforts of Great Britain, and by the dangers which threatened the nation, and in September, 1814, he volunteered to march to the defense of Washington. His name headed the roll of his neighbors and friends, who formed a rifle company commanded by Capt. William Purdy, in which he held the position of ensign. In 1815 he entered the State militia, and maintained an unbroken connection with it for thirty-five years; he filled every position from captain to major-general, and three times he was elected major-general of the division of militia belonging to Bucks and Montgomery Counties.

When Lafayette visited this country in 1824, Gen. Davis received him with his regiment, 600 strong, at the Trenton bridge, at Morrisville, and escorted him to the Philadelphia county-line, where he delivered the nation's guest to the authorities of Philadelphia. During the march from Morrisville, when the marquis learned that it was the general's father who assisted in carrying him from the field of Brandywine, he threw his arms around his neck and embraced him with every demonstration of gratitude and joy.

Gen. Davis was one of the most popular men in the State, and his fellow-citizens loved to place him in public positions; indeed, sometimes the difficulty was rather in avoiding than in securing responsible and lucrative offices. In 1833, Gov. Wolf appointed him a member of the board of appraisers of damages of public works of the State. In 1838 he was elected to the United States Congress, and he served his term in the House of Representatives, winning golden opinions from both political parties. In March, 1845, President Polk appointed him surveyor of the port of Philadelphia, which he held four years, and then retired to private life.

Gen. Davis was sprinkled in infancy among the Presbyterians, but in early life he adopted the sentiments of the Baptists, which he held very decidedly, and worshipped God among them ever after, though he always regarded his old friends with affection. After he formally united with the church, which occurred somewhat late in life, his piety shone forth over his whole movements, and his soul, with all its wealth of intellect, influence, experience, and resources, was devoted to Christ.

He contributed most generously to sustain the church, to support foreign and home missions, and to aid every worthy cause; and universal sorrow burdened the entire community when the noble old man fell into the sleep of death. Twelve ministers of different communities were at his funeral, and throngs of persons from Bucks and neighboring counties made it the largest assemblage ever gathered in Bucks County to honor the memory of one of its deceased sons.

Gen. Davis was a patriot of the most large-hearted order, a gentleman of unusual refinement and courtesy, a Christian largely endowed with the grace of God, and a citizen loved and honored by all that knew him.

Davis, Rev. John, was born in England, Nov. 8, 1803; studied at Horton College; ordained at Portsea, Hants; became pastor of the First Baptist church at Yarmouth, Nova Scotia, in 1853; pastor at St. George, New Brunswick, in 1857; next year took charge of the Baptist church at Charlottetown, Prince Edward Island, where he died, Aug. 14, 1875. He was a good thinker, a sound theologian, a strong Christian, and an able preacher.

Davis, Rev. Nathan M., long an efficient minister of Ouachita Baptist Association, La., was born in Mississippi, 1809, and died May 19, 1880.

Davis, Rev. Noah, was born in Worcester Co., Md., July 28, 1802. Being blessed with eminently pious parents, his religious training was specially cared for. His early education was such as the common schools of the neighborhood afforded. At the age of sixteen he was engaged as a merchant's clerk in the city of Philadelphia. While here he experienced a change of heart, and was baptized, July 4, 1819, by Dr. Stoughton, in the Sansom Street church. He longed to preach the gospel; removed to Maryland, and united with the church in Salisbury, and was licensed to preach July 9, 1820, being then only eighteen years of age. In November of the same year he joined the literary and theological institution in Philadelphia, under the care of Dr. Stoughton and Prof. Chase, and when the Columbian College opened in 1821, he entered upon the course of study there. His zeal to do something for Christ led him to leave the college in 1823, and to enter upon the work of the ministry at once. While pursuing his studies Mr. Davis preached frequently, and did much good by visiting poor families in the neighborhood, and especially by laboring in a Sunday-school organized for the instruction of the colored people. Shortly after leaving college he married Miss Mary Young, a pious and accomplished lady, who greatly aided him in his ministerial work. For a while he labored in Accomac Co., Va., and then in Norfolk, and in both places he was eminently successful in building up the churches with which he labored, and in counteracting the withering influence of Antinomianism so prevalent in those regions. While in Norfolk Mr. Davis became greatly interested in the welfare of sailors, formed a society to benefit them, and compiled an excellent selection of hymns for their use. Indeed, he was ever active in all plans of Christian benevolence. It was owing to Mr. Davis's suggestions that the Baptist General Tract Society was organized. A meeting was called to consider the subject, and a tract society formed in Washington, D. C., Feb. 25, 1824, which was placed under the supervision of Mr. George Wood. The society, however, was soon removed to Philadelphia, and Mr. Davis was invited to accept its management, for which position he was peculiarly adapted, inasmuch as his mind was of that energetic cast fitted to grasp and control the far-reaching interests of a national institution, and his views and aims were lofty and noble. But he was not permitted to labor long in this congenial field. Always somewhat feeble in health, he was suddenly taken sick, and after a very brief illness, died July 15, 1830, when not quite twenty-eight years of age.

As a student, Mr. Davis was diligent, and his progress rapid. His mind was strong, clear, and energetic. As a preacher, he was more than usually interesting. He spoke with great fluency and sometimes with much power and eloquence, while his simple and pointed diction always won its way to the conscience. As a Christian, he burned with zeal for the Master's service, his prayer being, "Anywhere, or anyhow, only let me serve my generation according to thy will." He lived much in communion with God, and the strength which he thus acquired flowed out in acts of love upon all who came within the reach of his influence. He lived but a little while on the earth, but his faithful labors have been made a blessing to many.

Davis, Noah Knowles, LL.D., son of Noah and Mary Young Davis, was born in Philadelphia, Pa., May 15, 1830. His father died when he was yet an infant. His mother married Rev. John L. Dagg, at that time a pastor in the city, and the family shortly afterwards removed to Tuscaloosa, Ala. In 1843, Dr. Dagg became president of Mercer University, then located at Penfield, Ga. Here young Davis was baptized, and in 1849 graduated with high honor. He then spent several years in his native city in the study of chemistry, supporting himself by teaching, by service in an architect's office, and by editing two books, the "Model Architect" and the "Carpenter's Guide." In 1852 he was appointed to the chair of Natural Science in Howard College, Marion, Ala. In 1859 he became principal of the Judson Female Institute, at the same place, which, under his management, attained its highest success, having during the six years of his presidency an average annual attendance of 225 pupils. In 1868 he was elected president of Bethel College, Russellville, Ky. He reorganized this institution, enlarged its curriculum, raised the standard of scholarship, and thus placed the college on a level with other similar institutions in the country. In his position as president of Bethel College he had an opportunity to give special attention to metaphysical studies, for which he always entertained a preference. In 1873 he was elected to the chair of Moral Science in the University of Virginia, recently made vacant by the death of W. H. McGuffey, D.D., LL.D., who had long filled it with distinguished success. This high position he still holds. As a teacher he is enthusiastic and thorough, and has made his course of instruction second to that in no institution of America. He is a clear and forcible, but not a prolific, writer. Besides articles in reviews, he published in 1880 (by Harper & Bros.) "The Theory of Thought, a Treatise on Deductive Logic." This work, while based on the writings of Aristotle, and aiming to reproduce his logical system, is yet both original and profound. Every principle enumerated is verified by the author's own processes: he has only followed Aristotle as he followed the laws of thought. It is not too much to say that he has produced by far the most acute, original, and satisfactory treatise on logic ever written in this country, and that his book deserves a place among the best on the subject in the English language. Space will not allow even a bare statement of the many excellencies of this admirable work. From the studies he has pursued and the positions he has filled, it may easily be inferred that Dr. Davis is a man of varied and high attainments. While not disposed to seek society, he is of a genial and social disposition, conversing readily and well on a great variety of subjects. His religious convictions are strong, and his piety deep, genuine, and unobtrusive. During the sessions of the university he lectures on Sunday afternoons on select portions of the Bible, and his lectures are largely attended by professors, students, and others. His presence in the Associational meetings of his denomination is always welcome; and his addresses on public occasions are heard with attention and profit. His own words, in a letter to a friend, will best indicate his spirit, and close this sketch: " A homeless wanderer and sojourner, yet ever abundantly blessed by a kind Providence all through an ill-spent life, grant me, my Master, to serve thee better in the few years or days that are left."

Davis, Rev. Stephen, was born at Andover, England, Oct. 30, 1783, of parents who were members of the Little Wild Street church, then under the charge of Dr. Stennett. His first deep impressions of religious truth he ascribed to a sermon by Samuel Pearce, of Birmingham, which he heard when he was about thirteen, but he was converted under Dr. Rippon's ministry, and was baptized in 1802. His gifts for public service being recognized by the church at Devonshire Square, to which he had united himself on his baptism, he was ordained July 11, 1816. His first labors were given to the Baptist Irish Society, then recently formed to aid in reviving the ancient Baptist churches in Ireland, and to diffuse a knowledge of the gospel among the people. He preached in Dublin for several months with great acceptance, and was invited to remain permanently independent of the society, but he proceeded to Clonmel, and during seven years evangelized in the county of Tipperary with apostolic zeal. His ability as an advocate of the claims of the work being discovered, he was frequently summoned to serve the society as its deputation. In the years 1832–33 he visited the United States, and was received with great pleasure. He obtained upwards of £1000, and diffused valuable information concerning Irish questions. In 1837 he became the traveling agent of the society, in which laborious vocation he spent the remaining years of his life. He fell asleep in Jesus Feb. 3, 1856, aged seventy-two. His sons, Dr. George Henry Davis and Stephen J. Davis, were for many years esteemed ministers among the English Baptists.

Davis, Rev. Wm. H., was born in Jasper Co., Ga., Aug. 18, 1826, and died Sept. 18, 1879, at his residence in Hephzibah. A graduate of Mercer University in 1853, he settled in Burke County in 1858, and in the course of time became one of the most prominent and useful ministers of the Rehoboth Association. He was often its moderator, and pastor of a number of its churches, including Bark Camp, Hopeful, Bottsford, and Rocky Creek. He was a trustee of Hepzibah High School from its commencement, except when a teacher and co-principal of it, from 1868 to 1875 inclusive. From 1877 until his death he was a trustee of Mercer University. He was licensed in 1847, and ordained in 1853. Wm. H. Davis was a man of classical education, a citizen of untarnished reputation, a teacher of rare ability, a Christian of most exemplary deportment, a pastor faithful to his obligations, a minister of the gospel surpassed in pulpit power by but few, if any, in the State. He was clear in the presentation of Scriptural truth, logical in his reasoning, and pathetic in his appeals.

Mr. Davis was of a commanding appearance, about medium height, weighing over two hundred pounds, of dark complexion, pleasant expression of countenance, kind and genial in spirit, and of polished manners.

Davol, William Hale, M.D., was born in Warren, R. I., July 3, 1823. He was fitted for college by Rev. Dr. Stockbridge, at the time principal of the Warren Ladies' Seminary. He graduated at Brown University, studied medicine in his native town, and received the degree of M.D. from the Massachusetts Medical School in 1850. After having practised in Fall River, Mass., for a short time, he removed to Brooklyn, N. Y. Here, for eleven years, he was occupied with the duties of his profession, in which he was rising to more than ordinary distinction, when he was arrested in the midst of his prosperous career by the disease which deepened into a settled consumption; and after resorting to all methods which his own skill and that of his brother physicians suggested to avert the dreaded calamity, he returned to his old home in Warren to die. Dr. Davol had professed his faith in Christ in Brooklyn, and joined the Bridge Street Baptist church in that city, becoming one of its deacons, and living the life and setting the example of a consistent Christian. His death took place in Warren, June 12, 1863.

Dawson, Hon. George, was born in Falkirk, Scotland, March 14, 1813. At eleven years of age he entered a printing-office, and was thus led to adopt the profession of journalism. He has a varied and accurate knowledge of the classics, sciences, philosophy, and history. He has been a reporter and editor for forty-four years; for thirty-nine years he has been the proprietor and editor of the Albany *Evening Journal.* Under his management that paper has held a high position among the dailies of the country. He is an ardent friend of his political party, but his paper has never violated the laws of pure and honorable journalism. He has made it the advocate of freedom, intelligence among the masses, and especially of free schools. He was converted and baptized in Rochester in 1829, by Rev. Dr. C. C. Comstock, pastor of the First Baptist church, and he was anxious to accompany his son, Grover S. Comstock, the missionary, to Burmah, as printer, but circumstances prevented him. In 1830 he entered a mission Sunday-school as teacher, and for the fifty years intervening he has not ceased to labor in that field. He has been for many years a liberal supporter of our great Baptist enterprises, and a helper of his pastors in their work. He is a member of the Calvary Baptist church, and he was regarded as a safe adviser and as an efficient co-worker by Drs. Welch and

Bridgman. Aside from his editorial duties, he has published "The Pleasures of Angling," a work highly prized by the disciples of Isaak Walton. For six years he filled the office of postmaster in Albany, N. Y., and for seven years that of park commissioner.

Dawson, Rev. Samuel G., was born in Virginia in 1834, and in early childhood removed with his parents to Zanesville, O. At the age of fifteen he became a Christian, and for some years was engaged in commercial life. Was ordained in May, 1859, as pastor of the Valley church, near Marietta, O., where he remained until 1863, when he became a missionary pastor in East Toledo, under the appointment of the Ohio State Convention. This pastorate was very successful. In the eleven years he held this position two meeting-houses were built, and the church grew from a membership of 8 to 125.

On the death of the lamented J. B. Sackett, Mr. Dawson was elected corresponding secretary of the Ohio State Convention. He began this work in January, 1875, and continued in it until September 5, when he was removed by death. His loss was deeply felt throughout the entire State. Affable, earnest, and consecrated, he was the object of much affection, and his early departure was regarded as a severe calamity to the cause of Christ. He was a conspicuous instance of the power of Christ in the human heart and life.

Dawson, Rev. Thomas, died at Pendleton, S. C., June 29, 1880, in his ninety-first year. He was born in England in 1790, and held a lieutenant's commission in the British army at the time of the battle of Waterloo, though he was not engaged on that decisive field. He was baptized Oct. 1, 1815, and came to the United States in 1818; he was ordained in 1819. The Triennial Convention sent him as a missionary to the Cherokee Indians in North Carolina. When they were about to be removed he came to South Carolina, where he spent the rest of his life. He preached for twenty years among the mountains, and he was for some time a missionary to the colored people along the coast. He was unable to preach for several years before his death.

Day, Hon. Albert, was born in Westfield, Mass., Nov. 29, 1797; settled in Hartford, Conn., in 1822; became a successful merchant; was converted, and united with the First Baptist church; was the leader in the formation of the South Baptist church in 1834; was chosen deacon at its organization, and was a pillar in the church in every respect to the end of his life; noted for his numberless acts of private benevolence; a remarkable friend to the poor; his house always open to ministers; a generous contributor to benevolent objects; was lieutenant-governor of Connecticut in 1856; was trustee of Brown University, also trustee of Connecticut Literary Institution; superintendent of the South Baptist Sunday-school from its formation till laid aside by infirmities, and distinguished in this position and in founding mission schools in the city of Hartford; left two sons and a daughter; died Nov. 11, 1876, nearly seventy-nine years of age.

Day, Charles B., for many years at the head of the large wholesale and retail dry-goods firm of Day Bros. & Co., of Peoria, Ill., was born in Chesterfield, N. H., in 1821, where he joined the Baptist church in 1850. The next year he removed to Brimfield, Ill., where he found a small Baptist church, to which, to its great joy, he immediately joined himself, though assured that such an alliance would not be favorable to his business. In 1860 he removed to Peoria, and became a member of the First church there, and continues one of its main supporters. Though not a man of fluent speech, he has always been regular in his attendance upon church appointments, and has ever been liberal in his contributions. He has also paid considerable sums to Christian education, in which cause his interest is intelligent and constant. He is well known in the State as a successful business man, a firm Baptist, an uncompromising friend of temperance.

Day, Rev. George E., M.D., was born in Sheffield, New Brunswick, Sept. 9, 1833; converted and baptized when young, he entered Acadia College, September, 1851; commenced preaching in 1852; taught in the Baptist Seminary, Fredericton, New Brunswick, also in a collegiate institute in New York; practised medicine in St. John, New Brunswick; was ordained pastor of the First Baptist church, Yarmouth, Nova Scotia, June, 1868, where he still ministers with success.

Dr. Day is a good preacher, and has labored assiduously and successfully to promote unity and efficiency in home mission work in the Maritime Provinces.

Day, Henry, D.D., oldest son of Rev. Ambrose and Sarah Day, was born in Westfield, Mass., May, 1818. His father, an earnest Christian (ordained when near middle life at the persistent request of his brethren), spent his life mainly upon a farm, and reared a large family. Having efficient helpers in his children, he was usually away from home, supplying feeble churches within a radius of forty miles, though receiving for the service but a pittance. All the entire youth of the oldest son was spent in farm-work, alternated with study, only interrupted by a single winter's teaching. When nearing his majority, with an iron constitution and perfect health, with little more than an ordinary New England country boy's culture, but with habits of industry, with a fair preparation for college, and a profession of faith in Christ, he entered the Freshman class of Brown University, where he found little time or inclination for anything but legitimate work. His sense of justice to

HENRY DAY, D.D.

parents and brothers would not allow him to remain dependent upon the limited means or strained credit of his father. At the close of his second year, he became assistant in the Worcester County High School, and spent in it one of the most profitable years of his life. Returning to his college studies, with the incubus of debt mostly removed, he graduated with honor in the class of 1843. Among his classmates were Profs. Huntington, of Columbian University, Washington; James, of Lewisburg University, Pa.; Robinson P. Dunn, Professor of Belles-Lettres, and Albert Harkness, for these many years Professor of Greek in Brown University; and Dr. Lyman Jewett, the Nestor of our foreign missions. Mr. Day had long purposed to preach the gospel; but justice to his creditors demanded immediate work more productive; and he accepted the position of first teacher in the Providence High School, in which he spent three and a half years. He shrank from incurring further liabilities until the means of meeting them, earned by his personal efforts, had been secured. He obtained from the First Baptist church of Providence, of which he was for ten years a member, a license to preach, and accepted the professorship of Mathematics in Georgetown College, Ky., then under the presidency of Dr. Howard Malcom. Two years later, he accepted a pressing invitation to the professorship of Physical Science, and returned to New England, where he spent the year under eminent instructors at Brown and Harvard Universities, in prosecuting the studies of his prospective chair. At the close of the year, he returned to Kentucky, his expectation being (in addition to his collegiate work) to preach whenever opportunity might be offered. But he found Dr. Malcom just retiring from the college; and at the close of yet another year such changes had occurred in the political world and in public sentiment as convinced him that he might anticipate a larger success in another latitude, and, as he hoped, exclusively in the pulpit. He returned to the North, and at once entered upon ministerial work as pastor of the church in Ashland, Mass. A year later, the impaired health of his wife, together with the advice of many brethren, induced him to accept the chair of Natural Philosophy, Astronomy, and Civil Engineering in Brown University. Two and a half years later, he accepted the pastorate of the Broad Street church, Philadelphia. This removal, however, came too late to prolong the life of his wife; but it availed to return Mr. Day to his best loved work in the pulpit. Two years afterwards, the gravest indications of serious throat and lung difficulties compelled him, after five years of service, to retire from this greatly endeared pastorate, with but small hope of ever again preaching Jesus. After two years of rest and change, however, his health was so far restored that he ventured to return to the pulpit; and in it was allowed to accomplish what he has of late regarded as the main work of his life. The pastorate of the First Baptist church, Indianapolis (made vacant by the resignation of J. B. Simmons, D.D.), was strongly urged upon his acceptance, and, for the accomplishment, as he thought, of one specific work, was cordially accepted. But, as years passed, the health of the pastor became confirmed; and the work, which, according to his plan, was to have lasted for two or three years only, continued pleasantly to himself and profitably as it seemed to the church, until Mr. Day found himself by many years the senior pastor in the city (outside of the Romish Church). The church, which he had found destitute of a house and much depressed, became one of the strongest and most efficient in the Northwest, setting an example of intelligent enterprise and large benevolence.

After fifteen years of uninterrupted work, with many tokens of divine as well as human favor, and especially many evidences of the sustaining power of the grace of God, he retired from the long pastorate which he dearly loved, and which he had repeatedly refused to exchange for others in distant States. In 1861 he received from Denison University the degree of D.D. He still resides in Indianapolis. In the city and in the State, and through the denomination at large, he enjoys the confidence and esteem due his transparent integrity, his clear judgment, his unselfish devotion to the general good, and his elevated piety.

Day, Larkin B., was born in Chesterfield, N. H., in December, 1831. Removing to Bromfield, Ill., in 1852, he was there converted and baptized; but in 1854 his residence having been changed to Peoria, he became a member of the First church there, Rev. H. G. Weston being the pastor. Although as a member of the firm of Day Brothers he has found the claims of business pressing, he has always found time to give needed attention to higher concerns. As a friend and leader of the young people in the church, as a free and cheerful participant in prayer and social meetings, as an occasional occupant of the pulpit, as a lay preacher, and as an ardent friend of the temperance cause, alike in private and in official positions, Larkin B. Day is held in high appreciation by the citizens of Peoria and throughout the State. He is at present (1880) a member of the city council.

Day, Rev. Samuel Stearns, was born in Leeds County, Upper Canada, in 1808. He became a student in the Hamilton Literary and Theological Institution in 1831. He shortened his term of study in order to accept an appointment as a missionary, was ordained at Cortland, N. Y., Aug. 3, 1835, and on the 20th of the next month sailed from Boston to Calcutta, arriving there in February, 1836. He spent one year at Vizigapatam in the study of the language, and at the expiration of this period removed to Madras, in which place and its neighborhood he spent several years, doing faithfully his missionary work. He took up his residence in Nellore in 1840, spending five years of earnest labor, which was accompanied with a rich harvest. Under the exhausting labors of so many years his health failed, and he returned to this country to recruit his wasted energies. A little more than two years were spent at home, when, leaving wife and children, he returned to the field of his former toil, to work on for five years as a missionary of the cross among the Teloogoos. It is not for us to say how intimate may have been the connection between the seed-sowing of Mr. Day and his associates and the glorious ingathering, of which we have heard so much. The end of these five years of consecration to his great work found Mr. Day once more prostrated, and compelled him to leave the field now ripening for the harvest, and seek in this country if possible, once more, restoration to health. What he sought he did not find. Several months were passed not so much doing as suffering the will of God. Death at last came to his relief, and he departed this life in 1871.

As one of the founders of the Teloogoo mission Mr. Day will always fill a conspicuous place in the history of Baptist missions. His field was a large one. The Teloogoos number more than 14,000,000 of people, occupying a territory extending about 600 miles upon the sea-coast, and 400 miles into the interior of Hindostan. To carry on missionary work alone among a strange people, subjected to the caste system in all its iron rigidity, with but little to encourage them from the sympathy of fellow-laborers, Mr. and Mrs. Day worked for years. They laid foundations upon which others have erected the structure which now is so rapidly going up. It has justly been said of him that "as an example of consecration, giving himself and all that he had to the mission; of strong faith, wavering not in purpose, nor ceasing in effort when other and strong hearts failed and strong hands were turned to other fields, his name justly deserves an honorable place in the list of missionary heroes."

Dayton, Rev. A. C., M.D., was born at Plainfield, N. J., near New York City, Sept. 4, 1813. When twelve years old he united with the Presbyterian church. At sixteen, on account of weakness of the eyes, he was obliged to leave the village school, which up to this time he had regularly attended. Afterwards he taught school, and continued in this occupation for a year. He determined to become a physician, and although he continued to teach at intervals, it was a long time before he could read the amount that was necessary, his sight being poor. He, however, employed a boy to read to him, and by continual effort acquired the habit of remembering everything he heard or read, so that he improved very rapidly. Slowly he thus worked his way through the Medical College of New York City, and received his diploma in 1834, in the twenty-second year of his age. He began at once the practice of medicine, but soon found the duties too great for his feeble health, and so the profession was relinquished. He then went South, seeking for a more congenial climate, and for a while was engaged in lecturing on phrenology and temperance; and, stopping in the town of Shelbyville, Tenn., he formed an acquaintance with Miss Lucie Harrison, which resulted in their marriage. Mr. Dayton not long after set out for Florida, hoping that its balmy air would restore his already diseased lungs. After a residence in that State of about three years, he removed to Columbus, Miss., and from it to Vicksburg. About this time he became dissatisfied with his church relations, and in 1852, after years of careful and prayerful investigation, he became a Baptist. In September, 1852, on the next Sabbath after his baptism, he preached his first sermon. His theme was, "The love of God," and it was his last as well as his first sermon. It was delivered with great unction and power. Afterwards he accepted the agency of the Bible Board of the Southern Baptist Convention, then located at Nashville, Tenn., and as corresponding secretary he soon became widely known throughout the South. In July, 1855, he removed to Nashville, Tenn., where, in connection with his duties as secretary of the Bible Board, he became associate editor of the *Tennessee Baptist*, and the author of several books. The first, "Theodosia," a denominational work, was received with unusual favor and rapidly ran through several editions, whose popularity is now evinced by its being eagerly sought for on both sides of the Atlantic. This was followed by the "Infidel's Daughter," a work of great ability. Several other publications in the Sunday-school department soon followed, all of which met with the most favorable reception everywhere. The war coming on, Dr. Dayton removed with his family to Perry, Ga., where he temporarily assumed the presidency of Houston Female College. He was also actively engaged with his pen as an editorial contributor of the *Baptist Banner*, then published at Atlanta, and in preparing a religious encyclopædia, which he designed to be the crowning work of his life. But consumption cut short his labors, and he died calmly, June 11, 1865, at his home in Perry, Ga. He was buried in the cemetery of that city, where his remains peacefully rest. His family reside in Shelbyville, Tenn.

Deacons.—The word *diakonos* means an attendant, a servant, one who waits upon guests at a table. The first deacons were elected at Jerusalem by the church of that city at the request of the apostles, that they might minister to the necessities of the poor saints, or as Luke says, that they might "serve tables." In Acts vi. 1–6, there is an account of the institution of this benevolent office. No doubt inspiration suggested it to "the twelve"; and ever since in each true church on earth there has been a class of men whose special duty it is to provide for the wants of the poor of the body to which they belong, and to administer the funds obtained as they are needed. The Scriptural deacon is not a preacher of the gospel in virtue of his deaconship; he may preach occasionally, and so may a private member.

Deacons, with the pastor, are often the disciplinary committee of the church; they frequently give invaluable assistance to the minister, and from an extended experience with deacons, we are prepared to say that they render immense service to the churches.

"Likewise," says Paul, "must the deacons be grave, not double-tongued, not given to much wine, not greedy of filthy lucre, holding the mystery of the faith in a pure conscience," etc.—1 Tim. iii. 8, 13.

Dean, Hon. Benjamin W., was born in Grafton, Vt., in 1827. He united with the Baptist church in his native place when he was but eleven years of age. He graduated at Dartmouth College in the class of 1848, in which he took high rank as a scholar. The profession of law had special attractions for him, and he pursued his legal studies at the law school in Ballston Spa, N. Y. Having practised law for a short time in Elmira, N. Y., he returned to Vermont, was appointed register of probate for the district of Westminster, and took up his residence in Bellows Falls for a time, and then returned to his native place, Grafton. He held several public positions, among them the office of Secretary of State for four years. He was highly respected as a citizen and a Christian. His death occurred July 6, 1864.

Dean, Rev. Myron M., was born in 1813; was a graduate of Middlebury College and the Newton Theological Institution. His first pastorate was with the Third Baptist church of Providence, R. I., where he enjoyed a revival of religion, the results of which were an addition to the church of more than one hundred converts. He remained in Providence three years, when he accepted a call to Marblehead, Mass., where he continued seven years. Trouble with his eyes obliged him to lay aside all ministerial work for a time. When his health was somewhat recovered, he accepted an appointment as agent of the Publication Society, and afterwards of the American and Foreign Bible Society. Hoping to be able to continue his ministerial work, he accepted a call to the pastorate of the Warren, R. I., church. Again, and for the same reason, he was obliged to give up the ministry. The last years of his life were devoted to secular business. He died at Cambridge, Mass., March 30, 1861.

Dean, William, D.D., was born in Morrisville, N. Y., June 21, 1807. He was a graduate of the Hamilton Literary and Theological Institution, and was ordained in his native town, Morrisville, in June, 1834. He received an appointment to the foreign mission field, and sailed from Boston, July 3, 1834. His destination was Siam; he was to be associated with Rev. J. T. Jones in Bangkok, and to direct his special attention to the Chinese in that city. He had so far learned the dialect—the Tie Chin—that he was able to preach in Chinese the last Sabbath in August, 1835, to a congregation of 30 persons. Dr. Dean had the usual experiences of missionary life for several years. The Word was preached; converts made from time to time; labor interrupted occasionally by sickness, and then resumed after a time; and thus the Chinese department of the Siam mission could show signs of progress from year to year. In 1842, ill health compelled him to retire from the field for a season. When he resumed missionary work, with special reference to teaching the

Chinese, he commenced his labors in Hong-Kong, in October, 1842. In the spring of 1845 he returned to the United States, after an absence of eleven years. Having spent a year in this country, he resumed his work in Hong-Kong in the fall of 1847, and remained abroad until 1854, when he again visited America, remaining here until 1865, when he once more took up the work in Bangkok. At the end of his first year's work he writes, "I expect not to be happier in the present world than I have been during the present year." His labors had been nobly blessed, and have continued to be up to the present time. His record, up to the report of 1876, was six Chinese churches gathered, the superintendence of the building of four Chinese chapels, the ordination of three Chinese pastors, and the training of two others, and the baptism of 339 Chinese disciples, twelve of whom became preachers of the gospel. In April, 1876, Dr. Dean left Bangkok and again visited his native land, and spent six months in it, embarking at San Francisco the following November for his home in Siam. Forty-four years ago he consecrated himself to his work. No missionary has more thoroughly won the respect and affection of his brethren than the now venerable and beloved missionary of Bangkok, whom God has so honored as a faithful ambassador of the Lord Jesus Christ.

Deane, John H., Esq., was born in Canada; removed to the United States at an early age; prepared for college in the Brockport Collegiate Institute, N. Y., and commenced his course in the University of Rochester. In 1862, the civil war having commenced, he enlisted as a private in the 140th Regiment N. Y. Vols. During the battle of Gettysburg he was captured, and after heroically enduring the hardships of prison life, he was exchanged. He then entered the navy, and faithfully served his country till the close of the war. After the required course of study was completed he was admitted to the bar, and choosing the real estate branch of the profession, he has pursued it with great success. For several years he has been an active member of the Calvary Baptist church of New York, and a member of its board of trustees. He is one of the most generous supporters of the church and the benevolent institutions of the Baptists. He has contributed $100,000 for the endowment of Rochester University, and $25,000 for the endowment of the Rochester Theological Seminary. He has given largely for the New York Baptist Home, for home and foreign missions, and for the work of church extension, especially in the city of New York. He is too modest to publish his gifts; and he has undoubtedly made large donations unknown to the public.

Deane, Richard, Major-General, and General at Sea, was born at Guyting Poher, England, in 1610. He had charge of the artillery at the battle of Naseby, and gave much help in securing the great victory achieved over Charles I. at that place. He was so completely in the confidence of Cromwell that he was taken by him to a celebrated private meeting composed of a limited number of chosen friends to discuss "The Settlement of the Kingdom." He was a member of "The High Court of Justice" that tried and condemned King Charles. A month after the death of the king, Deane was appointed one of the "Generals at Sea." The two others were Edward Popham and the brave Robert Blake. Gen. Deane contributed largely to the crushing victory of Worcester, where he held the rank of major-general and commanded a division. Soon after this battle he and Gen. Lambert were appointed to the civil and military government of Scotland, and on the retirement of Lambert he was elevated to the supreme command of Scotland by land and sea. The general was killed in the naval battle off North Foreland, June 2, 1653.

His enemies admitted his great courage, and while his friends rejoiced in his bravery, they gloried in "his deep-rooted piety." The periodical literature of the day described him as "a valiant and godly gentleman."

A descendant of the "General at Sea," a London Episcopal clergyman, published in 1870 "The Life of Richard Deane," etc., in which he thrice expresses the conviction that he was a Baptist.* He quotes one of the lampoons of the Royalists of 1649, written on the occasion of his appointment as a general at sea, in which the sailors are recommended to "*new dip Deane*" by throwing him overboard. This, as the Rev. John Bathurst Deane rightly judges, had reference to the general's immersion as a Baptist.

He held our doctrine of soul liberty as no one in that day but a decided Baptist grasped it. His form of expressing liberty of conscience was striking,—" Neither *to compel, nor to be compelled in matters of conscience.*"†

Gen. Deane had a public funeral in Westminster Abbey. "The hearse was received at the west door of the Abbey by the great officers of state, and the coffin was borne by a select party of soldiers to Henry the Seventh's chapel, and deposited in one of the royal vaults."‡ The general-admiral was the first and the last Baptist in England who slept, even for a few years, in a royal vault. But he gave the memorable chapel a holier consecration than any regal slumberer within its walls. Oliver Cromwell, the greatest king, with or without a

---

* The Life of Richard Deane, etc., pp. 248, 289, 536.
† Idem, p. 536.
‡ Idem, p. 676.

Dearborn, O. J.—A native of Tioga Co., N. Y., where he was born Aug. 21, 1823. When about twelve years of age he was hopefully converted. He commenced a course of study at the Literary and Theological Institute at Hamilton, N. Y., having the work of the ministry in view. Owing to the failure of his health he abandoned his purpose to enter the ministry, and turned his attention to business. He came to Janesville, Wis., in 1847. The Baptist church being without a pastor, in July, 1849, Mr. Dearborn, at the earnest solicitation of the church, consented occasionally to supply the pulpit. In February, 1850, he gave up his business and devoted himself to preaching the gospel. The church very soon called him to the pastorate. He was ordained in December, 1850. He held this position until May, 1854, when he retired from the pulpit. For nearly twenty-five years he was identified with the Baptist church in Janesville. He was its senior deacon, chairman of its board of trustees, its Sabbath-school superintendent. He gave time and consecrated his powers to the welfare of that church with rare devotion and self-denial. He was connected with all the denominational movements in the State, and no layman contributed more of time and wise counsel and performed more hard work in the establishment of Baptist interests in Wisconsin than Mr. Dearborn. He died June 6, 1872, in the city of his adoption, aged forty-eight.

De Blois, Rev. Stephen W., A.M., was born in 1827, in Halifax, Nova Scotia; graduated from Acadia College in June, 1846; studied theology at Newton; was ordained pastor at Chester, Nova Scotia, Feb. 26, 1854. He became, in 1855, pastor of the First Horton church, the pioneer church of the Maritime Provinces, and he has the distinguished honor of being the third pastor of that community since its organization in October, 1778. He has occupied this field of usefulness for twenty-five years. Mr. De Blois is a governor of Acadia College, and the worthy secretary of its board.

Deckmann, Rev. E. I., a useful and esteemed German Baptist pastor, was born in July, 1832, in Copenhagen, capital of Denmark. Mr. Deckmann received his early training in the German city of Schleswig, where his father subsequently resided as an officer of the crown. In 1853, as a youth of twenty-one years, he emigrated to America, and was converted and baptized at Piqua, Miami Co., O., under the labors of Rev. I. W. Osborn, becoming a member of the Calvary Baptist church at Piqua. From 1853 to 1862 he studied at Denison University, Granville, O.; from 1862 to the close of the war he served as a volunteer in the U. S. army. From 1865 to 1866 he studied in the German department of Rochester Theological Semi-

RICHARD DEANE, MAJOR-GENERAL AND GENERAL AT SEA.

nary. Since that time he has labored successfully as missionary and pastor with the German churches of Davenport, Iowa, Pittsburgh, Pa., New Haven, Conn., and Baltimore, Md., where he is at present. Mr. Deckmann is a member of the German Missionary Committee of the Eastern Conference, is energetic and laborious, exerts a good influence in the churches, and enjoys general esteem. He has frequently presided as moderator over the annual meetings of the Eastern German Baptist Conference.

De Laney, Rev. James, one of the best-known ministers in Wisconsin, was born in Ballymore, County of Galway, Ireland, in February, 1804. Here and at Castlereagh he passed his early childhood and youth. His parents were Catholics and of Celtic blood. In the faith of this church he was educated with the most painstaking care. Relations on his father's side were Roman Catholic priests. A brother ministers at a Catholic altar, and he himself was designed by a devoted mother for the same office, but being left fatherless and motherless while quite young, that hope sank with his mother into the grave. At the age of twenty-one he left his native land forever, and went to the city of London to seek a livelihood. After much hardship and many disappointments, and a sore struggle with poverty, in a moment of desperation he enlisted in the English army. His destination was Madras, one of the principal points occupied by the East India Company, which he reached with 224 comrades in January, 1827. These early steps in his life are only links in a wonderful chain of providences. Long and rigid discipline had made him an expert as an artillerist, and in 1830 he was detailed, with the corps with which he was connected, on special artillery service to Maulmain, in Burmah. This brought him under the influence and preaching of the American missionaries Judson and Kincaid, then located at Maulmain. In Mr. De Laney's early life, after the death of his mother, he enjoyed for a time the society and instruction of some devout Catholics,—mostly women connected with an orphanage. These teachings he regarded as of the highest value, and although his mind was dark as midnight on all the vital doctrines of God's Word, and especially on his plan to save sinners through the death of Christ, these early lessons in regard to his relations to his Maker and his law, his own depravity and corrupt nature, had much to do in restraining him from open vice, and prepared the way for his receiving the gospel. The earnest preaching of Mr. Kincaid at once found its way to his heart. After some weeks of most pungent conviction for sin, he obtained a joyful hope in Christ, and was baptized by Mr. Kincaid, March 23, 1831, in the Saluen River, about twenty-five miles from the "Hopia Tree." Subsequently, in conversation with Dr. Judson, he spoke to him of the work of the Christian ministry ; pointed out to him the broad valley of the Mississippi in his own land, and its great need of home mission labor, and urged upon him the work of preparation. He at once, through the influence of the American missionaries, secured his release from the English army and came to America. He entered Hamilton Literary and Theological Institution, and took the usual ministerial course provided at that early day. Upon leaving the institution at Hamilton he was called to the pastorate of the Baptist church in Broadalbin, N. Y., where he was ordained Jan. 10, 1838, and married to Tirzah A. Platt, April 2, 1839. In 1839 he was called to the pastorate of the Baptist church at Ticonderoga, N. Y. After serving the churches as pastor at Granville and Kingsbury, N. Y., he came to Wisconsin in 1844, and settled with the Baptist church at East Troy. Here he remained seven years, gathering one of the largest and most useful churches in the Territory. He was pastor at Horicon, Sparta, Port Washington, and Whitewater, Wis. For six years he was exploring missionary of the American Baptist Home Mission Society in the State at large. He was the general missionary of the Wisconsin Baptist State Convention for three years. In addition to these labors, Mr. De Laney supplied the vacant pulpits of a score or more of feeble Baptist churches, and in the early history of the State made frequent tours of exploration to visit the outposts and frontiers to find and feed the scattered flock of God. Many of these tours made along the Wisconsin and Mississippi are as full of wild adventure, thrilling incident, and heroic endurance as those made by his revered friend and father, Kincaid, along the Irrawaddy and the Saluen. Mr. De Laney's name stands connected with almost every institution bearing the Baptist name in the State. He was one of the founders of the State Convention, he took an active part in establishing Wayland Academy, and he was prominent in forming nearly all the Associations in the State. During the war Mr. De Laney was chaplain of the 18th Regiment of Wis. Vols. He was present with his regiment at Pittsburg Landing.

It is not possible to give the results of Mr. De Laney's labors, as he has not preserved all the facts of his long and useful services to the Master. Frequent revivals have blessed his ministry. Strong men in the pulpit, able professors in institutions of learning, and pillars in the churches East and West were led to Christ through his preaching. Missionaries converted by his instrumentality have been sent back to Asia, where he himself found a Saviour. But chiefly in his missionary labors will Mr. De Laney be best known and longest remembered.

Delaune, Thomas, was born at Brini, three miles from Riggsdale, Ireland. His parents were Roman Catholics. In his boyhood he showed remarkable talents, which led the landlord of his parents to send him to the friary at Kilcrash to be educated. He made the best of the advantages placed at his disposal in this institution, and left it with a superior knowledge of the Greek and Latin languages. His acquisitions he continually increased until he became a scholar in the tongues we have named, with few, if any, superiors, and not many equals.

About sixteen he was converted through the instrumentality of Mr. Bampfield, but persecution drove him from Ireland to England. In London he commenced a school for teaching the higher branches of an English education and the Greek and Latin tongues. His efforts were attended by a goodly measure of success. He united with the Baptists, and became speedily one of the most valued men among our brethren in London. He rendered scholarly aid to the Rev. Benjamin Keach in preparing the most popular of his works for the press. But Mr. Delaune lived in an unfortunate time for a learned, able, and conscientious Baptist.

In 1683, Dr. Benjamin Calamy, rector of St. Laurence, Jewry, London, in a printed sermon, invited non-conformists to examine the ceremonies imposed by the Church of England, and enforced by penal laws; and called upon them modestly to propose their doubts, and meekly to hearken to and receive his instructions. The proposition was extremely "modest," especially the last part of it. Mr. Delaune accepted the invitation, and gave to the nation his "Plea for the Nonconformists." He was speedily apprehended, and committed to Wood-street-Compter, where he had a bench for his bed and two bricks for his pillow. From it he was taken to Newgate, where he was thrust among felons whose dreadful words and acts continually reminded him of the abyss.

In one of his letters to Dr. Calamy, written from the prison, he says, "There is nothing (in his book) against the king's majesty, nothing against the civil government, nothing against the peace of this monarchy, there asserted. The only dispute is about the original of rites and ceremonies, and some things, which, under a show of truths, though not righteously, are charged on doubting persons. What the court will do with me I know not. The will of the Supreme Father be done." The letter from which this is a quotation was written in Latin. In another letter he says to Calamy, "I had some thoughts that you would have performed the office of a divine (minister) in visiting me in my place of confinement, to argue me out of my doubts, which, your promised 'Scripture and reason,' not a Mittimus or Newgate, could easily do. To the former I can yield, to the latter it seems I must. This is a severe kind of logic, and it will probably dispute me out of this world, as it did Mr. Bampfield and Mr. Ralphson lately, who were my dear and excellent companions in trouble" (in prison).

Daniel De Foe says of Delaune's book, "'The Plea for Nonconformists' is perfect of itself. Never author left behind him a more finished piece. I believe the dispute is entirely ended. If any man ask what we can say why the Dissenters differ from the Church of England, and what they can plead for it, I can recommend no better reply than this. Let them answer, in short, Thomas Delaune, and desire the querist to read the book." "They who affirm that the Dissenters were never persecuted in England for their religion (for their disloyalty, it was falsely said) will do well to tell us what name we shall give to this man of merit, than whom few greater scholars, clearer heads, or greater masters of argument, ever graced the English nation. I am sorry to say he is one of nearly eight thousand Dissenters who perished in prison in the days of that merciful prince, Charles II." "The Plea for Nonconformists," in 1739, had passed through seventeen editions, without an answer, except the crushing and deadly reply given by Newgate jail.

Ivimey says that Sir George Jeffreys was the judge before whom Delaune was tried, the judicial Nero whose "Bloody Assizes" will make his memory infamous throughout all time. The sentence of the court required Delaune to pay a fine of one hundred marks, and to find reliable security for his good behavior for one year afterwards, and his book was to be burned with fire before the Royal Exchange in London. He could not pay the fine, and he never left the prison alive. His wife and two children were compelled to live with him in the jail through the exhaustion of his means; and the hardships and the poisonous atmosphere of Newgate, which killed Delaune in fifteen months, sent them to the grave before him.

Delavan.—This well-known village was founded in 1836 by two Baptist brothers,—Henry and Samuel Phoenix, of Perry, N. Y. Nearly all the early settlers were Baptists. The Baptist church, now the largest in the State, was founded in 1838. It is the mother of four other churches in the immediate vicinity. It has received into its fellowship in its forty years' history 1141 members,—611 by baptism. Its present membership is 425, and its present pastor, Rev. D. E. Halteman, has been settled eleven years.

Delaware, Baptists of.—The churches of this State may be divided into the early and later, or anti-mission and mission. The Welsh Tract church was the first in the colony. It was formed in

Wales, and settled in Delaware in 1703. Their principles soon spread. In 1778, Rev. Elijah Baker, and in 1779, Rev. Philip Hughes, came from Virginia, preaching together the Word. There was a great quickening among the Baptists, and many were converted and baptized, and several churches were constituted. In this work these ministers received the hearty co-operation of the Baptist pastors and churches.

The first Baptist church in Wilmington was formed mainly through the efforts of Thomas Ainger, a Presbyterian, from Philadelphia, who became eventually a Baptist, and the pastor of the church. His wife was a Baptist. He maintained family worship, and Messrs. Fleeson and Boggs, Baptist ministers, preached by his invitation in his house. Rev. Philip Hughes preached in the town school-house and in the Presbyterian church. Several were baptized, and finally sixteen were constituted into a church. Their meeting-house still stands on King Street. The following is a list of the early churches, with the date of organization: Welsh Tract, New Castle County, 1701; Sounds, Sussex County, 1779; Broadcreek, Sussex County, 1781; Mount Moriah, Kent County, 1781; Brynzion, Kent County, 1781; Mispillion, Kent County, 1783; Gravelleybranch, Sussex County, 1785; First Wilmington, 1785; Bethel, New Castle County, 1786. Bethel, in Sussex County, Littlecreek, and Millsborough were of more recent date, and, with the Sounds and Broadcreek churches, belonged to the Salisbury Association, which was formed in 1782, composed mostly of churches in Maryland, and has since become anti-mission. The other churches were at first connected with the Philadelphia Association, but withdrew, with good feeling on both sides, to form the Delaware Association, which was organized in 1795. It was soon joined by several churches in Pennsylvania. Since 1856 it has taken the name of the Delaware *Old-School* Baptist Association. In 1801 it was composed of 5 churches, with 293 members; in 1825, of 9 churches, with 596 members; and in 1879, of 7 churches, with 197 members. Of the churches in this State belonging to the Delaware and the Salisbury Associations, six remain, with a total membership of 200. The Sounds, Mispillion, Gravelleybranch, Bethel, in New Castle County; Bethel, in Sussex County; and the Millsborough churches have ceased to exist. The minutes of the Delaware Association show that at one time both missions and missionary societies were approved of by that body. The Baptist Publication (then Tract) and the Home and Foreign Mission Societies and their work met with favor in the churches. It was not until after 1830 that a change took place in the Delaware Association and in the churches connected with it. They became anti-mission and anti-effort, which change led to the formation of the Second church, Wilmington, upon an avowed missionary basis. Among the many Baptist ministers of this period who were born, or converted, or ordained, or employed in the State were Rev. Enoch Morgan, Rev. John Davis, Rev. Jenkin Jones, Rev. David Jones, A.M., Rev. Abel Morgan, A.M., Rev. Morgan Edwards, A.M., Rev. Thomas J. Kitts, Rev. Joseph H. Kennard, D.D., and Rev. Daniel Dodge. The following is a list of the later churches, with the date of organization: Second, Wilmington, 1835; Dover, 1852; German, Wilmington, 1856; Delaware Avenue, Wilmington, 1865; Plymouth, 1867; Lincoln, 1869; Zion, Vernon, 1871; Wyoming, 1872; Magnolia, 1873; Milford, 1873; Elm Street, Wilmington, 1873; Shiloh (African) Wilmington, 1876; New Castle, 1876; Bethany, 1878. The old First was resuscitated for a while, but it and the Elm Street disbanded to form the Bethany and occupy the Elm Street chapel. A few old members hold on at King Street. The Lincoln church disbanded to form the Milford, and the Plymouth to form the Magnolia. In 1869 the Wyoming Institute was purchased (see article). A Baptist City Mission was formed in 1870 among the Wilmington churches, which bought a lot, built thereon the Elm Street chapel, which property they deeded to the Bethany church. In 1878 the Delaware Baptist Union was formed in the Second church, Wilmington. It is composed of eight churches in Delaware Co., Pa., and eleven in Delaware State. The objects of the "Union" are the promotion of fraternity among the churches composing it and the evangelization of the field. The Baptist churches not only of Delaware (except the Old School), but also those of the "Union," are connected with the Philadelphia Association.

The number of missionary Baptist churches in the State is 11, with a membership of 1924, and 2183 teachers and scholars in 14 Sabbath-schools. The benevolent contributions of the churches for 1879, for work at home and abroad, amounted to over $20,000.

Delke, James A., LL.D.—Prof. Delke was born in Sussex Co., Va., in 1821; was educated at Wake Forest and Chapel Hill, having graduated at the latter college in 1841; has taught in Virginia, Tennessee, and North Carolina, and for fifteen years has been Professor of Mathematics, Natural Science, and Belles-Letters at Murfreesborough Institute, N. C.

Prof. Delke received the degree of A.M. from Madison University, N. Y., and that of LL.D. from Southwestern University, Jackson, Tenn. He regards it as the chief boon of his life that he has always taken a lively interest in Sabbath-schools.

Dell, Rev. William, A.M., was educated at the University of Cambridge, England, and after receiving Episcopal ordination he became a clergyman of the Established Church. In the great awakening in England in the seventeenth century he adopted our views on the mode and subjects of baptism, and on the non-coercive authority of a gospel church.

He denounced all compulsion in matters of religion, and wrote a book against uniformity in religion secured by the persuasive force of legal enactments. This work stirred up the unhallowed wrath of the English Presbyterians, who were straining their powers to the utmost to make their church sole mistress of the consciences of her foes.

In 1645 he was appointed a chaplain in the army; in this position he attended constantly on Sir Thomas Fairfax, and preached at headquarters, where he exerted a powerful influence with leading men against Presbyterian legal intolerance, and in favor of religious liberty. Richard Baxter became a chaplain in the army to counteract the teachings of Mr. Dell and others, and he tried to induce some of his Presbyterian brethren to follow his example. Various efforts were employed to injure the character of Mr. Dell, by which he was subjected to much annoyance, but they were all failures.

On Nov. 25, 1646, he was appointed to preach before the House of Commons on the occasion of a public fast. His subject was *Reformation*, and in treating this popular topic he showed the folly and wickedness of trying to secure it by persecution. To many of his hearers this was extremely offensive, as the preacher well knew, but his conscience compelled him to tell these legislators some wholesome truths. The Rev. Mr. Love, a Presbyterian minister, was one of his hearers in the morning, and the preacher before the same body in the afternoon. Instead of delivering the sermon he had prepared for the occasion, he felt compelled to try and remove the deep impression left by the sermon of Mr. Dell. With much warmth and "many unhandsome reflections" he justified the punishment of heretics, and the authority of government to impose articles of faith and forms of worship. The two discourses created a sensation.

Mr. Dell was endowed with great mental powers, and he was possessed of extensive learning. In 1649 he was made master of Caius College, Cambridge, one of the numerous colleges constituting the University of Cambridge. He lost the rectory of Yeldon and the presidency of Caius College through his fidelity to Baptist principles by the Act of Uniformity in 1662. He was the author of several publications, a selection from which was issued in a handsome octavo volume in 1773.

De Mill, Rev. Elisha Budd, was born in St. John, New Brunswick, April 7, 1829. His college studies were pursued in part at Acadia College, Nova Scotia, and in part at Brown University. Two years were spent by him—1851-53—at the Newton Theological Institution. He was ordained as a minister of the gospel July 1, 1853, and became pastor of the Baptist church at Amherst, Nova Scotia. Here he remained not far from four years,—1853-57. On resigning his pastorate in Amherst he returned to his native city, and was city missionary for two years,—1857-59. Closing his connection with the society in whose service he had been during this period, he accepted a call to become the pastor of the Leinster Street Baptist church in St. John. This position he held during the remainder of his life. In connection with his ministerial duties he also discharged those of editor of the *Christian Watchman*, a religious paper, published at St. John. Mr. De Mill received the degree of M.A. from Acadia College in 1849, and from Brown University in 1853. He died at St. John, New Brunswick, in 1863. He was a preacher of ability, and a Christian without blame.

De Mill, Nathan S., an enterprising merchant of St. John, New Brunswick; he was baptized and joined Germain Street Baptist church in that city about 1842; was deacon of Brussels Street church and subsequently also of Leinster Street church; was a liberal friend of Acadia College, and a strong supporter of temperance and prohibition, and possessed sterling integrity. Died Dec. 26, 1864, aged sixty years.

Denison, Rev. Albert Edgar, son of William and Betsey Denison, was born in Saybrook, Conn., Sept. 12, 1812; his maternal grandfather was Rev. Eliphalet Lester, pastor of First Baptist church in Saybrook; was converted at the age of fifteen; baptized by Rev. Russell Jennings; united with First Baptist church of Saybrook (now Winthrop); studied at Connecticut Literary Institution, Suffield; graduated from Brown University in 1842; taught school in Chester, Conn., and preached in Saybrook (now Winthrop); ordained in his native town in 1843, and remained one year; in 1844 settled with the Baptist church in Wallingford, Conn., and labored successfully for seven years; in 1851 settled with the Baptist church in Clinton, Conn., and continued pastor with happy results for fifteen years; became for nearly three years agent for the American Baptist Home Mission Society; preached nearly three years for the Baptist church in Lyme; in 1871 settled with the Baptist church in Plainville, Conn., and remained until health failed in 1878; still resides there; renders occasional services to weak churches; has had a prosperous ministry; devout, scholarly, faithful, honored; very active in educational interests and all true reforms; served on school boards from 1844 to 1877.

Denison, Rev. Erastus, son of Frederick and Hannah (Fish) Denison, was born in Stonington, Conn., Dec. 22, 1791; baptized by Rev. John G. Wightman in 1814; began preaching in 1824; ordained by First Baptist church in Groton in 1826; labored as an evangelist; settled with Third Baptist church in Groton in 1831, and remained fifteen years; subsequent settlements and engagements: in Waterford four years; in North Lyme one year; in North Stonington three years; at East Marion, Long Island; on Martha's Vineyard; Charlestown and Hopkinton, R. I.; Montville, New London, East Lyme, and Stonington; preached 3878 sermons, baptized 311 persons. He was a pure man, devoted to the Master's work; died in Groton, Sept. 20, 1866, in his seventy-fifth year.

Denison, Rev. Frederic, son of Isaac and Levina (Fish) Denison, was born in Stonington, Conn.,

REV. FREDERIC DENISON.

Sept. 28, 1819; studied in Bacon Academy and the Connecticut Literary Institution; graduated at Brown University in 1847; in the same year settled with First Baptist church in Westerly, R. I., and was ordained; served that church, in two pastorates, for fifteen years; settled with Central Baptist church in Norwich, Conn., and remained five years; settled with Central Falls Baptist church in Rhode Island; served as chaplain in the army for three years, with 1st R. I. Cavalry and 3d R. I. Heavy Artillery; settled again in Westerly, then in New Haven, Conn., then in Woonsocket, R. I., and lastly in Providence, R. I.; baptized over four hundred persons; favored with special revivals; author of the following bound volumes: " The Supper Institution," " The Sabbath Institution," " The Baptists and their Principles in Norwich, Connecticut," " The Evangelist, or Life and Labors of Rev. Jabez S. Swan," " History of the First Rhode Island Cavalry," " Westerly and its Witnesses for Two Hundred and Fifty Years," " Picturesque Narragansett, Sea and Shore," " Illustrated New Bedford, Martha's Vineyard, and Nantucket," " History of the Third Rhode Island Heavy Artillery Regiment," " Picturesque Rhode Island," also of sermons and addresses; and of poems and articles numberless in secular and religious periodicals; a corresponding member of Rhode Island Historical Society, and Wisconsin Historical Society; member of Soldiers' and Sailors' Historical Society of Rhode Island; the first Baptist Historical Registrar of Rhode Island.

Denison, Deacon John Ledyard, A.M., son of Isaac and Levina (Fish) Denison, was born in Stonington, Conn., Sept. 19, 1826; studied at Connecticut Literary Institution and Worcester Academy; united with Third Baptist church in Groton, Conn., in 1839; became a successful teacher; established the Mystic River Academy; settled in Norwich, Conn., in 1855; received the degree of Master of Arts from Brown University in 1855; published " Pictorial History of the Wars of the United States," edited " Illustrated New World," in German, " Illustrated History of the New World," in English, and minor works; secretary and treasurer of the Henry Bill Publishing Company; superintendent of Central Baptist Sunday-school for about twenty-five years; very active with voice and pen in the religious affairs of the State, and in temperance reform; president of Connecticut Baptist Education Society, and a useful lay preacher.

Denison University is situated in the town of Granville, Licking Co., O., and was established by vote of the Ohio Baptist Education Society, May, 1831. Intended originally as a manual-labor school, it was at first located on a farm near Granville, and incorporated in 1832, under the name of Granville Literary and Theological Institution. This name was changed in 1845 to Granville College, and the manual-labor feature set aside. In 1856 it was removed from the farm to a beautiful hill site overlooking the town, and the name again changed to Denison University, in honor of one of its benefactors.

The first president was Prof. John Pratt, who took charge of the institution in 1831, and laid well the foundations of its success. He was succeeded, in 1837, by Rev. Jonathan Going, D.D.; in 1847, by Rev. Silas Bailey, D.D.; in 1853, by Rev. Jeremiah Hall, D.D.; in 1863, by Rev. Samson Talbot, D.D.; in 1874, by Rev. E. Benjamin Andrews; and in 1879, by Rev. A. Owen, D.D. The property of the university consists of a campus of twenty-four acres, nearly half of which is covered with a grove of forest-trees. The buildings are capable of accommodating 180 students, and are well provided with dormitories, study rooms, society halls, etc. Within the past two years a fine library building, called Doane Hall, after its donor, W. H. Doane, of Cincinnati, has been erected. The library numbers 12,000 volumes. The property, with its buildings and their contents, is estimated to be worth $105,000, and the productive endowment is $191,775, making a total of $296,775.

finally settled with the First Baptist church in Waterford; active, energetic, strong in faith, wise in council, beloved by all; one to whom Connecticut is under large obligations; died in Waterford, Oct. 26, 1877, aged seventy-one years; buried in Winthrop.

Denk, Hans, was a mystical Anabaptist who occupied an influential place among the Reformers of the sixteenth century. We first find him a young master of arts in Basle in 1522, and an intimate friend of the celebrated Œcolampadius. In 1523 he moved to Nüremberg and became rector of a

DENISON UNIVERSITY, GRANVILLE, OHIO.

The faculty of Denison consists of a president and nine professors. There is a regular classical course of study running through four years. There is also a scientific course, omitting the Greek and Latin languages, and a preparatory course of two years. The college has a high reputation. There are usually from 150 to 200 students in attendance in all the departments.

Denison, Rev. William, son of William and Betsey (Lester) Denison, was born in Saybrook, Conn., in June, 1806; converted when about twenty years of age; united with First Baptist church in Saybrook, March 25, 1827, being baptized by Rev. Joseph Glazier; licensed Dec. 20, 1828; preached a few years in Haddam; pastor for many years of the Baptist church in Easton; was appointed a State missionary in connection with Rev. N. E. Shailer, and nobly served for many years; assisted in improving meeting-houses; in Winthrop, where he resided, he established an institute for young ladies; meanwhile he supplied the First Baptist church;

school, where he met Münzer and Haetzer and adopted mystical and Anabaptist views. Driven from Nüremberg he went first to St. Gall, and afterwards to Augsburg, where by unceasing but cautious activity he contributed largely to make it a stronghold of Anabaptism. The publication of his book on "The Law of God" led to his expulsion in 1526. He next went to Strasburg, where he and Haetzer undertook the translation of the Hebrew Bible. Their version of the prophets was highly meritorious.

Driven from Strasburg, Denk labored in various places until 1527, when he died of the pest at Basle, in the house of his old friend, Œcolampadius. In the preface of his book already mentioned he says, "Whoever wishes to be of Christ must walk in the way that Christ has trodden, thus will he come to the habitation of God; he who does not walk in this way will err to all eternity." This sentiment is the cardinal doctrine which governs Baptists in regard to their practice everywhere, and which controlled them during their whole history.

In "An Exposition of Some Points of Belief," which he wrote, he says, "It grieves me to the heart that I must stand in lack of unity with many whom I cannot consider as other than my brethren, for they pray to the God to whom I offer supplication; they honor the Father whom I honor: the Father who has sent his Son into the world as a Saviour. Therefore, if God will, I will not make of my brother an adversary, and of my Father a judge, but I will reconcile myself with all my adversaries while I am in the way with them. Hereupon I beg them for God's sake to pardon me whatever I have, without my knowledge, done against them; and to promise besides to lift from me, and never to avenge any mischief, injury, or disgrace that may be laid up against me by them." Denk differed from the Reformers because truth compelled him. He was a Baptist because he could not help it, and like Baptists now, he was full of love for the children of God with whom he differed.

Denk was very popular in Augsburg. Urbanus Rhegius, a minister in that city while Denk resided in it, says of his influence, "It increased like a cancer, to the grievous injury of many souls." Throngs attended Baptist worship, the noblest and oldest families joined the movement, and some of them only left it for the martyr's crown. Before the truths and discourses of Hans Denk, the public sentiment of Augsburg seemed for a time to bow.

But his principles traveled "on the Rhine, in Switzerland, in Franconia, in Suabia, even as far as Moravia," and had his life been spared, and the favor of God still continued, the Reformation of Luther might have been a complete purification of Christianity.

The opinions of Denk in some respects differed from ours; his theology may be characterized as Origenistic; but he was largely with us; and he was a powerful advocate of the truth; "friend and foe rightly considered that his death was the severest blow" that the Baptist communities had received till 1527.

His knowledge of the Scriptures was profound, his theological information extensive, his learning great, his reputation as an author wide-spread, and his piety unquestioned. In him "his brethren had a prize that would have been an ornament to any party," and he became so easily and rapidly their chief that he was sometimes called their pope.

Denne, Rev. Henry, distinguished himself by his sermons, discussions, writings, sufferings, and heroism for the truth. Like many Pedobaptists he was designed for the ministry from childhood without any reference to conversion. He received his education at the University of Cambridge, and about 1630, he was ordained by the bishop of St. Davids.

He held the living of Pyrton in Hertfordshire for ten years, after receiving episcopal orders, and for his industry and earnestness in preaching he was highly esteemed by his people.

In 1641 he was appointed to preach the visitation sermon at Baldock to the clergy and gentry. The meeting was numerous and influential. The sermon was largely taken up with an exposure of the sin of persecution, the vices of the ministry, and the corruptions in doctrine and worship of the Established Church. Mr. Denne in his sermon showed no mercy to the pride, covetousness, pluralities, and non-residence of the clergy. The sermon produced a sensation among the hearers; the clergymen could scarcely keep their seats while their well-known offenses were set in order before them, and Mr. Denne preserved a good conscience and secured firm friends and lively enemies by his faithfulness. In studying the Scriptures he found that infant baptism was not enjoined by the Saviour, and in extending his researches he failed to discover it in the records of the first two centuries, and he felt bound to be baptized. He was immersed in London about 1643 by Mr. Lamb, pastor of the church in Bell Alley, Coleman Street, of which he became a member. Mr. Denne was regarded in his day as a man of extraordinary talents, and as an eminently fit person to win the perishing from iniquity. Like the apostles he journeyed much, and he preached the truth in many parts of England. He proclaimed the blessed gospel in London, in Cambridgeshire, in Lincolnshire, in Kent, and in other places, and he baptized many converts and founded churches wherever he went. This led to his arrest on several occasions, but he was not detained in prison for any considerable period by the efforts of his enemies.

Discouraged by persecutions and legal hindrances to his work as a minister, he entered the army as a cornet, in which his courage and intelligence soon made him a general favorite. He was in one of the twelve troops that mutinied at Burford, in Oxfordshire, and he and three others were condemned to death; the others were executed, but Cornet Denne when called out was pardoned. He came forward " expecting death with great composure of spirit," but he was spared. The troops thought that after the death of Charles I. there should be "liberty and a free commonwealth," but they were disappointed. And as twelve regiments were ordered for service in Ireland, under Cromwell, there was a revolt among the troops at Burford. Mr. Denne bitterly regretted the part he had taken in this transaction, and gave himself more heartily than ever to the spread of the gospel.

There was a lady in London greatly exercised on

the question, "Whether infant baptism were of God or not?" She desired that a friendly conference should be held in her presence that her mind might be relieved from doubts about her duty in reference to baptism. It was arranged that Mr. Denne and Dr. Gunning, subsequently bishop, first of Ely and then of Chichester, should present their respective views in St. Clement Dane's church, London, on the 19th and 26th of November, 1658. The discussion created so much interest that thousands of people flocked to hear it, and for a time it was an absorbing topic of conversation throughout all circles of society. During the second day Dr. Gunning took advantage of a tumultuous interruption in the church to decline further controversy, showing that he had an antagonist with whose blows he was wearied. The lady decided against the future bishop, and she was immersed on the 1st of December, by Mr. Denne.

Mr. Denne was the author of six works, which were widely circulated and highly esteemed. He died about 1661, and upon his grave a clergyman, one of his friends, put this epitaph:

"To tell his wisdom, learning, goodness unto men
I need say no more, but here lies Henry Denne."

He was a scholarly man, untiring in serving Jesus, of fine talents, and of a blameless life.

Denson, Rev. William, long an active and efficient Baptist minister east of Pearl River, in Mississippi, was born in Tennessee about 1805, but spent his boyhood in Alabama. He removed to Rankin Co., Miss., about 1820, and soon after began to preach. At first his education was defective, but by dint of close application he overcame these deficiencies and became one of the most influential preachers in his part of the State. He labored chiefly in the counties of Rankin, Madison, Scott, and Leake. Few men in the State have impressed themselves more upon the denomination than William Denson. He was many years moderator of his Association. He was accidentally thrown from his buggy and killed while attending a protracted meeting, in 1875.

Denton, Rev. Isaac, a distinguished pioneer preacher of Southeastern Kentucky, of French extraction, was born in Caswell Co., N. C., in September, 1768. He was ordained a Baptist minister, and preached several years in East Tennessee. He removed to Clinton Co., Ky., in 1798, and gathered Otter Creek, Beaver Creek, Clear Creek, and others of the first churches in this region of the State. After a long and useful ministry, he died Jan. 26, 1848.

Depravity, Total. See ORIGINAL SIN.

Desbrisay, James, is a retired merchant of Charlottetown, Prince Edward Island, who has taken a very active part for many years in promoting the progress of the Baptist denomination on that island, and in sustaining the missionary and educational institutions of the Baptists in the Maritime Provinces.

Des Moines, University of, Iowa, was founded in 1865. It originated in a conviction in the minds of many Iowa Baptists that they ought to have an institution of learning centrally located, and in one of the populous cities of the State. Des Moines had recently become the capital of Iowa, and by constitutional enactment was to remain the seat of government, and already had a population of about 10,000. It was near the centre of the State, growing steadily in population and mercantile importance, and was evidently to become the largest city in the State, the centre of great commercial, political, and moral influence. A building and campus, designed and partially prepared for educational purposes, were offered on reasonable terms. This property (which is beautifully located on an eminence overlooking the city, the rivers, the valley, and prominently seen from all approaches of the city) seemed then a little remote from the centre of population, but it is now surrounded by choice private residences, which are reaching far out beyond it.

The school was started in 1866. Limited resources have retarded the work, but there has been a gradual growth, until there is now a full college curriculum, classical and scientific, and also a ladies' course, occupying one year less than the full college course. Both sexes are equally admitted to all advantages and honors. Several classes, composed of both sexes, have already graduated from full courses of study.

The property of the university is valued at $50,000, and the endowment fund at $23,000. Located in the metropolis of the State, which has a present population of 23,000, a central point of railroads, in the midst of a vast coal-field, and in one of the best agricultural districts of the United States, with a healthful climate, there is no reason why, with earnest efforts, the university may not in the future rise to the position of one of the best seats of learning in the State.

J. A. Nash, D.D., who has been largely identified with the entire history of this university, is its present president, and he is assisted by a sufficient faculty of experienced teachers.

Devan, Thomas T., M.D., was born in New York City, July 31, 1809; graduated from Columbia College in that city in 1828, and later, at the College of Physicians and Surgeons. Early in life he became connected with the First Baptist church in New York, under the ministry of Dr. Cone, and he was a very influential helper. In 1844 he and his admirable wife, the daughter of David Hale, editor of the *Journal of Commerce*, went as missionaries to China. Mrs. Devan died within two years; the doctor's health failed so as to interfere with his preaching; he was transferred to the mission in France, where he remained through the stirring period from 1848 to 1853, when he returned home. Dr. Devan left a large remunerative practice to enter the ministry, and since his return he has continued to preach. He was army chaplain during the war; has been pastor at Nyack, N. Y., and West Hoboken, N. J.; has frequently supplied the churches of New Brunswick, where he resides, and is spending the evening of life doing good as he has opportunity, and beloved by his brethren.

Devin, Rev. R. I., of Huguenot descent, was born in Henry Co., Va., Aug. 14, 1822; baptized by Rev. John D. Handkins, May 18, 1839; educated at Rocky Spring Academy; ordained Aug. 11, 1845; labored in 1846–47 as a missionary of the North Carolina Baptist State Convention; settled in Oxford as pastor in 1848, and has spent most of a long and useful life in Granville County, where he has been instrumental in organizing a number of strong churches, and has baptized some 1600 or 1800 persons. He has been pastor of Mountain Creek church fifteen years, and of Grassy Creek church *twenty-nine* years. He has recently published a valuable and interesting history of this venerable church.

De Votie, J. H., D.D., was born in Oneida Co., N. Y., Sept. 24, 1813. He was baptized on

J. H. DE VOTIE, D.D.

the morning of Sabbath, Dec. 4, 1831, at Savannah, Ga., by Rev. H. C. Wyer. The First Baptist church of Savannah licensed him to preach the gospel on the 21st of October, 1832, immediately after which he pursued a course of study in theology at Furman Theological Seminary, located at High Hills of Santee, Sumter District, S. C., under the instruction of Jesse Hartwell, D.D., and Samuel Furman, D.D. He was ordained by Dr. Jesse Hartwell and Dr. Joseph B. Cook, at Camden, S. C., in 1833, and in this place he served his first pastorate of two years, while a student at the seminary.

He moved thence to Montgomery, Ala., preaching there one year; became pastor of the Tuscaloosa church, which he served four years; was then called to the charge of the Marion, Ala., church, remaining fourteen years; serving one year as financial secretary of the Domestic and Indian Mission Board of the Southern Baptist Convention, of which he was also president for a number of years. In 1856 he was called to Columbus, Ga., where he lived fourteen years, resigning the pastorship in 1870, and taking charge of the Griffin, Ga., church, which position he retained for two years,—1871 and 1872. He still resides in Griffin, although he has for several years been the able and efficient corresponding secretary of the State Mission Board of the Georgia Baptist Convention. Under his management that board has been very successful.

A strong Baptist, he never shuns to declare the whole counsel of God, yet Pedobaptists love and respect him. As a money-solicitor at our Conventions he has few equals, and his exquisite tact and inimitable humor make him a welcome and useful member of our religious assemblies. In person he is heavily built, rather beneath the average height, and dignified and deliberate in his movements.

No man possesses in a greater measure the love and confidence of his Baptist brethren, and at the same time the respect and esteem of other denominations, and of the community at large. His sermons are full of feeling, and are of that high order which comes from men of the loftiest intellect, culture, and sensibility, and while they affect the hearts of the humblest believers, they excite the admiration of the most fastidious and cultivated.

At the beginning of the war he served for a brief time on the Georgia coast as voluntary chaplain, declining from conscientious motives to receive pay. Though laboring in the ministry for more than forty years, he has not been without a field of labor for as much as two months at a time, having baptized not fewer than 1500 professed converts.

If there is any credit to be attached to the removal of Mercer University from Penfield, he is entitled to his share of it, for he offered to the board of trustees, of which he is a member, the first set of resolutions on that subject.

His influence in Georgia, as it was in Alabama, has always been commanding, resulting in a large measure from his great good sense, sincere piety, consistent life, ardent labors, and exalted intellectual powers. In his long experience he has been tried by many and deep afflictions, but all the while a spirit of sweet and pious resignation has thrown a mellow radiance around his life and character.

Dexter, Henry V., D.D., was born in Wayne, Me., April 3, 1815. He was a graduate of Waterville College in the class of 1842, and of the Newton Theological Institution in the class of 1845. His ordination took place in Brookline, Mass., Sept. 7, 1845, and he became pastor of the Second Baptist church in Calais, Me., where he remained nine years, and then removed to Augusta, Me. His connection with the Augusta church continued for six years, when, in 1860, he returned to Calais, and for the second time became pastor of the church with which he began his ministry, remaining with it for another period of nine years. Subsequently he was pastor of the church in Kennebunkport, Me., and of the church in Baldwinsville, Mass. Colby University, of which institution he is a trustee, conferred on Mr. Dexter the degree of Doctor of Divinity in 1870.

Dexter, Isaac, was born in 1751, at Dartmouth, Mass.; converted in Liverpool, Nova Scotia, under the preaching of the celebrated Henry Alline; baptized, in 1784, by Rev. Thomas Handly Chipman, the first Scriptural baptism administered in Queens County. Died in 1848. He was a worthy servant of the gracious Redeemer.

Dickenson, E. W., D.D., was born in Salem, N. J., Jan. 28, 1810; graduated at Hamilton in 1835; was ordained in Poughkeepsie in the autumn of 1836. For forty years he was a faithful minister of the gospel in the place of his ordination, and in Danvers, Mass., Burlington, N. J., Elmira, N. Y., Lewisburg, Pa., Dayton, O., and Marcus Hook, Pa., where he spent fourteen years in the service of his Lord. He was studious in his habits, careful in his pulpit preparations, attentive to the sick and the indigent, and interested in the religious welfare of the young. His ministry enjoyed much of the divine favor in his various fields of labor. He was moderator of the Philadelphia Baptist Association. He possessed the esteem of many of the best men in the Baptist denomination by whom he was known. He entered his eternal home Dec. 8, 1875. Lewisburg University conferred upon him the well-earned degree of Doctor of Divinity.

Dickerson, James Stokes, D.D., was born in Philadelphia, July 6, 1825. His boyhood was spent partly in Philadelphia and partly in New York; in the latter city with relatives of his mother, the daughter of Mr. Thomas Stokes, who, like Mr. Dickerson, the father of James, was remarkable for his devout spirit, and his active zeal in different

JAMES STOKES DICKERSON, D.D.

lines of Christian work. Three years were spent in study in Newburgh Academy. At the age of thirteen a position was secured him in a store in New York. His conversion took place in 1840, and he became a member of the Tabernacle Baptist church, receiving the ordinance at the hands of Rev. W. W. Everts. In 1842 he began his course of study preparatory to the ministry, which, even before his conversion, seems to have been his chosen sphere. At the age of about seventeen he entered the preparatory department of Madison University; after two years in it he entered the collegiate, and graduated in 1848. An affection of the throat interfered with his theological studies, and also with his plans for entering at once upon the active duties of the ministry. In 1850 he became associated with Prof. M. B. Anderson, then of Waterville College, Me., in the publication of the New York *Recorder*. This connection, mutually most pleasant, and of signal service in the journalism of the denomination, was brought to a close at the end of four years by Dr. Anderson's acceptance of the Rochester presidency. Mr. Dickerson engaged in the business of bookseller and publisher in New York, continuing in this two years, when he became depository agent of the Publication Society in Philadelphia. After four years in this service he became proprietor and editor of the Philadelphia

Christian Chronicle. It was while editing this paper that he began preaching at Wilmington, Del., first as supply of the Second Baptist church in that city. This ended in a call, which he accepted, and entered upon his new duties March 1, 1861. This pastorate he held five years; a pastorate fruitful in every way, a large number being added to the church,—200 at one time. It was also an eventful period to the country, by reason of the civil war, which in the mean time began and ended, and in which Mr. Dickerson, connected with the Christian Commission, rendered most important service. In May, 1865, he became pastor of the Fourth Avenue Baptist church, in Pittsburgh, Pa. It was again a five-years' service, with large results of lasting good. Besides the completion of the chapel of the present elegant house of worship, and the purchase of the ground upon which it stands, there were large ingatherings. In 1870 a call from the South Baptist church, Boston, took him to that city. It was while here that the rheumatic affection which caused his death became so serious as to occasion anxiety, and at length to necessitate a change of labor. The pastorate, which lasted until February, 1875, was a most happy and prosperous one, varied during the year 1871 by a visit to Europe with his wife, which he greatly enjoyed. Satisfied at length that further service in the pastorate had become impossible, through the almost complete failure of his health, he purchased an interest in the proprietorship of *The Standard*, of Chicago, and removing to that city in 1875, became joint editor of the paper, and co-proprietor with Mr. Edward Goodman. In spite of his rapidly failing health he rendered highly important service in his new relations, contributing valuable articles even while confined to his bed and suffering extreme pain. He died in the spring of 1876, and was buried, March 24, in the Oakwood Cemetery. He was "a man greatly beloved," and his death was felt as a severe denominational loss. His first wife, whom he had married in Utica, N. Y., as Miss Julia P. Spencer, the daughter of Mr. Julius A. Spencer, died at Philadelphia in 1864. In the autumn of 1866 he married Miss Emma R. Richardson, daughter of Prof. J. F. Richardson, of Rochester. Mrs. Dickerson with her son, J. S. Dickerson, succeeded him in the proprietorship of the *Standard*, having a connection also with its editorial staff.

Dickin, Rev. Edward Nichols, was born in Campbell Co., Ky., Sept. 26, 1835. He graduated at Georgetown in 1861. Was Professor of Greek and Latin from 1864 to 1870. At the latter period he took the pastoral charge of the Bethel Baptist church at Pembroke, Christian Co., Ky. Mr. Dickin is a fine scholar, a good preacher, and a most excellent pastor.

Dickinson, A. E., D.D., at present senior editor of the *Religious Herald*, published in Richmond, Va., was born December, 1830, in Orange Co., Va. Having pursued his studies both at Rich-

A. E. DICKINSON, D.D.

mond College and the University of Virginia, he became pastor of the Baptist church in Charlottesville, the seat of the university, where he was greatly blessed in his labors, influencing by his counsels many of the students for good, and building up the church of his charge into a strong and active body. He afterwards became superintendent of the Sunday-school and colportage work under the direction of the Board of the General Association of Virginia, in which position he organized many new Sunday-schools, strengthened those already in existence, enlarged their libraries, increased their facilities for carrying on their work more successfully, and preached the gospel in many places almost entirely destitute of these means of grace. After nine years' successful labor in this most important field of Christian activity, he became pastor of the Leigh Street Baptist church, Richmond, where, by means of his earnest and practical method of preaching, and his genial and sympathetic pastoral bearing towards, and intercourse with the people, he accomplished much good, and made his church a powerful instrument in spreading Baptist principles in the community. Afterwards he became joint owner and editor, with the Rev. Dr. Jeter, of the *Religious Herald*, a weekly journal, which for dignity of bearing, fidelity to old-fashioned gospel Baptist truth, for an earnest interest in, and advocacy of all denominational enterprises, and for largeness of circulation among an intelligent constituency, ranks among the best religious periodicals in the country.

Dr. Dickinson, too, does not confine himself to the seclusion of the editorial room. He is an interested attendant on Associational, educational, and other meetings, and is ever ready to encourage their efforts by his counsel and his contributions. Many a pastor has had his judicious help in protracted meetings, and numerous new converts can date their first quickenings of conscience, under the grace of God, to his earnest and pointed preaching, or the solution of their distressing doubts to his sympathetic and judicious counsel. Perhaps no editor of a denominational journal in the country is more widely and favorably known, or more cordially welcomed to all Baptist assemblies, than the "senior" editor of the *Religious Herald*. Furman University, of South Carolina, conferred upon him the honorary degree of D.D.

Dillahunty, Rev. John, was born in Kent Co., Md., about 1730. After his marriage he moved to the neighborhood of Newbern, N. C. The esteem of his new friends secured for him the sheriff's office for Craven County. The first sermon he ever heard was from George Whitefield, and it profoundly moved him. At a meeting conducted by Shubael Stearns and Daniel Marshall his soul was brought into the liberty of Jesus, and he was baptized. A church was organized in his neighborhood, which soon dissolved, but its members united again and elected him pastor. Near his church, in Jones County, was a fine Episcopal church edifice, erected by the government in colonial times, whose Tory rector fled to England in the beginning of the Revolutionary war. The members of this church attended the ministry of Mr. Dillahunty, and nearly the whole of them were converted, and the vestry met and gave the church edifice to him and his church, and to their successors forever. He went to Tennessee in March, 1796; the year after he was chiefly instrumental in organizing the church at Richland Creek, of which he became pastor, and in which he labored till his death, which occurred February 8, 1816. Mr. Dillahunty was an effective preacher, full of the spirit of God, a builder on the walls of Zion who needed not to be ashamed.

Dillard, Ryland Thompson, D.D., was born in Caroline Co., Va., November, 1797. He was educated at Rappahannock Academy, Port Royal, and he was a soldier in the war of 1812-15. At the age of twenty-one years he emigrated to Kentucky. He studied law, was admitted to the bar, and commenced the practice of his profession with Hon. Richard French at Winchester, Ky., in 1821. He had grown up and been confirmed in the Episcopal Church, but being convinced of the necessity of being born again, he sought and obtained hope in Jesus. He united with the Baptist church at Bryants, and was baptized by the venerable Ambrose Dudley in September, 1823. In 1824 he was or-

RYLAND THOMPSON DILLARD, D.D.

dained, and accepted the pastorate of East Hickman church, and a few years afterwards, in addition to his other charge, that of David's Fork, preaching to the former forty-seven years, and to the latter more than thirty years. During most of his ministry these two churches aggregated over 1000 members. In 1842, Mr. Dillard was appointed Superintendent of Public Instruction for the State, holding that position six years. He was active in originating the General Association of Kentucky, was many years moderator of Elkhorn Association, and was a trustee of Georgetown College. He wrote for the Baptist periodicals, and preached frequently to the destitute, especially among the mountains of Eastern Kentucky. During his ministry he baptized over 4000 people, and married 873 couples. He died Nov. 26, 1878, and was buried in the family grave-yard near Lexington.

Dimock, Rev. David C. W., son of Rev. Joseph Dimock, was born at Chester, Nova Scotia; studied at Horton Academy; ordained at Chester, Dec. 4, 1841; was for many years pastor at Onslow and Truro, Nova Scotia, and has labored extensively and prosperously in other parts of the Maritime Provinces.

Dimock, Judge Davis, was born at Rocky Hill, Conn., May 27, 1776. His father served as a lieutenant in the Revolutionary army. His parents moved into the Wyoming Valley, Pennsylvania, about 1790. Davis settled in Exeter, paid some attention to medicine, and became successfully engaged in business. He had imbibed infidel sentiments, but was converted in 1801, and ordained to the ministry in 1803. In 1808 he removed to Montrose, where he resided till his death, in September, 1858. For fifty years he was a leading Baptist minister in the Luzerne, Lackawanna, Susquehanna, and Wyoming region. For more than a quarter of a century he was an associate judge of Susquehanna County. In 1824 he commenced the publication of a monthly called *The Christian Magazine, or Baptist Mirror*, which he continued for three years. Mr. Dimock was fifty-eight years in the ministry, and by his talents and piety wielded an extensive influence for God and truth. His children inherited the genius of their father, and the Lord bestowed on them the same grace. His daughter, Mrs. Lydia C. Searles, is "a large contributor to current history."

Dimock, Hon. Davis, Jr., a son of the Rev. Davis Dimock, of Montrose, was born in 1807, and was blessed with the second birth at an early period in life, and united with his father's church in Montrose. He made the law his profession, and soon obtained such distinction in his calling that he was elected to the United States House of Representatives. While serving his country in this honored position he passed into the better land in 1842, in his thirty-fifth year.

Dimock, Rev. George, was born July 17, 1777, in Newport, Nova Scotia; converted 1789; baptized at Horton, 1799, by Rev. T. S. Harding, and united with the Baptist church formed at Newport in August, 1799; commenced preaching in 1818; ordained pastor of the church at Newport in 1820, and continued in this office till 1860; died Sept. 30, 1865. His life and ministry were marked by great usefulness.

Dimock, Rev. Joseph, son of Daniel Dimock, and prominent among the pioneers and founders of the Baptist denomination in Nova Scotia, was born in Newport, Nova Scotia, Dec. 11, 1768; converted July 17, 1785; baptized at Horton, May 6, 1787, by Rev. Nicholas Pierson; ordained pastor at Chester, Sept. 10, 1793, and so continued till his death, June 29, 1846; was active in forming the Baptist Association, June 23, 1800; evangelized and baptized in Cape Breton Island in 1825, 1826, and 1838, with gracious results; was a warm friend of education; eminently gentle and kind; sound in doctrine, strong in faith, and profound in Christian experience, Mr. Dimock's ministry was one of goodness and great spiritual results.

Dipping in the Westminster Assembly of Divines.—Dr. John Lightfoot, a Presbyterian member of the celebrated body just named, kept a journal of its proceedings, and of Aug. 7, 1644, he says, "And here fell we upon a large and long discourse, whether dipping were essential, or used in the first institution, or in the Jews' custom. Mr. Colman (one of the ablest Hebrew scholars in England) went about in a large discourse to prove *tauveleh* (Hebrew for immersion) to be dipping over head, which I answered at large. . . . After a long dispute it was at last put to the question whether the Directory (for public worship) should run, 'The minister shall take water and sprinkle or pour it with his hand upon the face or forehead of the child;' and it was voted so indifferently that we were glad to count names twice; for, so many were unwilling to have dipping excluded, that *the vote came to an equality within one;* for the one side was twenty-four, the other twenty-five,—*the twenty-four for the reserving of dipping*, and the twenty-five against it. And there grew a great heat upon it; and when we had done all, we concluded upon nothing in it; but the business was recommitted." (The Whole Works of Lightfoot, xiii. 300, 301. London, 1824.) The next day dipping was effectually voted down as one of the modes of baptism in the Presbyterian Church. At this period the immersionists had greater strength in that community than they have ever had since.

Disciples of Christ, The, or "Christians," or "Campbellites," as they are sometimes improperly called, are a religious community existing in Europe to a very limited extent, with a numerous membership on this side of the Atlantic.

Thomas and Alexander Campbell, father and son, Scotch-Irishmen by birth, connected originally with the Presbyterian church founded by the pious Erskines, in 1810 gathered a congregation at Brush Run, Pa., "which was designed from its very inception to put an end to all partisan controversies, and, far from narrowing the basis of Christian fellowship, to furnish abundant room for all believers upon the broad ground of the Bible, and a common religion upon the merits of Christ." In 1812 the congregation of Brush Run and the two ministering brethren were baptized by Elder Luse of the Baptist denomination, "upon the simple profession of faith made by the Ethiopian eunuch." In 1813 this body was received into the Redstone Baptist Association on the condition that "no terms of union or communion other than the Holy Scriptures should be required." After a connection with the Redstone Association of nearly ten years, rendered unpleasant by growing difficulties, Alexander Campbell was one of about thirty members who received dismission from the church at Brush Run to constitute a church at Wellsburg, Va. The new community was admitted into the Mahoning Baptist Association of Ohio. Nearly the whole Association by degrees adopted the views of Mr. Campbell. These sentiments became obnoxious to many neighboring Baptist churches, so that "the Beaver Association (of Pennsylvania) was induced to denounce them as heretical, and exclude from their fellowship all those churches which favored the views of" Mr. Campbell and his friends. The rent in the denomination was made wider, and the Disciples stood before the world as an independent community, differing from the Baptists chiefly about their "rejection of creeds, and baptism for remission of sins." The year 1828 was the time when the Mahoning Association adopted the doctrines advocated by Mr. Campbell, and as a consequence that year is commonly regarded as the commencement of the distinct denominational life of the "Disciples." The object of the movement of which Thomas and Alexander Campbell were the leaders, according to Prof. R. Richardson, of Virginia, was "to disinter the edifice of ancient Christianity from the rubbish which so many ages had accumulated upon it; and the beauty of those portions which were first exposed, only induced greater exertions to bring others into view. It was the unity of the church which first struck the attention; the subsequent submission to immersion is only one example among others of that progression which consistency with their own principles required. Thus, it was not until ten years after this that the *definite object of immersion* was fully understood, when it was recognized as the *remitting ordinance* of the gospel, or the appointed means through which the penitent sinner obtained an assurance of that pardon, or remission, procured for him by the suffering and death of Christ. Nor was it until a still later period that this doctrine was *practically applied*, in calling upon believing penitents to be baptized for the purpose specified. This view of baptism gave great importance to the institution, and has become one of the prominent features of this reformation." (Religious Denominations of the United States, p. 229. Philadelphia, 1859.)

They discard all human creeds and confessions, taking the Bible as their only religious authority; they regard all other denominations as imperfect, and claim that they have restored New Testament order in all things. They look upon the divisions of Christians as essentially wrong, and advocate the union of all believers on their platform. They insist on using Bible terms for Scriptural subjects, and therefore reject the words "Trinity, Triune, etc., (though) they receive everything which the Scripture affirms of the Father, the Son, and the Holy Spirit, giving to every expression its full and obvious meaning." They teach that when Christ is preached the hearers have ability to believe upon, and obey him; that baptism is immersion only, and should be administered to no one but a believer; that it precedes forgiveness and adoption; that the blood of Christ only cleanses from sin, but that God requires faith, repentance, *and baptism as the conditions* on which, for Christ's sake, he forgives and adopts his children; or as many state it, "*There are three steps necessary to salvation,—faith, repentance, and baptism.*"

They believe that conversion is a turning to the Lord, and that in the New Testament baptism is the outward act by which one who has faith and repentance manifests this great change. They believe that the Spirit operates on sinners through the Word of God, though some of them think that he acts directly on the guilty heart.

They object to relations of Christian experience as prerequisites to baptism, requiring nothing more than the brief confession made by the eunuch before Philip immersed him. They administer the Supper every Lord's day, to a participation of which with them Pedobaptists are not invited, but from which they are not excluded.

Their government is congregational; every church has elders to take charge of its spiritual affairs, and deacons to care for its temporal concerns. The official position of the preacher is not invested with quite as much authority as is accorded to it in other religious bodies, and the title of Rev. is never given him by his brethren.

In other particulars the Disciples are in harmony with evangelical Christians.

Their numbers in the United States are variously estimated at from 250,000 to 600,000. They have churches in almost every State and Territory of the Union, but they are most numerous in Illinois, Indiana, Kentucky, Missouri, and Ohio. They also have a few churches in the British American provinces, and in England, Ireland, Scotland, Australia, New Zealand, and Jamaica. They have a number of institutions of learning and several newspapers.

They are an active and moral people, some of whom occupy distinguished positions in the United States. Judge Jeremiah Black, of Pennsylvania, Gov. Bishop, of Ohio, and President-elect Garfield are citizens that reflect honor on the Disciples of Christ.

The editor places this sketch in the Encyclopædia because the Disciples of Christ are a considerable section of the great and growing immersion family. He has been at some pains to secure a fair representation of their opinions and practices. And he would add, that in common with his brethren, he dissents from all the peculiar opinions of Mr. Campbell and the special features of his reformation.

District of Columbia, The Baptists of.—The first Baptist church in the District was organized March 7, 1802, with six members. Washington at that time contained but 4000 inhabitants. The Rev. Wm. Parkinson, then chaplain to Congress, supplied the pulpit. In the following autumn a plain meeting-house was built at the corner of I and Nineteenth Streets. The church remained without a pastor five years, at the termination of which time the Rev. O. B. Brown was elected pastor (January, 1807), and continued such forty-three years. Spencer H. Cone, having abandoned the stage, was licensed by the church. In 1814 the Hon. O. C. Comstock, a member of Congress, was converted, baptized into the fellowship of the church, and licensed to preach. In 1833 the church built a meeting-house on Tenth Street. In 1859, in pursuance of an arrangement made with the Fourth church, worshiping on Thirteenth Street, the First church took possession of their building, the membership of the Fourth church uniting with them. Among its members were Cone, Rice, Cushman, Knowles, Howell, Stow, Chapin, Dodge, and others known and loved by the denomination. Its pastors have been Brown Hill, Cole, Samson, Gillette, and Cuthbert.

The Second (Navy-Yard) church was organized June 3, 1810, with five members. They first occupied a small frame building, in which Spencer H. Cone, at that time a clerk in the U. S. Treasury Department, preached his first sermon. The following year he was elected chaplain to Congress. In 1855 they finished their present house of worship, mainly the result of the faithful labors of Dr. I. Cole. Among the pastors or temporary supplies of this church were Lynd, Neale, Chapin, Maginnis, Poindexter, Bacon, Adams, Sydnor, Boston, and Cole.

The Third (E Street) church had its beginning in 1841; was organized Oct. 6, 1842, with twenty-one members, and took the name of the Third Baptist church of Washington. In January of 1843 a remarkable work of grace began among them, and soon extended to other churches. In April of 1843 the Rev. G. W. Samson became pastor, and from that time the church rapidly increased in numbers and efficiency. Up to August, 1846, the church had worshiped in public halls, but at that time they entered their new church edifice in E Street, and took the name of the E Street Baptist church. Dr. Samson continued pastor (with the exception of two years) until 1859. Since that time they have been served by Drs. Kennard, Gray, Parker, and the Rev. Messrs. Jutten and Mason.

In 1853 a number of brethren, mainly from the E Street church, under the Rev. T. C. Teasdale, erected a house of worship on Thirteenth Street. In 1859, under the ministry of Dr. Cole, this interest became merged in the First Baptist church.

In 1855 a mission was established on the "Island" by the E Street church, which, in 1857, was formally recognized as the Island Baptist church. The Rev. C. C. Meador was chosen pastor, and he has served them most faithfully and successfully from that time to the present.

The Calvary Baptist church (the Sixth Baptist church) was constituted June 2, 1862, with quite a large number of members dismissed from the E Street church. They worshiped in their beautiful new edifice for the first time in June, 1866. The cost of this building was about $115,000, by far the larger part of which was contributed by the Hon. Amos Kendall, the senior deacon of the church. Within eighteen months this beautiful building was destroyed by fire, and again Mr. Kendall furnished the means (added to the insurance of $50,000) to reconstruct it.

The North Baptist church, under the care of the Rev. Owen James, and the Metropolitan Baptist church, under the care of Dr. Parker, are both young churches, comparatively small in numbers, but constantly growing in strength and usefulness.

The Georgetown church, occupying a neat and commodious house, have had many difficulties to contend with, and have grown but slowly. There are two other points where preaching is regularly held, and where small neat buildings have been erected.

Most of the white churches in the District are connected with the Columbia Association, recently formed, the First church still retaining its connection with the Potomac Association of Virginia.

There are some six or eight colored Baptist churches in the District, most of them with a large membership, and occupying plain, neat meeting-houses.

Dixon, Rev. A. C., perhaps the most popular of all the young preachers of North Carolina. This gentleman, the son of Rev. T. Dixon, was born in Shelby, N. C., in 1854. He was graduated from Wake Forest College in 1875; read theology at Greenville, S. C., for a time, and was for three years pastor at Chapel Hill. He is now the pastor at Ashville, N. C., and has had much success in revival meetings.

Dixon, Rev. J. W., was born in Bladen Co., N. C., March 5, 1841; baptized by Rev. W. M. Kennedy in 1858; entered the army as a private and served through the war, attaining the rank of first lieutenant; was ordained in 1877 by Revs. H. and J. P. Lennon, and is at present the moderator of the Cape Fear Association. His principal service as pastor has been among the churches of Bladen and Columbus Counties.

Dixon, Rev. T., was born Dec. 24, 1820, in York Co., S. C.; was baptized by Rev. J. M. Thomas in 1838, and ordained in 1844, Revs. Wade Hill, T. K. Persley, and S. Morgan forming the Presbytery. Mr. Dixon has founded some large churches; served Buffalo church thirty years, and New Prospect for twenty-five, and baptized on an average 50 persons for thirty-eight years, making an aggregate of 1900 souls. He was the first moderator of the King's Mountain Association, and has served that body in the same relation many times. He still prosecutes his work as a pastor with vigor, and is a man of large influence in his Association.

Doane, William Howard, Mus. Doc., was born in Preston, Conn., Feb. 3, 1831. Received his education in the public schools and at Woodstock Academy, where he graduated in 1848. In 1851 took charge of the books and finances of the J. A. Fay Wood-working Manufacturing Company, and in 1860 became a partner in the firm, removing in the same year to Cincinnati, O., where he has since resided. Was converted in 1847, and baptized in 1851 by Rev. Frederic Denison into the fellowship of the Central church of Norwich, Conn. Has been all his Christian life an active worker in the Sunday-school.

Dr. Doane stands among the foremost musical composers of our day. He early developed a taste for music, and gave himself to its study. Among his instructors were C. W. Rouse, A. N. Johnson, and Kanhoyser, from whom he took a three-years' course of thorough-bass. In 1852–54 he was conductor of the Norwich Harmonic Society. In 1854 he assisted Prof. B. F. Baker in a musical convention. He began to compose Sunday-school music, in fulfillment of a covenant with God made during a severe attack of heart-disease in 1862, which brought him to death's door. His first book, entitled "Sabbath-School Gems," was published the same year. This was followed in 1864 by "Little Sunbeams." "Silver Spray" appeared in 1867, and "Songs of Devotion" in 1868. Since then, in connection with Rev. Robert Lowry, D.D., he has published "Pure Gold," "Royal Diadem," "Temple Anthems," "Tidal Wave," "Brightest and Best," "Welcome Tidings," "Fountain of Song," "The Devotional Hymn and Tune Book," and "Good as Gold." A large amount of sheet-music has also come from his pen. Some of his compositions have been sung in all parts of the world. Among those which have been particularly popular and useful may be mentioned "The Old, Old Story," "More Like Jesus," "Near the Cross," and "What Shall the Harvest Be?"

In 1875 Denison University gave him the honorary degree of Mus. Doc. In 1878 he returned this compliment by presenting the university with Doane Hall, a beautiful library building costing over $10,000. Dr. Doane is in the prime of life, and is characterized by abounding energy and enthusiasm. The head of a large and ever-growing business, he yet finds time for music and much public service for Christ. In the Robert Raikes Centenary in London (1880) he was one of the most prominent American delegates.

Dobbs, C. E. W., D.D., was born in Portsmouth, Va., Aug. 12, 1840. He was educated in the art of printing, and became editorially connected with the press of Norfolk and Portsmouth. He joined the Baptist church at Greensborough, N. C., in 1859, and in 1860 entered the theological seminary at Greenville, S. C., from whence he returned and preached to Court Street and Fourth Street churches in Portsmouth until 1866, when he moved to Kentucky. After serving several churches in Madison County he was called to the First church in Bowling Green, and was pastor six years. He now (1880) has charge of the Baptist church at Dayton, and has been for several years secretary of the Southern Baptist Convention, and of the General Association of Kentucky. Dr. Dobbs has written much for the periodical press, and published one or two small books.

Dockery, Gen. Alfred, was born in Richmond Co., N. C., Dec. 11, 1797. His great good sense

HON. OLIVER DOCKERY.

and extraordinary force of character enabled him to take a conspicuous part in the affairs of his State. When twenty-five years old he represented his native county in the House of Commons. He was a member of the Constitutional Convention of 1835; in 1836 he was in the State senate, and in 1845 he was sent to Congress from his district, and he was again in Congress in 1851. In 1854 he was a candidate for governor, and though defeated he made a fine canvass, reducing the majority of the successful party from 6000 to 2000.

After the close of the war he was, in 1865, a

member of the convention called by the provisional government of the State, and in 1866, against his wishes, he was made a candidate for governor. His last public position was that of president of the board of directors of the State penitentiary. Gen. Dockery became a Baptist early in life, and took an active part in our denominational movements. He died Dec. 3, 1873. His son, Hon. Oliver Dockery, is a man of culture, and of extensive legal attainments. He is recognized as one of the leading members of the bar in North Carolina. His integrity and ability secured his election as a Congressman from North Carolina.

Dodd, Rev. J. S., was born in South Carolina, Aug. 3, 1809; moved to Georgia in 1828 and settled in Fayette County, within two miles of where he now lives. In 1832 he united with Bethsaida church, where his membership still is (1880). In 1841 he was licensed, and in 1842 he was ordained. He at once took charge of four churches, and has never served fewer at a time. He has had charge of the Bethsaida church nearly forty years, and has baptized into its membership about 1000 persons, among them eleven of his own children and twenty-four of his grandchildren. He was pastor of Ramah church twenty-six years, Antioch church twenty-one years, Bethlehem church thirteen years, Fairburn church fifteen years, Ebenezer church eight years; and into these and other churches which he served he has baptized over 3000 persons. He has been for many years moderator of his Association, and wields a great and good influence in his community. His distinguishing trait is energy.

Dodge, Rev. Daniel, was born in Nova Scotia in 1775, and brought up in the United States. At eighteen he was converted, and united with the Baptist church of Woodstock, Vt. In 1801 he was ordained to the gospel ministry in Maryland. His convictions of duty for years led him to journey on horseback, preaching the gospel wherever he found an opening, in cities and villages, and in country barns. In Wilmington, where Mr. Dodge was settled for some years, he baptized 259 persons. He removed to Piscataway, N. J., in 1818, where he labored for nearly fourteen years, with continued manifestations of the divine favor. He accepted a call to Newark, N. J., in 1832, where he spent six years of successful toil as pastor of the First church. Afterwards he settled in Philadelphia, and became pastor of the Second Baptist church, a position that he retained till his death, which occurred in 1851.

One of his personal friends, who sat under his ministry for many years, says "his manner was easy and graceful, his sentences had force and application; he was impressed with the solemnity and responsibility of his sacred office; the simplicity and paternal style of his addresses lent a charm to his discourses." In his public ministrations it was evident to all that God was with him. He was an Israelite indeed, in whom there was no guile, a burning and a shining light, a minister of

REV. DANIEL DODGE.

Jesus who occupied probably the warmest place in the hearts of his brethren, and of some thousands of others, ever possessed by any pastor in Philadelphia. Though twenty-nine years in the grave, his memory is as fragrant in the Second Baptist church, and in the Philadelphia Baptist Association, as if he had only died a few months since.

Dodge, Ebenezer, D.D., LL.D., was born at Salem, Mass., April 21, 1819; graduated at Brown University, 1840; was principal of the Shelburne Falls Academy for two years; graduated at Newton Theological Seminary in 1845; was pastor in New London, N. H., from 1846 to 1853. Professor of Biblical Criticism in Hamilton Theological Seminary, and Professor of the Evidences of Christianity in Madison University, from 1853 to 1861. Since 1861 he has been Professor of Christian Theology. Since 1868 he has been president of the Madison University, and Professor of Metaphysics, and since 1871 president of Hamilton Theological Seminary.

Dr. Dodge spent fifteen months in theological studies in Europe, in 1858-59; was called to the chair of Ecclesiastical History at Rochester Theological Seminary, and also to the same chair at Newton Theological Seminary, and in 1868 he was invited to the professorship of Christian Theology at Newton.

He has published several reviews of a very high

order, among which may be noted one on the German school of theology. His work on the "Evidences of Christianity" has great and permanent value, in its method and its governing idea, that

EBENEZER DODGE, D.D., LL.D.

Christianity is its own best witness. His "Theological Lectures," published for the benefit of his students, are the result of the ripest scholarship, and reveal not only advanced theological study, but disclose a heart in deep sympathy with the spirit of the Word of God. These lectures are highly prized by those who have been his students. They are receiving constant revision and additions,—at present in the direction of the constitution of the Christian church and Christian ethics. It is hoped that the volume will be ultimately in the hands of the general public.

Dodge, Hon. George H., was born in Hampton Falls, N. H., Aug. 4, 1804. Both his parents were devout members of the Baptist Church. Mr. Dodge, as he grew up to manhood, merited and received not a few honors from his fellow-citizens. When but a little more than thirty years of age he was chosen for two years to represent his native town in the State Legislature, and later he was elected a member of the State senate. In 1850 he was chosen a member of the convention for revising the constitution of the State. In the deliberations of this body he took an active part. For four years he was president of the Manchester and Lawrence Railroad. His life was one of great business activity. When about thirty years of age; he was baptized by his brother, Rev. C. A. Dodge, and from the time of his public profession to his death he was a faithful member of the church, laboring in many ways to promote its prosperity. He died at Hampton Falls, Feb. 14, 1862.

Dodge, Rev. Oliver, was born at Hampton Falls, N. H., May 18, 1813. He entered Waterville College in 1829, graduating in 1833. While a member of college he was baptized by Dr. Chaplin. He studied theology at Newton, and then was ordained pastor of the church in Lexington, Mass., Jan. 7, 1835, when he was not quite twenty-two years of age. His pastoral life was a comparatively short one,—a little more than five years. He died May 22, 1840. He had gained a strong hold on the affections of his own people, and was greatly respected in the community in which he lived. His death, in the very morning of his ministerial life, was a sad blow to his church.

Dodge, Orrin, D.D.—This veteran district secretary of the American Baptist Missionary Union for the State of New York was born in Litchfield Co., Conn., in 1803. He was religiously educated in the Episcopal Church, and received its baptismal rites at the hands of Bishop Griswold, of Connecticut. He removed to Central New York in 1815. The days of his boyhood alternated between the farm and the school-room, in the latter of which he became a teacher at seventeen years of age, and followed that calling for nine years. Subsequently he spent three years in a public position at West Troy, N. Y., after which he went into mercantile business for a few years.

He was converted in 1831, and the same year he was baptized by Rev. Ashley Vaughn, and in 1833 he was licensed by the church in West Troy to preach the gospel. In May, 1834, he was ordained at Sand Lake Baptist church, east of Troy, where he served as pastor for three years. His next pastorates were at Maysville nine years, West Troy two years, and Ballston two years. In the year 1848 he was appointed collecting secretary for missions for the New York State Convention. He developed rare qualities for such a service, and at the expiration of ten months he was chosen by the board of the American Baptist Missionary Union as their agent for collecting funds for foreign missions. This service he has performed to this date (1879) with uncommon zeal, ability, and success; his fervid eloquence, and his absorbing sympathy with the missionaries, securing for him a hearty welcome among the churches.

Dodson, Rev. Elias.—No man is better known in North Carolina than Elias Dodson. He was born in Halifax Co., Va., Oct. 27, 1807; was converted under the preaching of Rev. John Kerr, and baptized by Wm. Blair, May 3, 1832; attended Richmond Institute, but graduated at William and Mary College, July 4, 1838, and was ordained in the Third church, Richmond, Va., September, 1838. Most of his life has been spent in North Carolina, in the work of an agent for some good cause, or as a missionary. Mr. Dodson has many peculiarities, but perhaps the greatest of these is his special consecration to the cause of his Master. He writes often and briefly for the press, and is remarkable for his memory. Not many better men live than Elias Dodson.

Dodson, Rev. Obadiah, an early preacher in Louisiana, and author of a useful book, entitled "Fifteen Reasons for the Proper Training of Children," was a native of Tennessee. He was employed for several years as a missionary by the Louisiana Baptist Convention. Died in 1854.

Donatists, The.—In North Africa, during the fierce persecution of Dioclesian, many Christians courted a violent death. These persons, without the accusation, would confess to the possession of the Holy Scriptures, and on their refusal to surrender them, they were immediately imprisoned and frequently executed. While they were in confinement they were visited by throngs of disciples, who bestowed upon them valuable gifts and showed them the highest honor.

Mensurius, bishop of Carthage, disapproved of all voluntary martyrdom, and took steps to hinder such bloodshed. And if he had gone no farther in this direction he would have deserved the commendation of all good men. But by zealous Christians in North Africa he was regarded as unfriendly to compulsory martyrdom, and to the manifestations of tender regard shown to the victims of tyranny. And by some he was supposed to be capable of a gross deception to preserve his own life, or to secure the safety of his friends. When a church at Carthage was about to be searched for copies of the Bible, he had them concealed in a safe place, and the writings of heretics substituted for them. This removal was an act of Christian faithfulness, but the works which he put in the church in their stead were apparently intended to deceive the heathen officers. Mensurius seems to us to have been too prudent a man for a Christian bishop in the harsh times in which he lived. In his own day his conduct created a most unfavorable opinion of his religious courage and faithfulness among multitudes of the Saviour's servants in his country. Secundus, primate of Numidia, wrote to Mensurius, giving utterance to censures about his conduct, and glorifying the men who perished rather than surrender their Bibles. Cæcilian was the archdeacon of the bishop of Carthage, and was known to enjoy his confidence and share his opinions.

Mensurius, returning from a visit to Rome, became ill, and died in the year 311. Cæcilian was appointed his successor, and immediately the whole opposition of the enemies of his predecessor was directed to him. In his own city a rich widow of great influence, and her numerous friends, assailed him; a synod of seventy Numidian bishops excommunicated him for receiving ordination from a *traditor* (one who had delivered up the Bible to be burned to save his life); and another bishop was elected to take charge of the church of Carthage. The Donatist community was then launched upon the sea of its stormy life.

Bishop Donatus, after whom the new denomination was named, was a man of great eloquence, as unbending as Martin Luther, as fiery as the great Scotch Reformer, whose principles were dearer to him than life, and who was governed by unwearied energy. Under his guidance the Donatists spread all over the Roman dominions on the African coast, and for a time threatened the supremacy of the older Christian community. But persecution laid its heavy hand upon their personal liberty, their church property, and their lives. Again and again this old and crushing argument was applied to the Donatists, and still they survived for centuries. Their hardships secured the sympathy of numerous bands of armed marauders called Circumcelliones, men who suffered severely from the authorities sustained by the persecuting church, "free lance" warriors who cared nothing for religion, but had a wholesome hatred of tyrants. These men fought desperately for the oppressed Donatists. Julian the Apostate took their side when he ascended the throne of the Cæsars, and showed much interest in their welfare, as unbelievers in modern times have frequently shown sympathy with persecuted communities in Christian lands.

There were a few Donatist churches outside of Africa, but the denomination was almost confined to that continent. They suffered less from the Vandals than their former oppressors, but the power of these conquerors was very injurious to them; and the victorious Saracens destroyed the remaining churches of this grand old community.

The Donatists were determined to have only godly members in their churches. In this particular they were immeasurably superior to the Church Universal (Catholic), even as represented by the great Augustine of Hippo. Their teachings on this question are in perfect harmony with our own. They regarded the Church Universal as having forfeited her Christian character by her inconsistencies and iniquities, and they refused to recognize her ordinances and her ministry. Hence they gave the triple immersion a second time to those who had received it in the great corrupt church. Their government was not episcopal in the modern sense. Mosheim is right in representing them as having at one time 400 bishops. The Roman population on the North African coast would not have required twenty diocesan bishops to care for their spiritual wants.

Every town, in all probability, had its bishop, and if there were two or more congregations, these formed but one church, whose services were in charge of one minister and his assistants. These church leaders were largely under the control of the people to whom they ministered. The Donatists held boldly the doctrine that the church and the state were entirely distinct bodies. Early in their denominational life, Constantine the Great, for the first time in earthly history, had united the church to the Roman government, and speedily the Donatists arose to denounce the union as unhallowed, and as forbidden by the highest authority in the Christian Church. No Baptist in modern times brands the accursed union between church and state with more appropriate condemnations than did his ancient Donatist brother. Their faith on this question is well expressed in their familiar saying, "What has the emperor to do with the church?" Soul liberty lived in their day.

It is extremely probable that they did not practise the baptism of unconscious babes,—at least in the early part of their history. It is often urged that Augustine, their bitter enemy, would not fail to bring this charge against them if they had rejected his favorite rite. His works now extant do not *directly* bring such an accusation against them, and it is concluded that they followed his own usage. This argument would have great weight if it were proved that all the Catholics of Africa baptized unconscious babes. But there is no evidence of such universal observance. Outside of Africa, in the fourth century, the baptism of an unconscious babe was a rare occurrence. Though born in it of pious parents, Augustine himself was not baptized till he was thirty-three years of age. His works are bristling with weapons to defend infant baptism; they are the arsenal from which its modern defenders have procured their most effective arms, and if the custom had been universally accepted, he would have seen no cause to keep up such a warfare in its defense. The frequency with which Augustine treats of infant baptism is striking evidence that its observance in his day and country was often called in question, and that had he directly pointed out this defect in the observances of the Donatists he would have been quickly reminded that he had better remove the opposition to infant baptism from his own people before he assailed it among the Donatists. This fact would account for the supposed silence of Augustine on this question. The second canon of the Council of Carthage, where the principles of Augustine were supreme, "Declares an anathema against such as deny that children ought to be baptized as soon as they are born." (Du Pin, i. 635. Dublin.) If this curse is against the Donatists, it shows that they did not practise the infant rite; if it is against other Africans, it gives a good reason why Augustine should be cautious in bringing charges against the Donatists on this account. Augustine wrote a work "On Baptism, Against the Donatists," in which, speaking of infant baptism, he says, "And if *any one seek divine authority* in this matter, although, what the whole church holds, not as instituted by councils, but as a thing always observed, is rightly held to have been handed down by apostolical authority." (Et si quisquam in hac re auctoritatem divinam quæret.—Patrol. Lat., vol. xlii. p. 174, Migne. Parisiis.) This book is expressly written against the views of baptism held by the Donatists; it was designed to correct their errors on that subject. And he clearly admits that some of them doubted the divine authority of infant baptism, and he proceeds to establish it by an argument from circumcision. Augustine was a powerful controversialist; to have charged the Donatists directly with heresy for rejecting infant baptism would have been an accusation against many in his own church, and he prudently assails his enemies on this point, as if only some of them regarded infant baptism as a mere human invention; and he boastfully and ignorantly, or falsely, speaks of it as always observed by the whole church, while one of his own African councils pronounces a curse upon those who "denied that children ought to be baptized as soon as they are born."

Doolittle, Hon. James R., LL.D.—Judge Doolittle was born in Salem, Washington Co., N. Y., Jan. 2, 1815, and was educated at Geneva College, in Western New York, graduating in the year 1834. Entering the legal profession, he practised law for several years at Rochester and Warsaw, serving at one period for some years as district attorney for Wyoming County, and also, at one time, under the old militia *régime*, as colonel of a regiment. Removing to Racine, Wis., in 1851, he was, two years after, elected to the bench, as judge of the first circuit. This he resigned in 1856, resuming the practice of law, and in January, 1857, he was elected to the United States Senate, and re-elected in 1863. At the end of his second term, in 1869, he retired from public life, and has since devoted himself to the practice of his profession at Chicago, his residence remaining at Racine. Judge Doolittle became a member of the Baptist Church early in life, and has, amidst all the vicissitudes of an active and varied public career, borne himself as a consistent Christian and a Baptist loyal to his convictions. He has been a trustee of the university at Chicago from the foundation of the institution; one year he served as its president, and during a succession of years as a professor in its law school. In respect to public affairs he is a man of large views, and his career, in that regard, has been characterized to an unusual degree by absolute personal integrity. In his own denomination he is held in high honor and esteem, as one true to its principles, and adding lustre to its annals.

Doom, Dr. Adam J., was born in Hopkinsville, Ky., May 13, 1813. At the age of sixteen he began the study of medicine at Nashville, Tenn., and became an eminent physician, and author of a medical treatise, which, when ready for the press, was accidentally destroyed by fire. In 1832 he was immersed. In 1834 he moved to Iowa, near Burlington; helped to organize a church; was active in religion, and, owing to the scarcity of preachers, was gradually led into the ministry; ordained in 1843, and immersed 26 converts on the day of his ordination. He helped to organize many churches and the first Association in Western Missouri, Eastern Iowa, and Nebraska, and after his removal to California, in 1859, was a leading citizen at Loyalton; its postmaster for eleven years; organized the church there; built its meeting-house, at a cost to himself of nearly $2000; finally located at Biggs' Station; gave much time to missionary work for new and poor churches, until 1877, when, aged and almost blind, he ceased active labor, waiting in the home of his children, and in the love of the churches, the Master's bidding to "come up higher." Dr. Doom is still one of the wise counselors and liberal supporters of Baptist interests in the Sacramento River Association, California.

Douglas, Hon. Stephen A.—Although Mr. Douglas was not himself a Baptist, yet his service to the denomination in the gift of a site for the University of Chicago, and his regard for it, for the sake of his first wife, who was a Christian lady and an earnest Baptist, make it suitable that he should have a brief record here. A native of Vermont, born at Brandon in that State in 1813, he received simply an academical education at Brandon and at Canandaigua, N. Y. Entering the legal profession, he removed to Illinois in 1834, establishing himself first at Jacksonville and afterwards at Chicago. His rise in his profession and in public life was remarkably rapid, in 1841 being chosen a judge of the Supreme Court of Illinois, in 1843 a Representative in Congress, in 1847 a United States Senator, which place he held until his death in 1861. The incidents of his career belong to the political history of this country, and cannot be detailed here. His gift to the denomination of ten acres of land for the site of a university is more particularly mentioned elsewhere. The terms of the donation were such as to enhance its value, securing the property to the denomination for the purpose named, and at the same time placing the institution in a position to command the support of intelligent friends of education of all religious views. The first wife of Senator Douglas was Miss Martin, of North Carolina, a most estimable lady, and mother of the two sons who survive as the only children of Judge Douglas.

Douglas, Rev. William, was born in Scotland, Dec. 25, 1812. He was a graduate of Brown University in the class of 1839. He spent one year at the Newton Theological Institution,—1839-40. He was ordained in Providence, Jan. 8, 1850. For eighteen years he was a city missionary in Providence, and has been chaplain of the Rhode Island State Prison for thirty-eight years. Since 1864, Mr. Douglas has been the registrar of Brown University.

Dowd, Rev. Patrick W., was born in 1799; was baptized into the fellowship of Friendship church by the elder Dr. W. T. Brantly; graduated at Columbian College, D. C., during Dr. Stoughton's administration, and was ordained as pastor of the Raleigh Baptist church, N. C., by Revs. Robert T. Daniel and Thomas Crocker. He was at one time pastor of the church in Tarborough, but the most of his pastoral labor was performed in the limits of the Raleigh Association, of which body he was for many years the moderator. He baptized Dr. William Hooper into the fellowship of Mount Carmel church in 1831. He was one of the founders of the Baptist State Convention, and the first president of that body. He died Aug. 28, 1866, and lies buried in the yard of Mount Pisgah church, of which he was pastor for twenty-seven years.

Dowd, Gen. Willis D., for many years moderator of the Sandy Creek Association, N. C., was born Oct. 25, 1805. Two of his brothers, William and Patrick W., were Baptist ministers, and he was an active and zealous Christian. For fifteen years he was chairman of the court of his county; was a member of the Legislature of his State in 1830, and was in the State senate in 1860. In 1875 he was chosen a member of the State Convention. He died April 10, 1879.

Dowling, Rev. George Thomas, was born in New York City, June 2, 1849; son of Rev. John Dowling, D.D.; converted at the age of thirteen, and baptized by his father; left the College of the City of New York to enter business life, but after two years consecrated himself to the ministry, and pursued courses of study at Madison University and Crozer Theological Seminary. After a short pastorate at Fellowship, N. J., in November, 1871, took charge of the Third church, Providence, R. I. In September, 1873, became pastor of Central church, Syracuse, N. Y., where he remained five years. His pastorate was very successful, though darkened by a terrible accident, by which a number of people were killed through the falling of the church floor. In 1877 he became pastor of the Euclid Avenue church, Cleveland, O., where he now remains. Has published sermons, and devotes considerable time to lectures. His present pastorate has been attended with great prosperity.

Dowling, John, D.D., was born at Pavensey, on the coast of Sussex, England, May 12, 1807. From the house in which Dr. Dowling was born may be seen the ivy-clad towers of Pavensey Castle, which was said to be an ancient ruin of Roman origin. Dr. Dowling's ancestors for generations were adherents of the Established Church of England. In early life he removed to London, and at the age of seventeen became a member of the Eagle Street Baptist church, whose pastor was the Rev. Joseph Ivimey, the historian of the English Baptists. In early youth he exhibited great fondness for books and literary pursuits. At nineteen he was tutor in the Latin language and literature in a classical institute in London, and at twenty-one he became instructor in Hebrew, Greek, Latin, and French in Buckinghamshire Classical Institute. In 1829 he established a classical boarding-school in Oxfordshire, a few miles from the city of Oxford, where he taught until 1832, when he embarked with his family for the United States. Soon after his arrival he settled with the Baptist church in Catskill, where he was ordained Nov. 14, 1832. In 1834 he removed to Newport, R. I., and in August, 1836, accepted a call to a church in New York worshiping in Gothic Masonic Hall. He also preached for two or three years as pastor of the Broadway church in Hope chapel, after which he went to Providence as pastor. In 1844 he first became pastor of the Berean church, in Bedford Street, New York, serving there eight years. In 1852 he accepted a call to Philadelphia, but returned in 1856 to the Berean church at their urgent and unanimous request. Here he continued to labor efficiently for twelve years. Afterwards he served the South church, Newark, N. J., and the South church of New York City. Dr. Dowling has been a prolific writer. In England he published three schoolbooks which were in general use for many years. In this country he has published "The History of Romanism," of which some 30,000 copies have been published and sold; "Power of Illustration," "Nights and Mornings," "Indoor Offering," and numerous pamphlets and tracts. One of the latest, if not the last of his tracts, and a most valuable treatise for ministers of the gospel, is an essay read before the New York Baptist Pastors' Conference in the fall of 1877, on "Humility as an Element of Ministerial Character." In 1846 he received the degree of D.D. from Transylvania University. For several years before his death Dr. Dowling, because of the infirmities of age, had no pastoral charge, but he preached in many pulpits of the city of New York of all evangelical denominations. No man was more cordially beloved than Dr. Dowling.

To a humble, generous, sympathetic spirit there was added a character of sterling and incorruptible integrity. His death occurred at Middletown, N. Y., July 4, 1878.

Downer, Prof. John Rathbone, was born of an honored and long-lived ancestry in Zanesville, O., Dec. 6, 1821; converted under the preaching of Rev. George I. Miles, and baptized in 1840; graduated at Madison University in 1845, and in the last class of the theological seminary at Covington, Ky., in 1848. From 1848 to 1850 was pastor at Xenia, O., when he settled with the Sandusky Street church, Alleghany City, Pa., where he remained three years. In 1853 was called to the chair of Rhetoric and English Literature in Granville College, O., a position which he held with unswerving devotion and eminent success until 1866, when he resigned. His health having become broken, he removed to Kansas and Missouri, where he spent eight years, partly in business and partly in missionary work. As a result of his efforts in this field, four churches were organized and three meeting-houses built. In 1875, with health still broken, he came East, and took charge of the Ridley Park church, near Philadelphia, Pa. Here he rapidly and thoroughly regained his health, and was successful in every way. In 1879 he resigned this position, and has since been residing in Philadelphia and doing general work.

Prof. Downer has spent the most of his mature life in the work of education, but has proved that he can be a successful pastor or executive officer as well as teacher. He has written considerably for the denominational papers, is in the prime of life, and is universally regarded as an energetic, consecrated, and capable man.

Downey, Rev. Francis.—This veteran preacher is now the oldest Baptist minister in Western Pennsylvania. He has entered his ninety-second year, and closes life surrounded by many comforts on his farm near Garrard's Fort, in Greene County. Mr. Downey was an actor in the scenes that transpired when Alexander Campbell left the Baptists and founded the denomination called "Disciples." He was also among the number who united to form the Monongahela Association. For many years, in the manhood of his strength, he traversed the country when rough roads and other difficulties would have cooled the zeal of many modern ministers. A crown awaits him when his work on earth is done.

Dozier, Rev. John, of Uniontown, Ala.; had some early advantages: a good reasoner; an eloquent preacher; holds a commanding influence among the colored Baptists who know him; he is well read and thoroughly posted in the Scriptures.

Drake, Rev. Jacob, was born in Connecticut, and removed from Windsor to Canaan, N. Y., in 1769. He was then a Congregational minister. In

1770 he formed a church of that denomination in his new home and became its pastor. Some years later he adopted Baptist principles, and organized a church after the Apostolic model. Mr. Drake was a minister of unwearied labors, and in ten years his church numbered more than 500 members. These were sometimes widely separated. At one period his church had eleven teachers and ruling elders, besides the pastor. The elders could administer baptism and the Lord's Supper. The church at Canaan established others in Great Barrington and Egremont, Warren's Bush, Coeyman's Patent, Duane's Bush, Rensselaerville, West Stockbridge, and New Concord. Eight churches were the fruit of twelve years of the successful labor of Jacob Drake. In 1792 he removed to the Wyoming region of Pennsylvania, where God continued to grant rich blessings upon his ministry.

Drake, Rev. Simeon J., was born in New York City, March 2, 1804. After studying at Columbia College he entered his father's store. At the age of seventeen there was a marked change in his life. Six years later, while in business at New Brunswick, he was greatly moved under the preaching of Rev. G. S. Webb. In 1832 he was baptized by Rev. Wm. Parkinson, and united with the First Baptist church, New York. In 1834 he was licensed, but continued in business. When called to the pastorate of the church at Rahway, N. J., the next year, it was a sacrifice to leave the bank of which he was an important officer for the meagre salary which a little church could give, but he did not hesitate. He was ordained in 1836. After serving the church for three years, during which the flock doubled its numbers, he was constrained by the call of the church and the providence of God to go to Plainfield, where his labors for nearly a quarter of a century were blessed to the conversion and edification of hundreds. His godly life, faithful preaching, and loving counsels will not soon be forgotten. Sunday morning, April 13, 1862, he died "in the midst of his brethren," after a short illness, beloved, and faithful to the last. He was prominent in State work, being secretary of the Convention for five years. His previous business training was very useful to him. The Baptists of New Jersey are greatly indebted to Mr. Drake for the efficiency of their benevolent enterprises and for the saintly example which he constantly set them.

Dudley, Rev. Ambrose, a distinguished Baptist preacher among the pioneers of Kentucky, was born in Spottsylvania Co., Va., in 1750. At the breaking out of the Revolutionary war he entered the army as captain. While stationed at Williamsburg he was converted, and on returning home was ordained and became pastor of the church at Spottsylvania. After preaching some years with much acceptance, he moved to Fayette Co., Ky., in 1786, and was immediately called to the pastoral care of Bryant's church. David's Fork church soon arose out of Bryant's, and called Mr. Dudley to its pastorate. His ministry at both of these churches was attended with extraordinary success. During the great revival of 1800–3, Bryant's church received 421 members. Mr. Dudley frequently acted as moderator of Elkhorn Association, and also of Licking Association. After a long life of great usefulness he died in 1825, leaving behind him eleven sons, three daughters, and nearly one hundred grandchildren. Among his sons was Benjamin Winslow Dudley, one of the most distinguished surgeons in the United States.

Dudley, Rev. John Hull, was a native of Andover, Vt., where he was born Sept. 7, 1803; educated at Madison University; ordained as pastor of the Baptist church in Victory, N. Y., in 1832. He came to Wisconsin in 1844 to take the pastorate of the Baptist church in Delavan. He was settled at Victory, N. Y., four years; at Sennett, N. Y., five years; at Arcadia, N. Y., two years; at Delavan, Wis., five years; and at Sugar Creek, Wis., thirteen years. He died at his home in Delavan, Feb. 7, 1868. He was a successful minister of Jesus Christ, and belongs to the class of pioneer and itinerant workers who laid the foundations in the early history of the State. He was the warm friend of education, and labored faithfully in connection with its early movements in Wisconsin. He was also the friend of missions and of temperance, and of human freedom. He died very suddenly, in the midst of his family, in the triumphs of the gospel he had so long proclaimed to others, at the age of sixty-five years.

Dudley, Richard M., D.D., is a great-grandson of Rev. Ambrose Dudley, a famous pioneer preacher of Kentucky, and the head of one of the most illustrious families of the State. He was born in Madison Co., Ky., Sept. 1, 1838. He entered Georgetown College in 1856, with a view to preparing himself for the practice of law. In 1857 he was converted to Christ, and united with the Baptist church at Georgetown. Being impressed with a sense of duty to preach the gospel, he abandoned his purpose of becoming a lawyer, and prosecuted his studies with a view to the ministry. He graduated at Georgetown College in 1860. Having been ordained to the ministry, he accepted the pastorate of East Baptist church, in Louisville, in the spring of 1861. In 1865 his voice failed, and he took editorial charge of the *Western Recorder*, a weekly Baptist paper published in Louisville, and soon afterwards purchased the paper. In 1871 he sold the *Recorder*, and moved to Fayette County, and became pastor of David's Fork church. Next year he accepted a professorship in Georgetown College, still continuing his pastoral relation. In

1877 he resigned his professorship, and gave himself entirely to the work of a pastor. In 1878 he took charge of the church at Georgetown. In 1879 he was elected chairman of the faculty of Georgetown College, and in June, 1880, was elected president of that institution. He is yet a young man, possessing good attainments, fine energy and zeal, and a varied experience, and will be likely to infuse new life into the college.

Dudley, Rev. Thomas Parker, son of Rev. Ambrose Dudley, is the most distinguished preacher among the Baptists of Kentucky. He was born in Fayette Co., Ky., May 31, 1792. In 1812 he entered the army, was made commissary of the Northwestern troops, participating in the battles of Frenchtown and the River Raisin; in the latter was wounded in the shoulder; taken prisoner by the Indians and carried to Detroit. In the fall of 1814 he was made quartermaster of a detachment which reinforced Gen. Jackson at the battle of New Orleans, and the same year was appointed quartermaster-general of Kentucky. From 1816 until 1824 he was cashier of a branch of the old Bank of Kentucky, located at Winchester, and for several years afterwards was engaged in settling up the business of these branch banks. He succeeded his father in the pastorate of Bryant's church in 1825. Of this church he has now (1880) been pastor fifty-five years, and of three other churches almost as long, and he has also been moderator of Licking Association forty-seven years. He resides in Lexington, Ky.

Dulin, E. S., D.D., LL.D., was born in Fairfax Co., Va., Jan. 18, 1821. His father died in Washington in 1823, and left his son when nine years of age. He was blessed with a Christian mother and with the grace of God, and he was converted and baptized in 1839. He entered Richmond College in 1841, and passed through a full course. After graduation he was Professor of Languages in Hollins Institute, Va. He spent a year in special study at the University of Virginia; was ordained in Baltimore in 1848, and in 1849 became pastor at Lexington, Mo.; was a member of the Convention which located William Jewell College, of which he was elected president the following October. In 1856 he was recalled to the Lexington church, and he accepted also the presidency of the Female College located there. In 1858 he became pastor of the church at Kansas City, and in 1859 of the Baptist church in St. Joseph, where he remained six years. After the war he reorganized the school at Lexington. He developed the plan for a Board of Ministerial Education for Missouri in connection with the college at Liberty. In 1870 he founded the Female College at Columbia, and gave six years' hard work to it. In 1876 he removed to St. Joseph, and founded the Female College there. He has received the degrees of D.D. and LL.D. He enjoys the confidence and love of his denomination and of many outside of it.

Dunaway, Thomas S., D.D., was born in Lancaster Co., Va., Nov. 5, 1829. He was the son of Col. Thomas S. Dunaway, a prominent Baptist of his time. His mother was Felicia T. Hall, the sister of Rev. Addison Hall, who was the father of two missionaries to China, Mrs. Shuck and Mrs. Tobey. Dr. Dunaway was baptized into the fellowship of the Lebanon Baptist church by his uncle, the Rev. Addison Hall, in September, 1848. His father dying in 1843, just as he was about to send the subject of this sketch, with his brother, to college, his education was afterwards completed at an academy of high grade in his own county. He continued for two years after 1850 to teach school; and subsequently filled for several years the offices of justice of the peace and county surveyor. During this period he determined to enter upon the study and practice of law, and to this end studied with Maj. Samuel Gresham, a prominent lawyer of the county. Just as he was ready to enter upon the labors of his profession his health failed, and for several years he continued quite feeble. In the mean time he recognized God's hand in his affliction, and he resolved to give himself wholly to the work of the Christian ministry. He was licensed by the Lebanon Baptist church in October, 1860, and immediately began to preach for the Lebanon and several other churches, in connection with their pastors, Hall and Kirk. He was ordained Nov. 23, 1862, still preaching without accepting the pastoral care of any church, until October, 1866, when he became pastor of the Fredericksburg church, Va. The honorary degree of D.D. was conferred upon him by Richmond College in 1877. Dr. Dunaway has been an occasional contributor to the public press, and has published "The Memoirs of Rev. A. Hall," an exceedingly interesting book, which has been well received by the public. No man stands higher in the esteem of his own community than Dr. Dunaway, and his labors in Fredericksburg have been greatly blessed in consolidating and strengthening the cause of the denomination.

Dunbar, Rev. Duncan, was born in the northern Highlands of Scotland about the year 1791. The days of his childhood and early youth were spent among the scenes of his birth upon the banks of the Spey. The Highland costume and customs prevailed in this region in Mr. Dunbar's boyhood, and the old Gaelic was still the language of the household. At the age of nineteen his serious attention was directed to the concerns of his soul. After a period of several months, during which he was the subject of deep convictions, he obtained peace through the blood of the Lamb. After his conversion he removed to Aberdeen and engaged in business, and shortly afterwards married Miss Christina Mitchel, a lady of a gentle, loving dispostion, and of deep, earnest piety. For several years Mr. Dunbar remained in Aberdeen, active and zealous in the cause of Christ, and preaching as a layman when opportunity offered. In 1817 he removed to America, and settled in the province of New Brunswick. Though not yet ordained, he felt constrained to preach the gospel. His labors in this field were incessant, and characterized by the same zeal and love for souls that marked his life ministry. After his conversion for a considerable period he was greatly exercised upon the Scriptural mode and subjects of baptism. At length his mind found rest in the adoption of believer's baptism, and he was immersed by the Rev. Mr. Griffis, of St. John, in the harbor of that city, Oct. 31, 1818. He was ordained at that time, or immediately after. Mr. Dunbar removed to the United States in December, 1823, and became pastor of the Baptist church at Nobleborough, Me. June 10, 1828, he accepted a call to the Vandam Street, subsequently called the McDougal Street, church, New York City. This settlement was the entrance into a great field of usefulness, and his pastorate with the McDougal Street church was the most important ministerial work of his life. In 1844 he removed to South Boston. After a pastorate of two years he returned to his church in New York, and remained with them until 1850, when he accepted a call to the Second church of Philadelphia. During his stay of two years with this church a large number of converts were added to it, many of whom lived to become useful and zealous Christians. In August, 1853, Mr. Dunbar ministered to the church at Trenton, N. J. After a service of fifteen months he returned to his old home with the McDougal Street church, and remained until the close of his earthly ministry.

As a man, Duncan Dunbar was remarkable for great kindness of heart, and manifested continually warm and practical sympathy for the distressed of every condition. As a preacher of the gospel he was energetic, earnest, and full of spiritual life. He was pre-eminently a man of prayer, and his long service in the ministry had abundant evidence of the blessing of God. He died July 28, 1864.

Duncan, Hon. James Henry, was born in Haverhill, Mass., Dec. 5, 1793. The fortunes of his ancestors on both his father's and his mother's side were for generations identified with the history of his native place. On his father's side he was of Scotch-Irish descent. The representatives of this race, who came from the famous Londonderry, in Ireland, were the worthy compeers of the early settlers of Plymouth. "In force of character," remarks the biographer of Mr. Duncan, "in zeal for religion, in previous preparation, in singleness of purpose, the Scotch-Irish were not inferior to the Pilgrims." The subject of this sketch was sent at eleven years of age to Phillips' Academy,

HON. JAMES HENRY DUNCAN.

at Exeter, N. H., at the time the best classical school in New England, if not in the whole country. Among his fellow-students were men who have risen to great distinction in the different professions which they followed. The names of Everett, Sparks, Buckminster, Palfrey, and Dix are among the most honored names in the annals of our country. Young Duncan was fitted to enter Harvard College when he was but fourteen years of age. He graduated in 1812, having passed through his course of study with credit to himself and honor to his friends.

Soon after his graduation he commenced the study of law, and was admitted to the bar in 1815, and opened an office in Haverhill, where for several years he devoted himself to the practice of his profession. The death of his father, in 1822, made it necessary for him to look after the affairs of his estate, and compelled him to withdraw from the active duties of his chosen calling. He took, however, a deep interest in public affairs and in the fortunes of the political party with which he identified himself. He was chosen a member of the House of Representatives and then a member of the senate of the Massachusetts Legislature. At different times during this period of his life he filled responsible places of trust and honor in his own State. In 1848 he was chosen by his district to represent them in Congress, and was re-elected in 1850. He exercised a commanding influence wherever he was called to act. The tribute of affection and respect which the poet Whittier paid to him after his decease makes honorable mention of him as a man in public life and in his social relations. "His Congressional career was a highly honorable one, marked by his characteristic soundness of judgment and conscientious faithfulness to a high ideal of duty. In private life as in public, he was habitually courteous and gentlemanly. For many years the leading man in his section, he held his place without ostentation, and . . . 'achieved greatness by not making himself great.'"

But it is time to turn from the consideration of Mr. Duncan's character as a public man. He took the most lively interest in the cause of education, and in the great religious organizations of his own denomination. Brown University was especially dear to him. Mr. Duncan was a member of the Board of Fellows of Brown University from 1835 till his death, a period which in many respects may be said to have been a "crisis period" in the history of the institution. It is needless to say that his name and influence were a "tower of strength" in the councils of the corporation. It is thus that Dr. Sears speaks of him as he appeared at its annual meetings or in the larger gatherings of the representatives of the Missionary Union: "Long will men remember the impression made on these and similar occasions by this Christian gentleman and scholar, with his finely-cut features and symmetrical form, his graceful and animated delivery, his chaste, beautiful, and musical language, his pertinent, clear, and convincing arguments, his unflinching fidelity, and his spotless integrity. So blended in him were these various attributes of body and mind that we can think of them only in their union, and it would seem that a mind of delicate mould had formed for itself a bodily organ suited to its own purposes. In him we see how much Christianity can do for true culture, and how beautiful an ornament culture is to Christianity."

Mr. Duncan was a sincere and earnest Baptist from his own honest, intelligent convictions, but like all Baptists he loved with a true Christian affection those who love the image of his Lord and Master of all denominations. He was forty years of age when he made an open avowal of his faith in Christ, but from the time of his public profession to his death men knew where James H. Duncan was to be found when the question was asked, "Is he or is he not on the Lord's side?" His love for his own church in Haverhill amounted almost to a passion. He lived for it and gave to it. He was sad when its spiritual life waned. He rejoiced when the signs of the presence of the converting and sanctifying spirit began to appear. To his pastors—and we include in them Drs. Hill, Train, Strong, and Bosworth—he was the confiding friend and the discreet counselor. "I can well remember," says Dr. Strong, "how he used to drink in the truth when I myself preached in the spirit of it, and how every such divine influence seemed to reproduce itself in his family and public prayers. With much of variation in his moods, with many doubts and conflicts in his inner life, it always gave strength and help to me to see how invariably principle and not feeling ruled him; how constant and devout was his attendance on the worship of the church, both social and public; and how bound up he seemed to be in all the interests of the Zion of God." Happy the pastor who has in his congregation even but one such man of whom things like these can truthfully be said!

But the interest which Mr. Duncan felt in the promotion of the Redeemer's kingdom went beyond the church of which he was a member. Every good cause had in him a friend. In this respect he resembled his fellow-laborer in "the kingdom and patience of the Lord Jesus,"—Gov. Briggs. For many years he was a member of the Board of Managers of the American Baptist Missionary Union, and for several years its chairman. The cause of home missions and ministerial education, and the publication of a sound religious literature, found in him an earnest advocate. Indeed, he gave himself with untiring zeal to all good objects by which humanity could be elevated and God be glorified.

The writer of this so imperfect sketch dares not trust himself in any attempt to lift the veil which shades from the public eye the domestic life of Mr. Duncan. Many times a recipient of his hospitality, and an eye-witness of what he was in the home circle, he can truly say that nowhere has he ever seen anything that came nearer to his ideal of what the family life of a cultivated Christian gentleman should be. Having said thus much he need say no more, but leave the imagination of the reader to fill up the outlines of the picture.

Having reached the age of seventy-five years, his strength not failing apparently, still fresh and strong, he was suddenly smitten with a malady which ended a useful and well-rounded life. After a brief illness, he died Sept. 8, 1869, and when he passed to his home in the skies a great void was made in his family, his church, and in the denomination, which to this day has never been filled.

Duncan, L. Alexander, a prominent layman and Sunday-school worker in Louisiana and Mississippi, residing at Meridian, Miss., was born in New York City in 1829; in 1847 associated with his brother, W. C. Duncan, D.D., in the publication of the *Southwestern Baptist Chronicle* in New Orleans; continued in 1852 under the name of *New*

Orleans Baptist Chronicle; superintendent of the American Tract Society in the Southwest from 1855 to 1861; published *Bible Student* at Memphis in 1878; subsequently agent of Ministerial Education Board of the Southwestern University; at present engaged in secular business at Meridian, Miss.

Duncan, Rev. Robert Samuel, was born in Lincoln Co., Mo., April 27, 1832. His father was a Baptist minister. His mother was Miss Harriet Kinnard. They were natives of Virginia. Mr. Duncan was converted at nineteen, and he was ordained in 1855 at Bethel church. He was fourteen years pastor of a country church, and a part of the time he was a missionary in Bear Creek Association. In 1869 he was appointed district secretary of the Southern Board for Missouri in the interests of foreign missions, and he still holds this position. He is the author of works entitled "The Primitive Baptists," "History of Sunday-Schools," and "The History of Missouri Baptists," soon to be issued. He lives in Montgomery City, Mo. He is of Scotch ancestry. He is one of the ablest men in our ministry in Missouri; his services to the denomination have been invaluable, and his writings should be read by all Baptists.

Duncan, Samuel White, D.D., son of Hon. James H. Duncan, was born at Haverhill, Mass., Dec. 19, 1838. At the age of twelve he was converted, and in August, 1851, was baptized by Rev. A. S. Train. His preparatory studies were pursued at Kimball Union Academy near Dartmouth College, N. H. In 1856 he entered Brown University, graduating with the honor of the Philosophical oration in 1860. After spending a year in travel, he entered in 1861 Newton Theological Seminary, but left in a little while to enter the U. S. army. Raising in two weeks a company in his native town, he became captain in the 50th Mass. Regiment, and served with honor in the army of Gen. Banks, then commanding the Department of the Gulf. Being mustered out with his regiment, he resumed his theological studies at Rochester Theological Seminary, graduating with the class of 1866.

Immediately after his graduation he was invited to supply for six months the Erie Street church of Cleveland, O. This led to his engagement as pastor. He was ordained in April, 1867, and remained in Cleveland until 1875, when he became pastor of the Ninth Street church, Cincinnati, O., a position which with great acceptance he continues to hold. One of the tangible results of his Cleveland work was the erection of a splendid new edifice on Euclid Avenue, to which the church removed and in which it now worships.

Dr. Duncan in 1879 was elected president of the Ohio State Convention as the successor of Hon. J. M. Hoyt. The honorary degree of D.D. was conferred upon him by the University of Chicago in 1878. He is a fine preacher, an earnest pastor, and is thoroughly interested in everything pertaining to the kingdom of Christ.

Duncan, William Cecil, D.D., was born in New York City in 1824; graduated at Columbia College, 1844; graduated at Madison University, 1846; went to New Orleans and engaged in publication of *Southwestern Baptist Chronicle;* succeeded Rev. I. T. Hinton as pastor of First Baptist church; in 1851 became Professor of Ancient Languages in the University of Louisiana; in 1853 pastor of Coliseum Place Baptist church, New Orleans; died in 1864. Dr. Duncan is the author of a valuable work on baptism, and a translation of Von Rhoden's "John the Baptist," besides other minor works.

Duncan, Col. Wm. H., was born and has always lived in Barnwell Co., S. C. Having in early life lost his father, he was in some measure thrown upon his own resources. He took a clerkship in a store at Barnwell Court-House, in which he became a great favorite. In the war he soon received a colonel's commission. His health having temporarily failed, and being unwilling to keep back others from promotion, he resigned. Having recovered his health, he returned to the service as a private, and rapidly rose again to his former rank.

After the war he studied law, and now holds a high position in the profession. He told the writer that he had never lost a case, simply because he would not take one till he was sure of its justice. He then frequently laid it before the court and submitted it without argument.

But the chief trait of his character is his zeal for Sunday-schools. No other man in the State has delivered so many Sunday-school addresses. His matter, language, and manner give a charm to his lectures seldom equaled. Were there a layman in every county in the Union laboring with equal zeal, the influence for good would be incalculable.

Dunegan, Rev. Jasper, a prominent minister in Northwest Arkansas, was born in North Georgia in 1825; removed to Arkansas in 1844; became a Baptist in 1845, and two years afterwards began to preach. By strong natural abilities he has acquired considerable local reputation as a pulpit orator and platform speaker. Through his instrumentality most of the churches north of Boston Mountain in the State have been planted or strengthened; long moderator of Bentonville Association; has served several terms in the General Assembly of the State, both in the lower house and the senate, during the most critical period since the war. For a number of years he was corresponding editor of the *Western Baptist* for the northwestern part of the State, to which he had been elected by several Associations.

Dungan, Rev. Thomas, was born in Ireland, and for some time he was a resident of Rhode Island, but in 1684, when advanced in years, he came into Pennsylvania. He settled three miles north of Bristol, at Cold Spring, and there he constituted the first Baptist church in Pennsylvania, built a meeting-house, and secured a burial-place for the dead. In 1688, Mr. Dungan was enabled to guide Elias Keach, when distressed by guilt, to the Saviour. He baptized him, and he was sent forth a minister of Jesus from the Cold Spring church. This was the most important event in the history of Mr. Dungan, or of his church, as will be seen by a reference to the memoir of Mr. Keach. He entered the heavenly rest in the year 1688; and before 1692 it is nearly certain that the church had ceased to exist. In 1770 "nothing remained of the Cold Spring church" but a grave-yard and the names of families that belonged to it: the Dungans, Gardeners, Woods, Doyles. He had five sons and four daughters, whose descendants in 1770 numbered between six and seven hundred persons. Mr. Dungan was the first Baptist minister in Pennsylvania. He was buried in the grave-yard surrounding the church. Nothing belonging to his church edifice or cemetery now remains to mark a spot so full of interest to Pennsylvania Baptists, except some foundations which can be distinctly traced across and on one side of a road which passes by the celebrated Cold Spring. The church site is two miles from Tullytown, Bucks County, and about two rods from the pike leading to it, and the same distance from the toll-gate on the Tullytown road. Some of the stones employed to mark graves in the burying-ground are in possession of persons in the neighborhood. The father of the celebrated Dr. Benjamin Rush is said to have been interred in this beautiful ground. Elias Keach, whom Mr. Dungan baptized, established the Lower Dublin church, now the oldest Baptist community in Pennsylvania.

Dunkards.—The word is a corruption of Tunkers, which signifies Dippers. (See GERMAN BAPTISTS.)

Dunn, L. A., D.D., was born in Bakersfield, Vt., June 12, 1814. In May, 1835, he went to Cambridge, Mass., and received private instruction in various branches. In May, 1838, he went to New Hampton, N. H., and devoted some attention to theology and to other branches of education, under the direction of Dr. E. B. Smith, Rev. J. Newton Brown, D.D., and Prof. Eaton. In 1841 he left New Hampton and taught in Bakersfield, Vt. In 1842 he commenced preaching at Fairfax, Vt.; was ordained in the October following, and remained pastor of that church twenty-nine years. He received the degree of D.D. from Hillsdale College, Mich. In 1861 he traveled through Europe, Egypt, and Palestine. On his return, under the direction of the Christian Commission, he visited the army three times. At the close of the war he was elected a member of the Vermont Legislature, and served three years. In 1869 he resigned his pastorate, having been elected president of the Central University of Iowa. In 1878 he made a second tour through Europe, Egypt, and Palestine, and since his return has published a work entitled "The Footprints of the Redeemer in the Holy Land."

Dunster, President Henry, was born in England probably in 1612. When about twelve years of age his attention was first called to the religion of Jesus. He was educated at the University of Cambridge, and he had among his fellow-students Ralph Cudworth, Jeremy Taylor, and John Milton. He was no doubt an Episcopal minister at first, and then a pious Puritan. He arrived in Boston in 1640.

Four years previous to the coming of Dunster the General Court had appropriated four hundred pounds to establish a college at Cambridge. Mr. Dunster became president of this institution on the 27th of August, 1640.

The new president was the friend of God and of his truth; he was a generous contributor to every good cause.

He was distinguished for his scholarly attainments in Latin, Greek, and Hebrew. In his day he was one of the greatest masters of the Oriental languages throughout the colonies, and Quincy, in his "History of Harvard University," says, "Among the early friends of the college none deserves more distinct notice than Henry Dunster. He united in himself the character of both patron and president; for, poor as he was, he contributed at a time of the utmost need one hundred acres of land towards its support, besides rendering it for a succession of years a series of official services well directed, unwearied, and altogether inestimable. The charter of 1642 was probably, and that of 1650 was avowedly, obtained on his petition. By solicitations among his friends and by personal sacrifices he built the president's house. He was instant in season and out of season with the General Court for the relief of the college in its extreme want." But Dunster was powerfully affected by the imprisonment of Messrs. Clarke, Holmes, and Crandal at Boston for worshiping God as Baptists without leave from the ruling powers; and after a full examination of the baptismal question, the first president of Harvard, a man of extraordinary learning, became a Baptist, and like a Christian man, despising financial losses and stripes and imprisonment, he boldly preached against infant sprinkling in the church at Cambridge, to the great indignation of its friends there and elsewhere. This sealed his career as president of Harvard. His years of service, marked by a success that created astonishment and gratitude, were quickly forgotten when, as Cotton Mather said, "he fell into the briers of anti-pedobaptism."

Quincy says, "Indicted by the grand jury for disturbing the ordinance of infant baptism in the Cambridge church, sentenced to a public admonition, and laid under bonds for good behavior, Dunster's martyrdom was consummated by being compelled to resign his office of president." "He found the seminary a school, it rose under his auspices to the dignity of a college. No man ever questioned his talents, learning, exemplary fidelity, and usefulness." Dunster deserves all this from the historian of Harvard. He was as noble a servant as ever followed Christ in times when truth demanded painful sacrifices. It is singular that such a man should become a Baptist. Brought up under other influences, having everything earthly to lose and nothing to gain, a profound scholar capable of weighing the merits of the controversy, nothing but the force of truth can account for his adoption of our sentiments. Like Alexander Carson, Adoniram Judson, Baptist W. Noel, and many others of culture and intellect, a tender conscience and the power of truth alone can account for the change. He died Feb. 27, 1659, and entered into that world where both the wicked and the godly cease from troubling and the weary are at rest.

Durfee, Job, Chief Justice, was elected a member of the corporation of Brown University to fill a Baptist vacancy. As the charter requires that persons so elected shall be Baptists, we take it for granted that he was a Baptist in sentiment. He was born in Tiverton, R. I., Sept. 20, 1790. His early days were spent upon his father's farm. When but quite a youth he began to develop those mental powers which afterwards gained him so much distinction in his native State. He entered Brown University in 1809. Dr. Messer was president of the college at the time. It is an indication of the position he held, that near the close of his college course Mr. Durfee prepared and delivered a Fourth of July oration to his fellow-citizens, which was so well received that a copy was requested for publication. He graduated among the foremost scholars of his class, "respected," says his son, "among his classmates for his vigorous powers of reason and imagination."

Mr. Durfee studied law, at the same time devoting himself to literary pursuits and cultivating his talent for poetry. He represented his native place in the State Legislature for six years, where he soon took the high position to which his abilities entitled him as an able debater and an accomplished legislator. From the representation of his State at home he passed to the House of Representatives at Washington, where he acquitted himself with distinction. He seems, however, to have become disgusted with Congressional life. At any rate, he would, with the independence of a citizen of the State of Rhode Island, whose best legacy was the spirit and honest freedom of its distinguished founder, speak out his own mind. Unfortunately, perhaps he may have thought fortunately for himself, his sentiments did not quite please his constituents, and he was defeated in the attempt to re-elect him. It was a relief from the excitements of political life to retire to his quiet farm, and amid the graver pursuits to which his attention was directed to woo his muse and indulge his poetic fancies, to the amusement and delight of his admiring friends. It was at this period of life that he laid the plan, and in due time carried it into execution, of writing a poem which should rehearse the fortunes of Roger Williams, for whose character he had the most profound regard. When the poem, to which he gave the title "What Cheer?" was completed, his modesty led him to conclude that it was not worthy of publication, "but," as his biographer remarks, "some lurking vanity of authorship—the hope to contribute 'something to the permanence of a genuine Rhode Island feeling'— or the praises of his friends overcame his modesty, and in 1832 a small edition was published by subscription." Its reception at home was anything but flattering to its author, but its merits were heartily recognized abroad, and that prince of reviewers, John Foster, was lavish in his praise of the production of the Rhode Island poet.

Mr. Durfee was appointed associate justice of the Supreme Court of the State in 1833, and two years after was made chief justice. It was while he was on the bench that Rhode Island passed through one of the great crises of its history. We refer to what is known as the "Dorr Rebellion." Judge Durfee was the firm friend of what he believed to be "law and order." He found time amid the pressure of other duties to prepare several valuable works, which were published. While engaged in his professional and literary work he was smitten down with disease, which ended his life July 26, 1847.

Durfee, Hon. Thomas, eldest son of Judge Job Durfee, was born in Tiverton, R. I., Feb. 6, 1826, and was a graduate of Brown University in the class of 1846. He was admitted to the bar in 1848, and in 1849 was appointed reporter of the decisions of the Supreme Court of Rhode Island, which office he held for four years. From 1854 to 1860, he served in the court of magistrates of the city of Providence, being for five years of this time the presiding magistrate. He was Speaker of the House of Representatives in 1863 and 1864. In 1865 he was chosen a State senator, and in June of this year was elected associate judge of the Supreme

Court of the State, which office he held until January 28, 1875, when he was chosen chief justice, which position he now (1880) holds. Judge Durfee, besides his valuable reports, has prepared jointly with Joseph K. Angell, Esq., a treatise on the law of highways, which was published in 1857.

HON. THOMAS DURFEE.

In 1872 he published a volume of poems. He is a member of the corporation of Brown University, of which he was chosen the chancellor in 1879, on the decease of the late Hon. B. F. Thomas. Judge Durfee is a regular attendant upon the worship of the First Baptist church, and identifies himself with the interests of that society.

Durham, Rev. C., was born in Rutherford Co., N. C., April 28, 1844. His mother was the sister of ex-Gov. Baxter, of Arkansas, and Judge John Baxter, of Tennessee. Mr. Durham was baptized in September, 1860; entered the army in April, 1861; was wounded four times; though but a boy, was blessed in conducting prayer-meetings in the army; was received by the Board of Education as a student at Wake Forest in 1867; graduated in 1871; was pastor in Goldsborough from August, 1871, to January, 1876, during which time the membership of the church more than doubled, an old debt was paid, and a pastor's study and parsonage were built; settled in Durham in 1876, where by his labors the church has been greatly strengthened, a new and beautiful house of worship has been built, also a parsonage. Mr. Durham has preached in twenty-five counties in North Carolina and three in South Carolina, and has baptized over 300 persons. He is a trustee of Wake Forest College.

Dutch Baptists in England.—About the seventeenth year of the reign of Queen Elizabeth a congregation of Dutch Baptists was found, without Aldgate, in London, twenty-seven of whom were cast into prison, and two of them were given to the flames. Fox, the author of the "Book of Martyrs," made an earnest appeal to Queen Elizabeth for these humble and harmless servants of the Saviour, but her majesty would not listen to the voice of mercy. This wicked event occurred in 1575.

Duval, Edmund Hillyer, was born in London in 1805; converted young, was baptized by Rev. J. Howard Hinton; was teacher and inspector of schools in England; came to New Brunswick in 1847; and as principal of the Normal School of St. John, and inspector of schools, Mr. Duval served the cause of education in New Brunswick well for thirty years.

Du Veil, Charles M., D.D., was trained from childhood in the Hebrew faith. His parents were evidently persons of intelligence and of ample financial resources, since they gave their son a thorough education.

Du Veil had a special taste for investigating every subject brought to his attention. It made no difference to him what others thought, even though they had been famous for learning, and united to him by the tenderest ties, he must examine everything for himself. A careful study of the prophets convinced him that Jesus was the Messiah; and with great independence of character he avowed himself a Christian. His father, whose hopes were so unexpectedly blighted, and whose heart was so deeply wounded, as he discovered the situation, seized a sword, and, if friends had not interfered, would have slain his son.

The form of Christianity which he embraced was the Roman Catholic. He was doubtless surrounded by nominal and earnest members of that apostate community. His literary attainments were so remarkable and his mental powers so great, that he was soon regarded with general favor as a popular preacher in the French Church. The University of Anjou gave him the degree of Doctor of Divinity, and appointed him Professor of Theology. The publication of his commentary on Matthew and Mark, in which, with great ingenuity, he defended the dogmas of Romanism, gave him the character of an able controversialist: and soon his belligerent talents were summoned into service against the Huguenots, then the chief friends of God, and the worst foes of Romanism, in France; but as he carefully examined the writings of the French Protestants he found that the truth was entirely on their side; and as it was his sovereign he immediately yielded to its precious sceptre. He fled to Holland to avoid persecution, and there abjured the heresies of the frail "scarlet lady" of the seven hills.

He came to England in search of truth, and a home; and in that country he became a favorite with some of the first men in the Episcopal Church, Stillingfleet, Tillotson, Patrick (Dean of Peterborough), Lloyd (Bishop of St. Asaph's), and Compton (Bishop of London). He was ordained an Episcopal clergyman, and became the domestic chaplain of an English nobleman.

He republished his commentary on Matthew and Mark in England in 1670, extensively revised and corrected. In 1679 he issued his "Literal Explication of Solomon's Song." This effort was highly appreciated by the English clergy, and by the Protestants on the Continent. In 1680 he published a "Literal Exposition of the Minor Prophets," dedicated to Lord Heneage Finch, the lord chancellor. The Bishop of London was so delighted with this work that he gave him the privilege of using his splendid library as freely as if it were his own. In that literary treasury Du Veil became acquainted with the works of the English Baptists, and speedily found that the Bible contained their doctrines; and that, notwithstanding the loss which the avowal would inflict upon him, he must proclaim himself a Baptist. A young woman in the service of the Bishop of London held Baptist principles, for which she was frequently annoyed by her companions; she discovered Du Veil's Baptist tendencies, and procured for him an interview with Hanserd Knollys, and subsequently with John Gosnold: and by Mr. Gosnold he was baptized. This act cost him all his Episcopal friends except Tillotson, the future Archbishop of Canterbury.

Some time afterwards he gave to the world "A Literal Explanation of the Acts of the Holy Apostles." It was published in London in 1685. In it he defends his new opinions with signal ability. It is the most valuable of his works. The celebrated French Protestant minister, Claude, for years Professor of Theology in the College of Nismes, whose reputation is still dear to all French Protestants, and to all sermonizers in England and America, whose knowledge of his writings only extends to his "Essay on the Composition of a Sermon," in a letter to Dr. Du Veil, says,—

"I have perused your Commentary, though it came but lately to my hands, and I have found in it, as in all your other works, the marks of copious reading, abundance of sense, right reason, and a just and exact understanding: and I do not doubt but that the Commentary will be kindly received by the learned, and prove very useful to all those who apply themselves to understand the Scriptures." Claude was a Pedobaptist.

Du Veil was familiar with all Jewish and Christian learning; and his departure from the Church of England and adoption of our sentiments and people, at a period when the Baptists were oppressed by the bitter hatred of James II., of the whole Episcopal establishment, and of nearly all English Pedobaptists, is a remarkable testimony to his conscientiousness, and to the truth of our doctrines.

Dwelle, Rev. George W., one of the most useful and prominent among the colored Baptists of Georgia, resides in Americus, and has charge of Shady Grove (colored) Baptist church, in Sumter County, and, also, of the Eureka (colored) Baptist church, at Albany. He stands high among his brethren, who repose great confidence in him. He is the clerk of the Ebenezer (colored) Baptist Association, and of the Missionary Baptist Convention of Georgia, having held each position since the organization of those bodies, in which he himself took a leading part. Under the appointment of this Convention he acted as an agent in collecting funds for the college building in Atlanta, and also as a State missionary. He was born in Augusta in 1833, and was converted in 1855. He joined the Springfield (colored) Baptist church at Augusta in 1856, and immediately, with great decision, entered upon religious duties; was in turn made superintendent of the Sunday-school and deacon of the church; was licensed to preach in 1873, and ordained in 1874. He has always been a steady worker in the church and Sunday-school; has strongly favored missions and education, and stands high in the estimation of both races, among the Baptists of Georgia, as a good preacher and a man of fine character.

Dye, Rev. Daniel, was born in Johnstown, Montgomery Co., N. Y. He was converted in 1823, and at once began to exhort men to repentance. In 1824 he was licensed to preach, and ordained in 1831 to the work of the ministry. Elder John Smitzer preached the sermon and Elder John Peck made the consecrating prayer. Mr. Dye has devoted his life to itinerant and pioneer labor almost exclusively. In the State of New York he labored at sixteen different places, either gathering churches or strengthening the feeble flock of God. Frequent revivals attended his ministry. In 1844 the American Baptist Home Mission Society sent him as its missionary to Davenport, Iowa, and Rock Island, Ill. The following year he entered the Territory of Wisconsin. He labored at Prairieville (now Waukesha), Raymond, East Troy, Darien, Walworth, and other places, confining his efforts mostly to Walworth and Racine Counties. He is eighty-one years old, and preaches still when called upon. During his ministry of over fifty years he has preached 6000 times, baptized 400 persons, attended 600 funerals, and married 400 couples.

Dyer, Rev. A. Nichols, was born in East Greenwich, R. I., May 1, 1803; was converted when very young; graduated at Hamilton in 1829; founded the church in Harrisburg, Pa., in 1830; was pastor of Roxborough in 1832; organized the church at Chestnut Hill; in 1837 was pastor in Phœnixville; aided in the formation of churches in East Nantmeal, Caernarvon, and West Calm, and afterwards was pastor of the former two; then of the Bethesda and Danville churches. He died in Philadelphia, Nov. 6, 1867.

Dyer, Rev. Sidney, Ph.D., was born at White Creek, Washington Co., N. Y., in 1814. He joined the army in the Black Hawk war of 1831, and was sent to fight the Indians. He continued in military life for about ten years, and rose to a position both pleasant and lucrative. But his desire to preach grew so overpowering that at twenty-two years of age he entered upon a course of study under the direction of Rev. Charles G. Sommers, D.D., then pastor of the South Baptist church, New York. He was ordained in 1842, and preached first in a church near his former residence at Brownsville, and afterward as a missionary among the Choctaws. Subsequently he occupied the office of secretary of the Indian Mission Board at Louisville, Ky. In 1852 he became pastor of the church at Indianapolis, and in 1859 was chosen district secretary of the American Baptist Publication Society at Philadelphia. He still remains in the service of the society, and continues with remarkable vigor his labors as preacher, author, and poet. He received the degree of A.M. from Indiana State University, and that of Ph.D. from the University at Lewisburg, Pa. His earlier contributions to poetry appeared in various literary journals, and were subsequently published in a volume entitled "Voices of Nature." Some of his verses embody very tender reminiscences of his early life and fellowships. He has also published "Dyer's Psalmist," "Winter's Evening Entertainment," occasional sermons, and a numerous collection of songs and ballads. Some of his sacred verses will doubtless occupy a permanent place in the services of the sanctuary. More recently he has contributed a charming and invaluable series of books for young people, among which may be mentioned "Great Wonders in Little Things," "Home and Abroad," "Black Diamonds," "Boys and Birds," "Hoofs and Claws," "Ocean Gardens," and "Elmdale Lyceum." These volumes evidence the author's wonderful tact and clearness in leading the mind through a knowledge of nature to the contemplation of nature's God.

His daughter, Mrs. Mattie Dyer Britts, is also widely known as a writer of marked ability. She has already published several juvenile volumes, and is a contributor to a number of literary and religious journals.

Dyke, Daniel, M.A., was born at Epping, Essex, about 1617. He was educated at the University of Cambridge. After receiving episcopal ordination he was appointed to the living of Great Haddam, Hertfordshire, worth about £300 per annum. He soon became noted as a man of great learning and deep piety, and speedily was invested with a very extensive influence. He was appointed by Cromwell in 1653 one of the Triers for the examination and admission of godly ministers into the national church. The Lord Protector also made him one of his chaplains. When Cromwell ordered a collection to be taken up in all the parish churches in England for the persecuted Waldenses, Mr. Dyke's name, with many others, appeared in the proclamation as commending the object. Cromwell himself gave £2000 on the occasion. Before the Act of Uniformity was passed, Mr. Dyke withdrew all his services from the national church, and preached wherever he had an opportunity until the year 1668, when he was appointed co-pastor with the celebrated William Kiffin. He retained this position for twenty years, when he entered upon his eternal rest, in the seventieth year of his age.

He was a man of great attainments, of extreme modesty, and of marked usefulness.

E.

Eaches, Rev. Owen P., was born at Phœnixville, Pa., Dec. 11, 1840; baptized Feb. 20, 1853; graduated at Lewisburg University in 1863, and from the theological department two years later. He taught in the university in 1865–66; was ordained at Nicetown, Philadelphia, October, 1866; became pastor of the old church at Hightstown, N. J., June 1, 1870. Here his labors have been very successful in building up the church and in the conversion of souls. His influence is largely felt in the affairs of Peddie Institute. He has been for a long time secretary of the board governing that academy, and when Dr. Fish resigned the secretaryship of the New Jersey Baptist Education Society, in 1873, Mr. Eaches was elected to that position, and still holds it. He is a close student, an active pastor, and a frequent contributor to the periodicals.

Eager, Rev. E. C., pastor at Brookhaven, Miss., was born in Vermont in 1813; graduated at Madison University, N. Y., in 1841; began his ministerial labors as a missionary at Memphis, Tenn., in 1842. Here he gathered about forty Baptists and preached to them three months; then he removed to Granada, Miss. He filled several other pastorates in the State, then accepted an agency of the Southern Baptist Publication Society, Charleston, S. C., in which he developed rare qualifications for raising money for benevolent uses; as an agent of Mississippi College he obtained one hundred and twenty thousand dollars; was the successful agent of the Bible Revision Association up to the war; after the war he again became agent of Mississippi College and the Domestic Mission Board of the Southern Baptist Convention until he settled in his present pastorate.

Eagle, Rev. J. P., a prominent minister at Lonoke, Ark., was born in Maury Co., Tenn., in 1837, but he was reared in that part of Arkansas where he has since labored; was a lieutenant-colonel in the Confederate army; since the war has served a number of terms in the State Legislature; began to preach in 1868, and has since supplied a number of churches in his region. Being a wealthy planter, he has preached without charge to his churches, but inculcates the duty of ministerial support and contributes largely to the cause. In a recent political State Convention, without being a candidate, he received a respectable vote for governor.

Earle, Rev. T. J.—This most estimable brother was born in Spartanburg Co., S. C., Dec. 23, 1824; baptized in 1845 by Rev. J. G. Landrum, and ordained in 1852. He took his literary and his theo-

REV. T. J. EARLE.

logical course in Mercer University. He was four years pastor at Pendleton, S. C., and left the church in a highly prosperous condition. He then settled in Gowensville, Glennville Co., S. C., where he has preached about twenty-four years, twenty-four at Holly Spring, and eighteen at Milford. He has taught for many years as principal of the Gowensville Seminary. He has baptized an unusual number of pupils, and many have been baptized by others. His countenance is a true index of his noble soul. Modesty is the crown of all his virtues. When the writer proposed to try to get him the title of D.D. he peremptorily refused. He is an accomplished scholar, a fine preacher, and one of the most perfect Christian gentlemen the writer has ever known.

Early, Rev. M. D., pastor at Dardanelles, Ark., was born in Georgia in 1846, but was reared in Clarke Co., Ark., whither his father removed in 1858; began to preach in 1870, and served a number of churches in the region of his home until 1875, when he was called to Hope, Hampstead County, where he did a noble work. In 1877 he was called to the Third Street church, Little Rock. With this feeble interest he labored successfully two years, and then removed to his present important field. Mr. Early is an acceptable preacher, and one of the rising young men of the State.

Eason, Rev. F. W., was born in Charleston, S. C., Oct. 31, 1837; baptized December, 1858, by Dr. Basil Manly, Sr.; entered the army April, 1861; surrendered under Gen. J. E. Johnston at High Point, N. C., May 15, 1865; was captain of infantry, and afterwards of artillery; was a merchant after the war; was called to ordination by Darlington church in 1867, Drs. J. O. B. Dargan, Richard Furman, and Geo. Bealer forming the presbytery. After seven years' service as pastor in Darlington, S. C., went to the theological seminary in Greenville, S. C., taking the full course. Mr. Eason has served the Fayetteville church, N. C., and is now pastor in Newberne. He was educated at Charleston College, S. C. He has a fine literary taste, and he is popular as a preacher, pastor, and lecturer.

East Alabama Female College, located at Tuskegee, was founded by the Tuskegee Association in 1850. The buildings were of the most beautiful and modern style, and cost not less than sixty thousand dollars. It had a brilliant career of twenty years. Dr. Bacon, Gen. W. F. Perry, Rev. A. J. Battle, D.D., Rev. E. B. Teague, D.D., and Prof. R. H. Rawlings, A.M., were presidents of this institution. By accident or by incendiary it was burned in 1870, and so ended its history.

Eastin, Rev. Augustine, a brilliant preacher of the last century, was one of the first converts to Baptist principles in Goochland Co., Va. He soon become a zealous minister, and was incarcerated in Chesterfield jail for preaching contrary to law. He moved to Kentucky in 1784, and was one of the constituents of Bryant's church, in Fayette County. Afterwards he moved to Bourbon County, where he formed Cowper's Run church, in 1807. He appears to have been popular and useful till he became an Arian, and was cut off from the Baptists. He maintained a good moral character to the end of life.

East Troy, a village of Walworth County. It was here that the Wisconsin Baptist State Convention was organized in 1846, and where Conrad, Delaney, and Miner toiled with great self-denial but unfaltering loyalty to Christ in the early history of the State.

Eastwood, Rev. Thomas Midgely, was born at Manayunk, Pa., May 11, 1848. He was baptized by Rev. Miller Jones, at Bridgeport, Pa., in March, 1863, and was received into the membership of the First Baptist church of that place. He was educated at the University of Lewisburg and at Crozer Theological Seminary. He graduated at Lewisburg in June, 1872, and at Crozer Theological Seminary in May, 1874. His ministry began with the First Baptist church, Wilmington, Del., May 1, 1874, and he was ordained in June of the same year. The chairman of the council of ordination was Rev. James Trickett, and the clerk Rev. W. R. McNeil; Rev. J. M. Pendleton, D.D., Rev. George W. Anderson, D.D., Rev. George W. Folwell, Rev. E. W. Dickinson, D.D., and Rev. Miller Jones participated in the exercises of ordination. During his ministry at Wilmington he has organized the Shiloh Baptist church, the first colored Baptist congregation in the State of Delaware. He assisted in the formation of the Delaware Baptist Missionary Union, which was organized September, 1874, and was its first secretary. He has also been actively engaged in furthering the interests of the Delaware Baptist Union. He was its first president, and has been three times elected to the office. At present he is pastor of the Bethany Baptist church, which is the outgrowth of a union of the Elm Street with the First Baptist church, effected in 1876. He has thus had at present writing a continuous pastorate of six years.

Eaton, Geo. W., D.D., LL.D., was born at Henderson, Huntington Co., Pa., July 3, 1804; family removed to Ohio in 1805; entered, 1822, Ohio University, at Athens, and remained two years; from 1824 to 1827 was engaged in teaching in Prince Edward Co., Va.; in 1827 entered junior class at Union College, Schenectady, and was graduated in 1829; in 1830 was elected tutor in the academy at Belleville, N. Y.; from 1831 to 1833 was Professor of Ancient Languages in Georgetown, Ky., and acted as president of the institution the last six months; in 1833 became connected with Madison University (see article MADISON UNIVERSITY), then Hamilton Literary and Theological Institution; from 1833 to 1837 was Professor of Mathematics and Natural Philosophy; from 1837 to 1850 occupied the chair of Ecclesiastical and Civil History; 1850-61, Professor of Systematic Theology and president of Madison University; Professor of Intellectual and Moral Philosophy, from 1856 to 1868; from 1861 to 1871 president of Hamilton Theological Seminary and Professor of Homiletics. Died Aug. 3, 1872. It is well-nigh impossible within brief limits to describe adequately this great man. In person he was tall, well formed, and pleasing in his movements, the features denoting great kindness of heart. In character he was gentle, unsuspicious, confiding, and hopeful,—a very Christian gentleman.

He was devoted to the interests of the institution, and when his failing health compelled his retirement he felt he was severing himself from his very life. Not an old man when he died, yet he had become aged by severe toil and faithful service in the interests of the university. By nature Dr. Eaton was an orator, and yet he possessed the best elements of a successful teacher. Few men have more deeply impressed themselves upon the character of their pupils than he. His influence, in connection with Dr. Hascall and Dr. Spear, carried the college through its darker hours, and to him the friends of education, and especially the Baptists of New York, owe a debt of gratitude which it will be impossible to pay.

GEORGE W. EATON, D.D., LL.D.

Eaton, Rev. Isaac, A.M., was the son of Rev. Joseph Eaton, of Montgomery, Pa.; was converted in early life, and joined the Southampton church, Pa. He soon began to preach, and when twenty-four years of age took charge of the church in Hopewell, N. J., Nov. 29, 1748. Rich blessings descended upon his pastorate, which ended only with his life, twenty-six years afterwards. He immediately became prominent in the Philadelphia Association, and the way was soon opened for his great work.

The "Elders and Messengers of the several congregations baptized on profession of faith in Pennsylvania, New Jersey, and Provinces adjacent," at Philadelphia, on Oct. 5, 1756, passed the following resolution:

"Concluded to raise a sum of money toward the encouragement of a Latin grammar school, for the promotion of learning among us, under the care of Brother Isaac Eaton, and the inspection of our brethren, Abel Morgan, Isaac Stelle, Abel Griffith, and Peter B. Van Horn."

The school was opened under this comprehensive resolution. While men who became eminent in divinity went out from the teaching and influence of that wonderful man, other professions were well represented. Eaton was the first teacher among American Baptists who opened a school for the education of young men for the ministry. Among his students were James Manning, D.D., first president of Rhode Island College (now Brown University), said to have been Eaton's first student; Samuel Jones, D.D., Hezekiah Smith, D.D., David Jones, A.M., Isaac Skillman, D.D., a number of physicians (Mr. Eaton had studied medicine, and practised among the poor), and several members of the legal profession. Mr. Eaton died before attaining old age. The tablet erected to his memory, first in the meeting-house, and now in the cemetery of the Hopewell church, has this inscription:

"To the front of this are deposited the remains of Rev. Isaac Eaton, A.M., who for upwards of 26 years was pastor of this church, from the care of which he was removed by death, on the 4th of July, 1772, in the forty-seventh year of his age.

In him with grace and eminence did shine
The man, the Christian, scholar, and divine."

He left little of his literary productions. There is a charge delivered at the ordination of his pupil and intimate friend, Rev. Samuel Jones, A.M., Jan. 2, 1763, which is full of wise counsels very happily expressed. Dr. Jones preached Mr. Eaton's funeral sermon. His subject was "Resignation," and his text Job i. 21. Toward the close of the discourse, having mentioned the intimacy between them, he says, "It might be expected I should say something concerning him; and verily much might be said with the greatest truth. The natural endowments of his mind; the improvement of these by the accomplishments of literature; his early, genuine, and unaffected piety; his abilities as a divine and a preacher; his extensive knowledge of men and books; his catholicism, prudence, and able counsels, together with a view of him in the different relations, both public and private, that he sustained through life with so much honor to himself and happiness to all who had connection with him, would afford ample scope, had I but abilities, time, and inclination, to flourish in a funeral oration. But it is needless, for the bare mentioning them is enough to revive the idea of him in the minds of all who knew him."

The house in which Mr. Eaton conducted the first institution for the education of Baptist ministers on this continent is still in the village of Hopewell, N. J., on the Bound Brook Railroad. The structure is a substantial frame building, in good condition, located near the Calvary Baptist church, and not far from the Old-School Baptist church edifice, in which the descendants of the people to whom he ministered are accustomed to meet for the worship of God.

Eaton, Rev. Jeremiah S., was born in Weare, N. H., in June, 1810. He was a graduate of Union College in the class of 1835. He took the full course of study at Newton, graduating in 1839. He was ordained as pastor of the First Baptist church in Hartford, Conn., Nov. 13, 1839. He remained in Hartford five years, and then accepted a call to the Free Street church, in Portland, Me., which connection he held for ten years. Ill health compelled him to resign in 1854. He died at Portland, Sept. 27, 1856.

Eaton, Joseph H., LL.D., was born in Berlin, Delaware Co., O., Sept. 10, 1812. His father died when he was a child, and he was brought up by his mother, a woman of great force of character and remarkable for her strong faith in God. Once during his childhood he was supposed to be dead, the physician pronounced him dead, and only the child's mother doubted the statement. She maintained, in despite of all appearances, that the boy still lived, because he was a child of too many prayers to die so young. She believed that God had a work for him to do, and the child recovered. He made rapid progress in his studies in the neighboring schools, and it was soon necessary for him to seek larger advantages for study. Being the youngest son, his mother parted with him with great reluctance, saying, "Joseph, I have but a little while to live. I believe God has a work for you, and you must be educated to fit you for it, and hence you must go." He accordingly left home and entered Worthington Academy. His brother, George W. Eaton, was at this time professor in Georgetown College, Ky., and afterwards in the Hamilton Literary and Theological Institution, N. Y. Joseph, after finishing his course at the academy, went to Georgetown, Ky., where he studied until his brother left, following him to Hamilton, where he graduated in 1837. In the same year he removed to Davidson Co., Tenn., where he taught school for six months, and thence went to Fayetteville, Tenn., to take charge of an academy. Here he remained three years. In 1841 he was elected a professor in the new Baptist institution at Murfreesborough, Tenn., and in 1847 he was appointed its president, it being named the Union University. He was ordained in 1843; was pastor in Murfreesborough, and of several country churches, preaching every Sunday, and faithfully teaching in the class-room, until he impaired his health by excessive labors, and died Jan. 12, 1859. Dr. Eaton was a man of great earnestness, laboring with an untiring zeal that nothing could thwart. As an educator he had but few equals, being distinguished for his power of imparting instruction and stimulating a love of knowledge; for a thorough control over students, shown in discipline and in influence upon their characters; and for his ability to win the affection of his pupils. As a preacher, Dr. Eaton was earnest and impressive, of impassioned utterance and rapid delivery. His power to fix attention and impress his thoughts upon his hearers has seldom been equaled. He won the enthusiastic devotion of those who knew him, of all classes and grades of society. His fellow-ministers, professors, the churches to which he preached, his many students, and his servants, all loved him as few men are loved. Handsome in person, gracious in presence, genial in manners, and winning in conversation, he was eminent in the qualities which make men charming in the home circle, as he was in those which make a great teacher and preacher. There was about him a sense of reserved power. The strength of the man was always felt beneath his genial graciousness. His children and his students would face any danger rather than have him know that they had been guilty of a dishonorable action, so much did they dread the glance of his eye, so much did they value his approving smile. His virtues live in the memories of all who knew him.

Eaton, Thomas Treadwell, D.D., was born in Murfreesborough, Tenn., Nov. 16, 1845, and was educated partly at the Union University, Tenn., partly at Madison University, N. Y., and partly at Washington College, Lexington, Va. Dr. Eaton was pastor at Lebanon and Chattanooga, Tenn., and he is now pastor of the First Baptist church, Petersburg, Va. From 1867 to 1872 he was professor in Union University, Murfreesborough, Tenn. He has published a small volume, "The Angels," issued by the American Baptist Publication Society, and he has contributed to many of the denominational papers, chiefly the *Religious Herald*, of Virginia. During 1870-71 he was one of the editors of the *Christian Herald*, of Tennessee, and he is prominent in all denominational meetings. He is a vigorous and polished writer, and a man of ripe culture. Dr. Eaton received the degree of D.D. from Washington and Lee University, Va., in 1878.

Eaton, William H., D.D., was born in Goffstown, N. H., Sept. 4, 1818, and was a graduate of Brown University in the class of 1845. He took the full course of study at the Newton Theological Institution, graduating in the class of 1848. His ordination took place in August, 1849, and he was pastor of the Second Baptist church in Salem, Mass., from 1849 to 1854. Having resigned his pastorate, he accepted an appointment as an agent to solicit funds for the endowment of the New London Academy. Returning to the active duties of the ministry, he became pastor of the Baptist church in Nashua, N. H., one of the largest and most flourishing churches in the State. Here he remained four years. He next accepted an appointment to act as an agent to raise funds for the better endowment of the Newton Theological Institution. "By his quiet, patient, and well-directed efforts," says Dr. Hovey in his historical address, "complemented at the last by the powerful exertions of a few distinguished brethren, the sum of $200,000 was raised by subscription, and in amounts varying from $1 to $18,000." Dr. Hovey also remarks, "A fortnight, more or less, before the time for completing this subscription expired, a meeting of the subscribers was held in Tremont Temple, Boston, at which Dr. Eaton stated that he had secured pledges to the amount of about $177,500, but could not obtain the required sum, $200,000. Thereupon Gardner Colby and J. Warren Merrill were appointed a committee to raise the subscription to $210,000. The time for doing this was short, but the task proposed was accomplished." Having completed his work as the agent of the Newton Theological Institution, Dr. Eaton returned to the active duties of the ministry by accepting, in 1872, an invitation to become the pastor of the Baptist church in Keene, N. H., where he is now living.

The degree of Doctor of Divinity was conferred on Dr. Eaton in 1867 by Brown University, of which he was appointed a trustee in 1876.

Eccles, Rev. Samuel, was born in the County of Roscommon, Ireland, and for a time was a merchant in his native country. Afterwards he went to France and took an active part in the terrible struggles of the revolution of 1792-93, until sickened by the enormities practised in the name of liberty, he resigned his commission and came to this country.

Soon after his arrival in South Carolina he was converted and united with the Baptists. Called of God to the ministry, he spent four years in literary and theological studies, and entered upon the active duties of the pastorate. His labors were greatly blessed for years, and when his prospects were unusually bright he passed into the heavenly rest, on the 12th of August, 1808.

As a preacher he was zealous and energetic, and manifested acquaintance with the heart and conscience, which he addressed with great power. He endured his last sufferings with calm submission to the will of Providence, and he died full of peace.

Eddy, Daniel C., D.D., was born in Salem, Mass., May 21, 1823, and was baptized July 3, 1842, into the fellowship of the Second Baptist church in that city. After the completion of his literary and theological education he was called to the pastorate of the First Baptist church in Lowell, Mass., Jan. 2, 1846, and was ordained in the same month. This relation continued for ten years, and they were years of great prosperity with the church. The whole number added to it was 1005, of which 637 were baptized. In 1850, Dr. Eddy went abroad to recruit his health, which was impaired by long-con-

DANIEL C. EDDY, D.D.

tinued ministerial labor. In 1854, a year which is embraced within the period when what was known as the American, or "Know-Nothing" party had so prominent a place in the politics of the country, Dr. Eddy was chosen as a representative from Lowell to the Legislature of Massachusetts, and, quite unexpectedly to himself, he was elected Speaker of the House. Without having had any experience in presiding over a deliberative assembly, he discharged the duties of his office so satisfactorily that the House passed a unanimous vote thanking him "for the promptness, ability, and urbanity with which he had performed the duties of presiding officer during the prolonged deliberations of the present session."

In 1856, Dr. Eddy was called to the Harvard Street church in Boston, and installed as pastor on the last Lord's day in December. Twice during this pastorate Dr. Eddy went abroad, extending his visit the second time to the Holy Land. Four hundred and seventy-eight persons were received by letter and by baptism into the Harvard Street church while Dr. Eddy was its minister.

In November, 1862, a call was extended to Dr. Eddy by the Tabernacle church in Philadelphia. He accepted it, and was installed Nov. 6, 1862, remaining there two years, when he was invited to the Baldwin Place church in Boston. The church for various reasons, chiefly on account of the unfavorable location of their house of worship, had become very much reduced in numbers. A change of location carried them to the "South End," where a new church edifice was erected in Warren Avenue, an almost entirely new congregation gathered, and prosperity attended the enterprise. Dr. Eddy was called from Boston to the First Baptist church in Fall River, Mass., and returned again to Boston to enter upon a work in which for many years he had taken a deep interest,—the opening of a place of worship at the "South End" on the free system. Various circumstances combined to make the enterprise not so successful as he desired, and it was abandoned. He is now the pastor of the church in Hyde Park, one of the pleasant suburban villages in the neighborhood of Boston.

Dr. Eddy has written a large number of books, some of which, especially his "Young Man's Friend," have had a very extended circulation. Several books, the result of his travels abroad, have also been widely circulated. Few of our ministers have had a more active and successful ministry than Dr. Eddy, and few ministers have superior ability, culture, and piety. Harvard College conferred on him the degree of A.M. in 1855, and Madison University the degree of D.D. in 1856.

Eddy, Herman J., D.D., was born in Marion, Wayne Co., N. Y., Dec. 10, 1810; baptized in 1827; studied at Hamilton Literary and Theological Institution; received the degree of A.M. from Madison University, and D.D. from Shurtleff College; was ordained at Marion in 1834. His first settlement as pastor was in Scipio, N. Y. After five years of successful labor he accepted the call of the church in Jordan. In 1849 he took charge of the Cannon Street Baptist church, New York. In 1856 he became pastor of the First Baptist church of Bloomington, Ill., where he founded the *Illinois Baptist*, which was subsequently consolidated with the *Christian Times*, now *The Standard*, of Chicago. In 1861 he was commissioned chaplain of the 33d Regiment of Ill. Vols., known in the West as the Normal Regiment. After two years' service becoming disabled he resigned and accepted the pastorate of the First Baptist church of Belvidere, Ill. In 1869 he was called to the Central Baptist church of Syracuse, N. Y. He was prospered in all his settlements; in the last three the churches built new and large houses of worship. When in New York he was a member of the board of the American and Foreign Bible Society, and afterwards of the American Bible Union, of which he was one of the founders. He is the author of several printed sermons and public addresses, and was the regular correspondent of the New York *Recorder* and the Michigan *Christian Herald*. He has also contributed to the *Standard*, of Chicago, the *Baptist Weekly*, and other journals of New York. An injury caused by a fall in 1873 induced him to retire from pastoral work, since which he has resided in the city of New York.

Eddy, Richard Evans, was born in Providence, R. I., July 19, 1802, and was a graduate of Brown University in the class of 1822. On leaving college he went into business in his native city, and continued in it till 1841, when he was appointed deputy collector of the port of Providence, which office he held for four years. In 1845 he was elected treasurer of the American Baptist Missionary Union, and removed to Boston, where he became an active and much beloved member of Dr. Baron Stow's church. For nine years he held the office to which he had been chosen, greatly to the satisfaction of the society. His official relations to his missionary brethren were of the most tender nature; he endeared himself to them by his interest in their work, and his sympathy with them in all their trials. The state of his health obliged him to resign his office in 1854, and he returned to his old home in Providence. For the last fourteen years of his life he held the office of deacon in the First Baptist church, of the Sabbath-school connected with which he had at an earlier period in his life been for nine years the superintendent. He died in Providence, April 29, 1870.

Edgren, John Alexis, D.D., the head of the Scandinavian department in the theological seminary at Morgan Park, Ill., was born in Wermland, Sweden, in 1839. After passing through the preparatory department of the elementary school of Carlstad he went to sea in 1852, sailing in ships of five different nations. In 1857 he was converted while at sea, and in 1858 was baptized. Entering the navigation school at Stockholm, he graduated in 1859 with the highest honors conferred in Sweden upon naval students. He then returned to the sea, sailing as mate and second mate of Swedish vessels. In 1862 he was examined as teacher of navigation, and passed successfully. In that year he came to this country, and as the war was in progress he entered the U. S. navy as acting ensign, and subsequently served as sailing-master. In 1863 he resigned and attended lectures in Princeton Theological Seminary. Again, in 1864, he entered the navy, and was placed in command of the U. S. steamer "Catalpa," sailing from Philadelphia to the Charleston blockade. Subsequently he volunteered for service at the naval battery on Morris Island, and participated in several engagements. In 1865 he finally resigned and left the sea, fully determined to obey the call he had long been conscious of, to preach the gospel. His first service was as colporteur and missionary of the American Baptist Publication Society. In the fall of 1865 he entered upon the study of theology at

Madison University, and in 1866 was appointed by the Missionary Union a missionary to Sweden. Upon returning to America in 1870 he was called to the pastorate of the Swedish Baptist church in Chicago, with an appropriation from the American Baptist Home Mission Society. In the fall of 1871 he began giving instruction at the theological seminary to Scandinavian students, himself pursuing study in the seminary at the same time, and graduating in 1872. The interest awakened by his work as instructor of Scandinavian students in various branches of theology eventuated in the founding of the Scandinavian department as a permanent branch of the seminary work.

At the present date (1880) 29 students have graduated from this department, and have become ministers of the gospel among their own people. Hundreds under their preaching have professed conversion and have been baptized. With the work of instruction Prof. Edgren has associated the editing of a Swedish religious paper. Six other religious publications are fruits of his pen.

Educational Institution for Ministers, The First American Baptist.—See article on REV. ISAAC EATON, A.M.

Edwards, Dr. Benjamin F., was born in Maryland, July 2, 1797, and converted in Kentucky in 1826. He removed to Illinois in 1827, and to St. Louis, Mo., in 1845. He died in Kirkwood, Mo., in April, 1877.

Dr. Edwards held a distinguished position as a medical practitioner. He had a superior intellect, richly furnished with the results of extensive reading and study. He was popular in social gatherings, and greatly beloved by a very numerous circle of friends and acquaintances. His golden wedding in 1869 was an occasion of great joy to the large numbers whose congratulations the aged and honored couple received at the time of its celebration, and to the whole community in which Dr. Edwards was so highly esteemed.

He loved the Saviour and his people, and cherished his own church with peculiar affection. To him there was no book like the Bible, reverence for which increased with his advancing years. He held tenaciously the doctrines and practices of the Holy Scriptures, and his faith was proved by a consecrated life.

While living in Edwardsville, Ill., the first missionary Baptist church in that State was formed in his residence, April 18, 1828. He assisted at the organization of the Edwardsville Baptist Association, Oct. 16, 1830. He was one of the original trustees of Shurtleff College in 1836. This great and good man expired in the triumphs of faith.

Edwards, Cyrus, LL.D.—Although Dr. Edwards became actually the member of a Baptist church only in his eighty-first year, he was the friend and supporter of such churches through many years, as also of Shurtleff College, in Upper Alton, which place was his home during the later portion of his life. He was born in Montgomery Co., Md., Jan. 17, 1793, his family being of Welsh origin, and residents of Virginia, until his father's removal to Maryland in 1750, from the earliest colonial times. In 1800 his father removed to Bardstown, Ky., in which place Cyrus attended a private academy kept by Mr. Daniel Barry. He began the study of law at the age of nineteen, and removing to Illinois, was in 1815 admitted to the bar at Kaskaskia. After this event he removed to Potosi, Mo., sixty miles south of St. Louis. In Missouri he became the personal friend of Thomas H. Benton and other eminent persons, and he acquired marked distinction in his profession. After some fourteen years' residence in Missouri, Mr. Edwards removed to Edwardsville, Ill., a town named for his brother, Hon. Ninian Edwards, one of the early governors of Illinois while yet a Territory.

In 1832 he became a member of the Illinois Legislature, and so continued until 1840, when he retired from politics until summoned again to public duties by the exciting events of 1860. His entire efforts for his fellow-citizens were characterized by integrity, high principle, and signal ability.

As a friend of education Dr. Edwards is especially remembered. He was one of the most liberal friends of Shurtleff College, having given to it at one time real estate valued at $10,000, besides other generous donations. For a period of thirty-five years he was president of its board of trustees. He was also most active in the origination of the State Normal School at Bloomington. In the eighty-first year of his age Dr. Edwards was baptized into the fellowship of the Upper Alton church, and remained in its communion until his death.

In 1837 he was a candidate for governor of Illinois, and he only failed because his political friends were in a hopeless minority.

The Alton *Weekly Telegraph* of Sept. 6, 1877, speaking of him, says, "With Hon. Cyrus Edwards has passed away one of the most prominent men in the early history of Illinois, whose residence therein was coeval with the existence of the State government. Of the famous men of earlier days who made the pioneer history of Illinois brilliant, few stand out with greater prominence, and few are more worthy of grateful remembrance than Mr. Edwards. In all the great movements in the early history of the State his name is conspicuous, and in all it is recorded with honor. He was the last survivor of the statesmen who, prior to the year 1840, wielded the destinies of Illinois." When he passed away a great American citizen fell, and an illustrious servant of Christ entered upon his reward.

Edwards, Hervey, a native of Onondaga Co., N. Y., better known as Deacon Edwards, a successful business man, a devoted Christian, and a zealous promoter of all the interests of the Baptist denomination. He was baptized in 1830 into the fellowship of the Fayetteville Baptist church by Rev. Charles Morton. He was specially conspicuous in his support of ministerial education, holding a position as member of the boards of the university and Education Society at Hamilton.

Edwards, Rev. James Jesse, a distinguished missionary, was born in Lee Co., Va., Dec. 30, 1824. In June, 1842, he obtained hope in Christ and joined the Methodist Church. Subsequently, upon a change of religious opinions, he united with a Baptist church. In June, 1850, he was ordained to the gospel ministry, and labored some years in his native county, his field being the mountainous districts of Western Virginia and Eastern Kentucky. Mr. Edwards received but little compensation for preaching, and his circumstances compelled him to adopt secular employment to support his family. His ministry was attended with the most wonderful results. After a few years he moved to Clay County, and finally to Estill Co., Ky., where his labors in the same rugged fields were greatly blessed. During a few years he received a partial support as missionary of the General Association of Kentucky, and his reports indicate that he traveled 36,730 miles. A large portion of this was accomplished on foot, and the remainder on horseback.

He has now been preaching thirty years, and has baptized over 5000 professed believers in Christ and organized 35 churches.

Edwards, Rev. Morgan, was born in Wales, May 9, 1722. He was educated at Bristol College under Bernard Foskett, its first president. He was ordained June 1, 1757, in Cork, Ireland, where he labored for nine years. He returned to England and preached for a year in Rye, in Sussex, when, through the recommendation of Dr. Gill and others, on the application of the Baptist church of Philadelphia, he came to that city and church, and entered upon the pastorate May 23, 1761.

In 1770 he preached a sermon on the text, "This year thou shalt die," which by many was regarded as his intended funeral sermon, as it is said that he expected to die on a particular day. But he was disappointed when the day of death dawned and departed, for instead of expiring he lived for nearly a quarter of a century after. Circumstances led to his resignation that year, though he continued to preach for a considerable period later.

After his departure from Philadelphia he never assumed the duties of the pastorate in any other church. He resided in Delaware. He supplied vacant churches till the Revolution, during which he gave up preaching, and after peace was proclaimed he gave lectures on Divinity in various parts of Pennsylvania, New Jersey, Delaware, and New England. He died at Pencador, Del., Jan. 28, 1795.

Mr. Edwards took the side of the mother-country during the Revolutionary struggle. One reason given for this course was that he had a son an officer in the service of Great Britain. He was the only Tory in the ministry of the American Baptist churches. The Baptists everywhere over this land, ministers and laymen, were enthusiastic friends of liberty.

Morgan Edwards was a man of refined manners, and shone to peculiar advantage in good society. He was the master of scholarly attainments, and he was accustomed to say, "The Greek and Hebrew are the two eyes of a minister, and the translations are but commentaries, because they vary in sense as commentators do." His attachment to Baptist principles was intense, and no man since the days of the Apostles ever showed greater love, or made more costly sacrifices for them than he did. He was full of generosity, he would give anything to a friend or to a cause dear to him. Edwards was a man of uncommon genius. In his day no Baptist minister equaled him, and none since his time has surpassed him.

He was the founder of Brown University, at first called Rhode Island College. It is well known that this enterprise was started in the Philadelphia Baptist Association in its meeting in 1762, and Morgan Edwards was "the principal mover in this matter," as he was the most active agent in securing funds for the permanent support of the institution. To Morgan Edwards more than to any other man are the Baptist churches of America indebted for their grand list of institutions of learning, with their noble endowments and wide-spread influence.

But we owe him another heavy debt for his "Materials Towards a History of the Baptists," etc. He journeyed from New Hampshire to Georgia gathering facts for a history of the Baptists, and these "Materials," printed or penned, are the most valuable Baptist records in our country. They show immense painstaking, they are remarkably accurate, they treat of points of great value. Morgan Edwards and Robert B. Semple, of Virginia, deserve the lasting gratitude of every American Baptist in a fervent measure. This great Welshman has conferred favors upon American Baptists not second to those of his illustrious countryman who founded Rhode Island.

Edwards, Prof. P. C., was born near Society Hill, Darlington Co., S. C., Feb. 8, 1819; was baptized in his seventeenth year; died in Greenville, S. C., May 15, 1867. He was graduated with honor in the South Carolina College, where he remained through the ensuing winter and spring, diligently studying as resident graduate. He took a full course at Newton, under Drs. Sears, Ripley, Chase, and Hackett, and spent a winter in New York, to enjoy the benefit of instruction by Dr. Robinson, of the Union Theological Seminary. In 1846 he became Professor of Biblical Literature and Exegesis in Furman Theological Institution, then located in Fairfield District, S. C.; after its removal to Greenville, and its expansion into Furman University, he became Professor of Ancient Languages in the collegiate department.

His intellect was massive, its movements not rapid. He never jumped at conclusions; often hesitated where men of less breadth of view would have terminated discussion. To this result his conscientiousness contributed. His regard for truth was reverential; patient and painstaking in investigation himself, he yet showed the most amiable deference for the opinions of others. His heart was formed for the tenderest and most enduring friendships; deeply humble and devout, he made the impression on all minds of a good minister of Jesus Christ. He died suddenly, in the very prime of his powers. On Sunday he preached a long and most impressive sermon on "Christ, the brightness of the Father's glory," etc., and on Wednesday he had gone to gaze with unclouded vision on the object of his adoring love.

Egan, Bartholomew, M.D., distinguished for his classical attainments and his professional skill, was born in Killarney, Ireland, in 1795, and graduated at Dublin University. He was the founder of Mount Lebanon University, La., and held many prominent positions in the State, as Presidential elector, surgeon-general of Louisiana, superintendent of the State Laboratory, and one of the board of supervisors of the State Seminary. He became a Baptist in Virginia in 1841, and from 1847 until his death, in 1879, he was prominently connected with the denomination in the State of Louisiana.

Elder, Joseph F., D.D., was born in Portland, Me., March 10, 1839. His early educational advantages were good. His academic studies were pursued at the Portland High School, in which he gave promise of ability to fill the positions which he has since attained. In 1860, when twenty-one years of age, he was graduated from Waterville College, now Colby University, with the highest honors. After his graduation he engaged in teaching, but his piety and ability as a speaker and writer led the Free Street Baptist church to give him a license to preach. This occurred in 1861. Afterwards he entered Rochester Theological Seminary, and was graduated from it in 1867. He was immediately called to the pastorate of North Orange Baptist church, N. J., where he was ordained, and where he remained two years. Such was his success as a preacher that in 1869 he was called to follow Rev. Dr. H. G. Weston, now president of

JOSEPH F. ELDER, D.D.

Crozer Theological Seminary, in the pastorate of Madison Avenue Baptist church of New York. The old and honored Oliver Street church had united with the Madison Avenue church, but when the courts decided that the Oliver Street church was not legally the owner of the church property, the latter withdrew with Dr. Elder, and are now building a church edifice which promises to be in all respects quite equal to the spacious and beautiful house which they left in Madison Avenue. Such was his popularity that nearly all the members of the church and congregation followed him to his new field in Fifty-third Street.

As a preacher he is an able advocate of Baptist principles, an eminently logical reasoner, dignified, earnest, and genial in manner. Standing calmly in his pulpit, he reminds one of the portraits of Napoleon Bonaparte. He is indeed an able leader and commander in the armies of Israel. He is still a student. His sermons, addresses, and essays give evidence of patient and thorough research. His conscientious presentation of the whole truth, as he and his denomination hold it, makes his ministry a force not only in his congregation, but in the city and country. His illustrations of obscure points show a wide range of reading and a familiarity with the mighty writers of the past ages. He has not yet reached the full measure of influence and usefulness which his present attainments promise to the churches.

Dr. Elder received the honorary degree of Doctor of Divinity from Madison University in 1865.

Elder, Rev. Samuel, A.M., was born in Halifax, Nova Scotia; converted and baptized in Cornwallis in 1839; graduated from Acadia College in 1844; ordained pastor of the Baptist church, Fredericton, New Brunswick, in November, 1845, and so continued until he died, May 23, 1852. Mr. Elder was a fine poet and an eloquent preacher, possessed an exquisite style and sound theology.

Eldred, Hon. Caleb, was born in Pownal, Vt., April 6, 1781, and died in Climax, Mich., June 29, 1876. On arriving at manhood he removed to Otsego Co., N. Y., where he engaged in farming; served his township as justice of the peace, and was president of the County Agricultural Society. He was two terms a member of the New York Legislature. In 1831 he removed to Kalamazoo Co., Mich., where he spent the remainder of his life. He was twice elected a member of the Territorial Legislature, and was a "side judge" of the Territorial court. As a Baptist he is best known as one of the founders of Kalamazoo College. For twenty-five years he was president of its board of trustees, and his contributions for its support were generous and continuous.

Eldridge, Rev. Daniel, was born in Washington Co., N. Y., in 1805, and died at Afton, Rock Co., Wis., aged seventy-one years. He was educated at Hamilton, N. Y. He was pastor of the churches in Hamilton, Broad Street, Utica, and Perry, N. Y.; Columbus, O.; Beloit, Clinton, Columbus, and Afton, Wis. He was a man of strong intellect, profound convictions, and an able defender of the faith and practice of Baptists. His last years were spent on his farm near Afton, Wis., where he died in great peace.

Election.—Every man that shall enter glory was elected of God to that blessed state, and because of such election is prepared by the Holy Spirit for its enjoyment. No elect person can be kept out of heaven.

When men repent and put their trust in Jesus they are "called according to God's purpose,"—Rom. viii. 28,—that is, according to his plan of election, or they would never turn to the Saviour. Hence Paul says, " Who maketh thee to differ?"—1 Cor. iv. 7. "By the grace of God, I am what I am."—1 Cor. xv. 10. The electing grace of Jehovah has placed every believer in saved relations with the Lamb.

The entire elect were given to Christ *to redeem,* " Christ hath redeemed us from the curse of the law, being made a curse for us,"—Gal. iii. 13,—*to intercede for,* " I pray for them, *I pray not for the world,* but for them whom thou hast given me, for they are thine."—John xvii. 9,—*to bring safely to heaven,* " All that the Father giveth me shall come to me, and him that cometh to me I will in no wise cast out."—John vi. 37. "My sheep hear my voice, and I know them, and they follow me, and I give unto them eternal life, and they shall *never perish,* neither shall any pluck them out of my hand."—John x. 27, 28.

God's election of believers took place in eternity, " According as he hath chosen us in him, before the foundation of the world that we should be holy and without blame before him in love."—Eph. i. 4. Before the existence of the earth, the fall was foreseen, and the salvation of the elect gloriously provided for.

Divine election in the Scriptures has to do exclusively with individuals. Paul speaks of those that love God as persons " called according to his purpose;" all men brought to embrace Jesus are drawn to him according to God's electing purpose. Saul himself, rushing with cruel haste to Damascus, " breathing out threatenings and slaughter" against the saints of Jesus and their Master, is called into the saved family. One moment he is a blind bigot full of murder, and the next, solely through God's call, he is a trembling penitent, crying for mercy. No one, when the Saviour found him, heard the voice of Jesus but himself. It is addressed to him alone, " Saul, Saul, why persecutest thou me ?"—Acts ix. 4. And when Ananias, who, by divine appointment, visited him a few days later, objected to call upon him on account of his persecuting reputation, the Lord said to him, " Go thy way, for he is a chosen vessel unto me, to bear my name before the Gentiles, and kings, and the children of Israel."—Acts ix. 15. Paul was an elect man, he was chosen and called as an individual. And so are all Christ's saints. Zaccheus was called by name out of the boughs of the tree, and found salvation that day, and this was according to God's purpose of election.—Luke xix. 5. An angel commanded Philip "to go unto the way that goeth down from Jerusalem unto Gaza," and seeing the eunuch, the Holy " Spirit said unto Philip, 'Go, man, and join thyself to this chariot.'"—Acts viii. 26–29. The eunuch hears the Word of life from Philip, and is saved and baptized. But an angel sends him to the road where he would find this solitary traveler; the Spirit orders him directly to the man, and the treasurer receives an individual call, according to God's purpose, for that purpose is the election of individuals to eternal life. At Antioch it is said, " As many as were ordained to eternal life believed," not a soul besides. The election of God had decreed the salvation of a number of persons who heard Paul and Barnabas at Antioch, and the elect ones only, received Jesus. The individual feature of election is strongly presented by the Saviour, where he says to his disciples, "Rejoice not, that the spirits (demons) are subject unto you, but rather rejoice because your names are written in heaven."—Luke x. 20. Election performed its work before the foundation of the world; the *names* of the saints were enrolled among the coming citizens of heaven before the birth of earthly ages, and the elect in God's great scheme of salvation are as much individualized as the legatees of a will. Eternal and personal election is the undoubted teaching of the sacred volume. When Moses in ancient times read the law to Israel, he took blood and scarlet wool and hyssop, and sprinkled the book and all the people with blood.—Heb. ix. 19. The Father, before suns sent forth light, prepared the Lamb's book of life, with the finger of everlasting love he wrote in it the names of all elect men and women, and youths and maidens; in the fullness of time the Saviour sprinkled the book and every name in it with his own blood, and now there is neither condemnation nor accusation for a single one of them in this or in any other world.

Men are elected that they may be made holy. Some have dreamt that they were chosen because they should become saints. This doctrine is like the baseless fabric of a vision. "God hath from the beginning chosen you to salvation through sanctification of the spirit and belief of the truth." —2 Thess. ii. 13. "According as he hath chosen us in him before the foundation of the world, that we should be holy and without blame before him in love."—Eph. i. 4. The *cause* of election was not the prospective holiness of the chosen, but the unparalleled love of God; and the chief object of election is to make men holy.

Men are elected *to salvation*. There is an "election of grace," but none to perdition. "For whom he did foreknow, he also did predestinate to be conformed to the image of his Son, *that he might be the first-born among many brethren*. Moreover, whom he did predestinate, them he also called: and whom he called, them he also justified: and whom he justified, them he also glorified."—Rom. viii. 29, 30. Predestination in this connection is the equivalent of election. And its first purpose is to make men like Christ, that he may be at the head, not of a handful of brethren, but of a multitude, and its other purpose is to call, justify, and invest with heavenly glory the Father's chosen hosts. There is no election to destruction; men are chosen to celestial crowns.

Election works in perfect harmony with the human will. Jehovah elected Saul king of Israel, and Samuel anointed him to the office. No descendant of Jacob, except Samuel and Saul, knew about God's choice, and yet all Israel convened and elected Saul their first king. The people were conscious of no interference with their will, and there was none, but, notwithstanding this, they simply ratified the appointment of Jehovah. So when God calls an elect one to repentance and faith he is made willing by matchless grace and by the mighty Spirit, and he feels a burning earnestness in his soul to follow Jesus Christ, though he would have fled from him forever if he had not given him a new heart.

"Chosen of him ere time began
We choose him in return."

The evidences of election in a believer's heart make him brave. Cromwell's warriors, consciously chosen to heavenly joys, were fitted for earthly victories, and filled Europe with enthusiastic admiration for their fearless valor; knowing themselves to be the elect of God, they feared nothing human or diabolical. A consciousness of election makes the Christian feel a burning gratitude in his heart for him that planned his salvation before stars twinkled in the heavens. An intelligent faith in election and in one's own choice of God leads to heroic works and sacrifices. A saved electionist knows that God has a people in the world, that this people in process of time, and in millennial days, will embrace the family of Adam, that God's whole power will be used to render the means successful to bring these hidden jewels of heaven into gospel light, and that instead of earthly uncertainties he has God's promises that his word shall not return unto him void, and he labors with untiring perseverance, confident of success. The greatest workers in Christ's vineyard have received the Scripture doctrine of election. Paul, Augustine of Hippo, Calvin, Cranmer, John Knox, Whitefield, the Evangelical Episcopalians, the Baptists, the Presbyterians, the Congregationalists, the men who have made this country what it is, who have given Britain most of her greatness, and Continental European Protestantism much of its glory, were firm believers in election. This Bible doctrine will yet bless the whole Christian family on earth with its light. Among the elect angels in heaven, the elect believers before the throne, and the elect infants in Paradise, from every land and age, it is a crowning joy.

El Karey, Rev. Youhannah, was born in Shechem, now called Nablous; this city lies at the base of Mount Gerizim, where the Samaritan temple, the rival of the temple of Jehovah in Jerusalem, stood. It has a population of about 20,000 persons, chiefly Mohammedans. There are a few of the Samaritans there still, the descendants of the people who owned the city in Christ's day, and they have not given up the religion of their fathers. Jacob's well is within a mile of Nablous, where the Saviour preached to the woman of Samaria.

Mr. El Karey was educated in England and married to a Liverpool lady. He and his wife are now missionaries in Shechem. This Baptist minister has a church of 16 baptized believers, and a congregation, meeting every Lord's day in a chapel dedicated in October, 1879. In their house of worship there is a day-school for girls with 100 scholars, and one for boys with 30. The Sunday-school has about 150 pupils. The Mohammedan mothers' meeting has an attendance of about 70. Mr. El Karey has been chiefly supported through the instrumentality of our brother, the Rev. Dr. Landels, of London.

Elkin, Rev. Robert, was a native of Virginia. He emigrated with a large company to the valley of the Holstein River in 1780. Here he constituted a church with the assistance of Lewis Craig and John Vivian, Sept. 28, 1781. In 1783 he led his flock to what is now Garrard Co., Ky. The next year he led them across the Kentucky River into Clark County, where the church took the name of Howard Creek, but in 1790 changed its name to Providence. To this prosperous old mother-church Mr. Elkin ministered until his death, which occurred in March, 1822.

Elliott, Hon. Victor A., was born July 23, 1839, in Tioga Co., Pa. He served in the Union army as captain and major during the war, where he contracted asthmatic difficulties, which were the occasion of his moving to Denver, Col., after practising law for a time in Nebraska. He followed the same profession in Denver till elected, in the fall of 1878, to the office of judge of the District Court. Judge Elliott is noted for promptness, carefulness, and integrity in his legal decisions, as well as for his spotless character and decided convictions in private life. He is one of the trustees of the Denver Baptist church.

HON. VICTOR A. ELLIOTT.

Elliott, Rev. Joseph, was born at Mason, N. H., in 1789. His father was a Baptist minister. Converted at the age of thirteen, Joseph almost at once became impressed that it was his duty to preach the gospel. Striving against such convictions he began the study of medicine, but abandoning it ere long, he became a preacher at the age of nineteen. At twenty he was ordained, and during forty-five years, in New England, New York, Ohio, and Illinois, exercised his ministry. With preaching he frequently associated the work of teaching, and in this was highly successful. He died at Monmouth, Ill., Aug. 17, 1858.

Elliott, Rev. W., was born in Adams Co., O., March 17, 1819. His parents belonged to the Scotch Presbyterian Church, for the ministry of which his father had been partly educated. Young Elliott received his education, literary and theological, chiefly from his father, who was an experienced teacher. When he was about seventeen years old, in October, 1836, he walked eight miles to receive baptism. He removed to Iowa, crossing the Mississippi at Burlington, on May 7, 1842, and immediately began to preach. He was present at the formation of the Iowa Baptist Convention, when there were but 350 Baptists in the State. He was ordained in October, 1842. He was employed eleven years by the American Baptist Home Mission Society. He has served churches as their pastor, but has generally labored as an evangelist, and in the latter calling he has traveled 100,000 miles, much of it on horseback, and often preaching three times a day for months in succession. In 1868 he was compelled to give up his exhausting labors for a time, only preaching occasionally as he was able. He devotes his feeble strength to protracted meetings in the winter. He has labored nearly forty years in Iowa, and he has been richly blessed in his saintly toils.

Ellis, Rev. Ferdinand, was born in Medway, Mass., in 1780; and graduated at Brown University in the class of 1802. For three years after the completion of his college studies he was a tutor in the university. At the end of this engagement he was ordained as a Baptist minister, and for a time was a colleague with Rev. Dr. Stillman, pastor of the First Baptist church in Boston. Subsequently he removed to Marblehead, Mass., and in 1817 to Exeter, N. H., where he was the pastor of the Baptist church for fifteen years. Having resigned his pastorate in Exeter, he preached for a short time in several towns in New Hampshire, and in Freeport, Me. Finally he returned to Exeter, where he died Feb. 20, 1858. Several of his sermons were published, and some theological writings which he prepared for the press. He was a very useful minister of the Saviour.

Ellis, Frank M., D.D., was born in Higginsport, O., July 31, 1838. He was educated at Shurtleff College, and has occupied several important points as pastor before settling at Denver, Col., where he commenced his labors March, 1876, which he prosecuted for more than four years, till called to the pastorate of Tremont Temple, Boston, in June, 1880. He is genial in his manners, and an able, efficient, and eloquent preacher. In descriptive powers, fluency of speech, and graceful manners he has few peers. His audiences in Denver were very large. His reputation in Boston as a preacher and as a Christian is very high, and extensive usefulness is expected from his ministry.

Ellis, Rev. Robert, was born in Wales, Feb. 3, 1812. In his twentieth year he connected himself with the Baptist Church. He commenced preaching not long after, and went through his preparatory studies under the preceptorship of the Rev. I. Williams, afterwards of Newtown, than whom there was not a more finished Greek scholar or a more able Biblical expositor within the boundaries of the principality of Wales. Robert Ellis served several churches with unquestioned ability, the last of which was Carnarvon, the scene of the ministry of the immortal Christmas Evans.

It was, however, as a bard and writer that Robert Ellis excelled. He published a commentary on the New Testament in three volumes, as well as several lectures and pamphlets bearing on ecclesiastical and theological subjects. He devoted much attention to Welsh literature. His productions are characterized by strength and purity, and that indefinable something which always accompanies genius. To the antiquarian and the bard, Robert Ellis was a consummate master and an acknowledged authority. As long as the Welsh language is spoken his name and memory will be held in veneration.

Ellison, Rev. Matthew, was born Nov. 10, 1804. He belongs to a family of preachers, his father, Rev. James Ellison, and three of his brothers having been Baptist ministers. He is now one of the oldest pastors in West Virginia, and is still actively engaged in the work of the Master. By close application in his youth he secured a liberal education, and has made good use of it. It is probable that he has traveled more than any other minister in the State. He has preached as supply for as many as nine churches at a time, and some of them sixty miles apart, and has had a meagre financial support.

Mr. Ellison is an author of some celebrity. He has written a book on "Dunkerism," a "Plea for the Union of Baptists," etc. He has baptized 2000 persons and organized 25 churches. He is one of the most prominent of our West Virginia ministers. He has an excellent reputation as a Biblical student and a controversialist.

When he was seventy-five years of age he gave up all his churches, spent the winter in writing, and in the spring he began to sell Bibles for the American Bible Society. His home is now at Raleigh Court-House, W. Va.

Ellyson, Hon. Henry K., was born in the city of Richmond, Va., on the 31st of July, 1823. When fourteen years of age he was apprenticed as a printer. While learning his trade his father died, and he had a mother and sisters to provide for. Having served his apprenticeship, he started a small job printing-office, and by the strict, methodical business habits, patient industry, and incorruptible integrity which have marked his entire life, he soon acquired a profitable business and the confidence and esteem of the city. In 1854 he was elected to the House of Representatives, and served for two terms. In 1857 he was elected sheriff of the city, then a lucrative and very responsible office. By successive elections he was continued in the same office until 1865.

After the fall of Richmond he and Jas. A. Cowardin re-established the *Daily Dispatch*, the most influential and widely-circulated journal in the State. In 1870 he was elected mayor of Richmond.

Mr. Ellyson joined the Second Baptist church in Richmond at an early age, and has been a model member ever since, punctual at all meetings, active in all work, liberal in his gifts, and pure in his life. For more than thirty years he has been superintendent of the Sunday-school, and for twenty years an active member of the Board of Foreign Missions of the Southern Baptist Convention.

In 1847 he was elected corresponding secretary of the State Mission Board of the General Association of Virginia, and in the administration of its affairs has displayed conspicuous tact, energy, ability, and faith. He has not received one cent as compensation for his services. To Mr. Ellyson's marvelous fitness for his office are the Baptists of Virginia largely indebted for their growth and influence. In 1851, excluding statistics that belong to the present West Virginia, there were in Virginia 471 ministers and 81,557 members. In 1880 there are 703 ministers and 205,909 members.

Mr. Ellyson has been long identified with the business interests of Richmond, being connected with the management of banks, railroads, steamboats, and insurance companies. His sons are active in religious and business matters. His home, where father, mother, daughter, sons, and their wives live as a happy Christian family, has been a home as well for hundreds of Baptist preachers. Mr. Ellyson's life is an example and a stimulus, showing how much consecrated time and property and talents, outside of the ministry, can accomplish for the Master.

Elton, Romeo, D.D., was born in Ellington, Conn., probably in 1790. He spent his early days on the farm of his father, but was unfitted by temperament and physical weakness for agricultural pursuits. He became a member of Brown University, and graduated in the class of 1813. Having devoted some time to the study of theology, he was ordained as the pastor of the Second Baptist church in Newport, R. I., June 11, 1817. He had a successful ministry, and greatly endeared himself not only to the people of his own church, but to the community in which he lived, by his gentleness and suavity, and his upright Christian deportment. Ill health obliged him to resign. The same cause also forced him to give up his ministry in Windsor, Vt., whither he had gone from Newport. An invitation having been extended to him to take the chair of Professor of the Latin and Greek Languages in Brown University in 1825, he spent two years abroad, chiefly in Germany, in preparing himself for the duties of his office. For sixteen years, from 1827 to 1843, he was connected with Brown University. He won the affection of his pupils by his kindness of manner, and no man could come under his influence without acknowledging him to be truly a Christian gentleman and scholar. He was peculiarly sensitive and delicate in his temperament, and was especially careful not to wound the sensibilities of those who came under his instructions.

After resigning his professorship and passing a few months with his relatives, he went to England, and resided in Exeter for twenty-two years, and in Bath two years. While abroad he devoted himself to literary pursuits, preaching for Baptist and Independent churches as occasion presented. His life in England seems to have been a singularly pleasant one, congenial with his tastes, and productive of great satisfaction to him, by bringing him in contact with literary people and scholars of similar temperaments with his own.

Dr. Elton returned to this country in 1869, and resided in Rhode Island and Boston, in which city he died, Feb. 5, 1870. He was the compiler of the "Remains of President Maxey," and wrote a memoir of Roger Williams while he resided in England. Among other bequests which he made was one of $20,000 to establish a professorship of Natural Philosophy in Brown University, and nearly as much more to Columbian College to establish a professorship of Intellectual and Moral Philosophy.

Elven, Rev. Cornelius, of Bury St. Edmund's, Suffolk, was for fifty years the most widely-known and esteemed Baptist minister in the eastern counties of England. He was born at Bury, Feb. 12, 1797, and received a good education. His family belonged to the Congregationalists, but in early manhood he was convinced of the Scriptural character of Baptist principles, and although the Baptist church in Bury was at that time very weak in numbers and influence, he loyally followed his convictions, and was baptized May 6, 1821. Displaying gifts which could not be hid, he was invited to preach, and on the retirement of the pastor the church called him to be his successor. He was ordained July, 1823. For nearly forty-nine years he actively labored in word and doctrine in this one field, winning in his native place universal esteem and affection, and crowned with ministerial success. Even in his declining years he was an attractive preacher. He had a rich fund of humor, and a most retentive memory, which he laid under tribute with remarkable effect in illustrating and pressing home divine truth. The common people heard him gladly, and the educated were charmed by his naturalness of manner, his fine appreciation of the best things in literature, and his transparent clearness of thought. In earlier life he was a bountiful helper of the poor, having then some private resources, and throughout his career his genial, kindly disposition was conspicuous. He was the firm friend of every good cause, and an effective advocate of liberty and progress. Very large in person, he frequently found it impossible to get into the box-pulpits with which country meeting-houses in England were usually furnished, and he pointed many a witticism at his own expense on such occasions. But although full of humor, and youthful in feeling even in old age, he was ever faithful to his calling as a minister of Christ, and by his pen as well as his voice delighted to proclaim the gospel of the grace of God. He died as he had lived, among his own people, Aug. 10, 1873, and the public demonstrations at his funeral showed that a prophet may sometimes at least be honored in his own city.

Ely, Hon. Lewis B., was born May 18, 1825, in Frankfort, Ky.; converted in 1841; baptized by Rev. W. C. Ligon in 1842, and united with the Baptist church at Carrolton, Mo. In 1844 he formed the mercantile firm of Hill & Ely in Carrolton, where he still lives, and has been a successful and honorable business man. He is a deacon of his church, and superintendent of its Sunday-school. He has been moderator of the Missouri Valley Association, a member of the executive board of the State Association, for ten years a trustee of William Jewell College, twice moderator of the General Association, and he is now financial agent of the college. He is unassuming, and his honors are pressed upon him. Self-denial, labor, benevolence, humility, and sincere devotion to Christ mark his character. He stands among the foremost of Missouri Baptist laymen as a brother beloved and as a servant of Christ worthy of the esteem and affection of all the friends of Jesus.

Emery, Rev. J. W., was born in Grafton, Vt., May 12, 1823. His father, James Emery, removed to the State of New York in 1831 and settled in Tioga County, then a thinly-settled community. Under the preaching of Elder Thomas S. Sheardown the subject of our sketch was converted, and was baptized by him in the fall of 1837. He was licensed to preach in 1851, and ordained in 1852. He gave himself with much fervor to the work, not only serving all his life since as pastor of some church, but doing the work of an evangelist almost constantly. Perhaps no man in the State has been more abundant in labors, or more largely blessed in the number of converts. He is a tower of strength wherever he has labored, and his services are in great demand. His pastorates have been in Barton, Candor, Caneseraga, Dansville, Big Flat, Cooper's Plains, North Parma, Walworth, Attica, Bath, with the last of which he has remained since 1870. He has been an earnest advocate of the strict old Baptist faith and practice for more than half a century, and a firm supporter of all Baptist institutions and enterprises. The dew of his youth is still upon him.

England, The Baptist of, a weekly family newspaper, was started about seven years ago as a low-priced Baptist paper of a strictly denominational character. It is now published at two cents a week by Elliot Stock, 62 Paternoster Row, London, and it has obtained an established position. Both sections of the English Baptists, the General or Arminian, and the Particular or Calvinistic Baptists, are represented by it.

England, The Baptist Magazine of, was commenced in 1809, and is the oldest of existing English Baptist periodicals. It is published monthly, and contains original articles on devotional, literary, and general religious subjects by leading members of the denomination. For many years it was edited by the Rev. William Groser, and was highly prized not only for the usual excellence of its contents, but especially for its biographical sketches. Several of the leading ministers of the denomination have at different times taken part in conducting the magazine. S. Manning, D.D., LL.D., now secretary of the Religious Tract Society of London, and the Rev. W. G. Lewis, the present editor, were notably successful in enlisting the services of able writers, including some of the most eminent pastors. From the commencement the profits arising from the sale have been given to the widows of Baptist ministers at the recommendation of the contributors. The total amount of these grants up to the present time (1880) is over $35,000. One excellent feature of the magazine is the publishing of the *Missionary Herald* under the same wrapper, so that its readers are put in possession of the facts of the work of the Baptist Missionary Society from month to month. It is published by Yates & Alexander, Castle St., Holborn, London.

England, The Baptist Missionary Society of, owes its origin, under God, to the energy and faith of William Carey. Although other men of similar mould had a share in the glory of reviving the missionary zeal of the churches of Christ, the name of Carey stands pre-eminent. It was while he was living at Moulton, Northamptonshire, as pastor of the feeble Baptist church in that village, and keeping school to make his income equal to his wants, that the great object of his life first presented itself forcibly to his mind. When teaching the village children geography, pointing out the different countries and peoples of the world on the map, and saying again and again, "These are Christians, and these are Mohammedans, and these are Pagans," it occurred to him, "I am now telling these children as a mere fact a truth of the most melancholy character." This simple thought was the germ of modern missions. His attention was arrested; his sympathies were aroused; he searched the Bible and prayed earnestly to ascertain what was the duty of Christians to the heathen world. After keeping his thoughts to himself for some time, he ventured to introduce it as a subject of conversation when he met his ministerial brethren. At a fraternal meeting of ministers at Northampton, he proposed as a topic for discussion, "The duty of Christians to attempt the spread of the gospel among heathen nations;" but he had hardly uttered the words when Mr. Ryland, Sr., sprang to his feet and denounced the proposition. "Young man, sit down; when God pleases to convert the heathen, he will do it without your aid or mine." Andrew Fuller, who was present, said that his own feelings respecting the proposal were very like those of the incredulous courtier in Israel, "If the Lord should make windows in heaven, might such a thing be!" Carey, however, was nothing daunted by the frowns and doubtings of his brethren. At length a few kindred spirits expressed sympathy, feeble at first, but gathering strength continually, and he prepared a pamphlet on the subject, which he showed in manuscript to Mr. Fuller, Mr. Sutcliffe, and Dr. Ryland. They urged him to revise it, and counseled deliberation, more in the hope of escaping from his importunities than from any serious purpose of encouraging his project. In 1789 Carey removed to Leicester, where his circumstances were somewhat improved, and his opportunities for prosecuting his missionary studies were multiplied. He continued to press the subject upon the minds of his brethren in the ministry, especially seeking to win the approval of the younger men who were rising into denominational influence. At a meeting held at Clipston in 1791, the discourses delivered appeared to bear a missionary aspect, and Carey urged that some practical steps should be taken then and there; but those who sympathized with him most shrank from the responsibility, and pronounced the plan too vast for their obscure position and limited resources. They advised him, however, to publish his manuscript, which he had revised and re-revised at their suggestion, before the next meeting of the Association, to be held at Nottingham, in May, 1792. It was arranged that Carey should preach, and having announced his text

ergy overcame all objections and difficulties, and under his influence, with fervent prayer for divine assistance, the Baptist Missionary Society was formed. A committee of five was appointed, consisting of Andrew Fuller, John Ryland, Reynold Hogge, John Sutcliffe, and William Carey. Mr. Fuller was made secretary, and Mr. Hogge treasurer, and a subscription was immediately taken up of £13 2s. 6d. No sooner was the subscription thus filled up than Carey offered himself as a missionary, ready to embark for any part of the heathen world to which they might choose to send him. As soon as Samuel Pearce came back from the Kettering meeting to his people at Birmingham, he aroused their interest so much that upwards of five times the

THE HOUSE IN KETTERING, ENGLAND, IN WHICH THE BAPTIST MISSIONARY SOCIETY WAS FORMED.

(Isaiah liv. 2, 3), he deduced the two propositions which have become familiar sayings all over the world, (1st) expect great things from God; (2d) attempt great things for God. Into this discourse he poured the long pent-up feelings of his soul with electrical effect. But when the excitement of the hour had passed away, the feelings of hesitation and doubt again appeared, and it needed an indignant expostulation from Carey to procure the passage of a resolution that a plan should be prepared against the next ministers' meeting for the establishment of a society for propagating the gospel among the heathen. This meeting in due time convened at Kettering, on the 2d of October, 1792. After the usual services of the day, the ministers, twelve in number, proceeded from the meeting-house to the parlor of the mansion of Mrs. Beeby Wallis, a widow lady, a member of Mr. Fuller's church, and there discussed the question of establishing a missionary society. Carey's en-

amount of the original subscription was forwarded from Birmingham alone, and an auxiliary society was formed. This example was followed by other churches, and the committee soon found themselves possessed of no inconsiderable resources. Still the interest felt in the movement was local, and limited to comparatively few churches. The ministers and congregations in London deemed it a mere burst of wild enthusiasm, which would soon burn itself out. Andrew Fuller afterwards described the situation in these words: "When we began, in 1792, there was little or no respectability among us; not so much as a squire to sit in the chair, or an orator to make speeches to him. Hence good Dr. Stennett advised the London ministers to stand aloof and not commit themselves." Indeed, the only minister from whom Carey received any sympathy in the metropolis was a clergyman of the Established Church, the venerable John Newton, the intimate friend of Dr. Ryland, of whom Carey said,

"He advised me with the fidelity and tenderness of a father." The determination to adopt India as the mission field was brought about by a communication from Mr. John Thomas, a physician, who had resided in Bengal for some years, and had long desired to promote Christian missionary operations in that country. On the receipt of Mr. Thomas's letter, Andrew Fuller went to London to make inquiries regarding him, which proving satisfactory, the committee invited Mr. Thomas to join the society and accompany Carey. But obstacles arose which were not surmounted until several months had passed. Funds requisite for the expense of the voyage were raised with considerable difficulty, the wealthier members of the London churches being either opposed to the scheme, or apathetic. Then the question of getting a passage had to be solved. No English vessels were then allowed to go to India except those of the East India Company, and the captains of the company's ships were strictly prohibited to take passengers without a license from the India House. The East India Company being resolutely opposed to missionary operations, and all attempts to procure a license for the missionaries having failed, it was finally determined to go without one. An arrangement was made, but at the last moment, after they had got on board the vessel, information arrived which compelled their leaving the ship. At length a Danish vessel bound to Calcutta was found, and terms being arranged through Mr. Thomas's energy, the party sailed on the 13th of June, 1793, and arrived safely in Calcutta on the 11th of November. New difficulties almost immediately arose. Their resources were inadequate, and Mr. Thomas's management of pecuniary matters was unfortunate. It became necessary for both missionaries to accept employment, which was providentially offered in connection with the indigo-factories of a Christian gentleman, who compassionated their situation. Carey, for the next five years, regularly devoted a fourth and upwards of his salary to the objects of the mission. As soon as he had acquired sufficient fluency in the native language, he daily assembled the laborers and servants of the factory for Christian worship and instruction, and constantly itinerated in the surrounding villages. He also began the translation of the New Testament, and procured a printing-press. In 1796 he was joined by Mr. Fountain, who had been sent out by the society, and two years later Carey wrote to Fuller that new missionaries might be introduced into the country as assistant indigo planters. Acting on this suggestion, and encouraged by the increase of the missionary spirit in the churches, the committee sent out four missionaries and their families in 1799, two of whom died soon after their arrival, but the two others, Joshua Marshman and William Ward, were destined, in the course of Providence, to share with Carey in the establishment of Christian civilization in India. But the jealous suspicions of the Indian authorities had by this time gathered around Carey, and the new missionaries were landed at Serampore, a Danish settlement, before the Calcutta officials could arrest them. All efforts failing to procure permission to join Carey, he determined to make Serampore the headquarters of the mission, and arrived there with his family on the 10th of January, 1800. For nearly twenty-five years Carey, Marshman, and Ward continued to labor unitedly in what was known throughout the world as the work of the Serampore mission. They threw all their earnings into a common fund, and from this resource contributed nearly £80,000 to the work. Mr. and Mrs. Marshman conducted flourishing boarding-schools for many years, which secured the mission from pecuniary destitution in its earlier history. Carey was appointed Professor of Bengalee in Fort William College, Calcutta, and devoted his salary to the mission work. Ward was a practical printer, and by his successful management of the printing department greatly aided the mission treasury. Providing thus for the permanent support of the mission, they gave opportunity for the sending out of other laborers, and attained a position of influence in the European community at Calcutta. Their residence under the Danish flag at Serampore secured them from the outbreaks of Anglo-Indian hatred of missions, and yet afforded all the advantages of a metropolitan position for their work. In March, 1812, the printing-office with all its contents was totally destroyed by fire, but the calamity only served to test and develop the strength of the missionary spirit. Contributions poured in upon Mr. Fuller and the committee in England until the whole loss was more than covered. The death of Fuller, in 1815, was a severe loss, and was keenly felt, particularly by the older missionaries. Dr. Ryland succeeded him as secretary, assisted by Mr. Dyer, and differences of opinion arose which ultimately led to the severance of the Serampore missionaries from the society. A separate organization in England undertook the charge of the Serampore work, and in 1818 the college was established. The abolition of the restrictions on missionary work in India now gave free scope to evangelical zeal, and other communions besides the Baptists entered in and possessed the land. But to Carey and his associates belongs the honor of "the forlorn hope." As Mr. J. C. Marshman, in his history of the Serampore mission, justly says, "They were the first to enforce the necessity of giving the Scriptures to all the tribes of India. Their own translations were necessarily and confessedly imperfect; but imperfections may be overlooked in the labors of men who produced the first editions of the New Testament in so many of the Oriental languages and dialects, and gave that impulse to the work of translation which still sustains it. They were the first to insist on the absolute exclusion of caste from the native Christian community and church. They established the first native schools for heathen children in Hindoostan, and organized the first college for the education of native catechists and ministers. They printed the first books in the language of Bengal, and thus laid the foundation of a vernacular literature; and they were the first to cultivate and improve that language and render it a suitable vehicle for national instruction. They published the first native newspaper in India, and issued the first religious periodical. In all the departments of missionary labor and intellectual improvement they led the way, and it is on the broad foundation which they were enabled to lay that the edifice of modern Indian missions has been erected." When the jubilee of the society was celebrated at Kettering in October, 1842, only one of its founders, Mr. Hogge, the first treasurer, remained alive. All the senior missionaries also had passed away, Dr. Marshman, the last survivor, having died in 1836. The breach which had taken place between the society and the Serampore brethren, after the death of Andrew Fuller, and which kept them apart for several years, had been healed. Missions had been established in the West Indies, which had been remarkably successful, also in the Bahamas and Central America. New stations had been opened in India and Ceylon, in connection with which many able and devoted missionaries, besides the Serampore band, had labored with encouraging results. At the end of the first fifty years the mission churches in India contained 978 native members, and about 300 Europeans in separate fellowship. In Jamaica there were upwards of 25,000 church members; in the Bahamas, 1176; and in Central America, 132. The work of translation had been continued by Dr. Yates and other brethren, so that the whole or part of the Scriptures, with myriads of tracts, in forty-four languages and dialects, attested their zeal and success. The funds contributed at the jubilee services enabled the society to enlarge its operations. New fields were opened in Western Africa, Trinidad, and Hayti. A mission in Brittany, France, which the Welsh churches had established, was adopted somewhat later, and a training college for the education of teachers and native ministers was founded at Calabar, Jamaica. In 1859 the China mission was entered upon, and help was rendered to sustain Baptist mission work in Norway, Canada, and Germany. In 1867 the membership of the native churches in India had increased to 2300, after deducting all losses. The entire number of persons in fellowship in all the mission churches connected with the society, exclusive of the Jamaica churches, which had become self-sustaining in a great measure, was 6500. The translating and printing of the Scriptures and Christian literature have been greatly prospered during the later period of the society's history. No Indian mission has so remarkable a record in this department of Christian work. Dr. Wenger, Rev. C. B. Lewis, and Rev. Mr. Rouse are on all hands recognized as worthy and distinguished successors of Carey and his coadjutors. In 1878 the report showed that the Indian mission still engaged the larger portion of the society's efforts, but that new fields had been opened up in Western Africa and Italy. The total receipts for all purposes for the year amounted to £50,068 17s. 10d., a large increase on the income of the preceding year. Among the more important features of the modern history of the society, the mission at Rome and in other parts of Italy is to be mentioned, and also the wonderfully laborious and successful career of Mr. Saker in Western Africa.

England, Legal Baptism in.—At this moment two clergymen of the Episcopal Church, established by law in England, are in prison for violating the ecclesiastical enactments and decisions which claimed their obedience. Outside of the state church they could practise any customs agreeable to themselves and not injurious to others. But the laws of the Church of England have the force of civil statutes, and inflict secular pains and penalties upon those who break them.

Dr. Richard Burn, a former chancellor of the diocese of Carlisle, compiled a body of ecclesiastical enactments, canons, customs, decisions,—a church code in short,—which he called "Ecclesiastical Law." He is an Episcopalian Blackstone very much in demand among the clergy of the English Church. Of the mode of baptism he says, "At first baptism was administered publicly as occasion served, by rivers. Afterwards the baptistery was built at the entrance of the church or very near it; which had a large basin in it that *held the persons* to be baptized, and they went down by steps into it. Afterwards, when immersion came to be disused, fonts were set up at the entrance of the churches.

"The priest taking the child into his hands, shall say to the godfathers and godmothers, 'Name this child;' and then naming it after them, if they shall certify him that the child may well endure it, he *shall dip it in the water*, discreetly and warily, saying, 'N., I baptize thee, in the name of the Father, and of the Son, and of the Holy Ghost;' but if the child is weak it will suffice to pour water upon it." (Burn's Ecclesiastical Law, vol. i. pp. 101, 103. London, 1787.) Until 1842 this work had passed through nine editions. The statement about the mode of baptizing in the above is the *doctrine* of the Church of England, and it is at the same time the *civil law* of England for the administration of baptism in the Established Church. Hence it follows, according to the highest authority on ecclesiastical law:

1st. That in England baptism, in the beginning, was administered at rivers, and afterwards in a baptistery at the entrance of the church or very near it, with a basin large enough to hold the baptized, to which they went down by steps, before *immersion was disused.*

2d. That if the godfathers and godmothers shall certify the clergyman that the child can well endure dipping, he must dip it, or risk civil penalties for his disobedience.

3d. That pouring is not the *proper* mode of baptism in the Church of England, but a mere makeshift, which may "*suffice*" for weak children, but should never be administered to the healthy.

English Baptists, Historical Sketch of.—The Christian religion was introduced into Britain in the second century, and it spread with great rapidity over the ancient inhabitants,—that is, over the Britons, or Welsh, not over the English, who came to their present home as pagans in the fifth century, and afterwards gave it their name. The ancient Britons, unlike the English, were not converted by missionaries from Rome, but apparently by ministers from the East, like Irenæus, the Greek bishop of Lyons, in France. The Britons refused obedience to the commands of the pope, and they observed some customs in opposition to the usages of the Romish Church. It is highly probable that when Augustine landed in Britain in the end of the sixth century, infants were not baptized in that country. "Pedobaptism was not known in the world the first two ages after Christ; in the third and fourth it was approved by a few. At length, in the fifth and following ages, it began to obtain in diverse places." Prof. Curcellaeus, of Amsterdam, a Pedobaptist, states the truth in the foregoing declaration. (Crosby, iii., Preface, p. xviii.) As the Britons had no relations with Africa, the birthplace of infant baptism, and no religious ties with Rome, and little intercourse with the distant East at that period, it is most likely that the infant rite was wholly unknown among them. When Augustine had his celebrated conference with the British bishops at Augustine's Oak, in 603, he demanded three things from them: "To keep Easter at the due (Roman) time; *to administer baptism,* by which we are again born to God, *according to the custom* of the holy Roman Apostolic Church; and jointly with us to preach the Word of God to the English nation." Bede's report of this meeting in his "Ecclesiastical History," lib. ii. cap. 2, is undoubtedly true. By some the demand about baptism is regarded as infallible testimony that the ancient British at this time did not baptize infants. This view lays too much stress upon the report of Bede. The ancient Britons had a different tonsure from the Romish monks and their English sacerdotal converts, and the lack of uniformity about this practice was the cause of bitter controversy; and so it is possible that the ancient Britons may have immersed infants, but with ceremonies obnoxious to Augustine. The probabilities, however, are altogether in favor of the view that they rejected the baptism of such children and unconscious babes as were immersed at that time in Rome. It should be remembered that in the Eternal City at this period, and for some ages later, little children were catechised and baptized twice a year. The truth about the Britons of Augustine's day is that they were most probably Baptists, and most assuredly not Roman Catholics. The Irish and Scotch in that day were in perfect harmony with the ancient Britons in wholly rejecting papal authority, and most probably infant baptism. St. Patrick was converted just as Christians are now, he baptized converts in rivers and wells, as may be seen in "The Baptism of the Ages," and to us he appears to have been a Baptist missionary; his religious successors in Ireland, and in the Scotch churches which sprang up from their missionary labors, and the ancient British churches, continued independent of Rome for a considerable period, and gradually fell into the papal apostasy, the Irish yielding last to the sacerdotal tyranny of the Seven Hills.

Among the people now called English, the Angles, Jutes, and Saxons, who first began to enter Britain in the middle of the fifth century, and whose conversion to Romish Christianity commenced in the end of the sixth, Baptist doctrines had no place for ages after the death of Augustine, their apostle.

In the twelfth century about thirty Publicans of foreign birth appeared in England. They were rustic in their manners, blameless in their lives, and their leader, Gerhard, was a man of some learning. They made one Englishwoman a convert to their doctrines. She was probably the first Baptist of Anglo-Saxon birth. These persons took "the doctrine of the Apostles as their rule of faith." They were orthodox about the Trinity and the incarnation, but "they rejected baptism and the holy Eucharist;" that is, they rejected infant baptism, like their Albigensian brethren on the Continent, and the Romish mass, together with the remaining papal sacraments. A council of bishops met at Oxford in 1160 to try these pious rejectors of papal authority, and when they were threatened with punishment for refusing to submit to the Catholic Church, they replied, "Blessed are they that suffer persecution for righteousness' sake, for theirs is the kingdom of heaven." The council condemned them. Upon this Henry II. ordered them to be whipped out of town after being branded in the forehead, and he forbade any one " to entertain them or give them any manner of relief." They endured their sufferings joyfully, and departed, led by Gerhard, singing, " Blessed are ye when men shall hate you." The severity of the winter, the superstitious dread of heresy, and the terror of the king, destroyed these poor people by hunger and cold. (Collier's Eccles. Hist. of Great Britain, ii. 262–63. London, 1840.)

That there were numbers who held Baptist sentiments among the Lollards and the followers of Wickliffe we have no reason to doubt. Robinson, the Baptist historian, says, " I have now before me a MS. register of Grey, bishop of Ely, which proves that in the year 1457 there was a congregation of this sort (Baptist) in this village where I live, who privately assembled for divine worship and had preachers of their own, who taught them the very doctrine which we now preach. Six of them were accused of heresy by the tyrants of the district, and condemned to abjure heresy, and do penance half naked, with a faggot at their backs, and a taper in their hands, in the public market-place of Ely and Cambridge, and in the church-yard of Great Swaffham." The charges against them in substance were, that " they denied infant baptism (item, quod puer . . . nec egeat, nec baptizari debeat . . .); that they rejected extreme unction; and said that the pope was antichrist, and his priests were devils incarnate." (Robinson's Notes on Claude's Essay, ii. 53, 55.) These Baptists held the truth before Luther preached the doctrine of justification by faith, or Cranmer favored the Reformation in England. We have reason to suppose that in the multitudes of English Lollards there were many Anabaptists, and not a few conventicles like the one at Chesterton.

In 1538, according to Bishop Burnet, " there was a commission sent to Cranmer, Stokesly, Sampson, and some others, to inquire after Anabaptists, to proceed against them, to restore the penitent, to burn their books, and to deliver the obstinate to the secular arm." At this period the Baptists in England were circulating their denominational literature, and were sufficiently numerous to disturb the head of the nation. In 1560 the Anabaptists were not only numerous in England, but some of them were " creeping into Scotland," and John Knox was afraid that they might " insidiously instill their poison into the minds of some of his brethren," and he lifted his powerful pen against our people, to refute their arguments, and to keep them out of Scotland. In 1553, when the great Scotch Reformer was in London, an Anabaptist called upon him at " his lodging" and " gave him a book written by one of this party, which he pressed him to read." (McCrie's Life of John Knox, p. 137. Philadelphia, 1845.) Ivimey (i. 138) says, " It is thought the General Baptist Church of Canterbury has existed for two hundred and fifty years (written in 1811), and that Joan Boucher was a member of it, who was burned in the reign of Edward VI." This would make 1561, the year when the church was founded, but it must have existed eleven years earlier if Joan of Kent belonged to it; and it may have been older than 1550. Ivimey represents the church at Eyethorne as formed before 1581. Dr. Some, an English Episcopalian, of great repute, wrote a treatise in 1589 against Barrow, Greenwood, and others of the Puritan sect, " wherein he endeavored to show what agreement there was between the opinions of the English Anabaptists and these men. Dr. Some acknowledges that there were several Anabaptistical conventicles in London and other places, that some of this sect, as well as the Papists, had been bred at the universities." (Crosby, i. 76.) At this period the Baptists with separate places of meeting and educated ministers must have been in the enjoyment of considerable prosperity.

In 1611, Thomas Helwys, pastor of the English Baptist church of Amsterdam, in Holland, concluded that it seemed cowardly to stay out of his country to avoid persecution, and that it was his duty to return and preach the truth at home, and cheer his suffering brethren; his church, when he gave his reasons, agreed to go with him; and probably in 1612 the Amsterdam English Baptist church was in London, and very soon became a strong community.

In 1620 the English Baptists presented King James I. a very able petition, in which they declare their loyalty, tell his majesty about their grievous imprisonment " for many years in divers counties in England," explain their principles, and appeal to the king, and to the Parliament then sitting, to relieve them from persecutions. At this period there was undoubtedly a considerable number of Baptists in England; some of them formed into churches, and others scattered throughout the nation. The foundation was in existence for that magnificent denominational success which thirty years later astonished Baptists themselves and utterly confounded those who disliked them.

PARTICULAR BAPTISTS.

In 1616 a Congregational church was established in London, of which Henry Jacob was the first pastor. His successor in 1633 was John Lathorp. At that time certain members of the church holding Baptist sentiments sought its sanction to form a church of baptized believers. The approval was given. The new church was organized Sept. 12, 1633. This community was the first English Calvinistical or Particular Baptist church whose special history we can trace with the greatest facility. John Spilsbury was its first pastor. (Crosby, i. 148.)

The Protectorate was a period of remarkable Baptist growth. Our brethren were full of zeal. They used the press in every direction; peddlers cried Baptist books for sale up and down the streets of cities and towns as newsboys invite customers among us for the daily papers; tracts were distributed in the army and elsewhere; sermons were preached in the streets by brethren and on the doorsteps by sisters, like the godly women of Bedford who told John Bunyan about the Saviour; soldiers preached to each other in the barracks and on the march; and the officers were heralds of salvation when they had an opportunity. And as a result Baptist principles triumphed to an extent that created wonder and alarm.

Maj.-Gen. Overton, according to Clarendon,* was a Baptist, a man of great religious fervor, and a fearless soldier. Gen. Lilburn was an enthusiastic Baptist. Lieut.-Gen. Fleetwood, the son-in-law of Cromwell, as the "Parliamentary History"† states, was a Baptist. Richard Baxter‡ represents Gen. Ludlow, the commander-in-chief of the forces in Ireland, as "the head of the Anabaptists in that country." Gen. Harrison was a Baptist worthy of immortal regard. Clarendon describes "Vice-Admiral Lawson as a notorious Anabaptist who had filled the fleet with officers and mariners of the same principles."§ Of the governors and colonels the number belonging to the Baptists was remarkable. And wherever the English army or fleet was found the Baptists made themselves felt. Ivimey|| quotes a letter from Capt. Richard Deane to Dr. Barlow, bishop of Lincoln, in which he says, "In the year 1649 the Baptists greatly increased in the country, and their opinions did likewise spread themselves into some of the regiments of horse and foot in the army; and in 1650 and afterwards some professing this opinion were called from their private employments and preferred to commands at sea. Among others Capt. Mildmay, to command the admiral's flag-ship, under the Duke of Albemarle (Monk), when he was one of the 'generals at sea'; Capt. Pack, to command the flag-ship under Sir George Ascue, rear-admiral; Sir John Harman to command the admiral's flag-ship under his royal highness the Duke of York." "In and after 1649 their numbers did increase, insomuch that the principal officers in divers regiments of horse and foot became Anabaptists, particularly Oliver Cromwell's own regiment of horse, when he was captain-general of all the Parliament's forces; and in the Duke of Albemarle's own regiment of foot, when he was general of all the English forces in Scotland." The writer of this letter was a Baptist, and a "general at sea" with Gens. Blake and Monk. In that day this title meant the highest grade of admiral. Gen. Lilburn's troops had a large representation of Baptists, who held religious meetings wherever they were on duty; and their denominational sympathies were as well known in England as the Presbyterianism of Sir Arthur Haslerig, or the Congregationalism of Oliver Cromwell. Thomas Harrison writing Secretary Thurloe from Dublin in 1655,¶ describing the Baptists in Ireland, says, "They have governors of towns and cities, twelve at least; colonels, ten; lieutenant-colonels, three or four; majors, ten; captains, nineteen or twenty; officers in the civil list, twenty-three; and many [others] of whom I never heard." The writer of this letter begins it with expressions of sorrow for a country with such a list of Baptists in official positions. These Baptists were all Englishmen temporarily located in Ireland. Probably in the list above Col. Sadler, the governor of Galway, is counted, who, according to Heath,** with all his officers, were Anabaptists. The most remarkable record of Baptist progress in the English army in Ireland we have from the ready pen of good, murmuring Richard Baxter. He says that in Cromwell's sway, "In Ireland the Anabaptists were grown so high that many of the soldiers were rebaptized [immersed] as the way to preferment; and they who opposed them were crushed with uncharitable fierceness." This is a proof of popularity and influence, the force of which we can easily appreciate. The unprincipled heathen enrolled themselves as Christians when Constantine the Great proclaimed himself a follower of the Redeemer. And in Ireland, as Mr. Baxter affirms, Baptist principles were so precious to men in power that Pedobaptist soldiers, with an accommodating conscience, professed to adopt them to secure higher positions in the army. In a letter addressed to Cromwell, and preserved by Thurloe,†† his principal secretary, written after he made himself a dictator, and after he began to persecute Baptist soldiers because they disliked his despotical assumptions, it is asked, "Have not the Anabaptists filled your towns, your cities, your provinces, your castles, your navies, your tents, your armies, except that which went to the West Indies, which prospered so well?" This army was shamefully

---

* Clarendon's History of the Rebellion, iii. 60, 728. Oxford, 1706.
† Evans's Early English Baptists, ii. 199, 209, 214. London.
‡ Baxter's Life, 69, 70.
§ History of the Rebellion, iii. 728. Oxford, 1706.
|| Ivimey's History of the English Baptists, i. 295, 296. London.

¶ Thurloe's State Papers, iv. 91. London, 1742.
** Heath's Chronicles, p. 438.
†† Thurloe's State Papers, iii. 150-1. London, 1742.

defeated at Hispaniola. The writer then puts some other questions to the Lord Protector: "1st. Whether you had come to that height you are now in if the Anabaptists had been as much your enemies as they were your friends? 2nd. Whether the Anabaptists were ever unfaithful either to the Commonwealth, &c., in general, or to your highness in particular? 3rd. Whether Anabaptists are not to be commended for their integrity, which had rather keep good faith and a good conscience, although it may lose them their employment [in the army], than to keep their employment with the loss of both? . . . 6th. Whether one hundred of the old Anabaptists, such as marched under your command in 1648, 1649, and 1650, &c., be not as good as two hundred of your new courtiers, if you were in such a condition as you were at Dunbar?" It was at Dunbar, near Edinburgh, where Cromwell gained a great victory over 30,000 splendid Scotch troops, with an army not more than 10,000 strong of all arms, and greatly discouraged by sickness and want, many of whom were valiant Anabaptists. From this letter, the truth of which cannot be questioned, the Baptists occupied many positions of great importance and power under the Commonwealth and under Cromwell.

But the most convincing evidence of the influence possessed by the Baptists just before the restoration of Charles II. is found in the efforts made by the Presbyterians to place that monarch on the throne. The first Stuart monarch of England renounced his Presbyterian education and professed principles, and ever, after he entered England, was a malignant enemy of the church of Calvin and Knox. His son, Charles I., was a wicked persecutor of everything bordering on Presbyterianism. Charles II. before he ascended the throne of his fathers showed no reliable mark of improvement to win the favor of an honest Presbyterian. Nor had he a single confidential friend whose character afforded one ray of hope that Charles was more favorably disposed to Presbyterianism than his father or his grandfather. The Presbyterians of England and Scotland restored Charles II. No one competent to give an opinion denies this. Why did they engage in such work? They have a grand character as the friends of liberty and of God. We have wept in reading the records of their martyrs, and gloried in the courage of their heroes. How came they to place on the throne of Great Britain and Ireland a treacherous Roman Catholic? Guizot,[*] the French Protestant statesman, tells the secret when he says, "The king's interest is also supported by the Presbyterians, although they are republicans in principle; and it is only the fear that the Anabaptists and other sectaries may obtain the government which leads them to oppose the present authorities." The Presbyterians at the period referred to by Guizot, just before the restoration, had only been placed in possession of the government for the first time in several years. The Episcopalians, when Richard Cromwell withdrew from the government, were of little account. The Independents and Cromwell had it for a long time; and the new rulers were alarmed lest the Anabaptists should seize the reins of state and give lasting liberty of conscience, which to them was odious, and spread their principles still more widely through all ranks of society; and they joined the old cavaliers to bring the royal exile from Breda because the Baptists were so numerous and powerful that they were afraid they might seize the government. The king, on obtaining the crown, crushed the Presbyterians without pity, and wickedly persecuted the Baptists. They were imprisoned in loathsome dungeons; in one place sixty of them were confined in a room nine feet wide and fourteen feet long; in many of the jails the Baptists were brought in such throngs that some had to stand while others lay down to sleep. Multitudes died through the foul air of the prisons. Others were kicked, beaten, and outrageously abused, until death came to their relief. Some were sold as slaves in Jamaica. Henry Forty was imprisoned twelve years in Exeter; John Bunyan, during the same period, in Bedford; another minister twenty years in the same place; and others were hung, drawn, and quartered. But the martyr spirit never exhibited itself more gloriously than among these Baptist worthies. Their enemies were confounded, if they were not conquered, by their blessed expressions and heroism, in losses, confinement, and agonizing pains.

Their love of the widest liberty of conscience, and of pure democracy, had unquestionably an extensive influence in shaping public opinion under Charles II. and James II. in Great Britain. So that at last the high-churchmen, whose fathers bled on many battle-fields for the divine right of kings and the passive obedience of subjects, began to believe that Englishmen had some rights which even kings should be compelled to respect; and James II., by the persuasive threatenings of an angry people, fled to France, and William III., the illustrious Hollander, ascended the throne of Britain with the joyful acclamations of most Englishmen, and the speedy obedience of all; and from him and the nation came "The Toleration Act," and an extension and consolidation of British liberty; results of a glorious revolution, many of the seeds of which were planted by the teachings and instructive sufferings of our British Baptist fathers of the seventeenth century.

From the persecutions of the last two Stuart kings the Baptists in England, for a long period, did not

---

[*] Guizot's Richard Cromwell, i. 407.

recover. They had been robbed, murdered, compelled to emigrate, and destroyed in prison in thousands, nevertheless they continued to hope, and they labored faithfully for the Master. A time of religious declension darkening the latter part of the seventeenth and more than a third of the eighteenth century was as great a calamity to our brethren. In 1720 the Bristol Baptist college was founded, and in succeeding years it largely blessed the churches; now there are five colleges in England among the Particular Baptists. The great awakening under the preaching of Whitefield exerted an immense influence over Great Britain, in the blessings of which the Baptists shared. The descending Spirit continued to favor them richly, and they projected the mission to India, and sent out Dr. Carey, the pioneer missionary of modern times. At present the English Baptists are doing a noble work for their own country, and for various quarters of the heathen world. In England proper there are 30 Associations, 1954 churches, 1385 ministers, 195,199 members.

It is probable that the first Baptist church in Ireland, since the decline of early Irish Christianity, was planted in Dublin by Thomas Patient. He was a minister of apostolic zeal, and for years co-pastor with William Kiffin, of London. In 1653 churches existed in Waterford, Clonmel, Kilkenny, Cork, Limerick, Wexford, Carrickfergus, and Kerry. But as the Baptist officers and soldiers of Cromwell's army left these localities the churches in some cases must have been immediately broken up. At present the churches in Ireland number only 29, with 1358 members. Baptist churches were planted in Scotland by Cromwell's soldiers. The church at Leith was among the very first. But, as in Ireland, our denomination has had little prosperity, so we have failed seriously to impress the Scotch. We have 90 churches, and 9096 members, in the land from which the immortal Knox warned us. Many distinguished men have been identified with the British and Irish Baptists, such as Hanserd Knollys, William Kiffin, John Milton, John Bunyan, John Gill, John Howard, William Carey, John Foster, Andrew Fuller, Robert Hall, Alexander Carson, the Haldanes, Sir Henry Havelock, C. H. Spurgeon, and others, sketches of whom will be found in this work. (See article on WELSH BAPTISTS.)

GENERAL BAPTISTS.

Until 1633 we have no distinct account of the existence of an English Baptist church resting on a basis wholly Calvinistical. After that period the points of difference between the Arminian and Calvinistical churches are clearly defined. The General Baptists were, and still nominally are, Arminians. Their first Confession of Faith was issued in Holland in 1611. In 1660 they published another, which received the sanction of 20,000 persons. At this period, just after the unhappy assumption of royal power by Charles II., they were quite numerous. In 1678 another creed was published by a section of the General Baptists, which was designed to approach Calvinism as closely as its compilers dared. In 1691 the members of this body living in Somersetshire and adjacent counties issued another Confession. After having done much for the cause of God and truth, and grown to considerable strength, some of the General Baptists adopted Unitarian sentiments, and others followed their example. The innovation led to bitter controversies, and as in the similar case of the old English Presbyterians, to the decay and dissolution of churches; this heresy caused deep sorrow to Christ's remaining friends, who mourned over the doctrinal errors and lax discipline of their churches, and at last, in 1770, they formed The New Connection of General Baptists, under the leadership of two pastors, Dan Taylor, of Wadsworth, Yorkshire, and W. Thompson, of Boston, Lincolnshire, for the purpose of reviving Scriptural piety and evangelical sentiments among the old General Baptists. Their first step was to send a deputation to the Assembly of General Baptists in London stating their reasons for separation, and bidding their former associates farewell. On the following day Dan Taylor preached to the new body from 2 Tim. i. 8: "Be not thou ashamed of the testimony of our Lord," and presided over the meeting which then formally initiated the New Connection of General Baptists. In order that there might be no uncertainty as to what they considered the faith and practice of primitive Christianity, a creed of six articles was proposed and adopted, not as a complete exposition of their whole belief, but as a declaration of their views on the points which had been often debated between them and their old associates. This creed was also intended to constitute a test, without agreement to which their former friends could not enter the new communion. It was also considered desirable that every minister should give an account of his religious experience at their next meeting in 1771, for their satisfaction concerning the reality of each other's conversion. The six articles expressed orthodox views concerning the fall of man, the nature and perpetual obligation of the moral law, the person and work of Christ, salvation by faith, regeneration by the Holy Spirit, and baptism. The last article reads as follows: "We believe that it is the indispensable duty of all who repent and believe the gospel to be baptized by immersion in water, in order to be initiated into a church-state; and that no person ought to be received into the church without submission to that ordinance." The number of churches uniting was seven only, some of them far asunder as to locality, but containing upwards of 1200 members. Repeated attempts were made to reunite the Old and New Connections, but without avail. The seceders went steadily forward in the work of edification and extension, providing a collection of hymns, and a catechism containing the most important principles of religion and reasons for dissent from state-churches. They agreed to hold an annual Association in different places, and to publish a Circular Letter, written by appointment, together with the minutes of each yearly meeting. In 1797 it was determined to provide assistance to candidates for the ministry. Pursuant to this resolution an academy was opened in January, 1798, in London, and placed under the care of the Rev. Dan Taylor. About the same time a magazine was started to aid in sustaining the academy. This enterprise having failed, another periodical was brought out, called the *Repository*, in which the general transactions of the body were recorded, and a medium of communication opened on subjects of common interest. The missionary spirit which had been aroused among the Particular Baptists found favor with many members of the New Connection, and contributions were made to the Baptist Missionary Society. In 1816, however, it was resolved to form a new mission, the operations of which should be under the supervision of the annual Association. The mission has labored with distinguished efficiency and success, mainly in the province of Orissa, Bengal. Its income from all sources for the year ending May 31, 1877, was £9332. Home missionary work is carried on in the districts where the churches are chiefly found, under the management of conferences, from which reports are made to the annual assembly of ministers and delegates. Most of the churches of which the New Connection was first constituted were located in the midland district of England, namely, Leicestershire, Nottinghamshire, Lincolnshire, and Derbyshire. Although they now number 184 churches, and are scattered over twenty counties, the strength of the denomination is still found in the midland district. All the churches still unite in one Association, meeting annually by their representatives for the transaction of business and for fraternal fellowship. The latest returns show a total membership of nearly 25,000. The annual assembly consists of ministers who are members *ex officio*, and of representatives sent from the churches in a certain fixed ratio. It is never held in any place oftener than once in seven years. The affiliated churches are expected to contribute to the support of the denominational institutions, such as home and foreign missions and the college. If any church declines to render this support, it forfeits its right of speaking or voting in relation to these institutions. Whilst acknowledging the perfect independence of the churches, and avoiding all synodic action which would infringe it, the assembly claims the right to guard the faith and morals of the Connection, and, if need be, to cut off a church from fellowship. In like manner any minister convicted of heresy or immorality, even if his church should adhere to him, would be disowned, and his name erased from the ministerial list. As the name "General Baptist" indicates, the body professes the doctrine of "general redemption," in opposition to the doctrine of "particular redemption," which is the tenet of the Particular or Calvinistic Baptists. It is commonly supposed that the designation General Baptist refers to the practice of open or free communion. But the article on baptism already cited is sufficient to show that the General Baptists restrict communion to the baptized. The practice of the churches of the New Connection is not, however, uniform in this matter. Another mistake is not uncommon, the origin of which is also traceable to the name. As "general" is sometimes taken in the sense of *universal*, it is presumed that the General Baptists are Universalists,—a mistake which receives countenance from the fact that the old body from which the New Connection seceded has now almost entirely merged into the Unitarian denomination. Efforts have been made from time to time to amalgamate the New Connection with the larger body known as the Particular Baptists, but no formal action has been taken by either section. Almost all the churches belong, however, to the Baptist Union of Great Britain and Ireland. Members are freely transferred by letters of dismission from one body to the other, and General Baptist churches sometimes choose Particular Baptist pastors, and some General Baptists have been settled over Particular Baptist churches. In later years some of the ministers and churches of the New Connection have approximated to the views of modern Calvinists. The college at Chilwell, near Nottingham, for the training of ministerial students, is well sustained. It has fine premises, including a detached residence for the president, and between seven and eight acres of land. Many eminent ministers and missionaries have been sent forth from this institution, and the standard of ministerial education has been raised to as high a level as in other theological seminaries. The missionary work of the body in Orissa has become famous through the zeal and success of such devoted laborers as Sutton, Peggs, Goadly, Buckley, Stubbins, Barley, and others. Among those ministers who have lately labored or are still laboring in the home field, the names of Pike, Stevenson, Hunter, Goadly, Burns, Matthews, Clifford, and Cox are widely known as preachers and writers of eminent ability and usefulness. Though possessing the field at an earlier day than their Calvinistical brethren, they have never obtained the same measure of success.

Ephrata is in Cocolico Township, Lancaster County, sixty miles from Philadelphia. In 1770 the village was frequently called Tunkerstown (Dipperstown), and it had about thirty or forty buildings. Conrad Beissel, a Seventh-Day Baptist, located here in 1733, and soon a community which he had formed at Mill Creek, Pa., gathered around him.

There were three places of worship in this village. One adjoined the apartments of the sisters, and it was regarded as their chapel, and one was near the house of the brethren for their use; the third was a common church built some distance from the chapels, where brethren, sisters, and the married people, with their families, met once a week for worship. The churches were called Sharon, Bethany, and Zion, and all belonged to the same small community.

The sisters adopted the dress of nuns, and the brethren that of White Friars, with some alterations. Both took the vow of celibacy, and when any one broke the vow he quitted the single men's house and lived among the neighboring married people. Those devoted to a single life slept at first on board benches with blocks for pillows, but a little later they became backsliders somewhat, and used beds. The men wore their beards. The brethren obtained a living by farming, a printing-office, a paper-mill, a grist-mill, and an oil-mill; and the sisters by spinning, weaving, and sewing. They kept the seventh day for the Sabbath. Their singing in worship was charming. Notwithstanding their peculiar appearance, a "smiling innocence and meekness grace their countenances and make their deportment gentle and obliging." This was their state in 1770 according to Morgan Edwards.

Errett, Hon. Russell, was born in New York in 1817, and removed to Pennsylvania in 1829. He is by profession an editor, and has held various public offices. In 1860 he was elected comptroller of Pittsburgh; he was clerk of the Pennsylvania senate for three different sessions; was appointed paymaster in the U. S. army in 1861, and served until mustered out in 1866; he was elected to the State senate of Pennsylvania in 1867; he was appointed assessor of internal revenue in 1869, serving until 1873. He was three times elected from the 22d district of the State as their Representative in Congress, in which capacity he is now doing good service.

Russell Errett was baptized in Pittsburgh, and held his first membership in the church of the Disciples, but coming to Mansfield, Alleghany County, he, together with his wife, united with the newly-formed regular Baptist church, and has found here a suitable home. His brother Isaac is editor of the *Christian Standard*, Cincinnati, O., and was baptized at the same time.

Mr. Errett is a conscientious Christian, a Representative of distinguished ability, and a public man of great purity of life.

Espy, T. B., D.D., was born in Cass Co., Ga., in 1837; educated at Howard College, Ala.; three

T. B. ESPY, D.D.

years a chaplain in Confederate army; pastor two years at Athens, Ga.; then became pastor two years of First Baptist church, Little Rock, Ark.; in 1873, in connection with T. P. Boone, became editor and publisher of the *Western Baptist*, at Little Rock, which was suspended in 1879. He then became connected with the *Baptist Reflector*, and at present is connected with the *American Baptist Flag*, St. Louis, Mo. Dr. Espy has engaged creditably in four public discussions. His residence is Little Rock, Ark.

Estabrooks, Rev. Elijah, was one of the pioneer Baptist ministers of New Brunswick, who often attended the meetings of the Baptist Association of Nova Scotia and New Brunswick in its early history, and was for many years pastor of the Baptist church at Waterbury, Queens Co., New Brunswick, and labored much in that county and in the settlements on the upper St. John, preaching the gospel earnestly and with marked tokens of God's approval.

Estee, Rev. Sydney A., was born in Salem, Washington Co., N. Y., in 1808. At twenty years of age he united with the Baptist church of his native town, and, deciding to prepare for the ministry, studied at Cambridge Academy, and afterwards at Hamilton. His first settlement as pastor was at Westport, N. Y., subsequently at Ticonderoga, in the same county. After several other pastorates in that State he removed to Illinois, and was located at York, Belvidere, and Aurora, where he died Dec. 7, 1872. His ministry was marked by great usefulness.

Estep, Rev. James.—For more than half a century this distinguished minister labored in Western Pennsylvania. Few men ever attained greater eminence as a clear thinker, a sound theologian, and an earnest preacher. He was born in Washington Co., Pa., Oct. 9, 1782. He died July 26, 1861. He was baptized into the fellowship of the Mount Moriah Baptist church in April, 1802, and by this church he was licensed to preach two years after his baptism. For eighteen months prior to his entering the ministry he was pursuing the study of medicine, but a sermon preached by the Rev. Morgan J. Rhees, then prothonotary of Somerset Co., Pa., led him to deep reflection as to personal duty, and in twenty days after he was found preaching. Long before he thought of entering the ministry he gave himself to reading works on divinity. In fact, from the first day of his conversion he was engaged in reading, meditation, and prayer. He was a warm friend of an educated ministry, and one of the most useful of Pennsylvania Baptist ministers.

His life was spent in an eventful period. In his day, and in his immediate neighborhood, the Campbellites, or to use their own distinctive term, the Disciples, and the Cumberland Presbyterians came into existence. The church required just such a man, and infinite wisdom provided for the hour of need in raising up James Estep.

Though years have rolled away since his death, no name is more frequently on the lips of surviving brethren than his. He honored God by a noble life, and he has honored his very memory to the present hour.

Estes, Rev. Elliot, was born in Caroline Co., Va., on the 23d of July, 1795. At fifteen he was baptized by Rev. Andrew Broadus, under whose direction he pursued his studies. About 1829 he came to South Carolina, and entered upon the work of the ministry with the Euham and Coosamhatchic churches.

He was remarkable for the firmness with which he held the leading doctrines of his denomination. No one in his section stood higher, intellectually or religiously.

He died June 9, 1849, leaving a son and a daughter, the latter of whom has since followed him. The former, Rev. Andrew Broadus Estes, still lives within a few miles of the old homestead.

Estes, Hiram Cushman, D.D., was born in Bethel, Oxford Co., Me., July 27, 1823. He was hopefully converted at an early age, and baptized in the spring of 1838. His preparatory studies were pursued at the Yarmouth Academy, and he

HIRAM CUSHMAN ESTES, D.D.

graduated at Waterville College in 1847. He went through the theological course of the divinity school at Harvard College, and was ordained pastor of the Baptist church in Auburn, Me., May 15, 1850, where he remained two years and a half. In October, 1852, he accepted an appointment as agent of the American Baptist Missionary Union in the eastern New England district, comprising the State of Maine. He continued in this service for three years. Returning to the active duties of the ministry, he was settled as pastor of the Baptist church in what was Trenton, now Lamoine, Me., from 1855 to 1860. After a settlement of two years in Leicester, Mass., he went to Jericho, Vt., where his pastorate continued ten years, from 1862 to 1872. On the 1st of January, 1873, he became pastor of the First Baptist church in Paris, Me., where he now lives.

Dr. Estes received the honorary degree of Doctor of Divinity from Colby University in 1872. He is the author of a volume entitled "The Christian Doctrine of the Soul," of several printed discourses, and of various contributions to periodicals. He has seen something also of public life, having been a member of the House of Representatives of the State of Maine, and chairman of the Committee on Education.

Esty, William S., was born in Queensburg,

York Co., New Brunswick, Oct. 4, 1797; was baptized and joined the Baptist church in Fredericton, New Brunswick; was chosen deacon in 1835, and still honors that office; he has been almost sixty years devoted to the service of Christ and the church. His life has been full of usefulness.

Eure, Hon. Mills S.—Judge Eure was born in Gates Co., N. C., Feb. 10, 1835; graduated at the University of North Carolina in 1859; was baptized by Dr. T. C. Teasdale at college, Oct. 6, 1856; read law with Judge Battle and Hon. Samuel F. Phillips at Chapel Hill; served the counties of Gates and Chowan in State senate in 1860–62 and 1865; was captain of Co. G, North Carolina Cavalry, 2d Regiment, and was captured at Hanover, Pa., in 1863. In 1865–66 was elected solicitor of the first judicial district, and in August, 1874, judge of same district. An upright judge and a good farmer.

Evans, Benjamin, D.D., was born at Bilston, England, May 13, 1803. In early life he became a

BENJAMIN EVANS, D.D.

member of the Baptist church in his native town, and in 1822 was received as a student for the ministry at Horton College, Bradford. He was invited to the pastorate of the church at Scarborough, and settled there in 1825. For thirty-eight years he labored in this charge with great acceptance and usefulness, and was throughout one of the most popular and influential ministers of the town and district. His labors were abundant in every sphere of activity into which his ardent and generous nature led him. He was for years the foremost champion of religious freedom in Scarborough, and was one of the first promoters of the anti-state-church movement. In philanthropic and benevolent efforts he was conspicuously useful, and in connection with the denomination and its interests his liberality and zealous devotion were everywhere spoken of. He was called to the chair of the Baptist Union in 1858, and delivered an address on "The early English Baptists, their principles, their struggles, and their triumphs," a subject to which in later life he devoted himself with special interest and fervor. His literary efforts were continuous. He wrote a vast number of pamphlets on subjects of passing interest, and published a number of occasional sermons. For some years he conducted a monthly magazine for Sunday-schools, and aided by pen and purse to establish the leading denominational periodicals. The *Freeman* newspaper was projected by him, and for many years he contributed regularly to its columns. His books on "Popery" and "The Early English Baptists" had a large circulation, and his literary and public services were recognized by the University of Rochester with the honorary degree of D.D. Dr. Evans took a lively interest in the American Baptist Historical Society's objects, and rendered it valuable services, which were most cordially appreciated. On his retirement from the pastorate in 1862 in broken health, he gave himself to benevolent enterprises which lay near his heart. He contributed generously both money and personal service to the interests of the National Society for Aged and Infirm Baptist Ministers. He also organized, under the auspices of the Baptist Union, the Society for the Education of Ministers' Children, and was its president until his death. In 1864 he took part in the founding of the new theological institution now located at Manchester, and undertook the professorship of Ecclesiastical History. He also edited a quarterly magazine identified with the principles on which the college was based, and to which he steadfastly adhered through life. In his long pastorate at Scarborough he maintained a reputation which reflected honor upon the denomination and materially promoted the cause of evangelical religion. When his resignation was announced, the high esteem in which he was held by the public manifested itself in the presentation of an address and testimonial, signed by the mayor of the town and a number of prominent citizens. In acknowledging the testimonial, Dr. Evans was able to note the fact that among the signers there were some who thirty years before would have rejoiced to banish him from the place on account of his principles as a Dissenter and a Baptist. His end came unexpectedly. He was in his usual health, and had retired to his study with one of his family at the close of the day. During conversation he suddenly reclined his head on the back of his chair and without a word or movement of any kind "fell asleep."

Evans, Rev. Benjamin, was born in Cardiganshire, Wales, within the second decade of the present century. He has been a conspicuous figure in all the great movements that have affected our denominational interests in the Welsh principality for the last forty years. Beside being a pastor of influential churches he has been a prolific writer. He was the originator of two monthly magazines, one of which he still edits with marked ability. His literary productions are highly appreciated for their keen analytical power. His "Key to the New Testament" passed through several editions and is still read. He is now engaged in preparing expositions of several of the books of the New Testament for a Family Bible, under the editorship of the Rev. Titus Lewis.

But it is as a preacher that Mr. Evans excels. In spite of a sharp, unmusical voice he commands enthusiastic attention. There is not a man within the boundaries of the country whom the ministry are more delighted to hear. He is original to the last degree, and his sermons are frequently master-pieces of analytical thinking. The high estimate in which he is held by the denomination was demonstrated a few years ago by the presentation of a superb address, together with a testimonial of £300.

Evans, Rev. Charles, was born in Bristol, England, April 14, 1791. Some time after his conversion he entered the college at Bristol. In 1819 he was sent as a missionary to Sumatra, where he labored for a few years, and then returned to England, and was for a time pastor of a church at Abergavenny, Wales, and afterwards in Dorchester, England, until 1840, when he came to this country and took charge of the church in South Reading, now Wakefield, Mass. Subsequently he acted for a time as pastor of two churches in Michigan, and for fifteen years was an agent of the New York American Tract Society. His death occurred May 28, 1869.

Evans, Christmas.—The Welsh pulpit found in Christmas Evans its brightest ornament. He was born on the 25th of December, 1766. In his early life there do not appear to have been any gleamings of power or genius.

It only needed, however, the proper influences to sweep over the as yet chaotic wastes of that young man's soul to call forth order and harmony. Like his native hills enveloped in the mists and snows of winter, he only needed the sunshine to liberate his imprisoned powers. Nor had he to wait long. What spring is to the ice-bound earth a religious awakening was to Christmas Evans. It subdued his nature, changed his life, and called into activity all the dormant faculties of his hitherto sluggish soul.

He learned to read his Welsh Bible in the course of a month, exulting not a little at the time in his achievement. His intense thirst for knowledge led him to borrow and read every book that the scant

CHRISTMAS EVANS.

libraries of the neighborhood afforded. It is noteworthy, in view of the imaginative brilliance which became the distinguishing characteristic of his mental processes, that one of the first books which he voraciously devoured was the "Pilgrim's Progress."

He soon cherished the fixed intention of entering the ministry. The first formal attempt which he made at preaching was in the cottage of a tailor in the neighborhood, who it would appear was a man of more than ordinary intelligence, and who took a lively interest in aspiring merit. This effort was in every respect successful.

Christmas Evans was a Baptist from conviction. He was for some years a member of a Pedobaptist community, and it was not until he began to study the New Testament carefully, with a view of exposing the Anabaptist heresy, as he was pleased to call it, that he discovered the utter untenableness of his position. He went into the royal armory to equip himself with weapons with which to slay an opponent, when to his dismay he found the edge of every blade turned against himself. "Having read the New Testament through," says he, "I found not a single verse in favor of infant sprinkling, while about forty passages seemed to me to testify clearly for baptism on a profession of faith." After a struggle, which, however, was not protracted, he was baptized in the year 1788 in the river Duar by the Rev. Timothy Thomas.

Some of the most exquisitely proportioned creatures are exceedingly ungainly when young and undeveloped. It was even so with Christmas Evans. For some time it was difficult to determine whether he was a genius or a fool. With a temperament intensely fervid and a mind vividly imaginative, his sermons at this early day were as disjointed and grotesque as his personal appearance. That great preponderating faculty of his mind which in after years, under the mastery of a keen and well-balanced judgment and strong common sense, gave him unrivaled popularity, now but infused a capricious wildness into his utterances which astonished rather than impressed, and exposed to ridicule rather than to admiration. He soon, however, acquired that mental elasticity which made him the Samson of the Baptist hosts.

The field upon which he expended well-nigh the whole of his fruitful life was Anglesea. Here he was for many years a quasi-bishop. But it would be impossible to form a correct idea of his labors without taking into account the frequent lengthened preaching excursions which he made into the most remote parts of the principality. It is said that he visited South Wales forty times in the course of his ministry, and preached one hundred and sixty-three Association sermons, each journey involving an absence from home of at least six or seven weeks, and occupied with incessant evangelistic work.

The influence which he exerted upon the churches, and upon the land, by these transient ministries, it is impossible to conjecture. Large congregations greeted him everywhere and at all seasons. The coming of Christmas Evans presaged a general holiday even in the midst of harvest. Whole neighborhoods flocked to hear him, and the effect of his preaching was such that the people, held by the spell long after the enchanter had left the scene, would continue sometimes weeping and rejoicing until the morning light reminded them that they were still in a world where ordinary duties demanded attention. Nor were the impressions thus made ephemeral. In some instances strong churches grew up and flourished as the result of a single sermon.

Forty years or more have passed since that voice which thrilled so many human hearts was hushed, but its rich melody remains as a grateful reminiscence. Old men revert to their hearing Christmas Evans as one of the most notable events in a lifetime. He could no more pass out of memory than could the everlasting hills amid which they were born. And no wonder. The genius of the Welsh character found in him its most perfect ideal. He embodied in his rugged honesty and fervent zeal, his clear penetration and poetic vision, the spirit and pathos of the Welsh mind.

He died in Swansea, at the home of the Rev. Daniel Davies, D.D., on the 20th of July, 1838.

Evans, Gen. G. W., of Augusta, Ga., was a prominent and useful deacon of unblemished character and high standing. He was intelligent, pious, and so uniformly courteous that he won the respect and esteem of all, and was universally popular. He took a deep interest in religious and denominational affairs, and was one of those men to whom a pastor could point and say with satisfaction, "That is a Baptist." He was a partner of the late William D'Atignac, the firm being D'Atignac, Evans & Co. Few men possessed more admirable traits for rendering them popular in the world or useful in the church.

Evans, Rev. Hugh, some time tutor and afterwards president of Bristol College, England, was descended from Welsh parents in easy circumstances, distinguished for their piety and benevolence. His grandfather, Thomas Evans, was elected a parish minister in Wales by the Board of Triers, appointed to license clergymen during the Commonwealth. After the restoration of the monarchy and the church establishment he joined the Baptist church at Pentre, and suffered much for conscience' sake as pastor of that church, in which office he was succeeded by his son. Thomas Evans died in 1688, and Caleb, his son and successor, in 1739. Hugh Evans, youngest son of Caleb, was carefully educated at a school of high reputation, and afterwards proceeded to the college at Bristol. He was baptized by Mr. Foskett at Bristol, Aug. 7, 1730. The Broadmead church, in that city, called him to the ministry in 1733, and at the close of the same year he accepted their invitation to become assistant to their pastor, Mr. Foskett. He soon became widely known as a preacher of extraordinary power and usefulness. In 1758, on the death of Mr. Foskett, with whom he had labored twenty-four years, he became president of the college and senior pastor of the church. He inspired his students with a remarkable affection and reverence, and the care of all the churches of the neighborhood came upon him. One of his most distinguished students, Dr. John Ripon, says of him, that "every one who knew him must admit that his gift in prayer was uncommon, his students thought it was unequaled. In the family, at occasional meetings, in the services of the Lord's day, and upon extraordinary occasions, with copiousness, dignity, and warmth of devotion he poured out his soul unto God, and yet with such variety that he was seldom, if ever, heard to pray twice alike. His pulpit compositions were clear, nervous, and pathetic. Few men were more capable of taking a large, comprehensive, masterly view of a subject, or of representing it with greater perspicuity, energy, and fervor. His language was striking, his voice clear, and his elocution manly. Nor did any preacher, perhaps, ever know better than he what it was to reign over his audience, enlightening their understanding, convincing their judgment, and then kindling all their noblest passions into a blaze of devotion." His characteristic spirit was evinced in his last discourse to the Western Association of Baptist churches, when he took a solemn leave of the brethren assembled in an affecting discourse from the words, "Be not deceived, God is not mocked." He closed his public ministry at Bristol shortly afterwards with a truly paternal address to his flock from the words, "My little children, of whom I travail in birth again until Christ be formed in you." He died in perfect peace, surrounded by his family and his students, on March 28, 1781.

Evans, John Mason, M.D., son of the Rev. Thomas B. Evans, was born in Urbanna, Middlesex Co., Va., March 22, 1829. He was educated at the Columbian College, graduating with the degree of A.B. in 1847. He studied medicine, and received the degree of M.D. at the Jefferson Medical School, Philadelphia, in the winter of 1849-50. He has practised his profession in connection with farming up to the present time. Since the inauguration of the public school system in Virginia, he has been the efficient county superintendent of public schools in King and Queen and Middlesex. Dr. Evans was baptized at the age of twelve, and has been an active and efficient member of the church. For more than twenty years he has been superintendent of the Sunday-school, and deacon of the church.

Evans, Rev. Thomas B., was born in the county of Essex, Va., Dec. 13, 1807. He was converted between the years 1830 and 1835, and was baptized by the Rev. R. A. Claybrook. He was ordained soon after 1837. At the organization of the Olivet church, in 1842, he was elected its pastor, and served it with great zeal and success till his death, Aug. 12, 1875. He was at one time pastor of Ebenezer, in Gloucester Co., and also of the Newington church, which he was mainly instrumental in constituting. He was also pastor of Exol, in King and Queen Co., and of Ephesus, in Essex Co. In 1855 he was elected pastor of Glebe Landing, in Middlesex, and served this church also until his death. He served as moderator of the Rappahannock Association, and was invited several times to preach the opening sermon. Mr. Evans was an earnest, plain, and successful preacher. He had a strong, logical mind, and a most retentive memory. He read much, thought profoundly, and could develop a subject clearly in all its important bearings. He accomplished much for the Master during his ministry of thirty-eight years, and was greatly esteemed by all who knew him.

Evans, Rev. Wm. L. T.—This devoted man was born in Maryland, Feb. 9, 1829. He spent his early years in Washington City, where he studied. In 1855 he moved to Landmark, Howard Co., Mo., and from it to Milton, where he died. He professed religion in 1857, and joined the Methodists; three years afterwards he united with the Baptists, and was baptized by Elder W. K. Woods, and was ordained by Elders Jesse Terrill and T. T. Gentry. He toiled faithfully in the ministry for nearly twenty years. He enjoyed the confidence of those with whom he labored in a marked degree. He was a man of prayer, richly endowed with the Holy Spirit. He died May 20, 1879.

Everett, Rev. John P., pastor at Shiloh, La., was born in Alabama in 1826, came to Louisiana in 1848 with his father, George Everett, who was a Baptist preacher, and labored in Union parish until his death, in 1855. The son was baptized in 1845; was a soldier in the Mexican war. In 1854 he was ordained to preach. From that time until the present he has been assiduous in his labors, which have been mainly confined to Union parish and the adjoining parts of Arkansas. He has been successful as a minister, and has greatly strengthened the churches; eleven years moderator of Liberty Association, Ark.; is at present chairman of the executive board of Louisiana State Convention. Has recently published a valuable work on "Bible Types."

Everts, Rev. Jeremiah B., was born in Granville, Washington Co., N. Y., in 1807. In 1829 he put his trust in Jesus as his Saviour, under the ministrations of Rev. Benjamin J. Lane, of Clarkson, N. Y. He first joined the Presbyterian Church, of which Mr. Lane was a minister. Subsequently, on examining the Scriptures about baptism, he was immersed, and united with the Baptist Church. He spent some time at Lane Seminary, in Ohio. He was ordained pastor of the church of Spafford, N. Y., in April, 1835. In this place his labors were largely blessed, his pulpit talents were highly appreciated, and his departure was greatly lamented. In Delphi, N. Y., and in Elbridge he enjoyed extensive revivals, and he had the same blessing in the New Market Street church, Philadelphia. In 1843 he accepted a call to Hartford, N. Y., where the love of the people and the prosperity of the church cheered his heart. After a lingering illness, produced by a painful accident, he entered the heavenly rest Aug. 26, 1846.

Mr. Everts had an original mind and a warm heart, he was wholly consecrated to God, and he lived in the hearts of throngs of friends. His death was full of peace.

Everts, William W., D.D., was born in Granville, N. Y., March 13, 1814, and united with the Baptist church of Brockport, N. Y. In 1830 the church licensed him to preach, and in 1831 sent him to Hamilton Literary and Theological Institution. In 1837 he was ordained at Earlville, N. Y., as its pastor. In 1839 he was settled as pastor of the Tabernacle Baptist church in New York City. After three years of extraordinary success he led out a colony and founded the Laight Street church. After eight years of labor his health was prostrated, and he settled at Wheatland, N. Y., as pastor. His ardent spirit and large plans of Christian work were felt by that country church, and three houses of worship were built for its branches in neighboring villages. In 1852 he accepted the pastorate of the Walnut Street church, in Louisville, Ky., and soon after it was enlarged and completed at an expense of $40,000. They organized the Broadway

WILLIAM W. EVERTS, D.D.

church of that city; the Portland church at the west end of the city, and built for it a house of worship; and a German church. In 1859 he accepted the charge of the First church of Chicago. During his twenty years of labor there, twenty Baptist church edifices were built in the city and vicinity. The Chicago University and Theological Seminary were founded and their superb buildings were put up chiefly by the contributions of the First church. In 1879 he accepted a call to the church on Bergen Heights, Jersey City, and during the first year a debt of $35,000 was paid and 67 members added to the church. Dr. Everts has not only devised plans for the multiplication, and the increased efficiency of the Baptists of America, in the realm of education, church extension, and the unity of the denomination in all its important Christian enterprises, but he has rendered great service with his pen. Many years ago he brought out his "Pastor's Hand-Book," which has been an invaluable helper to ministers of all denominations. He then brought out in succession the "Bible Prayer Book," "Scriptural School Reader," "Life and Thoughts of John Foster," "Voyage of Life," and "Promise and Training of Childhood." He also published a series of "Tracts for Cities," "The Theatre," "Temptations of City Life," and "The Great Metropolis," which, with tracts by Dr. Cheever and William Hague, D.D., were published in a volume entitled "Words in Earnest." He also wrote "Tracts for the Churches."

Dr. Everts has been for many years among the most prominent ministers of Christ in the United States. His great mind and heart, and his consecration to God, have made him a power among the Saviour's hosts. Few Baptist leaders in modern times have wielded such a mighty influence for God and his truth. Sacrifices to him have always appeared but trifles when great principles were called in question. We trust that his life and usefulness will be long continued to the denomination of which he is an ornament.

Everts, Rev. William Wallace, Jr., son of Rev. Dr. William Wallace and Margaret (Keen) Everts, was born in the city of New York, Feb. 10, 1849. He was a graduate of the Chicago University in the class of 1867. Immediately after graduating he went abroad for purposes of travel and study, and was absent three years, the larger part of which period he was at the Berlin University. Returning to this country in 1870, he became a student of the Union Theological Seminary in Chicago, where he was graduated in the class of 1873. He was ordained Dec. 23, 1873, as pastor of the Indiana Avenue branch of the First Baptist church in Chicago. He held an official connection with the Union Theological Seminary, Chicago, as teacher of Church History during the year 1875. He preached for the church at Morgan Park till 1877, when, coming East, he supplied the pulpit of the First Baptist church in Boston for four months as the assistant of Rev. Dr. Neale. In July of 1877 he was called to the pastorate of the Fourth Baptist church in Providence, R. I., of which he is now (1880) the minister. Mr. Everts is one of our most promising young ministers. His acquirements in ecclesiastical history are unusually extensive.

Ewart, Hon. Thomas W., LL.D., son of Robert H. and Mary C. Ewart, was born at Grandview, Washington Co., O., Feb. 27, 1816. When sixteen years of age he left school and became assistant in the office of the county clerk at Marietta, O. In December, 1836, he was appointed clerk of the court for Washington Co., O., and held this office until 1851. While in this office he was appointed a member of the convention which formed the present constitution of Ohio. At the expiration of his term he was elected probate judge of Washington County, but resigned after one year's service to engage in the practice of law, for which he had fully fitted himself in the office of Judge Nye. From the first he was very successful, and he has always held a prominent position in the legal profession of Ohio.

Converted and baptized at the age of sixteen, he has ever since been an active member of the Marietta Baptist church. For forty years he has been

HON. THOMAS W. EWART, LL.D.

superintendent of the Sunday-school, and for thirty-two years has been deacon. He has also been closely identified with general denominational interests. For many years he has been a trustee of Denison University. He was president of the Ohio Baptist State Convention for several years, and moderator of the Marietta Association twenty-five years in succession. As vice-president of the Missionary Union he occupied the chair of that body at Cincinnati and Philadelphia. Home missions have found in him a constant friend, and all good enterprises in the community a hearty supporter. The degree of LL.D. was conferred upon him by Denison University in 1878.

Ewing College is located in Ewing, Franklin Co., Ill., near the centre of that part of the State lying south of the Ohio and Mississippi Railroad. It is the only chartered college in that section of Illinois. It was founded in 1867 as Ewing High School by Prof. John Washburn. In 1874 it received a charter from the State under the title it now bears. Until 1877 it was undenominational, but during that year its charter was so changed as to place it under Baptist control. Its buildings, two in number, are substantial brick structures, and ample for the present uses of the college. It has a preparatory as well as collegiate department, the latter having two courses, classical and scientific. The college is open to students of both sexes. The number enrolled in the catalogue for 1879–80 is 150, of whom 32 were in the collegiate department. Its faculty numbers six teachers. Ewing College is performing a highly important educational service upon a field where it is greatly needed, and placing its rates of tuition and its other expenses within the reach of all classes of students, make its advantages available for all. At the present date (1880) an effort is in progress to raise for its endowment the sum of $50,000, with encouraging prospect of success.

Ewing, Hon. Presley Underwood, was the elder of two sons of the distinguished chief justice of Kentucky, E. M. Ewing, and was one of the most talented and brilliant young men his State ever produced. He was born in Russellville, Ky., Sept. 1, 1822. He graduated at Center College in 1840, and studied law under his father, graduating in the law department of Transylvania University in 1842. About this time, having become a member of the Baptist church, he was licensed to preach the gospel, and was soon afterwards invited to take the pastoral charge of the First Baptist church in Louisville. He accepted the call and preached a few times, but before ordination he resolved to spend some time in Germany. On his return from Europe he declined ordination to the ministry, and in 1848 was elected to the Kentucky Legislature, where he served two terms, being re-elected in 1849. In 1851 he was elected to the United States Congress, and re-elected to that position without opposition in 1853. He was chairman of a Congressional committee on the feasibility of constructing a railroad to the Pacific Ocean. His report on this subject gave him a wide reputation. As an orator he was regarded as the peer of the gifted John C. Breckenridge, whom he often met in debate in the legislative halls. But his career of almost unparalleled brilliancy was suddenly closed. He died of cholera while on a visit to the Mammoth Cave, in Kentucky, Sept. 27, 1854.

Examiner and Chronicle, The.—In June, 1855, Rev. Edward Bright, D.D., who had been for the preceding nine years the Home Secretary of the American Baptist Missionary Union, and Rev. Sewell S. Cutting, D.D., who was then one of the editors of the *Recorder and Register*, purchased that paper and became its editors and proprietors, changing the name to *The Examiner*. It was a four-page paper, and had at that time a circulation of about 10,000 copies. In the next year Dr. Cutting accepted the chair of Rhetoric and History in the University of Rochester, and Dr. Bright became the editor, a position which he has held from that time to the present. In the first ten years of his proprietorship the circulation had doubled. In March, 1865, the *New York Chronicle* was united with *The Examiner*, and the paper became *The Examiner and Chronicle*, which name it now bears. It was enlarged to a six-column eight-page paper in October, 1867, and again enlarged to seven columns a page in December, 1869. In 1868 *The Christian Press*, a Baptist paper of New York, conducted by Rev. W. B. Jacobs, was united with *The Examiner and Chronicle*, and in 1875 the small paper known as *The Outlook*, published in Brooklyn, was merged in it. *The Examiner and Chronicle* has attained the largest circulation of any Baptist newspaper in the world. It has always had a strong denominational character, and has fearlessly maintained the distinguishing doctrines of the old Baptist faith. Its aim has been to be as complete as it could be made in all the departments that belong to a first-class newspaper; to deal with the great questions of social and political, as well as Christian life; to present the news, with comments, from a Christian stand-point; and to do it with the fullness, freshness, and force that ought to characterize the very best class of religious newspapers.

The *New York Baptist Register*, afterwards united with the *Recorder*, was established in Utica late in 1823 or early in 1824 by Rev. Messrs. Willey, Lathrop, and Galusha, who issued it irregularly and edited it in turn. It subsequently passed into the hands of the managers of the Baptist Missionary Convention of New York, and became the organ of the Convention, with Alexander M. Beebee, Esq., as editor. In 1825 the *Register* absorbed a missionary newspaper in the form of a quarterly magazine, which, in 1814, was started and edited by Elders P. P. Root, Daniel Haskell, John Lawton, and John Peck. Its name, *The Vehicle*, was subsequently changed to the *Baptist Western Magazine*. Mr. Beebee was a gentleman of eminence in the bar of Onondaga County, and under him the *Register* was a most efficient advocate and helper in giving growth and strength to the denomination and its enterprises.

The *New York Recorder* was the outgrowth of *The Baptist Advocate*. The first issue of the *Advocate* was on May 11, 1839. It was founded by a number of leading Baptists in New York City, and the late Wm. H. Wyckoff, LL.D., was its editor. In about six months the *Advocate* Association purchased the *Gospel Witness*, the only rival of the new paper. But the *Advocate* was not a financial success, and was sold about the year 1842 to Messrs. Barker & Thompson. Mr. Barker soon withdrew, leaving Rev. James L. Thompson as the owner and publisher. A year or two later Mr. Wyckoff resigned the editorial chair, and Rev. S. S. Cutting, D.D., became the editor. The name was changed to the *New York Recorder*, and the paper subsequently became the property of Rev. Lewis Colby and Mr. Joseph Ballard. In February, 1850, the *Recorder* was purchased by Prof. M. B. Anderson, then of Waterville College, Me., now President Anderson, of Rochester University, and the late Rev. James S. Dickerson, D.D. When Prof. Anderson became president of the university in the autumn of 1853, the paper was again sold, Rev. L. F. Beecher being the purchaser. The *Register*, still published at Utica, and then owned by Rev. Andrew Ten Brook, D.D., was soon afterwards united with it, and the *Recorder* became the *New York Recorder and Register*, with Dr. Ten Brook as one of its editors.

The *New York Chronicle*, at first a monthly publication, was begun by Rev. O. B. Judd, LL.D., in 1849, and became a weekly paper in October, 1850. One of its distinctive features was its earnest advocacy of the Bible revision of the American Bible Union. About 1853 or 1854 the *Chronicle* was purchased by Rev. J. S. Backus, D.D., and at the beginning of 1855, Rev. Pharcellus Church, D.D., was associated with Dr. Backus as editor and proprietor.

In January of the next year Dr. Church bought the whole paper, and late in 1863 he purchased the *Christian Chronicle*, of Philadelphia, edited by the Rev. J. S. Dickerson, D.D., and continued to be the editor of the united paper until March, 1865, when the *Chronicle* was united with *The Examiner*.

Prior to the establishment of the *Baptist Advocate*, various attempts had been made to found a Baptist weekly newspaper in New York City. But it is difficult to learn the facts, even with the help of Mr. Geo. H. Hansell, who is probably more familiar with them than any other man. The first Baptist paper he has knowledge of in New York City was the *Gospel Witness*, started in 1835. The Directory for 1836 gives the name of *The American Baptist*, edited and owned by Rev. Jonathan Going, D.D. In 1837 the *Baptist Repository* appeared, edited by Rev. N. N. Whiting and Rev. David Barnard. But none of these newspaper ventures were successful, and the memory of them has been barely preserved. It cannot be said that *The Examiner and Chronicle* is a continuation of either of the papers named in this last paragraph.

Eyres, Rev. Nicholas, was born in Wiltshire, England, Aug. 22, 1691; came to New York about 1711; was baptized in 1714 by Rev. Valentine

Weightman, of Connecticut, and aided in founding the First Baptist church in that city and in the State; was ordained pastor of that church (then Gold Street) in September, 1724; in October, 1731, resigned and became co-pastor with Rev. Daniel Wightman of the Second Baptist church in Newport, R. I.; died Feb. 13, 1759; a man of great intelligence, benevolence, and piety. His associate in Newport, Rev. D. Wightman, was born in South Kingstown, R. I., Jan. 2, 1668; was ordained in 1701 as co-pastor with Rev. Mr. Clark, of the Second Baptist church in Newport, and remained as minister of this church till his death in 1750; a man greatly beloved and honored.

F.

Faith, Saving.—The majority of unconverted men in our country admit the divinity of Christ, and all the Scriptural facts in his earthly history, and some of them claim a considerable measure of orthodoxy, even according to recognized standards of sound religious belief. But these persons have not saving faith. It requires from a penitent that he *should intrust* his soul to Jesus for the removal of its iniquities. In John ii. 24, it is written, "But Jesus did not commit himself to them." The word translated "did commit" is ἐπίστυεν, "did believe," as it commonly means. But it is properly rendered in the quotation; John uses it in the sense of committing or intrusting himself. Saving faith is that act of a burdened soul by which it intrusts itself to Jesus that he might forgive and save it.

Saving faith rests upon these *foundations*. A man believes that God is inflexibly holy, that he hates sin, and that nothing can keep him from inflicting just but weighty punishment upon it; his conviction of Jehovah's holiness leads him to believe that it is a fearful thing to fall into the hands of the living God. He believes that he is guilty before the eternal judge, that his thoughts have been evil, his affections alienated, and his words and works sinful; and that he is hopelessly lost unless Jesus exercises his mercy towards him. He believes that God's love is the greatest blessing in any world. He thinks with hungering desire of that love that made Jehovah give up his most dear and only Son to be put to death instead of poor, guilty, perishing sinners. And he is fully assured that God has infinite pleasure in receiving and in forgiving penitent souls. He believes in the Saviour's merits; his obedience in life, and his fierce pangs in death. In the Saviour's blood he sees the only cure for his guilt, and a purifying element that will cleanse away all his sins. He also frequently seizes some encouraging promise, to which he tenaciously clings, such as "Him that cometh to me I will in no wise cast out." And as he fully believes in God's holiness and love, in Christ's blood and promise, and in his own guiltiness, he ventures to intrust his condemned soul to the Crucified, and the moment he commits it to the meritorious and loving Redeemer by faith he is forgiven. These are the bases of saving faith.

The owner of it is never entirely free from sinful tendencies. The young convert is apt to imagine that he ought to be wholly delivered from every sinful inclination. Satan encourages this impression, and tries to persuade him that he is not truly regenerated, or sin would cease to trouble him. The man has a new heart and hates sin; its power within him is broken; he loves Jesus, and he blames himself severely for not loving him more; he prays earnestly and his prayers have been answered; but he is not infallible, he finds he can be tempted, and he has to watch and pray against the Evil One. Sometimes Satan tries to make him proud, angry, covetous, forgetful of God and ungrateful to him; and he is full of grief over Satan's threatened or partial success. He finds constant need to watch his heart, and cling to Jesus for merits to justify, and grace to protect against his own weakness and Satan's wiles.

Nor is saving faith *always free from doubts*. It is the privilege of every Christian to have full assurance of faith, and many believers enjoy this treasure. But not a few are "weak in faith" who are certain to enter heaven: "Him that is weak in faith receive ye, but not to doubtful disputations."—Rom. xiv. 1. Doubts are sometimes thrust into the soul by the Tempter, just as he inspires blasphemous or other wicked thoughts which the believer rejects, and for which he is not responsible. Sometimes they come from a constitutional tendency to look on the dark side of everything. Sometimes they spring from a feeble condition of health. And very often they seize a believer who has fallen into worldliness, or some other breach of saintly fidelity. The Christian should aim at the strongest faith, and the Spirit will give it when he seeks it. But men are not saved by the *amount* of their faith, if they have true sorrow for sin, and a true reliance upon a crucified Saviour; the life of a babe is just as real as that of a giant; and the faith of a believer whose trust in Jesus is only like that of a "babe in Christ" will save him.

It gives the believer *great power with God*. The mightiest instrument ever used by mortals is a vigorous faith in Jesus. It not only removes the guilt of many years and of shocking vileness from the distressed sinner and gives him complete justification before the pure and piercing eye of the Omniscient, but it brings down harvests of answers to prayers which bless the soul, the family, and the church. It fitted Abraham to offer up Isaac in sacrifice to God, because it showed him his son in a figure restored from the dead. It gave courage to Moses, the timid fugitive who fled from Egypt to escape the weightiest penalty of its law, to confront and defy Pharaoh, his army, and his people. It enabled Shadrach, Meshach, and Abednego to be confident that God would protect them from the vengeance of Nebuchadnezzar, and, armed with this sublime conviction, they looked with contempt upon the intense heat of the fiery furnace, while they informed the king himself not only that they would not worship his image, but they also said, "Our God, whom we serve, is able to deliver us from the burning fiery furnace, and he will deliver us out of thy hand, O king." As the coupling of a railroad car links it to the locomotive and gives it all its power, so faith unites the soul to Jesus, and bestows upon it his divine righteousness, his almighty strength, his matchless wisdom, his all-prevalent intercession, the revelation of his great love, and his sure victory over all enemies. Truly faith can remove mountains, bring down rain-storms, divide oceans, and confer upon a terrified supplicant great deliverance, and the most glorious of titles,—*A Prevailer with God*.

Faith, in common with every grace in the renewed man, is the gift of God. It can be greatly strengthened by cultivating an earnest love for Jesus, complete consecration of heart, active efforts to glorify the Saviour, and constant struggles in the soul to resist doubting tendencies; by assiduous attention to closet exercises, Bible reading, and sanctuary privileges; by the utmost resistance to sin in every form, and by the frequently repeated prayer, "Lord, increase our faith."

Farmer, Hon. William, is one of the most widely known, generous, and influential Baptist laymen in California. He was born in Anderson Co., Tenn., in 1800; resided in Tennessee and in Cass Co., Mo., until 1857, when he moved to Santa Rosa, Cal., where he now lives. He has always been noted for his hospitality, and since his baptism, in 1838, as a prominent worker in the church. He has for many years been an upright and honored judge of the County Court. He is widely known in California as "Deacon Farmer."

Farnham, Jonathan Everett, LL.D., a distinguished scholar and educator, was born in Connecticut, Aug. 12, 1809. He finished his education at Colby University, where he graduated in 1833, and for two years was tutor in that institution. He then studied law three years at Providence, R. I., after which he went to Cincinnati, where he continued his legal studies. In 1838 he was elected Professor of Physical Science in Georgetown College, Ky., and has continuously occupied that position. For a number of years during this period he conducted the Georgetown Female Seminary, a school of high grade. In early life Dr. Farnham became a Baptist, and has been a valuable contributor to the periodical literature of the denomination.

Farnsworth, Hon. J. D., was born in Middletown, Conn., in 1771. When he was six years of age his parents removed to Bennington, Vt. He became a hopeful Christian at twelve. He completed his classical studies at Clio Hall, the first literary institution of the kind ever incorporated in Vermont. Having decided to be a physician, he entered upon the study of his profession, and at eighteen took his medical degree, and after practising for a time at Addison, Vt., he removed, in 1795, to the northern part of the State, where he spent the most of his life. For more than fifty years he was one of the most successful physicians in the northern section of Vermont. He was chief judge in Franklin County for fifteen years, and a member of the State Legislature for about twenty-seven years. He took a deep interest in the progress of the denomination. The constitution of the first Baptist Association ever formed in Northern Vermont, was drafted by him. Associated with Gov. Butler and several others, he took the first steps towards the organization of the Vermont State Convention. An act was passed in 1787 by the Legislature requiring the inhabitants of each town to support the "standing order," unless they could show that they were connected with some other religious organization. The Baptists, with their well-known sentiments on the right of private judgment in matters of religion, were led earnestly to oppose the act. The struggle lasted for many years, and the act was repealed in 1807. In all the controversy connected with the important subject Dr. Farnsworth took an important part. He was a decided Baptist for nearly seventy years, and boldly defended the peculiar views of his denomination. It is said that he had probably presided at more conventions, Associations, councils, etc., than any other Baptist who ever lived in the State of Vermont. He died at his residence in Fairfax, Vt., Sept. 9, 1857, honored and beloved by his own denomination and a large circle of his fellow-citizens.

Farrar, Rev. Wm. M., an aged minister in Mississippi, was born in Georgia; ordained in 1834, and the year following removed to Mississippi, where he has labored successfully forty-three years. He spent fourteen years in agency work, and raised in cash about $60,000, and in pledges about $20,000 more. Much of his time was devoted to missionary work, and about twenty years to the pastorate. He was two years associate editor of the *Mississippi Baptist*.

Farrow, Deacon D. T. C., was born in Wood Co., W. Va., Nov. 19, 1826. He was baptized Feb. 15, 1843. About 1849 he became deeply interested in Sunday-schools and missions. In 1866 he was appointed Sunday-School missionary for the State by the American Baptist Publication Society, and he is at present engaged in that work. He has organized 100 Sunday-schools, 8 Sunday-school conventions, and 1 church; has visited 47 of the 54 counties of the State; has sold and distributed $34,000 worth of publications of the American Baptist Publication Society. Mr. Farrow has been greatly blessed in his work, for which he is well adapted. He has acted as secretary and corresponding secretary of the General Association, and has long been a life-member, and has made all his family—wife and five children—life-members. Mr. Farrow has been of very great service to the denomination in West Virginia, and these services have been rendered whilst frequently suffering from severe physical disability.

Farwell, Hon. Levi, was born about the year 1784. He was baptized by Rev. Dr. Baldwin, Sept. 11, 1811, and was a constituent member of the First Baptist church in Cambridge, Mass. For many years he was the "steward" of Harvard College, and important civil trusts were committed to his hands. Prof. H. J. Ripley says of him, "He was a man of sound judgment, and an example of pure and consistent piety. Eminently discreet, he was also uniformly devotional. In church and in state his opinion was sought with profound respect. He and his wife can never cease to be held in the kindest remembrance. His funds, like those of Mr. Cobb, were liberally bestowed upon the institution at Newton." Mr. Farwell died May 27, 1844.

Faunce, Rev. D. W., was born in Plymouth, Mass. He was baptized at the early age of fourteen, by Rev. Ira Pearson. He was a graduate of Amherst College in the class of 1850, and pursued his theological studies for two years at the Newton Theological Institution. He was ordained pastor of the Baptist church in Somerville, Mass., in 1853, where he remained one year, and then removed to Worcester, Mass. His subsequent pastorates have been in Malden, Mass., Concord, N. H., and Lynn, Mass., where he now resides.

Mr. Faunce has written much for denominational papers, and prepared articles for the *Baptist Quarterly*. In 1874 he was awarded the "Fletcher Prize" at Dartmouth College, and his essay was subsequently published, under the title "The Christian in the World." He has published also "A Young Man's Difficulties with the Bible." Both of these volumes have been republished in London.

Fawcett, Rev. A. J., pastor at Hamburg, Ark., was born in Tennessee in 1845; after receiving a good education, he began to preach in 1867; was first pastor at Humboldt, Tenn., and continued to preach in West Tennessee until 1876, when he was called to Lake Village, Chicot Co., Ark.; in 1879 he was invited to his present work.

Fawcett, John, D.D., was born near Bradford, Yorkshire, England, Jan. 6, 1740. He was converted through the instrumentality of George Whitefield when he was about sixteen years of age, and at nineteen he was baptized into the fellowship of the Baptist church of Bradford. In 1765, Mr. Fawcett was ordained pastor of the Baptist church of Wainsgate, where his labors were greatly blessed. He removed from Wainsgate to Hebden Bridge, where he continued till his death, which occurred July 25, 1814. Near Hebden Bridge Mr. Fawcett conducted a flourishing academy, where John Foster, and others who subsequently gained great distinction, received their entire education, or a part of it. Mr. Fawcett had extensive culture and respectable talents; his reading was remarkable, and his standing in his own and other denominations high. When Dr. Gill died he was invited by his church to London, with a view of becoming his successor. He was offered the presidency of Bristol College in 1792.

His commentary on the Bible, in two folio volumes, is of great worth for its devotional character, and though now very scarce, it is highly prized by those who own it. He wrote a volume of original hymns, many of which are to be found in the sacred songs of various denominations. He was the author of eleven works.

A clergyman, preaching before George III., made a quotation from a small volume written by Mr. Fawcett, which attracted the king's attention; on inquiring, he found that Mr. Fawcett was the author of the book. Through the preacher he sent word that he would like to render Mr. Fawcett some service. The Baptist pastor declined the king's favor for himself; but afterwards turned it to account by saving one man from being executed, and several others from heavy legal penalties. In 1811, Mr. Fawcett was made a Doctor of Divinity. Dr. Fawcett had all the qualities that show a consecrated life.

Feake, Rev. Christopher, was a minister of the Established Church of England, who adopted the sentiments of the Baptists in the time of the Parliamentary war, and became one of the most noted leaders of our denomination. When a Baptist he preached in All-Saints' church, Hertford, the greatest church in the place; while there he opposed the Westminster Assembly of Divines, and treated their Directory with contempt. For these supposed heresies and for his Fifth Monarchy principles he was brought before the assizes, but the judges dismissed the charge. Afterwards he was appointed minister of Christ's church, in London; and he became the possessor of so much influence that Cromwell, who hated persecution, felt compelled to have him arrested and sent a prisoner to Windsor Castle for hostility to his government. He knew nothing of fear, and being a stern republican, he publicly branded Cromwell as "the most dissembling and perjured villain in the world;" and he made this charge at the period of Cromwell's greatest power. Feake was a skillful orator, a bold defender of the truth, a great sufferer for his principles, and he was held in high regard by the Baptists of his day.

Felder, Rev. Charles, a pioneer preacher in Mississippi and Louisiana, was born in 1783; began to preach in 1809; came to Mississippi in 1819, and was an active co-laborer with Cooper, Reeves, Courtney, and others, in South Mississippi; was often moderator of the Mississippi Association; died in 1843.

Felix, Rev. Joseph S., brother of William H., was born in Woodford Co., Ky., Aug. 19, 1851. He graduated at Georgetown College in 1871; then spent one year at the Southern Baptist Theological Seminary. He united with Hillsborough church, in his native county, where he was licensed to preach in 1871. He was ordained pastor of the Baptist church at Augusta, Ky., in 1872, where he still ministers. Mr. Felix is a young preacher of excellent gifts and attainments.

Felix, Rev. William H., was born in Woodford Co., Ky., Oct. 6, 1838. He united with Hillsborough Baptist church, in that county, in his youth. He was educated at Georgetown College, graduating in 1860, and was admitted to the bar and practised law at Shelbyville a short time. He was ordained to the pastorate of the Baptist church at New Castle, in August, 1860. He accepted a call to the First Baptist church in Lexington in 1863, and resigned, in 1869, to accept a call to Pilgrim Baptist church in New York City. In 1870 he returned to Covington, Ky., and became pastor of his present charge, the First Baptist church in that city. Mr. Felix's contributions to the Baptist periodical literature have been well received, and his book "True Womanhood," recently published, has met with popular favor.

Felton, Richard, was a deacon with C. E. Skinner, of the Hertford Baptist church, and like him was distinguished for his liberality. He gave $7000 to build the church in Hertford; he also gave $5000, at the convention in Raleigh, in 1856, to Wake Forest College, and about the same time he gave $2000 towards the erection of the First Baptist church of Raleigh, N. C. More than the example of his friend and brother, Deacon Skinner, prompting him to benevolence, was the sweet influence of his wife, Mary, whose noble heart consecrated all to Christ. Deacon Felton died soon after the close of the war.

Fendall, Rev. Edward Davies, was born at Churchtown, Lancaster Co., Pa., Aug. 6, 1814; was converted under the ministry of Rev. Leonard Fletcher, and by him baptized into the fellowship of the Great Valley church, Chester Co., Pa. Although reared in the Episcopalian Church, he became a Baptist through careful reading and study of the New Testament. With six other brethren, he was licensed to preach, Jan. 5, 1839, and entered upon a course of study at Haddington and Burlington Institutions, under the instruction of Revs. Henry K. Green and Samuel Aaron. Failing health compelled him to leave his studies, and he commenced his ministry at Cedarville, N. J.; was ordained May 17, 1839, and after a successful pastorate, he resigned April 1, 1843. He then became pastor of the venerable Cohansey church, at Roadstown, N. J., which was constituted in 1690, and was one of the five constituents of the Philadelphia Association, formed in 1707. Here he remained some three years and a half, during which the church attained its greatest number of members. After several years spent in teaching, he became pastor at Moorestown, N. J., May 1, 1852. Here his labors were greatly blessed, and he remained for twelve years, when failing health compelled his retirement from the pastorate. In 1854 he was chosen clerk of the West Jersey Association, which office he still holds. In 1864 he became Philadelphia editor of *The Chronicle*, the successor of the *Christian Chronicle*, which had been transferred to New York. In March, 1865, he was appointed superintendent of the sales department of the American Baptist Publication Society; and in 1876 was chosen assistant corresponding secretary, which position he still holds. He was a frequent contributor to religious newspapers; and wrote one or two tracts which have been widely circulated. By those who know him, he will always be kindly remembered as an exceedingly affable and exemplary Christian gentleman.

Ferguson, John, was converted in Halifax, Nova Scotia, and baptized July 9, 1826, by Rev. Edward Manning; joined Granville Street church, organized in that city in 1827, and became very influential in the church and denomination; a warm friend of education; one of the editors of the *Christian Messenger* from its commencement, in 1836, to his death, Feb. 10, 1855. Mr. Ferguson possessed fine talents, rare judgment and penetration, and holy enthusiasm in Christian and denominational enterprises.

Ferris, Rev. Ezra, M.D., was born in Stanwich, Conn., April 26, 1783. He came with his father to Ohio in 1789, and settled in Columbia, the first town in the Miami Valley. He joined the Baptist church there in 1801. He came to Lawrenceburg, Ind., in 1807, and preached the first sermon ever heard from a Baptist in the county. A few years afterwards he organized the Lawrenceburg Baptist church, and was its pastor for more than thirty years. He was prominent in the organization of the Laughery Association in 1816.

In his youth he had returned to the East to obtain an education. He was for many years a physician, having graduated at a Philadelphia medical college. He was a member of the first constitutional convention of Indiana, held at Corydon, was several times elected to the State Legislature, and was once nominated for Congress, but was defeated by five votes. He died at his home in Lawrenceburg, April 19, 1857.

Fickling, F. W.—Few, if any, of the sons of South Carolina have been endowed with nobler intellectual or moral faculties than F. W. Fickling, but his lack of "ambition," last infirmity of noble minds, is a real defect in his character. His practice as a lawyer before the war was very lucrative, and yet he never seemed to make the slightest effort to extend it.

The writer once heard him deliver an argument in court. In the beginning it was commonplace. But as his argument advanced his voice rose, his countenance brightened until it looked almost superhuman, and a mesmeric charmer has scarcely more complete control over his subjects than he had over his entire audience. He is now living in Columbia.

Had he sought fame, he might, instead of being but partially known in his native State, have ranked as one of the first lawyers of the nation. He is a Christian, with such a measure of piety as makes him a blessing to the church and to the world.

Field, Gen. James G., was born at Walnut, Culpeper Co., Va., Feb. 24, 1826. His father was Lewis Yancey Field, a justice of the county. After receiving the elements of an education, he was engaged for a while in a mercantile house in Fairfax (Culpeper). In 1845 he left this occupation, and entered a classical school, where he remained about one year. In 1847 he taught school, and was soon appointed clerk to Maj. Hill, paymaster in the U. S. army, with whom he went to California in 1848. There, in 1850, he was elected one of the secretaries of the constitutional convention, which formed the first constitution of that State. In

GEN. JAMES G. FIELD.

1850 he returned to Virginia, resigned his clerkship, and began the study of law with his distinguished uncle Judge Richard H. Field. In 1852 he was admitted to the bar, and began a professional career, which has continued to brighten to the present hour. In 1860 he was elected attorney for the Commonwealth in his native county, which office he held until 1865. Gen. Field took an active part in the Confederate service during the war, was wounded in the right hand at the first battle of Cold Harbor, and lost a leg at the battle of Slaughter's Mountain. Upon the close of the war he resumed the practice of law in Culpeper, occupying the first rank in his profession. He has been active in all the political contests in the State, and is one of the ablest debaters and most eloquent speakers in a commonwealth greatly gifted with such men. On the death of the lamented Mr. Daniel, attorney-general of the State, Gov. Kemper commissioned him to fill the unexpired term of Mr. Daniel. On the day previous to this appointment the Conservative party of Virginia nominated him for that distinguished position.

General Field was baptized May, 1843, into the fellowship of the Mount Poney church (Culpeper) by Rev. Cumberland George, where he has been a most active member for thirty-five years. He was for twenty years one of its deacons, and for many years superintendent of the Sunday-school. For successive sessions he served as moderator of the Shiloh Baptist Association. He has been deeply interested in all the enterprises of the denomination, aiding them by counsel and contributions. He has also been a frequent contributor to the secular papers, discussing with great legal acumen and vigor of style the current political questions of the day. One who knew him well characterizes him as "a sound lawyer, an able debater, an eloquent speaker, and a Christian gentleman."

Field, S. W., D.D., was born in North Yarmouth, Me., April 28, 1813. He was baptized by Rev. Alonzo King, pastor of the Baptist church, June, 1830; fitted for college at the academy in his native place, and entered Waterville College in 1832; completed a course of four years' study, but took his degree at New York University in July, 1836; was associate teacher with Rev. Nathan Dole one term in the North Yarmouth Academy; entered Newton Theological Institution, and graduated in 1839; was ordained at North Yarmouth as an appointed missionary to Assam, Oct. 3, 1839. Rev. Baron Stow, of Boston, preached the ordination sermon on the occasion. As the board were compelled for want of funds to inform him that no missionary could be sent out for two years, he was under the necessity of settling as a pastor. His first charge was in Methuen, Mass., of seven years; his second in Hallowell, Me., of three years. In his third and last, by the lamented death of his former pastor, Rev. L. Bradford, he became pastor of what was the Pine Street, now the Central Baptist, church, Providence, R. I. After ten years' labor he resigned in 1859. He was engaged in preaching in Providence and its vicinity till 1862, when he was appointed by the governor of Rhode Island chaplain of the 12th Regiment R. I. Vols. Served the full term of the enlistment, and was in the battle of Fredericksburg, Va. Heart and hand had full employ on that terrible day and for many days after. He was highly favored in his religious work by the co-operation of Col. Geo. H. Browne and Lt.-Col. James Shaw, Jr. He is still a resident in Providence, and a member of the First Baptist church, preaching in various places as occasion calls for his services. In 1877 the Central University of Iowa, Rev. L. A. Dunn, D.D., President, conferred on him the honorary degree of Doctor of Divinity.

Fifth Monarchy Men, The, for a considerable period, created great alarm in England to the government and to the people. Their name is taken from the dream of Nebuchadnezzar where he saw the golden image. The head of the image was the monarchy of the king who had the dream; the silver arms, that of the Medes and Persians; the brazen body, that of Alexander and the Macedonians; the legs of iron and the feet part iron and part clay, that of the Romans; and the stone, cut without hands, which smote and utterly destroyed the image, and became a great mountain, and filled the whole earth, was the monarchy of Jesus Christ which was to overthrow all earthly governments, and, under its divine sovereign, rule over all the nations of mankind. This was the "Fifth Monarchy" of Cromwell's day, and of the time of Charles II. The Fifth Monarchy men were in expectation of the coming of king Jesus, and of his glorious reign of a thousand years upon the earth. They aimed to destroy national church establishments and tithes, and to make religion free. And they were stern republicans, hating the one-man power of Cromwell a little more than they abhorred the tyranny of Charles I. If this had been all their faith many would not have found much fault with them. But unfortunately they came to the conclusion that they had to establish the government of king Jesus by force of arms. With this object in view, in 1657, according to Neal, 300 of them agreed to make an attempt to overthrow the government, kill the Protector, and proclaim king Jesus. Secretary Thurloe discovered the plot and seized their arms and standard. Their flag had a lion couchant upon it, alluding to the lion of the tribe of Judah, and this motto, "Who will rouse him?" The conspirators were arrested and kept in prison till Oliver Cromwell's death.

In 1660, Thomas Venner, a wine cooper, gathered about fifty Fifth Monarchy men, who were well armed, who set out to seize the government for king Jesus. Charles II. was on the throne, and he was no friend of king Jesus, or of Venner and his crazy followers. He sent the train-bands of London and portions of the regular army against them. The Fifth Monarchy men routed the train-bands, dispersed some soldiers in Threadneedle Street, but at last they surrendered, after losing about half their number, and eleven of them were executed. No Baptists had anything to do with Venner's mad outbreak, though not a few of them had some sympathy with the theory of the personal reign of Christ for a thousand years.

Finch, Rev. Josiah John.—This excellent man was born in Franklin Co., N. C., Feb. 3, 1814; attended academies in Louisburg and Raleigh, and spent two sessions at Wake Forest College. He became pastor of the Edenton Baptist church in 1835, removed in 1838 to Newbern, where for seven years he was the honored pastor of the leading Baptist church of the State. In 1845 he was called to Raleigh, where, in connection with his duties as pastor, he aided his wife in conducting a prosperous female seminary. He died of consumption Jan. 21, 1850. A volume of his sermons, published by his brother, Rev. G. M. L. Finch, after his death, shows that he was a preacher of more than ordinary merit.

Fish, Ezra J., D.D., was born in Macedon, Wayne Co., N. Y., Sept. 29, 1828. He was baptized in Medina, Orleans Co., in July, 1844. In the fall of 1847 he went to Hamilton to study for the ministry, and transferred his relations to Rochester University in 1850, graduating from the latter institution in 1853. He commenced study in the Theological Seminary at Rochester the same fall, but ill health compelled him to cease in the autumn of 1854, and he went to Michigan for rest and recuperation. The next spring he began pastoral work in Lima, Ind. Here and at Sturgis, Mich., he labored till the autumn of 1858, giving part of his time to each church. Then followed a rest of three years, made necessary by ill health, then a second pastorate of three years at Sturgis. From December, 1864, till November, 1874, he was pastor in Adrian, and was very successful in bringing the church into the front rank of the churches of Michigan. Sickness again compelled him to suspend work, and for nearly three years he was able to preach only a part of the time, making his home in Bronson, and supplying churches in the vicinity as his health allowed. From April, 1877, till July, 1878, he did the work of a pastor in Lansing, and in April, 1880, became pastor in Allegan.

For several years he has directed his attention largely to the study of church organization and officers, and he published a volume, soon after leaving Adrian, entitled "Ecclesiology: A Fresh Inquiry into the Fundamental Idea and Constitution of the New Testament Church." Kalamazoo College conferred on him the degree of Doctor of Divinity in 1874. He was president of the Michigan Baptist State Convention in 1867, and again in 1873.

Fish, Henry Clay, D.D., was born in Halifax, Vt., Jan. 27, 1820. His father was a Baptist pas-

HENRY CLAY FISH, D.D.

tor. He was converted at fifteen. He studied at the high school in his native town and at the Shelburn Falls Academy. He taught school in Massachusetts, and came to New Jersey in 1840 to pursue the same profession. While teaching he was a very severe student, as indeed he was ever after. He graduated from the Union Theological Seminary, New York City, June 25, 1845, and the next day he was ordained pastor of the Baptist church at Somerville, N. J. In January, 1851, he entered upon the pastorate of the First Baptist church at Newark. The degree of D.D. was conferred on Mr. Fish by the University of Rochester. He took a lively interest in educational enterprises, particularly in the Peddie Institute, at Hightstown, N. J. He was also a voluminous author. For more than twenty years he published an average of a volume a year. Among his works are "Primitive Piety," "Primitive Piety Revived," "The History and Repository of Pulpit Eloquence," "Pulpit Eloquence of the Nineteenth Century," "The Handbook of Revivals," and "The American Manual of Life Insurance." One of his last published volumes was "Bible Lands Illustrated," the result of an eight months' journey abroad in 1874.

He died at his home Oct. 2, 1877, after a pastorate over the First church of twenty-seven years. While Dr. Fish was well known throughout the land, and prominent in public assemblies as well as in his writings, he gave particular attention to the edification of his large church. In preaching he was very earnest and pointed. His capacious house was filled with listeners. He infused his spirit into every department of Christian work. He made free use of printed tracts and slips of his own composition, and had frequent ingatherings as the result of special meetings. The last year of his life was crowned with a great spiritual harvest.

For many years he was secretary of the New Jersey Baptist Education Society, and he rendered very valuable service in stimulating the churches to deeper interest in the rising ministry and in encouraging candidates for the sacred office in their efforts to prepare themselves for the noblest of callings.

Fish, Rev. Joel W., a native of Cheshire, Berkshire Co., Mass., was born Feb. 1, 1817. Educated at Madison University, from which he was graduated in 1843, and Hamilton Theological Seminary, from which he was graduated in 1845. He was ordained in September, 1845, at Mansville, N. Y.; soon after which he came to Wisconsin as a missionary of the American Baptist Home Mission Society, and settled at Geneva, where he was pastor of the Baptist church seven years. Subsequently he labored at Racine two years, Fox Lake eleven years, Waupaca as supply nearly two years, and at present he is pastor of the Baptist church in Augusta. He was general missionary of the American Baptist Home Mission Society for twelve years. During the war he was at the front in the service of the U. S. Christian Commission, caring for the sick, wounded, and dying. The ministry of Mr. Fish during his residence of thirty-four years in the State has been one of great growth with our people and churches. Even when pastor his labors and influence were not limited to his local field. He always took a deep interest in the progress and welfare of the denomination throughout the State. His influence as a herald of the cross is felt in all parts of Wisconsin, and he is held in high esteem by his brethren in the ministry. He has been a hard worker on an unproductive soil. While general missionary of the American Baptist Home Mission Society during twelve years of service he traveled over 40,000 miles. He has baptized 400 converts. At the age of sixty-three he is preaching the gospel with much acceptance and success.

Mr. Fish has had five children, only one of whom, a son, is living. Two highly gifted and accomplished daughters he buried after they had reached mature womanhood. His wife, a woman of fine mental and Christian culture, has been the sharer of his forty years of missionary labor, thoroughly in sympathy with him in his self-denying labors and often painful sacrifices.

Fish, Hon. Nathan Gallup, son of Deacon Sands and Bridget (Gallup) Fish, was born in Groton, Conn., Sept. 7, 1804; had a good education; became a distinguished sea-captain and ship-owner; also a merchant after leaving the sea; elected to the State senate; widely known and honored; president of the Mystic River Bank; a deacon of the Third Baptist church in Groton, now Union Baptist church; a man of wealth, but lost heavily by the Confederate cruisers during the war; a man of rare excellence and abilities; died in Groton, Aug. 1, 1870. His father was a greatly esteemed deacon of the First Baptist church in Groton.

Fisher, Abiel, D.D., was born in Putney, Vt., June 19, 1787. He was baptized into the fellowship of the church in Daville, Vt., Dec. 5, 1806. Having decided that he ought to be a minister of the gospel, he went through a preparatory course, graduating at the Vermont University in the class of 1811. He pursued his theological studies under Rev. Nathaniel Kendrick, then of Middlebury, and was ordained as an evangelist in Brandon, Vt., June 15, 1815. In January, 1816, he entered upon the duties of the pastorate of the church in Bellingham, Mass., where he remained twelve years. From Bellingham he was called to West Boylston, Mass., and continued as pastor of the church in that place for three years. After brief pastorates in Sturbridge, Mass., and Pawtuxet, R. I., he had the charge for several years of the church in Swansea, Mass., the oldest Baptist church in the State. His last pastorate was at Sutton, Mass., from which place he removed to West Boylston, where he died in the summer of 1862.

Dr. Fisher received his D.D. from Vermont University, and it was most deservedly bestowed. There was no good cause in which he did not take an interest. In connection with the Rev. Jonathan Going, he rendered the best service to the Baptist cause in the central sections of Massachusetts. He was a lover of learning, and quite a number of young men enjoyed the benefits of his instruction, among whom were Rev. Jonathan Aldrich and Hon. Charles Thurber. We may justly claim Dr. Fisher as having been one of the most useful ministers of the denomination in the State of Massachusetts.

Fisher, Rev. C. L., was born at Norwich, England, and is now pastor at Santa Clara, Cal. He was baptized in 1840 into the fellowship of the Broad Street church, Utica, N. Y., to which place the family removed from England in 1827. He was educated at Clinton, N. Y., the seat of Hamilton College. He began his ministry at Montello, Wis., where he was ordained in 1851. He labored in Wisconsin as pastor and missionary about ten years, organizing churches, building church edifices, and baptizing many converts. In 1859 he moved to Minnesota, and spent one year with the Meoney Creek and Centerville churches. He emigrated to Oregon in 1860, and was pastor seven years at Salem, where he built a house of worship. In 1869 he moved to California, and was pastor until 1875 at Sonora, Columbia, Santa Clara, and Marysville, and organized new churches at Camptonville and Yuba City. In 1875 he went to Virginia City, Nev., and in 1877 was at Reno. In these two cities he built houses of worship, and organized a church at Carson City. Returning to California, he organized a church at Holister, and in 1878 settled again at Santa Clara. His life has been a busy one in revival work. He has baptized about 600 converts, is an earnest preacher, and a constant contributor to the religious papers.

Fisher, Rev. Ezra, one of the pioneer Baptist missionaries to Oregon, was born at Wendel, Mass., Jan. 6, 1800, when Baptists were suffering much persecution in that State by the Established Church. In 1818 he was converted, and became a minister of the gospel. After many struggles for an education he graduated from Newton Theological Seminary in 1829, was ordained Jan. 17, 1830, labored with much success as pastor one year at Cambridge, and two years at Springfield, Vt., where he baptized 80 converts. As a missionary of the American Baptist Home Mission Society he preached for thirteen years at Indianapolis, Ind., Quincy, Ill., and Davenport, Iowa. In 1845 he crossed the plains with an ox-team for Oregon, and reached Tualatin Plains in the fall, and at once began to preach to the settlers. In 1846 he organized the first Baptist church west of the Rocky Mountains, in Washington Co., Oregon. He was full of zeal, and ready to sacrifice any comfort for Christ. He had special gifts for teaching, and in 1849 took charge of the Baptist school at Oregon City, out of which afterwards grew the college at McMinnville. In 1849 he resigned his chair in the institute, and gave himself to pastoral and missionary work until Oct. 18, 1874, when he preached his last sermon at the Dalles' church. A sudden illness prevented him from further labor. He was carried to his home from the church, and Nov. 1, 1874, he fell asleep in Jesus, and closed an unusually active and successful life, whose fruits are abundant everywhere in Oregon.

Fisher, John, was born in England, July 23, 1799; came to Philadelphia in 1817, and 120 miles from that city heard a sermon which changed his whole life; settled in St. John, New Brunswick, in 1828; became convinced that believers' baptism only is authorized by Christ, was baptized in 1842, and joined the Germain Street Baptist church; was soon appointed a deacon, which office he still honors. As a ship-builder and ship-owner Mr. Fisher has added greatly to the wealth of St. John, and the commerce of New Brunswick.

Fisher, Hon. Stearns, was born near Dover, Windham Co., Vt., Nov. 5, 1804. His father moved to Ohio in 1816. The son at the age of eighteen taught a school to the satisfaction of his patrons. He afterwards began to work on the Ohio Canal, and by dint of assiduous study he was able to step from the office of axeman to that of engineer. Hon. Alfred Kelly, who was chairman of the Ohio Board of Public Works, finding him one night after twelve o'clock studying algebra, took an especial interest in him and aided him. Having found employment on the Wabash and Erie Canal, he moved to a farm near Wabash, Ind., in 1833. He was afterwards appointed general superintendent of the canal. He had control of canal construction and land offices in the State, and although over one and a half million dollars passed through his hands, there was no charge nor thought of dishonesty. In 1846 he was again appointed general superintendent of the canal. He was for one term a member of the lower house in the Indiana Legislature. In 1868 he was elected to the senate of the Indiana Legislature. Here, as in the house, his ability and leadership were acknowledged. He was appointed paymaster of the Indiana Legion. In the dark days of the war he was a firm friend of the Union, and greatly aided Gov. Morton in his patriotic efforts in Indiana. He was converted, and joined the Wabash Baptist church in 1853, and was an earnest, consistent, benevolent Christian. Almost his whole life was spent in public service, and his integrity and wisdom were universally acknowledged. He died in Wabash, July 26, 1877.

Fisher, Rev. Thomas Jefferson, a strangely gifted orator, of German extraction, was born in Mount Sterling, Ky., April 9, 1812. At sixteen years of age he professed religion and joined the Presbyterian church at Paris, Ky., but soon afterwards becoming interested in the subject of baptism, he was led to unite with Davids Fork Baptist church, in Fayette County, where he was baptized in 1829, and in a short time licensed to preach. Having a great thirst for knowledge, he attended school at Middletown, Pa., and afterward at Pittsburgh, under the direction of Rev. S. Williams. In 1833 he returned to Kentucky, and was ordained to the ministry, entering the pastoral office at Lawrenceburg. This was soon abandoned for the work of an evangelist, to which he devoted most of the remainder of his life. He made his home in Kentucky, but traveled and held meetings in the towns and cities of many of the Southern States. Vast crowds thronged to hear him, and it is estimated that 12,000 persons professed conversion under his ministry. Whole congregations

REV. THOMAS JEFFERSON FISHER.

were frequently raised to their feet by the power of his eloquence. On the evening of Jan. 8, 1866, while walking along Eighth Street, in Louisville, Ky., he was struck on the head with a slung-shot, from the effects of which he died three days afterwards. His biography was written and published by J. H. Spencer, D.D.

Fitz, Hon. Eustace Cary, was born in Haverhill, Mass., Feb. 5, 1833. When a child his parents removed to Boston, where they resided until 1841, and then moved to Chelsea. He was a graduate of the Chelsea High School in 1847. Soon after leaving school he commenced mercantile pursuits, in which he has achieved a large success. In 1856 he took up his residence in Cambridge, Mass., where he lived till 1859, when he returned to Chelsea, where he has continued to reside until the present time. Mr. Fitz has been called by his fellow-citizens to fill various offices of civil trust. He was president of the common council of the city of Chelsea two years, mayor of Chelsea three years, a member of the Massachusetts House of Representatives two years, and a State senator two years. In the cause of Christian benevolence, he has proved himself an active and liberal friend. As a member of the executive committee of the Missionary Union, he has rendered good service to foreign missions. Mr. Fitz is in the prime of a busy life, and if it is spared he will continue to make his influence felt as a Christian citizen, and a loyal member of the denomination to which he belongs.

Fitz, Rev. H., was born in Charlton, Mass., Nov. 22, 1792. He received his education at Amherst College, where he graduated in the class of 1826. He pursued his theological studies at Newton, where he graduated in 1829. He was ordained as pastor of the Baptist church in Waterville, Me., Oct. 7, 1829, from which he removed to Hallowell, Me., and from thence to Middleborough, Mass., where he remained four years, from 1832 to 1836. He was subsequently pastor of the churches in Thompson, Conn., Marblehead, and Millbury, Mass. For more than thirty years, he was the missionary agent of the Massachusetts Baptist Convention, and came to be known everywhere as "Father Fitz." Among the feeble churches of the State, he did a work the influence of which will be felt for a long time to come. Mr. Fitz died at Middleborough in 1877.

Five-Mile Act, The, received the king's approval Oct. 31, 1665. By its provisions no minister was permitted to come within five miles of any city or corporation where he had preached after the Act of Oblivion, under very severe penalties, unless he should take the following oath: "I, A. B., do solemnly declare, that it is not lawful, upon any pretence whatsoever, to take up arms against the king; and that I do abhor the traitorous position of taking arms by his authority against his person, or against those that are commissioned by him, in pursuance of such commission. And I do swear that I will not at any time to come endeavor the alteration of the government, either in church or state. So help me God."

This act overflowed with cunning malice. The Non-Conformists of all sects, whose pastors had been removed from them by the Act of Uniformity, resided chiefly in corporate towns and cities, and, as a consequence, the execution of this law would drive the ministers from their only friends. Perhaps there was not a single Non-Conformist minister in England but believed that in some instances it was righteous to resist a wicked king by force of arms. So that on that ground alone he could not take the oath. And then all Non-Conformist ministers, as conscientious men, were bound to seek alterations in the government of a church so tainted with error that they preferred the loss of all their worldly goods to a confession of its purity by remaining in it. The Five-Mile Act was designed to subject them to the horrors of starvation, by cutting them off from their friends; or to the miseries of a dungeon if they ventured among them, for the king and Parliament well knew that they could never take such an oath. So that it was intended to destroy all Non-Conformist congregations.

Under this dreadful law, all Dissenting ministers suffered the most grievous wrongs; and not a few of them felt the pangs of hunger. Yet large numbers of them defied the act, and were thrust into foul prisons for their disobedience. The Baptist ministers were men of great courage, and soon after the enactment of this law many of them were in the jails of Christian England, for preaching Jesus and him crucified.

Flag, American Baptist, was established in La Grange, Mo., Jan. 1, 1875, by D. B. Ray, D.D., and removed to St. Louis in June, 1877. It aims to supply a place in religious journalism, occupied by no other paper, in views of the ordinances and church constitution, and in bold antagonism to error and latitudinarianism. The design of the editor is to interfere with no other religious journal of the denomination. It makes a specialty of ecclesiastical history and polemic theology. On Jan. 7, 1880, the name of the *Flag* was changed from *Battle Flag* to *American Baptist Flag*, and the paper was enlarged from 40 to 48 columns. It has able contributors, but only one proprietor and editor, Dr. D. B. Ray. Rev. D. B. Weber is the able business manager and a minister of promise. The *Flag* is not sectional, and circulates in all the States. It has a family and Sunday-school department.

Flagg, Rev. Wilkes (colored), a resident of Milledgeville, Ga., died Nov. 13, 1878, in the seventy-eighth year of his age, was universally respected and esteemed by all classes of the community. The white people had the highest regard for him as an honest man and a sincere Christian. He was converted, and joined the Baptist church at Milledgeville in 1834, was made a deacon, and soon after was licensed to preach to the colored people. He purchased his own freedom years before the war, and, while preaching, followed the trade of a blacksmith, being liberally patronized by the white people. He learned to read, and studied the Bible diligently, and became a most useful and consistent Christian, remaining so unto the day of his death, bold and zealous as a Christian, yet meek and humble as a disciple. After the war he organized the colored members of the Milledgeville church into a separate body, and was chosen their pastor, and so continued until his death. He was a prime mover in the organization of the Middle Georgia Baptist (colored) Association in 1866, of which he was annually elected moderator, while he lived. He was chairman of the Executive Board, and in 1873 was elected treasurer, which office he held at death. He was wise in counsel, pure in life, zealous in deed, and earnest and sincere in his religion. "He crystallized the teachings of his religion in his moral being."

Flanders, Charles W., D.D., was born in Salisbury, Mass., February, 1807, and was a graduate of Brown University in the class of 1839. He studied theology with Rev. John Wayland, D.D., at the time pastor of the First Baptist church in Salem, Mass. Dr. Flanders was pastor of the First Baptist church in Danvers, Mass., for almost ten years, and of the First Baptist church in Concord, N. H., for sixteen years. In both these places his labors were eminently successful. Waning health and strength, after so many years of almost uninterrupted ministerial and pastoral labor, warned him to resign the pastorate of so large a church, and the remainder of his life was passed in spheres of duty more limited and making less demand on his powers. The churches of Kennebunkport, Me., and of Westborough and Beverly Farms, Mass., were blessed with the ripe fruits of his Christian experience and knowledge, and held him in high esteem for the many excellent qualities which endeared him to them. Brown University conferred on him the degree of Doctor of Divinity in 1859. From 1854 to his death he was a member of the board of trustees. He died in Beverly, Mass., Aug. 2, 1875.

Fleet, Col. Alexander, the son of Capt. Wm. Fleet, was born on the 26th of April, 1798, at Rural Felicity, King and Queen Co., Va. He received instruction from Rev. R. B. Semple, D.D., and was graduated at William and Mary College. In 1831 he joined the Bruington church, of which he remained a member during his long life, and which he served as deacon more than forty years. He was one of the founders of its Sunday-school, and devoted his whole life to its prosperity, as well as organizing and assisting other schools. He was an active laborer in Associations, frequently presiding as moderator; was also interested in secular education, and after the close of the war taught a small white school at his own house, and subsequently a colored free school. He published no literary works, but many a troubled heart was made glad by the reception of letters of condolence and Christian sympathy from him. Col. Fleet did good service also as magistrate and as representative in the Legislature of his State. He was twice married, first to Mrs. Hoomes and then to Mrs. Martha A. Butler. His widow and four children are still living. This excellent man died on the 27th of September, 1877.

Fleischmann, Rev. Conrad Anton.—The name of this indefatigable and successful minister will ever remain dear to German Baptists in America, as he was the first German Baptist missionary in this country, and in some sense the founder of our German Baptist communities.

Mr. Fleischmann was born in Nuremberg, in the kingdom of Bavaria, April 18, 1812. He was early instructed in the tenets of the Lutheran creed, deeming himself to be a good Christian when as yet he knew nothing concerning regeneration. Having learned a trade, he left his native city in his nineteenth year to travel as a journeyman, ac-

REV. CONRAD ANTON FLEISCHMANN.

cording to the custom then prevalent among mechanics. Reaching Geneva, Switzerland, he came under the influence of earnest Christians, and soon found peace in believing. This was in 1831. He was subsequently baptized in Basle, Switzerland. After a severe inward struggle, Mr. Fleischmann yielded to the divine call and entered a theological school at Berne, Switzerland, then under the auspices of the Free Evangelical Church, an independent body to which Mr. Fleischmann at that time belonged. Three years later Mr. Fleischmann entered upon his labors in Emmenthal, canton of Berne. He labored amidst severe persecution, but with abundant blessing.

In 1837, Mr. Fleischmann revisited his native land, and in the following year, at the invitation of the well-known George Mueller, he came to Bristol, England, as his return to Switzerland had been providentially hindered. After remaining for some time under the hospitable roof of Mr. Mueller, in 1839 he left Bristol for the New World for the purpose of preaching the gospel to his countrymen in America, whose spiritual destitution touched his heart. He labored at first in New York, afterwards in Newark, N. J., where the first German converts were baptized by him. From Newark he removed to Reading, Pa. Then he preached in Lycoming Co., Pa., where his labors were abun-

dantly blessed. The spirit of God moved the whole region and many were converted and baptized.

In 1842, Mr. Fleischmann removed to Philadelphia, where a church was soon formed, which entered into fellowship with the Philadelphia Association in 1848. Although Mr. Fleischmann labored principally as pastor of this church, yet he continually made extensive missionary tours into different States. In 1852 the first Conference of German Baptists was held, and Mr. Fleischmann was appointed editor of the monthly paper. When in 1865 it became a weekly paper, he became associate editor. He presided at the first meeting of the General Conference in 1865. He was intimately identified with all the interests of the German cause in this land, and his efforts and advice seemed indispensable. When he was suddenly removed by death, Oct. 15, 1867, his departure spread intense gloom over the churches. All felt that a pillar in the denomination had been removed.

Mr. Fleischmann was a man of talent; he was winning, affectionate, and eloquent in his discourses, and indefatigable in his labors; just such a man as was needed to lay foundations for the German Baptist churches of America. His memory will ever remain precious to them, and to large numbers of American Baptists who appreciated his worth and honored him for his work.

Fletcher, Hon. Asaph, was born at Westford, Mass., June 28, 1746. He was the subject of very marked religious impressions when he was but ten years of age, and became a hopeful Christian when he was sixteen. His parents were Congregationalists, and he was sprinkled in his infancy. When he was old enough to make personal investigation of the subject, he adopted the sentiments of the Baptists, and was immersed at Leicester, Mass., May 15, 1768, being then not far from twenty-two years of age. For more than seventy years he was an active and intelligent member of churches in the towns where he had his residence. His fellow-citizens elected him to many positions of honor and trust. While living in his native place he was chosen a member of the convention which formed the constitution of Massachusetts in 1780. He used his utmost endeavor while thus acting to introduce into that instrument the Baptist principle that public worship ought to be sustained by voluntary contribution and not by taxation. Although he did not succeed in effecting his object, he tried to see it brought about at a subsequent period. In the month of February, 1787, Dr. Fletcher removed to Cavendish, Vt., where he continued to reside during the remainder of his life. Here, also, he became a man of note. He was a member of the Vermont convention which applied to Congress for admission into the Union. Shortly after he was a member of the convention which revised the constitution of the State. Here, as in the Massachusetts convention, he ably vindicated his Baptist sentiments on religious liberty. The citizens of Cavendish frequently elected him a member of the Legislature. For several years he was one of the judges of the County Court and a member of the governor's council. He was also one of the Presidential electors when James Monroe was chosen President of the United States. He held also many other civil offices, his election to which indicated the esteem in which he was held by his fellow-citizens. He died at the advanced age of ninety-two years, Jan. 5, 1839. Among the Baptists of his adopted State he held a high position, as one who was thoroughly loyal to his denomination.

Fletcher, Horace, D.D., was the son of Hon. Asaph Fletcher, and a brother of the late Judge Richard Fletcher, of Boston. He was born in Cavendish, Vt., Oct. 28, 1796. In 1813 he became a member of Vermont University at Burlington, and remained there until the college buildings were surrendered to the army. He entered Dartmouth College in the spring of 1815, joining the Sophomore class, and graduated in 1817. For a time he was principal of the Franklin County Academy at New Salem, N. H., and then commenced the study of law at Westminster, Vt. Being admitted to the bar, he commenced the practice of his profession in his native place, and continued in it for fifteen years. During this period he became a hopeful Christian, and was baptized into the fellowship of the Baptist church of Cavendish. He now felt it to be his duty to preach, and giving what attention he could to the study of theology, he was ordained pastor of the Baptist church in Townshend, Vt., where he remained until his death. His work as a minister was greatly blessed, and precious revivals were experienced during his long pastorate. He was a public-spirited citizen as well as a good minister of Jesus Christ. For some time he was a senator in the Legislature of Vermont. The honorary degree of Doctor of Divinity was conferred upon him by Madison University in 1860. Dr. Fletcher died Nov. 27, 1871.

Fletcher, Rev. John, was born July 9, 1832; was baptized by Rev. J. Inglis in February, 1851; was ordained pastor of the Baptist church in Ceresco, Mich., March, 1859. Subsequently he served the churches in Sturgis and Edwardsburg; was chaplain of the 9th Regiment of Michigan Volunteer Cavalry one year, ending with August, 1865; accompanied his regiment in Sherman's marches of that winter. Soon after leaving the army he became pastor of the church in Plainwell, and remains yet in that relation. In 1876 he had leave of absence for a few months, and meanwhile supplied the pulpit of the E Street church in Washington, D. C. That church called him to its pastorate, and he was inclined to accept the call. But the unanimous and earnest wish of the church in Plainwell, and a written petition signed by a large proportion of the citizens, and the action of a public meeting called to remonstrate against his leaving, changed his plans.

Mr. Fletcher, during the fifteen years of his pastorate in Plainwell, has performed an almost incredible amount of pastoral work, constantly maintaining several preaching stations besides filling his own pulpit. He is the only pastor the church has had, and he has seen it grow to one of the largest in the State. He is a true bishop after the apostolic model.

Fletcher, Joshua, D.D., was born in Kingsbury, Washington Co., N. Y., April 27, 1804; graduated at Hamilton in 1829; was ordained at Saratoga Springs the same year, where he continued pastor for nineteen years; has been pastor in Amenia and Cambridge, N. Y., in Southington, Conn., and he is now pastor of Wallingford, Vt. In 1866 Madison University conferred upon him the degree of Doctor of Divinity.

Fletcher, Judge Richard, was born in Cavendish, Vt., Jan. 8, 1788. At the age of fourteen he entered Dartmouth College, where he graduated in 1806. He studied law with Daniel Webster, and in 1809 was admitted to the bar. He commenced the practice of his profession in Salisbury, N. H., but like his celebrated teacher, he aspired after a wider sphere within which to exercise his vocation, and concluded to remove to Boston and try his fortunes there. Like so many others of his profession, he entered the arena of politics. He represented a section of his adopted home in the State Legislature. Then was chosen a representative to Congress. For many years he was a judge of the Massachusetts Supreme Court, and is best known in that State as "Judge" Fletcher. But his highest glory was that he was an earnest disciple of the Lord Jesus Christ. He was for many years a member of what was the Rowe Street church, and enjoyed the confidence and affection of his pastor, Rev. Dr. Stow.

After his decease, which occurred June 21, 1869, it was found that he had remembered with great generosity the college where he received his early education, having bequeathed to it the munificent sum of $100,000.

Flippo, Rev. Oscar Farish, was born at Lebanon, Lancaster Co., Va., Jan. 1, 1836, and educated at Kilmarnock Academy. He was licensed to preach in 1857, and was ordained in Salisbury, Md., in 1858, where he served as pastor nearly two years. From 1861 to 1868 he was pastor of the Newtown, Pitt's Creek, Rehoboth, and Chincoteague churches, and during that time baptized about 200 persons. From March, 1868, to September, 1870, he was pastor of the church in Dover, Del. During the following four years he served as general evangelist for the whole State of Delaware, and was remarkably successful in the work. The Wyoming Institute, at Wyoming, Del., passed into the hands of the Baptists mainly through his instrumentality. Mr. Flippo had the pleasure of seeing the entire Zion Methodist church, near Harrington, Del., change their views and adopt the principles of the Baptists, and he baptized every member of the church, including the pastor. During his pastorate in Dover he was elected chaplain of the Legislature of Delaware, in the winter of 1869. The failing health of Mrs. Flippo made it necessary that he should abandon his work as an evangelist, in which he had accomplished so much good, and he accordingly accepted the pastorate of the Waverly Baptist church, Baltimore, which he held for five years. In 1866 he started the *Baptist Visitor*, a monthly paper, which he continued to edit and publish for twelve years. In 1877 he returned to Virginia, and soon afterwards became pastor of the Baptist church in Suffolk, in that State. While in Baltimore he was elected moderator of the Maryland Union Baptist Association, in 1877. He has been quite successful as a public lecturer, and several of his addresses have been received with marked favor.

Flood, Judge Joseph, was born in Shelby Co., Ky. He removed to Callaway Co., Mo., in 1846, and settled near Fulton, where he lived for twenty years. In 1828 he removed to Clay County, and spent the remainder of his life in and near Kearney. He united early in life with the church in Christiansburg, Ky., and adorned his profession till the day of his death. He was connected with Westminster College, in 1866, as principal of the preparatory department, and held a like position in Stephens College, Columbia, in 1867. Few men surpassed him in zeal for Sunday-schools. He was superintendent at Richland, in Callaway County, for years, and also deacon in the church for a long time, and "used the office well."

At Kearney he was superintendent of the Sunday-school, and forty in it were converted just before his death. Joseph Flood was a man of sterling worth and unblemished reputation. He died Nov. 14, 1878, sixty-five years of age. His memory is fragrant wherever he was known.

Flood, Rev. Noah, was born in Shelby Co., Ky., June 14, 1809. He had marked talent from a child. He resisted his first religious impressions, and thought that God was harsh. He was converted in 1824. In 1828 he united with the Baptist church at Christiansburg, Shelby Co., Ky. In 1829 he came to Missouri. He attended Dr. Nelson's school in Marion Co., Mo. He was licensed in 1832 by Little Union church, near Palmyra, Mo. He spent 1834 and 1835 in Shurtleff College, Ill. After this he taught in Woodford Co., Ky. He was ordained in 1838. In 1839 he settled in Callaway Co., Mo. He organized Richland, Grand Prairie, Unity, Union Hill, Mount Horeb, and Dry Fork churches. In 1852 he removed to Fayette County. For six years he preached to Fayette, Walnut Grove, Mount Zion, and Chariton churches. In 1858 he removed to Huntsville, and labored there till 1863, and then removed to Roanoke. The war gave him trouble, but all parties respected him and became his friends before his death. In 1865 Brother Flood moved to Boone County, and died at Columbia, Aug. 11, 1873. The ministry of Missouri greatly honored him. Twice he was moderator of the General Association. He was a warm friend of William Jewell College. Rev. J. F. Cook, LL.D., his nephew, acknowledges his fatherly kindness to him. Noah Flood died in the enjoyment of perfect peace. Dr. S. H. Ford, Nathan Ayres, and his brother, Judge Flood, with his family, were present at his death.

Florida Baptist College.—The Baptists never made an effort to establish a denominational college, literary or theological, till very recently. Some six or eight years ago the Bethlehem Baptist Association, which possesses in the main the talents and numbers of the colored Baptists of the State, commenced to raise funds to found a theological school. They continued to contribute annually small sums, and purchased a lot at Live Oak for a site, but they have not yet been able to secure buildings. The Home Mission Society of New York have adopted the enterprise, and will commence to build in the fall of 1880. This is the first and only effort made by the denomination to secure a college in Florida.

Florida Baptist State Convention.—The Convention was organized in 1854, in the parlor of Rev. R. J. Mays, Madison County. Rev. David G. Daniel was the first secretary, but the writer is not able to give the name of the first president. Only a very meagre account of the Convention can be furnished.

The session for 1856 was held at Madison Court-House, in November. The attendance was not large. James Edmunds, of Kentucky, secretary of the Bible Revision Association, Rev. W. N. Chaudoin, agent of the "Bible Board" of Southern Baptist Convention, and Rev. T. J. Bowen, returned missionary of the Southern Convention from Central Africa, were visitors.

It is not known where the meetings were held in 1857, 1858, and 1859, but in 1860 a session was held in Jacksonville, with the Bethel Baptist church, in May. Joseph S. Baker, D.D., was then residing at Jacksonville, and his presence added interest to the meeting.

Of the next ten years no information can be given of the meetings, nor is it known whether there were meetings held every year.

A session was held in 1869, of which Rev. P. P. Bishop was elected president, and he was re-elected at Madison, in November, 1871, and Rev. H. B. McCallum was chosen secretary. From the minutes of that year it appears that at the previous meeting it was agreed to co-operate with the Home Mission Society of New York in missionary work, and under that arrangement F. C. Johnson labored at Jacksonville, Charles B. Jones at Palatka and vicinity, W. E. Stanton on the St. John's River, P. P. Bishop as general missionary, and H. B. McCallum at Lake City and vicinity.

The session was not largely attended, but was quite interesting, and the presence of such men as Bishop, McCallum, Smith, Tomkies, and C. D. Campbell made it strong. A report was made on ministerial education, and $63.50 raised to aid Brother Perry, who was in the theological seminary at Greenville, S. C., from Marion Co., Fla.

In 1872 the session was held at Lake City, in November. There was no report of missionary work, but the presence of W. N. Chaudoin was noted, in the capacity of district secretary of Home Mission Board of Southern Convention, and the desirableness of having a *general evangelist* was discussed, and Elder McCallum was requested to commence the publication of a Baptist paper.

November, 1873, the body met at Providence church, Bradford Co. Warren Randolph, D.D., of Philadelphia, and L. B. Fish, of Georgia, both in the interest of the American Baptist Publication Society, were present.

Probably a couple of years before this time the churches in several counties on the line of Georgia and Florida, in Georgia, but hitherto identified with Florida, organized an Association in Georgia, and it allied itself with the Georgia Convention. This materially weakened the Florida Convention, yet the meeting at Providence was well attended, and was one of more than usual interest. Elder Kinsey Chambers made a report as State evangelist.

The next meeting was held at Jacksonville, in February, 1875, Rev. J. H. Tomkies, President, and Rev. H. B. McCallum, Secretary. Elders Chaudoin, Fish, Gaulden, and Cawood were present from the Georgia Baptist Convention. In February, 1876, the meeting was held at Gainesville, at which time it was deemed best to change the time, and they adjourned to meet in December of the same year at Madison. In consequence of excessive rain the meeting in December was almost a failure, no business was transacted, and they adjourned to convene at the call of the Executive Committee, which was to meet at Tallahassee in January, 1879. That meeting was followed by another, at the same place, in January, 1880, which was the most important one held for several years. Dr. Graves, of Tennessee, added much interest to the meeting by his presence.

Florida Periodicals.—In 1860, Rev. N. A. Bailey, then pastor of the Baptist church at Monticello, Fla., and W. N. Chaudoin, then at Thomasville, Ga., issued a prospectus of a Baptist paper for Florida, but its publication was never commenced. In 1872, the Santa Fé River Association passed resolutions favoring a new paper, and their action was indorsed by the Florida Association. At the State Convention in Lake City, in November, the Committee on Publications also reported favorably, and a subscription was made to aid the enterprise. In February following the first number of the *Florida Baptist* was issued at Lake City, Rev. H. B. McCallum, Editor, with Elders T. E. Langley and J. H. Tomkies, Corresponding Editors.

The paper was published till 1875, but was never remunerative. During that year, or early in 1876, it was discontinued, and the subscription-list and good-will of the paper were transferred to the *Christian Index*, of Atlanta, Ga., and an arrangement made for a Florida department in that paper. The arrangement has been very generally approved, and the *Christian Index* has a considerable circulation. W. N. Chaudoin, Jacksonville, is Florida editor.

Florida, Sketch of the Baptists of.—The Florida Association was the first organized in the State, and the only one for four years after its formation. It has held its thirty-seventh annual session, and so was organized in 1841 or 1842. The territory covered by its churches is not known, but they were mostly in Leon, Jefferson, and Madison Counties in Florida, and Thomas Co., Ga.

Alachua was probably the next, and was organized in 1845 or 1846, and its churches were embraced in a territory reaching from the St. Mary's River to Tampa, on the Gulf coast.

The Santa Fé River Association was taken from the northern part of the Alachua, in 1854 or 1855, and its churches were located in Duval, Clay, Nassau, Columbia, Bradford, Alachua, Levy, and perhaps other counties.

West Florida Association, lying west of the Chattahoochee River, and occupying all that part of the State, was doubtless organized as early as the Santa Fé River, and may be earlier, but the date cannot be given.

Ten years elapsed before the organization of the South Florida, which was the next, and covers all the southern part of the territory of Alachua, viz., a part of Hernando and all of Hillsborough and Polk Counties. This was in 1866.

Suwanee and New River Associations were both made out of what the Santa Fé River included, mainly, in 1872. The year following, 1873, the St. John's River was organized.

Since that time Manatee, North St. John's River, Middle Florida, and Harmony Associations have been formed, and prior to these, but in what year is not known, the Wekiva Association was organized, and it includes most of the churches in Orange, and some in Volusia County. There is probably a small Association in Sumter County, but nothing is known by the writer of its condition, name, or numbers.

We are not able to give the number of the Associations of colored Baptists. Their principal strength is in the First Bethlehem, which has held its eleventh anniversary. The Bethlehem, No. 2, Jerusalem, Nazarene, and East Florida have all been organized since 1865. Others have recently been formed, but names are not known.

It is safe to say that there are more than 20,000 Baptists in Florida, somewhat more than half of whom are colored, in about 300 churches, and under the care of about 200 ministers.

Floyd, Rev. Matthew, was the son of Abraham Floyd, a native of Ireland, who with his father, Col. Matthew Floyd, came to America during the Revolutionary war; both entered the service of the colonies. At the close of the war Capt. Floyd settled in South Carolina, where his son Matthew was born. He came with his parents to Madison Co., Ky., in 1796. Here he joined the Methodists. But soon afterwards, having studied the subject of baptism, he was immersed, and joined the Baptists. This action greatly incensed his father, who was an Episcopalian, and young Floyd was expelled from his home. He was licensed to preach in 1811, and ordained the same year. He was pastor of White Oak church fifty-one years. He preached much among the destitute in his own and the surrounding counties, and is supposed to have baptized about 1500 persons. He was moderator of South Concord Association sixteen years, and of the South Cumberland twenty-one years. His life from the date of his ordination until his death, Aug. 19, 1863, was spent in Pulaski Co., Ky.

Foley, Rev. Moses, son of Rev. Moses Foley, an eminently useful preacher, was born in Washington Co., Va., Feb. 7, 1777. He professed conversion about 1801, and began to exhort before he was baptized. His usefulness was so apparent that he was ordained only a few months after his baptism. He labored about eight years in his native county, and in 1811 removed to Kentucky. He first settled in Pulaski County, but the next year took charge of the Baptist church at Crab Orchard, in Lincoln County, where he resided until his death. Under his ministry this church grew to a membership of over 400. He preached with success to several other churches. He died Nov. 6, 1858.

Foljambe, Rev. S. W., was born in Leeds, England, Oct. 14, 1827. His early associations were with the Methodists, his grandfather having for many years been a Methodist preacher. He re-

REV. S. W. FOLJAMBE.

ceived a liberal education. He came to this country in 1836, and for several years resided in Franklin, O. His early preaching was among the Methodists. While meeting an engagement in the Wesleyan church in Pittsburgh, Pa., he became a Baptist, and was installed as pastor of the Branch Street church in that city, remaining there until he removed to a village some fifteen miles north of Pittsburgh. His next settlement was with the Grant Street church in Pittsburgh. From it he went to Dayton, O., where he remained six years, then to Framingham and East Boston, Mass. From East Boston he accepted a call to Albany, where he remained but a short time, and then became pastor of the Harvard Street church in Boston, from which place he removed to Malden, Mass., where he now resides. Mr. Foljambe is an able preacher, whom the Saviour has honored and blessed.

Font, the name universally given to the vessel containing the water used in baptism in Episcopal and Catholic churches. It is the Latin *fons*, a spring, a fountain. It was employed first in early Christian times, when a well or spring was the common place for baptizing. Sometimes in primitive ages the baptistery was a bathing vessel, and the pool was called *lavacrum*, a bath. Baptism was administered in rivers and in the sea; but the bathing vessel and the spring were more accessible.

And, as the spring could be found almost everywhere, in process of time its name, *fons*, became the name of anything in which a person received baptism, whether it was the sea, a river, a tub, a spring, or a church basin. It is somewhat of a misnomer to call the small sprinkling vessel of a Pedobaptist church *a font, a spring;* but we admire the name; there is strong testimony in it about the primitive mode of baptism.

Fontaine, Rev. P. H., was born in King William Co., Va., Sept. 7, 1841; was educated at Rumford Military Academy and the University of Virginia; was baptized in 1854; ordained in 1863; moved to North Carolina in 1865, and he is now pastor of Reidsville and Leaksville churches. A descendant, on the part of father and mother, of Patrick Henry, after whom he is named.

Fontaine, Rev. Wm. Spotswood, was born in Hanover Co., Va., in 1811; studied medicine for two years, and afterwards obtained license to practise law; married his cousin, Miss L. L. Aylett, a granddaughter of Patrick Henry, he himself being a descendant of the Virginia orator; joined the Methodist Church at the age of thirteen; was baptized in 1842 by Rev. J. P. Turpin; was ordained in 1844, R. H. Bagby, J. P. Turpin, and a Mr. Bland forming the Presbytery. He was a country gentleman of very handsome estate, his residence costing $15,000, and his barn $5000. His library consisted of 5000 volumes. Ruined by the war financially, he came to Greensborough, N. C., in 1863, but returned to Virginia in 1866 to become president of Atlantic Female College; came back to North Carolina in 1867; went to Texas in 1872; returned after four years, and now resides in Reidsville, engaged in preaching and planting.

Foote, Rev. Elias J., was born June 22, 1824, in Olean, N. Y.; graduated from Union College in 1849; studied law; was seven years in California and Central America; graduated from Rochester Theological Seminary in 1860; was ordained in St. Louis in 1861. He afterwards labored in prisons and hospitals. After short settlements in Syracuse and Penfield, N. Y., he came to the church at Red Bank, N. J., in 1871. Upon the death of Rev. D. B. Stout, in 1875, he was called to the pastorate of the old church in Middletown, and now feeds that flock.

Forbes, Rev. W. A., pastor of the Eighth Street Baptist church, Little Rock, Ark., was born in Mississippi in 1844, but, deprived of his parents at an early age, he was reared by a maternal uncle at Lewisville, Ark. He served in the Confederate army as a private, after which he was employed in Tennessee, where he was converted and began to preach. He then entered Bethel College, Ky., from which he graduated in 1871, after which he returned to Arkansas and became pastor at Washington, and subsequently at Arkadelphia, where he continued, with the exception of one year in Kentucky, until 1878, when he was called to his present pastorate. For some years he has been connected with the State Mission Board, and is an active promoter of missions and ministerial education.

Force, William Q., was born in Washington, D. C., March 7, 1820. He was graduated at the Columbian College in 1839, and received the degree of Master of Arts in 1842. On the 23d of June, 1839, he was baptized by the Rev. O. B. Brown into the fellowship of the First Baptist church, Washington, of which he is still a most useful member. For many years he was a teacher in and also superintendent of the Sunday-school, as well as treasurer and deacon of the church. Mr. Force has always been a warm friend of the Columbian College, served as a trustee from 1851 to 1862, and was for several years its secretary and treasurer. He is a great lover of books, and one of the best-read laymen in the denomination. He edited and published *The Army and Navy Chronicle and Scientific Repository* from January, 1843, to July, 1845; compiled and published "The Builders' Guide," and also two editions of "The Picture of Washington." From 1845 to 1857 he aided his father, the Hon. Peter Force, so long and well known in Washington, in the preparation of that valuable work, "The American Archives." From 1857 to 1868 he had charge of meteorology at the Smithsonian Institution, which position, however, he was obliged to resign in 1868 in consequence of failing health. Mr. Force has a valuable library in which he spends much of his time, is a laborious student, and a frequent contributor to the newspapers, principally on religious subjects. His knowledge is varied, and at the same time accurate, and his articles are prepared with much care and always read with profit. Few men are as familiar with church history, Biblical interpretation, and the literature of the baptism question as Wm. Q. Force.

Ford, Rev. Samuel Howard, LL.D., son of Rev. Thomas H. Ford, was licensed in 1840, passed through the classes in the State University of Missouri, and was ordained in 1843, at Bonne Femme church, in Boone Co., Mo. He became pastor at Jefferson City, Mo., and in two years after of the North church in St. Louis for two years; also at Cape Girardeau, Mo., and the East Baptist church, Louisville, Ky. In 1853 he was associated with Dr. John L. Waller in the editorship of the *Western Recorder* and *Christian Repository*. Of the latter he is still the editor. His talented wife has written "Grace Truman," "The Dreamer's Blind Daughter," and other works of great value. At the breaking out of the war, Dr. Ford went to

Memphis, where he preached for some time. For two years he was in Mobile as pastor of the St. Francis Street church. At the close of the war he accepted the pastorate of the Central Baptist

REV. SAMUEL HOWARD FORD, LL.D.

church of Memphis, where he preached for seven years, till ill health caused him to resign. While in this church he was instrumental in building a capacious and splendid house of worship, upon which $75,000 were expended during his pastorate, and in increasing the membership from 75 to 450. Dr. Ford has received the honorary degree of LL.D. He preaches without manuscript, is earnest and eloquent, and many hundreds have been converted under his ministry. He is a firm Baptist, and he has had discussions with Alexander Campbell, Bishop Spaulding, of the Catholic Church, and Dr. N. L. Rice. Dr. Ford is a Hebrew and Syriac scholar; he is well read in general literature, and is specially familiar with the Romish controversy. In his theology he is a Calvinist. In the past twenty-seven years he has written upon almost every subject bearing on the religious issues of the times. He is now sixty years of age, and is as active, energetic, and laborious as ever. Baptists in all parts of our country and the British provinces, and in the British islands, wish length of years to the learned editor of the *Repository*, and to his cultured and talented wife.

Ford, Rev. Thomas Howard, was born about 1790, near Bristol, England. His ancestors were members of the famous Broadmead Baptist church of that city. He began to preach when eighteen years of age. He studied the ancient languages under Dr. Burnett, and was versed in Puritan theology. He often heard the celebrated Episcopalian Toplady preach, the author of "Rock of Ages, shelter me." His name appears in Illinois and Missouri minutes in the early history of these States. He supplied the Second church of St. Louis for a time, and was the guest of Samuel C. Davis. In 1844 he was pastor of the Baptist church in Columbia, Mo. The learning, piety, and pulpit power of Mr. Ford drew large congregations, William Jewell and Dr. Thomas attending his ministry. The church in Callaway County gave him a farm, and soon after he died in their midst in peace. Says Noah Flood, "I knew him well, and I have never been acquainted with a better man." His last words were, "Happy, happy, bless the Lord." He was about sixty years of age when he died. He left two sons and one daughter. One son is Rev. S. H. Ford, LL.D., of St. Louis. The brethren at Richland erected a monument at his grave, where he rests with his co-laborer, Noah Flood.

Ford's Christian Repository.—This popular magazine was established in 1852 by John L. Waller, LL.D., in Louisville, Ky. About that time Dr. S. H. Ford became assistant, and soon sole proprietor, and it speedily increased from 500 subscribers to 6000. In 1855, Dr. Ford married Miss Sallie Rochester, a lady of education and talent. She at once took a position as co-editor, and wrote the attractive and useful story of "Grace Truman." The war stopped the *Repository* for a time. It was re-issued in St. Louis in 1871, where it is now successfully established, and wields a powerful and an extensive influence. Its exegetical articles, popular sermons, and family department make it invaluable. It is distinguished for its biographical sketches. It is the chief source of such history in our denomination, and its absence would be a serious loss. Thousands of ministers commend it, and are aided by it.

Forgeus, Rev. S. F., was born in South Coventry, Chester Co., Pa., Aug. 19, 1844. He was baptized into the fellowship of the Vincent church, Jan. 15, 1860; was licensed to preach Jan. 21, 1871; served in the war in three different regiments; prepared for college at Conoquenessing Academy, Zelienople, Butler Co., Pa., and the University Academy, Lewisburg; spent one year and one term at Cornell University, N. Y., and graduated at Lewisburg, Pa., June 26, 1872, and from Crozer Theological Seminary, May 12, 1875; was ordained in August, 1875, as pastor of the Tunkhannock church; became pastor of Clark's, Green, and Mount Bethel churches in October, 1878; resigned the latter charges in June, 1879; accepted the call of the Roaring Brook church, in Lackawanna County, in April, 1880.

Mr. Forgeus was clerk of the Wyoming Association for two years ; and he has been secretary of the Northeastern Pennsylvania Baptist Ministerial Conference for five years. He is a popular minister, of large devotedness to the Master, whose past usefulness gives great promise for the future.

Fortiner, E. K., was born in Haddonfield, N. J., Aug. 12, 1820; was baptized by Rev. N. B. Tindall, Jan. 1, 1839, and received into the fellowship of the First church of Camden. At the age of twenty he was elected to the superintendency of the Sunday-school, a position he has held with occasional interruption for nearly forty years, either in connection with the First or Tabernacle church, and he is now the superintendent of the school of the Fourth Street church, formed by the union of the First and Tabernacle churches. About 1847 he was elected to the office of deacon of the First church of Camden. He was a constituent member and deacon of the Tabernacle church, and he is now a deacon of the Fourth Street church. Consistent in conduct, untiring in work, generous in giving, he has led a life of great usefulness.

Foskett, Rev. Bernard, was born March 10, 1684–85, near Woburn, England, of a family of wealth and high repute. He received a liberal education, and was trained for the medical profession. He became a member of the church in Little Wild Street, London, when he was seventeen, and formed an intimate friendship in his youth with John Beddome, who was then a member of Benjamin Keach's church. After Mr. Beddome was called to the ministry and settled at Henley Arden, in Warwickshire, Mr. Foskett abandoned his profession in London and joined his friend, assisting him in his ministry at Henley, Bengeworth, Alcester, and other places in the neighborhood. He had been regularly called to the ministry whilst practising as a physician, but did not devote himself entirely to ministerial work until 1711. In 1719 he received an invitation to become assistant minister of the Broadmead church, Bristol, and tutor of the academy for young ministers. He entered upon his duties there in 1720, and for thirty-eight years labored as pastor and tutor with distinguished ability and success until his death, Sept. 17, 1758, in the seventy-third year of his age. Under his wise conduct the college at Bristol gained the esteem of the churches, and became "the school of the prophets" to which they looked with confidence for a supply of competent pastors and teachers. Some sixty-four students were trained under Mr. Foskett and his colleagues. Among these were several of the most eminent Baptist ministers of the eighteenth century, including such men as John Ryland, Dr. John Ash, Dr. Llewellyn (esteemed the first scholar among the Protestant Dissenters of his day), Benjamin Beddome, Robert Day, Benjamin Francis, besides Hugh Evans and Dr. Caleb Evans, his successors in the presidency. Mr. Foskett's enlightened piety, generous disposition, and high character made the denomination influential in Bristol and the neighborhood.

Foster, Benjamin, D.D., was born in Danvers, Mass., June 12, 1750. He graduated from Yale College in 1774. He was appointed to defend the Pedobaptist view of the baptismal controversy in one of the college exercises. The result of his preparation astonished himself and others ; he became a decided Baptist. He united with Dr. Stillman's church in Boston shortly after his graduation. In October, 1776, he was ordained pastor of the Baptist church of Leicester, Mass. On the 5th of June, 1785, he became pastor of the First Baptist church of Newport, R. I. In the autumn of 1788 he took charge of the First Baptist church of New York, which position he retained as long as he lived. In 1792 he received the degree of Doctor of Divinity from Rhode Island College (Brown University). When the yellow fever visited New York he fearlessly kept his ground, and visited its victims until the disease sent him to the grave. He died Aug. 26, 1798.

Dr. Foster was distinguished for his knowledge of the Greek, Hebrew, and Chaldean languages. He was an able preacher, and the Lord blessed his ministry to many.

Foster, Rev. John, was born in the parish of Halifax, Yorkshire, England, Sept. 17, 1770. His parents were persons of deep piety and of strong mental powers. His father had a considerable library of Puritan theology, with which he was perfectly familiar. He occasionally conducted public worship in his church in the absence of the pastor. In boyhood he was retiring, and shunned society. He was exquisitely fond of nature ; a bird, a tree, a flower, beautiful scenery, filled him frequently with delight. He had, even in boyhood, his favorite authors, whose works fed his mind and charmed his heart. He early cherished a special admiration for the majestic, the rugged, the sublime. At fourteen he first felt the need of a new heart, and at seventeen he had a good hope through the great Saviour, and was immersed by Dr. Fawcett, and became a member of the Wainsgate Baptist church.

After his union with the church he soon began to exercise his gifts, and he felt convinced that God had called him to preach the gospel. To fit himself for this glorious work he attended the school of his pastor, Dr. Fawcett, at Brearly Hall, where he devoted his attention to classics and to such studies as would qualify him for his future profession. He made a free use of the valuable library at Brearly Hall, and sometimes spent whole nights in reading and meditation. From Dr. Fawcett's school he became a student in the Bristol Baptist College. From it he went forth to labor in the ministry in Newcastle, and subsequently in Dublin, in Chichester, in Dowend near Bristol, and in

REV. JOHN FOSTER.

Frome. His success in the ministry was not remarkable, and a serious disease in the throat, which was greatly aggravated by much speaking, publicly or privately, compelled him partially to relinquish a calling which he loved.

While he was a pastor he published his first Essays. There were four of them,—on "A Man's writing Memoirs of Himself," on "Decision of Character," on "The Application of the Epithet Romantic," and on "Some of the Causes by which Evangelical Religion has been rendered Less Acceptable to Persons of Cultivated Taste." In a little over a year the work passed through three editions, and the eighteenth English edition was published in 1845, and how many others since then we cannot tell. Immediately almost after the issue of these Essays the obscure Baptist pastor of Frome found himself ranked among the first literary men of his country, and he has retained that position ever since. No man of culture and means reckons his library complete without the works of John Foster. Sir James Mackintosh, after reading Foster's Essays, declared that they showed their author to be "one of the most profound and eloquent writers that England has produced." In this opinion the reading world have long since united. In 1819 his Essay on "The Evils of Popular Ignorance" appeared, and it added to the wide-spread popularity of its then celebrated author.

Besides other essays, Mr. Foster wrote one hundred and eighty-five articles for the *Eclectic Review*. On Sundays, as he had opportunity, when able, he preached in destitute churches. He also delivered a series of discourses in Broadmead church, Bristol, which were largely attended, and among the hearers were members of all denominations. These sermons are in print.

When Mr. Foster reached the close of life his faith in the blessed Redeemer was unwavering, and anxious to see him face to face, he fell asleep in Jesus Oct. 15, 1843.

Mr. Foster's piety was all-pervading and abiding. His mind, like the great cataracts and lofty mountains which he loved to think of in boyhood, possessed a massive grandeur, an originality, and a stately majesty only met at long intervals in the literary world. At his death all ranks of men united in paying honor to his memory and in deploring the loss of an intellectual giant.

Foster, Prof. John B., son of John M., was born in Boston, Jan. 8, 1822. In the seventh year of his age his father removed to Waterville, Me., where, until he was fourteen, he attended the public schools and the academy in that place. For two years—1836-38—he was occupied in mechanical pursuits, and then commenced preparation to enter college. He graduated at Waterville College, now Colby University, in the class of 1843. In the same year he entered the Newton Theological Institution with the intention of going through the three years' course of study. In the following spring, however, he left the institution, and engaged in teaching for some time. Subsequently he accepted a call to the pastorate of the Baptist church in Gardiner, Me., commencing his ministry in August, 1846. Ill health obliged him to resign after a brief period. Upon recovering he resumed his studies at Newton in the fall of 1847, and continued them until he was graduated in the class of 1850. A short time before completing his theological course he was called to Portland to take the editorial charge of *Zion's Advocate*, the organ of the Baptist denomination for the State of Maine. This position he held for eight years. In August, 1858, he was elected to the chair of the Greek and Latin Languages in Waterville College, to take the place of Dr. Champlin, who had been elected to the presidency of the college. In 1872 the department was divided, and since that time Prof. Foster has occupied the chair of Greek Language and Literature.

Foster, Rev. Jos. A., now pastor of the First African church in Montgomery, Ala., though without educational advantages while a slave, has since done much in cultivating his mind. He is regarded at this time as a fine preacher. He was one of the principal agents in originating the colored Convention, of which he was president for three years.

Foster, Rev. Joseph C., was born in Milford, N. H., April 16, 1818. Leaving a printing-office in 1835, he pursued studies preparatory to the ministry at Hamilton, N. Y., and New Hampton, N. H. He was ordained as pastor of the Baptist church in Brattleborough, Vt., Jan. 19, 1843. He closed his pastorate there July 1, 1856, after nearly fourteen years of service. He was elected pastor of the First Baptist church in Beverly, Mass., Aug. 7, 1856. This pastorate continued until Dec. 25, 1872, embracing more than sixteen years. Immediately entering upon the pastorate of the First Baptist church in Randolph, Mass., he was installed Jan. 23, 1873. During his ministry of thirty-six years he has baptized hundreds, and seen much development of the churches with which he has been connected, in various kinds of efficiency, including benevolent contributions and extensive improvement of church property. In two instances superior houses for worship have been built under his administration. He has been actively engaged in educational and denominational work, having served on school committees nearly thirty successive years, and held responsible positions on various boards of benevolent societies, especially in secretarial and financial service. Some of his publications have had extensive circulation, one of which, a tract on baptism and communion, has been in great demand. He has written much for the periodical press.

Foster, Prof. Joshua H., D.D., was born in Tuscaloosa Co., Ala., March 17, 1819, and has resided in that county to this date. After such advantages as could be had in the best country schools he graduated at the head of his class in the University of Alabama in 1839; was ordained as pastor of the Tuscaloosa church in 1853, Rev. B. Manly, Sr., Rev. T. F. Curtis, Rev. J. C. Foster, and Rev. R. Jones being the Presbytery; elected to a professorship in the university in 1841, when twenty-one years old; after three years, associated with Rev. E. B. Teague in a male high school in Tuscaloosa; re-elected to his former position in the faculty of the university in 1849, but soon withdrew in ill health; was several times offered positions in the faculty, which he declined, until in 1873 he accepted the professorship of Moral Science, and in 1874 that of Natural Philosophy and Astronomy, and filled both chairs for three years. He is still an honored member of the faculty of the State University; was for some years president of the Alabama Central Female College in Tuscaloosa. During his long career as a college professor he has been the useful pastor of neighboring country and village churches. Dr. Foster is profoundly intellectual, eminently learned, distinguished as a teacher, a sincere Christian, and a wise counselor among his brethren. The title of D.D. was conferred on him by Howard College in 1879.

Foster, Rev. L. S., Mississippi editor of the *Western Recorder*, of Louisville, Ky., was born in Alabama in 1847; educated in the University of Alabama; was baptized by Elder T. G. Sellers, in 1865, at Starksville, Miss., and began to preach in 1867; spent two sessions at the Southern Baptist Theological Seminary, and then spent two years preaching in Mississippi and Tennessee, when he returned to the seminary, where he graduated in 1875; has filled the pastorate at Okalona, Miss., and Camden, S. C., and was principal of Starksville Male Academy. As a writer he has contributed a number of valuable articles to the *Recorder*, and has also published an able sermon on "Truth Developed by Conflict."

Foster, Michael, M.D., of Huntingdon, England, an eminent physician of that district, was a member of the ancient Baptist family of the Fosters of Preston, near Hitchin, in whose house John Bunyan often found an asylum, and where the "Baptist bishop" preached sometimes at midnight in the times of persecution. Dr. Foster was a man of rare qualities, welcome and influential for good in every circle. When he settled in Huntingdon, in 1834, the Non-Conformist cause was almost extinct, but, notwithstanding obloquy, he followed the dictates of his conscience, and soon won his way to social eminence. For many years he took a leading part in promoting the evangelization of neglected districts, being welcomed as an acceptable preacher, and loved and trusted by all classes. His interest in the Baptist Missionary Society was intense. He served for many years on the Executive Committee, and endeared himself to missionaries and their families by his generous hospitalities and practical sympathy. In 1868 he was elected to the mayoralty of Huntingdon, being the first Non-Conformist since the days of Cromwell to occupy that position. As a deacon for forty-eight years his services were of the highest order, for he was one of the foremost in every onward movement of the denomination, and conspicuous for the saintliness of his character in a very wide circle. He died Jan. 7, 1880, aged sixty-nine years.

Foster, Rev. Nathaniel Greene, of Madison, was born July 25, 1809, in Greene Co., Ga. He had excellent instructors in youth, and in 1828 entered the State University at Athens, graduating in 1830. He studied law under his uncle, Seaborn Johnson, in Madison, and soon entered upon its practice. Converted in 1848, he united with the Madison church, and on the 10th of August of the same year he was licensed. On the 27th of January, 1849, he was ordained by the following brethren, who composed the Presbytery: B. M. Sanders, Jno. L. Dagg, V. R. Thornton, S. G. Hillyer, N. M. Crawford, S. S. Bledsoe, and C. M. Irwin. He soon accepted a call to the First church of Augusta, but resigned at the end of six months, convinced that his life as a lawyer had unfitted him for such a field of duty. He returned to the practice of law, preaching to country churches and serving the Madison church at times. His health began to fail in 1858, and on the 19th of October, 1869, he died. He served his district in Congress one session; was for many years a trustee of Mercer University; and was one of the founders of the Georgia Female College. He was a man of handsome appearance, of fine ability, and of good judgment, and when difficulties arose was always a peace-maker among his brethren.

Fountain, Rev. Ezra, was born in Bedford, Westchester Co., N. Y.; trained on a farm; mingled in the scenes of the Revolution; was converted in early manhood; ordained in 1802; was pastor of the Bedford Baptist church; was instrumental in organizing the Baptist church at Yorktown, and fostered it till his death; was fully up to his times; did very much pioneer work; strong, energetic, and devoted; he died of injuries received from being thrown from a wagon.

Fowler, Rev. T. J., a prominent young preacher in Attala Co., Miss., is a native of Georgia, where he was born in 1849. Having removed to Alabama, he became a Baptist shortly after. He began to preach in 1875, and was ordained the year following. He became pastor of New Bethel, Fayette Co., Ala., where he continued until he removed to Mississippi in 1877. He settled in Pontotoc County, and became pastor of Mount Moriah and Hosea churches in that county. He remained with those churches one year, then removed to Attala County, where he took charge of Providence church, of which he is still pastor, with a prospect of great good.

Fox, Rev. Jehiel, prominent among the pioneer Baptists of Northern New York, was born in 1760, at East Haddam, Conn. He was licensed to preach at Hoosick Falls, N. Y. In 1796 he removed to Chester, in the region of Lake George, which country was then a wilderness. Here a church was organized and he was ordained. At his own charges, Elder Fox traveled and preached throughout the surrounding counties, and under his ministry were organized most of the churches of the Lake George Association. He was a man of piety, energy, and wisdom, and of fine natural gifts. He had a great thirst for knowledge, and gave his children the very best educational advantages the times afforded. He died in 1823. His tombstone bears the quaint inscription, dictated by himself, "Jehiel Fox passes this way from the labors of the field and vineyard to his Master. Lo! Grace gives the triumph."

Fox, Rev. L. L., was born in Louisa Co., Va., in 1814. His grandfather, an officer in the Revolutionary war, was a near relative of Charles J. Fox, of England. He was baptized at sixteen years of age, and then resolving to prepare himself for a life of usefulness, he worked hard through the day and studied books at night. A few years being spent in this way, he then had three years of regular training at school. He was ordained to the ministry by a Presbytery consisting of Revs. James Fife, W. Y. Hyter, T. T. Swift, M. Jones, and Dr. S. B. Webb, and for four years served churches as pastor in his native county; then he was pastor for some years in Culpeper, Madison, and Louisa Counties. In 1846 he removed to Alabama, and located in Uniontown, where he remained as pastor until the close of the year 1865. 1866-67 he devoted to the religious interests of the colored people under appointment of the Home Mission Society, and would have continued this longer had not his flocks preferred men of their own color. From that time to this he has served churches in Marengo County. He has been moderator of the Bethel Association for fifteen years, and was previously moderator of the Cahaba. He has baptized about 1000 persons in his life. Mr. Fox is a cultivated man, an excellent preacher, and the most influential Baptist in his part of the State. He has a delightful family.

Fox, Rev. Norman, was sent by his father to Granville Academy, in those days one of the most prominent schools in Northern New York. In 1813 he entered Union College. Admitted to the bar, he was made judge of Warren County, and he was for several years a prominent member of the State Legislature. He was also extensively engaged in commercial affairs. Having been converted about this period, he began to address religious meetings. At his last election to the Legislature, the opposition members contested his eligibility to a seat on the ground that he was a clergyman, which class at that day were ineligible, but as he had been neither licensed nor ordained, the movement was unsuccessful. Soon after this he gave up secular pursuits entirely, and devoted himself to the work of the ministry alone. He preached at Kingsbury and other towns in Washington County, and was for twelve years pastor of the church at Ballston Spa. He stood aloof from politics after entering the ministry, declining even to vote. Remarkably able as a preacher, he was even more so as a private citizen. Few men have in their day commanded such profound respect from all classes of society. He died in 1863, aged seventy-one.

Among his sons the following have become prominent as influential Baptists: Alanson Fox, of Steuben Co., N. Y., a prominent business man and a member of the boards of management of several of our denominational corporations; also Prof. Norman Fox, of New York City.

Fox, Prof. Norman, son of the Rev. Norman Fox, a distinguished Baptist minister of New York,

PROF. NORMAN FOX.

who died in 1863, and grandson of Rev. Jehiel Fox, another honored minister of our denomination. Norman Fox received his literary education at Rochester University, and his theological training at its well-known seminary. He was ordained at Whitehall, N. Y. Afterwards he was associate editor of the *Central Baptist*, St. Louis, Mo. Subsequently he was Professor of History in William Jewell College, Mo. At present he resides in New York, and he devotes himself chiefly to denominational literature, writing for many religious journals.

Prof. Fox has read very extensively; his attainments in this respect are great. He has a mind of unusual clearness and power. He has the happy faculty of using the most fitting words to express important thoughts. He has a large heart. With the grace of God which he possesses he is a mighty power in the Baptist denomination, the force of which we trust will be long spared to us. Those who know him only by his writings, or by personal relations, admire and love him.

France, American Baptist Mission to.—The Triennial Convention projected a mission to France in 1832. The board sent out Prof. Ira Chase, of Newton Theological Institute, to explore the field, and M. Rostan, a native Frenchman, to make trial of mission work in Paris. A year later M. Rostan died of cholera. Rev. Isaac M. Willmarth, who had previously spent the greater part of a year in Paris, was appointed to take charge of the mission, and to instruct young men for the ministry, and he with his wife arrived on the ground in June, 1834. The design of the mission was to revive and strengthen the few small Baptist churches long in existence, to raise up an educated French ministry, and to diffuse the pure gospel in the nation. From French Protestants coldness and opposition were experienced. A chapel was opened, and services in French and English were maintained. M. Porchat was employed as a French preacher, but after a little he withdrew from the service. J. B. Crétin was the first student for the ministry. In 1835, Mr. Willmarth, in company with Prof. Barnas Sears, visited the churches in the Department du Nord, and they were welcomed everywhere. Two other students were received. An evangelist, M. Dusart, was ordained at Paris. In November, Revs. Erastus Willard and D. N. Sheldon joined the mission,—the latter to labor in Paris, the former with Mr. Willmarth to locate at Douay, in the North, to instruct students for the ministry. The missionaries ordained J. Thieffrey, at Lannoy. Religious services were sustained at Douay and Paris. There were four students, two pastors, and three colporteurs. A church was constituted at Genlis, and J. B. Crétin ordained pastor.

Mr. Willmarth by ill health was forced to leave the mission in 1837. In 1838 a church was constituted at Douay, and strict regulations introduced into the other churches. In 1839, Mr. Sheldon removed to Douay to aid Mr. Willard, but six months later resigned. In 1840 the whole number of Baptists was 180, and there were 33 baptisms during the year. Mr. Willard, now left entirely alone, had his hands and his mind fully occupied with the care of the churches and the instruction of his pupils. It was necessary for him to visit the different stations, to correct abuses and teach the principles of church order; but he bent his main energies to the training of young men for the ministry. "He was persuaded that the people could be more effectually reached by Frenchmen than by foreigners; but he was equally sure that they must be converted and trained, must understand the Scriptures and themselves, and have some acquaintance with the various forms of error with which they would have to contend. To prepare a body of men, able in the Word of God, and strong against the subtle influences of error, he bent" all the powers of his strong and energetic mind. "And God gave him some young men of rare promise, of genuine eloquence and power, who have since done," and are still doing, "noble service for the Master."* He thoroughly indoctrinated the students and the churches in the strict principles of American Baptists, and thus laid a solid foundation for the growth of Baptist churches in France. He watched with anxious care the conduct of his assistants, in its relation to an oppressive government, restraining the fiery zeal of those who would court a conflict with the civil power, and keeping all operations as far as possible within the limits of the law. To his faithful training and judicious care of the students and the churches, during more than twenty years, carrying forward under great difficulties the work begun by Mr. Willmarth, the French mission owes most of its subsequent success and present hopeful prospects. This was his great life-work, and will be an enduring monument to his memory.

In 1844, on the death of his wife, Mr. Willard visited America, still guiding the mission by correspondence through M. Foulbœuf, and after his lamented death through M. Thieffrey. On his return, in 1846, persecutions were rife all over the field. Some of the brethren were fined, others were imprisoned. Lepoids, Foulon, and Besin appealed to the highest court in the realm, and were defended by eminent French counsel, but before a decision was rendered Louis Philippe, the "citizen king," was driven from France by the revolution of 1848. The year was nevertheless prosperous. The number baptized was double that of any preceding year.

The revolution gave a respite to our persecuted brethren. The chapel at Genlis, which, as soon as built, was closed by government, and remained shut eleven years, was opened. Dr. Devan began work in Paris in 1848. A year later he repaired to Lyons, where he labored in the Southern Department of the mission till 1853, when he left the country. There were then 9 churches and 172 members in the South. In 1849 the first Association was formed at Verberie. From this period to 1856, Mr. Willard, again in charge of the whole work, resided in Paris, teaching the students, counseling and encouraging the pastors in the midst of persecutions and sufferings. Worn out with cares and anxieties, he then decided to return home, requesting the board to send some competent man to fill his place. To escape persecution numbers of the French brethren emigrated to the United States. The field having become too much enlarged for efficient supervision, the Southern Department was relinquished temporarily, and the number of stations reduced to 6, with a membership of 281. Around these stations meetings were held in many localities. The churches were animated with a spirit of piety and missionary zeal. Prayer-meetings were maintained in Paris almost every evening. There was an awakening among the soldiers in the garrison, and many Roman Catholics who had heard the gospel were visited on their death-beds and found rejoicing in Christ as their Saviour. "For this reason," says one of the pastors, "I believe that eternity alone will reveal the good which has been done to thousands who, during the last thirty years, have heard the Word of life from your missionaries."

Thus the work went on from year to year with alternations of successes and reverses. In 1866 the chapel at Chauny, which had been closed fourteen years, was re-opened with rejoicing, by decree of government. In 1870–71 all the operations of the mission were deranged by the Franco-Prussian war. Many young men from the churches were called into military service. The church in Paris lost nineteen members during the war, and a large number during the dreadful siege and the terrors of the Commune in 1871. The brethren carried forward their work as far as practicable, visited the soldiers, and circulated tracts among them, but war and its horrors absorbed the attention of the people, and little could be done except in spiritual efforts for the soldiers, the wounded, and the dying. After the war the churches slowly recovered from the evils it had caused, and as for a season there was entire religious freedom, the laborers were greatly encouraged, and with renewed zeal sowed the good seed among the people.

At the present date there are eight stations and numerous out-stations. The churches are sound in faith and strict in discipline, with a membership of about 760. Though generally poor they give largely according to their means, and since the mission was commenced have raised for the work and for benevolence $10,000 or $12,000. The pastors and evangelists are faithful and devoted men. Crétin, Mr. Willmarth's first student, still, at the age of sixty-four, pursues his work with ardor. The veteran Thieffrey still holds his post at Lannoy. The church in Paris has a large and beautiful chapel, and intends to keep a yearly feast on the 14th of September to celebrate its dedication, which occurred at that date in 1873. Our cause has gained greatly in public estimation, and is now treated with respect by other denominations and by public journals. Our pastors are invited to participate in ministerial conferences, and to explain their views of baptism and the communion. Our mission has given rise to discussions on these topics all over the country, and as a consequence, infant baptism is losing its hold on the Protestants of France. Several of the pastors have been baptized themselves and have baptized a large portion of

---

* C. E. Barrows, Commemorative Discourse on the Life and Character of Mr. Willard.

their flocks, and some of them have decided to admit in future, members to their churches only by baptism. Thus, since the mission was commenced in 1834, great progress has been made in Scriptural views of the ordinances. About 1200 have been baptized. The board has expended on the work probably over $400,000. The prospect for the future is encouraging. With a theological school at Paris now in operation, we shall be able to raise up useful pastors to succeed those devoted men now in the field. *This is indispensable.*

The time is propitious. Republicanism is in the ascendency; the enlightened classes are tired of the domination of the priesthood, and turn to Protestantism as the only force able to cope with the wily Jesuitism of the papacy. It seems the favorable moment for vigorous effort that France, one of the most influential of nations, may be wrested from the dominion of Rome; and being herself evangelized may become a centre of light for the world.

Francis, Rev. Benjamin, took charge of the church at Shortwood, England, in October, 1758. Under his unwearied labors the community became so numerous that it was necessary to enlarge the meeting-house before he was two years the shepherd of Shortwood. He preached regularly in four surrounding villages, in some of which chapels were built through his instrumentality; and he soon was summoned to minister in distant places, for his popularity increased with his years, so that before his death he was known throughout all the British Baptist churches as one of their ablest ministers. "His usefulness was so great, his talents so admired, and his character so revered that he shed a lustre over the denomination to which he belonged." He died Dec. 14, 1799. Mr. Francis was the author of some beautiful hymns. The following stanza is his, and the hymn to which it belongs:

> "My gracious Redeemer I love!
> His praises aloud I'll proclaim,
> And join with the armies above
> To shout his adorable name;
> To gaze on his glories divine
> Shall be my eternal employ,
> And feel them incessantly shine
> My boundless ineffable joy."

Franklin College, Indiana.—At the close of the first meeting of what is now called the Indiana Baptist State Convention, held in October, 1833, at Brandywine, Shelby Co., the friends of education met in conference and took steps looking to the establishment of an institution of learning. June 5, 1834, a meeting was held at Indianapolis for the purpose of forming an education society. Rev. Wm. Reese was elected chairman, and Rev. Ezra Fisher clerk. The following names were enrolled: William Reese, Ezra Fisher, Henry Bradley, John Hobart, Samuel Harding, Lewis Morgan, J. V. A. Woods, Eliphalet Williams, John L. Richmond, Nathaniel Richmond, John McCoy, John Mason, Moses Jeffries, and Reuben Coffey. Committees were appointed to call the attention of the brethren of the State, by means of correspondence and newspaper articles, and Jan. 14, 1835, was appointed as the time at which the formal organization of the Education Society should be effected. The immediate control of the institution was to be in the hands of a board of trustees elected by the society, it was to be on the "manual labor" plan, and it was by unanimous choice located at Franklin.

It was for years a "Manual Labor Institute" in fact as well as in name. In the language of Rev. T. C. Townsend, once agent for the institution, "I have known young men tie up their clothes in a handkerchief, walk through the mud one hundred miles, and when they reached the college they would borrow of President Chandler one dollar and twenty-five cents to buy them an axe, and work their way to an education. These boys are now the men that tell upon the interests of society throughout the West."

The first building was a frame, 26 by 38 feet, one story. It was used for chapel, recitations, and on Sundays for church service. It was built in 1836. In 1844 a three-story brick, 42 by 84 feet, was put up. In 1854 another brick, the copy of the first, was erected. The campus contains about twelve acres.

The first principal was Rev. A. T. Tilton, a man of large heart, great energy, and good taste. He was succeeded by Hon. W. J. Robinson, who conducted the school somewhat more than one year. In 1844, Rev. G. C. Chandler, pastor of the First church, Indianapolis, was called to the presidency, and the name was changed to Franklin College. He was a man of vast energy and great faith, and served the college zealously for eight years. The most that he and the professors could do barely enabled the board to meet current expenses. The work of instruction, however, went on, and the State was reaping the beneficial results.

The only respectable effort for endowment was made during the last years of Dr. Chandler's presidency. The plan was to raise $60,000; $10,000 was to be expended in canceling debts and meeting incidental expenses, the remainder was to be invested as a permanent fund. And the plan partially succeeded. The amount was subscribed. Unfortunately for the cause of education in the State, scholarships were issued as a reward to those who had made the subscriptions; hence while income as *interest* was assured, income as *tuition fees* was defeated. Almost every student in those days used a scholarship.

In the mean time Dr. Chandler resigned, and

Dr. Silas Bailey, late president of Granville College, was called to the presidency. He gathered about him an able faculty, and all would have gone well if the $60,000 had been collected, but it was not. The president labored with fidelity and marked ability till failing health compelled him to resign, and the war took the young men away from the pursuit of learning to the dangers and duties of the battle-field.

There was a suspension from 1864 to 1869. In 1869 the board again opened the institution. Rev. W. T. Stott was appointed acting president. In 1870, Rev. H. L. Wayland, D.D., was elected president. The endowment was small, the expenses rapidly outran the income, and in 1872 there was another suspension; the property of the college was taken for the debts and the organization dissolved. Immediately the citizens of Johnson County and other friends of the college proposed another kind of organization,—a joint-stock association,—over $50,000 was raised, and in the fall of 1872 instruction was begun, with Rev. W. T. Stott, D.D., as president.

The institution being now on a better financial foundation has bright hopes. Up to this time nearly $100,000 has been raised in cash, cash subscriptions, and real estate. The following is the treasurer's statement: Buildings, grounds, and equipments, $40,000; production endowment, $60,531; real estate, $10,652; beneficiary fund, $1250; Centennial Hall fund, $471; total, $112,904.

Of those giving the larger amounts, James Forsythe, Grafton Johnson, and William Lowe gave each $5000, in cash; Elbert Slink and J. L. Allen gave $5000 each, part cash and part in real estate. There are seven instructors, including the two teachers in painting and music. Another tutor will probably be added this year. Both sexes have had the advantages of the college since 1869. The standard of scholarship has been decidedly advanced. Rev. W. N. Wyeth is at present the financial agent.

The best men of the State have during all these years worked and prayed for the college; many of them died without seeing it in a prosperous state, but their prayers are being answered. Over 2000 young men and young women have been under the instruction of the college, and are now out in this and other States. An era of solid prosperity is at last dawning for Franklin College. Jubilee year will be celebrated in 1884.

Frear, George, D.D., son of the Rev. William Frear, was born in Eaton, Wyoming Co., Pa., June 21, 1831, and united with the Eaton church in February, 1849. He graduated from the University at Lewisburg in 1856, and from the theological department, before its removal to Upland, Delaware Co., Pa., in 1858. He was ordained in Reading in 1858.

FRANKLIN COLLEGE, INDIANA.

His first pastorate in the city of Reading was eminently profitable to both church and congregation. After several years of labor he resigned, and accepted the call of the Norristown Baptist church, and after two years of service, during which a handsome church was built, he was summoned to take the very important position he now holds, as pastor of the Lewisburg church, under the shadow of the university where he received his training for the work of the ministry.

Freeman, The, the oldest weekly newspaper of the English Baptists, was started in January, 1855, and has therefore had a continuous existence of more than a quarter of a century. Its beginning was due to the zeal of a few earnest Yorkshire and Lancashire Baptists, among whom Benjamin Evans, D.D., Revs. Francis Clowes, W. F. Burchell, Mr. John Heaton, and Mr. William Heaton were prominent in the inception and management of the paper, which was first published at Leeds, Yorkshire. Soon afterwards, having commended itself to the confidence and support of the denomination and won the approval of the Associations, the proprietors transferred the publishing office to London, the editorial department being then in charge of the Rev. F. Clowes, formerly classical tutor at Horton College. From the start the conductors of the paper declared it to be their object to foster an earnest denominational spirit among the Baptists, but proclaimed neutrality on the doctrinal and ecclesiastical differences by which they were divided into Particular and General, and Strict and Open-Communion Baptists. To both aims the paper has been faithful, and although the original proprietors are now merged into the Freeman Newspaper Company, it is still favored with the support of Baptists generally. Its price has been gradually lowered from fourpence halfpenny to the present popular price of one penny (two cents a week). It is understood to be under the direction of an editorial junto, of which Joseph Angus, D.D., president of Regent's Park College, is chief. For several years the late Rev. Edward Leach, who died April, 1880, was the laborious and faithful sub-editor. *The Freeman* may be obtained from the publishers, Yates & Alexander, 21 Castle Street, Holborn, London.

Freeman, Rev. Allen B., was born in New York in 1808, and converted at the age of about twelve years. He seems to have been licensed to preach by a church in Ohio, but returning to New York in 1827 or 1828, entered at the Hamilton Literary and Theological Institution, graduating in 1833, being ordained at Hamilton, with two or three others, immediately after his graduation. Having been offered an appointment as missionary of the American Baptist Home Mission Society, to be stationed at Chicago, he accepted, and proceeded immediately to his field of labor. His brief but active and useful ministry was not confined to Chicago. Previous to the organization of what is now the First Baptist church of that city, he had already formed one at the place now called Hadley. The first baptism in Lake Michigan was by him, occurring in April, 1834. A house was soon built at Chicago under his leadership, being adapted both for school and church purposes. At the end of November, 1834, Mr. Freeman went to Bristol to organize a church there, baptizing on the occasion, in Fox River, a young man afterwards a useful Illinois missionary and pastor, Rev. D. Matlock. His horse failing upon the return, the exposure of a long journey on foot brought on a fever, of which he died Dec. 15, 1834, greatly lamented. His name and memory are most affectionately cherished in Chicago and Northern Illinois.

Freeman, Joseph, D.D., was born in Colerain, Mass., Sept. 1, 1802. He pursued his education in Bethany College, and studied one year at Newton. He was ordained at Ludlow, Vt., June 11, 1826, where he was pastor for some time, as also in Concord, N. H. He was pastor of the church in Cavendish, Vt., four years; at Saxton's River four years; at Newport, N. H., three years. His other settlements were at New Hampton, N. H., again for a short time at Cavendish, Vt., Ballston Spa, N. Y., and Vergennes, Vt. His labors were owned of God to the joy of many souls.

Freeman, Rev. J. T., a prominent Baptist minister in Mississippi, and president of the Mississippi Baptist Convention, was born in Virginia in 1822; educated in Randolph Macon College, Va., and in Tennessee State Agricultural College; settled in Mississippi in 1846, and commenced the publication of a political paper; not long afterwards was converted and began to preach; in 1854–55 was pastor at Clinton, Miss. In 1857 was elected president of the State Convention, and appointed editor of the *Mississippi Baptist*, published at Jackson, until the war, during which he was pastor at Lexington and Durant; in 1865 removed to Corinth, where he was pastor nine years; is at present pastor at Starkville and West Point.

Freeman, Rev. Ralph, was born a slave in Anson Co., N. C. Showing fine gifts as a preacher, his white brethren bought his freedom, ordained him, and sent him forth to preach the gospel, which he did with great power in several counties. He was reckoned so good a preacher that he was often called on to attend the funeral services of white persons, and on several occasions was appointed to preach on the Sabbath at Associations. Rev. James Magee was his warm friend, and traveled and preached much with him. Such was their attachment for each other that they agreed that the survivor should preach the funeral sermon of the one who died first. Mr. Magee moved to the West and died first. On his death-bed he bequeathed to his colored brother his riding-horse, overcoat, Bible and fifty dollars, and requested his family to send for Mr. Freeman to attend his funeral. He went to Tennessee and buried Mr. Magee, and the large congregation which he addressed made him a present of fifty dollars. He lived to a good old age and died respected by all.

Freeman, Judge Thomas J., was born in Gibson Co., Tenn., four miles south of Trenton, the county-seat, July 19, 1827. In youth he had a ready memory, a great love for books, and he read extensively. At fifteen years of age he made a profession of religion, and joined Spring Hill Baptist church. He then commenced reading all kinds of theological works that came in his way, old books such as his father's library afforded, or could be had from neighbors. He read "Wesley on Original Sin," doctrinal tracts, "Fuller's Reply to Priestley," and other works of their character. When a young man, he was once reading in "Blair's Rhetoric" the chapter on "Eloquence of the Pulpit, Bar, and Forum," and his destiny was fixed. He decided to be a lawyer. This was in his seventeenth year. In March, before he was eighteen, he commenced the study of law. He followed this pursuit at home in the country, sometimes by the light of a splint-wood fire. While doing so he occasionally taught school. In January, 1848, he went to Trenton, and studied in the office of Mr. Raines. At twenty-one years of age he was licensed by Judge Calvin Jones, chancellor of his district, and Hon. W. B. Turly, one of the judges of the Supreme Court, and he opened an office at Trenton, with faint prospects of success. He studied closely, and read, he supposes, nearly every standard author in the language. His special taste, however, has been for metaphysical study and philosophic theology, the science, so to speak, of religion. He believes in the gospel of Jesus, and does not hesitate to avow it. At twenty-five years of age he ran against Mr. Etheridge for Congress, and greatly reduced his majority.

As a lawyer Judge Freeman stood very high. Under the new constitution, in 1870, he was elected judge of the Supreme Court, and after his first term he was re-elected, and he still holds this position with great honor and ability. In protracted meetings he is very efficient, leading in prayers and exhortations, and giving instructions and spiritual advice to inquirers. He is now, and has been for a number of years, an active member of the Trenton church, of which Rev. Dr. M. Hillsman is the pastor.

Free Mission Society, American Baptist.— This organization was an outgrowth of the more radical anti-slavery feeling among Baptists in the United States and their missionaries in Burmah.

In 1840, a convention of earnest men formed in New York a "Foreign Provisional Missionary Committee," which continued until May, 1843, when they took a wider range at a meeting held in Tremont Temple, Boston. They had sought to procure two changes in the organization now known as the "American Baptist Missionary Union." One was a pronounced severance from all slavery influence, and the other was a more strict recognition of church representation and control in the work of missions. They failed to gain either point. Seventeen of the number withdrew, and after earnest prayer signed the following declaration, drawn up by William Henry Brisbane, who had previously manumitted a large number of slaves inherited by him in South Carolina:

"We, whose names are undersigned, solemnly pledge ourselves to God and one another to unite in the support of a Baptist Missionary Society, with a constitution yet to be adopted, that shall be distinctly and thoroughly separated from all connection with the known avails of slavery in the support of any of its benevolent purposes."

Upon this platform a constitution was adopted and officers chosen. About the same time the Southern Baptists seceded from the national Baptist foreign mission organization, and formed the "Southern Baptist Convention."

The Free-Missionists went on with their work for over twenty-seven years. They established a mission in Hayti, and also in Japan. They sent nine missionaries to Hayti, and they had eleven in Burmah, some of whom had previously been in the service of the Missionary Union; they sent three to Africa, two to Japan, eighteen to the home field west of the Alleghany Mountains, and about thirty to the South, mostly during and shortly after the war.

In some departments of mental and moral progress the managers of the American Baptist Free Mission Society were emphatically pioneers. They aided English Baptists in sustaining the Dawn Institute, in Canada, composed of fugitives from the South. They founded the college at McGrawville, Cortland Co., N. Y., which was opened to students irrespective of color or sex. After the war, they aided in establishing Leland University, at New Orleans, largely endowed by H. Chamberlin and wife, of Brooklyn, N. Y.

The society was served by cultured and forcible writers, as Kazlitt Arvine, Cyrus Pitt Grosvenor, Warham Walker, John Duer, deceased, and Nathan Brown among the living.

While in active operation, the society raised and expended from $3000 to $22,000 per year. Its supporters were found among Baptists wherever the English language was read or spoken.

There were some differences between the Missionary Union and the society as to life-memberships, and also as to the relations between those dispensing the funds in trust and those at work on mission fields. Some preferred one and some the other medium. In the course of time this friction became less, and their relations became measurably adjusted.

The war rendered needless the existence of the society, and at a meeting in Laight Street chapel, New York, May, 1872, it was voted to suspend its operations, except so far as was necessary to execute trusts and perpetuate legacies. The Hayti mission was transferred to the "Consolidated Baptist Missionary Convention," and the Japan mission to the Union, which also cared for the Burman field.

The last president of the society, Albert L. Post, visited Great Britain in its behalf in 1865-66, and is commissioned to prepare its memorial volume, to which, when issued, the reader is referred for a more complete record. Most of its members were among the foremost promoters of temperance; they opposed secret societies, and the use of such titles as "Rev.," ' D.D.," etc., among Christian brethren; and they advocated higher recognitions of woman's work and wages. But these were rather incidental and personal matters, not included in the original definition of the specific object of the society.

Free-Will.—*Man is perfectly free to sin.* This statement is undeniable. When he becomes a drunkard it is to please himself; and when he is covetous to meanness, or dishonesty, when he is guilty of licentious acts, when he provokes God by his blasphemies, and when with wicked hands he slays his neighbor, he commits these crimes to gratify himself. And the same doctrine is true with reference to all his transgressions. No man on trial in court would venture to urge, as an excuse for his criminal acts, that he was compelled to commit them, unless indeed physical force was used; and if he offered such a plea every judge and jury in the world would regard this false pretense as an aggravation of his guilt. Satan can only tempt men to sin, he cannot coerce them to commit it. He possesses a great intellect, vast experience, unwearied perseverance, and hosts of agents; nevertheless, if men resist the devil he will flee from them. Every man's consciousness tells him that he sins because of his own personal wishes, and not because of outside force. Haman planned to murder Mordecai, not for Satan's pleasure but his own; Ananias and his wife kept back part of the price, not to gratify the prince of darkness, but to satisfy their own covetous hearts. The testimony of human consciousness proves that men sin because they themselves resolve upon it. And if we cannot believe our consciousness upon this question we cannot believe it about anything. We must reject its utterances when it tells us that we are living, or walking, or speaking, or working. To reject the evidence of our consciousness about our sins coming solely from ourselves, would compel us to discard belief in all our experiences. Either then our sins are our own, or we can believe nothing, and our consciousness is but a constant instrument of deception. From the fall of our first parents in Eden down to the last record of guilt in the Scriptures, God invariably assumes the responsibility of men for their sins; and in a great many instances he asserts it; and this responsibility rests upon their freedom to sin.

Man has lost his liberty to serve God. Paul says, Eph. ii. 1, "You hath he quickened who were *dead* in trespasses and sins." The death of which he speaks is a moral death; it represents men without Christ as destitute of all power to turn to Jesus. When a man is "dead drunk" he cannot reason, he cannot walk, he is stupid and helpless. So the unsaved are under the curse of sinful intoxication, and they are dead to all the claims of God, and to all the charms of a loving Saviour; and left to themselves, they would never seek or find salvation. The Saviour says, John vi. 44, "No man can come to me, except the Father who hath sent me draw him." There is a lack of moral ability in every human heart to come to Jesus till the drawings of grace lift the man from his helplessness and slavery and place him at the feet of Jesus. The impenitent man might be compared to Samson when his hair was shorn; the great Israelite was robbed of his eyes, thrust into prison, bound with fetters of brass, and he did grind in the prison: and the only power he had was to inflict death; for when the Philistines were feasting in the temple of Dagon, Samson seized two of the pillars and the house fell, killing himself and three thousand of his enemies. The unregenerate man has lost his moral eyesight, he is in the prison of unbelief, he is chained by sinful habits, he is grinding this world's grist, and he has only strength to destroy his own soul and the souls of others. The Philadelphia Confession of Faith, in Article IX., says truly, "Man in a state of innocency had freedom and power, to will and to do that which was good, and well pleasing to God. . . . Man by his fall into a state of sin hath wholly lost all his ability of will, to any spiritual good accompanying salvation, so as a natural man, being altogether averse from that good, and dead in sin, is not able by his own strength to convert himself, or to prepare himself thereunto."

The *palsied will of an unsaved man is made free* to serve God by the Holy Spirit. When the Comforter smote the heart of persecuting Saul his opposition to Christ instantly perished, and his earnest cry was, "Lord, what wilt thou have me to do?" An iron paralysis held the will of Paul in its resistless power, so that he was approvingly helpless to exercise any faculty of his soul for God until the Comforter made his heart the temple of Jehovah, and began to "work in him both *to will* and to do of his good pleasure." It is through this blessed working that God's "people are willing in the day of his power" to render obedience or to make painful sacrifices. The will of man, so free to sin, so powerless to decide for Christ's service, is strengthened and sanctified by the Spirit in conversion, and receives his assistance ever afterwards to steadfastly steer the soul for a heavenly port.

Men are conscious that they are free to sin, and when they are brought into the liberty wherewith Christ makes his people free, they are conscious that God's Spirit has given them deliverance from the bondage of unbelief, and they are conscious that their renewed hearts willingly love and serve the Saviour.

Free-Will Baptists, or (as some of them choose to be called) Free Baptists, are found chiefly in the northern portion of our country, particularly in New England, and extend into the British provinces. They now (1880) count 77,641 members, 1446 churches, 1280 ordained ministers, 162 licensed preachers, 2 colleges with theological departments, and 6 lesser schools. They have a weekly paper, *The Morning Star*, and a book-publishing house.

The denomination originated in 1780. Its founder was Benjamin Randall, of New Castle, afterwards of New Dunham, N. H., who was converted under Whitefield, and who at first united with "the standing order,"—Congregationalists,—then with the regular Baptists, till disfellowshipped for rejecting certain Calvinistic sentiments. He finally, June 28, 1780, organized the church at New Dunham. The denomination began with the simple name of Baptists, soon derisively styled "Free-Willers," but they shortly adopted the name Free-Will Baptists, as this best designated their marked peculiarity. They are Trinitarian, Arminian, evangelical; holding to immersion but practising open communion; in church government independent,—that is, strictly congregational; yet, for advice and helpfulness, having quarterly meetings of churches, yearly meetings of quarterly meetings, and a General or Triennial Conference of yearly meetings. They emphasize a free salvation and the freedom of the will, and reject the doctrine of the final perseverance of the saints.

From the New Dunham church, as a mother, their churches have sprung, though they have received additions from other quarters; notably from the Free-Communion Baptists of Central New York, who joined *en masse* in 1841; from the declining Six-Principle Baptists of Rhode Island; and from some churches once styled New Lights, or Separatists. Recently accessions have been received from churches at the South and West holding similar views. The early preachers were not as a rule educated men, but a great change has taken place in this particular. The leading ministers, now deceased, have been Benjamin Randall, John Burrell, John Colby, Daniel Marks, Martin Cheney, Elias Hutchins, Ebenezer Knowlton, George T. Day. Meanwhile gifted women have received recognition in the pulpit.

The General Conference was formed in 1827. The Free-Will Baptist Foreign Mission Society was organized in 1833, and has a vigorous mission in India, to which Rev. Jeremiah Phillips devoted his life (dying in 1879), and now reporting six stations and a training-school for native preachers. In 1834 was formed their Home Mission Society, in which the leader has been the venerable Rev. Silas Curtis, of Concord, N. H., and this society has done efficient work among the colored people of the South. An Education Society was organized in 1840, and has happily fostered learning in the denomination, so that it now claims Hillsdale College, Mich., and Bates College, Me., with theological schools attached; also schools at Pittsfield, Me., New Hampton, N. H., Rio Grande, O., Ridgeville, Ind., Milton Junction, Iowa, and Stover Normal School, at Harper's Ferry, W. Va., for colored students. Their periodical, *The Morning Star*, was started in 1826, published at Dover, N. H. William Burr was its originator, and for many years its able editor. It is issued by the publishing house of the denomination and managed by a board of thirteen corporators. Rev. J. M. Brewster, of Providence, R. I., is the author of the "History of the Free Baptists of Rhode Island and Vicinity," in an address delivered May 19, 1880, and published in the Centennial Minutes; also of the "History of the Missions of the Free-Will Baptists," published during their centennial year. The author is now one of the leading ministers and writers of the denomination, and to him we are indebted for the material of this sketch. The "History of the Free-Will Baptists for First Half-Century" was written by Rev. J. D. Stewart, and published in 1861. A volume entitled "Christian Theology," giving views from the denominational stand-point, was issued by Rev. John J. Butler in 1862.

French, George R., in his seventy-ninth year, but still active and useful, was born in Fall River, Mass., Jan. 24, 1802; lived in Darien, Ga., in 1819, and settled in Wilmington, N. C., in 1822; was baptized in 1827 by Rev. James McDaniel; was the leading spirit in building the first Baptist meeting-house of Wilmington, and next to Rev. John L. Prichard, is entitled to the largest measure of credit in the erection of the present edifice, very much the handsomest church edifice in the State. Mr. French is a very successful business man; has been director and president of the Bank of Wilmington, director in the Bank of Cape Fear, in Wilmington Gas Company, and other corporations. For many years he has been a trustee of Wake Forest College, and one of the vice-presidents of the American Sunday-School Union.

French, Rev. James, was born April 1, 1815, at North Hampton, N. H.; son of Rev. Jonathan French, D.D., Congregational minister in that town over fifty years, and grandson of Rev. Jonathan French, of Andover, Mass. He is a descendant in the eighth generation from John Alden and Priscilla Mullens of "Mayflower" fame. His mother was Rebecca Farrar, the only sister of Prof. John Farrar, of Harvard University. He went West as a teacher in 1835, became a Baptist from conviction while preparing for the ministry in the Presbyterian Church, was baptized by Rev. John L. Moore at Springfield, O., and ordained at Lima, O. He labored as missionary of the American Baptist Home Mission Society in Ohio and Indiana, then returned to New England, and was settled as pastor at Exeter, N. H., and afterwards at Holyoke, Mass., in which last-mentioned place the first Baptist house of worship was built during his pastorate. He has since for nearly twenty-five years been connected with the Baptist denominational mission societies in the capacity of financial agent or district secretary. During the last ten years he has labored more as superintendent of our Baptist missions on the frontier, with a field a portion of his time extending from the Mississippi River to the

REV. JAMES FRENCH.

Pacific Ocean. In connection with this work he had charge of a valuable tract of land known as the "Potter legacy," in and around Denver, from which he realized during the last year of his labors West, for both our Foreign and Home Mission Societies, some $45,000. He was called to superintend the Philadelphia Baptist City Mission, which call he accepted, and entered upon his new missionary work in Philadelphia on the 1st of August, 1880.

French, Judge Richard, a distinguished lawyer and statesman, was born in Madison Co., Ky., June 23, 1792. He was the son of James French, a prominent citizen among the first settlers of Kentucky. Richard French was educated at Mount Sterling, Montgomery Co., Ky. At an early age he established himself in the practice of law at Winchester. In 1820 he was a member of the Legislature, and again in 1822. In 1828 he was appointed circuit judge of his district, and served in that capacity till 1835, when he resigned, and was elected to a seat in Congress, where he served three terms. In 1840 he was the unsuccessful candidate for governor. After this he served two terms in Congress. In 1850 he removed to Covington, and engaged in the practice of medicine, but his health failing soon afterwards, he moved to the country, where he died, in Kenton Co., Ky., May 1, 1854.

Judge French was a man of great purity and integrity. He united with a Baptist church near his residence, and was baptized in 1847, by his early law partner, the distinguished Dr. Dillard. He left three sons, who are members of Baptist churches, two of whom are prominent lawyers in Winchester, and have served as judges of the County Court.

Frey, Rev. James, Sr., was born in Mifflin Co., Pa., Jan. 10, 1793. In 1822 he removed to Ohio. He was baptized in May, 1823. He was ordained to the work of the ministry by the Beulah church, in Muskingum Co., O. His field of labor, until 1863, was in Central Ohio, doing principally pioneer work and preaching to feeble churches. In 1863 he removed to Iowa, and settled near Sigourney, where he spent his declining years, preaching, as opportunity opened, until the close of his life. He died Jan. 3, 1880.

Frey, Rev. James, Jr., son of Rev. James Frey, Sr., was born in Clay, Knox Co., O., April 20, 1827. He was baptized in August, 1845. After completing his education he was ordained in the Hopewell church, Muskingum Co., O., in April, 1851. His first pastorate was with the Tomaka church, commencing in April, 1851, and closing in August, 1856. He then came to Iowa and settled in Sigourney. He has been identified with the Baptists of Iowa almost from their first settlement in the State. Few pastors remain in it who were there at the commencement of his ministry. He is still pastor at Sigourney.

Friley, Rev. William C., State evangelist and corresponding secretary of Louisiana Baptist Convention, was born in Mississippi in 1845; graduated at Mississippi College in 1871; was pastor at Yazoo City, Miss., three years; became pastor at Trenton, La., in 1876, and the year following organized a church at Monroe, on the opposite side of Ouachita River. These two churches greatly prospered under his ministry, and they surrendered him reluctantly to his present work. His labors as an evangelist have been eminently successful.

Fristoe, Prof. Edward T., LL.D., son of Joseph and Martha Fristoe, was born in Rappahannock Co., Va., Dec. 16, 1829. He received his early training at a school in the neighborhood, and at the age of seventeen entered the Virginia Military Institute, from which he graduated in 1846 with the highest honors. He was for ten years principal of an academy at Surrey Court-House, Va. In 1852 he entered the University of Virginia, and graduated in all the academic schools in three years, receiving the degree of Master of Arts in 1855. While at the university he excelled especially in mathematics and the natural sciences. During his residence there he was baptized by Dr. J. A. Broadus, and united with the Charlottesville church. In 1855, while yet a student, he was elected to the chair of Mathematics in the Columbian College, Washington, D. C., which position he held with great acceptance until 1860, when he resigned to accept the chair of Mathematics and Astronomy in the State University of Missouri. While there the war broke out, and Prof. Fristoe was offered several high positions in the Confederate provisional army of Missouri, which, however, for the time being he declined. In 1862 he left the university, and was appointed assistant adjutant-general in the Confederate army of South Missouri. In 1863 he was elected major of a battalion, and soon after appointed a colonel of cavalry. In 1864 he joined Gen. Price in his march from the Arkansas to the Missouri River. After the close of the war, in 1865, he was elected to the chair of Chemistry in the Columbian College, which position he still holds. In 1871 he was elected to the chair of Chemistry in the National Medical College of the Columbian University; and in 1872 he was chosen lecturer on Chemistry in the National College of Pharmacy, Washington, D. C. In 1872 he received the degree of LL.D. from William Jewell College, Mo., and in 1874 the degree of Ph.D. (Doctor of Pharmacy) from the National College of Pharmacy. Prof. Fristoe, owing to his pressing labors, has not published anything except a few occasional addresses before different societies. He is an active member of the First Baptist church, Washington, and one of its deacons.

PROF. EDWARD T. FRISTOE, LL.D.

Fristoe, Rev. William, was born in Stafford Co., Va., about the year 1742. He was baptized by the Rev. David Thomas at the age of twenty-one, and being apt to teach, he was soon ordained by the Chapawamsick church, of which he was called to act as pastor, after he had obtained a license from the legal authorities. His labors in the church were very successful, and large numbers were added to its membership. He also traveled extensively through Virginia, and was instrumental in forming several new churches. He attended the Buckmarsh church regularly once a month, although it was seventy miles distant from his home. Besides Chapawamsick, he supplied several churches regularly,—Brentown, Hartwood, Grove, and Rockhill. In 1787 he removed to Shenandoah County, and became pastor of the Broad Run church, in Fauquier County, which position he held until the year before his death. His influence was large among his fellow-ministers, and his practical sagacity and experience made him prominent at all public meetings, and particularly at the Ketockton Association, the first formed in Virginia. Mr. Fristoe was very skillful in discussions, which were often forced upon our pioneer ministers in Virginia, and impressive in preaching. He was thoroughly familiar with the Scriptures, as were all the ministers of that time; his language was plain, strong, and nervous, and his manner solemn, always speaking as one having authority. Some of the most prominent preachers of Virginia acknowledged him as their spiritual father,—Lunsford, Mason, and Hickerson receiving the tidings of peace from his lips. Mr. Fristoe was interested in missions, although the spirit of the times was generally indifferent or hostile to their prosecution, urging collections at different Associations for foreign and domestic missions. In 1809 he published a small work, entitled "The History of the Ketockton Baptist Association," which, in addition to the main object, refers to the history of the denomination throughout Virginia, and especially to the persecutions they suffered, and the sentiments for which they were distinguished. The work contains many interesting facts. He died Aug. 14, 1828, in his eighty-sixth year, having been laboriously and successfully engaged in the work of the ministry for more than sixty years. One who knew him well has said, "He was, perhaps, excelled by no man in the State in point of Biblical knowledge, and for pious walk and unblemished character."

Frost, Adoniram Judson, D.D., was born in Parishville, N. Y., Sept. 12, 1837; converted and baptized at eighteen; entered the St. Lawrence Academy at Potsdam at twenty; at twenty-four was licensed to preach; took the full college and theological courses at Hamilton, and graduated with high honor in 1867. He was pastor at Syracuse, N. Y., Bay City, Mich., and of the University Place church, Chicago, Ill. In 1876 he removed to

California; was three years pastor at San José, and in 1879 took charge of the First church at Sacramento. In 1878 California College conferred upon him the degree of D.D. Dr. Frost has a commanding presence and genial countenance; has a rich voice and magnetic eloquence: he instantly fastens the attention of his hearers, whether as preacher or presiding officer. His broad sympathies give him great influence over men; his independence inspires courage. His mind is vigorous, analytical, strong. He investigates his subject with resolution, pursues it to the end with fidelity, and forces conviction. His ministry is marked with great success in winning souls and strengthening churches. He has much influence among his brethren in all the churches of California, and is one of their most influential counselors and officers in Associational, educational, Sunday-school, and missionary organizations.

Frost, Rev. James Madison, a devoted and learned minister of Jesus, was born of pious Baptist parents, in Jessamine Co., Ky., Sept. 2, 1813. In his eighth year his parents removed to Washington Co., Mo., where he grew up to manhood. Here he was baptized by Joseph King, and joined Cartois Baptist church, Sept. 11, 1831. Was licensed to preach July, 1832, and ordained December, 1833. Feeling the insufficiency of his education, he entered Shurtleff College in 1834. Here he remained three years in the literary and theological departments. Two of his classmates were the learned Dr. Samuel Baker, now of Kentucky, and Rev. Noah Flood, late of Missouri. On leaving college, Mr. Frost accepted the pastorate of Potosi church, Washington Co., Mo. In September, 1838, he returned to Kentucky, where he took charge of Mount Vernon church, in Woodford County. In 1840 he became pastor of the church at Frankfort. His health failing, he removed to Georgetown in 1843, and became financial agent of the Baptist General Association of Kentucky. In 1846 he took charge of the First church, in Covington. After this he was at different periods pastor at Georgetown, Cave Run, New Liberty, Harrodsburg, Madison Street church, in Covington, and South Elkhorn, all in Kentucky. He died in Lexington, Ky., May 24, 1876. Few men were ever more sincerely lamented. His son, Rev. J. M. Frost, Jr., now of Virginia, is a brilliant preacher and author.

Fryer, Rev. R., a native of Bulloch Co., Ga., was born in 1800, and died in the beginning of 1879; was baptized in 1824 in Bryan Co., Ga. He was at once impressed that he should preach, but he rebelled, and moved away to South Georgia to avoid it. Reaching his destination, to his surprise the report had gone before him that he was a minister, and he continued his journey to the Territory of Florida. He located in what is now Hamilton County, and there commenced preaching, and was ordained in 1833. In an area of a hundred miles he labored zealously and successfully till he removed to South Florida, in 1870.

Mr. Fryer was in the unhappy controversy between the missionary and anti-missionary Baptists that occurred about the time of his ordination, and he was excluded for his missionary sentiments. He was a man of liberal views, and in full sympathy will all progressive measures of his denomination. He had great influence, for his mind was strong, his life blameless, and his heart large.

Fryer, Rev. R. C., was born in Alabama in 1821, baptized in 1837, became an active and zealous laborer, and on removing to California, was ordained pastor of El Monte church in 1854. Subsequently he was pastor at Santa Anna, and is now pastor at Spadra. He is a ready and effective preacher, and his home is one of the most hospitable and influential in Southern California. Yielding to the earnest persuasion of friends, he entered the State Legislature in 1869, and served in that body with distinguished ability and Christian fidelity.

Fuller, Rev. Andrew, was born in Wicken, Cambridgeshire, England, Feb. 6, 1754. When about fourteen years of age he first became the subject of religious exercises. This question arose in his mind, What is faith? He could not answer it, but he satisfied himself that it did not require an immediate response, and that he would learn in the future what it was. Nevertheless he was not as indifferent about his soul as in former times, and occasionally he was very unhappy. Once, with some boys in a blacksmith's shop, while they were singing foolish songs, the words addressed to Elijah seemed to pierce his soul,—What doest thou here, Elijah? And he arose and left his companions.

He was considerably affected at times by reading Bunyan's "Grace Abounding to the Chief of Sinners" and his "Pilgrim's Progress," and once he was led to weep bitterly in reading Ralph Erskine's "Gospel Catechism for Young Christians." A little later he was deceived by an imaginary conversion, which gave him great joy for a short time. But the joy departed and his sins returned, and for months they exercised dominion over him; then his convictions came back and filled his soul with misery continually; he saw that God would be perfectly just in sending him to the regions of despair. At this time Job's words came to him, and soon created the same resolution in him, "Though he slay me yet will I trust him;" and the words of Esther intensified his purpose, "'If I perish, I perish,' but I must go to Jesus;" and driven by his sins, and attracted by the redeeming power of the Lamb, he trusted Christ for the full salvation of his soul, and soon his guilt and fears were removed.

In March, 1770, he saw two young persons baptized.

REV. ANDREW FULLER.

He had never witnessed an immersion before, and it made such an impression upon him that he wept like a child, and he went away fully convinced that what he saw was the solemn appointment of the royal Saviour, disobedience to which would be rebellion in him. One month after this baptism he was immersed himself into the membership of the church of Soham.

In the spring of 1775 he was ordained pastor of the church of Soham. His income was miserably small, compelling him to resort to some secular pursuits to support his family. In October, 1782, he removed to Kettering, in Northamptonshire, where he spent the rest of his life. It gave him the greatest distress to leave the church of Soham, and nothing but a firm persuasion that he was following the will of God would have ever led him to Kettering.

A pamphlet published by Jonathan Edwards on the importance of general union in prayer for the revival of true religion, led to a series of prayer-meetings among the ministers of "The Northamptonshire Association" for this special purpose. Resolutions were passed by the Association at Nottingham, and at subsequent meetings held elsewhere, recommending that the first Monday evening of every month should be set apart for prayer for the extension of the gospel. It is with some reason believed that these prayer-meetings started that missionary tidal-wave that soon rolled over England and America, the surging waters from which reached India, and many other sections of the heathen world. At a meeting held in Kettering on the 2d of October, 1792, the Baptist Missionary Society was formed, and the first collection for its treasury, amounting to £13 2s. 6d., was taken up. Mr. Fuller was appointed its first secretary, and while others nobly aided, Andrew Fuller was substantially the society till he reached the realms of glory. Speaking of the mission to India, he says, "Our undertaking at its commencement really appeared to me to be somewhat like a few men who were deliberating about the importance of penetrating a deep mine which had never been explored. We had no one to guide us, and while we were thus deliberating, Carey, as it were, said, 'Well, I will go down if you will hold the rope.' But before he went down he, as it seemed to me, took an oath from each of us at the mouth of the pit to this effect, ' that while we lived we should never let go the rope.' " And Mr. Fuller held it fast till his hand fell powerless in death. He traveled all over England very many times, pleading for foreign missions; five times he journeyed through Scotland on the same errand of love; and he visited Ireland once to advocate the cause of the perishing. The noblest cause that stirred up Christian hearts, the cause that brought the Saviour himself from the heavens, found in Andrew Fuller its grandest champion, and to him more than to any other human being was the first foreign missionary society of modern times indebted for its protection in infancy, and the nurturing influences that gave it the strength of a vigorous organization.

His literary reputation spread all over his own country, and his name, long before his death, was as familiar in England and America as a household word. All denominations read his writings with profound interest, and they place the highest value upon them still. His "Calvinistic and Socinian Systems Examined and Compared, as to their Moral Tendency," and "The Gospel its own Witness; or, the Holy and Divine Harmony of the Christian Religion Contrasted with the Immorality and Absurdity of Deism," are works worthy of the greatest theologian of any age, and long since they have placed their author beside Dr. John Owen, Dr. John Gill, and John Howe, as one of the first expounders of the Bible of the Anglo-Saxon race. "The Franklin of theology," as he has been called. Mr. Fuller was a voluminous writer; and his works have passed through several editions. Though a staunch Baptist on the communion question, in 1798 Princeton College conferred on him the honorary degree of D.D., which he declined. Yale College, under the presidency of Timothy Dwight, followed the example of Princeton in 1805, with a similar declination from Mr. Fuller.

His death, on May 7, 1815, excited a profound sensation, and occasioned general grief. Throngs attended his funeral,—Episcopalian, Congregational, and other ministers vied with Baptist pastors in doing honor to his memory. His church erected a beautiful monument, which commemorates in glowing words their exalted appreciation of his great worth.

Mr. Fuller was "tall, broad-shouldered, and firmly set. The hair was parted in the middle, the brow square and of fair height, the eyes deeply set, overhung with large bushy eyebrows. The whole face had a massive expression."

He had great decision of character; he was usually very clear in his views of any subject that had occupied his attention. He was a natural warrior, ready to assail the foes of truth in every direction, but this characteristic was restrained and regulated by a heart filled with supreme love to Jesus, and by generous affections.

His style was clear as a sunbeam, with little effort at ornament. His arguments were commonly as forcible as the blow of a sledge-hammer, when delivered with all the power of a strong and practised hand. He was one of the few Englishmen that knew how to use the Scottish custom of expository preaching, and in this mode of applying the Word of God to men Mr. Fuller attained great distinction.

In general his theology is Calvinistic. His treatment of several of "the doctrines of grace" is such as to afford no comfort to the disciples of James Arminius. His views of the atonement, however, were innovations to the English Baptists of his day, which stirred up vigorous opposition. Dr. Gill was the theological teacher of one section of his denomination, and Mr. Fuller of the other. Mr. Fuller's doctrine of the great sacrifice is generally received by English and American Baptists, though there are still some among us who regard Dr. Gill, in the main, as approaching nearer to Paul's representation of the nature of Christ's glorious propitiation than the profound theologian of Kettering. These brethren agree with Mr. Fuller in using every Christian effort to bring sinners to Jesus, and to spread the gospel throughout the whole earth.

Fuller's views of substitution and imputation have had a far wider influence in the Presbyterian and Congregational denominations than the kindred opinions of Richard Baxter, of Kidderminster, conspicuous as their author and his doctrines have been for more than two centuries.

Andrew Fuller was one of nature's noblemen, and he was a blameless Christian; his life was eminently useful, and his death was full of peace.

Fuller, Rev. B. S., was born at Fitchburg, Mass., Sept. 3, 1806. He was the son of Joseph and Eunice Dodge Fuller. His mother was the sister of Daniel Dodge, who was the warm friend of Luther Rice, and a co-worker with him.

He was converted in his seventeenth year, and received into the church at Holden, Mass., of which Elder Walker was then pastor. From the time of his union with the church he was active and zealous. Soon after his conversion he removed to Boston, and labored in the South Boston Sunday-school, which only numbered about eighty at the commencement, but at the close of his labors had increased to three hundred.

The providence of God prepared the way for his removal to Florida, by afflicting him severely with asthma, and thus rendered it necessary for him to seek a milder climate. He came to Florida in 1837, but did not bring his family till he had remained two years, and became satisfied to live in the State.

While Florida was yet a Territory, he was licensed to preach by the Concord Baptist church, in what is now Madison County. This was done Jan. 15, 1843. He was at once requested to become pastor of the Hickstown church, and was ordained the 29th of the same month he was licensed. Alexander Moseley, Thomas Lang, R. J. Mays, and W. B. Cooper composed the Presbytery that ordained him. He was several years pastor of the church at Madison Court-House, and served several churches in the county contiguous; Monticello, the county town of Jefferson County, was his last pastorate.

Elder Fuller served the Florida Association efficiently as missionary and colporteur, and was agent for the Southern Baptist Publication Society, at Charleston, S. C. As pastor, missionary, and agent, he was active and faithful, and, as was truly said by the writer of an obituary notice of him, "He sympathized with every laudable effort to advance the cause of Christ." He possessed good natural endowments; was a great reader and student, and consequently was a strong man in the gospel and a popular preacher.

Though coming to the State an invalid, with not much prospect of recovery, and but little idea of preaching, his life was prolonged to nearly the "threescore and ten" allotted to man. The illness that terminated his life was protracted and painful, but it was borne with much submission, till death came to his relief, April 20, 1870, at his home in Monticello.

By a consistent life, and by earnestly speaking the truth in love, he did a good work for Christ and his beloved denomination in what is properly termed Middle Florida.

Fuller, Rev. Cyrenus M., was born in Grafton, Vt., March 24, 1791. His early childhood and youth were spent in the home of his parents, who were Congregationalists, and he received his early religious education in connection with them. From childhood he had serious impressions, and believed he would be converted and preach the gospel. In 1810 he obtained an assured hope in Christ, and in 1813 he was baptized and united with the Baptist church in Grafton, Vt. He was licensed to preach in 1814, and ordained in 1818 by the Baptist church in Dorset, Vt. Previous to his ordination he made his first journey with horse and carriage to Boston, and preached for Dr. Baldwin, and on his return he preached for Dr. Stephen Gano in the First Baptist church of Providence, R. I. He was pastor at Dorset ten years, supplying occasionally the churches in Middletown and Arlington, Vt. In 1826 he made a tour among the churches of Vermont and New York to collect funds for Hamilton Literary and Theological Institution, then in an embarrassed state. In 1827 he settled as pastor of the Baptist church in Elbridge, N. Y., remaining twelve years, and then removed to Pike, N. Y., where he continued pastor of the Baptist church four years. In 1843 he entered the service of the American Baptist Home Mission Society, and held this position until 1861. He traveled as financial agent in twenty-six States of the Union, and extensively in the British possessions,—in all about 120,000 miles. He came to Wisconsin in 1858, where he died in Darien, at the home of his son-in-law, Rev. E. L. Harris, June 6, 1865. His ministry was pre-eminently useful. While a settled pastor he baptized about 1000 persons into the churches. During his extensive travels in the service of the Home Mission Society, extending throughout eighteen years, his labors were very valuable to that society as well as to the thousands of churches which he visited. He did much in bringing the work of home missions prominently before the Baptist denomination. He was highly esteemed among the ministers and churches, not only for his works' sake, but also for his personal virtues and purity of character.

Fuller, Richard, D.D., was born in Beaufort, S. C., in April, 1804. His early education was conducted by the Rev. Dr. Brantly, father of the Rev. Dr. W. T. Brantly, now of Baltimore. In 1820 he entered Harvard University, Mass., and in his class, consisting of more than eighty, stood among the first for proficiency in his studies, for general culture, and for skill in debate. In consequence of ill health he was obliged to leave Harvard while still in the Junior year. On his return to Beaufort he entered upon a course of legal studies, and after being admitted to the bar, he became, by his talents, diligence, and force of character, one of the most accomplished and successful lawyers in the State. While thus in the full flush of professional distinction, Beaufort was visited by the celebrated revivalist, the Rev. Daniel Barker. During the meetings held at that time, and which were of remarkable interest and power, some of the most prominent and intellectual individuals of the place were brought to a consecration of themselves to the cause of Christ, among whom were Stephen Elli-

RICHARD FULLER, D.D.

ott, afterwards bishop of Georgia, and Richard Fuller. He had been up to this time a member of the Episcopal church. He felt it to be his duty to give himself entirely to the work of the Christian ministry, and in connection with the Baptist denomination. He had been previously immersed by the rector of the Episcopal church; but dating his real conversion from the influences of this revival season, and thoroughly convinced that believers' baptism only was Scriptural, he was rebaptized by the Rev. Mr. Wyer, then pastor of the Baptist church in Savannah, Ga. He at once entered, with all the glow and vigor of a new spiritual life, upon the congenial work of preaching the gospel. He was soon chosen pastor of the church in Beaufort, where he labored for some fifteen years, during which time the church was greatly strengthened in membership, character, and influence. Through his efforts, also, a handsome new church edifice was built. While in Beaufort he engaged in a memorable controversy with Bishop England, of Charleston, S. C., on the Scriptural principles and claims of the Roman Catholic hierarchy, and won, from all who read the able and polished arguments, the reputation of a thoroughly equipped and skillful controversialist. Then came that still more memorable dialectic contest between himself and the Rev. Dr. Wayland on the subject of slavery, in the conduct of which, whatever may be thought of the claims of the friends of either to a decided victory in the issue of the argument, there was such a uniform display of courtesy, kindness, and Christian manliness as is rarely witnessed in the discussion of such exciting questions. In the midst of these labors Dr. Fuller, in consequence of ill health, was obliged to suspend his pastoral labors, and, guided by the advice of his physician and friends, he, in the year 1836, made a visit to Europe. On his return he gave himself, with increased zeal and energy, to the one great work of his life,—preaching the gospel. His reputation had now become national, and many prominent churches in different parts of the country were anxious to secure his services. In 1846 he received and accepted a call to become pastor in Baltimore, where the remainder of his life was spent in pastoral duties. One of the conditions of his removing to Baltimore was that a new church edifice should be built, and accordingly a house of worship was erected on Paca and Saratoga Streets, where thronged congregations listened for so many years to his eloquent and impressive preaching, and where such large numbers were added to the church. After years of eminent success here, and partially in consequence of the very large number of members, a new enterprise was started, which resulted in the building of the beautiful house of worship at Eutaw Place, and the establishment of a strong church there. The same eminent success characterized his labors in this new field that had crowned his efforts in the old, and here, still apostle-like, doing "this one thing," he closed his useful life. Thorough Baptist as Dr. Fuller was in every fibre of his nature, his influence for good was felt through the entire Christian community, and his labors were abundant in all departments of Christian beneficence. No pastor in the denomination was more highly esteemed by the representative men of other churches than he, and none was more frequently urged to lend the influence of his name and counsel to those larger and more comprehensive benevolent organizations which embrace within their scope great communities and groups of churches. Though a slave-holder like Whitefield, he was a devoted master, as he lived among servants for whose religious and physical welfare he made the most ample provision, and who were strongly attached to him. Dr. Fuller died in Baltimore, Oct. 20, 1876, in the triumph of that faith which he had so earnestly and unremittingly preached through a remarkable and blessed ministry.

Dr. Fuller as a preacher had but few peers. Gifted with a rare, manly, and commanding presence; free in every movement from those restraints fatal to the orator, which necessarily arise from the use of manuscript; with a legal acumen that discriminated between the delicate shades of correlated yet of pregnant truths; with an imagination that embodied in forms of living beauty the personages, and places, and deeds of the far-off times and lands of the Saviour's earthly labors; and a voice whose tones could thrill the soul with heroic resolutions or melt it into tender pity,—he has taken his place among the few great pulpit orators whose names are embalmed in the memories of men. As a writer, too, Dr. Fuller had his excellencies. His style was tinctured by the influences of the past rather than by those of the present. The tendency of eminent living clergymen is to a scientific instead of a classical style,—scientific in form, in phraseology, and in illustration; whereas the style of Dr. Fuller's writings was saturated with the classic spirit, as seen in the well-balanced structure of his sentences, as well as in the affluence of his illustrations and allusions. The ennobling thoughts of the old Greek and Roman poets, historians, and orators, rather than the uncongenial dogmas of the present guiding lights of the scientific world, pulsate through all his sentences; and he has left us, in some of the latest articles he penned, examples of that chaste, symmetrical, and statue-like style of which Everett and Legare were such masters, but which is rapidly fading into an accomplishment peculiar to the past.

Fuller, R. W., D.D., was born in Beaufort, S. C., Nov. 27, 1824, and died in Atlanta, Ga., June 10, 1880. He was a nephew of Dr. Richard Fuller, from whom he received his theological training, at Beaufort, S. C. He came to Georgia to assume charge of the First Baptist church of Atlanta, but failing health caused his resignation. Consumption had fastened its fangs upon his vital organs. For years he acted as the successful agent for the Georgia Baptist Orphans' Home, and for Mercer University. But feebleness finally forced him to retire from all labor, and he gradually declined until the summer of 1880, when he peacefully fell asleep in Jesus.

Dr. Fuller was an exceedingly amiable and companionable man, full of humor and genial pleasantry. He had a superior education, a trained intellect, and strong mental powers. There was perhaps no abler preacher in the State, aside from mere delivery. His language was very choice; his thoughts were vigorous and clearly expressed; his logic good, and his spirit most devout. His piety was undoubted, and he commanded not only the respect and esteem, but the love of all.

Fuller, Rev. S. J., an aged, but still active minister in Logan Co., Ark., was born in Georgia in 1816; in 1849 he settled in Claiborne Parish, La., where he began to preach shortly afterwards. He labored in Louisiana fifteen or sixteen years, presiding seven or eight years as moderator of Concord (Louisiana) Association. He then removed to Arkansas, and after three years settled in his present field, where he has since labored. He soon gathered churches around him, and organized them into an Association, which he named Concord, of which he was moderator until compelled by the infirmities of age to decline re-election. He has accomplished great good as a pioneer.

Fulton, Rev. John, was born in Henderson, Jefferson Co., N. Y. When seventeen years of age he was baptized by Rev. Jacob Knapp. He graduated at Hamilton in 1843. He was ordained at Rensselaerville, Albany Co., N. Y., in 1844, and remained there three years. He served the church in Leesville, Schoharie Co., four years, and the First Cazenovia church nearly nine years. In 1859 he came to Iowa, under appointment of the American Baptist Home Mission Society, to the pastorate of the church at Independence, Buchanan Co., just organized with eleven members. He built the first Baptist meeting-house in the county, and the first erected by Baptists on the direct line from Dubuque to the Rocky Mountains. He remained on this field ten years, during which he built three meeting-houses,—one at Independence, one at Quasqueton, and one at Winthrop; and he secured a lot and made arrangements for the fourth at Jessup. From Independence he went to Belvidere, Ill., and remained there as pastor for eight years. Then he returned to Iowa as pastor at Winterset, still untiring in his labors. Since Jan. 1, 1880, he has been the pastor of the Olivet church, Cedar Rapids. He has been greatly blessed in working for the Master.

Fulton, Rev. John I., was born in Nova Scotia, Sept. 23, 1798; came to New York in 1802; was converted early in life and joined the church of North-East, Dutchess Co.; entered Hamilton in 1822; in 1824 was ordained pastor of Sherburne. He was pastor subsequently in Vernon, Mendon, and Stillwater, N. Y., and in several places in Michigan. He died in Tecumseh, Mich., Nov. 10, 1867. He was an able preacher and an exemplary Christian; one of his sons, Justin D. Fulton, D.D., is known throughout the United States.

Fulton, Justin D., D.D., was born in Sherburne, N. Y., March 1, 1828. He graduated at Rochester University in 1851, and pursued a theological course in the Rochester Seminary until June, 1853. At this date he was invited to St. Louis to edit the *Gospel Banner*, a paper devoted to the advocacy of Bible revision, and meantime to serve as pastor of one of the city churches, to which work he was ordained. In the fall of 1855 he resigned both of these positions, and took charge of the Baptist church at Sandusky, O., which was greatly prospered under his ministry. In 1859 he was solicited by two brethren, of whom George Dawson, of the Albany *Evening Journal*, was one, to assist in founding a new church. He accepted the call, and the result was the Tabernacle church of Albany, which soon became a power in that city. In 1863, Mr. Fulton became pastor of the Tremont Temple, Boston. His work here was so prospered that in a short time the spacious edifice was filled with attentive congregations. Here he labored for nine years, and built up a church of 1000 members, and one of the largest congregations in America. In 1872 he removed to the Hanson Place Baptist church, in Brooklyn. In 1876 the remnant of the Clinton Avenue church, of the same city, which had been struggling under financial embarrassments, invited Dr. Fulton to become their pastor. Members from other churches united with this interest, and a new church was formed, called the Centennial Baptist church. Here he still labors with his usual success, and the small band has increased manifold. Dr. Fulton is a prolific writer; the following works have proceeded from his pen: "The Roman Catholic Element in American History," "Rome in America," "The Way Out," "Show your Colors," "Woman as God Made Her," and "Life of Timothy Gilbert." The University of Rochester conferred the degree of D.D. upon Mr. Fulton in 1871. Dr. Fulton has great and varied ability, and unbounded energy.

Fuqua, Rev. J. B., was born Feb. 8, 1822, in Fluvanna Co., Va. He was converted when eighteen years of age, and ordained in Buckland Baptist church, Tenn., in December, 1851. He died Dec. 12, 1877. Was pastor at Cape Girardeau, Mo.; at Concord, and at Brush Creek. He was a missionary in the St. Louis Association for some time. He had a good mind and fair attainments. He was firm, cheerful, candid, cordial, and was very useful as a minister.

Furman, J. C., D.D., was born in Charleston, S. C., Dec. 5, 1809. He was educated at the Charleston College. In 1828 he was baptized by Dr. Manly. He then renounced the study of medicine for the ministry of the Word. He rendered efficient service in the great revivals in Edgefield, Beaufort, and Robertsville. During these meetings R. Furman, D.D., George Kempton, D.D., and Richard Fuller, D.D., were converted.

For several years he was pastor at Society Hill, one of the most refined communities in the State. At the earnest request of the Second church in Charleston he accepted a call as its pastor. But as the church at Society Hill resolved to renew their call annually, he felt it his duty to return to them.

In 1843 he entered upon a professorship in Furman Theological Institution, then offered to him a second time. In concert with Profs. Mims and Edwards he elaborated a plan for a broader system of education, which resulted in the establishment of the Furman University, of which he has long been president. He was for many years moderator of the Baptist State Convention.

During his whole connection with the university

J. C. FURMAN, D.D.

he has never neglected the ministry. He was pastor of the Greenville church at one time for two years, and at another for three and a half. Each resignation was tendered because he thought the church needed the entire time of a pastor. He is a son of Dr. Richard Furman, of Revolutionary fame. He has a fine intellect, broad culture, fervent piety, the love of all that know him, and a life fruitful in good works and influences.

Furman, Richard, Sr., D.D., was born in New York in 1755. His father removed to South Carolina while his son was an infant. Before he could hold the family Bible he would lay it on a stool and ask to be taught to read it, and as soon as he acquired the art, reading it was his chief delight. His education was almost entirely at home. When about seven years old he memorized, merely by reading, most of the First Book of the "Iliad," which he retained perfectly in middle life. In a short period at school having learned the rudiments of Latin grammar, he became quite a proficient in that language, and acquired a respectable knowledge of Greek and Hebrew.

He was baptized in his sixteenth year, and at once he began the work of instructing his father's servants. He also took an active part in what would now be called a Bible-class, and presently began to speak more publicly of the way of life.

Crowds flocked to hear the boy preacher, and his precocious intellect and profound piety produced a deep impression on those who heard him. In his nineteenth year he was ordained as pastor of the High Hills church. The sheriff once refused to allow him to preach in the court-house at Camden because he was not a minister of the Established (Episcopal) Church. Having preached in the open air, the court-house was ever after freely offered him. About the beginning of the Revolution a meeting of ministers and laymen of different denominations met at High Hills to concert measures to remove the odious discrimination restricting all offices to members of the Establishment. Here as everywhere the Baptists have led in the contest for religious freedom. So conspicuous was Dr. Furman from the commencement of the war, that Lord Cornwallis offered a large reward for his apprehension. He spent a part of the time of the war in Virginia, where Patrick Henry and family were regular attendants on his ministry. Mr. Henry presented him with a work on rhetoric and Ward's "Oratory," which are heir-looms of the family. After the war he returned to his church at High Hills. He was one of the most active and influential patriots throughout the Revolutionary war.

In 1787 he became pastor of the First church in Charleston. He found it enfeebled by the war. He

RICHARD FURMAN, SR., D.D.

left it, after thirty-seven years, strong and united. Never was minister more loved and venerated, not merely by his church, but by the whole city.

He was unanimously elected the first president

of the Triennial Convention in 1814. At this meeting he earnestly advocated the formation of an institution at Washington to educate young men for the ministry. At this time he gave a powerful impulse to the convictions from which have sprung Furman University, in South Carolina, Mercer, in Georgia, Hamilton, in New York, and finally the Southern Baptist Theological Seminary.

He was a member of the convention that formed the first constitution of South Carolina, and he strongly opposed the provision excluding ministers from certain offices. He was also president of the Baptist State Convention for several years.

He closed his long and eminently useful life in August, 1825. Probably no minister of any denomination has ever exerted a wider, more varied, or more beneficent influence.

Furman, Samuel, D.D.—"In this very name we are taught to honor the deceased, although we may have been strangers to his face on earth. Dr. Furman's life was long and faithful. God allowed his sun to travel from horizon to horizon. He died only when his work was done. He was a man of broad learning, deep piety, and of unparalleled reverence for his Master. His memory lies embalmed in the hearts of many who knew him, far and near. For almost two years before Brother Furman's death he was confined to his bed, and during a part of this time his suffering was great. He fell asleep peacefully on the 19th of March, 1877. His remains now rest in the grave-yard connected with the Sumter church."

Furman University, which has now (1880) been in operation about thirty years in Greenville, S. C., was founded by the Baptists of the State. It is the expansion of a seminary which had previously existed elsewhere, and which, under the name of Furman Theological Institution, was designed for the education of ministers. Embracing a theological, a collegiate, and an academical department, and contemplating a subsequent department of law, the establishment was chartered with its present title.

When it became expedient to provide a theological institution for the South, the Baptists of South Carolina made the largest offer for its settlement within their borders, proposing to give $100,000 to the enterprise, on the condition of an equal sum being raised by the other Southern States together. Their proposal was accepted, and this necessitated the withdrawal of the theological funds of the university and the closing of this department. Just before the war arrangements were on foot for opening the law department, Hon. B. F. Perry and C. J. Elford, Esq., having been appointed as lecturers. This purpose was put into abeyance by the war; the collegiate classes were broken up, and instruction was given only to such as were too young to bear arms.

When the havoc of war was over, amid all the discouragements arising from the fearful destruction of capital, the confused arrangements of social life, the loss of employment, and the difficulty of getting from one place to another, railroads having

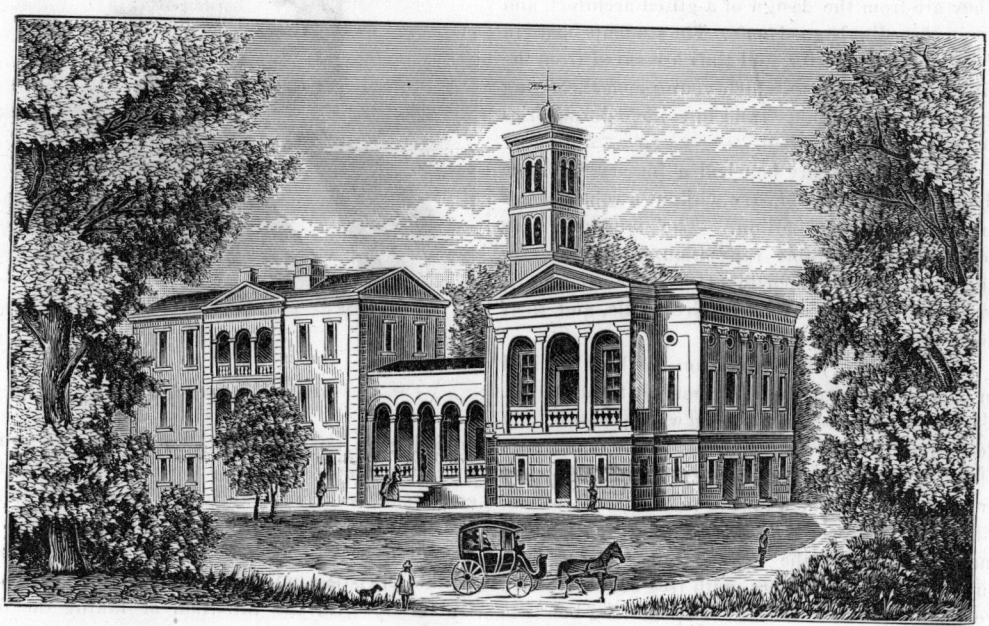

FURMAN UNIVERSITY.

been broken up, and mules and horses and conveyances destroyed, it was yet determined to keep within the reach of the young people the advantages of education. A few earnest-minded men convening at the time of the regular meeting of the Baptist Convention of the State, encouraged the professors to open the doors and resume the work of instruction. This was accordingly done.

The university owns a valuable site of about forty acres within the limits of the city of Greenville, one of the most beautiful locations for a seminary of learning to be seen anywhere, proverbial for its healthfulness, on the skirt of the mountains, accessible by different railroads. Its buildings are not spacious, but ample for all present purposes. They are from the design of a gifted architect, and are in exceedingly good taste. The students board in the families of the city, and thus are saved from the vitiating influences to which young men thronging together in "commons" and in college dormitories are more or less exposed.

Furman University has had a history for more than a quarter of a century without a rebellion, or an approach to rebellion. The students have achieved an honorable reputation for good order and gentlemanly deportment. Their coming is welcomed by the citizens of Greenville, and their departure regretted.

The support of the institution has been derived in part from vested funds, but mainly from tuition. The investments bearing interest were almost wholly destroyed by the war. Since that time bonds payable in a short series of years were procured; they entitled the bondsmen to the privilege of tuition. Then it was proposed to raise a permanent endowment of $200,000, the interest only to be used in supporting the professors, with free tuition for ten years. This was to be done by procuring bonds to be paid in five annual installments with interest. The bonds were procured, but unpropitious agricultural seasons, the fall in the price of cotton, and the general stringency in money matters up to a recent period, have made payments very slow. As a consequence the number of instructors, which ought to be six or seven, is only five. The vacancy occasioned by the death of Dr. Reynolds, Professor of Roman and English Literature, has not been filled, his duties being divided between two other professors.

The course of studies is equal to that commonly pursued in colleges of the best reputation. Graduation is awarded to success in closely written examinations.

The faculty are Rev. J. C. Furman, D.D., Chairman, and Professor of Intellectual and Moral Philosophy, Logic, and Rhetoric; C. H. Judson, Professor of Mathematics and Mechanical Philosophy; D. T. Smith, Professor of Ancient Languages; J. M. Harris, Professor of Natural Philosophy and Chemistry. There were eighty-six students in 1879–80.

Fyfe, Robert A., D.D., was born at St. André, near Montreal, Canada, Oct. 20, 1816. He was occupied with business avocations from his youth until the twentieth year of his age. His hopeful conversion occurred at about this time, when, under the impulse of his new love to Christ, he resolved to obtain an education and enter upon the work of the Christian ministry. He entered Madison University with the intention of taking the full course of study in that institution, but ill health compelled him to leave. His subsequent studies were pursued at the Worcester Academy, and at the Newton Theological Institution, where he graduated in the class of 1842, and at once he was ordained at Brookline, Mass., Aug. 25, 1842, entering immediately on his ministerial labors, as pastor of the Baptist church in Perth, Canada. Here he remained until the close of 1843, when he took charge of the Montreal Baptist College for one year, the arrangement being a temporary one. He then became pastor of the March Street church in Toronto, Canada, where he remained until 1848, when he returned to the church in Perth, and was its pastor for one year. From Perth he went to Warren, R. I., and was the pastor of the church in that place for four years. The next two years he was pastor in Milwaukee, Wis., and the next five years—1855–60—he had charge of the Bond Street church, Toronto, at the end of which time he ac-

ROBERT A. FYFE, D.D.

cepted an appointment as principal of the Literary Institute at Woodstock, Canada. It was an arduous undertaking, and it was only by the exercise of patience and rare executive abilities that the enterprise was carried on until it reached results which rewarded the labor and the sacrifice of its friends. "Never was man more devoted to his work; never was work done by a truer *man*. He has laid the Baptists of the British provinces under vast obligation, and his memorial can never perish while veneration and gratitude live in human hearts."

But it was not merely what Dr. Fyfe did as the head of an important institution of learning that made his influence to be so extensively felt in the provinces. Home and foreign missions, and the cause of ministerial education, found in him a warm friend. Everything connected with the prosperity of the denomination he so much loved was an object of interest to him. From the midst of his labors he was suddenly called to his reward. After an illness of but a day or two he died at Woodstock, Sept. 4, 1878.

G.

Gadsby, Rev. William, was born in Attleborough, England, in January, 1773. In early life he was remarkable for "frolic and mischief," and he was the undisputed leader of his companions. He found the Saviour's pardoning love before he was eighteen years of age, when in raptures of joy he could say, "He loved *me*, he gave himself for *me*." His first attempt to address the throne of grace in a prayer-meeting made him "tremble from head to foot," and feel so miserably ashamed of himself that he concluded he would never pray in public again. He was brought up among the Congregationalists, whose fellowship he left, and was baptized at Coventry in 1793. Mr. Gadsby was ordained at Desford, July 30, 1800. His first settlement was at Hinckley, where he remained till 1805, when he removed to Manchester. In that city he continued till his death, Jan. 27, 1844.

Mr. Gadsby was one of the most remarkable preachers of the first half of the nineteenth century. His pulpit eccentricities exceeded those of Rowland Hill, and his fame was as well known in his own country. He had a more original and powerful mind than Hill, and his genius was of the same order. Under his sermons very remarkable conversions occurred, and a great many of them. Numbers of persons entered his meeting-house with enmity to him and his doctrines, and went away rejoicing in his Master and full of affection for himself.

He believed that the children of God were not under the law, as a rule of life, but under the precepts of the gospel; for this he was branded as an Antinomian, as if the commandments of Christ did not embrace all that was moral in the law. He continually denounced "free-will," and in its stead he upheld sovereign grace. At a meeting of Dissenting ministers in Manchester during his pastorate there, it was resolved that the best method to further the gospel was "to preach in a way that the people could not discern whether they preached free-will or free-grace." When Mr. Gadsby heard the decision from a minister who was present, he quickly informed him that Satan was president of that meeting. He was an eloquent advocate of eternal and personal election, and the ultimate triumph of all the chosen of God, notwithstanding their own weaknesses, the world's attractions, and Satan's malicious cunning. He would say of the Saviour's loving scheme, "it is an everlasting gospel, proceeding from everlasting love, and ending in everlasting glory." The themes of his ministry were "the deceit, depravity, and helplessness of human nature; the first work of divine quickening in the cries, desires, and sensations of the living soul; the rich glories of eternal love and grace in the covenant purposes of God the Father, the mediatorial glories of the God-man, the inseparable union of the church with him, and her completeness in him, having all fullness treasured up there, and the effectual operations and sweet anointings of the Holy Ghost in the heart." He was a rigid Baptist. He stated to a Pedobaptist congregation to which he occasionally preached at their solicitation when he visited London, that "he was a Baptist to the backbone, and backbone and all." He had no sympathy with open communion, or with any other innovation upon the Saviour's doctrines and institutions.

He was bold as a lion, and he was meek as a little child. He led a life of holiness towards God, his enemies themselves being judges. He had a heart full of sympathy for the poor and the unfortunate, to whom his death was a great calamity.

He was an earnest friend of Sunday-schools, and in connection with his own church he was instrumental in establishing a school which flourished, and in securing a separate building for its accommodation. His labors were herculean; he preached three times on the Lord's day at home, and often six times in the week in other places; he traveled 60,000 miles, a considerable part of it on foot, to proclaim the unsearchable riches, and in four counties alone he was instrumental, directly and indirectly, in the erection of forty houses of worship. He kept distinct from the Regular Baptists in England, though his faith was substantially the creed of Dr. Gill.

He met with an accident in 1840, in alluding to which the Manchester *Times* says, "Any cessation of the activity of such a man is a public calamity. His preaching, though marked by some eccentricities, is of a high order, combining all the fervor of a deep devotion with the exercise of a vigorous, acute, and original intellect; and his active practical benevolence, manifesting itself not only by the relief of the distressed around him, but by his ardent desire to promote good legislation, and thus to advance the happiness of the whole human family, has endeared him alike to the sincere Christian, the philanthropist, and the reformer of political abuses. In any station he would have been a remarkable man."

Mr. Gadsby was the author of twenty-two works, some of which have been widely circulated.

Gage, Rev. Moses Dwight, was born Jan. 4, 1828, at New Woodstock, N. Y.; baptized at fourteen, and licensed in 1856; was educated at Alfred Academy and Rochester University. He became pastor, and was ordained at Bedford, Ind., in 1860, and in 1861 served the Pendleton and Muncie churches. From 1862 he was three years chaplain of the 12th Ind. Vol. Regiment, under Grant and Sherman, and wrote a history of the campaigns. In 1865 he became pastor at Franklin, Ind., for two years, helping to revive the college there. In 1867 became pastor for four years at Junction City, Kan., and built a $5000 church edifice. In 1873 he moved to California, and was three years pastor at Marysville, when he located at Camptonville as pastor and teacher. He is an able preacher, a fine scholar, and a popular educator; has written extensively for the religious and educational press, and served in various official positions in Baptist Associations and Conventions.

Gair, Rev. Thomas, was born in Boston, Feb. 5, 1755. He was baptized July 28, 1771. He was a graduate of Brown University in the class of 1777. He was ordained a few months before his graduation as pastor of the church in Medfield, Mass., where he remained until November, 1787, when he was called to the pastorate of the Second Baptist church in Boston. His ministry was successful, and its results were felt long after his decease. He died April 27, 1790. One of his sons, Samuel Stillman Gair, Esq., was connected with the famous house of the Baring Brothers, bankers, England.

Gale, Rev. Amory, was born in Royalston, Mass., Aug. 24, 1815. At the age of sixteen he experienced a hope in Christ. He was early called of God to the work of preaching the gospel.

REV. AMORY GALE.

His preparatory studies were pursued at Worcester Academy, from which he graduated in 1839.

He graduated from Brown University in 1843, and from Newton Theological Seminary in 1846. Under his labors while a student at Brown University an extensive revival was experienced in Royalston. His first settlement after graduating was at Ware, Mass. Here he was ordained Nov. 11, 1846. In the spring of 1857 he received a commission from the American Baptist Home Mission Society to visit the West, and settled with the First Baptist church of Minneapolis. He succeeded Rev. T. R. Cressey as general missionary for the State, July 1, 1858. For fifteen years he toiled in his missionary work, and reaped a glorious harvest. The Rev. Lyman Palmer collated many facts concerning Brother Gale's labors, from which we select the following: "Sermons, 5000; family calls, 16,000; books sold or donated, 25,000 volumes; miles traveled, 100,000,—more than 50,000 miles of his missionary journeyings were with Indian ponies, in a buggy or a sleigh." Large churches were anxious for his services, but his reply was, "The men are fewer who will take fields to be worked up, so I will take a new field." He had a strong physical frame, but it was the constraining love of Jesus that wrought within him an indomitable energy to grapple with and overcome great difficulties. He did not stop to look at obstacles, but to inquire for needed work. For years he suffered very much with asthma, and often slept leaning against the wall of his room. He had as true a missionary spirit as ever dwelt in a human heart. He organized Sunday-schools all over Minnesota. At the time of his death there were one hundred and sixty-nine Baptist churches in that State, more than one-half of which he had assisted in forming. His name will long remain a household word in Minnesota.

In the summer of 1874 he sailed for Europe. While abroad he visited the principal places of interest in Great Britain, many of the continental cities, Greece, Constantinople, and Palestine. At Jaffa, prostrated by Syrian fever, he was taken to the hospital, where he died, Nov. 25, 1874. During his travels a number of highly interesting letters from his pen were published in the *Watchman and Reflector*, of Boston. The death of no citizen of Minnesota ever occasioned more profound sadness. He was buried in the "American Protestant Cemetery," near the city of Jaffa.

At the annual meeting of the State Convention, held in St. Paul, October, 1875, the following resolutions were unanimously passed:

"WHEREAS, Rev. Amory Gale has fallen during the past year, having died at Jaffa, in Syria, just as he had fulfilled a long-cherished desire to make a tour of the Holy Land; and our brother beloved was one of the originators, and for fifteen years was the *efficient, self-sacrificing, hard-working*, and successful missionary of this Convention, and of the Home Mission Society; and there is one heart-throb of anguish among brethren and sisters throughout our entire State, especially among our Scandinavian and German brethren, to whom our brother was especially endeared by his great interest in their welfare; therefore,

"*Resolved*, That we express not only our deep grief for the loss we have sustained in the sudden and unexpected death of Brother Gale, but also our high appreciation of his many virtues, and of his unparalleled labors in severe pioneer work, which have been so effective in placing our denominational interests where they are in Minnesota to-day.

"*Resolved*, That we tender our sympathy to the family of our brother in their severe affliction."

Gale, Daniel B., was born in 1816, in Salisbury, N. H. He was educated at New Hampton Academy. He removed to St. Louis, Mo., and commenced business in 1837. He died Nov. 16, 1875. His widow has given expression to her love for him by the donation of a costly organ to the Second Baptist church of St. Louis, called the "Gale Organ."

Daniel B. Gale made a profession of religion in 1857, and was baptized by Rev. J. B. Jeter, D.D., into the fellowship of the Second Baptist church of St. Louis. He was an efficient and highly esteemed member of this community till his death. His firm became one of the most prosperous in St. Louis, with a very honorable reputation. He was a member of the common council, and a trustee of his church. His great modesty kept him from accepting offices that were pressed upon him. The community had the greatest confidence in him. His labors and benevolence were rarely surpassed. His memory will ever be tenderly cherished in St. Louis.

Gale, Rev. John, Ph.D., was born in London, England, May 26, 1680. His father, a distinguished citizen of London, gave him every facility for acquiring the best education. To this end he sent him to Leyden, in Holland, where he graduated with honor in the nineteenth year of his age.

On his return to England he pursued his studies with great diligence, especially in ancient literature, heathen and Christian, with which his acquaintance became very extensive.

The Rev. Dr. William Wall, an Episcopalian, wrote the "History of Infant Baptism," and received the thanks of both houses of Convocation for the work; and some years later, when he published a defense of his book, the degree of Doctor of Divinity from the University of Oxford. Dr. Wall's history is one of the ablest defenses of immersion as the Scripture mode of baptism that had appeared till that time; but its main design is to establish the authority of infant baptism. "This," as Crosby says, "Dr. Gale answered, before he was twenty-seven years of age, with so solid a judgment, such extensive learning, and so great moderation, that it gained him the esteem and affection not only of Baptists, but of all men of candor and learning on the opposite side." Dr. Whitby and Mr. Whiston both commend Dr. Gale's learned labors. And Lord Chancellor King, Dr. Hoadley, bishop of Bangor, and Dr. Bradford, bishop of Rochester, became his friends. He began to preach regularly in his thirty-fifth year, and he was favored with large and cultured audiences. He planned before his death to write an exposition of the New Testament, and a translation of the Septuagint; but a slow fever seized him in his forty-first year, and in about three weeks carried him to the grave. Dr. Gale's opinions on the Deity of Christ and on some other vital parts of the Christian system were not orthodox; though it is somewhat difficult to state his exact positions. His works, additional to his reply to Wall, were published in four octavo volumes after his death.

Gallaher, Rev. Henry M., LL.D.—Dr. Gallaher was born at Castlebar, Ireland, Sept. 11, 1833. He came to the United States in 1850. He was graduated from Shurtleff College, and the theological department connected with it. On leaving college he accepted the pastorate of the Vermont Street Baptist church of Quincy, Ill.

In 1864 he was called to the First Baptist church of Brooklyn, N. Y., which he served with marked success for several years. He then entered on an important field in Elizabeth, N. J., from which he went to New Haven, Conn., and in 1879 he accepted the call of the Hanson Place Baptist church, Brooklyn, N. Y.

Wherever he has been a pastor his congregations were large, often overflowing the commodious houses of worship where they were assembled. As a preacher and a lecturer he is equally popular. His Irish wit, his fervent zeal for Christ and his cause, his keen power of analysis, and the gathered results of industrious research in all the fields of learning give him an extraordinary influence over his audiences.

He generally writes his sermons, and closely follows the line of thought marked out, but he is not confined to his notes. He moves rapidly about his pulpit or platform, and some of the most brilliant passages in his discourses are not in his manuscripts. At New Haven, his meeting-house was generally thronged by the students of Yale College and other young men, many of whom were added to his church.

His warm heart makes him eminently social and attractive.

Galusha, Rev. Elon, a son of Gov. Galusha, of Vermont, began his ministry early in life, inspiring brilliant hopes, and fulfilling the expectations of his friends. He labored many years at Whitesborough, near Utica, N. Y., afterwards in Utica, and subsequently in Rochester, Perry, and Lockport. He was president of the Baptist Missionary Convention of New York, and he acted as agent for several local and national institutions. For years he was one of the best-known men in the State. He possessed a rich imagination, glowing enthusiasm, and, when his sympathies were thoroughly enlisted, pure eloquence. Few men could carry a large congregation with such overwhelming power as Mr. Galusha. He was one of the most unselfish and devout of Christians. He was a father and a leader in Israel, whose memory has a blessed fragrance. He died at Lockport, N. Y., Jan. 6, 1856.

Galusha, Gov. Jonas, was born in Norwalk, Conn., Feb. 11, 1753, and came to Shaftsbury, Vt., in 1775. From 1777 to 1780 he was captain of a militia company. In the famous battle of Bennington he led two companies. He was a representative from Shaftsbury in the Legislature of Vermont in 1800. He was councillor from October, 1793, until October, 1799, and again from October, 1801, to October, 1806. From 1781 to 1787 he was sheriff of Bennington County. He was judge of the County Court from 1795 until 1798, and again from 1801 until 1807; judge of the Supreme Court in 1807 and 1808. He was governor of Vermont from 1809 to 1813, and again from 1815 until 1820. In 1808, 1820, and 1824, he was an elector of President and Vice-President, and a member of the constitutional conventions of 1814 and 1822, of both of which he was the president. His services in public life covered a period of forty years.

Gov. Galusha, although not a member of the church, was a Baptist in sentiment, and took an interest in the affairs of the denomination in the State of Vermont. "He maintained family worship in all its forms, was known to observe private devotions, was an habitual attendant upon public worship and at social meetings, and frequently took an active part in the latter. When nearly seventy-nine years of age, he attended a protracted meeting at Manchester, and took an active part in its exercises; as a result of which he was aroused to a sense of the duty of making a public profession of religion, and announced his intention to do so, but was prevented by a stroke of paralysis, which he experienced soon after, and from which he never recovered. His children were well trained, and all of them who survived childhood became professors of religion; one of them, Elon, an eminent minister in the Baptist denomination." Gov. Galusha died at Shaftsbury, Vt., Sept. 24, 1834.

Galusha, Hon. Truman, was born in Shaftsbury, Vt., in October, 1786, and was the eldest son of Gov. Jonas Galusha. He was baptized by Rev. Caleb Blood, and united with the church in Shaftsbury. Subsequently he removed to Jericho, Vt. He held various offices of honor in his native State, among them that of associate judge of Chittenden County Court. As a Baptist layman he was highly respected in Vermont, where he did much to promote the interests of his denomination. He died at Jericho, Vt., June 13, 1859.

Gambrel, Rev. James B., editor of the Mississippi *Baptist Record,* and pastor at Clinton, Miss., was born in South Carolina in 1841, but was reared in Mississippi; held the rank of captain in the Confederate army; began to preach in 1867; after serving country churches two years he became pastor at West Point, Miss.; in 1872 became pastor at Oxford, Miss., and while supplying the church attended the University of Mississippi, which is located at this place. He sustained this relation five years, during which the church was much strengthened. Having acquired considerable reputation as a writer, he was chosen as editor of the

Mississippi *Baptist Record*, a position which he fills with ability.

Gammell, Rev. William, was born in Boston, Jan. 9, 1786. His early religious associations were with the Federal Street Unitarian church, which became so famous on account of the ministry in it of the celebrated Rev. Dr. William E. Channing. Of this church the parents of Mr. Gammell were members. Having experienced conversion, in the evangelical sense of that word, he was baptized in 1805 by Rev. Dr. Stillman, and united with the First Baptist church in Boston. He was educated in the schools of his native city, and studied theology under the direction of Rev. William Williams, of Wrentham, Mass. While devoting his attention to divinity, he was invited to supply the pulpit of the church in Bellingham, Mass., which gave him a call, and he was ordained as pastor in 1809. In 1810 he removed to Medfield, Mass. In this place there grew up under his ministry a flourishing church, which was gathered not only from Medfield, but from the adjoining towns. To it he ministered for thirteen years, and then resigned in August, 1823, and removed to Newport, R. I., and became the pastor of the Second Baptist church. Here his ministry was eminently successful, a large congregation was drawn to the house of worship by his attractive eloquence and his zeal for the honor of his Master. In the midst of his great usefulness and popularity he died suddenly of apoplexy, May 30, 1827, in the forty-second year of his age. He received the honorary degree of A.M. from Brown University in 1817, and in 1820 was elected a member of the corporation. "He was," says his son, Prof. W. Gammell, "a highly acceptable preacher, and an earnest friend of every object connected with the extension of Christianity."

Gammell, William, LL.D., was born in Medfield (where his father was the pastor of the Baptist church), Feb. 10, 1812. He entered Brown University in 1827, and graduated in 1831. The class numbered only thirteen, but several of its members arrived at considerable distinction in their different callings in life. Among them were Hon. F. W. Bird, Rev. Drs. Hoppin and Waterman, and David King, M.D. For three years Mr. Gammell was tutor in Brown University. In 1835 he was chosen Professor of Rhetoric and English Literature, and held the office for fifteen years, when he was transferred to the chair of History and Political Economy. His term of service in the college, which covered a period of thirty-three years, came to an end in 1864. He commenced his college life as a Freshman under Dr. Wayland, and was associated with him as a student or an instructor during his whole administration, which closed in 1855. He was also professor nine years under President Sears. During this long period Prof. Gammell conducted the studies of the two departments in which he was the professor with great ability and success, leaving the impress of his fine taste and rare skill in the elegant use of the English language on hundreds of young men, who, both consciously and unconsciously, were influenced by his instructions and his personal example. Prof. Gammell was not only a college professor, conducting the ordinary routine of hearing recitations and doing his part in maintaining discipline, but he found time to prepare a large amount of matter for the press. Sparks's "Biography" is indebted to him for lives of Roger Williams and Gov. Samuel Ward. He wrote a "History of Baptist Missions," which is a standard authority in matters of which it treats to this day. He was for some time one of the editors of the *Christian Review*, and the writer of many articles which have been given to the world through various channels.

Since his resignation in 1864, Prof. Gammell has resided in Providence and Newport, devoting his time and thoughts to the administration of his business affairs and to the oversight of charitable and educational institutions with which he is connected.

Gandy, D. R., a prominent Baptist layman in Sabine Association, La.; was sheriff of Sabine Parish many years, and in 1853 served one term in the Legislature of the State; born in Georgia in 1811; died in Louisiana in 1867.

Gano, Rev. John, was born in Hopewell, N. J., July 22, 1727. His family was of French origin, and its name Gerneaux. Mr. Gano's father was a pious Presbyterian, and he felt inclined to follow in his father's religious footsteps, but an examination of the subject of baptism led him to take the Saviour's immersion in the Jordan as his model and to unite with the Baptist church of Hopewell. With a new heart, a Scriptural creed, and a call from Christ to preach the gospel, he was ordained May 29, 1754, and became pastor of the Scotch Plains church. He removed to the South after a two years' settlement at Scotch Plains, where he remained till 1760. In June, 1762, the First Baptist church of New York was constituted, its members having received letters for this purpose from the parent church at Scotch Plains. Immediately after their organization they called Mr. Gano to be their pastor. He accepted the invitation, and held the position for twenty-six eventful years. His ministry was greatly blessed in New York, and the church that commenced its ecclesiastical life with twenty-seven members soon became a power in the future Empire City.

Mr. Gano was deeply interested in the Revolutionary struggle, and when fighting began he entered the army as chaplain to Gen. Clinton's New

York brigade, and performed services which rendered him dear to the officers and men with whom he was associated. Nor did he ever shun the scene of danger, though his duties were entirely peaceful. Headley, in his "Chaplains and Clergy of the Revolution," says, "In the fierce conflict on Chatterton's Hill, Mr. Gano was continually under fire, and his cool and quiet courage in thus fearlessly exposing himself was afterwards commented on in the most glowing terms by the officers who stood near him." In speaking of his conduct on that occasion, he said, "My station in time of action I knew to be among the surgeons, but in this battle I somehow got in the front of the regiment, yet I durst not quit my place for fear of dampening the spirits of the soldiers, or of bringing on myself an imputation of cowardice." Headley states that when he "saw more than half the army flying from the sound of cannon, others abandoning their pieces without firing a shot, and a brave band of six hundred maintaining a conflict with the whole British army, filled with chivalrous and patriotic sympathy for the valiant men that refused to run, he could not resist the strong desire to share their perils, and he eagerly pushed forward to the front." Any wonder that Washington should say of chaplains like Mr. Gano, and there were other Baptists of his spirit, that "Baptist chaplains were the most prominent and useful in the army"?

On the return of Mr. Gano to New York at the close of the war he could only find thirty-seven members of his church; these he gathered together again, and the Lord soon gave him and his people a gracious revival, which imparted strength and hope to his discouraged church. In May, 1788, he removed to Kentucky, and became pastor of the Town Fork church, near Lexington. He died in 1804.

Mr. Gano was the brother-in-law of Dr. Manning, the first president of Brown University, whose ordination sermon he preached. He was one of the earliest and most influential friends of Rhode Island College. He went everywhere to further Baptist interests. He had a fund of energy greater than most men, and an intellect which could grasp any subject. He was regarded in his day as "a star of the first magnitude," "a prince among the hosts of Israel," "a burning and a shining light, and many rejoiced in his light." One of his sons, Dr. Stephen Gano, was for thirty-six years the beloved pastor of the First Baptist church, Providence, R. I.

Gano, Rev. Stephen, M.D., was born Dec. 25, 1762, in the city of New York. His father at the time of his birth was the pastor of the Gold Street

REV. JOHN GANO.

Baptist church. He was a nephew of Rev. James Manning, and the purpose of his parents was to send him to the Rhode Island College, of which his uncle was the president, but so great were the distractions caused by the Revolutionary war that they were obliged to sacrifice their wishes in this respect. He was placed under the care of his maternal uncle, Dr. Stiles, and educated with special reference to the medical profession. Having completed his studies, and being desirous of entering the army, he was appointed a surgeon at the age of nineteen, and for two years was in the public service. The title of doctor which he received in his youthful days he bore in after years, and was called "Doctor" Gano. While occupied with his practice as a physician in Tappan, now Orangetown, N. Y., he became a subject of God's converting grace. At once he seems to have felt it to be his duty to give himself to the work of the Christian ministry, and was ordained on the 2d of August, 1786. After spending some time preaching in the vicinity of his native city he received, in 1792, a unanimous invitation to become the pastor of the First Baptist church in Providence, R. I. His ministry here was a long and remarkably successful one, from which he did not cease until three months before his death. His sickness was a distressing one, but he bore his pains with patience, and died in the triumphs of faith on the 18th of August, 1828. For thirty-six years he had been a power for good in the community in which he had lived for so long a time, and when he passed away devout men bore him to the grave, and his memory is still cherished with loving regard in the church he served with such rare devotion to their interests.

Dr. Gano was one of the most interesting and instructive preachers of the times in which he lived. "He possessed," says his son-in-law, the late Rev. Dr. Henry Jackson, "many qualities to render his preaching both attractive and impressive. He had a fine commanding figure, being more than six feet in stature, and every way well proportioned. His voice was full, sonorous, and altogether agreeable. His manner was perfectly artless and unstudied. He had great command of language, and could speak with fluency and appropriateness with little or no premeditation. His discourses were eminently experimental, and were adapted to every Christian, while they abounded in appeals to the careless and the ungodly." His confidence in the efficacy of prayer was remarkable, and his views of firmly trusting in the leadings of God's providence singularly clear and strong.

The Hon. James Tallmadge, LL.D., who was a relative of his second wife, and resided in his family while pursuing his studies in Brown University, thus speaks of Dr. Gano in a letter which may be found in Sprague's "Annals":

"Dr. Gano was admitted on all hands to hold a high rank among the ministers of his denomination. He devoted himself with great assiduity to the duties of his profession. Wednesday and Saturday he gave to the work of preparation for the duties of the Sabbath and other appointed services. It was his custom in studying his sermons to note on a small piece of paper his text and the general divisions of his discourse, with reference to passages of Scripture and other illustrations of his subject. This memorandum, placed in the book before him, was a sufficient guide to his thoughts, and it enabled him to speak with great promptness and fluency.

"His personal appearance was prepossessing, his voice manly, his articulation distinct, and his diction clear and impressive. His preaching was in turn doctrinal, practical, and experimental. His exhortations were often exceedingly earnest and pathetic, and, in the application of his discourse, it was not uncommon for a portion of his audience to be melted into tears.

"The administration of the ordinance of baptism in connection with the singing of a hymn at the water, according to the usage of the Baptist Church, afforded a fine opportunity for the display of his powers. His eloquence on these occasions was often greatly admired. He was a favorite among his friends, and had a high standing both as a man and as a minister in his denomination."

Gardner, Rev. Benjamin West, was born in Providence, R. I., July 4, 1822; graduated at Brown University in 1850, and at the Newton Theological Institution in 1853. He was ordained pastor of the church at Sheldonville, Mass., in September of the same year, and remained there two years. For three years he preached in Mansfield, Mass., and for nine years at West Dedham. The drafts made upon a constitution, never strong, were too great, and he was obliged to leave the pastoral office. North Marshfield was his home for the last five years of his life. He died July 6, 1874. He was a faithful, conscientious minister of Christ.

Gardner, George W., D.D., was born in Pomfret, Vt., Oct. 8, 1828. At the early age of fourteen he was baptized into the fellowship of the Baptist church in Canaan, N. H., by Rev. George W. Cutting. He was prepared for college at the academy in Thetford, Vt., and graduated at Dartmouth College in the class of 1852. For one year he was principal of the academy in Ludlow, Vt., and then took charge of the New London Institution, of which he was the principal for eight years. During this period over one thousand different students were connected with the school, and about one hundred and fifty young men were prepared for college under his immediate instruction. He was ordained as a minister of the gospel in September, 1858. In November, 1861, he was installed as pastor of the First Baptist church in Charlestown, Mass., where he remained eleven years. In September, 1872, he entered upon his duties as corresponding secretary of the American Baptist Missionary Union, of the Executive Committee of whose board he had been a member for the five years previous. He acted as corresponding secretary of the Union for four years, when the two secretaryships hitherto existing were merged into one, and Dr. Gardner retired and accepted a call to the pastorate of the First Baptist church in Cleveland, O. His connection with the church commenced in October, 1876, and continued between one and two years.

GEORGE W. GARDNER, D.D.

While residing in New Hampshire, Dr. Gardner was prominently connected with educational work in that State, and was a member of the State Board of Education for two years. In 1870 he made an extensive tour of Europe and the Holy Land. During the years 1873-76 he was the editor of the *Missionary Magazine*. He has contributed to the pages of the *Baptist Quarterly*, published several missionary tracts, and was the Sunday-school editor of the *Watchman and Reflector* for 1871 and 1872. He has published several sermons in pamphlet form, and has been a contributor to the religious papers.

Dr. Gardner, in February, 1881, was elected to the presidency of Central University, Iowa. Dartmouth College conferred upon him the degree of Doctor of Divinity in 1867.

Gardner, Rev. Solomon, a pioneer in Bradley Co., Ark., was born in Mississippi in 1824; came to Arkansas in 1844; served with distinction in 1st Miss. Regiment in the war with Mexico; began to preach in 1859; has at different times supplied most of the churches of his region; served with ability one term in the Arkansas Legislature at a most critical period; was commissary of the 9th Ark. Regiment in the Confederate army.

Gardner, William W., D.D., a pastor, educator, and author, was born in Barren Co., Ky., Oct. 1, 1818. In his eighteenth year he commenced the study of medicine. In 1838 he united with a Baptist church, and the following year entered Georgetown College, where he graduated in 1843. In 1844 he was ordained to the pastorate of the Baptist church at Shelbyville, Ky. In 1847 he took charge of the church at Maysville, Ky., where he remained until 1851, when he became agent of the Baptist General Association of Kentucky. At the close of the year he became pastor of the church at Mayslick. From 1857 to 1869 he was pastor of the church at Russellville, and Professor of Theology in Bethel College. At the latter date he resigned the charge of the church, and gave his time to the duties of his professorship. When the Southern Baptist Theological Seminary was removed from Greenville, S. C., to Louisville, Ky., the theological department of Bethel and Georgetown Colleges was abolished, and Dr. Gardner resumed the pastoral office at Glasgow, Ky. He has recently removed to Russellville, where he now resides.

Dr. Gardner has manifested especial excellence as a teacher of New Testament theology, and has published several books and pamphlets, among which is a volume on church communion, which has met with much favor.

Garlick, Joseph R., D.D., was born in King William Co., Va., Dec. 30, 1825. His early training was at the neighboring schools. In 1840 he entered the Virginia Baptist Seminary (now Richmond College), and remained there till the fall of 1841, when he matriculated at the Columbian College, and graduated in 1843. Being not quite eighteen years of age at this time, he engaged in teaching until January, 1849, when, having been ordained the year previous, he was elected pastor of the Hampton Baptist church, Va., remaining there four years. For two years he was connected with the Chowan Female Institute, Murfreesborough, N. C. He removed thence, in 1855, to Bruington, King and Queen Co., and established the Rappahannock Female Institute, over which he presided for fourteen years, and for ten years of that time was also pastor of St. Stephen's Baptist church, in that county. His present field is the Leigh Street church, Richmond, where he has labored for nearly nine years. This church numbers nearly 900 members, and is probably the largest white church in the South. It is a rigorous and busy hive of earnest Christian workers. Dr. Garlick received the degree of A.M. in course from the Columbian College in 1846, and the honorary degree of D.D. from Richmond College. He is also president of the State Mission of the Baptist General Association of Virginia. He removed from Richmond to King and Queen Co., Va., where he is now preaching.

Garnett, Judge James, was born of pious Baptist parents in Adair Co., Ky., July 8, 1834. After attending the common school of his neighborhood, he finished his education at a private academy conducted by Mr. Saunders. At the age of eighteen he was employed in the office of the county clerk of Adair, where he remained three years, industriously devoting his leisure hours to reading law. He completed his studies in the law-office of Judge T. E. Bramlette, and in November, 1856, was admitted to the bar in his native county. In August, 1871, he was elected to a seat in the Legislature of Kentucky, and served in one regular and one extra session of that body. In 1874 he was elected judge of the sixth judicial district of Kentucky, which position he has filled with ability until the present time. Judge Garnett was baptized into the fellowship of the Baptist Church at Columbia, Ky., in 1857, by Rev. H. McDonald, D.D., now of Richmond, Va.

Garrard, Gov. James, an eminent statesman, and a man of great purity of life and character, was born in Stafford Co., Va., Jan. 14, 1749. He entered the service of the colonies as a militia officer early in their struggle with the mother-country. He was called from the head of his command in the army to a seat in the Virginia Legislature, where he was a zealous and influential advocate of the passage of the famous bill for the establishment of religious liberty. He was among the early settlers of Kentucky, where he was a leading member of nearly all the political conventions of that district, including the one which formed the first constitution of the State. In early life he united with the Baptists in Virginia, at a time when they endured fierce persecution. After his settlement in Kentucky he was ordained to the ministry. In 1791, pending the convention which formed the first constitution of Kentucky, a committee, composed of James Garrard, Ambrose Dudley, and Augustine Eustin, reported to Elkhorn Association a memorial and remonstrance in favor of excluding slavery from the Commonwealth by constitutional enactment. After serving several times in the Kentucky Legislature, Mr. Garrard was elected governor of the Commonwealth in 1796, which office he held by re-election eight successive years. Kentucky has never had a citizen that stood higher in popular estimation than Gov. Garrard. He died at his residence in Bourbon Co., Ky., Jan. 9, 1822.

Garrard, Rev. John, was brought up, converted, and ordained in Pennsylvania, and he settled in Virginia in 1754 to preach Jesus. His labors were specially given to Berkeley and Loudon Counties. He assisted in the formation of the Ketocton Association, and his great love for souls was rewarded by the conversion of large numbers. He was one of those heaven-honored preachers whose memory should be precious to the Baptist denomination throughout all time. His brethren in the ministry gave him the most prominent place in their meetings, and his example and spirit were universally commended. He lived to be a very old man, and died about 1784.

Garrard, Rev. John, sometimes written Gerrard, was among the first preachers that settled in Kentucky. Where he came from is unknown. On the 18th of June, 1781, at the constitution of Severn Valley church, in Hardin Co., Ky., he was installed in the pastoral office of that body, and was consequently the first minister of any church in the Mississippi Valley. In May, 1782, he was captured by Indians, and never heard of afterwards.

Garrett, Rev. Hosea, was born in Laurens District, S. C., Nov. 26, 1800; ordained to the ministry in 1834. His first pastorate was in 1836. Removed to Texas in February, 1842, and settled in Washington County, near Independence, and has resided in the same county ever since. Preached to some of the most important churches. He has been always regarded as a remarkably sound and logical preacher. One of its original founders, he has been for nearly thirty-five years devoted to the maintenance of Baylor University, contributing liberally of his time and means for that object, acting as agent at one time, and as president of the trustees nearly all the time up to the present moment. As a preacher he is plain and perspicuous. In judgment and conservative policy he is the Nestor of Texas Baptists. He is well known as an officer of the State and Southern Conventions.

Garrett, Judge Oliver Hazard Perry, was born May 29, 1816, in Laurens District, S. C., and was educated in the district in which he was born. In December, 1833, he professed religion, and was baptized by Rev. Jonathan Dewees into the fellowship of the Warrior Creek Baptist church; removing to Texas, he was ordained, in 1844, a deacon of Providence Baptist church, Washington County, Rev. Wm. M. Tryon, Rev. R. E. B. Baylor, and Rev. Hosea Garrett acting as the Presbytery. He has continued in the office till this time. He served as clerk of Providence church from 1848 to 1868. In October, 1856, at Cold Springs, Walker County, he was elected clerk of the Union Association, and he is still clerk. In October, 1859, at Waco, he was elected recording secretary of the Texas Baptist State Convention, and continues still in the office. He has been a director of the Convention

JUDGE OLIVER HAZARD PERRY GARRETT.

since 1850, and a trustee of Baylor Female College from the date of its charter. In the mean time he has been an active farmer, a successful land surveyor, and he has served one or two terms as chief judge of the county. Few Baptists in Texas have been in labors so steady and abundant. He is now an active deacon of Brenham church, ready for every good word and work. Two sons are at the bar, and one a student at Louisville for the ministry, all Baptists, and his two daughters are Baptists and married to Baptists.

Garrott, Col. Isham W., was born in Wake Co., N. C., in 1816; educated at Chapel Hill; came to Alabama and settled in Greenville; moved to Marion in 1840; baptized in 1846; a distinguished lawyer; twice represented Perry County in the State Legislature; a Presidential elector in 1860; colonel of the 20th Ala. Regiment; killed at Vicksburg, June 17, 1863. His convictions were strong. He avowed them fearlessly and carried them out honestly. He was remarkable for his industry, uprightness, temperance, and courage; a consistent member of the church; liberal in the support of his church and of every worthy enterprise; unostentatiously kind to the poor; a warm friend of education; a trustee of Howard College at the time of his death and for many years previous.

Gartside, Deacon Benjamin, was born in England, May 26, 1794. His parents were members of the Baptist church of Ogden. Like his father he became a manufacturer in his native land. He came to this country in 1831. He first settled at Blockley, then at Manayunk, and finally, in 1852, at Chester, Pa. He has been greatly prospered in his business, and in his financial transactions he has an unsullied reputation.

He was baptized in 1839, and united with the Blockley church. When the First Baptist church of Chester was organized, in 1869, he became one of its constituent members. He gave more than half the money needed to pay for the erection of the new meeting-house, and he presented the parsonage as a free gift to the church. In his relations with the people of God he has always been the warm friend of the pastor. He began in early life to give to the Saviour's cause, and this spirit has grown with his means and years; he is a large-hearted benefactor of every department of our denominational work.

He is characterized by deep humility, sincere piety, an exalted sense of business integrity, and an abiding interest in the triumph of the Redeemer's kingdom.

Gaston, Rev. R., was born in England, Oct. 23, 1841, and came to America with his parents at the age of ten years. At seventeen years of age he entered the City Flouring Mills of Des Moines, Iowa, and continued in that business for five years. During this time he was converted, and united with the First Baptist church of Des Moines. In 1864 he entered Shurtleff College to prepare himself for the ministry. He graduated at the Baptist Union Theological Seminary of Chicago in 1871. He was settled at Winterset, Iowa. He afterwards took charge of the church at Waterloo, Iowa, where he still preaches. During this pastorate of six years many have been baptized. The church has grown numerically, financially, and spiritually, and is now one of the largest Baptist churches in the State. They are at present engaged in the erection of a church edifice, which when completed will be one of the finest in Iowa.

Gates, Rev. Alfred, was born in Granville, N. Y., Sept. 22, 1803; became a teacher; studied for the ministry at Hamilton Literary and Theological Institution, New York; ordained in Willimantic, Conn., in 1831; settled with the Baptist church in Preston, Conn., and with various churches, always with favor and success; something of an evangelist; ardent promoter of domestic, home, and foreign missions; died at Lake's Pond, Montville, Conn., Jan. 30, 1875, aged seventy-three years; a man very useful, and universally beloved.

Gates, Rev. George E., was born at Malvern Square, Annapolis Co., Nova Scotia. He graduated from Acadia College in 1873, and soon after was ordained as pastor at Liverpool, Nova Scotia, where he usefully labored until his acceptance of the pastorate of the Baptist church at Moncton, New Brunswick, June, 1880.

Gates, Rev. Oliver W., was born Feb. 24, 1830, at Preston, New London Co., Conn; converted at the age of twelve; baptized into the Preston church, Rev. N. E. Shailer pastor; conducted religious meetings when eighteen; soon after licensed to preach; entered Literary Institution, Suffield, Conn., in 1849; was a student four years, a teacher one; joined the Junior class of Madison University in 1854; graduated in 1856; was assistant teacher in Hamilton Female Seminary; spent one year in Theological Seminary, meanwhile supplying the Baptist church at Whitesborough, N. Y.; ordained Sept. 2, 1857, at Greeneville, Norwich, Conn.; pastor at Greeneville three years; supply at Hanson Place, Brooklyn, N. Y., one year; settled at Norwalk, Conn., as pastor, in 1861; remained there until 1873; removed that year to San Diego Cal., and served the San Diego church seven years. During his Norwalk ministry, spent part of one winter at Jacksonville, Fla., and assisted the church there. Mr. Gates has written several papers for the *Missionary Magazine*, sermons and a variety of articles in religious papers, "Glimpses of San Diego," a poem; "The Independence of Baptist Churches," "The Test; or, Have I the Spirit of Missions?"

At Norwalk was a member of the Board of Education, and for some years was secretary of the Norwalk and vicinity Bible Society. He is one of the most devout, earnest, and universally beloved of all the Baptist ministers on the Pacific coast. His wife is a highly gifted lady, thoroughly consecrated to Christ, and has charge of the Point Loma Seminary for young ladies, of which she is the founder.

Gaulden, Rev. C. S., pastor at Thomasville, Ga., was born in Liberty County, May 1, 1812, and was educated at Franklin College, now the State University, Athens. He professed faith, and was baptized by Rev. James Shannon, in 1826. He studied law and practised the profession twenty years, then was ordained, and began to preach about 1845, at Lumpkin. In 1859 he moved to Brooks County, organized the Baptist church at Quitman, and was its first pastor. He is now pastor at Thomasville, where he resides. Tall, and spare in form, earnest and straightforward in preaching, and rather vehement in manner, Mr. Gaulden is a man of influence and usefulness. For seven years he has been the moderator of the Mercer Association. He is a sound Baptist in doctrines and piety.

Gaunt, Mrs. Elizabeth, lived in London, England, in the dark days of wicked King James II. Mrs. Gaunt was a member of a Baptist church, and a lady of great benevolence. She was accustomed to visit the jails, and to relieve the wants of the victims of persecution of every oppressed denomination. Her reputation for generous acts was the cause of her martyrdom. The cruel king was greatly enraged that rebels against his authority should meet with a protecting roof and a little food from any of his subjects; and he resolved to be more severe to those who showed kindness to his outlawed enemies than to the traitors themselves. A rebel named Burton, hearing of the charitable deeds of Mrs. Gaunt, sought and found shelter and food in her house; but, learning the anger of the king against those who treated his enemies with humanity, with a depth of baseness seldom exhibited by the most abandoned of our race, he went and denounced Mrs. Gaunt to the authorities. She was seized and tried, and without the required number of witnesses was illegally condemned, and cruelly burned to death. She placed the straw around her at the stake so that she would be speedily reduced to ashes, and she behaved so gently, and yet so courageously, that "all the spectators were melted into tears." According to Bishop Burnet, she said to the spectators "that charity was a part of her religion, as well as faith. This, at worst, was the feeding of an enemy; so she hoped she had her reward with him for whose sake she did this service, how unworthy soever the person was that made so ill a return for it. She rejoiced that God had honored her to be the first that suffered by fire in this reign; and that her suffering was a martyrdom for that religion which was all love." She perished at Tyburn, Oct. 23, 1685. No doubt her holy blood was one of the powerful causes which summoned down the vengeance of heaven on the guilty king, and which sent him from his throne and country a crownless and cowardly fugitive. A writer familiar with the character of Mrs. Gaunt says, "She stood most deservedly entitled to an eternal monument of honor in the hearts of all sincere lovers of the Reformed religion. All true Christians, though in some things differing in persuasion from her, found in her a universal charity and sincere friendship, as is well known to many here, and also to a multitude of the Scotch nation, ministers and others, who, for conscience' sake, were thrust into exile by the rage of bishops. She dedicated herself with unwearied industry to provide for their support, and therein I do incline to think she outstripped every individual, if not the whole body of Protestants, in this great city [London]. Hereby she was exposed to the implacable fury of the bloody Papists, and of those blind tools who co-operated to promote their accursed designs; and so there appeared little difficulty to procure a jury, as there were well-prepared judges, to make her a sacrifice, as a traitor, to holy church."

Treacherous Burton must have set a high estimate upon the value of his life, when he was ready to offer this noble woman as a burned sacrifice for it. But long since in the eternal world he has learned that the preservation of the most precious life on earth is not worth one wicked act.

Gear, Rev. H. L., son of Rev. Hiram Gear, was born at Marietta, O., Dec. 1, 1842; graduated from Marietta College in 1862, and remained one year after as tutor; July 6, 1863, married Miss Cornelia, daughter of Judge P. Van Clief, of California; removed to California and practised law seven years in partnership with Judge Van Clief. In 1870 returned to Marietta, where he entered into law partnership with Hon. T. W. Ewart. In August, 1872, was ordained as pastor of the Newport and Valley churches. In July, 1875, became pastor of the church at Norwalk, O., and in February, 1876, was chosen corresponding secretary and superintendent of missions by the Ohio Baptist State Convention, which position he still holds.

Mr. Gear has published in the *Journal and Messenger* an extended reply to Dale's "Classic Baptism." The Publication Society has issued a treatise from his pen on "The Relation of Baptism to the Lord's Supper." He has also published various articles, sermons, and addresses. He is a thoughtful and earnest man, and is much esteemed for his work's sake.

General Baptists. See ENGLISH BAPTISTS.

Georgetown College, located at Georgetown, Scott Co., Ky., is the fifth Baptist university, in order of time, on the Western continent, and the first west of the Alleghanies and south of the Potomac. It was chartered by the Kentucky Legislature in 1829. On the 2d of September of that year Dr. Wm. Stoughton was elected to its presidency, but died before he reached Georgetown. In June of the next year Dr. Joel S. Bacon was elected president. The "Disciples" had just seceded from the Baptists in Kentucky, and were making a most determined and persistent effort to get possession of the college. After being perplexed and annoyed by lawsuits two years, Dr. Bacon resigned. The presidential chair remained vacant about four years, when, in 1836, Rev. B. F. Farnsworth was appointed to the position, but the controversy about the property, or rather the prerogatives of the college, still continued, and he resigned within a few months. In 1838, Rev. Rockwood Giddings was elected president, and within one year secured to the Baptists the peaceable possession of their college and a subscription of $80,000 towards an endowment, when he died. In 1840, Rev. Howard Malcom, D.D., was elected president, and served ten years, during which period the college was prosperous. He was succeeded by Rev. Dr. J. L. Reynold, who conducted the institution two years and resigned. Rev. D. R. Campbell, D.D., LL.D., became president in 1853. Under his management the college was prosperous in a high degree until the breaking out of the civil war, when its operations were again seriously embarrassed. In 1865, Dr. Campbell died, and was succeeded by Rev. Dr. N. M. Crawford. He presided over it for five years, when he resigned, and, in 1871, Rev. B. Manly, D.D., was chosen president. The course of the college was even and harmonious during his eight years' administration. In June, 1880, Dr. Manly having resigned, Rev. R. M. Dudley, D.D., was elected president. The college grounds and buildings are valued at $75,000, and its invested funds at $80,000. Since the college was established over 2000 students have been matriculated, and more than 200 of these have become ministers of the gospel.

Georgia Baptist, The, a weekly newspaper, published at Augusta, Ga., as the organ of the colored Baptists of Georgia, and under the auspices of the Missionary Baptist Convention (colored) of Georgia. It advocates Baptist principles, ministerial education, Sunday-schools, missions at home and abroad, and the temperance cause. It was commenced in 1880, and is a handsome four-page paper, ably edited by Rev. W. J. White, of Augusta, Ga.

Its existence manifests great zeal and intelligence among the colored Baptists in Georgia. Its editor is its business manager, and he says editorially, and it deserves to go on record, "We have tried to so manage the pecuniary part of the business as to have no failure, and we feel safe in saying that we consider the life of the *Georgia Baptist* now assured. We have bought and paid for the outfit of our office, and have as good material as there is in any printing-office in the State. We have a colored printer to superintend the work on our paper, and we have young colored men as compositors."

Georgia, Baptist Banner of, is a weekly paper published at Cumming, J. M. Wood and J. J. Morris, editors and proprietors. It was originated by the latter in the fall of 1876, and he became its chief editor in January, 1880. During its existence it has secured a good circulation. It is a paper of pronounced Baptist views, and reaches a large population of Baptists in Northeast Georgia.

Georgia Baptist Convention, History of.— In the year 1800 the Georgia Association met at Sardis, Wilkes Co., and adopted a resolution appointing a meeting at Powelton, in May, 1801, to consult in regard to mission work. The meeting was held, and the Association was advised to form a missionary society. This was approved by the Association, which appointed another meeting in

May, 1802, for consultation as to the proper steps to be taken. That meeting also recommended a General Committee to be appointed, to consist of three members of each Association. This was approved by the Associations of the State, and delegates were sent in May, 1803, and they elected a committee. The delegates appointed by the Georgia, Savannah, Hephzibah, and Sarepta Associations met again at Powelton, and chose a General Committee of twelve, as follows: Jesse Mercer, Henry Holcombe, Lewis C. Davis, James Matthews, A. Marshall, Charles O. Screven, Thomas Rhodes, Benjamin Brooks, Benjamin Moseley, Stephen Gafford, Joseph Clay, and Thomas Polhill. Henry Holcombe was made president, Jesse Mercer vice-president, T. Polhill secretary, and B. S. Screven treasurer, and a constitution was adopted. This committee continued for ten years, and was highly useful. It was the germ of the Georgia Baptist Convention. During its existence, besides encouraging mission work, it established and, in 1806, opened Mount Enon Academy, fourteen miles southwest of Augusta, mainly through the exertions of Henry Holcombe, sustained ably by Judge Clay, Jesse Mercer, and Joel Early, Sr., a committee appointed to act as agents by the General Committee. It passed out of existence in 1813, during the war, but was in a manner revived, through the influence and action of the Savannah Association. That Association organized a missionary society, called "The Savannah Baptist Society for Foreign Missions," under the form of a standing committee for missions in 1813, and, in 1814, sent a messenger bearing the constitution and a circular of this society to the Georgia Association, which met at Powelton, October 8. Jesse Mercer presented and read the circular and constitution, and the result was the formation, next year, 1815, of a strong missionary society in the Georgia Association, with a large amount in its treasury, and the name of "Mission Board of the Georgia Association" was given in 1816. The Ocmulgee and Ebenezer Associations followed the example of the Georgia, and in 1820 the three Associations united to send a missionary among the Creek Indians. A mission was established among the Cherokee Indians in North Georgia also, and a flourishing church was constituted and maintained there. In 1820, Dr. Adiel Sherwood offered a resolution in the Sarepta Association, through Charles J. Jenkins, the clerk, recommending to the Associations of the State the formation of a "General Baptist Association." Delegates appointed by the Georgia and Ocmulgee Associations met at Powelton, Hancock Co., and on the 27th of June, 1822, adopted a constitution drafted and supported by Wm. T. Brantly, the elder. Thus was formed and constituted the General Baptist Association of Georgia, which name, in 1828, was changed to "Baptist Convention of the State of Georgia." Its specific objects are:

"1. To unite the influence and pious intelligence of Georgia Baptists, and thereby to facilitate their union and co-operation. 2. To form and encourage plans for the revival of experimental and practical religion in the State and elsewhere. 3. To aid in giving effect to useful plans of the several Associations. 4. To afford an opportunity to those who may conscientiously think it their duty to form a fund for the education of pious young men, who may be called by the Spirit and their churches to the Christian ministry. 5. And to promote pious, useful education in the Baptist denomination."

The Convention had many difficulties to contend with at first, and for years the opposition to it was exceedingly bitter, but it gradually gained strength and efficiency, and so increased the number of its constituents, that at present it embraces thirty-seven Associations, besides various mission societies. As a mission body it sent delegates to the Triennial Convention, until the division in 1845. Since that time it has always been represented in the Southern Baptist Convention, and has been a liberal supporter of the mission work engaged in by its two boards. It has fostered education strongly, and has made the instruction of pious young men called to the ministry one of its leading objects. By the liberality of its early founders Mercer University has been established and sustained, and several high schools under its auspices are conferring great benefits upon the young of both sexes.

Georgia Baptist Seminary, The, for young ladies, is situated in the town of Gainesville, Hall Co., Ga. This institution arose from a desire on the part of the friends of education to establish a large female university in Georgia. The matter was broached in the Georgia Baptist Convention, and a committee of twenty was appointed to choose a location for it. In 1877, when the Convention met at Gainesville, as that town offered $25,000 to aid the enterprise, it was selected as the home of the institution. Work was commenced on July 4, 1878, and on the 11th of September following the school was opened with flattering prospects. During the first year of its existence it had in attendance 94 pupils, and during the second year 125. It has a full corps of experienced and popular teachers, and is presided over by Rev. Wm. C. Wilkes, an able educator.

Georgia Baptists, History of.—It is a historical fact that Baptists, whose descendants now dwell in Georgia, came over in the same ship with Oglethorpe, when he settled the province in 1733. Among the earliest settlers were Wm. Calvert, Wm. Slack, Thomas Walker, William Dunham, and a gentleman named Polhill, a well-known Baptist name in Georgia at the present time. These probably united with some of the converts of Nicholas Bedgewood and formed a branch of the Charleston Baptist church at Whitefield's Orphan House, nine miles below Savannah. Nicholas Bedgewood, an Englishman, came over with Whitefield about 1751, and was put in charge of the Orphan House. He was converted to Baptist sentiments in 1757, and joined the church at Charleston, being baptized by Rev. Oliver Hart, the pastor. Two years after this he was ordained, and in 1763 he baptized several converts among the officers and inmates of the Orphan House. Among these was Benjamin Stirk, who became a minister and settled at Newington, eighteen miles above Savannah, in 1767. He preached in his own house, and at Tuckasuking, about forty miles north of Savannah, where he constituted a branch of the church at Euhaw, S. C., with which he had connected himself, there being no Baptist church in Georgia. He died in 1770. The following year Edmund Botsford, from England, converted in Charleston, and a licentiate of the Baptist church there, sent out as a domestic missionary, came over from Euhaw, S. C., at the call of the Tuckasuking brethren. He began in June, 1771, a ministerial career of most zealous usefulness in Georgia, which continued without intermission for eight years. Ordained in 1773, he preached all over the country from Augusta to Savannah, baptized 148 persons, organized the Botsford church twenty-five or thirty miles below Augusta, and laid the foundations of future churches. Having embraced the American cause in the Revolutionary struggle, he fled first to South Carolina and then to Virginia, when, in the spring of 1779, Georgia was conquered by the British. This was the second source from which Baptist principles found an entrance into the State; a third was still farther northward.

In January, 1771, Rev. Daniel Marshall, an ordained Baptist minister of great piety, zeal, and ability, originally from Connecticut, moved into Georgia from South Carolina with his family, and settled on Kiokee Creek, about twenty miles northwest of Augusta. In the spring of 1772 he organized the Kiokee church there, the first Baptist church constituted in Georgia. Botsford church, formed the following year by Edmund Botsford, was the second. Daniel Marshall continued pastor of the Kiokee church until his death, in 1784, being succeeded by his son, Abraham Marshall, who was succeeded in turn by his son, Jabez P. Marshall, in 1819.

In 1784 the first Baptist Association, known as the Georgia, was formed in the State, probably at Kiokee church. At that time there were but six or eight Baptist churches in Georgia, and it is probable that the following were the original constituent churches of the body: Kiokee, Red Creek (now Abilene), Little Brier Creek, Fishing Creek, and Upton's Creek. To these were added next year Phillip's Mills and Whatley's Mills (now Bethesda). The principal ministers at that time were Abraham Marshall, Silas Mercer, Sanders Walker, Peter Smith, Lovelace Savidge, William Franklin, and Alexander Scott. The growth of the Association, which at that time embraced the whole denomination, was very rapid. In 1788 the churches numbered 31; in 1790 they numbered 32, with 2877 members, and 20 ministers, 17 of whom were ordained; and in 1792 the number of churches had increased to 56, scattered over a wide scope of country, some of them being in South Carolina. In 1794 the churches which were in the southern part of the Association were dismissed to form the Hephzibah Association, the second formed in the State. About this time the churches in South Carolina were dismissed also. In 1798 other churches obtained letters of dismissal, and formed, in 1799, the Sarepta Association. Notwithstanding all these withdrawals, the Georgia Association still contained 52 churches in 1810, when all south of the Oconee petitioned to be dismissed. These were constituted into the Ocmulgee Association, the third formed directly from the Georgia. The Savannah River Association had been organized in 1803; there were now five Associations in the State.

The early ministers of the denomination, impelled by a burning desire to preach the gospel, went everywhere proclaiming the Word, and the Lord blessed their work greatly. Again and again great and general revivals of religion swept over the State in consequence of their faithful preaching. In 1802 not less than 3345 new converts were added to the four Baptist Associations of the State. In 1812-13 over 1200 were baptized in the Sarepta Association alone, and a great blessing descended upon the entire State. In 1827 a memorable and most remarkable revival of religion commenced in Eatonton under the preaching of Adiel Sherwood, and resulted in the addition of not less than 15,000 or 20,000 to the Georgia Baptist churches. More than 5000 baptisms were reported that year in three Associations,—the Georgia, the Ocmulgee, and the Flint River. After a sermon preached in the open air by Dr. Adiel Sherwood at Antioch church, in Morgan County, during which the Holy Spirit gave him uncommon liberty, 4000 persons came forward for prayer, and for fifteen years afterwards persons who joined the Antioch and other churches referred to that sermon and time as the cause and date of their conversion.

A new and, in general, a more cultivated class of ministers, and, perhaps, not one whit behind the former generation in zeal and piety, next appeared;

and from that day to the present, the ministers, as a class, having better opportunities for education, have kept pace with the advancing intelligence of the age. Many of the Georgia Baptists, in their associational and conventional action, have manifested an ardent desire to promote the cause of missions in the world, and of education in the denomination.

Their organization for mission work extends back to the beginning of the century, while their efforts to promote education have resulted in the establishment and maintenance of one first-class university, two large high schools for young men, six colleges for young ladies, all of high grade, and one high school for the young of both sexes. These institutions have real estate and endowments worth at least $480,000. They have unflinchingly, and from the earliest period, shown themselves opposed to all union of church and state, the friends of entire religious liberty and of human rights. It was owing to a protest of the Georgia Association, in 1785, presented by Silas Mercer and Peter Smith, that the State Legislature repealed a law, then recently enacted, " giving two pence per pound to the minister chosen by any thirty families, for his support, to be paid out of the State treasury." At that time the Baptist denomination was largely in the ascendancy in point of numbers in the State ; its ministers were the most numerous, and, consequently, the largest amount of the State grant would have come to them.

It was owing to a petition drawn up by Dr. H. H. Tucker, and presented to the State Legislature, in 1863, signed by a number of distinguished Baptists, that the following section in the new code was immediately repealed : " It shall be unlawful for any church, society, or other body, or any persons, to grant any license or other authority to any slave, or free person of color, to preach or exhort, or otherwise officiate in church matters." The principal plea made was that the section was a violation of religious liberty, to which the Baptists of the State would never submit.

At its session in 1864, the Georgia Association adopted the following resolution unanimously ; it is condemnatory of the practice of separating husband and wife, which sometimes occurred during the slavery era :

"*Resolved*, That it is the firm belief and conviction of this body that the institution of marriage was ordained by Almighty God for the benefit of the whole human race, without respect to color ; that it ought to be maintained in its original purity among all classes of people in all countries and in all ages till the end of time; and that, consequently, the law of Georgia, in its failure to recognize and protect this relationship between our slaves, is essentially defective, and ought to be amended."

This resolution, also, was drawn up and offered by Dr. Henry H. Tucker.

In 1794, in the Georgia Association, which met at Powell's Creek meeting-house (now Powelton), Hancock Co., a memorial to the Legislature, that a law be made to prevent the future importation of slaves, was presented, read, and approved, and ordered to be signed by the moderator and clerk. Henry Graybill and James Sims were appointed to present the memorial to the Assembly. Abraham Marshall was moderator, and Peter Smith clerk.

In general, when a course of action has been decided, the Baptists of Georgia are harmonious. In regard to church order they are very strict, and in doctrine they are strongly Calvinistic.

The progress and growth of the denomination will perhaps be best exhibited by the following statistical table, which, though only approximately correct, is rather *under* than *over* the true figures :

Year.	Churches.	Ministers.	Members.	Associations.
1788	32	31	2,877	1
1790	42	72	3,211	1
1794	75	92	4,800	5
1812	163	109	14,761	5
1824	264	145	18,108	10
1829	356	200	28,268	16
1832	509	225	38,382	18
1835	583	298	41,810	22
1840	672	319	48,302	43
1845	771	464	58,388	46
1851	847	613	65,231	50
1860	996	786	84,022	65
1870	1218	831	115,198	70
1880	2663	1553	219,726	83

Of these, there are 27 Associations with 912 churches, 700 ministers, and 98,000 church members, who are colored Baptists. Of the remainder, about 10,000 are anti-mission, leaving the approximate number of white Baptists friendly to missions 112,000.

According to its report the State Mission Board of the Georgia Baptist Convention employed, during the last Convention year, twenty-four missionaries, for all or a part of the year, four of whom were colored. The present year it is employing about the same number, of whom five are colored. The Rehoboth Association sustains J. S. Morrow, white, as a missionary in the Indian Territory, and he has the guidance and supervision of many churches which have pastors.

Georgia, Cherokee Baptist Convention of. —On the 23d of November, 1854, a number of brethren appointed by the Middle Cherokee and Coosa Baptist Associations met at Cassville, Ga., to form an organization to take charge of the Cherokee Baptist College at Cassville. There were present John Crawford, J. W. Lewis, A. W. Buford, A. R. Wright, and Z. Edwards from the Middle Cherokee Association, and E. Dyer, W. Newton, J. M. Wood, C. H. Stillwell, W. S. Battle, and S. W. Cochran, from the Coosa Association. G. W. Tumlin from the Tallapoosa Association, and N. M. Crawford, J. S. Murray, Wm. Martin, J. D.

Collins, T. G. Barron, J. H. Rice, H. S. Crawford, and M. J. Crawford, were also present, and were invited to take seats and assist in the deliberations. Rev. John W. Lewis was elected moderator, and C. H. Stillwell clerk. On motion of C. H. Stillwell, "A Convention, to be known as the Cherokee Georgia Baptist Convention," was organized, and a constitution was prepared and adopted.

The principles upon which the Convention was constituted were those "exhibited in the Scriptures, and generally received by the Baptist denomination of Georgia;" the specific objects were declared to be, "1. To unite the friends of education, and to combine their efforts for the establishment and promotion of institutions of learning, where the young of both sexes may be thoroughly educated on the cheapest practicable terms. 2. To foster and cherish the spirit of missions, and to facilitate missionary operations in any or every laudable way." These objects were afterwards enlarged, and were made to include the distribution of the Bible and other good books, and the education of indigent young ministers and orphans.

There was no money basis to the representation, and Associations, churches, and societies approving and co-operating, might send messengers. The Convention grew to be a strong and useful body, very earnest in the advocacy and support of its measures, but was broken up entirely by the war. In sentiment it was what has been denominated as "landmark," generally. The following are the names of those who have officiated as president during its existence: J. W. Lewis, J. M. Wood, Edwin Dyer, and Hon. Mark A. Cooper.

Among the instrumentalities which this Convention put in operation for the promotion of its operations was a paper called *The Landmark Banner and Cherokee Baptist*, which it determined to publish at its session in Dalton, in the spring of 1859. Rev. Jesse M. Wood was selected for editor, and the first number was issued at Rome, in October, 1859. The paper was published in Rome until June, 1860, when it was removed to Atlanta, and the "Franklin Publishing House" was formed. Soon after, Rev. H. C. Homady was added to the editorial staff, A. S. Worrell becoming also the book editor. The paper had the service of much talent, and made itself felt in the denomination, being outspoken and very decided in some of its views. The war coming on, serious financial embarrassments occurred. The publishing house was sold to J. J. Toon, and the paper passed into other hands, and finally suspended, crushed out of existence by the exigencies of war. Before it expired its name was changed to *The Banner and Baptist*.

Georgia, Colored Baptists of.—In a work of this sort the distinction between white and colored Baptists must be preserved, since their organization, history, and operations are at present entirely distinct.

Previous to and during the war the colored Baptists were generally members of the white Baptist churches, although in many instances they had separate houses of worship, and sometimes their churches were independent. Their training, discipline, and religious worship were supervised by the white Baptists, who regarded them strictly as members of their churches. They assisted in their conferences, sustained their pastors in whole or in part, and aided by advice in troublesome cases of discipline. In many country churches a part of the building was assigned to the colored brethren, or else a time for their special services was given to them, when the pastor of the white church preached to them. No white pastor ever presumed to ignore or neglect the colored members. The Associations nearly always appointed missionaries to the colored people, and in the State Conventions their religious wants were sacredly regarded. The result was that at the conclusion of the war there was all over the South an immense number of colored Baptists, many of whom were organized into churches. These statements would hold good in regard to the Methodists of the South. There was no ecclesiastical separation of the races until after the close of the war. The colored Baptists were then "dismissed" from the white churches, generally in a formal and regular manner, at their own request, and they formed themselves into churches, being always advised and assisted when necessary by their white brethren. They were also aided by them largely in the formation of their Associations and Conventions, and in many cases the white ministers held Institutes for the instruction of colored ministers. The consequence in Georgia has been that the best feeling exists between the white and colored Baptists. The latter are organized very much after the manner of the white Baptists, and they have exhibited a zeal and intelligence in the highest degree commendable. All this, however, is largely to be attributed to the training received from the white Baptists, and to the good feeling and pleasant relations existing religiously between the two races. That the white Baptists have not done more for their colored brethren since the war has been solely because of inability on account of the generally impoverished condition of the country.

ORGANIZATION.

The colored Baptists of Georgia are formed into 28 Associations, which contain 875 churches, with a membership of more than 108,000. At least half of these churches maintain Sunday-schools. The Associations send delegates each year to a State Convention organized on missionary principles, called "The Missionary Baptist Convention of

Georgia," the main object of which is to organize and establish churches and Sunday-schools throughout the State and to promote theological education, as may be seen by the following:

"It shall be the object of this Convention—

"1. To employ missionaries to travel through the waste places of our State and gather the people and preach the gospel to them, and aid them in every way possible, and especially in organizing both churches and Sunday-schools.

"2. To establish a theological institute for the purpose of educating young men and those who are preaching the gospel and have the ministry in view, or any of our brothers' sons that sustain a good moral character, and to procure immediately some central place in Georgia for the establishment of the same."

Auxiliary to and a part of this State Convention is the "Missionary Baptist Sunday-School Convention," which is actually a separate body, though composed of the members of the State Convention, and governed by the same rules. It is well officered and is a very efficient body, and it is doing a good work in establishing Sunday-schools. Its last report embraces over 200 schools, containing nearly 1000 teachers and 14,000 scholars, which raised during the year $321.61.

The school at Atlanta for the education of colored ministers is doing a noble work for a large number of students, and through them for the numerous churches to which they shall minister.

Georgia Female College, which is situated in Madison, Morgan Co., Ga., 104 miles from Augusta and 67 from Atlanta, was incorporated by an act of the Legislature of Georgia on the 25th of January, 1850. At that time it was known as "Madison Collegiate Institute," but soon afterwards the board of trustees, by a legislative amendment, changed the name to "Georgia Female College." The institution was founded under the auspices of the Baptists, and the men mainly instrumental in establishing it were residents of Madison. George Y. Browne was called to the care of the institute in 1850, and assumed the presidency of the college in 1851, afterwards ably and successfully conducting its operations for ten consecutive years. In 1861 he removed to Alabama, but in 1870 returned to Madison and again accepted the presidency, which declining health compelled him to resign in 1878. As an instructor Geo. Y. Browne had no superior and but few equals, and those who enjoyed the benefit of his instruction received no superficial education.

Besides Mr. Browne, other distinguished men have as its presidents done honor to the institution. Notably among them may be named Rev. I. R. Branham, D.D., whose cultivated mind and heart left an indelible impress on all who came under his charge. Prof. A. S. Towns, of South Carolina, was also president for a brief period, and gave perfect satisfaction to his patrons. R. T. Asbury, late president of Monroe Female College, now has charge of this noble institution, having lately assumed the position. He has a widely extended reputation as a thorough and successful teacher, and is aided by an able corps of assistants. The main college building is a large and well-arranged brick edifice, situated in a beautiful grove, and presenting an attractive appearance. The college has a fine philosophical apparatus. The president of the board of trustees is Col. John B. Walker, a distinguished Baptist layman, who aided so largely in establishing the institution. The secretary and treasurer of the college is Rev. Samuel A. Burney, son of T. J. Burney, the former secretary and treasurer, who was also one of the warmest friends of the college. Perhaps no female college in the State has sent out more well-educated young ladies than this one.

German Baptist Publication Society.—This society was organized by the German Baptists in the United States and Ontario at the Triennial Conference held at Wilmot, Ontario, in 1866. It owed its origin to a deep conviction that the press should be more extensively used in disseminating Baptist principles among the Germans in this land. For some years previous to this there had been published a monthly paper, first under the editorship of Rev. K. A. Fleischmann, and subsequently under that of Rev. A. Henrich. This paper was adopted by the new society, and Rev. P. W. Bickel was appointed its editor and at the same time secretary of the society. The society progressed slowly for five years, when, through the activity of Rev. P. W. Bickel, a capital was raised for the more extensive prosecution of the work. Mr. J. T. Burghardt, a member of the German church at Louisville, Ky., proved himself a noble helper at the right time. He offered to give to the society a cash donation of $2000 on condition that the German churches would make up an equal sum. The condition was fully complied with. These donations were used in the year 1872 in buying a piece of property in Cleveland, O. A house was erected, types, presses, and machinery were bought, books, tracts, and papers explaining and defending our principles were published and spread broadcast over the land. These publications have given material help in spreading Baptist principles among the Germans and in increasing the membership. In 1874 *Der Sendbote*, the weekly periodical of the society, was enlarged to eight pages. The first accommodations becoming too small, in 1878 a large three-story building was erected at the corner of Jayne Avenue and Dayton Street (on a lot donated to the society by the Cleveland Baptist Union), where the business is now carried on, and where every facility is had for doing first-class work.

The society is sending forth its publications into many lands. Its weekly and Sunday-school papers circulate not only in this country, but also, to some extent at least, in Germany, Russia, and Australia, and even in South Africa, wherever in these lands German emigrants are found.

The regular publications of the society are *Der Sendbote*, a weekly paper, and three monthlies, *Der Muntere Saemann* (The Cheerful Sower), a child's paper, *Die Sonntagsfreude* (Sabbath Joy), a lesson paper, and *Der Wegweiser* (The Guide), a monthly tract for general distribution. There are also issued from time to time books and pamphlets for the use of the German Baptist churches.

In 1878, Rev. P. W. Bickel, D.D., having been sent by the American Baptist Publication Society to organize and conduct a Publication Society at Hamburg, Germany, Rev. J. C. Haselhuhn was elected to fill his place, and is now the chief executive officer.

German Baptists in America.—Rev. K. A. Fleischmann was sent by George Müller, of Bristol, England, to preach the gospel to the Germans in America. There existed at the time great religious destitution among the Germans in the New World. Mr. Fleischmann commenced his labors in Newark, N. J., where, in October, 1839, the first German converts were baptized. The believers whom he baptized were united in an organization for mutual edification, yet it seems that a regular Baptist church was not formed there until 1849, when this body of believers fully accepted the principles of the Regular Baptists, and united with the East New Jersey Baptist Association. Leaving Newark, N. J., Mr. Fleischmann labored successfully in the city of Reading, Pa., and especially in Lycoming Co., Pa., and then removed to Philadelphia, where through his zealous efforts a church of baptized believers was founded in May, 1843. This church was received into the Philadelphia Association in 1848. Subsequent to the formation of the church in Philadelphia, regular German Baptist churches were formed under the labor of godly men in New York in 1846, in Rochester, N. Y., in 1848, in Buffalo in 1849, in St. Louis, Mo., in 1850, in Chicago, Ill., in 1850, and in Bridgeport, Ont., in 1851.

In 1851 the number of missionaries and churches had so far increased that a Conference of pastors and churches was formed at Philadelphia, Pa. The ministers who attended this first Conference were J. Eschmann, K. A. Fleischmann, A. Henrich, A. Rauschenbusch, and A. von Puttkammer. A few delegates also were in attendance. Letters were sent by several missionaries who could not be present. It was indeed a day of small things, but foundations were laid in faith for the work of the future.

A hymn-book for the churches was projected and subsequently published by the American Baptist Publication Society. It was felt that a periodical was needed for the diffusion of Baptist principles among the Germans, and for the successful advancement of the missionary enterprise in the churches, and Rev. K. A. Fleischmann was appointed to edit a monthly paper for that purpose. Providentially, in the same year a way was opened by which young and older men in the churches, who felt themselves called to enter the harvest-field, could obtain the necessary preparation. A German department had been formed in connection with the Rochester Theological Seminary. The next annual meeting of the Conference, held in Rochester in 1852, proved that encouraging progress had been made in every direction.

In 1859 the number of the churches had so far increased that the Conference was divided into the Eastern and the Western, comprising the Eastern and Western States, each Conference restricting its special missionary work to its immediate field. Great help in the extension of the work came from three causes,—the services which the German theological department at Rochester rendered in furnishing men qualified to be pastors, the timely and continued aid and co-operation of the American Baptist Home Mission Society and kindred organizations, and the providential guidance through which such men of talent, zeal, and piety as Rev. A. Rauschenbusch, A. von Puttkammer, A. Henrich, H. Schneider, and a number of others, were led to accept Scriptural views concerning baptism. Thus faithful men, some of whom had been very useful long before they became Baptists, were called into this work, and doors of extensive usefulness were opened to them.

The denomination continued to spread, especially in the Western States, whither the tide of German immigration was moving. Since the separate organization of the Western Conference its work has extended into the States of Illinois, Indiana, Iowa, Kansas, Kentucky, Michigan, Minnesota, Missouri, Nebraska, Ohio, Wisconsin, Oregon, and Texas; and that of the Eastern Conference, though not embracing so large a territory, has been constantly growing.

It was soon felt that the interests of the German cause would be greatly aided by a Triennial Conference, embracing both Annual Conferences and all the churches. The first meeting of the Triennial Conference was held in September, 1865, with the church at Wilmot, Ontario. Rev. K. A. Fleischmann presided, and Revs. J. C. Haselhuhn and J. S. Gubelmann were appointed secretaries. A German Publication Society was formed, the religious periodical of the churches changed into a weekly paper, and placed under the editorship of Rev. P. W. Bickel.

When the first Conference met in Philadelphia, Pa., in 1851, there were in all 8 churches, 8 pastors, and 405 members. In 1880 there were 4 Conferences, or Associations, 130 churches, 115 pastors, and 9020 members. Counting those who were converted through the labors of German missionaries and who may now be members of English-speaking churches, the number of German Baptists must exceed 10,000. Considering the special difficulties in their way the growth of the German Baptists has been steady and cheering.

Much religious activity is manifested in the German churches. The Sunday-school work is actively carried on. The churches sustain a number of students preparing for the ministry in the theological school at Rochester, N. Y. They have also founded an academy. Their efficient Publication Society is disseminating Baptist literature in many forms. The German churches contributed in one year for the support of the gospel, and for benevolent purposes, $79,518.44, which is over $9 per member; for home missions alone they gave $3580.60, which is nearly 44 cents per member.

In doctrine and practice the German churches in this country are in accord with their English-speaking brethren; they generally belong to English Associations; their peculiar union as Conferences being simply for the effective prosecution of their special work.

German Baptists, or Brethren.—The German Baptists first became a distinct body of believers, separate from the corrupt elements by which they were surrounded, about the year 1708, near Schwartzenau, Germany.

They do not pretend to trace their line of succession up to the Apostles. They hold rather to the succession of the faith, practices, and rites of the Apostolic Church. They believe that the true religious succession consists not in personal contact, but in association with Jesus Christ, and in obedience to him in word and doctrine.

After their separate permanent organization they increased very rapidly. But they did not long enjoy prosperity, for the hand of persecution was lifted against them, and they were driven, some to Holland and Friesland, and many, in 1719–1729, to America. They established their first church in the United States at Germantown, Pa., from which the denomination has spread over the Middle, most of the Southern, and all of the Western States.

From 8, that composed the first congregation, there have now arisen 100,000 followers of Christ, with about 2000 ministers, 26 Annual District, and one General Annual Conference, which is composed of representatives chosen by the District Conferences. They control three excellent seminaries, which are now doing efficient educational work. Successful home and foreign missions have been established. The increase of the church of late years has been very rapid.

They have four weekly papers, one monthly magazine, and one weekly paper designed for the young, and intended to meet the demand of their rapidly-increasing Sunday-schools.

They believe in one true and living God, the Creator of the intelligent hosts of earth and heaven, of the universe visible and invisible, the omnipotent and omniscient sustainer and benefactor of all things.

They believe that Jesus Christ is the Son of the living God; that he was and will continue to be co-existent with the Father; that he is divine in his attributes; that he came to this world the incarnation of God; that he laid down his life for us, was buried, and rose again; that he ascended to the Father, where he is now the advocate of his people; that it is alone through his meritorious death and triumphant resurrection that his people have redemption and eternal life; that he will again personally come to this earth to gather his elect together.

They believe that the Holy Spirit is a divine personage, co-eternal in existence with the Father and the Son; that he was sent into the world to convince it of sin, of righteousness, and of judgment; that he is the guide, the enlightener, and the comforter of the people of God. They believe that these three divine persons, the Father, the Son, and the Holy Spirit, are one God, eternal and omnipotent.

They believe that the New Testament is the word and the will of God revealed through Jesus Christ, and by the inspiration of the Spirit through the holy Apostles; that the Old Testament is inspired, and the Scriptures are the only infallible rule of faith and practice to which the followers of Christ can look, and that they should strictly adhere both in letter and in spirit to their teachings.

They do not practise infant baptism. They believe that only persons who are competent to exercise intelligent, saving faith in Christ, and who repent of sin, are proper subjects of baptism. In baptism they are immersionists exclusively. They baptize into the name of the Father, and of the Son, and of the Holy Ghost, not by one action, but by three, thus constituting a triple immersion. During the observance of the rite the candidate kneels and is dipped face forward, the imposition of hands and prayer occurring while the candidate still kneels in the water.

They celebrate the communion of the bread and cup, commemorative of the death of Christ, in the evening, accompanied by the ancient love-feast. During this observance they eat as one family at the Lord's table, thus exhibiting a fraternal band of Christian believers.

Associated with the communion and Agapæ, they practise the washing of one another's feet as a Christian ordinance, and as a reason for such practice they refer to Jno. xiii. 1–17.

In connection with feet-washing, or while surrounding the table, they extend the hand of fellowship and salute one another with the holy kiss.—2 Cor. xiii. 12; 1 Pet. v. 14.

They also when called upon pray over their sick, anointing them with oil in the name of the Lord.—James v. 14, 15.

They hold very sacred the non-resistant principles of the Apostolic Church. They do not go to war, will not bear arms, nor even learn the art of war. Neither do they swear the civil or any other oath before magistrates or in courts of justice. They are noted for their modesty in apparel, plainness of speech, and distinguished hospitality.

Their church polity is not entirely Congregational. When differences arise in matters of expediency which cannot be disposed of satisfactorily by the individual community, they are referred to the Annual Conference for advice or adjudication. Thus they live together in communities, simple and harmless, adjusting their misunderstandings not by civil law, but by the gospel rule.—Matt. xviii. 15–17.

Germany, Baptists in.—The First Baptist church in Germany in modern times was constituted in Hamburg in 1834. Mr. J. G. Oncken, born Jan. 26, 1800, in the town of Varel, grand duchy of Oldenburg, Germany, came to England in his youth, and was there converted. Manifesting talent, he was sent back as a missionary to his native land in 1823, by a society in Great Britain which had been formed with special reference to the evangelization of the Continent. He labored zealously and effectively, preaching the gospel on the shores of the German Ocean, in the cities of Hamburg and Bremen, and in East Friesland. Everywhere open doors were set before him, and many were converted.

While Mr. Oncken was regularly and successfully preaching in Hamburg, the question of believer's baptism seems first to have occupied his attention. Without any influence from without, simply as a result of earnest study of the Scriptures, the conviction gradually grew upon him that the immersion of believers was the only Scriptural baptism. A strong impulse in this direction, however, was given him by his intercourse with a Baptist brother from America, Capt. Tubbs, a member of the old Sansom Street church, in Philadelphia, who was for some time an inmate of Mr. Oncken's family, and through whom communication between Mr. Oncken and the Baptists in America began.

On the 22d day of April, 1834, in the dead of night, Mr. Oncken and six others were baptized by Dr. Barnas Sears, then of the Hamilton Literary and Theological Institution, in the river Elbe, near Hamburg. On the following day the brethren were organized into a church. Mr. Oncken was soon after this set apart by solemn prayer and the laying on of hands to the work of the gospel ministry. In a chamber of Mr. Oncken's former residence, No. 7 Englische Planke, may be seen the spot where the Baptist church in Hamburg was organized, and where Mr. Oncken was set apart as its pastor. Here was laid the foundation of a work which, under the blessing of God, has extended through Germany and adjacent countries.

The baptism of Mr. Oncken and the founding of a Baptist church created a great sensation. The earnest preacher had suffered persecution before he became a Baptist, while yet in connection with the Independents, but now persecution rose to its height. The constant growth of the little church exasperated the clergy and the authorities. It was decided that this could no longer be tolerated. On a week-day evening police-officers came into the meeting and drove the members into the street, amidst the jubilant shouts of the populace. Mr. Oncken was arrested and conveyed to prison, where he was subjected to the treatment received by the lowest prisoners. After a few days he was tried, convicted, and sentenced to an imprisonment of four weeks. On other occasions he was fined, and, as his conscience did not permit him to pay them, his goods were seized and sold. Driven out from their place of meeting, the church secured another, where God wrought marvelously in their behalf. Through the great fire in 1842, and their generosity in offering an asylum to the destitute, the power of the persecutor was greatly weakened.

The work thus begun amidst strong persecution was destined soon to spread into other cities of Germany. The numerous connections Mr. Oncken had formed at the beginning of his evangelistic activities in 1823, and also as an agent of the Edinburgh Bible Society, naturally made his change of views a matter of conversation and consideration in different places. Here and there small bands of believers were formed who accepted these views as Scriptural, and gradually these bands grew into large and influential churches. The first instance of this nature was the organization of the church in Berlin, Prussia, in 1837. In 1830, Mr. Oncken had made the acquaintance, in Berlin, of Mr. G. W. Lehmann, a steel engraver. The subsequent baptism of Mr. Oncken led Mr. Lehmann to a prayerful and protracted consideration of the subject. As a result, in spite of much opposition and of the severe self-denial which such a step would cost, Lehmann and a few others felt that it was their duty to be baptized. On the 13th day of May, 1837, the first modern baptism in Prussia took place near Berlin. At three o'clock in the morning of that day a little group of believers passed out of the Stralauer gate to the Rummelsberger Lake, where, after fervent prayer, Mr. Lehmann, his wife, and four others were immersed by Mr. Oncken, at the very time when the first rays of the rising sun gilded the skies. On the following day Mr. Oncken preached a powerful sermon from John xiv. 16. In the afternoon of that day the little church of six members was constituted. Mr. G. W. Lehmann was appointed pastor. He assumed this office, and supported himself until 1838, when he received aid from the American Baptist Missionary Union. In 1840, Mr. Lehmann was formally ordained, and

organized in Copenhagen, but this beginning of the work in Denmark was made under severe trials. Rev. Peter Moenster, the pastor, was sentenced to ten weeks' imprisonment for preaching and administering baptism, and then banished. The same pastor, with his brother, Rev. Adolph Moenster, was afterwards confined in prison for an entire year. In the beginning of 1845 there were 17 preachers and assistants, 26 churches, and nearly 1500 members. Before 1849 the churches were formed into Associations; these Associations were united in a Triennial Conference, the first meeting of which was held in Hamburg in January, 1849.

MISSION CHAPEL, HAMBURG.

from that time the Saviour's kingdom began to prosper.

In the year following the organization of the church in Berlin, two other churches were founded, one in Oldenburg with 13 members, and one in Stuttgart, the capital of Würtemberg, with 23 members. It seems providential that in each church formed there was one among their own number capable of preaching the gospel.

We cannot follow minutely the progress of the Baptists in Hesse, Bavaria, Pomerania, Hanover, and Southern Germany. Though gradual, and amidst continual and often fierce opposition from the state church and the authorities, it was a constant and blessed triumph. In 1839 a church was

In 1851 there were 32 churches in the German mission, including 14 in Prussia, 5 in Denmark, and 2 in Switzerland. On the 23d of April, 1859, the church in Hamburg celebrated its twenty-fifth anniversary. "The original seven had grown to seven thousand, and stretched across the German states from the North Sea to Russia, from the Baltic well-nigh to Russia." At the eighth Triennial Conference, held in July, 1870, the German Baptists were reported "to have entered all quarters of the globe." They now possess churches or mission stations in most of the German states, in Switzerland, Holland, Denmark, Russia, Poland, Bulgaria, Turkey, Austria, and South Africa. In addition to this the denomination in Sweden owes its origin in part to the German mission. As early as 1841 the brethren in Germany reported a colporteur laboring in Norway, and in 1851 a church in Sweden with 58 members. In 1854 two brethren from Sweden were baptized in Hamburg and empowered to administer baptism to others. Besides, a large number of German Baptists have emigrated to America, and helped to increase the membership of the German churches here.

It will thus be seen that the German work from the beginning has been eminently of a missionary character, and that it has shared to a large extent the fostering care of American Baptists. The prospects for the future are encouraging. Divisions which some years ago seemed destined to retard growth have been healed. Pressing needs are gradually being supplied. One of these is a theological seminary for the adequate training of the ministry. Such an institution has just been founded, and steps are being taken to place it upon a permanent financial basis. Another is the preparation and spread of sound Baptist literature. For this purpose a Publication Society has been formed, the American Baptist Publication Society furnishing an able manager and editor in the person of Rev. P. W. Bickel, D.D. Doors are opening far and wide, and if men and means can be furnished the successes achieved promise to be but the small beginnings of a work of wonderful extent and power.

At the close of 1879 there were in Germany 16,602 members, and the gospel was preached at 1173 preaching stations. Adding the membership in Austria, Denmark, Switzerland, Poland, Russia, Turkey, South Africa,—countries to which German Baptists have gone, and whose churches are included in the German Baptist "Bund," or Union,—the total number cannot now be much less than 27,000. The increase is certainly cheering. It has been observed that since the first church was formed in Hamburg, every year but four has witnessed the organization of new churches. And yet the work is but begun. Millions upon millions have not yet been reached. Should not the abundant blessings of the past induce Baptists to aid in spreading the gospel throughout the whole of Germany?

Gessler, Rev. Theodore A. K., A.M., was born in Philadelphia, Oct. 16, 1841. He passed through the lower grades of the public schools and the High School. Subsequently he studied law. He was baptized in his native city by Rev. Benj. Griffith, D.D. Under a conviction of duty he abandoned the study of law, and entered Lewisburg University to prepare for the ministry, and was graduated in 1864. His first pastorate was at West Farms, N. Y., which continued four years, during which the church was greatly strengthened and a new house of worship built and paid for. From this charge he went to Elizabeth, N. J., and accepted a call from the First Baptist church. He remained on that field twelve years, during which large accessions were made to the church, and a handsome and commodious house of worship was built, costing about $60,000.

In 1874 he was chosen president of the New Jersey Sunday-School Union, which office he held until his removal from the State.

On the 1st of January, 1880, he entered upon the pastorate of the Central Baptist church of Brooklyn. Mr. Gessler is a zealous worker in the church, an interesting speaker, clear-headed, warm-hearted, eminently social, and has had unvarying success in all his settlements.

Gibson, Rev. J. G., of Crawfordville, Ga., an able and influential Baptist minister, was born March 29, 1832, in Morgan Co., Ala., where he lived for fifteen years. He removed to Oglethorpe Co., Ga., in 1847. He was converted, and united with Millstone church in 1850. He studied law in Lexington, and when the late civil war commenced he was clerk of the Inferior and Superior Courts, and also acting ordinary for his county, but resigned to enter the artillery service as lieutenant, in which he continued until the war closed. He served chiefly in Florida, and was for a time provost-marshal and commandant of the post at Tallahassee. After the war he was elected judge of the County Court, and held the position two years, but resigned that he might devote himself exclusively to the ministry. He was ordained in 1865, since which time he has served Millstone, Salem, Lexington, Crawford, and other churches in Oglethorpe County. Mr. Gibson is a man of marked ability and great strength of character. He is also well read, and a persevering student. Perhaps no minister in Georgia is more beloved by his churches, or more honored by the community in which he lives. There are few, if any, better preachers in the State; he is logical, earnest, and eloquent. An excellent organizer, he has trained all his churches in systematic benevolence, until they have attained a high degree of liberality, never failing to a full performance of duty, not merely in regard to church services, but in all those grand benevolent enterprises in which the denomination is interested.

Giddings, Rev. Rockwood, was born in New Hampshire, Aug. 8, 1812. He joined a Baptist church in his youth, and exhibited remarkable consecration from that time until his death. After a thorough preparatory course of instruction he entered Waterville College, graduating in 1833. He hesitated as to whether God had called him to preach the gospel. He removed to Virginia and commenced the study of medicine, and afterwards located in Warsaw, Ky. Here he had just completed his medical studies when he was impressed with a desire to preach the gospel, and accepted ordination in 1835. He became pastor of the Baptist church in Shelbyville, Ky. His success was almost marvelous. In the fall of 1838 he was made president of Georgetown College, which at that time was without a faculty or an endowment. He speedily organized the institution, with a full corps of professors, and gathered into it a number of students. He then exerted himself to raise an endowment, and in eight months he secured $80,000 in unconditional notes; he then attempted to secure half that amount in cash, and traveled long journeys, preaching everywhere as he went. But the constant strain was too much for his delicate constitution, and while preaching, he sank down in the pulpit, from which he was carried to Shelbyville, where he died on the 29th of October, 1839.

Gidney, Angus M., was born in New Brunswick, May 4, 1803; converted and baptized in Annapolis Co., Nova Scotia. He is a literary man and a poet; was for many years editor of a secular paper in Yarmouth and Bridgetown. Mr. Gidney was recently sergeant-at-arms in the House of Assembly in Nova Scotia.

Gifford, Andrew, D.D., was born in Bristol, England, Aug. 17, 1700. He was converted in his boyhood, and baptized in his fifteenth year. At the academy where he was educated there were some students who became noted men afterwards; and among these was Dr. Secker, who became archbishop of Canterbury.

Mr. Gifford, perhaps about his twenty-fifth year, became assistant minister to the Rev. George Eaton, of Nottingham. He subsequently sustained for two years the same relation to the Rev. Bernard Foskett, of Bristol. On Feb. 5, 1729, he became pastor of the church meeting in Little Wild Street, London. There was a division in Mr. Gifford's community in 1736, which led to the formation of a new church by the pastor and a majority of the members. Mr. Gifford and his friends erected a new meeting-house in Eagle Street, Red Lion Square, which was dedicated Feb. 20, 1737. During the ministry of Mr. Gifford this house was twice enlarged to accommodate the ever-increasing congregations.

Mr. Gifford early became celebrated for his acquaintance with and appreciation of ancient manuscripts and coins. His collection of rare coins was the most valuable in Great Britain; it attracted the attention of George II., who purchased it for his own cabinet. He became a recognized authority of national reputation upon subjects of this character. He was, of course, a member of the Antiquarian Society.

During a visit to Edinburgh he was honored with the freedom of that ancient city. In 1754 the degree of Doctor of Divinity was conferred upon him by Marischal College, Aberdeen. In 1757 he was appointed assistant librarian of the British Museum. His personal friends, Lord Chancellor Hardwicke, Archbishop Herring, Speaker Onslow, and Sir Richard Ellys, procured him this important position. He did not permit the duties of his place in the Museum to interfere with his pastoral labors. He had in his new station the best opportunity conceivable for increasing his vast knowledge, and adding to the list of his distinguished friends. The Marquis of Lothian, the Earl of Halifax, Lord Dartmouth, Lord Buchan, and others of the nobility were occasionally seen in the congregation of Dr. Gifford.

He was a zealous Baptist, and he permitted no aristocratic associations to turn him from the teachings of the New Testament. He was a firm Calvinist, and on all proper occasions proclaimed the doctrines of grace. He was a warm friend of George Whitefield and the Countess of Huntingdon, and gloried in seeing souls brought to Jesus. He died June 19, 1784.

Dr. Gifford bequeathed his library, pictures, and manuscripts, with a vast collection of curiosities, to the Bristol Baptist College. In the library and museum of that institution these valuable gifts are still to be seen; and no doubt they will long continue to impart instruction to the living, and to increase veneration for the learned and saintly donor, whose pictures and bequests claim their admiration.

Gifford, Rev. John, was at one time a major in the army of Charles I., king of England. In the unsettled condition of the times, while in the military service, he became restless, and he attempted to create an insurrection in the county of Kent. For this act of rebellion he was seized, and, after a summary trial, condemned to death. But he escaped from prison and fled to Bedford, where in safety he followed the medical profession; and in that town he persecuted godly persons with great fierceness.

By the power of Jehovah the heart of the major was broken, and he accepted Jesus as his Redeemer. He was immersed on a profession of his faith, and immediately began to preach. Converts were made by the Spirit's blessing upon his ministrations, whom he formed into a church about 1650. Of this church he became pastor, and he continued its under-shepherd till 1671, when he departed this life.

The "three or four poor women" of Bedford whose conversation about their sins and their Saviour first aroused John Bunyan to see the nature and blessedness of true religion were members of Mr. Gifford's church. Their pastor, by his sermons and pious counsels, was very useful in leading Bunyan to the Saviour, and it was by Mr. Gifford that he was immersed in 1655, when he united with the church at Bedford. On the 12th of December, 1671, just after Mr. Gifford's death, and while Bunyan was still in prison, he was elected Mr. Gifford's successor.

Gilbert, Hon. Joseph B., son of Capt. Joseph Gilbert, was born in Middletown, Conn., Oct. 10, 1787; converted about 1805, and united with a Baptist church; trained as a merchant with his father; in 1811 commenced business in Hartford, and united with First Baptist church; in 1817 was chosen deacon; held various public offices; elected to the State senate; for several years State treasurer; a long time treasurer of Connecticut Baptist State Convention; trustee of Connecticut Literary Institution; of sterling integrity, sound judgment, firmness of faith, humility of deportment, and marked hospitality; died June 2, 1857, in his seventieth year, leaving an honored name.

Gilbert, Rev. S. B., the pastor of the Baptist church at Normal, Ill., was born at Windsor, Broome Co., N. Y., Jan. 5, 1819, and was baptized at fifteen years of age into the fellowship of the church at Shelby, Orleans Co., N. Y., by his father, Rev. Samuel Gilbert, one of the pioneer ministers of Southeastern New York. He was ordained pastor of the Junius and Tyre Baptist church, Seneca Co., in 1846. His subsequent pastorates have been at Clyde, N. Y., Marshall, Mich., Mendota, El Paso, Freeport, and Normal, Ill. His removal to Illinois took place in 1855, when he settled at Mendota, then a small railway town on the newly-opened Chicago, Burlington and Quincy road. Here he remained fourteen years, the church which was in due time organized, growing to a membership of 200, and a second house of worship being under way as he left for another field. Mr. Gilbert is noted among his brethren for his thoughtful, judicious sermons, his excellent judgment, his steadiness of purpose, and genial, brotherly spirit.

Giles, Rev. John Eustace, for several years one of the most distinguished preachers among the English Baptists, was the son of the Rev. W. Giles, and was born at Dartmouth, April 20, 1805, where his father was pastor of the Baptist church. He was educated at the well-known school of the Rev. James Hinton, at Oxford, and in his twentieth year he was baptized and admitted into the church at Chatham, of which his father was then pastor. In 1825 he was entered as a student at Bristol College, and whilst there gave promise of eminent usefulness. His first settlement as pastor was at Salter's Hall chapel, London, where he remained six years. He accepted a pressing call from the church at South Parade, Leeds, in 1836, and during the next ten years he became a prominent leader in public and denominational affairs. In company with Dr. Acworth he visited Hamburg on behalf of Mr. Oncken and the persecuted Baptists of that city, and at a later period he was associated with the Rev. Henry Dowson as a deputation to the king of Denmark to plead for the Baptists of that country. In both cases the results were gratifying, although persecution for conscience' sake had not wholly ceased. In the Anti-Corn-Law struggle Mr. Giles played a prominent part, and during his residence in Leeds he was immensely popular. After his removal from Leeds he labored at Bristol for a short period, then for fifteen years at Sheffield; from thence he removed to Rathmines, Dublin, and finally settled as pastor of the church at Clapham Common, London, which position he held for thirteen years, until his death, June 24, 1875, aged seventy. His pulpit talents during his ministry at Leeds, in the prime of life, were of the highest order. Although he wrote much, he published nothing except occasional lectures and sermons. His baptismal hymn is a general favorite, and is found probably in every modern collection of hymns used by Baptists throughout the world, having been translated into several languages. It is perhaps not universally known that Mr. Giles was the author. No one can question that it has the ring of true poetry as well as of sound Baptist sentiments:

> "Hast thou said, exalted Jesus,
> Take thy cross and follow me?
> Shall the word with terror seize us?
> Shall we from the burden flee?
> Lord, I'll take it,
> And, rejoicing, follow thee."

Gill, John, D.D., was born at Kettering, Northamptonshire, England, Nov. 23, 1697. His father, Edward Gill, was a Baptist in the membership of a union church composed of Presbyterians, Congregationalists, and Baptists, in which, beside a Pedobaptist pastor, Mr. William Wallis, a Baptist was a teaching elder, with authority to immerse adults. As Isaac Backus found this system a cause of controversy and strife in New England, so it proved in Kettering, and Edward Gill, William Wallis, and their friends found it necessary to withdraw and form a Particular Baptist church. Edward Gill was elected one of the deacons. To the end of his life he obtained a good report for "grace, piety, and holy conversation."

His son John early showed uncommon talents, and quickly surpassed those of his own age, and many much older, in acquiring knowledge. Before he was eleven years of age, under the instruction of an Episcopal clergyman, who had charge of the grammar-school of which he was a pupil, he had read the principal Latin classics, and had made such progress in Greek that he became an object of wonder and admiration to several ministers who were familiar with his attainments. The bookseller's shop in the town was only open on the market-day, and by the favor of the proprietor John

Gill was continually found there on that day consulting various authors. This remarkable studiousness attended him throughout life. His teacher commenced the practice of requiring the children

JOHN GILL, D.D.

of Dissenters to attend prayers in the Episcopal church on week-days along with the youths that belonged to the Church of England. The law probably gave him authority to exhibit his mean bigotry in this way. But Dissenting parents properly resented this pious effort of the clerical teacher, and withdrew their children from his care. Deprived of an instructor, he studied with even increased industry, and soon became a proficient in logic, rhetoric, natural and moral philosophy, and Latin, Greek, and Hebrew. In Latin he read the hoarded treasures of ancient and modern divinity until he was conversant with all the great writers of Western Christendom.

When he was about twelve years of age, a sermon preached by Mr. Wallis, his father's pastor, on the words, "And the Lord God called unto Adam, and said unto him, Where art thou?" made a solemn impression upon his mind; his sins and the wrath of God alarmed him; and for some time he was in the deepest distress. But the Saviour drew near and showed him his wounds and dying throes, and everlasting love, and by grace he was enabled to trust him, and to find liberty and justification. On the 1st of November, 1716, he was baptized in a neighboring river, and received into the fellowship of the church of Kettering.

Almost immediately after, by the advice of friends, he began to preach, first at Higham Ferrers, and afterwards at Kettering. The Lord blessed these ministrations to the conversion of a considerable number of persons, and high hopes were cherished about the future usefulness of Mr. Gill.

He was elected pastor of the church at Horsleydown, Southwark, London, and ordained to the gospel ministry in its meeting-house March 22, 1720. Of this church the celebrated Benjamin Keach had been pastor, whose son Elias founded the oldest church now existing in Pennsylvania, the mother of all the Baptist churches in Philadelphia. Difficulties which met him on entering upon his pastoral life in London soon disappeared, his meeting-house was thronged with people, conversions were numerous, and for over fifty-one years he was a power in London, and a religious authority all over Great Britain and America.

In comparatively early life he began to collect Hebrew works, the two Talmuds, the Targums, and everything bearing on the Old Testament and its times, and it is within bounds to say that no man in the eighteenth century was as well versed in the literature and customs of the ancient Jews as John Gill. He has sometimes been called the Dr. John Lightfoot of the Baptists. This compliment, in the estimation of some persons, flatters Dr. Lightfoot more than Dr. Gill, great an authority as Dr. Lightfoot undoubtedly was on all questions of Hebrew learning. In 1748, Dr. Gill received his diploma of Doctor of Divinity from Aberdeen, in which his attainments are described "as extraordinary proficiency in sacred literature, the Oriental tongues, and Jewish antiquities."

His "Dissertation Concerning the Antiquity of the Hebrew Language, Letters, Vowel Points, and Accents," has been described as "a masterly effort, of profound research, which would have shown Dr. Gill to have been a prodigy of reading and literature had he never published a syllable on any other subject."

His "Body of Divinity," published in 1769, is a work without which no theological library is complete. His grand old doctrines of grace, taken unadulterated from the Divine fountain, presented in the phraseology and with the illustrations of an intellectual giant, and commended by a wealth of sanctified Biblical learning only once in several ages permitted to mortals, sweep all opposition before them, and leave no place for the blighted harvests, the seed of which was planted by James Arminius in modern times. In this work eternal and personal election to a holy life, particular redemption from all guilt, resistless grace in regeneration, final preservation from sin and the Wicked one, till the believer enters paradise, and the other doctrines of the Christian system, are expounded and defended by one of the greatest teachers in Israel ever called to the work of instruction by the Spirit of Jehovah.

Dr. Gill's commentary is the most valuable exposition of the Old and New Testaments ever published. In codices of the Scriptures, recently discovered, there are some more authoritative readings than those known in Gill's day; and light has been cast upon the inspired records by explorations in the East, lately undertaken, and still in progress. But except in these features, Gill's commentary has the largest amount of valuable information ever presented to Christians, in the form of "Annotations on the Bible." The work was republished in Philadelphia by a Presbyterian elder in 1811; and in Ireland by an Episcopal clergyman some years ago. His other writings are numerous and of great merit. His works are still in demand at large prices on both sides of the Atlantic.

He was among the first contributors to Rhode Island College, now Brown University; and in his will he bequeathed a complete set of his works and fifty-two folio volumes of the fathers to that institution. Dr. Manning stated at the time that "this was by far the greatest donation the little library of the college had as yet received." The works are still in the library at Providence.

Dr. Gill died in possession of perfect consciousness, and in the full enjoyment of the Saviour's love, Oct. 14, 1771. His death occasioned great sorrow, especially among the friends of truth throughout this country and Great Britain, and many funeral sermons were preached to commemorate his great worth.

Dr. Gill was of middle stature, neither tall nor short, he was well proportioned, a little inclined to corpulency, his countenance was fresh and healthful, and he enjoyed a serene cheerfulness which continued with him almost to the last.

He was one of the purest men that ever lived; the sovereign grace for which he so nobly waged war was his own refuge and strength, and it gave him a life-long victory over all outward and internal evils.

He was a man of great humility, though flattered by large numbers. He could honestly say, "By the grace of God I am what I am;" he felt the truth of this apostolic experience, and glorified sovereign grace.

He knew more of the Bible than any one with whose writings we are acquainted. "Dr. Gill," says John Ryland, "leads into an *ocean* of divinity by a system of doctrinal and practical religion, and by a judicious and learned exposition of the Old and New Testaments."

The profound and pious Episcopalian, Toplady, who was frequently at a week-night lecture of Dr. Gill's, the author of the hymn,—

"Rock of Ages, shelter me,
Let me hide myself in thee."

says of the doctor, "So far as the doctrines of the gospel are concerned, Gill never besieged an error which he did not force from its strongholds; nor did he ever encounter an adversary to truth whom he did not baffle and subdue. His doctrinal and practical writings will live and be admired, and be a standing blessing to posterity, when their opposers are forgotten, or only remembered by the refutations he has given them. *While true religion and sound learning have a single friend remaining in the British Empire, the works and name of Gill will be precious and revered.*"

Gill, Rev. Thomas A., the son of John S. Gill, of Philadelphia, Pa., was born in that city Feb. 8, 1840. After the usual preparatory training, he entered the Philadelphia High School, and was graduated in his sixteenth year. Soon after this, he entered successively for short intervals the offices of Francis Wharton and Wm. Henry Rawle, distinguished lawyers of his native city. On leaving the service of the latter, the next few years were spent with his father, whose purpose was to associate his eldest son with him in his business.

During this period—in his nineteenth year—he was converted under the ministrations of the Rev. Dr. Cathcart, and was baptized into the fellowship of the Second Baptist church, Philadelphia. In April, 1861, as the result of personal conviction, and the judgment of the church, he entered the university at Lewisburg to prepare for the gospel ministry. The late war being then in active progress, his collegiate course was interrupted by two short terms of service in response to the exigencies growing out of the invasion of Pennsylvania by the army of Gen. Lee, and the subsequent burning of Chambersburg. Graduating in the university at the close of the war, he entered the Theological Seminary at the same place, and completed the prescribed course in July, 1867. In July of the ensuing year he was called to the pastoral charge of the First Baptist church, Germantown, Philadelphia, and in October following ordained to the Christian ministry. Resigning his pastorate in impaired health in August, 1871, he sought the same month the benefits of a tour abroad, traveling extensively in Europe, Egypt, and the Holy Land. Reluctant, after his return, in 1872, to re-enter the pastorate, from considerations of health, he was at length nominated by President Grant as a chaplain of the navy, and confirmed by the Senate, Dec. 22, 1874. In the following year, April 8, he was married to Marie Antoinette, the daughter of the Rev. Dr. E. H. Nevin, of Philadelphia. On the death of his wife, in May, 1878, at Vallejo, Cal., while chaplain of the naval station there, he returned to the East, and was attached to the flag-ship "Tennessee," of the Atlantic Squadron, where he has been officiating as chaplain up to the present date. Mr. Gill possesses scholarly attainments, deep piety, a vigorous intellect, an unblemished reputation, and the warm regards of all that know him.

Gillette, A. D., D.D., was born in Cambridge, Washington Co., N. Y., Sept. 8, 1807; educated at Hamilton and Union College, Schenectady; ordained in Schenectady; pastor of the Sansom Street church (Dr. Staughton's), Philadelphia, for four years; founded the Eleventh Baptist church in the same city in 1839, and, under God, made it a large and prosperous community. He has been pastor of Calvary church, New York, the First church of Washington, D. C., the Gethsemane church of Brooklyn, and the church of Sing Sing, N. Y. He edited the "Minutes of the Philadelphia Association from 1707 to 1807," a work of great labor and of unusual value. He has baptized about 2000 persons. In 1856 he received the degree of Doctor of Divinity. Dr. Gillette is one of the most brotherly men the writer ever met; his friends are legion. He has been one of the most useful men in the Baptist denomination; his graceful manners, unselfish disposition, and cultured mind gave him access in Philadelphia, New York, and Washington to the best society. The denomination lamented the stroke of paralysis which re-

A. D. GILLETTE, D.D.

cently threatened his life in Saratoga. Dr. Gillette has always basked in the sunshine of Christianity, leaving its imaginary dark clouds to gloomy minds.

Gilmore, Gov. Joseph A., was born in Weston, Vt., June 10, 1818. Like many enterprising young men, he was not satisfied to remain in the quiet rural district where he spent his childhood, but sought a wider field of activity. In early life he

GOV. JOSEPH A. GILMORE.

went to Boston, and there for a number of years was engaged in mercantile pursuits. It was while he was thus occupied that he was brought under the influence of the ministry of Rev. Baron Stow, D.D., and became a hopeful Christian, and joined the Baldwin Place church, of which Dr. Stow was the pastor. After remaining several years in Boston, he moved to Concord, N. H., and for some time was engaged in the same business which he had pursued in the former city. Subsequently he became interested in railroads, for which he seems to have had special tastes. He was superintendent of the Concord, Manchester and Lawrence road, and afterwards of others leading out of Concord. He was chosen a member of the State senate in 1858, and in 1859 was elected president of the senate. In 1863 he became governor of New Hampshire, and held the office two years. Gov. Gilmore was a man of great energy of character, combining therewith the most tender domestic affections. He took a deep interest in the prosperity of the First Baptist church in Concord, of which Rev. Dr. C. W. Flanders was the pastor, and did what he could to promote its welfare. Prof. J. H. Gilmore, of Rochester University, is a son of the subject of this sketch. Gov. Gilmore died April 17, 1867.

Gilmore, Prof. Joseph Henry, was born in Boston, Mass., April 29, 1834; was graduated at

Phillips Academy, Andover, 1852, at Brown University in 1858, and at Newton Theological Seminary in 1861. During 1861-62 he was instructor in Hebrew at Newton, and pastor of the Fisherville, N. H., Baptist church. He served as private secretary to Gov. Gilmore, of New Hampshire, and as editor of the Concord *Daily Monitor* in 1864-65. The next two years he was pastor of the Second church of Rochester, N. Y., and during the latter year acting Professor of Hebrew in Rochester Theological Seminary. Jan. 1, 1867, he entered upon the professorship of Logic, Rhetoric, and English, which chair he still fills with great ability.

Prof. Gilmore is a scholarly writer. For the last ten years he has been a frequent editorial contributor to the *Examiner and Chronicle*. He has published an admirable treatise, entitled "The Art of Expression," intended as an elementary text-book on rhetoric. He has written some excellent poems, among which we mention "Little Mary" and "He Leadeth Me"; a part of the latter we give below:

> "He leadeth me! Oh, blessed thought!
> Oh, words with heavenly comfort fraught!
> Whate'er I do, where'er I be,
> Still 'tis God's hand that leadeth me.
>
> "Sometimes mid scenes of deepest gloom,
> Sometimes where Eden's bowers bloom,
> By waters still o'er troubled sea,
> Still 'tis his hand that leadeth me."

Gist, Hon. Joseph, was born in Union District, S. C., on the 12th of January, 1775. He was admitted to the bar in 1799, and attained such distinction in the profession that " his services were often sought by both parties to a dispute. An incident of two men of wealth and standing, in adjoining districts, after a hard ride meeting at his gate, to employ him in an important case, is remembered by his brother." " His influence with the juries was almost irresistible, and was very great with the judges."

He represented his district in the Legislature for eighteen years, and was then elected to Congress, of which he was a member for six years, after which he voluntarily retired on account of ill health.

The office of judge, which at that time was a very high honor, was once within his reach, but he declined in favor of David Johnson, then but little known, but afterwards one of the most honorable judges that ever occupied the bench in South Carolina. It is gratifying to claim such a man as an humble, pious Baptist.

Goddard, Rev. Josiah, was born in Wendell, Mass., Oct. 27, 1813, became a hopeful Christian in 1826, and was baptized in May, 1831. He graduated at Brown University in 1835, and at the Newton Theological Institution in 1838. Having been accepted as a missionary by the Board of the Missionary Union, he sailed, the December after he graduated at Newton, for the East, and landed at Singapore in June, 1839, and proceeded to the place of his destination, Bangkok, Siam, arriving there Oct. 16, 1840. He was to direct his special attention to the Chinese of that city, of whom there were many thousands. In 1842 he had so far made himself master of the language that he was able to take the pastoral charge of the church which had been gathered by Dr. Dean, where he was prospered in the work of preaching the gospel to the heathen. He also finished the translation of the Gospel of John, and it was printed. He prepared for the press some Christian tracts and an English and Chinese vocabulary. In 1848 he had a severe attack of bleeding at the lungs, and for some time his life was despaired of, but a change of climate, by his removal to Ningpo, arrested the progress of the disease, and he was able to resume his work. To do this he was obliged to learn an entirely new dialect of the Chinese language in order to be understood by the natives of Ningpo. For several years he was busily occupied with his missionary labors, and the Lord owned these efforts in the conversion of the heathen and the building up of his cause in the city where he had made his home. His work and life came to an end Sept. 4, 1854.

Dr. Dean accords to Mr. Goddard traits of character which rank him among the ablest of our missionaries. "His native endowments were superior; his education had been extended and thorough; his study of the Chinese language had been patient and successful; his knowledge of the sacred languages and literature was accurate and familiar, and he brought to his work a large share of common sense and sound judgment, and a warm heart and high-toned Christian principles."

Goforth, N. B., D.D., president of Carson College, was born in Sevier Co., Tenn., May 20, 1829. He made a profession of religion and joined the Baptist church at Boyd's Creek, Sevier County. He soon felt it to be his duty to preach the gospel and devote his life to the service of Christ as a minister, and in order to prepare himself properly for this work he entered Maryville College in 1851, and graduated in 1855.

In 1857 he was ordained to the work of the gospel ministry by a Presbytery consisting of Elders Wm. Ellis, Wm. Ballien, and W. M. Burnett. In 1855 he was elected to a professorship in Mossy Creek, now Carson, Baptist College, and was elected president of the same in 1859, but formally resigned that position in 1866, and was re-elected in 1870, continuing to serve in that capacity to the present time. His life for the most part has been devoted to teaching, believing that he can be more useful in this way than in any other department of labor, and he feels and his brethren know that God has greatly blessed his work. Dr. Goforth is regarded as one of our best educators, as well as one of the ablest ministers in Tennessee.

Going, Rev. Eliab.—At McHenry, Ill., Feb. 28, 1869, died one of that group of brothers to which belonged Jonathan Going, D.D., so well known in connection with the organization of home missions in this country, and as the founder of Granville College, now Denison University, Rev. Ezra Going, of Ohio, Rev. James Going, of Michigan, with Eliab Going, the subject of the present notice. Eliab Going was born in Reading, Vt., Dec. 5, 1790. His active life was spent chiefly in Western New York as missionary and pastor; for two or three years he was a missionary among the Seneca Indians. He came to Illinois in 1856 or 1857, residing with his children in McHenry County, and preaching occasionally, as opportunity served. Mr. Going's wife died only two days before himself, and they were buried at the same time and in the same grave. "Lovely and pleasant in their lives, in their death they were not divided."

Going, Jonathan, D.D., eldest son of Jonathan and Sarah K. Going, was born in Reading, Vt., March 7, 1786. In 1803 he entered the academy at New Salem, Mass., at which place and also at Middleborough, Mass., he prepared for college. In 1805 he entered Brown University, and during his Freshman year was converted to God and baptized into the fellowship of the First church, Providence, by the pastor, Rev. Stephen Gano, April 6, 1806. During his college course he was a most faithful and active Christian. After his graduation, in 1809, he spent a season in studying theology with Dr. Messer, the president of the university.

Returning to Vermont, he was ordained in May, 1811, pastor of the Baptist church at Cavendish. In December, 1815, he removed to Worcester, Mass., and remained pastor of the church in that city until 1832, a period of over sixteen years. This pastorate was one of the most successful and influential of that day. Sunday-schools, foreign missions, ministerial education, and reform movements had in Dr. Going a pronounced and able friend and advocate. During the later years of his ministry at Worcester he became profoundly interested in home missions, and in 1831 obtained leave of absence from his church to visit the Baptist churches in the Western States. May 25 of that year he attended the meeting of the Ohio State Convention at Lancaster, and gave great aid in the formation of the Ohio Baptist Education Society and the founding of Granville College.

As the result of this visit, Dr. Going was in 1832 made corresponding secretary of the Home Mission Society, a position which he held with signal ability and unwearied industry for five years. Much of the present prosperity and usefulness of the Home Mission Society is due to his wise plans and arduous toils.

In the autumn of 1837, Dr. Going accepted the presidency of Granville College, O., and removed from Brooklyn to the West. In this position he remained to the entire satisfaction of all the friends of the college until his death, which occurred Nov. 9, 1844. While in Ohio his influence was felt in every good work. He was profoundly interested in the growth of the denomination throughout the State, and gave much time and strength to securing funds for the education of young men. His death was regarded as the greatest loss that had befallen Ohio Baptists, and to this day his name and work are held in grateful remembrance.

Goodale, Rev. Hervey, was born in West Royalston, Mass., in 1822. He graduated at Georgetown College, Ky., in 1848. His heart was set upon being a foreign missionary, and he received an appointment from the Southern Board of Foreign Missions, and was ordained in 1848 with a view to going out as a missionary to China. Before his purpose could be carried into execution circumstances occurred which led to a change in his plans, and he decided to accept an appointment to Central Africa. With two others, fellow-laborers, he sailed from Providence, R. I., Dec. 17, 1849. On reaching the shores of Africa, he was seized with a fever early in March, 1850, and died on the 13th of April, at Sama, about ninety miles from Monrovia. Thus prematurely, as we judge, was cut off a young Christian hero in the bright hope of doing some service for his Lord on the coasts of dark heathen Africa.

Goodhue, Rev. Joseph Addison, was born at New Boston, N. H., about the year 1828. He was a graduate of Dartmouth College in the class of 1848, and of the Newton Theological Institution in the class of 1852. He was ordained as a minister of the Baptist denomination in October, 1852, and was pastor of the Central Baptist church, Norwich, Conn., for two years. He resigned his position to enter upon the duties of Professor of Languages in the Connecticut Literary Institution, where he remained only one year, and then accepted a call to South Boston, Mass. Here he remained two years, and then took charge of the church at Farmingham Centre, where he remained three years. He went from Farmingham to North Cambridge, Mass., from which in two years he removed to Westborough, Mass., where he was pastor three years. For a short time he was pastor of the churches in Shelburne Falls and Danversport. Mr. Goodhue was the author of a volume bearing the title "The Crucible," designed, like Edwards's immortal work "On the Affections," to furnish tests which would distinguish true from false conversion. It called forth considerable criticism at the time of its publication. He died at Hyde Park, Mass., Dec. 1, 1873.

Goodman, Edward, senior proprietor of the *Standard*, at Chicago, is a native of England, having been born at Clipstone, Northamptonshire, May 10, 1830. His education was directed with a view to the business of a druggist, and he became quite early in life connected with the establishment of Mr. Clark, one of the principal merchants in that line in Leicester. There he attended Robert Hall's church, at that time under the pastoral care of Rev. J. P. Mursell, Mr. Hall's successor. In 1846, at the age of sixteen, he was baptized by Mr. Mursell, and united with the Harvey Lane church. In June, 1852, Mr. Goodman left England for the United States, arriving in Chicago July 11, of that year. In August of the following year he took an agency for the *Christian Times*, now the *Standard*, visiting the churches in Illinois, Wisconsin, and Iowa with a view to introduce the paper. Some four years later, Jan. 15, 1857, he became one of its proprietors in association with Rev. Leroy Church. The changes which have since taken place in the proprietorship of the paper are noted elsewhere. It must suffice to say here that to the careful and wise business management of Mr. Goodman the *Standard* is greatly indebted for its financial success, especially in surviving the disasters and business reverses which have visited the city where it is published, and to his excellent taste for the neat and orderly style in which from week to week it is made to appear. Since 1863, Mr. Goodman has served as treasurer of the Baptist Theological Union, having the seminary under its care. In this office he has performed a vast amount of valuable though uncompensated service, the accounts of the seminary being invariably found in the best condition, and much complication and difficulty thereby saved. In 1854 he became a member of the First Baptist church, and eight years later, in 1862, was elected a deacon. an office which he still holds.

Goodman, Thomas, father of Edward Goodman, Esq., of the *Standard*, died at Chicago, in his son's family, Oct. 15, 1872, at the age of eighty-three years, during sixty of which he had been a consistent Christian and a useful member of Christ's church. He was born at Clipstone, England, Jan. 16, 1789. He was in his earlier life intimately acquainted with Andrew Fuller, Robert Hall, and William Carey. During twenty-five years he served as deacon of the church in Clipstone, and to the end of his life delighted in nothing so much as in what concerned the progress of Christ's cause.

Goodspeed, Edgar Johnson, D.D., was born at Johnsburg, Warren Co., N. Y., in 1833. He was the son of parents who, during a long life, have been examples of intelligent and earnest piety, and of fidelity to Baptist truth. The son of whom we now speak, one of four, all of whom are filling positions of usefulness, was converted early in life, and very soon after was led to consider the subject of personal duty with reference to the Christian ministry. He was encouraged to the necessary self-surrender by his mother. Entering the University of Rochester at the opening of that institution, in 1849, he graduated in 1853, winning during his course the character of one of the best scholars and most promising intellects then in the university. Entering the theological seminary at Rochester immediately, he graduated in 1856.

Dr. Goodspeed's first pastorate was at Poughkeepsie, N. Y.,—a successful one of two years. He was then called to Janesville, Wis., to the pastorate which Dr. Galusha Anderson had just left. There he remained seven years,—seven faithful years. In 1865 he was called to the Second Baptist church, Chicago. There he began a pastorate of eleven years' duration, which may justly be called a remarkable one. While gifted with unusual pulpit attractiveness, Mr. Goodspeed showed himself peculiarly suited to pastoral work in a large city. He was also fortunate in the supporters and co-workers whom he found in his church. The number had grown to some 1200 at the conclusion of his pastorate, while in every department of Christian enterprise the church had made its mark in an unusual degree. Dr. Goodspeed's health failing, he resigned his charge in 1876, and after one year of rest accepted, in 1877, the pastorate of the Central church, Syracuse, N. Y. There he remained until 1879, when he was tendered by the Home Mission Society the position of president of Benedict Institute, at Columbia, S. C. This place he still holds, his fine culture, teaching ability, and genial spirit eminently adapting him for it.

Dr. Goodspeed has written "The Life of Jesus for Young People," and various other works, the sale of which has been very large. The University of Rochester conferred upon him the degree of Doctor of Divinity.

Goodspeed, Rev. Thomas Wakefield, a younger brother of Dr. Goodspeed, was born at Glen's Falls, N. Y., in 1843. His early conversion, like that of his brother, illustrated the certainty with which pious parents may look for the prompt fruitage of the seed of Christian family influence and training. Deciding to prepare for the ministry, he studied first at the University of Chicago, graduating, however, at Rochester in 1863, and at the seminary there in 1866. His first ministerial service was with the North Baptist church, Chicago, to which he was called while still a seminary student at Rochester. In 1866, however, he accepted the call of the Vermont Street Baptist church, Quincy, Ill., an admirable church, between whom and its young pastor there grew up a deep and strong mutual attachment; so that when, in 1872, after an unusually successful service of six years, he felt it his duty to accept the call of the Second church in Chicago to become associate pastor with his brother, whose health had begun to fail, the sundering of the tie was an occasion of great mutual sorrow. Coming to Chicago at the date last named, Mr. Goodspeed continued in joint service with his brother until 1876, when the latter finding a change of residence and labor imperative, both pastors resigned. The secretaryship of the Baptist Theological Union, having in charge the Theological Seminary at Chicago, being now vacant, Mr. Goodspeed was called to this post, which he continues to hold; in 1879, that of financial secretary and treasurer of the Northwestern Baptist Education Society being associated with it. During Mr. Goodspeed's financial administration important progress has been made in placing the seminary upon a more secure financial basis, the removal to Morgan Park having materially contributed to that end.

Good Works.—In the Catholic Church some of the saints, it is supposed, performed more acts of obedience and charity than God demanded; these, for that reason, were called works of supererogation, and it was imagined that the grand aggregate of such good works constituted a treasury of merits, which the popes, as heads of the church, could transfer by indulgences to those whose guilty lives created a demand for them. Among Mohammedans, it is taught that on the day of judgment the good works of a true believer will be placed in one scale and his sins in another, and if the former outweigh the latter the man will be saved. Among the Burmese, the chief business of a pious man is to acquire merit; for this object he gives alms, attends to religious duties, and subjects himself to much self-denial.

Without reference to motives, almsgiving, patriotism, patience, kindness to the sick, and the worship of God seem good works; but to be sure of their real character we must know that they come from worthy motives. There can be no doubt about the excellency of the works that spring from affection to Jesus; he says, "If ye love me keep my commandments." If, because we cherish him in our hearts, we hearken to his teachings, obey his precepts, and bear the fruits of "love, joy, peace, long-suffering, gentleness, goodness, faith, meekness, temperance," then are we led by the Spirit of God. The Christian's controlling motive should ever be supreme love to the Lord Jesus. This will give the royal stamp of divine approbation to his works.

Good works are necessary to prove the new birth of a believer, and his freedom from the dominion of iniquity. "Every branch in me that beareth not fruit," says Jesus, "he taketh away, and every branch that beareth fruit he purgeth it, that it may bring forth more fruit." The heavenly husbandman, when he saw that the barren fig-tree in his vineyard was fruitless for the third year, said, "Cut it down, why cumbereth it the ground?"

The good works of a Christian have no part in his justification, "Therefore, we conclude," says Paul, "that a man is justified by faith without the deeds of the law." This inspired conclusion of the great apostle is infallible. "It is not by works of righteousness which we have done, but according to his mercy He saves us." The sufferings of Jesus are the Christian's justification,—his complete salvation. There can be no works of supererogation,—works beyond what God demands; where much is given much will be required; Jesus claims the love of our whole heart, and soul, and strength, and mind. We ought to be living sacrifices, lying every moment upon his altar, and wholly consecrated to him. We owe him this, and no work or woe of ours can ever exceed his constant claims.

Goodyear, C. B.—In the death of Mr. Goodyear, at Chicago, in 1875, the Baptist Theological Seminary in that city lost one of its most devoted and generous supporters. He had been for several years a resident of Chicago, and as a member of the Board of Trade had pursued a successful business career. In the Second church, where he held his membership, he was known as a man who regarded his gains in business as lent to him from the Lord for the uses of his cause. The annual report of the seminary for 1875 says of him, in his relations with that institution, "In providing for its endowment, in the erection of its buildings, in meeting its necessities, no one showed a more earnest zeal or ardent devotion than Mr. Goodyear." He was for some years president of the Theological Union, having the seminary under its care, and at his death was a member of the board of trustees.

Gordon, Adoniram Judson, D.D., was born in New Hampton, N. H., and graduated at Brown University in the class of 1860. He took the full course of theology at the Newton Theological Institution, and graduated in the class of 1863. He was ordained June 29, 1863, and became pastor of the church at Jamaica Plains, near Boston, Mass., where he remained six years, and then removed to Boston, where, since 1869, he has been the pastor of the Clarendon Street church, formerly Rowe Street, being the immediate successor of Rev. Dr. Baron Stow. Dr. Gordon was one of the compilers of the "Service of Song." He is also the author of one or two books of a devotional character, which have been favorably received by the religious public.

Dr. Gordon is a trustee of Brown University, and

received from that institution, in 1877, the honorary degree of Doctor of Divinity.

Though a comparatively young man, Dr. Gordon exerts a wide influence in Boston, and his name is favorably and deservedly known throughout the denomination in this country.

Gordon, Rev. Charles M., president of Meridian Female College., Miss., is a native of Mississippi, where he was born in 1839; educated at Mississippi College; began to preach in 1860; was chaplain of 36th Miss. Regiment in the Confederate army. After filling several important pastorates, and among them one at Natchez, Miss., he was called to Meridian in 1875. In connection with his pastorate he took charge of the female college, but at the end of two years gave up the church, and has since devoted himself to the college, preaching occasionally in the surrounding country.

Gorman, Rev. Samuel, is a native of Magnolia, Stark Co., O., where he was born in 1816. He passed his early youth in and near the place of his birth. He was converted when quite young, and united with the Baptist Church. Educated at Denison University (Granville College), Ohio, and at the Baptist Theological Institute, at Covington, Ky.; ordained at Keen, Coshocton Co., O., in 1842, where he began his ministry. He was subsequently pastor at Jefferson, Urbana, Muddy Creek, and Dayton, O. At each of these places he built meeting-houses, and at Urbana and Dayton gathered and organized churches. In June, 1852, he was commissioned by the American Baptist Home Mission Society to take charge of the home mission work of that society in New Mexico. He established missions at Laguna, both among the Indians and the Spaniards. Here he erected two chapels and a building for school purposes, and continued his missionary labors nearly seven years. At the end of which he took charge of the mission at Santa Fé, the capital of the Territory, leaving the gathered churches and mission work at Laguna in the care of native helpers, whom he had prepared for the work. At Santa Fé he preached to English-speaking congregations in the morning, and to Indians or Spaniards in the afternoon. Mr. Gorman remained here until 1861, when, upon the outbreak of the late war, the country was taken possession of by Confederate troops, and the mission broken up. The time given to this mission labor was ten years. Upon his return home he settled as pastor of the Baptist church in Canton, O., the seat of his native county. He remained here seven years, adding a large number to the membership of the church, and securing $17,000 to build a meeting-house. He labored one year in the service of Denison University, in raising its endowment, and then came to Wisconsin. He has had pastorates at Sparta more than four years, Monroe one year, Columbus four years, and Manston, his present home and field of labor, one year. He has been a laborious minister of the gospel, and has maintained throughout his long ministry of forty years a reputation unspotted and a life full of good works. At the age of sixty-four years he is in the active work of the ministry, and held in high esteem by his brethren.

Gosnold, Rev. John, was born in England in 1625. He received his education in the University of Cambridge, and became a clergyman of the Established Church. In the time of the Parliamentary wars he made the Bible his only guide to truth, and consequently he became a Baptist. He was chosen pastor of a church at Barbican, in London, where he soon had a congregation of nearly 3000, many of whom were persons of large means, and frequently seven or eight of them were Episcopal clergymen. He was a man of ability, learning, and piety; he was honored by the friendship of many distinguished persons, especially by that of Tillotson, archbishop of Canterbury. He was compelled to hide in times of persecution to escape the hands of Christ's enemies. He baptized the celebrated Israelite, Du Veil, who joined the Baptists from the Episcopal ministry. Mr. Gosnold belonged to the General Baptists, but he associated much with the Particular denomination. He was beloved by all good men, and he regarded with affectionate interest every child of Jesus. He was the author of two works.

Gotch, F. W., LL.D., president of Bristol Baptist College, England, was born at Kettering. Northamptonshire, in 1808. After the usual course of study for the ministry at Bristol College, he proceeded to Trinity College, Dublin, in 1832, and graduated M.A. His first charge was Boxmoor, Hertfordshire, where he remained several years. He then became lecturer in philosophy at Stepney College, London, and in 1846 accepted a professorship at Bristol as colleague of the Rev. Thos. S. Crisp. On the failure of Mr. Crisp's health, in 1861, he took charge of the institution, and some years later was elected president. Dr. Gotch's eminent scholarship was recognized by Trinity College, Dublin, in 1859, when he received the degree of LL.D. He was also elected examiner in Hebrew and New Testament Greek for several years successively by the faculty of the London University. When the Convocation of the Church of England resolved to invite the co-operation of learned men of various denominations in the revision of the authorized version of the Bible, Dr. Gotch was selected as a prominent representative of the learning and scholarship of the Baptists. In this important work he has labored from the beginning with enthusiastic devotion, and his rare gifts and acquirements have won universal respect.

He received the highest honor in the gift of his brethren by his election to the chair of the Baptist Union in 1868.

Goucher, Rev. John E., was born at Malvern Square, Annapolis Co., Nova Scotia; studied at Acadia College; ordained at Upper Gagetown, New Brunswick; and he has been pastor of the Port Medway and the North church, Halifax. He is now pastor at Truro, Nova Scotia. Mr. Goucher's ministry is devotedly earnest and useful.

Gould, A. A., M.D., was born at New Ipswich, N. H., in 1805, and received his collegiate education at Harvard University, where he graduated in the class of 1825. He also graduated from the medical school of Harvard, the degree of M.D. having been conferred on him in 1830. He devoted a life of more than thirty years to the practice of his profession, and stood high among the best physicians of Boston. He won also an enduring reputation as a laborer in different fields of natural science. We are told that when "Sir Charles Lyell visited this country in order to pursue his celebrated geological investigations, as soon as he touched the shore the first man from whom he sought aid as an 'expert' and co-worker was Dr. Gould, whose contributions to natural history, and at that time especially to conchology, furnished the light that was needed to mark out the programme of the explorer. From the years of his student life to the day of his departure his industry was incessant, sustained with manly vigor and scholarly enthusiasm." For a series of years he was vice-president of the Natural History Society, a member of the American Academy of Arts, of the American Philosophical Society, and of other kindred bodies. At the time of his death he filled one of the most honorable positions which a Massachusetts physician can occupy, that of president of the Massachusetts Medical Society.

Dr. Gould was a faithful and consistent member of the Rowe Street Baptist church, in Boston, during all his professional career. His death occurred Sept. 15, 1866.

Gould, Prof. Ezra Palmer, was born in Boston, Mass., Feb. 27, 1841. He graduated at Harvard University in the class of 1861, and at the Newton Theological Institution in the class of 1868. He was ordained in September, 1868. For three years he was assistant professor of Biblical Literature and Interpretation at Newton, and has been Professor of Biblical Literature and Interpretation (New Testament) since 1871. Prof. Gould has prepared articles for reviews on subjects pertaining to his department of study, and has been a frequent contributor to the columns of the weekly religious press.

Gould, Thomas, was famous in the annals of the early Baptists in Eastern Massachusetts for the persecutions he endured on account of his sentiments. He, like thousands in our own day not connected with Baptist churches, questioned the divine authority of infant baptism. Cotton Mather speaks of a "multitude of holy, watchful, faithful, and heavenly people among the first settlers of New England, who had scruples as to infant baptism." Mr. Gould was a man of very modest pretensions, a private member of a small country church, who declined to present his new-born child at the baptismal font, for which a crusade was opened against him by the whole Pedobaptist community, which in the end enlisted all the logic, the stratagems, and bigotry of the entire body of the clergy, and brought a long train of legal enactments from the secular powers.

Mr. Gould was a member of the Congregational church in Charlestown under the pastoral care of Rev. Mr. Sims, and this is his story: "On a first day, in the afternoon, one told me I must stop, for the church would speak with me. They called me out, and Master Sims told the church that this brother did withhold his child from baptism, and that they had sent to him to come down on such a day to speak with them, and if he could not come on that day to set a day when he would be at home; but he, refusing to come, would appoint no time; when we writ to him to take his own time and send us word." I replied that "there was no such word in the letter, for me to appoint the day; but what time of that day I should come." "Master" Sims told him he lied, but on reading the letter sent to him, it was found, somewhat to the confusion of "Master" Sims, that he was right. "They called me forth to know why I would not bring my child to baptism? My answer was, I did not see any rule of Christ for it, for that ordinance belongs to such as can make profession of their faith, as the Scripture doth plainly hold forth." No better answer could be given by the most learned divine. A meeting was appointed to be held the next week at "Mr. Russell's" to take further action on the matter. There seems to have been a four or five hours' hot discussion, when, as Mr. Gould tells us, "one of the company stood up and said, 'I will give you one plain place of Scripture where children were baptized.' I told him that would put an end to the controversy. 'That place is in the 2d of Acts, 39th and 40th verses.' After he had read the Scripture, Mr. Sims told me that promise belonged to infants, for the Scripture saith, 'The promise is to you, and your children, and to all that are afar off,' and he said no more; to it I replied, 'Even as many as the Lord our God shall call.' Mr. Sims replied that I spoke blasphemously in adding to the Scriptures. I said, 'Pray do not condemn me, for if I am deceived my eyes deceive me.' He replied again I added to the Scripture, which was blasphemy. I looked into my Bible, read the words again, and said it was so. He replied the same words the third time before the church. Mr. Russell stood up and told him it was so as I had read it. 'Ay, it may be so in your Bible,' saith Mr. Sims. Mr. Russell answered, 'Yea, in yours, too, if you will look into it.' Then he said he was mistaken, for he thought on another place; so after many words we broke up for that time."

For seven years this sort of controversy was kept up. All the powers of church and state seem to have been thrown into commotion because the child of a modest yet conscientious member of the church was not brought to the baptismal font. The very existence of the churches of the "standing order," it was believed, was imperiled by such wanton neglect. Well did Mr. Gould write, "If eight or nine poor Anabaptists, as they call them, should be the destruction of their churches, their foundation must be sandy indeed." Out of this persecution sprang the First Baptist church in Boston. Its members for years endured obloquy and shame. They were fined, and some of them sentenced to be banished, and because they would not go into exile they were imprisoned more than a year. It was in vain that some of the first men of the colony, like Gov. Leverett, Lieut.-Gov. Willoughby, and others opposed these persecuting measures. The English Dissenters at home protested against this harsh dealing as opposed to the very fundamental principles of religious toleration. But their protests availed nothing with the Boston Puritans. The sufferings of the martyrs of religious liberty continued for many years. Mr. Gould died in October, 1675. He had not lived and suffered in vain. The principles which he held, and for holding which he endured so much, are everywhere accepted, and the revolution which he started has secured wonderful victories for the cause of religious freedom not only in the old Bay State, but over the whole country.

Gove, Elijah, was born in Charleston, Montgomery Co., N. Y., in May, 1802. His father, who was a farmer, having become helpless through paralysis, important responsibilities devolved upon the son while yet very young. A mortgage upon the farm, large for that time, he paid off before he came of age. Leaving home without a trade or profession, we find him in a short time proprietor and captain of a boat on the Erie Canal. "On a trip from Albany to Rochester in 1824, he had a lady passenger who, two years later, became his wife." Soon after his marriage he removed to Ohio. Not yet having become a Christian, and ambitious to acquire a fortune, he became a distiller, engaging in this business at Mendosia, Ill., where at the end of seven years he had accumulated some thirty or forty thousand dollars. At the earnest solicitation of his wife he gave up this business, and in 1847 removed to Quincy. There, at the age of forty-seven, he became a Christian, uniting with the

ELIJAH GOVE.

Baptist church. He was one of those to whom the beautiful city which now became his home was most indebted for its early and rapid growth, and for the solid basis upon which its prosperity was made to rest. He became also greatly interested in church building, and gave large amounts towards enterprises of this kind in different Western States.

Mr. Gove's membership was at first with the First Baptist church in Quincy. In 1856 he went with others to constitute the Vermont Street Baptist church in that city, and was one of the few who erected its handsome house of worship. He remained a member here until his death, in 1874. Between the years 1856 and 1874 he gave about $18,000 to this church and its pastors. His gifts otherwise were very large. The first of all his many donations to various causes was made to Shurtleff College, while still living at Mendosia. To this institution, between the years 1849 and 1873, his gifts aggregated $59,285; including the legacy in his will, the whole amount given was about $75,000. In the twenty-five years from his conversion till his death, the sum of his gifts to various special objects was not far from $110,000, all in money. It has been said of him that "he gave more for the cause of Christian education than any other Baptist the West ever had." In this spirit of large benevolence his wife fully sympathized. She still lives in Quincy, a noble, generous, Christian woman.

Gow, Rev. George B., was born in Waterville, Me., and graduated at the college in that place in 1852. He went through the Newton course of theological study, graduating in the class of 1858. He was ordained September, 1858, and was the pastor of the church in Ayer, Mass., three years. He then became principal of the New London Institution, holding the position for three years, when he accepted a call to the pastorate of the church in Gloucester, Mass., where he remained three years. His next call came in 1867, from Worcester, Mass., where he continued for five years. Then he accepted an appointment as agent to raise a larger endowment for the Worcester Academy. In 1874 he became pastor of the church in Millbury, Mass., which relation he now sustains to the church.

Grace, Rev. William C., was born in Tippah Co., Miss., Jan. 19, 1844. He professed religion in the summer of 1857. In the month of September, 1865, he was baptized into the fellowship of the Pleasant Hill Baptist church, Miss. He subsequently united with the Flat Rock church, where he was licensed to preach the gospel.

He spent the next three years of his life as principal of Yorkville Academy. He was ordained by the Bethel church, Gibson Co., Tenn., Revs. M. Hillsman and R. A. Coleman constituting the Presbytery. In 1871 he was pastor of Spring Hill and Newbern churches. In 1875 he took charge of Humboldt and Pleasant Plains churches; having served the previous year with great success as financial secretary of the Executive Board of the West Tennessee Baptist Convention.

He is now pastor of the church at Sweet Water, East Tenn., one of the most important points in the State. He is a devoted Christian and a good preacher. May he long live to honor the Master!

Grafton, Rev. B. C., was born in Newport, R. I., Sept. 28, 1785. From the time of his hopeful conversion to the close of his life he was a cheerful, earnest Christian. Having formed an intimate acquaintance with Rev. Dr. Gano, of Providence, when he was not far from eighteen years of age, and engaged in active business in that city, he was wont to accompany that good man in his missionary tours, assisting him as occasion was given by offering prayer or speaking a word of exhortation to the people. By degrees he came to feel that perhaps he could serve his Master in the work of the Christian ministry. He studied for a time with Rev. Dr. Chapin, in Danvers, Mass., and subsequently with Rev. Dr. Benedict, in Pawtucket, R. I., and was ordained in Providence in August, 1818. He was called to the pastorate of the church in West Cambridge, Mass., and remained in this place for four years and a half, when he removed to Plymouth, Mass., and was pastor of the church in this old Pilgrim town for six and a half years. His next settlements were Leeport, Taunton, Mass., Wichford, R. I., Rowley, Mass., Stonington, Conn., Somerset and Medford, Mass. He spent the closing years of his life in Cambridgeport, Mass., where he died Jan. 12, 1858, in the seventy-third year of his age. Mr. Grafton was a useful, happy Christian minister, and formed many warm friendships in the places where he labored.

Grafton, Rev. Joseph, was born in Newport, R. I., June 9, 1757. His father, who had followed the seas for several years, on giving up the command of a vessel, removed to Providence and engaged in the business of sail-making, and at the age of fourteen Joseph began his apprenticeship with his father. Becoming a Christian, he united with the Congregational church in Providence, although nothing would satisfy him as baptism but immersion. Subsequently he became impressed with a conviction that it was his duty to preach the gospel. He was led through a severe discipline of sorrow before he finally yielded to the pressure of the duty which was laid on him. In the year 1787, finding his views were in harmony with those of the Baptists, he connected himself with the First Baptist church in Providence. Having received a call from the Baptist church in Newton, Mass., he was ordained as pastor of that church June 18, 1788, and continued to sustain the relation for almost fifty years. His labors were abundantly blessed, several revivals occurring during his ministry. Five hundred and fifty-four persons were received into the church during his connection with it.

Mr. Grafton was one of the best-known and honored ministers of his denomination in all the region where he labored so long as a servant of Christ. He was full of wit. To this day many anecdotes are related of him, showing what a vein of humor there was in him. Prof. Gammell, recalling the scenes of his own early childhood, when his father was the pastor of the Medfield church, remarks of him, in speaking of the little circle of excellent Christian ministers who were wont to meet at the parsonage, " No single form, after that of my own father, comes back to my memory with a distinctness so marked and life-like as that of my father's venerated friend, Rev. Joseph Grafton, of Newton. He was next to Rev. William Williams, of Wrentham, the oldest of them all; but he was, without exception, the sprightliest and wittiest in his conversation, and on this account the most interesting visitor in the estimation of the children. In dress he was extremely neat, and in person somewhat below the average stature; but of a firm, compact frame, and unusually flexible, easy, and quick in all his movements. His eye was dark and very expressive, and in its quick flashes, whether in the pulpit or at the fireside, there beamed forth a deep, spiritual intelligence and sincerity; while the tones of his musical and well-modulated voice did not fail to rivet the attention of all who heard him speak, whether in public or in private." He was an able minister of other days. He died Sept. 16, 1836.

Graham, Major W. A., the third son of Ex-Gov. Graham, was born in Hillsborough, N. C., Dec. 26, 1836; attended Chapel Hill for a term, but graduated at Princeton, N. J., in 1859; was baptized by Rev. L. Thorne in 1856; entered the army as first lieutenant; was wounded as captain at Gettysburg, and became assistant adjutant-general of North Carolina, with the rank of major. He was in the State senate in 1874–76–78, receiving every vote cast, and came within one vote of being chosen lieutenant-governor of the State. He was president of the Baptist State Convention in 1878, and is now the moderator of the South Fork Association.

Grammar, Rev. G. A., a missionary of the Arkansas Baptist Convention, living at Lonoke, Ark., was born in Mississippi in 1844; ordained in 1867; besides supplying a number of country churches he was pastor at Yazoo City, and supplied the Vicksburg church during 1878, passing through the terrible epidemic of that year, and losing most of his family by yellow fever; came to Arkansas in 1880 and engaged in his present work.

Grand River College is located at Edinburgh, in North Missouri. It has good grounds and buildings and is out of debt. Prof. T. H. Storts is principal; 131 students were enrolled the past year. P. McCullum is the financial agent. The school has flattering prospects and an important position in the State.

Granger, Abraham H., D.D., was born in Suffield, Conn., in 1815, and graduated at Waterville College in the class of 1839. He took the full course of theological study at Newton, and graduated in the class of 1843. He was ordained in November, 1843, as pastor of the church in Warren, Me., where he remained until called to take charge of the Fourth church in Providence, R. I., in 1854. He continued in this relation until 1876, when he resigned, and has since resided in Franklin, Mass. Dr. Granger is a trustee of Brown University and of Colby University. He received from the latter institution the degree of Doctor of Divinity in 1864.

Granger, James N., D.D., was born in Canandaigua, N. Y., in August, 1814. When he was seventeen years of age he received the appointment of a cadet at West Point, but before entering upon the studies of his chosen profession he became a subject of the renewing grace of the Holy Spirit, and a change in all his plans of life was immediately formed. At the age of twenty he became a member of the Hamilton Literary and Theological Institution, and graduated in 1838. He was ordained as pastor of the Baptist church in Avon, N. Y., in 1839. He accepted a call to the Washington Street church, Buffalo, after a residence of two years at Avon. His pastorate over the Buffalo church was a short one. Such was the reputation he had already gained that in October, 1842, the First Baptist church in Providence called him to be their minister. The position is one, in some respects, of peculiar difficulty, for the church has always sustained an intimate relation to Brown University, and its minister must accommodate himself to very wide extremes of character. Dr. Granger was quite equal to the demands made on him, and met them with satisfaction to his people as well as honor to himself. Ten years of persistent work were given to this important field of labor, under the exhausting toil of which his health became somewhat broken, and he decided to carry out a long-cherished purpose to spend several months abroad, and there secure needed relaxation and recreation. The Board of the American Baptist Missionary Union had decided to send a deputation to the East to look after their various mission stations, and they appointed Dr. Granger to accompany Dr. Peck, the foreign secretary, on this important journey. Eighteen months were spent in accomplishing the work which had been undertaken, and they were months of severe, unremitting toil, passed amid the heats and malaria of an Oriental climate. Dr. Granger returned to his church with the seeds of disease and death implanted in his system. He was not permitted long to labor as the faithful minister and the affectionate pastor. The disease which he had contracted in the East forbade the hope that he would rally from it. He lingered for some months, and then died Jan. 5, 1857.

Dr. Granger was one of the ablest, most pureminded, and unselfish ministers that has ever been raised up in the Baptist denomination. He was, in the best sense of the word, a wise man. His judgments about men and measures were generally proved to be correct. He possessed, to a remarkable degree, the elements of a noble Christian character. It is a good deal to be able to declare, as his most familiar friend, Dr. Caswell, has said of his pastor, " during a period of more than fourteen years of intimate, of unreserved, and confidential intercourse I never knew him utter a sentence or do an act which, if spread before the world, would in any manner detract from the purest Christian character. His purposes were all open and generous and good. In the very nobleness of his nature he was incapable of guile. He possessed, in an eminent degree, that attribute rarer than genius, rarer than high endowments of intellect,—an attribute almost unknown to the aspirants after worldly fame and joy,—a perfect candor and fairness of mind with respect to the claims of others."

It seems a mystery that one with such qualities of character, and capable of doing so much good, should have been taken away in the very ripeness and maturity of his powers. Cut off, however, so early, Dr. Granger has left to the denomination he served so faithfully the rich legacy of a bright example and a beautiful Christian character.

Grant, Stillman Bailey, D.D., one of four sons of a Baptist minister, all of whom became Baptist preachers, was born in Bolton, N. Y., Oct. 26, 1819; graduated from Madison University, N. Y.; the next year was ordained as pastor of the Baptist church in Granville, N. Y., and remained three years; settled in South Adams, Mass., and in Wallingford, Conn., then in New Haven, then in New London, where he remained nine years; in 1867 became pastor of the First Baptist church in Hartford, where he remained till his death, Dec. 17, 1874; positive yet tender, decided yet charitable, clear in his views, sound in the faith of Christ; his labors crowned with much fruit.

Graves, Rev. Absalom, a minister of Boone Co., Ky., distinguished for his zeal, piety, and great success, was born in Culpeper Co., Va., Nov. 28, 1768. He received a liberal education. In his twentieth year he professed religion, and united with the Baptist church at the Rapidan meeting-house. In 1797 he removed to Boone Co., Ky., and united with Bullittsburg church. He held some civil offices, the duties of which he discharged with wisdom and fidelity. He was licensed to preach in 1810, ordained in 1812, and became the stated preacher at Bullittsburg and some other churches, laboring extensively as an evangelist. He was among the first in Kentucky to espouse the cause of foreign missions, and was a zealous co-laborer of Luther Rice in this work. He compiled a hymn-book, known as "Graves's Hymns," that became popular. He died Aug. 17, 1826.

Graves, Alfred C., D.D., a great-grandson of Absalom Graves, was born in Boone Co., Ky., Jan. 5, 1838. He united with Bullittsburg Baptist church in 1853. In 1855 the church "encouraged him to exercise his gift." He was educated at Georgetown College, and finished his course in theology at the Western Baptist Theological Seminary, Ky., in 1860. He was ordained to the ministry, and took charge of the Baptist church at Harrodsburg, Ky., the same year. In 1863 he was pastor of Jefferson Street church in Louisville, also edited the *Western Recorder* several years, and supplied the pulpit of Portland Avenue church. While in Louisville, he wrote "La Rue's Ministry of Faith," which passed through two editions. In 1867 he took charge of Stamping Ground church, in Scott Co., Ky. In 1871 he accepted a call to the Baptist church in Manchester, N. H. He remained there about six years. During this pastorate the church built a house of worship, at a cost of $75,000, and received 171 members. In 1877, his health being impaired, he returned to his native State, and soon afterwards took charge of the Baptist church at Lebanon, Ky., where he now ministers.

Graves, Hon. Calvin.—The Graves family, of Caswell County, N. C., have long been distinguished for intelligence and virtue. The mother of the subject of this sketch was the daughter of Col. John Williams, who received his military appointment from the general Congress of the provinces in 1775, and afterwards was distinguished for bravery in the Revolutionary war. Mr. Graves was prepared for college by Rev. Wm. Bingham; spent but one year at Chapel Hill, and read law with Judge Thos. Settle and Chief Justice Leonard Henderson. He was admitted to the bar in 1827, and soon entered upon a large practice. He became a public man in 1835, having been elected a delegate to the convention called to revise the constitution of the State. He was chosen as a member of the House of Commons in 1840, and soon became a leader of his party. He was Speaker of the House in 1842. He was a member of the State senate in 1846, and again in 1848, when he gave the casting vote, as Speaker, in favor of the Central Railroad, and against the wishes of his constituents, because he thought it was for the good of the State. Mr. Graves became a Baptist in 1837, and preserved a consistent Christian character through all his professional and political career. He was twice married, and died Feb. 11, 1877, in his seventy-fourth year.

Graves, Rev. Henry C., was born in Deerfield, Mass. He pursued his academic studies at Shelbourne Falls and East Hampton Academies, and was a graduate of Amherst College in the class of 1856. He studied at Newton two years, and was ordained March 9, 1858. He was pastor of the Bunker Hill church, in Charlestown, Mass., five years, when he removed to Providence, R. I., and became pastor of what was then the Brown Street Baptist church, since united with the Third, to form the Union Baptist church of Providence. This pastorate continued for eleven years. Mr. Graves removed to Fall River, Mass., in 1874, and became pastor of the Second Baptist church in that city, where he now resides. In his fields of labor the Lord has greatly blessed his ministrations.

Graves, Rev. Hiram Atwell, was born in Wendall, Mass., April 5, 1813. He was a child of remarkable precocity. Within three months from the time his parents allowed him the use of a book, he had learned to read, and when he was four years old he had read the New Testament through. He might have been prepared for college when he was not much over twelve had he not been restrained by his parents. Soon after reaching the age of thirteen he gave good evidence of conversion, and was baptized by his father and received into the membership of the church of which he was pastor. He graduated at Middlebury College, Vt., in 1834. When twenty-three years of age he was ordained in Springfield, Mass. His pastorate was a brief one. Failing health compelled him to resign, and for the same reason he gave up his ministry in Lynn, whither he had gone on leaving Springfield. In 1842 he became the editor of the *Christian Reflector*, a Baptist weekly newspaper, published in Boston. He entered upon the duties of the office when the fortunes of the paper were at their lowest ebb. At once it was evident that an energetic man was at the helm of affairs. The moribund paper was lifted into new life. Its subscription list increased largely, and it was a power in the denomination, which made itself felt in every direction. At length it was united with the *Christian Watchman*, and under the new name of the *Watchman and Reflector* it was the most popular Baptist paper in all New England.

Such hard and constant strain on his nervous system, as he was forced to endure to bring his paper up to the point where he finally left it, thoroughly exhausted him, and he was compelled to retire from his editorial chair and seek rest and recuperation in a milder climate. Three or four years were spent in the island of Jamaica. His disease was probably held in check, but it was not subdued. Feeling satisfied that he could not recover, he returned to his native land, and after lingering a few weeks, he died at his father's house in Bristol, R. I., Nov. 3, 1850.

The fame of Mr. Graves rests upon his accomplishments as an editor. Of him, as working in this department of Christian labor, Dr. Turnbull says, "He formed the character and laid the foundation of the prosperity of the *Watchman and Reflector*, the leading Baptist journal in New England, and one of the best papers in the country. Easy, versatile, and graceful, apt, also, in a high degree, with sufficient spice of wit and vigor, always sensible and often eloquent, his leaders, short or long, were the first things caught by appreciative readers. In full sympathy with the spirit of Christianity and the progress of the age in all benevolent enterprises, he threw himself into the grand movement of the church for the salvation of the world. Our educational, missionary, and philanthropic schemes are largely indebted to his judicious, earnest advocacy."

Graves, Rev. J. M., was born in Shrewsbury, Mass., in 1794, and studied for the ministry with Rev. Dr. Going, of Worcester. He was ordained at Royalton, Mass., where he remained several years. He was pastor also for a time of the church in Wardell, Mass. Subsequently he devoted fifteen years of his life to pastoral work in Vermont. He was pastor also of churches in East Boston and Methuen, Mass. For a time he supplied the churches at Brighton and West Newton, and was in the service of the Massachusetts Baptist State Convention. He was a faithful minister of the gospel. His death occurred at Charlestown, Mass., Jan. 15, 1870.

Graves, J. R., LL.D., was born in Chester, Vt., April 10, 1820. On his father's side he descends

J. R. GRAVES, LL.D.

from a French Huguenot, who fled to America, most of whose family perished at the revocation of the Edict of Nantes, who settled in the village of Chester, Vt. His mother was the granddaughter of a distinguished German physician and scholar named Schnell. Dr. Graves is the youngest of three children. His father died suddenly when he was but three weeks old, and although a partner in a prosperous mercantile house, the business was so managed that but little was left to the stricken widow. Young Graves was converted at fifteen, and was baptized into the fellowship of the Baptist church of North Springfield, Vt. In his nineteenth year he was elected principal of the Kingsville Academy, O., where he remained two years, when with impaired health he went for the winter to Kentucky. There he took charge of the Clear Creek Academy, near Nicholasville, Jessamine

Co. About that time he united with the Mount Freedom church, and was soon licensed to preach without his knowledge, but he would not enter the ministry, feeling himself wholly disqualified for so great a work. For four years he gave six hours to the school-room and eight to study, going over a college course without a teacher, mastering a modern language yearly, making the Bible the man of his counsel, and Paul his instructor in theology. These years of hard study and self-reliant investigation gave the peculiar character which belongs to his preaching and reasoning. From the time of his conversion he was impressed with the duty of proclaiming the gospel, and always shaped his studies with a view to the ministry as his life-work, but breathed this secret to no one. He was called to ordination by his church against his desire. The venerable Dr. Dillard, of Lexington, Ky., was the chairman of the examining Presbytery, and preached the sermon on the occasion. He came to Nashville, Tenn., July 3, 1845. In a few days he rented a building and opened the Vine Street Classical and Mathematical Academy, and shortly afterwards united with the First Baptist church. In the fall of 1845 he took charge of the Second church, on Cherry Street, now the Central Baptist church, and the following year he was elected editor of the *Tennessee Baptist*, when his public religious career, with which all are more or less familiar, commenced. It is difficult to give even a brief summary of the work accomplished and the influence exerted by a mind so active, an intellect so great, and a genius so uncommon.

When in the autumn of 1846 he took charge of the *Tennessee Baptist*, it had a circulation of only 1000, and before the breaking out of the war it had attained the largest circulation of any Baptist paper in the world, and it is doubtful if any paper ever exerted a wider denominational influence. At the same time he edited a monthly, a quarterly, and an annual, besides editing all the books that were issued from the presses of the Southwestern Publishing House. In addition he has written and published the following works: "The Desire of All Nations," "The Watchman's Reply," "The Trilemma," "The First Baptist Church in America," "The Little Iron Wheel," "The Great Iron Wheel," "The Bible Doctrine of the Middle Life," "Exposition of Modern Spiritism," which, for originality and thoroughness, has received the commendation of the first scholars of the age, "The New Hymn and Tune Book," "The Little Seraph," and last, "Old Landmarkism, What It Is." He has edited and brought before the public, American editions of very valuable works,—Robinson's "History of Baptism," Wall's "History of Infant Baptism," Orchard's "History of Foreign and English Baptists," "Stewart on Baptism," and other minor works. But he considers that the great theological work of his life is now passing through the press, entitled "The Work of Christ in Seven Dispensations."

He originated the first Ministers' Institute. He raised without compensation the endowment of the theological chair in Union University, and without charge he established the Mary Sharpe College, Winchester, Tenn., securing the necessary funds, and he drafted its admirable curriculum.

In 1848 he originated the Southwestern Publishing House, Nashville, Tenn., for the dissemination of sound Baptist literature, and subsequently the Southern Baptist Sunday-School Union, both of which achieved great success, but were destroyed by the war. In 1870 he presented the plan of the Southern Baptist Publication Society to the Big Hatchie Association of Tennessee, by which it was approved; and in the summer of 1874 he turned over to the society $130,000, which he had raised in cash and bonds, as an endowment; but owing to the financial crisis which succeeded, and other causes, the society has suspended.

He is a great preacher, following unusual lines of thought. He is pre-eminently doctrinal, yet Christ crucified is the soul of every sermon. He is lengthy, yet he holds the attention of his audience to the last. He insists strongly upon the form, rights, and duties of the true church, and yet he always places Christ before the church, and upon water baptism, and baptism properly administered, yet he places the blood of Christ before water. In power of illustration, in earnestness of denunciation, in force of logic, in boldness of thought, and, at times, in tenderness of soul, he has few peers. His eloquence is sometimes overwhelming. A judge in the city of Memphis, on "brief day," in lecturing the bar upon the importance of a clear statement of propositions, once remarked, "The gift is as rare as genius, but is still susceptible of cultivation. Of living ministers I know of no one who possesses it in a higher degree than Dr. Graves, of the First Baptist church, in this city. He lays down his propositions so clearly that they come with the force of axioms that need no demonstration." It is not remarkable that a man of such force of intellect has taken bold and advanced positions, coming in conflict with the opinions of many even in his own denomination. He is the acknowledged head of the great movement among Baptists known as "Old Landmarkism." With all the strong blows he has inflicted upon error he is one of the kindest of living men.

In his early ministry, Dr. Graves had many converts under his preaching. The writer was with him on one occasion in Brownsville, Tenn., in 1849, where more than seventy persons, including the best men and women of the place, found the Saviour. His arguments, illustrations, and appeals were the most powerful he ever heard. Before he was thirty years of age over 1300 persons had professed religion in special meetings which he held.

In 1853 the Domestic Mission Board of the Southern Baptist Convention were exceedingly anxious to establish a strong Baptist church in New Orleans. To secure this object they invited Dr. Fuller, of Baltimore, to go to that city as a missionary. He was the most eloquent preacher in the South, and he had no superior in the North, but he declined the request. Then they formally appointed Dr. Graves to the position with a salary of $3000 per annum. The work to be done, the place where it was to be performed, and the extraordinary salary for that day which they offered, showed their great appreciation of his pulpit gifts. Dr. Graves has a wonderful command over his audience, holding them spell-bound for hours at a time. He is deeply in earnest, utters the strong convictions of his own mind, and carries his hearers with him as by the force of a tornado. And this is true of all classes,—teachers, doctors, lawyers, judges, statesmen. At a session of the Georgia Baptist Convention before the late war, Joseph E. Brown, then governor of Georgia, in a speech before the Convention upon the obligations of Baptists to give to the world a pure Bible literature, said, "There is one man who has done more than any fifty men now living to enable the Baptists of America to know their own history and their own principles, and to make the world know them, and that man is the brother on my right," bowing to the editor of the *Tennessee Baptist*, Dr. Graves, who was present.

As a presiding officer over deliberative bodies, Dr. Graves has often been honored, and no man more richly deserves it. Dr. Graves has had some eight or ten public discussions, to each of which he was challenged, and in every one of which his opponent felt sorry for inviting the conflict.

Dr. Graves in his peculiarities represents a section of the Baptist denomination, a conscientious and devoted portion of our great apostolic community, but in his earnest and generous zeal for our heaven-inspired principles he represents all thorough Baptists throughout the ages and the nations. In his literary efforts he has rendered immense service to the Baptist churches of America. The republication of Robinson's "History of Baptism" and Wall's "History of Infant Baptism," with his able introductions, and the other historical works which have been issued through his instrumentality, have exerted a vast influence in favor of the oldest denomination in Christendom. The fearless boldness of Dr. Graves in advocating the practices of Christ and his Apostles, his manly denunciations of that ungodly charity that would tread under foot a divine ordinance to please untaught professing Christians of Pedobaptist denominations, have aided mightily in suppressing lukewarmness, and in fostering zeal for the truth among us. The *Alabama Baptist*, Dr. E. T. Winkler editor, truly says, "Extreme as the views of Dr. Graves have by many been regarded as being, there is no question that they have powerfully contributed to the correction of a false liberalism that was current in many quarters thirty years ago." Dr. S. H. Ford, in his *Christian Repository*, gives his approval to this statement, saying, "We fully indorse this just commendation of the efforts of Dr. Graves. We differ with him in some things, but we honor his heroic life-work in meeting and exposing error wherever uttered."

Graves, Samuel, D.D., son of John and Betsey (Cilley) Graves, was born in Ackworth, N. H.,

SAMUEL GRAVES, D.D.

March 15, 1820. At the age of seventeen he was apprenticed to E. & T. Fairbanks & Co., scale manufacturers, in St. Johnsbury, Vt.; but at the end of two years his strong desire for an education led to the close of his apprenticeship, and he went to Madison University, N. Y. Here he remained until 1846, completing the collegiate and theological course of study. During the two years of his divinity course, and for one year following, he served the university as tutor in Greek.

In 1848 he became pastor in Ann Arbor, Mich. During three years of service in this field he saw the church increase from 62 to 216 members. In

1851 he became Professor of Greek in Kalamazoo College, and of Systematic Theology in the Theological Seminary. During the eight years that followed he rendered excellent service and had the fullest confidence of the friends of these institutions. In 1859 he took charge of the First Baptist church in Norwich, Conn., and enjoyed a prosperous pastorate of ten years.

January 1, 1870, he entered upon his work as pastor of the Baptist church in Grand Rapids, and has held the office till now. During his ministry the church has prospered far beyond its previous experience, and a commodious and elegant house of worship has been built. In 1872 he spent seven months in Europe and the Holy Land. In 1871-72 he was president of the Baptist State Convention of Michigan. In 1879 he preached the annual sermon before the American Baptist Missionary Union. He has an eminently catholic spirit, and is greatly respected and beloved by his brethren in the ministry.

Graves, Z. C., LL.D., was born in 1816, in Chester, Vt. He is the brother of Dr. J. R. Graves, of Memphis, Tenn. In early life he was frail, and unfitted to bear hardships, and by the advice of a physician he was sent to a farm to secure health from its pure air and strengthening exercises. Here he remained until his sixteenth year, working upon the farm during the summer, and attending the winter school for three or four months each year. It was in the latter part of this year that he united with the Baptist church in North Springfield. His insatiable thirst for books led to his return home, that he might enter Chester Academy. He prosecuted its classical and mathematical course for five or six terms. From it he went to the Baptist High or Normal School, at Ludlow, where he pursued his studies until twenty-one, supporting himself by teaching district schools three or four months each winter.

The wonderful success of the winter schools which he taught during these training years, the great interest taken in their studies by his scholars, and their proficiency, marked him out as the coming teacher before he had finished his education. At the age of twenty-one he went West, and opened a private school in Ashtabula, O., where becoming known as a successful teacher, upon the resignation of his brother, J. R. Graves, he was elected principal of Kingsville Academy, situated in a neat little village on the shore of Lake Erie, midway between Ashtabula and Conneaut. Here he married Miss Adelia C. Spencer, an intellectual and accomplished lady, who has been for thirty years associated with him as matron of the Mary Sharpe College, and known in literary circles as the authoress of "Jephtha's Daughter," a poem of rare excellence, and her master-piece, "Seclusaval; or, the Arts of Romanism."

As principal of this academy our young teacher achieved a success without a parallel in the history of Western schools and academies. His fame drew patronage not from surrounding counties only, but from adjoining States. Men who have become eminent as jurists and statesmen, missionaries, professors, and presidents of colleges, received their academic training under Mr. Graves in this school.

It was in 1850 that the Mary Sharpe Female College was founded in Winchester, Franklin Co., Tenn., to be what its name indicates, a college whose curriculum, with but few changes, is that of Brown University. It was intended that the graduates of this college should be able to pass an examination with the Seniors of that university, or of the University of Virginia, and this it has confessedly accomplished.

When this school was ready to be opened, the name of Z. C. Graves was placed before the trustees by his brother, J. R. Graves, through whose influence and labors mainly the college had been founded, and a correspondence opened which resulted in his election to the presidency, which position he has filled with distinguished ability for over thirty years. The high character of this institution is known North and South, and has justly won the title from scholars and educators of " The Female University of the South." Dr. Graves has made the success of this university his life-work, and his labors have been truly herculean. He attributes his iron constitution and unequaled powers of endurance in the class-room to the combined mental and physical training of his youth. He has in forty years lost but two or three days from the school-room from sickness, and fewer days from pleasure, and is now, at sixty-four, mentally and physically as active and vigorous as most men at forty. He has educated in part and graduated about four thousand young ladies at the Mary Sharpe College, who are occupying the first positions in social life, and not a few of them are among the noted teachers of the South. It is impossible to tell how much Dr. Graves has done for the higher education and elevation of woman during his long and unusually useful career as an instructor.

Dr. Graves is a man of great modesty, of a very penetrating mind, highly cultured, and beloved by all his pupils, and as widely as he is known.

Gray, Rev. Davis Dimock, was born in Windham, Wyoming Co., Pa., May 2, 1808. He was baptized and became a member of the Braintrim church, Wyoming Co., Pa., on Sept. 25, 1831. He was licensed by this church May 24, 1834, and ordained by the Bridgewater Association, acting as a council, Aug. 26, 1836. In the exercise of a long and useful ministry he has preached as supply, before ordination, to the Jackson, New Milford, and Union churches. Since his ordination he has served as pastor of the Union, in Luzerne Co., the Jackson and New Milford, in Susquehanna Co., Honesdale, Wayne Co., Penn's Neck (now Princeton), N. J., and in November, 1849, he returned to the place of his nativity, as pastor of the Braintrim church, which he still serves. During this last pastorate he has preached over 3000 sermons. While serving the Jackson church, Rev. D. D. Gray had the pleasure of baptizing his younger brother, H. H. Gray, who also became a prominent minister among the churches of the Bridgewater and Wyoming Associations. His death occurred in 1878. The influence of both these brethren has been only for good; it tended to promote a high standard of holy living. The life of the elder is still the heritage of the militant church, the death of the younger is precious in the sight of the Lord.

Gray, Edgar Harkness, D.D., was born in Bridport, Vt., Nov. 28, 1815. Having lost his father while only nine years of age, he was placed with a neighboring farmer until he was fourteen. He was converted at the age of twelve. At fourteen he was apprenticed to the printing business in Burlington, Vt. Subsequently he removed to St. Alban's, where, after a serious illness, he decided to prepare for the ministry. He left his business, retired to his native town, and attended a select school, paying his expenses by teaching primary classes in the school. In 1834 he entered Waterville College, Me. (Colby University). After graduating he studied theology with the Rev. R. E. Pattison, D.D., the president of the college, and the Rev. S. F. Smith, D.D., then pastor of the Baptist church in Waterville. Dr. Gray's first settlement in the ministry was at Freeport, Me., where he was ordained in 1839, being then twenty-five years of age. Here he remained five years, blessed in his labors. In 1844 he removed to Shelburne Falls, Mass. Subsequently, in 1847, he was settled at Bath, Me., and then, by unanimous request, returned to Shelburne Falls in 1850. In 1863 he accepted a call to the E Street Baptist church, Washington, D. C., where his labors resulted in the general prosperity of the church. In 1863, Dr. Gray returned again to his old field of labor, Shelburne Falls, and after three years' residence there, he removed again, in 1873, to Washington, to take charge of a new interest known as the North Baptist church. Here he remained until July, 1878, when he resigned to enter upon the work of church extension in California. In 1864 the University of Rochester, N. Y., conferred upon him the honorary degree of D.D. At the commencement of the Thirty-ninth Congress, Dr. Gray was elected chaplain of the U. S. Senate, and continued in that position four years. Dr. Gray was one of the four clergymen who officiated at the funeral of President Lincoln, and among others, conducted the services in connection with the burial of the Hon. Thaddeus Stevens, of Pa., pronouncing also a eulogy in the rotunda of the Capitol over the remains.

Grebel, Conrad. See article ANABAPTISTS.

Greece, Mission to.—The first Baptist missionaries sent to Greece were Rev. H. T. Love and Rev. C. Pasco, with their wives, who sailed from this country Oct. 24, 1836, and commenced their labors at Patras, where a school was opened in 1837, and the Scriptures and religious tracts were freely distributed among the people. Some opposition was manifested by the Holy Synod of the Greek Church, but this only stimulated the curiosity of the people to read the forbidden books. In September, 1838, a new station was established at Zante, one of the Ionian Islands. Mrs. H. E. Dickson, at one time a teacher in the Governmental Female Boarding-School in Corfu, arrived in Patras, Feb. 15, 1840, and commenced her labors as an assistant to Mr. and Mrs. Love. The health of Mr. Pasco having failed, the station at Zante was abandoned. For the same reason Mr. Love was obliged to leave Patras, and a new station was commenced at Corfu in April, 1840. The first Greek baptized by Mr. Love was Apostolos, who became his assistant. Rev. R. F. Buel and wife joined the mission June 18, 1841. Special hostility was awakened against Mr. Buel, who was falsely charged with having distributed tracts against one of the favorite saints of the people. A mob was raised, and Mr. Buel was compelled to leave Corfu. Mr. Love, in ill health, returned to the United States in the spring of 1843. Rev. A. N. Arnold and wife and Miss Waldo arrived at Corfu, Feb. 17, 1844. Together with Mrs. Dickson they labored for some time in Corfu; in 1851 they removed to Athens. Missionary work was carried on until their return to the United States in 1855. Mr. Buel soon followed them, and the mission ceased to be under the patronage of the Missionary Union until 1872, when Rev. D. Sakellarius was appointed a missionary. Mr. Sakellarius and his wife have with fidelity performed the duties which they have assumed, but the progress of evangelical religion in Greece has been slow.

Green, Rev. A. B., for many years a devoted and very successful missionary in the La Crosse and St. Croix valleys, Wis., was born in Warren, Vt., and died at Whitewater, Wis., Sept. 26, 1878, aged fifty-two years. He was converted when about thirty years old at Lakeland, Minn. He was ordained May 16, 1860, by the Baptist church at Prescott. He at once commenced with great zeal his work as a Christian minister. Before entering the ministry he practised law, and held the office of sheriff and judge in the county where he resided. After serving several churches as pastor he entered, in 1870, upon the great work of his life, that of pioneer missionary in the St. Croix and La Crosse valleys. It would be impossible to relate in the brief space allotted for the purpose his almost superhuman labors and grand triumphs on this field. He planted churches and built meeting-houses at almost every important point. His missionary tours extended over hundreds of miles, often through dense forests and wide unsettled districts, frequently made on foot, and requiring a physical fortitude and patient self-sacrifice almost unparalleled. He died in the full triumph of faith, having literally given his life to the work of missions.

Green, Rev. David, was born in Virginia. He was converted in youth, and gave himself soon after to the work of the ministry. In his early days he was very successful in the Carolinas. He removed to Kentucky. In 1805 he visited Missouri, and in 1806 settled in it, and in the month of June of that year he organized Bethel church, the first in Missouri. He served this church as pastor till 1809, when he ceased from his labors, and entered upon his eternal reward.

Green, Rev. Moses, pastor at Beebe, Ark., was born in North Carolina in 1818, and reared in West Tennessee, began to preach in 1844, was ordained in 1850; graduated at Union University, Tenn., and shortly afterwards became pastor at Somerville, Tenn., where he remained three years; was Professor of Greek in Madison College; removed to Arkansas in 1860, and settled at Austin, where he aided in the organization of a church; Mr. Green has filled a number of important positions in the State, and traveled much as an evangelist. He has been a constant contributor to the religious press, and has gained much reputation as a writer.

Green, Rev. William R., was born Jan. 24, 1823, in Tenn., and died Jan. 25, 1879, in Knobnoster, Mo. He was ordained at Murfreesborough, Tenn., by Rev. J. H. Eaton, LL.D. He graduated in 1854. He was pastor at Clarksville and Nashville, Tenn. About twenty years of his life were spent in Missouri. Rev. N. T. Allison, who knew him well, says he was sound in doctrine and pure in conduct. He fell from a railroad bridge, an accident which caused him years of suffering, yet he patiently performed his work down to the end of life.

Greene, Rev. G. W., was born in Watauga Co., N. C., June 27, 1852; baptized in 1865; graduated at Wake Forest College in 1870; graduated at Theological Seminary at Granville, S. C., in 1875, and is now master of the Moravian Falls Academy and pastor of several churches.

Greene, Rev. Jonathan R., was born in Chester, Vt., in 1801. He united with the church in Cavendish, Vt., in 1831. His business prospects were very flattering. He had a pleasant home in Cavendish, and the future of his life looked most hopeful. The call of God came to him in the midst of this worldly prosperity, to leave all and devote himself to the work of preaching the gospel. After some struggles, the call was obeyed. He removed to Newport, N. H., where he put himself under the tuition of Rev. Ira Pearson. His ordination occurred at Ackworth, N. H. He was pastor of the churches in Bradford, Ackworth, Unity, and Hanover, N. H., and Hardwich, Derby, and Passumpsic, Vt. He believed in revivals, and aimed to secure them in the churches of which he was the pastor. He died at Factory Point, Manchester, Vt., Sept. 19, 1852.

Greene, Judge Roger Sherman, chief justice of the U. S. Supreme Court, Seattle, Washington

JUDGE ROGER SHERMAN GREENE.

Territory, son of Rev. David Greene, a Congregational minister, was born at Roxbury, Mass., Dec. 14, 1840. His father was one of the corresponding secretaries of the American Board of Commissioners for Foreign Missions. His mother was granddaughter of Roger Sherman, of Connecticut. In 1848 his father retired to a farm in Westborough, Mass., where the mother died in 1850. In 1851 their home was burned, and the family settled at Windsor, Vt. Young Roger studied in the common schools of Roxbury, Westborough, and Windsor, and graduated at Dartmouth College in 1859. He engaged in teaching at Windsor, and Falmouth, Mass., and New London,

Conn., studying law until he was eighteen. He settled in New York City; was clerk and student in the law-office of Evarts, Southmayd & Choate until September, 1862; admitted to the bar in May, 1862. In October, 1862, he entered the army as second lieutenant, Co. I, 3d Missouri Inf. Promoted to first lieutenant; and in August, 1863, became captain of Co. C, 51st U. S. Colored Inf., holding the position until discharged, in November, 1865, for sickness contracted in line of duty. He took part in the battles of Chickasaw Bayou, Arkansas Post, Vicksburg, Fort Blakely, and other minor conflicts; was with his regiment in every Southern and border State, except Texas. At Vicksburg he was wounded in the right arm, May 22, 1863; was judge-advocate of the district of Vicksburg in 1864-65; held the same position in the Military Division of Western Louisiana. After the war settled, in 1866, at Chicago, practising law until 1870, when he was appointed by President Grant associate justice of the Supreme Court in Washington Territory, and settled at Olympia. In 1878 he was promoted to the office of chief justice by President Hayes, and moved to Seattle. In 1866 was married to Miss Grace E. Wooster, of Connecticut, a devoted Christian. In early life he had deep religious impressions, which recurred at different periods until his conversion, in 1868. From 1863 to 1868 he was exercised on the subject of baptism. His family were Pedobaptist, his wife a Baptist, both wished to be in unison, and believed they could be, but only in the truth. He saw that it was his duty and privilege to be immersed, and in 1871 he was baptized, and joined the newly formed Baptist church at Olympia. It was an occasion of great joy, enlarged Christian experience, and peace in the Lord. He was soon chosen deacon, and in 1874 was ordained pastor, serving one year, until ill health and overwork compelled him to resign. He had been clerk and moderator of the Puget Sound and British Columbia Baptist Association, and is now its treasurer. His membership is with the Olympia church. He is an upright judge, an earnest Christian, a Baptist from deep conviction, a brother whose praise is in all the churches.

Greene, Rev. Samuel H., was born in Enosburg, Franklin Co., Vt., Dec. 25, 1845. In 1847 his family removed to Montgomery Centre, Vt., and he continued to reside there until 1868. He pursued with great diligence his academic studies at the seminaries in Fairfax and Brandon, Vt., and also in Norwich University. Mr. Greene for some time engaged in mercantile pursuits, and in 1867 was elected superintendent of public schools, in which capacity he served with marked efficiency and success. He united with a Baptist church in 1866, and was licensed to preach in 1868. He pursued his collegiate and theological studies at Madison University, N. Y., graduating from college in 1873, and from the theological seminary in 1875. In the year of his graduation he was ordained as pastor of the Baptist church at Cazenovia, N. Y., where he labored with great success until December, 1879, at which time he resigned to accept the pastorate of the Calvary Baptist church, Washington, D. C. Mr. Greene is an earnest, polished, and interesting speaker, winning and holding the attention of an audience from the opening of his discourse; he is a pastor in whose visits old and young delight; and whose genial manners and gentle bearing make him a general favorite. Calvary church is growing both in numbers and strength under his faithful ministrations.

Greene, Samuel Stillman, LL.D., was born at Belchertown, Mass., May 3, 1810, and graduated

SAMUEL STILLMAN GREENE, LL.D.

at Brown University in the class of 1837. Prof. Greene has devoted his entire professional life to the cause of education in one form or another, and occupies a distinguished place among the educators of our country. He has taught in the grammar and English high schools of Boston, and has been superintendent of schools in the cities of Springfield and Providence. He was Professor of Didactics in Brown University from 1851 to 1855, when he was appointed Professor of Mathematics and Civil Engineering, and in 1864 Professor of Mechanics and Astronomy, which chair he now holds. Prof. Greene has occupied for many years a prominent place in several educational organizations, and by his pen has contributed largely to the cause of education. He has also prepared several text-books, his "Analysis" and Grammars having had a wide circulation all over the country. Brown University and the Worcester Academy are greatly indebted to him for the successful efforts he has made in many ways to add to their efficiency as institutions of learning.

Greene, Rev. Thomas Waterman, was born at Stamford, Conn., Feb. 10, 1837. He was a grandson of the revolutionary general, Nathaniel Greene. His father was a Congregational deacon, his mother a preceptress in the family of Rev. Dr. Wayland. In 1838 his parents settled at Metamora, Ill. Here he was converted at the age of thirteen, and was baptized in March, 1852. He graduated from Shurtleff College in 1860, and from Rochester Theological Seminary in 1863. April 21, 1864, he was ordained and became pastor of the church at Winchester, Ill. He baptized sixty converts during his three and a half years' pastorate at Winchester. Failing health compelled him to seek a more favorable climate. In 1867 he preached for a short time at Litchfield, Ill. In 1868 he settled at Lawrence, Kansas, where he remained until 1872, when he became pastor at Junction City; and in 1874 settled with the Fort Scott church. In 1875 he left Denver for California, and was invited to become president *pro tem.* of California College, and in May, 1876, he was elected its permanent president. In May, 1877, consumption had so fully got the mastery that he resigned his college work, and sought relief in the higher regions of the State at Camptonville, Cal., where he died Aug. 22, 1877. He was eminently spiritual, eloquent, conscientious, and consecrated to the work of the Lord.

Gregg, William Henry, was born Dec. 31, 1832, in Wilmington, Del.; was converted when seventeen years old, and baptized by Rev. Morgan J. Rhees, then pastor of the Second Baptist church. For a while he neglected the prayer-meetings, but returned resolving to fill his place always. His first contribution to foreign missions, which was one dollar, and nearly all he had, was made upon the presentation of the cause by Dr. Osgood. This gift did the donor more good than anything he ever bestowed afterwards. He has since been a member of the Board of the American Baptist Missionary Union.

He attributes his conversion to a faithful mother, who died when he was but thirteen years old. She was accustomed to take him to her room and pray with him. He was honored while a member of the Second Baptist church with all the offices within the gift of the church except that of deacon; remained until June, 1865, when, with the best of feeling, he, together with others, withdrew to form the Delaware Avenue church. While connected with the latter church he was superintendent of the Sunday-school and of the mission school at McDowellville; was deacon and treasurer of the church, and chairman of its building committee until the church edifice was erected and the basement occupied. Shortly after this, feeling that his day of usefulness with that church was over, he left it. During his short connection with the Delaware Avenue church he contributed to its treasury for building and other church purposes about $4000. Mr. Gregg was next instrumental in organizing a Sunday-school in a fire-engine house. It was soon removed to the building of the old First church, with which he and some others united, and new life was infused into the old body. Eventually the fresh element, under the leadership of the pastor, Rev. Thos. M. Eastwood, withdrew, removing to a more promising field of labor. Uniting with the members of the disbanded Elm Street church, they together formed a strong church, and now occupy the Elm Street chapel. Prior to this Mr. Gregg assisted in the formation of the Wilmington Baptist City Mission, and was the chairman of the committee on mission schools which selected and purchased the fine lot on Elm Street, and erected a chapel thereon. A Sunday-school, and then a church, were organized in the chapel, which gave place, in 1878, to the united churches under the name of the Bethany Baptist church, to which the property was transferred by the city mission. In this new interest Mr. Gregg takes a prominent part, both in the Sunday-school and church, besides contributing liberally for the extension of Christ's kingdom in our own country and in other lands.

Gregory, John M., LL.D., was born at Sand Lake, Rensselaer Co., N. Y., July 6, 1822, the son of Hon. Joseph Gregory of that place. His preparation for college, apart from such advantages as the schools of his native town afforded, was received at the Dutchess County Academy, in Poughkeepsie. Entering the Freshman Class in Union College at the age of twenty, he graduated there in 1846. Two years were spent in law study, but convictions of duty drew him into the ministry. After a brief pastorate in the East, removing to the West, he became principal of a classical school in Detroit, Mich. His marked success as an instructor soon fixed attention upon him as an educator. He was chosen Superintendent of Public Instruction for the State of Michigan. In the mean time, however, in association with President E. O. Haven, of the university at Ann Arbor, and Prof. Welch, of the Normal School, he had established the *Michigan Journal of Education*, having himself the entire editorial charge. In his capacity as State superintendent of instruction, he soon came to be recognized as one of the foremost educators in the country. His annual reports were characterized by remarkable breadth of view, and by their philosophical treatment of educational questions. He served three terms, six years in all, in this office, and in 1864, declining a re-election, accepted the presidency of the Kalamazoo College. Three years later, in 1867, he was called to the presidency of the Illinois Industrial University at Champaign, then just founded. This important post he held until the present year, 1880, when he resigned it, with a view to devote himself to the carrying out of some literary plans, impracticable so long as the cares and labors of such an office were pressing upon him.

While in previous spheres Dr. Gregory's power as an organizer and instructor was conspicuous, it was especially so in the position held at Champaign. The work of the university was adjusted upon a scale of comprehensiveness and efficiency unusual even in State institutions, while his personal power as the advocate of large views in education was felt throughout the West. Dr. Gregory, while as a speaker always commanding marked attention by the vigor and directness of his thought and his lucid diction, is also an excellent writer, and has already published quite extensively, mostly addresses and essays upon education, including, also, a valuable "Hand-Book of History." No man is more welcome in Baptist pulpits than Dr. Gregory, and though his service in the pastorate was not an extended one, he has, while so active in other spheres, enjoyed the privilege of extended usefulness as a Christian minister.

Gregory, Rev. O. F., is one of South Carolina's most energetic and useful ministers. He is a native of Charleston, S. C., born March 7, 1844, and baptized in 1858. He was educated in his native city, and ordained at the call of the old First church, by Revs. E. T. Winkler, D.D., L. H. Shuck, D.D., and T. R. Gaines, in 1871.

His first pastorate was at Mount Pleasant, near Charleston. He was called to Eufaula, Ala., in 1875, and thence to Tuscaloosa, in 1879. But in 1880 Cheraw and Florence called him back to his native State, where it is earnestly hoped he may spend the rest of his life. He is truly a great and successful worker, and, what is even more important, knows how to set his people to work.

He has missed preaching but four Sabbaths since he was licensed, except when attending Conventions and Associations. He has baptized over 500 in ten years; and fourteen Baptist ministers have arisen from his churches.

He was clerk of the Charleston Association eight years, of the Baptist State Convention six, and of the Southern Baptist Convention two, which office he now fills.

Gregory, Rev. Silas B., was the youngest of a family of ten children, whose father was for sixty years a Baptist deacon, and three of the sons entered the ministry. Silas B. was born at Sand Lake, N. Y., Oct. 28, 1827. His mother died when he was eight days old. Very early in life he was converted and baptized, and gave himself to the work of the ministry; for which he received a thorough classical and theological education, graduating at Madison University. After a successful pastorate of nine years at Little Falls, N. Y., he spent one year at Portsmouth, Va., and was pastor three years at Niles, Mich. He was then called to the chair of Theological Instructor at Wayland University, Washington, which he filled with marked ability. He resigned this position for the pastorate at Whitesborough, N. Y., where in two years he baptized sixty converts. He was a hard worker, and needing rest made the tour of Europe. On his return he was appointed by the American Baptist Home Mission Society president of Leland University, New Orleans, and proved himself eminently fitted for the position. He retired at the end of two years for the purpose of representing the society's missionary work, as secretary for New York State one year, which was followed by a year's pastorate at Lansingburgh, N. Y., where the wife of his youth (Miss Martha Huntington) died. He went to California, and after four years' arduous and successful toil as pastor of the Calvary church, Sacramento, he died May 7, 1880. He literally wore himself out in Christ's service.

URIAH GREGORY, D.D.

Gregory, Uriah, D.D., born at Sand Lake, N. Y., Oct. 4, 1823, was converted and baptized when ten years old. In early life he completed the classical course at the Armenia Seminary, N. Y., removed to Cincinnati, continued his studies, and taught school several years. He founded the Detroit College and Commercial Institute, and conducted it several years. During this period he studied law, and was admitted to the bar. Until 1870 he continued teaching in Michigan, Ohio, and Indiana; but early convictions of duty to preach forced him to give his life to that work. He was ordained at Rives, Mich., preached there for a time, became pastor at Leslie, and baptized nearly fifty during his first year in the ministry. He then studied theology two years, graduated at Rochester, supplied the Pittsford church a year, and was pastor at West Henrietta two years, both churches having revivals under his labors. For the benefit of his wife's health he went to California in 1875, where she soon after died, greatly beloved by all. He was pastor of the Fifth church, San Francisco, two years, during which time nearly one hundred were added to it. For a short time he was connected with the *Evangel*, the Baptist paper of California; was pastor at Santa Rica one year, when he resigned to engage in Sunday-school work, and was soon after called to the presidency of California College, over whose interests, in connection with his wife, a superior teacher, he is presiding with increasing favor. In 1876 he received the honorary degree of D.D. from the Baptist college in Arkansas.

Grenell, Rev. Levi O., was born at Mount Salem, N. J., Jan. 1, 1821, and is a son of Rev. Z. Grenell. He pursued a full course at Madison University, and graduated from the theological department in 1849. He was ordained at Elbridge, N. Y., and went as a missionary to San José, Cal., in 1850. After spending several years in the work on the Pacific coast, he returned East, and ministered successfully in New York and Pennsylvania. In 1865 he settled in New Market, N. J., and has been pastor of the Princeton church for the last seven years. The University of Rochester conferred on him the honorary degree of A.M. in 1855.

Grenell, Rev. Zelotes, was born in Kortright, N. Y., April 4, 1796; was converted and baptized when fourteen; was ordained August, 1819, as pastor of the Second Wantage church, N. J. He has been pastor of several churches in New York State and city, and in New Jersey. He has preached over 12,000 sermons, and delivered many temperance addresses. For several years he has been pastor of the Third church, Paterson, N. J., where his preaching commands attention. He is the oldest Baptist pastor in the State in actual service. On his eighty-fourth birthday he was visited by a number of his friends, and was congratulated on his vigor. Father Grenell has two sons in the ministry. He has been celebrated for the readiness with which any text or subject suggested to him falls into analytical order, so that he can preach from it in a few minutes. His brethren love to test him on this point, and rarely fail to elicit a prompt, original, full sketch.

Gressett, Rev. A., editor of the *Southern Baptist*, Meridian, Miss., was born in Mississippi in 1829; began to preach in 1858. His ministerial labors have been chiefly confined to country churches located in the counties of Lauderdale, Newton, and Kemper, Miss. He began the publication of the *Southern Baptist* in 1875.

Griffin, G. W., D.D.—This talented and cultivated brother was born in Southampton Co., Va., May 9, 1827. From early boyhood he had deep religious convictions, but did not make a profession of religion until 1843, and was baptized by Rev. Putnam Owen into the fellowship of the Black Creek Baptist church in 1844. He was ordained to the work of the gospel ministry by the Mill Swamp church, Elders G. W. Owens and J. K. Dougherty acting as the Presbytery. He immediately entered upon the pastorate of said church, which he served half his time for five years. He became the pastor of the church in Columbia, Tenn., in 1857, where he remained one year, since which time he has served churches at important places and towns with great acceptance. He is now one of the professors in the Southwestern Baptist University at Jackson. Dr. Griffin is regarded in literary circles as one of our best-educated men,—excels as a polemic, and is an able minister of the gospel, with the highest order of attainments.

Griffin, Rev. J. F., pastor at Selma, Ark., was born in Missouri in 1841. He began to preach in 1868. Since then he has labored in Arkansas, in the counties of Drew, Chicot, Ashley, Bradley, Dorsey, Desha, and Lincoln, and has baptized over 450 persons, and succeeded in erecting a beautiful house of worship at Selma.

Griffin, Rev. Richard, was born in Clinton, Conn. His first pastorate was at Granville, Mass. In 1836 he was sent by the American Baptist Home Mission Society as a missionary to Wisconsin. The Territory was then a wilderness, and Milwaukee a small village. He formed the first Baptist church in the State. He devoted the best part of his life to organizing churches and preaching the gospel in the early history of the State. His last years were marked by great suffering. He died at a ripe old age in the peace and triumph of that gospel which he had so long preached.

Griffing, William, a prominent Baptist layman in Southwestern Mississippi in the early part of the present century. He was a grandson of Rev. Samuel Swayze, the founder of the first Protestant church in the Natchez country. He was born in the Territory after its settlement. He at first united with the Methodists, but upon investigation his views underwent a change and he became a Baptist. He took an active part in all the movements of the Baptists. Towards the close of his life he was involved in the troubles growing out of the discussion of anti-Masonry and Campbellism, and for a time withdrew from the church, but he was afterwards restored, and to the close of his long and useful life abounded in every good word and work.

Griffith, Rev. Benjamin, was born in Wales, Oct. 16, 1688, and emigrated to America in 1710. He was baptized May 12, 1711. He was ordained pastor of the Montgomery church, Bucks Co., Pa., Oct. 23, 1725, and remained with this community till his death, which took place Oct. 5, 1768.

Mr. Griffith was an able minister, with a respectable education. He read extensively the works of the great Puritan divines, and he made considerable use of his own pen. He wrote a work in "Vindication of the Resurrection of the Same Body," an answer to "Simon Butler's Creed," and a refutation of a pamphlet called "The Divine Right of Infant Baptism." He also wrote "A Treatise of Church Discipline," which was published with the Philadelphia Confession of Faith, and which has been regarded as a work of very great merit. Mr. Griffith was among the foremost Baptist ministers in his day.

Griffith, Benjamin, D.D., was born in Juniata Co., Pa., Oct. 13, 1821; was converted in Baltimore, Md., and was baptized in November, 1839, by Rev. Stephen P. Hill, of Baltimore; graduated from Madison University, N. Y., in 1846; received the degree of Doctor of Divinity from the university at Lewisburg, Pa.; was ordained in 1846, and settled as missionary in Cumberland, Md. Here he organized a church, built a meeting-house, and enjoyed a successful pastorate of four years. In April, 1850, he settled with the New Market Street church in Philadelphia, where he remained six years. During this pastorate the name of the New Market Street church was changed to that of Fourth Baptist church of Philadelphia, and a large and attractive meeting-house was erected at the corner of Fifth and Buttonwood Streets. Here also his labors were abundantly blessed, and many were added to the church. On Oct. 17, 1854, he was married to Miss Elizabeth Crozer, daughter of the late John P. Crozer, Esq.

In May, 1858, he became corresponding secretary of the American Baptist Publication Society. To the work of this grand denominational enterprise he has given the best years and energies of his life, and his rare adaptation and varied talents still make him a tower of strength to the society. The vast and enlarging successes achieved by it are largely due to his wonderful administrative abilities. The entire management bears the impress of his intense concentration of purpose and effort. The erection of the magnificent and unencumbered building now

BENJAMIN GRIFFITH, D.D.

occupied by the society at 1420 Chestnut Street, Philadelphia, was the result of his wise counsel, unceasing toil, and great influence.

Much of his time and labor has been given to Sunday-school work. As editor of the *Young Reaper*, one of the Sunday-school periodicals of the Publication Society, he has cheered many youthful hearts with the gospel tidings; and as a Bible-class teacher in churches with which he has been connected he has been instrumental in making others wise unto salvation. He is a gifted preacher, a wise counselor, a "faithful steward," and one of the ablest and most popular secretaries any society ever had.

Griffith, Capt. H. P., was born in Laurens District, S. C., about 1835; baptized in 1860 by Dr. J. P. Boyce, and educated at Furman University.

In 1872, at the earnest solicitation of many leading citizens, he opened a high school at Woodruff, Spartanburg Co., five miles from his native place. Several families moved in to educate their children, others boarded. The school ran up to 75 or 80 scholars, sometimes nearly 100. It continued to flourish for three years, when his health compelled him to resign.

The school at once began to decline, and at the end of the second year it would have been closed, but his health having improved he returned in

February, 1880. Prosperity came with him. The place has grown from half a dozen houses to quite a flourishing village. Families are yet moving in to educate their children, business of all kinds is improving, the whole community is flourishing, and all from the influence of the school.

He was a captain in the late war, and is yet held in high esteem by the men of his former command. He was shot through the feet in the battle of the Wilderness, and the surgeons thought he would lose one or both. But he suffers little or no inconvenience from them now. "Whatsoever the king (David) did pleased the people." David was the representative of a class, and Capt. Griffith belongs to the class who are born to " please the people."

Griffith, Rev. R. H., was born in Henrico Co., Va., Oct. 7, 1825; baptized when thirteen by Rev. Eli Ball; spent a year at Richmond College, but took his degree at Columbian College, D. C., in 1849; after teaching for several years in Pennsylvania, New Jersey, and Virginia, he came to North Carolina, as a missionary of the State Convention, and labored for five years, when he was called to Charlotte, where he was pastor for eleven years. For four years Mr. Griffith has been agent of the Southern Theological Seminary, in North Carolina and Virginia, and a good one he is. He was for years the moderator of the South Yadkin Association.

Griggs, Samuel C., the Chicago publisher, so well known by his imprint upon a large variety of widely circulated books, was born in Tolland, Conn., July 20, 1819. While he was yet a boy the family removed to Hamilton, N. Y., where, at the age of eighteen, he was converted, and was baptized by Rev. Jacob Knapp. After a three years' course at the Hamilton Seminary, he taught the academy in that village one year, but preferring a business career, purchased a book-store in the place, and began the line of trade in which he has since won such distinguished success. In 1848, Mr. Griggs removed to Chicago. That city has since been his home. Resuming the book-trade there, at first upon a moderate scale, he prosecuted it with such enterprise and tact, steadily enlarging, that his establishment became for strangers an interesting feature of the young city in its marvelous growth. In a few years his book-store had become the largest in this country. On one occasion, Mr. Anthony Trollope, the novelist, visiting the store, expressed his great surprise at its dimensions, and the completeness of the literary assortment, declaring that while he had visited numerous similar establishments in England and on the Continent, he had seen none which equaled it in the particulars named. Mr. Griggs was the first bookseller to introduce theological works in Chicago, the first also to offer the public costly imported books with rich artistic embellishments, and the first Western publisher who succeeded in gaining for a Western book extended circulation. Three times Mr. Griggs has been burned out. On the last occasion of this kind, in 1871, the loss was so heavy, and his health had become so much impaired, that he determined to change the character of his business. He has since devoted himself to publishing exclusively, and in this line has been the means of bringing before the American public a large number of excellent books. Editions of classical works for use in colleges, prepared by such scholars as Prof. Boise, of Chicago, and Profs. Jones and D'Ooge, of Ann Arbor, have gained a wide popularity. The writings of Prof. Wm. Matthews are known and valued in every part of the land, as well as over the seas. Other authors of distinction have been glad to avail themselves of the well-known good taste as publishers, and enterprise and energy in pushing books, of the firm of S. C. Griggs & Co. The business in this form has grown to be a large one; the number of books made yearly exceeding 90,000. It is felt by literary people in the West that Mr. Griggs has rendered a great service to the cause of good literature and of culture in his section of the country; a service which is cordially appreciated and acknowledged. He is a valued and useful member of the First Baptist church, Chicago.

Grimmel, Rev. J. C., was born in the city of Marburg, Germany, May 30, 1847. His father was one of the first persons baptized by Mr. Oncken in that place, a godly man, who endured severe persecution for his faithful adherence to the truth. The example and influence of such a man must have been a blessing for the son. The father finally left his native land, and coming to America, settled with his family in Wilmington, Del., where through his efforts a German Baptist church was organized. His son was converted and baptized into the fellowship of that church Jan. 29, 1861. Early in life young Grimmel felt himself called to the work of the ministry. He pursued his studies at Rochester, N. Y., and graduated from the German department of Rochester Theological Seminary in 1866. In the year following he became pastor of the First German church, Buffalo, N. Y. In the year 1873 he accepted the pastorate of the First German church, Brooklyn, E. D. Mr. Grimmel was editor and publisher of the *Mitarbeiter*, an illustrated German monthly, from 1874 to 1879. As a preacher, Mr. Grimmel has been successful in leading many souls to Christ. He is a talented speaker, able to draw and instruct delighted hearers. In the general work, he occupies positions of trust and responsibility in the Missionary Committee of the Eastern German Baptist Conference, and in the School Committee, which has charge of the interests of theological training in the German ministry.

Grimsley, Rev. Barnet, was born in Culpeper Co., Va., Dec. 15, 1807. At nine years of age he entered school under the care of Mr. B. Wood, and remained during portions of four years. At this early age young Grimsley was remarkable for the strength of his memory, having, when about twelve years of age, at one of the school commencements, declaimed from memory alone an entire sermon on the Being and Perfections of God. Until about eighteen he assisted his father in his farm-work, devoting all his spare moments to reading and the improvement of his mind. His books were in a great measure committed to memory. At the age of twenty he chose as his life-work the occupation of milling, and with his characteristic energy he was soon at the very head of that business. In November, 1831, he was baptized by the Rev. Wm. F. Broaddus, and united with the Mount Salem church. His aptness for teaching was so marked that his brethren advised him to enter the ministry, and the church, in October, 1832, licensed him to preach. In June, 1833, he was appointed by the General Association to labor in the valley of Virginia. At this point he relinquished the occupation of milling, in which he had been so successful, and entered upon his real life-work, the preaching of the gospel. He soon gathered a small band of believers, organized a church at Cedar Creek, and on Nov. 25, 1833, was ordained to the ministry and became their pastor. After two years of successful labor under the patronage of the General Baptist Association he resigned his position as missionary and became pastor of the Liberty and New Salem churches. In January of 1836 he became pastor of Bethcar and Rapidan churches, the latter of which he was obliged to resign on account of the inconvenience of meeting with them. In September of 1833 he assisted in the organization of the Salem Union Association. In 1856 he took a prominent part in the uniting of that Association with the Columbia, from which sprang the present Potomac Association. On the retiring of Dr. W. F. Broaddus, in 1840, from the pastorate of Bethel church, Clarke Co., Mr. Grimsley became the pastor of it and of Long Branch church, resigning his care of Cedar Creek and Liberty. His ministry here, as elsewhere, was eminently successful, the church being greatly enlarged in numbers and strengthened in influence. In 1848, after a thirteen years' pastorate at New Salem, he resigned and took charge of Pleasant Vale, Fauquier Co., succeeding the eminent Ogilvie. In 1852, after a seventeen years' pastorate at Bethcar, and twelve at Long Branch, he resigned, and devoted all his time to Bethel and Pleasant Vale churches, still preaching, however, during the week, at Woodville. In 1854 he was called to preach to the newly-constituted church at Flint Hill, which he did during the week. In 1860 he took charge of the Mount Salem church, resigning Woodville, where he had labored for six years. In 1865 his labors were such that he was compelled to resign the care of Bethel, where he had preached to vast multitudes for a quarter of a century, and Pleasant Vale, where he had labored for seventeen years, and he became pastor of the Jeffersonton and Gourd Vine churches, which required much less physical labor in the way of horseback-riding, etc. He still serves these two churches, being abundant in labors and eminent in success.

Mr. Grimsley is one of the most remarkable men in the denomination in Virginia. As a preacher he has had but few equals. His reasoning is clear, consecutive, and closely logical; his language choice, chaste, and weighty; his descriptive power remarkably vivid; and his manner earnest and impressive. As a clear thinker and ready debater it is not too much to say that he had no equal in the local Association to which he belonged, while as a speaker on the platform or in the pulpit he had in the same field no compeer. He was the friend and advocate of all good movements, missions, Sunday-schools, temperance, education, church extension; and when the pernicious doctrine of Antinomianism rested like a blight over the valley of Virginia, Mr. Grimsley lent the strong powers of his mind, heart, and body to the destruction of the heresy. His labors, united to those of Dr. Wm. F. Broaddus, revolutionized the views of thousands, not only in the churches, but also out of the churches, of the most influential families in Clarke, Fauquier, and adjacent counties, and multitudes have arisen to call him blessed. When in the vigor of life nearly one-fourth of his time was spent in horseback-riding between his home and his churches. Exposure made him seem older than he really was, and yet with the infirmities of threescore years and ten upon him he preaches the unsearchable riches of Christ with much of the vigor, impressiveness, and eloquence of his earlier days. Mr. Grimsley is perhaps the only surviving minister in Virginia of that eminent circle of Baptist preachers that gave such celebrity to the Culpeper Baptist camp-meeting gatherings, in which Ryland, Jeter, Burrows, Poindexter, Taylor, and others engaged and accomplished so much good.

Grose, Rev. Henry L., was born at Minden, Montgomery Co., N. Y., Sept. 26, 1816. He early pursued a classical course, and at the age of seventeen began the study of medicine while editing a newspaper. Being converted soon after, he was baptized at Owego, entered Oneida Institute, and was licensed to preach by the Whitesborough church, C. P. Sheldon, pastor. He was ordained at West Danby, N. Y., Jan. 7, 1841, and held pastorates at Danby, Ithaca, Coxsackie, Athens, North

East, Galway, and Mannsville, where his health failed so completely in 1860 that he resigned and purchased the *Ballston Journal*, of which he is still editor and publisher. Leaving much of his business care to his sons, he has preached as supply at Burnt Hills, Saugerties, Saratoga, Middle Grove, and once leaving his native State, was pastor for six years at Hydeville, Vt., and has been pastor of the old Stone church, Milton, since 1878. Thus for forty years has Mr. Grose been a faithful minister of Christ, and during intervals of broken health has filled many other positions of trust, and made various contributions to Baptist literature. His oldest daughter is the wife of J. A. Smith, D.D., editor of the *Standard*, of Chicago; his oldest son is engaged in printing in Chicago; two sons conduct the *Ballston Journal*; and one son, H. B. Grose, a graduate of Rochester University, is on the staff of the *Examiner*.

Groser, Rev. William, editor of the *English Baptist Magazine* from 1838 to 1856, was born Aug. 12, 1791, in London. His parents then belonged to the Eagle Street church. Some years later his father was licensed to preach by that church, and removed to Watford to take charge of the Baptist congregation there. Mr. Groser assisted his father for a long time in the management of a flourishing school. Being a diligent student he made considerable progress in his studies, and his conversion when he was about nineteen led him to devote himself to theological reading. He began to preach in 1811, and was invited to become pastor of the church at Princes Risborough in 1813. Here he labored with much usefulness until 1819, when he removed to Battle, in Sussex, and in the following year settled at Maidstone, in which pastorate he remained nineteen years, until his removal to London. He occupied himself in editing the *Baptist Magazine* and in other literary engagements. In 1848 he accepted the pastorate of the Chelsea Baptist church, from which he retired to assume the duties of secretary of the Irish Society in 1851. His laborious and useful life was ended Aug. 6, 1856. Mr. Groser's services to the denomination were enthusiastically rendered and highly esteemed. His painstaking discharge of editorial duties spoke for itself, whilst his gentleness of spirit, Christian courtesy, and many personal excellencies endeared him to a very wide circle of friends.

Gubelmann, Rev. J. S., was born in the city of Berne, Switzerland, Nov. 27, 1836. He received his early training from his grandfather, a missionary among the Pietists. In the meetings, and under the influence of the Pietists, he received lasting impressions. In 1848 he followed his parents to the United States, and lived with them in New York. The next year, at the age of thirteen, he was converted and baptized, becoming a member of the First German Baptist church. Subsequently he lived some time in Ohio with his grandparents, his grandfather having accepted the charge of a German Reformed church in Monroe Co., O. Feel-

REV. J. S. GUBELMANN.

ing convinced that the Lord had called him to preach his gospel, on coming back to New York he was among the first German students who were sent to the theological seminary at Rochester, N. Y. Taking a full course, he graduated from the University of Rochester in 1858, and from the Rochester Theological Seminary two years later. From 1860 to 1862, Mr. Gubelmann labored successfully as pastor of the German church at Louisville, Ky.; from 1862 to 1868 he was pastor of the German church at St. Louis, Mo. During his pastorate there a new and commodious house of worship was erected, at a cost of some $30,000, of which a large amount was immediately collected. In 1868 he took charge of the First German church in Philadelphia, Pa., where he is still laboring.

Mr. Gubelmann stands foremost among the German ministers as a preacher. His superior gifts have been recognized among American churches and ministers wherever they have become acquainted with him. He is a thorough Bible student, and while his sermons are polished and scholarly, their greatest beauty is their evangelical simplicity. His remarkable talents, combined with his amiable disposition and childlike piety, have made him everywhere very successful. Hundreds have been given him as fruits of his labors. His great longing has always been for souls. The church at Philadelphia has been specially blessed, and a second flourishing German church, and also a mission, have been organized.

By his counsels and labors Mr. Gubelmann has rendered valuable service to the general cause, and his name will always be inseparably connected with the history of the German Baptist Mission in this country. He is one of the managers of the American Baptist Publication Society, and his standing in Philadelphia among its fifty-six Baptist pastors is highly creditable to his gifts and his grace.

Guild, Reuben Aldridge, LL.D., was born in West Dedham, Mass., May 4, 1822, and was fitted for college at the Baptist Academy in Worcester. He graduated at Brown University in 1847, and was appointed librarian of his *alma mater* in 1848, which office he now holds. During the thirty-three years of his connection with the library he has watched its growth, and in many ways contributed to it, until he has seen it transferred from its straitened quarters in Manning Hall to the elegant building recently erected for its reception by the munificence of the late Hon. John Carter Brown. Dr. Guild has found time, amid his numerous and pressing duties, to prepare and publish several works of great worth. Among them are his "Librarian's Manual," "Life, Times, and Correspondence of James Manning," and "The Early History of Brown University, a Biographical Introduction to the Writings of Roger Williams." In addition to these works, he has published an elegant edition of a full and exhaustive "History of Brown University." Few men in the Baptist denomination have rendered it such valuable services as Dr. Reuben A. Guild. As a writer of history about our distinguished men, and our first American college, he is without an equal among the living, and with very few among the dead.

Guirey, Rev. George, of French Huguenot descent, pastor of Trinity Baptist church, Oakland, Cal., was born at Princeton, Ind., Jan. 5, 1842; at the age of seven, on the death of his mother, he was placed under an Episcopalian guardian, and did not see his father afterwards until he had entered the ministry. He was baptized at sixteen, and joined the Little Union Baptist church, in Missouri. Studied at Bethel College, Ky., and was two years in Spurgeon's College, London, England. During the war he joined the Union army for the defense of Frankfort, Ky. He has spent fifteen years as pastor at West Troy, N. Y., Chelsea, Mass., Newark, N. J., and Oakland, Cal. He has been blessed with many conversions; is an extempore preacher, and impresses his hearers with a conviction that he believes what he proclaims. He is a writer of considerable vivacity, and is author of a book, entitled "Deacon Cranky," a plea for greater spirituality in Christians.

Gulley, Orrin S., was an apprentice in a printing-office in Detroit, became early a member of the church, and in it was ever faithful. When but eighteen he was the first printer of the *Michigan Christian Herald*, and either alone, or in company with Mr. Allen, he was its printer or publisher until it left Detroit, in 1862; more than twenty years of steady application and good judgment made his business yield him wealth; but, where others become haughty, he remained the plain, industrious man, using his means in generous gifts to deserving objects. He prosecuted business in the interest of those whom he employed, as well as in his own, and he is lovingly remembered by them, though sleeping in his grave. Ever pleasant, patient, and kind, the Sunday-school, the mission interests, the charities of the city, and all the denominational interests in the State, miss him as one of the best of the Lord's servants and stewards. His death occurred in 1878.

Gunn, Rev. Radford, was born in Virginia, May 13, 1797. At an early period in his life his parents removed to Georgia, and settled in Oglethorpe County. In 1820 he was converted and joined County Line church, in Oglethorpe County. His conversion was bright, clear, and joyous, "like a blaze of sunshine at midnight." With his heart overflowing with joy, he left his work and went among his neighbors, telling them what great things God had done for him. Not long afterwards he preached his first sermon from Rom. i. 15. He had a powerful memory, which enabled him to retain whatever he heard. He was ordained in 1822, and for forty years afterwards was an active, earnest, laborious preacher, very popular and influential, and in great demand as a pastor among the churches, the most prominent of which in his reach were glad to secure his services, and during his ministerial career he filled many pastorates in Oglethorpe, Taliaferro, Hancock, Warren, Lincoln, Columbia, and other counties, and always with success, for he was a most earnest and zealous worker. Those whose spiritual interests were committed to his care were daily in his prayers, his sympathies, and his affections, and he watched over their welfare tenderly, seeking to promote their happiness and usefulness.

He was a very effective and earnest preacher, his style being didactic, rather than hortatory. Unfolding his subject systematically and, frequently, with considerable logical effect, he would warm up as he proceeded, and at times would burst into an impassioned strain of oratory that would stir the feelings of his audience profoundly. His aim always was to present the truth as it is in Jesus, and his preaching was often followed by powerful effects; Christians were made to rejoice in the hope of glory, and sinners were made to weep over their sins. Under God, he was instrumental in the salvation of hundreds, while many Christians were strengthened and encouraged in the discharge of their duties.

It is not too much to say that Radford Gunn was a remarkable man. He possessed uncommon talents. In his community he was a leading man; and in his Association, the Georgia, he wielded a strong influence. He was a thorough Baptist, and all who knew him could bear witness to his many personal excellences. Rigidly honest and unflinchingly bold, he avowed his opinions on any subject and under any circumstances; still he was not obtrusive. He was generous to a fault, and he deemed nothing he had too good for his friends.

He spent a large part of the years 1862 and 1863 in the Virginia army, in evangelistic and charitable labors, breaking down his health and contracting the disease which ended his life. Unable to preach or do anything for his Master except exercise the grace of patience under suffering, he would frequently exclaim, "And now, Lord, what wait I for? My hope is in thee." "Lord, on thee do I wait all the day." "Now, lettest thou thy servant depart in peace, according to thy word, for mine eyes have seen thy salvation." When death did come he welcomed it with manifest joy; for his soul longed to escape from its crumbling tabernacle of clay. His work on earth was done, and he was anxious to depart and be with Christ. He died at his residence in Warren Co., Ga., June 15, 1866. His death was a very easy one, for he passed away as one falling into a sweet and peaceful sleep.

Gurney, William Brodie, was born in London in 1778. His father being a deacon of the Maze Pond church, he became acquainted in early life with the original members of the Baptist Missionary Society, and delighted them by the interest he manifested in the missionary enterprise. He followed his father's profession, stenography, and attained to such distinguished excellence in that art that at an early age he was appointed short-hand writer to the House of Lords, a lucrative office, which enabled him to give large sums for missionary and benevolent purposes. He took a leading part in the organization and direction of the Sunday-School Union, and liberally stimulated the production of a distinctive Sunday-school literature. This great and useful institution was in a large measure his creation. The Baptist Missionary Society was also greatly indebted to his enterprise and munificence for its present strength. As its treasurer for many years the duties of his office were no mere matters of finance. He took the liveliest interest in all the efforts of the society, and especially set himself to the development of a spirit of liberality towards evangelistic work at home and abroad. His example and influence produced a happy effect, which he lived to see. He died in London, March 25, 1855, aged seventy-seven.

Guthrie, Hon. James, an eminent lawyer, statesman, and capitalist, was born in Nelson Co., Ky., Dec. 5, 1792. He was educated at Bardstown, and studied law under the distinguished Judge John Rowan. He established himself in practice in Louisville, Ky., in 1820. Though not a communicant in any church, he was a Baptist in sentiment, and attended Walnut Street Baptist church, with his family, all of whom became eminently useful members of this church. He quickly established an extensive reputation as a lawyer, and acquired property with great rapidity. Was elected to the lower house of the Kentucky Legislature in 1827; was in the Kentucky senate from 1831 to 1840, and in 1849 was president of the convention that formed the present State constitution; was Secretary of the U. S. Treasury from 1853 to 1857, and in 1865 was elected U. S. Senator, which position he resigned in 1868, on account of declining health. From 1860 to 1868 he was president of the Louisville and Nashville Railroad. Besides these, he held many other prominent positions of trust and honor. He was a man of superior business qualifications, and was said to have become the wealthiest man in his State. He died in Louisville, March 13, 1869.

Gwaltney, Luther Rice, D.D., the son of Rev. James L. Gwaltney, was born in Isle of Wight Co., Va., and is now about fifty years of age. In early life he received a thorough collegiate education, graduating with distinction from Columbian University, Washington, D. C., thence he went forth as an ambassador of the Cross. Where his first pastorate was is not known to the writer of this sketch. He was called from Murfreesborough, N. C., in 1857, to take charge of the church in Edgefield village, South Carolina, where he labored with great fidelity and success for eleven years, both in his pastorate and in the educational interests of the community. In 1868 he left Edgefield and took charge of the church in the city of Rome, Ga., where he remained for eight years. Here he worked with the most constant zeal in the ministry, in the temperance cause, and in the interests of education, bearing a prominent part in the founding of Shorter Female College. In 1876 he was called to the presidency of the Judson Female Institute, in Marion, Ala., where he now labors with great acceptance. With the highest culture, a dignified and graceful appearance, a pure life and deep piety, the best kind of sense, and fine scholarly attainments, an earnest worker and an able preacher, Dr. Gwaltney has proven himself a success wherever he has been tried. He has the art of endearing himself in the lasting affections of his people. His *alma mater* in

Gwaltney, Rev. W. R., was born in Alexander Co., N. C., in 1834; graduated at Wake Forest College; taught in Wilkes and Alexander Counties; has served the churches of Hillsborough, Chapel Hill, Weeksville, and Winston, and is now the laborious and beloved and very successful pastor of the Second Baptist church of Raleigh. Mr. Gwaltney is a trustee of Wake Forest College.

Gwin, D. W., D.D., pastor of the First Baptist church, of Atlanta, Ga., is a Virginian by birth, and at the present time is about forty years of age. He is a man of fine person and splendid natural abilities, heightened by study and training. To unusual mental powers he adds eloquence, grace of action, a fine command of language, and large intellectual acquirements. He graduated at Richmond College, Va., before he was twenty-one years of age. Soon after graduating he was elected Professor of Ancient Languages by the Brownwood Institute, La Grange, Ga., where he speedily manifested his proficiency and his skill as an instructor. To an intimate knowledge of Greek and Latin, which he has studied enthusiastically, he has added an acquaintance with Hebrew since graduating. To learn a language is with him a pastime, and he ranks now with the first linguists of the land; and yet philosophy and theology are his favorite studies. He was called by the Baptist church at Rome, Ga., and was there ordained in 1861. Compelled to leave Rome on account of the war, he moved to Griffin, Ga., and took charge of the church there, remaining four years, during which he founded and conducted the Griffin High School. In 1868 he accepted a call from the First Baptist church of Montgomery, Ala., where he preached with distinguished ability and eloquence for six years. He then moved to Atlanta and assumed his present charge. He is a member of the board of trustees for the Southern Baptist Theological Seminary, and though a man of great modesty and diffidence, his worth and abilities are highly appreciated by his brethren, who have placed him upon the State Mission Board, situated at Atlanta. His wife is a daughter of the distinguished Dr. R. B. C. Howell, of Nashville, Tenn.

Gwynn, Hon. W., is a native of Kentucky, but has been in Florida many years. During the administration of Gov. Broome, Mr. Gwynn was a State-house officer, and was appointed State treasurer on the election of Gov. Drew, which important position he now holds. He is a man of spotless character and incorruptible integrity, and hence is much respected by the masses of the people in his adopted and beloved State.

Mr. Gwynn was converted under the ministry of Dr. E. W. Warren, and was baptized by him at Tallahassee. He took an active interest in the Baptist cause there, and has recently labored hard and contributed liberally to relieve the church property of an embarrassing debt, and to repair the house of worship and sustain the gospel. Not easily excited, very cautious and conservative, sagacious and discerning, he is a very safe adviser.

H

Hackett, Prof. H. B., D.D., LL.D.—Horatio Balch Hackett was born in Salisbury, Mass., Dec. 27, 1808. The Hackett family is believed to be descended from the Scotch and the Danes. Few of the name emigrated to America. During the Revolution, John Hackett, grandfather of Horatio, superintended the building at Salisbury of the Continental frigate "Alliance." His maternal grandfather, the Rev. Benjamin Balch, was chaplain on the same ship. Richard Hackett, a son of John, was also a ship-builder, and married Martha Balch, a daughter of the clergyman first mentioned, who was settled in Barrington, N. H. Horatio was the second of four sons. His father died in 1814, at the early age of thirty. In 1821 he attended the academy at Amesbury, under the charge of Michael Walsh, a graduate of Trinity College, Dublin, and a celebrated teacher. In September, 1823, he became a pupil in Phillips Academy, Andover, Mass., under John Adams. Among his schoolmates were Oliver Wendell Holmes, Ray Palmer, D.D., Jonathan F. Stearn, D.D., Wm. Newell, D.D., and H. A. Homes, LL.D., State Librarian at Albany, N. Y. He graduated in August, 1826, with the valedictory address. A month later he was admitted to Amherst College. It was while a student that he became a Christian. He united with the College church Nov. 2, 1828. Having graduated at Amherst, with the valedictory, Mr. Hackett returned to Andover and entered the theological seminary. At the end of his first year in the seminary Mr. Hackett was honored with an

PROF. H. B. HACKETT, D.D., LL.D.

appointment to a tutorship in the college which he had so lately left, and held this position during the year 1831-32. He then returned to theological studies at Andover, pursuing the course to the end, and engaging in some occasional literary work. He graduated in 1834, in which year he for some time ministered to the Congregational church in Calais, Me.

Mr. Hackett was married to his cousin, Mary Wadsworth Balch, Sept. 22, 1834, and spent the academic year of 1834-35 as a member of the faculty of Mount Hope College, Baltimore, in charge of the classical department. In the summer of 1835 he was baptized, and united with the First Baptist church of Baltimore, a step resulting from investigations about the proper subjects of baptism. In September, 1835, he became a professor in Brown University, Providence, R. I., with the title at first of Adjunct Professor of the Latin and Greek Languages, and in 1838 he was elected Professor of Hebrew Literature. Among his associates in the faculty were Drs. Wayland, Elton, and Caswell. Aug. 5, 1839, he was chosen Professor of Biblical Literature and Interpretation in Newton Theological Institution, becoming the colleague of Drs. Chase, Ripley, and Sears. Sept. 1, 1841, he sailed for Europe, and was absent a year, studying at Halle and Berlin, attending the lectures of Tholuck, Gesenius, Neander, and Hengstenberg. He also fulfilled a commission from the Board of Managers of the Baptist General Convention for Foreign Missions in behalf of Christian brethren in Denmark.

About a year after his return he published, with annotations, the treatise of Plutarch, "De Sera Numinis Vindicta" (1844). A revised edition, with notes by Profs. H. B. Hackett and W. S. Tyler, was published in 1867. In 1845 appeared his translation of Winer's "Chaldee Grammar," and in 1847 his own "Exercises in Hebrew Grammar." In 1852 he traveled in the East, and has given a record of his observations in the book entitled "Illustrations of Scripture, suggested by a Tour through the Holy Land." In 1858-59 he was abroad again, and resided six months in Athens, Greece, under the auspices of the American Bible Union. Shortly before this he published the second edition of his "Commentary on the Acts," the first having appeared nearly seven years earlier. This has been styled by Dr. Peabody, in the *North American Review*, "one of the very few works of the kind in the English language which approaches in point of massive erudition the master-works of the great German critics, differing from them only in possessing a soundness and accuracy which they sometimes lack." A few months after his return from Europe, Prof. Hackett delivered an able and eloquent address on Bible revision before the American Bible Union in the city of New York, Oct. 6, 1859. The society published the address, and also Dr. Hackett's "Notes on the Greek Text of the Epistle of Paul to Philemon," etc., in 1860. He contributed thirty articles to Dr. Wm. Smith's "Dictionary of the Bible," published in England in 1860-63, and in 1861 wrote an introduction to the American edition of Westcott's "Introduction to the Study of the Gospels." He compiled a volume entitled "Christian Memorials of the War," published in 1864. In 1866 he began to edit an American edition of "Smith's Dictionary of the Bible." Its publication took place between 1867 and 1870, and in this task he had the special co-operation of Prof. Ezra Abbot, D.D., LL.D., and some of the most able scholars of America. In 1868 appeared his translation of Van Oosterzee's "Commentary on Philemon," with additions, for Dr. Schaff's edition of Lange's Commentaries.

In the same year he terminated his professorship of twenty-nine years at Newton, intending, however, still to dwell there, and to labor more exclusively for the Bible Union. But after a year of literary occupation he listened with favor to an invitation made to him through the Rev. E. G. Robinson, D.D., LL.D., then president of the Rochester Theological Seminary, to resume there his career as a teacher. A year later, in September,

1870, he entered upon his duties as Professor of Biblical Literature and New Testament Exegesis, having just returned, with his daughter, from his fourth European trip. In 1870 was published his translation of Braune's "Commentary on Philippians," with additions, for Dr. Schaff's work before mentioned. He wrote an introduction to an American edition of "The Metaphors of St. Paul and Companions of St. Paul," by John S. Howson, D.D., dean of Chester, published in 1872, and in 1873 made additions, notes, and appendices to Rawlinson's "Historical Illustrations of the Old Testament." His many and valuable contributions to the "Bibliotheca Sacra," *Christian Review*, and kindred works cover a period of forty years from 1834. "The Book of Ruth," the common version revised, was a posthumous publication, in 1876.

His visits to the Old World were marked with attentions from eminent English and Continental scholars. A few weeks after this final one he died suddenly, Nov. 2, 1875, having just returned to his residence from an exercise with one of his classes.

Prof. Hackett was chosen to the membership of many learned societies in Europe and America, and only a few days before his death he attended a stated meeting of the New Testament Company of the American Bible Revision Committee. He received the degree of D.D. from the University of Vermont in 1845, and from Harvard University (where he was long an examiner) in 1861, and that of LL.D. from Amherst College in 1862. His memory was widely reverenced at the time of his death, and the tributes thus evoked were edited, some entire and others partially and in biographical connection,* by one who had been his pupil and colleague, and whom he had honored with his confidence and affection. In Newton's beautiful cemetery, not far from the spot and column consecrated by Prof. Hackett's patriotic discourse to the fame of her soldiers, a massive granite monument marks his own resting-place. Upon one side are the principal dates of his life and services. The reverse characterizes the writer and scholar who, fervent in spirit, serving the Lord, instructed a generation of Christian ministers.

Those who knew Dr. Hackett in later life will recognize the permanence of traits ascribed to him as a young man by the Rev. Ezekiel Russell, D.D.: "In character, H. B. Hackett was the beauty of our college Israel; modest, sincere, truthful, just, conceding to all their dues; claiming little for himself, and from his soul loathing everything in the form of affectation, intrigue, and selfish management."

He has a secure fame, and is held in the affectionate remembrance which he was himself so ready to accord. "Having once loved Andover as the place of his intellectual nativity, he loved it unto the end," said Dr. Park at his burial. At the centenary celebration of Phillips Academy, in 1878, a poem was delivered by Dr. O. W. Holmes, whose prose portrait of his schoolmate, the future great Biblical scholar, was published in 1869, and is well known. In commemorating

"The large-brained scholars whom their toils release,
The bannered heralds of the Prince of Peace,"

he laid these fresh *immortelles* upon the grave of Hackett,—

"Such was the gentle friend whose youth unblamed
In years long past our student-benches claimed;
Whose name, illumined on the sacred page,
Lives in the labors of his riper age."

Hackett, Rev. J. A., the present able pastor of the First Baptist church, Shreveport, La., was born in Illinois in 1832. When he was quite young his father removed to Mississippi, where he was brought up. He was educated at Mississippi College, in which he recently preached the commencement sermon, which has added greatly to his reputation as a clear thinker and forcible speaker. He served as pastor at Jackson, Miss., and at Clinton and Hazelhurst in the same State. He was called to Shreveport in 1876. During his present pastorate the church has erected a beautiful house of worship. He has also successfully established a mission station in the suburbs of the city at a former Sunday resort for amusement.

Hadley, Rev. Moses, a pioneer preacher in Southwestern Mississippi, came to the State some time previous to 1806, and at that time labored in Wilkinson County. The estimation in which he was held in that day is seen in the fact that he was chosen moderator of the Association at its second session, when both David Cooper and Thomas Mercer were present. In 1810 he wrote the circular letter of the body on religious declension, an able document, in which he treats of the causes and cure in a forcible manner. In 1812 he wrote again on "Union of the Churches." The same year he was sent to Opelousas to ordain Mr. Willis and constitute the First church in Louisiana. He was, in 1817, one of a committee to write a summary of discipline for the churches. He died in 1818, much regretted by his brethren, who by resolution expressed their high appreciation of his labors.

Hadley, Judge T. B., was born June 30, 1801, in Beaufort District, S. C. In childhood his parents moved to Woodville, Wilkinson Co., Miss., where he was educated; was admitted to the bar, and was sent to the Legislature of Mississippi. In 1830 he was auditor of public accounts for the State of Mississippi; in 1838 was State senator from Hinds

---

* Memorials of Horatio Balch Hackett. Edited by George H. Whittemore. 1876.

County, and he was greatly applauded for his indefatigable exertions in procuring a law for the "Protection of the Marital Rights of Women," long and familiarly known as "Hadley's Law." He moved to Houston, Texas, in 1844, and served his county as chief justice, and the city of Houston as recorder. He joined the Baptist church at Jackson, Miss., in 1839; served as clerk and deacon of the Houston church, and always took a deep interest in its prosperity and in the progress of Christ's cause. The Baptist ministry of Texas will ever remember the generous hospitality which his family at all times dispensed. A good man and an honored citizen, he passed to the rest which remaineth for the people of God, Sept. 25, 1869.

Haetzer, Ludwig, a Hebraist, an able polemical writer, a hymnist, and an Anabaptist. In 1523 we find him earnestly supporting Zwingli in his reformatory efforts. His writing against images did much towards securing their removal from the Zürich churches. When the Anabaptists come forward, in 1524, we find him sympathizing with them in their efforts to secure pure churches, but still seeking to maintain the favor of Zwingli, Œcolampadius, etc. In 1525 he published the ablest plea for temperance to be found in the literature of the Reformation period, in which he condemned unsparingly the social gatherings of the clergy, where wine was drunk immoderately, and where worldly talk, even indecent conversation, was freely indulged in. Driven from Switzerland, he labored in Augsburg, Strasburg, and Constance. In 1526, in connection with Hans Denk (see article), he published a meritorious translation of some of the prophetical books of the Old Testament. He was beheaded at Constance in 1529, ostensibly for adultery, but probably on account of his Anabaptist views.

Hague, Rev. John B., was born in New Rochelle, N. Y., in 1813, and was a graduate of Hamilton College in the class of 1832. He pursued his theological studies at Newton, graduating in 1835. His ordination took place at Eastport, Me., where he continued as pastor for ten years. Mr. Hague has devoted the larger part of his life to teaching young ladies. He has had schools in Jamaica Plain, Newton Centre for six years, at Hudson, N. Y., for ten years, and at Hackensack, N. J., where he removed in 1870.

Hague, William, D.D., was born in Pelham, Westchester Co., N. Y., Jan. 4, 1808, and was a graduate of Hamilton College, N. Y., in the class of 1826. He took his theological course at the Newton Institution, graduating in 1829. He was ordained Oct. 20, 1829, as pastor of the Second Baptist church in Utica, N. Y., the sermon being preached by Rev. Dr. B. T. Welch, of Albany. Here he remained until called to the pastorate of the First church in Boston, to fill the vacancy caused by the resignation of Rev. C. P. Grosvenor. His installation took place Feb. 3, 1831, Rev. Dr. Wayland preaching the sermon. His connection with this church continued until June, 1837, when he was dismissed to enter upon his duties as pastor of the First church in Providence, over which he was installed July 12, 1837, the sermon being preached by Rev. Dr. B. Sears. The church commemorated while he was pastor the second centenary of its foundation, Nov. 7, 1839, and he preached an historical discourse on the occasion, which was published. During nine months of the year 1838–39 he was abroad, the Hon. S. G. Arnold being his traveling companion. He resigned his office Aug. 20, 1840, and accepted a call to the Federal Street church, Boston, where he commenced his labors Sept. 20, 1840. His subsequent pastorates have been in Jamaica Plain, Mass., Newark, N. J., Albany, N. Y., New York City, and Boston. He is now pastor of a church at Wollaston Heights, one of the pleasant suburbs of Boston. Dr. Hague received the degree of Doctor of Divinity from Brown University in 1849, and from Harvard College in 1863. He was chosen a trustee of Brown University in 1837, and is now, with one exception, the oldest living member of the board. Among the productions of his pen are "The Baptist Church transplanted from the Old World to the New," "Guide to Conversation on the Gospel of John," "Review of Drs. Fuller and Wayland on Slavery," "Christianity and Statesmanship," "Home Life." He has also written much for the reviews and the periodical press, especially for the *Watchman*, of Boston, with which he was at one time connected editorially, and whose columns he has often enriched over his well-known signature "Herbert." Dr. Hague is justly regarded as one of the ablest and most scholarly ministers of his denomination.

Haigh, Deacon Daniel.—Mr. Haigh was born at Marsden, Yorkshire, England, in December, 1801. After his conversion he united with the Independent church at Huddersfield of which Dr. Boothroyd, the Bible commentator, was the pastor. He was afterwards baptized into the Baptist church at Wakefield, and served as deacon for some years. In 1847 he came to Illinois and settled near Long Grove. He was for many years an officer in the Pavilion and Bristol churches, and an active member of the Fox River Association, and helper in all denominational work. He still lives, retaining at advanced age his warm interest in the progress of Christ's kingdom.

Haigh, William Morehouse, D.D., was born at Halifax, Yorkshire, England, in April, 1829. Converted at the early age of thirteen, he was baptized at Wakefield by Rev. J. Harvey, in 1842. In

1852 the family removed to this country, settling at Pavilion, in the northern part of the State. He was licensed to preach by the Pavilion church in 1852, and began his pastorate over it in January, 1853, being ordained in November of that year. His subsequent pastorates were at Chillicothe, Bristol, Woodstock, Mendota, and Galesburg, in Illinois. In August, 1862, Mr. Haigh entered the army as chaplain of the 36th Regiment Ill. Infantry, continuing in that service until November, 1864. A year was then given to the service of the Baptist Union for Theological Education as agent for the seminary. In 1877, while pastor at Galesburg, having been tendered the appointment of district secretary of the Home Mission Society for Illinois, Iowa, Wisconsin, and Minnesota, he accepted the service, and is still prosecuting it with marked ability and success. His field has since been extended so as to include Nebraska, Dakota, and Kansas, a vast territory, which he nevertheless succeeds in reaching with measures promotive of missionary work.

Dr. Haigh has rendered important service in writings for the press. His "Letters to Young Converts," and his "Spiritual Life," first published in the Baptist paper at Chicago, have had a considerable additional circulation in more permanent forms.

Haile, Judge Levi, was born in Warren, R. I., and graduated at Brown University in the class of 1821. Having studied law, he practised his profession in his native town. From 1835 to the close of his life he was one of the judges of the Supreme Court of Rhode Island. For many years Judge Haile was a prominent member of the Baptist church in Warren. He died July 14, 1854.

Haldeman, Rev. Isaac Massey, was born at Concordville, Delaware Co., Pa., Feb. 13, 1845. He removed with his father in 1852 to West Chester, Pa., where he received a thorough academic education. From the age of nineteen to twenty-five he was engaged in business with his father. He was converted in 1866, and baptized by the Rev. J. A. Trickett into the fellowship of the West Chester church. From his conversion he was impressed with the conviction that it was his duty to preach, to which service his mother had from his infancy devoted him. His father designed him for business, but his own tastes were literary. He devoted his leisure hours to a course of study embracing the English classics and the ancient and modern languages, and he wrote for the magazines. Pursued by the "Woe is unto me if I preach not the gospel," he resolved to give himself to the ministry. He accepted the invitation of his pastor to preach during a revival, which lasted for thirty consecutive nights. He proclaimed also the gospel in other churches. He was called in April, 1871, to the pastorate of the Brandywine Baptist church, Delaware Co., in which he was ordained. Having remained there four years, preached to crowded houses, and baptized over 200 persons, he became pastor of the Delaware Avenue Baptist church,

REV. ISAAC MASSEY HALDEMAN.

Wilmington, Del., in April, 1875. Here again the house was thronged. Meetings held in the fall and winter resulted in the quickening of the members and in the addition of 400 to the church. The baptisms have since reached 800, and the membership over 1000. "As a speaker," says an intimate friend, "he is exceeding rich in imagery, clothing his ideas as they flow from a fountain of clear and logical thought with choice words and fitting metaphors. He always speaks extempore."

Hale, Rev. William, an early minister in Mississippi, whose labors laid the foundation of many of the churches in the northern part of the State, was born in Tennessee in 1801, and began to preach in his nineteenth year; came to Mississippi in 1835. He was a man of strong native abilities, and with his co-laborer, Martin Bull, abounded in evangelistic labors. He assisted in the organization of the Chickasaw Association, which has since grown into four large Associations, viz., Aberdeen, Judson, Tippah, and Tishamingo. He died Sept. 21, 1855.

Hall, Jeremiah, D.D., was born at Swanzey, N. H., May 21, 1805. He was religiously educated by his parents, and in 1816 was baptized at Colerain, Mass., by Rev. George Witherell.

His education was obtained in part at the academy in Ashfield, Mass., and at Brattleborough, Vt. But having prosecuted the studies of the college course as opportunity permitted, he was admitted in 1847, by Madison University, to the degree of Master of Arts, and in 1854 the degree of Doctor of Divinity was conferred on him by Shurtleff College.

In 1827 he entered the Newton Theological Institution, and finished the course of study in 1830. He was ordained a minister of the gospel, Feb. 3, 1831, in Westford, Vt. In his joint pastorate of the Westford and Fairfax churches he was greatly blessed, and large accessions were made to their numbers.

In the spring of 1832 he accepted the charge of the First Baptist church in Bennington, Vt. During this pastorate the church was greatly strengthened, and a flourishing Baptist Academy, originated by him, was established at Bennington, which for some years exerted a wide influence in promoting the cause of Christian education in that vicinity.

In the spring of 1835 he removed to Michigan, and settled at Kalamazoo. Here, in the following winter, under his labors was organized the First Baptist church, which he served as pastor till the close of the year 1842.

Soon after his arrival at Kalamazoo he learned that the Michigan and Huron Institute, which had been brought into corporate existence chiefly through the efforts of Rev. T. W. Merrill, was seeking a home in the western part of the State, and that strong inducements were offered to locate it about six miles east of Kalamazoo. Believing that it should be established in the town of Kalamazoo, he assumed such pecuniary obligations in the purchase of land for its site as induced the trustees to locate what is now Kalamazoo College at that town. The unredeemed pledges of others, and the financial depression which soon came on, caused him great embarrassment and loss.

Early in 1843 he became pastor of the church in Akron, O., and in 1845 he took charge of the church in Norwalk, O., with special reference to the founding of the Norwalk Institute, a flourishing Baptist Seminary, over which he presided five years. Though greatly prospered in this work, he resigned it to become pastor of the church in Granville, O.

In 1853 he was elected president of Granville College. Soon after he entered upon his duties the name of the college was changed to Denison University, and a new site was selected in the immediate vicinity of the village of Granville, handsome buildings were erected, a valuable library was procured, and additions were made to the faculty. He was subsequently pastor of the Tabernacle church in Kalamazoo, and of the churches in Chillicothe, Mo., and Shell Rock, Iowa. For the last few years he has resided in Port Huron, Mich. He has two sons in the ministry.

Hall, Rev. John P., was a brother of Rev. Wm. S. Hall. Both these brothers left their impress upon the denomination in Pennsylvania. John labored extensively and for many years in the eastern portion of Pennsylvania, where his consistent life won him many friends. His latter years were spent in the pastoral care of the Mount Moriah church, Fayette Co., Pa., and the Nixon Street church, Alleghany City, Pa. After a very short illness he fell asleep in Christ, and his departure cast a deep gloom over the entire church.

Hall, Rev. Robert, of Arnsby, England, was born April 15, 1728, old style; his birthplace was Black-Heddon, about twelve miles from Newcastle. His father was an Episcopalian and his mother a Presbyterian. The death of his father when he was a child removed him from his mother's care to the guardianship of an uncle. With his family he attended the ministry of an Arminian, whose teachings filled him with great distress without pointing him to the blood of atonement. His convictions were deepened by other causes, until, at twelve years of age, the lad was filled with "black despair, accompanied by horrid temptations, and by blasphemies which ought not to be uttered." And this unhappy state continued for more than seven years. For some time he thought that God would have been unholy to have saved him. Then he imagined that if he could live without sin there might be some hope for him. To secure this object he made a covenant with God, which was written with his own blood, agreeing to be lost eternally if he ever sinned again. This compact of course was soon broken, and he supposed now that his destruction was irrevocable. After some calculations he concluded that as his sins in a little while would soon exceed the crime of self-murder, he would commit suicide. He appointed a time to execute this design, but concluded that he would first look at the Bible, and as he opened it his eyes fell on the words, "Come, now, and let us reason together, saith the Lord; though your sins be as scarlet, they shall be as white as snow; though they be red like crimson, they shall be as wool." These words destroyed his plan to kill himself, though they gave him no solid hope. At another time as he was reading in the New Testament the words arrested him, "God sent forth his Son, made of a woman, *made under the law to redeem them that were under the law.*" Immediately this thought impressed him, "Christ was *made under* the law; then he was not under it originally; for what *end* was he made under the law? to redeem them that *were under the law; were* under the law! then they are not *under the law* now, but *redeemed.* There is, therefore, a way of redemption for sinners from the curse of the law by which it is possible even I may be saved;" and in a little time he soon put his entire trust in the Saviour; and ever after became valiant for the truth, and especially for the truth as Paul revealed it, and as John Calvin expounded it.

Mr. Hall's brother Christopher joined the Baptists, much to his indignation, for he regarded them with aversion. He and some friends had a discussion with a Baptist minister, in which they were silenced but not convinced; but on further examination Mr. Hall fully received believer's baptism, and like an honest man, and like so many other intelligent Pedobaptists, he came out publicly, and was baptized Jan. 5, 1752. The next year Mr. Hall became pastor of the church at Arnsby on a salary which seldom amounted to £15 a year. His family increased fast, until he was the father of fourteen children; and by the force of self-denial and the plans and cares of a good wife, he kept out of debt.

For a time after his settlement he was greatly troubled about his call to the ministry. One Sunday morning he came to tell the church that he could not preach. An aged brother asked him to enter the pulpit and pray, and if he obtained help then he could preach, and if not they would unite in prayer for him. He took the advice and soon found a text and a sermon. That season of prayer gave the death-blow to doubts about his call to preach.

He was blessed in winning many souls to Jesus Christ, in setting forth the glorious gospel in becoming and in heaven-given thoughts and words; and he was successful in leading a life of untarnished loyalty to his divine Master. His ministering brethren loved him, his church with which he labored for thirty-eight years was devoted to him, and even the ungodly regarded Mr. Hall with reverence.

He had a penetrating and clear mind, and a heart often overflowing with the love of Jesus. These qualities are strikingly exhibited in his little work, "Help to Zion's Travellers," which has had a wide circulation in Europe and America, and which has rendered great service to the children of God. Mr. Hall was an able and honored servant of the king of Zion. He died suddenly, March 13, 1791. His son, the celebrated Robert Hall, differed widely from the doctrines of his father, and obtained a distinguished reputation for eloquence.

Hall, Rev. Robert, of Leicester, England, was born at Arnsby, near Leicester, May 2, 1764. He was the youngest of fourteen children, and when two years old he could neither speak nor walk. He learned to read through the efforts of an intelligent nurse, who took him for air and exercise to a small cemetery near his father's residence. From its grave-stones she taught him the alphabet, spelling, and reading. Before he was nine years old he had become familiar with Jonathan Edwards on "The Freedom of the Will," and on "The Religious Affections," and with Butler's "Analogy." During his whole life Edwards was a favorite with him. Before he was ten years of age he had written many essays on religious subjects. When he was eleven his teacher, Mr. Simmons, dismissed him from his school because he was farther advanced in education than his instructor. Mr. Simmons, while young Hall was his pupil, had frequently to spend the night in preparation to keep up with him, and to relieve himself from this trouble Robert Hall was compelled to leave his school.

In his fifteenth year he entered Bristol College to study for the ministry. Here his progress was equally remarkable, and speedily inspired the brightest hopes for his future usefulness. During his first summer vacation he preached at Clipstone, in Northamptonshire, before his father and a number of ministers. His text was, "God is light, and in him is no darkness." The service was one of peculiar trial to him, and from which he earnestly begged to be relieved. Never till then had he assumed the responsibility of a preacher. But the effort was a success, and congratulations were showered upon him.

According to custom, while at Bristol he was required to give an address in the vestry of Broadmead church before his instructors and fellow-students. Its commencement was brilliant, but his nervousness overcame him, and "covering his face in an agony of shame, he exclaimed, 'Oh! I have lost all my ideas.'" He was appointed again to deliver the same address the next week, and a second time he made a worse failure than the first. Robert Hall was extremely sensitive, and these discouragements, while intensely mortifying, only summoned up or called down greater strength for the next trial, through which when it came he passed with flying colors.

After studying three years at Bristol he went, in 1781, to King's College, Aberdeen, where he remained four years. He pursued his studies in Greek and Latin, in philosophy and mathematics, with wonderful success. He was the first student in each of his classes, and the most distinguished young man in the college. While in Aberdeen Mr. Hall became acquainted with the celebrated Sir James Mackintosh, then a student in the same institution, and a young man of rare intellectual endowments. They discussed all important philosophical questions together on the sea-shore, or on the banks of the Don above the old town; they sat together in the class-room; they read Xenophon, Herodotus, and Plato together; and as their pursuits and friendships were well known, it was common for the students to say when Hall and

Mackintosh were seen together, "There go Plato and Herodotus." The regard that sprung up between them in Aberdeen lasted until death.

Immediately after leaving Aberdeen Mr. Hall became assistant to Dr. Caleb Evans, then pastor of Broadmead church, Bristol. The preaching of Mr. Hall speedily attracted very large congregations and an unusual amount of interest. Many of the leading men of Bristol, and quite a number of Episcopal clergymen, were occasionally among his hearers. His position, however, in the church, owing to misunderstandings between Dr. Evans and himself, and suspicions that the eloquent young preacher was not quite orthodox, became uncomfortable, and in 1791 he accepted a call to succeed the learned and erratic Robert Robinson as pastor of the church in Cambridge. In that city, famous for its Episcopal university, Mr. Hall soon acquired the reputation of being the most finished scholar and eloquent preacher in the British Islands. His "Apology for the Freedom of the Press," published in 1793, made him troops of friends and exhibited talents of the highest order. In 1801, Mr. Hall published a sermon on "Modern Infidelity," which carried his fame into every circle of society, and elicited the admiration and gratitude of the friends of Jesus throughout Great Britain. Dr. Gregory, his biographer, says, "The most distinguished members of the university were loud in his praises; numerous passages of the sermon that were profound in reasoning, or touching and beautiful in expression, were read and eulogized in every college (there are seventeen colleges in the University of Cambridge) and in almost every company;" and all over the land it was commended in reviews, periodicals, newspapers, and discourses. From this period Mr. Hall was at the head of the British pulpit; he was spoken of as "The prince of preachers," and his opinions and sayings were treasured up and quoted as if they had been the utterances of an inspired oracle. When his next sermon was printed, in 1803, which he named "Sentiments Proper to the Present Crisis," it was received all over the country with enthusiasm; and even England's great prime minister, perhaps her greatest, William Pitt, declared that "the last ten pages were fully equal in genuine eloquence to any passage of the same length that could be selected from either ancient or modern orators." His subsequent publications confirmed the splendor of his reputation. At Cambridge his intellect gave way twice for short periods from nervous prostration, but his recovery was perfect. He spent fifteen years at Cambridge and nearly twenty at Leicester, and then returned to Bristol in 1825, and entered the heavenly Canaan Feb. 21, 1831. His success in Leicester and Bristol was quite equal to his usefulness in Cambridge. He was the greatest preacher that ever used the English tongue, and his works will be read while the language of Britain is spoken. They were first published in six volumes, in 1833, and they have passed through eleven editions up till 1853.

Mr. Hall never read his sermons, and very seldom wrote them entire. He studied them with the greatest care, though his use of paper was exceedingly limited.

He was the victim of a painful disease from boyhood till death. His brothers had frequently to carry him part of the way to and from school; he was often in mature years compelled to lie down on his back on the floor to gain relief from his anguish. For more than twenty years he was unable to pass a whole night in bed. He carried with him continually "an internal apparatus of torture," ready for work any moment, and certain not to be idle for any considerable time; and yet when free from pain he was one of the happiest of men.

At thirty-three years of age he was "a well-proportioned, athletic man, with a deportment of unassuming dignity, with winning frankness in all that he uttered, and with a speaking countenance animated by eyes radiating with the brilliancy imparted to them by benevolence, wit, and intellectual energy." "His mind was equally distinguished by power and symmetry, where each single faculty is of imposing dimensions and none out of proportion to the rest. His intellect was eminently acute and comprehensive; his imagination prompt, vivid, and affluent." He had the readiest command of the most appropriate language and beautiful imagery ever given to a mortal. His reading was enormous, from six to eight hours a day he often spent at it, and it ran over the Greek and Latin poets, orators, historians, and philosophers; the early Christian fathers, the Reformers, the Puritans, and Episcopalians of the seventeenth century, and more modern theologians, French and English. Nor was there any branch of literature with which he had not a remarkable acquaintance.

His piety was deep and abiding. Soon after his first attack of mental aberration he felt in himself the most extensive change in his relations to Jesus. His heart became the Saviour's more unreservedly than ever; his habits were more devotional than they had been previously, and his spiritual exercises more fervent and more elevated. The light of God's countenance followed him, and the peace of God was continually with him, and when he came to die, though his was a death of extreme physical pain, his faith was triumphant, and strong in the Lord he passed away joyfully to his eternal home.

He held Arminian views of the atonement, and in a measure of some of the other doctrines of grace, and he spoke scornfully of the works of Dr.

Gill, a writer who knew immensely more of the languages and teachings of the Bible than himself; he believed that unbaptized persons might come to the Lord's table. He had other peculiarities of doctrine as unscriptural as those just named. But while we discard his errors without hesitation, notwithstanding the authority of his great name, and in disregard of the sublimest eloquence by which false doctrine was ever commended to human consciences, we rejoice in the mighty preacher of Cambridge, Leicester, and Bristol as an illustrious servant of king Jesus.

Hall, Rev. Robert S., a leading Baptist preacher and educator in Northwestern Louisiana, was born in Ireland, in 1825, of Presbyterian parents, who devoted much time to his religious culture. Being designed for the ministry, he received a liberal education at Queen's College, Belfast. He emigrated to the United States, and engaged in teaching. He united with the Baptists, and in 1852 settled in Caddo Parish, La. He began to preach in 1867, and from his talents and learning at once became a man of mark. He died much regretted in 1873.

Hall, Rev. Wm. S., was born of Quaker parentage, in Blockley, Philadelphia, Pa., Nov. 27, 1809, and died in White Deer Valley, June 8, 1867, in his fifty-eighth year. Converted at the age of sixteen, he was baptized by Rev. J. H. Kennard, D.D., and ordained Oct. 4, 1829. His labors were spread over Berks, Schuylkill, Lancaster, Chester, and the Northumberland region as a mission-field, and as a pastor they were given to Frankford and Milestown in Philadelphia, Zanesville, O., Ridley, Pa., Phœnixville, Pa., Laight Street, N. Y., and the North church in Philadelphia.

The peculiarities characterizing Brother Hall were uncommon energy, surprising fluency in language, suavity of manners, and great firmness in advocating and in defending unpopular sentiments. This led him to strongly press the claims of free missions, and the revision of the Bible. To his praise let it be said that in the hour when his position was deemed the very height of folly, he never gave up his principles, even at the period of his ministry when to be a free mission or Bible Union advocate was to invite bitter opposition. His record shows that he baptized 2459 persons, founded 9 churches, and built 8 meeting-houses.

Hallett, Capt. Benjamin, was born in Barnstable, Mass., Jan. 18, 1760. He saw active service, both in the navy and the army, during the Revolutionary war. He was among the most enterprising merchants of his time, and was recognized as a man of rare qualities. For nearly seventy years Capt. Hallett was a consistent member of a Baptist church. We are told that "when he visited Boston he was hailed with a welcome wherever he went, whether he made his appearance on the exchange, in marts of trade, or in Dr. Stillman's vestry, where his voice was often heard." He exerted his influence, and most successfully, in the Bethel, and stirred up the hearts of his Christian friends in Boston to labor and pray for the spiritual good of seamen. He died at his residence in Barnstable, Dec. 31, 1849, in the ninetieth year of his age.

Halliburton, Rev. Henry, an eloquent young Baptist minister of Northern Arkansas, was born in Tennessee in 1845. He began to preach in 1873, and developed rare abilities as an evangelist. At the time of his death, in 1877, he was a missionary in the White River region.

Halliburton, Col. W. H., is a distinguished lawyer at De Witt, Ark., who has taken an active part in the work of the Baptist denomination in the State for a number of years. He was born in Tennessee in 1815. He has never sought public position, but has filled several offices of trust with great credit to himself. During the war he was Confederate States marshal, and has always been efficient in church work.

Halteman, Rev. David Emory, pastor of the First Baptist church in Delavan, Wis., is a native of Montgomery Co., Pa., where he was born Aug. 28, 1834. His ancestors in the paternal line were

REV. DAVID EMORY HALTEMAN.

German Mennonites. The family came to America from Germany in 1698, and settled at Germantown, Pa. This old town was the birthplace of three successive generations of the family. His mother was Scotch by birth, although her parents emigrated to America when she was a child. When the subject of this sketch was four years old his father removed to Ohio and settled at Dayton, which became subsequently his home. Mr. Halteman's earliest religious instruction came from his godly Presbyterian mother. He attended the Sunday-school of the First Baptist church in Dayton, O. At twelve years of age he was converted and baptized into the fellowship of the First Baptist church in Dayton.

When seventeen years of age he was licensed by the church of which he was a member to preach the gospel. He was educated at Granville College (now Denison University) and Rochester University. He was formally set apart to the work of the Christian ministry by a council called by the Baptist church in Bloomfield, Ill., in December, 1857. This church he supplied six months. Having received an invitation to the pastorate of the Baptist church in Marengo, Ill., he entered upon his labors there in July, 1858, and continued in this relation eleven years. The church was small in numbers, and during his pastorate of eleven years it grew to be the largest in the Association, the membership being over 400 when he closed his labors there. The meeting-house and parsonage were built during his pastorate. Frequent revivals, in two instances of great power, blessed his ministry. In July, 1869, Mr. Halteman accepted a call to the pastorate of the First Baptist church in Delavan, Wis., one of the most important churches in the State. He began his ministry there in the autumn of the same year, and has continued it with fidelity and success up to the present time. Though it is of twenty-three years' duration it has been confined to two fields, and the results abundantly show the advantage of faithful labor in a prolonged term of pastoral service. He has frequently been tempted by calls to other important fields, but has uniformly declined to consider them, feeling that, as a rule, the more permanent the pastoral relation the better is the cause of Christ served. He has been an indefatigable worker in the study, in visits among his people, and in the State. During his ministry he has preached 4120 times, including sermons at Conventions, Associations, councils, dedications, and funerals. He has received 856 members into the two churches of which he has been pastor, 505 of whom were baptized by him; adding 180 persons baptized into other churches, he has immersed altogether 685 persons. His ministry builds up the churches strong doctrinally, develops generous habits of benevolence, and establishes the members in spiritual life and power. Just now his church is erecting a fine house of worship.

For eight successive years Mr. Halteman has been the president of the Wisconsin Baptist State Convention, and an active member of its board. As a presiding officer of a deliberative body he has few superiors, displaying rare tact, impartiality, and familiarity with parliamentary law. At the dedication of meeting-houses his services have been in frequent requisition.

During the war he served as chaplain of the 15th Regiment Ill. Volunteers one year, but his pastoral relation was not disturbed while he was absent.

Frank, open-hearted, generous to a fault, he has fulfilled in a high degree the promise with which he began his ministry. He has for many years taken a leading part in the denominational work of the State. If personal qualities, acquired knowledge, large experience, purity of aim and life, are of any value in the ministry, our brother is fitted to do the best work of his life in years yet to come.

Ham, Rev. Mordecai F., a prominent and useful minister in Southern Kentucky, was born in Allen County of that State, April 30, 1816. He united with Trammels Fork Baptist church, in his neighborhood, in April, 1838; was licensed to preach in 1842, and ordained in 1843, at which time he became pastor of Bethlehem, the oldest and largest church in his county, and has continued to serve in that capacity to the present time. He has preached stately to four churches, and, on account of the scarcity of preachers in his region, has sometimes supplied as many as six. He has received into the churches he has served over 2000 members, by experience and baptism. Mr. Ham has performed considerable missionary labor, and has, with the assistance of his co-laborers, formed several new churches. For some years he has been collecting at his own expense a library for the use of young ministers in his locality. He has expended several hundred dollars in this enterprise, and has commenced the formation of a valuable library, especially rich in the subject of Baptist history. He has been eighteen years moderator of Bays Fork Association. His only son, Rev. Tobias Ham, is a young preacher of excellent promise.

Hamberlin, Rev. John B., pastor at Vicksburg, Miss., a descendant of Deacon Wm. Hamberlin, who accompanied Richard Curtis and his company of Baptists to Mississippi in 1780; graduated at Mississippi College with the first honor of his class in 1856, and at Rochester Theological Seminary, N. Y., in 1858; pastor at Clinton and Raymond, Miss., from 1858 to 1862; two years chaplain in Confederate army, during the rest of the war was State superintendent of army missions. After the war he established Meridian Female College, and supplied Meridian and several surrounding churches, and edited *The Christian Watchman* and *College Mirror*. This excessive labor impaired his health, and he retired to the Gulf coast. Here he began a missionary work that resulted in the establishment of eight churches on the line of the New Orleans and Mobile Railroad, and the Gulf Coast Association. He became pastor at Vicksburg in 1880.

Hamilton, Rev. Alexander, was born in Ireland; his parents were Scotch-Irish; educated at the Royal College, Belfast, for the Presbyterian ministry, he embraced Baptist sentiments and united with that denomination in 1845; was employed by the Irish Missionary Society of the English Baptists, and labored at Conlig, Banbridge, and Belfast. He came to the United States through the influence of Spencer H. Cone, D.D., and Benjamin M. Hill, D.D., secretary of the American Baptist Home Mission Society. Soon after reaching this country he was ordained by the First Baptist church of New Haven, Conn., in 1851. He immediately went to Wisconsin as the missionary of the American Baptist Home Mission Society, where he has served in the Christian ministry until the present. He has been pastor at Barton, Appleton, Walworth, Eau Claire, and Waukau, spending twenty-eight years with these churches. He is living in retirement at Ripon, Wis. His ministry has been fruitful.

Hamilton, Rev. Hiram, was born Dec. 25, 1820, in Portage Co., O.; baptized in March, 1843, at Napoleon, Mich.; was soon after licensed. He studied at Madison University, and graduated at the University of Michigan in 1849. In 1850 he crossed the plains to California, and for eight years was at the head of the first Protestant female seminary in that State. In 1855 he was ordained, and served as pastor six months at San José. In 1864 he was appointed missionary to Idaho by the American Baptist Home Mission Society; organized a church and built a meeting-house at Idaho City. In 1866 he built a house at Boise City, at a cost of $3000, taught a school, and was chaplain of the first Legislature. He collected the Benneau and Shoshone Indians, and preached the gospel to them. In 1869 he returned to California, located in the San Joaquin Valley, began missionary work, established a church, into whose membership over fifty were soon baptized. His life-work is that of an educator. In this he is still active; is a member of the San Joaquin board of education, a zealous Christian, and ever ready to aid in advancing the interests of the denomination in California.

Hamilton Theological Seminary was founded at Hamilton, N. Y., May 1, 1820, by the Rev. Daniel Hascall as teacher in Ancient Languages, and Rev. Dr. Nathaniel Kendrick as teacher in Theology. It is certain, however, that as early as 1816 Daniel Hascall suggested the idea of a literary and theological institute to Nathaniel Kendrick. Out of this institution came Madison University, Hamilton Theological Seminary, and Colgate Academy. See these articles in this work, and also articles DANIEL HASCALL and NATHANIEL KENDRICK.

Hancock, B. F., Esq., was born in Philadelphia, Pa., Oct. 19, 1800, and he died Feb. 1, 1867. Two sons were born to him,—John Hilary, and Winfield Scott, now a major-general in the U. S. army, and lately a candidate for the Presidency of the United States. He served as deacon in the Norristown Baptist church, and also as superintendent of its Sunday-school for several years. He was a constituent member of the Bridgeport Baptist church, and served as deacon, church treasurer, and clerk, and he was Sunday-school superintendent until his death. He was regarded as a wise counselor, a conscientious, diligent, liberal, and faithful Christian. He loved the prayer-meeting, was invariably in his place, always prompt in taking part, and earnest and tender in urging his brethren to work for their blessed Lord and Saviour. Tears were often in his eyes while praying or speaking, or listening to the preaching of the gospel. At times, when pleading for his children, for the conversion of sinners, and for the prosperity of the church, his feelings would so completely overcome him as to compel an abrupt conclusion. He was not only uniformly present at all the services of the sanctuary and Sabbath-school, but was always in time. He was honored by the North Philadelphia Association with several successive elections as moderator.

No citizen of Norristown ever exerted a more decided Christian influence, or commanded more general respect. The Bridgeport Baptist church and Sunday-school are feeling the blessed influence of his counsels and prayers to-day, and will doubtless continue to be benefited thereby even to the end of time.

Hand, Rev. George, was born at Cape May, N. J., Sept. 2, 1821; graduated from the University of Pennsylvania with the first honor in 1849; was ordained pastor of the West Kensington church, Philadelphia, Pa., Nov. 7, 1849; was pastor of the Hatborough church, Pa., for ten years, from 1852. He has devoted much time to teaching, for which he has superior qualifications, but he has always maintained his calling as a preacher by proclaiming the Word of life on the Lord's day.

Mr. Hand is a scholar, a Christian, and a faithful laborer for Jesus in the seminary and in the pulpit.

Hand, Rev. Henry, was a native of New Jersey. He was converted Oct. 23, 1783, about which time he moved with his father to Georgia from South Carolina. He began to preach first as an itinerant minister, but afterwards had charge of a number of churches. He was a most laborious and zealous preacher, scattering the good seed of the gospel, on both sides of the Savannah River, from Savannah to Augusta, most faithfully and earnestly, during a period of not less than fifty years, from about 1785 to 1835. He died Jan. 9, 1837.

Hanks, Rev. Robert Taylor, was born April 23, 1850; a man of more than ordinary ability and of enviable reputation. His theological education was received in the Southern Baptist Theological Seminary at Greenville, S. C. After graduating he took charge of Barea church, near Greenville, having been ordained in 1871 at Dalton. In 1872 he went to Alabama, and entered Howard College, where he remained some time, but left that institution to enter Richmond College, Va., in 1873, where he spent three years. In the summer of 1875 he preached for the Petersburg church, in the interim between the resignation of Dr. Hatcher and the settlement of Dr. Eaton. On the 15th of October, 1876, he took charge of the Baptist church at Dalton, Ga., resigning in January, 1879, to assume the pastorate of the Albany church, where he is laboring most efficiently at present. As a preacher he is pleasant and graceful in manner, fluent in utterance, sound in his presentation of truth, and, at the same time, tender and pathetic. His social and genial disposition, combined with an earnest and sincere piety, has always won for him the affection, confidence, and esteem of those among whom he labors. He is an industrious worker, and fully abreast of the times in all the great benevolent schemes of the day.

Hanna, Judge William Brantly, was born Nov. 23, 1835, in the district of Southwark, now within the limits of the city of Philadelphia. His parents were, and still are, members of the First church, Philadelphia. He was educated at both private and public schools, and graduated from the Central High School of Philadelphia in July, 1853, when he determined upon a professional life; he began to study law in the office of his father, John Hanna, Esq. He graduated from the law department of the University of Pennsylvania, and was admitted to practise Nov. 14, 1857. He was subsequently appointed an assistant to the district attorney of the county, and remained in that position between two and three years. In 1867 he was elected to the common council of the city; was re-elected in 1870, and, before the expiration of the term, was chosen a member of the select council. In October, 1872, he was sent to represent the second senatorial district of the city in the convention that then assembled to revise and amend the constitution of the State of Pennsylvania. While serving as a member of the convention he was re-elected to the select council for the term of three years beginning Jan. 1, 1874. The new constitution having been ratified by the vote of the people, and having provided for the establishment of an orphans' court in the city and county of Philadelphia, he was nominated as one of the

JUDGE WILLIAM BRANTLY HANNA.

three judges who should compose the court. In November, 1874, he was elected for the term of ten years beginning Jan. 1, 1875, and he has been commissioned president judge, which office he still holds.

Judge Hanna is a member of the First church, Philadelphia, having been baptized April 3, 1859. He has served as clerk and trustee, and is at present one of the deacons of the church. He is also the president of the "Baptist Orphanage of Philadelphia," and a member of the board of managers of the "American Sunday-School Union." These varied and repeated appointments in secular and religious affairs are a fitting testimony to his marked ability, his sterling uprightness, and his exemplary Christian character. He is one of the best judges in the State.

Hanna, Rev. Thomas Alexander Thomson, son of Thomas Thomson and Matilda (Carson) Hanna, was born in County Derry, Ireland, Aug. 6, 1842; his grandfather, Surgeon Thomas Hanna, R.N., served under Nelson; his mother is a daughter of Rev. Alexander Carson, LL.D.; spent his childhood in Glasgow, Scotland; came to America at the age of seven ; converted in New York in 1858, and baptized by Rev. Ira R. Stuard; studied eight years in Hamilton, N. Y.; ordained in 1866 as first pastor of Central Baptist church, Williamsburg,

N. Y., and served about three years; then first pastor of Fifth church in same place more than four years; in 1874-75 traveled in Europe and the East; settled in Plantsville, Conn., in 1875; secretary of

REV. THOMAS ALEXANDER THOMSON HANNA.

Connecticut Baptist State Convention for past three years; has written small commentary for Bible Union, and numerous articles for leading Baptist periodicals; married, in 1870, Emily Frances, daughter of Dr. Adoniram and Emily Judson; a very scholarly man; a student in several languages.

Hannan, Rev. Barton, was a pioneer preacher in the Mississippi Territory, who suffered persecution under the Spanish rule. He was imprisoned for preaching soon after the government passed into the hands of the Spaniards, and remained several years in jail, until near the time of the change of government. When his wife went to the commandant, Don Manuel Gayoso de Lemos, and demanded the release of her husband, he endeavored to evade her demand by caressing her babe and making it rich presents. The resolute woman said to him, "I don't want your presents; I want my husband." He replied, "I cannot grant your request, madam." She answered, "I will have him before to-morrow morning, or this place shall be deluged in blood; for there are men enough who have pledged themselves to release him before morning or die in the attempt." The governor deemed it prudent to yield to the demand of this resolute woman, and Hannan was released. He lived to preach the gospel unmolested under the flag of the United States.

Hansard Knollys Society, The, was instituted by our English brethren to republish some of the valuable writings of their fathers, and to issue important records never printed before. Ten volumes are the results of its judicious efforts. The first appeared in 1846, and contains "Tracts on Liberty of Conscience and Persecution," from 1614 to 1661; the second, "The Unpublished Records of the Broadmead Church, Bristol," from 1640 to 1686; the third, "The Pilgrim's Progress," printed from the first edition; the fourth, "The Bloudy Tenent of Persecution," by Roger Williams; the fifth, "A Necessity of Separation from the Church of England," by John Canne; the sixth and eighth contain Van Braght's "Martyrology of the Churches of Christ," translated from the Dutch; the seventh contains Du Veil's "Commentary on the Acts of the Apostles"; the ninth, "The Records of the Fenstanton, Warboys, and Hexham Churches," from 1644 to 1720; the tenth, "Confessions of Faith and other Public Documents of the Baptist Churches of England in the Seventeenth Century."

These works are of rare value, and they have numerous and important notes. No Baptist minister who can secure them should be without them. Unfortunately, the Hansard Knollys Society is dead.

Hanson, James Hobbs, LL.D., was born in China, Me., June 26, 1816. His ancestors on both sides were of English origin, and among the early settlers of New England. His youth was spent amid the scenes and toils of farm-life, in the enjoyment of such intellectual advantages as the common school and an occasional term at the village academy were capable of affording. His earliest and strongest wish was to obtain an education. When he was eighteen years of age he became a hopeful Christian. Soon after he commenced his regular preparation for college. Even at that early period he had decided to make teaching the business of his life. He was a graduate of Waterville College, now Colby University, taking a distinguished position as a scholar in the class of 1842. The year after graduation was spent in teaching in Hampden, Me. In September, 1843, he entered upon his duties as principal of Waterville Academy, where he remained till March, 1853. At that time he took charge of the high school in Eastport, Me. In January, 1857, an invitation to become principal of the boys' high school in Portland, Me., was accepted. Here he taught for a little more than eight years, at the end of which he was urged to return to Waterville to take charge of the academy with which he had formerly been connected. Here he commenced anew his labors, and has continued at his post up to the present time. In addition to the discharge of his duties as a teacher,

Mr. Hanson has annotated and published Cæsar's "Commentaries on the Gallic War," Sallust's "Catiline," a volume of Cicero's orations in connection with Mr. J. W. Rolfe, of Cambridge, Mass., a volume of extracts from Ovid, Virgil, and Horace, called "The Hand-Book of Latin Poetry." In 1872 he received from his *alma mater* the honorary degree of LL.D.

Haralson, Judge Jonathan, a fine jurist, judge of the city court of Selma, a most useful member of the Selma Baptist church, and president of the Baptist Convention of Alabama, was born Oct. 18, 1830, in Lowndes County. Mr. Haralson graduated in the State University, under Dr. Manly, in 1851, and in 1852 in New Orleans in the law-school of Louisiana. In 1853 he settled in Selma, where he maintained a first-class practice until 1875, when he was appointed by the governor of the State judge of the city court of Selma. He is a trustee of Howard College and of the Agricultural and Mechanical Colleges of the State.

He united with the Baptist Church when fourteen years of age,—and he became a deacon of the Selma church in 1855; was the efficient superintendent of the Sunday-school for seven years; has been sent to Europe on important professional business twice. Judge Haralson may be reckoned among the most distinguished laymen in the State, and his brother Hugh is not less so.

Hardin, Charles Henry, ex-governor of Missouri and founder of the female college that bears his name, was born in Kentucky in 1820. His ancestors from colonial times lived in Fairfax Co., Va. His father removed to Kentucky, and afterwards to Missouri, where he settled in Boone County. Charles H. had good literary opportunities, of which he availed himself, and, after graduating with honor, pursued the study of law, and in 1843 commenced practice at Fulton. Being elected a justice of the peace, he was early noted for his correct decisions. His business increased, until he was recognized as one of the most laborious, efficient, and sound lawyers within reach. In 1852 he was elected to the Legislature, and afterwards re-elected; and he was chosen while there, with two others, to revise and compile the State statutes, and then to superintend their publication. After serving in the house of representatives six years he was elected to the senate, in which he was honored as chairman of the judiciary committee.

In 1861 he removed to his present home in Mexico, Audrain Co. Here his professional services were extensively sought. After a period of ten years he was again sent to the senate, and honored as before with the chairmanship of the judiciary committee, and also with that of the asylum committee. In 1874 he was elected governor of the State by a majority of more than 40,000, and by his wise management he was instrumental in restoring the credit of the State bonds. After serving out his term, he retired to his home, where he is honored and beloved for his great abilities, unswerving honesty, and Christian generosity. The cause of

GOVERNOR CHARLES HENRY HARDIN.

education finds in him a devoted friend. The female college, one of the results of his benefactions, which he has endowed, and which he continues to aid, exerts an extensive influence over the State. He is a member of the Baptist Church.

Hardin College.—This young ladies' school was founded in 1873, by Gov. Charles H. Hardin. He gave $40,000 in lands and cash to establish it. The college buildings are complete, and of modern style. The grounds are extensive and finely arranged. Mrs. H. T. Baird is the experienced and accomplished president. The course of study is comprehensive and thorough. Upwards of 100 students were in attendance last year. It is located at Mexico, Audrain Co., Mo.

Harding, Rev. Harris, one of the fathers of the Baptist denomination in Nova Scotia, was born Oct. 10, 1761, in Horton, Nova Scotia; converted under Henry Alline's preaching, in Cornwallis, in 1783; evangelized in 1785 in Colchester and Cumberland Counties; in Chester in 1788; in Annapolis County in 1789; in Yarmouth, Onslow, and Amherst in 1790; in Liverpool, Argyle, and Barrington in 1791; ordained at Onslow, Sept. 16, 1794; was immersed as a Baptist in Yarmouth, Aug. 28, 1799, by Rev. James Manning; took part in forming the Baptist Association, June 23, 1800; was a pioneer of the gospel in 1817 to Cape Canso, to Westport in 1818. Mr. Harding had a passion for the conversion of sinners; and to his labors, under God, is largely to be attributed the growth of the Baptist denomination in Yarmouth. Died March 7, 1854, in the ninety-third year of his age.

Harding, Rev. John, a prominent and useful preacher of Green Co., Ky., was born, of Baptist parentage, in Washington Co., Ky., Jan. 16, 1785. His education was finished under Rev. N. H. Hall. He joined Pitman's Creek Baptist church, in Green County, at the age of twenty-five. Two years afterwards he was ordained to the ministry, and became pastor of Pitman's Creek and other churches. He was a man of extensive reading, and he was a strong logical preacher and writer. He was a brother of Hon. Aaron Harding, and uncle of Chief-Justice M. R. Harding. Died Nov. 11, 1854.

Harding, John H., was born in St. John, New Brunswick; converted and baptized in Wolfville, Nova Scotia, while attending Horton Academy, in 1834; is a deacon of the Baptist church, Germain Street, St. John; was treasurer of the New Brunswick Baptist Home Missionary Board, and is a firm friend of all denominational enterprises.

Harding, Rev. Theodore Seth, a founder of the Baptist denomination in Nova Scotia, was born in Barrington, Nova Scotia, March 14, 1773; converted in 1787; commenced preaching in 1793; withdrew from the Methodist denomination, and was baptized at Halifax, May 31, 1795; ordained pastor of the Horton church, July 31, 1796; evangelized and baptized in Cobiquid, 1799; took part in forming the Baptist Association, June 23, 1800; ministered to the Baptist church, Fredericton, New Brunswick, three years from 1818; evangelized in Pictou and in Prince Edward Island in 1826. The church celebrated the jubilee of his pastorate Feb. 13, 1846; died June 8, 1855. Was a warm friend of Horton Academy and Acadia College. Strongly doctrinal, deeply emotional, quick and elastic, Theodore Seth Harding was pre-eminently the Baptist orator of the Maritime Provinces.

Hardwicke, J. B., D.D., was born in Buckingham Co., Va., Aug. 9, 1830. At the age of twelve he made a profession of religion, and united with the Enon Baptist church. In 1852 he was ordained at the Enon church, in order that he might accept calls to two churches in Campbell Co., Va. He at once became prominent among the young preachers of the country. In 1853 he accepted a call to Greenfield, Va., where he remained for seven years. Here his special mission seems to have been to aid in rescuing the churches from the growing influence of anti-mission teachers. His next call was from Danville, which he declined, and after the call was repeated, he agreed to divide his time with them until they could secure a pastor. In 1860 he accepted a call to the Second church of Petersburg, and remained there until 1864. Now his time was divided between his church and the hospitals that were established in Petersburg during the war. His next field was Goldsborough, N. C., where he spent several years of successful labor. Afterwards he removed to Parkersburg, W. Va. Here he commenced the publication of the *Baptist Record,* which he edited for five years. His efforts here aided in uniting the Baptists of West Virginia in their sup-

HARDIN COLLEGE.

port of one general organization, and in harmonizing churches that had been rent asunder by the civil war. In 1873 the College of West Virginia conferred upon him the degree of Doctor of Divinity. The year following he accepted a call to Atchison, Kansas. He served there for two years and nine months, was then called to Leavenworth, the largest city in the State. While in Kansas he was recording secretary, then president, and afterwards corresponding secretary of the State Convention. He was also a member of the board of directors, and a trustee of Ottawa University. He rendered valuable aid in freeing this school from financial embarrassments and difficulties that hindered its prosperity. At present Dr. Hardwicke lives at Bryan, Texas, and is pastor of a large and influential church. From early life he has been a regular contributor to various secular and religious periodicals, and he has published several sermons.

Hardy, Col. William H., a prominent lawyer at Meridian, Miss., was born in Alabama in 1837, and became a Baptist at the age of fourteen. He took a partial course at Cumberland University, Tenn. In 1856 he came to Mississippi and engaged in teaching. He began the practice of law in 1858, and at once became prominent at the bar, and he now occupies the front rank of his profession in Eastern Mississippi. He commanded a company in the Confederate army, and was afterwards on the staff of Gen. J. A. Smith as assistant adjutant-general. In 1872 he was elected grand master of the Masons; was tendered the nomination for governor of the State; was once elected vice-president of the Southern Baptist Convention; Presidential elector in 1876. Col. Hardy has always taken an active part in the denominational work in Mississippi.

Harkness, Prof. Albert, Ph.D., LL.D., was born in Mendon, Mass., and was a graduate of Brown University in the class of 1842. For nearly six years after his graduation he held an important position as an instructor in the Providence High School. In the fall of 1853 he went abroad to pursue his studies in the German universities, and was absent two years. He first attended lectures at the University of Bonn. From Bonn he went to Berlin, and from it to Göttingen. The degree of Doctor of Philosophy was conferred upon him by the University of Bonn. Returning home early in the fall of 1855, he entered upon his duties as Professor of the Greek Language and Literature in Brown University. In 1870 he went abroad the second time, and was absent a little over a year, studying at Bonn, Heidelberg, and Berlin, and making extensive tours through different parts of Europe.

Prof. Harkness has published several works connected with his special department, and others designed to aid the student in Latin. Of these the best known and most popular is his Latin grammar, first published in 1864, which has had a very large circulation. He was one of the founders of

PROF. ALBERT HARKNESS, PH.D., LL.D.

the Philological Association, and its president in 1876–77. It is matter for just pride that we have in the Baptist denomination so accomplished and well known a scholar as Prof. Harkness.

Harmon, Rev. G. W., was born in Davidson Co., N. C., March 29, 1847; baptized by Rev. Wm. Turner in 1866; attended Abbott's Creek Academy and New Garden College; was ordained in August, 1871, Revs. Wm. Turner, W. M. Bostick, Enoch Crutchfield, J. H. Brook, and J. B. Richardson forming the Presbytery; graduated at Southern Baptist Theological Seminary in May, 1874; settled as pastor at Wadesborough in January, 1875, where he still remains.

Harper, Rev. Pleasant Howard, is a leading preacher and missionary in Washington Territory. Born in Claiborne Co., Tenn., Feb. 1, 1836; educated in the public schools; baptized in 1860; licensed and ordained in 1871, he began his ministry at once in the Territory as pastor at Elma two years; labored two years as missionary of the Home Mission Society on the line of the Northern Pacific Railroad; organized the Centerville church, and was its pastor two years; then labored with the White River church two years; gave important help to the Brush Prairie church, and is now at Goldendale, where he is aided by the Baptist Convention of the North Pacific coast. He is a good scholar, a steadfast Christian worker, and has held important civil and military positions which were thrust upon him by the people. Throughout the Territory he is recognized as one of the most important men in that new and growing field, where the harvest is great and the laborers are few.

Harris, Rev. Austin, a teacher and preacher of prominence in North Louisiana, was born in Georgia in 1835; was ordained in 1858, and the next year removed to Louisiana. He founded a school at Arizona, in Claiborne Parish, where he has successfully taught, and preached to surrounding churches.

Harris, Rev. Benjamin N., was born in Brookline, Mass., in 1783. For twelve years he was a Methodist minister. He changed his views on the subject of baptism, and connected himself with a Baptist church in Wrentham, Mass. His service for Christ in the ministry of the gospel extended over a period of fifty years. He preached in all the New England States, in New York, and Canada, and came at last to be known everywhere as "Father" Harris, and was greatly beloved and esteemed. He died in Bolton, Mass., March 3, 1859.

Harris, Rev. David, was born in Cornwallis, Nova Scotia, in 1785; converted at Bridgetown, Nova Scotia, in 1806, and subsequently baptized; ordained July 23, 1814, pastor of the Baptist church, Sackville, New Brunswick. His pastoral and missionary labors were very successful in the Maritime Provinces, especially in Nova Scotia. Died April 15, 1853.

Harris, Rev. E. L., was born in Ira, Cayuga Co., N. Y., Jan. 12, 1816. In 1833 he united with the Baptist church at Cato. In 1839 he entered Hamilton Literary and Theological Institution, from which he graduated in 1843. He was ordained August 31 of the same year by the church in Pike, Wyoming Co., N. Y., which he served two and a half years, the church at Rushford, Allegany Co., five years, and in the fall of 1850 he came to Wisconsin and settled with the Baptist church in Beloit as pastor. Here his ministry was blessed with an extensive revival. He subsequently served as pastor the Baptist church in Walworth three years, the Baptist church in Darien ten years (this church he gathered and organized, and built their meeting-house), the Baptist church in Sugar Creek two years, the Baptist church in East Delavan one year, the Baptist church in Greenwood, Ill., nearly one year. He was called a second time by the Baptist church in Walworth, serving eighteen months.

During the war he spent some months as chaplain in the army.

Mr. Harris has frequently been moderator of the well-known Walworth Baptist Association, and he was for one year president of the Wisconsin Baptist State Convention.

His ministerial labors have often been interrupted by ill health. He resides near Delavan, Wis., which has been his family home for many years. He has been a faithful and devoted minister of the gospel.

Harris, Rev. George W., was born in Nassau, Rensselaer Co., N. Y., Jan. 8, 1813, the son of Rev. John Harris. He studied at Hamilton, completing the collegiate course in 1840 and the theological course in 1842. He was ordained in Pittsfield, Mass., in January, 1843, and the next year became pastor in Jackson, Mich. In 1848 he became editor of the *Michigan Christian Herald*, and served in that office fifteen years. Since 1863 he has resided in Battle Creek, writing for various periodicals, and preaching as opportunity has offered. He is a ready and perspicuous writer.

Harris, Henry Herbert, D.D., was born in Louisa Co., Va., Dec. 17, 1837. Trained by parents

HENRY HERBERT HARRIS, D.D.

of piety and intelligence, in consequence of early afflictions his mind frequently turned to Jesus, and in November, 1852, at the age of fifteen, he was baptized, and united with the Lower Gold Mine church, Va. He entered at once on active work in the Sunday-school and prayer-meetings, and in 1857 was licensed to preach. His preparation for his college course had been so advanced and thorough, that in October, 1854, he entered the Junior class of Richmond College, graduating with the degree of A.B. in July, 1856. In 1857 he entered the University of Virginia with his younger brother, Prof. J. M. Harris, now of Furman University,

S. C. At the termination of three years he received the degree of A.M., having studied Hebrew and applied mathematics in addition to the regular course. He was at this time invited to the chair of Greek in Richmond College, but having a strong predilection for scientific studies, he accepted a proffered position in the Albemarle Female Institute. At the close of the first session, July, 1861, though exempt from military duty and frail in health, he volunteered as a private soldier, and made the campaign of that summer and fall in the Kanawha Valley as an infantry rifleman, engaged in scouts and skirmishes. In December his company was disbanded, and, thinking the war already over, he entered, in January, 1862, the Southern Baptist Theological Seminary at Greenville, S. C. After one month's stay at the seminary he learned that his old regiment was in peril at Roanoke Island, N. C.; left at once to join them, and was prevented from doing so by their capture. He went to Virginia; joined a battery of field artillery, afterwards attached to the corps of Gen. Stonewall Jackson, and took part in most of the great battles fought under that leader, including his last at Chancellorsville. In June, 1863, he was honored with an unsought commission as first lieutenant in a regiment of engineer troops, about to be organized for the army of Northern Virginia, in which capacity he was engaged in the manifold duties of reconnoitring, selecting routes of march and lines of battle, bridging streams, running countermines, and, upon occasion, taking active part in engagements up to the time of Gen. Lee's surrender at Appomattox Court-House, in April, 1865. In the following October he resumed his former position as instructor in the Albemarle Female Institute; and, on the reorganization of Richmond College, in July, 1866, he was again invited to the chair of Greek, which he accepted, and has continued to fill up to this time, with the exception of an interruption of six months in 1878, spent in a visit to Palestine and Greece.

Prof. Harris began his ministry in 1859 by preaching to a congregation of colored persons. In 1860–61 he filled an appointment once a month at an old free church near Charlottesville. In 1864 the colonel of an infantry regiment applied to the War Department for his appointment as chaplain, but the application was refused, on the ground "that so good an officer could not be spared, and that he was already doing much of a chaplain's work in his own command." From 1868 to 1870, Prof. Harris preached regularly at a small house in the suburbs of Richmond, where he had gathered a Sunday-school and congregation. When a church was organized at this place, he was ordained, July 4, 1869, and became the pastor. In less than a year, in consequence of ill health, he was compelled to resign, and since that time he has been able to preach but seldom. In the field of literature, Prof. Harris is known by several admirable reports and addresses before educational meetings in his own State, at Marion, Ala., at Philadelphia, and also by contributions to periodicals, chiefly to the *Religious Herald*, Richmond, Va. From 1873 to 1876 he was the editor of the *Educational Journal* of Virginia, and in 1877 of the *Foreign Mission Journal*, the organ of the boards of the Southern Baptist Convention. Upon the organization of the Virginia Baptist Historical Society, in June, 1876, he was elected its secretary and treasurer, which offices he still holds. In addition to his other duties, Prof. Harris is now the junior editor of the Richmond *Religious Herald*.

Harris, Judge Ira, was born May 31, 1802, at Charleston, Montgomery Co., N. Y., and died in Albany, N. Y., Dec. 2, 1875. In 1808 his parents

JUDGE IRA HARRIS.

moved into Cortland County and settled on a farm. In 1815 he entered the academy in Homer, where he was prepared to enter college. In 1822 he joined the Junior class in Union College, and graduated with the highest honors in 1824. He commenced the study of law under Augustus Donnelly, Esq., of Homer, and subsequently entered the office of Chief-Justice Ambrose Spencer, at Albany, and was admitted to the bar in 1827. He soon rose to prominence in his profession. In 1844 and 1845 he represented Albany County in the Assembly, and in 1846 he was chosen to a seat in the State convention to revise the constitution.

In the autumn of the same year he was elected to the State senate, and in 1847 he was chosen to a seat on the bench of the Supreme Court of the State. At the expiration of four years he was re-elected for the entire term of eight years.

On leaving the bench, Judge Harris spent a year in foreign travel, and in 1861 was elected by the New York Legislature to the Senate of the United States to succeed William H. Seward, who had been called to Mr. Lincoln's cabinet. As a lawyer, a legislator, a judge, a statesman, Ira Harris was above reproach. In the dark days of the war he stood firmly by the government.

After the expiration of his term he was again elected to the State constitutional convention of New York, when he delivered the celebrated speech on the "Government of Cities."

He was an ardent promoter of higher education. He was president of the board of trustees of Union College, president of Albany Medical College, and of the board of trustees of Vassar College; also one of the founders of Rochester University. He also filled the chair of Equity, Jurisprudence, and Practice in the Albany Law School.

Judge Harris was a devoted Christian, an officer of the Emmanuel Baptist church, Albany, and for years was president of the American Baptist Missionary Union. He traced his ancestors back to the colonists in Rhode Island led by Roger Williams, whose principles of religious liberty he seemed to inherit. His lecture on the life and character of the great founder of the Baptist denomination in America will long be remembered by the people of Albany.

Harris, Rev. John, was born in Rensselaer Co., N. Y., Sept. 19, 1790, and died in Battle Creek, Mich., Oct. 11, 1864. In the summer and fall of 1812 he served in the army of the United States. In 1815 he was baptized by Rev. Enoch Ferris, whom he succeeded as pastor at Nassau, N. Y., the next year. For ten years he was pastor here, and for ten years following at South Ballston. He then settled in Battle Creek, where he spent the remainder of his life preaching to various churches in that vicinity during twenty-eight years of hard labor and privation. He was recognized as a representative Baptist clergyman of Michigan, and an earnest advocate of all beneficent and wholesome reforms.

Harris, Prof. J. M., is one of Virginia's many valuable gifts to South Carolina. Although the soil of the two States does not touch, "they have always," as Dr. Jeter once said in the South Carolina State Convention, "sympathized and generally gone hand in hand, and this is especially true of the Baptists of the two States."

Prof. Harris is now a little over forty years of age. His parents were pious, and tried to bring up their children in the ways of the Lord, and their son's conversion in his thirteenth year was the fruit of their training.

He entered the University of Virginia Oct. 1, 1859, and received the degree of A.B. in July, 1860, and of A.M. July 1, 1861. He served in the artillery during the war. In February, 1869, he became Professor of Natural Sciences in Furman University, and is still doing excellent service in that position.

Harris, Rev. Tyre, was born in Boone Co., Mo., Aug. 9, 1824. He made a profession of religion when seventeen years of age, and joined the Bethlehem Baptist church. He was baptized by the beloved Fielding Willhite, pastor of the church. He commenced preaching when nineteen years of age. He was a young man of brilliant talents and deep piety, and he was eminently successful in winning souls to Christ.

He was a warm advocate of missionary and benevolent efforts. He was pastor at Fayette, Mount Pleasant, Booneville, Big Lick, and Mount Nebo. He was president for one year of Stephens College, Columbia, and he was also pastor of the church in that place.

He afterwards took the care of the Baptist church in Lexington, Mo., and died a few months after, in September, 1854.

He was highly esteemed by all. Happy in his associations with the people, earnest and eloquent in his preaching, he was a great blessing during his ministry. It was thought that his zeal and labors shortened his life.

Harrison, Rev. Edmund, Professor of the Latin Language and Literature in Richmond College, Va., was born at "The Oaks," Amelia Co., Va., Feb. 17, 1837. He prepared for college in the Amelia Academy, an institution established and conducted by his father, Wm. H. Harrison. During the year 1854 he was engaged in studying law, and afterwards attended lectures at the law-school of the University of Virginia. During 1855 he was engaged in teaching school in Cumberland Co., Va., after which he returned to the university, took the literary course, and graduated in most of the schools. After graduation, Mr. Harrison was engaged in teaching in the Southern Female Institute at Richmond, where his scholarship was held in high esteem. The war breaking out about this time, he entered the Confederate army, joining the "Powhatan Troop" as a private soldier, and continuing in active service until failing health sent him to stationary duty in the Nitre and Mining Bureau. In 1864 he received the appointment of assistant in the Nitre and Mining Corps, with the rank of captain of cavalry, and was promoted, in 1865, to the rank of major, in consequence of a valuable report prepared and presented by him to Gen. St. John.

He was with the army under Gen. Johnston when it surrendered at Greensborough, N. C. During 1865 he was engaged in teaching in the Richmond Female Institute, and in 1866 was elected Professor of Latin in Richmond College, a position which he still holds, with honor to himself and advantage to the institution. Prof. Harrison was converted at the age of sixteen, and united with the Mount Tabor Baptist church, Amelia County. For some years he was actively engaged in Christian labors, and, feeling it to be his duty to consecrate himself to the ministry, he, in 1874, received ordination, and is now engaged in preaching regularly to two country churches. Prof. Harrison writes occasionally for different periodicals, secular and religious.

Harrison, Gen. James E., was born in South Carolina; early joined the Baptist Church; was prominent in Baptist affairs in Mississippi many years; served in the State senate of Mississippi; was attached to the Confederate army during the

GEN. JAMES E. HARRISON.

whole civil war, attaining the rank of major-general. In civil life he was occupied from boyhood to old age as a farmer. He was an earnest worker in all the missionary and educational enterprises of Texas, and was first president of the General Association. He died at Waco, about the sixty-fifth year of his age, in 1874 or 1875.

Harrison, Richard, M.D., was born in South Carolina; educated in Mississippi; received the degree of M.D., and successfully practised medicine in Mississippi and Texas. At an early age he professed religion, and joined the Baptist Church; zealously labored for benevolent enterprises, and served the Mississippi Baptist State Convention as its president. He represented Monroe Co., Miss., in the State senate. After moving to Texas he took an active part in Baptist affairs. He possessed high natural gifts as an orator. He was a younger brother of Gen. James E. Harrison, and twin-brother of Col. Isham Harrison, who fell at the head of his regiment during the civil war, in Mississippi. Dr. Harrison was married three times. His last wife was a daughter of Rev. Wm. C. Beech. Died at Waco, Texas, in 1877.

Harrison, Rev. T., was born in Sussex Co., Va., Dec. 9, 1839; graduated at Columbian College, Washington, D. C., in 1859; taught in Georgia two years; served through the late war in the cavalry; taught from 1865 to 1873 in Virginia and North Carolina; was ordained in Edenton, N. C., in 1872, and has been pastor at Hartford, Apex, Carthage, and Greensborough. Is now agent of Foreign Mission Board for North Carolina.

Harrison, Gen. Thomas, was born near Nantwich, Cheshire, England. His father, like the fathers of Henry Kirke White and Cardinal Wolsey, was a butcher, a circumstance that led such an excellent lady as Mrs. Lucy Hutchinson to say that " he was a mean man's son." He had a respectable education, and in early life he was a solicitor's clerk. His employer was on the side of Charles I.; but Harrison, from the beginning of the trouble, was with the friends of liberty. When the war commenced he became a cornet in the Parliamentary army. " He advanced," says Clarendon, " by diligence and sobriety to the grade of captain without any signal notice being taken of him, till the army was remodeled, when Cromwell, who possibly had knowledge of him before, found him of a spirit and disposition fit for his service, much given to prayer and to preaching, and otherwise of *an understanding capable of being trusted in any business;* and then he was preferred very fast, so that by the time the king was brought to the army he was a colonel of horse, and looked upon as inferior to few after Cromwell and Ireton in the councils of the officers and in the government of the agitators; and there were few men with whom Cromwell more communicated, or upon whom he more depended for the conduct of anything committed to him."* Lord Clarendon was no friend of Gen. Harrison, and his testimony to his ability and prominence may be taken at its full worth. Harrison was speedily known all over the United Kingdom as a soldier of skill and daring, and he was raised to the rank of major-general, and for a considerable period was justly regarded as second only to Oliver Cromwell. When Charles I. was to

---

* Clarendon's History of the Rebellion, iii. 247. Oxford, 1706.

be tried for treason against his subjects, Harrison was deemed the safest man to bring him from Hurst Castle to Windsor and London; for he was regarded as proof against bribery or fears for the future. The soldiers relied upon him for his well-known piety; he prayed in their meetings for religious worship, and sometimes delivered gospel addresses burning with holy fervor; and his life was without a guilty stain. And then he was a decided republican; so that the hero of Naseby, as long as he fought against tyranny, could trust Harrison, in whom, after himself, the army confided. "Harrison," says Hume, "was raised to the highest dignity, and was possessed of Cromwell's confidence."* By the favor of Cromwell, and of the Parliament, of which he was a very influential member, he had acquired an estate worth $10,000 a year, in addition to his professional income; and he lived in a style corresponding with his ample means. He was selected as one of the judges to try the king, and his name stands boldly at his death-warrant. He reluctantly consented to aid Cromwell in dispersing the Long Parliament. When the fatal day arrived, Cromwell, during the session, told him "that the Parliament was ripe for a dissolution," and the general tried to persuade him to give the subject further consideration; and when some time after, Cromwell declared the members "no Parliament," and called in soldiers to remove them, Gen. Harrison intimated to the speaker that he should leave the chair; he refused to vacate his position without force; "I will lend you my hand," says Harrison. Then, according to Gen. Ludlow, of the Parliamentary army, "putting his hand within his, the speaker came down."† This was the greatest mistake of Gen. Harrison's life, but Cromwell was a dear friend; and from no other man could he obtain such necessary assistance to shield him from the anger of his countrymen, who reverenced the very name of a Parliament, and abhorred a military despotism. His fervent piety, his warm regard for Cromwell, and his intimacy with him are strikingly expressed in the following letter, written him as he assumed the command of the army which, on Sept. 3, 1650, vanquished the Scotch at Dunbar:

"To spare you trouble, I forbear to give you my excuse for not waiting on you to Ware. *I know you love me*, therefore are not apt to except, though in this particular I had not failed, but that orders from the Council superseded me. Considering under how many and great burdens you labor, I am afraid to say any more, that I may not add to them, but love and duty make me presume. The business you go upon is weighty as ever yet you undertook. The issue plainly and deeply concerns the life or death of the Lord's people, His own name, and his Son's. Nevertheless may you rejoice in God, whose affair it is, who, having heretofore given you numberless signal testimonies to other parts of the work, will in mercy prosper this, that he may perfect what he hath begun; and to omit other arguments, that in Deut. xxxii. 27, hath much force on my heart, especially the last words, '*And the Lord hath not done all this.*'

"I believe, if the present enemy should prevail, he would as certainly reproach God, and all that hitherto has been done aforesaid, even as I now write; but the jealousy of the Lord of hosts, for his great name, will not admit it. My Lord, be careful for nothing, but pray with thanksgiving, to wit, in faith. Phil. iv. 6, 7. I doubt not your success; but I think faith and prayer must be the chief engines; as heretofore, the ancient worthies, through faith, subdued kingdoms, out of weakness were made strong, waxed valiant in fight, and turned to flight the armies of the aliens. Oh that a spirit of supplication may be poured forth on you and your army! There is more to be had in this poor simple way than even most saints expect. My Lord, let waiting upon Jehovah be the greatest and most considerable business you have every day; reckon it so, more than to eat, sleep, or counsel together. Run aside sometimes from your company and get a word with the Lord. Why should you not have three or four precious souls always standing at your elbow, with whom you might now and then turn into a corner? I have found refreshment and mercy in such a way. Ah! the Lord of compassion own, pity your burdens, care for you, stand by and refresh your heart each moment. I would I could in any kind do you good. My heart is with you, and very poor prayers to my God for you. The Almighty Father carry you in his very bosom, and deliver you, if it be his will, from touching a very hair of any for whom Jesus hath bled. I expect a gracious return in this particular.

"But I am sorry to be thus tedious. Pardon me. . . . The Father of mercies visit and keep your soul close to him continually, protect, preserve, and prosper you, is the prayer of, my Lord,

"Your excellency's loving servant, whilst I breathe, T. HARRISON.

"WHITEHALL, 3d July, 1650.

"For his excellency the Lord-General Cromwell, humbly present these."‡

That Gen. Harrison was in the closest relations with Cromwell and with Cromwell's Saviour is clear from every line of this letter. He was the right-hand man of England's great uncrowned

---

* Hume, Smollett, and Farr, i. 730. London.
† Memoirs of Ludlow, ii. 457. Vevay, 1699.
‡ Confessions of Faith, etc., pp. 315–17. Hansard Knollys Society, London.

ruler, loving him tenderly, and beloved by him in return, until he proclaimed himself Protector, or, as Gen. Harrison viewed it, Despot. From that moment, as Hume states, Harrison and the other Baptists deserted him. Rapin says, "The Anabaptists* were all of the republican party," and, having fought to dethrone a king, they had no intention of waging war to support the government of one man under any other name. Cromwell, afraid of the military talents and great popularity of Gen. Harrison, cast him into prison, until the masses of his country acquiesced in his dictatorship, when his former trusted friend was set at liberty.

The general and his wife were baptized† in the winter of 1657, though they held Baptist principles for years before their immersion. At the time of their baptism the cold was intense and the ice very thick.

The Protector's displeasure removed from the general the pretended friends who sought the patronage of Cromwell through him, but he still enjoyed the love of the hosts who appreciated patriotic worth, Christian character, and military genius.

When the English people for a season became demented, like the French in their great revolution, and showed their aberration of intellect by giving their throne to Charles II., the basest and the most immoral of men, Gen. Harrison was quickly sent to the Tower of London, and in due time he was brought before unprincipled judges for trial as a regicide. The court sat in the Old Bailey in London, and when he was required to answer, as Gen. Ludlow states, "He not only plead *Not Guilty*,‡ *but he justified the sentence passed upon the king*, and the authority of those who commissioned him to act as one of his judges. He plainly told them, when witnesses were produced against him, that he came not thither to deny anything he had done, but rather to bring it to light; he owned his name subscribed to the warrant for the execution of the king, as written by himself; he charged divers of his judges with having formerly been as active for the cause in which he had engaged as he or any other person had been; he affirmed that he had not acted by any other motive than the principles of conscience and justice, in proof of which he said it was well known that he had chosen to be separated from his family, and to suffer a long imprisonment, rather than to comply with those who had abused the power they had assumed (Cromwell) to the oppression of the people. He insisted that having done nothing, otherwise than by the authority of Parliament, he was not justly accountable either to this or any other inferior court, which, being a point of law, he desired counsel assigned upon that head; but the court overruled (the question); and by interrupting him frequently, and not permitting him to go on in his defense, clearly manifested a resolution to gratify the resentments of the court (the king) on any terms. So that a hasty verdict was brought in against him; and the question being asked, if he had anything to say why judgment should not pass, he only answered that, since the court had refused to hear what was fit for him to speak in his defense, he had no more to say. Upon which Bridgman pronounced the sentence. I must not omit (to state) that the executioner, in an ugly dress, with a halter in his hand, was placed near the general, and continued there during the whole time of his trial, but having learned to contemn such baseness, after the sentence had been pronounced against him, he said aloud, as he was withdrawing from the court, *that he had no reason to be ashamed of the cause in which he was engaged.*"

On Nov. 13, 1660, Harrison was executed at the place where Charing Cross formerly stood, that the king might have the pleasure of the spectacle, and inure himself to blood."§ In the "Trials of the Regicides"‖ the sickening scene is thus described: " He was drawn on a hurdle from Newgate to Charing Cross. Within certain rails lately there made a gibbet was erected, and he was hanged with his face looking toward the banqueting-house at Whitehall (the palace). Being *half dead*, he was cut down by the common executioner; his bowels were burned, his head severed from his body, and his body divided into quarters. His head was placed upon a pole on the top of Westminster Hall, and the quarters were exposed on some of the city gates." Ludlow declares that "he was cut down *alive*,¶ and saw his bowels thrown into the fire." It was intended that he should be alive and conscious of his pain when the human butcher of his most gracious majesty should thrust his knife into his body. Samuel Pepys, "Clerk of the Acts of the Navy" in 1660, writes:** "I went out to Charing Cross to see Maj.-Gen. Harrison hanged, drawn, and quartered; which was done there; he looking as cheerful as any man could do in that condition. He was *presently* cut down, and his head and heart shown to the people."

From Ludlow†† we learn that when Chief-Justice Coke was executed, he was drawn to the scene of death on a sled, upon the front of which was the head of Gen. Harrison, with the face uncovered and

---

* Rapin's History of England, ii. 603. London, 1733.
† Evans's Early English Baptists, ii. 254. London, 1864.
‡ Memoirs of Ludlow, iii. 61-64.
§ Idem, iii. 69.
‖ Trials of the Regicides, p. 282.
¶ Memoirs of Ludlow, iii. 63.
** Pepys's Diary, i. 146.
†† Ludlow's Memoirs, iii. 75.

directed towards him, the object being to fill him with terror; but there was an expression in the face of the brave warrior that filled the chief justice with heroism, and frustrated the designs of his cruel murderers.

Harrison was fully informed of the purpose to arrest and execute him; but he refused to fly from the deadly danger, "regarding* such an action as a desertion of the cause in which he had engaged." Gen. Ludlow, who knew Harrison better than most men of his day, commenting on this remarkable fidelity to principle, says, "I shall not take upon me to censure the major-general, not knowing what extraordinary impulse a man of his virtue, piety, and courage may have had upon his mind in that conjuncture. Sure I am, he was every way so qualified for the part he had in the following sufferings, that even his enemies were astonished and confounded."

As we think of the manly defense made by the general, with the executioner and his halter at hand all the time, and of his last words, which he uttered aloud as he left his judges, condemned to a frightful death by their wicked decree, "*that he had no reason to be ashamed of the cause in which he was engaged,*" and of his choice of martyrdom instead of flight, we are filled with admiration for the faith and the courage of the praying and preaching general. And then when we think of him, in full view of Charles II., and, no doubt, of several of his fair and frail companions, butchered and dressed, a victim of royal vengeance, full of the most triumphant endurance that ever made the death of a martyr glorious, we bless God for his invincible grace, and we praise him for our Baptist ancestry.

The enemies of Gen. Harrison were ready to confess his extreme conscientiousness, his fearless daring, and his fervent piety, and his memory should be cherished as a sacred legacy by his Baptist brethren while the world lasts.

Harriss, Col. Samuel, was among the most effective preachers that ever proclaimed the glad tidings in this country. He was born Jan. 12, 1724, in Hanover Co., Va. He was at one time church-warden, sheriff, justice of the peace, colonel of the militia, and captain of the Mayo Fort. His position was respectable, and his genial disposition made him exceedingly popular. His education had been liberal. He first became anxious about his soul in his thirty-fourth year. On one of his journeys to visit the fort officially he called at a small house, where he learned there was to be Baptist preaching; the ministers were Joseph and William Murphy. He seated himself behind a loom to hide his uniform. The eye of God, however, was upon him, and his heart was very deeply affected; but some time afterwards the Lord revealed his love to him in such fullness that, in an ecstasy of joy, he exclaimed, "Glory! glory! glory!" He was baptized by Rev. Daniel Marshall in 1758, it is believed. He forthwith, like converted Paul, began to preach Jesus. At first his labors were restricted to some neighboring counties of Virginia and North Carolina; but in process of time he preached throughout all Virginia and many parts of North Carolina. He was not ordained for years after he had been preaching. This event occurred in 1769; then he administered the ordinances. The first candidate he baptized was James Ireland, a much persecuted and very useful Baptist minister in Virginia. Mr. Harriss was the best-known man in his native colony, and it is doubtful if Patrick Henry could control a vast assemblage by a power superior to that of Samuel Harriss. His ministry was attended by conversions in very large numbers; churches sprang up on the line of his missionary travels; he was truly the apostle of Virginia. Not a few of his spiritual children became preachers after the order of Mr. Harris, and the aristocratic Episcopalian colony was agitated from one end to the other by these Baptist innovators.

Mr. Harriss feared nothing; legal prosecutions and private persecutions had no effect upon him. He was the owner of a respectable estate, and when he was converted he devoted the greater part of it to religious objects. He had been erecting a new and capacious residence before the Saviour called him, and when it was "covered in" he made it a meeting-house, and lived in his former confined abode. During the Revolutionary war, when salt was scarce, he kept two wagons running to Petersburg to bring it up for his neighbors.

When the Baptists in Virginia mistakenly supposed, in 1774, that the apostolic office still existed, Mr. Harriss was elected an apostle, but he held this honor for only a few months. At all meetings of delegates of the churches he was the presiding officer. Virginia Baptists loved to honor him, and, under God, he was chiefly instrumental in opening the prison-doors of the Old Dominion for the persecuted, and in sweeping away the foul ties uniting church and state.

He made a great mistake in the earlier part of his Christian life in denouncing the acceptance by ministers of any compensation for preaching the Word. This unscriptural and unjust doctrine nearly ruined some of God's faithful shepherds and their families; but Col. Harriss was led to see his error and renounce it. Take him "all together," he was a glorious man of God, a Virginia Whitefield, for which we gratefully bless our divine Redeemer. He died in the year 1795.

Hart, Rev. Jesse M., pastor at El Dorado, Ark.,

---
* Ludlow's Memoirs, iii. 12.

and president of the Arkansas Baptist Convention, was born in Alabama in 1838; began to preach in Louisiana in 1860, near the Arkansas line; has preached to a number of churches in both States, beside filling the important pastorates of Camden and El Dorado, Ark. By application Mr. Hart has made himself an effective minister.

Hart, John, a signer of the Declaration of Independence, was the son of Edward Hart, of Hopewell, a man of considerable importance, who raised a company of volunteers in the French war, and fought bravely in the campaign against Quebec.

John was born early in the last century at Hopewell, N. J., grew up in high esteem among his neighbors, and became eminent for his honesty, kindness, modesty, and benevolence. He had no taste for political life, made few speeches, but was ready with brave sacrificing deeds. Such a man could not remain in the background during the period preceding the birth of his country's nationality. He was identified with the cause of the patriots from the beginning. When he entered the Continental Congress of 1774 he was about sixty years of age. He resigned the next year, and became vice-president of the Provincial Congress of New Jersey. He was again elected to Congress in 1775, and he was re-appointed to the same body by the convention of New Jersey in 1776, and took his place among the signers of the Declaration of Independence. In the same year he was chosen Speaker of the Assembly, and re-elected in 1777 and 1778. He was also an important member of the Committee of Safety, and particularly obnoxious to the British and Tories. When, in 1776, the Legislature fled from Princeton to Burlington, to Pittstown, in Salem Co., and to Haddonfield, where it dissolved, Mr. Hart returned to find that his wife and children had fled to the mountains, that his crops were consumed, and that his stock had been driven away by the Hessians. Though the old man was a fugitive, pursued with unusual malice, sleeping in caves and in thickets, not permitted to visit his dying wife, his spirit was not broken, nor did he despair of the cause. After the battle of Princeton he came from his hiding-place, and convened the Legislature at Trenton. He died May 11, 1779, worn out by his labors and privations.

In 1865 a fine monumental shaft of Quincy granite was erected by the State of New Jersey near the old Baptist meeting-house in Hopewell to honor his memory. It was dedicated July 4, 1865, with imposing ceremonies, among which was an eloquent oration by Joel Parker, governor of the State, upon the life and services of John Hart. This monument prominently exhibits the words,

"HONOR THE PATRIOT'S GRAVE."

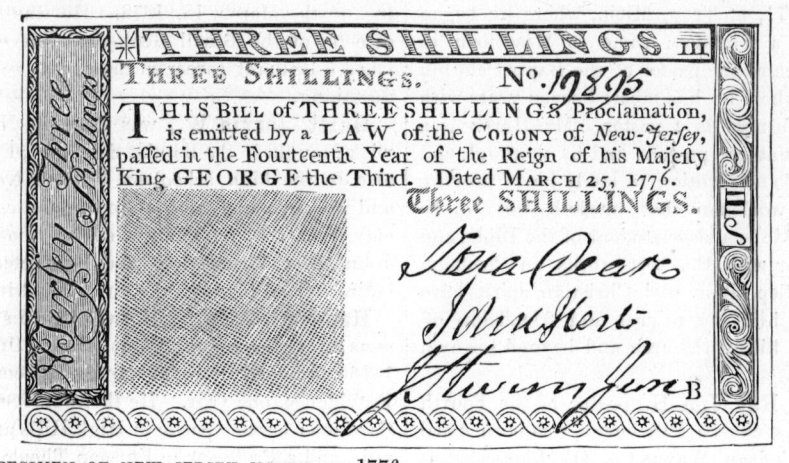

SPECIMEN OF NEW JERSEY MONEY IN 1776, BEARING THE SIGNATURE OF JOHN HART.

The following is an extract from Gov. Parker's address:

"As his public career was without blemish so was his private life pure and exemplary. He was a consistent member of the old Hopewell Baptist church, and gave to the congregation the land on which the meeting-house was erected, and in which his remains are now deposited. He was a true patriot. I am of opinion, after a careful examination of the history of New Jersey during and immediately preceding the Revolutionary war, that John Hart had greater experience in the colonial and State legislation of that day than any of his cotemporaries, and that no man exercised greater influence in giving direction to the public opinion which culminated in independence."

Hart, Rev. Oliver, A.M., was born in Warminster, Pa., July 6, 1723; made a public profession of religion in the eighteenth year of his age; was ordained at Southampton, Pa., Oct. 18, 1749. The same year he was called to the Baptist church in Charleston, S. C., where he continued thirty years. He was well acquainted with Whitefield and Tennent, and, as a patriot, traveled in South Carolina to enlighten the people in regard to their political interests. He was chiefly instrumental in establishing the Charleston Association. He became pastor at Hopewell, N. J., in 1780, and died there in triumph Dec. 31, 1795. Two funeral sermons were preached, one by Rev. Dr. Rogers, of Philadelphia, the other by Rev. Dr. Furman, of Charleston. The College of Rhode Island (now Brown University) constituted him M.A. at its first commencement. Among his publications are "Dancing Exploded," "A Discourse on the Death of Rev. Wm. Tennent, 1777," "The Christian Temple," "A Circular Letter on Christ's Mediatorial Character," and "The Christian Remembrancer."

Hartly, Rev. Wm., is a native of England; ordained, in 1871, at Troy, Mich., where he began his work as a minister; came to Wisconsin in 1873, and became the pastor of the Baptist church in Hudson, where he has labored seven years with growing usefulness as a pastor. Mr. Hartly is a man of fine natural powers, and by thorough and most industrious devotion to study he is proving himself a "workman that needeth not to be ashamed." He is a close student of the Bible, and he is familiar with the best works on theology. His genial disposition and Christian spirit have obtained for him the respect and friendship of many besides his own church and beyond his own denomination.

Hartman, Rev. Jno. H., pastor of the Fourth Avenue Baptist church, Pittsburgh, was born April 17, 1841, in Canaan, Wayne Co., O. Converted at the early age of nine, he soon after deemed it a personal obligation to devote his life to the work of the ministry. At the age of nineteen he entered upon his studies, and graduated at Vermillion College, O., in 1867, and from Newton Theological Seminary in 1870; ordained Nov. 17, 1870, in Canton, Mass.; baptized, while pastor in Canton, 71 persons; became pastor of Salisbury and Amesbury church in Massachusetts, June, 1874, where he baptized 99 on profession of faith; resigned June, 1878, and traveled in England and on the Continent. His present pastorate commenced, after three months of supply service, Oct. 1, 1880. Previous to his acceptance of the doctrines distinguishing the Baptists he was connected with the "Church of God," of which body his father was a licensed preacher.

Hartsfield, Rev. Green W., a prominent minister of Grand Cane Baptist Association, La., who resides at Mansfield, was born in Georgia in 1833; came to Louisiana in 1849; educated at Mount Lebanon University; ten years pastor at Mansfield; has devoted much of his time to the colored population, preaching to them, holding ministers' institutes, and aiding in the organization of the Northwestern Louisiana (colored) Baptist Association, of which he is secretary. As president of Grand Cane Sunday-School Convention he has promoted such interest in the work that every church in the Association has its Sunday-school. He is at present laboring successfully as an evangelist in the employ of the State Convention.

Hartt, Prof. Charles Frederick, son of Jarvis W. Hartt, was born at Fredericton, New Brunswick, Aug. 23, 1840; was baptized at Wolfville, Nova Scotia; studied at Horton Academy, of which his father was principal; graduated from Acadia College in June, 1860; studied geology extensively in the Maritime Provinces and the United States, and became Professor of Geology in Cornell University, N. Y., and continued in this position until his death, March 18, 1878. He was leader and director of the Brazil Geological Survey, and finished a brilliant career in that great scientific undertaking.

Hartt, Jarvis W., was born in New Brunswick; taught in the Baptist Seminary, Fredericton; also in the high school at Wilmot, Nova Scotia, and was principal of the Horton Collegiate Academy from 1851 to 1860, when he removed to St. John, New Brunswick, and conducted a young ladies' school for several years. Died in 1873.

Hartwell, Jesse, D.D., was born in Massachusetts in 1795; graduated at Brown University in 1816; ordained in 1821; supplied Second church, Providence, one year. He then removed to South Carolina; became pastor at High Hills and Sumterville, and a Professor in Furman Theological Institute. In 1836 he went to Alabama; was pastor at Carlowville, president of the Alabama Baptist Convention, Professor of Theology in Howard College, president of the Domestic Mission Board of the Southern Baptist Convention. In 1847 he removed to Arkansas, and founded Camden Female Institute. In 1857 he removed to Louisiana, and became president and Professor of Theology in Mount Lebanon University. He passed away Sept. 16, 1859.

Hartwell, Jesse Boardman, D.D., son of Jesse Hartwell, D.D., and grandson of Rev. Jesse Hartwell, of Massachusetts, was born in Darlington, S. C., Oct. 17, 1835. His father was an ardent friend of missions, and gave him to that work from his birth. When Luther Rice returned from India he called upon the father. At the door he met his friend, saying, "Brother Rice, my missionary has come," and that day the babe was dedicated as a missionary to the heathen. He was baptized July 14, 1850; studied at Howard College, Ala.; graduated at Furman University, S. C., in 1855; was Professor in Mount Lebanon University, La., until December, 1857. In 1858 he was appointed by the

Southern Baptist Foreign Mission Board a missionary to China, and sailed for his field in November, with his wife, Miss Eliza H. Jewett, of Macon, Ga., to whom he was married September 29. They labored two years at Shanghai; then for many years at Tung Chau Foo, in the Shantung province of Northern China, where they opened the first mission, organized a church, and Mr. Hartwell's first convert was ordained as a minister. Here they were alone for many years, until two Presbyterian families came to labor on the same field. Mrs. Hartwell died in June, 1870. She was one of the best female missionaries ever sent to the foreign field; she spoke the Chinese tongue fluently. On his return to the United States he married Miss Julia C. Jewett, his deceased wife's sister, in 1872, returned to China, but was compelled by his wife's health to come back to the United States. After four years he was appointed by the American Baptist Home Mission Society to mission work in California among the Chinese. His wife died Dec. 2, 1879, ten days after their arrival at San Francisco. Dr. Hartwell has a mission chapel in that city, and is an enthusiastic teacher and preacher to the Chinese of California in their own language.

Hartwell, John Bryant, was born in Alstead, N. H., Oct. 17, 1816. He became a member of the Freshman class in Brown University in September, 1838. It was his purpose to pursue a course of study in order to fit himself to enter the Christian ministry. Having changed his mind for reasons satisfactory to himself, he left college, and commenced business in Providence, and was a successful merchant, consecrating his talent and his property to the cause of his Master. He became a deacon in the Central Baptist church of Providence, and was an honor to the office. For six years he was a member of the board of trustees of Brown University. Death suddenly overtook him, and he passed away in the prime of a life of great usefulness, Dec. 9, 1872. "It is the testimony of those who knew him most intimately," says President Robinson, "that he was a man of deep religious convictions, gentle in spirit, persistent in purpose, active in life, and ready for death."

Harvey, Rev. Adiel, was born at Ashfield, Mass., July 29, 1805, and was baptized when twelve years of age. He graduated at Amherst College in the class of 1832. After teaching for a time, he entered Newton in 1835, and took the three years' course. On completing his studies at Newton, he settled over the church in Westborough, Mass., where he remained some eight years, and then went to Plymouth, Mass., where he was pastor for thirteen years. In the summer of 1858 he removed to Needham Plains, and took charge of a young ladies' school, and continued in his work until his death, which occurred June 23, 1864.

Harvey, Hezekiah, D.D., was born in Hulven, County of Suffolk, England, Nov. 27, 1821; came to America in 1830, and was graduated by Madison University and Hamilton Theological Seminary in 1847. It was his intention to become a foreign missionary, but poor health did not allow his cherished desire to have accomplishment. In 1847 he became tutor of Languages in Madison University, and pastor in Homer, N. Y., in 1849; pastor of the First church in Hamilton in 1857, and Professor of Ecclesiastical History in Madison University in 1858; Professor of Biblical Criticism and Interpretation and Pastoral Theology in 1861; pastor in Dayton, O., in 1864, when failing health compelled his resignation; re-elected to a professorship in 1869 in Madison University, where he still retains the chair of Pastoral Theology and New Testament Exegesis; received the degree of D.D. from Colby University in 1861.

Prof. Harvey has recently yielded to the desire of his students, and placed in the hands of the Baptist Publication Society his lectures on the Christian ministry and Baptist polity, and the society has given them to the public in two neat volumes bearing the titles of "The Pastor" and "The Church." The works have been most favorably received, and commended as invaluable alike to the minister and the layman.

Hascall, Rev. Daniel, A.M., was born in Bennington, Vt., Feb. 24, 1782, of Christian parents, originally from Connecticut. His father was a Baptist and his mother a Congregationalist. They were careful to give their children sound religious instruction, based upon their constant reading of Edward Hopkins and Bellamy, and paying particular attention to the Westminster Catechism. In 1785 his parents removed to Pawlet, Vt. Here the educational opportunities were very limited, being confined to school in the winter months, to a small public library, and to private instruction; but of these Daniel Hascall took the largest advantage, and laid the foundations of his future great and abiding usefulness. After some very serious and protracted religious struggles he was converted in 1799, and united with the Baptist church in Pawlet. At the age of eighteen he began teaching during the winter, and employed his evenings and free moments in hard study, so that in 1803 he entered the Sophomore class of Middlebury College, from which he was regularly graduated in 1806. During these years he defrayed his expenses by his own personal effort. From 1806 to 1808 he taught in Pittsfield, Mass., and, so far as his duties would allow, used his time in reading theology. In 1808 he became pastor of the Baptist church in Elizabethtown, Essex Co., N. Y. In 1813 he settled as pastor of the First Baptist church, Hamilton, N. Y., a place at that time described as located in a "region new and unsettled." In addition to his duties as pastor he was engaged in teaching, and he also edited in part the *Christian Magazine*. Feeling very deeply the need of an educated ministry for

REV. DANIEL HASCALL, A.M.

the Baptist denomination, he began to receive pious young men into his family about 1815, and through his efforts, in 1817, the Baptist Education Society of the State of New York was formed, which resulted in the establishment of the Hamilton Literary and Theological Institution, now Madison University (see that article). Until 1828 he continued as pastor and teacher, when he resigned the pastorate, giving himself more largely to the work of the institution and Education Society. In 1835 his relations with the institution were terminated, but he now gave his attention to the interests of an academy at Florence, Oneida Co.; removed in 1837 to West Rutland, Vt., and interested himself in the Vermont Baptist Convention; in 1848 became pastor at Lebanon, N. Y., and in 1849 resided in Hamilton amid scenes so dear to himself. At the time when the removal of the institution was debated, as one of the original founders, and being the only person who could properly stand forth as the legal representative of this location,—one of those who proposed to the citizens of Hamilton the raising of a certain sum of money for its location at Hamilton,—he plunged into the controversy, and at times alone, and at times reproached, he stood firm to his position, "It shall not be moved," and through his efforts a perpetual injunction against removal followed. His prophecy that he should live to see the institution saved and then die was fulfilled. He died June 28, 1852. His published works were a sermon, "Cautions against False Philosophy,"—Col. ii. 8 (1817); "Definition of the Greek Baptizo" (pamphlet, 1818); "Elements of Theology for Family Reading," pp. 260, and a smaller work for Sunday-schools. Daniel Hascall was a great man, deeply pious, versatile in his genius, heroic in his positions, sometimes risking his property to aid the enterprise in which he was engaged; industrious, and apparently possessing inexhaustible resources of physical strength and religious faith. To him more than to any other man does the denomination owe a debt of gratitude for the advance in the arts and sciences, and in Biblical scholarship of its ministry in the United States. (See Sprague's "Annals" and Dr. Eaton's "Historical Discourse in First Half-Century," Madison University.)

Haskell, Samuel, D.D., was born in Bridgeton, Me., March 20, 1818. While he was a child the family removed to Rockford, Ill., where he was baptized by Prof. S. S. Whitman, March 9, 1840. He fitted for college in Suffield, Conn., graduated from Brown University in 1845, and studied theology at Hamilton, finishing the course in 1847.

SAMUEL HASKELL, D.D.

He was ordained in Suffield, Aug. 4, 1847; was pastor of the First church in Detroit from 1847 to 1852, of the First church in Kalamazoo from 1852 to 1871, and in Ann Arbor from 1871 till now. Each of these churches grew in numbers and strength under his pastoral care. For thirty-three years he has been identified with every important enterprise conducted by the Baptists of the State. No man, living or dead, has had a larger share than he in the direction of our denominational work in Michigan. He was secretary of the State Convention in 1854, and president in 1866. Madison University conferred on him the degree of Doctor of Divinity in 1867.

Hastings, Rev. John, son of Rev. Joseph Hastings, was born in Suffield, Conn., in 1743; in early life he was worldly; became a true Christian; was settled as assistant pastor, with his father, by the First Baptist church of Suffield in 1775; became sole pastor after his father's death, in 1785, and so remained till his death; traveled extensively through the country, and aided in gathering a number of churches; his own became the most efficient church in Connecticut for the time; he baptized first and last about 1100 persons; a man of candor, kindness, strength, and fervor; died in Suffield, March 17, 1811, at the age of sixty-eight. His wife was Rachel Remmington, of Suffield.

Hastings, Rev. Joseph, of Suffield, Conn.; at first a member of the standing order; seceded in the Great Awakening; aided in forming a separate church in the west part of the town, of which he became pastor; immersed in 1752; in 1763 assisted in organizing the First Baptist church in Suffield, and became pastor; was at this time sixty-six years of age; remained pastor till 1775, when his son John was associated with him; traveled and preached in various places around; was a man of power; died in 1785, aged eighty-two years.

Haswell, James M., D.D., was born in Bennington, Vt., Feb. 4, 1810, and graduated at the Hamilton Literary and Theological Institution, now Madison University, in 1835. The question of his future service in the kingdom of his Lord having been settled by his decision to become a missionary to the heathen, he received his appointment from the Executive Board of the Missionary Union, Aug. 3, 1835, and sailed from Boston September 22, arriving at Maulmain in February, 1836. Having qualified himself for active service by mastering the language, he turned his attention to the evangelization of the Peguans, or, as they are more generally called, the Talaings. Into the language of this people he translated the New Testament, and wrote and published tracts for their religious benefit. For this people he always felt a deep interest even after he had learned the Burmese language, and performed missionary labor among the Burmese. He urged the appointment of a missionary to the people for whose spiritual welfare he had labored in some of the last letters he wrote home. "About the last work wrought by his trembling hand was the revision and preparation of tracts in their language." In 1849, Dr. Haswell visited the United States, and remained here not far from three years, and in 1867 he also made a short visit of nine months. More than forty years of his life, with the exceptions just referred to, he spent in missionary labors. He died Sept. 13, 1876.

The Executive Board, in their sixty-third annual report, speak of Dr. Haswell in terms of deserved commendation. "He was a man of high character, an industrious scholar, an adept in the languages and literature of the races for whom he labored, an able minister of the new covenant, and a devoted servant of Christ. He had few superiors in point of personal character and missionary efficiency."

Haswell, Rev. James R., son of Dr. James M. Haswell, was born in Amherst, Burmah, Sept. 4, 1836. It was his father's hope and prayer that in due time his son would be his associate in missionary labor among the Burmese. Accordingly he took special pains in his early days to make him thoroughly familiar with the language. He received his collegiate education at the Madison University, where he graduated in 1857, and from the theological school two years later. In September, 1859, he sailed for Burmah. It was not long after his arrival at his destined station that he was stricken down by disease, and left in so shattered a condition that it was deemed best for him to return to this country with the hope that he might recruit his health. He had in a measure lost his voice and his hearing was impaired. He recovered his voice in a good degree, but not his hearing. A few years having been spent in the United States, he returned once more to Burmah, and gave himself to his work as a missionary with great zeal and success. Again he was attacked with a violent disease,—the cholera,—and in a few hours was no more. His death took place May 20, 1877.

Hatch, Rev. E. B., was born in East Hardwick, Vt., Feb. 8, 1831; baptized at the age of sixteen, and educated in Williston and Johnson, and in the theological seminary at Fairfax; was licensed by the Johnson church in October, 1852, and ordained in Lowell, Vt., Jan. 3, 1856; labored as an evangelist at St. Armand and Standbridge, province of Quebec. In 1857 became pastor for one year at Lancaster, Wis. In 1858 settled at Clinton Junction, and remained there six years. In 1865 moved to Thorn Hill, N. Y. In October, 1870, moved to California, where he has labored one year at San Rafael, four years at Vallejo, and three years at Yountville. In the last two places he built two houses of worship. He is a good pastor and preacher, has baptized many converts, and is an earnest and zealous minister of the gospel.

Hatcher, Rev. Harvey, was born in Bedford Co., Va., July 16, 1832, in the same house in which

Dr. Jeter was born, of whom he was a near relation. He was baptized by Rev. Wm. Harris in 1849; was graduated from Richmond College in 1858; served the churches of Portsmouth, Va., Keytesville, Mo., Sidney, and Richmond, Va., and is now associate editor of the *Biblical Recorder*. Mr. Hatcher is an older brother of Dr. W. E. Hatcher, of Virginia, and possesses much of the wit and humor of that distinguished pastor. He has attained distinction as a newspaper writer under the *nom de plume* of G. Washington Jones.

Hatcher, William E., D.D., of Virginia.— Among the first men of Virginia stands Rev. Dr. W. E. Hatcher, pastor of the Grace Street Baptist church, Richmond. Born July 25, 1835, in the county of Bedford, Va., he passed his youth among those blue mountains where were raised such preachers as Dr. Jeter, the late Dr. Daniel Witt ("the golden-mouthed orator"), and a large number of the most distinguished ministers which Virginia ever produced. He entered Richmond College, and his native talent and close application soon enabled him to take rank among the best students in his class, and to graduate in June, 1858, among the first.

In August, 1858, he took charge of a very weak church in Manchester (opposite Richmond), and, by faithful, judicious, and most untiring work, he added 400 to the church, and made it not only self-sustaining, but one of the most efficient in the State.

From Manchester Dr. Hatcher went, in March, 1867, to the pastorate of the Franklin Square Baptist church, Baltimore. He had a pleasant and successful year with this church, but in October, 1868, he returned to his native State, and took charge of the First Baptist church in Petersburg. During his seven years' pastorate there Dr. Hatcher refused a number of most tempting calls to other pastorates, and labored on in his chosen field, where he added to the church 360, and built up the cause to an extent rarely equaled.

Besides his labors in the pastorate, Dr. Hatcher has been a remarkably successful preacher in protracted meetings, and several thousand persons have professed conversion in connection with his labors. In 1875 he accepted the pastorate of the Grace Street church in Richmond. Dr. Hatcher is a man of rare and varied gifts. As a preacher he is a remarkable sermonizer, and an earnest and most effective proclaimer of the soul-saving truths of the gospel. Able, simple, earnest, pathetic, and always *practical*, large and delighted congregations wait on his ministry.

But Dr. Hatcher is even more efficient in his pastoral work than in the pulpit. His genial humor, keen wit, and winning manners make him the centre of attraction to the social circle, while his devout piety, warm sympathies, and deep earnestness make him always a welcome visitor to the houses of his people and the "house of mourning." He is especially popular among the young, is a first-class Sunday-school man, and has had very large success in leading boys and girls to the Cross, and putting them to work for Jesus.

Dr. Hatcher has won a wide reputation as a writer of keen satire and a popular lecturer, and he is destined to still higher renown in this direction. He was one of the most untiring and successful workers in the great Virginia Memorial enterprise, and has won a place among the best collecting agents in the country. There opens up before few young ministers a brighter career of successful work for the Master whom he serves so faithfully.

Havelock, Maj.-Gen. Sir Henry, K.C.B., was born at Bishop Wearmouth, County of Durham, England, April 5, 1795. He had six brothers and sisters. It was the custom of his mother to assem-

MAJ.-GEN. SIR HENRY HAVELOCK, K.C.B.

ble her children in a room for the reading of the Scriptures and prayers, and as a result of this in early youth, Henry had serious religious impressions. When at the Charterhouse School, he and his companions met together regularly in one of the sleeping-rooms for religious reading and conversation. In 1814 he became a law pupil of Chitty, a distinguished "special pleader" of that day; the future Judge Talfourd was his fellow-student. Having a taste for the military profession, he obtained a commission in the English army about a month after the battle of Waterloo. To fit himself for his new calling he read every military work which he could procure, and made himself familiar with all the great battles in history and the tactics of all famous military commanders.

While sailing to India in the "General Kyd" in 1823 he first found peace with God through the blood of the Lamb. Until this time he had a great reverence for Jehovah and his religion, but he had never realized that his sins were blotted out by faith in the crucified Saviour. This rich revelation of divine love and grace in his soul was, as it is in every case, as lasting as life, and will be as continuous as eternity; and it produced the greatest results in his future career. In the first British war with Burmah, while in Rangoon his attention was attracted by the "magnificent Shway-dagong" pagoda. It had a chamber, with images of Buddha all around it in a sitting posture. Havelock selected this room for the prayer-meeting of his pious soldiers. An officer once heard the sound of "psalm-singing" coming from the pagoda, and, following it, he was led into the place of worship. Havelock was expounding the Scriptures; about a hundred soldiers were around him; the only light which they had came from lamps placed in the laps of the surrounding idols. The scene was a strange one in every way, and yet it was as glorious as it was remarkable. But in this fashion the young officer trained his men, and the result was that they became the bravest and the most moral soldiers in the army, in which they were called "Havelock's saints"; and they were often employed on occasions demanding special heroism. While on a mission to the king of Burmah, Havelock was "formally invested with a title of nobility and an official dress."

He was married Feb. 9, 1829, to Hannah, the third daughter of Dr. Marshman, one of the celebrated companions of Dr. Carey, the missionary. He was baptized April 4, 1830, at Serampore by the Rev. John Mack, and was ever after identified with the Baptists.

In Afghanistan, in 1842, after 13,000 English troops had been destroyed by a treacherous surprise, Havelock was with Sir Robert Sale at Jellalabad; famine stared the soldiers in the face; hosts of Afghan warriors surrounded them; retreat was certain destruction. Havelock commanded one of three columns, each of them five hundred strong, in an attack upon the besieging Afghans. After a short but fierce struggle his division routed the wing opposed to it, and, being speedily joined by the other two, the enemy, many thousand strong, fled in terror, leaving great numbers of their dead and wounded upon the field. He fought bravely in the Sikh war, but secured the greatest distinction in the Indian mutiny. When that frightful calamity fell upon the Europeans of India Havelock rushed to the scene of danger. He gained several victories near Cawnpore, and rescued it from Nana Sahib, the butcher of hundreds of European women and children, whom, wounded and dead, he cast into a great well. Then Havelock, in a second attempt, reached Lucknow, fighting, it is supposed, nearly 50,000 drilled Sepoys with 2500 men, and carrying on a battle through three miles of the city, "where each house formed a separate fortress," until he reached the British Residency, and gave ample protection to the women and children and the slender garrison, who expected death every day. He continued here until Sir Colin Campbell brought a powerful reinforcement, and rescued the Europeans in Lucknow. Brave Havelock after this deliverance sank rapidly under a deadly disease, and passed away Nov. 22, 1859.

In his last moments he said to Sir James Outram, "For more than forty years I have so ruled my life that when death came I might face it without fear. I am not in the least afraid; to die is gain. I die happy and contented." To his oldest son, who waited upon him with great tenderness, he said, "Come, my son, and see how a Christian can die."

Gen. Havelock believed that God was with him and that he ruled everything, and he was as cool in appalling dangers as if nothing could injure him. Wherever he was he found out the people of God and joined in their worship. He maintained his religious character among the most ungodly young officers of the English army in India, and he was always ready to confess his supreme attachment to the King of Kings. His death created the greatest gloom in the British Islands; as a Christian and as a military hero he is revered throughout his own country, and known and esteemed over the world. Just before his death he was made a baronet, with a pension of £1000 a year. A statue by public subscription has been erected to his memory in Trafalgar Square, London. Had this eminent Baptist lived a few years longer no doubt he would have risen to the highest grade of the British peerage; but the Lord elevated him to be a king and a priest with himself in the skies.

Hawthorne, J. B., D.D., pastor of the First Baptist church, Richmond, Va., was born May 16, 1837, in Wilcox Co., Ala. His father was a devoted Baptist minister of an old and honored family. Young Hawthorne was converted early in life, and after completing his literary studies at Howard College, in his native State, he spent about three years in the study and practice of law in Mobile. Under a conscientious sense of duty he decided to abandon his profession and engage in the ministry. He re-entered Howard College, and pursued a course of study in the theological department. On the 22d of September, 1859, at Friendship Baptist church, in his native county, he was ordained to the work of the ministry. Soon afterwards he became pastor of the Second Baptist

J. B. HAWTHORNE, D.D.

church in the city of Mobile. Here his reputation as a preacher and pastor was rapidly rising, when, in 1863, he entered the Confederate army as chaplain of an Alabama regiment, in which capacity his labors were very useful. At the close of the war he accepted the care of the Baptist church in Selma, Ala., where he remained two years, and was then called to the pastorate of the Franklin Square Baptist church, Baltimore. After a successful pastorate there of two years, he accepted a call to the First Baptist church of Albany, N. Y. From Albany he was called to the Broadway Baptist church, Louisville, Ky., where his labors were greatly blessed. While here a beautiful church edifice was erected, costing over $100,000, and dedicated entirely free of debt. From Louisville he was called to the pastorate of the Tabernacle Baptist church of New York City, which greatly prospered under his faithful labors. Failing health and the rigors of a Northern climate culminating in a sickness which was nigh unto death, compelled him reluctantly to leave this field of labor, and late in the year 1875 he accepted a call to the First Baptist church of Montgomery, Ala. Here in his native State his health greatly improved, and his ministry was largely blessed. The denomination increased in numbers and in influence, and the special tenets of the Baptist faith won their way to the favorable consideration of all sects. In the autumn of 1879, Dr. Hawthorne was invited to the pastorate of the First Baptist church, Richmond, Va., which he accepted. Succeeding such pastors as Manly, Burrows, and Warren, he has at once won the regard and admiration of the vast audiences which regularly crowd the church. Dr. Hawthorne is in the prime of life, tall, dignified, and of commanding presence. He has great power as an impressive speaker. His thoughts are fresh and stimulating, his language graceful, his utterance deliberate. He has considerable dramatic power, easily winning and holding the attention of his hearers. As a lecturer, also, he has secured a flattering reputation, and in evangelistic labors he has been greatly blessed by gracious revivals and numerous conversions.

Hawthorne, Rev. Kedor, was born in Robinson Co., N. C., in January, 1797, and moved to Alabama in 1817 and settled in Conecuh County; was baptized by the Rev. Alex. Travis in 1825, and began to preach two or three years afterwards; spent about fifty years in the ministry, planted many churches in South Alabama and West Florida, baptized about 4500 believers in Christ, and died in peace the latter part of August, 1877, at the age of eighty years. He was a pure man and an able minister of the New Testament. He reared a most interesting family, the gifted Rev. J. B. Hawthorne, D.D., now of Richmond, Va., and the Rev. Gen. Hawthorne, of Texas, being sons of his. The latter was a brigadier-general in the Confederate army, and the former has reached the highest celebrity as a preacher.

Haycraft, Rev. N. P., was born in Elizabethtown, Ky., April 9, 1797. He was converted in May, 1831; ordained in 1834 in Illinois. In 1835 he removed to Missouri and settled in Lewis County. He cultivated his farm, and was a missionary of the Bethel Association and of the General Association in North Missouri for six years from 1842. He baptized over 400 persons in the different churches in which he ministered. He endured heat and cold, toil and self-denial, for the Saviour's sake. In 1849 he went to California, and returning, began to preach Jesus. He has helped to organize thirteen churches and to ordain seventeen ministers. He is now eighty-four years old, and says, "My labors are well-nigh done."

Haycraft, Samuel, a distinguished citizen of Kentucky, was born in Elizabethtown, Aug. 14, 1795. He was clerk of the county and circuit courts, practised law, and represented his district in the State senate. Mr. Haycraft joined Severn's Valley Baptist church, the oldest congregation in the Mississippi Valley, in early manhood. He was one of the constituents of the Baptist Convention and General Association of Kentucky, and a generous contributor to its objects. He assisted liberally in the endowment of Georgetown College and the Southern Baptist Theological Seminary. He was connected with the Sabbath-school of his

SAMUEL HAYCRAFT.

church as superintendent and teacher forty years. He was a brilliant and humorous speaker and charming writer, a gentleman of superior culture, an almost unrivaled conversationalist, and during his long life made good use of his talents in devotion to Christianity and practical benevolence. He died Dec. 22, 1878.

Haycroft, Nathaniel, D.D., for several years one of the most eminent ministers of the English Baptists, was born near Exeter, Feb. 14, 1821. Having joined the church at Thorverton, Devonshire, in early youth, and manifesting a desire to enter the ministry, he was admitted to Stepney College, and subsequently studied at Edinburgh and Glasgow. His first settlement was at Saffron, Walden, in Essex, as co-pastor with the Rev. T. Wilkinson. Thence, after some years of successful labor, he was invited to the pastorate of the Broadmead church, Bristol. During this pastorate, which continued for eighteen years, he rose to the eminent place in the denomination which he held at his death. In 1866 he removed to Leicester to take charge of a new church, and in the midst of his work and the fullness of his powers, died Feb. 16, 1873, aged fifty-two. His indomitable energy and high culture secured him the respect of the community, whilst his services to the denomination endeared him to his brethren, and marked him as a leader to whom the highest trusts might be confidently committed. Though a prolific writer and a brilliant orator, he published little. He received the degree of D.D. from Glasgow University, with appropriate congratulations upon his high attainments.

Hayden, Lucian, D.D., was born in Winsted, Conn., in 1808; baptized in Bethany, Wayne Co., Pa., in August, 1830; was graduated in Hamilton, N. Y., in 1836; ordained in Dover, N. H., in June, 1838. He was pastor there four years, at Saxton's River, Vt., fourteen years, and at New London, N. H., eleven years; had charge of Theological Institute for Freedmen at Augusta, Ga., for a few months, and for three years of Indianapolis (Indiana) Female Institute; pastor at Grafton, Vt., for three years, and now is settled at Dunbarton, N. H.; was two years president of Vermont Baptist State Convention, and one year of New Hampshire State Convention; elected a member of New Hampshire Legislature from New London in 1865; author of "Pure Christianity Characterized by Spirituality," published by American Baptist Publication Society; received D.D. from Madison University. Dr. Hayden is an excellent pastor and preacher, distinguished for piety and practical wisdom, and has long been esteemed one of our prominent men in Northern New England.

Haygood, Rev. Francis M., of Lithonia, was born in Clark Co., Ga., Aug. 18, 1817. He professed a hope and united with Mars Hill church in 1835; was licensed in 1840; attended the theological department of Mercer University in 1840 and 1841, at Penfield, and was ordained at Canton in 1847. For a few years he taught school, but for forty years has been an evangelistic preacher, and a laborious and faithful colporteur and Sunday-school worker. He has had charge of several churches in different parts of the State; was for some years the depository agent of the Georgia Baptist Bible and Colporteur Society at Macon, and for many years the successful agent of the American Tract Society of New York, a position he fills at present. All his life he has been a hard-working and faithful Christian laborer.

Hayman, Rev. J. M.—Henry Hayman, paternal grandfather of our subject, was born on the Eastern Shore of Maryland. He was a lieutenant in the Revolutionary war, and after its close he married Mollie Goodall, and settled in Burke Co., Ga. Here he reared his family. James, his son, was the father of the subject of this sketch. His maternal grandfather, Rev. James Martin, of Bryan Co., Ga., was a Dunkard Baptist minister. James Martin Hayman, of whom we write, is the oldest child of James and Delila (Martin) Hayman, and was born in Bryan Co., Ga., Dec. 28, 1822. He professed religion and was baptized by Elder John Tucker, in

Hernando Co., Fla., Aug. 7, 1844, and was licensed to preach by Alafia church, of Hillsborough County, June 17, 1851, and at the request of the same church was ordained to the ministry Nov. 10, 1851, Elders John Tucker, Daniel Edwards, and M. N. Strickland constituting the Presbytery.

He informs the writer that his diary shows that he has traveled 25,000 miles in the discharge of ministerial labors, preached 500 sermons, besides lectures and other labor, and baptized 319 persons.

Elder Hayman moved to South Florida when it was almost a wilderness, and so sparsely inhabited that he would often ride forty miles from one community to another. He has lived to see the fruit of his labors to a considerable degree. Mr. Hayman is a prudent man, whose ministry has been a blessing.

Haymore, Rev. C. C., was born in Yadkin Co., N. C., in 1848; baptized in 1869 by Rev. J. H. Lewellyn; ordained in 1870; was a student for a while at Wake Forest College, and is now the efficient pastor of Mount Airy church.

Haynes, Albert G., was born in Greene Co., Ga., Aug. 1, 1805; was educated at Monticello, Jasper Co., Ga.; resided for two years in the forks of the Tallapoosa River, Ala.; resided seven years in Noxubee Co., Miss.; removed to Texas in the fall of 1842. He was a prominent participator in the efforts to establish the Baptist church at Independence. He served as moderator of the Union Association at one or two important sessions. He acted as deacon for nearly thirty years, and, besides contributing liberally of his means to the cause of Christ, dispensed a princely hospitality at his residence during his lifetime. He held the offices of notary and magistrate, and represented the county of Washington in the State Legislature, and was a trustee and treasurer of Baylor University for many years, aiding by all means in his power in promoting the cause of religion and education. He died May 22, 1870. He was a leading man in all religious and political assemblies in Texas from 1842 to 1870.

Haynes, Rev. Dudley C., was born in Portland, Me., Sept. 15, 1809. He was converted in the winter of 1831, and united with the First Baptist church of Portland, by which he was licensed to preach. He entered the preparatory department of Newton Theological Institution in 1832, and graduated from the seminary in 1837. He became pastor of the Baptist church at Marblehead, Mass., by which he was ordained immediately on leaving the seminary. He has also been pastor at Middletown, Conn., Utica, N. Y., Brunswick, Me., Hyannis, Mass., Philadelphia, Pa., Bainbridge and Union, N. Y., where now, in the seventy-second year of his age, he is actively engaged in pastoral work. During these forty-four years of uninterrupted labor, he has at different times served the American Baptist Missionary Union and American Tract Society. On resigning his pastorate at Philadelphia he became the district secretary of the American Baptist Publication Society for New England, in which work he was very successful. He was afterwards corresponding secretary of the American and Foreign Bible Society for four years. During the war he was engaged as the general agent of the American Freedmen's Relief Association and the American Freedmen's Union Commission, visiting California twice for these societies, and Europe once, and raising large sums of money.

He has also had charge at different times of the affairs of the American Colonization Society and of the American Peace Society in specially designated fields. During Mr. Haynes' secretaryship for the Publication Society he wrote "The Baptist Denomination," a book published by Sheldon & Co., which had a large sale previous to the war.

This is a brief sketch of a life of unceasing activity and usefulness. Few men have done so much hard work and enjoyed such remarkable health.

Haynes, Rev. Emory J, was born at Cabot, Vt., Feb. 6, 1846. His father and grandfather were Methodist Episcopal ministers of considerable note in that denomination. In 1863 he made a public profession of religion, and united with the Methodist Episcopal Church. In 1868 he was graduated from the Wesleyan University, of Middletown, and was immediately settled as pastor of a Methodist Episcopal church in Norwich, Conn. In 1870 he was put in charge of St. Paul's church, Fall River, and two years later he was transferred to Hanson Place Methodist Episcopal church, Brooklyn, N. Y. Here he drew great throngs of people, and the church found it necessary to increase the capacity of their house. In 1875 he took charge of the Seventh Avenue church in the same city. Two years later his convictions led him reluctantly to sever his connection with the Methodists and unite with the Baptists. He was baptized in the Fifth Avenue Baptist church by Thomas Armitage, D.D., and on that occasion made public his reasons for the change. He was very soon called to the pastorate of the Washington Avenue Baptist church, Brooklyn. During the three years of his labor a large number have been added to the church. He is a fluent and eloquent preacher, his discourses abounding in illustrations, showing a warm heart and an earnest desire for the spiritual welfare of the people. He is the author of a work entitled "Are These Things So?" gems of thought selected from his sermons.

Haynes, J. A., M.D., D.D., was born in King and Queen Co., Va., Dec. 13, 1822. He was educated by his father in part, and at the Virginia Baptist Seminary (Richmond College). He subsequently entered the Columbian College, where he graduated in 1843. After having served for a year as principal of the Bruington Academy, he attended lectures at the National Medical College (the Columbian College) during the session of 1844-45, and completed his medical course at the Jefferson Medical College, Philadelphia, where he graduated in 1846. After practising his profession in King and Queen and Clarke Counties, Va., for some time, he felt it to be his duty to preach the gospel, and was licensed by the Berryville church, Clarke County, in 1853, and ordained in 1857. After laboring for a while in behalf of the State Mission Board, he became principal of the Clarke Female Seminary, at Berryville. In the fall of 1860, Dr. Haynes removed to Loudon County, having accepted the pastorate of the Ebenezer and of Middleburg churches, the former in 1858, the latter in 1859. In 1867 he left Ebenezer and took charge of Long Branch. While residing at Middleburg, he also had charge of a young ladies' seminary until 1876. Dr. Haynes has preached frequently in the adjoining counties, assisting in protracted meetings, and rendering efficient services in Associational and kindred meetings, by means of his good judgment and independence. Richmond College conferred the honorary degree of D.D. upon him in 1877. Dr. Haynes died very suddenly in the early part of 1880.

Haynes, Lucius M. S., D.D., is the son of Rev. D. C. Haynes, and was born at Marblehead, Mass., in February, 1838. He was graduated at the High School, Philadelphia, and studied at Newton Theological Seminary. He was ordained as pastor at Augusta, Me.

Early in the war he enlisted in the army, and was commissioned first lieutenant of the 4th Maine Light Artillery. After serving one year he resigned, and accepted the pastorate of the Baptist church of Oswego, N. Y. He was afterwards induced to accept a call from Watertown, then from Norwich, and, after the death of the lamented Dr. Lyman Wright, he was called to the pastorate of the Binghamton Baptist church, N. Y. His earnest and faithful labor in all these leading churches in Central New York, his fidelity to his denomination, and his ability in the pulpit, have given him a high position in the estimation of his brethren. The honorary degree of Doctor of Divinity was conferred upon him by Madison University.

Haynes, Rev. Sylvanus, was born in Princeton, Mass., Feb. 22, 1768; commenced to preach in March, 1789; was ordained pastor of the Baptist church in Middletown, Vt., where he remained twenty-six years, his ministry being accompanied with abundant fruits. He removed to Elbridge, Vt., in 1817, and there preached with great success for several years. He died Dec. 30, 1826.

Hazen, Rev. J. H., for many years a pastor in Illinois, now laid aside in consequence of injuries received while a chaplain in the army, is a native of Pennsylvania, and was born Sept. 10, 1824, of Massachusetts Puritan stock on the father's side, and on the mother's of Scottish descent, his grandmother having come from the Highlands of Scotland. He was converted at twelve, and licensed to preach at seventeen, by the First church of Providence, into whose fellowship he had been baptized. He studied at Providence Academy and at the Northwestern Institute, Sharon, Pa., taking, subsequently, a two years' course in theology in a private class under Dr. John Winter. During the twenty-eight years of his pastoral service he has labored with churches at Salem, where he was ordained in 1844, Georgetown, and Meadville, Pa., and in Illinois at Brimfield, Peoria, and Amboy. During the war he served in the army both as chaplain and as surgeon, and by injuries and overwork was completely disabled. His present home is Amboy, where, though released from active service, he shares the sympathy and esteem of his brethren as a true man and " a good minister of Jesus Christ."

Heard, Rev. George Felix, son of Col. Abram and Nancy Heard, was born in Greensborough, Ga., Feb. 29, 1812; prepared for college at Athens, Ga.; entered University of Georgia in same place, and graduated with honor in 1829; joined the Presbyterian church at Athens in 1827; shortly after his graduation he entered Princeton Theological Seminary; remained a year; then went to Andover for a year; then returned to Princeton, and continued till May, 1833, when, convinced that the views of the Baptists could be sustained by the Scriptures, he was constrained to change his ecclesiastical relations and cast in his lot with the Baptists. Accordingly he left the Princeton Seminary, joined the First Baptist church in Philadelphia, and completed his studies under Rev. Wm. T. Brantly, Sr., D.D. He returned to Georgia, and in February, 1834, was called to Black Swamp church, S. C. But the next year he removed to Mobile, Ala., became pastor of the church, laboring with great zeal and fidelity five years, during the latter three of which he edited a Baptist paper called *The Monitor*. In 1841 he removed to Harrison Co., Texas, where his course was one of constantly increasing usefulness, until it was terminated by death in 1844. He was an admirable public speaker. Had he lived longer he would have produced a much deeper impression in reference to his powers as a scholar, a theologian, and a preacher.

Heath, Rev. Moses, A.M., was born in Kingwood, N. J., May 13, 1827, and graduated at Madison University, N. Y., in 1854. Having taught for two years, he was ordained in September, 1856, by the Baptist church at Flemington, N. J., where he had been baptized, licensed to preach, and married.

Immediately after ordination he became pastor at McKeesport, Pa. Sixty were added to the church during his pastorate there. In 1859 a long-cherished desire for missionary work induced him to remove to Minnesota. Commissioned by the American Baptist Home Mission Society, he settled at Belle Plaine, remaining six years as pastor of the church and missionary for the surrounding region. In this field he baptized about seventy. Compelled by ill health to leave it, he accepted the charge of the church at Anoka, Minn. There, amidst his pastoral duties, he served as county superintendent of public schools. After two years of happy labor he left a loved and loving people in order to take charge of the Minnesota Baptist school, then at Hastings, where he also became pastor of the Baptist church. In a few months, however, bronchial disease laid him aside from all labor and necessitated a change of residence. Benefited by climate and rest, he took charge of the Loller Academy, Hatborough, Pa., where he remained four years. Since 1872 he has been principal of Wyoming Institute of Delaware, preaching occasionally as health permits, and assisted in his educational work by members of his family.

Heath, Rev. William, was born in Newport, N. H., March 9, 1798. He graduated at Dartmouth College in the class of 1826. Among his classmates was the late Chief-Justice Chase. For a year after his graduation he was a tutor in the preparatory department of the Columbian College at Washington. He graduated at the Newton Theological Institution in 1832, and soon after became principal of the South Reading Academy. He was ordained as an evangelist July 1, 1835. His pastorates were with the churches in Shelburne Falls and North Reading, Mass. He was in the book trade for several years, having charge of the Baptist Sabbath-School Depository in Boston. His death took place Jan. 19, 1869, at Wakefield, Mass.

Hedden, Rev. Benjamin Franklin, son of Bartholomew, was born in Stonington, Conn., in 1803; was an excellent school-teacher; licensed and ordained by the First Baptist church in Groton, and succeeded Rev. John G. Wightman in its pulpit; labored in various fields with marked success,—Martha's Vineyard, Mass.; East Greenwich, R. I.; Manchester, N. H.; Mansfield, Conn.; Camden, N. J.; the Twelfth Baptist church in Philadelphia; an able and devout man. From ill health and a fall he resigned his pastorate in Philadelphia in 1871, and died Feb. 27, 1872, aged sixty-eight years. His brother, Rev. Harlem Hedden, was a useful preacher in different parts of New London Co., Conn.

Hedden, Rev. William D., the son of Presbyterian parents, was born at East Orange, N. J., Nov. 6, 1829. He was converted at seventeen, and being convinced that the immersion of believers only is New Testament baptism, he united with the church at East Orange. After pursuing studies at Hamilton he was ordained at Meridian, N. Y., in 1853. May 13, 1855, he became pastor of the church with which he first united, where, with the exception of a few months, he has continued to labor till the present time. Mr. Hedden has corresponded considerably for the religious press, and cultivates the poetic talent.

Helwys, Thomas, was a native of England, who went to Amsterdam, in Holland, and united with a church of English Separatists, founded in the early part of the reign of Queen Elizabeth. In this church a controversy arose about the validity of infant baptism, which led to the exclusion of those who rejected that unscriptural custom, and of Thomas Helwys with his Baptist brethren. While a member of the Brownist Church they looked upon him as a man of eminent faith, charity, and spiritual gifts.

In the Baptist church formed by the expelled Separatists, Mr. Helwys enjoyed the warmest regards of the entire people; and when, in 1611, their pastor, the Rev. John Smyth, died, Mr. Helwys was elected his successor.

Very soon after entering upon his office, probably early in 1612, Mr. Helwys became uneasy about staying out of England; it appeared to him to savor of cowardice, and he was convinced that it was his duty and that of his church to return home at once and bear testimony to the truth, since persecution threatened its extinction, and encourage and comfort their brethren who were suffering for Christ's sake. The church and pastor decided speedily, and soon commenced worship in London. The community flourished greatly in its new home, and its members were often the victims of royal and episcopal hatred. Mr. Helwys was a man of power, and his influence lived long after he slept with his fathers. His doctrines were said to be Arminian. His views of civil government in relation to religion were thoroughly Scriptural, and in that day were held by none but Baptists. In a Confession of Faith received by his people, and probably written by him, published about 1611, it is said, "The magistrate is not to meddle with religion or matters of conscience, nor to compel men to this or that form of religion; because Christ is the king and lawgiver of the church and conscience." (Crosby, i., Appendix, p. 71.) Nothing more emphatic was ever written on the question of soul liberty in any age or country. But in the days of Helwys this doctrine was denounced by Robinson, the father of the Puritans who founded New Plymouth in 1620. Mr. Helwys and his Baptist brethren were detested as much for the liberty of conscience for which they pleaded as for the believer's baptism which they practised.

Henderson, Rev. Samuel, D.D., a native of Jefferson Co., Tenn., was born March 4, 1817; united with the church in September, 1832. Reared to the business of a practical printer, when quite a youth he removed to Alabama, and established one of the first political newspapers of Talladega, which he published and edited for several years. He was ordained to the gospel ministry in the church in Talladega in 1840, this being his first pastorate. Moved to Tuskegee in 1846, where he was pastor for twenty-one years. To the Baptists Tuskegee was, during that period, one of the most important centres of influence in the State. In addition to its refined and wealthy church membership, it was the site of the East Alabama Female College, a property whose erection cost our brethren not less than $40,000. It was also the seat of publication of the *Southwestern Baptist*, the denominational organ of the State, which was conducted with marked ability by Dr. Henderson, it being then one of the most influential religious journals in the whole South. (See ALABAMA BAPTIST NEWSPAPERS.) In 1868, Dr. Henderson returned to Talladega County to the charge of several country and village churches, among the best country churches in the State, where he is pleasantly located on a handsome and fertile farm, and passes his time in visiting the churches, writing for the papers, being one of the editors of the *Christian Index*, of Atlanta, Ga., and in making further search into the contents of his splendid library. For the last thirty years Dr. Henderson has been among the most prominent and useful of Alabama ministers. Liberally educated at the start, he has become one of our erudite men, an able and distinguished preacher, an adviser of first-class judgment, a graceful, cultivated, and powerful writer, and withal a sound theologian, thoroughly *read-up*. Dr. Henderson has published a number of able sermons, review articles, and other strong and well-prepared documents. It was in his discussion with the Rev. Mr. Hamill of the Alabama Conference on "Methodist Episcopacy," more than twenty years ago, that he gained a distinguished reputation as a ready and cogent ecclesiastical controversialist. It was first published in his paper in Tuskegee, and subsequently in a book of 380 pages, by the Southern Baptist Publication Society at Charleston. Nothing can be found more satisfactory on that subject. His father, Deacon John F. Henderson, was for many years one of the most useful members of the church in Talladega. Of this church his younger brother, Hon. John Henderson, an able and upright judge of the Circuit Court, is now a member and a deacon.

Hendricks, Rev. John, who had been a Methodist minister, lived in Greensborough, Ga., where he was very useful as a preacher in the Baptist churches of that section. Becoming troubled on the subject of baptism, because of doubt as to its proper administration, and unwilling to remain in a state of uncertainty, he investigated the subject, and became convinced of the propriety of immersion. He was baptized by Dr. Adiel Sherwood about 1827. He afterwards removed to Cherokee, Ga., where he resided until his death.

Hendrickson, Charles R., D.D., was born Feb. 18, 1820, in Gloucester Co., N. J. His parents belonged to the Methodist Church, and, upon making a public profession of religion in the fifteenth year of his age, he identified himself with it.

He had early impressions that it was his duty to preach, and in the nineteenth year of his age he entered the Methodist ministry, and traveled one year in connection with the New Jersey Conference. He afterwards was transferred to the Kentucky Conference, and served two years in that connection. During his residence in Kentucky he was called upon to defend infant baptism and other doctrines of the Methodists; but the result of his investigations, instead of furnishing him arguments in favor of the tenets of his own church, caused him to see the error of his position and to adopt the sentiments of the Baptist denomination.

He immediately severed his connection with the Kentucky Conference, returned to Philadelphia, and was baptized by Rev. Dr. J. Lansing Burrows in 1842. Up to the time of his uniting with the Baptists he had never heard a sermon upon the subject of Scriptural baptism and the ordinances of the church, but at his baptism he preached upon this subject, setting forth the arguments that had led him to change his views.

He entered at once upon the work of an evangelist, and traveled extensively in Pennsylvania and Maryland. In 1846 he was called to the pastorate of the First Baptist church, Norfolk, Va. In 1852 he became pastor of the First Baptist church, Memphis, Tenn., where he was instrumental in building up a large and influential community. Owing to rheumatism, from which he has been a great sufferer, he left Memphis for California in 1859, and became pastor of the Baptist church at Stockton, and afterwards of the First Baptist church of San Francisco. He remained in California eleven years, and then returned to Philadelphia, and became pastor of the North church. He served it two years, during which time he baptized more than one hundred persons. In 1873 he accepted a call to the church at Jackson, Tenn., where he is now laboring with success.

Dr. Hendrickson is distinguished for his piety and the possession of those Christian graces that so beautifully adorn his life. While he is a sound Baptist, his gentleness and Christian charity secure for him the esteem and high regard of other denominations. His studies and varied reading have made Dr. Hendrickson a highly-cultured minister.

As a writer, his style is easy and natural, and his thoughts are forcibly and logically expressed. Few men are more completely at home in the pulpit. As a preacher, he is distinguished for his attractive delivery, his elegant English, his clear arguments, his honest sincerity, and his thorough comprehension of the subject.

The Southwestern Baptist University, located at Jackson, Tenn., owes much to Dr. Hendrickson. He has been chairman of the executive board of trustees from the date of its organization to the present.

Henricians, The.—Henry, a monk in the first half of the twelfth century, became a great preacher. He was endowed with extraordinary powers of persuasion, and with a glowing earnestness that swept away the greatest obstacles that mere human power could banish, and he had the grace of God in his heart. He denounced prayers for the dead, the invocation of saints, the vices of the clergy, the superstitions of the church, and the licentiousness of the age, and he set an example of the sternest morality. He was a master-spirit in talents, and a heaven-aided hero, a John Knox, born in another clime, but nourished upon the same all-powerful grace.

When he visited the city of Mans the inferior clergy became his followers, and the people gave him and his doctrine their hearts, and they refused to attend the consecrated mummeries of the popish churches, and mocked the higher clergy who clung to them. In fact, their lives were endangered by the triumph of Henry's doctrines. The rich and the poor gave him their confidence and their money, and when Hildebert, their bishop, returned, after an absence covering the entire period of Henry's visit, he was received with contempt and his blessing with ridicule. Henry's great arsenal was the Bible, and all opposition melted away before it.

He retired from Mans and went to Provence, and the same remarkable results attended his ministry; persons of all ranks received his blessed doctrines and forsook the foolish superstitions of Rome and the churches in which they occupied the most important positions. At and around Thoulouse his labors seem to have created the greatest indignation and alarm among the few faithful friends of Romanism, and Catholics in the most distant parts of France heard of his overwhelming influence and his triumphant heresy with great fear. In every direction for many miles around he preached Christ, and at last Pope Eugene III. sent a cardinal to overthrow the heretic and his errors. He wisely took with him, in 1147, the celebrated St. Bernard. This abbot had the earnestness and the temper of Richard Baxter, whom he resembled in some respects. He was a more eloquent man, and he was probably the most noted and popular ecclesiastic in Europe. He speaks significantly of the state of things which he found in Henry's field: "The churches (Catholic) are without people, the people without priests, the priests without due reverence, and, in short, Christians are without Christ; the churches were regarded as synagogues, the sanctuary of God was not held to be sacred, and the sacraments were not reckoned to be holy, festive days lost their solemnity, men died in their sins, souls were snatched away everywhere to the dread tribunal, alas! neither reconciled by repentance nor fortified by the holy communion. The life of Christ was closed to the little children of Christians, whilst the grace of baptism was refused, nor were they permitted to approach salvation, although the Saviour lovingly proclaims before them, and says, 'Suffer the little children to come to me.'"*

Elsewhere, St. Bernard, speaking of Henry and other heretics, says, "They mock us because we baptize infants, because we pray for the dead, because we seek the aid of (glorified) saints."† That Henry had a great multitude of adherents is beyond a doubt, and that he was a Bible Christian is absolutely certain, and that he and his followers rejected infant baptism is the testimony of St. Bernard and of all other writers who have taken notice of the Henricians and their founders. We incline to the opinion of Neander that Henry was not a Petrobrusian. We are satisfied that he and his disciples were independent witnesses for Jesus raised up by the Spirit and Word of God. The Henricians were Baptists, and their founder perished in prison.

Henricks, Rev. William, was born in 1800. His father was an Austrian, who emigrated to America to escape Romish persecution because of his conversion to Protestantism, and settled first in North Carolina and then in Greene Co., Ga., in 1808. Wm. Henricks was converted in 1826, under the preaching of Lovick Pierce, and was baptized in 1828 by Dr. A. Sherwood, after a thorough investigation of the subject of baptism. He was ordained in 1832. He became an able and zealous minister of the gospel, with few superiors as a revivalist. For eighteen years he preached among the churches of Greene, Morgan, Clarke, Monroe, and Walton Counties, with great power and usefulness. For fifteen years he was moderator of the

---

* Parvulis Christianorum Christi intercluditur vita, dum baptismi negatur gratia; nec saluti propenquare sinuntur; Salvatore licet pie clamante pro eis; *Sinite*, inquit, *parvulos venire ad me.* (Sancti Bernardi Genuina Opera, i. Ep. 241, p. 237. Parisiis, 1690.)
† Irrident nos, quod baptizamus infantes. Idem, i. p. 1497.

Appalachee Association; indeed, remaining so until his removal to Floyd County in 1850. He assisted in the organization of the Oostanaula Association in 1852, and was elected moderator. He died at Rome, Ga., June 18, 1856. He was a man of mark and of great usefulness in his day, and stood side by side with the first Baptist ministers of his time in promoting the interests of the denomination in Georgia.

Henry, Rev. Foster, was born in Perkinsville, Windsor Co., Vt., in 1817. He took the full courses of study at Brown University and at the Newton Theological Institution, graduating at the former in the class of 1845, and at the latter in the class of 1848. He was ordained to the ministry in November, 1852, and was pastor of the church in Tyringham, Mass., five years, when he removed to Pawtuxet, R. I., remaining there four years, then at Danversport, Mass., for three years, then at Newport, N. H., for six years. From Newport he went to North Bennington, Vt., and is at this time pastor of the church in that place.

Henson, Poindexter S., D.D., was born in Fluvanna Co., Va., Dec. 7, 1831; entered Richmond College in 1844, and graduated with the first

POINDEXTER S. HENSON, D.D.

class, in 1848, being then sixteen years of age. After teaching for one year in his native county, he entered the University of Virginia, and spent two years in that institution, graduating in various "schools." In the fall of 1851 he became principal of the Milton Classical Institute in North Carolina, and retained the position two years, in the mean while studying law with the Hon. M. McGee, and editing the *North Carolina Democrat*,—a weekly paper published in the town of Milton. When about entering upon the practice of law he was elected Professor of Natural Science in the Chowan Female College at Murfreesborough, N. C. This position he retained for two years, at the expiration of which he married Miss A. C. Ruse, of Hicksford, Va., and returned to Fluvanna County.

Was converted in 1846, while a student at Richmond College, and was baptized by Rev. J. B. Jeter, D.D., into the fellowship of the First church at Richmond. At the close of the year 1855 he abandoned the law and devoted himself to the ministry of the gospel; was ordained in February, 1856, and settled as pastor of the Fluvanna church. In connection with his pastorate he established the Fluvanna Female Institute, and remained there preaching and teaching until the summer of 1860, when he accepted a call to the Broad Street church, Philadelphia, and entered upon his labors Dec. 27, 1860. With this church he remained until September, 1867, when under pressure of demand for a new interest in a rapidly-growing section of the city, he, with others, went out to organize the Memorial church, where he still continues a faithful and efficient ministry. He received the degree of D.D. in 1867 from the university at Lewisburg. In 1878 he declined an urgent call to the presidency of that institution.

Dr. Henson possesses a keenly logical mind, and is thoroughly skilled in his methods of attacking error and defending the truth. As a preacher, he stands in the front rank of loyal and brilliant pulpit orators, and his sermons abound in the rich results of Bible study and devout piety. As a lecturer his services are in frequent requisition, and large audiences are ever ready to show their appreciation of his native wit and cultured scholarship. He is prominently and actively engaged in the management of local and general denominational societies, and as editor of the *Baptist Teacher* he continues to exert helpful and healthful influence upon Sunday-school work and workers. He has the largest Protestant congregation in Philadelphia.

Herndon, Rev. Thaddeus, was born in Fauquier Co., Va., May 9, 1807. He was the eldest of four brothers, all of whom were ministers of the gospel, and all of whom preceded him to their final reward. He was baptized by Dr. W. F. Broaddus in 1828, and united with the Long Branch church, being licensed to preach by it in 1833. For some years he was employed by the Salem Union Association as missionary, traveling over large districts of country in Loudon, Fauquier, Prince William, and Fairfax Counties. In 1837 he was called to the pastorate of Antioch church, Prince William Co., and about the same time to North Fork church,

Loudon Co., both of which he faithfully served for about forty years. He was the pastor also of two other churches. Although Mr. Herndon had the care of a farm and a large family, he very rarely failed in regularly meeting his church appointments, riding on horseback through the storms of winter and the heats of summer. He was an earnest gospel preacher and a welcome guest at many a fireside. He died June 2, 1878.

Herndon, Rev. Traverse D., the brother of the Revs. Thaddeus and Richard Herndon, was born March 11, 1810. His father was the Rev. John C. Herndon, a resident of Fauquier County. About the age of eighteen, being hopefully converted, he was baptized by Dr. W. F. Broaddus, and united with the Long Branch church. Being a young man of ardent piety, and longing to honor his Master by a life wholly consecrated to his service, he was persuaded to prepare himself for the work of the ministry. Having been for a short time engaged in mercantile business in Alexandria, Va., he relinquished his position in that place and entered the Columbian College, where he remained during five years, graduating in 1838, the year of his ordination. His first pastoral charge was the Falmouth church, which he held in connection with an engagement as missionary under the Salem Union Association. Owing to his precarious health, however, he was soon obliged to relinquish both these positions, and for nearly two years he was unable to preach. When he had recovered a good measure of health he took charge of four churches, Liberty, Mount Holly, Fiery Run, and Front Royal. These churches being too remote from his residence, he took charge of the Middleburg, Long Branch, and Ketocton churches, with which he labored up to the time of his death, which occurred Sept. 10, 1854. Mr. Herndon stood high among his brethren as a preacher. His sermons were plain, practical, and saturated with earnest descriptions of the love of Christ for sinners. Human guilt and divine redemption were the great themes upon which he loved to dwell, and his teachings were blessed to the conversion of many souls and the encouragement of God's people. More than three hundred were baptized by him during his ministry, while thousands of others who listened to him during his journeyings from home at protracted meetings were greatly quickened in their spiritual energies. As a Christian man in all the various relations of life he was a model. "His natural qualities, controlled as they were by a constant sense of the obligations on him as a Christian, made him, in the estimation of all who knew him well enough to appreciate his personal worth, most emphatically a Christian gentleman." Dr. Wm. F. Broaddus, who knew Mr. Herndon well, says, "But this I can say in all honesty, that after an acquaintance with him of nearly thirty years, and for many years an intimate acquaintance, such was his entire deportment both as a man and a Christian, that if he had faults, my admiration of the characteristics uniformly exhibited in his life and conversation so occupied me, that those faults entirely escaped my observation."

Herr, Joseph Daniel, D.D., was born in Sharpsburg, Pa., Feb. 23, 1837. At the age of seventeen he was converted and immersed as a member of the Methodist Protestant Church. In 1858, having completed a collegiate course at Madison College, Pa., he was ordained to the ministry. His reputation for ability in the pulpit led to his serving prominent churches in Pittsburgh and Cincinnati. He was also made secretary of the board of trustees of Adrian College, and of the Missionary Society of the Methodist Protestant Church. In August, 1870, in accordance with his early convictions, and impressed with the great truth that faith should precede baptism, he resigned the charge of the Second Methodist Protestant church of Pittsburgh, and immediately thereafter accepted the pastorate of the Union Baptist church of the same city. A few months later he assisted in the formation of the Penn Avenue Baptist church, and became its first pastor. Nov. 1, 1875, he resigned to take charge of the Central Baptist church of New York. Dr. Herr as a preacher is eloquent, and is noted for his fervor and earnestness. His pastorates have been marked by progress and spiritual prosperity. In 1876 he was made D.D. by Otterbein University, Ohio.

Hewes, Rev. and Prof., was born in Lynnfield, Mass., in 1818; converted and baptized at the age of fourteen; graduated at Brown University and the Newton Theological Seminary. In 1844 he was ordained as pastor at Lonsdale, R. I. In 1849 he began an eight years' pastorate at Lansingburgh, N. Y. In 1857–58 he was professor in the Troy University. From Troy he was called to the presidency of the Indianapolis Institute, holding his position there seven years. Removing to California, he was two years a professor in the Female College of the Pacific, two years pastor and lecturer on Natural Sciences in the Mills Seminary, five years pastor at St. Helena, and two years pastor of the Fifth church, San Francisco. Though much of his life has been spent in educating the young, he has baptized over three hundred converts. Since his arrival in California he has spent three years in extensive travels in Europe, Egypt, and the Holy Land.

Hewitt, C. E., D.D., was born Oct. 16, 1836, in Galway, Saratoga Co., N. Y., being a son of Deacon Edmund Hewitt, well known for more than half a century as a prominent member and officer of the Galway Baptist church, of which the son became a member at sixteen years of age. He graduated at the University of Rochester in 1860, and at the seminary in 1863. His pastorates have been at Ypsilanti, Mich., 1863–68; Bloomington, Ill., 1868–76; Centennial church, Chicago, 1877–79; and now (1880) he has charge of the First Baptist church, Peoria, Ill. During his service at Ypsilanti the membership of the church increased from 200 to 300, and at Bloomington from 300 to 500. His work in Chicago was in a time of great financial and spiritual depression, and though equally faithful, showed less of immediate result. Dr. Hewitt has always been active and interested in the general work of the denomination. In Michigan he was an influential member of the Board of State Missions, and one of the trustees of Kalamazoo College. In Illinois he has held like positions, especially as connected with the State missions and with the theological seminary; an ardent Sunday-school man; also for several years president and secretary of the State Sunday-School Association.

Hick, Col. J. M., was born in 1831, in West Virginia; was bred to the law; a member of the secession convention of Virginia in 1861; commanded a regiment at Cheat Mountain, and was captured there; was baptized in Raleigh, N. C., by Dr. T. H. Pritchard, in March, 1864; was president of the Baptist State Convention in 1875; was for several years chairman of the Sunday-School Board; is a trustee and a liberal benefactor of Wake Forest College, he and J. G. Williams, of Raleigh, having presented a building, known as the Library Building, to the college, which cost $10,000.

Hickman, David H., was born in Bourbon Co., Ky., Nov. 11, 1821. He died June 25, 1869. His father was a pioneer, having moved to Missouri in 1822. David was educated at Bonne Femme Academy. He was of studious habits, and for a time he was a teacher. He was delicate, but very energetic and successful. He was converted at seventeen, and united with the Bonne Femme church, and died in its membership. Mr. Hickman had no taste for public life, yet he served in the State Legislature of Missouri, and was moderator of the General Association when young. He framed the law for the common-school system of the State, which was adopted by the Legislature. He loved his home, and he was devoted to the church, in which he was a wise counselor and useful member. He was eminently successful in business, and gave $10,000 to Stephen College, of Columbia. He remembered in his will the poor of Bonne Femme and Columbia churches. Over the departing couch of David Hickman a voice from heaven said, "Blessed are the dead who die in the Lord."

Hickman, Col. H. H., for many years a deacon of the First Baptist church at Augusta, Ga., was born in Elbert Co., Ga., in 1818. He removed to Augusta when nineteen years of age. He was baptized in 1841, after a profession of faith, by Dr. William T. Brantly, Jr., then pastor of the church. Developing business talent early, he was admitted to membership in the firm, which was for many years known as that of Cress & Hickman. On the retirement of his partner, Mr. Hickman continued the business with uniform success until the close of the war between the States, although, like a host of others, he was injured financially to a serious extent. But after the return of peace his sagacity, his integrity, and his energy soon restored all that was lost. He became president of the Graniteville Manufacturing Company and of the Bank of Augusta, and was eminently successful in both of these positions.

Mr. Hickman was elected deacon of the Augusta (Greene Street) church more than twenty years ago, in which capacity he has served with great fidelity, always manifesting a deep interest in the welfare of the church, aiding it by his prayers, his counsels, and his substance. In the city with which he has been identified for more than forty years he has the highest standing as a business man of intelligent views and trustworthy character.

Hickman, Rev. William, one of the most famous of the pioneer Baptist ministers in Kentucky, was born in King and Queen Co., Va., Feb. 4, 1747. He was by early training an Episcopalian, and entertained great contempt for the Baptists. During a sermon by the renowned John Waller, in 1770, he was deeply impressed. After struggling with his sins and his prejudices about three years, he obtained peace in Christ and was baptized by Reuben Ford, in April, 1773. At this time he lived in Cumberland County. There being few preachers in that region, he, with others, established prayer-meetings. In February, 1776, he started to Kentucky, and arriving at Harrodsburg, he remained several weeks, and during the time, though not licensed, he attempted on one occasion to preach. Upon his return home to Virginia he was soon set apart for the ministry, and spent several years as a preacher in his native State. In 1784 he removed to Fayette Co., Ky., where he preached with great zeal and activity in the surrounding settlements. In 1788 he changed his residence to what is now Franklin County. Here, in the same year, he formed the Forks of Elkhorn church, and was chosen the pastor. From this place he made preaching tours among the settlers, often attended by a guard of soldiers to protect him from the Indians. The new churches he formed were watched over and nurtured until they grew strong and the savages were driven from the country. He was greatly blessed in his ministry. A contemporary supposes that in his day he "baptized more people than any other minister in Kentucky." He probably formed more churches than even the famous Lewis Craig. He "baptized over 500 during one winter." He died suddenly in 1830. His son William was long pastor of South Benson church, and Hickman Co., Ky., was named after his son, Col. Paschal Hickman, who fell in the battle of the river Raisin.

Hickson, Rev. Edward, A.M., was born Oct. 13, 1824, at New Bandon, County Gloucester, New Brunswick, and was converted when quite young. He was baptized at Wolfville, Nova Scotia, in 1855. He graduated from Acadia College in June, 1860. He was ordained as pastor of the North Esk church, New Brunswick, July 27, 1862, where he labored successfully for ten years. He was pastor at St. George, New Brunswick, and is now in charge of a church at Carleton, St. John.

Hiden, J. C., D.D., is a young man of uncommon native powers. To enjoy his conversation is a treat, and to hear him lecture, a feast. Born at Orange Court-House, Va., Nov. 5, 1837, he spent three years in the Virginia Military Institute as a cadet, graduating in July, 1857. Elected as Professor of Ancient Languages in the Chesapeake Female College of Virginia when nineteen, he occupied that chair one year, and then entered the University of Virginia, where he spent two years, pursuing a wider range of study. He was ordained at Orange Court-House, Va., in 1859, and served the Hillsborough Baptist church, Albermarle Co., as pastor during the last year he spent at the university. During 1860 and 1861 he taught a private school at Orange Court-House, then entered the Confederate army as chaplain, and served throughout the war. Afterwards he taught school at Orange Court-House, and at Staunton; in 1866 he was elected pastor of the Fourth Street Baptist church, Portsmouth, serving two years, when he was called to the care of the Wilmington, N. C., First Baptist church, which he served for more than six years. In March, 1875, he was called by the Greenville church, of South Carolina, which call he accepted. He is well read, a superior preacher, and a fine scholar. He possesses great physical strength and powers of endurance, and yet those who know him best would rather meet him in the field than on the platform or forum. His mother is a niece of Jas. Barbour, who was governor of Virginia, U. S. Senator, Secretary of War, and minister to England, and she is a sister of Philip P. Barbour, who was a member of Congress and justice of the U. S. Supreme Court. She is still living. Dr. Hiden has a fine fund of anecdotes, and tells them remarkably well. As a speaker, he is clear, vigorous, original, unique. He is a true and noble man, and those who know him best love him most. Still young, of good constitution, an ardent student and full of energy, he may naturally expect to attain a high degree of distinction.

Higgins, Rev. George, was born at Marcus Hook, Pa., Dec. 16, 1798; baptized in Spruce Street church, Philadelphia, in 1817; ordained in Reading, February, 1829. He was among the first missionaries in the service of the State Convention, now called the General Association, and had for his field the Schuylkill Valley, but soon after labored chiefly on the West Branch of the Susquehanna. The writer bears pleasant witness to his untiring zeal and fidelity during the ten years of service in this region. In this space of time he baptized nearly 500 converts, mostly gathered from regions where Baptist sentiments were unknown and opposition was strong. Several churches, now enjoying comparative strength, were planted by his labors, while other existing churches were much enlarged. In 1859 he returned to Philadelphia, and aided materially in founding the Calvary church in 1841. Here also his memory is fragrant. In 1850 he settled as pastor of the Montgomery church, Montgomery Co., Pa., and closed a useful and honored life March 9, 1869, in his seventy-sixth year. During his ministry he baptized nearly 1500 persons.

No discouragements dampened his ardor; he met all opposition with calmness. His blameless life disarmed adverse criticism of much of its force, and, though necessarily involved in frequent discussions during his missionary career, he never lost control of his temper. In argument he was clear and scholarly; in preaching, plain and simple. Even opponents were compelled to respect him, while friends loved him with great warmth.

Higgins, Rev. John S., was born in New Jersey, Dec. 29, 1789. His early life was spent in Ohio, and in Woodford Co., Ky. In 1813 he was converted and joined a Baptist church. In 1815 he removed to Lincoln Co., Ky., where he was ordained to the ministry, and became the stated preacher of McCormack's, Hanging Fork, and Forks of Dix River churches. He assisted in forming the Baptist church in Danville, Ky., and was for a time its pastor. He was active in the benevolent enterprises of his denomination, and eminently successful as a minister. He died in 1872.

Hill, Benjamin H., D.D., was born in Newport, R. I., April 5, 1793; studied in Newport Academy and at the University of Pennsylvania; took two courses of medical lectures; converted and baptized in Thompson, Conn., in 1812; licensed Feb. 5, 1815; preached two years in Leicester, Mass.; in 1818 was ordained pastor of Baptist church in Stafford, Conn.; was engaged for Connecticut Baptist Missionary Society; in 1821 settled with the First Baptist church in New Haven and was prospered; in 1830 took charge of the First Baptist church in Troy, N. Y.; in 1840 was chosen secretary of the American Baptist Home Mission Society, and served with remarkable success till 1862; in 1865 removed to New Haven, Conn., from which he was recently translated to the skies; received the degree of D.D. from Madison University in 1852; wise in judgment and in speech; a true man in the faith.

Hill, President David J., son of the Rev. Daniel T. Hill, was born at Plainfield, N. J., June 10, 1850. Received his early education in the public schools of Glen's Falls, N. Y., and Plainfield, N. J., and at the academy at Deckertown, N. J. Prepared for college at Suffield, Conn., and Cooperstown, N. Y. While at Cooperstown, in 1867–68, began writing for the press, the contributions consisting of short sketches and poems and a biography of Gen. U. S. Grant, in six numbers of five columns each. In April, 1870, was baptized by his father at Pauling, N. Y., and united with the church. In August of the same year entered the university at Lewisburg as a Freshman. Took the first "Lung Prize for Oratory" in 1873, and on graduating, in 1874, delivered the valedictory addresses, the first honor of the class. Was at once called to the pastorate of the Baptist church of Madison, Wis., but declined, accepting a call as tutor in Ancient Languages in the university at Lewisburg. At the close of the collegiate year 1874–75, Mr. Hill was appointed instructor in Rhetoric in the university, and in 1877, Crozer Professor of Rhetoric. At the same time he published, through Sheldon & Co., of New York, "The Science of Rhetoric," an advanced text-book for colleges, which was at once adopted in the University of Michigan, Vassar College, and other first-class institutions. At the request of Sheldon & Co., Prof. Hill prepared "The Elements of Rhetoric," for schools of lower grade, which is now used in every State of the Union. In 1879, Prof. Hill began a series of brief biographies of American authors, similar to Morley's "English Men of Letters." Two volumes, on Irving and Bryant, respectively, were issued by Sheldon & Co., and were widely accepted and highly praised. The preparation of this series was interrupted by his election to the presidency of the university at Lewisburg, in March, 1879, to succeed the Rev. Justin R. Loomis, LL.D., the position which he now occupies. Since his election to the presidency President Hill has confined his pen to lectures, sermons, and review articles. He has an engagement with Sheldon & Co. to prepare an elementary work on Logic as soon as his duties permit. President Hill, though quite young, is one of the ablest men in the Baptist denomination, with unusual prospects before him.

Hill, Rev. Noah, was born in Virginia, June 11, 1811; educated at Mercer University, Penfield, Ga.; commenced preaching in 1838; came to Texas in 1846, and prosecuted faithfully the work of the ministry at Brazoria, Matagorda, Wharton, and Brenham until 1869, when he was called away to his eternal home. He was a preacher of imposing personal appearance, and ably presented and enforced the great doctrines of the gospel. Few men in Texas labored under more difficulties and with more success.

Hill, Rev. Reuben Coleman, M.D., is one of the most distinguished and successful Baptists in Oregon. Born in Kentucky, March 27, 1808, of Baptist parents; baptized in 1833; ordained as deacon and licensed to preach by the Clear Creek church in 1835; ordained in 1845. He removed to Keetsville, Mo., in 1846; organized the church there, and increased its membership to 100. In 1851 he removed to Oregon; located at Albany, where he still resides; organized the Cowallis and Albany churches; was pastor of one church eighteen years, of the Albany church eleven years, and has served other churches shorter periods. He has baptized 1014 converts, among them six whole households. He is a physician as well as preacher; is liberal in his gifts; a member of all Baptist missionary, educational, and Bible organizations in the State, and has served two terms as a member of the Oregon Legislature.

Hill, R. J., M.D., was born in Ashland Co., O., June 15, 1836. He was educated at Vermilion Institute and Granville College. He was teacher and pupil till he closed his course. In 1859 he began a course of medical study with Drs. Rupert and

Thompson, of Mount Vernon, and graduated at the Starling Medical College, Columbus, O. In 1862 he became surgeon of the 45th Ohio Regiment of Volunteers; was captured in Tennessee by Gen. Longstreet in 1863; spent a month in Libby Prison; was exchanged November 20, and, after a brief visit home, re-entered the army, and remained till the end of the war. Came to St. Louis in 1866, where he has acquired an extensive practice and a flattering reputation. He is now president of the Public School Board of St. Louis. He was for years a deacon in the Baptist church in Green Town, O., and he is now a consistent and useful member of the Second Baptist church of St. Louis, Mo.

Hill, Stephen P., D.D., was born in Salem, Mass., April 17, 1806, and received his early education

STEPHEN P. HILL, D.D.

at the Salem High School. His parents and all his family connections were Unitarians. About the age of fourteen, casually entering a Baptist church, he heard a sermon from the venerable Father Grafton, of Newton, on the unbelief of the Apostle Thomas, which was instrumental in his conversion. He was baptized by the Rev. Lucius Bolles in June, 1821, being then about fifteen. At the age of twelve young Hill had entered the law-office of the Hon. David Cummins, but desiring a more active life, he was occupied for a while in mercantile pursuits. But his heart was in the work of the ministry. He began preaching at the early age of seventeen, and, in connection with the Rev. G. D. Boardman, then a student at Andover, he frequently preached for the colored people. Wishing to prepare himself more thoroughly for his life-work, he entered Waterville College in 1825, and in 1827 removed to Brown University, graduating in 1829. During his winter vacations he was engaged in teaching. He entered the theological seminary at Newton, and finished his course in 1832, at which time he was ordained as pastor of the First Baptist church in Haverhill, Mass. His connection with it, though pleasant, was short; he removed to a warmer climate in consequence of a threatened pulmonary complaint. He passed the winter of 1833-34 near Charleston, S. C., and, at the urgent request of Dr. Basil Manly, supplied the pulpit of the church in Georgetown in that State. On his return to the North, he was taken sick in Baltimore, and on his recovery he was invited to become pastor of the First Baptist church in that city, which position he accepted. His ministry here was long-continued and successful, the membership having increased during the first eight years of his pastorate from 80 to nearly 600. A Sunday-school numbering upwards of 500 was gathered, and several auxiliary schools organized in various parts of the city. After seventeen years of fruitful labor in this field, Dr. Hill removed to Washington, D. C., and took charge of the First Baptist church, in which relation he continued, greatly prospered, until 1861, when he resigned. Since that time he has had no regular charge, but has frequently preached to feeble congregations unable to support pastors. He has also taken a deep interest in the welfare and progress of the colored Baptist churches, often preaching for them, and always ready to give them encouragement and counsel. Dr. Hill has also added to the literature of the denomination. He is the author of several prize monographs,—one on "The Theatre," one on "The Church," etc., and has also published, among other works, an essay on "The Best Plan of an International Tribunal for Peace." He has also written some poetry,—"The Unlimited Progression of Mind," which was delivered before the literary societies of Brown University at the commencement in 1839; on "The Problem of Truth," delivered before the societies of Madison University in 1859; and on "The Triumphs of the Gospel," delivered before the Knowles Society of the Newton Theological Seminary in 1839. He has also written a number of shorter poems, published in various papers and periodicals. But few men are more familiar with the history of hymnology, and his refined taste in this department of literature led to his selection as one of the committee which had charge of the preparation of the hymn-book so extensively used at one time,—"The Psalmist." Dr. Hill is also the author of a collection of hymns under the title of "Christian Melodies," as well as of several small works for the young,—"Time, the Price of Wisdom," "The Youth's Monitor," and a "Comprehensive Catechism." He is an active member of the board of trustees of the Columbian University, and deeply interested in its welfare. Mrs. Hill is a sister of W. W. Corcoran, LL.D., the well-known and generous benefactor of so many good causes.

Hill, Rev. Thomas, was born Sept. 12, 1797. He was converted in 1822, and was ordained in 1825. He was the first missionary for Southern Indiana appointed by the American Baptist Home Mission Society. He served it and the Indiana State Convention thirteen years. He was pastor of the Coffee Creek church thirty years, and he was moderator of the Coffee Creek Association thirty-nine years. He was a strong thinker and an eloquent preacher. Hundreds have been led to Christ by his ministry. He died March 27, 1876.

Hillman, Walter, LL.D., a distinguished educator in Mississippi, was born on Martha's Vineyard, Mass., in 1829. After a preparatory course at the Connecticut Literary Institution and Worcester Academy, he entered Brown University in 1849. While in it he spent one year in teaching as sub-principal of Worcester Academy and as classical instructor in Pierce Academy. He graduated in 1854 with the degree of A.M., and was immediately elected Professor of Mathematics and Natural Philosophy in Mississippi College, at Clinton. In 1856 he became principal of Central Female Institute in the same town,—a connection he has retained until the present. During this time he also held the presidency of Mississippi College for six years. Under his administration these institutions greatly prospered. Ordained to the ministry in 1858, he has since occasionally preached.

Hillman, William, was born in the city of New York, Nov. 21, 1794, and died April 14, 1864. In his nineteenth year he was converted and baptized into the fellowship of the First Baptist church by the pastor, Rev. William Parkinson. For more than fifty years he was a member of that church. While a young man he was elected one of its deacons, and its honored pastors, Wm. Parkinson, Spencer H. Cone, A. Kingman Nott, and Thomas D. Anderson found him a safe adviser, an efficient helper, and a liberal supporter of the church and all the great evangelizing enterprises of the Baptist denomination. With Dr. Cone he entered heartily into the work of the American Bible Union. He was one of the eighteen men who on a stormy day met in Deacon Wm. Colgate's parlor and took preliminary measures for its organization. He paid the first hundred dollars into its treasury to make his pastor a life-director. He possessed a strong faith in God, was a man of ardent piety, and left this world by a death remarkable for its peaceful, joyful, triumphant demonstration of Christian victory.

Hillsman, Matthew, D.D., was born in Tennessee, near the town of Knoxville, Aug. 7, 1814.

MATTHEW HILLSMAN, D.D.

With the exception of two years in Talladega, Ala., he has spent all his life in his native State. Mr. Hillsman was converted at the age of nineteen, and was ordained in 1835. For many years he supplied Baptist pulpits in a number of cities and towns in Tennessee. Among his successful pastorates was the one with the church at Murfreesborough, from which there were sent out as foreign missionaries Dr. Burton, T. P. Crawford, and Rev. Mr. Gilliard. For one year he was president of Mossy Creek College, and subsequently for years corresponding secretary of the Bible Board of the Southern Baptist Convention. In 1862 he became pastor of the church at Trenton, Tenn., where he still resides, ministering to it and preaching with great acceptance in the surrounding country. As president of the board of the West Tennessee Baptist Convention, and sometimes president of the Convention itself, he has done much to promote its efficiency. A trustee of the Southern Baptist Theological Seminary, he was one of the committee who selected Louisville as its location; and he was also on the committee which presented a plan for the organization of the Southwestern Baptist University. For more than forty years he has been intimately connected with the educational, missionary, and benevolent enterprises of Tennessee, and he has always been zealous in aiding the

Domestic and Foreign Boards of the Southern Baptist Convention. Dr. Hillsman presides well over deliberative bodies, and is frequently called upon to act in that capacity, and is now the moderator of the Central Association. As a preacher he is widely known, and has great influence in all parts of Tennessee. As a teacher, editor, or pastor, he has been identified with all the great Baptist movements with credit to himself and honor to the denomination. No man has the confidence of his brethren more completely or stands higher in their estimation. In his sermons he is sound in doctrine, clear in exposition, and powerful in appeal, and entirely free from sensationalism. His style is plain, practical, and direct, his best efforts being those of his regular service. The degree of Doctor of Divinity was conferred on him by the Union University. He is at present one of the editors of the Nashville *Reflector*.

Hillyer, Rev. John F., LL.D., was born May 25, 1805, in Wilkes Co., Ga.; educated at University of Georgia and Georgia Medical College; practised medicine two years; professed religion in 1825, and soon thereafter commenced preaching; was connected as a professor with Mercer University, Penfield, Ga., from 1835 to 1839; preached and taught at Eatonton until 1847, when he became pastor of the Galveston Baptist church, Texas; was successful in establishing Gonzales College, of which he was first president. From 1860 to 1865 was Professor of Mathematics and Natural Philosophy in Baylor University. From the last-named institution he received the degree of LL.D.; was at the organization of the Georgia Baptist State Convention, the Southern Baptist Convention, and the Texas Baptist State Convention; has preached fifty-three years; is a brother of Rev. S. G. Hillyer, D.D., and Hon. Junius Hillyer, late member of Congress from Georgia; was chaplain of Texas house of representatives two sessions, and ministers now to two or three churches regularly. He has been a successful preacher and teacher, and always a hard worker.

Hillyer, Shaler G., D.D., president of Monroe Female College, Forsyth, Ga., stands among the first Baptist preachers and scholars of the State. For nearly fifty years he has been thoroughly identified with both the secular and religious affairs of the Baptists of Georgia, and he is universally recognized as a man of great ability, high culture, and deep piety, and of eloquence far above ordinary. He was born June 20, 1809, in Wilkes County, and was educated at the State University, graduating with the class of 1829. He united with the Baptist church at Athens in 1831, and was ordained in 1835. During his long life he has been the pastor of Baptist churches in all parts of the State,—at Athens, Milledgeville, Macon, Madison, Forsyth, White Plains, Rome, Penfield, Crawfordville, Cass Spring, Albany, and various other places; and his piety, zeal, amiability, scholarship, pulpit ability, and theological learning have united in making him both useful and successful. As a sermonizer and orator he has very few, if any, superiors in the State, for to a noble and dignified style, amounting often to striking eloquence, he unites a strong current of manly thought, arranged in a systematic train most attractive to cultivated minds. He was tutor in the State University during the year 1834, and Professor of Rhetoric and Belles-Lettres in Mercer University from January, 1847, to May, 1856. From September, 1859, to May, 1862, he was Professor of Theology in the same institution, and in both these positions he sustained himself with marked ability. When the war broke up Mercer University temporarily, his professorship ceased, and as it has never been re-established, his connection with Mercer University has not been resumed. He and Prof. Asbury, after the war, took charge of the Monroe Female College, at Forsyth, Ga., where he now resides. He is president of the college and pastor of the Forsyth church.

Dr. Hillyer is a devoted Christian, pure in heart, unselfish, confiding, and faithful. As a preacher, his sermons move the heart and excite the sensibilities. He is a guileless man, and stands high in the Christian confidence of his brethren.

Himes, Rev. Palmer C., was born in Clarendon, Vt., April 3, 1804. He was hopefully converted at the age of fifteen, and was baptized Dec. 19, 1824, by Rev. John Spaulding, and united with the Berkshire, Vt., Baptist church. He commenced preaching in Sheldon, and the seal of the divine blessing at once rested upon his labors. After preaching for a time, he went to the Madison Theological Institution, pursuing his studies a little less than two years. He was ordained at Enosburg in March, 1833. He labored as a minister of the gospel for forty-two years, in Vermont, New Hampshire, and Maine. It has been estimated that not far from one thousand persons were converted under his ministry. He died at Enosburg, Vt., March 5, 1871.

Hinckley, Rev. Abel R., was born in Livermore, Me., Dec. 24, 1809. He was converted in 1831, and joined the Baptist church in Augusta. He was licensed to preach by that church in 1832. Soon afterwards he began a course of study, spending some time in Waterville College, Newton, and New Hampton. Sept. 14, 1834, he was ordained by the Swanzey church, N. H., during the session of the Dublin Association, and shortly afterwards moved to Lawrenceburg, Ind. He was called to the pastorate of the Sparta church in 1836. After a few months he received a call from the church at Franklin, and his great interest in the "Manual

Labor Institute," then lately started, led him to accept it. He removed to Franklin in November, 1837. The church had no house of worship. Under his leadership it built a large, commodious edifice, and the membership rapidly increased. In July, 1842, he had a second attack of hemorrhage of the lungs, which obliged him to cease public labor. He died in the following September. He was for five consecutive years secretary of the State Convention. His efforts for the promotion of the institute were untiring. One of the present deacons of the Franklin church says that he was the best and purest man he ever knew.

He published in pamphlet form a series of letters on "Baptism," in reply to a sermon preached by Dr. Monfort, of the Franklin Presbyterian church. This pamphlet was extensively circulated and well received, and produced a good result in the State.

He was Indiana editor of the *Banner and Pioneer*, published at Louisville, Ky. He spent much of his time in planning for the enlargement of the Redeemer's kingdom among Indiana Baptists.

Hinton, Rev. Isaac Taylor, was born in Oxford, England, July 4, 1799. In 1821 he was baptized by his father. He sailed from London for Philadelphia, April 9, 1832. In June, 1833, he took the oversight of the First Baptist church of Richmond, Va. In 1835 he took charge of the First Baptist church of Chicago, then in its infancy. In 1841 he accepted a call to the Second church in St. Louis, Mo. In December, 1844, he received an invitation from the Baptists of New Orleans to labor in that city, and immediately removed to this new field. He was instrumental in building a church edifice for them, which was opened in February, 1846, and in greatly increasing their numbers, so much so that it was planned by the pastor and his people to erect a larger structure in the autumn of 1847. He died of yellow fever on the 28th of August, 1847.

Mr. Hinton was the author of a "History of Baptism," and of "Prophecies of Daniel and John, illustrated by the Events of History."

The churches over which Mr. Hinton presided, without exception, prospered, and he was instrumental in forming other churches in localities near these seats (cathedræ) of his ministry.

In fourteen years of his life in America he made a name as widely known as our country, and his memory is fragrant still in the land of his adoption. Like the saintly Wilson, a recent martyr, in the same city, by the same plague, Mr. Hinton left a numerous family. He possessed a remarkable amount of historical information and of Biblical knowledge, and he had a deep experience of the love of Christ.

He was invited to the presidency of Alton College, Ill., and he was justly regarded as one of the purest and most learned and talented ministers in the denomination.

Hinton, Rev. John Howard, M.A., was the son of the Rev. James Hinton, pastor of the Baptist church at Oxford, England, and was born in that city March 24, 1791. His father conducted a private school for many years with much credit and success, and was well known as an able and scholarly minister. Not a few men of brilliant reputation were educated by him. His mother was of the famous family of the Taylors, being the daughter of the eminent engraver, Isaac Taylor, the first of five in lineal descent of that name. Among Mr. Isaac Taylor's friends was John Howard, the philanthropist, and when he was about to take his last journey abroad, he said to his friend's daughter, "I have now no son of my own: if ever you have one, pray call him after me." Mrs. Hinton possessed much of the family ability, and her influence upon her eldest son, whom she named John Howard, determined him to devote himself to the ministry. At first he studied medicine, but when he was in his twentieth year, having been called by the church to exercise his gifts in the ministry, he was entered at Bristol College, then under the presidency of Dr. Ryland. Here he studied for two years, and proceeded to Edinburgh University in 1813. He had received an excellent scholastic training with his father's pupils at home, and the curriculum of the celebrated Scottish university, together with the theological studies of Bristol College, gave him a very complete furnishing for the work of his life. He took the M.A. degree at Edinburgh at the close of the third year of the academical course, and after preaching for some time in various places, he accepted a call to the Baptist church in Haverford-West, Pembrokeshire, and preached his first sermon there on May 19, 1816. After five years' ministry at Haverford-West, he removed to Reading, and in this more advantageous position he found scope for his great talents, and became prominent in the denomination. His native ability and very superior culture gave him a leading place among the foremost Non-conformist ministers in all public movements. In 1837 he entered upon the pastorate of the ancient church in Devonshire Square, Bishopsgate Street, in the very heart of London. In denominational work he was ever foremost. The Baptist Union, of which for many years he was the indefatigable secretary, would have miserably perished but for his persistence and faith in its utility as a means of securing denominational unity. In the operations of the Baptist Missionary Society he had taken the liveliest interest in his youthful days, when Andrew Fuller and other founders of the mission used to come to Oxford to confer with his father and pray together for divine direction. After coming to London he bore an influential part in the counsels of the Missionary Committee, and threw himself heart and soul into the enterprise of William Knibb to render the Jamaica Baptist churches self-supporting. His life of Knibb gives a lively and stirring presentation of the work and its claims upon Christian benevolence. For a quarter of a century, without any abatement of energy, he pursued these manifold labors, and all the while he was busy with his pen on theological and kindred topics suggested in the course of events. He entered warmly into controversies in which the fundamental truths of religion were assailed, and he enjoyed the remarkable experience of being suspected of heterodoxy in his youth for the maintenance of opinions which in his old age procured him the highest reputation for orthodoxy. He could boast that it was not he who had changed his sentiments. His collected works, published by himself, on his retirement from his London pastorate in 1863, form seven volumes. His intimate friend, the Rev. C. M. Birrell, says of his works, that "thousands could tell the tale of recovery from infidelity; of increased reverence for the authority of the Word of God; of the dispersion of sluggish formalism, and the creation of a vivid and vital realization of admitted truths, which had come to them through his penetrating and awakening pen." His figure was of commanding height, and his countenance was singularly calm and thoughtful. An admirable portrait of him hangs in the board room of the Baptist Missionary Society. He was "instant in prayer," steadfastly preserving the habits of devotion in the midst of exciting and absorbing public labors. During the last four or five years of his life his bodily powers gently and steadily diminished, until at last he fell asleep in Jesus in perfect peace, and with unclouded mind, on Dec. 22, 1873, aged eighty-two. As a preacher he excelled in analysis and exposition. His sermons were pre-eminently instructive, rich in argument, wrought in the fire of a fervid evangelical zeal for the salvation of men. Besides his collected works, in seven volumes, he edited the English edition of Dr. Wayland's "Principles and Practices of Baptists," Rev. Isaac Taylor Hinton's work on the "History of Baptism." He contributed several works to general literature, the most popular being the biography of William Knibb. In early life he published a work on the "History and Topography of the United States, from their First Discovery and Colonization to 1826," which was completed in 1832, and favorably received on both sides of the Atlantic. Later editions have been published in England and in America. His pamphlets on the voluntary principle and other stirring public questions were characterized by incisive force, with peculiar accuracy and lucidity of statement.

Hinton, James, M.D., eldest son of the Rev. John Howard Hinton, was for many years a distinguished London physician, and published several valuable works, some of which were widely known,—"The Mystery of Pain," "Man and his Dwelling-Place," "Life in Nature," etc. Dr. Hinton was baptized by his father in early life, and his writings are marked by a devout, reverent spirit, as well as high intelligence. His death, in London, was recently announced.

Hires, Rev. Allen J., was born in Bridgeton, N. J., Sept. 26, 1822. At the age of sixteen years he was baptized into the fellowship of the Baptist church in that town. After a course of study preparatory to the work of the gospel ministry he was ordained when twenty-five years old, and became pastor of the Vincent church, Chester Co., Pa. From his ordination up to the present time his life has been devoted to labor for the salvation of men and for the upbuilding of the cause of Christ. His pastoral relations have been, in addition to the above-named place, at Glen Run, Chester Co., Pa.; Jersey Shore, Lycoming Co., Pa.; Woodstown, N. J.; Cape May Court-House, N. J.; and with the Second church, Baltimore, Md. For four years he was also district secretary of the American Baptist Home Mission Society in Pennsylvania and New Jersey. Mr. Hires has been greatly honored of God in his ministry.

Hiscox, Edward T., D.D., was born in Westerly, R. I., Aug. 24, 1814. His mother was a member of the Society of Friends, and his father was a Seventh-Day Baptist. One of his ancestors, Rev. William Hiscox, was the first pastor of the first Seventh-Day church in America. In September, 1834, he was baptized by Rev. Flood Shurtleff, and became a member of the First Baptist church of Wakefield, R. I. He was graduated from Madison University in 1843, and in 1844 he accepted the pastorate of the First Baptist church of Westerly, R. I. During his three years of labor there the church had a rapid growth, built a spacious house of worship, and became one of the ablest churches in the State. In 1847 he took charge of the Central church, in Norwich, Conn., where, during five years, his labors were greatly blessed. In 1852 he accepted a call to Stanton Street church, New York. He remained there several years, during which about four hundred were added to the church, chiefly by baptism. At the present time he is pastor at Mount Vernon, N. Y., laboring with his usual vigor and success. He is an able preacher and a prolific writer. He is the author of "The Baptist Church Directory," a manual of Baptist Church order and polity, 30,000 copies of which have been sold. It has been translated into six foreign languages, and is generally used by our foreign missionaries; also, "The Baptist Short

Method," an examination of the characteristic features of the Baptists as distinguished from other denominations of Christians; "The Star Book for Ministers," a manual for ministers of all denominations; "The Star Book of Christian Baptism," a manual in reference to this ordinance. He is about to bring out "The Star Book on the Lord's Supper," "The Star Book on Baptist Councils," and a large volume on the mutual relations and responsibilities of pastors and churches, entitled "Pastor and People."

Historical Society, The American Baptist. —At the annual meeting of the American Baptist Publication Society, held May 4, 1853, in the Spruce Street Baptist church, Philadelphia, a special meeting was called for the next evening to organize a "Historical Department" in connection with the Publication Society. The motion to convene the meeting was made by John M. Peck, D.D., and the mover, together with Hon. H. G. Jones and Henry E. Lincoln, were appointed a committee to report a plan of organization. At the meeting of the Publication Society, on Thursday evening, the committee reported a constitution, which was unanimously adopted, establishing a national society, to be called "The American Baptist Historical Society," and they gave it "a separate and permanent form," and required "its officers to be elected by the Publication Society." William R. Williams, D.D., was its first president. "The objects of the society were to collect and preserve all manuscripts, documents, and books relating to Baptist history," etc.

The society made progress in various directions, but rather slowly until 1860, when the late Dr. Malcom became its president. Ardently attached to its objects, and free from public duties, he gave his entire time to the increase of its treasures, and in a few years its library was enriched by thousands of volumes, many of them of priceless value to our denominational history.

In 1861 the society was incorporated under a new constitution, which gives it as the constituency to elect its officers and board, not the Baptist Publication Society, "but all persons who pay ten dollars or more towards its objects." The secretary of the Publication Society and the president and secretary of its board of managers are *ex officio* members of the board of the Historical Society.

Constant accessions are made to the library, to the increase of which all the funds donated to the society are devoted.

The Historical Society has at least six thousand volumes, among which there are many rare works by the Baptist writers of other days,—books which it would be difficult, if not impossible, to replace; and it also has the writings of many Pedobaptists assailing our peculiarities. It needs financial support to secure the literary treasures which are frequently within its reach, and it should receive it liberally.

It is believed that the society should have a warm place in the hearts of our entire denomination, and that it should speedily be furnished with a fire-proof building to protect its invaluable collection of books and other treasures.

Rev. William Cathcart, D.D., is the president of the society, Rev. Job H. Chambers, secretary, and H. E. Lincoln, Esq., librarian and treasurer.

Hobart, I. N., D.D., for over ten years connected with the direction of State missions in Illinois, was born in Lyme, N. H., Feb. 20, 1812. His conversion took place July 4, 1831, and his baptism in August of the same year. In 1834 he was licensed, and on Aug. 12, 1841, he was ordained as pastor of the church at Radnor, Pa., Rev. Elon Galusha preaching the sermon. He remained pastor at Radnor nearly six years, returning to New England with impaired health in 1847, and for about two years remaining without pastoral charge. Jan. 1, 1849, he became pastor of the church at North Oxford, Mass., where he labored between three and four years, when he accepted the pastorate of the church at Bristol, R. I. Here his health failed again, and in 1855 he removed to St. Lawrence Co., N. Y. From Jan. 1, 1856, to Oct. 1, 1868, he labored in that State. At the last date he was appointed by the Home Mission Society to take charge of its work in Illinois. In the year following the society and the Illinois Baptist General Association adopted the co-operative plan in State missions, and Dr. Hobart was chosen superintendent of missions for that State. When the co-operative plan was discontinued he was appointed district secretary for the States of Illinois, Iowa, and Wisconsin. At the earnest solicitation of the Board of the General Association he decided to remain in the superintendence of its missions, and to this post has been elected from year to year to the present time (1880), conducting the Baptist missions of the State with marked self-devotion and administrative ability.

Hobbs, Smith M., M.D., an eminent physician of Mount Washington, Ky., was born in Nelson County in 1823. His early education was under the superintendence of Noble Butler, A.M., a well-known author, and was completed at St. Joseph's College, at Bardstown. He graduated at the Kentucky School of Medicine in 1852, and immediately commenced practice at Mount Washington. He is a gentleman of fine culture and a close student, a man of tireless energy, and has performed an incredible amount of professional labor. He was a member of the Kentucky Legislature in 1868, and was the author of a bill which largely increased the common-school fund of the State, and of a report in favor of "prohibiting the marriage of first cousins." In 1876 he was one of the two commissioners appointed to superintend the interest of Kentucky in the Centennial Exposition at Philadelphia. He

SMITH M. HOBBS, M.D.

became a Baptist early in life, and is a liberal contributor to Baptist enterprises.

Hobgood, Prof. F. P., was born in Granville Co., N. C., in 1846; was prepared by James H. Horner for college; graduated from Wake Forest College in 1869; taught an academy at Reidsville, N. C.; came to Raleigh and took the position of his father-in-law, Dr. Royall, as principal of a female college, which he conducted successfully until 1880, when he removed his school to Oxford, N. C.

Hodge, James L., D.D., son of Rev. William and Elizabeth Hodge, was born in Aberdeen, Scotland, in 1812, and at the age of twelve accompanied his parents to America. In 1831 he became a member of the First Baptist church of Hartford. In 1835, after graduating at the Literary Institution, Suffield, he was ordained pastor of the First Baptist church of that town. He was subsequently called to the First Baptist church in Brooklyn, which proved to be one of the longest and most successful settlements of his life. In the midst of his prosperity he was impressed with the importance of founding a church in the upper part of the city, on Washington Avenue. After a pastorate of some years with the new interest, which was crowned with success, Dr. Hodge was induced to settle in Newark, N. J. In 1864, after an absence of eight years, he was called to his present highly successful pastorate with the Mariners' church, New York. During his long experience as a minister, Dr. Hodge has been regarded as an eloquent champion of Scriptural truth, and has been especially fitted for the performance of his duties by his tender sympathies, magnetic nature, and analytical powers. In 1848 he was made D.D. by Madison University.

Hodge, Marvin Grow, D.D., was born in Hardwick, Vt., in 1822; educated at Derby Academy; ordained at Charleston in 1843, where he began his ministry. Subsequently he was settled at Colchester and Hinesburg, Stillwater and Brooklyn, N. Y., Kalamazoo, Mich., Beaver Dam, Janesville, and Milwaukee, Wis. At the last place he now resides, and is the pastor of the First Baptist church in that city. His pastorates at Hanson Place, Brooklyn, N. Y., Janesville, Wis., and Kalamazoo, Mich., were nearly seven years each. At Janesville he was very successful. He added not only large numbers to the church, but led the church to erect the finest Baptist meeting-house in the State. He left it a large, intelligent, and influential body. The church in Milwaukee is strengthening itself under his ministrations and entering upon a new era of usefulness. Dr. Hodge was one year district secretary of the New York Baptist Convention, and district secretary of the American Baptist Home Mission Society for New England two years. He received the honorary degree of A.M. from the University of Vermont in 1849, the like honor from

MARVIN GROW HODGE, D.D.

the University of Rochester in 1864, and the title of D.D. from the University of Chicago in 1867. He excels as an expository preacher. His sermons are nearly all clear expositions of the divine Word. Theologically exact and Scriptural, always thoroughly prepared with the riches of a ripe Christian experience, he brings to his people in his pulpit ministrations a gospel feast. His people love to see him in the pulpit. They are sure to be instructed. As the result, he indoctrinates his congregations and builds them up. Few congregations are better instructed in the doctrines of the Word of God than the churches at Janesville and Kalamazoo during his ministry over them. As a pastor, Dr. Hodge is wise, sympathetic, knows his people thoroughly, is their recognized leader and guide, and feeds his flock like a shepherd, gathering the lambs in his arms and carrying them in his bosom. With his fine abilities as a preacher, his decided executive talents, and excellent gifts for pastoral labor, he has for many years been regarded as one of the ablest of Christian ministers. In the State where he now resides, and where ten years of his life have been spent, he is known as a good man and a faithful herald of Jesus Christ, "watching for souls."

Hodgen, Rev. Isaac, "in some respects one of the most brilliant preachers of Kentucky," was the son of Robert Hodgen, a distinguished citizen and a leading Baptist among the first settlers of Kentucky. He was born in La Rue County about 1780, became a member of Severn's Valley church in 1802, and was licensed to preach at Nolin church in 1804. In 1805 he removed to Green County and united with Mount Gilead church, where he received ordination the same year. He devoted most of the energies of his life to the work of an evangelist, though he was stated preacher for several churches at different periods. He traveled and preached almost unceasingly, and multitudes were turned to the Lord wherever he labored. In 1817, accompanied by William Warder, he made a tour as far as Philadelphia, returning through Virginia. They traveled the entire distance on horseback, and preached almost every night. It was estimated that "over 600 were baptized who were awakened under their preaching in Virginia." Mr. Hodgen continued in this course of tireless zeal and energy till the Lord called him home in the maturity of his manhood, in 1826.

Hodges, Rev. Cyrus Whitman, was born in Leicester, Vt., July 9, 1802; became a Christian, and united with the Congregational church in Salisbury, Vt., in July, 1821. Within a few months, finding his views more in harmony with those of the Baptists, he joined the Baptist church in Brandon, and was licensed by them to preach in 1822. He was ordained at Chester, N. Y., in 1824, and remained there three years. His other pastorates were Arlington, Shaftsbury, and Springfield, Vt., Westport, N. Y., Bennington, and finally Bristol, Vt. In each of these places he rendered good service to the cause of his Master. He died April 4, 1851.

Holcombe, Henry, D.D.—Among those who took an active and beneficial part in shaping the destinies of the Baptist denomination in the State of Georgia was Henry Holcombe. Born in Prince Edward Co., Va., he moved to South Carolina, with his father, Grimes Holcombe, in early life. He was a captain of cavalry in the Revolutionary war, and, at the age of twenty-two, while in command of his company, was hopefully converted to God. He began at once to proclaim the unsearchable riches of Christ, making his first address on horseback, at the head of his command. He soon became distinguished as a preacher, and met with extraordinary success in his work. He was pastor of the Baptist church in Beaufort and other places in South Carolina until 1799, when he was invited to Savannah as "supply" to what is now known as the Independent Presbyterian church of that city, which then occupied the Baptist house of worship, having leased it for a number of years. In November of 1800 he, with his wife and ten others, united in organizing and constituting the First Baptist church of Savannah, which still exists. He became the pastor, soon gathered a large congregation, to which he ministered until 1811, when he accepted a call to Philadelphia. As pastor of the First Baptist church he preached in Philadelphia until his death, in 1824.

The degree of A.M. was conferred on him in early life by Columbia College, S. C., and the degree of Doctor of Divinity, which meant far more then than it does now, was conferred on him in 1810 by Brown University, R. I.

Dr. Holcombe never took any part in politics, but when quite a young man he was a member of the convention in South Carolina which ratified and adopted the Constitution of the United States. Several points in his life are worthy of mention:

1. He baptized the first white person ever immersed in the city of Savannah.

2. He was the originator of the penitentiary system of Georgia, *in lieu* of death, for ordinary crimes.

3. He was the founder of the Savannah Female Orphan Asylum, and wrote its constitution.

4. He published the first religious periodical in the Southern States, and one among the first in the United States,—a magazine called the *Analytical Repository*,—it was begun in May, 1802.

5. He was one of the Baptist ministers who met by appointment at Powelton, Ga., in May, 1802, and originated the "General Committee," which was the germ of the Georgia Baptist Convention.

6. He was the main instrument in the foundation of Mount Enon Academy, near the line of

Burke County,—a Baptist institution of learning, unfortunately located, but which prospered as long as Dr. Holcombe resided in Georgia. This was the first institution of the kind in the South established under the influence of Baptists, and it was the precursor of Mercer University.

Dr. Holcombe was a man of wide information and elegant culture. He was a great reasoner, mighty in the Scriptures, and a born orator. His bearing was dignified, his manners graceful, his presence commanding, and he had great personal magnetism. In its softer tones his voice was gentle and persuasive; at other times it was full of power and majesty. A man of very tender feelings and sympathetic nature, he was, indeed, a "son of consolation" to the poor, the widows, and the orphans, many of whom have been heard to speak with tears of his gentle ministrations a whole generation after his death. He condescended to men of low estate, was a friend to the friendless and the outcast, and would take to his home and to his bosom those who were spurned by society. On the very day when a man was put to death on the gallows in Savannah, his children were gathered together at Dr. Holcombe's house,—the abode of sympathy and love,—where they were cared for, comforted, counseled, and cherished with more than fatherly tenderness.

With these almost womanly qualities Dr. Holcombe's character possessed another side. He was a bold, brave man, immovably stern when occasion required, and at times imperial if not imperious in his bearing, and these qualities, in a man of herculean physique and of immense intellectual and moral momentum, inspired awe and even fear in the minds of many. He was a man of warm impulses, and, it is said, "liberal to a fault," lavishing his means with an almost reckless generosity. Add to all this wonderful preaching ability, intense zeal, and enthusiasm in the cause of Christ, and it need excite no wonder that he made a deep impress upon the State, and that his presence was felt as that of a great power. He died calmly, in possession of all his mental faculties, and fully aware of his approaching end; and the concourse of people attending his funeral was such, it is said, as was never before seen in Philadelphia. Dr. Holcombe was six feet and two inches in height.

Holcombe, Rev. Hosea, a native of North Carolina, was born about the year 1780. For some years a minister in upper South Carolina, he settled in Jefferson Co., Ala., early in the history of the State. Was unquestionably a leader in projecting the plans of the early Baptists of the State, taking a bold and aggressive part in everything that looked to the elevation of the Baptist cause, or to the progress of Baptist principles. Organized nearly all the churches for many miles around where he lived, and established them on a sound basis; and traveled and preached over a large part of the State; went to Associations far and near, and was universally regarded as able to guide them; was six years president of the State Convention; more than any other man in the State he withstood the anti-missionaries; was in the strength of his ministerial influence when the anti-missionaries were doing their work of mischief among Alabama Baptists. He was the man for the times, and performed his work well. One of the founders of our State Convention, and a most earnest advocate for the establishment of good schools by the denomination, and for ministerial education. He was an able minister of the New Testament, doctrinal and argumentative in preaching, clear and forcible in delivery, mighty in the Scriptures, a noble and impressive person, commanding respect and veneration everywhere; though not so great a man, he holds a position in the history of Alabama Baptists not unlike that of Dr. Mercer among the brethren of Georgia. He wrote a number of controversial pamphlets, compiled a hymn-book, and a history of the Baptists in Alabama,—a work of 375 pages, which brings its history down to the year 1840. He passed his ministry as pastor of a number of churches, and as a missionary evangelist. He died in 1841 at his home, and was buried on his farm, near Jonesborough. Two of his sons became Baptist ministers.

Holcombe, Rev. William H., a minister in Northeast Mississippi, distinguished for eloquence and piety, was born in Alabama in 1812. He began to preach very young; came to Mississippi at an early day; successfully filled the pastorate at Columbus, Aberdeen, Okalona, and at Pontoloc and Ripley. He died in 1867.

Holden, Rev. Charles Horace, of Modesto, Cal., is a young and most prominent Baptist pastor. He was born in West Milford, Va., Aug. 23, 1853; educated, converted, and baptized in Webster, W. Va.; removed to California; ordained in July, 1879, and became pastor at Modesto, where the baptism of converts, the awakened interest in the gospel, and other tokens of divine favor give great promise of increasing usefulness and power in connection with his ministry.

Holden, Charles N., was born at Fort Covington, N. Y., May 13, 1816, of parents who had emigrated to that place from New Hampshire, and were among the earlier settlers of Northern New York. His father, W. C. Holden, an energetic and patriotic man, was present and participated in the battle of Plattsburg, so important among the battles of the war of 1812–15. At twenty years of age, Charles N. Holden, the eldest son, having received such education as the opportunities of a new country afford,—though these were well improved,—engaged in teaching. Deciding at length to try his fortunes in the new West, Mr. Holden, in 1837, removed to Chicago. After a little time spent upon the farm of his uncle, P. H. Holden, in Will County, he returned to Chicago in the fall of the year just named, and in the spring of the following year began business as a lumber-dealer, afterwards as a grocer. In 1852, retiring from the business in which he had been so long engaged, he entered that of insurance and real estate ; was one of those who organized the Firemen's Insurance Company, holding in that company the office of secretary ; subsequently being elected treasurer of the Firemen's Benevolent Association, in which service he still remains. Mr. Holden has been called to repeated offices of trust,—as alderman, as commissioner of taxes for the city of Chicago, as city treasurer, and in other posts of important public service. Converted in early life, Mr. Holden has been during many years a valued and useful member of the Baptist denomination. In Chicago his church connection has been with what is now the Second church, always one of its most trusted and efficient members. He was also during many years a trustee of the university, and was one of those who laid the foundations of the theological seminary at Chicago. To no one man is it more due that the financial affairs of that institution have been always so judiciously guided, while his own donations to its funds have been ready and liberal. Held in high esteem by his fellow-citizens during his whole career, he has especially been remarkable for his firm, consistent, and useful course as a Christian, a friend of reform, and a worker in every good cause.

Holden, Gov. W. W., was born in Orange Co., N. C., in November, 1818 ; learned the printer's trade ; settled in Raleigh in 1836 ; was foreman of the *Raleigh Star* office four years, during which time he read law, and was licensed to practise 1st January, 1841. Became proprietor and editor of the *Standard* in 1843, which he conducted with distinguished ability for twenty-five years. He was a member of the House of Commons from Wake County in 1846 ; was several times State printer ; was for seven years a member of the State Literary Board ; elected a trustee of the State University in 1856 ; served several years as one of the board of directors of the insane asylum and the institution for the deaf and dumb ; was a member from Wake County in the secession convention of 1861 ; was provisional governor of North Carolina for seven months in 1865, having been appointed by President Johnson ; was elected governor of North Carolina in 1868 by a large majority, and served two years and six months, when he was impeached by the State Legislature ; was offered the mission to San Salvador by President Johnson, and that to Peru by President Grant, both of which he declined.

Gov. Holden professed faith in Christ in December, 1870, at a meeting held by Rev. A. B. Earle, in Raleigh, and was baptized by Dr. T. H. Pritchard, pastor of the First Baptist church of that city. He has been an active and useful church member, and has a Bible-class of young men in the Sabbath-school, which numbers 40 members. He has been the postmaster of Raleigh for six years.

Hollins Institute, Botetourt Springs, Va.— About the year 1841, the Rev. Joshua Bradly, of New York, went to Virginia. He was a Baptist minister, and enthusiastic on the subject of education. At this time Botetourt Springs, now the seat of Hollins Institute, was for sale, and Mr. Bradly at once conceived the plan of purchasing it for school purposes. Without a dollar in his possession he contracted for the purchase of the property, relying upon his own tact and energy to secure the necessary funds. He opened a school for boys and girls with the purpose of supplying the neighboring districts with good teachers. There was a large attendance of pupils, but financial and other troubles soon arising, he resigned at the end of a year and left the State. Before his departure he had formed an organization under the title of " The Valley Union Education Society of Virginia," which afterwards procured a charter as a joint-stock company, and continued the school. The Rev. George Pearcy, late missionary to China, and now deceased, was elected principal, and continued such for several years with varying success. Mr. Pearcy, about to leave for China, urged Mr. Cocke to take charge of the school, which, relinquishing his position in Richmond College, he consented to do on the following terms : that he would advance a sum sufficient to save the property from immediate sale ; he should be both principal and steward of the school, becoming responsible for all salaries of teachers whom he might employ ; and the society should furnish premises and buildings, but should be subjected to no liabilities whatever beyond the cost and repair of the premises. Mr. Cocke found the grounds and everything on them in a most unattractive condition, but by his untiring energy they were soon made to present a beautiful appearance. He opened the school, and the first year the number of pupils was small, but soon there was not room enough for all the applicants. Finding that the education of young men and young women together, and their living in the same building, was not desirable, Mr. Cocke advised the discontinuance of one class ; and as there was no chartered school in Virginia for young ladies, he counseled the continuance of the school as an institute of high grade for that sex, and in 1852 the change took place. The session of 1852–53 of the newly organized school for girls alone opened with cheering prospects. Soon the rooms of the institution were filled, and so great was the success, and so marked the interest in female education throughout the South, that there speedily rose into being Hampton Female College, Richmond Female Institute, Albemarle Female Institute, Warrenton Female Institute, and Danville Female College, all under the patronage of the Baptists, and a like number started by other denominations. In the year 1855, Mr. John Hollins, of Lynchburg, Va., at the suggestion of his wife, a pious Baptist lady, proposed to the company that if they would relinquish their stock he would give as much as all their shares aggregated, and place the institution in the hands of a self-perpetuating board of trustees. The proposition was accepted, and the amount given by Mr. Hollins was $5000, which in a few years was supplemented by a public subscription amounting to $10,000, Mr. Cocke acting as agent during vacation, and giving his services gratuitously. After Mr. Hollins's death his widow continued her donations, the whole amount from the Hollins family being about $19,000. With this assistance, Prof. Cocke managed to remove all the old buildings of the institute, which at this time, under the new charter, assumed the name of "Hollins Institute," and as such had perpetual succession. Handsome buildings were erected adapted to the wants of a school for young ladies, and the institution placed upon a new and higher career of usefulness. The exercises were continued throughout the long and weary years of the war, with an overflowing patronage, being the only institution in the State that preserved its organization during that terrible period of conflict and blood. Subsequent to the war the Virginia patronage diminished in consequence of the universal financial distress, but this loss was more than repaired by patronage from other States. Prof. Cocke's accomplished wife and daughters have been most efficient co-laborers with him in giving success to all departments of the institute, and they are highly appreciated by the public. The course of instruction is thorough and complete, and its certificates and diplomas are eagerly sought for. There are in the institute seven schools,—1. The English Language and Literature; 2. Ancient Languages and Literature; 3. Modern Languages and Literature; 4. Mathematics; 5. Natural Science; 6. Mental and Moral Science; 7. History. These schools constitute the collegiate department, besides which there is a normal department and an ornamental department. The faculty embraces fourteen experienced instructors.

Hollis Family, The.—Vice is often hereditary, and benevolence frequently descends from father to son; it remained in the Hollis family for generations, and we trust that it flourishes among the descendants of such worthy forefathers to-day.

Thomas Hollis was for more than sixty years a member of the church in Pinner's Hall, London. He was a man of unbounded liberality to benevolent and religious enterprises. Like many other persons who give away great sums, he systematically subjected his personal expenditures to the most rigid economy, that he might make larger donations to cherished objects. He died in September, 1718.

His son Thomas was baptized in 1680, when he was twenty years of age, and in gifts to sustain and extend education and religion he was the most prominent man of his day. He was a sagacious and successful merchant of London, who traded and toiled to make money that his resources might assist every noble cause.

He sent over a library of valuable theological books to the Philadelphia Baptist Association, which for many years was exceedingly useful to our fathers in the ministry. "The Assembly's Annotations on the Scriptures," a commentary in two folio volumes, now in possession of the American Baptist Historical Society, is supposed to have been one of the works given to the first Baptist Association in America. It bears his name, evidently in his own handwriting, and the date 1721.

Thomas and his brother John gave the Baptist church of Boston, Mass., £135 for repairing their meeting-house. Thomas Hollis founded a professorship of Theology in Harvard University, with a salary of £80 per annum, and an "exhibition" of £10 each per annum to ten scholars of good character, four of whom should be Baptists, if there were such persons there, and £10 a year to the college treasurer for his trouble, and £10 more to supply accidental losses or to increase the number of students. According to the charter, at the time Mr. Hollis made these gifts to Harvard the ministers of Boston (Congregational) were part of the overseers of the college, and when Mr. Hollis proposed the Rev. Elisha Callender, pastor of the Baptist church of Boston, as a fit person to have a seat in the board of overseers, Mr. Callender was refused the position, evidently because he was a Baptist. Isaac Backus gives this statement without expressing any doubt of its correctness, and he names his authority.

Six years after his first donation he founded a professorship of Mathematics and Experimental Philosophy in Harvard, with a salary of £80 a year, and he gave an apparatus for the professor which cost about £150, and he sent books for the library. Until that time, no man, according to Isaac Backus, who examined the records, had been so liberal to Harvard as this eminent Baptist. Mr. Hollis died in 1731. Prof. Wigglesworth, in a discourse which he published on the death of Mr. Hollis, says, "By his frequent and ample benefactions, for the encouragement of theological as well as human knowledge among us, who are Christians of a *different denomination from himself*, he hath set such an example of generous, catholic, and Christian spirit as hath never before fallen within my observation, nor, as far as I now remember, within my reading." We had no college in America at this period, and like a true Báptist, Mr. Hollis showed himself the friend of light.

The donations of this family of Baptists continued to enrich Harvard for nearly a century, and exceeded £6000. If the money was properly invested, it must to-day be worth many times more than $30,000.

We know nothing of the way by which these funds for Baptist students have been appropriated; for the honor of old Harvard we trust that the requisite number of Baptist students have regularly received the £10 per annum which Mr. Hollis left them. But we fear if the godly Calvinist, Thomas Hollis, heard the divinity taught in Harvard now he would bitterly regret his well-meant generosity. In a letter to Elder Wheaton, of Swanzey, Thomas Hollis writes: "God, that hath shined into our hearts by his gospel, can lead your sleeping Sabbatarians from the Sinai covenant and the law of ceremonies into the light of the new covenant and the grace thereof. I pity to see professors drawing back to the law, and desire to remember that our standing is by grace."

Hollis, Rev. J. A., was a native of South Carolina, but of English parentage. He was born in 1824. He graduated at Georgetown College, and subsequently entered the ministry in Mississippi. He removed to Missouri in 1844, and resided in that State till the time of his death, in 1870. He was pastor of several churches, and became president of Stephen Female College, at Columbia, in 1865, and held the office till his decease. He was a man of learning and ability, of eminent piety and noble characteristics, possessing a rare talent for the instruction of the young. He ended a laborious and useful life without a stain upon his memory. The institution, the church, and the community felt his loss deeply. His name will long live in the hearts of thousands.

Holman, Deacon James Sanders, a prominent and influential Baptist, died in Polk Co., Oregon, Jan. 14, 1880. He was born in Tennessee, Nov. 28, 1813; he moved to Oregon in 1847. He was baptized at Turnedge, Mo., at sixteen, and was for many years a deacon of that church. He was the first president of the Oregon Baptist Education Society, and a charter-member of McMinnville College. He was sheriff of Polk County several terms, and served two years in the Oregon Legislature. He carried his religion into public life, was honored by all, and spoken of by men as "the peace-maker." He was one of the first to plant the Baptist banner on the Pacific coast, and was faithful to God and his country until death called him to his rest.

Holman, Judge Jesse L., was born in Mercer Co., Ky., Oct. 22, 1783. He learned his letters while very young, and in his childhood was a daily reader of the Bible. He recollected a sermon that he heard when he was only four years old. He joined the Clear Creek Baptist church in his seventeenth year. After completing his studies he was admitted to the bar in New Castle, and afterwards practised in Frankfort. He, like his father, was an emancipationist, and he decided to remove north across the Ohio, and accordingly, in 1811, he passed over the river, and settled on a romantic bluff that he called Verdestan, and this was his home for the remainder of his life. When he removed to Verdestan the whole country was a wilderness, and Indians were roaming everywhere. At the time of his removal to Indiana he received from Gov. Harrison commissions for district attorney of the State for the counties of Dearborn and Jefferson. In 1814 he was elected a member of the house of representatives of the Territorial Legislature, and was chosen president by a unanimous vote. Near the close of the same year he was appointed the presiding judge of the district in which he lived, and in 1816, under the State government, he was appointed presiding judge in the second and third districts, and in the same year was chosen one of the electors of the President and Vice-President of the United States. In December, 1816, he was appointed judge of the Supreme Court of the State, which office he filled with great acceptance for fourteen years. In 1831 he was a candidate for the United States Senate, and was defeated by one vote. In 1835 he received the appointment of judge of the United States district for Indiana, which office he filled with singular ability till his death. He was a constituent member of the Laughery church. He also aided in gathering the Aurora church, and was a liberal giver to all worthy causes. In 1834 he was ordained, and thus entered upon a work that his soul longed to engage in. So unsullied was his public as well as his private life that men were always glad to hear him preach. While traveling the judicial circuit it was no unusual thing for him to address his fellow-citizens on Bible operations, missions, Sabbath-schools, general education, and temperance. So consistent and earnest was his life that there seemed no incongruity, but rather a singular harmony in his two offices of judge and minister. He was a leader in the organization of a Sabbath-school association in his own county. He took particular interest in the distribution of religious books and tracts. He was for many years vice-president of the American Sunday-School Union, and was president of the Western Baptist Publication and Sunday-School Society.

Mr. Holman was a warm and consistent friend of missions. Indeed, it may be said that in that time, when the gifts to missions were small in Indiana, a circuit of churches, of which Aurora may be said to be the centre, was the headquarters for missions. During the agency both of Dr. Bennett and Dr. Stevens, this portion of the State was always represented in donations. The Holmans, the Ferrises, the Hinckleys, the Dows, and others never refused or neglected to give. Judge Holman was for five years president of the Indiana State Convention. He was also from the first a member of the Indiana Baptist Education Society, and during several years was president of the board of trustees. His constitution was naturally feeble, and an attack of pleurisy caused his death, March 28, 1842. He knew that he must die, and expressed perfect confidence in the pardon and love and power of the Master.

Holman, Rev. John W., M.D., was born in Canaan, Me., in 1805; converted in 1818; studied at Waterville; ordained in 1824 in the Christian denomination; preached in Eastern Maine, New Brunswick, Philadelphia, and Boston; in latter city joined the Free-Will Baptists, and preached fifteen years; united with the regular Baptists at Mystic River, Conn.; settled with First Baptist church in Norwich, Conn., and with various churches in New York and Maine, with Franklin church, Mass., and finally with Third Baptist church in North Stonington, Conn.; in forty-nine years preached over 5000 sermons and organized 11 churches; was withal a poet, a painter, and a physician; a man of rare talents and great labor; left some interesting poetical and exegetical papers; while pastor in North Stonington was prostrated by sickness, and died May 16, 1873, aged sixty-eight years. All his four sons are Baptist ministers.

Holman, Russell, D.D., was born in Warwick, Mass., Aug. 14, 1812. The instruction and integrity of his parents gave him those virtues which made him a pure, conscientious man in after-life. He graduated at Brown University. He removed to Kentucky in 1839, and became pastor of two churches in Green County. Weak in body, he served there till 1842. He was ordained July 29, 1840. He performed missionary work in addition to his pastoral labor in these two churches.

In 1842 he went to New Orleans, and finding no Baptist church there, with great zeal, and against much opposition, he established what is now called the Coliseum Baptist church of New Orleans. In 1845 he was elected secretary of the Home Mission department of the Southern Baptist Convention. His skill and energy made the board efficient in home mission work. In 1851 he retired from this office from ill health, and left the work in the height of its prosperity. He became pastor till 1856, and was re-elected to the secretaryship, and held the office till 1862. Ill health caused him again to resign. During the war he tenderly ministered to the sick and wounded, and preached the gospel to them. Afterwards he was sent to collect the scattered flock of the Coliseum church in New Orleans. He succeeded in re-establishing the church six months after beginning his efforts. In 1867 he went to Illinois, and labored there and in Kentucky and Missouri till 1876, when a severe stroke of paralysis put an end to his active toils. His zeal and heart kept warm for the cause, and he patiently submitted to his lot. Says Dr. Wm. H. McIntosh, "As a preacher Dr. Holman was instructive, sometimes eloquent. He accepted the doctrines of grace, and enforced them upon the consciences of his hearers. His life was in constant conformity to the rule and spirit of the gospel. His heart was tender to all. In his family he was loving and true." His last days were spent in Miami and Marshall, Mo. On Dec. 2, 1879, he went to his eternal rest after a few hours of illness.

Holman, Judge William S., son of Hon. J. L. Holman, was born in Verdestan (now Aurora), Ind., Sept. 6, 1822. He had the advantages of the common schools and a partial course at Franklin College. Soon after he left college he was elected to the State Legislature. He was a member of the constitutional convention in 1850. He was elected judge of the Common Pleas, and served from 1852 to 1856. He was elected to the Thirty-sixth Congress, and made chairman of Revolutionary Claims. He was re-elected to the Thirty-seventh and Thirty-eighth, and served with marked ability. His untiring care for the expenses of the government has given him among the people the *sobriquet* "watch-dog of the treasury." He was elected again to the Fortieth Congress. He is a member of the Aurora Baptist church. He occupies the home of his father,—a beautiful spot on one of the hills on the Ohio River. No man has been so uniformly popular in his district as Mr. Holman.

Holme, Deacon George W., was a constituent member of the Baptist church at Holmesburg, and for thirty years one of its deacons. After a life of great usefulness, he died July 9, 1864, in his seventy-sixth year, in the house in which he was born.

Holme, Judge John, was one of the early settlers in Pennsylvania. He is supposed to have been the first Baptist, of any prominence at least, in the colony. Mr. Holme appears in the affairs of the colony in 1685-86. Whether he arrived in the country at this time, or earlier, is uncertain. Mr. Holme is said to have been a native of Somersetshire, England, on what authority it is not known. He does not seem to have been a relative of Thomas Holme, the surveyor-general, as

Thomas Holme, in one of his letters, addresses him as "namesake" merely. John Holme brought with him to this country four sons,—John, Samuel, Ebenezer, and Benjamin. He came hither by way of the Barbadoes, where he resided some time, and was engaged in sugar-planting. That Mr. Holme was a man of wealth and social standing appears from many circumstances. It was he who gave one-half of the lot on which the First Baptist meeting-house was erected, on Second Street near Arch Street. His name appears with that of Gov. Markham, and two or three men of prominence in the colony, to a petition to the council to put the colony in a state of defense against the hostile Indians, who, at the instigation of the French, were threatening it during the French and English war. His name is also found next to that of the mayor of the city as signer of a petition relative to "the cove at Blue Anchor,—that it should be laid out for a convenient harbor, to secure shipping against ice or other danger of the winter, and that no person for private gains or interests may incommode the public utility of a whole city."

John Holme was appointed justice in the County Court in 1690; and he represented the city of Philadelphia in the Assembly of 1692.

He married as his second wife, Mary, the widow of Nicholas More, the first chief justice of the colony, and president of the "Free Society of Traders of Pennsylvania." Chief-Justice More was a man of great legal acquirements and general learning. The closest friendship existed between him and John Holme. At the death of Judge More, Mr. Holme was made the executor of his estate and the guardian of his children. There is reason to believe that they had been acquainted before they came to this country, and if so, it would seem that they both came from Bristol.

That John Holme was himself a man of more than ordinary culture appears from his library, which for an emigrant at that time was certainly remarkably large and well selected. It must have contained several hundred volumes. In his will John Holme bequeaths to his eldest son, John, several large folios,—Wilson's "Christian Dictionary," Haak's "Dutch Annotations," and Newman's "Concordance." Besides these, there are still in possession of his descendants many books of great value that he owned, among which are Baxter's "Theology," Bunyan's works, a Baptist Confession of Faith (London, 1652), and the writings of many stalwart old Baptist worthies, such as "The Pulpit Guard Routed, by Thomas Collier, London, 1652;" "The Foundations of the Font Discovered, by Henry Haggar, London, 1653;" "The Storming of Antichrist in his Strongest Garrisons, Compulsion of Conscience and Infant Baptism, by Ch. Blackwood. Printed Anno 1644. *Being one of those years wherein Antichrist threatened the storming of the churches;*" "An Appeal for the Use of the Gospel Ordinances, by Henry Lawrence, Esq.," and the more generally known works of Hanserd Knollys and Benjamin Keath. Together with these are some controversial works of a more general character, such as "The Three Conformities, or the Harmony and Agreement of the Romish Church with Gentileism, Judaism, and the Ancient Heresies, by Francis De Croy G. Arth, London, 1620;" "A Large Examination taken at Lambeth, according to His Maiesties direction, taken point by point of M. George Blakwell, made Archbishop of England by Pope Clement 8, &c. Imprinted at London by Robert Barker, Printer to the Kings Most Excellent Maiestie, 1607;" "Triplicinodo, triplix cuneus, or an Apologie for the Oath of Allegiance, &c. Imprinted at London by Robert Barker, Printer to the Kings Most Excellent Maiestie, 1609." This book is supposed to have been written by King James himself. Among the general philosophical works in Mr. Holme's library are Bacon's "Essays," and among the devotional are works of Thomas Brooks, Thomas Vincent, and Thos. Dookitol, and others. But what is still more remarkable is that a copy of Milton's "Paradise Lost" is found among the books that belonged to him. Unfortunately the title-page of this book is gone, but it is undoubtedly among the earliest editions of the poems.

If the character of John Holme may be judged of from his books, he was a man of very much more than ordinary culture, for in the library of very few emigrants, in the seventeenth century certainly, were found the works of Lord Bacon, Baxter, Bunyan, and Milton. The writings of the last two mentioned were at that time scarcely known over half of England. No Macaulay had yet appeared to set forth their merits. We have from the pen of John Holme himself, in verse, a manuscript of some 20 pages (published in 1848, in the Bulletin of the Historical Society of Pennsylvania, vol. i. No. 13), entitled "True Relation of the Flourishing State of Pennsylvania."* This is probably the first metrical composition written in the State, and though worth little as poetry, it is valuable historically, as one of the earliest and most extended and accurate accounts of the condition of the colony; and as in it he avows himself a Baptist, it is a creditable testimony of an impartial witness to the general good government of the Quakers, and shows great foresight of the natural resources and coming greatness of the State of Pennsylvania.

But the incident which has given most interest

---

* The original manuscript of this work is lost. It was loaned by the family at Holmesburg to a gentleman for exhibition to the Pennsylvania Historical Society, and has never been returned.

and historic importance to John Holme is that he was one of the judges that presided at the trials of George Keith, William Bradford, and others, which may be considered the *causes cèlebre* of the administration of William Penn, and so serious in their consequences to Penn in England and here, as to occasion for a time the loss of the governorship to the proprietary. Of the eight judges that sat upon the bench at these trials, six were Quakers, Lacey Cock, a Lutheran, and John Holme, a Baptist. George Keith, who was a man of great ability, and previous standing and influence among the Quakers, was charged with defaming the character of Thomas Lloyd, the president of the council, in phrases, such as calling him an "impudent rascal," and saying "that his memory would stink," etc., of tending to encourage sedition and breach of the peace by his comments on the arrest of Babbit, a pirate, and also of aiming a blow at the proprietary's government. Judge Holme dissented from the majority of the bench on these charges, and boldly expressed his views, and was tacitly sustained in them by Judge Cock. Mr. Holme maintained that the whole affair was essentially a religious dispute, pertaining to matters of doctrine and practice among the Quakers, and was not fit to be adjudicated by a civil tribunal; that the arraignment was in effect a religious persecution, and without justification in a colony that proclaimed religious liberty. He especially maintained that the exceptions of Keith to the jury, as prejudiced and not impartial, ought to be admitted. But in this also he was overruled by the majority of the bench. In the trial of William Bradford he was again a dissentient. Mr. Bradford was the first printer in the colony, and was arraigned for unlawfully printing the appeals and attacks of George Keith upon the Quakers. And a tailor was also put on trial for posting one of Mr. Keith's protests in his shop. In all these matters Judge Holme persistently dissented from the majority of the bench, and it is said actually resigned his office rather than seem to be made a party in any degree to what he regarded a case of religious persecution, and of the infringement of the liberty of the press.

It is flattering to our denominational pride, that if you meet a Baptist you will find a friend both of religious liberty and the freedom of the press. It is not too much to say that in the person of Judge Holme, who stands as both the pioneer and the representative of the Baptists in this country, south of Rhode Island, is found a man of the broadest views, of a far-sighted state policy, of courage and patriotism and piety, a champion of religious liberty, even against the encroachments of the Quakers themselves, and the first fearless advocate of the freedom of the press, in his defense of William Bradford, the first printer of the colony.

Judge Holme removed in the latter part of his life to Salem, N. J., where he was again made a judge, which office he retained to the time of his death, in 1703. He was one of the constituent members of the Baptist church in Salem, and often exercised his gifts in religious meetings, but was at no time a minister. Many of the descendants of Benjamin Holme, his youngest son, still reside at Salem and in the vicinity.

His eldest son, John Holme, settled at Pennypack Mill, and his lineal descendants live in the very same town to this day. Every one, in line, having adhered strictly to the religious faith practised by their great Baptist progenitor.

Holme, John Stanford, D.D., was born in Holmesburg, now a part of the city of Philadelphia, March 4, 1822. His ancestors came to America from England in 1683, and purchased lands from William Penn. John Holme was a magistrate under Penn, but resigned by reason of what he deemed the intolerance of his Quaker associates. An ancestor named Rev. Abel Morgan was one of the earlier writers in defense of Baptist doctrines in the colonies, as appears by a volume which was published by Benjamin Franklin in 1747.

He prepared for college at New Hampton, N. H. He studied law in Philadelphia, but desiring to enter the ministry he graduated at Madison University in 1850, and was first settled over the Baptist church in Watertown, N. Y. Four years afterwards he accepted a call to the Pierpont Street Baptist church, Brooklyn, one of the most important churches in the denomination. He labored there ten years with marked success. He then devoted two years to literary pursuits. Afterwards he organized the Trinity Baptist church, corner of Third Avenue and Fifty-second Street.

Of his ancestors above mentioned, John Holme was the first Baptist of Philadelphia. Abel Morgan was from Wales, a talented minister, highly educated. He was the author of the first Welsh concordance ever printed.

Dr. Holme has a large library of choice and rare books, and is an enthusiastic student of history and of sacred learning.

While pastor of Pierpont Street, he adapted the Plymouth collection of hymns for the use of Baptist churches, which had a wide circulation. He also compiled a work entitled "Light at Evening Time," published by the Harpers. It is a collection of rare spiritual gems for the comfort of aged Christians. So great is the demand for it that already eight editions of it have been printed. He has recently organized the River-Side Baptist church, on the corner of Eighty-sixth Street and the Boulevard, in New York, of which he is pastor, and it gives promise of being a strong church.

Holmes, Rev. Obadiah, was born at Preston,

Lancashire, England, about 1606, and came to this country, as is supposed, about 1639. His religious connections were with the Congregationalists. At first, in Salem, Mass., from which he removed to Rehoboth, where for eleven years more he continued in the church of his early choice. He there became a Baptist, and united with the Baptist church in Newport, R. I. In the month of July, 1651, in company with Dr. John Clarke and Mr. Crandall, he made a visit to William Witter, a Baptist, who resided at Lynn, Mass., about twelve miles from Boston. The day after their arrival being the Sabbath, they arranged to have a religious service at the house of their host. In the midst of the discourse which Dr. Clarke was preaching two constables presented to him the following warrant: " By virtue hereof, you are required to go to the house of William Witter, and to search from house to house for certain erroneous persons, being strangers, and them to apprehend, and in safe custody to keep, and to-morrow morning at eight o'clock to bring before me. Robert Bridges." The three " erroneous persons, being strangers," were at once arrested and carried, first to " the ale-house or ordinary," and then forced to attend the meeting of the day. At the close of the meeting they were carried back to the " ordinary." The next morning they were taken before Mr. Bridges, who made out their *mittimus*, and sent them to prison at Boston. Having remained a fortnight there, they were brought before the Court of Assistants for trial, which sentenced Dr. Clarke to pay a fine of twenty pounds, Mr. Holmes thirty pounds, and Mr. Crandall five pounds, and in default of payment they were to be publicly whipped. Unknown to Mr. Clarke some one paid his fine, and Mr. Crandall was released on promise that he would appear at the next court. Mr. Holmes was kept in prison until September, when, his fine not having been paid, he was brought out and publicly whipped. Mr. Holmes says, " As the strokes fell upon me I had such a spiritual manifestation of God's presence as the like thereof I never had nor felt, nor can with fleshly tongue express; and the outward pain was so removed from me that indeed I am not able to declare it to you; it was so easy to me that I could well bear it, yea, and in a manner felt it not, although it was grievous, as the spectators said, the man striking with all his strength (yea, spitting in his hand three times, as many affirmed) with a three-corded whip, giving me therewith thirty strokes."—(Backus, i. 194. Newton.) Such was the charity of New England Congregationalists of that day. Gov. Joseph Jenks has left on record the following: " Mr. Holmes was whipped thirty stripes, and in such an unmerciful manner that in many days, if not some weeks, he could take no rest, but as he lay upon his knees and elbows, not being able to suffer any part of his body to touch the bed whereon he lay."

Mr. Holmes soon after removed to Newport. In 1652 he was ordained to preach the gospel, and took Dr. Clarke's place as pastor of the Baptist church in Newport. He died in 1682. He left eight children, one of whom, Obadiah, was a judge in New Jersey.

Holmes, Rev. O. A., was born in New Woodstock, Madison Co., N. Y., in 1825; joined the Baptist church in his native town when sixteen years of age. He was ordained pastor in La Fayette, O., when twenty-three. Five years after his ordination he came to Iowa, and has labored in the State as pastor for twenty-seven years,—at Maquoketa, Webster City, Marshalltown, and Tama City. While at Webster City, which was entirely a new field, he also organized a church at Boonsborough and one at Iowa Falls, supplying them until they became strong enough to secure pastors. His labors were extended through a wide range of country, and the results were marked and lasting. Mr. Holmes has given to the Baptist cause and to every good work in Iowa many years of efficient service. While faithful in his own field as pastor and preacher, he has contributed largely, by earnest labor, hearty co-operation, and wise counsel, to all the good results which have been accomplished by the Iowa Baptists in their general work.

Holmes, Willet, was born May 14, 1807, in

WILLET HOLMES.

Shelby Co., Ky.; was converted in 1847, baptized by H. L. Graves, and has been a deacon ever since;

was one of the three hundred colonists who, under Moses Austin's grant from Mexico, settled the province of Texas; was twice a member of the Congress of the republic of Texas, twice a magistrate, once a county commissioner, postmaster under the republic, and postmaster under Abraham Lincoln. His time, his talents, and his money have always been freely given to the church, the cause of missions, and as a trustee to Baylor University.

Home Mission Society, The American Baptist, and other Home Missions.—In the early history of the Baptists in this country most of our pastors were home missionaries. It was a common custom for the settled shepherd of one flock to make a tour through several counties in his own colony or State, or through other colonies or States, preaching the gospel almost every night in barns, private houses, school-rooms, or public halls. Months were spent frequently in this apostolic occupation. And many churches were founded and hosts of souls converted by these gratuitous labors of our saintly fathers in the faith. All the original colonies were frequently traversed by this almost extinct order of heaven-blessed home missionaries. Churches and Associations often rendered assistance in this form of home mission service. And nowhere on earth in any period of Christian history has Jesus had nobler missionaries among their countrymen, or grander results, than those furnished by the Baptist pioneers of the maritime provinces of Canada and of the country now called the United States.

In the year 1800 the *Boston Female Society for Missionary Purposes* was formed. It had at first only fourteen members, and of these some were Baptists and some Congregationalists. In its first year it raised $150 for home missions. This is said to have been the first society established in this country of a purely missionary character. It should not be forgotten when we award honors to the benefactors of their race, that *women* formed the first distinctively missionary organization in America.

Two years later the *Massachusetts Domestic Missionary Society* was founded. Among its first officers were Dr. Thomas Baldwin, Dr. Daniel Sharp, and Heman Lincoln. Its field included Massachusetts, Maine, Western and Southern New York, Pennsylvania, Virginia, Missouri, Ohio, and Lower Canada. Among the numerous missionaries of this society were John M. Peck, James E. Welch, and Nathaniel Kendrick.

In 1807 the *Lake Missionary Society* was organized in Pompey, Onondaga Co., N. Y. Its proposed field was the region of country adjacent to the lakes. Ashbel Hosmer was its first president and Elisha Payne its secretary. Among its early missionaries were John Peck and Alfred Bennett,—men whose names are still held in reverence for the divine power that attended their ministrations.

In 1822 the *Baptist Missionary Convention of the State of New York* was formed, and in 1825 the two New York organizations united, and in a few years the society had an income of $17,000, and missionaries in the Middle States, in some of the Western States, and in Canada.

The *American Baptist Home Mission Society* was formed in New York, April 27, 1832. Heman Lincoln was its first president, Jonathan Going its corresponding secretary, William R. Williams its recording secretary, and William Colgate its treasurer. Men mighty with God established one of the greatest agencies to spread the gospel that ever blessed any land. The Home Mission Society in 1880 had 285 missionaries and teachers, and, according to Dr. Morehouse, its secretary, an income of $213,821; and deducting $48,369.70 for loans repaid to the church edifice and trust funds, its remaining receipts from other sources were $165,452.11. Its missionaries during that year baptized 1160 persons, founded 67 churches, and organized 32 Sunday-schools. From its report in 1880 we learn that since its formation the society has commissioned 8301 missionaries and teachers, formed 2704 churches, and through its agents baptized 84,077 disciples. Many of the largest churches in the great cities of the West are the fruits of its wise efforts.

The church edifice fund, now amounting to $255,679, in 1880 was aiding by loans 213 churches in 34 States and Territories. The Home Mission Society in 1880 had eight institutions for the education of colored teachers and ministers. The Richmond Institute, located at Richmond, Va., has 5 instructors, 92 students, 61 of whom are candidates for the ministry, and a property valued in 1871 at $30,000 at least. Wayland Seminary, located at Washington, D. C., has 7 instructors, 92 students, 36 young men preparing for the ministry, and a property worth $40,000. The Benedict Institute, located at Columbia, S. C., has 6 instructors, 150 students, 50 of whom intend to preach the gospel, and a property valued at $43,700, with an endowment of $18,700. The Nashville Institute, of Nashville, Tenn., has 8 instructors, 231 students, 55 of whom are preparing for the ministry, and a property worth $80,000. Shaw University, of Raleigh, N. C., has 15 instructors, 277 students, 59 of whom intend to preach, and a property worth $125,000, with an endowment of $1000. The Atlanta Baptist Seminary, at Atlanta, Ga., has 4 instructors, 100 students, 60 of whom are candidates for the pulpit, and a property worth $12,000. Leland University, at New Orleans, has 5 instructors, 148 students, 41 of whom expect to enter the ministry, and a property worth $85,000, with an endowment of $10,000. The Natchez Seminary, of Natchez, Miss., has a property worth $15,000; 4 instructors and 120 students, 31 of whom, are studying for the ministry. The Home Mission Society in these eight institutions has property worth $430,700, and endowments amounting to $38,700; 54 teachers labor in them, 1572 young men and women pursue their studies in them, of whom 393 are qualifying themselves to preach Jesus. In these colored colleges the society is working gloriously for the salvation and education of our African millions. In the records of organized missionary effort few societies can show such a blessed series of successes and so grand a list of instrumentalities.

But we have other home missionary organizations. The *American Baptist Publication Society* in 1880 had 35 colporteur and 28 Sunday-school missionaries, with an income for all benevolent purposes of $68,321. The *Home Mission Board of the Southern Baptist Convention* had 34 missionaries and an income of $20,624. The *Women's* and the *Women's American Baptist Home Mission Societies* had 21 missionaries. From the "Year-Book," and from direct communications with brethren in various States, after making allowance for the union between the Home Mission Society and State organizations in the West, and for a similar connection between the Home Mission Board of the Southern Baptist Convention and kindred institutions in the South, we learn that the number of men receiving aid from State organizations to assist them in preaching the gospel in the United States is at least 766, and that the income of these State societies is $150,190. Many Baptist Associations and individual churches support additional missionaries.

This would give us a grand total of 1169 missionaries and teachers (missionary teachers in colored seminaries in the South), sustained by national and State organizations at an annual expense of $413,619.

Dr. G. W. Anderson, of Philadelphia, in a carefully prepared pamphlet, states that during the last fifty years (down to 1876), "nearly six millions of dollars had been raised by the Baptists of the United States for home mission work." The five years that have elapsed since would add more than two millions to that amount. For this liberality, and for the thousands of churches that have sprung from it, and from God's blessing upon it, millions of souls will praise Christ throughout all eternity. See articles on SOUTHERN BAPTIST CONVENTION, AMERICAN BAPTIST PUBLICATION SOCIETY, and the various State Conventions and General Associations.

Home Mission Societies, The Women's.— The organization and success of the Women's Baptist Missionary Societies for heathen lands drew the attention of Baptist ladies to the advantages to be secured by a similar agency for the necessities of the home field. The appeals of the devoted Miss J. P. Moore, in New Orleans, for help in prosecuting her mission among the colored people, and similar calls from other sections, together with the very able advocacy of the evangelization of the heathen Indians by Major G. W. Ingalls, led to the formation of the "Women's Baptist Home Mission Society," which took place Feb. 1, 1877. Subsequently the Women's American Baptist Home Mission Society was organized in Boston.

At first the Chicago Society adopted a constitution which placed it in close relations with the great Home Mission Society of the Northern Baptists, but six months later the constitution was changed and the institution became independent, with the avowed purpose of being a vigorous ally to the old society in its vast field, and of carrying on, according to its ability, the general home mission work.

The distinctive aim of the society is to perform women's work, through its missionaries, for women and children in the degraded homes of our country, especially among the colored people, the Indians, and the teeming foreign population of the West. "The (missionary) women visit from house to house, reading the Bible and familiarly teaching its truths to all who will listen." "They organize Sunday-schools, training the teachers for their work in teachers' meetings and Bible readings." They give lessons in cleanliness, industry, temperance, and purity.

At a meeting held in New York, Jan. 14, 1880, to secure union in labors between the Chicago and the Boston societies, it was

"*Resolved*, That the two societies should retain their separate existence; that the society located at Boston shall have New England for its territory, and that each society shall prosecute the work embraced in its constitution; that the missionaries appointed by the society located at Boston shall be commissioned by the society at Chicago and their salaries paid through its treasury; and that all missionary supplies shall be reported to the society at Chicago."

It was also resolved among other things that "Each society shall hold its own annual meeting, and that a yearly anniversary of the two societies shall be held at such time and place as may be agreed upon by their respective boards." These arrangements have been fully carried out, and harmony and success have marked the combined efforts of the two societies.

The Woman's Baptist Home Mission Society of Michigan and the Woman's State Board of Minnesota are earnestly toiling in the same glorious service.

The first home missionary society in the United

States was formed in Boston in 1800 by ladies, and it is a proper cause for thanksgiving that they have resumed the work once more, determined not to relinquish it while there is an unconverted woman or child within the broad limits of our mighty republic.

The receipts of the societies at Boston and Chicago in 1880 were $9098.66 in cash, and $2601.81 in goods and donations to missionaries and pastors on the frontier.

Twenty-one missionaries have labored under the auspices of the two societies during 1880.

Hooper, Wm., D.D., LL.D., was the ripest scholar North Carolina has yet produced. He was

WM. HOOPER, D.D., LL.D.

a grandson of Wm. Hooper who signed the Declaration of Independence for North Carolina, and was born near Wilmington in 1792; graduated at Chapel Hill about 1812, read theology at Princeton, N. J., and was elected Professor of Ancient Languages at the University of North Carolina at Chapel Hill in 1816. In 1818 he entered the ministry of the Episcopal Church, and was for two years rector of St. John's church in Fayetteville, when, because of a change of views on baptism, he resigned his position as pastor, and again became connected with the university as Professor of Rhetoric. In 1829 he was transferred to his old chair of Ancient Languages. He was baptized in 1831 by Rev. P. W. Dowd into the fellowship of Mount Carmel church, Orange Co. In 1838 he removed to South Carolina, and taught theology for two years in Furman Institute, when he became for six years Professor of Ancient Languages in South Carolina College, at Columbia, but was recalled to North Carolina to become the president of Wake Forest College in 1846. The financial embarrassments of the college discouraged him, and he did not remain in this position long. In 1852 he settled as pastor in Newbern; in 1855 became president of Chowan Female Institute; retired from this position in 1862; he taught school in Fayetteville for several years, and in 1867 became co-principal with his son-in-law, Prof. De B. Hooper, at Wilson, N. C.

A very important event in the history of Dr. Hooper was the killing of a young lady, his cousin, by the accidental discharge of a neglected gun, while playing with the children in his uncle's family. His whole life seemed from this circumstance to have been tinged with melancholy. The year before he died he addressed a letter to Prof. Hooper, while living in the same house with him, expressing the sadness that still weighed down his spirits as he looked into the years that were passed. He died at Chapel Hill, where so much of his life had been spent, Aug. 19, 1876, and if he had lived eleven days more would have been eighty-four. His remains were fittingly laid by the side of Dr. Joseph Caldwell, the founder of the college, in the campus of the State University at Chapel Hill.

It may well be questioned whether any man has lived in the South, or for that matter in America, who wrote better English than Dr. Hooper, and it is greatly to be regretted he died without issuing from the press a few volumes of his sermons or some other work by which future generations might have been certified of the lowly piety, exquisite taste, sparkling wit, and rich stores of learning of this great and good man.

Hooten, Rev. Enoch M., was born in Henry Co., Ga., June 30, 1837. At the age of fourteen he joined the Presbyterians, but in 1865 changed his religious views and united with the Baptists. On the 7th of November, 1866, he was ordained, and since then has served various Baptist churches in Middle Georgia, baptizing about 40 persons each year. For some years he taught school, and for several sessions was clerk of the Flint River Association. Mr. Hooten is a good pastor, a very clear and forcible preacher, and a graceful speaker. He enjoys the full confidence and esteem of all who know him.

Hopkins, Rev. Charles J., was the child of Quaker parents. He was born in Philadelphia, Pa., April 2, 1800. Converted in early life, he was baptized by Rev. Dr. Holcombe, and received into the First church, Philadelphia, in October, 1818. He was ordained at the First church, Camden, N. J., in 1824. From May, 1829, to April, 1835, he was pastor of the church at Salem, N. J. Then for five years he served the church at Bridgeton.

In the fall of 1843 he took the pastorate of Bethesda church, New York City. In October, 1859, he became pastor of the Salem church, which was his last charge. He died in Salem, July 14, 1863. Mr. Hopkins was a good, faithful, earnest minister of the gospel. His beaming countenance, ready wit, musical voice, and enthusiastic manner attracted attention. He was an ardent temperance man, and was in great demand as a speaker upon that subject.

Hopper, A. M., D.D., was born at Long Branch, N. J., Jan. 12, 1822; received his university education at Madison; ordained pastor of Academy Street church, New Haven, Conn., in the autumn of 1850; took charge of the First church of Charlestown, Mass., in 1855. He was also pastor in Auburn, N. Y., in Bridgeport, Conn., and in Scranton, Pa. In 1870 Madison University conferred upon him the degree of Doctor of Divinity. In 1872, Dr. Hopper had baptized more than 500 candidates. He is a genial, godly, and able minister of the Saviour.

Hopps, Herman K., one of the most interesting and promising of the early graduates from the University of Chicago, was drowned at Newport Beach, R. I., Aug. 1, 1873, while bathing. He was converted while a boy, and during his student course was remarkable not only for scholarly diligence and success, but also for his genial Christian spirit. He graduated in the class of 1870, and immediately entered the Rochester Theological Seminary. Spending a little time, however, with the church in Batavia, Ill., his preaching awakened so much interest that he found it his duty to remain for a year, in which time 70 were added to the church. He then entered the middle class at Newton. At the time of his death he was preaching for the church at Lynn, Mass., where a promising work was already in progress. His remains were taken to Lamoille, Ill., where his home had been, and where his parents still reside.

Hornady, Rev. Henry Carr, of Atlanta, Ga., is one of the most distinguished and influential ministers of the State. Born Feb. 22, 1822, in Jones County, he has spent all his life and exerted all his energies within his native State. He enjoyed excellent academical advantages and availed himself of them fully, until his twentieth year. Converted in 1843 and ordained in 1848, he became pastor of the Americus church, where he remained eight years. Since that time he has occupied various responsible positions in the denomination, as agent for Mercer University, editor of the *Cherokee Baptist*, and the pastor of various churches. He is now pastor of the Third Baptist church, in Atlanta. He is a Baptist in the strictest sense of the term, and consequently is a devoted Christian; he is a good pastor, and an earnest, tender, pathetic, and faithful preacher.

Hornberger, Rev. Lewis P., was born in the city of Philadelphia, Pa., Oct. 25, 1841. He was converted at the age of fifteen, and baptized one year after into the fellowship of the Olivet Baptist

REV. LEWIS P. HORNBERGER.

church, Philadelphia, by Rev. N. B. Baldwin, Oct. 4, 1857. On the 14th of October, 1858, he entered Madison University as a student for the gospel ministry, and graduated Aug. 2, 1865. On the 1st of July preceding he accepted the unanimous call of the Spring Garden Baptist church, Philadelphia. He entered upon the duties of his first charge Aug. 20, 1865.

The church had been for some time without a pastor. It had a membership of 279 and a debt of $7000. The young pastor entered with ardent zeal and vigorous faith upon his work. The church rallied nobly under the new leadership, and soon gave evidence of rapid and vigorous growth.

Mr. Hornberger remained with the Spring Garden church six years and nine months. During this period it was blessed with uninterrupted harmony and prosperity. The house was thoroughly repaired, the debt was paid, and 629 persons added to the membership, 415 of whom were baptized, 190 came by letter, 16 by experience, and 8 by restoration. Mr. Hornberger had a very pleasant trip to Europe during the summer of 1870. The membership and congregation having increased beyond the capacity of the house of worship, and the dimensions of the lot rendering an enlargement of it impossible, the project of a removal was seriously considered, but was afterwards dismissed as impracticable. Mr. Hornberger was finally induced, at the solicitation of many members of his church, as well as of a number of influential members of other churches, to undertake the establishment of a new church in the northwestern part of the city. Accordingly, in the early part of the year 1872, he retired from the pastorate of the Spring Garden church, and, with a constituency of 257 persons, 186 of whom were dismissed from the Spring Garden church for the purpose, he organized, March 28, 1872, the Gethsemane Baptist church. A lot was immediately secured at the northwest corner of Eighteenth and Columbia Avenue, and the work of building begun. It progressed rapidly, and the house was completed and dedicated April 30, 1874. The entire cost of the house and lot, with the furniture, was $100,000. The edifice is of brown-stone, substantially built, and handsomely furnished. It has a lecture-room which will comfortably seat 400 persons, and an audience-room seating about 1000. At the present date, 1880, the membership is 652, and the usual congregations are among the largest in the city. The Bible-school numbers 988, with an average attendance of 700.

As a preacher, Mr. Hornberger is eminently earnest and practical, sound in doctrine, clear in his statements of gospel truths, and uncompromising in their advocacy. He is a fluent, ready, and graceful speaker, equally good in extemporizing or reading.

As a pastor, he has unusual influence and power. Easily accessible and courteous, he is loved and respected by his people. He possesses a warm and sympathizing heart, and is ever a most welcome visitor in the homes of the sick and the sorrowing. His guiding hand is manifest in all the important movements of the church, and the almost unexampled success that has marked his career as a pastor is perhaps owing to a happy combination of qualities, shared in part by all, but not often so symmetrically united in one.

His church edifice is out of debt. Mr. Hornberger is one of the most useful ministers that ever labored in Philadelphia, and his talents and piety deserve the rich harvests he has garnered.

Horner, Rev. T. J., was born in Orange Co., N. C., Nov. 23, 1823; was baptized by Rev. Joseph King in 1855; was educated at the famous Bingham Academy, of Hillsborough; ordained at Mount Zion church, Granville Co., Rev. Joseph King and his son, Rev. Thomas King, forming the Presbytery, and has been pastor of this church for eighteen years. Mr. Horner has served other churches in Granville and Person Counties, and has taught for thirty-five years. He is now the senior principal of a flourishing academy at Henderson, N. C.

Horton, Hon. Albert C., was born about 1800, in Georgia; removed to Green Co., Ala.; engaged in farming and became wealthy; served in the Senate of Alabama; removing to Texas in 1835; commanded a company of cavalry, the advance-guard of Col. Fannin, whose force was savagely massacred at Goliad; narrowly escaping the same fate, his command being cut off from the main force. He was a member of the first Congress of the republic, with Houston, Rusk, Grimes, and Lester. He was a member of the convention which formed the constitution of Texas as a State, and was elected the first lieutenant-governor, and during the absence of Gov. J. Pinckney Henderson, who commanded the Texas troops during the war between the United States and Mexico, in 1846, he filled the chair of governor for several months with signal honor. The latter part of his life was spent in managing his large estate in Wharton and Matagorda Counties, dispensing a liberal hospitality to all classes, taking a deep interest in the religious welfare of his numerous slaves. Joining the Baptist church in his early days, he was to the end of his life a consistent, zealous, liberal, and active Christian. As a member of the body that formed the Texas Baptist State Convention, and as a trustee of Baylor University, his counsels and services will live as a heritage of blessings to education, and to the denomination of which he was so honored a member. He died in 1865.

Hoskinson, Thomas J., was born at Waynesburg, Greene Co., Pa., May 14, 1821; was baptized in 1855, by Rev. Thomas R. Taylor, into the fellowship of the Sandusky Street church, Alle-

THOMAS J. HOSKINSON.

ghany City, Pa. In 1871 he removed to Philadelphia, where he still remains an esteemed member of the Memorial church.

In early life he engaged in mercantile pursuits, and subsequently associated himself with others in the manufacture of iron. His enterprise and integrity enabled him to prosper abundantly, and others reaped the advantage of his benefactions. He has been long and prominently identified with the educational and missionary work of the denomination, and is widely known as a wise counselor and careful manager. As a trustee of the university at Lewisburg, and president of the Pennsylvania Baptist Education Society, he has especially aimed to advance and exalt the education of young men for the gospel ministry. Mr. Hoskinson is one of the leading Baptists of Pennsylvania; and he is known and honored by his brethren throughout the State.

Hotchkiss, V. R., D.D., was born June 5, 1815, in Spafford, Onondaga Co., N. Y.; was educated in Madison University; has been pastor in Poultney, Vt., in Rochester, N. Y., in Fall River, Mass., in Buffalo, N. Y., from 1849 to 1854, and from 1865 to the present time, 1880. He was a professor in Rochester Theological Seminary from 1854 to 1865. Dr. Hotchkiss is one of the strongest men in our denomination in the Empire State. Madison gave him his doctorate of divinity.

Hough, Rev. Silas, M.D., was born in Bucks Co., Pa., Feb. 8, 1766. He was thirty years of age before he exercised saving faith in the blessed Redeemer. He was baptized into the fellowship of the Montgomery church, in his native county, May 8, 1796. Dr. Hough was possessed of more than ordinary gifts for the ministry, and in June, 1804, he was ordained as pastor of the Montgomery church, which he served till December, 1821; eighteen months after his resignation, his spirit entered the heavenly rest.

Dr. Hough left $1000 to the Philadelphia Association, the interest of which is to be appropriated forever to the support of the widows of Baptist ministers. He was the first man to start this fund. Dr. Hough had a strong faith, an undying zeal, and a blameless life.

Hougham, John S., LL.D., a native of Indiana, graduated in Wabash College in 1846. In July, 1848, he was elected Professor of Mathematics and Natural Philosophy in Franklin College. He was after a short time transferred to the chair of Chemistry and Related Sciences. He built up an excellent laboratory, and, in addition to his teaching, established and superintended the manufacture of chemical and philosophical apparatus. He was also of great service to the institution by the aid he gave in its financial management. He is acknowledged to be a man of great practical ability. He made some original investigations in respect to the influence of mercury upon the body. He resigned in 1862, and several months later accepted a professorship in the Kansas Agricultural College. He accepted a professorship in the Indiana Agricultural College, and was appointed to superintend the laying out of the grounds and the structure of the buildings. He served the institution several years, and finally resigned to care for his real estate in the West. His home is in La Fayette.

House, Rev. Horace Lee, one of the youngest pastors in the State, a native of Otselic, N. Y., where he was born in 1850, was graduated from Cornell University, New York, in 1874, and from the Theological Seminary in 1877; ordained June 27, 1877. Mr. House's first pastorate was with the Fifth Avenue Baptist church in Minneapolis, Minn., from June 1, 1877, to Feb. 1, 1880, at which time he was called to the pastorate of the Baptist church in Racine, where he now resides. He has a fine field of labor and one of the best churches in Wisconsin.

Houston, Mrs. Margaret Moffette, daughter of Temple and Nancy Lea, was born in Perry Co., Ala., April 11, 1819. She belonged to a family of marked individuality. Her brother, Hon. H. C. Lea, was a distinguished member of the Alabama State senate. Her education was mainly received from Prof. J. A. McLain, a well-educated Scotch Baptist. She possessed poetical talent, which she occasionally exhibited by contributing articles for the journals of the day, and her conversational powers rendered her society attractive. Her views of Christian truth and duty were in full accord with the gospel. She was married to Gen. Sam Houston, in April, 1840. During the ministry of Rev. Peter Crawford at Marion she was converted and baptized. She was always ready to contribute of her means to the promotion of the cause of Christ. Eight children survive her,—Sam Houston, Jr., Mrs. Nannie Morrow, Mrs. Mary Morrow, Mrs. Maggie Williams, Mrs. Antoinette P. Bringhurst, Andrew Jackson Houston, William Rogers Houston, and Temple Houston. She died at Independence, Texas, Dec. 3, 1869. The following lines indicate both her Christian spirit and poetical gift:

A MOTHER'S PRAYER.

WRITTEN WHILE UNCERTAIN AS TO THE FATE OF HER SON, LIEUT. SAM HOUSTON.

O Thou! 'neath whose omniscient eye
 The footsteps of the wanderer roam
Far from his own loved native sky,
 Far from the sacred ties of home.
A captive on some hostile shore,
 Perchance his young heart pineth now
To join the household band once more,
 That 'round the evening altar bow;
Or, 'mid the cannon's roar again
 And gleam of clashing steel, perchance

Upon the bloody battle-plain
  Hath met the deadly foeman's lance.
I cannot tell: my dim eye now
  His wanderings may not trace;
But, oh! 'tis sweet to feel and know,
  Through every scene, in every place,
Thy glorious eye doth follow him.
  On toilsome march, 'mid prison gloom,
On Southern soil, through Northern clime,
  Or 'mid the cannon's dismal boom,
His life is safe beneath thy sight,
  As though a mother's love could soothe
And for the weary head each night
  With tender hand his pillow smooth.

Houston, Gov. Sam, was born near Lexington, Rockbridge Co., Va.; with his mother, six brothers, and three sisters he removed to Blount Co., Tenn., when about twelve years old; spent some time before his sixteenth year among the Cherokee Indians; entered the United States army in his nineteenth year; was under Gen. Andrew Jackson at the battle of Tohopeka, against the Creek Indians, serving as ensign, fighting heroically, and receiving two wounds from rifle-balls and one from a barbed arrow, from whose effects he never wholly recovered; was appointed a lieutenant, and stationed a while at Nashville and New Orleans; resigned when about twenty years of age; studied law at Nashville, Tenn., for about six months, under Hon. James Trimble; was licensed to practise, and in less than twelve months afterwards was elected district attorney of the Davidson circuit; settled first at Lebanon, and served as district attorney one year at Nashville; resigned, and devoted himself to the practice of law, until 1823, when hardly thirty years of age, he was elected to Congress without opposition, and also, in 1825, almost by acclamation, and in 1827 was chosen governor by 12,000 majority resigned Jan. 1, 1829, three months after his first marriage, leaving his wife, because she declared that neither at that time nor at their marriage did he have her heart; went among the Cherokees, and remained three years, with varying incidents of great political moment, then removed to Texas; aided in forming its first constitution, April, 1833; engaged in vigorous efforts for the liberation of Texas, until as commander of the Texan army, at the battle of San Jacinto, April 21, 1836, he succeeded in securing the freedom of the republic. At the battle of San Jacinto he received another wound. President of the republic from 1836–38; member of the Texan Congress from 1839–41; President of the republic from January, 1841, to January, 1845; Senator from Texas, in the United States Senate, from 1845–57; governor of Texas from January, 1859, to March, 1861; died July, 1863, at Huntsville, Walker Co. Married to Miss Maggie Lea, April, 1840; lived scrupulously devoted to morality, and his wife's views of religious truth, until he was converted. The influence of his wife over his later life was ever cheerfully and gratefully acknowledged by him. Was baptized at Independence, Texas, November, 1855, by Rev. Rufus C. Burleson, D.D.; regularly attended upon Dr. Geo. W. Samson's ministrations during the whole of his senatorial career at Washington. He took an active share in prayer-meetings, at Associations and Conventions when present, and delivered numerous lectures during the latter part of his life in aid of temperance. As a soldier, lawyer, general, President, Senator, governor, orator, Christian, he was one of the remarkable men of the nineteenth century.

Hovey, Alvah, D.D., LL.D., was born in Greene, Chenango Co., N. Y., March 5, 1820. In the autumn of that year his parents returned to their native place, Thetford, Vt., where his childhood and youth were passed, the summers mostly on a farm and the winters in a district school. He prepared for college in Brandon, Vt., and was graduated from Dartmouth College in 1844. He had been already principal of an academy in Derby, Vt., two years, and was principal of the academy at New London, N. H., one year. He studied at the Newton Theological Institution three years, and after graduating preached one year in New Gloucester, Me. Returning to Newton in the autumn of 1849, he has been engaged as a teacher in the institution from that time to the present (with the exception of ten months spent in Europe). From 1849 to 1855 he was tutor in Hebrew; from 1853 to 1855, Professor of Church History; from 1855 to the present time, Professor of Theology and Christian Ethics; and for the last twelve years president of the institution. Dr. Hovey has contributed a large amount of matter to the *Christian Review*, the *Baptist Quarterly*, the *Bibliotheca Sacra*, the

ALVAH HOVEY, D.D., LL.D.

Examiner and Chronicle, the *Watchman*, the *Standard*, and other papers. He is the author of the following books: "A Memoir of the Life and Times of Rev. Isaac Backus, A.M.," 1859; "The State of the Impenitent Dead," 1859; "The Miracles of Christ as attested by the Evangelists," 1864; "The Scriptural Law of Divorce," 1866; "God with us; or the Person and State of Christ," 1872; "Religion and the State," 1876; "The Doctrine of the Higher Christian Life, compared with the Scriptures," 1877; "Manual of Theology," 1878. Dr. Hovey has published several unbound discussions, as "Close Communion," "State of Men after Death," "Semi-centennial Discourse at Newton," etc. Brown University conferred on him the degree of D.D., and Richmond College and Denison University that of LL.D. He has been a member of the Executive Committee of the American Baptist Missionary Union for many years.

Howard, Rev. Amasa, son of Amasa Howard, was born in Woodstock, Conn., Sept. 9, 1832; converted in his twelfth year, at Slatersville, R. I.: baptized in North Uxbridge, Mass., in May, 1845: began to study with his brother, Rev. Johnson Howard, pastor of Baptist church in Dover, N. Y.; was at the academy at New Ipswich, N. H., and at Worcester Academy, Mass.; colporteur of American and Foreign Bible Society; connected with academy at Shelburne Falls for two years; entered Madison University; spent two years with a mission church in South Boston, Mass.; became city missionary in Hartford, Conn., in 1857, and labored eight years; ordained in 1861; in 1865 settled with Wethersfield church; in 1867 with Third Baptist church, Providence, R. I.; in 1870 returned to Hartford, Conn., and became pastor of the newly formed Washington Avenue church; resigned in 1877; supplied Bloomfield and other churches till health failed; in June, 1879, was chosen chaplain of Connecticut State Prison, where he is now laboring.

Howard College, located at Marion, is the Baptist male college of Alabama. It was founded in 1843. Prof. S. S. Sherman, Rev. H. Talbird, D.D., Rev. J. L. M. Curry, LL.D., Rev. S. R. Freeman, D.D., and Prof. J. T. Murfee, LL.D., have been presidents of this institution. Its buildings and grounds are estimated to be worth $150,000. And before the war its endowment was valued at as much more, which, however, was lost in that unhappy struggle. It belongs to the State Convention of Alabama, and that body appoints its trustees and devotes a great deal of attention to its welfare. It has a deep hold on the confidence and affection of the denomination in the State, as is seen in the fact that after its buildings had been twice destroyed by fire they were promptly rebuilt, with improvements, by the Baptists of the State; and in the further fact that although without an endowment, it is successfully competing with richly-endowed colleges in and out of the State. Dr. Murfee, the present president, who has occupied that position for eight years, has, with his able corps of professors, established for Howard College the reputation of imparting a thoroughness of scholarship and of manly deportment unsurpassed in the whole country. Besides, the moral tone and religious surroundings of the institution are of the first order. Every effort is made to develop the nobler traits of human character, and to bestow the best education that can be had. The graduates of Howard College are taking some of the highest stations in all the learned callings.

Howard, Hon. James L., son of Rev. Leland Howard, was born in Windsor, Vt., Jan. 18, 1818; settled in Hartford, Conn., in October, 1838; an extensive and successful merchant and manufacturer; well and widely known for ability, integrity, good judgment, and courtesy; largely trusted with public interests; to his fine taste Bushnell Park, Hartford, owes much of its attractiveness; baptized into the fellowship of the First Baptist church, Jan. 7, 1841; chosen deacon Sept. 4, 1857; active in this church and prominent in the denomination; president of Connecticut Baptist State Convention from 1871 to 1877; president of Connecticut Baptist Social Union from its origin in 1872, as he was its chief originator; president of American Baptist Publication Society from 1873 to 1878; for many years an efficient trustee of Connecticut Literary Institution; generous contributor to benevolent operations.

Howard, John, the Philanthropist, was born at Enfield, England, Sept. 2, 1726. His education

JOHN HOWARD.

was respectable. In his early manhood he traveled extensively in France and Italy, purchasing works of art, and inspecting the ruins of the glorious past and the creations of modern genius. In his travels he learned to speak the French language with great accuracy, which was of signal service to him in future life. Some time after his return from the Continent he became so ill that he was convinced that the attentions of his nurse alone saved his life, and as the only adequate expression of his gratitude he married her when she was fifty-three and he was twenty-five. She lived but a short time to enjoy her new position and the wealth of love in her husband's noble heart. On the 2d of May, 1758, he married Henrietta Leeds, with whom he spent nine happy years at Cardington. During this period his active mind found constant occupation in building school-houses and model cottages for the poor of the town, and in many other labors for the education and improvement of the neglected villagers. He was appointed sheriff in 1773. To accept this required him to produce a certificate stating that he had taken the Lord's Supper in an Episcopal church within a reasonable time. How- ard was a Dissenter, and he abhorred such contemptible methods of sustaining the interests of a church; neither would he decline the office and pay a fine as his father had done. He accepted the position, determined to contest to the uttermost any suit brought against him for breaking the law. No one prosecuted the good man. After the assizes were over he descended into the prison to see the condition of its inmates. It was the home of John Bunyan for twelve years, in which he wrote his immortal "Pilgrim's Progress." Everything in it was shocking, and appealed to his whole humanity to remove the horrid evils that reigned all over the place. From that moment he seems to have consecrated himself to fight prison abuses and the powers of the plague throughout the world. How he traveled, how he suffered, how he labored with kings, emperors, empresses, parliaments, and governors of jails; how he gave his money to relieve oppressed prisoners and victims of the plague; and how he risked his life times without number, it is not possible to tell in an article like this. It is sufficient to say that the name of Howard stands high above every other philanthropist to which our race has given birth. The Howard Associations of our country and of other lands show the extent and duration of his fame. He died at Kherson, in the Crimea, of camp fever, contracted in his warfare against that scourge, on the 20th of January, 1790. Mr. Howard's efforts have been followed by marvelous improvements in prison-life, and by a multitude of benevolent societies to aid the victims of the pestilence.

He was a member of the Baptist community of which Dr. Samuel Stennett was pastor, in London. On the 1st of March, 1790, Dr. Stennett preached a funeral sermon for his lamented friend. In that discourse, in describing Mr. Howard's faith, he says, "Nor was he ashamed of those truths he heard stated, explained, and enforced in this place. He had made up his mind, as he said, upon his religious sentiments, and was not to be moved from his steadfastness by novel opinions intruded upon the world. Nor did he content himself with a bare profession of these divine truths. He entered into the spirit of the gospel, felt its power and tasted its sweetness. You know, my friends, with what seriousness and devotion he attended, for a long course of years, on the worship of God among us. It would be scarcely decent for me to repeat the affectionate things he says, in a letter written me from a remote part of the world, respecting the satisfaction and pleasure he had felt in the religious exercises of this place."[*] The historian Ivimey gives the letter entire. It was written from Smyrna, on the 11th of August, 1786. In it he says, "The

---

[*] Works of Samuel Stennett, D.D., iii. 295. London, 1824.

principal* reason of my writing is most sincerely to thank you for the many pleasant hours I have had in reviewing the notes I have taken of the sermons I had the happiness to hear under your ministry; these, sir, with many of your petitions in prayer, have been, and are, my songs in the house of my pilgrimage. With undoubted pleasure I have attended your ministry; no man ever entered more into my religious sentiments, or more happily expressed them. It was some little disappointment when any one occupied your pulpit. Oh, sir, how many Sabbaths have I ardently longed to spend in Little Wild Street (Dr. Stennett's) : on those days I generally rest, or, if at sea, keep retired in my little cabin. It is you that preach, and I bless God I attend with renewed pleasure. I bless God for your ministry; I pray God to reward you a thousandfold.''

Mr. Howard had been a Congregationalist, but from "the many years" during which he had worshiped with Dr. Stennett, and the declaration that "no man ever entered more into his religious sentiments, or more happily expressed them," it is certain that John Howard was a Baptist.

Howard, Rev. Leland, was born in Jamaica, Vt., Oct. 13, 1793. During a revival in Shaftsbury he was hopefully converted, and baptized when about seventeen years of age, by Rev. Isaiah Madison. At an early age he commenced to preach. In 1814, having been invited by Gen. Abner Forbes, a wealthy citizen of Windsor, Vt., to come to that place to pursue his studies, he accepted the invitation. He was placed under the instruction of Rev. Joseph Bradley, pastor of the Baptist church, his board and tuition bills being paid by his kind friend. He completed his theological studies with Rev. J. M. Winchell, of Boston, and was ordained pastor of the church in Windsor, Vt., in November, 1817. In 1823 he became pastor of the First Baptist church in Troy, N. Y., where he remained five years. For a time he was again with his old church in Windsor, and then in Brooklyn, N. Y. He preached in Meriden, Conn., in the year 1837–38. Subsequently he was pastor in Newport, R. I., Norwich, N. Y., North church in Troy, then at Hartford, N. Y., and finally in Rutland, Vt., where his pastorate closed in 1852. He died May 6, 1870. Few men have left a better record in the places where he labored as a minister of the gospel than "Father" Howard. One of his sons is Hon. James L. Howard, of Hartford, Conn., president of the American Baptist Publication Society.

Howard, Rev. Mark William, was ordained at Ukiah, Cal., in 1859, and has been pastor of the Ukiah and other churches in that part of the State ever since. He was born in 1818, converted at nine, and joined his mother's church, the Methodist. In 1838 he removed to Fort Smith, Ark., three years after to Southwest Missouri. In 1844, having previously become a Baptist by studying the Bible, he was immersed and joined a Baptist church. In 1856 he removed to California, spent one year in San Joaquin County, one year in Sonoma County, and joined the Healdsburg church. In 1858 he settled near Ukiah, where he was soon after ordained. God has blessed him both in his business and in his labors in the pulpit, and given him great influence as a citizen and as a Christian pastor.

Howard, Wm., D.D., was born in Manchester, England, Dec. 17, 1828. In early life he ran away from home. For several years he was occupied as a cabin-boy in a sailing-vessel. While thus engaged he made the acquaintance of Rev. A. P. Repiton, D.D., at Wilmington, N. C. This good brother took him to his home and adopted him as a son. Through his instrumentality he was converted, and baptized in 1847. He early indicated strong powers of native intellect. Cherishing high desires for thorough education, he entered Howard College, Ala., in 1849, and graduated in 1852, receiving the degree of A.M. in 1854. In January, 1855, he became pastor of the Gainesville church, Ala., in the charge of which he continued until the close of 1866, when he assumed the pastorate of the First Baptist church in Galveston, Texas. At different times, while living in Alabama, he served as pastor at Providence and Sumterville churches, Ala., and Macon and Enterprise churches, Miss., preaching to them once a month. During the war he acted as a chaplain and general missionary in the Confederate army. For several years he was moderator of the Bigby River Association, Ala., and was for some months general agent in Texas of the Home Mission Board of the Southern Baptist Convention. He has represented Alabama and Texas in the Southern Convention, and in May, 1876, at Buffalo, N. Y., represented the same Convention in the general Baptist anniversaries. For several years he has been president of the Texas Baptist Sunday-School Convention. Baylor University conferred on him the degree of D.D. in 1870. He is a student, possessing a library rich in the variety, rarity, and number of its volumes. He is ranked by no minister of the "Island City." His commencement sermons at Baylor University and other educational centres have given him a prominent place among Southern ministers. He holds a warm place among the Galveston people.

Howe, Rev. Phineas, was born in Fitzwilliam, N. H., in 1792; was converted at the age of twenty-eight; licensed by the church in Fitzwilliam; studied with Rev. J. M. Graves, and was ordained

---

* Ivimey's "History of the English Baptists," iv. 361. London, 1830.

in 1824 to the pastorate of the Marlborough and Newfane, Vt., church, where he remained for seven years. After brief pastorates in one or two other places, he returned, in 1834, to the church which he had first served, where he continued his labors for another term of seven years. Broken down in his health, he suspended his ministerial labors for a season. His last settlements were in Hinsdale and Troy, N. H. He returned to spend the close of his life among his old friends, and died at Newfane, Vt., Jan. 17, 1869. During the nearly twenty-five years of his active ministry he baptized 308 persons, and was otherwise very useful.

Howe, Rev. Samuel, was pastor of the church meeting in Deadman's Place, London, for about seven years. Neal says that "he was a man of learning, and printed a small treatise called 'The Sufficiency of the Spirit's Teaching'" (vol. ii. 316, Dublin, 1755). Others speak of him as a cobbler, and, consequently, an illiterate person. He might have carried on the shoe business, because he could not support himself by preaching to a small persecuted Baptist church, and yet not be an ignorant man. Neither does the fact that his book seems to disparage learning prove that he was destitute of it. Many in his day represented learning as the CHIEF qualification for the ministry. Baptists never have entertained this opinion, though they regard learning in their pastors as of immense importance, and have given more money, perhaps, than any other denomination, with their numbers and resources, in this country to erect and endow institutions for the education of their ministry.

Mr. Howe attracted the attention of the persecuting clergy and their instruments, by whom he was imprisoned and excommunicated. Dying in jail, he was refused burial in consecrated ground; a constable's guard protected the parish cemetery at Shoreditch from profanation by the reception of his body. He was buried at Agnes-la-Clair; and several members of his church, at their own request, were buried afterwards with him.

Mr. Howe's people, after his death, according to Dr. Thomas Fuller, on Jan. 18, 1641, to the number of 80 meeting at St. Saviour's, Southwark, "preached," among other things, "*that the king was only to be obeyed in civil matters*." Crosby states that they were arrested while at their place of worship and committed to the Clink prison, and that the next morning six or seven of the men were taken to the House of Lords and strictly examined about their principles. They freely admitted that "they owned no other head of the church but Jesus Christ, *that no prince had power to make laws to bind the consciences* of men, and that laws made contrary to the law of God were of no force." Crosby states that this church was of the independent order. Fuller says they were Anabaptists; Crosby's and Mr. Howe's contemporaries represent him as a Baptist. The principles his people avow are emphatically the doctrines of the Baptists. They may have been Independents, who added believer's immersion to their Congregationalism. Mr. Howe was bitterly persecuted and deeply lamented. His reputation as a manly, talented, and learned Non-conformist was so favorably and widely known, that Crosby tells us "he was very famous for his vindication of the doctrines of separation."

Roger Williams, in "The Hireling Ministry," etc., says, "Among so many instances, dead and living, to the everlasting praise of Christ Jesus and of His Holy Spirit, breathing and blessing where He listeth, I cannot but with honorable testimony remember that eminently Christian witness and prophet of Christ, even that despised and yet beloved Samuel Howe, who, being by calling a cobbler and without human learning (probably he meant a university education, which Dr. Carey never had), which yet in its sphere and place he honored, who yet, I say, by searching the Holy Scriptures, grew so excellent a textuary, or Scripture-learned man, that few of those high rabbies that scorn to mend or make a shoe, could aptly or readily from the Holy Scriptures outgo him. And, however, through the oppressions upon some men's consciences, even in life and death, and after death, in respect of burying, as yet unthought and unremedied, I say, however, he was forced to seek a grave or bed in the highway, yet was his life and death and burial (being attended by many hundreds of God's people) honorable and (how much more on his rising again!) glorious."

It is probable that Roger Williams learned "soul liberty" from Samuel Howe, whose church believed that "the king was only to be obeyed in civil matters;" that "no prince had power to make laws to bind the consciences of men."

Howell, Judge David, was born in New Jersey in 1747, and graduated at Princeton in 1766. By the advice of President Manning he came to Rhode Island, and was his associate in the new Rhode Island College, just commencing operations in Warren. He was appointed Professor of Mathematics and Natural Philosophy in 1769, and continued to give instruction in his department until college exercises were suspended in consequence of the breaking up of the college in the Revolutionary war. He was Professor of Law in the university for over thirty years, and a Fellow for fifty-two years. For many years he ranked among the first lawyers of Providence, was a member of the Congress of Confederation, and in 1812 was appointed U. S. judge for the district of Rhode Island, holding the office until the time of his death, in 1824.

Prof. Goddard, in a sketch of Judge Howell, remarks, "He was endowed with extraordinary talents, and he superadded to his endowments extensive and accurate learning. Upon all occasions which made any demands upon him, he gave the most convincing evidence of the vigor of his powers, and of the variety and extent of his erudition."

Howell, R. B. C., D.D., was born in Wayne Co., N. C., on the 10th of March, 1801, and died in Nashville, Tenn., on Sunday, April 5, 1868. He commenced preaching about 1825, and was ordained, in 1827, in Cumberland Street church, Norfolk, Va., where he labored until 1834, after which he came to Nashville. Here he built for the First Baptist church of Nashville a fine house of worship, and gathered a membership of over 500. He resigned April, 1850, to take charge of the Second Baptist church of Richmond, Va., in which he labored until the 19th of July, 1857, when he returned to the scene of his early successes, where he had acquired the reputation of one of the most learned and eloquent divines in the country. Here his labors were again attended with the same blessings that crowned his efforts in past years, until paralysis obliged him to relinquish the pulpit he had filled so acceptably for more than a quarter of a century. In the earlier days of his ministry he had to contend with the anti-missionaries of his own denomination and with the followers of Alexander Campbell. He was often found in debate with them by voice and pen, and he always acquitted himself as a loyal disciple of our Lord Jesus Christ. At the request of the Tennessee Baptist Convention, in 1854, he wrote a work on the "Terms of Christian Communion," of 456 pages, which ran through several editions in this country and three or four in England. In 1846 he published a work entitled "The Deaconship: its Nature, Qualifications, Relations, and Duties," which was issued by the American Baptist Publication Society, and ran rapidly through six editions. "The Way of Salvation" was his next literary effort, which passed through several editions. A small work entitled "The Evils of Infant Baptism," followed, which caused a good deal of newspaper comment from Pedobaptist denominations. In 1854 he was the author of a work entitled "The Cross," which was published by the Southern Baptist Publication Society, at Charleston, S. C., and the Virginia Baptist Sunday-School and Publication Society, at Richmond. "The Covenants," published by the same societies, was written in 1856. These works evince a high order of learning, and some of them are authorities in the Baptist denomination. His scholarship was universally conceded. He was educated in Columbian College, Washington, D. C. The degree of Doctor of Divinity was conferred upon him by Georgetown College, Ky., about the year 1844. Besides the works of Dr. Howell just named, he died leaving four others in manuscript, upon which a great amount of thought and labor were bestowed. "The Early Baptists of Virginia," written in 1857, was printed by the American Baptist Publication Society, Philadelphia, for his children, and is the only one of the four that has been published. As a minister, he was regarded as one of the ablest and most learned men in the South, and no one exercised a greater or more beneficial influence within or outside of the church. His life was unspotted, his Christian course was marked by the highest virtues. His courtesy and kindness of heart made him a universal favorite, notwithstanding the fierce theological debates in which he was often engaged. He was a thorough Baptist, and always jealous of the fair fame of his denomination. Dr. Howell was for many years president of the Southern Baptist Convention, and one of its vice-presidents at the time of his death. He had filled also the post of vice-president of the American Baptist Historical Society. He was a member of the Historical Society of Tennessee, and was president of the board of trustees of the asylum for the blind, an institution endowed and sustained by the State of Tennessee. He administered the ordinance of baptism to an immense number of people, first and last, during the long course of his ministry. His death occurred on Sunday, about noon, at the very hour in which, for more than forty years, he had stood up for Jesus in the pulpit. For a week before his death he was speechless but conscious. He knew all that was said around him; and when the pastor of the First church of Nashville spoke of the infinite pity and compassion of the Saviour for his suffering servant, he burst into tears. On being asked if he saw Jesus, he answered by pointing first to his heart and then to heaven.

In addition to the positions held by Dr. Howell already mentioned, he was frequently the moderator of the Concord Association and other bodies. His capacity as a presiding officer of deliberative bodies was rare.

Howes, Prof. Oscar, A.M., was born near Carmel, N. Y., April 20, 1830; was converted while in college; graduated from Madison University in 1850; spent a year at Rochester University; went to Europe in 1852, and was abroad two years, devoting his time, with the exception of a few months spent in traveling, to the study of the German and French languages; in 1855 became Professor of the Greek and Latin Languages in Shurtleff College; in 1863 made a second visit to Europe, spending six months at Athens in the study of the Greek language, ancient and modern, attending daily lectures on the latter at the University of Athens.

After a tour through Greece, Egypt, and Palestine he returned to his duties at Shurtleff. In 1874 he accepted the chair of Latin and Modern Languages at Madison University, where he still labors. He went abroad for the third time in 1878, accompanied by his family.

Howlett, Rev. Thomas R., was born in Cambridgeshire, England, March 19, 1827. He was converted in Richfield, O., when fifteen. He graduated from Madison University in 1856, and from the seminary in 1858. He has been pastor in New Brunswick, N. J.; of the Pearl Street church, Albany, N. Y.; the Central, Trenton, N. J.; the Calvary, Washington, D. C.; in Hudson City, N.Y.; and of the Second church of Plainfield, N. J. During his seven years' pastorate in Washington, the Calvary church erected and paid for an edifice costing $120,000. Mr. Howlett is an able preacher, a sound theologian, a successful pastor, and a genial and loving Christian. In every way fitted to hold the conspicuous positions to which he has been called, and with many years apparently still before him, the denomination may yet expect much valuable services from him.

Hoyt, Col. James A.—Modestly declines to furnish any material for a biography. This notice will, consequently, be "short." Nearly fifty years ago the first Baptist newspaper was published in South Carolina. The numerous changes of name and place, proprietors and editors, tell the sad tale that not one of them was self-sustaining.

In 1878, Col. Hoyt became proprietor of the *Working Christian*, published in Columbia. He soon after removed it to Greenville, and called it the *Baptist Courier*. It has gradually improved until he has a paper sustained on business principles; and the brethren owe very much to him and his cultured coadjutor, Rev. J. A. Chambliss, D.D., for giving them an organ amply worthy of the liberal support it is receiving.

Col. Hoyt is a large-hearted Christian man, who enjoys the warm regards of all South Carolina Baptists, and of many outside our denominational fold.

Hoyt, James M., LL.D., was born in Utica, N. Y., Jan. 16, 1815; graduated from Hamilton College in 1834; read law in Utica and Cleveland, O.; engaged in the practice of law until 1853, when he turned his attention to the development and sale of real estate. In 1835 he united with the Baptist church at Utica, and on removing to Cleveland became connected with the First church of that city. For twenty-six years was superintendent of the Sunday-school, and subsequently teacher of a large Bible-class. In 1854 he was licensed to preach, but has never received ordination.

In State and national affairs Dr. Hoyt has been very prominent. In 1854 he was chosen president of the Ohio Baptist State Convention, and for twenty-five years was annually elected to that position. He was also chosen president of the American Baptist Home Mission Society, and was annually re-elected until his voluntary retirement

JAMES M. HOYT, LL.D.

in 1870. He was for thirteen years president of the Cleveland Bible Society. In 1870 he was made a member of the Ohio State Board of Equalization, —a body requiring great ability and worth. In 1873 he was appointed to represent the city on the Cleveland Board of Public Improvements.

Dr. Hoyt, while an active and successful lawyer and business man, has given himself largely to literary studies. His addresses before various bodies have always evinced wide study and the best taste. He published in the *Christian Review*, October, 1863, an analytical and exhaustive article on "Miracles." In September, 1879, he also published in the *Baptist Review* a defense of the intuitional philosophy, entitled "Theism Grounded in Mind," which has been very favorably received.

Dr. Hoyt was married in 1836 to Miss Mary Ella Beebee, in the city of New York. Of six children born of this union five are still living. Their eldest son, Wayland Hoyt, D.D., is pastor of the Strong Place church, Brooklyn, N. Y. Their second son, Colgate Hoyt, is in business with his father. James H. Hoyt, their third son, and Elton Hoyt, their fourth son, are practising law. In 1870 Denison University, in consideration of Dr. Hoyt's varied talents, services, and learning, conferred upon him the honorary degree of LL.D.

Hoyt, Wayland, D.D., was born in Cleveland,

O., Feb. 18, 1838. In 1860 he was graduated from Brown University, and in 1863 from Rochester Theological Seminary. He was ordained over the Baptist church of Pittsfield, Mass. After one year

WAYLAND HOYT, D.D.

there he removed to Cincinnati, O., and took charge of the Ninth Street Baptist church. Three years later he took charge of the Strong Place Baptist church, Brooklyn. It was a large and influential church, and in this relation began the development of his powers as a profound thinker, a scholarly writer, and an able preacher. In the hope of establishing a great Baptist tabernacle in New York, he accepted a call from the Tabernacle Baptist church, New York, and commenced services in Steinway Hall. It promised well in the beginning, but there were insurmountable difficulties, and the enterprise was abandoned. He then accepted a call to Shawmut Avenue Baptist church, Boston, Mass. The Strong Place church, Brooklyn, recalled him to that important field, where he now labors. He is a prolific writer. His contributions are eagerly sought by the great leading journals of the Baptist denomination. He is the author of "Hints and Helps of the Christian Life," and he is about to bring out a new work, the subject of which is not announced.

As a preacher, he is earnest, logical, and persuasive. He shows that he has thoroughly investigated the subject of his discourse. As a platform speaker, he is ready, clear, and forcible, and as a pastor he is faithful and successful.

Hubbard, Gov. Richard Bennett, was born Nov. 1, 1832, in Walton Co., Ga.; graduated with the degree of A.B. at Mercer University, Penfield, Ga., in 1851; pursued the law course at the University of Virginia, and graduated with the degree of LL.B. in the Law Department of Harvard University, Massachusetts; commenced practising law at Tyler, Texas, in 1854; was appointed United States attorney for the western district of Texas by President Franklin Pierce in 1856; resigned this office to accept a seat in the State Legislature of Texas in 1858–59; was a delegate to the convention which nominated President James Buchanan; during the war between the States he was colonel of the 22d Regiment of Texas Infantry; in 1872 was a Presidential elector; in 1874 was president of the Democratic State convention at Austin; during the same year was elected lieutenant-governor of Texas, and was re-elected to the same office in 1876; delivered by appointment Centennial oration for Texas at Philadelphia in 1876; became governor of Texas Dec. 1, 1876. All his ancestry and his immediate family belong to the Baptist Church. "The Baptists are the people of his fathers." At fourteen years of age he joined the church at Liberty, Jasper Co., Ga.

Gov. Hubbard is one of nature's noblemen. He is a thoroughly learned lawyer, an able statesman, and an orator of the highest order, whose utterances arouse intense enthusiasm among the people.

GOV. RICHARD BENNETT HUBBARD.

His administration of the executive office was remarkably popular with the people, and had he been a candidate for re-election he would have received fully two-thirds of the votes of the people at the polls. His earnestness in behalf of education, virtue, philanthropy, and religion make him a popular favorite; and as he is only yet in the prime of his powers, a brilliant and useful future may be anticipated for him.

Hubbard, Rev. William, was born in Boston, Mass., Jan. 28, 1778. His early associations were not with Baptists, his parents and friends being Episcopalians. When he became interested in the matter of his personal salvation, he was brought under the ministry of Rev. Dr. Stillman, and he united with his church. Encouraged by his pastor, he prepared for his life-work, and entered upon itinerant labors in Maine and Connecticut. The churches which he served as pastor were in the western part of Massachusetts, at Martha's Vineyard, the Third Baptist church in Middleborough, and fourteen years were spent at Goshen. He died at Lakeville, Mass., Jan. 3, 1858.

Hübmaier, Balthazar (Friedberger, Pacimontanus), is the most honorable name among the Anabaptists. He had not the impulsiveness of Grebel, nor the brilliancy of Hätzer and Denk ; but for calmness, soberness, logical clearness and consistency, absolute devotion to truth, and freedom from important errors, he stands unrivaled by any man of the Reformation time. Born in 1480, educated at the University of Freiberg, where his principal teacher was John Eck, he spent some years in school-teaching, then became tutor at Freiberg, and in 1512 followed Eck to Ingoldstadt, where he became preacher and Professor of Theology. Here he was created Doctor of Theology. In 1516 he was called to be preacher in the cathedral church in Regensburg. His great eloquence led to this appointment. Here he preached so powerfully against the Jews as to cause their expulsion from the city. In 1519 he declared himself for Luther, and was driven from Regensburg. In 1522 he became pastor at Waldshut, near Zürich. Here he was among the most zealous of the supporters of the Zwinglian doctrine ; but soon came to deny the Scripturalness of infant baptism. In 1524 he published eighteen axioms concerning the Christian life, in which he set forth his reformatory views, and he soon secured from the town council recognition and protection for the preachers. His writing on "Heretics and their Burners" soon followed. In this he shows that only those are heretics who contradict the Scriptures, especially the devil and the papists. This is the earliest and clearest plea for liberty of conscience of the Reformation time. He shows that heretics can be overcome by instruction only, and that to try to overcome them by violence is contrary to the teachings and spirit of Christ. In 1525 he wrote against infant baptism, and was elaborately answered by Zwingle and Œcolampadius. Hübmaier's tract against infant baptism is an admirable production alike in matter and in spirit. The straightforward earnestness and Christian courtesy of Hübmaier's tract are in striking contrast with the sophistry and reviling of Zwingle's reply. He was one of the chief participants in the disputations with Zwingle during this year. Assured of the support of the civil power, Zwingle, on these occasions, acted the part, not of a brother in Christ, but of a lord, and by his air of superior wisdom and authority, by his fluent sophistry, he easily persuaded the members of the council that his adversaries had been fairly vanquished. Hübmaier was imprisoned at Zürich, where he suffered great hardship. Having been released from prison, he went to Moravia (1526), where Anabaptists already existed in considerable numbers. At Nicolsburg he established a strong church, and published in quick succession a large number of tracts on ordinances, worship, and doctrine. Most of these have been preserved, and are among the choicest products of the Anabaptist movement. In 1527 he was taken to Vienna and thrown into prison. In 1528 he died heroically at the stake, a martyr to his Baptist principles.

Huckins, Rev. James, was one of the best men the writer has ever known. He was born in New Hampshire in April, 1807. He was left an orphan at four or five years of age, and was baptized at fourteen. He graduated at Brown University at an early age. He went among the first Baptist ministers to Texas, under the patronage of the Home Mission Society. His singular insight into human character, his high courage tempered finely with gentleness, and, what is no less important, his tact, fitted him peculiarly for usefulness among the frontiersmen.

After many years of incessant and successful labor as a missionary, he became pastor of the church in Galveston, where his influence over all classes was both wide and deep. The esteem in which he was held was manifested by the presentation of a heavy pitcher and pair of goblets of solid silver, on his departure, from the citizens at large.

In 1859 he accepted the pastorate of the Wentworth Street Baptist church, in Charleston, S. C. Here he was ready for every good word and work, especially among the poor. From the commencement of the war his labors in the hospitals in and around Charleston were incessant, and in the double toils of pastor and chaplain he fell on the 14th of August, 1863.

Hudson, Hon. Nathaniel C., was born in St. Johnsbury, Vt., Oct. 9, 1828. After receiving a common school education, he entered Leland Seminary, Vt., and prepared for the Sophomore class in college, but went south for his health. In 1852 he took charge of Twiggs Academy, in Georgia, where he proved a popular teacher. He studied law, came north, entered the National Law School at Poughkeepsie, and graduated in 1855. He then removed to Iowa, and entered upon his profession at Sioux City. He removed to St. Louis in 1866. Mr. Hudson was elected to the State Legislature in 1874 from St. Louis, and served on important committees. In 1876 he was elected a senator to the General Assembly of Missouri, and served on the committees of Ways and Means, Penitentiary, Bank and Corporations, Insurance, and Constitutional Amendments. He is courteous, frank, outspoken, cordial, and popular. His business relations are marked by integrity, and his church duties by fidelity. He is a member of the Second Baptist church of St. Louis.

Huff, Rev. Jonathan, a useful minister of the Hephzibah Association, was born in Warren Co., Ga., in August, 1789. Licensed by Little Brier Creek church, he was ordained in 1823. In 1829 he was elected moderator of the Hephzibah Association, in which capacity he served for thirteen years consecutively. His practical good sense and sterling integrity and unaffected piety gained him the confidence and esteem of his brethren. For thirty-one years he was pastor of Ways church, and of Reedy Creek church he was pastor thirty-seven years consecutively. In addition he labored with other churches to an extent which always occupied his whole time. A faithful student of the Bible, he was a safe expounder of its teachings; conscientious and tender of spirit, he was touching in his addresses to the unconverted; and hence he was very successful in winning souls to Jesus and in building up churches that were sound in the faith. He was indomitably persevering, and possessed an equanimity that nothing could disturb. He was usually slow of speech, yet few men have accomplished more good or exerted a wider influence. He was an ardent and intelligent supporter of the missionary and temperance causes, and heartily co-operated with the denomination in its benevolent enterprises. He died in the vicinity of his birthplace on the 25th of November, 1872, at the age of eighty-three.

Hufham, Rev. Geo. W.—Among the older living ministers of North Carolina is the Rev. Geo. W. Hufham, who was born in 1804; baptized in 1830 by Rev. Geo. Fennell, began to preach soon after, and has served many of the churches of Sampson and Duplin Counties. Mr. Hufham is a gentleman of respectable learning, and in his youth was a popular preacher. Ill health has prevented him from preaching as much as his heart desired. Honored and loved, this good man is resting in the Beulah Land, waiting for the call to pass over the river.

Hufham, J. D., D.D. The son of an esteemed minister, Dr. Hufham is one of the most noted of the living ministers of North Carolina. He was born in Duplin Co., N. C., May 26, 1834; was fitted

J. D. HUFHAM, D.D.

for college by the Rev. Dr. Sprunt, of Keenansville; graduated at Wake Forest College in 1856; was baptized at the college by Dr. Wingate in February, 1855, and ordained in 1857, Revs. A. Guy, B. F. Marable, and L. F. Williams comprising the Presbytery. In 1861 he purchased the *Biblical Recorder*, which he conducted with distinguished success till the close of 1867. For three years he was pastor of the Lanyino Creek church, Camden Co. He then became corresponding secretary of the Baptist State Convention, and, after four years' service in this position, became pastor of the Second church of Raleigh and associate editor of the *Biblical Recorder*. For the past three years Dr. Hufham has labored in Scotland Neck, and the adjacent country for a hundred miles up and down the Roanoke River, and so remarkable have been the results of his efforts, that it may be truly said that, though always active and useful, he never did such effective service in the cause of Christ as now. Dr. Hufham is a ripe scholar, refined and critical in his tastes, a born editor, and the prince of agents. He never seems so happy as when managing an Association or taking up a collection. He is the author of an admirable memoir of Rev. J. L. Prichard, is a trustee of Wake Forest College, and was for many years recording secretary of the State Convention. He received his D.D. from his *alma mater* in 1877.

Hughes, Rev. Joseph, was born in London, Jan. 1, 1769. He was baptized by Dr. Samuel Stennett into the fellowship of the church in Little Wild Street in his native city. He studied for the ministry at Bristol College, and at Aberdeen and Edinburgh, in Scotland. He was ordained in Battersea in 1797. He was appointed secretary of the Religious Tract Society of London in 1799, and continued to discharge the duties of that office during the remainder of his life.

In 1802 the Rev. Thomas Charles, of Bala, in Wales, came to London to secure, through private friends, a supply of Welsh Bibles. He appeared before the committee of the Religious Tract Society, and his appeal was the subject of deliberation at several of their meetings. At one of these meetings Mr. Hughes suggested that Wales was not the only part of the empire destitute of the written Word of God and requiring assistance; that Great Britain itself was not the only part of Christendom which needed to be supplied; and that it might be desirable to form a society which, while it met the demands of Wales and the necessities of all parts of the British Islands, might be comprehensive enough *to embrace within its scope the entire world.* Mr. Hughes was recommended to embody his thoughts in writing. In compliance with the request he prepared his celebrated paper entitled "The Excellency of the Holy Scriptures." In this document Mr. Hughes earnestly advocated the importance of forming an association of Christians of all denominations with the sole object of giving the Word of Life to the nations. The paper was widely circulated, and the plan was approved immediately by large numbers. After various preliminary arrangements, a meeting was held at the "London Tavern," March 7, 1804, consisting of about three hundred persons belonging to various denominations, at which the British and Foreign Bible Society was formally organized, and Mr. Hughes appointed one of its secretaries. This was the first Bible Society in the world, and the parent of all similar institutions everywhere. This noble organization received its origin and its very name from a Baptist. (History of the British and Foreign Bible Society, vol. i. pp. 4–9. London, 1859.) The thought that started this society on its career of usefulness and power was placed in the mind of our Baptist brother by the Comforter, the Guardian Spirit of revelation, and of the redeemed race.

In 1833 Mr. Hughes entered the eternal rest. The British and Foreign Bible Society passed resolutions expressing in the most touching and eloquent terms their appreciation of his exalted worth, and of the great loss their institution had suffered in his death. Evangelical Christians in throngs lamented the demise of one of the most useful men that had toiled for centuries for the spread of pure truth. The well-known Jay, of Bath, said of him, "I am thankful for my intimacy with him. My esteem for him always grew with my intercourse. I never knew a more consistent, correct, and unblemished character. He was not only sincere, but without offense, and he adorned the doctrine of God our Saviour in all things." His long pastorate at Battersea was a great blessing to the church which he loved, and by which to the last he was tenderly cherished, and it was only terminated by his death.

Hughes, Rowland.—This excellent brother had considerable property, which he used largely for benevolent purposes. Mr. Hughes was gentle in spirit and conservative in his views; he was ready for every good work, and he had the confidence of all his brethren and their highest esteem. After a protracted and painful illness he died of typhoid fever, Feb. 7, 1855. The Baptists of Missouri, where he so long lived, cherish his memory with great love.

Hulbert, E. B., D.D., was born at Chicago, Ill., July 16, 1841, and was baptized at Burlington Flats, N. J., in 1854. Entering Madison University, he continued in study there through his Junior year, taking his Senior year at Union College, where he graduated in 1863, and at the theological seminary in Hamilton in 1865. His first service was in connection with the Christian Commission, in Grant's army, while before Richmond, continuing in this until the close of the war. For three years from September, 1865, he was pastor at Manchester, N. H. In November, 1868, he began labor with the Rolling Mills Mission at Chicago, and continued there until its organization as a church, in March, 1870. In that year he accepted a call to the First Baptist church, St. Paul, Minn.; in 1874 was invited to the First Baptist church, San Francisco, Cal.; and in 1878 became pastor of the Fourth Baptist church, Chicago. Dr. Hulbert as a thoughtful, earnest, inspiring preacher, has great power with intelligent congregations, while as a lecturer before the theological seminary at Chicago, as well as before ministers' institutes, he has developed rare facility in handling profound and weighty subjects.

Hull, Rev. John, was born in Manchester, Nova Scotia. He was converted there in 1819; engaged in missionary labor in Cape Breton in 1821, where spirituality in religion was very little known or recognized. He was baptized by Rev. Joseph Dimock in 1825, and ordained at Wilmot, Nova Scotia, June 28, 1826. He died Aug. 13, 1829, at Sydney, Cape Breton.

Hull, Rev. Robert Bruce, pastor of the Tabernacle church of New York City, was born Jan. 12, 1841, in Kirkcudbrightshire, Scotland. His parents shortly after his birth removed to Liverpool, England, and after remaining there a few years came to America and settled at Buffalo, N. Y., where they now reside. His father, Robert Hull, while in Liverpool, was one of the preachers to a Scotch Baptist church in that city. In June, 1860, Robert B. was baptized into the fellowship of the Cedar Street Baptist church of Buffalo. He went to Tennessee in 1864, and there, with a relative, entered into business. Soon the conviction grew upon him that he must preach the gospel, and closing up a prosperous establishment, he returned to Buffalo to prepare for college. This was done, under a private tutor, in one year. In September, 1867, he entered the University of Rochester. While in his Freshman year he took charge of a mission Sunday-school, near the city, where, on Sunday evening, Feb. 16, 1868, he preached his first sermon. God set his seal on the work, and about twenty persons were converted. Finding that the preparation of sermons interfered with college studies, he ceased to preach, except in his vacations. His course in college was successful. He took the second prize for declamation in his Sophomore year; was honorably mentioned in connection with the Greek prize, and also for extra studies in French in his Junior year; and received a first prize for the Senior prize essay at his graduation. He then entered the Rochester Theological Seminary, and preached through the entire course, chiefly at Royalton and Dansville, N. Y. He supplied the Lockport, N. Y., Baptist church during his Senior year in the seminary, and accepted a unanimous call to become its pastor on his graduation. During this year a revival took place, and, at the request of the church, he was ordained Feb. 17, 1874. Over 100 were baptized as the result of the revival. He continued his studies, and graduated in May, 1874. During his pastorate at Lockport, the accessions to the church by baptism were continuous. Its membership was more than doubled. In March, 1877, the Tabernacle church of New York, hearing of his success, unanimously invited him to become its pastor. He accepted the call, and is now the honored successor of Everts, Lathrop, Kendrick, Hoyt, and Hawthorne.

Humble, Rev. Henry, a pioneer preacher in Louisiana, was born in South Carolina in 1765; settled in Catahoula Parish, La., 1822, and in 1826 gathered the First church on the Ouachita; was moderator of the Louisiana Association in 1828, and the following year died while attending the Association.

Humble, Rev. Thos. J., the leading minister of the Ouachita Baptist Association in Louisiana, was born in Caldwell Parish, La., in 1829; has long been the efficient clerk of his Association, and frequently its moderator.

Hume, Rev. Thomas, was the son of the Rev. Thomas Hume, of Edinburgh, Scotland, who, soon after his graduation from the university of that city, and his ordination as a minister of the Established (Presbyterian) Church, removed to the United States. Having settled in Virginia, he married there, and united to the duties of his sacred calling the office of classical teacher. His only child, Thomas, was born in Smithfield, Isle of Wight Co., Va., March 15, 1812. The sudden death of the father, while in the act of preaching the opening sermon as moderator of the Baltimore Presbytery, occurred when the son was scarcely six years of age. His education was interrupted in his sixteenth year by his acceptance of an assistant's place in a store in Petersburg, Va. At the age of eighteen he made a profession of religion, and joined the First Baptist church of Petersburg. His marked decision of character, his intellectual sprightliness, and his earnest piety attracted the attention of the devoted church, and he was soon licensed to preach. After a brief but fruitful training at the Virginia Baptist Seminary (now Richmond College), he made his first attempt at preaching in Chesterfield Co., Va. Just before his twenty-first year, he was called to the pastorate of the Court Street Baptist church, Portsmouth, Va., which was then small in numbers and influence, as well as burdened with temporal and spiritual troubles. His modest and scrupulous reluctance was overcome by the kind importunities of the community, and the rapid growth of the church, as indicated by the erection of a spacious and elegant house of worship within four years after his installation, and by the increase of the membership from a mere handful to 650, proved the wisdom of his choice. During this pastorate of nearly twenty-five years, his enlightened public spirit, his financial knowledge and administrative talent, gave him great influence in the commercial and charitable enterprises of the city. He was a director of the Seaboard and Roanoke Railroad Company, president of the Providence Society, general superintendent of education in Portsmouth and Norfolk Counties, president of the Portsmouth Insurance Company, and prominently connected, also, with other institutions. His reputation and usefulness in the denomination are attested by the number of important positions to which he was called. As president of the Virginia Baptist Bible Board, clerk and president of the Portsmouth Baptist Association, president of the Baptist General Association of Virginia, trustee of the Columbian College (from which he received the honorary degree of A.M.), and of Richmond College, owner (in part) and treasurer of the Chesapeake Female College, organizer and pastor of the Fourth Street Baptist church, Norfolk, Va., he was constantly active in the service of God and man. His self-sacrificing interest in the community to which he gave his consecrated life is specially remembered in connection with the yellow-fever epidemic, which, in 1855, desolated the twin cities of Norfolk and Portsmouth. He was the fearless, faithful pastor throughout all those sad and weary months, and the special guardian and friend of the many orphans, while his complete exemption in his own person from the pestilence enabled him to multiply his usefulness in every direction. As a preacher, Mr. Hume was marked for Scriptural soundness of doctrine, spiritual unction and pathos, and by practical wisdom. Great revivals of religion in his earlier ministry accompanied the orderly and successful administration of the work of the church and Sunday-school; while his financial skill was such as to distinguish him not only in his profession, but also in business circles, yet the sincere fervor of his piety restrained his undue absorption in worldly affairs, and kept his character and his reputation alike unsullied. In the vigorous maturity of his powers, he became suddenly enfeebled after exposure in the Virginia Baptist Memorial Campaign of 1872, and after two years died, lamented and beloved by all who knew him.

Hume, Rev. Thomas, Jr., son of the Rev. Thomas Hume and Mary Ann Gregory Hume, was born in Portsmouth, Va., Oct. 21, 1836. He enjoyed excellent opportunities both at home and at the collegiate institute of the city. At the age of fifteen he entered Richmond College, where he obtained the degree of A.B., followed by that of A.M. His studies were continued at the University of Virginia, where, after graduation in several schools, his course was interrupted by a serious illness. While at the university he was one of the editors of *The Literary Magazine*, and president of the Young Men's Christian Association. As he purposed devoting himself to the business of teaching, he accepted the professorship of Latin, French, and English Literature in Chesapeake Female College, near Old Point Comfort, but had not fairly commenced work when the war broke up that prosperous institution. During his residence there the church in Portsmouth, of which he was a member, corresponded with him with regard to his duty to enter the ministry, and learning that his informal services with the Christian Association had been blessed, urged upon him the propriety of accepting a license to preach. Having entered the Confederate service at the opening of the war, he was soon called by the 3d Va. (Infantry) Regiment to officiate for them, and he received an appointment as their chaplain. The authorities, however, soon transferred him to the post-chaplaincy at Petersburg, Va., a very important hospital station, around which the lines of a protracted siege were fast closing.

Since the war Mr. Hume has been at various times principal of the Petersburg Classical Institute (at the same time supplying country pulpits in Sussex and Chesterfield Counties, Va.), Professor of Languages and Literature in Roanoke Female College, Danville, Va., pastor of the Danville Baptist church, and of the Cumberland Baptist church, Norfolk, Va., and Professor of the English Language and Literature in the Norfolk (Female) Collegiate Institute. His interest in literary pursuits, especially in English studies, has accompanied but not interfered with his regular devotion to the higher work of the ministry. Mr. Hume is an earnest and forcible preacher and a successful pastor. As a writer he is vigorous, classical, and chaste, and among the younger of the Virginia ministers is marked for his genial social qualities, his intellectual acuteness, and his accurate and varied attainments.

Humphrey, Hon. Friend, was born in Simsbury, Conn., March 8, 1787; at nineteen he was

HON. FRIEND HUMPHREY.

converted and baptized; in 1810 he removed to Albany, N. Y., and commenced business for himself; in 1811 he was one of the constituent members of the First Baptist church of his adopted city; in 1834 he was one of the constituent members of the Pearl Street church. He was several terms mayor of Albany. He was also a member of the State senate. He was a man of great courage in times of pestilence, and as unselfish as he was brave. His liberality was universal; "no improvement, no enterprise, no mission, no charity that commended itself to the wise and liberal," was without his aid. It is supposed that his contributions to benevolent objects reached $100,000. " He was a noble specimen of a man, a universal philanthropist. The name of Friend Humphrey will never be forgotten in Albany." He died March 14, 1854. The stores of the city were closed during the services at his funeral; a profound stillness showed the love and sorrow of Albany; the city government and a large concourse of people followed the remains to their last resting-place, and tears fell from many eyes.

Humphrey, Rev. Luther, was born in Glover, Vt., Aug. 19, 1808; died at Augusta, Wis., Aug. 17, 1876; educated at Potsdam Academy and at Amherst College. After teaching as the principal of Southport Academy, N. Y., he prosecuted a course of theological study at Hamilton, N. Y. He was settled as pastor at Lorraine, Covington, and Massena, in New York, and at Mazomanie and Augusta, Wis. For a number of years he was not in the active work of the ministry owing to enfeebled health.

Humpstone, Rev. John, was born in Manchester, England, May 4, 1850. He is the son of Rev. William Humpstone, and came to America with his father when a lad. At twelve years of age he assisted his father in public worship in Music Hall, Worcester, England, by reading from the pulpit the Scriptures and the hymns, thus forecasting the work of his life. On the 25th of December, 1864, he was baptized by Rev. J. E. Cheshire, and became a member of the Baptist church of Falls of Schuylkill, Philadelphia. A few months later he gave promise of usefulness by the delivery of an address of remarkable ability for one of his age. In 1871 he was graduated from Lewisburg University, and in 1874 from Crozer Theological Seminary. Before his studies were completed he was compelled to leave school for a year, during which time he supplied the church in Galway, N. Y. A revival was the result, and 43 converts desired to be baptized by him, and for this reason a council was called and he was ordained at Galway in 1873. His first pastorate was at Manayunk, Philadelphia, where he was settled in 1874. In 1877 he accepted a call to the Calvary Baptist church, Albany, N. Y., where at the present writing his labors are greatly blessed.

Hunt, Rev. Abraham S., A.M., was born near Digby, Nova Scotia; converted and baptized in St. John, New Brunswick; graduated from Acadia College, June, 1844; ordained at Dartmouth the following November; became co-pastor, in 1847, with the venerable Edward Manning, of the Cornwallis church, and his successor in 1851; returned to Dartmouth in 1869; appointed superintendent of education in Nova Scotia in 1870, and conscientiously performed his duties till he died, in 1877.

Hunt, Rev. George, was born in Fayette Co., Ky., June 9, 1831. He united with East Hickman Baptist church in 1844; was educated at Georgetown College, and graduated in 1849. He was ordained to the pastorate of Maysville Baptist church in 1856. In 1858 he was elected Professor of Theology in Georgetown College, where he remained until 1861. In 1862 he was elected president of Bethel College, and occupied the position two years. He has since been pastor of Main Street Baptist church, in Bowling Green, the First Baptist church in Lexington, the church at Versailles, and is now pastor of the church at Hillsborough, Woodford Co., all in Kentucky. He has baptized about 400 persons into the churches of which he has been pastor. He is now conducting a school at Versailles in connection with his pastoral work.

Hunt, Judge Joseph D., was born in Fayette Co., Ky., in 1838. He is a brother of Rev. George Hunt, who, on the death of their father, became his guardian and superintended his education. He graduated with the honors of a class of forty-nine at Center College, Ky., in 1857. He graduated in the law department of the University of Louisville. In 1862 he entered the Confederate army as a volunteer, and remained until the close of the war. On the return of peace he resumed his profession. In 1873 he was appointed by Gov. Leslie judge of the tenth judicial district of Kentucky to fill a vacancy caused by the death of Judge Thomas. In 1874 he was elected by the people to the same position and served six years, but declined re-election and resumed the practice of law. He is an honored member of East Hickman Baptist church.

Huntington, Adoniram Judson, D.D., the youngest son of the Rev. Elijah Huntington, was born in Braintree, Vt., July 6, 1818. Though he lost his father before he was ten years of age, yet he was blessed, during his boyhood and youth, with the careful guidance of a mother eminent for prudence and tenderness, and for consistent and earnest piety. At the age of thirteen he united with the Baptist church in Braintree, of which his father was for a long period the pastor. He entered, in September, 1837, the Freshman class in Brown University. Here he remained less than a month, on account of that ill health which had before, as it has often since, been a serious obstacle to his intellectual pursuits, and from this cause he was compelled to suspend his studies for an entire year, the latter part of which he spent with a very kind relative and benefactor, the late Dr. Eleazer Parmly, in the city of New York. In the pleasant home of this gentleman he passed also the following year, at the same time pursuing his studies as a member of the Freshman class of the Columbia College. In this class he attained the second place in scholarship, the Hon. A. S. Hewitt having occupied the first. In September, 1839, he returned to Brown University, where he spent the Sophomore and a part of the Junior year, when failing health made it necessary for him again to leave college. Soon

ADONIRAM JUDSON HUNTINGTON, D.D.

afterwards he engaged as a teacher, as in those days so many Northern students were accustomed to do, in the more genial climate of the South, and in this occupation passed a year and a half in Middlesex Co., Va. Fearing the rigors of a Northern climate, he completed his collegiate course at the Columbian College, D. C., where he graduated in October, 1843. Immediately after he became tutor in the same institution in the Greek and Latin languages. In June, 1844, he married Miss Bettie G. Christian, the daughter of Dr. R. A. Christian, of Middlesex Co., Va. Having filled the office of tutor for three years, he was elected professor of the same departments, and after filling this position with great success for three years, he resigned it for the purpose of entering upon what he regarded as the chosen vocation of his life,—the ministry of the gospel,—and was ordained in June, 1849. His first pastoral charge was in Lexington, Va., which he relinquished (and to which he was afterwards again invited) for a wider field of labor in Chelsea, Mass. After a year of successful service in the First Baptist church of this place (having been called also at a later period to the Carey Avenue Baptist church of Chelsea), he received an unsolicited invitation to resume his former professorship in the Columbian College, which, from considerations of health, he accepted. After occupying this chair for seven years he again retired from it, in 1859, in hopes of being able to resume the duties of the ministry. After spending between one and two years in Farmville, Va., where his labors were signally blessed, he accepted, in September, 1860, a call from the First Baptist church of Augusta, Ga., and in this field, which was regarded as one of the most important in the denomination in the South, and in those troublous war times he so discharged the duties of his office for some five years that, with the divine blessing, the peace and prosperity of the church were promoted. Within this period he was selected to deliver, at the Georgia Baptist State Convention, an annual address before the Bible and Colportage Society, and again to preach the annual sermon on ministerial education. Soon after the resignation of the charge of this church, in August, 1865, he was again invited to the Columbian College to fill the Greek professorship, on which he entered in September, 1866. This position he has ever since occupied, excepting some fifteen months spent in Europe in 1867–68, partly in travel in pursuit of health as well as knowledge, and partly in study at Athens and Heidelberg. During the periods of his professorship he has given a considerable part of his Sabbaths to the preaching of the gospel. He published while in Augusta a tract of some thirty pages on the " Moral and Religious Training of Children," and in April, 1877, in the *Baptist Quarterly*, an article on " Ancient Attica and Athens ;" besides which he has made occasional contributions to religious journals. He received the degree of D.D. from Brown University in 1868. Dr. Huntington as an educator is clear, thorough, and exact; as a preacher impressive and instructive ; and as a man genial, affable, and of " good report of them which are without."

Huntington, Rev. Elijah, was born in Mansfield, Conn., Aug. 21, 1763. His ancestors settled in that State at an early period, and from them has sprung the numerous family of Huntingtons in Connecticut and other States. He was a soldier of the Revolutionary army, and soon after its close he removed to Vermont, where he was employed for a time as a teacher. When about twenty-seven years of age he was converted, and united with the Baptist church at Royalton. In June, 1800, he was ordained in Braintree, Vt., as an evangelist. Immediately he became pastor of the Baptist church in that town, and he held this office till his death, June 24, 1828.

Mr. Huntington had a strong, discriminating, and well-balanced mind. He was a successful teacher of youth, a forcible and acceptable speaker, and an instructive preacher of the gospel. In every relation of life he may be said to have been an example worthy of imitation.

In regard to his piety, it may probably be safely

asserted that no man in the region in which he lived was more distinguished for a holy and blameless life. It seemed to be his constant aim to know and to do the will of that Master to whom he had devoted himself without reserve. "The law of God seemed to be engraven on his heart." From the very thought of violating the divine commands he apparently shrunk with horror. And yet he placed a very low estimate upon his own piety; his humility was one of his most striking characteristics.

As a preacher he thoroughly and prayerfully studied the Bible, clearly expounded its doctrines, and faithfully enforced its precepts. His sermons were thoughtful, able, evangelical, earnest, and faithful. "Occasionally he rose above himself, and, as though endued with extraordinary power, presented truth in a manner the most clear and impressive."

His influence was extensive, permanent, and in every respect salutary. Nor were his efforts to do good limited to his own neighborhood. "He was an ardent friend of foreign missions, and prayed and labored, as well as gave of his substance, for the spread of the gospel. His end was peace. In view of it he said, "I wish not to choose for myself; I think it is my greatest desire that God may be glorified by me in life and in death."

A biographical notice of Mr. Huntington appeared in the *American Baptist Magazine* of February, 1829, written by Rev. A. Nichols, of blessed memory, then pastor of the Congregational church in Braintree, who, for twenty years, lived only three or four miles from Mr. Huntington. Appended to that obituary the following note appears: Mr. Huntington was at the house of a friend, when conversation was casually introduced respecting Mr. Nichols. Mr. Huntington remarked, "I do not know of a man I should be willing to exchange for Mr. Nichols." Not long after Mr. Nichols was at the same place, and conversation was in a similar manner introduced concerning Mr. Huntington. Mr. Nichols observed, "I do not know of a man I should be willing to exchange for Mr. Huntington." The references to each other mentioned in this note show both the high character of the two men and their mutual friendship.

Huntington, Rev. Joseph, son of Rev. Elijah Huntington, was born in Braintree, Vt., July 27, 1811. In the ordinary frivolities of childhood and youth he had little disposition to engage. He was habitually serious and contemplative, and often exhibited deep convictions of sin and anxiety for his salvation. It was not, however, till the revival of 1831 that he found peace in believing, and united with the Baptist church in Braintree. As he had felt a deep and most painful sense of his need of Christ as a Saviour, so his love to him was ardent and his consecration unreserved. Having determined to devote himself to the ministry of the gospel, he commenced the study of the Greek and Latin languages, in which he made great progress. He entered Middlebury College, in his native State, from which, at the expiration of four years (in 1837), he graduated, having maintained during his whole course a standing second to no one in his class. As a proof of the estimation in which he was held by his fellow-students they assigned to him the most honorable part in the anniversary exercises of their literary society on the day before commencement, while the offer of a tutorship in the college, soon after his graduation, showed the respect entertained for him by the faculty of the institution. This, however, he did not accept. In 1838 he entered the theological institution at Newton, Mass.; but, in hope of finding the duties of a country pastor more favorable to his declining health, and in consideration of the pressing need of ministers in his native State, he reluctantly returned to Vermont in less than a year, and was ordained as pastor of the Baptist church in East Williamstown. After a few months of very acceptable and useful service he was compelled to relinquish all ministerial duties. Soon afterwards, to recruit his health, he went to South Carolina and Georgia, where he passed a winter, but in the following spring he returned to Vermont without improvement. Here, at the home of his mother, he lingered for a year, and died of consumption April 26, 1843. Thus prematurely passed away this devoted servant of Christ, who nevertheless had lived long enough to secure the high esteem, the warm friendship, and the strong confidence of all who knew him well. His mind was strong and logical. He had great power of acquiring knowledge as well as untiring industry. He was a speaker of uncommon readiness, conciseness, earnestness, and force. His sermons were methodical, lucid, and pungent. His piety was ardent and consistent, characterized by deep feeling, and still more by inflexible principle. Nothing could make him swerve from what he deemed to be right. His conduct was not only above reproach, but also above suspicion. He seemed to have brought his passions and appetites, his heart, his intellect, and his will into subjection to Christ. The delineation, indeed, of his character would be an enumeration of the virtues that most adorn the man and of the graces that most closely liken the Christian to his Master.

As his grand aim in life was to do the divine will, so he cheerfully submitted to that will when he saw his earthly career coming to so early a close, and at last, knowing in whom he believed, he calmly and even joyfully committed his soul to his keeping.

Hurd, Rev. James Christie, M.D., was born in Nova Scotia, April 17, 1829. He early prepared himself for the practice of medicine, but soon felt that it was his duty to preach. In 1873 he became pastor of the Cedar Street Baptist church, Buffalo, N. Y. While residing in Buffalo he practised medicine for a time, and afterwards occupied an editorial position on the Buffalo *Express*. From Buffalo he went to St. Thomas, Ontario, as pastor of the Baptist church. He came to Iowa in 1876 and took charge of the Baptist church at Marshalltown, and soon became identified with his brethren of the State in all the general interests of the denomination. In October, 1878, he was elected president of the Iowa Baptist State Convention, and was re-elected in 1879, always meeting the duties of this position with signal ability. In 1878 he became pastor of the First Baptist church, Burlington. He died in the harness on Sunday, Dec. 21, 1879.

Hurley, Rev. William, was born in Warwickshire, England, Feb. 5, 1795. At eighteen he was converted and soon commenced preaching. He was ordained in 1822. Preached for ten years in England with marked success. In 1828 he came to America; preached a year in Providence, R. I., and afterwards came to St. Louis, Mo. In 1831 he took charge of the Fee Fee Baptist church. He was at the organization of the General Association of Missouri in 1835, and that year he became pastor of the Palmyra church, and afterwards of Bethel Baptist church. Subsequently for years he labored as an evangelist. He was earnest, self-denying, and very successful in leading souls to Jesus.

Dr. Fisk wrote his memoir, which shows that he was a man of unusual talent, culture, and eloquence. His last address was at the laying of the corner-stone of an institution of learning. He was a Mason of high standing and lectured eloquently to the "craft." He loved standard literature, and advocated its study. He was a man of deep piety; his memory will long be lovingly cherished in Missouri, and his influence for good be perpetuated. He died Aug. 3, 1856, in Troy, Lincoln Co., Mo., in the sixty-first year of his life.

Hutchens, Prof. Allen Sabin, a native of Spafford, Onondaga Co., N. Y., was born Dec. 8, 1817. He spent his early youth in Medina, N. Y. When but a boy his father removed to Adrian, Mich., where he grew up to manhood. He was educated at Denison University, Granville, O., from which he graduated in 1843. He subsequently studied theology at Newton, Mass. He taught at Denison University and at the Baptist Academy at Norwalk, O. But the chief work of his life has been done in connection with Wayland University, at Beaver Dam, Wis. He was called to the presidency of this institution in 1857, and has been connected with it, with the exception of a few years, throughout its entire history. Prof. Hutchens is a Christian teacher of fine culture and attainments. He stands high as a Greek scholar. He has been a hard worker, and in the very prime of his life, with health so impaired as to prevent his further labor in the class-room, at present he is living in retirement at Beaver Dam.

Hutchins, Rev. Hiram, was educated at Madison University; ordained in Richfield, N. Y., in August, 1840; served the church of Charlestown, Mass., as pastor, and the church of Roxbury, and in 1860 took charge of a church in Brooklyn, of which he is still the beloved pastor. For several years he was president of the American Baptist Free Mission Society. His long ministry of forty years has been blessed with many tokens of divine approbation.

Hutchinson, Rev. Elijah, was born in Marion, N. Y., June 7, 1810, and removed with his parents to Newport, N. H., when he was a child. He was baptized by Rev. Ira Pearson. Impressed that it was his duty to preach the gospel, he studied at New Hampton, and at Portsmouth, under the tuition of Dr. Baron Stow, and took the full course at Newton. In the autumn of 1834 he was ordained pastor of the church at Windsor, Vt., and continued in office for twenty years. After suspending his work for two years, he resumed his pastorate with the church at Windsor, where he labored for five years longer. This ministry of twenty-five years with one church, his only charge, was full of blessing to his people. His labors also, at times, extended beyond his more immediate field, and the feeble churches in his neighborhood enjoyed the benefit of his instructions. He came to be regarded as a leader in all good enterprises, and his counsels were sought and followed by those who asked his advice. He enjoyed a very large measure of the respect and esteem of his brethren in Vermont, and left the impress of his Christian influence upon the Baptist cause in that State. Mr. Hutchinson died at Windsor, April 5, 1872.

Hutchinson, Rev. Elisha, was born in Sharon, Conn., Dec. 22, 1749. After his conversion, at twenty, there seemed to be an awakening of his intellectual powers. He longed to preach the gospel, which had done so much for him. He commenced a course of preparatory study under the tuition of Rev. Dr. Wheelock, at Lebanon, Conn., and joined the Congregational church of which his instructor was the pastor. He was a member of the first class that graduated at Dartmouth College in 1775. Shortly after leaving college he was licensed as an evangelist, and preached some years, when he was ordained in the year 1778 as pastor of the Congregational church in Westford, Conn., where he remained five years. In 1785 he accepted a call to the Congregational church in Pomfret, Vt., where he remained for about ten years. For the next few years he supplied churches in Vermont and Massachusetts. In 1800 he changed his views on the mode and subjects of Christian baptism, and became a decided Baptist. After various charges he was invited to become the pastor of the Baptist church in Newport, N. H., in 1814. Four years after, he was blessed with a powerful revival of religion, and in about ten months 110 united with the church, adding very greatly to its efficiency. After this revival, feeling the infirmities of age, Mr. Hutchinson resigned his pastorate, but remained a resident in the place where his labors had been so signally blessed until his death, which occurred April 19, 1833.

Hutchinson, Rev. Enoch, was born in Marion, N. Y., in June, 1810, and was a graduate of Waterville College in the class of 1834, and of the Newton Theological Institution in the class of 1837. He was ordained in Boston, Nov. 26, 1837. He was pastor of the church in Framingham, Mass., one year, and Professor of Theology in the Maine Baptist Theological Institute at Thomaston, Me., for one year. For some time he was editor of the *Baptist Memorial*,—1846-51. The results of his Oriental studies are embodied in his "Syriac Grammar." He is the author of "Music of the Bible." Mr. Hutchinson has resided for several years in Brooklyn, N. Y.

Hutchinson, Gov. John, was born at Nottingham, England, in September, 1616. He was the son of Sir Thomas Hutchinson, and of the Lady Margaret, daughter of Sir John Biron, of Newstead. When he reached a proper age he spent five years in the University of Cambridge, where he greatly improved his opportunities for acquiring a superior education. After his marriage, which occurred July 3, 1638, he retired with his wife to Owthorpe, near Nottingham. There his mind became deeply exercised about religion, and he spent two entire years in the study of divinity. During this period he was enabled to put his whole trust in the Saviour, and he was led to see that salvation never entered a human heart through free will or creature merits, but through sovereign grace and the blood of Christ. From that period his faith warmly embraced the doctrine of God's election and of his minute overruling providence. He cherished a fervent love for the Saviour and his people, and a tender compassion for the impenitent and for personal enemies. The cavaliers and high-churchmen of his day, the men who caught the spirit of Archbishop Laud and his fellow-conspirators against Christ's truth and British liberty, were all Arminians, and Mr. Hutchinson was necessarily placed in the ranks of the defenders of the Commonwealth.

In the struggle which resulted in the overthrow and death of Charles I., he was made governor of the castle and town of Nottingham, and he became colonel of a regiment which he raised. The castle was a ruin and the town was full of traitors, some of whom were fitted by talents and malice to give

GOV. JOHN HUTCHINSON.

much trouble. Nottingham was a place of great importance to Charles and the Parliament. Under the care of the new governor the castle was greatly strengthened, and forts were erected to guard the town, malcontents were kept in check, the love of liberty was fostered, and the best interests of the people were secured. Repeated attacks of the foe were ignominiously defeated, and difficulties that overwhelmed others, and that would have crushed any ordinary leader, were surmounted with ease and honor. And when the sword of the king could not conquer the valiant governor and his men, immense sums of money were offered to corrupt Gov. Hutchinson and secure the stronghold. But it was held for the Parliament until Charles lost his head and the civil war was ended.

The fame of the governor spread all over his country. His skill, heroism, patience, and success made him dear to the hearts of all the friends of liberty in his native country. He was elected to the House of Commons, and he occupied a conspicuous and influential place in its debates. Cromwell early saw his extraordinary ability, and tried to enlist him on his side, but the governor quickly penetrated the selfish schemes of the future "uncrowned king" of England, and though Ireton, the son-in-law of Cromwell, was his cousin and trusted friend, he speedily informed the hero of

Marston Moor that he had not fought against one tyrant to assist in building the throne of another. And from that moment the coming Protector used every art to keep him from military promotion. Had it not been for Cromwell, Gov. Hutchinson would have been in a position, in all human probability, to have perpetuated a republic in the British Islands. He was one of the judges that tried Charles I., and signed his death-warrant.

After the return of Charles II. the English people for a time acted as if a wave of insanity had swept over the nation; the son of a deceitful and bloodthirsty despot, himself a treacherous libertine, was hailed with rapturous joy wherever he went; the enthusiasm was so general that hosts of the followers of Cromwell were carried away either through terror or a change of mind, and they made the air ring with their shouts for the king. The governor during this period of national madness kept his mind calm, and his heart courageous in his God, and while he took proper measures to protect himself he recanted no principle, he denied no act, he betrayed no friend. In a time when life could be purchased and large estates protected by information treacherously imparted, any amount of which was at his disposal, repeated opportunities to communicate which were given him by the attorney-general and others, he despised the meanness so common and so frequently commended of protecting himself by the sacrifice of others.

For a season he was unmolested at Owthorpe. He carefully attended to home duties, avoiding all connection with politics, expounding the Scriptures on the Lord's day to his family instead of attending the ministry of some semi-Catholic in the parish church. But at last he was arrested, and soon after he was removed to the Tower of London, and from it he was taken to Sandown Castle, in Kent, where he died Sept. 10, 1664, in the forty-ninth year of his age. During the eleven months of his imprisonment he enjoyed a large measure of the sustaining grace of God, and a foretaste of heavenly blessedness made his death-bed a scene of special joy.

Gov. Hutchinson believed that in religious affairs secular legislation had no place. He abhorred all persecution for conscience' sake. When George Fox, the founder of the "Society of Friends," was imprisoned in Nottingham, he extended to the persecuted Quaker his powerful protection.

He was a man of fearless courage, and when he saw his friends of the Commonwealth butchered by the bloody mandates of King Charles II., he was only restrained by his wife from giving himself up to die with them.

He and Mrs. Hutchinson became Baptists in this way: "When formerly the Presbyterian ministers had forced him, for quietness' sake, to go and break up a private (religious) meeting in the cannonier's chamber (of Nottingham Castle), there were found some notes concerning Pedobaptism, which were brought into the governor's lodgings, and his wife then having more leisure to read than he, having perused them and compared them with the Scriptures, found not what to say against the truths they asserted concerning the misapplication of that ordinance to infants; but being then young and modest, she thought it a kind of virtue to submit to the judgment and practice of most churches, rather than to defend a singular opinion of her own, she not being then enlightened in that great mistake of the national churches. But in this year, expecting to become a mother, she communicated her doubts to her husband, and desired him to endeavour her satisfaction; which while he did, he himself became as unsatisfied, or rather satisfied against it. First, therefore, he diligently searched the Scriptures alone, and could find in them no ground at all for that practice: then he bought and read all the eminent treatises on both sides, which at that time came thick from the presses, and was still more satisfied of the error of the Pedobaptists. After the confinement of his wife, that he might if possible give the religious party no offense, he invited all the ministers to dinner, and propounded his doubt and the ground thereof to them. None of them could defend their practice with any satisfactory reason but the tradition of the church from the primitive times, and their main buckler of federal holiness, which Tombs and Denne had so excellently overthrown. He and his wife then professing themselves unsatisfied in the practice, desired their opinions what they ought to do. Most answered, to conform to the general practice of other Christians, how dark soever it were to themselves; but Mr. Foxcraft, one of the Assembly (which framed the Westminster Confession of Faith), said that except they were convinced of the warrant of that practice from the Word they sinned in doing it: whereupon the infant was not baptized. And now the governor and his wife, notwithstanding that they forsook not their assemblies, nor retracted their benevolences and civilities from them, yet were they reviled by them, called fanatics and anabaptists, and often glanced at in their public sermons. And not only the ministers but all their zealous sectaries conceived implacable malice against them upon this account; which was carried on with a spirit of envy and persecution to the last; though he, on his side, might well have said to them, as his Master said to the old Pharisees, 'Many good works have I done among you; for which of those do you hate me?' Yet the generality even of them had a secret conviction upon them that he had been faithful to them and deserved their love; and in spite of their own bitter zeal, could not but have a reverent esteem for him whom they often railed at for not thinking and speaking according to their opinions." (Life of Colonel Hutchinson, by his Widow Lucy, pp. 299, 300, 301. London, 1846.)

This Christian hero, a graduate of Cambridge, like Judson, Noel, Carson, Dunster, and a host of others, sacrificed his feelings, his friendships, his interests, and his social comfort for no earthly gain, but for heaven-born truth. Gov. Hutchinson is an illustration of the resistless force of God's pure Word.

Hutchinson, Rev. John Blanchard, was born in Long Sutton, Lincolnshire, England, Dec. 16, 1825. His father was a respected minister of the Wesleyan body, and under his faithful labors his son was awakened. He also united with the Wesleyans, by whom he was licensed when but eighteen years of age. He came to America in May, 1856, and was minister in charge of the Methodist Episcopal church, South Orange and Jefferson Village, nearly three years.

His views of Bible truth becoming more matured he was baptized by Rev. William Hind, and entered into the membership of Northfield Baptist church, by which he was licensed to preach. On Oct. 1, 1860, he was ordained, and assumed charge of the Livingston church, in Essex Co., N. Y. Mr. Hutchinson has won for himself a strong place in the hearts of his brethren, and has rendered good service in the Olivet church, Philadelphia, the Centennial in Wilkesbarre, and in the Hatboro' church, Montgomery Co., Pa., where he now labors.

Hutchinson, Mrs. Lucy, was born the 29th of January, 1620, in the Tower of London. Her father was Sir Allen Apsley, governor of the Tower; her mother was Lucy, daughter of Sir John St. John, of Lidiard Treegooze, Wiltshire, England. Her parents were both the children of God, and by precept and example from her earliest years showed her the blessedness of a holy life.

When about seven years old she had eight teachers in as many different branches: languages, music, dancing, needlework, and writing. She hated needlework, and cared nothing for music and dancing. When children came to see her she wearied them with grave instructions, and treated their dolls so roughly that they were glad when she forsook their company for the society of older persons. Books were everything to her even in childhood; during hours intended for amusement she was reading, and at all other times when she had an opportunity. And when she reached womanhood her information was equal to that of any young lady in England, if she was not the best-informed woman in her country. Soon after she ceased to be a mere child she was called by Jesus into the kingdom of his grace; and she entered upon his service with a heart wholly his, and without a doubt of his love for her. This blessed condition fitted her to despise her own fancies, and every form of danger, and made Christ the Lord of

MRS. LUCY HUTCHINSON.

all her doctrines, and of her entire conduct. After her marriage with Mr. Hutchinson, when he was appointed governor of the castle and town of Nottingham, she went with him; and when the horrors of war visited Nottingham there was not a braver heart in the place than Mrs. Hutchinson's.

When five of her husband's soldiers were wounded and carried to the castle, and there was no surgeon to dress their wounds, with some assistance from a soldier, this young lady fearlessly bound up the bleeding limbs and bodies of the sufferers; and seeing some of the enemy carried in as prisoners in the same unfortunate situation, and consigned to a miserable dungeon, crowded with other prisoners, she sent for them and cleansed and bound up their wounds, while Capt. Palmer, an officer on her husband's side in the civil war, was helping her by declaring that "his soul abhorred to see this favor to the enemies of God."

Throughout life she ever showed a strong faith, a generous benevolence, and a lofty courage. She adopted Baptist sentiments from reading the notes found in the cannonier's room, in Nottingham Castle, where the Baptist soldiers had held a prayer-meeting; and from comparing them with the Scriptures; her husband, after careful and protracted examination, followed her example. But not all her quickness to perceive affronts; nor the exquisite pain inflicted by them upon her refined feeling; nor the certainty that insults, if not severe wrongs, would be heaped upon her for becoming a Baptist, could keep her from honoring and obeying her Lord. She confessed her principles in the most public way, in an age when Baptists alone understood Christ's law of religious liberty.

She helped her husband with more than the power of half a dozen ordinary men; and then she wrote his "Memoirs" in a style so charming and eloquent that it chains the reader from beginning to end. I doubt very much if in the seventeenth century, except the "Pilgrim's Progress," there was another book written in prose by such a masterly pen as that of Lucy Hutchinson. It is the best biography in the English language, and one of the most popular that ever was written in any tongue.

Hutchinson, Rev. William, was born in Drumlamph, Ireland, in August, 1795, of Scotch-Irish parents; came to the United States in 1818; entered Hamilton in 1821; ordained on leaving the institution, and labored as a missionary for three years in his native land; returned to this country in 1827, and has been pastor of seven churches in New York, and of Lower Dublin, Pa. Mr. Hutchinson has been blessed in delivering his glorious message, and he has walked with God in his own heart.

Hyatt, Rev. B. C., pastor at Monticello, Ark., was born in South Carolina in 1815; removed to Arkansas in 1846; ordained in 1857. His labors have been chiefly confined to the counties of Bradley, Drew, Ashley, and Lincoln; has gathered seven churches in his field, and baptized about one thousand persons.

Hyde, Rev. G. W., son of Richard and Eliza D. Hyde, was born near Chancellorsville, in Spottsylvania Co., Va., March 25, 1838. When a little more than one year old his parents removed to Missouri and settled near Keytesville, Chariton Co., where he was reared. He professed conversion and united with the Keytesville Baptist church in May, 1853. He entered the State University at Columbia, Mo., in September, 1855, and graduated with honors in July, 1859. In September, 1859, he entered the Southern Baptist Theological Seminary, then located at Greenville, S. C., and graduated in full in 1862. He was licensed to preach while a student at the university by the church in Columbia, and was ordained at Peterville church, Powhatan Co., Va., in August, 1863. He has twice been made financial agent of William Jewell College, and has been pastor at Keytesville and Brunswick, in Chariton Co., and also at Mount Nebo, Beulah, Concord, Mount Herman, and Boonville, in Cooper County. For ten years he has been an active member of the board of trustees of William Jewell College, and also a visitor of the Vardeman School of Theology. He has also been honored with the position of curator of Stephens College for a number of years.

Hyman, Rev. John J., was born Sept. 21, 1832. He is principal of the Mount Vernon Institute, at Riddleville, Ga. He was ordained April 12, 1863, and served all through the war as a chaplain of the 49th Ga. Regiment in Gen. Lee's army, and was considered one of the best chaplains in the army. During the war he baptized 260 soldiers, and since the war he has been a great worker both as pastor and teacher. He is an earnest, faithful pastor, a good preacher, and has served as moderator of Mount Vernon Association.

Hymns, and their Authors.—It is undeniable that in the infancy of the church, as Cave says, "It was usual for any person to compose divine songs in honor of Christ, and to sing them in the public assemblies." (Primitive Christianity, page 134, Oxford, 1840.) In the beginning of the second century, Pliny, in giving the emperor Trajan an account of the Christians, says, "They were accustomed to meet on a certain day before it was light and sing a hymn alternately to Christ as God." (Pliny, lib. x., Ep. 97.) This was evidently an uninspired composition. Eusebius, speaking of early hymns, says, "Whatever psalms and hymns were written by the brethren *from the beginning* celebrate Christ, the Word of God, by asserting His divinity." (Eccles. Hist., lib. v. cap. 28.) That there were many hymns written in the first and second centuries we have no doubt. These were all composed by Baptists. The oldest hymn now known among Christians in its most *ancient* form is, "Glory be to the Father, and to the Son, and to the Holy Ghost, world without end, Amen." In this form a Baptist was its author. And it was first given to the churches in the second century, or earlier. The additional words, "As it was in the beginning, is now, and ever shall be," were placed in this sacred song at an early period.

In modern times some of the most popular hymns in our language were written by Baptists. "My country, 'tis of thee," was written by Dr. S. F. Smith. This is the most popular patriotic hymn sung in the United States. "He leadeth me: oh, blessed thought," was written by Prof. J. H. Gilmore, of Rochester University. This is one of the finest hymns that ever was published. "Come, thou fount of every blessing," is from the pen of Robert Robinson. Rev. Dr. Fawcett wrote "Blest be the tie that binds." Dr. Samuel Stennett is the author of "On Jordan's stormy banks I stand," and the Rev. Edward Mote composed "My hope is built on nothing less." The following table gives the names of some Baptist authors of hymns, with their nationality, the date of their birth, and the first line of one of their hymns:

Name.	Born.	Country.	Hymns.
Adams, John	1751	England	"Sons we are through God's election."
Anderson, G. W.	1816	United States	"Onward, herald of the gospel."
Anderson, Mrs. G. W.	1819	France	"Our country's voice is pleading."
Balfern, W. P.		England	Author of a volume containing 139 hymns.
Baldwin, Thomas	1753	United States	"Come, happy souls, adore the Lamb."
Baxter, Mrs. Lydia	1809	"	"The Master is coming; he calleth for thee."
Beddome, Benjamin	1717	England	"Come, Holy Spirit, come."
Brown, J. Newton	1803	United States	"Go, spirit of the sainted dead."
Burnham, Richard	1749	England	"Jesus, thou art the sinner's friend."
Burton, John	1773	"	"Time is winging us away."
Cleveland, Benjamin		United States	"Oh, could I find from day to day."
Colver, Nathaniel	1794	"	"Weep for the lost; thy Saviour wept."
Cocks, Mrs. Sarah		England	Author of a volume of 216 original hymns.
Cole, Charles	1733	"	"Hark how the gospel trumpet sounds."
Cutting, S. S.	1816	United States	"Oh, Saviour, I am blind: lead thou the way."
Davis, Eliel	1803	England	"From every earthly pleasure."
Deacon, Samuel	1746	"	"To Jordan's stream the Saviour goes."
Denham, David	1791	"	"'Mid scenes of confusion and creature complaints."
Doane, W. H.		United States	"Safe in the arms of Jesus."
Draper, B. H.		England	"Ye Christian heralds, go proclaim."
Dracup, John	17—	"	"Thanks to thy name, O Lord, that we"
Dyer, Sidney	1814	United States	"Go preach the blest salvation."
Elvin, Cornelius	1797	England	"With broken heart and contrite sigh."
Evans, James H.	1785	"	"Faint not, Christian, though the road."
Evans, John M.	1825	United States	"Amid the joyous scenes of earth."
Fanch, James	1704	England	"Beyond the glittering, starry sky."
Fawcett, John	1739	"	"Blest be the tie that binds."
Fellows, John		"	"Jesus, mighty king in Zion."
Flowerdew, Alice	1759	"	"Fountain of mercy, God of love."
Fountain, John	1767	"	"Sinners, you are now addressed."
Francis, Benjamin	1734	Wales	"My gracious Redeemer I love."
Franklin, Jonathan	1760	England	"Thy church, O Lord, that's planted here."
Gadsby, William	1773	"	"Holy Ghost, we look to thee."
Giles, John E.	1805	"	"Thou hast said, exalted Jesus."
Gilmore, J. H.	1834	United States	"He leadeth me: oh, blessed thought."
Grace, Robert		England	Author of 240 hymns.
Groser, William	1791	"	"Praise the Redeemer, all mighty to save."
Groser, William House	18—	"	"Spirit of truth, celestial fire."
Harbottle, Joseph	1798	"	"See how the fruitless fig-tree stands."
Hinton, John H.	1791	"	"Once I was estranged from God."
Hill, Stephen P.	1806	United States	"The Lord is my shepherd and guide."
Horne, W. W.	1773	England	"Death is no more the frightful foe."
Hupton, Job	1762	"	"Jesus, omnipotent to save."
Ide, George B.	1805	United States	"Son of God, our glorious head."
James, R. S.	1824	"	"Hast'ning on to death's dark river."
Jessey, Henry	1606	England	"Unclean, unclean and full of sin."
Jones, Edmund	1722	"	"Come, humble sinner, in whose breast."
Judson, Adoniram	1788	United States	"Our Father God, who art in heaven."
Judson, Sarah B.	1803	"	"Proclaim the lofty praise."
Keach, Benjamin	1640	England	"My soul, mount up with eagle wings."
Keith, George		"	"How firm a foundation, ye saints of the Lord."
Knowles, J. D.	1798	United States	"O Lord, where'er thy saints apart."
Leland, John	1754	"	"The day is past and gone."
Lowry, Robert	1826	"	"Shall we gather at the river."
Lewis, W. G.		England	"Awake, my soul, thy God to praise."
Lawson, John		"	"Father of mercies, condescend."
Manly, Basil	1825	United States	"Holy, holy, holy Lord."
Medley, Samuel	1738	England	"Awake, my soul, in joyful lays."
Mote, Edward	1797	"	"My hope is built on nothing less."
Milton, John	1608	"	"Let us with a gladsome mind."
Needham, John	1710	"	"Holy and reverend is the name."
Newton, James	1733	"	"Let plenteous grace descend on those."
Norman, ——		"	"'Tis not as led by custom's voice."
Noel, B. W.	1799	"	"There's not a bird with lonely nest."
Pal, Krishna	1764	India	"O thou, my soul, forget no more."
Pearce, Samuel	1766	England	"In floods of tribulation."
Phelps, S. D.	1816	United States	"This rite our blest Redeemer gave."
Pledge, Ebenezer	1813	England	"I went alone: 'twas summer-time."
Poindexter, ——		United States	"Head of the Church, we bow to thee."
Rawson, George		England	"Cast thy burden on the Lord."
Rippon, John	1751	"	"There's joy in heaven and joy on earth."
Robbins, Gurdon		United States	"There is a land mine eye hath seen."
Robinson, Robert	1735	England	"Come, thou fount of every blessing."
Rowland, A. J.	1840	United States	"There is rest in the shadow."
Ryland, John	1753	England	"In all my Lord's appointed ways."
Saffery, Mrs. M. G.	1773	"	"'Tis the great Father we adore."
Scott, Jacob R.	1815	United States	"To thee this temple we devote."
Sherwin, W. F.		"	"Sound the battle-cry."
Smith, Samuel F.	1808	"	"My country, 'tis of thee."
Spurgeon, C. H.	1834	England	"The Holy Ghost is here."
Steele, Anne	1716	"	"The Saviour! Oh, what endless charms."
Stennett, Joseph	1663	"	"Another six days' work is done."
Stennett, Samuel	1727	"	"On Jordan's stormy banks I stand."
Swain, Joseph	1761	"	"Who can forbear to sing."
Sutton, Amos	1804	"	"Hail, sweetest, dearest tie that binds."
Thurber, Charles		United States	"From yonder Rocky Mountains."
Tritton, Joseph		England	"Spirit of glory and of grace."
Tucker, William	1731	"	"Amidst ten thousand anxious cares."
Turner, Daniel	1710	"	"Jesus, full of all compassion."
Turney, Edmund	1817	United States	"Oh, love divine! oh, matchless grace."
Upton, James	1760	England	"Come ye who bow to sovereign grace."
Wallin, Benjamin	1711	"	"Hail, mighty Jesus! How divine."
Washburn, H. S.	1811	United States	"Father, gathered round the bier."
Winkler, Edwin T.		"	"Our land with mercies crowned."
Wyard, George		England	Author of 140 hymns.
Ward, William	1769	"	"Oh, charge the waves to bear our friends."
Willmarth, J. W.	1835	France	"O Father! Lord of earth and heaven."
Yeager, George	1821	United States	"On the cross behold the Saviour."

I.

Ide, George B., D.D., was born in Coventry, Vt., in 1804, and was the son of Rev. John Ide, a Baptist minister of considerable reputation in the section in which he lived. Young Ide received an

GEORGE B. IDE, D.D.

academic and collegiate education, and he graduated at Middlebury College. It was his purpose to practise law, and he and his fellow-townsman Redfield, afterwards Judge Redfield, of Vermont, commenced a course of legal study in Brandon, Vt. Like Adoniram Judson, whose father also was a minister, Mr. Ide was inclined to be a skeptic, and did not hesitate sometimes to avow his infidel sentiments. But he was reached by the power of divine grace, and finally became settled in his belief of those doctrines which he so eloquently preached in after-life. At once he threw himself into the work of preaching the gospel, and as a revivalist preached with great power in different sections in Northern Vermont. For a short time in each place he was pastor of the churches in Derby, Passumpsic village, and Brandon, Vt., from which place he was called to the pastoral care of the First Baptist church in Albany, N. Y. Here he remained until, having completed a four years' pastorate, he was called to the Federal Street, now Clarendon Street, church, in Boston, where he continued for two years. He then went to Philadelphia to take charge of the First Baptist church in that city, where he remained for fourteen years, taking rank with the ablest and most eloquent preachers of any denomination in that city. From Philadelphia, Dr. Ide was called to the First Baptist church in Springfield, Mass., and was its pastor from 1852 to the time of his death, a period of nearly twenty years. Twice during this time he was called to important positions in New York, with double the salary he was receiving in Springfield, but he declined, not wishing to take upon himself the burdens of a large city church.

Without doubt Dr. Ide was one of the most vigorous and effective preachers that the Baptist denomination has had in this country. He has given to the public some of his more elaborate discourses in two volumes, bearing the titles "Bible Pictures" and "Battle Echoes," the latter a series of sermons preached during the late civil war. He was also the author of a Sunday-school book, which reached a considerable popularity, entitled "Green Hollow." He published also a missionary sermon, and several works of a denominational character.

Ide, Rev. John, was born in Vermont in 1785. For more than half a century he was a devoted minister of Christ. He was converted when he was about thirty years of age, and commenced his ministerial labors in Coventry, Vt. He was greatly prospered in his work. In one of the revivals which occurred under his ministry, six of his own children were converted and baptized together. In the different pastorates which he held, he was successful in the vocation upon which in early manhood he had entered. When he commenced his ministry the Baptists in Vermont were comparatively few in number, and were "everywhere spoken against." They were taxed to support the "standing order" by the laws of the State. In case of refusal to pay their taxes they were subject to the "pains and penalties" of the law, obedience to which they could not conscientiously render. In the meridian of his days Mr. Ide was associated with Gov. Butler, and men who sympathized with him, in fighting the battles of religious freedom in the Vermont Legislature. They were at last successful, and the Baptists were no longer compelled to support a ministry which did not preach what they regarded as the whole truth. Mr. Ide died at Potsdam, N. Y., July 27, 1860.

Illinois, Missionary Organizations.—What seems to have been the beginning of organized missionary work in Illinois was the appointment, by a meeting of Baptists held at Edwardsville in 1831, of a committee, instructed to arrange and superintend "a system of traveling preaching to promote the interests of religion within the limits of Illinois." The members of this committee were James Lemen, Paris Mason, George Stacey, James Pulliam, B. F. Edwards, J. M. Peck, and Hubbell Loomis. Rev. J. M. Peck was the missionary placed under appointment by this committee, receiving his support from the East, through an arrangement with the Massachusetts Baptist Missionary Society. The committee named above do not seem to have attempted independent work of any kind, but simply served as an agency for correspondence with the Massachusetts board, through Dr. Going.

Of the missionaries put into the field under this joint arrangement may be named, besides Mr. Peck, Alvin Bailey, Moses Lemen, Gardner Bartlett, Jacob Bower, and Elijah Dodson,—all names of note in the Baptist pioneer history of Illinois. The committee continued under appointment from year to year by what was called the General Union Meeting of Illinois Baptists, until October, 1834. At that time the Illinois Baptist State Convention was organized at Whitehall, Green Co. Three Associations and two churches were represented in its formation. The scope of the society was soon enlarged, so that at the third anniversary, which was held at Peoria, Oct. 12, 1837, eight Associations and ten churches were represented. The support of missions in the State was made a chief feature of the Convention's yearly plans, and at the anniversary just alluded to it was resolved to raise, in the ensuing year, $2000 for this purpose. Attention was also given to ministerial education, the institution at Upper Alton being one of the objects reported upon regularly at the yearly meetings.

At the anniversary of the Convention, held at Bellville, Oct. 3, 1844, a committee was appointed to confer with a committee of the Northwestern Baptist Convention upon the subject of a union of the two bodies. These committees met at Canton, November 21 following, and a new organization was made, called the Illinois Baptist General Association, covering the whole State. The Northwestern Convention had been formed in 1841, in consequence of dissatisfaction with the proceedings of the State Convention, "and to accommodate and bring into concerted action the brethren residing in Wisconsin, Iowa, and Northern Indiana," along with the Baptists in Northern Illinois. By the recent action, this body was now merged in the Illinois Baptist General Association, which has remained until the present date the missionary organization for the State. A "Baptist Convention for Southern Illinois," composed of churches and Associations declining to enter into the new organization, continued for some years to exist, but the strength of the Baptist body in the State has been concentrated in the General Association from the time of its organization at Canton, in 1844. Since that date, as nearly as can be ascertained, the number of missionaries bearing its commission has been about 600, the number of baptisms by these missionaries not far from 4000, and the amount of money raised and expended in salaries to missionaries nearly $125,000.

Illinois Woman's Baptist Missionary Society.—The Woman's Baptist Missionary Society of the West was organized at Chicago, May 9, 1871. Its first officers were Mrs. Robert Harris, President; Mrs. A. M. Bacon, Recording Secretary; Mrs. C. F. Tolman, Corresponding Secretary; Mrs. S. M. Osgood, Treasurer. The society is auxiliary to the American Baptist Missionary Union, having been formally accepted as such at the anniversary meeting in May, 1871. At the first annual meeting Mrs. A. L. Stevens was present, the first applicant for appointment to the foreign field. Since that time 24 missionaries have been sent out, of whom one has returned in feeble health, two have died, seven have, by marriage, been transferred to the service of the Missionary Union; leaving as missionaries of this society (1880), six in Burmah, three in India, and five in China. Miss Daniels, of Swatow, China, is the only medical missionary connected with the society of the West. During the year 1879–80 the society supported 13 missionaries, 17 schools, and 31 Bible-women. It sent within the year contributions to 18 missionaries of the Union, and to 2 supported by the Society of the East.

The contributions during the first year of the society were $4244.69. Those reported for the year 1879–80 amounted to $18,483.91. The present officers of the society are Mrs. A. J. Howe, President; Mrs. C. F. Tolman, Vice-President; Mrs. J. O. Brayman, Recording Secretary; Mrs. A. M. Bacon, Corresponding Secretary; Mrs. F. A. Smith, Treasurer.

Immersion.—We have a profound regard for the theology of John Calvin, and for many of his utterances. We view his declaration, "The word *baptize*, however, signifies *to immerse*, and it is certain that immersion was observed by the ancient church,"* as displaying sound learning, an accurate knowledge of church history, and fidelity

---
* Ipsum baptizandi verbum mergere significat, et mergendi, ritum veteri ecclesiæ observatum fuisse constat. Inst. Christ. Relig., lib. iv. cap. 15, sect. 19. London, 1576.

to truth. No man fully acquainted with the facts upon which the opinion of the great Genevan was based, could speak otherwise and maintain fidelity to the truth. Luther says, "Baptism is a Greek word; in Latin it can be translated immersion, as when we plunge something into water that it may be completely covered with water."* Luther and Calvin translate the Greek word baptism as it was understood by those who used the language of which it was a part, before Christ's days, and ever afterwards. In the sense of immersion it is employed in the New Testament. The whole church of Christ practised immersion for at least twelve centuries of our era, and several nations baptize in that manner still.

Tertullian, in the end of the second century, writes, "The act of baptism itself belongs to the flesh, because we are immersed in water."† Jerome, in his notes on Ephesians iv. 5, says, "We are immersed three times‡ to receive the one baptism of Christ." Ambrose, expounding the baptismal death in Romans vi. 3, says, "The death, therefore, is a figurative, not a real bodily death, for when you are immersing you present a likeness of death and burial."§ Pope Leo the Great, speaking of baptism in the fifth century, says, "Trine immersion is an imitation of the three days' burial (of Christ), and the emersion out of the waters is a figure (of the Saviour) rising from the grave."‖

According to Bede, who died in 735, Paulinus, the apostle of the north of England, "washed" some of his converts "in the river Glen," baptized others "in the river Swale" of Yorkshire," and a "great multitude in the river Trent."¶ Laufranc, archbishop of Canterbury in the eleventh century, commenting on Phil. iii. 10, says, "Being made conformable unto his death in baptism, for as Christ lay for three days in the sepulchre, so let there be a trine immersion in baptism."** St. Bernard, the most prominent ecclesiastic in France in the twelfth century, in his sermon on the Lord's Supper, says, "Baptism is the first of all the sacraments, in which we are planted together in the likeness of his (Christ's) death. Hence trine immersion represents the three days we are about to celebrate."††

There are many baptisteries in Italy that were used for centuries for the immersion of candidates for baptism. The most remarkable of these is in the catacomb of San Ponziano, Rome. It is on the right side of the Via Ostiensis, and at a short distance beyond the Porta Portese. Through this cemetery a stream of water runs, the channel of which is diverted into a reservoir, which was used for administering baptism by immersion from the first to the fourth centuries;‡‡ and within a few years candidates for primitive baptism have been buried under its waters once more. Dr. Cote§§ gives a list of sixty-seven of these baptisteries that exist in Italy now, some of them ready for service and others greatly changed. Not a few of the edifices reared to cover the baptismal pools are spacious and magnificent. The baptisteries above ground were erected from the fourth to the fourteenth century. The sacristan who shows the sacred structure has no hesitation in telling the visitor that the church formerly practised immersion. Until the beginning of the thirteenth century immersion was the mode of baptism of all Western Christendom, except in cases of sickness, and it was a common practice long afterwards in many parts of the papal dominions; it was the general usage in England until after the Reformation, and it was frequently observed down to the middle of the seventeenth century. There is a record of the immersion of Arthur and Margaret, the brother and sister of Henry VIII.,‖‖ and there is no doubt that immersion was the mode of baptism that prevailed all over his kingdom in Henry's day.

William Wall, the learned Episcopalian writer, says, that "in 1536 the lower house of Convocation sent to the upper house a protestation, containing a catalogue of some errors and some profane sayings that began to be handed about among some people, craving the concurrence of the upper house in condemning them. Some of them are these:

"'That it is as lawful to christen a child in a tub of water at home, or in a ditch by the way, as in a font-stone in the church.'

"I think," says Wall, "it may probably be concluded from their expressions, that the ordinary way of baptizing at this time in England, whether in the church or out of it, was by putting the child into the water."¶¶ He then proceeds to give the others.

In Tyndale's "Obedience of a Christian Man," published in 1528, he writes, "Ask the people what they understand by their baptism or washing, and

---

* Latine potest verti mersio, cum immergimus aliquid in aquam ut totum tegatur aqua. De Sacram. Bapt. Opera Lutheri, i. p. 319. 1564.

† In aqua mergimur. De Baptismo, cap. 7, pars ii. p. 37. Lipsiæ, 1839.

‡ Ter mergimur, tome ix. p. 109. Basle, 1516.

§ Cum enim mergis, mortis suscepis et sepulturæ similitudinem. De Sacramentis, lib. ii. cap. 7.

‖ Trina demersio, ep. 16, vol. liv. p. 699, Patrl. Lat.

¶ In fluvio Gleni . . . in Sualo fluvio. In fluvio Treenta. Hist. Eccles., ii. 14, p. 104; ii. 16, p. 107. Oxonii, 1846.

** Sic in baptismate trina sit immersio.

†† Trina mersio.

‡‡ Baptism and Baptisteries, p. 102. Amer. Bapt. Publication Society.

§§ Idem, 110–112.

‖‖ Cathcart's Baptism of the Ages, pp. 41–43. Amer. Bapt. Publication Society.

¶¶ History of Infant Baptism, p. 648. Nashville.

thou shalt see that they believe how that the very plunging into the water saveth them." . . . "Behold how narrowly the people look on the ceremony. If ought be left out, or if the child be not altogether dipt in the water, or if, because the child is sick, the priest dare not plunge him into the water, but pour water on his head, how tremble they! how quake they! 'How say ye, Sir John' (the priest), say they, 'is this child christened enough? Hath it his full christendom?' They verily believe that the child is not christened."[*] At this time plunging into water was the mode of baptism in England, and the exception of sick children was evidently unpopular; and the substitute for immersion, according to good William Tyndale, the translator of the English Bible, was regarded with grave suspicions.

The Book of Common Prayer, issued by the authority of Edward VI., in 1549, says, "Then the priest shall take the child in his hands, and ask the name. And naming the child, shall dip it in the water thrice. First, dipping the right side; second, the left side; the third time dipping the face toward the font; so it be discreetly and warily done. And if the child be weak it shall suffice to pour water upon it."[†] Immersion was still the custom as well as the law in England, with the exception for which the Prayer Book made provision.

On May 18, 1556, a complaint was made against a considerable number of persons who favored the gospel in Ipswich, before Queen Mary's council, sitting in commission at Beccles, in Suffolk. Among the charges preferred was a refusal to have children dipped in the fonts:

"Mother Fenkel, and Joan Ward, *alias* Bentley's wife, refused to have children dipped in the fonts. Mother Beriff, midwife, refused to have children dipped in the fonts."[‡]

There is no hint given by Fox, who records the names and accusations of these servants of God, that they preferred sprinkling or pouring for the children. They were Baptists undoubtedly, and dipping in the font was still the common mode of baptism.

Mr. Blake, vicar of Tamworth, in Staffordshire, the author of a pamphlet published in 1645, entitled "Infant's Baptism Freed from Antichristianism," writes on the first page, "I have been an eye-witness of many infants dipped, and know it to have been the constant practice of many ministers in their places for many years together." Mr. Blake is supposed to have been forty-three years of age when he wrote his pamphlet.

In the Westminster Assembly of Divines, on Aug. 7, 1644, according to Dr. John Lightfoot, when a vote was taken on the question, "The minister shall take water and sprinkle or pour it with his hand upon the face or forehead of the child," " it was voted so indifferently that we were glad to count names twice, for *so many were unwilling to have dipping excluded* that the vote came to an equality within one; for the one side was twenty-five, the other twenty-four, the twenty-four for the reserving of dipping and the twenty-five against it."[§] The question was finally decided against immersion the next day, and "it is said entirely by the influence of Dr. Lightfoot," as Ivimey states.[||] It seems surprising that an assembly of Presbyterians should be nearly equally divided about retaining immersion as a mode of baptism, and that "so many (in it), though none of them were Baptists, were unwilling to have dipping excluded." Learned Roman Catholics and Episcopalians have no prejudices against immersion; but, in 1876, Rev. J. H. Clark, of the Lackawanna Presbytery, Pa., immersed an applicant for membership in his church, for which he was censured by his Presbytery. His appeal to the Synod of Philadelphia resulted in the following decision: "In view of the teachings and principles entering into the doctrine of baptism, we judge that the administration of baptism by Rev. J. H. Clark, in the case excepted to came within the *possible limits of a permissible* administration of the rite, and although without *any sanction of command or fact in the Sacred Scriptures*, yet did not involve a moral wrong. The mode of administration, however, not being accordant with the distinctive mode of baptism accepted and appointed by the Presbyterian Church, we do approve of the spirit of the exception of the Presbytery of Lackawanna, as,"[¶] etc. The ministers composing the Synod of Philadelphia are men of broad culture and Christian integrity, but they differ widely from Mr. Coleman and Mr. Marshall and "many" others in the Westminster Assembly, who were "*unwilling to have dipping excluded;*" but the men of English birth who took part in framing the Confession of Faith of the Presbyterian Church in the United States, in 1644, had seen immersions all around them in the state church, the older men in large numbers, the younger men less frequently; and many of them loved the baptism of their fathers and of the Founder of Christianity.

Mr. Crosby mentions that "many sober and pious people belonging to the congregations of the Dissenters about London were convinced that

---

[*] Doctrinal Treatises, i. 276–77. Parker Society.
[†] Liturgies of King Edward VI., pp. 111, 112. Parker Society.
[‡] Acts and Monuments, viii. 599. London, 1839.
[§] The Whole Works of Lightfoot, vol. xiii. 301. London, 1824.
[||] History of the English Baptists, i. 183. London, 1811.
[¶] Burrage's Act of Baptism, p. 210. Amer. Bapt. Pub. Soc.

believers were the only proper subjects of baptism, and that it ought to be administered by immersion," and not being satisfied with the qualifications of any administrator in England, they sent Richard Blount to Holland, who received immersion there; and on his return he baptized according to the primitive mode Samuel Blacklock, a minister, and these baptized the rest of the company.* This event *may* have occurred, and if it did, it was probably about the beginning of the reign of Charles I.; no regular *Calvinistical* Baptist minister may have been permitted to live in England by the oppressions of the king and Laud, and though large numbers of persons then living in that country had been immersed, in the majority of cases it was not after believing. Mr. Hutchinson, from whom Crosby quotes, says about these persons, "The great objection was the want of an administrator, which, *as I have heard*, was removed by sending certain messengers to Holland." Crosby himself says, "This agrees with an account given of the matter in an ancient manuscript, *said to have been written* by Mr. William Kiffin." We would not bear *heavily* on the testimony adduced by these good men.

The Rev. John Mason Neale, a learned Episcopalian, whose "History of the Holy Eastern Church" is an authority on most of the topics on which it treats, writes, "The Constantinopolitan (Greek Church) ritual says, 'The priest baptizes him, holding him upright, and facing the East, and saying, "The servant of God is baptized in the name of the Father, and of the Son, and of the Holy Spirit," etc. At each sentence plunging and raising him up from the water.'

"The Coptic ritual says, 'He thrice immerses him, and after each immersion raises him up and breathes in his face.'

"The Armenian ritual says, 'Then the priest takes the child in his arms, and immerses him thrice in water, as an emblem of the three days' burial of Christ.'"†

In a celebrated Syriac liturgy it is written, "The priest stands by the font, and invokes the Spirit, who descendeth from on high, and rests on the waters, and sanctifies them, and makes new sons to God.

"When the child *is plunged into the water* the priest saith, 'N. is baptized for sanctity and salvation and a blameless life, and a blessed resurrection from the dead, in the name of the Father. Amen. And of the Son. Amen. And of the living and Holy Ghost for life everlasting. Amen.'"‡ "All the Syrian forms prescribe or assume trine immersion."§

Badger gives the baptismal ritual of the Nestorians, which says, "Then they shall take him (the child) to the priest, standing by the font, who shall place him therein, with his face to the East, and he shall dip him therein three times. . . . In dipping him he shall dip him up to the neck, and then put his hand upon him, so that his head may be submerged; then the priest shall take him out of the font and give him to the deacon." ‖

In Picart's description of Abyssinian baptism, we learn that "As soon as the benediction of the font is over the priest plunges the infant into it three times successively. At the first he dips one-third part of the infant's body into the water, saying, 'I baptize thee in the name of the Father;' he then dips him lower, about two-thirds, adding, 'I baptize thee in the name of the Son;' the third time he plunges him all over, saying, 'I baptize thee in the name of the Holy Ghost.'"¶

The same author, as quoted by Burrage, describing the baptism of "the Rhynsburgers, or Collegiants, a branch of the Mennonites, originating in Holland," says,—

"The candidate for baptism makes publicly his profession of faith on a Saturday, in the morning, before an assembly of Rhynsburgers held for that purpose. A discourse is pronounced on the excellency and nature of baptism. The minister and candidate go together to a pond behind a house belonging to his sect (we might call it a hospital, since they received for nothing those who had not wherewithal to pay their hotel bills). In that pond the neophyte, catechumen, or candidate is baptized by immersion. If a man, he has a waistcoat and drawers; if a woman, a bodice and petticoat, with leads in the hem."** Picart's work was published in Amsterdam in 1736.

The Russian Church, the Greek Church in Turkey and in the little kingdom of Greece, the Armenian, Nestorian, Coptic, Abyssinian, and the other Christian communities of the East, have always practised immersion, and that is their usage at this hour. About a fourth of the whole Christian people on earth still immerse in baptism; and counting the centuries when immersion was the mode of baptism used by all Christendom, and the millions that employ it still, we are safe in affirming that a majority of all Christians, living and dead, were immersed in baptism. (See articles on SCRIPTURAL MODE OF BAPTISM, BAPTISM OF CLOVIS, BAPTISM OF TEN THOUSAND ENGLISH.)

Immersions, Great European.—There are several remarkable baptisms which took place when Christianity was triumphantly introduced into some

---

* History of the English Baptists, i. 161-63.
† History of the Holy Eastern Church, p. 949. London, 1850.
‡ Neale's History of the Holy Eastern Church, pp. 992-93. London, 1850. § Idem, 950.

‖ The Nestorians and their Rituals, pp. 207, 208. London, 1852.
¶ Burrage's Act of Baptism, p. 182.
** Idem, p. 180.

of the European nations in which the mode was positively immersion. Saint Patrick baptized more than 12,000 men at one time in a spring in Ireland. (See article on PATRICK, THE APOSTLE OF IRELAND.) Clovis, king of the Franks, with 3000 warriors, his two sisters, and other women and their children, was baptized by "trine immersion" in 496. (See article on THE BAPTISM OF CLOVIS.) Ten thousand English were immersed in the river Swale, near Canterbury, in 597. (See article on BAPTISM OF TEN THOUSAND ENGLISH.) Three thousand English were baptized by Paulinus in 627, in a fountain in Northumberland, England. (See article on BAPTISTERY OF PAULINUS IN ENGLAND.) The whole population of the city of Kieff were immersed in the Dneiper at one time, about 988. (See article on BAPTISM OF THE POPULATION OF KIEFF.) These great baptisms must have conformed to the recognized mode of administering the ordinance.

Imposition of Hands after Baptism was a common custom among Baptists in the seventeenth century, in Europe and America, though it never was a general practice. Its observance often occasioned bitter controversies, which sometimes rent churches. The First church of Providence, R. I., continued the laying on of hands till the end of Dr. Manning's ministry; and the supposition that he held the observance of it rather to satisfy the consciences of others than to meet the demands of his own, subjected him to much opposition. When the Philadelphia Association adopted the English Baptist Confession of Faith of 1689, they added two articles to that document, one "On Singing of Psalms," and another on "Laying on of Hands." In the latter article the Confession of Faith says, "We believe that laying on of hands, with prayer, upon baptized believers, as such, is an ordinance of Christ, and ought to be submitted unto by all such persons as are admitted to partake of the Lord's Supper; and that the end of this ordinance is not for the extraordinary gifts of the Spirit, but for a further reception of the Holy Spirit of promise, or for the addition of the graces of the Spirit, and the influences thereof; to confirm, strengthen, and comfort them in Christ Jesus; it being ratified and established by the extraordinary gifts of the Spirit in the primitive times, to abide in the church, as meeting together on the first day of the week was, Acts ii. 1, that being the day of worship or Christian Sabbath, under the gospel; and as preaching the Word was, Acts x. 44, and as baptism was, Matt. iii. 16, and prayer was, Acts iv. 31, and singing psalms, etc., was, Acts xvi. 25, 26, so this of laying on of hands was, Acts viii. and xix.; for as the whole gospel was confirmed by signs and wonders, and divers miracles and gifts of the Holy Ghost in general, so was every ordinance in like manner confirmed in particular." This article was adopted with the Confession, Sept. 25, 1742. The Roxborough and Second Baptist churches of Philadelphia still practise this observance. Before the hand of fellowship is given to the newly baptized the pastor places his hands upon the head of each one and prays for the person.

By most modern Baptist churches the article quoted from the Philadelphia Confession of Faith is regarded as one of the unwise things received by our American religious ancestors. The few churches that still retain this usage see something in it to admire.

Imputed Righteousness. See article on JUSTIFICATION.

Index, The Christian, a weekly Baptist paper, has been published in the State of Georgia since the year 1833. It was first issued in Washington, D. C., under the auspices of the Baptist Board of Foreign Missions, under the name of *The Columbian Star*, and was removed to Philadelphia, where it was edited by Dr. Wm. T. Brantly, the elder, with the approval of the board. In 1833 it was transferred to Jesse Mercer, who began its publication in Washington, Wilkes Co., Ga., for his own convenience, securing the services of Rev. Wm. H. Stokes as assistant editor. In 1840, Mr. Mercer transferred the paper to the Georgia Baptist Convention, by which body it was published in Penfield until 1856, when it was removed to Macon. In 1861 it was sold to S. Boykin, at that time its editor. By him it was published until the close of the civil war, when he sold it to J. J. Toon, of Atlanta, who transferred it to that city. A few years ago Mr. Toon sold his entire publishing establishment, including the *Index*, to Jas. P. Harrison & Co., who now issue the *Index*. It is doubtful if there is any other one instrumentality by which the denomination in Georgia has been more benefited and united than *The Christian Index*. Its present editor is Dr. H. H. Tucker, a writer of great clearness and power, of extensive erudition, of mature judgment, full of love for the truth, one of nature's noblemen, whose journal is an honor to the Baptist denomination.

Indian Missions.—The attention of the Baptist Triennial Convention was early turned to the spiritual condition of the Indian tribes of North America. At the first meeting of the Convention after its formation in 1814, steps were taken to commence evangelical work among these "wards of the nation." In the directions given to Messrs. John M. Peck and James E. Welch, they were specially enjoined in the performance of their duties as domestic missionaries, stationed at St. Louis, to carry the gospel to the Indians with whom they might be brought in contact. The first person appointed to devote his whole time to this work was

Rev. Isaac McCoy, who was stationed at what was at that time—1818—the far West,—Fort Wayne, Ind. The several tribes of Miamies, Kickapoos, Ottawas, and Pottawatomies, all speaking dialects which had among them much that was common, came within the sphere of Mr. McCoy's labors. He was so far successful in his attempts to reach the people in the field of his missionary operations that he succeeded in gathering a school of 48 pupils, and in various ways had brought the truths of the gospel to the knowledge of these heathen of North America.

In 1822 a new station was established on the banks of the St. Joseph's River. This new station, which was named Carey in honor of the distinguished missionary, was a hundred miles from the nearest settlement of white men. To this place those who had been gathered under the fostering care of the missionary at Fort Wayne were removed, so that it was not long before there was a church at Carey of 30 or 40 members, many of whom were Indians, and it is said that "its exercises of public worship on the Sabbath often attracted large companies of natives from the adjacent settlements."

A third station was formed on the Grand River among the Ottawas, which was called Thomas, in honor of the English missionary of that name. When, in 1829, the station at Carey was partially abandoned, the missionaries withdrew to the new settlement, where the prospects of success were more hopeful. In 1832 several of the Indians gave such evidence of genuine conversion that they were baptized and received into the church. One of the principal chiefs of the Ottawas, Noonday, was among the number, and his after-life furnished proof that he was a sincere disciple of the Lord Jesus. While there were there things to encourage, there were others to depress. The Indians retire before the approach of civilization, and their territories fall into the hands of white men. The settlement at Thomas was broken up, and the mission, with the Indians connected with it, removed to Richland, fifty miles farther south. The most of the Ottawas have long ago disappeared from Michigan, and there is but little left to indicate what was done for their spiritual benefit by the self-denying missionaries who labored so earnestly to do them good.

The history of the mission among the Ojibwas deserves a passing notice. The board of the Triennial Convention, in 1828, accepted the funds appropriated by Congress to be expended for the benefit of this tribe, and established a mission at Saut Ste. Marie, one of the trading-places of the tribe, not far from fifteen miles southeast of Lake Superior. Rev. Abel Bingham was appointed missionary. His efforts were directed to both the whites and the Indians, and so successful was he that during a time of awakened religious interest, in 1832, forty persons were baptized and added to the church. Eleven of this number were Indians. A translation of the New Testament into Ojibwa was made and printed in 1833 in Albany, N. Y., and circulated among the people. The mission passed through various fortunes, adverse and prosperous, until 1857, when it was discontinued.

The mission among the Cherokees has yielded as much substantial fruit as any that has been attempted by the Baptists among the Indians. In the list of the early missionaries sent to this tribe we find the honored name of Evan Jones. Through his labors, and those of his associates, we find that up to the time of the removal of the Cherokees by order of the United States government, in 1838, hundreds of them had been converted and formed into Christian churches. Mr. Jones followed the Cherokees to their new home, and continued to labor for their spiritual good until his removal to Kansas in 1862. In 1842 all the churches were reported as having meeting-houses, and a printing-office had been furnished at the expense of the Cherokees. In 1846 the translation of the New Testament was completed. The progress of the mission was steadily maintained year after year, and the influence of the gospel in elevating and blessing the people was of the most marked character. In 1863 the estimate of the number of church members was 1500.

Other Indian tribes among whom Baptist missionaries have labored are the Choctaws, the Creeks, the Otoes, the Omahas, the Delawares, and the Shawanees. Among the honored servants of Christ who have labored among these different tribes may be mentioned Rev. Moses Merrill, Rev. Jotham Meeker, Rev. Leonard Slater, Rev. Thomas Frye, Rev. Jesse Busyhead, a native preacher, Rev. John B. Jones, Rev. Ira D. Blanchard, Rev. J. G. Pratt, Misses E. S. and H. H. Morse, Rev. J. Lykins, and Rev. Francis Barker.

The Home Mission Society has spent nearly $28,000 since 1865 in supporting missionaries among the Indians. It has at present three white missionaries, one colored, and six Indian, laboring among the Indians in the Indian Territory. It also supports the principal of a normal and theological school. In the Indian Territory there are 100 Baptist churches, with a membership of 6000.

See article on SOUTHERN BAPTIST CONVENTION.

Indiana Baptist Papers.—The *American Messenger* was first begun in Madison in 1843, with Rev. E. D. Owen as editor. It was then a bi-weekly, afterwards a weekly. In 1846 he removed it to Indianapolis, and after about one year sold it to the *Cross and Journal*, of Ohio, and it became a part of what is now the *Journal and Messenger*.

At a meeting of brethren attending commencement exercises at Franklin College, in June, 1856, it was unanimously resolved "that we make an effort to start a paper at Indianapolis," and "that the matter be put into the hands of a publishing committee, until such time as a suitable editor can be found." The paper was called *The Witness*. Very soon Rev. M. G. Clarke became editor. He was succeeded by Rev. E. W. Clark, who conducted it till 1867, when it was sold to the *Christian Times*, of Chicago, and became a part of what is now *The Standard*. Three different papers have been started by the presidents of Franklin College, as aids in their work. Dr. Chandler published a few numbers of *The Baptist Inquirer* in 1843. President Wayland issued twelve or fifteen numbers of the *Camp-Fire* in 1870, and President Stott has for three years conducted *The Link* in the immediate interests of the college.

Rev. A. R. Hinckley was for several years associate editor of the *Baptist Banner and Pioneer*, published in Louisville, Ky. Hon. J. L. Holman was likewise, for several years, associate editor of the *Baptist Advocate*, published in Cincinnati, O.

Rev. W. N. Wyeth, D.D., Indianapolis, is at present one of the editors of the *Journal and Messenger*.

Indiana Baptist State Convention, The, was organized at a church called Brandywine, in Shelby County, in April, 1833. Rev. Samuel Harding was elected President; Rev. J. L. Holman, Recording Secretary; Rev. Ezra Fisher, Corresponding Secretary, and Henry Bradley, Esq., Treasurer. The annual sermon was preached by Rev. Ezra Fisher. There were present 37 delegates, and the treasurer's receipts were $17.00.

The receipts in 1840 were $1265.05; 1850, $1139.73; 1860, $2464.23; 1870, $410.05; 1879, $3495.30.

The first policy adopted for the evangelization of the State was that each minister should spend several weeks in traveling, holding a series of meetings in destitute places.

These brethren received very little compensation, in some cases none. The next plan was to collect money in the several Associations, and employ a few men to travel and preach all the time. But little money was expended at any one point, and so the fruits of the labor were not apparent for any length of time. Next the "village fund" policy, introduced from Ohio by Rev. T. R. Cressy, who came into the State as pastor, was tried. In this plan men pledged themselves to give $5 or $10 per year for five years, to aid in planting Baptist churches in the villages. It did not contemplate the permanent settlement of a pastor over the church, and so it failed of any great fruit. Finally it was agreed that the money gathered should be expended only at such places as gave promise of success. For several years there was much discussion as to what points gave such promise. At the present time the settled policy of the State board is that no place shall be aided that does not give hopes of *becoming self-supporting* within a reasonable time, and the success of State missions was never so fully assured as now. The Convention at this time employs ten missionaries, and through the efficient labors of the general agent, Rev. A. J. Essex, the salaries are paid quarterly. The board is especially seizing opportunities to plant churches in country towns. Within five years a new departure has been taken as to the relation the State Convention sustains to foreign missions, home missions, education, etc.

It was formerly thought that the body having State missions in charge was the State Convention, and that the other organizations met with it for convenience, and by courtesy. The present conviction is that each of these organizations is a part of the State Convention. The Convention, through appropriate standing committees or boards, attends to State missions, home missions, foreign missions, publication society, education, etc. The organization under its present management seems to be in a high state of efficiency.

The past year 260 churches contributed to State missions; that was the largest number ever giving money for this purpose. This year the number will be 300.

Indiana Baptists, their Origin and Growth. —The first church organized in what is now the State of Indiana was originally called Owens, next Fourteen-Mile, and then Silver Creek. While bearing the name Silver Creek, the church was divided by the doctrines of A. Campbell; the portion holding fast the doctrines of the Philadelphia Confession of Faith retaining their organization, and finally becoming the Charlestown church. The original church was constituted in 1798, under the leadership of Rev. Isaac Edwards, a native of New Jersey. The church is best known in history by the name Silver Creek. Around it was gathered at length the Silver Creek Association, which in turn become three or four Associations. The first settlements were along the rivers, and so the centres of Baptist strength were at first along the Wabash on the west, the Ohio on the south, and White Water on the east, the main rivers of the State. The first Association in the State was White Water, formed in 1809, the next was Silver Creek, formed in 1812. As an indication of the unstable condition of affairs during the earlier history of Indiana Baptists, it may be stated that there have been formed in all, up to this time, sixty Associations.

There are now but thirty. Exact statistics as to membership can only be approximated. In

1812, 1376; 1832, 11,334; 1840, 16,234; 1845, 15,795; 1850, 18,311; 1857, 25,282; 1860, 28,038; 1866, 29,103; 1876, 40,015; 1880 (estimated), 42,159,—in 568 churches. The apparent decrease from 1840 to 1845 is to be accounted for by the fact that several *anti-mission* Associations withdrew from all correspondence with the State Convention. Indeed, it may be said that most of the thirty Associations dropped from the list have died because of their anti-mission policy and spirit. A few yet survive as working bodies, and some were merged into other missionary Associations. A brother, who is constantly traveling over the State, estimates the anti-mission membership at 5000. Their strength is now a mere fragment of what it once was. No account is made of them in the general statistics of the State.

Indiana, Educational Institutions of.—The first meeting having for its object the founding of an institution of learning for Baptists was held in Indianapolis, June 5, 1834. The final result was the establishment of Franklin College, which with a variety of experiences " continues to this day," and is now in a more prosperous condition than ever before. In 1848, Rev. J. G. Craven and his father founded a school at College Hill, Jefferson Co., for the education of all colors and both sexes. In 1849, Rev. J. C. Thompson, of Ohio, came to their assistance. The name given the institution was Eleutherean College. The Cravens put great energy at the service of the school, and for some time it prospered notwithstanding its persecutions. One of the most distinguished of its colored pupils is Rev. Moses Broyles, of Indianapolis. There have been several attempts to revive the school, but without permanent success. It had no endowment, and hence it could not live. About the year 1854, Revs. Anson Tucker and D. Taylor were appointed by the Education Society of Indiana to proceed in the work of founding a school for young women at La Fayette. They reported $12,000 pledged. Prof. W. Brand resigned his place in the faculty of Franklin College to enter upon his duties as agent of the school,—The Western Female Seminary. The effort finally failed, and the interest aroused in behalf of the enterprise was in a measure transferred to Ladoga in the Freedom Association. Ladoga Female Seminary, established in 1855, was intended at first to supply the wants of its own Association, but it was found that Northwestern Indiana was its appropriate field. It has done successful work under Principals Rev. G. Williams, M. Bailey, Rev. A. J. Vawter, and Rev. W. Hill. For lack of endowment it finally suspended.

The same may be said in general of Crown Point Academy, under the principalship of Rev. T. H. Ball, and Huntington Academy, founded by Deacon John Kenower. The lack of endowment, and the fact of the establishment of public high schools in the State within a few years, led to the suspension of all schools except the college at Franklin. The last to succumb was the Indianapolis Female Institute. This was founded in 1858. Rev. G. Williams was its first principal. The total expended for site and buildings was $53,000. Rev. L. Hayden, D.D., was the last principal. It suspended in 1872.

Indiana Baptists have also taken considerable interest in the Baptist Theological Seminary in Chicago, and contributed several thousand dollars to that institution. The largest sum given is $5000, by M. L. Pierce, Esq., of La Fayette.

Ministerial training is receiving new attention in the State. During the year there were 42 young men receiving education for the ministry, 23 of whom were at Franklin College.

Indiana, Publication Society in.—The American Baptist Publication Society began work in the State about the year that it took its present name. Revs. G. C. Chandler and T. C. Townsend took special interest in the circulation of its tracts, the one from Franklin as a centre, the other from Anderson. The State has made contributions to the society, giving in 1857, $85; 1865, $438; 1870, $663; 1875, $1081; 1880, $1873. Some legacies have been given, among the largest is one of $5000 from J. L. Allen. Rev. E. A. Russell is the Sunday-school missionary of the society for Indiana.

Indiana, The Sunday-Schools of, were not general before 1850. Many churches, however, had schools as early as 1833. Most of the schools at first, especially in the country, were *union schools*, and were what are now called "summer" schools. In 1848, the missionaries of the Indiana Baptist State Convention were instructed "to make it a prominent part of their business to establish Sabbath-schools, and labor to promote their interests." There was no persistent effort made to gather Sunday-school statistics till 1868, when Rev. E. A. Russell was appointed Sunday-school missionary for Indiana by the American Baptist Publication Society. His report for 1870 is as follows: schools, 285; officers and teachers, 1628; scholars, 22,369; converted during one year, 770; volumes in libraries, 17,111. Of the 285 schools, 51 were *union*. There is a marvelous increase since 1870. In 1878 there were: schools, 542; officers and teachers, 5000; scholars, 58,000; volumes in library, 30,000; benevolent contributions, $71,615. Indiana now comes to the front in the number of scholars.

Indianapolis, Ind., Baptists of.—The *First Baptist church* was constituted Sept. 28, 1822, with 17 members. The pastors have been Revs. B. Barnes, A. Smoch, J. L. Richmond, M.D., G. C. Chandler, D.D., T. R. Cressy, S. Dyer, Ph.D., J.

B. Simmons, D.D., H. Day, D.D. (who was pastor for fifteen years and built the present house of worship), W. Randolph, D.D., H. C. Mabie (present pastor). The church at present numbers 515. The superintendent of the Sabbath-school is W. C. Smoch. The church has planted three other churches in the city.

South Street was organized in 1869 with 73 members. Its pastors have been Revs. W. Elgin, H. Smith, G. W. Riley, J. S. Gillespie, and J. N. Clark (present pastor). Present membership, 217.

North Street was organized in 1871 with 27 members. Its pastors have been Revs. E. K. Chandler, J. B. Schaff, I. N. Carman, and G. H. Elgin (present pastor). Present membership, 120.

Garden church was organized in 1872 with 16 members. Its pastors have been Revs. S. Cornelius, D.D., P. Shedd, and C. B. Allen, Jr. Present membership, 112. Sabbath-school superintendent, H. Knippenberg.

Infant Baptism in all Ages has required Faith before its Administration.—This is one of the most remarkable features of that unscriptural practice. Neander alludes to this demand when he says, "Infant baptism also furnished probably the first occasion for the appointment of sponsors or godfathers; for as this was a case in which the persons baptized could not themselves declare their confession of faith, it became necessary for others to do it in their name." (Church History, i. 315. Boston.) From the first intimations of the existence of infant baptism the sponsor is spoken of, who professed faith for the child. Though it should be remembered that sponsors were required for others as well as infants, and that Neander was mistaken in saying that "infant baptism also furnished *probably* the first occasion for the appointment of sponsors." He only gives his opinion as a probability. As Bingham says, "There were sponsors for such adult persons as could not answer for themselves," who were speechless from some cause, and there were sponsors for persons of full intelligence, "whose duty was not to answer in their names" (the candidates for baptism), "but only to admonish and instruct them." (Antiquities of the Christian Church, pp. 526, 527. London, 1870.) Tertullian mentions the existence of sponsors in his day, when *child*, not *infant*, baptism was first proposed. (De Baptismo, cap. 18.) It is probable, since sponsors were in the church in the end of the second century, before infant baptism existed, that they were first used in times of persecution to guard the Christian communities against spies who sought membership in them to betray them, and that afterwards they were employed to instruct and guard those for whose character they had become responsible. There is no lack of evidence among early writers to sustain Bingham's three classes of sponsors, so that when the word sponsor is found in the fathers it may have no reference to infant baptism; but when infant baptism was introduced sponsors were always required to profess faith for the unconscious subjects of the rite.

When Augustine baptized an infant he asked, "Does this child believe in God? Does he turn to God?" And he declares expressly in another place that sponsors answered for the children. (Patrologia Latina, xxxiii. 363. Parisiis.) The great bishop of Hippo, the man who gave its chief impetus to infant baptism, insisted on faith before its administration. Martin Luther's "Smaller Catechism" has these questions and answers:

"When did the Holy Ghost begin this sanctification in you?" "In the holy ordinance of baptism the Holy Ghost began this sanctification in me."

"What did God promise you in holy baptism?" "God promised, and also bestowed upon me, the forgiveness of sins, life, and salvation."

"But what did you promise God?" "I promised that I would renounce the devil and all his works and ways, and *believe in God the Father, Son, and Holy Ghost.*"

"Through whom did you make this promise in holy baptism?" "I made this promise in holy baptism through my sponsors." (Catechism, p. 58. New York, 1867.)

"The Garden of the Soul" (pp. 184, 185. London), a popular English Catholic prayer-book, has these questions and answers about baptism:

"Dost thou renounce Satan?" "I do renounce him."

"And all his works?" "I do renounce them."

"And all his pomps?" "I do renounce them."

"Dost thou believe in God, the Father Almighty, creator of heaven and earth?" "I do believe."

"Dost thou believe in Jesus Christ, his only Son, our Lord, who was born into this world and suffered for us?" "*I do believe.*"

"Dost thou believe in the Holy Ghost, the holy Catholic Church, the communion of saints, the forgiveness of sins, the resurrection of the body, and life everlasting?" "I do believe."

It is stated at the commencement of these questions that "the priest interrogates the person to be baptized, or the sponsors, if an infant, as follows;" so that the sponsors not only make solemn renunciations for the infant, but profess a comprehensive faith for it before it can be baptized.

In the Greek Church the priest, as a prerequisite to baptism, asks, "Hast thou renounced Satan?" And the catechumen or *sponsor* replies, "I have renounced him."

"Hast thou joined thyself unto Christ?" And he answers, "I have joined myself."

"And dost thou believe on him?" The catechumen replies, "I *believe* on him as king and God." (Neale's History of the Holy Eastern Church, Part I. 956. London, 1850.) Of course, in the case of an infant the faith is professed by the sponsor, and it must be confessed before baptism.

In the Episcopal Church, when a child is brought for baptism, the minister asks each godfather and godmother the following questions, and receives the answers given to them:

"Dost thou, in the name of this child, renounce the devil and all his works, the vain pomp and glory of the world, with all covetous desires of the same, and the carnal desires of the flesh, so that thou wilt not follow nor be led by them?" "I renounce them all."

"Dost thou believe in God, the Father Almighty, maker of heaven and earth? And in Jesus Christ, his only begotten Son, our Lord? And that he was conceived by the Holy Ghost, born of the Virgin Mary; that he suffered under Pontius Pilate, was crucified, dead, and buried; that he went into hell, and also did rise again the third day; that he ascended into heaven and sitteth at the right hand of God, the Father Almighty, and from thence shall come again at the end of the world to judge the quick and the dead?" etc. "All *this I steadfastly believe*." (Book of Common Prayer: Public Baptism of Infants.) Such is the profession of faith made by sponsors for an unconscious infant in the Episcopal Church. The "Westminster Confession of Faith," chap. xxviii. sec. 4, says, "Not only those that do actually profess faith in and obedience unto Christ, but also the infants of one or both *believing* parents, are to be baptized." Here there is no provision made for the baptism of any infant unless one of its parents had faith in Christ; and upon that faith the baptism of any infant depends among the Scotch, Scotch-Irish, English, and American Presbyterians.

The British Congregationalists, though having the "Savoy Confession," prepared by their own brethren, according to Neale (History of the Puritans, iv. 164. Dublin, 1755), "have in a manner laid aside the use of it in their families, and agreed with the Presbyterians in the use of the Assembly's (Westminster) Catechism." Robinson gives an account of a Congregational baptism at which the minister stated that "not only those that do actually profess faith in and obedience unto Christ, but also the infants of one or both believing parents, were to be baptized." (History of Baptism, p. 681. Nashville.) These are the exact words of the "Westminster Confession of Faith," and they require faith in one parent for the baptism of an infant.

Throughout the Christian ages all the great churches that baptized infants before the Reformation, and all the large communities that were formed during or soon after it that followed that practice, insisted on faith as essential to baptism as strongly as the Baptists have ever done. When the "Episcopal Catechism," in answer to the question, "What is required of persons to be baptized?" says, "Repentance, whereby they forsake sin, and faith, whereby they steadfastly believe the promises of God made to them in that sacrament," it gives the doctrine held by all the great historic communities of the Christian world since infant baptism arose about the absolute need of faith before baptism. This has always been the teaching of Baptists during the Christian centuries when only believers were immersed, and throughout all the dark and enlightened ages since. The difference between us and Pedobaptists is that they are satisfied with healing faith in a sponsor, or in a parent, while the infant has the disease of sin and is without faith in Christ. If it reaches years of responsibility it will surely be without God and without hope in the world; and we want the healing faith in the heart of the candidate, according to the Master's saying, "He that believeth and is baptized shall be saved."—Mark xvi. 16.

We furnish candidates for immersion with suitable robes in which to receive Christian baptism; but we can only loan the garments, the needed faith is the gift of God. The five wise virgins in the parable, as they beheld their five foolish companions in the throes of despair because they had not the oil of saving faith in their lamps, full of compassion for them as they were, and enjoying the faith that gave everlasting life, had no faith to loan them or to profess for them. And no Christian ever had a faith which he could place to the credit of any one, infant or adult. A man might as well attempt to loan an unconscious child the vigor of his mature mind, or the power of his strong right arm, or a dozen of the heavenly worlds.

Infant Baptism in the first Four Christian Centuries.—There is not a single recorded case in the first two ages of Christian history of the baptism of an unconscious babe. Men have searched this period with a scrutiny and a measure of learning never surpassed to find one undeniable instance of the kind, but the literature of Christianity has been examined in vain, and it ever will be. Justin Martyr gives a full account of the manner of conferring baptism in the latter half of the second century. "As many," says he, "as are *persuaded and believe that the things which we teach and declare are true, and promise that they are determined to live accordingly, are taught to pray to God, and to beseech him with fasting to grant them the remission for their sins*, while we also pray and fast with them. We then *lead them* to a place where there is water, and there they are regenerated in the same manner as we also were; for they are there washed in that water in the name of God the Father and Lord of the universe, and of our Saviour Jesus Christ, and of the Holy Spirit." (Patrologia Græca, vol. vi. p. 240. Migne. Parisiis, 1857.)

In Justin's time candidates for baptism believed that the statements of Christian teachers were true; they promised to live according to gospel requirements, and they prayed for pardon. These were believers, and he names no other class of persons who were baptized. Tertullian, just at the close of the second century, while yet orthodox, says, "It behooves those who are going to be baptized to pray with frequent supplications, fasts, kneelings, and vigils, and with the confession of all past faults, that they may show forth even John's baptism; they were immersed," he says, "confessing their sins." (De Baptismo, cap. xx.) No unconscious babe could make these preparations, or at this period enjoyed Christian baptism. There was in Tertullian's time an effort made to introduce, not the baptism of new-born infants, but of little children, which he denounced. The learned Salmasius and Suicerus have been criticised by Bingham for the statement, "For the first two ages no one received baptism who was not first instructed in the faith and doctrine of Christ, so as to be able to answer for himself that he believed, because of those words, 'He that believeth and is baptized.'" (Antiquities of the Christian Church, Book xi. chap. iv, sec. 5.) But Bingham, profoundly versed as he was in the doctrines and practices of the early church, brings forward no case of the baptism of an unconscious infant during this period, or a positive account of the existence of the rite. *He could not.*

There is but one case of unconscious infant baptism in the entire third century. The facts about it are found—in the letter of Cyprian and sixty-six bishops addressed to Fidus—in the works of Cyprian bishop of Carthage. Fidus, an African bishop, living in scenes of rustic ignorance, wrote to Cyprian to learn the earliest time when an infant might be baptized. Cyprian could not answer the question; but a council of sixty-six bishops, of which he was a member, decided that it might be baptized as soon as it was born. They also gave their reasons for their conclusion. One was because the sins of a babe were not as grave as those of a man, and as baptism took away the greater sins it could remove the smaller; and another was that Elisha placed his body upon the lifeless body of the child which he restored, his mouth to its mouth, his eyes to its eyes, and his hands to its hands, *the spiritual sense of which was that infants are equal to men, and therefore should have their baptism.* This is the first record of unconscious infant baptism on the page of Christian history, and there is no other instance in the third century. The council was supposed to have been held about A.D. 256. This letter in Cyprian is supposed by many to be spurious; and we are inclined to that opinion, chiefly because the progress of the infant error was so very slow; the great theologian, Augustine, a North African by birth, who was born in 354, whose mother was the saintly Monica, was not baptized till he was thirty-three years of age,—an occurrence nearly impossible if the infant rite had been sanctioned by Cyprian and the other authorities of the North African Church a century before. The Christian writers of the East in the third century treat of *child*, not infant, baptism,—children of six years or more.

In the fourth century the greatest church leaders, and some of them the most eminent Christian authors of all the ages since Jesus, though the children of believers, were not baptized in infancy. Ambrose, whose family were all Christians, was governor of Milan, and elected to be its archbishop before he was baptized. In 381, Nectarius was elected archbishop of Constantinople, when, according to Sozomen, "he was of advanced age," and unbaptized. Gregory Nazianzen, who was born while his father was bishop of Nazianzum, was baptized in his thirtieth year, and he was archbishop of Constantinople. The eloquent John Chrysostom, both of whose parents were Christians, was baptized when he was twenty-eight, and he, too, presided over the See of Constantinople. Basil the Great, whose fathers were Christians for generations, who died in 379, was baptized in his twenty-eighth year. Jerome, the first Hebrew and Greek scholar among Christians in the fourth century, who was born of believing parents in 331, was not baptized till about 366. Theodosius the Great, after proving himself a valiant warrior, was baptized, though he had Christian parents, as Sozomen relates.

The baptism of the fourth century required candidates to profess faith in Jesus, as we learn from Ambrose in his "*De Sacramentis.*" "Thou wast asked," says he, addressing candidates, "'Dost thou believe in God, the omnipotent Father?' and thou saidst, 'I believe,' and thou was immersed, that is, thou wast buried. Again thou was asked, 'Dost thou believe in our Lord Jesus Christ, and in his cross?' And thou saidst, 'I believe'; and thou was immersed, and therefore thou wast buried with Christ. . . . A third time thou wast asked, 'Dost thou believe in the Holy Spirit?' And thou saidst, 'I believe'; and a third time thou wast immersed." (Patrol. Lat., vol. xvi. p. 448. Migne. Parisiis.) This faith was the general demand at the baptisms of the fourth century throughout Christendom. Masses of men whose parents were Christians, and who attended churches and loved Christ, had never been baptized either in childhood or in later years. They were waiting for baptism till the approach of death, that its waters might give full cleansing from sin and a perfect fitness for heaven.

The clergy of the fourth century were continually appealing to the regular members of their congregations to be baptized, throngs of whom had never received the rite; and in times of threatened war or pestilence multitudes hastened to baptism and the ministers could with difficulty immerse them. "Infant baptism," says Neander, "though acknowledged to be necessary, entered *so rarely and with so much difficulty* into the church life, during the first part of this period." (Church History, ii. 319. Boston.) The cases of infant baptism in the fourth century, outside of North Africa, are scarcely worthy of being named. And in that Roman colony the earnest appeals and arguments of Augustine show that its strength was not great. Dean Stanley only claims that "*after the fifth century* the whole Christian world . . . have baptized children." (*Nineteenth Century*, p. 39, October, 1879.) It is perhaps true that in all parts of Christendom *some* persons immersed children after the fifth century had entirely passed, but if the dean intends to state that the unconscious infants of Christians everywhere were baptized, his declaration is incapable of proof though the piercing eye of an archangel sought the evidence.

Infant Baptism, Unfit Supports of.—As Baptists view the bases upon which its friends place infant baptism, they seem wholly inadequate to sustain it.

Among the oldest of these is the assumption that baptism has come in the place of circumcision. Augustine of Hippo uses this argument as if it were infallible; and it is employed to-day with the same childlike confidence which marked the great African bishop when he framed it. But what Scripture confirms the statement? By implication or declaration the assertion has no more support in the New Testament than the claims of Leo XIII. to be the successor of Peter as the supposed prince of the apostles. If baptism took the place of circumcision, no man should have both rites. But Christ received both; so did the thousands of Pentecostal converts; so did Paul, the greatest of all the apostles. There is then no connection between the two ordinances. Dr. Halley, a distinguished English Congregationalist, in his celebrated work in defense of infant baptism, says, "The general opinion that baptism is substituted for circumcision, as a kind of hereditary seal of the covenant of grace, appears to be ill-sustained by Scriptural evidence, and to be exposed to some very serious, if not absolutely fatal, objections." (The Sacraments, p. 34. London, 1855.)

Another argument to sustain the infant rite is taken from Matthew's gospel, xix. 13, 14, 15: "Then were there brought unto him little children, that he should put his hands on them and pray; and the disciples rebuked them. But Jesus said, 'Suffer little children, and forbid them not, to come unto me: for of such is the kingdom of heaven.'" This passage is regarded by many as absolutely proving that infant baptism is invested with the sanction of Jesus. From it we learn that the apostles knew nothing of the baptism of children, for they would not let them approach Jesus till he commanded them to permit them to come; and, as baptism had been in existence for some time, it is quite clear infants had no part in the baptismal ordinance. Besides, they were only brought to him that he might "put his hands on them and pray," and it is said that "he laid his hands on them;" but he did not baptize them. The words "of such is the kingdom of heaven" do not mean that *of children is* the kingdom of heaven. If the Saviour had said of the little children, "of *them* is the kingdom of heaven," then no adult could have entered Christ's gospel kingdom of love. Jerome, in the fourth century, commenting on these words, in his Latin vulgate, observes, "Jesus said *of such*, not *of them*, to show that not *age* but *morals* should rule, and that to those who had *similar innocence* and *simplicity* a reward was promised." This is the Saviour's meaning, given by the famous monk of Palestine. This transaction has nothing in favor of infant baptism, and something against it.

In 1 Cor. vii. 12, 13, 14, Paul recommends a Christian not to put away an unbelieving husband or wife if the unbeliever will stay. Now the unbeliever might be a Pharisee or an idolater, and he adds, "For the unbelieving husband is sanctified by the wife, and the unbelieving wife is sanctified by the husband, else were children unclean; but now are they holy." The holiness spoken of here is not sanctification of the heart, but the legality of the wedded relations. The idolatrous companion or the unbelieving partner can be sanctified in no other way. Peter says, "Ye know that it is an unlawful thing for a man that is a Jew to keep company, or come unto one of another nation."—Acts x. 28. Paul tells these converted Israelites that they shall not forsake their Christ-rejecting partners, that their relations are proper, and their children legitimate. Because the children are said to be holy, it is argued that they should be baptized. For the same reason the ungodly idolatress or Jewess, the idolater or scornful Pharisee, should be baptized, for the adjective that describes the *children as holy is from the verb that sanctifies the unbelieving husband and wife*. The apostle is not treating of baptism, but of the sacredness of wedded relations and the legitimacy of children; and infant or unbelieving adult baptism can obtain no aid here.

The household baptisms furnish another argument for infant baptism. "There must have been infants in them," it is said, "and they must have been baptized, and therefore the children of all believers should be baptized." There is not a tittle of evidence that there was an infant in one of the households. Dr. J. H. Borum, of Dyersburg, Tenn., has baptized forty-six households in his ministry, and there was not an infant in one of them. And until it is proved that there were infants in these households, and that they were immersed, *infant baptism rests upon a supposition*,—a mere conceit, not worth the one-hundredth part of the chaffy covering of a corn of wheat. (See article on THE SCRIPTURAL SUBJECTS OF BAPTISM.)

Infant Salvation.—The following is from a tract entitled "Infant Salvation, Dedication, and Baptism," issued by the American Baptist Publication Society: " Are not infants, dying in infancy, saved? Certainly. Of a child which was the fruit of sin, David says, ' I shall go to him, but he shall not return to me.' 2 Sam. xii. 23. We have no reason to suppose that God will consign to hell infants who have never known good from evil. There is no controversy between Baptists and evangelical Pedobaptists on this point." If any statement could be regarded as authoritative for the whole Baptist denomination, this declaration might be received in that character. It comes from our great Baptist tract and book society, which is governed by the Baptists of America.

The doctrine of the quotation is held by all Baptists everywhere. Every child that dies before it knows "right from wrong," in any country under heaven, enters the regions of the blessed.

Ingalls, Mrs. M. B., the second wife of Rev. L. Ingalls, of the Arracan Mission, was born in Greenville, N. Y., Nov. 25, 1828. She was married in December, 1850, and sailed for the field of her labor July 10, 1851. Mr. Ingalls was transferred in 1854 to the Burmese department of the Rangoon Mission, where Mrs. Ingalls was his co-laborer until he died, March 14, 1856, after a faithful service of twenty-one years. Mrs. Ingalls superintended his schools for the education of Burmese girls, in 1857, and on one occasion, early in the year, made a tour of twenty-three days into the jungle in company with some of the native disciples, and found everywhere eager listeners. In April of this year she returned to America, remaining here until re-embarking for the scene of her former labors, Nov. 26, 1858, where she met a cordial welcome on her arrival in Rangoon from the missionaries and native converts. She took up her abode in the midst of a Burmese population, two miles north of the Kemendine Karen Mission, in a place called Zay-Ghee. In this place and at Thongzai her labors were greatly blessed. She removed to Thongzai in the latter part of 1860, from which place she wrote home a letter, soon after her settlement, full of hope and good cheer. The most remarkable success followed her labors,—a success in some respects unprecedented in the history of the Burmese Missions. One cannot but admire the good common-sense sort of way in which Mrs. Ingalls did, and always has done, her work. She wrote of herself, in 1864: "It is not a day of romance with me, but a day when my strength and trust in God must be tested." The trial came in one of the severest forms, in July, 1864, when the new and beautiful chapel was destroyed by fire. Mrs. Ingalls lost nearly all her personal effects, and among them various manuscripts which probably could never be replaced. The effect of this loss, in addition to the weight of the burdens she had so long carried, so prostrated her health that she returned to this country in 1865, remaining here until the fall of 1868, awakening a deep interest in the churches she visited in the cause of missions. On her return she found a new chapel nearly completed, and the church ready to give her a cordial welcome, and for several years the work went on hopefully and successfully, until the night of the 12th of March, 1876, when the torch of the incendiary was applied to the mission compound, and again nearly everything was destroyed except the chapel. But amid all these sorrows there were joys; so that of the year 1876 it could be said, "it was a year of troubles and a year of blessings." The last published report of the Executive Committee says that, "so far as outward circumstances are concerned, the mission under the charge of Mrs. Ingalls is in better condition than ever, and that the prospects of usefulness are as great as ever."

Ingels, Deacon George, was born in White Marsh Township, Montgomery Co., Pa., Feb. 26, 1746. When sixteen years of age he came to Philadelphia, and soon after the Holy Spirit made him the subject of serious religious impressions. In October, 1767, he was baptized into the fellowship of the First Baptist church of his adopted city. Five years after his baptism he was chosen a deacon by the church, and for fifty-five years he served the church in that honorable office.

He was a patriot full of self-sacrifice in Revolutionary times, and by his courage in the battle-field, and in the camp in the coldest of winters, he earned the character of a brave soldier and an unmurmuring sufferer. In civil life he was elected to various responsible offices by his fellow-citizens, and both the State and general government enlisted his services.

He was perhaps the most active man in Philadelphia in ministering to the victims of yellow fever in 1797. His efforts were unwearied, and brought comfort to the homes of suffering thousands in that visitation of terror and death.

Mr. Ingels had a strong faith in the Lord Jesus Christ, and a heart full of generous affections; and among the laymen connected with the "mother-church" of Philadelphia, in her long and honored history, no one rendered more efficient service to the Redeemer's cause than Deacon Ingels. He died in his eighty-first year, enjoying the confidence and love of the people of Philadelphia.

Ingersoll, Hon. George, of Marshall, Mich., was born in Victor, Ontario Co., N. Y., Feb. 5, 1819. He became a member of the Baptist Church in 1842, and has been a chief pillar of the church ever since. He has been superintendent of the Sunday-school fifteen years. He has also been president of the board of education of the city for fifteen years, and is now judge of probate for Calhoun County.

Ingham, Richard, D.D., author of the "Handbook on Christian Baptism," and "Christian Baptism, its Subjects and Mode," was born at Halifax, Yorkshire, England, in 1810. He was baptized Nov. 20, 1829, and received authority to preach from the General Baptist church at Slack, Yorkshire, in 1833. Relinquishing his business some time after, he studied for the ministry under the Rev. J. Jarrow, of Wisbeach, and was ordained pastor at Bradford in 1839. He spent the years of his ministry in Louth, Halifax, Vale, and Bradford, and died June 1, 1873. As a preacher he was highly esteemed, and his labors as a student were untiring and successful. His "Hand-book" is allowed to be a work of great value, carefully and thoroughly executed.

Inman, Rev. G., a native of Sumner Co., Tenn., was born in 1836; educated at Union University, Murfreesborough, Tenn.; ordained by the Hillsborough Baptist church in Washington Co., Ky., where he began his ministry in 1858; labored as pastor of the Baptist churches of Clarksville and Spring Creek, Montgomery Co., Ky., five years, of the Central Baptist church, Nashville, Tenn., five years, of the Baptist church in Decatur, Ill., three years, of the Baptist church of Fox Lake, his present field of labor, two years. His ministry has been fruitful in results. He has baptized about 500 persons into the fellowship of the churches of which he has been pastor. He is a very active and able worker in the temperance cause. In his native State he held a leading position in the ranks of temperance reformers, and no great temperance assembly was considered complete without his presence. By his pen and voice he has furnished to this important reform some of its most effective weapons. His own pulpit is always a stronghold of total abstinence, and from it are struck heavy blows against the sin of drunkenness and drunkard-making.

Installation in recent years has become general in large cities when an ordained minister enters upon a new field. The pastor and his people on such occasions commonly hear a sermon from some brother in the ministry, the hand of fellowship is given to the stranger, and a charge; a charge is also delivered to the church. The object of the service is to give a welcome to the pastor, and to stir up him and his people to appreciate the weighty responsibilities that rest upon them.

Intercessor, The.—A belief in intercessors is universal among the adherents of every false religion. Heathenism abounds in such mediators. Mohammed is supposed to intercede for all true Moslems. Tertullian expresses the conviction that Satan has something to imitate every institution of God. This observation is eminently true of intercession. Romanism has an intercessor in every canonized saint.

The Jewish high priest, by divine appointment interceded in the holy of holies for his nation. And God cannot be approached acceptably now, except through Christ the great intercessor, of whom the chief of the Jewish priesthood was an humble type. "For there is one God, and one Mediator between God and men, the man Christ Jesus."—1 Tim. ii. 5. "My little children, these things write I unto you, that you sin not; and if any man sin, we have an advocate with the Father, Jesus Christ the righteous."—1 John ii. 1. "Jesus saith unto him, I am the way, the truth, and the life; no man cometh unto the Father but by me."—John xiv. 6. God has appointed but one intercessor; every other claimant to that office is a sacrilegious impostor; and the fact that Jehovah ordained Christ as an advocate for all who ventured to approach him is infallible evidence that the purest and the foulest of our race, in their approaches to the eternal throne, need the all-prevailing Mediator.

Our intercessor bases his pleadings for us upon his expiatory sacrifice. When the high priest of Israel entered the holy of holies to plead for the Jews, he first sprinkled the mercy-seat with blood and then presented his supplications. Paul says, "Which hope we have as an anchor of the soul, both sure and steadfast, and which entereth into that within the veil (the holy of holies); whither the forerunner is for us entered, even Jesus, made a high priest forever after the order of Melchisedec."—Heb. vi. 19, 20. Christ enters into the holy of holies in paradise with his own blood, and, as the high priest of the whole elect family, he pleads its merits for them all.

He observes every supplicant who seeks his intercessions. His honored mother has no more power to see or hear than any other glorified believer, and, consequently, is totally unfitted to be an intercessor. But, "being in the form of God, and thinking it no robbery to be equal with God," he sees every petitioner at his throne, and he observes the prayerful desires of his heart before he clothes them in words.

He is unwearied in his intercessions. "He ever liveth to make intercession for us." Men die, and empires perish, and night hides the glory of the day, but the pleadings of our advocate are continually poured out in the ear of Deity; nor will they cease till the last gift needed by the last believer on earth has given him perfect preparation for heaven.

He is a tender-hearted intercessor. "Wherefore in all things it behooved him to be made like unto his brethren, that he might be a merciful and faithful high priest."—Heb. ii. 17. The fountain of compassionate love, from which all the affection of angels and men has streamed forth, is in his heart; and it exercises a boundless influence over his movements.

He will plead for *any penitent* who trusts his name, and he will seek *every needful gift* for each supplicating child; and his eloquent advocacy has such a power on high that the Father *always hears him*, and the trusting one who commits his case to him is invariably successful.

Iowa Baptists, History of.—There were some Baptists among the earliest settlers of Iowa. In succeeding years, as the tide of emigration flowed into the territory, Baptists were fairly represented. The fullest and most reliable account of Iowa Baptists in their earlier history is found in a paper carefully prepared by Rev. J. F. Childs some years ago, entitled "The History of the Rise and Progress of Iowa Baptists." This history is still unpublished, but, through the kindness of the author, it contributes largely to the facts of this sketch. The Danville, or, as originally called, the Long Creek, church, was the first Baptist church in Iowa. Brother and Sister Manly came from Kentucky, bringing with them the Articles of Faith adopted by the Bush Creek Baptist church, Green Co., Ky. They settled within six miles of Danville, where they continued to reside. Together with a few Baptists from Illinois, they organized a church, and invited Elders John Logan and Gardner Bartlett, of Illinois, to preach for them. Elder Logan preached in a log cabin the evening of Oct. 19, 1834, probably the first sermon by an evangelical minister in this part of the Territory. The next day the church was constituted and named "The Regular Baptist Church at Long Creek."

In 1838 another church was organized, about six miles southwest of Burlington, through the labors of Elders James and Moses Lemon and Clark, from Illinois. It was called "The Baptist Church of Christ, Friend to Humanity, at Rock Spring, Iowa." The Union and Pisgah churches were organized in 1839. In 1839 three churches, Long Creek, Union, and Pisgah, were organized into an Association, the first Baptist Association in the Territory. The meeting was held in a grove, west of what is now Danville Centre. The membership of the three churches was less than 90, and the number of delegates in attendance was 10. The organization was effected and the entire business of the meeting transacted while 9 of the delegates were seated in a row on a log and the moderator standing before them, supported by the back of a chair. The body was called "The Iowa Baptist Association." In 1843, after the organization of the Davenport Association, its name was changed to the "Des Moines Association."

The Baptists of Iowa went on gaining from year to year. Their strength and efficiency were increased by accessions to the ministry of able and earnest men, many of whom came under the appointment of the American Baptist Home Mission Society, by the constant tide of emigration from the older States bringing in many faithful Baptists, and by the conversion of souls. New fields of Christian labor were occupied, churches were multiplied, a general organization for missionary work was formed, additional Associations were established, the Sunday-school enterprise was pressed forward, means were proposed and devised for the advantages of higher education, and institutions of learning were founded.

Baptist churches are found in most of the principal cities and towns of the State. There are now in Iowa 24 Baptist Associations, 410 churches, having a membership of 24,700; over 1000 were added to these churches by baptism during the year 1879-80. They have about 250 Sunday-schools, with 20,000 pupils, and are well represented numerically in their institutions of learning now at work. The Baptist ministry of Iowa has many men of sterling worth. Not a few of them have supported their families in part or altogether by the labor of their own hands while preaching the gospel to others. Iowa Baptists have been, and they still are, represented in the civil and educational interests of the State and nation, holding places of prominence and trust in halls of legislation, in executive and judicial positions, and among professional men. Iowa Baptists have contributed some noble men and women for the work of foreign missions, and for missionary toils in the dark places of our own land. Among the biographical sketches of this work will be found the names of a few men who are now living in the State or are sleeping in its soil. These by no means exhaust the list of men worthy of special notice, but may be accepted as representatives of the different classes whose lives and labors occupy an important place in Iowa Baptist history.

Iowa Baptists have a future which has the promise of marked advancement and blessed results to those interests of Christ's kingdom committed to their trust.

Iowa, Baptist Centennial Academy of, is located in Malvern, Mills Co., Southwestern Iowa. The enterprise was begun mainly by Rev. J. W. Roe, pastor at Malvern, in 1876. The expense of building was borne almost wholly by the church. The subscriptions taken by Mr. Roe amounted to $8000, but he died before the edifice was begun. It was erected in 1877–78, during the pastorate of his successor, the Rev. O. T. Conger, the name of Mr. Roe being chiseled in the corner-stone. The building is a beautiful structure, and cost, as it now stands, about $12,000. The first and only principal the school has had thus far is R. M. Bridges, A.M., a man of scholarly attainments.

Iowa Baptist State Convention.—" In response to a call of the Des Moines Association, a Convention of brethren from the Baptist churches in Iowa Territory was held in Iowa City, June 3–4, 1842, to consider the expediency of forming a Territorial Association for missionary purposes." Twenty-five delegates were present. Some had walked seventy-five miles. Three of these delegates, C. E. Brown, William Elliott, and M. W. Rudd, are still living and in Iowa. B. Carpenter was made president, and W. B. Morey secretary, of "The Iowa Baptist General Association." In 1851 the name was changed to "Iowa Baptist State Convention." The constitution then adopted said, "The object of this Association shall be to promote the preaching of the gospel, ministerial education, and all the general objects of benevolence throughout this Territory." Though the name of the organization has been changed, the declared object has remained the same.

At the time of this organization there were about 380 Baptists in the Territory, and not more than 15 Baptist churches, while Iowa then had a population of about 52,000. For the first fourteen years of its history this Association was little more than an agent for the American Baptist Home Mission Society, to advise and assist that society in its work. In 1854 and 1855 the Convention attempted some direct labors in behalf of the German population. In 1856 the Rev. I. M. Seay received the first commission ever issued by this body. During the same year two other missionaries were sent forth, and the Convention entered heartily upon its declared work. During 1857 twenty-five missionaries were appointed, and Rev. J. Y. Aitchison was chosen agent. From 1858 to 1861, Rev. D. P. Smith labored in the interest of the Convention as financial agent, and a band of earnest-working missionaries were kept on the field. "In 1863, Rev. S. H. Mitchell became missionary agent, and labored till the fall of 1869. Other men have toiled in the general agency and missionary work of the Convention for shorter periods and rendered good service, while during all these years a number of noble, earnest-hearted men have been laboring as missionaries in the destitute and remote parts of the State. Among the secretaries have been Rev. T. S. Griffith, Rev. J. F. Childs, and Rev. T. F. Thickstun. Rev. J. Sunderland, the present missionary secretary and general missionary, in a recent circular says, "The Home Mission Society has aided missionaries in Iowa for forty-one years, issuing about 600 commissions. Besides all the churches organized, houses of worship built, Sunday-schools established, and souls saved, more than 5000 persons have been baptized into our churches in this State by its missionaries. Its work has equaled the labor of one man for four hundred and forty-two years, or an average of eleven missionaries constantly at work for the forty-one years. It has expended in this State $115,000. The State Convention has aided missionaries for the last twenty-five years, issuing 386 commissions. Its missionaries have baptized 3029 persons, organized 69 churches, and aided in building 66 meeting-houses. Their work equals the labor of one man for two hundred and sixty-one years, or an average of eleven men for the twenty-five years. There has been raised and expended in this work $65,300. In the whole work of Baptist missions in Iowa there has been expended $180,000.

The Convention is now prosecuting its missions in co-operation with the Home Mission Society,— holding the control of the work in its own hands with such guarantees of assistance from the Home Mission Society as enabled the Convention to extend it and increase its efficiency. There are at present thirty missionaries under appointment, including one Scandinavian and one German. There is a growing interest in this work, and a very deep conviction of the responsibility and promise of the present and future.

The Convention has its Sunday-school department and Sunday-school secretary. Formerly there was an organization called "The Iowa Baptist Sunday-School Union," formed in 1867, and having for its object "To promote the interests of Baptist Sunday-Schools in Iowa." This continued till 1878, and did good service. Now the Sunday-school work is a department of the Convention. It is put in the hands of a committee of five, known as "the Sunday-School Committee co-operating with the American Baptist Publication Society." The plan includes the employment of a Sunday-school missionary, "to do a general pioneer missionary work in destitute fields, by establishing Sunday-schools, organizing churches, holding meetings with feeble churches, holding Sunday-school institutes," etc. In the Baptist churches of Iowa there are about 250 Sunday-schools, having a membership of officers, teachers, and pupils of over 20,000. A number of the smaller churches join union schools, and some of the weaker, scattered churches have no schools. For two years the American Baptist Publication Society and the Iowa Baptist State Convention have sustained a Sunday-school missionary. Through the efforts of these missionaries new churches and schools have been organized, and twelve Associations have formed Sunday-school Conventions. Other Associations devote a part of their time to Sunday-school interests. Institutes have been held, awakening greater enthusiasm in the work. These Sunday-school missionaries have sold several hundred volumes of denominational works, besides giving away books, Testaments, and tracts.

In connection with their State Convention Iowa Baptists have "The Iowa Union for Ministerial Education," and "The Iowa Baptist Pastors' Conference." These assemble annually with the Convention, and also at the quarterly meetings of the board. The Union for Ministerial Education was organized in 1867. Its object is "the assistance of young men of Baptist churches in their educational preparation for the gospel ministry." The union has assisted over fifty brethren, several of whom are ordained pastors.

The Pastors' Conference was organized in 1867. Its object is "the mutual improvement of its members in Biblical knowledge and in the duties connected with the ministry." Ministers' institutes are occasionally held under the guidance of this Conference.

Ireland, Rev. James, was born in Edinburgh, Scotland, in 1748. He was brought up in the Presbyterian Church of his fathers. His education and talents were respectable. He came to America after reaching manhood, with pleasing manners, and without Christ in his heart. He was something of a poet, and in revising one of his religious pieces he was deeply convicted of guilt, from which faith in a suffering Saviour delivered him. He became eminent as a preacher soon after his baptism; his learning and the tenderness of his manner produced a powerful impression upon his hearers, and the Spirit's blessing upon the truth he proclaimed made him a great enemy of Satan's empire. He formed several Baptist churches during his ministry, which extended over forty years, and his influence in favor of truth was very great.

This led the Episcopal clergy of Virginia to stir up social and legal persecutions against him. He was thrust into jail in Culpeper for preaching without the authority of law; abuse was heaped upon him on his way to prison; within its walls an attempt was made to blow him up with gunpowder, and on its failure an effort was put forth to suffocate him by burning brimstone at the door and window of his jail. It was also planned to poison him. His persecutions permanently injured his health; two accidents completed the work begun by State church tyranny, and Mr. Ireland entered upon his rest May 5, 1806.

Ireland, Joseph Alexander, M.D., a distinguished physician and surgeon, was born in Jefferson Co., Ky., Sept. 15, 1824. At the age of seventeen he commenced studying, and graduated in the Kentucky School of Medicine in 1851, and immediately began the practice of his profession in the

JOSEPH ALEXANDER IRELAND, M.D.

city of Louisville. In 1854 he removed to Jefferson County, where he practised as a physician about ten years. In 1848 he was set apart for the ministry by a Baptist church, of which he had been a member from his youth, and preached statedly to several churches in his neighborhood. In 1864 he was elected Professor of Obstetrics and Diseases of Women and Children in the Kentucky School of Medicine, and afterwards was made a professor in the university at Louisville. Since 1875 he has filled the chair of Diseases of Women and Children in both the Kentucky School of Medicine and the Louisville Medical College.

Irish Baptists. See ENGLISH BAPTISTS.

Irwin, Rev. Charles Mercer, eldest son of Maj. Isaiah T. and Isabella Irwin, was born in Wilkes Co., Ga., Nov. 11, 1813. He was converted in early life, and was baptized into the fellowship of Sardis church by Rev. Enoch Callaway. His father, being wealthy, gave him the best educational advantages of the day. Prepared for college by Rev. Otis Smith at Powelton, he went through most of the regular course in the State University at Athens, and then studied law in the University of Virginia. On his return to Georgia he was admitted to the bar in 1834, married a most amiable lady, Miss Harriet E. Battle, settled in Washington, Wilkes Co., and for two years practised law successfully. He then settled on a plantation in Hancock County. There the Spirit of God met him and moulded him to his own sacred purposes. The feelings which made him say at sixteen, "If, when grown, I feel as I do now, I shall preach," constrained him to consecrate himself to the Lord for life. He entered the ministry and was ordained at Powelton. After devoting several years to missionary labor in the southern part of the State, he settled as pastor of the Baptist church in Madison, where he remained eight years, developing preaching talents of a high order, and manifesting remarkable executive ability. So successful were his labors that his church increased largely, and soon was regarded as a model. His next two pastorates were at Atlanta and in Albany, Ga., in which latter place he labored with wonderful success for three or four years. Broken down in health, he took a northern trip for recuperation in 1860. Then came sad years of war. Residing on his plantation in Lee County, he preached gratuitously to country churches until peace spread her balmy wings over the land once more. Although he has been a pastor twice since the war, his health has not been equal to the demands of the position, and he has devoted most of his time for the last ten years to agency work in the State of Georgia in behalf of foreign missions, for the Southern Baptist Convention. In this he has been faithful and efficient. Mr. Irwin is a man of fine and varied talents, he is modest as to his own merits, but a fluent speaker. By nature he is strictly honest, affectionate, and very devoted to his family, two children having blessed this union. In disposition, he is pleasant and genial; in manners, courteous and obliging. His piety is undoubted, and he has been a successful pastor and preacher, and a good business man. For several years he was clerk of the State Convention; has, for a long time, been a member of the board of trustees for the Mercer University. Few men are more generally beloved among the Georgia Baptists for their usefulness in the past, their excellence of character and qualities of sterling worth.

Irwin, Isaiah Tucker, a pious and wealthy deacon of the Sardis church, in Wilkes Co., Ga., who was born in Amherst, Va., Aug. 15, 1783, and died in April, 1856. His parents moved to Georgia when he was quite young, and, settling in Wilkes County, engaged in farming, which occupation he himself pursued, gradually accumulating a large landed property. At nineteen he married Miss Isabella Bankston, a woman in whom all the virtues of mind, heart, and person were blended, and who reached the age of ninety-one. Mr. Irwin was a very popular and useful man. He represented his county in the Legislature for many years, and served in the Creek war, rising to the rank of major. In 1827 the prayers of his pious wife were answered, and he was converted and united with the church of which he was afterwards an active, liberal, and useful member. He was ordained a deacon soon after uniting with the Sardis church, and filled the office well. His house was the seat of a princely hospitality; nor did he ever permit a minister who was his guest to leave without bestowing on him a pecuniary gift. To his children he gave the very best educational facilities that the country afforded, and he lived to see them all happily married and followers of Jesus. A daughter became the wife of the distinguished Baptist minister, Rev. J. L. Brookes; his second son was Speaker of the Georgia House of Representatives; and his eldest son, Rev. C. M. Irwin, a useful Baptist minister, is still living. To his servants Mr. Irwin was remarkably kind and considerate, providing liberally for their religious instruction. In return they almost idolized him. Affectionate and warm-hearted by nature, he was the tender husband, the kind and loving father, the sympathizing and generous neighbor, and faithful Christian. With full barns, he never forgot the poor, whether in the church or out of it, and at his mills the widows' sacks were always filled, and their wants were supplied in many other ways. When he died gloom pervaded the community, and at his funeral the poor exclaimed, "We have lost our best friend." In person he was tall and commanding, being in that, as in every other respect, one of nature's noblemen.

Ives, Dwight, D.D., son of Abraham and Eunice (Day) Ives, was born in West Springfield (now part of Holyoke), Mass., Sept. 20, 1805; pursued academical studies in New Ipswich, N. H., under Robert A. Coffin; graduated at Brown University in class of 1835, at the age of thirty; preached for the First Baptist church in Springfield, Mass., where he was ordained; settled with the Baptist church in Alton, Ill., where he won a high reputation, but was compelled from ill health to return to the East; settled with the Second Baptist church in Suffield, Conn., by the side of the Connecticut Literary Institution; guided in the erection of a beautiful church edifice, and drew a large congregation and built up a strong church; labored in this important field from 1839 to 1874 with most remarkable success, baptizing more than 1200 persons, and greatly aiding the Connecticut Literary Institution and benefiting the whole State; was a leading man in all ministerial circles and all educational and missionary affairs; received the honorary degree of Doctor of Divinity from Brown University in 1857; left two sons, the elder of which, William C., graduated at Brown University in 1865; resigning in Suffield in 1874, from age and ill health, he removed to Conway, Mass., and preached as he was able to the church in that place; died in Conway, Dec. 22, 1875, aged seventy years; one of New England's noblest men and most effective preachers.

DWIGHT IVES, D.D.

Ives, Rev. Jeremiah, was pastor of a General Baptist church in London, England, for more than thirty years. He had a peculiar talent for discussion, which enabled him to use with much readiness his great intellect and his stores of learning. He had controversies with the Quakers and the Presbyterians, in which he obtained considerable reputation. Crosby says that his fame reached Charles II., who sent for him to dispute with a Romish priest. Mr. Ives entered upon the discussion in the habit of an Episcopal clergyman, and pressed the priest very closely. He showed that the "pretended antiquity of their doctrines and practices fell short of the days of the apostles; for they were not to be found in any writings which remain of the apostolic age." The priest, after much wrangling, in the end replied "that this argument was of as much force against infant baptism as against the doctrines and ceremonies of the Church of Rome." To which Mr. Ives replied that he readily granted what he said to be true. The priest upon this broke up the controversy, saying "he had been cheated, and that he would proceed no farther, for he came to dispute with a clergyman of the Established Church, and it was now evident that this was an Anabaptist preacher." There is no community of Christians who are entirely invulnerable to the assaults of Rome except the Baptist denomination, a church ages older than the apostasy of the popes.

Ives, Moses Brown, was born in Providence, R. I., July 21, 1794, and was the son of Thomas Poynton and Hope Brown Ives. His father was the senior partner of the old and everywhere respected firm of Brown & Ives, and his mother the sister of the Hon. Nicholas Brown, the generous patron of the university which bears his name.

It was the intention of his father in due time to introduce him into the firm of which he was a member. Believing, however, that mental discipline and culture are not inconsistent with the calling of the merchant, he decided to give him a full collegiate education. He graduated at Brown University in 1812, and wishing to pursue his studies still farther, he entered the law-school at Litchfield, Conn., which then ranked among the best professional schools of its character in the country. On completing his course of study here he was still comparatively a youth, and it was deemed wise that he should reap the benefits of foreign travel, especially in so far as they had a bearing on his future calling in life. "While abroad," says Dr. Wayland, "his object seems to have been, not so much to see sights and walk through galleries, as to observe men and acquaint himself with the habits and manners of merchants of distinction. I have heard him frequently refer to this period of his life, but I think never for any other purpose than to illustrate the modes of doing business in the several capitals which he had occasion to visit."

Having passed through the preparatory training, he entered the counting-room of Brown & Ives, and at once applied himself to the work to which he proposed to devote his life, and he became, in the best sense of the word, "a model merchant." His opinion on all matters connected with his profession was received with the highest respect. He believed that there were great principles which were as certain and undeviating in business as the laws of nature, and he rigidly adhered to them. But it is not as a successful merchant that we wish to call attention to Mr. Ives, but to the deep interest he took both in popular and liberal education. The city of Providence owes to him a debt of gratitude for what he did in elevating the standard of common-school education which it can never pay. His relations to Brown University were of the most intimate character. He was elected a member of its board of trustees in 1822, and in 1825 he was chosen its treasurer, and without compensation, and as a labor of love to his *alma mater*, discharged its onerous and sometimes complicated duties for the long period of thirty-two years. "During the twenty-nine years of my connection with the university," says Dr. Wayland, "I do not remember an examination at some of the exercises of which he was not present unless detained by sickness, and in which he did not take a lively interest. His interest never flagged when anything could be suggested to improve the condition of the institution which he loved so well. If in any respect Brown University has gained in favor with the public; if it has taken a more honorable rank among the colleges of New England; if its means of education have been rendered, in any respect, ample, and its board of instruction such as would adorn any similar institution in our country; to no one are we more indebted for all this than to the late treasurer of the university."

Mr. Ives, although like his uncle, the Hon. Nicholas Brown, not a member of the church, was an habitual worshiper in the venerable meeting-house of the First Baptist church. He was not wont to give expression to his religious views, but as the shadows of time passed away, and the solemn realities of eternity rose to his view, he did not hesitate to make known the ground of his hopes. "I am now on my death-bed," said he, in a note dictated to a friend, "but my mind is perfectly clear. I am firm and unwavering in my belief in Jesus Christ and him crucified." To another he sent this message, "Give him this short message from me,—'Look unto Jesus.'" Such testimony to his firm and unshaken trust in his Redeemer, coming from the lips of such a man, meant all it expressed.

Ivey, Rev. F. H., was born in Fayetteville, N. C., in 1834; bred in the *Observer* office under the training of E. J. Hale, baptized by Dr. James McDaniel, and graduated at Wake Forest College, it is not strange that Mr. Ivey is a capital writer and an excellent preacher. He was for eleven years pastor of the Baptist church of Athens, Ga.; returned to North Carolina in 1873; did good work as agent for Wake Forest College for more than a year, and has been for the last four years pastor in Goldsborough.

Ivimey, Rev. Joseph, was born at Ringwood, Hampshire, England, May 22, 1773. When a youth he was convicted of sin, and a gospel hope first entered his heart through the stanza,—

"In the world of endless ruin
It shall never once be said,
There's a soul that perished suing
For the Saviour's promised aid."

This hope was soon after confirmed, so that he could regard the Saviour as his. He was baptized Sept. 16, 1790. He was ordained pastor of the Eagle Street church, Red Lion Square, London, Jan. 16, 1805. His labors were attended with great success. He was gifted with much energy, with

REV. JOSEPH IVIMEY.

an unusual power of gaining and keeping information, and with fearless faithfulness in proclaiming the whole truth of God. He had the happiness of baptizing his own father and mother. His father was seventy years of age at the time of his immersion, and only partook of the Lord's Supper once after he was received into the church.

Mr. Ivimey wrote a life of John Bunyan, which enjoyed considerable popularity, and "A History of the English Baptists," in four octavo volumes, the last two of which were published in 1830. This history is invaluable. It is only seldom for sale, and when it can be purchased it is held at a high price. He was also the author of other works.

Mr. Ivimey closed his useful life Feb. 8, 1834. A little before his departure he said,—

"Not a wave of trouble rolls
Across my peaceful breast."

J.

Jackson, Gov. Charles, son of Hon. Richard Jackson, and brother of Rev. Dr. Henry Jackson, was born in Providence, R. I., March 3, 1797, and was a graduate of Brown University in the class of 1817. He pursued his law studies in the office of Hon. James Burrill, of Providence, and was admitted to the bar in 1820. After practising his profession for three years, he retired from it, and devoted himself to the manufacture of cotton, and resided for several years in a village which took its name from him,—Jacksonville. He returned to Providence in 1839, and devoted himself during the remainder of his life to the manufacturing interests of the State and of the country at large. For several years he was a member of the General Assembly of Rhode Island, and Speaker of the House in 1841-42. He was chosen governor of the State in 1845, and held the office one year. His death occurred at Providence, Jan. 21, 1876. Although not a professor of religion, he had a pew in the First Baptist meeting-house in Providence, and regarded that place as his religious home.

Jackson, Henry, D.D., was born in Providence, R. I., June 16, 1798. By family connection he was related to some of the first people in the city of his birth and in Rhode Island. Having completed his preparatory studies in the university grammar school, he entered Brown University in 1813. During his second year in college he was baptized, and became a member of the First Baptist church in Providence, then under the pastoral charge of Rev. Dr. Gano. At once he took a decided stand as a Christian worker, and, obeying what he recognized as the call of God, he resolved to devote himself to the work of the Christian ministry. To fit himself for it he repaired to the Andover Theological Institution, and pursued the full course of study there. The First Baptist church in Providence, with which he was connected, gave him a license to preach the gospel in 1820. He was ordained as pastor of the Baptist church in Charlestown, Mass., Nov. 27, 1822. For fourteen years he labored with great zeal, and was rewarded by seeing the growth of his church, both in numbers and spiritual efficiency. It was largely owing to his influence and practical aid that the Charlestown Female Seminary was founded, an institution which did an incalculable amount of good in the intellectual training of young ladies, and fitting very many of them for positions of great usefulness in after-life. His ministry in Charlestown closed Oct. 19, 1836.

Dr. Jackson had received an invitation to take charge of the First Baptist church in Hartford,

HENRY JACKSON, D.D.

Conn., before his resignation of his pastorate in Charlestown. After a few weeks of cessation from his ministerial work, he was installed at Hartford. Serious illness interrupted his labors after he had been in his new field a little more than a year. After a season of rest, he was anxious once more to be engaged in the work of the ministry, and accepted a call to the First Baptist church in New Bedford, where he was installed Jan. 1, 1839. Seven years were spent in New Bedford. Once more he found himself overworked, and compelled, in comparative retirement, to recruit his wasted energies. He resumed his work in January, 1847, and was settled as the pastor of the Central Baptist church in Newport, R. I. The church had recently been formed, and he was its first pastor. This was his longest pastorate, extending from January, 1847, to the close of life, a period of a little more than twenty-three years. When the end of his long ministerial career came, he had been in the vocation which, in his young days, he had accepted with such a hearty consecration of himself to his Lord, nearly forty-one years. During this time he had welcomed into the different churches of which he had been pastor nearly 1400 persons, having administered the ordinance of baptism to 870 of this number.

Dr. Jackson was greatly interested in all forms of educational institutions. In 1828 he was elected a member of the corporation of Brown University. He was one of the founders of the Newton Theological Institution, and a trustee from 1825 through the remainder of his life. By his will he left generous bequests to both these seminaries of learning. He published a history of the Baptist churches in Rhode Island, and by his industry and diligent search gathered up materials which, but for his labors, might have been irrecoverably lost.

The death of Dr. Jackson was almost a translation. He was on his way to East Greenwich, R. I., going there on some errand of Christian love. While engaged in pleasant conversation with a friend who sat by his side, without a moment's warning, life was extinct, and he was transferred from the scene of his labors to that of his reward. It was without doubt a stroke of apoplexy. The event occurred March 2, 1863, at the age of sixty-four years and eight months and four days. He had filled so prominent a place in the denomination in which for so long a time he had exercised his ministry, that his sudden departure was a great shock to his friends. It is difficult to realize the sum total of the good which sprang from all those years of service for the Master. That he owned and blessed the service was the servant's exceeding great reward.

Jackson, Col. Moses, a member of the Mississippi senate from Wilkinson and Amite Counties, was born in Amite Co., Miss., in 1822; became a Baptist in 1852, and has since lived a consistent Christian life in the midst of public duties; twenty-two years a trustee, and twenty-four years a deacon, and twenty-five years clerk of his church. When the General Association of South Mississippi and Eastern Louisiana was formed, in 1866, he was elected moderator. He entered the Confederate army as a private, and was promoted through several grades to that of lieutenant-colonel of the 33d Miss. Regiment. Besides several minor offices which he has held, in 1861 he was elected to the State Legislature, and re-elected in 1863. In 1865 he was elected to the State senate, and re-elected in 1877.

Jackson, Hon. Richard, was born in Providence, R. I., July 3, 1764. His early boyhood brought him within the period of the Revolutionary war. When there were grave fears that Providence would be attacked by the British, the father of young Jackson removed his family to Pomfret, Conn., where they remained for some time away from the dangers and excitements of the war. Mr. Jackson early showed a taste for business pursuits, and embarked in mercantile and manufacturing enterprises, in the prosecution of which he was eminently successful. He also developed a taste for political life, and was honored several times with the votes of his fellow-citizens to fill places of important civil trusts. In 1815 he was elected a member of the Tenth Congress of the United States, and so acceptable were his services to a majority of the people of his native State that he was re-elected to the Eleventh, Twelfth, and Thirteenth Congresses. The whole period of his service as one of the representatives from Rhode Island was nearly seven years, covering the period between November 11, 1808, and March 4, 1815. In all matters affecting the welfare of his native town he took a great interest. Of one of the leading insurance companies of Providence—the Washington—he was the president for thirty-eight years. He took also an abiding interest in the affairs of the First Baptist church, in whose meeting-house he worshiped for so many years. Brown University chose him as a member of its corporation in 1809, and he held this office until his death, which took place at Providence, April 18, 1838. Mr. Jackson was the father of Rev. Henry Jackson, D.D., and of Hon. Charles Jackson, who was governor of Rhode Island during the gubernatorial year 1845–46.

Jackson, Rev. R. S., a gifted young minister, a native of Louisiana, was born near the mouth of Red River, Sept. 12, 1844; was educated at Mount Lebanon University and the State Seminary at Alexandria. He left school to enlist in the Confederate army, and rose to the rank of captain. After the war he engaged in teaching; began to preach in 1869 to the creoles in their vernacular; was subsequently tutor in Mississippi College; secretary of the Ministerial Educational Board of the Louisiana Convention, and missionary of Bayou Macon Association, La. After a successful pastorate at Bastrop, La., he entered the Southern Baptist Theological Seminary. As a contributor to the religious press he attained distinction. He died at the seminary from an old army wound in 1874.

Jackson, Thomas, a prominent Baptist layman in Eastern Louisiana, was one of "Marion's men" during the Revolution, and accompanied the old "Swamp Fox" throughout the war. It was he who prepared the dinner of roasted sweet potatoes for the British officers who visited Marion's camp under a flag of truce, and who reported that it was impossible to conquer men who fought for liberty and lived upon roots. He came to East Feliciana Parish, La., in 1806, and either united in the organization of the Hepzibah church in 1813, or became a member soon after. He died in 1844. Several of his descendants have been prominent Baptists in the State.

Jackson, Wade M., a pioneer among the Baptists of Missouri, was born in Fleming Co., Ky., Dec. 3, 1797, and died in Howard Co., Mo., March 22, 1879. He removed to Missouri in 1824, and settled on the farm where he died. He was the father of Mrs. Judge James Harris, of Boone Co., Mo., and brother of Claiborne F. Jackson, late governor of Missouri. As an honored citizen of Central Missouri he stood in the front rank. He became a Baptist forty-one years before his death, and consecrated his life to Christ, and served his denomination faithfully. He was a member of the Executive Missionary Board of the General Association for years, and a trustee of William Jewell College. He rendered valuable aid in drawing up the charter of that institution, and helped to organize it. Many old friends followed him to his resting-place in the family burying-ground near his home.

Jackson, Rev. Wingate, was born in 1776 in Virginia, and removed in early life to Kentucky, where he reached eminence as a preacher. He came to Missouri about 1809, and labored in and around Cape Girardeau and Jackson. He belonged to Bethel Association, and great success attended his ministry. He was clear in doctrine, eloquent in speech, wise in counsel, and untiring in labor. He died in 1835. His opinions for years after his death were quoted to settle controversies.

Jacobs, B. F., Esq.—This name is one well known among active and enterprising Christian workers throughout the land. Mr. Jacobs was born at Paterson, N. J., in September, 1834. He was baptized in Chicago in 1854, by Rev. J. C. Burroughs, then pastor of the First Baptist church, uniting with that church, of which he has remained a member until now. Previous to his removal to Chicago he had lived for some years in Detroit, where he was a member of the Bible-class of Mr. S. N. Kendrick. His conversion occurred while there. Immediately upon uniting with the church in Chicago he began active Christian work, at first as a teacher in the Taylor Street Mission School, the first of such schools established in Chicago, being engaged also in a similar way in the home school. In 1856 the first of the mission schools of our own denomination in Chicago was opened in what was then called New Street, now Seventeenth, and named the New Street Mission; subsequently, in recognition of the generous aid given it by Miss Shields, of Philadelphia, called the Shields Mission. Of this mission Mr. Jacobs remained the superintendent for eight years, and under his guidance it grew to be one of the most efficient agencies of the kind in the city. In 1865, when Deacon S. Hoard, by reason of his connection with the Second church, upon the west side of the river, left the superintendency of the school at the First church, Mr. Jacobs was elected superintendent in his place. The church was at that time building a new house of worship on Wabash Avenue, and was meeting meantime in Bryan Hall. On the first Sunday in January, 1866, it removed to the lecture-room of the new house, a room made for the accommodation of 800. The school numbered only 90, and seemed at first almost lost in the new quarters, but began at once to grow, and so continued until it had reached nearly 1200. During this time Mr. Jacobs remained the superintendent, and continued such until the house on Wabash Avenue had been destroyed by fire, in 1874. Upon the erection of a new house in the south part of the city, Mr. Jacobs, with others, organized a school and evening congregation upon Wabash Avenue near the site of the house that was burned. This, under the name of the Tabernacle, has been continued until the present time. The school at present numbers 400. There are 126 members of the organization holding their formal membership with the First church, but having otherwise a distinct identity. The weekly evening prayer-meeting numbers from 75 to 100, fully three-fifths of whom are men. Of those who have connected themselves with the organization most have come in by baptism, many of them rescued from the lowest depths of dissipation. At the evening service, which is always well attended, Mr. Jacobs preaches.

The large place which Mr. Jacobs has filled in general church work would deserve detailed record if space would allow. He was one of the founders, and has always been one of the most active members of the Young Men's Christian Association of Chicago, an organization which grew out of the revival of 1857–58. In 1861, Mr. Jacobs, Mr. Moody, and Mr. Tuthill King inaugurated the religious work at Camp Douglas, in Chicago, which was continued during the war with the happiest results. As one of the first who visited on a like errand the troops in service in the South, he may be said to have had a share in creating the Christian Commission, with which he remained connected to the end of the struggle, serving as its secretary for the West, and raising for its uses the sum of more than $100,000. In the general Sunday-school work, State and national, he has labored during many years; was the originator of the International Sunday-School Committee, and remains a member of that committee to this day. This is but the meagre outline of a career of remarkable Christian activity, carried on amidst the exacting demands of an engrossing business, and which, we rejoice to say, has still the promise of many years' continuance.

Jacobs, Capt. William S., commanded at sea

for many years, and on retiring, resided at Liverpool, Nova Scotia. He became a member of the Baptist church in that town; was liberal in support of all denominational objects, and at his death, in 1863, left handsome bequests to Acadia College, to home missions, and infirm ministers.

James, Prof. Charles Sexton, Ph.D., was born in Philadelphia, Pa., Feb. 6, 1820. He was prepared for college at the Haddington Institution, under the care of Rev. J. L. Dagg, D.D. He entered Brown University at sixteen, and was a member of the famous class of 1840, in which he was associated with James R. Boise, Wm. T. Brantly, Ebenezer Dodge, ex-Gov. Gaston, of Massachusetts, J. R. Kendrick, Heman Lincoln, and Henry G. Weston. His course was, however, interrupted by a three years' absence, and his graduation deferred until 1843. He distinguished himself as a student, and particularly in Greek. He was chosen to membership in the Phi Beta Kappa Society in his Junior year. He was converted during a revival at Brown University in 1835, and was baptized into the fellowship of the Tenth Baptist church, Philadelphia, by Rev. J. H. Kennard, D.D. After his graduation he became an instructor with his uncle, T. D. James, in the academy at Eleventh and Market Streets, Philadelphia, until 1851, when he was called to the Professorship of Mathematics and Natural Philosophy in the university at Lewisburg, Pa. As a scholar, Prof. James was exact and thorough. As a teacher, for more than a third of a century, he was enthusiastic and eminently successful. The dry problems of pure mathematics were poetry to him, and in his hands were clothed with unknown charms to his classes. Many of Lewisburg's best and most useful graduates refer to his class-room as the place of their first and lasting inspiration to exact reasoning and earnest scholarship.

As a student of the Bible and a member of the church, Prof. James was reverent and diligent. He was always an active worker in the Sunday-school. His knowledge of the New Testament was founded upon a thorough study of the original Greek. For years he has conducted a Sunday morning Bible-class of college students in his parlor, the New Testament being studied in Greek.

In 1859, the degree of Ph.D. was conferred upon him by Columbian College. Prof. James was singularly modest. In his class-room, and within the circle of his appointed labors, he was devotedly loved by those who knew him best, as a man of self-sacrificing generosity and earnest devotion to the cause of Christian education.

James, Rev. John, was pastor of the Baptist church meeting in Bulstake Alley, Whitechapel, London. In the latter end of 1661, Mr. James was rudely interrupted twice by officers of the law while preaching to his own people, and commanded to come down. Then he was dragged out of the pulpit. A perjured wretch named Tipler, a journeyman pipe-maker, charged him with uttering treasonable words against the king; and so disreputable a person was Tipler that the justice refused to commit Mr. James on his testimony, unless it was corroborated; but this was done, and the good pastor was sent to the Tower.

On the 14th of November he was brought before Chief-Justice Forster, and three other judges, at Westminster Hall, where he was charged with "endeavoring to levy war against the king; with seeking a change in the government; with saying that the king was a bloody tyrant, a blood-sucker, and a bloodthirsty man, and that his nobles were the same; and that the king and his nobles had shed the blood of the saints at Charing Cross, and in Scotland." To this indictment he pled "not guilty, neither in matter nor form." And there was not a tittle of evidence to substantiate one of the charges in any just court on earth. Mr. James was remanded to Newgate for four days, when the trial was to proceed. In the mean time he received a letter from a friend of distinction, who informed him that for many years there had not been such efforts to pack a jury, and that his only hope of safety lay in challenging them, or "most of the chief men of them." When Mr. James was brought before the court, the chief justice exclaimed, "Oh, oh, are you come?" "and this was a specimen of the way in which his trial was conducted." He was condemned according to the plot of those who planned his murder; and the next day, after the court had sentenced him, his wife presented a petition to King Charles II. proving his innocence, and appealing for mercy; but the only reply of his majesty was, "Oh! Mr. James, he is a sweet gentleman," "and the door was shut against her." The next morning she made another appeal to him; and his cruel response was, "He is a rogue, and shall be hanged."

When he was asked if he had anything to say why sentence of death should not be pronounced upon him, his answer was: "As for me, behold, I am in your hand: do with me as it seemeth good and meet unto you. But know ye for certain that if ye put me to death, ye shall surely bring innocent blood upon yourselves, and upon this city, and upon the inhabitants thereof. Precious in the sight of the Lord is the death of his saints. He that toucheth you toucheth the apple of mine eye." And when Mr. James heard his sentence, he immediately added, "Blessed be God, whom man hath condemned God hath justified."

At Tyburn, where he was *hung, drawn and quartered*, his remarks were gentle and loving, and his soul brave and full of hope. "His quarters were taken back to Newgate prison on the sledge which brought him to the gallows, and they were afterwards placed on the city gates, and his head was set upon a pole opposite his meeting-house."

John James was an inoffensive and benevolent man, free from any blemish in his character, and guiltless of every charge in the indictment. He was savagely murdered by Charles II., his courtiers, and his tools, the judges, to terrify the Dissenters, and especially the Baptists, into loyalty. Undoubtedly the vengeance of God, invoked by the innocent blood of John James, had something to do with driving the Stuarts from the throne of England. Mr. James was a Seventh-Day Baptist.

James, Rev. John Angell (colored), was born Nov. 5, 1826, in De Kalb Co., Ga. He was raised on a farm, but became a mechanic. He professed religion, and was baptized by Rev. S. Landrum in 1849, and joined the Cotton Avenue Baptist church in Macon, Ga., Feb. 10, 1850. He was licensed in 1856 by the Cotton Avenue church. In September, 1865, the Second Street (colored) church was formed by members who took letters from the Cotton Avenue church. They called Mr. James to ordination, and he was set apart to the gospel ministry by a Presbytery consisting of Rev. E. W. Warren (white), Rev. F. M. Haygood (white), and Rev. Frank Quarles (colored), on the 14th of October, 1866. He assumed the pastorate of the Second Street church in October, 1867, and served nine years with much success, and baptized over 300 persons. He then went to Houston County, where he organized the Springfield (colored) church, which he served sixteen months. Returning to Macon, he organized the Fulton church, which he served two years as pastor. He then went to Forsyth, Ga., and organized the St. James (colored) Baptist church in 1867, where he still labors industriously and usefully. He has baptized into the fellowship of that church 374 persons. The total number baptized by him during his ministry to the present time, 1880, is 738. Mr. James is one of the most intelligent, useful, and laborious ministers among the colored Baptists of Georgia, and one who stands high in the denomination. For years he was clerk of the Middle Georgia Association (colored), a large and working body. For eight years he has been assistant secretary of the Colored State Baptist Convention, and is a vice-president of that body and secretary of its executive board. He is liberal, earnest, and devout, and he is a faithful pastor, enjoying the confidence of all, and a man of marked ability as a preacher and writer among his race.

James, J. H., a banker of Atlanta, Ga., was born in Henry County, July 14, 1830. His father removed to Georgia from North Carolina, of which State he was a native. Until manhood Mr. James resided on his father's farm. There was, however, in him a genius for business that could not brook such a life, so, at twenty, he went to Atlanta and accepted a situation at $10 per month, which, before

J. H. JAMES.

a great while, was increased to $100 per month. In 1860 he opened a banking-house in Atlanta, and when the war began was wealthy; but the end of the war found him worth about $12,000 only. He opened his bank again, and prosecuted his business with such success that he is now one of the wealthiest men in Georgia. His business capacity and integrity are such that he enjoys the confidence of all who know him, and has now established for himself the reputation of a financier of the first order. In manner Mr. James is pleasant and friendly; free from affectation, and full of geniality. As a citizen, he is charitable and public-spirited; as a Christian, generous and sincere, taking part in all denominational affairs, and in the family circle he is kind, affectionate, and considerate. He has occupied the position of mayor of Atlanta, is a trustee of Mercer University, and a trustee and superintendent of the Baptist Orphans' Home of Georgia, located at Atlanta.

In 1876 his name was suggested in connection with the gubernatorial election, and many, desiring to secure for the State the benefit of his financial ability, entreated him to allow his name to be placed before the nominating convention, but this he declined.

Mr. James is a man of great liberality. At his individual expense he erected two Baptist houses of worship in Atlanta, at a cost of $2500 each; and to the completion of another he contributed the sum of $3500, besides generously aiding in the support of ministers for these churches. Thousands of his minor charities have relieved the necessities of the poor, and if the worth of men should be measured by their gifts to the needy, that of Mr. James would appear pre-eminent. His donations to churches since the war sum up more than $15,000, an amount considerably in excess of the entire capital with which he resumed business.

He is one of those noble men who win their way in life by capacity, integrity, and sound judgment, and who rise, not on the ruin of others, but through the legitimate exercise of their own abilities and good sense in the ordinary business affairs of life.

During the panic of 1873, when many of the wealthiest bankers were compelled to suspend, some going into bankruptcy, a heavy pressure was brought to bear upon the establishment of Mr. James, by the unexpected demands of depositors. At this juncture he closed his bank until he could collect assets, when a number of the wealthy men of Atlanta, voluntarily and through the press, proposed to assume, in his behalf, liabilities varying from five to fifty thousand dollars each. Such a manifestation of faith is seldom met in the history of bankers or banking institutions, and this was an expression of confidence unmistakably sincere, since it was based upon the advance of large sums of actual capital for immediate use.

Mr. James frequently attends the denominational gatherings of his brethren, and his speeches are always plain, practical, and full of good sense.

James, Rev. J. J., was born in Halifax Co., Va., Nov. 30, 1814; was for three sessions a student at Wake Forest Institute, and, after teaching for two years in Virginia, graduated at Columbian University, Washington, D. C., in 1841. Mr. James was baptized at the age of eighteen by the Rev. John G. Mills, and was ordained in 1842, Rev. J. G. Mills and Rev. A. M. Poindexter constituting the Presbytery. After laboring for many years with much success as pastor in Caswell Co., N. C., aiding in the organization of Oxford Female College, and being a useful member of the various boards of the Convention, he became editor of the *Biblical Recorder* in 1854, which position he held till 1861. He now resides on his farm in Caswell County, and preaches only occasionally.

James, Rev. Owen, was born Oct. 30, 1848, in the County of Carmarthen, Wales. Until his sixteenth year his time was spent partly at school and partly in agricultural pursuits. He was converted in the summer of 1864, was baptized, and became an active and useful church member. His marked ability at so early an age prompted the church to advise him to prepare for the ministry, to which his own inclinations strongly urged him; but circumstances for the time made it impracticable. Soon after this he united with another Baptist church, and here, again, after a most useful membership of nearly four years, the church urged him to devote himself to preparation for the ministry. Through the advice of Dr. Thomas Price, of Aberdare, Mr. James made his arrangements to come to the United States. He entered the preparatory department of Lewisburg University in September, 1870, and the college in 1872, from which he was graduated in 1876 with the highest honors of his class. In the fall of the same year he entered Crozer Theological Seminary, and was graduated from it in 1879. He was immediately called to the pastorate of the North Baptist church, Washington, D. C., which he accepted, where he was ordained, and where he still labors. Mr. James is an interesting and instructive preacher; is gifted with unusual logical and analytical power, and presents his themes in so fresh and original a manner that the most thoughtful minds listen to his expositions of Scriptural truth with both pleasure and profit. His congregation, though not very large, contains some of the most cultured of the denomination among its members.

James, Rev. Richard S., M.D., president of Judson University (Judsonia, Ark.), was born in Philadelphia, Pa., in 1824; educated at Brown University and Columbian College, Washington, D. C.; ordained in 1859; pastor nine years at Camden and Marlton, N. J.; was pastor at West Newton, Mass., and Market Street church, Zanesville, O.; and professor in Hillsdale College, Mich.; was pastor at Medina, Mich., where he was also principal of Oak-Grove Academy. At the beginning of the present year (1880) he was called to Judsonia, Ark., and soon after his arrival was elected president of the Judson University, located at Judsonia. Dr. James is an enthusiastic teacher, an eloquent preacher, and a sprightly writer.

Jameson, Ephraim H. E., D.D., was born at St. George, Me., May 19, 1835. His father, Rev. Thomas Jameson, was for many years a Baptist pastor in Maine, but removed to Illinois, where he died in 1870, at the age of eighty years. Mr. Jameson was educated at the Lebanon and South Berwick Academies, in Maine, and the Kingston Academy, N. H. He then entered upon the profession of teaching. In 1854 he was born into the kingdom of Christ. With a change of heart came convictions of duty in another direction, and he entered the New Hampton Collegiate and Theological Institution, at Fairfax, Vt., to prepare for the ministry. After completing his classical course, difficulties arrested his efforts, and he resolved to engage in secular pursuits till the way should open for him to preach the gospel. He went West, spent some time in teaching, and afterwards several years in the editorial profession in St. Louis, Mo. He bore an honorable part in the war as colonel of a U. S. regiment. He was elected to a seat in the Missouri Legislature, and being re-elected, filled the Speaker's chair one year.

EPHRAIM H. E. JAMESON, D.D.

During all this time the voice of conscience was calling him to his real life-work. He endeavored to compromise by engaging in Sunday-school and mission efforts, but this only led him to follow Christ more fully. He was licensed to preach in 1874, by the Park Avenue Baptist church of St. Louis, and on May 9, 1876, he was publicly ordained to the ministry.

Dr. Jameson was chosen pastor of the First Baptist church of Omaha, Neb., Aug. 1, 1876. He still continues in that office. The completion of their large church edifice will remain for years a monument to his indefatigable energy. Shortly after his settlement in Nebraska he was chosen corresponding secretary of the Baptist State Convention, a position which he still holds, and in which he has rendered the State valuable service. In June, 1880, he received from Central University, Iowa, the degree of D.D.

Jameson, Rev. J. D., late pastor at Camden, Ark., was born in Georgia in 1850; began to preach in Columbia Co., Ark., in 1870; after a course of study at Mississippi College, interrupted by bad health, he spent one year in the Southern Baptist Theological Seminary; was successful as agent of the Southern Baptist Publication Society; as pastor at Mineral Springs and at Camden, Ark.; at present he is State evangelist.

Janes, Col. Absalom, a prominent, consistent, and efficient member of the Baptist denomination in Georgia, was born in Wilkes County, June 8, 1796. In 1839 he took up his residence in Penfield, where he dwelt until his death, Sept. 25, 1847.

He was for eleven years treasurer of the Georgia Baptist Convention, and managed the finances of the body during years of extreme monetary depression with remarkable success. He was a trustee of Mercer Institute until it became Mercer University, and until his death, in 1847, he continued to be one of its trustees. In sustaining and in firmly establishing these two institutions, and all the other benevolent Baptist enterprises of Georgia, he was an active and most efficient co-laborer with Mercer, Mallary, Stocks, Sherwood, Dawson, Thornton, Battle, Davis, Campbell, and Walker. Col. Janes had talents of a high order, with a strong, active, discriminating intellect. He possessed great quickness of perception, excellence of judgment, and energy of character. He was liberal, public-spirited, and philanthropic, claiming and receiving nothing for his services while treasurer of the Convention. In practical financial affairs his judgment was inferior to that of no one. For several years he represented Taliaferro County in the State senate, and in 1844 he ran against Hon. A. H. Stephens for Congress, and, though defeated, he received a larger vote than any candidate who ever opposed A. H. Stephens. Col. Janes was distinguished for unvarying courtesy and kindness in all the relations of life, and he is justly considered one of the chief builders of the Baptist denomination in Georgia.

Japan, Mission to.—At the annual meeting of the Missionary Union in 1872, it was resolved to accept Rev. N. Brown, D.D., and Rev. Mr. Goble as their missionaries to Japan, they having been in the employ of the American Baptist Free Mission Society. These brethren returned to the field of labor to which they had been designated, arriving at Yokohama in February, 1873, and immediately entered upon their work. Mr. Goble's connection with the Union continued only for a short time. Rev. J. H. Arthur and wife were appointed as missionaries to Japan in 1873, and in December of the same year Rev. J. T. Doyen, formerly connected with the Episcopal Church, and a resident of Yokohama, was also appointed as a missionary of the Union. Dr. Brown entered, very soon after reaching the field of his labors, upon the work of translating the Scriptures into Japanese, and in 1876 was able to report good progress in this direction. From January, 1875, to April, 1876, there had been published 614,600 pages of various translations, including the gospels of Matthew and Mark, the

Epistle of James, and several distinct portions of the New Testament, as the parables, the sermon on the mount, etc., and other religious reading. A new missionary station was commenced in Tokio (Yeddo) by Mr. and Mrs. Arthur in 1876. Rev. F. S. Dobbins and wife were sent out by the Union in October, 1876, to be connected with Dr. Brown. Mr. Dobbins was obliged to return to this country in a few months, on account of the sickness of his wife. Mr. Arthur, one of the most promising of all the missionaries that have been sent to the foreign field, also, was compelled to retire from his labors, and sailed for California, hoping that a short respite from his work would restore his health. He died at Oakland, Cal., Dec. 9, 1877. The church which was formed by him in Tokio had, on the 1st of January, 1878, 23 members. The outlook for the mission in Japan is favorable. Dr. Brown says in his report to the Executive Committee, " here are 33,000,000 of people, all speaking the same language, and using the same written characters." Having referred to the fact that previous translations of the Bible had been made by those who were not favorable to Baptist views, he says, "We marvel that Baptists should for a moment hesitate as to the duty of giving this people a faithful translation of the New Testament. We have printed, within the last three years, over 1,000,000 pages of Scripture, including the first three gospels, and portions of the Old Testament."

In Yokohama in 1880 there were 7 male and female missionaries, and one church with 39 members. In Tokio there were 5 missionaries, one man and four women, and one church with 37 members.

Jarman, Prof. G. W., A.M., was born May 14, 1826, in Lawrence Co., Ala. He joined the Baptist church in 1843; graduated at La Grange College, Ala., in 1847. Before graduating he had employed his vacation and leisure hours in studying medicine with a view of becoming a physician. November, 1847, he was elected tutor in Union University, Murfreesborough, Tenn., and commenced teaching January, 1848. In 1850 was elected Professor of Latin in Union University, and in 1855 the professorship of Greek was added to that of Latin. He succeeded Rev. Dr. Jos. H. Eaton as president of Union University in 1860; resigned his position in Union University in 1873, and in 1874 was elected principal of the Southwestern Baptist University, Jackson, Tenn. In 1875 was elected Professor of Latin and Greek in the same institution, and in 1876 was elected chairman of the faculty, which position he now holds. He has had students from every quarter of the globe, and those who have attended his instruction number many thousands. With slight intermissions, has been engaged in teaching for thirty-three years. Prof. Jarman is still in his prime, and looks as though he might have another thirty years before him. Thorough in scholarship, skillful in discipline, dignified in bearing, he commands the respect and esteem of his students. He has left his impress upon great numbers who now occupy the higher walks of life as ministers, lawyers, physicians, teachers, and statesmen.

The Baptist churches of Tennessee and the Southwest are greatly indebted to this veteran teacher for his very efficient labors in their behalf. His name will be forever associated with the educational work of the denomination in Tennessee, and will grow brighter and brighter as his labors and sacrifices become better known in their far-reaching influence.

Jeffery, Rev. William, was born at Penhurst, England, about the year 1616. At Seven-Oaks he was one of the chief supporters, if he was not the founder, of the Baptist church. Of this church, then called Bradburn, he became the pastor, and under his zealous labors it enjoyed remarkable prosperity. Mr. Jeffery preached in various places in the county of Kent, and with some help from others was instrumental in founding more than twenty churches. He was the author of a valuable work called "The Whole Faith of Man," the second edition of which was issued in 1659. He was a gentle but steadfast Christian, and a very decided Baptist, never inviting controversy, and never permitting his heaven-born principles to lack a defender while he could wield a spiritual weapon to protect them.

Mr. Jeffery suffered much for his principles. On one occasion the magistrates of Seven-Oaks arrested all the men in his congregation while they were at worship, and kept them in prison an entire night. The next day the justices, after an examination, dismissed them. They returned to the church to thank God for their deliverance. To their astonishment, as they entered the house of God, they saw the women there, who, from the time of their arrest, had continued in fasting and prayer for their release until their supplications were visibly and joyfully answered. Mr. Jeffery was imprisoned after the restoration of Charles II., and subjected to many hardships.

After a life of great usefulness, of universal benevolence, and of abundant labors and sufferings, Mr. Jeffery rested from his toils in a good old age, and he was succeeded in his pastoral office by his son, the Rev. John Jeffery.

Jeffrey, Reuben, D.D., was born in Leicester. England, Feb. 15, 1827, and came to America when ten years of age with his parents, who settled in Geneva, N. Y. He was graduated from Madison University and the theological seminary connected with it. His first settlement was at Nantucket, where, in 1847, he was ordained and entered on a very successful ministry.

He has filled the pastoral office in the First church of Albany, N. Y.; the Fourth church in Philadelphia, Pa.; the North church in Chicago, Ill.; and the Ninth Street church, in Cincinnati, O. On the 14th of December, 1873, he accepted a call to the Marcy Avenue church, in Brooklyn, N. Y. It was a new and feeble organization, with about 40 members, meeting in a chapel. The house very soon became too small for his audiences. A new one was built, and that also in a few months was overflowing. It was enlarged, and more than a thousand people filled it at every service. The membership has increased to more than 600, the largest portion by baptism. Many of them are among the most substantial people in that section of the city. His friends regard this as the most successful work of his life.

Dr. Jeffrey's sermons are never sensational. He speaks without a manuscript or notes, yet his discourses are delivered with ease, force, and clearness. His rhetoric is good and his logic conclusive. He often thrills his hearers by impassioned bursts of eloquence, especially when presenting the great truths of the gospel.

Several of his sermons have been published. Recently he has removed to Denver, Col., where his new charge are building a spacious house of worship.

Jenckes, Gov. Joseph, was born in Pawtucket, R. I., in 1656. His grandfather, of the same name, was, without doubt, in the company of emigrants who came from England in 1630, under the leadership of Gov. Winthrop. The father of Gov. Jenckes is supposed to have taken up his residence in Pawtucket about the year 1655. He was a blacksmith by trade, and the articles of his manufacture were in ready demand in the section of the country where he lived. He was honored and respected in the colony, and filled several important offices of civil trust. Like his father, the subject of this sketch also took a prominent part in civil affairs. As early as 1705 he was a commissioner to aid in the settlement of the perplexing questions which arose about the boundary-line between Rhode Island and Massachusetts. He was elected, in 1715, deputy governor of Rhode Island, and was in office until May, 1721. Before he had completed his term of service he was sent, in 1720, to England to bring the boundary disputes between Rhode Island as the one party, and Connecticut and Massachusetts as the other, to the direct notice of the king. He was again re-elected deputy governor in 1722, and continued in this office for five years, making eleven years in all that he occupied this honorable position. In 1727, upon the death of Gov. Cranston, who had been in office for the long period of twenty-nine years, Mr. Jenckes was chosen as his successor, and occupied this post of honor for five years. During a large part of this time Gov. Jenckes resided, by the special request of the General Assembly, in Newport. When Gov. Jenckes completed his term of gubernatorial service he was well advanced in years. He is said to have been the tallest man of his time in Rhode Island, standing seven feet and two inches. His death took place June 15, 1740. Gov. Jenckes was a decided Baptist. Among other things we read from the inscription that was placed on his tombstone, that "he was a bright example of virtue in every stage of life. He was a zealous Christian, a wise and prudent governor, grave, sober, beautiful in person, with a soul truly great, heroic, and sweetly tempered."

Jenkens, Rev. C. A., was born in Benton, Miss., Jan. 20, 1850; educated at the University of Virginia; taught school in Virginia. He was a layman and vestryman of the Episcopal Church in 1875, when he was baptized by Dr. C. Manly in Staunton, Va. He came immediately to North Carolina, and took charge of Warsaw High School, and began to preach. He was at one time pastor of Louisburg church, then of Franklinton, and now of Oxford. Mr. Jenkens edited "Baptist Doctrines," published in St. Louis in 1880, a large and valuable work, several thousand copies of which have already been sold.

Jenkins, Charles J., was a prominent layman, for many years, among the Baptists of Georgia.

He was the father of ex-Gov. Chas. J. Jenkins of that State, who is still living. He was born in 1780, but moved from Georgia to Beaufort District, S. C., in 1804, on his marriage to Miss Susan Emily Kenny of that State. He resided in Beaufort District until the spring of 1815. Mr. and Mrs. Jenkins became deeply interested in the subject of religion, and both united with the Baptist church at Beaufort.

During several years of his residence in South Carolina Mr. Jenkins was ordinary of Beaufort District, an office then in the gift of the State Legislature, and always most carefully bestowed because of its great importance.

About the beginning of 1816 Mr. Jenkins removed to Jefferson Co., Ga., and united with the Providence Baptist church, on Rocky Comfort Creek, twelve miles above Louisville. He afterwards resided a short time in Washington County, near Fenn's Bridge; but, about the beginning of 1819, he removed to Madison County, where he built a Baptist house of worship and organized a Baptist church near his residence. In October of the following year, during the annual meeting of the Sarepta Association, at Ruckersville, Elbert Co., he, as clerk, presented the following resolution, drawn up by Rev. Adiel Sherwood, D.D.:

"*Resolved*, That we suggest for our consideration, and that of sister Associations in this State, the propriety of organizing a general meeting of correspondence."

The resolution was adopted, and resulted in the formation of the General Association on the 27th of June, 1822, at Powelton, which name was changed to the Baptist Convention of the State of Georgia in 1828.

In 1822, Mr. Jenkins was appointed surveyor and collector of the port of Apalachicola, in West Florida, where he remained three years, resigning and returning to Georgia on account of his deprivation of church privileges in Apalachicola. He settled in Jefferson County, where he had formerly resided, on his return to his native State, and there he died, in July, 1828, in his forty-ninth year. Mr. Jenkins was a quiet, unassuming man, very useful, kind and benevolent in disposition, and of the strictest integrity. He was exceedingly energetic and liberal, but seldom let his right hand know what his left was doing. He was a man of culture and refinement. He never sought office; and it was only because he positively declined that he was not elected State senator for both Jefferson and Madison Counties. His heart was in his religious denomination, and, outside of his domestic circle and private business affairs, all his efforts and energies were devoted to extending its borders, and widening its influence and power. In every community in which he dwelt he was a leading and an influential man, and enjoyed the respect and confidence of all who knew him. For years he was clerk of the Sarepta Association, and took hold of religious and educational measures with a strong hand, and he was able to accomplish much that was useful.

Jenkins, Rev. Nathaniel, was born in Wales in 1678; was converted, and began to preach in his native country. He settled at Cape May, N. J., in 1712, and became the founder and first pastor of the church at Cape May Court-House. He continued to preside over this church until 1730, when he took charge of Cohansey, where he died in 1754. His talents shone both in the church and state. He exemplified his belief in liberty of conscience on an important occasion. When he was a member of the Colonial Legislature of New Jersey, in 1721, a bill was introduced to punish all who denied the doctrine of the Trinity, Christ's divinity, and the inspiration of the Scriptures. He could not be persuaded to vote for it, but, rising in his place, said, among other things, with Welsh warmth and eloquence, "I believe the doctrines in question as firmly as the promoters of that ill-designed bill; but will never consent to oppose the opposers with law, or any other weapon save that of argument." The bill was defeated.

Jenkins, Samuel, was born in Wales, Feb. 12, 1789. At the age of six he was able to read in Welsh, and he loved to read the Bible. In 1801 his parents came to Philadelphia, and in 1804 he joined the Welsh Calvinistical church in that city, of which his father was pastor. Having settled in the Great Valley, Chester County, he was baptized, and united with the church in that place in 1816, and from that time to the day of his death he was a thorough Baptist.

Mr. Jenkins possessed a wonderful memory, and his knowledge of Welsh history was remarkable. He wrote much for the press. In 1852 he published a work entitled "Letters on Welsh History," which exhibited a thorough acquaintance with the records of that ancient people. He died Sept. 12, 1871.

Mr. Jenkins was a good man, a sincere Christian, and a friend to every worthy cause.

Jenkins, Rev. S. G., a native of Georgia, was ordained in that State by Elders Sanders, Lumpkin, Thornton, and Hillyer. In 1832 he removed to Mississippi, where he successfully served churches for some years. In 1840 he came to Alabama and settled on the picturesque spot where he now resides, in Talladega County. Soon he planted a number of churches. Has been pastor of Antioch and Cold Water churches, respectively, thirty-nine years, and has baptized 1006 members at these two churches, many of them from other denominations. He has been abundant in labors and success. He has baptized 13 households and 22 men who entered the ministry. He has always been a farmer, and before the late war was in good worldly circumstances. Has constantly been a fearless gospel preacher. Has reared an interesting family; is about seventy years old, and now often rides forty miles in a day, and preaches three sermons.

Jenks, Prof. John W. P., was born in West Boylston, Mass., May 1, 1819. He graduated at Brown University in the class of 1838. On leaving college he went to Georgia, where he taught four years, for a part of the time acting as colleague of Rev. Jesse Mercer, D.D., in the last year of his life in Washington, Wilkes Co., Ga. In 1842 he became the principal of the Peirce Academy, in Middleborough, and continued in that relation twenty-nine years. During his administration the academy rose to a high rank among the best institutions of its kind in New England. In 1872 he was elected Professor of Agricultural Zoology and curator of the Museum of Natural History in Brown University, which position he now holds. By his untiring efforts Prof. Jenks has brought his special department into a condition far in advance of what it was when he entered upon the duties of his professorship. Brown University has a museum of natural history of which it may justly be proud.

Jennings, Rev. John, was born in Danbury, Conn., Dec. 8, 1809; was hopefully converted at the age of fourteen, and baptized into the fellowship of the church in the place where he had passed his youthful days. He was licensed to preach when he was but seventeen years of age, June 17, 1826. He entered upon a course of preparatory study, and without going through college, he graduated at the Newton Theological Institution in the class of 1834. He was ordained pastor of the church in Beverly, Mass., Sept. 15, 1834, remaining here for two years, and then settling at Grafton, where he continued for six years, at the end of which period he was called to the pastorate of the newly organized Second Baptist church in Worcester, Mass. He commenced his labors here in March, 1842, and continued in this pastorate for eight years. For some time he was in the service of the American Tract Society. In 1852 he became the pastor of the Baptist church in Fitchburg, Mass., where he remained until 1859, when he was invited to Woonsocket, R. I., and labored there three and a half years. His last settlement was in Westfield, Mass., where he continued seven and a half years, when his failing health obliged him to resign, and he moved to Auburndale, Mass., where he died, June 26, 1871. An appreciative notice of this worthy minister of Christ, written by his friend, Rev. W. C. Richards, says of him, "Few men have lived more respected and beloved as a Christian man and a Christian minister by all who knew his virtues and piety. He leaves a clean record; his life was a success."

Jerome, Rev. Edward Miles, son of Chauncey and Salome (Smith) Jerome, was born in Bristol, Conn., June 15, 1826; removed to New Haven in 1843; graduated from Yale College in 1850; converted when a Sophomore, and united with Third Congregational church in New Haven; studied in Yale Law-School and in Baltimore, Md.; received LL.B. in 1852, and was admitted to the bar; manager of his father's business in New York; became a Baptist; baptized by Rev. R. Turnbull, D.D., and united with First Baptist church in Hartford, Conn., in 1856; licensed by that church and studied theology; ordained, in 1859, as an evangelist in Holyoke, Mass.; supplied First Baptist church in New Haven, Conn.; in 1861 settled as pastor in Northampton, Mass.; in 1862 settled with church in West Meriden, Conn., and remained four years, till disabled by throat affection; preached in New Haven occasionally; in 1869 settled in Westfield, Mass., but health again failed; in 1871 established the *Naugatuck Valley Sentinel* in Ansonia, Conn.; aided in gathering there a Baptist church, of which he became pastor; served as Sunday-school missionary of the Baptist State Convention; in 1879 returned as associate editor of the *Sentinel* in Ansonia; in April of present year (1880) became proprietor and editor of *The Shore Line Times*, in New Haven; good preacher and ready writer.

Jesse, Rev. John Samuel, one of the most influential young pastors in the Sacramento River Association, is located at Biggs Station, Cal. He was born in Missouri, Nov. 4, 1852. His father, W. M. Jesse, of Virginia, and five relatives were ministers. He was immersed in 1870; received a good education at Mount Pleasant College and the schools in Missouri; entered the ministry by license in 1873; was ordained in October, 1874. His preaching for three years in Missouri was greatly blessed. In 1877 he went to California, preached for a time for the Sutter and Calaveras churches, and in 1878 became pastor at Biggs Station, and he is also giving pastoral aid to the Virginia and Wheatland churches. He is a fine writer and liberal contributor to the religious press.

Jessey, Rev. Henry, A.M., was born at West Routon, Yorkshire, England, Sept. 3, 1601. When he was seventeen years of age he entered St. John's College, Cambridge, in which he continued six years. In his twenty-first year, while still at the University of Cambridge, the Spirit of God gave him a new heart, and a blessed hope through the Saviour's blood.

After leaving Cambridge he became a chaplain in the family of Mr. Brampton Gordon, of Assington, Suffolk, for nine years, during which he advanced rapidly in such knowledge as would qualify him for his holy calling. In 1627 he received episcopal ordination, and in 1633 he was appointed rector of Aughton, Yorkshire. In 1637 he became pastor of a Congregational church in London, in

REV. HENRY JESSEY, A.M.

which his labors were greatly blessed. But his church was repeatedly invaded and robbed by Baptist principles. In 1638 "six persons of note" were carried off; in 1641 a greater number still; and in 1643 the departing members were more numerous than ever. Many of those who joined the Baptists were persons of superior intelligence and piety. Mr. Jessey was forced to examine the Scriptures about the mode of baptism, and the result of his investigations was that immersion was the inspired mode of baptism, and that sprinkling was a modern innovation. From that time forward for two or three years he always dipped children when he administered baptism. In 1645, after an anxious examination of the subjects of baptism, and after earnest appeals to heaven for divine light, he became decided in the conviction that only believers should be baptized, and in the June of that year he was immersed by Hanserd Knollys. He was pastor for many years of the church meeting in Swan Alley, Coleman Street, London. He was one of the Triers appointed by Cromwell to examine candidates for the ministry in the national church, and to investigate the character and claims of "ignorant and scandalous ministers" with a view to their expulsion from the pulpits of the state church. He was rector of St. George's church, Southwark, London, and pastor of a Baptist church in the same city. In the morning of the Lord's day he preached at St. George's church, and in the afternoon he was among his own people. He was a man of great learning; he had an extensive knowledge of Greek, Hebrew, Syriac, and Chaldee. It was the ambition and labor of his life to produce a new translation of the Scriptures, which was about completed when the restoration of Charles II. poured a deluge of evils over the Non-Conformists of that country, and made worthless the labors of Mr. Jessey in revising the Scriptures. He was a man of boundless charity; he even employed efforts to send money to the poor Jews of Jerusalem to preserve them from threatened slavery.

His labors were unremitting, and they were attended with great success. He was the author of eight published works, and with some help from Mr. Row, Professor of Hebrew in Aberdeen, he was the author of a revised and unpublished version of the Scriptures. His literary labors were highly appreciated and widely known. His character was marked by unselfishness and an intense love for the truth and its Divine Author.

By the cruel Act of Uniformity he was ejected from St. George's church, Southwark, and soon after, through his zeal for the Saviour, he was cast into prison, where he died Sept. 4, 1663, full of peace, humility, and hope.

At his funeral, three days after his death, several thousand pious persons of various denominations attended, whose manifest grief showed the great esteem in which Mr. Jessey was held.

Jeter, Jeremiah Bell, D.D., was born in Bedford Co., Va., July 18, 1802. He was baptized on the first Sunday in December, 1821, by the Rev. Wm. Harris, in the North Fork of the Otter River. His first public address was made on the banks of this stream, in coming out of it, on the occasion of his baptism. On the evening of the 15th of January of the same year he preached his first sermon to a small congregation of mountaineers in the gorge between the Flat Top and Luck Mountains, in Bedford County. He was present at the organization of the Baptist General Association of Virginia in 1823, was the first missionary appointed by that body, and the last survivor of the men who formed it. On the 4th of May, 1824, he was ordained to the work of the ministry at High Hills church, Sussex Co., by the Revs. N. Chambliss and J. D. Williams, for the former of whom he acted as assistant. Leaving Sussex in the spring of 1826, his first pastorate was with Hills Creek and Union Hill churches, Campbell Co. In the autumn of 1827 he removed to the Northern Neck of Virginia, where he was installed pastor of Moratico church in Lancaster Co., and subsequently of Wicomico church in Northumberland Co. His ministry was eminently successful in this field of labor, he having baptized over one thousand persons in about nine years.

In the latter part of 1835 he became pastor of the First Baptist church, Richmond, Va., and was

JEREMIAH BELL JETER, D.D.

for nearly fourteen years its faithful and successful leader, baptizing into its fellowship nearly 1000 converts, among whom were the Rev. Dr. Garlick, of Richmond, and the Rev. Dr. Henson, of Philadelphia. During his pastorate the First church built the house of worship which it now occupies, and organized its colored membership of 2000 into the First African church of Richmond, since so well known for its large congregations, its efficient church regulations, and its excellent singing. The latter church was put into possession of the old house of worship at the corner of Broad and College streets.

In October of 1849, Dr. Jeter was invited to the pastorate of the Second Baptist church, St. Louis. He remained here three years, baptized 150 persons, and was instrumental in organizing two other churches in that city. In September of 1852 he returned to Richmond, and became pastor of the Grace Street Baptist church, whose membership was nearly doubled during his ministry, having increased from 322 to 600. About the close of the war he became the senior editor of the *Religious Herald*, and continued until his death, Feb. 18, 1880, to furnish for its columns the mature gleanings of his long, rich, and varied experience.

As preacher and pastor, Dr. Jeter was remarkably successful. His form was commanding, his face intellectual, and his eye expressive, all which secured for him marked advantages as a speaker. The interest of his preaching consisted in the earnest simplicity with which he presented and enforced the great truths of the gospel. He constantly aimed to establish from the Word of God some great doctrine, or to enforce some practical duty in gospel ethics. As a pastor, he was kind, genial, and gentle, welcomed alike by old and young, rich and poor, learned and ignorant. In the large deliberative assemblies of the denomination, Dr. Jeter always occupied a prominent place. As a debater, he was ready, self-possessed, courteous, wisely conservative, added to which qualities were a force and ability that won universal attention.

Dr. Jeter was quite successful as an author. In 1837 he published the "Life of the Rev. A. W. Clopton"; in 1845, "A Memoir of Mrs. Schuck, Missionary to China"; in 1850, the "Life of the Rev. Andrew Broaddus"; in 1854, "Campbellism Examined," which work won for him a wide reputation as a skillful polemic, and subsequently "Campbellism Re-examined"; in 1858, "The Christian Mirror"; in 1871, "The Seal of Heaven" and "The Life of the Rev. Daniel Witt," besides numerous tracts, sermons, addresses, and other works of minor importance. His writings were all characterized by that clearness and vigor, as well as that chivalrous courtesy, which won the regard of the most persistent opponents, and gained for him as a writer so wide a reputation.

Dr. Jeter was equally successful as an editor. For fourteen years the *Religious Herald* has been the medium of conveying his sage counsels, evangelical opinions, and earnest Christian appeals in behalf of everything noble, just, and good into thousands of Christian families. He displayed an excellent judgment and discrimination in selecting topics at once of genuine importance and yet of general interest.

Dr. Jeter also preserved an abiding and growing interest in all the great denominational movements of the day. Missions, education, a more thoroughly equipped ministry, higher schools for young women, reformatory movements, with kindred plans for the well-being of men and women, and the conversion of the world, always received his most cordial support. A long life was devoted to the cause of Christ and the good of the world, and it was as spotless to its protracted close as the perfect azure of a sunset flecked by no single cloud. "No one who knew Dr. Jeter would hesitate to put him among the aristocracy of the world. As a preacher, a pastor, an editor, a citizen, a Christian, he lived up to the measure of developed faculties, and was an Israelite in whom there was no guile."

Jewell, William, M.D., was born near Alexandria, Va., Jan. 1, 1779; removed with his father to Kentucky in 1800; graduated from Transylvania University with the degree of M.D. In 1820 he came to Missouri, and settled permanently in Columbia. He united with the Bonne Femme Baptist church. He had a capacious and acquisitive mind, and a fixed purpose to excel in his profession. His library was large and choice, and his practice was extensive. He was familiar with learned medical authors of all lands. He took a deep interest in his patients, and when his medical skill failed, he pointed them to the heavenly physician. He attained great eminence as a medical practitioner, citizen, and Christian. His gifts of more than $17,000 to the Baptist college at Liberty gave it the name of William Jewell. He superintended the erection of the college buildings, and at his death bequeathed his library and $3000 to the institution. He gave nearly half his property to benevolent objects. He died in Liberty, Clay Co., Aug. 7, 1852. He gave $1800 to the State University, at Columbia. He often represented Boone County in the State Legislature. He was a zealous student of the Bible. His religion was manifest at home, and in his professional experience, as well as in public worship. His death was deeply mourned, and deserved eulogies were pronounced over his Christian life.

Jewett, Lyman, D.D., was born in Waterford, Me., March 9, 1813. He was a graduate of Brown University and of the Newton Theological Institution. He served for some time as a supply of the Baptist church in Webster, Mass. His appointment as a missionary to the foreign field was made in 1847, and he was ordained to the work of the ministry in Boston, Oct. 6, 1848. Sailing a few days after for the East, he reached Nellore, April 16, 1849. For somewhat more than three years the mission had been without American helpers. Mr. Jewett found, at first, many things that were discouraging, but he addressed himself to his work with zeal, preaching his first regular Teloogoo sermon in the chapel Dec. 3, 1849. As he became more familiar with the language his ability to be useful increased, and his contact with the heathen was closer. Weeks and months passed in the usual routine of missionary labor. We learn from the report of 1852 that there was preaching in the chapel twice every Sabbath, the attendance varying from 40 to 150 persons. Considerable audiences were collected to listen to street preaching. Visitors calling at the mission house for instruction often received spiritual benefit. Excursions were made by Mr. Jewett to the neighboring villages and hamlets, and sometimes great crowds thronged to hear the Word, and receive Bibles and religious tracts. But while Mr. Jewett and his co-laborers were encouraged by these signs of outward success, and felt that could the mission be well reinforced and evangelical agencies plied with zeal, the best results would be secured, it was evident that many of the friends of missions at home were beginning to think that the Teloogoo Mission was not a successful one. The whole matter was submitted to the Missionary Union in 1853, and it was decided to continue to carry on the mission. The departure of Mr. Day from Nellore early in 1853 left Mr. Jewett the only American male missionary on the field. With what courage and hope he prosecuted his work appears from his own words, written Nov. 5, 1854: "The last month has been one of constant labor in preaching the gospel. I am earnestly looking for fruit. I feel in my soul that our labors will not be in vain." Again he writes with almost prophetic vision of the glorious ingathering of the harvests of souls which has been lately witnessed: "For the last few months I have felt more than ever not only the importance of the mission, but the certainty of accomplishing, in the Lord's good time, a great and glorious work for this people." Before this vision became a reality the faith of Mr. Jewett was often and most severely tried. Rev. F. A. Douglass joined Mr. Jewett, April 14, 1855, and the mission, thus reinforced, continued to enjoy a good degree of prosperity. In 1859 an increased interest in religion was reported. Mr. Jewett visited Ongole to see for himself what prospect of success there was in that place. In March, 1861, such was the state of his health that it was thought best that he should return to the United States and obtain needed rest and recuperation. He remained here until November, 1864, when he sailed the second time, and arrived at Nellore, April 22, 1865. He at once resumed his labors. Mr. Timpany became associated with him in missionary work in April, 1868. A part of the time of Dr. Jewett was occupied in the work of translating the Bible into the Teloogoo language. In 1875 he was again in his native country for the restoration of his wasted strength. He has returned to the scene of his labors, where he is now actively engaged in the service of him whose cause lies so near his heart.

Jewett, Prof. Milo P., LL.D., was born in Johnsbury, Vt., April 27, 1808. His father, Calvin Jewett, was an eminent physician of Johnsbury, and his mother was a highly cultivated lady. Milo was prepared for college at the Bradford Academy, Vt., and graduated from Dartmouth College in the class of 1828. Upon his graduation he became principal of Holmes Academy at Plymouth, N. H. Having the law in view as a profession, he spent a part of that year and of the following year in the office of Hon. Josiah Quincy, of Rumney, N. H. Abandoning the law in 1830, he entered the theological seminary at Andover, completing the course of study. Mr. Jewett, upon the invitation of Josiah Holbrook, of Boston, founder of the American lyceum system, spent his vacations during his theological course in lecturing in New Hampshire, Massachusetts, and Connecticut on "Common Schools." He had had much success in teaching, and his soul was full of his subject,—a higher grade of common-school education for the masses. His addresses on this subject are believed to have been the first of a popular character delivered in the country. They created extensive interest in the subject among our best educators. Through J. Orville Taylor, a fellow-student of Mr. Jewett, who became interested in the matter, a movement was started in New York City, which resulted in the establishment of the present common-school system of the Empire State.

Having decided that teaching and not preaching was the work for which God had fitted him, and in which he had already given him marked success, Mr. Jewett devoted himself to that profession, and in 1834 accepted a professorship in Marietta College, Marietta, O., just then founded. Before entering upon the active duties of his chair he spent some time among the Congregational churches of New England in soliciting funds for the college. He based his plea on " the perils which threaten our civil and religious liberties from the progress of Roman Catholicism in the Mississippi Valley." His addresses awakened a deep interest, and made the raising of funds an easy task. In 1836, Mr. Jewett was associated with Prof. Calvin E. Stowe and William E. Lewis by the State Educational Convention of Ohio to urge upon the Legislature the establishment of a new common-school system. He not only accomplished his object, but much more. Prof. Calvin Stowe went to Europe, under the direction of the State, to investigate the best school systems there, and Wm. E. Lewis became the first State superintendent of public schools in Ohio. But this was not all. His report on the subject created the deepest interest over the country, and resulted in the special educational mission and work of Horace Mann in New England.

In January, 1839, having changed his views on baptism, and united with the Baptist Church, Prof. Jewett resigned his professorship in Marietta College, and, going South, he established the Judson Female Institute in Marion, Ala. It soon became the most flourishing educational institution for ladies in the South. In connection with this school he established the *Alabama Baptist*, which became the Baptist organ of the State. In the autumn of 1855 he returned North, and purchased the Cottage Hill Seminary at Poughkeepsie, N. Y. Here he first met with Mr. Matthew Vassar. Their acquaintance ripened into friendship. Prof. Jewett found that Mr. Vassar proposed to leave his large fortune for benevolent purposes. He suggested to him the founding of a thoroughly furnished and endowed college for young women during his own life. It met with Mr. Vassar's approval. He changed his will, in which he had left his property for another object, and turned his attention to this new purpose. Thus originated Vassar College. It was incorporated in 1861. Prof. Jewett was the adviser of Mr. Vassar in everything relating to the establishment of the college, and was its first president. In 1862, at the request of the trustees, he visited Europe to inspect the universities, libraries, art-galleries, etc., in Great Britain and on the Continent to obtain information about the best educational systems in the old world, that Vassar might have the benefit of his observations and experience.

In 1864, having almost entirely lost the sight of his eyes, he resigned the presidency of the college, to the great regret of Mr. Vassar and the board, and in 1867 he removed to his present home in Milwaukee. Prof. Jewett devotes himself to the interests of education, philanthropy, and religion. He is held in high esteem in the First Baptist church, of which he is a member. He is the president of Milwaukee Female College, though not required to teach, chairman of the board of visitors of the University of Wisconsin, president of Milwaukee board of health, president of the Wisconsin State Temperance Society, president of the Milwaukee County Bible Society, and chairman of the State Baptist Educational Commission.

Prof. Jewett is a man of extensive literary attainments, and in addition to occasional articles in newspapers and magazines, has written several publications of marked character. In 1840 he published " Jewett on Baptism"; in 1863, " Report of the President's Visit to Europe" and " Report on the Organization of Vassar College"; in 1874, " Relation of Boards of Health to Intemperance"; in 1875, " A Plea for Academies"; and the same year, " The Model Academy."

Prof. Jewett, although never engaged in the active work of the ministry, received ordination at the hands of a council called by the Siloam Baptist church of Marion, Ala., in 1839. He received the degree of LL.D. from Rochester University in 1861.

He takes a very deep interest in everything pertaining to the growth of the Baptist denomination, especially in the State of Wisconsin. His efforts for the more thorough establishment of Wayland Academy have been of the highest value. He is an active member of its board, and contributes most generously both time and means to its increased usefulness.

Johnson, Rev. Cæsar.—A useful man among the colored Baptists of North Carolina is Cæsar Johnson, who was born in Warren Co., N. C., in 1833, and until the war was a slave of Mr. John

V. Canthorn. He was baptized by Rev. N. A. Purefoy in 1862; attended Shaw University in Raleigh for nine years; served as missionary of the Home Mission Board, New York, for eight years, and is now employed as colporteur by the American and Foreign Bible Society. Mr. Johnson has been moderator of the Convention of colored Baptists for four years, and is much interested in collecting historical and statistical data concerning his people.

Johnson, Col. Daniel D., a younger brother of Okey, was born in Tyler Co., Va., April 28, 1836. He was partly educated at Marietta College, and graduated a Bachelor of Philosophy from Columbian College, Washington, D. C., in 1860. He enjoyed the warm friendship, which yet continues, of Dr. Samson, then president of the college. In 1861, when the civil war broke out, as a firm friend of the Union he helped to raise the 14th Va. Regiment, of which he was elected major. He was soon promoted to the colonelcy, which post he filled until the close of the war. He participated in a number of hard-fought battles, among them Cloyd Mountain, Carter's Farm, Opequan, and Winchester. At the battle of Opequan he was severely wounded, and was granted leave of absence. At the battle of Winchester, on the 24th July, 1864, he commanded a brigade. When the Union forces were defeated and compelled to fall back, he covered the retreat in a masterly manner, for which the credit was unjustly given to another. Although a colonel, he commanded a brigade frequently. In 1865, after the close of the war, he received an honorable discharge, and at once set about the work of reconciliation with those against whom he had fought. He was an enemy in war, but in peace a friend. He received them cordially when they returned, and treated them as his equals in the government, being actuated by the same Christian spirit which had ruled his boyhood and manhood. He went to the Legislature in 1865, and served for several terms in the lower house. He was elected a member of the constitutional convention of 1872, where he distinguished himself as much perhaps as any member of that body, being an earnest, eloquent, and lucid speaker, and being by far the best parliamentarian in the State. In 1872 he was elected a member of the State senate, which position he yet holds, and for the whole time, except for two years, he has been president of the senate. He is one of the most active men in the State in the cause of education, and is now president of the board of regents of the West Virginia University. He is a thorough Baptist, and has been one for over twenty years. He has a number of times been moderator of his Association, and also president of the West Virginia Baptist Convention, and he is superintendent now of a Sabbath-school. In all these various relations he has shown himself a Christian gentleman.

Johnson, George J., D.D., was born in Vernon, N. Y., Oct. 9, 1824; was baptized before he was fifteen; studied at Madison University and Hamilton Theological Seminary, graduating from the latter institution in 1848; was soon after ordained at Trenton Falls, N. Y., and settled as missionary pastor in Burlington, Iowa. Here he organized a church of 12 members, which numbered 318 at the close of his pastorate in 1858. Among the converts was Rev. John E. Clough, present missionary to the Teloogoos at Ongole, Burmah. He also performed arduous and efficient labors in connection with the Burlington Collegiate Institute. He subsequently organized a church at Fort Madison, Iowa, and remained pastor five years. Returned to Burlington as district secretary of the American Baptist Publication Society for the Northwest, and afterwards became district secretary for the Southwest, with headquarters at St. Louis, Mo. In 1876-77 he engaged in celebrating the semicentennial of Shurtleff College at Upper Alton, Ill., by raising an additional endowment fund of $100,000. In this enterprise his incessant and self-sacrificing labors were crowned with magnificent success. In 1878 he was appointed missionary secretary of the American Baptist Publication Society, with headquarters at Philadelphia. This position he still holds, and the society is prospered by the large results of his faithful and unceasing toil. He received the degree of D.D. from Madison University in 1871.

Dr. Johnson has given the best years of his life to pioneer missionary work, and few men have accomplished such wide-reaching and abiding results. With varied and consecrated talents, and robust physical powers, and with an energy born of intense love for the truth, and an invincible determination to succeed, he has broken the soil and planted the seeds of the kingdom far and wide. The blessed and increasing fruitage of his past toil is a perpetual inspiration to his present unwearied and useful endeavors.

Johnson, Rev. Hezekiah, son of Rev. Eleazar Johnson and Martha Rounds, was born March 6, 1799, in Maryland; converted and ordained in Highland Co., O., in 1824. He was pastor at Frankfort and Greenfield, O., and labored in Iowa under the Baptist Home Mission Society from 1839 to 1844, and organized some of the first churches and Associations in that State. In 1845 he went, with Rev. E. Fisher, as missionary of the Home Mission Society, to Oregon, and settled at Oregon City, where he formed a church. This was his home until his death, in August, 1866. He traveled, preached, helped to organize churches and Associations, and lay the foundations of religious and educational institutions in the new State. He wrote and published many sermons and pamphlets in furtherance of the cause of religion and reform, completing the last on his death-bed. He was one of the strong Baptist leaders in the early days of Oregon. His faithful wife accompanied and upheld him in all his labors. They are buried near Oregon City. Over their graves a memorial stone bears this inscription,—" Pioneer Baptist Missionaries."

Johnson, Hon. James, a son of Col. Robert Johnson, and a brother of Col. R. M. Johnson, was born in Orange Co., Va., from which he removed with his parents to Kentucky. He united with Great Crossing Baptist church about 1801, of which he remained a faithful member until his death. He was a lieutenant-colonel in the war of 1812–15, and distinguished himself in the battle of the Thames. In 1808 he was elected to the State senate from Scott County. He was Presidential elector in 1821, and was elected to a seat in the U. S. Congress in 1825. He died at Washington while a member of Congress, in December, 1826.

Johnson, John L., LL.D., Professor of English Literature in the University of Mississippi, was born in Virginia in 1835. After receiving a liberal education at the University of Virginia, he was ordained in 1860. During the war he served as chaplain of the 17th Va. Infantry, and subsequently as pastor of the colored Baptist church at Lynchburg. After the war he was two years pastor at Portsmouth, Va., and about as long at Free Mason Street, Norfolk. He then retired to the country, engaging in literary pursuits, supplying some churches, and teaching in the Albemarle Female Institute. For some months he supplied Dr. Fuller's church in Baltimore. He also taught for a time in Roanoke Female College. He accepted his present position in 1873. While discharging the duties of his professorship he has also engaged in preaching at Oxford, Miss., and in the surrounding country. Dr. Johnson is the author of "The University Memorial" and a number of published sermons.

Johnson, Gov. Joseph, was born Dec. 19, 1785, in Orange Co., N. Y. His father having died when he was but five years old, his widowed mother soon after removed to Sussex Co., N. J., and from it, in 1801, to Harrison Co., Va. Here, at the age of fifteen, he was employed on the large farm of a Mr. Smith, whose chief manager he soon became, and at the age of twenty-one he married one of that gentleman's daughters. Four years after his marriage he purchased the estate on which he had been living, and continued to occupy the same until his death, a period of more than seventy years. Early in life Mr. Johnson became one of the most popular and influential men in the county. During the war of 1812 with Great Britain he organized a rifle company, was made its captain, marched to Norfolk, and continued in service until peace was secured, in 1815. His talents, decision of character,

GOV. JOSEPH JOHNSON.

and strict integrity forced him at this time into political life, and on his return from military service he was elected a member of the State Legislature, defeating his opponent, the distinguished Mr. Prunty, who had been in the Legislature during twenty-five consecutive years. Having served for four years in this body with great usefulness, he declined a re-election, and returned to the farm-life which he loved so well. In 1823 he was elected to Congress after one of the most exciting and thoroughly contested canvassings that Harrison County had ever witnessed, defeating his able and distinguished opponent, Mr. P. Doddridge. He was re-elected to Congress in 1825, returned to his home in 1827, and in 1832 was elected to fill the vacancy caused by the death of Mr. Doddridge. He was also elected to Congress in 1835, serving six years, and in 1845, serving two years. He had thus been elected to Congress seven times, and during his whole career in that body maintained the reputation of being one of the most punctual and laborious members of the body. In consequence of the urgent solicitations of his friends he served in the State Legislature during the session of 1847; was a member, in 1850, of the State convention which remodeled the constitution, and while a member of that body was elected governor of the State under the conditions of the old constitution, entering on his official duties in December, 1851. In the fall of 1851 he was elected governor by the popular vote for the term of four years. He was the first and only man ever elected governor of Virginia from that part of the State now comprised in West Virginia. As governor he took an active part in originating or carrying out greatly needed internal improvements, which, unfortunately, were sadly retarded by the breaking out of the war. At the close of 1855 he retired to his country home, having served his generation most faithfully in the State and national halls for more than forty years. Gov. Johnson followed Virginia during her terrible war experiences, and threw all the weight of his great influence and experience into the cause of the Confederacy. At the termination of that fearful contest, with the burdens of eighty years upon him, he withdrew, as much as such a man could, from public life. For more than ten years he enjoyed the coveted quiet of a lovely home, the attentions of kindred and loved ones, and the warm regards of troops of friends. He died Feb. 27, 1877, in the ninety-second year of his age, in the home which he had entered more than seventy years before, in the assured hope of a blissful immortality.

In private life, Gov. Johnson was modest, affable, genial, and kindly considerate of the interests of all. In appearance he was below the medium height, of a dark complexion, with a bright black eye that flashed as if on fire when in debate. During the last few years of his life his thoughts were almost constantly occupied with Biblical themes. He was punctual in the performance of religious duties, and would let nothing interfere with them. The last two years of his life were spent in superintending and liberally contributing to the rebuilding and furnishing of the Baptist meeting-house near his residence, where he was a member, and where his mother and wife had worshiped, frequently testifying himself in the meetings to the comfort, truth, and power of the gospel of Christ. As a man, he was beyond reproach, as a statesman, he was one of the strictest of the "Jacksonian" school, and as a follower of Christ, he adorned the doctrine of the Saviour by a "well-ordered life."

Johnson, Rev. J. E., was a native of Tolland, Conn., where he was born, Oct. 27, 1827. His early youth was spent in Willington, Conn., to which place his parents removed soon after his birth. He was baptized and united with the Baptist church in that place when but a mere lad. He was educated at Suffield Institute, Conn., and at Brown University, R. I., from which he graduated with honor in the class of 1853. He spent one year at Newton Theological Seminary. He was ordained by the Baptist church in Jackson, Mich., in 1855, and remained its pastor seven years. He was subsequently pastor of the Baptist church in Madison, Wis., four years, of the Baptist church in Delavan two and a half years, of the Grand Avenue Baptist church, Milwaukee, one year, and of the Baptist church at Beaver Dam three years, where he died Oct. 20, 1872. His ministry of seventeen years was highly successful. He was an excellent preacher, of clear, analytical mind, and of most earnest spirit. But he was pre-eminent in his simple, unostentatious piety, and devotion to the work of the ministry, to which he had consecrated his life.

Johnson, Rev. N. B., a distinguished missionary in the mountains of Kentucky, was born in Fayette County of that State, March 28, 1820. In early life he joined the Campbellites, but in 1842 he experienced a change of heart, was baptized, and united with the Baptist church at Georgetown. He was ordained to the ministry in 1862, and was pastor of several country churches along the border of the mountains. In 1866 he entered the mountain field as a missionary. During the thirteen years that followed he traveled, on horseback and on foot, 13,000 miles, preached 2800 times, besides delivering numerous addresses, visited a large number of families, organized 60 Sabbath-schools, baptized 1200 persons, and, with the assistance of proper helps, constituted 24 churches. He is, in 1880, pastor of four churches.

Johnson, Judge Okey, was born in Tyler Co., Va., March 24, 1834. His parents were both immersed into the fellowship of the Baptist Church over fifty years ago, by Rev. Jeremiah Dale, whose biography appears in "The Lives of the Virginia Baptist Ministers." Okey united with the Long Reach Baptist church on the 7th of July, 1849. He graduated at the Marietta High School in 1856. The same year he entered the law-school of Harvard University, where for two years he had the benefit of the lectures of those distinguished men Profs. Parsons, Washburne, and Parker, and graduated with the degree of LL.B. in July, 1858. He engaged in agriculture for nearly two years, and made two successful trading expeditions to Memphis and New Orleans, on flat-boats, in the fall and winter of 1859 and 1860, and left New Orleans on the 21st day of March, 1861. In May, 1862, he located in Parkersburg, Va., and commenced the practice of law in good earnest. On the 4th of July, 1862, at Parkersburg, while the United States troops were thundering at the gates of Richmond, he made an oration in favor of his candidate for the Presidency to a great multitude; and his effort was so full of lofty patriotism that it called forth the loudest plaudits, and on request of the vast throng it was published. Although a Union man, he was a decided Democrat, and very conservative on all questions involving the conduct of the war, and when that unhappy strife ended he was for general amnesty and peace, and did much in the State of West Virginia, which was the "Child of the storm," to arrest and repeal the legislation against the returned Confederate soldiers. In 1870 he was

JUDGE OKEY JOHNSON.

elected a member of the West Virginia senate. He was elected to the constitutional convention called by the Legislature of 1870, largely through his influence, by a triumphant majority. He was a very active and distinguished member of this convention, and when the new constitution was submitted to the people he was an eloquent advocate for its ratification, and it was adopted by a handsome majority.

In 1874 Marietta College conferred upon him the honorary degree of Master of Arts. From 1860 to 1870 he was annually elected moderator of the Parkersburg Association. And he was repeatedly elected president of the West Virginia Baptist Convention. Notwithstanding his political relations, he uniformly enjoyed the highest esteem of his brethren. His law practice was large and successful, rarely ever losing a case in the Supreme Court of Appeals. In 1876 he was nominated for the office of judge of the Supreme Court of Appeals, and elected for twelve years to that office, by a majority of 17,000 votes. He now holds that position, and fills it with fidelity and ability, and to the entire satisfaction of the people of West Virginia, by whom he is regarded as one of the purest men in the United States.

Johnson, Col. Richard Mentor, son of Robert Johnson, was born at Bryant's Station, Fayette Co., Ky., Oct. 17, 1780. He studied law after finishing his literary education at Transylvania, and was admitted to the bar at the age of nineteen. He was elected to the Kentucky Legislature in his twenty-first year, and was a member of the U. S. Congress, 1807-19. He accepted a colonel's commission, and was in active service in the war of 1812-15. In the battle of the Thames, Oct. 5, 1813, he rendered brilliant service, and was desperately wounded. He was, however, able to resume his seat in the House in February following. After serving several terms in the lower house of Congress, he was elected to the U. S. Senate in 1819, and remained a member of that body until 1829. After this he was again a member of the House in 1829-37. In 1837 he was elected Vice-President of the United States by the Senate, the choice having devolved upon them under the Constitution. In March, 1841, he retired to his farm in Scott County, where he spent the remainder of his life, except during two terms through which he served in the Kentucky Legislature. He died at Frankfort, Nov. 19, 1850, while a member of the Legislature. Col. Johnson appears to have been a member of Great Crossing church as early as 1801.

Johnson, Col. Robert, the head of one of the most distinguished families in Kentucky, was a native of Virginia. He removed to Kentucky during the Revolution and settled at Bryant's Station, but shortly afterwards he settled near the present site of Georgetown, in Scott County, where he was the principal instrument in organizing Great Crossing Baptist church, of which he was a member. He was prominent in the councils of the Baptists in the early settlement of the country, conspicuous as a leader in the Indian wars of the period, and a member of most of the councils of state. He was a member of the convention which formed the first constitution of Kentucky in 1792, and of that which formed the second constitution, in 1799. He was eight times elected to the Kentucky Legislature. Three of his sons were members of Congress from Kentucky, and several of his descendants have been members of Congress from other States. He died at a ripe old age at his residence in Scott Co., Ky.

Johnson, Rev. Thomas, was born in Georgia. He visited Missouri in 1799, and preached near Cape Girardeau ; one person at his first service made a profession of faith and was baptized, a Mrs. Blair. This is said to have been the first believer immersed west of the Mississippi River, in Missouri. The baptism was administered in Randal's Creek, where, in 1797, a number of Baptists settled near the village of Jackson. Here they built the first Baptist house of worship in Missouri. It was of logs, and was erected in 1806. Around this old church are graves with rough tombstones, which mark the resting-place of the first Baptists, and the first Protestants in Missouri.

Johnson, Rev. Thomas C., one of the best qualified and most successful ministers in the State, was born at Long Reach, Tyler Co., W. Va., Sept. 18, 1848. He is next to the youngest of nineteen children of Wm. Johnson, of Mineral County. In 1867 he entered college; was baptized the following April by Rev. J. D. Griebel, and graduated in 1872. He preached his first sermon in October, 1871, and was licensed to preach by the Long Reach church in the summer of 1872. He entered Crozer Theological Seminary in the fall of 1872, and graduated in 1875. He then took charge of the Willow Island church, in West Virginia, and the Valley church, in Ohio. He was ordained at Willow Island in 1875.

In December, 1877, he became pastor of the Baptist church in Charleston, W. Va., at which place he is now located. The church was in a low and scattered condition and deeply in debt, but he has, in less than three years, been instrumental in greatly promoting its efficiency and in enlarging its membership.

Johnson, Rev. Thomas Thornton, was born July 20, 1803, in Fauquier Co., Va. He was converted at the age of thirteen years, and baptized by Elder James Lugget, of Kentucky. He removed to Missouri in 1828. He contended for missionary principles against bitter opposition. Helped to form a missionary society in 1838, and labored much as a pastor, and was at home in protracted meetings. He was remarkably effective in exhortations. He aided in the formation of many churches in Ralls, Pike, Lincoln, and Montgomery Counties. He died at Truxton, Mo., Feb. 25, 1877.

Johnson, Rev. William, is a very remarkable man in some respects. He was born in Barnwell District, S. C., Jan. 9, 1803, and is related doubtless to Col. Richard M. Johnson, who killed Tecumseh in Kentucky. His father died before he was born, and his mother died when he was seventeen years old, at which time he was "bound" to a man in Augusta, Ga.

Here he remained till nearly twenty-one years of age, when he disagreed with his master for the first time, and leaving him, returned to South Carolina, and went to school a few months. He often quotes,—

"No mother to nurse and to guide,
No father to protect and provide,
No fortune to shield from hunger and cold,
A poor little orphan, cast on the world,"

as being almost literally true in his case.

Elder Johnson was converted and baptized about 1829, his baptism occurring at a branch of Darien church, and was performed by Prescott Bush, a Revolutionary soldier. He was ordained, while a member of Philippi church, by W. B. Johnson, D.D., Peter Galloway, John Landrum, and Joseph Morris. He was a constituent member in the organization of the Edisto Association, and was its moderator several times. He removed to Florida in 1854, and joined Pleasant Grove church, in Alachua County, and at different times has served that church, and Wacahoota, Eliam, and Ockwilla, in the same county; Paran, in Putnam County, and Providence, in Bradford County, besides aiding in building up some new churches. He aided in the formation of the Alachua Association, and has been perhaps its only moderator, and was for a few sessions moderator of Santa Fé River Association.

Mr. Johnson is strong in body and mind. His ancestors were Irish, and from them he inherited a robust constitution and a fondness for humor. In his preaching his favorite themes are divine sovereignty, election, grace, etc. He is a decided Baptist, and contends earnestly for the faith. He had a struggle before consenting to enter the ministry, and would never after take any civil office.

Mr. Johnson has been a tower of strength in Florida, and is yet popular and exerting a good influence, but he is not able to preach much.

Johnson, W. B., D.D., was one of the most active and useful ministers that ever labored in South Carolina. "Soon after 1820" he was a member of the Saluda Association, and presided over its deliberations for a number of years. Subsequently he was the acting pastor at Edgefield Court-House, and a member of the Association bearing the name of his church, and of this Association he was chosen moderator.

The State Convention founded in 1821 had a very warm friend in Dr. Johnson. He was one of a committee of three who drafted its constitution. In 1822 he preached the introductory sermon, and prepared the address of the Convention to the churches, which was printed in the minutes of that year, a document of great ability, and penetrated by a thoroughly missionary and evangelical spirit. In 1823 he was elected vice-president of the Convention. In 1824 he preached the annual charity sermon, and in 1825 he was chosen president on the death of the honored Dr. Richard Furman, whose name is justly venerated in South Carolina, and by hosts of Baptists all over our country. Dr. Johnson held this position for a great many years, an office the duties of which were discharged not only by Dr. Richard Furman, but by Dr. Basil Manly, Chief-Justice O'Neall, and other distinguished men. The reputation of Dr. Johnson spread over our whole country, and for three years he was president of our great national missionary society, "The Triennial Convention of the United States," and after the division in that body he was chosen the first president of the Southern Baptist

Convention. In no section of our country was any Baptist minister more highly honored by his brethren.

He was a solid and impressive preacher, deeply

W. B. JOHNSON, D.D.

versed in the sacred writings, and full of his Master's spirit. He was very hospitable, and his life was blameless. To the Saviour he rendered noble service, which was fruitful in an unusual measure.

Under Dr. Wayland's presidency Brown University gave him the degree of Doctor of Divinity. He died at Greenville, S. C., in 1862, when he was about eighty years of age.

The State Convention, in 1863, appointed its president, Dr. J. C. Furman, to preach a sermon "in honor of the memory of their venerable brother, the late Rev. W. B. Johnson, D.D.," and after the delivery of the discourse the Convention requested a copy for publication, and a committee was also appointed "to raise funds to erect a monument over his remains."

Johnson, Hon. William Carey, son of Rev. Hezekiah Johnson, was born in Ohio, Oct. 27, 1833. In 1845 he removed to Oregon with his parents, and has since then lived at Oregon City. He received a good academic education; was converted in 1854, and baptized by Rev. E. Fisher. He entered and attained a high position in the legal profession, and in 1866 became State senator. In 1868 he was married to Miss Josephine De Vore, the first woman to win the degree of A.B. on the Pacific coast, graduating with honor from the full course of Willamette University, at Salem, Oregon, in 1868. Mr. Johnson has continued one of the most active laymen in the work of the Baptists in his State, clerk of the Willamette Association, and for many years its moderator. In his church at Oregon City he has a leading influence, and in its Sunday-school is a devoted Bible-class teacher and superintendent.

Johnston, Judge James William, was born in 1791; studied law in Annapolis, Nova Scotia, and became distinguished in his profession; was converted and baptized in Halifax, Nova Scotia; strongly supported the educational movement which commenced among the Baptists of Nova Scotia in 1828, which resulted in the establishment of Horton Academy in 1829, and Acadia College in January, 1839; represented Annapolis County in the Provincial Parliament for twenty years; was leader of the government and attorney-general for several years; became, in 1865, judge of the Supreme Court, Nova Scotia, and judge in equity. James W. Johnston possessed a gigantic mind, unsullied integrity, indomitable energy, commanding eloquence, and Christian humility. On the death of Gov. Howe, Judge Johnston was appointed to succeed him as governor of Nova Scotia, but death interposed his veto Nov. 21, 1873.

Johnston, Judge James W., a son of Judge James W. Johnston, graduated from Acadia College in 1843; studied law with his father, and practised his profession in Halifax for many years; was appointed judge of the Halifax County Court in 1877, and performs his duties with ability. Judge Johnston is a member of the Dartmouth Baptist church.

Johnston, Col. John W., was born at Paltonsburg, Botetourt Co., Va., July 6, 1839. Having received his early intellectual training in the neighboring schools, he entered upon and finished his studies in law in Lexington, Va., and afterwards prosecuted his profession with great success. At the beginning of the war he entered the Confederate service, first as second lieutenant of riflemen of the 48th Regiment Va. Militia, and a few weeks after became second lieutenant of the 28th Va. Infantry, Provisional army of the C. S. A. Near the close of 1861 he became first lieutenant of Anderson's Battery, Light Artillery, and in the early part of 1863, captain of the Botetourt Artillery. During this year he served also as captain and inspector-general of artillery on Maj.-Gen. C. L. Stevenson's staff. During 1864 he held the position of major of artillery in the P. A. C. S., and until April, 1865, was in command of a battalion of light artillery, in all these positions he displayed the highest ability. During the sessions of 1875–77 Col. Johnston was a member of the house of delegates of Virginia from Botetourt County, and served with marked efficiency. April 24, 1877, he was elected president of the James River and Kanawha Company, and also president of the Buchanan and Clifton Forge Railway Company. Col. Johnston is a member of the Buchanan Baptist church, and actively engaged in all movements designed for the advancement and strengthening of the denomination.

Johnston, Rev. Jonas, was born in Beaufort Co., S. C., March 11, 1821; received a sound academic education; was converted and baptized in August, 1846. After ordination ministered to the following churches: Lawtonville, S. C.; Anderson, Bedias, Danville, Waverly, Bethel, Montgomery, Huntsville, Ebenezer, Planterville, and Navisota, Texas. He has been prospered in his worldly business beyond most ministers of the gospel, but at the same time he has been a laborious and very successful preacher, exerting extended influence and commanding general esteem. He is now the business manager of the Texas *Baptist Herald*, and is efficiently promoting the great educational and missionary operations of Texas. He is a sound theologian and an able counselor.

Jones, Rev. C. B.—For nearly twenty years the Baptist denomination in Florida had the valuable labors, influence, and advice of Rev. Charles B. Jones, who was born on Wilmington Island, near Savannah, Ga., in the year 1798, and died at Palatka, Fla., March 5, 1879. "In early life he was of a generous and jovial disposition, having plenty of money, and withal possessing a commanding personal appearance, he was not only a favorite, but an acknowledged leader among his associates."

He was deeply convicted by the killing of an uncle in a duel, he being present at the scene. He was soon after converted, and he united with the First Baptist church in Savannah. In a short time he began to preach, and was popular. He frequently filled the pulpit of the First Baptist church of Savannah during the annual vacations of the pastor, and at one time was its pastor. He was greatly beloved by all the churches he served.

"Few men could present the doctrines of the gospel with greater power. His favorite theme was the love of Christ, and when speaking upon this his countenance would become radiant, and he would seem to be almost inspired."

Upon going to Florida he settled in Marion County, and was for a time pastor of the church at Ocala. Soon after the close of the late war he moved to Palatka, where he labored as a missionary of the Northern Home Mission Society, preaching in Palatka and the surrounding country. Mr. Jones was a man of general intelligence and a ready use of language. He was tall, with a fine head, and a countenance that was a true index of his generous heart and noble impulses.

Perhaps his crowning gift was his power of conversation, in which he was ready, easy, and expressed himself in language well chosen, beautiful, and chaste. He was always welcome in every circle, and exerted a powerful social influence.

Jones, Rev. David, A.M., chaplain in the Continental army, was born in White Clay Creek Hundred, Newcastle Co., Del., May 12, 1736. His parents were Morgan and Eleanor (Evans) Jones, and his grandparents were David and Esther (Morgan) Jones. Esther Jones was a sister of Enoch and Abel Morgan, well known Baptist ministers, who were children of Morgan ap Rhyddarch, a famous Baptist minister, who resided in Llanwenog, South Wales. Mr. Jones was baptized May 6, 1758, joined the Welsh Tract Baptist church, and was one of the pupils of Isaac Eaton, at Hopewell Academy, N. J., but studied divinity with his cousin, Abel Morgan, at Middletown, N. J. He was ordained Dec. 12, 1766, as pastor of the Freehold Baptist church, Monmouth Co., N. J. While there he was impressed with a desire to preach the gospel to the Indians, and was the first Baptist missionary among that people.

REV. DAVID JONES, A.M.

No doubt the example of David Brainard influenced his heart, and the wretched condition of the poor red men for this and for the future life prompted his course. They then occupied what is now the State of Ohio, and he made them two visits. His first began May 4, 1772, and ended in August; his second began Oct. 26, 1772, and ended in April, 1773. He kept a journal of his missionary labors, which was published in 1773, and was reprinted in New York by J. Sabin, in 1865. Mr. Jones continued his pastorate at the village of Freehold until his outspoken views in favor of the rights of Americans rendered him unpopular, and in April, 1775, he became pastor of the Great Valley church, Chester Co., Pa. In that year the Continental Congress recommended a day of fasting and prayer, and he preached a sermon before Col. Dewees's regiment, entitled "Defensive War in a Just Cause Sinless," which was printed and extensively circulated. He took high ground even at that early day in favor of independence. In 1776 he was appointed a chaplain in Col. St. Clair's regiment, and was at Ticonderoga, where, just before battle, he delivered a patriotic address, which roused the courage of the soldiers to a high degree. Subsequently he served under Gen. Horatio Gates and Gen. Wayne, and was in many battles, and always proved himself to be a wise counselor and a devoted patriot. He was at the Paoli massacre, and narrowly escaped death. While the army was at Valley Forge he frequently showed his devotion to the cause, and was highly trusted by Washington. When news arrived that France had recognized our independence, he preached an appropriate sermon to the troops at the Forge. He continued in the army until the capitulation at Yorktown, and then retired to his farm in East Town, Chester Co., adjoining the farm of his old commander, Gen. Wayne. In 1786 he became pastor of the Southampton church, Bucks Co., where he remained until 1792, when he returned to the Valley church, with which he remained, part of the time as senior pastor, until his death. When Gen. Wayne was appointed to the command of the army, and undertook to put down the Indians in the Northwestern Territory, he induced Mr. Jones to accompany him as chaplain, and he acted in that capacity during 1794-95-96, and was present at the treaty of Greenville. When the war of 1812 broke out, although seventy-six years of age, he again volunteered his services, and was appointed chaplain by his old companion in arms, Gen. John Armstrong, then Secretary of War, and he served under Gens. Brown and Wilkinson until peace was declared. He then retired to his farm and devoted himself to its cultivation, and also to arboriculture, of which he was very fond. He thus passed the evening of a busy life, varying it with visits to his relatives, both near and far, preaching wherever he went, and often writing for the press on public affairs, in which he never ceased to take a deep interest.

Mr. Jones was a prominent member of the Philadelphia Baptist Association, of which he was moderator in the year 1798, and was often appointed on committees to answer queries or to settle difficulties among the churches. When the great Winchester defection occurred in the church of Philadelphia, and a majority of the members followed Elhanan Winchester, who had become a Universalist, or as he was then called a Restorationist, Mr. Jones was one of the ministers appointed by the church to advise them in their troubles.

Mr. Jones died at his farm, Feb. 5, 1820, in the eighty-fourth year of his age, and was buried at the Valley church-yard. The funeral services were conducted by Rev. Thomas Roberts, Rev. Wm. E. Ashton, and Rev. William Latta. The Rev. Dr. William Rogers delivered a funeral sermon on the next Sunday. The following notice of Mr. Jones appeared in Poulson's *Daily Advertiser:*

"In sketching the character of this venerable servant of the Cross, truth requires us to say that he was an eminent man. Throughout the whole of his protracted and eventful life Mr. Jones was peculiarly distinguished for the warmth of his friendship, the firmness of his patriotism, the sincerity and ardor of his piety, and the faithfulness of his ministry. In the army of the Revolution he was a distinguished chaplain, and was engaged in the same arduous duties during the last war. As a scholar he was accurate; possessing a mind of superior texture, he embellished it with the beauties of classical literature and the riches of general science. The Fellowship of Brown University, in the year 1774, as a testimony of respect for his learning and talents, conferred upon him the degree of Master of Arts."

In early life he studied medicine, and his services during the wars were often called for, and, although not a physician, yet he frequently prescribed when applied to.

Mr. Jones was the author of several works: 1st. A journal of two visits made to some nations of Indians on the west side of the River Ohio, in the years 1772 and 1773. 2d. A treatise on the work of the Holy Spirit. 3d. A treatise on laying on of hands. 4th. Another on the same subject, in reply to a broadside of Rev. Samuel Jones, D.D. 5th. "Peter Edwards' Candid Reasons examined."

Mr. Jones was married Feb. 22, 1762, to Anne, daughter of Joseph and Sarah Stilwell, of Middletown, N. J., and had issue: 1st. Morgan, who died near Wheeling, Va. 2d. Eleanor, who married John Garrett, and died at Garrettsville, O. 3d. Mary, who married Archibald McClean. 4th. Horatio Gates Jones, who died at Philadelphia. All his children left issue.

In danger he knew no fear, in fervent patriotism he had no superiors and few equals, in the Revolutionary struggle he was a tower of strength, especially in the section now known as the Middle States, and in piety he was a Christian without reproach.

Jones, Rev. David, was born in Wales, in April, 1785. Though bearing the same name, this is not the heroic David Jones, the Pennsylvania chaplain in the Revolutionary war. He landed in Philadelphia in 1803, when the yellow fever was raging;

he went to Ohio, and more than two years afterwards he was baptized into the fellowship of the Columbia church, near Cincinnati. He studied under Dr. Samuel Jones, of Lower Dublin, Pa., for some time. In January, 1814, he took pastoral charge of the church of Newark, N. J., where the Lord revived the church and converted many souls through his ministry. In 1821 he succeeded Dr. Samuel Jones as pastor of the Lower Dublin church, and he continued to serve it until the Lord took him home; in this church the Great Shepherd gave him several revivals, in one of which, in 1831, he baptized 65 persons, though the population around was small. He died April 9, 1833, in the enjoyment of a blessed hope through his Saviour's blood.

Jones, Rev. Evan, was born at Brecknockshire, Wales, in May, 1789. Previous to his coming to this country he was for thirteen years a merchant in London. He was appointed by the board of the Baptist Triennial Convention, July 24, 1821, a missionary among the Cherokee Indians. For several years before the removal of the Cherokees from North Carolina Mr. Jones labored with great success among them, establishing churches and schools, and proving that some of the Indian tribes of this country can be civilized and Christianized. In 1838, in carrying out the treaty of New Echota, the Cherokees were removed to what was known as the Western Territory, and Mr. Jones followed his flock to their new home, and in two years after their removal 130 persons were baptized and a new church formed. Mr. Jones's connection with the Cherokees covered a period of fifty years. It is said that "the confidence in which he was held by them was never impaired." He died at Tahlequah, Aug. 18, 1873, having reached the age of eighty-three years and three months. "He was a man of quiet home virtues, of unostentatious life, and of such purity of character that even suspicion presumed not to tarnish it."

Jones, Rev. F. H., was born in Surry Co., N. C., Sept. 4, 1836; educated at Union Academy, Davie Co., Beulah Institute, and Yadkin Institute; baptized by Rev. C. W. Bessant; has done much missionary work; is now pastor of the Yanceyville church, moderator of the Beulah Association, and the leading man in that body.

Jones, Rev. G. S., was born in Pasquotank Co., N. C., Dec. 23, 1837; graduated at Wake Forest College in 1860; ordained in 1861, Revs. T. B. Justice, Thomas Stradley, and Dr. J. D. Hufham forming the Presbytery; served the Hendersonville church as pastor from 1861 to 1868, since which time he has been in the employ of the American Sunday-School Union, and has organized and aided about 900 schools.

Jones, Rev. Henry V., was born in North Wales, Feb. 24, 1808. Left an orphan when four years old, he went to live with an uncle in London. After attending an academy, he entered mercantile life at seventeen. He was converted and baptized in August, 1826, into the fellowship of the Dean Street church, London, and was disowned by his uncle (an Episcopalian) the next day. He came to America in 1831, and was ordained in New York State, April 8, 1835. His first pastorate was in Palmyra. He held important positions in New York, New England, and New Jersey. In the latter State he accomplished a great work. When he took charge of the First church in Newark the cause was very low. Differences of doctrine and diverse views as to measures among the members had long prevented growth. Under his genial and loving preaching and administration union was secured, the congregation more than filled the house, a building for the South church was begun, and a colony was designated to occupy the new house. This was the beginning of church extension in Newark, and Mr. Jones was a moving spirit in the work. His health requiring a change, he accepted a call to the old church at Piscataway, N. J., where he spent six years of loving, successful labor. After good work was done at Rondout and West Troy, N. Y., and Noank, Conn., he served the church at Princeton, N. J. His brethren felt that his qualifications to incite the churches to benevolent work ought to be more extensively used, and he was persuaded to accept the position of district secretary of the Home Mission Society. He also acted at other times as financial secretary of Peddie Institute and South Jersey Institute, collecting large sums for these schools. He was a clear, sound, solid preacher, having the Welsh power of illustration blended with the sober judgment of a master in Scripture doctrine. He was a valuable helper in the First church, New Brunswick, of which he was a member the last seven years of his life. His last sermon was at the old church at Piscataway, on Sunday, June 16, 1878. He preached with great power, and seemed to be in usual health. The next evening, after two hours' sickness, he went to his heavenly home. A prominent periodical well spoke of him as "a man of strong common sense, singular magnanimity and devotedness, and great purity of character."

Jones, Hon. Horatio Gates, A.M., the youngest son of Horatio Gates Jones, D.D., was born Jan. 19, 1822, in Roxborough, Philadelphia. He graduated at the University of Pennsylvania in 1841; was admitted to the Philadelphia bar in May, 1847; formed an acquaintance early in life with the annalist of Philadelphia, John F. Watson, which in a great measure gave tone to the future studies of his life; in 1848 became a member of the Historical Society of Pennsylvania, and in 1849 its secretary, a position which he held for eighteen years, and in 1867 he was chosen one of its vice-presidents, and still holds that office; in 1856 he became connected with the Welsh Society of Philadelphia, of which he is now president; in 1858 he was elected clerk of the Philadelphia Baptist Association, and filled the office for fifteen years, when he was chosen moderator. He has been president of the board of trustees of the Philadelphia Association for thirteen years. He was elected in 1865 by the councils of Philadelphia a director of Girard College. He has been secretary of the board of trustees of Crozer Theological Seminary for thirteen years. In 1874 he was elected to the State senate from Philadelphia, and re-elected in 1876 and in 1878. Mr. Jones is a member of the historical societies of Rhode Island, New York, Delaware, Wisconsin, Minnesota, and Florida; and also of the Moravian Historical Society, the New England Historic Genealogical Society, and the American Antiquarian Society; and in 1877 he was elected an Honorary Fellow of the Royal Historical Society of Great Britain.

Mr. Jones was largely interested in the organization of the Baptist Home of Philadelphia, and he has been secretary of its board of trustees from its establishment.

Mr. Jones united with the Lower Merion church in 1840, of which his father was pastor, and he still remains a member of it.

He is the author of a number of valuable works, which show great research and literary ability.

In the senate of Pennsylvania, while not neglecting other interests of the State, he has devoted much time to religious liberty; his aim has been to secure freedom from the penalties of the Sunday law of April 22, 1794, for all persons who observed the seventh day as the Sabbath. In 1876-77-78-79, and in 1880, he introduced bills for this purpose into the senate, and though on each occasion he was defeated, yet the vote in favor of his motion was always larger. Mr. Jones cherishes an enthusiastic love for Baptist soul liberty; he understands the subject thoroughly, his efforts on its behalf have been well planned and valiant; and ultimate victory is certain under his generous leadership. He might justly be called the American champion of religious liberty.

Mr. Jones has an enviable reputation, an extensive influence, an unselfish disposition, and a heart full of love for his Master, his truth, and his servants.

Jones, Horatio Gates, D.D., of Roxborough, Philadelphia, Pa., youngest son of Rev. David Jones, of the Great Valley church, was born Feb. 11, 1777, at East Town, Chester Co., Pa., and passed his early youth there and at Southampton, Bucks Co. After acquiring such education as the schools there could give, when nineteen he was placed under the care of Rev. Burgiss Allison, D.D., who was principal of an academy at Bordentown, N. J. The celebrated Dr. Stoughton was one of the teachers, and the acquaintance then formed ripened into a friendship which lasted through life. The system of instruction was quite varied, and the attendance of many French refugees was of great advantage to the students, who could thereby acquire a knowledge of French. On his return from school, Mr. Jones devoted himself to farming. He also mingled in politics, and, being a fluent speaker, he soon acquired a prominent position, even before he had attained his majority. But about this time his mind was directed to religious concerns, and he made a public profession of his faith June 24, 1798, and became a member of the Valley church. He soon began to exercise his gifts as a speaker, and the church being satisfied with his efforts, licensed him to preach Sept. 26, 1801. The young man had before him the prospect of political preferment if he remained in civil life, but convictions of duty made him sacrifice all such aspirations, and he entered on his new work with an energy which proved the earnestness of his purpose. He preached in Chester and Delaware Counties, and also in the State of Delaware, where his Welsh ancestors had settled nearly a century before. Having been invited to preach at Salem, N. J., he visited that church, of which Rev. Isaac Skillman, D.D., had been pastor. His labors were appreciated, and on Feb. 13, 1802, he was ordained, and labored in Salem until April, 1805, when he was obliged to leave on account of enfeebled health; the climate not suiting him. He removed to a farm in Roxborough, Philadelphia, and preached every Lord's day, where an opening was had. Among other places he preached in "Thomson's Meeting-House," in Lower Merion, Montgomery Co., which belonged to Hon. Charles Thomson, first secretary of the Continental Congress. Mr. Thomson was a highly-educated man, had once been a tutor in the College of Philadelphia, was a thorough Greek scholar, and is well known as a translator of the Bible. He gave Mr. Jones a warm welcome, and in many ways exhibited an interest in the preaching of the gospel in that neighborhood. Although residing six miles from the meeting-house, yet he was generally the first person there, and for a period of three years he continued his labors without any signs of success. But in May, 1808, he was privileged to baptize the first convert in a small dam on Mill Creek, which he erected the previous day with his own hands. Other hopeful conversions and baptisms followed, until on Sept. 11, 1808, the Lower Merion Baptist church was organized with 19 members, with Mr. Jones as pastor. Rev. William Rogers, D.D., and Rev. William Stoughton, D.D., officiated on the occasion. In two years' time a meeting-house was built on a lot of ground the gift of Mr. Thomson, who, although a Presbyterian, ever continued to attend the Merion church, until over ninety years of age, and proved himself a warm friend of Mr. Jones. Notwithstanding Mr. Jones was a laborious minister, and was constant in visitations among his people, yet he took a deep interest in civil affairs, and to the close of his life filled many important posts of honor, but none of profit. For more than twenty years he was a director of the Bank of Germantown, and director and controller of the public schools.

In 1814, when the Baptist Board of Foreign Missions was organized in Philadelphia, he was present, aided in its formation, was one of the Board of Managers, and for many years acted as secretary of the board. He was warmly interested in the cause of education, and especially the education of young men for the ministry. It was chiefly through his influence that the Philadelphia Association was induced to organize a manual labor school at Haddington, Philadelphia Co., which afterwards became Haddington College. As long as the college existed he was president of its board of trustees, and spared neither time nor money in promoting its interests. In 1812, Brown University conferred on him the degree of Master of Arts, and in 1852 the university at Lewisburg bestowed on him their first degree of Doctor of Divinity, he being at the time the chancellor of the institution. In 1829 Mr. Jones was chosen president of the trustees of the Philadelphia Baptist Association, and he held that honorable position until 1853, a period of twenty-four years. He was chosen moderator of the Association in 1816 and 1822, and was clerk in 1808, 1810, 1813, 1815, and 1835.

The Lower Merion church, of which he was the first pastor, continued under his care for a period of forty-five years. It assisted all the benevolent and missionary organizations as they arose, and it was owing to a query from this church to the Association, that the Baptist State Convention, now known as the Pennsylvania Baptist General Association, for missionary purposes, was organized. Dr. Jones continued his active duties until 1845, when his health began to fail; but still he would not consent to give up his pastorate. And so he continued to preach and pray for his beloved Merion until called home to his reward on high, on the 12th of December, 1853, in his seventy-seventh year.

Mr. Jones was twice married, first to Miss Esther Righter, by whom he had three children,—Hon. John Richter Jones, Ellen Maria, married to Rev. George Higgins, Hetty Ann Jones, all of whom are deceased. His second wife was Miss Deborah Levering, and by her he had issue,—Sarah, married to Hon. Anthony D. Levering, Col. Charles Thomson Jones, Nathan Levering Jones, died April 19, 1879, leaving issue, Horatio Gates Jones.

Jones, Rev. Howard Malcom, son of the missionary, Rev. John Taylor Jones, D.D., was born in Bangkok, Siam. He was a graduate of Brown University in the class of 1853, and of Newton Theological Institution in the class of 1857. He was ordained pastor of the church in Schoolcraft, Mich., in 1858, where he remained one year, and then went to Racine, Wis., where he was a pastor four years. On leaving the Racine church, he settled in Fredonia, N. Y., where he was pastor six years, and then accepted a call to Bristol, R. I. Since 1869, Mr. Jones has been preaching in Bristol with much acceptance.

Jones, Hugh, D.D., president of Llangollen College, Wales, was born in Bodedern, Anglesea, July 10, 1831. He became the subject of religious convictions while yet a boy. When about twelve years of age he connected himself with the Welsh Calvinistic Methodist Church. In his sixteenth year he removed to the neighborhood of Llanfachreth, where the Baptists had a stronghold. His associations with them led him for the first time to examine the New Testament on the subject of baptism, and the result was his conversion to the Baptist faith. He was baptized in the river Alaw by the Rev. Robert D. Roberts in his seventeenth year. His abilities were soon discovered by the brotherhood at Llanfachreth, and he was urged to exercise his gifts as a preacher. Having spent some time in the grammar-school of the neighborhood, he entered Haverford West College in June, 1853. His progress in this institution was such as to command particular mention. In Hebrew, mathematics, and the classics he was the distinguished student of his class. In May, 1857, he settled as pastor over the Baptist church at Llandudno, Caernarvonshire. In a little over two years he was enabled greatly to strengthen the cause, leaving them on account of ill health in October, 1859.

In the same month he became co-pastor with the Rev. John Prichard, D.D., at Llangollen. This fellowship of service was most fruitful of good. The elder and the younger were true yoke-fellows in Christ. They had joint charge of the Welsh and English churches of Llangollen, as well as of a branch church at Glyndyfedwy, Merionethshire.

In 1862 the North Wales Baptist College was instituted at Llangollen, with Dr. Prichard as president, and Mr. Jones as classical and mathematical tutor. In 1866, Dr. Prichard resigned, and Mr. Jones became president, a position which he still holds with acknowledged efficiency.

Dr. Jones has not confined himself to his collegiate and ministerial duties. Some of the most valuable productions in the Welsh language are from his able pen. In 1862 he issued a small book on "The Mode and Subjects of Baptism, with the History of the Rise of Infant Baptism and Sprinkling," which has been widely read. In 1863 there appeared a volume on "The Act of Baptism, or an Enquiry into the Mode of Baptism." An abbreviated edition of this book has appeared in English, and has been very well received. It is in the Welsh language what Carson is in the English. Its excellence and value are universally recognized. Another volume which has been a rich boon to the Welsh people is a masterly production on "The Bible and its Interpretation, or an Introduction to the Holy Scriptures." Dr. Jones has done himself great credit both in the conception and execution of this work. It will do for the Bible-loving Welsh people what no other book could. There was nothing more needed in the vernacular of the principality than a scholarly treatise on Bible exegesis, and Dr. Jones has supplied the need in a manner that cannot fail to command the gratitude of every lover of the Book of books in the land. Several other minor productions have been issued from Dr. Jones's pen that have taken a high place in his country's literature: "The Church of Christ," being the inaugural address from the chair of the Welsh Baptist Union, 1876; "The History of the Protestant Reformation in Great Britain, with Special Reference to Wales;" "Popery: its History and Characteristics, with the Remedy Against It," being the inaugural address from the chair of the Welsh Baptist Union for 1877. He has also written many essays and sermons for the Welsh periodicals, together with a Commentary on Ecclesiastes for Mr. Gee, of Denbigh's family Bible.

Few men of this generation have done more to enlighten and elevate their countrymen than Dr. Hugh Jones, of Llangollen. His writings have all been of a sterling character.

Jones, Rev. Jenkin, was born about 1690, in Wales, and he came to this country in 1710. He took charge of the First church of Philadelphia, May 15, 1746, at the time the church was "reconstituted." Previous to that time the Philadelphia body was only a branch of the Lower Dublin church, and of it Mr. Jones had been pastor for twenty-one years. He died July 16, 1761.

Mr. Jones was "a good man," and performed valuable service to his church and denomination; he was the cause of changing the marriage laws of the colony, so that "dissenting" ministers might celebrate marriages; he built a parsonage largely at his own expense; he left "a legacy towards purchasing a silver cup for the Lord's table which is worth £60. His name is engraven upon it."

Jones, Rev. John, an eloquent colored Baptist minister, long pastor of the First African Baptist church in Shreveport, La., was a native of North Carolina, and came to Shreveport under the protection of Deacon John N. Howell about 1840. He was ordained in 1856 by a Presbytery consisting of Dr. W. H. Stokes, George Tucker, Jesse Lee, and A. J. Rutherford. In the early part of the civil war a law was passed requiring all free persons of color, not natives, to leave the State. Under the operation of this law he went to Ohio, but his loss was soon felt, and it was known that he could do more than all the police in keeping the Africans in order; consequently a special act of the Legislature was passed inviting his return, the terms of which he accepted, to the great joy of the people of both races. He was often invited to preach to the whites, and always drew large and interested audiences. He died in 1877, much regretted.

Jones, John Emlyn, LL.D., was born in the town of Newcastle, Emlyn, Caermarthenshire, Wales, on the 8th of January, 1820, and died at Ebbeo Vale on the 18th of January, 1873. He was a man of commanding presence and oratorical ability. He was editor at different times of the two leading organs of the Baptists of Wales. He was a voluminous contributor to various Welsh periodicals. He translated into the Welsh language Gill's Commentary and Hamilton's Grammar, and he wrote "The History of Great Britain for the Past Half-Century." During the last years of his life he was engaged in a work in the Welsh language called "The History of the World," one volume of which was published, and he had written about half of the other. He was likewise a poet of no mean order. He won during his lifetime a large number of prizes for poetical compositions. At the Abergavenny Eisteddfod, in 1838, he was invested with the degree of B.B.D. (Bard by Privilege and Usage). At the Denbigh National Eisteddfod, in 1860, he won the chair, with the accompanying prize, for the best ode on the "Pentecost," also at Llanerchymedd for the best ode on "Time." Among his poetical productions, "The Poor Man's Grave" is regarded for its pathos, simplicity, and heart-touching effect as equal to anything of its kind in the literature of the country.

Jones, Judge John Richter, the eldest son of Rev. Horatio Gates Jones, was born in Salem, N. J., Oct. 2, 1803, and was educated at the Germantown Academy, and was graduated from the University of Pennsylvania in the year 1821. He was admitted to the Philadelphia bar Nov. 17, 1827. For many years he was one of the judges of the Court of Common Pleas of Philadelphia County, during which time he lived at Roxborough. On retiring from the bench he settled in Sullivan Co., Pa. When the late war began he felt it to be his duty to devote himself to the service of his country, and with all the patriotic ardor of his renowned grandfather, Rev. David Jones, of the Continental army, Judge Jones immediately raised a regiment, the 58th Penna. Vols., of which he was commissioned colonel. He sought as soon as possible for active service, and was ordered to Norfolk, Va., and finally was sent to Newbern, N. C., where he soon achieved much renown for the boldness of his attacks. He did not know what fear was, and hence sought for the place of greatest danger. One of his last and most successful marches was made in May, 1863, against a force which had encamped at a place called Gum Swamp. He had placed at his command a number of regiments, over which he exercised the power of acting brigadier-general. After a long and arduous march he succeeded in capturing the whole of the force without losing a single man. But the song of victory was soon changed into a wail of sorrow, for shortly after his return to camp at Newbern his troops were attacked, and placing himself at the head of a force to reconnoitre, he was suddenly shot through the heart, and died without a groan. Most truly can it be said of him, *Dulce et decorum est pro patria mori.* Judge Jones was a devout Christian, and was a member of the Lower Merion church. He was a classical scholar, and carried with him to the camp his Septuagint version of the Old Testament, which he was accustomed to read daily. His death occurred May 23, 1863.

Jones, John Taylor, D.D., was born at New Ipswich, N. H., July 16, 1802. He joined the Congregational church in Ashby, Mass., when he was but fifteen years of age. He graduated at Amherst in 1825, and studied theology at Andover, where his views underwent a change on the mode and subjects of baptism, in consequence of which he thought it would be more expedient for him to complete his course of study at Newton. He was baptized by Rev. Dr. Malcom in 1828, and became a member of the Federal Street church, in Boston. He was appointed a missionary to Burmah, and reached Maulmain in February, 1861. He immediately addressed himself with great zeal to his missionary work. He was able to preach both in the Burman and the Taling languages before many months had elapsed. Believing that there was a favorable opportunity to preach to the Talings in the kingdom of Siam, it was decided by the board that Dr. Jones was the most suitable person to make the effort. To carry out this purpose he went to Bangkok. Providence soon pointed out to him what was to be his special mission to Siam. It was to translate the New Testament into the tongue of that country. He engaged in this congenial occupation with the greatest interest, and completed the work upon which he had set his heart in October, 1843. Meanwhile, circumstances brought him to his native land, where he remained for a short time, and then returned to the scene of his labors. Again, in 1846, the state of his wife's health led to another visit. He spent a year in this country, presenting everywhere, as opportunity offered, the claims of foreign missions to the churches, and in 1847 he returned to his post of labor. In Bangkok he was regarded with the highest respect. We are told that "the magistrates, and even the king, did not hesitate to consult him in cases of difficulty." He continued at his favorite work as a translator, and in the preparation of many books which he hoped would be useful to the natives. In the summer of 1851 he had an attack of dysentery, which so prostrated him that he died September 13, being a few weeks over forty-nine years of age.

His associates in missionary labor place Dr. Jones very high on the list of those who have devoted themselves to the services of Christ in the foreign field. His great work, the translation of the New Testament into the Siamese language, says Dr. Dean, "compares favorably with the translation of the New Testament made in any of the Asiatic languages, including the life-work of such men as Carey, Marshman, Judson, and Morrison, and their worthy successors." He adds, "I have met men on the missionary field who exhibited some stronger points of character, and some particular qualifications, or greater fitness for missionary usefulness, but, take him altogether, I have never seen his equal, and among more than a hundred men I have met among the heathen, I would select Dr. Jones as the model missionary."

Jones, Jonathan, A.M., principal of the University Female Institute at Lewisburg, Pa., was born in Chester County in that State, June, 1845. His early education was received in the schools of his native county, and in those of Reading, whither his family removed in 1860. Here he was fitted for college, but he did not enter the University of Lewisburg until 1864, having previously to this time served in the late war. He graduated from college in 1868 with high honors. The two succeeding years were spent in Minnesota in teaching and preaching. In the summer of 1870 he returned to Lewisburg, having been elected to take charge of the academy connected with the university. He remained here until 1873, when he accepted the principalship of the Classical and Scientific Institute at Mount Pleasant, Westmoreland Co., Pa. Here he remained five years. Although the school sustained great financial losses during that time, yet there was a steady increase in the attendance, largely due to his excellent management. In 1878 he accepted the principalship of the institute at Lewisburg,—the ladies' department of the university. Since his election to this position, the board of curators have introduced into the school, at his suggestion, a full classical course of instruction. The institute now confers on young women the advantages of a college, and it is the determination of the principal to keep the standard of scholarship equal to that of the most advanced institutions for women. His work as an instructor is in the line of psychology, ethics, and Greek.

Jones, Judge J. H. C., was born at Rockville, Md., July 31, 1823. He was educated at the Rockville Academy, and graduated at the Columbian College in 1841. He removed to King and Queen Co., Va., in 1842, where he taught school two years; he afterwards studied law, and was admitted to the bar in 1845. He was baptized into the fellowship of the Bruington church in October, 1842, of which church he has been clerk since 1861. He was elected clerk of the Rappahannock Association in 1863, which office he held continuously until 1869, when he was elected moderator of the body, to which office he has been annually re-elected ever since. He also filled the office of president of the Baptist General Association of Virginia at its annual sessions in 1875-76-77. In March, 1865, he was elected to represent the counties of King and Queen and Essex in the house of delegates of Virginia, but the failure of the Confederate cause shortly afterwards prevented the assembling of the body to which he was elected. He represented the counties of King and Queen and King William in the house of delegates under what was then called "the restored government of Virginia," during the sessions of the Legislature of 1865-66 and 1866-67. In April, 1870, he was elected by the Legislature of Virginia, under the new constitution, just then adopted, judge of the County Courts of King and Queen and Middlesex, and upon the expiration of his term of office, Jan. 1, 1874, he was re-elected by the same body judge of the County Courts of King and Queen and King William for six years, which office he holds at present. Judge Jones is warmly interested in everything pertaining to the progress of the denomination.

Jones, J. Wm., D.D., was born at Louisa Court-House, Va., Sept. 25, 1836, and was baptized Aug. 26, 1854, into the fellowship of the Mechanicsville church, Louisa Co. He received his literary and scientific education at the University of Virginia during the years 1855-59, and his theological education at the Southern Baptist Theological Seminary. He was ordained at Charlottesville, Va., June 10, 1860, with three well-known and beloved brethren, C. H. Toy, J. L. Johnson, and J. B. Taylor, Jr., all college-mates and intimate friends. On July 3, 1860, he offered himself to the Foreign Mission Board of the Southern Baptist Convention for appointment as missionary to Canton, China, was accepted, and had made arrangements to sail in the autumn with his friend (now Rev. C. H. Toy, D.D.), who was under appointment for Japan. The political troubles of that year caused the board to postpone their sailing, and the war finally prevented it. Dr. Jones's interest in foreign missions led him, in 1860, to visit many of the Associations and

J. WM. JONES, D.D.

churches to stimulate them to greater zeal in behalf of the cause, and he accomplished much good. During the winter of 1860-61 he became pastor of Little River church, Louisa Co., preaching once a month. In May, 1861, he enlisted as a private in the Confederate army, and followed its varying fortunes from Harper's Ferry to Appomattox Court-House. In 1862 he was made chaplain of his regiment, and in 1863 missionary chaplain to Gen. A. P. Hill's corps; and he was present and an active participant in all the great movements and battles from Manassas to the surrender. Dr. Jones knew intimately all the prominent officers in the Confederate service. He was an active worker in those great revivals in the army in Virginia in which over 15,000 of the soldiers under Gen. Lee professed conversion, baptizing himself 520 soldiers, and laboring in meetings which resulted in the conversion of at least 2000. In 1865 he took charge of Goshen and Lexington churches, Rockbridge Co., Va., and in 1866 devoted himself exclusively to the latter, remaining until July, 1871. His services here were greatly blessed. During his six years' pastorate in the valley he baptized 200 persons, and labored in meetings in which 250 others professed conversion. Dr. Jones's residence in Lexington opened up to him special opportunities for doing good, for he was one of the chaplains of Washington College, of which Gen. R. E. Lee was president, and also gave much time to the students of the Virginia Military Institute, where, during one session, there were over 100 professions of conversion in connection with a series of prayer-meetings which he conducted. Of those whom he baptized while at Lexington, eight have become useful Baptist ministers, and fifteen clergymen in other denominations. During 1871 he acted as agent for the Southern Baptist Theological Seminary, laboring mainly in Georgia and Alabama. In 1872 he became general superintendent of the Virginia Baptist Sunday-School and Baptist Board, and held the position until June, 1874. In 1875 he took charge of the Ashland Baptist church, of which he is still the pastor. Dr. Jones has performed some admirable literary work. In 1874 he published, through the Appletons, of New York, "Reminiscences, Anecdotes, and Letters of Gen. R. E. Lee," which received the warmest commendations of critics in all parts of the country, and which an accomplished scholar designates as "one of the most charming semi-biographies in the language." Of this work 20,000 copies have already been sold. He is diligently at work now on several historical works, among which are a "Life of Gen. Stonewall Jackson," and a "History of the Revivals in the Confederate Army," the latter of which, from the fact that he was actively engaged in them, will be looked for with eager interest by the Christian public. He is also at the present time secretary of the Southern Historical Society, and editor of their monthly paper. Dr. Jones also had the reputation of being one of the best "special correspondents" that prepared for the newspapers accounts of the terrible battle-scenes of the war. One who knows the subject of our sketch intimately describes him as "a noble man every way,—large in body and heart, liberal to a fault, the truest of friends, and a man of such strong will that he would die for his convictions on any point."

The honorary degree of D.D. was conferred upon him in 1874 by the Washington and Lee University, Virginia.

Jones, Rev. Miller, A.M., was born July 3, 1830, in Hilltown Township, Bucks Co., Pa. His father, John M. Jones, died Nov. 30, 1839; his mother, Mary Hines Jones, is still living, in her seventy-sixth year. Both parents were baptized at an early age by Rev. Joseph Matthias. The subject of this sketch was baptized by Rev. Joseph H. Kennard, D.D., in April, 1846. He was subsequently licensed by the Tenth Baptist church, Philadelphia, to preach the gospel; graduated from the university at Lewisburg in 1856, and from the theological department in 1858; ordained as a Baptist minister a few weeks afterwards by a council convened by the Marcus Hook Baptist church, Pa. He continued pastor of this church for three years and three months, and was greatly prospered. His second pastorate was over the Bridgeport Baptist church, Montgomery Co., Pa., and continued with most encouraging results for more than two years. The third settlement was with the Moorestown, N. J., Baptist church, which continued for four years. Here a most delightful and extensive revival was enjoyed. His fourth pastorate was with the Marlton, N. J., Baptist church, which continued, with many tokens of divine favor, for three years. His fifth charge was the Second Baptist church of Reading, Pa. Here a large number of conversions occurred, and much prosperity was enjoyed, but a call coming from the Bridgeport Baptist church to assume a second time the pastoral charge, his sixth settlement was with this beloved church. Here a steady and solid growth of the church was enjoyed during the eight years of a very happy pastorate. Jan. 1, 1880, he entered upon the pastorate at Village Green, Pa. A Baptist church has since been organized and recognized. A baptistery, with additional rooms for the convenience of the candidates, is now being constructed, and the whole property is being put in the best repair through the liberality of Mrs. J. P. Crozer. The prospects for growth are encouraging. About 300 persons have been baptized during his ministry.

Jones, Nathan Levering, A.M., of Roxborough, Philadelphia, Pa., was born Aug. 3, 1816, and was a son of Rev. Horatio Gates Jones, D.D. He received his early education at the Roxborough Academy, and also at Haddington College, and was one of its first students. Before graduating he entered into business, and located at Roxborough, in the lumber trade, which he continued to pursue during the remainder of his life. When quite young he joined the Lower Merion Baptist church, of which his father was pastor, and he was a constituent member of the Balligomingo church. His membership was finally removed to Merion, of which church he was a deacon at the time of his death. Mr. Jones was highly esteemed, and was elected to many offices of trust and honor. He was a director and also controller of the public schools of Philadelphia, a director of the Bank of Germantown, and of the Germantown Mutual Insurance Company. For over twenty years he was president of the Roxborough Lyceum. His death, which was sudden, occurred on Saturday evening, April 19, 1879. As a husband and father he was loving and affectionate, as a neighbor he was most highly esteemed, as a citizen he was honored, and as a Christian he was devoted. His memory is highly cherished in the community where he had so long lived. Mr. Jones for several years was active in the temperance work, and as a public man exerted a great influence in that direction among his associates. He was also largely interested in the cause of education, especially of ministerial, and was a manager of the Pennsylvania Baptist Education Society. In their obituary report for 1879, the committee, speaking of Mr. Jones, say, "He was a man of considerable prominence in the community where he was born and lived. He filled many positions of public trust with a fidelity which commanded confidence and inspired respect. His memory is blessed both in the church and in society, for he was a staunch Christian and a true and noble man." The honorary degree of Master of Arts was conferred upon him by the University at Lewisburg.

Jones, Rev. Philip L., was born in England in 1838; was baptized at East Clarence, N. Y., in 1854; was educated at the University of Rochester and at Rochester Theological Seminary, graduating from the latter institution in 1868; ordained the same year at Dunkirk, N. Y. In 1870 he was called to the pastorate of the South Broad Street church, Philadelphia, then a mission of the First church. He still continues to labor in this field, which has quietly and steadily grown under his efficient and faithful ministry. He is a member of the board of managers of the Pennsylvania Baptist Education Society, and was for several years the secretary of the Philadelphia Conference of Baptist ministers. He is a man of gentle and winning manners; and his sermons and writings are clear, forceful, and poetic.

Jones, Rev. Robert B.—The Baptists of North Carolina have produced no more remarkable man than Robert B. Jones. He was born in Person Co., N. C.; baptized into the fellowship of the Mill Creek church; went as a soldier to Mexico, to get rid of the duty of preaching; fought bravely till the army reached the city of Mexico, when he was pronounced an incurable consumptive, and told by the surgeons that he would never again see North Carolina. On his way to Vera Cruz, expecting to die, he promised the Lord that if he would allow him to reach North Carolina again he would preach as much as he wished. From this time he began to improve; he entered Wake Forest College in 1854, but after studying a year or two was obliged to leave on account of ill health. He went up on the Catawba River and did good service for the Master, and in 1858 returned to college, and graduated in 1861. He was pastor of Hartford church for several years, became agent of his *alma mater* in 1866–67, and died at the college in December, 1867.

Jones, Samuel, D.D., was born Jan. 14, 1735, in Glamorganshire, Wales, and was brought to this country two years afterwards by his parents. He received his education at the College of Philadelphia, and graduated in 1762; and in the beginning of the next year he was ordained to the ministry of the gospel. In 1763 he became pastor of the Lower Dublin Baptist church, and he held that office until his death, which occurred Feb. 7, 1814.

SAMUEL JONES, D.D.

Dr. Jones, if not superior in scholarly attainments to every other American Baptist of his day, was equaled by few, and surpassed by none. His wisdom in managing difficult matters was as striking as his learning was remarkable. At an early period of his life he became the most influential Baptist minister in the middle colonies, and probably in the whole country. Dr. Jones, when a young man, was sent by the Philadelphia Association to Rhode Island, to assist in founding Rhode Island College. At Newport he remodeled the rough draft of the college charter, which soon after obtained the sanction of the Legislature of Rhode Island. He prepared a new treatise of discipline for the Philadelphia Confession of Faith by request of the Association in 1798. Dr. Jones, Rev. David Jones, and Dr. Burgiss Allison compiled a selection of hymns for the use of the churches. In 1807 he preached the centenary sermon of the Philadelphia Association, which was published with the volume of "Minutes for One Hundred Years," by the Baptist Publication Society. His name occurs continually in the minutes of the Association for half a century, as moderator, preacher, committeeman, or writer of the circular letter. "Dr. Jones was a ready writer and a fluent speaker; he was a large and firmly-built man, six feet or more in height, and in every way well-proportioned. His face was the very image of intelligence and good nature, which, with the air of dignity that pervaded his movements, rendered his appearance uncommonly attractive."

He educated many young men for the Christian ministry, some of whom attained distinction for their talents, learning, and usefulness.

On the death of Dr. Manning, Dr. Jones received a letter from Judge David Howell informally offering him the presidency of Rhode Island College. Secretary Howell informed him that "the eyes of the corporation (of the college) seemed to be fixed on him for a successor to Dr. Manning."

This great and good man was largely blessed in his ministry; and he exerted a vast and useful influence over the rising Baptist churches of our country.

Jones, Rev. Thomas Z. R., was born in the parsonage of the Great Valley church, Pa., July 23, 1803, and died in Kalamazoo, Mich., July 2, 1876. His father was Rev. Richard Jones, a native of Wales. In 1835, Brother Jones came to Michigan Territory to take up his work. Years before he had selected that as his field of labor. He took the right wing of the little army of invasion that was strung along the rivers St. Clair, Detroit, Raisin, and Maumee. Up and down the St. Clair and back into the woods wherever a settler had pushed, he preached in the wilderness and sought the sheep. There he nursed his sick, and buried the members of his young family, and saw the salvation of God. The China church, as then called, was a visible result, and much seed for other harvests was sown. The missionary spirit thrusting him on, he reached the spiritual solitude between Jackson and Kalamazoo, and struck in on its eastern edge. Spring Arbor, Concord, Albion, Marengo, and Marshall in turn responded to his work, and he saw the churches in them planted and acquiring growth, and watered by gracious revivals. Then he struck through to Grand Rapids, and was one of the first and best master-builders on the Baptist foundation there. He went to Kalamazoo, from which he has gone to and fro in his agency services, with occasional short pastorates so mixed in as not to break up his home, where so many youth of the schools have been succored, and where he still lives. All older Michigan is a road where his wheels have made and worn marks as he sought supplies for domestic mission and educational works; also for our societies for evangelization, foreign as well as home.

His sympathies were broad as human want, his contributions from the smallest of incomes—with which he always seemed contented—were constant and liberal, his business habits painstaking and just, and his heart sincere. He gave forty-one years of good and faithful work to Michigan.

Jones, T. G., D.D., is a native of Virginia, and like many other Virginians, not a little proud of his State. His father, Wood Jones, of Nottoway, was a relative of U. S. Senator Jones, and of John

T. G. JONES, D.D.

Winston Jones, Speaker of the House of Representatives; and his mother, Elizabeth Trent Archer, of Powhatan, of U. S. Senator Wm. S. Archer, and of Branch T. Archer, who figured conspicuously in the earlier councils of Texas. He was early doubly orphaned, his mother dying when he was about three years old, and his father a few months later. In his boyhood he was with one of his brothers, who afterwards graduated at the University of Virginia and became a lawyer of distinction. When about eighteen years of age he entered the Virginia Baptist Seminary, now Richmond College. After being there some time he decided to devote himself to the ministry, and was licensed by the Second Baptist church of Richmond, whose pastor, the late revered James B. Taylor, had a few years before baptized him. Leaving that institution, he entered the University of Virginia, from which, after a two years' course, he went to William and Mary College, where he graduated. Immediately after taking his degree he went to Alabama, and for a year or two taught a few hours daily in a private family, devoting the rest of his time to theological study and occasional preaching. Returning to Virginia, he preached for a few months in Clarksville, on the North Carolina border; when, although not yet ordained to the full work of the ministry, he was elected the first pastor of the Freemason Street church of Norfolk, with which, though often invited to more prominent positions in the larger cities, he continued until the late war, when he was compelled to leave. He found an asylum in Baltimore as pastor of the Franklin Square church. When the war closed he was recalled to Norfolk, where he remained until he was elected to the presidency of Richmond College. Continuing at the head of that institution for several years, he was again recalled to his old charge at Norfolk. About ten years ago, having been elected pastor of the First Baptist church of Nashville, he removed to that city, where he still resides. Dr. Jones has been honored by the colleges. At the University of Virginia he was the valedictory orator of his society, and received the same honor upon his graduation at William and Mary College. While pastor of the church at Norfolk he was elected president of Wake Forest College, North Carolina, and a few years later, president of Mercer University, Ga. Both these appointments, however, he felt constrained to refuse from his reluctance to leave his first beloved and loving charge. Richmond College conferred upon him the degree of D.D., and, as already stated, called him a few years later to its presidency. Closely engaged in preaching and other pastoral work, he has not written much. Still, his pen has not been idle altogether. Besides a number of published addresses before literary and other bodies, unpublished lectures, and papers in various periodicals, he has written three small books, the first a prize essay, on "The Duties of Pastors to Churches," which was published in Charleston by the Southern Baptist Publication Society; the second on the "Origin and Continuity of the Baptist Churches," published by the American Baptist Publication Society; and the third entitled "The Great Misnomer, or the Lord's Supper, miscalled the Communion." These have met with a ready sale, and are highly commended. Dr. Jones is regarded as one of the finest pulpit orators of the nation, and highly esteemed by his charge in Nashville.

He has been for several sessions one of the vice-presidents of the Southern Baptist Convention, and is now first vice-president of the board of trustees of the Southern Baptist Seminary. He is possessed of rare dignity of manners, fine scholarship, and a blessed record.

Jones, Washington (son of William G. Jones), was born in Wilmington, Del., Jan. 5, 1818; commenced business for himself in his native place in November, 1839; was a director of what is now the National Bank of Wilmington and Brandywine for thirty years, of which he was elected president in 1868, which position he still holds. He is a manager of the Saving Fund, a prosperous institution, whose object is to help the poor to save their earnings; was prime mover in the introduction of gas into the city in 1850, and has been a director of the gas company since its formation.

WASHINGTON JONES.

The emperor Dom Pedro, of Brazil, when in this country in 1876, visited the factory of Mr. Jones, by whom he was shown through the establishment and the various processes explained to him. He seemed much pleased with the operations and took extensive notes.

Mr. Jones was converted in 1841, and baptized into the fellowship of the Second Baptist church on the 2d of January in that year; was elected a trustee of the church July 9 of the same year, and president of the board April 26, 1860, which office he held until 1876, when he resigned; was elected a deacon in June, 1853, which office he still holds; was treasurer of the church for seventeen years, and superintendent of the Sabbath-school fifteen years.

In 1852 the church resolved to rebuild in a new location, and Mr. Jones was made chairman of the building committee, and took an active part in erecting their present handsome and commodious house of worship, both by his own large contributions and zealous efforts in collecting funds from others. Besides, he gave much time and personal attention to the erection of the edifice, and when it was completed gave his individual note for part of the debt remaining upon it.

Mr. Jones is the largest contributor to the funds of the church of which he is a member, besides giving for missions and other benevolent objects at home and abroad. He has the respect of the whole community and the love of his brethren. A man of piety, he is active in church work, prompt and faithful in the discharge of his Christian duties, and speaks and prays with great acceptance in the public meetings of the church and of the denomination.

Jones, Rev. William, was born in the county of Denbigh, in Wales, June 17, 1762. When young he removed to Poulton, in Cheshire, where he received a classical education. In October, 1786, he was baptized by the Rev. Archibald McLean, of Edinburgh, then on a visit to Chester, in the river Dee.

In 1793 he established himself in Liverpool as a wholesale bookseller and publisher. In that city he began to hold meetings in his own spacious drawing-room, at first for his own family, for prayer, praise, reading the Scriptures, exhortation, and exposition. These assemblies were speedily frequented by neighbors and others, and soon they were transferred to a chapel, when a church was formed, and Mr. D. S. Wylie and Mr. Jones were appointed pastors.

Mr. Jones left Liverpool for London, and in 1812, soon after he went to the metropolis, he began his "History of the Waldenses and Albigenses."

In 1815 he started the *New Evangelical Magazine*, in London; this periodical, subsequently called the *New Baptist Magazine*, was conducted by Mr. Jones with great success for eleven years.

He spent three years in preparing a "Dictionary of the Sacred Writings," the first edition of which, consisting of 2000 copies, was quickly sold.

His Church History, of which his "History of the Waldenses and Albigenses" is not quite a half, is a work highly creditable to the research and candor of its author and worthy of a conspicuous place in every Baptist library.

Mr. Jones was the author of biographies of Rowland Hill, Edward Irving, Adam Clark, and of several other works.

He was a writer of great industry and conscientiousness; and in the latter part of his life his works were very popular among Baptists.

In 1843, when his means were very limited, the queen offered him a place in the Charterhouse, where all his wants would be cared for during the rest of his life; but, as the acceptance of it required him to become an Episcopalian, he declined the royal offer. The queen on learning the fact ordered £60 to be paid Mr. Jones in three annual installments. He died in January, 1846.

Jones, Rev. William, was born in Wake Co., N. C., about 1800; was graduated at Wake Forest in 1839, and for many years was the agent of the State Convention. He was a good and useful man.

Jones, William G., was born in Wilmington, Del., Sept. 3, 1784; was baptized April 3, 1803, upon profession of his faith, in the Brandywine, by Rev. Daniel Dodge, pastor of the First Baptist church. He was the first person baptized in Wilmington by Mr. Dodge, who afterwards became pastor of the Second Baptist church, Philadelphia.

About 1812 he, with others, united in the organization of another church, which disbanded after an existence of two years. He then united with the Marcus Hook church, and was at once elected deacon. For years he walked to and from "the Hook," a distance of twenty miles, to attend the services on the Sabbath.

In 1843, when Rev. Morgan J. Rhees became pastor of the Second church, Wilmington, Mr. Jones united with that body, by which he was chosen a deacon. He retained his membership and office until his death, Jan. 26, 1873. He died in the house in which he was born, and in which he lived nearly all his life.

Mr. Jones was to a large extent identified with the Baptist history of Delaware and Southeastern Pennsylvania. His house was a home for ministers, and among the many eminent men who enjoyed its hospitalities were John Leland, Dr. Staughton, Luther Rice, and Dr. J. L. Dagg.

His fidelity to truth was unswerving, and his business integrity unquestionable. He was urbane even in old age, and his conversation highly entertaining and instructive to the young. His Christian character was of the positive type, and the conversion of most of his children, and of many of his grandchildren, bears testimony to his domestic piety. By industry and economy he acquired the pecuniary means which he used to support and advance the cause of Christ, to which he also devoted his time, energies, and prayers.

Jones, Wm. P., M.D., of Nashville, Tenn., was born in Adair Co., Ky., Oct. 17, 1819. At the age of twenty he entered the Louisville Medical Institute, and subsequently received a diploma from the Medical College of Ohio and the Memphis Medical College. He first established himself in the practice of his profession at Edmonton, Ky., afterwards removing to Bowling Green, and finally to Nashville, Tenn.

Dr. Jones is a member of the American Medical Association, Association of American Superintendents of Hospitals for the Insane, American Association for the Advancement of Science, Tennessee State Medical Society, and the Medical Society of Davidson County. He was one of the editors of the *Southern Journal of the Medical and Physical Sciences* in 1853, and for several years thereafter; he established and edited the *Parlor*

Visitor in 1852, and in 1874 became associate editor of the *Tennessee School Journal.*

In 1858 he, with others, founded the Shelby Medical College, in which he was Professor of Materia Medica.

Academy Hospital, the first established in Nashville after the arrival of the Union forces, was

WILLIAM P. JONES, M.D.

under his charge. In 1862 he was elected superintendent of the Tennessee Hospital for the Insane. Through his persistent and earnest appeals to the State Legislature the funds were provided for, and Dr. Jones had the pleasure of erecting a separate and suitable building for the insane colored people, the first institution of the kind in America.

The affairs of the State institution were administered fairly and impartially, and Dr. Jones was unanimously re-elected for a period of eight years.

In 1876 he was elected president of Nashville Medical College.

The people have frequently demanded his public services, and he has rendered them with great distinction as president of Nashville city council and as State senator from Nashville. While acting in the last capacity he was made chairman of the school committee, and introduced the present public school law of Tennessee, which provides equal educational advantages for all the children of the State without regard to race, color, or previous condition.

Dr. Jones has been a member of the Baptist church since 1836, and he is now president of the Tennessee Baptist State Convention, and an honor to the Baptists in Tennessee.

Jordan, Rev. F. M., was born in Montgomery Co., N. C., June 4, 1830; was baptized by Rev. Eli Phillips in 1843; went to Wake Forest College in 1850, and was ordained in 1853. He has labored as pastor in Orange, Caswell, Person, and Davidson Counties.

For the last six years Mr. Jordan has given himself to the work of an evangelist; 1900 persons have professed faith in Christ under his preaching. He has been a laborious and useful minister of the gospel. He has one son in the ministry, W. T. Jordan, pastor at Lumberton.

Jordan, Hon. O'Bryan, was an active member of the Concord Association formed in 1823 at Mount Nebo church, in Cooper Co., Mo. He was appointed clerk of the Association at its organization. He was a member of the Mount Nebo church, and in 1824 he read a circular letter before it which he had prepared upon the Scriptural argument for the support of the ministry. The reasons were clear and convincing. He was a layman of remarkable devotion and purity of life. He was for years a member of the Legislature from Cooper County, and he came out unstained by the corruptions of politics.

Jordan, The.—From יָרַד, "yarad," to descend; "the river of God;" probably referred to in Ps. lxv. 9; the "Descender," now known among the Arabs as " esh Sheriâh," the watering-place. Three main sources of the river have been indicated: one at Tell-el-Kâdi, the site of the ancient Dan of the Israelites, where from the base of an oblong mound about eighty feet above the plain the water gushes out in rivulets numerous enough to form a considerable stream; another, a little northeast of this point, at Banias, the ancient Cæsarea Philippi, where the stream can be traced to a cave,—itself the outlet of a more remote *fons*,—whence it flows by a subterranean course, and reappears a considerable stream a short distance from the grotto. The third leading source of the river may be found, according to Lieut. Lynch, U.S.N., a short distance above the town of Hâsbeiyêh, where two copious streams burst from the base of a precipitous wall of rock, the immediate source of the river Hâsbeiyêh, which Lieut. Lynch regards, however, as the *true* Jordan, rather than as a tributary only.

From Tell-el-Kâdi the river flows for a few miles down the fertile valley, till it expands into Lake Hûlêh, "the waters of Merom" of Scripture, and about nine miles below this pours itself into the "Sea of Galilee." It emerges from the lake at its southern end, and finally buries itself in the Dead Sea. Lieut. Lynch, who gives us the natural history of the river and the region through which it passes, speaks of it at one stage of its course as describing "a series of frantic curvilinears, and returning in a contrary direction to its main course." Between the Lake of Tiberias and the Dead Sea, distant in latitude only about 60 miles, the river describes a course of fully 200 miles, through a valley averaging but 4 or 5 miles in width. The same authority represents it, in this part of its course, as ranging from 3 to 12 feet in depth, and in width from 25 to 180 yards, where it pours into the Dead Sea.

As "the Jordan" or "Descender," the river is most appropriately named. From the Lake of Tiberias to its final outlet in the Dead Sea its descent is over 1000 feet in the short distance of 60 miles. As a consequence, the American explorers encountered during the passage of the river between these points no less than twenty-seven threatening rapids, many others of lesser note, and numerous cascades and waterfalls. By its annual inundations the river appears to have burrowed out a channel above the one it ordinarily pursues, so that for a considerable part of its course there are plain indications of terraced or double banks. For some distance below the Lake of Tiberias, Lieut. Lynch found a luxuriant vegetation along its borders, while in patches here and there the valley bore traces of careful cultivation. But the lower Ghor, until the stream was lost in the Salt Sea, presented a picture of dreary sterility, and almost savage desolation. Tracks of the tiger and boar were clearly discerned, where the banks of the river were low enough to furnish a thicket for their lair. Numerous small islands, a number of tributaries, and the remains of several bridges of Roman and Saracenic architecture were passed in the descent of the river. But little need be said of the fords. There does not appear to have been at any time more than three or four places where the river could be safely forded when swollen after the winter rains. But two fords of any importance are indicated by explorers,—one at a point now known as Sûkwâ, in line with the road from Nâblûs to Es-Sâlt; the other, about five miles from the mouth of the river, and over against Jericho, now designated "El-Meshra," the Pilgrim's Bathing-Place. Boats may have been anciently used in crossing the river, but as an appliance now in going from bank to bank they are unknown. The course of the stream at times is between high banks of rock or alluvium; at other points, on one or both sides, they recede from the river, and in such cases are covered with thicket or jungle.

It is not necessary to dwell at length on the circumstances and incidents that lend such a peculiar and sacred interest to this river, or even to enumerate all of them. The Jordan was the eastern boundary of the Promised Land. Josh. i. 11. Abraham sojourned at a point where the fertile valley through which the river coursed could be seen. Gen. xiii. 3. Jacob, when he went into his long exile, crossed it with his staff alone, and recrossed it when he returned as two bands. Gen. xxxii. 10. His descendants, as they terminated their long wilderness pilgrimage, passed dry-shod through its waters. Josh. iv. 10. Elijah and Elisha successively smote it with their mantles, and it divided for their passage. 2 Kings ii. 8 and 14. Naaman dipped in it and was cleansed of his leprosy. 2 Kings v. 14. And last of all it was the stream where not only "all Judea and Jerusalem" were baptized by John (Matt. iii. 5, 6), but the Lord himself. v. 16. Here the interest of the sacred river fitly culminates. Enon, near to Salem (John iii. 23), where the Baptist in his later ministry baptized, cannot now with absolute certainty be identified. It appears, however, most probably to have been situated at a point a few miles below the ancient Bethshean, now Beisân, near or at one of the fords of the river, and where, either from the depth or quantity of water, or the nature of its banks, there were the desired facilities for the administration of baptism. Whatever the uncertainty, however, attending the site of Enon, manifold and unbroken tradition points to the ford nearly opposite Jericho, and about five miles from the Dead Sea, as the place hallowed by the baptism of the Messiah. Above and below this locality, now known, as intimated, as "the Pilgrim's Bathing-Place," the river flows through alluvial banks of considerable height, but at this point the western line of the stream forms a cove, where the strand and a convenient depth for immersion or bathing is at once reached by a gradual and easy descent. In the narrative of his expedition, Lieut. Lynch, who was an eye-witness, describes the annual ceremony of the baptism of the pilgrims. On this occasion, from 5000 to 8000 of them having come down from Jerusalem, plunged tumultuously into the stream, immersing themselves and each other three times, in the name of the Trinity. At this point he describes the river as 120 feet wide and 12 feet deep, the current dangerously swift, as the writer of this article himself discovered when bathing in the river but a few feet from the banks. Tradition locates the ancient Bethabara, "the House of the Ford or Passage," at a point near the eastern bank of the river, and opposite the Pilgrim's Bathing-Place.

Jordan, Rev. William Hull, was born in Bertie Co., N. C., Aug. 15, 1803. His mother afterwards married the Rev. Mr. Poindexter, and by him became the mother of Dr. A. M. Poindexter, and to the piety and force of character of this good woman, who consecrated her sons to God's service at their birth, is our Southern Zion indebted for two of the ablest and most eloquent ministers who have distinguished her annals. Mr. Jordan was educated at Chapel Hill, professed a hope in Christ on the 9th of December, 1823, preached his first sermon on the 25th of December of the same year, and was baptized by Rev. Reuben Lawrence, Jan. 25, 1824. It will thus be seen that Mr. Jordan was induced by the pressure of his brethren to preach before he was baptized. This has always been a source of sincere sorrow to him, but it may be doubted whether it should be, since it is said a great revival began from his preaching, spreading over several counties, and resulting in the conversion of 2000 souls. Besides serving a number of churches in the country, Mr. Jordan has been pastor of churches in Raleigh, Wilmington, Lilesville, and Wadesborough, N. C., Clarksville and Petersburg, Va., Norristown, Pa., and Sumter, S. C. He was for a long time the corresponding secretary of the Baptist State Convention; was twice agent for Wake Forest College, giving his time and money for its release from financial distress, and has worked faithfully for its prosperity as a trustee. Mr. Jordan calls himself a high-church Baptist, and has spent no small part of his life in vindicating by voice and pen Baptist and Calvinistic principles. He is a very devout man and a singularly eloquent preacher.

Joslyn, Rev. Adoniram Judson, during many years a denominational leader in Illinois, and one of the most effective preachers in the State, was born Oct. 5, 1819. He was baptized at the age of fourteen years, uniting with the Baptist church in Nunda, N. Y., where his early life had been spent. He removed to Illinois in 1838, settling at Crystal Lake, in the northern part of the State, where his first occupation was that of a farmer. Drawn to the ministry by his ardent love for the cause of Christ, he had a partial course of study with a neighboring pastor. His first pastorate was at Warrensville, where he was ordained in 1842. After two years he removed to Elgin, where he remained eleven years. In 1855 he accepted an agency for Shurtleff College, and in that form of labor, as well as in efforts of a like kind in behalf of the University of Chicago, he rendered important service in the cause of education. In November, 1856, he organized the Union Park church in Chicago, and became its first pastor, remaining in that relation three years. His health having become impaired, he returned to his old home in Elgin, and purchasing the *Gazette* in that city, entered upon journalism, holding at the same time the office of postmaster of the town; in the mean time preaching for destitute churches as his state of health would allow. The disease which had begun its inroads continued to make progress in spite of all efforts to check it. He lingered, however, until Oct. 9, 1868, when his labors and sufferings ended in rest. Mr. Joslyn was an ardent friend of reform, an outspoken temperance man, always bold, direct, and effective in his advocacy of whatever cause enlisted his zeal. In his relations with his brethren he was an acknowledged leader, with marked executive ability and rare powers of public speech.

Journal and Messenger.—The first number of a paper called the *Baptist Weekly Journal of the Mississippi Valley* was issued at Cincinnati, O., July 22, 1831. John Stevens, D.D., was the editor, and Noble S. Johnson publisher. It was a folio, 20 by 13 inches to the page, and the subscription price was $2.00 in advance or $3.00 at the end of the year. It had in three years a subscription list of 1300. In 1834 the *Cross*, the Baptist paper of Kentucky, was united with it, and it became *The Cross and Baptist Journal of the Mississippi Valley*. At the end of seven years it was removed to Columbus, and Rev. George Cole, D. A. Randall, D.D., and James Batchelder became the editors and publishers, the name being changed to *The Cross and Journal*. This name was subsequently still further changed to the *Western Christian Journal*. In 1850 *The Christian Messenger*, of Indiana, having been united with it, it was removed again to Cincinnati, and called the *Journal and Messenger*, Rev. E. D. Owen and J. L. Batchelder being the editors and publishers. In December, 1856, a stock company was formed called the Central Baptist Press Company, which bought out the interest of the former publishers, and Rev. George Cole again became editor, continuing in that capacity until 1865, when Rev. T. J. Melish succeeded him. In 1867 the form was changed from folio to quarto. In 1872, Rev. J. R. Baumes, D.D., became the editor, with Rev. W. N. Wyeth as associate editor. In 1876, having purchased all the stock and the entire interest of the paper, Rev. G. W. Lasher, D.D., became editor and proprietor, and so continues until the present time. The present form of the paper is a large quarto, 47 by 35 inches. In its circulation it ranks fourth among the Baptist papers of this country. It is devoted to the advocacy of Baptist principles, and is very enterprising in gathering denominational news.

Judd, Rev. J. T., a native of Canada, was born in Toronto Nov. 29, 1851, and became a graduate of Columbian University, D. C., in 1872, and of Crozer Theological Seminary in its full course in 1875. He was ordained at the call of the Harrisburg church Sept. 2, 1875. In this church he has remained ever since, and has succeeded where many others have failed. The church has become, after many years of painful struggling, a self-supporting body. Better still, it has developed the Christian grace of benevolence to a remarkable degree.

Judson, Adoniram, D.D., the eldest son of Adoniram and Abigail Judson, was born in Malden, Mass., Aug. 9, 1788. In the sixteenth year of his age, being sufficiently advanced in his studies, he entered the Sophomore class in Brown University, becoming a member of the institution on the 17th of August, 1804. He graduated in 1807 with the highest honors of his class. At the time of leaving college he was inclined to be skeptical in his religious opinions. The sudden death of a classmate, under circumstances of peculiar interest, was the means of arresting his thoughts and putting him upon a course of serious examination of the claims of religion to his personal attention. For the purpose of pursuing his inquiries, he was admitted as a "special student" into the Andover Theological Institution. He soon became a hopeful Christian, and was received into the fellowship of the Third Congregational church in Plymouth, Mass., of which his father was the pastor, on the

ADONIRAM JUDSON, D.D.

28th of May, 1809. Regarding himself now as not his own but the Lord's, he began to seek for light upon the pathway of his future career. The result of his prayerful deliberation was the determination reached, in February, 1810, to consecrate himself to the work of foreign missions. In the seminary he found other young men of kindred spirit, who joined with him in urging upon the Christian churches the claims of the heathen. The zeal and earnestness of these students gave power to the spirit of missions, which had already been aroused in the hearts of Christians. That honored society, the American Board of Commissioners for Foreign Missions, was formed June 28, 1810. Mr. Judson had been licensed on the 17th of May previous by the Orange Association of Congregationalist ministers, in Vermont. September 24 of this year he graduated at Andover. Soon after his graduation he was sent to England by the American Board to confer with the London Missionary Society on the matter of combining the efforts of the two societies in the work of carrying the gospel to the heathen. He embarked Jan. 1, 1811, in the ship "Packet." The vessel had not been long at sea when she was captured by the French privateer "L'Invincible Napoleon," and carried to Bayonne in France, where he was immured in a dismal dungeon. From his short confinement he was soon released, and, after various adventures, he reached England, presented his credentials, and was cordially received by the Christian friends to whom he had been commended. He and his fellow-students, Newell, Nott, and Hall, were appointed by the London Missionary Society as missionaries in India, with the expectation that their pecuniary support would be provided for by the friends of missions in America. The object for which he was sent to England having been accomplished, Mr. Judson returned to this country. The board, after mature deliberation, came to the conclusion that the wiser course to pursue was to enter upon the work of missions independently of any other organization, and they accepted as their missionaries the four young men, and pledged themselves to see that they were supported in the undertaking upon which they had embarked. Mr. Judson, with his wife, Ann Hasseltine Judson, and Messrs. Nott, Newell, Hall, and Rice, sailed Feb. 19, 1812, from Salem, Mass., and reached Calcutta the 17th of the following June. During the voyage Mr. Judson's views on the mode and subjects of baptism underwent a change, and, on reaching Serampore, he was baptized by Rev. William Ward, Sept. 6, 1812. This event severed his connection from the American Board of Commissioners for Foreign Missions, and led to the formation of the Baptist Triennial Convention, on the 18th of May, 1814, under whose patronage Mr. Judson and his Baptist associates were taken. After experiencing months of hardship, on account of the hostility of the East India Company, who opposed the establishment of his mission in India, Mr. Judson decided to commence his work among the Burmese. On the 14th of July, 1813, he reached Rangoon, and began at once the study of the language. It was a formidable task, and taxed all his powers to accomplish it. At nearly the end of his five years' residence in Rangoon a rayat was built, and opened with appropriate religious services, and Mr. Judson made this place his religious headquarters. Inquirers began to visit him, and he had the satisfaction of baptizing the first convert to the Christian faith, Moung Nau, on the 27th of June, 1819. No sooner, however, did there appear some signs of success than a spirit of opposition began to be awakened, and Mr. Judson had reason to fear that his work would be stopped by the arm of the civil power. With the hope of securing toleration, he went to Ava with Mr. Colman, and sought permission to preach the new faith in Burmah. But the king would not grant the request, and they returned to Rangoon, and continued the prosecution of their mission work regardless of the opposition which had been awakened. Mr. Judson devoted himself especially to the translation of the Scriptures and the preparation of religious tracts, to be circulated among the people.

We have now reached one of the most interesting periods of the life of Dr. Judson. Dr. Price, who had arrived at Rangoon in December, 1821, was summoned to the court of the king, in his capacity as a physician, and it was necessary that Mr. Judson should accompany him. His reception was favorable, and he had more than one opportunity to proclaim the gospel to the members of the royal family. The prospect for usefulness seemed so bright that he returned to Rangoon for Mrs. Judson, bringing her back to Ava, and began his missionary work, encouraged by the hope of greater success in his labors. But this hope was destined soon to meet with utter disappointment. War broke out between England and Burmah. Rangoon fell into the hands of the British on the 23d of May, 1824, and the tidings of its capture reached the capital two weeks after. The jealous Burman officers, regarding Dr. Price and Mr. Judson as spies, caused them to be arrested and thrown into a loathsome jail, where, for nine months, they were kept in the closest and most barbarous confinement. They were then sent to a wretched place called Oung-pen-la, where they were ordered to be put to death. The sentence, however, was not carried into execution. With the continued success of the English arms, the fears of the king and his court became so aroused that negotiations were entered into, in which Mr. Judson took a prominent part, and, as one of the results, he obtained his freedom. As soon as practicable he left Ava, and once more returned to Rangoon, and soon removed with his family to Amherst, designed henceforth to be the capital of British Burmah. For several months he was occupied with the English commissioner, Mr. Crawford, at Ava, in negotiating with the Burman government a commercial treaty. During his absence Mrs. Judson died at Amherst, Oct. 24, 1826. Dr. Judson removed to Maulmain Nov. 14, 1827, and entered once more upon his missionary work, which he carried on in Maulmain, Prome, Rangoon, and other localities, and he became especially interested in the conversion of the Karens. On April 10, 1834, he married Mrs. Sarah Boardman.

For many years Dr. Judson devoted a part of his time to the translation of the Scriptures into the Burmese language, and the compilation of a Burmese dictionary. On the last day of January, 1834, the closing page of the now wholly translated Bible was written by Dr. Judson. Many years were given to the careful revision of this work. In its completed state it is pronounced by competent judges to be nearly perfect. For several years Dr. Judson kept up his missionary labors, the blessing of God accompanying him in his toil. The failing health of Mrs. Judson forced him, in 1845, to leave Burmah for America. She died at St. Helena, where she was buried. Dr. Judson continued his voyage, and reached Boston in the month of October. During his stay in this country he was everywhere the recipient of the kindest attentions, and when, after a few months of residence in this country, he returned to his Oriental home, with the third wife, who was to share his fortunes, the prayers of thousands of Christian hearts followed him. "It was no sectarian adulation offered to a distinguished name, but rather the natural homage which Christian civilization pays to the cause of Christian philanthropy,—the instinctive admiration of an intelligent and religious people for the character of one who has proved himself a great benefactor of mankind." After this visit of Dr. Judson to his native land a few more years were allotted to him to render service to the cause to which he had given so large a part of his life. He hoped to live long enough to complete the Burmese dictionary, and was busily engaged in its preparation when he was attacked by the fever of the country, which completely prostrated him. A sea-voyage was recommended. The vessel sailed April 8, and four days after he died, and his body was committed to the deep.

Judson, Mrs. Ann Hasseltine, the first wife of Dr. Judson, was born in Bradford, Mass., Dec. 22, 1789. She received her early education at the academy in her native place. Her conversion took place when she was not far from seventeen years of age. The interest which she exhibited for religious reading of the most elevated character was remarkable in a person comparatively so young. She became a member of the Congregational church in Bradford Sept. 14, 1806. With a desire to be useful and to secure the means of an independent support, she engaged for several years, at intervals, in teaching. At the meeting of the Massachusetts Congregational Association at Bradford in June, 1810, Mr. Judson met his future wife. His persuasive words induced her to consent to share the fortunes of his missionary life, as well as to be the first American woman who "resolved to leave her friends and country to bear the gospel to the heathen in foreign climes." She was married to Mr. Judson Feb. 5, 1812. On the outward voyage to Calcutta she changed—as did her husband—her views on the mode and subjects of baptism, and was baptized with her husband by Rev. Mr. Ward. The missionary life of Mrs. Judson is so intertwined with that of Dr. Judson that the record of the latter contains all that needs to be said in that of the former. With the same fidelity and patience which characterized her husband, she applied herself to learning the language, and at the close of 1815 she states that she can both read and write it with a good degree of ease. She was the efficient helper of Dr. Judson for several years, when she was compelled by her failing health to return to her native land. On the 21st of August, 1821, she embarked for Bengal, and on reaching Calcutta took passage for England. The kindest attention was shown to

MRS. ANN HASSELTINE JUDSON.

her both in England and Scotland. She embarked on board the ship "Amity" at Liverpool, Aug. 16, 1822, and arrived at New York the 25th of the September following, and after a brief visit in Philadelphia she hastened to her old home in Bradford. The severity of a Northern climate to one who had lived so many years in the East was more than her enfeebled constitution could endure, and she was forced to make her winter home in Baltimore with her brother-in-law, Dr. Elnathan Judson. Here she rapidly improved in health, and was able to write an interesting account of the Burman mission. A few weeks of the following spring she spent among Christian friends in Washington, and then returned to Massachusetts. On the 21st of June, 1823, she embarked on her return voyage to Calcutta, having as her companions Rev. Jonathan Wade and his wife, and arrived at Rangoon on the 5th of the following December.

The narrative of the fortunes of Dr. and Mrs. Judson in Ava, to which city they proceeded soon after the arrival of the latter in Rangoon, is told in the sketch of the life of the former. The pitiful story of the dreadful sufferings of Oung-pen-la reads almost like a romance. The noble, heroic character of this most gifted woman has touched the sensibilities of thousands of Christian hearts, and the memorial of all that she did and endured for her husband will not soon be forgotten. When the anxiety and the intense and prolonged excitement connected with eighteen months of bitter trial had passed away, there came the natural reaction, and when the disease which forced her to return to her native land assumed a more violent type her weakened physical system was unable to endure the attack, and she yielded to its force. Early in the month of October, 1826, she was stricken with the fever which finally proved fatal, and died the 24th. The sad event was followed in a few months by the death of "little Maria," and together they were buried under the "Hopia" tree at Amherst. She was one of the noblest women that ever bore the Christian name. Her hallowed fame will be handed down with reverence to the last generation of Christ's followers on earth.

Judson, Prof. C. H., was born in Monroe township, Conn., in 1820. His early opportunities were limited to the common school. At eighteen his attention was powerfully turned to the subject of religion under the preaching of Rev. J. Robards. He became thoroughly convinced that the aim of man's life should be something higher than a mere subsistence. He resolved to seek the salvation of his soul, and soon he found peace in believing.

Some remarks of Mr. Robards called his attention to Locke's "Essay on the Human Understanding," which he read with eager interest, which opened up before him a new field of thought. He then resolved to secure an education. He spent two years at Hamilton Literary and Theological Institution. Afterwards he taught about three years, then he spent two years in the University of Virginia, graduating in five schools.

After leaving the university he taught in Virginia and North Carolina until 1851, when he was elected Professor of Mathematics and Natural Philosophy in Furman University, which position he held until 1861, when the war closed the university. In 1862 he was elected president of the Greenville Female College. He was recalled to his former position in the university in 1869, which he still holds.

He is singularly modest and retiring in his manners. His methodical habits fit him well for the post of treasurer of the university and of the Baptist State Convention. As a mathematician he probably has no superior in the South.

Judson, Rev. Edward, the son of Dr. Adoniram Judson, the missionary, was born at Maulmain, Burmah, Dec. 27, 1844. He graduated at Brown University in 1865. After teaching as principal of a seminary in Vermont he became tutor in Madison University, and in 1868 was appointed Professor of the Latin and Modern Languages. In 1875 he listened to the call of the church at North Orange, N. J., and was ordained pastor. He ministers to a large and intelligent audience in one of the finest meeting-houses in the State; and has seen a wonderful blessing upon his work. Between three and four hundred have been baptized by him within five years, and the denomination holds great prominence in the city of Orange. He has been often called to preach and speak before Associations, colleges, and denominational societies, and in 1880 he was elected a trustee of Brown University.

Judson, Mrs. Emily Chubbuck, was born in Eaton, N. Y., Aug. 22, 1817. Under the name of "Fanny Forrester" she wrote a number of articles in prose and poetry for the magazines of the day, which were afterwards collected together and published under the title of "Alderbrook," Boston, 1846, 2 vols. She became the third wife of Dr. Judson, being married to him June 2, 1846, and left the country the 11th of the month, reaching Calcutta the 30th of November following. Dr. Judson re-established himself in Maulmain, his wife submitting with courage to all the hardships and self-denials of a missionary's life. Dr. Judson found in her a sympathizing companion and friend, helping him to the utmost of her power in his missionary and literary work. She was not destined, however, to be long associated with him. In less than four years after their marriage he left her to enter upon that "long voyage" from which he never returned. After the death of her husband Mrs. Judson returned to this country, and died at Hamilton, N. Y., June 1, 1854. Besides "Alderbrook," she wrote an interesting biography of the second wife of Dr. Judson, Mrs. Sarah B. Judson.

Judson Female Institute, located at Marion, Ala., was first opened for students Jan. 7, 1839, with the Rev. Milo P. Jewett as president,—a position which he held for sixteen years with great distinction and a constantly increasing fame. Indeed, it is not too much to say that to Prof. Jewett, more than to any other man, the Judson is indebted for its existence and for the solid foundation on which its celebrity is laid. It is worthy of remark that the same distinguished gentleman was the first president of Vassar Female College.

After Dr. Jewett, Prof. S. S. Sherman, A.M., was president from 1855 to 1859. Prof. Noah K. Davis was president from 1859 to 1864. Prof. J. G. Nash was president in 1864–65. Prof. A. J. Battle, D.D., was president from 1865 to 1872. Prof. R. H. Rawlings was president from 1872 to 1875. Rev. M. T. Sumner, D.D., was president in 1875–76. Rev. L. R. Gwaltney, D.D., was elected president in 1876,—a position which he still holds to the universal satisfaction of the friends of that famous institution of learning. There have been but three presidents of the board of trustees of the Judson Institute,—Gen. E. D. King, for twenty-three years; Deacon W. W. Wyatt, for four years; and Hon. Porter King, from 1868 to this time. The Judson, one of the oldest, is confessedly one of the best, female colleges in the United States. While it does not neglect solid and thorough education, it has always given special attention to the esthetic branches, and as a consequence has gained great reputation for the accomplishments which it bestows upon and weaves into the character of young ladies who are educated under its management. Its buildings and property are worth at least $75,000. It reports annually to the Baptist Convention of Alabama.

Judson, Mrs. Sarah Boardman, the second wife of Dr. Judson, was born in Alstead, N. H., Nov. 4, 1803, and was the daughter of Ralph and Abiah Hall. At an early age she became a member of the First Baptist church in Salem, Mass., then under the pastoral charge of Rev. Dr. Bolles. Her thoughts began, soon after her conversion, to be turned towards the condition of the perishing heathen, and she longed to go forth and tell the story of a Saviour's love to those who were "sitting in darkness." While cherishing such desires as these she was introduced to George Dana Boardman, and found in him one whose tastes and wishes were like her own. Shortly before their departure from this country they were united in marriage, and took passage in the ship "Asia" for Calcutta, reaching the place of their destination Dec. 13, 1825, where they remained until March, 1827, and then proceeded to Amherst, at which they stayed for a few weeks, and then went to Maulmain to enter upon their missionary work in that place. Here, among some things to try their faith and others to encourage them, she continued a faithful helper to her devoted husband. Under date of Jan. 1, 1828, he writes, "Mrs. Boardman is now surrounded by a group of Burman girls, and is delighted with her employment." When it was decided to commence a station at Tavoy, in order that Mr. Boardman might be brought into closer contact with the Karens, she entered into the plan with all her heart. Again her husband writes under date of Aug. 17, 1828, describing the manner in which the Sabbath was observed, "After family worship and breakfast Mrs. Boardman and myself, with the Chinese

Christians, have worship, and a printed sermon is read. Mrs. Boardman is engaged in the afternoon in giving religious instruction to the scholars and domestics." A year from this date came the revolt of Tavoy, and Mrs. Boardman, with George, hastened away, amid many perils, to a place of safety at Maulmain, her husband joining her in a few days. They returned early the next October to the scene of their labors in Tavoy. An alarming illness of Mrs. Boardman, early in 1830, awakened the fears of her friends that she might soon be taken away. She rallied at length, and was able to resume her work for a time, but the state of her health was such that it was thought best that she should make a temporary home in Maulmain. After some months she returned again to Tavoy, and accompanied her husband on his last journey to the villages of the Karens, and was with him to close his eyes in death on the 11th of February, 1831.

Mrs. Boardman, after the death of her husband, continued to prosecute her missionary work as her health and strength permittted. On the 10th of June, 1834, she became the wife of Dr. Judson, and proved a most worthy successor of her who had so deservedly won his respect and love. For a little more than eleven years they shared each other's confidence and affection. After the birth of her last child, in December, 1844, she became the victim of a chronic disease, and the physicians decided that nothing would save her life but a long voyage. She embarked with her husband and three children April 26, 1845. Some encouraging symptoms were apparent in the early part of the voyage, but they proved deceptive, and she died on shipboard, in the port of St. Helena, Sept. 1, 1845. Mrs. Judson's knowledge of the Burmese language was singularly accurate. She translated the New Testament into the Peguan language, and the "Pilgrim's Progress" into Burmese. Dr. Judson, in the warmest terms, gave his testimony to her great worth. No one can read those charming lines of his commencing

"We part on this green islet, love,"

without feeling that hers was a character of singular grace and beauty. She was the mother of Dr. Boardman, the honored pastor of the First Baptist church of Philadelphia.

Judson University, located at Judsonia, White Co., Ark., was founded by some self-sacrificing Baptists, under the leadership of Prof. M. R. Forey, formerly of Chicago University, who became its first president. It was chartered in 1871, suitable buildings were erected, and an able Faculty organized. In 1874, Prof. Forey resigned, and Rev. Benjamin Thomas, D.D., late of Ohio, was elected in his place. Dr. Thomas continued to discharge the duties of the position until 1880. He was succeeded by Rev. R. S. James, M.D., a distinguished educator, whose enthusiasm has infused new life into the enterprise. The institution is yet young, but under its present able management bids fair to become permanently successful. The location is healthy, and it is surrounded by a thrifty population and superior lands.

Justice, Rev. T. B.—A great friend to missions is this venerable man, who was born in Henderson Co., N. C., July 27, 1813; was baptized by Rev. Benjamin King in August, 1835; ordained in 1842; has frequently been moderator of the Green River and other Associations. A man of faith and fervor, and greatly beloved.

Justification is not regeneration. A new heart lifts the affections from sinful objects, keeps them, by the aid of divine grace, from an immoderate love for proper earthly things, and fixes them supremely upon Jesus. It is not sanctification. It is a state in which holy principles, planted in the soul at the new birth, are cultivated and strengthened by the Spirit of God, until the disciple of Christ is fitted for the church in glory. It is not pardon. Barabbas, guilty of sedition and murder, was forgiven and set at liberty by Pilate. But no intelligent man would have said that he was justified by the governor of Judea when he was released from prison. Pardon and justification are great but widely differing privileges.

In justification the law underlies everything. It has been broken. and it must be satisfied. It was inscribed upon the human conscience by the Creator. The Saviour's version is no doubt the one received by Adam and revealed by Moses: "Thou shalt love the Lord thy God with all thy heart, and with all thy soul, and with all thy mind; . . . thou shalt love thy neighbor as thyself."—Matt. xxii. 37, 39. This law can never be abrogated or modified: "Till heaven and earth pass, one jot or one tittle shall in no wise pass from the law till all be fulfilled." Its requirements must be met to the very letter before a man can be justified, and without justification no one can enter heaven.

The judge who pronounces the sentence of justification is God the Father. "It is God that justifieth, who is he that condemneth? It is Christ that died, yea, rather, that is risen again, who is even at the right hand of God, who also maketh intercession for us."—Rom. viii. 33, 34. From this we learn that the Saviour, as advocate, moves the Chief Justice of the universe to give his decision of justification, and that the First Person of the Trinity, on hearing his appeals, pronounces the justification of all believers.

Forgiveness seems to be the special work of Christ, as the bestowment of the new birth is the peculiar office of the Holy Spirit. He gave the price of the soul, in obedience and sufferings, to the eternal Judge, the Vindicator of the holy law, and, after receiving this consideration of submission and dying throes, as a holy Jehovah he justifies all who receive Christ. The Saviour, who presented the redemption price, turns to those who have believed, and says, "I forgive you." Hence it is written, "Him hath God exalted with his right hand to be a Prince and a Saviour, for to give repentance to Israel, and forgiveness of sins."—Acts v. 31. The Father, who receives the payment of the debt, justifies the soul; the Son, who made it for men without a claim upon him, forgives them.

Christ is the occasion and the sole cause of our justification. The word צֶדֶק in the Old Testament, translated righteousness, and $\delta\iota\kappa\alpha\iota\sigma\acute{\upsilon}\nu\eta$, its representative in the New, describe Christ's grandest gift to his redeemed children. He imputes or reckons his righteousness to every one of them, and it becomes their own just as really as if they had "wrought it out" for themselves.

By the righteousness of Christ we are to understand his complete submission to the precepts and penalties of the law of God, his perfect earthly obedience, and his unparalleled anguish; these he places to the credit of each member of his elect family.

The law we have already described was only kept by Adam and Eve before their fall. The purest unregenerate man on earth would not claim to have observed it, and if he did the pretense would be baseless. The holiest saint of the entire Christian family, though stained with the blood of his own martyrdom, never fully kept the law, one breach of which, though no greater than a jot or a tittle, is death: "For whosoever shall keep the whole law, and yet offend in one point, he is guilty of all."—James ii. 10. Like a vessel anchored near the shore in a hurricane with one weak link in her anchor-chain, which breaks in the moment of greatest need, and destroys the ship, so one guilty act is an offense against the majesty of God and against his whole law, and it ruins the righteousness of its perpetrator. If one man had all the excellences of the whole American people from the landing of the Pilgrims or the first settlement of the Cavaliers, and, in addition, the good qualities of all the rest of Adam's children, past and present, there would be thousands of broken links in the chain of his righteousness, and the ship of his hopes would surely be dashed to pieces. "Therefore by the deeds of the law (human performances) there shall no flesh be justified in his sight."—Rom. iii. 20. Jesus became our substitute to obey the law and suffer its penalty. When God arrested the descending hand of Abraham, about to kill Isaac, he seized a ram caught by Providence in a thicket near by, and offered it up instead of his son; its blood was spilled instead of his, its life was sacrificed for his, its body was given to the flames which would have reduced Isaac's to ashes. And so "Christ also hath once suffered for sins, the just for the unjust, that he might bring us to God."—1 Peter iii. 18. He took our place before the violated law, and with it our guilt and pains, and he ended both, and gives the righteousness he acquired to every saint.

Paul says, "For he (the Father) hath made him (the Son) to be sin for us, who knew no sin, that we might be made the righteousness of God in him."—2 Cor. v. 21. The word $\dot{\alpha}\mu\alpha\rho\tau\iota\alpha\nu$, translated sin, means, in its New Testament use, sin, vice, wickedness. And it is without doubt properly translated in 2 Cor. v. 21. He was made sin, not by any guilty act of his own, but because the Lord laid on him the iniquities of us all. It was this that made the Father abandon him in death, and it was this that overwhelmed the glorious sufferer with horror as he realized the desertion. And just as he was made sin for us we are "made the righteousness of God in him." He creates a mutual exchange between himself and his redeemed ones; he takes their guilt, and they become the righteousness of God ($\delta\iota\kappa\alpha\iota\sigma\acute{\upsilon}\nu\eta$ $\Theta\epsilon\sigma\tilde{\upsilon}$), "For Christ is the end ($\tau\acute{\epsilon}\lambda o\varsigma$) of the law for righteousness (justification) to every one that believeth,"—Rom. x. 4,—that is to say, he has obeyed all its precepts, and suffered all its pains, for every trusting disciple, and he gives him this divine righteousness; this is "the righteousness of God, which is by faith of Jesus Christ, unto all and upon all them that believe."—Rom. iii. 22; of which the Psalmist speaks when it is said, "David also describeth the blessedness of the man to whom God imputeth righteousness without works."—Rom. iv. 6. The great apostle declares that this righteousness justifies without any of our own works: "Therefore we conclude that a man is justified by faith without the deeds of the law." —Rom. iii. 28.

In the New Testament, Christ and his people are represented as being one. Various figures are used to describe this union, but the most remarkable is that of a human body. "Now," says Paul, "ye are the body of Christ and members in particular." 1 Cor. xii. 27. Jesus is the head of this heaven-favored body, and, as a consequence, the acts of the head belong to the whole body, and its privileges, powers, and sacred attributes. According to this teaching Christ's obedience and death are as much ours as they are his. Hence Paul says, "For the love of Christ constraineth us, because we thus judge, that if one died for all, then were all dead."—2 Cor. v. 14. It follows from this undoubted and blessed union that we all died with Christ upon the cross, that the same spotless robe that belongs to the head flows down in unstained beauty and purity over the whole body of Christ, of all names, ages, and worlds.

It is no wonder then that Paul says, "There is, therefore, now no condemnation to them who are in Christ Jesus." "It is God that justifieth, who is he that condemneth?" "Who shall lay anything to the charge of God's elect?"—Rom. viii. 1, 33, 34. The righteousness of the holiest archangel is but the obedience and purity of a creature. The righteousness of a true believer is the immaculate robe of Immanuel, the righteousness of God, which shall for ever hide each moral defect, mortal weakness, and guilty stain. This robe envelops the soul and justifies it through the instrumentality of faith. As the hawser coming from a great steamship, when fastened to a dismasted and helpless vessel, gives her all the force of her powerful engines, and saves her, so faith binds the soul to Jesus, and gives it his justifying righteousness; and for this reason it is written, "Being justified by faith, we have peace with God, through our Lord Jesus Christ."—Rom. v. 1. Faith is one of the fruits of the Holy Spirit in the soul (Gal. v. 22), and whatever merit there is in it belongs to the Comforter, as the whole merit of our righteousness is Christ's. So that every ransomed man, as he enters the eternal world and examines his entire religious exercises, will feel and affirm, "By the grace of God I am what I am;" and his chief glory will be, "Jehovah *is* our righteousness."—Jer. xxiii. 6.

"Jehovah Tsidkenu (our righteousness)! my treasure and boast;
Jehovah Tsidkenu! I ne'er can be lost;
In thee I shall conquer by flood and by field,
My cable, my anchor, my breastplate and shield."

Jutten, David B., D.D., present pastor of the Sixteenth Street Baptist church of New York, was born in that city Jan. 7, 1844. His parents, Benjamin and Emma Jutten, were Baptists. His early education was received in the public schools. In 1859, at the age of fifteen, he united with the Berean Baptist church, having been baptized by the late Dr. Dowling. Soon after his membership was changed to the Bloomingdale Baptist church, now merged into the Central. From this church he received a license to preach in 1862. He entered Madison University in May of the same year, from which he graduated in 1867, and from the theological seminary in 1870. During this time he supplied for short periods, with acceptance, three churches, one in Connecticut, one in New Jersey, and one in New York State. After graduation, and in the same year, he was called to the E Street Baptist church, Washington, D. C. Here he passed three years in successful work.

In 1873 he received a unanimous call from the Sixteenth Street church of New York City, after having preached one Sabbath with great acceptance. The morning sermon on "The Office of the Spirit" indicated a man who realized the source of power in the church. In June, 1873, the new pastor was installed. Dr. Jutten preaches generally without notes. He is a man of large sympathy, and exhibits toward all a truly charitable spirit. He gives special attention to pastoral work. It is his endeavor to call upon every member of the church once a year, holding with all religious conversation and offering prayer with the family in accordance with the good old custom. He has been greatly blessed in his labors during the past five years, and is still prospering. During this time there have been added to the church about 300 members, of whom more than 200 have been received by baptism.

K.

Kalamazoo College.—For the beginning of the enterprise which resulted in the establishment of Kalamazoo College we must go back to the year 1829. In November of that year Thomas Ward Merrill, a graduate of Waterville College in the class of 1825, having finished the course of theological study at Newton in 1828, reached Michigan, seeking, as he then wrote, "to promote the intellectual as well as moral advancement of the people of the Territory of Michigan." He was the son of that Rev. Daniel Merrill who, in Sedgwick, Me., in 1805, became a Baptist, and was accompanied in his adoption of Baptist views by a large part of the Congregational church of which he had been many years pastor. The son was like his father in very hearty devotion to Baptist principles.

In the prosecution of his plans he opened a classical school in Ann Arbor. It, being the only one of the kind, as is supposed, in the Territory, was patronized by Detroit and the other early settlements, and enjoyed prosperity.

From it the next season, July, 1830, Mr. Merrill issued, and traversed the Territory with a petition, of which he was the author, asking the Territorial Legislature to charter an institution under the name of the Michigan and Huron Institute, and secure its control to the Baptist denomination by prescribing that three-fifths of its trustees should be of that faith. The object of the petition was favorably considered in the Legislature, but finally, meeting with objections from those opposed to its denominational features, the bill was laid over to the next session.

Meanwhile, under the influence of those who had opposed it, an academy was incorporated and started at Ann Arbor, of which Mr. Merrill was urged to take charge. But feeling that his Christian and denominational aims and hopes would thus be compromised, he declined.

And the same season, concluding that the eastern shore of the peninsula was to prove uncongenial to the growth of his cherished enterprise, he resolved to transfer it to the western shore. And as Kalamazoo was a forest through which but the smoke of one log cabin rose, he sought the older settlement of Prairie Ronde, among whose first settlers he assisted in building a house for schools and meetings, and occupied it for those uses as early as the winter of 1830-31.

The question now was where to drive the stake for the permanent institution, and how to purchase lands for its use, for it was then the design that it should incorporate the manual-labor system. And another question was how to reappear before the Legislature and secure the act of incorporation.

Fortunately the practical wisdom, the generous liberality, and the intelligent Christian citizenship of Caleb Eldred stood now waiting to ally themselves with the high aims and the unconquerable tenacity of Thomas W. Merrill. Judge Eldred was then just dragging his surveyor's chain through the untrodden grasses and the unbent bushes of the Western prairies and openings, and encamping with enthusiastic admiration beneath the majestic forests and beside the miniature lakes of Western Michigan. And among the waymarks which he was setting up, some of the first were those which, in his own mind, designated the places where his children should be baptized, his neighbors have their house of prayer and praise, and his denomination their Hamilton of Christian learning, for he had come from where the long shadow of the Hamilton of Hascall and of Kendrick had swept over him.

In the autumn of 1831 there were to be seen traces of these two pioneers coming together and planning methods by which to raise money to purchase land

![Kalamazoo College]

KALAMAZOO COLLEGE.

for the occupancy of the contemplated institution. And an appeal to the benevolent Baptists of the East was agreed upon. Accordingly, Mr. Merrill visited the meeting of the Michigan Association at Pontiac in September of that year, and secured the recommendation of that body for him to visit the East on such an agency. A month later he was at the Baptist Convention of the State of New York, and received a hearty commendation of his object signed by Elon Galusha, John Peck, C. M. Fuller, Archibald Maclay, Charles G. Somers, Jonathan Going, B. T. Welch, B. M. Hill, Philander D. Gillette, and others.

So far as appears, the first subscriptions paid in this work, except what Mr. Merrill paid in defraying his own expenses, were seven ten-dollar ones from these seven honored and ever to be remembered names: Jonathan Going, Nathan Caswell, James Wilson, John H. Harris, Byron & Green,

William Colgate, and E. Withington. This money went to purchase the property first bought for the institute in Bronson (now Kalamazoo).

Returning from this agency in 1832, Mr. Merrill, Judge Eldred, and others renewed the petition to the Legislature for the incorporation of the institution, under the name of the Michigan and Huron Institute, and without any provisions for denominational control, suggesting, however, the names of the petitioners and others as trustees. These names embraced the early ministers and active brethren of the Baptist denomination then resident in the Territory.

The bill, introduced in answer to the petition, had to work its way through some objections, but receiving the helping hand of Judge Manning, in addition to the watchful efforts of the petitioners, it passed, and, after lodging some time in the hands of the governor, was helped over his scruples by a committee, consisting of John Booth, F. P. Browning, and T. W. Merrill, and was finally approved April 22, 1833.

The first president of the board of trustees was Caleb Eldred, who for twenty-five years worthily filled the office, and was relieved of it only after his repeated and earnest solicitations.

As the charter did not locate the institute, a tedious work awaited the trustees in determining that important matter. There were long journeys over primitive roads to meetings in Clinton, Troy, Ann Arbor, Comstock, Whitmansville, and elsewhere, often resulting in a failure of the necessary quorum, and sometimes issuing in nearly a deadlock of rival contestants for the prize. But at length, in the autumn of 1835, Providence gave the weary fledgling a nest in Kalamazoo, through the subscription of $2500 by residents there, and the purchase of 115 acres of land in what is now the south part of the village, which property was afterwards converted into the site and building accommodations now occupied on the west side of the village, where, through favoring providences, no complaint of ineligibility has ever arisen, or can ever arise, to be among the embarrassments of the enterprise. Twenty years later the adjoining site was secured through the liberal and timely supply of $1500 by Mrs. H. E. Thompson; and the beautiful and commodious building which now graces it was entered and dedicated in the autumn of 1859.

No effort was made to endow the institution, nor was any debt suffered to accrue from its operation during the first twenty years of its history. Its expense for instruction was not large, as its course of study was chiefly preparatory. Moreover, the inferior condition of the public schools, and their lack of all high school facilities, left the people quite ready to extend to a good select school a remunerative patronage. And much of the time other corporations assumed the current expenses of the institute; for a while the State University supported it as one of its branches, and afterwards the Baptist Convention adopted it as the literary helpmate for its theological education. Yet the property of the institute always remained distinct, and its board of trustees allowed no intermission of their meetings and controlling care.

The privileges of the institute were free alike to both sexes from the first, except during, and for a little after, the time that the Baptist Convention paid the teachers; and, indeed, throughout this period, rooms were supplied free of rent, in which a school for young women was maintained.

In February, 1855, the charter was amended so as to confer full college powers, the name changed to Kalamazoo College, and the corps of instructors enlarged so as to meet the demands of the college course, which was required by the charter to be of as high grade as that of the State University.

The successive principal teachers from the establishment of the school till it became a college were Mr. Marsh, Walter Clark, Nathaniel A. Balch, David Alden, William Dutton, and James A. B. Stone. The last named of these had charge of the school from 1843, and, with the entrance of the institution on its career as a college, he was appointed its president, and remained until 1864. Mrs. Stone was associated with him during all these years.

From 1864 to 1867, Rev. John M. Gregory, LL.D., was president, and, after an interval of more than a year, was followed, in 1868, by the present president, Rev. Kendall Brooks, D.D.

In 1870 the "ladies' course," which prescribed a somewhat lower range of studies than the regular college course, was discontinued, and since that time both sexes have had equal admission to all the courses of study.

In 1853 the sum of $20,000 was secured by subscription towards the endowment of the college, and, in 1858, $10,000 for the new building. A few years later the sum of $30,000 was subscribed, and, immediately after the election of President Brooks, $50,000.

The ground and buildings occupied by the college are not wholly its property. The Baptist Convention of the State of Michigan owns the older edifice, used for students' dormitories, containing also the library and two halls for the literary societies of the young men. The new building, designated at its dedication as Kalamazoo Hall, in recognition of the fact that the expense of its erection was mostly paid by citizens of Kalamazoo, contains chapel, recitation-rooms, apparatus-room, and music-room. The whole real estate is estimated to be worth $100,000. The present endowment is about $80,000, of which a part is not now productive. There is nominally one endowed professorship of $10,000, established by Mr. Merrill, who also offered $15,000 as scholarships, the income to be given to students preparing for the ministry in Baptist churches. Of the whole sum, however ($25,000), only one thousand dollars was paid in cash, and the paper in which the rest was paid is not at present yielding any income. It is hoped that both endowments will become productive ere long.

Among those who have held professorships in the college the following may properly be named: William L. Eaton, Samuel Graves, D.D., Edward Olney, LL.D., Daniel Putnam, Edward Anderson, H. L. Wayland, D.D., Silas Bailey, D.D., LL.D., James A. Clark, Samuel Brooks, D.D., William C. Morey, Nathan S. Burton, D.D.

Honorary degrees have been very sparingly given. Only four men have received the degree of Doctor of Divinity, and three that of Doctor of Laws, from the college, during the first twenty-five years of its history.

We rejoice, in looking through the history of the college, that we are brought into something of the presence of an indwelling God. Revivals of religion have not been strange things in its history. For a long time nearly every year witnessed the cloud of God's saving and consecrating presence standing at the door of the institution. Some years the companies that have joined themselves to the Lord in covenant have been large. Fifty in a year have entered our Baptist family through the appointed door, while many more confessed Christ otherwise or elsewhere; and not a few have owed their call to the Christian ministry to these seasons of quickening from spiritual death.

Kalloch, Rev. Amariah, was born in 1808 at Warren, Me. He was one of the foremost ministers in his native State from 1830 to 1849, when he sailed for California. There having contracted a fever, and unwilling to remain quiet until fully restored, he set out upon a mission from Sacramento to Placerville, where he died in 1850. He belonged to a family of preachers well known in New England. He had great natural talents, and was distinguished for his piety, enthusiasm, and marked success in revival preaching and pastoral work. In 1832 he was ordained at Thomaston, where he organized a church at a small hamlet four miles distant, at Rockland. The church increased to 400 members under his oversight. In 1847 he was settled at Augusta, from which he removed to California. He was universally beloved. Many hundreds were baptized as the fruit of his labors.

Kane, Chaplain James J., U. S. Navy, was born in the city of Ottawa, Canada, Oct. 18, 1837; was sent to Europe at an early age; spent two years at a French, and four years at a leading English, college; in consequence of ill health was compelled to give up his studies, and went on a voyage to the Arctic regions. He followed the sea for several years, rising to the command of a vessel. In 1857 joined the Methodist Episcopal church. In 1861 was baptized in the Delaware River by Rev. Jos. Perry, pastor of the Mariners' Baptist Bethel of Philadelphia. Feeling called to preach the gospel, Mr. Kane made preparation to enter upon a theological course at Lewisburg, Pa. The civil war breaking out, he entered the naval service as an officer, and during the four years of the conflict performed the additional duties of a chaplain.

At the close of the war he entered the theological department of Lewisburg, Pa., and graduated in regular course in the class of 1867. He was ordained to the ministry the year previous in the Mariners' Baptist Bethel, in order to file his application for a chaplaincy in the navy.

By the special request of Admiral D. G. Farragut, Mr. Kane was commissioned as chaplain in June, 1868; has served in various ships and stations since that time. In 1870 he spent one year at Harvard Law-School. Chaplain Kane is the author of the work, "Adrift on the Black Wild Tide."

Kansas Baptist State Convention was organized in 1860, before Kansas became a State, and when there were only about 40 churches in the Territory. Its first officers were Rev. I. S. Kalloch, president; Rev. L. A. Alderson, vice-president; and Rev. E. Alward, secretary.

In 1861, Rev. A. Perkins, D.D., was present as pastor of Atchison church, and 26 Baptist ministers were reported as residing in the Territory, and about 1200 members.

In 1864 the churches were reported as numbering 54, and the additions during the previous year 191 persons.

In 1866 Leavenworth was represented by Rev. Winfield Scott, Ottawa by Rev. Isaac Sawyer, and Lawrence by Rev. E. D. Bentley. Rev. J. G. Pratt and C. Journeycake were delegates from the Delaware Reserve.

In 1868, Rev. C. A. Bateman was general missionary, and the names of Deacon S. J. Nugent, Prof. J. R. Downer, Hon. J. S. Emery, Rev. Robert Atkinson, and Rev. H. K. Stimson are reported among the active delegates at the Convention.

In 1869, Prof. Downer made an interesting report concerning church building along the line of the Kansas Pacific Railroad.

In 1870, Rev. Winfield Scott resigned his charge at Leavenworth to do general missionary work throughout the State. Judge Emery stated in his report on statistics that there were in the State 146 Baptist churches, of which 22, with a membership of 350 persons, had been organized during the year, and that of 84 ordained Baptist ministers in the State, and 9 licentiates, all but 2 or 3 were proclaiming the gospel. The aggregate membership at this time was about 6087, and great progress was made in erecting houses of worship.

In 1871 it was reported that nearly $60,000 had been expended in beginning or completing church edifices during the preceding year, and that the State contained 179 churches, with an aggregate of 7000 members. M. A. Clark was present this year as Sunday-school missionary for the State.

In 1872, Rev. Robert Atkinson was general missionary of the Home Mission Society, and Rev. F. M. Ellis, of Lawrence, was secretary of the Convention, and Deacon E. J. Nugent, of Ottawa, its treasurer. Mr. Atkinson reported that 3 general missionaries and 19 missionary pastors had been employed in the State during the year, at an expense of $6750, which was appropriated by the Home Mission Society for the purpose, the amount raised in Kansas for State purposes being included in this amount.

The decade from 1870 to 1880 began with a desire for church edifices far beyond the ability of the people to erect, and it had a very demoralizing effect on the churches, which were crippled greatly on account of it. Rev. E. Gunn labored faithfully as the district secretary of the Home Mission Society during a portion of this time, but under very great disadvantages. In 1879 and 1880, Rev. James French, who had been stationed at Denver, Colorado, as district secretary of the Home Mission Society over a large territory, including the mountain regions, was directed to include with his other work the attempt to liquidate the debts on Kansas church edifices. This, with the aid of pastors and others, was accomplished, and a new method of co-operation with the Home Mission Society was successfully inaugurated; so that with the beginning of a new decade, in 1880, and with a general missionary highly esteemed by the churches (Rev. Granville Gates), and Prof. Ward, of the State Agricultural College, as corresponding secretary, the Baptists of Kansas occupy a more favorable position than ever before. According to the "Year-Book" of 1881, the Baptists of Kansas had

Associations	21
Churches	441
Ordained ministers	309
Members	17,648

Karens.—See article on BURMAH.

Karen Theological Seminary.—Early in the history of our missions the conclusion was reached that the mission churches must be taught, as soon as possible, to be self-sustaining, and that a native ministry must be trained to take the pastoral oversight of them. The ministry thus raised up must be educated, and the necessary facilities furnished to secure the needed instruction. At the annual meeting of the board of the Missionary Union, in Albany, in 1843, Dr. Wayland, as chairman of a committee on the education of native teachers and preachers, reported in favor of the establishment of a theological school for the Karens. Immediate steps were taken to carry into effect this recommendation, and Rev. Dr. Binney and his wife sailed from this country in November, 1843, to take charge of the new institution. The location first selected for it was in the neighborhood of Maulmain, and it was named Newton. The first term was opened May 28, 1845, and thirty-six students were in attendance at the close of the first year. For the next few years the school was successful under the supervision of Dr. Binney. In September, 1850, Dr. Binney was obliged to leave, with Mrs. Binney, who was ill, for the United States, and the institution was left in charge of Rev. N. Harris, and in 1853 it was placed under the care of Rev. J. H. Vinton. In consequence of the ravages of the cholera, it was suspended at the close of the first term. When it was reorganized, in 1854, Dr. Wade was selected to take charge of it until the return of Dr. Binney, who resumed his old position May 25, 1860, the institution having been removed from Maulmain to Rangoon. In 1863, Rev. C. H. Carpenter was added to the corps of teachers, and Rev. D. W. Smith in 1865. After six years of faithful service, Dr. Binney was obliged again to return to this country on account of the impaired health of Mrs. Binney. For some two years Messrs. Carpenter and Smith had the oversight of the institution, and then Dr. Binney once more returned to his post, Mr. Smith retiring to Henthada, to fill the place made vacant by the removal of Mr. Thomas to Bassein. From the opening of the institution, in 1843, to Sept. 30, 1867, the sum of $12,330.16 had been expended in meeting its wants. The late Prof. Ruggles, of Washington, has been a liberal donor to the funds of the seminary, and to him more than to any other person is to be attributed, under God, its present prosperity. Mr. Smith returned to the seminary in 1869 and remained for a short time, and then resumed his duties at Henthada. For the past few years the institution has done its work with success. Dr. Binney's health failing, he left Rangoon Nov. 14, 1876. The seminary for more than a year was under the care of native teachers. Mr. Smith, who had again been placed on the corps of instructors, reached Rangoon in the latter part of 1876, soon after the departure of Dr. Binney, and at once entered upon the duties of his office as the presiding officer of the seminary. Its affairs are in a hopeful and prosperous condition, and the happiest results may be predicted for it in the future.

Kay, Robert G., was born in Culpeper Co., Va., Sept. 10, 1804. About the year 1825 he was converted, and united with a Baptist church in Christian County of which the lady whom he married, Miss Cynthia A. Burruss, and who survives him, was already a member. In October, 1833, he removed with his family to Illinois and settled at Payson, where he resided for more than forty years upon the same homestead. From this farm his family of eleven children, as they successively reached manhood and womanhood, went forth to do their life-work. Among these children was Mrs. E. P. Scott, well known as formerly a missionary, with her husband, Rev. E. P. Scott, in Assam. Mr. Kay always took an active interest in all public questions, but it was in the name of Christ that his energies were chiefly enlisted. Here he loved to bestow his prayers, his labors, and gifts. In donations he sometimes seemed almost prodigal, yet what he gave was always returned to him in larger measure. He was one of the constituent members of the Payson Baptist church at its organization, in 1834; was chosen to the deaconship in 1836, and continued in that office until his death. The Sabbath-school of the church was organized in 1840; he was its first superintendent, and while he lived continued to labor in the school either in this or in some other capacity. He also had an active share in the organization of the Quincy Baptist Association. His death occurred at Payson, Adams Co., Ill., May 12, 1877.

Keach, Rev. Benjamin, was born in Stokehaman, England, Feb. 29, 1640. He found peace through Christ in his fifteenth year; and being unable to discover infant baptism or baptism by sprinkling in the Bible, and being fully satisfied that every believer should be immersed, he was baptized after the Saviour's example by John Russel, and united with a neighboring Baptist church. This community, perceiving his remarkable talents, encouraged him, when he was eighteen years old, to exercise his gifts as a minister.

At first he was an Arminian about the extent of the atonement and free-will, but the reading of the Scriptures and the conversation of those who knew the will of God more perfectly relieved him from both errors. In 1668, in the twenty-eighth year of his age, he was ordained pastor of the church of Horsleydown, Southwark, London. The congregation increased so rapidly after Mr. Keach became pastor, that they had repeatedly to enlarge their house of worship.

Mr. Keach soon became a famous disputant on the Baptist side; he had taken Richard Baxter in hand, to the serious injury of the bishop of Kidderminster, and others had felt his heavy blows.

The Rev. John Tredwell, of Lavingham, a friend of Mr. Keach, was blessed in his ministry by the conversion of several vicious persons, who united with his church; this stirred up the indignation of the Rev. Wm. Burkitt, the commentator, a neighbor of Mr. Tredwell, who cast many unjust reflections upon the Baptists and their doctrines. Mr. Tredwell wrote Mr. Burkitt giving some reasons why he should abandon the unchristian course he was pursuing. Mr. Burkitt, at a time when Mr. Tredwell and his people were gathered in the sanctuary for public worship, with a number of his parishioners, entered the meeting-house, and demanded that Mr. Tredwell and his church should hear his view of the points in dispute. Mr. Tredwell, taken aback somewhat by "such a riotous and tumultuous challenge," agreed to let him speak against Baptist beliefs and usages, provided that he should have an opportunity to reply. For nearly two hours Mr. Burkitt sustained infant baptism, and then he and his "riotous company departed without giving Mr. Tredwell an opportunity of making any return, except to a few of his own

REV. BENJAMIN KEACH.

persuasion that were left behind." Mr. Burkitt speedily published the substance of the address so rudely intruded upon the Baptist minister and his people. Mr. Keach, as a valiant defender of the faith, was invited to reply to Mr. Burkitt's arguments, which he did effectively in "The Rector Rectified and Corrected." Mr. Burkitt was rector of Dedham.

He was challenged by some Episcopal ministers to discuss baptism at Gravesend, near London. As he went to that place in a boat with some friends, he incidentally alluded to the proposed meeting in a way that permitted a stranger, an Episcopal minister, to know that he was Mr. Keach. This person attacked him about infant baptism, and received such a complete drubbing that as soon as the boat touched land he started for his Episcopal brethren and informed them of the arguments which Mr. Keach would use and of his method of putting them. The result of the interview between Mr. Keach's fellow-traveler in the Gravesend boat and his brethren was that they went away as quickly as possible, leaving Mr. Keach without an antagonist.

Mr. Keach was often in prison for preaching, and his life was frequently in danger. Some cavalry sent down to Buckinghamshire to suppress the religious meetings of Dissenters found Mr. Keach preaching, and swore that they would kill him. He was seized and bound and laid on the earth, and four of the troopers were ready to trample him to death with their horses; but just as they were going to put spurs to their horses an officer who perceived their object rode up and stopped them. He was taken to prison, from which he obtained a release after suffering great hardships.

In 1664 he wrote "The Child's Instructor." For the heresies against the Episcopal Church in the little work he was arrested and bound over under heavy penalties to appear at court. The assizes began at Aylesbury Oct. 8, 1664. The judge was Lord Chief Justice Hyde, afterwards Lord Clarendon, who acted like Jeffreys at the "Bloody Assizes." He abused Mr. Keach outrageously, he threatened the jury, and he evidently wanted to have Mr. Keach executed if he could terrify him into making some unwise statements. The jury brought in a verdict that Mr. Keach was guilty in part. And when asked to explain their verdict the foreman said, "In the indictment he is charged with these words, 'When the thousand years shall be expired, then shall all the rest of the *devils* be raised'; but in the book it is, 'Then shall the rest of the dead be raised.'" The judge informed the jury that they could bring him in guilty of all the indictments but that sentence. They brought in the prompted verdict. And immediately the judge said: "Benjamin Keach, you are here convicted for writing, printing, and publishing a seditious and schismatical book, for which the court's judgment is that you go to jail for a fortnight without bail, and the next Saturday stand upon the pillory at Aylesbury in the open market for the space of two hours, with a paper upon your head with this inscription, 'For writing, printing, and publishing a schismatical book entitled "The Child's Instructor, or a New and Easy Primer,"'" and the next Thursday to stand in the same manner and for the same time in the market of Winslow; and then your book shall be openly burnt before your face by the common hangman in disgrace of you and your doctrine. And you shall forfeit to the king's majesty the sum of twenty pounds; and shall remain in jail until you find sureties for your good behavior and appearance at the next assizes, there to renounce your doctrines and make such public submission as shall be enjoined upon you." The sheriff was as rigorous in executing this infamous sentence as the judge was insolent in pronouncing it.

On the pillory at Aylesbury Mr. Keach defended himself and the truth with great boldness. The jailer frequently interrupted him, and finally the sheriff himself threatened to have him gagged. The people, contrary to custom, had no words of mockery for the good, persecuted minister, and no offensive missile was hurled at him. An Episcopal minister who ventured to assail Mr. Keach in the pillory was immediately reproached by the people with the ungodliness of his own life, and his voice was drowned in laughter. At Winslow, where he lived, he suffered the same shameful penalty, and a copy of his little book was burned.

Mr. Keach was a zealous Baptist; he aided ministers who came to him from all parts of his country, he had many meeting-houses built, and his works in defense of Baptist principles were read all over the kingdom. Before his death men spoke of him as the "famous" Mr. Keach, and he is still described by writers as a man of great celebrity. His two most popular works are "Tropologia, or a Key to open Scripture Metaphors," and "Gospel Mysteries Unveiled, or an Exposition of all the Parables." The latter work is more frequently offered for sale in the catalogues of the great London second-hand bookstores than any production of Richard Baxter, John Howe, or Jeremy Taylor. Mr. Keach was the author of forty-three works. He died July 18, 1704, in his sixty-fourth year. He was a devout Christian who led a blameless life and died in the triumphs of faith.

Keach, Rev. Elias, was born in 1667. He was the only son of the Rev. Benjamin Keach, a distinguished Baptist minister of London, England. He came to Philadelphia in 1686, when he was nineteen years of age. At the time of his arrival in this country he was a very ungodly young man. To make himself appear to be a clergyman he wore black clothing and bands, and he was at once taken for a minister. He speedily had an opportunity of showing his clerical talents by conducting a public service. He succeeded with his imposition until he had preached a considerable portion of his sermon. Then he stopped abruptly and "looked like a man astonished." The people supposed that he had been taken by some serious and unexpected complaint. But as they gathered around him they learned from him that he was neither a minister nor a Christian, and he made the communication with tears and "much trembling." Great was his anguish, and to obtain relief he went to Elder Dungan, of Cold Spring, near Bristol, Pa., who encouraged him to take his guilty soul to the sin-cleansing Redeemer. Soon the young man was a happy believer, full of ardent love to the Lord Jesus, and anxious to be a true preacher of his glad tidings. Elder Dungan baptized him; and from the Cold Spring church and pastor he went forth ordained to preach Jesus.

Mr. Keach constituted the Lower Dublin church in January, 1688. This church immediately elected him its pastor; and from it has sprung the wealthy and influential sisterhood of churches that now makes Philadelphia the home of the greatest number of Baptists in any large city in America. Mr. Keach labored in Pennsylvania and New Jersey with burning zeal, journeying far, preaching often, and succeeding marvelously. The Lower Dublin church at one time embraced in its membership all the Baptists in Pennsylvania and New Jersey; and to accommodate its widely scattered communicants the Lord's Supper was administered at Burlington and Cohansey, N. J., and at Chester, Philadelphia, and Lower Dublin, Pa. Lower Dublin at that time was the seat and centre of the Baptist denomination in several colonies, and from the community founded and extended so widely by Mr. Keach the Philadelphia Baptist Association arose, the first Association of our brethren on this side of the Atlantic.

Mr. Keach married Miss Moore, a daughter of Chief Justice Nicholas Moore, of Pennsylvania. Owing to some difficulties in the Lower Dublin church, Mr. Keach returned to England in 1792.

After his return to London he organized a church, of which he became pastor, into the membership of which he baptized about 130 souls in nine months after reaching London. He died in 1701 in the thirty-fourth year of his age.

He was a preacher of popular talents and of undoubted piety. He often had a congregation at the morning lecture, supported by the Baptists in Pinner's Hall, London, of 1500 persons. Mr. Keach published "Four Sermons on Justification," "A Treatise on Discipline," and "Two Sermons on the Nature and Excellency of the Grace of Patience."

Keachi Female College, located at Keachi, De Soto Parish, La., was chartered in 1857, with a capital stock of $18,000, and with buildings donated by Thomas M. Gattin, which cost $4500. The school opened in 1858 under Dr. J. S. Bacon, of South Carolina, who resigned in a short time, and Rev. J. H. Tucker succeeded him. At the beginning of the war 125 young ladies were in attendance. During the war the school was suspended, and the buildings used for a Confederate hospital. After the war it was reorganized, under Peter Crawford, who held the position until 1871, when he resigned, and Rev. J. H. Tucker was again called to the presidency, and has continued in office until the present time. The college has gradually regained its former prosperity.

Keely, Rev. George, was born at Walsham, County of Suffolk, England, July 26, 1772. Early in life he lost his father, and was thrown upon the care of an affectionate mother, whose instructions and wise counsels exerted an influence upon his youthful mind which was most salutary. When he was eighteen years of age he went to London, friendless and alone. By diligence and application to business he soon made for himself a position in which he bade fair to secure prosperity in his worldly affairs. The providence of God directed him to the place of worship where Dr. Rippon was the pastor, the same church of which Mr. Spurgeon is now the minister. Here he was converted and baptized. Soon after, he abandoned business, and prepared for the ministry at Bristol College under the charge of Dr. Ryland. He became the pastor of the Baptist church in Northampton in 1799, remaining there ten years, at the end of which period he became pastor of a church in Ridgemount, in the County of Bedford, and continued there until he resigned in 1818 to come to this country. Soon after reaching the United States he became the pastor of the First Baptist church in Haverhill, Mass., and was recognized as such Oct. 7, 1818. For nearly fourteen years he continued his labors in this important church, and established a reputation for being one of the ablest ministers in the denomination in Massachusetts. Upon his resignation he declined all overtures again to settle as a pastor. He passed the remainder of his life in such employments as were congenial with his tastes, and died, at the great age of ninety-four years, at Hampton Falls, N. H.

Keely, Prof. George Washington, LL.D., was born in Northampton, England, Dec. 25, 1803. His father, Rev. George Keely, came to this country in 1818, and for several years was pastor of the First Baptist church in Haverhill. George entered Brown University in 1820, and graduated with the highest honors of his class in 1824. He was appointed tutor of the Latin and Greek Languages in Brown University in 1825, and continued in the office for three years, and gained for himself a high reputation as an accomplished instructor. Having taught a private school for a year, he was appointed in 1829 Professor of Mathematics and Natural Philosophy in Waterville College. A new direction was soon given to his studies, which hitherto had been in the department of languages. He had so vigorous a mind that it was not difficult to turn his intellectual energies into new channels, and he soon mastered the more abstruse studies to which he now directed his attention, and proved himself to be one of the ablest scholars in the land in the special direction to which he applied himself. For twenty-three years he held the office of Professor of Mathematics and Natural Philosophy, securing for himself the sincere respect and the warm admiration of the students who came under his supervision. He resigned his professorship in 1852, and returned to more private life. He was employed for several years in the United States Coast Survey, and was also a correspondent of the Royal Observatory of England. Prof. Keely combined in himself what might be regarded as opposite traits of character. He was modest almost to timidity and lived the life of a scholastic recluse, and yet no man in the community kept himself better informed as to what was going on in the world, or was more entertaining and instructive in his conversation with those who were the sharers of his hospitality or casually met him in the ordinary walks of life.

Prof. Keely was an habitual worshiper at the First Baptist church in Waterville, in whose prosperity he always felt interested. The writer of this sketch, once his pastor, cherishes for him a regard and an affection which he has felt for but few men. Brown University conferred upon him in 1849 the honorary degree of Doctor of Laws. His death took place almost without a moment's warning, at Waterville, June 13, 1878.

Keely, Rev. Josiah, son of Rev. George Keely, was born in England May 26, 1806. He was baptized by his father June 18, 1826, ordained Dec. 21, 1843, as pastor of the church in Wenham, Mass., where he remained until called to the church in Saco, Me. He continued to act as pastor of this church for eleven years, when he resigned, having received an appointment as chaplain of the 13th Maine Regiment, Jan. 1, 1864. The hard service of military life undermined his health, and suffering from disease, he was taken to St. James Hospital, New Orleans, where he died June 24, 1864.

Keen, Joseph.—Jöran Kyn (Keen), the ancestor of Joseph Keen, came to this country from Sweden at about the age of twenty-three with Gov. John Printz in 1643. He was the founder of Upland, now Chester, Delaware Co., Pa.; and the Crozer Theological Seminary (in which Dr. W. W. Keen, the grandson of Joseph Keen, is one of the constituent trustees) stands on a portion of what was once his land. (See "The Descendants of Jöran Kyn," in the *Penna. Mag. Hist. and Biog.*, 1878–81.) Like not a few of his descendants, Jöran Keen was of such eminent piety that he is referred to in early colonial documents as "the pious." The family were originally Swedish Lutherans, and the grave-stone of Matthias Keen, the great-grandfather of Joseph, is (with the exception of that of two children) the oldest in the old Swedes' (Gloria Dei) church-yard, Philadelphia.

The father of Joseph Keen, Matthias, of Tacony, Oxford township, near Philadelphia, was a member of the Church of England (as most of the Swedish Lutherans became), and was a vestryman for many years of Trinity church, Oxford. His mother, through whose influence Joseph became a Baptist, was Margaret Thomas, whose father, John Thomas, came to America from Wales, settled near Philadelphia, and died in 1747. Joseph was born July 14, 1762. At the age of eighteen he left Tacony, and was apprenticed to George Oakley, a tanner and currier, for £150, which sum, with characteristic integrity, he worked out. He continued in this business to the end of his life in co-partnership with John Sellers, an eminent and devoted Quaker. He was married by Dr. Rogers, Jan. 24, 1788, to

JOSEPH KEEN.

Margaret Williams, a woman of superior character and eminent worth, who died Oct. 16, 1815. He related his personal Christian experience before the First Baptist church, Philadelphia, April 5, 1790, was unanimously elected a deacon Nov. 25, 1799, and served as such for nearly twenty-two years until his death, May 12, 1821, at the age of fifty-nine.

"No one can peruse the minutes during his long connection with the church without being impressed with the variety and intensity of his Christian activities, the kindliness of his heart, the loyalty of his faith, and the high esteem in which he was held by the entire church." When the Baptist Sunday-school enterprise was first started in Philadelphia it was approved by some, mildly countenanced by Dr. Holcombe, the pastor, but heartily encouraged by Deacon Keen, and when, in October, 1815, the first session was held, he "opened the school with the first public prayer connected with the Baptist Sunday-school enterprise in this city" (see Spencer's "Early Baptists of Philadelphia," pp. 186–8),—a service he repeatedly rendered to the cause in its early days.

Keen, William Williams, son of Joseph and Margaret (Williams) Keen, was born Sept. 4, 1797, in Tacony, near Philadelphia. His mother had taken refuge there during the epidemic of yellow fever, and he was born in a house built by his great-grandfather, John Keen, on a tract of 300 acres of land originally obtained from Sir Edmund Andros in 1676. He was associated with his father

WILLIAM WILLIAMS KEEN.

in business at the age of nineteen. At his death he succeeded him, with his brothers Joseph and Samuel W., and was for many years one of the most prominent men in his branch of trade. He retired from active business in 1851. He was married Feb. 20, 1823, by Dr. Holcombe, to Susan Budd, a descendant of William Budd, who came over from England and settled in Burlington Co., N. J., in 1678. She came of a robust religious stock. Rev. Thomas Budd, the father of William, while rector of Martock, Somersetshire, England, in 1660, under Charles the Second, became a Quaker. In 1662, on account of his religious opinions, he was thrown into jail at Ilchester, and remained there, resolutely adhering to his conscientious convictions, till liberated by death June 22, 1670, after eight years of imprisonment. After an honored and most useful life, she died Oct. 27, 1877, in the seventy-fourth year of her age. He became a member of the First Baptist church, Philadelphia, Oct. 24, 1831, he and his wife being baptized with a large number of candidates, including seven married couples, by Dr. Brantly. As was then the custom, the whole company, in baptismal robes, attended by the members of the church, marched to Arch Street wharf, crossed to Cooper's Point, Camden, and were there baptized in the Delaware. Both his personal and his family ties have ever bound him closely to this ancient church. His father was a deacon in it for nearly twenty-two years; his brother Joseph was a deacon for twenty years; his brother Samuel a trustee and church clerk; and he in his turn became a trustee Jan. 20, 1834, and a deacon Nov. 22, 1838.

In May, 1843, he removed to West Philadelphia. Here he quickly gathered a few scattered brethren into a determined and hopeful band, and in October, 1843, less than five months after their first meeting, they laid the corner-stone of a neat building for the First Baptist church, West Philadelphia, on a lot given to the church by him, and afterwards repurchased on their removal to the present site at the corner of Thirty-sixth and Chestnut Streets. In 1860 the present handsome brownstone church and chapel were erected. Few who have never gone through the trials of building two churches know what zeal and determination, and often what real sacrifices, are necessary to carry them through. His brethren deserve all praise for their heroic endeavors to carry the load, but the main burden, financially at least, fell upon him, and when failure threatened he sold his horses and his carriages, curtailed family expenses in every direction, often at personal discomfort, and made even his garden and his grapery aid in the work of building the Lord's house. Most men settle on a scale of expenses, family and personal, suitable to their means and social position, and give away what they can afford out of the remnant of their income, but with him the sum devoted to the Lord was the standard by which all expenses, family and personal, were regulated, and many a debate was held with his conscience before a grapery, a greenhouse, a coachman, or a pair of horses was decided upon, lest the unusual expense should curtail his beneficence. When he retired from business he resolved on his knees never to lay up another dollar, a resolution he has fulfilled for more than twenty-seven years. He has frequently given away more than half his income, and an aggregate sum amounting to more than all he is worth at present. Next to his church, the American Baptist Publication Society was his cherished field of denominational work. In 1837, while it was a feeble institution, occupying a small building belonging to his father's estate on Fourth Street above Chestnut, he became its treasurer, and faithfully administered its finances for eighteen years. He was one of the most earnest advocates of its removal to 530 Arch Street, and headed the subscription list with $5000. After serving the society as treasurer, vice-president, and manager from 1837 to 1872, his joy has been great in its removal to such a splendid home as the exceptional liberality of its friends has now provided for it. More than usually trusted by his brethren, he has been called to many offices of usefulness and responsibility in the denomination. Besides his service in the Publication Society, he was a constituent trustee of the university at Lewisburg, and served for three years (1846–49); a member of the first and most carefully chosen board of managers of the Missionary Union, organized in 1845 after the dissolution of the Triennial Convention, a position he filled for two years; manager of the Philadelphia Baptist Association since 1856; trustee of the Ministers' and Widows' Fund since 1858; manager of the Pennsylvania Education Society for twenty-five years (1842–67), to which society he gave, in 1856, its first scholarship; manager of the Pennsylvania Baptist General Association for twenty-two years (1832–54); and in the two churches of which he has been a member a deacon for nearly forty-three years.

Not only in the church, but also in the commercial community, he has been confided in, having been a manager in the Woodlands cemetery for nineteen years, a director in the Bank of North America, the oldest bank in the country, for nearly twenty years, and as a constituent manager of the Western Saving-Fund since 1847, has served nearly thirty-four years.

Now, in a ripe though feeble and blind old age, honored by all who know or know of him, he is awaiting with expectation and delight the summons of his Lord, "Well done, good and faithful servant; enter thou into the joy of thy Lord."

Keen, William Williams, M.D., son of William W. and Susan (Budd) Keen, was born in Philadelphia, Jan. 19, 1837. Graduated from the Central High School, January, 1853. Entered Brown University in 1855, and graduated in 1859. After pursuing scientific studies as a resident graduate for one year in Providence, entered Jefferson Medical College in 1860, and graduated M.D. in March, 1862.

During several years of the war, as Assistant-Surgeon, U.S.A., Dr. Keen discharged duties belonging to his office both on the battle-fields and in the general hospitals with great success. Resigning from the service in 1864, he went abroad and pursued his studies in Paris, Berlin, and Vienna. In 1866 he settled in private practice in Philadelphia, where he has remained, chiefly devoting himself to anatomy and surgery, and has attained an enviable reputation for skill and ability in his profession. Dec. 11, 1867, he married E. Corinna, daughter of Jefferson Borden, of Fall River, Mass.

As a medical teacher, especially of anatomy, and as an author, Dr. Keen is widely known throughout this and other countries. He was appointed Lecturer on Pathological Anatomy in the Jefferson College from 1866 to 1875. During the same period he occupied the chair of Anatomy and Operative Surgery in the Philadelphia School of Anatomy, in which institution he gathered the largest private anatomical class ever assembled in this country. In 1876 he was appointed Professor of Artistic Anatomy in the Pennsylvania Academy of Fine Arts, and in 1878 was made Lecturer on the Anatomy of Animal Forms as applied to Decorative and Industrial Art in the schools of the Pennsylvania Museum. He has also for five years been special Lecturer on Clinical Anatomy in the Woman's Medical College of Pennsylvania.

Dr. Keen has made extensive contributions to medical literature. Among his principal works are "Gunshot Wounds, and other Injuries of Nerves," 1864; "Reflex Paralysis," 1864 (both with colleagues); "Clinical Charts of the Human Body," 1872; editor of the "American Health Primers, vols. i.–xii.," by various authors; Heath's "Practical Anatomy," 1870; Flower's "Diagrams of the Nerves," 1872. In 1876 he delivered the fifth Toner Lecture before the Smithsonian Institution on the "Surgical Complications and Sequels of the Continued Fevers." He has published also interesting lectures on the "History of Practical Anatomy," 1870; the "History of the Philadelphia School of Anatomy," 1875; and on "Medical Missionary Work in Japan," 1878. In addition to these he has contributed a large number of articles to journals and reviews.

His activities are by no means confined to his professional sphere. As a manager of the American Baptist Publication Society, a trustee of Crozer Theological Seminary and of Brown University, and as a deacon and trustee of the First Baptist church of Philadelphia, Dr. Keen gives a practical illustration of the vast influence that may be exerted by men who, while serving suffering humanity, are led by the teachings of Jesus.

Keith, Hon. George H., was born in Randolph, Orange Co., Vt., May 4, 1825. He is of Scotch descent. His ancestors came to this country early in the seventeenth century. He received his elementary education at the public school in his native town. At the age of sixteen he entered the Kimball Union Academy at Meriden, N. H. Here he devoted four years to study and teaching. He then received the appointment of superintendent of the primary department of Franklin College, Ind. After holding this position one year he commenced the study of medicine, and graduated from the medical college at Woodstock, Vt., in 1852. In 1855 he came to Minneapolis, Minn., where he now resides. He was elected to the first Legislature of Minnesota in 1858 and 1859. In 1862 he was appointed surgeon of the expedition sent to relieve Fort Abercrombie. In 1863 he was appointed provost marshal for the second district of Minnesota, which position he filled until the close of the war. In May, 1871, he was commissioned by President Grant postmaster of Minneapolis, which office he yet honorably fills.

HON. GEORGE H. KEITH.

He was converted in October, 1838, and applied for membership in the Free-Will Baptist church, of which his parents were members. His experience was satisfactory, but the pastor and church thought him too young to make a profession of religion, and advised him to wait six months. At the end of that time he was baptized and received into the fellowship of the church. In 1846 he united with the First Baptist church in Indianapolis, Ind., Rev. T. R. Cressey pastor. He has ever been an earnest worker in all departments of Christian labor. He was the first president of the Minnesota Baptist State Convention, and has been a continuous member of its board of trustees, except when absent during the war. He was active in the establishment of the Minnesota Academy at Owatouna.

Keithian Quaker Baptists.—In the early history of William Penn's colony a serious controversy broke out among the Quakers about "the sufficiency of what every man naturally has within himself for the purpose of his own salvation." Some denied this sufficiency, and, as a consequence, exalted Christ and the Scriptures more than Barclay had done. George Keith, an impetuous and talented Scotchman, was the leader in resisting Quaker orthodoxy. The dispute was carried on with much bitterness, and in 1691 it led to a division and the establishment of separate meetings in Pennsylvania and New Jersey. Keith and his friends published a confession of their faith, and other works in favor of their views, and in denunciation of "the slanders, fines, imprisonments, and other persecutions which they endured from their brethren." Keith soon turned Episcopalian; others were reconciled to their brethren; and many became Baptists, Seventh-Day and Regular. According to Morgan Edwards, the Keithian Quakers started the Seventh-Day Baptist denomination in Pennsylvania. The Regular Baptists obtained valuable accessions from the Keithians in Philadelphia, Lower Dublin, Southampton, and Upper Providence. They were called Quaker Baptists because they retained the language, dress, and manners of the Quakers.

Kellar, Rev. William, an eminent pioneer Baptist minister, of German extraction, was born in Shenandoah Co., Va., in 1768. His early life was spent in East Tennessee, and afterwards in what is now Oldham Co., Ky. He was instrumental in forming Harrod's Creek church in 1797, Eighteen-Mile church in 1800, and Lick Branch (now Lagrange) church in 1802. In 1803, Long Run Association was constituted, of which he was chosen moderator, and filled that office four years. In 1812 he raised a company of volunteers, of which he was commissioned captain. At the close of the war he resumed his pastorates, and labored diligently in his profession. He was greatly beloved by the people, and led many souls to Christ. He died Oct. 6, 1817.

Kelley, Rev. Edwin D., was born in North Clarendon, Vt., June 18, 1846, pursued his preparatory studies at Rutland, Vt., and graduated at the University of Michigan in 1866. After teaching a while in Granville, O., he entered Newton Theological Institution, and graduated in June, 1871. He was appointed a missionary to the Shans, and reached Toungoo Feb. 20, 1872. He had so far made himself familiar with the language, that he was able to teach and to preach in it in less than one year, which was all the time that he had to devote to his missionary work. He was drowned in Shanland, Jan. 1, 1873. The editor of the *Missionary Magazine* says of him: "Mr. Kelley was a good scholar, and possessed a remarkable aptness for the acquisition of languages. He was also a well educated theologian, and a devout and earnest Christian. He was modest and firm in following his convictions, a man of sound and discriminating views of truth, and of much promise as a missionary."

Kellis, Rev. Lewis C., an active and efficient minister, who resides at Monroe, La., but supplies the churches at Bastrop, Oak Ridge, Delhi, and Wynn Island, situated between the Ouachita and Bayou Macon Rivers; was born in Mississippi; educated at Summerville Institute and Mississippi College. He removed to Louisiana in 1874, and became pastor at Alto. In the fall of the same year he became pastor at Trenton and Delhi. Mr. Kellis has been successful in his work. He is a ready writer, and has contributed largely to the Baptist papers of Mississippi and Louisiana. He is about thirty years of age.

Kelly, Robert, son of Robert Kelly, an Irish patriot, who in 1796 emigrated to New York, was born in the city of New York, Dec. 15, 1808. From early youth Robert Kelly was inclined to study. He was diligent, pure-minded, and honorable. He entered Columbia College the first of his class, and maintained that position to his graduation in 1826. In mercantile life he was distinguished by industry and energy. His integrity and sense of honor were utterly beyond the reach of temptation. He learned the French, Spanish, Italian, German, and Hebrew languages. On retiring from business he followed this bent of his mind, and remained to the end of life a student. Naturally, he became a leader in all matters pertaining to higher education. He was conspicuous in the organization of the institution now known as the College of the City of New York.

For many years he was a trustee of the University of New York, and also of Madison and Rochester Universities, which institutions are largely indebted to his generosity, his judgment and labors. He was chairman of the committee which organized the course of study in the University at Rochester. His services in education were recognized by his election as one of the regents of the University of the State of New York. In the House of Refuge and in the Institution for the Benefit of Merchants' Clerks he took a leading part. At the time of his death he was chairman of the board of trustees of the New York Society Library. There was scarcely a form of public activity in the city, whether financial, fiduciary, charitable, commercial, or literary, in which, in some way, he did not bear a prominent part.

Without political office, except that of city chamberlain, he was fitted to adorn any civic station, and, at the time of his death, at the height of his powers, he was without question one of the very foremost citizens of New York. He never made a public profession of religion, but was a Christian man, a Baptist by conviction, and a devoted attendant on the ministry of Wm. R. Williams, D.D., his lifelong friend. He died in New York City, April 27, 1856.

Kelly, Hon. William, son of Robert Kelly, an Irish patriot who fled from his native land in 1796 to find liberty in the New World, was born in the city of New York, Feb. 4, 1807. His father became a very prosperous merchant, and died in 1825, leaving three sons, John, William, and Robert. They continued his business for several years with great success. In 1836 John died, and in 1837 William and Robert retired, each with an ample competence. In all their arduous business days the brothers maintained a love for literature, refinement, and the high moral and religious tone for which their early home had been so long conspicuous. In 1842, William purchased a property on the Hudson, near Rhinebeck, which he made his permanent residence, and which his energy and taste invested with every attraction. For two years he was a member of the senate of the State of New York, and he was a candidate for governor against Edward D. Morgan, his successful competitor. Mr. Kelly was a man of large heart, and constantly, though silently, dispensed his gifts and charities. He was trustee at the beginning, and for some years after, of Cornell University, the mathematical portion of which bears his name in acknowledgment of a generous donation. He was also a trustee of Vassar College and of Rochester University at the time of his death, of the first from its inception, and of the last from the death of his brother Robert, whose vacant seat he was called to fill. He was a liberal contributor to Rochester, a final subscription of $20,000 being made not long before his decease. He was a member of the Baptist church at Rhinebeck, where his widow still resides. He died in Torquay, England, whither he had gone in hope of restoration to health, Jan. 14, 1872.

Kelton, Rev. William H., was born in 1835; entered the New Hampton Institution in 1855, having previously spent some time in the Bangor Theological Seminary, and graduated in 1858. He was ordained, soon after his graduation, as pastor of the church at Bluehill, Me., and subsequently was pastor for a time at West Waterville, Me. His health was broken down in consequence of his hard experience in the army as a worker, sent to the seat of war by the Christian Commission, and he did not attempt ministerial labor until 1865, when he took charge of the church in North Scituate, Mass. Here he did excellent service for the cause of Christ until the Master called him to his reward. He died April 4, 1871. He was very greatly beloved by a large circle of friends, who sincerely mourned over what to them seemed his untimely end.

Kemper, Rev. Burdette, a popular and useful minister of Garrard Co., Ky., where he was born Feb. 24, 1788, was of German extraction. He was converted, and became a member of Forks of Dix River church in 1830, and at the age of forty-five was ordained to the ministry. He was immediately associated with John S. Higgins in ministering to the church of which he was a member. On the resignation of Mr. Higgins, in 1839, Mr. Kemper became the pastor, and under his ministry the church greatly prospered and increased in numbers, until it embraced a membership of more than 500. Besides performing his pastoral labors, Mr. Kemper preached to several of the churches of South District Association, of which he was moderator twenty-five years. He died March 18, 1876.

Kempton, George, D.D., was born in South Carolina in 1810. He graduated from Hamilton Literary and Theological Institution in 1839. After preaching a few years in the South he became pastor of Spruce Street church, Philadelphia, and remained for eight years. He also had charge of the Lower Dublin church, in Philadelphia, for five years. He presided over the First church in New Brunswick, N. J., for five years. From a partial failure of health, in 1863 he located in Hammonton, N. J., and has preached for the church there with great acceptance. In 1859 Madison University gave him the degree of D.D. He is a sound theologian and a logical preacher.

Kempton, Rev. S. Bradford, A.M., was born in November, 1834, at Milton, Queens County, Nova Scotia; converted and baptized there in 1853; graduated from Acadia College in 1862; ordained pastor at New Minas, Sept. 16, 1863; took charge of the First Cornwallis church in 1868, being the third minister that has held that position since 1808; sound theologian, good preacher, and pastor.

Kendall, Hon. Amos, was born near Woburn, Mass., Aug. 16, 1789. By great self-denial and perseverance he prepared for college, and entered Dartmouth in the spring of 1808, from which he graduated with distinction. After leaving college he entered the law-office of W. M. Richardson, at Groton, Mass., but, encountering numerous perplexing difficulties, he made preparations for leaving New England. Accordingly he removed to Kentucky, and engaged as tutor in the family of Henry Clay, then residing near Lexington. After continuing in this position for a few months, he became editor of a newspaper in Georgetown, and at the same time opened a law-office there. In 1816 he became co-editor and proprietor of the *Argus*, a journal published at Frankfort. He held this position for several years, and became one of the most influential writers on local and State politics in Kentucky. In 1826 he was appointed fourth auditor of the treasury by President Jackson, and in consequence removed to Washington. This position he filled with great advantage to the government and honor to himself for five years, when, through his great executive ability, and the vigorous aid which he gave to the administration, he was appointed, in 1835, postmaster-general. The energy with which he carried on this important department of the government was soon evident, but the fidelity with which he managed its affairs subjected him to some vexatious and damaging prosecutions at the hands of his enemies. In 1840, in consequence of impaired health, he sent to the President his resignation from the office, and was thus relieved of the

HON. AMOS KENDALL.

great burden. Mr. Kendall while residing in Washington was connected with several different daily journals, in which many of the absorbing questions of the day were discussed with much pungency and power. He became interested at a very early day in Prof. Morse's telegraph operations, and by his business energy and tact gave a great impetus to the movement. In 1857 he gave a house and two acres of land, near the boundary-line of the city of Washington, for an institution for the deaf and dumb, which, under the judicious guidance of its superintendent, Edward M. Gallaudet, LL.D., and the generous appropriations of the United States government, has become the only college in the world with a regular and full curriculum for deaf mutes.

Mr. Kendall, although indulging the thought that he had been converted early in life, was not baptized until April, 1865, the ceremony taking place in the E Street church; he became a member, however, of the Calvary Baptist church, whose pastor at the time was the Rev. J. S. Kennard. He took a deep interest in securing a church edifice for the society with which he became thus connected, and contributed for the purpose nearly $100,000. On the 3d of June, 1866, the new house was dedicated, and the church entered at once on a most prosperous career. In June of 1866, feeling the need of rest and recreation, Mr. Kendall visited Europe, being absent about fifteen months. On Sunday morning, Oct. 15, 1867, the beautiful edifice of the Calvary church was destroyed by fire, nothing being left but the blackened walls. Encouraged by Mr. Kendall, a new structure was soon reared, towards the cost of which (the insurance money received being $80,000) he gave upwards of $15,000. This new building was dedicated July 11, 1869. He gave to the Columbian College, of which he was always a stanch friend and counselor, $6000, to purchase a classical scholarship, which should be enjoyed during six years by the best-prepared pupil in any one of the public schools of Washington. He also endowed two mission Sunday-schools, his contributions to them amounting in all to about $25,000. He died in Washington, Nov. 12, 1869.

Kendrick, Adin A., D.D., the present president of Shurtleff College, was born at Ticonderoga, N. Y., Jan. 7, 1836. He was the son of Dr. Albert Kendrick. Dr. Kendrick is of the family to which have belonged several eminent men of that name, including Adin Kendrick, M.D., of Poultney, Vt., his grandfather; Rev. Ariel Kendrick, of New Hampshire; Rev. Nathaniel Kendrick, D.D., the first president of what is now Madison University, and one of its founders; and Rev. Clark Kendrick, of Vermont; with whom may be included, as still living, Prof. A. C. Kendrick, D.D., of the University of Rochester, and the Rev. J. R. Kendrick, D.D., of Poughkeepsie.

President Kendrick received his education at Granville Academy, in Washington Co., N. Y., at Middlebury College, Vt., and at the Rochester Theological Seminary. Upon leaving college, and before commencing his theological course, he studied law, and was admitted to the bar, practising that profession at Janesville, Wis., and afterward for a short time at St. Louis. Deciding to study for the ministry, he went to Rochester for his theological course, graduating there in 1861. His first pastorate was in Chicago, where he served in that capacity the North Baptist church until 1865, when he returned to St. Louis as assistant pastor of the Second Baptist church, Rev. Galusha Anderson being the senior pastor. After a year and a half he became pastor of the Beaumont Street church. In 1872 he was chosen president of Shurtleff College.

Although comparatively a young man, Dr. Kendrick discharges the duties of his present responsible post with marked efficiency and success. With unusual gifts of attractive public address he combines studious habits, a special taste for the high themes which belong to his chair as instructor, and qualities as a teacher and disci-

ADIN A. KENDRICK, D.D.

plinarian which give him every year a stronger hold upon his work and upon those under his care. The college has never prospered more than under his administration; year by year it is taking higher rank upon the roll of American colleges. Dr. Kendrick is always cordially received on the various public occasions, in his own State and elsewhere, when service is required of him, and invariably acquits himself in a way which commands the respect of all.

Kendrick, Albert, M.D., of Waukesha, Wis., is a native of Vermont, and a son of Adin Kendrick, a prominent physician of Poultney, where the subject of this sketch was born Aug. 1, 1813. At the age of seven years Albert had his right hand nearly severed from the arm, disabling him ever afterward for all kinds of manual labor. He was therefore kept at school through the early years of his life. He studied at Hamilton Literary Institution (now Madison University). He graduated from the medical school in Woodstock, Vt., when twenty years of age. He commenced the practice of his profession in Poultney, Vt., where he resided three years. Subsequently he removed to Ticonderoga, N. Y., and remained three years. He then settled in Granville, N. Y., and practised medicine for sixteen years, and in June, 1855, he located in Waukesha, Wis., which has since been his home.

Dr. Kendrick is a man of fine standing in his profession, and thoroughly conscientious. He has been a member of the Baptist Church since he was sixteen years of age. He is a nephew of Nathaniel Kendrick, D.D., once president of Madison University, a cousin of A. C. Kendrick, D.D., the eminent Professor of Greek in the University of Rochester, and the father of A. A. Kendrick, D.D., the president of Shurtleff College, at Upper Alton, Ill.

In the Baptist church at Waukesha he is a trusted pillar. In the denomination of the State he is highly esteemed for his wise counsels and intelligent views. He is a liberal contributor to the religious and benevolent work of his denomination.

Kendrick, Asahel C., D.D., LL.D., was born in Poultney, Vt., Dec. 7, 1809. When thirteen years of age he went to Hamilton, N. Y., where his uncle, Nathaniel Kendrick, D.D., held the presidency of Hamilton Literary and Theological Institution. He pursued a course of study to prepare himself for college. He entered the junior class of Hamilton College, at Clinton, N. Y. At the end of one year he returned to Hamilton, and was employed as teacher in the village academy. He then re-entered Hamilton College, and was graduated in 1831. He was appointed tutor in the literary and theological seminary at Hamilton (now Madison) University, and the next year he was elected Professor of Greek and Latin. Relieved after a few years of the Latin department, he held the Greek chair until 1850, when, on the establishment of the University of Rochester, he accepted the Greek professorship in that institution, which he still continues to fill. In 1852 he went to Europe, perfecting his knowledge of Greek in the University of Athens. He also visited several Italian and German universities, studying the educational methods of those celebrated centres of learning. After two years he returned to his duties at Rochester. While he is an admitted authority in Greek, he is not lacking in other languages, ancient and modern. For many years he has been employed in the revision of the New Testament. He is the author of several Greek text-books. He brought out a revised edition of Olshausen's "Commentary on the New Testament." He is also the author of a memoir of Mrs. Emily C. Judson, wife of Dr. Judson, the missionary. His poetic talent was shown when a mere lad by anonymous contributions to the village papers of Hamilton, which created considerable discussion among the students and people as to their authorship. In later years he has brought out a volume of poems entitled "Echoes," some of which were greatly admired in literary circles. As a teacher of the Greek language he has no superior in America. He has made that a specialty. He has never been a pastor, but he has often, to the great satisfaction of the churches, supplied the pulpits of pastors. His profound learning, especially in the field of New Testament exegesis, gives his discourses a value and a public interest rarely found in sermons.

Kendrick, Rev. Clark, was born in Hanover, N. H., Oct. 6, 1775. The death of his father was the occasion which led to his removal to Vermont, in which State most of his life was spent in constant efforts to advance the Redeemer's kingdom. His conversion took place in 1797. He seems at once to have been impressed with the conviction that it was his duty to prepare himself for the Christian ministry. Although at first shrinking from assuming the responsibilities of the sacred office, he concluded, after much struggle, to obey what he regarded as a divine call, and, with such preparation for the work as he could obtain, he entered upon his ministerial labors, and was ordained April 20, 1802, at Poultney, Vt. Revivals of religion followed his preaching, one of which, that in 1816, resulted in an addition of more than 100 persons to his church.

Mr. Kendrick possessed in an eminent degree the missionary spirit. The religious destitution of his adopted State deeply touched his sympathies. He made tours to different sections of Vermont, the northern parts of New York and Canada, and labored most zealously to give the gospel to multitudes who were deprived almost wholly of the means of grace. His interest in missions extended to heathen lands, and he was among the most efficient agents in giving momentum to the efforts of the Baptist churches—aroused to new life by the stirring appeals of Luther Rice—to carry the news of salvation to the dark corners of the earth. Ministerial education also was another cause which enlisted his zeal and called forth his earnest efforts. The Vermont Baptist Education Society was formed mainly through his instrumentality, and he was chosen its president, and became its agent to visit the churches. To provide an educational home for these young men, the Baptists in Vermont proposed to start an institution of learning having special reference to the training of indigent students to become preachers of the gospel. The Baptists of the central and western districts of the State of New York had a similar plan in their minds. It was decided at length to unite efforts and establish the desired institution in some locality that would be convenient to all the parties concerned.

This locality was Hamilton, N. Y., the seat of the now flourishing Madison University. Mr. Kendrick was selected as an agent to solicit funds for the new institution, and for the remainder of his life devoted himself with great singleness of purpose to this work, and to him the infant seminary owed a debt of gratitude larger than it could ever repay.

Thus it was that the life of Mr. Kendrick was filled with deeds of Christian benevolence and unwearied activity in the cause of his Master. He was a recognized power in his State, greatly honored and respected wherever he was known. Middlebury College conferred on him the honorary degree of Master of Arts in 1819. His death occurred Feb. 29, 1824. The loss of the denomination by this premature cutting down of one of its strongest pillars was very great. It was not easy to supply the vacancy thus made. It is pleasant to know that the mantle of the father fell on sons who have risen up to render honor to their beloved parent. The influence which he so widely exerted has been extended in many directions by those who bear his venerated name and inherit the virtues which shone so brightly in his character.

Kendrick, James Ryland, D.D., youngest child of Rev. Clark and Esther Thomson Kendrick, was born in Poultney, Vt., April 21, 1821. He pursued his early studies at Hamilton Seminary, N. Y., where he made a profession of religion and joined the church, February, 1837. He entered the Junior class of Brown University in September, 1838, and graduated with the "classical oration" in 1840. In the latter part of the same year he removed to the State of Georgia, where he taught school for two years, having been licensed and ordained at Forsyth in the autumn of 1842. In the spring of 1843 he entered on his first pastorate in Macon, Ga. After a ministry of nearly five years in Macon, Dr. Kendrick was called, in 1847, to the First Baptist church in Charleston, S. C., where he remained for nearly seven years. He left this position to accompany a little colony of Baptists who established what is now known as the "Citadel Square church," of Charleston, and who built what is probably the best Baptist house of worship south of the Potomac. The civil war having straitened his flock, he retired from this field in May, 1862, after a pastorate of nearly eight years. During the further continuance of the war he preached for the Baptist church in Madison, Ga. At the close of the great struggle his Union sentiments led him North, and he settled with the Tabernacle Baptist church, New York City, in November, 1865, where he remained nearly seven years. In September, 1873, he became pastor of the church in Poughkeepsie, where he still labors, having secured the building of a fine and commodious house of worship. He has no living children. The degree of Doctor of Divinity was conferred on him by Rochester University in 1866. He was for some time associate editor of the *Southern Baptist* newspaper, published in Charleston, S. C. Several tracts from his pen have been published, among them the following: "Responsibility for our Belief," "Human Depravity," "Address to Christians on the Subject of Temperance." He has also published several sermons on a variety of subjects. Of late years he has been a frequent contributor to the *Examiner and Chronicle*, New York. He is a brother of Prof. A. C. Kendrick, D.D., LL.D., of Rochester University. He is noble-minded, generous, cordial in his manners, of commanding presence, devout in spirit, and a good preacher.

Kendrick, Nathaniel, D.D., was born in Hanover, N. H., April 22, 1777. His parents, among the first settlers of the town, were both members of the Congregational Church. He labored on the

NATHANIEL KENDRICK, D.D.

farm until he was twenty, and then, with his father's consent, divided his time between teaching a school and attending the academy. About this period he was converted, through a revival that occurred in a small Baptist church; but, not being ready to give up the faith of his childhood, he sought from both a Baptist and a Congregational minister a statement of their views, and their reasons for holding them. Not satisfied by this method, he resolved to examine the New Testament, and after prosecuting his studies for nine months he became satisfied that the peculiarities of the

Baptists were derived from and supported by the New Testament, and he was immersed in April, 1798.

During the succeeding four years he engaged in farm labors and academic studies, uncertain as to his permanent life-work, feeling a strong disposition to enter the ministry, but shrinking from its responsibilities. Satisfied at length that it was his duty to preach, he spent some time in studying with Rev. Mr. Burroughs, of Hanover; with Rev. Dr. Asa Burton, of Thetford; with Dr. Emmons, of Franklin; and with Drs. Stillman and Baldwin, of Boston. By the church of the latter he was licensed to preach in the spring of 1803, at the age of twenty-six.

He began preaching as a supply at Bellingham, Mass., where he remained one year. Declining their call, he was ordained at Lansingburg, N. Y., in August, 1805. In 1810 he settled at Middlebury, Vt., dividing his time between this and three other feeble churches.

In 1817 he settled with the churches at Eaton and Morrisville, N. Y., resigning the latter in 1820 to lecture in the Hamilton Literary and Theological Institution. In 1821 he was elected Professor of Systematic and Pastoral Theology. In 1823 received D.D. from Brown University. In 1824 he located in Hamilton Village. In 1825–37 was one of the overseers of Hamilton College, at Clinton, N. Y. In 1836 was chosen president of the Hamilton Literary and Theological Institution, but, while acting as such, did not formally accept the office; corresponding secretary of New York Baptist Educational Society from 1834 to 1848; died Feb. 11, 1848, after a lingering and painful illness caused by a fall in 1845.

Dr. Kendrick's great work was in the Hamilton Institution. In his manners he was a dignified Christian gentleman. His theology belonged to the Edwards form of Calvinism. As a counselor he was wise and safe. See also article MADISON UNIVERSITY, and for a complete sketch see "Nathaniel Kendrick" (American Baptist Publication Society); consult also "Sprague's Annals," jubilee volume Madison University.

Kennard, Joseph Hugg, D.D., was born in Haddonfield, N. J., April 24, 1798; baptized by Rev. Daniel Dodge, at Wilmington, Del., July 3, 1814; began to preach when but seventeen years of age, and attracted at once great attention on account of his youth and fervor; was licensed in September, 1818, and in 1819 undertook an agency to present the claims of missions, under the direction of Luther Rice. Became pastor at Burlington, N. J., Nov. 14, 1819; at Hopewell, N. J., January, 1822; and at Blockley, Pa., in October, 1823. In 1832 took charge of the New Market Street church, Philadelphia, Pa., where he remained six years. In 1838 went with a colony from the New Market Street church to form the Tenth church, and remained pastor of it until his death, June 24, 1866,—a period of twenty-eight years. A natural, graceful and vigorous style in presenting doctrinal as well as practical truths, united with tenderest sympathies, made Dr. Kennard one of the most successful preachers of his day.

During his ministry of nearly fifty years he was the means of the conversion of over 3000 people, 2500 of whom he himself baptized. No man in Philadelphia was more sincerely loved, or is more affectionately remembered. Nor was he merely a pastor. All agencies for the redemption of men had his sympathy and support. In his early life he traveled much in destitute regions to preach

JOSEPH HUGG KENNARD, D.D.

Christ and establish Baptist churches. He was one of the founders of the Pennsylvania General Association, and a life-long member of the Board of the Publication Society. He was among the first to advocate the temperance cause. In the great noonday prayer-meetings of 1857 he was a most conspicuous leader. A number of the Baptist churches of Philadelphia owe their origin to him. No man was more earnest in his advocacy of foreign and home missions. He sought in every way to secure a first-class education for the rising ministry.

Dr. Kennard was married June 27, 1822, to Miss Beulah E. Cox, of Burlington, N. J., who died June 26, 1862. He left six children, five daughters and a son, Rev. J. Spencer Kennard,

D.D., who in 1867 edited a memoir of his father, which was issued by the American Baptist Publication Society.

Kennard, J. Spencer, D.D., was born in Philadelphia, Sept. 24, 1833. He was converted when twelve years old; baptized by his father, Rev. Dr. Jos. H. Kennard, in April, 1846, and united with the Tenth Baptist church, Philadelphia.

After graduating from the Philadelphia High School, he entered the senior class of Lewisburg University. Here he consecrated himself to the ministry New Year's Eve, 1852. Graduating with honor, he entered Princeton Theological Seminary, and, completing a two years' course, accepted the pastorate of the First Baptist church of Bridgeton, N. J., October, 1856. After three years of successful work he became pastor of the E Street church, Washington, D. C., in 1859, succeeding Dr. George W. Samson. The church suffered distraction during the civil war, the flock being scattered North and South. The shepherd remained with his charge, working in a government clerkship during the week, preaching on the Sabbath, laboring for the sick and wounded on the battle-field; but health failed, and the Woburn church, Mass., called him in 1862 to that field.

He removed from Woburn to Albany, N. Y., after gathering a rich harvest of souls. In 1865, Dr. Kennard accepted the pastorate of the Calvary Baptist church, Washington, D. C. The new interest became a vigorous church. On the death of his father he was called to the Tenth church, Philadelphia, in April, 1867. After four prosperous years, 196 converts having been added to that church by baptism, and various mission enterprises successfully started, he removed to New York, and became pastor of the Pilgrim church. Here 300 persons were baptized by him. In 1879 a call from the Central Square church, East Boston, was accepted, and he is now the pastor. The doctorate was conferred on him by Madison University, N. Y., in 1879.

Dr. Kennard's literary labors have been the memoir of his father, many contributions to the press, especially a series of articles on "Pulpit Eloquence," and a work, in preparation, on the "Relation of Oriental Religions to Christianity."

During his ministry Dr. Kennard has baptized 1100 converts.

Kennedy, Rev. W. M., was born in Duplin Co., N. C., Aug. 26, 1825; baptized by Rev. Jesse Howell, Feb. 14, 1847; ordained by Revs. G. W. Hufham, G. W. Wallace, L. F. Williams, and Jesse Howell, in November, 1849; has been a pastor for thirty-one years; was moderator of Easton Association two years; was for many years president of the board of trustees of Warsaw High School; has baptized 1800 persons, traveled over 90,000 miles in preaching the gospel, and he is as full of zeal and efficiency as ever.

Kentucky Baptists.—" The Baptists were the pioneers of Kentucky." The first explorers of its territory were the brothers Daniel and Squire Boone. The latter was a Baptist preacher. The first settlement was made at Boonsborough, in what is now Madison County, in the summer of 1775, by Col. Daniel Boone, his wife and daughters being the only women in the small colony. Col. Richard Calloway and his family joined the settlers the first day of September. They also were Baptists. The same fall a small settlement was made at Harrodsburg, some thirty miles southwest of Boonsborough. Early in the spring of 1776, Thomas Tinsley and William Hickman, Baptist ministers, came to Harrodsburg. "Mr. Tinsley," says Mr. Hickman, "preached almost every Sunday." Hickman also preached. Nothing more is known of Mr. Tinsley except that "he was," says Hickman, "a good old preacher." Mr. Hickman returned to Virginia the following summer. Emigrants, principally from Virginia, now began to pour into the new country rapidly. Among these were Gen. Henry Crist, Gen. Aquilla Whitaker, Gen. Joseph Lewis, Col. Robert Johnson, Col. William Bush, Hon. James Garrard, Gabriel Slaughter, the Clays, and many others, who became prominent in the camps and councils of the State. These were all Baptists.

During the years 1779 and 1780, William Marshall, John Whitaker, Benjamin Lynn, John Garrard, and Joseph Barnett, Baptist ministers, settled in the new country. John Taylor and Joseph Reding visited it and preached during this period.

The first Baptist church formed in Kentucky, or in the great Mississippi Valley, was constituted of 18 members by Joseph Barnett and John Garrard, on the present site of Elizabethtown, forty miles south of Louisville, June 18, 1781. It still bears its ancient name, Severn's Valley. The second church was constituted by the same ministers, July 4, 1781. It is called Cedar Creek, and is located forty miles southeast from Louisville. The third church in Kentucky was Gilbert's Creek, in Garrard County. It was constituted in Spottsylvania Co., Va., and removed to Kentucky, under the pastoral care of Lewis Craig, in the fall of 1781. Here it held its first meeting the second Sunday in December of that year.

Then followed Forks of Dix River, in 1782; Providence, in 1783; South Elkhorn, in 1783; Gilbert's Creek (Separate Baptists), in 1783; Beargrass, in 1784; Cox's Creek, Clear Creek, Great Crossings, Tate's Creek, Limestone, Brashear's Creek, Rush Branch, Pottinger's Creek, and Head of Boone's Creek, in 1785.

In 1785 three Associations were formed, Elkhorn and Salem of Regular Baptists, and South Kentucky of Separate Baptists. In 1793 an effort to form a union between the Regular and Separate Baptists failed in its object, and resulted in the formation of Tate's Creek Association of United Baptists. From this period till 1799 religion was at a low ebb, and open infidelity much abounded. In 1800 the religious awakening known as "The Great Revival in Kentucky" began, and continued three years. In this period the number of Baptists in the State was more than doubled. It was at this time that the jerks and the barking and dancing exercises prevailed in some degree among the Baptists, but much more extensively among the Presbyterians and Methodists.

In 1801 the Regular and Separate Baptists formed a union, and all assumed the name of United Baptists. From that time until 1818 the Baptists of Kentucky continued to prosper, with little to interrupt their harmony. About this period Daniel Parker introduced his two-seed doctrine, and with it the anti-mission spirit. This caused much trouble, dividing many churches and Associations. These factions still exist, but have become weak and insignificant. In 1823, Campbellism began to disturb the denomination, and continued to distress the churches until the Campbellites were cut off. The formal separation began in 1829, but was not completed till 1835, when the Campbellites became a distinct sect, known by various names in different localities.

In 1832 the Baptist State Convention was organized. Its operations were unsatisfactory, and, after a trial of four years, it was dissolved. In 1837 the General Association of Kentucky Baptists was constituted. Its special object was to promote the spread of the gospel in the State. Its success was encouraging from the beginning. It is estimated that 50,000 persons have been baptized under its auspices. Meanwhile, the anti-missionary spirit, which had first manifested itself in the churches about the year 1818, was fully aroused by the organization of the General Association. Divisions were produced in many churches and Associations. In not a few of these a majority was on the anti-missionary side. The formal division began in 1840. Since that time the Baptists of Kentucky have been divided into missionary and anti-missionary churches. The latter have now an aggregate membership of about 7000.

Since the division last referred to the denomination has enjoyed a good degree of harmony and prosperity. Until the close of the late civil war, the white and colored people worshiped together in the same churches. Since that period the colored people have formed churches and Associations of their own. The separation was harmonious, and the feeling between the brethren of the two races is kind, and their correspondence is fraternal.

The subjoined table will show the growth of the Baptist denomination in Kentucky from 1790 to 1880:

Date.	Population of the State.	Number of Baptists.	Date.	Population of the State.	Number of Baptists.
1790	73,677	3,105	1850	982,405	69,894
1810	406,511	......	1860	1,155,684	81,262
1812	......	21,666	1870	1,321,011	......
1830	687,917	......	1875	......	144,269
1831	......	34,827	1878	......	159,743
1840	779,828	47,325	1879	......	161,190
1846	......	60,991	1880	......	163,696

Kentucky, General Association of.—The first general organization of the Baptists in Kentucky was effected in 1832 at Bardstown. It was styled "The Kentucky Baptist Convention." There was much opposition to it among the churches. It continued to meet for about four years, and then dissolved. In 1837 "The General Association of Baptists in Kentucky" was organized in Louisville. Its leading objects were to promote preaching among the destitute within its bounds, to encourage literary and theological education, and to foster foreign missions. The churches watched its movements with doubt and suspicion, and some of them openly opposed it. But immediately after its organization an extensive revival swept over the whole State, and the General Association grew rapidly in favor. It employed a large corps of missionaries, and built up many churches that were weak, and constituted a large number of new ones. It is estimated that its missionaries, and those of its auxiliary societies, have averaged at least a thousand baptisms a year, from its organization until the present time. It has stimulated the churches to support their pastors, kindled the spirit of home and foreign missions, encouraged the building up of schools and colleges, and checked the ravages of intemperance, and has been in every way of incalculable advantage to the denomination in Kentucky.

Kenyon, Rev. Archibald, as the pastor during three years and a half of the Tabernacle church in Chicago, and afterwards for several years of the Berean Baptist church, is to be remembered with those who have contributed to build up the Baptist denomination at important points. He was born in Athol, Warren Co., N. Y., July 31, 1813. Until eighteen years of age his home was at Hague, on the west side of Lake George. His conversion occurred in the fall of 1831, and he was baptized by Elder Daniel Tinkham July 6, 1832. Feeling himself called to the work of the ministry, he was licensed by the church at Hague. He studied at the Sandy Hill Academy, also at East Bennington, then conducted by Messrs. A. Macomber and A. N.

Arnold. He was ordained in 1836. His first pastorate was at Lakeville and Shushan, in Washington County. Subsequently he was engaged at White Creek, Shaftesbury, and Hoosac. During the years 1840-41 he had the care of a Baptist church in Providence, R. I., but in 1842 the relation was dissolved. After a year at Vernon, Oneida Co., N. Y., and three and a half years at Clinton, eight miles away, he came West, and accepted pastorates in Chicago as above mentioned. From 1852 to 1856 he served the Tabernacle church, and later the Berean. His subsequent pastorates have been at Iowa City, at Peoria, and other places in Illinois. Though his pastorates have for the most part been brief, they have been fruitful, in nearly every instance considerable accessions being made to the church. He has been an active champion of every kind of reform, in that department of effort being a valued associate and co-laborer of Dr. Nathaniel Colver. He now suffers a great affliction in nearly a total loss of sight, but continues in service as pastor of two small churches near the central part of the State.

Kerfoot, Franklin H., D.D., was born in Clarke Co., Va., Aug. 29, 1847. Until the age of fourteen he was educated at schools in Berryville. He was engaged in the Confederate service during the war. In 1866 he entered the Columbian University, graduating in the college with the degree of Bachelor of Philosophy, and in the law school with the degree of Bachelor of Law, in 1869. He spent a year and a half at the Southern Baptist Theological Seminary, but, his health failing, he was obliged to suspend all study for nearly a year. Subsequently he entered the Crozer Theological Seminary, and after one year's study graduated in 1872. Afterwards he traveled over Europe, Egypt, and Palestine, and spent a year at the University of Leipsic. On his return to this country he became pastor of the Midway and Forks of Elkhorn churches, Ky., entering on his labors in those fields Feb. 1, 1875. On the death of the lamented Dr. Richard Fuller, of the Eutaw Place Baptist church, Baltimore, Mr. Kerfoot was elected his successor, and he entered on the pastoral charge of that church in November, 1877. While in Kentucky, Mr. Kerfoot held for one session the professorship of German in Georgetown College, Ky.,—a position for which he was admirably fitted by his studies in Germany. During his absence in the East he published in the *Religious Herald* some interesting letters descriptive of classical and Biblical scenes. The Columbian College conferred upon Mr. Kerfoot, in 1872, the honorary degree of A.M.

Kermott, Rev. Wm. Judson, was born in Carrolton Co., New Brunswick, in 1833. In his infancy his parents removed to Canada West, where he remained until twelve years of age, when he became a member of the family of his brother-in-law, Rev. E. J. Scott, a Baptist minister. He made a profession of religion at fifteen years of age, and united with the Baptist church at New Market, Canada West. He very early in life felt that God called him to preach the gospel, and made preparation for it as opportunity afforded up to manhood. He was ordained by the Baptist church in Almond, Allegany Co., N. Y., in 1857, and at once became the pastor of the church. This pastorate he resigned after two years' labor to accept an appointment from the American Baptist Home Mission Society as general missionary for Kansas. This position he held for eleven years, accomplishing during the time a very successful and important work. In 1866 he became the pastor of the First Baptist church in Omaha, Neb. The church there was largely gathered through his labors, and its fine meeting-house built and completed so as to enable the church to meet for worship in the basement. In 1870 he removed to Chicago, Ill., where he was pastor of the Coventry Street Baptist church six years, and of the Halsted Street Baptist church two years. This last pastorate Mr. Kermott resigned for the purpose of again entering the service of the American Baptist Home Mission Society as district missionary for Southwestern Wisconsin, which is his present field of labor.

During his ministry of twenty-three years, devoted largely to the new States and Territories, Mr. Kermott has been an indefatigable worker and a highly successful minister. He has organized a number of churches, built several meeting-houses, aided in the formation of the Kansas and Nebraska Baptist State Conventions, assisted struggling churches encumbered with heavy debts to provide the means for their payment, and all his work is of a substantial character. He has fine acquisitions in literary and theological learning, and is a highly esteemed minister of Christ.

Kerr, Judge John, LL.D., distinguished as a jurist, orator, statesman, and above all as a devout Christian, was born in Pittsylvania Co., Va., Feb. 10, 1811, and was the son of the Rev. John Kerr, the most eloquent preacher of the gospel who has yet appeared in North Carolina or Virginia. Mr. Kerr was educated in Richmond, Va.; was the first law student of the late Chief-Justice Pearson, and settled in Caswell, N. C., his father's native county, at the age of twenty-one, and was baptized in 1832 into the fellowship of the Yanceyville Baptist church by the Rev. J. J. James. Mr. Kerr was a decided Baptist, and was called on by his brethren to fill many important positions. He was a trustee of Wake Forest College, vice-president of the Southern Baptist Convention, president of the Baptist State Conventions for many sessions, and frequently moderator of the Beulah Association. He represented his county in the State Legislature; was in the Congress of the United States in 1852–53, and again in 1858–59; was judge of the Superior Court during the war, and was again elected judge by the people in 1874 for eight years. He was the orator of the Mecklenburg Centennial, celebrated May 25, 1875.

He was also a trustee of the State University, president of the North Carolina Historical Society at the time of his death, and received the title of LL.D. from both Trinity College and the State University.

When a young Christian his faith and zeal were so great that many predicted that he would follow his father into the pulpit, but worldly ambition tempted him into politics. God, however, was gracious to him and restored his first love, and for many years before his death he became eminent for godliness. He loved the society of Christ's children, and while he was attending to his judicial duties it was a common thing for this magnificently endowed man to forsake the fashionable circles which eagerly courted his society and find his chief delight in some humble prayer-meeting. He was never ordained as a preacher, but no Sabbath was permitted to pass, no matter where he was, without his bearing witness to the love of Jesus, and his exhortations were all the more forcible because of his position on the bench. He died Sept. 5, 1879, at his home in Reidsville, N. C., after a protracted illness.

JUDGE JOHN KERR, LL.D.

Kerr, Rev. John, was born in Caswell Co., N. C., Aug. 4, 1782. His father was of Scotch descent, and was eminently pious. His early education was superior to that of most of those by whom he was surrounded. He was converted under the preaching of Rev. Wm. Paisley, a Presbyterian clergyman, and was baptized Aug. 12, 1801. Shortly afterwards he was licensed to preach, and was everywhere listened to with the most earnest attention. Having been engaged in teaching previous to his conversion, he now abandoned it and gave himself wholly to the ministry. He made extensive tours in all directions, visiting South Carolina and Georgia, and preaching to large assemblies of people. Lower Virginia, also, was the scene of his labors. About the year 1811, Mr. Kerr, at the earnest solicitation of friends, allowed himself to become a candidate for Congress. At first he was defeated, but he was subsequently elected, and continued to serve his constituents in that body during the war of 1812. Mr. Kerr always regarded this step as a grievous error, inasmuch as it diminished his own spirituality and injured his influence as a minister of the gospel; and his belief was that he was brought back from political life only by a painful special providence. In March of 1825 he removed to Richmond, Va., and took charge of the First Baptist church in that city. During the six years he spent as pastor of this church, nearly a thousand persons were baptized by him, so powerfully did the Word of God prevail. Mr. Kerr was deeply interested in all the benevolent movements of the day, and for many years presided over the General Association of Virginia, as well as over the Dover Association. He took an active part also in protesting against the dangerous errors of Alexander Campbell. In 1832 he resigned the care of the church in Richmond in order to devote himself more especially to evangelistic labors. His time was thenceforth given to protracted meetings and visiting destitute churches. In the year 1836 he removed to a farm near Danville, Va., still prosecuting his labors among the feeble churches, and accomplishing much good. He died Sept. 29, 1842. As a preacher Mr. Kerr was greatly gifted. With a fine person, a well-modulated voice, and a graceful manner, he won and held the attention of the largest assemblies for hours. His sermons were exceedingly interesting and impressive, and one who knew him has said, "Under his stirring and almost seraphic appeals I have frequently, I judge, seen thousands at one time bathed in tears." "Thousands have acknowledged him," says the same writer, "as their spiritual father; and in Virginia and North Carolina multitudes were turned to righteousness through his labors."

Keyser, Charles, D.D., was born at Albany, N. Y., May 13, 1827; received his literary and theological education at Madison University and

Rochester Theological Seminary; ordained at Wallingford, Conn., in 1851; was pastor at Mount Norris, Niagara Falls, and Binghamton, N. Y., in Providence, R. I., in Philadelphia, Pa., in Trenton, N. J., and in Wakefield, Mass., where he died. In 1865 he received the prize offered by the American Baptist Publication Society for the "Baptist Catechism." Lewisburg University conferred upon him the degree of Doctor of Divinity.

Dr. Keyser was the owner of a clear, powerful intellect; he was logical, orthodox, fearless, and faithful. The writer lamented his early and unexpected death, and thousands shared in his sorrow.

Kidder, Rev. Wm. S., of Igo, Shasta Co., Cal.; born in Charing, County of Kent, England, Nov. 15, 1834; came to New York in 1842; was converted at fifteen, and baptized into the fellowship of the Morris church, N. Y.; removed to California in 1858, and was ordained at Sacramento in 1860. He is a devoted pioneer preacher in Northern California,—almost the only Baptist minister in that wide and destitute field. He has acted as pastor at Red Bluff, Weaverville, Mount Shasta, and Eagle Creek, laboring with his own hands for his bread, and riding forty or fifty miles at his own expense to serve some poor church or minister to the afflicted, looking for his reward on high. He has been greatly blessed in his work and has secured much influence among the people, who have honored him with some of their most important offices.

Kieff, Baptism of the Population of.—Vladimir the Great, Prince of Russia, was a heathen until he married the Princess Anna, of Constantinople, when he repudiated his god Perune, and about A.D. 988 ordered the entire inhabitants of Kieff to be baptized. The proclamation stated that "Whoever, on the morrow, should not repair to the river (Dnieper), whether rich or poor, he should hold for his enemy." . . . "Some stood in the water up to their necks, others up to their breasts, holding their young children in their arms. The priests read the prayers from the shore, naming at once whole companies by the same name."—Mouravieff's "History of the Church of Russia," pp. 13, 15. Oxford, 1842. In this baptism thousands were immersed, and Christianity of a certain kind was triumphantly introduced into Russia.

Kiffin, Rev. William, was born in London in 1616. In 1625 the plague, which swept over his native city, deprived him of both his parents and left him with six plague sores, the cure of which was regarded as impossible. Through two sermons preached by Mr. Davenport and Mr. Coleman, in London, Mr. Kiffin obtained from Christ a divine life which defied the evils of seventy stormy years. He united with a Congregational church, by which he was first called to the ministry. In 1638 he joined the Baptist church of which the Rev. John Spilsbury was pastor. From this community a colony went forth in 1640 which formed another church. The new organization met in Devonshire Square. It elected Mr. Kiffin pastor,—an office which he retained for sixty-one years, the duties of which three assistant pastors at different times aided him to discharge.

Mr. Kiffin was a merchant, carrying on business with foreign countries, and especially with Holland. He conducted his mercantile affairs with so much skill that in a few years he was among the wealthiest men in London, and known by all classes of society throughout the kingdom as one of the greatest of English merchant-princes. This made him a conspicuous object for persecuting spite, and

REV. WILLIAM KIFFIN.

it stirred up the cupidity of a base horde of informers, whom the Stuarts employed to ruin Dissenters. Lord Arlington, one of the secretaries of Charles II., told Mr. Kiffin that he was on every list of disaffected persons whose freedom was regarded as dangerous to the government.

He was arrested many times. Once he was committed to the White Lion jail in London, where some prisoners formed a conspiracy to murder him, but he was unexpectedly set at liberty. Gen. Monk arrested him for an alleged conspiracy against the king, but the charge was shown to be false, and he was released. About midnight, on another occasion, he was taken into custody, accused of having hired two men to kill the king, but soon after this wicked fabrication was exposed, and he was permitted to depart. His position among Dissenters exposed him to extreme peril for many years.

Kiffin's influence was very great. Macaulay says, "Great as was the authority of Bunyan with the Baptists, William Kiffin's was greater still." He had talents of the highest order; his education was respectable; his sagacity was uncommon; his manners were polished; his piety was known everywhere; and for half a century he was the first man in the Baptist denomination. With the business community of London, or with the great trades of other cities, the credit of Kiffin stood higher than the financial promises of kings. Even the haughty nobles of Britain were not too proud to be his friends, and among these Clarendon, the Lord High Chancellor, stood the first. Thurloe, the chief secretary of Cromwell, in his "State Papers," frequently mentions Mr. Kiffin's name with respect, and the "Whitlocke's Memorials" are equally just to the great and good Baptist. Even King Charles himself, as far as his heartlessness would permit him to show affection, was the friend of Mr. Kiffin. There were ten Baptist men and two women arrested at a Dissenting religious meeting at Aylesbury, for which offense against the Church of England they were sentenced to three months' imprisonment. At the expiration of that time they were brought before the court and commanded to conform to the Episcopal Church or to leave the country immediately. These sturdy Baptists refused to do either, and they were sentenced to death *according to law.* A man forthwith started off to Mr. Kiffin, in London, who interceded with the king, and saved their lives. And on several other occasions the king gave substantial proofs of his regard to the great city merchant. He was so friendly to Mr. Kiffin that he sent to borrow £40,000 from him, no doubt as a return for favors he had granted his brethren, which Mr. Kiffin compromised by a gift of £10,000, and felt that he had saved £30,000 by the arrangement. When King James II. abolished the charter of the city of London he wanted to make Mr. Kiffin an alderman to secure the influence of his great name to help him in his illegal suspension of many charters, and of all penal laws against Dissenters and Catholics. But he disliked the king's illegal measures, and lent him no willing aid, direct or indirect, to assist him in their execution.

Mr. Kiffin's ample means were chiefly used in works of benevolence. He gave large sums to the poor; he contributed with great liberality to the feeble churches and their persecuted ministers; he assisted in the education of young men for the ministry, and he was ever ready for any labor or gift of love.

The only work he ever published was a treatise in favor of "close communion," the arguments in which are as sound as the principles that governed his pure and noble life.

One of the sons of Mr. Kiffin was poisoned by a Catholic priest in Venice because he had been too free in denouncing his religion. Two of his grandsons, the Hewlings, were murdered by Jeffreys, the basest of judges, and James II., the meanest of kings. Macaulay speaks of them as "the gallant youths, who, of all the victims of the Bloody Assizes, had been most lamented." Their sister Hannah married Major Henry Cromwell, the grandson of the great Protector.

Mr. Kiffin was evidently raised up by the providence of God and invested with his talents, influence, and wealth to shield his persecuted brethren in times specially calamitous; and in a spirit of supreme love to Jesus, for half a century, he was the father of the English Baptists. He died Sept. 29, 1701, when the sword of William III. of blessed and of "Boyne Water" memory had terrified the last Stuart from the English throne.

Kilborne, Rowley, was born in the town of Bristol, Addison Co., Vt., Sept. 28, 1780. He removed to Canada in 1820. Converted with his wife in the winter of 1827–28, he joined the Baptist church in the township of Lobo. In 1832 he removed to Beamsville, and two years after was chosen deacon of the church there, in which office he continued to the day of his death, Oct. 17, 1880. He was the first president of the Baptist Missionary Convention of the Province of Ontario. For forty years he was a magistrate, and in several other official positions he served the public with rare skill and fidelity.

Killingsworth, Judge Thomas, was probably a native of Norwich, England, and came to this country very soon after his ordination. We find him at Middletown and Piscataway exercising his ministry in 1688 and 1689. His name was prominently associated with Baptist movements in New Jersey, and especially in Piscataway. He was the first pastor at Cohansey, continuing for nineteen years, until his death. The destruction of the old church records for the first century of its existence deprives us of facilities for securing information about him. Mr. Killingsworth was appointed judge in Salem County, and discharged the duties of the bench as well as those of the pulpit satisfactorily. He died in 1709. He was a firm Baptist, but avoided any rash illegal act; so we find that in 1706 at a court held in Salem he took out a license under the Toleration Act for a preaching-place at the house of one Jeremiah Nickson.

Kilpatrick, Rev. J. H. T., was one of those who aided greatly in elevating our denomination in Georgia to its present high standard in a missionary point of view. He was born in Iredell Co., N. C., June 24, 1793. In his younger years he had excellent educational facilities, received an exceptionally classical education, and prior to his permanent settlement in Georgia he taught school in several places in Louisiana. While in that State he married his first wife, and also took an active part in the campaign of 1814 and 1815, participating in the battle of New Orleans, Jan. 8, 1815. He was converted in 1817, and joined the Baptist church at Cheneyville, La., June 22. In 1820, after the death of his wife, he returned to the East, was prevailed upon to remain and preach at Robertvill, S. C., from whence he removed to Burke Co., Ga., where he married Miss Harriet Eliza Jones, June 23, 1822. Afterwards he removed to Richmond County, and at once identified himself with the most prominent Baptists in the State, taking a high

REV. J. H. T. KILPATRICK.

position among them. His field of labor lay within the Hephzibah Association, which, when he first became connected with it, was violently anti-missionary. With great zeal and prudence he promulgated missionary sentiments, and after the lapse of thirteen years had the pleasure of seeing it entirely revolutionized on the subject of missions. A tract written by him in 1827 or 1828, entitled "A Plain Dialogue on Missions," which was afterwards published in the "Baptist Manual" in connection with denominational articles by Pengilly, Booth, and Andrew Fuller, was prepared specially for the Hephzibah Association, and had a most salutary influence. Mr. Kilpatrick was, through the force of circumstances, a great champion of baptism and temperance in his Association, and to him those two causes owe much able and eloquent support by both pen and voice. He aided, too, greatly in promoting the Baptist educational interests of Georgia. The land upon which Hephzibah High School is situated was donated by him, and at the State Convention of 1829, at Milledgeville, he, Sherwood, Sanders, and Mercur promptly raised the $2500 necessary to secure the Penfield legacy,—an action which proved to be the inception of Mercer University. His life was prolonged until Jan. 9, 1869, and was one of remarkable usefulness.

The following is part of a sketch of Mr. Kilpatrick, written by Gen. G. W. Evans, of Augusta, which appeared in the minutes of the Hephzibah Association for 1869:

"As a citizen, he was quiet, retiring, and unobtrusive; as a man, open, honest, and unsuspecting; as a friend, true but undemonstrative; as a pastor, laborious and constant, always punctual to his appointments; as a preacher, he was logical and profound, and when aroused oftentimes sublimely eloquent; as a writer and controversialist, he was true, accurate, and resistless; as a Christian, uniform and faithful; and in his expiring moments, as if to seal the holy record of his life with his dying testimony, his last words were 'Precious Jesus!'

"Such, brethren, is the brief and imperfect record of the man now gone to his reward, who, before many of us were born, became, by the power of his intellect, we might almost say the father of this Association, and who, by pen and voice, aided by the late Rev. Joshua Key, was the main instrument of building up the missionary interest among us, and who for years was the triumphant defender of our peculiar views and the eloquent vindicator of our denominational honor. Gifted with a massive intellect and an iron constitution, he literally wore out in the service of his Master. We deem it no injustice to the living or the dead to express our honest conviction that in his death is extinguished the brightest intellectual light which it has ever been our pride to honor."

Kilpatrick, Rev. James Hines, youngest son of Rev. J. H. T. Kilpatrick and Miss Harriet E. Jones, was born in Burke Co., Ga., Oct. 18, 1833. He entered Mercer University in 1849 and graduated in 1853, sharing the highest honors of his class. While at Mercer he made a public profession of religion and united with the church, and was called to ordination by the White Plains church, Greene County, in 1854. He began his labors as pastor of that church in 1855, succeeding Rev. V. R. Thornton. Since that time his energies have been concentrated upon the White Plains church, of which he has been the pastor ever since, though he has had charge of other churches, and he has succeeded in so developing its capabilities that it has become one of the most spiritual, efficient, liberal, and enlightened churches in the State. For years it has been regarded as a model church, and Mr. Kilpatrick as the model pastor of the State. In his preaching he makes no effort at display, his aim being to present gospel truth in such a manner that all may understand and few fail to appreciate it; and perhaps no minister in the State is uniformly heard with more interest and profit.

In public life he is very quiet and unobtrusive, but is ever ready to maintain his opinions with ability. He has always taken a prominent part in the affairs of the Georgia Association, and since his majority has invariably occupied a seat in the Georgia Baptist and Southern Baptist Conventions.

In private life he is simple in his habits, affable in manners, and pleasant in social intercourse. He is fond of books and study. He has published several valuable sermons and a series of articles in the *Christian Index* on the subject of "Baptism," which were masterly in character and exhaustive in execution. He exerts a strong influence in the denomination within his own State, and might deservedly occupy a much more prominent position were it not for his modesty. He is a strong, terse, sensible writer, a forcible speaker, and a man of great power every way.

Kilpatrick, Rev. Washington L., eldest son of Rev. J. H. T. Kilpatrick, was born in Burke Co., Ga., Oct. 18, 1829. He was graduated from Mercer University, with the first honors of his class, in 1850; was ordained in 1852, entered upon the duties of a country pastor, and to the present time, with persistent and untiring energy and faithfulness, has labored in the ministry, serving different churches within the bounds of the Hephzibah Association. So eminent have been his abilities, so exalted his character, so uniform his courtesy and kindness, and so efficient have been his labors and so Christian his deportment, that he wields an influence possessed by no other in his Association. He is commanding in person, with a fine open countenance, great benignity of expression, and a pleasing address that secures the confidence of strangers. Having a tender heart and liberal impulses, the suffering have ever found him a ready friend and the poor a generous almoner. As a preacher, he speaks extemporaneously, is always practical, pointed, and clear. Too deeply concerned in presenting sound and wholesome instruction, which he does in a solemn and impressive manner, to seek for mere ornamentation in speech, he makes no special effort to embellish his sermons. By his preaching he has attained the most gratifying results, and has secured for himself an enviable reputation; for, while an unflinching Baptist, and ardently devoted to the spread of Baptist sentiments, he seeks for success more by the firm maintenance of truth than by directly combating error.

But other labors pertaining to the welfare of our Baptist Zion, besides those of a pastor, have engaged his attention. For twenty-two consecutive years he managed the mission and colporteur work of the Hephzibah Association. Chiefly through his instrumentality the Hephzibah High School was established in 1861, and that school he taught, as president, with eminent success, from 1866 to 1876. In 1868 he organized the Walker Colored Association, and since its formation he has been the chief and trusted counselor of its ministers and churches. Prior to emancipation the members of those churches belonged to the Hephzibah Association. Since 1869 he has faithfully discharged the duties of a trustee of Mercer University; and in 1878 he succeeded in securing the organization of the Georgia Baptist Historical Society, of which he is the efficient corresponding secretary.

Mr. Kilpatrick has sought to make his attainments more and more available for wide-spread usefulness; and, whatever his influence may be as a public man,—and unquestionably it is very great,—it is but the natural and logical sequence of an unblemished private record and consecrated talents.

Kimbro, Rev. W. C., M.D., a prominent minister and physician in Drew Co., Ark., was born in North Carolina in 1835; came to Arkansas in 1860 and settled near his present residence, and engaged successfully in the practice of medicine. He united with the church in 1868, and was soon after licensed to preach, and ordained in 1870. While pursuing his profession he has done much to relieve the destitute around him. Hopewell and Centre Point churches have enjoyed his labors, and have been much blessed under his efficient ministry.

Kimbrough, Rev. Bradley, son of Rev. Duke Kimbrough, was born in Jefferson Co., Tenn., Nov. 3, 1799. He studied and practised law for a time, and was regarded as one of the first lawyers of the State.

In 1834 he was a leading member of the convention which revised the constitution of the State of Tennessee. He afterwards refused political preferment and became a minister of the gospel, and was ordained by the Madisonville Baptist church in the year 1835. His efforts as a pastor were very successful; he assisted in the organization of a number of churches, and labored in protracted meetings, which were abundantly blessed of the Lord.

His ministerial gifts were of a high order. In 1845 he was chosen agent to endow Union University, located at Murfreesborough, Tenn. He accepted, and completed the work in 1847. At one time he was agent of the Bible Board. He was successful in whatever he undertook. For many years he was moderator of the Liberty Association, and he was also president of the General Association. He closed his earthly labors June 30, 1874. While living he was one of the brightest lights in our beloved Zion.

Kincaid, Eugenio, D.D., was born in the State of Connecticut, and brought up in Southern New York; was one of five students who formed the first class in Madison University, Hamilton, N. Y. Under the influence of sermons preached by Dr. Carey, during his second year at Hamilton, he determined to become a missionary. At the time of his leaving college there was war between the English and Burman governments, which led to the breaking up of the Burmese mission and delayed his departure for heathen lands. He then became pastor of the church at Galway, N. Y., where, however, he became dissatisfied, and resolved that if no door was yet open for labor among the heathen, he would find some destitute region in his own country where he could do missionary work. His attention being directed to the mountainous districts of Central Pennsylvania, he commenced work at Milton, where at that time there was but one Baptist, and she a poor widow with six children. He preached in court-rooms, school-houses, and occasionally in groves, for four years, with manifold tokens of the Divine favor.

While thus engaged he received a letter from the executive committee of the Missionary Union asking him to go to Burmah. He replied at once that he would. In the spring of 1830 he sailed from Boston, and towards the close of the year he reached Maulmain, where he found Drs. Judson and Wade and Mr. Bennett.

Dr. Kincaid commenced the study of the language under a native preacher, giving twelve hours every six days of the week to the work. Meanwhile, he preached for the English soldiers then stationed in those parts. After a year of preparation he went to Rangoon and gave his entire time to work among the Burmans. In a little more than a year he left the Burman church at Rangoon under the care of a native pastor, and proceeded to Ava, the capital, and subsequently spent three months in visiting every town and village along the banks of the Irrawaddy. For nearly two months he lived in his boat, subjected to severe hardships; but he heroically continued his work among the natives, and at the end of fifteen months had baptized eleven converts and organized them into a church.

He continued his labors for many years in foreign lands, and subsequently returned to America broken in health by his incessant toil. At his quiet home in Girard, Kan., the enfeebled body detains a little longer "the hero missionary" from his home beyond the skies.

Kincaid, Rev. J. P., was born in Garrard Co., Ky., March 4, 1848. In 1852 his parents removed to Danville, where, at the age of thirteen, he united with the Baptist church. In 1868 he transferred his membership from the church at Danville to New Providence church, in the same county, where, July 14, 1872, he was ordained to the gospel ministry in the Baptist church by the following Presbytery: T. M. Vaughn, R. L. Thurman, W. P. Harvey, I. M. Sallee, and A. D. Rash. About this time he was called to the pastoral care of the Drake's Creek church, in Lincoln Co., Ky. After this he took charge of the Logan's Creek church also. About forty persons were added to the Drake's Creek church during his first year's labors there. In the latter part of 1873 he resigned the care of these churches, and removed to Covington, Tenn. During the summer and fall of the year he labored in protracted meetings in Topton, Lauderdale, and Dyer Counties, and in October, 1874, was called to the care of the Elam Baptist church, Durhamsville, Tenn.

He is a decided Baptist. He is now pastor of the church in Gallatin, Tenn. Mr. Kincaid, though a young man, stands among the first preachers of our State; he is a reasoner, and knows how "rightly to divide the word of truth."

"Kind Words" and "The Child's Gem."—*Kind Words* is the Sunday-school paper of the Southern Baptist Convention. It is published at Macon, Ga., and edited by Rev. S. Boykin. This useful paper wields a strong, extended, and healthy influence. Its lesson expositions of the "International Series" are studied to advantage by perhaps 200,000 persons each week in all the editions, counting the Lesson Leaflets. Its tone is highly evangelical, and at the same time it is strikingly denominational and a decided advocate of the mission cause. It first appeared in January, 1864, in the very midst of the throes of war, and was originated by Mr. C. J. Elford, of Greenville, S. C., assisted by Rev. Basil Manly, D.D., president, and Rev. John A. Broadus, corresponding secretary, of the Sunday-School Board of the Southern Baptist Convention, and soon reached a circulation of 25,000. For years it was a small monthly sheet, and its price was ten cents. It was then published at Greenville, S. C. In 1868 the Sunday-School Board was removed to Memphis, Tenn., and *Kind Words* was transferred to that city, where, in 1870, it was consolidated with the *Child's Delight*, a Sunday-school paper published by Rev. S. Boykin, at Macon, Ga., who was employed as editor. The *Child's Delight* was a semi-monthly paper, and thus *Kind Words* became a semi-monthly. Two years later a weekly edition was also issued, and its circulation became very extensive throughout the South and Southwest. In 1873 the Sunday-School Board was merged into the Home Board of the Southern Baptist Convention at Marion, Ala., and *Kind Words* was transferred to the care of that board, by which it has been issued ever since. Its publication office was changed to Macon, Ga., where satisfactory printing arrangements were made with the firm of J. W. Burke & Co. by the secretary of the Home Board. It is beautifully illustrated and elegantly printed, and yields the Home Board of the Southern Baptist Convention an income of $1000 per annum above expenses. The different editions of the paper are a weekly, semi-monthly, and monthly. The monthly issue contains no lessons; the weekly and semi-monthly issues contain them. Four-page Lesson Leaflets are also published.

The Child's Gem, a beautiful little four-page weekly illustrated Sunday-school paper for infant classes, is published by Rev. S. Boykin, Macon, Ga. It contains appropriate matter for the very young, with the lesson-story and questions adapted to the capacity of children unable to read. It has now been in existence two years, and has quite a wide circulation. It was first published under the title of *The Baptist Gem*.

King, Rev. Alonzo, was born in Wilbraham, Mass., April 1, 1796. When he was three or four years of age his family removed to Newport, N. H. He pursued his studies preparatory to college at the Newport Academy, and under the tuition of Rev. Leland Howard, of Windsor, Vt., and was a graduate of Waterville College, now Colby University, in the class of 1825. He was invited, immediately on his graduation, to become pastor of the church in what is now Yarmouth, Me., then North Yarmouth, which had become vacant by the removal of its pastor, Rev. Stephen Chapin, D.D., afterwards president of Columbian College, Washington, D. C. He was ordained Jan. 24, 1826, and was eminently successful in his ministry till failing health forced him to resign, in the spring of 1831. A year afterwards he was so far recovered that he was able to accept a call to the pastorate of the Baptist church in Northborough, Mass. While residing at Northborough he was for a time agent of the Massachusetts Baptist Convention, and also soliciting agent to raise funds for the endowment of the Newton Theological Institution. He was several times urged to take charge of important churches in cities and large towns, but his modest estimate of his abilities led him to decline all these overtures. In the spring of 1835 he removed to Westborough, Mass., where he died November 29 of the same year. As an author he is known by his "Memoir of George Dana Boardman." "In my own memory," says Baron Stow, "and in that of every one who knew him, his name is fragrant."

King, Rev. Daniel, was born July 1, 1803, on what was then the disputed border line of Kentucky and Tennessee. He was converted and baptized in 1831, and soon began missionary work in Mississippi. For twenty-five years he was a most faithful and successful evangelist and pastor, conducting many revivals, building up new churches, and baptizing large numbers. He was robust and had great natural force, swaying large audiences with the powers of a splendid eloquence. In 1853 he went to California and located on the Solano plains, where he built up one of the strongest and wealthiest churches, now known as the Dixon church. He died at Dixon, Oct. 3, 1877. He was honored and loved by all, and his influence on the Baptist cause, in its missionary and educational departments, will be felt for many generations on the Pacific coast.

King, Gen. E. D., was born in Greene Co., Ga., April 12, 1792; was a captain in the command of Gen. Floyd in the principal Indian war, fought in several battles, and was twice wounded. He removed to Alabama while it was yet a Territory, commenced life there in a log cabin, and became princely wealthy. For many years he was a trustee of the University of Alabama, one of the projectors of Howard College and of the Judson Female Institute, and president of the board of trustees of the last-named institution from its beginning to his death; contributed liberally of his time and means to the cause of education and religion; deacon in the Baptist church at Marion, and one of its most useful members; ardent and sincere in his attachments and convictions; of a strong and determined will; noted for his eminently practical judgment and good sense. He was the father of the Hon. Porter King.

King, Rev. Eustace E., pastor at Senatobia, Miss., was born in Mississippi in 1850; graduated at Mississippi College in 1873; began to preach at the age of eighteen; spent two years at the Southern Baptist Theological Seminary, then located at Greenville, S. C.; after which he was called to his present pastorate, where his labors have been eminently successful.

King, Rev. G. M. P., principal of the Wayland Seminary, Washington, D. C., was born at Oxford, Me., in 1833. He was fitted for college at Hebron Academy, and graduated from Colby University in 1857. He spent one year at Newton Theological Seminary. For the school year of 1858–59 he had charge of the rhetorical department of the Maryland Agricultural College. In 1860 he became pastor of the Baptist church in East Providence, R. I., and remained there five years. In April, 1865, while spending a few weeks with the army, in the service of the Christian Commission, he became interested in the education of the colored people of the South. He wrote and urged the granting of the first request to be allowed to open a school in Richmond, Va., for the teaching of the freedmen. In 1867 he took charge of the National Theological Institute, Washington, D. C.,—a school for their education. After two years it was united with Wayland Seminary, and Prof. King became the principal,—a position which he still holds. In the beginning they had no building and but few students; now they have a property free from debt, worth nearly $50,000, a handsome building in a beautiful location. It has numbered nearly 100 students annually for the last ten years, about half of whom have been connected with the theological department, and already more than 50 of the students are doing effective work as pastors, while a much larger number have engaged in teaching. The last class numbered 17, the largest ever graduated at this excellent institution.

King, Rev. H. M., was born in Ralls Co., Mo., April 8, 1839. He attended for some time the Shelbyville Seminary, at Shelbyville, Mo., and afterwards continued his studies under a graduate of Berlin, and finally with a Presbyterian minister of Kentucky. He was converted at Shelbyville, Mo., in 1859, in February, and baptized the same month. In August of that year he commenced to preach, and in the December following was ordained.

Mr. King labored for some years acceptably in Missouri, when, on account of being frail, he removed to Texas, hoping that its milder climate would suit him better. He was quite successful at Chapel Hill, Texas. Here his health gave way again, and he concluded to go to Florida. He arrived there a few years ago, and settled at Gainesville. His first pastorate was at Fernandina. He has been constantly engaged in the ministry, and his health is restored.

Mr. King is a man of fine intelligence, and as a preacher he has few equals. He thinks closely and clearly, and expresses himself perspicuously. He is remarkably prudent, conservative, and firm. He is able to adapt himself to the various classes of society, and he is beloved alike by all, which, in a country with such a complex population, adds very materially to his usefulness. He is one of the most valuable men in the denomination in Florida.

King, Rev. I. D., was born in Baltimore, Md., Feb. 4, 1824; was baptized into the fellowship of the Spruce Street church, Philadelphia, by Rev. T. O. Lincoln, May 8, 1842; was ordained in May, 1854, and settled as pastor of the church at Smithfield, Pa., where he remained two years; was subsequently pastor of the churches at Uniontown, Pa., Portsmouth, O., Granville, O., Phœnixville, Pa., and Chestnut Hill, Philadelphia. In 1876 he took charge of a new mission interest in Philadelphia, which, under his efficient labors, soon became the Centennial church. With this church he still continues as pastor, and God is still blessing his ministry.

King, Hon. Judge Porter, was born in Perry Co., Ala., April 30, 1824; educated at the University of Alabama and at Brown University, R. I., whilst under the presidency of Dr. Wayland; studied law under Thos. Chilton, Esq.; was judge of the circuit court of one of the judicial circuits of the State before the late war, and held the office until deprived of it by Federal authority in 1865; for many years a trustee of the State University and of the Hospital for the Insane, taking a deep interest in these institutions; deacon in the Baptist church at Marion, trustee of Howard College, and president of the board of trustees of the Judson Female Institute. Judge King is a wealthy, cultivated gentleman, a lawyer of distinction, and a Baptist of sterling worth. He is a son of the late Gen. E. D. King.

Kinnear, Judge William Boyd, was born in St. John, New Brunswick, Oct. 12, 1796; converted in that city, and baptized in Halifax, Nova Scotia, in 1827; was one of the founders of the Baptist seminary at Fredericton; elected member of the Provincial Parliament in 1832; appointed to the Legislative Council in 1838; was judge of probate in St. John for many years, and was deacon of Brussels Baptist church. Judge Kinnear possesses a keen, well-cultured mind, accurate knowledge of law, deep Christian experience, zeal for education and other denominational enterprises, and the strictest integrity.

Kinnersley, Rev. Ebenzer, was born in Gloucester, England, Nov. 30, 1707. He arrived in America Sept. 12, 1714, was ordained in 1743, and ministered in Philadelphia and elsewhere until 1754. He had serious doubts about the character of Whitefield's preaching, and involved himself in grave trouble with the Baptist community in Philadelphia by proclaiming in the pulpit his convictions.

"In 1746," says Senator Jones, of Pennsylvania, "his attention was first directed to the wonderful and unknown properties of the electric fire, as it was then termed, and he was brought into close companionship with Benjamin Franklin. He was intimately associated with Franklin in some of his most splendid discoveries, and he more than once gratefully acknowledged his aid. He attracted the attention of many of the most eminent philosophers on both sides of the Atlantic, and he was chosen a member of the American Philosophical Society, which was then composed of the most learned and scientific men in the city." He was elected Professor of the English Tongue and of Oratory in the University of Pennsylvania in 1755. He held this position with advantage to the institution for eighteen years, and resigned it to the great regret of the students and their teachers. He died July 4, 1778. In the splendid building recently reared for the University of Pennsylvania a beautiful memorial window commemorates the worth of Ebenezer Kinnersley.

Kinney, Deacon Albert William, eldest son of Hon. R. C. Kinney, is deacon of the Baptist church of Salem, Oregon. He is successor to his father in an immense business at Salem, is noted for his devotion to Christ and for his lovely spirit. He is a large contributor to Baptist benevolent objects and other charities on the Pacific Coast. He was born at Muscatine, Ia., Oct. 3, 1843, became a Christian in early life, and is a zealous and steadfast member of the Baptist church.

Kinney, Hon. Robert Crouch, one of the most distinguished of Baptist benefactors in Oregon, was born July 4, 1813, in St. Clair Co., Ill.; removed to Muscatine, Ia., in 1838, and to Oregon in 1847; successful in large business enterprises, kind to the poor, just in his dealings, liberal to all, especially

HON. ROBERT CROUCH KINNEY.

to churches and colleges. He died at Salem, Oregon, March 2, 1875; all business was suspended, the Capitol was in mourning, and State officials wept as for a brother at the funeral. When death was near, his son, Dr. Kinney, was summoned at midnight to a distant town. The night was stormy, and the son, being reluctant to leave his father, was urged to go. "It may be some poor man that cannot pay you, Alfred; but go; don't let him suffer."

His marriage in early life was a happy one. He and his wife were Baptists; their children illustrated their parents' piety in the consecration of their wealth to the upbuilding of McMinnville College, the support of missions, and all other objects of benevolence. Mr. Kinney was a member of the Iowa Constitutional Convention; also a member of the Territorial Legislature, and of the Constitutional Convention of Oregon.

Kirk, Rev. A. G., is of Scotch origin on his father's side, and of English on his mother's. He was born in Lancaster Co., Pa., Nov. 14, 1809, of Quaker parentage. His great-grandfather, Benjamin Gilbert, and his family, were taken prisoners by the Indians in April, 1780, and suffered a miserable captivity, passing their days in constant terror of being killed, but, in the language of the chief, Rowland Mintour, "The Great Spirit would not let us kill you."

The son remained with his father's family until his marriage, in 1833, and in the subsequent year removed into Ohio, and engaged in teaching until 1845. On Jan. 15, 1843, he was baptized, and made his first public speech to a large assembly, partly composed of his scholars and of skeptical friends attracted to the solemn scene. He was ordained Jan. 12, 1845, at Salem, Columbiana Co., O. He was the first resident pastor of the church in New Castle, Lawrence Co., Pa., and the first pastor of the Nixon Street church, Alleghany City, Pa. At New Castle he enjoyed a prosperous ministry of eleven years. In Alleghany City and other churches he was highly favored. His entire ministry has been richly blessed. In labors he has been abundant, having preached during thirty-three years about 5000 sermons, and during the entire period losing only eight Sabbaths by any indisposition of the body. He is still in service.

Kirtley, Rev. E. N., a prominent minister in Louisiana, is a native of Virginia, and nearly fifty-five years of age. He came to Louisiana about 1850 as a licensed preacher in the Methodist church. He was convinced of the truth of Baptist sentiments from reading "Pendleton's Three Reasons." He was ordained as a Baptist minister in 1854, and became a missionary of the Grand Cane Association. He labored here until the war. About 1863 he removed to Springville, in Red River Parish, and engaged in teaching and preaching. He then removed to Ringgold, in Bienville Parish, where he taught and preached until he was called to Minden, in 1873. He then took a school at Red Land, in Bossier Parish, where he still lives, supplying the church at Bellevue, the capital of Bossier Parish.

Kirtley, Rev. Robert, was born in Culpeper Co., Va., May 30, 1786. In 1796 he with his parents emigrated to Boone Co., Ky., where he spent the remainder of a long and eminently useful life.

He professed religion and united with the Baptist church at Bullittsburg in 1811. In 1812 he entered the army as a lieutenant, and at the close of the campaign returned home and engaged in the active duties of religion. He was licensed to preach in 1819, ordained in 1822, and in 1826 he succeeded the beloved Absalom Graves in the pastoral care of Bullittsburg church. He was the leading preacher for years in North Bend Association, of which he was moderator thirty-one years. He died April 9, 1872.

Kitchen, Hon. W. H., who represents the Second District of North Carolina in the U. S. Congress, was born in 1837; received a collegiate education in Virginia; read law; entered the army in 1861, and attained the rank of captain of infantry, 12th Regiment N. C. troops; was baptized by Rev. C. Durham in 1876. Mr. Kitchen is a man of great worth.

Kitts, Rev. Thomas J., was born in 1789, and was licensed to preach by the First Baptist church of Wilmington, Del. He was ordained to the pastorate of the church of Canton, N. J. In 1823 he took charge of the Second Baptist church of Philadelphia. This office he held for nearly sixteen years, till death summoned him to the skies.

His preaching was able and his ministry successful. He was a man of prayer; he was thoroughly conversant with the Word of God; he lived near the Eternal, whose love lifted his heart above the world and gave him the warm regards of all the friends of Jesus with whom he came in contact. He died Jan. 26, 1838, in the forty-ninth year of his age.

Knapp, Halsey Wing, D.D., was born in the city of New York in October, 1824. His father, Rev. Henry R. Knapp, was a successful Baptist minister, and his mother a woman of piety and force of character. In his youth and early manhood he was impulsive, energetic, and jovial, leading a restless life, some years of which were spent at sea. In 1846 he settled in business in New York. He was converted in 1857, and in 1858 was ordained to the ministry by a Council of the Baptist churches of New York. From this time his career has been especially eventful. His pastorates have been at West Farms and Hudson City, and in New York City with the South, Pilgrim, and Light Street churches. These important positions he has filled and at the same time conducted an extensive business. During nineteen years of pulpit service he has given away his entire salary to religious and benevolent objects. He daily transacts business, preaches every night in the week, during revival seasons traveling at night to keep his appointments, without any expense to the churches, and he often gives largely of his own means to assist new churches. His donations are without ostentation, and aggregate many thousands of dollars. As a preacher Dr. Knapp is eloquent and impressive, and he is greatly beloved by his denomination. A Western college conferred upon him the degree of D.D. in 1876.

Knapp, Rev. Henry Reynolds, was born in the city of New York Dec. 6, 1800; converted at the age of twenty-four; with his half-brother, William, organized a Sunday-school and preaching service in the basement of his father's house, out of which grew the Sixteenth Street Baptist church; licensed by McDougal Street Baptist church in 1832; ordained pastor of Greenport church, L. I., Oct. 8, 1834; having evangelistic gifts, afterwards settled with Baptist church, Essex, Conn.; First Baptist church, New London; Baptist church, Preston City; Second Baptist church, Groton; church in Rockville; church at Rondout, on the Hudson; returned to Greenport, L. I.; with church at Noank, Conn.; with the church at Hastings, on the Hudson; clear and forcible preacher; sound in doctrine and devoted in labors; his ministry crowned with many and happy revivals; occupying different fields in order to do the most good; in every place honored and held in sweet remembrance; has three sons now living, Rev. Halsey W. Knapp, D.D., Rev. Samuel J. Knapp, and Prof. Knapp of Yale College; had in his wife an eminent helpmeet; died May 13, 1862, in his sixty-second year, and the thirty-first of his ministry.

Knapp, Rev. Jacob, was born Dec. 7, 1799, in Otsego Co., N. Y., and died at Rockford, Ill., March 3, 1874. He studied at Hamilton in 1821–25, and was ordained August 23 in the year last named. Entering the pastorate at Springfield, Otsego Co., N. Y., he remained there five years; then removed to Watertown, N. Y., where he remained three years. Entering there upon the work of an "evangelist," he continued in that service during the remaining forty-two years of his public ministry. Fifteen years he resided at Hamilton, N. Y., twenty-five upon his farm near Rockford, Ill. In his revivalist work he ranged widely over New York, New England, and the Western States, including California. "He preached about 16,000 sermons," says Prof. Spear, of Madison University, "led about 200 young men to preach the gospel, and baptized 4000." Mr. Knapp's physique was in some sense a type of his mental and spiritual habit. He was of moderate height, strongly built, with broad shoulders and a muscular frame capable of great endurance. His conspicuous physical, like his mental, quality was that of robustness, while the business-like air with which he moved about in his ordinary avocations was typical of the serious, earnest, unflinching way in which he preached and toiled in the face of severe personal exposure and reproach. His preaching was doctrinal, direct, unsparing, even sometimes to the verge of coarseness; but his power over audiences was remarkable, and the fruits of his long toil in his chosen sphere, while not always genuine, were believed in many cases to be so, and always abundant. Among his last words were, "Oh, I have come to the everlasting hills!"

> "On Christ the solid rock I stand,
> All other ground is sinking sand."

He was buried at Rockford, Ill., Drs. Cole and Osgood and Hon. Messrs. Fulton, of Belvidere, and Holman, of Rockford, participating in the service.

Knapp, William J., Ph.D., was born at Greenpoint, Long Island, March 10, 1835; received his collegiate education in Madison and New York Universities. At graduation, in Madison, he was elected Professor of Modern Languages, for which he possesses remarkable qualifications. For a time he was Professor of Ancient and Modern Languages in Vassar College. In 1867 New York University conferred upon him the honorary degree of Doctor of Philosophy. For some years he was engaged in successful missionary labors in Spain. He is now a professor in Yale College.

Kneeland, Rev. Levi, was born in Masonville, N. Y., in 1803; converted at the age of fifteen, and united with the Baptist church in Masonville; at twenty licensed to preach; in 1824 entered Hamilton Literary and Theological Institution, and remained four years; ordained at Packerville, Conn., Oct. 8, 1828, with church just formed; held meetings in remote neighborhoods; established branch church at Voluntown; preached at Jewett City, Sterling, and Plainfield; assisted in protracted meetings at Norwich and elsewhere; held protracted meetings at Packerville every year; bold, aggressive, mighty in prayer, powerful in exhortation, full of illustrations, affable, sociable; intent on saving souls and greatly beloved by his brethren; in the six years of his ministry baptized more than 300; died at Packerville, Aug. 23, 1834, aged thirty-one.

Knight, Rev. Aaron Brightwell, A.M., was born in Todd Co., Ky., Feb. 24, 1824. He united with the Baptist church at Russellville in 1842, was licensed to preach in 1846, and was ordained in 1850. He was educated at Centre College, Ky., and graduated in 1845, after which he pursued a three years' course at Princeton Theological Seminary, in New Jersey. He received several flattering calls to city and village churches, but preferring the quiet of a country home, after preaching a short time for Salem church in Christian County, in his native State, he settled on a farm in Shelby Co., Ky., in 1858, where he still resides. He has been pastor of Burk's Branch church since 1858, and for a short time of Clay Village church. Since 1871 he has been pastor at Simpsonville church. In 1863 he was moderator of the General Association, and has been thirteen years moderator of Long Run Association, which includes the churches of Louisville. He was active in establishing the Kentucky Female College at Shelbyville; was its first president, and chairman of its board of trustees until it was destroyed by fire. He is a good preacher, and is much beloved and honored by his people.

Knight, Rev. Richard, author of the "History of the General and Six-Principle Baptists in England and America," in two parts; and the son of Deacon Stephen Knight, was born in Cranston, R. I., Oct. 5, 1771; a descendant of Richard Knight, one of the first settlers of Cranston; united with the Six-Principle Baptists in 1804; ordained pastor of the church in Scituate, R. I., Oct. 19, 1809, by Revs. Westcott, Manchester, and Sprague; served this church till his death; favored with powerful revivals; his church finally numbered over 400 members; published his history (8vo, 370 pages) in 1827; occupied his pulpit for fifty-three years; a man of great worth, industry, and strength; died in Cranston, R. I., April 10, 1863, in his ninety-second year.

Knollys, Rev. Hanserd, A.M., was born at Chalkwell, in Lincolnshire, in 1598. His parents gave their son religious instruction and a superior education. He was sent to the University of Cambridge, where he remained until he graduated. He had some religious exercises before he came to Cambridge, but sermons which he heard during his residence there were blessed to his conversion.

In June, 1629, he was ordained by the Bishop of Peterborough, and soon after he received the living of Humberstone from the Bishop of Lincoln. While at Humberstone he preached in many parishes beside his own, and at several hours in the day. He frequently proclaimed Christ at Holton at seven in the morning, at Humberstone at nine, at Scartha at eleven, and at Humberstone again at three in the afternoon, besides preaching on every holiday. After he became a Non-conformist he was in the pulpit just as frequently. For above forty years he delivered three or four sermons a week, and when he was in prison he preached every day. While he was a clergyman of the National Church and a Conformist he knew of no case of conversion resulting from his labors, but when he set out without state support he had throngs of converts.

He was convinced that many things in the Episcopal Church were destitute of Scripture warrant, and he first resigned his parish, and then two or three years afterwards his ministry and membership in the Anglican Church. This event occurred in 1636. That year he was arrested by order of "The High Commission Court," a tribunal second only to the Inquisition in wickedness, but by the connivance of the man who had him in charge he escaped. He started for New England by way of London. There he had to wait so long for a vessel that his entire money was spent except six brass farthings. His wife, however, was able to give him five pounds. They were twelve weeks on their passage, and their provisions became nearly unfit for use.

When he arrived at Boston, which was in 1638, he was speedily and falsely denounced as an Antinomian, and though he met with some kindness he had to work with a hoe to secure his daily bread. He was there but a brief time when he had an opportunity to go to Dover, then called Piscataway, in New Hampshire, and preach the gospel to the

REV. HANSERD KNOLLYS, A.M.

people of that place. That he was a Baptist at this time we see no reason to doubt. Mr. Mather says in his "Ecclesiastical History of New England," "I confess there were some of those persons (more than a score of emigrant ministers that had arrived in Massachusetts) whose names deserve to live in our book for their piety, although their particular opinions were such as to be disserviceable unto the declared and supposed interests of our churches. Of these there were some godly Anabaptists; as namely Mr. Hanserd Knollys, of Dover, who, afterwards removing back to London, lately died there, a good man, in a good old age." That Mr. Mather was acquainted with the religious opinions held by Hanserd Knollys when he was in Dover is evident to us. There was a bitter controversy between two sections of Mr. Knollys' church during his residence there, and his doctrines unquestionably were well known, and Mather speaks of him as an Anabaptist when he came. We wish no better testimony to the good character of Hanserd Knollys whilst in Dover, and to his Baptist principles, than Mather furnishes. Knollys probably had a sort of union church there for a time, such as Backus had for a short period at Middleborough. Mr. Lechford, an Episcopalian, visited Dover in April, 1641, and he describes a controversy existing between Mr. Knollys and a ministerial opponent there as being about baptism and church membership. "They two," says he, "fell out about baptizing children, receiving of members," etc. And Mr. Knollys' section of the Dover church evidently held Baptist sentiments. The Baptists taught by Knollys, to escape persecution from Massachusetts, to which Dover was recently united, removed, in 1641, to Long Island. After Long Island fell under the power of the English and of Episcopalianism they removed again, and located permanently in New Jersey, near New Brunswick, and they called their third American home Piscataway, after their first on this continent. The Piscataway church is to-day as vigorous a community as bears the Baptist name in any part of our broad country.

Mr. Knollys was summoned to England by his aged father, and on his return immediately commenced to preach in the churches. For this he was drawn into frequent troubles. At last he set up a separate meeting in Great St. Helen's, London, where the people thronged his house, and his congregations commonly numbered a thousand. For this innovation he was summoned before a committee of " The Westminster Assembly of Divines," by whose chairman he was commanded to preach no more. But his ready reply was that " he would preach the gospel publicly, and from house to house."

In 1645 he was formally ordained pastor of the Baptist church which he had gathered in London. This position he retained till his death. His popularity as a preacher was very great, and it continued till a late period of life.

He was imprisoned frequently for breaking the laws against the worship of Dissenters. Even in his eighty-fourth year he was in jail six months, and just before his incarceration he refused to employ his immense influence with the Baptists to secure their approval of the suspension of the penal laws by James II.

He was a strong Calvinist, a devoted servant of God, a decided Baptist, a firm friend of every true Christian, and a man of great learning in the ancient languages and in general literature. He was the author of eleven works, among which was a grammar of the Latin, Greek, and Hebrew languages. He was regarded, and he is still revered, as a shining light by the denomination whose name he honored and whose bounds he extended. He died in London, Sept. 19, 1691, in the ninety-third year of his age.

Knowles, Prof. James Davis, was born in Providence, R. I., in July, 1798. His father having died when he was but twelve years old, he was left to the care of an affectionate mother, who lived to see the successful career of her son. He was placed when quite young in a printing-office in Providence, which became to him an excellent school for the acquisition of knowledge. At the age of twenty-one he became the co-editor of one of the leading journals of Rhode Island.

It was about this time that he made a public profession of his faith under Rev. Dr. Gano's ministry, and he became a member of the First Baptist church in Providence, and soon after was licensed to preach the gospel. All the previous plans which he had formed with reference to his future life were abandoned, and he resolved to give himself to the work of the ministry. To prepare for it he pursued a course of theological study with Dr. Stoughton, first in Philadelphia, and then in Washington when his teacher removed to that city to take charge of Columbian College.

Along with his theological studies he was able to pursue a collegiate course with such success that at the end of two years he graduated with the highest honors of his class. He was at once appointed tutor in the college, which office he held until the summer of 1825, when he returned to New England, having received a call to become the pastor of the Second Baptist church in Boston, as the successor of the venerated Dr. Baldwin. He was ordained Dec. 28, 1825. After a pastorate of seven years he felt compelled to resign his charge, and by a change of occupation relieve his overtaxed energies. Having been appointed Professor of Pastoral Duties and Sacred Rhetoric in the Newton Theological Institution, he retired from the church, between which and himself there was the warmest affection. He found renewed health in the position to which the providence of God had called him, and made his experience as a minister of Christ of the highest importance to him in his new field of labor. It was during his connection with the seminary that he conducted the *Christian Review* with an ability that placed it among the best quarterlies in the country. Prof. Knowles was the author of the biography of Mrs. Ann Hasseltine Judson, one of the most finished memoirs ever published in America. He was also author of a memoir of Roger Williams.

The connection of Prof. Knowles with the Newton Theological Institution terminated very suddenly. While on a visit to New York he contracted the smallpox, and shortly after his return sunk under the attack and died May 9, 1838, being within a few weeks of forty years of age. His apparently premature decease was lamented by all who knew him. Prof. Knowles was a man of great energy and indomitable will. His life was one of diligence, and of quiet but persistent work. He was not to be led aside from the performance of his duties by the temptations of ease or by difficulties besetting his path. The denomination has cause for rejoicing in his devotedness to the service of Christ.

Knowles, J. Sheridan, author of "Virginius" and other dramas of great literary excellence and celebrity, joined the Baptist church at Torquay, Devon, England, in 1847, when he was about sixty years of age. He had maintained a high moral character throughout his literary career, but received no serious religious impressions until late in life. The semi-popery prevalent in the Established Church at Torquay, where he resided, disgusted him, and he resorted to the Baptist meeting-house, where, under the ministry of the late Rev. J. King, he found the joy of salvation. Soon after his conversion he went forth as an evangelist, and crowds came together to hear him. Always a graceful elocutionist, his reading of the Scriptures was very impressive. Until his death, which took place Nov. 30, 1862, he manifested the deepest interest in evangelical Christianity and a firm attachment to Baptist principles. His eminent literary services were recognized by the government, and a pension was awarded him, which, after his death, was continued to his widow.

Knowles, Deacon Levi, a merchant of Philadelphia, was born in New Jersey in 1813. He early commenced business, and determined to pursue it with energy and industry. He began life without the advantage of capital, but resolved to use all the talent he possessed to succeed. He joined the church in his youth, adopting the Baptist faith, that had been handed down through two generations in his family. He gave some of his best efforts to the Sunday-school cause and other objects of benevolence. He was unanimously elected a deacon in three different churches while he was in their membership. His services were sought for to take charge of the funds of various organizations, for twelve of which he is now treasurer, and in none of which is any compensation given. His firm has maintained its credit through all the vicissitudes and panics of years. Mr. Knowles is familiar with the great writers of the past and present. He married wisely and was blessed with children, in whose society he spends many of his happiest hours. He is strong in his friendships, liberal in his gifts, and one of the pillars of the Baptist denomination in Philadelphia. Mrs. Knowles, with rare wisdom and generous giving, has made the Baptist Home of Philadelphia, of which she is president, one of the most successful institutions of its class on either side of the Atlantic.

Knowles, William B., son of Deacon Levi and Mrs. E. A. Knowles, was born in Philadelphia, Feb. 20, 1848, and died Sept. 22, 1875, at the early age of twenty-seven years. Mr. Knowles was possessed of fine natural abilities, and, in addition to a liberal education, he received a thorough training for mercantile pursuits, enabling him in early manhood to occupy a prominent position in the business community of his native city. As a member of the firm of L. Knowles & Co., so widely and honorably known, he was brought into relations with merchants in all parts of the country, and gained by his deportment and honorable bearing a wide circle of friends.

The Christian character of William B. Knowles was an exemplification of the great beauty and usefulness that the Lord often causes to be manifested in a life devoted from tender years to his service. Very early he gave clear evidence of a change of heart, and at the age of twelve he spoke of his love for Jesus to the Tabernacle church of Philadelphia, and on the last Lord's Day in February, 1860, he was "buried with Christ in baptism."

From this date until his triumphant death his life was one of faith manifested by works. Clerk of Beth-Eden church from its organization, active in the Sunday-school, young people's association, and in the prayer-meetings of the church, he was always solicitous for the spiritual interests of Zion. In his daily life he commended to others the religion of the Lord Jesus by maintaining a high Christian reputation. In his early bloom, just as the promise of his youth began to be fulfilled, he passed away, and, to use his last faint words, he was "Safe, safe in the arms of Jesus."

His loss was severely felt, and the most tender sympathy was expressed for his parents and loving wife by the Commercial Exchange of Philadelphia, merchants in this and other cities, and by ministers and hosts of brethren in the Christian faith.

Knowlton, Miles Justin, D.D., was born in West Wardsborough, Vt., Feb. 8, 1825. Both his parents were persons of more than ordinary excellence of character, and took the deepest interest in the early development of their son. He prepared for college at West Townsend, and completed both his collegiate and his theological course at Hamilton. Near the close of his college course he seems to have had a fresh baptism of the Holy Ghost, which was followed by a new and thorough consecration of himself to any work which his Lord had for him to do. A missionary life, either at home or abroad, appeared to him to be that to which he regarded it both as a privilege and a duty to devote himself. At length his mind settled upon the foreign field, and he offered himself to the Missionary Union and was accepted, and China was designated as the field of his labor. He was ordained in his native town Oct. 8, 1853, and soon after sailed for China, arriving at Ningpo in June, 1854, which henceforth was to be his home, and where he was to labor as a servant of the Lord Jesus Christ. There he continued for a little more than twenty years, deducting two years for his temporary sojourn in this country, whither he had come to recover his shattered health. With singleness of aim and the utmost persistency he gave himself to the one great business of preaching "the glorious gospel of the blessed God" to the Chinese. In season and out of season he determined to know only one thing among the heathen, and that was the gospel of Christ. He was full of energy and moral heroism, and he knew how to kindle the enthusiasm in the souls of others which he felt in his own.

Dr. Knowlton, in Ningpo, did not spare himself if he might but win souls to Christ. At the post of labor he was found when death came to him, on the 10th of September, 1874. It is thus that the executive board speak of him in their sixty-first annual report: "With what earnestness, what zeal, what love for Christ and the souls of men, what devotion to the special evangelization of the great empire of China, and with what success in his personal work as a missionary of the cross, our lamented Brother Knowlton gave himself to his life-work for twenty years, is partially and imperfectly recorded in the history of your work in China, but it is all registered in completeness in the book above. He died in the city of Ningpo, on the 10th of September last, in the very midst of his usefulness. China mourns."

Knox, Rev. George, was born in Saco, Me., Oct. 24, 1816, and fitted for college at the academy in Yarmouth, Me. He graduated at Waterville College, in the class of 1840. Having spent a year at the Newton Theological Institution, he was ordained as pastor of the Baptist church in Topsham, Me., where he remained for four years, when he removed to Cornish, where he was pastor two years, and then to Lewiston, where his relation with the Baptist church in that city continued for thirteen years. He had two brief pastorates after leaving Lewiston, one at Brunswick, and the other at Lawrence, Mass. While acting as chaplain of the 3d Me. Regiment in the late war he died, in Virginia, Oct. 31, 1864.

Krishna Pal was the first Hindoo led into the

baptismal waters by Dr. Carey; he had courage and faith to stand alone in renouncing the abominations of his countrymen in the presence of his kindred. He was born about 1764, at Chandernagore, Bengal.

Krishna was by trade a carpenter; and in listening to a discourse on the folly of idolatry and the great truths of Christianity, he became deeply affected and shed tears. He visited the missionaries soon after for religious instruction, and received with great eagerness the truths which they communicated. Soon he felt that he had put his trust in Jesus, and that he was a Christian. He then requested baptism, and laid aside openly his allegiance to idolatry. He sat down at the table of the missionaries in presence of their Hindoo servants, and by this act renounced caste. The news spread rapidly, and soon Krishna was besieged by a mob of 2000 persons, who poured out torrents of maledictions upon him, and then dragged him to the magistrate, who immediately released him and commended him for the piety of his course, and commanded the mob to disperse. The magistrate placed a Sepoy at Krishna's house to guard him, and offered armed protection to the missionaries during the celebration of the rite of baptism. The immersion occurred in the Ganges, on the 28th of December, 1800. Mr. Carey walked to the river from the chapel with his eldest son, Felix, on one side, and Krishna on the other. At the landing there were gathered the governor and a number of Europeans, and a great throng of Hindoos and Mohammedans. Mr. Ward preached a sermon in English from John v. 39, " Search the Scriptures." Dr. Carey delivered an address in Bengali after a Bengali translation of the hymn was sung,—

> " Jesus, and shall it ever be,
> A mortal man ashamed of thee?"

Then he baptized Felix Carey and Krishna amid profound silence and deep solemnity. Krishna was the first baptized convert after seven years of labor. Krishna the same day partook of the Lord's Supper, and he enjoyed an unusual measure of the love of God as he waited upon Him in both ordinances. For more than twenty years Krishna Pal preached the blessed gospel to his countrymen with great success and ability. He led a holy life and he possessed a strong faith, and when he came to the end of his earthly journey his heart was full of peace, and of the light of a bright hope of immediate entrance into heaven. A European who was present at his dying couch says, " I myself witnessed the last moments of Krishna, and heard his aged and quivering lips speak of the preciousness of Christ." Krishna composed the beautiful hymn from which the following stanzas are taken:

> " O thou my soul, forget no more
> The Friend who all thy misery bore;
> Let every idol be forgot,
> But, O my soul, forget Him not.

> " Jesus for thee a body takes;
> Thy guilt assumes, thy fetters breaks,
> Discharging all thy dreadful debt;
> And canst thou e'er such love forget?"

Kutchin, Rev. T. T., was born in Philadelphia, Pa., Nov. 5, 1815, died at Dartmouth, Wis., Aug. 7, 1877. He entered the ministry at New Britain, Pa., at the age of twenty-one, and at once became popular as a preacher. He came to Wisconsin in 1855. For many years he was the editor of the *Milwaukee Sentinel*, and subsequently of the *Fon du Lac Commonwealth*. He was distinguished for remarkable intellectual power united with great kindness of heart. His two sons are esteemed ministers of the gospel, occupying important pulpits in the State.

L.

La Grange College was chartered in 1859, and a commodious brick building was erected, 90 by 70 feet, which was finished in 1866. It had superior chemical and philosophical apparatus when J. F. Cook, LL.D., became president. Both sexes are admitted to this institution. In the fourteen years of his presidency there have been more than two thousand matriculations, and among the number about sixty students for the ministry. Nearly $15,000 have been raised for improvements and for the removal of debts during the administration of Dr. Cook. One hundred and fifty children of ministers have been gratuitously educated in La Grange. Dr. Sawyer is now vice-president of the institution. It has eleven able instructors, who render excellent service, as the character of their graduates testifies. This college is beautifully located on the bluffs of the Mississippi, one hundred and thirty-seven miles north of St. Louis. (See page 668.)

Lailey, Thomas, was born Aug. 29, 1820, in the parish of Poplar, London, England. When quite young he came with his parents to Canada. He owns the largest wholesale house in his business in the province of Ontario. He united, by baptism, with the Bond Street church, Toronto, in 1849. In 1867 he, with several others, left this old mother-church to form a new interest on Alexander Street. The cost of the neat and comfortable edifice which they at once proceeded to erect was chiefly borne by him; and he has been from the first by far the largest contributor toward the current expenses of the church. The erection of the College Street and Lewis Street church edifices was also mainly due to his enterprise and liberality, and he is now (1881) promoting a scheme of church extension in the western part of the city. He has purchased an eligible site, on which a mission chapel is to be commenced immediately. He was president of the Home Mission Convention of Ontario in 1868–69.

tions, which he has filled with great ability and fidelity.

For forty years Mr. Lain has been a member of the Baptist church in Waukesha. He is known as a man of great purity of character, and of blameless Christian life. Until the failure of his health, which occurred a few years ago, he was very efficient and active in promoting the Baptist cause in his city, and in strengthening the denomination in the State.

Lake, Rev. J. B., was born in Fauquier Co., Va., May 4, 1837; attended school in Alexandria, Va., where he received a thorough training at the hands of the well-known Benjamin Hallowell, and afterwards studied at the University of Virginia, where he was graduated from several of its schools. While still at the university he was elected to a professorship in Edgeworth Female College, Greens-

LA GRANGE COLLEGE.

Lain, Hon. Isaac, of Waukesha, was born in Orange Co., N. Y., Dec. 18, 1820. His ancestors were from England, and settled at an early day on Long Island, N. Y. Isaac Lain's father was a farmer, and to this calling the son devoted himself until 1833. He then learned the business of architect and builder. In June, 1842, he settled in Waukesha, Wis., where he still resides. Here he engaged extensively for many years in his new business. In 1852 he established a real estate and insurance agency, and in 1860 he took an active part in founding the Waukesha County Manufacturing Company, of which he is now a heavy stockholder and secretary. In 1861, at the outbreak of the civil war, Mr. Lain was a member of the State Legislature, and took an active part in the measures which placed Wisconsin in the front rank of States for the promptness and efficiency with which her regiments were raised and sent to the front.

Mr. Lain has held many local and county posi-

borough, N. C. Subsequently, Mr. Lake held a professorship in Chesapeake Female College, Va., four years, and then had charge of the Roanoke Female College, at Danville, Va., nine years. In 1872 he left Danville to become pastor of the church in Upperville, Va., where he still remains as a most successful preacher and pastor. His mind is vigorous and logical, and his sermons are filled with cardinal doctrinal truths and enriched by apt and numerous historical illustrations.

Lake, Rev. P. W., came to Wisconsin in 1839, and settled in Walworth County, and performed much foundation work in the early history of the State. He was an interesting preacher. Earnestness and spirituality were distinguished characteristics in his ministry. He died many years ago, but his name and labors are held in remembrance in many of the churches of Walworth County.

Lamar, Rev. A. W., editor of the *Baptist Courier*, was born at Leavenworth Mills, S. C.,

March 30, 1847. His father was Col. Thomas G. Lamar, who distinguished himself in the late war as commander at the battle of Secessionville, near Charleston, in June, 1862, and who died soon after. In honor of his memory the State Legislature sent the subject of this sketch to the State Military School to be educated. Being strongly impressed that it was his duty to preach, he sold a tract of land—obtained from his father's estate—to procure means for educating himself. Entering first Furman University, and then the theological seminary at Greenville, he afterwards accepted a call of the Mount Zion church in Newberry County, where he was ordained Jan. 15, 1871, at the age of twenty-four. At the meeting of the State Convention in November, 1871, he was elected its general agent. In November, 1873, the State Convention manifested its appreciation of his ability and success by electing him both corresponding secretary and general agent, charging him with all the work of the body during its recess. He was converted when at the military school, and began at once to work for Jesus among the cadets, praying with and for them, holding prayer-meetings, and reading Spurgeon's sermons to them. At first he met with much opposition, was treated with every indignity, but in the end those who led in these things asked him to pray for them. He has met with extraordinary success in the work assigned him, being imbued with zeal, perseverance, and earnestness, and blessed with great tact and good judgment. He is a young man, self-reliant and with good judgment, who takes hold of his work and does it like a veteran, having the confidence and esteem of all. His present field of labor is Camden.

Lamb, Rev. Amherst, was born in Phillipston, Mass., July 28, 1796, and spent his childhood and youth in Guilford, Vt. Soon after making a public profession of faith he commenced to preach, but, feeling the necessity of a better preparation for his work, he placed himself under the tuition of Rev. Dr. Young, then of Worcester, Mass. He was ordained in December, 1821, as pastor of the church at Guilford, Vt., and remained there for six years, when he became pastor of the church in Whitingham, September, 1827, and continued there until 1836. He then went to Charlemont, Mass., and preached there for nine years, having charge of the church in Buckland during a part of this period,—for half the time. Recalled to the church in Whitingham in 1845, he gave it twelve years of additional service, after which he supplied churches in his neighborhood, where his labors were much blessed. He died at Whitingham, May 29, 1870. His record was one of a high character wherever he was known.

Lamson, William, D.D., was born in Danvers, Mass., Feb. 22, 1812. He prepared for college at the academy in South Reading (now Wakefield), Mass., and graduated at Waterville College in the class of 1835. After his graduation he served as tutor for one year. In the autumn of 1837 he was ordained as pastor of the church in Gloucester, Mass. Wishing to pursue a more extended course of theological study, he entered the Newton Theological Institution in 1839, and remained until 1841, when he was settled as pastor of the church at Thomaston, Me. He returned to Gloucester, where he continued until called to Portsmouth, N. H., in 1848. He was pastor of the church in Portsmouth for eleven years. The church in Brookline, Mass., called him in 1859, and he was their pastor until 1875, when failing health obliged him to give up his ministerial work. Since his resignation he has lived chiefly in Salem and Gloucester, Mass.

Dr. Lamson has been one of the most useful and acceptable ministers in the denomination. By his pen, as well as his voice, he has made his talents subservient to promote the interests of truth.

Lancaster, Rev. William, was born in Warren Co., N. C., in 1753; was baptized by Rev. Wm. Walker; was the founder of the churches at Maple Spring and Poplar Spring, Franklin Co., about 1793; was a member of the State Convention, of the convention to ratify the Federal Constitution, and for many years chairman of the Court of Pleas and Quarter Sessions of Franklin County. He closed his long and useful life Sept. 16, 1826.

Landrum, Rev. John G., was born in Tennessee in 1810. At eighteen he removed to Union Co., S. C., and the next year began to preach. His slender form made him look much younger than he was, and for some years he was called the boy preacher. He became pastor of the Mount Zion and Bethlehem churches, in Spartanburg County, in 1830, and still serves them. He has had charge of the New Prospect church since 1835. The Baptist church at Spartanburg Court-house was organized under his ministry, where he preached for twenty-five years.

He has baptized about 5000 persons in fifty years. He exercises a very extensive influence in Spartanburg and the surrounding counties. Perhaps he could not say that his "natural force is not abated," but his labors are as abundant as ever.

Landrum, Sylvanus, D.D., pastor of the Baptist church at Savannah, Ga., has exerted a strong influence among the Baptists of Georgia. For many years he has been on the board of trustees of Mercer University, and for a long time acted as secretary of the board, and, besides, he has served the denomination in various positions with much success. He is a courteous gentleman, with a sound judgment, sincere piety, and intellectual ability.

He is an eloquent speaker. His congregations love and respect him. He was born in Oglethorpe Co., Ga., Oct. 3, 1820; his parents came from Virginia. He was educated at Mason Academy, Lexington, Ga., and at Mercer University. Ordained Oct. 23, 1846, he became, in January, 1847, pastor of the Baptist churches at Lexington and Athens, Ga.

SYLVANUS LANDRUM, D.D.

In December, 1849, he became pastor of the Macon (Ga.) Baptist church, where he served ten years, being instrumental there in the erection of a handsome and costly Gothic church edifice. In December, 1859, he accepted a call to Savannah, Ga., and there he remained twelve years, building up and uniting the Baptist cause in the city. He was there during the war, and never lost a single service on account of hostilities,—his was the only white Baptist church on the coast line from Baltimore to Texas which did not close at all during the conflict. He preached on one Sabbath to Confederate and the next Sabbath to Federal soldiers, at the time of the city's capture.

In 1871 he removed to Memphis, and became pastor of the Central Baptist church, remaining until after the severe yellow-fever scourge of 1878, during which he lost two sons, both prominent and talented young men. In 1879 he returned to Georgia, and again took charge of the Savannah church, where he is doing an admirable work.

Two colleges in one year conferred on him the Doctorate in Divinity,—Georgetown, Ky., Dr. Crawford president, and Columbian College, Washington, Dr. Samson president.

He is a man of national views, whose heart is in the pastorate, and whose chief aim is the advancement of Christ's kingdom on earth. His sermons are always good and never disappointing. To great administrative ability he unites remarkable excellence of judgment and a good knowledge of men and human nature. He is a wise and safe counselor, and makes his influence for good felt in the assemblies of his denominational brethren.

Landrum, Rev. William Warren, son of Dr. Sylvanus and Eliza Jane (Warren) Landrum, was born in Macon, Ga., Jan. 18, 1853. He was converted at the age of ten, and baptized in his fourteenth year. His early education was received at Chatham Academy, Savannah. He entered Mercer University, but subsequently went to Brown University, where he was graduated with distinction in 1872. He then became a student in the Southern Baptist Theological Seminary, at Greenville, S. C., from which he graduated in 1874, in nine of the thirteen schools in the institution.

At the call of the Central church of Memphis, he was ordained in May, 1874. His first pastorate was at Shreveport, La., where he labored with success for two years. He then accepted a call from the First Baptist church in Augusta, Ga., and removed to his native State in February, 1876. Of that church he is still the pastor. He was married Sept. 21, 1875, to Miss Ida Louise Dunster, a descendant of Henry Dunster, first president of Harvard University.

Mr. Landrum is a good preacher and pastor, and a man of more than ordinary abilities. He hates controversy, has great faith in the power of gospel preaching and the efficacy of a cheerful, loving piety, and his highest ambition is to be a consecrated and successful minister of Jesus Christ.

Lane, Rev. Dutton, was born Nov. 12, 1732, near Baltimore, Md. He was baptized by Shubael Sterns in 1758, and ordained to the ministry in October, 1764. He had a vigorous constitution, a powerful voice, and a heart on fire with the love of Jesus, and he was greatly blessed by his Master. In the Dare River church, Va., of which he was pastor, and for many miles around, the fruits of his ministry were visible to the whole community. His father, impelled by hatred to his religious fervor, tried to kill him, but "he himself was slain by the sword of the Spirit, from which he soon after revived with the hope of eternal life," and was baptized by his son.

Mr. Lane continued in the ministry till death, but the latter part of his life was marred by certain strange opinions which he adopted.

Lane, Rev. Thomas Jefferson, one of Tennessee's veteran Baptist ministers, was born in Jefferson (now Hamilton) Co., East Tenn., Oct. 9, 1804; son of Aquila and Agnes Lane, and grandson of

Elder Lane, one of the first Baptist ministers that settled in East Tennessee, in 1785.

Mr. Lane professed religion in 1834, and was baptized by Andrew Coffman, and regularly set apart to the ministry on the second Saturday in October, 1839, by the Bent Creek Baptist church, Elders Joseph Manning and Hugh Woodson acting as the Presbytery. From that time Mr. Lane has been doing effective service for the Master in the same section of country. Eternity alone will reveal the good he has accomplished for the cause of Christ and the salvation of sinners.

Lankershim, Deacon Isaac, is the Baptist benefactor of California. He is of Jewish birth; was converted to Christianity, baptized in Missouri, and removed with his wife, a converted Jewess, to California at an early day; joined the First Baptist church; was one of its deacons; became a constituent member of the Tabernacle church in 1865, and is still a member, the church having changed its name to Metropolitan in 1875. He is a large benefactor of Baptist institutions; purchased lots for the Second, Fifth, and Tabernacle churches; was a chief contributor to the building of the Tabernacle, and in 1875 provided the money, nearly $200,000, for the Metropolitan church lots and building. In 1874 he gave the second large subscription for California College, nearly $13,000. Always successful in business operations, careful, prudent, and conscientious, quiet and unassuming in manner, he is everywhere loved and honored. He has large city properties and immense farms in the country. His home is at Los Angeles. Though a converted Jew,—"an Israelite in whom there is no guile,"—giving quietly from principle, and not from impulse, he has never lost the respect of his Jewish kindred, with whom he is associated in many business enterprises. Deacon Lankershim is for California what the Crozers, Colgates, and Colbys are for the Atlantic States.

La Rue, Rev. Alexander Warren, whose ancestors were French and Irish, and firm Presbyterians, was born in La Rue Co., Ky., Jan. 23, 1819. He united with Severn's Valley church while attending an academy at Elizabethtown in 1837; was licensed to preach in November, 1838. In 1839 he entered Georgetown College, graduating in 1842. During the latter year he was ordained for the pastorate of Flemingsburg church. This church was in the Bracken Association, among the churches of which Mr. La Rue held many protracted meetings with encouraging success. In 1849 he removed to Louisville and became associate editor of the *Baptist Banner*, a weekly religious paper, since called the *Western Recorder*. While in this position he preached a short time to Bank Street Baptist church in New Albany, and afterwards to East Baptist church in Louisville. Having resigned his editorial office, he accepted the pastorate of the church at Harrodsburg in 1853, where he remained three years, and then accepted a call to the church at Georgetown. Subsequently he was pastor of the church at Stanford, and finally at Salem, in Christian County. At the latter place he died, Sept. 11, 1864, after a life of singular consecration, devotion, and fruitfulness. His biography was written and published under the appropriate title of "La Rue's Ministry of Faith," by Rev. A. C. Graves, D.D.

Lasher, George William, D.D., was born in Schenectady Co., N. Y., June 24, 1831. His father

GEORGE WILLIAM LASHER, D.D.

was a farmer of Holland ancestry, and his mother traced her descent from a member of the "Boston Tea Party." He was converted at Hamilton, in 1853, while attending the academy, and in the same year entered Madison University, graduating in 1857. In 1859 he graduated from Hamilton Theological Seminary, and at once entered upon the pastorate of the Baptist church of Norwalk, Conn., where, on September 30, he was ordained. In 1860 he married Miss Lizzie C., daughter of Dr. G. W. Eaton, president of Madison University. In July, 1861, he became chaplain of the 5th Conn. Regiment, and served for six months on the upper Potomac, when he became pastor of the Baptist church at Newburg, N. Y. From 1864 to 1868 he was pastor of the Portland Street church, Haverhill, Mass., from 1868 to 1872 of the First church of Trenton, N. J., and from 1872 to 1875 was corresponding secretary of the New York Baptist Education Society. In 1875 he made a tour of Europe,

Egypt, and Palestine, and in August, 1876, became editor and proprietor of the *Journal and Messenger*, at Cincinnati, O. In 1874 he received the degree of D.D. from Madison University. Dr. Lasher has a commanding presence, and is a vigorous and successful preacher and editor. The *Journal and Messenger* under his management has a wide influence in the Central West.

Lathrop, Edward, D.D., son of Burel Lathrop, who early removed from Norwich, Conn., to Georgia,

EDWARD LATHROP, D.D.

was born in Savannah, Ga., March 14, 1814; baptized by Rev. H. O. Myer into the Savannah Baptist church in June, 1827; commenced study for the ministry at Furman Institution, S. C., in 1832; on the closing of that institution went to Hamilton, N. Y., and graduated in what is now Madison University in 1840; pursued a course of theological study at Hamilton; was called as assistant of Rev. Richard Fuller, D.D., at Beaufort, S. C.; in 1844 settled as pastor of the Tabernacle Baptist church in New York City, and labored with distinguished success for twenty-two years, until health failed; granted a long furlough by the church, but finally resigned; in 1866 became pastor of the Baptist church in Stamford, Conn., where he still labors with great honor; received the honorary degree of Doctor of Divinity from Rochester University; has been a trustee from the beginning of Vassar College, N. Y., and is now president of the board of trustees; is also president of the board of trustees of Connecticut Literary Institution; is one of the trustees of Madison University; engaged in all benevolent objects; a strong preacher and able counselor; he has published several sermons by request.

Lattimore, Rev. Samuel S., was born in Rutherford Co., N. C., March 9, 1811; removed with his father while yet a child to Jennings, Ind. At fourteen years of age became a member of the literary institution at South Hanover, Ind. Supporting himself by his own exertions, he remained at this institution for nine years, until he completed his course, in July, 1833. During this period he became a member of the Presbyterian church, and remained in this connection for six or seven years. Leaving college soon thereafter, he went to Vicksburg, Miss., thence to Clinton, and shortly afterwards taught in the school at Society Ridge. In 1834 he joined the Baptist church. In 1835 he was ordained to the gospel ministry, and became general agent for the Mississippi Baptist State Convention. In December, 1837, he settled at Middleton, Carroll Co., Miss., where he engaged in preaching, and in teaching a school under Baptist auspices until 1840, when he removed to Sumter Co., Ala., where he preached to Providence and other churches. In 1845 he was again general agent of the Mississippi Baptist State Convention. In 1847 he was called to the pastorate of Macon church, Noxubee Co., Miss. Remaining there one year, he accepted a very urgent call from the Aberdeen church, with an understanding that he should return to Macon after the lapse of a year. Accordingly he returned to Macon, and remained till he again accepted an invitation to take charge of the Aberdeen church. In this relation he continued until his death. From 1849 to 1854 he was president of the Mississippi Baptist State Convention. He had various controversies on the principles and practices of the Baptists, and endured no little persecution. He was a man of marked ability, of warm and generous affections, eloquent as a preacher, able as a controversial writer, and eminently successful as a minister of the gospel.

Law, Rev. Francis Marion, was born in Sumter District, S. C., May 15, 1828; was educated for a physician, and received his diploma from the Medical College of Georgia, at Augusta; practised medicine at Wetumpka and Selma, Ala.; ordained in 1855; for five years financial secretary of Alabama Baptist Bible and Colportage Society; one year missionary and surgeon on the Bethel ship "Mobile Bay," under auspices of American Seamen's Friend Society; removed to Texas in November, 1859; pastor of Chapel Hill, Bellville, Brenham, Plantersville, and Bryan churches from 1860 to 1876; is a man of vigorous intellect and indomitable energy; now engaged in raising $250,000 for Texas Educational Commission.

Law, Rev. Josiah S., son of Samuel S. Law, was born in Saulsbury, Ga., Feb. 5, 1808. He received a classical education, and succeeded Rev. James Shannon as a teacher in Liberty County, when Mr. Shannon was called to Augusta, in 1827. It was while teaching at Sunbury that he was converted and joined the Baptist church there. He then took a three years' theological course at Newton Theological Seminary. In 1831 he entered upon his ministerial duties at Sunbury, and for twenty years served that church and neighborhood with great usefulness, except during two short intervals when he accepted calls to Macon and Savannah.

The colored people received great benefit from his preaching, among whom he was very successful. He died on the 5th of October, 1853. At that time sixty colored candidates were awaiting baptism at his hands.

Law, Rev. Samuel Spry, was born in Liberty County in 1774. He moved in the best society all his life, his family and connections being cultivated and wealthy. For forty years he lived a worldly-minded man and a moralist, but was converted in his forty-first year, and joined the Sunbury Baptist church on the 30th of April, 1815. He was ordained to the ministry Dec. 27, 1827, at the age of fifty-three. After laboring on the coast for some time, he was called to succeed Dr. C. O. Screven, at Sunbury. This connection continued for a year or so only, and he devoted his whole time to the colored people, and to the poor white churches of Liberty County. This work he continued with great usefulness for six or seven years, when his health began to fail gradually, and he expired on the 4th of February, 1837.

He was a man of great fervor and spirituality; prepared his sermons carefully, and became a good preacher. He was well acquainted with the Scriptures, and was much gifted in prayer. Few ever made more progress in piety and in the knowledge of our Lord Jesus Christ than he.

Lawler, Rev. B. F., was born in West Tennessee, Jan. 1, 1834; baptized in 1858; ordained in 1860; labored a number of years at Windsor, Mo. He is at the present time pastor of the Salem and Prairie Union Baptist churches, Neb. In connection with his ministerial labors, Mr. Lawler, while in Missouri, devoted a part of his time to teaching. In 1880 he published a volume of sermons, addresses, and letters.

Lawler, Judge Jacob, was born in North Carolina in 1796; while a youth his father removed to Tennessee, and the son subsequently located in North Alabama, and about the year 1820 settled in Shelby County. He held various offices of trust: judge of the county court, member of the House of Representatives of the State Legislature from 1826 to 1831, and was then elected to the State Senate; resigned that position to accept that of receiver of public moneys for one of the land districts of the State, tendered him by President Andrew Jackson; held that office at Mardisville, in Talladega County, where it was located, until he was elected to Congress in 1835; was re-elected to Congress in 1837, and died on the 8th of May, 1838, in the city of Washington, while Congress was in session, and his remains now rest in that city. He was in office continuously from 1822 to 1838, never having suffered defeat or reproach.

In 1826, Jacob Lawler united with the Baptist church, and in a short time was ordained to the ministry. From the time of his ordination to his election to Congress he filled the office of pastor. The Talladega (now Alpine) and the Talladega town churches were originated by his ministry, and he was their pastor. It was characteristic of Mr. Lawler not to allow his secular duties to interfere with his religious obligations when it could be avoided.

Lawler, Gen. Levi W., was born in Madison Co., Ala., in 1816; with his parents, settled in

GEN. LEVI W. LAWLER.

Talladega County in early life; united with the Talladega church, of which his father was pastor, in 1835. After Judge Lawler resigned the office of receiver of public moneys at Mardisville he was succeeded by his son Levi, under appointment of President Jackson, and, though only nineteen years of age, he easily obtained the required bond of $100,000. After four years he was suspended on account of his opposition to the administration of President Van Buren, but was restored to the position by President Tyler in 1841, and held it for another term of four years. In 1848 he located in Mobile, and engaged in the commission business, which he has not yet relinquished. In 1861 his friends elected him to the Legislature without consulting him; was returned in 1863; was a member of that body during the whole period of the civil war, and he was three years chairman of the committee on ways and means. In 1874, Gen. Lawler was appointed by Gov. Houston one of the State commissioners to adjust and liquidate its burdensome debt. He drafted the plan of settlement, and performed the principal labor in its execution among creditors of the State,—a work which brought great relief to the people of Alabama. For many years he has been one of the trustees of Howard College, and of the Agricultural and Mechanical College of the State. He has been and is still a man of handsome fortune, of great energy, industry, and financial skill; liberal to objects of benevolence and to public enterprises. It is conceded that the gubernatorial honors of Alabama have been within his reach for years, but he has declined them. His vast influence affects for good all the higher relations of life, political and civil, social and educational, financial and denominational, in the State. He maintains the constant confidence of all grades of society. When a master he was famous for his tenderness to his slaves, and now that they are free he has their uniform confidence and highest regard. He has no superior in Alabama.

Lawrence, William Mangam, D.D., was born in Washington, D. C., May 11, 1848; was converted in early youth, and entered college at Amherst, Mass.; graduated from Madison University and Hamilton Theological Seminary; settled with the church at Amsterdam, N. Y., where he was ordained in August, 1871. The following year he received an urgent call from the Spring Garden church in Philadelphia, which he accepted, and entered upon his labors in October, 1872. It was an important period in the history of the church. A large colony had just gone out to form the Gethsemane church in a new and rapidly-growing neighborhood. A pastor was needed with power to hold and strengthen "the things which remained," and in this work he has, under God, been eminently successful.

Mr. Lawrence throws the vigor of his early manhood into all that he says and does. His sermons and occasional contributions to religious journals give evidence of an observing and thoughtful mind. His systematic methods enable him to accomplish a vast amount of pastoral work, and to render valuable service to other denominational interests with which he has become connected. His powerful intellect, scholarly attainments, and Christian spirit make him a power in the community. In 1880 he became pastor of the Second Baptist church of Chicago.

WILLIAM MANGAM LAWRENCE, D.D.

Laws, Rev. M. L., was born in Virginia, Aug. 21, 1842. He made a profession of religion when eighteen years of age, and was baptized by Rev. J. S. Kennard in the E Street Baptist church, Washington, D. C., in November, 1859. He was ordained in 1871 at the Rehoboth Baptist church in Saline Co., Mo. Brother Laws has been pastor at Glasgow and Booneville, and of the Park Avenue church in St. Louis. He is now secretary of the Missouri Baptist Sunday-School Convention, and he is rendering efficient service in this position. He is a man of ability, industry, and usefulness.

Lawson, Rev. Albert G., was born in Poughkeepsie, N. Y., Jan. 5, 1842. In 1858 he made a public profession of religion, and was baptized by Rev. John Q. Adams, and became a member of the North Baptist church, New York. He studied in the College of the City of New York and in Madison University, and was ordained as pastor of Perth Amboy Baptist church, N. J., in June, 1862. In 1867 he took charge of the Greenwood Baptist church, where he still labors with marked success.

He is one of the most able laborers in the temperance cause. He is the author of "Methods of Church Work," "Duty of the Christian Church in Relation to Temperance," and the "Peace and Power of Temperance Literature," also an address on "Self-Culture." His discourses are clear, logical, and earnestly delivered.

Lawson, Admiral Sir John, was born near

Scarborough, Yorkshire, England. From very early life he was on the ocean. When the Parliament resolved to fight for the liberties of England, Lawson entered its naval service. His intelligence, faithfulness in executing orders, and religious behavior soon attracted attention and secured promotion. Having obtained the command of a small vessel, he made himself so useful that he was soon the captain of the finest ship in the British navy; and in process of time he became an admiral, and occasionally had the whole fleet placed under his authority. He fought under Blake in all the battles which gave him and his country so much naval glory. Cromwell looked upon him with special favor, and was always ready to promote his interests, until he became a king in everything but the name.

On the 2d of June, 1653, the British fleet attacked the Dutch off the coast of Flanders. Deane and Monk were admirals, Sir William Penn was vice-admiral, and Sir John Lawson was rear-admiral. Lawson charged through the Dutch fleet with forty ships, pouring destruction into the enemy, and so disabling De Ruyter's squadron that Van Tromp had to come to his relief; and after a hot engagement, in which Lawson was the foremost fighting man, the Dutch withdrew. The next day the battle was renewed and the enemy was routed. Six great ships of the Dutch were sunk, two blown up, and eleven of the largest and two smaller vessels were captured, with thirteen hundred prisoners, and nothing but flight saved the other Dutch vessels.

As soon as the power of Richard Cromwell ended, and the Parliament of the country had reassembled, the officers of the fleet, being largely Baptists, and consequently strong republicans, acknowledged the authority of Parliament in terms of loyal satisfaction. Immediately after, the Committee of Safety appointed by the Parliament ordered the equipment of six frigates to be ready for any emergency, and, to show their appreciation of our gallant brother, Sir John Lawson, they gave him the command of this squadron and created him vice-admiral of the fleet. For a considerable period after this Sir John had control of the whole British navy, and he was known throughout his country as a supporter of a free Parliament whom no bribes or persuasions could turn from his patriotic convictions.

The Parliament in power at this period was the Long Parliament dispersed by Oliver Cromwell, and recalled once more to the exercise of legislative and executive powers. Against this body the army determined to wage war, and they hindered the speaker and the members from reaching the house. Lambert and the principal officers of the army were bent on ruling the nation by the sword. Lawson brought his fleet into the Thames and declared for the Parliament by a voice which the Dutch had respected on the ocean, and which his countrymen reverenced everywhere. And his timely assistance, with the aid of Monk, overcame the friends of the sword, and the Parliament resumed its meetings and its authority. On the 3d of June, 1665, in a great naval battle between the English and the Dutch, in which the Duke of York was the nominal and Lawson the real commander of the British fleet, and in which the Dutch lost thirty-two ships and six thousand men, Sir John Lawson received a shot in the knee in the middle of the battle; the wound gangrened, and he died a few days after on shore, rejoicing in the blessed Saviour whom he was going to meet.

Lord Clarendon, a bitter enemy of Baptists and republicans, says of the admiral: "He was, indeed, of all the men of that time, and of that extraction and education, incomparably the modestest and the wisest man, and most worthy man to be confided in. He was in all the actions performed by Blake, some of which were very stupendous, and in all the battles which Cromwell had fought with the Dutch. He was commander-in-chief of the fleet when Richard (Cromwell) was thrown out; and when the contest grew between the Rump (the Long Parliament) and Lambert, he brought the whole fleet into the river and declared for that which is called the Parliament (Clarendon did not recognize this body as a Parliament), which broke the neck of all other designs, though *he intended only the better settlement of the Commonwealth.*" He had no wish to aid the Stuarts to mount the throne forfeited by Charles I. Elsewhere he says: "The present fleet, prepared for the summer service, was under the command of Vice-Admiral Sir John Lawson, an excellent seaman, but then *a notorious Anabaptist;* and they well remembered how he had lately besieged the city (London), and by the power of his fleet given that turn which helped to revive the 'Committee of Safety' (the government set up by the army) and restore the Rump Parliament to the exercise of their jurisdiction." Granville Penn, in his "Memorials of Admiral Sir William Penn," speaks of "the renowned Sir John Lawson," and he states that Oliver "Cromwell set aside Major Bourne and appointed Lawson rear-admiral of the fleet in his place." The great Protector held Sir John Lawson in the highest esteem. Except Cromwell himself, in his day no soldier stood higher than Gen. Harrison. And during the latter part of Lawson's life he was regarded as one of the greatest heroes in the naval history of Britain, and his death was felt to be a national calamity. These brave men were both decided Baptists. See "Memoirs of Ludlow," ii. 466, 666, 726, 736, 855, Vevay, 1699; Southey's "Lives of the British Admirals," v. 269, note,

London, 1837; Clarendon's "History of the Rebellion," iii. 728, Oxford, 1706; Rapin's "History of England," ii. 639, 640, London, 1733; "Memorials of Sir William Penn, Knt.," i. 312, 469, 470, London, 1833.

Lawton, Col. Alex. J., who died some three years ago, spent his life, which, "by reason of strength was fourscore and four years," in Beaufort, S. C. He was long a deacon of the Black Swamp church, and repeatedly a member of the State Legislature. He was dignified but extremely pleasant, especially among the young, with whom he was a great favorite. The writer met him about a year before his death, and found him the same genial Christian that he had always been. Few masters were so considerate of their slaves, and few had their affection in an equal degree. He used much of his large property for benevolent objects. Few have spent a life so long and so well regulated.

Lawton, Rev. Joseph A., may be called the Baptist patriarch of Barnwell, S. C., and of the surrounding counties. He held and used his large fortune, before the war, as a steward who must give an account. He now lives, in advanced years, in the midst of his spiritual children, white and colored, who revere him. Prudence and moderation have marked his whole life. His numerous servants, at the close of the war, cherished him in their hearts, and quite a number of them still live with him, and manifest the same respect as they did in the time of slavery. Baptist ministers in his section owe him much, because he refused to preach for wealthy churches unless they paid a salary in proportion to their ability, saying that if he preached for nothing it should be to churches not able to compensate him. They complied, and many brethren have been less stinted than they would have been had Mr. Lawton not insisted that "the laborer is worthy of his hire." He always gave his salary, and much more, to some worthy object. He has long been pastor of the Allendale church, one of the most active and liberal in the Savannah River Association.

Lawton, Rev. W. A., was born in Beaufort Co., S. C., in 1793. He was in the ministry fifty-five years, and at the time of his death, in 1878, he had been pastor of the Pipe Creek church for twenty-seven years. His remarkably strong constitution bore him up in good health almost to the close of life, which "by reason of strength was fourscore and five years." Next to Thomas Dawson, he was probably the oldest Baptist minister in the State.

Lea Female Seminary, located at Summit, Miss., on the line of the New Orleans and Jackson Railroad, Rev. Charles H. Otken, principal, is an admirable institution.

Lea, Hon. Fryer, was born in Tennessee, and is now nearly eighty years of age; joined the Baptist Church in Tennessee, where he practised law with success and distinction. Represented Tennessee in the Congress of the United States. He afterwards removed to Mississippi, and practised law at Jackson. Has served as State superintendent of public instruction in Texas, and now lives at Goliad. He has been a consistent Baptist under all circumstances.

Lea, Rev. Wm. M., a prominent minister in Arkansas, was born in North Carolina in 1817, but reared and educated in Tennessee. He came to Arkansas in 1851 as missionary of the Marion Board Southern Baptist Convention, and began his labors at Helena. The following year he severed his relations with the board, and boldly entered the State as an independent missionary, relying upon his field for support, and, with the exception of a few years, has ever since continued there to labor. Helena, Pine Bluff, Little Rock, Forest City, and other places have received the benefit of his labors. Just before the late conflict he raised a subscription of $75,000 towards endowing a State college, which was unfortunately lost by the war. Mr. Lea has distinguished himself as a polemic, having engaged in many debates, and considers himself specially set for the defense of the truth.

Leach, Beriah N., D.D., was born in Middletown, Vt., April 28, 1801; converted at fourteen; ordained pastor at Cornwell, Vt., in October, 1826; pastor at Middlebury, Fredonia, Wyoming, Hamilton, and Brooklyn, N. Y., and in Middletown, Conn. He received the degree of Doctor of Divinity from Madison University in 1859. He died Jan. 23, 1869, strong in his Redeemer's supporting grace. Dr. Leach was full of labors and of love for the Redeemer, and the favor of heaven rested upon his toils for Jesus as well as upon his own soul.

Leach, Rev. William, was born in Shutesbury, Mass., in 1804, and baptized by Rev. David Goddard, of Wendall. Relinquishing the business in which he was engaged, he pursued a select course of study at the Shelburne Falls Academy, and took a partial course at Newton. In 1840 he was ordained in Paterson, N. J. Subsequently he removed to Newark, N. J., and then to Wendall and South Hanson, Mass., and Omaha, Neb. To this latter place he had gone on business, but, seeing the destitution of the gospel in that rising city, he preached for some time there without compensation, and for two years as a missionary of the American Baptist Home Missionary Society. The Baptist church of Omaha is the child of his prayers and labors. Returning East, he had charge of the churches in East Stoughton, Holmes' Hole, South

Yarmouth, Harned, and Still River, all in the State of Massachusetts. He died at Still River, Mass., March 30, 1871.

Learning, Baptist Institutions of.—Preceding and during the Commonwealth in England, large numbers of our ministers in that country were graduates of Oxford and Cambridge. After 1660, when Charles II. ascended the throne, the necessity for seeking education for Baptist pastors in some new quarter forced itself upon the attention of our brethren. Various plans were discussed in London and elsewhere to secure an object so dear to the churches. Edward Terrill, of Bristol, in 1679, set apart a portion of his property for the instruction of students for the ministry, which did not become available until the death of his wife. Though some aid was received from it for five years preceding 1720, it was in that year, under Rev. Bernard Foskett, that Bristol Baptist College was formally established.

In 1756, Rev. Isaac Eaton, of Hopewell, N. J., opened the first Baptist Seminary in this country "for the education of youth for the ministry." In the progress of this institution the Philadelphia and Charleston Baptist Associations took the deepest interest. They appointed trustees to watch over its affairs; and the Philadelphia Association raised about £400 to aid it in its work. The principal was a scholarly man, and he had the art of imparting knowledge to others. His school was in existence only eleven years, and in that time the following were among its pupils: Dr. James Manning, Dr. Samuel Jones, Dr. Hezekiah Smith, Dr. Isaac Skillman, and Revs. David Thomas, David Jones, the celebrated Revolutionary chaplain, and Charles Thompson. The distinguished Judge David Howell was also a student at Hopewell. The frame house in which Mr. Eaton presided over his seminary is still standing, and in excellent condition.

ISAAC EATON'S ACADEMY.
THE FIRST BAPTIST SEMINARY FOR THE EDUCATION OF MINISTERS IN AMERICA.

On the 12th of October, 1762, the Philadelphia Baptist Association, with twenty-nine churches in its fellowship, met in the Lutheran church on Fifth Street above Race Street, Philadelphia. Rev. Morgan Edwards was chosen moderator, and Rev. Abel Morgan clerk. At this session of the mother Association of American Baptists it was decided that it was "expedient to erect a college in the colony of Rhode Island, under the chief direction of the Baptists." Morgan Edwards was "the principal mover in this matter," and to him and Dr. Samuel Jones the grand educational project was referred.

In 1763 an effort was made to secure the confirmation of a charter for the new college in the Rhode Island Assembly. The charter had been prepared by Dr. Ezra Stiles, of Newport, a Congregational minister, and it "was so artfully constructed as to throw the power into the Fellows' hands, whereof eight out of twelve were Presbyterians, usually called Congregationalists." "The trustees were presumed to be the principal branch of authority, and as nineteen out of thirty-five were to be Baptists, the Baptists were satisfied, without sufficient examination into the authority vested in the fellowship, which afterward appeared to be the soul of the institution, while the trusteeship was only the body" (Manning and Brown University, pp. 48–49). This unworthy effort of Dr. Stiles was frustrated by Daniel Jenckes and others in the Assembly. The amended charter was confirmed by the Legislature of Rhode Island in 1764. In that year the Philadelphia Association recommended the churches to be liberal in placing the new college upon an efficient basis; and in 1766 the Association "agreed to recommend warmly to the churches the interests of the college, for which a subscription is opened all over the continent." Dr. James Manning was the first president of Rhode Island College, now Brown University. This institution to-day has nineteen instructors, property valued at $1,750,000, an endowment of $650,000, a library of 53,000 volumes, 247 students, and a history of usefulness of which Americans, and especially American Baptists, may justly be proud. The Baptist colleges, theological seminaries, and academies of the United States, according to the report of the "Baptist Year-Book" for 1881, have property worth $11,988,883, and endowments of $4,960,730,—that is to say, these institutions own assets amounting to $16,959,613, nearly seventeen million dollars. Their reported income last year was $679,178, to which may be added $160,000 from 36 of them from which we have no report of receipts. They had, during 1880, 667 teachers, 8749 students, of whom 1532 were preparing for the Christian ministry.

In the United States most Pedobaptist communities receive large accessions from European emigration; the Baptists gain comparatively few members from this source. Besides, they have had to contend against powerful prejudices from the earliest period in the history of this country, prejudices which for a long time in several colonies clothed themselves in persecuting legal enactments, and which exist to-day, without the force of law, in unfounded charges of bigotry and saving sacramentalism. Nevertheless, by the favor of God, they have been able not only to rear a multitude of church edifices, but to invest seventeen million dollars in institutions of learning. Indeed, we have reason to believe that if all our educational enterprises were *reported*, and an exact examination of their property and endowments made, that the result would show an investment in these fountains of light of a sum little less than twenty million dollars.

BAPTIST INSTITUTIONS OF LEARNING.

UNITED STATES. IN 1881.

COLLEGES AND UNIVERSITIES.

Name.	When Founded.	President.	Location.	Instructors.	Students.	Property.	Endowment.
Brown University	1764	E. G. Robinson, D.D., LL.D.	Providence, R. I.	19	247	$1,750,000	$650,000
Madison University	1819	E. Dodge, D.D., LL.D.	Hamilton, N. Y.	10	90	640,000	480,000
Colby University	1820	Henry E. Robins, D.D.	Waterville, Me.	8	148	300,000	200,000
The Columbian University	1821	J. C. Welling, LL.D.	Washington, D. C.	25	343	370,000	110,000
Shurtleff College	1827	A. A. Kendrick, D.D.	Upper Alton, Ill.	7	128	175,000	150,000
Georgetown College	1829	R. M. Dudley, D.D.	Georgetown, Ky.	6	119	125,000	75,000
Denison University	1831	Alfred Owen, D.D.	Granville, O.	9	173	300,000	190,000
Franklin College	1834	W. T. Stott, D.D.	Franklin, Ind.	8	85	120,000	80,000
Wake Forest College	1834	T. H. Pritchard, D.D.	Wake Forest, N. C.	8	171	86,000	46,000
Mercer University	1838	A. J. Battle, D.D.	Macon, Ga.	9	108	300,000	100,000
Richmond College	1832	B. Puryear, A.M.	Richmond, Va.	8	125	300,000	95,000
Howard College	1843	Col. J. T. Murfee.	Marion, Ala.	8	125	50,000	....
Baylor University	1845	W. C. Crane, D.D., LL.D.	Independence, Texas.	6	119	70,000	26,000
University at Lewisburg	1846	Rev. D. J. Hill, A.M.	Lewisburg, Pa.	7	66	250,000	121,769
William Jewell College	1849	W. R. Rothwell, D.D.	Liberty, Mo.	7	145	175,000	100,000
University of Rochester	1850	M. B. Anderson, LL.D.	Rochester, N. Y.	9	146	846,443	255,540
Mississippi College	1850	W. S. Webb, D.D.	Clinton, Miss.	7	200	50,000	20,000
Carson College	1850	N. B. Goforth, D.D.	Mossy Creek, Tenn.	4	185	50,000	....
Furman University	1851	J. C. Furman, D.D.	Greenville, S. C.	5	86	100,000	....
Central University	1852	L. A. Dunn, D.D.	Pella, Iowa.	7	121	....	....
Kalamazoo College	1855	Kendall Brooks, D.D.	Kalamazoo, Mich.	9	169	175,000	75,000
Bethel College*	1856	Leslie Waggener, LL.D.	Russellville, Ky.	5	105	175,000	75,000
University of Chicago	1859	Galusha Anderson, D.D.	Chicago, Ill.	16	250	150,600	600
McMinnville College	1858	Rev. G. J. Burchett, A.M.	McMinnville, Oregon.	4	100	30,000	20,000
Waco University	1861	R. C. Burleson, D.D.	Waco, Texas.	10	190	50,000	13,000
Vassar College	1861	S. L. Caldwell, D.D.	Poughkeepsie, N. Y.	31	303	992,154	281,250
University of Des Moines	1865	J. A. Nash, D.D.	Des Moines, Iowa.	4	78	70,000	20,000
La Grange College*	1859	J. F. Cook, LL.D.	La Grange, Mo.	8	131	36,000	....
Monongahela College	1867	H. K. Craig, D.D.	Jefferson, Greene Co., Pa.	6	108	40,000	20,000
California College	1871	U. Gregory, D.D.	Vacaville, Cal.	4	60	30,000	20,000
Southwestern Baptist Univ.	1874	Prof. G. W. Jarman, A.M.	Jackson, Tenn.	6	185	105,000	55,000
Total number 31				280	4609	$7,910,597	$3,279,159

* From previous reports.

THEOLOGICAL INSTITUTIONS.

Name.	When Founded.	President.	Location.	Instructors.	Students.	Property.	Endowment.
Hamilton Theological Sem.	1819	E. Dodge, D.D., LL.D.	Hamilton, N. Y.	5	36	$70,000	$32,750
Newton Theol. Institution.	1825	Alvah Hovey, D.D.	Newton Centre, Mass.	6	67	426,878	314,801
Rochester Theological Sem.	1851	A. H. Strong, D.D.	Rochester, N. Y.	8	70	450,000	300,000
Southern Baptist Theol. Sem.	1858	Jas. P. Boyce, D.D., LL.D.	Louisville, Ky.	4	89	300,000	300,000
Shurtleff Theological Dept.	1862	A. A. Kendrick, D.D.	Upper Alton, Ill.	...	...	....	....
Baptist Union Theol. Sem.	1867	G. W. Northrup, D.D.	Morgan Park, Ill.	7	78	....	....
Crozer Theological Seminary.	1868	H. G. Weston, D.D.	Upland, Pa.	4	42	403,000	244,130
Vardeman Sch. of Theology.	1868	W. R. Rothwell, D.D.	Liberty, Mo.	3	48	40,000	....
Total number............8				37	430	$1,689,878	$1,191,681

BAPTIST INSTITUTIONS OF LEARNING—Continued.

ACADEMIES, SEMINARIES, AND FEMALE COLLEGES.

Name.	When Founded.	President.	Location.	Instructors.	Students.	Property.	Endowment.
Alabama Central Female Col.	1857	Prof. A. K. Yancey, Jr.	Tuscaloosa, Ala.	12	110	$100,000	
Atlanta Baptist Seminary†	1870	Rev. J. T. Robert, LL.D.	Atlanta, Ga.	4	100	12,000	
Baptist Female College	1855	John F. Lanneau, A.M.	Lexington, Mo.	12	133		
Bardstown M. and F. College.	1842	H. J. Greenwell, A.M.	Bardstown, Ky.	7	85	10,000	
Baylor Female College	1846	J. H. Luther, D.D.	Independence, Texas.	10	100	20,000	
Benedict Institute†	1870	E. J. Goodspeed, D.D.	Columbia, S. C.	6	150	43,700	$18,700
Bethel Female College	1852	J. W. Rust, A.M.	Hopkinsville, Ky.	8	100	30,000	
Broaddus Female College	1871	Rev. E. J. Willis, LL.D.	Clarksburg, W. Va.	7	75	10,000	
Burlington Colored Institute.	1852	Prof. E. F. Stearns.	Burlington, Iowa.	6	60	50,000	20,000
Cedar Valley Seminary*	1863	Rev. A. Bush, A.M.	Osage, Iowa.	6	172	22,000	9,000
Central Female Institute	1853	Walter Hillman, LL.D.	Clinton, Miss.	7	104	20,000	
Chowan Baptist Female Inst.	1848	Dr. A. McDowell.	Murfreesborough, N. C.	8	60	50,000	
Colby Academy	1836	James P. Dixon, A.M.	New London, N. H.	6	76	181,000	81,000
Colgate Academy	1872	Rev. F. W. Towle, A.M.	Hamilton, N. Y.	5	111	125,000	55,000
Connecticut Lit. Institution.	1833	Martin H. Smith, A.M.	Suffield, Conn.	7	110	100,000	28,000
Cook Academy	1872	Prof. A. C. Hill.	Havana, N. Y.	10	120	168,708	
Georgetown Female Sem.	1846	Prof. J. J. Rucker.	Georgetown, Ky.	10	115	25,000	
Georgia Female College	1850	Mr. P. F. Asbury.	Madison, Ga.	5	70		
Grand River College	1859	Prof. T. H. Storts.	Edinburg, Mo.	4	131	10,000	
Greenville Baptist Fem. Col.	1854	Prof. A. S. Townes.	Greenville, S. C.	10	153	20,000	
Hardin Female College*	1873	Prof. A. W. Terrill.	Mexico, Mo.	8	160	68,000	40,000
Hollin's Institute	1841	Prof. Chas. L. Cocke.	Botetourt Springs, Va.	12	114	75,000	
Howe Literary Institute	1874	Prof. S. F. Holt.	East St. Louis, Ill.	4	84	25,000	
Judson Female Institute	1839	L. R. Gwaltney, D.D.	Marion, Ala.	10	115	50,000	
Keystone Academy	1868	Rev. J. H. Harris, A.M.	Factoryville, Pa.	7	145	30,000	
Leland University†	1870	Rev. Seth J. Axtell, Jr.	New Orleans, La.	5	148	85,000	10,000
Lea Female College	1877	Rev. C. H. Otken, A.M.	Summit, Miss.	6	75	10,000	
Mary Sharp College	1850	Z. C. Graves, LL.D.	Winchester, Tenn.	8	110	16,000	
Minnesota Academy*	1877	S. H. Baker, A.M.	Owatonna, Minn.	6	173	12,000	5,190
Mount Pleasant Institute	1873	Rev. Leroy Stevens, A.M.	Mount Pleasant, Pa.	6	60	25,000	
Nashville Institute†	1865	D. W. Phillips, D.D.	Nashville, Tenn.	8	231	80,000	
Natchez Seminary†	1877	Rev. Charles Ayer.	Natchez, Miss.	4	120	15,000	
Normal and Theol. School.	1878	Rev. H. Woodsmall.	Selma, Ala.	6	250	8,000	
Peddie Institute	1865	Rev. E. J. Avery, A.M.	Hightstown, N. J.	10	125	125,000	1,000
Reid Institute	1862	C. A. Gilbert, A.M.	Reidsburg, Pa.	3	68	10,000	
Richmond Institute†	1867	Rev. C. H. Corey, A.M.	Richmond, Va.	5	92		
Shaw University†	1865	Rev. H. M. Tupper, A.M.	Raleigh, N. C.	15	277	125,000	
South Jersey Institute	1870	Prof. H. K. Trask.	Bridgeton, N. J.	10	150	75,000	
Stephen's Female College	1856	Prof. R. P. Rider.	Columbia, Mo.	14	170	50,000	20,000
University Academy	1846	W. E. Martin, A.M.	Lewisburg, Pa.	4	65		
University Female Institute.	1846	Jonathan Jones, A.M.	Lewisburg, Pa.	10	72	75,000	
Vermont Academy	1872	H. M. Willard, A.M.	Saxton's River, Vt.	8	125	142,000	100,000
Wayland Seminary†	1865	Rev. G. M. P. King.	Washington, D. C.	7	92	40,000	
Wayland University	1855	N. E. Wood, A.M.	Beaver Dam, Wis.	6	120	50,000	19,000
Worcester Academy	1834	Nath. Leavenworth, A.M.	Worcester, Mass.	4	58	200,000	83,000
Wyoming Seminary	1867	Rev. M. Heath, A.M.	Wyoming, Del.	5	88		
Young Ladies' Institute	1832	D. Shepardson, D.D.	Granville, O.	9	100		
Total number.....48				350	5522	$2,388,408	$489,890

* From previous reports.   † Under the auspices of the American Baptist Home Mission Society.

ENGLAND, WALES, AND SCOTLAND.*

Name.	When Founded.	President.	Location.	Instructors.	Students.	Property.	Endowment.
Bristol College	1720	F. W. Gotch, LL.D.	Bristol.				
Chilwell College (Gen. Bap.).	1797	Rev. F. Goadby, B.A.	Nottingham.				
Rawdon College	1804	Rev. T. G. Rooke, B.A.	Rawdon, Yorkshire.				
Pontypool College	1807	Rev. W. M. Lewis, A.M.	Pontypool, Wales.				
Regent's Park College	1810	Joseph Angus, D.D., M.R.A.S.	London.				
Haverfordwest College	1839	Thomas Davies, D.D.	Haverfordwest, Wales.				
Theol. Institution of Scotland.	1856	James Culross, D.D.	Glasgow.				
Pastor's College (Spurgeon's).	1856	Rev. C. H. Spurgeon.	London.				
Llangollen	1862	Hugh Jones, D.D.	Llangollen, North Wales.				
Manchester Bap. Theol. Inst.	1866	Rev. Edward Parker.	Brighton Grove, M'ch't'r.				
Total number.....10							

* These institutions had an income of $80,000 in 1880.

BAPTIST INSTITUTIONS OF LEARNING—Continued.

CANADA.—ONTARIO.

Name.	When Founded.	President.	Location.	Instructors.	Students.	Property.	Endowment.
Canadian Literary Institute..		Rev. John Torrance, M.A.	Woodstock, Ontario	10			
Toronto Theol. Institution....	1881	J. H. Castle, D.D.	Toronto, Ontario	3			
Total				13			

NOVA SCOTIA.

Name.	When Founded.	President.	Location.	Instructors.	Students.	Property.	Endowment.
Acadia College		A. W. Sawyer, D.D.		8	75		

In addition to these, we have missionary colleges and theological institutions in Jamaica, Burmah, India, France, Germany, and Sweden.

The Hollis family of London, earnest Baptists, were such generous friends of education, that down to 1735 they gave more than "£6000 currency of Massachusetts" to Harvard College, then a Congregational institution, that New England might have literary advantages. We had no American Baptist colleges in that day to receive such benefactions.

In establishing and sustaining institutions of learning, and in extending general education throughout our entire country, no denomination occupies a more honored place than the Baptists.

Leavitt, Rev. Samuel K., was born at Levant, Me., June 23, 1830; graduated at Colby University in 1855; after graduation taught in the literary and scientific institution at New London, N. H., in the high school at Holyoke, Mass., and at Halliwell, Me. In 1857 removed to Evansville, Ind., where he studied law and remained in the legal profession until the spring of 1870, with an interruption of three years' service in the army as captain in the 65th Regiment of Ind. Inf. Vols. Was converted in college in 1852, and baptized at Holyoke in 1855 by Rev. James French. In the spring of 1872 was ordained to the work of the ministry at Evansville, Ind. Has had only two pastorates, the first at Keokuk, Iowa, and the second at First church, Cincinnati, O., from December, 1872, to the present time. He is an earnest, thorough-going man, and he is profoundly interested in the reformatory as well as the religious movements of the day.

Lecompte, Rev. Edwin Augustus, was born in Boston, Sept. 14, 1835. He was religiously trained at home, and in the Sunday-school of the Charles Street Baptist church, under the ministrations of the Rev. Dr. Sharp. Having gone through the course of study pursued in the excellent schools of his native city, he decided to devote himself to business. When but fifteen years of age he was hopefully converted, and was baptized by Rev. A. H. Burlingham, then pastor of the Harvard Street church, Boston. His attention was now turned to the Christian ministry, and in order to fit himself for his chosen work he pursued his preparatory studies in part at the Middleborough Academy, under the tuition of Prof. J. W. P. Jenks, and graduated with honor at Harvard University in the class of 1862. "His subsequent work proved that his intellectual as well as moral culture was broad and thorough." He was ordained as pastor of the Fourth Street church, in South Boston, July 30, 1862. For seven years he labored successfully with this church, and then accepted a call to the pastorate of the First Baptist church, in Syracuse, N. Y., where he remained until 1864, when he was called back to his native State and became pastor of the Worthen Street church, Lowell, Mass. Here for fifteen years he "made full proof of his ministry," and his work was respected in the community in which he lived, inasmuch as he brought to the discharge of his duties a well-cultivated intellect and a warm, gentle, and guileless heart. "He was one of those men for whom we are never called on to explain or apologize." He died March 2, 1880, not having quite reached the forty-fifth year of his age.

Lee, Rev. David, was born in Johnston Co., N. C., Feb. 4, 1805. With his father, Joel Lee, and family, he removed to Alabama and settled in Conecuh County in 1817. David Lee was happily converted, and in November, 1827, was baptized by Rev. Alex. Travis, and the next year began to exhort sinners to repentance. Was ordained in 1833 by Revs. David Peebles and Alexander Watson. Has been pastor of Hopewell church, at Mount Willing, ever since he entered the ministry, and from time to time of other churches. Has attended every meeting, save one, of the Alabama Association since 1833, and has been moderator of that body for about thirty-five years, and is one of the best presiding officers in the State. All his life as a man and a minister he has exerted a commanding influence in that large and powerful Association. Has written extensively and ably for our religious papers; has ever been in good worldly circumstances.

Lee, Franklin, Esq., was born in New Jersey in 1787; was a member of the Second Baptist church, Philadelphia, Pa., for more than fifty years,

FRANKLIN LEE, ESQ.

and for about thirty years an honored deacon. He was treasurer of the Philadelphia Baptist Association for many years. He was a representative from Philadelphia in the Pennsylvania Legislature, and he held other public positions of importance in times when such offices sought the men to fill them. In his own church he was familiarly known as "Father Lee," and every member of it felt a special interest in him. He was known and venerated by the whole denomination in Eastern Pennsylvania; he held a high place in the regards of all the leading citizens of Philadelphia among whom he mingled in business pursuits and in patriotic efforts.

His doctrinal sentiments accorded with those proclaimed by Dr. Gill and taught by inspired Paul; he was deeply devotional in his religious exercises, a generous friend of missions at home and abroad, and a liberal contributor to the necessities of the poor. While broad in his charities, Mr. Lee was a strong Baptist, and no struggling community of his denomination ever vainly appealed to him. For years before his death his ordinary gifts to the poor and the cause of Christ were about two thousand dollars annually.

Intimately conversant with God's Word, of which he was a diligent and intelligent student, he was strengthened by its doctrines and its promises, and led a life marked by unspotted purity. His hope was unusually bright; he often quoted the words of the poet to express his experience,—

"More happy, but not more secure,
The glorified spirits in heaven."

He entered the eternal inheritance Dec. 13, 1861, mourned by throngs in whose hearts he will ever live, and from whose memories the records of his worth can never be obliterated.

Lee, Rev. Hanson, distinguished as an educator, preacher, and editor, was born in North Carolina, but reared in Alabama, where he received a fine classical education, and afterward graduated at the Southwestern Theological Seminary, Marysville, Tenn. After several successful pastorates in Alabama, he became president of Mossy Creek College, Eastern Tennessee. In 1854 he came to Mount Lebanon, La., where he founded the *Louisiana Baptist*, which took rank among the best Southern religious journals. In connection with his intelligent wife he also founded Mount Lebanon Female College. He died May 7, 1862.

Lee, Rev. Jason, son of Rev. Joseph Lee, of Long Island, N. Y., was ordained pastor of the First Baptist church in East Lyme, Conn., in 1774, and with great honor sustained this relation till his death, which occurred in 1810, in the seventieth year of his age, and the thirty-sixth of his pastorate.

Lee, Rev. Jesse, was born in Alabama in 1803; became a preacher in 1837. He removed to Caddo Parish, La., in 1847. Through his labors the Shreveport church was greatly strengthened, and a large church built up at Summer Grove, of which he was pastor more than twenty years. He died Oct. 9, 1872.

Lee, Rev. S. C., pastor at Farmersville, La., and editor of the *Baptist Messenger*, was born in Alabama in 1826; has served several churches in

Concord Association, La., and has been often elected moderator of that body. He conceived the idea of establishing the Concord Institute, and as agent secured in a few months an endowment of $14,000.

Leigh, Hon. John T., is descended from Revolutionary stock. He was born in New Jersey in 1821. At twelve years of age he went into a store at New Brunswick as clerk. In 1844 he began business at Clinton, N. J., and has risen to a prominent place among business men in the community. He was one of the founders of the Clinton National Bank, has been twice mayor, and he has been a member of the Legislature. He is a deacon of the Baptist church in Clinton.

Leland, Rev. Aaron, lieutenant-governor of Vermont, was born in Holliston, Mass., May 28, 1761. He became a member of the Baptist church in Bellingham, Mass., in 1785, and soon after was licensed by that church to preach. He removed to Chester, Vt., where, in 1789, a small church of only ten members was formed, of which he took the pastoral charge. In ten years the church had grown so large, in consequence of a great revival which spread through that section, that it became necessary to divide it, and four churches were set off from the parent stock.

Mr. Leland did not confine his ministerial labors to his own vicinity, but went out, as our fathers in the ministry were wont to do, into the surrounding districts, making disciples and then gathering them into Christian churches. "It was not uncommon for him during the early years of his ministry to go from fourteen to twenty miles through the wilderness to attend a funeral."

Mr. Leland, from his known intelligence, and because in his political sentiments he harmonized with the people of the district in which he lived, was often called upon to act in civil affairs. For nine years he was representative in the General Assembly. He was speaker of the House for three years, and one of the governor's council for four years. For five years he was lieutenant-governor of the State, a part of the time being associated with Rev. Ezra Butler, who was governor. Probably this is the only instance in the history of the country where two Baptist ministers occupied together the two highest posts of honor within the gift of their fellow-citizens, as officers of a State government. For eighteen years he was one of the assistant justices of the County Court. He was proposed as a candidate for governor in 1828, but feeling that he must separate himself too much from the work of the ministry if he accepted the position, he declined to run for the office. We are told that "he had high qualifications for a popular and effective preacher. He had a noble form; a mind of a powerful cast, that perceived quickly and composed easily; a voice of vast compass, but smooth and mellow; great facility of utterance, and great fervor of spirit; clear, but impassioned, he would carry with him the multitude irresistibly." With such traits of character, and ready to enlist heartily in any and every good cause, it is no wonder that he wielded an extensive influence throughout the State of Vermont. "He had great influence among his brethren, and commanded their high respect, as was evident from their almost uniformly making him the moderator of their meetings. He was a wise and safe counselor, always bringing to his aid the best light he was able to command, and forming his judgment with a discreet reference to all the circumstances of the case." He was one of the Fellows of Middlebury College, and received from that institution in 1814, and from Brown University in 1815, the honorary degree of Master of Arts. He died Aug. 25, 1833.

Leland, Rev. John, was born in Grafton, Mass., May 14, 1754. At the age of eighteen he passed through an experience not unlike that of John

REV. JOHN LELAND.

Bunyan, coming out gradually into the liberty of the gospel. Within a month after his conversion, in June, 1774, he made his first attempt at public speaking. Having connected himself with the church in Mount Poney, Culpeper Co., Va., he was ordained by the choice of the church. He preached from place to place, everywhere proclaiming "the unsearchable riches of Christ." Wonderful revivals everywhere followed the labors of Mr. Leland in Virginia. Hundreds came under the power of converting grace, and professed their faith in

Christ. The summary of his labors during the fifteen years of his ministry in Virginia is thus recorded,—3009 sermons preached, 700 persons baptized, and two large churches formed, one of 300 members, and another of 200.

Having finished the work which he thought his Master had given him to do in Virginia, Mr. Leland returned to his native State, and made his home for the most of the remainder of his life in Cheshire, Mass. Here, and in the region about, the same power and the same success followed his ministry. He reports the whole number of persons whom he had baptized down to 1821 as 1352. "Some of them," he says, "have been men of wealth and rank, and ladies of quality, but the chief part have been in the middle and lower grades of life. Ten or twelve of them have engaged to preach." Missionary tours were made in almost every direction, and multitudes crowded to hear him. The story of the "mammoth cheese" sent by the people of Cheshire to President Jefferson belongs to this period. He was the bearer of the gift to Washington. "Mr. Jefferson," remarks Rev. J. T. Smith, "treated him with much deference, among other things taking him into the Senate chamber." Year after year he went on doing that special work to which he believed the Lord had called him. "From seventy to beyond eighty years of age he probably averaged more sermons a week than most settled pastors." And it is interesting to have the following recorded of him by one who could speak intelligently about him, "The large attendance on his preaching was as creditable to the hearers as to the preacher. A sensational preacher he was not, nor a mere bundle of eccentricities. The discriminating and thoughtful listened to him with the most interest and attention." He was evidently "a born preacher." The life of a settled pastor would have been irksome to him. He wanted freedom from all restraint, and to do his own work at his own time and in his own way. In politics he was a Democrat of the Jeffersonian school, a hater of all oppression, whether civil or ecclesiastical. His warmest sympathies went out to his Baptist brethren in their efforts to secure a complete divorce of the Church from the State. Everywhere he pleaded with all the energy of his soul for civil and religious liberty, and he had the satisfaction of seeing it at last come out of the conflict victorious over all foes. Among the class of ministers whom God raised up during the last century to do the special work which it was given the Baptist denomination to perform, John Leland occupies a conspicuous place. We doubt if his equal will ever be seen again. Mr. Leland died Jan. 14, 1841.

Leland University, located at New Orleans, La., was founded by the munificence of Holbrook Chamberlain, under the direction of the Home Mission Society. It is devoted to the education

LELAND UNIVERSITY, NEW ORLEANS, LA.

of freedmen. Mr. Chamberlain first gave $12,500 to found it, and the amount was duplicated by contributors to the society. He then gave $5000 more towards the buildings. He and his wife not only donated money to this noble object, but lent also their hearty personal efforts. This school has now been in successful operation several years, and has the warm sympathy of the Baptists of the city, and indeed of the Southwest. It is an important factor in the evangelization of the freedmen of the South.

Lemen, Rev. James, was born in Berkeley Co., Va., in 1760. In early life he was one of those who went North from Virginia with Gen. Washington, and was in some of the noted actions of the war of the Revolution. Returning to Virginia he settled near Wheeling, but in 1786 removed to Illinois, being one of the earliest settlers in that region of then almost unbroken wilderness. He went down the Ohio River in a flat-boat, with his family, and after much exposure and disaster arrived at length, though with a loss of all his household goods, which the river in the wrecking of his boat had swallowed up. His first home in Illinois was near Kaskaskia, at New Design, on the road from Kaskaskia to St. Louis. For many years his house was a stopping-place for travelers between the two places, and they were always entertained with Western hospitality. Under the preaching of Rev. James Smith, the first evangelical minister to visit Illinois, Mr. Lemen experienced conversion in 1787, but did not make a profession of his faith in baptism until 1794, when with his wife and two others he was baptized by Rev. Josiah Dodge. This was the first instance of the administration of baptism in what is now the State of Illinois. Two years later Mr. Lemen and his wife united with a few others in forming the first Christian church in Illinois, their minister being Rev. David Badgley. The Baptists thus led the way in the work of establishing churches in the great Prairie State. Even before Mr. Lemen had experienced conversion he had been one of a small company who met together on the Lord's day to read the Scriptures, with a sermon whenever one could be procured. After his conversion he was able to accompany these exercises with prayer. Finally, in 1808, he was licensed to preach, being now nearly fifty years of age. From that time until his death he was an active, zealous, and useful minister of the gospel, associating this with other public duties, such as, for some years, justice of the peace, and also as one of the judges of the County Court. He died Jan. 8, 1823, aged sixty-two. His son, James Lemen, Jr., who was in the ministry before him and assisted at his ordination, also preached his funeral sermon.

Lemen, Rev. James, Jr., third son of the foregoing, was born at New Design, Ill., Oct. 8, 1787. Converted at the age of twenty, he immediately began preaching, even before he had united with any church. Joining the church at New Design, he was by that church ordained, and he continued in the duties of an active ministry in various parts of Southern Illinois for more than sixty years. He took an active part also in public affairs; was during sixteen years a member of the Legislature, both as representative and as senator. An election to the U. S. Senatorship was offered him but declined. He died Feb. 8, 1870, aged eighty-two.

Lemen, James H., was one of the family of Lemens who came into Illinois among its earliest settlers. He died in O'Fallon, Madison Co., Sept. 12, 1872, at the age of sixty-five. He had been a member of Bethel church since the age of twelve, was for many years clerk of the church, and for twenty years clerk of the South District Association.

Lemen, Rev. Joseph, was the second son of James Lemen, Sr., and was born near Harper's Ferry, Va., Sept. 8, 1785. He was only nine months old when his parents removed to Illinois. He was converted at a camp-meeting near Edwardsville, Ill., conducted by the Methodist bishop, McKendree, and by two Baptist ministers,— "Father Clark" and James Lemen, Sr. He was ordained Feb. 4, 1810, and was an active and useful minister for fifty-one years. He died June 28, 1861, at the age of seventy-five.

Lemen, Rev. Josiah, was born Aug. 15, 1794, at New Design, Ill. He was the sixth child of James Lemen, Sr. He also, like his brothers Joseph, Moses, and James, became a minister of the gospel. He was baptized May 2, 1819, by Rev. John Clark, known in the former history of Illinois as "Father Clark," and united with the Canton, now Bethel church, near the place of his birth. He died July 11, 1862, aged seventy-two.

Lemen, Rev. Moses, was the youngest son of James Lemen, Sr., and he was born at the Illinois home of that remarkable family, Sept. 3, 1797. Though converted at ten years of age, he did not unite with the church until his twenty-second year. He was then baptized by "Father Clark." He and his brother Josiah were both baptized and ordained at the same time, their ordination occurring March 24, 1822. Moses Lemen, during thirty-six years, was one of the most laborious and useful ministers in Illinois. He died March 5, 1859, aged sixty-one.

Lemen, Rev. Sylvester, was also of the famous Lemen family, of Illinois, and he was for many years a member of the Bethel church. He died at Belleville, Ill., Sept. 28, 1872, at the age of fifty-six. He was, during some thirty-five years, one of the active and useful members of the South District Association.

Lennon, Rev. Haynes, was born Dec. 15, 1816; was deeply impressed with a desire to seek the Saviour at four years of age, but did not join a church till twenty-three; was baptized by Rev. Wm. Ayers, in June, 1839; began to preach in May, 1841, and was ordained in March, 1842, Rev. Wm. Ayers and Rev. Dwight Hayes forming the Presbytery. He has been the pastor of the Antioch church, in Robinson County, N. C., for thirty-eight years, and of several others nearly as long. He was moderator of the Cape Fear Association, the second largest in the State, from 1850 to 1878, with the exception of the sessions of 1864 and 1865, when he was absent on account of sickness. In 1870 he became general superintendent of missions in his Association, and has been eminently useful in developing a missionary spirit among the churches. He is still an active and effective minister.

Lenox, Judge David T., whose parents were Scotch Methodists, was born at Catskill, N. Y., in 1801. He was baptized at Rushville, Ill., in 1832, with his wife (Miss Louisa Swan, of Lexington, Ky.). He organized and superintended two Sunday-schools; he removed to Missouri in 1840; joined the Todd's Creek church; was clerk of the church and Association until 1843, when he removed to Oregon, and located on the Tualatin Plains; found five other Baptists in the wilderness, invited them to his house and there organized the West Union church, the first Baptist church west of the Rocky Mountains. In 1852 he spent $1500 of his own money, and raised $1200, to build a church edifice. He was deacon of the church. He was district judge and judge of Probate Court many years. In 1856 he removed to Weston, Eastern Oregon, where he closed a useful and consecrated life, Nov. 4, 1873.

Leonard, Rev. George, was born in Raynham, Mass., Aug. 17, 1802. He entered Brown University and graduated in 1824. He studied subsequently at the Newton Theological Institution, and was one of the first students who graduated from that seat of sacred learning. He was ordained pastor of the Second Baptist church in Salem, Mass., in August, 1826, where he labored until compelled to resign on account of ill health. On the 4th of July, 1830, he began his ministry as pastor of the First Baptist church in Portland, Me. Again his health failed. He gave up all ministerial work, and died at last, Aug. 11, 1831, in Worcester, Mass. If Mr. Leonard had been blessed with good health, and had lived longer, it may be safely predicted that he would have taken a high place among the ablest ministers of his denomination. Both the churches he served revere his memory.

Leonard, Judge John, was born in Knox Co., O., Aug. 20, 1825. He attended Denison University, at Granville, O. On leaving college he located in Morrow County, and at the age of twenty-three was elected county surveyor. While holding this office he devoted his spare time entirely to the study of law, and in 1852 was admitted to the bar in Wooster, Wayne Co., O. In the summer of 1853 he came to Iowa, and settled at Winterset, where he opened a law-office, and gradually built up an extensive practice. In 1862 he was elected district attorney, but resigned in 1864. In January, 1874, he entered upon his duties as judge of the Fifth Judicial District, to which he had been recently elected, and in which he continued to serve till the expiration of his term of office. He is an earnest and studious reader, especially in the line of his profession, and has one of the best libraries of any lawyer in Southwestern Iowa. He has long been a member of the Baptist church, and he is exemplary and faithful in his life and church relations. He still resides in Winterset, where his home has been for more than twenty-seven years. His eldest son, Byram Leonard, an attorney of much promise, a man of sterling Christian worth, and an earnest worker in the Baptist church of which he was a valued member, died in 1879, in his early manhood, and in the midst of a useful life.

Leonard, L. G., D.D., was born in Monson, Mass., Jan. 6, 1810; graduated at Newton in 1836; the same year became pastor of the church in Webster, Mass., where he remained nearly seven years. After two short pastorates in Thompson and New London, Conn., he took charge, in 1848, of the Market Street church, Zanesville, O. From 1855 to 1863 was pastor at Marietta, O., where he was the means not only of greatly strengthening the home church, but was instrumental in forming several new churches in the surrounding country. In 1863 he took charge of the church at Lebanon, O., remaining until 1872, when he became pastor of the church at Bucyrus, a position which he still holds.

Dr. Leonard has been closely identified with Baptist interests in Ohio. For thirty years he has been a member of the board of trustees of Denison University. His pastorates have been long and fruitful. A wise counselor and a faithful toiler for Christ, he has received during his many years of service the highest esteem and affection.

Leslie, Gov. Preston H., was born in Clinton Co., Ky., March 8, 1819, and was educated in the schools of his vicinity until the age of sixteen. Upon leaving school he spent a portion of his time

GOV. PRESTON H. LESLIE.

upon a farm near Louisville. At the age of eighteen he accepted a position in a store in Clinton County, and shortly afterwards entered the county clerk's office as a deputy. After this he attended a school of higher grade, and applied himself to study with great diligence, committing to memory the whole of a text-book on logic within a few weeks. When he left this school he entered the law-office of Gen. Rice Maxey, since Judge Maxey, of Texas, and father of United States Senator S. B. Maxey, of that State. In 1841 he was admitted to the bar. While a law-student, or just before he began the study of law, he professed religion and joined a Baptist church, and from that time made the Bible his study and his guide. When he commenced the practice of law he formed a resolution not to advocate knowingly an unjust cause for any consideration, and he determined never to neglect his duty to God for any worldly advantage however great. On these principles he began the business of life, and it is believed that he has adhered to them with unyielding tenacity. His success was assured from the beginning. From 1842 until 1853 his residence was upon a farm on Cumberland River, in Jackson Co., Tenn. Here he divided his time between farming and his profession. A few years later he removed to Glasgow, Ky., where he now resides. He was first elected to the Legislature from Monroe County in 1844, and was re-elected in 1850. He represented Barren and Monroe Counties in the State Senate from 1851 to 1855, and again in 1867, occupying the speaker's chair in the Senate in 1869. On the resignation of Gov. Stevenson he became governor *ex-officio* until the expiration of the term, in 1871. During that year he was elected governor by the extraordinary majority of 37,156. In the discharge of his duties as chief magistrate he attained a national reputation for diligence, wisdom, and integrity. At the close of his term, in 1875, he returned to his home in Glasgow and resumed his legal practice. Gov. Leslie is as faithful to his church as to the State, and he allows nothing but Providential circumstances to detain him from public worship or to prevent him from taking an active part in the business of his church. He superintended the Sunday-school at the Baptist church in Frankfort while he was governor, and was frequently moderator of the General Association of the Baptists. The State and the Church alike are justly proud of this pure statesman and devoted Christian.

Leslie, Rev. Robert, was born in Edinburgh, Scotland, in 1838, and came with his parents to the United States in 1851, stopping at Chicago, Ill., but subsequently locating at Schenectady, N. Y. In 1856 the family again removed to the West, establishing their home this time at Clinton, Iowa. According to the old established rule among the Scotch Presbyterians, the parents of Mr. Leslie designed him for the ministry, and while yet quite young he attended for some time the Rev. Dr. Andrew Thompson's school in Edinburgh. The conversion of his parents to Baptist views, and their removal to the United States, somewhat modified and changed these early purposes and also interrupted his education. Converted at the age of sixteen, he made a profession of religion in 1854, and united with the Baptist church in Clinton, Iowa. After his union with the church he prosecuted, in connection with his father, the business of architect and builder. During a number of years he had a painful conflict with his convictions with reference to the Christian ministry, which finally culminated in his happy and entire consecration to that work. He was educated at the University of Chicago, graduating in the class of 1869, and at the Chicago Theological Seminary, graduating in 1870. He was ordained Oct. 12, 1870, as pastor of the Baptist church at Anamosa, Iowa. He was subsequently settled at Joliet, Ill., and in Waverly, Iowa. He took charge of the Baptist church in Waukesha, Wis., Aug. 1, 1879, where he is now the highly esteemed and useful pastor of the church of which Dr. Robert Boyd was pastor emeritus until his death. Thoroughly educated, fully consecrated to the work of the ministry, sound in his views of truth, and the pastor of one of the best churches in Wisconsin, Mr. Leslie has before him a bright and most promising future.

Lester, James S., was born in Virginia; is now over eighty years old; was a soldier against the Indians and Mexicans in Texas in 1842; was a member of the convention and signed the declaration of independence of Texas, March 2, 1836; has been a consistent Baptist all his life; a trustee of and liberal contributor to the endowment of Baylor University; joined the Baptist church in Texas at an early age, and lives now among his old friends in the enjoyment of their warm regard. He is one of the remarkable men of Texas.

Letters of Dismission are granted to members to unite with other churches of the same faith and gospel order. A letter of dismission is only a recommendation to the brother in whose favor it is granted. No church is obliged to receive it or him. It is found by experience that a letter should always be addressed to a particular church. General letters are unfavorable to permanent church relations. The letter is wisely limited in time, expiring in three, six, or twelve months. Until the accceptance of the letter by another church the person in whose favor it has been issued retains his membership in the church granting it unless a by-law provides otherwise. Authority to unite with another church ceases when the date of limitation in the letter is passed. According to Baptist usage the applicant for a letter should pay his church dues, if he is able, before he receives it. After receiving his letter of dismission, if he changes his mind about uniting with another community, he should return the letter to the church or its clerk. While retaining the letter, and before its date of limitation is reached, though still a member of the church, he should not vote at church meetings or take any part in the regular business of the church.

Every Baptist has a right to obtain a letter to unite with a regular Baptist church unless there is a charge against him. And this privilege, it is believed, would be sustained by the civil courts. And for the same reason, if a member is excluded from a church contrary to its by-laws, or, if it has none, against the usages of the denomination, the courts would order his restoration. An English authority recently makes the following statement on this question: "The courts say to a church, chapel, company, club, or partnership, Make what contract you please, but *when the agreement is made we will see that it is kept.*" There is no reason to doubt but that this is the law in every State of the Union for every association, secular and religious, legally holding real estate. When a member asks for a letter, and there is no accusation against him before the disciplinary committee or the church, unless some grave breach of duty has been committed no charge should be brought then. Baptist usage requires the clerk of a church receiving a letter to notify the church granting it that the brother commended by it has been received into fellowship. Regular Baptist churches do not grant letters of dismission to Pedobaptist religious communities. Neither do they receive letters from these bodies except as testimonials.

Form of a Letter of Dismission.

The Baptist church of ——— to the Baptist church of ———

DEAR BRETHREN:

This is to certify that ——— is a member with us in good standing and full fellowship; and at his own request he is hereby dismissed from us to unite with you. When received by you his connection with us will cease.

By order of the church.

——— ———, *Church Clerk.*

This letter will be valid for six months.

Leverett, Prof. Warren, was born Dec. 19, 1805; he and his twin-brother, Prof. Washington Leverett, are sons of William and Lydia (Fuller) Leverett, of Brookline, Mass. At the age of fourteen the two brothers went to live with Samuel Griggs, Esq., a brother of Mrs. Leverett's second husband, a farmer residing in Rutland, Vt. Here they remained until they reached their majority. In the mean time they had experienced conversion, and leaving the home in Vermont that they might pursue study under the direction of their eldest brother, Rev. William Leverett, of Roxbury, they united with the Baptist church in Cambridgeport. September, 1828, they entered Brown University, graduating in 1832. For a time the brothers were separated, Washington becoming one of the faculty of Columbian College, Washington, D. C., and Warren being compelled by broken health to travel, though engaged occasionally in teaching. He removed to the West and opened a school in Greenville, Ill, and successfully carried it on for a year and a half, when he removed to Upper Alton, becoming connected with Shurtleff College, and remaining in that service until 1868. He died at Upper Alton in November, 1872. Prof. Leverett's department in Shurtleff College was that of ancient languages, in which studies he was a thorough, proficient, and an admirable instructor. While a member of the church in Cambridgeport he was licensed as a preacher, and frequently during his life officiated as such with much acceptance.

Leverett, Washington, LL.D.—Some account of the early life of Washington Leverett, professor in Shurtleff College during so many years, is given in connection with the notice of his twin-brother, Prof. Warren Leverett. Washington Leverett, after two years spent as teacher in Brown University, and in Columbian College, Washington, D. C., entered at Newton, where he graduated in 1836. Receiving at that time a call to the chair of Mathematics and Natural Philosophy in Shurtleff College, he accepted it, and removing to Illinois entered at once upon his duties. This post of service he continued to fill with marked acceptance for thirty-two years, resigning it in 1868. Since that date he has continued his connection with the college as a member of the board of trustees, and as librarian and treasurer. It is justly written of him that "as a teacher he was eminently successful, and possessed a thoroughness of scholarship and real worth that never failed to command the respect of his pupils, and which has endeared him to a large circle of warm friends."

Levering, Judge Charles, associate judge of the Circuit Court of Allen Co., O., was a lineal descendant of Wigard Levering, one of the pioneer settlers of Roxborough, in Philadelphia County, who emigrated to this country from Germany in 1685.

He was born in Roxborough township, Dec. 8, 1782.

Mr. Levering received the common rudiments of an English education at the district school of his native place.

In 1805 he indulged a hope in Christ, and was baptized into the fellowship of the Roxborough Baptist church, of which he was elected deacon March 24, 1821.

On Sept. 24, 1812, he was married to Esther Levering, eldest daughter of Deacon Anthony Levering, of Roxborough, a most estimable Christian wife and mother.

Mr. Levering was a patriot, and during the war of 1812–14, although he was major of a regiment, yet when he found his command was not to be ordered into active service until after six months, he enlisted as a private in the Roxborough Volunteers, of which company he subsequently became captain.

In 1822 he removed into the district of Southwark, and united with the Third church; subsequently he joined the Second church, during the pastorate of the Rev. Thomas J. Kitts.

In 1835, Mr. Levering removed to Allen, now Auglaize Co., O., soon after which he was appointed

JUDGE CHARLES LEVERING.

associate judge of the Circuit Court for that county, which position he held for several years.

He was active in everything pertaining to the success of our denomination. He was a constituent member and deacon of the Amanda and Wapaukoneta churches, and held the office of deacon in the latter until his death, which occurred March 14, 1860. His remains lie in a country churchyard, on the State road, about five miles north of Wapaukoneta, the county seat of Auglaize Co., O.

Levering, Eugene, Sr., was born in Baltimore, Md., April 24, 1819. He traced his family for seven generations to Rosier Levering, born probably in France about 1600, who fled to Holland or Germany on account of religious persecutions, and married Elizabeth Van De Walle, of Wesel, Westphalia. They had two sons,—Wigard and Gehard. The former, Eugene's ancestor, was born at Gamen, Westphalia, about 1648, and married, in 1671, Magdalene Böker. In 1685, accompanied by his wife and their four children, he came to America and settled at Germantown, Pa. In 1692 he removed to Roxborough, where he bought 500 acres of land. Wigard and his wife had ten children. Their son William, of the third generation, was born at Mulheim, in Germany, May 4, 1677, and came to America with his parents. He died in 1746, leaving five children. The eldest, William, of the fourth generation, was born at Roxborough, August, 1705. He married, May 2, 1732, Hannah Clement. He built the first hotel at Roxborough, now known as the "Leverington," which he carried on together with blacksmithing and farming, his farm embracing 250 acres. He died March 30, 1774. The first school-house in Roxborough was built through his exertions, and he gave the ground for it in 1748. It is now called "The Levering Primary School." William and Hannah had nine children, one of whom, Enoch, of the fifth generation, was born in Roxborough, Feb. 21, 1742. After conducting his large tannery there for many years, he removed to Baltimore, Md., between the years 1773 and 1775. Here he entered extensively into the grocery business. He married Mary Righter, and died aged fifty-four. They had nine sons. Peter was the first-born. Enoch's brother, Nathan, born in Roxborough, May 19, 1745, gave the lot on which the Roxborough Baptist church is built, and superintended its erection. This church, of which he was a constituent member, met at his residence prior to the erection of their house of worship. He also gave the ground for their cemetery. He was father-in-law to H. G. Jones, D.D., son of Rev. David Jones, A.M., a famous Revolutionary chaplain. Hon. H. G. Jones, the son of Dr. Jones, is the author of "A Genea-

EUGENE LEVERING, SR.

logical Account" of the Levering family, from which many of the facts of this article are taken. Peter, of the sixth generation, was born in Roxborough, Feb. 14, 1766, and removed to Baltimore with his parents, where he became engaged in the shipping and commission business. He married, May 22, 1798, Hannah, only daughter of William Wilson, of the firm of William Wilson & Sons, one of the most extensive shipping-houses of Baltimore. They both were members of the First Baptist church. Mr. Levering united with it late in life, but was a prominent member of the congregation, and his house was headquarters for the denomination. He died Dec. 7, 1843. They had fourteen children, Eugene being the twelfth, and the 455th descendant of Rosier Levering. He was born in Baltimore, April 24, 1819. After spending some years in preparation in private schools in Baltimore, he went to college, but his health compelled him to relinquish his intention. At an early age he was converted, and united with the First Baptist church, of which he became a most useful member. Subsequently he became a valued member of the Seventh Baptist church, Richard Fuller, D.D., pastor, of whom he was an intimate friend. He was for many years the treasurer of the Maryland Baptist Union Association. He married, Oct. 4, 1842, Ann, daughter of Joshua and Mary E. Walker, of Baltimore, and a descendant of Henry Sater, who came from England in 1709, and through whose liberality and efforts the first Baptist church in Maryland was formed. They had twelve children, nine of whom are now living. In 1842 he commenced business, in partnership with his brother, Frederick A., who married Martha E. Johnson, grandniece of the first governor of Maryland. Levering & Co. soon became a leading house in their business, and not only established for themselves an enviable reputation, but also added much to the prosperity of Baltimore. In 1861, when the war began, owing to their extensive trade with the Southern States, where they were unable to collect their debts, they were compelled to suspend and to compromise with all their creditors for fifty cents on the dollar. But near the close of the war, so successful and conscientious were they, that they paid the entire obligation, from which they had been legally released, with interest, amounting to nearly $100,000. In 1866, upon the death of his brother, Eugene took into partnership with him his sons William T., Eugene, and Joshua. The house took a position at the head of their special trade, and has been greatly instrumental in making Baltimore second in importance in their branch of business in the United States. Mr. Levering died, after an illness of four months, in June, 1870. He left $30,000 to charitable and religious objects. He made his three sons his executors, and left them in charge of the business. The present firm, composed of his sons William T., Eugene, Joshua, and Leonidas, succeeded the old firm in January, 1875, upon the settlement of their father's estate. It is the largest house in their business in Baltimore, and the third or fourth in the United States. Eugene is president of the National Bank of Commerce. Following in the footsteps of their fathers, the sons are living for Christ, being active in church and denominational matters, and being also among the largest contributors to the cause of Christ in the Baptist denomination North or South. Mr. Levering's widow survives him. She and her children—eight sons, one daughter, and four daughters-in-law—are all members of the Eutaw Place Baptist church. These children are left to testify by their worth of character and their noble deeds to the true principles and exalted reputation of their parents.

Levering, Franklin, was born in Baltimore, March 9, 1811. He united in early life with the First Baptist church in Baltimore. He removed to Clark Co., Mo., and united with Fox River church, and organized the first Sabbath-school in the county. In 1843 he located at Hannibal, and entered upon mercantile pursuits. He was a successful business man, and a zealous Christian, given to hospitality. His house was the home of visiting ministers. He united with the church in Hannibal, and was clerk, deacon, and Sabbath-school superintendent. The last office he held twenty-six years.

He left his children the heritage of an unblemished character, and was held in the highest esteem as a citizen. He died July 26, 1870, and was deeply mourned in the church and in the community. His daily life exemplified the beauty of holiness. When dying he was asked if he wanted anything, he shook his head and replied, "Jesus is coming." When asked if he had any message to leave, he said, "Live holy lives."

Levy, Edgar Mortimer, D.D., was born in St. Mary's, Ga., Nov. 23, 1822; was converted when thirteen years of age, and united with the Presbyterian Church. After pursuing studies for two years in a private classical school, he spent three years in the University of Pennsylvania, and studied theology under the late Rev. Albert Barnes; was licensed to preach in 1843; became deeply interested in the subject of baptism, and after a year of prayerful study, was baptized April 14, 1844, by Dr. G. B. Ide, of Philadelphia. In the autumn of 1844 he was invited to supply the First West Philadelphia church, and soon after became pastor. After fourteen years of abundant labor he accepted a call to the South church, Newark, N. J., where he remained ten years. In 1868 he returned to Philadelphia, and became pastor of the Berean church, where he still remains, and where many have been gathered into the church under his ministrations. He received the degree of D.D., in 1865, from the university at Lewisburg. Dr. Levy has had much to do with the prosperity of the Baptist church in West Philadelphia.

Levy, Capt. John P., was born in St. Mary's, Ga., July 25, 1809; learned the trade of ship-carpenter, and on completing his apprenticeship shipped as a sailor on a Liverpool packet; was soon made commander of the vessel, and spent a number of years in seafaring life. At length he returned to Philadelphia, and established the well-known ship-building firm of Reaney, Neafie & Levy, which undertaking was attended with rapidly increasing success. In the spring of 1855 he was baptized by his brother, Rev. E. M. Levy, D.D., and united with the First church, West Philadelphia, of which his brother was at that time pastor. He subsequently became impressed with the necessity of establishing another interest in this rapidly growing section of the city, and united with others in organ-

CAPT. JOHN P. LEVY.

izing the Berean church. The beautiful meeting-house of this church was secured mainly through his munificent benefactions, and was dedicated free of incumbrance June 22, 1860. As a thank-offering for continued prosperity, he built an attractive parsonage adjoining the sanctuary, and conveyed it to the church, together with an annuity of $600. Nor were his benefactions confined to the church of which he was a member. He was a man full of generous impulses, and his wealth was largely distributed. He died at Aiken, S. C., whither he had gone to recruit his feeble health, Dec. 26, 1867.

Lewis, Rev. Cadwallader, LL.D., an eminent scholar, and one of the most eloquent pulpit orators of the South, was born in Spottsylvania Co., Va., Nov. 5, 1811. He was educated by his father, who conducted a classical school many years at Llangollen, Va., but finished his course of study, which was a very full one, at the University of Virginia. In 1831 he went to Kentucky, and taught school in Covington. The following year he took charge of the preparatory department of Georgetown College. In 1844 he commenced the study of medicine, but his health failed, and he located on a farm in Franklin County, where he has lived until the present time. During the same year he made a profession of religion, and united with Buck Run Baptist church, near his home. He was very soon after licensed to preach, and was ordained in 1846. He was invited to take pastoral charge of the Baptist church at Frankfort, but his health would not admit of his leaving his farm. He took charge of country and village churches convenient to his residence, preaching one Sunday in the month to each, and has thus employed himself to the present time, except when, in consequence of a crushed limb, he was unable to travel. He occupied the chair of Theology in Georgetown College four years. He is a strong, logical writer, and exercises a leading influence in the councils of the denomination in his State.

Lewis, Rev. Charles Casson, son of Horatio and Betsey Lewis, was born in Stonington, Conn., June 8, 1807; became a sea-captain; converted in 1842 under the preaching of Rev. J. S. Swan; joined Third Baptist church in Groton, Conn.; began preaching at Key West, Fla., where he planted a church and was ordained; afterwards settled with the following churches: First Groton, Conn.; Lisbury, Mass.; Second Hopkinton, Exeter, North Kingstown, Block Island, and Lattery Village, R. I.; and Second North Stonington, Conn.; from Block Island he was elected to the senate of Rhode Island; was a man of fervor and power; died in the pastoral office with the Second Baptist church of North Stonington, Conn., March 10, 1864, in his fifty-seventh year.

Lewis, Rev. Daniel D., was born in Barnstable, Mass., July 21, 1777. He was converted in early life, and joined the First church in Portland, Me., then composed of nine members. These persons were full of the grace of Christ, and the church soon became numerous and widely influential.

Mr. Lewis took charge of the church at Ipswich, Mass., on first entering the ministry. He was subsequently pastor of the Second church of Providence, R. I., of the church in Fishkill, N. Y., in Frankford, Pa., in Wilmington, Del., and in Paterson and Piscataway, N. J. In Piscataway he spent years rich in divine blessings, and from it he entered the "general assembly and church of the first-born," Sept. 25, 1849. He delivered his last sermon on Sunday evening, and died on the following Tuesday.

Mr. Lewis was an able preacher, full of the Spirit and Word of God, and a successful pastor of the churches for whose welfare he labored. He healed church wounds, built up disciples in the glorious doctrines of grace, led throngs of converts to Jesus, and enjoyed the warm affection of large numbers. His memory is precious still in the churches for whose eternal interests he employed his time and talents, and his fervent prayers.

Lewis, Rev. Geo. W., was born in Ellisburgh, Jefferson Co., N. Y., April 14, 1822, where he was baptized in March, 1833; ordained in Lowell, Ind., Jan. 18, 1866; labored in Indiana, Illinois, and Iowa; and became pastor of the Aurora Baptist church, Neb., in 1878. Mr. Lewis has enjoyed the divine blessing in his pastorates.

Lewis, Hon. Henry Clay, of Coldwater, Mich., was born in Orleans Co., N. Y., May 5, 1820. He has resided in Coldwater since 1844, where he has been engaged in business, first as a merchant and afterwards as a banker. He is president of the Coldwater National Bank, and has been mayor of the city. He has been a member of the Baptist Church nearly twenty years. He is chiefly known as the owner of an art-gallery, which he founded in 1868, which is open to the public without charge. It is larger than any other art-gallery on this continent. Mr. Lewis takes great pleasure in affording

HON. HENRY CLAY LEWIS.

enjoyment to others, and has made his gallery, in its surroundings as well as in itself, beautiful and attractive, and a most important element in the educational influences of the city of Coldwater.

Lewis, Prof. John J., A.M., was born in Utica, N. Y., Dec. 25, 1843, of Welsh Congregational parentage; entered the grammar school of Madison University in 1859; entered Madison University, and afterwards Hamilton College (Clinton), and was there graduated in 1864; Professor of Belles-Lettres and Elocution in Brooklyn Collegiate and Polytechnic Institute from 1864 to 1866. In the fall of 1866 he removed to Syracuse, and began preaching in a small mission chapel; was settled March, 1867, as pastor of First Baptist church, Syracuse; was very successful, the increase in sixteen months being over 140. In 1868 he became Professor of Belles-Lettres in Madison University, which position he still retains, to the great satisfaction of students, alumni, and friends of the institution; has contributed largely to the press, many of his articles being founded on his travels in Japan, Burmah, India, and the Orient.

Lewis, Rev. John W., one of the most distinguished Baptist ministers of North Georgia, was born near Spartanburg, S. C., Feb. 1, 1801. Educated at a classical academy near Spartanburg, he studied and practised medicine at Greenville, S. C., becoming a skillful and popular physician. He united with the Baptist church of that town. During the years 1830 and 1831 he was a member of the South Carolina Legislature. About that time he began to preach, and was ordained in 1832. He removed to Canton, Ga., in 1839 or 1840, becoming pastor of that and other churches in Cherokee, Ga., and acquiring a great influence. He was a preacher of much force and energy; a strong and bold defender of the faith; an able expounder of the Word, and an eloquent advocate of the truth. A man of fine practical sense, he had a strong mind, and was a deep, original thinker. He had a benevolent heart, and was steadfast in his friendships. He had extraordinary forecast, and managed business matters with great ability and success. In 1857 he was appointed superintendent of the State road by Gov. Brown, and his management was eminently successful. During the war he served in the Congress of the Confederate States, as Senator, with great ability, and previous to the war he served in the State senate, and was instrumental in the establishment of the Supreme Court of Georgia. His character stood extraordinarily high in Georgia. A man of firm faith, deep piety, and unabated zeal, he won many souls to Jesus. After a life of great usefulness, he died in Cherokee County, in June, 1865.

Lewis, Rev. Lester, was born in Suffield, Conn., Oct. 15, 1817; baptized by Rev. Henry Jackson, D.D., and united with First Baptist church in Hartford, Feb. 11, 1838; studied in Connecticut Literary Institution; ordained pastor of the church in Agawam, Mass., Oct. 7, 1840; in 1846 began to labor for Connecticut Baptist State Convention, but soon settled with the church in Bristol; in 1853 became pastor of the church in Middletown, where, after great success, he died, Feb. 7, 1858; large-hearted, sound in the faith, a clear and forcible preacher, fervent in prayer, and beloved by all who knew him.

Lewisburg, Pa., the University at.—In the year 1845, some intelligent Baptists of the Northumberland Association saw the need of higher education for their sons and daughters, under the religious auspices of their own denomination. Their perception of this need at first took form in a plan for a first-class academy. The natural beauty, healthfulness, and economic advantages of the borough of Lewisburg, in Union Co., Pa., on the West Branch of the Susquehanna, and in the geographical centre of the State, determined the location of the school in that village. Through the Rev. Eugenio Kincaid and the Rev. J. E. Bradley, Stephen W. Taylor, who had recently resigned his professorship in Madison University, became enlisted in the new enterprise. Under the principalship of Prof. Taylor, assisted by his son, Alfred Taylor, A.M., and I. N. Loomis, A.M., a school was opened in the fall of 1846 in the basement of the Baptist church, since destroyed.

Prof. Taylor combined prophetic insight with the powers of a rare teacher, and saw in the new school the germ of a university. Others approved the project of founding at Lewisburg such an institution as would meet the higher educational demands of the whole State. A charter incorporating "The University at Lewisburg, Pa.," was approved on the 5th day of February, 1846, with the following trustees: James Moore, James Moore, Jr., Joseph Meireell, William H. Ludwig, Samuel Wolfe, Levi B. Christ, Henry Funk, Joel E. Bradley, Eugenio Kincaid, Benjamin Bear, William W. Keen, William Bucknell, Thomas Wattson, James M. Linnard, Lewis Vastine, Oliver Blackburn, Caleb Lee, Daniel L. Moore.

It was provided in the charter that ground should be purchased and buildings erected when $100,000 had been raised, that a fourth part should be permanently invested in a productive form, that the property should not be mortgaged or debt incurred under any pretext whatever, that no misnomer should defeat or annul a grant or bequest, and that ten acres of ground with improvements should be exempt from taxation. The management was committed to two boards: 1st, a board of trustees, not to exceed twenty members, all of whom must be Baptists; and, 2d, a board of curators, not to exceed forty members, the majority of whom must be Baptists. Both boards are self-perpetuating.

The subscription of $100,000 was declared to be secured on the 17th day of July, 1849, through the efforts of Drs. Eugenio Kincaid and William Shadrach, who traversed the State soliciting funds. Previous to this a tract of land to the south of the borough of Lewisburg, including a fine hill of nearly a hundred feet elevation, covered with a beautiful natural grove, and commanding extended views over river and valley, had been secured for the university. In 1848 an academy building was begun and nearly completed. In January, 1849, the trustees felt justified in electing professors for the college, and in commencing a college building. Two graduates of Madison University, the Rev. G. W. Anderson, A.M., editor of the *Christian Chronicle*, of Philadelphia, and the Rev. G. R. Bliss, of New Brunswick, N. J., were appointed, respectively, to the chairs of Latin and Greek. Both soon afterwards began their labors, the students of the academy and the college, consisting of both sexes, reciting together in the academy building, Prof. Taylor still acting as principal.

In 1851 the west wing of the college building was completed, and the college students moved into dormitories and studies regarded at the time as "unsurpassed in pleasantness by those of any institution." In the spring of this year Prof. Taylor resigned his position to accept the presidency of Madison University, but remained to preside at the first Commencement, August 20, 1851, when a class of seven was graduated in the chapel of the academy. It is but just to the memory of this good man and great teacher to quote the words of a co-worker who knew him well: "Without him it is almost certain that our university would never have existed, and existing in an essential measure by his agency, it is well for us that that agency was not only earnest, benevolent, laborious, and pious, but also in the main judicious and beneficial."

The Rev. Howard Malcom, D.D., of Philadelphia, an alumnus of Princeton, and ex-president of Georgetown College, had been chosen president of the university, and Charles S. James, A.M., a graduate of Brown, and Alfred Taylor, A.M., a graduate of Madison, were added to the faculty of the college, the former as Professor of Mathematics and Natural Philosophy, and the latter as Professor of Belles-Lettres. With these additions began the collegiate year 1851–52. The college now became a distinct department of the university, the academy became gradually a preparatory school for boys only, while, in 1852, the "University Female Institute" became a separate department. A theological department was added in 1855. From this point, therefore, we may consider the departments separately.

THE COLLEGE.

The presidency of Dr. Malcom continued from 1851 to 1857, during which the college building was completed, consisting of a main building 80 feet

THE UNIVERSITY AT LEWISBURG, PA.

square, of three stories, for recitation-rooms, chapel, society halls, library, cabinet, and Commencement Hall, and two wings, each 120 feet long and 35 feet wide, of four stories, for students' study-rooms and dormitories. In 1852 the sum of $45,000 was added to the funds by a few friends without a general canvass. About $20,000 were received from lands sold from the original campus, leaving finally about twenty-six acres as university grounds.

Thus established, the college began a work of incalculable value to the intellectual and spiritual progress of the denomination in Pennsylvania. On the resignation of President Malcom, in 1857, the Rev. Justin R. Loomis, Ph.D., who had been called from Waterville, Me., in 1854, to fill the chair of Natural Sciences, succeeded him as president. During twenty-five years President Loomis devoted his best energies to the work of building up the college, and establishing the youth who came under his moulding hand in the principles of a deep Christian philosophy. The invasion of Pennsylvania by Lee's army, in 1863, caused the closing of the college during a campaign of six weeks, officers and students uniting to form Company A of the 28th Regiment of Pa. Vols. A memorial tablet in Commencement Hall commemorates the names of those who fell in the war for the Union. In 1864, President Loomis increased the funds of the university by collecting subscriptions amounting to $100,000. In 1876 an attempt was made to secure additional endowment, but owing to other interests in the field the effort was abandoned after about $20,000 had been promised, mostly in private subscriptions offered by a few liberal friends.

In 1879, President Loomis resigned the presidency, and Prof. David J. Hill, A.M., a graduate of the college, and at the time of his appointment Crozer Professor of Rhetoric, was chosen president of the university, a position which he still occupies.

The following were presidents and acting presidents from the foundation of the college to the year 1880:

PRESIDENTS.

Elected.		Resigned.
1851.	Rev. Howard Malcom, D.D., LL.D.	1857
1857.	Rev. Justin R. Loomis, Ph.D., LL.D.	1879
1879.	Rev. David J. Hill, A.M.	

ACTING PRESIDENTS.

Stephen W. Taylor, LL.D., prior to 1851.
Rev. Geo. R. Bliss, D.D., LL.D., during 1871-72.
Rev. Francis W. Tustin, Ph.D., for six months in 1879.

The university has an endowment of $121,000, and property worth $117,000, and an effort is now started by which its endowment is certain to be greatly increased. The institution has no debts.

The college is now in possession of a fine library of nearly 10,000 volumes, a museum of about 10,000 specimens for the illustration of the sciences, a chemical laboratory and apparatus. There are two flourishing literary societies with libraries of their own. They publish a monthly journal called *The College Herald*. There is also a "Society for Moral and Religious Inquiry." There are two prizes for preparation for college and one for excellence in oratory in the Junior year. Tuition is free to the sons of ministers. The expenses range from $125 to $250 per annum.

The courses of study have expanded greatly since the opening of the college, as shown in comparative tables published in "A Historical Sketch of the University at Lewisburg," edited by O. W. Spratt, LL.B., in 1876, and printed by the Society of Alumni. There are now two courses leading to a degree: (1) The classical course, of four years, leading to the degree of A.B., and (2) the Latin scientific course, leading to the degree of S.B. Both courses have been brought up to the standard of the best Eastern colleges, and have recently given some scope to the optional element. Anglo-Saxon, American literature, comparative zoölogy, analytical chemistry, and constitutional law have been added to both courses. A good collection of engravings, heliotypes, and casts has stimulated the study of the fine arts, and illustrated lectures are given to the Senior class. Lectures on Grecian history, life, and literature; Roman history, life, and literature; mediæval history; English history and literature; the history of philosophy; natural theology; and the evidences of Christianity are regularly delivered. The introduction of a short course of lectures on practical ethics and hygiene for the Freshman class is believed to be distinctively peculiar to this college. The government is thus based on ethical ideas, and so far has proved that an appeal to manhood develops it and secures self-government.

The graduates of the college number 322. Honorary degrees have been bestowed as follows: LL.D., 12; D.D., 36; Ph.D., 10; A.M., 52.

Since 1851, when the first class was graduated, important changes bearing upon the prosperity of the college have gradually taken place. The Philadelphia and Erie Railroad runs within one mile of Lewisburg, and the Lewisburg and Tyrone Railroad passes through it. The town is lighted with gas, and contains several miles of well-paved sidewalks. A new church edifice, costing nearly $60,000, has been built by the Baptists. The natural beauty of the place has been enhanced by these improvements, yet it remains a quiet, moral, and rural retreat admirably adapted to the seclusion which thorough study demands for the young.

THE INSTITUTE.

This department of the university began its separate organization as a school in 1852, under the principalship of Miss Hadassah E. Scribner, of

Maine, who retained her position for two years. In 1854 two young ladies, the first class of the institute, were graduated. At this time all the teachers resigned, and Miss Amanda Taylor, of Easton, Pa., with a new corps of assistants, undertook the work. Strong prejudices existed in the community against the liberal education of women, but this was gradually overcome by persistent effort, and in 1858 fifteen young ladies were graduated in the presence of an audience of 1500 people. Since then classes ranging from ten to twenty have been graduated every year. In 1857 six acres of a beautiful grove were appropriated for a suitable building on the university grounds. The building is pleasantly and healthfully located, warmed with furnaces, and lighted with gas, and it will accommodate ninety boarders. In 1869 a wing was added, at the cost of $10,000, containing rooms for students and a large gymnasium, which has been suitably fitted up.

In 1863, Miss Taylor resigned, and was succeeded by Miss Lucy W. Rundell, of Alden, N. Y. She continued her work ably until 1869, when she was succeeded by Miss Harriet E. Spratt, daughter of the Rev. Geo. M. Spratt, D.D., and a graduate of the institute. This rare Christian woman had already spent fourteen years in the school as a teacher. She continued as principal until the Commencement of 1878. A few months later she ended a career of extraordinary usefulness by death, having been made Emeritus lady principal after her resignation. For twenty-four years her life was devoted to the successive classes of young women that passed through the institute, and hundreds mourned for her as for a sister.

In 1878, Jonathan Jones, A.M., was elected principal, a position which he now holds. The institute is provided with an able corps of instructors, who live in the institute building and make it a school home. There are five courses of study, ranging from a preparatory English course to a full classical collegiate course. The young ladies recite in their own building, apart from the young gentlemen, but attend the lectures of the college, enjoy the use of the library and museum, and witness the experiments of the professor of natural sciences. There are excellent advantages for instruction in music, drawing, crayoning, and painting. The graduates number 293.

THE ACADEMY.

When, in 1849, the college emerged into a distinct department of the university, the academy was intrusted to the principalship of Isaac N. Loomis, A.M., sharing the new academy building with the college. This arrangement continued until the college building was completed, H. D. Walker, A.M., succeeding Principal Loomis in 1853, and George Yeager, A.M., following in 1857. Isaac C. Wynn, A.M., became principal in 1859, and in January, 1860, the academy building being used then solely for that department, it was fitted up for a boarding-school for boys and young men. Until 1868 the academy embraced the classical preparatory classes of the university, but in that year "The Classical Preparatory Department" was organized, with Freeman Loomis, A.M., as principal, the academy being confined to English branches only. This arrangement continued, the English academy having in the mean time a succession of separate principals, until 1878, when the departments were reunited under the principalship of William E. Martin, A.M. "The Classical Preparatory Department," from 1868 to 1878, was established in the west wing of the college building.

The academy, as reorganized in 1878, is a thorough English and classical school, designed to prepare young men for college, for business, or for teaching in the common schools. The students have access to the college library and reading-room. When prepared they are admitted to the college upon the certificate of the principal, without examination. Special attention is given to English and commercial branches. Many improvements have been made in the building, rendering it a pleasant home for boys. Students of small means are allowed to board in clubs, which reduces their expenses considerably.

THE THEOLOGICAL DEPARTMENT.

The charter of the university permits the establishment of any professional school by the corporation. A school of theology, however, is the only department of this kind so far attempted. This was opened in 1855 under the charge of Thomas F. Curtis, D.D., and continued during thirteen years. On the resignation of Prof. Curtis, in 1865, the school was reorganized, with Lemuel Moss, D.D., as Professor of Theology, and Lucius E. Smith, D.D., as Professor of Sacred Rhetoric and Pastoral Theology, Geo. R. Bliss, D.D., being continued as Professor of Biblical Interpretation. In 1868 the department was removed to Upland, Pa., and reorganized by the family of the late John P. Crozer as "The Crozer Theological Seminary," under a new corporation, but still retaining a close connection with the university at Lewisburg, whose graduates supply its classes in a large measure. While at Lewisburg the department enrolled 38 graduates. These have been received and enrolled among the alumni of the Crozer Seminary.

Liberia.—The people of Liberia are of the African race, by the way of the United States. They are very enterprising, and there is reason to believe that the providence of God designs to accomplish great spiritual good for the country of their fathers through their instrumentality. There are 26 Baptist churches in the republic with a membership of about 2000. At the last meeting of "The Liberia Baptist Association," in December, 1879, a considerable amount of prosperity among the churches was reported. The Providence church in Monrovia had received 56 by baptism, the Arthington church 24, and the First church in Edina 39; 275 baptisms were reported for the year.

At the annual meeting of the Liberia Baptist Association the members agreed to form another Association and a national organization.

Liberty, American Religious.—Much has been said and written about the originator of our religious freedom. Some have zealously claimed Lord Baltimore as its author. This nobleman was a Roman Catholic, and on that account a large amount of very clear evidence is necessary to establish his right to this honor. He was a talented man, with many of the qualities of a statesman. He knew that the English people in 1633, when his first settlers left their country for the New World, would never tolerate a colony in the British dominions where the Protestant religion was excluded, and, as a matter of absolute necessity, he had to permit its existence in Maryland. He deserved no credit for showing common sense. His first settlers were Catholics, and to them his colony appealed for recruits; and nothing in the history of Maryland shows him to be an unselfish friend of religious liberty. He simply appears as a yielding statesman bending to the necessities of the times.

John Leeds Bozman's "History of Maryland" was published by the General Assembly of that State in 1837. It is derived largely from "the written memorials which then existed in the public archives of the State," to which the author had free access, and it bears the authority of the government of Maryland. In 1639, Bozman says, "A very short bill was introduced into the house (the Legislature), entitled 'An act for church liberties,' and was expressed nearly in the following words: '*Holy Church* within this province shall have all her rights, liberties, and immunities safe, whole, and inviolable in all things.' When we reflect on the original causes of their emigration (the colonists of Maryland), we cannot but suppose that it was the intention of those in whose hands the government of the province was, a majority of whom were without doubt Catholics, as well as much the greater number of the colonists, to erect a hierarchy, with an ecclesiastical jurisdiction similar to the ancient Church of England *before the Reformation*."* "Holy Church" is the Catholic Church, and this was but the entering wedge of a Romish persecuting religious establishment.

Another bill of the same session provided, that "eating flesh in time of Lent, or on other days, Wednesdays excepted, wherein it is prohibited by the law of England, without case of infirmity, to be allowed by the judge; and the offender shall forfeit to the lord proprietary five pounds of tobacco, or one shilling sterling, for every such offence."† This is liberty of conscience at the expense of a shilling, or five pounds of tobacco, for each indulgence in such freedom. In 1640, Bozman says, "The *first of the acts* passed at this session, entitled 'An act for church liberty,' is nearly *verbatim* the same as the first section of the second act of the preceding session;"‡ that is, that "Holy Church within this province shall have all her rights, liberties, and immunities safe, whole, and inviolable in all things;" and the Catholics of Maryland would probably have given force to their law, and erected a persecuting popish established church in their colony, if they had not heard the commencing thunder that roared with such fury a little later at Marston Moor and Naseby. Their church act was the second of the preceding Legislature, and the first of this, showing their great earnestness on the subject.

Cromwell wrought wonders in England; the Church was completely overthrown, Satan was as popular in Great Britain as a Catholic, and Lord Baltimore, certain to lose his province unless he suited his sails to the fierce hurricane then raging, at once appointed a Protestant governor (Stone) instead of Gov. Greene, a Catholic; he also appointed a Protestant secretary of the province and a Protestant majority in the council. Bozman, speaking of the change, says, "In this measure of his lordship we discern *the commencement* of that general toleration of all sects of religion which prevailed under the early provincial government of Maryland."§ No principle of toleration required Baltimore to place Protestants at the head of his government. He certainly did not love Protestantism at this very time, for he required Gov. Stone to take the following as a part of his official oath: "And I do further swear that I will not, by myself nor any person directly or indirectly, trouble, molest, or discountenance any person whatsoever in the said province professing to believe in Jesus Christ, *and in particular no Roman Catholic for or in respect of his or her religion, nor in his or her free exercise thereof within the said province.*"‖ A councillor had to take the same oath. It certainly was not love for the men or their religion that led Baltimore to make his new appointments. It was "an enlightened measure of state policy" to save his province from Cromwell.

With this change in the rulers of Maryland his

---

* History of Maryland, ii. 107–9.
† Idem, 137.
‡ Idem, 174.
§ Idem, 336.
‖ Idem, 648, note lxi.

lordship proposed, and his Legislature enacted, a law with the following clauses in it: "Whatsoever* person or persons within this province and the islands thereunto belonging shall from henceforth blaspheme God, that is, curse him, or shall *deny our Saviour Jesus Christ to be the Son of God, or shall deny the Holy Trinity, the Father, Son, and Holy Ghost,* or the Godhead of any of the said three persons of the Trinity, or the unity of the Godhead, or shall use or utter any reproachful speeches, words, or language concerning the Holy Trinity, or any of the said three persons thereof, shall be punished with death and confiscation or forfeiture of all his or her land and goods to the lord proprietary and his heirs." "Whatsoever person or persons shall from henceforth use or utter *any reproachful words or speeches concerning the blessed Virgin Mary,* the mother of our Saviour, or the holy apostles or evangelists, or any of them, shall in such case for the first offence forfeit to the said lord proprietary, and his heirs lords proprietaries of this province, the sum of £5 sterling, or the value thereof, to be levied on the goods and chattels of every such person so offending; but in case such offender or offenders shall not then have goods and chattels sufficient for the satisfying of such forfeiture, or that the same be not otherwise speedily satisfied, then such offender or offenders *shall be publicly whipped, and be imprisoned during the pleasure of the lord proprietary,* or the lieutenant or chief governor of this province." For the second offense the fine is £10, *or a public and severe whipping,* and imprisonment as for the first. For the third offense, *the forfeiture of all lands and goods, and expulsion from the province.* A subsequent part of the *same law* says, "*Except as in the act is before declared and set forth,* no person or persons whatsoever within this province, or the islands, ports, harbors, creeks, or havens thereunto belonging, professing to believe in Jesus Christ, shall from henceforth be anyways troubled, molested, or discountenanced for or in respect of his or her religion, nor in the free exercise thereof within this province, or the islands thereunto belonging, nor any way compelled to the belief or exercise of any other religion against his or her consent." The penalty for breaking this enactment is "treble damages to the party wronged," and a fine of 20*s.*; and in case of failure to pay the fine, a severe public whipping, and imprisonment at the pleasure of the proprietary or his governor. This is the celebrated toleration law of Lord Baltimore for which his liberality has been lauded extravagantly, and for which Catholics have been represented as the first founders of religious liberty on this continent. The act was passed in the end of April, 1649, and Charles I. was executed three months before. This event, and the motives that prompted it, and the men whom they governed, account wholly for Lord Baltimore's liberality. The toleration was partial and poor. Those who denied the Trinity—all Jews, Unitarians, and Arians—were condemned to death. The gallows was the liberty it gave them. Respect for the Virgin Mary was encouraged by fines and whippings, and, in obstinate cases, by the loss of all property, and by exile. There was, indeed, some liberty in this law, accompanied by cruel and wicked limitations; and for this liberty no thanks are due to Lord Baltimore or his Maryland Catholics.

Bozman, in another work† published in 1811, truly says, "In most of the States the penalties of the common law in matters of religion still subsist. The *bloody statutes* also of some of them only *sleep.* Not being repealed, they are liable to be called up into action at any moment when either superstition or fanaticism shall perceive a convenient time for it. *What Jew, Socinian, or Deist, possessing a sound mind, would venture, in the State of Maryland for instance, to open his lips in defence of his own religion?*" Even in 1811 the statute book of Maryland contained cruel, persecuting enactments; and only by asserting what is flagrantly untrue can the Baptist State be robbed of her just glory to bestow it upon the founder of Maryland, or upon his colony.

The "Colonial Records of Rhode Island" were published by order of the Legislature in 1856, and in them we learn that Roger Williams landed on the site of Providence in the month of May or early in June, 1636, and that he and his friends on their "first coming thither did make an order that *no man* should be molested for his conscience," even though he was an Israelite, a Unitarian, or an infidel. And a woman had her religious freedom protected by the same law. In August, 1636, the celebrated compact was entered into and signed at Providence, by which its people "subjected themselves in active and passive obedience to all such orders or agreements as shall be made for public good of the body in an orderly way, by the major consent of the present inhabitants, masters of families, incorporated together in a Town fellowship, and others whom they shall admit unto them, *in civil things only.*" No laws for favoring or prohibiting any form of religion were to be enacted. On the 21st of May, 1637, Joshua Verin was sentenced to lose the right of voting "for restraining the liberty of conscience" of his wife.‡ On the 27th of May, 1640, among certain proposals agreed upon at Providence to form a government, these words are found: "We agree, as formerly

---

* History of Maryland, 662, 663, note.

† A Sketch of the History of Maryland, during the Three First Years after its Settlement, p. 374. Baltimore, 1811.

‡ Colonial Records of Rhode Island, printed by order of the Legislature, i. 13, 14, 16. 1856.

have been the liberties of the town, so still, to hold forth liberty of conscience."*

The first charter of Rhode Island was signed March 14, 1643, and adopted in the colony in May, 1647. Arnold, in his "History of Rhode Island," truly says, "The use of the word *civil* is everywhere prefixed (in the charter) to the terms 'government' or 'laws' wherever they occur . . . to restrict the operation of the charter to purely political concerns. In this apparent restriction there lay concealed a boon of freedom such as man had never known before. They (Rhode Islanders) held themselves accountable to God alone for their religious creed, and no earthly power could bestow on them a right which they held from heaven. . . . At their own request their powers were limited to *civil matters*."† The first instrument of government in the world's history disavowing all right to make laws for or against religion, and thereby giving the widest religious liberty, was adopted in Rhode Island two years before Lord Baltimore's bigoted toleration act was passed in Maryland. After making a code of laws for the *civil affairs* of the colony occur these striking words: "These are the laws that concern all men, and these are the penalties for the transgression thereof, which by common consent are ratified throughout the whole colony; and otherwise than thus what is herein forbidden (*non-religious crimes only*), all men may walk as their consciences persuade them, every one in the name of his God. And let the saints of the Most High walk in this colony, without molestation, in the name of Jehovah their God, for ever and ever,"‡ etc.

Roger Williams gives a striking view of liberty of conscience in his letter to the town of Providence in 1654. "It hath fallen out," says he, "sometimes that both Papists and Protestants, Jews and Turks, may be embarked in one ship, upon which supposal I affirm that all the liberty of conscience that I ever pleaded for turns upon these two hinges: that none of the Papists, Protestants, Jews or Turks, be forced to come to the ship's prayers or worship, nor compelled from their own particular prayers, if they practise any."§ In the charter of 1663, inspired by their convictions and their Baptist agent in London, it is written, "*No person* within the said colony, at any time hereafter, shall be anywise molested, punished, disquieted, or called in question for any difference of opinion in matters of religion."‖ Even the Quakers, as may be seen in "Laws agreed upon in England by the Governor of Pennsylvania (William Penn) and Divers Freemen thereof," restrict their legal toleration to "all persons who confess and acknowledge the one almighty and eternal God to be the creator, upholder, and ruler of the world."** The Baptists of Rhode Island had no laws upon religion, the greatest infidel of the human race carried no *legal* stigma in that colony for his opinions from its first settlement by our Baptist fathers; it had the only government in the world where religion was entirely free. Maryland's mean toleration was *not* freedom of conscience, except for certain classes, and poor as it was, Rhode Island gave full liberty thirteen years sooner. In 1789, Washington, at the request of the Virginia Baptists, recommended to Congress that amendment to our national Constitution which says, "Congress shall make no law respecting an establishment of religion, or prohibiting the free exercise thereof." It was through their influence that grand article was added to our great instrument of government.†† The religious liberties of our country were first established in Rhode Island by our Baptist fathers, and only through Baptist channels have the nations of the earth learned soul freedom.

Liberty of Conscience among the English Baptists before the Publication of "The Bloudy Tenent" of Roger Williams.—In 1589, as Crosby states, Dr. Some, a man of great reputation in England, wrote a work against certain prominent Puritans, whom he compares in some things to the Anabaptists. In his book he represents the Anabaptists as holding, among their doctrines, that ministers of the gospel ought to be maintained by the voluntary contributions of the people, and that the civil power has no right to make and impose ecclesiastical laws. This is the great Baptist doctrine of soul liberty, the proclamation of which about fifty years later has given undying fame to the illustrious founder of Rhode Island. These men in demanding that religion should be completely delivered from state patronage and persecution were the successors of a line of Baptists who claimed the same privileges in every Christian age up to the Teacher of Galilee. Leonard Busher, a citizen of London and a Baptist, presented to James I. and to Parliament his "Religious Peace, or a Plea for Liberty of Conscience," and published it in pamphlet form in 1614. The work of Mr. Busher is both able and eloquent, and, considering his times, one of the most remarkable productions ever printed. He says,—

"Kings and magistrates are to rule temporal affairs by the swords of their temporal kingdoms, and bishops and ministers are to rule spiritual affairs by the Word and Spirit of God, the sword of Christ's spiritual kingdom, and not to intermeddle

---
* Colonial Records of Rhode Island, i. 28.
† History of Rhode Island, i. 200. ‡ Idem, 201.
§ Idem, 255. ‖ Idem, 292.

** Minutes of Provincial Council of Pennsylvania, p. 41. Published by the State. Philadelphia, 1852.
†† Cathcart's Baptists and the American Revolution, pp. 97–111. Philadelphia, 1876.

one with another's authority, office, and function." Again, "All those bishops that force princes and people to receive their faith and discipline by persecution do, with Judas, go against Christ in his members, with swords, staves, and halberds, who, seeing God's Word will not help them, betake themselves with all haste and hazard unto the authority of the king and magistrate." Again, "It is not only unmerciful, but unnatural and abominable, yea, monstrous, for one Christian to vex and destroy another for difference and questions of religion." Again, "Neither suffer the bishops with persecution to defend their faith and church against their adversaries. If they have not anything from God's Word against us, let them yield and submit themselves. If they think they have anything against us, let them betake themselves only to God's Word, both in word and writing." Again, "By persecution are the Jews, Turks, and Pagans occasioned and encouraged to persecute likewise all such as preach and teach Christ in their dominions; for if Christian kings and magistrates will not suffer Christians to preach, and preach the gospel of Christ freely and peaceably in their dominions, how could you expect it of the infidels? . . . And the king and Parliament may please to permit (liberty to) ALL SORTS OF CHRISTIANS; YEA, (to) JEWS, TURKS, AND PAGANS, so long as they are peaceable and no malefactors, as is above mentioned." This is the true liberty for which our denomination has always contended,—liberty of conscience for all mankind. Busher says, "Persecution for difference in religion is a monstrous and cruel beast, that destroyeth both prince and people, hindereth the gospel of Christ, and scattereth his disciples that witness and profess his name. But permission (liberty) of conscience in difference of religion saveth both prince and people; for it is a meek and gentle lamb, which not only furthereth and advanceth the gospel, but also fostereth and cherisheth those that profess it."* Leonard Busher delivered a noble testimony for liberty and truth.

His work was speedily followed by another treatise on the same subject, entitled "Persecution for Religion Judged and Condemned." It was published in 1615 "by Christ's unworthy witnesses, his majesty's faithful subjects, commonly, but falsely, called Anabaptists." No writer in the nineteenth century, in Europe or America, has a clearer conception of religious liberty than the author of this book. He says, "The power and authority of the king are earthly, and God hath commanded me to submit to all ordinances of man, and therefore I have faith to submit to what ordinance of man soever the king commands; if it be a human ordinance, and not against the manifest Word of God, let him require what he will, I must of conscience obey him with my body, goods, and all that I have. But my soul, wherewith I am to worship God, belongeth to another King, whose kingdom is not of this world, whose people must come willingly, whose weapons are not carnal but spiritual." Again, "The whole New Testament throughout, in all the doctrines and practices of Christ and his disciples, teaches no such thing as compelling men by persecutions to obey the gospel, but the direct contrary." Again, "I unfeignedly acknowledge that God hath given to magistrates a sword to cut off wicked men, and to reward welldoers. But this ministry is a worldly ministry, their sword is a worldly sword, their punishments can extend no further than the outward man; they can but kill the body. And therefore this ministry and sword are appointed only to punish the breach of worldly ordinances, which is all that God hath given to any mortal man to punish." Again, "Christ's kingdom is spiritual, his laws are spiritual, the transgressions are spiritual, the punishment is spiritual, everlasting death of soul, his sword is spiritual; no carnal or worldly weapon is given to the supportation of his kingdom. The Lawgiver himself hath commanded that the transgressors of these laws should be let alone until the harvest, because he knows that they that are now tares may hereafter come to repentance and become wheat." Again, "Magistracy is a power of this world; the kingdom, power, subjects, and means of publishing the gospel are not of this world." Again, "But if I defend the authority of Christ Jesus over men's souls, which appertaineth to no mortal man, then know you that whosoever would rob him of that honor, which is not of this world, he will tread them underfoot. Earthly authority belongeth to earthly kings, but spiritual authority belongeth to that one spiritual King, who is King of kings. . . . I have showed you *by the law of Christ that your course is most wicked, to compel any by persecution to perform any service to God*, as you pretend."†

The Anabaptists presented James I. a petition in 1620 pleading for liberty of conscience and deliverance from persecution. The soul freedom, so dear to Baptists in all ages, is conspicuous in this "Supplication." The writer of this document says, "The vileness of persecuting the body of any man, only for cause of conscience, is against the Word of God and law of Christ." Again, "Oh, be pleased to consider, why you should persecute us for humbly beseeching you, in the words of the King of kings, to give unto God the things which are God's, which is to be Lord and Lawgiver to the soul in that spiritual worship and service which he re-

---

* "Religious Peace," in Tracts on Liberty of Conscience, Hansard Knollys Society, pp. 23, 24, 25, 33, 41. London, 1846.

† Persecution for Religion Judged and Condemned. Idem, pp. 107, 108, 120, 121, 122, 133, 135.

quireth. If you will take away this from God, what is it that is God's? Far be it from you to desire to sit in the consciences of men, to be lawgiver and judge therein. This is antichrist's practice, persuading the kings of the earth to give him their power to compel all hereunto. You may make and mend your own laws, and be judge and punisher of the transgressors thereof, but you cannot make or mend God's laws, they are perfect already. You may not add nor diminish, nor be judge nor monarch of his church; that is Christ's right. He left neither you nor any mortal man his deputy, but only the Holy Ghost, as your highness acknowledgeth; and whosoever erreth from the truth, his judgment is set down and the time thereof."* The author of the "Humble Supplication," according to the famous Roger Williams,† was committed "a close prisoner to Newgate, London, for the witness of some truths of Jesus, and having not the use of pen and ink, wrote these arguments in milk, in sheets of paper brought to him by the woman, his keeper, from a friend in London as the stopples of his milk-bottle. In such paper written with milk nothing will appear; but the way of reading it by fire being known to this friend who received the papers, he transcribed and kept together the papers, although the author could not correct nor view what himself had written." From the "Humble Supplication" were taken the arguments, which, being replied to by Mr. Cotton, gave rise to the work of Mr. Williams, and which he has so significantly called "The Bloudy Tenent of Persecution Discussed." This theory, so nobly advocated by English Baptists, so ably defended by the illustrious founder of Rhode Island in his celebrated work, was carried out in practice by the Baptists in England. In 1655, John Biddle, a Socinian, was arrested on the charge of heresy in London; his danger was very great; with his opinions Baptists had no sympathy; but for his liberty of conscience they cherished a profound regard, and many Baptist congregations petitioned Cromwell for his release. They made common cause with the man whose life was endangered by an attack upon his rights of conscience. How the theory of Roger Williams has been carried out first in Rhode Island, and now in every State in the Union, all the world knows.

In 1644, when "The Bloudy Tenent" was published in London, the Baptists were the only advocates of full liberty of conscience on earth, that year Mr. John Goodwin, a Congregationalist, came to their help. The Congregationalists as a body, in England and America, were willing to grant liberty only to those "sound in fundamentals."

Daniel Neal, an Independent (Congregationalist), says, "The Independents pleaded for a toleration so far as to include themselves and the *sober* Anabaptists, but did not put the controversy on a general foot (ing). They were for tolerating all that agreed in the fundamentals of Christianity; but when they came to enumerate fundamentals they were sadly entangled, as all those must be who do not keep the religious and civil rights of mankind on a separate basis." Neal writes of his brethren in 1645, and from the last sentence we quote, he would have given them a better character as friends of true liberty if the facts would have permitted him. The Parliament of Scotland appealed to the legislature of England, and declared their conviction "that the piety and wisdom of the honorable houses (of Parliament) will never admit toleration of any sects or schisms contrary to our Solemn League and Covenant." This covenant was taken in England in the end of 1643 and in the beginning of 1644. Neal says that "at the same time they appealed to the people, and published a declaration against toleration of sectaries and liberty of conscience, in which, after having taken notice of their great services, they observe that there is a party in England who are endeavoring to supplant the true religion by pleading for liberty of conscience, which, say they, is the nourisher of all heresies and schisms. They then declare against all such notions as are inconsistent with the truth of religion, and opening a door to licentiousness, which, to the utmost of their power, they will endeavor to oppose; and as they have *all entered into one covenant*, so to the last man in the kingdom they will go on in the preservation of it. And however the Parliament of England may determine in point of toleration and liberty of conscience, they are resolved *not to make the least start*, but to live and die for the glory of God in the entire preservation of the truth;"‡ that is, in suppressing liberty of conscience. This was the spirit of Presbyterian Scotland in 1645.

Richard Baxter, the most influential Presbyterian minister in England, as quoted by Crosby, writes, "My judgment in that much debated point of liberty of religion I have always freely made known; I abhor unlimited liberty, or toleration of all." The Westminster Assembly of Divines, which framed the creed of all British Presbyterians, Dec. 15, 1645, in response to an application of the Congregationalists for a very moderate toleration for themselves, declared that "this opened a perpetual gap for all sects to challenge such a liberty as their due; that this liberty was denied by the churches of New England, and that they have as just ground to deny it as they; that this

---

* An Humble Supplication to the King's Majesty. Idem, pp. 192, 230.

† Bloudy Tenent, page 36, Pref. 30, 35. London, 1848.

‡ Neal's History of the Puritans, iii. 244, 240. Dublin, 1755. See also Collier's Ecclesiastical History, viii. 300, 301. London, 1841.

desired forbearance is a perpetual division in the church, and a perpetual drawing away from the churches under the rule; for upon the same pretense those who scruple infant baptism may withdraw from their churches, and so separate into another congregation. Are these divisions, say they, as lawful as they are infinite? or must we give that respect to the errors of men's consciences as to satisfy their scruples by allowance of this liberty to them? That *scruple of conscience is no cause of separation;* nor doth it take off causeless separation from being schism, which may arise from errors of conscience as well as carnal and corrupt reason." The Assembly flatly denied the toleration solicited by the Congregationalists; and for the moment the English government was ready to enforce their decision. These godly men in the Assembly and the leading ministers and laymen of their denomination in London, and in the country at that time, were fierce enemies of liberty of conscience. To-day our Presbyterian brethren are friends of true liberty, secular and sacred. But down to 1644 the Baptists were the only advocates of liberty of conscience for all Christians, and *all other men on earth.* They have the honor of being the first preachers of this doctrine, and of converting the masses of other denominations to this part of their creed; and they have the glory of founding Rhode Island, the first State on earth where this doctrine received legal recognition; and through Rhode Island the Baptists have given this doctrine a place in the Constitution of the United States, and in the legal enactments of every State in the American Union.

License, A Form of.—As a Baptist church is the highest ecclesiastical authority in the denomination, or in the Sacred Book, upon whose teachings our churches are built, the church, after hearing a brother exercise his gifts as a preacher, gives him a license, not to administer baptism and the Lord's Supper, but to proclaim the blessed gospel. This license gives him no ministerial standing, and no position beyond that of a layman, except that it expresses the opinion of the church of which he is a member that he has qualifications for preaching the gospel. The following form of license has been used:

"*To all whom it may concern.* The Baptist church of Blanktown sends greeting: Our beloved brother, Joshua Smith, a man of good repute, undoubted piety, and sound knowledge of divine things, after exercising his ministerial gifts in private and in public to our entire satisfaction, is hereby licensed to preach the gospel, wherever the Lord may open a door for him. We recommend him to the favor of our brethren; and we pray that the Lord may greatly bless him.

"Done at our regular meeting for business, etc."

Ligon, William Claiborne, was born in Prince Edward Co., Va., Dec. 18, 1796. He studied at Golgotha Academy; was converted at eighteen years, and ordained in 1825 by Elders P. P. Smith and Clapton. He came to Missouri in 1841, and settled near Carrollton. For thirty years he labored in that part of the State; was pastor at Lexington, Dover, Liberty, Richmond, and Carrollton. He gave much time and effort to the establishment of William Jewell College. He was successful as an evangelist, in Clay, Ray, Lafayette, and Saline Counties. He died in Dover, April 13, 1877.

Lilburn, Maj.-Gen. Robert, was a soldier of great daring. When the Earl of Derby placed himself at the head of 1500 horse and foot in Lancashire, Lilburn met him near Wigan, and with 800 men routed his forces, though they fought bravely for about an hour. Lilburn killed many of the enemy, captured between 300 and 400 prisoners, and lost only 11 men.

In Scotland his military administration was marked by a spirit of devout piety, and of great kindness. The Baptist church of Hexham, Northumberland, England, has several allusions to the general in old letters belonging to its records; and one of its letters written to the general is still preserved. In this epistle the church writes:

"Honored Sir,—It hath been matter of great joy and consolation to our spirits, ever since we heard of the glorious appearances of the divine nature in you, which manifests itself through your love, which you have towards all saints, and particularly towards us. We desire to admire the good hand of our God in it, that we, who are less than the least of saints, should have favor given us in your eyes, whom God has so highly honored to set in a place of so great eminency."[*] They then proceed to thank him for his great kindness to three of their brethren,—Edward Hickhorngill, Charles Bond, and Thomas Stackhouse,—and for his great love to their entire church. Ten of the brethren sign the letter on behalf of the church. It is dated the 22d day of the Fourth month, 1653. Gen. Lilburn had Baptist chaplains, and maintained loving relations with the churches of that denomination wherever he was stationed. In 1647 he was governor of Newcastle; next year he was one of the judges that tried Charles I. and condemned him to death; and the name of Robert Lilburn is appended to the warrant for his execution.

Cromwell for a time imprisoned him because of his inflexible republicanism, as he served Harrison and others. But this only showed the immense influence wielded by Gen. Lilburn; for it was not to punish him that Cromwell subjected him to arrest, but to protect himself from the attacks of a powerful military leader, who was opposed to all govern-

[*] Fenstanton Records, etc., 328. London, 1854.

ments administered* by "one man." Cromwell knew his great worth, and it was he who made him a major-general.

Lilburn† was very active in securing the recall of the remnant of the Long Parliament, when the system of government instituted by Oliver perished in the hands of Richard Cromwell. Largely through his great influence in the army was this course pursued. He felt that no military chieftain should exercise dominion in his country, nor any committee of generals; and that government was the creation of the people themselves; and as the Long Parliament was the only fragment of legal government in England capable of being invested with life, he lent effectual aid in giving it the sceptre of power once more.

When Charles II. was placed upon the throne Lilburn was tried as a regicide; he offered no defense, and of course was condemned; he was exiled to the Isle of St. Nicholas, off Plymouth, where he died in 1665. Why he was not executed we cannot conceive; it was not because of any mercy possessed by Charles II., nor on account of any bribe given to the frail but all-powerful companions of the king's dearest pleasures. Probably, legal murder, accompanied by the horrible custom in treason cases of "drawing and quartering," had begun to arouse the indignation of the nation against the Stuarts; and Lilburn's life was spared because its sacrifice might cost too much. We love the memory of Maj.-Gen. Robert Lilburn, the "fanatic Anabaptist," as Guizot, in his Memoirs of Monk, is pleased to call him.

Lillard, Rev. Jas. M., was born in Mercer Co., Ky., Sept. 27, 1806, and has been a Baptist minister for forty-seven years. He removed from Kentucky to Lewis Co., Mo., in 1832, being the first Baptist preacher north of Palmyra, Mo. He traveled far and near, traversing large prairies in the severest weather, preaching the gospel and receiving little or no compensation. He was truly a missionary. He often went down the Mississippi River, and occasionally returned to Kentucky, where he held, and assisted his father in conducting, a number of great revival meetings, in which hundreds professed faith in Christ. He has exerted a wonderful influence for good throughout all Northeast Missouri, and though now old and much afflicted, often preaching while sitting, he travels almost continually, laboring for Christ. He has organized a great many Baptist churches; assisted in ordaining at least twenty-five Baptist ministers, and has baptized more than 3000 persons.

Lillard, Rev. Robert Rodes, A.M., a man of remarkable gifts and attainments, was born in Anderson Co., Ky., Jan. 10, 1826. After a preparatory course he entered Georgetown College as a Sophomore in 1842, and graduated in 1845. Having professed religion and united with the Baptist church at Lawrenceburg, in his native county, in 1841, he was licensed to preach the following year, and was ordained to the ministry in 1846. He now placed himself under the instruction of the distinguished Dr. J. L. Waller, and the following year became associated with his preceptor in the editorship of the *Western Baptist Review*, at that time the ablest periodical in the West. His career was a most brilliant one, and within a few months he was placed among the ablest periodical writers of his time, but shortly after, death closed his too brief career, on June 7, 1849.

Lincoln, Ensign, was born in Hingham, Mass., Jan. 8, 1779. He enjoyed good educational opportunities in his youthful days, and the inestimable blessing of an early religious training. When he reached the age of fourteen he was placed as an apprentice at the business of printing. Having become a Christian he was baptized by Rev. Dr. Baldwin in 1799, of whose church he was a member until he transferred his relation to the Third Baptist church, for so many years under the pastoral charge of Rev. Dr. Sharp. As he had evidently gifts which fitted him to preach the gospel, he was induced to exercise them. The churches at Lynn, East Cambridge, Cambridgeport, Roxbury, South Boston, and Federal Street, Boston, owe to him a great debt of gratitude for what he did among them in the days of their early weakness. While engaged in promoting the Redeemer's kingdom by the use of the talents which God had given him as a preacher of righteousness, he was also in another way accomplishing a vast amount of good. As the leading partner in the publishing house of Lincoln & Edmunds, he was instrumental in sending out from the press a healthful religious literature, which proved a blessing of great value to multitudes of people. He spent a life of purity and blamelessness among his fellow-men, until God took him home to receive the reward of a faithful servant. His death occurred Dec. 2, 1832. Dr. Wayland says of him, "Since his death was mentioned to me, I have been striving to think of one who was of more value to the church as a layman. I could not think of one. I have thought of clergymen, and the result was the same. You may look over a dozen cities before you find a man in a private station who has cleared away around himself so large and so fertile a field of usefulness. I know of no man to fill up his place."

Lincoln, Hon. Heman, was born in Hingham, Mass., Jan. 7, 1779. He was one of a family of eleven children, whose parents were honored and loved in the community in which they lived for their consistent piety. When Heman was fourteen

---

* Hume, Smollett, and Farr, i. 730. London.
† Rapin's History of England, ii. 605. London, 1733.

years of age he was apprenticed to a carpenter in Boston. He was baptized by Dr. Baldwin, May 19, 1799, and in 1809 he was chosen a deacon of the church.

A man of his sterling worth could not remain long in private life. His fellow-citizens, recognizing his abilities, were not backward in soliciting him to occupy public positions. At different times, as representative and senator, he served in the Legislature of Massachusetts. He was chosen a member of the convention for the revision of the State constitution, and, as an intelligent Baptist, he made an earnest plea in behalf of religious liberty and the rights of conscience. Ten years, however, passed before the cause which he so earnestly advocated triumphed over the prejudices with which it had been called to contend.

Deacon Lincoln was among the earliest and most steadfast friends of home and foreign missions. For several years he was the president of the American Baptist Home Mission Society, and when the conversion of Mr. and Mrs. Judson to Baptist sentiments called forth an appeal to the churches in this country for help in the establishment of the missions in Burmah, he was among the first to respond. In 1824 he was chosen treasurer of the Baptist General Convention, and he held the office twenty-two years. So deep was his interest in the cause that he gave up his regular business, and spent his time at the mission rooms in Boston, and proved himself a most valuable assistant to Rev. Dr. Bolles, at the time the corresponding secretary of the Convention.

But it was not merely the two great denominational organizations for the prosecution of home and foreign missions that awakened the regards of Deacon Lincoln. He was ready to unite with all good men for the advancement of any cause which aimed at the improvement of mankind and the glory of God. He was a steadfast friend of the American Bible Society, the American Tract Society at New York, the American Temperance Society, and kindred organizations. For twenty-seven years he was a trustee of Brown University. He was one of the founders of the Newton Theological Institution, and for several years one of its trustees. For twenty-two years he was chairman of the executive committee of the American Baptist Missionary Union. The missionaries under appointment found in his hospitable dwelling a happy home while waiting the time of their departure to the distant fields of their labor, and when, worn down with protracted toil, they returned to recruit their wasted strength in their native country, Deacon Lincoln was among the first to give them a hearty welcome under his own roof. A life of more than ninety years was consecrated to the service of his Master, and when he died, Aug. 11, 1869, it was felt that a good man had gone home to heaven. Most truthfully was it said of him, "The cause of Christ was dearer to him than personal reputation or any earthly good. His record was remarkably unsullied, and all the churches with which he was connected may count that record as among their choicest ornaments."

Lincoln, Heman, D.D., was born in Boston, Mass., April 14, 1821. He graduated at Brown

HEMAN LINCOLN, D.D.

University in the class of 1840. Among his classmates were Prof. J. B. Boise, LL.D., Rev. Dr. W. T. Brantly, President E. Dodge, LL.D., Rev. Dr. J. R. Kendrick, and President H. G. Weston, D.D. He graduated at the Newton Institution in the class of 1845, and was ordained immediately after his graduation, in Boston, September, 1845. He was pastor of the church in New Britain, Pa., for five years, when he removed to Philadelphia to take charge of the Franklin Square church. After three years of service he was called to Jamaica Plain, Mass., where he continued six years. He accepted a call to the Central Baptist church in Providence, of which he was pastor for eight years, the connection being terminated by his appointment to the professorship of Ecclesiastical History in the Newton Theological Institution, the duties of which he performed for five years, when he was transferred to the chair of Homiletics and Pastoral Duties, which position he now holds. Dr. Lincoln has had much experience in writing for the press during all his professional life. For five years he was editorially connected with the *Christian Chronicle*, and for thirteen years with the *Watchman and Reflector*. Rochester University conferred upon Dr. Lincoln the degree of Doctor of Divinity in 1865.

Lincoln, Prof. John, LL.D., son of Ensign Lincoln, was born in Boston, Mass., Feb. 23, 1817, and was graduated at Brown University in the class of 1836. Immediately after which he was chosen a tutor in Columbian College, Washington, D. C., where he remained during the academic year 1836-37. In the fall of 1837 he entered the Newton Theological Seminary, where he remained until the fall of 1839, when, having been elected a tutor in Brown University, he removed to Providence. He held this office two years, at the end of which he went abroad, in company with Prof. H. B. Hackett, in order to pursue his studies at the German universities. He spent the academic year 1841-42 in Halle, studying theology with Tholuck and Julius Müller, and philology with Gesenius, in Hebrew, and with Barnhardy in the classics. The vacation of July and August was spent in an excursion through Switzerland and Northern Italy, with Tholuck as a companion. The second academic year, 1842-43, was spent in Berlin, under Neander, in church history, Old Testament history with Hengstenberg, and the classics with Boectch. The fall of 1843 he spent in Geneva, where he devoted himself to the study of French, and then went to Rome, where he remained until May, 1844. In the fall of 1844 he entered upon his duties as Assistant Professor of the Latin Language and Literature in Brown University, and was appointed full professor in 1845. In 1857 he went abroad a second time, and was absent six months, a part of which was passed in Athens. Again in the summer of 1878 he took a third trip to the Old World. Prof. Lincoln has prepared editions of Livy and Horace, which have been well received. He has also contributed able articles for reviews, magazines, and the religious papers.

Lincoln, Mrs. Nancy Hanks, the mother of Abraham Lincoln, was born in Virginia, and when quite young removed to Kentucky with some members of her family. In 1806 she married Thomas Lincoln, of Hodgenville, Hardin Co., Ky.

In 1843 La Rue County was created, which included the home of Thomas and Nancy Lincoln. This county was named after John La Rue, and Hodgenville after Thomas Hodgen. A biographer of Abraham Lincoln says, "Both these pioneers were men of sterling integrity and high moral worth; they were consistent and zealous members of the Baptist church, and one of their associates, Benjamin Lynn, was a minister of the same persuasion. Such were the influences under which, more than twenty years before Thomas Lincoln settled there, this little colony had been founded, and which went far to give the community its permanent character." In this Baptist settlement Abraham Lincoln, afterwards President of the United States, was born, Feb. 12, 1809.

Nancy Hanks Lincoln was a woman of rare qualities of mind and heart, and though she died in 1818, when her son was only nine years old, she left impressions upon him which could never be effaced, and which directed his whole future movements. "All that I am on earth," said President Lincoln to Rev. Dr. A. D. Gillette, then of Washington City, "I owe to my Baptist mother. I am glad to see you, doctor; you remind me of my Baptist mother."

Mrs. Lincoln lived and died unknown beyond a very limited circle, but her light has been carried over this land and over all the world by the fame of Abraham Lincoln, her distinguished son.

Lindsay, Edmond J., a well-known Christian business man of Milwaukee, was born in Dundee, Scotland, in 1838. His father, in 1841, emigrated with his family to New York, and in 1843 came to Dodge Co., Wis., where he engaged in farming. He was a prominent member and officer in a Scotch Baptist church in Dundee, a man of decided Christian influence. When he came to Wisconsin and found himself in a newly-settled country, where the institutions of religion were not yet established, he had a church in his home, teaching his children the way of God, expounding the Scriptures, and holding regular worship until churches were established.

It was in this Christian atmosphere young Lindsay's childhood and youth were passed. He obtained his education in the log school-house of the newly-settled neighborhood, and an occasional term of study in the classical schools at Waupun and Fox Lake. But Mr. Lindsay has been a student all his life, having a fine library and other facilities for the acquisition of knowledge.

When eleven years of age his father died, and the care of the farm devolved upon him.

Mr. Lindsay is the senior member of the firm of E. J. and W. Lindsay. The business was established by Mr. Lindsay in 1869, and is now one of the most extensive establishments of its class west of the Lakes, having relations with every State and Territory in the Northwest. As its manager Mr. Lindsay displays qualifications of a high order.

But it is chiefly as a Christian that he has become widely known. He made a profession of religion when fourteen years of age, and united a few years later with the Baptist church at Fox Lake. He is one of the best-known members of the First Baptist church in Milwaukee, a member of its board of trustees, has been its Sabbath-school superintendent, and in all the work of the church a chief actor. In the city, outside of his church, he is a leader in all benevolent enterprises. In the denominational work of the State he takes a prominent part. He is a member of the board of the Wisconsin Baptist State Convention, and of its Executive Committee, and he is its efficient treasurer.

Lindsay, Rev. W. C., was born in Virginia in 1840. He spent four years at a literary and two at a medical college, and afterwards three in the study and practice of law. At the close of the war he resumed the study of medicine, but having "tasted and seen that the Lord is good," "immediately he conferred not with flesh and blood," but came to the Southern Baptist Theological Seminary, and spent four years and graduated.

His first pastorate was at Wilson, N. C., where he had the society and warm friendship of the celebrated Dr. Hooper. In five months his health failed, pneumonia contracted in camp having left his lungs in a diseased condition. Having rested a few months, he took charge of the church at Barnwell Court-House, when, as an evidence of their appreciation, they almost doubled the compensation they were accustomed to give. The young men who avoided the church not only went, but contributed liberally to his salary. Five years in the pine belt, as frequently happens, restored his health. He next spent a year, 1876, as agent for the Southern Baptist Theological Seminary and Furman University, and then settled in Columbia, S. C., where he is now pastor.

He probably has not an enemy in the world.

Lindsey, Rev. E. H., a prominent minister of Dallas County, Ark., was born in Alabama in 1831. He embraced Christ and united with the Methodist Church in 1848, and was a preacher in that denomination for seven years. A careful examination of the subject of baptism led to a change of views, and he united with the Baptists in 1859, and in the following year was ordained to the ministry. He came to Arkansas and settled in Dallas County, where he has remained ever since, having served the following churches in Dallas and the adjoining counties: Cold Water, ten years; Hampton, nine years; Millville, seven years; Holly Springs, three years; Edinburg, two years; Chambersville nearly twenty years. During the time he has baptized about 400.

Lineberry, Rev. William, a useful minister in the Sandy Creek Association, N. C. He had been a minister of the Protestant Methodist Church, but became a Baptist, and was baptized by Rev. Enoch Crutchfield in 1843. He was agent for the State Convention in 1845 and 1846. He died in 1875.

Link, Rev. J. B., was born in Rockbridge Co., Va., May 7, 1828; converted in October, 1840; baptized at the Natural Bridge, Va., in October, 1841; ordained at Mount Pleasant, Jessamine Co., Ky., in 1852, Drs. D. R. Campbell and Wm. M. Pratt acting as the Presbytery; prosecuted the four years' course of study at Georgetown College, Ky., graduating in 1853; studied theology at, and graduated from, Rochester Theological Seminary, after a two years' course, in 1855; pastor of the churches at Paris, Ky., and Liberty, Mo.; acted as agent for William Jewell College for nearly two years, and raised $20,000 for that institution; entered the Confederate army, spent most of the time as a chaplain; went to Texas as agent of the Home Mission Board of the Southern Baptist Convention, especially for army missions. At the close of the year was occupied in efforts to establish the *Texas Baptist Herald*. Since 1866 has published and edited that journal with indefatigable energy, placing it upon a solid foundation. He is a man of indomitable will and courage, clear-headed,

REV. J. B. LINK.

patient, wise, and logical. He has been a vice-president of the Southern Baptist Convention, and is now laboring for the "Texas Educational Commission," in connection with his editorial management of the *Texas Baptist Herald*.

Linnard, James M., was born in September, 1784; was baptized about the year 1830, by Rev. Gideon B. Perry, into the fellowship of the Spruce Street church, Philadelphia, Pa. He continued in membership with this church until his death, which occurred Oct. 16, 1863. Few men have left behind them the record of a Christian life more abundant in the blessed results of intense consecration and large-hearted benevolence. Nor do these results pertain to his own life alone; for it appears to be well and widely known that his example and influence were agencies divinely employed to inspire similar consecration and benevolence among others possessed of greater wealth, whose princely benefactions still continue to aid the advancement of the Redeemer's kingdom. He was for many years, and up to the time of his death, the president of the Pennsylvania Baptist General Association. The growth and usefulness of this organization were largely due to his love for Christ and zeal for his cause. He had a clear, sound mind, and was a warm friend and wise counselor in every department of benevolent and religious effort. He was one of three laymen who have been moderators of the Philadelphia Baptist Association.

Linsley, Rev. James Harvey, son of James and Sarah (Maltby) Linsley, was born in North Branford, Conn., May 5, 1787; in 1809 went South; converted in 1810; taught school in Cheshire, Conn.; baptized in 1811 in North Haven; studied in Wallingford Academy; graduated from Yale College in 1817; taught in an academy at New Haven, also at New Canaan, also in a select school at Stratford; began to preach in 1828; ordained, in 1831, as an evangelist, at Meriden; preached in Milford and Stratfield; in 1835 was delegate to Triennial Convention in Richmond, Va.; health failed in 1836; went to Florida; was a member of Yale Natural Historical Society, of Connecticut Academy of Arts and Sciences, of Hartford Natural Historical Society, of Boston Society of Natural History; published valuable scientific papers. He died Dec. 29, 1843, leaving a precious record as a scholar and as a Christian.

Lisk, Rev. James, was born near Coshocton, O., Oct. 16, 1839; was baptized April 27, 1855, by Rev. A. W. Odor; graduated from Denison University in 1862, and from Rochester Theological Seminary in 1865; was ordained in June, 1865, and settled with the Second church, Cincinnati, O.; removed to Rockford, Ill., in 1867, and remained for two years; accepted a call to his present field of labor, the Second church, Germantown, Philadelphia, and entered upon his duties June 1, 1870. He is an able and impressive preacher and a faithful pastor, diligent in personal efforts for the salvation of souls, and strong in defense of "the faith once delivered to the saints." He is actively identified with the educational and missionary work of the denomination, and is conscientious in the performance of duties assigned to him in the management of important trusts. In 1879 he was made moderator of the Philadelphia Baptist Association. His people, after worshiping for years in a neat chapel, are now building a handsome church edifice.

Literature, Baptist.—The list of authors in this article contains the names of only a portion of the great body of Baptist writers; and often but one book is mentioned where several came from the same hand; or three, as in the case of Benjamin Keach, where forty-three were the fruits of his active mind.

THE SACRED TEXT AND WORKS UPON IT.

Our Lord was immersed in the river Jordan when he reached adult years, and founded the Baptist denomination. The writers of the New Testament, like the Saviour, were Baptists, whose "one (material) baptism" is believer's immersion. In translating the New Testament into the language of a heathen people, Baptists have always insisted upon *translating* Βαπτίζω, instead of transferring it. The first versions of the Scriptures followed this plan. The Peshito, a Syriac version, made early in the second century for the Jews in Palestine, renders the act of baptizing by the verb ܥܡܕ, to immerse.

About the same time a Latin translation was prepared for the people who used that tongue. Probably from this first version Tertullian quotes the Saviour's commission, "Go, teach the nations, immersing them in the name of the Father, and of the Son, and of the Holy Spirit."—Matt. xxviii. 19. (Ite, docete nationes, tinguentes eas in nomen Patris, etc. De Baptismo, cap. 13.) In the next chapter Tertullian quotes Paul's statement, that he was "not sent to baptize, but to preach," and he uses the words *ad tinguendum*, to immerse, to describe the baptismal act. The men who made these earliest translations, like the inspired writers of the New Testament, were Baptists. Jerome, in his Vulgate, uses *baptizo*, instead of *tinguo* or *immergo*, not because immersion was abandoned, but on account of a mass of ceremonies that in his day burdened the baptismal rite, authority for which could readily be claimed under a foreign word, the meaning of which was only known to scholars. What was true of the Syriac and Latin versions is true of other primitive translations of the New Testament; and from these and other considerations we claim the versions of the first three centuries as substantially Baptist productions. Like modern Baptists, the early Christians multiplied versions of the Scriptures, and distributed the Word as widely as possible. Augustine says, "Those who have translated the Bible into Greek can be numbered, but not so the Latin versions, for in the first ages of the church whoever got hold of a Greek codex ventured to translate it into Latin, however slight his knowledge of either language."

In 1229, at a Catholic council held in Thoulouse, in France, a canon was passed prohibiting "laics from having the books of the Old or New Testament, unless it be a Psalter, or a Breviary, and the Rosary, and it does not permit them so much as to *translate them into the vulgar tongue.*" Du Pin after recording the above adds, "This restraint was doubtless founded on that frequent abuse which was made of them in that country." (Eccles. Hist., ii. 456. Dublin, 1724.) This canon was enacted to rob our Baptist Albigensian fathers of the Scriptures, parts of which they had for a time in French, and subsequently the whole of them. Their version was a Baptist work. In 1526, Denk and Haetzer, two Anabaptists, commenced the translation of the Hebrew Bible in Strasburg, and succeeded well with the prophets, which were published early in the following year, nearly five years before Luther's Bible. The Rev. Henry Jessey had a translation of the Scriptures prepared in 1660, when the persecutions that followed the accession of Charles II. to the throne of England rendered its publication impossible, and resulted in its destruction.

Dr. William Carey translated the Scriptures into Sanscrit, Hindu, Brijbbhassa, Mahratta, Bengali, Oriya, Telinga, Karnata, Maldivian, Gurajattee Bulooshe, Pushtoo, Punjabi, Kashmeer, Assam, Burman, Pali, or Magudha, Tamul, Cingalese, Armenian, Malay, Hindostani, and Persian. Before the death of Dr. Carey the mission press at Serampore had sent forth the Scriptures in forty different languages and dialects, the tongues of 330,000,000 of human beings.

Dr. Judson translated the Scriptures into Burmese, Dr. Marshman into Chinese, Dr. Mason into Sgau Karen, Dr. Nathan Brown into Japanese. Dr. H. F. Buckner translated the gospel of John into the language of the Creek Indians. The New Testament, " with several hundred emendations," was edited by Spencer H. Cone and William H. Wyckoff. The American Bible Union, controlled by Baptists, though not exclusively composed of them, revised the entire English New Testament, and a large part of the Old; and they also revised the Spanish and Italian New Testaments, and made a new translation into the Ningpo colloquial dialect of China. It may be added that the Bible Union did much to create the public opinion that has resulted in the movement in England to make a revision of the Bible of 1611. The Rev. Joseph S. C. F. Frey edited an edition of Van Der Hooght's Hebrew Bible.

Dr. John Gill was the author of a commentary on the Old and New Testaments, in nine quarto volumes. This great work was republished in Philadelphia by a Presbyterian in 1819, and in Ireland many years later by an Episcopal clergyman. It is the richest treasury of Biblical and Oriental learning and of gospel truth which exists in the form of a commentary. Dr. John Fawcett was the author of a commentary in two folio volumes. The Baptist Publication Society is preparing a commentary under such auspices as will secure the fruits of the ripest scholarship and of the most recent discoveries in Bible lands. Robert Haldane was the author of " Notes on the Epistle of the Romans," and a work upon " The Verbal Inspiration of the Scriptures." Dr. C. M. Du Veil, a converted Israelite, led to embrace Baptist sentiments when an Episcopal clergyman, by reading our books in the library of the bishop of London, to which he had access, in 1685, published " A Literal Explanation of the Acts of the Apostles." James A. Haldane wrote an " Exposition of the Epistle to the Galatians." Prof. H. J. Ripley prepared " Notes on the Gospels and Acts," and on the " Epistle to the Hebrews." Prof. Hackett wrote a commentary on the " Acts of the Apostles ;" Spurgeon has a commentary upon the Psalms, called " The Treasury of David," in six volumes. Dr. Adiel Sherwood was the author of " Notes on the New Testament." Dr. George W. Clark has prepared " Notes on the Gospels."

Rev. William Jones was the author of " A Dictionary of the Sacred Writings." Dr. Hacket edited an American issue of Smith's " Dictionary of the Bible," to the English edition of which he contributed thirty articles. John Canne spent " more than thrice seven years" in preparing marginal references for the English Bible. A marginal Bible, printed in 1747, now before the writer, after the dedication to King James, presents Mr. Canne's " Letter to the Reader." Dr. Malcom's " Dictionary of Names, Objects, and Terms Found in the Holy Scriptures" has had a circulation of nearly 200,000.

Dr. Samuel G. Green's " Handbook to the Grammar of the New Testament, Together with a Complete Vocabulary (Lexicon) and an Examination of the Chief New Testament Synonyms," is a work of great learning and value.

RELIGIOUS WORKS.

In this list we might include a large number of the books written by primitive Christians, whose authors, like Justin Martyr, speak only of the " washing in water," of " persuaded believers" (Just. Philos. Mart. Apol. I. Pro Christ. Patrol. Græca VI. p. 240, Migne), or of trained catechumeni. Tertullian in his orthodox days wrote on the mode and subjects of baptism like a very zealous Baptist, and a part of his works might be legitimately reckoned to the credit of Baptists. The Confession of St. Patrick, and his Letter to Caroticus, are Baptist productions ; he immersed throngs of believers in wells in various parts of Ireland. The Swiss Anabaptist Confession of 1527, as far as it goes, is almost entirely in harmony with modern Baptist opinions. The religious literature of this period, of the sober Anabaptists of the Continent of Europe, may be largely claimed by our denomination to-day. The writings of Leonard Busher and others " On Liberty of Conscience," from 1614 to 1661, published by the Hanserd Knollys Society, are vigorous Baptist productions. The Confessions, issued by the same society, beginning with 1611 and ending with 1689, belong to us.

"Tropologia, or a Key to Open Scripture Metaphors," and "Gospel Mysteries Unveiled, or an Exposition of all the Parables," are the two most popular works of the celebrated Benjamin Keach. The "Exposition of all the Parables" is more frequently offered for sale now in London catalogues of second-hand books, than any of the works of John Howe, Dr. John Owen, or Bishop Jeremy Taylor. John Bunyan's works, in 761 royal octavo double-column pages, of which the "Pilgrim's Progress" occupies but 120, are not as well known as they should be, except "Grace Abounding," "The Holy War," and "The Pilgrim's Progress." Of the last, we may truly say that it is the most popular book ever written. Until 1847 it had been translated into French, Flemish, Dutch, Welsh, Gaelic, Irish, Hebrew, Spanish, Portuguese, Italian, Danish, German, Armenian, Burmese, Cingalese, Orissa, Hindostani, Bengali, Tamul, Mahratta, Canarese, Gujaratti, Malay, Arabic, Samoan, Tahitian, Pehuana, Behuana, Malagasy, New Zealand, and Latin; and undoubtedly it has been translated into several languages since that time. The prose writings of John Milton were numerous and popular. Some of these were political, like his first and second "Defence of the People of England;" but a number of them treated of ecclesiastical questions, like his "Reformation in England," his "Prelatical Episcopacy," his "National Establishments of Religion," his "True Religion, Heresy, Schism, and Toleration;" others were devoted to "Education," "The History of Britain," and to miscellaneous subjects. His Treatise "On Christian Doctrine," edited by Charles R. Sumner, librarian and historiographer to his majesty, and prebendiary of Canterbury, and published in 1825, is a very remarkable work. In it there are some opinions from which we decidedly dissent, but upon many questions, and conspicuously about the mode and subjects of baptism, Milton was a strong Baptist. "Anti-Christ Unmasked," by Henry Denne; "The Necessity for Separation from the Church of England," by John Canne; Delaune's "Plea for Nonconformists," according to Daniel De Foe, "perfect in itself; never author left behind him a more finished piece;" in 1739 it had passed through seventeen editions; "Ill News from New England, &c.," by John Clarke, a celebrated work in defense of liberty of conscience.

"Gill's Body of Divinity" and his other theological works are invaluable. The works of Andrew Fuller, in 1012 double-column imperial octavo pages, are necessary to the completeness of any Protestant theological library. The works of Robert Hall, in six 12mo volumes, breathe the eloquence which made their author the greatest preacher of his day, and the equal of any orator of the Anglo-Saxon race. The following works are favorably known: Buck's "Philosophy of Religion," Pendleton's "Christian Doctrines," "Baptist Doctrines," edited by C. A. Jenkens; Dagg's "Moral Science," "Evidences of Christianity," and "Manual of Theology," Stock's "Handbook of Revealed Theology," Carson on "The Knowledge of Jesus, the Most Excellent of the Sciences," and "The Providence of God Unfolded in the Book of Esther." The works of Archibald McLean, in six volumes, 12mo; "Help to Zion's Travelers," by Robert Hall, Sr.; "Exhortations Relating to Prayer and the Lord's Supper," by Benjamin Wallin; "First Fruits," and "Primitive Theology," by Henry Holcombe; Edmund Botsford's "Spiritual Voyages;" "Writings of John Leland," by L. F. Green; complete works of Abraham Booth; "Church Order," "The Election of Grace," "Internal Call to the Ministry," and "Sermons," by Isaac Backus; "Treatise on Various Subjects," and "Vindication of Natural Religion," by John Brine; Magowan's "Dialogues of Devils," "The Deity and Atonement of Christ," by John Marshman; the works of John H. Hinton, in seven volumes 12mo; the writings of Dr. Francis Wayland, educational, philosophical, and religious; the "Miscellanies," and "Lectures on Baptist History," of William R. Williams; Angus's "Handbook of the Bible," "The Power of the Cross," by Richard Fuller; "Apostolic Church Polity," by William Williams; "Preaching: its Ideal and Inner Life," by Thomas Armitage; "Preparation and Delivery of Sermons," by John A. Broadus; "Wheat from the Fields of Boaz," by A. G. Thomas; "Christian Experience," by D. W. Faunce; "The Atonement," by Octavius Winslow; "The Atonement," by J. A. Haldane; "Soul Prosperity," by C. D. Mallary; "Maxcy's Literary Remains," by Romeo Elton; "Lectures on Biblical Antiquities," by F. A. Cox; "Christ in History," by Robert Turnbull; "The Apostolical Constitutions, including the Canons," by Irah Chase; "Internal Evidences of Christianity," by John Aldis; "Book of Worship for Private Families," "The Sanctuary, Its Claims and Power," by W. W. Everts; "Pulpit Eloquence," by Henry C. Fish; "The Spirit, Policy, and Influence of Baptists," by T. G. Jones; "Black Diamonds," "Great Wonders in Little Things," and "Ocean Gardens," by Sidney Dyer; "A Pedobaptist Church no Home for a Baptist," by R. T. Middleditch; "Baptist History, Faith, and Polity," by D. B. Cheney; "Encyclopedia of Religious Knowledge," by J. Newton Brown; "Campbellism Examined," by J. B. Jeter; "Morning by Morning," and "Evening by Evening," by C. H. Spurgeon; "The

Church, its Polity and Ordinances," by H. Harvey; "Baptist Short Method," by Edward Hiscox; "The Papal System from its Origin to the Present Time," "A Historical Sketch of Every Doctrine, Claim, and Practice of the Church of Rome," by William Cathcart; "History of Romanism," by John Dowling; "The Pernicious Effects of Infant Baptism," by Norman Fox; "The Philosophy of Atheism Examined and Compared with Christianity," by B. Godwin; "Duties of a Pastor to his Church," by Franklin Wilson; Dr. Malcom's "Travels in South-Eastern Asia," "A Year's Tour in the Holy Land," by S. D. Phelps; "Plea for Baptist Principles," by G. W. Anderson; "Text-Book of Campbellism," by D. B. Ray; "Text-Book of Popery," by J. M. Cramp; Dr. J. R. Graves is among the first of living Baptist writers, his last work is "Old Landmarkism, What is it?" "Religious Denominations in the United States and Great Britain," by Joseph Belcher; "The Creative Week," and "The Mountain Instruction," by George Dana Boardman; "Priscilla," by Joseph Banvard; "Western Empire, or the Drama of Human Progress," by E. L. Magoon; "Corrective Church Discipline," and "Parliamentary Practice," by Chancellor P. H. Mell.

Sermons in volumes have been published very extensively by Baptists. In 1876, Spurgeon had issued twenty-one volumes. Some of his sermons have been translated into German, Danish, Swedish, French, Italian, and Welsh. Maclaren has published sermons which have been very popular. We shall only add the following as authors of volumes of sermons: Dr. Samuel Stennett, Dr. William T. Brantly, Sr., Dr. Samuel Stillman, Rev. Oliver Hart, and Rev. William Parkinson.

The following are among a large number of works on baptism and the Lord's Supper: "Anti-Pedobaptism," by John Tombes (Mr. Tombes wrote fourteen distinct works on baptism); "A Treatise of Baptism, wherein that of Believers and that of Infants is Examined by the Scriptures," by Henry D'Anvers; "Anti-Pædo-Rantism, or Mr. Samuel Finley's Charitable Plea for the Speechless Examined and Refuted, the Baptism of Believers Maintained, and the Mode of it by Immersion Vindicated," by Abel Morgan, Philadelphia, printed by B. Franklin, in Market Street, 1747; Mr. Finley was subsequently president of New Jersey, now Princeton, College; "The Baptism of John" and "Letters on Baptism," by Thomas Baldwin; "Pedobaptism Examined," by Abraham Booth; "Infant Baptism a Part and Pillar of Popery," by John Gill; "History of Baptism," by Robert Robinson; "Scripture Guide to Baptism," by Richard Pengilly; Gale's "Reflections on Wall's History of Infant Baptism;" "Baptism, a Term of Communion at the Lord's Supper," by Joseph Kinghorn; "Baptism in its Mode and Subjects," by Alexander Carson; "Infant Baptism an Invention of Men," by Irah Chase; "Essay on Christian Baptism," by B. W. Noel; "Baptism and Terms of Communion," by Richard Fuller; "Doctrine of Baptism on the Principles of Biblical Interpretation," by J. J. Woolsey; "Baptism," by F. W. Broaddus; "Handbook on the Mode of Baptism," and "Handbook on the Subjects of Baptism," by Robert Ingham; "Theodosia Ernest," by A. C. Dayton; "Grace Truman," by Mrs. S. R. Ford; "Baptism and Baptisteries," by W. Cote; "The Meaning and Use of Baptizein Philologically and Historically Investigated," by T. J. Conant; Howell on Communion; "Immersion Essential to Christian Baptism," by John A. Broadus; "Church Communion as Practised by the Baptists," by W. W. Gardner; "Studies on the Baptismal Question," by D. B. Ford; "Baptism in Harmony in the East and in the West," by J. C. Long; "The Position of Baptism in the Christian System," by Henry H. Tucker; "History of Baptism," by Isaac T. Hinton; "The Act of Baptism," by Henry S. Burrage; "The Baptism of the Ages and of the Nations," by Wm. Cathcart.

The following histories were written by Baptists: Keach's "History of the English Baptists," Crosby's "History of the English Baptists," Ivimey's "History of the English Baptists," Orchard's "History of the English Baptists," Taylor's "History of the General Baptists," Robinson's "Historical Researches," Backus's "History of the Baptists," Cramp's "Baptist History," Benedict's "History of the Baptists," "Materials for a History of the Baptists in Delaware and in other States," by Morgan Edwards; Semple's "History of the Rise and Progress of the Baptists in Virginia," Cook's "Delaware Baptists," Orchard's "History of Foreign Baptists," "Historical Vindications," by S. S. Cutting; Duncan's "History of the Baptists," "The Early English Baptists," by Benjamin Evans; Asplund's "Baptist Register," Hague's "Historical Discourse," Callender's "Historical Discourse on the Civil and Religious Affairs of Rhode Island and Providence Plantations;" the materials gathered by John Comer for a history of American Baptist churches are of great value to all who have engaged in the undertaking, from which death removed the talented collector; Curry's "Struggles and Triumphs of Virginia Baptists," Hayne's "Baptist Denomination, its History and Doctrines," Ford's "Origin of the Baptists," Wm. Jones's "Church History," "Sketch of the Lower Dublin, or Pennepek Church," by H. G. Jones; "History of the First Baptist Church of Newport," by C. E. Barrows; "Religious Liberty and the Baptists," by C. C. Bitting; Anderson's "Annals of the English

Bible," Ray's "Baptist Succession," Mrs. T. J. Conant's "History of the English Bible," Curtis's "Progress of Baptist Principles," Cox's "History of English Baptist Missions," Gammel's "History of American Baptist Missions," McCoy's "History of Baptist Missions among American Indians," "Baptists and the American Revolution," by Wm. Cathcart; "Annals of the Christian Commission," by Lemuel Moss; "History of Missions," by John O. Choules; "Bunhill Memorials," by J. A. Jones; Bunhill is the London cemetery for Dissenters, where the ashes of Bunyan repose; "Manning and Brown University," by Reuben A. Guild; "The Baptist Encyclopædia," edited by William Cathcart.

BIOGRAPHIES.

"Life of Colonel Hutchinson, 'written by his widow Lucy;'" Ivimey's "Life of John Milton;" "Life of Henry Dunster," first president of Harvard College, by Jeremiah Chaplin; "Life of William Kiffin," by Joseph Ivimey; "Virginia Baptist Ministers," by J. B. Taylor; Hovey's "Life and Times of Isaac Backus;" Lives of Roger Williams, by J. D. Knowles, Romeo Elton, William Gammel, and Benjamin Evans; Wallin's "Life of Dr. John Gill," Wilkin's "Life of Joseph Kinghorn," Gregory's "Life of Robert Hall," Fuller's "Life of Samuel Pearce," "Memoirs of Mrs. Ann Hasseltine Judson," by J. D. Knowles; "Memoir of Dr. Judson," by Francis Wayland; "Memoir of Dr. Wayland," by F. and H. L. Wayland; a "Biographical Sketch of Sir Henry Havelock," by William Brock; "Life of Mrs. Lydia Malcom," by H. Malcom; "Life of Jesse Mercer," by C. D. Mallary; "Life of Luther Rice," by James B. Taylor; "Life and Times of James B. Taylor," by George B. Taylor; "Life and Writings of Robert Robinson," by George Dyer; "Life of Joseph Stennett," by D. Turner; "Memoirs of Mrs. Theodosia Dean," by Pharcellus Church; "Life of Rev. Duncan Dunbar," by Jeremiah Chaplin; "Life of William Knibb," by J. Howard Hinton; "Life of Rev. Thomas Burchell," by W. F. Burchell; "Life of Dr. Eugenio Kincaid," by Alfred Patton; "Life of Joseph Ivimey," by George Pritchard; "Life of Dr. Richard Fuller," by J. H. Cuthbert; "Life of Mrs. Shuck," "Life of Andrew Broaddus," and "Life of Daniel Witt," by J. B. Jeter; "Life of John Thomas," by C. B. Lewis, the first Baptist who preached the gospel in India; "The Life of John Bates," by Justin A. Smith; "Memoir of Andrew Fuller," by A. G. Fuller; "Memoir of Dr. William Stoughton," by S. W. Lynd; "Life and Correspondence of John Foster," by J. E. Ryland; Lives of Carey, Marshman, and Ward, by J. C. Marshman; "Life of John P. Crozer," by J. Wheaton Smith; "Life of Dr. Joseph H. Kennard," by J. Spencer Kennard; "Life of Spencer H. Cone, D.D.," by Edward and S. W. Cone; "Autobiography of John Gano," "Memoir of Dr. Baron Stow," by J. C. Stockbridge; "Life of Mrs. E. C. Judson," by A. C. Kendrick; "Memoir of Governor George N. Briggs," by W. C. Richards; "Life of John M. Peck, D.D.," by Rufus Babcock; "Life of William Colgate," by W. W. Everts; "Life of Joseph G. Binney, D.D.," by Mrs. J. G. Binney.

GENERAL LITERARY WORKS.

Hanserd Knollys wrote a Hebrew, Latin, and English grammar; Dr. Carey a Mahratta grammar, a Sanscrit grammar extending over a thousand quarto pages, a Punjabi grammar, a Telinga grammar, and a Mahratta dictionary, a Bengali dictionary, and a Bhotanta and a Sanscrit dictionary. Dr. Judson made a Burmese dictionary, and Dr. Mason a Pali grammar. Dr. J. Wade was the author of a Karen dictionary, and Dr. H. F. Buckner prepared a grammar of the language of the Creek Indians. The "Essays" of John Foster are among the finest productions in the literature of our tongue. Sir James Mackintosh justly describes their author as "one of the most profound and eloquent writers that England has produced." Dr. Gill's "Antiquity of the Hebrew Language, Letters, Vowel Points, and Accents" has been properly represented "as a masterly effort of profound research, which would have shown Dr. Gill to be a prodigy of learning, of reading, and of literature had he never published a syllable on any other subject." "Orators and Oratory" is one of several able works from the pen of William Matthews, LL.D. John M. Gregory, LL.D., wrote "A Handbook of History." Dr. Mason wrote "Burmah, its People and Natural Productions, or Notes on the Natives, Fauna, Flora, and Minerals, &c.;" F. S. Dobbins, "False Gods;" James De Mille, "The Dodge Club;" John Ash, LL.D., "A Grammar and Dictionary of the English Language;" Rev. F. Denison, the "History of the First Rhode Island Cavalry," and the "History of the Third Rhode Island Heavy Artillery;" Col. C. H. Banes, the "History of the Philadelphia Brigade;" Dr. James T. Champlin, a "Text-Book of Intellectual Philosophy." Prof. Cleveland Abbe for ten years has been meteorologist of the bureau of the army signal office, in which he compiles the published weather probabilities, the storm signals, monthly reviews, and international bulletin. He has made numerous contributions to the *American Journal of Science, Monthly Notices*, Royal Astronomical Society, the Smithsonian Annual Reports, and to Appleton's and Johnson's Encyclopædias. Rev. John Howard Hinton wrote a "History of the United States;" Lieut.-Gov. Arnold, a "History of Rhode Island;" Dr. Joseph Angus, "The Handbook of the English Tongue," "The Handbook of English Literature," and "Specimens of English Literature;" Dr. Hackett translated Winer's Chaldee Grammar and published his own exercises in Hebrew grammar; Dr. Benjamin Davies prepared a "Student's Grammar" and a "Student's Lexicon" of the Hebrew language; Dr. T. J. Conant translated Gesenius's Hebrew grammar, which he enlarged and improved; this work is now the standard of the schools in America and Europe. Joseph S. C. F. Frey was the author of a Hebrew grammar, the ninth American edition of which appeared in 1835; he also compiled a Hebrew lexicon. Dr. Leechman wrote a work on logic. Prof. Noah K. Davis has published "The Theory of Thought, a Treatise on Deductive Logic;" and President D. J. Hill has issued "The Elements of Rhetoric" and "The Science of Rhetoric." Dr. K. Brooks, in "Baptists and the National Centenary," says, "Dr. William Stoughton prepared an edition of Virgil, which had extensive use in his day. Adoniram Judson published an English grammar before he turned his attention to the Christian ministry. Dr. Francis Wayland was the author of very popular treatises on moral science, intellectual philosophy, and political economy. Dr. A. C. Kendrick has published introductory text-books in Greek and an edition of 'Xenophon's Anabasis;' Dr. Hackett, 'Plutarch on the Delay of the Deity in Punishing the Guilty;' Dr. John L. Lincoln edited Livy and Horace. Dr. J. R. Boise has given to the public seven volumes of Greek text-books, and Dr Albert Harkness eight volumes of Latin text-books and one of Greek. Dr. J. T. Champlain has published a large number of school-books, including treatises on ethics and intellectual philosophy, and editions of Demosthenes and Æschines. Dr. J. R. Loomis is the author of treatises on geology, anatomy, and physiology. Dr. S. S. Greene has published a series of English grammars; Prof. S. P. Sanford, a series of arithmetics; Prof. J. F. Stoddard, a series of arithmetics and algebras; and Dr. Edward Olney, a series of mathematical text-books, covering the whole ground of school and college study. Dr. J. H. Hanson has edited two volumes of the Latin authors usually read in preparation for college. Dr. G. W. Sansom is the author of a volume on art criticism; Dr. S. H. Carpenter, of an Anglo-Saxon grammar; and Prof. James G. Clark, of a treatise on the 'Differential and Integral Calculus;' Dr. A. A. Gould was associated with Agassiz in preparing a treatise on geology;" and Prof. S. M. Shute, D.D., "A Manual of Anglo-Saxon, comprising a Grammar, Reader, and Glossary."

The amount of secular literature coming from the intellect and the learning of Baptists is immense. They have written a multitude of books, and control many influential secular newspapers.

POETICAL WORKS.

"Paradise Lost," by John Milton; Miss Ann Steele's "Hymns and Poems" were published in three volumes in 1780. Dr. John Fawcett was the author of 156 hymns which were printed in 1782. Benjamin Beddome wrote many precious hymns; Benjamin Wallen, a book of hymns, published in 1750; Samuel Medley, a work with 232 hymns; John Fellows, a book with 55 hymns. Turner's "Divine Songs, Hymns, and Other Poems" were published in 1748. Joseph Swain wrote 129 hymns, which were issued in 1792. Samuel Stennett furnished 40 hymns to Dr. Rippon in 1787 for his "Selection." Edward Mote published a "Selection" of hymns in 1797, 108 of which were written by himself; and Dr. Edmund Turney wrote "Baptismal Harmonies," containing 36 hymns and chants; Richard Furman was the author of "Pleasures of Piety, and Other Poems;" but no considerable part of our poetical treasures can be recorded in this article; with Dr. S. F. Smith, Hon. Charles Thurber, Prof. J. H. Gilmore, Dr. Robert Lowry, Dr. Sidney Dyer, and others among the living, and Milton and a large number among the dead, we have great reason to bless God for our gifts. (See article on HYMNS AND THEIR AUTHORS.)

SUNDAY-SCHOOL LITERATURE.

The American Baptist Publication Society has 1326 works on its list, of which 444 are for Sunday-school libraries. These were written with great care and ability. Many others have been issued by private publishers in different sections of our country. In foreign lands Baptists are equally interested in providing religious books for the young, and the efforts which they have used for this object have been attended with great success.

In periodicals for the religious instruction of the young the Baptists have shown great enterprise. The *Young Reaper* is probably the most popular paper in existence; its pages are eagerly read by hundreds of thousands. *Our Young People*, intended for the period between childhood and adult years, is edited with great ability, and has a large circulation. The Baptist Publication Society has a list of periodicals, only two of which we have named, whose pages show remarkable adaptation to the various stages of childhood and youth for which they are intended. *The Teacher*, designed to benefit the young through their instructors, is one of the best Sunday-school papers in existence. *Kind Words*, issued by the Southern Baptist Convention, is a great blessing to throngs of the young. Baptists of all nationalities have numbers of religious papers for the enlightenment of the rising generation.

AMERICAN PERIODICALS.

Name.	Editor.	Issued.	Where Published.
Advanced Bible Lesson Quarterly	Dr. C. R. Blackall	Quarterly	Philadelphia, Pa.
Alabama Baptist, The	E. T. Winkler, D.D.	Weekly	Marion, Ala.
American Baptist Flag	D. B. Ray, D.D.	"	St. Louis, Mo.
American Baptist, The	A. C. Caperton, D.D.	Monthly	Louisville, Ky.
American Baptist Year-Book	Rev. J. G. Walker	Yearly	Philadelphia, Pa.
Baptist, The	J. R. Graves, LL.D.	Weekly	Memphis, Tenn.
Baptist Banner	James I. Morris	"	Cumming, Ga.
Baptist Banner	Rev. W. P. Throgmorton	"	Benton, Ill.
Baptist Beacon, The	Rev. W. J. Crawford	Monthly	Albany, Oregon.
Baptist Courier, The	Rev. A. W. Lamar	Weekly	Greenville, S. C.
Baptist Family Magazine	J. Eugene Reed	Monthly	Philadelphia, Pa.
Baptist Journal, The	Rev. A. R. Griggs	"	Dallas, Texas.
Baptist Missionary Magazine	S. F. Smith, D.D.	"	Boston, Mass.
Baptist Pioneer, The	W. H. McAlpine	"	Marion, Ala.
Baptist Record, The	Rev. J. B. Gambrell	Weekly	Clinton, Miss.
Baptist Reflector, The	J. B. Chevis	"	Nashville, Tenn.
Baptist Review, The	J. R. Baumes, D.D.	Quarterly	Cincinnati, O.
Baptist Signal	J. J. Spelman	Monthly	Jackson, Miss.
Baptist Teacher	P. S. Henson, D.D.	"	Philadelphia, Pa.
Baptist Weekly, The	A. S. Patton, D.D.	Weekly	New York, N. Y.
Biblical Recorder	Rev. C. T. Bailey	"	Raleigh, N. C.
Bible Lesson Monthly	Rev. J. W. Willmarth	Monthly	Philadelphia, Pa.
Canadian Baptist, The	Wm. Muir	Weekly	Toronto, Ontario.
Canadian Missionary Link	Mrs. H. J. Rose	Monthly	" "
Central Baptist, The	Wm. Ferguson	Weekly	St. Louis, Mo.
Children's Picture Lesson	Mrs. M. G. Kennedy	Monthly	Philadelphia, Pa.
Christian Helper	H. E. Buchan, M.D.	"	Toronto, Ontario.
Christian Index, The	H. H. Tucker, D.D., LL.D.	Weekly	Atlanta, Ga.
Christian Messenger, The	S. Seldon	"	Halifax, Nova Scotia.
Christian Monitor, The	Dr. D. M. Breaker	"	Gainesville, Ga.
Christian Repository	S. H. Ford, LL.D.	Monthly	St. Louis, Mo.
Christian Secretary	S. D. Phelps, D.D.	Weekly	Hartford, Conn.
Christian Visitor	Rev. J. E. Hopper	"	St. John, New Brunswick.
Der Muntere Säeman (German)	Rev. J. C. Haselhuhn	"	Cleveland, O.
Der Sendbote (German)	Rev. J. C. Haselhuhn	"	" "
Die Sonntags Freude	Rev. J. C. Haselhuhn	Monthly	" "
Der Wegweiser	Rev. J. C. Haselhuhn	"	" "
Evangel, The	Rev. J. T. Prior	Weekly	San Francisco, Cal.
Evangel, The Arkansas	{ B. R. Womask / J. B. Searcy }	"	Little Rock and Dardanelle.
Evangelisk Tidskrift	Prof. J. A. Edgren	Monthly	Chicago, Ill.
Examiner and Chronicle, The	E. Bright, D.D.	Weekly	New York, N. Y.
Foreign Journal	H. A. Tupper, D.D.	Monthly	Richmond, Va.
Georgia Baptist, The	Rev. Wm. J. White	Weekly	Augusta, Ga.
Helping Hand		Monthly	Boston, Mass.
Herald of Truth	G. S. Abbott, D.D.	Semi-monthly	Oakland, Cal.
Intermediate Lesson Quarterly	Mrs. M. G. Kennedy	Quarterly	Philadelphia, Pa.
Journal and Messenger	G. W. Lasher, D.D.	Semi-monthly	Cincinnati, O.
Kind Words	Rev. S. Boykin	Weekly	Macon, Ga.
Le Moniteur	T. Amyrauld	"	Granby, Quebec.
Michigan Christian Herald	Rev. L. H. Trowbridge	"	Detroit, Mich.
Missionary Baptist	C. C. Dickinson	Semi-monthly	Memphis, Tenn.
National Baptist, The	H. L. Wayland, D.D.	Weekly	Philadelphia, Pa.
National Monitor, The	Rev. R. L. Perry	Semi-monthly	Brooklyn, N. Y.
National Watchman	Howard Bunts, Jr.	Monthly	Albany, Ga.
New Jersey Baptist, The	John W. Moody	"	Trenton, N. J.
Our Little Ones	Dr. C. R. Blackall	Weekly	Philadelphia, Pa.
Our Young People	A. J. Rowland, D.D.	Monthly	" "
Picture Lesson Cards	Mrs. M. G. Kennedy	Weekly	" "
Religious Herald	{ A. E. Dickinson, D.D. / Prof. H. H. Harris, D.D. }	"	Richmond, Va.
Standard, The	J. A. Smith, D.D.	"	Chicago, Ill.
Texas Baptist, The	Rev. R. C. Buckner	"	Dallas, Texas.
Texas Baptist Herald	J. B. Link, D.D.	"	Houston, Texas.
Vermont Baptist, The	Rev. J. K. Richardson	Monthly	Rutland, Vt.
Watchman, The	Lucius E. Smith, D.D.	Weekly	Boston, Mass.
Watch Tower, The	J. W. Olmstead, D.D.	"	New York, N. Y.
Western Recorder	A. C. Caperton, D.D.	"	Louisville, Ky.
Young Reaper	B. Griffith, D.D.	Semi-monthly	Philadelphia, Pa.
Y Wawr (Welsh)	O. Griffith	Monthly	Utica, N. Y.
Zion's Advocate	Rev. H. S. Burrage	Weekly	Portland, Me.

BRITISH PERIODICALS.

The Baptist Handbook, yearly; *The Baptist Almanac*, yearly; *The Baptist Year-Book and Almanac*, yearly; *The General Baptist Almanac*, yearly; *Spurgeon's Illustrated Almanac*, yearly; *The Quarterly Reporter of the German Baptist Mission*, quarterly; *Baptist Magazine*, monthly; *Baptist Messenger*, monthly; *The Church*, monthly; *General Baptist Magazine*, monthly; *Earthen Vessel*, monthly; *Gospel Herald and Voice of Truth*, monthly; *Missionary Herald*, monthly; *Juvenile Missionary Herald*, monthly; *Sword and Trowel*, monthly; *The Irish Baptist Magazine*, monthly; *The Freeman*, weekly; *The Baptist*, weekly.

WELSH.

The Welsh Baptist Handbook, yearly; *Y Greal (The Magazine)*, monthly; *Yr Athraw (The Teacher)*, monthly; *Cydymaith Y Plentyn (Child's Companion)*, monthly; *Seren Cymru (Star of Wales)* weekly.

SCOTLAND.

The Scottish Baptist Magazine, monthly.

Littlefield, Gov. Alfred Henry, was born in Scituate, R. I., April 2, 1829. Several of his ancestors occupied prominent positions in the administration of the civil affairs of Rhode Island. He was one of a family of eleven children. In the spring of 1851 he entered into partnership with his brother. The business of the firm was so successful that it has become one of the most prominent in the State. Gov. Littlefield had an appointment in the civil war as brigade quartermaster on the staff of Brig.-Gen. O. Arnold, and in various ways rendered efficient aid to the government, and extended his sympathy and pecuniary help to the families of the soldiers. He has filled, and continues to fill, important positions in different corporations in Pawtucket, R. I. He has represented the town of Lincoln in both branches of the General Assembly. He was chosen governor in 1880. Gov. Littlefield is an habitual attendant on the ministry of Rev. George Bullen, pastor of the First Baptist church in Pawtucket, of which his wife is a member.

Lloyd, Rev. W. B., the oldest Baptist minister in Mississippi, was born in Georgia in 1809; became a Baptist in 1825, and at once began to preach; was ordained the following year. He settled in Noxube Co., Miss., in 1830, where he engaged actively in the ministry. He was an able preacher and a successful revivalist, having baptized about 3000 persons during the fifty-five years of his ministry.

Lloyd, Rev. W. S., was born in Hyde Co., N. C., Feb. 27, 1811; ordained in South Carolina in 1835; educated in Furman University, in both the literary and theological courses. After a useful ministry of ten years in that State, he settled in Macon Co., Ala., in 1845, where he remained until his death. Soon attracting general attention, he became one of the most popular and useful, as he was one of the most gifted ministers in the State. A striking form, excellent social qualities, with the spirit of a Christian, he made friends of all with whom he came in contact. His churches were among a wealthy and highly-cultivated people. He fell dead in the pulpit in the midst of one of his eloquent sermons, at Mount Meigs, Ala., at eleven o'clock on Sabbath, March 12, 1854. Rev. W. E. Lloyd, of Auburn, one of the best preachers in Alabama, is his son, possessing many of the striking and noble traits of his brilliant father.

Locke, Rev. Jacob, an able and useful preacher of the Old Green River Association in Kentucky, was born in Berkeley Co., Va., about 1768. He removed to Mercer Co., Ky., in 1789, and subsequently to Barren County of that State about 1799. Here he was ordained to the ministry in 1801, and became pastor of the Mount Tabor Baptist church in 1803, besides supplying several other churches. Mr. Locke was a man of wisdom, piety, and zeal. He was the leading man in planting and establishing the young churches and guiding their associational councils. He was moderator of Green River Association for more than twenty years, and then of Liberty Association from its constitution until his death, which occurred Jan. 18, 1845.

Lofton, George Augustus, D.D., pastor of the Third Baptist church, St. Louis, Mo., was born Dec. 25, 1839, in Penola Co., Miss. He finished his education in 1859–60 at Mercer University. It was his purpose to enter the Methodist ministry, but in 1859, from the study of the Greek New Testament, he was convinced of the Scripturalness of Baptist views, and was immersed into

GEORGE AUGUSTUS LOFTON, D.D.

the fellowship of the Second Baptist church, Atlanta, Ga. In 1861 he entered the service of the Confederacy, and continued through the war as an officer of artillery. He entered the Baptist ministry at Americus, Ga., in 1868; and since that time Dr. Lofton has served as pastor, principally, the Baptist church at Dalton, Ga., the First Baptist church at Memphis, Tenn., and the Third Baptist church at St. Louis, Mo. These churches have all flourished under his care, numerically, spiritually, financially, and socially. He has baptized some 600 converts in his churches; and he is regarded as a devoted, able, and successful pastor, a sound and practical preacher, an indefatigable worker, a friend to the poor, a popular speaker. Besides many articles and sermons for the periodical press, he has written and published some bound volumes, which have received favorable criticism, and which indicate culture and originality. He is in the prime of life, and has the promise of many years of usefulness. He and his present charge are in close bonds of sympathy, and are co-operating most successfully in religious work of all kinds in St. Louis, in the State, and in the regions beyond. Thoroughly evangelical, Dr. Lofton leads any church he serves as pastor in the most efficient methods of work, and into the widest fields of usefulness. He served faithfully and suffered greatly through the yellow fever scourge of 1873 in Memphis; and in 1875 he led his brethren in the centennial effort to endow the Southwestern Baptist University at Jackson, Tenn. He was also president for two years of the Southern Baptist Publication Society, located at Memphis. Dr. Lofton is especially prominent and well known in the South, and he is rapidly acquiring a national reputation.

Long, Rev. F. M., traces his ancestry to the "Mayflower" and Plymouth Rock. He was born Sept. 30, 1839, in East Tennessee, where he was converted. He was baptized in Macoupin Co., Ill., licensed in 1864, ordained in 1865 by the Honey Creek church, and preached with great success for ten years in Madison, Bond, and Montgomery Counties, Ill. In 1874 he removed to Oregon, and has since then been connected with the Oak Creek church, giving occasional aid to the Providence, North Palestine, and Lacreole churches. He is an earnest, doctrinal extempore preacher, and is one of the most logical reasoners in the Oregon pulpit. He does not put himself forward, but when called out carries all hearts with him. A diligent student and active pastor, he deserves the love of the brethren and the churches, which he possesses to an unusual degree.

Long, Prof. J. C., D.D., LL.D., was born in Campbell Co., Va., Nov. 28, 1833; graduated at Richmond College in June, 1856. The month following his graduation he was appointed tutor in the college, but resigned at the close of the first session; was ordained in Grace Street church, Richmond, Va., July 5, 1857. In the summer of 1857 he was elected teacher in the Florida State Seminary, and held the position for one year in connection with the pastorate of the Tallahassee church. He then became pastor of the Cumberland Street church, Norfolk, Va., and remained until 1861, when the relationship was broken up by the war. From 1861–65 he resided in Goochland Co., Va., and during part of the year 1863 was teacher of a school in Danville, Va. He subsequently became pastor of the Fine Creek and Mount Tabor churches. From 1866–68 he was pastor of the Scottsville and Hardware churches in Albemarle County. In 1868 he became pastor of the church at Charlottesville, Va., where he remained until April, 1875, when he was elected Professor of Ecclesiastical History in the Crozer Theological Seminary. In this position he continues to render valuable service to the cause of ministerial education. He received the degree of D.D. from Richmond College in 1872, and that of LL.D. from Baylor University in 1880.

Dr. Long is a man of ripe scholarship, unassuming manners, and most genial social accomplishments. His writings evince the results of long-continued and patient research, and display his marked ability to interpret the facts of history in their relation to the church of Christ. His sermons are rich in the clear, simple, and devout exposition of the Word of God.

Long, Nimrod, a banker, merchant, and manufacturer, was born in Logan Co., Ky., July 31, 1814. At the age of fourteen he went to Russellville, the seat of justice of his native county, and entered a store as clerk. Three years afterwards he became a partner in the house. In a short time the senior partner died, and Mr. Long took his brother into the partnership. They were very successful. After some years Mr. N. Long withdrew from the business, and became a commission merchant, and afterwards established the banking-house of N. Long & Co., and in 1870 built the largest flouring-mill in the State. This, like all his enterprises, proved a success, and Mr. Long is now a wealthy capitalist. He became a member of the Baptist church in Russellville in early life, and has used his business talent and growing capital for the cause of Christ with rare liberality. He was ordained a deacon of his church in 1832, was made its treasurer in 1838, and has for many years been superintendent of the Sunday-school. He has been the leading spirit in founding and endowing Bethel College, one of the best and most flourishing institutions of the West. After contributing largely to the erection of its buildings, he endowed the chair of English, known as the N. Long professorship. In 1870 he conceived the idea of boarding students at actual cost, and, to carry it out, caused the erection of the N. Long Boarding Hall, capable of accommodating 100 students. He has also been a liberal patron of Georgetown College and other institutions of learning in his denomination.

Longley, Avard, M.P., was born in Wilmot, Annapolis County, Nova Scotia; is a member of the Wilmot Baptist church; represents the county of Annapolis in the Parliament of Canada. Mr. Longley has been much in political life; is a governor of Acadia College, a strong advocate for prohibition of all intoxicating liquors, and a friend of all denominational enterprises.

Loomis, Rev. Ebenezer, was born in 1794; baptized in 1809; preached first in Tolland Court-

House, Conn., in 1821; ordained in New London, Conn.; labored as pastor, exploring agent, and evangelist in Richfield, Otsego Co., N. Y.; First Newark, N. J.; Hudson, N. Y.; Springville, Boston, and Evans, Western New York; Detroit, China, and Coldwater, Mich.; Cincinnati, O.; North Lyme; First Colchester, Brooklyn; First North Stonington, Preston, and Killingly, Conn.; Fredonia, N. Y.; finally Bradford Co., Pa.; gifted, scholarly, amiable, devoted; gave thousands of dollars to churches, to Connecticut Literary Institution, and to the missionary press in Burmah; always traveled on foot; died in Bradford Co., Pa., in 1872, in his seventy-ninth year.

Loomis, Prof. Freeman, was born in Waterville, Me., May 21, 1844. His studies preparatory to admission to college were pursued mostly at the academy connected with the university at Lewisburg, and he was admitted to Freshman standing in June, 1862. He graduated in 1866, taking the second honors of his class. He passed at once to theological studies, the course in that department then occupying two years. Having finished his theological course, he was temporarily appointed to the principalship of the academy in the spring of 1867. At the commencement in June the board of trustees elected him principal, which position he held for two years. In 1869 the preparatory department became distinct from the academy, and he was placed at the head of it. In 1879 the preparatory department again became a part of the academy, and Prof. Loomis resigned his connection with it. In 1870 he obtained leave of absence, and occupied himself for two years in the study of French and German in Berlin and Paris. During his absence, in 1871, the trustees appointed him to the chair of Modern Languages in the university. This position he held in connection with that of head of the preparatory course till his resignation of the latter in 1879. Since that time he has held only the professorship of Modern Languages. In this department his instruction is faithfully given, and he is deservedly popular with his classes.

Loomis, Rev. Hubbell, died Dec. 15, 1872, in his ninety-eighth year, at Upper Alton, Ill. He was an example alike of the physical vigor and of the intellectual and spiritual robustness of the New England stock. He was born at Colchester, Conn., May 31, 1775. As his father, a descendant of Joseph Loomis, who emigrated from England to this country in 1638, was in moderate circumstances, he was thrown chiefly upon his own resources in procuring his education, graduating at Union College, Schenectady, N. Y., in 1799. Having studied theology under Rev. Joel Benedict, of Plainfield, Conn., he was licensed as a Congregationalist minister in 1801. His first pastorate was at Willington, Conn., where he continued twenty-four years, uniting with his pastoral duties the work of a teacher, one of his pupils being Jared Sparks, afterwards so eminent as president of Harvard College and author of "The Life of Washington," and other valuable works. In the later years of this pastorate, as a result of earnest study of the Scriptures with reference to questions of denominational difference, he became a Baptist, and united with the Baptist church of Willington; this event, of course, dissolving his connection with the church he had served so long, and necessitating great self-denial in other respects.

In 1829, Mr. Loomis removed to Illinois. After some months spent in Kaskaskia and Edwardsville, he settled in Upper Alton, and then founded the seminary which in 1835 became incorporated as Shurtleff College. His name stands first on the list in the college charter of incorporation. He was a liberal donor to the college, and to the end of his life its earnest friend, while in the various exigencies of its history his counsel was often sought. He was remarkable for conscientiousness; an ardent advocate of human rights, and a warm friend of moral reforms. One of his sons, Prof. Elias Loomis, of Yale College, ranks with the eminent men of science in this country, while others of his children have filled stations of great usefulness, one daughter, Sophia, having been the wife of Hon. Cyrus Edwards, another, Caroline, was married to Prof. Newman, of Shurtleff College, who died in 1844; a son, David B., residing in Minnesota, has filled several terms as a member of the Legislature of that State; while another, John Calvin, was at one time Professor of Languages in the Alabama University.

Loomis, Justin R., D.D., LL.D., was born in Bennington, Vt., Aug. 21, 1810. At the age of seventeen he went to Hamilton Literary Institution, and at a subsequent date he entered Brown University, and graduated with marked honor in 1835. Shortly after his graduation he was elected professor in Waterville College, now Colby University.

Determined to thoroughly inform himself in the field of his chosen studies, he visited South America, where he spent a profitable year in scientific explorations through Bolivia, Peru, and Chili. Thus prepared for more efficient service, he was elected Professor of Natural Science in the university at Lewisburg, Pa., and in 1858 succeeded to the presidency. This office he held with singular ability for twenty years, retiring from it in January, 1879.

His consistent and blameless life, his many acts of benevolence, his indomitable will, combined with practical good sense, his warm interest in the welfare of the university, and especially in the students, his influence in shaping the character of the town, and in making the Baptist church edifice, which was mainly erected by his own exertions, among the best in the State, have left a stamp of permanent value upon the history of the university.

As an author, he has prepared various standard

JUSTIN R. LOOMIS, LL.D.

works: "Principles of Geology," "Physiology," and "Anatomy," are works of great value, while various essays, lectures, pamphlets, and sermons attest the possession of talents of a high order. While he could lay no high claim to oratorial power as a public speaker, yet his presence and counsel at the meetings of the Associations and other bodies were always welcome, and were much desired.

His son, Freeman Loomis, is a professor in the university at Lewisburg.

Lord, Edward C., D.D., was born at Carlisle, N. Y., Jan. 22, 1817, and was a graduate of Madison University. He was ordained at Preston Hollow, N. Y., Aug. 27, 1846, having previously received an appointment as a missionary to China. He reached Ningpo June 20, 1847, and was connected with Dr. Macgowan in the care of that station. Having acquired the language, he was able to preach to the natives and hold conversation with them on religious subjects. The health of Mrs. Lord made it necessary for him to return to the United States, which he reached at the close of 1851. Remaining here a little less than two years, he returned to Ningpo. Arriving there June 1, 1854, he commenced again his missionary labors, taking, as far as possible, the place of the lamented Goddard, and having Mr. Knowlton as a co-worker with him. While occupied with these evangelical labors, Mr. Lord performed some work in his study. Writing to the Executive Committee, in 1860, he says, "My notes on the Epistles to the Hebrews and Romans have been completed, and considerable other labor of a similar kind has been performed." And the next year he writes, "My notes on the First Epistle to the Corinthians have been completed and put to press. My notes on Ephesians have been carefully revised, and those on Second Corinthians are in course of preparation." In 1863 he writes, "At Ningpo, in my own neighborhood, I have plenty of work, and I am thankful to say there is much encouragement. At the communion season, about three months ago, I baptized five persons, three men and two women, and I have at present several applicants." The connection of Mr. Lord with the Missionary Union closed in July, 1864. He was in the diplomatic service of the United States in China, and performing more or less of missionary service for several years. His formal connection with the Missionary Union has been resumed. He has had charge of two chapels in Ningpo, being aided in his work by three native preachers.

Lord's Supper, The.—The Lord's Supper, in its *form*, must be bread and wine; for Matthew says that Jesus took bread and blessed it, and brake it and gave it to the disciples and said, "Take, eat; this is my body. And he took the cup, and gave thanks, and gave it to them, saying, Drink ye all of it."—Matt. xxvi. 28. The retention of the cup from the laity in the Church of Rome, deprives her Eucharist of every divine sanction, and reduces it to a mere human invention.

The Supper is a *memorial* or *remembrancer* of a *slain* and *absent* Saviour. His wounds and death are shown by the broken bread and the flowing cup. His *bodily* absence is proved by the object of the Sacrament. Speaking of the bread Jesus says, "This is my body which is given for you; this do in *remembrance* of me."—Luke xxiv. 19. We can only *remember* absent persons. So that the purpose of the Eucharist as a remembrancer makes it certain that Christ's body is not in it. And Paul teaches the same truth when he writes, —"For as often as ye eat this bread and drink this cup, ye do show the Lord's death till *He come*."—1 Cor. xi. 26. In body, he is not in the Supper, for it is intended to be observed till Jesus, whom "the heaven must receive until the times of restitution of all things" (Acts iii. 21) shall come in the glories of his final advent. His humanity is now at the right hand of God. His Deity is everywhere, but peculiarly near the devout worshiper. The transubstantiation* of Rome, and the consubstantiation† of Luther are, therefore, without foundation either in Scripture or in fact.

The sole direct teaching of the Supper is: *The agony of Jesus the sustenance of redeemed men.* Strange that *bread* should be the figure to represent the body of Christ. Why not his image in gold or silver? His statue in marble or wood? His picture on canvas? Then each wound might have been seen, and every writhe of anguish. But no, bread, the *food of the world,* and wine, the beverage of many nations, are chosen to exhibit the wounded body of Jesus. Food and drink, the support of all human life, constitute the *monument* erected by Jesus for himself,—the food, *broken* bread, to remind us of his torn body—the cup, wine, to represent the purple current drawn from his veins. And these emblems are not *to be viewed, simply,* in solemn sadness, nor even in joyful faith,—we are *to partake* of them. Thus teaching that as food and drink sustain men, without which their bodies must perish, so the sufferings of Jesus *are the bread and the beverage* of the soul. And as it would be madness to try to support flesh and blood on anything but food and drink, so it is insanity to look anywhere but to Christ's woes for the nourishment of the undying spirit. And the true disciple, by a hungering faith, ought to make these sorrows bread for his soul; while by a thirsting frame of spirit he ought to drink at these crimson streams of divine torture. And as we need bread and drink *all the time,* the choice of these emblems by the Saviour proclaims to us that his wounds and death **are a** constant supply for the necessities of a soul perpetually in want. What other doctrines could be designed by such emblems? Beyond all doubt God speaks to us through them, and says, Like the body needing bread several times *every* day, so your souls require atoning blood each instant, and like the food of mankind there is an everlasting supply for all the weaknesses and criminal experiences that mark each footprint of your earthly journey, to which you are as welcome every moment as to the food that covers your own tables, or the fruits that wave in golden beauty on your own abundant harvest-fields. " He that spared not his own Son but delivered him up for us all, how shall he not with him also *freely give us all things?"*—Rom. viii. 33. "By one offering he hath *perfected forever* all them that are sanctified."—Heb. x. 14. " I give unto them *eternal life;* and they shall *never perish,* neither shall any pluck them out of my hand."—John x. 28. Thank God for the Lord's Supper!

The Supper has no commission to teach us charity for each other. Examine the descriptions given of it in Matt. xxvi. 26–28, in Mark xiv. 22–23, in Luke xxii. 19, 20, in 1 Cor. xi. 20–29, and allusions made to it elsewhere, and in *every instance* it is a memorial of the Saviour's *wounds and blood,*—a picture of Christ's only *food* for perishing souls, and in each case *destitute* of any other allusion. Many Christians turn it into a feast of charity for members of their own and of other sects, and speak *with unloving harshness* of those who observe it solely as a remembrancer of a Saviour in the throes of death. Charity in its own place is a truly blessed grace; he is not Christ's who has not a goodly measure of it; it is the chain whose golden links bind together the whole heavenly throng, from the Mighty One wielding the sword of Omnipotence to the lowliest shining spirit. From the depths of our hearts, *enthusiasm* surges up in a mighty current around charity, the darling of heaven,—the element of which God himself is composed. But we have a fervent love for the truth of God,—for that whole body of revelation, one fragment of which exceeds in worth the riches of time, and all the material splendors of the universe. And as the Lord's Supper, according to Jesus, has nothing to do with charity, as it is a MONUMENT upon which is sculptured the ANGUISH OF JESUS, THE FOOD AND DRINK OF THE SOUL, and a monument from which the most dazzling glories in the universe shine forth, and around which the most thrilling melodies of heavenly harmony shall ever float, why obliterate its *divinely* appointed inscription to trace upon it any other writing, even though you inscribe upon it man's love to his fellow,—where Christ's love *in lines of blood* was once read? Surely this is an impious act in any one, and peculiarly so in the adherents of that Protestantism which boasts that the " Bible and the *Bible alone* is its religion." You might with as much propriety assemble the pious business people of several localities together on New Year's day, who manifested the grace of Christian integrity by paying their debts, and induce them to celebrate the Supper as an exhibition of their uprightness and probity. And if it might be said, the cross shows Christ's love for us in the Supper, the example of which commands us to love one another, it might with equal justice be affirmed, the sufferings of Jesus seen in the Supper *as our surety,* show him as wonderfully honest in paying our debts to the violated law, and following in his footsteps, we should refuse all gains not righteously secured.

Lorimer, George C., D.D., was born near Edinburgh, Scotland, in 1838, and in that city he spent

---

* The Council of Trent decrees, "If any man shall deny, that in the sacrament of the most holy Eucharist, there is contained really, truly, and substantially, *the body and blood, together with the soul and divinity* of our Lord Jesus Christ, and so *whole Christ,* but shall say he is only in it in sign, or figure, or power, *let him be accursed.*" De Eucharis, Can. i. Less. xiii. p. 63. Canones et Decreta Concilii Trid. Lipsiæ, 1863.

† The body and blood of Christ truly present in the Supper. Augsburg Confession, Article x.

the early part of his life. For a short time he followed the sea, then for a brief period he had some business connection with a theatre, and occasionally performed some parts, but God had something higher

GEORGE C. LORIMER, D.D.

and better for him than the stage. He came to the United States when he was about eighteen years of age, and having been providentially led to the city of Louisville, Ky., he was brought under the influence of the preaching of the pastor of the Walnut Street Baptist church. That preaching was blessed to him, and he became a hopeful Christian. The whole purpose of his life was at once changed. He entered upon a course of study in Georgetown College, Ky., preparatory to the Christian ministry, and in 1859 was ordained pastor of the church at Harrodsburg, Ky. He remained there until called to Paducah, Ky., and from there to Louisville, where he was a pastor for eight years. The degree of Doctor of Divinity was conferred upon him by Bethel College while he was in Louisville. From Louisville he was called to Albany, N. Y., where he remained two years, and then accepted an invitation to the Shawmut Avenue church, Boston. While in the midst of a successful ministry with this church, the attention of the Tremont Temple church was directed to him, and he was urged to occupy that central and important position, in which, for several years, his labors have been so much blessed. About eighteen months ago he took charge of the First church, Chicago. Dr. Lorimer is in the prime of his life, and, it is to be hoped, of his usefulness. His ministry is a popular one, in the best sense of the word. He believes in a genial religion, and seeks to draw men to Christ by the sweet words of a Saviour's love. His preaching has been blessed to the building up of a large church and congregation in Boston; and it has been equally effective in his present charge.

He has just sundered his happy relations with the First church to minister to a new community occupying the field vacated by the Michigan Avenue Baptist church.

Lothrop, Rev. J. Grafton, was a brilliant young minister in Eastern Louisiana, who died, very much regretted, at Greensburg, La., June 16, 1868. He began to preach in 1861.

Louisiana, one of the Gulf States, was long a part of the territory of France, but was purchased by the United States in 1803. It has about 20,000 white Baptists and about 30,000 colored.

The sentiments of the Baptists were first propagated in this State by preachers from the contiguous parts of Mississippi. Rev. Bailey E. Chaney removed with his family into Eastern Louisiana, then called West Florida, in 1798, and settled with a number of other South Carolinians not far from Baton Rouge. He began to preach to his American neighbors, but he was not long without molestation. He was arrested and imprisoned at Baton Rouge by the Spanish authorities. But he purchased his liberty by promising to abstain from preaching in the future, and subsequently returned to Mississippi.

Soon after the cession of the French portion of the Territory, Joseph Willis, a mulatto, who was a licensed Baptist preacher, and who had been a colaborer with Richard Curtis in Mississippi, boldly crossed the Mississippi River, and in 1804 preached at Vermillion and Plaquemine Brulé. The following year he returned and settled on Bayou Chicot in St. Landry Parish, where he began to preach, and in 1812, with assistance from Mississippi, organized a church, of which he became pastor.

About the beginning of the present century a number of young ministers crossed into West Florida, at the peril of their liberty. By the labors of these, two churches were gathered on Pearl River, called Mount Nebo and Peniel, which were constituted in 1813.

Previous to 1806, Ezra Courtney, who had settled in Mississippi in 1802, made frequent visits into the Felicianas and East Baton Rouge, and about that time removed and settled near the present town of Clinton, and in 1814 Hepzibah church was constituted. In 1819 West Florida was ceded to the United States. Other ministers came into this part of the State. Elisha Anders settled in West Feliciana, Howell Wall and W. B. Wall in St. Helena. As early as 1818 a small church was gathered in New Orleans, and enjoyed the labors of Benjamin Davis.

West of the Mississippi Joseph Willis continued for several years to labor alone, and organized churches at Cheneyville, Vermillion, Plaquemine Brulé, and Hickory Flat. In 1816 he was joined in this field by Ezekiel O'Quinn and Isham Nettles. On the 31st day of October, 1818, six churches met by delegates at Cheneyville, and organized the Louisiana Baptist Association, of which Joseph Willis was elected moderator. Other ministers were ordained, and churches increased, mainly through the zealous labors of Mr. Willis.

In 1822, Rev. Henry Humble settled on the Ouachita River, in the parish of Catahoula, and in 1826 the First church in Catahoula was established. Here, at a somewhat later day, labored Asa S. Mercer, John Hill, the Merediths, Thomas and James, and many churches were gathered in the Ouachita region.

In 1820, Rev. James Brinson, with a number of other Baptists, settled at Pine Hills, not far from the present town of Vienna, and organized a church in 1821. Here they were joined by John Impson. They extended their labors westward, and gathered a church about four miles east of Mount Lebanon, called Providence. It was afterwards removed to Athens. Not far from the present town of Minden they found a few Baptists, whom they gathered into a church called Black Lake.

In 1837 a colony, most of whom were Baptists, removed from South Carolina and settled at Mount Lebanon, in Bienville Parish. In the company was Henry Adams, a colored man, who was an ordained Baptist preacher. A church was organized, and Mr. Adams became pastor. He was a man of some education, and was very much respected by the community. This church became one of the most active and influential in the State.

About the same time Elias George, Samuel J. Larkin, and William B. Larkin began to preach in Union Parish, and many churches were gathered in a few years.

In 1843, Rev. John Bryce, an eminent Baptist minister, was sent to Shreveport as collector of customs on imports from the republic of Texas. While discharging the duties of his office he preached in Shreveport and the surrounding country. In 1845 a church was gathered in Shreveport, and Mr. Bryce became pastor. His office of collector of customs having expired by the annexation of Texas, he continued to labor in this region until 1850. He was joined in 1847 by A. W. Jackson and Jesse Lee, two able ministers from Alabama, and on Dec. 21, 1849, the Grand Cane Association was organized.

In the Sabine region the churches were principally planted and consolidated by the labors of Nathan H. Bray after 1847. There were a few churches before this planted by Willis and his co-laborers, but they were feeble and scattered. In 1848, Mr. Bray formed them into an Association called Sabine.

The Bayou Macon region, between the Ouachita and Mississippi Rivers, had but few Baptists previous to 1850. Shortly after this J. P. Blake and D. D. Swindall began their labors there, and in 1855 organized the Bayou Macon Association.

Louisiana Baptist, a weekly newspaper, was started at Mount Lebanon, La., in 1855, by Rev. Hanson Lee, and conducted with such ability that it ranked with the ablest religious journals of the South. In 1862, Mr. Lee died, and the paper was continued by W. F. Wells, with Dr. Courtney as editor, and subsequently as part owner. At the close of the war Rev. A. S. Worrell bought it, but after a short connection, resold to W. F. Wells, and Dr. Courtney became editor, with W. E. Paxton associate. At the end of the year 1869 Mr. Wells sold his subscription to Rev. J. R. Graves of the *Memphis Baptist*, and the *Louisiana Baptist* was discontinued.

Louisiana Baptist Convention was organized in 1848. Its leading objects were educational and missionary. Under its fostering care Mount Lebanon University came into existence and other schools were encouraged. Its missionaries have penetrated into many destitute parts of the State, and laid the foundation for numerous churches now flourishing. With an active mission board, inspired by Rev. W. C. Friley, the State evangelist, the work of the Convention has greatly prospered for the last two years. Its operations during the past year secured about $6000.

President, Rev. J. P. Everett, Shiloh, La.; Recording Secretary, Rev. G. W. Hartsfield, Mansfield, La.

Louisiana, Baptist Messenger of, is a weekly paper published at Farmerville, La., Rev. S. C. Lee editor. It started in 1879 as a semi-weekly. It began its second year as a weekly. It is well conducted, and it is rapidly growing in public favor.

Louisville, Baptist Orphans' Home of, was established through the efforts of the ladies of Walnut Street church, in Louisville, in 1866. The building first occupied was a rented one. Soon after the house was opened, however, Mrs. J. Lawrence Smith, a member of the Walnut Street church, donated to the Orphans' Home Society $5000 in money and a lot of ground valued at $15,000, provided a sufficient amount should be raised to erect suitable buildings thereon. The sum of $22,000 was speedily secured, and in March, 1867, the ground was broken for the foundation. The new home was dedicated Dec. 19, 1870. During its existence 280 children have been received; 171

of these have been placed in good homes, 62 have been legally adopted in Christian families, and 41 remain in the home. The object of the home is to receive such orphans as cannot be well provided for otherwise, and to educate and train them for useful employments until such time as suitable homes can be procured for them in private families, or until they are able to take care of themselves. Under the management of Miss Mary Hollingsworth, who has been matron since its organization, the home has been very popular, and has been well sustained by voluntary contributions.

Louisville, Walnut Street Baptist Church of.—The First Baptist church in Louisville was organized by Rev. Henson Hobbs in 1815, and consisted of 14 members. In 1839 the church numbered 539. Eighteen withdrew and formed the Second Baptist church. In 1849, when both churches were without pastors, they invited Rev. Thomas Smith, who accepted both calls on condition that the churches would unite and build a good house in an eligible locality. On Oct. 29, 1849, both churches dissolved and formed the Walnut Street Baptist church, and the present magnificent house was erected the following year on the corner of Fourth and Walnut Streets. The first public meeting held in the finished house was the funeral of the pastor. The edifice cost $105,000. Since its erection it has been altered at considerable expense several times. At one time $20,000 was expended upon it. Its seating capacity is 1300. It is the mother of the other Baptist churches of Louisville,—a goodly family.

Lovelace, Rev. Colmore, was born in Maryland, Nov. 26, 1795. At five years of age his parents removed to Kentucky. At the age of fourteen he united with Mount Moriah Baptist church, in Nelson County. He was licensed to preach at Severn's Valley church, in Hardin County, in 1822, and ordained in 1823. He was pastor of several churches in Salem Association, and devoted much time to the work of a missionary. He was distinguished for his piety, zeal, and philanthropy. Few men were more devotedly loved or more extensively blessed. He baptized more than 1200 persons. He died in Hardin Co., Ky., March 16, 1864.

Lovell, Rev. Andrew Sprague, son of Stephen and Rhoda (French) Lovell, was born in Braintree, Mass., in September, 1807; converted in 1825; studied at Maine Wesleyan Seminary, Kent's Hill, Readfield, Me., at Connecticut Literary Institution, Suffield, Conn., and at Newton Theological Seminary, Mass.; chosen associate principal of the Connecticut Literary Institution in 1837; principal of the city high school in Middletown, Conn., for two years; for a time the editor of *The Ægis*, published in Worcester, Mass.; in 1847 became pastor of the Baptist church in Mansfield, Conn.; ordained in 1848; in 1853 accepted a call to Bloomfield, Conn.; in 1857 settled with the Baptist church in East Longmeadow, Mass.; during the war was an agent for the Christian Commission at Newbern, N. C.; in 1868 settled with the Baptist church in Tariffville, Conn.; now living in Andover, Conn.; very scholarly, calm, penetrating, thorough in thought, elegant in style, eminently sound in the faith; mightier with his pen than with his voice; a poet of unusually delicate taste; a man of great purity and integrity.

Lovell, Rev. N. G., was born in Rowley, now Georgetown, Mass., in 1806. He graduated at Brown University in 1833, and in the following October entered Newton Theological Institution. He was ordained pastor of the Baptist church in Princeton, Mass., in July, 1834. His subsequent settlements were at Amherst, Bellingham, and North Attleborough. Seventeen years of his life were thus devoted to the ministry. His labors were blessed in all his pastorates, especially in that of Bellingham, where there was an interesting revival of religion, followed by large additions to his church. He died at Valley Falls, R. I., Nov. 15, 1851.

Lowry, Gen. M. P., president of Blue Mountain College, Miss., ten years president of Missis-

GEN. M. P. LOWRY.

sippi Baptist Convention, distinguished as an educator, preacher, editor, and as a brigadier-general in the Confederate army, was born in Tennessee in 1828. He began to preach in Mississippi in 1852; supplied the churches at Farmington, Corinth,

WALNUT STREET BAPTIST CHURCH, LOUISVILLE, KY.

Rienzi, Ripley, and other places; in 1861 entered the Confederate service as a captain, was elected colonel, and for gallant conduct was made brigadier-general, and although he refused further promotion, he was often assigned to the command of a division, and served with distinguished ability at Corinth, Perryville, where he was wounded, and in that terrible succession of battles that followed Sherman's advance into Georgia. During the war he preached regularly to the soldiers, and at its close resumed his old field; founded Blue Mountain Female College; contributed two years to *Georgia Index*, and was six years associate editor of the *Memphis Baptist*. He is also a Doctor of Divinity.

Lowry, Rev. Jennings O'Bannon, pastor of Coliseum Place Baptist church, New Orleans, was born in Georgia in 1851, but reared in South Carolina. He took a literary course at Erskine College, S. C. After a course in theology at the Southern Baptist Theological Seminary, he spent some time at Leipsic, Germany; was pastor of St. Francis Street church, Mobile, Ala., five years; called to New Orleans, in December, 1879.

Lowry, Robert, D.D., was born in Philadelphia, Pa., March 12, 1826. His parents were members of the Associate Presbyterian Church. At the age of seventeen he became a subject of divine grace. After reading the New Testament, he was convinced that it was his duty to follow Christ in baptism. He was immersed April 23, 1843, by Dr. George B. Ide, pastor of the First Baptist church, Philadelphia. He began his religious life with Christian work in helping to organize a Sunday-school in a destitute part of the city. For several years he felt an irrepressible drawing towards the ministry, but did not venture to disclose it until his pastor probed his feelings and encouraged him to begin a course of study. In 1848 he entered the university at Lewisburg, Pa., and was graduated in 1854, receiving valedictory honors. In the same year he was ordained, and called to the pastorate of the First Baptist church, West Chester, Pa. Here he remained four years, during which time a new church edifice was built. In 1858 he was called to the Bloomingdale Baptist church, New York City. A movement for a new church edifice was interrupted by the breaking out of the civil war. In 1861 he accepted a call to the Hanson Place Baptist church, Brooklyn, N. Y., where he labored over eight years. During this pastorate about 400 members were added to the church. In 1869 he was induced to accept the professorship of Belles-Lettres in Lewisburg, and the pastorate of the Baptist church. While here the new church edifice was dedicated. After performing this double work for six years, he retired, with the honorary title of D.D., to Plainfield, N. J. He was subsequently elected chancellor of the university.

Shortly after reaching Plainfield a new church was organized, which called him to its pastorship. This movement led to the erection of the Park Avenue church at a cost of $40,000. He has always been an active worker in the Sunday-school. He preaches extemporaneously, and holds tenaciously to the distinctive views of Baptists. Multitudes know him as a composer of sacred song rather than as a preacher. His melodies are sung in every English-speaking land. Some of his hymns have been translated into foreign tongues. Music and hymnology are favorite studies with him. Of five sons, three of whom are living, the oldest has given himself to the work of the ministry.

Loxley, Col. Benjamin, was born in Yorkshire, England, Dec. 20, 1720; came to Philadelphia at the age of sixteen, and served five years at the carpenter's trade. Married first Jane Watkins, sister of his master, and on her death, Catherine Cox, of Upper Freehold, N. J. He had fifteen children. About 1755 he helped to form the 1st Artillery Company of Philadelphia, and went as lieutenant into the service under Gen. Braddock, sharing his defeat at Great Meadows. In 1758, Gen. Forbes appointed him to take charge of the king's stores in the province, which he did for seven years. In 1764 he had command of the artillery which awaited the invasion of the "Paxton boys," of which Mr. Graydon gives an amusing account in his "Reminiscences." He describes Capt. Loxley as a very honest little man, "who was always put foremost when great guns were in question." In 1775, Col. Loxley was on the Committee of Safety for Dock Ward, and served in the Provincial Conference and Convention of the times. Commanded the artillery at Amboy, at Germantown, and was constantly engaged in casting and in supplying various munitions of war. While driven out of Philadelphia by the British, they burned five of his buildings and destroyed other property. Some of his family also served in the army. Col. Loxley was early a member of the First Baptist church, and liberal and conspicuous in erecting its meeting-house at La Grange Place. Among other Baptist houses, public or private, where Whitefield preached in Philadelphia, was Loxley's residence, near 177 South Second Street, then said to be in the country. The front of the house was arched, and there the great preacher addressed thousands on the gentle hill, whose slope afforded a resting-place. The neighborhood was where Cadwallader drilled his "silk-stocking company," some of whom proved doughty warriors in times that tested men's souls. About opposite was the house of William Darrah, whose wife (Lydia) overheard a plot laid by certain British officers, quartered upon them, to surprise Washington at Whitemarsh. She "went to mill" early next morning, and contrived to convey information whereby the danger was averted, the British not knowing why their plans failed. Col. Loxley died in the fall of 1801, aged about eighty-one years, leaving many of his name and blood in Pennsylvania and New Jersey. One, Benjamin R. Loxley, was long a useful home missionary in Philadelphia. Another is wife of Robert Lowry, D.D.

Lucas, Rev. Elijah, was born in Plymouth, England, in December, 1828. When quite a lad he accepted Christ, and united with the Wesleyan Methodists. In the spring of 1850 he came to

REV. ELIJAH LUCAS.

America, and having been for a long time troubled on the subject of baptism, and being convinced that the law of Christ required immersion, he offered himself to the First Baptist church of Troy, N. Y., as a candidate for baptism, and was baptized by Rev. Geo. C. Baldwin, D.D., and some time afterwards that church licensed him to preach. Mr. Lucas always shrank from the work of the ministry, and was at last almost thrust into it by the providence of God.

His first settlement was at Waterford and Half-Moon, in Saratoga Co., N. Y. He served both those churches, preaching three times each Lord's day. After laboring for about two and a half years, he removed in 1855 to Stanford, in Dutchess Co., N. Y. In 1859 he accepted a call from Greenport, and continued there three years. He served the First Baptist church in Harlem, New York City, nine years, after having labored about two and a half years in Hastings, on the Hudson. On returning from Harlem he went to Europe, and on his return he accepted the unanimous call of the First Baptist church of Trenton, N. J., and began his labors there in 1873, and he is still with that church.

Mr. Lucas has baptized a large number at Trenton. His church has over 1000 members, being the largest Baptist church, except the First of Newark, in the State. Mr. Lucas is an able preacher and a devoted servant of the Redeemer.

Luck, Rev. William Francis, was born Nov. 7, 1801, in Campbell Co., Va., in 1827. He removed to Tennessee, and lived there thirty years. In 1857 he located in Lincoln Co., Mo. He professed religion in 1830, and joined the Pleasant Valley church, Tenn. At one time he was missionary of the General Association of Middle Tennessee and North Alabama. He preached until within a few days of his death, and chiefly to four churches. As a preacher, he was bold and impressive. As an evangelist, he was efficient. In Missouri he labored much in revivals. He died Dec. 26, 1878. Rigid in discipline, prompt in reproof, and full of the spirit of Jesus, he commanded the confidence and love of his brethren.

Ludlow, Gen. Edmund, was born at Maiden-Bradley, in Wiltshire, England, in 1620, and educated at Trinity College, Oxford. He was one of the judges that condemned Charles I.; he was a distinguished general in the Parliamentary forces, and for a time at the head of the large English army necessarily kept in Ireland. He was endowed with a penetrating and independent mind; and he could not be moved by fear for the mighty power of Cromwell, or by a desire for the great favors he had to bestow, to change the course he had selected for himself. Ludlow was a decided republican, and when Cromwell assumed the Protectorate, he made a vigorous protest against the step, and gave up his command in Ireland. After the return of Charles II. to England, he went to Vevay, in Switzerland, where he died in 1693. His "Memoirs" are necessary to complete the history of the Parliamentary war in England.

Richard Baxter, speaking of Cromwell, says, "He sent his son Henry into Ireland, who mightily suppress the Anabaptists, . . . so that Maj.-Gen. Ludlow, who headed them in Ireland, was forced to submit."* Ludlow was a Baptist, and worthily he walked in days of danger and temptation.

Ludlow, Rev. James Peter, grandson of Rev. Dr. Stephen Gano, of Rhode Island, was born at Charleston, S. C., Jan. 5, 1833. He was converted at sea, on the whale-ship "Helen Augusta"; baptized at Honolulu, Sandwich Islands, in February,

---
* Baxter's Life, pp. 69, 70.

1853, by the seamen's chaplain, S. C. Damon; the first immersion ever witnessed at Honolulu. He graduated at Rochester, in 1861 from the university, and in 1864 from the theological seminary, and was ordained in 1864 by the Central church, Newport, R. I.

The American Baptist Home Mission Society sent him to San Francisco, Cal., in 1864, at which place he organized, in 1865, the Tabernacle church, and was for six years its successful pastor. In 1872 he was pastor of Calvary church, Sacramento. Failing health induced him to take a sea-voyage around the world. With health restored, he became pastor at Olympia, Washington Territory, where he served with great success. In 1879 he became missionary for Puget Sound, with residence at Seattle. He is deputy clerk of the U. S. District Court of Washington Territory, over which the Hon. Judge Roger S. Greene, his friend, and also a Baptist preacher, presides with marked ability.

Lumpkin, Rev. John, the third of eight brothers, all of whom attained prominent positions, was the son of John and Lucy Lumpkin, who removed from Virginia and settled in Oglethorpe Co., Ga. He was born in Pittsylvania Co., Va., Nov. 4, 1785, but was brought to Georgia in his infancy, and in Oglethorpe County he was reared and educated, and in it he labored and died. He was a Baptist minister of prominence, usefulness, sterling worth, ability, and conscientious rectitude. Gov. Wilson Lumpkin, of Georgia, was his elder brother, and Judge Joseph Henry Lumpkin, chief justice of the Supreme bench, was his younger brother. He united with County-Line church, Morgan Co., in 1808, and was ordained the same year, and immediately was called to the care of churches. During his ministry he constituted the churches at Antioch and Salem, in Oglethorpe County, and Sardis, in Wilkes County; and at the time of his death, Aug. 1, 1839, the buildings of these three churches were draped in mourning.

His life was a shining example of true Christianity. As a preacher, his sermons were more remarkable for their practical bearing than for brilliancy. In his ministerial career he labored diligently and persistently to win souls for Christ; and God blessed his labors wonderfully. By conforming his example to his precepts he made a deep impression upon the community where he lived, and left to his children a spotless name. During his last moments an aged minister stepped in to bid him a final adieu, and said, "Brother Lumpkin, you are now entering Jordan, how do you find it?" "The deeper I wade the firmer the bottom," was the reply.

Lumpkin, Ex-Gov. Wilson, of Georgia, was born in Pittsylvania Co., Va., Jan. 14, 1783, and died at Athens, Ga., on the 28th December, 1870, at the age of eighty-seven.

In 1786 his parents moved to Georgia, bringing with them the infant destined to fill so many conspicuous positions in the State of his adoption. At eighteen years of age his mind became awakened to the great importance of salvation, and he experienced peace through faith. Personal investigation of the Scriptures led to his adoption of Baptist views, although his parents were Methodists, and his predilections were towards the Presbyterians. In the course of time his parents, affected by his baptism, became Baptists themselves, after searching the Scriptures. Subsequently, others of the

EX-GOV. WILSON LUMPKIN.

family followed the parents into the waters of baptism, and in a short period all the adult members of the family united with a Baptist church. "God made me a Baptist," said Gov. Lumpkin to a friend, in after-life, "and I can never be anything else. I must be of this faith, if I am the only person in the world professing it," and to the end of his long life he remained steadfast to his convictions.

Hardly had he attained his twenty-first year before he was elected a member of the Legislature of Georgia, which met in 1804, and he discharged his responsible duties so satisfactorily that he was elected for several consecutive sessions. In 1814 he was chosen to represent his district in the national councils, and took his seat at Washington the same year,—a year memorable for the destruction of the national capital by the British troops.

For several sessions Mr. Lumpkin was returned to Congress, bearing off the prize from all competitors. In 1831 he was so prominent with his party—the old Union party, as it was then termed—that he received the nomination for governor, and his election followed. Having served the State for two years, he was triumphantly re-elected in 1833. On retiring from the gubernatorial chair he received, from Gen. Jackson, an important commission in connection with Indian affairs, after the discharge of which duty he became, in 1838, a United States Senator.

He had now enjoyed all the political honors the State could bestow, and being nearly threescore years of age, he sought retirement; and, purchasing a comfortable home in the vicinity of Athens, Ga., he spent in that locality the remainder of his days. The only public service he afterwards rendered was as a member of the board of trustees of the State University, of which he was the senior member and honored president for many years.

Few men have lived in Georgia more universally popular than Gov. Lumpkin. He never failed to secure any office for which he was a candidate before the people. For forty consecutive years he was retained in positions of high trust and honor, and for a much longer period, if we include his service as trustee of the State University. His popularity was due, in a good degree, to his unswerving fidelity to the trusts he had received. If not a bold and dashing leader, he was a prudent officer, and the people felt that the public interests were safe in his hands. He was always ready to serve his friends at any reasonable sacrifice, whilst towards his political opponents he deported himself with so much courtesy that he was constantly disarming their opposition and winning them to his support.

He was endowed by nature with an active and inquiring mind. He early learned to think for himself, and by this process his fine intellectual gifts were drawn out or educated. There were few subjects of importance connected with the science of government which had not been carefully examined by him, and his opinions were promptly forthcoming whenever required. His official papers while governor, and his speeches while a member of Congress, are able and statesmanlike, evincing a thorough knowledge of the subjects discussed; and they are written with the perspicuity and good sense characteristic of a man who has something to say and is intent only in lodging his meaning in the minds of those whom he addresses.

But it was the elevated moral and religious character dignifying and adorning the life of Gov. Lumpkin which constituted his highest excellence. He was a Christian statesman, not indifferent to the approbation of his fellow-men, but far more anxious for the honor which comes from above. With some honorable exceptions, politicians make poor church members; but Gov. Lumpkin never furled his religious colors for fear it might lose him the votes of those who were of a different religious faith. Whether at his country home, where he first professed faith in Christ, or at Milledgeville, or in Washington City, or Athens, he always took his stand for Christ, identifying himself with his Baptist brethren, however obscure they might be. Assuming nothing on account of the high honors he had received from the State, he took his place among the humblest members of the church, ever counting it a privilege to be even a door-keeper in the house of God. When the work of the Lord was revived, no one rejoiced more than he; and it was a touching sight to see him exhorting the youthful converts to be faithful to their vows, when they presented themselves for church-membership. His silvery locks and tearful eye and tremulous voice emphasized his pious advice with a power and pathos which subdued every heart.

He courted the confidence of his brethren more than the praises of politicians. Late in life he attended a meeting of the Sarepta Association, and, quite unexpectedly to himself, was elected moderator. His heart was touched by the respect thus expressed, and he subsequently remarked that no office which worldly men had conferred ever gave him such pleasure as the confidence thus exhibited by his brethren in calling him to preside over their deliberations. He was a man of great faith and large heart, and with a nature as tender and sensitive as a woman's. Afflictions severe and frequent kept his heart soft. "He had," said one who knew him most intimately, "as much real, heart-breaking, continued trouble as any one I have ever known, yet such was his faith in God that he could rejoice at all times." He was accustomed to say, "I would rather walk in the dark with God than go alone in the light. My dear Lord appoints all my troubles, and I brush away the coming tears when I think that it is his will."

At the time of his death he was probably the oldest Baptist, as he was certainly among the oldest citizens, of the State. He served his generation faithfully, by the will of God, and then fell asleep,—that
"blessed sleep,
From which none ever wakes to weep."

Lung, Rev. A. H., was born in Rush, Susquehanna Co., Pa., Nov. 1, 1826. He received his first lessons at school from Benj. F. Bently, now Judge Bently, of Williamsport, Pa.

At the age of eleven years he found Christ, and was baptized at thirteen by Rev. Davis Dimock, and became a member of the Rush Baptist church.

For two years he taught school. He then became a student in Hartford Academy, in Northeastern Pennsylvania, and after two and a half years was admitted into Lewisburg University, and graduated in 1853. He entered the theological seminary at Rochester, N. Y., and completed his course in the class of 1855.

Acting as a supply, he preached as opportunity offered until May, 1857, when he became pastor of the Baptist church at Canandaigua, N. Y., and was ordained the following August.

Here he labored with marked success until the breaking out of the war. In January, 1862, he was commissioned as chaplain of the 33d Regiment N. Y. Vols. While on the Peninsula, Va., he was attacked with severe illness, and for several days lay in the hospital at Fortress Monroe at the point of death. Recovering, he remained with his regiment until it was mustered out of service, a little before the battle of Gettysburg, after which he resumed his pastorate at Canandaigua. In September, 1864, he was called to the pastorate of the First Baptist church of Germantown, Philadelphia. Here his ministry was signally blessed in the conversion of many souls. In 1866 he laid the corner-stone of the chapel now known as the Second Baptist church of Germantown, and his church dismissed a colony to aid in forming the organization.

In 1867 he was permitted to enjoy the most gracious revival of his whole ministry. In a single year he gave the hand of fellowship to 202 new members, 179 of whom were received by baptism.

In 1868 he planted a mission in Lower Germantown, erected a chapel, and organized a church, which became the Third Baptist church of Germantown.

He became its pastor, and remained with it with much success until June, 1872. In that year he was called to take the pastorate of the Trinity church of Camden, N. J. He is now in his ninth year with this church, which has grown from 90 to about 400 members. Mr. Lung has baptized 712 persons during his ministry.

He is a member of the board of trustees of Lewisburg University and of South Jersey Institute. He is also a member of the board of managers of the New Jersey Baptist Education Society and of the American Baptist Historical Society. He is a diligent worker, a conscientious Christian, and a successful pastor.

Lunsford, Rev. Lewis, was born in the county of Stafford, Va., about the year 1753. He was baptized by the Rev. Wm. Fristoe, and, uniting with the Potomac church, now Hortwood, he began at once to preach. His labors in the Northern Neck of Virginia were greatly blessed, and many were added to the churches which he himself had organized. In the year 1778 he was chosen pastor of the Moratico church, just then constituted, and he continued in that relation until his death, which occurred Oct. 26, 1793. Mr. Lunsford, in many respects, was a remarkable man. His zeal in the work of his Master is seen in the fact that he would sometimes rise from his sick-bed and preach a thrilling sermon to the waiting crowds; also in the fact that he would start on long and wearisome journeys in the most stormy weather to meet either regular or special appointments. His journeyings took him three different times as far as Kentucky, preaching the gospel everywhere, and he was listened to by thronging crowds of anxious and delighted hearers. In his spare hours he was a diligent student, and among his acquirements was quite an accurate knowledge of medicine, which made him specially useful among families to whom he might, otherwise, not have had access. As a man, Lunsford stood among the foremost in his State for consistency of character, amiability of deportment, and an example of all the nobler traits of human nature; while his powers of reasoning, the keenness of his sarcasm, and his undaunted spirit, made him a terror to the wicked. As a preacher, he had but few equals in his day. His presence was commanding; his voice strong and well modulated; his conceptions quick and elevated; and his whole manner attractive in the highest degree. Lunsford, with other Baptists of those days, met with considerable persecution at the hands of the ignorant and the bigoted. He was frequently threatened, sometimes assaulted, and more than once in great danger; but his prudence and perseverance overcame, in a measure, this hostility. Dr. Jeter has said of him, "He was eminently useful, and the churches which he founded have enjoyed a large measure of prosperity.... He would have been distinguished in any age and country;... and, though taken from the field of labor in the vigor of his days, but few have accomplished more than he for the extension of the Redeemer's kingdom."

Lush, The Right Honorable Sir Robert, a lord justice of the English High Court of Appeals, has been for many years a prominent member of the Baptist denomination in England. He was born at Shaftesbury, Wiltshire, Oct. 25, 1807, and was educated in his native town. He was called to the bar in 1840, and practised with success in the Chancery courts, his professional services being held in high esteem by the leading commercial men of the metropolis. In 1857 he obtained the dignity of Queen's counsel, and in 1865 he was elevated to the bench and received the honor of knighthood, to which has since been added the dignity of a Privy Counsellor. Sir Robert Lush married the daughter of the Rev. Christopher Woollacot, many years pastor of the venerable church in Little Wild Street, London, and with that church he was associated until the organization of the Regent's Park church, under Dr. Landels, in 1857. Since that time he has served the church in the office of deacon with zeal and devotion, and has been a ready helper of the pastor in every good work. He has also taken a lively interest in the Missionary Society, and has been for several years one of the treasurers of the Particular Baptist Fund. Several treatises on points of law attest his professional eminence, and he was gazetted in 1878 as one of the members of the Royal Commission appointed to inquire into the provisions of the Draft Code relating to Indictable Offenses.

THE RIGHT HONORABLE SIR ROBERT LUSH.

Luther, John Hill, D.D., was born in Warren, R. I., June 21, 1824. On his mother's side he is of Huguenot origin, while his ancestors on the father's side were among the Welsh emigrants who founded one of the earliest Baptist churches on the American continent, the Rev. Samuel Luther being the second pastor of the Swansea Baptist church. He graduated at Brown University in 1847. Among his classmates were Prof. G. P. Fisher, of Yale College; Dr. J. P. Boyce, of the Southern Baptist Theological Seminary; R. A. Guild, LL.D., of Providence; and Benjamin Thomas, a missionary to Burmah. He graduated at Newton Theological Seminary in 1850; taught three years in Georgia before ordination; was pastor of Blackswamp and Old Pendleton churches, S. C., 1854–58; president of Young Ladies' Seminary in Kansas City, Mo., 1858–61; pastor of Miami church during the war, 1861–65; of Palmyra church, 1865–68; established *The Central Baptist* in St. Louis, Mo., in 1866, and edited it for nine and a half years; pastor of Fee Fee church in St. Louis Co., Mo., the oldest Protestant church west of the Mississippi; pastor of Second Baptist church, Galveston, Texas, one year, ending August, 1878; now president of Baylor Female College, Independence, Texas. His training under Wayland, Sears, and Hackett, his association with Sherwood and Campbell, of Georgia, Johnson and the elder Manly, of South Carolina, have fitted him for extended usefulness. The journals of Louisville and Boston speak of him as a fine rhetorical scholar, a thorough theologian, and an accomplished editor. William Jewell College conferred on him the de-

JOHN HILL LUTHER, D.D.

gree of D.D. He is also a member of the Phi Beta Kappa Society. He is in the prime of his powers.

Luther, Rev. Robert M., was born in Philadelphia, Pa., in 1842. At the age of fifteen he united with the Chambers Presbyterian church, in Philadelphia. For more than two years he continued his connection with this body, and pursued preparatory studies with a view to entering the Christian ministry. In August, 1859, through witnessing a baptism in the Tabernacle church, Philadelphia, administered by Rev. W. T. Brantly, D.D., he was led to be baptized according to the requirements of the Scriptures.

This course involved a temporary separation from his relatives, and gave him a practical experience of the blessedness of putting his whole trust in the Lord, which determined to some extent his after-course.

He was licensed to preach by the Nicetown church of Philadelphia in 1860, and after completing his studies at Princeton, N. J., was ordained April 4, 1864, by a council called by the Nicetown church. About a year previous to this time he had decided to enter the foreign mission field. In May, 1864, having recently married Calista, only daughter of Rev. Dr. J. H. Vinton, our sainted missionary to the Karens, Mr. Luther and his wife sailed for Burmah, and having joined the Rangoon mission to the Karens, they began there the work of educating the future preachers and teachers of the mission. Mr. Luther was chosen president of the Pegu High and Normal School. The mathematical department was committed to Mrs. Luther. The theological class numbered usually about 25 members, and was conducted entirely by Mr. Luther. The vacation of four months was spent in jungle work and in conducting a series of evangelistic labors among the heathen. Having studied medicine, much of the influence attained over the heathen communities was due to Mr. Luther's medical skill, and thus by a combination of labors he and his faithful wife were enabled to do good service for Christ and the church. They were not appointed by any society, preferring to labor independently, and upon the work of the Rangoon mission they expended their entire property. Excessive labor and exposure ruined Mr. Luther's health, and he was carried on board ship in January, 1870, and supposed to be at the point of death. The voyage, however, and the unwearied care of his devoted companion, saved his life, and he landed, after more than six years' absence, in July, 1870, upon his native shores.

He has since been actively engaged in the work of the ministry in this country. He served the Fifth Baptist church of Philadelphia for seven months as stated supply, during which period about 100 were led to Christ, principally from the Sabbath-school. Needing a colder climate in order to control the frequent attacks of the malarial disease contracted in the Burmese jungles, he accepted a call to Bennington, Vt., where he remained for more than nine years, having a very successful pastorate. He resigned his charge at the request of the Executive Committee of the American Baptist Missionary Union, at the same time declining a call from the church at Waltham, Mass., to accept the position of district secretary of the Missionary Union for the Southern District. He entered upon his labors Oct. 1, 1880.

Lyndon, Gov. Jonas, was born in Newport, R. I., March 10, 1704. His relatives were among the honored and respected citizens of his birthplace, and he received in early life a good education. At the age of twenty-six he was chosen clerk of the lower house of the General Assembly, and of the Superior Court of the county of Newport, which offices he held for many years, discharging his duties with great fidelity. The year 1758 is memorable in Rhode Island history, it being the year in which commenced an exciting struggle for the governorship between the friends of Samuel Ward and Stephen Hopkins. Strife raged with great violence until, as we are told, "such was the heart-burning hostility of the belligerent parties as very greatly to impair the enjoyment of domestic tranquillity and interrupt the hospitalities of social life." Success and defeat at different times fell to the lot of the rival candidates, and for ten years the State was the scene of bitter animosity. At last the parties interested seem to have been aware that the time had come to put an end to the quarrel, and amicable arrangements were made for the election of a governor, both Mr. Ward and Mr. Hopkins stepping aside to give place for the introduction of a new name. It is an indication of the esteem in which Jonas Lyndon was held by his fellow-citizens that he was at once selected as a candidate to fill the most important position in the State, and chosen by them to occupy the gubernatorial chair, his term of service commencing May 1, 1768. Gov. Lyndon came into office at a time of great interest in the colonies. Signs of growing hostility to the arbitrary measures of the British government were exhibiting themselves on all hands. In Rhode Island, where there was the declaration of sincere loyalty to the crown, there was no hesitancy in giving utterance to an earnest protest against the infringement of the rights of the citizens. In Bartlett's "Records of the Colony of Rhode Island" we find a lengthy correspondence between Gov. Lyndon and the Earl of Hillsborough touching matters in which the citizens of Rhode Island felt the deepest interest, and a letter also which the governor wrote to the king. In the letter, after giving expression to the most loyal affection for "His Most Excellent Majesty," Gov. Lyndon and the "Company of the English Colony of Rhode Island and Providence Plantations in New England in General Assembly convened, beg leave with great humility to lay before your majesty a representation of our grievances, and to offer our humble supplications for redress." After alluding to the close ties which unite them to the mother-country, and briefly rehearsing the history of the events which led to the establishment of the New England colonies, and dwelling with emphasis on the rights and immunities guaranteed to Rhode Island by the charter of King Charles II., especially the "exclusive right of giving and granting their own money by themselves or by their representatives," the letter of Gov. Lyndon goes on to say, "It is with the greatest concern and grief that your majesty's loyal subjects in this colony find their property given and granted by your majesty's Parliament without their consent. Although we have the highest veneration for that most august body, to whom we cheerfully and readily submit, as to the supreme legislature of the whole empire, in all things consistent with the first and most fundamental rights of nature, yet we humbly conceive that the late acts of Parliament imposing duties and taxes upon your majesty's subjects in America, not for the regulation of commerce merely, but for the express purpose of raising a revenue, thereby giving and granting the property of the Americans, without their consent, to be an infringement of those rights and privileges derived to us from nature, and from the British constitution, and conformed by our charter, and the uninterrupted enjoyment of them for more than a century past." This letter, expressive of the sentiments of the General Assembly of Rhode Island, and signed by its patriotic governor, was accompanied with two others to the Earl of Hillsborough, in which the same views were presented. The three communications were sent to Joseph Sherwood, Esq., the agent of the colony in London, to whom the governor wrote, "By these you will know the sentiments of the General Assembly upon the late acts of Parliament for raising a revenue upon the free inhabitants of the colonies without their consent. They look upon them as incompatible with their rights, and with their existence as a free people; and they have no doubt but that you will exert your utmost endeavors to obtain a repeal of these acts." Those letters to the king and the Earl of Hillsborough produced no change in the policy of the British Parliament. Mr. Sherwood in communicating the circumstances that he had delivered the documents forwarded to his care, writes, "We learned yesterday from one of his majesty's ministers that the legislature is determined not to repeal those acts for the present, but to enforce the execution of them; yet such enforcement is intended to be executed with lenity and mildness if it can; but at all events the execution of those acts will at present be enforced, according to the best information we can get."

The administration of Gov. Lyndon continued but for one year, from May 1, 1768, to May 1, 1769. His declination for another term seems to have been a voluntary act on his part. It may be that he saw that difficulties and dangers were gathering around the colony, and he shrank from the grave responsibilities which might fall upon him as the chief magistrate of the State. His habits of life rather fitted him for the quiet clerical pursuits in which he had so long been engaged. The Hon. J. R. Bartlett speaks of him as "of an amiable and something of a literary character; he had been many years clerk of the Court of Common Pleas for the county of Newport, which place he held undisturbed by either party. He was of mild and inoffensive manners; moderate in politics, as well as in his general deportment. He held the place of governor only one year, when, by his own consent, he left the gubernatorial chair to resume his former office of clerk of the Common Pleas, which place he held until his death."

Although not a communicant, Gov. Lyndon was a warm friend and supporter of the First Baptist church of Newport, and a constant attendant on its worship. In conjunction with another person, Hezekiah Carpenter, he gave the lot on which the church edifice stands, and also a parsonage, which stood on the lot on which the "Perry House" was subsequently built. Upon the occupancy of Newport by the British he removed to Warren, R. I., where he died of smallpox, March 30, 1778.

Lynn, Rev. Benjamin, "the Daniel Boone of the Kentucky pulpit," is known only as the hunter-preacher of Southern Kentucky. The earliest account we have of him is that he was a wandering hunter in the Green River Valley before its settlement. As soon as a few people had settled in stockade forts along the river to which he had given his name, he formed No-Lynn (now called South Fork) church of Separate Baptists, in 1782, according to tradition, in what is now La Rue County. Three years after he gathered Pottingess Creek church, in Nelson County, and a little later Levelwoods church, in La Rue County. His name is connected with the traditions and, in some cases, with the earliest records of the oldest churches located in Southern Kentucky, near the Tennessee line. His name is preserved in No-Lynn (now written Nolin) River, *Lynn* Camp Creek, *Nolin* church, *Lynn* Association, and other localities and religious bodies.

Lyon, Rev. Albert Jonathan, was born in Sturbridge, Mass., July 11, 1848. When he was ten years of age his family removed to Newport, Minn. He was prepared for college by Rev. Dr. Drury. While pursuing his studies he became a Christian, and was baptized by his father, Rev. A. S. Lyon, in June, 1863. One year of his university course was spent in Shurtleff, and the last three in Rochester University, where he graduated in 1871. He entered the Rochester Theological Seminary to prepare for the ministry, and decided to offer himself as a missionary. He sailed from New York Oct. 24, 1877, and arrived at Rangoon December 27. He reached Bhamo Feb. 13, 1878. He was soon attacked by a fever, and died March 15. Thus, on the threshold of life a promising young missionary was cut off. His loss was deeply felt by his companions in Christian labor.

47

M.

MacArthur, Robert Stuart, D.D., was born at Dalesville, Quebec, Canada, July 31, 1841. His parents came from the Highlands of Scotland to Canada. His father is a Presbyterian, but his

ROBERT STUART MACARTHUR, D.D.

mother and other members of the family are Baptists. He was converted at the age of thirteen, and baptized at Dalesville. He was zealous as a church member, and at eighteen began to hold religious meetings and address the people. He prepared for college at the Canadian Literary Institute at Woodstock, Canada; was graduated at the University of Rochester in 1867, taking in the course the Sophomore prize for declamation, and the gold medal for the best written and delivered oration at graduation. He was licensed to preach Sept. 25, 1868; was graduated in the theological seminary at Rochester in 1870. While in the seminary he preached on Sunday evenings at Lake Avenue chapel, which resulted in many conversions and the organization of a church now flourishing.

In June, 1870, he accepted the call of the Calvary Baptist church, on Twenty-third Street, New York, where he has since labored with marked ability and success. He is now one of the leading ministers in that city.

Macgowan, Rev. John, was born in Edinburgh, Scotland, about 1726. He was converted among the Wesleyan Methodists, and by them ordained to the ministry. Discovering the unscriptural character of Arminianism, he left the Methodists and united with the Congregationalists; light continuing to increase upon him, he followed the Saviour in immersion. In July, 1767, he was ordained pastor of the Devonshire Square church, London. He continued in this office till his death, which occurred Nov. 25, 1780.

Mr. Macgowan had a powerful imagination, a clear intellect, and a heart full of love to Jesus.

As an author, he became well known beyond the limits of his own denomination. His "Dialogues of Devils" has passed through a number of editions, and its pages are well known on both sides of the Atlantic; this book deserves a place in the library of every Christian. His other books are "The Shaver, or Priestcraft Defended; a sermon, occasioned by the expulsion of six young gentlemen from the University of Oxford for praying, reading, and expounding the Scriptures; humbly dedicated to Mr. Vice-Chancellor and the Heads of Houses;" "Sermons on the Book of Ruth;" "The Arian and Socinian Monitor."

Mackenzie, Hon. Alexander, ex-prime minister of the Dominion of Canada, was born Jan. 28, 1822, in Logierait, Perthshire, Scotland. In his boyhood he attended the public schools of Moulin, Dunkeld, and Perth; but at the age of fourteen the death of his father made it necessary for him to engage in industrial pursuits. He learned the business of an architect and builder, which he followed for a time in the neighborhood of Irvine, on the coast of Ayrshire. During his stay there he became the subject of saving grace, and united with the Baptist church in Irvine, then under the pastoral care of the late Dr. Leechman. In 1842 he emigrated to Canada, and settled in Sarnia, on the St. Clair River, where he commenced business as a contractor, meeting with well-merited success. This was a period of great political excitement in the Canadian colony, on the subject of Responsible Government. The masses of the people, in opposition to the ruling faction, demanded that public affairs should no longer be managed under the irresponsible control of Downing Street nominees, but that Cabinet ministers should have seats in the Canadian Legislature, and be responsible to the Parliament of Canada for every executive act.

The contest was long and bitter; but at a general election, in 1848, the Reformers were completely victorious, and popular government became firmly established. It was not possible for a man

HON. ALEXANDER MACKENZIE.

of Mr. Mackenzie's strong political convictions and sympathies to stand idly by when such a struggle was in progress. Very shortly after his arrival in the country he espoused the cause of the people, and was soon recognized as one of its most earnest and fearless advocates. In process of time he became the acknowledged editor of the *Lambton Shield*, a Liberal paper, which he conducted for several years in Sarnia with distinguished ability. He was first elected to Parliament in June, 1861, as member for the county of Lambton, of which Sarnia is the county town, and at every succeeding election he has been returned for the same constituency. From the beginning of his parliamentary career he has taken a prominent part in the councils of the nation. He contributed very largely to the success of the scheme of British American confederation, which was accomplished in 1865. In the fall of that year he was offered a seat in the Federal Cabinet, which he declined because he could not approve the commercial policy of the government. In 1871 he was elected to the local Legislature of Ontario, as representative of West Middlesex, and soon after became a member of the Provincial Administration. But finding it inexpedient for a member of the Federal Parliament to busy himself with local legislation, he resigned both seat and office in 1872, and has since given his undivided attention to the politics of the Dominion. Soon after this he became the recognized leader of the Liberal party, and in 1873 he was made prime minister of Canada. For five years he discharged the duties of this exalted position with rare wisdom and fidelity, laying the country of his adoption under a debt of gratitude, which history will not fail to record. In 1875–76 he visited Great Britain, where he was warmly welcomed by Queen Victoria and the leading statesmen of the empire. In Scotland his visit was a series of ovations, men of all ranks and parties uniting to do him honor. He received the "freedom" of several Scotch burghs, and many other marks of popular appreciation; but the order of knighthood, tendered him by her majesty in recognition of his distinguished public services, he felt himself obliged to decline.

Mr. Mackenzie is a man of superior mental culture and of great intellectual power. In private life he manifests the most kindly disposition, without the slightest ostentation or assumption. He is (1881) a member of the Jarvis Street Baptist church, Toronto, Ontario, a trustee of the Toronto Baptist College, and a warm friend to the work of the denomination generally.

Maclaren, Alexander, D.D., was born in Glasgow, Scotland, in 1825. His father was for many years a pastor of the Scotch Baptist church in that city, and was held in high reputation by his brethren as an expositor of the divine Word. On his father's removal to Australia, he attended the ministry of Dr. James Paterson, for forty-six years pastor of the Hope Street Baptist church in Glasgow, and was baptized on May 7, 1840. When not much more than sixteen years of age he was entered at Stepney College, London, as a student for the ministry. He made thorough and honorable progress in all the studies of that seminary, and at the close of the course took the B.A. degree at the London University, with the prize for proficiency in the Hebrew and Greek Scriptures. His first settlement was at Portland chapel, Southampton, where a notable minister, Rev. John Pulsford, had preached for a few years, and a very mixed congregation had been gathered. At the time of Mr. Maclaren's settlement the attendance was small, and for some years few, if any, signs of progress appeared. The young minister was for a time uncertain whether his ministry should be continued, but he persevered in his course, making for himself the reputation of an original and reverent thinker. His peculiar treatment of sacred themes in the pulpit, and his unclerical attire, led some of his neighbors to think he was heterodox. But Mr. Maclaren lived down all suspicion of heterodoxy, and it became evident to all that the town possessed in the young Baptist pastor a public teacher of great gifts. The church was filled, and ultimately crowded. In 1858 he was induced to remove to Manchester, to become pastor of a church founded on similar principles of organization to that at Southampton. Since that time his fame as a preacher and writer has steadily risen. The great mercantile city cherishes his name as one of her choice possessions, while the literary and theological world esteems Dr. Maclaren one of the foremost preachers of the age. By the denomination he is regarded as a tower of strength; his attachment to the distinctive tenets of the body being known to all. He filled the chair of the Baptist Union in 1875, and is a zealous promoter of the missions and other denominational enterprises. He is in great request as a lecturer, but for the most part he gives himself to pulpit and pastoral work. A very large edifice recently built is already too small to accommodate the congregation, and the church is the centre of evangelistic activity. Several editions of his sermons have been published on both sides of the Atlantic. He has also written a little book on Italy, which attracted favorable notice. The Edinburgh University gracefully tendered him the degree of D.D. in 1878, in recognition of his distinguished ability as a theologian and a preacher.

Maclay, Archibald, D.D., was born in Killearn, Scotland, May 14, 1778, and died in New

ARCHIBALD MACLAY, D.D.

York, May 2, 1860. The family removed to Glasgow, where he formed the acquaintance of the learned Christian philanthropist, Robert Haldane. To him he made known his wish to prepare for the ministry, and Mr. Haldane gave him the means to procure an education. In 1802 he commenced preaching as a Congregationalist at Kirkcaldy, in Fifeshire. In 1804 he was appointed a missionary to the East Indies, but the British government interfered and the project was abandoned. Then, through the advice of Mr. Haldane, he sailed for New York; commenced preaching in Rose Street, and soon organized a Congregational church. Three years later his investigations and convictions led him to unite with the Baptists, and the majority of his church in Rose Street followed him.

A Baptist church, now known as the Tabernacle church, was organized, of which he remained pastor until 1837, when he resigned, to become the general agent of the American and Foreign Bible Society. He labored with great success in this work for thirteen years, traveling over all parts of the United States and the British provinces. The Bible Translation Society of England was one of the results of his labors. In 1850 he assisted in organizing, and became the general agent of the American Bible Union, whose main object was the revision of the English Bible. Becoming dissatisfied with its management, he withdrew from it in 1856, and published his reasons for so doing.

One of his addresses in favor of faithful translations was issued in several languages, and more than a hundred thousand copies of it circulated. He was a superior preacher, an able writer, and a successful minister.

Maclay, Hon. William B., son of Archibald Maclay, D.D., was born in New York in 1812. After four years at the University of New York he was graduated with the highest honors of his class in 1836, the valedictory being awarded to him by the faculty. He was immediately elected a member of the council of the university, which position he still holds. He was elected to the Legislature of New York in 1840, 1841, and 1842. He is known as the author of bills which passed the Legislature which greatly improved the facilities of the higher courts in their work, and lessened the expenses of litigation. In 1842 he drafted a bill, which became a law, establishing the present system of public schools of New York, of which he has the honor of being the founder. Mr. Maclay has been five times elected a representative in Congress from his city. With great credit he served on the Committee of Ways and Means, on the Committee on Naval Affairs, and on other important committees. He was prominent in securing a reduction of letter postage, and published his views in *Hunt's Merchants' Magazine*. He had the faculty of stating his opinions on all public questions with clearness and force, and therefore carried his points in State and national legislation. It is admitted by statesmen that he has given the clearest account of our title to Oregon of any man, and put that matter beyond dispute. Since his retirement from Congress he has held no office except that of commissioner of the New York and Brooklyn Bridge Company. He is a member and supporter of the Madison Avenue Baptist congregation.

Maclay, William W., a grandson of Rev. Dr. Archibald Maclay, was born in the city of New York, March 27, 1845. He was graduated from the U. S. Naval Academy in 1863, and was immediately commissioned ensign in the navy. For gallant conduct he was promoted to the grade of master in 1865. He served with Admiral Porter in both bombardments of Fort Fisher, in 1864 and 1865. In 1867 he was commissioned lieutenant, and in 1868 was again promoted, to lieutenant-commander. In the same year he was made fleet-lieutenant and acting fleet-captain in the U. S. Asiatic Squadron. Again, in 1868, he was appointed instructor of mathematics in the Naval Academy at Annapolis. In 1870 he was elected corresponding member of the U. S. Geographical Society, and was awarded the gold medal by the society on practical engineering, and was then appointed an engineer of the dock commission of the city of New York, which position he still holds. His rapid promotion was the result of his peculiar fitness and ability for the service assigned him. His essay was published in a pamphlet of over fifty pages in the "Transactions of the American Society of Civil Engineers," and shows great industry and remarkable talent in that field of labor.

Macon, Hon. Nathaniel, was born in Warren Co., N. C. He was a soldier of the Revolution, and a member of the U. S. Congress for thirty-six years; whom John Randolph, his life-long friend, remembered in his will, describing him as "the wisest man I ever knew;" and whom Jefferson characterized as "the last of the Romans." He was a great reader of the Bible and a staunch Baptist, because the New Testament made him one. While in college at Princeton, N. J., nigh the then seat of war, in 1777, he enlisted in the Continental army for a short term. When the emergency passed he studied law, but when the seat of war was transferred south he again enlisted. Refusing a commission, he served as a private; was at the fall of Charleston and the defeat at Camden, S. C.; retreated with Greene before Cornwallis in Virginia, but saw his surrender at Yorktown; retired from the army only when the preliminary treaty of peace was signed in 1782, and refused all pay during his service and a pension after the war. His ability and integrity led to his choice, while a youth and in the army, in 1780, as a State senator, where he served till 1785. He opposed the payment of the depreciated State currency except at its market value, on the ground that speculators from covetousness had robbed the soldiers in their need. From 1787 to 1789 he opposed the adoption of the U. S. Constitution as giving a power liable to be abused to the oppression of the people. In 1791 he entered the U. S. Congress; was a member of the lower house till 1815, and Speaker from 1801 to 1806, and was then in the U. S. Senate from 1816 to 1828, serving as president *pro tem.* from 1825 to 1827. He steadily declined cabinet positions, twice refusing Jefferson's efforts to secure his services as postmaster-general, and remonstrating when, in 1824, Virginia cast her twenty-four electoral votes for him as Vice-President. In Congress, as in his State, he opposed speculators in the Continental currency. He supported the second war with Great Britain only on the ground that defensive, not offensive, war was justifiable. He voted for the embargo, but against privateering, the increase of the navy, and the building of forts, except for home defense. From the conviction that true philanthropy, as well as patriotism, could not be mercenary, he voted in 1795 against a grant of lands to the Count de Grasse, and in 1824 to the Marquis de La Fayette. When his principles triumphed in the election of Gen. Jackson, he felt that he could withdraw from national affairs. During his long public life, the sagacity as well as integrity of Mr. Macon won the esteem of all parties. Called in 1835 to preside in the convention that revised the constitution of North Carolina, his marked consistency again appeared. He opposed the "freehold" qualification of voters because it fostered a landed aristocracy. An avowed and devout Christian believer, he opposed all religious tests from official candidates, since the conscientious doubter was more reliable than an unscrupulous taker of an oath. The last public position held by Mr. Macon was that of Presidential elector in 1836, when Mr. Van Buren was chosen. To a friend who blamed his independent course, he explained in these memorable words, under date Warren Co., N. C., Oct. 6, 1836, "I think better of the people than most men. I have tried them in every way, and never found them wanting." He was taken sick only a few hours before his death. He had ordered a plain wooden coffin, and had directed that he should be buried on a rocky knoll, where the plow could never find soil to tear, and that a heap of loose stones only should mark his grave. The only memoir of his life, that of Edward R. Cotton, Baltimore, 1840, is out of print. He died June 29, 1837. The *Democratic Review* for October, 1837, Washington, D. C., thus opens its notice: "There is no man in the history of this country who is destined to a higher or a more perpetual fame than Nathaniel Macon of North Carolina." The pupils of Dr. Wayland will imagine his ethical views echoed as by telephone from

Rhode Island to North Carolina. The line of Christian heroes is not broken in this New World.

Madison University, Hamilton, N. Y., overlooks a village of rare beauty and healthfulness. It is near the geographical centre of the State, and near the centre of a new net-work of railways, which give easy communication with every part of the State. In all of its forms it is sixty years old; was opened as a school in 1820; organized as a seminary, college, and academy in 1834; chartered as a university in 1846. As a university, it at once appropriated the patronage, organism, faculty, classes, alumni, and what of property and other resources there then were in the Hamilton Literary and Theological Institution, and thus were united the vigor of a young life with the strength and prestige of the old.

Early patronage was wide-spread,—drawn not from New York only, but from Vermont, Massachusetts, Connecticut, New Jersey, Pennsylvania, Ohio, and Michigan. The body that founded it was at the time energetic and diffusive. It looked to this school with great hope, and on it concentrated its best offerings and fervent prayers. The school was strictly indigenous, springing up from the smallest of beginnings, brought from no foreign land, borrowing its plan from no existing institution. It grew under the pressure of an outward need and the workings of an inward zeal, and became the expression of a denominational sentiment. Free in its blessings to all, it yet acknowledged its chief allegiance to those representative Baptists who founded it.

The times that gave birth to this enterprise were eventful. The second war with England had closed with the Treaty of Ghent, Dec. 24, 1814, and English domination in the colonies had ceased. The country was stimulated by a new sense of freedom, and the American idea of independence and undisputed sovereignty in the Western World was for the first time having full scope. Emigration, with a fuller tide, was flowing west of the Hudson, and carrying New England arts, manners, education, religion, and thrift over this State, and through it into the Western States.

One of these tides moved down the beautiful valley of the Chenango, and towns, villages, schools, and churches sprung up in the valley and on the hill. Baptists had no college in the State of New York, nor had they any schools for common education or for the education of the ministry. But no Convention was called, no general concert of action, no resolutions passed determining when, where, or how. Almost unconsciously a seed was dropped, a prayer was offered,—

> "Sink, little seed, in the earth's black mould,
> Sink in your grave so wet and so cold;
> Earth I throw over you, darkness must cover you,"—

and the seed germinated and grew, almost unobserved, but vigorously.

In 1817 thirteen men met. They gave one dollar each, and these thirteen dollars were the beginning of the endowment. Soon Dr. Baldwin, of Boston, and thirty others gave 238 volumes, and this was the beginning of the library. A room was given in the chamber, and this was the beginning of the college buildings. Two students came in poverty,—Wade and Kincaid,—and these were the beginning of generations of students. True, such beginnings did not seem auspicious. But faith gave them superhuman energy. This energy had push, and this again, vitalized by the idea that Baptists must have an institution that furnished a complete education, gave unexpected development and growth.

The alumni, most of whom have graduated from some one of the courses,—academical, scientific, collegiate, or theological,—number about 2700. The first two students, Rev. Jonathan Wade, D.D., and Rev. Eugenio Kincaid, D.D., and 80 others, went out as foreign missionaries; 21 are counted as presidents of colleges; 88, professors and principals; 63, authors, legislators, and Congressmen. The alumni are found in all the professions, but the largest number are ministers of the gospel; 130 have been honored with the Doctorate from different colleges and universities, and these alumni are found in every quarter of the globe as true representative men. The three schools have graduated about as follows: from the theological seminary, 700; from the college or university, 830; from the academy or grammar school, 1200.

The annual average of students in attendance is about as follows: in the theological seminary, 35; in the college or university, 102; in Colgate Academy, 100. Ladies not counted in. The first class that took the full college course of four years, and graduated in 1836, numbered 26, 9 of whom are still alive, and 8 of these now living have been honored with the Doctorate. This class entered about fifty years ago.

If you inquire after the faculty that has taught this large body of students, you will find that many are gone,—Rev. Nathaniel Kendrick, D.D., Prof. Daniel Hascall, Prof. Seth S. Whitman, Prof. Joel S. Bacon, D.D., Rev. George W. Eaton, D.D., LL.D., Stephen W. Taylor, LL.D., Rev. John S. Maginnis, D.D., John H. Raymond, LL.D., Rev. Edmund Turney, D.D., Prof. John F. Richardson, Ph.D., Rev. David Weston, D.D., Rev. Barnas Sears, D.D.

The following have resigned: Rev. Thomas J. Conant, D.D., Rev. Asahel C. Kendrick, D.D., William Mather, M.D., Rev. George R. Bliss, D.D., Rev. Albert N. Arnold, D.D., Rev. Prof. Ezra S. Gallup, Prof. Wm. I. Knapp, Prof. Edward Judson, Prof. A. S. Bickmore, Ph.D.

EAST COLLEGE.

WEST COLLEGE.

ALUMNI HALL.

MADISON UNIVERSITY, HAMILTON, N. Y.

The following are the present faculty: Rev. E. Dodge, D.D., LL.D., Professor of Metaphysics and Theology and Præses; Rev. P. B. Spear, D.D., Professor of Hebrew and Latin Emeritus; Rev. A. M. Beebee, D.D., Professor of Logic and Homiletics; Rev. H. Harvey, D.D., Professor of New Testament Exegesis and Pastoral Theology; L. M. Osborn, LL.D., Professor of Natural Sciences; N. L. Andrews, Ph.D., Professor of Greek Language and Literature; J. J. Lewis, A.M., Professor of History, Literature, and Oratory; J. M. Taylor, A.M., Professor of Mathematics; O. Howes, A.M., Professor of Latin and Modern Languages; Rev. W. H. Maynard, D.D., Professor of Moral Philosophy and Ecclesiastical History; Rev. W. R. Brooks, D.D., Lecturer on Natural History; Rev. S. Burnham, A.M., Professor of Hebrew and Old Testament Exegesis; Rev. F. W. Towle, A.M., Professor of Greek Language and Principal of the Colgate Academy; E. P. Sisson, B.P., Professor of Mathematics; J. W. Ford, A.M., Professor of Latin Language; Geo. H. Coffin, Professor of English and Natural Sciences.

The four Presidents.—There have been four presidents. Dr. Nathaniel Kendrick, the first, died Sept. 11, 1848, from a fall and lesion of the spine, being seventy-two years old. He was elected in 1836, but was virtually president during the twenty-eight years of his connection with the institution. He was tall, six feet four, well proportioned, of large brain, lofty forehead, and benevolent expression. He was easily *primus inter pares*, and, of natural right, presided everywhere. His influence was as far-reaching as his name. He had a clear voice, an earnest look, and was truly eloquent. He is well described by B. F. Taylor, the "Jubilee" poet,—

> "I see Kendrick's grand form towering up like a king's,
> I hear accents at first like the waving of wings;
> Now he warms with his theme into true welding weather,
> And the word and the blow are delivered together.
> The thought and the thinker are all in a glow,
> The glasses he whirls from his dome of a brow.
> His words that were halting grow freer and bolder,
> And he strikes for the truth straight out from the shoulder.
> It is Gabriel's trumpet and Gideon's sword,
> 'Tis the pillar of fire and the breath of the Lord;
> It is crash after crash with the tables of stone,
> 'Tis the thrill of the thunder, the dread of the throne.
> Then softer and sweeter his cadences grow;
> It was Sinai before, it is Calvary now."

Standing by Dr. Kendrick is Rev. Prof. Daniel Hascall, who came to Hamilton in 1812, and settled as the pastor of the Baptist church. To him is accredited the original idea of a seminary in Hamilton. Dr. Kendrick, in 1816, became pastor of the church at Eaton. These two men supplemented each other, and harmonized in every good work. In 1820, when the "school" was opened, Hascall became Professor of Languages, and Kendrick of Theology. Hascall continued eighteen years and resigned. Kendrick remained till his death.

Around these men rallied other stalwart men, pioneers in the forest, in the churches, and in great enterprises,—Hon. Jonathan Olmsted, Judge Samuel Payne, Deacon William Colgate, Hon. Seneca B. Burchard, Judge James Edmunds, and others,—men ready at all times for great sacrifices and great achievements.

In 1851, Prof. Stephen W. Taylor, LL.D., was elected second president. He was graduated at Hamilton College; had made teaching his life-work; had been from 1834 to 1836 professor or principal of the academy at this institution; had in the mean time founded the university at Lewisburg, Pa., and, after the settlement of the question of removal, returned to Hamilton. He was of the English type, square, strong built, methodical, firm of purpose, a good organizer, and strong executive officer. He was connected with the university in different departments of instruction for eighteen years, and left his mark on its history. He died of disease of the spine, Jan. 7, 1856, at the age of sixty-five.

In 1856, Rev. George W. Eaton, D.D., LL.D., was elected the third president. In mind and body he was cast in a large mould. His features symmetrical, movements graceful, sympathies large, of good nature, in satire powerful, his language felicitous. He was a natural orator. In memory, imagination, and description he was masterly. A scene once before him, he could reproduce with all the freshness and vividness of the reality. His religious emotions and convictions were strong, and constituted the underlying current of his life. He was connected with the university in different capacities—as Professor of Mathematics, of History, of Philosophy, of Theology, and as president—for forty years, and died Aug. 3, 1872, at sixty-eight years of age.

The fourth president is Rev. Ebenezer Dodge, D.D., LL.D., elected in 1868. He has been connected with the university twenty-seven years as Professor of the Evidences of Christianity, of Metaphysics, of Biblical Interpretation, of Theology, and as president. He was graduated from Brown University and Newton Theological Seminary, and has earned a reputation as scholar, teacher, and author that places him among the best thinkers of the age.

The present faculty are well known among the educators of our country. Some who have left us deserve mention. Dr. Barnas Sears, the secretary of the Peabody Fund and former president of Brown; Dr. Thomas J. Conant, a well-known exegete and translator; Dr. A. C. Kendrick, a Greek scholar and author, have helped to make this university. Then the writer's room-mate and classmate and colleagues in the faculty, Dr. John H. Raymond and Prof. J. F. Richardson, the one president of Vassar and the other Professor of Latin in Rochester, now both departed, have been free to acknowledge their indebtedness chiefly to this university for their success in life's work, and to accept the credit in turn given for their hand in this enterprise. What the university has done for them it can do for all the loyal.

Financial Condition.—The finances of themselves would make a history, for these are the rock-bottom on which human endeavor builds. It should be noticed that since 1846 two corporations have a hand in this enterprise. The Baptist Education Society for twenty-seven years had the sole responsibility and management. For the last thirty-three years the Madison University has had the same in all except the nomination of theological professors and the support of needy young men for the ministry. All the salaries and running expenses of these three schools fall upon the Madison University. The annual income needed for this corporation is now about $40,000, the salaries alone being $30,000.

It were vain to attempt a history of the night and day struggles, of men who have had to dig a channel and create a depth of current sufficient to float this great enterprise. It were as easy to tell of the hidden forces of nature which underlie all her operations. Only results are known or seen.

When the university was chartered it had no property. It had none in 1850 on the adjustment of the removal controversy. It had only about $52,000 in 1864 when the war closed. Without a hired agency, the most quiet and energetic measures were prosecuted to fill the treasury. The old policy of borrowing and paying was set aside, and the university put upon the most rigid cash system. For seventeen years, without debt or outside assistance, except from liberal donors, the university has each year balanced its accounts, drawing nothing from endowment funds. No pledges were counted or even reported till they were turned into cash or its equivalent. The progress has not been rapid, but of steady growth. In round numbers: in 1864, $62,000; in 1865, $121,000; in 1868, $177,000; in 1870, $255,000; in 1874, $304,000; in 1876, $405,000; in 1880, $430,000, for endowment, without debt.

Then the unproductive property, buildings, grounds, library, museum, apparatus, president's house, which have come of gifts within the last sixteen years, amount to $120,000 more, making the whole sum raised since the war $550,000. These figures are independent of the Education Society's accounts of scholarships, beneficiaries, and agencies. Deacon Alva Pierce has been treasurer of the Baptist Educational Society of New York for the last forty-three years, and P. B. Spear treasurer of Madison University for the last seventeen years.

This university has acted directly and indirectly on the schools and systems of instruction in our country to stimulate the standard for higher attainments. It has acted on its own denomination to lift it to a higher plane of moral power. It has given origin to three other universities of similar type, and has co-operated with like institutions to mould the national mind and to give Americans an enviable name among the nations of the earth.

To the above account of the financial prosperity must be added a gift of $50,000, one-half to go to Colgate Academy, given at Commencement in 1880 by Mr. James B. Colgate, of New York, as a thank-offering for his rescue at sea in the winter of 1879–80. See also articles HAMILTON THEOLOGICAL SEMINARY, COLGATE ACADEMY, and the biographical articles of persons alluded to in this sketch. For a full history, see also the historical discourse of President Eaton in Jubilee volume, or "First Half-Century of Madison University."

Magazine, Massachusetts Baptist Missionary, has the honor of being the first periodical publication by the Baptists of this country. It was established by the Massachusetts Baptist Missionary Society in September, 1803. The society was organized somewhat more than a year before its executive officers announced a periodical which was felt to be necessary as a medium of communication with the churches, to awaken interest in the cause of missions, and to give publicity to the reports and letters of the missionaries in their employ in different sections of the country. Only two numbers, of thirty-two pages each, were issued the first year, and two the second year. The twelfth number of the volume was published Jan. 1, 1808. The second volume was completed in the next two years. The issues were somewhat irregular until a new series was commenced in 1817, the numbers being issued in alternate months till the close of 1824. Since that time it has been published each month down to the present time. The area of its operations was enlarged in 1826, after the removal of the Foreign Mission Board to Boston, and it became the organ of the Triennial Convention, and when the Missionary Union was formed it held the same relation to the new society. Until the close of 1835 the contents of the magazine were of quite a miscellaneous character, being largely biographies of distinguished ministers and laymen, not always Baptists, but persons of note in the other denominations, essays on literary subjects, reviews, letters, journals, etc. From the commencement of 1836 down to this date it is devoted to the publication of articles bearing directly or indirectly on the cause of foreign missions. As the organ of communication between the missionaries and the churches it has rendered invaluable service to the noble cause which it advocates. It is not easy for us to appreciate the eagerness with which in thousands of Baptist families the letters and journals of Boardman and Judson, in the earlier history of foreign missions, and those of Wade and Kincaid, and Dean and Bixby, and very many others in later times, have been read, and what an impulse has been given by their perusal to the great work of evangelizing the nations of the earth. Steady improvement in the magazine has been the aim of its editors. It may safely be said to take a high rank among the class of publications of which it is so good a representative, comparing favorably with the organ of the American Board of Commissioners for Foreign Missions, the *Missionary Herald.*

Magazine, The Baptist.—Our English brethren were occasionally troubled by their relations with *The Evangelical Magazine.* The profits of that publication were to be divided among the widows of Congregational and Baptist ministers. And it was sometimes unkindly hinted that Baptist widows needing its aid were more numerous than those of Independent ministers. Besides, our English brethren felt a crying need for a magazine to spread the tidings of their missions fully before their churches, and to discuss many denominational questions. *The Baptist Magazine* was established in 1809, and it has rendered immense service to our British brethren and to the cause of truth.

Magazine, The Baptist Family.—This pictorial monthly is published in Philadelphia, Pa. J. Eugene Reed, Esq., is editor and proprietor. Its contents include tales, biographical sketches, notes of travel, essays, poems, and editorials. It devotes special attention to the following departments: the young folks, literature, popular science, health in the home, music and art notes, farm and kitchen, and church and ministerial record. The pictures are numerous and well chosen. The editor is one of the most talented young men in the denomination, he is an earnest Baptist, and his magazine is full of interest and instruction. The young and the old read it with delight and profit.

Magee, Rev. John, son of Rev. Thomas Magee, was born in Cork, Ireland, but converted and baptized in St. Stephen, New Brunswick; studied at the Baptist Seminary, Fredericton; was ordained pastor of the Baptist church, Mangerville, New Brunswick, in 1840; was pastor at Macknaquack and Nashwaak, and performed much missionary work. Died Dec. 23, 1861, after a useful ministry of twenty years.

Magee, Rev. Thomas, was born in Ireland; converted and baptized in the city of Cork; ordained in New Brunswick, March, 1831; labored as an evangelist extensively, not only in New Brunswick, but also in the State of Maine. He served the Baptist denomination in a faithful ministry of over twenty years.

Maginnis, John Sharp, D.D., was born of Scotch-Irish parents, in Butler Co., Pa., June 13, 1805. He was brought up a Presbyterian. He was converted young, in Vernon, O., and united with the Baptist church in that place. He received his literary and theological training in Waterville College, Brown University, and Newton Theological Seminary. In October, 1832, he was ordained pastor of the Baptist church of Portland, Me., and soon the community had such an increase that a second church was established. In 1838 he accepted the professorship of Biblical Theology in the institution at Hamilton. In this position he continued with great usefulness until he accepted the chair of Biblical and Pastoral Theology in the new seminary connected with the University of Rochester, and the professorship of Intellectual and Moral Philosophy in the university at the same time. He died Oct. 15, 1852.

In 1844 he received the degree of Doctor of Divinity from Brown University.

Dr. Maginnis was a vigorous Calvinist, and his students went forth with Paul's doctrines enshrined in their hearts or living in their minds to confound the Arminianism which they brought to the seminary, and which prejudice would not permit them to renounce.

He was a man of very extensive and varied learning, often reaching into the distant Christian past, so largely given up to Romanists and Anglicans. He had a powerful and penetrating, as well as a highly-cultured mind. He had not many equals in his day, and very few superiors, as an acute reasoner. While not offensive in his independence, he was unbending when truth required it, or wisdom seemed to demand it.

He was a devout Christian in the minute as well as in the grandest relations of the soul. The churches lost a noble leader and heaven gained a mighty soul when John Sharp Maginnis left his frail body for the skies.

Magoon, Elias Lyman, D.D., was born in Lebanon, N. H., Oct. 20, 1810. His grandfather was a Baptist minister, and a participator in the scenes of the Revolution; his father an architect, who enjoyed considerable success in his profession and endured protracted sickness.

At sixteen years of age young Magoon was apprenticed to the bricklayer's trade, which he followed to his twentieth year, and by the use of his trowel during his vacations, and in the intervals of study, supported himself through ten years of preparatory studies at New Hampton Academy, Waterville College, and Newton Theological Institution.

He was ordained the night after graduating, in 1839, and he immediately settled at Richmond, Va., as pastor of the Second Baptist church, where he remained six years. A beautiful new edifice was

ELIAS LYMAN MAGOON, D.D.

erected, and all was prosperous until the division arose in the denomination on the question of slavery, which took place while the young pastor was in Europe.

Returning speedily, he quietly resigned, and was at once called to the Ninth Street Baptist church, Cincinnati, but remained in Richmond until a successor was procured. He served in Cincinnati four years, and in 1849 removed to New York, as pastor of the Oliver Street Baptist church. In 1857 he took charge of the First Baptist church in Albany, where he remained ten years, and from it removed to the Broad Street Baptist church, Philadelphia, where he still labors.

Rarely sick, this busy preacher has not been out of employment a single Sunday for forty years. His large and liberal congregation have just celebrated his seventieth birthday with unanimous congratulations, and both leader and people seem never to have been under more favorable auspices than now.

The usual honors of A.B. and A.M. were conferred at Waterville, now Colby University; and, in 1853, Rochester University added the D.D.

Dr. Magoon's published works are "Orators of the American Revolution" (New York, 1848); "Living Orators in America" (New York, 1849); "Proverbs for the People" (Boston, 1848); "Republican Christianity" (Boston, 1849); and "Westward Empire" (New York, 1856). In their day many of these books were sold, but now are out of print.

Dr. Magoon possesses extensive culture, manly independence, a large heart, an unsullied record, and the warm love of throngs in and out of Philadelphia. His ministry has been greatly blessed, and his name is favorably known all over the land.

Main, A. H., is a native of Plainfield, Otsego Co., N. Y., where he was born June 22, 1824. His parents were Alfred and Semantha Main. His father removed from Connecticut to New York in his youth, and thence, in 1846, to Dane Co., Wis., which has since been the family home. Mr. Main was educated in the common schools of New York. He engaged in mercantile business, and continued it after his removal to Madison, Wis., in 1856, until 1860. That year he became cashier of the Sun Prairie Bank, which position he held until he closed the business, in 1863. For many years Mr. Main has been at the head of one of the largest insurance offices in Madison, and in fact in the Northwest.

When quite young he united with the Baptist church. He is well known by the denomination in the State, and in his own Association, as well as in the State work, he has borne a generous and active part. In his own church at Madison he is a trusted leader; and in the Christian and philanthropic enterprises of the city he is one of the most able and earnest workers.

Maine Baptists.—The oldest incorporated town in what is now the State of Maine was Kittery. The presence of Baptist sentiments was recognized not far from the year 1681. A few Baptists were among the earlier settlers of this place. Among the more prominent of these was William Screven, who suffered no small amount of persecution from the "standing order" on account of his persistent adherence to Baptist principles. A church was formed in 1682, but in less than a year it was broken up and its members scattered. From the dissolution of the church in Kittery, a period of eighty-five years elapsed before the appearance of any other organized body of Baptists. In 1768 a church was formed in Berwick from persons converted under the preaching of Rev. Dr. Hezekiah Smith. That church lived through all the fiery trials of persecution, and is to-day the flourishing church of South Berwick. In a few years other churches were formed. As the district of Maine was settled, Baptist principles everywhere spread and new churches were organized. In the State there are now 13 Associations, embracing 261 churches, with a membership of nearly 21,000 persons.

The Maine Baptist Convention was formed in 1824. Its officers are: President, Rev. H. E.

Robins, D.D.; Vice-President, Rev. S. L. B. Chase; Recording Secretary, Rev. H. S. Burrage; Corresponding Secretary, J. Ricker, D.D. Its permanent invested funds are $9700, and its income from all sources as reported at its last meeting $8400.91.

The Maine Baptist Charitable Society has for its object to contribute to the wants of indigent ministers and to the needy families of deceased ministers. The president is P. Bonney, Esq.

The Maine Baptist Education Society furnishes aid to young men in a course of preparation for the Christian ministry. Its funds amount to nearly $3000. The president of the society is Rev. J. McWhinnie.

The Baptists of Maine constitute one of the strongest and most efficient denominational bodies in the country. Their college, Colby University, with the three academic institutions having a vital connection with it, the Waterville Classical Institute, Hebron Academy, and Hootton Academy, furnish the best facilities for the higher education of the young. An able ministry is guiding and moulding the churches. The spirit of benevolence pervades these churches, and they will compare favorably with other churches in their contributions to all good causes. Every year marks progress and religious enterprise. The Baptists of Maine have no reason to be ashamed of their past record, or of the position which they now hold among the other religious communities of the State.

Major, Samuel C., a deacon of the Fayette church, was born in Franklin Co., Aug. 26, 1805. In 1826 he removed to Fayette Co., Mo. Seven of eleven children survive him. One of them is Hon. Samuel C. Major, Jr. In 1832, Mr. Major was elected a justice of the peace, and held the office for thirteen years. In 1840 he was appointed public administrator. At different times he was mayor of the city of Fayette. He was alive to the public good and to religious interests.

In 1843 he made a profession of faith in Christ, and united with the Fayette Baptist church. He was for years the efficient president of the executive board of the General Association of Missouri. He left for his family the rich legacy of a well-spent life, whose characteristics were unfeigned modesty, strict integrity, genuine friendship, and devoted piety. He died March 13, 1880, aged seventy-five years.

Malcom, Howard, D.D., LL.D., was born in Philadelphia, Pa., Jan. 19, 1799. His father was of Scotch descent, and his mother a lineal descendant of Hugh Roberts, a distinguished Welsh Friend preacher, who was on terms of intimacy with Wm. Penn. Howard's father died at the age of twenty-three, in 1801, leaving his wife and child to the care of her father, John Howard, a retired merchant. This grandfather died when Howard was nine years of age, and Mrs. Malcom devoted herself to the education of her only child. In 1813 he was placed at school in Burlington, N. J., to be prepared for college, and in September, 1814, he

HOWARD MALCOM, D.D., LL.D.

entered Dickinson College, at the age of fifteen. Most of the students here were insubordinate, and a serious difficulty between students and professors terminated, in April, 1815, in the closing of the institution. In 1815, Howard entered a counting-house to prepare for the life of a merchant, which had long been his ambition. While here, he says in his diary, August, 1815, "I have for some time past been tormented with the fear of dying," the first indication of an awakened conscience. In December an accident to his knee confined him to his room for three weeks, and he says, "This was one of the most merciful providences of God to me. The pain was not so great as to prevent my reading. . . . I learnt more about the Bible than I knew before altogether." On January 1, 1816, he related his experience before the Sansom Street Baptist church, and on the 16th of January this entry appears in his diary, "Have been much disturbed lately with an idea that intrudes itself upon all occasions, viz., that I must shortly quit the counting-house and prepare to go out and proclaim the glad tidings." . . . He was licensed to preach in 1818; entered Princeton Seminary soon after, where he remained until 1820. During these formative years, from 1816 to 1820, young Malcom's experiences, as given copiously in his diary, were most deep and interesting, and characterized by a singular maturity of thought and independence of action. But space here only permits a very brief sketch. He was ordained in April, 1820, was married to Miss Lydia Sheilds May 1, 1820, and in the same month became pastor of the Baptist church at Hudson, N. Y. Here he remained until 1826, when he became first general agent of the American Sunday-School Union. In this capacity he spent nearly two years, and visited all the principal cities of the country in establishing auxiliary societies and local depositories, in raising funds, and in the performance of the varied duties of this responsible mission. In November, 1827, Mr. Malcom became pastor of Federal Street church in Boston. His success with this church was very great. He was also a member of various boards and societies, and he delivered a great many lectures. He was the author, in 1828, of his "Bible Dictionary," which was immensely popular, reaching a circulation of over 200,000 copies, and it is still sold. He also prepared for the press a work on the "Extent of the Atonement," and one on "The Christian Rule of Marriage," both of which had a large sale. He edited "Law's Call," Henry's "Communicant's Companion," and Thomas à Kempis's "Imitation of Christ." Under these labors his health gave way, and in 1831 he spent eight months with his wife in visiting the countries of Europe. In December, 1833, his beloved wife died. In 1835, Mr. Malcom was obliged to resign his pastorate because his voice failed him, and in September, having been chosen to visit foreign missionary stations by the Triennial Convention in Boston, he sailed for Burmah, remaining two and a half years. The issue of this important journey was in the missionary field a cementing and unifying of the labors of our missionaries, and in this country, upon his return, the result was a general increase of interest and contributions for missionary purposes. These were accomplished by his numerous lectures in different parts of the country, and the publication of "Malcom's Travels," a work of 600 pages, which at once became a standard both in this country and Great Britain. Upon his return he could not resume his pastorate, as his voice had not been restored. In 1838 he married Miss Anne R. Dyer, of Boston, and in 1840 he was simultaneously elected to the presidency of Shurtleff College, Ill., and Georgetown College, Ky. He accepted the latter early in 1840. Under his fostering care and indomitable industry the institution received a great impulse. In 1842 he received from Dickinson College the degree of A.M., and the degree of D.D. at the same time from the University of Vermont and Union College, New York. In 1849 he resigned the presidency of Georgetown College, and within a few weeks was called to the pastorate of the Sansom Street church, Philadelphia, and again to the presidency of Shurtleff College. He accepted the former. This church of his youth was not long permitted to have the benefit of his labors, for in 1851 he became the president of the university at Lewisburg, Pa. About this time he edited "Butler's Analogy," with a very full conspectus, which is now used largely as a text-book. After six years of successful labor for the university, Dr. Malcom resigned to complete his "Index to Religious Literature," which was published in 1869. During these years he became deeply interested in building up the American Baptist Historical Society, and to this noble work he was devoted to the end of his life. He was for many years the president of this society, as well as of the American Peace Society, senior vice-president of the Pennsylvania Colonization Society, and was one of the founders of the American Tract Society. In 1878 he sustained a severe trial in the loss of his esteemed and beloved wife, and from this time all his powers rapidly failed, and he died in Philadelphia in March, 1879, in the eighty-first year of his age, a member of the church in which he was converted, baptized, licensed, and ordained. A noble eulogy was pronounced by one in the expressive words, "It would be difficult to name any good cause to which his heart had not been given."

Mallary, Charles Dutton, D.D., was born in West Poultney, Vt., Jan. 23, 1801, and died July 31, 1864. He graduated with the first honor at Middlebury College, Vt., in August, 1817; was baptized and joined the church in 1822; and the same year moved to South Carolina, where he was ordained in 1824, at Columbia. There he married Miss Susan Mary Evans, granddaughter of Rev. Edmund Botsford. In 1830 he removed to Augusta, Ga., and took charge of the Augusta Baptist church. Four years afterwards he became pastor of the church at Milledgeville, but resigned to become the agent for Mercer University, in 1837, laboring as such for three years, when he began a life of evangelistic and pastoral labors for various churches in Middle and Western Georgia, which continued until 1852, when he retired to his farm, near Albany, where he resided, in feeble health, until his death, in 1864. In 1840 he married his second wife, Mrs. Mary E. Welch, a lady of superior worth and talents, who preceded him to the skies by two years.

Dr. Mallary was a man of most uncommon piety, and exerted a more wholesome influence than any other man of the denomination in the State. No other stood higher in the esteem of the brethren; nor did any other of his day, in the truest sense, do more for the cause of God and the denomination in the State. Dawson was a more brilliant orator, and Crawford was more learned and scholarly, but neither surpassed him in the highest and best characteristics, as a preacher. He had clear views of divine truth, and a deep experience of its sanctifying power in the heart. His voice was commanding; his elocution distinct and forcible; his

CHARLES DUTTON MALLARY, D.D.

imagination splendid; his language chaste, and his address affectionate and persuasive. While eminently pure and clear, his style was often ornate, and sometimes arose to sublimity. He loved to preach Christ crucified as the only foundation of a sinner's hope, and to exhibit a sovereign God, working all things after the counsel of his own will. These high themes he discussed with a clear head and a warm heart, and rendered them eminently practical by the manner in which he pressed them on the consciences of his hearers. Thoroughly instructed in the Scriptures, profoundly conversant with the workings of experimental religion, and knowing well "the windings and doublings" of man's deceitful heart, he was exactly fitted to take it captive with the sweet influences of revealed truth.

He had the happy talent of introducing religious subjects in his conversation with others, and of directing their attention to the great interests of eternity. To those who knew him intimately his conversation was simply delightful, for a spirit of piety pervaded almost every sentence of his discourse; and the power of a well-cultivated mind added interest and instruction to the other charms of his conversation. In all that he did and said his profound spirituality shone conspicuously as the distinguishing feature of his character. If any man ever had the full assurance of hope it was he, for his faith in God seemed to know no misgiving. His chief joy was in the worship of God, and scarcely any possible contingency was permitted to interrupt his family and private devotions. At the domestic altar and in the closet he held sweet communion with the Father of spirits, and came forth to his public ministrations and religious efforts richly imbued with the spirit of his divine Master. Everywhere he exhibited a beautiful consistency of Christian character. He maintained always a close walk with God. His aim in life was to promote the glory of God and the good of mankind. Every personal interest was subordinated to this sublime purpose. No narrow-mindedness checked his expansive charity, for his benevolence embraced the whole human race,—the needy at his own door, and the heathen at the ends of the earth.

His private life was as pure as his sentiments were exalted, and in all his relations with his brethren he was a model of gentleness and unselfish Christian courtesy. He was distinguished for his controlling and peaceful influence in our denominational councils. He was most skillful and prompt to adopt measures in promotion of harmony and efficiency, and, by word and deed, led his brethren onward in the way of truth and righteousness, and in extending the Redeemer's kingdom throughout the world. When money was needed for the interests of the churches and for the spread of the gospel, he was a liberal contributor and a most successful agent in procuring the gifts of others. His example and influence survive in the memory of thousands; the seeds of truth which he has sown are still growing and bringing forth fruit in the lives and hearts of many who heard his voice. Besides these he has left written memorials which will be read with interest and profit for many years to come, among which are his memoirs of Mercer and Botsford, and that most excellent book entitled "Soul Prosperity." While a man of strong convictions and determined purposes, he was as meek and gentle as a lamb. With a will as determined as ever moved a despot, it was so tempered and subdued by grace that it would bear all things, believe all things, hope all things, endure all things. His self-control seemed to be complete; no unkind word or hasty speech, or anything to stain a most consistent and holy life, ever escaped his lips or characterized his actions. He never entered the arena of strife, but would pour oil on the troubled waters, and turn away anger by soft words, and with melting tenderness reprove the erring. So profound was his piety that nothing ever seemed to disturb it. The expression of his countenance when in the pulpit was tender and heavenly. While replete with doctrinal truth, his sermons were full of tenderness and pathos, his greatest strength consisting in what rhetoricians have denominated *unction;* for, as he stood in the pulpit, his audience *felt* that they were in the presence of a man of God. It was this, united to his native good sense, which gave him such influence in religious deliberative assemblies, and secured for him the most profound attention, and rendered his suggestions most likely to meet the approval of his brethren; and it was this, imbuing all his words and actions, which gave him such spiritual power among his brethren, and made him a pillar in the denomination, and which yet gives his memory a fragrance among Georgia Baptists.

Dr. Mallary was a warm advocate of temperance, missionary societies and Sunday-schools, and to the very end of life continued to preach whenever physically able. Though so energetic and laborious during his whole ministry, his services to God and his generation were performed with a feeble body, especially in the last years of his life, when he was subject to frequent attacks of nervous disease, attended with violent pain in the head. His death was peaceful and happy, and his last expression, uttered while gently clapping his hands, was, "Sweet, sweet home!"

Mallary, Hon. Rollin C., was born in Cheshire, Conn., May 27, 1784. Ten years after his birth his parents removed to Poultney, Vt. He was a graduate of Middlebury College, in the class of 1805. He studied law with Horatio Seymour at Middlebury, and Robert Temple at Rutland, and was admitted to the Rutland County bar in March, 1807. He soon became a leading lawyer in the county, and for five years was State attorney. He was elected a member of Congress in 1819, and took his seat in the House of Representatives Jan. 13, 1820. He had several re-elections, and remained a member continuously until his death. He gained a prominent position in Congress, second, perhaps, to no other member from New England in his time, and particularly distinguished himself as a friend and advocate of the "protective system." At the commencement of the Twentieth Congress he was made chairman of the Committee on Manufactures, and reported the tariff of 1828, and his efficient efforts doubtless contributed largely to secure its passage.

Mr. Mallary died at Baltimore, Md., in 1831, while on his return home from Washington.

Maltby, Rev. Clark O., was born in Rutland, N. Y., July 19, 1836; educated at the Normal College at Albany, from which he graduated in 1858. Mr. Maltby devoted a number of years to teaching and mercantile pursuits, in both of which he was very successful. Hearing the call of God to preach the gospel, he entered Rochester Theological Seminary in 1874, and graduated in 1877. Before he completed his course he received the unanimous call of the Baptist church in Madison, Wis., to its pastorate. He entered upon his labors here in the autumn of 1877. The church had been in a very dispirited condition for a number of years. Through Mr. Maltby's pastorate a great change has been effected. The house of worship has been thoroughly repaired, a new organ purchased, a fine congregation gathered, and the future of the church is full of promise. He occupies one of the most important fields in the State,—the capital of the Commonwealth. He is bringing to his work the practical wisdom gained by large experience with men in business relations, mature and finely cultured intellectual powers, and a heart aglow with love for the highest and holiest calling. He has won in his brief ministry the place of a trusted shepherd in his flock, that of a Christian gentleman in the city, and that of a useful and respected minister of Christ throughout the State.

Mangam, William D., was born in Croton, Westchester Co., N. Y.; an uncommon man, with acute, strong, comprehensive mind, and noble, generous impulses; started in the city of New York without capital, and became one of the largest and most successful commission merchants; but lived not for himself; was an unswerving Baptist in his principles; bequeathed to the Clinton Avenue Baptist church of New York City, of which he was a member, a property worth $60,000; was habitually benevolent, and always active and noble.

Manly, Basil, D.D., was born in Chatham Co., N. C., Jan. 25, 1798; baptized Aug. 26, 1816, and licensed to preach in 1818. He graduated at the College of South Carolina, Dec. 3, 1821, with the first honor, when honors were given to such men as Preston, Pettigrew, and O'Neal. He was ordained in 1822. His first settled pastorate was at Edgefield Court-House, S. C., where the savor of his influence is yet felt. In March, 1826, he became pastor of the First Baptist church in Charleston. Seldom has a pastor been so loved by all, saint and sinner, old and young.

After about ten years of most successful labor in Charleston he became president of the State University of Alabama. He was the controlling spirit of the university, and it enjoyed unwonted prosperity for eighteen years under his administration.

In 1855 he returned to Charleston as pastor of the Wentmouth Street church. After four years of fruitful toil, he was again recalled to Alabama as State evangelist, a position for which he was peculiarly fitted, and his labors were abundantly blessed.

He spent the close of his life with his son, Rev. B. Manly, Jr., professor in the Southern Baptist Theological Seminary, at Greenville, S. C. It was a great pleasure to him to see the institution in successful operation for which he had so long labored and prayed. Doubtless he could have adopted the language of Simeon: "Lord, now lettest thou thy servant depart in peace, for mine eyes have seen thy salvation."

BASIL MANLY, D.D.

Dr. Manly was one of the most distinguished ministers with which the Spirit of God ever blessed the Baptist denomination.

Manly, Basil, Jr., D.D., LL.D., son of the distinguished Dr. Basil Manly, of South Carolina, was born in Edgefield District, S. C., Dec. 19, 1825. After attending a preparatory school in Charleston, he became a student at the State University of Alabama, where he graduated in 1843. He then entered Newton Theological Seminary, where he remained for a time, and subsequently graduated at Princeton. He was licensed to preach at Tuscaloosa, Ala., in 1844, where he was ordained in 1848. He preached two years to several country churches in Alabama. In 1850 he accepted a call to the First Baptist church in Richmond, Va. His health failing, in 1854 he superintended the erection of a building, costing $70,000, for the Richmond Female Institute, of which he became principal. In 1859, when the Southern Baptist Theological Seminary was established at Greenville, S. C., he was elected one of its original professors. While the seminary was suspended during the war he preached to several churches in the neighborhood. Upon the re-opening of the seminary he resumed his professorship, in addition to which he collected money for the support of students, by means of which nearly a hundred young men were enabled to attend the institution. In 1871 he accepted the presidency of Georgetown College, which position he occupied until 1879, when he again accepted a professorship in the Southern Baptist Theological Seminary, now located at Louisville, Ky. He is regarded as a man of extensive learning and critical scholarship, and is still more highly esteemed for his "meek and quiet spirit" and his constant devotion to the cause of Christ.

Manly, Rev. C. G., was born in Hamden, Geauga Co., O., Jan. 14, 1834; converted and baptized in 1851. He attended the district school and Burton Academy, and studied at Kalamazoo and Franklin Colleges. He was ordained at Rolling Prairie, Ind., in February, 1865, and was pastor of the church there one year; was missionary colporteur of the Baptist Publication Society for Northern Indiana to Southern Michigan one year; organized the church at Three Oaks, Mich., during this year and became their pastor, and continued with them four years. He came to Kansas in November, 1869, and organized the second Baptist church west of Emporia; assisted in constituting what is now known as the Southwestern Kansas Baptist Association, in October, 1871. He has been pastor of the Augusta church four years. During the fifteen years that he has been in the ministry he has supervised the building of three meeting-houses and the repairing of two. He is a modest, but faithful and efficient pastor.

Manly, Charles, D.D., was the son of Dr. Basil and Sarah M. Manly, May 28, 1837, in Charleston, S. C. He was prepared for college at Tuscaloosa, Ala., in the school of R. Furman, and was graduated from the University of Alabama July 11, 1855; was baptized April 24, 1853; licensed to preach by the Tuscaloosa Baptist church Oct. 2, 1855; was graduated from the Princeton Theological Seminary, N. J., April 29, 1859, and was ordained pastor of the church in Tuscaloosa, Ala., June 19, 1859. Dr. Manly continued in this field of labor until called to the pastorate of the church in Murfreesborough, Tenn., Sept. 24, 1871, whence he removed to Staunton, Va., as pastor of the church there, Oct. 12, 1873. Dr. Manly was connected, either as professor or president, from 1860 to 1873, with the Alabama Female College; and, as president, with Union University, Murfreesborough, Tenn., from September, 1871, to September, 1873. The degree of A.M. was conferred upon him by the University of Alabama in 1859, and the degree of D.D. by William Jewell College in 1872. Dr. Manly has contributed frequently to the *Religious Herald*. In his pastoral labors he has been very successful, and is a polished and vigorous preacher. He is now pastor of the church at Greenville, S. C., where he labors with great acceptance and usefulness.

Manning, Rev. Edward, pre-eminent among

the founders of the Baptist denomination in the Maritime Provinces, was born in 1766, in Ireland; brought up in Falmouth, Nova Scotia; awakened by hearing Henry Alline pray, in 1784; converted April 29, 1789, under the ministry of Rev. John Payzant, and soon began to evangelize; had a revival at Kingsclear, New Brunswick, 1793; ordained Oct. 19, 1795; renouncing Pedobaptism, was immersed, in 1797, in Lower Granville, by Rev. Thomas Handley Chipman; became pastor of the Regular Baptist church, Cornwallis, Nova Scotia, Jan. 27, 1808, and continued in it till his death, Jan. 12, 1851; united in forming the Baptist Association, June 23, 1800; was a firm friend of Horton Academy and Acadia College. Edward Manning possessed a massive and powerful intellect, much firmness, keen penetration, great administrative ability, deep Christian experience; was a profound theologian and a very useful minister of Christ.

Manning, James, D.D.—So identified was the life of James Manning with Brown University that the history of the earlier years of that institution is also the history of his life. He was its first president, we might almost say its founder, and he ceased not from laboring for it till the hand of death interposed. The twenty-six years of his connection with the college were years calling forth the highest administrative and financial ability, the utmost prudence and indomitable perseverance; years always crucial to a young and financially feeble institution, but doubly so by the poverty consequent on the war of the Revolution. How ably he accomplished the arduous task that befell him the high position that Brown University occupies among the colleges of our country sufficiently attests.

James Manning was the son of Isaac and Catherine Manning, and was born at Elizabethtown, N. J., Oct. 22, 1738. About the age of eighteen he went to Hopewell, N. J., to prepare for college, under the instruction of the Rev. Isaac Eaton. In 1758 he entered the College of New Jersey, where he graduated four years later with the highest honors of his class. It was at the beginning of his college course that he made a public profession of his faith, and shortly after his graduation he entered the ministry. His marriage to Margaret Stites occurred in 1763, and a year was spent by him in traveling extensively through the country.

There was a strong feeling among the Baptists of their need of an educated ministry, and the Philadelphia Association, which met in 1762, resolved to attempt the establishment of a denominational college in Rhode Island, and to Mr. Manning was intrusted the carrying out of this object. A charter was obtained from the General Assembly in 1764 authorizing the establishment of the College of Rhode Island.

Mr. Manning then removed to the town of Warren, about ten miles from Providence, where he established a grammar-school, which soon became a flourishing institution. It was removed to Provi-

JAMES MANNING, D.D.

dence in 1770, and is now in existence as the University Grammar-School. A church was organized in Warren the same year,—1764,—and Mr. Manning was called to the pastorate. In 1765 he was formally appointed " President of the College of Rhode Island, and Professor of Languages, and other branches of learning, with full power to act in these capacities at Warren and elsewhere." The college opened at Warren in 1766 with one student. Three others, however, joined within a few days, and at the first commencement—1769—a class of seven was graduated.

In 1767 was formed the Warren Association, comprising at first but four churches, but it soon extended over New England. Mr. Manning was a prominent and useful member of this body, several times being chosen moderator. The Association was of much benefit to the college, giving it material aid and strength.

It was decided in 1770 that the time had come for the erection of a college building, and Providence was selected for the site, the town and county subscribing £4200 as an inducement thereto. The officers and under-graduates accordingly removed from Warren to Providence, and during the course of the year University Hall was erected. Mr. Manning having resigned the pastorate of the Warren church, and the pastor of the First Baptist church of Providence being desirous of retiring from the duties of his office, that church invited President Manning to preach for them, and in 1771 called him to be their pastor. His power in the pulpit was great, and during his pastorate the church was much blessed. Many additions were made to its membership, and several revivals were experienced, that of 1774 resulting in 104 conversions. The increased prosperity and membership of the church under Mr. Manning's charge made necessary the erection of a new house of worship. With the view also of holding there the commencement exercises of the college, the church was designed and made to be the largest and finest church edifice of the denomination in the colonies.

President Manning continued his arduous and multifarious duties as president, professor, and pastor till the breaking out of the war of the Revolution. The college had been growing in reputation and usefulness, and was fast attaining that high position and influence it now occupies. But the capture of the town by the British forces necessitated the closing of the college, the building being occupied by them as barracks. After their departure it was used as a hospital by the American and French forces, and not till 1782 was the course of instruction permanently resumed. Meanwhile, President Manning occupied himself with his pastoral labors, and efforts for the amelioration of the distress so prevalent during that period.

In 1786, President Manning was chosen by the General Assembly to represent Rhode Island in the Confederation of the States. He was induced to accept the position in the hope of gaining from Congress an appropriation for the use made of the college by the allied forces during the struggle for independence. He was granted leave of absence by the college and church from March until September, when he returned and resumed his duties.

The articles of the Confederation of the States proving inadequate for the purpose designed, a union upon a new basis was proposed. Our national Constitution, framed at Philadelphia in 1787, was adopted by a few of the States with serious opposition, but in some of them, and especially in New England, there was great danger of its final rejection. Dr. Manning, though holding no political office, was deeply interested in the result, believing that upon the adoption of the Constitution the future prosperity of the country depended. He attended the debates on the measure in Boston, and the favorable action of Rhode Island was in a large degree due to his counsels and influence.

Dr. Manning had long felt that his collegiate duties were too great to allow him to give the care his church required, and in 1791 he requested the appointment of a successor. In April of this year he preached his farewell sermon. He had the year previous expressed a desire to be relieved from his collegiate duties, but before the request had been complied with he was stricken with apoplexy, and his useful life was ended July 29, 1791, in the fifty-third year of his age.

Manning, Rev. James, another founder of the Baptist denomination in Nova Scotia, was born in Ireland in 1764; brought up in Falmouth, Nova Scotia, and awakened under Henry Alline's ministry; converted in 1789, and joined the Congregational church, Rev. John Payzant, pastor; commenced to preach in 1792; evangelized with his brother Edward in New Brunswick, in 1793; in 1796, James, renouncing Pedobaptism, was immersed by Rev. Thomas Handley Chipman. After returning from a second tour with Edward in New Brunswick and Maine, he was ordained pastor of the church in Lower Granville, Sept. 10, 1798, and continued in this position to his death, May 27, 1818. James Manning was an earnest Christian and a faithful minister, a wise counselor and peacemaker in the church of God. His grandson, Rev. J. W. Manning, is now the useful pastor of the North church, Halifax, Nova Scotia.

Manning, Rev. Reuben Elias, late one of the principals of Wayland Academy, a native of Penfield, Monroe Co., N. Y., was born March 31, 1840. His parents removed while he was quite young to Salem, Mich., where he spent his childhood and youth, receiving in the common schools of the neighborhood the rudiments of an education. He devoted himself for a number of years to agricultural pursuits with marked success. As the result of his excellent management he became the owner of a fine farm, and was one of the most successful men in that calling in his neighborhood. He obtained a hope in Christ in 1858, and united with the Baptist church. He had frequent convictions that he was called to preach the gospel, and finally, in 1869, he abandoned farming and began to prepare for the work of the ministry. He graduated from Kalamazoo College, Mich., in 1873, and from the Baptist Theological Seminary at Chicago in 1874. Before graduating he received a call to the pastorate of the Baptist church in Beaver Dam, Wis., and was ordained by this church Feb. 28, 1874. His pastorate here was one of marked success, the church growing in numbers and efficiency, and obtaining through his influence a prominent position in the community.

In September, 1877, having become associated with Prof. N. E. Wood in the principalship of Wayland Academy, he resigned his pastorate to engage in the work of teaching in that institution. He was associate principal with Prof. Wood, and Professor of Mathematics until June, 1880, when he retired from the school with a view of again entering the pastorate.

He is a man of splendid executive abilities, with superior qualities as a pastor.

Mansfield, Rev. David Logan, a distinguished minister in Gasper River Association, was born in Logan Co., Ky., June 8, 1797. In early manhood he became a member of Stony Point church, in his native county. His education was completed at Glasgow, Ky., under the direction of that famous instructor, Rev. R. T. Anderson. He was ordained to the ministry in November, 1823; soon after which he became pastor of Providence church, in Warren County, to which he removed in 1825, and there he settled for life. He was pastor of several other churches, and was very successful in leading sinners to Christ. In the winter of 1832–33 he baptized over 300 persons. He died about 1850.

Mansfield, Rev. James W., the most prominent minister of his day in Little River Association, in Kentucky, was born in Albemarle Co., Va., March 18, 1794. In 1815 he settled in Kentucky, stopping for a few months in Mercer County, where he was baptized, and then locating in Christian County. In 1819 he removed to Caldwell County, where he made his home. In May, 1820, he was licensed to preach, and was ordained pastor of Donaldson church in 1827, in which office he served twenty-five years. At the same time he had charge of three other churches, and from the scarcity of ministers, for a considerable period he preached to several other churches on "week-days." Among the churches he formed is that at Princeton, the county seat of Caldwell. He was fourteen years moderator of Little River Association. He died Oct. 15, 1853.

Manton, Rev. Joseph Randall, A.M., son of Dr. Shadrach and Amey Randall Manton, was born in Providence, R. I., Sept. 28, 1821; graduated at Brown University in 1842; united with the Fourth Baptist church in Providence; taught in Worcester Academy; studied theology at Hamilton, N. Y.; ordained to the Baptist ministry at Gloucester, Mass., in 1848; from delicate health left the New England coast and settled with the church in Clarksville, Tenn., from 1850 to 1857, also preaching widely as an evangelist; settled with the Vermont Street Baptist church in Quincy, Ill., from 1857 to 1860; from impaired health removed and settled with the Baptist church at Minneapolis, Minn., in 1860, and remained till 1865; removed to St. Joseph, Mo., and remained four years; in 1869 settled with the church at Richfield, Minn., where he now labors; a man of marked talents, true devotion, uncommon culture, and great eloquence, of delicate health, successful in his labors, and greatly esteemed.

Manz, Felix.—See article ANABAPTISTS.

March, John, was born in England; removed to St. John, New Brunswick, in 1854; is a prominent Baptist of that city; was connected for several years with the press; is now the efficient secretary of the board of school trustees for St. John; is earnest and liberal in support of all denominational objects.

March, Rev. Stephen, brother of John March, was born March 28, 1832, in England; came to New Brunswick in 1854; was ordained at St. Francis, New Brunswick, July 5, 1856; became, in 1858, pastor of the Baptist church in St. George, New Brunswick; took charge of the church in Bridgewater, Nova Scotia, in 1862; Onslow in 1874; Canning in 1877; returned to Bridgewater in 1879. He is a good preacher and pastor.

Marchant, Judge Henry, was born at Martha's Vineyard, Mass., in April, 1741. His early education was the best that could be obtained in the schools of Newport, R. I. He completed his studies at Philadelphia, in the institution which subsequently became the University of Pennsylvania. He spent five years in the study of law, and having been admitted to the bar, commenced the practice of his profession at Newport, R. I. Early in his career he advocated the rights of his country against the oppressions of Great Britain. At the October session of the General Assembly, in 1770, he was elected attorney-general of the State, and held this office until May, 1777. In 1771 he went to England in his official character to look after some matters affecting the interests of Rhode Island. While abroad he was brought into intimate relations with gentlemen of the Whig party, upon whom he exerted no little influence in favor of his country. Returning to his home in 1772, and anticipating the troubles which his sagacity told him would soon befall a town so exposed as was Newport, he purchased an estate in Narragansett, whither he moved his family. He was a delegate to the Continental Congress for three years, and was one of the signers of the Articles of Confederation. After the war he returned to Newport, which place he represented for a time in the General Assembly. President Washington appointed him judge of the District Court for Rhode Island, which position he held until his death, Aug. 30, 1796. In his religious sympathies Judge Marchant was a Baptist, and shared, with Roger Williams, an intense love of civil and religious liberty, which was transmitted to his posterity.

Marcom, Rev. J. C., was born in Orange Co., N. C., in 1814; baptized in June, 1835, by Thomas Freeman; ordained in 1847, Revs. J. S. Purefoy, W. T. Brooks, W. A. Atkinson, and T. B. Horton forming the Presbytery; has served many churches in Wake, Chatham, and Harnett Counties; was reading clerk of Raleigh Association for thirty years, and moderator for two sessions; has taught school, and is still active and useful.

Marcy, Gov. William Learned, was born in Southbridge, Mass., Dec. 12, 1786, and died at Ballston Spa, N. Y., July 4, 1857. He was graduated at Brown University, removed to Troy,

GOV. WILLIAM LEARNED MARCY.

N. Y., studied law, and was admitted to the bar. He served as lieutenant in the war with England, in 1812. In 1816 he was appointed recorder of Troy, and in 1818 he became editor of the *Troy Budget*, a leading daily newspaper. In 1821 he was appointed adjutant-general of the State militia, and in 1823 was elected by the Legislature comptroller of the State, and removed to Albany. In 1829 he was appointed one of the associate justices of the Supreme Court of the State, which office he held till 1831, when he was elected United States Senator. He served as Senator two years, when he resigned to accept the office of governor of New York. He was re-elected in 1834, and again in 1836. In 1845 he was made Secretary of War by President Polk, a post made peculiarly difficult by hostilities with Mexico. As a member of President Polk's cabinet he distinguished himself in the settlement of the Oregon boundary question, and other matters which engaged the attention of the government. In 1853 he was called into the cabinet of President Pierce to fill the high office of Secretary of State. In his correspondence with Austria, his state papers on Central American affairs, and the Danish Sound dues, his great ability as a writer, a statesman, and diplomatist was demonstrated to the world.

He was a constant attendant and liberal supporter of the Pearl Street Baptist church of Albany, and an ardent admirer of Dr. Bartholomew T. Welch. In all the varied relations of life, public and private, there is no stain on his memory. His wisdom, his faithfulness, and his integrity stand unchallenged, and his memory is justly revered by all who knew him.

Margrave, Rev. William G., was born in Lexington, Va., Nov. 23, 1793. The death of his father when he was an infant left his education entirely to his faithful mother, who was a member of the Presbyterian Church. When seventeen years of age he located in the town of Lewisburg, W. Va., where he spent the remainder of his life.

He was for a long time one of the most ungodly men in Lewisburg, a common drunkard, and a reproach to his neighbors. While engaged in his dissolute pleasures he was powerfully convicted of sin and was converted. It was with difficulty that he found a Baptist preacher to receive him. At length Rev. James O. Alderson heard of him, and came to his home and baptized him, and at once he began to preach. Whatever he did he performed with all his might. And such was the strength of his faith that he never doubted the reality of his conversion, and to the day of his death his zeal knew no abatement. His ministry was greatly blessed. An attack of pneumonia ended his work on the 24th of February, 1867. He died exhorting sinners to repent.

Marsh, Ebenezer, is one of the men long identified with Baptist progress in Southern Illinois. He has been for many years president of the Alton Bank, and a pillar in the Alton Baptist church. He was born in Sturbridge, Mass., Sept. 16, 1806. He was educated at Dudley Academy in that State, but in early life removed to Illinois, being one of the first settlers in Madison County in that State. His first occupation was that of teacher in the Rock Spring Seminary, St. Clair County, an institution founded by Dr. John M. Peck. In 1832 he removed to Alton, engaging first in the insurance business, subsequently as a banker. As a member of the church in Alton, of the Shurtleff College board of trustees, and in other positions of service, he has done much to promote denominational growth in his own section of the State.

Marsh, Rev. J. B., was born in Collisville, N. Y., May 26, 1830; converted at nine; baptized by A. B. Earle in May, 1848; was licensed by the Collisville church, but fearing that he was not called he returned the license; came to Virginia as a missionary of the Sunday-School Union in 1854; to North Carolina in April, 1855; was ordained in Ashville in September, 1858; preached for several years in Western North Carolina, but since 1868 has served churches in Catawba, Iredell, and Davie Counties.

Marsh, Rev. R. H., was born in Chatham Co., N. C., Nov. 8, 1837; graduated at Chapel Hill in 1858; was baptized by Dr. T. C. Teasdale at Chapel Hill, in October, 1856; spent two years at the Southern Baptist Theological Seminary in Greenville, S. C.; was tutor at Wake Forest College in 1859; professor in Oxford Female College in 1862–63; preached in Granville County until 1864, when the death of his father recalled him to Chatham; returned to Oxford in 1868, where he still resides, the blessed pastor of several excellent country churches. Mr. Marsh was for several years the pastor of the Oxford and Henderson churches; was for two sessions moderator of the Flat River Association, and has been for ten years a trustee of Wake Forest College.

Marshall, Rev. Abraham, to whom belongs the highest place among the Baptist pioneer preachers of Georgia, was born April 23, 1748, in the town of Windsor, Conn. He was the son, and probably the oldest, of Daniel Marshall, by his second wife, Martha Stearns. Although he was the subject of deep religious impressions from early childhood, yet it was not until he was about twenty-two years of age that he entertained well-grounded hopes of salvation. At that time his parents were living on Horse Creek, S. C., a few miles north of Augusta, and there, about 1770, he united with the church, and was baptized in the Savannah River. He was immediately seized with a desire to lead others to the Saviour, and soon began to call sinners to repentance. In January, 1771, in company with his parents, he removed to Columbia Co., Ga., and settled on Big Kiokee Creek, about which time he was regularly licensed to preach. He was not ordained, however, until May 20, 1775.

Just as he had chosen his life-work the Revolutionary war broke out, and Georgia became a scene of violence and blood. During almost the entire struggle the people were subject to the combined outrages of Britons, Tories, and Indians. Many sought safety in flight, among whom were those noble and useful men, Edmund Botsford and Silas Mercer, the former never to return as a permanent laborer, and the latter not until after an absence of six years. Abraham Marshall and his venerable father, however, remained at their posts, faithfully preaching the gospel. Sometimes they were taken prisoners, and subjected to great indignities, but through all God mercifully preserved them.

On the 2d of November, 1784, soon after the war closed, Daniel Marshall was called to his reward on high, and his son Abraham succeeded him as pastor of Kiokee church. In May, 1786, some business affairs, in connection with his father's estate, rendered it necessary for Abraham Marshall to visit his native town in Connecticut. He made the trip on horseback, and was absent several months, preaching almost every day during his journey. In New England his sermons drew together vast crowds, some comparing him to Whitefield in the fervor and power of his eloquence.

On his return, in November, 1786, he entered upon his ministerial labors with greater zeal than ever, and, being free from the care of a family, he engaged much in itinerant work, visiting various parts of the State, and preaching the Word with great power. In the spring of 1787 a wonderful revival began, and spread far and wide: thousands attended the ministrations of the gospel, and multitudes were converted. During the year more than 100 were baptized at Kiokee church alone, and the church membership soon increased to more than 300.

Now in the zenith of his powers, Abraham Marshall went everywhere throughout the State, preaching, baptizing, organizing churches, and ordaining ministers. So much assistance did he render in the work of constituting churches, and setting men apart to the ministry, that it was said to be "his business, his trade." This language will not appear extravagant when it is remembered that in three years the number of churches in the Association increased from 7 to 31, and in seven years to 56, while during the same period the ministers had increased from 6 to 36.

Mr. Marshall married Miss Ann Waller, of Virginia, in 1792, being then forty-four years old, and for twenty-three years they lived happily together, she preceding him to their heavenly home by four years only. Four sons were the issue of this marriage, only two of whom attained to manhood.

He retained the pastorship of the Kiokee church until his death,—a period of thirty-five years,—during which it kept its high position as the mother of churches and ministers. He from time to time had the oversight of other churches. In addition, during the whole course of his ministry, he continued his itinerant labors, his praise being emphatically in all the churches.

In the old family mansion, near the Kiokee meeting-house, Mr. Marshall, full of years and honors, ended his earthly life on Sunday, Aug. 15, 1819.

It is not too much to say, in conclusion, that for abundance of labors and general usefulness the first place among the pioneer Baptists of Georgia belongs to Abraham Marshall.

Marshall, Rev. Andrew, was for many years pastor of the First African church of Savannah, Ga. He was born in South Carolina about 1755. He was owned by different masters, and he acted as "body-servant" to President Washington when he visited Savannah. Andrew was a witness of many of the exciting events of the American Revolution and of the war of 1812, and in the latter war he showed a patriotism which proved him to be above the love of money.

Andrew purchased his liberty about the time he was converted, and he joined the church in 1785, and not long after he was licensed to preach. In 1806 he became pastor of the Second Baptist church of Savannah. This was a colored church; the First church was a white community, of which Dr. Henry Holcombe was pastor. Mr. Marshall's church increased from 1000 to 3000 members, when he led off a colony and formed the First African church. Here his popularity was extraordinary, and his influence and usefulness unbounded. His congregations were overflowing; his reputation was carried over the whole country, and it was known even in Europe. Andrew Marshall became one of the noted ministers of America. Every visitor who came to Savannah was likely to hear him, and when he was going to officiate in Augusta, Macon, or Charleston, throngs greeted his ministrations, many of whom were respectable white persons. It is said that "the Legislature of Georgia at one time gave him a hearing in an entire body." Sir Charles Lyell and Miss Frederika Bremer attended his church, and published sketches of him. But his wide-spread fame did not injure him. He was an intelligent man, and he was deeply pious; he had wonderful executive ability in managing his immense church and his secular business; he had great good sense and untiring perseverance; he was endowed with a keen perception and with ready arguments, and he would have been a leader in any age or country.

He read and owned many books, among which was Gill's "Commentary," which shaped his theology and gave perseverance and stability to his converts.

"His voice was so deep, sonorous, and tender that its capacity for the expression of pathos was unsurpassed."

He baptized nearly four thousand converts.

He died in Richmond, Va., Dec. 8, 1856, and he was buried in Savannah on the 14th of the same month.

"An immense procession about a mile long, with fifty-eight carriages, either loaned by families in the city to their servants or other colored friends, or occupied, as in many instances, by respectable white people themselves, followed him from his church to his grave." So Andrew Marshall, a colored friend of law and order, a man of genius, a grand Calvinistical Baptist, a man upon whose ministry the broad seal of divine approval conspicuously rested, was honored in life and in death in his native South.

Marshall, Rev. Asa M., for many years one of the most beloved ministers of Georgia, was born in Jones County, Dec. 20, 1832, of parents who were pious and consistent Baptists. A. M. Marshall was left an orphan at seven; at twenty he professed religion and united with the church; entered the Freshman class of Mercer in 1856, and graduated in 1860, studying with a view to the ministry. He was ordained in the fall of 1860, and in the following year became chaplain of the 12th Ga. Regiment, and served through the entire war, preaching to the soldiers, nursing the sick, and taking part in those grand revival movements that occurred among the troops which resulted in the salvation of so many. After the war he returned home and entered upon pastoral duty, which he has continued to the present time, serving various churches in Putnam and Greene Counties. As a preacher, he is plain and unaffected, earnest, and forcible. His whole aim seemed to be to edify his churches, hold up the Cross, and win souls to Christ. He is a man of genuine piety, and during his entire ministry has maintained a consistent and godly character. He is a strong friend of missions and Sunday-schools.

Marshall, Rev. Jabez P., eldest son of Rev. Abraham Marshall, was converted after leading a wild life in youth, and became an able and useful minister. He succeeded his father in charge of the Kiokee church, which he served usefully until his death, which occurred in 1832, closing a period of sixty years, during which father, son, and grandson presided over the same church. He wrote a life of his father, and served as clerk of the Georgia Association for a number of years.

Marshall, Rev. William, belonged to one of the most distinguished families of Virginia, and one that has been equally famous in Kentucky. He was a brother of Col. Thomas Marshall, so noted among the pioneers of Kentucky, and an uncle of Chief-Justice John Marshall of the Supreme Court of the United States. He was born in Fauquier Co., Va., in 1735. He grew up to be a brilliant young man, and gave himself much to fashionable amusements. Upon his marriage with the daughter of Rev. John Pickett, a pioneer Baptist minister of that region, he was brought under the influence of the gospel. In 1768 he was converted and baptized. In a short time he began to preach with mighty power, and multitudes were converted. He was a singularly gifted orator, and continued to labor here about twelve years. Meanwhile he was ordained, and became pastor of South River church. As early as 1780 he removed to Kentucky, and settled in Lincoln County. He was active and diligent in the ministry, and in a short time aided in building up a number of churches. After a few years he settled in Shelby County, where he raised up Fox Run church, and became its pastor. He died in 1813.

Marshman, John C., son of the distinguished

missionary, Dr. Marshman, of Serampore, accompanied his parents to India in early childhood, and spent many years in that country in various secular employments, especially identifying himself with Christian journalism. While a mere boy he devoted himself with remarkable zeal and fidelity to the work in which the Serampore missionaries were engaged. In conjunction with his father he labored in producing the Chinese version of the Scriptures. He established the first paper-making works in India, issued the first newspaper published in the Bengali language, and founded the English weekly newspaper, the *Friend of India*, which in his hands became one of the most influential journals in the world, and a potent factor for good in the Indian dependencies of the British crown. In its early days this newspaper escaped suppression from the British authorities by the protection of the Danish government, under whose flag it was published at Serampore. It was outspoken in its denunciation of official misdoings, and fearlessly advocated the civil rights of the native population. But whilst Mr. Marshman continued to be a layman he did efficient work in connection with the Baptist missions, especially devoting himself to the interests of Christian education. He gave a very large proportion of his increasing income year by year to the maintenance of Serampore College and other educational institutions. He became in later life the friend and trusted adviser of the government in important affairs, and few men exercised a greater influence upon the rulers and the ruled. His literary labors also procured him high standing. The lives of Carey, Marshman, and Ward, together with his history of India, will long perpetuate his name. His eminent services were recognized by the English government by the bestowment of the honor of C.S.I. (Companion of the Order of the Star of India). He spent the closing years of life in his native land, enjoying the esteem of a large circle of friends, and serving the cause of Christian missions and philanthropy. He died July 8, 1877, in his eighty-third year, and was followed to his grave by many distinguished men, including Lord Lawrence, formerly governor-general of India, and other famous Anglo-Indian statesmen, who had personally known his character and worth. Mr. Marshman's views concerning missionary methods of operation occasioned much discussion. He held with tenacity the opinion that India and the other Eastern nations could not be converted to Christianity by Europeans, and that the business of missionaries was to raise up "native apostles." When he died he was engaged upon a series of biographies of the viceroys of India, a work for which he was universally regarded as better qualified than any man living.

Marshman, Joshua, D.D., was born at Westbury Leigh, Wiltshire, England, April 20, 1768. He received such education as the village school afforded, and eagerly perused all the books that came within his reach. His love of reading was so notorious, that when he proposed to join the Baptist church, the members were afraid he had too much head knowledge of the gospel to have much heart experience of it, but their apprehensions in time passed away. In 1794 he removed to Bristol to take charge of a school supported by the Broadmead Baptist church, and was soon afterwards baptized and received into church fellowship. He joined the classes of the theological seminary, and for upwards of five years studied the classics, and also Hebrew and Syriac. The periodical accounts which recorded the labors of Carey awakened in him a missionary spirit, and in 1799 he and his wife offered themselves for service in India. Three other missionaries embarked with him in an American ship, the "Criterion," on the 29th of May, 1799, and landed at Serampore on October 13, seeking protection under the Danish flag from their anti-missionary countrymen in Calcutta. When the authorities found that the missionaries had arrived without a permit from the India House, they threatened Capt. Wickes, of the "Criterion," that his vessel should be refused entry unless the four missionaries appeared at the police-office, and entered into engagements to return forthwith to England. Representations were, however, made to the governor-general, Lord Wellesley, which resulted in the abandonment of all hostile proceedings against the vessel, but the missionaries were compelled to remain at Serampore. After the establishment of the mission in Serampore, Mr. and Mrs. Marshman opened boarding-schools, which soon attracted large numbers of scholars, and were a source of permanent income to the mission. In association with Mr. Marshman, Carey labored on translations of the Scriptures, preaching, and other missionary work. In 1806, Mr. Marshman commenced the study of Chinese, with the view of translating the Scriptures into that language, and, after fifteen years of arduous toil, he carried through the press the first Chinese Bible. He received the diploma of D.D. from Brown University in June, 1811. In 1814 he published "Key to the Chinese Language," towards the expense of which the government of India voted £1000. On the 31st of May, 1818, the first newspaper ever printed in any Eastern language was issued from the Serampore press, and was very popular among the natives. After the death of Dr. Carey, his already enfeebled constitution gave way, and although he rallied for a time, the capacity for work was exhausted. He died on Dec. 4, 1837, and his remains were laid in the cemetery with his departed colleagues.

Marston, Rev. Charles C., pastor of the Baptist church in Clinton, Wis., a native of West Medway, Mass., was born in 1849. When he was but a child his parents removed to Washington Co., Iowa. At the age of twelve he made a public profession of faith in Christ. His parents were Baptists, and he had been from early youth instructed in this faith. But no Baptist church had yet been organized in the vicinity where he resided, and he united with the Winebrennarians,—a denomination holding views of faith and practice in some respects similar to those of Baptists. By them Mr. Marston was licensed in 1865, and ordained to the work of the ministry in 1866. He held pastorates at Boiling Springs, Spring Grove, and Lanark, Ill. In 1876 he united with the Michigan Avenue Baptist church of Chicago, Ill. He has since been fully identified with the Baptist denomination. He completed the usual course of study in the University of Chicago, preaching for the Norwood Park Baptist church while prosecuting his studies in the university. In 1878, having been called to the pastorate of the Baptist church in Clinton, Wis., he removed to that place, which continues to be his field of labor. His ministry has been more than usually successful, having been attended with revivals of considerable power. He is doctrinal in his preaching, a close student of the Bible, and one of the promising young ministers of the State.

Marston, S. W., D.D., was born in York Co., Me., July 23, 1826. He studied in academies in Maine and New Hampshire, and for four years in New Hampton Institute, and graduated with honor in 1852. He was baptized by Rev. Abner Mason in 1847, in Medway, Mass.; was pastor at Brookfield in 1852, and in 1853 went South for his health, and in a short time returned to Middleborough, Mass., and taught two years, and preached during this time at New Bedford. Subsequently he taught in Greenville, Ill., and in Burlington, Iowa. In 1860 he became pastor at Plainfield, Ill. In 1865 he took charge of the Boonville Institute in Missouri. In 1868 he began his Sunday-school labors in Missouri, and in five years he increased the number of Baptist schools from 74 to 603, and organized a Sunday-school Convention in each of the 59 Associations of the State, auxiliary to the State Sunday-school Convention, of which he was the secretary. In October, 1873, he became superintendent of State missions for Missouri, which position he held for three years, and then was appointed by President Grant United States agent for 57,000 civilized Indians in the Indian Territory, whose affairs he managed with great satisfaction to the government. In 1879 he was appointed by the American Baptist Home Mission Society superintendent of freedmen's missions in the South, which position he now holds. Dr. Marston is a thorough Baptist, a logical thinker, an able preacher, and a successful minister of Jesus.

Martin, Rev. A. F., was born in 1812 in Missouri, and converted in 1830; has been preaching forty-seven years in Linn Co., Mo.; has served as missionary of the General Association of Missouri, and performed evangelistic work, through which many have been converted. He was ordained in 1833. His parents were constituent members of the Fee Fee church, St. Louis County, and his brother, Dr. Martin, was a constituent member of the Fourth Baptist church of St. Louis.

Martin, Hon. Isaac L., was born in New Brunswick, N. J., Jan. 11, 1829. He early entered into business with his father, a merchant in his native city. After years of success his father transferred the business to his sons. Mr. Isaac Martin has long been a director of the National Bank of New Jersey and of the New Brunswick Fire Insurance Company. After serving in the Legislature two terms he was, in 1879, elected senator from Middlesex County for three years. Mr. Martin while yet a youth united with the First Baptist church in New Brunswick; has been in the board of trustees, the Sunday-school, and other departments of church work.

Martin, Rev. James, B.A. (of London University), late president of the Baptist Association, Victoria, Australia, and distinguished among scholars and theologians for his translations from the German, was born in London, England, in September, 1821, and at an early age joined the church at Hackney. He studied at Stepney College, and then proceeded to Bonn, in Germany. Having completed his course with success, he settled first at Lymington, and subsequently at Stockport, Edinburgh, and Nottingham. During his nine years' pastorate at Nottingham he rose rapidly to distinction as a preacher and theologian. He translated upwards of twenty volumes of Clark's Foreign Theological Library, including several of the best works of Keil, Delitzsch, Kurtz, Ebrard, and Hengstenberg. In 1869 he received a pressing call from Melbourne, Australia, which at length he accepted. The position involved the honor and responsibility of denominational leadership in that rapidly growing city and colony, and high expectations were cherished by all who knew him, which, in his brief Australian career, were in no scanty measure fulfilled. But in the full tide of success and honor he was stricken down, and died Feb. 13, 1877, in his fifty-sixth year. Both in England and Australia his death was keenly felt as a severe bereavement to the denomination and the Christian church at large. Mr. Martin published little except an able treatise on "The Origin and History of the New Testament."

Martin, Rev. M. T., proprietor of *Baptist Record*,

Jackson, Miss., was born in 1842; was nine years Professor of Mathematics in Mississippi College; acted as agent of the college after the war; redeemed the property from mortgage; added $50,000 to the endowment, and extinguished an incumbrance in the form of scholarships, amounting to $42,000; began to preach in 1877, and is one of the most efficient evangelists in the State.

Martin, Rev. Robert, a prominent minister in North Louisiana Association, La., was born in South Carolina in 1814; began to preach in Georgia in 1841; removed to Bossier Parish, La., in 1852, and became the successful missionary of the Baptist State Convention, and was instrumental in planting most of the churches in Bossier Parish. After three years in this relation he became supply for a number of the churches which were planted by his instrumentality, and he has since labored in that capacity, supplying Salem, New Hope, Sarepta, and Spring Branch, in the parish of Bossier.

Martin, Rev. Samuel Sanford, was born April 15, 1820, in Colisville, Broome Co., N. Y., and was baptized at the age of sixteen. After a three years' course at Hamilton, he was ordained at Colisville, Sept. 27, 1843. Removing to Illinois, he became pastor of the Knoxville, now Galesburg, Baptist church. His pastorates since have been at Lamoille, where he helped to build the first Baptist house of worship, at Dixon, Tremont, Delavan, —where also under his labors the first meeting-house was built, and Rev. D. H. Drake, missionary to Kurnool, India, was baptized,—Washington, Forest City,—a church being here gathered,—and San José. Mr. Martin is numbered with those in Illinois whose chief work has been the laying of foundations.

Martin, William E., A.M., principal of the University Academy, Lewisburg, Pa., was born in May, 1845, in Saltsburg, Indiana Co., Pa. Here he received his academic training. In 1868 he was baptized by Rev. Azariah Shadrach, and united with the Saltsburg Baptist church. In the following year he entered the Junior class in the university at Lewisburg, from which he was graduated in the class of 1871.

After a year spent in teaching in the preparatory department of the university, he entered the Crozer Theological Seminary, in fulfillment of his original purpose to prepare himself for the ministry. After a single session, however, he was recalled to the work of instruction at Lewisburg. He was principal of the English Academy until 1878, when the classical and English departments of the preparatory work of the university were consolidated into the University Academy, with Principal Martin at its head. He has been very earnest in his purpose to elevate the standard of scholarship. Under his excellent management, and with his constant and self-denying labors, the academy is a success.

Maryland, The Baptists of.—The first Baptist church in Maryland was formed in 1742, at Chestnut Ridge, about ten miles north of Baltimore City. Its founder was Henry Sator, or Sater, a General Baptist, who came from England in 1709. It has ever since been known as "Sater's" church. It has a small brick meeting-house in a beautiful grove of about four acres, containing numerous graves of the Baptist fathers and their descendants. This church at first increased rapidly. In four years it numbered 181 members, and extended into Opeckon and Ketockton, in Virginia. In 1754 a church, principally originating from Sater's, was founded at Winter Run, in Harford County, which has since borne the name of the Harford church. For forty years it was under the pastoral care of the Rev. John Davis, who died in 1809, in the eighty-eighth year of his age, venerated and beloved. "Sater's" became nearly extinct under Antinomian influence, and is now a very feeble body.

The First Baptist church of Baltimore was organized Jan. 15, 1785, with 11 members, all of whom, except its pastor, the Rev. Lewis Richards, were dismissed from the Harford church. From the Harford church also arose the churches at Taneytown and Gunpowder. The First church worshiped until 1817 in a small house on the corner of Front and Fayette Streets. In that year they completed the edifice in Sharp Street, so long known as the "Old Round-top," at a cost of $50,000; but the debt thereby incurred was not entirely removed for thirty-five years, and seriously hindered the prosperity of the church. During ninety-five years it has had only five pastors, viz.: Lewis Richards, thirty-three years; E. J. Reis, three years; John Finlay, thirteen years; Stephen P. Hill, sixteen years; and J. W. M. Williams, the present pastor, nearly thirty years. From it originated several churches, principally the Waverly church, and the Seventh church in 1845, and the Lee Street church in 1854. In the year 1878, the vicinity of the meeting-house having become almost entirely occupied by warehouses, the church removed to Lafayette Avenue, near Tremont Street, where, in a new and beautiful house of white marble, renewed prosperity has been enjoyed.

The Second church of Baltimore was founded in 1797, by Elder John Healey, from Leicester, England, who with five others came to Baltimore in 1795. Elder Healey remained as pastor for *more than fifty years*, and died June 19, 1848. To this church belongs the honor of having established the first Sunday-school in the State of Maryland, in the year 1804.

The High Street Baptist church was constituted

Feb. 14, 1835, of 10 members, six of whom were Wm. Crane and his family, and two, the Rev. J. G. Binney, its first pastor, and his wife. It was at first called the "Calvert Street church." Mr. Binney remained but a few months, and in January, 1836, the Rev. George F. Adams became the pastor, and continued as such for about seven years, during which time the church increased to nearly 300 members. In 1843, the Rev. Jonathan Aldrich succeeded Mr. Adams, and in 1844 the church left the Calvert Street house and built a new one on High Street, first occupied in November of 1845. A crushing debt had been incurred in its erection, and in July, 1846, the pastor resigned and the house was offered for sale. After months of anxious solicitude relief was obtained by the concessions of creditors, the extra efforts of the church, the liberality of friends, and the election of a pastor, the Rev. Frankin Wilson, who served without salary, thus permitting the entire income to aid in reducing the debt. In November, 1850, a disease of the throat compelled Dr. Wilson to suspend his labors; but, in a large measure owing to his liberality, the house was saved, and the church has continued to prosper under his successors, the Revs. H. J. Chandler, John Berg, L. W. Seeley, E. R. Hera, Geo. P. Nice, R. B. Kelsay, M. R. Watkinson, and J. T. Craig. The above named may rightly be called the "mother-churches," as most of the others (except the Nanjemoy and Good Hope churches in Charles County) sprang from them either directly or indirectly.

ASSOCIATIONS.

The Salisbury Association, on the eastern shore of the Chesapeake Bay, was formed in 1782, under Elijah Baker and Philip Hughes. It probably never had over 600 members, and, having adopted anti-mission views, has almost dwindled into nonentity.

The first meeting of the *Baltimore Baptist Association* was held at Fredericktown, in August, 1793. Six churches, with 226 members, were represented there. It increased slowly, until, in 1820, it had 18 churches, with 1362 members. It was decidedly in favor of domestic and foreign missionary operations for more than forty years, with a few dissentients on the part of some pastors and churches. The anti-missionary spirit culminated at the meeting held in May, 1836, at Black Rock, in the adoption, by a vote of sixteen to nine, of resolutions against "uniting with worldly societies," and in a declaration of non-fellowship with those who had done so. By "worldly societies" were meant missionary, Sabbath-school, Bible, tract, and temperance societies. The Association was at once divided, and the two sections have since had only a nominal existence.

The Maryland Baptist Union Association was organized Oct. 27, 1836, with only 6 churches, 4 ministers, and 345 members. The ministers were Stephen P. Hill, Geo. F. Adams, Thos. Leahman, and Joseph Mettam. From the beginning it was a missionary body, and in favor of all the objects denounced by the "Black Rock" resolutions. For many years it included several churches in the District of Columbia; but in 1877 six white churches there withdrew to form a separate Association, and in 1879 the few colored churches of the District also withdrew, so that the Association is now confined to Maryland alone. Its present statistics will be found below. The largest number ever reported was in 1877, before the withdrawal of the District churches, viz., 51 ministers, 60 churches, 10,716 members. Nearly all the churches outside of Baltimore have been aided more or less by its contributions, and several of those within the city. During the forty-four years of its existence it has disbursed, in sustaining missionaries and aiding feeble churches, $130,518, besides assisting indirectly in the erection of a large number of meeting-houses, the education of young men for the ministry, the support and endowment of the Columbian University, and the distribution of Bibles and religious publications. A weekly paper, the *True Union*, was originated under its auspices in 1850, and continued until suspended by the war in 1861. Afterwards, in 1865, the *Maryland Baptist*, a monthly, was issued for one year. Subsequently, the Rev. O. F. Flippo for several years published a monthly,—the *Baptist Visitor*. The Association has an invested fund of $11,205 derived from special legacies, a "Superannuated Ministers' and Widows' Fund" of $3061.22, and a "Church Building Loan Fund" of $606.81.

The Baltimore Baptist Church-Extension Society, organized in 1854, has been of much value in planting churches in the city. The Lee Street and Franklin Square meeting-houses were built under its auspices, and more recently the Leadenhall Street house; and a new and handsome edifice for the First Colored church has been partly erected by this society aiding the members of the church. The recent progress of the colored Baptists in Baltimore has been wonderful. The First church, founded in 1836, had only 80 members in 1868, after an existence of thirty-two years; it now has 350. In 1848, the Rev. Noah Davis, then a slave in Virginia, was aided by Baltimore Baptists in purchasing his freedom. He became a missionary of the Association, and a small church was organized under his ministry in 1852. That church, united with fragments of others, has now grown to be the largest one in the Association; and the colored Baptists, who, twelve years ago, were comprised in 2 churches, with 273 members, have now 5 churches, with 2726 members.

REVIVALS.

Many revivals have occurred at intervals in separate churches, but some have had a general and marked influence on the denomination. The first was in 1839, when the additions by baptism (606) were more numerous than the whole previous aggregate of members (565). In 1857 the baptisms reported were 559. From 1870 to the present time (except in 1871-72) the annual additions have ranged from 531 to 1085.

EMINENT MINISTERS.

This sketch would be very incomplete without further reference to at least two brethren whose labors, under God, have been greatly blessed in building up the cause of truth in Maryland,—the Rev. George F. Adams and Richard Fuller. To Brother Adams was largely due the origin of the Maryland Baptist Union Association. As pastor of two churches in the city, and two or three in the country, as general State missionary for several years, as editor, historian, as a faithful, zealous, wise, consistent, devoted man of God, his labors and his character contributed much to the extension of our principles and the establishment of the churches in the faith. He died April 16, 1877, universally lamented, leaving behind him a precious memory, and a rich treasure in the "History of the Maryland Churches," carefully prepared by him.

The Rev. Richard Fuller, D.D., entered upon the pastorate of the Seventh church, Baltimore, June 1, 1847. After twenty-four years' labor there, during which the church increased from 104 to 1170 members, he went out, in 1871, with 134 members, to establish the Eutaw Place church. At the time of his death, October, 1876, that church had increased to 468 members. But his usefulness must not be measured by the hundreds converted and baptized under his ministry. The influence of his noble character, his splendid talents, his impassioned eloquence, his fame as one of the greatest pulpit orators of the age, his powerful advocacy of every philanthropic and Christian enterprise, did much to give his beloved denomination and the truth it maintains a higher estimate in the public mind, and to win for it a wider sway. Such transcendent abilities so thoroughly consecrated to Jesus, and permitted for nearly thirty years to shed their sacred lustre upon Baltimore and the surrounding country, formed indeed one of the richest gifts of God to the Baptists of Maryland.

Quite a large number of ministers have gone forth from the Maryland Baptist churches, many of them to do good in other States. Among them are the honored names of Spencer H. Cone, Bartholomew T. Welsh, Wm. Carey Crane, Elijah S. Dulin, Noah Davis, the founder of the American Baptist Publication Society, and Benjamin Griffith, for so many years its efficient corresponding secretary; the missionaries Rosewell H. Graves, Brethren Bond and Rohrer, whose mysterious loss at sea occasioned such profound sorrow; J. L. Holmes, murdered by the rebels in China; Jno. A. McKean, J. H. Phillips, J. B. T. Patterson, Levi Thorne, Isaac Cole, S. C. Borton, J. W. T. Boothe, J. L. Lodge, J. T. Beckley, C. J. Thompson, Richard B. Cook, J. H. Brittain, George McCullough, H. W. Wyer, W. S. Crowley, and many others.

CONDITION IN 1880.

Nearly all the Baptist churches in Maryland are connected with the Maryland Union Baptist Association. At its session in November, 1879, reports were received from 47 churches, 14 of them being in Baltimore City, and 33 in the country or in the smaller towns. The strength of the denomination is in the city of Baltimore. Ten of the city churches are white, numbering 3641 members; four colored, numbering 2686 members. Twenty-three of the other churches are white, numbering 1386 members; ten colored, numbering 605. In other words, there are in Maryland 8318 Baptists, of whom 5027 are white, 3291 colored. Of these, 6327 are in 14 churches in Baltimore, averaging over 452 members to each church, while only 1991 are in the 33 churches of the State at large, averaging about 60 members to each church. The largest church is the Union Colored church of Baltimore, with 1497 members. The largest white church is the Seventh, with 590 members, though several others nearly equal it; for instance, the First church, 528; the Eutaw Place, 519; the Franklin Square, 494; the High Street, 438; the Lee Street, 407; the Second, Broadway, 328.

All the city churches have good substantial houses of worship, none very large, but several of considerable architectural beauty. They are well located, at proper distances from each other, so as to reach all parts of the city. All except four, one German and one colored, are self-supporting and liberal in benevolent contributions. With each is connected a flourishing Sunday-school.

Many of the churches in the State are not well located. Of the 23 white churches only 7 are in towns or cities of over 2000 population, the remainder being in small villages or country places. All of them have suitable meeting-houses, generally paid for. Partly for want of material, their growth has been slow, and their struggles for existence severe. Several have become extinct.

Mason, Alanson P., D.D., was born in Cheshire, Mass., Jan. 19, 1813. He was graduated from Madison University in the class of 1836, and from the Hamilton Theological Seminary in 1838. He was pastor of four churches in the State of New

York,—Clockville, Groton, Binghamton, and Williamsburg, and of the First Baptist churches in Fall River and Chelsea, Mass. After serving the latter church for thirteen years, he resigned his pastorate to enter upon the duties of district secretary for New England of the American Baptist Home Mission Society. In this position he is now serving his thirteenth year. While pastor in Chelsea he was for seven years a member of the board of overseers of Harvard University by appointment of the Massachusetts Legislature. He received the degree of Doctor of Divinity from Madison University in 1859.

Mason, Rev. Auguste Francke, pastor of the Baptist church in Milwaukee, Mich., was born in Clockville, N. Y., Nov. 17, 1839. He is a descendant of sturdy old Samson Mason, a dragoon of the republican army of Oliver Cromwell, who came to America in 1650, and concerning whom the records of Rehoboth, Mass., contain the following curious mention: " Dec. 9, 1657.—It was voted that Samson Mason should have free liberty to sojourn with us, and to buy house, lands, or meadow, if he see cause for his settlement, provided that he lives peaceably and quietly." Anabaptist as he was, this permission was regarded a peculiar act of grace on the part of the New England Puritans. For generation after generation the descendants of Samson Mason were pastors of the Baptist church in Swanzey, Mass. The Rev. Alanson P. Mason, D.D., the sixth generation from the old Cromwellian, and Sarah Robinson Mason, were the parents of Auguste Francke Mason. Mr. Mason's father, an able and prominent minister of the Baptist church, after a pastorate at Clockville, N. Y., was settled for six years at Brooklyn, N. Y., and thirteen years at Chelsea, Mass. Mr. Mason's mother was the daughter of a New England farmer, and a woman of superior intelligence and great force of character. She was educated at Mrs. Willard's well-known seminary, Troy, N. Y., in which institution she afterwards became a teacher. Mr. Mason was educated at Chelsea, Mass. After leaving the high school he became a clerk in the counting-room of a mercantile house in Boston, where his energy and business aptitude pointed to a successful career. In 1857, during the great religious awakening, he was the subject of deep religious convictions, which caused him to withdraw from mercantile life and to turn his attention to the gospel ministry. After a course of study at Madison University, from which he afterwards received the degree of A.M., he was ordained at Barnstable, Mass., in June, 1859. Although comparatively a young man, his ministerial labors extend over a period of nearly twenty years, and have been attended with marked success. He has been settled as pastor at Meriden, New York City, Leominster, and Washington, D. C. Mr. Mason is an earnest and forcible speaker, and his sermons exhibit much originality of thought and scholarly research.

Mason, Rev. Darwin N., was born in Indiana, and reared in New York, on the shore of Lake Erie, on a farm. He graduated at the State Normal School in Albany in 1856. He was ordained, and settled as pastor at Rochester, Minn., in 1861 ; removed to Iowa in 1868 ; served as pastor in Cedar Falls, as principal in Des Moines University, as pastor in Indianola, Boone, Marshalltown, and Marion. He was secretary of the Iowa Baptist State Convention 1874–77. He has been in his present pastorate at Marion since 1876.

Mason, Francis, D.D., was born in York, England, April 2, 1799. In early life there was developed in him a remarkable taste for mathematical studies. A love for the English classics was also awakened, and he made himself familiar with the works of the best authors in his native tongue. He came to this country in 1818. After his conversion he could not rest satisfied with the routine of his daily life. He wanted to do noble things for his Master. He was licensed to preach Oct. 1, 1827, and became a member of the Newton Theological Seminary in November following. Two years afterwards he received an appointment from the executive board of the Missionary Union, and sailed May 26, 1830, in company with Rev. E. Kincaid and wife, for Calcutta, and arrived in Maulmain in November. He joined Mr. Boardman in Tavoy in 1831, and was with him during the last weeks of his life, administering the ordinance of baptism to the Karen converts on the memorable occasion when, as a dying man, the worn-out missionary reclined on the banks of the stream in whose waters the new disciples were " buried with Christ by baptism." Dr. Mason's connection with the Tavoy mission continued for about twenty-two and a half years, or one-half of his whole missionary life. While at Tavoy Dr. Mason's life was an exceedingly active one, and the visible results of his labors were manifest in many directions. For some time the superintendence of the station rested on him. A seminary for the education of teachers and preachers was also under his charge. He translated the Scriptures into the Sgau Karen and Pwo Karen languages. He also made his collections for his " Notes on the Fauna and Flora of Burmah," published in 1852, and for a similar work which was published some time later.

Dr. Mason having obtained permission of the board, proceeded to Toungoo to commence a mission in that place, where he arrived Oct. 22, 1833. In a few weeks he was joined by San Quala, " the Karen apostle," and two assistants. The most remarkable success followed the labors of these devoted missionaries. Although Dr. Mason was obliged to leave Burmah for this country in the early part of 1854, the work went on with marvelous strides, so that when, three years later, he returned to Toungoo, there were 2600 baptized Christians and 35 churches connected with the mission. In ten years from the establishment of the station more than 6000 converts had been baptized and 126 churches had been formed.

In the midst of this wonderful prosperity occurred those singular circumstances which those who have made themselves familiar with the history of this mission will recall. Mrs. Mason, the wife of Dr. Mason, came under the influence of certain strange delusions, and through her teachings of the new converts the most lamentable defections from the simple gospel were the result. The peculiar hallucination which seemed to have taken possession of her mind was this: "She pretended to have found the language in which God spoke to Adam, the 'God language' as she called it, in the embroideries of the Karen women's dresses, in the pagodas, and other appendages of Buddhist worship, and claimed that all nations have this language, and that what is needed only is to read it according to the key which she stated she had received." It was in vain that the executive board protested against the inculcation of these wild vagaries, and set forth the great injury which the Karen churches must suffer from the propagation of such sentiments. Dr. Mason did not see fit to interfere in the matter, and there was no alternative but that his connection with the Missionary Union must cease. For a little more than seven years this separation continued, but at last the extravagant conduct of his wife forced him to believe that she must be laboring under a form of insanity, and he could no longer sanction the course which she was pursuing. His relation to the Missionary Union was restored July 11, 1871, and continued harmonious and pleasant until his death, which occurred March 3, 1874.

From the foregoing sketch it is evident that Dr. Mason was no common man. Placed in any position he could not fail to secure respect for his ability. He created a new literature for the Karens, giving to them the Word of God and other devout and instructive books in their own tongue. He was a careful observer of the natural history of the country in which he passed so many years of his life. Sir J. D. Hooker, an eminent English naturalist, says of his "Fauna and Flora, etc., of British Burmah and Pegu," "F. Mason, D.D., has made the most valuable addition to the history of the fauna and flora of British Burmah of any man of modern times." In many respects Dr. Mason will be regarded as holding a first place in the ranks of American missionaries.

Mason, Rev. J. O., D.D., was born in Fort Ann, Washington Co., N. Y., Dec. 25, 1813. His parents were active members of the Baptist Church, and lived until a ripe old age. Their influence and training during his early years very largely moulded his subsequent life and character. When about to enter college, in his eighteenth year, he was converted, and began to prepare for the gospel ministry. In 1833 he became a student in the Literary and Theological Institution at Hamilton, N. Y., graduating in 1836. Shortly after appointed by the Foreign Mission Board as a missionary to the Creek Indians beyond the Mississippi. He was ordained Aug. 30, 1838, and, accompanied by his wife, started for his field. The unsettled state of the Indian tribes rendered mission work almost impossible, and, after many attempts to gain a foothold, he was compelled to abandon it. In May, 1840, he settled as pastor at Fort Ann, and remained with much success nearly four years. Sept. 1, 1844, he entered upon the great work of his life, as pastor of the Bottskill Baptist church, in Greenwich, N. Y. With an occasional brief intermission on account of ill health, he has labored with this honored church until the present time. During all these years he has been blessed in leading souls to Christ and in breaking the bread of life to a people in whose hearts he is held with affectionate regard.

Mason, Deacon John R., son of Deacon Mason, of Warren, R. I., is a member of the Central church, Oakland, and treasurer of the California Baptist State Convention. He was born at Warren, R. I., in 1826; spent some years at St. Louis, Mo.; crossed the plains for California in 1849; and has been a successful merchant. He was converted in 1868, and baptized by Rev. J. P. Ludlow, and has ever been active in church and denominational interests on the Pacific coast.

Mason, Rev. J. P., was born in Chatham Co., N. C., March 13, 1827; baptized by Rev. Johnson Olive, November, 1848; ordained in January, 1856, Revs. G. W. Purefoy, B. J. Hackney, and Thomas Yarboro forming the Presbytery. Mr. Mason has served Lystia church for twenty-two years, and served other country churches nearly as long. He is a good pastor.

Mason, Prof. Otis Tufton, was born in Eastport, Me., April 10, 1838; was baptized in 1856, and united with the First Baptist church, Washington, D. C., and was licensed to preach by the First Baptist church in Alexandria, Va., in 1859. Prof. Mason was educated at the Columbian College, where he graduated in 1861 with the degree of A.M. From that time to the present he has been the successful principal of the preparatory school of the university. He is superintendent of the Sunday-school of the First Baptist church,

Washington, D. C., and a deacon in the same. He is a collaborator of the Smithsonian Institution in anthropology, joint editor of the scientific department of Harpers' serials, and anthropological editor of the *American Naturalist*. He is the author of several papers on anthropology, published in the "Smithsonian Reports," and in the "Proceedings of the American Association." Prof. Mason is, at present, engaged in collating materials for an encyclopædia of the North American Indians, an atlas of the archæology of the United States, and a grammar and dictionary of the Southern Indian languages, a department of research in which he is deeply interested, and for which he has special aptitude.

Mason, Sumner R., D.D., was born in Cheshire, in the western part of Massachusetts, June 14, 1819. He was a lineal descendant of Samson Mason, who was at one time an officer in Cromwell's army, a radical in politics and a Baptist in religion. He came to America about 1650. For assisting in the building of the Baptist meetinghouse in Swansey he was summoned before the authorities of Plymouth colony, fined fifteen shillings, and warned to leave the jurisdiction. When the subject of this sketch was about seven years of age his parents removed to Penfield, in the western part of New York. His father died in 1828, leaving a widow and a large family. Dr. Mason pursued his preparatory studies in Cincinnati, and entered Yale College in 1838, where he remained two years. He was baptized and united with the First Baptist church in New Haven, March 1, 1840. For the next seven years he was engaged in teaching in Cincinnati and in Nashville, Tenn. He was licensed to preach by the First Baptist church of Nashville when Dr. Howell was pastor, Sept. 7, 1844. He pursued his theological studies under the direction of Dr. Howell, and was ordained pastor of the First Baptist church in Lockport, N. Y., Aug. 22, 1849, where he remained until called to the First Baptist church in Cambridge, Mass., where he commenced his ministerial labors March 4, 1855. Here he proved himself to be "a workman that needed not to be ashamed, rightly dividing the word of truth." The church under his ministry of sixteen years grew not only in its membership, but in sound doctrine and active benevolence, and every year added to its pastor's reputation and the weight of his influence in every direction in which that influence was exerted. It might have reasonably been predicted that many years of active service and great usefulness were before this devoted minister of Christ, but in the very prime of life he was suddenly cut down. What at the time was known as the "Revere disaster" sent a great shock through the minds of people residing in the neighborhood where the frightful event occurred. Dr. Mason was on his way to Beverly, Mass., to exchange pulpits with Rev. J. C. Foster. It was on Saturday evening, Aug. 26, 1871. At the Revere station, a few miles out of Boston, an express train from Portland met the outgoing train, and Dr. Mason, with a score of others, was instantly killed.

In an appreciative sketch of the life of Dr. Mason, his friend, Dr. O. S. Stearns, says of him, "He was a sincere friend, an earnest, sympathetic Christian, a truth-searching theologian, an effective preacher, a wise and judicious pastor. To his family he has bequeathed a life full of sunny memories. By his people his name will always be honored. In his denomination he will long be considered one of its choicest ornaments. By all who knew him he will be esteemed as a *prince in Israel*."

Massachusetts Baptists.—We can trace the history of the denomination in the State of Massachusetts nearly to the settlement of Boston in 1630. Among the earlier inhabitants of the district taken possession of by Gov. Winthrop, and the nearly fifteen hundred people who accompanied him, there were found some who had grave doubts about the divine authority of the rite of infant baptism, and refused to have it performed in the case of their own children. The first president of Harvard College, Rev. Henry Dunster, took a decided stand on the subject, and openly avowed his sentiments against infant baptism. Then came the persecution of Thomas Gould, and the troubles through which the First Baptist church in Boston passed, beginning with the formation of the church in 1665 and extending through several years. Two years previous, in 1663, the church in Swanzey was formed, it being really a transfer of the Swansea church in Wales, organized in 1649, to this country. From the Boston church there were formed, from time to time, churches in different sections of the State, made up chiefly of members who, having been connected with that church because it was the only church of their faith which they could conveniently join, desired to enjoy church privileges in the locality where they lived. In this way commenced the church in Kittery, formed in Maine in 1682, and about the same time the church in Newbury. Thomas Hollis, an eminent merchant of London, proved himself the warm friend of his denomination by making generous provision for Baptist young men to be educated for the ministry in Harvard. As early as 1727 we find that there were Baptists in Springfield, the pastor of the First church in Boston, by special request, visiting that place to administer the rite of baptism to several persons. Before the close of the century there were about 50 churches in different sections of the State. Among the oldest of these we mention the church in Wales, 1736; Bellingham, 1737; the Second church, now Warren Avenue church, Boston, 1743; First Middleborough, 1756; West Harwich, 1757; Third Middleborough, 1761; and the First church in Haverhill, 1765. With rare exceptions very few of these 50 churches were churches of much pecuniary ability. But they were earnest followers of Christ, and contended for what they believed to be "the faith once delivered to the saints." They encountered persecution, they suffered many civil disabilities, and yet they continued to grow and multiply until they have reached a high rank among the other denominations of Christians in the State.

The latest statistics give us the following figures: There are 14 Associations, embracing 289 churches, with 232 pastors. The number of ordained ministers in the State is 328. The total membership of the churches is 48,764, and the amount of money raised for various purposes, so far as reported, for the year covered by the statistical tables to which we refer, was $713,125. The church having the largest membership is the Union Temple, Boston, the number being 1501.

Of the State denominational societies the Convention may be first mentioned. It was formed May 26, 1802, and was incorporated Feb. 28, 1808. It is authorized to hold real estate to the amount of $200,000. The receipts for 1880 were $13,800. The officers of the Convention at the present time are Eustace C. Fitz, president, and four vice-presidents, all laymen, Rev. G. W. Bosworth, D.D., secretary, and Rev. Andrew Pollard, D.D., treasurer.

directors is made up of 50 ministers and laymen, who represent the different sections of the State. Another organization is "The Baptist Charitable Society for the Relief of Widows and Orphans of Deceased Baptist Ministers." Rev. G. G. Fairbanks is its president. Its receipts in 1880 were over $2550. This society was formed in 1821. "The Massachusetts Baptist Pastoral Conference" was formed in 1829, its object being the relief of aged and indigent ministers. It is authorized to hold property to the amount of $75,000. The president is Rev. C. M. Bowers, D.D. "The Northern Baptist Education Society" was formed in 1814. It has a permanent fund of $32,400. The president is Rev. Henry M. King, D.D., and the secretary Rev. J. C. Foster. The society has aided during the year 52 young men studying for the ministry. Its income in 1880 was $6774.91. (See articles on FIRST BAPTIST CHURCH OF BOSTON, FIRST BAPTIST CHURCH OF SWANZEY, NEWTON THEOLOGICAL SEMINARY, PIERCE ACADEMY, WORCESTER ACADEMY, and THE WATCHMAN AND REFLECTOR.)

Mather, Rev. Asher E., was born in Canada in 1823; son of Deacon Alonzo T. Mather. The

REV. ASHER E. MATHER.

family removed to St. Lawrence Co., N. Y., in 1828, and to Michigan in 1836. He devoted some time to teaching, and then engaged in business in the city of Detroit. His attention was early turned to the gospel ministry, and many of his brethren thought he was called of God to this work before he could overcome his fear lest he was not qualified for it. At length, in 1851, turning away from pursuits that promised large pecuniary returns, he became pastor in Mount Clemens, where he was ordained in August, 1851. This pastorate continued only for a year, but was specially attended with the blessing of God. The Tabernacle church, in Detroit, of which he had been a deacon, called him to be its pastor, and he accepted the call. But the plans of the church could not be carried out with the means at its command, and after a brief period he removed to Romeo, where a small church was in a depressed condition. During the next four years his work was greatly blessed, a good house of worship and a parsonage were built, and the church, which had been aided by the American Baptist Home Mission Society, became self-supporting. His next pastorate was in Pontiac, and continued nine years. These were years of prosperity. At the opening of the war he rendered valuable service in raising a regiment of volunteers, and became its chaplain. He was absent from the church a year in this service.

In 1866 he became district secretary of the American Baptist Home Mission Society, and for ten years engaged in work for that society with great earnestness, and with constant tokens of divine approval. Having led in the organization of the church in Caro, in 1876, and the erection of its house of worship, he became, soon after, pastor in Portland, where he is now engaged in earnest work.

No Baptist in Michigan is more fully acquainted with the churches throughout the State, and none have rendered a service more widely felt. He has assisted at the dedication of more than fifty houses of worship. It was at his suggestion that the Woman's Baptist Home Mission Society of Michigan was formed,—the first society of its kind in the country. He served the State Convention as its secretary for seven years, and in 1879 was made its president.

Mathews, William, LL.D., is by far the best and most successful writer the West has yet produced. Having enjoyed in early life the culture of New England, and, later, having breathed for many years the stimulating atmosphere of the West, he combines with the finished scholarship of the one, the vigorous vitality of the other. He was born at Waterville, Me., July 28, 1818. His taste for study, and his proficiency in whatever in that way was undertaken, were shown very early in life. At the age of thirteen he entered Waterville College, now Colby University, and in 1835, at the age of seventeen, graduated. Two years were then spent in the Harvard Law School, and two years more in the office of Hon. Timothy Boutelle, of Waterville. Having been admitted to the bar, he first taught for a year in Virginia, but returning to Waterville in 1841, he began the practice of law, associating with that, however, the editorship of a literary paper,—*The Yankee Blade*. This latter proved to be for him the more congenial sphere. After two years the paper was removed to Gardiner, Me., where for some four or five years its publication was continued with marked success; subsequently to Boston, in which city it achieved a circulation and popularity in all parts of the United States scarcely equaled by any other literary paper. As editor of the *Blade*, Mr. Mathews formed many interesting and valuable literary acquaintances, including several of the best known and most eminent of American writers.

In 1856, Mr. Mathews sold his paper and removed to Chicago. His work here was at first in the form of contributions to various journals; but in 1859 he was appointed librarian of the Young Men's Association, holding that office some three years. He was then elected Professor of Rhetoric and English Literature in the University of Chicago. This place he filled with eminent success until 1875, when he resigned it, with a view to devote himself entirely to authorship. In this new line of work he has been remarkably successful. His writings for the most part have the form of essays, upon subjects literary, biographical, and practical, covering a wide range, but so grouped as to give each of his volumes admirable unity of direction and general topic. His style is a model of elegance and vivacity, while his method, being largely illustrative, enables him to utilize the results of an almost ubiquitous reading and study. The titles of his principal books, and nearly in the order of their appearance, are "Getting On in the World," "Words, their Use and Abuse," "Orations and Orators," and "Monday Chats," the last named being a translation of Sainte-Beuve's "Causeries du Lundi," introduced by an appreciative biography of the great French *littérateur* and critic. Dr. Mathews's home is still in Chicago, where he enjoys the warmest esteem of a wide circle of cultured friends.

Mathias, Rev. Joseph, of Hilltown, Bucks Co., Pa., was born May 8, 1778. He was baptized on a profession of his faith in his twenty-second year. He was ordained to preach the gospel July 22, 1806, and he continued in the work of the ministry for more than forty-six years as pastor of the same church. He possessed a vigorous intellect, a spirit of stern loyalty to Jesus, and a heart overflowing with love to the Redeemer.

He was a strong Calvinist, fully persuaded that each believer owed his salvation to a gospel springing from the everlasting and personal love of God, a gospel bearing the whole treasures of grace to every heart that received it, and a gospel surely carrying each recipient to the world of glory.

He was untiring in the use of means to bring men to the Saviour. His prayers for the salvation of his people were marked by a fervor and a faith that nothing could surpass. His public appeals to saints and sinners to follow Jesus were unusually tender and earnest.

He preached three times on the Lord's day, and several times during the week. And it was his regular custom to make a tour annually, at a convenient season of the year, extending over several weeks, and to preach every night at the place where he stopped. To gather a congregation he sent word beforehand, and the people thronged to hear the gospel. In a brief account of one of these apostolic trips before me, it is stated that he preached in ten different places, and baptized ten persons at three of his meetings. Only one of these services was held in a church, the others were conducted in barns and school-houses. The labor performed for the Saviour in this way was effective and very extensive. Many were born again, and united with other denominations, and many others formed Baptist churches, several of which are in a flourishing condition at this time.

In one of his preaching journeys he tells of two persons "who requested baptism, but the relation they gave was not satisfactory, and their request was not granted." Mr. Mathias built up Christian churches in the truth, and with soundly converted members, whose future experience would encourage their brethren and commend the gospel.

He was an earnest advocate of missions all over our own country, and away to the ends of the earth. He was ever ready to speak for missions in his own church and in the region around. And it was his custom to commend Christian love for the perishing at home and abroad by a liberal contribution of his own, which gave him freedom of utterance in appealing to others, and which imparted a peculiar power to his missionary arguments.

He had five sons and three daughters, every one of whom was converted under his ministry, and buried in the waters of baptism by his hands.

No man was loved more in the old Philadelphia Association than Father Mathias. His fame had traveled over the entire State and a large section of New Jersey. Wherever he was known he had a warm place in the hearts of the friends of Christ.

He was a firm Baptist, and while he loved all Christians, he knew nothing of that charity that would sacrifice the smallest part of God's truth. Not for empires, nor for mines of gold, nor for worlds, would he slight his Lord that he might bribe the servants of that Master for their good will.

Mr. Mathias preached three times the Sunday before his death; on the following Tuesday evening his spirit suddenly entered the heavens. On Friday an immense concourse of people gathered at his funeral services, every one of whom felt that a father and a friend had been borne to the skies when Father Mathias fell asleep. And though this event occurred thirty years ago the memory of our venerable friend is as fragrant as ever, not in Hilltown only, but for hundreds of miles around it.

Mattoon, Rev. C. H., of Albany, Oregon, is an earnest and influential preacher, and known as the Baptist historian in that State. There is hardly any pastor or prominent Baptist in Oregon whose history is unknown to Mr. Mattoon. He has preached in nearly every part of the State. Born at Canastota, N. Y., of Old-School Presbyterian parents, he became a Baptist, and was immersed at Genoa, O., in 1844. He obtained a good education at Central College, O. He went to Oregon in 1851; was licensed in 1853; published *The Religious Expositor* six months; was Professor of Mathematics in McMinnville two years; and in agency work became familiar with Baptists in the State and adjacent Territories. In 1871 he was ordained by the Pleasant Butte church; is a strong Baptist writer of the Landmark school; in 1874 held a written discussion on that subject; is more logical than rhetorical in preaching; is positive, and so full of the facts in Baptist history that he is sometimes called "the Baptist Encyclopædia of Oregon." He is historical secretary of the Baptist Convention of the North Pacific coast.

Maxcy, Jonathan, D.D., was born in Attleborough, Mass., Sept. 2, 1768. In his case the moulding influence of a highly gifted mother was felt in the formative period of his life. Such was the intellectual development of young Maxcy that his parents determined to secure for him all the advantages of a liberal course of study. Having been prepared for college in the academy of Rev. William Williams, of Wrentham, not far from his native place, he became a member of the Freshman class in Brown University in 1783, when he was but fifteen years of age. All the hopes which had been cherished with reference to him were abundantly realized. He made rapid progress in the acquisition of knowledge and in mental discipline, and graduated with the highest honors of his class in 1787. His talents were brought into immediate service in the college where he had gained his laurels. He was appointed a tutor, and for four years devoted himself with great success to the duties of his office. But his Master had a higher service for him. Having become a subject of the converting grace of God, he was baptized by Rev. Dr. Manning, and connected himself with the First Baptist church in Providence. The church at once gave him a license to preach, and he was invited to supply the pulpit which President Manning had recently vacated. From the outset of his public efforts as a preacher of the gospel his rank as a pulpit orator was established. So pleased was the church with these efforts that he was solicited to resign his office as tutor in Brown University and accept a call to the pastorate of the flock to which he had ministered with so much satisfaction. The call was accepted, and Mr. Maxcy was ordained Sept. 8, 1791, when he was but twenty-three years of age, the Rev. Dr. Stillman preaching the ordination sermon. He was also appointed a professor in Brown University on the same day, as well as a trustee of the college.

In the midst of most congenial employments, and when he was constantly developing his powers as a preacher and a pastor, Dr. Manning was suddenly smitten down by a fatal disease and died. All eyes were at once turned to Maxcy as the most suitable person to fill the vacancy created by the decease of the lamented Manning, and he was unanimously elected president. He resigned his pastorship just one year from the day he was ordained, and entered upon his duties in the university. He was only twenty-four years of age, the youngest man, if we mistake not, that was ever called to fill so responsible a position in this country. His youth probably brought him in closer and more intimate relations with the students of the college than if he had been older. At any rate, he was from the first very popular, and the young men were proud of their youthful president. Several discourses which he published within a few years after he took charge of the university added greatly to his reputation as an able divine. In 1801 Harvard University conferred on him the honorary degree of Doctor of Divinity. He was at the time only thirty-three years of age. His official connection with Brown University continued for ten years, when he was called to the presidential chair in Union College, where he remained two years. Finding our Northern climate too severe for his delicate constitution, he accepted an invitation to take the presidency of the South Carolina College, where he remained for sixteen years, and was the means of raising the institution to a high rank among the colleges of the country.

From all the traditions that have come down to us there is reason to believe that Dr. Maxcy was one of the most eloquent preachers, not merely of his own denomination, but of any, in the country. It is said that " a profound and breathless silence, an intense feeling, and a delight amounting to rapture were the almost invariable attendants of his preaching. His manner was emphatically his own. There was no labored display, nothing turgid or affected, but everything was easy, graceful, dignified, and natural. His general manner of delivery was rather mild than vehement, and rather solemn than impetuous ; commencing in a moderate tone of voice, but becoming more animated and impassioned as he proceeded, he gradually influenced the hearts and feelings of his audience." Says Hon. Jas. L. Petigru, of South Carolina, " Never will the charm of his eloquence be erased from the memory on which its impression has once been made." Hon. Senator Evans, of South Carolina, " He was the greatest orator I have ever heard in the pulpit." Judge O'Neall, of South Carolina, " His were the finest specimens of eloquence and truth to which it has been my privilege to listen." Dr. Maxcy died June 4, 1820.

Maxey, Gen. Rice, was born in Barren, Ky., July 23, 1800. In 1829 he became a member of Mill Creek Baptist church, Monroe Co., Ky. Practised law from his twenty-first to his fiftieth year; removed to Paris, Texas, Nov. 20, 1857 ; elected to the State senate to succeed his son, Gen. S. B. Maxey, in 1862. He lived to see his son, Samuel Bell Maxey, a U. S. Senator from Texas. He was a leader in Kentucky and Texas, both in religion and politics, and exerted great influence both by his lofty character and fine abilities. He was twice married. After a painful illness, borne with Christian fortitude, he died Jan. 11, 1878.

Maxey, U. S. Senator Samuel Bell.—The Maxey family are of Huguenot descent, having settled on James River soon after the revocation of the edict of Nantes. His great-grandfather, Radford Maxey, became a planter in Halifax Co., Va., and his grandfather, William Maxey, removed to Kentucky in the last century. His father, Rice Maxey, was born in Barren Co., Ky., in the year

GEN. SAMUEL BELL MAXEY.

1800, and was a lawyer by profession. His mother was the daughter of Samuel Bell, a native of Albemarle Co., Va.

Samuel Bell Maxey was born at Tompkinsville, Monroe Co., Ky., March 30, 1825. His father removed, in 1834, to Clinton County, where he was clerk of the Circuit and County courts. In 1857 he removed to Texas and settled at Paris. Samuel was educated at the best schools, studying Latin, Greek, and mathematics until he was seventeen years old, when he was appointed a cadet in the Military Academy at West Point. He was graduated there in 1846, and assigned to the 7th Infantry as a brevet second lieutenant. That fall he went to Mexico. He first joined Taylor at Monterey, and when Scott organized a new offensive line from Vera Cruz, Maxey went in Twiggs' column to Tampico. He shared in the siege of Vera Cruz, and was with Harvey's brigade at the battle of Cerro Gordo. He was brevetted a first lieutenant for gallant conduct at the battles of Contreras and Churubusco, and was also engaged at Molino del Rey and in the engagement which resulted in the capture of the city of Mexico. After the city fell into his hands Gen. Scott organized a battalion of five companies of picked men under Col. Charles F. Smith as a city guard. Maxey was assigned to the command of one of these companies, and he was thus provost of one of the five districts of the city. Maxey had learned French at West Point. While in Mexico he became familiar with the Spanish tongue, which subsequently proved useful to him in the practice of the law in Texas. He returned to the United States from Mexico in the summer of 1848, and was stationed at Jefferson Barracks, but finally resigned Sept. 17, 1849. He returned to his father's home, studied law, and in 1850 began the practice at Albany, Clinton County.

In 1857 he settled at his present home in Paris, a promising town in Northeastern Texas, and practised law until 1861. About the opening of the war he was elected to the State senate, but never took his seat, as he thought he ought to be in the army. He raised the 9th Texas Infantry for the army under Gen. Albert Sidney Johnston. In December, 1861, it marched by land and reached Memphis in time to join the army at Corinth. In the mean time he had been made a brigadier-general. He joined Gen. Johnston at Decatur, and was sent by him to Chattanooga to collect and reorganize troops there.

Gen. Maxey's services in the Confederate army were many and important. On the direct application of Gen. E. Kirby Smith, then in command of the Trans-Mississippi Department, in the fall of 1863 he was ordered to take command of the Indian Territory. Everything there was in terrible confusion. Maxey, with very little aid from headquarters, put eight or ten thousand troops under arms. In the spring of 1864 he advised Gen. Smith of Steele's advance, and moved into Arkansas, where he joined Price and shared in his fight at Prairie Danne to check the enemy. He fought Steele at Poison Springs, April 18, 1864, and captured his entire train of 227 wagons. The loss of his transportation compelled Steele to retire. For his conduct on this occasion Maxey was made a major-general.

Gen. Maxey went to his home and devoted himself to the practice of the law, which soon proved both laborious and lucrative to him. He was appointed judge, but declined. In 1874 he was elected to the United States Senate, and took his seat March 5, 1875. Gen. Maxey undoubtedly owes his election to the popular conviction that he is stanch, diligent, and a representative man.

At first Gen. Maxey was placed on the Committee on Territories, but was transferred the same year, 1875, to that on Military Affairs. He has served continuously on the Committee on Labor and Education, and on Post-Offices, of which latter he is now chairman. He has had more than ordinary success in practical legislation. He has never made a report from any committee which was not sustained. The post-office committee is a very important one to a frontier State. Gen. Maxey has aided greatly in increasing the postal facilities of Texas. Among others, he has had established the stage route from Fort Worth to Fort Yuma, the longest stage line in the world.

Gen. Maxey is a member of the Baptist Church, to which his family has belonged for four or five generations. He is a gallant, genial gentleman, and a hard-working, useful Senator. Very few Senators enjoy so generally the affection and esteem of their colleagues.

Maxson, Rev. John, the first white child born on the island of Rhode Island, was born in 1638, shortly after his father had been killed by the Pequots. He was one of the purchasers of Westerly, R. I., in 1661, and one of the freemen there in 1669; ordained, when seventy years of age, "to the place and office of an elder" in the First Westerly (now Hopkinton) Seventh-Day Baptist church; had as assistants, in 1710, John Maxson (2d), William Davis, Joseph Clarke, Sr., George Stillman, Joseph Clarke, Jr., and Joseph Crandall, and in 1712 the church numbered about 130 members; died Dec. 17, 1720, aged eighty-two.

Mayfield, W. D., D.D., pastor of Central Baptist church, Little Rock, Ark., was born in South Carolina in 1837; began to preach in 1856; chaplain of the 3d S. C. Regiment, in the Confederate army; after filling several important pastorates in his native State he became pastor at Helena, Ark., in 1868; from 1874 to 1877, corresponding secretary of the Southern Baptist Publication Society; then removed to Nashville, Tenn., and began the publication of the *Baptist Reflector;* he also published a literary magazine called *Happy Home;* at the close of the year 1879 he removed to Little Rock. Dr. Mayfield is a fine writer, and as he is yet in the prime of life, much may be expected from his vigorous pen.

Mays, Rev. John L., a pioneer preacher in North Louisiana, by whose zealous labors many churches in Union, Claiborne, and Jackson Parishes were founded, was born in 1814, and died in the pulpit, Nov. 16, 1866.

Mays, R. G., M.D., was born in Edgefield Co., S. C., Oct. 5, 1800. "After finishing his regular course of study," writes his sister, Mrs. Judge Brevard, "he decided on medicine as his calling, and graduated at the medical college in Baltimore in 1822." Not caring for his profession, he devoted himself to farming and became a very successful planter.

In the extensive revival of 1831, Dr. and Mrs. Mays were converted, and baptized into Edgefield church by the Rev. Mr. Hodges. From his conversion to his death he was an earnest, zealous Christian. He was a natural orator, readily using beautiful expressions with a voice full of melody, and he was almost irresistible in exhortation. His prayers were from a heart imbued with the Spirit of God, and could scarcely be heard without emotion. His manners were genial and kind, and his hospitality overflowing and refined.

He was ready to aid every good work, and being blessed with a competency, and coming to Florida when the denomination was young and weak, he did much to build it up. He was specially interested in the spiritual welfare of his slaves, and employed ministers to preach to them.

He was called to pass through deep waters. Seven of nine children were taken from him, and in April, 1878, the wife of his youth died at their home at Orange Mills. Since that time Dr. Mays himself has gone to his eternal home.

McAlister, Rev. I. N., an active minister of Sabine Association, La., was born in Mississippi in 1813; came to Louisiana in 1853; was employed as a missionary of the State Convention, and did good service. He died Jan. 27, 1874.

McAlpine, Rev. Wm. H., is about thirty-six years old; reared as a slave in a cultivated family; received instruction and good breeding; entered school at Talladega soon after he became free. Took a liberal course in the Congregational College at that place; at the same time received instruction in theology from Dr. J. J. D. Renfroe, by whom he was baptized, ordained, and installed pastor of the colored church in the city. He has been State evangelist for his race; now pastor of the large colored church at Marion. No man has done more for the elevation of the colored people in Alabama. He is an excellent preacher, and a rising man.

McArthur, Joseph Benjamin, was born Nov. 25, 1849, in the township of Lobo, County of Middlesex, Ontario, Canada. He attended the public school until fifteen years of age, and, after an interval of two years spent upon a farm, went to the Middlesex Seminary. In 1868 he matriculated into the Law Society of Upper Canada, and was entered as a student at Osgoode Hall, in the city of Toronto. He was called to the bar of Ontario in November, 1873, and was invited to join the eminent legal firm to whom he had been articled. The retirement of a member of the firm on Jan. 1, 1881, led to the formation of the present firm of Mulock, Tilt, McArthur & Crowther. Mr. McArthur was baptized in 1873, and united with the Alexander Street church, Toronto, of which he has been for several years a deacon. He is superintendent of the Sunday-school, one of the trustees of the Toronto Baptist College, and a vice-president of the Home Mission Board. For personal consecration and liberal giving he is conspicuous among the laymen of Canada.

McCall, Rev. G. R., of Hawkinsville, Ga., is one of the ablest, most prominent, and influential of the younger generation of Georgia Baptist ministers,—a man whose modesty equals his merit, and whose ability as a preacher is second to few of his age. He was born Feb. 7, 1829, in Screven Co., Ga., and was educated at Mercer University, graduating with the third honor, in a talented class, in the year 1853. He then spent one year in the same university studying theology. He joined the church at fifteen, was licensed at eighteen, and ordained Sept. 24, 1854, when nearly twenty-five. In January of 1855 he was called to preach once a month to the Richland church, Twiggs County, and has continued its pastor ever since. After the war he settled in Hawkinsville, and took charge of the Baptist church there in October, 1866, to which church he is still preaching. He has been a diligent and successful pastor. For years Mr. McCall has acted as the moderator of the Ebenezer Association, and his influence in all the region where he lives is very great, especially in the Baptist churches. For ten years in succession he has been the clerk of the Georgia Baptist Convention, and for two years was clerk of the Southern Baptist Convention. He has been a member of the board of trustees for Mercer University, acting as secretary of the board. He is a strong friend of missions, Sunday-schools, and of education. He is an excellent preacher and a wise counselor. He ranks very high in the estimation of his brethren.

McCallum, Rev. H. B., was born in Knox Co.,

Tenn., Jan. 9, 1837, and spent his childhood at Gravesville, in the northeastern part of that county. In his thirteenth year his father removed to Knoxville. Here Hugh spent his time from 1849 to 1853.

In 1852 he entered East Tennessee University, and remained several terms. During the fall of 1852 he was converted, and was baptized by Dr. Matthew Hillsman in December of that year. He was soon impressed with the duty of preaching the gospel, and resolved to devote his life to that work. In 1854 he entered Union University, Murfreesborough, Tenn., intending to take a full course, but his health declined so rapidly that he remained but ten months.

By advice of his physicians he visited Florida in December, 1856, and remained till spring. By doing this for two or three years he was restored to comparatively good health.

In 1859 he settled in Camden, S. C., and continued meanwhile to study theology. The following year he enlisted as a private, and was mustered into service in the Confederate army. In 1861 he was called to the chaplaincy of his regiment, and was ordained at the call of his church, and served as chaplain during the war.

At the close of the war he settled in Sumter District, S. C., and preached to country churches. In 1867 he removed to Florida, and in 1869 he located at Lake City, and was soon chosen to the pastorate of the church there. The little organization, with no house, was soon built up to an effective church, and one of the best houses of worship in the State erected. In 1873 he was induced to commence the *Florida Baptist*, and published it two years, and then transferred it to the *Christian Index*, of Georgia.

Mr. McCallum is a man of ability and energy. He is a ready, forcible writer and speaker, and by his pen and his preaching has done much to strengthen the Baptist denomination in the State.

McCloud, Rev. Constant S., a native of Vermont, was born in 1818; graduated at Georgetown College in 1846; removed to Mississippi, and became successively pastor at Starkville, Vicksburg, and Raymond. After the war he became pastor at Jefferson, Texas, where by his indefatigable labors he increased the membership from a mere handful to about two hundred, and erected one of the handsomest church edifices in the State, and a comfortable parsonage. In 1872 he became missionary of the Grand Cane Baptist Association, La. He fell a victim to yellow fever at Shreveport, Oct. 17, 1873.

McCoid, Hon. M. M., member of Congress from Iowa, was born in Logan Co., O., Nov. 5, 1840. His father, Robert McCoid, was of Irish, and his mother, Jane Bain, of Scotch, descent. Her father came from Ayrshire, Scotland, and was a Revolutionary soldier in the Virginia troops. McCoid removed with his parents to Iowa when he was eleven years old. He received a common-school education, and then attended Fairfield University, and Washington College, Washington, Pa., until the Junior year, leaving because of ill health. He soon after entered upon the study of law. He was admitted to the bar in 1861, but immediately enlisted as a private in Co. E, 2d Regiment Iowa Vols., in which he served for the full time of enlistment, being discharged May 28, 1864. He was promoted to be second lieutenant, and was for a considerable time acting adjutant of the regiment. He was in seven battles, including Fort Donelson, Shiloh, Corinth, and Stone River. In 1864 he returned to civil life, and began the practice of law. In 1866 he was elected district attorney of the sixth Iowa judicial district, and served for four years. In 1870 he was elected State senator, and re-elected in 1875; in 1878 he was elected from the first district as a member of the Forty-sixth Congress, and he was re-elected to the present Congress. He was brought up a Presbyterian, and learned the Shorter Catechism before he was able to read, but on his conversion, in 1865, he embraced the Baptist faith, and has been a member of the Fairfield Baptist church ever since. He is a man of great ability, integrity, and piety.

McConnico, Rev. Garner, was a native of Lunenburg Co., Va., where his family occupied a high social position. He became hopefully pious, under the instructions of an excellent mother, at a very early age, and united with the church; and such were the spirit and the ability which he manifested in the part he occasionally took in the social religious exercises that the church in due time licensed him to preach, and ordained him as a minister of the gospel before he had reached his twenty-eighth year. As the beautiful valley of the Cumberland presented extraordinary attractions as a place for settlement, Mr. McConnico sold his property in Lunenburg County near the close of the last century, and selected as his future home a spot in Williamson County than which it would be difficult to find another more beautiful. Here he secured a large tract of land, and spent thirty-five years rearing a large and estimable family, some of whom have since reached positions of usefulness and honor. His mansion was ever the scene of a profuse hospitality. In it was found the best society then in the West; and especially was it the home of ministers of the gospel. Mr. McConnico immediately commenced among the settlers his appropriate work. He was a diligent student of the Bible, and of standard theological writings, with which his library was furnished. He clung with unyielding tenacity to the great doctrines of the

Cross, and had an intelligent and definite view of the whole evangelical system. He prepared his discourses with much care, and they were characterized by remarkable perspicuity and directness, and they were delivered with graceful elocution and impressive fervor. For years he preached often in all parts of the middle district, and sometimes beyond it. Many professed religion, and a large number of churches were raised up mainly through his instrumentality. Of the Harpeth church, which was in his immediate neighborhood, and which was large, intelligent, and wealthy, he became the regular pastor, and continued in the office until the end of his life. Of seven other churches around him he was the stated supply, according to the practice of the times. His popularity was almost unbounded. He died suddenly, full of faith and hope, in the year 1833.

His piety was deep, and his presence neutralized every tendency to levity. Listening to him beneath the shade of the gigantic forest-trees, where he so often preached, you would have felt coming over you a strange reverence for his mighty mind. His memory and influence can never die.

McCoy, Rev. Isaac, the great apostle to the American Indians, was born in Fayette Co., Pa., June 13, 1784. He came with his father to Kentucky in 1790. In 1801 he was converted and joined the Buck Creek Baptist church. In 1803 he was married to Christiana Polk, daughter of Capt. Polk, whose wife and several children were captured by the Ottowas. Mr. McCoy and his wife were afterwards missionaries to that tribe.

In 1804 he came to Vincennes, Ind., and in 1805 removed to Clarke County, same State. He had a marked influence upon the churches and Associations of that part of the State. No one of the great benevolent enterprises of the denomination was allowed to pass unnoticed. Living in a part of the country where Antinomianism was industriously taught, he exerted himself to counteract its baneful influence. He was licensed to preach by the mother of all Indiana Baptist churches,—Silver Creek. In 1810 he was ordained by the Maria Creek church. In 1817 he received an appointment as missionary to the Indians of Indiana and Illinois. After his departure for his work the influence of Daniel Parker grew rapidly in the southwestern part of Indiana, and the missionary spirit waned. Mr. McCoy was appointed for one year, but had no thought that he should cease to labor for the red man at the expiration of that time; his plans embraced many years. After spending some time in Western Indiana, it occurred to him that he should move to Fort Wayne and establish a mission. He labored there till 1822, when he established a mission about one mile west of where Niles (Michigan) now is. He named it Carey, after the English missionary. Mr. McCoy and his wife entered upon this missionary work with all the zeal and strength of faith that characterized the life and labors of Mr. and Mrs. Judson. And their faith did not fail. Deprivations, sicknesses, and sorrows such as but few mortals know were not strangers to them. Mr. McCoy rode hundreds of miles through the wilderness, and swam the swollen streams, lying on the wet ground at night, for the sake of carrying forward his missions. He went on horseback to Washington several times to interest Congress in measures beneficial to the Indian. Many months would be occupied in these journeys. One of the severest trials that Mr. McCoy was called to bear was that during his absence from home sickness and sometimes death would visit his family. Five of his children were called by death at different times while he was absent from home. Persons of narrow selfish views would readily call him cruel and indifferent, but men who could rise to his plane of devotion to the work that he believed God had given him can see that his loyalty to the Master was superior even to parental affection. No man loved his wife and children more than he.

Many conversions occurred at the Carey mission. The hymns composed by him on the occasion of the first baptism at Fort Wayne and at Carey are expressive at once of his great joy and his great hope of what would yet be done for the Indian.

He records that the greatest obstacle by far that he was obliged to meet in his labors for the conversion of the Indians was the introduction of whisky among them by white men. So great were his annoyances at one time that he decided to send several of his Indian pupils East to be educated, so that they might become teachers for their own people. They found a ready welcome at Hamilton, N. Y.

His labors at Washington were to secure a territory for the Indians into which the white man might not intrude his wicked commerce. This he regarded as the only sure hope for the Christianization or civilization of the red men. He lived to see some of the tribes settled on their own territory, industrious and happy. In his labors for the passage of such acts as he recommended to Congress he speaks of the sympathy and co-operation afforded him by Spencer H. Cone, William Colgate, and others of his brethren.

Oct. 9, 1825, Mr. McCoy preached the first sermon in English ever delivered in Chicago or near its site. In 1826 he gave up the personal superintendence of the Carey mission for the purpose of selecting lands for the Indians farther West. He made surveys west of the Mississippi River, and several times went to Washington to communicate facts to Congress and to lay his plans before that body. In 1840 he published his "History of Indian Affairs," a volume of 600 octavo pages, and full of interest. In 1842 the American Indian Mission Association was formed, and he was made secretary, with headquarters at Louisville, Ky.

In June, 1846, as he was returning from Jeffersonville, where he had preached, he was caught in a rain-storm, from the effects of which he died in a few days at his home in Louisville.

"His life and labors were truly the connecting link between barbarism and civilization in this region of the country and over a large portion of the West. His perseverance and devotion were morally and heroically sublime. For nearly thirty years he was the apostle to the Indians of the West." His last words were, "Tell the brethren, never to let the Indian mission decline."

McCoy, Milton, M.D., was born in Kanawha Co., West Va., in January, 1824. He professed conversion, and joined the Hansford Baptist church in 1847, being baptized into the fellowship of that church by Rev. M. M. Rock. He commenced the practice of medicine in 1849; removed to Moniteau Co., Mo., in 1853, and to Boonville in 1863. He was a constituent member of the First Baptist church in Tipton, Mo., which was formed in 1858, and of which he was made a deacon. Upon his removal to Boonville he was made a deacon there, and has held the office ever since. For years he has been one of the main pillars in the church.

McCraw, Rev. A. G., a native of Newberry District, S. C., was born June 4, 1803. He is of Scotch descent. In 1818, with his father, he removed to Alabama, and located in Perry County. An industrious student, he pursued an extensive range of historic reading; was baptized at Ocmulgee church in May, 1828, and began at once to preach the gospel; was ordained in 1831, Rev. George Everett receiving ordination at the same time; these two labored much together, mainly as evangelists. They planted a number of churches, had many revivals, and baptized large numbers of converts; in one of their revivals 200 were baptized in Shelby County in 1832. In 1835 he became pastor of the large and influential church at Ocmulgee,—a position which he held for many years. In 1851 he became pastor in the growing city of Selma, where he led a career of success until his death, which occurred Jan. 14, 1861. Always in easy circumstances, Mr. McCraw labored constantly in the ministry, and with but small remuneration. He was prominently connected with the leading interests of Alabama Baptists, earnestly pleading every cause fostered by our State Convention. He was several years president of that body. He reared a highly accomplished family.

McCraw, Rev. N. F., an active and efficient minister of the Bayou Macon Association, La., was born in Tennessee in 1828; did much to strengthen the Baptist churches between the Mississippi and Ouachita Rivers. Died in 1874.

McCulloch, Rev. Jno. V., a pioneer preacher in Arkansas, was born in Tennessee in 1820. He settled in Dallas County, Ark., in 1839, and shortly afterwards began to preach, though not ordained until 1851. Abounding in labors in the gospel, he preached in all the surrounding country; was instrumental in forming most of the early churches in the region between the Ouachita and Saline Rivers. He even extended his labors into the region between the Bayou Bartholomew and the Mississippi River, where he died from malarial fever in 1874. This useful minister is affectionately remembered by the people.

McCully, Judge Jonathan, son of Rev. Samuel McCully, was born in Nappan, Nova Scotia, July 25, 1809. He was converted and baptized in 1849. He removed to Halifax soon after, and became deacon of the North Baptist church in that city, which office he held until his death, Jan. 2, 1877. He was a member of the Nova Scotia Legislative Council and of the Senate of Canada, and judge of the Supreme Court of Nova Scotia. He was an able lawyer, statesman, and judge. He left bequests to Acadia College and foreign missions.

McCully, Rev. Samuel, was born in Nova Scotia. He was converted under the ministry of Rev. Joseph Crandall, and embracing Baptist principles, was immersed by him in 1813. He was ordained at Sackville, New Brunswick, in 1820. From 1827 he was associated in labor with Rev. Charles Tupper at Amherst, Nova Scotia, but preached frequently in Cumberland and Westmoreland Counties. Faithful and earnest, firm yet pacific, his labors were highly prized.

McCune, Hon. Henry E., deacon of the Baptist church at Dixon, Cal., a man of great social, political, and religious influence, an intelligent Christian and generous Baptist. Through his liberality the large college property at Vacaville, worth $20,000, was secured for California (Baptist) College. He is president of its board, and a large contributor to its funds. The Dixon house of worship, an elegant edifice, was erected by his aid as a chief contributor. He was born June 10, 1825, in Pike Co., Mo.; baptized in March, 1840, and joined the Peno church; removed to California, and settled near Vacaville, Solano Co., in 1854; went into the organization of the Vacaville Baptist church in 1856; was ordained as deacon in 1863. In 1873 he was elected to the State senate of California, and served two terms. By occupation he is a farmer, and holds several thousand acres of fine land. Deacon McCune has been greatly prospered; but he holds his wealth as a trust for the Lord, and, though he gives wisely and largely for church and denominational enterprises, and is loved and honored by all who know him, he is one of the most modest and unassuming of men. His home and heart and purse are all for Christ.

HON. HENRY E. M'CUNE.

McDaniel, James, D.D., was one of the men whom the Baptists of North Carolina delighted

JAMES M'DANIEL, D.D.

to honor. He was born near Fayetteville, N. C., in 1803; was baptized in 1827, and began to preach the same year. He was chiefly instrumental in the organization of the Fayetteville Baptist church, of which he was pastor for thirty-two years. For six years he was pastor of the First Baptist church of Wilmington, N. C., during a part of which time he was also editor of a religious journal.

Dr. McDaniel was one of the founders of the Baptist State Convention, being present at its organization in Greenville, Pitt Co., in 1830, and he had the honor of presiding over its deliberations for nineteen years. He was a trustee of Wake Forest College for many years, and his zeal in the cause of missions was ardent and unremitting. He was clerk of Cape Fear Association for fourteen years. Dr. McDaniel possessed in a rare degree the gifts and graces of the orator, and many are the traditions of the pathos and power of his preaching in his younger days. At a good old age, and with his natural force unabated, this eminent divine was gathered to his fathers in 1870. Wake Forest College conferred the degree of Doctor of Divinity upon him in 1868.

McDonald, Rev. Alexander, was born in 1814, in Scotland. He was converted at Margaree, Cape Breton, and baptized by Rev. Wm. Burton. He studied at Acadia College from 1838 to 1841. He was ordained pastor in Prince Edward Island. He was pastor of Carleton Baptist church, St. John, New Brunswick, from 1846 to 1849. He died Jan. 27, 1851. He was an earnest, faithful, and useful minister.

McDonald, Gov. Charles J., was born in Charleston, S. C., in July, 1793. His parents removed to Georgia during his infancy. In his youth he was sent to a classical school in Hancock Co., Ga., and was graduated at the University of South Carolina during the presidency of Jonathan Maxey, who at twenty-four years of age was president of Brown University. Returning to Georgia, young McDonald studied law, and even in his early manhood took rank with the best lawyers in the State. In a short time he was elected by the Legislature to a judgeship of the Superior Court. Though his duties were confined to a district, he acquitted himself in this office so handsomely that he became known throughout the State as one of its ablest jurists. Having previously been a member of the Legislature, he had acquired some standing among politicians, and in 1839 was elected governor of the State by a handsome majority. In 1841 he was re-elected to the same office, although the State, at an election held for President of the United States only a short time previously, had given a large majority to his political opponents. The fact shows that he was a far more popular man with the people than the party with which he was identified. Retiring from the gubernatorial chair, and being still in the vigor of his days, he resumed the practice of law. But in a short time the people called him to be a judge of the Supreme Court of the State, and he continued in the office until disabled by the illness which

GOV. CHARLES J. M'DONALD.

terminated in his death. He died at his beautiful home in Marietta, Ga., in December, 1860.

Perhaps no man was more popular in his day than Gov. McDonald. Besides commanding all the votes of his party when a candidate for office before the people, he was sustained, from personal considerations, by many who dissented from his political views. This was not because he descended to the low expedients of the partisan in seeking supporters. He utterly despised all unworthy means. It was his fine character which commanded universal respect. His integrity was above reproach, whilst as a politician he always aimed at the general good. On one occasion during a heated canvass, a friend suggested a method by which he might gain a great advantage over his opponent. "It is not honorable," said the governor. "What of that? It will never be known." "I shall know it myself; and a man cannot afford to know anything mean of himself."

The confidence which the people reposed in his judgment was another source of the support he enjoyed at their hands. His mind was remarkably well-balanced. He was singularly sagacious and discriminating; and had he been connected as intimately with the national as with State politics, would have left the impress of his wisdom on the legislation of the country. Throughout life he was a man of the strictest probity and morality. It is believed by those who knew him best that he had experienced converting grace, and, though not baptized, he was a decided Baptist, and like Nicholas Brown, was closely identified with the Baptists.

McDonald, Rev. D. G., was born Feb. 15, 1843, at Uigg, Prince Edward Island, where his conversion and baptism took place in 1863. He studied at Acadia College, and was ordained at Newport, Nova Scotia, Jan. 16, 1873. He labored as a missionary for some time on Prince Edward Island. Subsequently he became pastor of the Baptist church at Charlottetown, the capital of that province, where his ministry proved highly beneficial.

McDonald, Henry, D.D., was born in the county of Antrim, in the north of Ireland, Jan. 3, 1832. He was nurtured in the Roman Catholic Church, to which his parents and ancestors all belonged. He was educated in the national schools of Ireland, and afterwards passed through the regular course of the Normal School, Dublin. In 1848 he left his native country in consequence of the failure of the patriots to throw from them the yoke of British oppression, and reached New Orleans, which city he left, after a few weeks, to visit Kentucky. He taught school for some time in Greensburg Co., Ky., and afterwards studied law and was admitted to the bar. During his residence in Greensburg County he made a thorough examination of the doctrines of Roman Catholicism, the result of which, after a severe mental struggle, was the rejection of the whole system as unscriptural. Abandoning his faith in the church's dogmas, he was led to a complete trust in Christ alone for salvation. In consequence of this radical change in his religious views and feelings, he publicly professed his faith in Christ, and united with the Baptist church in Greensburg, having been baptized by the pastor, the Rev. George Peck. He soon felt it to be his duty to devote himself to the ministry, and was accordingly licensed by the church and subsequently ordained, in May, 1854. He was invited to the pastorate of the church in Greensburg, and served it with great success for nearly ten years. During this period he was also pastor, at different times, of the Friendship and Campbellsville churches, in Taylor County, and the Mount Gilead church, in Greene County. For one year he was pastor of the Tate's Creek and Waco churches in Madison County, and for six years of the Danville church. He was afterwards pastor of the church in Georgetown, Ky., and at the same time elected to a professorship of Theology in the Western Baptist Theological Institute, from which position he subsequently retired to fill the chair of Moral Philosophy in the Georgetown College, Ky. The honorary degree of A.M. was conferred upon him by the Georgetown College, and the degree of

D.D. by both the Georgetown and Bethel Colleges, Ky. Several years ago, Dr. McDonald was invited to the pastorate of the Second Baptist church, Richmond, Va., which he accepted, and where he still labors with eminent success. In 1856 he married, in Greensburg, Miss Mattie Harding, daughter of the Hon. Aaron Harding, for several successive terms a representative in Congress from Kentucky. Dr. McDonald is greatly gifted as a preacher, impassioned, eloquent, and a master of men's emotional nature. Those who know him intimately honor him greatly.

McDougal, Rev. Alexander, was born in Dublin, Ireland, about 1738. In his twenty-first year he came to America and settled in Wilmington, N. C., from which he soon afterwards removed to Union District, S. C. He and his wife were Presbyterians, but about 1770 he became convinced that he was without Christ. He was deeply convicted of sin. When he found peace in Jesus he united with a Baptist church, and soon began to exhort. He was ordained to the ministry about 1775. This was at the commencement of the Revolution. Warmly espousing the cause of the colonies, "he divided his time, during the war, between cultivating his farm, preaching the gospel, and fighting the Tories." He continued preaching in his adopted State until about the year 1800, when he removed to Kentucky, and settled in Hardin County. Here, in 1803, he became pastor of Nolin church, and he was also pastor of Severns Valley church. He continued to serve these communities until his ninety-fifth year, when he resigned. He died March 3, 1841, aged one hundred and three years.

McDowell, Archibald, D.D., was born in Kershaw Co., S. C., in 1818; became a Christian early; graduated at Wake Forest College in 1849; was for a time tutor in that institution, then took charge of the new enterprise since known as the Chowan Female Institute, at Murfreesborough, and afterwards removed to Milton, where he preached and taught. In 1853-54 he taught in Raleigh, but returned in 1855 to the Chowan Institute, where he has been ever since, having become president in 1862. He received his degree of D.D. from Wake Forest College, of which he has long been a trustee.

McFarland, Rev. Arthur, a pioneer preacher in North Louisiana, was born in Tennessee in 1793; removed to Louisiana in 1821, and with his father-in-law, Elder James Brinson, united with the Pine Hills Baptist church, the first gathered between the Ouachita and Red Rivers. Shortly after he began to preach, and continued to labor in the region where he resided until disabled by age. He died at Athens, La., Aug. 21, 1878. He is mentioned by Benedict as one of his correspondents in Louisiana.

McGee, Rev. W. H., pastor at Minden, La., and secretary of Louisiana Baptist Convention, was born in Mississippi in 1846; graduated at Mississippi College in 1876; in 1877 called to his present field, where his labors have been greatly blessed.

McGuire, Rev. John A., a veteran Baptist minister, residing at Monroe, La., was born in Kentucky in 1799; began to preach at the age of seventeen. He labored successfully in his native State until 1850, when he settled permanently at Monroe, La., where he gathered a few Baptists into a church and became their pastor. The circumstances were most unfavorable, but he labored with such success that a comfortable house was built, and another church gathered at Trenton, on the opposite side of the river. He has lived to witness a commodious brick edifice take the place of the first humble house of worship, and two strong churches grown up from the seed he sowed.

McIntosh, W. H., D.D., a descendant of Gen. McIntosh of American Revolutionary fame, was

W. H. MCINTOSH, D.D.

born in McIntosh Co., Ga., April 4, 1811. After thorough preparation for college, he finished his education in Furman Institution, S. C., under the Rev. Samuel Furman and Dr. Jesse Hartwell. Preached for some years as voluntary missionary, under a license from the Sunberry Baptist church, and was ordained by the South Newport church in 1836. Became pastor at Darien in 1838, where he remained for eleven years. In 1849 he was called to the pastorate in Eufaula, Ala., and remaining there six years, in 1855 he accepted the call of the Siloam church in Marion; and, after a pastorate there of seventeen years, he was, in 1872, called to Macon, Ga., from which he returned to Marion, Ala., in the fall of 1875, to assume the corresponding secretaryship of the Home Mission Board of the Southern Baptist Convention, of which he was president during his long pastorate in that place. The degree of Doctor of Divinity was conferred on him by two institutions in 1868,—Columbian College, Washington, D. C., and Baylor University, Texas. Dr. McIntosh is a man of dignified presence, engaging manners, and high character. There is no minister in our acquaintance more widely honored and beloved. His letters and discourses are traced by a remarkably graceful and vigorous pen; and rare tact, energy, and executive power are displayed in the discharge of the duties of his responsible office.

McIver, Hon. Alex. M., a native of Darlington District, S. C., was born on the 21st of February, 1799. He graduated at the South Carolina College in 1817. He was admitted to practice in the law court in 1820, and in that of equity in 1828. He was a member of the Legislature from 1830 to 1833, and in 1841 was elected solicitor of the northern circuit. He was twice re-elected, and died in his third term, on the 10th of July, 1850. His descendants are among the most honorable in the State. As a Christian and a Baptist he adorned his profession, " walking in all the statutes and ordinances of the Lord blameless."

McIver, Rev. D. R. W., was born in Charleston, S. C., in 1794; was educated at the University of South Carolina. Being a man of large property his early labors were devoted to the poor, preaching on the plantations to the slaves. He filled a successful pastorate at Prattville and Wetumpka, Ala. In 1856 he removed to De Soto Parish, La. Here he labored with great success until 1862. He died Feb. 10, 1863.

McKay, Rev. Uriah, was born in the State of Indiana in 1821. At the age of eighteen he was baptized. He went to Franklin College to obtain a better education, to prepare for usefulness in the world without having the ministry in view; spent some time preaching and teaching in Indiana. He went to Illinois in 1854, and was ordained the next year. He spent fourteen years in Effingham Co., Ill., preaching most of the time for but little compensation. He came to Iowa in 1868, and is now living on a farm at Elm Grove, near Des Moines. He has been employed chiefly since coming to Iowa in preaching to feeble churches in destitute fields, doing good service for the cause of Christ by his earnest labors, his consistent and cheerful Christian life, and hearty co-operation in all denominational works. He represents a class of men in the ministry found in Iowa who, while supporting themselves by the labors of their own hands, have contributed largely to the growth and prosperity of the denomination.

McKenzie, Rev. David Banks, was born in Liverpool, England, June 26, 1836, and came to America, arriving at Boston April 15, 1848. In 1853 he became the subject of religious impressions, and was immersed by Rev. Mr. Pierce, at Gloucester, Mass. He had a natural love for the ocean, followed the sea in early youth, and during the civil war in the United States entered the navy, and was three times promoted for meritorious service. For many years, though he had professed Christianity, he lived in sin, gave himself to the world, was very intemperate, and apparently a moral wreck, until, in December, 1871, he was rescued by sovereign grace, and gave himself fully to the Saviour. He began his real religious life as a temperance preacher, and had immense success in New England, where thousands were reclaimed. He enlisted benevolent persons in the work, and built reformatories in many places. In 1877 he extended his mission to California, and in April, 1880, after two years' absence, returned to that State to labor permanently in the gospel, as temperance reformer and pastor. He possesses unusual gifts for persuading men to forsake their evil ways, and in all places stirs the people to active and earnest work to save the fallen and rescue the perishing from temporal and eternal ruin.

McKenzie, William S., D.D., was born in Liverpool, Nova Scotia, Feb. 29, 1832. He was a graduate of Harvard University in the class of 1855. He was ordained in April, 1857, and was pastor of the church in Abington, Mass., one year, and of the church in Andover, Mass., for two years. For six years he was pastor of the Friendship Street church in Providence, R. I., and was pastor in St. John, New Brunswick, also six years. In 1872 he received an appointment as district secretary of the American Baptist Missionary Union, which position he now holds.

McKinlay, Rev. John, was born in Alexandria, Dumbartonshire, Scotland, March 6, 1831. He came to this country in 1855, and was employed as a designer in the Pacific Mills, Lawrence, Mass. While thus occupied he became a subject of converting grace, and feeling it to be his duty to preach the gospel, he pursued his studies at Fairfax, Vt., and at Andover, Mass. He was ordained pastor of the church in Lebanon, N. H., in November, 1862, where he labored with great acceptance until his death, which occurred Sept. 20, 1868.

"He was a close and diligent student of the Scriptures, always bringing well-beaten oil to the sanctuary. Every sermon bore the stamp of his own genius. He could not be a servile copyist.

He was always John McKinlay, and Scotch at that. He had the Scotch acumen to detect the truth, the Scotch tenacity to hold it, the Scotch wit to garnish it in impressive style, and he had withal the Scotch energy and accent of speech to apply it."

McLafferty, Rev. B. S., educated for the law, dedicated himself to the ministry, and was pastor in Illinois. Under appointment of the Home Mission Society he went to the Pacific coast in 1864–65; was pastor at Virginia City, and preached at Carson, the capital of Nevada, until ill health forced him to settle in the better climate of Petaluma, Cal. He had great success here as pastor; sought to establish a Baptist institution at Petaluma; traveled for a time, and did much to enlist the churches in education and in missionary work. He is a busy worker and a vigorous preacher. Continued ill health led him after brief pastorates to take an ocean voyage to China, where he visited missionaries and mission stations. After his return he was pastoral supply of the First Baptist church, San Francisco, for a time pastor at San Diego, and afterwards at Oakland for several years, until near the close of 1878. The Oakland church had large accessions during his ministry. In 1879 he visited the Atlantic States, and on his return made the tour of Oregon, preaching to the churches and assisting in revival meetings. The church at Eugene, the southernmost city in Oregon, and seat of the State University, called him to its pastorate in June, 1879.

McLean, Rev. Thomas George, was born May 18, 1843, of Presbyterian parents, at Montreal, Canada; spent his youth at Chicago and Waukegan, Ill. He was converted at fifteen, and after six years' struggle with doubts as to Presbyterianism, finally yielded to his convictions, was immersed by Dr. Everts, joined the First church of Chicago in 1864, and enlisted in the U. S. army; decided on his return home to enlist in the ministry; graduated in 1869 at the Chicago Theological Seminary, and during his studies had charge of the Erie Street Mission, and preached at Englewood. He settled and was ordained pastor at Cordova, Ill., in 1870. After three years' service at Cordova, with health impaired, he removed to California; was five years pastor at Brooklyn; and in 1878 became missionary and pastor in Santa Barbara County, where he has the oversight of the Carpenteria and Santa Paula churches; preaches at four stations, labors in revivals, and is moderator of Santa Barbara Association.

McLearn, Rev. Richard, was born in Rawdon, Nova Scotia; was converted and baptized when a youth; ordained March 10, 1828, as pastor of the Rawdon Baptist church; subsequently served the church in Windsor, Nova Scotia, as pastor for twelve years, when bronchial disease compelled him to withdraw from the pulpit, but his integrity, piety, and prudence continued to serve the church of Christ until called hence, Aug. 17, 1860.

McLeod, Sir Donald F., Companion of the Bath, and Knight Commander of the Star of India, was born in Fort William, Calcutta, May 6, 1810; his family were Scotch, and to their country he was sent for his education. At eighteen he returned to India, and some time after he was appointed an assistant magistrate.

When about twenty-one, while stationed at Monghir, on the right bank of the Ganges, midway between Calcutta and Allahabad, the Redeemer found and saved him, gave him a new heart and character, and fresh aims and motives. The instrument used in this work was Rev. A. Leslie, a devoted Baptist missionary. Speaking of this change just after it occurred, Sir Donald says, "I have attained a confidence and tranquillity in regard to my worldly duties from which the weakness of my character formerly debarred me, and I have now been freed from despondency and gloominess of spirits, to which for the five previous years I was continually a martyr." And on another occasion, speaking of prayer, he says, "I resort to it in the morning, not only as the most delightful but as the most necessary act of the day, for without it I should have no peace, no power, and during the remainder of the day, whatever of difficulty or annoyance presents itself, my mind flies up to its Creator and is at rest." After obtaining mercy through the blood of the Lamb, he solicited baptism. Mr. Leslie warned him of the contempt which would meet him from the circle in which he moved, but he was ready to follow Christ in the baptismal waters regardless of all consequences, and he was duly immersed in the name of the adorable Trinity, and he continued to the close of his life in communion with the Baptist denomination.

Sir Donald immediately after his conversion began to plan for the secular and religious enlightenment of the people among whom he lived, whose heathenism deeply moved his heart. He gave large sums of money to assist educational efforts and benevolent movements, and his whole soul was enlisted in the work of the missionaries. Rev. Behari Lal Sing, for many years a missionary of the Free Church of Scotland among his countrymen in India, in relating his conversion from heathenism, tells about his education in Dr. Duff's celebrated school, where he read the Bible, and in a medical institution, without any inclination to Christianity, and then says, "It was the pious example of Sir Donald F. McLeod, his integrity, honesty, disinterestedness, and active benevolence, that made me think that Christianity was something living, that there was a loving power in Christ. Here is a man in the receipt of 2000 or 3000 rupees a month ; he spends little on himself and gives away the surplus for education and for the temporal and spiritual welfare of my countrymen. This was the turning-point in my religious history, and led to my conversion."

Sir Donald was specially interested in missions to some of the aboriginal races of India, to be found in large numbers in the hilly regions. These being neither Hindoos nor Mohammedans, are held in contempt by both, and as they have neither literature nor a priesthood, they are far more accessible to the gospel. Among them he sustained missionaries at his own expense, and though death hindered the work, yet many of them have been brought to Jesus.

In his official career his fidelity and talents gradually secured his promotion in the civil service, until he became lieutenant-governor of the Punjab; and in the alarming times of the mutiny, when butchery and terror made the bravest British hearts in India tremble, McLeod, like his Baptist brother, Havelock, felt courageous in the Lord his God, and rendered services to his country which will never be forgotten by natives or Britons while the history of English rule in India is read; for these he was made a Companion of the Bath and a Knight Commander of the Star of India.

He died in London, Nov. 28, 1872, full of the peace of God.

McMaster, Hon. Senator William, was born in 1811, in the county of Tyrone, Ireland, and came to Canada at the age of twenty-two. After a short clerkship in a leading Toronto establishment, he became a partner in the business, and ultimately started for himself as a wholesale merchant. The career thus commenced has been eminently successful, and to-day Mr. McMaster's name is almost a household word in the Dominion, as one of its greatest merchants and bankers. For many years past he has given his attention to purely financial, far more than to commercial, transactions. He is officially connected with several great monetary institutions, the most important of which is the Canadian Bank of Commerce. He has held the presidency of this corporation during a period of twenty years, and its splendid success is largely due to his sagacity and prudence. He was also, for many years, chairman of the Canadian board of directors of the Great Western Railway.

In 1862, at the solicitation of friends, Mr. McMaster reluctantly consented to enter political life, and was elected a member of the upper house of the Canadian Legislature by an overwhelming Liberal majority. Immediately after the confederation of the British American provinces, in 1865, he was chosen Senator of the Dominion, and in that capacity he still continues to serve his country. He was appointed a member in the same year of the council of public instruction, and in 1873 of the senate of Toronto University.

Mr. McMaster was converted in early life, and

HON. SENATOR WILLIAM M'MASTER.

united with the Baptist church in Omagh, about forty miles from Belfast, in his native land. To the denomination in Canada he is a tower of much strength. His generous aid secured the erection and re-erection of the Canadian Literary Institute at Woodstock; and he was chiefly instrumental in the formation of the Superannuated Ministers' Society, of which, from its inception, he has been the honored president. Of home and foreign missions he is a steadfast friend; and to many a feeble church, struggling with a building debt, he has rendered timely help. A leading Toronto paper remarks that "the Jarvis Street Baptist church (in which he worships) is one of the costliest and handsomest in the city, and will as long as it stands remain a memorial of his liberality, and of that of the equally liberal-minded lady who has, since 1871, been his wife." But the crowning achievement of his well-spent life is the erection, at his own cost, of the Toronto Baptist College, which occupies a beautiful site in the Queen's Park.

Mr. McMaster has reached the age of threescore years and ten, but "his eye is not dim, nor his natural force abated." He has been twice married, his present wife being Sarah Moulton, widow of the late James Fraser, Esq., of Newburgh, in the State of New York.

McMinnville College is centrally located for

the Baptists of Oregon, at McMinnville. Chartered in 1852, with Rev. G. C. Chandler as president, in spite of many changes it has continued to gain strength, and now is enlisting the hearty support of all the churches. It has already educated some of the most useful men and women in the State. It has a modest building, a college campus of five acres, $15,000 in endowment funds, and nearly $20,000 already secured for the erection of a brick building. It has four professors, and last year there were 100 students. Rev. G. J. Burchett, the president, is one of the best educators on the Pacific coast. He has the confidence of the churches, and under his administration the college is doing good work for the denomination.

McPherson, Hon. William, was born in Boone Co., Ky., Feb. 15, 1813. His father died

HON. WILLIAM M'PHERSON.

when he was a boy, and left him to care for his mother and her little children. While he met this responsibility nobly, at the same time he obtained a good education. In connection with school-teaching he studied law, and mastering all difficulties, he was admitted to the bar at the age of twenty-one. He first practised law in Burlington, Ky., and from it he removed to Helena, Ark., in 1836, and was successful. From Arkansas he removed to St. Louis, Mo., and remained there till his death, in 1872. Mr. McPherson was a man of commanding presence and strong common sense. He took a prominent place among men by general consent. He was a man of vast information. He had one of the finest private libraries in the West. He was noted for his quick penetration and well-considered plans. He had great magnetic power to sway men, of which he seemed to be unconscious.

He was a decided Baptist. On Jan. 8, 1843, he was baptized by Rev. J. T. Hinton, and united with the Second Baptist church of St. Louis. He was an unconscious leader in Zion. His gifts to his church were large. He inaugurated the building of the house of worship at the corner of Sixth and Locust Streets, and gave to it over $6000. He held official positions in our State and national denominational societies.

The great bridge across the Mississippi at St. Louis was built by capital which he secured in New York, which was necessary to its success, and he was president of the company. The first railroad to St. Louis was established by his aid. He was president of the North Missouri Railroad, and was a prominent mover in the establishment of the Bellefontaine Cemetery. His labors for the growth of the city of St. Louis were not surpassed, if equaled, by any other man. His will to accomplish great things, through difficulties, was imperial.

After a long illness, he came to church for the last time borne in a chair. Strong men wept as he came in. Dr. G. Anderson, his former pastor, preached. Dr. Burlingham, pastor at the time, said, "We fear this is too much for you." He answered, "I was determined to come." Just before he died, he replied to a question in reference to his future hope, "I think I stand on granite." These words are inscribed on his tombstone. There the brave man reposes. "Peaceful be his rest!"

McWhorter, A. B., M.D., a native of Sumterville, S. C., was born Jan. 26, 1791; departed this life Sept. 19, 1859; resided in Montgomery, Ala., from 1830 to his death, and constantly secured in that city the universal regard of the people. It is conceded that the Baptist cause at the capital of our State is more indebted to him for the strong position which it has sustained for forty years than to any other person now living or dead. This is the testimony of Dr. Tichenor, who was his pastor for many years. He was conscientiously particular to meet all his obligations, and a more hospitable home was never kept in that city of rare hospitality. Liberal with his money, generous to the poor, kindly affectionate to all men, wise in counsel, and watchful of the interests of the church and of the pastor, it is but just to say that he was a Christian prince among his brethren.

Meacham, Rev. A. W., an able and eminently successful minister of Little River Association, Ky., was born in Christian Co., Ky., Feb. 13, 1818. He was baptized into the fellowship of Pleasant Hill Baptist church in 1838, where he was licensed to preach in May, 1839, and ordained in December of the same year. A few months after his ordination he accepted a call to the church at Paducah, Ky. From Paducah he removed to Middle Tennessee, where he spent some years in evangelizing. In 1844 he took charge of the church at Shelbyville, Tenn. While laboring with it and with several other churches he was attacked with hemorrhage of the lungs, and was so prostrated that he despaired of life, and returned to his native home, expecting to die. In 1854, having partially recovered, he was called to the care of West Union church, in his native county, to which he still ministers. He has aided in the constitution of 25 churches, and has baptized 4000 persons, 20 of whom are known to have entered the ministry. While he was in Tennessee he was two years moderator of Salem Association and twice moderator of the General Association. Since his return to Kentucky he has been seventeen years moderator of Little River Association.

Meachum, Rev. John Berry, was born May 3, 1789; died Feb. 19, 1864. He was pastor of the First African Baptist church of St. Louis. A marble monument marks his grave in the Baptist burial-ground in Bellefontaine cemetery, erected by the First and Second African churches of St. Louis. He took charge of the First Colored church in 1828; was twenty-five years its pastor. He was born a slave; bought his own freedom, then his father's, a Baptist minister in Virginia. He lived in Kentucky, and married a slave-woman. He worked at the carpenter's trade, and purchased the freedom of his wife and children. He came to Missouri in 1815. He built a steamboat in 1835, and furnished it with a library, and made a temperance boat of it. He was worth $25,000 when he died. He was ordained in 1825, gathered a large church and Sabbath-school, and a deep religious and missionary spirit pervaded his church. He died in his pulpit, with armor on.

Meador, Rev. Christian C., was born in Bedford Co., Va., receiving an elementary education in the common schools of the neighborhood. He was baptized into the fellowship of the New Hope Baptist church, then under the care of the Rev. James Leftwich, in 1844. At this time he was farming, and regarded it as his life-work. Being actively engaged in the prayer-meetings and Sunday-school work of the church, he felt it to be a duty to prepare himself to enter into the Christian ministry. He was licensed to preach by the Mount Hermon church in 1849, and in 1850 went to the school at Botetourt Springs, where he remained for about fifteen months. He then returned to his home, and taught school for nearly a year, frequently preaching in destitute neighborhoods. In 1853 he entered the Columbian College, and graduated in 1857. In 1856, still a student, he started a Sunday-school in South Washington, which was quite successful, and a church was organized in 1857, of which he became the pastor, and which he still serves. Mr. Meador has been greatly blessed in his labors, nearly 500 persons having been added to the church through his instrumentality. His pastoral labors are quite onerous, frequently being called upon by members of other denominations in the neighborhood to visit their sick and bury their dead. Twenty-two years of continuous toil among the same people have given him a strong hold upon their affections. Columbian College conferred upon him in 1860 the degree of A.M. in course.

Medbury, Rev. Arnold Rhodes, missionary secretary of the Wisconsin Baptist State Convention, is a native of Seekonk, R. I., where he was born Dec. 10, 1837. His childhood was spent on a farm in his native town. When seven years old he suffered an irreparable loss in the death of his mother, who was a devoted Christian. He obtained a hope in Christ in 1855, and united with the Third Baptist church in Providence, R. I., of which Rev. Jas. B. Simmons was pastor, and by whom he was baptized. Very early in his Christian experience he had strong impressions that it was his duty to preach the gospel, and began preparation for the work. But in this purpose he met with many hindrances, having to depend upon his own resources to obtain means to secure an education. After a two years' struggle, with but little progress, he determined to join two older brothers in California, hoping the more speedily to obtain the means to educate himself. At the end of six years of varied experiences of success and defeat, he found himself deeply in debt, and apparently farther than ever from realizing his cherished plan for study. At this time the Baptist church of Sonora, Cal., to which he had removed his church membership from Rhode Island, licensed him to preach the gospel, and invited him to do such pastoral work as he could without ordination. This experience only deepened his conviction of his need of more thorough preparation for the Christian ministry, and he gladly availed himself of an offer of pursuing a private course of study, under the direction of Rev. D. B. Cheeney, D.D., pastor of the First Baptist church in San Francisco. This arrangement having been suspended, owing to Dr. Cheeney's extended visit in the East, he entered the University of the Pacific, completing about two-thirds of its prescribed course of study. Leaving the university to engage in mission work in Petaluma, he found himself again, in the autumn of 1865, under the private instruction of Dr. Cheeney, and performing pastoral work for the Third Baptist church of San Francisco. He was ordained by a council convened at the call of the First Baptist church, San Francisco, in March,

1867. In the autumn of the same year he entered the theological seminary at Newton, Mass., and graduated in the class of 1870. Receiving the call (which he accepted) of the First Baptist church in San Francisco, he returned again to California to enter this new field of labor. In 1872, Mr. Medbury became the pastor of the First Baptist church in Portland, Oregon. His pastorate here was in every way successful, the church was greatly strengthened, and reached a highly influential position in the city through his ministrations. From this charge Mr. Medbury was called to the Grand Avenue Baptist church, Milwaukee. After five years of successful pastoral labor with this church he accepted a call to the State Street Baptist church, Rockford, Ill., and entered upon his labors there.

When Mr. Medbury came to Wisconsin, in 1874, he was almost immediately made corresponding secretary of the Wisconsin Baptist State Convention, and secretary of the board and its Executive Committee, for which position he had unusual qualifications. During his entire pastorate at Grand Avenue Baptist church he devoted much time to this important missionary work. It is owing largely to his influence that the State Convention reached its high degree of prosperity and accomplished so much successful missionary work. He gave such value and character to the annual reports of the Convention, especially in its statistical tables, conveying such exact information on all Baptist matters in the State, as to awaken a wide-spread interest not only in the State but in neighboring States. While pastor at Rockford, Ill., the board of the Wisconsin Baptist State Convention extended to him an urgent invitation to take charge of its mission work in the State as missionary superintendent and secretary. He has accepted the position, and entered in September, 1880, upon its duties.

Mr. Medbury is a man of fine native powers, and thorough attainments in literary and theological learning. He is a vigorous thinker and an earnest preacher of the gospel. He has qualifications that fit him pre-eminently for the position he now fills. He brings to it the best of executive and organizing powers, and a supreme love for the work, combined with an unquestioned consecration to Christ and his cause on earth.

Medley, Rev. Samuel, was born at Cheshurst, England, June 23, 1733. In his seventeenth year he entered the British navy as a midshipman. He was full of mirth and frolic, and as a consequence he was a great favorite with his ungodly associates. He was wounded in an action with the French when on service in the Mediterranean, and the opportunities he had for serious reflection during his enforced leisure were of lasting benefit to his soul. Some time afterwards he was led to put his trust in Jesus, and he united by baptism with the church of Dr. Andrew Gifford, in London.

His first settlement in the ministry was at Watford, where he was ordained in July, 1768. In April, 1772, he removed to Liverpool, and in it he labored till his death, in 1799. When Mr. Medley entered upon his pastoral duties at Liverpool the church was small, but under his efficient ministry it prospered greatly, and the house was soon enlarged. Mr. Medley was for some years one of the most influential ministers in Liverpool, or in the north of England. He was greatly beloved by the whole denomination, and by large numbers outside the community whose denominational name he bore and whose principles he ardently loved. He enjoyed great faith, and much of the presence of his Redeemer. His last words were, "Dying is sweet work, sweet work, my Father! my heavenly Father! I am looking up to my dear Jesus, my God, my portion, my all in all, glory! glory! home! home!" He was the author of two works, and of some precious hymns, one of which is familiar wherever the English language is spoken:

"Awake, my soul, in joyful lays,
And sing thy great Redeemer's praise;
He justly claims a song from me;
His loving kindness, oh, how free!"

Meech, Rev. Levi, son of Capt. Daniel and Zerviah (Witter) Meech, was born in North Stonington, Conn., Feb. 14, 1795; baptized by Rev. Roswell Burrows in 1811, and united with the Baptist church in Preston, Conn.; served in the war of 1812; licensed to preach in 1820; ordained in 1824; an evangelist in spirit from the beginning; served as pastor or supply of churches in Preston, Bozrah, Andover, Salem, Packersville, Voluntown, Colchester, Lebanon, Suffield, Second and Third North Stonington, Mystic, Conn., and Exeter, R. I.; organized the Union Baptist church of Montville, Conn.; greatly blessed in all his work; a wise and successful revivalist; earnest and firm in all reforms; benevolent and devoted to missions; mighty in the Scriptures; strong thinker and sound reasoner; full of sympathy and tenderness; baptized 400 persons; had three sons and two daughters; his oldest son, Levi Witter, a graduate of Brown University, is a distinguished mathematician and actuary; his youngest son, Rev. William W., has been an earnest Baptist minister for thirty years. He died at the homestead in North Stonington, Conn., June 4, 1873, in his seventy-ninth year.

Meek, Rev. John, M.D., a pioneer preacher in South Arkansas, was born in South Carolina in 1791; was first a Methodist preacher, then became a Baptist, and began to preach as such in 1837; removed to Union Co., Ark., in 1840. Here he soon organized a church, the first of the missionary Baptist faith in his region. While supporting his family by the practice of medicine, he was indefatigable in his ministerial labors, and was instrumental in planting many churches and organizing several Associations. He died in 1873.

Mell, Patrick Hughes, D.D., chancellor of the State University, and for many years a leading and

PATRICK HUGHES MELL, D.D.

influential Baptist of Georgia, was born in Walthourville, Liberty Co., Ga., July 19, 1814. In his boyhood he studied in the academies in Liberty County and near Darien, Ga., and then he spent two years at Amherst College, Mass., afterwards teaching in the academy at Springfield, Mass., and in the high school at East Hartford, Conn. In 1838, at twenty-four years of age, he returned to his native State, and, after teaching school in lower and middle Georgia for five or six years, was elected to the professorship of Ancient Languages in Mercer University. He entered upon his duties in February, 1842, and continued a professor in that institution for thirteen years, during which time he became noted for his ability as a professor and for the firmness and excellence of his discipline. His connection with Mercer University was dissolved in November, 1855, but in August, 1856, he was elected Professor of Ancient Languages in the State University at Athens. When Dr. Alonzo Church resigned the presidency of the State University, in 1860, Dr. Mell was elected to the chair of Metaphysics and Ethics, which he still holds, although he was, in August, 1878, elected chancellor of the university, and *ex-officio* president of the State College of Agriculture and Mechanic Arts. His position is one of great dignity, and has been filled by him with distinguished ability and success.

Dr. Mell's religious life began in the summer of 1832, when he was baptized by Rev. Samuel Law, at North Newport church, Liberty Co., Ga. He began to preach at Oxford, Ga., in 1840, and was ordained by order of the Penfield church at the request of the Greensborough church, Nov. 19, 1842, at Penfield. From that time to the present he has preached almost without intermission, having charge of various churches, and some of his pastorates continuing for remarkably long periods. He was pastor of the Greensborough church for ten years; of the Antioch church, in Oglethorpe County, twenty-eight years; and of the Bairdstown church, on the line between Greene and Oglethorpe Counties, thirty-three years. Since his election to the chancellorship of the State University he has resigned all his pastorates and has devoted himself exclusively to the duties of his office.

As a preacher, he is logical and argumentative, delighting in the deep doctrinal subjects of the Bible, and rendering them simple and clear to the comprehension of his hearers. The power and penetration of his intellect enable him to grasp a doctrine forcibly and present it clearly; and his skill in the art of thinking and reasoning is so great that he always speaks logically, his conclusions having the force of demonstrations.

As an author, Dr. Mell has issued several works which have been accepted as standards, among which are his works on "Baptism," on "Corrective Church Discipline," and on "Parliamentary Practice." He has also published small works on "Predestination," "Calvinism," "God's Providential Government," the "Philosophy of Prayer," and part of a work, "Church Polity," which promises to be of great value.

As a presiding officer, Dr. Mell has manifested pre-eminent excellence, which has been recognized by his repeated re-election to the presidency of the Southern Baptist Convention and of the Georgia Baptist Convention.

During the late civil war, in response to a call by the governor of the State for six months' troops, Dr. Mell, although professor in the State University, raised a company, of which he was elected captain, and when the regiment to which he belonged was organized, he was elected colonel. As such he remained in actual service six months at different points within the State.

Few, if any, have exerted a wider and more healthful influence in the denomination in Georgia than Dr. Mell.

Melvin, Rev. R. E., a preacher and writer of note in Mississippi, was born in Pennsylvania in 1811; received a good education, and engaged in teaching; made a profession of Christ in 1852, and was baptized near Brandon, Miss.; engaged in the practice of law in the city of Jackson until the close of the war. He then again commenced teaching near Meridian, where he soon began to preach, although not ordained until 1878. Recently a number of well-written articles in the *Mississippi Baptist Record* have attracted notice, and given him reputation as a writer of ability.

Menno and the Mennonites.—Simon Menno was born in Witmarsum, near Bolswert, in Friesland, in 1505. His education must have been of a high order, and his talents were such as to have given boundless success in any worldly calling, or in the leadership of any community except his Anabaptist disciples. He was persuasive and eloquent. He was familiar with the springs that open the hearts of men, and he wielded an astonishing influence for years over large numbers of persons scattered over several countries of Europe, many of whom would have died for him without murmur, and some of whom were martyred because they entertained him, and they knew the penalty before they gave him a hearty welcome to refresh himself in their homes.

In 1529 he became a priest of the Catholic church at Pinningen, in Friesland. At this time he had never read the Scriptures lest they might draw him away from his fidelity to Rome. In this respect he was even more hostile to God's Word than some other priests of his acquaintance. In celebrating mass the question naturally came into his mind, Can the bread and the wine be the real body and blood of the Son of God? At first he imagined that this suggestion came from the Wicked One, and he resorted to the confessional and other papal methods to chain and silence common sense, but Menno was too gifted for the successful use of such instrumentalities. He had been accustomed to spend his time with two priests in "playing, drinking, and other indulgences," but these sacerdotal exercises failed to satisfy him about transubstantiation. He finally concluded that he would despise the curses of lordly prelates, and search the New Testament to solve his doubts. In its light the falsehood of the mass vanished like the shades of night before the rising sun, and its brazen idolatry excited his indignation.

On the execution of Seicke Snyder, at Leeuwarden, for being "rebaptized," he was filled with astonishment to hear of a second baptism and the reason for it, that infant baptism had no warrant from the Word of God. As he read the Scriptures he saw that it had no divine authority. Then he says, "As I remarked this I spoke of it to my pastor (the rector of the church in which he was an assistant), and, after several conversations, he acknowledged that infant baptism had no ground in the Scriptures. Yet I dared not trust so much to my understanding. I consulted some ancient authors, who taught me that children must by baptism be washed from their original sin. This I compared with the Scriptures, and perceived that it set at naught the blood of Christ. Afterwards I went to Luther, and would gladly have known from him the ground, and he taught me that we must baptize children on their own faith, because they are holy. This also I saw was not according to God's Word. In the third place I went to Bucer, who taught me that we should baptize children in order to be able the more diligently to take care of them, and bring them up in the ways of the Lord. But this too I saw was a groundless representation. In the fourth place I went to Bullinger, who pointed me to the covenant of circumcision, but I found, as before, that, according to Scripture, the practice could not stand. As I now on every side observed that the writers stood on grounds so very different, and each followed his own reason, I saw clearly that we were deceived with infant baptism." Menno had no temptation to give up infant baptism, and his prejudices and interests, and even his bodily safety, were linked to it. But the truth was not in it, and the truth, which he loved, drove him into the ranks of the Anabaptists. No denomination at this hour has so many men, like Dunster, Judson, and Noel, as the Baptist, whose convictions have constrained them to renounce the most cherished ties, and make other weighty sacrifices.

Menno for a time was rector of the village church where he had been an assistant, and preached the Word of Life to his parishioners with acceptance; but finally, in 1536, his conscience would permit him no longer to retain any connection with Rome, and he withdrew from the priesthood and communion of the popes. In 1537 he listened to the appeal of a few godly Anabaptists and became their religious leader, an office which he held till he fell at the feet of the great Teacher in Paradise.

Menno was twenty-two years younger than Luther, whom he greatly respected, and whose writings he carefully studied, but his supreme regard for the Scriptures kept him from adopting any guide except revelation.

When he accepted his new office he knew the fierce cruelties and the violent death which it invited, and which it was likely to bring upon him, but washed in the Saviour's blood himself, he could not withhold the glorious gospel from the millions of doomed papal bondmen, whose present darkness and prospective torments enlisted the deepest sympathies of his soul. He went everywhere preaching Jesus. As a distinguished writer says, "For about five-and-twenty years he traveled with his wife and children amid perpetual sufferings and daily perils of his life over many districts of country,—first in West Friesland, the territory of Groningen, and East Friesland, and then in Gelderland, Holland, Brabant, Westphalia, and the German provinces along the shores of the Baltic as far as Livonia, and in this way he gathered an immense number of followers." Menno was one of the master-spirits and master-builders of the sixteenth century, whose immediate disciples were multitudes, and whose influence has journeyed far beyond the borders of the religious community bearing his name.

He died in 1561 at Oldesloe, in Holstein, where his ashes rest in peace.

Menno had a new heart given him in 1535. God "led him from the way of death, and through mere mercy called him upon the narrow path of life;" "he was graciously forgiven of his impure conduct, and loose, vain life through the merit of the blood of Christ," and he went in a mightier power than even Whitefield to proclaim the efficacy of atonement to perishing men. The churches he instituted were composed of professed believers alone, and these were the only subjects of his baptism. He disclaimed the use of force to support, spread, or defend his religious opinions. His views of the Lord's Supper were Scriptural. He denounced wars, self-defense, and oaths, and insisted on personal piety with great and appropriate zeal. While in many highly important things Menno agreed with us, facts incline us to the conviction that the mode of baptism with him was indifferent. He was almost a Baptist, though a very decided Anabaptist.

The Mennonites, or the communities founded by Menno, survive the fury of persecution, the hatred of state churches, and the evils that dwell in the heart and tempt in the world. The chief strength of the Mennonites in Europe is in Holland, where, in 1846, they had about 130 churches, and a seminary for ministerial education. They had also communities at that time in East Prussia, in Alsace and Lorraine, in Switzerland, and in the south of Russia. In the United States the Mennonites have about 120 churches and 20,000 members. There are three sects of Mennonites in this country,—the Mennonites, the Reformed Mennonite Society, and the Omish Church. The first and last communities hold the same Confession of Faith, which was adopted in Dortrecht, in Holland, in 1632. The Omish Church differs chiefly from the regular Mennonites in their greater simplicity of dress and strictness of discipline. The Reformed Mennonite Society was instituted to pay special attention to the religion of the heart, and in this respect to restore the spirituality of early times. This denomination has condensed the old creed, but with the other two its members profess to believe that the first lesson of the New Testament is repentance. They baptize only penitent believers (no children); they practise feet-washing; they believe that they should not discharge the duties of a magistrate, or "elevate others to a magisterial office; they forbid the use of carnal weapons and oaths," and "they administer baptism (in the United States) by sprinkling or pouring" ("Confession of Faith of the Mennonites," p. 458, Winchester), though the Rynsburgers, or Collegiants, a branch of the Mennonites, originating in Holland, according to Picart, in 1736, practised immersion (see Burrage's "Act of Baptism," p. 180). The Mennonites of to-day are a little nearer us than orthodox members of the Society of Friends, but they are not Baptists.

Mercer, Rev. Asa S., was born in Georgia in 1790; began to preach in Mississippi in 1812; removed to Louisiana in 1823, and settled on the Ouachita. He long exercised a wide influence, and held many prominent positions. He died in Texas in 1850.

Mercer, Jesse, D.D., was the most distinguished and influential Baptist minister ever reared in the

JESSE MERCER, D.D.

State of Georgia; and it is doubtful if any one, under the providence of God, ever exerted a more beneficial influence among the Baptists of Georgia, or as an instrument in the divine hands ever accomplished more beneficial results for the denomination in the State. "How is Mr. Mercer?" asked Dr. Staughton of a gentleman from Georgia. "He is well," was the answer. "He exerts a great influence in your State," continued Dr. Staughton.

"His word is *law*," the other replied. "I am sure," said the doctor, in return, "it is *gospel*."

Jesse, the son of Silas Mercer, was born in Halifax Co., N. C., Dec. 16, 1769. His father removed to Georgia about 1775, and settled in Wilkes County, but fled to North Carolina at the outbreak of the Revolution, and did not return until after the war, when Jesse was about fourteen years old. From that time until his death, on the 6th of September, 1841, Jesse Mercer resided in Georgia. His youthful character was free from stain; not even a profane word was ever used by him, nor was he ever guilty of any deviation from strict truthfulness. He was a sober, staid, discreet youth; even-tempered in his conduct, never dejected nor morose. He had great command of his passions, and was never known through life to have a personal quarrel with any one. He was a pattern of filial obedience, submitting cheerfully to every command of his parents. He was converted at fifteen, was baptized in his eighteenth year, and soon after began to preach. On the 31st of January, 1788, in his nineteenth year, he was married to Miss Sabrina Chivers; and before he was twenty years of age he was ordained, on the 7th of November, 1789, by Silas Mercer and Sanders Walker. In succession he then took charge of the churches at Hutton's Fork, Indian Creek, in Oglethorpe County, Sardis, Phillips' Mill, Powelton, Whatley's Mill (now Bethesda), Eatonton, and Washington, his pastoral services extending over a period of fifty years. He by no means confined himself to the churches of his charge, however, but, traveling far and near, he preached the gospel everywhere, with a power never surpassed in the State, and with a pathos and unction productive of the best results.

As a Preacher.—Long will he be held in honorable estimation as a truly able, pious, instructive and powerful minister of the gospel. Said Dr. Basil Manly, Sr., of him, "In his happy moments of preaching he would arouse and enchain the attention of reflecting men beyond any minister I have ever heard. At such times his views were vast, profound, original, striking, and absorbing in the highest degree; while his language, though simple, was so terse and pithy, so pruned, consolidated, and suited to become the vehicle of the dense mass of his thoughts, that it required no ordinary effort of a well-trained mind to take in all he said." His voice was neither very strong nor distinguished for its compass and melody; his gesticulations were rather clumsy, and the fastidious could find fault with his manner; but, notwithstanding all, his appearance in the pulpit was far from being uninteresting.

The fair and comely baldness of his head, his venerable mien, his portly frame, his countenance clothed with meekness, benevolence, intelligence, and devotion, rendered him an object of peculiar interest and respect wherever he stood forth

> "To negotiate between God and man,
> As God's ambassador, the grand concerns
> Of judgment and of mercy."

Whilst he seemed untrammeled by the laws of criticism, he violated not the principles of true taste. His sermons were for the most part doctrinal, yet always tending to practical results. His language had a noble bearing, which made it a suitable vehicle for his noble thoughts. The accurate principles of sound logic ran through his addresses, though its forms were not at all times visible. Ungodly men of cultivated minds listened to his sermons as to an intellectual treat. Religious men enjoyed them as affording a spiritual feast. To the graces of oratory Mr. Mercer made no pretensions, but there was an unction from the Holy One, that breathed from his spirit and beamed from his sweet and heavenly eye, which enchained and animated the hearer, and thus more than supplied the absence of oratorical grace. His words did not often flow down upon the people in a rushing torrent, but rather fell like a refreshing shower. No useless verbiage encumbered his topics. Some preachers are occasionally great because, like a small stream, with a shallow and narrow channel, swollen by a sudden shower, they sometimes dash and roar; but Mr. Mercer's preaching was like a stream whose channel is wide and deep: it embraced a large scope of religious instruction, exhibited a great variety and richness, and flowed onwards with a mighty and increasing volume.

The Cross of Christ was the fixed, luminous centre of his preaching. He delighted in contemplating the gospel as a scheme which honored God and abased the creature. Upon the majesty of the law; the exceeding sinfulness of sin; the amazing obligations of the sinner, and his total inability to rescue himself from his ruined and guilty state; and upon the infinite virtue of the atonement, and the uncontrolled sovereignty of God, and the glorious efficiency of divine grace, he was truly great. Never was a minister more immovably rooted in the respect, confidence, and affection of his people than was Mr. Mercer, while to all classes of the community he was an object of admiration, reverence, and love.

About 1818 he removed from Greene County to Powelton, where he resided until the end of 1826 or beginning of 1827, when he removed to Washington, which remained his home until death. Of the church at the former place he was pastor for twenty-eight years, and of the church at the latter he was pastor about seventeen years; but after removing to Washington he resigned the charge of most of his other churches.

Connection with the Index.—In the year 1833 the

Christian Index, published by Dr. Wm. T. Brantly, Sr., at Philadelphia, was purchased by Mr. Mercer and removed to Washington, Ga. For several years he was the editor of the *Index*, assisted by Rev. Wm. H. Stokes, and was the means thus of greatly benefiting the denomination in the State by his wise counsel and skillful expositions of discipline and doctrine. But editorial duties were not congenial to him, and the paper became a pecuniary disadvantage. In 1840 he tendered the *Index*, and all its appendages, to the Georgia Baptist Convention. The gift was accepted, and it was published by the Convention, through a committee, until 1862, when it was sold to Rev. S. Boykin, who for several years had been employed as editor. To Mr. Mercer the denomination in the State is indebted for much of its harmony and prosperity, through the influence exerted for many years by that paper.

Efforts in Behalf of Education.—The cause of education has had no more indefatigable, successful, and liberal advocate in the State of Georgia than Jesse Mercer. He took an active part in the establishment of Mount Enon Academy, in Richmond County, in 1807. He was one of the most munificent supporters of Mercer University from its very inception, and the institution was accordingly named after him. His donations, including legacies to the university, did not amount to less than $40,000.

His Efforts in the Missionary Cause.—No object was dearer to Jesse Mercer than the cause of missions. Through his influence the Powelton Baptist Society for Foreign Missions was established, May 5, 1815; and in the year following he procured the appointment of the Mission Board of the Georgia Association to be a component member of the General Missionary Convention of the Baptist denomination, which board existed for many years, and prosecuted its business with much success. He was uniformly appointed a member of the board, was generally its president, and always one of its most liberal and efficient supporters. In 1820 and in 1826 he represented this board in the General Convention. Not until merged into the operations of the State Convention was this board dispensed with.

For some years Mr. Mercer was an active member, and for a while corresponding secretary of the Board of Trustees of the Co-operating Baptist Associations for Instructing and Evangelizing the Creek Indians, organized under the direction of managers appointed by the Ocmulgee, Georgia, and Ebenezer Associations. By his pen, in the pulpit, and with his purse Mr. Mercer strenuously advocated the mission cause throughout his whole career, and was one of those who organized, and for the ten years of its existence was the master-spirit of, the General Committee of the Georgia Baptists, which resulted in the establishment of the Georgia Baptist Convention, the grand missionary body of the Georgia Baptists. For eighteen years in succession he was elected president of the Georgia Baptist Convention, and for more than twenty years he was successively elected presiding officer of the Georgia Association.

In the discussion of all weighty and difficult subjects in the religious bodies which he attended he usually took a prominent part, and his views generally decided the question under discussion. On one occasion some important subject was discussed for a considerable time, when a worthy brother rose and said, "Well, I now move that Brother Mercer give us his views, and that the question then be put, without any further debate," intimating that it would be improper for the question to be taken until the Gamaliel of the meeting had expressed his opinion, and that after he should speak little more of importance could well be said.

His Liberality.—He gave hundreds and thousands and tens of thousands. To home and foreign missions, to the Bible, tract, Sunday-school, and publication societies, to Columbian College, and to Mercer University he dedicated many thousands of dollars. His bequests to Mercer University amounted to more than $40,000, and to various other benevolent objects not less than $20,000 or $25,000.

His Character.—With all his greatness and reputation he was lowly and humble. His modesty was conspicuous; yet, though eminently meek and gentle in spirit, he was a man of uncommon firmness and of great moral courage. In matters of principle and conscience he was immovable as a rock. His heart was remarkably tender and sympathetic, and he was kind, courteous, and hospitable. He treated his servants with the greatest humanity and with the most judicious consideration. The mental elevation, the distinguished piety, and the ministerial excellence which were combined in Mr. Mercer partially account for the extensive and wonderful influence he exerted over the minds of men, for no other man has wielded the same power over the Baptists of Georgia, nor is any other Baptist who has ever lived in the State to be compared to him in the beneficial results accomplished by his long ministry. In the denomination in Georgia he stands as a bright and shining light, and while it exists in that State his exalted merit and faithful services will cause him to be held in affectionate and sacred remembrance.

Mercer, Rev. Thomas, an able and zealous Baptist minister, who removed from Georgia in 1818 and settled in Southwestern Mississippi; was an early laborer in spreading Baptist sentiments. To facilitate the cultivation of the song-service of the churches he compiled a collection of excellent hymns. He aided in the formation of the Mississippi Association in 1806. In 1817, Thomas Mercer and Benjamin Davis were requested by the Association to visit the Creek Indians and inquire what could be done towards the establishment of schools and the introduction of the gospel among them, and the funds of the Association were applied for their use, and they were required to account to the Mississippi Society for Baptist Missions, Foreign and Domestic. Upon this journey Mercer died, and was buried among strangers.

Mercer University.—One of the objects of the Georgia Baptist Convention, when organized, as set forth in its constitution, was " to afford an opportunity to those who may conscientiously think it their duty to form a fund for the education of pious young men, who may be called by the spirit and their churches to the Christian ministry." From 1826 to 1832 several beneficiaries were adopted by the Convention, and no less than eight received aid from the Convention in the last-named year. In 1828, Josiah Penfield, a devout deacon of the Savannah Baptist church, offered to give $2500 towards a fund for the education of young ministers, provided the Convention would contribute an equal amount. More than $2500 was subscribed by the delegates at the Convention, in Milledgeville, in March, 1829. From this Penfield legacy, and from annual additions, grew the permanent fund for the education of young ministers, which amounted at one time to $33,400, but which now, owing to losses during the civil war, amounts to about $24,000. Having an educational fund, the Convention resolved, in 1831, to establish a classical and theological school, to be connected with manual labor. This resolution was offered by Dr. Adiel Sherwood. Lands and money were subscribed, a site was chosen, and on the second Monday in January, 1833, Mercer Institute was opened, so named in honor of Jesse Mercer, who has been called " the most influential minister of his day, and, perhaps, the most distinguished minister of the denomination ever reared up in the State." (Campbell's " Georgia Baptists.")

When it grew into a village the site was named Penfield, in memory of Deacon Penfield. Rev. Billington M. Sanders presided over the institute, and brought to the work indefatigable industry. Under his care the institute attracted students from all parts of the State, and contributed greatly to popularize education in the minds of the people. It was not intended to impart a collegiate education, and its elevation to the dignity of a college was an after-thought, started by the failure to establish the Southern Baptist College at Washington, Wilkes County, for which an endowment fund of $100,000 had been subscribed. Of this sum $20,000 had been contributed by the Central Association, a body of intelligent and liberal brethren, to endow the Central Professorship of Languages and Sacred Literature. That body suggested that Mercer Institute be elevated into a college, and this solved a problem which was puzzling the denomination. The Executive Committee of the Convention took the matter in hand, changed the name of Mercer Institute into Mercer University, procured the transfer of most of the subscriptions which had been made to the Southern Baptist College, and, in December, 1837, obtained a charter for the new university. At its next session, in May, 1838, the Georgia Baptist Convention ratified this charter and elected the first board of trustees. The first meeting of this board was held at Penfield, in July, 1838, when they assumed the management of the institution; and this date may be regarded as the official beginning of Mercer University, though the college classes were not organized until January, 1839.

The board of trustees was composed of the following brethren: Jesse Mercer, C. D. Mallary, V. R. Thornton, Jonathan Davis, John E. Dawson, Malcom Johnson, W. D. Cowdry, J. H. T. Kilpatrick, J. H. Campbell, S. G. Hillyer, Absalom Janes, R. Q. Dickinson, William Richards, Thomas Stocks, T. G. Janes, J. M. Porter, Lemuel Greene, James Davant, F. W. Cheney, E. H. Macon, William Lumpkin, J. G. Polhill, Lott Warren, Mark A. Cooper, John B. Walker, I. T. Irwin, W. H. Pope, men who were representatives of the denomination in piety, wealth, intelligence, and in social and political influence. They gave shape to the institution, and to their wise counsels much of its success is due. Thomas Stocks, a layman, who had labored in building up the institute, was the first president of the board of trustees, and was continuously re-elected for about twenty-five years, until failing health unfitted him for the duties of the office. The university entered upon its career with a liberal endowment for the times. Four agents—Posey, Connor, Davis, and Mallary—were employed in getting the subscriptions to the Washington project transferred, and in obtaining new pledges. In this work Rev. C. D. Mallary was engaged during the years 1837, 1838, and 1839. Rev. Jesse Mercer was by far the largest contributor, as he gave during his life and by will about $40,000. Among those who donated from $1000 to $5000 were Cullen Battle, R. Q. Dickinson, W. H. Pope, James Boykin, T. G. Janes, Absalom Janes, W. Peek, Solomon Graves, and John B. Walker. Within the last twenty years several legacies have been left to the university.

In December, 1844, the manual labor system was indefinitely suspended by the trustees, with the concurrence of the contributors to the university.

The first diplomas were conferred in 1841, and since then there has been a regular succession of graduating classes, with the exception of seven years. An efficient faculty was gradually enrolled. One, Prof. S. P. Sanford, entered the institute as a teacher in 1838, and has served continuously down to the present time. Another, Prof. J. E. Willet, an alumnus of 1846, was elected professor in 1847, and has served continuously since that time. In both Mercer Institute and the university a theological education was a primary thought, and was specifically provided for in donations and legacies. Very appropriately, therefore, Rev. Dr. Adiel Sherwood was, in 1840, elected the first theological professor, a position which he occupied three years only, as he then accepted the presidency of Shurtleff College, Ill. In 1845 the theological department was fully organized, embracing Greek, Hebrew, systematic and pastoral theology, ecclesiastical history, and Biblical literature, and it was extended over three years. Two professors usually gave most of their time to instruction in this department of the college. The exigencies of the civil war, in 1862, caused a suspension of the theological department, which has never been revived, owing to a general

MERCER UNIVERSITY.

desire to build up the Southern Baptist Theological Seminary.

The curriculum of the classical department in Mercer University embraces the studies usually taught in colleges of respectable grade. The regular course requires four years, and leads to the degree of A.B. A scientific course, including the regular course except ancient languages, is completed in three years, and leads to the degree of B.S.,—Bachelor of Science. Seven have graduated in the scientific course and 440 in the regular course, of whom 77 became ministers of the gospel. Add to these the 12 theological graduates and the

75 who have taken a partial course in the institute and university, and we have a total of 164 Baptist ministers who have received their education in this "classical and theological school" instituted by the Baptist fathers nearly half a century ago.

The law school was organized in 1873. Its course extends through one year, and thus far 24 graduates have received the degree of B.L.

The disasters to the college caused by the civil war led to its dissolution in May, 1865, and the faculty reluctantly closed its doors. The two senior members of the faculty, however, opened a school in the college buildings, and carried on the mixed studies of preparatory and college classes until the close of the year, when the trustees began again the rehabilitation of the university.

There had always been differences of opinion as to the location of the college, and in 1850 a feeble effort was made to remove it to Griffin. About 1853 the Baptists of Northwestern Georgia established the Cherokee Baptist College at Cassville, and soon after those of Western Georgia instituted another at Griffin,—Marshall College. Both failed to secure endowments and passed away. Not long after the war the question of removal was re-opened; several cities offered valuable pecuniary inducements; and in April, 1870, the Convention, by a vote of 71 to 16, resolved to remove the university from Penfield; and at a subsequent conference of a committee of the Convention and the Board of Trustees, it was decided to locate it at Macon, which city gave the university $125,000 of her bonds and seven acres of land on Tatnall Square. A modification of the charter was secured, and the university was removed to Macon in 1871. A large four-story brick building, containing over thirty rooms for recitation purposes and for the library and philosophical apparatus, was erected by the trustees. Another brick building was also reared as a dormitory and dining-hall for the students. A chapel, and a building to contain the museum and to furnish lecture-rooms, were in contemplation also, but the financial panic of 1873 caused a suspension of further building operations.

For more than a quarter of a century the endowment and funds of the university were managed by Thomas J. Burney, treasurer of the Convention, than whom a more faithful and efficient officer never lived. To his discretion the trustees confided the finances of the institution entirely, and that so large a proportion of its funds was saved during the war is due to his wisdom and foresight.

The presidents have been as follows: Rev. B. M. Sanders, 1839; Rev. Otis Smith, 1840–43; Rev. John L. Dagg, D.D., 1844–54; Rev. Nathaniel M. Crawford, D.D., 1855–56 and 1858–65; Rev. Henry Holcombe Tucker, D.D., 1866–71; and Rev. Archibald J. Battle, D.D., 1872 to date, 1880.

Administration.—Rev. Billington M. Sanders, who had been the central figure in the institute, consented to remain one year as president of the university. It was fitting that he should launch upon its new career of usefulness the bark which he had guided so successfully for six years. Rev. Otis Smith succeeded him, and remained three years. He gave diplomas to the first two graduating classes.

Rev. Dr. Dagg succeeded, in 1844, to a presidency of ten years. With superior mental endowments, solid scholarship, venerable presence, affable manners, aptness in teaching, and steadiness in discipline, he commanded the love and reverence of the whole institution. To the new college he gave dignity and character; and he made its friends feel that it deserved to take rank among the colleges of the State.

Rev. Dr. Crawford inherited much of the massive intellect of his father, Hon. Wm. H. Crawford. His mind mastered, with equal ease, almost every department of thought. Modest, sincere, sagacious, companionable, independent, and with great clearness and coolness of judgment, he won the respect of his students; and was a beloved and wise counselor in the assemblies of his brethren. Rev. Dr. Tucker was a president of remarkable originality, acuteness, and readiness. Clear, brilliant, magnetic, he "enthused" his classes as few have the power to do. "You are gentlemen, and the sons of gentlemen," was the key-note of his discipline, which banished from the college all silly tricks and pranks, and encouraged true manliness of character among the students. The fresh vitality of his administration is still felt in the institution.

Rev. Dr. Battle, though a native of Georgia, came from another State, Alabama. His father, Dr. Cullen Battle, had been a prominent Baptist in Georgia until his removal to Alabama, and had been a liberal donor to the university, and his son received a warm welcome on returning to his native State; and he found friends in all. A Christian gentleman of the highest tone and cultivation, with fine social powers, he has strongly attached to the college the community which contributed so liberally to its endowment.

The university, thus founded in the prayers, sacrifices, and best purposes of the denomination, the centre of its intellectual culture, has ever been the rallying-point of the Georgia Baptists. Sprung from a desire for an educated ministry, it has expanded into a fountain of knowledge for Baptists of every calling. Enlisting their minds and hearts in its great work, the Georgia Baptists have brought to it their offerings of time, money, and wisdom, and when necessary have sacrificed their preferences for locations and measures. Such a fusion of mind and heart has unified and consolidated the denomination, and girded it for the great religious work which it has wrought in the State.

Meredith, Rev. James J., an able minister of Ouachita Baptist Association, La., was born Oct. 27, 1810, and died in Caldwell Parish, La., June 27, 1870.

Meredith, Rev. Thomas, was beyond question the ablest man who has yet appeared among the Baptists of North Carolina, and as the founder, and for nineteen years the editor, of the *Biblical Recorder*, probably did more to develop the denomination than any man who has ever lived in the State. Mr. Meredith was born in Pennsylvania in 1797; came to North Carolina as pastor of the Newbern church in 1820; removed to Georgia in 1822; settled as pastor in Edenton, N. C., in 1825; originated the *Baptist Interpreter* in 1832, which was changed to the *Biblical Recorder* in 1834; removed to Newbern in 1835, and was pastor as well as editor till 1838, when he removed to Raleigh, and taught a female school in connection with editorial labors. Mr. Meredith was the author of the constitution of the North Carolina Baptist State Convention, and of the masterly address of that body when organized in 1830. He was elected a Professor of Mathematics in Wake Forest College in 1835, but did not accept the position. He died in Raleigh in 1851. As an editor, he was the equal of any man in the United States in his day.

Meridian Female College, located at Meridian, Miss., was founded by J. B. Hamberlin since the war. From one to two hundred young ladies are annually taught in this institution. Rev. C. M. Gordon, A.M., is the principal, with whom is associated Rev. M. T. Martin as agent.

Merriam, Rev. Asaph, was born in Gardiner, Mass., in March, 1792; hopefully converted at the age of twenty-five, he united with a Congregational church. Subsequently he became a Baptist, and in 1825 was ordained at Royalston, Mass., and remained here five years. He was afterwards settled over churches in New Ipswich, Canton, Athol, and Bolton. He also supplied one or two churches for a time. His entire ministry extended over a period of about forty years. He died at Bolton, Sept. 19, 1868. He was a useful minister of Christ.

Merrifield, Rev. A. S., was born in Newfane, Vt., April 1, 1837. He belongs to a family of eleven children, all of whom are active members of Baptist churches. Two are in the ministry, three are deacons, and three are ministers' or deacons' wives. He was converted to Christ while a student at Leland Seminary, Townshend, Vt., at the age of seventeen. At this academy he prepared for college, and entered Madison University in 1860. He graduated from college in 1864, and from the theological seminary in 1866. He accepted a call from the Baptist church at Sherman, Chautauqua Co., N. Y., where he was ordained to the ministry Oct. 17, 1866. His pastorate with this church lasted for three years and a half. After this he was pastor at Morris and Sablette, Ill.

Feeling that he might accomplish more good in a new and rising field, he accepted an invitation from a few Baptists in the city of Newton, Kansas, to aid them in starting and building up a Baptist church. With no church organized, no house of worship, and no specified salary, he began labor in this new field in November, 1877. Having no place to hold meetings, these brethren commenced to build a house for that purpose. In January it was completed, and dedicated to the worship of God, free of debt. At that time the church was organized. The preaching of the Word was attended by the power of the Spirit, and many souls were saved. Special meetings were held both in the town and in the country. Thirty persons were baptized, and a goodly number were received by letter and experience. These were the first baptisms that ever took place in the town of Newton. The Baptist church of Newton is a little more than two and a half years old. He has baptized into this church 56 converts, and there have been added in all 164 members.

Mr. Merrifield while in Kansas has, under God, made his own field, and is one of the most judicious, devoted, successful, and able workers in the State.

Merrill, Rev. Daniel, was born March 18, 1765, in Rowley, Mass. He was converted in his thirteenth year; he enlisted in January, 1781, when only fifteen years of age, and fought to the close of the Revolutionary war. He graduated at Dartmouth in 1789 with high honor. He began to preach in 1791, and his first sermon commenced a revival of religion which in a short time brought nearly 100 souls to Jesus. He preached with similar success in several places, staying but a short time in each. In 1793 he formed a church in Sedgwick, Me., of 20 members, on the Congregational platform, and in 1805 it was the largest church of any denomination in the State. Mr. Merrill at this period of great prosperity was filled with doubts about the divine origin of infant baptism, and months after, when he declared himself a Baptist, it produced a great commotion. A Baptist church was then organized of 85 members, and Mr. Merrill was ordained as its pastor. He continued in this field till 1814, when he took charge of a church in Nottingham, N. H., in which he remained seven years. He returned to Sedgwick and again enjoyed extensive revivals, until his death, in June, 1833.

Merrill, Rev. Eliphalet, was born in Stratham, N. H., April 7, 1765. His name is intimately associated with that of Dr. Samuel Shepard, who was the pastor of the church in Brentwood, N. H.

This church has several branches, one of them being in Northwood. Over this branch Mr. Merrill was ordained colleague pastor with Dr. Shepard in 1804, and for thirty years he was the minister of this branch church. He was especially useful in revivals, and made many missionary tours, preaching the gospel and gathering a large number of converts into the churches of New Hampshire. He died in Northwood, Feb. 7, 1853.

Merrill, Rev. Thomas W.—A graduate in the first class that took its full course in Waterville College, and of one of the earliest classes at Newton; commenced missionary work in Michigan in May, 1829. He was the son of Rev. Daniel Merrill, of Maine, who, when a Congregational pastor, was converted to Baptist sentiments, and baptized by Dr. Baldwin, and who was followed by a large part of his church. It was the mission of the son to lead in the commencement and establishment of the educational work of the denomination in Michigan. After teaching in Ann Arbor and Schoolcraft, he enlisted the co-operation of others and gained the charter of what is now Kalamazoo College in 1833. From that time until his death, in 1878, he devoted his life largely to the cause of education, performing gratuitous agency service, and consecrating the accumulations of his life to the endowment of the institution. This is his monument.

Merritt, Rev. W. H., was born in Chatham Co., N. C., in February, 1779; professed faith in Christ in 1801, and began to preach in 1824. He died July 3, 1850, and left $1000 for the erection of a Baptist church at Chapel Hill, and $2000 to Wake Forest College to be appropriated to the education of young ministers.

Merry, Rev. N. G., was born in Christian Co., Ky., July 10, 1824; removed from Kentucky to Tennessee in 1826, where he lived until 1836, when he returned to Kentucky, and remained there until 1840. On the 15th day of May of that year his mistress died, and he was brought again to Tennessee, where he has lived ever since. He removed to Nashville, and resides there at this time. He was converted, and Nov. 1, 1845, he was baptized in the Cumberland River by Dr. R. B. C. Howell. From his conversion he was impressed that he must preach the gospel. He commenced, although with great fear and trembling, to exhort. He tried to shrink from duty, but the more he tried the more forcible became the conviction that of necessity he must preach. In March, 1853, he received a license to fill the pulpit of the colored branch of the First Baptist church. A request was made for his ordination, and a council was called on the 29th of November, 1853, which set him apart to the Christian ministry. Rev. S. Baker, D.D., delivered the ordination sermon. Since then he has preached to the First Colored Baptist church successfully. He began with 100 members; the church now numbers 2300. During this time he has organized 13 churches. He has had occasion to build four times for his congregation. The present church cost $26,000, and will seat about 1300 persons. The labors of Brother Merry have been wonderfully blessed of the Lord. His influence for good is wide-spread.

Messer, Asa, D.D., LL.D., the third president of Brown University, was born in Methuen, Mass., in 1769. He graduated from Brown University in 1790. He was a tutor in the college for six years. In 1801 he was publicly ordained as a minister of the gospel. Upon the resignation of President Maxcy he was elected to fill his place. He resigned his office in 1826, after having been connected with the university as student and officer nearly forty years. His death occurred at Providence, Oct. 11, 1836.

The estimate in which President Messer was held as a man of scholarly attainments may be inferred from the fact that his own university conferred upon him the honorary degree of Doctor of Divinity in 1806, and Harvard University in 1820. In 1812 the University of Vermont conferred upon him the degree of Doctor of Laws.

His published writings are discourses delivered on different occasions when he was called upon to officiate, on account of his position and his reputation.

Prof. Park and Hon. W. L. Marcy have left on record testimony to the ability and the peculiarities in the character of President Messer, which no one can read without reaching the conclusion that he was a man of mark in the community in which he lived.

Metcalf, Rev. Whitman, was born in Royalston, Mass., Nov. 16, 1797. At an early age he was the subject of serious convictions, and devoted himself to the Lord. It was the desire of his heart that the Lord would honor him by calling him to the work of the ministry. But it was not until June, 1821, that he preached his first sermon by appointment of the Royalston church. The result was a license to preach, which he did as opportunity offered, pursuing his studies at Amherst and Waterville meanwhile. In September, 1825, he was ordained, and sent out by the Baptist Missionary Society of Massachusetts to preach as their missionary in Western New York. He was soon recognized as a leader of the new interests in the western counties of New York, and his services were sought far and near in establishing and fostering churches. He spent six years in Sardinia, Erie Co., building up not only the church there but other flourishing churches in neighboring towns.

The next five years he gave to the church in

Albion, when he returned to Sardinia for three years. He was then appointed by the New York State Convention as their financial secretary, in which service he remained for three years. From 1844 to 1848 he served the church in Brockport, when he was again called from the pastorate by the New York Baptist Education Society to assist for one year in raising funds for her beneficiaries. At the close of this year's service he was employed for one year by the American Baptist Publication Society for New England, when he was called to the church in Springville, which he served from 1850 to 1854, and then removed to Nunda, where he preached with his wonted power and success until 1863, when the infirmities of age compelled him to retire from pastoral work. He resided here, however, until his death, which occurred Nov. 7, 1877. He lived an eventful life, as a missionary, a pastor, and a builder of churches. He came to the close of his earthly career in full age, seeing many communities bearing the precious fruits of his prayers and toils, and loved and lamented by a host of friends.

Michigan, The Baptists of.—The earliest trace of Baptists in the Territory of Michigan is found in Oakland County, in 1818, where the city of Pontiac now stands. Orison Allen and his wife are the first names that appear. In their hands our denominational flag seems to have been brought into the Territory, and over their rude cabin that symbol of our faith and love was first displayed. Others of the same faith accompanied this honored pair, and united with them in efforts to serve the same blessed Master.

After four years, during which these brethren and sisters on this wild shore must have often, like the man of Macedonia, turned wistful looks and pleading calls to the ministers and churches across the lakes for some one to come over and help them, the Paul came over. Rev. Elon Galusha was that Paul. He was the ardent and gifted missionary of the New York Baptist Convention. Brother Galusha reached Pontiac on an itinerant mission in 1822. Here he preached in the wilderness, and led in the organization of the first Baptist church of the Territory.

The population of Michigan, when our first church was planted in it, was about 9000. Detroit was a muddy village of some 1500 inhabitants, among whom, if there was a Baptist, as doubtless there was, his or her memorial has perished.

The first resident Baptist preacher that we learn of in the Territory was Lemuel Taylor, who settled at Stony Creek, in Oakland County. He held the deacon's office, and preached as a licentiate, never desiring ordination. He was a good and useful man, the head of a large family, for whom his hands were diligent, and who perpetuated his usefulness by their own worth in the churches. As far as in him lay he preached the gospel to his neighbors and in the settlements around, seeking earnestly to plant the virgin soil with true religion and the true church.

The church at this place—Stony Creek—was the second one formed in Michigan. Rev. Nehemiah Lamb and his sons, Revs. C. A. and R. P. Lamb, visiting Pontiac in June, 1824, and breaking bread to the shepherdless flock, organized the brethren at Stony Creek into a church.

The first ordained minister who settled as pastor in our Territory was Elkanah Comstock. As missionary of the New York Convention he volunteered for this remote and solitary service, and took charge of the church in Pontiac in the summer of 1824.

In connection with the labors of Elder Comstock a church was constituted at Troy in 1825, and another at Farmington in 1826, making four churches in the Territory, all in Oakland County.

The Michigan Baptist Association was formed in 1826 of the above four churches, with their two or three ordained ministers.

The second pastor that we learn of was Rev. John Buttolph, who was settled in Troy in 1826. He died with this church the same year. His memory was long perpetuated as that of a loved and successful pastor, a character that was reproduced in his son, also one of the early ministers in the State, who died while yet young, and sleeps by his father's side in Troy.

In Detroit, the year 1826 set the Baptist elements astir, and while they were moving towards securing preaching, Brother Henry Davis, in his studies at Hamilton, was feeling strong impressions impelling him to attempt missionary work in their city. Accordingly, in the summer of this year, he visited Detroit for exploration, and became interested in its few Baptists. The next season (1827) we find him early on the ground with the wife who had given herself to share his life and work. Meetings were established in the academy, and soon baptisms were drawing the interested people to the great river-side to see the new spectacle. The church having formed under covenant, was approved by council of recognition, Oct. 20, 1827. No minister of the Territory was present. The New York Baptist Convention stood nurse to the babe, Elisha Tucker, of Fredonia, presiding and preaching, Jairus Handy, of Buffalo, giving the hand of fellowship, and Asahel Morse, of Ohio, the charge.

Brother Davis, as pastor, addressed himself with enterprise to the building up of the interest. Under his leadership, and with the friendly sympathy and co-operation of Gov. Cass, the grant was secured of the valuable lots, so long occupied, on the corner of Fort and Griswold Streets. But sickness seized and disabled the young pastor, compelling him to abandon his Western work before a year of it was finished.

The next tributary to Baptist influence in Michigan had its rise in the coming of Thomas W. Merrill to this as his adopted field of pioneer work. He entered the Territory in May, 1829, and enjoyed the longest ministerial life in the State which our entire ministry presents. He was from the State of Maine, where his father, a Congregational minister, turned a piece of the world upside down by becoming a Baptist, and by treating his church as "a cake not turned," an "Ephraim who had mixed himself among the people." Thomas had graduated at Waterville College and Newton Theological Seminary. Taking his appointment "not from men nor through man," he started at his graduation from the seminary, and made his way to Michigan at the date aforesaid.

It was his mission, as he had conceived it, and as the event has proved, to start and aid in rearing the Michigan Baptist Institution of Christian and Ministerial Learning, the history of which is detailed in another paper.

Looking across the Territory there is one other quarter in which light was newly breaking at this date, showing that torch-bearers were there setting the fires. It is at the southwest corner, and it reveals Rev. Jacob Price in Cass County. He entered there from Wales in 1831 or 1832, having been furthered on his way by Dr. Cone and others in New York. A Brother Miller, from Virginia, was also working along the Indiana border, adjoining Brother Price's field; and Brother H. J. Hall, from Vermont, was the same year sent as a missionary into that vicinity, and labored with Brother Price happily, and with some cheering ingatherings of souls churches were formed at Liberty, Lagrange, Niles, Edwardsburg, and perhaps over the Indiana line.

Elder Price was the unremitting toiler on that field for forty years. He was benevolence and work personified. God anointed him with the Holy Spirit, and he went about doing good. His kindly countenance was the first preacher's face seen in the cabin doors of the new settlers over a large portion of Southwestern Michigan. Under him numerous churches rose up, and by his wise counsels and Christ-like spirit they guided their affairs with discretion. One generation after another saw his familiar appearance passing along the roads to his scattered preaching-places, and leading the funeral processions of many surrounding towns; and then "he was not, for God took him."

At Comstock, the mother of all the churches in the Kalamazoo River Association was formed by Brother Merrill, Judge Eldred, and others. It is now the Galesburg church.

In 1831 the churches associated in organizing the Michigan Baptist Domestic Mission Society, which kept up its annual meetings, inspired the formation of auxiliaries in all the churches, solicited and appropriated funds, and was in fact what later took the name and form of the State Convention. Foreign missions were alike cared for, and Christian education. Tract circulation was also organized and urged with intelligent liberality and personal labor from the first.

In 1832 there were twenty churches in the Territory and twelve pastors.

Rev. Robert Turnbull became pastor in Detroit in November, 1834, soon after which time the church dedicated their permanent house of worship. During the two and a half years of this pastorate our cause in Detroit advanced well.

At Kalamazoo and vicinity, in 1835, Rev. Jeremiah Hall commenced preaching, and the church was formed the ensuing February. He labored as pastor eight years with discretion and faithfulness, and the church became a steady and central light. The Literary Institute fixed there its permanent location, and began its school-life.

At Schoolcraft, Rev. William Taylor was setting on the candlestick that pure and beneficent light which shone there in such blessing while he lived; ay, and is phosphorescent from his grave there yet, though the storms of more than twenty years have drenched it.

Under these laborers and their co-workers in the churches our growth spread widely. The second Association was called for and formed in 1833 or 1834, bearing then the name of Lagrange, but now the St. Joseph River. And the third, first called the river Raisin, now the Washtenaw Association, was formed on the 14th of January, 1835.

Now came the building and launching of the Baptist Convention of the State of Michigan; for Michigan was becoming a State just in time to allow this name. The story of its organization and growth is reserved for another article.

Of the number of churches and members in the State at the date of the Convention's formation we can only have approximate knowledge. We judge there were about 35 churches and nearly 2000 members.

A large number of ministers came in or were raised up in the churches from 1836 to 1840: Brethren Weaver, Curtiss, Hamlin, J. Harris, N. G. Chase, M. Allen, L. H. Moore, G. B. Day, O. C. Comstock, Fulton, Hendee, Pennell, Rummerey, Wisner, Piper, and others. The American Baptist Home Mission Society came promptly on the field at its origin in 1842, and has been at the front ever since. Almost all the churches, both older and newer, have felt its ready and steady hand of help in their time of need.

In all their efforts, and in general co-operation with missionary, Bible, and other causes, there has been remarkable freedom from partisan divisions and strifes in the churches, Associations, and Conventions. The Baptists of Michigan have been a homogeneous people, respectful towards each other's opinions and modes of action, and determined that no incompatibility should divorce what God had joined together.

The largest number of baptisms in a year was in 1876, when it lacked but little of 3000. The average for fifteen years is a little over 1400. Membership, 27,064. Number of churches, 341, constituting eighteen Associations. For benevolent objects of all kinds, not including what has been done by contributors for their own local churches, they must have given not less than $600,000, all of it in comparatively small sums,— the drops that make the ocean.

Michigan, The Baptist Convention of the State of.—The oldest Baptist church in Michigan —that in Pontiac—was formed in 1822. The first ordained Baptist minister residing in the State entered it in 1824. The first Association was organized in 1827, but no general convention of the Baptists in the State was attempted till 1836. In that year a call was issued to the churches to send delegates to Detroit for a State organization, and in response to the call 26 churches were represented by 55 delegates in Detroit on the 31st of August. Dr. Nathaniel Kendrick, Archibald Maclay, Elon Galusha, Elisha Tucker, and eight others, not residents of the State, were present, and invited to aid the delegates in their work.

The plan of organization then adopted was almost exactly the same as that now in use, after an experience of forty-three years. The design of the Convention was declared to be "to carry out the commission of Christ in giving the gospel to every creature; by multiplying and circulating copies of the Holy Scriptures; aiding home and foreign missions; encouraging Sabbath-school instruction; promoting the circulation of religious tracts; and the cause of education, especially that of the rising ministry." The constitution further provided that the objects contemplated by the Convention " shall be classed in the following order: Bible efforts; home missions; foreign missions; education; general benevolence; and each of the foregoing objects respectively shall be assigned to a specific committee appointed by the Board of Managers."

How little change has been introduced into the general plan of organization after nearly half a century will appear from the following statement of the present plan of work, contained in the by-laws as last printed:

"The board, at its first meeting after its election, shall appoint special boards, consisting of not less than five, nor more than nine members, as follows:

"1. The Board of State Missions.

"2. The Board of Christian and Ministerial Education.

"3. The Board of Foreign Missions.

"4. The Board of Bible Publication and Sunday-school work.

"5. The Board of Home Missions.

"These special boards shall be regarded as co-operative respectively with the general societies of the Baptist denomination for the same objects."

As a result of this organization the American Baptist Missionary Union, and the American Baptist Home Mission Society, and the American Baptist Publication Society, have at their service organized committees to commend their interest to the churches of the State, while other committees are intrusted with the care of new and feeble churches, and with the duty of aiding young men whom God has called to prepare for the gospel ministry. At each annual meeting these subjects come up in turn for consideration, not as intruders, nor simply as welcome visitors, but as the very interests which the Convention was organized to serve.

At the first election of officers, Rev. Robert Powell was chosen president, and Rev. Robert Turnbull secretary, and the Convention entered on its work with hopeful zeal.

Among the objects for which the Convention was formed State missions have naturally occupied a prominent place, both because the demand for missionary work in the State has been great and constant, and because in this work the board was not auxiliary to any broader organization, but responsible for the whole direction and accomplishment of the enterprise. For a few years it co-operated with the American Baptist Home Mission Society in the care of the churches in the State, as was the case in other States, but in 1875 returned to the former plan of separate control. A large proportion of the ablest and largest churches in the State have been fostered by the Convention, and are now glad to recognize their indebtedness.

A second branch of the Convention's work is that of Christian and ministerial education. At the organization of the Convention appreciative recognition was made of the institution at Kalamazoo, and the policy was indicated of having a college with full powers. Funds also were then proposed for theological education. In 1837 a theological school was resolved upon. Funds for beneficiaries were raised and appropriated to students at Hamilton.

In 1846 the establishment of a theological seminary was determined, grounds were purchased in Kalamazoo, and preparations were made for building. The seminary was not, and never became, a separate corporation, but was directly controlled by the Convention, which owned the property, and by its board governed the institution. Prof. James A. B. Stone, pastor at Kalamazoo, and principal of the institute, was placed in charge of the work in the beginning, and retained this place for seventeen years. Instruction began in 1849, and Rev. Samuel Graves was added to the faculty in 1851. After the institute became Kalamazoo College, its professors taught in the seminary as occasion required. In 1866, Dr. Silas Bailey became the principal teacher in the seminary, and remained in this service till the fall of 1869, when the failure of his health compelled him to retire from all severe labor. The funds of the Convention for the support of the seminary had never been adequate, and after the retirement of Dr. Bailey, the seminary at Chicago having been established, it was thought not to provide at present for distinctively theological education. Meanwhile the funds of the Convention which were given for ministerial education are sacredly kept for that purpose, and the income is appropriated in aiding young men in their preparation for the ministry. While the seminary was maintained between 50 and 60 students passed from its studies into the ministry.

In 1869, Rev. Thomas W. Merrill offered to the Convention the sum of $8000 for the support of a professor in Kalamazoo College, who must be a Baptist minister and serve as college pastor. The original endowment was to remain on interest till it should amount to $10,000. In 1874 the same brother proposed to add $14,000 to a previous gift of $1000, for the endowment of scholarships in Kalamazoo College, this addition to become available in 1880 or at his death. These endowments are not at present available, as the notes in which Mr. Merrill made payment are not now paying interest. For one year, however, Rev. Dr. N. S. Burton served in the Merrill Professorship. The funds now in possession of the Convention for educational purposes, besides the Merrill endowments, are about $6000. The Convention also owns the grounds on which the upper buildings of Kalamazoo College are situated, worth about $60,000.

Another enterprise of the Convention was the establishment of a weekly religious paper. Contemplated in the origin of the Convention, and agitated at each of the annual meetings for six years, it was undertaken at the meeting in 1841, and the first number was issued in January, 1842, bearing the name of the *Michigan Christian Herald*. It was put in charge of a committee, of which Rev. Andrew Tenbrook, pastor in Detroit, acted as editor, and R. C. Smith and S. N. Kendrick as publishers. The second year Rev. Miles Sanford performed editorial work. After Prof. Tenbrook was called to the university, Rev. J. Inglis succeeding him as pastor, also filled the editorial chair. With the year 1848 began Rev. Marvin Allen's proprietorship of the paper, and Rev. Geo. W. Harris assumed editorial care of it. Thence to the death of Mr. Allen, in 1861, these co-laborers supplied the State with the *Herald*. The editor gave eminent satisfaction in his department, and the publisher threw his tireless zeal and rare executive abilities without reserve into the enterprise. On the death of Mr. Allen it was difficult to find a man ready to do his work. The orphaned *Herald* was taken up in Kalamazoo by Brethren Olney, Curtiss, Walden, Clark, and Cadman, and continued to serve the churches well but its publishers ill. In 1867 it was deemed expedient to consolidate the *Herald* with the *Christian Times*, of Chicago, and the *Witness*, of Indianapolis, under the name of the *Standard*, which has since been published in Chicago.

The publication of a weekly Baptist paper for Michigan was, however, commenced again in January, 1873, not by the Convention, but by Rev. L. H. Trowbridge as both publisher and editor. This paper, which bears the name of the *Christian Herald*, is issued from Detroit, and has had a constantly increasing circulation and a continuous growth in power among the churches till now.

Most of the influence which the Convention has exerted has not been of a nature to be easily stated. It has produced unity of action among the churches, has steadily aided in the collection of funds for foreign missions, home missions, and the circulation of religious books, has provided for the support of candidates for the ministry, and has collected and published statistics of the denomination in Michigan. The meetings from the very beginning have been characterized by harmony and an earnest desire to serve the interests of Christ's kingdom.

In Michigan there are 18 Associations, 352 churches, 307 ordained ministers, and 27,285 members.

Middleditch, Robert T., D.D., was born in Bedfordshire, England, May 22, 1825. His father and a brother were Baptist ministers. He became a member of a Baptist church at sixteen years of age, and was educated at an English seminary for missionary students, and in 1844 was sent as a missionary to Jamaica, West Indies, by the English Baptist Missionary Society.

In 1846 he came to the United States, and settled at Lyons Farms, N. J., where he was ordained in 1848. In 1850 he settled at Red Bank, N. J., where he remained as pastor till 1867. He also served the churches of Nyack and Flushing, N. Y., as pastor. In all his settlements he met with success. Since 1872 he has been associate editor of the *Baptist Weekly*. He received the honorary degree of Doctor of Divinity from Madison University.

He is the author of that widely-circulated work, "A Pedobaptist Church no Home for a Baptist;" also a premium mission tract, "The World's Revolution," published for the Southern Baptist Board; "A Baptist Church, the Christian's Home," and "Burmah's Great Missionary." Several sermons preached by him have been published. He is an able and industrious writer and preacher, as his works attest.

Mikels, Wm. S., D.D., was born in Orange Co., N. Y., May 18, 1820. He was graduated from Madison University in 1843, and the theological seminary at Hamilton, N. Y., in 1845. He was ordained pastor of the Baptist church at Rondout, N. Y. After four years of service he then settled in Sing Sing, where he labored six years. In 1856 he accepted the pastorate of the Sixteenth Street Baptist church, New York, which position he filled for seventeen years. This was the great work of his life. It was a continuous revival, and many hundreds were added to the church. Dr. Mikels is a plain, earnest speaker, appealing directly to the hearts of the people. As a friend in need, a counselor in trouble, and as a peace-maker, he has few equals. For some years he has been the pastor of the East Baptist church, located in the Seventh Ward.

Miles, Rev. Edward, was born in the arsenal at Philadelphia, Nov. 15, 1812; baptized in Milesburg, Pa., Nov. 25, 1832; ordained at Milesburg, May 15, 1837, and at different periods served the following churches in Pennsylvania: Alleghany, Meadville, Freeport, Loyalhannock, Uniontown, Zion, Kittanning, New Castle, Brownsville, and Red Stone in Union County. June 4, 1852, he took charge of the Second church in Davenport, Iowa, where he still resides.

Miles, Rev. Frederick W., was born in New Brunswick; was a graduate of King's College, Windsor, Nova Scotia, and was converted while attending that institution. Subsequently adopting Baptist principles, he was baptized. He was for some time pastor of the Baptist church in St. John, New Brunswick, and afterwards pastor of the church at Fredericton, New Brunswick. At the opening of the Baptist seminary, in January, 1836, in Fredericton, Mr. Miles became its principal, and so continued till, to the regret of all, sickness compelled him to resign. Enthusiastic and energetic in his work in the seminary and in the gospel, he had the entire confidence of the Baptist denomination, and their highest commendation. He died February, 1842.

Miles, Rev. George Frederick, was born in Mangerville, New Brunswick; converted and baptized in that province; ordained pastor in 1846, and has been pastor at St. George, Moncton, and Sackville, New Brunswick, and also at Amherst, Nova Scotia, and now performs a vast amount of pastoral and missionary work in Cumberland and Colchester Counties, Nova Scotia.

Miles, Rev. John, in 1662, was ejected from the living of Ilston, in Wales, by the Act of Uniformity. Like a considerable number of Baptists in the time of Cromwell's protectorate he was probably pastor of a Baptist church, and officiated as a preacher in one of the state churches. The law, in 1662, compelled him to surrender his relations to the Establishment, and subjected him otherwise to great sufferings if he would carry out his conscientious convictions. He had been a very active and successful Baptist minister. Backus represents him as the "father of the Baptist churches in Wales, which began in 1649." This statement requires some modification, but it is certain that he was exceedingly useful in spreading the truth in the principality. And had he not been a man of strict conscientiousness he would have retained his living in the national church and sacrificed his religious principles. Many followed this course.

In 1663 he and his Baptist friends of Swansea, in Wales, came to Massachusetts, and located at a place to which they gave the name of their old home. They brought their church records with them, and they joined together "in a solemn covenant" (in a church organization) in the house of John Butterworth. Mr. Miles was the pastor of the American Swanzey church. He was a minister of great industry and zeal, and of fearless courage. When the Boston brethren suffered heavily from the persecuting laws of their Puritan brethren, Mr. Miles went to succor them, and give such counsel and encouragement as his wide experience would readily furnish. He stood his ground in Swanzey against all discouragements and threatenings, and proved himself a tower of strength to the abused and persecuted Baptists. He remained the pastor of Swanzey till his death, in 1683.

Mr. Miles was distinguished for his learning, and remarkable for his piety, and such was the blessed influence which he exerted, and the deep impression which he left, that Backus writes of him in 1777, nearly a hundred years after his death, "his memory is still precious among us." And Mather is compelled to place him and Hanserd Knollys among "some godly Anabaptists" who came from England. "Both of these," he says, "have a respectful character in the churches of this wilderness."

Miles, Gen. Samuel, was born at White Marsh, Montgomery Co., Pa., 1739. His grandfather, one of the first settlers of this State, was a native of Wales. In his sixteenth year Samuel Miles joined a company of militia which was ordered to Northampton County to defend its inhabitants from hostile Indians. In his military duties he showed such skill and courage that the governor of the colony, in 1757, sent him an ensign's commission in the troops of Pennsylvania. He was three

GEN. SAMUEL MILES.

years in active service, during which he was advanced to the command of a company; and he was only once slightly wounded.

At the close of the war he married Catharine, daughter of John Wistar, Esq., and entered upon housekeeping and commercial pursuits in Philadelphia. His talents and industry secured for him such a measure of prosperity that in 1774 he retired from business.

When the Revolutionary agitation began Capt. Miles was among the first to show his patriotic ardor. In 1776 he became colonel of a regiment of riflemen, formed by himself, and composed of his neighbors and friends. This body of brave men, one thousand strong, was attached to the regular army under Washington. On the 28th of August, 1776, he fought with great gallantry at the battle of Long Island, and his riflemen showed a heroism worthy of the glorious cause which they represented. But the army of freedom was not equal to the forces of oppression, and for the time being they were compelled to give way. With Col. Miles, Gens. Sullivan and Stirling, and eighty-one other officers were captured. During his imprisonment he was made a brigadier-general for distinguished services in the field. After his release he was for a time deputy quartermaster of the American army for the State of Pennsylvania. His military services were of the highest importance in the Revolutionary struggle; and his patriotic example exerted an immense influence in stirring up the lukewarm, and in putting the disloyal to shame.

After the conclusion of peace he was elected mayor of Philadelphia, a position which, for generations, has been regarded by its citizens as an honor of unusual magnitude, the duties of which have generally been discharged by distinguished men. The picture of Gen. Miles adorns the office of the chief magistrate of Philadelphia at this time, surrounded by the portraits of his predecessors and successors; and his biography may be consulted in the archives of the mayor's office. Gen. Miles was an alderman of Philadelphia, a member of the Colonial and State Legislatures, and a judge of the Court of Errors and Appeals. He was a man whom his fellow-citizens delighted to honor.

In 1792 he retired again, to a country-seat in Montgomery County. Of this place President Manning, of Rhode Island College (now Brown University), says, "Col. Miles has a most elegant seat, gardens, meadows, etc., and a most remarkable spring, which turns three wheels in one-fourth of a mile from its source. I spent three days very agreeably" (there). In that beautiful home, in gratifying refined tastes, and in extending a generous hospitality to his numerous friends, he spent the remainder of his days. He died Sept. 29, 1805, in the sixty-seventh year of his age.

Gen. Miles was a zealous Baptist, and a warm friend to every Baptist interest. A lady, a relative of the general, who wrote a sketch of his life for *The Assembly's Magazine* of 1806, a Presbyterian periodical, says, "A Scotch nobleman was once complimented upon the number of offices he had filled under the British government, each of which was mentioned to him; 'You have forgotten,' said he, 'to mention one of my honors, which I prize more than all the rest, and that is the office of an elder in my parish church, which I have filled for many years.' The same pre-eminence in ecclesiastical over civil honors was possessed by Gen. Miles for many years in the Baptist church of Philadelphia."

The writer means that the general was a Baptist deacon, and that he esteemed that office his chief honor. Grace had so completely moulded the heart and character of Gen. Miles, that an intimate friend of nearly twenty years' standing "had never once seen him angry." "He loved and cherished his country as if he expected to live in it forever, and yet he served his God as if he constantly felt that he was a stranger in this world, and that his citizenship and home were in heaven."

Miller, Rev. Andrew Jackson, was born in Hardin Co., Ky., Jan. 7, 1839. He was educated at Madison College, Tenn.; was baptized into the fellowship of Mount Zion Baptist church, in Ohio Co., Ky.; licensed to preach in 1859, and was ordained at Cool Spring church, in the same county, in 1861. He was pastor for a time at Henderson, Ky. Afterwards he preached several years at Carrollton, Mo. In 1877 he returned to Kentucky, and took charge of the church at Cloverport. At present he is pastor of Zion church in Henderson County. He has baptized over 1000 persons, and has served the Henderson County Association as moderator during the last three years. He is a brother of Rev. Dr. A. B. Miller, of Evansville, Ind., an able preacher and an efficient pastor.

Miller, D. Henry, D.D., was born in the Isle of Jersey, Oct. 31, 1827. His mother was the daughter of one of the heroes of Bunker Hill. His father was a native of England. On the death of his father Mrs. Miller returned to Boston, where her son received his first training. He was graduated from the Wesleyan Institution in 1845. In 1849 he received the degree of A.M. from Madison University. Soon after the time of his graduation he embraced the views of the Baptists, and was licensed to preach by the Stanton Street Baptist church in New York. In 1847 he was ordained as pastor of the Baptist church in North Stonington, Conn. In 1849 he organized a church of seven members under an old elm-tree in Yonkers, N. Y., where he remained until 1857. In that year he settled in Meriden, Conn., and in 1861 was commissioned as chaplain of the 15th Regiment Conn. Vols. After two years of service in the field, he settled as pastor of the First Baptist church of Trenton, N. J. In 1866 he received the degree of D.D. from Lewisburg University, Pa. In 1867 he accepted the pastorate of the Broad Street church of Elizabeth, N. J. In 1872 he settled with the Worthen Street church in Lowell, Mass., and in 1873 accepted a call from the Plymouth church in New York. In 1875 he took charge of the Noble Street church, Brooklyn, where he has been eminently successful.

Dr. Miller succeeded Rev. Dr. Dowling, some years since, in the editorship of the *Baptist Memorial*, in which he continued for several years, until its sale and removal from New York.

Miller, Rev. Harvey, son of Rev. Samuel Miller (pastor of old Wallingford church, and first pastor of Meriden church in 1817), was born in Wallingford, Conn., April 3, 1814; baptized on the day he was seventeen years of age by Rev. Simon Shailer; soon began to preach; in 1832 entered Hamilton Theological and Literary Institution, and remained four years; ordained at Ann Arbor, Mich., Nov. 23, 1836; returned to Connecticut in 1838, and became pastor of Baptist church in Meriden, where he successfully labored eighteen years till his death; died Aug. 27, 1856; had an active and quick mind; an extensive reader; often quaint in his mode of expression; laborious worker; realized excellent results in his ministry; beloved and honored.

Miller, Hon. James, was born in West Philadelphia, Pa., Oct. 22, 1822; was baptized into the fellowship of the Blockley church, Philadelphia, by Rev. Joseph Hammett, Oct. 22, 1843. He soon after became one of the constituent members of the First church, West Philadelphia; but subsequently returned to the Blockley church, where for many years he was a faithful member, an honored office-bearer, and an efficient Sunday-school superintendent. In 1872 he connected himself with the Mantua mission interest in West Philadelphia, and by his labors and benefactions largely aided the organization and growth of the present Mantua church. He was prominently identified with the establishment of the Baptist Home of Philadelphia, and is still a member of its board of trustees. He is also a member of the board of curators of the university at Lewisburg, and is treasurer of the Pennsylvania Baptist General Association and the Philadelphia City Mission. In other religious and secular enterprises he is officially connected with the management of important trusts. For several years he was editor and proprietor of the *Philadelphia Progress*. In 1864–65, and again in 1869–70, he was chosen to represent his fellow-citizens in the Pennsylvania State Legislature. In all these varied and responsible positions he has shown himself to be an able officer, a wise counselor, an upright man, and a consistent Christian. He was especially devoted to Sunday-school work, and much of his time has been spent in earnest and successful efforts to so address himself to the young as to make early religious impressions upon their hearts. Of those whom he has thus influenced many will doubtless shine as stars in the crown of his rejoicing.

Miller, Rev. John, was born at Voluntown, Conn., Feb. 3, 1775; experienced a saving change in his eighteenth year; removed to Abington, Luzerne Co., Pa., Feb. 18, 1802. Here he lived and labored until his decease, Feb. 19, 1857, in his eighty-third year. His wife was the fifth lady in the settlement. On the 18th of October, 1802, the Abington Baptist church was recognized, and the same day he was ordained as its pastor, and he served them with singular ability and success until 1853,—a period of over fifty years. But service in this single church was not enough to satisfy the longing desires of his heart. "He cultivated as his field the northern part of Luzerne County, with portions of Wyoming and Susquehanna Counties, embracing the large area commencing on the summit of the Moosie Mountain on the northeast, and extending down its southwestern slope over the Abington hills, and beyond the waters of the Susquehanna." The immense labor required for the work could not easily be conceived, much less performed, by ministers used to the ordinary comforts of the present day. Benton, Blakely, Clifford, Carbondale, Eaton, Exeter, Newton, Northmoreland, Pittston, Providence, Greenfield, and Tunkhannock are churches located now in what was then the geographical field of this hardy missionary and pastor. Such were the herculean labors of this man, performed without remuneration, amid winter's cold and summer's heat, on foot or on horseback, in dangers seen and unseen, but with unfaltering faith and glowing desire to fulfill the ministry given him in the dispensation of grace. And the fruits were more abundant than the labor. He baptized not far from 2000 converts, attended nearly as many funerals. Six whole churches, and parts of six others, the results of his ministry, have become independent bodies; seven preachers of the gospel have been raised up in the one church, and an influence all-pervading had leavened the entire field.

After a ministry of fifty-three years he lingered for a few weeks in great pain, but was calmly released, in the full possession of his mental powers, on Thursday, Feb. 19, 1857.

Miller, Col. John Blount, was born in Charleston, S. C., on the 16th of September, 1782. He studied law at an early age, and was the first notary public ever appointed for Sumter County. His diligence and accuracy in business soon gave him a large and lucrative practice, and the highest respect of the bench and bar.

He joined the Baptist church, High Hills of Santee, in early life, and his devotion as a Christian was even greater than he had exhibited in his legal profession.

In 1817 he was appointed commissioner and register in equity, which office he held until his death, on the 21st of October, 1851. He was elected to the Legislature in the next winter, and re-elected for each term while he lived.

He was a captain, major, and lieutenant-colonel successively in the war of 1812. Hence the title of colonel, by which he was ever afterward known.

Miller, Rev. Manoah D., of Madison, Wis., was born Feb. 15, 1811, in Elizabethtown, N. J. His parents were Manoah and Elizabeth Miller. They were Baptists, and their Christian lives and example made a deep impression on him, and contributed largely in shaping the future of their son. His father was a judge of the Supreme Court of New York. In early life he obtained a hope in Christ and united with the Baptist Church. He completed the full literary and theological course of Hamilton Literary and Theological Institution. He was ordained at Monkton, Vt., and became the pastor of the Baptist church in that place. He subsequently served as pastor the churches at Springfield, Danville, Windham, Wilmington, and Addison, in Vermont. He received the honorary degree of A.M. from Middlebury College. In January, 1853, he came to Madison, Wis., which has been his place of residence since that time. When he came to Madison the Baptist church there had no church edifice. He at once led the church in the work of building, and succeeded in enlisting the city generally in the movement to such an extent as to secure the best edifice for the church, and the most centrally located of any in the place. He was in that early day an active and very useful pastor. He did much outside of his church to organize the missionary and educational work of the State.

In June, 1857, owing to impaired health requiring his retirement from the active work of the ministry, he organized the Wisconsin Bank of Madison, which institution he managed with honor and success until 1861, when he closed it. He continued banking in other forms and connected with other business until 1876, when he withdrew from active business. He is now living in retirement near the city of Madison. He has always taken the liveliest interest in the Baptist church of which he was the pastor, and of which he has continued an active and useful member.

Miller, Rev. R. M., was born in Sevier Co., Tenn., Nov. 3, 1815. He died April 22, 1871. Professed religion when fifteen years of age, and began to preach in early life. He was ordained July 8, 1843. Revs. John Woody, Thos. Jackson, and John Avery composed the Presbytery. Mr. Miller labored in Johnson, Cass, and Pulaski Counties. He was unwearied in work, and he was successful. He was stricken with paralysis, and died soon after.

Miller, Rev. T. Doughty, was born in New York, Sept. 19, 1835. He was brought up in the Episcopal Church. He was converted in 1850; shortly afterwards he pursued classical and theological studies at St. Augustine's Institute, N. Y., with a view to the ministry of the Episcopal Church. He was principal of a public school in Trenton for three years, and he held the same position subsequently in Newburgh, N. Y. In 1856, having learned the truth more perfectly, he was baptized in the Hudson River with his wife at Newburgh. In August, 1858, he was ordained pastor of the Mount Zion Colored Baptist church, of New Haven, Conn. In this church and in Albany his labors were greatly blessed in winning souls to Jesus.

In 1864 he accepted a call from the First African Baptist church of Philadelphia. In this old community he soon became a great favorite, and the seal of the Spirit was given to his ministrations. The membership is three times more numerous than when he assumed the pastorate. Under his guidance the church purchased a larger edifice in a better locality, which is now entirely paid for through the liberality of the members and the generous gifts of friends in the white churches, who appreciate the talents and piety of Mr. Miller. His enlarged edifice is filled, and his usefulness is visible to all that know the community over which he so worthily presides.

Since his settlement in Philadelphia the First African church has sent out a missionary to the land of their fathers, and four young men who have become successful pastors in Wilmington, Baltimore, New Bedford, and in the Indian Territory.

Mr. Miller was appointed to preach the introductory sermon before the Philadelphia Association in 1879; he was the first colored man that ever occupied the position, and he was not placed in it through political bias, but as a simple recognition of his Christian worth; his sermon showed the propriety of the choice. Mr. Miller is a man of scholarly tastes; he is the best colored preacher ever located in Philadelphia, and his piety is of a high order.

Millett, Rev. Joshua, was born in Leeds, Me., Jan. 26, 1803. He took part of the collegiate course of study at Waterville, and then went to the Newton Theological Institution, where he graduated in the class of 1835. His ordination took place at Charleston, Me., Jan. 6, 1836, where he remained two years, and then went to Cherryfield, where he was pastor five years. Afterwards he removed to Wayne, where he continued until his death, March 10, 1848.

Mr. Millett was the author of "A History of the Baptists in Maine," in which he has gathered up many facts about men and things in that State which were fast passing into oblivion. Future historians of denominational matters in Maine will be grateful for the careful and useful work which he has done.

Milliken, Rev. L. H., was born Aug. 21, 1813, in Logan Co., Ky. He was educated in Nashville, Tenn., graduating Oct. 3, 1838. He professed religion Dec. 27, 1832, in Logan Co., Ky., and was baptized into the fellowship of the Whippoorwill Baptist church, Law County, by Rev. R. T. Anderson, and ordained at the instance of Pleasant Grove church, by Revs. Wm. Warder, O. H. Morrow, and R. T. Anderson. Mr. Milliken spent a year in evangelistic labors in North Alabama; came to Memphis, Tenn., in the winter of 1839, and took charge of the First Baptist church one year. In the winter of 1841 went to Somerville, Fayette Co., Tenn., where he remained teaching, and preaching to Somerville Baptist church until the winter of 1851, when, upon invitation of the church of that city, he removed to Aberdeen, Miss., where he labored six years. In the spring of 1856 he accepted a call to Jackson, Miss., where nearly four years were spent. In 1860 he removed to his plantation in Hardeman Co., Tenn., near Grand Junction, to recruit his health from excessive and long-continued labor. In 1862 he became chaplain of the 13th Tenn. Regiment, C. S. A., and he continued in that office until the winter before the close of the war.

Since the war he has been engaged in teaching and preaching the gospel. Through his efforts a substantial house of worship has been built in La Grange, Tenn., costing $5000, and the foundation of another has been laid in Somerville, Tenn., the county seat of Fayette County, the estimated cost of which is $8000, with a fair prospect of completion. Mr. Milliken is possessed of more than ordinary ability and of great piety.

Mills, J. H., was born in Halifax Co., Va., July 9, 1831; was baptized by his father; graduated with first distinction at Wake Forest in the class with Judge W. T. Faircloth of the Supreme Court of North Carolina and Dr. T. H. Pritchard; became president of Oxford Female College in 1855; bought the *Biblical Recorder* in 1867, which he conducted with success for six years; organized the Oxford Orphan Asylum in 1873, of which he has been the superintendent ever since. This noble charity, which has fed, clothed, and educated hundreds of poor orphan children, has been sustained almost altogether by the unaided efforts of this most benevolent and energetic man, and a rich heritage of blessing will rest upon him and his forever for his "works of faith and labors of love."

Mills, Prof. L. R., was born in Halifax Co., Va., Aug. 17, 1840; baptized by Dr. Wingate, Oct. 19, 1859. He graduated at Wake Forest College in 1861, and served four years in the late war. He has been Professor of Mathematics in Wake Forest College since 1871. Prof. Mills was for several years secretary of the board of education, and is a very effective speaker. He is now bursar of Wake Forest College, and one of the rising men of the State.

Milton, John, was born in London, Dec. 9, 1608. His father was a man of taste and of ample resources, and John had everything to contribute to his proper training. When he was only twelve years of age he had an irresistible desire to acquire information, and would sit up till midnight reading, though seriously afflicted with weak eyes and with severe pains in the head. At fifteen he turned some of the Psalms into beautiful stanzas. Before he went to the University of Cambridge, which he entered when he was sixteen years and two months old, he was an advanced classical scholar, and he was well acquainted with ancient and modern theories of philosophy. He studied seven years in Cambridge.

JOHN MILTON.

When he left the university he came to reside with his father at Horton, in Buckinghamshire, with whom he stayed for several years. This period he spent in reading, in learned investigations, and in giving to the world several pieces of exquisite poetry. He could translate with the greatest ease Hebrew, Greek, Latin, French, Italian, and Spanish, and his works carried marks of the wealth of universal learning. They speedily became known all over Europe, and especially in Italy, so that when he visited that country, in 1639, he was received with extraordinary enthusiasm and honor, the leading men in literary and scientific pursuits treating him as if he were Virgil or Dante returning to visit the glorious land in which they spent their earthly lives. Milton was rudely recalled from his Italian ovations by the fierce conflicts of his countrymen, and for twenty years he wielded his pen for liberty with a power almost surpassing that of the sword of Cromwell, the greatest warrior of the whole Anglo-Saxon race. Milton was a republican arsenal stored with intellectual weapons, which he could use with so much ease, and with such fatal effect, that no man could stand before him. Among his countrymen there was not another with his intellect, his culture, and his skill in using his mighty arms. The royalists, with good reason, dreaded and hated him. Cromwell and his followers cherished him with a tender affection.

He was the Latin secretary of Cromwell during his entire protectorate. Latin was the language of diplomacy and of courts in their business relations with each other. It was Milton that wrote the dispatches which made the Duke of Savoy tremble on his petty throne and drop the bloody sword with which he was inflicting martyrdom upon the godly Waldenses. If Cromwell forged his own thunderbolts, his Latin secretary hurled them forth with such a force that their execution was fatal to every plot conceived against Protestantism or England.

Milton was married three times. His last wife survived him for many years, and was buried in Nantwich, Cheshire, in the Baptist chapel. She had been for a long period a member of the Baptist church of Nantwich.

The work with which Milton's fame is now chiefly connected is "Paradise Lost." It was published in 1667. The author was paid £5 for it, and he was to receive £5 more for every 1300 copies sold. He received £10 from the immortal poem, and his widow sold the copyright for £8. "Paradise Lost" altogether brought the author and his wife less than ninety dollars! Such compensation for the most sublime production ever created by human genius!

How Milton escaped the axe or the halter of Charles II. history does not tell. It is a circumstance so singular that it seems almost miraculous.

Milton had very decided religious convictions. His principal error was a peculiar view about the person of Christ, tending somewhat towards Arianism. His general opinions, however, were those of the Baptist denomination. He believed, for example, that it was not lawful for any power on earth to exercise compulsion over the conscience in religious matters; that the Word of God was the only authority in Christ's earthly kingdom; that the government of a church was purely congregational, as contrasted with the usurpations of popes, prelates, and presbyteries; and that the members of a church should be regenerated persons. His opinion about imputation is sounder than the doctrine of the great theologian of Kittering. He says, "As therefore our sins are imputed to Christ, so the merit or righteousness of Christ is imputed to us through faith. It is evident therefore that this justification, in so far as we are concerned, is gratuitous; in so far as Christ is concerned, not gratuitous, inasmuch as Christ paid the ransom for our sins, which he took upon him by imputation." The great poet and the great apostle see alike on this blessed subject.

In his "Treatise on Christian Doctrine" Milton

gives a clear account of his views of the mode and subjects of baptism. He says, "Under* the gospel the first of the sacraments, commonly so called, is baptism, wherein the bodies of believers who engage themselves to pureness of life are immersed in running water to signify their regeneration by the Holy Spirit, and their union with Christ in his death, burial, and resurrection. Hence it follows that infants are not to be baptized, inasmuch as they are incompetent to receive instruction or believe, or to enter into a covenant, or to promise or answer for themselves, or even to hear the Word. For how can infants that understand not the Word be purified thereby, any more than adults can receive edification by hearing an unknown language? For it is not the outward baptism which purifies only the filth of the flesh, but the answer of a good conscience, as Peter testifies, of which infants are incapable." The poet then proceeds to refute the arguments, now threadbare, by which Pedobaptists in that day urged the baptism of children. And when Milton concludes he has left infant baptism without any authority or even pretext for its existence.

In regard to the mode and subjects of baptism, Milton, in "Paradise Lost," expresses the same opinion as he gives in his "Treatise on Christian Doctrine,"—

.... "*them who shall believe
Baptizing in the profluent stream*, the sign
Of washing them from guilt of sin to life
Pure, and in mind prepared, if so befall
For death, like that which the Redeemer died."
xii. 441.

His "Treatise on Christian Doctrine" was written in Latin, and translated in 1825 by Sumner, who afterwards became bishop of Winchester.

Milton in his old age was blind. The Conventicle Act suspended heavy penalties over all who attended religious services other than Episcopalian, for which Milton had no relish, and he stayed at home and read his Bible, determined to give the government no opportunity to inflict vengeance on the most talented enemy of the house of Stuart. He died Nov. 8, 1674. Macaulay says, "Though there were many clever (talented) men in England during the latter half of the seventeenth century, there were only two minds which possessed the imaginative faculty in a very eminent degree; one of these produced 'Paradise Lost,' the other 'The Pilgrim's Progress.'" John Bunyan and John Milton† were both Baptists.

Mims, Prof. James S., was born in Columbus Co., N. C., Feb. 10, 1817. He wished to be baptized before he was twelve years of age, but his father, fearing he might be acting prematurely, kept him back until he was about thirteen.

He desired immediately to commence preaching, but his father again restrained him for a short time. Having heard his son speak in a prayer-meeting, he gave his consent, and the church at Fayetteville licensed him to preach.

He went first to Chapel Hill, but close application injuring his health, he was compelled to return home. He next studied privately with Prof. J. C. Furman for eighteen months, and then entered Furman Theological Institution. Having spent a year there, he went to Newton, where he graduated in 1842.

In the autumn of the same year he was elected Professor of Theology in Furman University, and entered on the duties of his office in January, 1843, and continued there until his death, which happened in June, 1855.

He was ordained at Society Hill, S. C., in July, 1843, by Brethren J. C. and Richard Furman, J. O. B. Dargan, and John Culpepper. Although eminently fitted for the pastorate, his brethren claimed his services in preparing others for that office.

His face correctly and plainly indicated the leading features of his mind,—gentleness and firmness, native talent and high culture, in short, every characteristic of the highest order of a Christian gentleman. But his "sun went down while it was yet day."

Miner, Rev. Ashur, was born in North Stonington, Conn., Jan. 30, 1772; ordained in 1805; for ten years associate pastor with Rev. Simeon Brown of the Second Baptist church in North Stonington; on the death of the aged minister, Nov. 24, 1815, he became sole pastor, and continued in that office until his death; was the cotemporary of Revs. Jonathan Miner, John G. Wightman, Roswell Burrows, Elihu Chesebrough, John Sterry, Wm. Palmer, the Darrows, and the Babcocks; enjoyed a number of powerful revivals; received nearly 500 into the church; died Sept. 1, 1836, in his sixty-fifth year.

Miner, Rev. Bradley, was born in North Stonington, Conn., July 18, 1808. He joined the Baptist church in his native place when he was but thirteen years of age. He began to preach at seventeen. He taught for four or five years, combining study with teaching. He was for some time at Newton, and then went to Hamilton, N. Y. His ordination occurred in 1830, when he accepted a call to the First Baptist church in Fall River. After three years of service with this church, he spent the next three years partly in Pawtucket and partly in Woonsocket, R. I., from which place he removed to Neponset, Mass., and was pastor of the church in that village for nine years. In 1846 he went to Pittsfield, Mass., and, as in other places,

---

* Treatise on Christian Doctrine, pp. 431-2. London, 1825.
† Ivimey's Life of Milton, p. 104. London, 1833.

a rich blessing attended his labors. He removed to the South Baptist church in Providence, with which the Fifth Baptist church united, and the church thus composed, under the guidance of their energetic pastor, erected the Friendship Street church. After a ministry of nearly twenty-eight years, Mr. Miner died in October, 1854. With a warm, ardent temperament, and thoroughly consecrated to his work, he was the means of accomplishing no small amount of good in the different fields in which he was called to labor.

Miner, Rev. George Herman, son of Deacon Leland and Bridget W. (Main) Miner, was born in North Stonington, Conn., Sept. 15, 1835, of a historic Baptist family; well trained; taught two years in Bacon Academy, Conn., and two years in Marion Collegiate Institute in New York; prepared for college in the Connecticut Literary Institution, at Suffield; graduated with honor from Brown University in 1863; studied theology; ordained as pastor of the Central Falls Baptist church in Lincoln, R. I., in August, 1864, and remained four years; in September, 1868, became pastor of the Second Baptist church in Cambridge, Mass., and continued until 1872; in October of that year settled as pastor of the Baptist church in Newburyport, Mass., and labored four years; in October, 1876, accepted the pastorate of the Baptist church in New Britain, Conn., where he is now laboring with his characteristic ability and wonted success; devoutly wields a ready eloquence and good pen.

Miner, Rev. Jonathan, was ordained by the First Baptist church in Groton, Conn., in February, 1814; the same year settled as fourth pastor of the First Baptist church in North Stonington, Conn., and remained twenty years; his labors were followed by very powerful revivals in 1814, 1822, 1828, and in 1831; a man of strong native talents, fervent piety, and clear doctrinal views; a superior preacher; died in 1844. The second pastor of this church was Rev. Eleazar Brown; ordained Jan. 24, 1770; died June 20, 1795. The third pastor was Rev. Peleg Randall; ordained Oct. 25, 1792; settled, 1795; resigned, 1813.

Miner, Rev. Simon G., was born in Brookfield, Madison Co., N. Y., March 8, 1808, being the son of Absalom and Mary Miner. He believes that his conversion took place when he was at the age of five years. When twelve years old he was strongly convinced of his duty to be baptized and unite with the church; but the scruples then so common with reference to early conversion caused a postponement until his twenty-first year. He was then baptized into the fellowship of the church of his native town by Rev. Mr. Kelsey. The family having removed to Friendship, Alleghany Co., his impressions, for some time entertained, as to his duty to preach the gospel, then took more decided form. They were shared also by the deacons of the church, in which he was at length, in the absence of the pastor, quite unexpectedly called upon to fill the pulpit. He complied, and was then regularly licensed by the church, the date of this official act being January, 1830. Up to this time he had been engaged in farming. He now abandoned this business, and began a course of study at Hamilton. His health failing, by advice of the faculty and of his physician he left the institution and began the active duties of the ministry, being ordained at Rushford in August, 1834. His pastorates in the State of New York were with the Rushford, Farmerville, and Penfield churches, some months, meanwhile, being spent in the service of the Genesee Sunday-School Union. In 1837, in association with Rev. Alfred Bennett, he was appointed by the New York State Convention a delegate to the General Convention of Western Baptists, held that year in Cincinnati. This resulted in his removal to the West. His first field of labor was at Lafayette and Crawfordsville, Ind. In July, 1841, he became pastor of the church in Franklin, after one year being recalled to Lafayette, where his labors were resumed, and a house of worship built. In 1847 he accepted an appointment as agent of the Missionary Union, serving one year. He then became pastor of the church in Canton, Ill., the pastorate continuing some ten years, characterized by rich blessings, so that the church grew to be one of the strongest in the State, 490 being added by baptism. After a year of service as secretary of the General Association, Mr. Miner was recalled to Canton, and continued in this second pastorate until 1861. He then entered the service of the Union as a chaplain in the army, remaining in it three years. His health becoming impaired, he engaged in business at Bloomington at the close of the war, and has since served churches as a supply, or acting pastor. His whole period of service has been one of signal usefulness, alike in the gathering of converts and the successful administration of church affairs.

Ministers.—The office of the Christian minister was created by God himself, and its existence is to be defended by all the power of the churches. It is the province of the minister to feed the flock of Christ committed to his charge, to preach the glorious gospel of the blessed God to the perishing, to see that the church is kept free from heresy and sin, and to administer baptism and the Lord's Supper. The minister should be "blameless, the husband of one wife, vigilant, sober, of good behavior, given to hospitality, apt to teach." He should be free from all vices, and "have a good report of them who are without."

The official authority of all ministers is exactly

equal; they are all bishops, and each bishop is but an elder. Prelacy and diocesan episcopacy are unknown in the New Testament. The church of Ephesus, a single congregation, recent in organization, had elders or presbyters, and these elders were called overseers (πρεσβυτέρους επισκόπους) by the apostle Paul, that is, *bishops*, as the Greek text informs us, Acts xx. 17, 28. A bishop, like a Romish, Greek, Anglican, or Methodist prelate, had no existence among the officers of apostolic churches, as there were several bishops in one congregation. St. Jerome, in the fourth century, repeatedly confirms this statement, one quotation from whom we will give. Commenting on Titus i. 5, 7, he says, "A presbyter is the same as a bishop, and until, by the instigation of the devil, there arose divisions in religion, and it was said among the people, 'I am of Paul, and I of Apollos, and I of Cephas,' churches were governed by a common council of the presbyters. Afterwards truly, every one reckoned those to be his, not Christ's, whom he baptized. Then it was decreed over the world that one of the presbyters should be placed over the rest, to whom the whole care of the church should belong,"* etc. Jerome was undoubtedly right about the original equality of gospel ministers, and about the agency which reared Christian hierarchies.

Ministers should be supported by the people for whom they labor. "Even so," says Paul, "hath the Lord ordained that they who preach the gospel should live of the gospel."

Ministers are chosen by the churches, and ordained by brethren summoned for that purpose by the authority and invitation of the churches. God calls every true minister to his work, the churches recognize his voice and obey it, by placing those whom he has selected as watchmen upon the walls of Zion.

Minnesota Baptists, Historical Sketch of.—The First Baptist church of St. Paul was the first church of our denomination organized in the State of Minnesota. The Rev. John P. Parsons, under the appointment of the Baptist Home Mission Society, came to St. Paul in May, 1849. After a search of six months for Baptists he found twelve persons in St. Paul and vicinity who were ready for the formation of a church. The organization took place Dec. 30, 1849. The first baptism was administered in April, 1851. The first meeting-house was built the same year, and the funeral service of its pastor was the first held within its walls.

The church grew in numbers, both by conversion and by letter, until they were compelled to build a larger house of worship, which they entered on New Year's morning, 1863. The little Indian trading-post had now become a commercial city. The church continued to enjoy the divine presence until it was again found necessary to erect a more spacious house, which was built, and for the first time occupied May 30, 1875. The edifice cost $130,000, and it is now free from debt, with money in the treasury of the church. This church is a child of the American Baptist Home Mission Society, as indeed most of the churches in Minnesota are. It has had eight good pastors. The longest pastorate was that of Rev. J. D. Pope, covering a period of nine years. Some of the membership have fallen asleep. Prominent among these we mention the name of the Hon. Horace Thompson, a brother of great wealth, and a generous giver to the cause of Christ. Others who have gone to the better land have left a worthy record. Among the living we mention Deacon A. H. Cavender, a constituent member, and D. D. Merill, who for a period of about sixteen years has held the position of treasurer of the Minnesota Baptist State Convention. Many others are worthy, and would receive honorable mention if space permitted. Five of the Sunday-school scholars and one Sunday-school superintendent are now preaching the gospel.

The First Baptist church, Minneapolis, was organized March 5, 1853, with ten members. It was publicly recognized June 23, 1853. For one year it was supplied with occasional preaching by Rev. Edwin W. Cressey and Rev. T. B. Rogers, both of whom were missionaries of the Baptist Home Mission Society. They have since enjoyed the labors of seven worthy pastors, viz.: Rev. A. A. Russell, Rev. Amory Gale, Rev. J. R. Manton, L. B. Allen, D.D., Rev. W. T. Lowry, Rev. T. W. Powell, Rev. H. C. Woods. This church and the First church of St. Paul are and have been towers of strength to the cause of Christ in Minnesota.

In June, 1852, Rev. T. R. Cressey became pastor of the Baptist church of St. Paul, and incipient measures were taken by him for the organization of the Minnesota Baptist Association. A call having been extended, delegates from four churches convened in St. Paul, Sept. 24, 1852. The churches represented were St. Paul, St. Anthony, Stillwater, and Willow River, now Hudson, Wis. The combined membership of these four churches was 82; 60 of this number were residents of Minnesota. This was the entire number of Baptists then in Minnesota so far as known. At the second annual meeting the aggregate membership of the churches was 180. The third annual meeting showed a constituency in the churches of 202. The fourth a membership of 331. The fifth anniversary was held in Minneapolis, at which sixteen churches were represented, having in all 349 members.

---

* Idem est ergo presbyter, qui et episcopus et antequam diaboli instinctu, studia in religione fierent, et diceretur in populis . . . communi presbyterorum concilio, ecclesiæ gubernabantur. Hierom., tom. vi. 198. Coloniæ, 1616. For a full discussion of this subject, see Cathcart's "Papal System," p. 57. Philadelphia.

STATE CONVENTION.

The following statement pertaining to the organization of the Minnesota Baptist State Convention we copy from the minutes of the Convention of 1861:

"As early as the summer of 1858, many brethren thought that a State organization was demanded by the interests of the denomination. At the anniversary of the Minnesota Baptist Association of that year a committee was appointed to take the matter into consideration. This committee recommended the formation of a State Convention, and immediately after the adjournment of the Association a meeting was called for that purpose, when a preliminary organization was effected, of which Hon. J. H. Keith was President, Rev. J. D. Pope, Secretary, and William Wakefield, Esq., Treasurer."

But little was done that year, except to procure a charter and prepare the way for future operations.

The first annual meeting was held at Winona, Aug. 29, 1859, when the Convention assumed a permanent form by the adoption of the charter and constitution. The principal officers were re-elected. The board agreed to raise $200 towards the salary of Rev. A. Gale, exploring missionary of the American Baptist Home Mission Society for Minnesota.

The second anniversary of the Convention was held at Minneapolis, Sept. 7, 1860. The meeting was largely attended, and manifested a commendable interest in the work of the Convention. J. D. Ford, M.D., was elected President, Rev. J. D. Pope, Secretary, and Wm. Wakefield, Esq., Treasurer. The members of the Convention pledged $200 for colporteur work, with the understanding that two colporteurs would be employed through the year. The services of Rev. B. Wharton and Brother G. L. Case were secured in connection with the American Baptist Publication Society.

The third anniversary of the State Convention was held in Owatonna in 1861, and reveals a gratifying advance. The number of ministers then in the State was 68; number of churches, 96; number of Associations, 6; with a total membership of 2384. At the close of the first decade of conventional work (1868) the statistics show seven Associations, with a membership of 3940. In 1869 the board report that ten of the churches in the State are self-supporting. The whole number of Associations reported at the last anniversary (1879), counting the Scandinavian Baptist Conference as one, is eight, and the total membership in the State is 6854. The three churches reporting the largest membership are First Minneapolis, 421; First St. Paul, 346; First Rochester, 245.

EDUCATIONAL HISTORY.

Early in the history of the State an effort was made to found a university. A charter was obtained and a primary building erected in the city of Hastings, but the financial embarrassments which occurred in 1857 and 1858 were so severe as to fatally cripple the enterprise. For a number of years no further effort was made to found a literary institution, but at the annual meeting of the State Convention, in the autumn of 1874, a "centennial committee" was appointed, who reported favorably, and at the annual meeting of the Convention, in 1875, three committees were appointed: 1. On location for an academy. 2. On finance. 3. On charter. The committee on location recommended the city of Owatonna as an eligible place for Minnesota Academy. The report was adopted. The committee on finance were authorized at the same meeting to erect an academic building, and if their judgment approved, to commence a school. At the next Conventional meeting (1877) a building had been erected at an expense of $4400, five teachers were employed, and a school in successful operation having 101 students. During the following winter the committee on charter obtained from the Legislature a revision of the old university charter, under which the Minnesota Academy was organized. The finance committee is to be perpetual, having entire charge of the pecuniary affairs of the institution. The endowment fund now amounts to $5500. The academy is already doing a noble service for sound learning. It receives much encouragement from Congressman M. H. Dunnell, a member of the Baptist church in Owatonna, who is deeply interested in the educational affairs of the State, and from other enlightened and liberal Baptists.

In 1880 there were in Minnesota 9 Associations, 154 churches, 112 ordained ministers, and 7056 church members.

Mirick, Rev. Stephen H., was born in Salem, Mass., Jan. 9, 1819. After having been prepared for college in the Latin grammar-school in his native town, he entered Waterville College, Me., and graduated in August, 1838, receiving in course the degree of A.M. in 1841. Removing South, he taught school in St. Helena Parish, La., during 1839; and during 1840 was engaged in the preparatory department of the University of Louisiana. In the fall of 1840 he entered Newton Theological Seminary, and finished the course there in 1843. After leaving the seminary, he preached for the Central Baptist church, Philadelphia, for six months, and was ordained in November, 1843, the sermon being delivered by the Rev. R. E. Pattison, D.D., and the charge by the Rev. Stephen Chapin, D.D. Removing to Charlottesville, Va., he supplied the Baptist church in that place for some months, after which he opened a seminary for young ladies, in 1845, which he conducted with much success during eight years. He then removed to Washington, D. C., where he succeeded the Rev. R. W. Cushman, D.D., as principal of a young ladies' school. After four years' labor in this field, he felt it to be his duty to relinquish teaching and give himself wholly to the work of the ministry. Accordingly he became pastor of the First Baptist church in Camden, N. J., remaining a year, and removed, in 1859, to Lewisburg, Pa., where he took charge of the Baptist church, continuing pastor until 1866. During his pastorate in Lewisburg, he acted as Professor of Greek in the university at that place, while the president was absent completing the endowment fund. Owing to a bronchial disease contracted mainly by exposure during the war, he removed to Washington, D. C., where he entered into government employ in February, 1867. Mr. Mirick has frequently contributed to our religious newspapers and periodicals; was the Washington editor of the *True Union*, Baltimore; and has contributed to the *Religious Herald* Expositions of the International Sunday-School Lessons for the past seven years. The same Expositions have also been furnished for the *Index and Baptist*, of Atlanta, Ga. During his residence in Washington, Mr. Mirick has been quite active in promoting Sunday-school interests and in supplying churches destitute of pastors. He is now pastor of the Metropolitan Baptist church, a body gathered and organized under his lead, and in a part of the city where a Baptist church is greatly needed.

Missionary Union, American Baptist.—The General Missionary Convention of the Baptist denomination in the United States of America for Foreign Missions, sometimes called the Triennial Convention, was established in Philadelphia, May 18, 1814, and it continued under that name until 1845.

The agitation produced by the slavery question led to an amicable separation of the Southern and Northern Baptists in their foreign mission efforts, after which, at a Convention held in the Baptist Tabernacle, New York, on the third Wednesday of November, 1845, the present Foreign Missionary Society of the Northern Baptists was organized, and it went into operation in May, 1846, under the name of the "American Baptist Missionary Union." The new body assumed all the indebtedness of its predecessor, and became heir to all its effects. Our Southern brethren, immediately after retiring from the General Convention, formed the Southern Baptist Convention, an honored society, a record of whose toils and triumphs is to be found in another part of this work. The Missionary Union has had its representatives preaching Jesus in several quarters of the world, and rich blessings have descended upon its self-sacrificing men and saintly women as they have carried the tidings of salvation to the perishing. The missions to the Karens and Teloogoos are the most prosperous fields of labor at this moment in the heathen world; the seal of heaven rests upon them in a more signal manner than upon any other organized efforts upon earth to bring pagans to Jesus. Marvelous success has attended the labors of our missionaries in Germany and Sweden.

The Missionary Union in 1880 had in Burmah 88 missionaries, 448 native preachers, 433 churches, and 21,594 members.

In Assam there were 17 missionaries, 49 native preachers, 13 churches, and 1331 members.

Among the Teloogoos there were 21 missionaries, 77 native preachers, 11 churches, and 15,660 members.

Among the Chinese there were 24 missionaries, 37 native preachers, 16 churches, and 1426 members.

In Japan we had 12 missionaries, 5 native preachers, 2 churches, and 76 members.

In all our Asiatic missions there were 162 missionaries, 616 native preachers, 475 churches, and 40,087 members.

In Sweden we had 150 native ministers, 298 churches, and 18,851 members.

In Germany there were 270 native ministers, 121 churches, and 25,497 members.

In France there were 12 native ministers, 9 churches, and 726 members.

In Spain there were 3 native ministers, 4 churches, and 140 members.

In Greece there was 1 native minister and 1 church, with 7 members.

In our various foreign missions we had 162 American missionaries, 1052 native preachers and pastors, 908 churches, and 85,308 members. In 1880 there were 8419 converts baptized in our different mission stations. The income of the Missionary Union in that year was $290,851.63.

See separate articles on the missions just named, and on AFRICA, ASSAM; and for foreign missions conducted by our brethren of the South, see article on SOUTHERN BAPTIST CONVENTION, and the TRIENNIAL CONVENTION.

Mississippi, The Baptists of.—In 1780 a company of Baptists from South Carolina and Georgia settled on Cole's Creek, about twenty miles southeast of Natchez, and in the latter part of the same year organized a church, which they called Salem. These consisted of Richard Curtis, Sr., and his wife, Phebe Curtis, his stepson, John Jones, and his wife, and his three sons, William, Benjamin, and Richard Curtis, Jr., with their wives, together with John Courtney, who married Hannah Curtis, and John Stampley, who married Phebe Curtis, Daniel Ogden and wife, and a man named Perkins and his wife; Jacob Stampley, the brother of John, and James Cole, who married Jemima Curtis, probably accompanied them. Most of these were church members. Richard Curtis, Jr., was a licensed preacher, and John and Jacob Stampley both became ministers afterwards. Upon the organization of the church Richard Curtis, Jr., was chosen pastor. His labors were greatly blessed, and in a short time sinners were converted and desired baptism. As Mr. Curtis was only a licentiate some perplexity arose about the propriety of his administering the ordinance. But it was very properly decided that Curtis, under the authority of the church, might lawfully baptize them. Among the converts baptized was a Spanish Catholic named Stephen de Alvo, who publicly renounced Catholicism. This greatly incensed the Catholics, but as yet they had no power to punish the offense. At this time the country was nominally under the government of Great Britain, but at the peace of 1783 the territory passed for a time into the hands of the Spanish.

People continued to come into the country, and among them some Baptists. William Chaney, a Baptist deacon, and his son, Bailey E. Chaney, a licensed preacher, came from South Carolina. There came also one Harigail from Georgia, and also Barton Hannon and William Owen, all of whom were, or became, Baptist preachers. Harigail proved to be a man of more zeal than discretion, and proceeded to denounce the Catholics in unmeasured terms. This, together with the conversion and active labors of De Alvo, who had become a deacon, incensed them, and they determined to make an example of some of the leaders. William Hamberlin, Richard Curtis, Jr., and Stephen de Alvo were selected as the chief offenders. This was about 1793 or 1794. A letter was written by Gayoso, the Spanish commandant, to Curtis, expostulating with him upon his course. To this Curtis replied bluntly, and an order for his arrest was issued, and he was brought before Gayoso, April 6, 1795. After threatening to send Curtis, Hamberlin, and De Alvo to work in the mines of Mexico, they were discharged, with an injunction not to offend again. An edict was also issued that "if nine persons were found worshiping together, except according to the forms of the Catholic Church, they should suffer imprisonment." But the church continued to meet privately for worship, and Mr. Curtis officiated publicly in a marriage ceremony in 1795. This was considered a violation of the law, and an attempt was made to arrest him, but he made good his escape, in company with Hamberlin and De Alvo, and they made their way on horseback across the country to South Carolina, where they arrived in the fall of 1795. A number of others were also persecuted. At the end of two years and a half Curtis returned, having been ordained during his stay in South Carolina. The country having passed into the hands of the United States, the Baptists henceforward had rest, and prospered greatly. In 1798 an arm of Salem church was extended into Williamson County, and "the Baptist church on Buffaloe" was constituted. Another church was formed in the same county in 1800, called Good Hope, and two in Amite County, Providence, in 1805, and Ebenezer in 1806. These churches, in 1806, united, and formed the Mississippi Baptist Association. Thomas Mercer came into this region in 1800, and David Cooper, a learned and pious man, in 1802. They were soon joined by a number of young ministers, who afterwards distinguished themselves in this part of the State, and through whose instrumentality Baptist sentiments were propagated in Mississippi and Louisiana. The Association became an active body, and its missionaries penetrated to the remotest settlements.

In 1820 the churches contiguous to Pearl River were dismissed to form the Pearl River Association. In the decade from 1830 to 1840 the churches were torn by internal dissensions, on account of Masonry, missions, and Campbellism. In the conflict old Salem suffered her light to be extinguished. From that time forward population rapidly increased, and many able and zealous ministers entered the field, and Baptist sentiments took a deep hold upon the people.

In 1880 there were in Mississippi 59 Baptist Associations, 1537 churches, 831 ordained ministers, and 122,369 members.

Mississippi Baptist, a religious paper, established by the Mississippi Baptist Convention about 1857. Previous to this it had been struggling for existence as a private enterprise. Under the patronage of the Convention a new life was infused into the paper. Rev. J. T. Freeman, an able writer and an editor of experience, was secured to take charge of it. It was removed to Jackson, the capital of the State, and under the management of Mr. Freeman it was winning a fine success, when it was suspended by the events of the war.

Mississippi Baptist Convention.—This body was organized in 1839. Its object has been to foster a missionary and educational spirit. As the fruit, a number of missionaries are laboring in foreign fields, and one of the best colleges in the South has been built up.

The officers elected in 1880 were Col. W. H. Hardy, of Meridian, President; A. J. Miller, Port Gibson, Recording Secretary; J. T. Buck, Jackson, Corresponding Secretary; W. T. Ratcliff, Treasurer. The Convention, through its Board of Ministerial Education, contributed $800 to aid thirty ministerial students, and contributed $6000 to support twenty missionaries, three district evangelists, and one State evangelist. Eastern Louisiana and New Orleans are embraced in their field.

Mississippi Baptist Record is published under the patronage of the Mississippi Baptist Convention. It was started in 1876 to promote the work of the State Convention, and J. B. Gambrell, formerly pastor at Oxford, was selected as editor. It was at first issued at Clinton, but subsequently removed to Jackson. Its circulation is full of encouragement.

Mississippi College, located at Clinton, Hinds Co., Miss., was chartered as Hempstead Academy in 1826. In 1827 the name was changed to Mississippi Academy, by an act of the Legislature authorizing the board of trustees to raise by lottery $25,000. The rents of thirty-six sections of the school land, donated by the United States to the State, were given to the academy for four years. In 1830 the name was changed to Mississippi College, and in 1842 it was transferred to the Presbyterians, and remained under their control until 1850, when it was again surrendered to the people. The Baptist State Convention met that year in the city of Jackson, when the college was offered to the Baptists, and accepted by them. An agent was placed in the field, and by 1860 a cash endowment of $100,000 was raised, with $30,000 more pledged, and buildings costing $20,000 erected. Unfortunately the whole endowment was lost by the war, and the college suspended. In 1867, Dr. Walter Hillman found it disorganized, with a mortgage of $10,000 resting upon it, and only eleven students in attendance. At the end of his administration, in 1873, the debts had all been paid, the building thoroughly repaired, $40,000 towards an endowment raised, a faculty of eight professors engaged, and 190 students in attendance. He was succeeded by W. S. Webb, D.D., under whom the institution has continued to prosper until the present time. From 20 to 30 young ministers have been educated annually for some time, many of whom are now filling the most prominent pulpits in Mississippi, Louisiana, and Arkansas; 191 students were in attendance during the term ending in June, 1880.

Mississippi General Association.—This body operates in the eastern part of the State of Mississippi, and was organized some years ago in opposition to the State Convention. But it is believed that a better state of feeling is beginning to prevail, and the two bodies now seem to be co-operating. The jealousies out of which the division grew are passing away, and the day of entire unification is not far distant. The work of the Association is missionary. A long neglected tribe of Indians in their bounds is receiving special attention, and a converted Indian is employed to preach to them. We have not received the data to be able to state particulars of their work.

Missouri Baptist General Association.—In the year 1833 an informal and small meeting of Baptists was held in the town of Columbia, Mo., to devise ways and means for further promoting Christianity in that State. The anti-mission spirit then ruled the Baptist churches of that region, and the few who possessed the progressive spirit of the gospel labored under great disadvantages in all efforts and plans for the spread of divine truth. They were met at every step by the violent and almost virulent opposition of anti-mission brethren.

The meeting at Columbia was composed of Ebenezer Rogers, Thos. Fristoe, Roland Hughes, Joseph Hughes, Tilman Bell, and Wm. Mansfield. These men of God resolved to secure the services of some good minister of the gospel to do missionary work in the central counties of the State. They contributed of their own limited resources the sum of $600 for the remuneration of the men who might be secured for the work. Rev. Wm. Mansfield was selected to correspond with suitable persons until a missionary should be obtained. He wrote to Anderson Woods and Wm. Duncan, both of whom responded favorably to the call. The duty of making arrangements for the proposed mission work was intrusted to Mr. Mansfield. He attended a meeting of the Mount Pleasant Association for the purpose and in the hope of securing some co-operation. At that meeting he was informed by anti-mission Baptists that if he went on the "stand" he should be forcibly ejected from it. At a convenient time in the progress of the meeting he took a position near the stand and read aloud a list of appointments for Woods and Duncan, and then quietly gave a statement of the reasons why he was not on the stand. Mr. Mansfield was a good man, a plain, earnest, and effective preacher, who supported a large family by successful farming. Woods and Duncan were preachers of no mean ability, and while the work they did under Mansfield's arrangements was much opposed, it was greatly blessed in the conversion of souls and in awakening the spirit of missions.

As a result of this effort a meeting was held at Providence church, in Calloway County, in 1834, to effect a permanent organization for doing mission work. The anti-mission spirit was still rife. In this year the churches and Associations were much troubled with contentions and divisions. At the Providence meeting, Thos. Fristoe, Ebenezer Rogers, Wm. Suggett, Noah Flood, and others were present. The meeting adopted preliminary measures for the permanent organization of the Baptist Central Society. This organization was completed the subsequent year. Out of the Central Society grew the present Missouri Baptist General Association, which held its forty-third annual session in October, 1879.

The objects of the General Association are to promote the preaching of the gospel and the spread of divine truth in the State. For the attainment of these objects the constitution provides mission work, Christian education, and the circulation of religious literature.

A mission board of seventeen members and a corresponding secretary have the management of the missionary department. The board endeavors to develop and enlarge the spirit of progress and beneficence, procure the preaching of the gospel to the destitute, and help weak churches to become self-sustaining. This work has contributed largely to making the Baptist denomination the largest and most influential in the State. From $3000 to $5000 are annually expended by the board in State mission work. The local Associations expend about the same sum in their missionary efforts.

William Jewell College—a history of which is given in another part of this work—is an outgrowth of the progressive spirit of the General Association, and is provided for by its constitution. Stephens College, for the education of young ladies, is likewise organically recognized. At each session of the Association a report is heard from a standing committee on schools and colleges, in which the condition of Baptist institutions of education within the State is made known. Of such institutions there are nine in number, each doing a good work.

The Association at each session hears a report on denominational publications, and seeks to encourage religious literature as a means of spreading divine truth. The American Baptist Publication Society receives encouragement, and Baptist journals in the State in harmony with the purposes and plans of the Association, receive a hearty moral support. At this writing (1880) *The Central Baptist*, an able weekly journal, conducted by Rev. Wm. Ferguson, and *Ford's Christian Repository*, edited by Rev. Dr. and Mrs. S. H. Ford, an excellent magazine of long standing, both published in the city of St. Louis, are indorsed and commended.

All along the history of this organization down to the present time its records are adorned by the names of the best men of the denomination in and out of the ministry. Of ministers who have gone to their reward are such names as Wm. Suggett, Wm. Thompson, D.D., Thos. Fristoe, I. T. Hinton, James E. Welch, S. W. Lynd, D.D., Noah Flood, J. B. Jeter, D.D., X. X. Buckner, Wm. Crowell, D.D., Y. R. Pittz, Jerry Vardeman, and A. P. Williams, D.D. Of deceased laymen there are such men as Judge R. E. McDaniel, Hons. Wade Jackson, David Hickman, Wm. Carson, Marshal Brotherton, Jos. Flood, and Wm. Jewell, M.D., D. L. Shouse, Wm. McPherson, and others, the presence of any of whom would have adorned the most honorable assembly on earth.

The chief living Baptists of the State, ministers and laymen, and honorable women not a few, are now the active friends and hearty supporters of the General Association, which is, no doubt, the organization through which the power and usefulness of an influential denomination in a great State are to reach their highest and broadest development.

Missouri, Baptist Sunday-Schools in.—The Missouri Baptist Sunday-School Convention was organized in August, 1868. Rev. S. W. Marston, D.D., served as the secretary during the first five years.

The following table will show how he found Sunday-school work in Missouri, and how it has increased for eleven years:

Year.	Number of Associations.	Number of Churches.	Number of Preachers.	Number of Church Members.	Net Gain.	Number of Bible-Schools Reported.	Number of Officers and Teachers.	Number of Scholars.
1868...	45			52,996		74		
1869...								
1870...	50	1003	506	57,089	4,091	430	3494	25,781
1871...	57	1166	846	67,501	10,414	754	5873	44,871
1872...		1210		71,717	4,216			
1873...	60	1212	920	74,274	2,557	806	6247	48,261
1874...		1264	706	76,072	1,798	816	6250	49,260
1875...		1274	750	78,144				
1876...								
1877...	66	1328	802	79,546				
1878...								
1879...	66	1381	823	88,491		450	3076	41,173
1880...						820	6300	50,000

There were about 5937 church members working in the schools during 1879, and 4605 conversions among the scholars. The libraries comprise 26,000 volumes. The churches expended on their own schools, in 1879, $9997; for organs and other objects, $7687; for State Bible-school work, $1023.96.

In 1873 about two-thirds of all the district Associations had within them organized Sunday-school Conventions.

The Rev. M. L. Laws is the able corresponding secretary of the society at this time, upon whose noble work so rich a blessing has descended.

Missouri Baptists, Sketch of.—The first Christians of any denomination, save Catholic, that ever set foot upon the soil of Upper Louisiana, now the State of Missouri, were Baptists. So far as we have been able to learn, Thomas Bull, his wife, and her mother, Mrs. Lee, were the first to come. They settled in Cape Girardeau County in 1796. The following year they were joined by Enos Randall and wife, and Mrs. Abernathy. At that time Missouri was under the dominion of Spain, and the Roman Catholic was the established church. In 1799, Rev. Thomas Johnson, of Georgia, visited these pioneers, preached the gospel to them and their neighbors, and baptized one woman. This was the first administration of baptism west of the great river, and Elder Johnson was the first Baptist minister of the *regular* order who ever visited the Territory.

Rev. David Green removed from Kentucky and settled in Cape Girardeau County in 1805, and commenced at once to gather together the Baptists. He organized, in 1805, the Tywappity Baptist church, in Scott County, of eight or ten members. For want of succor it soon became defunct, but was reorganized in 1809. The Bethel church was the first permanent church organization in the State. It was formed with fifteen members, July 19, 1806, near the town of Jackson, Cape Girardeau Co. Elder Green was the first pastor of these churches. For some years the Bethel church was an aggressive missionary body, and greatly prospered. It afterwards opposed missions, and as a consequence withered, and finally died. From it sprang, directly or indirectly, all the churches that formed the first Association. Five other churches originated prior to the date next to be mentioned, and together with the two first named, met at the Bethel meeting-house, near Jackson, on the last Saturday in September, 1816, and organized the Bethel Association, the first in the Territory. The constituent churches were Bethel, Tywappity, Providence, Barren, St. François, Bellview, and Dry Creek. The ministers present were Henry Cockerham, John Farrar, Wm. Street, and James P. Edwards. Bethel Association adopted the appellation of "United Baptists."

In 1796 and 1797 a number of Baptist families removed from North Carolina, South Carolina, and Kentucky, most of whom settled in the present limits of St. Louis County. Among them we notice the names of Abraham and Sarah Musick, Jane Sullens, Sarah Williams, and R. Richardson and wife. They came in the face of Catholic restriction. The law said, "Liberty of conscience is not to be allowed beyond the first generation; the children of emigrants must be Catholics." And further, "No preacher of any religion but the Catholic must come into the province." John Clark, a Baptist in sentiment, though not a member, and Thomas R. Musick visited and preached in Missouri in these times of proscription. Clark's first trip was made in 1798; Musick's not long after. Clark was, we presume, the first Protestant minister that ever preached the gospel west of the Mississippi River. Musick settled in the St. Louis district in 1803 or 1804,—the first minister other than Catholic to locate in the Territory. He organized the Fee Fee church, the first in St. Louis County, in 1807, of eighteen members, and became its pastor. This is now the oldest church in the State. Cold Water, the next church in the county, was organized by Musick in 1809.

In November, 1817, at the house of Thomas R. Musick, the Missouri (now St. Louis) Association was formed with the following as constituent churches, viz.: Fee Fee, Cold Water, Bœuf, and Negro Fork, in St. Louis County; and Femme Osage, St. Charles County, and Upper Cuiver in Lincoln County; the aggregate membership of which was 142.

In the autumn of 1817, Revs. John M. Peck and James E. Welch, missionaries of the Baptist General Convention, arrived in St. Louis, then a little French village on the west bank of the Mississippi River. St. Louis is now the fourth city in the Union, extending some fifteen miles up and down the river, with a breadth of four to three miles. Messrs. Peck and Welch organized the First Baptist church of St. Louis, Feb. 8, 1818, with a membership of eleven persons.

Mingled with the tide of emigration westward we find Baptists. Nineteen persons formed a Baptist church near Loutre Island, in Montgomery County, in 1810. Joseph Baker was their pastor. The war of 1812-15 soon afterwards broke out, and most of the membership took refuge in the forts of Howard County. Mount Pleasant church was the first in the upper county. It was organized by Revs. Wm. Thorp and David McLain, near old Franklin, Howard Co. Few meetings for business were held during the war. Thorp and McLain preached to the people in the forts. When the war was over the people began again to hold meetings. The Mount Pleasant Association was formed July 25, 1818, at the old Mount Pleasant meeting-house. The constituent churches were Mount Pleasant, Concord, Cooper Co., organized May, 1817; Bethel, Boone Co., formed June, 1817; and Mount Zion and Salem; their aggregate membership was 161. Ministers present, David McLain, Wm. Thorp, Luke Williams, Edward Turner, and Colden Williams. In less than five years this associational community had extended its limits as far west as Clay and Lafayette Counties, and an average of twenty-five miles on either side of the Missouri River. At its meeting in 1823 it divided its territory, and formed the Fishing River Association, in Clay County, and Concord Association, in Cooper County, in the autumn of that year. Seven churches and six ministers were set off to organize the former, and seven churches to the latter. This left Mount Pleasant with seventeen churches. In 1827 the Mount Pleasant Association again divided for convenience, and the formation of the Salem Association the same year was the result. The new Association took thirteen churches, with 513 members, leaving the old Association with sixteen churches and 734 members.

The Cuivre Association was formed in 1822, of churches in St. Charles, Lincoln, and Warren Counties, eight in number, most or all of which had been dismissed from the Missouri Association for the purpose.

The gospel was early preached in Pike County

by Leroy Jackson, J. M. Peck, and Davis Biggs. Churches were organized as follows: Ramsey's Creek, prior to 1818; Peno, Dec. 25, 1819; Stout's Settlement (now New Hope) Lincoln Co., in 1821. On the 23d of August, 1823, the three churches last named, together with Bethlehem, New London, and Beer Creek, met on Big Peno and organized the Salt River Baptist Association. In 1834 this body sent out a colony of fourteen churches, and formed the Bethel Association, at Bethel meeting-house, Marion Co., the aggregate membership of which was 589. By churches gathered mainly by Elders Lewis and James Williams, situated mostly in Franklin, Washington, and Jefferson Counties, the Franklin Association was organized in 1832, at the house of J. C. Duckworth.

The Cape Girardeau Association, a daughter of the Bethel, was organized in 1824, at Hebron church.

We now pass to Western Missouri. In 1834 the Fishing River Association embraced all the churches west of a line indicated by Grand River. This year it was divided, the Missouri River being made the line, and the ten churches south of the river met in the following October at Little Snibar and organized the Blue River Association. Their total membership was 384.

The twelve Associations now named embraced, in 1834, nearly 200 churches, with a membership of some 7000, scattered over a vast extent of country from St. Genevieve County on the south to Lewis County on the north, from two to three counties deep west of the Mississippi River; and on either side of the Missouri River one to three counties deep, from the eastern to the western boundary of the State.

The General Association for missionary purposes was organized in 1835. This was made the occasion of a fierce and strong war upon boards and benevolent institutions by the anti-missionary party.

In the contest on missions in Missouri the anti-missionaries refused absolutely to fellowship under any circumstances those who favored the missionary enterprise. At the time of the division the regulars numbered over 5000, and the anti-missionaries upwards of 3000. The present strength of the former in the State is 90,000, and of the latter about 6000. (See article on MISSOURI BAPTIST GENERAL ASSOCIATION.)

The Missouri Baptists are warm friends of education.

INSTITUTIONS OF LEARNING.

William Jewell College, with its school of theology, is located at Liberty. Founded by the General Association; chartered February, 1849, and opened about one year after. This is the State denominational school for young men.

Stephens College, for females, is at Columbia. It was established in 1856 as a "Baptist Female College;" chartered in 1857; adopted by the General Association in 1870. R. P. Rider, President.

Mount Pleasant College, a mixed school, is located at Huntsville. A. S. Worrall, D.D., President.

La Grange College, at La Grange, is for male and female students. J. F. Cook, LL.D., President.

Lexington Baptist Female College is located at Lexington. President, Jno. F. Lanneau.

St. Joseph Female College, at St. Joseph. E. S. Dulin, President.

Hardin College, located at Mexico; female. Mrs. P. A. Baird, President.

Grand River College, at Edinburg. The president is T. H. Storts.

South-West Baptist College, located at Bolivar. J. R. Maupin, President.

These are the Baptist institutions of learning of this State, the most or all of which are doing a noble work.

NEWSPAPERS.

The first Baptist newspaper published in Missouri was issued in 1842 under the auspices of the General Association, called the *Missouri Baptist*. I. T. Hinton and R. S. Thomas were editors. It was abandoned in 1844, and in 1848 it was succeeded by the *Western Watchman*. Another *Missouri Baptist* was established by the Missouri Baptist Publication Society in 1860, edited by S. H. Ford. Both the last-named papers were suspended early in the war. In 1865, John Hill Luther commenced the publication, at Palmyra, of the *Missouri Baptist Journal*, which was recognized as the "State paper" by the General Association in 1866. This is now the *Central Baptist*, published at St. Louis, by Wm. Ferguson. In 1875, Dr. D. B. Ray established the *Baptist Battle-Flag*, now the *Baptist Flag*, devoted to church history and polemic theology. It was first issued from La Grange, but was subsequently removed to St. Louis. And last, *Ford's Christian Repository*, a monthly, is published at St. Louis, and edited by S. H. Ford, LL.D., and Mrs. S. R. Ford.

The Baptists of Missouri have an important position in this great central State, and are wielding a potent influence for good in the evangelical and educational enterprises of the West.

Baptist Progress in Missouri by Decades.

Date.	Number of Associations.	Number of Churches.	Number of Ministers.	Number of Communicants.
1796............	...	...	...	12
1806............	...	2	3	50
1816............	1	14	11	426
1826............	8	91	52	2,984
1836............	18	230	126	8,723
1846............	...	410	201	19,667
1856............	31	539	349	31,358
1866............	37	749	432	44,877
1876............	65	1284	842	89,786
1880............	70	1449	839	95,967

Missouri, Central Baptist of.—The first number of the *Missouri Baptist Journal* was issued Jan. 1, 1866, in Palmyra, Mo., as the acknowledged organ of the General Association. About a year later the *Baptist Record* made its appearance in St. Louis, under the editorial conduct of Rev. A. A. Kendrick, D.D. In 1868 these two papers were consolidated, and the name of the *Central Baptist* was given to the journal, whose chief aim was to unite the Baptists of Missouri on a common platform of doctrinal truth, missionary effort, and educational interest.

The result of the consolidation was most gratifying. The circulation of the *Central Baptist* soon reached 8000. Its conciliatory spirit, sturdy defense of our distinctive principles, and the literary ability of its contributors, representing every section of our country, won for it the confidence of Missourians and the respect of Baptists throughout the land. Its principal editors have been successively Dr. J. H. Luther, Dr. W. Pope Yeaman, and Rev. W. Ferguson, aided at different periods by Rev. Norman Fox, President A. A. Kendrick, and Rev. J. C. Armstrong.

The aim of the managers of the *Central Baptist* has always been to establish for the valley of the Missouri a journal of conservative character, maintaining in its editorial conduct pronounced views on every question relating to evangelical religion, and encouraging a spirit of free inquiry in the ministry and among the masses. The enlightened and working element of the denomination has recognized it as a necessity in the region of which St. Louis is the centre, and has generously supported it as one of the permanent agencies in the furtherance of the grand mission intrusted to us as a people. It has an honorable record, with the promise of a brilliant future.

Rev. Wm. Ferguson, the present proprietor and managing editor of the *Central Baptist*, was born in Saline Co., Mo., July 15, 1845. In early life he found the Saviour, and, being impressed with the duty of preaching the gospel, in 1868 he gave up the study of law and entered William Jewell College, at Liberty, Mo., to prepare for the ministry. Here, from the very start, he took the first place in his classes, and secured the abiding love and respect of his instructors and fellow-students. On his graduation, in 1873, he was united in marriage to Miss Florence M. Chandler, of Liberty, and assumed the pastorate of the Baptist church at Fulton, Mo. After one year of successful labor he was elected to the responsible position of financial agent of the Missouri Baptist Ministerial Education Society, and of William Jewell College, which position he held with great acceptance and success until January, 1877, when he purchased a partnership interest with Rev. W. P. Yeaman, D.D., in the *Central Baptist*, of which, in 1878, he became sole proprietor. Under his management of rare tact and ability the paper has been lifted out of financial embarrassments and placed within the

REV. WILLIAM FERGUSON.

first rank of denominational exponents. He possesses many qualifications which mark the born journalist. To a well-balanced mind, holding decided convictions, and exercising a positiveness in their maintenance, he joins a heart of keen sensibilities and broad sympathies, which enable him to weigh and deal fairly with all the questions which interest the church and humanity. These qualities, combined with unassuming modesty and geniality, secure the respect, esteem, and love of all who know him.

Missouri, Colored Baptists of, are a significant force. They have a State Convention and six district Associations, and claim 30,000 members, with 300 ministers. Among the leaders now living are W. W. Brooks, W. T. Jones, Thos. Jefferson, John Marshall, Henry Burton, L. T. Vealman, Samson Lewis, Hardin Smith, and Daniel Sawyer, men of piety and influence. Some of their churches have a thousand members. Four of their ministers have sketches in this work.

Missouri, Southwest, Baptist College of, is located at Bolivar, Southwest Missouri, and was founded by the Southwest Baptist Convention. It opened at Lebanon, Sept. 17, 1878. Rev. J. R. Maupin, A.M., a graduate of Lagrange College, Mo., is its first president. He was chosen for five years. The curriculum of the institution compares favorably with other colleges. It has a three years' preparatory course and a four years' collegiate. The faculty is composed of ten able instructors. The charter of the college was granted March 19, 1879. It is one of the most liberal in the State. The school is open to male and female students. One hundred and thirty-nine students attended the first year. A large number of students have been converted the past year. The college has a new and beautiful building and six acres of ground. Rev. N. T. Allison is principal of the preparatory department.

Mitchel, Rev. George, was born in England, Sept. 5, 1820. He was converted and baptized in 1838. He studied at Horton College, in Bradford, England, and in Edinburgh University, Scotland. He was ordained in England in July, 1847, and became pastor of the Baptist church at Horsforth, England, where he labored four years, and three at Irwell, Terrace chapel, Bacup. He came to America in 1855; had charge of the church at Beverly, N. J., for three years; was pastor of the Fourth Baptist church of St. Louis, Mo., for two years, in which he built the present house of worship; the church prospered under his ministry. In 1860 he became pastor at Lebanon. During the war he practised medicine and preached Christ. After the war he organized churches in Southwest Missouri. He was pastor at Bolivar, Mo. In 1874 he went to California, and returned soon after to Kansas, and preached at Hiawatha for two years with success,—a stroke of palsy closed his labors there. He returned to Bolivar, Mo., and bore his affliction with patience. He died May 27, 1879.

In both his pastorates in England he was popular and useful, and in this country his labors were successful.

Mitchell, Rev. Edward, was born in the island of Martinique in 1794. He followed the sea in his early life, but having been hopefully converted and baptized by Rev. Dr. Staughton, his attention was at once turned to the Christian ministry. He entered Dartmouth College, and graduated with honor in 1828. Soon after leaving college he was called to become pastor of the Baptist church in Burke, Vt. In 1834 he became pastor of the church in Eaton, Canada East, where he remained until 1838, when he was called to the church in West Hatley, Canada East, where he continued until his death, which occurred March 31, 1872. "He was regarded as the most profound theologian ever settled in the section in which he passed so many years of his useful life."

Mitchell, Edward C., D.D., was born at East Bridgewater, Mass., Sept. 20, 1829. His early religious training was of the Unitarian type. While a student in Waterville College, Me., he was converted, and became a member of a Baptist church.

He was graduated in 1849. He entered Newton Theological Seminary, and was graduated in 1853. He was first settled as pastor in Calais, Me., where he was ordained in 1854. After three years he removed to Rockford, Ill., where he founded the State Street Baptist church, and remained the pastor for five years. In 1862 he was appointed Professor of Biblical Interpretation in the theological department of Shurtleff College, in Illinois, which position he filled during seven years. In 1870 he was elected to the professorship of Hebrew and Old Testament Literature in the Baptist Union Theological Seminary, Chicago. He filled this chair eight years. Then he accepted an appointment to the professorship of Biblical Interpretation in Regent's Park Baptist College, in London, England. He then became the president of the Baptist Theological School of Paris, France. He is the author of "The Critical Hand-Book, a Guide to the Study of the Authenticity, the Canon, and the Text of the Greek New Testament," also "Gesenius's Hebrew Grammar, Translated by Davis, thoroughly Revised and Enlarged." He is a fine scholar, and eminently successful in the line of labor to which he has devoted his life.

Mitchell, John, D.D.—This gentleman, known as "the beloved disciple," was born in Bertie Co., N. C., in 1829; professed faith in Christ at Wake Forest College in 1851; graduated in 1852; studied theology at Greenville, S. C.; was agent for the endowment of Wake Forest College in 1856-57; was pastor at Hillsborough and Greensborough; settled as pastor in Chowan Association after the war; took charge of the Asheville church in 1875; returned to Murfreesborough in 1879, where he now resides. Dr. Mitchell is a trustee of Wake Forest, and also of Chowan Female Institute, and was made a D.D. by his *alma mater* in 1876.

Mitchell, Rev. J. F., a leading minister in Spring River Association, Ark., was born in North Carolina in 1823. He subsequently removed to Georgia, where he began to preach in 1853. He spent five years preaching in that State, and just at the commencement of the civil war he was called to the pastorate at Jacksonville, Florida, but owing to the disturbed state of the country he removed to Texas, where he remained until after the war. His labors were greatly blessed in that State. After laboring in Texas five years, he removed to Benton Co., Ark., where he has been an active co-worker with Jasper Dunegan. He has baptized during his ministry 615 persons.

Mitchell, Rev. S. H., was born in Washington Co., Ind., Feb. 20, 1830. He removed to Iowa in 1855. He was baptized at Oskaloosa in 1859. At the time of his baptism he looked upon teaching as his probable life-work. In 1862 he was licensed to preach, and not long after he was ordained. In

1863 he was appointed general missionary and financial agent of the Iowa Baptist State Convention, and continued in this position till October, 1869. During this period he traveled 30,000 miles over the State, 25,000 of which were by horseback and buggy. It was a time of great activity and growth in the Convention work, as is shown by the increased number of missionaries employed, and the amount of funds collected. In 1862 there were only six missionaries employed, and less than $1000 collected. In 1868 there were thirty, and nearly $6500 were collected.

Jan. 1, 1870, Mr. Mitchell settled as pastor at Ames, Iowa, and remained five years, doing a good work. Lots were purchased, and a substantial meeting-house built. During 1875 he labored as financial agent for the University of Des Moines. In February, 1876, he became pastor at Shell Rock, Iowa, and in July, 1877, began his ministry at Grundy Centre, Iowa, where he still labors, having now entered upon his fourth year of service. There are few men in Iowa so well and favorably known among the Baptists, or whose labors have had as wide a range or as marked effects in State missions.

Mize, Rev. T. S., was born Jan. 29, 1840, at Carrollton, Carroll Co., Ill. He made a profession of religion at the age of twelve years; was graduated at Shurtleff College at twenty years of age; pursued his theological studies at Rochester, N. Y.; ordained at Faribault, Minn.; settled at Clinton Junction, Wis., January, 1867, and died April 29, 1872. Great humility and modesty, and great fidelity to Christ and the church were his crowning characteristics.

Moffat, Judge John S., a well-known Baptist layman of Hudson, Wis., was born on the 25th of November, 1814, in Lansing, Tompkins Co., N. Y. His grandfather, Rev. John Moffat, emigrated from Ireland with a colony, with which also came the Clintons, who settled in New York. He was a Presbyterian clergyman of fine classical and theological attainments. Judge Moffat's parents were Samuel and Ann (Shaw) Moffat. They were Christians, and early in life began to instruct him in the principles of morality and religion; he received his education in the schools of the neighborhood. At eighteen he entered the counting-room of a merchant in Dryden, N. Y., as assistant. Here he remained two years. At twenty he entered the academy at Homer. He also studied at the academy at Groton.

In 1840, Mr. Moffat entered the law-office of Coryden Tyler, of Dryden, and, although admitted to the bar, he engaged for several years in mercantile pursuits. In 1854, Mr. Moffat came to Hudson, Wis., which has since been his home. Upon his arrival here he obtained a position in the land-office, which, together with the position of police justice, he held for many years. Since January, 1870, he has held the office of county judge. He also practises extensively in the courts, and presides over one of the largest insurance and collecting agencies in the Northwest.

Judge Moffat is a thorough-going Christian gentleman. For many years he has been a member of the Baptist church. In the church at Hudson he is a deacon and Sunday-school superintendent. He is a man of commanding influence, which he devotes to the best interests of the community where he resides. Temperance and public virtue and morality have in him an ardent friend. He exemplifies these, as well as the graces of pure religion, in his own daily life.

Mrs. Moffat's maiden name was Nancy Ann Bennet. She is a daughter of Phineas Bennet, a well-known inventor of New York. They were married Jan. 24, 1844. She is in perfect accord with Mr. Moffat in all his Christian and philanthropic labors, and an active and influential member of the Baptist church in Hudson.

Monroe Female College.—This institution, situated in the village of Forsyth, Monroe Co., Ga., was founded in the year 1849, under the title of Forsyth Female Collegiate Institute, Rev. E. J. C. Thomas being the first president. A few years afterwards Rev. Wm. C. Wilkes, a graduate of Mercer University, was elected president, and he managed the college with great energy and success until the close of the year 1866, except when it was temporarily suspended during the war. Rev. S. G. Hillyer, a graduate of Franklin College, and for many years a professor in Mercer University, was its next president. Dr. Hillyer, who is both an excellent scholar and an eminent divine, administered its affairs with great success until 1872, when R. T. Asbury succeeded, only to give way in turn to Dr. Hillyer, in the spring of 1880.

The management of this excellent college has always been in Baptist hands, and year after year has sent out large classes of well-educated young ladies. In 1879 its beautiful building was consumed by fire, but it is now being rebuilt in a more handsome style. The exercises, in the meanwhile, are still continued.

Monroe, Rev. John.—No minister in North Carolina of any denomination is more respected for his piety and usefulness than this venerable man. He was born in Richmond Co., N. C., in October, 1804. His parents emigrated from the Highlands of Scotland in 1 03. He was baptized into the fellowship of the Spring Hill Baptist church in 1819; began to preach in 1825; has labored extensively in the counties of Anson, Richmond, and Robeson, N. C., and Marlborough, S. C., and during the fifty-five years of his ministry he has been pastor of the Spring Hill church. For twenty years he was moderator of the Pedee Baptist Association, and would still fill that place did the infirmities of age permit.

Monroe, Rev. William Y., was born in Oldham Co., Ky., April 3, 1824; removed with his father to Scott Co., Ind., in 1834, and joined the Methodist church in 1842. About this time his mind was exercised in respect to his entering upon the work of the ministry. He began a thorough search of the Bible; the result was that he became a minister and a Baptist. He was ordained in 1850, and has been the pastor of the North Madison Baptist church for twenty-three years. He was elected treasurer of his county two consecutive terms, and has been sent to the State Legislature two sessions. He was elected president of the Indiana State Convention in 1878. He is a man of deep piety, modesty, and profound convictions.

Montague, Rev. Howard W., the eldest son of the Rev. Philip Montague, was born in Middlesex Co., Va., Oct. 10, 1810. He was baptized by his father in November, 1831. In 1838 he married Miss Mildred C. Broaddus, daughter of the Rev. Andrew Broaddus. He was ordained to the ministry in 1840. During his ministerial career of thirty-six years he was at different times pastor of the following churches,—Mount Zion, Ephesus, Howerton's, and Upper Essex, in the county of Essex; Bethel, in the county of Caroline; and Shiloh and Round Hill, in King George. In addition to these he had stated appointments at several other churches, besides being a frequent and zealous worker in protracted meetings in his own and neighboring churches. The one great object of his life was to preach the gospel plainly and faithfully to men, and he did it with great earnestness, power, and success. He was a laborious worker in the ministry, forgetting himself and laying all his energies on the altar of the Master. He possessed a vigorous intellect, was a strong thinker, and in his style of preaching was impressive and stimulating. His own life exemplified the doctrines of godliness, and all who were acquainted with him knew that Christ was the moving spring of his entire actions. He died June 9, 1876, leaving to the churches of his love and labors the memories of a character fragrant with the graces of the Spirit.

Montague, Rev. J. E., was born in Granville Co., N. C., in 1818; baptized in 1839; educated at Wake Forest College; was ordained in 1850, Revs. R. I. Devin and S. Creath forming the Presbytery; and has been the successful pastor of Mill Creek and Bethel churches, Person County, for twenty-six years.

Montague, Judge Robert L., was born in Middlesex Co., Va., May 23, 1819. His parents were zealous members of a Baptist church. His education was begun at a small country school. He was afterwards sent to Fleetwood Academy, in the county of King and Queen, conducted by that accomplished teacher, Oliver White, to be prepared for college. From this school he went to William

JUDGE ROBERT L. MONTAGUE.

and Mary College, where, in July of 1842, he received the degree of Bachelor of Laws, graduating also in the school of political economy. He returned to the college the next session, and continued his studies in legal and political science, and then entered upon the practice of law. He was baptized in August, 1842, by the Rev. Mr. Street, and united with the Glebelanding church, of which he has continued a member till the present, being actively identified with all the movements of the denomination, and serving most efficiently for several years the General Baptist Association of Virginia as its president. Having begun the practice of law in 1844, Judge Montague was appointed, in 1845, the Commonwealth's attorney for Middlesex County, which position he held with efficiency and honor for nineteen years and then resigned. In 1850 he was elected a member of the Virginia Legislature, and was re-elected in 1851, but he resigned without serving. In 1852 he was a Presidential elector, and was the messenger of the electoral college to convey the vote of Virginia to Washington; and in 1856 he was again a Presidential elector. In 1859 he was elected lieutenant-governor of the State. This office he held for the constitutional period of four years. In February, 1861, he was elected by the people of Middlesex and Mathews Counties to represent them in the secession convention; and in April of the same year he was chosen by the convention a member of the executive council to aid the governor in his arduous and responsible duties. He was elected president of the convention at its last session, and it is a singular fact that Judge Montague while presiding over this body was also the president of the Virginia senate for nearly a month, both bodies sitting in the same building, so that, in order to accommodate the presiding officer, the hours of meeting for both bodies had to be changed. In 1863 he was elected a member of the Confederate Congress, and served in that body till its last session; after which time, until 1873, he remained in private life, giving himself entirely to the practice of his profession. In 1873 he was elected a member of the Virginia Legislature by the people of Middlesex County, and in March, 1875, he was elected by the Legislature judge of the eighth judicial circuit. Although Judge Montague's numerous official duties prevented him from adding much to the literature of the denomination, he made a great many public addresses on various subjects, many of which have been published and widely read throughout the State. Although much in public and political life, no man sustained a more honorable reputation. He died during the summer of 1880.

Montanye, Rev. Thomas B., was born Jan. 29, 1769, in New York. When seventeen years of age he was baptized by the Rev. John Gano into the fellowship of the First Baptist church of that city. He was ordained pastor of the Baptist church of Warwick, N. Y., when only nineteen years of age. In 1801 he became pastor of the Southampton church, Bucks Co., Pa. He held this position till death summoned him to the church in glory, Sept. 27, 1829. Mr. Montanye was one of the most popular Baptist ministers in the eastern part of Pennsylvania, where his name was familiar to most professors of religion. No man in the Baptist ranks stood higher than he. His church trusted and loved him, and he and his Southampton brethren walked in harmony with the Baptist brotherhood everywhere. In preaching, his theme was the cross, and he possessed great power in setting forth the matchless glories of the suffering Saviour. His memory is tenderly cherished all over Bucks County at this day.

Montgomery, Rev. W. A., was born in Jefferson Co., Tenn., Nov. 16, 1829. He was converted and baptized in his fourteenth year. He entered the University of Tennessee, at Knoxville, in 1845, and graduated with the first honor of his class in 1850; read law with the Hon. E. Alexander, judge of the Knoxville Circuit Court. He was admitted to the bar in the fall of 1851. He removed to Texas in 1855. He served as a member from Washington County in the secession convention in 1861. He was licensed to preach while in the Confederate army in 1862. He continued in it until the close of the war; removed to Leadvale, Tenn., in 1867. He was ordained to the work of the ministry in 1868. He received his D.D. from Carson College in 1870, and from the University of Tennessee in 1876. He was pastor first of Leadvale and Dandridge churches from 1868 to 1872; then of First church, Lynchburg, Va., until 1877. He was corresponding secretary of the Southwestern Board for eighteen months. He is now the pastor of the First Baptist church of Memphis, Tenn.

Dr. Montgomery possesses rare ability as an evangelist. The numerous protracted meetings held by him, in which his labors were singularly blessed, abundantly show this. In the pulpit his manner is solemn; his words and arguments are logical, instructive, and convincing. He is among the most prominent preachers in the State.

Montreal College.—This institution owes its origin to the conviction among the Baptists of Canada that, in order to prosecute their denominational work in the provinces, a native, educated ministry must be raised up to do this work. The funds necessary to commence the undertaking having been secured, Dr. Benjamin Davies, then living in England, came to Montreal in 1839, and took charge of what was called the Baptist Theological College, the original design being to have but two instructors, a principal and a tutor, to train the young men who proposed to enter the Christian ministry. Buildings were secured, the necessary preparations made, and a few students connected themselves with the new institution. In 1843, Dr. Davies was called to England to take the presidency of Stepney College, now Regent's Park College, London, and Rev. Dr. Fyfe occupied the place thus made vacant for one year. In 1844, Dr. J. M. Cramp entered upon his duties as president of the college. A fine, cut-stone building was erected on a commanding site in the city of Montreal, and the prospects of the institution wore an encouraging aspect. But it was not long before financial embarrassment crippled the energies of those who had been foremost in promoting the interests of the college. The "hard times" of 1848-50 destroyed all hope of raising funds, which it had been thought could be obtained in England. There was no alternative but to sell the college property, to pay off, as far as possible, the debts of the institution. Apparently the experiment to establish a Baptist theological college in Montreal had proved a failure, and the friends of ministerial education must look for success in some other quarter. (See article on CANADIAN LITERARY INSTITUTE.)

Moody, Lady.—This titled lady lived at Lynn, Mass., in 1640. She purchased the estate of Mr.

Humphrey, one of the magistrates, and intended to become a permanent resident. Soon after making her abode at Lynn she embraced the principles of the Baptists; and then neither her character nor her position in society could avail her anything. She was compelled to withdraw from the Congregational citizens of Lynn and seek a home on Long Island among the Dutch, who, like their liberal countrymen in Holland, gave her a generous welcome. And when the Indians came to Long Island to kill its Dutch settlers, forty of them defended the house of Lady Moody at the peril of their lives. In that day to embrace Baptist principles was to invite expatriation, if not something worse, even from American Christians.

Moore, David, D.D., was born in Northumberland, England, March 28, 1822. He came to the United States in 1834. He received a superior education, and being called of God to the ministry, he was ordained, in June, 1852, as pastor of the Gaines and Murray churches, N. Y. In 1855 he accepted a call to the Le Roy church in the same State; in 1860 he became pastor of the Washington Street church, Buffalo; and in 1864 he took the oversight of the Washington Avenue church, Brooklyn, from which he retired, through impaired health, in 1876. He is now pastor of the church of Geneva, N. Y.

He has published several occasional sermons, essays, and addresses, and was, till the failure of his health, an active manager of the American Baptist Home Mission Society, the Long Island Mission Board, and of other denominational institutions.

Few men in the Baptist denomination have wielded a wider or more beneficial influence. As a preacher, he is lucid, sound, earnest, and eloquent. As a pastor, sympathizing, magnetic, and faithful, and, in all the councils of his brethren, capable, practical, and prudent.

Moore, Rev. Ferris, was born in Putney, Vt., Dec. 31, 1796, united by baptism with the church June 24, 1816, and was ordained Dec. 30, 1819, at Keene, N. H., where he was the pastor of the church for two years. Subsequently he was settled at New Ipswich, N. H., Canton, Mass., and at Saratoga, N. Y. From April, 1846, to the fall of 1857 he preached every alternate Sabbath at South Lee, Mass., where he died April 7, 1858.

Moore, John L., D.D., one of the pioneer Baptists of Ohio, was born in Lewis Co., N. Y., Feb. 17, 1803, and was converted at the age of twenty-two. In 1831 he graduated from Hamilton, and one week after his graduation was ordained at Watertown, N. Y., with special reference to the Western field. In October of the same year, in company with three of his classmates, William Choffee, Alvin Bailey, and G. Bartlett, he visited Cleveland, then a village of 1000 inhabitants. From it he went to Columbus, where there was a small Baptist church, and thence to Cincinnati, where there were then three Baptist churches. After a short stay in Cincinnati he visited the towns of the Miami valley. At Hamilton he met with a very severe accident, by which his face was terribly burned and the sight of his eyes greatly injured. Nothing daunted at this, however, he accepted in the spring of 1832 an appointment by the Home Mission Society, then just organized. After general missionary work he became pastor of the church of Piqua, and in 1834 gave half his time to the new church at Troy. His next pastorate was with the church at Dayton, where he remained two years.

For eight years subsequent to this Dr. Moore was the general agent for the Ohio State Convention. Part of his time was, however, devoted to the interests of the college at Granville, of which he was a trustee for more than thirty years. On resigning his agency he took pastoral charge of the church in Springfield, O., which position he held for nearly two years, when he gave himself to the work of establishing a theological institution at Fairmount, near Cincinnati. In 1855 he was appointed an exploring missionary for Ohio by the State Convention, and did much effective work. His health becoming greatly impaired he relinquished this position, and gave himself thenceforward to a more quiet life, preaching, however, as he found opportunity, and making himself useful in the general denominational work. In the same year Denison University conferred upon him the degree of D.D. In 1870 he removed to Topeka, Kan., where he remained until his death, Jan. 23, 1878.

Dr. Moore was one of the most influential and wealthy of the early Baptist ministers of Ohio. His memory is treasured by thousands in that State. He was a very acceptable preacher, and a man of most excellent spirit. He leaves a son in the ministry, Rev. A. S. Moore, of Salem, O.

Moore, Rev. Wm., was born near Pisgah, Butler Co., O., Dec. 8, 1821; was baptized by Elder Daniel Bryant at the age of twenty; studied at Farmer's College, and also at Granville; took his theological course at the Covington Institute, under Dr. Patterson; was ordained to the ministry in the autumn of 1847, at the Ninth Street church, Cincinnati, and shortly afterwards was married to Miss E. W. Forbes. In company with Dr. Jewett, of the Teloogoo Mission, he was set apart as a foreign missionary, first to Assam, and afterwards, at the death of Mr. Bullard, to the Pwo Karens, Burmah.

He sailed with his wife from Boston, in the ship "Cato," Nov. 2, 1847, in company with Brethren Danforth, Stoddard, and their wives, and also Brethren Simons and Brayton. On reaching the heathen land he entered with energy upon the arduous labor of acquiring a foreign language. This he soon accomplished, and was permitted to visit the Karens in their distant homes, and tell them of a Saviour's dying love. After about five years of labor his health began to fail, and before the sixth year was completed it was manifest to all that his missionary toils were ended, at least for a time. His voice entirely failed, so that he could speak only in a low whisper. With great reluctance he bade adieu to the chosen labors of his life, and returned to this country. He located first at Cincinnati, but, not being able to preach, he went to Middletown, and entered into business, in which he continued twenty-six years, until his death. Being prompt, reliable, and enterprising, he secured a flattering position in the commercial world. His word was the synonym of honor and fair-dealing.

His influence was always on the side of right and morality, and in this direction it was mighty and constant, and it was felt for the improvement of the community. He was a member of the school board for twelve years, and president of the board of education when he died. In the church he was looked upon as one of the main pillars, holding the office of deacon from 1867 until the close of his life. He was also church clerk for fifteen years, until the time of his death, and during his membership he was a constant attendant at the Sabbath-school, having in charge the adult Bible-class. In his teaching he was clear and methodical, and eminently useful. He was not only a faithful teacher, but a true friend, and a wise counselor to all his class. Even after they left the school he never lost sight of them, but watched his opportunity to do them good. It brightens our appreciation of his goodness to remember that he himself was never conscious of its possession, but labored diligently each day as though the results of eternity depended upon the passing hour. Few men have been more honored for Christian integrity. His unfaltering devotion to the church, his familiarity with men, his sound judgment, and his kindness won many hearts to trust the Saviour whom he loved and honored. With an unblemished reputation, he filled up the measure of his days. He died Sept. 29, 1880, in the full enjoyment of the Saviour's love.

Moran, Rev. M. Y., an able minister in Lincoln Co., Ark., was born in North Carolina in 1818; at the age of twenty-two professed Christ, and soon after began to preach. Having settled in Somerville, Tenn., in 1844, he studied for three years, and obtained a fair knowledge of Greek, Latin, and mathematics. He was ordained in 1855; after preaching in Tennessee three years he removed to Bolivar Co., Miss., where he organized the first church in the county. Here he continued to labor until the war. In 1862 he came to Arkansas and settled at his present place of residence, where he has preached successfully until the present time. He has presided several times as moderator of Bartholomew Association, of Arkansas Baptist Convention, and the General Association of Southeast Arkansas.

More, Godwin C., M.D., was born in Hertford Co., N. C., Nov. 7, 1806; graduated at Chapel Hill; read medicine with his brother-in-law, Dr. Fletcher, and graduated in medicine at Transylvania University. In 1831 he represented his native county in the State Legislature; ran for Congress in 1837, and in 1838 became moderator of the Chowan Association, the largest body of the kind in the State, and he held this honorable position for thirty years. He was elected a member of the Legislature again in 1842, and also in 1867. He was a trustee of Wake Forest College, and for many years president of the board of trustees of the Chowan Female Institute. He died in 1880, loved and lamented by all who knew him.

Morehead, Gov. James T., an able lawyer, and one of the most brilliant orators that Kentucky has produced, was born in Bullitt Co., Ky., May 24, 1797. He attended school at Russellville, and completed his education at Transylvania University. He was raised in the faith of the Baptists, but delayed uniting with the church until late in life, for which he expressed much regret. He studied law at Russellville, and commenced practice at Bowling Green in 1818. He was elected to the Legislature in 1828, and served several terms in that body. He was elected lieutenant-governor of Kentucky in 1832, and became governor of the State upon the death of Gov. Breathitt, in February, 1834. He was several years president of the board of internal improvements. In 1841 he was elected to the U. S. Senate, and at the close of his term, in 1847, he located in Covington, Ky. He died Dec. 28, 1854.

Morehead, Rev. Robert W., A.M., was born in Logan Co., Ky., April 13, 1834. He entered Bethel College in 1854, and remained two years. In 1856 he entered Union University, Tenn., where he graduated in 1859. His theological studies were pursued under the supervision of Dr. J. M. Pendleton. He united with Union Baptist church, in his native county, in 1849; was licensed to preach in 1856, and ordained in 1859. In 1860 he took charge of Bethel church, in Christian County. For several years he has been the beloved and honored pastor of the Baptist church at Princeton, Ky. He is a man of culture and great moral worth.

Morehouse, Henry L., D.D., was born in Stanford, Dutchess Co., N. Y., Oct. 2, 1834. Mr. Morehouse was graduated at the University of Rochester in 1858. He entered Rochester Theological Seminary in 1861, and was graduated in 1864. His first settlement was at East Saginaw, Mich., where he remained from 1864 to 1873, when he was called to the pastorate of the East Avenue Baptist church, in Rochester. Mr. Morehouse was prominently identified with educational and State missionary work in Michigan. He was for some time corresponding and financial agent of the New York Baptist Union for Ministerial Education, which has charge of the theological seminary at Rochester. He was elected to that position in 1877. His report in "Vindication of the Beneficiary System" won for him high encomiums from the first educators of the country. He has also published several able sermons. He was poet of the alumni of Rochester University in 1874. His racy and very readable contributions to the *Examiner and Chronicle*, over the signature "Helmo," have earned him a good reputation. His church has greatly prospered under his ministry, and his earnest labors for the seminary have secured for him the respect of all the friends of ministerial education in the State and in the many States where Rochester is represented. He is now the able corresponding secretary of the American Baptist Home Mission Society.

Moreland, Rev. W. C., for nine years pastor at Arcadia, La., was born in Georgia in 1824; for nineteen years a preacher in the Methodist connection; in 1864 he was ordained as a Baptist minister. He came to Louisiana in 1848. He has served the following Baptist churches acceptably: Homer, Rock Spring, and Antioch, in Claiborne Parish, and Liberty, Mount Gilead, and Arcadia churches, in Bienville Parish.

Morell, Rev. Z. N., was born in Tennessee; is now about eighty years old; commenced preaching at an early age after his conversion, and was successful as a minister in Tennessee and Mississippi; removed to Texas in 1835; was intimately associated with the early warriors, civilians, and ministers who founded the republic of Texas and organized the State. He was one of the originators of the State Convention and Education Society of Texas. His book, "Flowers and Fruits; or, Thirty-six Years in Texas," published in 1872, by Gould & Lincoln, Boston, is full of remarkable incidents touching religious, civil, and martial life, written in a style of masculine vigor.

Morey, Rev. Reuben, a native of Fabius, Onondaga Co., N. Y., where he was born Feb. 21, 1805, obtained a hope in Christ in early life, and united with the Baptist Church. Having strong convictions that it was his duty to preach the gospel, he soon after his conversion began the work of preparation. He was educated at Hamilton Literary and Theological Institution and at Brown University. Dr. Wayland was president at Brown while he was there, and he left upon his student the impress of his own strong intellect and powerful grasp of truth. Dr. J. R. Loomis, president of Lewisburg University, Dr. Ives, of Suffield, Conn., and Dr. William Dean, of Bangkok, Siam, were among his intimate friends at college. After his graduation from Brown University he was ordained and settled as pastor of the Baptist church in Madison, Ind. His subsequent pastorates were at Louisville, Ky., North Attleborough, Mass., Homer, Wyoming, and Arcade, N. Y., Delavan and Tonica, Ill., and Merton, Wis. His longest pastorate was at North Attleborough, Mass., where he remained eight years. His preaching was analytical and doctrinal. He had a profound reverence for the ministerial office, and this imparted depth and solemnity to his public services. As a pastor he was peculiarly gifted for efficient labor in the family and with the individual. He was a tower of strength in all his pastoral labors with his flock. His home during the closing years of his life was in Waukesha, Wis. Here he fell asleep in Jesus, Feb. 17, 1880. "Mark the perfect man and behold the upright, for the end of that man is peace."

Morgan, Rev. Abel, was of Welsh descent, and was born at Welsh Tract, Del., April 18, 1713. He was baptized when about twenty years of age, and was soon afterwards ordained. He had laid the foundation of the learning which he subsequently evinced at the academy in Pencador. In 1739 he took charge of the church in Middletown, N. J., and continued there until his death, in 1785. The period of his life was an important one, and he was equal to the work demanded from him. His influence and the history of the denomination in New Jersey and America are inseparably connected. He had a good judgment, unusual literary attainments, a logical mind, and a very valuable library. He was powerful in debate; he was also unsparing in labor by night and by day. In his old springless cart he rode long distances to preach Jesus. Dr. Jones, in his century sermon, called him "the *incomparable Morgan*." Edwards says of him, "He was not a *custom* divine, nor a *leading-string* divine, but a BIBLE DIVINE." He was on different occasions challenged to debate on doctrine, and always maintained his position. In 1742 there was a great revival at Cape May, in which Baptist and Presbyterian ministers preached. Too many of the converts "took to the water" to suit the Presbyterians. Mr. Morgan accepted a challenge from Rev. Samuel Finley, afterwards president of Princeton College, to discuss the baptismal question. He gained a signal triumph. Mr. Finley tried his pen, and wrote "A Charitable Plea for the Speechless." Mr. Morgan had a reply printed, under the title "Anti-Pædo Rantism, or Mr. Samuel Finley's Charitable Plea for the Speechless examined and refuted, the Baptism of Believers maintained, and the Mode of it by Immersion vindicated, by Abel Morgan, of Middletown, in East Jersey. Philadelphia, printed by B. Franklin, in Market Street. MDCCXLVII." This little work is so valuable and scarce that it sells for $12 or more.

REV. ABEL MORGAN.

As a patriot, his trumpet gave no uncertain sound. Even while the royal troops were moving through his neighborhood, after the battle of Monmouth, he was outspoken. The next Sunday he had for his text, "Who gave Jacob for a spoil and Israel to the robbers?" He says in his diary, that the Sunday after that, "Preached in mine own barn, because the enemy had taken out all the seats in the meeting-house." He baptized many persons, and was the means of converting and edifying many more. He wrote some of the most important documents issued by the Philadelphia Association, and was frequently called by it to preach and preside. His many manuscripts, neatly written, show careful preparation, sound doctrine, and practical application. The inscription upon his plain tombstone at Middletown is, " In memory of Abel Morgan, pastor of the Baptist church at Middletown, who departed this life Nov. 24, 1785, in the 73d year of his age. His life was blameless, his ministry was powerful; he was a burning and shining light, and his memory is dear to the saints."

Morgan, T. J., D.D., Professor of Church History in the Baptist Union Theological Seminary at Chicago, is of Welsh descent. His father was Rev. Lewis Morgan, a pioneer Baptist preacher in Indiana, and he was born at Franklin, in that State, Aug. 17, 1839. His collegiate course he pursued at Franklin College, graduating in 1861. The war being then in progress, he entered the Union service as a private, and, after three years and four months, at the close of the war, resigned as colonel of the 14th U. S. Colored Infantry. He commanded a division at the battle of Nashville, and was made, subsequently, brevet brigadier-general for " gallant and meritorious service during the war." The struggle having closed, Gen. Morgan decided to enter upon study for the ministry, and graduated at Rochester in 1868. His first service was as secretary of the New York Baptist Union for Ministerial Education. At the end of three years he resigned this position, and, removing to Nebraska, served in that State as pastor for one year, and two years as president of the Nebraska State Normal School, being complimented, in 1874, with an appointment by President Grant as a member of the Board of Visitors at West Point. In September of the year last named he entered upon his duties as professor in the theological seminary at Chicago, holding, first, the chair of Homiletics, and at present that of Church History. In the year 1879 Dr. Morgan spent four months in study at the University of Leipsic, Germany, and in the year 1880 five months in European travel and in

T. J. MORGAN, D.D.

the prosecution of historical studies. To his fine scholarly attainments and ability as a teacher Dr. Morgan adds the talent of a "ready writer," and has contributed largely and most acceptably to the denominational press.

Morgan, Rev. William D., was born in Wales; educated at Pontypool College; came to America, and was ordained as a Baptist minister in Plymouth, Pa.; settled in Chester, Conn., in 1875, and with the Third Baptist church in North Stonington, Conn., in the spring of 1877; here he was thrown from a carriage and instantly killed, May 7, 1878, aged thirty-four years.

Morrill, Rev. Abner, A.M., son of Deacon John Adams and Mary McDonald Morrill, was born in Limerick, Me., Aug. 18, 1827; was converted while a student in college, and, though educated a Pedobaptist, united with the Main Street Baptist church in Brunswick, Me. To this step he was led by a careful study of God's Word, overcoming much opposition. He graduated from Bowdoin College in 1850. He was called to the chair of Mathematics and Natural Sciences in Midbury Academy the same year. In 1852 he became tutor in the West Tennessee College, Jackson, Tenn. After spending several years in teaching in connection with various institutions in the South, he returned to Maine in 1859, and became pastor of the Baptist church in Farmington. He was afterwards pastor at Turner and Mechanic Falls. In 1865 he came to New York, and has been pastor of the churches in Warsaw and Arcade. He is now settled in Painted Post. He is a faithful minister, a good preacher, and a noble-minded citizen.

Morrill, Rev. D. T., the present (1880) pastor of the Upper Alton Baptist church, Ill., was born Oct. 24, 1825, in Danville, Caledonia Co., N. Y. When he was about three years of age the family removed to Potsdam, St. Lawrence Co., in the same State. His preparation for college he received at the St. Lawrence Academy, in Potsdam. In September, 1847, he entered Union College, intending at first to take an eclectic course, but changed his plans subsequently, entering the Junior class, and graduating in 1849. His conversion took place while in college, without apparent special human agency, and partly in connection with a struggle against doubts even of the truth of the Christian religion. Earnest study of the evidences, accompanied by manifest strivings of the Spirit, ended not only in entire acceptance of the Christian system, but also of Christ as a personal Saviour. Deciding to enter the ministry, he took his theological course at Rochester, entering the seminary in 1851 and graduating in 1853. The interval of time since leaving college and before entering the seminary had been spent in teaching in Rahway, N. J., where he was baptized by Rev. W. H. Wines. Mr. Morrill's desire had been towards foreign missionary work, but a field of missionary labor opening to him at Newark, N. J., he decided to enter it. The mission so undertaken in that city resulted in the organization of the Fifth Baptist church, in March, 1855. This church he served as pastor fourteen years. The church grew into a strong one, built a meeting-house and parsonage, and took its place among the vigorous and efficient churches of the city and State. In 1869 he accepted a call to the Fourth Baptist church, St. Louis, continuing there six years, until 1874. Two hundred accessions by baptism were fruits of this ministry. A year and a half as pastor of Park Avenue church and superintendent of missions in St. Louis Association, and nearly a year in the service of the Publication Society as district secretary, brings the record to 1876, when Mr. Morrill accepted the call of the Upper Alton Baptist church, a field made especially interesting by the close relations into which the pastor of that church is necessarily brought with the students and faculty of Shurtleff College.

Morrill, Rev. J. C., was born in Amesbury, Mass., Aug. 16, 1791. Until he was about forty years of age he was in secular business. Impressed that it was his duty to preach the gospel, he received from the First Baptist church in Lowell a license, and was ordained as an evangelist at Waterville, Me., Oct. 25, 1832. He devoted himself with great zeal and energy to the work for which he had thus been set apart, and his preaching was accompanied by the conversion of souls. His successive pastorates were with churches in Augusta, Sidney, Freeport, Wiscasset, and Corinth, in Maine, Manchester, N. H., and Somerset, Mass. For four years he was in the service of the American and Foreign Bible Society. He died at Taunton, Aug. 22, 1858.

Morris, C. D., D.D., of Toledo, O., was born in North Wales, June 6, 1839. His parents, who were Calvinistic Methodists, removed to America in 1840, and settled in Ohio in 1841. In his eleventh year he united with a Presbyterian church, but in 1860, through independent investigation of God's Word, he became a Baptist, and united with the Baptist church at Urbana, O. In 1859 he became a public school teacher, and followed that calling for three years, when he gave himself entirely to preaching, and became pastor of the Baptist church at Fairfield, O. After remaining here a little while, he took a selected course of study in the university and a full course in the theological seminary at Rochester, N. Y., graduating in 1867. Shortly after graduation he became pastor of the First church, Toledo, O., where he still remains, the oldest pastor in the continuous service of one church in Ohio.

Dr. Morris is a scholarly and strong preacher, and makes himself felt not only in the growing city of Toledo, but throughout the State. He received the degree of D.D. from Chicago, Ill., in 1879.

Morris, Rev. Joshua, a celebrated pioneer Baptist preacher of Kentucky, was born in James City Co., Va., about 1750. He was baptized by Elijah Baker about 1773. He preached for a time in the country, and subsequently in Richmond, where he formed the first Baptist church in that city, in June, 1780. Of this church he became pastor, and ministered to it about seven years. In 1788 he removed to Kentucky, and became the pastor of Brashear's Creek church, in Shelby County. Besides ministering to this body about ten years, he constituted several churches in the regions around him. In 1798 he located in what is now Carroll County, and established Ghent church, and two years afterwards he removed to Nelson County, where he ministered to Cedar Creek and Mill Creek churches, and formed one or two new churches. He was a man of high respectability, and was eminently useful. He died about 1837.

Morris, Rev. William La Rue, was of Irish extraction, and was born in Hardin Co., Ky., Jan. 10, 1821. He was educated as a lawyer, and entered upon the practice of his profession at Hodgensville, Ky. He was a fine speaker, and a young man of strict honesty and integrity, and readily gained a good patronage. At this period his conscience was deeply impressed with a call from God to preach the gospel. To this conviction he finally yielded, and having joined a Baptist church while he was a law student, he was ordained pastor of the Baptist church at Hodgensville in January, 1851. He was remarkably active and zealous in his holy calling, and his improvement was such that he soon became one of the most eloquent preachers in the Kentucky pulpit. In 1866 he was appointed by the board of the General Association, general evangelist for the State. He died June 13, 1867.

Morrison, Judge A. W., was born in Jessamine Co., Ky., Nov. 25, 1802; removed to Missouri and settled with his mother and family in Howard County, his father having died in Kentucky. He was liberally educated. His known ability and integrity commended him to the people of his county for almost every office at their disposal. He was for four years receiver of the United States land-office for Missouri, under appointment of President James K. Polk. In 1851 he was appointed State treasurer by Gov. King to fill the vacancy occasioned by the death of Peter G. Glover. So thorough was his efficiency in this department, and so great his personal popularity, that he was elected by the people for three succeeding terms to the same office. He was the incumbent at the breaking out of the civil war, and Gov. Gamble insisted on his holding the position, but this he declined, refusing to take the "test oath."

Judge Morrison's ancestry were of the highest respectability in Wales, and afterwards in Virginia and Kentucky. He still lives on a beautiful and valuable estate in Howard Co., Mo.

In 1873 the judge made a profession of faith in Christ, and united with the Baptist church at Glasgow, in Howard County. His integrity as a man and citizen has marked his course as a Christian. He is intelligently active in every good work, a strong friend of his pastors, a liberal helper in missions and Christian education, and he is a member of several denominational boards. He is remarkably active in mind and body, and still wields a mighty influence in public matters.

Morrow, Rev. Orson Holland, a popular, useful, and much esteemed minister of Bethel Association, was born in Rutherford Co., N. C., Nov. 10, 1800. He was taken by his parents to what is now Simpson Co., Ky., in 1807, where he still lives. He was baptized in 1827, licensed to preach a few months later, and ordained in 1833. He became a close Bible student, and was very thorough in his researches. He has been pastor of four churches most of the time since his ordination, until the feebleness of old age rendered him incapable of the work. He has performed a great amount of missionary labor, and has organized a number of new churches.

His pastorates have been Pleasant Grove, Union, Warren Co., and Sulphur Spring, Simpson Co. During his long and faithful service he has been the means of the conversion of large numbers of souls, eighteen of whom are known to have become active ministers of the gospel. Mr. Morrow has been a frequent contributor to the periodical press.

Morse, Rev. Asahel, son of Rev. Joshua and Susannah (Babcock) Morse, was born in Montville, Conn., Nov. 10, 1771; removed with his parents to Landisfield, Mass., in 1779; was a lover of good books and an apt scholar; taught schools with success; was converted in 1798; was baptized Nov. 9 of that year, by Rev. Rufus Babcock, of Colebrook, Conn.; licensed to preach in the spring of 1799; removed to Winsted, Conn., in 1800, where he was ordained in May, 1801; traveled and preached in almost every town in Connecticut; settled with the Baptist church in Stratfield, Conn., in 1803, and remained more than nine years, preaching most of the time six sermons a week; meanwhile he made a missionary tour, by appointment of the Shaftesbury Association, into Upper Canada, and attended fifty-four meetings; in 1812 settled in Suffield, Conn., as successor to Rev. John Hastings; in 1818 was a member of the State convention to frame a new State constitution, and penned for it the article on religious liberty,—a marked event in the State's history; was a man of great power, and a typical Baptist; in 1820 went to Philadelphia as delegate from the Connecticut Baptist Missionary Board to the Baptist General Convention; for a time supplied a church in Colebrook, and in 1832 became pastor of the Second Baptist church in that town; returned to Suffield in 1836, where he died June 10, 1838, in his sixty-seventh year. He married, Aug. 24, 1795, Rachel Chapel, of New Marlborough, Mass., and had eight children,—all sons. His was a noble life.

Morse, Rev. John Chipman, was born in Annapolis Co., Nova Scotia; converted and baptized when a youth; ordained pastor over the Digby Neck church March 31, 1842, and continues still in that happy relation. Mr. Morse is a deep and enthusiastic student of the Bible and of nature, and a very useful preacher of the gospel.

Morse, Rev. Joshua, was born in South Kingston, R. I., April 10, 1726; was converted under the preaching of Whitefield at the age of sixteen, and commenced preaching the next year as an itinerant; gathered a church in Montville, Conn., where he was ordained May 17, 1751; for aiding the New Lights and preaching Baptist doctrines in North Stonington, he was opposed, arrested, and abused; the distresses of the Revolution on the coast occasioned his removal to Landisfield, Mass., in 1779, where he gathered a church that he lived to see enrol a hundred members. He was an able, zealous, and faithful minister. He died in 1795, in his seventieth year.

Morse, Rev. Levi, was born in Jefferson, Schoharie Co., N. Y., Aug. 23, 1817; was born again, as he trusts, in December, 1835; baptized into the Jefferson Baptist church in 1838; commenced his studies preparatory to the ministry at Jefferson Academy in 1839, and graduated from Madison University in 1844; settled as pastor of the Baptist church of Athens, Pa., Sept. 8, 1844, the church having been raised up under his labors previously, during one of his vacations; remained as pastor five years, leaving a united church, with 112 members and a convenient house of worship. He has since been pastor at Franklin and Deposit, N. Y., of the North Baptist church of Newark, and at Newton and Pittsgrove, N. J., at Unionville, the Orange Baptist church, and the Franklindale Baptist church, New York, and he is now pastor of the Baptist church of Burlingame, Kansas. His settlements have all been pleasant and prosperous.

During the thirty-seven years of his ministry he has baptized into the churches he has served about 800 converts. In his sixty-fourth year, he is still able to undertake as much public speaking as at any previous period of his history.

Morse, Rev. Samuel B., is one of the most successful and beloved pastors in California. He was born Oct. 26, 1834, in Fayette, Me.; was baptized when scarcely twelve years old, by Rev. John Butler. He graduated at Colby University and at Newton. Having special gifts for teaching, he engaged in that work for a time in Kentucky and at Vacaville, Cal., the seat of the Baptist College in that State, while it was in the hands of the Methodists. He returned East for some years, and was ordained at Newton in August, 1869. Coming back to California, he became pastor at Stockton nine years, and was remarkably blessed in his work. While pastor there he made the tour of Europe, Egypt, and Palestine, and gathered materials for several instructive lectures on the Holy Land, and has given them over one hundred times with ever-increasing favor. Feb. 1, 1878, he accepted the pastorate of the Brooklyn church, which up to that time was greatly discouraged. His unusual pastoral gifts and spiritual power as a preacher have made the church one of the best in California. He occupies a conspicuous position on missionary and college boards, and as moderator of the San Francisco Association and presiding officer at other public meetings he shows fine executive ability.

Morton, Rev. Salmon, was born in Athol, Mass., May 11, 1767. He was convicted of sin in his sixteenth year, and invested with justifying faith several years later. He was baptized at Madison, N. Y., in 1799, and he was ordained in June, 1802, as pastor of the Madison church, for which he labored for eleven years. In 1816 he took charge of the church in Marcellus, Onondaga Co., but he resigned in 1818 to preach as a home missionary. He died at Marcellus, Jan. 22, 1822. By the people among whom his ministry was exercised he was regarded as a great preacher. His usefulness was very extensive, and his Christian worth was of a high order.

Moss, Lemuel, D.D., was born in Owen Co., Ky., Dec. 27, 1829. His father, Demas Moss, was well known among the pioneer Baptists of Southern Indiana as a man of unusually strong native powers. His mother was a woman of fervent piety as well as mental energy. He came with his parents to Dearborn Co., Ind., in 1833. He was converted at the age of thirteen, and joined the Baptist church at Milan. When he was fourteen he entered the office of the *Lawrenceburg Register*. He spent nine years in printing, part of the time as foreman of a stereotyping establishment. While yet a youth his membership was removed to the First Baptist church, Cincinnati, where his prayer-meeting talks and other earnest religious services led his brethren to think that he ought to enter upon the work of the ministry. As this persuasion accorded with his own convictions he decided to give himself to the Master as a minister. He entered Rochester University, N. Y., in 1853. The select course marked out for him by President Anderson was abandoned after a year's preparatory work, and he entered upon the full course. He graduated in 1858, and two years later graduated in Rochester Theological Seminary, under President Robinson. As a student he was always remarkably diligent, and won and held the confidence of his teachers and fellow-students. He was awarded all the honors of the class. His high moral tone and strict integrity were characteristic during his whole course of study, as they have been ever since. He began preaching during his Sophomore year, and soon exhibited rare power as a public speaker.

Immediately upon his graduation from the seminary he was called to the pastorate of the First Baptist church of Worcester, Mass. In 1868 his *alma mater* conferred upon him the degree of Doctor of Divinity. Upon the organization of the United States Christian Commission by Mr. George H. Stuart and others, in 1864, he was chosen its home secretary, and charged with the responsible duty of interesting the people of the North in the work of the Commission. By request of the Commission he wrote and published "Annals of the United States Christian Commission,"—a book full of interesting facts and inferences, and the only authentic record of the doings of the Commission. The work has received the highest praise. In 1865 he accepted the chair of Systematic Theology in the University of Lewisburg, Pa., and, after three years' service, resigned to accept the position of editor of the *National Baptist*, the organ of the American Baptist Publication Society. His editorship was a marked success. After four years he resigned this work to accept the chair of New Testament Interpretation in Crozer Theological Seminary, Pa. While occupying this position he came to Indiana, and was the principal lecturer for a State ministers' institute. During the course it was very manifest that he was able to answer difficult questions in both systematic theology and exegesis.

In the National Baptist Educational Convention, held in Brooklyn, N. Y., in 1870, he presented a paper on "The Organization of our Educational Work." He has also written for the *Baptist Quarterly* two articles,—one on "Our Schools and Foreign Missions," the other on "The Final Condition of the Unregenerate." In 1876 he edited a book entitled "Baptists and the National Centenary," a book of vast value to those who would know the origin and progress of the various enterprises taken up and carried forward by the denomination.

In 1875 he was elected president of Chicago University, Ill. In 1876 he was elected president of the Indiana State University, and he is still carrying forward its work with a vigor and wisdom that give great promise for the future of the university. He was in 1879 made president of the Indiana State College Association.

He is a clear thinker, a genial friend, an inspiring teacher, and a public speaker of rare power.

Mother-Churches among American Baptists, Some.—The First church of Providence, R. I., is regarded by the majority of Baptists as the oldest church of our denomination in America. That venerable community has been the mother of many churches. The First church of Newport, R. I., with John Clarke, the sturdy old Calvinist, and the enlightened statesman, as its founder, has been the mother of a goodly family of churches. Apart from New England successes, from it Thomas Dungan came to Pennsylvania, who formed the first Baptist church in that State; and by him Elias Keach was encouraged to trust Christ when convicted of sin and baptized, and by his church he was ordained. Mr. Keach founded the Pennepek church, the oldest church now existing in Pennsylvania, of which the First church of Philadelphia was a branch, and also some of the oldest churches in New Jersey, the communities that organized the Philadelphia Association. What these churches have done for the States in which they are located, and through communities springing from them, as well as directly in several other States, only the students of Baptist history know. The church at Swanzey, Mass., was constituted by John Miles in 1663. When he and his Welsh brethren came to New England they brought their church records with them. Their American community was a church like the First Newport, with no dependence upon the First church of Providence. The Welsh Tract church, in Delaware, was formed in Wales in the spring of 1701. Thomas Griffith was the first pastor, and he emigrated with the church to Pennepek, Pa., and subsequently removed with it to Welsh Tract, Del., where the church prospered, and exerted an extensive influence in favor of truth and righteousness. These were the most noted of the mother-churches that came into existence in America *independently of each other*.

It should be remarked that the First church of Providence was not the mother of any of the churches named; that the First church of Newport had some connection with the Pennepek church through Thomas Dungan, but no similar relationship with any of the others, and that the Swanzey and Welsh Tract churches had a European existence before they came to America. A sketch of all the great mother-churches of America would be of unspeakable interest, but in this article we can only notice those already mentioned.

Mott, Judge Frederick, was born near Montrose, Susquehanna Co., Pa., Jan. 14, 1828. Longing for an education beyond that afforded by common schools or the neighboring academy, he entered Brown University, from which he graduated in 1851. He was principal of Derby Academy, Vt., for three years, reading law at the same time, and was admitted to the bar in Vermont. In 1854 he took charge of a union school in Upper Sandusky, O., where he remained two years, and then came to Iowa, located at Winterset, Madison Co., and immediately commenced the practice of law. In September, 1862, entered the army, and was made adjutant of the 39th Iowa Infantry in 1863, and was commissioned by President Lincoln as assistant adjutant-general in 1864, serving as such until the close of the war. Returning home in August, 1865, he resumed the practice of law. In 1868 he was elected judge of the fifth judicial district of Iowa, serving the full term of four years. In October, 1870, was elected president of the Iowa Baptist State Convention, and re-elected to that position at each of the three succeeding annual meetings. In 1873 he was appointed to the professorship of Pleading and Practice in the law department of the State University, which position he held for two years, and resigned to accept the presidency of the University of Des Moines. At the close of the centennial year, his health failing him, he resigned his position, and returned to his former home at Winterset, where he now resides, engaged in his profession. He was a Baptist from his youth up, and has always been a persistent worker in the church and Sabbath-school. While devoted to his own church and the general work of his own denomination, he is deeply interested in every good cause, and is regarded by the community in which he has so long lived as an earnest Christian worker and a public-spirited and invaluable citizen.

Mount Carroll Seminary, now exclusively for young ladies, is located at Mount Carroll, in Carroll Co., Ill. It was founded in 1853, by Miss F. A. Wood and Miss C. M. Gregory, graduates of the Normal School at Albany, N. Y. Beginning with 11 pupils, the school has grown to an average yearly attendance of nearly 200. In 1878 Miss Gregory's connection with the institution ceased, and it has since remained under the principalship of her associate, now Mrs. F. A. W. Sheiner, with whom Miss C. A. Jay is at present associated. The school, which opened in a small and inconvenient room, is now accommodated with extensive buildings, three separate additions having been made to that which the principals erected, in the early history of the seminary, upon the delightful and healthful site still occupied. The grounds are very extensive, consisting of twenty-five acres, and are laid out in orchards, gardens, vineyards, botanical garden, conservatory, with a great variety of shade and ornamental trees. The department of instruction consists of a preparatory, a regular four years', and a normal course. The seminary is incorporated by charter, with full college power to confer degrees.

It is proper to say that this institution has been founded and built up entirely by private enterprise. Superior executive ability has characterized its administration from the beginning. It has grown simply through the public appreciation of its merits, no agents having been at any time employed, either to solicit pupils or to raise funds. Apart from the five acres of ground on which the buildings stand, with the sum of $1000 given at the foundation of the school, no aid from either private or public funds has been received. It is gratifying to have this example of a school built up simply through the good management of those in charge, with the appreciative patronage of a discerning public.

Mount Lebanon Female College, Mount Lebanon, La.—Simultaneously with the movement to establish Mount Lebanon University the Mount Lebanon Female College was organized, and the accomplished wife of Rev. Hanson Lee became principal. At the beginning of the war there were over 100 young ladies in attendance. Mrs. Lee was succeeded by Rev. John Q. Prescott, and upon the suspension of the university Dr. Crane became principal. Finally the buildings were sold to the State for a laboratory, where medicines were manufactured, under the direction of Dr. Egan. About the close of the war an effort was made by Mr. Prescott to revive the school. The buildings were destroyed by fire in 1866, and no attempt has since been made to rebuild.

Mount Lebanon University, Mount Lebanon, La.—About 1847, Dr. B. Egan began to agitate the question of a school of high grade at Mount Lebanon. His efforts resulted in the organization of Mount Lebanon University, which was chartered in 1854. A donation of $10,000 was obtained from the State, and about $50,000 raised in subscriptions; a commodious college building and president's house were erected, a large boarding-hall provided, and an able faculty secured. Rev. Jesse Hartwell, D.D., accepted the presidency, and in a short time nearly 200 students were in attendance. Dr. Hartwell died in 1859, and Rev. W. C. Crane, D.D., LL.D., now president of Baylor University, Texas, was called to the presidency. But in the midst of its prosperity the war began, and the students and faculty were dispersed. Early in the war the endowment notes matured, and were paid in Confederate money, invested in Confederate bonds, and consequently lost. After the war an effort was made to revive the institution, but after a few years' struggle the enterprise was virtually abandoned. The academical department is still maintained, but with some irregularity. The revival of prosperity in the State has awakened a new interest in education, and the question of reviving the university is receiving serious attention.

Mount Pleasant College was founded in

Huntsville, Mo., in 1854. A. S. Worrell, D.D., is the president. He is an admirable teacher, and the institution is rapidly advancing. It is for both sexes; 138 were matriculated last year. The instruction includes all, between the lowest primary and a full college course.

The degrees of A.B. and A.M. are conferred, according to the scholarship of the candidates. The students are pledged to temperance and good conduct. This college is in Randolph County, in a fine portion of the State, and it is doing a needed and noble work.

church, Cleveland, O., where he still remains. In June, 1879, was graduated with the degree of A.B. from the University of Rochester. Has published sermons and reviews, and he is regarded as a young man of great energy and promise.

Muir, Rev. William, was born in Scotland in February, 1829. His parents were Presbyterians, and he received a careful religious training from them. For several years he devoted himself to agricultural pursuits. When he was seventeen years of age he was apprenticed to learn a trade, and continued at the same until 1860. When he

MOUNT PLEASANT COLLEGE.

Moxom, Rev. P. S., was born in Palermo, Canada, Aug. 10, 1848. Removed when a child to Ogle Co., Ill. In January, 1862, went out with the 78th Ill. Regiment, as page to Capt. Bewley. A few days after the battle of Fort Donelson, at the age of fifteen, he enlisted in the 17th Ill. Cavalry, and served until Nov. 28, 1865. Jan. 1, 1866, he entered Kalamazoo College, Mich., where he was converted and baptized into the fellowship of the Battle Creek church by his father, Rev. J. H. Moxom. In the autumn of 1868 he entered Shurtleff College, where he remained until 1870, when he returned to Michigan to teach. In 1871 engaged in the study of law, but in a little while abandoned that for the ministry. His first settlement was at Bellevue, Mich., where he received ordination. In October, 1872, became pastor of the church at Albion, Mich., and in 1875 removed to Rochester, N. Y., to pursue theological studies. During the period of his studies in Rochester was pastor of the church at Mount Morris. Was called, in November, 1879, to the pastorate of the First

grew up to manhood he connected himself with the Presbyterian Church, although, as he subsequently had reason to believe, he knew nothing of experimental religion. In 1852 he left his native country and came to Canada, taking up his residence near Toronto. Early in the year 1855 he met with a severe accident, which laid him aside from labor for two months. Having recovered measurably from its effects, he returned to his usual employment. Two days after recommencing work he was caught in the machinery, and came to all appearance within a hair's breadth of losing his life. These providences of God aroused his attention, in connection with the warm appeals of a personal friend, and he became a hopeful Christian. In a little more than a year he and his wife were baptized and joined the church at Cheltenham. Here he remained four years, when he was licensed to preach the gospel. At once he went to the Canadian Literary Institute to acquire an education, in which he spent three years, and then was ordained to the work of the gospel ministry. Having devoted seven years to the pastoral work, he became, in April, 1871, office editor and business manager of the *Canadian Baptist*, the recognized organ of the Baptist denomination in the provinces of Ontario, Quebec, and Manitoba. In 1874 he became managing editor, and virtually, proprietor, which position he still retains.

Mulcahy, Rev. Michael, was born in Fermoy, County of Cork, Ireland, in 1842. He received a good education in England, where he spent his youth; in 1867 he emigrated to Canada, was converted in 1869, and joined the Baptist church at Boston, where his natural eloquence and pleadings for Jesus led many to believe. He prepared for the ministry at Woodstock, preaching to destitute churches while pursuing his studies. He was successively pastor at Grand Blanc, Canada; Ovid, Mich.; South Bend, Ind.; and Little Rock, Ark., where he was also chaplain of the State senate. An attack of hemorrhage compelled him to seek health in California. Reaching San Francisco, Sept. 4, 1873, he was called to the vacant pulpit of the First church. His fervid eloquence drew large audiences to the church, and he was on the eve of an evident revival when a return of his old disease brought him to an early grave. He died Jan. 4, 1874.

Mulford, Rev. Clarence W., was born at Salem, N. J., June 8, 1805; was converted and baptized at nineteen; studied at Princeton for a time; was ordained pastor of the Baptist church at Pemberton, N. J., in November, 1830. He was five years there, and nearly ten at Hightstown. His pastorates at Flemington and Holmdel yielded much fruit. He was particularly blessed in leading souls to Christ. He frequently assisted neighboring pastors. His voice had unusual power to attract and impress. He was one of the early friends of the New Jersey State Convention, was for several years its secretary, and its president from 1843 to 1849. In the early days of the temperance reformation he stood almost alone, but he was a brave advocate in the face of opposition. Through failure of health he was obliged to give up preaching for the most part in the latter years of his life, but having studied medicine, he was very useful in that profession, at the same time ministering to the spiritual comfort of his patients. He died June 28, 1864, at Flemington, N. J.

Mulford, Hon. Horatio J., was born at Canton, N. J., Jan. 16, 1818. He was trained to business, and has been engaged for many years in the management of his own, and in taking part in public affairs. He was baptized at Bridgeton, and united with the First Baptist church in 1853. He was elected deacon in 1856, and still holds the office. He was for a long time superintendent of the Sunday-school. He is a member of the university board at Lewisburg, a trustee of the Crozer Theological Seminary, and a manager of the Baptist Publication Society. He is greatly interested in the education of the ministry; has been president of the

HON. HORATIO J. MULFORD.

New Jersey Baptist Education Society since 1857, and still holds that office. His earnestness, executive ability, and liberality have been particularly prominent in bringing the South Jersey Institute to its present prosperity. Mr. Mulford's sympathies go far beyond the societies with which he is officially connected. His help is relied upon by those who take the largest views of spreading the gospel.

Mundy, Rev. J. A., was born in Virginia about 1835; graduated at Richmond College in 1858, and was pastor of several important churches in Virginia before he removed to North Carolina, in 1875. He has been for more than four years pastor of the Warrenton church. Mr. Mundy is regarded as one of the finest preachers in the State.

Munro, Rev. Andrew Heber, was born in Surrey, England, in 1827, of Scotch parents. He was chiefly educated at home, but went for a time to a private institution in the south of London, and from thence to the Normal College of the British and Foreign School Society. After a short attendance at the college, he was sent out by the society as one of the teachers of a Model and Normal School established by the government of New Brunswick. He afterwards taught for a time in the Methodist College at Sackville, and subsequently became Latin and mathematical tutor in the Baptist Seminary at Fredericton, New Brunswick, where he also read theology with Dr. Spurden. While at the seminary he began preaching, the scene of his labors being the Welsh settlement of Cardigan, nineteen miles distant, and was instrumental in the conversion of a large number of persons. He was ordained at Digby, Nova Scotia, in 1857. In 1860 he took charge of the North Baptist church, Halifax, Nova Scotia, where he remained nearly seven years. From thence he went to the First church, Yarmouth, Nova Scotia, and after a short pastorate removed to Liverpool, in the same province. In 1869 he accepted a cordial invitation to Alexander Street church, Toronto, Ontario, where, during seven years, his ministry was highly appreciated by the church and community. He then entered upon his present charge, the pastorate of the First church, Montreal, and shortly after his settlement the church received into its fellowship nearly the entire membership of the St. Catharine Street church. During his ministry of twenty-four years he has been permitted to see several extensive revivals of religion.

As a public speaker, Mr. Munro is one of the most attractive and popular men in the Dominion of Canada. Both in the pulpit and on the platform he is at once powerful, graceful, and eloquent. He is one of the trustees of the Toronto Baptist College, and secretary of the Eastern Missionary Convention and of the Baptist Union of Canada.

Munro, Rev. James, was born in Scotland in 1784; converted in 1806 in Chester, Nova Scotia; baptized in New York in 1807; returned to Nova Scotia, and commenced preaching in Halifax; evangelized with Rev. Joseph Crandall, in 1815, to the east of Halifax; ordained in 1816, and evangelized on eastern shores of New Brunswick, and in 1818 up the St. John River; became pastor at Onslow in 1819, and continued in this relation until his death, July 3, 1838. Possessing a keen, logical mind, sterling integrity, fervent piety, and sound theology, Mr. Munro's ministry was highly useful.

Munster, The Uproar at.—See article on ANABAPTISTS.

Münzer, Thomas.—See article on ANABAPTISTS.

Murch, William Harris, D.D., was born at Honiton, England, May 17, 1784. He was entered as a student for the ministry at an Independent college when he was quite a lad. Here that most charming little book, Fuller's "Life of Samuel Pearce," fell into his hands, and led him to abandon the Arian belief, in which he had been brought up, and to embrace evangelical truth. In May, 1802, he was baptized by Dr. Rippon, at Carter Lane meeting-house, London, being then seventeen. He continued his studies for two years longer, and subsequently preached in several places without any stated charge. On John Foster's retirement from the pastorate of Sheppard's Barton church, Frome, Mr. Murch succeeded him, having previously supplied the pulpit for six months during Mr. Foster's affliction. He remained pastor, with many evidences of usefulness, for twenty-one years, when he was invited to the presidency of Stepney College, the Baptist theological seminary in the metropolis. He entered upon his work there in 1827. During his presidency the interests of the college were diligently advanced, and a large number of students prepared for the ministry. When he retired from this position, in 1844, after seventeen years' service, the tutors and students of the colleges at Bristol, Bradford, and Stepney combined to do honor to him for his worth and usefulness. The degree of D.D. was conferred upon him by Brown University during his presidential course. He presided over the church at Rickmansworth for a short time, and rendered occasional services to churches in and around London until compelled by illness to retire from public employments. He died at Bath, July 12, 1859, and was buried at Frome, the scene of his early labors. During his residence in London he identified himself with all the literary and religious institutions of the denomination. He was one of the secretaries of the Baptist Union from 1834 to 1846, secretary of the Baptist Board from 1837 to 1843, and gave his care and interest to the "New Selection Hymn-Book" for several years. His end was peculiarly peaceful and edifying. His mind was unclouded and serene to the last. He had made daily allusion to his approaching departure for several months, and expressed himself as ready and waiting. His last words, an hour before his death, were, "Precious Saviour! all is right; precious Saviour!"

Murdock, John Nelson, D.D., was born in Oswego, N. Y., Dec. 8, 1820, and received his early religious education among the Methodists. His devoted Christian mother named him after one of the co-laborers of John Wesley, and her earnest prayer was that he might become a minister of the gospel. He was fitted for college by teachers well qualified for their work, one of them, Master Hogan, having been educated at Oxford University. In consequence of his father's death he was obliged to give up the idea of taking a collegiate course. Having chosen the legal profession for his future vocation, he commenced his law studies, and while engaged in them carried on special courses of mathematics and languages, including French and German. Having completed his law studies, he was admitted to the bar. At the age of seventeen he became a hopeful Christian, and united with the Methodist Church in his native city. Not long after commencing the practice of his profession his religious life was greatly quickened, and the duty and privilege of serving his Master in the ministry of the Word was so impressed upon him that he was licensed to preach. While supplying the pulpit of a Methodist church in Jordan, N. Y., in 1841, his attention was drawn to the subject of baptism,

JOHN NELSON MURDOCK, D.D.

and as the result of his investigations he was baptized in 1842, at Durhamville, N. Y., by Rev. Seymour W. Adams, late of Cleveland, O. His ordination as a Baptist minister took place at Waterville, N. Y., in May, 1842, when he was but a few months beyond his majority. Here he remained until January, 1846, when he became pastor of the church in Albion, N. Y. In April, 1848, he entered upon his duties as pastor of the South church, in Hartford, from which place he was called to the pastorate of the Bowdoin Square church, Boston, his service there commencing Jan. 1, 1857, and continuing until Jan. 1, 1863, a period of just six years. In July of this year he was elected secretary of the Missionary Union, which position he now holds.

During a part of the time of Dr. Murdock's ministry in Hartford—i.e., 1853–56—he was joint editor with Rev. Dr. R. Turnbull of the *Christian Review*. The number of his published sermons is twenty-one. All of these were called for by the bodies before which they were delivered. The amount of literary work which he has done in his extensive and varied correspondence, and in the preparation of his valuable reports and special papers in his official relations to the Missionary Union, it is impossible to compute. Honored and beloved by the denomination which he has so long and so faithfully served, Dr. Murdock takes a high place in the front ranks of her most worthy and distinguished members. He received the honorary degree of Doctor of Divinity from Rochester University in 1854.

Murfee, James T., LL.D.—His paternal grandfather was the Rev. Simon Murfee, a prominent Baptist minister of the Portsmouth Association, Southampton Co., Va. His ancestors were a pious people, and they were Baptists. The subject of this sketch was born in Southampton Co., Va., Sept. 13, 1833. His early home surroundings were of the best character. He graduated from the Virginia Military Institute at Lexington in 1853, without a single demerit and with the highest honors of his class. Soon after graduating he was elected Professor of Mathematics and Natural Sciences in Madison College. Thence called to Lynchburg College, where he united with the Baptist Church in 1857; was called to the University of Alabama in 1860 as Professor of Mathematics, and became commandant of cadets in that institution. At the close of the war he was employed as architect to design and erect new buildings for the institution. He then recommended "a new scheme of university organization," which was adopted by the trustees, but was defeated by State reconstruction. He was called to the presidency of Howard College to put in operation a plan which promised results so long felt as most desirable. The work accomplished at Howard College since the introduction of the system of college administration originated by James T. Murfee bears testimony to the superiority of the method employed. This position he still holds to the universal satisfaction of the denomination.

Murphy, John R., D.D., was born Dec. 8, 1820, in Cape May Co., N. J. As he approached manhood he concluded to study law, but after his conversion felt constrained to devote his life to the ministry. He was baptized, in 1841, by Rev. J. H. Kennard, D.D., and united with the Tenth Baptist church, Philadelphia. He pursued his studies for a time at Branchtown, Pa., and at the old Germantown Academy. He graduated from Madison University in August, 1849, and was ordained in Philadelphia in 1849. From 1850 to 1852 he was pastor of the Greenwich Baptist church, Cumberland Co., N. J. From 1853 to 1859 he was pastor of the Marlton church, Burlington Co., N. J. From 1859 to 1872 he was pastor of the First Baptist church, Salem, N. J. During these years of labor in New Jersey he was closely identified with the Baptist enterprises in the State. During 1864 he spent some time at White House and City Point, Va., with the Union army, as a member of the Christian Commission. In 1872 he accepted a call to the pastorate of the First Baptist church, Des Moines, in which position he remained till September, 1879, sharing with his brethren in Iowa the responsibilities of the general work. At present he is residing near Winterset, Iowa, waiting for improved health to resume pastoral work. During his twenty-seven and a half years of ministerial labor he has received into the four churches he has served nearly 1000 members, over 600 of whom came by baptism.

Murphy, Rev. Joseph, like his brother William, was made a happy subject of redeeming grace in early life, and a preacher of the blessed gospel. He and his brother were sneeringly called "the Murphy boys," because of their youth. Joseph gave great diligence to his education after his conversion, that he might be fully qualified to preach the gospel. He had mental power, ready wit, and fearless courage, and he had a heart in which Christ reigned supreme. After preaching with much success in his native Virginia, he took charge of the church in Deep Creek, Surrey Co., N. C. In his new home he was eminently useful, and soon became the leading minister in the Yadkin Association. His influence also had weight in South Carolina. He was living in 1803, and had passed his eightieth year, an honored and happy Christian.

Murphy, Rev. William, was led to the Saviour and baptized by the celebrated Shubal Stearns. His talents were respectable, his faith vigorous, and his zeal burning. He was the chief instrument in leading Col. Samuel Harris to Jesus, and he was also favored in bringing a whole harvest of souls to the same blessed Redeemer. Mr. Murphy had not only a sound Christian experience, but his doctrines were those of Calvin, Augustine, and Paul. In the year 1775, when the churches were agitated by the Arminian controversy, Mr. Murphy, with great ability and success, defended sovereign and efficacious grace. He went to Kentucky for a permanent home, where he labored with the divine approval for a few years, and then was transferred to the church in glory.

Murphy, Hon. William D., was born in New York, June 4, 1796; died Aug. 26, 1877. A full record of the life of Mr. Murphy would present an illustration of the success and intellectual development that so often attend upon young men whose hearts are influenced by correct religious principles, and who are diligent in business. He had received an English education, but with a wonderful memory, great power of observation, and remarkable conversational abilities, he was enabled to make up for any deficiencies in his earlier opportunities. His life was one of continuous study as well as activity. He was greatly respected in his native city, and was often called to fill important trusts. As member of common council in 1841 and 1842, and of the board of education for several years, he manifested great interest in the schools, and conscientiously discharged his duties. In public discussions he displayed much ability, and was full of quiet wit and humor, and master of an audience.

He was hopefully converted in June, 1813, and joined the Mulberry Street church, New York. In 1828 he removed his membership to the Oliver Street church, of which he was made a trustee, and for many years took a deep interest in its welfare. As a lay preacher, he often delighted in bringing the consolations of the gospel before the destitute in the asylums of New York, and few men were more widely known or more warmly welcomed. He enjoyed a happy old age in the bosom of his family, where he was greatly beloved by an affectionate household. He published, as the result of the leisure of his later years, a volume entitled "The Advent, and other Poems and Hymns." He represented a New York district in the United States Congress for two years.

Murrow, Rev. Joseph Samuel, a missionary to the Choctaw Indians, in the Indian Territory, sent out and supported by the Rehoboth Baptist Association of Georgia, was born in Jefferson Co., Ga., June 7, 1835. He became a Christian at a very early age, and received academical instruction in youth. He joined Green Fork Baptist church, in Burke Co., Ga., at nineteen; was licensed at twenty. In 1855, at the age of twenty, he entered Mercer University, where he pursued his studies diligently until ordained and sent out as a missionary to the Indian Territory in the fall of 1857. In November of that year he began what has proved to be a long, laborious, and useful missionary life, in which much of hardship and suffering has been mingled with great success and joy.

He settled at North Fork town, and began his missionary work among the Creeks, among whom he labored most assiduously for two years. He then removed to Little River, Creek Nation, and began a work among the Seminoles. In 1861 he constituted the first Baptist church ever formed among that tribe. During the war the Seminoles selected him as their agent, in transactions with the government, to receive their food and supplies; and, as he was cut off from the Association which sustained him, he was thus supported; but he never forgot his character as a missionary, nor ceased to maintain it, while performing his official duties to the satisfaction of both the government and tribe. One of the first structures built always was a bush arbor for preaching services. For several years he and his wife lived thus with the Seminoles, during which period he baptized 200 of that nation, and may thus be considered the father of the mission work among the Seminoles. Three-fifths of the adults of that nation are now Baptists.

The war closed in 1865, and his duties as Indian agent came to an end. Being still cut off from his Association, he took refuge for a year in Texas,

53

but returned in 1866, settling at Atoka, Choctaw Nation, the first missionary to return to the Indian field after the war. He found the Choctaw mission in a very demoralized condition, and proceeded at once to reorganize the churches, in which he was very successful, constituting a large Association, and putting the Sunday-school work on a healthy basis. The Baptist Theological School, for training teachers and preachers, now being established at Tallequah, Cherokee Nation, by the Home Mission Society of the North, is the conception of his brain. He has now been a missionary among the Indians for twenty-four years, has preached thousands of sermons, traveled hundreds of thousands of miles, and baptized over a thousand Indians, yet there is no abatement in his desire to live and labor for the triumph of the gospel among the red men of the West.

Mursell, Rev. James, the eldest son of the Rev. J. P. Mursell, was born at Leicester, England, July 22, 1829. He received a liberal education, and after two or three years of secular employment, in connection with the great railway works of Sir Morton Peto, he determined to give himself to ministerial work, having previously been baptized and received into his father's church at Leicester. After a brief period of study and tutorial work at Aberdeen, he entered Bristol College, and at the conclusion of the college course he was invited to the pastorate of the church at Kettering, as successor to the Rev. William Robinson, who had recently removed to Cambridge. For seventeen years Mr. Mursell labored at Kettering, with a zeal, devotion, and power which attracted general interest and encouraged the highest expectations. Few men were more genial in manners, or had more attached friends. A new edifice was erected more worthy of the denominational celebrity of the town, and better adapted to the wants of the congregation. He removed from Kettering to Bradford in 1870, and after a brief pastorate there, settled at Newcastle-on-Tyne in 1872. In the fullness of successful labors and growing influence he died, May 28, 1875, in his forty-sixth year.

Mursell, Rev. James Philippo, was born at Lymington, England, in 1800. His father, Rev. William Mursell, labored for many years in that town and neighborhood as a Baptist pastor. Mr. James P. Mursell was educated at the famous Baptist school conducted by the Rev. James Hinton, of Oxford, and having given abundant evidence of ministerial gifts in village preaching, he was entered at Bristol College in 1822. His remarkable ability as a preacher procured him several overtures from pastorless churches before his course of study was completed, and in 1825 he commenced his stated ministry as pastor of the church at Wells, Somersetshire. In 1826, on the removal of Robert Hall from Leicester to Bristol, the attention of the church at Leicester was directed to Mr. Mursell, and in the following year he entered upon his ministry as Mr. Hall's successor in the pastorate. For nearly fifty years Mr. Mursell continued to minister to the same church, and he was the recognized leader of the denomination in the midland district. In conjunction with Mr. Edward Miall he took a conspicuous part in organizing the anti-state-church movement, in 1843. He occupied the chair of the Baptist Union in 1864, and presided over the first of the autumnal assemblies of that body. Throughout his long and honorable career Mr. Mursell rendered valuable service to the denominational interests, particularly in connection with the foreign missions, of which for many years he was one of the Committee of Management.

Muscatine, Iowa.—The Baptist church at this place is among the oldest churches of the State. It was constituted in 1841, and has always held a good position among the churches of Iowa. It has a substantial meeting-house, valued at $14,000, and 202 members.

Muse, Rev. Thomas, of Cuthbert, Ga., was born in Middlesex Co., Va., Jan. 6, 1810. His grandparents were natives of England. At seventeen years of age Mr. Muse began to engage in mercantile pursuits, which he continued for fourteen years. In 1832 he was baptized, and four years after removed to Georgia, settling in Blakely, Early Co. While still merchandising he gradually entered into the duties of a minister, led on by his zeal and the necessity for ministerial labor in his neighborhood. In consequence he was licensed May 7, 1837, and ordained in December, 1840, to take charge of a church organized in Blakely out of material resulting from his own personal labors, and which before he left its service numbered 200 members. Mr. Muse moved to Cuthbert to take charge of a church there, and also of one in Randolph County; and has continued to the present time a faithful, laborious, and successful minister and pastor. He has succeeded in winning souls to Christ far beyond what is granted to most pastors, for more than 4000 have been baptized by his own hands. He has been greatly beloved by his churches, and his pastorates have lasted from four to twenty years. He aided in establishing the Baptist Female College in Cuthbert, and became president of its board of trustees. For twenty years he has been moderator of the Bethel Association, and for forty years has been actively engaged in all its interests.

Musgrove, Rev. Thomas Jefferson, was born in Mason Co., Ky., Jan. 30, 1837. His parents removed to Clark Co., Mo., in 1840. The subject of this sketch finished his college course when twenty-four years of age. In May, 1861, he was ordained to the ministry. In 1867 he took charge of the public schools in Alexandria, Mo. Afterwards he established the Pleasant Hill Academy, where he taught for four years. Then he accepted the charge of the schools in Alexandria a second time. After laboring for two years in this capacity he established Alexandria College, of which he is the president. He is a Baptist, and a man of energy, character, and usefulness.

Music, Rev. Thomas R., was born Oct. 17, 1756; was converted at the age of seventeen. He spent his early life in North Carolina. He came to Missouri with his family in 1803. He lived in St. Louis County. In 1807 he organized the Fee Fee church, among the constituent members of which were Adam Martin and his wife Mary, Richard and Jane Sullens, Thos. R. Music and his wife Sarah. Elder Brown, from Kentucky, and John Clark, labored with Mr. Music, who died in 1842. Mr. Music preached in Missouri, where he was persecuted by Catholics, and needed a gun to guard him from Indians. He is buried in the church grounds at Fee Fee. The old people still cherish his memory.

Mynatt, Rev. Wm. C., was born in Knox Co., Tenn., Nov. 16, 1808, and was baptized by Rev. Samuel Love, in 1832; removed to Asheville, Ala., in 1833, and that year he began to preach, and was ordained in 1836, in Cherokee County, where, in connection with other counties, he spent his best days as a minister, living ten years of that time in De Kalb County; spent several years as missionary of the Domestic Mission Board, and was unquestionably the leading minister in that part of the State. In 1857 he removed to Calhoun County, where he still resides and labors for Christ; though seventy-two years old he is constantly active. He has baptized large numbers of converts, and has been a most trustworthy and gifted minister of the gospel. His son, Rev. J. B. Mynatt, and his brother, Rev. Gordon Mynatt, are also worthy Baptist ministers.

N.

Nash, Rev. C. H., was born at North Granville, Washington Co., N. Y., Dec. 6, 1835; and nine years from that time was born again; but for want of proper instruction and encouragement, was not baptized until 1850. He became impressed that it was his duty to preach the gospel, and in 1857 commenced a preparatory course at Troy Conference Academy, Poultney, Vt.; and two years later entered on the regular course at Madison University, Hamilton, N. Y. Completing his studies at Hamilton, he was called, in 1864, to the pastorate of the Baptist church at Westport, N. Y. Here he was ordained. He remained at Westport four years and a half, during which the church was considerably increased and strengthened. In 1869 he visited Glen's Falls, N. Y., and after supplying the pulpit of the Baptist church there for a few months, accepted the call of the church to the pastorate, and labored with much success for ten years and a half. In 1879 he resolved to enter some mission field in the great West. Finding a little discouraged, scattered church at Concordia, Kansas, he commenced labor there under the appointment of the Home Mission Society. During two years this church has doubled in membership, and has now a neat brick edifice nearly completed. With the advantage of this new church, centrally located, and with the Lord's blessing, there is a good work in prospect at Concordia.

Nash, John Anson, D.D., was born in Shelburn, Chenango Co., N. Y., July 11, 1815. In his sixteenth year he united with the Methodist Church, and soon after he embraced Baptist views. Feeling called to preach the gospel, he entered Madison University in 1836, and graduated from college in 1842, and from the seminary in 1844. Having accepted a call from the Baptist church at Watertown, N. Y., he immediately entered upon the duties of his pastorate, and was ordained in September, 1844. He remained at Watertown about six years. In 1850 he came to Iowa. He has preached to the Baptist churches in Des Moines about seventeen and a half years; has extended his labors far into the surrounding country, gathering and organizing nearly thirty Baptist churches. In 1865, on the starting of the University of Des Moines, by the advice of the movers in this enterprise, he resigned his pastorate and entered upon its work; first as financial agent, then as professor, and for several years he has been its president, which office he now holds. Much of this time, however, he has spent in supplying destitute churches in the surrounding region. In 1877 he received the degree of D.D. from the University of Chicago.

Nashville, First Colored Church of.—Rev. N. G. Merry became pastor of this community in 1853, when it was a branch of the First church of white Baptists. Since that time the organization has be-

FIRST COLORED BAPTIST CHURCH, NASHVILLE, TENN.

come independent, and it has been unusually prosperous. The church has grown from 100 to 2300 members, and it has built four times since 1853. Their present edifice cost $26,000, and it will seat 1300 persons. It is an honor to the colored Baptists of the State.

Nashville Institute is situated one mile from Nashville, Tenn., upon a property containing thirty acres, adjoining the Vanderbilt University grounds. The site is high, and commands an unsurpassed prospect of the city and surrounding country. The estate was bought in the spring of 1874 for the American Baptist Home Mission Society, at a cost of $30,000. At the time it had a mansion upon it, 48 by 80 feet, and two stories high. The Society spent about $45,000 in additional buildings, exclusive of the cost of furnishing. The Institute took possession of its home in October, 1876.

The mansion-house now has four stories, and furnishes apartments for the teachers and dormitories for the young women. Centennial Hall, 49 by 185 feet, and four stories in height, in its ample basement provides accommodations for the boarding department. The first story is devoted to public rooms, and the three stories above it furnish dormitories for about 140 young men. For this building the Institute is chiefly indebted to Mr. and Mrs. Nathan Bishop, of New York.

The institute has a "Normal," an "Academic," a "Scientific," a "Classical," and a "Theological" course. It prepares young men and women for teaching, and it educates students for the Christian ministry. For 1880-81 the institute had 8 instructors and 249 students of both sexes. Nashville Institute has been and is now a rich blessing to the colored Baptists of this country.

Natchez Seminary.—This institution is devoted to the instruction of freedmen. It is located at Natchez, Miss., and is doing a noble work. The spring term of 1880 closed with 117 matriculates, of whom 31 were preparing for the ministry, and 46 design to become teachers. The institution has the hearty sympathy of the Baptists of Mississippi, and is destined to become an important factor in the elevation of the colored race.

National Monitor, The, Brooklyn, N. Y., was established in 1870 by Rev. Rufus L. Perry as the official organ of the colored Baptists of the United States. The condition of the colored people made it necessary for this paper to be of a politico-religious character, which it still maintains. It circulates among the prominent colored people North and South, and is read in Canada, Hayti, and Africa. It is now one of the leading and most influential papers among the colored people. Rev. Rufus L. Perry is still editor.

NASHVILLE INSTITUTE.

Neale, Rollin Heber, D.D., was born in Southington, Conn. He prepared for college in his native town, and graduated at Columbian College, Washington, D. C., in the class of 1830. While a student

ROLLIN HEBER NEALE, D.D.

in college he was ordained as pastor of the Second Baptist church in Washington, and preached there the last two years of his course. While pursuing his studies at the Newton Theological Institution he was the pastor of the South Boston Baptist church. He graduated at Newton in 1833. From the spring of 1834 to September, 1837, he was the pastor of the First Baptist church in Needham, Mass., from which place he was called to the pastorate of the First Baptist church in Boston, Sept. 17, 1837, and continued in that relation until June, 1877, a period of nearly forty years. Few pastorates in Baptist churches have been so long, and few have been more harmonious. The labors of Dr. Neale, extending on through all these years, have been greatly blessed, his church, under the ministrations of their pastor, having been favored with many precious revivals of religion.

The degree of Doctor of Divinity was conferred upon Dr. Neale by Brown University in 1850, and by Harvard College in 1857. He has published a few sermons, a Harvard College Dudleian lecture, a little volume called the "Burning Bush," and he has written much for the public press. Many of the addresses which he made (and in the making of which he had a most happy gift) on funeral occasions of dear friends have found their way into print. They were the outgushings of a warm, sympathizing heart, and were exceedingly appropriate to the occasions upon which they were uttered.

Dr. Neale visited Europe four times, one of which was in company with Rev. Dr. Kirk, the late eloquent pastor of the Mount Vernon Congregational church, who was his companion while traveling in the Holy Land.

For many years he was a "visitor" and an overseer of Harvard University. He always took an interest in public affairs, and from the pulpit expressed his views upon the great moral questions of the day. He was known to be a minister of a kind and catholic spirit, and while he held a very warm place in the hearts of his own brethren in the ministry, he had the respect and affection of the clerical profession of all denominations in Boston and its vicinity. He entered upon his eternal reward in 1879, from the city where he lived for so many years.

Nebraska.—Nebraska occupies a position near the centre of the republic. Bounded north by Dakota, east by the Missouri River, south by Kansas, and west by Wyoming. It was originally a part of the Louisiana purchase. It was organized as a Territory May 30, 1854, by the Kansas and Nebraska Act. It was admitted into the Union as a sovereign State in March, 1867. The extreme length of the State from east to west is within a fraction of 413 miles, and its extreme width from north to south is 208 miles. In area the State contains nearly 75,995 square miles, or about 48,636,800 acres. The area of Nebraska is 12,359 square miles larger than all the New England States combined.

Emigration into the Territory began in 1849. The first settlements were confined to the neighborhood of the Missouri River and a narrow strip on one side of the Platte. Here were, therefore, laid the foundations of the future churches in Nebraska. For religious enterprises the circumstances were unfavorable. The population was unstable. Some came to speculate in land, whose stay was transient. But others came to remain. These were poor and scattered, but unity in religious beliefs brought these settlers together, at convenient centres, for the service of God and for mutual edification.

THE BAPTIST ASSOCIATION.

The few Baptists who had come to the Territory to remain formed themselves into churches at various points. On the 28th and 29th of May, 1858, at Nebraska City, the Nebraska Baptist Association was organized by seven churches, which had been previously formed. These were, in the order in which they were constituted, Nebraska City, Peru, Plattsmouth, Fontenelle, Cumming City, Rock Bluff, and Florence.

The First Nebraska City church was recognized Aug. 18, 1855.

At the organization of the Nebraska Association the names of only two ordained ministers appear on the minutes,—Rev. J. M. Taggart and Rev. J. G. Bowen, missionaries of the American Baptist Home Mission Society. If the members were few in number, the records of the first meeting show that they were men of large ideas, strong faith, and a clear insight into the future greatness of the Territory. At this meeting vital questions were discussed,—education, Baptist literature, benevolence, temperance. Among the resolutions passed we find the following, so full of wisdom:

"*Resolved*, That we recommend to the churches of this Association, when practicable, to erect their meeting-houses within the limits of incorporate towns, and that measures be taken at an early day to secure eligible sites for building purposes."

The first effort at church-building by the Baptists in Nebraska was at Omaha in 1860. For years the growth of the churches was slow; the faith of the early laborers was severely tested.

At the fifth annual meeting of the Association there was an increase of one church and of 84 members. In 1867 four churches were dismissed with prayers, and the Omaha Association was formed. Since then God has greatly blessed our struggling brethren in Nebraska.

STATE CONVENTION.

The Nebraska Baptist State Convention was organized in 1868 to take the place of the Domestic Mission Board, which had been organized under a resolution adopted by the original Association Sept. 10, 1864.

The resolution reads as follows: "*Resolved*, That a missionary board of five members be appointed at each annual meeting of this Association, whose duty it shall be to ascertain the destitution of Baptist preaching as far as possible, and by corresponding with the American Baptist Home Mission Society, and appealing to the churches composing this Association, to make arrangements for its supply; and that we recommend to the churches the penny-a-week system for the purpose of carrying out this resolution."

Article 2d of its constitution states the object of the State Convention: "The object of this body shall be to unite the Baptist churches of the State in the dissemination of the principles of the gospel as understood by them into all parts of the State, and especially, in the prosecution of domestic mission work, to co-operate with the Baptist Home Mission Society." In the revised constitution of 1879 the object is substantially the same.

At the annual meeting in 1872 the following resolution was carried:

"*Resolved*, That for the purpose of carrying out more fully the objects of the Nebraska Baptist State Convention we hereby incorporate ourselves in accordance with the laws of the State, so that we may acquire and hold property with which to educate and sustain ministers, build or aid in building church edifices, make provision for superannuated pastors or preachers, and sustain all other institutions by which the churches may be united in the dissemination of the principles of the gospel as understood by them in all parts of the world."

The aim of the Convention has been hitherto to assist and co-operate with the Baptist Home Mission Society. At each of its annual sessions questions of vital importance to the home field have been discussed. At no meeting has the work abroad been forgotten.

At a meeting of the board held in October, 1877, it was resolved to hold a historical meeting in June, 1878, at Nebraska City. The object of the meeting was to bring the Baptists together and to review the past. An interesting programme was prepared. Eminent men from abroad lent their aid. Rev. J. M. Taggart, the only remaining pioneer missionary, read a historical paper of much interest, in which he reviewed the growth and development of the denomination for twenty years. The meeting resulted in imparting new zeal to the brethren and new life to the State Convention. At the annual meeting in 1879, Rev. H. L. Morehouse, corresponding secretary of the American Baptist Home Mission Society, submitted to the board of the State Convention a plan for practical co-operation with that society, which was adopted. The third and fourth specifications are as follows:

"The Home Mission Society shall appropriate to the mission work in Nebraska a definite sum *pro rata* to receipts from the State for the fiscal year of the Convention ending Nov. 1, 1880, four dollars additional to each dollar received from the State; the apportions to be made, so far as possible, at the beginning of the year, upon a reasonable estimate of probable receipts, and to be corrected by actual experience.

"The Convention shall superintend the work in the State, determine fields, nominate missionaries, name their salaries, and determine the time of labor; the Home Mission Society to appoint and pay those nominated so far as they approve such nominations and terms."

The existence and growth of the Baptist churches in Nebraska are due largely to the American Baptist Home Mission Society. There is scarcely a church in the State which it has not aided. The number of self-supporting churches as yet is small. The majority of the pastors in active service are sustained in part by this society. The need for enlarged liberality in this field is very great.

EDUCATION.

Recognizing the need and value of an educated ministry, the question of higher education received attention in the early history of this Territory. We find the following in the minutes of the State Convention for 1870:

"Your Executive Board, to which was referred, by a resolution passed at the last annual session, the subject of a denominational educational institution for the State, respectfully report that the duty charged upon them has been fulfilled, as will be seen by referring to the proceedings of the board meeting published in last year's minutes. So far as the members of the Executive Board have knowledge, no definite propositions for the location of a Baptist college have as yet been received which were of such a character as to warrant your committee in recommending a location, as was contemplated in that resolution.

"Your committee would further add that the subject of the founding of a Baptist college in Nebraska, while it is one of the greatest importance to our interests, is one which should demand and receive the most careful deliberation at our hands. We are warned on every hand by the experience of our brethren in other States, as well as by that of other denominations in our own State, that the attempt to build up at too early a day in the history of a State such an institution as is contemplated in your resolution of last year is not only full of difficulty, but of real danger to the interests it is designed to support. It imposes a pecuniary burden not easily borne even in wealthy communities and with favorable surroundings,—a burden which, in our estimation, it would be unwise for us at present to assume.

"Your committee are of opinion that the following are essential to success in a denominational college enterprise in Nebraska:

"1st. That it be located in the midst of earnest and able friends.

"2d. That it have sufficient local subscriptions to erect suitable buildings in which to open the school, and a fair sum towards an endowment.

"3d. Denominational unity in the State in reference to its support as a part of the list of agencies for carrying on the work of this Convention.

"We therefore recommend that further action in this matter be dispensed with until God by his providence shall show us that we are in possession of the conditions which will insure success; and that in the mean time the brethren residing in localities where circumstances are favorable aim at the establishment of local seminaries and academies mainly self-supporting, which may in the future, when our wants and our ability warrant it, become the nuclei of such an institution as shall reflect credit upon our denomination and our State."

This question was considered each subsequent year until the meeting of the Executive Board of the State Convention held in Hastings in May, 1880, when Mr. Eddy, a Baptist of Gibbon, was present to invite the attention of the Educational Committee to an opportunity offered at that place. After correspondence on the subject, the chairman of the committee visited Gibbon, and learned that there was a prospect of obtaining a good donation if we would locate our Baptist school there. A report was made at the meeting of the Executive Board in Blair, Aug. 4, 1880, and the following resolution was passed:

"*Resolved*, That we locate our Baptist school at Gibbon, provided the citizens of Gibbon and vicinity will donate a certain brick building, three stories high, 40 by 60 feet, together with five acres of land, and $1000 for repairs and alterations; also $1000 per year for three years as tuition for pupils of the district above the primary department."

A request was made by the Executive Board that the Educational Committee proceed at once to secure the property and open a school as soon as possible.

A special meeting of the Executive Board was called to meet at Lincoln, Aug. 16, at which resolutions were passed appointing the Rev. G. W. Read as principal of the school, and giving it the name of Nebraska Baptist Seminary. The appointment was accepted, and a meeting arranged between the Educational Committee and the citizens of Gibbon for Aug. 23. At this meeting the citizens agreed to comply with the conditions expressed in the resolution.

Papers were drawn and the building transferred to the Nebraska Baptist State Convention. The money promised for repairs was paid, and the building is now undergoing repairs. School will be commenced about Nov. 1, 1880. The property is valued at $15,000.

Statistical Report of Associations.

Associations.	Number of Churches.	Number of Members.
First Nebraska	13	690
Omaha	15	693
Nemaha Valley	16	575
Blue River	11	458
York	21	607
Republican Valley	15	306
Grand Island	17	672
Loup and Elkhorn Valley	11	201
Scandinavian	9	428
German	3	145
Unassociated	7	80
Associations, 10.	138	4855

The following ministers have done noble work in other States, and are at present in active service in Nebraska: Rev. O. A. Buzzell, Juniata; Rev. W. S. Gee, Lincoln; Rev. J. Gunderman, Central City; Rev. N. P. Hotchkiss, Pawnee City; Rev.

J. Lewelling, Weston; Rev. S. B. Mayo, Beaver City; Rev. J. W. Osborn, Fremont; Rev. Amos Pratt, Exeter; Prof. C. C. Bush, St. Edward's; Rev. I. R. Shanafelt, Macon; Rev. G. W. Taylor, Blair; Rev. E. D. Thomas, Liberty; Rev. T. K. Tyson, Wahoo; Rev. A. Weaver, Loup City; Rev. F. M. Williams, Ashland.

Nelson, Rev. Ebenezer, was born in Middleborough, Mass., Nov. 9, 1787, and received his early education in Taunton and South Reading, and entered upon mercantile pursuits in Providence, R. I. At the age of twenty-nine years he made a public profession of his faith, and was baptized by Rev. Dr. Gano. Soon after he commenced to study for the ministry, being for a part of the time a pupil of Rev. Dr. Chaplin, afterwards president of Waterville College. He was ordained as pastor of the Baptist church in Lynn, Mass., July 26, 1820, where he remained seven years. His health failing, he resigned his pastorate, and was employed for a year in raising funds for the endowment of the Newton Theological Institution. His term of service being completed, he accepted a call to become the pastor of the West Cambridge church, and was installed Sept. 9, 1828. He remained here six years, and was then appointed the secretary of the Northern Baptist Education Society, holding this position for two years and a half, during which time he rendered most efficient service in the cause of ministerial education. A vacancy having occurred in the Central Baptist church in Middleborough, Mass., he accepted a call to that church, and for fourteen years was their pastor, his labors being greatly blessed in the conversion of sinners and the building up of the church. He took also a deep interest in promoting the prosperity of Pierce Academy, an institution which accomplished so much good in the mental and moral training of scores of both sexes. His health failing again, he resigned his ministry. He continued to perform such service as he could for the cause he so much loved, but gradually he wasted away under the disease which finally proved fatal. He died at Lynn, whither he had removed from Middleborough, April 6, 1852.

Few ministers in Massachusetts labored more faithfully or accomplished more good than Ebenezer Nelson. His name and memory are greatly revered to this day in the places where he labored as an ambassador of the Lord Jesus Christ.

Nelson, Rev. James, was born in Mississippi in 1841; was educated at Center College, Danville, Ky. His great work was in connection with the board of ministerial education of Mississippi College. His field was Mississippi, Arkansas, and Louisiana, where his name will long be affectionately remembered. Through his instrumentality a large number of young ministers were stimulated to strive for higher education, and provided with the means to meet their expenses. Some of these have proved to be the most efficient ministers in the Southwest. He died at Clinton, Miss., Jan. 21, 1876. In connection with his educational work he performed a vast amount of evangelical labor.

Nelson, Rev. James, was born in Louisa Co., Va., Aug. 23, 1841; was converted at the age of fourteen, and joined the Elk Creek church. He was educated at Richmond and the Columbian College, graduating at the latter in 1866, with the degree of A.M.; was licensed in 1859, and ordained in 1863. While a chaplain in the Confederate army the great revival which occurred among the troops of Northern Virginia had its origin in his labors in connection with those of the Rev. Mr. Marshall, of Georgia. Immediately after his graduation Mr. Nelson became pastor of the Baptist church in Georgetown, D. C. In 1871 he resigned his charge there, and became the evangelist and Sunday-school missionary for Maryland and the District of Columbia, and during the four years of his services in this capacity hundreds were converted and baptized, and a number of new churches formed. He is at present the useful pastor of the Farmville Baptist church, Va. He is a forcible writer, and occasionally contributes to the religious papers of the denomination.

Nelson, Rev. Stephen S., was born in Middleborough, Mass., Oct. 5, 1772, and became a member of the celebrated Rev. Isaac Backus's church when he was sixteen years of age. He graduated at Brown University in 1794 with the first honors of his class. He pursued his theological studies with Rev. Dr. Stillman, and was licensed to preach in the twenty-fourth year of his age. He was ordained by a council selected from the Warren Association. His first pastorate was in Hartford, Conn., where his labors were greatly blessed. In a memorable revival which occurred in Hartford in 1798 more than 100 were baptized into the fellowship of the Baptist church. While in Connecticut, Mr. Nelson proved himself the warm friend of religious liberty, and took an active part in urging the Baptist petition or remonstrance, addressed to the Legislature of Connecticut, against the unjust law which compelled Baptists and others to contribute to the support of the "standing order." The restrictions were finally removed by the new constitution, which went into force in 1818.

Mr. Nelson received and accepted, in 1801, a call to become pastor of the church in Mount Pleasant, N. Y., and to take charge of a literary institution in that place. In this new relation he met with deserved success. His subsequent pastorates were in Attleborough and Plymouth, Mass., and in Canton, Conn. Having resigned the pastorate of the church in this latter place, he removed to Amherst, Mass., for the purpose of giving his sons an opportunity to take a course of study in Amherst College. Declining again to become a pastor, he preached whenever opportunity presented in the neighboring villages. His closing days were days of peace and religious enjoyment. He died Dec. 8, 1853, at the ripe age of eighty-one years.

Nelson, Rev. W. A., D.D., was born in Jefferson Co., Tenn., July 1, 1837; baptized by M. Cate; graduated at Carson College, Tenn., in 1859; ordained in 1860; was missionary during the war; did good work as a pastor at Shelbyville, Tenn., and was very successful at Edgefield, Nashville, where, under his pastorate, the church increased from 31 to 350, and built a fine house and parsonage; came to North Carolina in search of health in 1879; became president of Judson College, and has gone into the pastorate again at Shelby; a very successful man. He received D.D. from his *alma mater*.

Nevada, one of the States of the American Union, lying east of California, noted for its immense silver and gold mines, yielding many millions every year. Several Baptist churches have been organized. Only two remain, and give promise of permanence and growth,—one at Virginia City, formed in 1873, with eighteen members, and one at Reno, organized about 1875. Both are making good progress. There are only two Baptist ministers in the State engaged in the ministry,—Rev. H. W. Read, of Virginia City, and Rev. Dr. D. B. McKenzie, at Reno. Both churches have good meeting-houses. There are many Baptists in the towns and mining-camps of Nevada, but they are members of churches elsewhere. This great State is ripe for cultivation by faithful Baptist missionaries.

New Birth, The.—Nicodemus, a cultured Israelite, a sincere inquirer after truth, a loved, honored, and blameless citizen, at the time when he came to Jesus first, knew nothing of the second birth, and was destitute of all title to heaven. And the same thing is true of many of the enlightened and worthy of our age. Without this birth there can be no love for Jesus, and no taste for the gratifications of heaven.

God is the author of the second birth: "As many as received him, to them gave he power to become the sons of God, even to them that believe on his name, who were born, not of blood, nor of the will of the flesh, nor of the will of man, but of God."—John i. 12, 13. In these words it is emphatically denied that regeneration springs from any fleshly or human agency, and it is ascribed wholly to God. Again, it is said, "The wind bloweth where it listeth, and thou hearest the sound thereof, but canst not tell whence it cometh, and whither it goeth: so is every one that is born of the Spirit."—John iii. 8. The Spirit is the regenerator of every believer. The Lord says, in Ezekiel xxxvi. 26, "A new heart also will I give you, and a new spirit will I put within you: and I will take away the stony heart out of your flesh, and I will give you a heart of flesh." The new heart, the new birth, is the work of God's Spirit altogether.

The new birth requires no lengthened preparation; the Spirit, with his instrument, the truth, can complete it in a second in the worst specimen of humanity. When the Spirit enters the heart the second birth is the work of a moment, no matter how long penitential sorrow, unrelieved by justifying faith, may continue.

The new birth is not Christian baptism, in which it has been said that a person is "made a member of Christ, the child of God, and an inheritor of the kingdom of heaven;" not a single one of these blessings was ever conferred by that solemn rite. It is a change of affections; the regards of the soul are lifted by the Spirit of God from ourselves, the world, and sinful objects, and they are made to hunger for the Saviour. This produces an extensive alteration in the internal and external condition of the man. He does not delight in what he once loved. His chief pleasure is the favor of Christ, for which, or for the fuller enjoyment of which, his soul is constantly craving. "He is a new creature: old things are passed away; behold, all things are become new." His mind is enlightened, his will is corrected, his sins are loathed and forsaken, and his affections are turned Christward.

The regenerated man when he is first born again feels repentance for sin in his heart; this accompanies the new birth invariably. He always feels a desire to trust in Jesus when he is born again, and he never rests till he has committed his soul to Christ.

The regenerate man loses his old hopes and their foundation as soon as he is born again. His expectations of divine favor were once built upon his good qualities, blameless acts, or commendable intentions. The regenerating grace of the heavenly Spirit sweeps away all his imaginary merits and false hopes, and for a foundation he sees only the crucified Saviour full of gospel hopes.

The new birth removes old treasures and bestows new riches. The wealth of unbelieving days no longer has power to fascinate the soul, and Calvary becomes the pearl of great price for which the regenerated person counts all things but loss.

And the new birth dethrones old despots in the soul,—the world, sinful habits, covetousness, and superstition,—and it never rests until Christ is Master of mind, heart, and life.

A new heart is demanded by the sinner's reproaching conscience, and by the God of infinite goodness. "Heaven is a prepared place for a prepared people," without a taste for the enjoyments of paradise a man cannot be happy in it. An unregenerate man could not gather satisfaction from the religious pleasures of the celestial home; and if he were to enter it he would be rendered still more miserable by its holy conversation and occupations. For him there is no rest in any world without a new heart. Besides, a holy law must hurl its anathemas forever at the man who cherishes sin in his heart. And as his "carnal mind is enmity against God," he would feel himself at war with God in any quarter of his wide dominions, and in any section of everlasting duration. The Saviour utters the doctrine of the glorified in heaven, of all holy angels, of the entire earthly believing family, of the Holy Word, and of the adorable Trinity, when he says, "Marvel not that I said unto thee, Ye must be born again."—John iii. 7.

New Brunswick Baptists.—See article on NOVA SCOTIA BAPTISTS.

Newell, Rev. I. D., was born in Rushville, Schuyler Co., Ill., July 2, 1837; baptized in Upper Alton in 1849; ordained in Moline, Oct. 13, 1871. He is the son of Rev. I. D. Newell. Mr. Newell spent nearly four years in the Union army during the war, being the first to enlist in Bunker Hill, under the President's first call. He served two years in the ranks, during which time he participated in the battles of Fort Henry, Fort Donelson, Pittsburg Landing, and the siege of Corinth, bearing the colors of the regiment in the last-named conflict. At the end of two years' service he was transferred to Ellet's fleet, on the Mississippi River, and promoted to a first lieutenancy, and one month later to a captaincy, both commissions coming from President Lincoln. At the close of the war he entered Shurtleff College. He completed his theological course at Crozer Seminary, graduating in 1871. He was pastor of the Baptist church of Moline, Ill., for one year. Failing in health, he removed to Nebraska, and preached three years in Clay and Adams Counties. At present he gives but a part of his time to the ministry, being county superintendent of public schools in Clay County.

Newfoundland Baptists.—See article on NOVA SCOTIA BAPTISTS.

New Hampshire Baptists.—Hanserd Knollys founded the First church in Dover, N. H., in 1638. A little later he preached Baptist doctrines; and in 1641 he was recognized by the people of Dover as a decided exponent of our principles; the result was two religious communities. After his return to England, the Baptists, it is said, fled to Long Island to avoid persecution, and for the same reason, in 1644, they removed to the neighborhood of the present New Brunswick, N. J., and called their new home Piscataway, after the original name of Dover. It is not certain that these Baptists were regularly organized into a Baptist church in Dover.

The first church of our faith in New Hampshire, of whose regular formation there are no doubts, was founded at Newton in 1755. In 1770 it is supposed that there were but three Baptist churches in New Hampshire,—Newton, Madbury, and Weare.

In 1770, Rev. Dr. Hezekiah Smith, an able and devoted minister, settled in Massachusetts, preached extensively in New Hampshire, and great blessings attended his ministrations. He baptized the Rev. Eliphalet Smith, a Congregational clergyman, and thirteen others, who the same day were formed into a Baptist church at Deerfield. Two days after Mr. Smith baptized seven persons, among whom was Dr. Samuel Shepard, who became one of the most active and useful ministers that ever labored in New Hampshire. He was afterwards, till death, the pastor of a church gathered in Brentwood, in 1771, with branches at one time in more than twelve different towns, and a membership of nearly 1000. During this year churches were formed in Richmond, Hinsdale, and Chesterfield. In 1780, Dr. Shepard baptized 44 persons at Meredith, and constituted them into a church. Drs. Hezekiah Smith and Samuel Shepard were apostles in New Hampshire, whose labors enjoyed a remarkable measure of the divine favor. There were other early preachers and churches in New Hampshire worthy of our denominational name; and upon them and their brethren the Spirit of God fell, and converts were gathered and churches formed in all directions, until to-day we have 7 Associations, 86 churches, ministers, settled and without charge, 103. The number of members is 9210. In the department of Sunday-schools we find that there are 72 schools, with 814 teachers and 9319 scholars.

In education the Baptists of New Hampshire have taken an active interest. In 1826 they founded the "New Hampton Literary and Theological Institution," at New Hampton. Dr. B. F. Farnsworth was its first principal and Professor of Theology. Dr. E. B. Smith succeeded him in 1833, and retained his position until 1861. In 1838, Dr. J. Newton Brown was made Associate Professor of Theology, and discharged the duties of the office until 1845, when Dr. James Upham was appointed to the professorship. At the death of Dr. Smith, Dr. Upham became president of the institution, and retained the position until 1866. Owing to inadequate financial support the seminary was removed to Fairfax, Vt., in 1853. This institution gave instruction in the higher branches of a general education, and prepared young men for the ministry; and it had in connection with it an academy of a high order for young women. In its two locations it had about 200 theological students, most of whom became very useful in the pastorate and in other departments of Christian work. Few seminaries with its means have rendered such important service.

After the removal of the New Hampton Institution to Vermont in 1853, the Baptists of New Hampshire took immediate steps to establish an academy at New London, which was opened in 1853; it now bears the name of Colby Academy. (See article on COLBY ACADEMY.) The report of the benevolent operations for the year covered by the statistics here given is, for the Missionary Union $1848.11; for the Woman's Foreign Mission Society, $1074.06; home missions, $863.26; for the Convention, $2581.19; for home objects, $82,114.04. The total for all purposes, $92,254.03.

The State Convention was founded in 1826. It has accomplished great results in New Hampshire, and its affairs have been managed with much ability. In 1880 it aided seventeen churches and two missions, which have become churches. Its officers were Rev. W. V. Garner, President; Rev. W. Hurlin, Secretary; A. J. Prescott, Treasurer. While in New Hampshire very many of the churches suffer constant diminution by emigration, a review of the last half-century presents many facts, showing how the denomination has grown in that State. Fifty years ago there were in New Hampshire seventy churches and forty-one ministers. The greater part of these churches were poor, and pastors that were settled received but a scanty support. Moreover, there was more or less direct oppression which Baptists were compelled to endure from the "standing order." They were the "sect everywhere spoken against." But a most happy change has taken place in all these respects. The statistics given above will show the present situation of the denomination. Baptists have places of worship which will compare favorably with those of any other denomination. They are firmly planted in all the prominent cities and villages of the State. In the valley of the Merrimack they were but little known fifty years ago; "Now the churches which occupy that valley," says Dr. E. E. Cummings, in his "Ministry of Fifty Years," "are the pride and strength of the denomination throughout the State." There is every reason to expect that continued prosperity will attend the churches in the future as it has in the past, and that the sentiments and practices of the Baptists will continue to have strong hold on the intelligent convictions of no small part of the community.

New Jersey, The Baptists of.—A goodly number of those who came to the early settlements in the New England colonies held our views of Bible doctrine. They found on their arrival that freedom of conscience was only for Puritans. Persecutions led them to desire a better country, and they warned their friends in Europe to steer for another destination. When Lord Berkeley and Sir George Carteret obtained possession of "Nova Cesarea," or New Jersey, about 1664, they formed a "Bill of Rights," by which "liberty of conscience to all religious sects who shall behave well" was guaranteed. Speedy immigration followed. The Baptists of New Jersey, except a church or two in the northern hill-country, which sprang out of the religious reconstruction following the revivals under Edwards and the men of his time, came from the old country seed. While there may have been isolated Baptist settlers elsewhere, the first companies of baptized believers located at Middletown, near the entrance of New York harbor, at the territory on the lower Delaware, and at "Piscataqua," on the Raritan River.

The churches at Middletown, "Piscataqua," "Cohansick," and Cape May are called original because they are the mothers of the other organizations.

MIDDLETOWN,

in order of time, stands first. The date assigned it is 1688, but there are good reasons for believing that it originated earlier. In 1648 one Richard Stout and five others appear to have settled in Middletown. The Indian title was purchased previous to the patent from "Nicolles," about 1667. This title is said to have been made to thirty-six men, of whom eighteen were Baptists. They seem to have come from the west end of Long Island, and there is a strong probability that some of them were connected with the people who were dealt with in Massachusetts for Baptist sentiments about 1642, and took refuge at Gravesend, Long Island. Tradition states that they consorted for mutual edification, but there is no church record previous to 1688, when they "settled themselves into a church state," after consultation with the brethren at "Pennepek," Pa., who had just taken that course. There were several gifted brethren among them, of whom John Brown, James Ashton, and George Eaglesfield are mentioned.

Thomas Killingsworth was at the constitution of the church, but there is no evidence that he became its pastor. Obadiah Holmes, who was whipped at Boston, Mass., for his Baptist sentiments, was one of the patentees of Monmouth County, but it is not known that he ever resided here, though his son Jonathan did, and in 1668 was a member of Assembly.

Very little is known of the church during the first generation of its existence, except that an unhappy division occurred, which resulted (in 1711) in each party excommunicating the other, and the silencing of two of their gifted preachers,—John Bray and John Okison. They agreed to call a council of neighboring churches, which met May 25, 1711. The ministers who convened were Messrs. Timothy Brooks, of Cohansey; Abel Morgan and Joseph Wood, of Pennepek; Elisha Thomas, of Welsh Tract, and six elders. The office of elder, in distinction from pastor, is referred to frequently as existing among the old churches in the State. It may be interesting to read the finding of this first council probably in New Jersey, convened in a case of church difficulty. Advice was given (1) "to bury their proceedings in oblivion and erase the record of them." This was done, and four leaves are torn out of the church book. (2) "To continue the silence imposed on the two brethren the preceding year." (3) "To sign a covenant relative to their future conduct." Forty-two signed this, and twenty-six did not, though many of them came in afterwards. The first forty-two were declared to be the church to be owned by sister churches. Another direction of the council was, "That the members should keep their places and not wander to other societies." Peace and prosperity followed, and the gospel soon spread over a wide territory.

PISCATAWAY.

A large tract on the east side of the "Rarinton" was bought of the Indians in 1663. Among the first settlers were people from Piscataqua (now Dover, N. H., then in the province of Maine). It is claimed that of these early settlers at least six were Baptists. (Hanserd Knollys preached Baptist sentiments in Piscataqua, N. H., as early as 1638.) These six were constituted into a gospel church by Rev. Thomas Killingsworth in 1689.

Three of the constituents—John Drake, Hugh Dunn, and Edmund Dunham—were lay preachers. Mr. Drake was ordained pastor at the constitution of the church, and continued until his death, fifty years afterwards. His descendants are numerous and influential.

The first meeting-house, by order of the town-meeting, was "built forthwith as followeth: dimensions, twenty foot wide, thirty foot long, and ten foot between joints."

COHANSEY.

In 1683 a company of immigrants, members of Cloughketin church, in the County of Tipperary, Ireland, landed at Perth Amboy, and traveled across the country to the "Cohansick" Creek. In 1685, Obadiah Holmes (son of Obadiah who was persecuted) arrived from Rhode Island. His influence was soon felt. He became judge of the Court of Common Pleas for Salem County, and preached acceptably, though he was never ordained. In 1688, Rev. Elias Keach, of Pennepek, administered baptism to three persons. Thomas Killingsworth having moved into the vicinity, united with the nine males in constituting the church, and he became the first pastor, continuing nearly nineteen years, until his death. He was appointed judge of the court, and served honorably, while he preached faithfully and successfully. He was succeeded by Rev. Timothy Brooks, who died after serving the church six years, and his successor, a young man of much promise, passed away after a two years' pastorate.

The church records for the first hundred years were burned, but Mr. Kelsay, a subsequent pastor, preserved some minutes, among them the following:

"In 1710, Timothy Brooks, with his company, united with the church. They had come from Swanzey, in Plymouth government, about 1687, and had kept a separate society for twenty-three years, on account of difference in opinion relative to predestination, singing of Psalms, laying on of hands, etc.; the terms of union were *bearance* and *forbearance*."

Mr. Kelsay says that Mr. "Brooks was a useful preacher, of a sweet and loving temper, and always open to conviction."

CAPE MAY.

Among some who came over in 1675 were two Baptists,—George Taylor and Philip Hill. Taylor held Bible readings and expositions at his own house. After his death, in 1702, Mr. Hill continued the meeting. Mr. Keach visited the place, and preached as early as 1688, and others labored with success. Most of the converts went to Philadelphia for baptism. In 1712, by advice of the pastor and two deacons of Cohansey, thirty-seven persons constituted themselves into a church, under the pastorate of Nathaniel Jenkins, one of their own number.

Before 1707 there was no Association in America. We find, however, an institution called a yearly meeting, which fostered communication. From one end of Jersey to the other pastors and devoted brethren went by Indian trails and rough roads to these immense gatherings. There are traditions concerning these fraternal "great meetings" that are full of tender, touching memories.

When, at the suggestion of the Pennepek church, the Philadelphia Association was formed, in 1707, three of its first churches were in New Jersey, viz., Middletown, Piscataway, and Cohansey. There are no extended early records of the Association, but the usual heading of the earliest is "The Elders and Messengers of the Baptized Congregations in Pennsylvania and the Jerseys."

The Associational fellowship led to greater interest among the ministers and churches, an increase of doctrinal strength, and a spreading of

Bible sentiments, which took deep root, and in the succeeding half-century brought forth abundantly.

The New Jersey Baptists have had in their ranks some of the strongest men among the early Baptists of this country, and among them have arisen brethren to whom the whole denomination is indebted. Oliver Hart performed a work of the highest importance in South Carolina; James Manning, the first president of Rhode Island College, laid all Baptists under lasting obligations to himself for his services to general and ministerial education; Abel Morgan was a man of learning, and of immense influence for good over the Middle States; Hezekiah Smith, of Hopewell, N. J., was settled in Haverhill, Mass., and was blessed with great success in winning souls to Christ; John Gano, the most eloquent preacher among the Baptists of his day, and a man greatly honored of God in extending his kingdom, was a native of New Jersey; our first institution of learning was located in New Jersey, and worthily conducted by Isaac Eaton, at Hopewell. Quite a number of distinguished men have been identified with the Baptists of New Jersey.

For a long period the New Jersey churches belonged to the Philadelphia Association. Their representatives in that body exerted such an influence that they had no desire to sunder the ties that united them to it until their great growth compelled them.

Their first Association was formed in 1811; it consisted of fourteen churches, and was called the New Jersey Association. The Central New Jersey Association was formed in October, 1828, by the representatives of seven churches. The Sussex Association was formed in 1833, by four churches. The Delaware River Association was constituted in 1835, by Old-School, or Anti-Missionary Baptists; its members were less than five hundred when the Association was organized, and they have not increased since that time. The East New Jersey Association was established in November, 1842, by fourteen churches. There are at present in New Jersey the following five Associations: the Central, East, North, Trenton, and West, representing 178 churches, with 31,936 members.

From their early history the Baptists of New Jersey have been the intelligent and generous friends of education, and at present they have two seminaries of a high order, with spacious and beautiful buildings, known as Peddie Institute and South Jersey Institute, the former with 10 instructors, 125 students of both sexes, property worth $125,000, and an endowment of $1000; the latter with 10 instructors, 150 students, and a property moderately estimated at $75,000. These institutions are owned by the denomination in New Jersey. In addition to the money invested in Peddie and South Jersey Institutes, the New Jersey Baptists gave liberally to Hamilton and Lewisburg.

New Jersey Baptist Education Society is forty-two years old. It has aided many students who are doing successful work in the ministry. Its officers for 1880 are: President, H. J. Mulford; Vice-Presidents, R. F. Young, W. H. Parmly; Secretary, O. P. Eaches; Treasurer, W. V. Wilson. Income, $1922.65.

New Jersey Baptist State Convention was organized in 1830. There were then 55 churches in the State, with a membership of 4164.

OFFICERS OF THE CONVENTION FROM ITS ORGANIZATION TO THE PRESENT TIME.

Presidents.—Daniel Dodge,* 1830 to 1839; G. S. Webb, 1839 to 1843; C. W. Mulford,* 1843 to 1849; S. J. Drake,* 1849 to 1853; D. B. Stout,* 1853 to 1854; C. E. Wilson,* 1854 to 1855; D. M. Wilson,* 1855 to 1873; James Buchanan, 1873 to ——.

Vice-Presidents.—Joseph Maylin,* 1830 to 1834; Henry Smalley,* 1830 to 1834; G. S. Webb, 1834 to 1839, 1849 to ——; J. M. Challiss,* 1847 to 1848, 1849 to 1868; John Rogers,* 1839 to 1848; J. C. Harrison,* 1839 to 1844; J. E. Welch,* 1844 to 1847; D. B. Stout,* 1868 to 1875; J. M. Carpenter, 1875 to ——.

Secretaries.—M. J. Rhees,* 1830 to 1840; C. W. Mulford,* 1840 to 1843; S. J. Drake,* 1843 to 1848; J. M. Carpenter, 1848 to 1865; H. F. Smith, 1865 to 1879; T. E. Vassar, 1879 to ——.

Treasurers.—P. P. Runyon,* 1830 to 1871; S. Van Wickle, 1871 to 1879; A. Suydam, 1879 to ——.

Income in 1880 was $4429.55.

Within the last fifty years about 54,000 hopeful converts have been added to our churches by baptism. Our present membership is 31,936. Fifty years ago we had but 2 churches, with a membership of only 200 each. Now we have 1 with over 1100, 1 with 1000, 1 with 800, 1 with 600, 5 with 500, 8 with 400, 14 with 300, 24 with 200, and 53 with over 100 each.

New Jersey Baptist Sunday-School Union is only nine years old, but in gathering statistics of the work, awakening interest, organizing mission schools, as well as in helping the weak, it has entered upon a field of great usefulness.

Newman, Prof. Albert Henry, was born in Edgefield, S. C., Aug. 25, 1852; entered the Thomson, Ga., high school, then in charge of Rev. E. A. Steed, now a professor in Mercer University, by whom he was baptized into the fellowship of the Thomson Baptist church in 1868.

Called to the Christian ministry, and encouraged by brethren of wisdom and piety, he took a place in the Junior class in Mercer University in 1869.

* Deceased.

Here he was specially indebted to Prof. H. H. Tucker, D.D., LL.D., for his inspiring instruction in metaphysics and logic, and to Prof. J. J. Brantly, D.D., who, at great personal cost, gave him private

PROF. ALBERT HENRY NEWMAN.

instruction for a year and a half in the German language. He entered the Rochester Theological Seminary in 1872; in it his favorite studies were Biblical interpretation, under the direction of the learned Dr. Hackett, and systematic theology, under President A. H. Strong, D.D. He spent a year at Greenville, S. C., at the Southern Baptist Theological Seminary, 1875–76, studying Hebrew, Chaldee, Syriac, and Arabic, under Dr. Toy. He also was greatly aided in Greenville by the lectures of Dr. Broadus on the New Testament, the Septuagint, Josephus, and the early Greek fathers. In 1880, Prof. Newman was elected "Pettengill Professor of Church History" in the Rochester Theological Seminary, after he had served as temporary instructor in, and acting professor of, Church History in the same institution.

Prof. Newman, while a careful student of general church history, is devoting himself specially to the records of the Baptists and related bodies. Prof. Newman not long since was offered the professorship of Hebrew in one of our institutions. His attainments are remarkable; his pen is in demand in various parts of the country as contributor to works on theology and church history. The highest estimate is placed upon his acquisitions and talents by competent judges who are familiar with his worth. Before him, if his life is spared, there is undoubtedly a bright future. He has recently accepted a professorship in the Toronto Theological Seminary.

Newman, Judge Thomas W., was born in Somerset Co., Md., Jan. 23, 1829. He pursued his studies in Washington Academy, Princess Anne, Somerset Co., Md., until he removed to Baltimore, and there studied law under Levin Gale, Esq., and was admitted to the bar in 1850, after which he at once removed to the West, and established himself in his profession the same year at Burlington, Iowa, where he still resides. In 1855 he was elected county judge of Des Moines County for two years. When the civil war broke out he warmly embraced the Union cause, and was appointed by President Lincoln captain in the 11th Regiment of the regular army, and commissioned Aug. 1, 1861. He served until the spring of 1863, when, on account of impaired health, he resigned his commission and returned home, and, after six months spent in recuperation and rest, he again entered upon the practice of his profession. From 1855 to 1857 he was a director of the Burlington and Missouri River Railroad, and aided by an active canvass over the entire line, by speeches and otherwise, in raising means for its construction. He was appointed district judge of the first judicial district of Iowa, in 1874, to fill a vacancy. At the October

JUDGE THOMAS W. NEWMAN.

election of the same year he was chosen for the unexpired term of Jan. 1, 1875, and for a full term of four years, to Jan. 1, 1879, which office he filled with credit, and at the end of the term, though strongly urged to continue, declined on account of the inadequate salary. As a judge he was noted for kindness of heart, urbanity of manner, legal acumen, and loyalty to justice. He has been an active director in the Merchants' National Bank of Burlington since its organization, and for some years past its attorney. He became a Baptist the first year of his manhood, in 1850, and has ever since been closely and warmly identified with the interest of the church and denomination. He was president of the State Convention for some years. He has been a trustee in the Burlington Collegiate Institute since its organization, in 1852, and has filled the office of secretary or treasurer of said institution all the time except when in the army.

New Orleans Baptist Chronicle was published at New Orleans, La., by L. Alex. Duncan from 1852 to 1855. Dr. Duncan, having recovered his health, was the principal editor. It was in quarto form and published weekly. Although it had a considerable circulation in the Southwest, it yielded so little profit to the publishers that its publication was discontinued.

Newport, R. I., The First Church of, had its rise in the very beginnings of New England colonial history. The exact date of its origin, however, is *not definitely known.* Those who have studied the subject the most carefully have reached the conclusion that the *probable* date is early in 1638. As this differs from the traditional one (1644), it may be pertinent to give some of the reasons on which this conclusion rests. (1) From the outset the people statedly assembled for public worship, but it is uncertain whether for this purpose they gathered in several congregations, or, as is more probable, they all met in one. (2) There was certainly a church on the island in 1638. Its members were drawn from various sources. Some had been connected with a Congregational church in Boston. It is, however, well known that the church formed here disclaimed any ecclesiastical fellowship with that church. It was of a different order. And if it was the only church on the island, it is certain that there were Baptists among the members, and that they had a Baptist for their minister. (3) Of the church thus formed Mr. Clarke was the pastor or teaching elder. Gov. Winthrop, writing in 1638, speaks of him as "preacher to those of the island." In 1640, Mr. Lechford writes, " On the island there is a church where one Master Clarke is pastor." Describing the controversy which arose shortly after the foregoing sentence was penned, Mr. Hubbard says " their minister, Mr. Clarke, . . . dissented and publicly opposed." (4) The pastor, Mr. Clarke, was undoubtedly a Baptist before leaving England, and as a Baptist refugee came to this country. (*a*) He is known to have held, and on his arrival, one distinctively Baptist tenet, viz., that of religious liberty ; a tenet as distinctively Baptist at the time as is a converted church membership to-day. (*b*) In the discussion which arose in 1640–41, he contended for another Baptist tenet, viz., the sufficiency of Scripture as a rule of religious faith and practice. (*c*) We have no record of any change in his religious views after his arrival in this country, as we should in all probability have had if any such change had taken place. (*d*) Just as soon as he touched shore at Boston he was ready for the sake of his principles to remove into the wilderness. (*e*) He was not caught in a current which was already setting towards a new settlement; the proposition came from himself. (5) Those who during this early period became Baptists in the neighboring colony of Massachusetts gravitated naturally to Newport, and there sought a church home. (6) Mr. Comer, who has given us the traditional date of 1644,—a mere conjecture of his,—and whom almost all subsequent authors have followed, although painstaking and accurate as a writer, had not access to all the sources of knowledge since put within our reach. (7) Finally, Mr. Backus, who made later researches and with better facilities, inclined to the opinion that an earlier date was the probable one.

The history of the church may be considered as falling into five periods. (I. 1638–1682.) The first pastor, John Clarke, born in Suffolk, England, Oct. 8, 1609, and educated at one of the ancient universities, arrived at Boston, November, 1637, near the close of the famous Antinomian controversy. Because his opinions were obnoxious to the magistrates he proposed to a number of kindred spirits to withdraw and plant a new colony, which they did the following March, on the island of Rhode Island. He at once assumed the functions of a minister, conducting the public religious worship of the inhabitants. The sense of freedom which the settlers enjoyed led some of them into theological vagaries. They broke not only from the authority of the church, but from the authority also of the Scriptures. They claimed to be led by an "inner light." They were ably controverted by " their minister, Mr. Clarke," who was strongly seconded by Mr. Lenthall, Mr. Harding, and others. The Baptists maintained the binding authority of the Bible and the existence upon earth of a visible church with visible ordinances. This controversy gave rise to the " Seekers," many of whom afterwards became " Quakers."

A visit paid to William Witter, a member of the church, during the summer of 1651, by delegates appointed by the church, may be noticed, since it has been rendered memorable both on account of the treatment received from the Massachusetts authorities and of the results that followed. The truths presented by these confessors—John Clarke,

Obadiah Holmes, and John Crandall—led to a serious examination; "divers," as Obadiah Holmes said, "were put upon a way of inquiry." It is interesting to know that among the number of these was the scholarly Henry Dunster, then president of Harvard College, who became convinced of the unscripturalness of infant baptism. These events were preparing the way for the formation of the First Baptist church in Boston, with which this church for several years held correspondence.

In the year 1652, the year after Mr. Clarke went to England as agent for the colony, the question of "laying hands on" all baptized believers began to be discussed in the church, and four years later, in 1656, several members withdrew and formed a church of the "Six Principle" order. The year after Mr. Clarke's return from England, namely, in 1665, the Sabbath question was agitated in the church, and a few members supposing they were thus following still more closely the teachings of the Spirit in his Word, began to observe the seventh day, and in 1671 a small number drew off and formed a Sabbatarian church. On the 20th of April, 1676, Mr. Clarke died, after a laborious life devoted to an extension of the Redeemer's kingdom, and having from its very beginning served the colony with almost unexampled fidelity and distinguished success.

He was succeeded by Obadiah Holmes, who, born in Preston, England, in 1606, and educated at Oxford University, came to this country in 1629 and united with a Congregational church in Salem, Mass., and ten years later, in Rehoboth, was baptized by Mr. Clarke, and with several others formed a Baptist church. Removing to Newport, he united, late in 1650 or early in 1651, with this church. He was one of the delegates to Lynn in 1651, where he severely suffered for the sake of his faith. He assisted in ministering to the church during Mr. Clarke's prolonged absence in England, and finally succeeded to the pastoral office, in which he continued till his death, which occurred October 15, 1682.

Singing in public worship was from the beginning approved and practised. Four members were disfellowshiped in 1673 for denying the deity of Christ. The doctrinal position of the church was strongly Calvinistic. Both pastors, Clarke and Holmes, left on record confessions of their faith. The distinction which appeared in England dividing the Baptists into two bodies, described as "Particular" and "General," obtained likewise in this country. This was from its organization a "Particular" or "Calvinistic" church, and has continued so ever since. It was in early correspondence with the Particular Baptists of London, and with the churches of Swanzey and Boston. It made efforts to disseminate Baptist principles both at home and throughout the neighboring colonies. The church was furnished with a board of elders; among the earliest were Joseph Torrey, Obadiah Holmes, Mark Lucar, and John Crandall, the first of whom held many offices of trust in the colony. The first deacon was William Weeden, who died in 1676; the second was Philip Smith. It should be mentioned, further, that Robert Lenthall attempted in 1638 to form a Baptist church in Weymouth, Mass.; that Thomas Painter had been publicly whipped in Hingham, Mass., for refusing to carry his child to the baptismal font; that John Cooke, once a Congregational minister in Massachusetts, and the subject of a letter from John Cotton to his nephew, Cotton Mather, "was living in 1694, probably the oldest survivor of the male passengers in the Mayflower;" that Philip Edes was a friend and helper of Oliver Cromwell; that Samuel Hubbard did much by his letters and other manuscripts to preserve the early history of the church and denomination.

(II. 1683–1732.) The third pastor was Richard Dingley, who, coming from England, was received into the Baptist church in Boston in 1684, and four years later was ordained pastor of this church; in 1694 he resigned and went to South Carolina. In November, 1711, William Peckkam, one of the members of the church, was ordained to the pastorship, and continued in office until his death, in 1732. His ministry was disturbed by a headstrong elder, Daniel White, who had been procured as an assistant, but who drew off a few members and set up a separate meeting, which, however, continued but a little while. John Comer, the fifth pastor, born in Boston, Aug. 1, 1704, and educated at Yale College, was baptized into the Baptist church in Boston, Jan. 31, 1725, and May 19, 1726, ordained pastor of this church, colleague with Elder Peckham. His change of views respecting the rite of the imposition of hands, and his preaching it as obligatory on the church, led to a severance of the pastoral relation, Jan. 8, 1729.

During this period there were two interregna in the pastoral office, the second extending to more than a decade of years. During the first, however, the church improved its material condition, and during the second for most of the time sat under the ministry of Mr. Bliss, a Seventh-day Baptist preacher. The church not only had a name, but had, and for a long time possessed, a local habitation. The meeting-house in which the church had long worshiped was sold in 1707, and during the following year a new one was built. Though a salary was voted him at his settlement, Mr. Comer early made an effort to induce the church to adopt the method of weekly offerings for the support of the ministry. The church voted, Sept. 8, 1726, "that a weekly contribution for the support of the ministry should be observed." Singing having

54

fallen into disuse, Mr. Comer re-introduced it. He commenced also regular church records, and gathered much material towards a history of the church. Of members during this period we may mention James Barker, an elder in the church; Peter Taylor and Samuel Maxwell, made deacons in 1724, and William Peckham, in 1732; Peter Foulger, the maternal grandfather of Benjamin Franklin, and a successful missionary to the Indians; Thomas Dungan, the first Baptist minister in Pennsylvania; also three sons of the second pastor, namely, Obadiah, John, and Jonathan Holmes, one or two of them pioneers in New Jersey. The church was thus through its members extending its influence; as during the former period throughout New England, so during this to provinces more remote.

(III. 1732–1788.) John Callender, the successor of Mr. Comer, born in Boston in 1706, and graduated at Harvard College in 1723, and the same year baptized into the Baptist church of his native town, was, Oct. 13, 1731, ordained as pastor of this church. The one hundredth anniversary of the settlement of the island was celebrated by the building of a new house of worship, and by a historical discourse of great fullness and accuracy, preached March 24, 1738, by the pastor, in which he reviewed the events of the century. The entire colony was brought under obligation to him for this first history of its beginnings and early progress. His pastoral labors continued till death, Jan. 26, 1748. Before the close of the same year the church called to the pastorship Edward Upham, born in Malden, Mass., in 1709, and graduated at Harvard College in 1734. It was during his term of service that the Baptists of America made an effort to establish a college within the colony, for which Newport made a strong but unsuccessful bid. There were cogent reasons why it should be located elsewhere. Mr. Upham resigned his charge in 1771, to be succeeded by Erasmus Kelley, who was ordained on the 9th of October. He was born in Bucks Co., Pa., July 24, 1748, and received his education at the University of Pennsylvania. His ministry was interrupted by the Revolutionary war and the British occupancy of the town. He died Nov. 7, 1784, and the pastoral office thus made vacant was filled by the choice of Benjamin Foster, who began his labors on the first Lord's day in January, 1785. He was born in Danvers, Mass., June 12, 1750, graduated at Yale College in 1774, and September 4 of the same year was baptized into the Baptist church in Boston. Mr. Foster severed his pastoral relations Sept. 15, 1788, and removed to New York.

The doctrinal position of the church remained unchanged. The last pastor was very pronounced in his Calvinism. Under his leadership the church united with the Warren Association. So early in this period as 1733–34 the church had agreed upon the desirableness of coming into an association with the churches with which it was in ecclesiastical fellowship. We do not know why the idea was not then realized. During Mr. Foster's administration, Tate and Brady's collection of hymns was in the service of song superseded by Dr. Watts's psalms and hymns. A few names may here be mentioned, as follows: Samuel Fowler, member of the last colonial Assembly which passed the bold act that severed the colony from Great Britain; William Claggett, an ingenious maker of astronomical and musical clocks, and who anticipated Franklin in some of his experiments with electricity; Hezekiah Carpenter and Josias Lyndon, both generous benefactors of the church, though the latter, Gov. Lyndon, was never a member; Benjamin Hall and Joseph Pike, made deacons in 1785.

Reviewing the history of the church thus far traversed, we find a noble record made. Strong were many of the men connected with the church, worthy to be leaders in Zion; and the ministry was able and cultivated. With scarcely an exception the pastors were men of university training. Benedict, having in his history (1848) brought his account of this church down to the close of this period, 1788, adds this remark: "We have now followed the succession of pastors of this ancient community for about a century and a half, . . . and of these nine pastors all but Mr. Holmes (he means Mr. Peckham) were men of liberal education."

(IV. 1789–1834.) The next pastor's term of service extended through nearly a half-century. Michael Eddy, born in Swanzey, Mass., in 1760, and ordained in the same town in 1785, was called to the pastorship of this church Aug. 10, 1789. In 1792 the church, without assigning any reason for the action, voted to withdraw from the Warren Association, and it remained unassociated during the remainder of Mr. Eddy's long pastorate. For a number of years a union Sunday-school was maintained by the several churches in town. Subsequently the different churches organized schools of their own. That in connection with this church was formed in 1834, and the same year the First Baptist Society was incorporated. During this period we seem to pass from the ancient into the modern world. Rapid changes were taking place in modes of life. And changes even in matters of faith were beginning to appear. Suspicions of unsoundness in the faith clouded the closing years of the pastor's life. A loosening in the spiritual temple was manifest. Some members became Arminians, a few were tinctured even with Socinianism. Dr. Channing was welcomed to preach in the pulpit. One sermon of his made a strong impression. Nevertheless, the majority of the church, it is believed, remained true, though it is known that a few in their love for pure orthodoxy left the church. James A. McKenzie was chosen assistant minister in 1833, and the following deacons were elected: Jethro Briggs, in 1803; George Tilley, in 1813; Abner Peckham and Arnold Barker, in 1822; Benjamin W. Smith and Peleg Sanford, in 1833. Mr. Eddy died June 3, 1835.

(V. 1834–1880.) Already the church had called to the pastoral office Arthur Amasa Ross, born in Thomson, Conn., in 1791, and ordained in his native town in 1819, who entered upon his duties as pastor of this church Nov. 9, 1834. His preaching produced consternation among those who had received "another gospel." In 1836 the church reunited with the Warren Association. In commemoration of the two hundredth anniversary of the settlement of the island the pastor preached, April 4 (March 24, O.S.), 1838, a historical sermon, in which he reviewed the second century of progress. He resigned his charge Nov. 1, 1840, and Joseph Smith was invited, Jan. 2, 1841, to succeed him. He was born in Hampstead, N. H., June 31, 1808, studied a year (1831–32) at the Newton Theological Institution, and was graduated at Brown University in 1837, and the same year ordained as pastor of the Baptist church in Woonsocket, R. I. During his pastorate a new meeting-house was built, with galleries on three sides, and containing 120 pews on the floor. It was dedicated, May 13, 1846, "to the worship of God, the Father, the Son, and the Holy Ghost." The Psalmist displaced in the service of song Winchell's edition of Watts. On the 19th of August, 1849, Mr. Smith resigned the pastoral office, and was succeeded by Samuel Adlam, who was called to the pastorship the 14th of the following October. He was born in Bristol, England, Feb. 4, 1798, and at the age of twenty-two came to Boston, where he was baptized into the First Baptist church. He was ordained pastor of the Baptist church in West Medway, Mass., and after two other settlements was graduated at the Newton Theological Institution in 1838. It was during his ministry that twenty churches, of which this was one, withdrew from the Warren Association and formed a new body, which was called the Narragansett Association. Mr. Adlam resigned his charge June 27, 1864, and March 12, 1865, was succeeded by Rev. C. E. Barrows, D.D., who was graduated at Brown University in 1858, and the Newton Theological Institution in 1861, and on the 25th of December of that year was ordained pastor of the Baptist church in Peabody, Mass. The following brethren have during this period been elected deacons: Benjamin B. Howland, in 1837; Samuel S. Peckham, in 1847; Stephen S. Albro and Samuel Eyles, in 1857; Gilbert Tompkins, George M. Hazard, Thomas H. Clarke, and George Nasen, in 1867; and in 1874, Ara Hildreth. Mr. Howland was deacon for forty years, and for fifty years was clerk of the town and city of Newport.

C. E. BARROWS, D.D.

During the nearly two centuries and a half which have elapsed since the first members of the church entered into solemn covenant with one another to observe the public worship of God and keep the ordinances as given by the Head of the church, this body has remained true to its early confessions of faith. Slight changes have been made in the statement of some of the doctrines, nevertheless the essential principles on which the church rests are the same now as at the first. Among the principles at the beginning were these: that Christ " may alone lay commands upon the church with respect to worship;" that " dipping in water is one of these commands, and that only a believer may be baptized;" that "baptized believers have the liberty to speak in the assemblies of the saints for the edification of the whole;" and that "no disciple of Christ has a right to constrain or restrain the conscience of another, or to seek by physical force to compel men to worship God." The church still believes that Christ alone is the rightful sovereign in the realm of religious faith; that his will has been recorded in Holy Scripture, which is a sufficient rule of doctrine and duty; that it is the will of Christ that those who have by faith accepted him as their Saviour should identify themselves with his people by church relations; that the ordinances of baptism and the Lord's Supper belong to the church, and are designed to set forth great spiritual facts,—the first the origin, and the second the maintenance of the new life in the soul, and each in intimate and vital connection with the death of Christ; and finally, that Christ's church, deeply imbued with his Spirit, is the divinely appointed agency for the evangelization of the world.

Newton, Prof. Calvin, was born in Southborough, Mass., Nov. 26, 1800. He entered Brown University in 1820, and graduated at Union College in 1824. While in Brown University he became a Christian and was baptized. He was licensed to preach by the church in Southborough; graduated at Newton in 1829, and was ordained pastor of the church in Bellingham, Mass., the same year. He remained here three years, and then accepted an appointment, in 1832, as professor in Waterville College. He occupied the chair to which he had been elected for five years. Resigning his position in Waterville, he was appointed professor in the newly established theological institution in Maine. With this institution he was associated for four years, when he became pastor of the church in Grafton, Mass. Having decided to become a physician, he pursued his medical studies until he received the degree of M.D. from the medical institution in Pittsfield, Mass. During the remainder of his life, he was for the most of the time a lecturer or professor in the Worcester Medical Institution, and finally its president. He died Aug. 9, 1853.

Newton, Matthew Turner, M.D., son of Deacon Israel and Harriet T. Newton, was born in 1830 in Colchester, Conn.; fitted for college at Bacon Academy; in 1848 chose the medical profession, and in 1851 graduated from the medical department of Yale College; commenced practice in Salem, Conn.; represented Salem in the General Assembly in 1853; at the close of the Legislature removed to Suffield; in the civil war was assistant surgeon of 3d Conn. Vols.; afterwards surgeon of 10th Conn. Vols.; resumed practice in Suffield; elected deacon of Second Baptist church in Suffield in 1875; has been a trustee of Connecticut Literary Institution since 1872; occupies a high position in society, and exerts a broad and happy influence.

Newton Theological Institution commenced its first session on the 28th of November, 1825. The plan for the foundation of a theological institution of a high order had long been under contemplation, but did not take definite shape until the 25th of May, 1825, when at a large meeting of Baptist ministers and laymen, representing different sections of New England, it was decided to establish such an institution, and commence operations at Newton Centre, Mass. The new seminary was opened, with Rev. Irah Chase as the first instructor of its students, with whom was associated, at the beginning of the second year, Rev. Henry J. Ripley. These two professors constituted the faculty of instruction for six years. In 1834 the trustees added Rev. James D. Knowles to the corps of instructors, and in 1836, Rev. Barnas Sears. Upon the death of Prof. Knowles in 1838, Prof. H. B. Hackett, then a professor in Brown University, was called to Newton. The early history of the institution was marked by the usual experiences of such seminaries of learning. Interest was awakened, some funds raised, students increased faster than there was ability to meet their wants; then a troublesome debt oppressed the hearts of friends and well-wishers; then came attempts to secure, first, an endowment of $30,000, then of $50,000, both of which attempts failed; then another effort to secure $100,000 was made, and that was successful. But the amount was not yet deemed sufficient to meet the wants of the institution, and there followed a scheme to add $200,000 to the endowment already existing, and success crowned the effort, thus placing Newton on such a foundation that there was every reason to believe its future prosperity was placed beyond all ordinary contingencies.

More than 700 students have enjoyed the advantages of the institution, having obtained their theological education in part or wholly within its walls. Of this large number more than three-fourths have been pastors of churches in this country, and about 60 have received appointments as missionaries to the foreign field. Not far from 55 students have been called to occupy prominent positions in our colleges or theological seminaries, either as presidents or professors, while a large number have been useful as authors or editors. The institution has done a noble work for the cause of Christ in connection with the denomination, to whose ministry it has been such a rich blessing.

New York Baptist Home for Aged and Infirm Persons is the name of one of the best institutions in New York. It is the outgrowth of the Ladies' Home Society, organized in 1869 to provide the aged, infirm, or destitute members of the Baptist churches of New York with a comfortable residence, with board, clothing, skillful medical attendance, with their accustomed religious services, and, at their death, with respectable burial. In its application for means to accomplish its end the society met with a generous response, and speedily erected a large building in Sixty-eighth Street. It is six stories high, and nicely furnished. It does not belie its name. It has rooms for the accommodation of over a hundred inmates. To obtain the position applicants must be recommended by the pastor and deacons of the church to which they belong, or shall give other satisfactory evidence of their good standing in a regular Baptist church for

NEWTON THEOLOGICAL SEMINARY, NEWTON CENTRE, MASS.

five years, must have no means of support, nor relatives who will provide for them, and must pay to the treasurer $100. "Patrons," who have paid $1000, can enter one person without the entrance fee, and, in exceptional cases, the trustees may admit applicants without the fee. A matron presides over the institution, who is chosen for her gentleness, piety, and fitness for such a responsible position. It is her duty each day to inquire after the comfort and health of the inmates, and provide promptly all that may be necessary for them. Both male and female members of the churches, becoming poor, and with no friends to support them, find in this building a home in which, to abide with comfort until called to the eternal rest.

New York Baptists, Historical Sketch of.—In the latter part of the seventeenth century Rev. William Wickenden, of Rhode Island, a Baptist minister, visited the little town of New York to preach Christ. He labored for two years, meeting with discouragements and persecution. Without a license from the representatives of the British government, he was regarded as a law-breaker, and thrown into prison, where he lingered for months. For several years afterwards no Baptist minister made New York the scene of his labors. In 1712, Rev. Valentine Wightman, of Groton, Conn., came to New York for a short period; during his ministry about a dozen persons were baptized. After his removal Mr. Nicholas Eyers preached to the struggling community which he left. The following petition of his is on record:

"To His Excellency William Burnet, Esq., Captain-General and Governor-in-Chief of the Province of New York and New Jersey.

"The humble petition of Nicholas Eyers, brewer, a Baptist teacher in the city of New York:

"Sheweth unto your Excellency that on the first Tuesday of Feb., 1715, at a general quarter sessions of the peace, held at the city of New York, the hired house of your petitioner, situated in the broad street of this city, between the houses of John Michel Eyers and Mr. John Spratt, was registered for an Anabaptist meeting-house within this city; that the petitioner has it certified under the hands of sixteen inhabitants, of good faith and credit, that he had been a public teacher to a Baptist congregation within this city for four years, and some of them for less; that he has it certified by the Hon. Rip Van Dam, Esq., one of his Majesty's council for the province of New York, to have hired a house in this city from him January, 1720, only to be a public house for the Baptists, which he still keeps; and as he has obtained from the Mayor and Recorder of this city an ample certificate of his good behavior and innocent conversation, he therefore humbly prays:

"May it please your Excellency,

"To grant and permit this petitioner to execute the ministerial function of a minister within this city to a Baptist congregation, and to give him protection therein, according to his Majesty's gracious indulgence extended towards the Protestants dissenting from the Established Church, he being willing to comply with all that is required by the Act of Toleration from dissenters of that persuasion in Great Britain, and being owned for a reverend brother by other Baptist teachers.

"As in duty bound the petitioner shall ever pray.
"Nicholas Eyers."

After this petition was granted the community to which Mr. Eyers ministered enjoyed considerable prosperity, and in 1724 a church was formally organized, and subsequently a meeting-house was built on Golden Hill, near John Street, of which they were deprived in a few years by the action of one of their own trustees, who had the house sold. Mr. Eyers was pastor of the church for seven years. After 1732 the community disbanded. The church of Mr. Eyers is described as an "Arminian" community.

In 1745, Jeremiah Dodge, a member of the Fishkill Baptist church, who lived in the city of New York, opened his house for the Baptist worship, instituted by his Master and precious to himself. Benjamin Miller, of New Jersey, was accustomed to preach in the house of Mr. Dodge. Some of the members of the Free-Will Church, whom the Lord had taught to renounce Arminianism, joined Mr. Dodge in sustaining the new movement. Joseph Meeks, who was baptized the first year that Mr. Dodge had preaching in his house, greatly contributed to the continued existence of this Baptist enterprise. John Pine, a licentiate of the Fishkill church, preached for them for some time. In 1747 the Scotch Plains church, New Jersey, was constituted, and in 1753 the thirteen New York Baptists united with the community at Scotch Plains. Benjamin Miller, the pastor of the church, needed more room for his New York hearers than a dwelling-house could afford, and a rigging-loft was secured in Cart-and-Horse Street, now William Street, in which the future First church of New York held its meetings for several years. They erected their first church edifice on Gold Street, which was opened in March, 1760. On the 19th of June, 1762, twenty-seven persons, who had received letters of dismission for the purpose from the Scotch Plains church, formed the First Regular Baptist church of New York City. The same day John Gano, of New Jersey, entered upon his duties as pastor of the church, and in two or three years the membership exceeded two hundred. The house had to be enlarged, and soon it was filled to overflowing. The eloquence and piety of Mr. Gano made him one of the most popular ministers in the colonies.

During the Revolution the church was dispersed; baptism was not administered from April, 1776, to September, 1784. Mr. Gano was a brave patriot, and he entered the army as a chaplain. This position he held throughout the war. When the enemy evacuated New York he returned, to find only thirty-seven members of his church. The church edifice had been used as a stable, but it was soon renovated; and on the resumption of divine worship the Lord visited them again, and in two years the church numbered more than two hundred. Mr. Gano left it in 1788 for Kentucky, and he continued there until his death, in 1804.

In 1788, Rev. Dr. Benjamin Foster, of Rhode Island, became pastor of the church, who died of yellow fever in 1798, after exercising his ministry with much acceptance and success for nearly ten years. The Rev. William Collier, of Boston, accepted the pastorate in 1800, and in 1803 the church opened a new stone meeting-house, 65 by 80 feet, which cost $25,000. Mr. Collier resigned in 1804. In the same year the Rev. William Parkinson succeeded Mr. Collier, and continued pastor till 1840. In 1841, Rev. Dr. Cone took the oversight of the First church, and held that office till 1855. The Rev. A. Kingman Nott was elected his successor, and was drowned July 7, 1859, and the Rev. Dr. Anderson followed Mr. Nott. Dr. John Peddie is the present pastor. This mother of churches has had an illustrious succession of shepherds, men of God and men of remarkable talents; and she has had, and has still, a membership worthy of her pastors.

In New York, and in its suburbs and surrounding cities, there are now more than one hundred churches, where a century ago our single Baptist church edifice was a stable for British cavalry horses, and its male members were in the Revolutionary army or in the graves of patriots.

There were Baptists settled at Oyster Bay, Long Island, probably not many years after William Wickenden preached in New York City. They were found here in 1700, with William Rhodes, a licentiate, as their preacher, under whose ministrations converts were brought to Jesus, and among them Robert Feeks, who was ordained pastor in 1724. Fishkill had a Baptist church in 1745, of which Jeremiah Dodge was a member, who had removed to New York, and in that year opened his house for Baptist worship. Northeast church was founded in 1751, by men who had been brought to Christ in the great revivals in the time of Whitefield; Simon Dakin was their first pastor. The First church of Dover was constituted in 1757, and the next year Rev. Samuel Waldo became their pastor, and held that position for thirty-five years. In 1759 the church at Stanford was organized. The Warwick church was formed in 1766, by Rev. James Benedict, and from a small membership it soon began to prosper, and early in its history it established several new churches. From these seed-scattering communities, and from Baptists coming from New England, our principles soon after this date, at the close of the Revolutionary war, began to spread with extraordinary rapidity, and this was especially true in the western part of the State.

The first Baptist meeting in Western New York was held at Butternuts, in 1773, within the present limits of Otsego County. In 1776 another meeting for worship was established by six baptized Indians, at Brothertown, now in the county of Oneida. These red brethren came from Connecticut and Long Island, N. Y. The community at Butternuts was scattered by the Revolutionary war, but four of the families composing it returned after the proclamation of peace, and the next year revived their meetings for public worship, and in August, 1793, they were recognized as a regular Baptist church. In 1789, Rev. William Furman settled in Springfield, Otsego Co., and at once began the preaching of the gospel, which was soon made powerful to the conversion of souls, and a church was formed, consisting of 30 members, in 1789; the church in Franklin, Delaware Co., was constituted in 1792; in 1794 the Kortright church, Delaware County, and the First, Second, and Third Burlington churches, Otsego County, were organized. And the word of God had free course, and was glorified in the conversion of throngs and in the formation of great numbers of churches. On Sept. 2, 1795, under the leadership of Rev. William Furman, the ministers and messengers of thirteen churches met at Springfield and formed the Otsego Association. The sessions were full of joy, hope, and the love of Christ. In 1800 this body contained 37 churches, with 1718 members, nearly two-fifths of all the Baptist church members in the State of New York. The advantages conferred by the Otsego Association led to the formation, in 1801, of the Cayuga Association, and similar needs and benefits resulted in the organization of others, and such an era of almost unbounded prosperity blessed the denomination in Western New York that in 1846 there were thirty Associations in that field.

Among the instrumentalities greatly favored of God in spreading the gospel in Western New York was the "Lake Missionary Society," founded in Pompey, Onondaga Co., in the house of Rev. Jonathan Baker, Aug. 27, 1807. This body, at its meeting in German in 1808, assumed the name of the "Hamilton Missionary Society." It employed men of great zeal and ability to preach Christ, and its success was very great. It was nobly assisted by the "Hamilton Female Society" and other women's organizations existing for the same purpose; the first contribution from this source came on Feb. 19, 1812. The Massachusetts Baptist Missionary Society sent laborers into this field. The "New York Missionary Society" performed some mission service among the Tuscarora Indians. On Nov. 21, 1821, at Mentz, Cayuga Co., the "Baptist Domestic Missionary Convention of the State of New York" was founded, and for an account of its growth, changes, and great usefulness, see article on NEW YORK STATE MISSIONARY CONVENTION.

An educated ministry for our rapidly-increasing churches was long felt to be an absolute necessity. To meet this pressing demand, on Sept. 24, 1817, the "Baptist Education Society of the State of New York" was formed. The first applicant for its patronage was Dr. Wade, subsequently of Burmah. Dr. Kincaid, a member of the same class, and a laborer in the same heathen field, was among the earliest to receive its advantages. For two years the students were taught by private instructors, and at academies, until the spring of 1820, when the Hamilton "Literary and Theological Institution" was founded, which finally became Madison University, Hamilton Theological Seminary, and Colgate Academy. The institutions at Hamilton have done more for New York, New England, the Middle and Western States, and Burmah than any human pen will ever record. Rochester University, with its brilliant history, came from Hamilton.

For the Baptist newspapers of New York, see articles on THE EXAMINER AND CHRONICLE, THE BAPTIST WEEKLY, and THE WATCH-TOWER.

The "New York Association" is the best-known body of that character in the State. In the minutes of the Philadelphia Baptist Association for 1790 we find the following: "The request of the churches at Stamford, Warwick, First and Second of New York, King Street, and Staten Island, for permission to join other Associations if it should be found more convenient, is granted." The Association was formed Oct. 19, 1791. The Rev. Elkanah Holmes was chosen moderator, and the Rev. Dr. Foster, pastor of the First church, clerk. Dr. Foster preached the first sermon before the Association from the text, "Many shall run to and fro, and knowledge shall be increased." The meeting was held in the First church of New York. On May 2, 1805, the Fayette Street, better known as the Oliver Street church, was received into the Association; the messengers representing it on that occasion were John Williams, pastor, and John Withington, Jacob Smith, John Cauldwell, and Francis Wayland. The New York Association has been remarkably active and useful in extending the Redeemer's kingdom throughout the State, and its members have ever shown a spirit of enlightened liberality in their contributions to spread the gospel all over this and many other lands.

There are now 44 Associations in the State of New York, 877 churches, 801 ordained ministers, 114,094 church members, and 878 Sunday-schools, with 13,161 officers and teachers, and 91,217 scholars. In New York the Baptist denomination is but of yesterday, and yet its numbers, intelligence, resources, piety, and influence exhibit a miracle of prosperity.

New York, The First Baptist Church of.— This splendid edifice was dedicated to the worship of Almighty God in October, 1871. The church and chapel, with their ground and furniture, cost $197,500. The edifice is free from debt. The spire, like the whole structure, is of brownstone. Dr. John Peddie is the devoted and popular pastor of the venerable community worshiping in the superb edifice represented in our picture.

New York State Missionary Convention, The.— Availing ourselves of facts stated at the annual meeting of the Convention for 1880, it may be interesting to say that the first Baptist church organized in New York State west of the Hudson was in 1789, at Springfield, Otsego Co., and in 1795 the Otsego Association was organized with 13 churches and 5 ministers. In 1802 its churches had increased to 42, and its ministers to 9. There were at this time in the whole State of New York only 86 churches, with not more than 5000 members. In 1817 the number of churches was 310, with 28,000 members. Now, in 1880, the number of churches is 877, with nearly 115,000 members. In 1802 the population of the Empire State was about 650,000; in 1880 it is fully 5,000,000. The Baptist denomination in the same years has increased more than three times faster than the population, and in the decade ending with 1880 the growth has been more rapid than that of the population.

To no other cause than to the character of the first and second generations of pioneer Baptist ministers can this large growth be ascribed. Most of the first generation died early in this century, and few of them lived later than 1825. But how can this generation estimate the debt it owes to such ministers of the Lord Jesus as Joseph Cornell, Ashbel Hosmer, William Furman, Salmon Morton, Obed Warren, David Irish, Emory Osgood, John Lawton, Joel Butler, Sylvanus Haynes, Ora Butler, Lemuel Covill, and Jonathan Ferris? And to such laymen as Squire Munro, Jonathan Olmsted, Samuel Payne, Ebenezer Wakely, and John Keep? These were noble men of the first generation of Baptist pioneers, and before they had entered into rest another generation on whom their mantle had fallen took up their work and bore their responsibilities. They included such ministers as

FIRST BAPTIST CHURCH, NEW YORK.

Alfred Bennett, Nathaniel Kendrick, Daniel Hascall, John Peck, Caleb Douglass, John Blodgett, Lewis Leonard, Cornelius P. Wyckoff, Elon Galusha, John Smitzer, Bartholomew T. Welch, Spencer H. Cone, Oliver C. Comstock, and Elisha Tucker, and such laymen as William Colgate, Friend Humphrey, Alexander M. Beebee, Seneca B. Burchard, Asa Bennett, Oren Sage, and William Cobb.

These men knew how to discern the signs of coming events and obligations, and to make ready for them. In 1807 they formed the Hamilton Missionary Society, and its field was wider than the State. In 1812, Mrs. Betsey Payne and Mrs. Freedom Olmsted attended the annual meeting of the society as delegates from what was called the Hamilton Female Missionary Society, and carried with them twenty yards of fulled cloth as their society's contribution to the larger treasury. This was the first woman's Baptist missionary society known west of the Hudson, but it soon became the mother of a large number of like societies over all the State. In 1814, Rev. John M. Peck attended the annual meeting of the Hamilton Society as the representative of Luther Rice, and the society took immediate measures to awaken a spirited co-operation in the work of foreign missions. In the same year the necessity of a religious paper, devoted largely to religious news, was felt, and a quarterly paper, called *The Vehicle*, was set agoing, which was subsequently merged in the *New York Baptist Register*. In 1817 the New York State Baptist Education Society was organized, and in 1820 the Hamilton Literary and Theological Institution was started upon its beneficent career. In 1821, prompted by the Hudson River Association, the State Missionary Convention was organized at Mentz, near Auburn, and in 1825 the long-desired union of the Hamilton Missionary Society and the State Convention was effected.

What this State Convention, dating back by this union to the year 1807, has done appears in its helping to make strong and self-supporting such churches as Binghamton, Owego, Waverly, Corning, First and Emmanuel, Buffalo, First and Second, Rochester, Ogdensburg, and scores of others in every part of the State. But, like most other good movements, the Convention has had a checkered history. It took several years to bring about a union between it and the Hamilton Missionary Society. But some years after the union was effected a new and rather sharp trial came in settling the relations that should exist between the Convention and the American Baptist Home Mission Society. An auxiliary relationship was finally fixed upon, and it was made the duty of the Convention to act as a collecting agency for the Home Mission Society, so as to avoid two sets of appeals to the churches. But it was found, after some years of trial, that the plan did not work well. Then came the conflict of a re-adjustment, which ended in making the State of New York open to the agents of both organizations. But the Convention continued to do good work for the means at its command under this arrangement to the year 1868, when the co-operative system was adopted, by which all the home and domestic money of the State went into the Home Mission Society's treasury, and the State missionaries were paid out of that general fund. The effect of this was to make the State Convention less influential and successful as a purely State organization.

In 1874 the Convention was reorganized at Hornellsville, N. Y., under a new constitution, the main purpose of which was to make it a strictly State organization, more distinctively representative in its character and less complicated in its structure. It was provided that its sole object should be to promote the interests of the State missionary, educational, and Sunday-school work, and that its efforts should be directed by an executive committee of seven men living in the city of New York and vicinity. In these six years a larger and better work has been done within the State than in any other corresponding period in the Convention's history. Each year has been an advance over the one preceding it in the number of missionaries commissioned, the work done, and the amount of money received. In the year closing with October, 1880, the total receipts and disbursements were $11,978.31. During the year 73 missionaries were commissioned, as against 61 the previous year; and from 70 of these reports were received quarterly up to October 1. These show a total of 2344 weeks' labor performed, 6230 sermons preached, 3931 prayer-meetings held, 12,476 religious visits, 242 churches and out-stations supplied, and 260 persons baptized by the missionaries themselves. The late annual meetings of the Convention have been distinguished for their unity and ability, and for their benign influence on all the denominational interests of the State.

New York Watch-Tower, The, is a weekly journal devoted to Christian work in the Baptist denomination. It was at first called *The Baptist Outlook*, edited by Justin D. Fulton, D.D., but in 1878 its name was changed, and John W. Olmstead, D.D., became the editor and proprietor. It appeared at first in the quarto form, but increase of patronage led to enlargement and a change to the folio form. Its plan is to furnish a good Baptist newspaper at so low a price that the less able members of our churches will be induced to take it. In November, 1880, the paper was further enlarged and improved under the auspices of *The Watch-Tower* Publishing Co., Dr. Olmstead, editor-in-chief, with able assistants. It is loyal to Christ and the Baptist faith and practice. It is the special champion of the "Bible Union" principles, of pure versions in the English as well as foreign tongues. As a journalist, Dr. Olmstead, so long the editor of the *Watchman and Reflector*, of Boston, stands deservedly high. A large part of his paper is filled with carefully-written editorial matter. His discussions of religious and denominational matters are calm, dignified, and forcible. *The Watch-Tower* is growing in public favor and patronage.

Niles, Rev. Asa, was born in North Middleborough, Mass., Feb. 10, 1777. He was baptized by Rev. Dr. Baldwin in 1800, and united with the Second Baptist church in Boston. He studied for a time with Rev. W. Williams, of Wrentham, Mass., and at a meeting of the Warren Baptist Association at Warren, R. I., in 1805, he was ordained as an evangelist. He commenced at once to preach, and labored in several places, not remaining long in any one of them. He was also a missionary of the Rhode Island Convention for some time, doing the work of an evangelist in different parts of the State. In 1832 he removed to North Middleborough, and preached there for two years. His death occurred April 15, 1849.

Nisbet, Ebenezer, D.D., was born June 20, 1826, in Edinburgh, Scotland. He came with his

EBENEZER NISBET, D.D.

parents to America in 1834. The family settled in Broome Co., N. Y. After some years they removed to the neighborhood of Owego, N. Y., at whose academy Ebenezer prepared for the University of Rochester, in which he graduated in 1853. He entered Rochester Theological Seminary the same year, and graduated in 1855. He remained as a resident graduate at Rochester for a year, and then settled at East Avon, N. Y., and was ordained Sept. 5, 1856. He was pastor at East Avon and Brockport, N. Y., at Fond du Lac, Wis., at Rochester, N. Y., at Rock Island, Ill., and he is now pastor at Leavenworth, Kansas. During his labors at East Avon the membership nearly doubled, large accessions were made at Brockport, 342 were admitted to the Fond du Lac church, and above 200 at Rochester. At Rock Island he was instrumental in largely relieving the church of a burdensome debt, while at Leavenworth under his administration a debt of above $16,000 has been removed. The University of Chicago bestowed upon him, in June, 1868, the degree of Doctor of Divinity. He delivered the following year in the university building, before the Ministers' Institute of the Northwest, a course of lectures on "Science and Religion." He was appointed, in 1881, by the governor of Kansas, one of the regents of the State University. He is the author of an able work on the Resurrection, and he has also written several review articles. Quite a number of his sermons have been published by request.

Nix, Rev. Allen, an able pioneer preacher of Ouachita Baptist Association, La., died in Catahoula Parish in 1847. At the time of his death he was pastor of the First Baptist church on Little River.

Noble, Rev. Mark, was born in Old Charlton, Kent, England, Nov. 25, 1836; was converted under the preaching of Rev. C. H. Spurgeon, by whom he was baptized Dec. 1, 1859. He was ordained at Necton, Norfolk, England. Mr. Noble was brought up by his maternal grandparents. In early life he studied architecture. He entered Mr. Spurgeon's college in 1862. He had charge of the Baptist church at Carleton Road, Norfolk, which he resigned to come to America, in 1870. He arrived in Fairbury, Neb., March 10, 1870. Under his labors the Baptist church in Fairbury was organized, July 3, 1870; also, July 5, 1870, the Dry Branch Baptist church. Mr. Noble has served these churches since their formation, and has organized other churches. He has labored industriously and successfully amid many privations.

Noel, Hon. and Rev. Baptist W., was for many years an eminent clergyman of the Church of England, but from 1848 he was identified with the English Baptists. He was the brother of the Earl of Gainsborough. He was educated at Trinity College, Cambridge, graduating with distinction in 1826. Having been ordained, he became minister of St. John's, Bedford-row, London, where he preached to a very numerous audience of the upper classes until his secession from the Established Church.

He was universally regarded as one of the most eminent preachers in the metropolis, and a leader of the evangelical party. He was one of the royal chaplains, and according to common report more

HON. AND REV. BAPTIST W. NOEL.

than once declined promotion to the Episcopal bench. His secession was the leading event in English ecclesiastical affairs for some time. The publication of his book on the "Union of Church and State" excited much curiosity concerning his future course. At length he avowed himself convinced of the Scripturalness of Baptist principles, and was publicly baptized in London, Aug. 9, 1849. He published two essays about the same time on the "External Act of Baptism" and "Christian Baptism." Soon after, he entered upon his ministry in John Street Chapel, as successor to the venerable John Harrington Evans, near the scene of his labors as a State Church clergyman. Here he ministered until 1868, when, having attained his seventieth year, he resigned his pastoral charge, and engaged occasionally in evangelistic services in different parts of the country, as he had done for some time after his retirement from the Church of England. As an Episcopal minister he had wielded a moral influence scarcely second to that of any of his contemporaries. This was due to the fine blending of dignity and independence in his character with high spirituality. When he joined the Baptists these qualities were irradiated by the sacrifices he had made for conscience' sake. Wherever he went to preach, immense throngs, belonging to almost every denomination, assembled to listen to a man whose sincerity of motive was beyond suspicion, and whose whole demeanor and action seemed a vivid embodiment of the noblest Christian manhood. When he was invited by the Baptist Union to accept the highest honor which his brethren have it in their power to bestow, he willingly, but with characteristic modesty, accepted the position. He filled the chair in 1867, the year preceding his retirement from the pastorate, and at the autumnal meeting at Cardiff, his unwritten address on the work of the ministry produced a singularly powerful impression. When he retired from the pulpit at John Street in the following year, his text at both services was Gal. vi. 14: "God forbid that I should glory, save in the cross of our Lord Jesus Christ," and he uttered scarcely a word of personal reference during the whole day. It is a remarkable fact that until the time of his departure drew near, he was never known to have a day's illness in his life. Dr. Tyng, in his "Recollections of England," published in 1847, described Mr. Noel as "certainly a most interesting and delightful preacher; altogether extemporaneous; mild and persuasive in his manner, yet sufficiently impressive and sometimes powerful, having a very clear and consistent flow of thought." In addition to a variety of occasional sermons, and sermons on special occasions, Mr. Noel published numerous works of greater or less celebrity. Besides his well-known book on Church and State, and the volumes on Baptism, he published "Sermons on the First Five Centuries of the Church," 1839; "Sermons to the Unconverted," 1840; "Sermons at St. James's," 1842; "Sermons at the Chapels Royal," 1842 and 1848; "Case of the Free Church of Scotland," 1844; "Notes of a Tour in Switzerland in 1847;" "Letters on the Church of Rome," 1852, etc. Among pamphlets which excited considerable attention, his letter to the bishop of London on the spiritual destitution of the metropolis was particularly effective for good. Also his publications on the Jamaica Massacres; on the "Duty of Englishmen towards the Hindoos," and on "American Freedom and Slavery," during the civil war in this country, were widely read. He died Sunday afternoon, Jan. 19, 1873, in his seventy-fifth year. His amiable spirit, exemplary character, fidelity to conviction, and complete and life-long consecration to the work of the Lord, are a precious possession to the whole church, and particularly to the Baptist body, with which, constrained by conscience, he spent his maturer years.

Noel, Silas Mercer, D.D., son of Rev. Theodoric Noel, was born near Richmond, Va., Aug. 13, 1783. He received a classical education, after which he studied law, and entered on the practice of his profession at Frankfort, Ky. After a prosperous career of a few years, he abandoned the law for the gospel ministry, and was ordained pastor of the Big Spring Baptist church in Woodford County. A few years later he was appointed judge of the Circuit Court about the year 1817, which position he filled several years, when he resigned and resumed the active duties of the ministry. He traveled and preached extensively, and, during a number of years, his success was so great that it was said " he baptized more people than any other preacher in Kentucky." In 1827 he became pastor of Great Crossing church in Scott County, and during the following year baptized into its fellowship 359 persons. He was an author of more than ordinary ability, and he wrote extensively for the periodicals of his time. He was the publisher of a Baptist monthly in 1813, which, however, was suspended for want of patronage. In 1836 he was called to the pastorate of the First Baptist church in Lexington. His death occurred May 5, 1839.

Noffsinger, Rev. M. V., pastor at Macon, Miss., was born in Virginia, and educated at Union University, Murfreesborough, Tenn. He professed faith at the age of sixteen, and was ordained in 1862. He has labored successfully as pastor at Marion, Va., four years; Jonesborough, Tenn., four years; Morristown, Tenn., four years; agent of Union University, one year, adding $25,000 to the endowment. He has been some time in his present pastorate. He has been successful as a church builder, and in removing debts from churches. He is about forty years of age.

Norris, S. M., an active Sunday-school laborer at Kingston, La., was born in South Carolina in 1813. He came to Louisiana in 1853. Has accomplished great good as colporteur and Sunday-school agent.

Norsworthy, Rev. Galbanum, M.D., a leading minister of Liberty Association, Arkansas, was born in North Carolina in 1815; removed to Arkansas in 1848, and engaged successfully in the practice of medicine; began to preach in 1868, and has done much to supply the destitution about him; is an able preacher and forcible writer.

North Carolina, The Baptists of.—

THEIR ORIGIN.

Moore, in his " History of North Carolina," says, " Sir William Berkeley, governor of Virginia, drove out of that colony, in 1653, the Baptists and Quakers, who found a refuge in the Albemarle region of Carolina." Morgan Edwards says there were Baptists in North Carolina as early as 1695, and Dr. Hawks, in enumerating the freeholders in several eastern counties of North Carolina, mentions the names of many Baptists, and among them two preachers,—Paul Palmer and William Burgess. The first church, however, of which we read was not organized till 1727,—some authorities say 1729,—in the county of Camden, by Paul Palmer, and was called Shiloh. This church still exists. Palmer was a native of Welsh Tract, Del.

In 1729 the Meherrin church, which still exists, and is located near Murfreesborough, N. C., was constituted by Joseph Parker, who was ordained by Paul Palmer, of Camden County. In 1750 the Meherrin church gave letters for the formation of the Sandy Run church, in Bertie County, and from these three original churches Baptist principles were gradually but slowly disseminated through the eastern part of the State.

In 1742, Elder William Sojourner came with a colony from Berkeley Co., Va., and settled on Kehukee Creek, in Halifax County. In 1752 the church they founded had multiplied into sixteen churches.

It would seem from what Benedict says that the Baptists of both these settlements were Arminian, or Free-Will, for some time, and were accustomed to baptize, certainly in some cases, without requiring regeneration. In 1775, Miller and Vanhorn were sent down by the Philadelphia Association to look after these irregular Baptists, and with the blessing of God were enabled to effect a great reformation among them. They adopted the London Confession of Faith, published in 1689, and in 1765 formed the Kehukee Association.

The reformation of doctrine alluded to above must have been but partial, however, as we find a resolution adopted at a large meeting held at the Falls of Tar River in 1775, described at length by Burkett and Read in their " History of the Kehukee Association," in which non-fellowship was declared with those churches whose members were not converted *before* baptism. Gradually the churches came to the old landmarks of Baptist faith and were united, though for a long time Joseph Parker and the Meherrin church did not come into the union.

The third, and by far the most prosperous, colony of Baptists who settled in North Carolina also came from Berkeley Co., Va., led by Elder Shubal Stearns, and settled on Sandy Creek, then in Guilford, now in Randolph.

Daniel Marshall, the brother-in-law of Mr. Stearns, before a Congregationalist, became a Baptist, and was very successful as an evangelist. The Sandy Creek was a most fruitful mother of churches, though originally composed of but 16 members. In seventeen years it had organized 42 churches, had ordained 115 ministers, and gathered a membership of 600 communicants.

The first Association formed in this State was the Sandy Creek, in 1758. In 1792 the Arminian Baptists of the eastern part of the State united with the Calvinistic Baptists of this Association, and thus the denomination became united, to remain so till

1827, when the Kehukee and Country Line Associations left the Old-School Missionary Baptists and became a new sect of Anti-Missionary Baptists.

In Dr. G. W. Purefoy's "History of the Sandy Creek Association," pp. 51-57, it is abundantly shown that in 1821 the Country Line Association was a Missionary body, and in favor of Sabbath-schools, and the "History of the Kehukee Association," by Burkett and Read, shows that that body was composed of Missionary churches for many years after its organization. The Portsmouth and the Chowan were both daughters of the Kehukee Association, and were in their origin, as they still are, Missionary organizations.

FORMATION OF THE STATE CONVENTION.

There seems to have been no general effort to unite the denomination till about the years 1814-16, when the North Carolina Baptist Society for Foreign and Domestic Missions was formed. Who were the leaders in this movement does not appear, but we find that the address to the churches was written by the Rev. Josiah Crudup, and that the famous Robert T. Daniel was its agent. This effort at organization having failed, another society was formed about 1826, called the Baptist Benevolent Society. It drew together a number of prominent men in Greenville in 1829, and after talking the matter over it was pretty well agreed that they would make an effort to form a State Convention at their next meeting. In a journal of Dr. Samuel Wait it is stated that Rev. Thomas Meredith prepared the constitution of the new Convention before he left his home in Edenton, and that when the Convention was formed, in the barn of Dr. J. C. Gorham, a leading Baptist of Greenville, Pitt Co., March 20, 1830, that constitution was substantially adopted, and that is still the constitution of the North Carolina Baptist State Convention. Its second article reads as follows: "The primary objects of this Convention shall be the education of young men called of God to the ministry and approved of by the churches to which they respectively belong, the employment of missionaries within the limits of the State, and a co-operation with the Baptist General Convention of the United States in the promotion of missions in general."

At the time of the adoption of this constitution the Baptists of North Carolina, including Primitive, or Anti-Missionary, and Free-Will Baptists, numbered but 14 Associations, 272 churches, and 15,360 members. They had no denominational paper, and no school, male nor female, under control of the denomination. Many of the Associations scarcely raised more money at their annual meetings than was necessary to defray the expenses of printing their minutes, but the founders of the Convention were men of large brain, unflagging zeal, and earnest piety. They were the strongest men of their denomination, and some of them the peers of any men in the State. They planned largely, and worked zealously up to their plans.

The officers of the Convention were P. W. Dowd, President; W. P. Biddle, Thomas Meredith, and C. McAlister, Vice-Presidents; R. S. Blount, Recording Secretary; and H. Austin, Treasurer.

The first Board of Directors of the Convention consisted of Charles W. Skinner and Henry A. Skinner, of Perquimans; Elder Thomas D. Mason, of Greenville; Daniel Boon, of Johnson County; Elder Samuel Wait, William Sanders, and Elijah Clark, of Newbern; Elder James D. Hall, of Currituck County; Peter B. Lawrence and James Hartmers, of Tarborough; James B. Outlaw, of Bertie County; W. B. Hinton, I. Holliman, and Elder John Purefoy, of Wake; Elder Jacob Rascow, of Edenton; Samuel Simpson, of Craven; Elder James McDaniel, of Cumberland; and G. Hukeby, of Orange.

The following ministers were appointed as agents of the Convention, and served without pay, viz.: P. W. Dowd, Raleigh; Thomas Meredith, Edenton; William P. Biddle, Craven County; James McDaniel, Cumberland County; John Armstrong, Newbern; Reuben Lawrence, Bertie County; Robert T. Daniel and Eli Phillips, Moore County; James D. Hall, Currituck County; John Purefoy, Wake County; John Culpepper, Montgomery County; William Dowd, Stokes County. Samuel Wait was appointed general agent of the Convention, at a salary of $1.00 a day, and John Armstrong, corresponding secretary.

An address, wise and masterly in an extraordinary degree, was prepared by the Rev. Thomas Meredith and sent forth to the churches, showing the advantages of such an institution, answering objections, and inviting them to unite in the organization. The Convention was a bond of union and a source of development, and thus proved a great blessing to the denomination.

The Convention has three boards or Executive Committees to attend to the four special departments of work, the Board of Missions, Home and Foreign, located in Raleigh; the Board of Education, located at Wake Forest College; and the Sunday-School Board, also located in Raleigh. These boards are composed of prominent men, laymen as well as ministers, chosen from different parts of the State, enough, however, residing in the vicinity of the location of the board to constitute a quorum.

NORTH CAROLINA BAPTISTS WHO HAVE BECOME DISTINGUISHED IN OTHER STATES.

As in the field of politics North Carolina has produced three Presidents of the nation, Jackson,

Polk, and Johnson, each of whom attained distinction in other States, so in the realm of religion it is not immodest to say that many of the wisest and ablest men who have adorned the Baptist Zion of the South have gone forth from this State. Silas Mercer, of Georgia, was a preacher in North Carolina for years before he went South, and his nephew, Jesse Mercer, the leader of the Georgia Baptists and the founder and benefactor of Mercer University, was a native of Halifax Co., N. C. The elder W. T. Brantly and the elder Basil Manly were born in Chatham Co., N. C., within five miles of each other, and entered the ministry in this State. John Kerr, who as an orator was pronounced by Dr. Jeter as first, and no man was second, and who became so celebrated in Virginia, was born in Caswell Co., N. C., where he began to preach, and he died in North Carolina. Dr. R. B. C. Howell, so long identified with Virginia and Tennessee, and among the most distinguished Baptist authors of the South, was a native of Wayne Co., N. C., and began his ministry in North Carolina. Dr. A. M. Poindexter, the prince of agents, and the most eloquent man the writer ever heard, was born in Bertie Co., N. C. And J. S. Mims, the learned professor, and Iverson L. Brooks, the successful pastor, both of South Carolina, were born, the first in Cumberland County, the second in Caswell Co., N. C. All these, with Saunders, the first president of Mercer University, Georgia, and Emerson, of William Jewell College, Missouri, and Solomon, of Kentucky, and hundreds of other useful and honored men among the Baptists, have gone forth from this great Baptist State.

PROGRESS OF THE BAPTISTS IN NORTH CAROLINA.

In 1770 there were but 9 churches in the State. In 1784 there were 42 churches, 47 ministers, 3776 members. In 1812 there were 204 churches, 117 ministers, and 12,567 members. In 1832 there were 332 churches, 211 ministers, and 18,918 members. In 1851 there were 599 churches, 374 ministers, and 41,674 members. In 1860 there were 692 churches, 374 ministers, and 59,778 members. In 1876 there were 1442 churches, 793 ministers, and 137,000 members. Their statistics as reported for 1880 foot up 77 Associations, 1905 churches, and 172,951 members.

These figures place North Carolina third among the States as regards Baptist strength. Georgia is first, Virginia second, and North Carolina third.

North Carolina, The Biblical Recorder of.— No single agency has done so much to unite and develop the Baptists of North Carolina as the *Biblical Recorder*, which for forty-six years has been their State organ. In 1833, Rev. Thomas Meredith, then pastor in Edenton, issued *The Baptist Interpreter*, a monthly publication, in pamphlet form, with a list of less than a hundred subscribers. In about two years there was a call for a weekly paper, and in January, 1834, *The Biblical Recorder* was originated by the same man, beginning with nearly 1000 subscribers. The paper was removed to Newbern in 1834, and to Raleigh in 1838, where it is now issued. About this time the *Recorder* and *Southern Watchman*, of Charleston, S. C., were united, and, until 1842, it was published under the style of *The Recorder and Watchman*. In 1842 the *Recorder* was suspended for six months, being superseded by a monthly periodical entitled *The Southern Christian Repository*. After six months, however, the publication of the *Recorder* was resumed, and it continued under the management of Mr. Meredith till his death, in 1851. For two or three years it was edited by Rev. T. W. Toby, D.D., pastor of the Raleigh church, and was still the property of Mrs. Meredith. In 1854 the paper was purchased by a joint-stock company, and Rev. J. J. James, one of the proprietors, became editor. Two years afterwards Mr. James bought out his partners, and associated Rev. J. S. Walthal with himself as editor, and they continued these relations until 1861, when Rev. J. D. Hufham, D.D., bought the journal, and edited it throughout the war. In April, 1865, by reason of a want of postal facilities, the *Recorder* was again suspended for a time, but its publication was resumed in the fall of the same year.

In 1867, Dr. Hufham sold the paper to Dr. Walters and Mr. J. H. Mills, who were its joint editors for a time. Mr. Mills, however, became sole proprietor in a few months, and continued to conduct the paper till 1873, when the *Recorder* passed into the hands of Prof. A. F. Read, who, after two years' experience as editor, sold it to Rev. C. T. Bailey, who still owns it, in connection with C. B. Edwards and N. B. Broughton. Dr. J. D. Hufham was associate editor with Mr. Bailey for more than a year after he took charge of the *Recorder*. Dr. T. H. Pritchard was also employed on the editorial staff for two years, and the Rev. Harvey Hatcher is now the associate editor.

The *Recorder* has a subscription-list of about 4500, and is regarded not only as a means of eminent usefulness, but a good property, yielding a handsome income to the proprietors.

North Carolina, The Colored Baptists of.— There are probably 80,000 colored Baptists in North Carolina in regular Baptist churches. A considerable number also are to be found in Methodist churches who have been immersed, and who do not believe in or practise infant baptism. Up to the close of the war the colored people in most cases were members of the same churches with the whites, having a portion of the meeting-houses set apart for their use, though in a few instances they had distinct organizations and their own pastors. As was naturally to be expected, they withdrew from their white brethren after their liberation, though not in all cases, for the colored members of the First Baptist church of Raleigh did not retire till nearly four years after the war closed.

Since the war they have grown rapidly, and have now 30 Associations, with about 750 churches, and a membership of 80,000, and with probably 30,000 teachers and scholars in their Sunday-schools.

CONVENTION.

Their State Convention was organized at Goldsborough, N. C., Oct. 17, 1867, and they were aided on this occasion by a committee appointed by the Convention of their white brethren, consisting of Revs. J. S. Purefoy, W. M. Young, A. D. Cohen, and C. J. Nelson. Rev. William Warwick was chosen President, and L. W. Boone, Secretary. The objects of their Convention are the promotion of missions, ministerial education, and Sunday-schools. This Convention met in Newbern in October, 1879, and its officers are Rev. Cæsar Johnson, President; Rev. H. A. Powell, Vice-President; E. E. Smith, Secretary; Rev. John Curly, Corresponding Secretary; Rev. A. B. Williams, Treasurer; Rev. G. W. Perry, Auditor.

They also have a Sunday-school Convention, which meets annually, the last session having been held in September, 1879, in Goldsborough. They have a church organ, called the *African Expositor*, which is issued monthly.

Their corresponding secretary travels as an agent, collecting money, and doing missionary work also.

As early as 1868 the Convention voted that a chair of theology should be established for the training of their ministers, and the Rev. H. M. Tupper, of the Shaw University, was chosen to fill this chair.

In addition to the Shaw University they have three academies,—one at Plymouth, one at Garysburg, and one at Goldsborough; the first two are paid for and the other nearly so.

North Carolina, Western Convention of.— In 1789 the French Broad Baptist church was organized in that part of North Carolina known as west of the Blue Ridge. Big Ivy church also claims to have been constituted about the same time. The first Association organized in the west was the French Broad, in 1807, and was formed by the union of six churches,—Little Ivy, Locust's Old Fields, New Found, Caney River, French Broad, and Cane Creek. The first three were dismissed from the Holston Association of Tennessee; the other three from Broad River, in South Carolina. Its ordained ministers were Thomas Snelson, Thomas Justice, Sim Blythe, Benjamin King, Humphrey Posey, and Stephen Morgan.

Other churches and Associations having originated in this part of the State, the Western Baptist Convention was organized in 1845 as an auxiliary of the State Convention. In 1857 it became an independent body. At first its territory extended as far east as the Yadkin, but since the late war it has confined its labors principally to the fourteen counties west of the Blue Ridge. This territory contains 9 Associations, representing about 20,000 Baptists. The Convention has three boards,—a Sunday-school board, located at Asheville; a Mission board, located at Waynesville; and an Education board, whose headquarters are at Hendersonville. In 1853 the *Carolina Baptist*, a weekly newspaper, was started at Hendersonville, with Rev. James Blythe as editor. It suspended in 1856, but resumed publication in 1857. Soon afterwards it was succeeded by the *Baptist Telescope*, W. A. G. Bunn editor, but this paper lived only a few years. Rev. N. Bowen originated the *Cottage Visitor*, which continued until 1871. The *Baptist Gleaner*, edited by Rev. John Ammons, appeared in Asheville in 1877, but lived only a year. The *Baptist Telescope* has been revived, and is edited by Rev. N. Bowen.

The Baptists sought to establish a college at Mars Hill, in Madison County, before the war, but the prevalence of hostilities caused the enterprise to be abandoned, and it has not since been revived. A school at Holly Springs, in Macon County, has been under the patronage of the denomination for several years.

In 1858 it was determined to build a Baptist female college at Hendersonville. Rev. N. Bowen, as agent, pushed the work, until stopped by the war. A granite building, three stories high, nearly complete, owned at present by a joint-stock company, but controlled by the Baptists, is the result of this effort. This institution, known as the Judson College, has a patronage of a hundred students of both sexes, and is presided over by Rev. W. A. Nelson, D.D., aided by a competent corps of teachers. The present officers of the Convention are: President, Rev. N. Bowen; Vice-Presidents, Rev. S. M. Collis, Rev. John Ammons; Secretary, Columbus M. Williams; Treasurer, John L. Pleasants; Historian, Rev. D. B. Nelson.

Northrup, G. W., D.D., LL.D., the able and distinguished president of the theological seminary at Chicago, was born at Antwerp, Jefferson Co., N. Y., Oct. 15, 1826. From his earliest childhood he was under strong religious influences, his father being a man of singularly devout character and life. Though converted, as he believes, at the age of twelve, it was at the age of sixteen that he received baptism, at the hands of Rev. Wilbur Tillinghast, becoming a member of the Baptist church in his native town. The school advantages in Antwerp were of an inferior character. His scholarly tendencies, however, very early showed themselves,

G. W. NORTHRUP, D.D., LL.D.

and he began the study of Latin, with such imperfect helps as he could secure, while but a boy. At the age of eighteen he left home, with a view to make a career for himself, though as yet with no distinct purpose as to the line of life he should choose. Some years were spent in teaching at Trenton, near Utica, and at Granville and Hartford, Washington Co. When at about the age of twenty-one a visit to relatives living in Watertown, N. Y., was the means of deciding him to enter upon a regular course of study. He had already, in connection with his teaching, but mainly through private study, become so much a proficient in mathematics that he had in that department passed over most of the ground of a college course. In Latin he had done something; in Greek he had not made even a beginning. Setting himself resolutely to private study, partly under the tuition of A. C. Beach, Esq., since lieutenant-governor of the State of New York, he made such progress that in a year and a half he was prepared to enter the last term of the Sophomore year at Williams College in Massachusetts. At his graduation, in 1854, he took the metaphysical oration, perhaps the highest of the college honors at Williams. Entering the theological seminary at Rochester, he graduated there in 1857.

Immediately upon the conclusion of his theological course he was appointed instructor in church history in the seminary at Rochester, and at the end of the year full professor in that department. The ten years of service, until his call to Chicago in 1867, made their lasting impression in the seminary and upon the numerous young men who came under his tuition. Better work in church history has probably never been done in any theological seminary in this country. During this period, besides, Dr. Northrup won distinction as a preacher. For one year and a half he supplied the pulpit of the First church in Rochester, 165 being in that time added to the church by baptism. In 1867 he was called to the presidency and the chair of Theology in the seminary about to be organized at Chicago. Marked as had been his adaptation to the form of work assigned him at Rochester, for this at Chicago he was perhaps still better suited. While yet a youth he had become an enthusiastic student of metaphysics. Previous to entering college he had read "Rational Psychology" (not an easy book to master) through no less than five times, and knew pages of it by heart. This intellectual learning and capacity qualified him in an especial manner for a mastery of systematic theology; and his classes at Chicago enthusiastically testify to the grasp he has, and in their measure enables them to take, of the whole subject of Christian doctrine in its classification and in its verification. Although he has not as yet become known as an author, his lectures, alike in church history and in theology, have been made so complete and so full that, if they could be given to the world, they would rank with the most valued of the many books in these lines of theological study. As a preacher and lecturer Dr. Northrup renders eminent service, alike to the denomination and to the general cause of truth, in those departments of it which it is the fashion of these times especially to assail,—more particularly what concerns the relations of science and philosophy with the doctrines of the Christian faith.

Norton, Charles C., D.D., was born in Washington, Conn. He was brought up in the Protestant Episcopal Church. After his conversion his convictions of duty led him to unite with a Baptist church, and he was baptized into the fellowship of the church in Carmel, Putnam Co., N. Y. Soon after his connection with the church he was licensed to preach, and entered the University of New York, and afterwards the University of Rochester, from which he was graduated. He then entered the theological seminary there, and was graduated in 1854. In 1855 he accepted a call from the Sixth Street Baptist church in New York, where he was ordained and commenced his ministerial work. His connection with that church continued nine years, during which a pressing church debt was removed, and about 400 converts were added to it by baptism. For the past seventeen years he has been the successful pastor of the Central Park Baptist church of New York. He is a fine scholar and an able preacher. The honorary degree of D.D. was conferred on him by Shurtleff College. During his ministry he has baptized 704.

Norton, Judge E. H., was born in Logan Co., Ky., Nov. 21, 1821. He entered Centre College, at

JUDGE E. H. NORTON.

Danville, at seventeen years of age. In 1842 he graduated from the law department of Transylvania University, and located in Platte City, Mo., and rapidly built up a legal practice. In 1852 he was elected circuit judge over a district of seven counties. He was re-elected in 1857 without opposition, and served until sent to Congress, in 1861. At this time he was elected to the State convention to consider the relations of Missouri to the general government. In that body he opposed the ordinance of secession. In 1875 he was elected a member of the convention which framed the present constitution of Missouri, and was chairman of the committee on representative districts. In 1876 he was appointed to the Supreme bench by Gov. Hardin to fill a vacancy occasioned by the death of Judge H. M. Varis. He united with the Baptist Church, in Kentucky, when fourteen years of age. In 1853 he aided to organize a Baptist church in Platte City. He is a trustee of William Jewell College, and takes an interest in his denomination in the State. He is an upright and talented judge.

Nott, Rev. Abner Kingman, son of Rev. Handel G. and Lydia C. Nott, was born at Nashua, N. H., March 22, 1834, being the fourth son in a family of fifteen children. His early preparation for college was carried on partly under the tuition of Mr. J. H. Hanson, principal of the Waterville, Me., Academy, and partly under the instruction of his father. While thus engaged in study his conversion took place, in January, 1849. His later preparation for college was made at the Connecticut Literary Institution at Suffield, where he spent a little over one year. The question of his future vocation was settled when he entered Rochester University, in the fall of 1851. He was graduated in the class of 1855. Two years were devoted to theological study in the seminary at Rochester. His life both in college and in the seminary was one of constant and unceasing activity, for he was largely dependent on his own efforts to secure the funds needed for the payment of his bills. He preached, taught, and lectured, and thus acquired a remarkable facility as a public speaker. He preached the first time for the First Baptist church, New York, in the fall of 1856, and Dec. 29, 1856, was unanimously called to the pastorate of the church as the successor of Rev. Dr. Spencer H. Cone. This call he accepted, and a few weeks after his graduation, in July, 1857, was ordained. With the most brilliant prospects before him, and in the midst of a career of usefulness such as few young ministers are permitted to see, he was suddenly

REV. ABNER KINGMAN NOTT.

called to his reward while bathing near Perth Amboy, N. J., July 8, 1859. His goodness, intellectual powers, and eloquence gave him immense popularity in New York City, and made his death a public calamity.

Nott, Rev. Richard M., died at Wakefield, Mass., Dec. 21, 1880, after several months of suffering from extreme nervous prostration. He was born in Nashua, N. H., in March, 1831, where his father, Rev. Handel G. Nott, was then a prominent Congregational minister, settled over the leading church in that rapidly-growing place, from which situation he retired a few years later upon becoming a Baptist, in which character his first settlement was over the Federal Street, now Clarendon Street, Baptist church, Boston. At the age of eleven years Richard was converted, and soon after baptized by his father. He graduated at Waterville College when about nineteen years old. During the next five years he taught school in Red Creek, N. Y., three years, and Calais, Me., two years. Then he entered the theological seminary at Rochester, where he graduated in 1859, and entered immediately upon the pastorate of the First Baptist church in Rochester, N. Y., to which he had been called several months before his graduation. In this important position he continued six years. During this time he wrote the exceedingly interesting memoir of his younger brother, A. Kingman Nott, who suddenly closed in death a most brilliant earthly career in July, 1859, while pastor of the First Baptist church in New York City. At length his health failed, and his appreciating people sent him abroad for recuperation, but he never regained the physical vigor then lost. After his return from his foreign tour, having resigned at Rochester, he labored three years at Atlanta, Ga., where he was successful in gathering what is now the Second Baptist church in that city. Next he was pastor of the church in Aurora, Ill., three years. In 1872 he was called to the pastoral charge of the church in Wakefield, Mass., which he accepted and held about two years, when he resigned; but he continued to reside there until his death, supplying most of the time since his resignation the church in Brookville, formerly South Randolph, where his labors were highly valued, and a good work was done by him. In the summer of 1880 his health so failed that he was obliged to abandon his supply at Brookville, and also his valuable work in the Sunday-school department of *The Watchman*, the "Lesson Helps," which were very satisfactorily prepared by him. After this he gradually declined, till his earthly end was reached at the age of nearly fifty years. He was a superior scholar and a clear thinker. His early promise was uncommon. Few men were his equals in critical scholarship and logical acumen. He would have graced a position as a professor or president of a college or a theological institution. In the Boston Ministers' Meeting, which he constantly attended, he was justly esteemed as a most serviceable member. Probably there was no place during the last five or six years of his life in which he appeared to better advantage than there. His utterances were real contributions, the great worth of which was readily conceded by all his brethren, among whom he is greatly missed.

Nova Scotia, New Brunswick, Prince Edward Island, and Newfoundland, Historical Sketch of the Baptists in.—From the cession of Acadia,—Nova Scotia and New Brunswick were originally included under this designation,—by France to Great Britain, in 1713 till 1776, when Henry Alline, the celebrated New Light preacher, entered on his fervid, trumpet-toned, evangelistic ministry, a dead formalism in religion almost universally prevailed in these provinces, with only here and there a faint glimmer of evangelical doctrine and spiritual experience.

But amid this moral desolation three or four Baptist ministers appeared almost simultaneously in Acadia,—Rev. John Sutton, with a company of emigrants from New Jersey, settled at Newport, Nova Scotia, in 1760, and there preached and baptized converts, and Daniel Dimock also. Rev. James Sutton, brother of John, was also at Newport. Rev. Ebenezer Moulton, of South Brimfield, Mass., came with the first settlers to Yarmouth, Nova Scotia, in 1761, and preached among them, and baptized a Mrs. Burgess, and probably other converts; and his preaching subsequently in Horton, Nova Scotia, was attended with great success. Rev. Nathan Mason, with a number of Baptists in church order, emigrated from South Swanzey, Mass., and settled at Sackville, New Brunswick, in 1763. No church, however, appears to have been formed here by either of them, and in a few years they returned to their own country.

In 1776, Henry Alline came forth from obscurity like John the Baptist to prepare the way of the Lord; many were converted under his ministry, and churches, composed of Baptists and Pedobaptists, were formed. The time, however, soon came for a distinct Baptist movement.

The pioneer Baptist church of the Maritime Provinces was formed of ten members, at Horton, Nova Scotia, Oct. 29, 1778. Rev. Nicholas Pierson, one of their number, was ordained as their pastor Nov. 5, 1778. The Second Baptist church in the provinces was formed at Halifax, Nova Scotia, in 1795, Rev. John Burton being pastor. The Third church was organized at Newport, Nova Scotia, in August, 1799; and the Fourth Baptist church was organized at Sackville, New Brunswick, in October, 1799, Rev. Joseph Crandall being ordained their pastor. Six others must have been formed previous to 1800.

The Nova Scotia and New Brunswick Baptist Association, the first in these provinces, was formed at Lower Granville, Nova Scotia, June 23, 1800, and comprised ten churches,—Upper Granville, Lower Granville, Digby, Digby Neck, Yarmouth, Cornwallis, Horton, Newport, Chester, and Sackville. Mixed communion was allowed for a time in some of these churches, but was soon discontinued.

The ministers who united in forming this Association were Thomas Handley Chipman, James Manning, Enoch Towner, Harris Harding, Edward Manning, Theodore Seth Harding, Joseph Dimock, and Joseph Crandall.

These churches, located thus widely apart in the two provinces, were true Baptist Christian centres, whence spiritual knowledge and influence were diffused through the surrounding communities; and the ministers were true watchmen and evangelists, who bore abroad the torch of divine truth and the message of the gospel to guide the perishing to Christ.

The Baptist denomination, whose origin in these provinces has now been briefly traced, is a large and influential body; and the movements and events which will now be mentioned will indicate its progress, and also the means of its further expansion.

Organized home missionary efforts were originated at the meeting of the Nova Scotia and New Brunswick Association in 1815, and were immediately followed by the most encouraging success, and home mission work has ever since been carried on in Nova Scotia and New Brunswick with great spiritual results.

The Nova Scotia and New Brunswick Association, composed of 31 churches, with 1827 members, and 22 ministers, was divided into two in 1821, the churches in Nova Scotia forming one Association, and those in New Brunswick forming the other. As in 1810 the membership of the Association was 924, the above figures show that it was nearly doubled in eleven years.

In 1825, Rev. Dr. Tupper, from Nova Scotia, and Rev. Joseph Crandall, from New Brunswick, evangelized on Prince Edward Island, and were the first associated Baptist ministers to labor in that gem of the St. Lawrence, though Rev. A. Crawford, a Scotch Baptist, had successfully commenced operations there as early as 1811.

In 1825, 1826, and 1838, Rev. Joseph Dimock evangelized for several months in Cape Breton, and with the happiest results. Now our home missionary enterprise is one of the most interesting and important of the denomination, and the field is as large as the three provinces and Newfoundland.

The use of the press for denominational and Christian purposes indicates life and progress.

The Nova Scotia and New Brunswick *Baptist Magazine* was commenced in St. John, New Brunswick, in 1827, and continued to be the organ of the denomination in the provinces till 1836, when the *Christian Messenger*, published weekly at Halifax, Nova Scotia, took its place.

In 1847 the *Christian Visitor* was issued at St. John, New Brunswick, as the organ of the denomination in that province. Both these papers continue as Baptist organs, and have been very influential in promoting denominational interests.

Education.—The Baptist Association at Horton in 1828 adopted measures for establishing an institution of learning for our youth, and especially with a view to the proper training of young men called of God to the gospel ministry; and as a result Horton Academy was opened in May, 1829, with more than 40 pupils, under charge of Rev. Asahel Chapin as principal.

In 1833 the New Brunswick Baptist Association originated a similar movement; and as a result the Baptist Seminary at Fredericton was opened in January, 1836, with Rev. F. W. Miles as principal.

In the autumn of 1838 circumstances in Nova Scotia impelled the Baptists to make a further advance in the work of higher education; and Acadia College sprung from the resolve then taken, and was opened in January, 1839, with Rev. E. A. Crawley and Rev. John Pryor as professors, to which Prof. Isaac Chipman was added a year later, and continued his valuable services until he was drowned in the basin of the Minas, in June, 1852. Notwithstanding opposition, difficulties, and loss, Acadia College has grown and attained a leading position among the colleges of these provinces. It has now an endowment of $84,112.46, with other sources of income, and six professors, with Rev. Dr. Sawyer as president. Though the college building at Wolfville was destroyed by fire in December, 1877, a new edifice soon adorned College Hill, flanked on the east by Acadia Seminary, a high school for young ladies, and by Horton Collegiate Academy on the west. The Baptists of New Brunswick and Prince Edward Island have an equal share with those of Nova Scotia in the ownership and government of these institutions.

Foreign Missions.—The organized movement to send out missionaries to the heathen world commenced, like that for home missions in 1815, at Chester in 1838, and in this action the New Brunswick Baptist Association cordially concurred, and Rev. R. E. Burpe, of the latter province, was accordingly sent out to Burmah in 1845 by the Baptists of these provinces,—their first missionary to the heathen. The denomination has now four missions established among the Teloogoos, with native preachers and assistants, under the direction of the missionaries.

The New Brunswick Baptist Association, comprising 50 churches, with 4806 members, and 29 ministers, was divided in 1847 into two Associations,—the Eastern and Western. The figures indicate an increase of over ninefold in the membership of that body in twenty-five years.

The Nova Scotia Baptist Association, comprising 72 churches, with 8967 members, and 54 ministers, was also divided in 1850 into three Associations,—the Western, Central, and Eastern.

In July, 1868, the Prince Edward Island Baptist Association was organized, with 13 churches, containing a membership of 600, dismissed for the purpose from the Nova Scotia Eastern Association, and the membership of the denomination in that island is 1622, or nearly three times what it was twelve years ago.

Union.—The leaders of the Baptist denomination in these provinces provided for the union of all the churches and Associations in denominational work, and through their wise forethought the Baptist Convention of Nova Scotia, New Brunswick, and Prince Edward Island was organized in the city of St. John, New Brunswick, in September, 1846. This Convention is now the most influential of the Baptist organizations in the Maritime Provinces. To its direction and management are committed the great public benevolent enterprises of the denomination,—home missions, education, and foreign missions,—and the greatest care is exercised to conduct matters wisely and efficiently, and yet not to intrench on great denominational principles.

Revivals of a genuine type have all along been a vast means of growth, and they are still needed to promote healthful enlargement. Our churches and denomination should aspire wisely and well to realize the highest ideal of Christian life, activity, and progress.

Newfoundland.—There are a few Baptists on this great island, but no Baptist church or minister. Revs. J. B. McDonald, M.D., and George Armstrong, spent a few weeks in missionary work there in 1875, and Rev. George Armstrong evangelized for nine weeks in 1879.

The following figures show the numerical progress of the Baptist denomination in the Maritime Provinces for the past eighty years:

Year.	Churches.	Ministers.	Members.
1800	10	8	*600
1810	14	9	924
1820	29	19	1,785
1830	70	40	4,633
1840	115	64	9,041
1850	....	....	13,773
1860	260	139	21,579
1870	257	145	27,460
1880	356	195	36,700

* About.

Novatians, The.—Novatian, the distinguished founder of the community that bore his name, is known among Greek ecclesiastical writers as Novatus. He was not Novatus of Carthage, a presbyter of that city, who sorely vexed the imperious soul of Cyprian, and who came to Rome and united with Novatian in efforts to maintain gospel purity in the churches.

Novatian, before he professed conversion, was a philosopher of remarkable ability, culture, eloquence, and powers of persuasion; he was a natural leader of men. When attacked by a dangerous disease, from which death was apprehended, in accordance with the opinion then commonly held by Christians, it was judged that he should be baptized to make heaven certain, and, as his weakness rendered immersion impossible without risking his immediate death, he was subjected, on his couch, to a profuse application of water. We are not informed that Novatian desired this ceremony himself, without any persuasions from his alarmed friends. The writer was once sent for to see a dying lady, and, after praying with her, was earnestly pressed by a follower of Irish Romanism, the perverted faith of St. Patrick the Baptist, " to *reginerate* her ;" he declined to exercise the powers of the Spirit of God and the functions of a Pedobaptist minister; had he yielded, the lady was in a condition in which she could not be held responsible for the act. And it is not improbable that this was the situation of Novatian. He was spared by the providence of God for a mighty work in the churches, and when restored to health he became very active in advancing the interests of Christianity in Rome.

At that period the church, in the capital of the world, as Eusebius records, had 46 presbyters, 14 deacons and subdeacons, 50 minor ecclesiastical officials, and widows and sick and indigent persons, numbering in all 1500, whose support had to be provided for. And partly to assist in bearing this burden, but chiefly through a lack of faith and of complete consecration to God, the door of the church was kept very wide for the admission of unconverted professors, and when these persons betrayed the Saviour by sacrificing to idols in times of persecution, their conduct was excused by their lax brethren; and the excommunication, necessarily pronounced upon them immediately after their apostasy, was speedily removed.

Cornelius, a Roman presbyter, with an eager eye to the support to be gathered from restored apostates, strongly advocated their forgiveness by the church. Novatian very strenuously resisted it; and when a successor to Bishop Fabianus was to be elected, Cornelius was properly made a predecessor of a long line of coming popes, who loved gold more than anything in the Christian religion.

Novatian was condemned by Cornelius and by all his episcopal friends; and the bishop of Rome sent letters everywhere, bringing the most grievous charges against him, and giving the names and positions of the bishops who united with him in his efforts to crush the first great reformer.

Novatian had been made a presbyter by Fabianus against the custom of the church, for, as Cornelius says, in Eusebius,* "It was not lawful that one baptized in his sick-bed by aspersion, as he was, should be promoted to any order of the clergy. . . . If, indeed, it be proper to say that one like him did receive baptism." But this only shows his extraordinary talents and influence.

After Cornelius became bishop Novatian was elevated to the same office by three Italian bishops, and at once founded the purer community, for whose advancement he labored with great success until martyrdom removed him from the presence of wicked church members in full ecclesiastical standing.

Among the charges brought by Cornelius against Novatian, a list of which can be found in Eusebius, was an accusation of cowardice for refusing to perform the duties of his ministerial office in a time of persecution. Novatian set up a new community in defiance of Cornelius and of nearly all the Christian bishops on earth; and in this he showed unusual courage. Opposition to the treachery, charged upon himself by Cornelius, was the chief instrument which he used to establish his pure church, and it is not in human nature to believe that any man could found a new community in Rome itself by denunciations of a cowardly crime of which he himself had given a conspicuous example. Besides, he left the world as a martyr.

It was customary in the time of Ambrose, when the minister distributed the Lord's Supper to the faithful, to say, "The body of Christ," and the recipient answered, "Amen."† Cornelius, in the same calumnious letter in Eusebius, states that Novatian, when he gave a portion of the Eucharist to a communicant, instead of permitting him to say "Amen," according to the usage no doubt then in existence, seized his hand in both of his hands, before he partook of the symbolic bread, and made him "swear by the body and blood of our Saviour, Jesus Christ, that he would never desert him, nor turn to Cornelius." This story carries its own refutation; the idea that the founder of the purest Christian community then in existence should resort to such an infamous procedure is simply incredible. Cornelius, in the same connection, makes slanderous statements about the extraordinary ambition of Novatian, which have come down to us through the "Ecclesiastical History" of Eusebius; and his vanity is frequently given as the motive that led to his assumption of the bishop's office, and to the reformation inaugurated by Novatian.

The Novatians called themselves Kathari, or Puritans. The corner-stone of the denomination was purity of church membership. Novatian charged Cornelius and his followers with dishonoring the church of God, and destroying its divine character by admitting apostates into its membership. He maintained that those who had sacrificed to the idols to save their lives should never be permitted to come to the Lord's table again. This theory became popular with the saintly heroes and heroines, who suffered terribly at the hands of Christ's persecuting enemies, but whose lives were spared. And all true Christians felt a strong leaning towards the holy religion advocated and exhibited by Novatian and his followers. Socrates,‡ a candid and intelligent Greek historian, says, "Novatus (Novatian), a presbyter of the Romish Church, separated from it because Cornelius, the bishop, received into communion believers who had sacrificed (to idols) during the persecution which the emperor Decius had raised against the church. . . . On being afterwards elevated to the episcopacy by such prelates as entertained similar sentiments, he wrote to all the churches, insisting that they should not admit to the sacred mysteries those who had sacrificed (to idols), but exhorting them to repentance, leave the pardon of their offense to God, who has the power to forgive all sin. . . . The exclusion of those who, after baptism, had committed any deadly sin from the mysteries appeared to some a cruel and merciless course; but others thought it just and necessary for the maintenance of discipline, and the promotion of greater devotedness of life. In the midst of the agitation of this important question letters arrived from Cornelius the bishop promising indulgence to delinquents after baptism. . . . Those who had pleasure in sin, encouraged by the license thus granted them, took occasion from it to revel in every species of criminality." The Novatians permanently excluded from their community all who were guilty of deadly sins and second marriages, as well as those who sacrificed to idols to save their lives; and they regarded the church universal as having lost the character of a church of Christ by receiving such persons into her membership. As a result of this conviction they baptized again all who came from the old church to them. Their baptism was immersion, the "pouring around" of Novatian on his sick-bed is the only transaction of that kind in their history now known; and as their leader suffered so much from the unscriptural performance, his followers had little encouragement to imitate such an unfortunate example.

---

* Eccles. Hist., lib. vi. cap. 43.
† Ambros. De Sacram., lib. iv. cap. 5.
‡ Eccles. Hist., lib. iv. cap. 28.

The general doctrines of the Novatians were in perfect harmony with those received by the church universal; they only differed from it on questions of discipline, and chiefly on the great subject of consecration to God.

It is creditable to the piety of the centuries during which the Novatians existed that great numbers of Christians adopted their sentiments and their fold; though hated, wickedly calumniated, and fiercely persecuted for a long time, they spread, and they found adherents not only in rural regions, but in great cities and in the palaces of the emperor. Speaking of the law of Constantine the Great by which heretics were forbidden to meet "in their own houses of prayer, in private houses, or in public places, but were compelled to enter into communion with the church universal," Sozomen says, "The Novatians alone, who had obtained good leaders, and who entertained the same opinions respecting the divinity as the Catholic Church, formed a large sect from the beginning, and were not decreased in point of numbers by this law. The emperor, I believe, relaxed the rigor of the enactment in their favor. . . . Acesius, who was then the bishop of the Novatians in Constantinople, was much esteemed by the emperor on account of his virtuous life."*

Novatian himself was a man of fervent piety; and his life after his conversion was above reproach, unless when accusations came from a calumniator whose charges were incapable of proof. He was the author of works on "The Passover," "Circumcision," "The Sabbath," "High-Priests," "The Trinity," and on other subjects. He had many distinguished men among his disciples. His community spread very widely, and enjoyed special prosperity in Phrygia; but declined rapidly in the fifth century. The Novatians, as a people, were an honor to Christianity, and their teachings and example exercised a powerful restraint upon the growing corruptions of the old church.

The Novatians commenced their denominational life when the baptism of an unconscious babe was unknown outside of Africa; and there it had a limited, if not a doubtful, existence. Indeed, if a celebrated letter of Cyprian, about a council of bishops, said to have been held in Carthage half a dozen years after Novatian set up his banner of church purity, be a forgery, and the supposition is by no means an improbable one, unconscious infant baptism has no proof of its existence in the literature of the world. The infant rite, according to the letter of Cyprian just referred to, had Cyprian for its patron, and as he had shown the utmost hostility to Novatian, he and his followers would not be

* Eccles. Hist., lib. ii. cap. 32.

very eager to adopt a ceremony of which his letter, if genuine, shows that he was the special friend. These considerations, together with the holiness of life demanded by Novatian churches, have led many persons to regard them as Baptists. Of the truth of this opinion in the early history of this people there can be no doubt; and that the majority of their churches baptized only instructed persons to the end of their history is in the highest degree probable.

Nowlin, Rev. David W., was born in Pittsylvania Co., Va., April 11, 1812, and died in Montgomery Co., Mo., Oct. 17, 1865. He was educated for the bar, and was noted for clear views of the law, and for a sound judgment. He taught the Bible in his schools where he gave instructions in science, because he believed it to be the foundation of sound civil law. Hence when he was converted he was familiar with Scriptural knowledge. He found the Saviour in 1849, under the preaching of Rev. William Vardeman, by whom he was baptized, in November, 1851, into the fellowship of Zion church. In 1856 he was ordained by Revs. Jas. E. Welch, W. Vardeman, and the venerable J. T. Johnson. Mr. Nowlin's culture, talent, and piety made him exceedingly acceptable as a preacher. He was frequently moderator of his Association. He was honored and loved as a faithful and successful minister of Jesus.

Nugent, Deacon E. J., was born on the 13th of March, 1812, near Philadelphia, Pa. He grew to the age of sixteen and a half years without religious training. In the year 1831 a lady invited him to accompany her to hear a sermon in the First Baptist church of Philadelphia. A stranger, Rev. N. Colver, preached, and for the first time in his life he was awakened to an alarming consciousness of his sinfulness, and was so exercised that he could not work for several days. He was enabled through grace to repent of sin and to embrace Jesus Christ by a living faith, and was baptized by the pastor, W. T. Brantly, Sr., D.D., with thirty-one others, in the river Delaware. He was immediately set to work as a teacher in the Sunday-school, where he served the church for some years. At this period he was led to consider seriously the impropriety of using intoxicating liquors as a beverage, and he has been an earnest advocate of the cause of temperance ever since. He regarded the Lord's day as a sacred time for moral and religious improvement, bodily rest and recuperation, and under the influence of this view he was early led to fixed habits of constant attendance upon the social and public worship of God. In connection with others he conducted religious services in the suburbs of the city. In March, 1835, he removed to Springfield, O. Mr. Nugent assisted in organizing a Baptist prayer-meeting and Sunday-school, and in January, 1837, a church was formed consisting of thirteen members, of which he was chosen a deacon. The church continued public worship, meeting in school-houses until permitted to worship in an old court-house, where, in the year 1841, a series of meetings was commenced, resulting in the first great revival ever experienced in the town. Over 100 were converted, about 50 of whom joined the Baptist church. The deacon, with a few others, was engaged in conducting meetings for prayer and exhortation in country school-houses, thereby creating an interest in the farming community for the Baptist church. This custom, under the blessing of God, was the secret of the remarkable growth and influence of this church. The deacon afterward wrote a history of the church.

About this time he asked a young Presbyterian brother whom he had heard declare that infant baptism was taught in the Scriptures to point out to him some of the proof texts, and promised to pay him handsomely for his time if he would produce them. But the young man never demanded the reward. Conversations were continued on the subject for several months, resulting in his union with the Baptist Church. On the day he was baptized he preached a sermon on the subject of baptism, giving reasons for his change of views, and was baptized in Buck's Creek by Rev. J. L. Moore, and was licensed to preach the gospel by the Baptist Church. That young man is now the beloved and honored superintendent of Baptist Missions of the city of Philadelphia, Rev. James French. The deacon was either a teacher or superintendent of the Sunday-school during his residence in the place. When it became possible for the church at Springfield to build a house, he was appointed on a building committee of two, and they succeeded in erecting a very commodious brick church edifice and parsonage. Mr. Nugent continued his membership there until the church numbered over 300.

In 1852 he removed to Marysville, O. There being no Baptist church in the town, and only four Baptists, he commenced prayer-meetings in private houses.

In the month of March, 1865, he and his family removed to Ottawa, Kansas. The next day after reaching Ottawa was the Lord's day, and the deacon went to the Baptist Sunday-school and into the young men's Bible-class. On the following Sabbath he was appointed teacher of the same class. At the time he arrived in Ottawa the Baptist church had no edifice. The question of building one was discussed, and he was appointed on the building committee. A house was completed at a cost of $3700. In 1872 he was elected to a seat in the Kansas Legislature. He was also chosen to several offices of trust and honor in his own city. Mr. Nugent has led a godly and useful life.

Nugent, Deacon George, was born in Philadelphia, Pa., May 3, 1809. He received a liberal education in Clermont Academy, in the vicinity of the city. Many of his fellow-students have risen

DEACON GEORGE NUGENT.

to distinguished positions; among these may be mentioned the Hon. John Welsh, late minister to England. His father was George Nugent, a highly respected and influential merchant of Philadelphia.

At the age of twenty-three he was converted, and from careful study of the Scriptures was led to unite with the Lower Merion Baptist church, under the pastoral care of the Rev. Dr. Horatio Gates Jones, by whom he was baptized in 1832. From that time he has proved himself a faithful and devoted Christian. He has been a deacon for more than forty years. While visiting among the poor, and witnessing the destitute and sad condition of many aged saints, he conceived the idea of a home for them. This thought was the primal inception of the Baptist Home. Originated by him, it has also received largely of his gifts.

He has been a member of the boards of the American Baptist Publication and Historical Societies for many years, and has also been long identified with the American Sunday-School Union as chairman of its Missionary Committee. He has taken great interest in the education and moral training of the young. Many churches have shared in his practical benevolence. He was one of the founders of the Second Baptist church, Germantown, and a large contributor to its funds. Of this community he is now a member.

Mr. Nugent is one of the leading citizens of Philadelphia,—public-spirited, benevolent, and universally respected.

Nunnally, Rev. G. A., was born in Walton Co., Ga., March 24, 1841. In youth he was very precocious. At fourteen he entered the University of Georgia, and was the youngest graduate that ever received a diploma at the State University. Before his nineteenth year he was elected Professor of Mathematics in Hamilton College, and for ten years he was principal of Johnson Female Institute. He entered the ministry in 1865, preaching in the same field for eleven years. In 1876 he was elected pastor of the Rome Baptist church, which position he still holds. He is a trustee of Mercer University, and, though young, one of the most influential ministers of Georgia. He is a fine orator, and a man of genius. As a preacher he is surpassed by few, and as a worker his zeal, energy, and capacity make him pre-eminent. In the Appalachee Association, of which he was formerly a member, his influence was unbounded, and he was frequently its moderator.

Mr. Nunnally is a thorough friend of education, missions, and the Sunday-school, and he is possessed of great administrative ability. His fine command of language and brilliancy of intellect make him an able and ready debater, and, with his zeal and earnestness, give him great influence in our denominational gatherings.

Nutter, Rev. David, a useful minister in Nova Scotia and New Brunswick, was ordained at St. John, New Brunswick, June 24, 1819; organized the Baptist church at Windsor, Nova Scotia; labored as a missionary in Canso, Greysborough, and Antigonish; organized the Baptist church at Liverpool, Nova Scotia, in 1821; was pastor of the Baptist church in Portland, St. John; died Jan. 15, 1873.

Nutting, James Walton, LL.D., was one of the first graduates from Windsor College, Nova Scotia; was bred to the bar, and became prothonatory of the Supreme Court of Nova Scotia. His conversion was thorough; he was baptized at Halifax, 1827, and became a member of Granville Street church in that city; was the originator of the system of education among the Baptists of Nova Scotia, which took form at the Baptist Association at Horton in 1828. He was a warm friend of Horton Academy and Acadia College; was co-editor with Mr. Ferguson of the *Christian Messenger* until his death, in 1870, aged eighty-three years. Dr. Nutting possessed great integrity of character, and was universally beloved.

O.

Oates, Rev. Samuel, charged with Murder for Baptizing a Lady, who died soon after, was a minister of popular talents, and a disputant whom it was better for antagonists to shun. Visiting Essex, England, in 1646, he preached in several places, and baptized large numbers of people. This created great indignation among Pedobaptists, and especially among the ministers. They endeavored to stir up the magistrates to arrest Mr. Oates, but they had no charge against him, and they were afraid to imprison him.

Among those baptized by Mr. Oates was a young woman, named Anne Martin, who died a few weeks after her baptism. This furnished the clergymen the charge which they required, and forthwith Mr. Oates was sent to jail, accused of murdering Anne Martin by administering immersion to her. He was actually tried for his life at Chelmsford assizes for this dreadful crime. In that day in the writings of Pedobaptists immersion was frequently denounced as a very dangerous practice; and some branded the Baptists as " a cruel and murdering sect for using it." If the trial against Mr. Oates had been successful it would not only have sent him to the gallows, but it would have been a heavy blow at the administration of the Saviour's only baptism. Great efforts, Mr. Crosby tells us, were made to secure the conviction of Oates; it was asserted that he held Miss Martin so long in the water that she immediately became sick, and stated on her death-bed that the dipping caused her fatal illness; all the falsehoods told about her case, on the trial, were completely exposed. Several witnesses were produced, and among them her own mother, whose testimony proved that she had better health for several days after her baptism than she had enjoyed for years before.

Crosby mentions an essay of Sir John Floyer to prove the advantages of bathing in cold water, in which he gives a catalogue of diseases for which it is a remedy. Sir John closes his essay by observing " that the Church of England continued the use of immersion longer than any Christian church in the West. For the Eastern Church yet uses it; and our church (the Episcopal) still recommends the dipping of infants in her Rubric, to which, I believe, the English Church will at last return, when physic has given them a clear proof by divers experiments that cold baths are both safe and useful. And," he says, "they did great injury to their own children, and to all posterity, who first introduced the alteration of this truly ancient ceremony of immersion, and were the occasion of a degenerate, sickly, and tender race ever since." (Crosby's History of the English Baptists, i. 236–240. London, 1738.)

Ober, Levi E., M.D., a native of Vermont, was born at Rockingham, Windham Co., July 31, 1819, and is the son of Wm. and Fanny (Fairbanks) Ober. In 1830 his father's family moved to Claridon, Geauga, O. Here Levi remained on his father's farm until eighteen years of age, in the summer assisting his father and during the winter attending school. He continued his literary and scientific studies, interspersed with manual labor, until 1845, when he began the study of medicine with Dr. Storm Rosa, of Painesville, O. He took medical lectures at the Western Reserve College, Cleveland, and at the Eclectic Medical College, Cincinnati, from which last-named college he received a diploma in March, 1850. He subsequently attended a course of lectures in the Jefferson Medical College of Philadelphia. Dr. Ober began practice in Moline, Ill., in 1850. He came to La Crosse, Wis., in 1857, where he has since resided. He stands at the head of his profession in the State. He has a very extensive practice, reaching far beyond the city of his residence. In 1872 he went to Europe, traveling extensively in England, Belgium, Switzerland, and parts of Germany, and spending the winter of 1872–73 in Italy. He availed himself of every facility for visiting hospitals, attending lectures, and for making the personal acquaintance of the most eminent medical men in the old country, that he might extend and perfect his medical knowledge.

He was one of the founders of the Illinois Homœopathic Medical Association, and also a founder of the Wisconsin Homœopathic Society, and has been president of both organizations. Once he was called upon to preside over the National Society.

But in Wisconsin Dr. Ober is no less widely known as an eminent medical practitioner than as an earnest and active Christian. He is a member of the Baptist church in La Crosse, one of its deacons, and one of its large-hearted, liberal supporters. In all the religious and benevolent work of his denomination in the State he takes a deep interest. He is a member of the board of the State Convention, and is nearly always present at its annual meetings.

Offer, George, was born in London in 1796. In early life he became a member of the Baptist church at Bow, and subsequently attached himself to the congregation at Mare Street, Hackney. Although actively engaged in business during the greater part of his life, and rendering valuable public services as a magistrate of London, and as member of the metropolitan board of works, he devoted himself with such ardor and persistence to the history of two books,—the English Bible and the "Pilgrim's Progress,"—that he became a chief authority with all students and inquirers, with book-buyers and booksellers. His collection of Bibles and Testaments, and of the works of the Puritan divines, especially of John Bunyan, was without a rival. Mr. Offer's library was the resort of scholars and divines of all ranks and denominations. He edited the works of Bunyan in three volumes, and wrote a memoir which is allowed to be the most complete biography of that illustrious man. He also wrote the "Life of William Tyndale," published by Bagster. He left in manuscript the largest production of his pen, entitled "The History of the Great Bible," embracing the history of Coverdale's translation, Tyndale's, Cranmer's, and the Genevan, each profusely illustrated with fac-similes carefully made by himself. His death took place at his home in London, Aug. 4, 1864.

Ogilvie, Rev. John, was born in Stafford Co., Va., in the year 1793. He seemed inclined at different times to prepare himself for the profession of the law, and again for that of medicine. He taught school for a short time in Culpeper County, then at Jeffersonton, and subsequently in Fauquier County, having taken charge of the New Baltimore Academy. In early life he was quite skeptical in his views, but in 1823, having heard a sermon by Rev. C. George, his conscience was quickened, he saw the folly of his views, and was led to give himself to Christ. One month after his baptism he was licensed to preach, and one year after was ordained to the work of the ministry and became pastor of the Goose Creek (Pleasant Vale) church. With this church he labored most faithfully for more than twenty-five years. Teaching school and at the same time preaching regularly for three or four churches, his labors were necessarily very onerous, and his exposure to all kinds of weather terribly exhausting. The great majority of the Baptist ministers of Virginia twenty-five years ago, supplying as they did five or six churches, often spent at least one-third of their time on horseback, riding to and from their various appointments for preaching, and Mr. Ogilvie had his full share of these wearying labors. As a preacher, he was endowed with rare gifts. His mind was strongly logical, and he could divest a subject of all its ambiguities and present it so plainly to his hearers as to make the most abstruse subjects clear to the humblest capacities. One who knew him well has said that he never heard him preach a sermon from which a man who had never heard the gospel before, and should never hear it again, might not learn enough about the plan of salvation by the cross of Christ to save his soul. In all the relations of life his character was irreproachable. As a citizen, a neighbor, and a friend he was esteemed by all who knew him, while as a Christian he was revered for his unaffected piety and devotion. He died June 2, 1849, in the fifty-sixth year of his age, and his memory is fragrant among the people who knew him and loved him so well.

Ohio Baptists.—The first church of any denomination in Ohio, or the Northwestern Territory, as it was originally called, was a Baptist church. This was organized at Columbia, then five miles above Cincinnati, and now a part of that city, in 1790. A year and a half previous to this twenty-five persons from Pennsylvania and New Jersey had come down the Ohio River to this point. Six of these were Baptists. This number had increased to nine, when Rev. Stephen Gano, subsequently pastor of the First church of Providence, R. I., who was then visiting the colony, one Saturday at the house of Benjamin Davis, presided over their organization, and the next day baptized three believers. The first pastor of the church was Rev. John Smith, who afterwards became a member of the Senate of the United States. A meeting-house—the first Protestant place of worship in Ohio—was built in 1793.

From this point Baptists soon began to scatter through lower Ohio. After Wayne's victory over the Indians, in 1794, it was safer to leave the river, and the Miami valley rapidly became settled. A Baptist church was formed at Staunton, near Troy, in 1804. About the same time the King's Creek and Union churches were organized, as were also the churches at Middletown and Lebanon. In 1808 the Columbia church removed to Duck Creek, and has ever since borne the name of the Duck Creek church. The Miami Association, containing originally but four churches, was formed in 1797, and for several years included all the Baptist churches in Ohio.

The origin of Baptist churches in other parts of the State was somewhat later. One of the oldest of the churches is that at Marietta. The First church, Dayton, O., was constituted and recognized in 1824, though as early as 1806 there are traces of Baptists in the place, and for some time there had been preaching by traveling ministers. The First church in Cleveland was organized in 1833, the First church in Columbus three or four years earlier, and the First church, Toledo, not until 1853. The oldest Association after the Miami is the Scioto, and the next oldest the Mad River.

The progress of the denomination in Ohio was greatly retarded by what is known as the Campbellite schism in 1827–30, which divided a number of churches and carried away some prominent ministers, notably Rev. D. S. Burnett, of Dayton. In the reaction following this movement, Old-School or Anti-Mission tendencies were developed, which produced divisions and resulted in loss of numbers and power.

In later years, however, there has been great progress. The largest contributors to this have been the State Convention, established in May, 1826, Granville College, opened for students December, 1831, and the Education Society, organized in 1834. At present the Baptists in Ohio number 49,950. There are 633 churches and 469 ordained ministers. Connected with the churches there are 645 Sunday-schools, with 6800 officers and teachers, and 58,500 scholars. Granville, Licking Co., is the literary centre of the denomination, being the seat of Denison University, of which Rev. A. Owen, D.D., is president, and of a young ladies' institute, under the charge of Rev. D. Shepardson, D.D. There are other schools in the State also in which Baptists have a controlling interest, notably the Mount Auburn Young Ladies' Institute, Cincinnati, O., and Clermont Academy, in Clermont County.

Old-Landmarkism.—The following sketch was written at the editor's request by one of the ablest Baptist ministers in this country. His account of the opinions of all landmarkers is entirely reliable:

The origin of the term old-landmarkism was as follows: about the year 1850, Rev. J. R. Graves, editor of the *Tennessee Baptist*, published at Nashville, Tenn., began to advocate the position that Baptists cannot consistently recognize Pedobaptist preachers as gospel ministers. For several years he found but few to sympathize with this view. Among the few was Rev. J. M. Pendleton, then of Bowling Green, Ky., who in 1854 was requested by Mr. Graves to write an essay on this question, "Ought Baptists to recognize Pedobaptist preachers as gospel ministers?" The essay was published in four consecutive numbers of the aforesaid paper, and afterwards in the form of a tract. The title given to it by Mr. Graves was "An Old Landmark Reset." The title was considered appropriate, because there had been a time when ministerial recognition and exchange of pulpits between Baptists and Pedobaptists were unknown. This was an old landmark, but in the course of years it had fallen. When it was raised again it was called "an old landmark reset." Hence the term "old-landmarkism," and of late years, by way of abridgment, "landmarkism."

That the doctrine of landmarkism is not a novelty, as some suppose, is evident, because William Kiffin, of London, one of the noblest of English Baptists, advocated it in 1640, and with those who agreed with him formed a church, of which he was pastor till his death, in 1701,—a very long pastorate. These facts are taken from Cramp's "Baptist History," and he refers to Ivimey's "Life of Kiffin."

Benedict, in his "Fifty Years among the Baptists," in referring to the early part of this century, says, "At that time the exchange of pulpits between the advocates and the opponents of infant baptism was a thing of very rare occurrence, except in a few of the more distinguished churches in the Northern States. Indeed, the doctrine of non-intercourse, so far as ministerial services were concerned, almost universally prevailed between Baptists and Pedobaptists." pp. 94, 95.

Truly the old landmark once stood, and having fallen, it was deemed proper to reset it.

The doctrine of landmarkism is that baptism and church membership precede the preaching of the gospel, even as they precede communion at the Lord's table. The argument is that Scriptural authority to preach emanates, under God, from a gospel church; that as "a visible church is a congregation of baptized believers," etc., it follows that no Pedobaptist organization is a church in the Scriptural sense of the term, and that therefore Scriptural authority to preach cannot proceed from such an organization. Hence the non-recognition of Pedobaptist ministers, who are not interfered with, but simply let alone.

At the time the "Old Landmark Reset" was written the topic of non-ministerial intercourse was the chief subject of discussion. Inseparable, however, from the landmark view of this matter, is a denial that Pedobaptist societies are Scriptural churches, that Pedobaptist ordinations are valid, and that immersions administered by Pedobaptist ministers can be consistently accepted by any Baptist church. All these things are denied, and the intelligent reader will see why.

Olmstead, John W., D.D., was born in Saratoga Co., N. Y., Nov. 13, 1816. His parents were members of the Methodist Episcopal Church. When converted his convictions led him to the Baptists, and he was baptized in Schuylerville, N. Y., in 1836, by Rev. C. B. Keyes. He pursued academic studies in Johnstown, N. Y. The honorary degree of A.M. was conferred on him by Yale College, and afterwards that of D.D. by the University of Rochester. He was first, in 1837, settled over the Baptist church of Little Falls, N. Y., where he remained five years. He then became pastor in Chelsea, Mass., where he continued five years. In 1846 he became editor of the *Christian Reflector*, of Boston. In 1848 the *Watchman* was united with it, and he filled the editorial chair of the consolidated papers until 1877. His ability as a religious journalist was fully demonstrated in his long and successful management of that paper. In 1878 he commenced the New York *Watch-Tower*, a popular Baptist paper, and he is confident of success. He held prominent positions in Roxbury, Mass., in educational work, and was on the executive committee of the Missionary Union. His life has been one of great usefulness and honor.

Olney, Edward, LL.D., Professor of Mathematics in the University of Michigan, and author

EDWARD OLNEY, LL.D.

of a complete set of mathematical text-books, is descended from the Rhode Island Olneys, and was born in Moreau, Saratoga Co., N. Y., July 24, 1827. During most of his childhood and youth he resided in Ohio. His early opportunities for an education were very slight, but he made the most of them. Beginning to teach at the age of nineteen, he prosecuted his own studies with great energy and success, and early became eminent as a teacher. From 1853 to 1863 he was Professor of Mathematics in Kalamazoo College, and acquired a reputation as teacher in this department almost unequaled. In 1863 he became professor in the State University, and still holds that position; but his interest in Kalamazoo College remains unabated. He is a member of its board of trustees, and among its most liberal supporters. He has the warmest interest in Sunday-school work, and is always ready to serve the temperance enterprise. From 1875 to 1879 he was president of the Baptist State Convention, and has since been its treasurer. Although not an ordained minister, he sometimes conducts religious services. No one would deny that his influence is very great, and always on the side of justice and religion. He was made A.M. by Madison University in 1853, and LL.D. by Kalamazoo College in 1874.

Oncken, Rev. John Gerhard.—No one will refuse to this eminent man the designation of

REV. JOHN GERHARD ONCKEN.

apostle of the German Baptists. His life being so intimately connected with the rise and progress of the Baptist denomination in Germany, the reader is referred to the account of them in this work, and this article will confine itself to some brief biographical data.

Mr. Oncken was born in Varel, in the grand duchy of Oldenburg, Jan. 26, 1800. In his youth he came to England, where, by the grace of God, he became a true Christian. Manifesting a peculiar fitness for evangelistic labors, he was sent to Germany in 1823 as a missionary of the British Continental Society,—a society formed in England for the purpose of spreading the gospel on the continent. Filled with zeal and fervent love, he went back to his native land a joyous herald of the truth which he had learned in a foreign clime. He first preached the gospel on the coasts of the German Ocean, in the cities of Hamburg and Bremen, and in the province of East Frisia. His strong religious convictions, his clear insight into the Word, united with a deep spirituality, a pleasing appearance, and considerable oratorical talent, gave him a welcome reception among the people everywhere. Many were converted, and a powerful religious movement manifested itself in all that region. Mr. Oncken labored as a missionary of the British Continental Society till 1828, and then became the agent of the Edinburgh Bible Society.

As a result of faithful Bible study, Mr. Oncken gradually reached the conviction that baptism belongs only to believers, and that immersion is the only Scriptural mode of baptism. After having long waited for an opportunity to receive baptism, Mr. Oncken was at length baptized, together with six others, by Rev. Barnas Sears, then of Hamilton Institution, on the 22d of April, 1834, in the river Elbe, near Hamburg; these seven believers were the first fruit of thousands yet to follow. On the succeeding day these seven were constituted a church, the First German Baptist church in *modern* times; Mr. Oncken was chosen pastor.

Mr. Oncken's baptism created a great sensation in all circles where he was known, and the persecutions which he formerly endured now became still more violent. The clergy, in harmony with the police, were determined to destroy the work in its inception, but all their efforts proved unavailing. Mr. Oncken, full of love and zeal, proved himself a man of firm determination and undaunted courage; he could not be intimidated nor silenced; he paid no heed to the prohibitions of the authorities; he dreaded not the dungeon, and yielded not, even when incarcerated. Under God, the continuance and the prosperity of the work in Germany is due largely, first of all, to the endurance, fearlessness, and determination, and, secondly, to the untiring labors, of this remarkable man. From that day until now Mr. Oncken's life has been one of apostolic toil and blessed success in spreading the gospel through Germany.

Mr. Oncken has always remained pastor of the church in Hamburg, and has made Hamburg the centre of his evangelistic labors, being enabled to do this through the faithful aid of helpers like Koebner and Schauffler and others, who supplied the church in his absence. In addition to his evangelistic labors in Germany and adjoining countries, Mr. Oncken has frequently visited England in the interest of the German Baptist cause, and in 1853, by invitation of the executive committee of the American Baptist Missionary Union, he visited the United States, traveling extensively in the Northwestern as well as in the older States. On that memorable journey Mr. Oncken's life was wonderfully preserved in a fearful railroad accident at Norwalk, Conn. As a result of Mr. Oncken's visit the committee voted to aid the mission in erecting chapels to the extent of $8000 a year for five years.

Looking over his eventful and useful life, it may be said that Mr. Oncken's piety, courage, untiring energy, and his strong organizing faculty have been the foundation-stones of his great success. His influence over the churches and pastors in Germany has been powerful. They have looked upon him as a father, have greatly revered him, and highly respected his judgment. The weakness of advanced age hinders Mr. Oncken engaging any longer in his loved employ; but while he still lingers amid the scenes of his former conflict, throngs of blessings cheer his declining days, and when he shall be no longer walking among his brethren, the memory of his faithful and successful service will be embalmed among the Baptists of Germany in all succeeding generations.

O'Neall, Chief-Justice John Belton, was born on the 10th of April, 1793, near Bobo's Mills, in

CHIEF-JUSTICE JOHN BELTON O'NEALL.

Newberry District, S. C. He was the son of Hugh O'Neall and Ann Kelly, his wife,—his ancestors on both sides being of ancient Irish families. In his youth he had facilities for education that were unusual for that period. In February, 1811, he entered the Junior class of South Carolina College, and in December, 1812, graduated with the second honor of that institution. He devoted himself to the profession of the law, and from the commencement obtained a large and lucrative practice. In 1816 he was elected to the House of Representatives in the Legislature of South Carolina. He was again elected in 1822, 1824, and 1826, and during the last two terms was the Speaker of the House. In December, 1828, he was elected an associate judge, and in 1830 a judge of the Court of Appeals. On the abolition of that court he was transferred to the Court of Law. In 1850 he became president of the Court of Law Appeals and of the Court of Errors. Upon the reorganization of a separate Court of Appeals, he was with great unanimity appointed chief justice of South Carolina. It would be superfluous to attempt to describe the manner in which these several offices of public trust have been filled. His thorough business habits, his untiring industry, his incorruptible integrity, his conscientious discharge of the duties of every office, together with his great learning, enabled him to establish for himself a position unequaled by any chief justice in the history of this State.

It might seem that surrounded by such cares he would have no time for the performance of other public duties. But, on the contrary, we find him devoting himself in various other ways to what he deemed the vital interests of the country. His attention to agriculture contributed in great part to its advancement in South Carolina, but especially in his native district of Newberry. To his labors and personal influence, too, is the State indebted for the successful completion of the Greenville and Columbia Railroad. His activity in these respects was but an index of his more private labors in every way in which the material prosperity of the State could be advanced.

Outside of his official labors, perhaps Judge O'Neall was known in no respect so well as in the character of an ardent advocate of total abstinence from all intoxicating liquors. To this work he devoted himself during the most vigorous years of his manhood, and continued his efforts until the time of his death. He became known as the apostle of temperance in South Carolina, and occupied the highest position among its most distinguished advocates in North America. No one man has performed more voluntary labor in this cause than he.

It was the privilege, however, of those who knew Judge O'Neall in his private life to appreciate most highly the true worth of his character. His public life displayed the sterner, his private life the gentler, traits of true and noble manhood, each in equal perfection. God blessed him in the selection of a companion whom he spared until the end of his life. On the 25th of June, 1818, he was married to Helen, eldest daughter of Capt. Sampson and Sarah Strother Pope. All the children of this marriage preceded their honored father to the grave. He himself died on Sunday, the 27th of December, 1863, being seventy years, eight months, and seventeen days old.

The Convention of the Baptist denomination in South Carolina suffered a great loss in the death of Chief-Justice O'Neall, because he was an ardent co-worker with his brethren in the advancement of Christ's kingdom. His parents were Friends, or Quakers, but from the time that Brother O'Neall made a profession of Christianity he was an earnest advocate of the religious views held by the Calvinistic Baptists. A great revival in the town of Newberry, in 1831, gave origin to the Baptist church of that place, on the records of which, under date of Saturday, Jan. 26, 1833, is the following: "Received by experience, John B. O'Neall." In the minutes of Saturday, March 22, 1834, is another item of importance: "Resolved, that it is expedient to appoint three additional deacons of this church, who are requested to conduct all prayer-meetings from time to time, and to take part in any other religious exercises to which they may be prompted by the Spirit in aid of the pastor of this church." Under the above resolution were appointed John B. O'Neall, M. T. Mendenhall, and Drayton Nance. In compliance with the above resolution religious meetings were conducted by the brethren named with great regularity for a considerable time. Judge O'Neall's addresses, lectures, and exhortations are still remembered by those who used to hear them. They were characterized by all the vehemence and earnestness which at a later period marked similar efforts in the cause of temperance. He was at that time very active in the church. Afterwards the judge was often absent discharging his official duties, but whenever at home he was a constant attendant upon the public ministry of the gospel, and felt much interest in all that concerned the welfare of the church.

He carried into it the same characteristics which distinguished him in other important relations,—great zeal, energy, ardor, and devotion. These qualities, connected with unusual ability, made him the effective Christian he was. Judge O'Neall was remarkable for his humility as a Christian, and though occupying prominent positions in the State, and receiving at times an homage which was well calculated to foster worldly pride, he always retained that humility which condescends to small things and to men of low estate. His piety, as exhibited at home, around the fireside, and in private life, displayed this quality most strikingly. It was his custom to erect a domestic altar night and morning, when, gathering his family, white and black, around him, he invoked the blessings and pardon of heaven upon them in a most simple and touching manner, and if a friend or stranger happened under his roof, he invariably prayed for him personally. His fervid manner of addressing a throne of grace showed his strong faith in a special providence. He was remarkable for a tender regard for all around him. If his humblest servant was seriously sick, he exhibited a strong sympathy for him and made him a subject of prayer at the family altar, and followed the remains of a servant to the burying-ground, and stood by the grave during the funeral service with a reverence, humility, and awe which showed how deeply his heart was imbued with the spirit of Christ, and how surely he felt that God was no respecter of persons. He was loved and revered in his own district as the friend of the widow and orphan. Indeed, this was his character throughout the State. Enjoying a reputation for liberality, and occupying a position which exposed him to calls of this kind, it is not too much to say that he expended a small fortune in responding to such appeals. He was quite as well known for that charity which marked the good Samaritan,—that gentle and kind sympathy which will observe and even hunt out and relieve the wants and distresses of others by counsel, advice, and sympathy as well as donations of money.

But Judge O'Neall's most distinguishing trait as a Christian was that he was not ashamed of the religion of Christ. It was this that made him so eminently useful. No man, certainly no layman in the Baptist denomination, nor in any other, has exerted so wide-spread an influence for good. Before assembled multitudes, in charging juries, in sentencing criminals, or in making temperance speeches, he always made it a point to enforce directly or indirectly the truths of Christianity.

At home, in his own church, he was in the habit for many years of conducting prayer-meetings and delivering addresses when there was no preaching in the church. He continued this until he was seriously injured by an accident on the railroad, after which he discontinued public speaking of all kinds. His prayers and lectures on such occasions were warm, fervent, and effective. He would usually take a chapter or a portion of one, and make a running comment. Often he would select a psalm, the fervid eloquence, poetic sentiment, and language of which seemed congenial to him, and gave him an opportunity, which seemed to delight him, of expatiating on the goodness, power, and glory of God.

With all his honors he cherished most his privileges as a servant of Christ, who, amid the many duties of a life of extraordinary activity, has always remembered his dependence upon God, and sought his aid, and strove to guide others, too, in the way of life.

It is not surprising that where such piety is united with such greatness his brethren should have loved and honored him. At the session of the Southern Baptist Convention, held in July, 1858, he was elected president, an office in which he continued until July, 1863, when his failing health forbade his further attendance upon its meetings.

Ontario and Quebec, Baptists of.—It is difficult to trace the history of the introduction of Baptists into these provinces, as until a comparatively recent date no attempt was made to preserve the denominational records. But as Baptists are always found wherever the Word of God is freely circulated and devoutly studied, it is to be presumed that there were many converts to our principles, in the upper province at least, before the arrival of Baptist preachers. So far as can be ascertained, the first churches were planted by itinerant missionaries from Nova Scotia, New Brunswick, and the United States. None of these churches has a history extending over a much longer period than eighty-five years. According to a brief sketch published by the late Rev. Dr. Fyfe, in 1859, the first church in the eastern section of the country of which there is any authentic account was formed in Caldwell's Manor, by Rev. E. Andrews, of Vermont, in 1794. This section is indebted to missionaries sent out by a society of which the late venerable Dr. Sharp, of Boston, was secretary. In the same year (1794) the first church in the western section was formed under Elders Hamilton and Turner, at Thurlow, in the county of Northumberland; and about the same year Elder Winn commenced to labor in the district of Prince Edward. Through this region there once flourished many churches,—in the townships of Rawdon, Sidney, Cramahe, Murray, etc.,—but chiefly through emigration westward some of them have become extinct, and others have languished for years.

In 1800 a brother named Finch, from New Brunswick, began to preach at Charlotteville, and in 1804 a church was formed there, of which several neighboring churches are the thriving daughters. Soon after this the church in Beamsville was formed, under the missionary labors of Elders Covell and Warren, from the Shaftsbury Association, Vt. This church has also been a fruitful mother. Beyond these outlines it would be scarcely possible to trace the influences (they have been so varied) which have raised up Baptist churches in different parts of the country. The Baptists were the first anti-Roman Catholic missionaries to Canada, as they were the first missionaries to the heathen, and it is to be regretted that the history of their early trials and labors is so little known.

The numerical increase of the denomination will be indicated by the following statistics: in 1828 there were in Ontario (then called Upper Canada) 45 ministers, 1435 communicants, and 5740 regular hearers. The Baptists in Quebec, or Lower Canada, at that time were very few, and would not have materially altered the above figures. In 1842 the census gave 19,623 Baptists in the two provinces; six years later they numbered 28,503; in four years more (1852) they numbered 49,846; and in 1860 the number of ministers was about 190, of communicants 13,715, and of adherents 60,000. Now (1881) there are not fewer than 250 ministers, 356 churches, a membership of more than 27,000, and at least 125,000 adherents. Of these, by far the greater number belong to Ontario. The "Canadian Baptist Year-Book" for 1881 gives the Baptists of Quebec only 26 English-speaking churches, with a total membership of about 2000. If the members of the Grande Ligne Mission churches (French) are added, the number of communicants will not even then exceed 2400. These figures need occasion no surprise, when it is remembered that the entire Protestant population of that province is exceedingly small. The largest churches in the two provinces are Jarvis Street, Toronto, with 751; First Brantford, with 525; and First Montreal, with 479 members. Several others have from 200 to 350 members. There are 14 Associations.

For Christian enterprise and liberality the Baptists of Ontario and Quebec will compare favorably with their brethren in any part of the world. Their Literary Institute, at Woodstock, for which an adequate endowment is nearly raised, and the new Theological Seminary at Toronto, the land and buildings of which are the donation of one man, stand as monuments of princely giving on the part of the rich, and of the munificence of the body generally. Home mission work is done under the direction of two boards, representing the East and the West respectively. The new province of Manitoba receives missionary aid through a separate organization. A Foreign Missionary Society is also maintained, with which are connected two Women's Auxiliary Societies. Besides these the aid of the denomination is claimed by a Church Edifice Society, a Society for the Relief of Superannuated Ministers, and the Grande Ligne Evangelical Society.

Two weekly newspapers, the *Canadian Baptist* and *Christian Helper*, are published at Toronto; and also a monthly, the *Canadian Missionary Link*, devoted to the interests of the Women's Foreign Mission Societies. (See also the article BAPTIST UNION OF CANADA.)

O'Quin, Rev. Ezekiel, a pioneer preacher in Rapides Parish, La., was born in North Carolina in 1781, and died in 1823.

O'Quin, Rev. John, son of Ezekiel O'Quin, was born in South Carolina in 1808, and settled in Rapides Parish, La., in 1815; began to preach in 1834, and became a pioneer in the St. Landry region. While preaching constantly he engaged successfully in planting, and amassed a large fortune. Since the war he has engaged actively in politics, and has served with ability several terms in the Louisiana Legislature.

Ordination.—When a brother is set apart to the work of the gospel ministry, if he is ordained by the authority of the church to which his services are to be given, his membership is first transferred to that community. They pass resolutions declaring their conviction that he should be ordained, and they summon a council to meet for that purpose on a designated day. They appoint brethren to represent them in the council. The clerk of the church presents the council with its resolutions, a list of the churches invited, and the names of the representatives of the church. When the council is organized, and opened with devotional exercises, the candidate gives an account of his conversion, call to the ministry, and views of doctrine and church order. After a searching examination from the ministers and laymen of the council, he is requested to retire, when his conversion, divine call, character, orthodoxy, and talents are carefully scrutinized. If he is approved by the council a resolution to that effect is passed, and another that the council proceed to his ordination. The candidate is then brought before the council, and the moderator announces to him its decision. A committee is then appointed to arrange for the ordination services; this committee always includes the candidate. The moderator of the council presides at the ordination. Its services include a sermon, the imposition of hands on the head of the kneeling candidate by all the ministers in the pulpit, the hand of fellowship as a herald of the gospel, a charge to the candidate and to the church. If the minister is not yet a member of the church of which he is to become pastor, the church to which he belongs calls the council, and he is ordained by its request and under its authority.

Oregon, a rich agricultural and mining State, with many prosperous cities. It has four universities and colleges, and a splendid common school system. On May 25, 1844, "The West Union Baptist church" was formed on the Tualatin Plains, with eight members. It was the first Baptist church at that date in the United States west of the Rocky Mountains. They met regularly for years to study the Bible and hear a sermon read by one of their number. In February, 1845, Rev. V. Snelling preached the first sermon to the little flock, joined them, with his wife, and David T. Lenox was ordained a deacon. In May, 1845, they celebrated the Lord's Supper for the first time. Other ministers began to arrive, new churches were organized, until now Oregon has nearly eighty churches, five Associations, a monthly paper, *The Beacon*, one college, at McMinnville, its State Convention, Mission, Education, and Sunday-school Conventions and Boards, a Woman's Missionary Society, and about 3000 Baptist members. There is also a flourishing mission for the Chinese in Oregon, located at Portland; the soul of this mission is a converted and ordained Chinaman, Rev. Dong Gong, who became a Christian and a Baptist almost at the peril of his life.

Origin of Infant Baptism, The. — Infant baptism came into life in Africa, the country of slavery, cruelty, and ignorance. In the Roman colony stretching along the coast of the Mediterranean Sea, where the warlike and ferocious Carthaginians built up their commerce and sovereignty, this superstitious rite was born. Never in human history is it heard of until African writers mention it. Tertullian, at the very close of the second century, discountenances the baptism of *children*,— not unconscious infants. Speaking of them he says, "They know how to ask for salvation (baptism) that you may seem to have given it to one seeking it." (Norint petere salutem, ut petenti dedisse videaris. De Baptismo, cap. 18. Lipsiæ, 1839.) These candidates for baptism could ask for it, and consequently were not unconscious babes, and he opposes its administration to them on account of their early years. There is no hint given that it was customary to baptize intelligent children of several years of age. Tertullian's little book was written against the Quintillianists, who suffered women to preach and baptize, and who were regarded as heretics. His work affords no hint of the existence of the baptism of unconscious babes. The first case of that sort, if real, in the literature of Christianity, is to be found in a letter of Cyprian, bishop of Carthage, written about A.D. 256, giving an account of the proceedings of a council of sixty-six bishops held at that time in Carthage. Fidus, a country bishop, wanted to know if an infant might be baptized before it was eight days old. There is not a Sunday-school teacher in a Pedobaptist school in Christendom who could not answer that question in a moment, but Fidus, a bishop, could not decide what to do, and Cyprian, a man of superlative presumption, feels compelled to seek the wisdom of sixty-six bishops to guide Fidus. If the letter of Cyprian is genuine, this is the first distinct evidence of the existence of infant baptism among the Saviour's followers; no other intimation of its occurrence in the third century is given, but few instances of it can be found in the fourth, and the baptism of catechized persons was common for ages after; but we doubt the genuineness of this letter.

Beyond all question infant baptism began in Africa, and Augustine of Hippo was the man who lent it the force which gave it victory. Africa had been cursed for ages with human sacrifices to Saturn,—little children were placed in the arms of a metal image intensely heated, with a blazing fire underneath its outstretched arms. Many persons who became nominal Christians practised this ancient and horrid abomination; backsliders from Christianity followed this hideous rite of the Phœnician colonists of North Africa. Robinson has a theory about the origin of the infant ceremony which may contain some truth. His idea is that it was probably used to place God's mark upon the infants, and thereby to protect them from the bloody arms of infamous Saturn, to whose frightful embrace their superstitious parents would consign them. After mentioning various matters connected with his theory, he says, "Collecting into one point of view all the forementioned facts, the eye fixes on Fidus, the honest and humane bishop of a company of Christians in a country place of Africa, where some of his neighbors bought, stole, captured, and burnt children; where some of his flock returned to paganism; others intermarried with pagan families and went with them into the old practices of sacrificing children to the gods; himself filled with Jewish ideas of dedicating children to the true God, and marking them by circumcision; and sending for advice to Cyprian, exactly such another confused genius as himself, is it a very improbable conjecture that Fidus bethought himself of baptizing new-born infants as an expedient to save the lives of the lambs of his flock? . . . To prevail with such savages to dedicate their infants to God; to take possession of them by the soft method of dipping them in water; to procure some persons of more influence than the parents to become sponsors for the babes (adults required sponsors in order to be baptized soon after the apostolic age, to instruct them, and probably to protect persecuted Christians from baptizing spies); this resembles the great Alfred's uniting Britons into tens, and forcing every nine to pledge themselves that the tenth should enjoy his liberty and his life." (History of Baptism, 248–9. Nashville.) Whether Cyprian's letter is genuine or a forgery, and whether or not such a man as Fidus ever lived, it is extremely probable that Mr. Robinson's conjecture had some truth in it. The writer, however, is of the opinion that the grand forces which gave success to infant baptism after the application of the rite to them was conceived, were the pernicious falsehoods that Adam's guilt would keep every unbaptized infant out of heaven, and that his iniquity was washed from the soul of the infant by baptism. So soon as these fables were received, men, and surely women, were inclined to favor the dipping of new-born babes.

Original Sin.—Adam and Eve were created in perfect innocence. They could not be invested with infallibility, for that attribute belongs to God alone, and Jehovah could not create a deity; but they were summoned into life without a tendency to sin, and they were as holy as the angels of God.

The human race was created in Adam and Eve, just as millions of oaks were created in the first tree of that kind. Physical defects or material beauties have been transmitted down from the first two parents of our race; they could come from no other source. When Adam sinned he forfeited his title to the tree of life in Eden, and as a consequence its leaves and fruit no longer healed his wounds, acted as an antidote against his diseases, and arrested the decay that ever since has wasted declining years. He lost Eden with the tree of life at the fall, and so did his posterity in him. The head of the family recklessly squandered his rich inheritance, and as a matter of course those who were born to him afterwards never enjoyed any part of it. The same thing was true of the divine favor which he forfeited in Eden; it was lost to him for the time being by the use of the forbidden fruit, and it was never restored unless he repented, and through divinely-appointed sacrifices turned to the Lord his God.

He left Eden with a heart vitiated by sin, and his children subsequently born came into the world with his spiritual defects and temporal disadvantages. He once bore the image of God, but sin destroyed it, and all his descendants have been marked by a guilty likeness to him.

Original sin vitiates the moral tastes of each man; it leads him to prefer the world, fleshly gratifications, and even the snares of the tempter, to the service of God. And as there is not in human nature a counteracting agency to subdue guilty tastes and restore the transgressor to Jehovah, he must continually sink deeper into sin unless sovereign grace restores him.

Original sin leads directly and surely to total depravity. We prefer *total perversion* as a better description of this sad state. Good and gentle and moral persons who have not been born again are totally perverted from God. If the heart is for Christ, the whole being is on his side; if the heart is against him, the whole man is his enemy. When Anne Boleyn had the heart of Henry VIII., he slighted Queen Catharine, hurled aside the authority of the pope and the claims of his religion, in the defense of which he had written a book, defied all Europe in his determination to marry her, and befriended the Bible, which he had burned, and the Protestants, whom he had slandered and persecuted, because of his regard for her. But when his heart turned to a rival of Anne, then he was wholly alienated from her. This is the exact situation of each unsaved man: his heart and life are wholly perverted from God. What was true of ancient Israel may be justly applied to all unconverted persons, " Ye will revolt more and more: the whole head is sick, and the whole heart faint. From the sole of the foot even unto the head there is no soundness in it; but wounds, and bruises, and putrefying sores."—Isa. i. 5, 6.

Original sin has extended over the whole race. Dreadful and undeniable facts prove this statement, and inspiration asserts it. Paul says, " We have before proved both Jews and Gentiles, that they are all under sin; as it is written, 'There is none righteous, no, not one: there is none that understandeth, there is none that seeketh after God. They are all gone out of the way, they are together become unprofitable; there is none that doeth good, no, not one.'"—Rom. iii. 10–12. When he speaks of Jews and Gentiles he intends to describe all men. The race in unbelief is in a state of total perversion from God.

Original sin paralyzes the moral powers of the soul, and forbids any man, unaided by divine grace, to go to Jesus. A young French ecclesiastic, years ago, was supposed to have died, and was in his coffin when the mass for the dead was being read. He heard every word of it, knew his situation exactly, but could not move a finger, nor an eyelid, nor utter a word. Something led to an inspection of the face, when a slight flush was discovered, and the heart was found to be beating. The man was restored to his family, and by proper remedies speedily became well. But without help he would have been buried. So the entire impenitent are dead in sin. "You hath he quickened who were *dead* in trespasses and sins."—Eph. ii. 1. And under the influence of this moral death of themselves they will never go to Jesus. "No man," says Jesus, "can come to me except the Father who hath sent me draw him." Original sin has the first hold of a human heart, and it will never let it go till the all-powerful hand of grace destroys its dominion.

Original sin has doomed the race except where the Spirit of Christ has given a new heart and saving faith. "By the offense of one judgment came upon all men to condemnation."—Rom. v. 18. "He that believeth not is condemned already."—John iii. 18. This is the condition before God of all who have kept away from Jesus over the whole earth: they are in a state of total perversion from God.

Osage, Iowa, the county town of Mitchell County, is widely known and honored for its adherence to temperance principles and the high moral tone of its people. The Baptist church was organized in 1862. It has grown into an efficient body of 170 members. The Cedar Valley Seminary, one of the Baptist schools of Iowa, under the care of the Cedar Valley Baptist Association, is located at Osage.

Osborn, Rev. John W., of Scio, Linn Co., Oregon, was born Oct. 18, 1838. His father was a laborious and successful preacher. He was in his youth wild, worldly, and loved to ridicule religion; but in 1859, during one of his father's meetings, he was converted, and two months later, while studying at Pella University, was baptized by Rev. Elihu Gunn, and joined the Pella church. He was ordained at Concord, Iowa, in March, 1864, preached in many places for two years in Iowa, Nebraska, and Colorado, and in 1866 removed to Oregon, and preached in Polk County until 1873, when he removed to the Forks of Santiam. In 1878, on account of sickness he removed to Eastern Oregon, and spent some time in Washington Territory, doing missionary work at Dayton, Grande Ronde, the Cove, Indian Creek, and other places. Returning in February, 1880, he settled at Scio, and is pastor of the Providence and Union churches, where he has had his greatest successes. Brother Osborn has always preached without a stated salary; he has done a vast amount of mission work in Central Oregon for the Yamhill, McMinnville, Union, Dallas, Lacrole, Providence, Antioch, Oak Creek, Pilgrim's Home, Pleasant Valley, Shiloh, Scio, and other churches; organized many new churches; helped to organize the General Baptist Association of Oregon, in 1868; has been active on missionary boards, and is one of the most earnest, self-denying, and influential Baptist preachers in the Central Association of Oregon.

Osborn, Rev. John Wesley, Sr., was born of Methodist parents, Aug. 19, 1802. His parents afterwards became Baptists, and the father a Baptist minister. The son was converted and baptized in 1821, in St. Clair Co., Ill.; licensed in 1826, ordained in 1830. He traveled extensively in Central and Northern Illinois, Southern Wisconsin, and Iowa, with little or no salary; organized many permanent churches, and baptized over 3000 converts. He preferred to go where there was no preaching, and build up churches from his own labors. He was often bitterly opposed; sometimes his life was threatened; some of his enemies were converted, and became powerful helpers of the truth. In 1866 he removed to Oregon; served the Union, Lacrole, Antioch, Dallas, North Palestine, Providence, and Scio churches. He was doctrinal in preaching, using only brief notes, and swayed his audiences with the eloquence of truth. Died Oct. 16, 1875, and left his youngest son in the work of the ministry; one of Oregon's successful Baptist preachers.

Osborn, Lucien M., LL.D., was born in Ashtabula, O., in 1823; graduated at Madison University in 1847; principal of the grammar-school of Madison University, 1851–56; Professor of Mathematics and Natural Philosophy in the university, 1856–68. Since 1868, Professor of Natural Sciences; degree of LL.D. conferred by Denison University in 1872; associated for some time with the president of Madison University "to take charge of the internal discipline of the university, which delicate and difficult task was performed with high credit." Dr. Osborn has a high standing in the Baptist denomination, and he is among the purest and most useful men in it.

Osgood, S. M., D.D., died at Chicago, July 9,

1875. He was born at Henderson, Jefferson Co., N. Y., March 2, 1807, being the son of Rev. Emory Osgood. At the age of nine years he became a Christian, and was baptized by his father. He entered active life as a printer, in Watertown, N. Y., and in this place, with the exception of brief intervals, lived some ten years, at the end of that time becoming connected with the office of the *Baptist Register*, in Utica, N. Y., uniting with the Broad Street Baptist church in that city. After one year in Utica he removed to Cortland, N. Y., and, in company with Mr. Rufus A. Reed, took charge of the *Cortland Chronicle*. Returning to Watertown in 1831, he had for his pastor there Rev. Jacob Knapp, and was made a deacon in the church. In 1834 he was appointed missionary printer at Maulmain, Burmah, and on July 3 of that year sailed from Boston in the ship "Cashmere." His associates on the voyage were Jonathan Wade, Grover S. Comstock, William Dean, and Miss Ann Gardner. There were, besides, three missionaries of the American board.

Mr. Osgood remained at Maulmain until 1846, rendering most valuable service. One of his reports, covering a period of two years, "showed that in that time the seven iron hand-presses of the mission had turned out nearly seven hundred thousand copies of different publications, including almost nine million pages of the Scriptures in the New Testament and different books of the Old." Returning to this country in 1846, Mr. Osgood was appointed an agent of the Missionary Union for Western New York; after seven years his field was changed to that of New Jersey, Pennsylvania, Delaware, and the District of Columbia, his residence being at Philadelphia. In 1860 he was appointed district secretary for the West, with his residence at Chicago. This was his work until his death,—a period of fifteen most laborious and useful years. He was a man greatly beloved in all relations, a devout Christian, a judicious adviser, energetic, indefatigable in service, with a singular faculty for engaging the confidence and interest of all whom he approached.

Ottawa University was originated in 1860, under the name of the Roger Williams University. During the meeting of the Kansas Baptist State Convention, held in Atcheson in 1860, the location of the institution was discussed. Several places desired to secure it. Rev. John T. Jones, a delegate from the First Baptist church of Ottawa (Indian), informed the Convention that his people for some time had felt the need of a school of high grade, and, as they were all Baptists, they would unite with their white brethren in their educational efforts. In December, 1860, the trustees of the projected university visited the Ottawa nation, and after a full conference with these Indian Baptists they agreed to give 20,000 acres of their land, then worth something over $20,000, to aid in the new educational enterprise. This proposed contract became a law in 1862. In 1865 the name of Roger Williams was dropped, and the institution incorporated under the name of the Ottawa University. The change took place in compliance with the express wish of the Ottawas, who desired to perpetuate their name. Owing to the disturbed state of the country the institution was greatly impeded in its progress until 1865. The college edifice was completed in 1869, at a cost of $40,000.

It is located near the thriving city of Ottawa, Kansas, some fifty-five miles southwest of Kansas City. It has an endowment of 640 acres of choice land, on a part of which the university stands. The buildings are large and substantial stone structures. There were ninety-three students in attendance last year, to whom Dr. P. J. Williams, the president, and his able assistants gave thorough instruction. The institution needs an endowment that would enable it to increase the faculty and to meet all current expenses without annual appeals to the churches and its friends. Dr. Williams is unusually well qualified, by talents, acquirements, facility for imparting instruction, and executive ability, for the position he occupies. The vigorous and expanding Baptist denomination of Kansas is in great need of the university. The friends of truth could not make a better investment than to place a generous endowment at the service of Ottawa University.

Ottumwa, Iowa (pop. 9018), county-seat of Wapello County, has two Baptist churches. The First was constituted in 1855, and has a present membership of 139. The Second was constituted in 1869, and is still a small company. There is also a colored Baptist church of twenty-one members.

Overby, Rev. R. R., was born in Dinwiddie Co., Va., Oct. 12, 1827; was a licensed preacher in the Methodist Church; he was baptized in Petersburg, Va., in July, 1850; spent two years at Richmond College, and served as pastor of two colored churches in Petersburg while at college; served as agent of Murfreesborough Female Institute in 1858; settled as pastor in Elizabeth City in 1859, and, with the exception of a year spent as agent of Wake Forest College, has lived and labored for twenty-one years in the section where he now resides. A man of power with the people, and possessing many noble qualities.

Owen, Alfred, D.D., was born in Chiva, Me., July 20, 1829, where he spent his boyhood and received his academical education; graduated from Waterville College after a four years' course of study, in 1853; taught an academy two years at Bridgeton, Me., and in 1855 entered Newton Theological Seminary; supplied the High Street church, of Lynn, Mass., during a large part of his seminary course, and became pastor of this church on his graduation, in 1858. In 1867 he left Lynn and

ALFRED OWEN, D.D.

became pastor of the Lafayette Avenue church, Detroit, Mich., where he remained until July, 1877. The following two years he was pastor of the University Place church, Chicago, Ill. In 1879 he was elected president of Denison University, O., which position he still holds.

Dr. Owen has written much for the papers, and has given courses of lectures in Ministers' Institutes, as well as before the students of Chicago and Newton Theological Seminaries. He has had large experience in educational work, is a scholarly writer and preacher, and gives great satisfaction as a college president. Kalamazoo College conferred the honorary degree of D.D. upon him in 1871.

Owen, Rev. Ezra D., was born near Norristown, Pa., in 1809. His parents came to Scipio, N. Y., in 1810. He was converted and joined the Baptist church of Venice in 1826. He studied in the common schools and under Dr. Smith, and was ordained at Branchport in 1830. He was pastor at Branchport five years. In 1835 he and his wife came by carriage to Springfield, O., where he served as pastor one year. He came next to Cincinnati, and soon had an appointment from the American Baptist Home Mission Society to go to Richmond, Ind. He labored there two years, and was called to the pastorate of the church at Madison. He served this church as pastor ten or twelve years, in the mean time undertaking the issuing of an Indiana Baptist newspaper,—the *American Messenger*. After publishing it at Madison for about three years, he removed it to Indianapolis in the fall of 1846. During the time of his editorship at Indianapolis he was also under appointment by the American Baptist Home Mission Society, and founded the Baptist church at Evansville. The *American Messenger* was sold to the *Cross and Journal*, of Ohio, and thenceforth the name was the *Journal and Messenger*. He then was called by the Lafayette church, which he served three years, after which he was invited back to Madison, which he served till his death, Sept. 26, 1852.

Owens, Deacon Benjamin W., was born in South Carolina in 1818, lived in Alabama and Arkansas, where he was baptized in 1835, and settled at Stockton, Cal., in 1850. He helped to organize the first Baptist church in that city, bought a house for its worship, helped to build another, and paid several thousand dollars for erecting another. In 1868 he settled in San Francisco, and was a deacon of the Tabernacle and Columbia Square churches many years. He is a generous layman, active on mission and educational boards, and never more happy than when engaged with others in revivals.

P.

Page, Rev. J.—Few ministers in Florida have been more useful than Rev. James Page, pastor of the Baptist (colored) church at Tallahassee. For about forty years he has labored in the city and vicinity, and whether as a slave or freedman, has commanded the respect and confidence of all classes. Nor is his influence confined to his immediate section, it is felt for good among the colored Baptists nearly all over the State. He visited Thomasville, Ga., in 1860, and, by invitation, preached acceptably to the white congregation. Mr. Page is a man of good sense and observation; he is an earnest student of the Bible, and he has long been an acceptable preacher of the gospel. He is a man of large frame, robust constitution, and though now quite an old man, is the unaided pastor of a church numbering some 1200 members.

He has been for several years the clerk of the Bethlehem Association, a very large body, and the first organized by the colored Baptists of the State. He is a progressive man, the friend of education, and has earnestly favored the effort to build up a school for the special benefit of the ministry of his race.

Page, Lady Mary, the wife of Sir Gregory Page, was brought to the Saviour in early life. She examined the baptismal question, and the grounds for dissenting from the Episcopal Church, for five years, and, having decided that she could not make any improvement upon the Saviour's example, she was immersed by Mr. Maisters, in the presence of more than two hundred spectators. Further reading, especially during a protracted sickness, but confirmed her in her religious principles and in her attachment to her church home. Says one who knew her, "Her constant regard for the church, her tender concern for pastor and people, her uncommon benefaction upon their removal hither, deserve a particular acknowledgment, as does also her further bounty given in her last will for the relief of the poor members. She distributed vast sums of money in so silent a way that 'her left hand knew not what her right hand did.'" She endured severe afflictions with heaven-given patience. She enjoyed a clear hope through the blood of the Lamb, and without a struggle she fell asleep in Jesus, March 4, 1728. She was buried in Bunhill-fields, in London, in which city she died. She was a great ornament to her holy profession; she lived in the hearts of the members of her church, and in a multitude of other hearts. Mr. Richardson, her pastor, preached a funeral sermon for her. Mr. Harrison, a neighboring Baptist minister, preached another funeral sermon to commemorate God's grace in her holy life and death. And he delivered a funeral oration when she was interred; he also composed an ode in honor of the deceased, in which he says,—

> "At length the heroine's crowned. Her numerous foes,
> With whom she long conflicted, are subdued;
> Under her feet they're laid, while she, in strains
> Angelic, sings the praises of the Lord."

Page, Stephen B., D.D., was born in Fayette, Me., Oct. 16, 1808; spent his early life in the family of Rev. Justin Edwards, D.D.; was converted at the age of eighteen, and united with the Baptist church at Hartford, Conn., being the first person baptized by Barnas Sears, D.D., then just ordained; pursued his preparatory studies at Hamilton, N. Y., and graduated at Waterville, Me., in 1835. After spending one year in teaching, entered Newton Theological Seminary, which he left in 1839. In September, 1839, became pastor at Masillon, O., and in 1844 at Wooster, O., where he remained six years. In 1850 took charge of the Norwalk, O., Baptist church, and in 1854 of the Third church, in Cleveland, where he continued with much success until 1861, when he assumed the pastoral care of the Second (now Euclid Avenue) church of Cleveland. This church at the time of his settlement was heavily in debt and apparently near extinction, but under his well-directed labors grew largely in numbers and strength. In 1866 he resigned this pastorate, and engaged in a successful effort to complete an endowment of $100,000 for Denison University. Shortly after this he was appointed by the American Baptist Home Mission Society district secretary for Ohio and West Virginia, this latter State being subsequently, however, given to another, and Indiana and Michigan added to his field. In this work he continued nearly twelve years, during which time he collected over $100,000 for home mission work.

Feb. 1, 1880, Dr. Page resigned his secretaryship. He continues to reside in Cleveland, being with one exception the oldest resident minister in the city.

Paine, Rev. John, was born in Pomfret, Conn., in 1793; baptized in 1813, by Rev. Amos Wells; united with the Baptist church in Hampton, Conn.; ordained and settled pastor of the same church in

1819, and remained eight years; in 1827 removed to Auburn, Mass., then to Ward, Mass., where he labored ten years; subsequent pastorates were in Bozrah, Conn., four years; in South Woodstock, eleven years; in Packersville, Conn., five years; always a close student, clear thinker, instructive preacher, judicious pastor; removed to Preston, Conn., in 1863, where he died April 29, 1864, aged seventy-one years. His daughter Mary married Rev. O. W. Gates, now of California.

Painter, Mr., and the Persecuting Laws of Massachusetts.—In 1644 the General Court of Massachusetts decided "That if any person or persons within this jurisdiction shall either *openly condemn or oppose the baptizing of infants, or go about secretly to seduce others from the approbation or use thereof, or shall purposely depart the congregation at the ministration of the ordinance*, or shall deny the ordinance of magistracy, or their lawful right and authority to make war, or to punish the outward breaches of the first table (of the ten commandments), and shall appear to the court wilfully and obstinately to continue therein after due time and means of conviction, every such person or persons shall be sentenced to banishment." Mr. Backus, speaking of this wicked law enacted by our Congregational brethren, says, "I have diligently searched all the books, records, and papers I could come at upon all sides, and have found a *great number* of instances of Baptists suffering for the above points that we own." Baptists "refused to countenance infant baptism and the use of secular force in religious affairs," and Backus found many cases of persons persecuted by law for opposing infant baptism in the methods specified. Painter, in 1644, "a poor man, was suddenly turned Anabaptist, and having a child born, would not suffer his wife to carry it to be baptized. He was complained of for this to the court, and enjoined by them to suffer his child to be baptized. And because he refused to obey them therein, and told them it was an antichristian ordinance, *they tied him up and whipped him*, which he bore without flinching, and declared he had divine help to support him." Gov. Winthrop says that "he belonged to Hingham, and that he was whipped for denying the Lord's ordinance." (History of the Baptists in New England, by Isaac Backus, i. 127–8. Newton.) This stinging argument brought no conviction to the mind of Mr. Painter, and it only showed the dearth of Scriptural reasons for the infant rite, and the lack of justice and common sense in those who tried to secure persuasion with the lash. More than a hundred years earlier the same kind of argument was freely used in Switzerland, and in our own times force has brought the Baptist infant to the font in Germany. But this old argument of the highwayman will gradually fall into disuse as men see its worthlessness and its thorough wickedness.

Palen, Rev. Vincent, was born Jan. 17, 1810, in Poughkeepsie, N. Y., of Methodist parents. He experienced religion in 1828, although he did not then make a public profession. In 1833 he became a full member of the Methodist Episcopal Church, and a preacher. After filling a circuit appointment he held a protracted meeting at McAllister's church, near Harrisburg, Pa., at which 120 persons professed conversion. From these converts a church was organized, of which he was chosen pastor. Some of the candidates for membership refusing to accept sprinkling as baptism, he was led carefully to investigate the subject of baptism, and became convinced that immersion is the only Scriptural mode. He was baptized in the Susquehanna River at Harrisburg, by Rev. E. Thomas, a Winebrennarian minister, and was ordained to the ministry in that body. After a pastorate here of sixteen months (during which a meeting-house was built), followed by a brief engagement at Baltimore, he united, in 1843, with the High Street Baptist church in that city, May 25, 1845, after which he was ordained, Rev. S. P. Hill, D.D., preaching the sermon. From this time until the outbreak of the war his time was divided among evangelistic, missionary, and pastoral labors. The beginning of the war found him at Portsmouth, Va., from which he was sent to Richmond, and imprisoned as an "alien enemy." He was, however, soon released, and on reaching Washington was appointed a hospital chaplain. He discharged the duties of this office with efficiency and unflagging zeal. In this and other ways he rendered very important service to the government during the great struggle. At the close of the war he was, with one exception, the last hospital chaplain mustered out of the service, and he was then transferred to the regular army as post chaplain. In December, 1869, in consequence of chronic ill health, he was at his own request retired from active service. He has since resided in Camden, N. J. As his health permits he continues to fill up the measure of his usefulness by preaching and other Christian ministries.

Palmer, Albert Gallatin, D.D., son of Luther and Sarah (Kenyon) Palmer, was born in North Stonington, Conn., May 11, 1813; experienced religion at nine years of age; baptized by Rev. Jonathan Miner, in 1829; joined First Baptist church in North Stonington; began early to preach, and supplied for a year the church in Andover, Conn.; pursued academical studies at Kingston and Pawtucket, R. I., and Andover, Mass.; preached for First Baptist church in North Stonington, by which body he was ordained in 1834; was pastor of First Baptist church in Westerly, R. I., from 1837 to 1843, and blessed in his work; pastor of

Stonington Borough church, Conn., from 1843 to 1852, and prospered; enjoyed three revivals of power; pastor of the church in Syracuse, N. Y., for three years; pastor at Bridgeport, Conn.; pastor for three years at Wakefield, R. I., and shared large revivals; in 1861, by urgent solicitation, returned to Stonington Borough; rich and constant blessings followed; he is here now laboring with great honor, having served at this post twenty-seven years; received from Madison University the honorary degree of Doctor of Divinity; in 1844 published a small volume, "The Early Baptists of Connecticut;" in 1872, a "Historical Discourse" (Centennial), given before the Stonington Union Association; above one hundred sermons and sketches in the *Christian Secretary*, of Hartford, various missionary papers of worth, numerous poems and sonnets, and a superior translation of "Dies Iræ;" is a preacher of remarkable gravity, unction, and earnestness; possesses marked talents, guided by strong faith; for years was president of the Connecticut Baptist State Convention; always a strong advocate of education, temperance, and missions; a leader among Connecticut Baptists.

ALBERT GALLATIN PALMER, D.D.

Palmer, Ethan B., D.D., was born in Austerlitz, N. Y., March 12, 1836; baptized at East Hillsdale in 1852; graduated from Madison University in 1860, and from the seminary in 1863; was ordained in the city of New York, Jan. 6, 1864; labored in Newbern, N. C., and at other places. In March, 1872, he began his pastorate of the First church, Bridgeton, N. J., where he continues. Nearly 200 have been baptized since his labors in Bridgeton began, the membership has almost doubled, and the work of the church has been very much enlarged. In connection with the South

ETHAN B. PALMER, D.D.

Jersey Institute, Mr. Palmer has found a large field for his labors, and his counsels on the denominational boards are very serviceable.

Palmer, Henry, M.D., an eminent and widely-known physician and surgeon of Janesville, Wis., was born in New Hartford, Oneida Co., N. Y., July 30, 1827. He is a son of Deacon Ephraim Palmer, a well-known Baptist of Edgerton, Wis. His father was a farmer, and Henry assisted in the management of the farm until he was nineteen years of age. During the winter he attended the district schools of his neighborhood. He subsequently completed a full course of studies at the Academy of Cazenovia, N. Y. From his early boyhood he earnestly desired to prepare himself for the medical profession. Owing, however, to his want of pecuniary resources he was obliged to delay his cherished plan, and several years were devoted to other pursuits, chiefly teaching school. In 1851 he entered the office of Drs. March and Armsby, at Albany, N. Y., both of whom were distinguished physicians and professors in the Albany Medical College, from which he graduated in 1854. In 1857 he established himself in Janesville, Wis., where he has built up a very extensive local practice, and in surgery his field covers the State at large. Since the death of Dr. E. B. Wolcott, of Milwaukee, he ranks as the leading surgeon in Wisconsin.

On the outbreak of the civil war in 1861, Dr. Palmer offered his services to the State, and was commissioned surgeon of the 7th Wis. Regiment. Subsequently he was appointed director of the hospital service in Baltimore. He was afterwards transferred to the same service in York, Pa. At this post he remained two years. When Gen. Lee's army commenced the invasion of Pennsylvania, York fell into their hands, and he was taken prisoner, but escaped during the progress of the battle of Gettysburg, and immediately took possession of his hospital, filling it with the wounded from the battle-field. In March, 1864, he was assigned to duty as medical inspector of the 8th Corps of the Army of the Potomac. He continued in this position until the end of the war, when he was ordered to Chicago to close up the medical department of the Western district. This service performed, he returned again to the practice of his profession in Janesville, Wis., having won honorable distinction in the army, and the highest place in his profession.

For many years Dr. Palmer has been a Baptist. The numerous demands made upon his time by his professional engagements prevent his sharing largely in the active work of the church of which he is a member. He is a man of exemplary life, thorough conscientiousness, and earnestness in his profession. Twice his fellow-townsmen have elected him mayor of the city. During the late war between Turkey and Russia, Dr. Palmer went to Europe for the purpose of visiting the hospitals of the contending armies, to acquaint himself with the latest results of the science of surgery attained by the profession in those countries. He was freely passed through the lines, and allowed every facility for accomplishing his object.

Dr. Palmer has won an enviable position, but at fifty years of age, in fine physical health, with unimpaired mental powers, he may be said to have but entered upon his professional career. His past splendid success justifies the hope of his friends that his future will be brilliant, and of still larger usefulness to his fellow-men.

Palmer, Rev. Lyman, was born in Dutchess Co., N. Y., Aug. 19, 1818; his parents were both Baptists, and their home was a place of hearty welcome for ministerial brethren at all times. In his early years he listened to many theological discussions in the quiet old farm-house of his parents. After repeated struggles with his conscience, aroused by the truth and the Holy Spirit, he became a subject of redeeming grace at the age of nineteen. He at once united with the Baptist church in East Hillsdale, Columbia Co., N. Y. Soon after making a profession of religion, he had deep convictions of duty in reference to preaching the gospel. The salvation of his soul was so precious an event that he felt he owed his best services to the Saviour, who had redeemed him. A sense of unfitness and of the magnitude of the work at first appeared an impassable barrier. Through increasing light he was brought to say

REV. LYMAN PALMER.

from the heart, "Yes, Lord, I will do anything thou requirest." After a few months he received a license from the church and a call to supply their pulpit.

He entered Madison University in the autumn of 1843. He had previously attended an academy, where he had made some proficiency in Latin and Greek. After one year of close application to study his health became so precarious that he left the university, and read Greek and Hebrew with a private teacher, and at the same time studied theology with his pastor. On Lord's day he supplied destitute churches. In February, 1845, he was ordained, that he might go to Iowa as a missionary of the American Baptist Home Mission Society. Before he was ready to journey West he was prostrated by fever, and thus prevented from entering his chosen field. With returning health he entered upon missionary work in Columbia Co., N. Y. Here the work of the Lord prospered in his hands, blessed results crowning his labors. He organized a church, nearly all of whom were converted and baptized under his ministry. In 1851 he received an appointment from the American Baptist Home Mission Society to labor in the Territory of Minnesota. In November, 1851, he started for the falls of St. Anthony, but having to cross the State of Illinois with a wagon, he did not reach the Mississippi at Galena until after the last boat of the season had gone up the river. He remained in Galena during the winter and supplied the Baptist pulpit. His first sermon in St. Anthony was preached on Lord's day, April 24, 1852. The church was small, and in debt for their unfinished chapel. After three years' hard labor the church increased to a membership of 67. He then went up the river fifteen miles, to the town of Anoka. Here he preached in private houses, or in school-houses, or on board of steamboats, as opportunity presented. After three years' untiring labor a good meeting-house was dedicated, and, by the generosity of friends, was soon free from debt. He served the Anoka church eight years, leaving them with a good working membership of 50. A part of the time during the war, teachers being very scarce, he engaged in teaching. In August, 1864, he commenced labor as colporteur of the American Baptist Publication Society. With the exception of about one year, he labored either as colporteur or Sunday-school missionary until 1875. While in the employment of the society he traveled 36,700 miles, distributed by sale and donation 12,700 books, 423,000 pages of tracts, besides selling and giving away many Bibles and Testaments. These were years of severe service, traveling in all weathers, by night and by day, summer and winter, lodging in all manner of places, yet they were happy years, for much good was accomplished in them. Many Christians were strengthened, the weary and heavy-laden were pointed to Christ, and Sunday-schools and churches were organized for the Master.

Palmer, N. J., Esq.—Among the departed worthies of our Zion this earnest man deserves honorable mention. He was a lawyer, an editor, and sometimes preached. For many years he was secretary of the Baptist State Convention, North Carolina, and a trustee of Wake Forest College. He was a devoted Christian, and died where he had lived for many years, in Milton, in 1855.

Palmer, Rev. Wait, the first pastor of the First Baptist church in North Stonington, Conn., was ordained in 1743, at the same time that the church was organized; remained pastor twenty-two years; preached often in destitute regions; baptized Rev. Simeon Brown and Rev. Shubal Stearns; was an actor in the great "New Light," or Separatist movement; also an active patriot in the Revolution, soon after which he died. The Baptist ministry in Connecticut has been honored by the Palmers: Christopher Palmer, ordained in 1782; Abel Palmer, in 1785; Reuben Palmer, in 1785; Gresham Palmer, in 1805; Phineas Palmer, in 1808.

Palmer, Rev. William, son of Rev. Abel and Lois Palmer, was born in Colchester, Conn., Sept. 10, 1785; was a student from boyhood; was converted and baptized at the age of eighteen; received a license and commenced preaching at the age of twenty; in 1807 was married to Sarah Bennett, sister of Revs. Alfred and Alvin Bennett; in 1809 was ordained at Colchester, sermon preached by Rev. Samuel Bliss, of Stafford; settled in Ashford, Conn., and labored three years; settled in his native town and preached ten years; from 1824 to 1834 was pastor of the First Baptist church in Norwich, Conn., succeeding Rev. John Sterry; blessed with remarkable revivals in 1829 and 1832, in which he baptized more than a hundred; three years with the church in East Lyme, Conn.; four years with the church in North Lyme; revivals attended his labors; again filled the pastoral office in Norwich from 1841 to 1845, when impaired health compelled his retirement from the pulpit except occasionally. He was lovely and loved, meek, quiet, fervent, and faithful. Passionately fond of study, he held a high rank as a preacher. For twenty-five years he was the clerk of the New London Baptist Association. He died in Norwich, Dec. 25, 1853, at the age of sixty-eight, and after a ministry of forty-eight years, and was buried in Yantic cemetery.

Parker, Rev. Carleton, was born in Hopkinton, Mass., Nov. 30, 1806, and was fitted for college at South Reading and Amherst Academies. He graduated at Waterville College, now Colby University, in the class of 1834. He intended to have entered the ministry on graduating, but the state of his health forbade him, and he devoted himself to teaching for nearly twenty years. Four years he was the principal of the Vermont Literary and Scientific Institution at Brandon. From 1841 to 1844 he had charge of Groton Academy, in the State of New York. For three years he had a "Home School for Boys" in Framingham, Mass. Feeling that the state of his health now warranted his entering the ministry, he was ordained pastor of the Baptist church in Wayne, Me., in May, 1852. He held this relation until September, 1856, then went to Hebron, Me., where he was the pastor for seven years. His other pastorates were in Maine, at Canton, Norridgewock, and North Livermore, where he died, Aug. 22, 1874. By his will he bequeathed several thousand dollars to four of the benevolent societies of the denomination which he had served so long and so well.

Parker, Hon. D. McNeil, M.D., deacon of the Baptist church, Granville Street, Halifax, Nova Scotia, was born in 1822, at Windsor, Nova Scotia; graduated M.D. from the University of Edinburgh, Scotland, in 1845; returned immediately to Nova Scotia, and has ever since been practising his profession in Halifax with high reputation for skill; is a member of the Legislative Council, a governor of Acadia College, and a liberal supporter of all denominational objects.

Parker, H. I., D.D., was born of pious parents at Cavendish, Vt., Nov. 12, 1812. At the age of eighteen he was converted, and four years later was baptized by Rev. Joseph Freeman, D.D. After two years' study at the Norwich and the Black River Academies, and one year at Dartmouth College, he spent two years as instructor at "The Old Cambridge Latin School," graduated at Harvard University in 1840, and studied theology at Newton. He was ordained at Factory Point, Vt., in January, 1842, and was pastor at Burlington, Vt., from 1844 to 1854, when he removed to Wisconsin to aid in establishing the Baptist Institution at Beaver Dam, and was pastor there from 1856 to 1861, when, on account of ill health, he removed to Austin, Minn. Here he preached at six different stations, where as many churches were afterwards organized. In 1872 he settled in California, and has ministered to the churches at Visalia, Santa Barbara, and Santa Anna. During the thirty-eight years of his ministry he has enjoyed many revivals, laid the spiritual foundations of many new churches, built four church edifices, helped to endow and manage two institutions of learning, and was for eight years a member of the Minnesota State Normal Board. In May, 1880, California College conferred upon him the degree of D.D.

Parker, Rev. James, was born in 1812, in Aylesford, Nova Scotia; converted and baptized in 1828; he was ordained May 19, 1842, and became in 1843 pastor of the Baptist church of Brookfield, Queen's Co., Nova Scotia; of the Third Cornwallis church in 1855; of the Third Horton church in 1870; of the Kentville church in 1874; died June 26, 1876. His was a useful life and ministry.

Parker, J. W., D.D., was ordained and settled as pastor of the First Baptist church in Cambridge, Mass., in 1836, and continued to serve in that relation with success during twenty years. At the close of that long pastorate he became secretary of the Northern Baptist Education Society, which position he held about ten years, five of which he was pastor of the Shawmut Avenue Baptist church, in Boston. In January, 1865, he resigned the pastorate of this church, and entered upon the work of establishing schools for training colored men as preachers, and young men and women as teachers, among the freedmen of the Southern States. In this labor Dr. Parker continued about five years, visiting all the Atlantic States many times, introducing teachers into destitute fields, and organizing schools in many towns and cities. While thus occupied his health failed, owing to overwork, hardships, and exposures. Settling down for a while on a small farm in Maryland, he engaged in constant out-door work, and soon regained his usual health. He was then invited to accept the pastorate of the Calvary Baptist church in Washington, D. C., which he did, occupying the pulpit for about six years with marked success. At the close of this period, feeling the need of rest and change of climate, he visited Europe, where he remained upwards of a year. Soon after his return he was urged to become the pastor of the E Street Baptist church, Washington, D. C., which he consented to do, and he still holds that position. While residing in Massachusetts, Dr. Parker acted for a period of sixteen years as a member of the executive committee of the American Baptist Missionary Union, and in 1849 he was delegated by that body to represent them at the first Baptist Association held in Germany, at the old city of Stettin. Accompanied by that pioneer German missionary, the Rev. J. G. Oncken, he visited the Baptist missions in Denmark and Germany. The missionary stations in France he visited with the Rev. Erastus Willard. From these visits he gleaned many interesting facts which were of great use to the committee in the prosecution of their work in those fields. Dr. Parker stands deservedly very high among his Baptist brethren, as well as among his friends in other denominations, who have long known and acknowledged his sterling worth.

Parker, Rev. Uriah H., an aged Baptist minister residing in Bradley Co., Ark., settled in this part of the State about 1846, and shortly after gathered Shady Grove church in the southern part of Bradley County, the oldest missionary Baptist church between the Ouachita and the Mississippi Rivers. An anti-mission church was gathered at Warren a few years before, but it is long since extinct. Mr. Parker also gathered another church in Bradley County, which was afterwards dissolved. He united his labors with Royal in Drew County, and Tommie in Bradley, and by their common labors the foundations of many of the oldest churches in Bartholomew Association were laid. He often preaches yet with great earnestness and power.

Parker, Rev. Willard G., was born in Annapolis Co., Nova Scotia, April 4, 1816; converted and baptized in 1828; ordained pastor at New Albany, Jan. 28, 1843; was pastor at Sackville, New Brunswick, seven years, and in Nova Scotia at the following places: Nictaux, seventeen years, also of Mitton, Queen's County, Lawrencetown, Valley West, and Pine Grove churches; baptized over a thousand converts; died Dec. 6, 1878; an eminent minister of the gospel.

Parkerism in Indiana.—1. *The Doctrine.*—God never made a creature that will suffer eternally. All the elect were created in union with Christ, and so he was bound by covenant to redeem them. These are the "good seed." The non-elect are the children of the devil, begotten in some mysterious manner of Eve. These are the "bad seed."

2. *The Man.*—Reared on the frontiers of Georgia, "he was without education, uncouth in manners, slovenly in dress, diminutive in person, and unprepossessing in appearance." His enthusiasm bordered on insanity. In 1819 he came into Indiana from his home in Illinois, and at once began to attract attention. He opposed missions, education, and Sunday-schools.

3. *The Motive.*—He sought notoriety as a writer, and was anxious to use the columns of the *Columbian Star*, published in Washington City. His articles were rejected. In his revenge he attacked not only the paper, but all it advocated, such as missions, education, etc.

4. *The Effect.*—Scores of churches and hundreds of members were drawn away after him. And they went so far as to pass resolutions denouncing missions, etc. But finally those churches died as a proper result of their heinous heresy. Parker was excluded from his own church.

Parkhurst, Rev. Jabez W., was born in Middletown, Conn., Jan. 10, 1806. At the age of twenty-two he united with the Baptist church in his native town. In the fall of 1831 he removed to Newton, Mass., fitted himself to enter the theological institution there, and graduated in 1836. For seven years after his graduation he was the pastor of the church in Tyngsborough, Mass., and at the end of this period became pastor of the church in West Dedham, Mass. His pastorate of this church continued for six years, and was closed in consequence of his ill health. He was chosen an agent of the American Baptist Home Missionary Society, and performed the duties of his office for fourteen years. Having closed his relations with the society, he supplied different churches for a time, hoping that his health would be so far restored that he would be able to resume his pastoral work. This hope not being realized, he accepted an appointment as an agent of the Hancock Mutual Life Insurance Company, a position which he occupied until his death, March 19, 1871.

Parkinson, Rev. William, was born in Frederick Co., Md., Nov. 8, 1774. He was convicted of sin in his twentieth year, and in June, 1796, he was baptized by the Rev. Absalom Bainbridge, in Israel's Creek, in his native county. He was ordained to the Christian ministry in April, 1798. He delighted in preaching as an itinerating home missionary, a practice very common among our Baptist fathers, and greatly blessed. In December, 1801, and for "three successive seasons," during Jefferson's administrations he was "a chaplain to Congress." He was chosen to this position by a large majority, and without solicitation on his part. On Lord's day morning he preached in the Capitol, and in the afternoon in the Treasury. He says, "The members of Congress attend abundantly better than I expected; I have, moreover, the pleasure of stating that the President has missed but one of my meetings at the Capitol."

On the 20th of December, 1804, Mr. Parkinson came on a visit to the First Baptist church of New York; after preaching to their great satisfaction for about six weeks, he received an earnest call to become their pastor. Early in April he accepted the call, and very soon after a powerful revival of religion came down upon the church from the throne of grace, and it continued for several years, adding large numbers to the membership of the church, and giving a glorious impetus to Baptist influence, and efforts, and prayers in New York. His congregations were very large, and his sermons swept the people along with him with resistless force. He continued pastor of the First church for thirty-five years, and then resigned, after which he went to Frederick, Md. In 1840 the Bethesda church of New York City, composed chiefly of warm friends of Mr. Parkinson, recently connected with the First church, invited him to become their pastor. He accepted the call, and in 1841 commenced his labors. But soon a fall seriously impaired his health and largely unfitted him for future pulpit efforts; he lingered along for several years, and died March 9, 1848. The last words he uttered were a declaration that "he was in the arms of his precious Saviour." Daniel Dodge, of saintly memory, pastor of the Second church of Philadelphia, preached his funeral sermon in the First Baptist church of New York.

Mr. Parkinson was endowed with a powerful mind, a voice said to be like Whitefield's, and with a large measure of the grace of God. He had some enemies that possessed a great faculty for hating, and he did not always try to disarm them, but he had throngs of warm-hearted friends who loved him living and who bitterly lamented his death.

His published writings were "A Treatise on the Ministry of the Word" and "Sermons on XXXIII. Chapter of Deuteronomy," in two volumes.

Parks, Rev. Harrison H., son of Rev. Benj. M. Parks, was born in Ontario Co., N. Y., March 1, 1815; joined Athens church, O., in 1832; removed to Illinois in 1834; helped to organize the Whitney Grove church and the Old Salem Association; entered upon the work of pioneer preaching in "the far West"; and was ordained in 1847 by the Black Creek church, Mo., of which he became pastor. He subsequently preached for the Quincy, Warsaw, Fall Creek, Lamarsh, Union, and Howard Grove churches, Ill.; was missionary of the Burlington Association, Iowa, and of Bethel church, Ill., until 1876, when he removed to California; has done much to encourage and build up feeble churches; is now serving as pastor the church at Willows, Colusa Co., Cal.

Parks, Rev. James H., was born in New York City, July 13, 1829. He was converted in the year 1847, and united with the Reformed Dutch Church. Soon after he commenced a course of preparation for Rutgers College, having the Christian ministry in view. But health failing, and a series of circumstances arising which brought the subject of Christian baptism to his attention, he was compelled to make a thorough examination of Scriptural teachings upon this subject, which resulted in his being immersed on profession of faith on the 2d of July, 1854.

He afterwards pursued a post-graduate course at Columbian College, Washington, D. C., and received the degree of Master of Arts from that institution upon examination. He was also honored with the degree of A.M. from Princeton College, N. J. He was ordained to the ministry May 28, 1856. He has been pastor of the Baptist churches at Stamford, Conn., Bedford, N. Y., Pemberton, N. J., Manayunk and Calvary, Philadelphia, and is now successfully laboring with the Linden Avenue Baptist church at Dayton, O. He also performed faithful service as a chaplain in the army at Washington, D. C., during the late war. His pastorates have been successful and efficient. His views of doctrine are clear, strong, and Scriptural, and are always fearlessly enunciated. He is a positive Baptist, perhaps the more so because his own prejudices, instilled from early childhood, were each successively removed by a specific investigation and a conscientious study of the Word of God.

Parmly, Wheelock H., D.D., was born in Braintree, Vt., July 27, 1816; graduated at Columbia College, New York City, in 1842, and from the theological department at Hamilton in 1844; a classmate of George C. Baldwin, of Troy, and others; spent several years preaching in Louisiana and Mississippi, and for three years was pastor at Shelburne Falls, Mass. In 1850 he took charge of the church in Burlington, N. J., and in 1854 he accepted a call to the First church of Jersey City, of which he remains the beloved, honored, and successful pastor. The city has grown rapidly, and the First church has become large and influential, sending out other churches, which are useful and prosperous. He received the degree of Doctor of Divinity from Madison University in 1867. Dr. Parmly has exercised an extensive influence in the moulding and upbuilding of the missionary and educational institutions of the State. He has a place on the board of the American Baptist Home Mission Society. He is loved by his own people and honored by the denomination in the State.

Patch, Rev. George Washington, was born in Boston, April 30, 1817; pursued his preparatory studies in Wakefield, Mass., and New London, N. H. He was a graduate of Brown University in the class of 1839. Having taken the course of theological study at Newton, he was settled first at Wenham, Mass., and then at Sharon, Mass. From this latter place he was called to Marblehead, Mass., where he had a long and most useful ministry of twenty-six years, and ceased to preach only under the pressure of fatal disease. He died, with scarcely a moment's warning, Dec. 25, 1875. Few ministers have left behind them a better record than he.

WHEELOCK H. PARMLY, D.D.

Paterson, James, D.D., of Glasgow, Scotland, was for fifty years pastor of the first regular Baptist church in that city. He was born in 1801 at Dumbarton, and received his early education at the burgh school, then, as now, of considerable reputation. At first he thought of devoting himself to the medical profession, but during his university course he connected himself with the Glasgow City Mission, and eventually entered the ministry. He had joined the Scotch Baptist Church, but never embraced their views of church polity. In 1829 he hired a room and began to preach. A number of university students came to the poor room, a kind of loft, and, after seeing the place and the congregation, they said, "You never mean, Paterson, to make a kirk out of that!" But he did, and the church which originated with three members gradually grew strong and influential, and is now the largest Baptist church in Scotland. He rendered eminent service to the interests of the denomination, and for many years superintended the theological education of students for the Baptist ministry in Scotland. In 1850 he undertook the editorship of the *Scottish Temperance Review*, and subsequently he edited the *Scottish Review*. His ministry was characterized by solidity and strength, and his life was singularly upright, and marked by a severely conscientious regard for duty and integrity. In everything he put his hand to Dr. Paterson proved himself "a workman who needeth not to be ashamed." In the later years of his life he was aided in the pastoral care of the church by the Rev. James Cubross, D.D., as junior pastor, but he continued to minister to his charge until within a short period of his departure, which took place on Jan. 29, 1880.

Patient, Rev. Thomas, was born in England, and educated, we have no doubt, in Oxford or Cambridge. He became a Congregationalist, and emigrated to New England. After laboring in the ministry on this side of the Atlantic, he was convinced that the Saviour and his apostles were Baptists, and he frankly avowed his convictions. He was immediately subjected to violent persecutions, and to escape them he returned to England.

In 1640 he was appointed co-pastor with Mr. Kiffin in London, where he labored for some time. Parliament having voted that six able ministers should be appointed to preach in Dublin, at a salary of £200 per annum, to be paid from the lands formerly owned by bishops, deans, and chapters, Mr. Patient accepted one of these positions, which was offered to him. In the capital of Ireland he became a very popular preacher, and so gifted was he as an eloquent speaker that at times he traveled much through the country, preaching Jesus wherever he went to delighted throngs of British settlers.

In Dublin he acted as chaplain of Col. John Jones, who was married to a sister of the Protector, and who occupied a seat in his "House of Lords." And such a favorite was he with Col. Jones that he selected him to preach before him and the council every Sunday in Christ church cathedral. This church was completed in 1038, and it was repaired and extensively improved by the celebrated English invader of Ireland, Strongbow. In it he was buried in 1176, and his monument is the chief attraction at this day of a superb church. In this grand old temple, before the governor of Dublin and the *élite* of Anglo-Irish society, Mr. Patient proclaimed a living gospel. He was on friendly relations with Oliver Cromwell himself, as the following quotations from a letter written to the Protector by him will show:

"My Lord,—From that little acquaintance I had with your excellency before you went out of Ireland, and the suitableness I found in that letter of your experiences, of which I was made a partaker, compared with my observation of the goings of God with you for many years, in this great work in which God hath made use of you, it hath, indeed, very thoroughly confirmed my heart in charity and love towards you, as one elect and precious in the sight of God. . . . Truly God hath kept the heart of my lord deputy close to himself. . . . I am at present, and have been at the headquarters ever since a little before my Lady Ireton (Cromwell's daughter) came over. I do by good experience find, so far as I can discover, the power of God's grace in her soul, a woman acquainted with temptations and breathing after Christ. And I am persuaded it hath pleased God to begin a work of grace in the soul of Col. Henry Cromwell, your son. . . . I watch him, and he is crying much to God in secret. . . . Your grandchild hath been very weak, but it is recovered. . . . I think I shall be at Dublin with my lady (Ireton) this summer."

This letter shows that Mr. Patient had received an epistle from Cromwell, and that he was intimately and religiously associated with several members of his family at that time in Ireland.

Mr. Patient baptized a large number of persons in Dublin. He was a wise and experienced Christian, and he rendered substantial service to the Saviour's kingdom in Ireland. He died July 30, 1666, and the Lord was with him as he passed from this world of the dying into the heaven of the living. His only published work was a quarto volume on baptism.

Patrick, Prof. John B., is a native of Barnwell County, the garden spot of South Carolina. He graduated in the State Military Academy in 1855. From 1856 to 1858 he was tutor in Furman University. In 1859 he was second lieutenant and Assistant Professor of Mathematics, and then Professor of Mathematics and first lieutenant, until the war closed the academy. He was with the cadets during their active service.

In 1866 he was principal of the preparatory department of Furman University. In 1870 he opened the Greenville High School, and in 1878 he converted it into the Greenville Military Institute. He is a very modest man. Those who know him think that few men in the State have exercised a better or more extensive influence over the young men who are assuming the places of the old as they pass away.

Patrick, Saint, the Apostle of Ireland, was of Scotch birth. His proper name was Succathus; the name by which we designate him is of Latin origin; *patricius* means noble, illustrious; it was a surname and a title of honor at the same time given to him by his grateful admirers. Patrick was wild and wicked until his sixteenth year, when he remembered the God of his fathers and repented him of his sins, and enlisted in the divine service. There is no ground for doubting but that he preached the gospel of repentance and faith in Ireland, and that his ministrations were attended by overwhelming success. There are accounts extant of a number of his baptisms, but they are all immersions. There is one baptism mentioned by Nennius (History of the Britons, p. 410. Bohn, London) and by Todd (St. Patrick, Apostle of Ireland, p. 449. Dublin), and found in many other histories, of which O'Farrell writes (Popular Life of St. Patrick, p. 110. New York, 1863), "When the saint entered Tirawly the seven sons (of Amalgaidh) assembled with their followers. Profiting by the presence of so vast a multitude, the apostle entered into the midst of them, his soul inflamed with the love of God, and with a celestial courage preached to them the truths of Christianity; and so powerful was the effect of his burning words that the seven princes and over twelve thousand more were converted on that day, and were soon after baptized in a well (a spring or fountain) called Tobar Enadhaire, the well of Enadhaire." A number of other fountain baptisms of St. Patrick may be found in "The Baptism of the Ages," pp. 62–70. Publication Society, Philadelphia. We have strong reasons for regarding St. Patrick as a Baptist missionary, and beyond contradiction his baptism was immersion.

Patterson, Rev. John W., was born in New Kent Co., Va., Dec. 14, 1850. He was baptized in 1868, entered the Richmond Institute, and was graduated from the same in 1874. He served as missionary of the American Baptist Home Mission Society for some time, and was ordained in July, 1872. He was soon called to the pastorate of the First Baptist church (colored), Danville, Va., where, during five years, he has had abundant success, having baptized nearly one thousand persons. He has been greatly honored by his people, and fills a wide sphere of usefulness. He is an excellent preacher, and quite a vigorous writer, several of his sermons having been published and widely circulated. He is deeply interested in all good movements, and is a trusted leader among his people.

Pattison, Robert E., D.D., was born in Benson, Vt., Aug. 19, 1800. His mother was Sarah Everett, daughter of a physician; his father was a Baptist minister, and Robert was his second son. He united with the Baptist Church when a young man, and soon gave up business for an education to enter the ministry. He prepared for college, and entered Amherst in 1826; stood second in a class of forty. He was tutor in Columbian College, Washington, D. C., then Professor of Mathematics in Waterville College, Me. He was pastor in Salem, Mass., then at Providence, R. I. In 1836 he became president of Waterville College until it suspended for want of means, in 1839. He occupied the pulpit of the Second Baptist church for a year, and returned to his former charge in Providence. In 1842 he became secretary of the home department of the American Baptist Missionary Union. This position was urged upon him, and he reluctantly left his

ROBERT E. PATTISON, D.D.

church in Providence to fill it. After three years of service he was re-elected secretary, but accepted, in 1845, the presidency of the Western Baptist Theological Institute, at Lexington, Ky. This school was suspended by local difficulties, and Dr. Pattison for six years was a professor at Newton Theological Seminary. Then he resumed, by request, the presidency of Waterville College, and held the office until failing health caused him to retire from labor for a time. He removed to Worcester, Mass., to pass his days free from care, but in two years he assumed the proprietorship of Oread Institute.

In the fall of 1864 he was a Professor of Theology in Shurtleff College. In 1870 he removed to Chicago to become a professor in the Union Baptist Theological Seminary, where he remained until his last illness. In the summer of 1874 his energies began to give way, and after a protracted illness he died at the residence of his eldest son, in St. Louis. Dr. Pattison left as his only literary monument a "Commentary on the Epistle to the Ephesians." Few men have impressed their views more deeply upon others. In all circumstances he possessed a resolute hopefulness and a firmness in adhering to his convictions of right and duty. His powers of persuasion were remarkable, and his life was one of great usefulness and of devoted piety.

Pattison, T. Harwood, D.D., was born in England in December, 1838. He was educated by private tuition, and at the London University School; studied architecture for four years in London; spent

T. HARWOOD PATTISON, D.D.

four years at Regent's Park Baptist College, London, from which he graduated in 1862; was pastor at Newcastle-on-Tyne and Rochdale, in England.

In 1874, during a tour in the United States, he received a call to the pastorate of the First Baptist church of New Haven, Conn. After returning to England he accepted the invitation, and came to this country again in March, 1875, and settled in New Haven. His brilliant pastorate in that city attracted the attention of intelligent Baptists everywhere, and when, in 1879, the Pearl Street church of Albany, N. Y., wanted an under-shepherd to succeed Dr. Bridgman, and fill the position which had been occupied by some of the first ministers in the Baptist denomination, they extended a call to Mr. Pattison. His labors in that city have increased his reputation as a fine scholar, an eloquent preacher, a judicious pastor, and a gospel laborer upon whose efforts the favor of heaven specially rests. He received in 1880 the degree of Doctor of Divinity from Madison University, and he has just been chosen to fill one of the most important chairs in Rochester Theological Seminary.

In the history of our denomination in this country no man has ever acquired such distinguished success in a shorter time than Dr. Pattison, and no one more richly deserves it. Those best acquainted with him anticipate an unusually bright future for him, rich in the fruits of ripe scholarship, great modesty, ardent piety, and intellectual powers of a high order.

Dr. Pattison, in 1872, published "Present Day Lectures." He is the American correspondent of *The Freeman*, one of the organs of the English Baptists.

Patton, Alfred S., D.D., was born in Suffolk, England, Dec. 25, 1825, came to America when a child, and was educated at Columbian College, Washington, D. C., and Madison University, N. Y. He received the degree of Master of Arts from the former, and Doctor of Divinity from the latter. After graduating he spent some months in Europe.

He was settled as pastor in West Chester, Pa., then in Haddonfield, N. J., then for five years in the First Baptist church of Hoboken, N. J.

In 1859 he accepted the pastorate of the church in Watertown, Mass., and for 1862 and 1863 was the chaplain of the Massachusetts senate.

In 1864 he accepted a call from the old Broad Street church of Utica, N. Y. While there the church built the spacious and attractive house of worship known as the Tabernacle Baptist church. It is located in one of the finest sections of the city. His labors in the new field met with marked success. Dr. Patton is an able preacher, and was a good pastor, possessing remarkable tact and superior

ALFRED S. PATTON, D.D.

social qualities. He has been industrious with the pen. He is the author of the following works: "Kincaid, the Hero Missionary," "The Losing and Taking of Man-Soul, or Lectures on the Holy

War," "Light in the Valley," "Live for Jesus," "My Joy and my Crown," and smaller works published by the American Tract Society. He also contributed articles for the *Christian Review* on "The Influence of Physical Debility on Religious Experience," and "Dreams, their Nature and Uses," also for the Boston *Review*, an article on "Liberal Religion," and for the *Congregational Review*, one on "The Temptation."

In 1872 he purchased the *American Baptist*, and soon after changed its form to a quarto and the name to the *Baptist Weekly*, since which time that journal has taken high rank among Baptist periodicals. He is a firm supporter of all the great enterprises of his denomination, and though kind and considerate to all Christian communities, he is a strenuous supporter of Baptist doctrines and polity.

Patton, Rev. Garrett R., pastor of the Baptist church in Juda, Wis., was born in Fayette Co., Pa., in April, 1811. He passed his youth in the place of his birth, and was educated in the common schools of his neighborhood. In 1830 he made a profession of religion, and united with the Baptist church in Smithfield, Fayette Co., Pa. He was licensed to preach the gospel in 1839, and ordained by the church with which he united when converted. He was pastor of the Monongahela Baptist church in 1839. In 1845 he removed to Juda, Greene Co., Wis., and became pastor of the Baptist church in that place, in which relation he has remained until the present time. He gathered and organized churches in the same county at Monticello, Wyota, and Monroe. He has held the same pastorate longer than any minister in Wisconsin. He is a faithful and successful preacher of the gospel. His ministry has been frequently blessed with revivals of great power. In his seventieth year he is preaching with much acceptance to one of the largest churches in the State.

Patton, Rev. John, was born in 1752, in Kent Co., Del. He was baptized by the Rev. Abel Griffith, of Welsh Tract, in 1789. In 1793 he settled in Shamokin, Pa., and became pastor of the church formed the following year in that place. In 1809 he removed to Fayette Co., Pa., and assumed pastoral care of the Mount Moriah Baptist church. This relation continued until his death, in 1839, aged eighty-seven. Half a century was given to the ministry, and judging from the warm expressions of aged members, both in the Eastern and the Western field he occupied for so many years, he must have been a man of more than ordinary ability and of great activity. As the founder of the ancient church of Shamokin his memory will not perish. Thirteen children and a very large circle of grandchildren, as well as the church he so faithfully served, mourned his loss. One son, James, became a preacher, as did also three grandsons,—John P. Rockafeller, G. R. Patton, and Wm. R. Patton. The latter is a graduate of the university at Lewisburg, and a graduate of the Crozer Theological Seminary. He is now pastor of two churches, the Flatwoods, Fayette Co., and the Greensborough, Greene Co., Pa., and is highly respected as a Christian, a minister, and a citizen.

Paul, Rev. Thomas, a gifted and eloquent colored preacher, was born in Exeter, N. H., Sept. 3, 1773, and at the age of sixteen became a Christian. At the age of twenty-eight he commenced preaching, and was ordained at Nottingham West, N. H., May 1, 1805, and soon after became the pastor of the African Baptist church in Boston, where he remained for more than twenty years. He had a fine, commanding presence, and a fervent, pleasing address, so that his preaching was exceedingly attractive, and crowds came to hear him when he preached, as he frequently did, in the towns about Boston. Genuine revivals of religion occurred under his ministry, and he was highly respected and beloved wherever he went.

Mr. Paul was much impressed with the need of evangelical labor in the island of Hayti, and in 1823 he offered himself to the Massachusetts Baptist Missionary Society as a missionary to the people of that island. He was accepted, and on reaching the field of his labor, addressed himself with great earnestness to his work. But his ignorance of the French language made it impossible for him to reach the people whom he was especially desirous of influencing, and he returned to this country, once more to preach the gospel here. It has been said of him, "He was not an ordinary man. For without the advantages of a good education in early life he became distinguished as a preacher. His understanding was vigorous, his imagination was vivid, his personal appearance was interesting, and his elocution was graceful. We have heard him preach to an audience of more than one thousand persons, when he seemed to have command of their feelings for an hour together. On baptismal occasions he was truly eloquent. His arguments were unanswerable, and his appeals to the heart were powerful. The slow and gentle manner in which he placed candidates under the water and raised them up again produced an indelible impression on the spectators, that they had indeed seen a 'burial with Christ in baptism.'" Mr. Paul died April 14, 1831.

Paulicians.—See ALBIGENSES.

Paullin, Rev. James Stratton, was born in Eufaula, Ala., June 7, 1837, and united with the Baptist church in that place in 1853; ordained in 1858; then became pastor of the church in Clayton, where he remained until 1873; removed to Midway, and was pastor there for four years; then pastor of Broad Street church, Mobile, one year; then returned to his old charge at Clayton, where he remains. Mr. Paullin is an earnest Christian and a thorough Baptist, a working pastor, and a good preacher of the gospel.

Pavey, Rev. Charles, was born in England, and licensed to preach by the Fifty-third Street church, New York, in 1849. In 1860 he was ordained, and he took charge of the Hilltown church, Bucks Co., Pa., where he died in 1871. His ministry as a licentiate and as a pastor was greatly blessed. He had an unusual measure of consecration to God. His views of the doctrines of sovereign grace were eminently Scriptural, and his presentation of them was very earnest and effective. The Hilltown church, so blessed by the labors of Father Mathias, felt the death of Mr. Pavey to be a heavy affliction. His memory is warmly cherished by the people and church of Hilltown.

Paxton, Rev. James Edwards, a useful pioneer Baptist preacher in North Louisiana, by whose labors many of the churches in Bienville, Natchitoches, Jackson, Claiborne, and Bossier Parishes were founded, was born in Kentucky in 1820; aided in the organization of Red River Association and the Louisiana Baptist State Convention, and as financial agent of Mount Lebanon University raised the principal part of the endowment of that institution. Removing to Texas, he became in succession pastor at Anderson, Washington, Independence, and Brenham; died in 1876.

REV. WILLIAM EDWARDS PAXTON.

Paxton, Rev. William Edwards, was born in Little Rock, Ark., in 1825; graduated at Georgetown College, Ky., under the presidency of Howard Malcom, D.D., by whom he was baptized in 1845; removed to Louisiana in 1853, and engaged in the practice of law; during the war served, with the rank of captain, in the Confederate army; entered the ministry in 1864 and became pastor at Minden; in 1873, president of Shreveport University; in 1877, corresponding secretary of the Southern Baptist Publication Society; in 1878, took charge of the Centennial Institute, Warren, Ark., where he now (1880) teaches and preaches. He has contributed largely to the denominational literature of the South. Besides many articles as contributor or editor, he is the author of the following works: "Rights of Laymen," "Apostolic Church," "Faith a Prerequisite to Church Membership," a premium essay published by American Baptist Publication Society, and "Endless Retribution." He is one of the ablest and most cultured ministers in the Baptist denomination.

Pearce, Rev. Samuel, of Birmingham, England, was born in Plymouth, July 20, 1766. In boyhood he occasionally had distressing convictions of sin. When he was fifteen years of age he was in the house of a dying man, who, in despair, exclaimed, "I am damned forever." As the words fell upon the ear of the youth he was filled with horror for the fate of his father's dying friend, and with anguish for his own guilty state; and though his distress on account of sin grew less, it was not until about a year after, when the sermon of a man of God made him grieve over sin more deeply than ever, and pointed out to his hopeless soul the wounded Saviour, that the truth as it is in Jesus gave him peace. His heart was full of Christ, and completely relieved of all fears. He was blessed with full assurance of faith, and as a result, with joy unspeakable and full of glory.

Soon after this he made a covenant with Jehovah, signing it with his own blood, pledging himself completely to the Lord. But though his heart was full of ardor, and his resolution firmly taken, it would seem that he trusted too much to himself, and he partly broke his vows; in consequence of which he was overwhelmed with despair, until the cross with the agonizing Redeemer took the place of his violated covenant as his great source of comfort.

He was educated for the ministry at Bristol College, and during his stay there he was often engaged in preaching Jesus to the poor and neglected in and around that city, and his grand theme on these occasions was "The Sacrifice of Calvary."

In the latter part of 1789 he was ordained pastor of the Cannon Street church, Birmingham, where his ministry was continued till he rested from his labors and his pains.

At one period his mind was a little agitated in

reference to Arminianism and Socinianism: he was then a young man weighing for the first time the shrewdest sophistries of the enemies of truth. But he was completely cured by a dangerous malady which seized him, in the distresses and apprehensions of which he saw that "his diligence, faithfulness, and unspotted life" were no props to sustain a departing soul, that only the omnipotent and guilt-atoning Saviour could protect him, and from that moment the perfect Lamb of his first religious experience was his whole trust till he met him face to face.

He was the friend of Carey and Fuller before Carey went to India, and he was one of the warmest advocates of foreign missions that dwelt on earth since the Son of Mary came from his heavenly home on a foreign mission to this lost world. During his whole life after entering upon the ministry, and while his health was unbroken, he had a continual struggle about going out as a missionary to India. His popularity as a minister was immense, his people loved him tenderly, his usefulness showed that the seal of God was deeply impressed upon his ministry. The board of the Missionary Society, at his request, gave an opinion upon his duty to go to the heathen, and their decision was that as he was more useful to foreign missions in England than he could be in India, he should remain in Birmingham; nevertheless, his heart was in India with his friend Carey until he was carried by angels to his Saviour's presence in glory. He rendered effective service to the cause of missions by his eloquent appeals in Birmingham and in various parts of England, and also in Ireland. And in 1794 he wrote to Dr. Rogers, of Philadelphia, and made a rousing appeal to him to try and secure the formation of an American Baptist Foreign Missionary Society.

Mr. Pearce died of consumption, Oct. 10, 1799, after a ministry of only ten years. His last illness was full of hope, patience, and the love of Christ.

He had great faith in prayer, and he carried everything to the Saviour, with whom he wrestled with persevering importunity till the Lord revealed his will. He continually thirsted for the presence of God; life was nothing without it, nor any amount of earthly success or joy. His peace was unusual, and it was apparent to all that knew him. He was sure that his Saviour loved him, that nothing could hurt him, and that he had a home and a divine welcome awaiting him in the heavens, and he was one of the happiest of men. His love for God was all-engrossing and ever-enduring, and his love for men embraced every one, and in needful situations would give everything. He was like Fenelon, Robert Murray McCheyne, of Dundee, or the apostle John, the friend of God and the friend of man. And in his ten years' ministry he left an impression that lives in Birmingham, and in many parts of England to-day, though he has been in his grave for eighty-one years. Measured by usefulness instead of years this young pastor preached for at least a century.

Peat, Rev. J. B., was born in England, Sept. 24, 1816. His father died in 1818, and his mother in 1824, and he was thus left an orphan at an early age. America had such attractions for the boy that he emigrated to the New World in his young manhood, and when converted gave his whole heart and service to the cause of Christ, and won for himself much esteem as a zealous and conscientious preacher in some of the Western States. About the year 1870 he visited California for his health, and received much benefit. He became pastor at the city of Red Bluff, where he died, Nov. 15, 1876. He was very active in temperance and other reform movements. He was the author of the following published works: "The Baptists Examined," "Sure," and "Parsonage Pencillings."

Peay, Rev. John M., was born in Rutherford Co., Tenn., May 19, 1832. He removed to Kentucky in his youth. After attending the common schools, he finished his education, under the supervision of Rev. Dr. J. S. Coleman, at Beaver Dam, Ohio Co., Ky. He united with the Sandy Creek Baptist church in 1853, was licensed to preach in 1854, and was ordained at Beaver Dam in 1857. In 1858 he took charge of the Baptist church at South Carrollton, where he still labors. He has been pastor of three other churches most of the time since he was ordained. He is a powerful and practical preacher, and has been a very successful pastor. He is a vigorous writer, and has published several works, which have met with popular favor. He is also senior editor of *The Student*, an educational journal, published in South Carrollton.

Peay, Rev. Richard Dawson, A.M., brother of John M. Peay, was born in Coffee Co., Tenn., Nov. 10, 1846. He was baptized into the fellowship of Green River Baptist church, in Ohio Co., Ky., in 1864. Entered Bethel College in 1866, graduated with the honor of his class in 1871, was ordained at South Carrollton in 1872, and immediately took pastoral charge of the Portland Avenue Baptist church in Louisville, Ky. After remaining three years he accepted a call to the church in Henderson, Ky. In 1879 he became the principal of the high school in Henderson, meanwhile preaching on the Lord's day to the church at that place.

Peck, Rev. A. C., was born June 25, 1846, at Munson, Geauga Co., O.; graduated at the University of Wisconsin in 1866; taught high school at Freeport, Ill., one year; united with the Baptist church there, and was licensed to the ministry; took a three years' course in the theological seminary at Rochester, N. Y., graduating in 1870; was called to the pastorate at Mumford, N. Y., but, on account of ill health, did not enter upon it; came to Kansas in 1871; engaged in teaching and farming. In 1872 taught in the university at Ottawa, and was called to the pastorate of the Baptist church there; ordained in January, 1873; resigned on account of failing health in 1874; elected superintendent of schools of Franklin Co., Kansas; called to the First Baptist church, Lawrence, Kansas, in October, 1875, where he still ministers.

Peck, Rev. Elijah, was born May 3, 1767, in Warren, Conn. Early in the spring of 1795 he removed from Cooperstown, N. Y., into the "Beech Woods," and settled in Mount Pleasant, Wayne Co., Pa. This journey, in company with his wife and three children, he performed with an ox-team and sled; modern luxuries were then unknown. In June, 1806, he received ordination. From March 3, 1808, until his decease, March 16, 1835, he was the esteemed pastor of the Mount Pleasant church, but, like all pioneer ministers, he performed a vast amount of work in regions round about. "His general appearance indicated great activity and power of endurance. His voice was musical and pleasant, and his manners affable and modest." "He moved in a sphere of great usefulness," and "served his own generation by the will of God."

Peck, Rev. John, was born in Milan, Dutchess Co., N. Y., Sept. 11, 1780. He found full relief from sin, through faith in Jesus, in his eighteenth year, and was baptized. On the 11th of June, 1806, he was ordained as pastor of the First church in Cazenovia, after preaching to the people for eighteen months. This relation continued until 1835, when he resigned to give himself to more extended usefulness. There was spiritual prosperity among his people when he left them, and his ministry among them had been greatly blessed. Six churches were organized chiefly from members dismissed from Cazenovia, and fifteen of her young men had been ordained as pastors of other churches. It was the greatest trial of his life to break the holy tie that united him to his dear people.

He was a warm friend of the Baptist Education Society of the State of New York, which established the Hamilton Literary and Theological Society, now Madison University. He was an active supporter of the Hamilton Baptist Missionary Society, which accomplished a great work for the Saviour over an extensive section of New York; and when it was merged into the Baptist Missionary Convention of the State of New York, he became the general agent of the new body, and served for fifteen years with abounding success. Mr. Peck was a good man, full of the Holy Spirit, whose name will ever be remembered with gratitude in the wide sphere in which his labors were performed. He died Nov. 15, 1849.

Peck, John Mason, D.D., was born in the parish of Litchfield, South Farms, Conn., Oct. 31, 1789. His conversion took place in 1807, when he was eighteen years of age. He first united with the Congregational church in Litchfield. Removing, in 1811, to Windham, Greene Co., N. Y., he became acquainted with the Baptists through the church, and through the pastor, Rev. H. Harvey, in the adjoining town of New Durham. He had already become doubtful of Pedobaptist views and practices, and now, after further inquiry, having fully abandoned those views, he was baptized, Sept. 14, 1811, uniting with the church in New Durham. On the next day, by invitation of the church, he preached his first sermon, and was immediately licensed, and in 1813 was ordained as pastor of the Baptist church in Catskill. After a brief pastorate here, and another at Amenia, in Dutchess County, he accepted an agency in behalf of foreign missions, laboring under the guidance of Rev. Luther Rice. He then, 1816–17, had a year of study under Dr. Stoughton, of Philadelphia. He was then appointed a missionary of the board of the Triennial Convention, to labor in St. Louis and vicinity. Thus began his Western career. July 25, 1817, he set out, with his wife and three children, in a covered wagon, upon the long journey of 1200 miles to his field of labor, and on the 1st of December reached St. Louis. His associate, Rev. James E. Welch, had reached the field before him. In 1822 he became a resident of Rock Spring, Ill., and this remained his home until his death.

At Rock Spring, Dr. Peck, in connection with his missionary labors, now under the appointment of the Massachusetts Baptist Missionary Society, established a seminary for general and theological education, being aided in this, to some extent, by Eastern friends. The seminary was certainly a successful one. It is said to have had at one time one hundred students. As another sphere of auxiliary labor, he began, April 25, 1828, the publication of a paper,—the *Western Pioneer and Baptist*. His work in preaching, meantime, covered a very wide region; while all the affairs of the Territory, soon to become the State of Illinois, engaged his intelligent and active interest. In due time the Rock Spring Seminary became united with the seminary at Upper Alton, now Shurtleff College. Dr. Peck, aside from other labors, wrote largely. Among his works were "A Biography of Father Clark," "Emigrant's Guide," "Gazetteer of Illinois," "Annals of the West," and other works. He died at Rock Spring, March 24, 1857, in the sixty-eighth year of his age. He was a man of many remarkable qualities, robust in intellect, strong in purpose, positive in his opinions, and bold in their advocacy, a born missionary, and a thorough-going Western man.

Peck, Solomon, D.D., was born in Providence, Jan. 25, 1800. He early developed a taste for study, and was sufficiently advanced to enter the Sophomore class in Brown University when he was but thirteen years of age. He graduated in 1816, taught in the University grammar-school and in the college three years and a half; was a student at Andover four years, and was ordained a minister of the gospel in 1823. He preached for a short time in North Yarmouth, Me., and subsequently for one of the churches in Charleston, S. C. He was appointed Professor of the Latin and Hebrew Languages in Amherst College in 1825. In 1832 he visited France in the service of the American Baptist Board of Foreign Missions. A connection was thus commenced with foreign missions which had its influence on what proved to be the great life-work of Dr. Peck. As the secretary of the executive board for twenty hard-working years he performed an amount of clerical work of the magnitude and importance of which few persons can form any conception. He performed not only this home work, but, as an associate with the Rev. Dr. James N. Granger, he traveled extensively in Europe and Asia, visiting the stations of the Missionary Union, suggesting plans, setting things in order, and in many ways doing what lay in his power to advance the cause he so much loved.

After resigning his position as secretary of the board in Boston he spent some time at Beaufort and Edisto Island, S. C., laboring for the mental and spiritual improvement of the colored race. His last public service was as chaplain to the Home for Disabled Soldiers, in Boston, and as secretary of the Freedmen's Aid Society. Dr. Peck died June 12, 1874.

Peckham, Rev. William Augustus, was born in 1810, in Euclid, O., where he lived until he reached manhood, when he removed with his parents to Ontario, N. Y. In early life he experienced religion, and united with the Methodist Episcopal Church. But about the year 1836 his religious views changed, and he united with the Baptist church in Lyons, N. Y., where he was then residing. In 1840 he was licensed to preach, and in 1845 was ordained by the Baptist church in Cassadaga, N. Y., where he was settled as pastor. In 1847 he came to Wisconsin and settled in Jones County, devoting his ministry to the churches in Franklin and Highland. The following year he removed to Aztalan, Jefferson Co., Wis., where he shortly afterwards died. He is remembered by the older ministers of the State as a very earnest and devout Christian minister, from whom much was hoped in those early pioneer days.

Peckworth, Rev. John P., was born in England about 1770, and came to this country when he was thirteen years of age. He united with the First Baptist church in Wilmington, Del., but afterwards he removed to Philadelphia, and joined the First church in that city. He was ordained in 1808, and the next year he and others formed the Third Baptist church of Philadelphia, of which he became the pastor. The new community prospered greatly under his earnest and godly ministrations, and became a strong body. In 1823 he went to Baltimore, and after some other changes of residence and scenes of labor he died at Wilmington, March 7, 1845, in his seventy-fifth year, in the full enjoyment of a blessed hope through the blood of the Lamb.

Peddie Institute.—Eaton's school at Hopewell was not forgotten when Brown University flourished and academies grew in other States. In 1848 the subject of academic education was agitated in New Jersey, and schools were begun at Salem and Plainfield.

"In 1863 the following decisive action was taken" by the Baptist State Convention held at Bordentown:

"*Resolved*, That a committee be appointed to take into consideration the desirableness and propriety of making arrangements immediately for establishing a *Literary Institution* under the patronage of our denomination in New Jersey."

The next year, 1864, the following was adopted:

"*Resolved*, That the efforts of brethren to establish a first-class school at Hightstown, to be under the control of the Baptists, meet the hearty approval of this body, and that we pledge to it our cordial support."

In the month of March, 1866, a charter was first obtained. In 1867 the subject of a new building began to be earnestly considered, and (two years after) on Oct. 26, 1869, it was formally opened as "The New Jersey Classical and Scientific Institute."

In 1872 the charter was so altered as to change the name to that of Peddie Institute, in honor of its munificent donor, Hon. T. B. Peddie, of Newark. Mr. Peddie's gifts and subscription to this institute now amount to more than $50,000. And besides him the names of such men as Colgate, Trevor, Wyckoff, Van Wickle, Judges Runyon and Cook, Hon. D. M. Wilson, Rev. W. V. Wilson, and many others good and true, are to be remembered for their large donations, as well as the masses of Baptists who gave liberally to secure the valuable property at Hightstown. During its brief existence it has furnished many students who in the professions and in mercantile life have been a credit to the school and the denomination. Under

PEDDIE INSTITUTE, HIGHTSTOWN, N. J.

Prof. E. J. Avery and his corps of teachers it is steadily progressing.

The building consists of a centre and wings in line. It is 255 feet in length, five stories high, including basement and attic. The three middle stories of the wings contain eighty-four rooms for students and teachers, each room designed to accommodate two occupants. In the attics are the rooms for the literary societies, and in the ladies' building, the music-rooms; the rest is occupied for dormitories. The basement in the north wing contains the school-room for the primary department, artists' rooms, suite of rooms for teachers, and four rooms for students.

The kitchen, laundry, steward's private rooms, servants' sleeping-rooms, and steward's office are situated in the basement of the south wing. The basement of the centre contains the dining-room; the first story, the small chapel in the rear, and the parlors in front; the second story, two school-rooms in front, and three recitation-rooms in the rear; the third story, the laboratory and lecture-room in the rear, and three rooms for library cabinets in the front. The attic is designed for a large chapel or temporary gymnasium. Water-tanks are situated at the extreme ends of each wing, under the roof, supplying water to each story, by means of pipes, furnished with faucets, passing down through the end rooms in front. These are also designed for bath-rooms. The whole building is heated by apparatus in the cellar.

Peddie, John, D.D., was born of Scotch parents, in Ancaster, Ontario, May 24, 1838; was converted when seventeen years of age, and pursued a full course of study at Madison University and Hamilton Theological Seminary, graduating from the latter institution in 1865. Settled at Watertown, N. Y., in 1865, and remained nearly three years. Became pastor of the Calvary church, Albany, N. Y., in May, 1868, and remained until March, 1871, when he entered upon the pastorate of the Fourth church, Philadelphia. Here he remained for seven years and a half, when he received and accepted a pressing call to the Second church of Chicago, Ill. In the spring of 1880 he became pastor of the First church of New York City. Received the degree of D.D. from Madison University.

Dr. Peddie possesses remarkable pulpit power. His originality of thought, his clear and manly utterances, and his strong sympathetic nature enable him to present the "glad tidings" with an almost irresistible magnetism. He has already baptized nearly 1000 converts, and has cheered and strengthened the faltering faith of many of God's children. The weak and the unfortunate always find in him a true friend, and few men have so largely won the love and regard of others. His services have been in frequent demand on special occasions, and by his sermons and lectures he has been a generous helper to many enterprises beyond the boundaries of his immediate church work. The close of his pastorate in Philadelphia was made the

JOHN PEDDIE, D.D.

occasion for a special meeting of the Philadelphia Baptist Social Union, at which the farewell greetings were mingled with many tender and eloquent testimonies to the value of his ministry and friendship.

Peddie, Hon. Thomas B., is a native of Edinburgh, Scotland. He received a good education, and in his youth was a great reader. He came to this country in 1833, and settled in Newark, N. J. By strict habits of industry and by remarkable ability his manufacturing establishment is now among the largest of the kind in the country. He has been twice mayor of Newark, the largest city in the State, twice in the State Legislature, and he served in the United States Congress of 1876–78, in which he was placed upon important committees. He has also been president of the board of trade, and in foreign travel has ably represented business interests. When a young man Mr. Peddie made a profession of religion, and was baptized by Rev. Mr. Brown. He united with the First Baptist church in Newark, and as a trustee was particularly active in the building of their fine commodious meeting-house. He takes a deep interest in all the affairs of the church.

When the academy at Hightstown was in great straits Mr. Peddie's sympathies were enlisted, and he gave it at one time a donation of $25,000. His benefactions since have increased this sum to more than $50,000. Mr. Peddie is a generous benefactor

HON. THOMAS B. PEDDIE.

of the Baptist denomination, whose record is an honor to us.

Peirce Academy, Middleborough, Plymouth Co., Mass., was founded by deacon Levi Peirce, of Middleborough. Two purposes were kept in mind in the erection of the academy building in 1808,—one was to furnish a hall suitable to hold public worship in, and the other to secure rooms for the use of the teachers who might have charge of the academy. Like so many institutions of a similar character, the first few years of its existence were years of struggle and varied fortunes. Its history furnishes another illustration of the saying, that "it is hard to get up a Baptist institution, and harder yet to kill it." In 1828, a place for public worship having been built by Deacon Peirce on the lot adjoining the academy, the meeting-house and the academy, with the lots on which they stood, were deeded to the Central Baptist Society; and subsequently the academy passed into the hands of trustees, an act of incorporation having been obtained from the Legislature of Massachusetts for this purpose in 1835. In 1842 it came under the control of Prof. J. W. P. Jenks, and it is due to his energetic efforts and most persistent labors that the institution rose to the high rank which it attained among the academies of New England. A new school building was erected, valuable apparatus and cabinets were secured, and the institution in all its departments was pervaded with new life. Hundreds of young men and young ladies have been educated within the walls of the academy, and to the entire section of country in which it is located it has proved to be the source of untold good. Too much praise cannot be awarded to Prof. Jenks for the efforts he has put forth and the personal sacrifices he has made in behalf of the institution, to which he has given twenty-nine of the best years of his life. He closed his connection with it in 1871. Its present principal is Mr. George H. Coffin.

Pella, Iowa,—" The City of Refuge,"—was settled by Hollanders. A Baptist church was early organized in it, which has grown in usefulness and numbers. It has a good edifice, recently erected, and its prospects are very encouraging.

The Iowa Central University, one of the educational institutions of the Iowa Baptists, has been located at Pella, and for years has been successfully prosecuting its work.

Pelot, Rev. Francis, a native of Switzerland, was born March 11, 1720. His parents were Presbyterians, and gave their son a fine education. He came to South Carolina in 1734, and joined the Baptists about 1744. He was probably the first pastor of the Euham church, and he continued in the office until his death, in 1774. He held a very high place in the denomination, as was to be expected because of his talents, piety, and wealth. Mr. Edwards once said of him, "He possesses three islands and about 3785 acres on the continent, with slaves and stock in abundance. This (said he) I mention, not to flatter my friend Pelot, but in hope that his conduct may influence other wealthy planters to preach the gospel among the poor Baptists when God inclines their hearts to it." He was very useful in spreading the gospel in South Carolina.

Peltz, George Alexander, D.D., was born in Philadelphia, Pa., May 2, 1833. His ancestry was German on his father's side, and Scotch on his mother's. His father, Alexander M. Peltz, died at an early age, but he had become prominent as a State politician, and especially as an acceptable political speaker. Under the care of a pious mother the subject of this sketch became an attendant at the Spruce Street Baptist church and Sunday-school. This was under the pastorates of the Rev. Dr. Rufus Babcock and the Rev. Thomas O. Lincoln. He subsequently attended the Second Baptist church of Southwark, Philadelphia, afterwards known as the Calvary Baptist church. Here he found the Lord, and was baptized by the Rev. John A. McKean, Jan. 5, 1851. One year later he began preparation for college, and entered the Freshman class at Lewisburg, Pa., in the fall of 1853.

During his college course he labored quite extensively among the churches of the vicinity, especially at Sunbury, Northumberland, Muncy, and Hughesburg. He also took the lectures and other studies of the theological department begun at Lewisburg in 1855. He graduated as valedictorian of his class in 1857, and at once proceeded to New York City, where, on August 1, he took charge of a mission interest founded by two generous Baptists, and located in Continental Hall, corner of Eighth Avenue and Thirty-fourth Street. From this mission the Pilgrim Baptist church was organized, Oct. 7, 1857. Mr. Peltz remained here as pastor for eight years, leaving a united church of 402 members, with a good house of worship and a hopeful outlook.

In October, 1865, he became pastor of the Tabernacle Baptist church of Philadelphia, remaining there until March 31, 1871. During his pastorate the church cleared off its entire indebtedness, thoroughly revised its roll, and was largely increased in membership. Mr. Peltz then devoted himself entirely to Sunday-school work until the end of 1872. In Convention and Institute efforts he traveled over nearly all the States east of the Mississippi. In January, 1873, he settled with the South Baptist church of Newark, N. J. In January, 1876, he returned to Philadelphia to assume the associate editorship of the *The Sunday-School Times*. In November, 1877, he removed into the Chautauqua region, so famous in Sunday-school work, and became pastor of the First Baptist church of Jamestown, N. Y.

In 1869, Mr. Peltz edited the first series of lessons issued by the American Baptist Publication Society. He was the first editor of *The Baptist Teacher*, and held that post for three years. He previously edited a Sunday-school department in *The National Baptist*, and subsequently a similar department in *The Independent*. He contributed largely to the leading Sunday-school papers and lesser publications of the land. He was a member of the Executive Committee of the International Sunday-School Convention for ten years. He presided over this body at its session in Baltimore, in April, 1875. He was chairman of the Baptist National Sunday-School Convention at St. Louis in 1869. For three years he was president of the Pennsylvania State Sunday-School Convention, and for two years its corresponding secretary. He was for nearly two years associate editor of *The Sunday-School Times*. At present he resides in Philadelphia.

Pemberton Baptist Church, at Pemberton (formerly New Mills), a pleasant village in Burlington Co., N. J., surrounded by a rich and beautiful farming country. Its real founder was Francis Briggs, probably a member of the Cohansey church, who settled at New Mills in 1750; invited Baptist ministers to preach at his house; seven were converted and baptized, and a small meeting-house erected in 1752. A noble example of fidelity and activity worthy of imitation by every isolated Baptist! He died in 1763. In 1764 the church was constituted with nine members, Rev. Peter P. Van Horn pastor. It is counted as the eleventh, as to date of constitution, among existing regular Baptist churches in the State. It immediately united with the Philadelphia Association; in 1812 transferred its membership to the New Jersey Association (now West New Jersey), formed in 1811. Prior to 1816 the following were pastors: Revs. Peter P. Van Horn, David Branson, David Loughborough, Alexander Magowan, Isaac Carlile, Isaiah Stratton. At that date the membership was 164. Rev. John Rogers, who was successful in doctrinating and building up the church, was pastor from 1816 to 1828. A second and larger house of worship was erected in 1823. Then the following pastors: Revs. C. W. Mulford, 1830–35, a time of ingathering; Timothy Jackson, two years; J. G. Collom, seven years, chapel erected in a more central location, for evening meetings and Sunday-school; D. S. Parmalee, about five years; L. C. Stevens, very brief pastorate; S. M. Shute, three years, during which the present parsonage was bought; Thomas Goodwin, three years. Rev. Levi G. Beck's pastorate (1859–64) was signalized by the erection, in 1861, of the present pleasant and commodious house of worship, centrally and conveniently located. Rev. J. H. Parks was pastor from 1864 to 1869; Rev. James W. Willmarth from 1869 to 1878. Various improvements made. Present pastor, Rev. J. C. Buchanan.

From the constitution of the church until now (May, 1880) 911 have been baptized. Present number, 184.

This ancient church is the mother of several churches in the vicinity, has always been self-supporting, has had no debts or mortgages on its property, and has been favored repeatedly with precious revivals. Its membership has been loyal to Baptist principles, kind to pastors, and interested in the general work of the denomination. The field does not, perhaps, give promise of specially rapid growth, but the church is firmly established, has had much faithful instruction, and will doubtless live and prosper. It has sent out several able ministers, has had among its lay members men of steadfast piety and of influence and usefulness, and is dear to all who have been connected with it or have labored with it in the ministry.

Pendleton, James Madison, D.D., was born Nov. 20, 1811, in Spottsylvania Co., Va. His parents, John and Frances J. Pendleton, removed to Christian Co., Ky., when he was one year old, and settled upon a farm near the present village of Pembroke. Upon this farm he lived until he was twenty years old. During the winter seasons he attended the best schools the community afforded, and with the judicious training of his excellent parents he was better educated than the average farmer boy.

At fifteen he became interested in the subject of religion, but his convictions did not result in conversion until he was seventeen, when he united with the Bethel church, near Pembroke. He was baptized by Rev. John S. Wilson, April 14, 1829.

In February, 1831, he was licensed to preach, and began the work of the ministry before he was twenty years of age.

He is the only licentiate ever sent forth by the Bethel church to this date (1878). *Unum sed Leonem.* In 1833 he entered the Christian County Seminary at Hopkinsville, and took a three years' course of instruction in the Latin and Greek classics, meantime preaching for the Hopkinsville and Bethel churches alternate Sundays. At the former church he was ordained Nov. 1, 1833. In 1837 he accepted the call of the church in Bowling Green, Ky., and entered upon a pastorate of twenty years. Soon after this settlement he formed the acquaintance of Miss Catharine Stockton Garnett, of Glasgow, Ky., who became his wife in 1838. By her piety and abounding good works she has proved herself to be a model pastor's wife. They have four children living, three of whom are wives of professional gentlemen, and the other, a son, is a lawyer in the city of Philadelphia.

During his twenty years' pastorate at Bowling Green, in 1849, Dr. Pendleton cordially espoused Henry Clay's gradual emancipation measures, and supported them by many newspaper publications. The vote of the State, however, was largely against those measures, and slavery remained unchanged till the "civil war" wrought its overthrow.

In 1857, Dr. Pendleton was elected Professor of Theology in Union University, Murfreesborough, Tenn. He had ever esteemed the pastorate his office and preaching his function in life, and would accept the professorship only with the proviso that he should have a pastorate also. Arrangements were made at once that he should become pastor of the Baptist church in Murfreesborough, and he removed to his new field, where he remained until the civil war laid its paralyzing hand upon church and college. The unquenchable loyalty of the man made it necessary for him to remove to the Northern States. After a short settlement of three years, from 1862 to 1865, at Hamilton, O., he removed, in November, 1865, to Upland, Pa., where he has ever since been the highly esteemed and faithful pastor.

At an early day, Dr. Pendleton became an almost constant writer for the denominational press and for the local papers of his community. Of this kind of literature few men except editors are so prolific. Besides, he has published many books, pamphlets, tracts, and sermons, such as "Three Reasons why I am a Baptist," "Church Manual," "Treatise on the Atonement," "Sermons on Important Subjects," "Christian Doctrines, a Compendium of Theology," the last of which is generally conceded to be a masterly production, concise, logical, orthodox, and comprehensive, and supplying a long felt want in the curriculum of theological education and in the libraries of Christian households.

Dr. Pendleton is a hard student, devoting his morning hours to his study, which he keeps well stocked with only the best and most approved evangelical literature, and history, biography, and philosophy. His impatience with irreverence and looseness guards his library from the intrusion of liberalism and trash.

He preaches as he writes, after a well-defined model or plan, from which he seldom swerves even in the most impassioned efforts. He is methodical in his work, and resolutely follows his prearranged plans, alternating study with pastoral visitation with a regularity few men can maintain. He is devout, serious, conscientious, and yet highly appreciates good wit and humor, and is ready and judicious in the use of them. He is of medium height, well proportioned, firm of step as of convictions, a sincere friend, generous to every good cause according to his ability, unostentatious and affable with his friends, reserved among strangers, and cautious of his associations. His integrity of character and honesty of conviction are absolutely above suspicion, and are due to his abiding, unshaken trust in God.

Pengilly, Rev. Richard, author of the "Scriptural Guide to Baptism," was a native of Penzance, Cornwall, England, where he was born Sept. 14, 1782. In early life he was a member of the Wesleyan Methodist body. Like Samuel, he was devoted to God in his childhood. A baptismal service and a sermon by the Rev. Isaiah Birt attracted his attention to the principles of the Baptists, and in 1802 he was baptized, and became one of the constituent members of the newly-formed Baptist church at Penzance. He had been licensed as a local preacher among the Methodists, and his Baptist brethren encouraging him to exercise his gifts, he was received as a student at Bristol College, and pursued the usual course of study until 1807, when he was sent to Newcastle-on-Tyne as a probationer. Having received a call to the pastorate there, he was ordained Aug. 12, 1807, and continued to minister to the same church until 1845, when he retired from all pastoral work. Although he never accepted another charge, he occupied himself with various evangelical and benevolent engagements which his strength permitted until his death, March 22, 1865, in his eighty-third year. During his long pastorate at Newcastle he did good service. He established the first Sunday-school in the town among the evangelical Non-Conformists, and promoted the formation of the local Bible and tract societies. His denominational work was of great value in the district. He published "Seven Letters to the Society of Friends on the Nature and Perpetuity of Baptism" and several tracts, some of which had a wide circulation. His "Scripture Guide to Baptism" has passed through many editions, and has been translated into the German and other European tongues. Probably no other book on the subject has had such a wide diffusion, or been more generally useful.

Penick, Rev. Wm. Sydnor, was born in Halifax Co., Va., May 12, 1836. His father, William Penick, being a planter in easy circumstances, his early educational advantages were the best that could be secured. After prosecuting his studies for four years under a tutor employed in the family, he entered a school under the care of the Rev. A. M. Poindexter, D.D. At the age of fourteen, his father designing him for mercantile life, he was placed in a store, where he remained for three years. About this time he was converted, and was baptized by the Rev. James Longanacre. At the close of his three years' service in business he resolved to pursue his studies, and entered an academy in his native county. Afterwards, in 1855, he became a student in Richmond College, where he graduated in 1858, with the degree of A.B. In the fall of 1858 he was ordained to the work of the gospel ministry, and early in 1859 took charge of the Baptist church in Chatham, the county-seat of Pittsylvania, Va. In the summer of 1861 he entered the army of the Southern Confederacy as captain of a company. In 1868 he resigned the care of the church in Chatham, and, having removed to the Shenandoah Valley, became pastor of several churches in Jefferson and Berkeley Counties, W. Va. In 1870 he settled in Martinsburg, taking exclusive charge of a church which he had organized there, and directing the building of a handsome house of worship. While a resident of this place he was elected superintendent of the public schools in Martinsburg and Berkeley Counties, and served for two years with great efficiency. About this time Richmond College conferred on him the honorary degree of A.M. In 1874 he entered upon his present field of labor as pastor of the First Baptist church in Alexandria, Va., where his labors have been greatly blessed in enlarging the membership and increasing its influence for good. Mr. Penick is honored for his worth and labors not only by his own congregation but by all who know him.

Penn, Admiral Sir William, was born in England in 1621. His father, the captain of a merchant vessel, taught him his own profession so thoroughly that early in life he was one of the ablest mariners in the British islands. The Mediterranean at that period was full of pirates, whose vessels were the swiftest that plowed its waters; the crews of these ships were skillful and reckless men, who shed blood without pity, and enslaved freemen without remorse. The son of Captain Giles Penn learned his calling in the ocean specially scourged by the pirates, and as a matter of necessity he was a fighting mariner. At the age of twenty-three William was appointed a captain in the Royal navy, and was ordered to take charge of the "Fellowship," of twenty-eight guns. He rose rapidly to the highest commands in the navy; before he was thirty years of age he was vice-admiral of the Irish seas; and, though he died when he was only forty-nine years of age, he was an admiral and general of the British fleet, and had rendered brilliant services to his country.

Some Baptists for years have been under the impression that Penn held their faith. David Benedict and Curtis make this statement; and many others in comparatively recent times. Crosby and Ivimey do not. Neither does a single writer competent to bear testimony on such a question. Southey says that "Sir John Lawson was a rigid Anabaptist," others of an earlier day assert the same thing. But while the religion of the one distinguished admiral is frequently stated, the denomination of the other during the doubtful period of his life is not named. Granville Penn, the great-grandson of Sir William, says, "His church was the Church of England, by whose services he was baptized and buried, and to which he adhered when *it could be found.*" He, no doubt, was baptized in the Episcopal Church, but so were many thousands of Baptists in his day. And his being buried with the Episcopal service affords no evidence that he was an Episcopalian. He died in 1670, under the restored Stuarts, when nothing but the Episcopal service would be tolerated in the parish church of Redclyffe, Bristol, where he was interred. Moreover, a man of Sir William's character under the Stuarts was certain to be a member of the church patronized by the powerful. Granville Penn states that Sir William adhered to the Church of England (Episcopalianism) "when it could be found." Daniel Neal says that in 1641 "the old English hierarchy was suspended, and lay prostrate for about eighteen years." Macaulay says, "The Puritans interdicted (in England), under heavy penalties, the use of the Book of Common Prayer, not only in churches, but even in private houses. It was a crime in a child to read, by the bedside of a sick parent, one of those beautiful collects which had soothed the griefs of forty generations of Christians." Episcopalianism was outlawed in England for years. During this period Sir William Penn never hinted that his preferences were for the Episcopal Church. He would have been, during a large part of the interregnum, instantly removed from his command if he had. It is extremely probable that the politic admiral, especially just before the Protectorate, was a friend of the Baptists. His interests required him to be a Congregationalist or a Baptist, and these were of supreme moment with Sir William Penn. Baptist principles were extensively held in the navy, and they were entertained by his chief friends. So that it is not unlikely that he pretended to favor Baptist doctrines. But we know of no *authority* for the common tradition that Penn was a member of any Baptist church or congregation.

Sir William Penn owed his entire position in the navy to the enemies of the Stuarts. The Parliament first, and Cromwell afterwards, gave him promotion and wealth. When he was about to leave for the West Indies in charge of a fleet of thirty-eight vessels of war, according to Granville Penn, at his own request, he received from Cromwell lands in Ireland worth £300 per annum, "as they were let in 1640," to make up for his losses. On the 4th of December, 1654, the Protector himself wrote to the Lord-deputy and Council in Ireland ordering the speedy selection of the lands given to Penn, and Cromwell directs that they should be chosen "where there is a castle, or convenient house of habitation upon them, and near to some garrison for security." Cromwell gives as a reason for the special interest which he showed in Penn's lands, that the admiral "is now engaged in further service for the Commonwealth in the present expedition by sea, and cannot himself look after the settling of the said estate." The expedition was the disastrous West Indian undertaking led by Penn and Venables.

After all the favors which the Parliament and Cromwell could grant Penn, on the 25th of December, a few days after he left Spithead, he sent word to Prince, subsequently Charles II., that he was ready to place the whole fleet at his disposal, and run it into any port he might designate. Granville Penn admits this, and accounts for it by the desire of his ancestor to see the king supplant Cromwell "as the only means of restoring health and soundness to his disordered country." Clarendon records Penn's treacherous act. Penn's acceptance of the command of the expedition, and his seeking and obtaining a very valuable grant from Cromwell, make the proposed surrender of his fleet to Charles II. an infamous offer. It was the deliberate and wicked expression of a deceitful and selfish heart.

Penn was thrown into prison after his return from the West Indies, and, according to Dixon, he sent a humble petition to the Council, in which he confessed his faults and threw himself upon the mercy of Cromwell, who generously restored him to freedom. After this, pretending to give up politics, he retired to Ireland, and upon the very estate given him by the Protector "he used his whole influence to prepare in secret a way for the return of the exiled princes." And on the deposition of Richard Cromwell, even Monk was not a more unblushing betrayer of the liberties of his country than Admiral Penn. Charles II. knighted him in Holland for his treason to the people of England. Dixon, in his "Historical Biography of William Penn," says of the admiral, "The cavalier who stood by his prince through all the changes of fortune may be admired, even by a Republican; but for the man who seeks a trust merely to betray it, who uses the sword to strike the hand he voluntarily swears to defend, no term of reprehension is too strong. Admiral Penn's case was one of peculiar baseness, for he added ingratitude to treason." The American army, in the Revolution, had one notorious general who tried to serve the king of England in the spirit which governed Admiral Penn.

William Penn, the founder of this State, learned his ideas of liberty from Algernon Sidney, and not from his father, who never was a Baptist. His views of freedom were broad and generous for that day. But the Baptists before and during his time were far in advance of Penn or his teachers in their knowledge and application of religious liberty. Hepworth Dixon says that at Chester, in 1682, Penn's first legislative assembly met in the Friends' meeting-house with the great Quaker, and they passed laws in conformity with Penn's "Frame of Government," issued by him in London some time before. One of these gave liberty to the people to believe "any doctrines not destructive to the peace and honor of civil society," and another declared "that *every Christian man* of twenty-one years of age, unstained by crime, *should be eligible to elect* or *be elected* a member of the Colonial Parliament." According to this law, no Israelite or unbeliever in Christ could vote in Penn's territories. This was William Penn's own doctrine. In Rhode Island, in 1647, under the guidance of Roger Williams, laws were made giving equal liberty to men of all creeds and of none. And this was the doctrine of Baptists for ages before that time.

See Southey's "Lives of the British Admirals," v. 240. London, 1837. "Memorials of Sir William Penn," by Granville Penn, i. 94; ii. 17, 20; ii. 15, 141. London, 1833. Neal's "History of the Puritans," ii. 466. Dublin, 1755. Macaulay's

"History of England," i. 125. Boston, 1854. Clarendon's "History of the Rebellion," iii. 576. Oxford, 1706. William Hepworth Dixon's "Historical Biography of William Penn," 23, 25, 27, 201, 202.

Pennepek, or Lower Dublin Church.—This is the oldest Baptist church in Pennsylvania. The Cold Spring church existed before it, but dissolved in a few years. Its edifice is in the twenty-third ward of Philadelphia, in a beautiful rural region, a few rods from the Pennepek Creek, where candidates have been immersed from the organization of the church. This church is the *seat* (cathedra) from which the influences and the men went forth who organized the earliest churches in Pennsylvania and in New Jersey.

It was founded by Elias Keach, whose father was a distinguished Baptist minister and author in London, in the month of January, 1688. Its constituent members were Elias Keach, John Eaton, George Eaton and Jane, his wife, Sarah Eaton, Samuel Jones, John Baker, Samuel Vaus, Joseph Ashton and Jane, his wife, William Fisher, and John Watts. Mr. Keach was elected pastor, and Samuel Vaus was chosen and ordained a deacon. Mr. Keach was an apostle in zeal and labors to win souls to Jesus. He preached in Philadelphia, Chester, Salem, Middletown, Cohansey, Burlington, Trenton, and elsewhere. The Lord greatly blessed these missionary efforts, and a branch of the Pennepek church was formed in each preaching station. Morgan Edwards says of these branches, "They were all one church, and Pennepek the centre of union, where as many as could met to celebrate the death of Christ; and for the sake of distant members they administered the ordinance quarterly at Burlington, Cohansey, Salem, and Philadelphia." In about three years Middletown, Piscataqua, and Cohansey became churches. Mr. Keach returned to England in 1692. John Watts, a member of the church, succeeded Mr. Keach as pastor. In 1700, Mr. Watts, at the request of the church, prepared a catechism, which was also intended for a confession of faith, and the work was published that year. In 1707 a house of worship was erected near the site of the present church; the building was 25 feet square. In 1770 a new house was built, 33 by 30. The third church edifice was reared in 1805, and it stands to-day a substantial and capacious structure, around which hallowed memories cluster. Many other churches, including the First Baptist church of Philadelphia, owe their origin to the Pennepek community.

During a period of six years there were no baptisms in the Pennepek church, though it was favored by the pastoral labors of Dr. Samuel Jones, one of the most talented and godly men that preached the gospel in the United States. At the close of this time of barrenness a revival commenced in 1804, which lasted for about six years.

The Pennepek church is a member of the Philadelphia Association at this day, which came into existence under her auspices. The church has had twenty pastors, and has sent forth twenty-two persons to preach the gospel.

Pennsylvania Baptists.—Thomas Dungan, an old minister, came from Rhode Island to the colony of Penn in 1684. He gathered a church at Cold Spring, near Bristol, Bucks County, "of which," says Morgan Edwards in 1770, "nothing remains but a grave-yard and the names of the families that belonged to it,—the Dungans, Gardners, Woods, Doyles, etc." He died in 1688, and was buried at Cold Spring. Even the grave-yard has disappeared now, and only the foundations of a wall can be traced, which formed a part of the church or a portion of the cemetery wall. The church itself disbanded after a brief but useful existence.

The second church founded in Pennsylvania was the Lower Dublin, or Pennepek. In the year 1686, Elias Keach, of London, a wild young man, arrived in Philadelphia. He dressed in black and wore bands to pass for a minister. He obtained an opportunity to preach in the house of a Baptist in Lower Dublin, and when he had spoken for some time he "stopped short, looked like a man astonished, and the audience concluded that he had been seized with some sudden disorder." But they speedily learned that he was deeply convicted of sin. He went to Father Dungan, of Cold Spring, who pointed him to Jesus; he soon had peace in believing, and he was baptized and ordained by Mr. Dungan. He formed a church of twelve persons at Pennepek in January, 1688, and became their pastor. He labored with burning zeal, and, considering the difficulties, with astonishing success, through Pennsylvania and New Jersey, and established missions at "the Falls (Trenton), Burlington, Cohansey, Salem, Pennsneck, Chester, and Philadelphia," and he maintained preaching at Cold Spring and Middletown. He had the zeal of an enthusiast, and "he was considered the chief apostle of the Baptists in these parts of America." He returned to his birthplace in 1692, but the missions in several cases became churches, and the spirit he planted in these communities created the Philadelphia Association a few years after he left the colony.

The Great Valley church was constituted in 1711. The Brandywine church was formed in 1715. The Montgomery church was organized in 1719. The Tulpehocken church was founded in 1738, and the Southampton in 1746. The Philadelphia church had an existence either as a branch of Lower Dublin or as an independent community from 1698, the former is the more probable. But in 1746, to settle doubts on this question and to protect legacies, the church was formally incorporated. The New Britain church was organized in 1754, and the Vincent in 1770.

Since our national independence was secured, about 200 churches have arisen in the counties east of the Susquehanna River and its North Branch. Some of these became extinct, or changed names and locations, so that a clear and complete sketch of them all, however interesting, would be entirely impracticable in this work.

The first known English Baptist preacher on the Susquehanna was the first person named as slain in the first Wyoming massacre, in 1763. He was William Marsh, a New England Separatist, but came from Wantage, N. J., into Pennsylvania. The first church was formed in Pittston, in December, 1776. The first Baptists in Northern Pennsylvania were from Connecticut, Rhode Island, Massachusetts, Virginia, New York, and New Jersey. They were Revolutionary soldiers and pioneers of the settlements, both ministers and private members.

A portion of Southwestern Pennsylvania was taken up by Virginians. There were Baptists among them, and a church was founded at Aughwick, Huntingdon Co., in 1776; at Konoloway, Bedford, in 1764; at Sideling Hill, Fulton, in 1790; at Turkeyfoot, Somerset, in 1775; at Great Bethel (Uniontown), Fayette, in 1770; at Goshen, Greene, in 1773; at Peter's Creek, Washington, in 1773; at Pigeon Creek, in 1775; Loyalhanna, in 1775; Forks of Yough, in 1777. Enon church arose in 1791; Beulah, Cambria Co., in 1797; Pittsburgh in 1812. These facts show the progress of settlements, without attempting details of the scores of churches which have arisen on and west of the Susquehanna.

ASSOCIATIONS

are yearly meetings of messengers of churches combining for spiritual improvement, to ascertain changes, and to confer as to measures for promoting their sentiments. Their powers are advisory. The following are the regular Baptist Associations in Pennsylvania:

1707.—Philadelphia, the first Association in America, now 174 years old.

1776.—Redstone, in Southwestern Pennsylvania, finally absorbed by others about 1841.

1807.—Abington, in Lackawanna County, and west and north of it.

1809.—Beaver, on west central border of the State.

1821.—Northumberland, in the east-central (Lewisburg) region.

1823.—French Creek, in the northwest corner of the State.

1826.—Bridgewater, out of old Susquehanna, in Susquehanna County and eastern Bradford.

1830.—Centre, a missionary body in the Juniata River region.

1831.—Central Union, in and west of Philadelphia.

1832.—Monongahela, a missionary body, southward of Pittsburgh.

1835.—Bradford, North, mostly from Old-School Chemung.

1837.—Clarion, north-central, west of the Alleghany Mountains.

1839.—Pittsburgh, in and around that city.

1843.—Wyoming, from Bridgewater, in Wyoming and Luzerne Counties.

1843.—Tioga, from Bradford, mostly in Tioga County, northern tier.

1847.—Clearfield, central, both sides of the Alleghanies.

1848.—North Philadelphia, from Philadelphia and Central Union.

1859.—Ten-Mile, southwest corner of the State.

1865.—Oil Creek Association was formed.

1870.—Wayne, from Abington, northeast corner of the State.

1875.—Reading, in east-central, or Schuylkill coal region.

1876.—Indiana, south of Clarion, west of the Alleghanies.

1878.—Wheeling, in Western Pennsylvania and West Virginia.

East Pennsylvania Welsh Association is more than twenty years old.

There are about forty Welsh churches, and half a dozen German, of the regular Baptist faith not connected with English Associations

All our churches in Potter and McKean Counties, and a number of the others on the northern tier, associate with bodies in New York State.

There are 23 Associations in this State, 568 churches, and 64,572 members. There are 503 Sunday-schools reported, with 6120 officers and teachers, and 50,860 scholars. Six Associations make no report of Sunday-schools, when most probably every church has one.

When it is remembered that Pennsylvania was chiefly settled by Scotch-Irish and Germans, that is, by people intensely Presbyterian or tenaciously Lutheran, nearly the most difficult material on earth out of which to make Baptists, and that few members of our denomination, comparatively, came from Europe, the progress of the Baptists is remarkable.

EDUCATION.

Pennsylvanians led in forming the first Baptist academy in this country,—Isaac Eaton's, at Hopewell, N. J., 1756,—and also in establishing their first college,—Brown University, Providence, R. I., in 1766. Dr. Samuel Jones conducted an academy at Lower Dublin from 1766 to 1794. In 1814 an education society for the Middle States was formed in Philadelphia. Its master-spirit, Dr. William Staughton, had for some years taken ministerial students to his home for private instruction, and in 1818 he and Prof. Irah Chase hired rooms for the same object. The institution was removed to Washington City, and in 1821 appeared as Columbian College. The Hamilton (N. Y.) Institution, now called Madison University, received material aid from Pennsylvania. In 1832 the Northumberland Association proposed a Manual Labor Academy, principally to aid ministerial students, but waived it in favor of the proposal of Philadelphia brethren to found an institution at Haddington. And when the Haddington effort failed, the Northumberland friends rallied, and in 1846, Prof. S. W. Taylor opened a high school, which developed into a college, with academic and theological departments, and a female institute, now called the University of Lewisburg. By amicable arrangement, the theological department was, in 1868, transferred to Crozer Theological Seminary, at Upland, Delaware Co.

The academies under the direct control of the Baptists of the State are five in number: the University Academy, at Lewisburg, founded in 1846; the Reid Institute, in Clarion County, established in 1863; Monongahela College Academy, in Greene County, instituted in 1867; Keystone Academy, in Wyoming County, opened in 1868; and Mount Pleasant Institute, in Westmoreland County, founded in 1873. The University Female Institute at Lewisburg is not included in the above list. It is the only ladies' institute within the State, and is connected with the university, thus enjoying peculiar advantages. It embraces a regular college course, and has hitherto been awarded a large share of public patronage.

During the past year the number of instructors attached to these academies was 37, and the number of students 641. At a very low valuation, the amount invested in these schools is $160,000. These institutions are of recent origin, and it is believed that the Baptists of Pennsylvania will soon start new schools in other localities.

LITERATURE.

The first known American work in favor of distinct Baptist principles is attributed to John Watts, of Pennepek, and was printed in the year 1700. It was designed mostly for children and youth. No copy of it is known to the public. Morgan Edwards, of Philadelphia, wrote historical sketches of priceless value of the Baptists in several of the colonies. Doctors S. Jones, Rogers, Staughton, Holcombe, Belcher, Malcom, Curtis, Brantly, Sr., Ira M. Allen, Geo. B. Ide, and J. Newton Brown among the dead, and H. G. Jones, Jr., Anderson, Magoon, Cathcart, Pendleton, Dyer, Spencer, J. Wheaton Smith, Dr. W. W. Keen, Francis Jennings, J. Spencer Kennard, Justin R. Loomis, and others among the living. Robert Lowry's hymns are sung around the world. Any attempt to name the books, or other most worthy products from the pen of our people, might seem invidious, and it is hardly possible to make such a record complete.

The following are names of Baptist periodicals that have been or are still issued in Philadelphia: *Latter-Day Luminary, Christian Index, The World as it is and as it should be, Religious Narrator, Christian Gazette, Baptist Record, Christian Chronicle, National Baptist, Baptist Quarterly,* and several for children and Sunday-schools, with millions of pages of tracts and books from the American Baptist Publication Society.

From 1825 to 1827, at Montrose, Davis Dimock issued the *Baptist Mirror, or Christian Magazine.* In 1827, Eugenio Kincaid, at Milton, published a *Literary and Evangelical Register.* And Pittsburgh has furnished one or more periodicals adapted to the wants of Western Pennsylvania.

BENEVOLENCE.

Early minutes of the Philadelphia Association are very meagre, yet they give proofs of efforts to send the gospel to the destitute at home, to use the press for the common good, and to aid young men in preparing to be able ministers of the New Testament. Before and after the Revolution they sent evangelists into the new fields on the Susquehanna, and at an early day they transmitted money to Hindoostan, and to Burmah soon after missions were opened there.

In 1800 a Philadelphia Domestic Mission Society was formed. In 1810 they reported seven men in their service,—Thomas Smiley, on the West Branch; Thomas G. Jones, in Pennsylvania and Ohio; Henry George, at Owl Creek, in Ohio; William West, near Lake Erie; and Brethren Montague, Bateman, and Cooper on both sides of the Delaware. In 1827 the Philadelphia and other similar local societies began their union as the Baptist Missionary Association of Pennsylvania. At its semi-centennial, in 1877, it reported a total expenditure of $282,189 in its fifty years' work, during which it had aided 233 churches and made 1430 appointments of home missionaries, who had reported about 17,000 baptisms.

The Baptist General Tract Society, formed in Washington City in 1824, came to Philadelphia in 1826, and is now known as the American Baptist Publication Society. It has constantly enlarged its power in the production of wholesome reading, its business department aiding its large outlays in benevolence. It was many years located at 530 Arch Street, but now has spacious and eligible accommodations, as denominational and book headquarters, at 1420 Chestnut Street.

The Pennsylvania Baptist Education Society, founded in 1839, has vigorously prosecuted its aims, with great advantages to the rising ministry, and through them to the church and to the world.

Among the promoters of every good enterprise may generally be found a fair proportion of Pennsylvania Baptists. In the first national foreign mission meeting were Staughton, Rogers, Holcombe, Proudfoot, Randall, White, Peckworth, H. G. Jones, Sr., Hough, and Mathias. The Baptists of Pennsylvania are generous contributors to home and foreign objects.

The university at Lewisburg has extensive and beautiful buildings and a handsome endowment. Crozer Theological Seminary, in its home and in its endowment, is a monument of liberality. The white marble house of the American Baptist Publication Society cost $258,000, is entirely out of debt, and was paid for chiefly by Pennsylvanians. The fifty-six Baptist churches of Philadelphia have a greater number of splendid church edifices than any one of the other denominations in the city, and they are nearly all free from debt.

The Baptists of Pennsylvania are thoroughly united, and they are praying, working, and giving to spread the knowledge of Jesus in a way that inspires the hope that in twenty years, with God's blessing, they will double their numbers.

Pennsylvania Baptist Education Society, The, was organized Sept. 18, 1839, in the First Baptist church in Philadelphia. It has extended aid to about 500 students. It is believed that over 300 ministers thus aided are now in active service in home and foreign fields. The experience of the past forty years fully justifies us in stating that such organizations are of vital necessity. In the workings of this society, each year is strictly probationary, and students failing to meet just expectations are dropped from the list. The society is not in formal connection with any institution of learning, but holds itself at liberty to give aid to students studying outside of Pennsylvania, when adequate reasons for the selection are given. The appropriations given to students are designed to cover the cost of cheap boarding and the expense of tuition. They have varied in different periods from $80 annually to $150. The present maximum grant is $110.

The officers for 1881 are Thomas J. Hoskinson, President; Levi Knowles, Treasurer; Rev. G. M. Spratt, D.D., Corresponding Secretary; Rev. Jacob G. Walker, Recording Secretary. Twenty members constitute the board of managers.

Dr. Spratt has made the society, in his many years of service, the most successful agency for its object in this country. The receipts last year were $12,000, and there were 63 students who received assistance.

Pennsylvania Baptist General Association was founded July 4, 1827, in the Blockley Baptist church, Philadelphia. The organization of the society was perfected in the autumn of the same year. It is purely a State missionary institution. Rev. William E. Ashton was its first president. Hon. James M. Linnard held that office with remarkable usefulness for twenty-seven years. During the first half-century of its existence it has had on an average 29 missionaries a year in its employment, and it issued 1430 commissions. In that period it formed or fostered 233 of the Baptist churches of the State, some of which today are the strongest and most flourishing in Pennsylvania. During the fourteen years' secretaryship of the Rev. L. G. Beck the sum of $172,000 was raised for the Association, and the churches increased from 424 to 553, and the members from 40,000 to 63,500. The Association has accomplished a grand work, and it is, at this time, in a state of efficiency that inspires exalted hopes for coming days.

In 1880 it employed 42 missionaries. Its income was $14,914.43. Rev. R. H. Austin was its president, and Rev. W. H. Conard its corresponding secretary.

Pennsylvania, Western, Classical and Scientific Institute is located at Mount Pleasant, Pa., about forty miles southeast of Pittsburgh, with which it is connected by rail. The academy is at the foot of the mountains, in a rich farming region. Its site affords a commanding view of the town and the surrounding country. Its buildings are spacious, and possess every convenience and comfort.

Mount Pleasant has seven evangelical churches, with a substantial membership in each, and other religious bodies, with regular preaching. No intoxicating liquors, according to law, can be sold in Mount Pleasant, or within two miles of it.

The school was organized under the auspices of the Pittsburgh, Monongahela, and Beaver Baptist Associations. It was opened in 1873, and its growth has been constant until it is now self-sustaining. Both sexes are admitted to its advantages, and they are about equally represented in its classes. It has usually six teachers. It imparts a first-class academical education, and it is now a blessing to the section of the State where its advantages have been so extensively enjoyed.

Pentecost, Rev. Hugh O., son of Hugh L. and Emma (Flower) Pentecost, was born Sept. 30, 1848, at New Harmony, Ind.; educated at Madison University, N. Y., where he took a select course; ordained in 1871, at Rockville Centre, Long Island, and settled as pastor; second settlement was with the Calvary Baptist church in Westerly, R. I., Aug. 4, 1875; third settlement with South Baptist church, Hartford, Conn., May 1, 1878; has recently become pastor in Brooklyn, N. Y.; an able, successful, and devoted minister.

Pepper, Prof. George Dana Boardman, D.D., the youngest son of John and Eunice Hutchinson

PROF. GEORGE DANA BOARDMAN PEPPER, D.D.

Pepper, was born in Ware, Mass., Feb. 5, 1833. His parents were members of a Baptist church in which his father was a deacon, so that from infancy the future professor lived in an atmosphere of Christian influence. Though the subject of positive religious experiences when not more than seven or eight years old, it was not until May 4, 1856, that he publicly professed faith in Christ by baptism, and became a member of the Baptist church in his native town. After a thorough academical preparation for college he entered Amherst, in which he graduated in 1857, ranking third in his class. He entered Newton Theological Seminary after leaving Amherst, and took the full course. After leaving Newton he became pastor of the First Baptist church of Waterville, Me., the seat of Colby University. In 1865 he accepted the chair of Ecclesiastical History in Newton Theological Seminary, which he occupied with so much acceptance and success that he was elected to the professorship of Christian Theology in the newly established school at Upland, Pa., the Crozer Theological Seminary. He spent one year in preparation for the duties of the new position, upon the discharge of which he entered in the autumn of 1868; and he continues in that institution still, giving his able co-operation in moulding the principles and characters of men, not a few of whom have already taken an honored place in the Baptist ministry.

Several of his discussions of denominational and other theological questions have been published in reviews, in pamphlets, and otherwise. For eight years he prepared for the *Baptist Teacher* the expositions of the International Sunday-School Lessons. This effort involved and exhibited great learning, given in wisely simple terms. And it is doubtful if the same work was ever performed as well by another. He is the author of a volume of respectable dimensions on "Outlines of Theology," which he has not given to the public, and which he uses in his class with so much success that his students leave him the equals of the best-trained theological graduates in our country, and the superiors of many of their young brethren. Prof. Pepper is a man of extreme gentleness and modesty, of the highest culture, the deepest piety, and the greatest worth. Mrs. Pepper is well and widely known as a very able and efficient worker in every department of the Master's kingdom, especially in the cause of missions.

Periodicals.—See article on BAPTIST LITERATURE.

Perkins, Rev. Isaac, a native of Georgia, removed to Arkansas about 1830, and gathered the first Baptist church in Southwestern Arkansas. He died in Hempstead County in 1852. He was moderator of Saline Association for about twelve years.

Perren, Rev. Charles, the pastor of the Western Avenue Baptist church, Chicago, was born Oct. 22, 1839. His conversion took place when he was fourteen years of age. Deciding to study for the ministry, he entered the Canadian Literary Institute, at Woodstock, Ontario, where he graduated from the department of Arts, and that of Theology. In 1862 he was ordained at Vienna, Ontario. Subsequently, upon passing the senior examination of the theological seminary at Chicago, he received the degree of B.D. in that institution. His former pastorates have been at Georgetown and St. Catherine's, Ontario. He has held his present one in Chicago some three years, enjoying to an unusual degree the confidence and affection of the people he serves.

Perry, Hon. Eli, was born in Cambridge, Washington Co., N. Y., Dec. 25, 1799, and died May 17, 1881. In early life he was baptized by Dr. Bartholomew Welsh into the fellowship of the Pearl Street church, Albany. He was possessed of a large mind and a generous heart. Christ was everything to him, and to his cause he consecrated his means and his efforts. He was for many years the personal friend of the strong men who gave a high character to the Pearl Street church, in the Baptist denomination, among whom were Judge Ira Harris, Friend Humphrey, and John N. Wilder. Possessing great force of character, uncommon sagacity, and irreproachable integrity, combined with quiet simplicity and humility, he became an eminent citizen whom every one delighted to honor. For seventeen years he was mayor of Albany, a longer period of service in that office than was rendered by any of his predecessors since the incorporation of the city. As a member of the Legislature, and of Congress for two successive terms, he enjoyed the confidence of the bodies in whose deliberations he shared, and of his constituents. For many years he was president of the board of trustees of his loved church, and for some time an honored deacon. For this community he cherished a warm and an abiding affection. He left $16,000 to Emmanuel church and Sunday-school, and to the Albany Baptist Missionary Union and the Rochester Theological Seminary, at his death; and he made provision in his will that at the decease of his widow, after the payment of several legacies of $1000 each to distant relatives, his entire estate, estimated to be worth $400,000, should be divided into five equal parts, and distributed as follows: one-fifth each to Rochester and Hamilton Theological Seminaries, and one-fifth each to the Hudson River Baptist Association North, the American Baptist Missionary Union, and the American Baptist Home Mission Society. In life, Mr. Perry was a generous contributor to all denominational and charitable objects, and he made arrangements that after death his gifts should send forth streams of beneficence for generations. Few men were more loved in life or more lamented after death.

Perry, Prof. Herman, A.M., was born in Wyoming, N. Y., Feb. 12, 1824. Converted and baptized in early youth, and having remarkable natural grace and great persuasive force in addressing religious meetings, he was believed to be destined to the work of preaching. With the approval of the church he studied for the ministry, graduated at Madison University in 1846, received the degree of A.M. from Rochester University in 1850, and commenced to preach; but was compelled by his delicate health to discontinue. He took charge successively of the academies at Richburgh, N. Y., and Allegan, Mich. For the sake of his health he removed to California in 1863, and established at Sacramento "The Young Ladies' Seminary," which took rank among the best educational institutions of the State. He died Jan. 18, 1876, and his death was felt to be a great loss by the Baptists of the Pacific coast, in whose educational and benevolent enterprises he had been a wise counselor and generous supporter.

Perry, Rev. Joseph, was born in Stanhope, N. J., in November, 1806. While yet a young man he was converted, and united with the First Baptist church of Newark, N. J., Rev. D. Dodge, pastor.

Soon after his marriage he removed to Paterson, N. J., and took a most prominent part in the great Washingtonian temperance movement. Here he was licensed to preach by the First Baptist church. Afterwards removing to Washington, D. C., he was ordained as a minister of the gospel.

Accepting an appointment as a home missionary, he went to Fairfax, Va., his circuit extending to Richmond. From this field he removed, and took charge of the Haverstraw, N. Y., Baptist church. From Haverstraw he was called to New Durham, N. J., where he toiled with wonderful courage to redeem the place from the control of rum. After a struggle such as few men have encountered, with his life almost constantly in danger, he overthrew the liquor power, and transformed the village from a state of riotous Sabbath-breaking to a lovely and quiet abode. After building, by strenuous efforts, a beautiful church, he closed a pastorate of six years, and removed to Manahawkin, N. J., and spent two years of hard and successful labor for Christ.

In 1859 he accepted a call to the Mariners' Baptist Bethel, of Philadelphia, where for twenty years he labored unceasingly among the sailors of the merchant service, and among the seamen of the U. S. navy on the receiving-ship at the Philadelphia navy-yard. At this port, through the generosity of Wm. Bucknell, Esq. (still living), John P. Crozer, Capt. John Levy (both deceased), and others, he built a neat church for seamen. At last, after baptizing hundreds of sailors, and many others, he was compelled by failing strength to retire from the active ministry. Recovering his health soon afterwards, he entered with renewed energy upon general and heaven-blessed work for his divine Master.

Two years of happy unflagging toil followed, when a sudden and fatal attack of pneumonia ended his earthly work, and he went to his reward Feb. 14, 1881, closing a life filled with most thrilling incidents and adorned with Christian graces.

Mr. Perry was one of the best men in the Baptist ministry in Pennsylvania.

Perry, Rev. Lewis.—Lewis Perry, a well-known colored Baptist preacher of North Carolina, was born in 1804, and became the body-servant of Dr. Wiley Perry, an eminent physician of Franklin County, about 1820. He became a lover of Jesus at an early age, and during the great revival which visited the village of Lewisburg in 1830, he was eminently useful in instructing and encouraging struggling penitents. He possessed a voice of great pathos and power, which he used with fine effect in singing and prayer, and his preaching, especially when touching on religious experience, was impressive in a high degree.

His education was quite limited. By his own unaided efforts he learned to read and write, and attained a useful knowledge of the simpler rules of arithmetic. He was a close student of the Bible for many years, and few men were better acquainted with the teachings of the New Testament.

This good man had secretly acquired from his master's books, and a close study of his practice, a very respectable knowledge of medicine; and such was the esteem in which he was held by the people, and the confidence of his master in his judgment, that when Dr. Perry had become quite old, he would frequently send Lewis to see his patients, especially when called out at night. Indeed, the old Baptist preacher was familiarly known all over the county as "Doctor Perry"; and so much esteemed was he as a physician and a nurse that a young man of his native county left him a legacy of a thousand dollars for his attention to him during his last illness.

He died at the age of fifty-eight, and the respect in which he was held was manifested by the very large number of persons of all classes who attended his funeral services.

Perry, Rev. Rufus L., was born a slave in Smith Co., Tenn., March 11, 1834. He learned to read and write in early life, which inspired him with an irrepressible abhorrence of slavery, and he ran away to Canada in August, 1852. He went to Windsor, opposite Detroit, and by hard study soon became a schoolmaster among the large body of fugitives who had escaped from slavery.

He was hopefully converted in 1854, prepared for the ministry at Kalamazoo Theological Seminary with the class of 1861, and was ordained as pastor of the Second Baptist church of Ann Arbor, Oct. 9, 1861, by a council, of which Rev. Samuel Cornelius was moderator, and Prof. James R. Boise clerk. He afterwards served as pastor at St. Catharines, Ontario, and Buffalo, N. Y. In 1865 he entered upon a general missionary and educational work among the freedmen, and has, until the present, labored for the education, evangelization, and general elevation of his race, serving as superintendent of schools for freedmen, as editor of the *Sunbeam*, co-ordinate editor of the *American Baptist*, editor of the *People's Journal*, and editor and publisher of the *National Monitor*. He was for ten years corresponding secretary of the consolidated American Baptist Missionary Convention, and he is at present corresponding secretary of the American Educational Association and of the American Baptist Free Mission Society, and editor of the *National Monitor*, of Brooklyn, N. Y.

Perryman, Rev. Elisha, one of the most useful pioneer preachers of the Georgia Baptists, was born in Halifax Co., Va., Feb. 6, 1769, of Welsh ancestors, all of whom, on both sides, as far back as known, were stanch Baptists. His father commanded a company, raised by himself, in the Revolutionary war, and, besides other engagements, was present at the battle of Guilford Court-House. Cornwallis's army, and especially Tarleton's troopers, in their ravages, so completely destroyed his property, when encamped within six miles of his house, that he removed to Georgia with his family, and settled on Big Kiokee Creek, twenty-two miles from Augusta. Here Elisha Perryman, after much mental distress, was gloriously converted in May, 1799. On the third Sabbath in August, 1801, he was baptized by Abraham Marshall, and joined Kiokee church. Gradually the conviction that it was his duty to preach grew upon him. He studied by firelight at night; and he made it a point to accompany Jesse Mercer and Abraham Marshall to their appointments, in order to learn the doctrines of Christianity. He gave himself entirely to the work of an evangelist, confining himself to no one section of the country, but going wherever destitution abounded. In January, 1810, he removed to Warner County, and often would make preaching tours afterwards through Montgomery, Emanuel, Tatnall, and Bullock Counties, and, at other times, would make tours through Richmond, Burke, Jefferson, and Severn Counties. Again, he would sally forth among the northern counties, and even sometimes into South Carolina, traveling up and down the Savannah River. It was thus that the Baptist pioneer preachers of Georgia established their principles in the State.

The Lord blessed him with a strong constitution, and, though he died Dec. 1, 1857, in his eighty-ninth year, he continued to preach with vivacity and vigor to the last, calling upon sinners to flee from the wrath to come.

Persecution of Baptists in America.—John Waller, Lewis Craig, and James Childs, three Baptist ministers, were arrested in Spottsylvania Co., Va., "for preaching the gospel contrary to law," and while in prison they proclaimed the good news to listening throngs through the doors and windows of the jail. In Middlesex and Caroline Counties, Va., many Baptist ministers were imprisoned for preaching; they were subjected to the treatment of common felons, and if possible to worse indignities. William Webber and Joseph Anthony were imprisoned in Chesterfield Co., Va., for telling the story of the Cross. James Ireland suffered imprisonment in Virginia, and illegal and wicked efforts were made to kill him in jail because he was a herald of Calvary. To keep the people from hearing the imprisoned preachers, walls were sometimes built around the jails in which they were confined, and half-drunken outcasts were hired to beat drums to drown their voices. When out of prison in the Old Dominion they were mobbed; while immersing converts men on horseback would ride into the water to create a disturbance. They were often interrupted in their discourses and insulted, but they despised the jail, the lash, and the malicious jeers. When hunted like wild beasts, and denounced as wolves in sheep's clothing, they meekly replied, "That if they were wolves and their persecutors the true sheep, it was unaccountable that they should treat them with such cruelty; that wolves would destroy sheep, but that it was never known till then that sheep would prey upon wolves." (Semple's History of Virginia Baptists, p. 21.)

In New England, outside of Rhode Island, our brethren were frequently arrested for not paying taxes to support the Congregational clergy. Women, too, had their rights recognized, and they were arrested and robbed to support the ministers of their neighbors. The sacred tax-gatherers took from the Baptists "pewter dishes, skillets, kettles, pots and warming-pans, workmen's tools, and spinning-wheels; they drove away geese and swine and cows, and when there was but one it was not spared. A brother recently ordained returned to Sturbridge, Mass., for his family, when he was thrust into prison and kept during the cold winter, till some one paid his fine and secured his release. Mr. D. Fisk was robbed at Sturbridge of five pewter plates and a cow, J. Perry of the baby's cradle and a steer, J. Blunt of andirons, shovel, and tongs, and A. Bloice, H. Fisk, John Streeter, Benjamin Robbins, Phenehas Collier, John Newel, Josiah Perry, Nathaniel Smith, John Corry, and J. Barstow of spinning-wheels, household goods, cows, and of their liberty for a season." (Backus's Church History, ii. 94, 95. Newton.) Sturbridge was but a specimen of what was taking place all over New England, and of the love cherished for our Baptist fathers by men who only differed from them about baptism. Early the persecution of Baptists was commenced in New England; Roger Williams was compelled to fly from Salem to escape illegal violence in 1635; the meeting-house of the First Baptist church of Boston, in 1677, was closed by order of the General Court of Massachusetts, and after a little, when they ventured to use it again, the doors were nailed up and a paper fastened on them, which read, "All persons are to take notice that by order of the court the doors of this house are shut up, and that they are prohibited from holding any meeting therein or to open the doors thereof without license from authority till the General Court take further order, as they will answer the contrary at their peril." (Hildreth's History of the United States, i. 497–499. New York.)

The town of Ashfield, Mass., was settled by Baptists, and when it had a few Congregational families in it they built a church, called a minister, and then laid a tax upon the land to meet the cost of the one and the support of the other. The Baptists refused to pay the church bills of their Puritan neighbors, and immediately the best portion of the cultivated land in the town was seized and sold for trifling sums to pay their iniquitous dues. The house and garden of one man were taken from him, and the young orchards, the meadows, and the cornfields of others. The grave-yard of the Baptists was actually sold to liquidate the debts of a church with which they had nothing to do, and to support a minister with whom they did not intend to worship. These properties were sold in 1770 for £35.10, and they were worth £363.8. The Congregational minister was one of the purchasers. This was but the first payment, and two others were to follow. (Minutes of the Philadelphia Baptist Association for 1770, p. 160.) Such were some of the countless wrongs which our fathers suffered even in this land.

Perseverance, Final.—The Saviour is *the Shepherd* of his believing flock. He says, "The hireling fleeth, because he is a hireling, and careth not for the sheep. I am the good shepherd, and know my sheep, and am known of mine."—John x. 13, 14. Peter, speaking of Jesus, says, "For ye were as sheep going astray; but are now returned unto the Shepherd and Bishop of your souls."—First Epistle ii. 25. Christ will never leave nor forsake his flock. Besides, "He that keepeth Israel shall not slumber nor sleep. The Lord is thy keeper." —Psalm cxxi. 4. Now, as the Saviour is the shepherd of his flock, as he knows every one of them, is always with them, and never slumbers, he can never lose a sheep. David risked his life when a mere stripling in killing a lion and a bear to protect his flock, and is there any likelihood that the omnipotent Master of heaven will be a poorer shepherd than David, and suffer the old lion of the pit to rob his flock?

"His honor is engaged to save
The meanest of his sheep;
All that his heavenly Father gave
His hands securely keep."

Christ never changes. He knows everything in the most hidden recesses of the pit, in the secret parts of Satan's heart, in the lurking-places of earth, and in the concealed quarters of heaven. He has a perfect knowledge of the past and the present; and the entire future lies bare before him. "All things are naked and opened unto the eyes of him with whom we have to do." He is without any motive to change, and change with him is impossible, unless, indeed, some human weakness should overtake the intellect that has planned and executed the creation. He commands Philip to join the eunuch's chariot and preach to him; the evangelist obeys, and soon the traveler believes and is baptized. Now, why does the Spirit begin this work if it is ever to be abandoned? Could it agree with Christ's wisdom and purposes of love to begin a temple of salvation in the soul which Satan was soon to pull down and destroy? He takes the same interest in every believer which he showed in the eunuch; and as he is the Father of lights, without variableness or the shadow of turning, the work of grace will be carried on in every soul till the man reaches the heavenly rest.

The love of Christ is fixed upon each one whom his Spirit calls to repentance. This is the only reason for the regeneration of a single human being. This love was born in Christ in the distant morning of a past eternity; it led to the election of each believer from everlasting, as Paul says, "According as he hath chosen us in him before the foundation of the world, that we should be holy and without blame before him in love."—Eph. i. 4. What Jehovah declared in ancient times about Israel is true of all the spiritual Israel to-day, "Yea, I have loved thee with an everlasting love, therefore with loving-kindness have I drawn thee."—Jer. xxxi. 3. As Paul says, "But God, who is rich in mercy, for his great love wherewith he hath loved us, even when we were dead in sins, hath quickened (made alive) us together with Christ."—Eph. ii. 4, 5. The love that gave Jesus for us is God's, the love that made us alive as believers when we were dead in sins is Christ's, will that love ever give up one soul which it cherished in its everlasting regards? Will the Saviour permit one chosen and eternally loved friend to drop out of his heart into the abyss? Who shall separate us from the love of Christ? Shall tribulation, or distress, or persecution, or famine, or nakedness, or peril, or sword? Nay, in all these things we are more than conquerors through him that loved us. For I am persuaded that neither death, nor life, nor angels, nor principalities, nor powers, nor things present, nor things to come, nor height, nor depth, nor any other *creature* (creation) shall be able to separate us from the love of God, which is in Christ Jesus our Lord. Nothing created can separate the saint from his Saviour's love, nor shall the Uncreated One.

The believer in his second birth *is made a new creature*, he receives a new heart with new tastes, and while his old love of sin, not wholly subdued, may for a time, through the arts of the tempter, lead him from God, yet he cannot remain in sin, he will one day become dissatisfied with its husks, and feel the famishing pangs of spiritual starvation; and he will hunger for the soul-bread, which abounds in the house of his Saviour-Father; and will arise and go to his Father. The carrier-pigeon taken five or six hundred miles from its home and set at liberty, immediately and swiftly returns; and so a soul, born from above, will surely awake to its wants and dangers, and nothing out of heaven can keep it from the throne of grace, and no one in the skies shall cast it out.

God's Word speaks of the eternally enduring life given in conversion. In Rom. viii. 29, 30, we read, "Whom he did foreknow, he also did predestinate to be conformed to the image of his Son, that he might be the first-born among many brethren. Moreover, whom he did predestinate, them he also called: and whom he called, them he also justified: and whom he justified, them he also glorified." According to this inspired statement every soul whom God calls to repentance shall be glorified in heaven. The Saviour generally connects faith in himself with everlasting life: "My sheep hear my voice, and I know them, and they follow me: and I give unto them eternal life; and *they shall never perish*, neither shall any pluck them out of my hand. My Father, who gave them to me, is greater than all; and none is able to pluck them out of my Father's hand."—John x. 27, 28. "None," neither the believer himself, nor any one else, shall tear a redeemed soul from the protecting hand of the great Redeemer's Father.

Several Scriptures are supposed to contradict the passage just quoted, and others of kindred meaning, one of which will fully represent the others. It is, "For if we sin willfully after that we have received the knowledge of the truth, there remaineth no more sacrifice for sins, but a certain fearful looking for of judgment and fiery indignation, which shall devour the adversaries."—Heb. x. 26, 27. That these words threaten eternal death to believers who sin *willfully* there is no doubt; but they do not declare that any one ever did sin willfully, or that any one ever shall. They simply warn the children of God of the dreadful results of such a crime, with a view to protect them from it; and this warning and others like it show that the good Shepherd will use every effort to keep his word, in which he declares that he gives them eternal life, and they shall never perish. Paul, in the ocean-storm, received the assurance from God that there would be no loss of any man's life, but of the ship. But when near the shore the sailors were deserting, he said to the soldiers, "Except these abide in the ship ye cannot be saved." Paul in this declaration did not contradict his favorable prediction, he was taking steps to have it fulfilled; and every warning like Paul's in Hebrews x. 26, 27, is but putting forth efforts to make the saints persevere, and to prove the truth of Paul's assurance in Philippians i. 6, "Being confident of this very thing, that he who hath begun a good work in you will perform it, *will complete it* (ἐπιτελέσει), until the day of Jesus Christ." The Saviour never began the needless work of saving a man in part; there is no sinner once truly converted among the myriads of the lost. Every elect soul is regenerated, and every man whom the Spirit calls will be glorified.

Peto, Sir Samuel Morton, Baronet, was born at Woking, England, on Aug. 4, 1809. He served

SIR SAMUEL MORTON PETO, BARONET.

an apprenticeship of seven years with his uncle, a builder engaged in extensive operations, at whose death, in 1830, he succeeded to a moiety of the business. His firm took part in the great work of erecting the new Houses of Parliament at Westminster, and other important undertakings. On the dissolution of his partnership, in 1845, Mr. Peto engaged extensively in railroad-building in England and other countries. In some of these enterprises he was associated with the eminent railroad-builder Thomas Brassey. Towards the close of the Crimean war, he undertook, without prospect of profit, the construction of a railway from the harbor of Balaklava to the British camp before Sebastopol, and most expeditiously accomplished this valuable work, thereby facilitating the military operations and relieving the hardships of the soldiers. In appreciation of this patriotic service he was made a baronet of the United Kingdom, by a royal patent dated Feb. 22, 1855. His conspicuous ability as a man of business had been recognized some years earlier by the citizens of Norwich, who elected him to Parliament in 1847, and also in 1852. He was one of the members for the metropolitan borough of Finsbury from 1859 to 1865, and in the latter year was elected for Bristol, which seat he held until the bankruptcy of his firm in the financial troubles of 1866-67. Sir S. Morton Peto joined the Baptist church at St. Mary's, Norwich, during the pastorate of the Rev. William Brock, and soon won a distinguished name in the Baptist body. On the death of W. B. Gurney, Esq., he was chosen treasurer of the Missionary Society, and by his zeal and munificence gave a great impetus to the missionary cause. Feeling the need of an enlargement of denominational effort in the metropolis, he built Bloomsbury Chapel at his own cost, and united with the church which Dr. Brock gathered there in 1848. He also purchased the building known as the Diorama, in Regent's Park, and, having converted it into a commodious and elegant place of worship, induced the Rev. Dr. Landels to become the minister of the church afterwards formed there. Both these enterprises soon became prosperous, and the rapid growth of the Baptists in London and the neighborhood during the last twenty-five years is largely due to the liberality and energy of Sir Morton Peto. He was one of the first to discern the remarkable gifts of Mr. Spurgeon, and gave largely towards the erection of the Metropolitan Tabernacle. Regent's Park College and other Baptist institutions of learning shared in his generous regards, and he has latterly taken a deep interest in promoting the efficiency of the schemes of the Baptist Union for a suitable provision for aged and infirm ministers. Whilst in Parliament, Sir Morton Peto was recognized as a leader of the Nonconformists, and was held in high esteem by all parties for his fidelity to his principles and his unfailing courtesy of behavior. He published in 1863 a book on "Taxation, its Levy and Expenditure," and in 1866 "Resources and Prospects of America," the fruit of a sojourn of several weeks in this country.

Petrobrusians, The.—Peter de Bruys was the Catholic priest of an obscure parish in France, which he left, early in the twelfth century, when he became a preacher of the gospel. How he unlearned the gospel of the Seven Hills and was instructed in that of Calvary we cannot tell, but he was educated in both directions. Many Romanists, like Staupitz or Fenelon, have received the saving knowledge of Jesus and retained their connection with the papal church; but Peter abhorred popery.

He taught that baptism was of no advantage to infants, and that only believers should receive it, and he gave a new baptism to all his converts; he condemned the use of churches and altars, no doubt

FIFTH BAPTIST CHURCH, PHILADELPHIA, PA.

for the idolatry practised in them; he denied that the body and blood of Christ are to be found in the bread and wine of the Supper, and he taught that the elements on the Lord's table are but signs of Christ's flesh and blood; he asserted that the offerings, prayers, and good works of the living could not profit the dead, that their state was fixed for eternity the moment they left the earth; like the English Baptists of the seventeenth century, and like the Quakers of our day, he believed that it was wrong to sing the praises of God in worship; and he rejected the adoration of crosses, and destroyed them wherever he found them.

It is said that on a Good-Friday the Petrobrusians once gathered a great multitude of their brethren, who brought with them all the crosses they could find, and that they made a large fire of them, on which they cooked meat, and gave it to the vast assemblage. This is told as an illustration of their blasphemous profanity. Their crucifixes, and along with them probably the images of the saints, were the idols they had been taught to worship, and when their eyes were opened they destroyed them, just as the converted heathen will now destroy their false gods. Hezekiah did a good thing in destroying the serpent of brass, which in the wilderness had miraculous powers of healing, when the Israelites began to worship it as a god.

Peter's preaching was with great power; his words and his influence swept over great masses of men, bending their hearts and intellects before their resistless might. "In Provence," says Du Pin, "there was nothing else to be seen but Christians rebaptized, churches profaned or destroyed, altars pulled down, and crosses burned. The laws of the church were publicly violated, the priests beaten, abused, and forced to marry, and all the most sacred ceremonies of the church abolished."

Peter de Bruys commenced his ministry about 1125, and such was his success that in a few years in the places about the mouth of the Rhone, in the plain country about Thoulouse, and particularly in that city itself, and in many parts of "the province of Gascoigne" he led great throngs of men and women to Jesus, and overthrew the entire authority of popes, bishops, and priests.

Had the life of this illustrious man been spared the Reformation probably would have occurred four hundred years earlier under Peter de Bruys instead of Martin Luther, and the Protestant nations of the earth would not only have had a deliverance from four centuries of priestly profligacy and widespread soul destruction, but they would have entered upon a godly life with a far more Scriptural creed than grand old Luther, still in a considerable measure wedded to Romish sacramentalism, was fitted to give them.

Peter and his followers were decided Baptists, and like ourselves they gave a fresh baptism to all their converts. They reckoned that they were not believers when first immersed in the Catholic Church, and that as Scripture baptism required faith in its candidates, which they did not possess, they regarded them as wholly unbaptized; and for the same reason they repudiated the idea that they rebaptized them, confidently asserting that because of the lack of faith they had never been baptized.

Peter the Venerable, abbot of Cluny, was born in 1093, and died in 1157. He was distinguished by scholarship, acuteness of mind, and Biblical knowledge. He and St. Bernard were the two leading ecclesiastics of France. Peter would rebuke a pope if he deserved it without hesitation, and no other human being was above his authority. The abbot had assailed the Jews and the Saracens in two distinct works. And such was the extraordinary success of the Petrobrusians, and the great difficulty of refuting their arguments from the Scriptures, that Peter felt compelled to come forth and defend the deserted ecclesiastics and the church threatened with ruin. We shall quote somewhat freely from the abbot to show the doctrines of these grand old Baptists. At the beginning of his pamphlet he states the five heads of the heresy of the Petrobrusians.

In the first he accuses them of "denying that little children under years of responsibility can be saved by the baptism of Christ; and that the faith of another (alienam fidem, the faith demanded from popish sponsors when a child was christened) could benefit those who were unable to exercise their own (faith); because, according to them, not another's faith, but personal faith, saves with baptism, the Lord saying, 'He who shall believe, and be baptized, shall be saved, but he that believeth not shall be condemned.'" This is the abbot's first and heaviest charge against these ancient Baptists. This accusation means that the Petrobrusians refused to baptize children because they were destitute of faith. The charge is repeated frequently by the abbot of Cluny.

"The second *capitulum* says that temples or churches should not be built, and that those existing should be torn down; that sacred places for praying were unnecessary for Christians, since God when addressed in supplication heard equally those who in a warehouse and in a church deserved his attention, in a market-place and in a temple, before an altar or before a stable." By this we understand that the Petrobrusians did not believe in the sanctity of bricks and mortar, and probably thought that as Romish churches were nests of idols and scenes of blasphemous superstition, their destruction would be no crime.

"The third *capitulum* requires holy crosses to be broken and burned, because that frame, or instrument, on which Christ, so fiercely tortured, was so cruelly slain, is not worthy of adoration, or veneration, or of any supplication; but to avenge his torments and death, it should be branded with disgrace, hacked to pieces with the sword, and consumed in the flames." The Petrobrusians detested the worship of the crucifix, and prayers offered to it, and, like the Scotch Covenanters, they urged its destruction as a Christ-dishonoring idol.

"The fourth *capitulum* denied not only the reality of the body and blood of the Lord, as offered daily and constantly in the sacrament (Eucharist) in the church; but judged that it was absolutely nothing, and should not be offered to God." In this opinion all Protestants concur.

"The fifth *capitulum* holds up to ridicule sacrifices, prayers, charitable gifts, and the other good works performed by the faithful living for the faithful departed." Peter then states that he had answered "these five heads," or heresies, "as God had enabled him." He might have added a sixth *capitulum*, that the Petrobrusians wanted Scripture for everything and not the sayings of the fathers. This is admitted in his discussion of their errors. The creed given by Peter to these Baptists is excellent as far as it goes. It is the faith of their brethren to-day. The abbot then proceeds to refute these imaginary heresies separately. And under the heading, "Answer to the Saying of the Heretics that Little Children should not be Baptized (Responsio contra id quod dicunt hæretici parvulos non posse baptizari) he commences his attack on the first *capitulum*. Peter assumes without evidence that the Petrobrusians believed that baptism was essential to salvation; and he takes up their declaration that faith was necessary to baptism, and that not the faith of another but the faith of the subject of baptism, and then he proceeds with great ingenuity to show how the faith of others " saved" persons, as he says, in the Saviour's day. Among the cases which he brings forward is that of the paralytic let down through the roof of the house to the Saviour who was inside, and Peter quotes the gospel narrative. "And when he (Jesus) saw *their faith* he said, Thy sins are forgiven." . . . Peter then says, "What do you say to these things? Behold, I relate this not from Augustine (the godfather of infant baptism, whose arguments have been its defensive weapons for ages, and were very useful to the abbot) but from the Evangel, which you say you trust most of all. At length either concede that some can be saved by the faith of others (aliorum fide alios tandem posse salvari concedite), or deny if you can that the cases I brought forward are from the Evangel." This and several similar instances of healing in the New Testament where the faith of another exercised an influence in securing healing, make the abbot jubilant over the Petrobrusians. But the paralyzed man had faith himself, as well as those who brought him to Jesus.

This theory is probably borrowed entirely from Augustine. In his day the baptism of adults demanded faith continually, and when he put forth enormous efforts to change the subjects of baptism, he still insisted upon faith, the faith of sponsors for unconscious babes. Hence he says, "A little child is benefited by their faith by whom he is brought to be consecrated" (in baptism) (prodesse parvulo eorum fidem a quibus consecrandus offertur*); "a little child believes through another (the sponsor) because it sinned through another" (Adam) ([parvulus] credit in altero quia peccavit in altero†). Again, speaking of a little child, he says, "It has the needful sacrament of the Mediator, so that what could not as yet be done by its faith is performed by the faith of those who love it" (necessarium habet Mediatoris sacramentum, ut quod per ejus fidem nondum potest, per eorum qui diligunt, fiat‡). Speaking of baptism, Augustine says, "Mother-church loans them (little children) the feet of others that they may come (to it), the heart of others that they may believe, and the tongue of others that they may make confession" (accommodat illis mater ecclesia aliorum pedes ut veniant, aliorum cor ut credant, aliorum linguam ut fateantur§). Augustine was in arms to compel all Christendom to adopt infant immersion. He was almost constantly declaring, "Without baptism little children can have no life in themselves" (sine quo [baptismo] nec parvuli possunt habere vitam in semetipsis‖); and as Peter the Venerable is fighting a similar battle with the Petrobrusians, he stores his memory with Augustine's arguments. No doubt it was this that led him to say about the faith of those who carried the palsied man to Jesus, "Behold, I relate this not from Augustine, but from the Evangel."

Another common Pedobaptist argument is presented by Peter, the abbot, in these words, "The unbelieving husband is saved by the believing wife, and the unbelieving wife is saved by the believing husband." This he gives as a quotation from 1 Cor. vii., and commenting upon it, he says, "If the unbelieving wife is saved by the faith of the husband, and the unbelieving husband is saved by the faith of the wife, why should not the child be saved by the faith of husband and wife together?" This is a very natural question. But unfortunately for the abbot, Paul does not speak of either husband or wife as being saved by the faith of the other. He represents the one as being

---

* Augustini Opera Omnia, i. 1304. Migne, Parisiis, 1842.
† Idem, v. 1342. ‡ Idem, iii. 418.
§ Idem, v. 950. ‖ Idem, x. 615.

SANCTIFIED by the other. And the sanctification he refers to after its work is done leaves its subject an unbeliever. It is the legal righteousness of their wedded relations and the legitimacy of their children of which the apostle is speaking. If indeed a Christian lady could give not only her own heart but the love of Christ and the heavenly inheritance to her unbelieving husband, and allow him still to remain in unbelief and sin, it would make a union with her an unheard-of attraction. And the same would be true of the believing husband. But Peter misquotes the Vulgate, the only copy of the Scriptures which he had. It has not his *salvatur*, but *sanctificatus* and *sanctificata est*.

In ancient times, after the heresy sprang into existence that water baptism was necessary to salvation, it was believed that martyrdom, or a baptism in one's own blood, would supply the place of the saving immersion. Peter turns this to ingenious account. He says, "If the martyrs by a personal faith are saved without baptism (in water), why may not little children, as I have said, be saved by baptism without a personal faith?" Or WE might add, Why may they not be saved like the martyrs without any baptism? Treating of the commission of the Saviour, the baptismal creed of the Petrobrusians, he says, "'He who believeth not shall be damned.' You think, forsooth, that little children are held by this chain, and because they are not able to believe, that baptism will profit them nothing. But it is not so; the sacred words themselves show this; they do not show it to the blind, but to those who see; they show it to the humble, not to the haughty. 'Go,' says the Lord, 'into all the world, and preach the gospel to every creature. He that believeth and is baptized shall be saved; he that believeth not shall be condemned.' These words terrify the rebellious; they do not condemn the innocent, they strike iniquity; they do not strike irresponsible infancy, they destroy despisers of grace; they do not condemn the simplicity of nature (innocent children). . . . Restrain, therefore, the excessive severity which you assume, and do not aim to appear more just than him, all whose ways are mercy and truth, nor shut out little children from the kingdom of heaven (by refusing to baptize them), in reference to whom he has said, 'Of such is the kingdom of heaven.'" Peter's interpretation of the condemnation of the commission is correct; it does not condemn any who cannot believe. But his inference from it that infants should be baptized is childishness for the imaginary advantage of infants. All infants are saved without baptism, as the Petrobrusians believed. The commission has only to do with believers and their baptism, and the penalty of unbelief when persons have heard the gospel in years when faith is possible.

Peter proceeds to take up the old argument which Augustine uses, and which has such a modern and familiar sound: "For thus afterwards Christ the Lord placed holy baptism in his church, the sacrament of the New Testament for the circumcision of the flesh." (Sic etiam postquam Dominus Christus in ecclesia sua sacramentum Novi Testamenti pro circumcisione carnis sanctum baptismum dedit. Augustini Opera Omnia, ii. 1087. Migne, Parisiis, 1842.) And he says, "For it is very disgraceful and impious that we should refuse that to the little children of Christians which we grant to the little children of Jews, . . . for neither does the law prevail over the gospel nor Moses over Christ. . . . The little children of the Hebrews were circumcised by divine command on the eighth day, and *purged from original sin*. Where, then, was the faith of the boys? What was their understanding of the sacrament which they received? What was their knowledge of divine things? Where are you who condemn Christian little children? The little children of Jews *are saved* by the sacrament of circumcision, and shall not the little children of Christians be saved by the sacrament of baptism? The Jew believes, and his son is cleansed from sin; the Christian believes, and shall not his child be freed from similar guilt? There is no faith in the little children of Christians, but neither is there any faith in the little children of Jews, yet they are *saved* by the faith of another when circumcision is received, and these (little children) are saved by the faith of another (the sponsors) when baptism is received."*

We have made these quotations to show how vigorously the Petrobrusians denounced baptism on the "*faith of another*" and insisted on personal faith. Much more might be introduced from the celebrated assault of the abbot of Cluny, but from what has been placed before the reader from Peter the Venerable, it is clear that the Petrobrusians were very decided Bible Baptists,—Baptists ready for anything on earth except a renunciation of their Scriptural principles. The other four charges of Peter are quite as favorable to the general orthodoxy of these ancient brethren.

Their immense strength to resist the church and make converts is seen in the extraordinary pains Peter takes to arm himself with all the weapons of Augustine and with such as he had made himself, and in the extremely skillful use which he makes of them. It is refreshing to read a treatise written seven hundred and thirty-six years ago against a powerful body of Baptists by a very able theologian. Augustine directed the most subtle arguments against the men who held Baptist principles in his day; but our people, when crushed, have

---

* Patrl. Lat., clxxxix. pp. 722, 729, 752, 754, 755, 757, 758. Migne, Parisiis, 1854.

MEMORIAL BAPTIST CHURCH, PHILADELPHIA, PA.

only been overcome for a time, and then received fresh life again; and beyond a doubt our doctrines will finally seize the whole race and bless all nations.

Phelps, Mrs. Sophia Emilia, a daughter of Rev. James Harvey Linsley, a Baptist minister, was born Nov. 16, 1823; married, Aug. 26, 1847, Rev. S. D. Phelps, D.D.; a graceful and popular writer; author of a memoir of her father; frequent contributor to journals, especially to the *Christian Secretary;* writer of the expositions of the Sabbath-School Lessons of the International Series in the *Christian Secretary;* successful teacher of Bible-classes; gives to Sunday-school teachers weekly lectures in Hartford, before members of different denominations.

Phelps, Sylvanus Dryden, D.D., editor of *Christian Secretary,* son of Capt. Israel and

SYLVANUS DRYDEN PHELPS, D.D.

Mercy (Stevens) Phelps, grandson of Deacon Judah Phelps, of the Revolutionary war, was born in Suffield, Conn., May 15, 1816; worked on farm and taught winter schools; had great fondness for books; converted in 1834; baptized, in 1838, by Rev. M. G. Clarke; united with Second Baptist church in Suffield while a member of the Connecticut Literary Institution, where he fitted for college; licensed to preach in 1840; taught in Connecticut Literary Institution and Southwick Academy, Mass.; entered Brown University, and graduated in 1844; same year entered Yale Theological Seminary; supplied Baptist church in Bristol, and afterwards First Baptist church in New Haven, where he settled as pastor Jan. 21, 1846, and remained twenty-eight years, during which time 1217 united with the church, 615 by baptism, and four colonies went out to form new churches. In 1871 the present church had 800 members,—largest evangelical church in the State; called at same time to two churches, but settled, in 1874, with Jefferson Street church in Providence, R. I.; on death of Rev. E. Cushman became proprietor and editor of *Christian Secretary,* Hartford, Conn., for which he had previously largely written; in 1859–60 spent about a year in Europe and the East; a brief trip to Europe in 1872; has written and published; a volume of poems in 1842; another, "Eloquence of Nature, and Other Poems;" yet another, in 1855, "Sunlight and Hearthlight;" in 1865, a volume of selections from previous volumes, with new poems; in 1862, a prose volume, "Holy Land," etc., passing through nine editions; "Sermons in the Four Quarters of the Globe;" delivered poems at college commencements; written numerous articles for reviews and periodicals; often lectured on Egypt and the Nile; easy and graceful writer of prose and poetry; popular and honored preacher; received degree of D.D. from Madison University in 1854; married, Aug. 26, 1847, Sophia Emilia Linsley, of Stratford, Conn.

Philadelphia Baptist Association, The, was formed on the "twenty-seventh day of the seventh month, on the seventh day of the week," in the year 1707. The meeting lasted till the third day of the week following. Before the formation of the Association the churches had a general meeting for preaching and administering the ordinances, which was held in different places. The first was held at Salem, N. J., in 1688; this was about three months after the Lower Dublin church was constituted. The next was held at the latter church, the next at Philadelphia, and the fourth at Burlington. Others were held in various places. The people with whom the brethren met called the gathering a yearly meeting because it met with them but once a year, but those who attended all the sessions of this body spoke of it as a quarterly meeting. The Association was designed to differ from the yearly meeting chiefly in this, that it was to be a body of *delegates representing* churches, and the yearly meeting had no representative character.

The brethren who constituted the Association came from Lower Dublin (Pennepek), Middletown, Piscataqua, Cohansey, and Welsh Tract. The Philadelphia congregation, though giving its name to the Association, is not represented as a constituent member, because it was regarded as a branch of the Lower Dublin church. Morgan Edwards mentions with evident satisfaction, that though the Association was formed of but five churches, "It has so increased since as to contain thirty-four churches (in 1770), exclusive of those which have been detached to form another Association." In 1879 the Association had 81 churches, with a membership of nearly 24,000.

The influence of the Philadelphia Association has been greater in shaping Baptist modes of thinking and working, than any other body in existence. It is older by nearly fifty years than any other Association. Its "Confession of Faith" and "Treatise of Discipline" have wielded an immense power in favor of orthodoxy and piety among our rising churches. It has ever been the warm friend of missions at home and abroad, its ministers making missionary tours all over our country. It has always been the friend of Sunday-schools since the system was first presented to its churches. It encouraged the school of Isaac Eaton, of Hopewell, N. J., for the preparation of young men for the ministry, the first Baptist institution of that character in America; and it founded Brown University, formerly Rhode Island College, and through it, indirectly, all our seminaries of learning. As early as 1788 it took its stand in favor of temperance. It was a tower of strength to our persecuted brethren in other colonies in times when they suffered great legal oppression. It gave them financial aid and good counsel, and lent the weight of its great influence in seeking a redress of grievances from men in power, and it has ever demanded liberty for all men to worship God according to the dictates of their consciences.

What our denomination would have been in this country without the Philadelphia Association is an interesting question. We cannot suppose that the Associational institution would have had no existence among us. It flourished in England long before 1707. But this mother Association had men of learning even in her early history, with sound Baptist principles, great practical sagacity, and with a love for struggling Baptists in the farthest East and in the most distant South; and, as a consequence, the Associational plan became popular, and the spirit of the old Philadelphia body was grafted upon every kindred institution all over the land. Nor did this ancient body look coldly upon the crushed liberties and the struggling warriors of their country in Revolutionary times. On the 19th of October, 1781, our army made its victorious entry into Yorktown; on the 23d the Association was in session; on the night of that day the old watchmen of Philadelphia cried, "Twelve o'clock and all is well, and Cornwallis has surrendered." The next morning the Association met *at sunrise* to bless God for the glorious news, and to record their gratitude in appropriate resolutions. The mother Association of our land has a precious record.

Philadelphia, Baptist Home of, was chartered in 1869. Its object is "to provide a place of residence for members of Baptist churches who may, by reason of age, infirmities, or poverty, become

BAPTIST HOME OF PHILADELPHIA.

incapable of supporting themselves and their families, and also to afford such persons other relief, and in such other way, as the trustees may deem prudent and advisable." The trustees have authority to admit members of other Christian churches whenever special contributions are made for that purpose.

The management consists of a board of trustees, who must be members of Baptist churches, and of a board of lady managers, consisting of representatives from the Baptist churches of Philadelphia and vicinity. To the former belongs the duty of securing titles, investing trust funds, and other legal matters, and to the lady managers is assigned the entire management of the institution, the admission and care of the inmates, and the procuring of funds to meet the required expenses above the amount furnished by the partial endowment of $30,000.

Mr. George Nugent, President; Hon. H. G. Jones, Secretary; and Mr. Levi Knowles, Treasurer, of the board of trustees, have served from the date of organization with great zeal and fidelity. The officers of the lady managers are Mrs. L. Knowles, President; Mrs. John Mustin, Vice-President; Mrs. P. G. McCollin, Corresponding Secretary; Miss Anna E. Friend, Recording Secretary; Mrs. C. H. Banes, Treasurer. Mrs. Knowles and Mrs. McCollin have filled the offices assigned to them from the founding of the institution, and to the wonderful executive ability of the former and the enthusiasm and persevering zeal of the latter, aided by a noble band of Baptist sisters, the home is largely indebted for its success and popularity.

The building is located at Seventeenth and Norris Streets, upon a plot of ground valued at $30,000, the generous gift of Deacon Joseph F. Page, of the First Baptist church. It has a handsome exterior, and is especially adapted by its plan for the purpose for which it is used. Built with wings forming three sides of a square, and surrounded by ample grounds, laid out with walks and shrubbery, its appearance is one of great beauty. There are rooms for 85 inmates. The charge for admission is $200 when under seventy years, and $150 when over that age.

As its name indicates, it is a home, and it is remarkably free from the cheerlessness that too frequently mars places of public charity, and, on the contrary, it possesses an air of comfort and contentment that reflects the highest credit upon the Christian benevolence of the denomination.

Philadelphia, The Fifth Baptist Church of, was founded in 1824, by members of the Sansom Street church, organized by Dr. Staughton. It cost about $100,000, and was dedicated to the worship of Almighty God, Oct. 13, 1864. It was paid for before it was used for divine service. Its membership, as reported to the Philadelphia Association in October, 1880, was 584. Rev. B. D. Thomas is its highly esteemed pastor. (See illustration, p. 911.)

Philadelphia, Memorial Baptist Church of, was organized in July, 1868, by Rev. P. S. Henson, D.D.; its chapel was built soon after the formation of the church. The main edifice was completed and dedicated in February, 1876. The latter building will seat 1500 persons. Both structures and lots cost $165,500, and the church has no debt. It had in October, 1880, a membership of 642. (See illustration, p. 915.)

Philadelphia, Second Baptist Church of, was organized in March, 1803. It has had seven pastors since it was formed, six of whom have left the church militant for the heavenly assembly. William Cathcart, D.D., the seventh pastor, has held his office since April, 1857. The church is strongly Calvinistical and warmly missionary. It has paid the present pastor's salary *every month* since April, 1857, a few days before the time, except on two occasions, when it was received on the day it was due. It had a membership in October, 1880, of 707. Its present church edifice is a two-story building, 65 by 100, with a front 76 feet 6 inches wide. It was dedicated in March, 1875. It cost $93,500, and it is entirely paid for. The design of its magnificent front was evidently taken originally from the ancient church of the Abbey of Sainte Geneviève, in Paris, founded by Clovis, and rebuilt from the eleventh to the thirteenth century, an engraving of which is in Lacroix's "Manners, Customs, and Dress of the Middle Ages," p. 40. London.

Philips, Prof. G. Morris, A.M., was born at Penningtonville (now Atglen), Chester Co., Pa., Oct. 28, 1851. He was fitted for college in his native village, and entered the university at Lewisburg in 1867. Having completed the regular classical course, he graduated in 1871, taking the second honors of the largest class which has ever graduated from the university. In the ensuing autumn he assumed the chair of Mathematics in Monongahela College, which position he filled most acceptably for a year and a half. From 1873 to 1878 he held the chair of Higher Mathematics in the State Normal School at West Chester, Pa., where he soon became known most favorably as an enthusiastic and successful instructor. While in that position he declined an appointment to the county superintendency. In 1878 he was appointed Professor of Mathematics and Natural Philosophy in the university at Lewisburg.

Prof. Philips is a most careful and accurate scholar, with great breadth of mind, and a large acquaintance with literature, especially in the line of science. As an instructor he has few equals for clearness of statement, earnestness of manner, and

SECOND BAPTIST CHURCH, PHILADELPHIA, PA.

ability to awaken enthusiasm. His genial manners, thoroughness of work, and large Christian sympathy endear him to all who come under his influence. At the present writing he is engaged with Prof. Sharpless, of Haverford College, in preparing a new text-book on astronomy.

Philips, Judge John W., was born in Wilson Co., Tenn., July 1, 1837. He graduated at Alleghany College, Pa., in 1860. Made a profession of religion in Meadville, Pa., while at college, in the spring of 1859, and joined the Baptist church. He took his letter from the Meadville church to the Round Lick Baptist church in Wilson Co., Tenn., and from it he came to the Second Baptist church of St. Louis, in 1873, of which he is now a member and a deacon. He superintends the Olivet Mission of the Second church.

He was elected judge of the seventh judicial circuit of Tennessee, by the people of that circuit, by a large majority; every vote in the county where he lived was cast for him except six. There were four counties in the circuit. Judge Philips raised a company for the Union army and performed honorable service, and was made colonel of his regiment. He is now a lawyer of successful practice in St. Louis, in the firm of Philips & Stewart.

Philips, Dr. M. W., the veteran agricultural editor of the South, was born in South Carolina in 1806; graduated at South Carolina College in 1826; graduated in the medical department of Pennsylvania University in 1829; settled in Mississippi in 1830; soon became distinguished as a scientific farmer, and contributor to agricultural journals; became a Baptist in 1849, and at once took an active part in church work, especially in the promotion of education, and was chiefly instrumental in the purchase of Mississippi College and the establishment of Central Female College at Clinton, Miss. After the war he removed to Memphis, Tenn., and became editor of the *Southern Farmer*. This he gave up in 1877 to take charge of the Farm and the Agricultural professorship of the University of Mississippi, a position he still holds.

Phillips, Rev. William, was born in Provincetown, Mass., Aug. 24, 1801. In his boyhood his family removed to Pawtucket, R. I. At the age of seventeen he became a Christian, and was baptized by Dr. Benedict, then the pastor of the Baptist church in Pawtucket. At once he began to speak and perform other service in the social meetings, and was so acceptable to his brethren that his pastor sent for him, and asked him if he had ever thought it would be a privilege to preach the gospel. The young man replied that it was a pleasure to him to take part in the religious meetings which he attended, but he felt that an insuperable obstacle lay in the way of his obtaining an education, as he was the sole stay and support of a widowed mother. In the providence of God it was found that this obstacle could be removed, and the way was opened for him to fit for college, under the tuition of Dr. Benedict. He entered Brown University in 1822, and graduated in 1826. In the class were several members who were afterwards distinguished in their professions in life. Among these may be mentioned Rev. George Burgess, D.D., the Episcopal bishop of Maine, Hon. John Kingsbury, LL.D., and Prof. Edwards A. Park, D.D. On leaving college Mr. Phillips did not take a course of theological study, but in the March following his graduation he was ordained pastor of the church in North Attleborough, Mass. He remained here until the fall of 1828, when he accepted a call to the Third Baptist church in Providence, R. I., and commenced his ministry there the first Sabbath in November, 1828. He continued with this church eight years, when he was invited to become the pastor of the First Baptist church in Charlestown, Mass. He remained here until the fall of 1841, when, his health having failed, he resigned his office and removed to Providence, R. I., where he has lived ever since. For one year he suspended regular ministerial labor. At the end of that time his health was sufficiently restored to enable him to supply churches, although he has never been a regular pastor since he left Charlestown. For five and a half years he thus supplied the church at Fruit Hill, in the neighborhood of Providence, and for eight years the church at Lonsdale, R. I. While filling this last engagement he went abroad, extending his trip up the Nile as far as Thebes, and visiting also the Holy Land, spending several weeks in Jerusalem.

Mr. Phillips resides at his pleasant home in the suburbs of Providence, respected and beloved by a large circle of friends. He was made a member of the corporation of Brown University in 1836.

Phippen, Rev. George.—At the residence of his daughter, Mrs. J. W. Mills, in Chicago, May 15, 1873, died Rev. George Phippen, in the eighty-fourth year of his age. He was born in Salem, Mass., Feb. 2, 1790, baptized into the fellowship of the Baptist church there by Rev. Lucius Bolles, Aug. 25, 1805, and ordained at Middletown, Conn., June 11, 1812, after graduating at Brown University. His successive pastorates were at Middletown Centre and Suffield, Conn., West Troy and Newburgh, N. Y., Tyringham and Lee, Mass. He had an influential share in the establishment of the Connecticut Literary Institution at Suffield, and was successively secretary and president of the Education Society in that State. He closed, in the peaceful joy of one departing to be with Christ, a long life of marked fidelity and usefulness.

Picket, Rev. John, was born in King and Queen

Co., Va., Jan. 14, 1744. In early life he was fond of sports and frivolous amusements. On a visit to North Carolina the Saviour called him into his peace. He was baptized in 1766. A year after he returned to Virginia. In 1768 a church was formed in Fauquier, Va., chiefly through his instrumentality; the church was called Carter's Run. Mr. Picket was ordained its pastor in 1772. His prosperity in winning souls soon drew persecution upon him. A mob broke into the meeting-house and split the pulpit in pieces. The magistrates sent the pastor to prison, where he preached God's Word to the salvation of great numbers. When he was released from prison he proclaimed Jesus with greater zeal than ever, extending his labors into Culpeper and over the Blue Ridge, where at the first baptism that ever took place in Shenandoah fifty were immersed. Mr. Picket loved the Saviour intensely, was never weary in laboring for him, was honored by great usefulness in the service of Jesus, and he led a saintly life. He died in June, 1803.

Pidge, Rev. John Bartholomew Gough, the son of Edwin and Mary E. Pidge, was born at Providence, R. I., Feb. 4, 1844; was educated in public and private schools at Providence, and subsequently entered Brown University, graduating therefrom in 1866; graduated also at Newton Theological Institution in 1869. While a student at Newton he translated Braune's "Commentary on Philippians," from the German, under the supervision of Dr. Hackett; was ordained Sept. 8, 1869, and became pastor of the church at Lawrence, Mass. In 1871 he declined a call to the professorship of New Testament Exegesis from Crozer Theological Seminary. In April, 1879, he accepted a call to the pastorate of the Fourth church, Philadelphia, in which field of labor he continues a ministry that has greatly endeared him to one of our largest churches.

Mr. Pidge is a man of studious habits, of scholarly attainments, and of marked pulpit power. His sermons are fruitful in the results of close application, and are well calculated to enrich the minds of those who wait upon his ministrations.

Pierson, Rev. Nicholas, an English Baptist, who settled in Horton, Nova Scotia, about 1775; was ordained, Nov. 5, 1778, pastor of the Baptist church at Horton, formed seven days previous; the first Baptist church organized in the Maritime Provinces. Mr. Pierson continued pastor till his removal to New Brunswick in 1791, where he died some years after.

Pike, Rev. James C., an eminent minister of the English General Baptists, and for twenty-two years secretary of their Foreign Missions, was born June 26, 1817. His father, the author of "Persuasives to Early Piety," was gratified to see in his own son what he so earnestly commended to the young generally. After a course of study at Stepney College, he commenced his ministry at Wisbech, as assistant to the Rev. Joseph Jarrom. He labored here fourteen years, and then removed to Leicester, where, in two pastorates, he spent the remaining years of his life. In 1855 he was chosen secretary of the Foreign Missions, in the place of his father, to whose faith and zeal it owed its origin. His industry and courage, as well as bodily strength, were severely taxed by the burdens laid upon him as a pastor of a large church and the responsible director of the missionary work. But he was a workman who needed not to be ashamed. He died August, 1876, aged fifty-nine years.

Pike, Rev. John G., was born at Edmonton, England, April 6, 1784. His father, the Rev. Dr. Pike, had formerly been a clergyman of the Established Church, from which he seceded for conscience' sake, and became the minister of a Presbyterian congregation in the neighborhood of London. When in his eighteenth year he was entered as a student for the ministry at an Independent college. Whilst pursuing his studies the subject of baptism powerfully attracted his mind, and he was led by his convictions to abandon the Pedobaptist sentiments in which he had been brought up. He was baptized by the only Baptist minister he was acquainted with in August, 1804, but did not join any Baptist church until 1808, when he was received into the church in London under the pastoral care of the eminent General Baptist minister, Dan Taylor, by which he was soon after formally licensed to preach. After preaching for some time without a fixed engagement, he accepted a call to the General Baptist church in Derby. His success was attested by the rapid increase of the congregation and numerous baptisms. The church edifice was inadequate, and, notwithstanding the commercial depression of the period, a new and much larger building was erected. His scanty income obliged him to commence a boarding-school for the support of his family, but his ministerial labors were abundant in Derby and all the neighborhood. He threw himself heartily into the work of foreign missions, and co-operated with Andrew Fuller and the Particular Baptists until the General Baptist Mission was organized. Mr. Pike was immediately chosen secretary of the society. Besides these labors his pen was ever busy. His "Persuasives to Early Piety" and "Guide for Young Disciples" had a wide circulation and were eminently useful. Besides these works, which are everywhere known and deservedly esteemed, he wrote other practical works of great value. During his long pastorate at Derby, which was terminated only by his death, he lived in the affection of his people and enjoyed the esteem of all classes of the community. He died suddenly, seated at his desk with his pen in hand, Sept. 4, 1855, aged seventy.

Pilgrim, Rev. Thomas J., was born in Middlesex Co., Conn., Dec. 19, 1805; was licensed to preach, and spent a time at Hamilton, N. Y., under the tuition of Nathaniel Kendrick and Daniel Hascall. His health failing him, in 1827, he left Hamilton, and by the Western waters came to New Orleans, where, after waiting some time, he succeeded in getting a passage on a schooner to the mouth of the Brazos River, in the then Mexican province of Texas. He accepted service as a teacher of the children of Mexican hidalgos, and assisted Stephen F. Austin in translating from Spanish into English the laws of Mexico, thus acquiring a thorough command of the Spanish language. For the most of his life he was occupied as a teacher with signal success, instructing such men as James H. Bell, M. Austin Bryan, and Guy M. Bryan. He organized and conducted the first Sunday-school ever originated in Texas. In establishing Sunday-schools, teaching Bible-classes, distributing the Bible, and managing Gonzales College he spent most of his life. After coming to Texas he gave up the duties of the ministry, but lived and acted as a consistent, devoted Christian, taking a deep interest in the education of the young men proposing to enter the Christian ministry, and giving liberally to their support. He died at Gonzales, Texas, Oct. 29, 1877.

Pillsbury, Rev. Stephen, was born in Amesbury, Mass., Oct. 30, 1781. Hopefully converted at the age of twenty-one, he was baptized into the fellowship of the church in Sutton, N. H. Having decided to give his life to the work of the ministry he preached as a licentiate in different places. He was ordained in Hebron, N. H., where he remained fifteen years. In 1830 he became pastor of the church in Sutton, where his labors were much blessed during his five years' pastorate. His next pastorates were at Dumbarton and at Londonderry, N. H. In the latter place he died, Jan. 22, 1851.

Pingry, Judge William M., was born at Salisbury, N. H., May 28, 1806, and was admitted to the bar in Vermont in June, 1832. He was baptized in 1831, and at once identified himself with the interests of his denomination in the State of Vermont. In 1841 he removed to Perkinsville, and became a deacon of the Baptist church in that place. He has occupied several of the most prominent positions in Baptist organizations in the State. From 1838 to 1840 he was judge of the Washington County Court. He was a member of the Vermont constitutional convention in 1850, State auditor from 1853 to 1860, a member of the Vermont house of representatives in 1860, 1861, and 1868, and of the senate in 1869, 1870. He has practised his profession since June, 1832, excepting that from November, 1854, to August, 1857, he was cashier of a bank. Dartmouth College con-

JUDGE WILLIAM M. PINGRY.

ferred on him, in 1860, the honorary degree of Master of Arts.

Pitman, Judge John, the son of Rev. John Pitman, was born in Providence, Feb. 23, 1785. Such was his precocity that he entered Brown University before he had completed his eleventh year. He graduated in the year 1799, and though but a mere lad of fourteen, commenced the study of law, which he pursued for two years and a half, at the end of which time he was prepared to be admitted to the Rhode Island bar. He was too young, however, to practice his profession, and in order to perfect himself in his studies he was placed under the direction of an eminent lawyer of Poughkeepsie, N. Y., Hon. Theodorus Bailey. After various fortunes in different localities he returned to his native city and opened a law-office, and for several years practised in the Rhode Island courts. He then took up his residence in Salem, Mass., and subsequently in Portsmouth, N. H., and thus became familiar with the practice of law in the courts of those States. Once more he returned to Providence, and continued his residence there from 1820 to the close of his life. In 1824 he was appointed U. S. district judge for the district of Rhode Island. During this long period of professional service he proved himself a public-spirited citizen, always throwing the weight of his influence on the side of any plan or organization which had for its object the improvement of his fellow-men. He was a member of the corporation of Brown University for thirty-six years, six years as a trustee and thirty years as a Fellow. His college conferred upon him the degree of Doctor of Laws in 1842.

JUDGE JOHN PITMAN.

Few men have more thoroughly won the respect and affection of the community in which they lived than Judge Pitman. Loyal to the faith of his fathers, he was a firm Baptist, and a devout worshiper in the venerable church in which for so many years he had a seat. Although, like his long cherished friend, Nicholas Brown, he never made a public profession of his faith, he nevertheless "illustrated the strict integrity, the devout humility, and the exemplary life of a Christian man." His death took place in Providence, Nov. 17, 1864, when he was within less than four months of being eighty years of age.

Pitman, Rev. John, was born in Boston, April 26, 1751. Early in life he was apprenticed to learn the business of a rope-maker. He was baptized by Rev. Dr. Stillman, Feb. 24, 1771, and became a member of the First Baptist church in Boston. He removed to Philadelphia in 1774. For some time he was in the Continental army during the Revolutionary war. He began to preach probably in 1777, and in October of this year became pastor of the Baptist church in Upper Freehold, N. J., where he remained until March 10, 1780. For two or three years he was without a settlement. He removed to Providence, R. I., in 1784, and was occupied with secular pursuits and preaching for the next two years, and in October, 1786, was called to the pastorate of the church in Warren, R. I., where he continued until 1790, when he returned to Providence, where he resided for several years, during a few of which he was the pastor of the church in the neighboring town of Pawtucket. In 1797 he became pastor of the church in Rehoboth, Mass., where for nearly all the rest of his life he lived, dying July 22, 1822.

Pitts, Rev. Y. R., was born in Scott Co., Ky., Nov. 8, 1812. His parents were Younger and Elizabeth T. Pitts. His father died when he was but twelve years of age; his mother was left a widow with eight children. She was a remarkable Christian woman, and she was much assisted by her son; between them there existed a tender relation of heart devotion. He removed to Missouri in 1860. He was ordained to the ministry of the Baptist denomination in Georgetown, Ky., Nov. 23, 1841. The ordaining council were J. D. Block, J. M. Frost, Howard Malcom, D.D., president of Georgetown College, R. T. Dillard, B. F. Kinney, and William Craig. He was pastor at Elkhart, Ky., thirteen years. He labored also at Williamstown, Blue Creek, and elsewhere. In Missouri he was pastor at Fayette. At the time of his death he was about to enter upon an agency for William Jewell College. He died at Clinton, Mo., in October, 1870, to which place he had gone to attend the General Association of Missouri. A neat marble monument marks his resting-place in the city cemetery at Huntsville, Mo. He was a man of high character, and a faithful minister of Christ.

Platt, Rev. Edward Francis, was born at Schroon Lake, N. Y., Dec. 16, 1821, and was baptized into the fellowship of the Baptist church of the same place in 1838. At an early period in his Christian life he made choice of the ministry, and pursued a course of studies under the instruction of Rev. W. W. Moore, of Lansingburg, N. Y. He commenced preaching in Cairo, N. Y., in 1845, and in the following year was ordained at that place to the work of the ministry. In 1847 he became pastor of the First church, Catskill, N. Y., where he labored with great success for five and a half years. Being obliged by ill health to resign this pastorate, he went West, and in 1853 became pastor of a young and struggling church at Toledo, O., under the direction of the Home Mission Society. Here he labored with untiring zeal until his death, which occurred Nov. 21, 1866. During this period of thirteen years he won the hearts of all by his purity of life, his devotion to the cause of Christ, and his pulpit abilities. His death was felt to be a great loss not only in Toledo, but in the entire State.

Poindexter, Abram Maer, D.D., was born in Bertie Co., N. C., Sept. 22, 1809. His father was the Rev. Richard Poindexter, of Louisa Co., Va., who, on the occasion of his marriage with Mrs. Jordan, of North Carolina, removed to that State. Young Poindexter's early educational advantages were good, and he applied himself closely to the ordinary studies preliminary to a college course. While still quite young he entered the Columbian College, but owing to feeble health his studies there were interrupted, and after a brief period he was compelled to abandon them and return to his home. In 1831 he made a profession of religion; in 1832 he was licensed to preach, and in 1834 he was ordained to the work of the gospel ministry. For some time before his ordination he was the companion, student, and co-laborer of the Rev. A. W. Clopton, the popular and useful pastor of Baptist churches in Charlotte Co., Va., from whose gifted mind and heart, as well as varied and ripe experience in pastoral duties, he derived valuable and life-long impressions for good. Quite early in life Dr. Poindexter married Mrs. Eliza Craddock, a lady of great excellence of character, after which he resided in Halifax Co., Va., where most of his mature life was spent. From the very beginning of his ministry he displayed unusual talents, and was esteemed the most promising young minister of his time. As a preacher, Dr. Poindexter was deservedly held in very high regard, especially with large out-door assemblies, such as convene at Associational meetings. On such occasions his preaching was frequently distinguished by great fluency and power of speech, unusual vigor and depth of thought, a beautiful logical consecutiveness in the development of truth, and an earnestness and impetuosity of manner that swayed and moved the masses with resistless power. As a thinker he had but few equals. His intellect was clear, active, strong, and original. His thoughts were pre-eminently his own. He called no man master, excepting always the great Teacher. As an extemporaneous debater he stood almost alone among disputants; and so accurate was his method, so precise his arguments, so correct his style, that a *verbatim* report of his remarks would rarely require the least revision for publication. As an agent for the Columbian and Richmond Colleges he was greatly successful, while as secretary of the Southern Baptist Publication Society, and afterwards as co-secretary of the Foreign Mission Board of the Southern Baptist Convention, he won a noble reputation for energy and executive ability. His impressive appeals in behalf of missions and education stimulated the zeal, enlisted the interest, and secured the contributions of large numbers throughout the South, and gave an impetus to those causes which they still feel. He was a man of deep convictions and intense feeling. His words were indeed the outer image of his inmost soul. He believed, and therefore he spoke; and when he spoke men had no hesitation in saying, here is a Christian man who will part with his life rather than with his convictions of right and duty. Dr. Poindexter, like many of his brethren in the ministry, was called, in the providence of God, to pass through dark waters of affliction. Two promising sons were taken from him during the war, one by the accidental discharge of his own pistol, and the other at the head of his company, by a bullet of the enemy. The ravages of war swept away his estate; and to crown his sorrows his estimable wife soon passed away from his desolated home, leaving among the wrecks an only daughter, who has since died, who was married to the Rev. J. B. Taylor, Jr., now of Wilmington, N. C. In 1843 the Columbian College conferred upon him the degree of D.D. He died May 7, 1872.

Pollard, John, Sr., was born in Goochland Co., Va., July 14, 1803. The maiden name of his mother was Catherine Robinson, of the same family with Speaker Robinson, of the house of burgesses of Virginia, who was presiding over that body at the time Patrick Henry made his celebrated speech against the British crown, and who was the first to cry "treason!" when the great orator closed with the startling utterance, "Cæsar had his Brutus, etc." One of his uncles was private secretary to Chief-Justice Marshall, and one of his aunts, wife of the distinguished Judge Pendleton, of the Virginia Court of Appeals. His education was received in a school at Hanover Court-House, and comprised the ordinary English branches and some acquaintance with Latin. He learned much afterwards in the office of his uncle, R. Pollard, clerk of King and Queen Co., Va., with whom he served as deputy from his seventeenth to his twenty-first year. When of age he settled in King and Queen County, farming and practising law. In 1826 he was baptized into the fellowship of the Lower King and Queen church by Rev. Wm. Todd. Subsequently he withdrew, with others, to form the Mattapony church, of which he continued a member until his death, having been thirty-five years one of its deacons, and thirty-four years the superintendent of its Sunday-school. He was an ardent supporter of denominational enterprises, and was noted for his hospitality, especially to Baptist ministers, many of whom, such as Luther Rice, Eli Bell, Valentine Mason, Andrew Broaddus, and William F. Broaddus, were frequently found at his cheerful fireside. He was at different times commissioner of revenue, a justice of the County Court, and high sheriff. Mr. Pollard was very strong in his attachments to the Columbian College, to which he contributed liberally and frequently, and at which institution four of his sons were educated; while at the same time friendly to other institutions of learning. He was a man of very decided principles, and of remarkable liveliness of temperament. He died Sept. 13, 1877. It is a noteworthy fact, that of his seven children and twenty-eight grandchildren surviving him, all that have attained the age of twelve years are useful members of Baptist churches.

Pollard, John, D.D., son of John Pollard and Juliet Jeffries, sister of Judge J. M. Jeffries, of the second judicial circuit of Virginia, was born Nov. 17, 1839, in King and Queen Co., Va. He began his education at Stevensville Academy, and completed it at the Columbian College, Washington, D. C., where he graduated with the highest honors in 1860. After his graduation he remained as tutor of Greek and Latin in the college during the session of 1860-61, and also took a private course in theology under Rev. G. W. Samson, D.D., at that time president of the college. He was ordained to the ministry July 14, 1861, and became pastor of Hermitage and Clarke's Neck churches, Middlesex Co., Va., with which he remained nine years, until October, 1870, when he accepted a call to the pastorate of Lee Street Baptist church, Baltimore. Mr. Pollard has published a compendious history of the Lee Street church, and was appointed by the Executive Board of the Maryland Union Association to finish the "History of the Churches" connected with that body, begun by the late Dr. G. F. Adams, in which desirable work considerable progress has been made. He has contributed occasional articles also to the religious papers. For three successive sessions of the Maryland Union Association, embracing not only the churches of the whole of Maryland, but also those of the District of Columbia, he has been its efficient moderator. The Columbian College conferred upon him, in 1867, the degree of A.M. in course, and in 1877 the degree of D.D. In 1880, Dr. Pollard became a pastor in Richmond, Va., leaving throngs of friends in Baltimore.

Pomeroy, Caleb M., was born at old Salem, Mass., Aug. 8, 1810. His father died when he was nine years of age. In 1831 he removed to Cincinnati. He became a resident of Quincy, Ill., in 1837, and that city has since been his home. During twenty-four years he was a successful pork-packer; then for fourteen years president of the First National Bank in Quincy. In 1842 he united with the First Baptist church of Quincy, and was elected one of its deacons in the same year. His membership and office he continued to hold until 1857, when he united with others in forming the Vermont Street church, where again he was called to the office of deacon. For thirty-three years he was a teacher in the Sunday-school. Mr. Pomeroy has always been a very liberal man, giving largely to many and various objects of Christian enterprise, in the time when his business prospered making these gifts in hundreds and thousands of dollars. Reverses in business have reduced his ability, but in no degree affected his interest or his readiness to give. He is, and has always been, a pillar in the church.

Pools of Jerusalem.—Of all cities of antiquity, in proportion to area and population, Jerusalem seems to have been the most abundantly supplied with water. In the worst straits of siege, drought, or famine, during its checkered and eventful history, it seems never to have suffered from such a curtailment of its water-supply as to amount to a serious calamity. While there is no stream in the near vicinity of the city to account for this abundance, the Kedron being but a brook in name, yet such sources of supply as were available seem to have been so utilized that the city could always be guarded against so grave an evil as an inadequate supply of water. The sources of this supply were the natural springs without, and perhaps within the city, and the drainage of the winter rains, gathered into public and private pools, tanks, wells, and cisterns. In most cases the ultimate and most copious source of supply for the larger reservoirs were the springs or fountains mentioned. For ordinary domestic uses the winter rains seem to have been stored in private cisterns and tanks. Public institutions appear to have had larger cisterns and reservoirs for their special wants. Modern exploration beneath the traditional temple area has fully brought to light the elaborate system of water-supply for the wants of the ancient temple service and worshipers. But the public reservoirs or pools, to which we now confine our attention, were the receptacles where the waters were most abundantly collected, and most freely used by the people. Outside the walls of the modern city traces of several large pools can now be discerned which indicate their early existence; but those that remain, in their varying degrees of preservation, fully show the important part they must have performed in the water-supply of the city. For the purposes of convenience we may begin at the large pool located in a valley or basin to the northwest of the modern city. This pool was most probably built by Solomon, and is characterized by the prophet Isaiah as "the old pool" (Isaiah xxii. 11), and also as "the upper pool, which is in the highway of the fuller's field" (2 Kings xviii. 17). It is excavated out of the earth and limestone rock, the walls, like these structures in general, being built up of stones and cement. Here, by the conduit of this upper pool (2 Kings xviii. 17), the envoys of the king of Assyria stood when they delivered the message of their master to Hezekiah. Dr. Robinson carefully measured this pool, and found the length 316 feet; breadth, 218 feet at one end, and 200 feet at the other, with a depth of 18 feet. Steps were found at the corners leading down to the bottom of the reservoir. Originally, the pool received most of its supply, in all probability, from the neighboring springs or fountains that the king sealed when the city was besieged during his reign; but now the drainage of the winter rains from the adjacent hills appears to be the only source of supply. From the dilapidated condition of the pool, this, however, soon disappears. At the northwest angle of the city, within the modern walls, and near the Church of the Holy Sepulchre, is the "Pool of Hezekiah," supposed to be referred to in 2 Kings xx. 20, where the king is represented as making a pool and conduit, and bringing water into the city. The modern name is Birket-el-Hummam,—the Pool of the Bath,—from its supplying a neighboring bath. During the rainy season the water is brought down from the Upper Pool referred to by a small aqueduct that enters the city near the Yâfâ Gate. In October, 1871, when the writer of the present article saw this pool, the quantity of water did not suffice to cover the floor, which sloped considerably from north to south. At the northwest angle there is the usual descent by steps to the bottom of the reservoir. The people of the neighborhood, at the present time, freely use the pool to wash and fill their water-jars. The length of the pool, according to Dr. Robinson, is 240 feet; its breadth, 144 feet. On the opposite side of the city, north of the Mosque of Omar, and near the eastern wall, is an immense excavation, with walls of stone and cement, known as Birket Israel, or Pool of Israel. Almost uniform tradition identifies the modern Birket Israel as the "Pool of Bethesda," in our Lord's time described as having five porches, and where he performed a striking miracle.—John v. 2–7. Dr. Robinson, though standing alone among ancient and modern authorities in his views respecting the identity of the modern pool with "Bethesda," yet admits that it was once used as a reservoir. The limits of this article will not permit any reference in detail to the testimony of such witnesses as Eusebius, Jerome, and others, who describe the pool as, in their time, divided into two sections, filled with water, but evidently the same structure as the single pool that in our Lord's day was surrounded by covered colonnades. In superficial area this pool covers more than an acre of ground. It is 360 feet long, 130 feet broad, and 75 feet deep, now partly choked with rubbish. Emerging from St. Stephen's Gate, and passing a short distance down the bed of the Kedron, the modern traveler comes to a natural cave or grotto, from the bottom of which, reached by a flight of steps cut in the rock, issues a copious supply of water. This fountain at present is known as the "Fountain of the Virgin," and is the same, in all probability, as the King's Pool mentioned by Nehemiah.—Neh. ii. 14. The general dimensions of the grotto are 15 feet in length, 5 or 6 feet in width, and 6 or 8 feet in height. The water in the basin varies in depth from one to three feet, but can be indefinitely increased in quantity by slightly damming or obstructing the outlet. This fountain is much resorted to by the poorer classes of the modern city. Recent discoveries leave little room to doubt that the "Fountain of the Virgin" derives its supply from the reservoirs beneath the temple area, in turn replenished, it is believed, by subterranean conduits, not yet discovered, from the springs that were sealed by King Hezekiah when the ancient city was besieged. By an underground passage of little more than a quarter of a mile in length, the "Fountain of the Virgin" pours its surplus waters into the Birket-es-Silwân,—the ancient "Pool of Siloam." Accepting the measurement of Dr. Barclay, the pool is 17 feet at the upper end, 14½ feet at the lower, and 18½ feet in depth. It is now never filled, the water easily passing through it by an outlet at the lower end. The walls are very much out of repair, so that it would be impossible for the pool, under existing circumstances, to be charged with the volume of water it must have originally received. A short distance back of the pool, up the hill, is a smaller reservoir, 6 or 8 feet wide by 8 or 10 feet in length. This tank receives first the overflow from the "Fountain of the Virgin," and then pours it into the adjoining "Pool of Siloam." The bottom of this upper basin, or that of the adjacent pool itself, may be reached by a flight of steps, and the water graduated in depth by temporarily damming the outlet of one or the other. "The Lower Pool of Gihon," situated to the west of the city, in the valley of that name, and now known as Birket-es-Sultan, was the largest in or near the city. This pool, or lake, was formed by damming up the bed of the valley, so as to confine the overflow of the Upper Pool, described as situated to the northwest of the city. Dams across the valley form the ends, while its bed, sloping gently on either side, forms the sides of this immense reservoir. By a careful measurement, Dr. Robinson found the length along the centre, 592 feet; the breadth at the north end, 245 feet; at the south, 275 feet. The depth at the north end is 35 feet; at the south, 42 feet. This pool owes its construction most probably to Hezekiah, and may be referred to in 2 Chron. xxxii. 30. It is now dry, and is not unfrequently used as a corral for camels. In the time of the Crusades, from the accounts that have been transmitted, it was abundantly charged with water, and appears to have been a great watering-place for horses. From the Upper Pool, the rains, and the aqueduct passing near by from the pools near Bethlehem, the volume of water in this great reservoir, derived from these several sources, must have been practically inexhaustible. This, of course, could have only been the case when the pools and aqueducts were very different in condition and repair from that seen at the present day.

In any enumeration of the public pools of the ancient city mention at least must be made of three immense pools situated near Bethlehem, constructed by Solomon, and known as "Solomon's Pools." They are fed by natural springs in the vicinity. They were built for the use of the Holy City, and as they now, by an aqueduct, send their wholesome waters within its walls, so in the past they must have played an important part in the water resources of the city.

The pools in or near Jerusalem known to have existed in the time of our Lord, where they can with sufficient positiveness be identified, have now been considered. That they were all in good repair and thoroughly fitted, in the days of the Apostles, to serve the purposes of their construction, there is scarcely reason to doubt; for a generation had not elapsed since Herod carefully repaired and strengthened the pools and reservoirs in and near the capital of his kingdom. The assumption by Pedobaptists that the rite of immersion could not have been administered in connection with the 3000 converts of Pentecost on a single day, because there could have been no facilities for baptism on such a scale, is not only untenable, but preposterous in the light of what has been advanced. These pools at that time, even under unfavorable circumstances, must not only have contained a sufficient *depth* of water for the purpose, but, as a necessary appliance, steps appear to have been built for entering them. In the case of the largest of them, the "Lower Pool of Gihon," the sloping sides of the valley were peculiarly fitted for entering the pool to any required depth. The multitude of sick people lingering and waiting at the "Pool of Bethesda" when the impotent man was healed, indicates that in one of the largest reservoirs, if it does not establish the fact respecting the others, the people were accustomed freely to enter. Even *now* the comparatively small basin at the bottom of the "Fountain of the Virgin" would furnish an excellent baptistery, if there were need of so employing it. The "Pool of Siloam" near by, must have been, as it would be now if in repair, still better fitted for the purpose. Moreover, the sloping floors of "the Upper Pool of Gihon" and the neighboring "Pool of Hezekiah" show conclusively that these pools could be entered to any depth suitable for bathing, and hence for immersion. The first converts appear at the outset to have worshiped in the temple unmolested. "They grew in favor with all the people." Popular sympathy was with them. The spirit of intolerance had hardly begun to manifest itself, as it did so virulently afterwards. It is not likely, therefore, there was any opposition to the use of the public pools in administering the rite of baptism to the Pentecostal converts, or the multitudes subsequently. In the "Lower Pool of Gihon" alone,—the largest, and the one perhaps most extensively used,—with the Apostles and the Seventy as possible administrators, any reasonable objection against the immersion of the 3000 on the day of Pentecost, or any number later, at once vanishes; and when the facilities furnished by the other pools are taken into consideration, the absurdity of the objections against the immersion of a large number, as to time and quantity of water, becomes still more apparent.

Pope, Rev. George.—This useful minister was pastor of Abbott's Creek Church, Davidson Co., N. C. He was repeatedly moderator of the Sandy Creek Association, and during the great revival of 1800 baptized 500 persons. He baptized the elder Dr. W. T. Brantly into the fellowship of May's chapel.

Pope, John Francis, was born in New Bedford, Mass., Jan. 22, 1823; was converted at the age of sixteen, and baptized by Dr. Henry Jackson. He was a graduate of Harvard. Mr. Pope was among the early pioneers to California, arriving there in August, 1849, and, with his wife, joined the First Baptist church, San Francisco, and became one of its most influential members, holding the position of deacon from July, 1854, twenty-five years. He occupied important positions in the school department of the city, and assisted in establishing its high schools. In denominational matters he held high official positions in the Associations, Conventions, and college boards, and did much to impress upon the State his own character as a Christian and an enlightened Baptist. At the quarter centennial of the organization of the San Francisco Baptist Association, in 1874, he was the moderator.

Pope, Rev. O. C., the managing editor of the *Texas Baptist Herald*, was born Feb. 15, 1842, in Washington Co., Ga.; was educated at Mercer University, Penfield, Ga., and graduated regularly from its theological department; connected himself with the Baptist church in August, 1858. Since entering the ministry he has served Louisville church, Ga., Morristown, Tenn., and Central Baptist church, Nashville, Tenn. He has acted as secretary of Mercer Association, Ga., Nolachucky Association, Tenn., and corresponding and recording secretary of the General Association of East Tennessee. He founded and edited for two years the *Baptist Reflector*, at Nashville, Tenn. He is in the vigor of his manhood, and promises to make the *Herald* a power for good in Texas.

Porter, Rev. William, was born in Erie Co., Pa., May 3, 1803, of Congregational parents; was married, converted, and baptized in Delaware Co., O.; joined the Mill Creek church, and was ordained by it in 1838. He was pastor and missionary in and around the region of the church till 1847, when he moved to Oregon, settled on the "West Plain," near Forest Grove; served the West Union church,—the first Baptist church organized west of the Rocky Mountains,—the West Tualatin and other churches, and for twenty years kept alive (with the aid of Deacon D. T. Lenox) the Baptist denomination in the lower part of the Willamette Valley, west of the river. He was both doctrinal and practical, extempore and pathetic, swaying his hearers with a wonderful power. Having done much work for Christ, he died Nov. 29, 1872, mourned by a multitude who revered him as their spiritual father and guide in religious life.

Posey, Rev. Humphrey, an eminent Baptist minister, was distinguished for his benevolent spirit

REV. HUMPHREY POSEY.

and great abilities. He was above the ordinary size, with a large frame and fine face and head. Born in Henry Co., Va., Jan. 12, 1780, he commenced preaching in 1803, and was ordained in 1805, in Buncombe Co., N. C., and, among others, preached to the Cherokee Indians. He was regularly appointed a missionary to the Cherokees at Valley Town, in North Carolina, by the Baptist Mission Board, of Philadelphia, in 1817, and maintained his connection with the mission until 1824, accomplishing great good. In 1824 he settled in Cherokee, Ga., and became a very successful agent for the Hearn School, relieving it of much pecuniary embarrassment. In 1844 he married a second time, and removed to Newnan, where he died, Dec. 28, 1846. Dr. J. H. Campbell, in his "Georgia Baptists," records it "as his deliberate conviction that Humphrey Posey was naturally one of the greatest men, and, for his limited opportunities, one of the greatest preachers he has ever known. His person, his countenance, his voice, the throes of his gigantic mind, the conceptions of his large Christian soul, —all proclaimed him great." The first time Dr. Campbell ever met him was at the Georgia Baptist Convention, in 1835, near Penfield, and the doctor says, "Such men as Mercer, Sanders, Dawson, Thornton, Mallary, Brooks, and others were there, but Posey was a giant among them all." Dr. C. D. Mallary wrote and published a "Life of Humphrey Posey."

Post, Rev. Albert L., was born in 1809, at Montrose, Pa. Montrose was founded in 1800 by Capt. Bartlett Hinds, who survived the storming of Stony Point, a worthy pioneer magistrate and Baptist. His daughter, Susanna, and his stepson, Maj. Isaac Post, were the parents of the subject of this sketch. He was educated at Union College, Schenectady, N. Y.; was admitted to the bar, and soon after became prosecuting attorney for Susquehanna County. In 1836 he started *The Spectator*, a paper devoted to the freedom

REV. ALBERT L. POST.

of the colored race. In 1841 he was ordained to the ministry at Montrose, which has still continued to be his residence. He has rendered valuable service in protracted meetings and in partial pastorates. He was president for many years of "The American Baptist Free Mission Society," in whose interests he visited England. He is a vigorous opponent of secret societies. Mr. Post is a man of mind and a model of Christian integrity. He would suffer the loss of everything, and the worst form of death, rather than sacrifice a principle. Stern, the embodiment of the martyr spirit, with a keen intellect and a generous heart, all men love him, though not a few differ from his opinions. Pennsylvania never had a purer Baptist.

Post, Rev. John Clark, was born at Montpelier, Vt., April 20, 1814; spent most of his childhood and early youth in Connecticut; went West in 1832; was converted and baptized into the fellowship of the Baptist church of Aurora, Ind. (the pastor being Rev. Jesse L. Holman), on Nov. 4, 1838; was licensed there to preach in 1839; was ordained at Charlestown, Ind., in 1840. He has been pastor at Charlestown, Franklin, Delphi, and other places in Indiana; of Aledo, Edgington, Andalusia, and other churches in Illinois, and was settled at Fort Scott, Wichita, Hutchinson, and other places in Kansas; has been blessed with extensive revivals, and built several meeting-houses. At sixty-six years of age he enjoys good health, and occupies an extensive mission field in Southwest Kansas.

Potter, Albert K., D.D., was born in Coventry, R. I., and was a graduate of Brown University in the class of 1859. He studied at the Newton Theological Institution, and was ordained Sept. 27, 1860, as pastor of South Berwick, Me., where he remained for four years. He removed to Springfield, Mass., in 1864, and became pastor of the State Street church in that city. He has held this position ever since.

Dr. Potter is endowed with a fine intellect, whose vigorous power is unsurpassed in the State which his labors have long blessed. His reading extends over a very wide range; he is one of the most cultured men in the Baptist ministry; his usefulness in Springfield and in the denomination generally is very great. As a writer he is regarded with admiration. The friends of truth wish him a long life for the exercise of his great talents in the Master's cause.

Potter, Rev. C. W., was born in Voluntown, Conn., in 1821; at the age of fourteen united with the Baptist Church; baptized by Dr. A. G. Palmer,—his first candidate; studied in Bacon Academy; licensed in Colchester in 1842; preached two years in East Haddam; ordained at Avon, Sept. 23, 1846; subsequent settlements were at North Haven, Cromwell, Lee, and Sturbridge, Mass.; at Willington, Suffield, and other places in Connecticut; has had five sons and a daughter; one son, Rev. George B., was pastor of Baptist church in Ashland, but is now dead; one son, Rev. Lester L., is now pastor at Everett, Mass.

Potter, Rev. Daniel C., was born in Stonington, Conn., March 15, 1850. He was baptized in Jersey City in 1865, into the North church. He graduated at Madison University in 1873, and was settled and ordained as pastor in the Sixth Street Baptist church, New York, in 1873.

Special public attention has been called to him by his series of illustrated lectures, by the aid of stereopticon views, on European manners, art, and architecture. By travel abroad and by correspondence he has secured photographs of rivers, pools, and baptisteries in Oriental countries, which, with the temples connected with them, make his lectures on the mode of baptism of the ancients interesting and convincing. By an invention of his own, not yet disclosed, his magic lantern gives a better representation than any other in use. His pastorate in Sixth Street is successful, and promises to be a long one. For several years he has officiated as secretary of the New York Baptist Ministers' Conference. Mr. Potter's ministry is marked by talent and spirituality.

Potter, Deacon Giles, son of Elisha P. and Abigail (Lathrop) Potter, was born in Lisbon, Conn., Feb. 22, 1829; educated in common schools and at Leicester Academy, Mass., and graduated at York College in 1855, and converted in same year; baptized by Rev. S. D. Phelps, D.D., and united with First Baptist church in New Haven; taught in the academy in East Hartford, in Connecticut Literary Institution, Suffield, and in Hill's Academy and Essex Seminary; chosen superintendent of Sunday-school in Essex in 1860, and remains in that position to the present (1880); chosen deacon in 1865, and now holds the office; represented Essex in the Legislature for three years,— from 1870 to 1873; selectman and justice of peace in Essex; school visitor for fourteen years; elected in 1873 agent of State board of education, and still holds the position; of marked abilities, energy, prudence, and fidelity.

Potter, Rev. Lester Lewis, son of Rev. C. W. Potter, was born in Colebrook, Conn., March 30, 1858; educated at Connecticut Literary Institution, and at Rochester, N. Y.; baptized at the age of ten; licensed by the Baptist church in Willington, Conn., at the age of sixteen; during studies at Rochester supplied churches in Avon and West Somerset, N. Y.; in April, 1879, settled with the Baptist church in Everett, Mass.

Potter, Rev. Walter McD., was a native of Rhode Island. He graduated the second in his class in Brown University, and pursued his theological studies in Andover and Rochester. He was the first Baptist minister in Colorado. The Baptist church at Denver was gathered under his labors. He collected the means for, and superintended in the construction of, the basement of the first Bap-

REV. WALTER M'D. POTTER.

tist house of worship, when his health failed; he returned to Providence, where he died, April 9, 1866, aged twenty-nine years and eleven months. Few men have accomplished so much in so short a time. With a remarkable foresight he secured lands in and around Denver, which he bequeathed to the Home and Foreign Mission Societies, out of which they will realize together probably nearly $100,000. On account of the great interest that he felt in the Denver church, the Home Mission Society has transferred a large portion of its share of their legacy to this church, which has enabled it to pay some $12,000 of debts, leaving a handsome balance of about as much more as a beginning towards the erection of another church edifice as a monument to its founder's memory. He was noted for positive convictions and a conscientious adherence to what he believed to be duty. He had tact to adapt himself to circumstances, so as to be successful in whatever he undertook. His life was brief, but long enough to form an established character as an able, devoted servant of Jesus Christ.

Potter, Hon. William H., was born on Potter Hill, in the town of Westerly, R. I., Aug. 26, 1816. His father, Col. Henry Potter, commanded the 3d R. I. Regiment in the war of 1812. Col. Potter was a warm friend of education, and he took great pains to secure its advantages for his only son, William. He sent him to Yale College, after he had been for years at schools and academies, that he might receive the best culture that New England could impart. He was compelled, through impaired sight, to leave Yale before he graduated, but that institution recognized his literary standing, and in 1852 bestowed upon him the honorary degree of A.M.

For many years he made teaching his profession, and he obtained such a measure of success in that calling as cheered himself and gratified his friends, and bound the hearts of throngs of the young to him for life.

By President Lincoln he was appointed assistant United States assessor of internal revenue, an office which he held for several years. He was State senator in the Connecticut Legislature from the seventh district for some time, and during that period his great worth as an instructor was abundantly proved. He was appointed chairman of the committee on education, and took an important part in the revision of the school code of his adopted State. So satisfactory were his labors in connection with legislation for education that he was appointed one of the four elective members of the State board of education. This position he held for two successive terms of four years each. He is now judge of probate for the district in which he resides. He has been for many years a deacon of the Union Baptist church of Mystic River, Conn.; loved and honored by the entire community in which he lives.

He is a vigorous Baptist. While his love for other Christians is large, his admiration for the Baptist denomination, the first community that bore the name of Christ, is unbounded. He knows the history of his religious ancestors, and can write it better than almost any other man in the "Land of Steady Habits;" he knows their principles of liberty and love, and he would like to spread them everywhere; he is a worthy man in all the relations of life.

Potts, Col. D. G., was born in Sussex Co., Va., Aug. 27, 1810, and was educated in the neighboring schools. He served for several years most efficiently as sheriff of the county, being also engaged in farming and merchandising until 1844, when he removed to Petersburg, Va., and engaged in the commission business. In 1856 he was elected treasurer of the Petersburg Railroad Company, which position he held with rare fidelity during nineteen years, up to 1875. In 1877 he was appointed by the President postmaster at Petersburg, which office he still holds. Col. Potts has always taken a deep interest in the well-being of the communities where he has lived, and his integrity and experience have made him a valuable counsellor in public affairs. He served in the city council of Petersburg from 1853 to 1868, and was senior alderman and chairman of the committee on public property during all that long period. He is as active and useful in church affairs as he is in public. In 1836 he united with the Baptist church at Newville, Sussex Co. When he removed to that neighborhood in 1834 there was but one professor of religion there. Through his efforts and the preaching of Rev. J. L. Gwaltney, a church building was erected and a church organized, and when he left there, in 1844, there was a large and flourishing congregation, and one of the most prosperous county Sunday-schools in the State. For more than forty years Col. Potts has been an active worker in the Sunday-school as teacher or superintendent, and, what is something worthy of special mention, he was never once late at school. He has also served as deacon during all his long Christian life, and in all the spheres in which he moves no man is more highly honored and justly esteemed.

Powell, Rev. Joab, was one of the most remarkably successful and eccentric preachers in Oregon. Whenever it was known that he would preach the entire population crowded to hear him. He was born in Claiborne Co., Tenn., July 16, 1799. He was baptized in 1824, and joined the Berean church; removed to Missouri; licensed in 1830, and soon after was ordained by the Salem church, which was anti-mission, while he was a missionary Baptist. Soon after he went to the Blue Springs. The county judge, Richard Stanley, said to him, as he had said to others, supposing that he also was anti-mission, "If your mission is only to preach to the sheep and lambs, you need not come here, for we have no sheep and lambs." Mr. Powell replied, "My mission is to poor sinners." The judge said, "Then you can preach for us." He did so, built a large church, and baptized 150. He continued many years as a frontier preacher; removed to Oregon in 1852; went about everywhere, sometimes acting as pastor, but was almost constantly doing the work of an evangelist. His discourses were earnest and full of sharp points. His audiences were kept in tears and smiles, and when the sermon was over he would sing, exhort, pray, and entreat by times, until the most obdurate would yield. After a long and useful life, beloved by his church, he died Jan. 25, 1873.

Powell, Rev. Robert, was a native of Massachusetts, but removed with his parents to Hamilton, N. Y., in 1805, where he experienced religion while yet a child. He commenced preaching when young, and was permitted to enjoy the service nearly sixty years. In 1817 he was one of the thirteen who in prayer together, and the offering of a dollar each to the object, organized the Hamilton Institution. He was for some years the last survivor of that honored band. Coming to Michigan in 1832, he was, until his death, in 1875, one of the most trusted and loved standard-bearers of the denomination. Highly gifted in voice and song, of an excellent spirit, with clearness of reason and native eloquence, he was a good and able minister of Christ. He died at Clinton, his home in Michigan, in his eightieth year.

Powell, Rev. Thomas.—No name is linked in more interesting ways with early Baptist history in Illinois than that of Rev. Thomas Powell. He was born, Dec. 9, 1801, in the town of Abergavenny, Monmouthshire, South Wales. In his fifteenth year he experienced conversion, and united with the Baptist church in his native town. In the year 1818 he emigrated to New York, and united with the Mulberry Street Baptist church in that city, under the pastoral care of Dr. Archibald Maclay. At that time there were in the city only six Baptist churches, namely, Gold Street, Fayette Street, afterwards called Oliver Street, Mulberry Street, Van Dam Street, Broome Street, and Anthony Street. In Brooklyn there was no Baptist church. In the year 1822, Mr. Powell was licensed by the Mulberry Street church, and although not ordained, was called out and encouraged to preach in Hoboken, Brooklyn, Newark, and other places in the vicinity. He had enjoyed advantages of education, which enabled him then to begin at once an active ministry, which may be said to date from the year named, 1822. Subsequently he was ordained, and appointed a missionary to labor at Newburgh and Cornwall, in Orange County. He was later called to the pastorate of the church in Hudson, but after some months resigned, and became pastor in Milton, Saratoga Co., where he remained in care of the church nearly ten years.

While Mr. Powell resided in Milton members of the church and others were from time to time removing to the West. This circumstance, and the representations then made as to the religious destitution of the Valley of the Mississippi, induced him, contrary to the opinion and advice of many warm friends in the church at Milton, to volunteer as missionary of the Home Mission Society. He accordingly removed to Illinois in 1836. Rev. Jonathan Going, D.D., was at that time the corresponding secretary of the society. He made his home at first in La Salle County, although the first churches organized by him were in Putnam County, at Hennepin and Granville. At this time there was no Association organized between the northern boundary of the State and Springfield save one, the Northern Association, including the one church in Chicago. Nearly all the churches now included in the Ottawa Association were organized by Mr. Powell, and some connected with other Associations. He shared also in organizing the Illinois

River Association. In the various forms of denominational activity within the State he has actively shared, while engaged during many years in fruitful missionary labors over wide districts of country. To no man is the denomination more indebted for its prosperity and growth, especially in the earlier history of the State.

Powell, Rev. T. W., was born Sept. 12, 1836, at Chesterville, O. He graduated at Denison University, Granville, O., in 1863, having paid his way mostly by teaching. He took a select course in theology at Hamilton Theological Seminary, N. Y. He became pastor at Tiffin, O., in 1865. He was called to Davenport, Iowa, in September, 1868. Here the church enjoyed almost a constant revival for a year and a half, during which time he baptized over 130 persons. From overwork in long continuous meetings his health gave way, and he resigned in the autumn of 1870. After a year's rest, during which he did some mission work at Tama City, he settled with the First Baptist church in Minneapolis, Minn., in October, 1871. After two and a half years his health failed again, and he spent a year and a half in recruiting, mostly in the South. In the summer of 1875 he once more returned to Iowa. After supplying the church at Pella for a few months, he was recalled to Davenport. After three years in a second pastorate with this church, he resigned to enter upon work at Marshalltown. Here the church has paid a cumbersome debt of many years' standing, and is enjoying prosperity.

Powell, Vavasor, was born in Radnorshire, Wales, in 1617. Through his parents he was connected with the first families in North Wales. When young he was taught the learned languages, and he became a successful student in pursuit of general knowledge. He received his university education at Jesus College, Oxford. In his youth he was the most mischievous boy in the neighborhood in which he lived. When he first officiated as an Episcopal minister, he says that "he was a reader of common prayers, in the habit of a foolish shepherd, that he slighted the Scriptures, was a stranger to secret and spiritual prayer, and a great profaner of the Sabbath."

By reading Puritan books, hearing sermons which they preached, and by conversations with them, Mr. Powell was led to the Saviour, and his heart and character were completely changed. Soon after this he forsook the Episcopal Church. His preaching now became the most powerful agency in Wales. Wherever he went multitudes waited upon his ministry, and large numbers were renewed by the Holy Spirit and became followers of the Lamb. Opposition was stirred up by his burning eloquence and his unexampled success; and in 1642 he went to London, where his popularity was nearly as great, in a little time, as it was in Wales. He received a pressing invitation to settle in Dartford, in Kent, which he accepted, and there he founded a church, and brought many souls to the Redeemer.

In 1646, Mr. Powell was frequently importuned to return to Wales. He knew its language better than he understood any other. The people regarded him as an apostle. That country seemed more free from a persecuting spirit than it had been, and its people were in the most deplorable ignorance about the salvation of the Saviour, with but few ministers to point them to the light of Christ; and having received a testimonial to his godly life, and to his "able gifts for the work of the ministry," signed by Charles Herte and seventeen members of the Westminster Assembly of Divines, he returned to Wales and resumed his labors among his countrymen. Crosby says that "he frequently preached in two or three places in a day, and he was seldom two days in a week throughout the year out of the pulpit; nay, he would sometimes ride an hundred miles in a week and preach in every place where he might have admittance, either night or day; so that there was hardly a church, chapel, or town hall in all Wales where he had not preached." He proclaimed Jesus at fairs, markets, and wherever there was a gathering of people. He preached the glorious gospel upon mountains, in jails, and even in the houses of persecuting magistrates. He was once arrested in Brecknockshire, about 10 P.M., with fifty or sixty of his hearers, and confined during the night in a church. At midnight he preached a sermon to his companions and captors from the words, "Fear not them who kill the body." During the service the most malevolent of his persecutors wept bitterly. Next morning when brought to the house of the justice that functionary was temporarily absent, and while waiting for his return Mr. Powell preached again. The justice was indignant to find his house turned into a conventicle, but two of his daughters were deeply moved by the truth which fell from the lips of the fearless man of God. Before 1660 Mr. Powell had formed more than twenty churches, of which some had two, some three, and some four or five hundred members. Mr. Powell at one time had 20,000 followers in Wales, and has been properly designated the Whitefield of that principality.

Mr. Powell was a Calvinist, holding and preaching election, effectual calling, final perseverance, full justification by faith, and the absolute need of the Divine Spirit to give a man power to will and to do the things that please God. He was also a Baptist.

He had no fear of men, or jails, or death in his heart. He was a strong republican, and he openly denounced the protectorship of Cromwell when his power was dreaded by all Europe; and Cromwell was so apprehensive of his influence that he arrested him. He spent eight years in thirteen prisons. And he died in the Fleet jail, in London, in the eleventh year of his incarceration, Oct. 27, 1671. His death was unusually blessed; the power and love of God filled his soul with enthusiasm in the miseries of a cell and in the agonies of a distressing complaint.

He was the author of nine works, one of which was a Concordance. Mr. Powell was an ardent lover of the Bible.

The footprints of Powell are seen all over Wales to-day, and many of his religious descendants have crossed the Atlantic to build up the mighty denomination whose name is dear to us, and whose liberty of conscience has given freedom to the churches of America.

Powers, Rev. J. Pike, a talented minister, and one who is greatly esteemed for his piety and usefulness, was born in Westmoreland Co., Va., Aug. 4, 1842. He removed to Kentucky in 1855, was engaged some years in mercantile business at Augusta, and was afterwards president of the Exchange Bank of Kentucky at Mount Sterling. He was educated at Augusta and Georgetown Colleges, and afterwards spent two years at the Southern Baptist Theological Seminary. He united with the Baptist church at Georgetown, Ky., in 1857, and was ordained to the ministry at Augusta in 1869, and immediately appointed missionary of Bracken Association. Among the churches he founded while acting in this capacity was the church at Mount Sterling, of which he was chosen pastor, in which capacity he has since labored. Mr. Powers has performed much missionary work, and caused to be erected three good houses of worship and one parsonage.

Pratt, Rev. Dura D., was born in Marlborough, Vt., July 13, 1806. Having removed to Worcester, Mass., he was brought under the influence of the ministry of Rev. Jonathan Going, by whom he was baptized into the fellowship of the First Baptist church in that city. Called of God, as he believed, to the ministry of his Son, he prepared himself for his work, and in 1832 was invited to take the pastorate of the Baptist church in Nashua, N. H., where he had a most successful ministry for twenty-three years, baptizing during that period not far from 600 individuals. He died of paralysis Nov. 13, 1855. "Mr. Pratt was among the best ministers of the Baptist denomination in the State of New Hampshire. He was uncompromising in his opinions and fearless in defending them, yet kind and conciliatory in treating of the views of others. He was remarkable for his clear foresight and judicious management in times of difficulty and trial. He studied to know his people and adapt his labors to their wants. He was highly evangelical and practical in his preaching, seizing on those points of Scripture with great vigor which were appropriate to the existing state of affairs." These are words of warm commendation, but justly deserved.

Pratt, John, D.D, educator, and founder of Denison University, O., was born in Windham Co., Conn., Oct. 12, 1800. He spent most of his early life on a farm and in a mill. By dint of undaunted energy and much lonely night study he succeeded in fitting himself to teach a public school. At the age of twenty he went to Amherst Academy, Mass., where he prepared for college. After spending nearly four years in Columbian College, Washington, D. C., he entered Brown University, and graduated in 1827, and, after a short professorship in Transylvania University, Ky., became pastor of the First church, New Haven, Conn. In 1831 he was principal of South Reading Academy for six months, and then accepted a call from the trustees of Granville Literary and Theological Institution to take charge of the same. In 1833 this school, then very weak and badly housed, was incorporated, and Prof. Pratt was made president. In 1837 he resigned the presidency, and became Professor of Ancient Languages, which position he retained, with slight interruptions, until 1859, when he retired to private life. In 1878 the degree of D.D. was conferred upon him by Denison University. He has been twice married. His first wife, Miss Mary Glover Corey, to whom he was married in 1830, was a sister of Mrs. Dr. B. Sears. In 1855 he married Susan C. Wheeler, of Licking Co., O.

Dr. Pratt has been one of the most prominent and foremost of Ohio Baptists. His work in Denison University is his monument. As a teacher, he was unrivaled. Dr. Turney, late of Washington, D. C., said of him that he had no superiors and but few equals in the professor's chair. His long life has been characterized by signal devotion to the cause of education and religion, and his sacrifices for these objects have been numerous and great. Taking in view the struggles of his early life, his career has been very remarkable. His closing days are being spent on his farm near Granville, the scene of his life-long toil.

Pratt, William M., D.D., was born in Madison Co., N. Y., Jan. 13, 1817. After a common school and academic preparation, he entered Hamilton University, where he took the full course in letters and theology, graduating in 1839. He married Miss Julia A., daughter of Rev. John Peck, and subsequently removed to Crawfordsville, Ind., where he preached, and taught a school for young ladies. In 1845 he took charge of the First Baptist church in Lexington, Ky., to which he ministered seventeen years. He was several years corresponding secretary of the board of the General Association of Baptists in Kentucky. In 1869 he removed to New Albany, Ind., where he preached two years to Bank Street church, after which he located in Louisville, Ky., and engaged in the book-trade, at the same time preaching on the Lord's day for Broadway and Walnut Street churches. In 1871 he became pastor of the church at Shelbyville, Ky. In a few years he returned to Lexington, where he now lives, and is supplying several churches in the vicinity. He is an able preacher, an excellent business man, and has contributed largely towards establishing Baptist interests in Kentucky.

Predestination is one of the revealed doctrines of God's Word. Moses says, "Secret things belong unto the Lord our God, but those which are revealed belong unto us and to our children forever."—Deut. xxix. 29. Predestination is frequently noticed by the inspired writers, and consequently, as a portion of God's revelation, it belongs to us. We should lovingly receive it, and try to understand it, and never slight the Mighty One by whose authority prophets, apostles, and evangelists penned the sacred writings, by attempting to argue it out of the Scriptures, or to pass it by as a dreaded mystery, of which we should not think, and which the Spirit ought not to have revealed.

$προορίζω$ in the New Testament means to predetermine, to predestinate. Paul says, "In whom also we have obtained an inheritance, being *predestinated*, according to the purpose of him who worketh all things after the counsel of his own will."—Eph. i. 11. According to this statement saints enjoy an inheritance because God predestinated them to it, and the same Almighty Ruler "worketh *all things* after the counsel of his own will," in heaven and on earth. Predestination is the foreordination of believers to heaven, and the instrumentalities by which they are to be converted, preserved, and rendered triumphant, and it is the foreordination of all the occurrences of earth. The celestial worlds are governed by laws ordained ages ago, and constraining such exact obedience that men can tell everything, with unerring certainty, about various changes that are to take place in the sun, moon, and stars from the past movements of these heavenly bodies. Calvin beautifully says, "There is no power among all the creations more wonderful or illustrious than that of the sun; for, besides his illumination of the whole world by his splendor, how astonishing it is that he cherishes and enlivens all animals by his heat; with his rays inspires fecundity into the earth; from the seeds genially warmed in her bosom produces a green herbage, which, being supported by fresh nourishment, he increases and strengthens until it rises into stalks; feeds them with perpetual exhalations till they grow into blossoms, and from blossoms to fruit, which he then by his influences brings to maturity; that trees likewise and vines by his genial warmth first put forth leaves, then blossoms, and from the blossoms produce their fruit." But the sun, and every plant and animal on earth, are governed by predestinated laws, enacted at their creation. This doctrine applies to all human events.

Speaking of the decrees of God in reference to the transactions affecting men for good or evil in this life, the celebrated Jonathan Edwards says, "Whether God hath decreed all things that ever came to pass or not, all that own the being of a God, own that he knows all things beforehand. Now it is self-evident, that if he knows all things beforehand, he either doth approve of them, that is, he either is willing they should be, or he is not willing they should be. But to will that they should be is to decree them. . . . That we should say, that God has decreed every action of men, yea, every action that is sinful, and every circumstance of those actions, that he predetermines that they shall be in every respect as they afterwards are; that he determines that there shall be such actions, and just so sinful as they are, and yet that God does not decree the actions that are sinful, *as sin*, but decrees them as good, is really consistent. For we do not mean by decreeing an action *as sinful* the same as decreeing an action so that it shall be sinful. . . . So God, though he hates a thing as it is simply, may incline to it with reference to the universality of things. Though he hates sin in itself, yet he may will to permit it for the greater promotion of holiness in this universality, including all things, and at all times. So, though he has no inclination to a creature's misery, considered absolutely, yet he may will it for the greater promotion of happiness in this universality. . . . He wills to permit sin, it is evident, because he *does* permit it."* This account of predestination is clear, almost complete, and in harmony with the Word of God. It may be summed up in these words: God governs the world by decrees of *permission* for evils, and of appointment, for proper things, and in this way he foreordains everything on earth, and is the absolute ruler of all things.

The late Dr. Richard Fuller says, "The Libertarians reject the doctrine of predestination; they deny that God has foreordained all things. But how can this negation be even mentioned without shocking our reason and our reverence for the oracles of God? I might easily show that nothing is gained by this denial, that it only removes the difficulty a little farther back. This system rejects predestination, and maintains that God has left all

---

* Works of Jonathan Edwards, ii. 525, 527, 528. London, 1840.

men to act as they choose. But what is meant by a man's acting as he chooses? It is of course that he obeys the impulses of his own feelings and passions. Well, did not God endow him with these passions? Did not God know that if certain temptations assailed the creature to whom he had given these passions he would fall? Did he not foresee that these temptations would assail him? Did he not permit these temptations to assail him? Could he not have prevented these temptations? Why did he form him with these passions? Why did he allow him to be exposed to these temptations? Why, in short,—having a perfect foreknowledge that such a being, so constituted and so tempted, would sin and perish,—why did he create him at all? None will deny the divine foreknowledge; and I at once admit that the mere foreseeing an event, which we cannot hinder, and have no agency in accomplishing, does not involve us in any responsibility. But when the Creator, of his own sovereign pleasure, calls an intelligent agent into being, fashions him with certain powers and appetites, and places him amid scenes where he clearly sees that temptations will overcome him,—in such a case it is self-evident that our feeble faculties cannot separate foreknowledge from foreordination. The denial of preordination does not, therefore, at all relieve any objection, it only conceals the difficulty from the ignorant and unthinking.

"But even if the theory of the Libertarians were not a plain evasion, it would be impossible for us to accept such a solution; for it dethrones Jehovah; it surrenders the entire government of the world to mere chance, to wild caprice and disorder. According to this system, nature, providence, are only departments of atheism; God has no control over the earth and its affairs; or, if that be too monstrous and revolting, he exercises authority over matter, but none over the minds and hearts of men. 'The king's heart is in the hands of the Lord, as rivers of water he turneth it whithersoever he will,'—such is the declaration of the Holy Spirit; but this theory rejects this truth. God exercises no control over men's hearts, consequently prophecy is an absurdity, providence is a chimera, prayer is a mockery, since God does not interfere in mortal events, but abandons all to the wanton humors and passions of myriads of independent agents, none of whose whims and impulses he restrains, by whom his will is constantly defeated and trampled under foot. A creed so odious, so abhorrent to all reason and religion, need only to be carried out to its consequences and no sane mind can adopt it."*

The Scriptural authority for this doctrine is unquestionable. Nebuchadnezzar dreams of a great image (Daniel ii.) with a golden head, the breast and the arms of silver, a brazen body and thighs, legs of iron, and feet part of iron and part of clay; a stone cut without hands destroys the image, becomes a great mountain, and fills the world. The golden head was the kingdom of Nebuchadnezzar, the silver arms the Medo-Persian empire, the brazen body the Macedonian dominion, and the iron legs, and feet partly iron and partly clay, the government of Rome. The stone cut without hands was Christ's coming kingdom and conquests that would destroy all existing empires and fill the whole world with the agencies of its universal authority. These events, except the destruction of Nebuchadnezzar's kingdom, were ages in the future, but they were predetermined and absolutely certain. The same thing was true of the second dream of the king,— the dream of the cutting down of the great tree "whose height reached unto heaven, and the sight unto the end of all the earth." It foretold the insecurity of the king and his removal from the throne for seven years; this heaven-preordained calamity fell upon the king soon after. The present condition of the Jews, and their state for ages, was preordained of God: "I will deliver them, saith the Lord, to be removed to all the kingdoms of the earth, to be a curse and an astonishment, and a hissing, and a reproach, among all the nations whither I have driven them."—Jer. xxix. 18. "I will sift the house of Israel among all nations, like as corn is sifted in a sieve, yet shall not the least grain fall upon the earth."—Amos ix. 9. Isaiah (vi. 11, 12) foretelling evils for the Jews, says, "Lord, how long? And he answered, 'Until the cities be wasted without inhabitant, and the houses without man, and the land be utterly desolate.'" "Be not dismayed, O Israel, for, behold, I will save thee from afar off, and thy seed from the land of their captivity; and Jacob shall return, and be in rest and at ease, and none shall make him afraid. I will make a full end of all the nations whither I have driven thee: but I will not make a full end of thee, but correct thee in measure; yet will I not utterly cut thee off, or leave thee wholly unpunished."—Jer. xlvi. 27, 28. The Jews have been scattered into all lands, and they are everywhere unjustly regarded as a "reproach and a hissing"; they have been sifted among the nations, but no grain of Israel has taken root in the lands of their exile; their country and their cities are desolate; he has not wholly cut off Israel, and he is evidently awaiting the right time to restore them to their country and their God. These events were predestinated and foretold thousands of years ago.

In the fifth chapter of Revelation, the Lamb standing in the midst of the throne took the wonderful book with seven seals, the book of providential decrees; for he has all power in heaven and on earth, and he opened seal after seal, ushering

---

* Baptist Doctrines, pp. 483–85. St. Louis, 1880.

in a vast train of events running over many ages; but these great issues were all predestinated, foretold, and recorded in a book before any of them became realities. Peter, addressing the Jews, says of Christ, "Him, being delivered by the *determinate counsel and foreknowledge of God*, ye have taken, and by wicked hands have crucified and slain."—Acts ii. 23. "For of a truth against thy holy child Jesus, whom thou hast anointed, both Herod and Pontius Pilate, with the Gentiles and the people of Israel, were gathered together, for to do whatsoever *thy hand and thy counsel determined before* (literally, *predestinated*) *to be done.*"—Acts iv. 27, 28. Every item in the Saviour's death occurred by the determinate counsel and foreknowledge of God, even to the carrying out of the prophetic record, "A bone of him shall not be broken." The Jews actuated by malice, Satan prompted by murderous hate, Pilate controlled by cruel selfishness, and the people misled by base slanders, demanded the Saviour's blood, and without intending or desiring it, they inflicted upon Jesus "Whatsoever God's hand and counsel determined before should be done;" and what occurred in the Saviour's death governs the whole transactions of earth; as Augustine, quoted approvingly by Calvin, says, "Nothing could be more absurd than for anything to happen independently of the ordination of God, because it would happen at random."* "Our days are determined, the number of our months is with him, he has appointed our bounds that we cannot pass, he doeth according to his will in the army of heaven, and among the inhabitants of the earth."

The Philadelphia Confession of Faith says, "God hath decreed in himself from all eternity, by the most wise and holy counsel of his own will, freely and unchangeably all things whatsoever comes to pass; yet so as thereby is God neither the author of sin, nor hath fellowship with any therein, nor is violence offered to the will of the creature, nor yet is the liberty or contingency of second cause taken away, but rather established, in which appears his wisdom in disposing all things, and power and faithfulness in accomplishing his *decree.*

"Although God knoweth whatsoever may, or can come to pass upon all supposed conditions, yet hath he not decreed anything, because he foresaw it as future, or as that which would come to pass upon such conditions."—Chap. iii. 1, 2.

The Westminster Confession of Faith† has the two clauses of the Philadelphia Confession just quoted; the only change is "ordain" for "decreed," in the first section of the Philadelphia article, and the words "in which appears his wisdom in disposing all things, and power and faithfulness in accomplishing his decree."

The seventeenth article of the Episcopal Church of England says, "Predestination to life is the everlasting purpose of God, whereby, before the foundations of the world were laid, he hath constantly decreed by his counsel, secret to us, to deliver from curse and damnation those whom he hath chosen in Christ out of mankind, and to bring them by Christ to everlasting salvation, as vessels made to honor. Wherefore they which be endued with so excellent a benefit of God be called according to God's purpose by his Spirit working in due season; they through grace obey the calling; they be justified freely; they be made sons of God by adoption; they be made like the image of his only-begotten Son Jesus Christ; they walk religiously in good works, and at length by God's mercy they attain to everlasting felicity."

Predestination, the foreordination of all the elect to heaven, and of all the instrumentalities to secure their conviction and preservation until they reach the skies, and the preappointment of all earthly occurrences, is the doctrine of all British Presbyterians, and their American religious descendants, of all regular Baptists, and of the celebrated Thirty-Nine Articles of the Episcopal Church.

In no sense does this doctrine interfere with our responsibility for our acts. The Jews on the day of Pentecost who heard from Peter that by "the determinate counsel and foreknowledge of God" they had killed the Lord, gathered no comfort from the divine predestination of the Saviour's death; on the contrary, as they heard Peter's sermon "they were pricked in their heart, and said unto Peter, and to the rest of the apostles, 'Men and brethren, what *shall we do?*'" They knew the act was theirs, and nothing in the universe could make them think otherwise.

Dr. Thomas Reid,‡ one of the most eminent mental philosophers of modern times, says, "We have by our constitution a natural conviction or belief that we act freely; a conviction so early, so universal, and so necessary in most of rational operations, that it must be the result of our constitution, and the work of him that made us. If any one of our natural faculties be fallacious there can be no reason to trust to any of them, for he that made one made all." We are conscious that a particular sin is ours; *if we cannot believe our consciousness about that, we can be sure of nothing, we must doubt everything.* Men sin because they desire to do it; they transgress without constraint, and they know it. Judas did not pretend to charge

---

* Calvin's Institutes, lib. i. cap. 16, sec. 8.
† The Constitution of the Presbyterian Church in the United States of America, p. 256. Philadelphia.

‡ Essays on the Powers of the Human Mind, vol. iii. p. 245. London, 1822.

his crime on predestination, nor did the three thousand on the day of Pentecost, and no man true to his own consciousness ever will in this or any other world.

The Scriptures assume that all sinners perpetrate their iniquities of their own free will, and hence the publican is represented by the Saviour as praying, "Lord, be merciful to me, a sinner," and the prodigal, " I have sinned against heaven and in thy sight, and I am no more worthy to be called thy son." This language would be absurdly false if the publican and prodigal were compelled by a decree of God or man to sin. If he who made a mother's heart, and gave a Saviour to die for us, by his undoubted predestination of all events compelled men to sin, there would be pity for unfortunate and unwilling transgressors in his bosom, but no pains from him for them in any world, and no day of judgment. But our *own consciousness*,—by which we are aware that we see, hear, feel pain, and have the Saviour in our affections,—the instrumentality by which we learn everything outside of ourselves, tells us that we sin of our own choice, and that the guilt is ours. It makes each of us say, "Against thee, thee only, have I sinned and done this evil in thy sight." And its statements must be true. The whole Scriptures charge their iniquities upon men, and it would indicate insanity, or a hypocrisy never developed in the most outrageous deceivers of our race, to charge them upon others than those who perpetrate them.

We do not pretend to reconcile predestination and human freedom to sin. God asserts both, and has not seen fit to show us how they agree; and while we are absolutely certain that both doctrines are true, we leave any *apparent* lack of harmony between them to the light of an eternal morning. As Dr. Richard Fuller, speaking of these two great facts, says, " I have shown that both these doctrines are true, and of course that there is no discrepancy between them. I have shown that it is impossible for us to resist either of these great truths, and it is equally impossible for our minds to reconcile them. But here, as everywhere, faith must come to our aid, teaching us to repose unquestionably upon God's veracity."

God has predestinated the continuance of harvest while the earth remaineth, but he has also predestinated the perpetual return of seed-time, and both are preappointed together. If a farmer were to say, " God has foreordained the annual coming of a harvest forever, therefore I shall sow nothing," his Scripture-reading neighbor would inform him that he had also foreordained the planting of seed just before and in connection with the predestinated harvest. "While the earth remaineth, *seed-time and harvest*, and cold and heat, and summer and winter, and day and night, shall not cease."

So is it with spiritual blessings, and the means of securing them. If a man is predestinated to eternal life, it is foreordained that he shall repent, that he shall strive to enter in at the strait gate, that he shall believe upon Jesus, that he shall lead a holy life, that he shall be a man of prayer, that he shall be anxious to lead sinners to Christ, and that he shall in some measure be faithful unto death. Paul, in his passage to Rome, when the storm was very alarming, said to his companions in peril, " there should be no loss of any man's life among you, but of the ship." God had predetermined this; but when the sailors were about to desert the vessel, he said to the soldiers and prisoners on board, " Except these abide in the ship, ye cannot be saved."—Acts xxvii. 22, 31. It was also foreordained of God that the sailors should stay and work the vessel. So is it with the saint's predestination to life eternal; with this there are the following foreordinations of God: " I am the vine, ye are the branches: He that abideth in me, and I in him, the same bringeth forth much fruit: for without me ye can do nothing. If a man abide not in me, he is cast forth as a branch, and is withered; and men gather them, and cast them into the fire, and they are burned. If ye abide in me, and my words abide in you, ye shall ask what ye will, and it shall be done unto you. Herein is my Father glorified, that ye bear much fruit; so shall ye be my disciples. Ye have not chosen me, but I have chosen you, and ordained you, that you should go and bring forth fruit, and that your fruit should remain."—John xv. 5-8, 16. And when a believer sees these evidences of predestination in himself, the words of the poet are true of him,—

" More happy, but not more secure,
The glorified spirits in heaven."

Prescott, Rev. John Q., a distinguished preacher and educator in Louisiana, was born in New Hampshire in 1820; while teaching in Alabama was ordained to the ministry; for six years at the head of a large school at Macon, Miss.; removed to Louisiana in 1852; was successively financial agent of Baptist State Convention, Professor of Mathematics in Mount Lebanon University, and principal of Mount Lebanon Female College; died in 1867.

Pressley, Judge B. C., was born in York County, S. C. He is between fifty and sixty years of age, and has long been regarded as one of the ablest lawyers in the State. Gen. Connor, for some time attorney-general of South Carolina, once said to the writer, " Mr. Pressley prides himself on his skill in planting, at which he has never succeeded, and thinks very little of himself as a lawyer. But I would as soon encounter any other man at the bar." This is not the first instance in which men of high order of talent have mistaken both their strong and their weak points. He has been a circuit judge for several years, and there is not an abler or a purer on the bench. He carries his natural urbanity and kindness into his high position as well as into private life. He is everywhere the same Christian gentleman, and never ashamed of being a Baptist.

Pressley, Judge John Gotea, was born in Williamsburg Co., S. C., May 24, 1833; descended on his father's side from the Scotch Covenanters, and on his mother's from the French Huguenots. His father was an eminent citizen and Presbyterian ruling elder. His mother, a woman of great piety. In 1851 he graduated high in his class from the South Carolina Military Academy, at Charleston. Studied law with a relative, Judge Benjamin C. Pressley, a man of great piety, through whose friendly conversation he was led to investigate the faith of Baptists, in order to vindicate the faith of his ancestors, but the result was that he became a Baptist, and joined, by baptism, the Second church of Charleston, in 1854. In June, 1854, he was admitted to the bar before he was of age, by special dispensation of Presiding Judge J. B. O'Neall, a name dear to all Baptists in South Carolina. He settled in Kingstree; joined the Baptists; helped to make the Bethlehem church respected and influential; was ordained a deacon in 1856; had a fine legal practice; became a member of the State Legislature in 1858; and at the beginning of the war, in 1861, joined the Confederate army as a captain; rose to the rank of lieutenant-colonel of 25th S. C. Vol. Regiment; commanded it in every battle but one, until disabled by wounds, and often prayed with his men around the camp-fire. He was a brave soldier. He was trustee of Furman University, a frequent member of Baptist State Conventions, and in 1868 a member of the Southern Baptist Convention at Baltimore, which inaugurated the good feeling then fast growing between Southern and Northern Baptists. In 1869 he removed to California; located at Suisun City; joined the Dixon church; entered into a lucrative practice; helped to organize California College; was a trustee and secretary of the college board until his removal to Santa Rosa, in 1873, when he joined the church there; was chosen deacon and Sunday-school superintendent, and is a leader in the church. Moderator of Association, and known everywhere as an earnest Baptist. In 1875 he was elected county judge. In 1879 he was nominated by Democrats, and indorsed by Republicans, Workingmen, and the Temperance parties for superior judge, and elected, which position he occupies with distinguished ability. There are few happier Christian homes than the one occupied by Judge Pressley and his wife at Santa Rosa, Cal.

Prevaux, Rev. Francis Edward, was born in Amesbury, Mass., in 1822, and was a graduate of Brown University in the class of 1846, and pursued his theological studies at Newton. On leaving the institution he received an appointment from the American Baptist Home Missionary Society to go to California as a missionary to the new settlements of that State. He not only preached but engaged also in the work of teaching. Although his connection with the Home Missionary Society was not of long continuance, he remained in the vocation to which he deemed himself called by the voice of Providence. Ten years were devoted to his work, when the disease which terminated fatally compelled him to return to his Eastern friends in Salisbury, Mass., where he died May 12, 1860.

Price, Rev. Jonathan D., in early life was a Presbyterian, and had studied at Princeton College. He was born and reared in New Jersey. Expecting to go as a missionary, in order to increase his usefulness he took a course in a medical college at Philadelphia. While reading the news from the Baptist missions he was led to investigate the subject of the ordinances, became a Baptist, was ordained at Philadelphia, shared with Judson the savage barbarities of Oung-pen-la, afterwards had a prospect of great influence with the king and court because of his medical skill, but died in 1828. His wife was the first female missionary laid in the grave in Burmah. This early link between the Baptists of New Jersey and foreign missions is calculated to animate zeal and activity in conquering the world for Christ.

Price, Rev. Thomas, Ph.D., was born in Breconshire, Wales, on the 17th of April, 1820. He was baptized into the fellowship of the Watergate Baptist church, Brecon, by the Rev. John Evans. At the age of twenty-one he left the rural scenes of this ancient Welsh town for the metropolis. Here he united at first with the Welsh church at Moorfields, and subsequently with the Eagle Street church, whence, in 1841, he was sent to Pontypool College to pursue his studies for the Christian ministry.

In 1845, Mr. Price was invited to assume the pastoral charge of the Calvaria Baptist church in Aberdare. It was at the time a feeble interest, and the only church of the Baptist faith (with perhaps one exception) in the whole of that vicinity. The growth of the town, in consequence of the development of large iron and coal interests, was rapid and substantial, but not more so than the growth of the Baptist cause under the vigorous administration of Mr. Price. In 1851 a new building was decided upon, with a seating capacity for 1000 hearers. The work of the succeeding ten years is unprecedented in the history of the denomination in Wales. Large and commodious churches were built at Llwydcoed, Mill Street, Cwmdare, Gadlys Ynislwyd, Aberaman, Cwmaman, Capcouch, and the edifice previously occupied by the Welsh church was fitted up and used by a flourishing English congregation.

In 1862 there were 3096 members in full communion in the Aberdare Valley, over 1000 at Calvaria, the parent church, alone. No such record of aggressive work can be instanced of any other single pastor within the boundaries of the principality.

Nor has the great strength of this indefatigable worker been confined to the interests of his own church. All the great movements of a social and political character find in him an energetic and commanding supporter. He has been, and still is, a prominent leader and moulder of public sentiment on every great question of social, national, and religious interest. The citizens have on frequent occasions testified their appreciation of his services in a befitting manner. His pleasant home is a perfect gallery of costly testimonials, indicating a life of remarkable activity and a versatility of talent rarely found in the same person.

Dr. Price has been for many years on the staff of the *Seren Gomer*, and was for a considerable period co-editor of the *Gweon*, an undenominational newspaper of wide influence. He was likewise joint editor of the *Gweithewo*, a social and political paper, devoted mainly to the interests of the working classes. He was principal promoter and one of the editors of the *Gwyliedydd* and the *Medelwo Iewane*, and was for many years chief editor of the *Seren Cymru*, the leading organ of the Welsh Baptists in the principality.

As lecturer and preacher, Dr. Price is known throughout the length and breadth of Great Britain. His realistic power is remarkable. He speaks of the remote past with a quaint familiarity which sometimes borders on the grotesque, but which is immensely effective on the popular mind. The simple narratives of Scripture seldom glow with a purer lustre than when garnished with his peculiar genius. In every form of descriptive speech he is an accomplished master.

Long life and a glory-tinted old age to the veteran who has been so true and brave in the moral and spiritual conflicts of his country and his times!

Price, Rev. Thomas Jones, was born in the town of Hay, Breconshire, North Wales, March 9, 1805; came with his parents to America in 1818, and settled in Clark Co., O.; was converted at the age of fifteen, and soon after began to preach, being then known as the boy preacher. His work was for the most part within the bounds of the Mad River Association, Ohio, over which he presided for thirty-nine years, and in which he exercised a controlling influence. He was somewhat eccentric in his methods of work, and had a special liking for the itinerant system, preaching at the same time for a number of churches. Being blessed with a competency, it was his delight to supply feeble churches, to help the poor, and to give to the cause of missions at home and abroad. Under the title of "Elder" Price he was known far and near, and is remembered most affectionately by thousands of people. He died April 15, 1876, and was buried at Urbana, O.

Prichard, John, D.D., was born in the parish of Llaneilian, near Amlwch, Wales, in the month of March, 1796. He was led to the acceptance of the Baptist faith from hearing a sermon preached by a distinguished Calvinistic Methodist (Rev. John Prytherch) on the sufferings of Christ, from the text, "I have a baptism to be baptized with, and how am I straitened until it is accomplished?" He was immersed by the Rev. Thomas Rees Davies. He entered the college at Abergavenny at the age of twenty-five. His first and only settlement was Llangollen. He was a most indefatigable worker in the cause of Christ. His influence was felt more widely than that of any other pastor in the northern counties of the principality for many years. He labored diligently to establish an English church in Llangollen, and not without effect. In 1862 a college for the training of young men for the Christian ministry was established largely through his influence, of which he became the president.

Dr. Prichard wrote much for the press. Early in his ministry he started a monthly magazine for the use of Baptist Sunday-schools, called *Yr Athraw* (The Teacher), which he conducted single-handed for many years. He likewise published a compendium of doctrines, called "The First Catechism," upwards of thirty thousand copies of which were sold, not to mention the reprint of the same in this country. Many pamphlets of great value were likewise the production of his pen.

He was an able and instructive preacher. Many of his contemporaries exceeded him in brilliancy, but in sanctified common sense and exalted piety he was unsurpassed. Few men served their age more faithfully and well. He died on the 7th of September, 1875, in his eightieth year.

Prichard, Rev. John Lamb, was born in Pasquotank Co., N. C. Prof. John Armstrong found him, at the age of twenty-three, a carpenter, and awakened in him a thirst for knowledge. The next year, 1835, he presented himself at Wake Forest Institute, then a manual labor school, with his kit of tools on his shoulder, and asked the privilege of working for an education. In 1840 he graduated with honor, spent a year as master of an academy in Murfreesborough, N. C., and then, at the instance of the Rev. John Kerr, settled as pastor of the Danville Baptist church, in Virginia. Here he remained ten years, preaching a part of the time for the churches of Yanceyville and Milton, in North Carolina. In 1852 he removed to Lynchburg, Va., where for four years he labored with intense ardor and distinguished success.

In 1856 he became pastor of the First Baptist church of Wilmington, N. C., and at once entered upon the enterprise of erecting a new house of worship. He was not permitted to finish this work, but he lived long enough to see that his labors would be rewarded by giving the Baptists of Wilmington the handsomest church structure in the State.

In 1862 the little blockade steamer "Kate" brought the yellow fever to Wilmington, and among its last and noblest victims was this great and good man. He died a hero and a martyr, and his virtues have been fittingly commemorated in an admirable memoir by the Rev. J. D. Hufham, D.D. Mr. Prichard was twice married, first to Miss Mary B. Hinton, of Wake Co., N. C. His second wife was Miss Jane, eldest daughter of Dr. James B. Taylor, of Richmond, Va. His eldest son, Robert, graduated at Wake Forest College, and was an accepted missionary to China, where he died. His eldest daughter, Mary, is the wife of Prof. Charles E. Taylor, of Wake Forest College.

Prime, Rev. George M., was born in Vermont in 1802; received a liberal education, and entered upon the practice of medicine first in Mississippi and Louisiana. In 1830 he settled in Little Rock, Ark., where he continued some years, and then removed to Camden. He became a Baptist about 1858, while practising his profession in Franklin Parish, La. He was soon after ordained to the ministry, and in a few years returned to Arkansas and devoted himself entirely to the ministry. Dr. Prime was a fine writer, and at one time paid much attention to art as an amateur portrait-painter. He died at Eldorado, Ark., March 1, 1869.

Prince Edward Island Baptists.—See article on Nova Scotia Baptists.

Prior, Rev. John Thomas, a native of Georgia, was born in Madison, Morgan Co., Feb. 27, 1847. At the age of fifteen he was immersed, and joined the Bethlehem church, of which his father was an honored deacon. At the age of twenty-one he entered Mercer University, and graduated from the full course in 1870. He began preaching early in life, under a license from the Bethlehem church. In 1871 he was ordained, and engaged in teaching in important schools of the South. In 1872 he accepted a call from the Dixon church, California, acting as associate pastor for fifteen months. In 1874 he was pastor at Grand Island. The next five years he was pastor of the Hopewell and Woodland churches. In California he gained general confidence as a writer, and was cordially welcomed to the business and editorial control of the *Evangel*, the duties of which he assumed in 1879. As a pastor and preacher he has been very successful.

Pritchard, T. H., D.D., was born in Charlotte, N. C., Feb. 8, 1832; baptized by Dr. W. T. Burke in 1849; graduated at Wake Forest College in 1854; served the college one year as agent; was ordained pastor of Hartford church, N. C., November, 1855, Dr. Wm. Hooper preaching the sermon; read theology for a while with Dr. J. A. Broadus, in Charlottesville, Va.; was pastor of the Franklin Square church of Baltimore from January, 1860, to July, 1863; filled the pulpit of First church, Raleigh, N. C., from November, 1863, to May, 1865, during the absence of pastor, Dr. T. E. Skinner, in

T. H. PRITCHARD, D.D.

Europe; settled as pastor of First church, Petersburg, Va., in July, 1865; resumed care of the Raleigh church in February, 1868, and remained in this position till called to the presidency of Wake Forest College, in July, 1879. For seven years Dr. Pritchard was chairman of the Board of Missions of State Convention; and was for several years associate editor of *Biblical Recorder*. He received the title of D.D. from the University of North Carolina in 1868. His father, Rev. J. P. Pritchard, has lived in Texas for twenty-five years.

Dr. T. H. Pritchard is doing a noble work for Wake Forest College, and his great ability and piety qualify him for eminent success in any department of ministerial labor.

Progress of Baptist Principles in other Denominations.—The Baptists have increased at a rate within a hundred years which is fitted to excite astonishment. In 1784 we had 471 churches and 35,101 members in this country, now we have 26,060 churches and 2,296,327 members. But our principles have spread very widely in other religious communities.

Ever since the Saviour said, "My kingdom is not of this world; if my kingdom were of this world, then would my servants *fight*," Baptists have repudiated the connection between church and state, by which the latter supports the former. About the middle of the seventeenth century the Quakers and Baptists were severely persecuted in Massachusetts, and numbers of both communities were banished. "Toleration was preached against as a sin in rulers, that would bring down the judgment of heaven upon the land. Mr. Dudley (the deputy governor) died with a copy of verses in his pocket, of which the two following lines make a part—

'Let men of God, in court and churches, watch
O'er such as do a *toleration* hatch.'"*

John Adams, subsequently President of the United States, while he was at the Continental Congress, in 1774, declared that it was against the consciences of the people of Massachusetts to make any change in their laws about religion; that Israel Pemberton the Quaker, and Isaac Backus the Baptist minister, who were seeking deliverance for their brethren, suffering imprisonment in Massachusetts jails for their religious opinions, might as well think they could change the movements of the heavenly bodies as alter their religious laws.† This was the doctrine of American Congregationalists during the struggle for independence.

In Virginia the Episcopal state church levied taxes to support her ministry, with an oppressive severity from the settlement of the colony down to the time when Revolutionary liberty and Baptist and Presbyterian growth deprived her of her unjust exactions. But after this an insidious effort was made to pass an assessment law, by which each man should be compelled to pay a tax to support his own minister. Patrick Henry‡ favored the assessment, and Washington and John Marshall, the future chief justice of the United States,§ and the Presbyterian ministers of Virginia, and, of course, the Episcopal Church. But the Baptists and Presbyterian laymen finally secured the rejection of the assessment in 1785. Thomas Jefferson, the great friend of liberty in worshiping God for the Baptists of Virginia, says, in a letter to Dr. Rush, "There was a hope confidently cherished about 1800 that there might be a state church throughout the United States, and this expectation was specially cherished by Episcopalians and Congregationalists."‖

To-day, in our broad country, in every denomination of Protestants, the Baptist doctrine, that religion should be free from state guardianship and financial support, is universally accepted.

In the time of Jonathan Edwards, one of the greatest of American thinkers, and one of the most devout Christians that ever ministered in a Congregational meeting-house, his church in Northampton, Mass., admitted to the Lord's Supper "those who really rejected Jesus Christ and disliked the gospel way of salvation in their hearts, and knew that this was true of themselves;" and the church had a method of admitting such members "without lying and hypocrisy." This system "spread very much among ministers and people in that county and in other parts of New England."¶ When Mr. Edwards, in 1749, felt compelled to take the ground that none but real Christians have a right to come to the Lord's Supper, his Baptist platform for the communion table created a great ferment throughout the town, and a general cry for his dismissal was heard, and the next year he was driven from a church where the Lord had so signally honored his ministry. Isaac Backus brought the same charge against the First Congregational church of Norwich, Conn., in 1745. As Dr. Hovey relates it, "Men who entertained no hope themselves, and who gave no evidence to others that they had been renewed by the Spirit of God, were often, if not generally, admitted to all the privileges and ordinances of the Christian church."** This system, out of which Unitarianism grew in New England, was a wide-spread and malignant evil one hundred and thirty years ago.

The Presbyterian Church in America was in the same situation. The Larger Catechism of that church says of baptism, "Whereby the parties baptized are solemnly *admitted into the visible church*, and enter into an open and professed engagement to be wholly and only the Lord's."†† In the time of Edwards this article, framed by the Westminster Assembly, was in full force, the child of church members was admitted into the church by baptism, and in youth on merely repeating the catechism, without any reference to a new heart, was permitted to go to the Lord's table. Curtis states that at the time when Princeton Seminary was founded, "so far from conversion being es-

---

* Grimshaw's History of the United States, pp. 57, 58. Philadelphia, 1836.
† Life and Works of John Adams, ii. 399.
‡ Wirt's Life of Patrick Henry, p. 263. Hartford.
§ Rives's Life and Times of James Madison, i. 601–2.

‖ Memoirs, Correspondence, etc., iii. 341. Charlottesville, 1829.
¶ Works of Jonathan Edwards, i. Pref. clvii. London, 1840.
** Life and Times of Isaac Backus, p. 44. Boston, 1859.
†† The Constitution of the Presbyterian Church, pp. 341–42. Presbyterian Board of Publication Philadelphia.

teemed necessary to full communion, it was a matter of formal discussion whether it was proper to require the credible profession of a change of heart in the ministry, and considered that it was not. Yet even now there is nothing in their Confession of Faith to prevent the reception of unconverted persons as communicants. The Established Church of Scotland, with a similar confession [the same], does not require conversion."*

As late as the Revolution the Episcopalians were lamentably indifferent about the conversion of the clergy as a qualification for their sacred office, and about the regeneration of the laity as a needful preparation for the Eucharist.

In our day the Congregational ministry and membership stand on the Saviour's platform of conversion. No one can unite with the Presbyterian Church of this country without satisfying the minister and elders that he has a new heart. And even in evangelical congregations of the Episcopal Church the godly rector in preparing his "confirmation class" for the bishop will exercise much vigilance to see that each of them is born "from above."

Infant baptism is suffering from a rapid decline. In the time of Edwards every infant in the colonies, whose parents were not Baptists or Quakers, was duly christened shortly after birth, just as every similar child in England is baptized in our day. But with us now there are hosts of unsprinkled children whose parents are pious Pedobaptists. Many of the most devoted members of non-Baptist communities leave their children to select their own form of baptism when they are converted. Curtis, whose work was published in 1855, among other evidences of the decline of infant baptism quotes from a "recent number" of the *Journal of Commerce* the statement of its Boston correspondent, who says, " In our Congregational churches we fear that there is considerable indifference and neglect in reference to infant baptism. In one of our oldest churches in this State there had not been a few years since an instance of infant baptism for the seven preceding years. Last year there were seventy Congregational churches in New Hampshire that reported no infant baptisms. This year ninety-six churches report none. If this indifference continues the ordinance will become extinct in the Congregational churches."

In 1827, Curtis states that there was one infant baptized in the Presbyterian Church in the United States to every $13\frac{1}{5}$ communicants, and in 1853 the tables of the Old and New School Presbyterians being counted together, infant baptism had decreased from $13\frac{1}{5}$ to $22\frac{3}{10}$. This is a reduction of not quite a half in a few years.† Among the Methodists the ceremony is treated with even less consideration, and the decay is still in rapid progress.

Our principles have invaded the churches of our brethren of the evangelical denominations, and they have expelled state-churchism from every one of them; they have shown them the Saviour's grand doctrine that a church should be composed of converted members, which has been adopted extensively, and they are breathing a withering decline over the practice of infant baptism. In our own denominational fold, by the blessing of God, we have gathered a host of converts and trained them for the highest usefulness. We have reared many noble institutions of learning, sent out missionaries whom God has greatly blessed, and exerted a powerful influence in favor of true liberty on the State and National institutions of our country, and outside of it in America our work has been almost as great. And it is likely that our influence in other denominations will continue, and even spread, until " alien baptisms" will equal Baptist immersions, and children will be relieved from the initiatory rite altogether, and one great fold will embrace the whole regenerated followers of the Lamb.

Proper, Rev. Datus D., was born in Van Buren Co., Iowa, Jan. 31, 1844. In 1862, during his academic course at Mount Pleasant, he entered the army and served three years. In January, 1866, he united with the Baptist Church. He afterwards engaged for a time in teaching school and farming, and while thus occupied he was impressed with the conviction that it was his duty to preach the gospel. In 1872 he was ordained. In 1873 he went to the Theological Seminary, Chicago, where he graduated from the special course in 1875. In 1875 he settled as pastor at Ames, Iowa, where he remained two years. During this time 56 were added to the church. In 1877 he accepted a call to the church at Iowa Falls. He resigned this pastorate to become State Sunday-School missionary of the American Baptist Publication Society and of the Iowa Baptist State Convention. He gave to this work fifteen months of earnest and successful labor, and then returned to the pastorate, settling with the East Des Moines Baptist church, his present field of labor.

Proselyte Baptism of the Jews is still a living institution, and occasionally in the United States it is administered. Dr. Lightfoot says that " As soon as the proselyte grows whole of the wound of circumcision they bring him to baptism, and placed in the water, they again instruct him in some weightier and in some lighter commands of the law; which being heard, he plunges himself, and comes up, and behold he is an Israelite indeed in all things." To explain what the plunging is he quotes from Maimonides, " Every person baptized must dip his whole body, now stripped and made

---

* Progress of Baptist Principles, p. 66. Boston, 1855.
† Idem, pp. 131-35. Boston, 1855.

naked, at one dipping." (Whole Works, vol. xi. pp. 59, 61. London, 1826.) This complete dipping is still required for a Pagan or a Christian embracing Judaism. (The Baptism of the Ages, p. 192. Publication Society, Philadelphia.)

Proudfoot, Rev. Richard, was born in the city of London in 1770. He came to America prior to the war of 1812, and became a student under the celebrated Dr. Staughton, of Philadelphia. Soon after his course of preparatory study for the work of the ministry, he settled in Cambria County, when that section was almost an unbroken wilderness. His field of labor stretched over the Alleghanies and eastward to Huntingdon, Stone Creek, Mill Creek, Shirleysburg, and parts adjacent. In all these places the fruits of his labor are very apparent in churches still existing. He traveled over this immense region, sometimes on foot or in the saddle, amid all conditions of weather, until called home to his reward, May 2, 1845, aged seventy-five years. His place of burial is at Three Springs, Huntingdon County. Brother Proudfoot stands among the honored band of twenty-six ministers, from eleven different States, who assembled in Philadelphia, May 18, 1814, and organized the Baptist Triennial Convention, and, at the same time, recognized and appointed Judson and Rice as missionaries in Burmah.

Providence.—That God created the world and everything in it we assume, and that he exercises dominion over these works of his hands his Word unmistakably teaches. His government of the world is plainly to be inferred from the vast and diversified interest he has shown in summoning it into existence. The maker of a powerful engine, requiring great skill and patient toil, would not leave it at work without superintendence, and without protection from the efforts of the evil disposed, who might readily destroy its efficiency. Jehovah has complete control of the world and all its movements, and his government is in continual exercise for the best interests of our race.

The supreme *reason* for each earthly act is the order of Jehovah. We do not speak of the *causes* of events, but the *reasons*, without which they cannot exist in this world. God has two classes of orders, *decrees of permission and decrees of appointment*. By the former he allows men and demons to commit acts of wrong which they have planned, and for the conception and execution of which they are solely responsible. By the latter he directly ordains the existence of pure and merciful events. And by these two classes of divine orders Jesus rules the world. Job's experience furnishes an illustration of God's decrees of permission and of appointment. When Satan turned the fury of the tornado upon the house in which his children were feasting, and his sons were killed, he said, "The Lord gave and the Lord hath taken away, blessed be the name of the Lord." By divine *appointment* Job's sons came to him ; by divine *permission* Satan destroyed his young men, and Job recognizes the dominion of God in both events. The Saviour says, "All power is given unto me in heaven and in earth." The word power ($\dot{\varepsilon}\xi o v\sigma \acute{\iota}\alpha$) used by Matthew means authority, sovereignty, dominion. Christ, then, has entire control of the birds of the air, the fish of the sea, the beasts of the field, and the whole movements of human beings, and of all the elements, and of all the worlds, of everything, and of every one that can influence mortals favorably, unfavorably, or indifferently. He received this authority to use it, and he cannot be unfaithful to his trust. " He doeth according to his will in the army of heaven, and among the inhabitants of the earth."

Instruments of the Saviour's Providential Government.—He uses what we call *accidents as the instruments* of his providential government. When the voice of God arrested the knife with which Abraham was going to kill Isaac, he found a ram caught in a thicket ready for the altar from which his only son was released. No human being enticed the ram to the thicket, or drove, or bound it there; Jehovah drew it by the attractive shrubs, or the sweet grass, and unconsciously it pressed forward until its horns were firmly held by the tangled brush ; and by this apparent accident the Lord provided for the necessities of Abraham's situation, as he has done myriads of times since for the needs of others.

The *worst crimes of men are instruments* of God's government. The special love which Jacob cherished for Joseph stirred up the fierce malice of his brothers, and at first they proposed to murder him, and then they concluded to sell him into slavery and tell his father that a wild beast had killed him. A band of Ishmaelites going down to Egypt, no doubt knowing that he was as free as themselves, agreed to buy him and to aid his brothers in their great crime. When Potiphar bought Joseph the wickedness of his wife soon covered the young Hebrew with infamy and cast him into prison. Three parties, by as many distinct iniquities, lent their aid to place Joseph in jail. There he interpreted the dream of a high officer in Pharaoh's palace, he in process of time mentioned Joseph to the king, whose mysterious visions he explained, and Joseph became governor of all Egypt, and saved its people and the inhabitants of the adjacent countries, including his father and brothers, from the horrors of a seven years' famine. The basest passions of men's hearts are often turned by Jehovah into channels of benevolence.

Henry VIII., of England, wrote a book against Luther, and was the strongest partisan of the papacy in Europe. But the Lord determined to bring him and his people from the odious tyranny of Rome. Henry fell in love with a young lady of his court, and for certain reasons he sought a divorce from his wife Catherine; the pope was afraid to offend Charles V., a near relative of the queen, and a neighbor of his holiness, and he refused Henry's application. The king secured a divorce from his Parliament and married Anne Boleyn. Upon the new marriage the wrath of papal Europe was expended, and Queen Anne, who loved the Bible, led her husband and his kingdom into the ranks of the Reformation. Before, and since, the Jews, out of envy and hatred, were employed by Jehovah to shed the blood of atonement and to purchase our redemption by the wounds they inflicted upon Jesus; in innumerable cases God has used the dark passions of men to execute his plans of love.

The *towering ambition of men* is another agency of his providence. The Medes were once lying outside of Babylon, resolved to increase their glory and their empire by the capture of the mightiest and most magnificent city on earth. Within its walls their power and threats were regarded with contempt. One night the king made a great feast for a thousand of his lords, and during the joyful excitement the sacred vessels carried from the temple of God in Jerusalem by the plundering Babylonians were brought to the favored guests, and they drank wine out of them in honor of the gods of Babylon, and they blasphemed Jehovah. Soon the terrible hand and writing were seen, and speedily the ambitious Medes were in that palace, and that night guilty Belshazzar was slain, and Darius sat upon his throne.

The *suggestions of Jehovah* influence men to perform the behests of his providence. Just as evil spirits can make suggestions in our minds without our knowledge of their presence, so can Jehovah. When Achan concealed the precious metals and the rich robe at the capture of Jericho, his brethren knew nothing of his crime. The rout at Ai proclaimed the fact that some one had sinned, but said nothing about the transgressor. The lots were cast, and Achan was unmasked and he confessed. But the suggestions of God himself were required to guide those who cast the lots. So when Haman was going to hang Mordecai, the man of God, the night before the king's consent was to be solicited, Ahasuerus could not sleep, and instead of music or wine he had the chronicles of his kingdom read, and, singularly enough, that section of them narrating that Mordecai had saved the king from assassination, and that he had never been rewarded. Mordecai was honored the next morning by Haman leading him through the principal street of Babylon with the king's crown upon his head and a royal robe around him, and making proclamation that he was the man whom the king delighted to honor. God disturbed the king that sleepless night; he suggested the chronicles of his kingdom, and the section about Mordecai, and his providence protected his life and honored him. It was Jehovah that suggested modern missions to William Carey, and by suggestion, beyond all doubt, harvests of acts of God's government are summoned into life. These are some of the agencies employed by divine providence.

Character of the Government.—It *applies to everything* affecting human life, even the smallest matters. The Saviour says, "Are not two sparrows sold for a farthing? And one of them shall not fall on the ground without your Father; but the very hairs of your head are all numbered; fear ye not, therefore, ye are of more value than many sparrows."—Matt. x. 29–31. From the falling of a sparrow to the jar which makes a globe tremble the Saviour's providence controls everything.

It *rules everything wisely*. The wheels of providence, according to Ezekiel, are full of eyes, and they give such abundance of knowledge that there is no room for mistakes; and, according to the same writer, the God-man, enthroned, sat on a crystal firmament, watching every movement of the great wheels of providence, and rendering mistakes impossible. The Stamp Tax and the Tea Duty created the American Revolution, extended and secured the liberties of this land, and have made our country a miracle of progress, without a parallel in human history. Our independence gave the Reform Bill and vastly extended liberty to England and to all her colonies. It gave freedom to all the republics on this side of the Atlantic; and it has given the same blessing to France and Italy, and, in some measure, to Spain, Prussia, and Austria. The providence of God makes no mistakes.

It *draws blessings from all sources*. The foul waters that flow from the sewers of a large city reach the river and the ocean, and the sun draws them up in vapors into the clouds, but in their journey they lose everything poisonous and offensive, and they descend in sweet rains to fill the fountains and the rivers. So the events of providence are all turned into favors for the children of God, "*All things* work together for good to them that love God, to them that are the called according to his purpose." "No weapon that is formed against them shall prosper." While the hands that were pierced with the nails of Calvary hold the reins of earthly movements, started by material, satanic, or human agencies, the child of God is safe; his wants shall be supplied, and his Master will continually, as well as finally, give him the victory.

Providence, First Baptist Church of, was

founded in 1639. This ancient church has a grand history, and deserves a conspicuous place in the "Baptist Encyclopædia." In March, 1639, Ezekiel Holliman baptized Roger Williams. Mr. Williams, immediately after, immersed him and ten others. The church was constituted at this time. Mr. Williams, whose ministerial character was recognized by his brethren in receiving baptism from him instead of Mr. Holliman, after he submitted to the rite, became the minister of the infant community. Some time afterwards he withdrew from them, and was succeeded by Chad Brown, a man of steadfastness, wisdom, and great influence, the founder in America of the distinguished Brown family of Providence, one of whom, Nicholas, gave his name to our oldest university. William Wickenden followed Chad Brown as pastor of the First church of Providence. Gregory Dexter, after Wm. Wickenden, held the same position. Thomas Olney took charge of the church after Mr. Dexter. The Rev. Pardon Tillinghast ministered to the old church after Mr. Olney. This generous man gave his ministerial services for nothing, and at his own expense built a house of worship and presented it as a gift to the church. Ebenezer Jencks was the successor of Pardon Tillinghast, his ministry continuing some seven years. The little church, like a good many other small churches, had its controversies. The question which disturbed it was one to which is attached very little importance in these days. It was whether the "laying on of hands" was necessary to constitute a person a valid member of a church formed, as was believed, after the divine apostolic model. James Brown, the grandson of Chad, succeeded Ebenezer Jencks, and Samuel Winsor followed him. In 1726 a better and more commodious house of worship was erected, through the zeal and enterprise of some of the members of the church, and under the ministry of Samuel Winsor, Jr., the discordant elements appeared to be blending more harmoniously together.

"For one hundred and thirty years," says the historical sketch prepared by Dr. Caldwell and Prof. William Gammell, "the church has been going on, receiving neither from within nor without any strong impulse. Its ministers were natives, bred on the spot, generally advanced in years, at work for their daily bread, and with no special training. The church had been content with their unpaid services, and with such growth as came. It had a small meeting-house. It had but 118 members in a population of 4000, with 400 families. The time had come for advance and enlargement."

The establishment of Rhode Island College, as it was then called, in Providence, and the coming to the town of so gifted a scholar and so eloquent a preacher as Rev. James Manning, the first president of the college, were the harbingers of better days to the church. The weight of Mr. Manning's influence was thrown in the scale against those who insisted on "the imposition of hands" being a prerequisite to full church membership. Mr. Winsor and those who sympathized with him withdrew from the church, determined to have no fellowship with those who either denied or questioned the permanent obligation of those who were to enter a Christian church " passing under hands," as it was termed. Dr. Manning had the rare gift of enlisting the sympathy and co-operation of others in aiding him to carry out the plans upon the accomplishment of which he set his heart. He elevated the tone of public sentiment in the matter of sustaining religious worship. A house "for the public worship of Almighty God, and also for holding commencement in," was erected. Modeled after that of "St. Martin-in-the-Fields" in London, it is a gem of architectural beauty, which even to this day wins the admiration of all persons of good taste, and will ever remain as an illustration of the large benevolence and the generous self-sacrifice of those who were chiefly instrumental in rearing a structure of such noble dimensions and eminent fitness for the purposes for which it was built. It cost not far from £7100, a sum which represents, we venture to say, more than twice that amount in these days.

President Manning died July 29, 1791, in the fifty-fourth year of his age. In spite of the heavy weight of care which rested on him as the presiding officer of an institution which was struggling for life, no ministry of the church in all its previous history had been so successful as his. Although he never regarded himself, in the proper sense of the word, as the pastor of the church, he performed for it a service of great value, and left an impress upon it which is felt to this day.

The pastorate of the next minister, Rev. John Stanford, and that of his successor, the eloquent Maxcy, were of comparatively brief duration. Upon the election of Maxcy to the presidency of the college, a nephew of President Manning, the Rev. Stephen Gano, M.D., was called to succeed him. His ministry continued for thirty-five years, and was blessed as that of few servants of Christ has been. Remarkable revivals attended his preaching. The first one of them, that of 1820, brought an addition of 147 persons to the church by baptism. Dr. Gano died Aug. 18, 1828. The church more than quadrupled during the pastorate of Dr. Gano.

Rev. Robert Everett Pattison was called to fill the important place made vacant by the death of his predecessor, and entered upon the duties of his office March 21, 1831. For a little more than five years he preached and performed the work of a pastor with distinguished success, in building up his people in Christian knowledge and the development of the graces of the Christian character. Such a ministry as that of Dr. Pattison's was most fruitful for good, and its results are felt down to the present hour. Called to the presidency of Waterville College, now Colby University, he resigned his office Aug. 11, 1836. Rev. William Hague was elected pastor of the church June 1, 1837, and sustained that relation to it a little more than three years. Over one hundred persons were received into the fellowship of the church by baptism and by letter during his ministry. Upon the resignation of Dr. Hague, Dr. Pattison for a short time performed again the duties of pastor, when his election as one of the secretaries of the Baptist Board of Foreign Missions once more dissolved his connection with the people of his charge. His successor, whose memory is still so greatly revered in Providence, was the Rev. James Nathaniel Granger, who commenced his labors Nov. 13, 1842, and remained pastor of the church until his death, which occurred Jan. 5, 1857. Having been appointed in connection with Dr. Solomon Peck as one of a deputation to visit the Baptist missionary stations in the East, he was absent from his people a little more than a year and a half. The larger part of this time the pastoral care of the church devolved on the Rev. John Calvin Stockbridge, until his call to succeed the venerable Dr. Sharp as pastor of the Charles Street church, in Boston, brought the engagement to a close. During the remainder of Dr. Granger's absence the Rev. Francis Smith supplied the pulpit. After the return of Dr. Granger from the East, the Rev. William Carey Richards was his assistant for a brief period, until the formation of the Brown Street church, of which he was chosen the pastor, dissolved the connection. The Rev.

FIRST BAPTIST CHURCH, PROVIDENCE, R. I.

Francis Wayland, D.D., on the death of Dr. Granger, acted as pastor of the church for somewhat more than a year with rare fidelity, and the most conscientious application to the discharge of the duties of what he ever regarded as the most solemn and responsible position to which a mortal can be called, that of a minister of the Lord Jesus Christ. The Rev. Samuel Lunt Caldwell, who for twelve years had been the pastor of the First Baptist church in Bangor, Me., was invited to become the pastor of the church. He commenced his ministry in Providence June 13, 1858, and ended it Sept. 7, 1873. His pastorate covered a period of more than fifteen years, and was closed that he might accept the professorship of Church History in the Newton Theological Institution. The successor of Dr. Caldwell was the present pastor, the Rev. Edward Glenn Taylor, D.D., who commenced his labors April 18, 1875.

The above sketch presents but a meagre outline of the history of what in some respects may be regarded as one of the most prominent Baptist churches in the country. As one proof of the influence for good which has gone forth from it, it is stated that since 1775 sixty ministers of the gospel have been connected with it, besides its pastors, in addition to fifty persons who have received license of the church to preach, all of whom have entered the ministry. Nearly all of these persons have been connected with the college as officers or students.

For more than one hundred years the First church of Providence has enjoyed an unusual amount of peace. In 1774 there was a signal illustration of this union. The church wished to erect the noble edifice to which allusion has already been made, a house 80 feet square, with a spire 196 feet high, a magnificent structure for the 4321 persons who then dwelt in Providence. In such a great enterprise every one commonly has advice to give, and opinions to be respected; John Brown, however, the brother of the celebrated Nicholas, was appointed "a committee of one" to build one of the most spacious and beautiful temples for the worship of God in America. Unity of purpose and feeling have characterized this community in an extraordinary measure for many years.

Patriotism has had its warmest friends in the First church. John Brown, the "committee of one," was a fair representative of the people for whom he built a house of worship. He owned twenty vessels at the commencement of the Revolutionary war, every one of which was likely to be captured or destroyed by the British fleet, if he opposed the measures of the mother-country, and he uttered his Declaration of Independence four years before the document of Jefferson was issued. He destroyed the British armed schooner "Gaspee" in June, 1772, which was sent from Boston to enforce obnoxious revenue laws in Narragansett Bay; Lieut. Duddingston was wounded in the encounter which resulted in the blowing up of his vessel; and his blood was really the first shed in the war of independence.

This church never began to prosper thoroughly until it gave a stated income to its pastors. Nicholas Brown, whose gifts to Brown University amounted to nearly $160,000, belonged to the congregation of this church; and his munificent donations to advance higher education have raised up for it liberal friends in all denominations. Many of the first men in Rhode Island have descended from the pastors and members of the First church.

In the words of the historical sketch to which reference has been made, "For three-quarters of a century this church stood alone, or the same as alone, the only church of its own persuasion, or perhaps of any persuasion, within the large territory then included in the town of Providence. It has held its place and held on its way while a populous city has grown around it, and churches of many names have multiplied on every side. It has twelve sisters of the same polity and faith, all of them organized since the beginning of the present century; the thirteen having 3377 members. Eighty-eight churches, of at least thirteen different denominations, the major part of which have arisen since that time, now occupy the ground where once and for two generations it stood alone. It was either the first in this country, or it stood side by side with Newport in the van of a numerous succession of similar churches, amounting in 1880 to 26,060, with 2,296,327 members."

Pruett, Rev. William Harrison, is one of the pioneer Baptist preachers in Eastern Oregon and Washington Territory, where since his ordination, in 1871, he has traveled extensively, preached the gospel in new settlements, organized many new churches and baptized many converts; labored as pastor or missionary at Weston, Mount Pleasant, Pilot Rock, Walla Walla, Dayton, Pendleton, Butte Creek, Meadowville, Mountain Valley, Heppner, and other places; built several church edifices; and has been one of the most influential and successful laborers in all that new and needy field. He is still in the vigor of manhood. He has a good education, having studied at Jefferson Academy and McMinnville College, Oregon. At the age of three years he removed from Ray Co., Mo., where he was born, to Oregon, in 1847. In 1861 he professed Christianity, and was baptized; but in 1862, believing he had been deceived, he was again baptized, on the confession of what he was sure was the work of the Holy Spirit in his salvation.

Pryor, John, D.D., was born in Halifax, Nova Scotia, and pursued his studies at King's College,

Christ Church College, Oxford, and at the Newton Theological Institution. He was ordained in Providence, R. I., in 1830. For some time he was principal of the Horton Academy, Wolfville, Nova Scotia, and subsequently professor and president of Acadia College. He was associate pastor at Horton, then pastor of the old Cambridge church, the church in Halifax, Nova Scotia, and the churches in Randolph and Lexington, Mass., in which latter place he now resides.

Publication Society, The American Baptist.—On the 25th of February, 1824, a company of twenty-five Baptists met at the house of Mr. George Wood, in Washington City, D. C., to consider the propriety of the formation of a Baptist General Tract Society. The call which brought them together was the result of a letter sent by the Rev. Noah Davis, of Maryland, to his classmate, the Rev. James D. Knowles, then living in Washington City. Mr. Davis had been deeply impressed with the desirableness of such a tract society, and of its importance for the promotion of the welfare of the Baptists in this country, and for the prosecution of their special Christian work. Hence his letter to Mr. Knowles, the call for the meeting at Mr. Wood's, and the organization of the society. It began its work at once, though in a modest way. The receipts of the society for the first year of its existence amounted to $373.80, and it issued 696,000 pages of tracts.

In the year 1826 the society was transferred to Philadelphia, because that city offered greater advantages for publishing and distributing its tracts throughout the country. Its growth from this date was slow but steady. It at length began to issue bound volumes; then to care especially for Sunday-schools, and to prepare books and other publications to meet their needs. In 1840 it was led to employ colporteurs for the circulation of its publications, and for the performance of necessary pioneer Christian work. At length, in 1845, the name of the society was changed, and it became The American Baptist Publication Society, whose object, according to its constitution, is "To promote evangelical religion by means of the Bible, the printing-press, colportage, and the Sunday-school."

The total number of publications on the catalogue of the society on April 1, 1881, was 1326. This was after a thorough examination of the list and the dropping of a number that were once issued. These publications include books, tracts, and periodicals. A few figures will exhibit the increase of its issues from its origin, and show the magnitude of this part of its work. The issues are all reduced to 18mo pages.

In 1824, total issues..................................	696,000
From 1824–1840, average annual issues......	7,840,198
" 1840–1857, " " "	22,110,645
" 1857–1860, " " "	61,856,066
From 1860–1870, average annual issues......	198,382,395
" 1870–1880, " " "	381,829,429
" 1824–1880, " " "	94,845,010
" 1824–1880, total issues.....................	5,311,320,610

In regard to the character of the publications of the society, George W. Anderson, D.D., in his little work, "The Baptists in the United States," says, "If the excellence of a denominational literature is to be determined by the strong common sense which pervades it, its reverence for the sacred Scriptures, and habitual and thorough deference to its teachings, by its complete and scholar-like examination of the Word of God, and by its calm, candid, and courteous tone, then the works issued from the press of this society will bear comparison with those of any denomination in the world."

The progress of the society will further appear from a glance at the receipts into its treasury at different periods of its history. These receipts include both those in its business department and the funds specially contributed for its missionary work. The former is self-sustaining; hence all the funds contributed to the latter are used exclusively for that object.

In 1824, total receipts............................	$373.80
" 1830, " "	3,094.09
" 1840, " "	12,165.77
" 1850, " "	40,579.71
" 1860, " "	84,783.91
" 1870, " "	332,149.59
" 1880, " "	349,564.46

The increasing work of the society demanded from time to time larger accommodations. At length, in 1876, the present building at 1420 Chestnut Street was completed, at a cost of $258,000, the whole of which was provided for by the liberality of its friends and the proceeds of the sale of its former building. The last $100,000 of the cost was given by Wm. Bucknell, Esq., and members of his family, and by the various members of the family of the late J. P. Crozer, Esq. It is thought that the accommodations furnished in this edifice will be sufficient for many long years to come.

During the fifty-six years of its existence, the society has fulfilled the expectation of its founders, and has proved an efficient means of promoting the unity of the Baptists of the United States in feeling, in doctrinal views, in Scriptural practices, and in the promotion of missionary work at home and abroad. Its publications have gone throughout the land into every State and Territory, as also have its colporteurs and Sunday-school missionaries. Its power for good has been steadily developed, and everything indicates that under the blessing of God it will continue to enlarge its work as the demands of the wide field in which it is called to labor become more numerous and pressing.

MISSIONARY WORK
OF THE AMERICAN BAPTIST PUBLICATION SOCIETY.

This department of the society has been developed to meet the wants which from time to time claimed recognition. At first the gratuitous distribution of tracts, and, subsequently, of books, was undertaken; then the missionary colporteur agency was originated. At length the demands for systematic efforts to increase the number of Sunday-schools, and to promote their efficiency, led to the employment of Sunday-school missionaries. The work, as now carried on, consists in three things:

1. In preaching the gospel *from house to house* by a band of missionary *colporteurs*, who unite with personal efforts to convert the inmates, the circulation of the Holy Scriptures, and the dissemination of a gospel literature.

2. In sustaining *Sunday-school* missionaries to form new schools, to strengthen and improve old ones, and to organize the forces of the different States for efficient Sunday-school work.

3. In making grants of small libraries to poor ministers and Sunday-schools, and of tracts to pastors and to missionaries of other societies and Conventions.

Colporteur missionaries were first employed by the society in 1840, about one year before any other society in this country entered on a similar work. During the forty years that have since elapsed it has employed nearly 1500 such laborers, in the various fields in this country, as well as in Canada, Sweden, Norway, and Italy. In 1880 there were 34 employed in as many States and Territories of our country.

The work in Sweden was commenced in 1855, when the Rev. Andreas Wiberg was sent to that country to originate and direct a system of missionary colportage. His efforts were very successful, and when, in 1866, the work was transferred to the American Baptist Missionary Union, there were in Sweden 176 Baptist churches and an aggregate of 6606 members, and the work had extended into Norway and other adjacent countries. This was all the development of the work undertaken by the society in 1855, when there were only forty Baptists in the kingdom. At the present time there are nearly 300 Baptist churches, with about 20,000 members, though they are sending hundreds of their young and enterprising members to this country every year.

The Sunday-school missionary work was first inaugurated in 1867. In 1880 there were under appointment 21 such missionaries, laboring in as many of our States and Territories, all of them, with one exception, in the South or the West.

The society's donations of tracts and books have been steadily increasing in number from the earliest years of its history, and this work might with great benefit be still vastly enlarged were the necessary means at its disposal.

The extent and results of the work may be partially understood on an examination of the following table, which shows the statistics from the beginning until 1880:

Days of service	262,342
Miles traveled	2,998,492
Books sold	171,987
Books given away	92,139
Pages of tracts distributed	6,937,445
Sermons and addresses delivered	620,417
Prayer-meetings held	53,086
Families visited	664,580
Persons baptized	13,446
Churches constituted	499
Sunday-schools organized	3,955
Conventions and institutes held or addressed	4,674
Sunday-schools aided by donations	7,931
Pastors and ministerial students furnished with grants of books for their libraries	1,710

It is proper to remark that all the contributions to the society are used exclusively for its missionary work, unless specially directed by the donors to some other end.

PERIODICALS.

In common with religious publication societies in this country and abroad, the society at an early period in its history recognized the periodical press as a powerful agency for the promotion of Christian work. Soon after its organization it began the monthly issue of *The Tract Magazine*, which, during its short life, was a means of extending the circulation of tracts. This was followed by *The Monthly Paper*, afterwards the *Baptist Record*, which was first published in 1836, and was suspended in 1855.

Since that date the periodical department has been gradually becoming more comprehensive in its issues, while their circulation has largely increased, as the following figures will show. They indicate the total number of copies of each periodical issued, from the time of its establishment until April 1, 1881:

Young Reaper, monthly and semi-monthly, 1857–1881	56,445,930
National Baptist, weekly, 1865–1881	5,307,481
Baptist Quarterly, 1867–1878	59,383
Baptist Teacher, monthly, 1869–1881	4,189,400
Baptist Lesson Monthly, 1869–1881	47,263,500
Baptist Primary Lesson Monthly, 1874–1881	17,791,200
Bible Lesson Quarterly, 1879–1881	1,205,500
Intermediate Lesson Quarterly, 1881	235,000
Our Little Ones, monthly, 1873–1881	15,958,000
Our Young People, monthly, 1881	215,000
Total number of copies issued	148,670,394

Purefoy, Geo. W., D.D.—The Rev. John Purefoy, a wise and good man, gave three sons to the Baptist ministry of North Carolina,—Geo. W., James S., and N. A. Purefoy. George was the oldest of them, and was born in 1809; was baptized in 1830, and began to preach at once. In early life he preached much, but for many years before his death his health did not allow him to preach often. He was the author of the "History of the Sandy Creek Association," and of several works on the baptismal controversy. He died in 1880. The State University at Chapel Hill gave him the title of D.D. in 1870.

Purefoy, Rev. James S., the third son of Rev. John Purefoy, was born in 1813, baptized in 1830, began to preach in 1835, and was ordained in 1840, Dr. Samuel Wait and Rev. P. W. Dowd constituting the Presbytery. Most of the pastoral labor of Mr. Purefoy has been performed in Wake and Granville Counties. No man, living or dead, has done so much for Wake Forest College as this unpretending brother. When plowing in the field, before he was twenty-one, he gave $25 to this institution, and through all its checkered history he has been its unfaltering friend. For many years he was its treasurer, without salary. He secured for it, since the war, a contribution of $10,000 from the Baptists of the North, and to him, more than to any other, is due the credit of rescuing the college from loss when it was heavily involved in 1848–49, and by his energy and liberality the handsome Wingate Memorial Hall was erected in 1879–80. Early in life Mr. Purefoy married Mary, the daughter of Deacon Foster Fort, and a kindred spirit, ready for every good work, she proved to be. Many poor young men, and especially many young ministers struggling to obtain an education, have found in this man and his wife friends ready and willing to help them, and it gives the writer of this sketch peculiar pleasure to leave on record the fact that by money voluntarily loaned by Mr. Purefoy he was enabled to complete his course in college. Mr. Purefoy is still a vigorous man, and seems to reckon it the highest glory of his life to labor and sacrifice for Wake Forest College.

Purefoy, Rev. N. A., was born in Wake Co., N. C., in 1811; attended Wake Forest College, but took his degree of A.B. from Columbian College, Washington, D. C. He served the Fayetteville church and the church in Warrenton each for several years, but most of his pastoral life has been spent in preaching to country churches. Quiet and unobtrusive, this good man has long been regarded by his brethren as a fine illustration of almost every Christian virtue.

Purinton, Jesse M., D.D., was born in Coleraine, Mass., Aug. 12, 1809; baptized in Truxton when eleven years of age; educated at Hamilton, N. Y., and ordained in 1834; was pastor in Coleraine, and in Arcade, N. Y., in Forestville and Mount Moriah, Pa., and in Morgantown, W. Va. He was for several years a missionary in Northwest Virginia. He aided in many revivals, and was instrumental in leading large numbers to Jesus. In 1860 the degree of Doctor of Divinity was conferred upon him. He died at Morgantown, June 17, 1869. Dr. Purinton was an able minister and a devoted follower of the Saviour.

Putnam, Daniel, professor in the Normal School at Ypsilanti, Mich., was born in Lyndeborough, N. H., Jan. 8, 1824. Having fitted for college at New Hampton, he entered Dartmouth College, and graduated in the class of 1851. During the next two years he taught in the New Hampton Academy, as he had done a part of his Senior year. He remained with it a short time after its removal to Fairfax, Vt., but came to Michigan in 1854, as professor in Kalamazoo College. He resided in Kalamazoo till 1868, but did not hold his professorship the whole interval. For seven years he was superintendent of public schools, for eighteen months county superintendent, and for one year served as president of the college *ad interim*. In 1868 he became professor in the State Normal School at Ypsilanti, and still holds that position. He is a preacher, but was never ordained. He has been chaplain of the State Insane Asylum at Kalamazoo the last eighteen years, and has often preached in other pulpits. He has rendered abundant service to the Baptist State Convention on its different boards, and is at present a valuable member of the Board of State Missions. Mrs. Putnam is a daughter of the late Rev. E. B. Smith, D.D., of Fairfax, Vt.

Puryear, Bennet, LL.D., Professor of Chemistry in Richmond College, Richmond, Va., was born in Mecklenburg Co., Va., July 23, 1826. He graduated at Randolph Macon College, in June, 1847, with the highest honors of his class. After leaving college he taught school one year in Monroe Co., Ala.; then returned to his native State, and during the session of 1849–50 attended lectures at the University of Virginia. In July, 1850, he was appointed tutor in Richmond College, and in the year following was elected Professor of Natural Science in that institution. In 1859 he resigned his professorship in Richmond College to accept the chair of Chemistry and Natural Philosophy in Randolph Macon College, where he remained until 1866, at which time he was recalled to his former position in Richmond. In 1868, when the college was reorganized and the office of president abolished, he was elected chairman of the faculty, which position he has continued to hold until the present time, being annually chosen thereto by his colleagues. In 1873 the school of natural science was divided into physics and chemistry, and the school of chemistry was assigned to him. At college, Prof. Puryear was distinguished for his attainments in the classics as well as in natural science, and when circumstances have required him to take charge of a class in Greek, or Latin, or mathematics, he has done so with distinguished success. His acquaintance with the subjects of his own school is broad and thorough. As a lecturer, his style is clear and pointed, and often enlivened by sallies of genial humor. The matter of his lectures is so admirably arranged that they are felt to be a growth, and not a mere aggregation of facts. In the experiments of the laboratory he is unusually successful. Prof. Puryear has not given much attention to popular lectures or addresses, but whenever he has spoken in public he has been heard with pleasure. Besides occasional contributions to various periodicals, he published, in 1866–

BENNET PURYEAR, LL.D.

67, in the *Farmer*, a series of articles on "The Theory of Vegetable Growth"; in 1875, in *The Planter and Farmer*, papers on "The Public School in its Relation to the Negro," since printed in pamphlet form; in the same year, in the *Religious Herald*, a series of articles on the "Public School"; and in 1878, also in the *Religious Herald*, papers on the "Virginia State Debt," and also on "The Atmosphere." With the exception of the first series, these papers were all published under the signature of "Civis." These articles evinced ability and fullness of information, but those relating to the public school are specially noticeable. No newspaper articles on questions of public State policy ever awakened in Virginia a more general interest, or produced a profounder impression. Questions which seemed to be settled, and whose discussion was unthought of, were brought again into the field of controversy; and the public school system, established by constitutional enactment, fostered by the spirit of the times, and appealing to the interests of the masses of the people, was shaken to its foundation. The articles were everywhere talked of, and called forth able replies. It was the opinion of many that no papers so fundamental in scope, so vigorous in statement, so brilliant in rhetoric, and so instinct with passion had appeared in Virginia for a long time. Although these articles discussed questions which were largely local, they exerted much more than a local interest. In a few weeks the hitherto but slightly known professor became one of the most widely known men of the whole South; and in acknowledgment of the learning and ability shown in the "Civis" articles, Georgetown College, Ky., and Howard College, Ala., conferred on him the honorary degree of LL.D. (June, 1878). Dr. Puryear is president of the Tuckahoe Club, an association of farmers in the vicinity of Richmond College, and his eminent success in cultivating a small farm is a practical illustration of the value of science in agriculture. Notwithstanding Dr. Puryear's opposition to public schools, he is an earnest advocate of education, and has contributed much to the prosperity of Richmond College. He is among the most honored and influential citizens of Richmond, a man of sound judgment, genial disposition, and inflexible integrity. He is an active member of the Grace Street Baptist church in Richmond.

Q

Quarles, Rev. Frank (colored), is a Baptist minister of great worth, now about sixty years old. He was born in Caroline Co., Va., and came to Georgia in 1850. He was a faithful slave until the close of the war, but his character and abilities may be estimated when it is stated that he was licensed and ordained by the First Baptist church in Atlanta in 1863, previous to emancipation, the Presbytery being composed of Rev. H. C. Hornady and Rev. William T. Brantly, D.D. Since 1863 he has lived in Atlanta, and has served the Friendship Baptist church as pastor since 1866. For twelve years in succession he has been moderator of the Ebenezer (colored) Association, and since the organization of the (colored) Missionary Baptist Convention at Augusta, Ga., in 1868, he has been its president. He exerts a wide and healthful influence in the State, and uses it freely for religious and educational purposes. He married in Virginia, and lived with his wife thirty-eight years, raising two children,—a son and a daughter. He is a man of ability and piety, and as a man and preacher is highly esteemed by all who know him.

Quincy, Hon. Josiah, was born in Lenox, Mass., March 7, 1793. His father, Samuel Quincy, was a lawyer in Roxbury, Mass., where he acquired a large property in the practice of his profession. He indorsed heavily the paper of several mercantile firms in Boston, and the commercial disasters of 1777–78 swept away nearly every vestige of his estate. He then retired to a little cottage among the Berkshire hills, where he soon died of a broken heart. His son Samuel, the brother of Josiah, with a dollar and a half in his pocket, but rich in spirit, left on foot for Boston to seek his fortune. He became in due time a flourishing shipmaster and owner of vessels, and filled many offices of trust and responsibility in that city. Josiah, from a lameness caused by sickness in infancy, was unable to perform much manual labor. He accordingly turned his attention to study as a necessity for his future support. Under many discouraging circumstances he prepared himself at the Lenox Academy to enter as a Sophomore in college. Circumstances prevented him from carrying out his plan to take a full collegiate course, and on leaving his academic studies he entered upon the study of law with Samuel Jones, Esq., of Stockbridge, Mass. He taught school during the day, and his law studies were necessarily carried on at night. It was by these fierce battles with indigence that the latent powers of his nature were largely developed, that his invincible determination for ultimate success was strengthened, and that, by heroic effort, he laid broad and deep the foundations of his future eminence.

On being admitted to the bar, Mr. Quincy practised his profession a few months at Stockbridge, and removed from that place to Sheffield, where he remained a short time, and then went to Rumney, N. H., ever afterwards his home. Soon after settling in Rumney he was married to May

HON. JOSIAH QUINCY.

Grace, daughter of Jabez Weed, of Plymouth. Rumney is a small town among the hills of New Hampshire, but the young lawyer, by industry and perseverance, soon gained a high rank in his profession, his practice extending for a long distance in all directions. Not many years elapsed before he was known as one of the most eminent lawyers of the State, and when he retired from practice in 1864, his professional business was said to have been as large as that of any legal gentleman in New Hampshire. For years he was president of the Grafton County bar. He had under his tuition many law students, and among them the eminent Judge Clifford, of the United States Supreme Court. Mr. Quincy was a prominent politician, and filled many public offices. He was several years a member of the New Hampshire house of representatives, and was twice elected to the State senate, the latter year filling the office of president of that body. He was also a member of the first board of trustees of the State Asylum for the Insane. In financial matters he was favorably known, and for years was one of the directors of the Pemigewassett Bank, in Plymouth, N. H. He was one of the most active of that persevering band of men who originated and carried forward the building of the Boston, Concord and Montreal Railroad, and for fourteen years was the president of its board of directors. The herculean labors he performed in the progress of this enterprise, and the intense anxieties he endured in its behalf, had much to do with the completion of the work upon which he and the gentlemen associated with him had embarked, and with its final, successful accomplishment.

Mr. Quincy was very active in educational matters. Remembering his own early struggles, the needy student always found in him a friend and counselor, and many will always remember with gratitude his generous gifts in their extremity. He was much interested in the schools of the county and the town in which he lived. He was a trustee of the Newton Theological Seminary, and for years was president of the trustees of the New Hampton Academy. He took the deepest interest in the latter, as for many years it was the leading Baptist institution in the State, and had connected with it a theological department. At one time, by his own funds, he removed from it a debt amounting to several thousand dollars.

In his religious belief Mr. Quincy was thoroughly a Baptist, although he had, like all Baptists, a wide catholicity of feeling for true believers of any name. He was converted under the faithful ministry of Rev. Noah Nichols, pastor of the Baptist church in Rumney, and by him was baptized in 1831. He remained a prominent member of this church until his death, always ready to aid it with his wise counsel, and contributing largely to its support. As it had been his early religious home, during his long and eventful life he cherished for it a strong and increasing affection. He loved to attend the gathering of the Associations and the State Conventions, and found these meetings a refreshing rest from the laborious cares of his profession. He was a life member of the Missionary Union, and other Baptist organizations formed for the advancement of the Redeemer's kingdom. In his domestic life he was a kind and indulgent parent, and made home attractive by an exhibition of its sweeter charities. He died in Rumney, his residence for sixty years, Jan. 19, 1875, being almost eighty-two years of age. He passed away as he had lived, in the full hope of a blessed immortality. Two sons and three daughters survive him.

One of the most prominent traits in the character of Mr. Quincy was his invincible and unbending integrity. No temptation could swerve him a hair's breadth from a stern and incorruptible honesty. In his profession he was keen and sharp, but with no smirch of trickery. He was an eminent lawyer, a faithful public officer, an upright business man, and a generous and valuable citizen. In private life he was a most courteous gentleman, highly beloved by a very extensive circle of acquaintances. In his religious faith he was firm and unwavering, trusting for salvation alone in the Lord Jesus Christ, and at the close of his long and active life could well say, " I have finished my course ; henceforth there is laid up for me a crown of righteousness."

R.

Rabun, Gov. William, one of the noblest and purest of men, was born in Halifax Co., N. C., April 8, 1771. When he was about fourteen his father, Matthew Rabun, removed to Georgia, and, after residing a short time in Wilkes County, settled in Hancock County. In the year 1788 young William professed faith in Christ, and united with the church at Powelton, having been publicly baptized by Silas Mercer.

Growing up to man's estate he took a high position, both as a church member and a citizen. Without solicitation on his part, he was, for many years, sent to the Legislature from Hancock County, then one of the most influential counties in the State. Being president of the State senate, in March, 1817, he became *ex-officio* governor of the State, on account of the resignation of Gov. Mitchell, and in the following November he was elected governor of Georgia. He died Oct. 24, 1819, while occupying that exalted position.

He was a man of singular piety. Though highly honored by his fellow-citizens, he was not made vain by it; and, though heavily burdened with the affairs of state, he never forgot the claims of his Master's cause. Up to the time of his death he was a regular attendant upon the sessions of the Georgia Association, taking an active part in the deliberations and workings of the body. Even while governor of the State, in the years 1817, 1818, 1819, his familiar name still appears in the minutes of the Association, and it was a pleasing and common sight to witness the governor of the State fulfilling the duties of chorister and clerk in the Powelton church. He was a man of prayer, and his house was the house of prayer. To all the benevolent institutions of the day he gave his influence and his purse. Wise in counsel, firm in purpose, upright in dealing, he was possessed of a piety transparent, unaffected, deep, and ardent; all the elements of true greatness were in him beautifully blended.

Upon the death of Gov. Rabun, Rev. Jesse Mercer, by request of the Legislature, preached before them a memorial sermon, in which occurs the following tribute to his piety and worth: "Your late excellent governor was the pleasant and lovely companion of my youth; my constant friend and endeared Christian brother in advancing years; and until death my unremitting fellow-laborer and able supporter in all the efforts of benevolence and philanthropy in which I had the honor and happiness to be engaged, calculated either to amend or ameliorate the condition of men."

During the Seminole war, in 1818, Gov. Rabun called out the militia, and placed them under the command of Gen. Gaines. They were ordered, under command of Maj. Wright, of the U. S. army, to discover the course of the Indians who had been committing depredations. Capt. Obed Wright, of the Chatham militia, had positive orders from Gov. Rabun to destroy Hoponee and Philemi towns, for committing atrocities on the frontier. By mistake Chehaw town was taken, partly burned, and some Indians killed. An angry correspondence ensued between Gov. Rabun and Gen. Jackson in regard to the matter, a part of which is given. Gen. Jackson wrote, May 7, 1818, "Such base cowardice and murderous conduct as this transaction shows have no parallel in history, and shall meet with their merited punishment. You, sir, as governor of a State within my military division, have no right to give a military order while I am in the field; and this being an open and violent infringement of the treaty with the Creek Indians, Capt. Wright must be prosecuted for this outrageous murder, and I have ordered him to be arrested and confined in irons until the pleasure of the President of the United States is known upon the subject." In his reply, after referring to the communication of Gen. Glasscock, upon which Gen. Jackson based his answer, Gov. Rabun says, "Had you, sir, or Gen. Glasscock, been in possession of the facts that produced this affair, it is to be presumed, at least, that you would not have indulged in a strain so indecorous and unbecoming. I had, on the 21st of March last, stated the situation of our bleeding frontier to you, and requested you, in respectful terms, to detail a part of your overwhelming force for our protection, or that you would furnish supplies, and I would order out more troops, to which you have never yet deigned to reply. You state, in a very haughty tone, that I, a governor of a State under your military division, have no right to give a military order whilst you are in the field. Wretched and contemptible, indeed, must be our situation if this be the fact. When the liberties of the people of Georgia shall have been prostrated at the feet of a military despotism, *then, and not till then*, will your imperious doctrine be tamely submitted to. You may rest *assured* that if the savages continue their depredations on our unprotected frontier, I shall think and act for myself in that respect."

Rambaut, Thomas, D.D., LL.D., is of French descent. He was born in the city of Dublin, Ireland, and was regularly educated in the liberal arts, having studied in the celebrated school of Rev. Henry Lyon, of Portington, and at Trinity College. He came to Savannah, Ga., on attaining his majority, with the intention of studying law, and was converted under the preaching of Rev. Richard Fuller, D.D., of Baltimore, and baptized by Rev. W. T. Brantly, D.D., then in Augusta, Ga. On the Wednesday following he preached his first discourse. He has successively filled the positions of pastor of the Blackswamp church, S. C., Savannah Baptist church, Ga., president of Cherokee Baptist College, Professor of History and Roman Literature in Georgia Military Institute, president of William Jewell College, Mo., and pastor of Tabernacle Baptist church, Brooklyn. He was called to be the successor of Rev. Henry C. Fish, D.D., as pastor of the First church, Newark, N. J., in March, and entered upon this charge on the 1st of April, 1878. He received the degree of LL.D. from Madison University in 1860, and of D.D. from William Jewell College in 1873.

Rand, Theodore Harding, A.M., D.C.L., was born in Cornwallis, Nova Scotia, and is a graduate

THEODORE HARDING RAND, A.M., D.C.L.

of Acadia College; was converted and baptized in Wolfville in 1855, while attending college; taught in the Provincial Normal School, Truro, from 1861 to 1864; then he was chief superintendent of education in Nova Scotia until 1870, and rendered important services in that department; traveled in Europe and observed methods and results of teaching in the best schools there; was appointed, in 1871, chief superintendent of education in New Brunswick, and has there performed similar services to those rendered in Nova Scotia. Admirably adapted for educational work, Dr. Rand performs his responsible duties with enthusiasm and efficiency.

Rand, Rev. Thomas, was born in Manchester, N. H., May 21, 1776, his father being a Presbyterian minister. He was hopefully converted when he was twenty-two years of age, and baptized in Alstead. He began to preach at once, but wishing to secure a better preparation for his work, he entered the school of Rev. William Williams, of Wrentham, and subsequently graduated at Brown University in 1803. He was ordained pastor of the church in Holyoke (then Ireland Parish, West Springfield, Mass.), Oct. 6, 1803. At the time of his ordination his church was the only Baptist church in a circle the diameter of which would be thirty miles, including Hampshire and Hampden Counties. Here he performed his work for twenty-five years, during six months in the year having the charge of a school, in which not a few persons whose after-lives were very useful received their education. In October, 1828, he became the pastor of the church in New Salem, N. H., where he remained six years, then went to Hinsdale, continuing here two years. For five years he was a city missionary in New York City. His closing years were passed in Holyoke, among his former parishioners, where he died, May 31, 1857.

Rand, Rev. Thomas, the son of a minister of the same name, was born in West Springfield, Mass., July 10, 1813; licensed to preach in 1836; graduated at Hamilton Theological Seminary in 1838; ordained at Bayou Chicot, La., in 1841; died at Lake Charles, La., July 1, 1869. He devoted his life to teaching and preaching, and did much to build up the Baptist cause in the Opelousas region. He was a ripe scholar and fine preacher.

Randall, David Austin, D.D., was born in Colchester, Conn., Jan. 14, 1813. At the age of fourteen made a public profession of religion; was licensed to preach June 30, 1838; ordained in Richfield, O., Dec. 18, 1839, where he was pastor of the Baptist church for five years, and where he edited a Washingtonian paper, and gave much time to the temperance cause. In 1845 removed to Columbus, O., and became one of the editors of the *Journal and Messenger*. For several years, after severing his connection with this paper, he engaged in the book business. In 1858 was called to the pastorate of the First Baptist church, Columbus, O., and continued in that position eight years. During this pastorate he made an extensive journey through Oriental countries, the results of which he embodied in a royal octavo volume of 720 pages, entitled "The Handwriting of God in Egypt, Sinai, and the Holy Land." This book has had an extensive sale, and is said by competent critics to be one of the best works on the East. Subsequently he made a minute and extensive tour through continental Europe, and England, Scotland, and Ireland.

Dr. Randall was for six years corresponding secretary of the Ohio Baptist State Convention, and subsequently its treasurer. In 1870 Denison University conferred upon him the honorary degree of D.D. He still resides at Columbus, O., where he devotes his attention to literary pursuits, though he gives much time to lecturing, preaching, and the various educational and missionary enterprises of the day.

Randall, Rev. Nelson Birney, was born in Springville, N. Y., June 14, 1838. After graduating from Hamilton College, Clinton, N. Y., in 1858, and from Rochester Theological Seminary in 1869, he was ordained at Ypsilanti, Mich., the following October. Four years of his previous life had been spent in the practice of law in Gloversville, N. Y. He has sustained with eminent success the relation of pastor in Ypsilanti, Mich., Vineland, N. J., Providence, R. I. (Jefferson Street), and Norristown, Pa., where he now ministers, deeply intrenched in the affections of the church and congregation. No small service has been done in the wiping out of debts, aggregating $16,000, and in important improvements inaugurated under his ministry.

Randall, Judge Samuel, was born in Sharon, Mass., Feb. 10, 1778. A pupil of Rev. William Williams, of Wrentham, Mass., he fitted for Brown University, and graduated in the class of 1804. Hon. Virgil Maxcy and Gov. Marcus Morton were members of the same class. Mr. Randall read law with Judge Howell, but before completing his studies he removed to Warren, to take charge of an academy in that village. Quite a number of his pupils were subsequently students in college, and were an honor to their faithful instructor. For many years he acted as a judge in different courts in Rhode Island. For forty-four years he was a member of the Baptist church in Warren, and took a deep interest in its material and spiritual prosperity. He died at the advanced age of eighty-six, March 5, 1864. Judge Randall was the father of Rev. George M. Randall, D.D., the Episcopal bishop of Colorado. Prof. Gammell says of him, "He died as he lived, universally respected as an upright magistrate, a useful citizen, and a consistent Christian."

Randall, Rev. William H., was licensed to preach in his native town,—North Stonington, Conn.; graduated at Hamilton Theological Seminary, N. Y., in 1850; settled in Frensburg, Phillipsville, and Williamsville, N. Y.; in the late war raised a company, and entered the service as a captain, performing also the duties of a chaplain; for gallant conduct at Chancellorsville he was raised to the rank of major; wounded at Gettysburg, and obliged to leave the field; in 1865 resumed his pastorate at Williamsville; while seeking restoration to health, died at Lake Maitland, Fla., May 7, 1874, in the fifty-sixth year of his age; a pure, noble spirit.

Randall, Rev. William Henry, son of William P. and Marie L. Randall, was born in Groton, Conn., Aug. 23, 1840; converted in February, 1855, and baptized March 25 of same year by Rev. Harvey Silliman, uniting with the Second Baptist church in Groton; graduated with special honor from Brown University in 1861; spent another year at the university in post-graduate studies; taught schools in Mystic and Suffield, Conn., and Providence, R. I., from 1865 to 1872, with the exception of one year—1870-71—spent in travel in Europe and the East, visiting specially the Holy Land; studied at Newton Theological Institution in 1873-74; ordained pastor of Windsor Avenue Baptist church, Hartford, Conn., Dec. 15, 1874; settled with Central Baptist church, Thompson, Conn., in June, 1877, where he is now (1880) laboring; married, July 1, 1874, Mary F. Gallup, daughter of Deacon John Gallup, of Groton, Conn.

Randolph, Judge Joseph F., was born in Plainfield, N. J., about 1800. He was the son of Rev. Robert Randolph. He was baptized at Freehold by Rev. J. M. Challiss. He opened a law-office in Freehold, and afterwards resided and practised in New Brunswick, Trenton, and Jersey City, where he died at an advanced age. He was first elected to Congress in 1838, and served two terms. He also was honored with an appointment to the judgeship of the Supreme Court in New Jersey.

Randolph, Warren, D.D., son of Lewis S. and Hannah (Gilman) Randolph, was born at Piscataway, N. J., March 30, 1826. He was a graduate of Brown University in the class of 1851. Among his classmates were Prof. J. L. Diman, D.D., and Rev. J. B. Simmons, D.D. Soon after his graduation he was ordained as pastor of the High Street Baptist church, Pawtucket, R. I., where he remained but a short time, and then accepted a call to become pastor of the Eighth (now Jefferson) Street church, Providence. He removed to Philadelphia in 1857, and became pastor of the First Baptist church in Germantown, which office he held until 1863, when he was called to the Harvard Street Baptist church, Boston. Four years later, in 1867, he returned to Philadelphia, and was pastor of the Fifth Baptist church until 1870, when his health failing he resigned, and spent not far from a year in foreign travel, extending his trip

WARREN RANDOLPH, D.D.

as far as to Egypt and Palestine. On his return, in 1871, he became Sunday-school secretary of the American Baptist Publication Society. In the discharge of his official duties he traveled very extensively over the United States, and proved himself a most useful agent in promoting the interests of the society which he served.

In 1872 a committee was appointed, by a Sunday-School Convention representing the evangelical denominations of the United States and Canada, to select lessons for a seven years' course of study. Dr. Randolph represented the Baptists in this committee. Its labors were so successful that before the seven years had expired it was calculated that about eight millions of persons were reaping the advantages of the lessons. A second international lesson committee was appointed to serve for the ensuing seven years; of this committee Dr. Randolph was a member. He resigned his secretaryship in 1877, to the sincere regret of the Publication Society, to accept the pastorate of the First Baptist church of Indianapolis, where he remained a little more than two years. On his return to the East he became pastor of the Central Baptist church of Newport, R. I.

Dr. Randolph has been in almost constant service since his ordination, in 1851, and he is admirably qualified for the work of the gospel ministry.

Rangoon Karen College.—In the fifty-sixth annual report presented to the Missionary Union in 1870, among other suggestions Dr. Binney made the following: " Whether we ought not to make some provision for general education for Karens, by which this institution" (the Karen Theological Seminary) " might be relieved of that department." The suggestion of Dr. Binney met with a prompt response, and in the annual report of the executive committee for 1871, we are told that " the effort begun the past year, for the founding of a Karen College at Rangoon, is the logical result of the general educational impulse, which has been felt at the missionary stations." The college was opened on the 28th of May, 1872, Rev. Dr. Binney, president, with three native teachers and seventeen pupils. Rev. John Packer, who had been professor in the State University of Missouri, sailed in October, 1872, to be connected with Dr. Binney, both in the theological institution and the college. The second year of the college opened April 1, 1873, two weeks after the arrival of Prof. Packer, and, with the exception of two weeks' vacation in October, was in continuous session until Jan. 28, 1874. The whole number of students in attendance during the session was 39, of whom 36 were boys. Of course, the work done was of a very elementary character, but it was work well done, and designed to be the foundation work preparatory to something higher in the future. Rev. C. H. Carpenter was appointed president in 1873, and left the United States in January, 1874, to take charge of the college. He remained in office but a short time, when Prof. Packer was chosen in his place. Several circumstances conspired for a year or two to hinder the progress of the college. The report at the end of the session of 1876–77 was more favorable, the number of pupils having been 109, and the last year the number had risen to 127. Through the generosity of one individual an ample site and buildings for the college, including a dormitory, have been secured. A good beginning has been made in the life of the Rangoon College, and the prospect of its future usefulness is very bright.

Rangoon Mission Press.—The first printing-press of which the Baptist missionaries made use was a gift from the English Baptist Mission at Serampore, in 1816. It was sent to Rangoon and placed under the charge of Rev. G. H. Hough, who had learned and practised the trade of printing in the United States. At once Mr. Hough put to press Dr. Judson's " Luminary of Christian Doctrines," a catechism, and a translation of the gospel of Matthew. After the war between England and Burmah, Maulmain became the chief seat of printing operations. In 1861 the Mission Printing-Press, with all that pertained to it, was again established at Rangoon, under the charge of Rev. C. Bennett, and the mission printing was constantly and vigorously prosecuted in the line of Scriptures, books, and tracts. All the movable portion of Mr. Ranney's printing establishment at Rangoon was purchased by the Missionary Union in 1862, and proved a valuable addition to the facilities needed for the publication of a religious literature. From Oct. 1, 1861, to Sept. 30, 1862, there had been published 2,113,000 pages of matter, religious and secular, and during the next year the amount was more than doubled. When Mr. Bennett, who had spent some time in this country, returned to Rangoon in 1865, he was the bearer of important additions to the working material of the printing-office and bindery, which had cost over $6000. During the two years, 1863–65, 8,751,900 pages had been printed. The books and tracts were upon a great variety of subjects, and varied in size from a 16mo to an 8vo,—a revival hymn-book representing the first, and a Burmese and English dictionary the second. The report of the Executive Committee for 1867 estimates the value of the investments made to carry on printing at Rangoon at $18,736.56. From Oct. 1, 1867, to Sept. 30, 1868, the number of pages printed was 10,678,000. Besides the printing done to meet the wants of the missions, a large amount of job work, also, was done, thus enabling the Union to reduce the expenses of running the establishment. Mr. Bennett, who again made a visit to this country, returned to the scene of his labors in the fall of 1872. During his absence the work went on under the superintendence of Rev. I. D. Colburn. In the annual report of the Executive Committee for 1877 the announcement was made that Mr. Bennett had resigned his connection with the press the fall previous. It was stated that "he had been more or less intimately connected with the press for forty-seven years, and during the greater part of this time had taken charge of it. He developed excellent business qualities, and managed its affairs with great prudence and skill till it has become one of the most important factors of our mission work in Burmah." Upon the resignation of Mr. Bennett, Rev. W. H. Sloan was appointed superintendent. He remained in charge for some time, and on returning to this country on account of the health of his family, Mr. Bennett consented, temporarily, to occupy the position he had held for so many years. The report for the year ending Oct. 1, 1877, presents the names of a long list of books and pamphlets printed in the following languages and dialects: English, Burmese, S'gan Karen, Pwo Karen, and Bghai Karen. The number of pages in these books and pamphlets was 4693, and the total of pages printed was 5,843,974. Among the more important of these publications we notice, in Burmese, Judson's English-Burmese Dictionary, completed, royal octavo, the Four Gospels, the Acts, and several of the Epistles, each in royal quarto, together with the Pentateuch in quarto. In S'gan Karen, the English-Karen Dictionary, in medium quarto, several books of the New Testament, and the minutes of six Associations.

Rathbone, Maj.-Gen. John T., was born in Albany, N. Y., Oct. 18, 1821; was educated in the academy at Albany and the Collegiate Institute of Brockport, N. Y. His father died when he was fifteen years old, when he left school and accepted a clerkship in Rochester. At seventeen years of age he united with the Baptist church of Brockport. At eighteen he returned to Albany. In 1845 he built his foundry in Albany, which, with the additions since made, is one of the largest in the world.

In 1861, Mr. Rathbone was appointed brigadier-general of the Ninth Brigade of the National Guards of New York, and on the breaking out of the civil war he was appointed commandant of the Albany Depot for Volunteers. On being relieved from this command Gen. Rathbone was highly complimented, not only by the adjutant-general, but by the commander-in-chief, for his great success in raising recruits and performing all the duties of his office. He sent to the front thirty-five regiments from his depot. In 1867, Gen. Rathbone resigned his position as commandant of the Ninth Brigade. When John A. Dix was elected to the governorship of New York he appointed Gen. Rathbone adjutant-general of the State, with the rank of major-general. He served under Gov. Dix's administration with credit to himself and great advantage to the State. He has been asked to accept political nominations, which he invariably declined, ambitious only to serve his fellow-men as a private citizen. He is one of the founders of the Albany Orphan Asylum, of which he has been a trustee for thirty years, and for many years the president. For thirty years he has been superintendent of the Emmanuel Baptist Sunday-school, and he has been a working member of the church for forty years. He founded the Rathbone Library of the University of Rochester, of which he is a trustee, to whose funds he has contributed about $40,000.

Gen. Rathbone is one of the noble Baptists who have conferred honor upon our denomination in the State of New York.

Rauschenbusch, Augustus, D.D., was born at Altena, province of Westphalia, Germany, Feb. 13, 1816. He was the son of A. E. Rauschenbusch, Lutheran pastor in that city, a learned and highly esteemed clergyman, from whom also he received his earliest instructions. In his fifteenth year he entered the gymnasium (college) at Elberfeld, and, having graduated, he went, in his nineteenth year, to the University of Berlin for the purpose of studying for the ministry. Through the instructions of his teacher, the venerable Dr. Neander, and through the influence of pious friends, he was awakened to a sense of his guilt before God, and, after a severe

AUGUSTUS RAUSCHENBUSCH, D.D.

inward struggle, at the age of twenty, he became a decided and joyful believer. Having spent some time at home, he went to the University of Bonn, where he devoted his time both to natural science and theology. At the death of his father, in 1841, the son was chosen by the congregation as his successor. As that congregation numbered about 3000 souls, an important field was thus opened to the youthful minister. His earnest pleading aroused great opposition on the part of the worldly-minded, but, at the same time, it proved the means of awakening many hundreds of persons at Altena and at various places in the vicinity.

After four years of successful labor, Mr. Rauschenbusch felt himself more and more hampered by his ecclesiastical relations, and, after much prayer, he resolved to go to a land where he could preach the gospel untrammeled and unmolested. Having heard of the great religious destitution among the Germans in America, he emigrated to this country in 1846, and immediately went to Missouri to preach to the numerous Germans settled there. In 1847 he was invited by the American Tract Society to come to New York to conduct the publication of their German tracts. Here he became acquainted with Dr. Somers, a Baptist pastor, and a member of the publishing committee of the Tract Society. Through him he was led to consider the question of baptism. After a long and prayerful investigation of it, he was baptized in May, 1850. He continued his connection with the Tract Society until August, 1853, superintending their seventy German colporteurs, editing their German monthly, the *Botschafter*, and preparing books and tracts. At the same time his influence was strongly and effectively exerted in furthering the Baptist cause among the Germans. In 1851, withdrawing for a time from the Tract Society, he labored as a preacher in Canada, and organized the first German Baptist churches there. Having visited his native land, he returned to this country in 1854 with a number of emigrants, and settled with them in Missouri. In 1855 he organized a German Baptist church in Gasconade Co., Mo., and preached to it until 1858, when, in obedience to a call from the New York Baptist Union for Ministerial Education, he took charge of the German department of the Theological Seminary at Rochester, N. Y. Since that time he has fulfilled, with much ability and success, the duties of his professorship. He is doing a great work. His influence on the young men going forth from Rochester as evangelists and pastors of the German Baptist churches is strongly felt, and his valuable services are gratefully acknowledged by all the churches.

Rawdon College, Yorkshire, England, the theological seminary originally called "the Northern Baptist Education Society," was founded in 1804. Until 1859 the college was located at Horton, near Bradford, and was known as Horton College. Its first president was the Rev. William Steadman, D.D., whose eminent services established the reputation of the seminary and won the confidence of the churches. Dr. Steadman was succeeded by Dr. Acworth, during the latter part of whose presidency the present handsome and commodious building was erected and paid for. The Rev. S. G. Green, D.D., was elected president on the retirement of Dr. Acworth. In 1876, Dr. Green accepted the position of literary editor of the Religious Tract Society, and was succeeded by the Rev. T. G. Rooke, B.A., the present head of the seminary. About 350 ministers and missionaries have been trained in this institution, many of whom have distinguished themselves by faithful and successful service in England, the United States, the British colonies, and in heathen lands. Rawdon College is affiliated to the University of London, and during recent years several students have graduated with distinction. Two scholarships, the "Acworth" and the "Steadman and Godwin," have been founded recently. (See illustration on next page.)

RAWDON COLLEGE, YORKSHIRE, ENGLAND.

Ray, Rev. Ambrose, a distinguished co-laborer with Martin Ball, W. H. Holcome, and others in North Mississippi, was born in South Carolina in 1798. He began to preach about 1833, and, after a successful ministry of seventeen years, he removed to Mississippi in 1850, where he took a high rank among his co-laborers, and was often called to positions of honor and trust among his brethren. He died in 1873, and his remains rest at Union church, Tippah Co., Miss.

Ray, D. B., D.D., was born in Hickman, Ky., March 30, 1830. He was converted, and baptized by Elder White, into the Little Albion Baptist church, Oct. 16, 1844. He was ordained in 1856. He labored in Kentucky and Tennessee till 1870, and then became associated with President Worrell in the editorship of the *Baptist Sentinel* at Lexington, Ky. In 1873 he became pastor at La Grange, Mo., and removed to St. Louis in 1880. He studied in Clinton Seminary, Ky., until ill health compelled him in two years to leave school. His ordination took place in 1856. After this he devoted much time to theological studies, history, and the sciences. Thousands have been converted under his ministry. Not only as an evangelist is he known, but more as a debater on religious questions. He has held forty oral discussions. Most of these have been with Campbellite and Methodist leaders. His discussions have been frequently followed by revivals, as well as by the discomfiture of his opponents.

In 1867 he published his "Text-Book on Campbellism." Seven editions have been issued, and this blighting error has been exposed. In 1870 he issued his "Baptist Succession." It is a convenient

D. B. RAY, D.D.

hand-book of Baptist history, to meet objections against Baptists. Eight editions of it have been issued. "The Church Discussion" is another book he has issued, containing a debate with the Campbellites. He now resides in St. Louis, and is editor and proprietor of the *American Baptist Flag*. He is a man of marked ability and of great courage.

Raymond, John Howard, LL.D., was born in the city of New York, March 7, 1814. His father, Eliachim Raymond, a merchant, was distinguished for his active interest in every religious enterprise, and was a leader among the Baptists of his day. In his earliest school-days J. H. Raymond was the pupil of Gould Brown, and the influence of this master may be traced in his early acquisition of a taste for analytical thinking and correct expression. He was prepared for college at the Hamilton Academy and at the High School of New York. In 1828 he entered Columbia College. Four years later he was graduated at Union College, and immediately began the study of law at New Haven. It was during this period of his life that he was led to an abiding faith in the teachings of the Bible and to an acceptance of Jesus as his Saviour. He united with the First Baptist church of Brooklyn, and shortly after his convictions led him to the study of theology, with the intention of preparing for the ministry. In 1834 he entered the Theological Seminary at Hamilton, N. Y. His talent for acquiring languages made it easy for him to gain distinction as a student of Hebrew, his progress being so marked that he was appointed a tutor of the language at the seminary before he had completed its course of study. In 1839 the chair of Rhetoric and English Literature was established in Madison University, and he was called to the new professorship. He had rare qualities for the work,—habits of thoroughness in study, brilliant oratorical powers, fine rhetorical taste, winning social ways, keen sympathies, ready wit, and the art of teaching. He soon came to believe that he had found his calling, and that he saw his work for life in the profession of the teacher. For ten years Prof. Raymond continued at Madison University, winning reputation as an orator and as a teacher.

He accepted the professorship of Belle-Lettres in the University of Rochester at the time of its organization, in 1850. He remained at Rochester until 1856, when he was selected to organize the Collegiate and Polytechnic Institute in Brooklyn. This work brought him prominently before the educational profession, for he had a difficult task assigned to him, and he accomplished it with brilliant success.

When Matthew Vassar sought the advice of prominent American teachers in selecting the man who should be intrusted with the work of organizing the first great college for women, he found it to be the general opinion that the temperament, the accomplishments, and the experience of Dr. Raymond made him the man for the position. He was promptly appointed to the presidency and professorship of Mental and Moral Philosophy at Vassar College. His work there began in the summer of 1865. To his task he brought unwearying patience, close observation, and the cautiousness of a man who appreciates the sacredness of a great trust. No man connected with educational institutions in this country has shown more talent for organization than was exhibited by President Raymond. The Collegiate and Polytechnic Institute at its inception was looked upon as a dubious experiment. He there demonstrated that by new and improved organization elements of culture seemingly incongruous could be made coalescent, and that institution became the model after which many high schools and academies have been patterned. This royal talent was yet more brilliantly displayed by him in the organization of Vassar College. His work was accomplished, not by spasmodic efforts, but by patient industry. A careful process of reasoning brought him to a conviction, and for that conviction he could toil unceasingly. Popular appreciation was not a powerful incentive to him. Respect for his own well-considered opinions and faithfulness to trusts placed in his keeping were the constant motives of his earnest life. Such a life gave him an ever-growing influence and an unsought eminence. But success did not dim the glow of his spiritual graces. Humility, calmness, trustfulness, catholicity, and the consecration of his industry and his influence shone brighter and brighter in him till the end of his life.

He gave himself so exclusively to his official work that his graceful pen had little opportunity for exercise. Save a few pamphlets and sermons, all marked with dignity and finish of style, he left no published works. Never physically strong, Dr. Raymond broke down under his labors, and though his physician warned him that he must have rest, he could not release himself from the work he loved. After a year of much suffering, in which his quiet patience and geniality shone brighter than ever before, with no definable disease, but worn out, he died on the 14th of August, 1878. His last words fittingly closed his earnest life as he quietly said to his family, "How easy, how easy, to glide from the work here to the work in heaven!" His death summoned attention to his dignity and worth, calling forth a general tribute of respect to his memory. "His fame, like the fame of Arnold, of Rugby, will live and grow through generations of those to whom and to whose fathers and mothers he was strong guardian, wise guide, dear friend."

Raymond, Rev. Lewis, was born Aug. 3, 1807, at Walton, Delaware Co., N. Y. When he was about seven years of age the family removed to

Sydney, in the same county, now called Sydney Centre. His conversion occurred at twenty-three, when he was baptized by Rev. S. P. Griswold, one of the veteran ministers of New York. In July, 1831, he was licensed by the Sydney church, and for a while united preaching with his business as a builder. His first pastorate was at Laurens, in Otsego County. After two years of successful labor he removed to Cooperstown, where he remained eight and a half years. By this time his brethren had found in him uncommon qualifications for usefulness in revival labor, and in 1841 called him to that sphere of service. Three years were spent in such labor in New York and in Northern Pennsylvania. In June, 1844, he removed to the West, being called to the pastorate of the Baptist church in Milwaukee. The church was very small and feeble, but grew under his ministry, and erected its first house of worship. After four years in Milwaukee he was called to Chicago as pastor of the Tabernacle church, succeeding Rev. H. M. Rice, who had died of cholera. After three years he again engaged in revival labors. In 1854 he removed to Sandusky, O., organizing a church there, which, however, after one year, he gave up to Rev. J. D. Fulton, and he entered the service of the Ohio State Convention. In 1857 he accepted a call to a new organization in Aurora, Ill., the Union Baptist church; in 1859 he went to another new church at Peoria; at the end of a year he entered the army as a chaplain, continuing in that service to the end of the war. Since that time he has been engaged as an evangelist, and in labor with feeble churches. His life has been one of energetic service in a spirit of great enthusiasm and personal devotion. And the fruit, in souls added to the Lord, has been abundant.

Raynor, Samuel, was born on Long Island, Aug. 10, 1810. He was baptized by Dr. Spencer H. Cone in 1833, and became a member of the Oliver Street church, New York, of which he has been a deacon over a quarter of a century. He is a well-known business man in New York. He is distinguished for his liberal support of the great institutions of the Baptist denomination. He is a manager of the American and Foreign Bible Society and of the New York Sunday-School Union. He was for years president of a benevolent institution in New York known as the "Eastern Dispensary," and has official connection with several insurance companies and the Metropolitan Savings-Bank of New York.

Read, Daniel, LL.D., was born in Orangeville, N. Y., April 11, 1825. He was educated at Madison University, and settled at first as pastor of the Big Flats Baptist church, in New York, where he was ordained to the work of the gospel ministry. He was next pastor of the Medina Baptist church, N. Y., and was then induced to accept the pastorate of the Second Baptist church of St. Louis, Mo. In 1856 he was elected president of Shurtleff College, in Illinois. This old institution was patronized by the Baptists of St. Louis, which enabled Dr. Read to render the special service to it that his influence in that city and his learning promised. Under his charge the college was placed on a firm financial basis, and rose to a position it had not hitherto attained.

In 1873, Dr. Read resigned the presidency of the college and accepted a call of the First Baptist church of Williamsburg, N. Y. He is a faithful pastor and an able preacher. His study of the Bible in the languages in which it was written makes him one of the most instructive expounders of its sacred truth.

Read, Rev. George R., of Alameda, Cal., was born at Attleborough, Mass., March 5, 1841; baptized at North Attleborough in October, 1856; served in the army under Gen. Banks at New Orleans until 1863; studied at Pierce Academy, Mass.; graduated at Brown University in 1868, and at Newton Theological Seminary in 1871; settled as pastor for five years at Lisbon Falls, where he was ordained, Oct. 25, 1871. The church grew under his ministry; many were baptized. He removed to California in December, 1876, and supplied the Stockton church six months, during the pastor's absence in the Holy Land. In July, 1877, he settled at Alameda, organized a church, built a house of worship, and has been favored with growing prosperity. He is greatly beloved, is a self-denying pastor, and zealous worker. He has acted in honorable official positions in Associations and Conventions, and is numbered with the brethren of influence on the Pacific coast.

Read, Rev. Geo. W., was born at Frankfort, Ky., Jan. 16, 1843. Mr. Read spent nearly three years and a half in the Union service during the war, receiving a wound from which he still at times severely suffers. He was baptized Dec. 1, 1866. He entered Shurtleff College preparatory to the work of the ministry, and was ordained at Kinmundy, Ill., June 11, 1871. He was pastor of the Baptist church in Clayton, Ill., five years, and the Union Avenue church, Litchfield, Ill., one year. He removed to Peru, Neb., Jan. 1, 1878. Through his labors a commodious church edifice has been built. He preaches to the Brownville Baptist church in connection with that of Peru.

Read, Rev. Hiram Walter, was born in Jewett City, Conn., July 17, 1819; baptized March 11, 1838, at Oswego, N. Y.; educated at Oswego Academy and Madison University; began his ministry in 1844, at Whitewater, Wis. He was pastor, and chaplain to Wisconsin senate, and labored in many revivals. In 1849 he went to New Mexico, and in 1852 preached to U. S. troops and to the Indians and Mexicans; organized churches, located missionaries, and established schools, explored adjacent Territories, and laid foundations for mission work. Returning East, he labored for the Home Mission and the American and Foreign Bible Societies, and settled for a time in Virginia, near Washington; built the Falls Baptist church, and helped others in revivals. During the war he served the U. S. government at Washington, in the field, and in hospitals; was taken prisoner, and exchanged for Dr. Broaddus, of Fredericksburg, Va. Assisted to establish the Territorial government of Arizona, and held positions of great pecuniary trust, under direction of the U. S. treasurer. Visited California in 1864. In 1865 settled at Hannibal, Mo., and soon after was engaged in many revivals as an evangelist. His labors have been greatly blessed in Eastern cities and many of the larger towns of the country. He has baptized nearly 1000, and led thousands more to Christ, who were baptized by others. While in New Mexico he was captured by Indians, and threatened with death by fire, but was graciously saved. He is now pastor at Virginia City, Nev.

Read, Rev. Isaiah W., was born at Frankfort, Ky., May 25, 1848; baptized Dec. 2, 1866. He was ordained at Roanoke, Ill., June 10, 1873, and became pastor of the Baptist church of that place. He afterwards had charge of the Baptist churches in Kingsbury and Elkhart, Ind. He graduated from the Baptist Theological Seminary in Chicago, May 8, 1879, receiving the degree of B.D. He had previously accepted a position under the American Baptist Publication Society as their general missionary in Nebraska and Dakota. Efficient and valuable work has been already done by him in this new field.

Read, Rev. James C., was born at Frankfort, Ky., April 18, 1845. Mr. Read spent two years and eight months in the Union service during the war. He was baptized Dec. 2, 1866; educated at Shurtleff College, Upper Alton, Ill., and the Baptist Theological Seminary in Chicago. He labored with the Baptist churches in Fairbury, Washington, and Metamora, Ill., and in Westville, Ind. He removed to Nebraska in 1879, and became pastor of the Baptist churches at Tecumseh and Sterling, in which field his toils have been incessant and his labors greatly blessed. He is at the present time engaged in building a church edifice in Tecumseh.

Read, Rev. John C. H., was born at Frankfort, Ky., May 5, 1857; baptized in 1866; ordained at Roanoke, Ill., Dec. 30, 1875, from which he removed to Edwardsburg, Mich. In 1879 he accepted a call from the Baptist church in Blair, Neb., where he has met with much success.

Blessed are the parents who have given to the cause of Christ four efficient and faithful ministers, men who are deeply interested in all questions pertaining to the progress of the church and the denomination, not alone in their immediate fields, but also in the State and throughout the world.

Read, Rev. Wm. E., was born in Missouri, Feb. 4, 1845; removed with his parents to California in 1852; was converted, and joined the Methodists in 1855. In 1862 he was appointed to take charge of the Carson Valley Circuit, Nevada Territory. During the war he was three years in the U. S. army. At its close he continued in the Methodist ministry, and was located in California, at Cache Creek, Rio Vista, Capey, and Colusa. In 1873 he joined the Baptist church at Newville; was licensed, and ordained in 1875; labored as a missionary of the Sacramento River Association; traveled and preached in the mountain regions and mining camps; organized Sunday-schools, and preached to feeble churches. He has been for three years clerk of the Sacramento River Association, and in 1880 was enrolling clerk of the California Legislature. Conscientious, finely educated, easy in public address, and logical in preaching, he is held in high esteem, and is known as an earnest and successful advocate of the ordinances and faith of the Baptists.

Reding, Rev. Charles W., was born in Portsmouth, N. H., Sept. 21, 1811, and was a graduate of Brown University in the class of 1837, and of the Newton Theological Institution in the class of 1840. He was ordained as pastor of the church in West Townsend, Mass., May 12, 1841, where he remained for three years, and then removed to Yarmouth, Me., where he was pastor also for another three years. From Yarmouth he went to the Second church in Beverly, Mass., where he continued until 1856, and then removed to Manchester, where he was pastor five years; then two years at Beverly, with his former church; then at Webster, from 1863 to 1869; and then at Milford, for two years. Since 1874 Mr. Reding has resided at Beverly, and has supplied the church which he formerly served since 1874.

Reding, Rev. Joseph, a distinguished pioneer preacher in the South and West, was born in Fauquier Co., Va., about 1750. He was converted under the ministry of the eloquent William Marshall, and baptized in 1771. He commenced preaching immediately, and with such success that a large number of people were converted. In 1772 he removed to South Carolina. The next year he returned to his old home, where he was ordained at Happy Creek church. Soon after this he located in Hampshire County, where he founded several churches, there being no other preacher in the county. In 1779 he started with his family to Kentucky. His boat was wrecked, and he did not reach the present site of Louisville until the following April. In a short time after he landed one of his children died. The Indians were so troublesome that he could preach but little, and in the fall he returned to Virginia. In 1784 he again removed to South Carolina, where he traveled and preached extensively, occasionally supplying the pulpit in Charleston, before Dr. Furman took charge of it. In the fall of 1789 he settled in Scott Co., Ky. He preached there with the same zeal and constancy that he had exercised elsewhere, and became the most popular preacher in the new settlements. He was called to the care of Great Crossing church, to which he preached with great success sixteen years. During the years 1800 and 1801 he baptized 361 persons into the fellowship of the Great Crossing church. In 1810 he took charge of Dry Run church, which he had formed in Scott County. Here he remained until his death, which occurred in December, 1815.

Reed, N. A., D.D., was born in Lynn, Mass., Jan. 20, 1815. He was early ambitious for an education, and availed himself, with that view, of such opportunities as offered during intervals of labor on the farm or in the store, for private study. In 1832, in a revival at Andover, he was converted. Though educated as a Congregationalist, the study of the Greek New Testament made him a Baptist. He was baptized in 1833 into the fellowship of the Andover Baptist church. Deciding to enter the ministry, he studied at Brown University, graduating in 1838, and was ordained at Wakefield, R. I., soon after. His successful pastorates have been at Wakefield, Suffield, Conn., Bedford and Franklindale, N. Y., Winchester, Mass., near Boston, Wakefield a second time, Bristol, R. I., Middletown, N. Y., Zanesville, O., Grand Rapids, Mich., Hamilton, O., Muscatine, Iowa, Centralia, Ill., and the present one at Amboy, in the same State. At these important points his work has always been fruitful in conversions and additions to the churches, while the influence of his public ministry has been ever promotive of harmony and the spirit of church enterprise.

Rees, Rev. Cyrus William, A.M., was born in Guernsey Co., O., Jan. 2, 1828; son of Rev. Wm. Rees, who did so much for missions and education in Indiana; has two brothers in the Baptist ministry, Rev. Eli Rees, of California, and Rev. Jonathan H. Rees, of Texas. In early life he studied for the medical profession. At eighteen he was converted, and baptized by his father at Delphi, Ind. Studied at Franklin and Kalamazoo Colleges, graduating at Kalamazoo in 1855. Offered himself as a foreign missionary, and was accepted by the board at Boston, but the $60,000 debt prevented the Union from sending him. In 1855 he settled as pastor of the Mount Clemens and Macomb churches, Mich., and was ordained November 15, precious revivals attending his work at both churches. In 1856 he settled at Fort Wayne, built a meeting-house, and baptized sixty. Losing his voice, he removed to Texas. In 1859 he removed to California, regained his voice, settled at Petaluma, and built a meeting-house costing $1500; removed to Nevada in 1861; was the first Baptist preacher at Carson, Virginia City, Silver City, Dayton, and Fort Churchill, and school superintendent for Lyon County. Until 1869 he labored in Nevada and Eastern California, and organized more new churches than any other pastor or missionary on the Pacific coast. He has labored at Sacramento and Red Bluff in California, built new meeting-houses, organized the Eastern Association in 1873; moved to Oregon in 1876; was pastor at Eugene City, the seat of the State University; is now pastor at the Dalles; has baptized 300 converts. He is author of a "Chronological Historical Chart" of the leading events of the world; also author of a similar "History of the American Civil War," a "Baptist Chronological History from the Days of Christ," and now has a work nearly ready for the press, containing nearly four hundred Pedobaptist concessions to Baptist principles, arranged denominationally. He is a good preacher and lecturer on reformatory subjects, and a number of his discourses on special subjects have been published.

Rees, Rev. Eli, eldest son of Rev. Wm. Rees, was born in Ohio, Jan. 11, 1821. Two of his brothers are Baptist ministers, C. W. Rees, of Oregon, and Jonathan H. Rees, of Texas. Educated at Denison University, O.; ordained as pastor at Huntington, Ind., Jan. 16, 1848. After two years he became general agent of the Indiana State Association, and did much to arouse a mission spirit; organized and served the Brookville church, baptizing many converts, until 1854, when health required him to go to the warmer climate of Texas, where he taught and preached; was president of the Margaret Houston Female College; held protracted meetings, baptized many converts; and in 1859 crossed the plains to California, preaching on the journey. During twenty years he has given himself to mission work, laboring almost alone in the San Joaquin Valley, raising up several Baptist churches, and training them for future pastors. He is the inventor of a patent which promises fine pecuniary returns, which he has dedicated to home and foreign missions, and the endowment of a Baptist paper on the Pacific coast. His residence is Merced, Cal.

Rees, Rev. George Evans, was born near Haverford-West, South Wales, in the year 1845;

was baptized at Pembroke Dock in the eighteenth year of his age; studied at Bristol College, England, under the presidency of Rev. F. W. Gotch, LL.D.; settled in his first pastorate at Truro, Cornwall, England, and remained more than three years and a half. He came to the United States in June, 1872, and soon after accepted a call to the Tabernacle church, Philadelphia, in which field of labor he still continues in the esteem and co-operation of a large and influential membership. He is also connected with the boards of management in city and State mission work. Mr. Rees is a man of genial temperament and robust intellect, and a preacher whose words are spoken with great clearness and force. The blessing of God has rested upon his labors in an unusual measure.

REV. GEORGE EVANS REES.

Reese, Rev. Joseph, was born in Delaware in 1736. His father came to South Carolina during his childhood. He was for many years pastor of the Congaree church. He was, in a great measure, instrumental in the revival from which the noted church, High Hills of Santee, sprang. The people of the vicinity had been singularly careless about religion, until their interest was awakened by Mr. Reese, and greatly increased by Dr. Furman.

He was in feeble health for years before his death. "His last attendance at church was about twelve months before his decease, at which time, in great pain and weakness, he administered the Lord's Supper."

Reeves, Rev. James, was born in Wilkes Co., Ga., in 1783, and died in Carroll County, April 6, 1858, in the seventy-fifth year of his age. He was most decidedly a praying man and a student of the Bible. From his entrance into the ministry he was devoted to its sacred duties, and gloried in being a pioneer preacher. He removed successively to Jasper, Butts, and Troup Counties, following the tide of immigration, and with John Wood and other zealous ministers planted the cross in what was then, comparatively speaking, a wilderness. Preaching in log cabins and under temporary arbors, they supplied the people with Bibles and tracts, and established Sunday-schools and temperance societies. Some of the most flourishing churches in Troup and the adjoining counties were established by Reeves and his coadjutors. In those days the anti-mission war raged, and John Reeves was one of the firmest defenders of missions. He was benevolent and exceedingly punctual, and no one enjoyed more the confidence of those who knew him. To the very last he was faithful and devoted, old age neither dampening his ardor nor restraining his zeal, and death found him "as a shock of corn fully ripe."

Reeves, Rev. Jeremiah, Sr., was born in Halifax Co., N. C.; brought up in the Episcopal Church; his painstaking in the acquisition of knowledge gained him the office of clerk, whose business it was to assist the rector in public service; but upon hearing the Baptists preach he entered into their views with all his heart. This was a source of deep mortification to his father, who remarked, "Jerry, I am the more astonished at you, seeing you have labored through so many difficulties to inform your mind, and have obtained more knowledge than the rest of the family, that you should now turn fool and follow after these babblers." Nevertheless, Jerry connected himself with a Baptist church on Mars' Fork of Haw River before the Revolutionary war. He removed to Georgia in 1784, and settled in Wilkes County, on the Dry Fork of Long Creek, and was among the early members of Sardis, then Hutton's Fork church. As a Christian, he was zealous, pious, and devoted; as a church member, he was constant, stable, and persevering; as a preacher, he was ardent in spirit and sound in the faith; and as a man, he was industrious, courteous, and honorable.

Mr. Reeves raised a fine family of children, most of whom grew to maturity and became useful Christians. Four of them, Malachi, Jeremiah, John, and James, became ministers of the gospel.

Reeves, Rev. Jeremiah, Jr., son of Rev. Jeremiah Reeves, Sr., was born in North Carolina in 1772, and removed with his father to Georgia in 1784, settling in Wilkes County. He was ordained a deacon in 1806, and set apart to the ministry in 1813. He labored long and faithfully in the northeast part of the State, being one of the first pioneers in that section, aiding in the constitution of various churches. In sentiment he was strongly missionary, and encountered some persecution on account of his stern advocacy of missionary and temperance principles. He was a man of great piety, and eminent for his devotional spirit and for promoting missions in the Sarepta Association. He died on the 27th of January, 1837, in the sixty-fifth year of his age.

Reeves, Rev. John, third ministerial son of Jeremiah Reeves, was born in Georgia about the year 1790, and was a very useful man in his day.

Reeves, Rev. Malachi, son of Jeremiah Reeves, Sr., was born in Halifax Co., N. C., about the year 1770, and removed with his father to Georgia in 1784. At maturity he joined the church at Sardis, Wilkes Co., and was introduced into the ministry through the following train of circumstances: About the year 1808 he, in company with his brother Jeremiah and Pitt Milner, another member of the church, instituted a series of prayer-meetings to be held at their houses. About a dozen attended the first appointment, and it was agreed to continue the meetings so long as one dozen should attend. At each consecutive meeting a larger number was in attendance, until both house and yard were full. Soon it became apparent that the Spirit of the Lord was in the design, and for the accommodation of an anxious multitude the meeting-house was put into requisition. Naturally such an attentive multitude of inquirers rendered necessary the reading and expounding of the Scriptures and exhortation, in which exercises Malachi Reeves took the lead, and soon gained for himself the title of preacher. Pitt Milner was called the exhorter, whilst Jeremiah Reeves, Jr., was called the praying man, on account of the fervor of his petitions.

From this commencement a glorious revival ensued, and about 100 were added to the church. The Sardis church saw fit to license Malachi Reeves to preach, which was done in 1809, and the following year he was ordained to the full work of the ministry, and ever afterwards, to his death, in 1826, he proved a good and useful minister of Christ, greatly beloved by all. He was a man of good natural talents, clear judgment, and discriminating understanding.

Reeves, Rev. Zachariah, a distinguished pioneer preacher in South Mississippi, was born in South Carolina in 1799; came to Pike Co., Miss., in 1811; began to preach in 1832; was a man of great power, and exerted a wide influence in the southern part of the State; planted many churches; and was for twenty-four years moderator of the Mississippi Association; died in 1871.

Regent's Park College, one of the finest educational edifices in London, England, is the home of the Baptist theological seminary formerly known as Stepney College, which was founded in 1810, under the presidency of the Rev. W. Newman, D.D. Since the removal to Regent's Park, in 1856, lay students have been admitted, and the institution has won a high position in public esteem. The Rev. Joseph Angus, D.D., LL.D., has been president upwards of thirty years. In commemoration of his personal worth and eminent services to the Baptist denomination and to education, the "Angus Lectureship" has been founded during the present year (1880). Regent's Park College is affiliated to the University of London, and a large number of students have graduated, several of whom have taken high honors and valuable prizes. During the last twenty years about $50,000 have been contributed by friends of the college to found scholarships. More than 300 ministers have gone forth from the college to labor in different parts of the United Kingdom, the British colonies, the United States, and heathen lands.

Register, The Baptist Annual.—This work was first issued in 1790, in London, by Dr. John Rippon. Until this period the Baptists in Europe and America were destitute of any organ. The *Register* had articles from both sides of the Atlantic, and it was a creditable forerunner of the long list of periodicals and newspapers that now give a knowledge of our doctrines and movements to millions of readers.

Reid, Judge Jacob P., departed this life Aug. 19, 1880, in his sixty-sixth year. He was solicitor of the western circuit of South Carolina for sixteen years, and was accounted one of the ablest in the State. In 1868 he was elected to Congress from the third district, but was not permitted to take his seat. In 1874 he was elected judge of the first circuit, and served with great ability until he resigned the position in 1878.

He was a member of the Anderson Baptist church for many years. He was a man of much force of character, and of great liberality and public spirit. The influence of his useful life will long survive him.

Reid, Rev. Samuel Ethelred, of African descent, was born of Baptist parents at Browstown, Jamaica, West Indies, May 22, 1840. He graduated at Lady Mico Institution, Kingston, then engaged in mission work. He removed to California in 1865; preached for the Second Baptist church, Stockton, four years; was ordained at Stockton in October, 1867, and had marked success. Removing to Virginia City, Nev., his talent and integrity led to his employment in a responsible position in one of the gold-mining companies of that city. But he preaches frequently, is an official member of the church, a man of influence, and deeply interested

REGENT'S PARK COLLEGE, LONDON, ENGLAND.

in the welfare of the scattered colored Baptists on the Pacific coast.

Reid, Rev. T. A., was born in Hall Co., Ga., March 28, 1828. He studied and taught alternately until 1853, when he entered Mercer University. That great and good man, Rev. P. H. Mell, D.D., entered his room and said, "I and my wife have determined to take you as a member of our family and incur all your college expenses."

He had long felt it a duty to preach, and soon after going to Mercer he told Dr. Mell of his desire, and soon after he received a license.

In 1856 the Rehoboth Association in Georgia determined to send him as a missionary to Africa. He and his wife sailed from New York on the 7th of August, 1857, and landed in Africa in the following September. In 1858 he lost his wife. In loneliness, in perils of a native war, and amid great privations, he still labored for the Master in Awyaw, the capital of the Yoruba country. In 1864 the feebleness of his health made it necessary for him to return to his native country. Having spent some time in England he landed in New York. For several years he preached in South Carolina and in other States with acceptance, waiting till the board could send him to his chosen foreign field. The board, however, having at length determined not to send any more married missionaries to Africa, as he was now married a second time, he reluctantly gave up Africa, and he is now preaching with characteristic zeal and success at Millway, S. C.

Reid, Rev. William, was born in Ayrshire, Scotland, in 1812. His parents were Presbyterians, but at the age of seventeen he was baptized by Rev. James Blair, and joined the Baptist church of which he was pastor. His father soon afterwards also united with the Baptist Church. He was licensed by the church to preach. In his twentieth year he came to the United States, and engaged in secular business; but by the advice of friends he resolved to devote himself to the work of the ministry. For several years he studied in the Connecticut Literary Institution at Suffield. He was ordained in East Windsor in 1839, and was first settled as pastor at Wethersfield. After two years he accepted the pastorate of the church at Tariffville. During this settlement of five years large additions were made to the church. He then became pastor of the church at Bridgeport, where he remained nine years; then he took charge of the First Baptist church of New London, where he remained eight years. He was then pastor at Green Point, Brooklyn, four years. From thence he was called to the McDougal Street church in New York. After a pastorate of several years he accepted the call of the Herkimer Street church in Brooklyn, N. Y. In all these settlements he met with great success.

He is a fluent, calm, deliberate speaker, showing clearly, by his style and accent, that his early training was in Scotland. He has a clear head and warm heart. Often there is a grandeur in the sweep of his thought that thrills and charms his hearers. As a Baptist, he is conservative, and eminently sound in the faith taught by the fathers of the denomination.

Reinhardt, Rev. J. J., was born a slave, Aug. 15, 1828, in Lawrence Co., Miss.; had no early advantages of education. He made use of all the opportunities which came in his way, and he is now prepared to study any book in the English language. He has given some attention to New Testament Greek, receiving occasional assistance and advice from Rev. R. Andrews, Jr., and Rev. W. C. Crane, D.D., LL.D. He was born from above April 7, 1849, and was licensed and encouraged to preach to his race in the summer of 1849. He was ordained to the full work of the gospel ministry in the fall of 1866. He has baptized 300 persons in Walker County, 400 in Grimes County, 200 in Brazos County, 400 in Robertson County, 60 in Houston County, 100 in Leon County, and 100 in Washington County, Texas; total, 1560. He has been pastor of 21 churches, all organized by his agency, with such help as he could procure. He now resides at Navasota, and is pastor of two churches. He has held three offices,—1. Supervisor of public schools for Grimes, Walker, Madison, and San Jacinto Counties; 2. School director for Grimes County; 3. Alderman for the city of Navasota for five years. At present he holds no office except that of a minister of the gospel. He is a man of fine natural sense, clear and sound judgment, using good language in expressing his ideas, and commanding the respect and confidence of both the white and colored races. In the councils of his people he holds a high rank, and is exerting a healthful spiritual influence in the community where he resides.

Reinhart, President H. W., was born in Charlottesville, Va., July 4, 1833; graduated in a number of the schools of the University of Virginia; was baptized by Dr. Jeter; has taught twenty-four years in Virginia and North Carolina, in Albemarle Military Institute, Richmond College, Roanoke Female College, as co-principal with Rev. J. B. Lake, at Fredericksburg, Va.; came to Yanceyville, N. C., in 1859; served as captain of cavalry till health gave way, in 1864; taught in Danville Va., Raleigh, N. C., and now for several years has been president and proprietor of a prosperous female college at Thomasville, N. C. Mr. Reinhart has never been ordained, but sometimes preaches.

Religious Denominations in the United States.—The following statistics are from the "Baptist Year-Book:"

Denominations.	Churches.	Ministers.	Members.
Adventist	80	120	10,000
Anti-Mission Baptist	900	400	40,000
Baptists	26,060	16,596	2,296,327
Church of God, Winebrennarians.	400	350	30,000
Congregationalists	3,674	3,536	382,920
Disciples, Campbellites	2,366	2,000	350,000
Episcopal, Protestant	2,996	3,435	345,841
Episcopal, Reformed	64	100	5,000
Free-Will Baptists	1,471	1,294	74,851
Friends	800	....	100,000
Lutherans	5,697	3,225	712,240
Mennonites	120	90	20,000
Methodist Episcopal	17,111	11,811	*1,723,147
Methodist Episcopal, South	....	3,867	828,301
Methodist Episcopal, African	....	1,418	214,808
Methodist Episcopal, Zion African.	....	1,500	190,900
Methodist Episcopal, Colored	....	638	112,300
Methodist Evangelical Association	....	893	112,197
Methodist, Free	....	271	12,642
Methodist, Independent	....	24	12,550
Methodist, Primitive	....	196	3,210
Methodist Protestant	....	1,314	113,405
Methodist Episcopal Union, American (colored)	....	101	2,550
Methodist, Wesleyan	....	250	25,000
Moravian	75	....	9,212
Presbyterian, Cumberland	2,000	1,239	100,000
Presbyterian, North	5,489	5,044	578,671
Presbyterian, Reformed	153	128	10,250
Presbyterian, South	1,928	1,000	120,028
Presbyterian, United	798	625	77,414
Reformed Churches in America (Dutch)	510	545	80,208
Reformed Churches in United States (German)	1,374	714	151,761
Roman Catholic (said to be)	6,920	4,873	†6,000,000
Seventh-Day Baptists	84	80	8,548
Six-Principle Baptists	20	12	2,000
Tunkers	500	1,200	50,000
United Brethren	3,079	2,196	157,835

* Including 179,029 members on probation.
† Entire Roman Catholic population.

Relyea, Rev. S. S., was born in New York in 1822; spent two years at Waterville College, Me., and graduated at New York City University in 1846, and Hamilton Theological Seminary in 1849. After filling a number of prominent pastorates in New York he removed to Mississippi, and subsequently to Louisiana, where he was actively employed in teaching and preaching; nine years in charge of Silliman Institute, Clinton, La.; eight years at Woodland Institute, East Feliciana Parish, La. Subsequently he returned to Mississippi, and became connected with a school at McComb City, Miss., and associate editor of the *Southern Baptist*. He died in 1877. He left a manuscript work on church polity.

Remick, Rev. Timothy, was born in Kittery, Me., Sept. 30, 1775; was hopefully converted at the age of twenty-three, and having become a Baptist from his personal study of the Bible, joined the Baptist church in Parsonfield, Me. Feeling it to be his duty to preach the gospel, he commenced his work as an evangelist in the neighborhood in which he lived, his labors being followed by rich fruits. He was ordained in Cornish, Me., in June, 1804, as pastor of the church in that place, where he remained the rest of his life. His ministry was one of blessing to his church and to the community in which he lived for so many years. He died Dec. 27, 1850.

Renfroe, J. J. D., D.D., was born in Montgomery Co., Ala., Aug. 30, 1830. He was baptized by A. N. Worthy, Aug. 30, 1848; ordained at Cedar Bluff in 1852. The earlier years of his life

J. J. D. RENFROE, D.D.

were spent among a rude, uncultured people. Entering the ministry when young, with great difficulties in his pathway, he has by persistent and faithful effort made his way to the front rank of preachers in the South. During the first years of his ministry he was eminently successful as pastor and preacher, baptizing large numbers into the various churches in Cherokee and Calhoun Counties of which he was pastor. While diligently engaged in leading sinners to Christ, he was earnest and aggressive in his defense of "the faith once delivered to the saints." This led him into frequent controversies with ministers of other denominations. The results of these conflicts never made his brethren blush for his defeat, but his almost uniform success made them confident when their cause had been committed to the strong young pastor.

Unusual native ability, hard study, faithful, effective service, commanded the attention of the denomination, and on the 1st of January, 1858, he was called to the pastorate of the church in Talladega. The last three years of "the war between the States" he spent in Virginia, the efficient and beloved chaplain of a regiment in the Confederate army. At the close of the war he returned to Talladega, resuming his pastorate. The beautiful brick building in which the church in Talladega now worships is a lasting monument of his indomitable energy and untiring zeal. He is still the pastor of the church in Talladega, enjoying the unquestioning confidence and deepest Christian affection of the entire membership.

His practical, pointed, and able contributions to various religious periodicals during almost the entire term of his public life have given him a wide reputation, and made him a power in the denomination. The current questions of the day always command his attention, and he is ever ready to defend the tenets of his church.

In 1875 Howard College conferred upon him the degree of Doctor of Divinity.

To him more than to any other is due the credit of inaugurating the State mission work in Alabama. When almost all were opposed he stood firm, and contended earnestly for what he conceived to be best. Results have demonstrated his wisdom and rewarded him for all the efforts made in this direction.

Dr. Renfroe is a man of strong convictions, with courage to follow wherever they lead without hesitation and without wavering. An humble man of God, who has spent his life and sacrificed himself in the service of his Master.

The latter years of his life have been made bitter by severe bereavements and affliction. Amid repeated sore troubles and hard trials, rapidly recurring, he has made it manifest that he is a trusting child of God, a good servant of Christ, who can endure hardness as a good soldier of the Cross.

To-day no minister in Alabama occupies a larger or more tender place in the affections of his brethren, no man has more of the confidence and respect of the denomination to which he belongs.

Renfroe, Rev. N. D., was born in Macon Co., Ala., Oct. 7, 1833; united with the Baptist Church, and was baptized by Rev. J. R. Hand in 1848; educated in the Cedar Bluff Academy and in Union University, Tenn.; spent four years in the university under Rev. J. W. Eaton, LL.D., also took the theological course under Rev. J. M. Pendleton, D.D.; ordained as pastor of the church in Jacksonville, Ala., in 1859, where he manifested superior tact as a young pastor, and far more than ordinary ability as a preacher; entered the Confederate service at the opening of the war, and was killed, in command of his company, in the battle of Fredericksburg, Va., Dec. 13, 1862. From childhood he was distinguished for the purity of his personal character, and after becoming a Christian his life was nearly faultless. At the time of his death he was popular, and growing in popularity in the army as a soldier, as an officer, and as a minister, for he frequently preached to his comrades. When on the march, when in hard service, when in need, and when any were sick, he was constantly watchful for them and tender of their interests, though rigid in duty. After he fell the Rev. Dr. Henderson edited a tract of sixteen pages on his life, entitled "The Model Confederate Soldier," which was published in thousands by the Virginia Tract Society, and circulated among the soldiers; it consisted mainly of articles which appeared in the papers about him. He was one of the purest and most spotless soldiers in the Confederate army. His remains were carried to Alabama and buried in Talladega, where his elder brother, the Rev. J. J. D. Renfroe, has long been pastor. Mr. Renfroe was twenty-nine years old, and unmarried.

Repentance is indispensable to the blotting out of our sins and to the possession of that holiness without which no man shall see the Lord. It was frequently on the lips of John the Baptist, and of the Saviour and his apostles, and it should be in the heart of every member of Adam's guilty race.

Repentance is not merely fear for God's anger, coming from a consciousness of our guilt. The five foolish virgins, when death came, were filled with apprehensions in view of meeting God, and they immediately sought pardon, and failed to find it because the Saviour knew nothing about them as penitent persons.

Repentance is not mere grief for the consequences of sin. Esau sold his birthright, and for an insignificant price he gave up the honor of being the father of the coming Messiah, of many kings, and of a great historic nation, stretching over thousands of years of human history. When he came to see the full measure of his folly, he was filled with bitter grief for the consequences of his sin. So are convicts in view of the scaffold, and so are hosts of men drawing near the eternal world who have never repented.

Repentance is not despair in view of some great wrong which the soul has committed. Judas was guilty of an act of atrocious baseness in betraying Jesus for thirty pieces of silver. He evidently had no idea that the Jews intended to proceed to such extreme measures with his late Master, though he knew full well that they wanted to perpetrate some outrage upon him. And when he learned that Jesus was condemned to be crucified he was filled with maddening despair and he destroyed himself. He seems to have had no regret for any other sin of his hypocritical and dishonest life. He solicited no pardon. He was simply overwhelmed with a consciousness of his great guilt in betraying the sinless Redeemer to a violent and cruel death. The Saviour says about this false apostle, "Woe unto that man by whom the Son of man is betrayed; it had been good for that man if he had not been born." The fierce anguish of his soul was not repentance for his great sin, nor for any other of his iniquities; it had no appeals for mercy in it, and the man was abandoned by his fellows and by himself as worthy to feel forever in his soul the woe pronounced by Jesus upon him by whom the Son of man was betrayed. In many similar cases of despair, and sometimes of suicide, there has been no repentance, no supplication, and no forgiveness. It is a delusion to suppose that agonizing despair for sin is that repentance which secures salvation.

Repentance has nothing in common with Catholic penance. Fastings, flagellations, hairy garments to sting the skin, and other forms of penance are foreign to the nature of gospel repentance. When it is said, "Repent ye therefore, and be converted, that your sin may be blotted out," we are not to imagine that Peter enjoins any penance, any physical application to secure the removal of our iniquities.

Repentance is a change of mind or purpose. This is the meaning of μετάνοια, the Greek word translated repentance in the New Testament. There is implied in it sorrow for unbelief and sin, and a turning from them unto God. Until a man repents he commonly feels comfortable about himself and his ways; but when the Saviour, through the Spirit, gives him repentance he changes his mind about himself, and seeing nothing good in his heart or in his works, his whole soul cries out, "Lord, be merciful to me a sinner."

Repentance is a change of mind about God's relations to the soul. Before its existence in the heart the unbeliever feels as if Jehovah had little, if anything, to do with him or his acts. When the Spirit gives him penitential light he sees immediately that every sin against himself or others is a crime against God. And his soul, as he considers each transgression, is ready to cry out before the Lord, "Against thee, thee only have I sinned, and done this evil in thy sight." Before he repents the justice of God seems to him very pure, but distant, and in a large measure powerless. When he is first illuminated by the Spirit the justice of God appears to him to be the most active attribute of Jehovah, and he is certain that it must be satisfied before his conscience can enjoy rest. This change of mind is instantly attended by a change of heart, and like the prodigal loathing his husks, the penitent abhors his sins, and his whole soul turns from them. Repentance is always accompanied by a conviction that the soul is in a lost condition. "How many hired servants of my father," saith the prodigal, "have bread enough and to spare, and I perish with hunger?" The penitent always desires to go to the Saviour after receiving the heaven-given "change of mind." The decision of his soul is, "I will arise and go to my father." As the penitent man thinks of his wasted life, of the privileges he has abused, of the Redeemer against whom he has madly fought, of his numerous and aggravated iniquities, his heart is filled with grief, it is a broken and a contrite heart, and he feels resolved that nothing shall keep him from Jesus. And nothing can; the unchanging Spirit who has commenced the work of saving his soul, by giving it repentance, will never cease his loving toils till the soul rejoices in the dazzling light of the day of Christ in heaven.

Repentance never saved a soul by its merits; it lays the needful foundation for the temple of faith in the heart. But all the penitential sorrows of Adam's family would not remove one faint stain of sin. If a man borrowed five thousand dollars, for which he gave security, and squandered it most foolishly, and afterwards, filled with true repentance, he solicited and expected the forgivenness of the debt because he was sorry for it, the spendthrift would only meet with contempt in his application; his sureties would have to pay the money. Faith alone in the Crucified cleanses from all sin, and repentance is God's instrumentality for leading the sinner to the Lamb of God, the Great Remover of sin.

Restoration.—It is the privilege and duty of every Baptist church to restore to its fellowship any of its own fallen members who lament and renounce their backslidings. When an excluded and reclaimed brother seeks restoration to church relations in a strange church, it has a right to receive him on the broad ground of the independency of Baptist churches, but this right should be exercised with prudence. Our churches owe each other fraternal courtesy in matters of discipline as well as in other things; and, as a consequence, many of our Associations have a resolution declaring that the churches composing them will respect each other's discipline, and all of them have an understanding of kindred import.

It is desirable, therefore, in every case, that the excluded person should be restored by the church which expelled him from its membership. But as he sometimes has decided and well-founded objections to connect himself with his former friends, the church of his new choice should gain their concurrence to his restoration, if possible; and failing, and thoroughly satisfied of the piety of the applicant and of the justice of his objections, they may call a council, and receive him on its recommendation,—if it is an important case this is the wiser course,—or they can admit him to their fellowship without any external advice.

It is extremely desirable that Baptist churches should act in harmony in everything; but it is of great importance that no disciple of Jesus should suffer wrongfully.

Resurrection, The, was one of the chief elements in apostolic preaching. Wherever Paul went in his missionary journeys he proclaimed Jesus and the resurrection,—the complete redemption of soul and body by the Saviour's cross. The doctrine of the resurrection was one of the great agencies in making the early Christians fearless of bodily danger and death. As the flames, the sword, or the wild beasts threatened them, they felt confident that the body would spring from the dust of death with immortal vitality, and in the wondrous glory which the Saviour's body wore when he took his place in paradise, and they were ready to defy death in its most hideous forms, and bid it welcome in any situation. We can scarcely conceive the extraordinary joy which the resurrection gave Christ's first followers; the cross with its fierce agonies, its ghastly death, its darkened sun, its rent rocks, its cleansing blood, its intense love, and the hopes which it kindled in the believer's heart, was only a little dearer to primitive Christians than the resurrection. They loved to think of the bursting graves, of the saints in glorified bodies, of routed and conquered death, of persecutions, diseases, and the decay of years crushed; of the saintly victims of infuriated soldiers invested with spiritual and glorious bodies. To them the cross was the fountain of all blessedness, and the resurrection the richest stream of hope that flowed from the cross.

They refused to continue the word sepulchre (a place of concealment) as a designation for the resting-place of a dead believer; they used the word cemeteries (κοιμητήρια), that is, *dormitories*, to describe the scenes where the holy dead were sleeping, until the trumpet of the archangel should banish their slumbers and arouse their bodies from the sleep of years or ages.

In the ordinance of baptism there is a distinct announcement of the resurrection as well as of death and burial. Paul says, "Therefore we are buried with him by baptism into death: that like as Christ was raised up from the dead by the glory of the Father, even so we also should walk in newness of life. For if we have been planted together in the likeness of his death (in the baptismal immersion), we shall be also in the likeness of his resurrection" (by rising up from the waters of baptism).—Rom. vi. 4, 5. Paul uses baptism as an argument in favor of the resurrection. "Else what shall they do who are baptized for the dead (who profess faith in the resurrection of the dead by the very form of baptism), if the dead rise not at all? why are they then baptized for the dead?"—1 Cor. xv. 29. That is, "Why does baptism proclaim the resurrection of the dead if there is no such thing?" Just as the Lord's Supper shows the wounds and blood of Jesus, so baptism teaches the resurrection of the dead.

The Philadelphia Confession of Faith says, "At the last day such of the saints as are found alive shall not sleep, but be changed, and all the dead shall be raised up with the self-same bodies, and none other, although with different qualities, which shall be united again to their souls forever. The bodies of the unjust shall, by the power of Christ, be raised to dishonor; the bodies of the just, by his Spirit, unto honor, and be made conformable to his own glorious body." (Article XXXIII. 2, 3.)

The resurrection body, as the Confession says, will have "different qualities"; in fact, the qualities are just the opposite of the body deposited in the grave: "it is sown in corruption, it is raised in incorruption; it is sown in dishonor, it is raised in glory; it is sown in weakness, it is raised in power; it is sown a natural (animal) body, it is raised *a spiritual body*."—1 Cor. xv. 42-44. This resurrection body will be a wonderful structure, entirely unlike any other human body except the one now worn by the Saviour in the heavens. Paul's idea seems to be that as a grain of wheat planted in the earth has a germ of life in it, which makes a stalk and, in due time, grains of wheat exactly like itself, so from the human body, at the resurrection, shall spring up a spiritual body, with every feature of the " natural" body once deposited in the grave, but with wholly " different qualities." A distinguished Baptist clergyman, commenting on Paul's resurrection theory in the fifteenth chapter of the first epistle to the Corinthians, says, " As the wheat germ controls the form, not the material, of the plant, so, as to its form, though not its material, will the germ of each human body, fashioned alike in infancy, youth, maturity, and decay, produce for itself its own body,"—that is, a body exactly like the one smitten by death, and reduced to dust by the grave. This sublime victory over death and the grave fills the apostle with jubilant exultation, and inspires rapture in the heart of the intelligent and devout Christian. When Pharaoh proposed to Moses to let the children of Israel depart on condition that they should leave their flocks and herds in Egypt, Moses replied, "Our cattle also shall go with us; there shall not a hoof be left behind." So our redemption shall be completed by the recovery of the whole man, both soul and body, from the havoc of sin, the blows of the Destroyer, and the power of the grave; there shall not an atom of the man be left behind.

Some believe that there will be two resurrections at distinct periods of time, the " dead in Christ rising first" (1 Thess. iv. 16), "obtaining a better resurrection" (Heb. xi. 35), and enjoying the apocalyptic benediction, " Blessed and holy is he that hath part in the first resurrection" (Rev. xx. 6); but the object of this article forbids us to treat of the second resurrection in this place. It is proper to state that the doctrine is held by not a few Baptists, among whom there are men of unsurpassed piety and intelligence.

Review, The Christian, was commenced in 1836. The design was to make it a literary and religious quarterly, which, under its varying fortunes, and lately under the name of the *Baptist Quarterly*, it always has been, with the exception of a brief period, when it was issued bi-monthly. Prof. J. D. Knowles was its first editor, and continued such to the time of his death, when Rev. Dr. Sears took charge of the editorial department, his connection with it dating from the second number of the third volume. This relation continued until the close of the sixth volume, when it passed into the hands of Rev. Dr. S. F. Smith, where it remained to the end of volume thirteen. The fourteenth volume was edited by Rev. E. G. Sears. Rev. Dr. S. S. Cutting, with several assistant editors, carried it to volume eighteenth, and Rev. Drs. Turnbull and Murdoch to volume twenty-first. Rev. J. J. Woolsey was the editor of the twenty-first volume, and Rev. Drs. Wilson and Taylor editors of the next three volumes. Dr. E. G. Robinson was its next editor, and had the charge of the next four volumes, bringing it down to 1863, when it was merged into the *Bibliotheca Sacra*, with Dr. Sears as one of the editors. The union of the two periodicals continued for one year, when it ceased, and the *Baptist Quarterly* occupied the position which the *Christian Review* had held, as the sole organ of its kind in the Baptist denomination in this country.

"The *Review*," says Rev. Dr. Crowell, to whom we are indebted for the above facts, "has maintained a highly respectable position among the literary and theological quarterlies of the day. It has been an able exponent of Baptist principles, though catholic in its tone." It has added some 23,600 pages to the permanent literature of American Baptists.

It seems unnecessary to mention the names of its contributors, as they include those who will be recognized as leading Baptist scholars and divines, and some who are not Baptists, in different sections of the country.

Revolution, The, and the Baptists.—When the Legislature of Massachusetts, in 1778, forbade the return of 311 public enemies to their government, the historian Backus, who was acquainted with the facts, declares that not one of them was a Baptist. (Church History, p. 196. Philadelphia.) In Sabine's "History of American Loyalists" (Tories), with its 3200 brief biographies, we find 46 clergymen of one denomination, 6 of another, 3 of another, and but 1 Baptist minister. This was Morgan Edwards, a man of great genius and worth, who was born in the Old World, and who failed to honor the patriotism of the Baptists of his *native* country by adopting it. We can discover no layman in Sabine's list who was a Baptist. Christopher Sower, of Germantown, Pa., is represented by Sabine as a German Baptist minister and a Tory. Sower was a printer and bookseller, and unbound Bibles belonging to him, because of his loyalty to King George, furnished cartridge-paper for the Continental troops at the battle of Germantown. Sower was not a Baptist, but a member of a respectable German community that has no relations with the Baptists.

In the work of the Tory exile, Judge Curwen, of Salem, Mass., there are the names of 926 persons who fled from Boston with Gen. Howe when he sailed for Halifax; there are also the names of many others who left their country by the persuasion of State laws, committees of safety, or their own just fears. Among these are persons of all occupations, and of all positions in colonial society, 46 clergymen keeping them in company. In this singular work (Curwen's "Journal and Letters." Boston, 1864. Written in England, while its author was living on British alms), in which are the names of many American Tories, the gossiping ex-judge treats of literature, war, politics, theatres, and *theology*, but no hint is given that one of the Tories mentioned in it was a Baptist. Nor can we learn from other sources that any of them inflicted such a disgrace upon us.

President John Adams, in some respects an enemy of the Baptists, gives our people credit for bringing Delaware from the gulf of Toryism to the platform of patriotism. And he charges the disloyalty of her people on "the missionaries of the English Episcopal Society for the Propagation of the Faith." (Life and Works, by Charles Francis Adams, vol. x. p. 812.)

George Washington, in his reply to the "Committee of the Virginia Baptist Churches," which expressed to him grave doubts about the security of religious liberty under the Constitution of the United States, just adopted, said, "I recollect with satisfaction that the religious society of which you are members has been throughout America, *uniformly and almost unanimously*, the firm friends of civil liberty, and the persevering promoters of our glorious Revolution." (Writings of George Washington, Sparks, vol. xii. 154–55. Boston.) With such a testimony from the noblest patriot of the whole human race, we may well bless God for our religious ancestry, who were among the most active builders of our country's great temple of liberty. (See articles on VIRGINIA BAPTISTS AND THE REVOLUTION, and RHODE ISLAND BAPTISTS AND THE REVOLUTION.)

Revolution, The, and the English Baptists. —When Robert Hall, the future great preacher, was a little boy, he heard the Rev. John Ryland, Baptist minister of Northampton, say to his father, "If I were Washington I would summon all the American officers, they should form a circle around me, and I would address them, and we would offer a libation in our own blood, and I would order one of them to bring a lancet and a punch-bowl, and we would bare our arms and be bled, and when the bowl was full, when we all had been bled, I would call on every man to consecrate himself to the work by dipping his sword into the bowl, and entering into a solemn covenant engagement by oath, one to another, we would swear by him that sits upon the throne and liveth for ever and ever that we would never sheath our swords while there was an English soldier in arms remaining in America." (Robert Hall's Works, vol. iv. 48, 49. Harper, N. Y.)

Dr. John Rippon, of London, in a letter to President Manning, of Rhode Island College (Brown University), written in 1784, says, "I believe all our Baptist ministers in town (London) except two, and most of our brethren in the country, were on the side of the Americans in the late dispute. . . . We wept when the thirsty plains drank the blood of your departed heroes, and the shout of a king was amongst us when your well-fought battles were crowned with victory; and to this hour we believe that the independence of America will for a while secure the liberty of this country. But if that continent had been reduced, Britain would not have been long free." (Backus's History of the Baptists, vol. ii. p. 198. Newton.) Dr. Rippon and John Ryland were two of the leading Baptist ministers in England; and there is no doubt that the spirit of our brethren in England was in harmony with these noble utterances, with a few insignificant exceptions.

Revolution, The, and Rhode Island Baptists.—Before the Revolution Rhode Island was the freest colony in North America, or in the history of our race. Her founders had made her a real republic while under the nominal rule of a king, a government with which there could be no legal interference by any power either in the Old World or in the New. Before the Revolution Rhode Island had no viceroy, and the king had no veto on her laws. In 1704, Mompresson, chief justice of New York, wrote Lord Nottingham that "when he was in Rhode Island the people acted in all things as if they were outside the dominion of the crown." (Sabine's American Loyalists, p. 15. Boston, 1847.) Bancroft justly speaks of Rhode Island at the Revolution "as enjoying a form of government, under its charter, so thoroughly republican, that no change was required beyond a renunciation of the king's name in the style of its public acts." (History of the United States, ix. 261.) As Arnold says, Rhode Island, when the United States Constitution was adopted, "for more than a century and a half had enjoyed a freedom unknown to any of her compeers." (History of Rhode Island, ii. 563.) In the Revolution the little colony had everything to lose by its failure, and nothing in liberty to gain by a successful revolution.

And yet the colony of Roger Williams was the most enthusiastic friend of the Revolution on this side of the Atlantic. On May 4, 1776, Rhode Island withdrew from the sceptre of Great Britain; this was two months before the adoption of the Declaration of Independence. Scarcely had the retreating troops of Gen. Gage reached Boston when recruits from the nearest Rhode Island towns marched to the Massachusetts patriots who fought at Lexington and Concord; and the Legislature soon after voted fifteen hundred men, to be sent to the scene of danger. When the Declaration of Independence was read in Providence, Newport, and East Greenwich, it called forth outbursts of delight and shouts for "liberty o'er and o'er the globe." A British historian says, "The Rhode Islanders were such ardent patriots that after the capture of Rhode Island by Sir Peter Parker, it required a great body of men to be kept there, in perfect idleness for three years, to retain them in subjection." (Hume, Smollett, and Farr, iii. 99. London.) Gov. Green, in a dispatch to Washington in 1781, reports that "*sometimes every fencible man in the State*, sometimes a third, and at other times a fourth part was called out upon duty." (Collections of the Rhode Island Historical Society, vi. 290.)

With scarcely fifty thousand people of all ages and of both sexes the little State supported three regiments in the Continental army throughout the entire war, an immense number for her when we remember the demands for local defense. Rhode Island began the war early by declaring her independence thirty-two days before the brave Virginians renounced allegiance to George III., and she continued inflicting her heaviest blows until the United States were free from the yoke of Great Britain.

We have special pleasure in Rhode Island patriotism, because, while noble men of other denominations honored that State in the Revolutionary war, the ruling portion of the people were Baptists. Morgan Edwards, who died in 1795, whose statement cannot be questioned, says, "The Baptists have always been more than any other sect of Christians in Rhode Island; two-fifths of the inhabitants at least are reputed Baptists. The governors, deputy governors, judges, assemblymen, and officers, civil and military, are chiefly of that persuasion." (Collections by the Rhode Island Historical Society, vi. 304.) The spirit of liberty ruled the Baptist founders of Rhode Island, and in the Revolution held supreme sway over her Baptist people, who controlled the destinies of the State, and never did a people make greater sacrifices or more heroic efforts for liberty. (See articles on VIRGINIA BAPTISTS AND THE REVOLUTION, and BAPTISTS IN THE REVOLUTION.)

Revolution, The, and the Virginia Baptists.—The Baptist General Association of Virginia notified the Convention of the People of Virginia, "That they had considered what part it would be proper to take in the unhappy contest, and had determined that they ought to make a military resistance to Great Britain in her unjust invasion, tyrannical oppression, and repeated hostilities." (Headley's Chaplains and Clergy of the Revolution, p. 250. New York, 1864.) And they proclaimed to the world that "to a man they were in favor of the Revolution." (Semple, p. 62.) Preachers and people, Semple declares, were *engrossed* with thoughts and schemes for effecting the Revolution. Howison, in his "History of Virginia," ii. 170, says, "No class of the people of America were more devoted advocates of the principles of the Revolution, none were more willing to give their money and goods to their country, none more prompt to march to the field of battle, and none more heroic in actual conflict than the Baptists of Virginia."

Had it not been for the Baptists of Virginia it is probable that the "mother of Presidents" would have sided with Great Britain in the Revolutionary war. The leading men of the Old Dominion were the descendants of English aristocratic families, whose guiding principle for centuries was loyalty to the king. They were rigid Episcopalians, and so were the sovereign of England and the majority of his influential subjects in his home kingdom. The rectors of Virginia were native Englishmen, and bitter Tories, many of whom were specially acceptable to gay young Virginians, because they frequented the race-course, betted at cards, and rattled dice like experts. One of them was president of a jockey club, and another fought a duel. These men present a perfect contrast to their successors in the Episcopal Church of the Old Dominion in our day. Virginia proclaimed Charles II. before he was king in England. (Howe's Virginia Historical Collections, p. 133. Charleston, 1846.) When Patrick Henry introduced his five celebrated resolutions into the Virginia Assembly, in 1765, in connection with the Stamp Act, the men of influence in that body were opposed to his movement, and intended to submit to that iniquitous measure. (Campbell's History of Virginia, p. 541. Philadelphia.) Henry's fifth resolution, which recognized the great doctrine that their Legislature alone could tax its inhabitants, was carried by but *a single vote;* and yet this principle was the mainspring of the American Revolution. "Speaker Robinson," says Campbell, "Peyton Randolph, Richard Bland, Edmund Pendleton, George Wythe, and all the leaders of the House and proprietors of large estates, made a strenuous resistance." (History of Virginia, pp. 541–42.) Jefferson says, "The Resolutions of Henry were opposed by Robinson and all the cyphers of the aristocracy." It was in advocacy of these resolutions that Henry used the words, "Tarquin and Cæsar had each his Brutus, Charles I. his Cromwell, and George III.——" "Treason!" shouted the Speaker; "Treason, treason!" was echoed around the house; while Henry, fixing his eyes on the Speaker, continued, without faltering, "may profit by their example." (Bancroft, v. 277.) The next day the men who voted for the fifth resolution, alarmed by their own manly patriotism, actually had it expunged from the journals of the House. (Howison's History of Virginia, ii. 52. Richmond, 1848.) Eleven years later Virginia withdrew from the British crown on the ground which she took, by a majority of one, in 1765, and from which she shamefully withdrew the next day. What made the great change in Virginia?

"In 1774," says Howison, "the Baptists increased on every side. If one preacher was imprisoned, ten arose to take his place; if one congregation was dispersed, a larger assembled on the next opportunity. The influence of the denomination was strong among the common people." (History of Virginia, ii. 170.) At the Revolution, Jefferson tells us that in Virginia two-thirds of the people were dissenters. (Jefferson on the State of Virginia, p. 169. Richmond.) These were chiefly Baptists. A small portion of them were Presbyterians, of Scotch-Irish ancestry, brave men of eminent worth. But the Baptists were sweeping Virginia with a heavenly whirlwind, and their love of liberty and denominational success brought Virginia into the ranks of the Revolution. Under God our honored brethren were instrumental in placing the grand Old Dominion on the ground which her aristocratic rulers would never have selected for themselves. Without them Patrick Henry and Thomas Jefferson would have expended their eloquence and statesmanship in vain. And as Massachusetts and Virginia were the two principal sources of Revolutionary regiments, it is extremely probable that the liberty and triumphs of the Revolution, as far as we are indebted to Virginia for them, sprang chiefly, under God, from the extraordinary increase of the freedom-loving Baptists in the Old Dominion just before the great struggle. (See articles on BAPTISTS IN THE REVOLUTION, and RHODE ISLAND BAPTISTS AND THE REVOLUTION.)

Reynolds, J. L., D.D., a native of Charleston, S. C., was born on the 17th of March, 1812. He graduated with the first honor at Charleston College, and from it went to Newton Theological Seminary, where he took the full course. His first pastorate was in Columbia, S. C. Thence he was called to the presidency of Georgetown College, Ky. After a successful service in that position, he became pastor of the Second Baptist church in Richmond, Va. He was called from Richmond to the professorship of Latin in the South Carolina College in the palmiest days of that renowned institution. "For nearly twenty-five years the handsome, intellectual face and courtly manners of Dr. Reynolds were familiar in those classic halls, and hundreds of young men who read these lines will have tender memories revived of the genial and elegant Latin professor of their college days." He was at length, at his own request, transferred to the chair of Moral Philosophy. After the war political changes dismissed him and the entire faculty of the college. In 1874 he became Professor of Latin in Furman University, from which position he was called to "come up higher" on the 19th of December, 1877.

He was one of the most genial and delightful of companions. As a classical scholar, the Baptist ministry of South Carolina has not had his superior, if, indeed, his equal. As a preacher he was always instructive, and at times overwhelmingly eloquent and pathetic. The great gulf which he left has not yet been filled. His wife, a fit helpmeet in talent and accomplishments, survived him but a short time, so that it might almost be said "in death they were not divided."

Reynolds, Rev. P. B., was born in Patrick Co., Va., Jan. 9, 1841. At the age of seventeen he began to teach a few months in each year; entered the Confederate army in 1861, and was a private soldier until the close of the war; was captured in the Valley of Virginia in 1864, and spent the following winter as a prisoner at Point Lookout; was converted in the woods on the Rapidan River, in Virginia, while in the army, in November, 1863, and was baptized in May, 1865. He was licensed to preach in June, 1865; ordained in May, 1868. After preaching a short time in his native county he entered Richmond College in 1866, and remained until 1872. In 1872 he took charge of Coalsmouth High School, now Shelton College, of which he is now (1880) the president. Shelton is the principal Baptist college of the State, and Prof. Reynolds is striving to build it up. He has sacrificed much time and money, and has every prospect of success. He is a fine scholar, a most excellent preacher and pastor, an untiring worker, and capable of filling almost any position of usefulness. He is president of the West Virginia Baptist Educational Society.

Reynolds, Maj. Walker, was born in Columbia Co., Ga., Aug. 28, 1799; settled in Talladega Co., Ala., in 1833, where he accumulated a large fortune; was worth several hundred thousand dollars at the breaking out of the late war, and after the war was still quite wealthy. Maj. Reynolds was eminently a public-spirited man; contributed liberally to denominational enterprises, and invested largely in secular corporations. The Selma, Rome and Dalton Railroad owes more to him for its existence than to any other person. He was a wise man, an extensive planter, and a good church member. One of the last acts of his life was to give $1000 to the building of a new house of worship for his church at Alpine. He was twice married, and reared a most interesting family. He died at his home in January, 1871.

Rhees, Rev. Morgan John, Sr., was born in Wales, Sept. 8, 1760. He was converted in early life, and educated at Bristol College for the ministry. He was a pastor in Wales for some time, but concluded to lead a little colony of his countrymen to America in 1794. Dr. Rogers, pastor of the First Baptist church of Philadelphia, gave him a cordial welcome on his arrival, and soon his eloquence gathered throngs wherever it was known that he would preach. He traveled extensively through the Southern and Western States proclaiming the blessed gospel, and gathering converts into the kingdom. In connection with Dr. Benjamin Rush he bought a large tract of land in Pennsylvania, which he called Cambria, after his native Wales. In 1798 he took his own family and a company of his countrymen to the new settlement. He located at Beulah, and became pastor of the church formed there. He subsequently removed to Somerset, in the county of that name, where he died Sept. 17, 1804. He was married to a daughter of Col. Benjamin Loxley, a distinguished officer of the Revolution; and he was the father-in-law of Dr. Nicholas Murray (Kirwan), of Elizabeth, N. J., and Dr. Benjamin Rush was his special friend.

Rhees, Morgan John, Jr., D.D., was born at Somerset, Pa., Oct. 25, 1802. On reaching twenty-one he studied law under the celebrated David Paul Brown, of Philadelphia, and after being called to the bar he soon secured a respectable standing in his profession. In 1827 the Saviour found him, and "chosen of him ere time began, he chose him in return," and was baptized into the fellowship of the First Baptist church of Philadelphia. He was ordained in September, 1829. His first fields of labor were Bordentown and Trenton. While in New Jersey he assisted in the formation of the State Convention for missions, and was its secretary from its organization until he left the State. In 1840 he accepted the invitation of its board to become corresponding secretary of the Baptist Publication Society. In February, 1843, he took charge of the Second Baptist church of Wilmington, Del.; of this church he retained the oversight for seven years, during which he baptized nearly 300 persons. In 1850 he became pastor of the First church of Williamsburg, N. Y., where he died Jan. 15, 1853. He received the degree of Doctor of Divinity from the University of Rochester in 1852.

Dr. Rhees was greatly blessed in every pastorate, and he rendered valuable services to the Publication Society. His calls to churches seeking the best gifts were numerous. He had a fine intellect, the polish of a gentleman, the courage of a brave man, the piety of a saint, and the tenderness of a woman. He was loved by many hundreds while he lived, and his memory is still revered by the churches for which he labored, and by many admiring friends.

Rhode Island Baptists.—To most Baptists the evidence is conclusive that the First Baptist church of Providence, formed in 1639, is the oldest Baptist church in Rhode Island, and the first church of our denomination in America. Roger Williams was baptized by Ezekiel Holliman in March, 1638–9, and about that time the First church of Providence was founded. Soon after the origin of this church, as Baptists generally believe, the First church of Newport was organized. John Clarke, M.D., came from England in 1637, and not long after, taking up his residence in Newport, he became the public instructor of a congregation out of which, in 1644, according to tradition, a church was formed "on the scheme and principles of the Baptists." (For the arguments favoring 1638 as the time when this church was founded, see article on THE FIRST CHURCH OF NEWPORT, R. I.) Rev. Dr. Henry Jackson says of this church, "It occupied a high rank in the community, and drew members from towns remote."

The second church in Newport was established in 1656. These three communities comprised all the regular Baptist churches in Rhode Island for many years. The next in age are the churches in Richmond, Warwick, and East Greenwich, constituted in 1743, Exeter in 1750, Warren in 1764, and Shoreham in 1780. Rhode Island is everywhere permeated by Baptist principles, and churches of the denomination are found in all parts of the State. The rights of conscience are everywhere respected, and protected by public opinion and legislative enactments.

There are three Associations of Baptist churches in Rhode Island, the oldest being the Warren, formed in 1767; the next in the order of time is the Providence, formed in 1843; and the third the Narragansett, formed in 1859. The last report of the Warren Association, in 1880, gives 21 churches, 24 ordained ministers, and 4036 members. In the Providence Association there are 15 churches, 21 ordained ministers, and a membership of 2953. The Narragansett Association has 24 churches, 20 ordained ministers, and a membership of 3850.

There are 60 churches, with 10,839 members, in Rhode Island. The Rhode Island Baptist State Convention was made a corporate body by an act of the General Assembly, passed in October, 1826, and is authorized to hold in trust an amount not exceeding $300,000. The Convention gave to feeble churches in the State nearly $2500 during the year. The Rhode Island Baptists contributed funds for the education of ministers from 1792; the plan for starting a society for this purpose originated with President Manning, and two months after his decease it was submitted to the Warren Association by Rev. Dr. Stillman, of Boston. Up to 1816 the concerns of ministerial education formed a part of the regular business of the Association. In that year a separate education society was formed, at which time there was placed in the treasury, in the form of bank stock, the sum of $1800, from which amount various sums have been withdrawn, until there now remains $1350. Some of the most distinguished Baptist ministers in the country have been among the nearly 150 beneficiaries who have been aided by this society.

The Baptists of Rhode Island legally proclaimed absolute religious liberty for men of all creeds when no government in the world but the one which they controlled pretended to confer such a boon, or regarded it as either wise or just to give it. Roger Williams, in his "Bloudy Tenent," defended this doctrine of his Baptist fathers in the faith with a power which no mind governed by intelligence could permanently resist, and finally that doctrine swept from the statute books of American persecuting States every intolerant enactment. The freedom of conscience demanded by Roger Williams has effected a greater change in the relations between Church and State on this continent than the Declaration of Independence, the armies of the Revolution, and the Constitution of the United States have made in the secular liberties of this great republic. A moral cable, stretching from the Teacher of Nazareth, in Palestine, across the ages, the countries, and the oceans, kept in order by our Baptist fathers of all preceding Christian time, to whom it communicated its blessed news, *landed at Providence, R. I., in* 1636. Roger Williams received and put in circulation its divine dispatches, and by the authority of the King Eternal, immortal and invisible, demanded liberty for all men to pay their devotions to Deity, without State laws commanding or prohibiting religious worship. All Rhode Island received and obeyed the divine message coming through this glorious cable. Baptists everywhere respected it, and now our whole country has yielded obedience to the heavenly teaching. And, as Rhode Island was the American landing-place of this blessed cable, and her Baptist people the interpreters and propagators of its precious communications, we would honor them as the best friends of American liberty and of the universal rights of men. (For further information about Rhode Island, see articles on FIRST BAPTIST CHURCH OF PROVIDENCE, FIRST CHURCH OF NEWPORT, THE WARREN BAPTIST CHURCH, RHODE ISLAND AND THE AMERICAN REVOLUTION, JAMES MANNING, D.D., BROWN UNIVERSITY, and THE BROWN FAMILY, OF PROVIDENCE.)

Rhodes, Rev. Christopher, was born May 20, 1821. His parents were James E. and Mary A. Rhodes. At the date of his birth they were members of the First church, Providence, R. I. His ancestors had been in the State from its earliest settlement. He was baptized in February, 1839, and united with the Third church. After pursuing a collegiate course until 1843, he was licensed to preach, and at once commenced a series of revival services, assisting churches in Rhode Island and Massachusetts. His first charge was the church in Allendale, near Providence. He assisted in organizing this church, and was ordained its first pastor in May, 1850. The subsequent pastorates of Mr. Rhodes have been Phœnix church, Warwick, R. I., 1855-61; Stewart Street church, Providence, 1861-64; First church, South Kingston, 1864-66; Stanton Street, N. Y., 1866-74; Central church, Williamsburg, 1874 to present date. During these years he has devoted himself almost exclusively to pastoral work, and he has received many evidences of the divine blessing. Through his preaching converts have been added to the churches, and he has had great success in building up weak interests and relieving them from financial embarrassment. Mr. Rhodes is a strong man mentally and physically, and one whose counsel is held in high esteem by ministers and churches.

Rhodes, Gen. Elisha Hunt, son of Capt. Elisha H. and Eliza (Chase) Rhodes, was born in Pawtuxet, R. I., March 21, 1842; had an academical education; entered the Union army as a corporal in June, 1861; was with his regiment in most of the great battles in Virginia; rose to be the colonel of the 2d R. I. Inf. Regiment; brevetted brigadier-general for gallant conduct; since the war has filled some of the highest offices in the Grand Army of the Republic; is collector of United States revenue for the district of Rhode Island; brigadier-general of the militia force of Rhode Island; a member of the Central Baptist church in Providence, R. I.; a man of talent and sterling worth.

Rice, Rev. Francis, was born in Logansport, Ind., Nov. 27, 1853. His family came to Kansas in the year 1858, settling at Oskaloosa, Jefferson Co. In 1865 they removed to Topeka, where he received his education. He passed through the regular classic course at Washburn College. He also took a business course in a commercial college in the same city, employing for this purpose his summer vacations. He was baptized, and united with the First Baptist church of Topeka in January, 1870. He had experienced conversion several years before, when about the age of eleven. He became interested in the Sunday-school, and did what he could in the Master's cause, but had no serious thought of entering the ministry until January, 1877, when he received an invitation to visit the church at Valley Falls, and he was ordained their pastor May 16, 1877. His ministry has been attended by good results. He has been for several years clerk of the Missouri River Association.

Rice, Rev. John, was born in Virginia in 1759. He removed to Kentucky; was baptized and brought into the ministry at Gilbert's Creek church, in Garrard Co., Ky. He was a constituent of Shawnee Run, for a long time the largest church south of the Kentucky River. Of this church, in Mercer County, he was pastor from its organization, in 1788, till his death, March 19, 1843. He was eminent among the pioneers of Kentucky, and greatly beloved for his piety, faith, and usefulness.

GEN. ELISHA HUNT RHODES.

Rice, Rev. Luther, was born in Northborough, Worcester Co., Mass., March 25, 1783. His parents were members of the Congregational Church, his mother being a woman of remarkable intellectual vigor. He attended the public schools of the neighborhood, and was apt in acquiring knowledge. While still a mere youth, the wonderful self-reliance, for which he was always distinguished, displayed itself; for, at the age of sixteen, he entered into a contract to visit the State of Georgia to assist in obtaining timber for ship-building, without consulting his parents, and was absent six months. Soon after this he became greatly concerned about his soul, and suffered the acutest mental agony for many months. At the age of nineteen, in March of 1802, he united with the church at Northborough. He was from the beginning a most consistent and active Christian worker. He infused a new and higher type of piety into his own family and the church, and made it a special duty to converse frequently with the impenitent. He was from the start of his Christian career deeply interested in missions and missionary publications. During all this time he was laboring upon his father's farm. His mind was now directed to the Christian ministry, and he resolved to secure a collegiate and theological education. He spent three years at Leicester Academy, and paid his expenses by teaching school during the vacations and giving lessons in singing at night. He made such rapid progress at the academy that he was able to complete his collegiate course in three years, having entered Williams College, Mass., in October of 1807. While in college he became deeply interested in missions, and he infused the same enthusiasm into the minds of his friends, Mills and Richards. In a letter, written March 18, 1811, he says, "I have deliberately made up my mind to preach the gospel to the heathen." A society of inquiry on the subject of missions was formed through his instrumentality, and about the same time a branch society at Andover Seminary, where Judson and his friends caught the new awakening. They must preach the gospel to the pagan nations. Judson, Nott, Mills, Newell, Richards, and Rice prepared a memorial to the General Association of all the evangelical ministers of Massachusetts, convened at Bradford in 1810, urging the pressing claims of the heathen, and asking an appointment in the East. The names of Richards and Rice were omitted from the memorial at its presentation, the number being so large. The result of these efforts was the formation of the American Board of Commissioners for Foreign Missions; and, later, the Baptist General Convention of 1814, the American Bible Society, the American Tract Society, the Baptist General Tract Society, the Columbian College, the Newton Theological Seminary, and other kindred organizations. Judson, Nott, Mills, and Newell were appointed by the board as missionaries, Rice and Richards being omitted. But Rice had set his heart upon going, and he was permitted to do so upon the condition that he would himself raise the money necessary for his outfit and his passage, which he did within a few days. Having been previously licensed, he, with his companions, was ordained at the Tabernacle church, Salem, Mass., Feb. 6, 1812, and sailed from Philadelphia, February 18, in the packet "Harmony," destined for India. Dr. Judson and wife, who had sailed from Salem, having changed their minds on the subject of baptism, were baptized by Dr. Carey soon after their arrival at Calcutta; and Mr. Rice, having also been led, after a thorough investigation, to change his views on the same subject, was also baptized, on Nov. 1, 1812, by Mr. Ward, a few weeks after Mr. and Mrs. Judson. Owing to the continued and bitter opposition of the English authorities in India, Mr. Rice concluded to sail for the Isle of France, and thence to the United States, to adjust his relations with the Congregational board, to enlist the Baptist churches in the cause of missions, and to recruit his health. He arrived at New York, Sept. 7, 1813; went immediately to Boston, and communicated with the board, who, however, received him with much coldness, and, rather rudely, dissolved his relations with themselves. Mr. Rice now completely identified himself with the Baptists. At a consultation, in Boston, it was determined to appoint him an agent to visit all parts of the country, and enlist churches and individuals in the cause. He journeyed throughout the entire length of the country, and met with the most encouraging success. Delegates were appointed from all parts of the land to meet for conference, and on the 18th of May, 1814, a large number assembled at Philadelphia, Dr. Richard Furman presiding. After several days' deliberation the General Convention of the Baptist Denomination in the United States for Foreign Missions was formed, that organization which has accomplished so much in heathen lands for the glory of God and the good of men. On his Southern tour Mr. Rice collected about $1300, made arrangements for future contributions, and organized about twenty missionary societies, and throughout the country about seventy societies. At the meeting of the Triennial Convention in Philadelphia, in 1817, he reported that he had traveled, during a very short time, 7800 miles, collected nearly $3700, and aroused a warm interest in missions everywhere. These journeys were "through wildernesses and over rivers, across mountains and valleys, in heat and cold, by day and by night, in weariness and painfulness, and fastings and loneliness."

To Mr. Rice, more than to any other man, is due the awakened regard in ministerial education. He was deeply interested in the school opened in Philadelphia, under Staughton and Chase, for the instruction of young men for the ministry. Eighteen were in course of preparation there. He urged the founding of a college at Washington, D. C., and through his efforts forty-six and a half acres were purchased adjacent to the city of Washington, and a building capable of accommodating eighty students was begun. The Convention took the new institution under its supervision, and in the report made to the Convention in 1821, there was set forth a most gratifying statement of the progress of the college. Mr. Rice was appointed its agent and treasurer. About this time he originated the *Columbian Star*, published at Washington. Still serving as missionary agent, his additional labors as agent for the college were overwhelming. Difficulties arose; the expenses of the college were not met; and Mr. Rice was prostrated by sickness arising out of his terrible anxieties. The college seemed threatened with ruin in its very inception. A warm discussion arose in the Convention which met in 1826, and it was determined then to separate the educational movement from the missionary operations. Other financial agents were appointed by the college, but Mr. Rice still collected money for its funds, and labored earnestly with an unshaken faith in its final success; and before he died he had the pleasure of seeing his wishes partially fulfilled. Mr. Rice sacrificed his life for the welfare of the institution which he originated, and which he loved so well. During a collecting tour through the South he was taken seriously ill, and soon after died at the house of his friend, Dr. Mays, Sept. 25, 1836. He was buried at Point Pleasant church, Edgefield District, S. C. The following is the memorial inscription on the marble slab erected by the Baptist Convention of the State of South Carolina, written by men who knew him well and loved him dearly for his self-denying labors in the cause of Christian missions and ministerial education:

Born } Beneath this marble { Died
March 25th, } Are deposited the remains of { Sept'r 25th,
A.D. 1783. } Elder LUTHER RICE, { A.D. 1836.

A minister of Christ, of the Baptist Denomination.
He was a native of Northboro', Massachusetts,
And departed this life in Edgefield District, S. C.
In the death of this distinguished servant of the Lord, "is a great man fallen in Israel."

Than he,

Perhaps no American has done more for the great Missionary Enterprise.

It is thought the first American Foreign Mission, on which he went to India, associated with Judson and others, originated with him.

And if the Burmans have cause of gratitude towards Judson, for a faithful version of God's Word, so they will thro' generations to come "arise up and call Rice blessed;" for it was his eloquent appeals for the Heathen, on his return to America, which raised our Baptist churches to adopt the Burman Mission and sustain Judson in his arduous toils.

No Baptist has done more for the cause of education. He founded the "Columbian College, in the District of Columbia," which he benevolently intended, by its central position, to diffuse knowledge, both literary and religious, through these United States. And if for want of deserved patronage that unfortunate Institution, which was the special subject of his prayers and toils for the last fifteen years of his life, fail to fulfil the high purpose of its founder, yet the spirit of education awakened by his labors shall accomplish his noble aim.

Luther Rice,
With a portly person and commanding presence,
Combined a strong and brilliant intellect.
As a theologian he was orthodox;
A scholar, his education was liberal.
He was an eloquent and powerful preacher;
A self-denying and indefatigable philanthropist.
His frailties with his dust are entombed;
And upon the walls of Zion his virtues engraven.

By order of the Baptist Convention for the State of South Carolina,
This monument is erected
To His Memory.

His love for the Columbian College is seen in his dying request,—" Send my sulky, and horse, and baggage to Brother Brooks, with directions to send them to Brother Sherwood, and say that *all belong to the college.*"

As a preacher, Mr. Rice was rarely excelled. He was dignified in appearance, and unusually attractive in his style. His sermons were characteristically doctrinal, and weighty in fundamental truths. He was eminently gifted also in prayer. He wrote a work on Baptism, which, however, was not published. He was elected in 1815 to the presidency of Transylvania University, at Lexington, Ky., and also to that of Georgetown College, Ky., both of which he declined, as the two great objects of his life—missions and ministerial education—absorbed all the energies of his soul and body.

Rice, Rev. Thomas Moor, a distinguished preacher and educator, was born in Jessamine Co., Ky., Dec. 7, 1792. He was a soldier in the war of 1812–15, and soon after its close united with the Methodist Church, and became a circuit preacher. After a few years he was compelled to desist from regular preaching on account of physical disability. Mr. Rice was a linguist and mathematician, and adopted the profession of a teacher, and became very successful. In 1838 he was elected to the chair of Mathematics in Georgetown College, but declined the position, and remained the teacher of a private school. He continued to exercise his gifts as a local preacher among the Methodists, and engaged in several public debates on religious doctrines, one of which was with President Fanning, a distinguished Campbellite preacher of Tennessee. About 1839 he decided to preach an argumentative sermon on the "mode of baptism." In his preparation he became convinced that immersion alone was Scriptural baptism, and soon afterwards united with the Baptist church at Pleasant Grove, Ky., and was ordained to the ministry. He served two Baptist churches until his death, which occurred Oct. 3, 1842.

Richards, Rev. Humphrey, was born in Rowley, Mass., Sept. 17, 1818. Having completed his preparatory studies, he entered Brown University in 1833. While in college he became a Christian. Ill health obliged him to abridge his course of study. It was a sad disappointment to him to be compelled to renounce his long cherished hopes and give up the plans of years; for he was a good scholar, and was distinguished in his class. Having spent a year at the Suffield Literary Institution, Conn., he entered upon a course of theological study at Hamilton, N. Y., which he completed in 1842. He was ordained pastor of the First Baptist church, Springfield, Mass., May 10, 1843, where he remained three years. He became pastor of the First Baptist church in Dorchester, Mass., in the summer of 1846. This relation he sustained to the people, who were warmly attached to him, for eight years. Long continued application to his ministerial and pastoral work told at last on a constitution never strong, and he declined rapidly, and passed away Sept. 4, 1854. His ministry was fruitful for good, especially in building up his church in knowledge and in the graces of the Christian character.

Richards, Rev. James, was born Jan. 28, 1804, at Llanddarog, Carmarthenshire, Wales. He began preaching about the year 1819. He received his theological training at Horton, now Rawdon, College, under the presidency of Dr. Steadman. He had not been long in the ministry before his reputation as a preacher of the first rank was established. His style was exceedingly ornate. With a weak voice and quiet manner, he was nevertheless thrillingly eloquent. A volume of his sermons has recently been published, which amply sustains the reputation which he enjoyed. His principal pastorates during a long and useful life were Fishguard, Pembrokeshire, and Pontyprydd, Monmouthshire. He departed this life Sept. 22, 1867.

Richards, Rev. William, LL.D., was born in South Wales in 1749, and educated at Bristol College. He became pastor of the Baptist church in Lynn, England, in 1776, where he spent the rest of his life, though only about half the time as pastor of the church. He died in 1818.

Dr. Richards was deeply learned in English and Welsh history, and in other departments of literature. His talents and culture were of eminent importance to his brethren in the British Islands in defending their principles against Pedobaptist assailants. He sympathized with our Revolutionary fathers so strongly that he expressed a preference for the union of Wales (his country) with the United States rather than with the British empire. He was the author of several works of great value.

Brown University conferred upon him the degree of LL.D. In accordance with a purpose which he formed more than a quarter of a century before his death, he left his library of 1300 volumes to Brown University. This treasure enriches our oldest college to this day.

Richards, William C., A.M., Ph.D., was born Nov. 24, 1818, in London, England. His father came to this country in 1831, and settled in Hudson, N. Y., as pastor of the Baptist church. There the son joined the church in 1833, and in 1834 entered Hamilton Institution with a view to the ministry, from which he was graduated in 1840. In 1869 Madison University conferred upon him its first degree of Doctor of Philosophy, upon the occasion of his delivering the semi-centennial poem. After his graduation he went South, and was for ten years engaged in literary and scientific and educational work in Georgia.

In 1849 he transferred his literary efforts to Charleston, S. C., and became associated there with the *Southern Quarterly Review*. In 1852 he returned to the North, with the understanding that he should at length enter the ministry. After two or three years of varied work he began to preach, and early in 1855 he went to Providence, R. I., as associate pastor of the First Baptist church. He was ordained in New York in July of that year. Resigning his position in October, he was pressed to accept the charge of a new interest to be immediately formed in the city, and for seven years was pastor of the Brown Street Baptist church. In 1862 his health failed. He then began his public lectures on physical science, which have since engrossed the most of his time. From 1865 to the end of 1868, however, he was pastor of the Baptist church in Pittsfield, Mass., and while residing in Berkshire was elected Professor of Chemistry in the Berkshire Medical College, and filled the chair for two years.

In 1876 he removed to Chicago, and was pastor there for a year, but he was constrained reluctantly to resume his scientific work. His literary labors have been varied and voluminous. In 1856 he prepared the memoir of Gov. Briggs, of Massachusetts. He had previously published "Harry's Vacation," a very successful book on every-day science for the young. His contributions to the leading magazines of prose and verse are numerous. He has printed several anniversary and college poems. His editorial labors have covered, at intervals, a period of forty years, and for four years past he has been connected with the Chicago *Standard*. In addition to his popular lectures—chiefly under the auspices of the Young Men's Christian Association from the Atlantic to the Mississippi—he has preached twice nearly every Sabbath, and frequently at night, to large assemblies on religion and science.

Richards, Zalmon, A.M., was born at Cummington, Mass., Aug. 11, 1811, and graduated at Williams College, in the same State, in 1836. Being interested in the cause of education, he has devoted much of his life to teaching. He was at one time principal of the Cummington Academy, Mass., of the Stillwater Academy, N. Y., and subsequently of the preparatory school of the Columbian College. At present he is principal of the Eclectic Seminary, in Washington City, D. C. Mr. Richards was the first president of the National Educational Association, and also of the Young Men's Christian Association of Washington. He has contributed various articles to the *American Journal of Education*, and also to other periodicals. He has also filled various municipal offices, having been president of the common council and of the board of aldermen, auditor under the District government, and the first superintendent of public schools in Washington. He received the degree of A.M. in course from Williams College.

Richardson, Rev. Horace, a native of New Hampshire, was born about 1820; gave himself to Christ, and was baptized in his youth. He graduated with honor at Dartmouth College in 1841, and from Newton in 1844, and was ordained at Keene, N. H., in 1845, where he was pastor one year. In 1846 he settled at West Acton, Mass., and remained pastor there seven years. In 1853 he arrived in California, and spent twelve years in teaching and preaching at various places. In 1865 he was appointed general distributing agent of the American Bible Society, and spent ten years in that service. He distributed personally over sixty tons of Bibles, preaching everywhere in the destitute regions, doing the work of an evangelist, and leading many to Christ. He died at Brooklyn, March 15, 1876.

Richardson, Rev. J. B., was born in Montgomery Co., N. C., June 16, 1839; was baptized by Dr. Wingate, at Wake Forest College, in 1857; graduated at Wake Forest College in 1862; was ordained at Litchville in 1862, his father, Rev. Noah Richardson, Rev. John Minsor, and Rev. B. G. Covington constituting the Presbytery; was nearly four years corresponding secretary of the State Convention, and has been pastor of Greensborough, High Point, and Catawba churches. Mr. Richardson is widely known and greatly beloved by his brethren.

Richardson, Prof. John F., was born in Oneida Co., N. Y., in February, 1808; was a graduate of Madison University and its Professor of Latin for fifteen years. In 1850 he accepted the same chair in the University of Rochester, where he remained until his death, Feb. 11, 1868. He was the author of a work entitled "The True Roman Orthoepy," for which the Right Honorable W. E. Gladstone, now Prime Minister of Great Britain, and one of the finest scholars in England, thanked him in an autograph letter. Prof. Richardson was eminently a learned man, of great refinement, and of superior qualifications for imparting instruction.

Richardson, Rev. Noah, was born in Moore Co., N. C., June 30, 1804; was converted under the preaching of the celebrated Robert T. Daniel; baptized by Elder Farthing, and ordained in 1827 by Elders Swaim and Hymer. His father died when he was a child. His reading was extensive, and his talents superior. His control over an audience was sometimes wonderful, and many are the traditions of his extraordinary powers as a pulpit orator. He preached for forty-five years, and his great popularity is evidenced by the fact that for twenty-seven successive years he was elected to preach on Sunday at the sessions of his Association.

Dr. James McDaniel, of Fayetteville, and Mr. Richardson were devoted friends, and in delivering his funeral sermon, Dr. McDaniel said, "That in his prime Noah Richardson was the best preacher in North Carolina."

He was especially effective in revival meetings, and is said to have baptized thousands during the long course of his ministry. He died May 9, 1867. He left a son, Rev. J. B. Richardson, who was for several years corresponding secretary of the Baptist State Convention.

Richardson, Rev. Phineas, was born in Methuen, Mass., Feb. 2, 1787. When he was seventeen years of age he was baptized by Rev. Joshua Bradley, and united with the church in Londonderry, N. H. He longed to be able to preach the gospel, but many years passed before his wish was gratified. He studied for a time with Rev. Jeremiah Chaplin at Danvers, and was ordained at Methuen in November, 1817. His first pastorate was in Gilmanton, N. H., where he commenced his labors in March, 1818, and continued as the minister of the church for eighteen years. After acting as a missionary for the Convention for two years, he was instrumental in gathering a church in Hollis, of which he was the pastor for eleven years. He was then pastor of the church in New Hampton, N. H., for four years. The last two years of his life were passed in Lawrence, Mass., where he died in January, 1860. During his long ministry he was honored of God, as the instrument of doing a good work for the Master whom he delighted to serve.

Richmond College.—Virginia Baptists, very soon after the war of independence, began to consider the question of founding a seminary of learning. In 1778 a committee was appointed to further the scheme, and upon their recommendation, in 1793, the General Committee of the Denomination, which had charge of the matter, appointed trustees to carry into effect what had been proposed. For some cause, however, no practical solution of the question was found, and while from time to time the subject was agitated, still it was not until 1830 that an earnest and successful effort was made to establish a school of high grade, which should be under the control of Baptists, and which should be used directly to advance the interests of their special work in the State. The General Association met in Richmond in June, 1830, and it was while this body was in session that the friends of education met, and, after free discussion, organized the Virginia Baptist Education Society. The prime consideration which prompted the movement was the necessity felt on all sides by the churches for the improvement of their rising ministry.

During the first and second years of the operations of the society thirteen young men were received for instruction. These were placed in private schools. At the close of the second year it was found that the number of students would be considerably increased, and that the location of the school with permanent teachers was therefore necessary. Accordingly, a farm was purchased, and the institution assumed the name of the

VIRGINIA BAPTIST SEMINARY.

The location of the seminary was about five miles from Richmond. It was opened on the 4th of July, 1832, under Rev. Robert Ryland. The scheme of student training combined manual with intellectual labor. An opportunity occurring soon after for securing a more eligible site for the seminary, in the most beautiful section of the western suburbs of Richmond, it was removed to the present location of the college. From this time, under the judicious and efficient management of its principal, upon whom, from the inception of the enterprise, had devolved an unusual share of anxious solicitude and self-denying labor, the number of students, which before had been comparatively small, rapidly increased. Of these, many have become widely influential and useful ministers of the gospel, some at home, others in foreign lands, while others still as teachers, members of the legal and medical professions, and men of business, have won an honorable reputation in their several vocations.

RICHMOND COLLEGE.

Desiring still further to enlarge the influence and usefulness of the institution, its founders applied to the General Assembly of the State for a college charter, which, in 1840, they secured. Rev. Robert Ryland continued in the presidency under the new corporate organization. Efforts were made to secure a permanent endowment with considerable success, and the college seemed to be placed upon a broad and firm foundation, with encouraging prospects of an extended and enduring prosperity.

During the recent war the exercises of the institution were suspended, and the greater part of its endowment fund lost.

In 1866 the college was again opened. The alumni and other friends, sustained by the warm love and determined zeal of the denomination which had founded the institution in the past, rallied to the support of the trustees, and vigorous efforts were made to raise the loved school from its prostrate condition and restore it to more than its former efficiency and usefulness. A good degree of success has rewarded these efforts. The gifts of a people suffering severely from a disastrous war have been freely and generously offered, and the college, with its present fair but still insufficient

RICHMOND COLLEGE.

equipment, is a monument to the faith, love, and generosity of that noble brotherhood, the Virginia Baptists.

In reorganizing the college in 1866 the trustees determined to remodel their former plans, and adopted the organic change which at present marks its successful scholastic career. The plan is that of *independent schools*, of which at present there are eight in the academic department and a school of law. The faculty of instruction and government consists of co-equal professors, one of whom is annually chosen to be their chairman and chief executive officer. To them as a body is committed all that pertains to the discipline and interior management of the institution, while each professor is responsible for the efficient conduct of his own school. Eclecticism in studies, under certain restrictions, prevails with satisfactory results. There are five academic degrees conferred by the trustees on the recommendation of the faculty, viz., Bachelor of Literature, Bachelor of Science, Bachelor of Arts, Master of Arts, and Bachelor of Law. There are also school diplomas for those who graduate in the school, and *certificates of proficiency, promotion, and distinction* when a certain measure of success is attained in the regular examinations.

It has been the aim of the trustees to secure superior scholarship in the faculty, and the vigorous, accomplished, and faithful men who compose the board of instruction have so administered their trust as to prepare their students for and require at their hands a high standard of excellence for graduation.

Prominent among the many special features of

the organization and work of this college is the school of English, with its separate professor, in which our mother-tongue is carefully and elaborately studied.

The college lost her library, museum, and apparatus among the other calamities of war, but good foundations are already laid for increased excellence in each of these important departments. The literary societies are vigorous, and encourage a worthy emulation in the arts of writing and speaking among the students.

ENDOWMENT.

The property of the corporation consists of a most excellent plat of ground just within the corporate limits of the city, sufficiently ample for all needed improvements. On this campus there are buildings well adapted to the purposes of the college and capable of yet wider extension. Besides this realty, which is justly considered very valuable and eminently adapted to its purpose, there is an invested fund of some $75,000, whose income is applied to the purposes of education. The corporation is not encumbered by debt, the property is clear and the investments well placed. So that it may be justly seen that this institution, so long the pride and hope of Virginia Baptists, is doing the work of a college, and gives promise of wide future usefulness.

It is important to notice that amid all the changes of fortune and the gratifying development which has marked its course, there has been no departure from the plans and purposes of its founders. Ministers of the gospel are still and must ever be "privileged students." On the recommendation of the Education Board of the Baptist General Association of Virginia, all young men having the ministry in view are received free of all college fees. The ties which bind the school and the churches of Virginia are tender and yet powerful. Purely literary in its work, yet eminently Christian in all its influences, the college meets the expectations and claims of an enlightened constituency, and receives at their hands a united and cordial support.

Richmond Female Institute.—This excellent school for young ladies was chartered by the Legislature of Virginia, March 2, 1853. It was a joint-stock enterprise, and cost, including lot, building, and apparatus, about $70,000. Its beginning was remarkably successful. During its first session of 1854–55 it had 191 students, and during its second session 268. Until the war its average number of students annually was about 200, and since that time about 100. The Rev. B. Manly, Jr., was its organizer and first president, holding that position during 1854–59. Prof. Chas. H. Winston succeeded Dr. Manly, and held the position of president from 1859 to 1873, during two years of which period, however,—1863–65,—the school was closed in consequence of the war. Prof. John Hart held the presidency from 1873 to 1878, since which time Miss Sallie B. Hamner has filled the position of principal most successfully. The institution has been greatly impeded in its movements by pecuniary difficulties, but still, as an educational enterprise of the denomination, it has been of incalculable value to the Baptists of Richmond and of the State. Its boarding patronage has fallen below the expectation of its founders, because of the competition of cheaper schools in country districts, but it has always commanded an excellent day patronage, and the superiority of its course of instruction has made it an object of interest and just pride to the denomination. It has usually had a large number of accomplished instructors, sometimes as many as twenty, and has aimed to cover the whole period of a girl's education from the most elementary studies of the preparatory school to the most advanced branches of the collegiate department. Much attention has always been given to music and art. The institute, like the University of Virginia, is made up of "schools," of which there are eight; and one can become a "full graduate" only upon the completion of all the studies of all the schools, after a satisfactory examination. So rigid is the course, and so thorough the examination, that but comparatively few students attain this honor, perhaps, on an average, only about two each year. As a consequence, the diploma of the Richmond Female Institute is held in the highest esteem by those who have been so faithful as to secure it.

Richmond, Va., First Baptist Church of, was constituted in 1780, when Richmond was a village, with a population of about 1800, half of whom were Africans.

Its present spacious edifice, on the northwest corner of Broad and Twelfth Streets, was dedicated Oct. 17, 1841. It was designed by Thomas U. Walter, Esq., of Philadelphia. In 1858 the seating capacity of this large meeting-house had to be increased by adding to the rear about fourteen feet. The original cost of the building, and its subsequent enlargement, amount to $49,000.

According to Dr. Burrows (First Centenary of the First Baptist Church of Richmond, p. 29), "This church of fourteen members in 1780 has swelled into nineteen churches in Richmond and Manchester in 1880, with 16,847 members."

J. B. Hawthorne, D.D., is the present pastor of this venerable mother-church.

Richmond Institute, The, for the training of colored preachers and teachers, is located in the city of Richmond, Va. The Rev. Dr. Binney, under the patronage of the American Baptist Home

FIRST BAPTIST CHURCH, RICHMOND, VA.

Mission Society, opened in November, 1865, a school in that city for the preparation of colored men for the ministry. He began with a class of about twenty-five, whom he could instruct only at night. He remained in charge, however, but a short time, and soon after returned to Burmah. The Congress of the United States chartered, May 10, 1866, the National Theological Institute of Richmond, the object of which was "the judicious training of men of God for the Christian ministry," and this charter, by an act passed May 2, 1867, was amended, and the name changed to that of The National Theological Institute and University. Of this institution the Rev. J. D. Fulton, D.D., was made president, and the Rev. J. W. Parker, D.D., corresponding secretary. The Rev. N. Colver, D.D., of the Chicago Theological Seminary, was subsequently invited to the presidency of the institute, which he accepted, and entered upon his duties May 13, 1867. He leased for three years, at a rent of $3000 per annum, the establishment known as Lumpkin's Jail. The school opened in its new location with about thirty pupils, two-thirds of whom were preparing for the ministry. The Rev. Robert Ryland was associated with Dr. Colver in the management of the school from September, 1867, to June, 1868, when he resigned. Dr. Colver, also, resigned in June, 1868, in consequence of failing health. Mr. Corey, then in charge of a similar school at Augusta, Ga., was invited to take charge of the Richmond Institute, which invitation he accepted, entering upon his duties in October, with Miss H. W. Goodman as chief assistant. In November and December of 1868 a ministers' institute was held, the principal lecturers being the Rev. Dr. Parker and Mr. Corey; it was attended by eighty-one ministers and church officers, in addition to the regular students. During this winter about sixty pupils attended the daily sessions of the schools, and at night the principal gave instruction to another class, consisting of sixty-eight men. In May, 1869, the institute passed into the hands of the American Baptist Home Mission Society, and since that time has been under the care of that society. On the expiration of the lease of Lumpkin's Jail, in 1870, it became necessary to secure a more permanent location. The United States Hotel, on the corner of Nineteenth and Main Streets, was purchased Jan. 26, 1870, and in the fall of the same year it was occupied by the school. This building was erected in 1818, and was at one time the most fashionable hotel in Richmond. It is four stories high, and contains about fifty rooms. It is said to have cost originally $110,000, and it was purchased for $10,000. The building needed extensive repairs, and the students collected for this purpose more than $1000 from the citizens of Richmond, white and colored; they also gave of their own means, and in addition rendered valuable service by their daily labor on the building. One hundred and two of the students subscribed, each, $100 to the endowment of the school,—$10,200, paid in monthly instalments. The entire amount expended in repairing the building and in fitting up the school-rooms, up to April 1, was upwards of $11,000. The value of the building and furniture is estimated at $50,000. Since the close of the war about $80,000 have been expended in building up the school and in carrying on its work. Six hundred students have enjoyed its educational advantages for a longer or shorter time. The library contains about 2200 volumes. The number of students in the institute during 1878 was 103, 70 of whom were preparing for the ministry.

The school for a time was known as the Colver Institute, but for satisfactory reasons the more general name, the Richmond Institute, was inserted in the deed which conveyed the property to the trustees, and under that name it was incorporated by an act passed by the General Assembly of Virginia Feb. 10, 1876. Dr. Colver's connection with the institute continued less than a year. Since 1868 the Rev. C. H. Corey, D.D., has filled the position of president. The following persons have, at different times, been its instructors: the Rev. Robert Ryland, D.D., Miss H. W. Goodman, Rev. S. J. Neiley, Mr. Sterling Gardner, Rev. J. E. Jones, Mr. D. N. Vassar. The following students have also served, temporarily, as teachers: I. T. Armistead, Wm. Cousins, B. J. Medley, A. H. Cumber, H. B. Bunts, H. H. Johnson, and Chas. J. Daniel.

Richmond, Rev. John L., M.D., was born in Hampshire Co., Mass., April 5, 1785. He was converted at the age of thirteen, but did not make a profession of faith, because there was no Baptist church in the vicinity. He joined the Onondaga church in 1802. He studied at home, and gained a considerable mastery of Latin, Greek, and mathematics. It was his habit to read the New Testament in the Greek. He was ordained in 1817 at Camillus, N. Y. He became pastor of East Fork church, O., in 1818, and of Clough Creek church in 1819. Having already engaged in the practice of medicine, he entered the Ohio Medical College, and graduated in 1822. He became a physician that he might support his family, while he preached to the feeble churches. In 1832 he removed to Cincinnati, practised medicine, lectured in the Ohio Medical College, and preached as opportunity offered. In 1824 or 1825 he performed the "Cæsarian section," saving the life of the mother. This is said to be the first time that the operation was ever performed in this country. (*Indiana Journal of Medicine*, July, 1872, also

Western Journal of Medicine and Physical Science, 1830, vol. iii. p. 485.) In 1833 he removed to Pendleton, Ind. While living here he preached for the churches of Fall Creek and Anderson, and continued the practice of medicine. In June, 1835, he was called to the pastorate of the Indianapolis Baptist church, which, to use his own language, "contained at that time about twenty-six available members." He continued pastor of the church until it was united and strong, then he resigned, and was followed by Rev. G. C. Chandler. In 1846 he had a paralytic stroke, that forbade his further practice of medicine for the time, and in 1847 he removed to Covington, Ind., and became a member of the family of Albert Henderson, his son-in-law.

He was a commissioned surgeon in the war of 1812, and was in service on the lakes. He was a member of the first meeting that was called to organize an Indiana Baptist Education Society, and was for several years a member of the board of the Indiana Baptist Manual Labor Institute (afterwards Franklin College). He was a member of the committee appointed to obtain a college charter. He loved to study, he loved to preach, and he proclaimed Christ several times after he became too feeble to stand. One of his remarks, remembered by his brethren, is that "twenty persons could support a pastor if they were willing and united, and a hundred could starve him as easily." He died in Covington, Oct. 12, 1855.

Richmond, Va., Religious Herald of.—In the year 1826 the Rev. Henry Keeling commenced in Richmond the publication of a small monthly magazine, with but few subscribers. At that time there were only four Baptist weekly journals in the United States. The magazine was soon merged in the *Religious Herald*, which made its first appearance Jan. 11, 1828. The plan of this paper originated with Deacon Wm. Crane, who invited Mr. Wm. Sands, an English printer residing in Baltimore, to assist in establishing it. Of this paper Keeling was the editor, Sands the printer, and Crane the financial supporter. It was small, neat, and well conducted. After a short time the Rev. Eli Ball became the editor, who held the position, however, only a year or two. The editorial labor then devolved upon Mr. Sands, who, in consequence of his experience and judgment, as well as his thorough acquaintance with the denomination and its wants, made the paper quite popular. Its subscribers gradually increased in number until, in 1857, owing to the feeble health of Mr. Sands, the Rev. David Shaver became associate editor. Dr. Shaver wielded a polished and vigorous pen, and in written argument had but few equals. The *Herald* continued to grow in favor, influence, and pecuniary prosperity until the war. During the disasters of that period nearly every religious journal in the South was suspended. The *Herald* was reduced in size to half a sheet, and issued monthly or semi-monthly; and, on April 3, 1865, when Richmond fell, the office of the *Herald*, with all its types, papers, and fixtures, was burned, its mailing list only escaping the flames. Rev. J. B. Jeter, D.D., and Rev. A. E. Dickinson, D.D., purchased the subscription list, issued a specimen number of the new series Oct. 19, 1865, and began its regular publication on the 16th of the following month. The paper was greatly improved in every respect under their management, and was characterized by an unusually moderate, conservative, and dignified tone. Its columns for many years have advocated peace within our borders, and much of the fraternal feeling which has grown up between the Northern and the Southern Baptists since the close of the war is due to its kindly and judicious course. As a representative of Baptist doctrine it stands among the very foremost. It treads unfalteringly the old paths, and gives no uncertain sound in the advocacy of gospel truth. Every good cause receives its cordial and constant support. The Rev. Drs. Fuller and Furman were, for some years, associate editors of the *Herald*, and their elegant and vigorous articles have been read with delight by multitudes. Its present associate editors are the Rev. Dr. Broadus, of Louisville; Dr. Brantly, of Baltimore; Dr. Upham, of Boston; and Prof. Puryear, of Richmond,—all of whom bring to the pages of the paper an experience in authorship, and a brilliancy and vigor of style, that make the *Herald* one of the most attractive and instructive of our denominational journals.

Since the death of Dr. Jeter, Prof. H. H. Harris, D.D., has become junior editor, and his scholarly pen increases the attractions of the *Herald*.

Ricker, Joseph, D.D., was born in Parsonsfield, Me., June 27, 1814. At the age of fifteen he was hopefully converted, and was baptized by Rev. Willard Glover, and became a member of the Parsonsfield church. He graduated at Waterville College, now Colby University, in the class of 1839. In May of this year he took the editorial charge of *Zion's Advocate*, in Portland, Me. Having connected himself with the First Baptist church in Portland, he was licensed by that church, in the spring of 1840, to preach the gospel. He was ordained as an evangelist May 12, 1842, and accepted a call to the pastorate of the Baptist church in New Gloucester, Me., entering upon his duties Jan. 1, 1843. He remained in New Gloucester between four and five years, and then became pastor of the church in Belfast, Me., where he continued until the fall of 1852, when he removed to Woburn, Mass., to take the pastoral charge of the church in that place. His relation with this church continued for more than five years. Having resigned, he accepted an invitation to become chaplain of the Massachusetts State Prison, which position he held for two years and a half, and then returned to the pastorate, having accepted a call from the church in Milford, Mass., where he remained five years, at the end of which time he became pastor of the church in Augusta, Me., acting for two years— 1870 and 1871—as chaplain of the Maine Insane Hospital.

For several years Dr. Ricker was the corresponding secretary of the Maine Baptist Convention. The duties of the office requiring the services of some one all the time, he resigned his pastorate of the church in Augusta, and gave his entire energies to the work assigned to him by the State Convention. In this position, which he continues to hold, he has labored since Jan. 1, 1872. Through his life Dr. Ricker has done a large amount of clerical work, having been the clerk of two Maine Associations for fourteen years and of the Maine Sabbath-School Union for five years. He was the secretary of the Massachusetts Baptist Convention from 1858 to 1865, and of the Maine Baptist Convention from 1869 to the present time. He has also been instrumental in the erection of several houses of worship, and in raising the necessary funds to enable more than one church to pay off its debts. To such objects as these he has himself been a liberal donor. Colby University, of which Dr. Ricker was made a trustee in 1849, conferred upon him the degree of Doctor of Divinity in 1868.

Riddell, Mortimer S., D.D., was born at East Hamilton, N. Y., May 8, 1827. His pious mother consecrated him to the Christian ministry while he was an infant. He was converted and baptized at the age of fifteen. He studied three years at the Hamilton Academy. In 1844 became clerk in a store in Hamilton, and subsequently its proprietor. After that he carried on the same business in Watertown, N. Y., for nine years. "Impressed by the long-cherished wish of his mother, and by the appeals of a faithful pastor," he entered the theological seminary at Hamilton in 1858. On his graduation he was ordained pastor of the church at New Brunswick, N. J., and immediately entered the first rank of preachers in that college town. Of small stature and delicate constitution, he had an active brain and a large heart. His attractive style of sermonizing, clear and accurate judgment, strong sympathy with the people, and full recognition of duty as a Christian pastor and a patriotic citizen, marked him for a leader. In social power, spiritual earnestness, and intellectual activity he excelled most men, and his eight years' pastorate was full of deserved success. In the spring of 1867 there was a precious revival, into which Dr. Riddell threw his whole soul. His delicate health gave way. There were long months of absence for health. The church showed great kindness and affection, and only accepted his resignation after he pressed it repeatedly. He did not long survive. Feb. 1, 1870, he peacefully fell asleep at Ottawa, Kansas. His body was sent, according to his wish, "to lie among his dear people in New Brunswick."

Madison University conferred upon him the degree of D.D. in 1867. Several of his sermons and addresses were published by request.

Rigby, Rev. N. L., was born in Skelmersdale, Lancashire, England, April 21, 1839. At the age of twelve he formed the purpose of coming to America, and on the 4th of April, 1856, at the age of sixteen, he started alone for this country. Two years later he found Christ, and on the 4th of April, 1858, he was baptized in Bloomington, Ill. In two years more he had his "commission to preach the gospel," and in September, 1860, entered Shurtleff College, from which he graduated in 1866, and from the seminary in 1869. He graduated from both institutions with honor. On June 25, 1869, he was ordained at Fairbury, Ill. In October, 1870, he located as pastor of the Baptist church at Chetopa, Kansas. In two years at this point he baptized seventy-five persons, fifty of whom were Delaware Indians, living in the Territory. On the 22d of June, 1873, he became pastor of the church at Winfield, Kansas, his present home. In 1876 his health failed, and since then he has had no regular charge.

Riggs, Rev. Bethuel, a pioneer minister in Missouri, was born in 1760, in New Jersey. Not much is known of his early life; nearly half of which was spent out of Missouri. When about eighteen he enlisted in the army to fight for American independence. He married, early in life, Miss Nancy Lee, sister of a celebrated pioneer Baptist minister, James Lee, who preached with his gun by his side when fearing an attack from Indians. At the age of eighteen Bethuel Riggs was converted, and became a Baptist minister. Soon after he removed to North Carolina, and then to Georgia, where he traveled extensively, and preached with great success. Subsequently he removed to Kentucky, and settled opposite Cincinnati. In 1809 he settled in Missouri, and lived in St. Charles County for eight years. He thence removed to Troy, the seat of Lincoln County, near a sulphur spring, and a church was organized in 1823 at his house, called after the name of the spring, and for years he was its pastor. He traveled much over Warren, St. Charles, Lincoln, Montgomery, and Pike Counties, preaching Christ. He finally removed to Monroe County, where he died, and was buried beside his faithful wife.

Riley, Rev. Garrard W., has been connected with the Baptist ministry of Illinois since the year

1836, and is therefore at the present time one of the oldest, as he is one of the most respected, ministers in the State. His father, John W. Riley, his grandfather, Garrard Riley, and his great-grandfather, Ninian Riley, were all earnest and useful Baptist ministers in Virginia, Kentucky, Ohio, and Illinois. He is himself one of four brothers, all of whom are Baptist ministers,—Rev. C. L. Riley and Rev. A. J. Riley in Indiana, Rev. J. W. Riley in California, himself, for a period of forty-four years, in Illinois. He was born Sept. 2, 1813, and was baptized at the age of nineteen by Rev. Aran Sargent into the fellowship of the Bethel church, Clermont Co., O. In 1836 he was ordained as pastor of the Bloomfield church, Ill., where he remained ten years. At that time he removed to Paris, the county-seat of Edgar County, where he enjoyed a pastorate of marked success for twelve years, the church, organized with eight members at the beginning of his ministry, growing to a membership of 160. His work since has been chiefly at Urbana, Champaign, Indianapolis, Ind., and a second pastorate at Paris. During his ministry he has baptized more than 2000 persons, organized about 40 churches, built and dedicated about 20 meeting-houses, his work always branching out from the main points held into the region round about. A man of singular enterprise and self-devotion in his work, and held in high esteem in every community where his name is known.

Riley, Judge Richard, was born Sept. 14, 1735. His early life was blameless. In 1765 he was made a magistrate, and he held the office until our national independence was declared. He was a member of the Committee of Safety for Pennsylvania. He served in the Legislature for two terms. In 1791 he was appointed to the office of assistant judge, a permanent position.

He made a profession of religion about 1772, and was baptized into the fellowship of the First Baptist church of Philadelphia. He subsequently united with the Sansom Street church, and continued in its fellowship till the formation of the Marcus Hook church, of which he was a constituent member, and with it remained until death opened for him a blessed entrance into the general assembly and church of the first-born in glory. He died Aug. 27, 1820; his venerable companion rejoined him in the skies just one month afterwards.

Judge Riley was a great friend of missions, and took an active part in the formation of a local society to send the gospel to the heathen before the establishment of the General Convention. He was a man of broad views, of great benevolence, of extensive information, and of ardent piety. His connection with the denomination was an honor, and his influence on its behalf at the mercy-seat was a power.

He endured with great patience the weakness and pains of a two years' sickness before his death, and he left this for the better world, cheered by the holiest expectations and the sweetest peace. The Philadelphia Baptist Association, in its session of 1820, passed a resolution in which it "condoles with the church at Marcus Hook in the removal of our venerable brother, Richard Riley."

Ripley, Henry Jones, D.D., was born in Boston, Jan. 28, 1798, and was of a family more than one member of which was remarkable for great gentleness and sweetness of temper and manners. He enjoyed the best facilities which his native city afforded for the acquisition of a thorough preparatory education to fit him for college. To say of him that he was a "medal scholar" of the Boston Latin School, and was fitted to enter Harvard University at the early age of fourteen, is to speak in high terms of his scholarship. It was safe to predict that, if his life should be spared, he would win distinction in whatever profession he might select as his calling in life. He graduated at Harvard University in 1816, and soon after, having become a hopeful Christian, he repaired to the Andover Theological Institution to fit himself for the work of the Christian ministry. At the close of his Andover course he was ordained as an evangelist in the Baldwin Place church, Boston, Nov. 7, 1819, and commenced his ministry among the colored people in Georgia. After some months of evangelical labor in the South he returned North, and for a year preached in Eastport, Me. Prevented by the severity of the climate from making a permanent settlement in Eastport, he returned once more to Georgia, and for nearly five years labored most faithfully in that section, until an invitation was extended to him to become Professor of Biblical Literature and Pastoral Duties in the Newton Theological Institution. Such a call brought him back to the scenes and associations of his younger days, and he was not unwilling to respond affirmatively to it. He entered upon his work as professor at Newton in 1826, and remained in the institution until his resignation in 1860, a period of thirty-four years. He did not confine himself to the special department of which he had been called to take the charge, but as, from time to time, emergencies arose, he took his classes over ground outside of his appointed field of labor. "By a careful survey of his professional life," says Dr. Stearns, "it appears that he taught more or less in every department of the institution's curriculum. He did this diligently and laboriously." While he was performing the duties of his office, his busy pen was at work on the magazine and review articles, and on the more elaborate volumes which he committed to the press. Among the latter which have been received with much favor, not only by his own denomination but by Christian scholars of other names, we mention his "Notes on the Four Gospels," "Notes on the Acts of the Apostles," "Notes on the Epistle to the Romans," "Notes on the Epistle to the Hebrews, with new translation," "Sacred Rhetoric; Composition and Delivery of Sermons," and "Church Polity; a Treatise on Christian Churches and the Christian Ministry."

Several years were passed in the quiet of his study, after his resignation, devoted to literary work. His old love for the colored people of Georgia seems to have been again awakened, and he accepted an appointment which carried him back again to Georgia, where he labored with great zeal and fidelity the better part of a year, when he returned once more to his beloved Newton home, never again to leave it. He found most congenial employment in the institution library, for which he cherished an affection bordering on that which a mother feels for the child of her love and care. He labored in many ways to increase its efficiency and make it a model of what the library of a theological institution should be; and in this he was singularly successful, and if Newton may boast of its well-selected collection of some of the best books in all the departments of Biblical science, she will never forget the mind and the heart which had so much to do in making the library what it now is.

Dr. Ripley died at his residence at Newton Centre, the modest, unpretending home which his pupils so well remember, May 21, 1875, having reached the ripe and well-rounded age of seventy-seven years and four months. His memory is very fragrant in the hearts of hundreds who knew him but to love and revere him.

Ripley, Rev. Thomas Baldwin, was born in Boston, Mass., Nov. 25, 1795. Like his brother, Prof. Henry J. Ripley, he received his early training in the excellent schools of Boston, and graduated at Brown University in the class of 1814. He was a pupil of Rev. Dr. Staughton, of Philadelphia, for one year, and then was ordained as pastor of the First Baptist church in Portland, Me., July 24, 1816, and for twelve years held the office to which he had been chosen. His labors were much blessed in the conversion of sinners and the building up of the church. From Portland he was called to take charge of the First Baptist church in Bangor, Me. Here he remained for five years. On leaving Bangor he supplied for a time two or three churches, his connection with them all being a comparatively short one, and then removed to Nashville, Tenn. He preached for a brief period in several places in the Southwest, and then came back to New England and passed the remainder of his days in Portland, Me., where, among his old parishioners and friends, he came to be recognized by the affectionate name of "Father Ripley." As a city missionary he rendered an acceptable service in the place of his former residence, and, respected and beloved by the community in which he had lived so many years, he at length passed away on the 4th of May, 1876.

Mr. Ripley was a man of almost childlike guilelessness and transparency of character. He loved the cause of Christ with a strength and tenderness of affection seldom equaled. He lived to do good and to commend the gospel to others by his holy teachings and his pure, blameless life. He walked among men, his head always lifted upward, literally as well as spiritually, as if in the clouds he saw the gates of the celestial city, and, "a pilgrim and stranger" here, was hastening thither. For more than eighty years his Master kept him here, and always found some congenial work for him to do. The church of God is the richer for such men. So much real goodness in this wicked world could be no other than a blessing to humanity and a glory to him whose divine nature was so largely reproduced in one of whom it could so truly be said, "he walked with God, and he was not, for God took him."

Rippon, John, D.D., was born at Tiverton, in Devonshire, England, in 1751. When about sixteen years of age he was called by divine grace to follow Jesus. When a little over seventeen he entered Bristol Baptist College. When about twenty-one he became the successor of the great Dr. Gill, in London. Mr. Rippon had neither the talents nor the learning of his illustrious predecessor, but he was bold, witty, and ready in speech; his "preaching was lively, affectionate, and impressive;" his administration of church affairs was marked by great prudence, and he soon became very popular. The church edifice was enlarged, and the community over which he presided was "one of the wealthiest," according to Spurgeon, "within the pale of Nonconformity." Dr. Rippon was a great friend of missions, and his church gave large sums to the home and foreign Baptist missionary societies.

He projected and edited the *Baptist Register*, to give our brethren in Europe and America an organ through which they might address each other.

Dr. Rippon was engaged in preparing a work commemorating the saintly worthies who were interred in Bunhill Fields, but the book never was published. His plan embraced the records on every stone. J. A. Jones, in his "Bunhill Memorials," in which he gives sketches of three hundred ministers and other persons of note buried in Bunhill Fields, produced probably a much more valuable book than Dr. Rippon's time would have permitted him to write.

Dr. Rippon is best known by his "Selection of Hymns." This work for a long period, with the hymns of Dr. Watts, was used in Baptist churches. Mr. Spurgeon says that his "'Selection of Hymns' was an estate to him." And he adds, "In his later days he was evidently in very comfortable circumstances, for we have often heard mention of his carriage and pair."

He was a friend to America in the Revolutionary struggle, as the English Baptists generally were.

He was pastor of the community now worshipping in the Metropolitan Tabernacle, over which Rev. C. H. Spurgeon at present presides, from 1773 to 1836, a period of sixty-three years.

Ritner, Rev. I. Newton, was born near Malvern, Pa., Feb. 22, 1841. "Born again" in December, 1857, during revival meetings held at a Lutheran church. Declined to be sprinkled on account of Bible convictions, and was subsequently baptized in Philadelphia by Rev. Dr. D. B. Cheney, April 4, 1858. His father was baptized at the same time, he having been led to accept Christ through words written by the son. Was educated for a business life, but was diligent in labors for souls in connection with business pursuits. Declined an offer to provide for his liberal education on condition of entering the Presbyterian ministry. Entered the army in 1861, and became brevet captain "for faithful and meritorious services." After four years of service he returned to Philadelphia, and became book-keeper in a large mercantile house. United with the Fifth church, and soon gathered a large and interesting Bible-class, more than forty of whom were led to Christ. He also served as deacon and trustee. During the summer of 1873 he was impressed with the thought that the Lord desired him to preach the gospel. With his slowly and prayerfully reached convictions he found the church in hearty accord, and he was ordained Feb. 12, 1874. He began his ministry first as "stated supply," then as pastor of the Eleventh church, Philadelphia, in whose meeting-house he had previously put on Christ by baptism. In this field of labor he continues to glorify God in both body and spirit. He is a faithful, conscientious, self-sacrificing servant of the Lord Jesus, and his labors are marked with manifold tokens of divine favor. He has served as secretary of the Philadelphia Conference of Baptist Ministers since 1875, and is associated with his brethren in other important trusts.

River Baptisms in Venerable Bede's Ecclesiastical History.—This distinguished Christian, the first English historian, died in 735. His "Church History" gives an account of the conversion of the "Angles, Jutes, and Saxons," his English fathers. In it he says, "Paulinus, coming with the king and queen of the Northumbrians to the royal country-seat of Adgfrin (Yeverin, in Glendale), stayed there with them thirty-six days, fully occupied in catechising and baptizing, during which days, from morning till night, he did nothing else but instruct the people resorting from all the villages and places in Christ's saving Word, and when instructed *they were washed* (abluere) *in the river Glen,* which was near by, with the water of absolution. These things," he says, "happened in the province of the Bernicians; but in that of the Deiri also, where he was accustomed often to be with the king, he *baptized in the river Swale* (in Sualo fluvio), which flows past the village of Cataract" (Carrick, in Yorkshire). He speaks also of an old man who said that "he and a great multitude were baptized at noonday in the presence of King Edwin in the river Trent by the bishop, Paulinus" (*in fluvio Treenta*). (Eccles. Hist., lib. ii. 14, p. 105; lib. ii. 16, p. 107. Oxonii, 1846.) Paulinus, like John and the Jordan, used the flowing river for his font.

Robbins, A. C., deacon of the First Baptist church, Yarmouth, Nova Scotia, was born, Oct. 19, 1819, in Chebogue, Yarmouth Co., Nova Scotia; is one of Yarmouth's largest and wealthiest ship-owners and most influential citizens. In 1876, Mr. Robbins contributed $10,000 towards the endowment of Acadia College.

Robert, Rev. Baynard C., a pioneer preacher in Rapides Parish, La., was born in South Carolina in 1800. He came to Louisiana in 1818; was ordained in 1821,—the second Baptist minister ever ordained in the State. He was a man of intelligence and ability, and was instrumental in founding many churches in his region. He was often moderator of the Louisiana Association. He died in 1865.

Robert, Maj. Henry Martyn, U.S.A., is a native of Robertville, Beaufort District, now Hampton Co., S. C., where he was born May 2, 1837. His father is Rev. Joseph T. Robert, Sr., LL.D., president of Atlanta Baptist Theological Seminary. His mother, who has been dead several years, was a descendant of the well-known Lawton family of South Carolina, being a daughter of Gen. Lawton, U.S.A., for many years commander at West Point. Maj. Robert's paternal ancestors were French Huguenots, who settled in his native town and gave it its name in 1680. His paternal grandfather was an Episcopal clergyman, but became a Baptist, and with him the Baptist element in the family begins. When thirteen years of age Henry made a public profession of religion, and was baptized by his father into the fellowship of the First Baptist church in Portsmouth, O., of which he was then pastor. Having completed his primary education, and having spent one year at Denison University, he entered West Point Military Academy in 1853, when sixteen years of age. He graduated at twenty, the youngest member of his class. He received his commission with the rank of lieutenant in the corps of engineers, U.S.A., in which he has served ever since. After graduating he was appointed assistant professor of Natural Philosophy at West Point, and subsequently he was transferred to the department of Practical Engineering. In 1858 he was ordered to the Department of the Pacific, and stationed at Fort Vancouver, Washington Territory. During the critical period of the Northwest boundary difficulty between our country and Great Britain, Maj. Robert was put in charge of the defenses and troops on San Juan Island.

When the civil war broke out Maj. Robert, although of Southern birth, and although all his relatives resided in the South, and were in sympathy with Southern sentiments, hesitated not a moment as to his duty. He heartily espoused the Union cause, and devoted his services to the government which had educated him, and which he loved. He served on the staff of Gen. McClellan, the commander of the Army of the Potomac. He had charge of building the fortifications around Washington. During this service his health was so seriously prostrated as to require less fatiguing duty, and he was accordingly transferred to Philadelphia, to erect fortifications for that city, and subsequently he had charge of a similar service at New Bedford, Mass.

At the close of the war he was again placed at the head of the department of Practical Military Engineering at West Point. In 1867 he was assigned to the Military Department of the Pacific, serving as chief engineer on the staff of Maj.-Gens. Halleck, Thomas, and Schofield, successively. In 1871 he was put in charge of the fortifications, light-houses, and river and harbor improvements in Oregon and Washington Territories, with headquarters at Portland. In 1873 he was transferred to Milwaukee, Wis., and put in charge of a like service on Lake Michigan. He has in charge all the government improvements and expenditures on Lake Superior, except at Duluth and Superior City, and all the western shore of Lake Michigan north of Milwaukee.

Maj. Robert is the author of the article on Parliamentary Law in "Appleton's American Cyclopedia," and of "Robert's Rules of Order," a standard authority on parliamentary law, used as a text-book in many of the schools and colleges of the country, and adopted by many of the most important civil and religious deliberative bodies. He is also the author of "An Index to the Reports of the Chief Engineers of U.S.A. on River and Harbor Improvements," being an analytical and topical index to the public documents relating to the system of internal improvements carried on by the U. S. government. He is the author of the very complete system of statistical blanks for the use of Baptist State Conventions, Associations, churches, and Sunday-schools, together with a church record to be used in connection with the blanks, all of which he prepared as a gratuitous service for the Wisconsin Baptist State Convention, and which has resulted in great denominational efficiency, and which he has just placed at the disposal of the American Baptist Publication Society for future publication for the Baptist denomination throughout the land.

As a Christian, Maj. Robert is an earnest worker in the church of which he is a member, and in the denomination, notwithstanding the numerous duties and responsibilities connected with his official position, without neglecting a single one of which he has always found time to devote to the interests of his church and the claims of his Master. In the Grand Avenue Baptist church, Milwaukee, of which he is a member, he is chairman of the board of trustees, one of the deacons, and superintendent of the Sunday-school. He is a decided Baptist, and insists with military precision that everything in the conduct of the church shall be according to Scriptural Baptist faith and practice. Though sometimes supposed to be a little rigid,—a quality of character acquired in his long military experience,—he is of a most kind and generous spirit, and always wise in counsel. In the denomination in the State his labors are invaluable. He is an active member of the board of the State Convention and of its Executive Committee. In the Bible-school work he is one of the soundest thinkers and most thorough workers in the State.

Robert, Rev. Joseph T., LL.D., president of the Atlanta Baptist Seminary, Ga., an institution for the classical and theological instruction of colored people of both sexes, was born at Robertville, S. C., Nov. 28, 1807. He received his ante-collegiate education in that place, and there he professed conversion and was baptized, in October, 1822. In February, 1825, he entered Columbian College, at Washington, D. C., where he studied some time, taking the very first rank in his classes, and he was graduated with the first honors of his class at Brown University, R. I., in 1828. He was a resident graduate and medical student at Yale College, New Haven, during the years 1829 and 1830. In 1830 he returned to his native State and entered the South Carolina Medical College, graduating the following year, 1831. In 1832 he was licensed to preach by the Robertville church, and then went to Furman Theological Seminary, in order thoroughly to prepare for the ministry, in 1832, remaining two years. He was ordained pastor of the Robertville church in 1834, but removed to Kentucky in 1839 to become pastor of the Baptist church at Covington; afterwards, in 1841, he took charge of the Lebanon Baptist church, in Kentucky. About 1848 he returned South and took charge of the First Baptist church of Savannah, Ga., where he resided a year or two. But in 1850 he was called to the Portsmouth church, O., continuing in that position until 1858, when he became Professor of Mathematics and Natural Science in Burlington University, Iowa. In 1864 he was secured by the Iowa State University as Professor of Languages, but accepted the presidency of Burlington University in 1869. The necessity for returning to a milder climate carried him to Georgia in October, 1870, and in July, 1871, he accepted the care of the Augusta Institute for colored ministers, a school established by the Home Mission Society of the Northern Baptists. The institute was removed to Atlanta in 1879 and incorporated with the Atlanta Baptist Seminary, under the presidency of Dr. Robert. In this position he is exerting a great influence for good and is doing a most invaluable work. A scholar of the highest order and a perfect Christian gentleman, he is admirably adapted to his position, and it is doubtful if a better selection could be made. Dr. Robert is of Huguenot descent. As a preacher and theologian he is sound and learned, and as a scholar he possesses a wide proficiency.

Roberts, Rev. Benjamin, was born in North Carolina, July 21, 1794. He removed to Georgia when quite young; was baptized in 1822 by Rev. Jas. Barnes, and was received into the fellowship of the Beulah church, which he afterwards served, as pastor, for twenty-three years consecutively. Shortly after his baptism he was chosen clerk of the church, and the next year was ordained a deacon. In a few years he was licensed to preach, and in August, 1829, was ordained to the full work of the ministry. He was most widely known as clerk of the Washington Association, in which capacity he served during almost the entire period of his ministry, exerting a wide and very beneficial influence. He was a man of few words, but they were always to the point, his chief characteristics being simplicity and meekness.

Roberts, Rev. Joseph, was born in Virginia in the year 1770. Some time about the close of the last century he left his native State in company with his father and settled on Little River, Greene Co., Ga. He had married before leaving Virginia, but had lost his wife, and therefore resided with his father for some years; but at that time neither he nor any of the family cared for religion, being intent upon the world and its pleasures and follies. Arrested in his wild career by the grace of God in the year 1803, Mr. Roberts united with the church at Whatley's Mills, now Bethesda, and at once took a high stand as a member, attending the Georgia Association as a delegate in 1804. He married in 1805, and settled in Powelton, Hancock Co., where he was the companion and fellow-laborer of William Rabun, the two representatives for a number of years of the Powelton church in the Association. He soon manifested the possession of decided ministerial talents, and in 1811 was licensed to preach; two or three years afterwards he was ordained, and immediately entered upon a course of extensive and useful labor. The churches at Powelton, Horeb, Bethel, and White Plains, besides others, enjoyed the benefits of his ministry, the last mentioned, perhaps, sharing most largely in his godly labors. For eighteen consecutive years he preached to the White Plains church, being much esteemed by it and by all the other churches he served. Few ministers possessed to the extent he did the faculty of endearing their people to them, and this, perhaps, was one secret of his usefulness. The doctrines of grace were his delight, and furnished the staple of his sermons; yet, like Paul, he dwelt much upon practical godliness. He ended his useful life on the 22d of October, 1837, in the sixty-seventh year of his age.

Roberts, Rev. McCord, was born in Wilkesborough, Wilkes County, N. C., March 28, 1810. He became early inclined to close study, a habit which he has always cultivated, and has become one of the best thinkers of his day. He was at first a Methodist minister for twenty years, and has preached for thirty years in the Baptist denomination. He was very popular among the Methodists, and he is no less so among the Baptists. He is a man of rare attainments, especially in metaphysics.

He has shunned the walks in life which bring men into prominence. His career has been remarkably useful; he is most favorably known throughout the State of Missouri and in the Southwest. Men of talent and education respect and honor him, and the people are glad to hear him.

His labors have been great and self-denying for the cause of Christ in Missouri. He is deeply interested in education. He now resides in Bolivar, and is one of the board of directors of the Southwest Baptist College located there.

Roberts, Rev. Thomas, was born in Wales on June 12, 1783; came to this country in 1803; was baptized in New York by Rev. John Stephens, March 8, 1807. When speaking of that going down into the East River, he said, "God be thanked that a creature so unworthy was permitted to follow his blessed Son." He studied under Dr. Staughton, and in 1814 became pastor of the church at Great Valley, Pa. After remaining there for seven years he became a missionary to the Cherokees. In 1825 he took charge of the church at Middletown, N. J., where for thirteen years he was wonderfully blessed in bringing hundreds to Christ and in building up the church. After serving in New York and Pennsylvania, he returned to Monmouth Co., N. J., and preached as long as the burdens of age would permit. At eighty-two he passed peacefully away. The gentle, loving spirit of Mr. Roberts enabled him to be very useful in settling difficulties, and his Welsh fervor, combined with an unusual power of illustration, made him very popular as a preacher. After his death a volume containing some of his sermons was published, and several articles of his appeared in periodicals while he was yet living.

Roberts, Rev. W. S., pastor of the Spruce Street Baptist church, Philadelphia, Pa., was born in New Carlisle, Clarke Co., O., April 1, 1846. His father, bearing the same name, was an honored Baptist minister; two younger brothers are in the same holy calling.—Rev. Charles B. Roberts is pastor of the Baptist church in Englewood, Ill., and Rev. John E. Roberts serves the First Baptist church of Kansas City, Mo.

William commenced his higher studies at Kalamazoo, and completed them at Shurtleff College, in the literary course in 1872, and in the theological department in 1875. He was ordained as pastor of the church in Janesville, Wis., in July, 1875. He retained this position for three years, during which the church enjoyed much spiritual prosperity and removed a burdensome debt. He entered upon his present charge July 1, 1878.

In each of his fields of labor Mr. Roberts succeeded some of the most distinguished ministers in the Baptist denomination. Mr. Roberts is a man of culture, a student, a faithful pastor, and an able preacher. He possesses much of the spirit of his loving Master, and he enjoys the affection of his own people and of all his brethren in the ministry.

Robertson, Rev. Norvell, an eminent Mississippi minister, the author of an excellent "Hand-Book of Theology," was born in Georgia in 1796. His father, also named Norvell, was a Baptist preacher, who spent fifty-one years in the ministry in Georgia and Mississippi, and died at the advanced age of ninety-one years. His distinguished son professed Christ in 1830, and was ordained in 1833. He was soon called to take charge of the Leaf River Baptist church, where he continued as pastor to the time of his death, in 1879, about forty-five years, steadily refusing the most tempting offers to leave this country church. His "Hand-Book of Theology" is a lasting monument to his memory.

Robey, Rev. Geo. W., pastor at Bedford, Iowa, was born May 27, 1838, in Marion Co., Mo. His father was an infidel, his mother was a member of the Presbyterian Church. His mother's prayers saved him from infidelity; the New Testament made him a Baptist. He was converted at the age of fourteen, baptized at seventeen, and licensed to preach at eighteen. He graduated from Bethel College in 1860. In 1859 he was ordained pastor of Union church, in his native county, where he was baptized. Here with the people among whom he was brought up his labors were wonderfully blessed. His father was converted and became a zealous Baptist, and the young pastor was permitted to lead " down into the water" for baptism, as his first subject, his own mother, whose views on this ordinance had changed. Other churches in Northeast Missouri were blessed under his ministry, until 1867, when he settled as pastor at Shelbina, Shelby Co. In 1872 he accepted a call to Hamburg, Iowa, where he remained three years, and resigned the pastorate to become associate editor of the *Baptist Beacon*, published at Pella, Iowa. In September, 1875, he accepted a pressing invitation to settle at Bedford. Here he is held in high esteem as pastor of one of the largest congregations in the State. Though possessing a weak constitution, and all the time in feeble health, yet he has been " in labors abundant," and already over 1000 have been added to the churches under his ministry.

Robins, Rev. Gurdon, son of Ephraim Robins, was born in Sheffield, Conn., Feb. 6, 1786; his parents, Congregationalists, became Baptists; all removed to Hartford in 1796, the father becoming a local preacher; Gurdon was converted in 1798, baptized by Rev. S. S. Nelson, and united with the First Baptist church; in 1814 was chosen deacon; was a merchant; in 1816 removed to Fayetteville, N. C.; began to preach; invited to a church at Cape Fear, but health forbade settlement; was active in reviving the North Carolina Baptist Mission Convention; became judge of the county court; in 1823 returned to Hartford, Conn.; five years editor of *Christian Secretary*; in June, 1829, ordained pastor of South (then East) Windsor church; in 1832 returned to Hartford; established a store; became a publisher; supplied churches at Avon, Canton, Bloomfield, Bristol; active in Connecticut Baptist State Convention, Connecticut Baptist Education Society, Connecticut Literary Institution, and every good work; familiar with Baptist history; sound in the faith. His son, Dr. Robins, is president of Colby University. Died Jan. 2, 1864, in his seventy-eighth year.

Robins, Henry E., D.D., was born in Hartford, Conn. He pursued his studies at the Suffield Literary Institute and at the Fairmount Theological Seminary, Ky. For three years he was connected with the Newton Theological Institution. His ordination took place Dec. 6, 1861, and he became pastor of the Central Baptist church in Newport, R. I., where he remained five years, when he removed to Rochester, N. Y., where he was pastor six years. He was elected president of Colby University in 1873. Under the administration of President Robins the university has been greatly pros-

HENRY E. ROBINS, D.D.

pered. The position to which he was called in 1873 he still holds. He is a fine scholar, with a powerful intellect, and a very flattering record. No man in the denomination has earned a higher reputation for usefulness in his noble calling than Dr. Robins.

Robinson, Rev. Asa A., son of Gordon and Lydia Robinson, seventh generation from "John, the Puritan," was born in Windham, Conn., in May, 1814; converted in 1828; baptized by his father-in-law, Rev. Esek Brown, in 1829; educated at Connecticut Literary Institution; studied awhile in Brown University; acted as merchant with his father; was school visitor, postmaster, town clerk, and treasurer; ordained in 1849 in Agawam, Mass.; afterwards settled in Wales, in Suffield, in Mansfield, and in Willington, Conn.; in Russell, Mass.; in North Sunderland; in Saybrook, Conn., where he is now (1880) laboring; has served efficiently on school boards; been moderator and clerk of Associations; served on board of trustees of Connecticut Literary Institution; has a son, Julius B., born in Lebanon, Conn., in 1842; graduated at Newton Theological Seminary in 1873; settled at Milford, Mass., and now (1880) pastor at Fisherville, N. H. He is the eighth generation from "John, the Puritan."

Robinson, Prof. D. H., was born June 24, 1836, in Cayuga Co., N. Y. His boyhood and early manhood were passed on his father's farm in Central New York; was converted and joined the Weedsport Baptist church in the spring of 1854. His ancestors for generations were church members, mostly Presbyterians, running back to John Robinson, the famous Puritan pastor; prepared for college at Elbridge Academy, and entered the University of Rochester in 1855, graduating in 1859; chose the profession of teaching as a life-work. After teaching several years in high schools and academies in New York and Michigan, was elected, in the summer of 1866, to the professorship of Ancient Languages and Literature in the University of Kansas. This professorship was subsequently divided, Prof. Robinson retaining the chair of the Latin Language and Literature. The institution has grown from a small school of 55 pupils, the first year, with three professors and a very meagre equipment, to a strong, healthy university of 450 students, with fourteen instructors and a pretty full apparatus for instruction.

Robinson, Rev. Edwin True, was born in Monroe Co., N. Y., July 24, 1833; converted at the age of seventeen, and soon afterwards felt himself called to the work of the ministry; pursued his studies at Hamilton and Rochester, and graduated at Rochester Theological Seminary in 1859. In May, 1860, was ordained pastor of the Ninth church, Cincinnati, O., where, after a short and brilliant ministry of two years, he died July 21, 1862.

Mr. Robinson was a man of exceptionally fine gifts and gave the largest promise for the future. As a preacher he was greatly admired, and as a man universally beloved. It was probably his all-absorbing devotion to his work which shortened his life, and was the cause of the sickness which swept him off. His early death was lamented not only by the church of which he was pastor, but by multitudes of others to whom he had endeared himself by his genial Christian character, his eloquence, and his devotion to Christ and the souls of men.

Robinson, Ezekiel Gilman, D.D. (Brown University, 1853), **LL.D.** (Brown University, 1872), was born at Attleborough, Bristol Co., Mass., March 13, 1815. He graduated in 1838 at Brown University, where he also spent the following year as resident graduate. In 1842 he graduated at Newton Theological Institution. He was pastor at Norfolk, Va., 1842–45. During eight months of this time (being an academic year) he served as chaplain at the University of Virginia, having received from the church leave of absence for this purpose. He was pastor at Cambridge, Mass., 1845–46. In 1846 he became Professor of Biblical Interpretation in the Western Theological

Seminary, Covington, Ky. From 1850 to 1853 he was pastor of the Ninth Street church, Cincinnati. During all these years he had been steadily growing in power and reputation, and when he became

EZEKIEL GILMAN ROBINSON, D.D.

Professor of Theology in Rochester Theological Seminary in the spring of 1853, the feeling was general that the field was the one above all others for which his abilities, his acquirements, and his mental traits peculiarly fitted him. The resignation of Dr. Conant in 1857 left Dr. Robinson the senior professor and virtual president, though the title of president was not conferred upon him till 1868. During the nearly twenty years of his connection with the seminary Dr. Robinson achieved a work the arduousness and the influence of which cannot easily be overestimated. The increase of students, the growth of the library, the enlargement of the endowment (chiefly through his personal exertions), the addition of new professors, the erection of adequate buildings, the extension of the course of study from two years to three, and above all the accession to the Baptist ministry of a large body of men, thoroughly equipped, mighty in the Scriptures, full of zeal for the truth and of love for God and man, and animated with a lofty sense of duty,—these were among the visible results of his labors. In 1867–68, Dr. Robinson traveled quite extensively in Europe. In 1872 he became president of Brown University. In this position he has shown not only the high, broad, and exact scholarship which had already been universally recognized, but also great executive ability and power of leadership. The university has advanced in all the elements of prosperity, maintaining the position which naturally belongs to the oldest Baptist college in America. As an educator, Dr. Robinson's power lies not alone in the knowledge which he communicates, but in the mental and spiritual quickening which he imparts, in the example which is presented to the pupil of logical acuteness, of mental independence, of reverent love for truth, of loyalty to duty. He has been a peculiarly wise counselor to those who were of an inquiring disposition, and who were pressing their inquiries in a manner that was perilous to their faith. He has not repelled or awed them by the parade of authority, but he has pointed out to them the real sources of knowledge, and has so wisely guided their inquiries as to lead them to an intelligent and well-grounded faith. His labors as an instructor have not wholly withdrawn Dr. Robinson from the pulpit. His preaching is marked by logical power, singular clearness of definition and statement, directness of appeal to the conscience, a vivid presentation of the great facts of religion and the great lessons of duty. Dr. Robinson has not felt that his position as a minister of the gospel made it his duty to withdraw himself from all concern in public affairs. At critical times in the national history, especially when the existence of the nation was at stake, his utterances from the platform and the pulpit have been stirring beyond expression, arousing, deepening, and intensifying the spirit of patriotism. Dr. Robinson has not published largely. His addresses and sermons, though the result of intense and careful thought, have usually been unwritten in form. Some of his sermons and lectures have been reported with varying degrees of correctness. His most elaborate work was the revision of the translation of Neander's "Planting and Training of the Church" (which, in fact, amounted to a new translation). While at Rochester he was for several years the editor of the *Christian Review*, and wrote extensively for it.

Robinson, Jabez, was born in Bedford, Westchester Co., N. Y., in 1787; converted in early life; united with the Bedford Baptist church; kept a free "Baptist Inn" for preachers and others; given to hospitality; occupied positions of responsibility in the church and in civil affairs; was justice of the peace for more than thirty years; was clerk of the Bedford church until his death; a man of wide influence; died full of honors in 1873.

His brother, Henry Robinson, was born in 1791; converted early; member of the Bedford Baptist church, a pillar in the church, and a father in Israel.

Robinson, Robert, one of the most eminent names in Baptist history, was born at Swaffham,

Norfolk, England, Oct. 8, 1735. He received for a few years excellent instruction at the endowed grammar-school at Scarning, Norfolk; but the death of his father compelled him to leave school in

ROBERT ROBINSON.

his fourteenth year. He was bound apprentice in Crutched Friars, London, in 1749. Although it was evident that literary pursuits were much more congenial to him than business, he won the esteem of all around him. He kept up his acquaintance with the classical languages and French, by early rising, and finding time for reading everything that came in his way. When in his seventeenth year, he went one Sunday evening to hear the celebrated George Whitefield, who was then preaching in London. The preacher's text was Matt. iii. 7. Writing of the event, Robinson says, " Mr. Whitefield described the Sadducean character: this did not touch me. I thought myself as good a Christian as any man in England. From this he went to that of the Pharisees. He described their exterior decency, but observed that the poison of the viper rankled in their hearts. This rather shook me. At length, in the course of his sermon, he abruptly broke off; paused for a few moments; then burst into a flood of tears; lifted up his hands and eyes, and exclaimed, 'Oh, my hearers, the wrath's to come! *the wrath's to come!*' These words sank into my heart like lead in the waters. I wept, and when the sermon was ended, retired alone. For days and weeks I could think of little else. Those awful words would follow me wherever I went." The convictions of sin thus aroused held possession of his mind, and he obtained no relief until Dec. 10, 1755, when, to use his own words, " he found full and free forgiveness through the precious blood of Jesus Christ." Having attained his majority in the autumn of 1756, his indentures were given up to him, and he was free. For some time he remained at his employment, associating constantly with Mr. Whitefield's congregation at the Tabernacle. Many of his friends thought that he had the qualifications of a preacher, but, although he felt strongly drawn towards the ministry, he left London without making his case known to Mr. Whitefield, in the winter of 1758, on a visit to his relatives in Norfolk. At Mildenhall, in that county, he found " many souls awakened who had the Word preached but now and then; we met of evenings to sing and pray and speak our experience." At their repeated requests he began to preach. From that time his course was decided. His reputation as a preacher rapidly extended over the whole district, and in the summer of 1759 he wrote to Mr. Whitefield from Norwich, " We have near forty members in the church which I preach to, and many more are desirous of being received. We have on the Lord's day several hundred hearers who seem very serious and inquiring the way to Zion. On the week-days we have abundance of people to hear. The days I do not preach in Norwich the country people frequently send for me, and multitudes come to hear, so that the preaching-houses will not hold them." Whilst preaching in Norwich he had not formally separated from the Established Church, any more than Whitefield or Wesley had, and a rich relation promised to provide liberally for him if he would leave " the Methodists" and enter the ministry of the establishment. But he declined the offer, and forfeited the favor of his relative by so doing.

He had not questioned hitherto the propriety of infant baptism, but one day he was invited to the christening of a child, and the ceremony being delayed by the absence of the officiating minister, one of the company expressed doubts concerning the benefit of infant baptism. Mr. Robinson from that time investigated the whole subject, and became convinced that the Scriptures taught only the baptism of believers. He was baptized at Ellingham, and soon after left Norwich, accepting an invitation from the Baptist congregation at Cambridge to visit them. He continued preaching to them without accepting the pastoral office for nearly two years, until May 28, 1761. He was publicly ordained June 11, following. His success in Cambridge was marvelous. The meeting-house, which had been " first a barn, afterwards a stable and granary, then a meeting-house, and, notwithstanding its pews and galleries concealed its meanness within-side a little, it was still a damp, dark, cold, ruinous, contemptible hovel," became too strait for the audiences which assembled there. Members of the university and other hearers who had never in their lives entered a Baptist meeting-house, became regular attendants. In 1764 a new edifice, capable of seating 600 persons, was built and paid for. Whilst thus prospering in his ministry in the university town, he enlarged the circle of his influence by extensive village preaching in the surrounding country, and wherever he went "the common people heard him gladly." In 1774 he had a congregation of 600 or 700 persons. His popularity occasioned numerous preaching engagements beyond his own sphere of labor, yet by his methodical habits and incredible industry he found time for extensive reading, and few years passed without some publications from his pen. His translations of Saurin's "Sermons" and Claude's "Essay on the Composition of a Sermon," in two octavo volumes, with copious annotations, are widely known. Besides numerous sermons, lectures, and brief essays in illustration and defense of the principles of Nonconformity, he was occupied for several years with a history of the Baptists, undertaken at the suggestion of the Rev. Dr. Gifford and other prominent members of the denomination. The fruit of this study appeared in the two volumes of "Ecclesiastical Researches" and the "History of Baptism," published after his death. Excessive labor, with unhappy complications in his private affairs, doubtless undermined his constitution and hastened his death, which took place suddenly June 8, 1790, in his fifty-fifth year. The later period of Robinson's life was clouded not only by private sorrows, but also by his aberration from orthodoxy, and the consequent withdrawal from him of many attached friends and brother ministers. His enthusiastic devotion to liberty, civil and ecclesiastical, attracted to him many persons of skeptical opinions, whose influence was injurious to his spiritual health. His most recent biographer, the late Rev. William Robinson, also a pastor of the church at Cambridge, says in a memoir published in the "Bunyan Library" (London, 1861), "He was one of the most decided Unitarians of the age, but never a mere Humanitarian. No man has the right to call him either Socinian or Arian. He held apparently the indwelling hypothesis to the end of his life, but became vague and confused in its application. He was like a noble vessel broken from its moorings and drifting out to sea amidst fogs and rocks without a compass or a rudder." His mind may have been somewhat impaired in his later years. A current tradition reports that on one occasion when he was preaching from home his two well-known hymns were sung, "Mighty God, while angels bless thee," and "Come, thou fount of every blessing." After the service he expressed very strongly his wish that he could feel as he did when he wrote them. A memoir of Robinson by Mr. George Dyer was published in 1796, and another by Mr. Benjamin Flower in 1804, but the most complete and trustworthy account of this remarkably gifted man was given by the late Rev. W. Robinson in the volume referred to above, in which are interesting extracts from the church book, from Robinson's own hand, and a large collection of his letters arranged chronologically, together with selections characteristic of his genius from several of his works, including "The History and the Mystery of Good-Friday," "A Sermon on a Becoming Behavior in Religious Assemblies," "Morning Exercises," etc. It is well known that the celebrated Robert Hall succeeded Robinson as pastor of the church at Cambridge. Soon after his coming he was shown the copy of an epitaph which it was proposed to inscribe on a tablet in the meeting-house at Birmingham where Mr. Robinson last preached. Dissatisfied with the inscription proposed, Hall consented to write a substitute, and produced the following choice eulogium: "Sacred to the memory of the Rev. Robert Robinson, of Cambridge, the intrepid champion of liberty, civil and religious. Endowed with a genius brilliant and penetrating, united to an indefatigable industry, his mind was richly furnished with an inexhaustible variety of knowledge, his eloquence was the delight of every public assembly and his conversation the charm of every private circle. In him the erudition of the Scholar, the discrimination of the Historian, and the boldness of the Reformer were united in an eminent degree with the virtues which adorn the Man and the Christian. He died at Birmingham on the 8th of June, 1790, aged 54 years, and was buried near this spot."

Robinson, Rev. Samuel, was born, in 1801, in Ireland; settled in Charlotte Co., New Brunswick, in 1830. Rev. Thomas Ainslie, who evangelized there about that time, saw the young Irishman, and intimated that God designed him for a Baptist minister. He was baptized in 1831 by Mr. Ainslie; ordained pastor at St. George, New Brunswick, Aug. 4, 1832; became, in 1838, pastor of the Baptist church, Germain Street, St. John, and subsequently pastor of Brussels Street church, and continued in this position till he died, Sept. 19, 1866.

Mr. Robinson's ministry was a power in St. John, and, indeed, in New Brunswick. He was distinguished for urbanity, administrative ability, sympathy, tact, indomitable energy, and successful work.

Robinson, Rev. William, late of Cambridge, England, was commended to the authorities of the Bristol College in 1826, as a student for the ministry, by the Baptist church at Dunstable. After a full course of study he received, in 1830, an invitation to the church at Kettering, a church which, through its connection with the Missionary Society and Andrew Fuller, held a conspicuous position in the denomination. But the young pastor soon proved his fitness, and during the twenty-two years of his ministry at Kettering his reputation as a scholarly and able minister was fully established. In 1851 he accepted the call of the church at Cambridge, and for twenty-two years more ministered in the pulpit formerly occupied by those far-famed preachers, Robert Robinson and Robert Hall. He received in 1870 the highest honor the Baptist denomination in England has to bestow, when he was elected president of the Baptist Union, and it was a significant token of the esteem in which he was held by the public that, when the autumnal meeting of the Union took place in Cambridge, the Episcopalian heads of several of the colleges of the university tendered hospitalities to the delegates. Mr. Robinson was a man who had the courage of his convictions; but his straightforward plain speaking was perfectly blended with courtesy and Christian simplicity. Pre-eminently an expositor, he was mighty in the Scriptures, and even aimed at the nicest accuracy in stating doctrine. His studies were not exclusively Biblical or ecclesiastical. Physical science was specially attractive to him, one of his last efforts being a review article on Lyell's arguments concerning the antiquity of man. He died in Iowa, while on a visit to his children settled in that State, in the autumn of 1873. He published several pamphlets and a work entitled "Biblical Studies."

Roby, Z. D., D.D., was born in North Carolina, Feb. 9, 1838. Baptized in Georgia in 1855; ordained at the call of the Second Baptist church of Columbus, Ga., in 1865; was pastor of that church and the church in Girard, Ala., dividing his time between them. In 1868 he removed to Salem, Ala., and became pastor there and of neighboring churches. At the beginning of 1875 he accepted the call of the church in Tuskegee, where he still resides and labors among an intelligent people. The degree of D.D. was conferred on him in 1879. Dr. Roby ranks with the best preachers in the State.

Rochester Theological Seminary was founded in 1850. Up to this time the only Baptist school for literary and theological training in the State of New York was Madison University, situated at Hamilton. In 1847 many friends of education throughout the State, with a view to securing for this university a more suitable location and a more complete endowment, sought to remove the institution to Rochester. This project was opposed by friends of Hamilton, legal obstacles were discovered, the question was carried into the courts, and the plan of removal was finally abandoned as impracticable. Not so, however, the plan of establishing a theological seminary and university at Rochester. Rev. Pharcellus Church, D.D., and Messrs. John N. Wilder and Oren Sage devoted much time and energy to awakening public sentiment in behalf of the new enterprise. A subscription of $130,000 was secured for the college. Five professors in Hamilton—Drs. Conant and Maginnis of the seminary, and Drs. Kendrick, Raymond, and Richardson of the university—resigned their places, and accepted a call to similar positions in the new institutions at Rochester. In November, 1850, classes were organized in the Rochester Theological Seminary as well as in the University of Rochester, and instruction was begun in temporary quarters secured for the purpose. Many students came with their professors from Hamilton. The first class graduated from the Theological Seminary numbered 7 members, and the first published catalogue, that of 1851–52, enrolls the names of 2 professors and of 29 students.

Although the early history of the Seminary was intimately connected with that of the University of Rochester, and the two institutions at the beginning occupied the same building, there has never been any organic connection between them, either of government or of instruction. While the University has devoted itself to the work of general college training, the Rochester Theological Seminary has been essentially a professional school, and has aimed exclusively to fit men, by special studies, for the work of the ministry. It has admitted only college graduates and those who have been able successfully to pursue courses of study in connection with college graduates. Beginning with the two professorships of Theology and of Hebrew, it has added professorships of Ecclesiastical History, of New Testament Greek, of Homiletics and Pastoral Theology, and of Elocution. Besides its two original professors,—Rev. Thomas J. Conant, D.D., and Rev. John S. Maginnis, D.D.,—it has numbered in its faculty the names of John H. Raymond, Velona R. Hotchkiss, George W. Northrup, Asahel C. Kendrick, R. J. W. Buckland, Horatio B. Hackett, William C. Wilkinson, Howard Osgood, Wm. Arnold Stevens, T. Harwood Pattison, and Benjamin O. True. To Rev. Ezekiel G. Robinson, D.D., LL.D., however, professor in the seminary from 1853 to 1872, and from 1868 to 1872 its president, the institution probably owes more of its character and success than to any other single man. His successor in the presidency and in the chair of Biblical Theology is Rev. Augustus H. Strong, D.D., who has now (1881) for nine years held this position.

In 1854 a German department of the Seminary was organized. The German Baptist churches of the country, which in 1850 were only ten in number, have now increased to more than one hundred. This constant growth has occasioned a demand for ministers with some degree of training. The German department is designed to meet this necessity. In 1858, Rev. Augustus Rauschenbusch, D.D., a pupil of Neander, was secured to take charge of this work, and in 1872, Rev. Hermann M. Schäffer was chosen as his colleague. The course of studies in the German department is four years in length, and being designed for young men who have had little preparatory training, is literary as well as theological. This course is totally distinct from the regular course of the Seminary, which is accomplished in three years.

When the Seminary began its existence it was wholly without endowment, and, dependent as it was upon the churches for means to defray its current expenses as well as to support its beneficiaries, the raising of a sufficient endowment in addition was a long and arduous work. In fact, it has only now, after thirty years of effort, been accomplished. The sum first sought to be secured was $75,000. This was not obtained until after ten years had passed. In 1868 the funds of the Seminary had reached $100,000; in 1874, including subscriptions of $100,000 yet unpaid, they amounted to $281,-000; in 1881, including subscriptions of $179,000 yet unpaid, they amount to $512,000. Adding to this sum the real estate of the Seminary, valued at $123,000, its library valued at $32,000, and other property to the extent of $6500, the total assets of the institution may now be stated as amounting to $674,000, from which, however, is to be subtracted an indebtedness of $21,000, leaving its net property $653,000. When all subscriptions are paid in and its debts are cancelled, the institution is expected to have a productive endowment of $450,000, an amount sufficient to maintain its operations only upon condition that the churches shall continue to provide, as they have hitherto done, by annual contributions for the support of students preparing for the ministry. This comparative prosperity of later years has been due, under Providence, to the wise and liberal gifts of a few tried friends of the seminary, among whom may be mentioned the names of John B. Trevor, of Yonkers, N. Y.; Jacob F. Wyckoff, of New York City; John D. Rockefeller, of Cleveland, O.; William Rockefeller, of New York; Charles Pratt, of Brooklyn; Joseph B. Hoyt, of Stamford, Conn.; Charles Siedler, of Jersey City, N. J.; William A. Cauldwell, of New York; Mrs. Eliza A. Witt, of Cleveland, O.; Jeremiah Milbank, of New York; and others.

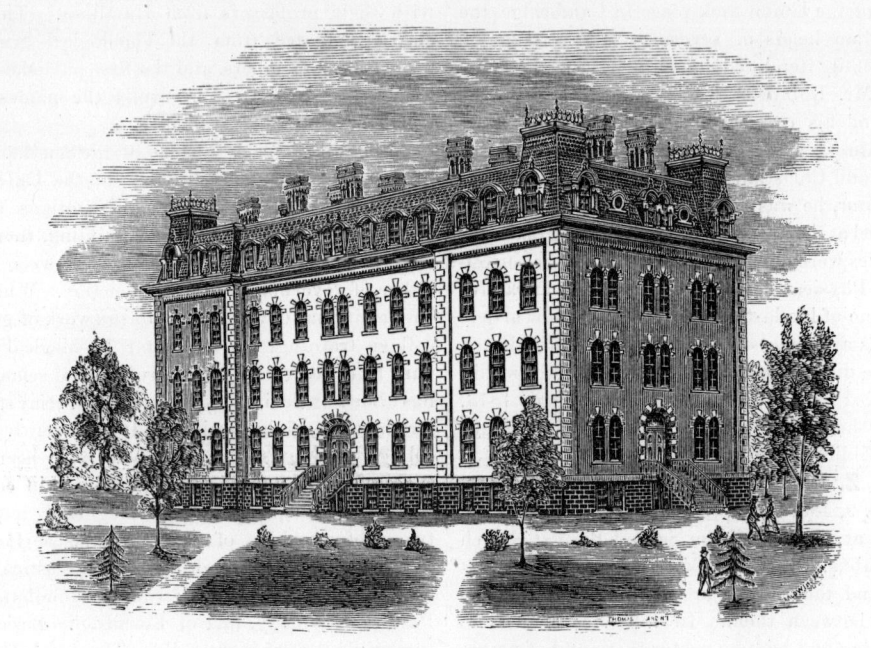

TREVOR HALL, ROCHESTER THEOLOGICAL SEMINARY.

The Seminary instruction was for some years given in the buildings occupied by the University of Rochester. In 1869, however, the erection of Trevor Hall, at an expense of $42,000, to which John B. Trevor, Esq., of Yonkers, was the largest donor, put the institution for the first time in possession of suitable dormitory accommodations. The gymnasium building, adjoining, erected in 1874, and costing with grounds $12,000, was also a gift of Mr. Trevor. In 1879 Rockefeller Hall, costing $38,000, was built by John D. Rockefeller, Esq., of Cleveland, O. It contains a spacious fire-proof room for library, as well as lecture-rooms, museum, and chapel, and furnishes admirable and ample accommodation for the teaching work of the seminary. In addition to these buildings the German Students' Home, purchased in 1874, at a cost of $20,000, furnishes a dormitory and boarding-hall for the German department.

The library of the seminary is one of great value for theological investigation. It embraces the whole collection of Neander, the great German church historian, which was presented to the seminary in 1853 by the late Hon. Roswell S. Burrows, of Albion, N. Y. It also contains in great part the exegetical apparatus of the late Dr. Horatio B. Hackett. Valuable additions have been made to it from the "Bruce Fund" of $25,000, subscribed in 1872 by John M. Bruce, Esq., of Yonkers, and further additions from this source are hoped for. The generous subscription in 1879 of $25,000, by William Rockefeller, Esq., of New York City, has furnished means for extensive enlargement, so that the library now numbers over 18,000 volumes, and it is well provided in all the various departments of theology. In 1880 the "Sherwood Fund," contributed by the late Rev. Adiel Sherwood, D.D., of St. Louis, Mo., furnished the means for beginning a Museum of Biblical Geography and Archæology, intended to provide, in object lessons, valuable aids for the study of the Holy Land, its customs and its physical features.

Thus the Rochester Theological Seminary has grown from small beginnings to assured strength and success. Its early years were years of trial and financial struggle; but, founded as it was in the prayers and faith of godly men, it has lived to justify the hopes of its founders. Of those who took a deep interest in its feeble beginnings should be mentioned the names of Alfred Bennett, William R. Williams, Justin A. Smith, Zenas Freeman, Alvah Strong, Friend Humphrey, E. E. L. Taylor, E. Lathrop, J. S. Backus, B. T. Welch, William Phelps, Lemuel C. Paine, H. C. Fish, A. B. Capwell, N. W. Benedict, G. C. Baldwin, G. D. Boardman, A. R. Pritchard, Henry E. Robins. All these have been officers of the New York Baptist Union for Ministerial Education, or members of its board of trustees. The financial management of this board has been such that no loss of funds, of any significance, intrusted to its care has ever occurred.

The results of the work of the Seminary can never be measured by arithmetic. As its purpose has been to make its graduates men of thinking ability and of practical force, as well as students and preachers of the word of God, it has leavened the denomination with its influence, and has done much to give an aggressive, independent, manly tone to our ministry. The names of some of its former students, such as J. H. Castle, J. B. Simmons, J. V. Schofield, J. D. Fulton, R. J. Adams, P. W. Bickel, G. W. Clarke, B. D. Marshall, E. Nisbet, E. J. Fish, J. B. Thomas, Galusha Anderson, E. J. Goodspeed, E. G. Taylor, C. D. W. Bridgman, Norman Fox, G. W. Northrop, A. Kingman Nott, J. C. Haselhuhn, R. M. Nott, C. B. Crane, J. S. Gubelmann, Lemuel Moss, Thomas Rogers, J. C. C. Clarke, J. H. Griffith, A. A. Kendrick, Wayland Hoyt, A. J. Sage, H. L. Morehouse, Wm. A. Stevens, J. W. B. Clark, S. W. Duncan, A. J. Rowland, J. F. Elder, T. J. Backus, C. J. Baldwin, T. J. Morgan, Wm. T. Stott, W. R. Benedict, R. S. Macarthur, E. H. Johnson, W. C. P. Rhoades, R. B. Hull, A. J. Barrett, O. P. Gifford, T. S. Barbour, and many others, are enough to show that its training has combined in equal proportions the intellectual and the spiritual, the theoretical and the practical. During the thirty years of the seminary's existence, and up to the present year (1881), 745 persons have been connected with the institution as students, of whom 590 have attended upon the English and 155 upon the German department. Of the 590 in the English department, 444 have been graduates of colleges, and 54 have pursued partial courses in colleges. Sixty-five different colleges and 42 different States and countries have furnished students to the seminary. Three hundred and sixty-nine persons have completed the full three years' course, including the study of the Hebrew and Greek Scriptures; 221 have pursued a partial course, or have left the seminary before graduating. The average number of students sent out each year has been 19. The number of students during the last seminary year has been 70, of whom 50 were in the English department. Of its former students, 41 have filled the position of president or professor in theological seminaries or colleges; 31 have gone abroad as foreign missionaries; and 25 have been missionaries in the West; 20 have been secretaries or agents of our benevolent societies; and 4 have become editors of religious journals. With such a record in the past, and in the present more fully equipped than ever before for its work, there seems to open before the seminary a future of the utmost promise. It remains only to state that the Rochester Theological Seminary is maintained and controlled by the New York Baptist Union for Ministerial Education, a society composed of contributing members of Baptist churches, and that the actual government and care of the seminary is in its details committed to a board of trustees of thirty-three members, eleven of whom are elected by the Union annually. The present president of the board of trustees is John H. Deane, Esq., of New York, and the corresponding secretary is Rev. William Elgin, of Rochester, N. Y.

Rochester, University of.—This institution is situated in Rochester, N. Y., a city of 90,000 inhabitants, on the Genesee River, six miles south of Lake Ontario. It has no preparatory department, and no organic connection with the flourishing theological seminary in the same city; nor has it as yet organized schools of law, medicine, or applied science. Its purpose—so far as that purpose has been attained—is simply to superinduce upon the instruction given in the academy or the high school, such broad and generous culture as is essential to the successful prosecution of any of the learned professions, and indisputably useful to the merchant, the farmer, or the mechanic.

III. The eclectic course, designed for students who may desire to receive instruction in particular departments without becoming candidates for degrees. Such students are admitted, provided they have the requisite preparation for the studies of those departments and become subject to the laws of the university. This arrangement is intended to meet the wants of those whose age or circumstances may prevent them from pursuing either of the regular courses, but who are desirous of obtaining the liberal culture which the studies of a portion of the course will give them. Special care

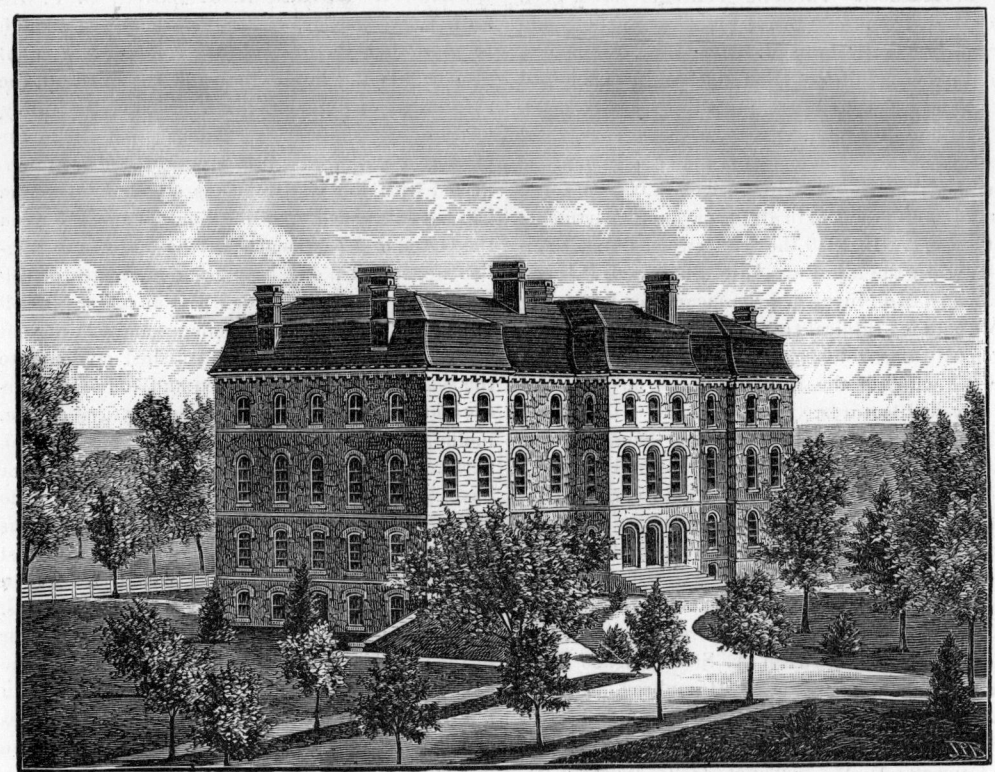

UNIVERSITY OF ROCHESTER.

Three courses of study are open to the members of the university:

I. The classical course, extending through four years,—at the expiration of which time those who have satisfactorily met the requirements of the faculty are admitted to the degree of Bachelor of Arts.

II. The scientific course, extending through four years,—requiring Latin as essential to the successful prosecution of the modern languages and the mastery of scientific terminology; but prescribing, in the place of Greek, a more extended course of study in the physical sciences. Those who satisfactorily complete this course are admitted to the degree of Bachelor of Science.

is taken to give such pupils the instruction which they require.

The number of students in attendance upon the university in 1880 was 160, of whom 105 were pursuing the classical course, 16 the scientific course, 19 the eclectic course, while 21 were special students in the department of chemistry. These students were distributed into classes as follows: Seniors, 30; Juniors, 26; Sophomores, 32; Freshmen, 53. Of the whole number of students, 46 were from Rochester; 83 from places in the State of New York outside of Rochester; while the remaining 31 were divided among 14 different States, as follows: Pennsylvania, 5; Michigan, 4; New Jersey, 4; Illinois, 4; Connecticut, 3; Ohio,

3; Maine, Massachusetts, Iowa, Minnesota, California, Wisconsin, Kentucky, Georgia, 1 each.

The faculty of instruction includes the following names, twelve in number: Martin B. Anderson, LL.D., President, Burbank Professor of Intellectual and Moral Philosophy; Asahel C. Kendrick, D.D., LL.D., Munro Professor of the Greek Language and Literature; Isaac F. Quinby, LL.D., Harris Professor of Mathematics and Natural Philosophy; Samuel A. Lattimore, Ph.D., LL.D., Professor of Chemistry and Curator of the Cabinets; Albert H. Mixer, A.M., Professor of Modern Languages; Joseph H. Gilmore, A.M., Deane Professor of Logic, Rhetoric, and English Literature; Otis H. Robinson, A.M., Professor of Mathematics and Librarian; William C. Morey, A.M., Professor of Latin and History; Henry F. Burton, A.M., Assistant Professor of Latin; George M. Forbes, A.M., Assistant Professor of Greek; E. R. Benton, Assistant Professor of the Natural Sciences; Herman K. Phinney, A.M., Assistant Librarian.

Notices of President Anderson and several of his colleagues will be found in this work, under their respective names.

The buildings of the University of Rochester are situated in the eastern part of the city, about a mile from the business centre, on a handsomely adorned and well-kept lot, embracing twenty-three and a half acres.

The principal building, Anderson Hall, was designed almost exclusively for recitation-rooms, although it affords temporary accommodations for the chapel, cabinets, and chemical laboratory of the university, and includes, in the basement, apartments for the janitor and ample facilities for storage. It is a severely plain but very substantial structure, of brownstone, three stories in height, and 150 feet in length by 60 in breadth. The cost of the building, which was completed in 1861, was $39,000.

Sibley Hall, the gift of the Hon. Hiram Sibley, of Rochester, is a strictly fire-proof building, designed for the accommodation of the library, and capable of affording shelf-room for 250,000 volumes. It is 125 feet by 60, with a projection 20 feet square in the centre of the front, and has only two floors, though its walls are 52 feet in height.

SIBLEY HALL, UNIVERSITY OF ROCHESTER.

The material is brownstone, with white trimmings; the style of architecture is somewhat ornate; and the building cost about $100,000. The lower story is at present all that is needed for the accommodation of the library, and the upper story will, it is hoped, soon be fitted up to receive the valuable cabinets of the university.

On the university campus there is also a small

building erected for the accommodation of the Trevor telescope,—an instrument designed mainly for use as an adjunct to class-room instruction, though sufficiently powerful for purposes of special investigation. And, but a few steps from the campus, on a plot of ground four acres in extent, is the president's house, which was presented to the university by the citizens of Rochester and others in 1868.

The library of the university has been acquired mainly by purchase, and includes few duplicates, and still fewer trashy and ephemeral publications. It contains more than 18,000 volumes, and especial care is taken to make its contents practically available by a card catalogue, and by indexes of periodical and of miscellaneous literature, all of which are constantly kept up to date, and accessible to every student. Provision is made for the annual increase of the library by a fund of $50,000, which was presented to the university by Gen. John F. Rathbone and Lewis Rathbone, of Albany.

The cabinets of geology and mineralogy were collected by Prof. Henry A. Ward during ten years of extensive foreign travel and during many careful visits to the most fruitful American localities. They were purchased by the citizens of Rochester, in 1862, for $20,000 (a sum far less than their present estimated value), and presented to the university. Dr. Torrey, of Columbia College, says that "no geological cabinet in the United States can compare, in magnitude and value, with this;" and that the mineralogical cabinet, "although it is not the best in the United States, is excelled by very few, and is admirably selected for the purpose of instruction." "For fullness and perfection of specimens," says President Loomis, of Lewisburg, "it is superior to any cabinet that I have ever seen." Prof. Silliman (Jr.) characterizes it as "the most extensive geological museum in the United States," and predicts that "it will ultimately attract students from all parts of the country,"—a prediction which is already realized. Similar opinions have been expressed by Prof. Hitchcock (Sr.), President Winchell, and Profs. Agassiz, Hall, and Orton.

The value of the unproductive property of the university (including land, buildings, library, cabinets, and apparatus) was, in June, 1881, $408,405.05. The interest-bearing funds were, at the same date, $435,007.15. The expenses of the university for the year ending June 5, 1881, were $30,616.34. Its receipts from students' tuition were $5485; from other sources, $28,121.34; making a total of $33,507.83,—being an excess of income over expenses, for the last academic year, of $2891.49.

The university year begins twelve weeks after commencement-day, which occurs on the second Wednesday before the first of July, and is divided into three terms. Each student is charged, for tuition and incidentals, $25 a term. Forty scholarships, yielding free tuition, are, however, set apart for candidates for the Baptist ministry, twelve similar scholarships for graduates of the Rochester city schools,. four similar scholarships (endowed) for graduates of the Brockport State Normal School, and six similar scholarships (endowed) for indigent students who fall under neither of these categories. The university also has a fund of $50,000 (the gift of John H. Deane, Esq., of New York), the interest of which is available for the assistance of the sons of Baptist ministers,—preference being given, other things being equal, to students from the States of New York and New Jersey. In point of fact, tuition is remitted to every student of promise who really needs such remission, and the number of those who do need it is about one-third the whole number in attendance. The university also distributes about $300 a year in prizes, the most important of which is the Stoddard medal, valued at $100, for proficiency in mathematics; and there are, in addition, two post-graduate scholarships,—the Sherman scholarship in the department of political economy, and the Townsend scholarship in the department of constitutional law,—each of which yields, to some member of the graduating class, $300.

The University of Rochester has no "dormitories," its custodians regarding them as of questionable value so far as economy is concerned, and a positive detriment to the student physically, morally, and intellectually. In a city of the size of Rochester it is not difficult for the university to find suitable accommodations for its students in Christian homes; and they are taught to regard themselves as members of the community in which they temporarily reside, subject to its laws and amenable to its usages. The price which the individual student pays for room and board varies from $3 to $6 per week, making his total expense, on this account, for the forty weeks during which the college is in session fall between $120 and $240 a year. The students of the university are addicted to no expensive amusements, and are, as a rule, economical in their habits. Some of them, no doubt, with the help of free tuition, get through the year for $250 apiece; and the faculty would regard $500 as a liberal allowance for any one of them. Meanwhile, students for the ministry receive aid—in some cases to the amount of $100 a year—from the "Union for Ministerial Education;" and in a city whose industries are so numerous and varied as those of Rochester, frequent opportunities for remunerative employment that will not seriously interfere with one's studies present themselves.

The discipline of the university, which is administered by the president, is that of the family rather than that of the police station. Young men are put, as far as possible, upon their honor, and encouraged to become, in a high and noble sense, a law unto themselves. They are encouraged fully to communicate with the members of the faculty upon all matters connected with their intellectual and religious culture, as well as with reference to their pecuniary difficulties, their plans and purposes. The necessity for discipline is thus very largely forestalled by establishing, in place of the time-honored antagonism between teacher and pupils, relations of personal friendship which will enable the instructor to exert a constant influence for good.

The discipline, as well as the instruction of the university, is facilitated by the fact that it has no "tutors" or "instructors;" that each student, so soon as he enters the university, is brought in personal contact with men who have made the discipline and training of youth a life-study. The time-honored American college course—a distinctive outgrowth of American society, which has proved its usefulness too conclusively to be lightly set aside—forms the basis of instruction in the university; but the course is, in accordance with the demands of the times, enlarged in the direction of the modern languages and the physical sciences, and is subject to some variation, to adapt it better to the wants of the individual student during the Junior and Senior years. Special encouragement is given to the best men in each class to pursue extra studies under the immediate supervision of the Faculty; and many of the students, in this way, practically add a fifth year to their undergraduate course. Great freedom of discussion is permitted in the class-room, and the utmost pains is taken in every department of instruction to trace the growth of principles and the bearing of conflicting opinions on the vital questions of the present day. It is a definite purpose with the corps of instructors not merely to store the mind with facts, but to develop the capacity to accumulate and co-ordinate facts, and give expression to the principles which underlie them. Their paramount object, however, is to fit the students intrusted to their charge, morally as well as intellectually, to acquit themselves as *men* in any station that they may be called to fill; and it is believed that the graduates of the University of Rochester, wherever they are found, evince an independence of thought, a breadth of culture, and an adaptation to the exigencies of practical life with which college graduates are not, as a class, accredited.

It is necessary to supplement the cursory view that has been taken of the University of Rochester as it is, by an outline sketch of its history, which will still further illustrate its distinctive character.

As early as 1820 the Baptists of the State of New York established at Hamilton, in Madison County, an institution of learning which "had one object exclusively, namely, to furnish means for the education of young men who shall give evidence of a call to the Christian ministry." The object and methods of instruction at Hamilton gradually broadened in the lapse of time, but not to a degree commensurate with the growing interests of the New York Baptists in general, as distinguished from distinctively ministerial, education. Meanwhile, objection was made to Hamilton as an unsuitable site for such a college as the Baptists of New York would inevitably demand, and attention was called to the fact that west of Cayuga Bridge there was a large section of the State—populous, intelligent, wealthy, and rapidly being brought into railroad communication with Pennsylvania, Canada, and the great West—which was utterly destitute of collegiate facilities.

The result was a determined effort, which took definite shape in 1847, to remove Madison University to Rochester, give to its course of study a broader and more generous character, and secure for it an adequate endowment. Into the heated controversy between the friends and opponents of removal to which this proposition gave rise it is not necessary or desirable to go. The removal of Madison University to Rochester was authorized by the Legislature of the State, voted by its board of trustees, and approved by a large convention of New York Baptists assembled at Albany in 1849. Legal hindrances were, however, thrown in the way of the desired change, and the advocates of removal made application to "the Regents of the University of the State of New York" for a charter for a new college at Rochester. This application was granted Jan. 31, 1850, subject to the proviso that $130,000 be raised for the new college within two years. On the 2d of December, in the same year, satisfactory proof was submitted to the regents that this provision had been complied with; and, Feb. 14, 1851, the regents issued that charter under which the university is now organized.

This charter did not vest the control of the university in any religious denomination. It simply created a self-perpetuating board of trustees,—twenty-four in number,—who hold office for life, but may be removed, by vote of their associates, for non-attendance at five successive annual meetings. Twenty of the trustees named in the charter were Baptists, and the Baptists have thus maintained an effective control over the university. Different religious denominations have always, however, been represented in its board of trustees and faculty of instruction; and Methodists, Presbyterians, Episcopalians, Romanists, and Jews meet on an equal footing with Baptists in its chapel and recitation-rooms.

It must not be inferred that either the legal guardians of the University of Rochester or its corps of instructors regard with indifference any of the truths inculcated in the Christian Scriptures. They simply feel that the college class-room is no place for the discussion of those truths respecting which Christians themselves are unhappily divided; that the true aim of a denominational college is not to proselyte, but to protect. Instruction is given in every department from a Christian stand-point, and in a Christian spirit; and it is the aim of the faculty, in connection with the discipline of the intellect, to inculcate a pure morality and those truths and duties respecting which all evangelical Christians are agreed. The students, whatever their religious proclivities, are expected to attend morning prayers in the university chapel, and attendance upon that exercise is, in point of fact, as regular as at any other.

The University of Rochester was organized, under the provisional charter granted by the regents, on the first Monday in November, 1850, having attracted to itself five professors—Thomas J. Conant, John S. Maginnis, A. C. Kendrick, John H. Raymond, John F. Richardson—and a considerable number of students from the older institution at Hamilton. The first catalogue reported 8 instructors and 71 pupils; and in July, 1851, it graduated its first class of 10. In 1853, Martin B. Anderson, LL.D., assumed the presidency of the new institution, and its ultimate success was from that time assured. Still, it has passed through many periods of adversity, during which its very existence seemed imperiled; and those periods of adversity have corresponded very closely to our periods of national depression and gloom. In 1856, when the university was but six years old, its students numbered 163, and it seemed destined speedily to take rank with institutions that could boast of a century's growth. Then came the financial crisis of 1857, attended by pecuniary embarrassment for the university, and a diminution of its Freshman class from 47 in 1856 to 28 in 1858. In 1860 the university seemed to have measurably recovered its lost ground. The entering class numbered 45, and the whole number of students was 168. Then came the civil war. The first two years' regiment raised in New York to recruit the Union army was raised and commanded by Professor (afterwards General) Quinby. Of the 198 alumni of the university (including the class of 1861), 25, or about one in eight, entered the service, and these were speedily joined by 29 of the lower classmen. Three undergraduate members of the university and seven of its alumni died of wounds or disease in the service of their country, and their names are commemorated by a memorial tablet in the university chapel. So far as is known, only one graduate of the university entered the Confederate army; and he was faithful to the cause that he espoused, and sealed his devotion by his death. Not only were the classes of the university, but the classes of the preparatory schools on which it relied for students, thus depleted by the civil war; and a tendency was developed among the young men of the country towards active rather than student life, which has hardly yet been outgrown. As a natural consequence, the entering class fell as low as 19 (in 1864), and the whole number of students as low as 100 (in 1866). With the return of peace there was a gradual increase in the number of students, however, until, in 1873, the Freshman class included 53, and the whole number of students in attendance was 173. It was not long before the financial distress of the nation again interfered with the pecuniary prosperity of the university, and sensibly diminished the number of its students, who, in 1878, were only 146, though there are cheering indications of returning prosperity.

During all these vicissitudes the University of Rochester has been sustained by the devotion of its noble-hearted president, supported by a body of friends and benefactors of whom any institution of learning might well be proud. Prominent among the early friends of the university stood John N. Wilder, Pharcellus Church, and Oren Sage, of Rochester; William L. Marcy, Ira Harris, and Friend Humphrey, of Albany; William R. Williams, Sewall S. Cutting, and Robert and William Kelley, of New York. With these names may properly be associated that of William N. Sage, who has from the first had charge of the finances of the university, and has contributed more efficiently to its success than any other man save its first and only president. The names of the principal pecuniary benefactors of the university may be ascertained from the following list, which includes the names of all persons who have subscribed $10,000 or more to its funds. The sums affixed to their respective names are all the eulogy they require: Hon. Hiram Sibley (library building), $102,000; John B. Trevor, $113,000; John H. Deane, $100,000; Hon. William Kelley and family, $38,550; Gen. John F. Rathbone (library fund), $42,575; Tracy H. Harris (chair of Mathematics), $30,250; Joseph B. Hoyt, $27,600; Charles Pratt, $25,500; Jeremiah Millbank, $25,000; John D. Rockefeller, $25,000; State of New York (Anderson Hall), $25,000; Jacob F. Wyckoff, $22,000; James B. Colgate, $20,000; Gideon W. Burbank (chair of Metaphysics), $17,500; Lewis Rathbone (library fund), $12,500; Deacon Oren Sage and family, $11,765; Lewis Roberts, $10,925; John N. Wilder, $10,000; Hon. Azariah Boody (land), $10,000.

The number of students who since the organization of the university have completed the classical course and received the degree of A.B. is 707. The number who have completed the scientific course and received the degree of B.S. is 39. The whole number of graduates, down to and including 1881, is 746. Of the graduates of the university, 181 had, in 1878, entered the Christian ministry, including such men as the lamented Kingman Nott; Bridgeman, MacArthur, and Hull, of New York; Crane, of Boston; Fulton, of Brooklyn; Goodspeed, of Chicago; Sage, of Hartford; Telford, Chilcott, and Kreyer, of China; Jameson, of Bassein; and Comfort, of Assam. One hundred and nineteen (represented by such men as Judge Bailey, of the Appellate Court of Illinois; Judge Tourgee, of the Superior Court of North Carolina; Judge Macomber, of the Supreme Court of New York) had studied law; 19 had studied medicine; 18 (including such names as Manton Marble, Joseph O'Connor, and Rossiter Johnson) had attained to a prominent position as journalists; 90—or nearly one in seven of the entire number of graduates—had, as professional teachers, transmitted the spirit and methods of the University of Rochester to other institutions of learning. Among them we may mention Prof. S. H. Carpenter, LL.D., of the University of Wisconsin; President A. A. Brooks, of Goliad College, Texas; President Lemuel Moss, D.D., of the University of Indiana; President Galusha Anderson, D.D., and Prof. A. J. Howe, of the University of Chicago; President Sylvanus Taft, of California College; Prof. Wm. C. Wilkinson, D.D., of the Rochester Theological Seminary; Prof. Wm. Wirt Fay, of the United States Naval Academy; Prof. Wm. Harkness, of the United States Naval Observatory; Prof. John C. C. Clarke, of Shurtleff College; Prof. Norman Robinson, of Bethel College, Ky.; Prof. Norman Fox, of William Jewell College, Mo.; Prof. D. H. Robinson, of the University of Kansas; Prof. John C. Overhiser, of the Brooklyn Polytechnic Institute; Profs. Otis H. Robinson and William C. Morey, of the University of Rochester; Prof. Truman J. Backus, of Vassar College; Prof. Carl T. Kreyer, of Kau-Chang Miau College, China; Prof. Albert T. Barrett, of Mary Sharpe College, Tenn.; Principal Malcolm McVicar, LL.D., of the Potsdam (N. Y.) Normal School; Principal William J. Milne, of the Geneseo (N. Y.) Normal School; Principal F. B. Palmer, of the Fredonia (N. Y.) Normal School; Prof. Frank S. Capen, of the Cortland (N. Y.) Normal School; Principal A. C. Winters, of Cook Academy; Principal Merrill E. Gates, of the Albany Academy.

About one-third of the graduates of the University of Rochester have, it will be seen, devoted themselves to active rather than professional life,— a fact which abundantly vindicates the wisdom of its founders when they recognized the demand for a college that should educate its students as *men*, rather than as ministers, doctors, or lawyers in embryo; and make equal provision for the sons of the rich and the sons of the poor. To such men as the Hon. Henry Strong, of Chicago; the Hon. Moreau S. Crosby, of Grand Rapids; Isaac E. Sheldon, of New York; Edwin O. Sage, of Rochester; Lieut.-Col. Elwell S. Otis, of the U. S. army; William H. Harris, of Cleveland; George F. and William H. Davis, of Cincinnati, the university points in exemplification of the practical benefits of the culture she affords. Upon them she confidently relies for the means to do more and better work in the future than she has done in the past.

Rockefeller, John D., a resident of Cleveland, O., and one of the most successful business men of the day, began life with few advantages save honesty of purpose and a determined Christian character. With a small capital he commenced business, and now the company of which he is the head employs thousands of men, and as a result of his skill and economy Mr. Rockefeller has amassed for himself a very considerable fortune.

In his business success, however, Mr. Rockefeller has not forgotten his obligations to God. He has been for years a most faithful and valued member of the Euclid Avenue Baptist church of Cleveland, and has given large sums to this body, to missionary and other benevolent societies, and to educational institutions. One of his latest and most princely acts of beneficence was the presentation to Rochester Theological Seminary, at a cost of about $40,000, of a new building for lecture-rooms, library, and chapel, which, in grateful recognition of his services, has been called Rockefeller Hall. Mr. Rockefeller is in the prime of life, and is constantly proving himself a "good steward" for the Master of souls.

Rockwell, Rev. Cortland Butler, the pastor of the Baptist church in Merton, Wis., was born in New London, Conn., Nov. 10, 1841. Here he spent his early life until about nine years of age, when his father's family removed to Rome, Bradford Co., Pa. Eight years afterwards he returned with his parents to his native city. He obtained a hope in Christ in 1854, and the same year united with the Baptist church in Rome, Pa. At the breaking out of the war, in 1861, he entered the U. S. navy, and served in the position of paymaster's steward, on board the U. S. sloop "Granite," for a term of three years. Mr. Rockwell's conviction that he was called to preach the gospel began soon after his conversion, and it was only after a struggle extending through years that he became obedient to the call of God. In October, 1867, when twenty-six years of age, he was licensed by the Second Baptist church in New London to preach the gospel. Having received a call to the pastorate of the Baptist church in Warrenville, in the town of Ashford, Windham Co., Conn., he was ordained by that church Dec. 3, 1868. He was subsequently pastor of Second Woodstock, Eastford, Union, Plainfield, and East Killingly, Conn. In 1879, having received a call from the Baptist church in Merton, Wis., he accepted, and removed to Merton, where he now labors. While in Windham Co., Conn., he was a member of the Legislature one year from the town of Eastford. Mr. Rockwell's ministry has been marked by success. The churches have been strengthened and many souls led to Christ under his labors.

Rockwood, Rev. Edwin J., was born in Remsen, Oneida Co., N. Y., Oct. 25, 1835; baptized in May, 1852. He was educated at Rochester University, graduating with honors. He was ordained at Waterloo, N. Y., Nov. 17, 1863. From Waterloo he removed West. He was pastor of the Baptist churches in Sioux City and Logan, Iowa, Bellevue and Hastings, Neb. At the present time he is preaching to the Glenville Baptist church. Mr. Rockwood has labored for years under great disadvantage, on account of failing health.

Roe, Charles Hill, D.D., who died at Belvidere, Ill., June 20, 1872, was a native of King's County, Ireland, where he was born Jan. 6, 1800. He was the son of a clergyman of the Established Church, and was educated by his father in English and classical studies, with a view to a course at Trinity College, Dublin, and to orders in the English Church. When he was fourteen years of age his father died, and the plan of study thus made for him was interrupted. Through the instrumentality of an Irish Baptist minister he was converted, and became a Baptist. In 1822 he entered Horton College, Bradford, Yorkshire, England, then under the presidency of Dr. Steadman. Having completed his course there, he became pastor of the church at Middleton, a daughter of Dr. Steadman having become his wife. With the work of this pastorate he associated extensive preaching tours in the surrounding country. This service brought him so much in contact with the destitution of right religious teaching as to interest him greatly in the aims and measures of the English Baptist Home Mission Society. In 1834 he became secretary of that organization, and remained in that office until 1842, when he became pastor of an important church in Birmingham. Here, as in former spheres of service, his labors were richly blessed. He was a co-laborer in Birmingham with the well-known John Angell James, who, in his book entitled "Nonconformity in Birmingham," speaks of the 700 new members added to the church under Mr. Roe's ministry, of the 1200 children in the Sunday-school, and of the various organizations of Christian labor which had been formed under his guidance.

In 1851, Mr. Roe came to this country, and, after a brief stay in New York and Milwaukee, settled in Belvidere, Ill., as pastor of the Baptist church there. Here, again, his work was fruitful, and the church grew not only in numbers but in spirituality. During the war he was for a portion of the time chaplain of a regiment. He also, later. visited England in behalf of the educational work among the freedmen. Upon his return to this country he served two years as pastor at Waukesha, Wis., succeeding Dr. Robert Boyd. Two years subsequently were spent in the service of the University of Chicago, of which he was one of the founders, and with this his public life ended, the final close coming soon after. The funeral at Belvidere was very largely attended, the sermon being by Dr. J. C. Burroughs, who was followed in an address by Gen. S. A. Hulburt, Gen. A. C. Fuller, and other eminent citizens of Illinois.

Dr. Roe, while beloved for his Christian virtues, and as a spiritual, eloquent preacher, was honored by all classes of men for his sterling manhood. In both England and the United States he stood among the stalwart men, and achieved a work whose fruits, in the long succession of seed-sowing and harvest, must be permanent.

Rogers, Rev. John, was born in Ireland, of English parentage, in November, 1783. He was converted in his seventeenth year, and joined the Presbyterian Church, of which his parents were members. He was educated for the ministry in Edinburgh, Scotland, and became pastor of an Independent church near Belfast in 1807. At his first baptism his mind became unsettled on that and kindred topics, and, after a long investigation, he embraced the views of the Baptists, and candidly informed his people that he could not administer the ordinances according to their mode. The church invited him to remain, and exchange with other ministers when those rites were to be administered. In 1811 he was baptized by Rev. Mr. Cook, and resigned his charge. Six weeks afterwards he baptized his wife. Some other members of the church also changed their views. He intended to come to the United States, but the war detained him until 1816. Soon after reaching New York he attended an Association in New Jersey, which led to his settlement with the church at New Mills (now Pemberton), where for thirteen years he ministered, greatly to the increase and efficiency of the church. In 1829 he accepted a call from Scotch Plains, where he remained twelve years, during which there were two powerful revivals. After a few years' pastorate at Perth Amboy he removed to Paterson, where he "fell asleep," Aug. 30, 1849.

One who knew him well has described Mr. Rogers as kind, courteous, hospitable, free-hearted, an excellent sympathetic pastor, an instructive preacher, an able divine. He was a warm advocate and supporter of missionary movements. He always maintained the dignity of a man, a Christian, and a minister. His son, A. W. Rogers, M.D., still living in Paterson, N. J., is not only a useful and beloved physician, but is a licensed preacher, and a liberal giver to the cause of God.

Rogers, Rev. John, was for a time rector of Purleigh, in England, during the Parliamentary war, then lecturer in the church of St. Thomas the Apostle, in London, and subsequently minister of Christ's church, Dublin, a building containing the remains and monument of the celebrated Strongbow, and attended, during the ministry of Thomas Patient and John Rogers, by the *élite* of English society in Ireland. Mr. Rogers was a Baptist. His wife, whom he married in 1649, was the daughter of Sir Robert Paine, of Huntingdonshire. Mr. Rogers adopted the principles of the Fifth-Monarchy men, and he became very unfriendly to Cromwell's government. He was a popular speaker, with many friends, and with a dangerous candor in expressing his sentiments. He would utter petitions like this in his public prayers: "O Lord! hasten the time when all absolute power shall be devolved into the hands of Christ; when we shall have no lord protector but our Lord Jesus Christ, the only true protector and defender of the faith;" and he would publish such doctrines by the printing-press. The result was the imprisonment of the bold Baptist. It could not be otherwise in the case of a man possessed of such influence. Cromwell's order to the officer who arrested him ran: "Sir, I desire you to seize Maj.-Gen. Harrison, Mr. Carew, Portman, and such as are eminent Fifth-Monarchy men, especially *Feake* and *Rogers*: do it speedily, and you shall have a warrant after you have done." The form of this order shows the powerful influence wielded by the two Baptist ministers, and it proves that they had inspired the great Protector with alarm. Brook says, "After Cromwell had deserted these sectaries, he took umbrage at the great popularity and enterprising spirit of Rogers; and was little less apprehensive of Feake, who was also regarded as a leader of that party."* Mr. Rogers was the author of several works. These were issued in a thick quarto in 1653.

Rogers, Rev. Peter, son of Peter, a descendant of John, the martyr, was born in New London, Conn., in 1754. In the early part of the Revolution he served on a privateer, later he entered the army, and won distinction in the Washington Life-Guard. In March, 1790, he was ordained pastor of the Baptist church in Bozrah, Conn. His first wife was Miss Green, his second was the daughter of Rev. Zadoc Darrow, of Waterford, Conn. He died in Illinois in 1849, in the ninety-sixth year of his age, and the sixtieth of his ministry.

Rogers, Lieut. Robert, was born in Newport, R. I., April 19, 1758. Converted at the age of sixteen, he joined the First Baptist church in Providence. He was a graduate of Brown University in the class of 1775, and a member of the corporation for nearly forty-nine years. He was connected with the American army as a lieutenant, and fought for the liberty of his country during the Revolutionary war. On leaving his military life, he devoted himself to studies congenial with his tastes, and conducted for many years, in his native town, a classical school of a very high character. He was intimately connected with the Redwood Library, as its secretary, treasurer, and librarian. He was a most devoted member of the church. Respected and beloved in the community in which he had so long lived, he died Aug. 5, 1835.

Rogers, William, D.D., was born in Newport, R. I., July 22, 1751. It is stated that he was the first, and for several days the only student of Rhode Island College. He was then but fourteen years of age. He graduated in 1769. A comparison has been drawn between Archbishop Ussher and Dr. Rogers in their talents and in their relations to the universities in which they studied. Ussher, it is asserted, was the first student of Trinity College, Dublin. He says himself that he was "among the first." The archbishop was one of the most learned men that ever lived; and Dr. Rogers, with no claim to his great learning, reflected the highest honor upon his *alma mater*. In 1770 the Saviour revealed his pardoning love to him, after which he united with the Second Baptist church of Newport. In May, 1772, he was ordained pastor of the First Baptist church of Philadelphia. He sustained this new relation for three years, with great advantage to the struggling church; its congregations were largely increased, and men like Dr. Benjamin Rush came to hear the eloquent young preacher. When Pennsylvania raised three battalions of foot for the Revolutionary war, the Legislature appointed Dr. Rogers their chaplain. Afterwards he was a brigade chaplain in the Continental army. For five years he followed the fortunes of the Revolutionary army as an unwearied and honored chaplain.

His relations with Washington were intimate and cordial. Dr. Reuben A. Guild quotes the following from an English gentleman who visited Philadelphia in 1793: "After traveling through an extremely pleasant country we arrived in Philadelphia and waited on Dr. Rogers. Dr. Rogers is a most entertaining and agreeable man; we were with him a great part of the time we remained in the city, and were introduced by him to Gen.

---

* Brook's Lives of the Puritans, iii. 327, 328. London, 1813. Evans's Early English Baptists, ii. 214. London, 1846.

Washington. The general was not at home when we called, but while we were talking with his private secretary in the hall he came in, and spoke to Dr. Rogers with the greatest ease and familiarity. He immediately asked us up to the drawing-room, where were Lady Washington and his two nieces.''

Dr. Rogers was for many years Professor of Oratory and Belles-Lettres in the University of Pennsylvania, a position which was never more worthily filled by any of his honored successors. His popularity in Philadelphia and throughout the country was remarkable, and it was limited to men of no special opinions, religious or political.

He belonged to the Masonic fraternity, and frequently addressed his brethren on public occasions. He was in the General Assembly of his adopted State during the sessions of 1816 and 1817. He was a member of the various societies in Philadelphia which existed to promote knowledge, relieve misery, and spread gospel light.

A gentleman of refinement, with learned attainments, a large heart, and an unswerving faith in the blessed Redeemer, Dr. Rogers necessarily lived in the affections of all that knew him. And when he passed away, April 7, 1824, it was universally felt that our country had lost one of its best citizens, and our denomination one of its brightest ornaments.

Rose, Rev. A. T., was a graduate of the Hamilton Literary and Theological Institution, and was appointed a missionary to Burmah in October, 1851. He sailed for the place of his destination Jan. 17, 1853, arriving in Akyab the following May. Before him was every prospect of a healthful and agreeable residence, but a sad cloud was thrown over these prospects by the sudden death of Mrs. Rose, who was attacked with the cholera, and died after a short illness. In accordance with his own request, Mr. Rose's connection with the Union in 1854 was dissolved, and he was a government school-teacher until 1861. He was re-appointed in October of this year, and commenced his labors in the Burmese department of the Rangoon Mission. He engaged in the usual routine of missionary labor, and, judging from the reports we have, he was successful, by the living voice and the printed page, in reaching a large number of persons. The report of 1867 speaks encouragingly of his excursions in various directions from Rangoon. In some of these trips he was absent six or eight weeks. A visit of this kind to Thongzai is spoken of as one of great interest. Such labors Mr. Rose speaks of as "the cream of missionary work, both as to usefulness and enjoyment." While on one of these tours to the north in 1868, he contracted a fever, which so enfeebled him that he was obliged to return to this country, where he remained for several years. A part of this time he was the pastor of the Jefferson Street church in Providence, R. I. Having been re-appointed by the Union, he returned to Burmah in 1874, and resumed the work of former years. During 1875 he was absent nearly six months on a missionary tour to Northern Burmah. The reports of what has been accomplished the last two years are full of interest and hope. Mr. Rose is one of the busiest and most active of the missionaries of the Union.

Rose, Rev. Frank Bramwell, was born in Tuckerton, N. J., April 5, 1836. At the age of six he removed to Philadelphia, receiving a public-school education, finishing at the High-School in 1852. He was converted at the age of twelve, in the Methodist Episcopal Church. He resigned a responsible position in a bank in 1859 to enter the ministry of the Methodist Church; was ordained thereto by Bishop Levi Scott, and appointed first to Freehold and subsequently to St. James' church, New Brunswick, N. J. In September, 1862, he was appointed by Gov. Olden, of New Jersey, chaplain of the 14th Regiment N. J. Vols., serving as such for three years, until the close of the war, participating in the battles of Locust Grove, Wilderness, Spottsylvania, Cold Harbor, Monocacy, Winchester, Fisher's Hill, Cedar Creek, etc. At the close of the war he announced his clear conviction of the more Scriptural faith and practice of the Baptists, and received baptism on profession of faith, in the winter of 1865, at the hands of Rev. William S. Hall, in the Enon church of Philadelphia. The same year he was duly ordained to the ministry by direction of a council of which D. Henry Miller, D.D., was moderator, and accepted a call to the pastorate of the First Baptist church of Camden, N. J., serving it four years. In 1870 he was appointed by President Grant chaplain in the U. S. navy, and has since served in the South Atlantic and Pacific, upon the flag-ships " Lancaster" and " Pensacola," and upon the " Potomac" and " Constitution." Whilst unassigned to active naval duty, in 1879–80, he served the Second church of Camden as pastor for eighteen months. Now (1880) he is on board U. S. training-ship " Constitution," the "*Old Ironsides*" of the war of 1812. Mr. Rose is a cultured and talented minister, who enjoys the confidence and affection of his Baptist brethren.

Ross, Rev. Michael, was born in England. In youth he was thoroughly instructed in the ritual and doctrines of the Church of England. Coming to America in early manhood, he was converted; entered the ministry of the Baptist Church; served important churches in Alabama and Mississippi many years with signal ability and success. Removing to Texas, he faithfully served the Texas Baptist State Convention as general agent. He was pastor of the Independence church from 1858 to 1864, serving the church acceptably, proving himself to be a workman that needeth not to be ashamed. Few men had a more thorough knowledge of the Holy Scriptures, or could quote them more accurately. He died at Independence, Texas, in December, 1865, in the sixty-sixth year of his age.

Rothman, Bernard.—See article ANABAPTISTS.

Rothwell, Andrew, was born in Ridley township, Delaware Co., Pa., Nov. 11, 1801. His father

ANDREW ROTHWELL.

was a native of Cecil Co., Md., whence he removed in his youth to Tinicum Island, Pa. Mr. Rothwell's mother died while still young, leaving eight small and helpless children, who were placed for care and protection in several families of their friends. The subject of this sketch resided with Dr. Henry Paschall, of Kingsessing, where most of his time was occupied with farming, spending only three months in the year at school. In his seventeenth year he entered the printing-office of Wm. Frey, Philadelphia, remaining five years and acquiring an unusually accurate knowledge of the business. When nine years of age he became deeply impressed with religious convictions, and, while engaged in his business in Philadelphia, he was converted and baptized by Dr. Staughton, becoming a member of the Sansom Street church in that city. At the age of twenty-one he removed to Washington, and was employed in the office of Gales & Seaton, printers to Congress, and publishers of the *National Intelligencer*. In 1828, associated with T. W. Ustick, he commenced in Washington the publication of a newspaper, *The Washington City Chronicle*, which was discontinued after a few years. In 1831, Mr. Rothwell entered the service of the city government as receiver of taxes, which position he retained for nearly twenty years. Subsequently he occupied for a number of years a position in the U. S. Navy Department. On his removal to Washington he became a member of the Second Baptist church (Navy-Yard), with which he was connected for a long time. In 1842, associated with a few others, he took a leading part in the formation of the E Street Baptist church, where his membership still is, having, during the entire period, filled important offices, including that of deacon. He has done much for this church, both by his labors and his liberal contributions. Since the year 1835 he has been continuously a member of the board of trustees of the Columbian College, portions of the time occupying the offices of secretary and of treasurer. He has always manifested a deep interest in the college, and has generously contributed to its funds. He is also an active promoter of various benevolent institutions, and has been for more than thirty years a zealous member of the board of managers of the Washington Bible Society. In 1833 he prepared a valuable compilation of the laws relating to the city of Washington and the District of Columbia; and in 1867 he prepared and published a valuable pamphlet, "History of the Baptist Institutions of the District of Columbia."

Rothwell, W. R., D.D., was born in Garrard Co., Ky., Sept. 2, 1831. He was the son of the late Dr. John Rothwell, of Callaway Co., Mo. His mother was China Renfro. Both of his parents were of Virginian birth and British descent. His father's family removed to Missouri after his birth in 1831. He graduated in 1854 at the University of Missouri with the first honors in a class of ten members. In 1874 his *alma mater*, in honorable recognition of his distinction as a man of letters, conferred upon him the degree of D.D.

Every moment of Dr. Rothwell's time since his graduation has been one of intellectual activity and usefulness. From 1854 to 1856 he was principal of Elm Ridge Academy. He was the first president of the Baptist Female College at Columbia, Mo. (now known as Stephens College), and after one year of service there he was elected to succeed the Rev. Wm. Thompson, LL.D., as president of Mount Pleasant College. In 1860 he was ordained to the ministry of the gospel, and was successively pastor of the Baptist churches at Huntsville and Keytesville, Mo. During the years 1871 and 1872 he was corresponding secretary of the Baptist General Association of Missouri, in which position he acquitted himself with marked ability. His letters and communications while corresponding secretary are noted as being among the most graceful and forcible that have advocated the interests of that body. In 1872, Dr. Rothwell was unanimously elected Professor of Theology and Moral Philosophy in William Jewell College, a place which he still fills with great distinction.

In his eight years' professorship of Theology he has instructed for a longer or shorter time 150 young ministers of Missouri and the West. Since 1874 he has been chairman of the faculty.

Dr. Rothwell is in the prime of life and mental vigor. He is one of the most modest and unassuming of men, but his very high sense of duty always impels him to the front whenever principle or honor calls. He is a "scholar and a ripe one," of elegant culture, and a man of liberal, expansive views. Probably no man in the State stands higher in the love and confidence of his denomination.

Roussy, Rev. Louis, was born in the canton de Vaud, Switzerland, and died in 1880 at Grande Ligne, province of Quebec, in the sixty-ninth year of his age. Converted when very young, Mr. Roussy early in life felt his heart drawn out towards the cause of missions. At the age of nineteen he commenced the work of colportage in France, which he carried on for two years. But when a missionary seminary was opened at Lausanne in his native land, the object of which was to prepare young men for the foreign field, he discontinued his work in France, and was one of the first to enter the seminary. In 1835, Mr. Roussy accompanied Madame Feller to Canada, arriving in Montreal on the 31st of October, 1835. After a few months spent in the work of French Canadian evangelization in Montreal and St. John, province of Quebec (where, especially in St. John, he met with violent opposition), he went to Grande Ligne. On the 30th of June, 1837, he baptized four converts, who, with himself and Madame Feller, were organized into the first French Protestant church ever founded in Canada. (For fuller information respecting the mission which Mr. Roussy assisted in establishing, and in connection with which he labored forty-five years, see article GRAND LIGNE EVANGELICAL SOCIETY.) Courageous and courteous, patient and loving, full of faith, and ever zealous for his Master's glory, Mr. Roussy was a most efficient and devoted missionary of the Cross.

Rowan, Rev. Thomas J., the youngest of nine children, was born in Copiah Co., Miss., Dec. 9, 1854. He was always considered a pious and model boy, but was not converted until sixteen years of age. Having the ministry in view, he became a student of Centenary College, Jackson, La., under the care of Rev. C. G. Andrews, a distinguished Methodist divine. By his brilliant intellect and studious habits he soon won the esteem and confidence of all the professors, especially the president, who invited him to his home and into his family, treating him more like a son or companion than as a pupil. Possessing as he does an ardent love for God's Word, regarding its teachings as above the opinions of men, and knowing that the Master whom he had professed to love preferred obedience to sacrifice, he began to pass through the bitterest and yet sweetest experience of his life when he undertook a prayerful investigation of the subjects of baptism and communion. Here he had to pass through deep waters, which caused an illness so severe that it took months to recover. Deliberate in reaching his conclusion, he asserted his indisputable right in maintaining it; and in his eighteenth year, while a student of Centenary College, he united with the Baptist church at Jackson, La., and was baptized by Rev. S. A. Hayden. By the same church he was ordained, Revs. S. A. Hayden and George Hayden constituting the Presbytery. After changing his faith he entered Mississippi College. His deep-toned piety, brilliancy, eloquence, and modesty, as well as manliness, secured for him the admiration of the whole school and community. He was elected orator for his literary society several times, and was considered its brightest star. He completed the A.B. course at Mississippi College at the age of twenty-one.

Elder Rowan spent three years and a half in the Southern Baptist Theological Seminary, completing the full course, except a small portion of the Hebrew and Latin.

His sermons are noted for brevity (scarcely ever exceeding thirty minutes), unity, simplicity,—within the grasp of a child,—accuracy, and much thought for a young man.

He succeeded Dr. Landrum as the pastor of the Central Baptist church, Memphis, Tenn., where his labors are much blessed, and a hopeful future is opening to his view.

Rowden, Philip, M.D., D.D., was born in England in 1828. In early life he came to New York. He was converted, and joined the church in Newark, N. J. He was pastor in Newark, in Bronson, Mich., and in Chili, Ind. The churches enjoyed many genuine revivals during his pastorates. He was a man of studious habits and deep research. At the time of his death he was vice-president of the American Anthropological Association. He died at his home in Rochester, Ind., April 4, 1875.

Rowland, A. Judson, D.D., was born at Valley Forge, Pa., Feb. 9, 1840; was baptized at Lawrenceville, Pa., by Rev. W. H. H. Marsh, Jan. 6, 1858; entered the Sophomore class of the university at Lewisburg in 1859, and graduated with first honors in 1862; was ordained at Lawrenceville, October, 1862; was chaplain of the 175th Regiment Pa. Vols. from September, 1862, to July,

1863; entered Rochester Theological Seminary in the fall of 1863, and completed the full course of study in 1866. In July, 1866, became pastor of Mount Auburn church, Cincinnati, O., which po-

A. JUDSON ROWLAND, D.D.

sition he resigned in 1868 to assume the presidency of the Mount Auburn Institute,—a school of high grade for young women. In 1870 he became pastor of the First church, Pittsburgh, Pa. In 1872 he accepted a call to the Tenth church, Philadelphia, where he still remains. He has for years been a regular correspondent for several denominational journals, and has published a number of sermons and reviews. In 1879 he preached the doctrinal sermon before the Philadelphia Baptist Association. He is a member of various educational and missionary boards, and is prominently and actively engaged in the general work of the denomination. He received the degree of D.D. in 1880 from the university at Lewisburg.

Dr. Rowland is a man of superior mind, pleasing manners, studious habits, extensive learning, and exemplary piety. As pastor of a large and influential church, he magnifies his office, and is very highly esteemed in love for his work's sake. His sermons are rich in original thought and Bible knowledge, clear in expression, and impressive in delivery. His writings show enlarged acquaintance with books and men. He has gathered a large library of choice and standard works, which he utilizes with rare ability. He is the first and the successful editor of *Our Young People*, a very able monthly journal for the older scholars in our Sunday-schools. This paper deserves the great circulation it has already secured, and under its gifted editor it will be a still greater power among the young.

Rowley, Rev. Moses.—This pioneer missionary, now residing at Mazomanie, Wis., at the advanced age of eighty-four years, is a native of Swanton, Vt. He was born again and baptized into the fellowship of the Baptist church in Gouverneur, N. Y., in 1817; commenced preaching in 1830, in Erie Co., N. Y., and was ordained at Evans, N. Y., in 1833. He has been in the active work of the ministry fifty-one years. He was pastor of twenty churches, none of which was able to support him when settled. As soon as the church he served was able to give him a competent support he resigned his pastorate, after having provided an acceptable successor. With his call to the ministry he had clearly indicated to him that his work was to preach the gospel to the feeble churches and to collect the scattered members of Christ's flock on the frontiers. "Christ sent me," he writes, "not to baptize, but to preach the gospel to his poor." And of these, multitudes have heard the pure gospel of Christ from his lips. He gave thirty-two years of his life to strictly itinerant and missionary labor. Of these, thirteen years he was in the service of the New York Baptist Convention and the American Baptist Home Mission Society. He organized seventeen churches, nearly all on the frontier, and baptized about 400 persons. He has been a resident of Wisconsin thirty-two years. In 1876, when nearly eighty years of age, he went to Nebraska to engage again in the work to which he had given the best part of his life,—to preach the gospel to Christ's poor and gather the scattered believers into churches. Thus for four years longer he engaged in his loved work,—organizing churches in Hamilton and York Counties, and providing for them houses of worship. The Lord has granted this minister of the gospel a long and very useful life, and he is now waiting to hear the Master call, "Give an account of thy stewardship."

Royal, Rev. Young R., a pioneer preacher in Arkansas, was born in North Carolina in 1812. He professed religion in 1838, and in 1840 was licensed to preach. In 1842 he removed to what is now Drew Co., Ark., and was ordained in Mississippi the following year. In 1848 he was one of a Convention that organized the Bartholomew Baptist Association, of which he was chosen moderator, a position he continued to hold until his death. He labored very assiduously in the gospel, and many churches were gathered through his instrumentality. He also filled one term of clerk of the District Court of Drew County. He died in 1867.

Royall, Wm., D.D., was born July 30, 1823, in Edgefield District, S. C. From six to thirteen resided in Charleston, S. C. For two years was a pupil of Furman Institution, Fairfield District, S. C., then under charge of his uncle, Prof. W. E. Bailey. Entered South Carolina College, Colum-

WM. ROYALL, D.D.

bia, Sophomore class, when fifteen years old, and graduated in 1841 in a class of sixty. He enjoyed the rare advantages of instruction, under Dr. James H. Thornwell, in logic and metaphysics; Dr. Wm. Hooper, in languages; Bishop Stephen Elliott, in evidences of Christianity; and Dr. Francis Lieber, in political economy; to the instructions of the last named he has ever felt most deeply indebted. After graduating, taught as an assistant in a high school in Charleston, and studied law two years under Hon. Henry Bailey, attorney-general of South Carolina. Trained by a grandfather, an elder in the Presbyterian Church, and taught by Rev. Charles Lanneau, in a Sunday-school class out of which came six preachers. He does not remember the time when he was not the subject of religious impressions. In the great revival of 1835, under the fervent preaching of Richard Fuller, D.D., he became a subject of God's saving power. Always satisfied that it was his duty to preach, he was so impressed with the idea of ministerial sanctity, as illustrated by that devout and eminently holy man of God, Basil Manly, Sr., who baptized him, that not until he had studied law two years did he fully determine to heed the call to preach. For one year he studied theology under Dr. W. T. Brantly, Sr., and Dr. Thomas Curtis, Sr. He supplied Dr. Brantly's place each Sabbath morn-

ing while that good man was lying on a bed of death, stricken with paralysis; was ordained in Charleston in 1844; preached four years to five different churches in Abbeville and Edgefield Districts, S. C., two years in Georgia, and four years in Florida. In 1855 was elected to a professorship in Furman University, and continued to preach to three churches for five years. In 1859 was elected Professor of Languages in Wake Forest College, N. C.; resigned his professorship in 1872. In 1872 founded Raleigh Baptist Female Seminary; and, when his health failed, transferred it to his son-in-law, Prof. F. P. Hobgood, under whose administration it has become a noted seat of learning. During the war served for fourteen months in Virginia and North Carolina as chaplain of 55th N. C. Regiment. Has baptized over 1500, of these about 400 in connection with one church, which he served ten years, in North Carolina, named Flat Rock,—a mother of churches; baptized 220 whites and blacks during one revival in Wayneville church, Ga., which he served; was pastor of twenty churches, for terms varying from two to ten years; has taught successfully in the seminaries of Bryan and Calvert, Texas, and since September, 1875, has been president of Baylor Female College, Independence, Texas. As a scholar and a preacher he stands in the first rank. Is now head of a female seminary at San Antonio, Texas.

Rucker, James Jefferson, A.M., was born in Randolph Co., Mo., Jan. 27, 1828. After receiving an academic education, and teaching school for a while in Missouri, he entered Georgetown College, Ky., in 1852, where he graduated in 1854. In 1855 he was elected Professor of Mathematics in Georgetown College, and has filled that position twenty-five years. He has also been principal of the Georgetown Female Academy since 1869. He united with a Baptist church in his youth, and has been very active in promoting the interests of his denomination, especially in the departments of education and Sunday-schools.

Ruggles, William, LL.D.—In the list of co-workers always ranked with Baptists, though never having made a public profession of the Christian faith, Prof. Wm. Ruggles, LL.D., has a high place. He was born in Rochester, Mass., Sept. 5, 1797. Of quiet and studious turn, he fitted for college under the parish minister, a graduate of Brown University in 1796, whose course showed that Massachusetts clergymen of the "standing order" appreciated the Baptist college, since not only many of them, but many pupils educated by them sought this seat of non-sectarian learning. Entering Brown at the age of seventeen, young Ruggles graduated in 1820. In 1822, with his life-long friend, President A. Caswell, LL.D., he became tutor at Columbian College, Washington, D. C., at its opening. He became Professor of Mathematics and Natural Philosophy in 1827, remaining at the college during the years of suspension, when all others left it for more lucrative fields. In 1859, at the accession of its fifth president, he was transferred to the chair of Political Science. No man could have been called to a more important and influential post at so critical a juncture. An unusual number of students from the Gulf States, as well as from the other Southern States, were thoroughly instructed in the principles and history of the American Constitution. Absent during the first year of the war, 1861-62, Dr. Ruggles returned in 1862, and retained his college connection, after the accession of the sixth president in 1871, as Professor Emeritus, up to the time of his death, Sept. 10, 1877, at the ripe age of eighty years.

During his perhaps unparalleled life of fifty-five years as teacher in the same college, Dr. Ruggles was universally esteemed by the trustees, faculty, and pupils. He was ready for any service. Three times he acted as president *ad interim.* Though firm in his opinions, he was deferential to his fellow-officers, both in his earlier and later years. His clear analysis and his wide experience during two-thirds of the nation's history at the seat of government, gave force and effectiveness to his later instructions. The appreciation in which he was held by his *alma mater* was indicated in 1852, when the degree of LL.D. was conferred upon him by Brown University.

Though a constant attendant on religious services, and at times free to converse on his own religious experience, strong convictions as to the spirituality of the Christian faith, and high conceptions of Christian integrity, deterred him from an open profession. His contributions to every Christian charity were numerous and unostentatious, his gifts to Baptist churches and missions having the first place.

His intimate relations with Rev. Dr. Binney and his accomplished wife during his presidency of Columbian College, from 1855 to 1858, fixed his special attention on the Karen Theological School, of which, in 1843, Dr. Binney became the founder, and to which, after an absence of five or six years, he returned in 1858. Dr. Ruggles was the virtual founder, with Dr. Binney, of the school, as he gave during his life nearly $15,000 to the mission, and left at his death a legacy of $25,000,—about one-half his estate. He used to say privately to those who sought large donations to home colleges, that " to mould the young ministry of a recently Christianized nation was the most comprehensive work possible for any man."

During his summer vacation, spent at his usual retreat on Schooley's Mountain, N. J., after a last and lingering visit to the graves of his vacation associates, Dr. S. H. and Mrs. Cone, Dr. Ruggles was prostrated by general debility, and in seven days he was laid beside them. Two views from the Mountain House always charmed him,—the " valley" and the " sunset" views. His first words to his old associate and executor, who visited him on his death-bed, were, " I have come to look within the last few weeks on the future world, as compared with this, in a very different light from what I ever did before." His pilgrimage of fourscore years made the "valley" view to him a long one, but the closing, the " sunset" view, was to have no end.

Runyon, Judge Peter P., was born at Long Hill, N. J., May 19, 1787. He used to speak with

JUDGE PETER P. RUNYON.

much affection of his *good* mother. After his marriage and a brief period of school-teaching in Plainfield he removed to New Brunswick, where he spent the vigor of manhood and the evening of his life. His character and abilities could not be hidden, and his fellow-citizens honored him, while he honored the offices he held. As alderman and recorder of the city, justice, freeholder, and for thirteen years judge of the Court of Common Pleas, he sustained a high reputation for fidelity, sound discretion, legal wisdom, and an amiability that was often brought into requisition as a peace-maker. He thought he was made a subject of grace when he was fifteen years old, after a severe season of conviction lasting six weeks; but he did not join the church until 1811, when he was baptized by Rev. Thomas Brown, pastor of the church at Scotch

Plains. When he removed to New Brunswick and united with the church there, which was weak, he was constrained to use his gifts. His financial abilities were drawn upon during his forty-seven years of membership. As trustee, church treasurer, Sunday-school superintendent for twenty-two years, he had much to do with the moulding of the church. But his influence reached beyond his own city. Sympathizing most heartily with the work of the Baptist State Convention, he became its treasurer in 1830, and was continued by the suffrages of his brethren for the remaining forty-one years of his life. When he died he left the Convention a handsome legacy. His business promptness, his liberal sympathy with the missionaries, his wise counsels in the board, were very valuable. He took an active interest in the great national missionary societies, while he loved the work about his own home. He spent his eighty-fourth birthday attending the missionary meetings at Chicago, filled his place in the meeting of the board of managers, after his return attended an educational convention in Richmond, prepared his report for the State Convention, but was not able to attend its meeting. After a short illness he breathed out his life; his last words were, "The bliss of dying."

Russell, Rev. A. A., was born in Albany, N. Y., July 7, 1823, and baptized in 1841 in the fellowship of the First Baptist church in that city. His attention having been already directed towards the work of the ministry, he was soon after his baptism sent by the church just named to Hamilton. His term of study here was brief, yet subsequently he enjoyed good educational advantages under Profs. Walker and Canning at Stockbridge, Mass., and before his conversion his school privileges had been excellent at the Albany Academy, under Dr. T. Romeyn Beck. He was ordained at Austerlitz, N. Y., Aug. 19, 1844. He has had one pastorate in Massachusetts, five in New York, two in Minnesota, three in Illinois, and one in Iowa. In the spring of 1854, under appointment of the Home Mission Society, he became the first pastor of the First church in Minneapolis, Minn. The church then had 11 members. At the end of three years he left them with 100, with Amory Gale for his successor. His pastorates have all been successful, marked to an unusual degree with revival influence. Fifty such revival seasons he has been permitted to enjoy, either in his own pastoral labors or when assisting his brethren. "The sermons I have preached"—these are his own words—"with most satisfaction to the people and to myself are those which have presented Christ as 'all and in all' to Christians, and the all-sufficient Saviour for all sinners."

Rust, Jacob Ward, an active and efficient educator, was born in Logan Co., Ky., Feb. 14, 1819. His early opportunities were limited, but by diligent and constant application he has become a scholar of considerable reputation. Teaching has been his profession from his youth, and he has been principal of Mount Carmel Academy, Springfield Academy, Clarksville Female Academy, and Lafayette Female Institute. In 1864 he was elected president of Bethel College. This institution had been prostrated during the war, but Mr. Rust speedily brought it up to as high a degree of prosperity as it had ever attained. In 1868 he resigned on account of impaired health. After a brief rest he, with Prof. Dudley, became joint editors and proprietors of the *Western Recorder*. In 1871, having sold his interest in the paper, he became financial agent for the Orphans' Home in Louisville. The next year he was elected principal of Bethel Female College. He is a consistent Baptist, a man of great energy, and rarely fails in any enterprise in which he engages.

Rutherford, Rev. A. J., a pioneer minister of ability in Northwestern Louisiana, was born in Vermont in 1815; taught in Alabama from 1837 to 1843; practised law in Arkansas, and became probate judge; ordained in 1846, removed to Louisiana in 1851, and settled in Caddo Parish, and founded many strong churches; was for years moderator of Grand Cane Association; died in 1863.

Rutherford, Prof. Williams, of the State University of Georgia, a most worthy deacon of the Baptist church at Athens, Clarke Co., is the son of Williams Rutherford and Eliza Boykin, and was born near Milledgeville, Ga., Sept. 3, 1818. Until sent to Franklin College, as the State University was then called, he was educated by Rev. C. P. Beman, a famous teacher at Midway, near Milledgeville. He graduated in 1838, and, after devoting some years to farming and railroad business, opened a preparatory school in Athens, Ga. In January, 1856, he was elected Professor of Mathematics by the trustees of the State University, which position he still holds.

He joined the Baptist church at Milledgeville in 1836, in his eighteenth year, when C. D. Mallary was pastor, and just after a sermon preached by Adiel Sherwood, relating a very satisfactory experience; and from that time forward his life has been as the sun that shineth more and more unto the perfect day. He began at once to labor in the Sabbath-school as a superintendent, and nearly every year since has continued to occupy the same post of honor and usefulness.

In the year 1856, Gov. Lumpkin, then a deacon of the Baptist church at Athens, of which Prof. Rutherford was also a member, asked to be discharged from the duties of his office, on account of age and infirmities, and moved that Williams

Rutherford be appointed to the deaconate in his place. The church consented unanimously, and Prof. Rutherford still retains the office, which he has filled most usefully and efficiently. For many years he has thus, as clerk and deacon of the Athens church, been a "living epistle," known and read of all men, highly respected and esteemed by the community at large. For twenty-four years he has held an important position in the faculty of the State University, and has always exerted a marked influence in the religious gatherings of the denominations which he has attended.

He was married to Miss Laura Cobb, sister of Gov. Howell Cobb, in 1841, a lady of remarkable mental powers and great moral excellence. Noted for his piety, Prof. Rutherford is a man of great humility, and the length of time he has retained his professorship argues the excellence of his scholarship.

Rutland, Judge W. R., an active Baptist and prominent lawyer at Farmerville, La., was born in 1836. He took an irregular course in Mount Lebanon University, La., which was interrupted by the civil war, in which he took an active part, being a lieutenant in the Confederate army. After the war he studied law, and has since distinguished himself at the bar and on the bench. Judge Rutland is at present doing a good work for the denomination by writing "Pen Sketches" of useful ministers.

Ryals, J. G., D.D., was born in the southern part of Georgia, April 3, 1824. His parents came from North Carolina. Mr. Ryals is a graduate of Mercer University, taking the first honor in the class of 1851, which was more than usually brilliant in the intellectual ability of its members. After graduation he taught school one year in Columbus; then he studied law for one year under the celebrated lawyer, Judge Cone, of Greene County; and about 1856 was admitted to the bar in Cass County. He practised law successfully, and carried on farming operations for some seven or eight years in the same county. In 1859, after a long struggle, he became thoroughly converted to Jesus, united with the church, and was baptized by Dr. Thomas Rambant. In early manhood Mr. Ryals was tinctured with skeptical sentiments, which were obliterated by a perusal of the theological works of Jonathan Edwards, which also imbued him strongly with Calvinistic sentiments. Two or three years after his union with the church he began to take part in public religious exercises, and his efforts were so blessed that he became powerfully impressed with the conviction that it was his duty to preach the gospel. He lost his interest in the law, and soon abandoned its practice and devoted himself wholly to the ministry. In 1863 he succeeded Dr. Rambant as pastor of the Cartersville Baptist church, and since that period, as the pastor of several churches in the neighborhood of his home, he has been very useful in the Master's cause. In order to educate his children he has been compelled, besides preaching and farming, to teach school in Bartow County. He has long been recognized as one of the best, strongest, and most influential Baptist preachers in Georgia. For many years he has been the moderator of the Middle Cherokee Association and a member of the board of trustees for Mercer University. He is also a member of the State Mission Board of the Georgia Baptist Convention.

Ryan, Rev. Joseph, was born in Fairfield District, S. C., Oct. 3, 1782. A soldier in the war of 1812, as was his father in the Revolution. He united with the Baptist Church in 1814, and soon after entered the ministry. Came to the Territory of Alabama and settled in Greene County in 1815. He originated and was the first pastor of Salem church, near Greensborough, then a most wealthy church; he was its pastor for twenty-one years. Other strong churches in West Alabama grew up under his eminent ministry. The Cahaba and the Tuskaloosa Associations had the assistance of his wise counsel in their formation. He was a firm and intelligent advocate of the cause of missions. In 1837 he removed to Sumter County, where his ministry again was a grand success. Many great revivals followed his preaching. He educated his seven children liberally. One of them is an able minister of the gospel,—Rev. J. K. Ryan, of Pushmataha, Ala. The father died in 1848, leaving a spotless name and a precious memory.

Ryland, Rev. Charles Hill, was born in King and Queen Co., Va., Jan. 22, 1836. After a thorough training at Fleetwood Academy, he entered Richmond College in 1854, and the Southern Baptist Theological Seminary in 1859. During the war, he was for two years with the Confederate army in Virginia as evangelist and colporteur, and subsequently the depositary and treasurer of the Army Colportage Board. He was ordained in 1863 at the Bruington church, and became pastor, after the close of the war, of Burruss's church, Mount Carmel, succeeding the distinguished preachers, Andrew Broaddus and A. M. Poindexter, in that venerable church. In 1866 he was made general superintendent of the Sunday-schools in Virginia under the General Association, and succeeded in reorganizing and equipping the schools, and in bringing their work to a high degree of proficiency. In 1869, when the first National Sunday-School Institute was held in St. Louis, under the American Baptist Publication Society, Mr. Ryland took a leading part, delivering the opening address, on "Our Aims in this Institute." In 1869 he became pastor of the church in Alexandria, Va.; in 1874 was elected financial secretary of Richmond College, Va., which position he still holds. He is a trustee of Richmond College, a member of the corporation of the Columbian University, and the founder of the Virginia Baptist Historical Society, organized in 1876. Mr. Ryland is actively identified with every good work which the denomination has at heart.

Ryland, John, D.D., was born Jan. 29, 1753, at Warwick, England, where his father, the able and scholarly John Collett Ryland, was pastor of the Baptist church. The study of Hebrew was his father's ruling passion as a teacher, and Mr. Ryland was not a little elated at his child's early proficiency in the language, for when only five years old he was able to read and translate the twenty-third psalm to the celebrated Hervey, with whom his father was intimately acquainted. When he was about fourteen years old his religious impressions became fixed, and he was baptized by his father on Sept. 13, 1767. He was recommended to preach by vote of the church at Northampton, to which his father had removed from Warwick, when he was about eighteen years of age, and was fully engaged in the villages around for several years. During this time he assisted his father in his private school, which had stood high under Mr. Ryland's management. In 1781 the church invited him to become co-pastor with his father, and five years later sole pastor, Mr. Ryland, Sr., having removed to the neighborhood of London. His labors at Northampton were greatly blessed. He took a deep interest and a leading part in the formation of the Missionary Society, and at the close of his life he became its secretary. In April, 1792, he received a unanimous invitation to the two offices of pastor of the Broadmead church, Bristol, and president of the Baptist college in that city. After prolonged consideration he at length decided to accept the call, and entered upon his duties at Bristol at the beginning of 1794. For upwards of thirty years he was the most eminent Baptist minister in the west of England, and was greatly esteemed by men of all ranks and denominations. The college flourished under his presidency, and for a long time he exercised by common consent a kind of episcopal supervision over a large number of churches. His correspondence was extensive. An ardent Liberal in political and ecclesiastical principles, he felt a lively interest in American matters, and had frequent communications with American correspondents respecting them, and also concerning missionary work. He wrote and published a considerable number of special discourses and tractates on important subjects, and also several hymns now in general use in public worship.

John Foster says of him, that as a preacher "he excelled very many deservedly esteemed preachers in variety of topics and ideas. To the end of his life he was a great reader, and very far from being confined to one order of subjects, and he would freely avail himself of these resources for diversifying and illustrating the subjects of his sermons. The readers of the printed sketches of his sermons, who never heard him, can have no adequate idea of the spirit, force, and compulsion on the hearer's attention with which the sermons were delivered." He died at Bristol on May 25, 1825, in his seventy-third year. The funeral sermon, preached by Robert Hall, is well known as one of the choicest specimens of pulpit eloquence in our literature.

Ryland, Robert, D.D., a distinguished minister and educator, was born in King and Queen Co., Va., March 14, 1805; was baptized into the fellowship of Bruington Baptist church in 1824, licensed to preach in 1825, and ordained in 1827. After studying the Latin and Greek languages, he entered Columbian College, Washington, D. C., where he graduated in 1826. The next year he became pastor of the church at Lynchburg, and filled the position for five years. In 1832 he took charge of the manual labor school at Richmond, Va. This institution developed into Richmond College, which was chartered in 1844, with Dr. Ryland as president. In 1866 he resigned and was made pastor of the First African Baptist church, in Richmond, serving it for twenty-five years, during which time he baptized into its fellowship over 3800 persons. In 1868 he removed to Shelbyville, Ky., where he taught a female school and preached to several country churches. He has since been similarly engaged at Lexington, and is now president of a female seminary, and preaches to the church at New Castle, Ky.

Dr. Ryland is one of the most distinguished Baptist ministers in this country. His services to the cause of truth have been invaluable, and he occupies an affectionate place in the regards of his brethren in every State of the Union.

S.

Sackett, Rev. John Buell, was born in Tobias, N. Y., Jan. 8, 1812; under the labors of Dr. Vinton, missionary to Burmah, was converted and baptized in 1831; studied at Hamilton, and entered the pastorate at Kingsville, O., where he continued with great success nine years; was subsequently pastor of the churches at Mount Vernon, Lancaster, and Fredericktown. In 1862 he became corresponding secretary of the Ohio State Convention, assuming later, in connection with this office, the duties of superintendent of missions and financial agent. From October, 1869, to October, 1870, while retaining the office of corresponding secretary, gave most of his time to the struggling church at Oberlin, but, on the completion of their house of worship, resumed his full duties, and remained in the State service until his sudden death, at Clyde, Dec. 24, 1870. Mr. Sackett was a man of sterling worth, and has left the impress of his genial Christian character on many of the Ohio churches.

Sacred Scriptures, Inspiration of the.—In saying that the Scriptures are inspired we mean the Scriptures in the languages in which they were originally written. We do not claim that the transcribers and translators of the original Scriptures enjoyed the same divine protection from error which controlled the original writers. It is well known that the first manuscripts of the New Testament, for instance, have all been lost. It is also evident that the work of transcribing and retranscribing subjected the text to possible variations. No supernatural aid was given to shield the transcribers from such mistakes. Then any translation of the New Testament could be valuable and accurate only in so far as it reproduced most faithfully the language and spirit of the original text. No one will claim that in translating the Scriptures the same divine aid is enjoyed which was given to holy men of God in writing them. The fact then that in the determination of the original text we are left to the comparison of the different transcriptions yet extant with the ancient versions and quotations that give them support, and that more perfect translations and revisions are continually needed, does not in the least militate against the doctrine that the original Scriptures were inspired.

Of course the oldest manuscripts existing have the greatest authority in determining the accuracy of the text. There are several manuscript copies of the New Testament extant, but the number of the oldest, and consequently the most valuable, may be reduced to four.

1. The Sinaitic manuscript (Codex Sinaiticus), probably the most ancient of New Testament manuscripts, was discovered by Tischendorf, in 1859, at the convent of St. Catherine, near Mount Sinai. It is now at St. Petersburg. Tischendorf thinks it was written about the middle of the fourth century.

2. The Vatican manuscript (Codex Vaticanus) is also of the fourth century. It is in the Vatican library of Rome. It is not so complete as the Sinaitic manuscript. Schaff judges it to be more correct.

3. The Alexandrian manuscript (Codex Alexandrinus) was brought from Alexandria in Egypt by Cyril Lucar, patriarch of that city. It was presented by him to Charles I. of England in 1628. It is now in the British Museum. It is of the fifth century probably.

4. The manuscript of Ephraim the Syrian (Codex Ephraimi Syri). The name of this manuscript is derived from the fact that the divine Word was partly erased, and that some of the works of Ephraim the Syrian were written over it. It is of the fifth century, and is now in the library of the Louvre at Paris.

These four are *uncial* manuscripts,—that is, they are written in capital letters of a large size,—while later, or *cursive*, manuscripts, are written in a running hand Greek.

"If these four manuscripts agree in support of a reading, their testimony outweighs that of all the others."

Granting that the Scriptures contain a divine revelation, the question remains, Are these Scriptures an infallible communication of that revelation? It is not enough for us to be convinced that God revealed himself to chosen men, and that these men communicated his revelation to others by writing. We ask, Did they communicate it correctly and fully? Did they enjoy such a degree of divine aid as was sufficient to preserve them from all error, and to render their communication infallible and authoritative? The question is not, How did the sacred writers *obtain* the truths they record? but, How did they *transmit* that truth to their fellow-men?

We hold that the Scriptures are divinely inspired,—that is, *that in writing them the sacred penmen enjoyed the supernatural influence and guidance of the divine Spirit in a measure sufficient to secure its end,—the infallible communication of divine truth.* This is what we mean by inspiration. The inspiration of the Scriptures has to do with its writers simply as the recorders of the truth. In the words of Dr. Hovey, "The sacred writers were moved and assisted by the Holy Spirit to put on record all which the Bible, apart from errors in the text, now contains." We hold such assistance by the Spirit to have been necessary, because without it it would be impossible for erring man to give us an infallible record, and without an infallible record we could possess no reliable authoritative rule of faith and practice.

In determining whether such supernatural assistance was given to the writers, we refer to the exalted character of the Word of God and to the testimony of the Scriptures themselves.

Apart from direct Scripture testimony, there are weighty considerations which lead us to expect that God would provide for man a perfectly infallible record of his revealed will. The very fact that God has given a revelation to man furnishes presumptive proof that he has secured an infallible and perfect record of it. What advantage would there be in a revelation imperfectly transmitted? Could it demand our trust and obedience? Would not such a revelation be practically worthless? And can we believe that God would suffer his design in giving a revelation to be utterly frustrated by neglecting to provide for its perfect transmission? Are we not compelled to believe that God would complete this work and secure to us its perpetual benefits by means of an infallible record?

Everything that goes to prove that the Bible contains a revelation from God furnishes evidence of the completeness of its inspiration. There is, we claim, no rational way of accounting for the wonderful character of the Scriptures unless they are divinely inspired. Such truths, thus written, must have been not only divinely given, but divinely recorded.

As regards the New Testament, it is plainly promised to the apostles by the Master that through the power of the Holy Spirit they would be enabled to convey the divine truth given to them in an infallible manner. (Compare Matt. x. 19; Luke xii. 12; John xiv. 26; xv. 26, 27; xvi. 13; xiii. 20; xx. 21–23.)

In relation to the New Testament writers who were not apostles, it is true that the promise of immediate divine guidance was not primarily given to them, but they must have shared in it. Their fellowship and intimate intercourse with the apostles lead us to accept the generally-received opinion that they wrote under the direction and supervision of apostles. The character of their writings proves their equal inspiration.

Accepting the fact that the New Testament Scriptures were inspired, the inspiration of the Old Testament necessarily follows. The Old Testament is the basis of the New. The New Testament writers constantly refer to the words of the Old Testament as the words of the Spirit, the words of God. (Compare Luke i. 70; Heb. i. 1; 1 Peter i. 10–12; 2 Peter i. 21.) In 2 Tim. iii. 16, the testimony regarding the inspiration of the Old Testament is emphatically asserted by Paul, "All Scripture is given by inspiration of God." Evidently the apostle here refers to the Old Testament, and speaks of it as inspired of God.

But what is the nature and extent of that influence which the Holy Spirit exerted over the writers in producing the sacred books? What is implied in a guidance sufficient to secure its end,— the infallibility of the record? What kind and amount of influence are needed to secure this end?

In approximating an answer, the human element in Scripture must be taken into consideration and given its due weight. The individuality of each writer stands out plainly in his writings. Any theory of inspiration which ignores this fact is defective.

But the human element must ever be held in subordination to the divine element.

Taking both points into consideration, the only adequate explanation of the phenomena before us can be this,—that while the writers were left to the free exercise of their individual faculties, they were at the same time so influenced, guided, and controlled in the use not only of their thoughts but also of their words, that their writings may be truly said to be the word not of men but of God.

If the Spirit's work in regeneration and sanctification does not restrict the free exercise of our own personal activities, why should it do so in inspiration? If God can guide minutely and absolutely our purposes, affections, and destiny in the new birth without interfering with our personal freedom of volition and action, why should we conceive it to be incredible that he should guide men minutely in writing his revelation without such an interference?

If preservation from error is to be secured by inspiration, it is absolutely necessary that the assistance, influence, and guidance granted by the Spirit should extend to the words as well as the thoughts communicated. Thought is clothed in words, language is the garment, the incarnation, so to speak, of thought. How can they be separated? How can thought be infallibly conveyed unless it is clothed in infallible language?

The very idea of inspiration involves divine assistance and guidance. A divine influence which does not extend to the language is not sufficient to secure its end,—the perfect infallibility of the Scriptures. If the writers had been left to themselves in the choice of words, it does not appear how they could have been preserved from error. Without a special divine protection the sacred writers were liable, as other writers are, to employ inadequate and erroneous expressions. Nothing short of a special divine interposition was sufficient to preserve them from all such errors in language. Either the divine influence exerted was sufficient to protect the writers from all error in language, or it was not sufficient to do this. If it was not sufficient, we have no assurance that the record is reliable; if it was sufficient, then the inspiration was verbal.

The apostle in 2 Tim. iii. 16, speaks of the "*Scripture*" as inspired,—that is, the *writing*, not the thoughts simply. We have to do then with the inspiration of a *book*, the inspiration of certain *writings;* but the inspiration of a book, the inspiration of a certain writing, necessarily involves the inspiration of its language. How can a *book*, a *writing*, be inspired of God unless its words are the product of a divine influence and guidance? If all Scripture is given by inspiration of God its written words are inspired.

Accepting, then, heartily, the fact that the Scriptures do not only contain a divine revelation, but that they are the infallible record of that revelation; that both as to thought and expression they were penned under the guidance, influence, and protection from error of the Holy Spirit; that they reveal to us God's thoughts in the words he has chosen to convey them; that though the Bible is given through man it is not to be taken as the word of men, but, as it is in truth, the word of God; holding firmly that the influence exerted by the Holy Spirit in recording the Scriptures is an influence differing in manner and degree from the general influence of the Spirit; that it is a special and gracious influence restricted to the sacred writers exclusively; we believe that we have in these Scriptures the sole and sufficient divine authority and rule regarding the way of salvation, and regarding every Christian doctrine, duty, and hope. Christians ask no other standard. No human authority can for a moment take its place. What it teaches they feel bound to believe; what it commands they feel bound to practice, and that only.

Sage, Adoniram Judson, D.D., was born in Massillon, O., in 1836; removed to Granville; in 1844 settled with parents near Cincinnati; attended school for three years in Covington, Ky.; at fifteen served one year as private tutor; gave three years to teaching school; fitted for college; entered Rochester University, and graduated in 1860; entered Rochester Theological Seminary, and graduated in 1863; pastor of Shelburne Falls Baptist church, Mass., from 1863 to 1867; supplied Strong Place church, Brooklyn, N. Y., four months; pastor of Fourth church, Philadelphia, Pa., from 1868 to

ADONIRAM JUDSON SAGE, D.D.

1869; supplied Pierpont Street church, Brooklyn, N. Y., five months; Professor of Latin in Rochester University, 1870–71; settled with First Baptist church, Hartford, Conn., in 1872, where he is still preaching with marked success. In his ministry thus far (1880) he has baptized about 300 persons; wields an unusually elegant and effective pen; has written important articles for *The Examiner* and other leading periodicals; delivered addresses at commencements; is president of Connecticut Baptist State Convention, and trustee of Connecticut Literary Institution; received honorary degree of D.D. from Rochester University in 1872; for talents, attainments, and character honored as a leader in Connecticut and as a prominent minister out of it.

Sage, Deacon Oren, son of Giles Sage, was born at Middletown, Conn., Dec. 25, 1787, and died at Rochester, N. Y., Sept. 12, 1866. At sixteen years of age he was converted. In 1809 he settled at Ballston, but in 1827 transferred his business to Rochester, N. Y., where he permanently settled. He made himself felt at once as a Christian and a Baptist. To him more than to any other one man our denomination owes its successful start and career in Rochester. His growing means gave him a commanding position, which he faithfully used for the promotion of religious work in general and his own loved denomination in particular.

All classes of men in the city knew and loved him. In his own church every member was his personal friend. During the pastorates of five successive ministers, through a period of forty years, Deacon Sage was a pillar of the church.

At the age of sixty-three he became one of the prime movers of the project of establishing the University of Rochester. He appreciated the value of education, and was always deeply interested in the welfare of students. The Theological Seminary of Rochester received his close attention; the education of the ministry was always near to his heart.

The cause of city missions received much of its best support from him, and the development of the Baptist interest from one to six churches in Rochester is largely due to the impulse which he gave it.

His character showed a remarkable combination of qualities. Strength and sweetness, justice and mercy, force and patience, were united in it. His temperament was at once ardent and enduring. He could work and wait. He was wise and also childlike. The spirit of the Master seemed to have possessed him wholly. For him to live was Christ, and his last words were, "As for me, I am going to glorify God."

Sage, William Nathan, second son of Deacon Oren Sage, was born at Ballston, Saratoga Co., N. Y., July 15, 1819. At the age of eight, in 1827, he removed with his parents to Rochester. He was converted at eleven, and united with the First Baptist church of Rochester, Jan. 2, 1831, and was identified from his childhood with the growth and prosperity of that church; for fifty-one years in its Sabbath-school as a scholar, secretary, teacher, superintendent, and Bible-class instructor, for forty-eight years in the church, and for nearly twenty years a deacon. At the age of twenty-one he graduated from Brown University, in the class of 1840, with Drs. E. Dodge, H. G. Weston, W. T. Brantly, J. R. Kendrick, H. Lincoln, and Franklin Wilson, and a number of others who have been prominent in political life. He was one of the prime movers in the organization and establishment of the Rochester Theological Seminary and the University of Rochester. He has been secretary and treasurer of the latter from the commencement, and financial agent since 1850. These trusts he has filled with eminent ability and sagacity.

In 1855, Mr. Sage was elected for three years as county clerk, and although often solicited, after filling that office with great credit, to accept other political offices, he has firmly refused. He has often been honored with positions of high trust, such as manager of the House of Refuge, a State institution, president of Rochester Orphan Asylum, president of the Sage Deposit Company, president and trustee of the Dime Savings-Bank, president of the Citizens' Association, executor of several estates, president of the Christian Union Association at Martha's Vineyard, and numerous other responsibilities. In a report by President M. B. Anderson to the trustees of the University of Rochester is found this testimonial: "The first twenty years of growth and prosperity on the part of this university have been greatly due to the skill, judgment, and self-sacrificing labor of William N. Sage.

Saker, Rev. Alfred, for more than thirty-seven years a missionary of the English Baptist Missionary Society in Western Africa, will in after-ages be remembered with Livingstone and Moffat and Mackenzie among the founders of African Christian civilization. When the mission to Western Africa was commenced, Mr. and Mrs. Saker, then members of the Morice Square church, Devonport, offered themselves for the work. It was the purpose of the missionary executive to use a small steamer in connection with mission work, and Mr. Saker went out in the position of assistant missionary, combining with that the duties of engineer. This plan, however, was not carried out, but Mr. Saker's trained capacity found ample scope in the circumstances of the mission. Shortly after his arrival at Fernando Po, the headquarters of the Baptist missionaries, he visited the tribes on the mainland at the mouth of the Cameroons River. Here he built a house suitable for the work, with his own hands, and gradually acquired acquaintance with the language of the people. Within two years of the commencement of his labors he had reduced their language to writing and prepared a lesson-book for the school which he had formed. With the printing-press and material sent to him by the church at Devonport he printed school-books for the use of his scholars and portions of the New Testament. In 1849 the church at Cameroons was formed, and a Christian civilization began to spread itself there through Mr. Saker's efforts. He induced the people to labor with something like regularity in agriculture, introducing various plants, such as bread-fruit, mangoes, oranges, and other fruits and vegetables for daily sustenance. These productions, moreover, enabled them to obtain manufactured articles from the ships frequenting the river, and in the course of a few years a civilized community was established. He taught his converts the industrial arts, and soon found himself surrounded by artisans of all sorts,—carpenters, smiths, bricklayers, etc. The more forward scholars soon became helpful in the printing-office work, and aided in the translation and printing of the Scriptures in the Dualla tongue, which was his life-long task. In 1851 the mission was reduced by death to such a degree that not a single fellow-laborer remained of those who went out with him, except one or two colored brethren. All his European colleagues were gone, and he was left alone. Hitherto he had been in a subordinate position, but now from necessity he was obliged to take the lead. In 1853 the Spanish government, instigated by the Jesuit missionaries, insisted on the departure of the Baptists from Fernando Po, and suppressed all Protestant worship. The converts resolved to accompany their teachers, and the whole Baptist community removed under Mr. Saker's guidance to Amboises Bay, on the mainland. He purchased a tract of land on the coast from the Bimbia chief, and mapped out the new colony of Victoria. Under his energetic superintendence and untiring personal labor the ground was soon covered with houses and gardens for the exiles. Mr. Saker's influence upon the native chiefs and their people was most successfully exercised in suppressing many of their cruel and sanguinary customs. Indeed, if he had chosen, he might have made himself their king in the later years of his residence among them. Although he lived so long in a climate deadly to Europeans, he suffered greatly from fever and debility. Few who saw him when occasionally visiting England to recruit his strength, can forget the look of extreme emaciation which always characterized him. But his soul was full of indomitable vigor, and it was not until 1878 that he finally gave up the work and returned to England. As opportunity offered, he visited the churches in the interest of missions until March, 1880, when he entered into rest, aged sixty-five years. His devoted wife yet survives him.

Salin, Rev. Lewis H., a learned and talented Israelite, was born in the kingdom of Bavaria, Germany, July 2, 1829, and is the son of Rabbi Henry B. Salin. He was educated in his native country. He came to the United States a young man, and engaged in the mercantile business in Cincinnati. In 1852 he was converted to Christ, and united with Longridge Baptist church in Owen Co., Ky., where he has since resided. He was licensed to preach in 1855, and ordained in 1857. He has usually been pastor of four country and village churches, but he has also labored extensively and very successfully as an evangelist in the towns and cities of the State.

Sallis, James G., M.D., a prominent physician in Attala Co., Miss., deacon in the Baptist Church, and one of the most efficient Sunday-school workers in his part of the State, was born in Alabama in 1825. He has resided in Mississippi since 1848.

Salter, Lieut.-Gov. Melville Judson, was born in Sardinia, Wyoming Co., N. Y., June 20, 1834, and was one year old when his parents removed to Battle Creek, Mich. They removed again, in 1840, to Marshall, Mich., where he was converted at the age of sixteen, and united with the Baptist Church. He is a self-educated man. He removed to California, where he spent some time. On hearing of

LIEUT.-GOV. MELVILLE JUDSON SALTER.

the death of his mother in Michigan, he took passage on the steamer "Cortez" to Nicaragua, where the vessel was seized, and the whole crew came near being pressed into the service of Gen. Walker, and but for the prompt action of Capt. Collins the object might have been accomplished. At Panama about forty of the passengers stopped at the "Ocean House." In a mere freak, Mr. Salter suggested to a comrade that they board a train just leaving for Aspinwall, and in twenty minutes after a riot broke out in which every American guest at the "Ocean House" was killed. He and his comrade only escaped. In 1871 he removed with his wife and three sons to the neighborhood of Thayer, Neosho Co., Kansas. In 1872 great excitement prevailed among the settlers on the Osage ceded lands. A protective association was formed, and he was elected chief counselor. Here his executive abilities were demonstrated. The settlers triumphed in the contest for their homes. In 1874 he was elected lieutenant-governor of Kansas, and in 1876 was re-elected, and also appointed regent of Manhattan College. In 1877 he was appointed register of Independence land-office. He is also a deacon of the Baptist church. While the church was unable to support a pastor he led in the services and read sermons on the Sabbath, and superintended the Sunday-school with acceptance and success. Lieut.-

Gov. Salter's religion is of that kind that will bear transportation without yielding.

Samson, Rev. Abisha, was born at Woodstock, Vt., Sept. 28, 1783. He was hopefully converted when about seventeen years of age, and joined the Congregational church in Halifax, Mass. In the spring of 1805, finding his views more in harmony with those of the Baptists, he united with the First Baptist church in Providence, R. I., where he was then residing. In 1804 he commenced to study with Rev. W. Williams, of Wrentham, Mass., with the intention of entering the Christian ministry. He was licensed by the First church, in Providence, in April, 1805, and was ordained in June, 1806, in the meeting-house of the church of which he was a member, and at once entered upon his work as pastor of the church in Tisbury, Martha's Vineyard, Mass., in which place, and in adjoining places, his ministry was very successful. Circumstances which he could not control led to his resignation and acceptance of a call to Harvard, Mass., in 1812, where he remained, a most useful pastor, for twenty years. In 1832 he took charge of the church in Southborough, Mass., remaining there for eight years, when he removed to Worcester, Mass., and after four years to Washington, D. C., to reside with his son, Rev. Dr. Samson, then president of Columbian College, where he died, June 24, 1861.

Samson, George Whitefield, D.D., was born Sept. 29, 1819, at Harvard, Mass. His father, Abisha Samson, was the sixth in descent from Abraham Samson, who came to Plymouth among the earliest Pilgrims; and his mother, Mehetable Kenrick, was the sixth in descent from one of the earliest Puritan settlers at Boston, Mass. From the age of eight young Samson was his father's chief reader,—his eyesight having failed entirely,—and by this means, before he was thirteen years old, he became familiar with Scott's "Commentary," Gill's "Divinity," Buck's "Theological Dictionary," and such early Andover press-issues as Jahn's "Old Testament Introduction," "Biblical Archæology," etc. At the age of twelve, during a series of "four days' meetings" held in 1831, he was hopefully converted, and was baptized by his father in November of that year. The reading of the memoir of the first Mrs. Judson led him to resolve to study for the ministry, having in view the foreign mission work. In the spring of 1832 he began to prepare for college under the Rev. Chas. Train, of Framingham; and in June, 1833, at the opening of the Worcester Manual Labor School, under the charge of Silas Bailey, he became one of its first pupils, and a favorite of the Hon. Isaac Davis, one of its chief patrons. He entered Brown University in September, 1835, and graduated in 1839. In the mean time he was an occasional correspondent of, and reporter for, the *Christian Watchman*, Boston. During 1839-40 he was assistant principal, under Prof. S. S. Greene, at the Worcester Manual Labor School, during which

GEORGE WHITEFIELD SAMSON, D.D.

time he was licensed to preach by the First Baptist church, Worcester. He entered Newton Theological Seminary in September, 1840, and graduated in 1843. Meanwhile he preached in the summer vacation of 1841 at Martha's Vineyard, and in the spring and summer of 1842 at Washington, D. C., the E Street church being constituted at his second visit, Oct. 6, 1842, with twenty-one members. In the autumn of 1842 he was invited by the Baptist General Convention to take charge of the Karen College, about to be organized, but circumstances prevented, and Dr. Binney accepted the appointment. During the winter of 1842-43, Rev. Jacob Knapp was preaching for the new church in Washington, and M. B. Anderson, now of Rochester University, and at that time tutor in Waterville College, was with the church during December and January. At the solicitation of the church, Mr. Samson spent three months with them following up the work, which resulted in the addition of 120 new members. Returning to Newton, he finished his course, and graduated in 1843, and was ordained at Washington in August. After four years of arduous labor, having specially prepared himself for the study of art and of Biblical archæology, he spent a year in the East and in Western Europe, devoting half a year to Goshen, the Desert of Sinai, and Palestine; following the route of Napoleon's engineers in 1798-99 through the delta retraced by Seetzen in 1810, and personally finding the valley east of Jebel Mousa, regarded by early Christians as the place of Israel's encampment, and since his visit recognized by French and German scholars. He satisfactorily identified also the sites of Christ's birth, baptism, transfiguration, death, ascension, and other localities. A series of letters was written for the *Watchman*, of Boston; three articles on Goshen were prepared for the *Christian Review*; one on Sinai for the *Bibliotheca Sacra*; a treatise on the places of New Testament baptisms; a small volume on spiritualism,—all appearing between 1848 and 1851. Returning to Washington, he remained with the E Street church from 1848 to 1850, when he became, for two years, the successor of Dr. Hague at Jamaica Plain, Mass. Returning again to Washington, he continued pastor of the church for eight years, having among his regular hearers Amos Kendall, Sam Houston, W. L. Marcy, Thos. Corwin, W. A. Graham, Duff Green, Stephen A. Douglas, and other prominent statesmen. In 1858 he was elected president of the Columbian College, Washington, D. C., and within two years the number of students was considerably increased, many donations were made, and the legacies of Prof. R. Elton, D.D., John Withers, and James McCutchen given. At the opening of the war the main college edifice was rented to the government as a hospital, and it was the only building thus occupied for which a written lease was given. Prior to the war, as early as 1845, when the Southern Baptist Convention was formed, the E Street church, at the suggestion of the pastor, voted that in missionary collections all who chose might designate their contributions, while undesignated funds should be equally divided between the North and the South. Dr. Samson was associated with the boards of the Northern and the Southern organizations, and was a trustee of the Southern Theological Seminary at Greenville. Prior and up to the opening of the war, the most extreme political partisans met at the communion table in his church. During the war he was permitted by President Lincoln and his cabinet, and especially by the Secretaries of State and of War, and by the Postmaster-General, to keep alive all possible religious and missionary exchanges between the North and the South. At the close of the war everything connected with the college needed improvement. W. W. Corcoran, LL.D., since a most munificent donor, gave a building for the medical department; a law-school of marked efficiency was organized, and a building purchased and fitted for the purpose, and made to pay for itself; the college building improved, a new preparatory school built, and a theological department organized for young men, white and colored, temporarily residing in Washington. The increasing labors and cares of President Samson led him, in 1871, to resign, after twelve years' arduous service as president, and twenty-five as a trustee, in order to accept the presidency of Rutgers Female College, New York City. In 1873 he accepted the pastorate of the First Baptist church, Harlem, now Mount Morris Baptist church, New York, though retaining his connection with Rutgers College as president up to 1875, and as lecturer on art up to the present time. Dr. Samson has, notwithstanding his arduous labors, written much. In addition to the writings already mentioned, he published, in 1866, "Elements of Art Criticism," and in 1868 an abridged edition of the same; numerous small treatises and articles in weeklies, monthlies, and quarterlies, especially on the subjects of "Evolution" and the "Future State." A small volume on the "Atonement Historically Considered" has just been published, and a treatise on "Wine in Religious Uses" has been prepared by him at the request of two Conventions. No Baptist clergyman in the country is perhaps better known throughout the denomination than Dr. Samson.

Sanctification.—Sanctification ($ἁγιασμός$) is separation from the world, purity of heart and life, holiness.

The inspired truth of God is the instrument by which the soul is sanctified, and the Spirit of God is the author of that blessed work.

It commences in the soul when the Comforter gives a new heart, and when he imparts that faith in Jesus which enables the believer to shake off the allurements and power of sin.

Its *nature* is often misunderstood by Christians. In the unconverted man there is but one bent, one inclination, and it always points to some form of selfishness or sin. He forgets God, or only thinks of him to resist him. And though his conscience may occasionally remonstrate with him, yet he has but one purpose in life. The Christian *has two dispositions*: the controlling one is governed by love to Christ and hatred of sin; the inferior one is composed of the remains of his corrupt nature, and it is full of hatred to Jesus and a holy life. These opposite inclinations are found in some measure in every regenerated member of Christ's family, from the most perfect disciple, ready for heaven, to the most defective believer, just born of the Spirit. There never was a true believer on earth entirely free from the abiding evil of which Paul speaks in Romans vii. 23: "But I see another law in my members, warring against the law of my mind, and bringing me into captivity to the law of sin which is in my members." This law of sin needs continual watching, and it needs resistless grace; and it only perishes in a child of God when death destroys the life of the body.

Sanctification, after it is commenced by the new birth and a firm reliance upon Christ, consists in a constant growth in faith and in love to Christ; these developments of the religious life impose increased restraints upon our evil tendencies, and give additional power to our earnest and frequent prayers for grace to overcome every foe of Jesus within and around us.

We should aim at *complete consecration* to God. The Saviour says, "Be ye perfect even as your Father who is in heaven is perfect;" that is, "Be fully developed (τέλειοι) or complete (in the graces of the Spirit) as your Father who is in heaven is complete (in all the grand attributes of his being)." Paul says, "I beseech you therefore, brethren, by the mercies of God, that ye present your bodies a living sacrifice, holy, acceptable unto God, which is your reasonable service." When any creature was given to a Jewish priest to be offered up to God in sacrifice, nothing was retained by the worshiper, not even a portion of the hair or of the wool. A Jewish altar must be built not of hewn, but of whole stones (Joshua viii. 31); the priest must not be deformed or injured: he must be a perfect physical man; and the sacrifice must be without blemish, and must be given whole to the priest. And we are required to present our bodies a *living sacrifice*, an enduring and complete offering to God.

Sanctification is a *progressive work*. Paul says, "Leaving the principles (rudiments) of the doctrine of Christ, let us go on unto perfection;" that is, unto the full development of Christian graces. An intelligent patriot, in a time of war, enlists; but though he loves his country, and has a strong body and a vigorous mind, he needs drilling to make him useful. Five thousand veterans could chase one hundred thousand warriors of his order. But let him be drilled for six months, and pass through two or three battles, and he is fitted for anything which the experienced and brave patriot can achieve. So the believer, as he journeys along the narrow way, learns more every day of the cunning and perseverance of sin, and of the power of grace to resist it; and while he may never be freed from the attacks of the tempter, nor from his internal weaknesses, till death, yet he may become a powerful veteran in watching, fighting, and routing sin; and he may become strong in the Lord and in the power of his might, so that sin shall never have dominion over him.

A holy heart and life *give the richest pleasure*. When the believer falls he prepares for the most miserable doubts, and for bitter repentance. Soon he will be crying, "Has God forgotten to be gracious?" "Cast me not away from thy presence and take not thy Holy Spirit from me." "Restore unto me the joys of thy salvation and uphold me with thy free Spirit." And, besides, the chastising hand of God may fall heavily upon him and his, to make him renounce sin. But if he is only faithful to Jesus, grace equal to every trial will be given him; Jesus will walk with him in every furnace of affliction, and give him joy when the most acute anguish shall scourge others. So Paul was blessed in his sorrows, and as a result, he says, "We glory in tribulations also;" and so the martyrs have been favored as their bodies were subjected to the worst woes that human cunning could invent; the Saviour filled them with his love, and they had overflowing pleasures in their agonies.

Holiness of heart *pleases God*. The sin of the angels drove them from heaven. The guilt of our first parents expelled them from Paradise. The sinful pride of Moses, when he smote the rock for water, shut him out of the earthly Canaan. We should follow after holiness, without which no man shall see the Lord, and without which our prayers will not be heard, for David says, "If I regard iniquity in my heart the Lord will not hear me."

It gives the world the noblest *testimony to the power of Christ*. A community of holy persons attracts the attention of all around them. Their purity of life and love to Jesus become proverbial, and with the greatest eloquence and success they preach the Cross of Jesus, even when they do not utter a word. In this way they keep the Saviour's words, "Let your light so shine before men that they may see your good works, and glorify your Father who is in heaven."

Sanders, Rev. B. M., was born in Columbia Co., Ga., Dec. 2, 1789, and was left an orphan at an early age. Previous to his entrance upon college life in the State University at Athens, in 1806, he studied in Kiokee Seminary, under good instructors. Leaving Athens, he entered the South Carolina College, at Columbia, S. C., April 4, 1808, and was graduated Dec. 4, 1809. His education was thus far above the generality of the young men of Georgia in that day. Returning to his native State, he taught in the Columbia County Academy two years, and then engaged most successfully in the occupation of farming for many years. Mr. Sanders united with Kiokee church in 1810, and was baptized by Abram Marshall. He was licensed to preach by Union church, Warren Co., in 1823, at which church he was ordained in 1825, after a call by the Williams Creek church, the Presbytery being composed of Jesse Mercer, Malachi Reeves, Joseph Roberts, John H. Walker, J. P. Marshall, and Elisha Perryman. In 1832 he removed to Penfield to take charge of Mercer Institute, the manual labor school established by the Georgia Baptist Convention in January, 1833. Under his energetic and wise administration the institute prospered greatly. Dr. J. H. Campbell, in his volume entitled "Georgia Baptists," says of Mr.

Sanders, "He was not merely the general superintendent of the seminary, but he was teacher, steward, and farmer. He had accounts to keep, buildings to erect, lands to clear, fence, and cultivate, financial plans to evolve, discipline to administer, studies to review, an extensive correspondence to keep up, besides preaching to the churches around, and attending to his own private and agricultural interests. He proved himself to be the very man for the position, and in all his various duties he sustained himself most successfully. God smiled upon his endeavors, public favor was conciliated for the institution, the number of students increased, pecuniary aid flowed in, and precious revivals of religion were enjoyed from year to year. When the institute was elevated to the rank of a college, Mr. Sanders was elected its first president, which position he accepted only on the condition that the trustees would procure a successor at their earliest opportunity. A successor having been obtained, he resigned at the close of 1839, having conducted the institution successfully through the first seven years of its existence. Though no longer the president, he continued, in other relations, his untiring efforts for its prosperity. He was about five years its treasurer, without compensation; and he was a member of the board of trustees, and secretary of that board up to the time of his decease. He did more to establish the university than any other individual."

With all these duties he did not diminish, but rather increased his ministerial labors, preaching to various churches. "For more than a quarter of a century he was a burning and a shining light in the Georgia Association, was its clerk for several years, and for nine years its moderator. For many years he was more fully identified with all the important measures of the Georgia Baptist Convention, at least as far as their practical execution was concerned, than any other man in the State." For six years he was its president, and for a series of years was chairman of its Executive Committee. For a time he was editor of the *Christian Index*, and generally attended the old Triennial Convention, and the Southern Baptist Convention, as a delegate. Decision of character, punctuality, indomitable energy, and great moral courage were his distinguishing characteristics. During his whole Christian life he seemed to make but one contribution to the cause of human happiness, and that was—*himself*. He will long be held in honor for the distinguished part he took in building up the Baptist denomination in Georgia; and by the hundreds of young men whom he guided so faithfully and successfully in the paths of education and religion, his memory is cherished with the highest esteem. He departed this life, after a lingering illness, which he endured with cheerful resignation, on the 12th of March, 1852, and his remains very appropriately repose in the grave-yard at Penfield.

Sanders, Rev. Henry Martin, pastor of the Warburton Avenue Baptist church, Yonkers, N. Y., was born in New York City, Nov. 20, 1849. His father is the author of the well-known series of school books of that name. He received a thorough common-school education in the public schools of New York City; prepared for college in Homer, N. Y.; entered Yale College in 1868, and graduated in 1872. While in college Mr. Sanders was successful in taking several prizes in composition and oratory. After graduation, feeling it his duty to enter the ministry, he gave a year to wide reading and study, entered the Union Theological Seminary, of New York City, in 1873, and graduated in 1876. While in the seminary he received a call to the church of which he is at present pastor, and in September, 1876, was ordained to the gospel ministry at that church. For so young a man Mr. Sanders has a wide reputation as an orator and scholar, and is destined to wield a great power among Christians of every name.

Sanderson, Deacon Daniel, was born in Rindge, N. H., in 1798. He was left an orphan in his childhood, and was obliged to work his way, by his own energies, through the world. Having been baptized by Rev. Charles Train, he united with the Baptist church in Weston, Mass. He was one of the constituent members of what are now the flourishing churches in Brookline and Jamaica Plain, Mass. Removing from the latter to the former place, he was made a deacon of the church, and for seventeen years was one of its most active and useful members. For many years he was on the board of the Massachusetts Baptist Convention, and for two years was its president. He was also for several years one of the trustees of the Newton Theological Institution, and a member of the executive committee of the American Baptist Missionary Union. In all these relations Deacon Sanderson performed good service for his Master. He died July 26, 1863.

Sanford, Vincent.—This truly excellent and godly man was born in Loudon Co., Va., in April, 1777; when about twenty-six years old he was converted, and joined the Ketockton church, in his native State. In the fall of 1810 he removed to Georgia and settled in the town of Greensborough, where for some time he engaged in merchandising. At that time he was a member of the Shiloh church, seven miles distant, there being no Baptist church in Greensborough; but in 1821 a Baptist church was constituted in that place, largely through his influence, in which church he remained until his death. He was elected clerk of the Inferior Court in 1829, and soon after, clerk of the Superior Court, which position he retained by successive elections as long as he lived.

In many respects Vincent Sanford was a remarkable man, being noted chiefly for his purity of character; and perhaps no public man ever had more friends or fewer enemies. "Uncle Vincent," as he was familiarly called, was a general favorite. To singular piety he united extreme and unpretending modesty. He loved to pray, and he loved the house of prayer; and the longer he lived the nearer to God did he approach. With a clear intellect and a still clearer hope, he died May 27, 1859, in the eighty-third year of his age. He was one of the many remarkable laymen of Georgia whose godly influence did much to give tone and character to the denomination in the State.

Sanford, Rev. J. W., a gifted young preacher in Mississippi, was born in Ripley Co., Miss., in 1848. After thorough preparation in Ripley Male Academy, he entered Mississippi College in 1870. His remarkable gifts as an orator soon attracted attention, and he was frequently called upon to deliver public addresses. He united with the church in 1866, and was at once licensed to preach. While in college he supplied several churches in the vicinity of Clinton, and after his graduation, in 1875, he became pastor at Corinth, Miss., in connection with Baldwyn in the same State. But, after a brief and brilliant career, he fell a victim to consumption in 1877.

Sanford, Miles, D.D., was born in Connecticut, and preached for a time in the Methodist denomination, but changing his views, he became pastor of the First Baptist church in Chicago, then editor in Detroit. He afterwards returned to Massachusetts, and labored in the pastoral office at Boston, Gloucester, and North Adams, and during this latter pastorate he also served as chaplain in the army. Following this he served the American Bible Union as financial secretary, and after retiring from this position he accepted the pastoral charge of the First church of Salem, N. J., where he labored for about two years. During this period he was a member of the board of trustees of the South Jersey Institute. He had fine talents and high culture, was an able preacher and an efficient pastor, and he was loved and honored by all who knew him. He died at Salem, N. J., while pastor of the First church, Oct. 31, 1874.

Sanford, Prof. S. P., LL.D., a professor in Mercer University, at Macon, Ga., a son of Vincent Sanford, was born in Greensborough, Ga., Jan. 25, 1816. His parents were natives of Loudon Co., Va. In 1810 they moved to Georgia and settled in Greensborough. His grandfather, Jeremiah Sanford, was a neighbor and intimate friend of George Washington, under whom he served at the siege of Yorktown, witnessing the surrender of Lord Cornwallis.

Prof. Sanford took a full course in the State University, graduating in 1838, sharing the first honor with Hope Hull, Isaiah Irwin, and B. M. Palmer. While the languages and mathematics were his favorite studies, he acquired a particular fondness for mathematics under the tuition of Prof. C. F. McCay. Three months before his graduation he was elected tutor in Mercer University, in which institution he has been an instructor since August, 1838. He was elected Professor of Mathematics in 1840, a position he still holds. As an educator in his particular department, he probably has no superior in the country. Besides instructing, he has made his mathematical knowledge generally serviceable by the publication of a series of arithmetics, which have a very extended circulation, both North and South. He has lately published also an elementary algebra for schools and academies, which has already secured a wide circulation.

Prof. Sanford is energetic and elastic in both mind and body. Good-natured, even-tempered, vivacious, and cheerful, he is popular with students, whose attention during recitation he never fails to arrest and hold. For more than forty years he has been either a Sunday-school superintendent or teacher, and much of that time, also, a faithful and useful deacon. The degree of LL.D. was conferred upon him by Mercer University. Outside of his particular department he is an accomplished scholar, and has, during more than one *interregnum*, officiated as president of the university.

San Francisco, Cal.—The First Baptist church of San Francisco is the mother of 120 churches in the State. It was organized July 6, 1849, with six members. It was the first Protestant church

FIRST BAPTIST CHURCH, SAN FRANCISCO.

edifice erected in California. In size it was 30 by 50 feet, built of rough joists and sides, roofed with ship's sails, walls and ceilings of cotton-cloth, and cost, with the ground, $6000. In this building the first public school of San Francisco was held. The church has rebuilt or enlarged its houses of worship four times, and now occupies a beautiful edifice in the heart of the city. There are now five Baptist churches, two missions, and a Chinese mission in the city. The number of Baptists is 1310. (See article METROPOLITAN TEMPLE.)

San Francisco, Metropolitan Temple of, is occupied by the Metropolitan church, the result of a union in 1875 of the Second and the Tabernacle churches. In five years the number of members increased from 231 to 563. The temple was completed in 1877, at a cost, including the lots (75 by 100 feet), of $200,000. It is mainly the benefaction of Deacon Isaac Lankershim as a free place of worship. The main auditorium, amphitheatre in form, beautifully finished and furnished, accommodates 3000 hearers; lecture-room and parlors, 1000 persons. It has eleven other rooms, for pastor, libraries, classes, etc., and two large stores. The church meets all expenses of free public worship. Rents of stores, and the hall for concerts and lectures, are used as a sinking fund to pay for the building, in the expectation that all will be eventually paid, when the property will be a perpetual source of revenue for mission purposes. The Sunday evening services are always largely attended; the morning congregations are from 600 to 1000. This church is now the largest Baptist church, and its congregation the largest Protestant one on the Pacific coast. (See article LANKERSHIM.)

Sarles, John Wesley, D.D., was born in Bedford, N. Y., June 26, 1817; became a member of the Oliver Street church, New York; was baptized by Dr. Cone, April 5, 1835. He pursued the full eight years' course at Hamilton, graduating in 1847. He became pastor of the newly-formed Central church, in Brooklyn, N. Y., and remained there for thirty-two years, enjoying an unusually successful pastorate. It was supposed that he was too firmly rooted to be moved, but the old church at Piscataway, N. J., gave him a hearty call, and in 1879 he accepted it. His talents and piety are well adapted to the important position which he is called to fill. In 1860 Madison University gave him the degree of D.D. He has by request permitted several able sermons to be published, and his memorial of his excellent wife has been widely circulated. Dr. Sarles is one of the purest and best ministers in the Baptist denomination.

Saunders, Rev. Edward Manning, A.M., was born Dec. 20, 1829, in Aylesford, Nova Scotia; taught in Milton Academy, Queen's Co., Nova Scotia; entered Acadia College in 1854; graduated there in June, 1858; ordained pastor of the Baptist church in Berwick, Nova Scotia, Dec. 15, 1858; subsequently studied theology at Newton; became pastor, in 1867, of the Baptist church, Granville Street, Halifax, Nova Scotia, where he still ministers. Mr. Saunders is a sound theologian and an able preacher.

Sau Quala is a S'gan Karen, and was among the earlier converts from that interesting people. Eminently successful as he was in the commencement of his Christian life as a preacher of the gospel, the missionaries thought him to be a most suitable person to be ordained to the work of the Christian ministry in 1846, and he soon came to be regarded as the leading Karen minister in the Tavoy Mission. At a meeting of an Association of Karen churches, held at Mata for several days in January, 1851, we find that "the annual sermon, a pertinent and practical discourse, was preached by Sau Quala at the opening." The report of the Executive Committee for 1852 alludes to a remark of one of the Tavoy missionaries, who is speaking, without doubt, of Sau Quala, as "a good man in whom people repose unbounded confidence. They fear they can do nothing without him." For some time he was pastor of the church at Pyeekhya. The true missionary spirit was in Sau Quala, and he yielded to the strong desire he felt to reach his countrymen in other parts of Burmah. When Dr. Mason commenced the mission at Toungoo, being obliged on account of ill health to be absent for a time, the whole responsibility of conducting the mission devolved on Sau Quala and his native assistants. Dr. Mason had great confidence in him. He had been his teacher in Karen, and had rendered him aid in translating the Scriptures. He commenced his work at Toungoo with apostolic zeal, making tours into the adjacent country, and preaching, in connection with his assistants, so effectually that at the end of their first year's labors there were 12 preachers, 14 churches, and 741 members, besides hundreds who had asked to be baptized but had been advised to wait for a season. The tribes of Karens among whom he labored were a nation of drunkards and gamblers, exceedingly quarrelsome and vindictive. After five years of evangelical labor with these savage tribes, as the result of the missionary work which had been done, there was a Christianized population of 26,000 souls, of whom nearly 4000 were members of churches. Year after year we find the name of Sau Quala among the list of native preachers in the Toungoo station, and we know he did good work in the field of his labors. During all the troubles which wrought such havoc with the Karen Christians in the Tavoy station, in connection with the eccentric movements of Mrs. Mason, he was not seduced from his allegiance to the cause he so much loved. Said Dr. Warren in his appeal to the Karen Christians, "Sau Quala stands firmly; follow him." Mr. Cross says of him, "Quala's character appears grandly in the fires of this furnace." Among Mr. Bunker's "First Impressions" we find the following: "The good old Quala is here. Were there no other fruit save Quala for a fifty years' sowing, missions would be a glorious success. He is a monument of grace, and a bright example of God's love and the elevating influence of the gospel." In September, 1878, Mr. Carpenter, in giving an account of the jubilee to commemorate the conversion of Ko-Thah-Byu, writes, "The aged Quala had been invited, but suffering as he is from partial paralysis, he was unable to come so far. He wrote a long letter, however, telling what he knew of Ko-Thah-Byu and the early work in Tavoy, which was read to the congregation at this season."

Savage, Rev. Eleazer, was born in Middletown, Conn., July 28, 1800; entered Hamilton in 1820; was ordained in Rochester in 1824; was pastor in several other communities in New York, in which he baptized more than 400 souls; published a valuable work on Church Discipline. Mr. Savage was a very useful minister, and an honored and faithful servant of Jesus; one of his daughters is the wife of the able president of the Rochester Theological Seminary.

Savage, Rev. R. R., was born in Nansemond Co., Va., in 1835. He was fitted for college at Reynoldson Institute, N. C., and graduated at Wake Forest College in 1858. He labored for some time in Halifax Co., Va., but for many years has been one of the wise and mighty men who have guided the counsels of the Chowan, the largest Association in North Carolina. He is a trustee of Wake Forest College, and also of the Chowan Female Institute. He is a man of great worth.

Savannah, The Baptist Church of.—In 1794 the few Baptists who were in Savannah, Ga., proposed the erection of a house of worship. The following year, by the assistance of general contributions from different denominations, a house 50 by 60 feet was erected on Franklin Square, under the superintendence of Ebenezer Hills, John Millen, Thomas Polhill, John Hamilton, Thomas Harrison, and John H. Robards as trustees. There seems to have been some sort of church organization in 1795, as in that year the city conveyed a lot to the church, the petition for which was drawn by Robert Bolton. The house, in an unfinished state, was rented to the Presbyterians, who had lost their church edifice by fire. They completed it, and occupied it three years. In 1799, while the house was still under lease to the Presbyterians, Rev. Henry Holcombe, of Beaufort, S. C., was chosen pastor of the congregation, then consisting of different denominations. His salary was $2000 per annum. The house of worship was dedicated by the Baptists on the 17th of April, 1800, and on the 26th of November in the same year the church was fully organized and constituted, the membership then consisting of fourteen persons.

The charter of incorporation was drawn by John McPherson Berrien, and was signed by Gov. Josiah Tatnall, in the year 1801. Dr. Henry Holcombe was called to the pastorate of the new church on the 25th of January, 1802, and he accepted the invitation on the 24th of March of the same year. The church worshiped on Franklin Square till 1833, and then removed to the building on Chippewa Square. In 1839 the edifice was enlarged, during the pastorate of Rev. J. G. Binney. The improvements cost about $40,000. The church still worships in this house.

Pastors of the First church from 1800 to 1847: Henry Holcombe, D.D., Wm. B. Johnson, D.D., Benjamin Screven, James Sweat, Thomas Meredith, Henry O. Wyer, Josiah S. Law, Chas. B. Jones, J. G. Binney, Henry O. Wyer, Albert Williams.

On the 4th of February, 1847, the church divided, Rev. Albert Williams pastor, after which the two branches were known as the First and Second Baptist churches, though the first never changed its name. The Second Baptist church dissolved on the 6th of February, 1859, and reunited with the old church, and invested its improvements on the church building and in the purchase of the pastor's home.

The pastors of the First church from 1847 to 1859 were Albert Williams, Joseph T. Robert, Thomas Rambaut, J. B. Stiteler, and S. G. Daniel. Of the Second church, the pastors for the same time were Henry O. Wyer, J. P. Tustin, Henry O. Wyer, and M. Winston.

After the reunion the church called Rev. Sylvanus Landrum, of Macon, Ga., in November, 1859, and in the December following he settled with the church as pastor. His first pastorate terminated Oct. 1, 1871. From that time until May 1, 1879, Timothy Harley was pastor. The second pastorate of Dr. Landrum began Sept. 1, 1879, and he still occupies the position.

The deacons now acting are Wm. H. Stark, John B. Howard, Charles W. West, Robert N. Reed, David B. Morgan, and Wm. O. Van Vorst. The membership is about 500. The church has adopted the New Hampshire Confession of Faith and the covenant attached to it.

Sawtelle, Henry Allen, D.D., was born in Sidney, Me., Dec. 11, 1832. Until he was sixteen years of age he lived on a farm. He then fitted for college at Waterville, under the tuition of J. H. Hanson, LL.D. He entered what is now Colby University in 1850, and graduated with the honors of his class in 1854. Immediately on graduating he was appointed tutor in his *alma mater*, and held the office for one year, at the end of which he entered the Newton Theological Institution, and graduated in regular course in 1858. Soon after leaving Newton he was ordained and became pastor of the church in Limerick, Me. He remained here but one year when, having received an appointment from the Missionary Union, he resigned the pastorate of the Limerick church, and sailed for the field of his destination in China, Oct. 5, 1859, and joined the mission among the Tie Chin, established near Swatow. Here he remained until severe illness compelled him to resign his position in the fall of 1861. In 1862 he became the pastor of the Second Baptist church in San Francisco, and in this and the Union Square Baptist church of the same city he performed a continuous pastoral service of fourteen and a half years. While living in San Francisco, besides performing his ministerial duties, he edited the *Evangel* for three years jointly with Rev. D. B. Cheney, D.D., and edited and published the *Spare Hour* for the same length of time. At the termination of his ministry in San Francisco, Dr. Sawtelle returned to his Eastern home with the highest testimonials of his ability and success as a minister of Christ. In 1877 he accepted a call to become the pastor of the Cary Avenue church in Chelsea, which position he now holds.

Dr. Sawtelle has made diligent use of his pen during his ministerial life. Besides the numerous articles he published while he was editing the *Evangel* and the *Spare Hour*, he issued a volume entitled " Things to Think of," a valuable work in theology and literature. While pursuing his studies at Newton, at the suggestion of Prof. Hackett he prepared and published in the *Christian Review* an extended article on the " Straussian Theory." He has also been an occasional contributor to the *Bibliotheca Sacra* and the *Baptist Quarterly*, and is one of the writers of the new Commentary on the New Testament to be published under the supervision of Dr. Hovey, by the American Baptist Publication Society.

The honorary degree of Doctor of Divinity was conferred upon Dr. Sawtelle by Hillsdale College, Mich., in 1874.

Sawyer, Artemus W., D.D., was born in West Hanover, Vt., and graduated at Dartmouth College in the class of 1847. He pursued his theological studies at Newton, graduating in the class of 1853. He was ordained in December, 1853. For six years he was professor in Acadia College,—1855–61; pastor of the Baptist church in Saratoga, N. Y., three years,—1861–64. Dr. Sawyer retired from the active duties of the pastorate in 1864, and became principal of the New London Literary and Scientific Institution, which position he held for five years,—from 1864 to 1869,—when he was appointed president of Acadia College. He received the degree of Doctor of Divinity from Colby University in 1867. He is one of the most useful men in the Maritime Provinces.

ARTEMUS W. SAWYER, D.D.

Sawyer, Conant, D.D., was born in Monkton, Vt., May 23, 1805; converted and baptized in early life; graduated at Hamilton in 1826; ordained in 1829 in Keesville, N. Y.; was settled as pastor in Jay, Schenectady, Lowville, Canton, Gloversville, and Bedford, N. Y., and in Randolph, Mass. Large gatherings of souls have followed his ministry. In 1869 he received the degree of Doctor of Divinity. His present field of labor is Albion, N. Y.

Sawyer, Rev. E. H., D.D., was born in Milford, Oakland Co., Mich., Dec. 18, 1843. Professed religion when sixteen years of age, and was baptized by the Rev. John Boothe. He was mainly educated at Kalamazoo, Mich.; graduated at La Grange College, Mo., in 1870, and from the Baptist Union Theological Seminary of Chicago in 1873. He was pastor of the Baptist church in Kirkwood, Mo., and he is now pastor at Macon City. Mr. Sawyer received the honorary degree of Doctor of Divinity from La Grange College in 1879. He has just been appointed vice-president of La Grange College. He is a man of culture and talent, and he enjoys the confidence of all who know him.

Sawyer, Rev. Isaac, was born in Hoosick, N. Y., Nov. 22, 1770, and was left an orphan at the age of fourteen. In 1786 he removed to Monkton, Vt. The whole country being little better than a wilderness, he devoted himself to the toils of a pioneer's life. Here the young man lived until he was twenty-one years of age. In 1793 he was hopefully converted. All his relatives were Congregationalists, and he himself had been sprinkled in infancy. He was not satisfied, however, with receiving a traditional faith, and after examining the subject became a decided Baptist, and united with ten others in the formation of a Baptist church, of which, although the youngest member, he was made the deacon. In 1797 the church of which he was a member urged him to enter the Christian ministry. He heard, as he believed, besides the call of the church, that higher call of the Spirit of God, upon which our Baptist fathers laid so much stress, and he would not resist that call. His ordination occurred June 29, 1799, and he remained the pastor of the church in Monkton for thirteen years. In addition to his home work, he performed, as was the custom of the ministers of his day, no small amount of missionary labor, and we are told that "many of the large and flourishing churches in the northern counties of New York were gathered through his instrumentality. He was generally sent out by the Association to which he belonged, and was absent from home six or eight weeks at a time. He was accustomed as long as he lived to revert with great satisfaction to these missionary labors as having been among the most pleasant and successful of his whole ministry."

Mr. Sawyer's pastorate at Monkton closed in 1812. Having passed a year in Fairfield, he spent the next four years at Orwell, and was greatly prospered in his ministry there. In 1818 he became pastor of the church in Brandon, and remained here for seven years, when he removed to Bethel, supplying the church in that place and acting for a part of the time as an agent of the Hamilton Literary and Theological Institution. His next settlement was in Westport, N. Y., where during his pastorate of six years he baptized 150 persons. On leaving Westport he preached in several places, being but a short time in any one of them. His death occurred Sept. 30, 1847. Upwards of 1100 persons were baptized by Mr. Sawyer during his ministry, and "among them a greater number who became ministers than have been baptized by any other pastor in Vermont." Five of his own sons became ministers of the gospel. The name of a servant of Christ so active and so useful deserves to be held in everlasting remembrance.

Saxton, J. B., D.D., was born in Northumberland Co., Pa.; baptized in December, 1835, and was soon after licensed by the Shamokin church. He entered Madison University, and graduated with honor in 1845. During his college course he spent sixteen months at Somerville, N. J., organized a church there, and built a house of worship. He was pastor at Towanda, Pa., where he was ordained, at Lancaster, supply to the Fourth church, Philadelphia, and pastor at Hightstown, N. J., until 1852. He went to California as home missionary, arriving at San Francisco Jan. 11, 1853. He organized and was pastor of the churches at Stockton three years, Oakland and Brooklyn four years, Healdsburg seven years, and has been pastor at the seat of the college, at Vacaville, two years, where he was president of the college board and librarian for the college; has labored at Red Bluff, and is now pastor at Grand Island. He is a strong preacher, a good moderator, having presided over the San Francisco and other Associations. He has done much mission work in California, organizing many churches and building houses of worship. In war times he collected $12,000 in aid of the Sanitary Commission. For a considerable time he edited the Esmeralda *Daily Union*, and served as superintendent of public schools. He received the degree of D.D. from California College in 1878. Nearly 1000 persons have been converted under his ministry, 600 having been baptized by himself. Few men in California have done more hard work or been more successful than Dr. Saxton.

Scammon, Mrs. Rachel T., a native of Rehoboth, Mass., married a Mr. Scammon, of Stratham, N. H., about 1720. She was a decided Baptist, and cared nothing for the opposition of the Pedobaptists among whom her new home was located. Backus says, "The country around her was so full of prejudices against Baptist principles that in forty years she could gain no more than one person to join with her therein, and that was a pious woman in the neighborhood who traveled fifty-five miles to Boston, and was baptized by Elder Bound."

Mrs. Scammon had such a desire to have others enlightened, that having obtained Norcott's "Plain Discourse upon Baptism," she carried it to Boston with a design to get it reprinted at her own cost, but when she came to a printer about it he informed her that he had then 110 copies of that book on hand; whereupon she purchased them all, and came home and gave them away to her acquaintances and to any persons who would accept them; by which means they were scattered through the country and among poor people in new plantations. She often said to her pious neighbors that "she was fully persuaded that a church of Christian Baptists would be formed in Stratham, though she might not live to see it. This came to pass soon after her death, and the like happened in other places." (History of the Baptists, by Backus, ii. 167–69. Newton.)

Chiefly through one of Mrs. Scammon's copies of Norcott's work Dr. Samuel Shepard became a Baptist and a Baptist minister, and Baptist churches were formed in Stratham, Brentwood, and Nottingham, of which Dr. Shepard became the pastor; and he founded branch churches in more than a dozen places in the region around, and at one time had more than a thousand church members under his care. "Thus," as Backus says, "Mrs. Scammon's bread, cast upon the water, seems to have been found after many days, the books that she freely dispensed being picked up and made useful to many."

Had Mrs. Scammon been a weak woman she would have sacrificed her Baptist principles and joined some Pedobaptist community. She no doubt regularly attended a Congregational church: this was her manifest duty; but she always protested against their infant baptism in modest Christian words, and by refusing to unite with them. And though her arguments seemed to bear little fruit, the book she circulated was greatly blessed of God. The Baptist church of Allentown, Pa., was founded by a lady a member of the Second Baptist church of Philadelphia, who for a time worshiped with the excellent Presbyterians of that town. And as she felt that she could not and ought not to sacrifice her Baptist principles—her Saviour's teachings—for anything under heaven, she enlisted aid and commenced a Sunday-school, out of which grew a flourishing church, from which two little churches sprang and set up their banner in Bethlehem and Catasauqua. Many Baptist women have honored the Saviour in this way.

Scandinavian Baptists in the United States.—In 1852 nine Swedish Baptists arrived in America. The first Swedish Baptist church in this country was formed in Rock Island, Ill., Aug. 13, 1852; it had only three members. In 1855 Swedish churches were organized at Houston and Scandia, Minn. In 1856 the first Danish Baptist church on this side of the Atlantic was established at Raymond, Racine Co., Wis. In 1857 a Swedish church was gathered at Galesburg, Ill. In Chicago the first Swedish church was founded Aug. 19, 1866; it began with 36 members, and it now numbers nearly 300. A little before 1866 the first Danish church was constituted in the same city. Small churches have gradually sprung up in all the States in which a Scandinavian population exists.

In Minnesota a vigorous State Conference was early formed, one in Illinois followed, then one each in Eastern Iowa, in Nebraska, in Western Iowa, and in Dakota, and preliminary steps have been taken for a similar organization in Kansas. Two years since a General Convention of all the Swedish Baptists in America was established. The Danish and Norwegian Baptists have a similar institution.

In 1871, Rev. Dr. J. A. Edgren commenced the publication of a monthly Swedish Baptist paper. About the same time Dr. Edgren began a course of instruction for Scandinavian ministers, in connection with the Baptist Theological Seminary of Chicago, as its Scandinavian department. From this school twenty-nine ministers have gone forth, representing Sweden, Norway, and Denmark. These brethren have been faithful laborers, and some of them have been very successful in winning souls to Jesus.

Religious tracts, pamphlets, and books, written by Dr. Edgren, have been published in the Swedish language. A Danish graduate of the department, N. P. Jensen, has done excellent service to the cause among the Danes as a translator, publisher, editor, and pastor. The Danish monthly is edited by Rev. P. H. Dam, and the Swedish by Rev. E. Wingren.

There are now 80 Scandinavian churches in the United States, with 5000 members. These churches are located as follows: in New York City, 1; in Boston, 1; in Illinois, 6; in Michigan, 6; in Wisconsin, 10; in Minnesota, 38; in Iowa, 4; in Dakota, 5; in Nebraska, 7; in Kansas, 4; and in Missouri, 1. Of the 5000, 3500 are Swedes; of the remainder, the Norwegians are but a small minority.

The Scandinavian emigration is large, and new fields for mission work among them are rapidly increasing; the demand for laborers is greater than can be supplied. Dr. Edgren is the distinguished leader of these pious and thriving communities. Other brethren of talent and consecrated lives are working nobly for the Master, and the approval of Jesus rests conspicuously upon these godly ministers and the communities of which they are the chosen leaders.

Scarboro, Hon. J. C., was born in Wake Co., N. C., in September, 1842; served as a soldier through the war; graduated at Wake Forest College in 1869; has taught school for several years, and is now the superintendent of public instruction, having been elected to that office in 1876.

Scarff, E. H., D.D., was born in Virginia in 1821. In 1841 he entered the preparatory department of Granville College, O., and graduated in 1847. After teaching a year in Jefferson, O., he entered the theological department of Madison University, N. Y., and graduated in 1850. He was ordained at New Carlisle, O., July 18, 1850. For two years he had charge of Judson College, West Jefferson, O. He was pastor at Gallipolis, and afterwards at Delphi, Ind. In 1854 he came to Iowa, and took charge of the academic department of the Central University at Pella. The university was just starting into life, and he was its first teacher, and continued his labors as teacher for over twenty years, much of this time serving as pastor of the First Baptist church in that town. He still resides in Pella, disabled in body, but strong in mind, patient and cheerful in suffering God's will, and awaiting his pleasure.

Schaeffer, Prof. Hermann Moritz, was born Aug. 22, 1839, in Lage, Lippe-Detmold, Germany. He graduated at the rectoral school (academy) in his native place. In his fifteenth year he emigrated to this country. In Boston, where he first fixed his abode, he pursued studies in the English language at evening schools, while following a mercantile career. In the year 1857 he was converted and baptized by Rev. Wm. Howe, joining the Union Baptist church at that place. In 1858 he removed to New York, where he joined the Second German Baptist church. Feeling prompted to devote his life to the work of the ministry he went to Rochester, N. Y., in 1860, and pursued studies at the University of Rochester, and in the German and English departments of Rochester Theological Seminary. After preaching for the German churches in Holland, N. Y., and New Haven, Conn., he settled as pastor of the First German Baptist church in New York City. During his efficient pastorate the church erected its present excellent house of worship. After six years of pastoral labor in New York, Mr. Schaeffer was called to the chair of Biblical literature in the German department of Rochester Theological Seminary in the year 1872. While engaged in teaching, Prof. Schaeffer succeeded in procuring the present German Students' Home at the cost of $20,000. By his energy the larger proportion of that sum has already been obtained, and the building bids fair to be free from debt very soon. Mr. Schaeffer has also been very active in establishing a German-American Academy. Perfect in health and untiring in labor, Prof. Schaeffer has been very useful in the German work in this country, and his old days are yet before him.

Schism Bill, The.—See CORPORATION AND TEST ACTS.

Schofield, Rev. James, Sr., was born in Penn Yan, Yates Co., N. Y., June 7, 1801. He removed to Chautauqua County when eighteen years of age; made a profession of religion in 1826; was ordained to the ministry in 1835; was pastor in Sinclairsville until 1842. He married into the family of John McAllister,—Miss Almira for his first, and Miss Caroline for his second wife. Of these marriages six children are now living,—Lieut. C. Schofield, Col. G. W. Schofield, and Maj.-Gen. J. W. Schofield, all of the U. S. army, and two of them graduates of West Point, also Rev. J. V. Schofield, D.D., of St. Louis, and two daughters. The subject of this sketch removed to Illinois in 1843; labored for many years in the cause of the Home Mission Society; built houses of worship in Freeport, Galena, and Rossville, Ill. He removed to Missouri in 1867. In Southwest Missouri thirteen houses of worship have been built through his instrumentality, one of which is in Dallas County, his home, called Schofield chapel. He is a member of the board of the Baptist college at Bolivia, Mo. He is now in his eightieth year, awaiting his appointed time till the change comes.

Schofield, J. V., D.D., was born in Chautauqua Co., N. Y., Dec. 4, 1825. He was converted in 1843,

J. V. SCHOFIELD, D.D.

and baptized by Rev. Orin Dodge in Lake Chautauqua. In 1844 he removed to Chicago, and by invitation spent two years in the family of Dr. L. D. Boone, and commenced studying for the ministry. In 1847 he entered Madison University, and in 1850 Rochester University, where he graduated in 1852, and also from the Theological Seminary in 1854. Dr. Schofield was ordained in Louisville, Ky., in 1854, and was the first pastor of the new Chestnut Street Baptist church of that city. In the four years of his pastorate 181 joined the church.

In 1858 he became pastor of the First Baptist church of Quincy, Ill. In his four years' pastorate here 150 united with the church. In 1862 he accepted the pastorate of the Third Baptist church, St. Louis, Mo., and for seven and a half years was the efficient and beloved minister of this church. It was a critical period. Civil strife divided families and former friends, yet under his wise administration the church prospered. The present edifice was built at a cost of $50,000. Dr. Schofield inaugurated the movement, and raised nearly all the money. The house was dedicated May 12, 1866. During his pastorate the whole amount was nearly paid and the balance provided for, and the church took rank with the first churches in the city. In 1869 he took the pastorate of the Baptist church of Des Moines, Iowa. In one year their house of worship was completed and a debt of $5000 provided for, then a revival followed for three months, in which eighty were baptized, forty of whom were heads of families.

In 1871 he became pastor at New Britain, Conn. In four and a half years there were 305 additions, 225 by baptism, 150 of whom were immersed during the last six months.

In 1876 he removed again to St. Louis, and November 6 became pastor of the Fourth Baptist church, his present field. By his persistent labors much has been done. The edifice has been thoroughly repaired, debts paid, and the church improved, financially, socially, and spiritually. In May, 1880, La Grange College conferred on him the honorary degree of Doctor of Divinity, and June 24 of the same year Chicago University conferred upon him the same degree. Dr. Schofield is a clear thinker and an able preacher, he is an earnest and efficient pastor, has baptized over 600 persons, and he has held many successful meetings with neighboring pastors. His works commend him, and his reward is sure.

Schulte, Rev. G. A., was born in Neustadtgodens, East Frisia, Germany, Nov. 30, 1838. His parents were pious Lutherans, who instructed him in the way of salvation from his earliest youth. In the year 1850 he came to this country with his parents, who settled near Buffalo, N. Y. When twenty years of age he was converted, and being baptized in April, 1858, he was received into the fellowship of the First German Baptist church in Buffalo. Feeling the call of God within, he entered the German department of Rochester Theological Seminary in 1860. After pursuing theological studies for three years, he yielded to an urgent call from the Second German Baptist church, Buffalo, N. Y. He was ordained in October, 1863. After serving this church acceptably as pastor for eight years, Mr. Schulte, by the choice of his brethren, was made general missionary and evangelist of the Eastern German Baptist Conference. After filling this responsible position faithfully for two years he returned to the pastorate, accepting a call from the First German church, New York City. Since then he has been its efficient and loved pastor. Mr. Schulte enjoys the esteem and affection of his German brethren throughout the land. He is closely identified with all the interests of the German work, being the active secretary of the Missionary Committee of the Eastern German Baptist Conference. His presentations of the gospel are clear, forcible, and instructive, his tact is admirable, and his services in the general work make him one of the most valuable men in the German ministry.

Scotch Baptists.—See ENGLISH BAPTISTS.

Scott, Rev. Jacob Richardson, was born in Boston, March 1, 1815. His preparatory studies for college were pursued at South Reading, now Wakefield, Mass. He entered Brown University in 1832. After his graduation in 1836, he spent two years in teaching, at the end of which time he became a student at the Newton Theological Institution. He graduated at Newton in 1842, and was immediately ordained and became the pastor of the Market Street Baptist church in Petersburg, Va. For several years he was the minister of this church, and then became the pastor of the Baptist church in Hampton, Va. Such was his reputation as a preacher that he was chosen chaplain of the University of Virginia, and had the honor of having a re-election to the office at the close of his one year's service, being the first clergyman who for a second year was invited to fill the important position. At the end of this second engagement, he found his health so shattered that he concluded to return North. He had the charge of churches in Portland, Me., Fall River, Mass., Rochester and Yonkers, N. Y. During all this period his health was precarious, and he concluded that it was his duty to give up the ministry. Accordingly he resigned his office as pastor of the church in Yonkers and removed to Malden, Mass., where, having received an appointment as superintendent of schools, he performed his duties in that capacity until the time of his death, which took place Dec. 10, 1861. "In every part of his career," says Prof. Gammell, "he won the confidence and respect of all with whom he was connected, and proved himself a faithful and useful minister of the gospel. His only publications are a few hymns and several articles in the magazines of the day."

Scott, Rev. Kemp, was born in Washington Co., Va., June, 1791. His father died when he was a child. He came to Kentucky when nineteen years of age, and lived in Barren County. In 1820 he confessed Christ, and was soon after ordained. In 1824 he came to Missouri, and lived in Cooper County. Then there were 30 ministers in the State and 2000 members. He preached east and west from St. Louis to Leavenworth. He was pastor of Mount Pleasant church nineteen years. He aided in constituting fifteen churches, and baptized about 1500 persons.

In 1864 he removed to Carroll County, and was pastor of Bethel church. When the war broke out he arranged to have a meeting at his own house, and he preached. All his children had professed faith in Christ, and one was a successful minister. At this meeting a grandson was converted, and the aged grandfather went trembling into the stream and baptized him. This was the last act of his life. April 12, 1864, he died.

"Soldier of Christ, well done!"

Scott, Rev. Winfield, was born in West Novi, Mich., Feb. 26, 1837; son of Jas. B. and Margaret E. Scott; converted and baptized at Farmer, N. Y., in February, 1853; graduated at Rochester University, N. Y., in 1859, and from Rochester Theological Seminary in 1861; ordained as pastor of Second church, Syracuse, N. Y., in December, 1861; raised a company and was commissioned captain in U. S. Volunteers in 1862, and was in active service in Second Army Corps of the Potomac until wounded and discharged, in October, 1864. In 1865 he became pastor at Leavenworth, Kansas, building there a house of worship costing $65,000. The church grew under his six years' pastorate from 19 to 250 members. He organized three other churches near Leavenworth, built three meeting-houses, and baptized 500 converts. From January, 1872, to September, 1875, he was pastor at Denver, Col., and built a meeting-house and parsonage costing $20,000; the church increased from 40 to nearly 300 members. In 1875 he removed to California, and edited the *Evangel* from February to October, 1876, when he resigned this work and became pastor at Los Angelos one year, during which 50 were added to the church. In 1878 he was for a time associate pastor of the Metropolitan church, San Francisco. He afterwards supplied the Petaluma and the Central Oakland churches, and in February, 1880, became pastor at San José, where in four months 60 new members were added to the church, of whom 48 were baptized. He is an earnest worker, a faithful preacher, and ready writer, fully devoted to the cause of Christ.

Screven, Charles O., D.D., son of Gen. James Screven, who was killed in the Revolutionary war, was born in 1774, and was baptized at twelve by Dr. Furman, at Charleston, S. C. He was licensed by the Charleston church in 1801, and began to preach at Sunbury, his large patrimony lying in Bryan Co., Ga. He was ordained by Dr. Furman, Mr. Botsford, and Mr. Clay, of Savannah, in 1804, and from that time until disabled by disease, in 1829, he labored faithfully and most ably as the pastor of Sunbury church. Compelled to resign, on account of cancer in the eye, May 16, 1829, he expired July 2, 1831, at the age of fifty-seven. He did a vast amount of good during his ministerial life, and his name is still held very precious in the region where he lived.

Screven, Rev. Wm., was the founder and first pastor of the Charleston, S. C., church. "He was a native of England, where he was born about the year 1629. When he settled at Piscataway, N. H., cannot be ascertained. The sufferings which he and his brethren endured in that place drove them to seek an asylum in the more tranquil regions of the South. After his removal to South Carolina, the Baptist church in Boston sent for him to be their pastor. His answer, dated June, 1707, contains this passage, 'Our minister, who came from England, is dead, and I can by no means be spared. It is a great loss, but the will of the Lord is done.' Aug. 6, 1708, he wrote to them as follows, 'Our society are for the most part in health, and I hope thriving in grace.' He wrote 'An Ornament for Church Members,' which was printed after his death. In the latter part of his life Mr. Screven removed to Georgetown, about sixty miles to the north of Charleston, where he died in peace in 1713, having arrived at the good old age of eighty-four years. He is said to have been the original proprietor of the land on which Georgetown is built." Some of his descendants still live in the lower part of the State.

Scrivenor, Rev. Thomas, a noted and eminently useful preacher of Southern Kentucky, was born in Rowan Co., N. C., Feb. 25, 1775. He removed to Kentucky in 1796, and the same year united with Tate's Creek Baptist church, in Madison County. After residing in a number of localities he settled in Barren County, where he was licensed to preach in 1827, and in 1829 was ordained to the ministry in the fifty-fifth year of his age. Within less than a year after his ordination he founded three churches, all of which he served until advanced years unfitted him for pastoral work. He was also pastor of Dover church, near his home. Besides ministering to four churches, he preached among the destitute and the feeble churches in his own and the adjoining counties with great success. Although he began his work late in life, he is supposed to have baptized over 2500 people. He was moderator of Barren River Association fifteen years. He resigned his pastoral charges in 1858, and died in great peace July 16, 1864.

Scruggs, Rev. John, was a citizen of Monroe Co., Tenn., and for many years pastor of Madisonville and Mount Harmony churches, and others. He was a good pastor and a man of education. He was a close Bible student and a fine reasoner. He had many able and learned discussions with Methodists and Presbyterians. He was regarded by the Baptists as their standard-bearer. He has been dead about ten years.

Scruggs, M. D., was born in Scott Co., Ky. Mr. Scruggs studied at Georgetown and Bethel Colleges, Ky., and at William Jewell, Mo. He came in 1855 to Missouri with his father, and settled in Clay County. He entered the Southern army for a year. He came to St. Louis in 1871. He professed religion in 1873, and was baptized by Rev. D. T. Morrell into the fellowship of the Fourth Baptist church of St. Louis. He has rendered valuable services to this church through his wise counsels and generous gifts. His integrity and business capacity give him high standing in circles of trade; his devotion and benevolence give him influence as a Christian.

Seagrave, Rev. Edward, was born in Chester, Vt., July 15, 1797. He was a graduate of Brown University of the class of 1822, and studied theology under Rev. Calvin Park, D.D., a professor in the university, and was ordained at Scituate, Mass., March 30, 1830. He served two or three other churches, and for several years performed missionary labors in Kansas. The last sixteen years of his life were passed in Pawtucket, R. I. As a member of the First Baptist church in that place he greatly endeared himself to his brethren by his unaffected Christian humility and his readiness to perform such service as he could render to the cause of Christ. He lived to a good old age, and departed with the respect and love of all who knew him. His death occurred in Pawtucket, Aug. 18, 1877.

Searcy, Rev. James B., a prominent minister in Arkansas, was born in Alabama in 1838; in

REV. JAMES B. SEARCY.

1857 removed to Bradley Co., Ark.; was ordained in 1860; and was chaplain of the 26th Ark. Regiment in the Confederate army. In 1872–73 he traveled over the State as superintendent of missions and ministerial education; has filled the important pastorates of Warren and Monticello, but his labors have been mostly confined to country churches; wrote for *Arkansas Baptist*, and attracted attention as a vigorous writer and clear reasoner; wrote one year for *Central Baptist*, St. Louis, Mo.; a regular contributor to *The Baptist*, Memphis, Tenn., for ten years; corresponding editor of *Western Baptist;* at present Arkansas editor of *The* (Memphis) *Baptist*. He is a very able minister and a devoted Christian.

Searle, Rev. David, of Puritan stock, was born in Vermont in 1798. He removed to Western New York, and married Emily, daughter of Hon. Jas. McCall. His family were Pedobaptists, but when converted he united with a Baptist church in Rushford in 1825. In 1830 he was licensed; he studied at Hamilton Literary and Theological Institution; was ordained in Rushford in 1831. He preached in Morrisville and vicinity. Studied and supported himself, so that, though a husband and father, he was never a beneficiary. He graduated in 1833, and dedicated himself to the home mission work in Western New York; was pastor in Springville and Boston; was Sunday-school agent, then pastor again in Springville, Portage, Franklinville, and Arcade. Afterwards he was for many years agent for the Home Mission Society, his field being Western New York and Eastern Ohio, Western Pennsylvania, Northwest Virginia, and Canada West. In his declining years he went to Missouri. He died suddenly in 1861, aged sixty-three.

Judge Rowden, of Maries Co., Mo., writes: "He was a man of extensive information. His arguments were logical, and always explanatory. He was a devoted Christian, and said on his death-bed he had long been ready whenever it should be the will of God to call him home."

Sears, A. D., D.D., was born in Fairfax Co., Va., Jan. 1, 1804. In 1828 he married Annie B. Bowie, who is still alive. Two years ago they celebrated their golden wedding in Clarksville, Tenn., where they have long resided. The occasion was one of festive joy, the venerable pair receiving many attentions and valuable presents. They are both in good health, and he ministers regularly to the Baptist church in Clarksville, where he has been eminently useful in building up the cause of Christ. He has a large active membership, who greatly admire him, and give him a bountiful support. He has been the pastor of but three churches,—one at Louisville, Hopkinsville, and Clarksville. He has been very successful both as an evangelist and pastor, having baptized about 2000 persons. He took charge of the church in Clarksville, in January, 1866. It then numbered 25 members. It now numbers 225, or more. They have built a handsome church edifice at a cost of $25,000.

The doctor, though seventy-six years old, walks erect, and is full of vigor and elasticity, promising many more years of useful service in the Master's vineyard.

Sears, Barnas, D.D., LL.D., was born in Sandisfield, Mass., Nov. 19, 1802. After a thorough preparation in the best schools in the vicinity he entered Brown University, and graduated with the highest honors of the class in 1825. He en-

BARNAS SEARS, D.D., LL.D.

tered upon and completed his theological course at the Newton Theological Institution, Mass. After leaving the seminary he became pastor of the First Baptist church of Hartford, Conn., in which relation he remained two years. In 1829 he accepted a professorship in the Hamilton Literary and Theological Institution (Madison University), where he remained until 1833, when he went to Germany for the purpose of prosecuting his studies. While there he baptized the Rev. Mr. Oncken, whose zealous and self-denying labors have been so abundantly blessed in the spread of a pure Christianity, and in the gathering together of so large a Baptist membership. On his return, his ripe and thorough scholarship led to his choice as a professor in the Newton Theological Seminary, of which he was also for several years president. In 1848 he was chosen secretary and executive agent of the Massachusetts board of education, in which position his wide and varied experience of methods of education in Europe made him especially useful. In August of 1855 he was elected president of Brown University, in which position he gave new life and vigor to the institution, and elevated its standard of scholarship. In 1867 he became the general agent of the Peabody education fund, which responsible position he held until his death in 1880. Dr. Sears resided for a number of years at Staunton,

Va., greatly beloved by all who knew him. In 1841 Harvard College conferred upon him the degree of D.D., and Yale, in 1862, the degree of LL.D. Dr. Sears published, in 1844, "Ciceroniana, or the Prussian Mode of Instruction in Latin;" in 1846, "Select Treatises of Martin Luther in the Original German," with valuable philological notes; in 1850, "Life of Luther," with special reference to its earlier periods and the opening scenes of the Reformation; and in 1854 a revised edition of Roget's "Thesaurus." He also edited for several years *The Christian Review*, in which may be found some very valuable papers written by himself. In the large yearly assemblies of the denomination Dr. Sears rightfully held a conspicuous place in view of his wide experience and his attachment to the tenets of our churches.

Sebree, Capt. Uriel, a native of Orange Co., Va., was born July 15, 1774; left an orphan at the age of ten years. Soon after the death of his father he went to live with his uncle, Cave Johnson, in Boone Co., Ky. He commanded a company in the war of 1812. He was in the disastrous battle of River Raisin, where he was made a prisoner. He returned to Kentucky and served several sessions in both branches of the Legislature. In 1819, Capt. Sebree was sent on an expedition to Council Bluffs with government stores, which duty he performed with great satisfaction. He was appointed to similar service in 1820. He was a man of great skill and perseverance. He was for years receiver of public moneys in the land-office at Fayette, Mo., and in all these stations he had the reputation of an upright and efficient man.

As a Christian he was marked for consistency and usefulness. He became a member of the Baptist Church in early life, and for more than forty years took an active part in all the interests of the denomination. He co-operated in the organization of the General Association, frequently was its moderator. His house was a home for his brethren. He died May 18, 1853.

Secretary, Christian, the Baptist weekly published at Hartford, Conn., was first issued Feb. 2, 1822, for the Connecticut Baptist Missionary Society; in 1824 it was transferred to the Connecticut Baptist State Convention, then organized; in 1829 it was given to the Christian Secretary Association, which conducted it till July, 1837, Deacon Philemon Canfield, publisher; the first editor was Rev. Elisha Cushman, Sr., two years; then Rev. Gurdon Robins, five years; then Deacon Canfield, the acting editor. In July, 1837, it was united with the *Gospel Witness*, a paper of New York, which movement gave dissatisfaction; in March, 1838, on the return of Rev. E. Cushman, Sr., to Hartford, it was resuscitated, he becoming editor and proprietor, and on his death, Oct. 26,

1838, his son, E. Cushman, Jr., continued it till July, 1840. Normand Burr, in company with Walter S. Williams, and later with Almond A. Smith, edited and published it till 1850, when Mr. Burr became sole proprietor, and so remained till his death, Dec. 5, 1861. Rev. E. Cushman, Jr., who in July, 1861, became associate editor, on Mr. Burr's death became editor and proprietor, and continued such till his death, Jan. 4, 1876, when S. D. Phelps, D.D., succeeded him in ownership and editorship, who still has charge of the paper. It was at first a sheet 16 by 19 inches; it was enlarged in 1824, and again by Mr. Cushman, Sr., in 1838, and still further by Dr. Phelps; it now measures 28 by 42 inches; it is true to the denomination and holds a high rank for ability.

Sedgwick, Rev. George Cook, was born in Calvert Co., Md., Nov. 3, 1785. Reared in the Church of England, but at an early age became a Baptist. Leaving a successful business to enter the ministry, he took a course of study under Dr. Wm. Staughton; was ordained pastor of the Hartwood church, Va., but being attracted to the West, removed to Zanesville, O., in 1820, where, in 1821, he organized the First Baptist church, and remained its pastor for sixteen years. During this pastorate he taught a select school, and published a monthly paper called *The Regular Baptist Miscellany*, probably the first Baptist paper published in Ohio. He was also instrumental in establishing the Meigs' Creek Association, and, in company with his brother, William Sedgwick, and with brethren Dale, McAvoy, Spencer, Calver, Rees, Berkley, and others, traveled most, and he laid the foundation of Baptist churches. The Ohio State Convention was born in his church, and he aided largely in the establishment of Granville College. After leaving Zanesville, in 1837, he served churches in Kentucky and West Virginia, but in his later years returned to Ohio, where he died Aug. 25, 1864. He was a man of large influence, and his name is widely revered.

Sedgwick, Rev. William, A.M., brother of George Cook Sedgwick, was born in Calvert Co., Md., Feb. 7, 1790; baptized in 1812 by Rev. Jeremiah Moore. Like his brother, left a successful business to enter the ministry, and fitted himself for his life-work by a course of hard study, pursued under the greatest difficulties. Was ordained pastor of Bethel church, Va., Oct. 21, 1821, to which place he returned after a short pastorate at the Navy-Yard church, Washington, D. C. In November, 1823, went to Ohio, and took charge of a large school in Cambridge, where he organized a church, and preached in all the regions round about. In 1828 he removed to Salt Creek, Muskingum Co., O., preaching not only at Salt Creek, but at Brookfield and McConnellsville and many other places. In 1837 he succeeded his brother George as pastor of the First church, Zanesville, and, after two years, took charge of the Adamsville church, where he labored for eighteen years.

During his long ministry of fifty-six years, forty-three years of which were spent in Muskingum Co., O., Mr. Sedgwick baptized over 1000 persons. He was greatly interested in the missionary and educational enterprises of Ohio, and assisted in the organization of the Meigs' Creek Association in 1825 and the State Convention in 1826. He died Nov. 30, 1871, revered and mourned by old and young. A son, Rev. G. C. Sedgwick, of Martin's Ferry, O., succeeds him in the work of the gospel.

Seely, Hon. Alexander McL., was born in St. John, New Brunswick, in 1812; commenced to attend Baptist preaching in 1835; was subsequently converted, and was baptized with eighteen others at Indiantown by the late Rev. Samuel Robinson, March 25, 1842; was deacon in Portland church, and Germain Street church, St. John, and is now deacon in Leinster church in that city. Became a member of the Legislature in 1854, and is now president of the popular branch of the New Brunswick Legislature. He is conscientious, urbane, and faithful in the performance of all his church and public duties.

Seemuller, Mrs. Anne Moncure, daughter of Wm. Crane and Jean Crane, and great-granddaughter, on her mother's side, of Thomas Stone, a signer of the Declaration of Independence, was born in Baltimore, Jan. 7, 1838. She was educated with superior advantages in the city of her nativity. She early gave herself to literary composition, contributing to the *Galaxy* and other periodicals. Three novels of remarkable characteristics are from her pen,—"Emily Chester," "Opportunity," and "Reginald Archer." She married Mr. Augustus Seemuller, of New York. Her health failing, she went to Stuttgart, Germany, where she died Dec. 10, 1877. She early became a member of Dr. Richard Fuller's church in Baltimore, and died in its communion. Her remains, as well as her husband's, repose beside her father's, in Green Mount Cemetery, Baltimore.

Seger, Rev. John, was born Feb. 14, 1786. He was baptized in the North River, in April, 1803; licensed to preach by the First Baptist church of New York, June 17, 1813. He took charge of the Hightstown church in May, 1818. Here he spent the vigor of his manhood. For eighteen years he was pastor of this church; during part of this time he was also the pastor of the Hamilton Square church. Great spiritual awakenings followed his ministry. Many were led by him into the light. Large portions of New Jersey, from the Delaware to the coast, were traversed by him in preaching Jesus. He was moderator of the first State Convention of New Jersey, held at Nottingham Square, in 1830. He was settled for a time at Lambertville, subsequently on Long Island. From this time he lived in retirement, among the people of his first love. He was a godly man, whose life was made beautiful by the Saviour's presence. He died in a good old age, Nov. 15, 1870, leaving the heritage of a blessed memory.

Sellers, Rev. T. G., principal of Starkville, Miss., Institute, was born in South Carolina in 1831; began to preach in Alabama in 1850, and graduated at Union University, Tenn., in 1854; two years pastor at Athens, Ala.; since 1857 has supplied the church at Starkville, Miss.; has been several times moderator of the Columbus, Miss., Association; in 1869 established the Starkville Female Institute, which ranks among the first schools in the State.

Semple, Robert B., D.D., the youngest son of John Semple and Elizabeth (Walker) Semple, was born at Rose Mount, King and Queen Co., Va., Jan. 20, 1769. His father dying while he was still an infant, he was left to the faithful care of his mother, a stanch adherent of the Episcopal Church. He was educated at the well-known academy conducted by the Rev. Peter Nelson, and he made such progress in his studies that at the age of sixteen he became a valuable assistant teacher. Having finished his course of study here, he was employed as tutor in a private family, and at the same time entered upon the study of law. At this period he was troubled with grievous skeptical views as to religious truth, but through the prayers of an humble friend who was very familiar with the Bible, and with whom he held many conversations and protracted arguments, he was led to realize his errors, and was brought, by the grace of God, to feel his sinful condition. Immediately on his conversion, he felt it to be his duty to connect himself with a Baptist church, although the denomination in his neighborhood was but lightly esteemed. He was baptized in December, 1789, by the Rev. Theodoric Noel, and joined the Upper King and Queen church. He began immediately to speak for Christ, and preached his first discourse at the house of Mrs. Loury, Caroline County, December 24, the same occasion on which the Rev. Andrew Broaddus made his first effort at preaching. He gave but little evidence at that time of any special "aptness to teach." He persevered, however, in his efforts, and when, in 1790, the Bruington church was constituted, Mr. Semple became its pastor, having been ordained Sept. 26, 1790. This church he served until his death, a period of forty years. In 1793 he married Miss Ann Loury, daughter of Col. Thomas Loury, of Caroline County, and settled in King and Queen County, on a farm named "Mordington," where for many years, in addition to preaching, he taught school. Mr. Semple soon became one of the most

ROBERT B. SEMPLE, D.D.

useful and popular men in the State. He made frequent and extensive tours throughout lower Virginia, strengthening the churches and proving a great blessing to the people. He had the gratification of baptizing converts frequently and in large numbers. He was an active member of the Dover Association, and its efficiency was, in a great measure, owing to his zeal and labors in its behalf. He was deeply interested in the cause of missions, and was one of the first in Virginia to advocate their claims. He enlisted the prayers and labors both of individuals and churches in them; attended the first meeting of the Baptist General Convention; was an active friend of the Richmond Foreign and Domestic Society, and labored for the General Association of Virginia. Mr. Semple was also an ardent friend of education. At a very critical period in the varied history of the Columbian College he was persuaded to become its financial agent and president of its board of trustees. He subjected himself to numerous inconveniences in accepting this trust, and his death soon after frustrated the hopes which the friends of the college had indulged from their knowledge of Mr. Semple's prudence and energy. As an author, he won the regards of the denomination. In 1809 he published a Catechism for the use of children, which was extensively used and highly commended. In 1810 his "History of Virginia Baptists" was published. This work must have cost the author much time and trouble, but it conferred an important benefit on the churches, in enabling them to become familiar with each other's rise and progress, and in its tendency to bind them more closely together. This is an invaluable volume. He also wrote a biography of the lamented Straughan. He was frequently called on to write the circular letters of the Dover Association, all of which were marked by rare excellence of style and matter. As a minister of the gospel Mr. Semple was eminently successful. The secret of his usefulness lay in his great prudence and decision of character; in the unwearied diligence with which he discharged his ministerial duties, and in the marked practical character of his preaching. No one knew better than he how to counsel persons under conviction of sin, or how to advise under any perplexing circumstances. His congregations were always large, because he never failed to fill his appointments; while his discourses were remarkable for appropriateness, and were always delivered in simplicity and sincerity. The Rev. Andrew Broaddus, who knew him intimately, said of him, "The distinguishing excellence of our brother in his ministerial capacity appeared to me to consist in a fund of knowledge of human nature, applied, as occasion called for it, to the various workings of the heart, and in what the apostle calls 'instruction in righteousness;' or an exhibition of the duty and advantage of practical godliness." Mr. Semple was invited, in 1805, to become the president of Transylvania University, which honor he declined. In 1815 Brown University conferred on him the honorary degree of A.M. It also conferred on him the degree of D.D., which honor was also given to him by the college of William and Mary, both which, however, he felt constrained respectfully to decline. He died Dec. 25, 1831, and "in his removal," says his biographer, "the whole denomination sustained a loss."

Senter, Deacon James M., of Trenton, Tenn., was born in Cumberland Co., N. C. His father removed to Tennessee in 1831. He professed faith in Christ and joined Liberty Baptist church, and was baptized by Rev. S. P. Clark in 1846. He united with the Trenton church, where he still retains his membership, in 1858. He was ordained to the deaconship in said church in February, 1860, which position he still holds, to the pleasure and profit of both church and pastor. His pastor, Dr. M. Hillsman, one of our ablest ministers, speaks of him always in the most complimentary terms. It is the opinion of the writer that he has but few, if any, equals as a deacon. He is the deacons' treasurer. They assess the membership, the amounts to be paid quarterly, the sum is promptly given, and handed over to the pastor. Everything moves regularly like a clock; there is no friction in the machinery. If all our churches had such deacons our ministers would all fare well. Dr. Hillsman has no fears that his salary will fall short. Deacon Senter is a man of much prayer, consequently ready for every good word and work. He attends our anniversaries, and is always found upon important committees. He is now treasurer of the Central Association. He not only works and gives himself, but encourages others to labor and give. The churches should implore the Lord from day to day to raise up more such deacons.

Senter, Deacon William M., was born at Lexington, Henderson Co., Tenn., April 11, 1831. He was converted and united with the Baptist church at Bluff Springs, and was baptized by Rev. Jas. Hurt, D.D., in 1850. In 1854 he united with the church at Trenton, Tenn. He united with the Third Baptist church of St. Louis, Mo., in 1870. He was elected trustee in 1871, and deacon in 1878. He is now president of the financial board of the church, composed of deacons and trustees; has been treasurer of the executive board of the General Association of the State. He is president of the Cotton Compress Company of St. Louis. By integrity, energy, and skill he has built up from small beginnings one of the largest establishments in the West. He is a man of admirable social, religious, and benevolent qualities. Mr. Senter has given thousands of dollars to our Baptist cause, and he is a pillar of strength in his church and in our denomination in the city and State.

Separate Baptists.—When George Whitefield preached in New England, as elsewhere, many were converted to God; and as in the State Congregational churches religion was in a very low condition, the new disciples were regarded as a strange element, except by those in them, ministers or laymen, who had been blessed with new hearts. These persons for a time were called Newlights; but, as their treatment by the old religious communities was cold and sometimes unfriendly, and as the truth was frequently neither loved nor preached in the churches of the "standing order," the Newlights established religious services of their own, and in process of time they organized churches, into which only regenerated members were received. These communities were first established about 1744, and they were pious Congregational churches, as distinguished from the formal legalized bodies of the State. Baptists and Pedobaptists were often found in the Separate churches. Isaac Backus and Shubal Stearns were ministers among them. This union, however, was not permanent. The Baptists did not care to see a child sprinkled in a church to which they belonged, and the Congregationalists were not happy when one of their believing brethren was immersed. Open communion, instead of fostering charity, promoted discord, and ultimately either the Baptists or the Congregationalists withdrew from the church which they had formed and organized another on the basis of the truth as they held it. Mr. Stearns was ordained among the Separates; and after he had been immersed and ordained as a Baptist minister, impressed with what seemed to him the call of God to remove far to the West to perform a great work for his Master, he and a few of his members, in 1754, departed from Connecticut. He stopped on the way before he reached the home selected for him by the providence of God, Sandy Creek, Guilford Co., N. C., when, on Nov. 22, 1755, he and his companions formed a church of sixteen members. The first Separate church in Virginia was constituted in 1760, with Dutton Lane as its pastor. Daniel Marshall, Dutton Lane, and Col. Samuel Harriss enjoyed extraordinary success in their ministrations, converts came to Christ in throngs, churches were constituted, Associations were formed, the first of which was established among the Separates in North Carolina in 1758. In 1770 there were but two Separate churches in Virginia north of the James River, and about four south of it; in 1774 there were thirty south and twenty-four north of it that sent letters to the Association, and there were probably several others not yet identified with the Association. The ministers traveled extensively and preached everywhere. Messrs. Harriss and Read baptized 75 at one time on a preaching tour, and in one of their journeys they immersed 200. Sometimes the floor of the house where the meeting was held was covered with persons struck down with conviction of sin, and frequently the ministers were raised up at night to point weeping penitents to Jesus. A torrent of saving grace descended on Virginia, North Carolina, and other States through the labors of the Separate Baptists, which has never been exceeded in saving power in one section of country since the Saviour ascended into heaven. The Separate Baptists did not lay so much stress upon an educated ministry as their Regular brethren; they were unwilling for a time to be bound by any creed, and finally, only with explanations, accepted the Philadelphia Confession of Faith on Aug. 10, 1787, as one of the terms of a union with the Regular Baptists, consummated at that time, after which the Baptists of the Old Dominion were known as the United Baptist churches of Virginia. The Separate Baptists had some leaders who were strongly inclined to Arminianism, though generally they were sound on the doctrines of grace; and they were for a time regarded by their Regular brethren as somewhat loose, and lacking in order in their religious meetings. We heartily approve of the old Calvinism of the Regular Baptists of Virginia, and as heartily commend the holy fervor and boundless zeal of their Separate brethren. United, they have planted churches all over Virginia, swept out of existence the union between Church and State, and secured through James Madison and George Washington the religious amendment to the United States Constitution. The Separate Baptists had for a time a distinct and vigorous existence in several other States besides Virginia, and wherever they were found they were the most aggressive and successful body of Christians ever known in our country. No effort or sacrifice stood in their way where souls were to be saved or Christ's truth honored. The Separate Baptists were divinely prepared agents, exactly suited to the people among whom they labored to accomplish a gigantic work for God and for the Baptist denomination in the Southern and Southwestern States of this country; and whatever may have been their deficiencies as compared to their Regular brethren of their own day, or to the Baptists of our times, they are worthy of grateful and everlasting remembrance by their present successors and by the Saviour's friends of every name.

Long since the chasm between them and the Regular Baptists has been bridged, and the two bodies everywhere are now one in name and in religious principles.

Settle, Judge Thomas, Sr.—For a series of years Judge Settle was the moderator of the Beulah Association. He was born in Rockingham Co., N. C., March 10, 1789. The law was his chosen profession, though he was a politician during a part of his life, having served in the United States Congress in 1817, and also in 1819, when he declined re-election. He was Speaker of the House of Commons of North Carolina in the sessions of 1826–27, and in 1832 was elected a judge of the Superior Court, which office he filled till his resignation in 1854. He died Aug. 7, 1858. His last official position was that of chairman of the court of his county. He was the father of Hon. Thos. Settle, at one time on the Supreme Court bench of North Carolina, and now United States district judge in Florida, and of Mrs. Gov. D. S. Reid.

Seventh-Day Baptists, The, are distinguished from the Regular Baptists mainly by their views of the Sabbath. They believe that the seventh day of the week was sanctified for the Sabbath in Paradise, and was designed for all mankind; that it forms a necessary part of the Ten Commandments, and is as immutable as they; that it was not changed by divine authority at the introduction of Christianity; that passages in the New Testament, speaking of the first day of the week, do not imply its substitution for the Sabbath, or its appointment as a day of worship; that early Christians continued to observe the seventh day as the Sabbath till the edicts of emperors and decrees of councils suppressed it; that, finally, "The seventh day of the week, and not the first, ought now to be observed as the Sabbath of the Lord our God." Notices of people holding these sentiments are found in the first six Christian centuries, also during the dark period intervening between the establishment of papal dominion and the dawning of the Reformation. In the seventh century, under Pope Gregory I., the Sabbath was much discussed, a class declaring "it was not lawful to do any manner of work on the Saturday, or the old Sabbath." In the eleventh century, under Gregory VII., the same was preached. In the twelfth century there existed a large community in Lombardy who kept the seventh day as the Sabbath. The Reformation introduced a new era. In the sixteenth century, Baptists who kept the seventh day were quite common in Germany. In the beginning of the seventeenth century they made their appearance in England, but did not begin to organize churches until 1650. Within fifty years from the latter date there were eleven Sabbatarian churches in England, and scattered Sabbath-keepers in many parts of the kingdom. Nine of the eleven churches have become extinct, one remaining in London and one at Walton, near Tewksbury. They enjoyed the ministry of distinguished Dissenters, as Francis Bamfield, founder of Cripplegate church in London; Edward Stennett, ancestor of the famous Stennett family; Joseph Stennett, author of the reply to Russen's "Fundamentals without a Foundation, or a True Picture of the Anabaptists;" Joseph Stennett, D.D., and Samuel Stennett, D.D., of the Little Wild Street Baptist church in London.

Seventh-Day Baptists made their appearance in America in the latter part of the seventeenth century. The first church was organized at Newport, R. I., in 1671. With this church for many years united the scattered Sabbatarians in Rhode Island and Connecticut, the pastors holding meetings in distant places. In 1708 a church was organized in Hopkinton, R. I.; in 1784, another in Waterford, Conn. There are now eight in Rhode Island and two in Connecticut. In New Jersey the first church was embodied at Piscataway in 1705; from this sprang the church at Shiloh in 1737. Now there are four churches in that State.

In New York there are thirty-three churches. The church at Berlin was gathered in 1780, and formed a branch in Stephentown, and then a church at Petersburg. Then followed the churches at Adams, and at Hounsfield, and Brookfield, in 1797. This last church gave rise to two others in the same town. Then there are churches in Verona, Watson, Preston, Otselie, Lincklaen, De Ruyter, and Truxton. One in New York City, twelve in Allegany, Steuben, and Cattaraugus Counties, and several others in Western New York. Churches are now found over the South and West; 4 in Pennsylvania, 6 in West Virginia, 2 in Ohio, 7 in Wisconsin, 8 in Illinois, 2 in Iowa, 1 in Missouri, 1 in Kansas, 2 in Nebraska, 4 in Minnesota, and 1 in Dakota Territory. There are also 2 in England, previously named, 1 in Holland, and 1 in China, which report to the General Conference.

The Yearly Meeting in America was early established, which gave rise to the General Conference, held annually in September. In connection with this are held the Missionary, Tract, and Education Societies. In 1835 the churches organized into Associations; these are now the Eastern, Central, Western, Northwestern, and Southeastern. The Missionary Society was organized in 1843, operating at home and abroad. Its foreign mission is located at Shanghai, China, having a church, chapel, and dwelling-house. The foreign work is conducted by Rev. David H. Davis and wife and Miss E. A. Nelson, aided by two native preachers. The society has a charter from Rhode Island, and is located at Westerly. The Tract Society manages the denominational issues, and publishes the weekly paper, *The Sabbath Recorder*, with headquarters at Alfred Centre, N. Y. The Education Society is located at Alfred Centre, and largely aids the Alfred University at that place in carrying on its classical, mechanical, and theological instruction. *The Sabbath Recorder* was established in 1844. The denomination also publishes a Sabbath-school paper. Much of the substantial history of the churches and ministers may be found in the *Seventh-Day Baptist Memorial*,—a quarterly. The literature of the denomination is fairly represented in the volumes published by the Tract Society. In revival efforts the churches and ministers very heartily unite with the laborers of other evangelical denominations.

The following statistics are taken from the returns of 1879: Associations, 5; churches, 90; ordained ministers, 105; total membership, 8605.

The above, somewhat condensed, is from the pen of a leading member of the Seventh-Day Baptist denomination. The editor gives it as an expression of the opinions of these brethren, not as a declaration of his views.

Shadrach, Wm., D.D.—This name is a household word among the Baptists of Pennsylvania. If fidelity to truth, earnest convictions, impassioned eloquence, and active zeal through half a century entitle a clergyman to peculiar prominence among his brethren, such prominence must be awarded this veteran minister.

Dr. Shadrach is a fine specimen of the Welsh people, of whom there have been not a few highly distinguished ministers in the State of Pennsylvania. He was born in Swansea, Glamorganshire, South Wales, Dec. 4, 1804, and came to America, landing at Pictou, Nova Scotia, when fifteen years of age. After spending some time in Baltimore, Md., he removed to Pennsylvania, and on the 22d of May, 1825, was baptized into the fellowship of the Two Lick Baptist church, Indiana Co., by Rev. Thomas E. Thomas. He received ordination Dec. 10, 1828, and became pastor of the Mount Pleasant Baptist church, Westmoreland Co. From this date to 1837 he served with much acceptance and signal success the churches of Mount Pleasant, Loyalhannah, Peters' Creek, and Alleghany City. In 1837 he settled with the New Market Street church (now Fourth) in Philadelphia.

After a service of more than three years he accepted the agency of the Pennsylvania Baptist State Convention (now the General Association), and labored with great success for three years. After a brief connection with the Grant Street church in Pittsburgh, he was called in 1844 to the Fifth Baptist church, Philadelphia, where he remained until 1847, resigning in order to devote himself to the work of assisting to found the university at Lewisburg. For six years he devoted himself with untiring energy and eminent success to this great undertaking. In 1853 he was chosen corresponding secretary of the American Baptist Publication Society, and continued in this service until July, 1860. In that year he received the honorary degree of Doctor of Divinity from Madison University. In 1840, and also in 1841 and 1846, he was elected moderator of the Philadelphia Baptist Association.

From 1860 to the present date Dr. Shadrach has led an active life as a pastor of several important churches, giving also portions of his time to the interests of the denomination at large in labor for the Publication Society and the university. In a serene old age he is still honored as the devoted pastor of the church in the county-town of Indiana, Pa. Long may the shades of night be deferred!

Shailer, Rev. Nathan Emery, son of Rev. Simon Shailer, a stanch, old-time representative Baptist minister, who left an excellent record in Haddam, Conn., where he died, was born in Haddam, June 17, 1803; studied in Bacon Academy, Colchester, and became a teacher; converted under the preaching of Rev. William Bentley; commenced mercantile life, but yielded to the ministry; studied theology at Hamilton, N. Y., under Dr. Kendrick, with the missionaries Haswell and Vinton as fellow-students; ordained in New Britain, Conn., in the autumn of 1829, and remained three years; in 1832 became pastor of the Baptist church in Chesterfield, which, with the church in Voluntown, he served three years. He then settled with the church in Preston, where he had an unusually happy and prosperous pastorate of eight years; in 1844 was chosen State missionary by the Connecticut Baptist State Convention, which responsible position he filled with admirable tact, fidelity, and success for thirty years, visiting annually all parts of the State, and laboring with feeble churches and in destitute regions; held protracted meetings; organized churches; aided ministers; collected funds; and settled difficulties. He was unwearied in his devotion; genial and ready; an engaging preacher; mighty in prayer; wise in council; pure in doctrine and in life; kind to all, but firm as a rock for the truth; the co-laborer of Cook, Denison, Bailey, Steward, Ives, Swan, and Turnbull; full of honors and virtues as of years, he died July 10, 1879, aged seventy-six.

Shailer, William H., D.D., was born in Haddam, Conn., Nov. 20, 1807. Having enjoyed such

WILLIAM H. SHAILER, D.D.

advantages as could be secured in his native town for obtaining an education, he began to teach at the early age of seventeen. His desire was to fit himself eventually for the profession of law, but having become a hopeful Christian all his life-plans at once underwent a change. He was baptized into the fellowship of the church in Deep River, Conn., and soon after completed his preparatory studies at Hamilton. He then entered Madison University, and graduated in the class of 1835. While pursuing his studies at the Newton Theological Institution he was chosen principal of the Connecticut Literary Institution at Suffield. He commenced his labors there in December, 1835, teaching during the week and preaching on the Sabbath. He was ordained as an evangelist at Deep River, Conn., Feb. 26, 1836. Having occupied the position to which he had been called in Suffield for nearly two years, he accepted an invitation to become pastor of the Baptist church in Brookline, Mass., and began his ministry there Sept. 1, 1837. For sixteen years and a half he continued pastor of that church, though frequently invited and urged to accept other and seemingly more important positions. During that period he was connected with various denominational organizations,—was ten years secretary of the Massachusetts Baptist Convention, thirteen years recording secretary of the American Baptist Missionary Union, nearly eight years a member of the Executive Committee of the Union, and was connected with the boards of several other denominational institutions, attending their meetings with great regularity.

In March, 1854, Dr. Shailer became pastor of the First Baptist church in Portland, Me., a position to which he had been invited twelve years before. In 1858 he became the proprietor and editor of *Zion's Advocate*, of which paper he was the publisher for more than fifteen years, in addition to his pastoral labors. His connection with the church in Portland continued for the unusually long period of twenty-three and a half years. He resigned his pastorate in 1877, his resignation taking effect August 1 of that year. It thus appears that Dr. Shailer has had but two settlements during forty consecutive years.

Dr. Shailer was a trustee of the Newton Theological Institution from 1848, and of Colby University from 1855. The honorary degree of Doctor of Divinity was conferred upon him by Madison University in 1853.

He resided in Portland, active in various ways in promoting the cause of Christ and the interests of the denomination to which he was so long attached, and enjoyed the respect and confidence of his brethren and friends until his death, which occurred Feb. 23, 1881.

Shallenberger, Aaron T., M.D., eldest son of Abram Shallenberger, was born at Mount Pleasant, Westmoreland Co., Pa., Feb. 20, 1825, and was baptized into the fellowship of the Baptist church in 1842; studied medicine in the office of W. C. Reiter, M.D., of Mount Pleasant, and graduated at Jefferson Medical College, Philadelphia, March 20, 1846; married Miss Mary Bonbright, of Youngstown, Pa., Sept. 1, 1846; removed to Rochester, Pa., Jan. 7, 1847, where he has since resided in the practice of his profession. He is a member of the Baptist church at Rochester and president of its board of trustees. He has been prominent in the local and educational interests of the county, a constant reader of general and professional literature, and especially interested in scientific investigations and discoveries.

Shallenberger, Deacon Abram, was born in 1797, of Swiss ancestry. He was baptized in early manhood into the fellowship of the Baptist Church. He married Rachel Newmyer, and settled in Mount Pleasant, Pa., where he carried on an extensive business for many years; was a constituent member of the Mount Pleasant Baptist church, and was elected its first deacon in November, 1828, which office he filled until he removed to Beaver County in 1856. He passed away very suddenly in December, 1868, dropping dead while walking home from church at New Brighton, Pa., where he had greatly enjoyed a communion service.

Deacon Shallenberger was a man of great natural endowment, force of character, and information. He found time for much study and general reading. He was, indeed, mighty in the Scriptures, and had a reason for the faith that was in him. He was a terse and vigorous writer, contributing occasionally to the religious weeklies. He was active in every good work, a shining light in the church, a tender and affectionate husband and father, universally esteemed for the purity and probity of his character. He died in the triumph of the Christian's hope.

His wife, a noble Christian woman, survived him a year and a half, then fell asleep in Jesus. Twelve children were born to these parents, eight of whom are still living, all married, teaching their children the religion of Jesus.

Shallenberger, Hon. William S., was born at Mount Pleasant, Westmoreland Co., Pa., Nov. 24, 1839; received his education at the university at Lewisburg; was baptized into the fellowship of the Mount Pleasant Baptist church in 1857; enlisted, in August, 1862, in the 140th Regiment Pa. Vols., in which he was afterwards appointed adjutant; was wounded slightly at Chancellorsville, and severely at Gettysburg and at the Wilderness; was discharged from the service on account of wounds.

Since the war he has been active in business pursuits. He is a deacon of the church at Rochester. He was the first president of the Beaver County Sunday-School Institute. He has been moderator of the Pittsburgh Association for the years 1877 and 1878, and he gained signal reputation for his judicious rulings. He was elected to the Forty-fifth Congress in 1876, at the early age of thirty-seven, from the twenty-fourth district of Pennsylvania, and re-elected to the Forty-sixth Congress in 1878.

He married Josephine, daughter of Gen. Thos. J. Power, of Rochester, in 1864.

A Washington journal represents him as possessing "a reputation for personal integrity that has secured for him the esteem and confidence of his peers, and has given him an influence with the various departments of the government that has made him one of the most useful members of the

HON. WILLIAM S. SHALLENBERGER.

House of Representatives. There is not, we venture the remark, a more industrious or painstaking man in Congress at this time than Mr. Shallenberger, a more obliging representative, or a more upright Christian gentleman."

Shanafelt, Rev. A. H., passed from labor to the refreshing blessedness and the unbroken rest of heaven in 1875. Mr. Shanafelt was a native of Pennsylvania, and he died when about forty years of age. He had a vigorous constitution, and looked as if designed by the Creator for a long and arduous life.

He was called by the Spirit into the kingdom of grace and peace in early life, and united with the Methodist Church; but he soon learned the truth more perfectly about free-will and the ordinance of baptism, and he was immersed on a profession of his faith. He was a graduate of Lewisburg University. After laboring in the interior of Pennsylvania, he settled in Chester in 1867, where his efforts were sanctioned by the divine Spirit, and where the laborer was tenderly loved. Few men enjoyed in a greater measure the confidence of his brethren, and few men so richly deserved it.

Shannon, Rev. James, a distinguished scholar, a graduate of Belfast College, Ireland, who came to Sunbury, Ga., to assist Dr. McWhirr in the academy. He became a candidate for the ministry among the Presbyterians, and for a trial thesis was given the subject, "Did John's baptism belong to the Jewish or Christian dispensation?" His examination of the subject of baptism led to his becoming a Baptist, and he was baptized by Rev. C. O. Screven, D.D., in 1822 or 1823. He became the successor of the elder Brantly, as pastor of the Augusta church, in May, 1826, and his pastorate extended through three and a half years, his acceptance of the professorship of Ancient Languages in the State University, at Athens, causing his resignation. During his pastorate—in the year 1827—there was a powerful revival in the church at Augusta, and Mr. Shannon baptized many, who became faithful and useful church members. While at Athens, he was instrumental in the organization of the Baptist church in that city, on the 31st of January, 1830, and was elected pastor on the 20th of March following. This relation existed until 1835, when he removed to Missouri, and became president of William Jewell College in 1844 or 1845. He died about 1853. He was a man of great zeal, an unblemished reputation, and fine scholarship; but he became somewhat erratic before his death, and joined the "Campbellites."

Shans, Mission to the.—The Shans, with their kindred races, are spread over a large territory of Burmah, and are found in great numbers in Siam, Cochin China, Assam, and the adjacent countries. As far back as 1836 they were supposed to be ten times as numerous as the Burmese. Their general character is regarded as much superior to that of the Burmans. In religion they are supposed to be Buddhists. The spiritual wants of this widely scattered people attracted the attention of the friends of missions in this country more than forty years since, but comparatively little was done to save them until 1859. Rev. M. H. Bixby, who had been a missionary among the Burmans and Talings, was appointed to the new field of labor among the Shans. The most encouraging indications met Mr. Bixby from the very outset of his work. Having made Toungoo his headquarters, he commenced to preach and make himself better acquainted with the language, and many inquirers came to him to learn of Jesus. The first highly raised expectations were not met. Various causes conspired to hinder the progress of the work. In 1863 the prospect seemed more encouraging. Conversions occurred, and the belief was strengthened that the blessing of heaven would largely rest on the labors of the missionaries. On Sunday, the 22d of May, 1864, Mr. Bixby baptized fifty-five converts in a deep gorge between two mountains, on the sides of which were two villages of the Shans. At the end of four years' work he reports one hundred baptisms and the formation of three churches. The constant labor of so many years at last so undermined the health of Mr. Bixby that he returned to the United States in the summer of 1868, and the care of the mission devolved on Rev. Mr. Cushing, who was joined by Rev. E. D. Kelley in the spring of 1872. Mr. and Mrs. Cushing returned to their native country in 1875. During the absence of Mr. Cushing the mission to the Shans was put in charge of Rev. Mr. Eveleth. On his return, in the latter part of 1877, Mr. Cushing established a new station in Upper Burmah, at Bhamo, where he could come in contact with many of the Shans. He was hopeful of good results from his labors.

Sharp, Daniel, D.D., was an Englishman by birth, the place of his nativity being Huddersfield,

DANIEL SHARP, D.D.

in the county of York. He was born Dec. 25, 1783. From his pious parents he received a religious education, and always spoke of them in terms of the highest affection. Having become a hopeful Christian, he joined a Congregational church, but a change in his sentiments having taken place as to the proper mode and subjects of baptism, he united with a Baptist church. Turning his attention to mercantile pursuits, he was sent to this country as the business agent of a large firm in Yorkshire. On reaching New York, in the autumn of 1805, he identified himself at once with the church under the pastoral charge of Rev. John Williams. In the social meetings of the church he developed such gifts at public speaking, and showed such a love for the work to which he devoted the energies of his life, that it was the conviction of his brethren that he ought to prepare for the Christian ministry. After deliberating prayerfully over the matter, he decided to obey what seemed to be a call from the Master, and without delay put himself under the careful training of the Rev. William Staughton, D.D., of Philadelphia, and received ordination May 17, 1809, as pastor of the Baptist church in Newark, N. J. For nearly three years he occupied this position, when he was invited to take the pastoral charge of the Charles Street church in Boston. The services of his recognition took place April 29, 1812.

The great executive talents of Dr. Sharp found a larger development and a wider sphere within which to exercise themselves when he was thus transferred to the metropolis of New England. Dr. Baldwin and others of kindred spirit were laying the foundation and enlarging the usefulness of organizations which have since become a power for great good in the denomination. He interested himself in these various organizations. For a number of years he was one of the editors of the *American Baptist Magazine*. The intelligence that Rev. Messrs. Judson and Rice had become Baptists and had thrown themselves on the sympathy and aid of the churches stirred all the generous impulses of his susceptible nature, and he was among the foremost and the most earnest of his brethren to respond to the call made upon the benevolence of the denomination. In April, 1814, the General Convention of the Baptist denomination in the United States was formed. Almost from the outset he was one of its officers, and for many years president of its acting board. Upon the formation of the American Baptist Missionary Union he was chosen its first president, a distinction which showed in what estimation he was held by his brethren.

Dr. Sharp was a warm friend of every movement which looked to the education of the ministry. With others he took the incipient steps which resulted in the formation of the Northern Baptist Education Society. The Newton Theological Institution found in him a stanch supporter. For eighteen years he was the president of its board of trustees. His long pastorate of the Charles Street church, extending from April, 1812, to June, 1853, made him so well known in Boston that his straight, commanding form and dignified bearing were held in remembrance by citizens of all classes and denominations long after he had passed away.

Dr. Sharp was eminently conservative in his tastes and habits. His long experience and wide observation made him suspicious of the permanent results of those spasmodic religious movements which stir whole communities from their profoundest depths. He was a believer in the worth of steady, every-day work, and he thought more of harmoniously developed, well-rounded Christians than of those whose zeal so often outruns a wise discretion. In the city of his adoption he was known and respected as few clergymen of any denomination were in his day. Brown University honored him by making him a Fellow of her corporation, and in 1811 by conferring upon him the honorary degree of Master of Arts, and in 1828 that of Doctor of Divinity. He was one of not more than eight or ten Baptist ministers in the country who have received this latter degree from Harvard University, which conferred it upon him in 1843, at a time when he was a member of its board of overseers. He left behind him a stainless Christian reputation and an honored memory as a minister of that gospel which he preached for more than forty years.

Shaver, David, D.D., late editor of the *Christian Index*, and for years editor of the *Religious*

DAVID SHAVER, D.D.

Herald, of Richmond, Va., was born in Abingdon, Va., of Presbyterian parents, in November, 1820. He professed religion early in life, but was not permitted to unite with a church. At sixteen he joined the Methodist Protestant Church, and was licensed to preach, and entered the itinerant ministry when nearly twenty, in connection with the Virginia Annual Conference. Previous to that time he had read theology one year; subsequently he devoted three years to the study of theology, suspending the active discharge of ministerial functions for the purpose.

In November, 1844, he adopted Baptist sentiments openly, after mature investigation, and was baptized at Lynchburg by Rev. James C. Clopton, and was ordained to the ministry of the Baptist denomination. In June, 1845, he became pastor of the Lynchburg Baptist church, where he remained until called to succeed Dr. Jas. B. Taylor as pastor of the Grace Street church, Richmond, Va., in October, 1846. At the end of two years, on account of throat disease, he was compelled to accept an agency for the Domestic Mission Board of the Southern Baptist Convention. Again entering the ministry, he served the Baptist church at Hampton, Va., from 1853 to 1857, when he became editor of the *Religious Herald*, which he held until the surrender of Richmond. In 1867 he went to Atlanta, Ga., to assume the editorship of the *Christian Index*, from which position he retired in 1874. He then took charge of the Third Baptist church in Augusta. In 1878 he was elected professor in the colored theological seminary, now in Atlanta, which position he still holds. This institution is maintained by the American Baptist Home Mission Society, and was removed from Augusta to Atlanta in 1879.

Dr. Shaver is one of the finest scholars in the South, and possesses a mind of extraordinary acuteness. As a sermonizer he perhaps has no superior, and his acquaintance with the whole range of theological investigation renders him perfectly at home on any subject, and entitles his opinions to the highest respect. He is a most polished writer and an excellent editor. Of unquestionable piety and surpassing abilities, he would be fitted to adorn any ministerial position were it not for the failure of his voice, by which his usefulness as a public speaker is impaired.

Shaw, Benjamin F., D.D., was born in Gorham, Me., Oct. 26, 1815. He fitted for college at the academy in Yarmouth, Me., and pursued his collegiate studies at Waterville and Dartmouth Colleges, graduating from the latter in the class of 1837. He spent one year at the Newton Theological Institution. His ordination occurred March 16, 1843. He has been pastor of the churches in China, Thomaston, and Waterville, Me. The state of his health has obliged him during his life to retire altogether at times from ministerial work and devote himself to more active pursuits. In different sections of his native State he has performed missionary labor among feeble churches, and been successful in promoting revivals of religion. Colby University, of which he is a trustee, conferred on him the degree of Doctor of Divinity in 1872.

Shaw, Rev. J. F., editor of the *Baptist Index*, published at Texarkana, Ark., was born in Georgia in 1845; was ordained in Alabama in 1866; after filling important positions in North Alabama came to Arkansas and founded the Arkadelphia Baptist High School, and supplied the church in that place two years; in 1879 traveled as State evangelist; in 1880 began the publication of the *Baptist Index*.

Shaw, Rev. John, was born in Scotland in 1796, and converted there in 1812; emigrated to Prince Edward Island in 1819, and was baptized there by Rev. T. S. Harding in 1832; ordained at Three Rivers, Oct. 14, 1832. Mr. Shaw evangelized much, and with great success, particularly in Cape Breton Island. He died June 4, 1879.

Shaw University.—This school had its origin in the formation of a theological class of freedmen in the old Guion Hotel, now the National Hotel, in the city of Raleigh, N. C., Dec. 1, 1865, and taught by Rev. H. M. Tupper, of Massachusetts, in the employ of the American Baptist Home Mission Society of New York. The following year it was removed to a large wooden building, corner of Blount and Cabanas Streets, where it continued as the Raleigh Institute till 1870. Some 2000 men, women, and children were enrolled on the books of the institute from its commencement. In 1870 the Barringer property was bought for $15,000. In 1872 the Shaw building was finished and furnished, at a cost of $15,000, and in 1874 the Esty building, a school for girls, was completed, at a cost of $25,000. Mr. Shaw, of Wales, Mass., from whom the school is named, has been one of its largest benefactors, having given $8000 towards the original purchase, and the erection of the Shaw building. Towards the erection of the Esty building the J. Esty Company, of Brattleboro', Vt., gave $8000; George M. Morse, of Putnam, Conn., gave $2000; $5000 were raised by the North Carolina Jubilee Singers, and various persons in the North gave smaller sums. About $3000 a year have been spent in the erection and furnishing of buildings since 1870, from money saved out of the receipts of the school. From 1870 to 1874 about 600 pupils attended, and the school was known as the Shaw Institute. In 1875 the school was incorporated as the Shaw University. In 1879 the university hall was completed, at a cost of about $6000, all the money, except $650, having been saved from tuition and the boarding department. The number of pupils enrolled from 1875 to 1880 is 900.

At a recent meeting of the board of trustees a separate theological course was established for advanced students, also a medical department, which will go into effect Nov. 1, 1881. Funds to erect a medical dormitory, and also a necessary medical building, have recently been received, and this department will be known as the Leonard Medical School, named in honor of the largest donors, the Leonard family, of which family Mrs. Tupper, the wife of the president, is a member.

The students pay annually, for board and tuition, about $6000 in cash and $2000 in work.

The school has five departments,—normal, scientific, collegiate, theological, and medical.

It will be seen that the property has cost more than $70,000, and that great good has been done, and will be accomplished, by its establishment, and it is proper to say, that while much credit is due to the friends who have so generously aided it, its success is still more largely due to the energy, business talents, faith, and perseverance of Rev. H. M. Tupper, the founder and president of the university.

The students in 1880, of both sexes, numbered 277; these were under the care of fifteen instructors.

Sheardown, Rev. Thomas Simpson, was born Nov. 4, 1791, in the County of Lincoln, England; baptized in the fall of 1812, settled in the United States, October, 1820, and was ordained in December, 1828.

The field occupied by this eminent servant of Christ was in Northern Pennsylvania and Southern New York. Almost his entire ministry was spent on horseback, gathering churches in new settlements. Necessarily such a field, in its roughness and great privations, involved much self-denial. But rewards follow great sacrifices, and are correspondingly great. Revival succeeded revival. Churches were organized, and others built up. The number baptized by his own hands exceeded 1400, while many others, converted under his labors, received baptism at the hands of pastors in whose churches he labored as an evangelist. With the single exception of the Troy church, in Bradford Co., Pa., he never settled over a church formed by other men's labors. His public life covered more than half a century, and, to the very last of his long career, both old and young were deeply attached to him, and even venerated him. His name had become a household word in the entire field he occupied, and Father Sheardown's advice almost became a law.

The writer well remembers the earliest and the latest impressions made upon his own mind in listening to his earnest and glowing utterances. Traveling from Hamilton Seminary, N. Y., into Pennsylvania, during a vacation, he reached the waters of Crooked Creek, in Tioga Co., Pa. Dusty, footsore, and discouraged beyond measure, he halted at a country house, where a crowd had assembled in the afternoon of a very hot day. Father Sheardown was preaching. The theme of his sermon was the familiar words, "Christ is all and in all." Never can he forget the glow of his countenance as he held spellbound his rustic congregation. Every eye seemed suffused with tears. The writer forgot dust, heat, soreness of feet, and discouragements in the entrancing picture he drew of the moral worth of Christ, and each man's need of such a Christ. Years after, on his dying bed, he said to him, "Do you recollect the sermon you preached on Crooked Creek when the writer was but a boy?" He referred him to the text. "No; not the sermon," he replied, "but the theme. Why, that supported me long before. It has ever since, and never more than now, while on this bed, a mere wreck on the shore of time. 'Christ *is all!*' Preach it, brother!" In such a spirit lived and died this man of power with God, and this prince among preachers. Let the pulpits continue the blessed theme, "Christ is all and in all."

Shedden, Capt. James, whose memory is dear to the Baptists of Western Pennsylvania, was born in the County of Derry, Ireland, April 27, 1833. He belonged to a Scotch-Irish family which for generations had held high positions in the British army. His father having removed to this country, died when James was yet young, thus throwing him upon his own resources. His early years were spent in the unsettled life of a riverman, and yet amid the busy scenes of steam and gunboat service the teachings of a pious mother were not forgotten. In later and more settled life these instructions resulted in his conversion. In the year 1873 he was baptized, and entered into fellowship with the First Baptist church of Sharpsburg, Alleghany Co., Pa.

His life knew no idleness. At his death he held various offices,—deacon, trustee, church clerk, treasurer, and superintendent of the Sabbath-school. In the Association he also held the office of treasurer and assistant clerk. At the same time he was honored in being vice-president and a director of the Pittsburgh Baptist Social Union. His fellow-citizens also honored him by his election as a school director, and by constituting him burgess of Etna Borough. Capt. Shedden died suddenly Aug. 23, 1878. His prayer has been answered, that when it should please the Lord to take him into rest the community might be all the better for his having lived among them.

Sheffield, Rev. Charles Smith, was born at Jewett City, New London Co., Conn., Oct. 13, 1833. He was baptized into the fellowship of the Butternuts Baptist church, Gilbertsville, Otsego Co., N. Y., April 24, 1853; prepared for college at Gilbertsville Academy and Collegiate Institute; entered the Freshman class of the University of Rochester, Sept. 10, 1856, and graduated July 11, 1860; entered Rochester Theological Seminary, Sept. 13, 1860, and graduated July 2, 1863; received a unanimous call from the church at Newfane, Niagara Co., N. Y., and was ordained at Newfane, Oct. 1, 1863, Rev. E. G. Robinson, D.D., LL.D., preaching the sermon. December, 1866, resigned the pastorate at Newfane, on account of throat disease, and in the following spring became teacher of natural sciences in Buffalo Central School, where he taught about four and a half years. In August, 1871, removed to Kansas City, where he taught, with an interval of one year, for a period of seven years, most of the time as principal of the Kansas City High School. On July 1, 1878, he became superintendent of public schools at Atchison, Kansas, and served in that capacity for two years. In August, 1880, became president of Pierce City Baptist College, of Pierce City, Mo. Since resigning the pastorate he has preached occasionally for various churches, acting as pastor of the Pleasant Grove Baptist church from January, 1874, for one year, and supplying the Ottawa Baptist church for some months.

Sheldon, Clisson P., D.D., was born in Bernardstown, Mass., May 9, 1813; pursued academic studies at Hamilton, N. Y., until compelled by diseased eyes to discontinue; ordained pastor at Whitesborough, Oct. 21, 1836, where he remained seven years. He then re-entered Madison University, where he graduated in 1846. During the year 1845 he served as pastor of the First church, Hamilton, N. Y. Upon his graduation he settled with the Niagara Square church, Buffalo, which he served until, in 1854, he became a second time pastor in Hamilton. In 1856 he accepted a call to the Fifth Street church, Troy, N. Y., which church he served nearly twenty years, during which it grew in numbers and influence until it has become a leading church in the State. Nov. 1, 1875, at the request of the American Baptist Home Mission Society, he closed his pastorate at Troy and became district secretary of the society for New York and Northern New Jersey.

His life has been that of a preacher and pastor. He has written, however, a number of excellent articles for newspapers and reviews, among them an "Historical Sketch of the Baptist Missionary Convention of the State of New York." He has frequently served the State Convention as corresponding secretary, as a member of its board, and as president. He has baptized 762 persons. He is a hard worker at whatever he undertakes, and a man of fine judgment. He is eminently qualified for the important office he now fills. He still resides at Troy, and is honored as one of its most worthy citizens.

Sheldon, D. Henry, was born in Union Village, Washington Co., N. Y., in March, 1830. At the age of fourteen he was baptized into the fellowship of the Prattskill Baptist church of that place, Dr. Isaac Wescott being the pastor. In the beginning of his course of study he was prepared at Rochester for West Point, but that purpose having been changed, he removed to Racine, Wis., in 1849, where he went into business. Still having his mind upon study, he returned to Rochester in 1854, and entering the Sophomore class in the university, graduated in 1857. Having chosen a business career, he went first to St. Louis, where he was engaged in successful pursuits of that nature until 1861. At that date he removed to Chicago, which has since been his home. Mr. Sheldon was one of the first to enlist in the work of founding a theological seminary at Chicago, was one of the earliest chosen on the board of trustees, and during the whole history of the institution has been one of its influential, generous, and judicious friends. His donations in money have amounted to $10,000; besides which he gave $20,000 more in property. In other relations Mr. Sheldon has been known during his residence in Chicago as a devout Christian and the zealous friend of every good cause.

Shelton College is located at St. Albans, in Kanawha Co., W. Va., on the Chesapeake and Ohio Railroad. Steps preliminary to its establishment were taken by the Teays' Valley and Guyandotte Associations in 1871. It was first called Coalsmouth High School. Rev. J. C. Rice was the first president, and Rev. B. Cade the first financial agent. Rev. P. B. Reynolds was elected principal of the school in 1872. A building for the institution was begun in 1873, and the first regular session of the school commenced Oct. 1, 1875. An effort was made in 1876 to raise an endowment of $50,000, and Rev. W. P. Walker acted as agent, but owing to the stringency of the times and other causes the effort had to be abandoned after securing $4000 or $5000.

In consideration of gifts by Mr. T. M. Shelton, amounting to about $10,000, the name was changed to Shelton College. The institution owns property worth from $15,000 to $20,000, and after a hard struggle of ten years is nearly out of debt, and ready to begin the work for which it was established.

The course of instruction in the college comprises mathematics, modern and ancient languages, and sciences. Each department is a distinct, complete school in itself, under a competent head, with necessary assistants. There is also a practical Biblical course for the special benefit of theological students. A number of very useful young preachers have been educated at this school.

Shelton, William, D.D., son of James and Nancy Shelton, was born in Smith Co., Tenn., July 4, 1824. In his youth he attended the common schools of the country, in the vicinity of his home, until he acquired the rudiments of a common-school education. In the fourteenth year of his age he entered a high school, then taught at Big Spring, Wilson Co., Tenn., where he commenced the study of Latin, Greek, and mathematics.

In his seventeenth year he entered the Junior class of the University of Nashville. While a student in that institution he made a profession of religion, and joined the First Baptist church of Nashville, and was baptized by Rev. R. B. C. Howell, D.D., then pastor of the church, and was soon afterwards licensed to preach. In 1843 he graduated from the University of Nashville, in his nineteenth year. He next became a student, in 1844, in the theological department of Madison University, N. Y., from which he graduated in 1846.

Immediately after his graduation he was called to the pastoral care of the Baptist church in Clarksville, Tenn. Having accepted the call, he was ordained to the work of the gospel ministry; the Presbytery consisting of Rev. R. B. C. Howell, D.D., Rev. Samuel Baker, D.D., Rev. Reuben Ross, Rev. Robert Williams, and Rev. R. W. Nixon.

In 1850 he resigned the care of the church in Clarksville, and accepted the professorship of Greek and Theology in Union University, Murfreesborough, Tenn.

In 1851 he accepted the pastorate of the Baptist church in that place, performing the double work of pastor and teacher. He continued in these positions till 1855, when he was offered the presidency of Brownsville Female College, and was called to the pastorate of the Baptist church in that place. Having accepted these offices he removed, and entered upon his work. Under his pastoral care the church was greatly enlarged and strengthened, and under his administration the college grew to be one of the largest and most flourishing schools of the South up to the civil war.

Immediately after the close of the war he was elected president of West Tennessee College, Jackson, Tenn. Having accepted the position, he removed with his family to that city. He succeeded during the four following years in building up that institution to a high degree of efficiency and success. In 1869 he resigned the presidency of West Tennessee College. In 1873 he became financial agent and Professor-elect of Moral and Intellectual Philosophy in the University of Nashville.

At the organization of the Southwestern Baptist University, in 1876, he was elected its first president.

In 1878 he was elected president of Ewing College, Ill., and has succeeded in imparting to it a high degree of prosperity. His home is still near Nashville, Tenn., six miles from the city.

Dr. Shelton is regarded as a fine educator, and a good and useful preacher, as was demonstrated in his pastorate at Brownsville, Tenn., when large accessions were made to the church. At one protracted meeting, in which the writer assisted, between sixty and seventy were added. His son, Wm. Shelton, Jr., has entered upon the ministry, and bids fair to make a useful preacher.

Shepard, Rev. Samuel, M.D., was born in Salisbury, Mass., June 22, 1739. He studied medicine, and practised his profession at Brentwood, N. H., and rose to distinction as a physician. The perusal of "Norcott on Baptism" led to a change of sentiments, and he left the Congregational Church and connected himself with the Baptists. Rev. Hezekiah Smith, of Haverhill, baptized him in June, 1770, and, soon after his public profession of faith in Christ, he began to preach. Within a year three small churches were formed in three different but neighboring towns, and he was invited to take the pastoral oversight of them. The number of members in the three churches was small. Dr. Shepard accepted the invitation, and was ordained at Stratham, N. H., Sept. 25, 1771. Blessed with a good physical constitution, and more than ordinary intellectual ability, he was able to accomplish a large amount of ministerial work, and was instrumental in advancing the interests of religion over a wide extent of country. In the double office of minister and physician, he came in contact with a large number of families, and, literally, looked after the cure of both soul and body. As illustrating the character of his work, and the success which followed his labors, we quote an extract found in Sprague's "Annals," from a letter written by Dr. Shepard to Rev. Isaac Backus in 1781 :

"Some hundreds of souls are hopefully converted in the counties of Rockingham, Strafford, and Grafton, in New Hampshire, within a year past. In the last journey I made before my beloved wife was taken from me, I baptized seventy-two men, women, and some that may properly be called children, who confessed with their mouths the salvation God had wrought in their hearts to good satisfaction. I baptized forty-three in the town of Meredith in one day, and such a solemn weeping of the multitude on the shore I never before saw. The ordinance of baptism appeared to carry universal conviction through them, even to a man." He then goes on to describe the great blessing which had followed the outpouring of the Spirit in different towns in New Hampshire, and the glorious results in the formation of seven Baptist churches within a period of about one year, and closes by saying, "There appears to be a general increase of the Baptist principles through all the eastern parts of New England."

Dr. Shepard was a man of rare executive ability, and adopted a plan with reference to churches gathered in a sparsely settled country worthy of imitation in sections similarly situated. His own home was where he commenced his professional life as a physician,—Brentwood. Of the Baptist church in this place he was the pastor, and had the oversight of several other churches which were branches of the Brentwood church. In the best sense of the word he was a bishop without Episcopal consecration. We are told that " in his active days he was accustomed to visit all these churches, making a circuit of about two hundred miles ; and they all looked up to him with grateful and reverential regard."

Dr. Shepard was the author of several works, which had considerable circulation at the time of their publication. These were "A Scriptural Inquiry respecting the Ordinance of Water Baptism," "A Reply to Several Answers in Defense of this Inquiry," "A Scriptural Inquiry concerning what the Friends or Quakers call Spiritual Baptism, being an Answer to a Work published by Moses Brown, of Providence, R. I.," "The Principle of Universal Salvation examined and tried by the Law and the Testimony," "An Examination of Elias Smith's two Pamphlets, respecting Original Sin, the Death Adam was to die the Day he eat of the Forbidden Fruit, and the Final Annihilation of the Wicked."

In Sprague's "Annals" we find one or two incidents which are worth preserving, as illustrative of the character of the subject of this sketch : " He was a man of extraordinary presence, and could almost by a look exert great power over other minds. On one occasion he was called to visit a suffering woman, a member of his church, whose husband, wealthy but penurious, did not allow his family necessary comforts. After calling for different things, and being told there were none in the house, Dr. Shepard rose upon his feet, indignantly stamped upon the floor, and said, " Mr. ——, do you go at once and tackle your horse, and purchase the articles, and a tea-kettle." The man started as if electrified with terror, and obeyed the command, to the great comfort of his sick wife.

No man in the history of the Baptist denomination in New Hampshire stands out more prominently to our view than Dr. Shepard. His death occurred at Brentwood, Nov. 4, 1815.

Sheppard, Rev. Joseph, was born in Greenwich, N. J., Jan. 9, 1786. He was the son of a respectable farmer. At the age of eighteen he attended Dr. Staughton's school at Burlington. He united with the Burlington church May 1, 1804, was licensed to preach May 4, 1805, and, after studying a little longer with Dr. Staughton, he entered the University of Pennsylvania, where he graduated in 1808. He was ordained pastor at Salem, N. J., April 19, 1809, by Wm. Staughton, D.D., Wm. Rogers, D.D., and Rev. Henry Smalley. He labored hard and successfully there for more than twenty years, baptizing many. In 1829 he became pastor at Mount Holly ; he also supplied Marlton every third Sabbath, and taught a private school. Six years of this work wore upon his health, and he was obliged to give up the pastorate, but he supplied churches as his strength permitted, and engaged in evangelistic labor. On Dec. 9, 1838, he preached at Pemberton three times, and walked several miles visiting the sick. On Tuesday he reached his home, and was taken with apoplexy, from which he died on Thursday. Preaching was his delight, and he was very fond of instructing youth. He was faithful, kind, and beloved.

Shermer, Rev. Henry B., was a native of Philadelphia, Pa., who graduated at Madison University in 1850, and from Rochester Theological Seminary in 1852. He went as a missionary to the Bassa tribe in Africa in 1852, but fell a victim to the African fever, and was obliged to return to this country in 1854. Though in broken health, he served the church at Newton, N. J., for four years, and at Schooley's Mountain, N. J., for five years. He died in triumph there on March 22, 1869.

Sherwood, Adiel, D.D., a most distinguished minister and educator, a man of remarkable piety,

ADIEL SHERWOOD, D.D.

zeal, humility, and learning, was born at Fort Edward, N. Y., Oct. 3, 1791. He died at St. Louis, Mo., Aug. 18, 1879, when he had nearly completed his eighty-eighth year. His father was a member of the New York Legislature, a Revolutionary soldier, and a personal friend of Gen. Washington, whom he had the pleasure of entertaining twice after independence was secured.

Adiel Sherwood studied three years in Middlebury College, and then, after an honorable dismissal, entered Union College, Schenectady, in 1816, and was graduated in 1817. The following fall he entered Andover Theological Seminary, remaining one year. He then went to Georgia for his health, where he resided for many years, taking his place side by side with Abram Marshall, Jesse Mercer, Henry Holcombe, William T. Brantly, Sr., Gov. Rabun, Charles J. Jenkins, Gov. Lumpkin, Thomas Stocks, B. M. Sanders, and a host of others who built up the Baptist denomination in that State and gave it tone and direction. Entering at once upon evangelistic labors, he became one of the foremost workers in the State. In 1820 he, through the clerk, offered a resolution which led to the formation of the Georgia Baptist Convention in 1822. In 1823 he attended the Triennial Convention, in Washington City, and introduced a resolution urging all the States to form Conventions, which was accomplished in a few years. He was, also, one of the founders of the American and Foreign Bible Society.

His pastorates in Georgia were many, his first being that of Bethlehem, near Lexington. It was at the request of the Bethlehem church that he was ordained in March, 1820, at Bethesda, Greene Co., Mercer, Reeves, Roberts, and Matthews forming the Presbytery. Afterwards, during a period of many years, extending to 1865, most of which time was spent in Georgia, he was the pastor of many churches in the State, a mere list only of which can be given: Freeman's Creek, Clarke Co.; Greensborough from May 1821 to 1832 or 1833, which church he and Jesse Mercer organized; New Hope, Greene Co.; Eatonton from 1827 to 1837; Milledgeville, 1827 to 1834; Macon, 1829; Monticello, 1829; Indian Creek, 1831–33; Penfield, 1839; Bethesda, Griffin, Greenville, and others.

In 1827 he took charge of the academy in Eatonton, Ga., becoming pastor of the Baptist church also; and in that year a most memorable revival commenced at Eatonton, spread all over the State, and resulted in the conversion and baptism of many thousands, during the two years it lasted. The numbers may be surmised when it is stated, in his own records, that 16,000 persons were baptized in three Associations only. His labors may be computed when it is stated that, besides all his other official and ministerial labors, he preached, during 1828, 333 sermons, in as many as forty counties. At the session of the Georgia Baptist Convention, in 1831, he offered the resolution in favor of a theological institution, that resulted in the establishment of Mercer Institute, which, finally, merged into Mercer University. He himself had a small theological school at Eatonton in 1831, and in 1832 opened a manual labor school, but discontinued it in January, 1833, when Mercer Institute was established at Penfield.

Elected a professor in Columbian College, Washington, D. C., he spent 1837 and 1838 in Washington, but returned to Georgia to accept the professorship of Sacred Literature in Mercer University, in which institution he spent 1839, 1840, and 1841. He was then elected president of Shurtleff College, Alton, Ill., where he remained for years. During 1846 and 1847 he served as secretary of the American Baptist Indian Missionary Society, and during 1848 and 1849 he was president of the Masonic College, Lexington, Mo. He then accepted the charge of the Baptist church at Cape Girardeau, Mo., where he remained until 1857, when, on account of rheumatism, he returned to Georgia, and became the president of Marshall College, Griffin. This position he filled, while serving various churches, until the war commenced. After the war, in 1865, he returned to Missouri, where he resided until his death, on Aug. 18, 1879, preaching constantly.

To Dr. Sherwood much of the credit is due for the high position in point both of numbers and intelligence attained by the Georgia Baptists. He was learned and eloquent, an earnest and incessant worker, wise and prudent, and an able financier. He did much to elevate the standard of education in Georgia; he strenuously promoted unity of action in the denomination; his missionary zeal was second to that of none; and when the anti-missionary and antinomian spirit aroused such bitter dissension in the State, from 1827 to 1837, ending in division, he stood side by side with those who rolled back the tide and made Georgia what she has been nearly ever since,—the banner mission State of the South.

All his life Dr. Sherwood was an indefatigable writer, and his articles and sermons have appeared in nearly every Baptist paper in the country. His "Gazetteer of Georgia" is a valuable book, and so is his "Christian and Jewish Churches," but his most important work is his "Notes on the New Testament," written almost entirely while confined to his bed by rheumatism. In his preaching he was systematic and concise, and in his young days very vehement and impressive. His character was altogether above reproach, and his spirit much resembled that of the Master he served. In appearance he was tall and commanding, with noble and dignified features.

Shirley, Rev. Philemon Perry, was born Dec. 16, 1827, in Hancock Co., Ind. He was converted and baptized in 1840. In 1841 his parents removed to Iowa. His mother died in 1848. Thirsting for knowledge, he left home at the age of twenty-one, without money or helper, and studied, taught, and preached for four years among the destitute. With a fair knowledge of natural sciences he entered Madison University, N. Y., and in 1854 became pastor at Grafton, where he was ordained. A year later he returned to Iowa, and labored in that State and in Illinois, preaching for many of the important churches, partly as a pastor, and much of the time as an evangelist, helping other pastors. He has baptized about 1000 converts, and seen many others baptized by their pastors, with whom he has labored. In 1879 he removed with his family to California, and became pastor of the church at Petaluma; but poor health prevents his continuous work in the pulpit. He is sympathetic, genial, and eloquent whenever he is able to plead with men, in the pulpit, for the gospel of Christ.

Shorter, Alfred, the son of Jacob Shorter and Adelpha Bankston, was born in Wilkes Co., Ga., on the 23d of November, 1803. During his infancy he lost his mother, and before he reached the age of manhood he was made an orphan by the death of his father. At sixteen he found employment as a clerk in Monticello, Jasper Co., and developed such extraordinary business qualifications that, besides gaining the respect and confidence of the community, he became, at the age of thirty, one of the substantial men of the town, noted for his honor and strict integrity. About that time he was fortunate enough to secure the affections of one of the most beautiful and charming ladies of the State, Mrs. Martha Baldwin, who became his wife. In 1837 he removed to Rome, Ga., where he has resided to the present time, amassing a fortune sufficient to class him among the most wealthy men of his State. For the past fifty years he has been a Baptist, ever most liberal in his contributions to charitable institutions and benevolent objects. In 1877 he founded the Shorter College, of Rome, Ga., and presented it as "a gift to our daughters," —a deed accompanied by a degree of enlightened liberality which places him among the great benefactors of the day. Mr. Shorter is a gentleman of modesty, acknowledged piety, and great generosity. Since the death of his wife, which occurred in 1877, he has lived quietly and alone at his retired but elegant mansion near the city of Rome, Ga.

Shorter College.—This Baptist institution of learning for young ladies, at Rome, Ga., was organized as the Cherokee Baptist Female College, in October, 1873. In 1877 the property was transferred to Alfred Shorter, whose name the college now bears. He paid its debts, demolished the old buildings, and erected others larger and far more elegant. After their completion he selected a board of trustees, to whom he committed the property in trust for the daughters of the land. The buildings stand upon an eminence, and command views of charming landscapes in all directions. The grounds have been laid out in beautiful walks and carriage-drives, and have been artistically terraced. The entire premises are inclosed by a beautiful iron railing. The buildings themselves are magnificent structures of brick, of the latest and most approved style of architecture, and elaborately finished. The memorial chapel, with its windows of stained glass, and its walls and ceiling superbly adorned with fresco-paintings, has been pronounced the most elegantly finished room in the Southern States.

Pennington Hall, the principal boarding-house, a fire-proof brick edifice, four stories high, crowns the summit of the beautifully terraced hill. Its large apartments are all neatly finished and thoroughly warmed and ventilated, and are supplied with everything necessary for the convenience and comfort of the inmates. The buildings are all supplied with gas-pipes and steam-pipes, which are used for lighting and heating the various apartments. The institution is furnished with an excellent chemical and philosophical apparatus, and with a cabinet of minerals and fossils.

Though young in years, Shorter College is already known throughout the land as one of the best public institutions of learning in the country, and is classed with the first colleges for females in America. It is a noble monument of the munificent liberality and enlightened zeal in the cause of education of him whose name it bears, and whose donations, to the extent of more than a hundred thousand dollars, have made him one of the greatest benefactors of Georgia.

Shorter, Col. Eli, was a leading lawyer, a man of the first order of culture, a member of the United States Congress before the war, colonel of a Confederate regiment during the war, and prominently connected with Alabama politics since. Col. Shorter was an orator of a high order, and every way a brilliant man. He was a brother of the late Gov. Shorter, of Alabama, and otherwise honorably connected in family relations. He was a member of the Eufaula church, and an officer of the Alabama Baptist Convention. He died in 1878.

Shorter, Gov. John Gill, was born in Jasper Co., Ga., in 1818, and graduated at the university of that State in 1837. His father having previously removed to Eufaula, Ala., the son followed, and began the practice of the law. In 1842 he was appointed State's attorney for a circuit composed of nine counties. In 1845 he was elected to the senate, and in 1851 to the house. In 1852 he was appointed by the governor circuit judge. The appointment was ratified by the people, and Judge Shorter continued on the bench nine years. He was an able and upright judge, administering the law fearlessly and impartially, exerting a healthful influence on the bar, and creating by his charges to the grand juries and intercourse with the people, a sound public opinion. The law in Alabama then required alternation of circuits, and Judge Shorter became the most popular man in the State.

When the troubles between the North and the South began, he was appointed commissioner from Alabama to Georgia, and in 1861 was appointed by the Convention a deputy in the Provincial Confed-

GOV. JOHN GILL SHORTER.

erate Congress. He was then elected governor, and served with ability for two years. When he retired from public life he resumed the practice of the law, and continued in it until May 29, 1872, when he died, his last words being

"'To Canaan's fair and happy land,
Where my possessions lie,'

I want to be off."

Gov. Shorter was a deacon in the Baptist church at Eufaula, the moderator of his Association, a liberal contributor to all benevolent enterprises, and universally beloved as a man of God.

The death-bed of this Christian lawyer, patriot, and statesman bore clear testimony to the truth and comforts of the religion of Jesus. It was illumined by celestial radiance. The atonement of Christ was the basal truth of his religious creed. Repeatedly, in his last days, he said, "I have no fear, nor doubt, nor anxiety, *none whatever*. The atonement of Christ, oh, it is a rock, a refuge!" With undimmed faith, he said, "There *is* a truth in religion; it is all true; and a power in the atonement of Christ. It is a reality, a glorious reality. As sure as the sun shines, so sure is my faith in the plan of redemption and in the atonement of the Lord Jesus Christ, which will stand firm as the everlasting hills."

Shouse, Daniel Lewis, was born in Shelby Co., Ky., April 5, 1827. He left his father's home at nineteen years of age, and taught a district school. He taught also in Shelby Co., Ky. He united with the Baptist church in Fisherville, Ky., and engaged in business. He became active in the Sabbath-school, the chief work of his life. In 1855 he removed to Missouri, and became a resident of Kansas City, where he lived until his death. At first he was a merchant, then cashier of the Mechanics' Bank for several years, till he organized the Kansas City National Bank, of which he was cashier till he died. He was a power in advancing the growth of the city, its banks, schools, and churches. His church, the Baptist, owes much to his toils, prayers, and gifts. The Baptist college at Liberty, the General Association, and the Sabbath-School State Convention, of which he was so long the efficient secretary, all were aided in no ordinary degree by him. For years he was the efficient and loved superintendent of the Sabbath-school in Kansas City. By the advice of his physician he gave up its care. In peace and war he was with it, and it was the largest and best in the city. In his last days he was patient, waiting for the Master's call. He was cheerful and hopeful in the darkest hour. Rarely has a death produced such a feeling in the community as Mr. Shouse's. The influence is still felt. Rarely is a man so sincerely and universally honored and loved by man, woman, and child. Truly "a good name is rather to be chosen than great riches."

Shreveport University, Shreveport, La.—In 1870 an association of gentlemen at Shreveport purchased the Helm School property, with seventy acres of land attached, in the suburbs of the city, intending to develop the value of the property, and devote the proceeds to the establishment of a university. A company was organized to extend the street railroad to the property. An arrangement was made with the Southern Life Insurance Company by which policies were to be taken in favor of the university, and the insurance company advanced money to put up buildings. A large brick edifice was erected, and nearly completed. The school was opened in 1871, under Rev. M. S. Shirk. In 1872, Rev. W. E. Paxton was elected president. But in 1873 the city was ravaged by yellow fever, succeeded by a financial panic. The insurance company failed, the property depreciated, and a collapse was the result.

Shuck, Rev. J. Lewis, was born at Alexandria, Va., Sept. 4, 1812. In early life he became a Christian. He was ordained in 1835, and at once went as a missionary to China, sent by the Triennial Convention. In 1837 he baptized his first convert at Macao. In 1840 the agent from whom he received support failed. He removed to Hong-Kong and supported himself by editing a paper, but did not suspend his work as a missionary. In 1843 the church he had organized numbered twenty-six.

His wife died in 1843, and in 1845 he returned to the United States to make provision for his children. In 1846 he went back to Shanghai, China, under the patronage of the Southern Baptist Convention, taking his second wife with him.

He returned to the United States in 1853, having lost his second wife. In 1854 he was sent by the Southern Baptist Convention as a missionary to the Chinese in California, taking his third wife with him. Here he spent seven years, discharging the double duties of missionary and pastor of Sacramento church. He organized the first, perhaps the only, Chinese church on the continent.

Having spent twenty-five years in laboring among the Chinese, he returned to Barnwell Court-House, S. C., in 1861, where he spent the remainder of his life, preaching to the surrounding churches. In 1863 he rested from his labors, in the fifty-first year of his age. His son, Rev. L. H. Shuck, D.D., pastor of the First Baptist church in Charleston, received the mantle of the ascending father.

Shuck, L. H., D.D., was born at Singapore, on the Malay Peninsula, while his parents were on their way to China as missionaries, in 1836. After the death of his mother, in 1844, he was sent back to his grandfather, Rev. Addison Hall, in Virginia, where he was prepared for college. He graduated at Wake Forest College, N. C., from which he received the degrees of A.B., A.M., and D.D.

After his graduation he spent a year as professor in the Oxford Female College, N. C., and then became principal of the Beulah Male Institute, in the same State.

On the death of his father, Rev. J. L. Shuck, the son took his place as pastor of several churches in Barnwell Co., S. C. He was next chosen pastor of the Baptist church at Barnwell Court-House, and from it he removed to Charleston, and took the pastoral care of the old First church, in 1869, which position he now holds.

Shuey, Gen. Martin, was born in Lebanon Co., Pa., Sept. 28, 1785, of Lutheran parents; entered the military service, passed through various official grades, until he was promoted to the rank of brigadier-general for his eminent services. In 1825 he entered into business and settled in Indiana, and subsequently in Illinois, and upon his conversion, in 1826, examined the subject of baptism; became an active Baptist and liberal supporter of all benevolent and church enterprises. In 1859 he crossed the plains, and settled at Brooklyn, Cal.; aided in organizing the church there, in 1860; was its first deacon, and held that office until he was over ninety years old. He died Feb. 12, 1876.

Shurtleff, Benjamin, M.D., was born in Boston in 1775. He graduated in 1796, and commenced at once the study of medicine. Having received the degree of M.D., he was appointed to a situation in the medical department of the naval service of the United States. He returned to Boston after a brief period of service, and gave himself with untiring energy and success to the practice of his profession for fifty years. He possessed those traits of character which made him from the outset a popular and acceptable physician.

In 1835. Dr. Shurtleff made a donation to Alton College, Ill., of $10,000. As a token of their appreciation of the value of the gift the trustees named the institution Shurtleff College. His death occurred in Boston, April 12, 1847.

Shurtleff College.—The first suggestion of Upper Alton, Ill., twenty-five miles north of St. Louis, as a suitable place for a Baptist college seems to have been made by Dr. Jonathan Going, who visited it in 1831. Special attention had only in the previous year been directed to Alton itself as a possible commercial centre, and the two towns, two and a half miles apart, were then in their infancy. The suggestion of Dr. Going, however, was received with approbation, and on June 4, 1832, the seminary at Rock Spring having been removed to the new point, seven gentlemen " formed a compact to establish a college to be under the supervision of Baptists, and engaged in a written obligation to advance each $100, which was subsequently increased to $125, and to become jointly obligated in the loan of $800 more." We quote the words of Dr. John M. Peck. These seven, with James Lemen and J. M. Peck, added in 1833, were the original trustees of the Alton Seminary. With a part of the sum named above a tract of 122 acres was purchased adjoining the town of Upper Alton; with the remainder and added donations from citizens a building was erected. The school opened with twenty-five students, with Rev. Hubbell Loomis as principal, and Rev. Lewis Colby as professor in the theological department. The college charter was granted by act of the State Legislature in 1835. In its original form this charter forbade the establishment of a theological department, but a modification of it, by act of the Legislature in 1841, removed that restriction. The institution, at first called Alton College, received the name it now bears through Dr. Benjamin Shurtleff, of Boston, who, in 1835, made to the college the donation, very liberal at that time, of $10,000.

Instruction in theology has always been an important feature of the college work, and a few years since, chiefly through the liberality of Mr. Elijah Gove, a theological department was formally organized, with Dr. R. E. Pattison and Prof. E. C. Mitchell as instructors. The president of the college now gives instruction in Systematic Theology. Justus Bulkley, D.D., is Professor of Church History and Church Polity, and Rev. J. C. C. Clarke, Acting Professor of Biblical Literature and Interpretation. The successive presidents of the college have been Prof. Washington Leverett (acting president), 1836–40; Rev. Adiel Sherwood, D.D., 1840 –46; Prof. Washington Leverett (acting president), 1847–49; Rev. N. N. Wood, D.D., 1850–55; Rev. Daniel Read, LL.D., 1855–69; at which last date the present president, Dr. A. A. Kendrick, came into the office. Upon the faculty, besides those already named, are Orlando L. Castle, LL.D., Shurtleff Professor of Oratory, Rhetoric, and Belles-Lettres; Charles Fairman, LL.D., Hunter Lecturer on Chemistry, Geology, and Mineralogy; J. C. C. Clarke, Gove Professor of the Latin and Greek Languages and Literature; Charles Fairman, LL.D., Professor of Mathematics and Natural Philosophy; John D. Hodge, A.M., M.D., instructor in Botany, Zoology, and Physiology; Charles B. Dodge, A.M., principal of the preparatory department.

In the year 1876 a centennial fund of $100,000 was raised for the college by Dr. G. J. Johnson, which has greatly relieved the college by placing its finances upon a sounder basis. In all respects Shurtleff College is a prosperous institution, holding a high rank among the colleges of the West. Its past record is one for which any institution may cherish abounding gratitude to the God of goodness.

Shute, Samuel M., D.D., was born in Philadelphia, Pa., Jan. 24, 1823; prepared for college in the academy of Dr. Wm. Curran; entered the Sophomore class of the University of Pennsylvania in 1841; graduated, with the degree of A.B., in 1844, and received the degree of A.M., in course, in 1847; was baptized, in the fall of 1845, by the Rev. Dr. Shadrach, and united with the Fifth Baptist church, Philadelphia; licensed by the same church to preach, July 26, 1847. Prosecuted his theological studies in the seminary of the Reformed Presbyterian Church, Philadelphia, at that time under the supervision of the Rev. S. B. Wylie, D.D., vice-provost of the University of Pennsylvania, Dr. Crawford, Dr. Theo. T. Wylie, and others. While engaged in his theological studies he was chosen instructor of English literature in the Sigoigne (French) Academy for young ladies, in Philadelphia, which position he held for several years, until his ordination. During one year of this period he also served as assistant editor of the *Christian Chronicle*, a Baptist religious journal, published in Philadelphia, under the auspices of the American Baptist Publication Society, and conducted by the Rev. Heman Lincoln, D.D., and the Rev. W. B. Jacobs. In the fall of 1852 he received a call to the pastorate of the Baptist church in Pemberton, Burlington Co., N. J., which he accepted, entering on his labors there Jan. 1, 1853, and receiving ordination on the 17th of the following

SAMUEL M. SHUTE, D.D.

February. He remained in Pemberton three years, and at the termination of that period, in consequence of the ill health of his wife, he prepared to remove to Alexandria, Va., having been invited to the pastorate of the First Baptist church in that city, on the resignation of Rev. H. H. Tucker, D.D. He remained here three years, during which time a beautiful church edifice was built, and about 100 baptized and added to the church. In the fall of 1859 he was elected to the chair of the English Language and Literature in the Columbian College, which position he accepted, and still holds, having given the institution up to this time a continuous service of twenty-two years. During his connection with the college he has spent most of his Sabbaths in preaching, although having charge of no churches, except for short periods, and while they were endeavoring to secure regular pastors. In addition to his one year of editorial labors in Philadelphia, Prof. Shute has written quite a good deal, having contributed frequently to monthly and weekly periodicals, to *The Nation*, of New York, and occasional articles to the *Southern Review* and to the *Baptist Quarterly*. In 1865 he published an "Anglo-Saxon Manual," the second text-book of the kind issued in this country, and the first to reject the primary English methods of grammatical exposition of the language, and to base it on the more scientific plan of Heyne and other German scholars. This book has passed to a third edition, and has been extensively used in the high schools and colleges of this country. Prof. Shute, at the request of Rev. Dr. Cathcart, the editor of the "Baptist Encyclopædia," has prepared the biographical sketches contained in this work of the ministers and laymen of Maryland, Virginia, and the District of Columbia.

His first wife, who lived only three years after their marriage, having died before the close of his pastoral labors in Pemberton, was Miss Phebe H. Taylor, of Taylorsville, Bucks Co., Pa.; his present wife was Miss Jane C. Kerfoot, daughter of Daniel S. Kerfoot, of Fauquier Co., Va.

The degree of D.D. was conferred upon him by Mercer University, Ga.

Dr. Shute is a man of a quick and penetrating intellect, and of a sound judgment, and to these gifts of nature years of diligent study have added a wide and varied culture. He has been not only a successful professor of the Greek, Latin, Anglo-Saxon, and German languages, but also a careful student in other departments of knowledge, and especially in English literature and in theology.

As a professor, in the branches above referred to, as well as in rhetoric and in kindred studies, he has been able, faithful, successful, and popular.

As a writer, he is forcible and chaste.

As a preacher of the gospel, he is instructive, and there is a frequent demand for his pulpit services in Washington and in the neighboring cities.

Sibley, Rev. W. L., a pioneer preacher in Louisiana, was born in Georgia in 1795; settled in Washington Parish, La., in 1825. In 1847 he removed to Sabine Parish, and became a co-laborer with Father Bray. He was instrumental in building up many churches both in Eastern and Western Louisiana. He died Oct. 21, 1861.

Sicklemore, Rev. James, was a clergyman of the Episcopal Church of England, and became a Baptist about 1640.

His change of views about baptism occurred singularly, and yet very naturally. He was rector of Singleton, Sussex, and in catechising the young people of his parish he took occasion to speak of the promises made by godfathers and godmothers on behalf of children at their baptism. One of those who were present inquired if the Holy Scriptures gave authority for anything he said. For the moment he defended himself by the general practice of the Christian Church, but, after examining the Word of God and other ancient Christian documents, he saw that infant baptism was a mere human tradition, without the authority of inspiration or of the apostolic age. He disapproved of tithes, and gave away most of his income to the needy. He was "famous for his piety and learning," and under God he was the founder of the Baptist churches of Portsmouth and Chichester.

Simmons, James B., D.D., was born in the township of Northeast, N. Y., April 17, 1827. He made a profession of faith in Christ at the age of sixteen years, was graduated from Brown University in 1851, and in Newton Theological Seminary in 1854. He was pastor of First Baptist church of Providence, R. I., three years; of the First Baptist church of Indianapolis, Ind., four years; and of the Fifth (old Sansom Street) church of Philadelphia, Pa., five and a half years. In Indianapolis he established a mission, which has grown into the South church. In Philadelphia he set in motion the celebrated adult "Bible schools" now so common in the churches. In 1867 he was elected corresponding secretary of the American Baptist Home Mission Society, in which capacity he served for seven years. He had special charge of the freedmen's department, establishing seven schools for their education. He received the degree of D.D. in 1870. In 1877 he accepted the pastorate of Trinity Baptist church, New York, which he still retains. His special labor for the salvation of Chinamen has resulted in the conversion of a few of them, and about twenty are members of his Bible schools. He is the author of several tracts published by the American Baptist Publication Society.

Simmons, Lockey, was born in Montgomery Co., N. C., April 14, 1796; baptized by Noah Richardson at the age of twenty-three; was county surveyor for many years; accumulated a good estate, and was a great friend of education. He aided several young ministers in their studies. He died at Wake Forest College, at the house of his son, Prof. W. G. Simmons, Jan. 23, 1880.

Simmons, Prof. W. G., was born in Montgomery Co., N. C., March 4, 1830; graduated with high honor at Wake Forest in 1852; read law at Chapel Hill with Judge Battle and Hon. S. F. Philipps; came to Wake Forest College in 1855 as Professor of Mathematics; is now Professor of Natural Science in the same institution and a man of undoubted learning.

Simonson, Rev. George A., is of Baptist ancestry. His grandfather, Rev. George Allen, was pastor at Burlington, N. J., and his father, Rev. P. Simonson, at Providence, R. I. He was born at Providence. His father dying early, George's boyhood was spent in Burlington, N. J. Baptized at twelve years of age, George, by the loss of his mother, was an orphan at thirteen, passing his three following years in a boarding-school. The remaining years of his youth he was in the West, learning practical surveying and civil engineering, though he afterwards returned and graduated at the Polytechnic College of the State of Pennsylvania. He then resumed the practice of his profession as division engineer on the Pittsburgh, Fort Wayne and Chicago Railroad. In 1856 he taught the high school at Indianapolis. Here, feeling called to the ministry, he gave up teaching to take the full theological course at Rochester, graduating in the class of 1864. The seven following years were given to incessant labors in the Western ministry, most of them in the State of Illinois. Leaving his last settlement there of nearly four years in Pontiac, Ill., he became pastor of the Windsor Avenue church of Hartford, Conn., in 1871. He entered upon the pastorate of the Fifth church, Newark, N. J., in the spring of 1874, since which time the meeting-house has been enlarged and beautified at considerable expense, and many members have been added to the church.

Singing in Public Worship.—In the end of the seventeenth century singing was introduced among the English Baptists. Probably persecution had much to do with its general omission in their religious assemblies. Nothing more useful to the informer could have been contrived than songs of praise from a large congregation. In Benjamin Keach's church, for some years before the happy revolution which placed William III. upon the throne and gave the Dissenters restricted religious liberty, singing was practised at the close of the Lord's Supper, even when it was used as a guide to the informer. It is thought that church music was first employed in divine service among the Baptists in Mr. Keach's meetings. He introduced it among his people gradually. At first, after the celebration of the Supper; and they had no singing but this for six years, then on public thanksgiving days, and this continued for fourteen years, and then the church solemnly agreed to sing the praises of God every Lord's day. But some of his people withdrew and founded the Maze Pond church on the principles of the mother-church, but they formally prohibited singing in their worship.

In 1691, Mr. Keach wrote a work called "The Breach Repaired; or, Singing of Psalms and Hymns and Spiritual Songs proved to be a Holy Ordinance of Jesus Christ." It seems strange that such a book was necessary, and more remarkable that it met with bitter opposition for a season.

When the Second church in Newport, R. I., was formed, in 1656, among the reasons given by the twenty-one persons who founded it for leaving the First church was that they disapproved of psalmody which the parent community used. Dr. Guild, speaking of the First church in Providence, R. I., when Dr. Manning settled in that city, and of Mr. Winsor, who preceded Dr. Manning as pastor, says, "The true cause of opposition to Dr. Manning was his 'holding to singing in public worship, which was highly disgustful to Mr. Winsor.'

On this point the sentiments of the Quakers appear to have prevailed in the church, and singing was discarded as unauthorized by the New Testament." Mr. Winsor and his friends seceded from the church because of the supposed departure of Dr. Manning and the church from the six principles laid down in Hebrews vi. 1, 2: "Not laying again the foundation of repentance from dead works, and of faith toward God, of the doctrine of baptisms, and of laying on of hands, and of resurrection of the dead, and of eternal judgment."

Sioux City, Iowa, with a population of 7246, is on the east side of the Missouri River, about 1000 miles above St. Louis. It is the county-town of Woodbury County, and the largest city of Northwestern Iowa. The Sioux City Baptist church was organized in 1860, but remained a feeble interest for several years. In 1871, when Rev. James Sunderland became pastor, there were only 14 members, but in 1876 the number had increased to 90. They have recently enlarged and improved their meeting-house, and now have 144 members.

Sisty, Rev. John, was born March 26, 1783; baptized July 4, 1802, by Rev. Thomas Ustick, of Philadelphia, Pa.; and in August, 1817, he began to hold meetings at Haddonfield, N. J., which resulted in the organization of the church there in 1818. He continued as pastor there for twenty-one years, and was greatly prospered and beloved. He was instrumental in forming the Baptist church at Moorestown. He died Oct. 2, 1863.

Six-Principle Baptists.—These churches of the great Baptist family hold, as their distinguishing doctrines, the six principles mentioned in Heb. vi. 1, 2. They claim a history running far back into the past, as may be learned from Rev. Richard Knight's "History of the General or Six-Principle Baptists in Europe and America," published in 1827. In this country, at first, they did not differ from the Particular or Regular Baptists, save in the matter of the laying on of hands; but later they swerved to Arminianism, yet remained strict communionists. They were once comparatively strong in Rhode Island, being among the first to establish themselves in the soul-free colony; and for a time they claimed the First Baptist church in Providence, the Second Baptist church in Newport, and the first churches in many of the towns. They once had the lead in thirteen of the present thirty-six towns of the State. Near the year 1700 they formed a Yearly Meeting; indeed, they now date their annual meeting from 1670. This Yearly Meeting embraces their churches in New England. In 1729 it counted twelve churches and eighteen ordained elders.

As a people they flourished until about the period of the Revolution, when failing to manifest a proper degree of enterprise, and neglecting education, literature, and an aggressive spirit, they began, prior to 1800, to decline in popularity and numbers, and have rapidly decreased within the last sixty years. A number of their once strong churches have become Regular Baptists. A few from sheer feebleness have fallen into the arms of the Free-Will Baptists. They are now, as they have always been in this country, without an academy or college, or periodical organ or distinctive literature, or missionary society for home or foreign work. They seem to have waned on account of their inactivity; yet they have ever been a pure, sincere people.

At present, in New England, they count less than a dozen small, expiring churches, and a roll of hardly more than a thousand active members. They, however, maintain a Yearly Meeting. A small—very small—Association of this order is reported in Pennsylvania and New York, where their existence is like a flickering lamp. In New England we can find at present (1880) but two churches outside of Rhode Island,—one in Connecticut and one in Massachusetts.

Skinner, Deacon Charles W., was born, in 1780, in Perquimans Co., N. C. The death of his first wife led to his conversion, and he is said to have been comforted in reading the fortieth chapter of Isaiah. He joined the Presbyterian church at Princeton, N. J., where his brother Thomas was studying theology, but afterwards connected himself with Bethel Baptist church in Perquimans County, and was baptized by Rev. Robert F. Daniel. He was one of the founders of the Baptist State Convention, and used to ride hundreds of miles in his sulky to attend its sessions. He was one of the first and best friends of Wake Forest College, pledging his personal property for its debts, and giving it at one time as much as $5000.

Mr. Skinner was remarkable for his benevolence, and probably gave to the cause of Christ more money than any Baptist who ever lived in North Carolina. He gave $2000 towards building the church at Bethel; he gave $7000 towards the beautiful church in Hertford, which cost $16,100; he gave $2000 to erect the house of the First Baptist church of Raleigh, and he probably gave, all told, $10,000 to Wake Forest College. It has been said that he gave not less than $50,000 to the various objects of benevolence in North Carolina. His brother, Thomas H. Skinner, D.D., was so eminent a Presbyterian minister that, when he died a few years since in New York City, hundreds of ministers attended his funeral. Dr. Thomas E. Skinner, pastor of the First Baptist church of Raleigh, is his son. Deacon Skinner died April 15, 1877.

Skinner, Thomas E., D.D., youngest son of Charles W. and Mary C. Skinner, was born in Perquimans Co., N. C., April 29, 1825; graduated at the University of North Carolina in 1847; began life as a planter; was baptized at Bethel church, by Rev. Q. H. Trotman, Jan. 19, 1851; graduated at the Union Theological Seminary, N. Y., May 8, 1854, his uncle, Dr. T. H. Skinner, being a professor in that institution; settled as pastor in Petersburg, Va., in November, 1854; became pastor of First Baptist church, Raleigh, in November, 1855; settled as pastor of First Baptist church, Nashville, Tenn., November, 1867; removed to Columbus, Ga., in November, 1870; to Athens, Ga., in August, 1871; to Macon, Ga., in December, 1875, being pastor in each of these places; and in September, 1879, became pastor the second time of the First church in Raleigh, being both the predecessor and successor of Dr. Thomas H. Pritchard, D.D. Besides being the pastor of the largest and most influential church in the State, Dr. Skinner is the president of the board of trustees of Wake Forest College. He was made a D.D. by Furman University, S. C.

Slack, Mrs. Mary, was born in New Castle Co., Del., Nov. 18, 1809. Died in Philadelphia, Pa., Sept. 12, 1878.

She commenced business in a limited way, in Wilmington, Del., in 1840, and was so successful as to retire in 1873 with a small fortune.

She was baptized March 13, 1842, upon profession of her faith in Christ, by Rev. Sanford Leach, then pastor of the Second Baptist church, with which church she united. Withdrew, in 1865, with others, from the Second church to form the Delaware Avenue church, Wilmington, Del.

Rev. Geo. W. Folwell, first pastor of the Delaware Avenue church, and her pastor for some years, says of her: "I believe Sister Slack gave about $10,000 to the Delaware Avenue Baptist church. During most of my pastorate she rented two of the most expensive pews in the church, for which she paid $80 per year. This she did not only to increase the revenue of the church, but also to have the privilege and pleasure of inviting friends and visitors to sit with her. She was very seldom absent from any of the services of the church. She was unostentatious and unobtrusive, simple and sincere in her professions and practices, and evidently constrained by the love of Christ. On more than one occasion, when offering to add one or more thousand dollars to her contributions to the building fund, and I questioned whether or not it was her duty to do so, she said, 'I was awake nearly all night praying about it, and I believe my heavenly Father wants me to give it.' When she thought I was trying to check her liberality, she said, 'Do you want to rob me of the pleasure of doing good?'"

The last large contribution she gave, one of $2000, she procured by giving a mortgage on her home for the greater part of it, and paid the interest herself.

In addition to her larger donations, she gave liberally to every benevolent object presented in the church, besides giving to our denominational societies, sometimes, one-fourth of the church's annual contribution. She was decidedly the largest contributor to the funds of the Delaware Avenue Baptist church.

The number and extent of her private benefactions no man knows. The writer frequently heard of them as he visited among the sick and poor. Her pastor and his family, and even their friends who visited them, were many, many times refreshed by her gifts.

Slack, Rev. W. L., M.D., a distinguished preacher and teacher at Pontotoc, Miss., was born in Cincinnati, O., in 1819. His father was an eminent Presbyterian minister, and president of Cincinnati College, under whose careful training Dr. Slack became a fine classical scholar, and in 1846 received the degree of A.M. from Miami University. Having studied medicine, circumstances diverted him from his original plan, and he engaged in teaching in Tennessee. While giving instruction in Greek he was led to change his views on baptism. The reasons for this change he has given in a little work entitled "Slack's Reasons for becoming a Baptist," which has been widely circulated. He united with the Baptists, and was ordained in 1852, at Denmark, Tenn., where he was teaching. Subsequently he became president of Mary Washington College, Pontotoc, Miss. The buildings having been destroyed by fire during the war, he founded the Baptist Female College at the same place, with which he remained until failing health compelled him to desist. He has also supplied the Pontotoc church twenty-five years.

Slade, Rev. T. B., for many years principal of a high school for young ladies in Columbus, and a distinguished and successful educator, was born in North Carolina. He graduated at Chapel Hill, taking the first honor. He came to Georgia, and opened a school at Clinton, Jones Co.; helped to organize the Wesleyan Female College at Macon; took charge of a female seminary at Penfield; and then removed to Columbus, about 1842, where he has resided ever since. Few men, if any, in the State have sent forth into society more well-educated young ladies than Rev. Thomas B. Slade, of Columbus. At present he is an octogenarian.

Slater, Rev. Franklin S., was born in St. Lawrence Co., N. Y., Feb. 11, 1823; graduated from Madison University in 1850; had brief settlements in Connecticut and New York, but most of his ministerial life has been spent in New Jersey. During his six years' pastorate at Keyport a fine church edifice was built, and at Matawan, where his pastorate has extended to fifteen years, the church has grown, and the name of the good pastor is a household word in the community.

Slater, Rev. Leonard, missionary to the Ottawa Indians, was born in Worcester, Mass., Nov. 16, 1802; was converted at the age of sixteen, and studied for the ministry with Dr. Going. He was appointed missionary to the Indians by the board of the Triennial Convention in 1826. After reaching Detroit, in company with Mrs. Slater, he traveled on horseback 200 miles through the woods to Carey Station, near where Niles now is, and began his missionary work. The next year he was transferred to Thomas Station (now Grand Rapids), where he remained nine years, teaching and preaching. He learned their language so as to use it as readily as English. The progress of white settlements made necessary a change of residence for the missionary, and in 1836 he removed to Barry County, near Prairieville, and continued his work among the Ottawas for the next sixteen years. The Indians became greatly attached to him, and many of them were hopefully converted. In 1852 he retired from active missionary labor, with a constitution greatly impaired, and resided in Kalamazoo till his death, April 27, 1866. A firm friend of all our denominational enterprises, he contributed largely of his earnings for their promotion.

Slaughter, Gov. Gabriel, was born in Virginia in 1767. He was an early settler in Mercer Co., Ky., where he united with Shawnee Run Baptist church, and was prominent in his church, his Association, and all the enterprises of his denomination, as well as in the councils of state. He was elected to the Legislature in 1799, and re-elected in 1800. He served in the State senate from 1801 to 1808, and was during the following four years lieutenant-governor. He held a colonel's commission in the war of 1812–15. In 1816 he was again elected lieutenant-governor, and, on the death of Col. Madison, the governor-elect, became governor of the State, in which capacity he acted four years. At the close of his gubernatorial term he retired to his farm in Mercer County, where he died in 1830.

Slocum (Frances) Mission.—In the year 1780 a little girl about six years old, Frances Slocum, was stolen by the Indians from Wyoming, Pa. Her father and brothers followed as far north as Niagara Falls, but could find no clue to her whereabouts. Sixty years passed away. Washington Ewing, a member of Congress, and a trader among the Indians, stayed one night at the house of one of the Indians, near Peru, Ind. He saw there an elderly white woman. He inquired about her history. She remembered that her first name was Frances, and that she was taken from a place called Wyoming. Within about one year it was established that she was the same Frances Slocum.

She was wealthy, but said she never could again become accustomed to civilized life. She wished to adopt her brother's son. He and his wife came to the settlement, went through the form of adoption, and settled near their aunt. They were Baptists, and began Christian work on behalf of the Indians. Rev. T. C. Townsend assisted them in organizing a Sunday-school. The two sons-in-law of Frances Slocum—Capt. Bruillette and Peter Bundy—were the first to join the church that had been organized. A church house worth $1500 was built. The church grew. Bruillette and Bundy were licensed to preach. A general revival was enjoyed, and another Baptist church was formed. Christian Indians, of their own accord, went as missionaries to their people in Kansas. In 1858 the Indiana Baptist State Convention resolved "that the mission heretofore sustained among the Miami tribe of Indians by the board of the Huntington and Weasaw Associations be now transferred to the board of the State Convention, and that the school, mission-house, land, and all other property belonging to the mission, be henceforth under their patronage."

By removals and deaths the tribe gradually declined, and the mission declined also. In the death of George Slocum, in 1860, the mission sustained a great loss.

Small, Rev. J. S., was born in Guilford, N. H., Aug. 16, 1826. The progress which he had made in his youthful studies is shown by the circumstance that when he was but fifteen years of age he began to teach in the public schools. It was his early ambition to be a lawyer, and with this end in view he began to fit for college, but his health failing he was obliged to give up his plan. His hopeful conversion took place when he was twenty-three years of age. At once his thoughts were turned to the Christian ministry, and he became a student in the Fairfax Institution, Vt., and was graduated in the class of 1858. His ordination took place at Williamstown, July 9, 1837. In 1859 he went to East Wallingford, Vt., where he remained about a year. Wishing to pursue still further his theological studies, he returned to Fairfax, where he remained some time as a resident graduate. He preached in Montgomery, Vt., and Lowell, Mass., in 1861, and was settled, July 15, 1862, at Enosburg, where he remained four years, leaving his pastorate to accept a call to the Fairfax Institution, to act as president after the removal of Dr. Upham. This position he occupied about three years, when, feeling the want of a more thorough intellectual training, he decided to take a full college course of study. He was a graduate of Dartmouth College in the class of 1872, preaching more or less during his four years' residence in Hanover. His pastorates after leaving college were at Bristol and Felchville, Vt. He died very suddenly, after preaching the annual sermon before the Woodstock Association, Vt., Sept. 22, 1880.

Smalley, Rev. Henry, was born in Piscataway, N. J. He was baptized by Rev. Reune Runyon in 1781, at the age of sixteen. He studied at Queen's College, New Brunswick, and at the College of New Jersey, in Princeton, where he graduated in 1786. In 1788 he was licensed; in 1790 he was ordained pastor of the Cohansey Baptist church, N. J., where he exercised an able and successful ministry of forty-nine years, and died Feb. 11, 1839, in his seventy-fourth year. Mr. Smalley was abundant in labor, adding to his stated preaching and catechising, services in neighborhoods beyond the bounds of his own congregation. His judgment was excellent, his success in peacemaking and settling difficulties was prominent; he rightly divided the word of truth, and the fruits of a judicious and long pastorate are abundant.

Smiley, Rev. Thomas, was born in Dauphin Co., Pa., in 1759; baptized in 1792, in Wyoming Co., Pa.; licensed December, 1796, by the Braintrim church; ordained December, 1802, when forty-three years of age; died in 1832 in White Deer, Lycoming Co., Pa., in his seventy-third year. In two things he was quite distinguished,—controversies about land titles in the northern portion of the State between the Pennymites, as they were called, and the Connecticut claims, and in his fearless defense of the cardinal doctrines of the Word of God. No minister held more tenaciously to the doctrines of grace.' In these sentiments he had been reared from childhood, his father being a rigid Presbyterian of the Scotch Seceder branch. In his day the conflict between Arminianism and Calvinism was peculiarly marked and bitter. Elder Smiley, as he was generally called, held to the less popular side of both questions, and while failing to secure applause, he nevertheless won for himself in his advocacy of sovereign grace what is infinitely better, the plaudit of his Lord when called to his rest. His work as a minister was in sowing seed. The harvest came in due time, but others, the writer included, were permitted to gather it. His character was of the purest type, and his constant and earnest exhortations to practical godliness, as well as his appeals to the unconverted, proved him to be far from fatalism, and entirely forbade his relation to such as claim him for saintship in the dogmas of " old-schoolism." His advocacy of sovereign grace in election was pure and thoroughly Biblical.

Smith, Hon. Almerin, died on the 31st of June, 1854, at Savanna, Ill., at the age of seventy-one years. He was a native of Manchester, Vt., and of a patriotic ancestry, his father, Maj. Nathan Smith, having been one of those who accompanied Ethan Allen in his memorable expedition against Ticonderoga. He himself, immediately upon the breaking out of the war of 1812, joined the army, with the commission of lieutenant, and served until the close of the war, chiefly in the northern part of the State of New York. His services were so highly appreciated that he was offered a desirable post in the regular army at the close of the war, which he declined, as he had other aims in life. He had married previous to the breaking out of the war, and upon the conclusion of peace he purchased a farm and made his home in Ticonderoga, N. Y., where most of his life was spent. His fellow-citizens expressed their trust in his capacity and integrity by calling him to various posts of civil service. During thirty years he was successively elected justice of the peace. Various county offices were given him, besides one term of service as a member of the State Legislature. He refused a renomination when tendered him, as a political life was not his choice. About the year 1850 he removed to Illinois, and there died, as mentioned at the beginning of this article. In his earlier life he was skeptical, but when nearly fifty years of age he became convinced of the truth of Christianity, and sought and found a personal participation in its benefits. One who knew him well says of him, " In the army, in the halls of legislation, in the courts of justice, he was faithful, wise, impartial, and capable. Three sons survive him; the eldest being Dr. J. A. Smith, editor of the *Standard;* the others, John L. Smith, Esq., of Omaha, and Prof. E. C. Smith, of Dixon, Ill. One daughter of four is left,—Mrs. Lucy M. Olin, widow of J. R. Olin, Esq., a son of Hon. Henry Olin, of Vermont, and brother of Dr. Stephen Olin, so well known as president of Wesleyan University. The youngest daughter, wife of Rev. W. W. Harsha, D.D., of Jacksonville, Ill., died a few years since ; another, wife of Dr. A. Kendrick, of Waukesha, Wis., died some years before; while the second daughter has slept during more than a generation in the soil of Vermont.

Smith, Dester P., D.D., was born in Tully, N. Y., Dec. 16, 1810; entered Madison University, N. Y., in 1831, and remained some time in the theological department after graduation. He had consecrated himself to the foreign mission work, but enfeebled health prevented him entering upon this service. For a year and a half he was pastor of the Baptist church of Manchester, Vt. He was also pastor in Strykersville, N. Y., where he baptized 200. In 1845 he came to Iowa City, Iowa, and was pastor of the church there until 1851, during which time a good meeting-house was erected and the church gained a commanding position. From 1851 to 1859 he was the general agent for Sunday-schools for the State. From 1858 to

1861 he served as financial agent of the Iowa Baptist State Convention, and for a number of years he was the secretary of the Iowa Baptist Union for Ministerial Education He still resides in Iowa City, where for thirty-five years he and his honored wife have commanded the respect of that community and exercised a saving influence over many hearts. Though not now engaged in any consecutive labors, he is doing good service for Christ and the Baptist cause in Iowa. Conciliatory in spirit, earnest in purpose, and wise in counsel, his usefulness continues with declining years, and makes his presence an impulse and power in the deliberations and plans of his brethren in the State.

Smith, Prof. D. Townsend, was born on Edisto Island, near Charleston, S. C., Aug. 9, 1842. He left the Junior class in the South Carolina College to join the army near the commencement of the late war, and served as a private until its close. His early conversion is but one of the many illustrations of the truth of Solomon's adage, "Train up a child in the way he should go, and when he is old he will not depart from it."

Soon after the war he resumed his studies in Furman University. On the death of Prof. Edwards in 1867 he took the lower classes in Latin and Greek. He was retained after his graduation the same year as Professor of Languages, and has occupied that position ever since.

Smith, Eli B., D.D., was born in Shoreham, Vt., April 16, 1803. While preparing for college he was hopefully converted at the age of fourteen, and united with the church Feb. 3, 1817. He graduated at Middlebury College in 1823; spent two years at Andover in theological study; and, as a member of the first class at Newton, graduated from that institution in 1826, the other member of the class being Rev. John E. Weston. In September, at the meeting of the Boston Baptist Association held in South Reading, he was ordained as an evangelist, and entered at once upon his duties as pastor of the Baptist church in Buffalo, N. Y. At this time it was a small church, numbering but a little over thirty members, and had no house of worship. Under his energetic efforts a meeting-house was erected, and dedicated in the summer of 1828. Dr. Smith continued with the church in Buffalo until June, 1829, when he resigned and accepted a call to Poultney, Vt. He had the satisfaction of seeing his labors blessed in that place, and large numbers were converted under his ministry. Dr. Smith was called away from this happy and successful pastorate to take charge of the New Hampton Academy, upon the resignation of its principal, Rev. B. F. Farnsworth. He entered upon the duties of his office in May, 1834, and found himself associated with teachers who stood in the first rank of their profession, among whom were Miss Martha Hazeltine, for twelve years the lady principal of the institution, and Miss Sarah Sleeper, afterwards the wife of Rev. Dr. Jones, of Siani, and, after his decease, the wife of Rev. S. J. Smith. The special department which came under the supervision of Dr. Smith was that of theology, and in conducting that department he performed a service for the churches the value of which cannot be easily estimated.

President Smith, for twenty years, gave himself with the utmost enthusiasm to the great work to which he had been called. The discouragements were many, owing to the want of pecuniary endowment, but they were met with a heroic spirit of sacrifice for the cause of education. In the fall of 1853 the institution was removed to Fairfax, Vt., and it seemed as if its future prosperity was guaranteed at once by the change of location. Unexpected difficulties arose, and new burdens came upon its presiding officer. Domestic sorrows also added to the weight of his cares. He resigned his office as president of the New Hampton Institution in October, 1860. He died Jan. 5, 1861, at Colchester, Vt. In summing up the traits of character which were most conspicuous in Dr. Smith, his associate in office, the Rev. Dr. James Upham, selects the following as deserving of special notice: "his fixedness of purpose, his self-control, his wisdom in council, his administrative talent, and his practicalness of mind." The influence he exerted directly and indirectly on the Baptist churches in Vermont and New Hampshire was very great. He left the mark of his own sterling mind upon a multitude of others, who, in the ministry and occupying important posts in Church and State, have served faithfully their God and the generation.

Smith, Rev. Eliphalet, was the minister of a Presbyterian church in Deerfield, N. H., in 1770. At that time he was a young man, distinguished for talents, piety, and success. While preaching on the words, "If ye love me keep my commandments" (John xiv. 15), the truth about baptism flashed into his mind so clearly that he felt compelled to proclaim it to his people; and President Manning says that "he convinced the church of which he was pastor that believer's baptism, by immersion, *only* is a divine institution." And he further states that "they sent a messenger to him to come and administer the ordinance to both minister and people, the most of whom expected immediately to submit thereto." Dr. Manning, on account of the distance, requested Dr. Hezekiah Smith, of Haverhill, Mass., to take his place. On Thursday, June 14, 1770, Dr. Smith baptized the pastor and a portion of his people; on the same day a church was formed, and two days later the ex-Presbyterian minister baptized seven persons into the fellowship of the Baptist church, of which he had been elected the pastor. Eliphalet Smith had the strongest reasons for retaining his old faith, and nothing but the force of truth can account for a change so remarkable. In other denominations the Lord has trained throngs of Baptist ministers and multitudes of Baptists.

Smith, Rev. Francis, was born in what is now Wakefield, but was formerly South Reading, Mass., July 12, 1812. He graduated at Brown University in the class of 1837, and at Newton in the class of 1840. He was ordained as the pastor of the Fourth Baptist church in Providence, R. I. For thirteen years he continued the minister of the church. Happy in his residence in Providence he did not remove from the city, but, while living here, supplied, one after another, several small religious societies, and for about two years the church in Rutland, Vt. For three years he was the district secretary for New England of the American Baptist Publication Society. The closing part of his life was spent in the most acceptable missionary labors in and about Providence. He died Jan. 29, 1872.

Smith, Maj.-Gen. Green Clay, was born at Richmond, Ky., July 2, 1832. After attending a preparatory school at Danville, he entered Transylvania University, graduating in 1850. He studied in the office of his father, Hon. John Speed Smith, and graduated in a law-school at Lexington, in 1853. After a partnership of several years with his father, which terminated in 1858, he commenced business in Covington. In 1860 he was elected to the Kentucky Legislature. In 1861 he entered the army as a private, and during the civil war attained the rank of major-general. In 1863 he was elected to Congress, and served two terms. At the close of his second term he was appointed governor of Montana, in which position he acted until the fall of 1868, when he resigned for the purpose of entering the gospel ministry. He united with a Baptist church, of which his mother (a daughter of Gen. Green Clay and sister of Hon. Cassius M. Clay) was a member. He was licensed to preach, and ordained in 1869. He was called to the Baptist church in Frankfort, and served as pastor several years, when he resigned, and engaged in the more laborious work of an evangelist. He afterwards took charge of the Second church in Frankfort, to which he now ministers. He was elected moderator of the General Association of Baptists in Kentucky in 1879, and was re-elected in 1880. He is a chaste and pleasing orator, has been very successful in his holy calling, and is much beloved by his brethren.

Smith, Hezekiah, D.D.—Fortunately for the writer of this sketch of Dr. Smith, the materials for doing it are abundant in the interesting memorials furnished by Dr. S. F. Smith for Dr. Sprague's "Annals," and in the centennial discourse of the late Dr. Arthur S. Train, of Haverhill.

The birthplace of Hezekiah Smith was Long Island, N. Y. He was born April 21, 1737. His college life was spent in Princeton, N. J., where he graduated in 1762, under the presidency of that prince of pulpit orators, Rev. Samuel Davies. He was ordained at Charleston, S. C., but assumed no pastoral charge at the South, although he preached constantly as opportunity presented. In 1764 he came to New England, and preached for some time in the west parish of the town of Haverhill, Mass., to a Congregational church, where his labors were greatly appreciated and much blessed. As, however, he was a most conscientious Baptist, it could not be expected that he could long sustain such a relation as this. The circumstance which led him to make Haverhill the scene of what proved to be a most successful ministry is thus related by Dr. S. F. Smith :

"Mr. Smith now resolved to return to New Jersey, where several of his relatives resided. The day was fixed for his departure from the scene of his labors and successes. In the morning several young persons came to visit him, deeply affected by the prospect of losing their loved and revered teacher, by whose instrumentality they had been brought to believe on the Lord Jesus Christ. They exhibited their ardent affection towards him, and expressed the wish that he would baptize them. Still they found him fixed in his determination. Notwithstanding, they ventured to utter their conviction that he would soon return and be their minister. He replied, 'If I return, your prayers will bring me back.' The same day he proceeded to Boston, and the day following commenced his journey to Providence. But after he had advanced eighteen or twenty miles, the words were impressed with unusual weight on his mind, 'Strengthen ye the weak hands, and confirm the feeble knees. Say to them that are of a fearful heart, Be strong, fear not : behold, your God will come with vengeance, even God with a recompense; he will come and save you.' Stopping his horse, he mused awhile on the occurrence. He soon proceeded, but was shortly after arrested again by the same passage. Yielding to the impulse, he turned his horse, and rode back to Boston. Here he found two persons, sent by his friends in Haverhill to solicit his return. He readily accepted their invitation, and went back the next day to Haverhill, where he was received with many expressions of affection and gratitude."

The church in Haverhill was organized May 9, 1765, and its pastor publicly recognized Nov. 12, 1766, and he held that position for forty years. Faithful to the trusts that were committed to his hands, he felt it to be his duty no less than his privilege to preach the gospel in the regions beyond the field of his own special cultivation. Accordingly, acting under the direction and by the advice of his church, he would start out, accompanied by one or two of his members, to make evangelizing tours through destitute sections of New Hampshire and the district of Maine. Returning from these towns, he would call the church together, as the apostles did in primitive times, and rehearse the wonderful things which God had wrought by their hands. Persons holding Baptist views, but living too far away from any church of their own faith and order, would be brought into vital relations with the Haverhill church. In the course of time the population would increase in the places where these persons lived, and there would be encouragement to form Baptist churches out of these scattered materials. "Thirteen churches" we are told were thus established by the action of the Haverhill church and the evangelizing labors of its ministers and members.

In connection with such friends of religious freedom as Backus, President Manning, his friend and college classmate, and others of kindred spirit, he labored incessantly to have the Baptists delivered from the oppression which they suffered from the standing order. He took, moreover, the deepest interest in the prosperity of the new college which had been established in Rhode Island, and at one time was absent nearly nine months collecting funds for it. When the war of the Revolution broke out, he was appointed chaplain in the American army. Here he was brought into terms of intimate relations with Gen. Washington, and enjoyed the confidence and friendship of that great and good man. As soon as he could be released from his duties in the army he gladly returned to his beloved church, and took up his ministerial and pastoral work where he had laid it down. Preaching in the sacred desk, and from house to house, literally "in season and out of season," making his evangelical tours through different sections of New England; his coming was everywhere hailed with delight, now in the "backwoods" of Maine, now among the grand old hills of New Hampshire, and now attending the meetings of the corporation of Brown University in Rhode Island; such is a picture of the life of one of the busiest ministers of his times. "He often expressed the wish," says Dr. S. F. Smith, "that he might not outlive his usefulness, and his desire was graciously fulfilled. He preached for the last time, among his people, on the Sabbath, from John xii. 24: 'Except a corn of wheat fall into the ground and die, it abideth alone; but if it die, it bringeth forth much fruit.' The sermon was unusually impressive, and a revival of religion followed, to which it seemed introductory. On the Thursday succeeding he was seized with paralysis, and spoke no more. His life-work was finished and its record complete. He lay a week in this condition, and died Jan. 22, 1805, in the sixty-eighth year of his age and the forty-second of his ministry."

It is not difficult to assign the place which Hezekiah Smith will always be regarded as having held among the Baptist fathers of New England. It is safe to say that no man did more than he to give character to the denomination which had to fight every step of its way in securing for itself a foothold, and at last a permanent home in the Eastern States. There was no good cause in which he did not take an interest. He lived a most useful life. Like one of kindred spirit who came after him,—Dr. Baldwin, —the summons to depart and be with Christ came suddenly, but found him prepared for it. Devout and loving hands laid him away in his grave, with many of his own parishioners sleeping by his side, and his own dust mingling with that of the friends of his youth and the co-workers of his riper years.

Smith, Rev. James, widely known as the author of the "Daily Remembrancer" and other evangelical works of large circulation, was born Nov. 19, 1802. When he was eighteen years of age he was baptized and admitted into the Baptist church of his native place,—Brentford, England. Manifesting gifts of utterance, he was encouraged to preach; but he was slow to yield to the solicitations of his pastor and the brethren. In 1829 he was invited to become pastor of a congregation in Cheltenham, to which he had preached as a probationer for several months. Soon after his settlement in Cheltenham he was convinced of the duty of pointedly addressing the unconverted, to which many of his friends vehemently objected. He therefore withdrew from the edifice where he had hitherto ministered and organized a new church in 1835. His ministry was remarkably successful until 1841, when he removed to the New Park Street church, London, now the Metropolitan Tabernacle. His London ministry was not unsuccessful, but he never felt the comfort and encouragement he had enjoyed in his old field. Failing health at length led him to leave London. He preached at Byrom Street, Liverpool, in 1850 for a short time, and subsequently at Shrewsbury. At length, in 1852, he returned to Cheltenham. Here old friends rallied around him, many new friends were raised up, and the remainder of his life till the period of his final illness was spent in building up a large and important church, and in every good word and work. A new edifice, called Cambray chapel, was built and opened in 1855. In 1861 he was attacked by paralysis, and, although he partially recovered, and his life was prolonged, his public labors were ended. He died Dec. 14, 1862. Only great energy of character and earnestness of purpose could have sustained him amidst such multifarious exertions, and doubtless his constitution, though naturally vigorous, succumbed to a pressure too great for its strength. He had the pen of a ready writer. No fewer than forty distinct productions were given to the press, and he was a constant and always acceptable contributor to several religious periodicals. His writings are characterized by great plainness of diction, remarkable felicity of Scripture quotation and illustration, and an exuberant richness of Christian experience. Cultivated persons of all ranks as well as unlettered Christians bought James Smith's little books. They had an immense sale; but as he wrote mainly with a view, as he said, to the poor of the Lord's flock, his books were published at a very cheap rate, and the author's profits were not large. By his preaching and his pen he turned many to righteousness, and few ministers of any denomination, who were contemporary with him, were worthier to be considered a master in Israel.

Smith, Rev. James F., was born in Jessamine Co., Ky., in 1811; made a profession of religion when twenty-four years of age, and was baptized by Rev. Jeremiah Taylor, of Marion Co., Mo., who was the first pastor of the Bethel Baptist church.

Brother Smith was ordained in 1843. He has helped to organize many churches, and has labored a great deal in revival meetings. Over 1200 persons have been baptized by him upon a profession of faith, and as many more have been converted in meetings he has held who were baptized by other pastors. He has for nearly forty years been a standard-bearer of the Cross in North Missouri, where he is now an active and highly esteemed Christian minister.

Smith, James Wheaton, D.D., was born at Providence, R. I., June 26, 1823. His father, Hon. Noah Smith, served the State in both branches of the Legislature, was a member of the governor's council, secretary of state in Maine, and candidate for governor, and at the time of his death, in 1867, was chief legislative clerk in the United States Senate. His mother's maiden name was Hannah D. Wheaton, a near relative of Mr. Henry Wheaton, author of "International Law" and "History of the Northmen."

His parents removed to Calais, Me., when he was ten years of age. He was baptized in his twelfth year by Rev. James Huckins, and united with the Calais church, then recently formed, of which his father was a deacon and his mother a devoted member. He was one of sixty children baptized about the same time into the fellowship of that church. Entered Brown University in 1844, and graduated in 1848, receiving the "Jackson premium" for the best essay on Moral Philosophy; graduated from Newton Theological Institution in 1851. While yet a student at Newton was ordained pastor of the Worthen Street church, Lowell, Mass. In 1853 he became pastor of the Spruce Street church, Philadelphia, and has remained in con-

JAMES WHEATON SMITH, D.D.

tinuous pastoral relations with that people to the present time. In 1870, under his efficient leadership, a colony went out from the Spruce Street church to a growing and important centre of population and organized the Beth Eden church, whose beautiful sanctuary at the corner of Broad and Spruce Streets, one of the most attractive church buildings in the city, was recently burned down. In this new field of labor he continued in pastoral service until 1880, when his impaired health induced him to tender his resignation; whereupon the church immediately elected him "Pastor Emeritus." He continues in their fellowship, and his increasing strength gives promise of many years of useful labor. He received the degree of D.D. in 1862 from the university at Lewisburg.

Dr. Smith has been long and prominently identified with the various educational and missionary societies of the denomination, and has frequently been called upon to aid in the management of important secular and religious trusts. During what may be called the forcing period in Philadelphia no man has exerted a wider influence. It was often his to set the key-note of denominational thought and feeling, and shape some of the grandest enterprises in the State. He is a man of commanding presence, and is possessed of rare pulpit talents. His manners are easy and graceful, and his diction fluent and elegant. He preaches without notes, and develops his subject with logical clearness and magnetic power. He is an adept in polemics, and, although his discourses are marked by a fullness of catholicity, he is nevertheless quick, forceful, and tender in his defense of "the faith once delivered to the saints." He has been a frequent contributor to denominational literature, and the "Life of John P. Crozer," published in 1868, is a beautiful product of his graphic pen.

Smith, Judge J. B., an eloquent preacher and distinguished jurist at Clinton, La., believed to have been a native of Virginia, came to Louisiana in 1832 as a missionary of the American Baptist Home Missionary Society, and labored in the Red River region; in 1836 he aided in the constitution of the church at Clinton, La. He located here and engaged successfully in the practice of the law, preaching in the surrounding country; was district judge for one or more terms; fell a victim to yellow fever in 1868.

Smith, J. Byington, D.D., was born in Scroon, N. Y., May 1, 1830. He was baptized by Rev. John Smitzer into the fellowship of the Baptist church of Elbridge, N. Y., in 1846. He was graduated from the University and the Theological Seminary of Rochester. He labored awhile in Dunkirk, where he was ordained to the work of the ministry in 1854. In 1855 he settled at Fayetteville, N. Y., where he remained five years, during which many additions were made to the church by baptism.

In 1860 he settled with the Farmerville Baptist church, where his pastorate continued six years, during which a fine house of worship was built. From 1866 to 1869 he filled the office of chaplain of the prison at Sing Sing, on the Hudson. The other officers in charge said he was the most successful chaplain ever chosen to fill that place.

In 1869 he accepted the pastorate of the Baptist church of Geneva, N. Y., which continued seven years. He then spent a year traveling in Europe, and on his return settled as pastor of the church of Peekskill, N. Y. While chaplain in Sing Sing he published the "Prison Hymn Book," a selection well adapted to prisoners, which is still in use in some of the prisons. He is also the author of "Sayings and Doings of Children," published by U. D. Ward, and "Sunday-School Concert Exercises." Several of his sermons and public addresses have also been published.

Smith, Hon. John, the first pastor of the First Baptist church in Ohio, organized at Columbia, near Cincinnati, in 1790. Mr. Smith was a man of fine natural abilities and most pleasing address, and became so popular in the new State that he was elected a United States Senator during the administration of Jefferson, and spent the rest of his life in political and public affairs.

Smith, John Lawrence, M.D., LL.D., one of the most distinguished scientists in the United States, and equally distinguished in Europe, was born near Charleston, S. C., Dec. 16, 1818. He

JOHN LAWRENCE SMITH, M.D., LL.D.

was educated in Charleston College and in the University of Virginia. At first he selected civil engineering for his profession. After devoting two years to the study of its various branches, including geology and mining, he was employed as assistant engineer on the Charleston and Cincinnati Railroad. This pursuit proving uncongenial, he commenced the study of medicine, and graduated in the medical school of the University of South Carolina, and then pursued his education for three years in France and Germany. Upon returning to the United States, in 1844, he commenced the practice of medicine at Charleston, and shortly afterwards received the appointment of assayer of bullion for South Carolina. At the request of the sultan, he was selected by the President of the United States, in 1846, to instruct Turkish agriculturists in the methods of cultivating cotton. On his arrival in Turkey he was appointed mining engineer to the Turkish government, and occupied the position four years, made extensive mineralogical explorations, and published a report "On the Thermal Waters of Asia Minor" in 1849. On his return from Turkey he was instrumental in the discovery of deposits of emery and corundum in the United States. He invented, in 1851, the inverted microscope, and in that year was elected Professor of Chemistry in the University of

Virginia. He was married to the daughter of Hon. James Guthrie, of Louisville, Ky., and settled in that city about 1850, and was appointed to the chair of Chemistry in the medical department of the University of Louisville. He held this position several years, and then resigned to take charge of the scientific department of the Louisville Gas-Works, which position he still retains. About 1855 he made a profession of religion, and united with the Walnut Street Baptist church in Louisville, of which he has since been a pious, faithful, and useful member. Adding his own fortune to that of his most excellent Christian wife, he possesses abundant means for indulging his fondness for study, investigation, and scientific labor. He has made many discoveries and inventions. His original researches are embraced in upwards of seventy papers, a list of which has been published by the Royal Society of England. He is a member of the American National Academy of Sciences, etc., membre correspondant de l'Institut de France (Académie des Sciences), etc., member of the Chemical Society of Berlin, of the Chemical Society of Paris, of the Chemical Society of London, of the Société d'Encouragement pour l'Industrie Nationale, of the Imperial Mineralogical Society of St. Petersburg, corresponding member of the Boston Society of Natural History, of the American Academy of Arts and Sciences, of the American Philosophical Society, American Bureau of Mines, the Société des Sciences et des Arts de Hainaut, etc., Chevalier de la Legion d'Honneur, member of the Order of Nichan Iftahar of Turkey, member of the Order of Mijiddeh of Turkey, Chevalier of the Imperial Order of St. Stanislaus of Russia.

Smith, Rev. Joseph, was born in Hampstead, N. H., Jan. 31, 1808. He worked on his father's farm until he reached the age of nineteen. Feeling it to be his duty to prepare for the Christian ministry, he commenced his studies at the New Hampton Academy, and then repaired to the Newton Theological Institution with the purpose of completing them there. Impressed, however, with the conviction that it would be wise to extend his course of study, he went through Brown University, graduating in 1837. On leaving college he was ordained pastor of the church in Woonsocket, R. I., where he remained until 1841, when he removed to Newport, R. I., where he was the pastor of the First Baptist church for nine years. It was a season of prosperity with the church. He resigned his pastorate in 1850, and after two years he became pastor of the church in Grafton, Mass., and remained such for five years. After a brief connection with the "Female Collegiate Institute," in Worcester, he took charge, in 1852, of the church in North Oxford, Mass., where he remained until his death, which occurred suddenly, April 26, 1866.

Smith, Rev. Josiah Torrey, was born at Williamstown, Mass., Aug. 4, 1815. He made a profession of faith at the early age of fourteen, being baptized in December, 1829. He fitted for college at Cummington and Williamstown, and graduated at Williams College in the class of 1842. His theological studies were pursued at Newton, and he was ordained at Lanesborough, Mass., in 1845. Mr. Smith has served the following Baptist churches: Lanesborough, Sandisfield, and Hinsdale, in Massachusetts; Bristol, in Connecticut; Amherst, Mass., Woodstock, Conn., and Warwick, R. I. Besides performing his ministerial and pastoral work, he has found time for the preparation of articles for some of our leading quarterlies, and for the daily secular and weekly religious press. He has written for the *Biblical Repository*, the *Christian Review*, the *Congregational Review*, the *Baptist Quarterly*, and the *Baptist Missionary Magazine*. He has also contributed to the *Watchman*, the *Christian Era*, the *Christian Secretary*, and the New York *Examiner*. He has published the following treatises on subjects connected with Baptist sentiments: "Review of Peters on Baptism," "The Covenant of Circumcision, Considered in its Relation to Christian Baptism," "New Testament and Historical Arguments for Infant Baptism Considered." One or two other pamphlets, the production of his pen, have been published. The present residence of Mr. Smith is Warwick, R. I.

Smith, Justin A., D.D., was born on the 29th of December, 1819, at Ticonderoga, N. Y. His father, Almerin Smith, was a man of influence and ability, and encouraged the literary tastes early developed in his son. At the age of fifteen he studied one year at New Hampton Literary and Theological Institute. Soon after his return home he was converted, and united with the Baptist church in Ticonderoga. After three years' suspension of study, save such as could be carried on privately, and a few months of study in North Granville Academy, he entered Union College, Schenectady, N. Y., graduating in 1843, Dr. Alonzo Potter being then acting president, although Dr. Nott, so famous in his time, was still alive, and by no means past service. After graduation he served one year as principal of Union Academy, at Bennington, Vt. His thoughts, however, had been directed towards the ministry, and at the solicitation of the people he preached a few times for them. The church of North Bennington having urgently called him to the pastorate, he at once relinquished his project of teaching, and assumed the pastoral care of the church. Here he remained five years. From it he was called to the pastorate of the First Baptist church of Rochester, N. Y., where he labored for five more years. In 1853, having resigned his charge at Rochester, he removed to Chicago, Ill., and became associated with Rev. Leroy Church in the editorship of the *Christian Times*. Here he found the sphere of labor to which his tastes and

JUSTIN A. SMITH, D.D.

talents most adapted him, and in the management of this paper he has continued up to the present time. Dr. Smith, after twenty-eight years of editorship, still maintains the principal editorial control of the paper, now called the *Standard*, and with no less vigor and ability than at his first connection with it.

Besides his journalistic labors during this period, he has engaged extensively and influentially in church work. It has been his privilege to lead in the organization of three Baptist churches of the city which have had creditable histories: the North Baptist church, in 1857, the Indiana Avenue, in 1863, of which he was pastor five years, and the University Place church, which he served for some months, leaving it for an extended European tour for travel and study, and also in part for attendance at the Vatican Council at Rome in 1869.

Not a few excellent books have come from Dr. Smith's pen, the best known being the "Memoir of Nathaniel Colver," the "Shetland Apostle," the "Spirit in the Word," and "Patmos; or, the Kingdom and the Patience." One or two other works are now in process of preparation. He has devoted no little time and energy to the educational interests of the denomination, having been connected as a trustee with the University of Chicago and the Theological Seminary from their foundation. He is at present giving two courses of lectures each year in the seminary, and is thus enabled to meet personally and to strongly influence many of the young men who assume the care of churches. His writings are in a marked manner chaste and elegant in diction, comprehensive in thought, while the spirit is that of an humble disciple of the Master.

Smith, Rev. Lewis, was born in Chester Co., Pa., July 20, 1820. His father was Rev. Samuel Smith, a Baptist pastor. When twenty years old he was converted, and baptized by Rev. A. D. Gillette; studied at Hamilton; became pastor of the church in Hatborough, Pa.; spent several years as a missionary in New Mexico; returned in 1855, and settled with the First church of Trenton. In 1858 he became pastor of the large and prosperous church at Hightstown. In 1864 his failing health warned him to seek a change. While on a journey in Minnesota he departed to his rest on Aug. 24, 1864. He was an eloquent and powerful preacher. A number of his sermons have been published in a memorial volume. His brotherly affection, outspoken patriotism, glowing devotion to the missionary cause, and deep personal piety were well known to all who were acquainted with him.

Smith, Rev. Lucius, the pastor of the Baptist church in Verona, Wis., is a native of Westmoreland, Oneida Co., N. Y., where he was born in 1830. He was educated at Phillips Academy, Exeter, N. H., and ordained to the work of the Christian ministry at Bristol, Wis., in 1866. In April, 1868, he was called to the pastorate of the Baptist church in Stoughton, Wis., where he remained five years, developing fine abilities as a preacher and pastor. In 1873 he was called to the vacant pastorate at Verona, Wis., and his second pastorate still continues. He is an earnest, natural, simple, and strong preacher of the gospel.

Smith, Lucius E., D.D., was born in Williamstown, Mass., Jan. 29, 1822, and graduated at Williams College in the class of 1843. He read law in the office of Hon. D. N. Dewey, of Williamstown, and was admitted to the bar in 1845. He was associate editor of the Hartford *Daily Courant* for a time, and editor of the *Free-Soil Advocate* in 1848. In 1849 he was associated with Hon. Henry Wilson in editing the Boston *Republican*. During the years 1849–1854 he was assistant in the secretary's department of the American Baptist Missionary Union. The next three years he spent at Newton, graduating with the class of 1857, and was ordained pastor of the Baptist church in Groton, Mass., in 1858, continuing in office until 1865, when he was appointed Professor of Rhetoric and Pastoral Theology in the University of Lewisburg, Pa., which position he held until 1868. During one year of this time he was the editor of the *Bap-*

tist Quarterly. In 1868 he entered upon his duties as literary editor of the *Examiner and Chronicle*, and held that office until 1876, when he was called to the chair of editor of the *Watchman*, which place he now occupies.

Dr. Smith's editorial calling seems to be the one for which he has special and most superior qualifications. His experience in this line goes back to his student days, when for a year he was editor of the *Williams Miscellany*, a college magazine. President Hopkins said at the expiration of that year's work, "I do not believe you are done with editing. I am inclined to think it is your vocation." The event has justified the correctness of his confident assertions. Besides articles contributed to reviews, magazines, and various newspapers, Dr. Smith published, in 1852, "Heroes and Martyrs of the Missionary Enterprise, with an Historical Review of Earlier Missions." The degree of D.D. was conferred upon him in 1869 by Williams College. Dr. Smith is one of the ablest and best men in the denomination.

Smith, Martin Henry, A.M., present principal of the Connecticut Literary Institution, eldest son of Henry and Lydia Smith, was born in Suffield, Conn., Aug. 5, 1833; converted at the age of sixteen; baptized by Dr. Dwight Ives into the fellowship of the Second Baptist church in Suffield; prepared for college at the Connecticut Literary Institution; entered Williams College in 1853, and graduated in 1857; for two subsequent years taught mathematics in Connecticut Literary Institution; in 1859 was elected principal of Maysville Literary Institute, at Maysville, Ky., a high school chartered with collegiate privileges, and remained until June, 1880, when he was elected principal of the Connecticut Literary Institution; was prominently identified with the Baptists of Kentucky; has contributed valuable articles to denominational and educational journals.

Smith, Judge Perrin M., was born in Middlebury, N. Y., in 1811. At the Wyoming Academy, at the age of nineteen, he was converted, and joined the Baptist Church; studied law, and entered upon its practice in Leroy; came to Centreville, Mich., in 1849. He was the chief supporter of the church in that place, and a brotherly helper in all the churches. As a trustee of Kalamazoo College, he was earnest and judicious, expecting great things from it, and attempting great things for it. Added to the contributions of his life were large bequests for the college in his will, which, unhappily, failed of realizing his designs through disastrous litigations. He was honest and manly in his profession, and incorruptible upon the bench, from which death suddenly took him in 1866.

Smith, Robert, the Martyr, was in the employment of Sir Thomas Smith, provost of Eton College in 1555. Then he came to the Windsor College, where he had a clerkship of ten pounds a year. He was tall and slender in stature, very active in his labors, and invested with great powers of mind. The ferocious Bonner, bloody Mary's principal inquisitor in murdering the saints of Jesus, met in him an intellectual giant, who could expose his sophistries in a moment and defy his rage. When he found Christ precious to his soul he was filled with a glowing enthusiasm and a fearless courage which made him despise danger and death. He was deprived of his clerkship by Mary's visitors, and brought to Newgate by command of the council.

He was led in due time before Bonner, and we give a few of the questions and answers of his examination:

BONNER.—"How long is it since you confessed to any priest?"

SMITH.—"Never since I had years of discretion. For I never saw it needful, neither was I commanded of God to show my faults to any of that sinful number whom you call priests."

BONNER.—"How long is it since you received the sacrament of the altar?"

SMITH.—"I never received the same since I had years of discretion, nor ever will by God's grace; neither do I esteem the same in any point, because it hath not God's ordinance, neither in name, nor in other usage, but rather is set up to mock God."

BONNER.—"You must be burned."

SMITH.—"You shall do no more to me than you have done to better men than either of us. But think not thereby to quench the spirit of God, or make your case good; for your sore is too well seen to be healed so privily with blood. For even the very children have all your deeds in derision; so that although you patch up one place with authority, yet shall it break out in forty to your shame."

BONNER.—"I believe, I tell thee, that if they (infants) die before they be baptized, they be damned."

SMITH.—"Ye shall never be saved by that belief. But I pray you, my lord, show me, are we saved by water or by Christ?"

BONNER.—"By both."

SMITH.—"Then the water died for our sins; and so must ye say that the water hath life, and it being our servant and created for us, is our Saviour. This, my lord, is a good doctrine, is it not?" (Acts and Monuments, vii. pp. 348, 352. London, 1838.)

The protracted examination of this great man shows a marvelous acuteness of mind and lofty heroism in danger. He was given to the flames at Uxbridge, and out of their midst he discoursed to the spectators. *When black with smoke and almost roasted, drawn into a shapeless mass, and regarded as dead, he suddenly rose up before the people, lifting the stumps of his arms, and clapping the same together,* he told them of his triumphant joys, and then, bending down over the fire, his spirit soared away to the everlasting glories of heaven.

Smith, Samuel Francis, D.D., was born in Boston, Oct. 21, 1808. He was fitted for college in

SAMUEL FRANCIS SMITH, D.D.

the Boston Latin School, and graduated at Harvard College in the class of 1829. Among his classmates were Judge G. T. Bigelow, Dr. James Freeman Clarke, Judge B. R. Curtis, Oliver Wendell Holmes, M.D., Prof. Benjamin Pierce, and Dr. Chandler Robbins. Immediately on graduating he went to the Andover Theological Seminary, and completed his course of study there in 1832. For the next year and a half he was the editor of the *Baptist Missionary Magazine.* He was ordained pastor of the Baptist church in Waterville, Me., in February, 1832, and elected at the same time Professor of Modern Languages in Waterville College. He remained in Waterville eight years, and then removed to Newton Centre, Mass., where he was pastor of the Baptist church twelve years and a half. During this period he was the editor of the *Christian Review* from the commencement of the seventh volume to the close of the thirteenth, writing for it about sixty articles, making 1380 pages. In addition to all this, he prepared nearly all the literary notices which were published while he was editor. He has been editor of the publications of the American Baptist Missionary Union for about seventeen years.

Dr. Smith was the author of the national hymn "My Country, 'tis of Thee," and of the missionary hymn "The Morning Light is Breaking," and of many other familiar hymns. In connection with Rev. Dr. Baron Stow, he compiled the "Psalmist," which for many years was a standard hymn-book in the denomination throughout the country. He has also published "Lyric Gems" and "Life of the Rev. Joseph Grafton." Dr. Smith continues to reside in Newton Centre, supplying a neighboring church, and occupied with such literary work as he finds congenial with his tastes.

Smith, Prof. S. K., D.D., was born in Litchfield, Me., Oct. 17, 1817. He became a Christian early in life, and made a profession of religion in his twentieth year. His studies preparatory to college were pursued at the Monmouth and Waterville Academies. He was a graduate of Waterville College in the class of 1845. Soon after his graduation he took charge of Townsend Academy, Vt., where he remained until he was appointed tutor of Waterville College, in 1846. He spent one year at the Newton Theological Institution, and then became editor of *Zion's Advocate.* He occupied this position two years, at the end of which he was chosen Professor of Rhetoric in Waterville College. In 1872 he was ordained as a minister of the gospel, and the same year received from Colby University the degree of D.D. Dr. Smith is still connected with Colby University in the chair to which he was called in 1850.

Smith, Rev. Thomas, one of the most brilliant, popular, and consecrated young preachers that Kentucky has ever produced, was born in Henry County, of that State, in June, 1827. His father was a Baptist, and a man of great wealth. In 1845, while studying law at Georgetown College, he professed religion, and joined the Baptist Church. He graduated in 1846, and was licensed to preach. He spent three years in Princeton Theological Seminary. On his return to Henry County he commenced holding meetings in the churches around him. He labored with consuming zeal and great power, and his ministrations were blessed in the conversion of hundreds. He went to Louisville, united two small churches, formed Walnut Street Baptist church, and became its first pastor. After a few months of labor with his new charge his health failed, never to be restored. He died in Florida, March 8, 1851

Smith, Gov. Wm. E., was born in Scotland in 1824. His parents were Alexander and Sarah Grant Smith; both are dead. He came with them to America when a boy, and spent his youth in New York and Michigan. He was married to Mary Booth in 1849, and soon afterwards removed to Wisconsin. He settled at Fox Lake, Dodge Co., and engaged in business. Like many Western men of activity of body and mind, Mr. Smith took practical hold of political matters as soon as he could vote. In 1851 he was elected a member of

GOV. WM. E. SMITH.

the Legislature and re-elected in 1871, when he was chosen Speaker of the house. In 1858-59 he was State senator from his district, and he occupied the same position in 1864-65. He was elected State treasurer in 1866, and held the office for four consecutive years. In 1858 he was appointed by the governor of the State a member of the board of regents of normal schools, which position he held until 1876. In 1874 he was appointed a director of the State prison, and retained this position until 1878. Mr. Smith was chosen governor of Wisconsin in 1877, and entered upon the duties of his office in January, 1878. He was re-elected in 1879, receiving the largest majority ever given to a governor in Wisconsin. In addition to these public trusts, Gov. Smith has often been chosen to county and municipal offices, and to the position of director in banks, insurance companies, and institutions of learning. In his important and responsible office his conduct is visible to all men, and it is without reproach. His intimate friends, and indeed the whole people of the State, fully appreciate the rare talents which he so ably exercises in his administration. Gov. Smith has through his many years of public service not only maintained but increased his reputation as a wise and just legislator, and faithful and conscientious executive officer. He has shown in all his public duties courage, integrity, justice, and a steady and untiring industry. Immediately upon his settlement at Beaver Dam he united with the Baptist church, having been previously converted and baptized. Of this church he was an active and useful member until his removal to Milwaukee in 1871. Gov. Smith is well known throughout the State as an exemplary and laborious Christian, a practical and consistent temperance man, and a generous giver to every good cause. In all the political controversies of his day no attack has been made upon his private character. Few men in his position have received such considerate treatment in this respect as Gov. Smith. In the early history of the church of which he was for many years a member he was one of its most useful men. When weak and struggling for existence he was its sexton, usher, Sunday-school superintendent, and deacon. He has been a Sunday-school teacher nearly all his Christian life. In the early educational and missionary work of the State he has taken a deep interest. For many years he was the treasurer of the State Convention, and has always been a member of its board.

Smyth, Rev. E. T., was born in Lawrence District, S. C., June 3, 1828; removed with his parents to Calhoun Co., Ala., in 1837, where he has resided ever since; was baptized by Rev. W. R. Harris in 1843; ordained in 1849. His culture is of a highly useful character. The first ten years of his ministry were spent with village and country churches, and attended with gratifying success. For twenty years he has been a popular pastor in the flourishing town of Oxford, where he has established a strong and working church, gaining for himself the honor of being recognized as one of the best pastors in the State, and he is also usefully connected with the general interests of the denomination. A good preacher, with great energy, gifted in the details of pastoral work, and distinguished for sound judgment in whatever he undertakes, his life has been eminently successful.

Smyth, Rev. John, was a beneficed clergyman of the Church of England, holding the living of Gainsborough, in Lincolnshire. After Robert Brown gave his religious doctrines to his countrymen, Mr. Smyth adopted them, and he became very hostile to Episcopalian ceremonies and prescribed forms of prayer. He suffered heavily from the persecuting spirit of the times, and to escape its evils he and a great company of his followers fled to Holland in 1606, where they united with the English Brownist Church, of which Mr. Johnson was the pastor, and Mr. Ainsworth the teacher.

Mr. Smyth adopted sentiments that rendered him liable to the charge of Arminianism; and he also rejected infant baptism. The Brownist congregation was filled with agitation about him; many received his principles, but the greater number expelled him and his friends; they charged him with being "a murderer of the souls of babes and sucklings, by depriving them of the visible seal of salvation." Several works were written against Mr. Smyth's real and imaginary errors. Mr. Ainsworth, teacher of the Brownist congregation of Amsterdam, wrote one, Mr. Johnson, the pastor, published another, Mr. Robinson, minister of the Brownist congregation of Leyden, issued a third. Even the good bishop, Joseph Hall, printed a work against him and other Nonconformists.

Mr. Smyth's enemies bring several charges against him which look frivolous and ridiculous. The most important one was that he had baptized himself, and this they denounce as a dreadful heresy. We see no evidence to substantiate the charge.

Mr. Smyth was a great man among the Dissenters of his day; Bishop Hall bears emphatic evidence on this question; and others speak with equal force about his prominence. " He was accounted," says Ephraim Paget, " one of the grandees of the separation, and he and his followers did at once, as it were, swallow up all the rest of the separation." He was the author of four works. He died in 1611.

Sneed, Rev. Robert, was a native of Virginia, and removed to Tennessee some forty years ago; was then a deacon of the Baptist church. He united with the old Sweetwater church, under the pastorate of Rev. Eli Cleveland, and soon after this was ordained to the work of the ministry. He was a man of giant mind. He preached extensively in East Tennessee; was a good pastor, a fine presiding officer, and for many years was moderator of the Sweetwater Association, and also of the General Association. He was doctrinal in his style of preaching. His influence was deeply felt in his days of usefulness. He died March 29, 1878, in Knoxville, Tenn. He labored most zealously for the salvation of men until the last few years of his life, during which he suffered great affliction. He fell asleep in Jesus in the full assurance of the Master's approbation. His last words were, "Glory to God!"

Snelling, Rev. Vincent, was the first Baptist minister on the Pacific coast. He was born March 15, 1797, in Christian (afterwards Caldwell) Co., Ky., of Baptist parents. At the age of thirteen he was baptized, suffering much ridicule from his companions, some of whom he afterwards led to Christ. He was ordained in Missouri. In 1844 he removed to Oregon, and gave himself fully to the ministry. Soon after his arrival he organized a church at West Union,—the first Baptist church west of the Rocky Mountains. In 1846 he organized the Yamhill and Lacreole churches, and afterwards assisted in forming several others. In 1848 he helped to organize the Willamette Association, the oldest Baptist Association on the Pacific coast. In preaching he was earnest and practical, with doctrinal tendencies. He was a thorough pioneer Bible Baptist, and traveled extensively through Oregon and California, convincing men mightily by the multitude of his Scripture proofs and his positiveness in stating the truth. About the beginning of 1856 he died at Yreka, Cal., in the triumph of Christian faith. The Willamette Association, at its meeting in 1856, made this record of him: he was "a pioneer in the Baptist cause in Oregon, a strong pillar, and active co-laborer in the cause of Christ."

Snyder, Rev. Frederick, was a graduate of Union College, N. Y., and pastor of the First church, Dayton, O., from 1844 to 1851; subsequently pastor of churches in Terre Haute, Ind., and Williamsburg, N. Y., where he died July 2, 1853; was buried at Dayton, O., where he had been greatly successful and much beloved.

South Carolina, The Baptists of.—The First Baptist church of Charleston, S. C., the first in the colony, was probably founded in Kittery, Me., by Rev. William Screven, Deacon Humphrey Churchwood, and eight other brethren, with some sisters, in September, 1682. Persecutions in Maine, it is said by some, dissolved the community, and it is certain that they drove away the leaders and others from that territory. In the same, or in the following year, Mr. Screven, with a number of his Kittery brethren, arrived in South Carolina, and either regarded their Eastern church organization as still in force or formed a new one. They settled first on the west side of the Cooper River, and soon after removed to Charleston, then a village.

The second, the Ashley River church, was formed in 1736, with Rev. Isaac Chanler as pastor.

The third, the Pee Dee, now the Welsh Neck church, was organized in 1738. James James, Esq., was the leader in the movement, whose son Philip soon after became the pastor.

The fourth church was the Euhaw, formed in 1746 as an independent body, having for some years been a branch of the Charleston church. The old building was burnt during the war. The old barrel-like pulpit and the sounding-board were still preserved because Whitefield had once preached there. The writer saw them shortly before they were consumed.

THE CHARLESTON BAPTIST ASSOCIATION

was formed in 1751, the first meeting being held in Charleston, Oct. 21. Rev. Oliver Hart was the moving spirit. They obtained from the Philadelphia Association Griffith's " Essay on the Nature, Power, and Duty of an Association" as the basis of union. The object was declared to be the promotion of the Redeemer's kingdom by the maintenance of love and fellowship. The independence of the churches was asserted, and the power of the body restricted to an advisory council.

MISSIONS.

In 1755 they began to collect funds to supply the destitute places with preaching in their own and in the adjoining provinces, and the next year Rev. John Gano was sent by the Philadelphia Association to the Yadkin settlement, in North Carolina, and wherever Providence might direct his steps, and his labors were eminently successful.

CONFESSION OF FAITH.

In 1767 the Association adopted the Confession of Faith published by the London Assembly in 1689. That year there were 8 churches, with 390 members, in South Carolina.

CONTRIBUTIONS.

In 1774 a resolution was adopted by the Association recommending the churches to contribute funds for the Rhode Island College, now Brown University. The body also urged the churches to send funds to the brethren in Massachusetts, then suffering for righteousness' sake.

The Religious Society and, afterwards, the General Committee were the agencies through which funds for missions and the education of young ministers were collected and disbursed. Probably nearly one hundred young men have from time to time shared in its benefactions. Among these were the elder Dr. Brantly, Rev. J. L. Brooks, the venerable Jesse Mercer, and the writer, who most gratefully acknowledges his obligation to the same source.

RELIGIOUS LIBERTY.

It is pleasing to find here, as everywhere else, our brethren contending for complete religious liberty. In 1779 the Charleston Association appointed a standing committee for several purposes, and "particularly to treat with the government in behalf of the churches" for complete freedom from political control.

NEW ASSOCIATIONS.

Churches having sprung up here and there in the "backwoods," the distance sometimes traveled to reach the Association, and the want of facilities for traveling, led to the formation of the Bethel Association in 1789. In 1800 the Broad River was constituted. In 1802 the Savannah River, the Saluda in 1803, the Edgefield in 1808, and the Moriah in 1815. Thus did our Zion "lengthen her cords and strengthen her stakes," until, in 1819, the letter of the High Hills church suggested to the Charleston Association the formation of

THE SOUTH CAROLINA BAPTIST STATE CONVENTION.

From their settlement in South Carolina its Baptist people took an active interest in ministerial education and missions. In colonial times they gave a large sum to aid in establishing Rhode Island College, now Brown University. "The Religious Society" was founded, in 1755, in the First church of Charleston to aid missions and ministerial education. This society rendered efficient help to ministers preaching among whites and Indians, and it sustained, in whole or in part, a number of candidates for the ministry who were under the instruction of Rev. Oliver Hart and others.

In 1819 both the Charleston and High Hills churches suggested to the Charleston Association the propriety of forming a more general union of the churches for this double purpose. The plan had been drawn by Dr. R. Furman, then pastor in Charleston. This led to the meeting of delegates from the Charleston, Savannah River, and Edgefield Associations, in Columbia, in December, 1821, who formed the Baptist State Convention. Dr. Richard Furman was its first president, and held that position until his death, Aug. 25, 1825. His successors have been W. B. Johnson, Basil Manly, J. C. Furman, J. B. O'Neall, E. T. Winkler, J. P. Boyce, J. L. Reynolds, J. A. Broadus. No Convention can show a more distinguished list of presiding officers.

The Convention founded the Furman Theological Institute, which has grown into both Furman University and the Southern Baptist Theological Seminary.

The State Board of Missions employed last year (1880) about thirty missionaries, and not only paid them, but reserved sufficient funds to pay the first quarter's salary for 1881 in advance.

There are now twenty-eight white Associations in the State co-operating with the Convention.

There is great harmony and hearty effort in sustaining the Convention.

The present officers are Col. B. W. Edwards, President; T. P. Smith, Vice-President; Capt. A. B. Woodruff and Rev. Luther Broadus, Secretaries; and Prof. C. H. Judson, Treasurer. Executive Board: Rev. Charles Manly, D.D., President; Rev. A. W. Lomax, Vice-President; Rev. W. H. Strickland, Corresponding Secretary and Treasurer.

In 1880, according to the "Baptist Year-Book," there were in South Carolina 44 Baptist Associations, 1126 churches, and 140,442 members. The white and colored Baptists are included in these statistics.

South Carolina, Baptist Journalism in.—Rev. Joseph A. Lawton distinctly remembers that Rev. W. H. Brisbane, M.D., was publishing a paper in Charleston in 1836. It is probable that

Dr. Manly assumed the editorship when Dr. Brisbane retired.

There are now two copies of *The Southern Watchman and General Intelligencer* in existence, dated Feb. 3 and Feb. 10, 1837, printed in Charleston by James S. Burges, and edited by the late Basil Manly, D.D. These numbers belong to the fourth volume. The terms were $3 in advance, $3.50 in six months, and $4 afterwards.

From among many interesting items we select the following statistics of South Carolina Baptists for 1835: Associations, 14; churches, 336; ordained ministers, 158; licentiates, 55; baptisms, 1985; members, 33,486. There is an extract from the *Religious Herald*, and one from the Mississippi *Christian Herald*.

Rev. T. W. Haynes published a monthly in Charleston, and in 1843 he began the *Carolina Baptist*, which was published for some years.

The Southern Baptist was first published in 1846. It was for years edited by a committee of brethren, consisting of Rev. J. R. Kendrick, James Tupper, Esq., and others. Next by Rev. E. T. Winkler, D.D., then by Rev. J. P. Tustin, and finally by Rev. W. B. Carson. At the beginning of the war the paper was suspended on account of the uncertain future, and never resumed.

It was succeeded by the *Confederate Baptist*, published in Columbia, and edited by that accomplished scholar and Christian gentleman, Rev. J. L. Reynolds, D.D.

Soon after the war *The South Carolina Baptist* was started; it was edited and published by Rev. W. E. Walters, at Anderson Court-House; and *The Baptist Church and Sunday-School Magazine* (monthly), edited and published by Rev. T. R. Gaines, gave us a tenfold blessing. The latter did not continue long. In about three years Brother Walters sold the subscription-list and good-will to the *Religious Herald*, of Richmond, Va.

After an interregnum of about a year, Brother T. R. Gaines began to publish the *Working Christian* at Yorkville. A year or so afterwards he removed to Charleston, and then to Columbia. He sold out to Mr. Junkin, who, again, transferred it to the present proprietor, Col. James A. Hoyt. Brother Hoyt removed it to Greenville, and soon after exchanged the name of *The Working Christian* for that of *The Baptist Courier*, and placed it under the editorial management of Rev. J. C. Hiden, D.D. It is now edited by the proprietor and Rev. J. A. Chambliss, D.D., whose classic pen is certainly not inferior to any of its predecessors.

South Jersey Institute, The.—The idea that gave birth to this noble academy was first seriously entertained by that veteran and honored pastor, the Rev. R. F. Young, of Haddonfield. At his suggestion, when settled at Salem, in 1849, a convention of churches connected with the West New Jersey Baptist Association was held in his meeting-house, at which resolutions were passed commending the project for establishing a first-class academy.

The church at Salem, through an educational committee, fitted up a room in the rear of their lecture-room in 1852, and secured the services of the Rev. Samuel Richards and his wife, of Providence, to take charge of the infant enterprise.

SOUTH JERSEY INSTITUTE, BRIDGETON, N. J.

They were specially qualified for the work, and their success was in the highest degree flattering. But Mr. Richards accepted another position in Salem, which resulted in the closing of the school.

On Sept. 12, 1865, the West New Jersey Baptist Association appointed a committee to consider this question and report during the Association. The committee was numerous, earnest, and able, and their report, which was adopted, recommended immediate efforts to secure a suitable building. A committee was appointed to carry out the decision of the Association. They selected Bridgeton as the place where the school should be located, and a first-class academy for the education of both sexes as the institution to be founded.

Bridgeton lies at the head of navigation on both sides of the Cohansey River. It contains about 8000 inhabitants. It has two Baptist churches. The character of its population specially fits it to be the seat of a large academy. The scenery around it is charming, and the health of its residents makes it peculiarly desirable for those who wish long life. The site of the academy is one of the most beautiful, for educational purposes, in the whole country. Forests, rich farms, and the winding Cohansey are spread out before the spectator as he looks down from the grounds of the institute. These grounds were given by H. J. Mulford, Esq., of Bridgeton; they contain about ten and a half acres.

The structure consists of a central building 43 by 58, with an east and west wing, each 57 by 41, making the entire length 157 feet. It is built of brick, lighted by gas, and heated by steam; and it is five stories high. Its appearance is imposing, and it has every convenience for carrying out the aims of its Christian projectors. It is fitted to accommodate one hundred and twenty-five boarders. It was opened for pupils in October, 1870. The buildings and grounds are valued at $75,000. Ladies and gentlemen bearing the honored name of Mulford have on various occasions given $50,000 to the institute. Many others in New Jersey, and some friends in Pennsylvania, have contributed liberally in the erection of the building and in centennial gifts.

The principal, H. K. Trask, LL.D., by scholarship, talents, and experience is fitted for the marked success that has attended his labors in the institute. In 1880 ten instructors assisted the principal in training one hundred and fifty pupils for the toils of coming life.

Southern Baptist, a Baptist paper published at Meridian, Miss., by Rev. A. Gressett. Circulation encouraging.

Southern Baptist Convention.—That Adoniram Judson and Luther Rice by independent study of the Scriptures should become Baptists, while voyaging to India, was a singular fact in the history of missions. This change of opinion necessitated their support by the Baptists of the United States. Luther Rice returned to America to arouse among the Baptist churches increased missionary ardor. Traveling much in the South, he so enlisted an interest in behalf of the work of missions that, when the General Missionary Convention was formed, Southern Baptists participated largely in the movement. Dr. Richard Furman, of South Carolina, was the first president. Under the constitution and proceedings of that body, for thirty years no discrimination was made in favor of or against either section. Northern and Southern Baptists acted in entire harmony. In course of time the anti-slaveholding sentiment became so strong that the Board of Foreign Missions declared, in response to a demand for an explicit avowal of opinions and purposes, that a slaveholder offering himself as a missionary would not be appointed. The Home Mission Society, organized for domestic mission work, avowed practically a similar opinion, and declared in favor of a separate missionary organization at the South and at the North.

In view of this antagonism of opinion, the board of the Virginia Foreign Mission Society suggested a convention to confer on the best means of promoting the foreign mission cause and other interests of the Baptist denomination in the South. Augusta, Ga., and Thursday before the second Lord's day in May, 1845, were suggested as a proper place and a proper time for the meeting; on May 8, 1845, 310 delegates from Maryland, the District of Columbia, Virginia, North Carolina, South Carolina, Georgia, Alabama, Louisiana, and Kentucky met at Augusta. Among these men, who came together to deliberate, were Fuller, Manly, Furman, Johnson, Jeter, Robinson, Howell, Curtis, Brantly, Taylor, Mell, Crawford, Dagg, Lumpkin, Hillyer, Cooper, Dockery, Witt, Hume, Mallary, Winkler, etc.

Wm. B. Johnson, D.D., of South Carolina, was chosen president. A resolution was unanimously adopted that "To accomplish the greatest amount of good, and for the maintenance of those Scriptural principles on which the General Convention of the Baptists was originally formed," the Convention should organize a society for the propagation of the gospel. A constitution, precisely that of the original union, was adopted, "for eliciting, combining, and directing the energies of the whole denomination in one sacred effort for the propagation of the gospel." A board for foreign missions was appointed and located in Richmond, Va., and a board for domestic missions at Marion, Ala.

No good would come of a discussion of the causes of the origin of the Southern Baptist Convention. Property in slaves has now happily ceased to disturb political and religious assemblages. The separation was reluctant and painful, but God has brought good out of apparent evil. A separate organization has developed the resources and energies of Southern Baptists, quickened a sense of responsibility, and trained to more active beneficence. Baptist societies for the spread of the gospel, existing in different portions of the Union, are now working without jar or discord, the most fraternal feelings are cherished, and few desire an organic union co-extensive with our territorial limits. Southern Baptists have contributed for foreign missions from 1845 to 1879, $939,377.23. In the last seven years $284,010.99 have been given for foreign missions, $72,000 more than the whole amount raised during the thirty years' connection with the Triennial Convention.

The Board for Foreign Missions had J. B. Jeter, D.D., for its first president, and James B. Taylor, D.D., for its corresponding secretary. J. L. M. Curry, D.D., LL.D., is the present president, and H. A. Tupper, D.D., the corresponding secretary.

Dr. Tupper, the scholarly secretary, has recently published, with the imprimatur of the Publication Society, a very valuable book, giving full information of the past and present work of the board.

The Home Mission Board at Marion, Ala., formerly called the Domestic Mission Board, has E. T. Winkler, D.D., for its president, and W. H. McIntosh, D.D., for its corresponding secretary. This board seeks to remedy religious destitution in the Southern States and among the Indian tribes adjacent to its territory. It has also a mission among the Chinese in California. During the war a valuable work was done in the Confederate army in supplying the soldiers with the Scriptures and religious literature, and in supporting seventy-eight missionaries.

In 1863 the Convention established a Sunday-school board at Greenville, S. C., and, under the efficient secretaryship of C. J. Elford, Esq., and C. C. Bitting, D.D., did active and valuable service. In 1868 it was removed to Memphis, and in a few years was discontinued.

The Southern Baptist Theological Seminary, now at Louisville, Ky., while not under the control of the Convention, is regarded with peculiar favor, and receives at every meeting attentive consideration.

Since the war the Convention meets annually. The boards submit to the Convention reports of their operations, receipts, and expenditures, and the officers and members are annually appointed.

Organized to "promote foreign and domestic missions and other important objects connected with the Redeemer's kingdom," and respecting fully "the independence and equal rights of the churches," the Convention consists of members who contribute funds, or are delegated by religious bodies contributing funds, on the basis of one delegate for every $100 given within the twelve months next preceding the meeting of the body. To bring the Convention into still closer affiliation with State Conventions and General Associations, representatives from those bodies are also admitted on the basis of $500 expended for objects similar to those in the promotion of which the Convention is engaged.

Between the Southern Baptist Convention and the three great Baptist organizations at the North —the Missionary Union, the Home Mission Society, and the Publication Society—the utmost harmony and fraternity exist. Each working in its own approved way has the good will and prayers of the others.

FOREIGN MISSIONS AND MISSIONARIES.

BRAZILIAN MISSION.—This mission in the province of San Paulo, adopted in 1879, has a church of thirty members at Santa Barbara, and another of twelve members at "Station." Rev. E. H. Quillan has been teacher and preacher. On Jan. 13, 1881, Rev. W. B. Bagby and wife, of Texas, were sent to reinforce the mission. In 1859 the Convention started a work in Rio de Janeiro, under Rev. and Mrs. T. J. Bowen, former missionaries to Africa. The mission was abandoned in 1861, on account of obstacles that do not now exist and the wrecked health of Mr. Bowen. The present outlook is promising, though the field is hard.

MEXICAN MISSION.—The Convention had but recently accepted as their missionary Rev. J. O. Westrup, stationed at Muzquis, in the State of Coahuila, when, on Dec. 21, 1880, he was murdered by a band of Indians and Mexicans. Another missionary will be soon appointed, and probably stationed at Monterey, where there is a Baptist Missionary Society. Rev. T. M. Westrup, of Corpus Christi, brother of the murdered missionary, writes, Feb. 5, 1881: "I sometimes think Catholic fanaticism or national prejudice had more to do with the case than appears so far." This blood may be seed.

ITALIAN MISSION.—This work was organized in Rome, in the fall of 1870, by Rev. W. N. Cote, M.D., who labored, with marked success, until 1873, when he was succeeded by G. B. Taylor, D.D. Dr. Cote died in Rome in 1877. Rev. J. H. Eager and wife joined the mission in 1880. The chapel at Rome cost some $30,000. To build one at Torre Pellice $3000 have been collected. This mission has prospered from the beginning, and is in a flourishing condition. There are five schools, with some 150 pupils: the church membership is about 175. The stations and laborers are as follows:

At Rome, G. B. Taylor, Mrs. Taylor, J. H. Eager, Mrs. Eager, and Signor Cocorda; Torre Pellice,

Signor Ferraris; Milan, Signor Paschetto; Modena and Carpi, Signor Martinelli; Naples, Signor Colombo; Bari and Barletta, Signor Volpi; island of Sardinia, Signor Cossu; Venice, Signor Bellondi; Bologna, Signor Basile.

A sketch of Dr. G. B. Taylor, whose praise for eminent wisdom is in all the churches, appears elsewhere in this "Encyclopædia."

AFRICAN MISSIONS.—*Liberian and Sierra Leone Mission.*—The First Baptist church of Monrovia, Liberia, was organized with twelve members, in 1821, in a private dwelling in Richmond, Va., Feb. 2, 1846, the Board of Foreign Missions of the Southern Baptist Convention having resolved to start a mission in Africa. That year two colored brethren, Rev. John Day and Rev. A. L. Jones, were appointed missionaries. From 1846 to 1856 many others were appointed, and churches and schools were established in fourteen villages of Liberia and two in Sierra Leone. In 1852 and in 1854 the mission was visited respectively by Rev. Eli Ball and Rev. John Kingdon in the interest of the board. In 1860 there were 24 stations and churches, 18 pastors, 1258 members, 26 teachers, and 665 pupils. During our civil war the mission suspended, and resumed in 1871, under Rev. A. D. Philips, who had been identified with the Yoruban Mission of the Convention. Eight stations were established in Liberia and the Beir country, and fifteen missionaries and teachers were appointed. The stations in Liberia were posts for the interior work in the Beir country, through which it was hoped that access might be had again to Yoruba, from which the missionaries had been driven in 1867. In 1873 the missionaries were expelled from the Beir country. Our country being under a fearful monetary pressure, the missionaries, except the supervisors,—B. P. Yates and J. J. Cheeseman,—were dismissed. A gratuity of $500 was distributed among them. They acted with noble Christian spirit. Jan. 8, 1875, Rev. W. J. David and Rev. W. W. Colley (colored) sailed for Africa. Finding Yoruba reopened to missionaries, they, according to instructions, settled all accounts, and closed the mission in Liberia, and in October, 1875, resumed work in Yoruba. From 1845 to 1875 thousands had been converted and taught through the Liberian and Sierra Leone Mission, and many strong and godly men and women of the African race were developed. Among the colored missionaries publicly recorded are F. S. James, who left in his churches the savor of a holy life; B. P. Yates, J. H. Cheeseman, J. J. Cheeseman, noted respectively for financial ability, spiritual devotion, and uncommon culture; A. P. Davis, B. J. Drayton, J. T. Richardson, R. E. Murray, J. M. Harden, J. J. Fitzgerald, Lewis K. Crocker, Jacob Von Brunn, Milford D. Herndon, and Josephine Early. John Day, the first missionary, was born at Hicksford, Va., Feb. 18, 1797; was baptized in 1820; licensed to preach in 1821; went to Liberia in 1830; resigned a judgeship, and was elected, without his consent, lieutenant-governor, in 1847. In 1849 he established a manual labor school of fifty pupils at Bexley. In 1854 he became pastor of the church at Monrovia, where he founded and presided over a high school, known as "Day's Hope," in which were departments elementary, classical, and theological. As superintendent of the mission, he made extensive preaching tours, and reported "a Sunday-school in every village, and the Word preached stately to more than 10,000 heathen." This remarkable man was gathered to his fathers in 1859. Prof. E. W. Blyden, the learned African linguist, in pronouncing an eulogy on Mr. Day, considered his subject thus: 1. His love of metaphysics; 2. His burning zeal for the gospel; 3. A household word; 4. As judge and statesman; 5. The good physician; 6. As a soldier; 7. His moral and religious character; 8. As educator and theologian; 9. His life and death a legacy.

THE YORUBA MISSION was founded in 1850 by Rev. T. J. Bowen. In 1853 it was reinforced by Rev. Messrs. J. S. Dennard and J. H. Lacy, with their wives; in 1854 by Rev. W. H. Clarke; and in 1856 by Rev. Messrs. S. Y. Trimble, R. W. Priest, J. H. Cason, and their wives, and Mr. J. F. Beaumont. Stations were opened in Lagos, Abbeokuta, Ijaye, and Ogbomishaw. Residences and chapels were built, churches and schools were established, the heathen were soon preached to in their own language, and not a few of them were saved. The labors in Africa of all these missionaries, except Mr. Bowen, were brief. Rev. Henry Goodale, who accompanied Mr. Bowen, was buried at Golah, before Yoruba was reached. Dennard and his wife were put under the sod; Clarke, Trimble, and Beaumont came home to go to their reward. Priest and Lacy and Cason toil on in their native land. In 1855, Rev. J. M. Harden, a colored missionary, was transferred from the Liberian to the Yoruban mission, and died in Lagos in 1864. His wife is now in the employ of the board. Rev. A. D. Philips entered the field in 1855, and labored with signal success until 1867, when he was driven out of the country by war and persecution. He retired from the service of the board in 1872, and preaches in Tennessee. Rev. T. A. Reid labored at Awyaw and elsewhere, and was devoted to the work from 1857 to 1864. Like Mr. Philips, he left his noble wife a sleeper in Afric sands. Rev. R. H. Stone worked from 1863 to 1869. He is a faithful minister in Virginia. As has been stated, the mission was reorganized by Messrs. David and Colley in 1875. They found a number of the native Christians steadfast, and overjoyed at the answer of their prayers through long years for the return of "God's men." A chapel and residence, at the cost of some $4000, have been erected at Lagos, and buildings put up at Abbeokuta and Ogbomishaw. The last station is occupied by a native missionary, Rev. Moses L. Stone. Rev. S. Cosby, missionary of the Colored Baptist Convention of Virginia, is associated with Mr. David in the mission. Mr. Colley was recalled by the board in 1879. On Dec. 22, 1879, Mr. and Mrs. David lost their infant daughter. In the mission there are 60 scholars and 80 church members. Some further record of Mr. Bowen, the founder of the mission, is fitting. He was born in Georgia, Jan. 2, 1814; was a gallant soldier in the Creek-Indian and Texas wars; studied law, but abandoned it, in 1841, for the ministry; traveled extensively in Central Africa, and was the soul and inspiration of the Yoruban Mission from 1850 to 1856. He married, May 31, 1852, Miss L. H. Davis, of Greensborough, Ga., who shared his toils and successes in his second missionary campaign in Africa. Mrs. Bowen resides in Greensborough, loved and honored for her own sake, and for her good and great husband. He entered his heavenly rest Nov. 24, 1875. He was the author of an admirable work on "Central Africa," and a quarto volume on the Yoruban language, published by the Smithsonian Institute.

CHINA MISSIONS.—*Canton Mission.*—Rev. J. L. Shuck and Rev. T. J. Roberts, missionaries of the Triennial Convention, transferred themselves to the Southern Convention soon after its organization. The former had constituted the First Baptist church of Canton, and traveling in this country in 1846 with a native convert, Yong Seen Sang, raised for a chapel $5000. This chapel fund, with the consent of the donors, was transferred with the missionary, in 1847, to Shanghai. Mr. Roberts had preached six or seven years to lepers at Macao. In 1847 his chapel was destroyed, and the mission property of the Missionary Union was bought by the Southern Convention. Mr. Roberts raised much money on the field, and published and distributed large numbers of tracts and portions of the Scriptures. In 1850 the mission had been reinforced by Messrs. S. C. Clopton, George Pearcy, F. C. Johnson, B. W. Whilden, and Miss H. A. Baker. There were three preaching-places. A union effected between Mr. Roberts's (Uet-tung) church and the First church was not happy. In 1852 "the relation between Mr. Roberts and the board was dissolved." He had done some good foundation-work. He remained an independent missionary until 1866, when he returned to America. He died of leprosy, Dec. 28, 1871, at Upper Alton, Ill. Mrs. Roberts lives at St. Louis, Mo. Mr. Clopton was born in Virginia, Jan. 7, 1816, fell asleep July 7, 1847, lamented as a choice spirit. Mr. Pearcy and Miss Baker were transferred to the Shanghai Mission. Mr. Johnson went as "Theological Tutor and Missionary," and after making great progress in the written language, returned, in 1849, with broken health. He resides in Marietta, Ga. In 1848 the native assistants, Yong and Mui, went to Canton. In 1850, Mrs. Whilden died, and Mr. Whilden brought home his children. The health of his second wife failing, they retired from the field finally in 1855. Mr. Whilden, much beloved, resides in his native State, South Carolina. In 1854, 1856, 1860, Rev. Messrs. C. W. Gaillard, R. H. Graves, and J. G. Schilling joined, respectively, the mission. In 1856, Mr. Gaillard reported "69 Sunday-school scholars, 32,200 tracts and Scriptures distributed;" and in 1860, "40 baptisms and 58 church members." July 27, 1862, he was killed by the falling of his house in a typhoon. Mr. Schilling made "good progress in the language," but after the death of his wife, in 1864, came home with his children. He practises law in West Virginia. Rev. N. B. Williams, whose wife is the daughter of the returned missionary, Rev. B. W. Whilden, went to China in 1872, accompanied by his wife's sister, Miss Lula Whilden, who, supported by the women of South Carolina, is doing a grand work among the women of Canton. Mr. Williams had a school of forty pupils, and was treasurer of the mission. In 1876, Mrs. Williams's failing health compelled their return to the United States. Mr. Williams preaches in Alabama. In 1874, Wong Mui died. Yong Seen Sang, supported by the Ladies' Missionary Society of the First Baptist church of Richmond, Va., since 1846, still labors for the Master. Rev. E. Z. Simmons and wife arrived in Canton Feb. 6, 1871, and are doing good work for the Lord. Miss Sallie Stein, sustained by the Young Ladies' Missionary Society of the First Baptist church, Richmond, Va., joined the mission in 1879. Rev. R. H. Graves, D.D., was born in Baltimore, May 29, 1833; was baptized by Dr. R. Fuller, Oct. 15, 1848; graduated at St. Mary's College in 1851; arrived at Canton 14th August, 1856. For twenty-five years he has been consecrated to his mission, in which he has achieved great success, and has won, as many a brother missionary has done, a name for purity of character and ability as a gospel laborer which is imperishable. He married first the missionary Gaillard's widow, who died Dec. 12, 1864. His present wife, daughter of G. W. Norris, Esq., of Baltimore, has been, since 1872, a self-sacrificing and successful missionary worker for Jesus. In the last eight years Dr. Graves has published, in Chinese, two hymn-books, a work on the Parables of our Lord, a book on homiletics, a work on Scripture geography, and will soon publish a "Life of Christ." In the same time "a dwelling has been built in Canton, one chapel finished, and money raised for another in the country, six country stations have been opened, and two native brethren ordained to the ministry. The Chinese Native Missionary Society has also a station and two assistant preachers, supported mainly by contributions from Chinese Christians in Demerara and the United States." The results of the preaching and Scripture distribution and holy living of this long line of missionaries in the city of Canton, and among the dense masses of the interior of Southern China, can never be estimated. The statistics reported in 1880 are as follows: 2 churches, 230 members, 52 baptized, $255 annual contributions, 9766 tracts and Bibles distributed, 4514 medical cases, 5 schools, with an average attendance of 121, 6 foreign missionaries and 12 native assistants, $5585.35, cost of house recently built, $4591.87 house fund in Canton treasury.

The *Shanghai Mission* was started in 1847 by Rev. Messrs. M. T. Yates, J. L. Shuck, and T. W. Tobey. Mr. Yates was the first on the ground. Nov. 6, 1847, a Baptist church of ten members was founded. Two natives—Yong and Mui—were licensed to preach. In April, 1848, a gloom overspread the infant church by the drowning of Dr. and Mrs. J. Sexton James, who were daily expected at Shanghai. Mr. Pearcy, from Canton, joined the mission in November, 1848. The meetings were attended by "500 or 600 natives." In 1849 Mr. and Mrs. Tobey, very useful missionaries, were forced home by the ill health of the latter. In May, 1850, a mission building was erected at Oo-Kah-Jack. Mr. Shuck wrote, "Our board is the first Protestant board of missions in the world which ever held property and gained a permanent footing in the interior of China." In 1851, Mrs. Shuck died. Her biography was written by Dr. Jeter. Mr. Shuck returned with his children to America. In China he had been very "faithful and effective." In 1854 he went to California, where he labored for seven years, baptizing sixteen Chinese, and organizing a Chinese church. He died in Barnwell, S. C., Aug. 20, 1861, aged fifty-one. His widow resides in Charleston, S. C., with his son, Rev. L. H. Shuck, D.D. In 1852, Rev. and Mrs. Crawford and Dr. G. W. Burton reinforced the mission, and early in 1853, Rev. and Mrs. A. B. Cabaniss arrived. In the city there were three schools and six places of worship. In 1854, Miss H. A. Baker, who came from Canton in 1851 and opened a boarding school, was recalled by the advice of her physician. She lives in California, and is the author of the "Orphan of the Old Dominion." Mr. and Mrs. Pearcy, on account of his shattered health, returned home in 1855. He passed away July 21, 1871, "mildly and grandly as the setting sun." That year, 1855, there were "eighteen public services per week, with an average attendance of 2500 souls; five day schools, with an average attendance of 100 pupils. This year was signalized by *the first baptism of a Chinese woman*. The board reported, "The gospel has won glorious triumphs in China.... Multitudes having given evidence of saving faith in the Redeemer." The next year the board commended the missionaries as performing "almost superhuman labors in their wide-opened field." In 1859, Rev. and Mrs. J. L. Holmes came to Shanghai, and the next year were settled in the Shantung province. In 1859, Rev. J. B. Hartwell and wife arrived, and in 1860 joined Mr. Holmes in Shantung. In 1860, Mr. and Mrs. Cabaniss, after eminent service, returned home. The same year Rev. and Mrs. A. L. Bond, assigned to this mission, were lost at sea, with Rev. and Mrs. J. Q. A. Rohrer, assigned to Japan, in the ill-fated "Edwin Forrest." In 1863, Rev. and Mrs. T. P. Crawford, having done a good work in Shanghai, went to Tung-Chow. In 1861, Dr. Burton, a great benefactor of the mission, returned to America, and is practising his profession in Louisville, Ky. In 1865, Mr. and Mrs. Yates were alone in Shanghai, and have remained so until now. To sum up the labors and holy influences of these missionaries, and of this great man and his noble wife, would be impossible. Dr. Yates wrote,—

"Sept. 12, 1877.—This is the thirtieth anniversary of our arrival at Shanghai. At first our way was in the dark; but every successive decade has shown marked progress in our work. To-day the missionary influence in China is a mighty power. The leaven of divine truth has been deposited in this mass of error and corruption, and its irresistible force is beginning to be seen and felt far and wide. The Bible has been translated into the literary or dead language of the whole country, and also rendered into the spoken language or dialects of many localities,—a style in which the Chinese have not been in the habit of making books. Places of worship have been secured, where multitudes come to the sound of the church-going bell to hear the word of God. Churches of living witnesses have been established. Tens of thousands have been convinced of the truth of the gospel, who have not had the moral courage to make a public confession of their faith in Christ. Thirty years ago, when the prospect was *so* dark, and the darkness seemed *so* impenetrable, I would have compromised for what I now behold as my life-work. Now my demand would be nothing less than a complete surrender. I am in dead earnest about this matter, for I fully realize that God is in Christ reconciling the world unto himself, and has committed unto us the word of reconciliation, and that he has commanded us to make it known to all nations. I not only do not regret devoting my life to the mission work, but I rejoice that he counted me worthy to be his embassador to the greatest empire on the globe. Now my one desire is that he would give me wisdom to do his will and be a faithful steward. The Lord be praised for all his goodness and mercy to us in our hours of darkest affliction."

Statistics, 1880: 2 churches, 100 members, $273.17 contributions, 2 important out-stations.

A sketch of Dr. M. T. Yates, whose reputation is as broad as the earth, is found on another page of this volume.

The *Shantung Mission* has had two main stations, viz., at Chefoo and at Tung-Chow. In 1860, Rev. and Mrs. J. L. Holmes settled in the former, and Rev. and Mrs. J. B. Hartwell in the latter. The next year Mr. Holmes was brutally murdered by the rebels. He was born in Preston County, now in West Virginia; was graduated from Columbian College in 1858. In "Our Life in China" Mrs. Nevins describes him as "handsome, talented, ardent, with very winning manners, and peculiarly fitted for usefulness among the Chinese." Mrs. Holmes removed to Tung-Chow, where she is still doing heroic work. She has issued several editions of "Peep of Day." In 1871, Mr. Hartwell re-opened the station in Chefoo. In 1872 he located in Chefoo, which, he said, had "sextupled itself" since 1860, and asked the board "to appropriate $4000 for a residence and $4000 for a chapel." He rented a commodious dwelling, where he had "at evening family prayer a company of twenty Chinese," and used the chapel of the English Baptist mission, kindly offered by Dr. Brown of that mission. In 1875 he wrote, "I think the people are receiving the ideas of the gospel." That year he was forced home by the ill health of his wife, who died Dec. 3, 1879, in California, where Dr. Hartwell has a mission under the home board of the Convention. Dr. Hartwell was born in Darlington, S. C., in 1835; graduated with distinction from Furman University in 1856. In 1858 he married Miss Eliza H. Jewett, of Macon, Ga., who died in China in 1870, greatly lamented. His second wife, Miss Julia Jewett, was her sister. With sixteen years' experience in China, Dr. Hartwell is eminently adapted to the work in California, where he has organized a Chinese church. The Doctorate was conferred on him by Furman University.

Tung-Chow Station.—Mr. Hartwell, as has been stated, located there in 1860, and constituted a church of eight members, Oct. 5, 1862. It was known as the North Street church. In 1864 there were eighteen members. Mr. Crawford, coming to Tung-Chow, took charge of the church, while Mr. Hartwell supplied a temporary absence of Mr. Yates from Shanghai, and baptized eight converts. There were two schools there, and some "6000 books had been printed and distributed." In 1866, Mr. Crawford constituted a second church, of eight persons, known as the Monument Street church. In 1868 "a deep religious revival" arose in neighboring villages, through the instrumentality of a native baptized by Mr. Hartwell, and twenty were baptized. In 1869, Mr. Hartwell reported his church contributions to be $127. In 1871 the membership was fifty-six. In 1870, Woo was ordained a native pastor. In 1872, Mr. Hartwell wrote, "Woo has managed the church with great discretion and propriety. . . . He tells them that instead of their being dependent on the missionaries, the missionaries should be dependent on them." In 1873 the statistics were: membership, 63; connected with the church from the first, 81; income of church, $224. The church bears its own expenses, except chapel rent. In 1875 the board reported, "Rev. Woo is pastor, but Brother Hartwell, though living in Chefoo, kept an advisory relation to it, and aided it by his constant counsel and occasional presence." After sundry vicissitudes this church is virtually merged in the Monument Street church.

In 1871, Mr. Crawford, greatly encouraged, wrote, "Christianity gains ground day by day. The government and people all feel that their ancient strongholds are giving way." In 1873 he built a chapel for $3000. In 1872, Miss Edmonia Moon joined the mission, but, after remarkable progress in the language, she had to yield in 1876 to broken health and quit the field. In 1873 her sister, Miss Lottie Moon, a woman of distinguished ability, joined the mission, and, with Mrs. Crawford and Mrs. Holmes, is teaching in the city, and telling of Jesus far in the country. In four years the ladies made 1027 visits to country villages. In 1879 the schools numbered 56, the church 115. In 1880 "more than a thousand visits were made for preaching the gospel and distributing books in villages around Tung-Chow." Dr. Crawford adds, "May God bless the seed thus sown under many difficulties!"

T. P. Crawford was born in Warren Co., Ky., May 8, 1821; graduated from Union University, Tenn., in 1851, "at the head of his class, and with the first honors of the institution." He was ordained in 1851, and married Miss Martha Foster, of Alabama, daughter of the late Deacon J. L. S. Foster. The same year he was appointed a missionary; labored in Shanghai until 1862, when he went to Tung-Chow, where he has toiled indefatigably ever since. Mrs. Crawford has published several books. The last work of Dr. Crawford's is "The Patriarchal Dynasties." In 1879 the degree of D.D. was conferred on him by Richmond College, Va.

RECEIPTS AND EXPENDITURES.

From 1846 to 1881 the Convention has received and expended for foreign missions $1,029,920.90.

HOME MISSION BOARD.

The home mission work of the Baptists of the South in the United States is mostly performed by State Mission Boards. Still, a large measure of general evangelical labor has been accomplished, and is still being performed, by the Home Mission Board of the Southern Baptist Convention. This evangelical labor may be divided into the following departments: 1. Home mission work; 2. Indian missions; 3. Chinese Mission, in California; 4. Work of the Bible Board; 5. Work of the Sunday-School Board. (See articles on those topics.) The Southern States, properly speaking, are Maryland, Virginia, North Carolina, South Carolina, Florida, Georgia, Alabama, Mississippi, Louisiana, Texas, Arkansas, Missouri, Tennessee, and Kentucky. The Southern Baptist Convention and its two mission boards—domestic and foreign—were formed at Augusta on May 8, 1845. The first officers of the Domestic Board, as it was then called, were Rev. Basil Manly, Sr., President; Rev. J. L. Reynolds, Corresponding Secretary; Rev. M. P. Jewett, Recording Secretary; Thos. Chilton, Treasurer; and Wm. N. Wyatt, Auditor. The board was located at Marion, Ala. Owing to the distance of his residence, Dr. Manly resigned, and Dr. Hartwell was elected president. Prof. Reynolds also declined, and, in November, Rev. Russell Holman became corresponding secretary, and Mr. Wm. Hornbuckle was elected treasurer, as Mr. Chilton removed from Marion. For many years Mr. Holman and Mr. Hornbuckle filled their respective positions with honor to themselves and to the satisfaction of their brethren, nobly sustained by a board of managers which contained such men as J. H. De Votie, E. D. King, and Wm. N. Wyatt. In 1851, Mr. Holman resigned, in consequence of feeble health, and Rev. Thomas F. Curtis was elected secretary; but he retired, after two years' efficient service, and was succeeded, in 1853, by Rev. Joseph Walker. In 1855 the American Indian Mission Association of Kentucky transferred its work to the Southern Baptist Convention, together with a heavy debt, which was promptly paid. Thenceforth the Domestic Board was designated as the Domestic and Indian Mission Board until 1874, when its name was changed to Home Board. This union and transfer gave a mighty impulse to the work of the board, and a great enlargement to its field. The sympathies of the denomination were strongly enlisted, and its liberality largely increased. At the close of 1856, Rev. Joseph Walker resigned the secretaryship, a position he had filled with eminent ability, and Rev. R. Holman was again called to the position, but, after prosecuting his labors with much consecration, he was compelled by ill health to retire in 1862. Rev. M. T. Sumner, who had entered the service of the board as financial secretary in 1858, succeeded Mr. Holman, and conducted the affairs of the Home Board with wonderful ability and success until 1875, when he resigned. Wm. N. Hornbuckle, Treasurer, and Wm. N. Wyatt, Auditor, both efficient, faithful, and beloved, were respectively succeeded by J. B. Lovelace and S. H. Fowlkes, who have given their valuable services to the present time. Dr. Basil Manly, Jr., was elected to succeed Dr. Sumner, but declined, and Dr. Wm. H. McIntosh, the present most able and efficient secretary, was elected to fill the vacancy, and entered upon his duties Oct. 1, 1875. He reported the board almost entirely free from debt in 1877, and since that time it has enlarged its work to the full extent of the means furnished.

The Home Mission Board has sustained missionaries in every Southern State, has planted churches, and fostered interests that needed support. Weak churches, in most of the large cities of the South, have been assisted by it, until able to sustain themselves. Notably among these cities are Baltimore, Washington City, Richmond, Petersburg, Fredericksburg, Raleigh, Augusta, Atlanta, New Orleans, Galveston, Houston, Texas, Mobile, St. Louis, Memphis, Knoxville, and many others. Young and growing cities on the frontiers have contained its missionaries. Especial attention has been paid to Texas, into which a rapid tide of population from other States has flowed constantly. Among the many missionaries employed in that State may be mentioned Rev. Wm. M. Tryon, Rev. James Huckins, Rev. R. C. Burleson, Rev. J. W. D. Creath, Rev. Z. N. Morrell, Rev. Jesse Witt, and Wm. M. Pickett; and the work accomplished by these and others in Texas is now seen in a membership, in that State, larger than that claimed by any other denomination, in a numerous, devoted, and most efficient ministry, and in male and female Baptist colleges of a high order. The board, in connection with Associations and State Conventions, has always labored most earnestly and energetically in bestowing religious instruction upon the colored people. It has ever found the Christian masters and mistresses keenly alive to the moral responsibilities growing out of their relations to their servants, and ever ready to aid in giving them gospel privileges. Generally, all the missionaries of the Home Board had colored interests in connection with their charges, and, in many instances, rich blessings crowned their labors in the conversion of colored people. The wonderful success of this evangelical labor among the colored people of the South is clearly demonstrated by the existence, after the war, of hundreds of thousands of colored Baptists in those States where emancipation occurred, not to mention the numerous colored church members of other denominations. In the State of Georgia alone there are over 30 colored Associations, about 900 churches, and 110,000 church members. During the war the work of the board was necessarily suspended in many parts of the country, but effective service was done by its missionaries among the soldiers of the Confederate armies, many professing conversion through their instrumentality. During the war one hundred and fifty-one commissions were issued by the board to chaplains and missionaries to the armies and hospitals.

The conclusion of the war left the board prostrate. Gradually it has resumed and enlarged its home mission work, as vigorously as its means allowed, adding to its other efforts the holding of ministers' institutes for the benefit of colored Baptist ministers. Its report for 1880 shows twenty missionaries and three missionary agents in the field, as follows: six in Florida, four in Arkansas, two in Georgia, two in Texas, one in California, three in Alabama, one in Tennessee, one in Virginia, and a missionary agent and evangelist in each of the States of North Carolina, Kentucky, and Alabama. It also kept employed one white and four native missionaries in the Creek nation, two natives in the Choctaw nation, one, Rev. A. Frank Ross, an intelligent educated man, one white missionary in the Chickasaw nation, and a Seminole Indian missionary among the wild tribes.

CONTRIBUTIONS.—The contributions to the Home Board from 1845 to 1859, inclusive, $266,358.13. During the last twenty years its receipts have been $739,483.64, so that the total receipts from 1845 to 1880, inclusive, were $1,005,841.77.

GENERAL SUMMARY.—Since its organization the Home Board has issued 1893 commissions. To the year 1881 the total number of the weeks of labor performed by its missionaries makes a period of 506 years. The number of baptisms performed by its missionaries is 36,874, an average of 1053 annually. Five thousand and fifty churches and stations were supplied with preaching, and many churches were constituted and Sunday-schools organized.

INDIAN MISSIONS.—From the beginning of the century Southern Baptists have manifested much interest in the reformation and evangelization of the Indians. Organized efforts were made first in Kentucky and then in Georgia for their education and Christianization, and were carried on, partly, through the Mission Board of the General Convention, at Philadelphia, until 1842, when a Western Baptist Convention met at Cincinnati, and the result was the formation, in 1843, of the American Indian Mission Association. This association established missions in the Choctaw and Creek nations, sending as missionaries to them Rev. Sidney Dyer, Rev. Joseph Smedley, Rev. Ramsey Potts, Rev. A. L. Hay, and Rev. H. F. Buckner, who was sent in 1848, and who is still laboring successfully in the Creek nation. These missionaries, aided by faithful native preachers, baptized many converts and established various churches. In 1854 the American Indian Mission Association, through its Mission Board at Louisville, transferred all its Indian mission work to the Domestic and Indian Mission Board of the Southern Baptist Convention, which accepted the charge in 1855, at Montgomery, Ala. Since that time this board has been most earnestly and zealously engaged in the Indian mission work, and wonderful success has crowned its efforts. From time to time the board has sent out various missionaries to labor in the Indian Territory, among whom were Rev. R. G. Moffatt, sent in 1853; Rev. R. J. Hogue, sent in 1858; Rev. A. E. Vandivere, in 1858; Rev. J. A. Slover, in 1859; Rev. Willis Burns, in 1859; Rev. J. A. Preston, in 1860; Rev. J. S. Murrow, of Georgia, a most efficient and faithful missionary, was sent out in 1857, and, supported by the Rehoboth Association, has continued to labor most efficiently until the present time. From first to last, however, Dr. H. F. Buckner has remained in connection with the Convention, and his laborious faithfulness constitutes him the "Judson" of the West.

Among the missionaries were many half-breed and full-blood natives, whose long and faithful labors in the employ of the board have aided immensely in making the Cherokees, Creeks, Choctaws, Chickasaws, and Seminoles what they are to-day, a civilized, Christian people; and their names should be put on record,—Peter Folsom, Simon Hancock, Lewis Cass, William Cass, John Jumper.

A few figures will give an idea of the number of missionaries employed, the amount disbursed for their support, and the nature and result of their labors as employés of the Domestic and Indian Mission Board. In 1856 and 1857, 26 white and native missionaries were employed, at a cost of $16,780.26, among the Creeks, Cherokees, and Choctaws. Several schools, also, were maintained in successful operation. In 1858–59, 35 missionaries were sustained,—19 among the Creeks, 10 among the Choctaws, and 6 among the Cherokees,—and $18,019.77 were expended. The amount collected for Indian missions in five years was $61,641.74. The work performed was the supply of preaching to 135 churches and out-stations, 355 converts baptized, 5 churches constituted, 5 meeting-houses built, 4 Sabbath-schools organized, with 13 teachers and 117 pupils, and 2 ministers and 10 deacons ordained. In 1860 and 1861, 31 missionaries and 8 interpreters were employed, at a cost of $23,835. During the two years 171 churches and stations were supplied with preaching, 20 churches were constituted, 23 ministers and 8 deacons were ordained, 3 temperance societies were formed, and 400 persons were baptized, while both Sunday-schools and secular schools flourished.

The war then came on, and finally caused a total suspension of Indian missions. Previous to 1870 about half a dozen missionaries only were kept employed. In 1875 there were sixteen,—two in North Carolina among the Cherokees in that State. In 1876 eleven were sustained in the Indian Territory; but of late years the board has been gradually increasing its operations and enlarging its field among the Indians.

Results.—As late as 1845 the Creeks had laws in force to punish "praying people," and in that year four Christians were whipped. Now, the Baptists alone have among the Creeks 2 Associations, 32 churches, with 17 Sunday-schools, about 30 native preachers, and a membership of 1500. Among the Seminoles there are 700 members and several native preachers; and yet, except for a few years only, H. F. Buckner has been the only white missionary of the board to these two tribes, containing a population of 14,500 Creeks and 2500 Seminoles. Among the Choctaws and Chickasaws there are 2500 church members. The Choctaw and Chickasaw Baptist Association, connected with Southern Baptist Missions, had 29 churches, with 1300 members, and 16 Sunday-schools, with 626 scholars and 45 teachers, in 1880. Among the Cherokees there is a Baptist Association comprising a membership of more than 1000. In connection with its Creek mission the board has a manual labor school, capable of educating at one time 50 girls and 50 boys; and it has, also, a church with 69 members among the wild tribes, the pastor of which, John Jumper, is a full-blooded Seminole.

MISSION TO THE CHINESE IN CALIFORNIA.—In November, 1879, the Home Mission Board sent Rev. J. B. Hartwell, D.D., as a missionary to the Chinese in San Francisco, Cal. Immediately after his arrival Dr. Hartwell entered heartily into his work, and soon baptized a convert. He employed a hall for preaching, and he opened a night school for the Chinese. His labors gradually extended successfully, and he at length united the Chinese Baptist converts into a church, having baptized one woman, who is, perhaps, the first Chinese female convert ever baptized in the United States.

Rev. J. B. Hartwell has fine talents. He spent twenty years in Northern China; but being compelled by the ill health of his family to return to America, he was thus providentially at hand, well prepared for this important mission in California. It is thought that it will assist greatly in the evangelization of China by the return to that country of converts from California.

THE BIBLE BOARD.—In 1846 the Southern Baptist Convention constituted its two boards its agents for Bible operations, and in the next four years $10,000 were contributed and disbursed in the distribution of the divine Word. During the same time the Southern Baptists gave more than twice as much—that is, $20,308.89—to the American and Foreign Bible Society. In view of this and similar circumstances, the Convention organized a Bible board, in 1851, for the purpose of more effectually circulating the holy Scriptures at home and abroad. The four great objects designed by the origination of the board were,—"1. To aid our Foreign Mission Board in the translation and distribution of the Scriptures in foreign lands; 2. To co-operate with the Domestic Mission Board in the home distribution of the Scriptures; 3. To concentrate and develop the liberality of the Southern Baptists; 4. To supervise and provide for the vast moral destitution at home and abroad."

The board was located at Nashville, Tenn. Its first president was Dr. Samuel Baker. The other officers were W. C. Buck, Corresponding Secretary; W. P. Jones, Recording Secretary; and C. A. Fuller, Treasurer. The first biennial report, in 1853, showed over $8000 collected and $6920 expended.

The report of 1855 exhibited $10,126.90 received and $8862.40 disbursed, of which $3254 were expended in sending copies of the Bible to foreign countries.

In the mean time, Dr. S. Baker had resigned, and W. H. Bayliss was elected President, and A. C. Dayton had become Corresponding Secretary, and J. J. Toon, Recording Secretary.

The third biennial report, in 1857, showed an income of $33,135.27, collected and disbursed partly through State societies, with the exception of $2115.38 in the treasury. The report exhibited the existence of various strong and active State Bible societies in different States.

In 1859, Dr. R. B. C. Howell was elected president of the board, and in the next two years about $8000 only were collected, due partly to the want of a corresponding secretary a large portion of the time, and partly to political agitation. The report, rendered at Savannah in the spring of 1861, manifested that over $8000 had been collected, Rev. L. W. Allen being the corresponding secretary, and the successor of Rev. Matt. Hillsman; and although Rev. C. D. Mallary brought in a special report advocating a continuance of the board, and although the secretary made a strong report in favor of the operations of the Bible Board, it was apparent that its days were numbered.

A committee was appointed to arrange some plan, if possible, by which a union might be effected between the Bible Board and the Southern Baptist Publication Society, at Charleston. Many consultations took place; but before any arrangements could be effected the storm of war fell upon the South, the corresponding secretary became an officer in the Confederate army, Nashville fell into the hands of the Federal army in February, 1862, the president of the board was imprisoned, and, of course, the active operations of the board ceased. It had, however, by means of stereotype plates, which had "run the blockade," printed 20,000 small neat Testaments, 14,000 of which had been distributed in the Confederate armies, chiefly in Virginia, Kentucky, South Carolina, and Georgia. Some colportage work was done in 1861, but war disturbances soon caused a suspension of it. It, however, continued to hold its regular meetings until April, 1863. The board met on the 13th of April, 1863, and made a report, which was sent to Dr. Fuller, at Baltimore, to be forwarded through the lines, but it did not reach the Convention until its session at Russellville, Ky., in 1866. In the mean time, at the session of the Southern Baptist Convention in 1863, in Augusta, Ga., a committee, composed of James P. Boyce, B. Manly, Sr., and A. M. Poindexter, recommended the abolition of the board. Their report was adopted, and the churches were recommended to send their contributions for Bible distribution to the two boards of the Convention,—Foreign and Domestic,—according to the field they wished to supply.

Of this action the board remained in ignorance until the 10th of April, 1866, when a meeting was called by the president, and its dissolution was announced. Its final report was made in May, 1866, when it reported $2148.74 in the treasurer's hands to the credit of the Southern Baptist Convention.

SUNDAY-SCHOOL BOARD.—In 1863, at the session of the Southern Baptist Convention, held at Augusta, Ga., Dr. B. Manly, Sr., chairman, rendered a special report strongly advocating the creation of a board of Sunday-schools of the Southern Baptist Convention. A committee was appointed, by whose advice the following officers were elected, besides the board and vice-presidents: Basil Manly, Jr., President; C. J. Elford, Corresponding Secretary; Rev. John A. Broadus, Recording Secretary; J. C. Smith, Treasurer; and T. Q. Donaldson, Auditor. The board was located at Greenville, S. C. Soon Rev. John A. Broadus was made corresponding secretary, with a small salary. The board within three years published several excellent little question-books and catechisms, works by Drs. Boyce, B. Manly, Jr., and Rev. L. H. Shuck, which still retain a position as favorites in the South. In January, 1866, the board began the publication of a small monthly Sunday-school paper called *Kind Words for the Sunday-School Children*, at the price of ten cents a copy. Its first editor was Basil Manly, Jr. In the year 1870 this paper was united to *The Child's Delight*, purchased from S. Boykin, of Macon, Ga., and the two papers united bore the name of *Kind Words*, which now maintains a vigorous and useful existence as a Sunday-school paper, and which still remains the property of the Convention, with a wide circulation. Its editor since 1872 has been Rev. S. Boykin. During the first three years of its existence the Sunday-School Board collected $47,684.10, most of which was expended in publishing *Kind Words*. This was in Confederate money, however, of which $4583.45 remained on hand in Confederate treasury notes at the end of the war. In the fourth year of its existence the board collected $7308, including subscriptions received for *Kind Words*, which had reached a circulation of 25,000. It continued to publish various useful catechisms, question-books, and a Sunday-school hymn-book. It employed several evangelists, who organized many Sunday-schools, and performed evangelistic labors in Missouri, North Carolina, Tennessee, and Kentucky. It is pleasing to record that in the year 1866 the American Bible Society made the board a grant of 25,000 Testaments, equivalent to a donation of $2025.16.

The fifth year of the board's existence showed some vitality and afforded cause for encouragement, yet the States manifested comparatively little interest in it. Rev. C. C. Bitting had become its corresponding secretary, and served with great efficiency. In 1868 the board was removed to Memphis, Tenn., and united with the Southern Baptist Sunday-School Union. In 1870, with Dr. T. C. Teasdale for its corresponding secretary, new life was infused into this board. Its receipts ran up to about $8000, and it had come into possession of the stereotype plates of many Sunday-school books, through its consolidation with the Southern Sunday-School Union. It consequently soon issued many valuable Sunday-school books. It also employed various colporteurs and missionaries in different States, and appeared to enter upon a grand and good work.

Its receipts during the eighth year of its existence were $18,807.09, the monetary contributions from the different States amounting to about $8000. Still it was found that the board was in debt to the amount of $4500. Dr. T. C. Teasdale resigned his position Sept. 15, 1871. No other corresponding secretary was ever secured, but the business affairs of the board were very successfully managed by S. C. Rogers, acting corresponding secretary and business manager. The receipts for 1872 were $14,240.65; and the receipts for 1873 were $16,449.25, of which $4551.27 were general contributions from the States, and $11,426.82 were received as subscriptions for *Kind Words*. In the report to the Southern Baptist Convention for that year, the editor of *Kind Words*, S. Boykin, who was acting as corresponding secretary *pro tem.*, made suggestions which led to the consolidation of the Sunday-School Board with the Domestic and Indian Mission Board of the Southern Baptist Convention, at the session which met in Mobile. It was understood that this board, now called the Home Board, should continue the publication of *Kind Words*, the Sunday-school paper of the Convention, which had attained a very large circulation. The paper was removed to Macon, Ga., in 1873, where it has been published ever since, and has been of valuable assistance, by its lesson expositions, to the Baptist Sunday-schools of the South; and it has been beneficial in indoctrinating the Sunday-school children of the Southern States in Baptist principles, and in inculcating missionary sentiments. Its management has been such that for five years in succession it earned $800 net per annum, and the contract for the next five years secured for the Convention $1000 per annum.

The Sunday-School Board of the Southern Baptist Convention was greatly needed during the war, when it was originated. After the war, the necessity for its existence was not generally acknowledged, and hence it was not adequately sustained. The field of operations was entirely too large for the instrumentality employed, and it was discerned that the Sunday-school work should properly be left to the denominational machinery of each State. Hence the State Conventions, Associations, and churches were earnestly exhorted to take in hand and perform a work far too great for any one agency, with very limited means. The result has been that each Southern State, through its State Mission, or Sunday-School Board, is now diligently, zealously, and prosperously carrying forward the Sunday-school work within its own borders.

Southern Baptist Theological Seminary, The, at present located at Louisville, Ky., was first opened at Greenville, S. C., the first Monday in October, 1859, with four professors,—James P. Boyce (chairman of the faculty), John A. Broadus, William Williams, and B. Manly, Jr. Twenty-six students attended the first session, thirty-six attended the second session, but the war diminished the number during the third session, and the conscript act of the Confederate Congress caused the suspension of the institution until the close of the war. Its property and a large subscription for its support were rendered almost valueless by the results of the conflict. At the close of the war, Oct. 1, 1865, the seminary was reopened with a full faculty and *eight* students. It was largely sustained for a time by the private fortune of Prof. Boyce. In 1866 the institution, which had hitherto been under the direction of the board of an educational society, sought and obtained the fostering influence of the Southern Baptist Convention. From this period till 1871 no attempt was made to raise an endowment. The institution was supported by annual collections. According to a resolution of the board of trustees at that date bids were received for a new location for the seminary. The Baptists of Kentucky pledged $300,000 for its location in that State. The proposition was accepted, and Louisville selected for its home. Nearly the amount pledged, which was to be supplemented by $200,000 from the other Southern States, was raised in stocks, individual bonds, and real estate, when a financial crash again blasted the prospective endowment, and the institution was saved from destruction only by a prompt subscription, in 1874, of $90,000, to be paid in five annual installments for its current expenses. In 1879 the last of what was secured of this subscription was exhausted, and little of the remains of the prospective endowment having been collected, the seminary was again brought to a great strait. But once more its friends were encouraged by the endowment of a professorship by Gov. Joseph E. Brown, of Georgia, who donated $50,000 for that purpose. The board resolved to put forth an earnest effort to add to this $150,000, previous to June, 1881. George W. Norton, Esq., of Louisville, has pledged $10,000 of this sum, provided the whole amount shall be raised. This accomplished, an endowment of at least $500,000 will be speedily completed. Through all its struggles for existence the seminary has continued to hold its usual sessions, with its full corps of professors and a regularly-increasing number of students. It was removed to Kentucky, and opened its first session in Louisville, Sept. 1, 1877. Since that time it has had an average attendance of about seventy-five students. Its present faculty are James P. Boyce, John A. Broadus, B. Manly, and W. H. Whitsitt. It is but just to say that Dr. Boyce, who is chairman of the faculty, treasurer of the board, and general financial agent for the seminary, has been the life-power of the institution from its conception to the present, notwithstanding his co-laborers have been great, good, and faithful men.

Southern Female College, The, La Grange, Ga., was organized in 1843 by Rev. J. E. Dawson, D.D., as a school of a high order for the education of young ladies. Dr. Dawson, however, was shortly succeeded by Milton E. Bacon, A.M., whose first class of five young ladies graduated in 1845. Under Mr. Bacon's administration the college rapidly grew into favor, the graduating classes and the attendance on the various departments of instruction increasing from year to year. Large and beautiful buildings were erected for the various departments of instruction and for the accommodation of the boarders, who came in large numbers from this and adjoining States. President Bacon retired from the college in 1855, and was succeeded by John A. Foster, A.M., who, remaining in charge till 1857, was succeeded by I. F. Cox, A.M., the present president.

During the administration of Mr. Bacon the Western Baptist Association purchased a half interest in the property, and secured the appointment of half the trustees, the other half remained with the president and proprietors of the remaining half interest. The college buildings were destroyed by fire, but President Cox with persistent, indomitable energy kept up the organization of the college, in spite of obstacles that seemed insurmountable, and with the returning prosperity of the country, assisted by the liberal and progressive citizens of La Grange, he erected the magnificent buildings now used by the college, and supplied the various departments—literary, music, and art —with an outfit commensurate with the demands of this age of progress and intellectual activity.

The college for nearly a quarter of a century has been under its present management. Its influence extends to all parts of the South. The graduates, to the number of 400, are found in every part of the country, filling the highest social positions, and in their literary, music, and art training beautifully illustrating the work done by their *alma mater*.

The last catalogue of the college, for the year closing in June, 1880, gives the names of 148 pupils, with unusually large classes in the various styles of painting, and in music on the different instruments. The advantages for music offered here are believed, by the best critics, to be unequaled in the South.

Spain, Mission to.—In the latter part of November, 1869, a letter was received from Rev. W. J. Knapp, asking aid of the Missionary Union in his gospel work at Madrid. On the 10th of August, 1870, the First Baptist church in Madrid was constituted with a membership of thirty-three persons. The enterprise was now taken under the charge of the Missionary Union, and Rev. John W. Terry was appointed as the assistant of Mr. Knapp, but his connection with the mission continued for only a short time. Mr. Knapp labored with great zeal and earnestness, and at times with good prospects of success. Several missionary stations were established, conversions took place, and a considerable number were baptized. Having accomplished what he regarded as his special mission in Spain, Mr. Knapp resigned and left Madrid late in the fall of 1876. The Executive Committee of the Union, referring to his work in Spain, say, "He labored with zeal and industry to plant missions in various parts of the country; but owing to the unsettled state of Spain, the frivolous character of the people, and the inefficiency of the native preachers, one promising interest after another dropped out of sight." Notwithstanding the discouragements connected with the carrying on of the mission in Spain, the Executive Committee have not felt justified in abandoning the field at present. The work is now carried on entirely by native agency. There are four churches, three ordained ministers, and 140 church members in Spain.

Spalding, Albert Theodore, D.D., pastor of the Second Baptist church, Atlanta, Ga., is a man

ALBERT THEODORE SPALDING, D.D.

of ability and administrative capacity; possesses great courteousness of demeanor, and is especially beloved by the young. He is a very ready speaker, has a fine command of language, and his pulpit manner is agreeable, even to the most fastidious. He was born in Elbert County, Oct. 20, 1831, his parents being Rev. A. M. Spalding, A.M., M.D., and Lucinda Burton. Mr. A. T. Spalding was graduated with one of the honors of his class, in 1851, from Mercer University. Impressed with the duty of preaching the gospel, he spent two years more at Mercer, in the theological department, receiving instruction from Dr. John L. Dagg and Dr. N. M. Crawford. In 1854 he was ordained as pastor of the church in Aiken, S. C., where for two years he was pastor; then he was pastor at Madison, Ga., for four years. Called to the charge of the Berean church, in West Philadelphia, he served two years, and returned South on account of the civil war, then in progress. His services were soon put in requisition at the South. The Selma, Ala., church called him, and had his labors for four years. Mobile then demanded his time and talents, and he preached for the St. Francis Street church four years. A call by the Walnut Street church, Louisville, Ky., drew him to that large church, of which he was pastor four years, succeeding Dr. G. C. Lorimer. His native State once more claimed his services, and, in response to an invitation of the Second Baptist church, he moved to Atlanta in 1871, becoming the successor of Dr. Wm. T. Brantly, who had been called to Baltimore.

He is still residing in his elegant home in that famous city of the South, the successful pastor of one of the largest, richest, and most prominent Baptist churches in the country. The degree of Doctor of Divinity was conferred upon him by Georgetown College, Ky., in 1869.

Dr. Spalding has been well educated, and is a fine scholar. He is a man of cultivated tastes and gentlemanly instincts, and, as a preacher, sustains a good reputation admirably. His churches always grow, and they contribute liberally to our benevolent projects. Wherever Dr. Spalding has labored his natural abilities, force of character, independence of spirit, and unflagging zeal have enabled him to sustain himself well. He is a member of the State Board of Missions and of the Georgia Baptist Convention, and is a trustee of Mercer University. Besides being an able preacher, he is the author of a work called "The Little Gate, an Allegory," that was published by Gould & Lincoln, of Boston.

Spalding, Rev. Amos Fletcher, was born in Boston, Mass., Jan. 12, 1821. His intention was to devote himself to mercantile pursuits, but having been called of God, as he believed, to the work of the ministry, he prepared for college at the Worcester Academy, entered Brown University in 1843, and graduated in 1847. Three years were spent in theological studies at the Newton Theological Institution, and in March, 1851, he was ordained, and settled as the pastor of the Baptist church in Montreal, Canada. He remained here but a short time. The next eight years of his ministerial life were equally divided between the churches in Cambridge, Mass., and Calais, Me. Having been called to Warren, R. I., he was pastor of the Baptist church there for ten years. He was subsequently pastor at Norwich, Conn., and Needham, Mass. The only thing Mr. Spalding published was an interesting centennial discourse on the history of the Warren church, to which reference is made in the historical sketch of this church found in this volume. He died at Chelmesford, Nov. 30, 1877. He was one of our best ministers, respected and beloved by a large circle of friends.

Spear, Prof. Philetus B., D.D., was born at Palmyra, N. Y., May 23, 1811; prepared for college at Ostrander's Mathematical School and Palmyra High School; came to Hamilton Dec. 1, 1831; entered the first class that took a full college course; graduated from college in 1836, and from the theological seminary in 1838.

He became classical teacher in 1835, tutor of mathematics in 1837, then Professor of Hebrew, and in 1850 Professor of Hebrew and Latin; has taught over forty years; was punctual, methodical, thorough, inspiring his classes with high motives, and with enthusiasm.

After the charter of 1846 he was a sort of committee of ways and means to the treasurer. Two emergencies outside of his chair taxed severely his energies:

First. The removal controversy, in the midst of the highest prosperity, was suddenly sprung upon the university, running through three years, with divided counsels and legal proceedings. His position was moderate but firm: "That a *new* institution was better for the Western field, that the possibility of removal was doubtful, and therefore Madison University should be let alone." He made a historical and legal "Brief" that became the basis of all the injunctions against removal. The positions taken in it were sustained by the courts, and a perpetual injunction issued. Twice he stood alone, once when the "compromise scheme" was urged to take away the university charter and leave "another school." He insisted that it meant death to the Hamilton enterprise, and that the charter must stay or all go. Then again, when all other questions were settled, and by deaths and resignations not even a quorum of Hamilton men were left on the university board, he took the responsibility, pecuniary and otherwise, of "negotiation and adjustment," at an hour when all that had been contended for might have been lost by losing the university charter and board; and thus the university was saved by passing through the narrowest strait possible, there being but a bare quorum to act in the adjustment.

The controversy ended, around Drs. Eaton and Spear rallied the old enthusiasm and patronage, and in three years brought back more than the old prosperity. This success brought large accretions of work and responsibility, and for ten years, besides his chair of Hebrew and Latin, he was librarian, and secretary of both boards, and of the executive and provisional committees. This outside work he discontinued when the necessity ceased.

Second. The necessity for an endowment brought another emergency. Salaries were small, income inadequate. To push out with larger plans required larger means. Hired agencies for this specific work had nearly proved a failure. Forced by the logic of circumstances, he undertook this outside work. He had already, in 1850, engineered the first subscription for $60,000, then near the close of the war he had organized and started the Colgate plan for $60,000 more. In 1864 he took more earnest hold of endowment as a voluntary and gratuitous service, but making it a side-issue for recreation. The first year $82,000 came in; for the "Jubilee," 1869-70, $220,000; for the "National Centennial," 1876, $102,000; and other sums straggling in, made for all purposes about half a million in cash since the war. This should be said to recognize the aid of those whole-souled men and women, without whom no success could have followed, namely, the Colgate Brothers and a thousand others, Trevor, with Mrs. Dr. Somers, and many new-comers, Mrs. King, D. Munroe, Cornell, and scores doing equally well.

As a student and professor he has kept pace with the university life for nearly half a century, having personally known every member of the faculty, and being familiar with the different phases of university history. He has used his pen with effect, especially in the removal controversy. He drew up the "Fraternal Address" to Baptists, issued June 9, 1849; also the "Address to the Albany Convention" of Oct. 4, 1849; and then the "Answer to Dr. Williams's Compromise Scheme" of Oct. 22, 1849,—all of which did much to settle mooted questions, and to establish the old devotion, enthusiasm, and patronage.

Speight, Gen. Joseph Warren, was born in Greene Co., N. C., May 31, 1825. His father, Hon. Jesse Speight, was a member of Congress from North Carolina, and U. S. Senator from Mississippi. His early education was obtained at Stony Hill High School. After the family removed to Mississippi, which occurred when he was twelve years old, he completed a higher course of study under the tuition of Rev. R. C. Burleson, then teaching in Mississippi. At the age of twenty he commenced the practice of law in Aberdeen, Miss., and continued it with profit and distinction until failing health induced him to turn his attention to farming. In the fall of 1853 he removed to Waco, then a village in McLennan Co., Texas, and ever since has been constantly employed in agricultural pursuits. His connections and early predilections were Methodist, but "the plain, unmistakable, and irresistible force of God's holy truth compelled him to become a Baptist." Soon after his baptism, in 1857, he was chosen a deacon, clerk of the Waco church, and superintendent of the Sunday-school, and has continued in these offices up to this time. He has served as moderator of Trinity River Association, twice as president of the General Association of Texas, and he is now moderator of Waco Association. He was grand master of the Grand Lodge of Masons in Mississippi when about twenty-seven years old. His father named him Joseph Warren from a twofold admiration of the distinguished general who fell at Bunker Hill, and who was the

GEN. JOSEPH WARREN SPEIGHT.

first Masonic grand master in North America. The son has ever been a prominent Mason. At the opening of the civil war he raised the 15th Regiment Texas Infantry, and was appointed its colonel, serving with it exclusively in the trans-Mississippi Department. He was promoted to the command of a brigade, and continued to be its general until after the battles of Mansfield and Pleasant Hill, La., at the latter of which he was wounded. His health failing, he surrendered his brigade to Gen. Polignac, and was relieved from field duty till the war closed. From its origin he has been president of the board of trustees of Waco University, and perhaps the best service of his life has been in behalf of that important institution, in whose prosperity he manifests all a father's love. Blessed in his married life, prosperous in secular pursuits, and in the prime of manhood, the church and the world will, Providence favoring, witness yet much work for man and his Creator.

Spence, Rev. George Sumner Goddard, was born in Boston, Dec. 21, 1819; fitted for college at the academy in New Hampton, N. H.; graduated at Brown University in 1839; and, after teaching four years, went to the Newton Theological Seminary, where he graduated in 1846. He was ordained as pastor of the Baptist church in West Wrentham, March 31, 1847, where he remained a year and a half, and then became pastor of the church in Augusta, Me. Such was the state of his health that he was obliged to give up the ministry and devote himself to business pursuits. He died at Salem, Mass., Sept. 7, 1863.

Spencer, Rev. David, A.M., youngest son of Charles W. and Mary Spencer, was born at Enderby, Leicestershire, England, May 23, 1839. His parents, on coming to the United States, settled in Germantown, Philadelphia, where, in 1852, they became constituent members of the First Germantown church. Into the fellowship of this church the subject of this sketch was baptized May 1, 1853. He entered upon his studies at the university at Lewisburg, March, 1857, and remained until 1862; was licensed to preach in 1859, and was ordained at Point Pleasant, Pa., Aug. 6, 1862, where he entered upon his first pastorate. He remained until March 1, 1865, when he became pastor of the Roxborough church, Philadelphia. Here he continued in abundant and fruitful labors until Oct. 15, 1877, when he accepted an appointment as district secretary of the American Baptist Missionary Union. This position he filled with remarkable ability and untiring devotion until Sept. 1, 1880, when he accepted an urgent call to become pastor of the Penn Avenue church, Scranton, Pa., in which field of labor he still remains. He served the Philadelphia Baptist Association for eleven years as clerk or associate clerk, and, as a fitting testimony to the value of his services, his letter of declination was placed upon the minutes of that body for 1878. He has also served as secretary and president of the Philadelphia Conference of Baptist ministers, and has been constantly and zealously engaged in promoting the local and general interests of the denomination. He received the degree of A.M. in 1868 from the university at Lewisburg.

Mr. Spencer is an effective preacher, a faithful pastor, and a devout Christian. He is deeply interested in all that pertains to the history and growth of the denomination, and in 1877 he published an interesting volume entitled "The Early Baptists of Philadelphia."

Spencer, Rev. James, was born in Cape Breton; was baptized, and united with the Baptist church at Sydney, the capital of that island; ordained pastor at Chester, Nova Scotia, May 17, 1853; filled useful pastorates in Nova Scotia, at Lower Granville, Digby, Tusket, and Chebogue. Mr. Spencer is now seamen's chaplain in St. John, New Brunswick.

Spilsbury, Rev. John.—In 1616, in London, England, a Congregational church was formed, of which Henry Jacob was the first pastor. His successor was John Lathorp, who presided over the church in 1633. During 1633 several persons, dissatisfied with the loose way the church held its dissenting principles, and convinced that baptism should be administered to all believers and to no babes, sought and obtained the authority of Mr. Lathorp's community to found a distinct church, in accordance with their own principles. The church was constituted Sept. 12, 1633. The Rev. John Spilsbury was elected its first pastor. William Kiffin and others, in 1638, came from the old Congregational home and united with the Baptist church. This was a Calvinistical church, and by some is supposed to have been the first church of the Particular Baptist order in modern England. This view lacks evidence. Mr. Spilsbury attained great eminence as a minister of our denomination, and was long the honored pastor of this people. He was alive in 1660.

Spotts, Rev. John, was born Oct. 8, 1784. He was of German descent, and lived in Lewisburg, Greenbrier Co., W. Va. At the age of thirty he joined the Presbyterians, and became a zealous worker in the church and Sunday-school. It is a matter of record that twenty-one of the young men connected with his Sunday-school became preachers, and one of them, Rev. J. L. Shuck, a missionary to China. Upon changing his views on the mode of baptism, he gave up his connection with the influential and popular Presbyterian church, and became a member of the small Baptist church in Lewisburg.

Not long after this he was licensed to preach, and in 1832 was ordained, and appointed to travel as a missionary.

Mr. Spotts was distinguished for his ardent love of Christian people, and for earnest piety and zeal in his work. Though called home in the very strength of his manhood, being but forty-four years of age, yet he did a grand and glorious work, and many will rise up in the last day and bless God that he lived. He was cheerful in his work, and when the summons came he met it with exclamations of triumph. "Blessed are the dead."

Spratt, George M., D.D., was born in Quebec, Canada, April 7, 1813; was converted when seven years old; entered upon his studies at Hamilton, N. Y., in 1830, having walked all the distance from his home in Pennsylvania; was afterwards ordained as a missionary in Central Pennsylvania. During his labors he organized three churches, built three meeting-houses, and baptized many converts. He subsequently became pastor of the church at Towanda, Pa., where he remained four years; was also pastor of the churches at Elmira and Fairport, N. Y.; received the degree of D.D., in 1869, from the university at Lewisburg. In the establishment and growth of this institution he contributed a large measure of efficient service. In 1851 he was made corresponding secretary and financial agent of the Pennsylvania Baptist Education Society. This position he still holds, and to the work of ministerial education he has given the best years and energies of his life. His name and his praise are in all the churches. He has labored

GEORGE M. SPRATT, D.D.

long and well, but his eye is not yet dimmed nor his natural force abated. He is an instructive and earnest preacher, and carries forward his work with intense devotion and efficiency. His daughter, Miss Harriet E. Spratt, was for several years before her death the principal of the University Female Institute at Lewisburg, Pa.

Spratt, Geo. S., M.D., was born in Winchester, England, July 8, 1787. Jan. 11, 1811, he married Miss Elizabeth Main, and three days after set sail as a medical missionary for the East Indies. Providence, however, guided him to Quebec, Canada, where he labored as pastor of an "Independent" church. Removing to Philadelphia, he became thoroughly convinced of the truth of Baptist sentiments, and received not only Scriptural baptism, but also ordination, the brethren of that day being unwilling to recognize the orthodoxy of an alien administration of either baptism or the official act of consecration to the functions of the gospel ministry. His first pastorate in his new connection was over the recently-formed church in Bridgeton, N.J. Subsequent labors were given to the churches of Shamokin and vicinity. The church of Covington, Tioga Co., was formed through his labors; Alleghany and Mead Corners, churches in the northwestern portion of the State, shared in his pastoral efforts. The last church he served as pastor was the Great Valley, in Chester County. After closing his labors here, the growing infirmities of years precluded any change, but he supplied occasionally the Valley Forge church, until his sudden death,

GEORGE S. SPRATT, M.D.

Jan. 28, 1863, in the seventy-sixth year of his age and the fifty-third of an acceptable ministry. "A sinner saved by grace" was the memorial he ordered in his will to be engraved on his tombstone. A son, the corresponding secretary of the Pennsylvania Baptist Education Society, and a grandson, John Spratt Weightnour, pastor in Pittsburgh, Pa., are in the active service of the ministry.

Spurden, Charles, D.D., was born May 25, 1812, near London, England, where he was converted in 1832; was baptized by Rev. Edward Steane, D.D., of Camberwell; studied four years at the Baptist College, Bristol, under the presidency of Dr. Crisp; ordained in 1841 pastor of the Baptist church of Hereford; became principal of the Baptist Seminary, Fredericton, New Brunswick, in 1843, and continued ably to discharge the duties of his office till his resignation in 1867. Eminently gentlemanly and Christian, sound in theology, earnest and clear as a teacher and preacher, Dr. Spurden's work and ministry in New Brunswick proved a blessing to the denomination and the public.

Spurgeon, Rev. Charles Haddon, the most widely-known preacher of the age, was born at Kelvedon, County of Essex, England, June 19, 1834. At an early age he was removed to his grandfather's house at Stambourne, in the same county, and remained there several years. His grandfather, who was the pastor of the Independent church of that place, and a man of considerable note for his long-continued and useful labors, was

REV. CHARLES HADDON SPURGEON.

soon impressed with the child's thoughtfulness and keen moral perceptions. Most of the pious people who were acquainted with the family seem to have anticipated a remarkable career for him, and the well-known Rev. Richard Knill, when visiting at Stambourne in 1844, was so struck with the boy's ability and character that he declared to the assembled family his " solemn presentiment that this child will preach the gospel to thousands, and God will bless him to many souls." Having received a liberal education at a private academy at Colchester, he engaged himself in his fifteenth year as assistant in a school at Newmarket conducted by a member of the Baptist denomination. This engagement led to his first associating himself with Baptists, his family and friends being all Independents. At this time, however, he had not found peace in Christ, although deeply convinced of sin. About the close of the year 1850 his distress of soul greatly increased, and he attended religious services in various places, seeking salvation in vain, until on December 15 he happened to go into a Primitive Methodist chapel in Colchester, and heard a sermon on the text, " Look unto me, and be ye saved." From that hour he rejoiced in salvation. He now felt it his duty to make a profession of his faith in Christ, and to unite himself with the Baptists. Although this step was not altogether pleasing

to his family, his father and his grandfather being Pedobaptist ministers, they at length yielded to his wishes, and he was baptized May 3, 1851. A year afterwards he removed to Cambridge, still continuing to teach as an usher, or assistant master. Having joined the old Baptist church in St. Andrew's Street, of which Robert Hall and Robert Robinson had been pastors, he soon found a congenial sphere of work in connection with "The Lay-Preachers' Association." He became a welcome visitor at the thirteen village stations supplied by this body, and in 1852 he was invited by the little church at Waterbeach to assume the pastoral charge. His family and friends wished him to enter a theological seminary, and steps were taken to introduce him to Dr. Angus, the distinguished president of Regent's Park College. Through a misunderstanding the proposed meeting did not take place, and he continued at Waterbeach. His ministry there was so eminently successful that in the autumn of 1853 the deacons of the ancient church in Southwark, London, the church of Benjamin Keach, Dr. Gill, and Dr. Rippon, were led to invite him to supply the pulpit. For some time the congregation there had been dwindling away, and at his first service there were only 200 attendants in a building capable of holding 1200. The result of the first sermon was a great increase in the evening attendance, and an invitation to come again as soon as possible. After three more Sundays he was asked to supply for six months with a view to a permanent settlement as pastor. He agreed to come for three months. Before the three months had passed away the small minority who had opposed the motion to call him to the pastorate were absorbed into the majority, and on April 28, 1854, he accepted their cordial and unanimous call. His metropolitan ministry was a grand success from the start. All London was soon talking of the youthful Whitefield who had been discovered in a Cambridgeshire village. From London his fame spread throughout the land. Within a year the church edifice had to be enlarged. During the alterations Exeter Hall was hired, and overflowing congregations in that spacious and central place attracted towards him the attention and criticism of the press. His " Exeter Hall Sermons" were published and had an extensive sale. Invitations to preach flowed in upon him from all quarters, to which he readily responded. In 1856, the enlarged chapel having proved utterly inadequate to accommodate the crowds who flocked to hear him, he commenced preaching in the Music Hall of the Surrey Gardens, an immense building, which, although capable of seating 7000, was always densely crowded. Here notable persons of all sorts were frequently seen curiously studying this pulpit phenomenon. But, of course, the Music

SPURGEON'S TABERNACLE, LONDON, ENGLAND.

Hall could not be the home of a church, and in August, 1859, the foundation-stone of the Metropolitan Tabernacle was laid. The structure was completed in March, 1861, and at the conclusion of a series of opening services the entire cost, £31,000 ($150,000), was contributed. Subsequent improvements have enlarged the accommodations, and there are now seats for 5500 persons, and standing-room for 1000 more. It is well known that the congregations always fill the place on Sundays when Mr. Spurgeon preaches. When the church took possession of the Tabernacle there were 1178 members on the roll; there are now upwards of 5500. Mr. Spurgeon's frequent attacks of illness, and the great increase of the membership, led the church, in 1868, to appoint his brother, the Rev. James Archer Spurgeon, as co-pastor, and this fellowship in service is still harmoniously and prosperously maintained. Besides his pulpit labors, Mr. Spurgeon's pen is ever busy. His contributions to the press and to theological literature rank him with the most eminent masters of style, and are scarcely less effective than his preaching. He is also among the most active leaders in philanthropic work, and princely in his gifts. An orphanage for boys was commenced in 1867, and one for girls in 1880, at Stockwell, London. In these buildings 500 or 600 fatherless children are received, being admitted between the ages of six and ten years, and remaining until they are fourteen. The most needy applicants are generally preferred by the trustees, without regard to sectarian distinctions. Mr. Spurgeon's remarkable faculty of administration has made the Stockwell Orphanage famous among works of benevolence. Early in his ministry he commenced at his own charge the enterprise which has developed into the Pastors' College, from which institution some hundreds of students have gone forth as preachers and missionaries. In 1865 he started a monthly magazine, the *Sword and Trowel*, purposing to make it the foster-parent of the college and orphanage, and the project has proved every way successful. A Colportage Association and Mrs. Spurgeon's Book Fund to provide free gifts of books for poor pastors, are valuable adjuncts to the colossal work of which the Tabernacle is the centre. Week by week for upwards of twenty-five years a sermon by Mr. Spurgeon has been published, and not a few of them have had a remarkably large sale. They have been translated into several languages, and their entire circulation is probably unparalleled. Mr. Spurgeon has two sons, twins. Both are preachers, and one is pastor of a Baptist church at Greenwich, near London.

Spurgeon, James Archer, co-pastor of the Metropolitan Tabernacle, London, and only brother of the senior pastor, studied at Regent's Park College, and began his regular ministry at Southampton in 1859. Subsequently he became pastor of a church at Croydon, near London, at the same time assisting in tutorial work at the Pastors' College. In 1868 he was invited to his present position, in which he has won the confidence and esteem of the denomination.

Stackelford, Josephus, D.D., was born in Portsmouth, Va., Feb. 6, 1830; baptized by Rev. Martin Ball, in Mississippi, in 1849; graduated from Mercer University in 1855, and ordained the same year at Pontotoc; after a brief missionary work in Memphis, Tenn., he accepted the presidency of the Baptist Female College at Moulton, Ala., in 1856, which was flourishing until broken up by the war. He then entered the army of the Confederate States as captain of cavalry, and became chaplain in 1863. Retiring from the army in 1864, he reopened his school; constantly had charge of churches while he was teaching. In 1865 he commenced in Moulton the publication of the *Christian Herald*, then the only Baptist paper in the State. It was published for some time in Tuscumbia, and then in Nashville, until purchased by the proprietors of the *Christian Index*. He was pastor in Tuscumbia for quite a number of years. In 1876 he removed to Forest City, Ark., as pastor, and was president of the Baptist College in that place. Returned to Alabama in 1879, and took charge of the high school at Trinity, where he still presides, having charge of several churches. The degree of Doctor of Divinity was conferred on him by the Alabama Agricultural College in 1872. Dr. Stackelford stood for many years as our most distinguished minister in North Alabama.

Stallings, Rev. J. N.—The son of a useful Baptist minister, Mr. Stallings was converted at the University of North Carolina; read and practised law for several years before he began to preach, and has combined in himself several different pursuits at the same time. Just now he is pastor, teacher, and editor; for many years he was pastor, attorney, and editor, and has been in politics somewhat, having represented his county, Duplin, in the State convention of 1875. He is principal of the Warsaw High School and a very useful man.

Standard, The.—In the year 1853 the subscription list of the *Watchman of the Prairies*, published at Chicago, was purchased from Rev. Luther Stone by Rev. J. C. Burroughs, then pastor of the First Baptist church in Chicago. The new paper, *The Christian Times*, was for some months conducted by Mr. Burroughs, in association with Rev. H. G. Weston, of Peoria, and Rev. A. J. Joslyn, of Elgin. In November, 1853, Rev. Leroy Church and Rev. J. A. Smith became joint proprietors and editors of the paper, the proprietary interest of the latter, however, being soon transferred to Rev. J.

F. Child, who was succeeded in the proprietorship by Edward Goodman. By Messrs. Church & Goodman the paper continued to be published until Jan. 1, 1875, when the interest of Mr. Church was purchased by Dr. J. S. Dickerson, of Boston, who removed to Chicago and became connected with the paper as joint editor and joint proprietor. Upon his death, in March, 1876, his proprietary interest passed to his widow, Mrs. Emma R. Dickerson. His eldest son, J. Spencer Dickerson, has since become also a member of the firm, which is now known as Goodman & Dickerson.

During the twenty-seven years of its history the paper has consolidated with itself *The Illinois Baptist*, published for several years at Bloomington, Ill., by Dr. H. J. Eddy ; *The Witness*, at Indianapolis, by Rev. M. G. Clarke,—at which time its name was changed to *The Christian Times and Witness*,—and *The Michigan Christian Herald*, of Detroit. At the time of the last-named consolidation the name was changed to *The Standard*, the name by which it is now known.

The Standard is the denominational organ for Illinois, Indiana, Michigan, Wisconsin, Minnesota, Iowa, Kansas, Nebraska, Colorado, Dakota, and Wyoming, with a circulation, also, in all the States and Territories of the Union ; its circulation, in fact, having become strictly national. It now ranks second in the number of its subscribers and readers in the list of American Baptist journals. Rev. J. A. Smith, D.D., has been connected with the paper since 1853 either as associate editor or editor-in-chief, in which latter capacity he still serves.

Stanford, John, D.D., was born Oct. 20, 1754, in Wandsworth, Surrey, England. In early life the Saviour found him, and revealed himself to him. He united with the Baptist church in Maze-Pond, London. He was ordained, and served the church at Hammersmith for a few years as pastor. In 1786 he arrived in Norfolk, Va., but soon after sailed for New York ; there he opened a seminary, and he received the patronage of many respectable families. He preached for the Rev. John Gano and others with such power that his time on Lord's days was continually occupied in that blessed work. For one year he was pastor of the First church of Providence, R. I., to their great satisfaction. He, however, felt a peculiar call to preach for nothing, and to teach for a living. He returned to New York, and carried out his plan for thirty-six years.

In 1813 he was appointed chaplain of the almshouse and city hospital and of the State prison ; along with these institutions he regularly ministered at the orphan asylum, the penitentiary, lunatic asylum, debtors' prison, and the house of refuge. Several of the benevolent institutions of New York were largely indebted to him for their existence. His influence was so great that the city authorities and the citizens generally were prompt in carrying out his plans. He was justly regarded as "one of the most practical and distinguished philanthropists of modern times." He died Jan. 14, 1834. In 1830 Union College, Schenectady, conferred upon him the degree of Doctor of Divinity.

Stapp, Hon. Milton, was born in Scott Co., Ky., in 1793. He studied and practised law ; was for a number of years a member of the Indiana Legislature, and was Speaker of the house, first at Corydon and afterwards at Indianapolis. He was regarded as the leader of the internal improvement system of the State. He was for four years lieutenant-governor, and was the first fund commissioner. He was for several years internal revenue collector at Galveston, Texas. He was for a number of years' mayor of Madison, Ind., his home. He became a member of the Madison Baptist church in 1844, and was an active Christian. He was for six consecutive years president of the Indiana Baptist State Convention, and was president of the board of trustees of Franklin College during several different years. He was sanguine, and scarcely ever failed in accomplishing what he undertook. "He did more for his city and county than any other man who ever lived in it."

He died in Galveston, Texas, in 1870, in his seventy-seventh year, and his remains were brought to his old home for burial.

Starkville Female Institute, located at Starkville, Miss., was founded by Rev. T. G. Sellers, who is principal.

Staughton, Wm., D.D., one of the first of American preachers and educators, was born at Coventry, England, Jan. 4, 1770. At the age of twelve he wrote poems from Goldsmith's "Animated Nature," which were published, and thought to indicate great native talent. Having been baptized at the age of seventeen by Rev. Samuel Pearce, of Birmingham, he turned his attention to the ministry, and took a thorough course of study at Bristol College, graduating about the year 1792. At this time he was called to succeed Dr. Ryland at Northampton, but feeling drawn towards America, he left England in 1793, and became pastor at Georgetown, S. C., where he remained eighteen months. Becoming dissatisfied with the Southern climate he went North, and became pastor of the church and principal of the seminary at Bordentown, N. J. This was followed by pastorates at Jacobstown and Burlington, N. J., at which latter place he remained until 1805, when he became pastor of the First church, Philadelphia, Pa., a position which he retained until 1811, when he resigned to accept the pastorate of a colony from the First church, called the Sansom Street church. In this latter position he remained with wonderful success until 1823, when he removed to Washington to assume the presidency of Columbian College, to which he had been elected in 1821. Here he continued until April 3, 1829, when he resigned his connection with the college, and returned to Philadelphia. In August of the same year he was elected president of Georgetown College, Ky., and in October started for this new field of labor. At Washington, D. C., he was taken sick, and died Dec. 12, 1829, in the sixtieth year of his age.

Dr. Staughton was a man of wonderful eloquence. During his long ministry in Philadelphia he was recognized as the leader of his profession, and invariably preached to crowded houses. He was profoundly interested in education. Before coming to Philadelphia he was constantly engaged in teaching, and while in Philadelphia was principal of a Baptist theological institution for the training of ministers. It was his custom also to deliver lectures in select schools on various subjects, particularly the subject of botany, in which he was an adept. He was the first corresponding secretary of the American Baptist Board of Foreign Missions, and through his whole life gave much time and toil to the missionary cause. He was also the father of the Philadelphia Bible Society, the first female Bible society in the world. In all this varied work he exhibited a zeal and industry which made him the admiration of his time. Traditions of his eloquence and power still linger about the scenes of his active life, and keep alive the memory of his name. (See portrait in Appendix.)

At the early age of twenty-eight he received the degree of D.D. from Princeton College. He was twice married. His first wife, Maria Hanson, died in January, 1823, and his second wife, Anna C. Peale, who survived him, in 1878. A memoir of Dr. Staughton was published by his son-in-law, Rev. S. W. Lynd, D.D., in 1834.

Stearns, Rev. Harrison William, was born in Conway, Mass., in October, 1848; educated at Brown University, from which he graduated in 1867, and at Newton Theological Seminary, from which he graduated in 1870, and was ordained the same year. He was settled as pastor at Minneapolis, Minn., two years, and at Clinton, Wis., six years. He has been the pioneer church and Sunday-school missionary of the Wisconsin Baptist State Convention two years, and holds the position now. He has planted a number of churches and organized Sunday-schools in the new settlements in the northern portion of the State. He is giving his best strength to the mission work of the State. His ideal of a new church, founded according to the New Testament model, is lofty and grand. He delights in this foundation work, and he is pre-eminently fitted for it. He is a safe, devoted, and consecrated servant of Jesus Christ.

Stearns, Prof. John William, son of Rev. O. O. Stearns, of Lodi, Wis., is a native of Sturbridge, Mass., where he was born in 1840. In 1852 his father removed with his family to Racine, Wis., and assumed the pastorate of the Baptist church in that place. Here young Stearns was fitted for college at the Racine High School. In 1854 he entered the Freshman class at Harvard University, Mass., from which he was graduated in 1860. In 1865 he received the appointment of Professor of Latin in the University of Chicago. In 1874, having been tendered the position of director of the National Normal School at Tucuman, in the Argentine Republic, he resigned his professorship in the University of Chicago to accept one in the National Normal School in the Argentine Republic. Returning in 1878, after having spent some months in Europe, he was elected, in August of the same year, president of the State Normal College at Whitewater, Wis., the oldest and most important of her four normal colleges.

Prof. Stearns published in the *North American Review* for July, 1860, "Homer and his Heroines;" in the *Christian Review* for 1864, "The Miltonic Deity;" and in the *Baptist Quarterly*, "The Emperor Marcus Aurelius."

Prof. Stearns is a fine specimen of thorough scholarship and noble character. His rise to eminence is the result of hard study in his early youth, laying a thorough foundation for the future structure, and subsequent intense study and application. He is æsthetic in his tastes, refined in his ideas, and profoundly consecrated to his profession. At the age of forty years he has succeeded in taking a place in the front rank of American educators.

Stearns, Rev. Myron N., was an earnest, able, and evangelical missionary, pastor, and preacher in Oregon. He was born at Monkton, Vt., Jan. 1, 1812, and was baptized at the age of seventeen in Essex, N. Y. Having a great desire to preach the gospel, he obtained a good education at Brown University and at Denison, O. He served for some years successively the churches at Londonville, O., Jericho, Vt., and Plattsburg, N. Y. In 1854 he accepted a call to the Table Rock church, Oregon, where he was pastor four years. In 1858 he accepted the position of principal of the Roseburg Academy. Two years later he settled upon a farm in order to support his family, preaching nearly every Lord's day to the poor in the destitute regions of the State. In 1864 he settled at Oregon City, and gave himself wholly to the work of a missionary evangelist until, in 1867, he removed to Santa Clara, Cal., and was pastor of the church in that city until his death, Dec. 29, 1868.

Stearns, Oakman S., D.D., a son of Rev. Silas Stearns, was born in Bath, Me., in 1818, and graduated at Waterville College in the class of 1840, and at Newton in the class of 1846. He was instructor in Hebrew at Newton one year, 1846-47. His ordination took place May 19, 1847, and he became pastor of the Baptist church in Southbridge, Mass. The relation continued for seven years. For one year he was pastor in Newark, N. J., and then became pastor of the church at Newton Centre, where he remained thirteen years. In 1868 he was appointed Professor of Old Testament Interpretation, which position he now holds.

The degree of Doctor of Divinity was conferred on Dr. Stearns in 1863 by Colby University, of which he is a trustee.

Prof. Stearns has eminent qualifications for the position he occupies, and enjoys the grateful love of the students, to whom his instructions have been of priceless value.

Stearns, Rev. Orrin Orlando, is a native of Monkton, Addison Co., Vt., where he was born in February, 1810. His childhood was spent in and near the place of his birth. He entered Brown University in 1833, and graduated in the class of 1837. Having, soon after his conversion, felt it his duty to preach the gospel, he devoted himself to the work of the Christian ministry. Soon after graduating at Brown University he received an invitation to the pastorate of the Baptist church at Sturbridge, Mass., and was ordained by that church Sept. 28, 1837. He held pastorates in New England at Sturbridge, Mass., and at Hancock, Deerfield, Milford, Manchester, N. H., and at Thomaston, Me. In these pastorates his ministry was very much blessed, the churches were strengthened and built up in doctrine and practice, and numerous additions were made to the membership. Mr. Stearns's ministry in New England was, however, several times interrupted by ill health, requiring him to abandon temporarily the work of preaching. He employed these intervals chiefly in teaching. He was principal of the Hancock Literary and Scientific Institution two years, and of the Rockingham Academy at Hampton Falls two years. While principal of the Hancock Academy he also served the Baptist church in Hancock as pastor. In 1854, having received an invitation to the pastorate of the Baptist church in Racine, Wis., he removed to that State. This pastorate continued four years. In 1858 he became the pastor of the Baptist church in Winona, Minn. At the end of three years, owing to the failure of his health, he retired to his farm near Lodi, Dane Co., Wis., which has since been his home. His health having improved, in 1863 he became the pastor of the Baptist church in Lodi, and remained in that relation ten years, when he retired from the active duties of the ministry, having devoted thirty-six years to pastoral work.

Mr. Stearns has always taken a deep interest in the work of education. During his pastorate in Racine he was superintendent of schools, and has acted in the same position in Dane County, his present place of residence. One of his sons, Prof. J. W. Stearns, is president of the Normal College at Whitewater, Wis., and another of his sons, C. M. Stearns, is a professor in the University of Chicago.

He is thoroughly educated, and has made extensive acquirements in the knowledge of God's Word. Although the full results of his ministry cannot be known here, enough fruit appeared in connection with his work to attest his eminent usefulness as a faithful servant of God, destined to be crowned with honor in the day of his Lord's appearing.

Stearns, Shubal, was born in Boston, Mass., Jan. 28, 1706. He was the son of Shubal Stearns and Rebecca Larriford. About 1745, Mr. Stearns joined the New Lights, as the converted Congregational communities that originated from the ministry of George Whitefield in New England were designated. Called of God to proclaim the unsearchable of Christ, he speedily became a minister among the pious New Lights, and exercised his gifts among them until 1751. At this time, like many of his brethren, he was constrained by reading the Scriptures to accept believer's immersion as the baptism of the New Testament; and after receiving this conviction, as the Saviour alone was his Master, he came out boldly as a Baptist. He was immersed on a profession of his faith, in Tolland, Conn., by Rev. Wait Palmer, in 1751, and on May 20th of that year he was ordained to the Baptist ministry by Mr. Palmer and Rev. Joshua Morse.

Mr. Stearns received an impression, as he thought from God, that there was a great work for him to do outside of New England, and he obeyed what was undoubtedly a divine call, and started in 1754 for his expected field of labor. He had no definite section to which he directed his steps, but expecting divine guidance, he was constantly looking out for providential openings. He stopped for a time at Opeckon Creek, Va., where there was a church under the pastoral care of Rev. S. Heton. Mr. Stearns rested for a short time at Cacapon, near Winchester, but anticipating greater success in his ministry than he enjoyed in that place, he removed, with his relatives, to Sandy Creek, N. C. There, as soon as he arrived, he constituted a Baptist church of sixteen persons, "Shubal Stearns and wife, Peter Stearns and wife, Ebenezer Stearns and wife, Shubal Stearns, Jr., and wife, Daniel Marshall and wife, Joseph Breed and wife, Enos Stimpson and wife, and Jonathan Polk and wife" being its constituent members. Shubal Stearns was elected pastor of the infant church. These devoted servants of God immediately built a meeting-house for public worship. Daniel Marshall and Joseph Breed were appointed to assist the pastor in his ministerial duties.

In the region around Sandy Creek the people knew nothing of the Christian religion except what they had learned from Episcopal clergymen, who in that section, at that time, were unconverted men, and their irreligious darkness was dense. The new heart to them was an unknown mystery, and paltry and commonly unpractised duties, instead of the Saviour's sufferings, were the only known means of salvation. The instructions of Mr. Stearns and the godly lives of the church members were an astonishing revelation to their neighbors. Soon some of them were called by the Spirit into the liberty of the gospel, and their experience filled their acquaintances with even greater wonder. A mighty outpouring of the Holy Spirit fell upon the truth proclaimed by the pastor and the licensed preachers of Sandy Creek church, and as a result throngs of converts surrounded the gospel banner, and mission communities were organized far and near. The parent body in a few years had 606 members, and in seventeen years from its origin it had branches southward as far as Georgia, eastward to the sea and the Chesapeake Bay, and northward to the waters of the Potomac. It had become the mother, grandmother, and great-grandmother of forty-two churches, from which 125 ministers were sent out as licentiates or ordained clergymen. And in after-years the power that God gave Shubal Stearns and his Sandy Creek church in its early years swept over Virginia, North Carolina, Georgia, and South Carolina with resistless force, and brought immense throngs to Christ, and established multitudes of Baptist churches. There are to-day probably thousands of churches that arose from the efforts of Shubal Stearns and the church of Sandy Creek.

Mr. Stearns traveled extensively in his own region, preaching Jesus, organizing churches, and giving counsel to the new communities which were formed. And his labors in every department of his work were remarkably blessed. Through him, in 1758, three years after the Sandy Creek church was formed, the Sandy Creek Association was organized. For twelve years all the Separate Baptist churches in Virginia and the Carolinas were members of this body. All who were able traveled from its remote extremities to attend its annual meetings, which were conducted with great harmony, and afforded such edification as induced them to undertake with cheerfulness long and laborious journeys. By means of these meetings the gospel was carried into many new places where the fame of the Baptists had previously spread. As great multitudes attended from distant places, chiefly through curiosity, many of them were charmed with the piety and zeal of this extraordinary people, and petitioned the Association to send preachers into their neighborhoods. In these Associational meetings Shubal Stearns exerted an immense influence. Other men among the Separate Baptists were conspicuous for their ability and usefulness, but in the entire body in the several States Mr. Stearns wielded a founder's authority. Elder James Read, in speaking of the first meeting, says, " The great power of God was among us, the preaching every day seemed to be attended with God's blessing. We carried on our Association with sweet decorum and fellowship to the end. Then we took leave of one another with many solemn charges from our reverend *old father, Shubal Stearns*, to stand fast until the end." This Association conducted its annual meetings without a moderator for several years after it was formed, which shows the extraordinary modesty of Mr. Stearns; its harmony, when we remember that its members and ministers were nearly all new converts without experience, proclaims the great power possessed by Mr. Stearns in its deliberations.

The founder of Sandy Creek church "was of small stature, had a very expressive and penetrating eye, and a voice singularly harmonious; his enemies, it is said, were sometimes captivated by his musical voice. Many things are related of the enchanting sound of his voice, and the glance of his eyes, which had a meaning in every movement." "He managed his voice in such a way as to make soft impressions upon the heart and bring tears from the eyes, and anon to shake the very nerves and throw the physical system into tumults and perturbations. All the Separate Baptists copied after him in tones of voice and actions of body." "When the fame of the preaching of Mr. Stearns reached the Yadkin, where I lived," says Mr. Tidance Lane, " I had a curiosity to go and hear him. Upon my arrival I saw a venerable old man sitting under a peach-tree with a book in his hand and the people gathering about him. He fixed his eyes upon me immediately, which made me feel in such a manner as I never had felt before. I turned to quit the place, but could not proceed far; I walked about, sometimes catching his eyes as I walked. My uneasiness increased and became intolerable. I went up to him thinking that a salutation and shaking hands would relieve me, but it happened otherwise. I began to think that he had an evil eye, and ought to be shunned, but shunning him I could no more effect than a bird can shun the rattlesnake when it fixes its eyes upon it. When he began to preach my perturbations increased, so that nature could no longer support them, and I sank to the ground." Mr. Lane afterwards became a very useful Baptist minister.

It is related on the best authority that "Elnathan Davis had heard that one John Steward was to be baptized by Mr. Stearns on a particular day, and, as Steward was a large man and Stearns of small stature, he concluded that there would be some diversion, if not drowning. Therefore he gathered about eight or ten of his companions in wickedness and went to the spot. When Mr. Stearns began to preach Elnathan drew near to hear him, while his companions kept at a distance. He was no sooner among the crowd than he perceived that some of the people began to tremble as if in a fit of the ague. He felt and examined, to see if it was not a pretense. Meanwhile one man leaned on his shoulder, weeping bitterly. Elnathan, perceiving that he had wet his new white coat, pushed him off, and ran to his companions, who were sitting on a log away from the congregation, to one of whom, in answer to his inquiry, he said, 'There is a trembling and crying spirit among them, but whether it be the Spirit of God or the devil, I do not know. If it be the devil, the devil go with them, for I will never more venture myself among them!' He stood awhile in that resolution, but the enchantment of Mr. Stearns's voice drew him to the crowd once more. He had not been long there before the trembling seized him also. He attempted to withdraw, but his strength failing, and his understanding being confounded, he, with many others, sank to the ground. When he came to himself he found nothing in him but dread and anxiety, bordering on horror. He continued in this situation some days, and then found relief by faith in Christ." Mr. Davis afterwards became a successful minister of Jesus. We mention these two well-known cases as illustrations of the extraordinary power attending the preaching of Shubal Stearns.

That he had a remarkable voice and eye is unquestionable; but he was eloquent, wise, humble, pathetic, full of faith, and wholly consecrated to God, and few men ever enjoyed more of the Spirit's presence in the closet and in preaching the gospel. He was undoubtedly one of the greatest ministers that ever presented Jesus to perishing multitudes, and one of the most successful soul-winners that ever unfurled the banner of Calvary. Had he been a Romish priest, with as flattering a record of service to the church of the popes, long since he would have been canonized, and declared the "patron saint" of North Carolina, and fervent supplications would have ascended to the most blessed of American intercessors from devout Catholics, and stately churches would have been dedicated to the holy and blessed St. Shubal Stearns, the apostle of North Carolina and the adjacent States.

Mr. Stearns died Nov. 20, 1771, and his remains were interred near the Sandy Creek church.

Stearns, Rev. Silas, was born in Waltham, Mass., July 26, 1784. In the year 1804 he was baptized by Rev. Dr. Stillman, of Boston, and, impelled by the warmth of his newly-found love for the Saviour, he longed to preach the gospel and win souls to Christ. He spared no pains in faithful preparation for the ministry, devoting such spare time as he could secure for several years to earnest study, until, in the judgment of his friends, he was deemed to have made sufficient progress to justify his receiving a regular license from the church in North Yarmouth, Me., to do the work of an evangelist. Having done good service for his Master in Freeport, Me., he removed to Bath, then a pleasant town on the Kennebec River, and there gathered a small Baptist church, which was recognized Oct. 30, 1810. For over thirty years he preached to the church in Bath, and was honored and loved for his great sincerity and unwearied devotion to his work. It can with truth be said of him, he was a good man and full of the Holy Ghost and of faith.

Steele, Miss Anna, was the daughter of a Baptist minister of Broughton, England. In early life she learned to cultivate the poetical taste with which her Creator had endowed her, and she succeeded so well that some of her hymns have been regarded by competent judges as equal to the sacred songs of Charles Wesley or Augustus Toplady; and of her psalms it has been said that "in literalness, smoothness, and evangelical power they may almost compare with those of Dr. Watts."

The first lines of some of her hymns will be recognized by almost every Christian who speaks the English language,—"The Saviour! oh what endless charms," "Come, weary souls, with sins distressed," "Jesus, the spring of joys divine," "Father of mercies, in thy word," "He lives, the great Redeemer lives," "The Saviour calls, let every ear," "Jesus, in thy transporting name," "Come ye that love the Saviour's name," "Stretched on the cross, the Saviour dies," "While my Redeemer's near," "How oft, alas! this wretched heart," "Ye glittering toys of earth, adieu!"

While her productions were chiefly devotional, she composed other poems of great beauty. Miss Steele possessed talents of a high order, and has wielded over the hearts of Christians a vast influence for more than a century; and such are the beauty and sweetness of her sacred songs that they will guide the thoughts and affections of Christians while the Anglo-Saxon tongue is spoken by mortals. She died about 1779. Two volumes of her poetry were published during her life, and a third soon after her death.

Steele, Rev. D. A., A.M., was born in Herefordshire, England, in 1838; converted and baptized in Halifax, Nova Scotia, in 1857; is a graduate of Acadia College; ordained June 20, 1865, at Wolfville, Nova Scotia; pastor at Canso, 1865-67; became, in 1867, pastor of the Baptist church of Amherst, Nova Scotia, where he continues to minister with ability and success.

Stennett, Rev. Joseph, was born at Abingdon, County of Berks, England, in 1663. His father, Edward Stennett, was a clergyman of some distinction and of considerable suffering during the Parliamentary war. With the blessing of God upon the prayers and efforts of his pious parents, Joseph Stennett was born again in very early life.

After finishing the ordinary branches of his education he mastered the French and Italian languages, acquired a thorough knowledge of Hebrew and other Oriental tongues, and successfully studied philosophy and the liberal sciences.

He came to London in 1685, and on the 4th of March, 1690, he was ordained pastor of the Seventh-Day Baptist church, meeting in Pinner's Hall. He preached on Sunday to other Baptist churches, but he remained the faithful pastor of the Pinner's Hall church till his death. His polished manners, ready address, fine intellect, and extensive learning speedily gave him a high position among the Baptists, and, a little later, in other denominations. At the request of the Baptists he drew up and presented an address to William III. on his deliverance from the "Assassination Plot." This document was highly commended. When he published his thanksgiving sermon for the victory at Hochstedt, in 1704, a nobleman, without his knowledge, presented a copy of it to the queen (Anne), with which her majesty was so pleased that she sent a gift to the eloquent and patriotic minister. He composed beautiful hymns, which are still used in the churches, which drew forth commendations from Mr. Tate, the poet laureate. His version of the "Songs of Solomon," and his hymns, secured such a reputation for him as a poet and Hebrew scholar that he received an application to revise the English version of the Psalms of David. Dr. Sharp, archbishop of York, speaking of this proposition, declared that "he had heard such a character of Mr. Stennett, not only for his skill in poetry, but likewise in the Hebrew tongue, that he thought no man more fit for that work than he." In 1702, when David Russen assailed the Baptists in his book "Fundamentals Without a Foundation, or a True Picture of the Anabaptists," Mr. Stennett was invited to refute the work; and he accomplished the task with so much learning, such solid reasoning, and such an utter rout of all the forces of Mr. Russen, that he was satisfied never again to meddle with the Baptists. The reputation he acquired by quieting David Russen prompted his friends to secure his services to write a complete history of Baptism. He intended to comply with this service if his life should be spared, and for some years he collected materials for it, but he was unable to carry out his design.

He was offered preferment in the Episcopal Church, and there is reason to believe that he could have reached an exalted position in it, but the conscience of Mr. Stennett was not for sale, though all the wealth of earth had been offered for it. He died July 11, 1713. His works, in four octavo volumes, were published in 1732, and a fifth, containing his reply to Mr. Russen, was designed to follow.

Stennett, Joseph, D.D., was born in London, Nov. 6, 1692. His educational advantages, of which he made the best use, were of the highest order. At fifteen he gave himself to the Saviour, and he was baptized. At twenty-two he entered upon the Christian ministry; twenty-three years afterwards he came to London as pastor of the church in Little Wild Street. Dr. Gill preached one of the two sermons delivered on the occasion of his settlement in London. At that time he was in possession of splendid powers, matured by a wide range of experience, and by information from all ages and regions. He was among the most eloquent preachers of the day, and soon his talents were recognized all over the metropolis of Britain. He was on agreeable terms with Dr. Gibson, bishop of London, a true follower of Jesus. He was personally known to King George II., who cherished a warm regard for him. He was an eloquent defender of the doctrines of grace against Socinianism. On behalf of the Dissenting ministers of the "Three denominations in London (Congregational, Baptist, and Presbyterian), on Oct. 3, 1745, Mr. Stennett presented an address to the king, congratulating his majesty on his return to England, on the triumph of his arms in America, and on his successes on the continent of Europe." The address also deprecated "the present unnatural and rebellious attempt to impose upon these kingdoms a papist (Charles Edward) and an abjured Pretender."

The University of Edinburgh, in 1754, created him Doctor of Divinity on the "recommendation of his royal highness the Duke of Cumberland, their chancellor," who sent Mr. Stennett the diploma by his secretary.

Dr. Stennett died Feb. 7, 1758, in the sixty-sixth year of his age. His funeral sermon was preached by Dr. Gill, and in it he stated that "his death was a public loss, particularly to the whole Dissenting interest." Dr. Stennett was a Seventh-Day Baptist, though pastor of a regular Baptist church. He was the author of eight small works.

Stennett, Samuel, D.D., was born in Exeter in 1727, and converted and baptized when young.

Like his father, he was a man of superior talents and of great erudition. Ivimey says, "His proficiency in Greek, Latin, and the Oriental tongues, and his extensive acquaintance with sacred literature, are so abundantly displayed in his valuable works that they cannot fail to establish his reputation for learning and genius." He had been accustomed to move in the society of persons of refinement, and, on entering upon his pastoral duties in London, he was remarkable for the ease and suavity of his manners, for the good breeding, the polished language, and the graceful ways of the true gentleman. He was frequently in company with persons enjoying the highest social distinction, and in such situations as gave him an opportunity to commend Baptists and aid Dissenters of all denominations. In 1763 he was made a Doctor of Divinity by King's College, Aberdeen. Among the noble men who waited upon his ministry and loved him with the affection of a friend was John Howard, the philanthropist. In a letter from Smyrna, written to Dr. Stennett Aug. 11, 1786, Mr. Howard says, "I bless God for your ministry; I pray God to reward you a thousandfold. My friend, you have an honorable work; many seals you have to your ministry."

The meeting-house was rebuilt during the ministry of Dr. Stennett. He fell asleep in Jesus Aug. 24, 1795, in the sixty-eighth year of his age. He ministered to the Little Wild Street church, as assistant and successor to his father, for forty-seven years. His father, Joseph Stennett, D.D., his grandfather, Joseph Stennett, his great-grandfather, Edward Stennett, his brother, Joseph Stennett, and his son, Joseph Stennett, were all Baptist ministers.

Most of the works of Dr. Samuel Stennett were reprinted, in 1784, in three octavo volumes. In 1772 he published a work entitled "Remarks on the Christian Minister's Reasons for Administering Baptism by Sprinkling." This was a duodecimo of 170 pages. In 1775 he issued a volume of 300 pages, called "An Answer to the Christian Minister's Reasons for Baptizing Infants." He was also the author of two productions treating of appeals to Parliament by Protestant Dissenters for relief from persecuting enactments; these are not found in his collected works.

Stephens College is located at Columbia, Mo., and has for years ranked among the first ladies' schools of the State. Prof. R. P. Rider is the principal.

The literary course is divided into seven distinct schools. Its students are admitted to lectures in the State University. Teachers of ability and experience are employed. In 1880 it had 14 teachers and 170 students.

Stephens, James L., was born in Garrard Co., Ky., Nov. 17, 1815. His father was of English descent and his mother of Scotch. His father removed to Missouri in 1819, and located in Boone County. He was a man of culture, with a fine library. His son, James L., was a clerk, in 1836, in a store in Columbia, where he has resided ever since, except for a short time. J. L. Stephens has been a leading man in Central Missouri in business, educational, and religious interests. He was active in securing the location of the State University at Columbia, and his liberal donation caused Stephens College, of Columbia, to be named after him. He also contributed generously to William Jewell College, at Liberty. He was nominated for governor of Missouri, and made an honorable canvass.

He married Amelia Hockaday, daughter of Judge J. O. Hockaday, of Fulton, Mo. Mr. Stephens and his family are members of the Baptist Church, and to religious and educational interests he gives much of his time.

Sterry, Rev. John, son of Roger and Abby (Holmes) Sterry, was born in Providence, R. I., in 1766. His father was an Englishman, but his mother was from Stonington, Conn. Related to Gov. Fenner, he had good educational advantages, and studied for a time in Brown University. He and his brother, Consider Sterry, were eminent mathematicians, and published a volume on mathematics, at which time John learned the printer's trade. Near 1790 he removed to Norwich, Conn., where he established himself as a printer, book-binder, bookseller, paper-maker, author, and publisher. On his conversion, after settling in Norwich, he became a Baptist, and in 1800 founded the First Baptist church in that city, of which he was ordained the pastor Dec. 25, 1800. Under his ministry were revivals of power in 1816, 1817, and 1819. He was the joint author with his brother of two mathematical works, "The American Youths' Arithmetic and Algebra," and "Arithmetic for the Use of Schools in the United States," favorably noticed in England. He assisted Mr. Nathan Daboll in his almanacs, and Rev. William Northup in preparing his hymn-book. He invented the art of marbling paper, and an improved method of bleaching cottons, that was adopted in Rhode Island. He was the chief party in editing and publishing *The True Republican*, a paper that was strongly Republican in doctrine, and did service in securing the full recognition of religious liberty in the constitution of Connecticut. Mr. Sterry was a strong thinker, able writer, logical preacher, devoted Christian, and faithful advocate of all the interests of the people. In his day he was an efficient toiler and wise leader. He died in Norwich, Nov. 5, 1823, in his fifty-seventh year.

Stevens, Rev. Adoniram Judson, was born at

Gaspereaux, Nova Scotia, Dec. 26, 1848. He was converted and baptized in Wolfville, Nova Scotia. He was a graduate from Acadia College in June, 1873; studied theology at Newton; was ordained at Kentville, Nova Scotia, in 1873; became pastor of the Baptist church, Fredericton, New Brunswick, in 1878, whence he exchanged a useful and happy pastorate for higher and unwearying service in the upper sanctuary, March 15, 1880.

Stevens, Rev. Carlos W., was born in Sunbury, Liberty Co., Ga., Sept. 30, 1823. His parents, Oliver and Eliza S. Stevens, were members of the Baptist Church, and were distinguished for their many Christian virtues. From early childhood the fruits of his Christian training were manifested in Carlos's exemplary deportment at home and among his schoolmates. Truthfulness and conscientiousness in the discharge of every duty were as distinctive characteristics of his youthful days as of his manhood in all the varied relations of life. About the fourteenth year of his age he experienced converting grace, and his whole subsequent life was an illustration of vital godliness. He was prepared for college at the Wasthourville Academy, and entered Franklin College, where he remained two years, and finished his course preparatory for the ministry at Mercer University.

The greater portion of his life was spent in preaching the gospel and teaching, in each of which vocations he met with commendable success. As a teacher, his discipline was mild, yet decisive; as a pastor, he was indeed the good shepherd, and he secured the love and admiration of all with whom he associated, and by whom even now his memory is cherished with peculiar tenderness. Charity in its broadest significance, that of love for all, was the crowning glory of his life. In the midst of his usefulness, and in the vigor of his manhood, after a short illness, he died, at Sparta, Ga., Oct. 31, 1866.

Stevens, E. A., D.D., was born in Liberty Co., Ga., Jan. 23, 1814. He was a graduate of Brown University and of the Newton Theological Institution. His appointment to the foreign mission field bears the date of June 27, 1836. His ordination took place at Ruckerville, Ga., May 6, 1837, and he sailed the 28th of the October following from Boston for the East, arriving at Maulmain Feb. 19, 1838. While studying the language he preached for a while to the English congregation in Maulmain. The theological school for native assistants was placed under his charge, and was reopened on the 4th of March, 1839, and continued in active operation until August, 1841, when it was suspended for want of funds to carry it on, but it was reopened in the summer of 1844. Dr. Stevens edited the *Religious Herald* for several years, besides attending to all his other duties as pastor, preacher, and teacher. The pastorate of the Burman church was transferred, in 1851, to Dr. Wade, thus allowing Dr. Stevens to devote himself more closely to the completion of the Burmese dictionary, which was left unfinished by Dr. Judson. In 1854, Dr. Stevens returned to his native land. He had been transferred to the Rangoon, Burman, mission previous to his departure, and on his return to Burmah, early in 1857, he commenced again his labors. A brick chapel was completed and dedicated Oct. 30, 1859. Year after year Dr. Stevens prosecuted his work with untiring industry and zeal, and was rewarded by seeing the abundant success of his labors. In the early part of 1867 he had the pleasure of welcoming his son, Rev. E. O. Stevens, and wife to be his helpers. In 1875 he once more returned to this country to recuperate his health, remaining here until the fall of 1877. He arrived in Rangoon Dec. 27, 1877, and once more resumed the busy life he has always led in Burmah.

Stevens, Rev. George Dana Boardman, the pastor of the Baptist church in Bloomington, Wis., is a native of South Paris, Me., where he was born Sept. 5, 1838. He obtained a hope in Christ at the age of twenty, and united with the Baptist Church. He graduated from Colby University in the class of 1863. In January, 1868, he came to Richland Centre, Wis., and engaged in teaching as the principal of the public school in that place. He was made superintendent of public instruction for Richland County, which position he held for several years. It was through his earnest efforts that the Baptist church—the first Baptist organization in the county—was organized in Richland Centre, and its meeting-house built. Having strong convictions that it was his duty to preach the gospel, he abandoned teaching and was ordained to the work of the Christian ministry by the Richland Centre Baptist church, April 6, 1871, and at once became the pastor of the church. Dr. Wm. H. Brisbane was moderator of the council, and Rev. Joel W. Fish preached the sermon. He remained pastor at Richland Centre four years, building up the church and doing an immense amount of pioneer work in the county and surrounding counties. He has been for six years the useful and highly esteemed pastor of the Baptist church in Bloomington, Wis.

Stevens, John, D.D., for nearly half a century identified with the leading educational and missionary movements among the Baptists of Ohio, was born in Townsend, Mass., June 6, 1798. At the age of seventeen he was taken by his father, Solomon Stevens, a man of the New England type, intelligent and strong, to Middlebury, Vt., where, in 1817, he entered college, and graduated in 1821. After a year of teaching as principal of the Montpelier Academy, though not then a professing

Christian, he entered Andover Theological Seminary, where he greatly enjoyed the instruction of Moses Stuart. He had been reared a Congregationalist, but being convinced of the truth of Baptist doctrines while yet in the seminary, in 1823, he was baptized by Dr. Lucius Bolles at Salem, Mass. In 1825, at the urgent solicitation of President Bates, he broke off his theological studies, in which, by extreme assiduity, he had injured his health, and became classical tutor in Middlebury College, where he taught with great success for three years. For another three years he was classical tutor in the academy at South Reading (now Wakefield), Mass. This position he resigned to go to Ohio.

JOHN STEVENS, D.D.

His first service in Ohio was rendered as editor of the *Baptist Weekly Journal*, a new religious newspaper for the Mississippi Valley, established in 1831. He continued in this position seven years, and did a generally successful work in the midst of much difficulty and opposition,—the Ohio Baptists of that day numbering less than 10,000, and a large proportion of them being opposed to Sunday-schools, missions, and an educated ministry. In 1828 he became Professor of Moral and Intellectual Philosophy in Granville College. Dr. Going was at that time president of the college, but as he was expected to give his time to theological instruction and public efforts, the main duties of the presidency fell on Prof. Stevens. Much of the early success of the college is therefore due to him. In 1843 he was engaged by the American Baptist Missionary Union to be its district secretary for Ohio and Indiana, and for the following twelve years he continued in this work, raising the collections for foreign missions from an annual average of $962 to nearly $5000.

In 1834 a society called the Western Baptist Education Society was formed at Cincinnati. Prof. Stevens acted as the secretary of this society until 1856, when its work passed into the hands of the Ohio Baptist Education Society. He was also largely engaged in the establishment and support of the Western Baptist Theological Institute, which was opened for students at Covington, Ky., in 1845, under the presidency of Rev. R. E. Pattison, D.D., and subsequently, when disagreements occurred and a separation took place, in the founding of a similar institution at Fairmount, near Cincinnati. Throughout all this period he was unceasingly active both in the cause of education and of missions, and made many personal sacrifices of time and money.

In 1859 he was made Professor of Greek and Latin in Denison University. In 1868, the two departments having been separated, he took the chair of Latin, which he retained until 1875. During all these years he maintained the fresh zeal and enthusiasm of youth, and kept himself fully abreast with the age. His hours of leisure and his vacations were spent in the service of the Education Society. In 1875 he resigned his professorship, but by the unanimous vote of the trustees was continued as Emeritus Professor. Two years afterwards, April 30, 1877, he died at the house of his son in Granville, after a single day's illness.

Prof. Stevens was ordained in the Ninth Street church, Cincinnati, in 1844. In 1873 he received the degree of D.D. from the University of Rochester. He was married in 1836 to Mary, daughter of Deacon Wm. Arnold, of Charlestown, Mass., a woman rarely endowed in heart and mind. He leaves two sons, one, George E., in business in Cincinnati, O., and the other, Wm. A., professor in Rochester Theological Seminary.

Stevens, Hon. Thaddeus, was born in Peacham, Caledonia Co., Vt., April 4, 1793. He graduated with honor at Dartmouth College in 1814. He removed to York, Pa., where he practised law, and soon became a prominent man in the public affairs of his adopted State. He came to reside permanently in Lancaster in 1842. He was elected to the U. S. House of Representatives in 1848, and again in 1850. He was re-elected in 1858, and to every subsequent Congress until his death, which occurred in Washington, Aug. 11, 1868.

Mr. Stevens was for some time the leader of his party in the House of Representatives, and its chief man throughout the free States. Since the days of Henry Clay no man had a larger or more devoted throng of followers. They admiringly spoke of him as "The great commoner."

He was a member of no church, but he was brought up in the principles of the Baptists by his godly mother, and to his latest breath he proclaimed himself a Baptist. About twenty years before his death, Mr. Stevens and another gentleman united, in purchasing a church edifice for a small Baptist community then organized in Lancaster. The church had the use of this building free until they disbanded. In his will he left $1000 to the Baptists to assist in building a meeting-house in Lancaster, provided the work should be undertaken not later than five years after his decease. In recording the bequest he declared that the gift was in honor of his mother, to whom he was indebted for his attainments and usefulness. "To-day there stands in Lancaster a beautiful and substantial meeting-house, largely growing out of Mr. Stevens's bequest," and within its walls a hopeful Baptist church meets to worship God.

"His name is dear to the people of Lancaster. He was very liberal; it is commonly reported that he never refused to respond to the appeals of any needy person." He and President James Buchanan sleep in cemeteries within a few rods of each other.

Stevenson, Rev. Samuel, a distinguished educator and friend of Sunday-schools in Arkansas, was born in Philadelphia, Pa., in 1815, and took an irregular course in Georgetown College, Ky., where he graduated in the English course in 1847. He came as a pioneer educator into the State shortly after his graduation and established at Arkadelphia the "Arkadelphia Institute," the first Baptist school in the State; was present and participated in the organization of the State Convention in 1848, and became an active promoter of missions and Sunday-schools at a time when these objects were but little understood. He was ordained after he came to the State, and preached occasionally. After the war he removed to Little Rock, and engaged in business. He died in 1878.

Steward, Rev. Ira R., son of Nathan and Drusilla (Rogers) Steward, was born in New London, Conn., April 3, 1795; served in the war of 1812; was converted in 1816; baptized same year by Rev. Francis Darrow, and united with First Baptist church in Waterford, Conn.; ordained deacon in New London; ordained in same city to the ministry March 26, 1833; assisted Rev. Roswell Burrows, in Groton; settled in Waterford and Montville; succeeded Rev. R. Burrows, in Groton, for eleven years from 1837; in 1842 received 260 members; also labored as an evangelist at Norwich; at the solicitation of Dr. Spencer H. Cone and others, settled with the Baptist Bethel in New York City, and labored with remarkable success for twenty years, and became known over the world; having in early life been at sea, and knowing sailors and human nature, and having a deep Christian experience, his ministry in New York was one of great power; "previous to his entering upon the ministry he had memorized the entire New Testament and a large part of the Old;" retired from the pastorate in 1865, and died Dec. 26, 1867, aged seventy-two years; was buried in New London, Conn.

Stewart, Rev. Henry Greene, was born in East Clarendon, Vt., April 25, 1811. He graduated at Brown University in the class of 1839; studied at Newton; accepted a call to the Baptist church at Cumberland Hill, R. I., where he remained for about nine years. He became pastor of the Baptist church in Seekonk, Mass., in 1859. For eight years he was in the service of the American and Foreign Bible Society. At the end of this period he accepted a call to the church in Warwick. During the late war he was employed by the "Freedmen's Bureau," and in his official capacity made extensive tours through the South and West, gathering what information he could concerning the condition and the wants of the colored people. The service he performed was arduous, but of great value. Returning to his home, he acted for some time as the missionary of the Rhode Island Baptist Convention in the destitute sections of the State. His health was seriously impaired by the hardships he had passed through in his labors for the "Freedmen." Hoping that he might be benefited by a residence in Nevada, he secured an appointment which took him to that State. Scarcely had he reached his new home when he died, July 6, 1871.

Stewart, Rev. J. L., was born in Mississippi about the year 1833. He was graduated from the University of North Carolina, read law at Chapel Hill, and was ordained in 1864, Rev. N. W. Wilson, D.D., Geo. W. Purefoy, D.D., and T. H. Pritchard, D.D., forming the Presbytery. He removed to Sampson County soon after his ordination, where he has since resided, and has obtained an enviable reputation as a lawyer and preacher, both of which professions he has successfully prosecuted. He has been for years moderator of the Eastern Association, and is one of the best presiding officers in the State.

Stewart, William, D.D., was born in the parish of Haddam, Dumfriesshire, Scotland, on July 27, 1835. He studied at Annan Academy and the University of Glasgow, at which latter institution he obtained by competition two of the highest scholarships. Having removed to Canada, he was engaged for a time in teaching a high school, and when the Canadian Literary Institute was opened, in July, 1860, he was appointed Professor of Classics. In the same year he was admitted to an *ad eundem* degree in the University of Rochester. He has been pastor successively of the First Baptist church, Brantford; of the Bond Street church, Toronto; and of the Park Street church, Hamilton,—three of the largest churches in the province of Ontario. He was also for three years editor, and for nearly seven years editorial contributor, to the *Canadian Baptist*. In 1876 Knox University conferred on him the degree of D.D. In addition to taking an active part in the societies charged with the great work of ministerial education, foreign missions, and home missions, for each of which he has at times been secretary, Dr. Stewart has published several pamphlets and discourses, among which are a prize essay on the "Officers of the New Testament Church," and a sermon on "Future Punishment." At present (September, 1880), owing to failing health, he is in California.

Stifler, William H., D.D., was born in Blair Co., Pa., in 1841, and left home in 1857 for the West. He entered the preparatory department of Shurtleff College, Upper Alton, Ill., in 1858. He was converted in 1859. On account of interruptions in his course of studies by time spent in teaching and in the United States service, he did not graduate until 1866 in the college department, and 1869 in the theological department. He was ordained pastor of the Pana Baptist church, Pana, Ill., in 1869. In May, 1872, he became pastor of the Baptist church at Cedar Falls, Iowa. In May, 1876, he became pastor at Cedar Rapids, and in October, 1879, he became pastor of the Calvary Baptist church, Davenport, where he is now laboring. During his ministry in Iowa he has been prominently connected with all the denominational interests in the State, and has rendered efficient service, especially in the Sunday-school work.

Stiles, Ezra, D.D., a Congregational minister of Newport, R. I., in 1763, a leader of distinction in his denomination, who was subsequently president of Yale College, had much to do with the charter of our first American college.

Dr. Manning, the first president of Rhode Island College, now Brown University, arrived at Newport in July, 1763. At the house of Col. Gardner, deputy governor of the colony, and a Baptist, a meeting of about fifteen Baptist gentlemen was held to arrange about framing a charter for the new Baptist college. Dr. Manning was requested to prepare a sketch for examination on the following day, when the brethren present should again meet. At the next meeting Dr. Manning's "rough" draft was read, the tenor of which was, that this institution was to be a Baptist one, but that as many of other denominations should be taken in as was consistent with the said design. Hon. Josias Lyndon and Col. Job Bennet were "appointed to draw a charter," with a petition that it should be approved by the Legislature, to be laid before the next General Assembly; they, pleading inexperience, requested permission to solicit the assistance of Dr. Stiles. Their request was granted, and the whole matter was left to Dr. Stiles, after he was informed that "the Baptists were to have the lead in the institution, and the government thereof forever, and that no more of other denominations were to be admitted than would be consistent with that."

Dr. Stiles undertook the matter, and received some help from Mr. William Ellery. The day when the charter was to be read to its Baptist friends Dr. Manning had to sail for Halifax, so that he could not remain long enough to see that the intentions of the founders of the proposed college were carried out. Besides, the document was difficult to understand without careful examination. The corporation of the projected college was to consist of trustees and fellows, and these boards were "to sit and act by distinct and separate powers." The Baptists thought that the trustees were "the principal branch of authority, and as it was provided that nineteen out of thirty-five were to be Baptists, the Baptists were satisfied," without a proper examination of the deceptive document. But Dr. Stiles had so "artfully constructed the charter as to throw the power into the fellows' hands, whereof eight out of twelve were Presbyterians, usually called Congregationalists, and that the other four might be of the same denomination for aught that appeared in the charter to the contrary."

When the charter came before the Assembly, and a vote was demanded, Daniel Jenckes, whose daughter Rhoda was the mother of Nicholas Brown, and who was afterwards chief justice of the Providence County Court for nearly thirty years, demanded time to examine it; he was allowed, after some opposition, to take it home while the Assembly was at dinner; and comprehending the real wickedness of the charter, he went to consult Gov. Lyndon, who was a Baptist, and the governor understanding its character immediately called on Dr. Stiles and demanded why he had perverted the design of the charter. His answer was, "I gave you timely warning to take care of yourselves, for we had done so with regard to our society" (denomination). He finally added that "he was not the rogue." Mr. Jenckes succeeded in having the charter confirmation postponed for that session, "*notwithstanding the attempts of Mr. Ellery and others of the Presbyterians to the contrary.*" Before the breaking up of the Assembly, by order of the house, at the request of Mr. Jenckes, the Speaker gave him the charter on his promise that it should be forthcoming at the next meeting of the Assembly.

Mr. Jenckes showed the charter to many, and loaned it to others for examination; and when he needed it he sent for it to Dr. Ephraim Brown, who had borrowed it last, and then to Samuel Nightingale, to whom he had loaned it; but it could not be found, "Neither do I know," says Mr. Jenckes, "to this day what became of it." The Baptists prepared another charter, and when it was presented to the next Assembly, it was warmly opposed by the Congregationalists; the charter intrusted to Mr. Jenckes was demanded, and when he explained the way in which it was lost he was rudely charged with secreting it, and with being guilty of a breach of trust; and such clamorings and bickerings came from the enemies of the Baptists in the Assembly that they gave up their efforts to secure the confirmation of their charter for that session. In the mean time an advertisement was posted up in the most public places, and the most diligent efforts employed to secure the lost charter, but it could not be found for nearly a century. The new charter was granted in 1764 "by a great majority," after much opposition and many unjust reproaches against Mr. Jenckes. He richly deserved the abuse of the Congregationalists of Rhode Island; for when they and their religious leader, Ezra Stiles, had determined to "*confiscate*" by stealth a Baptist college charter, he saw the treachery and frustrated its success.

Strange to say, the lost copy of Dr. Stiles's charter, for the failure to return which to the Assembly Mr. Jenckes suffered so unjustly in his feelings and reputation, "*was recently found,*" Dr. Guild writes in 1864, "*among the archives of Dr. Stiles's church, and is now in the possession of the university*" (Brown). These facts are taken from statements of Dr. Manning, Daniel Jenckes, and Dr. R. A. Guild in "Life, Times, and Correspondence of James Manning," pp. 46-49, 52-54, 56.

Stillman, Samuel, D.D.—Among the honored names that have been handed down to us in the annals of the eighteenth century, that of Samuel Stillman is not the least worthy of mention. Born of respectable parents, in the city of Friends, Feb. 27, 1737, and spending the first eleven years of his life in the atmosphere of that city, he was surrounded by influences that were conducive to both moral and intellectual growth, and in very early childhood these influences made noticeable impressions upon his character.

In his eleventh year he went with his parents to Charleston, S. C., where was laid the foundation upon which he afterwards built the magnificent superstructure of his life. His teacher, a Mr. Rind, was celebrated as an instructor, and under his guidance he made rapid progress in his studies.

His childhood seems to have been not uncommon. While at times under deep religious convictions, he was not permanently affected by them until he had nearly passed out of his boyhood. A

SAMUEL STILLMAN, D.D.

youth of earnest character, he was not hasty in deciding the great question that troubled him, but, having decided it, he was not slow in obeying the Word of God and the voice of conscience. He was, therefore, soon received by baptism into the church of which the Rev. Oliver Hart was then pastor, and under whose preaching he had been converted.

At this time his mind was directed towards the work of the ministry, and he determined to enter at once upon the preparation necessary for that service, which seemed to him of all others most imperatively to demand his attention.

His theological studies, which he began immediately upon the completion of his classical course, were carried on under the direction of his pastor, and his earliest sermons were preached in the church of which he was a member. The first of these was delivered on the 17th of February, 1758. One year later he was ordained to the work of an evangelist. An index to his character, and the impression he had made at this early date, is given in the recommendation of the Charleston Association of 1758, wherein they speak of him as "an orderly and worthy minister of the gospel."

Soon after his ordination he took charge of the church at James' Island, near Charleston, and, when comfortably settled, he visited Philadelphia, and took back with him to his Southern home a helpmeet in the person of Miss Morgan, a daughter of Dr. John Morgan, a distinguished surgeon and professor of that city.

It was at this time also that the degree of A.M. was conferred upon him by the College of Philadelphia. He received the same honor from Harvard University in 1761.

Upon his return to James' Island he entered with zealous spirit upon the duties of his pastorate, but his labors were seriously interfered with by ill health. After a year and a half of unsatisfactory toil, he was obliged to resign his charge, and went with his family to Bordentown, N. J., at which place he preached for two years. In October, 1763, he received an invitation from the Second Baptist church of Boston to assist their pastor, Rev. James Bound, whose health had been impaired by a paralytic affliction. In response to this invitation, he left Bordentown, became Mr. Bound's assistant, and continued to preach for the Second church until November, 1764, "when he accepted an invitation to the pastoral office of the First Baptist church, made vacant by the resignation of Mr. Condy." He was installed pastor of this church Jan. 9, 1765, and here he spent the remainder of his life. Only once during a pastorate of forty-two years was he away from his church for any great length of time. "During the occupancy of the town by the British troops, in 1775, the church was in a dispersed condition," and Dr. Stillman removed his family to Philadelphia. In June, 1776, however, he returned to his post of duty, and gathered together his little flock, assembled them in their house of worship, and continued regular services until the close of the war. During all this time the church was almost the only one in the city in which public worship was held. In passing, be it observed, that this meeting-house was, in 1830, "taken down, removed, and rebuilt, with a new and neat finish," and became the property of the South church.

Dr. Stillman's ministry was long and remarkably successful. Revivals in his church, of unusual importance, were of frequent occurrence, and became the subject of deep interest throughout the country. Especially noticeable were the outpourings of grace in 1804 and 1805, and the *Baptist Magazine* for those years comments upon the wonderful dignity of the work.

Throughout his long pastorate Dr. Stillman was not at any time a hale, hearty, and vigorous man, and yet he lived to be the last of his contemporaries in the ministry in and around Boston. For a year previous to his death he had looked forward to that event, and even desired his church to call a colleague, in order that, in case of his death, they might not be without a shepherd. Nor were his apprehensions groundless, for before Mr. Clay, whom they invited to assist Dr. Stillman, had completed his arrangements for leaving his church in Georgia, the aged warrior passed to his rest.

His last sermon was from Luke xxiv. 50, 51, and his theme was "The Saviour's Ascension." He had preached every Sabbath until within two weeks of his death, having had the prayer of his life answered,—that his ministry and his life might end together. His last sickness was paralysis, and he lived only twelve hours after receiving the stroke. He died on the 12th of March, 1807, and on the Monday following, in the meeting-house where he had preached so earnestly, services were held over his remains, at which his old and dear friend and co-worker, Dr. Baldwin, officiated. The last words of Dr. Stillman were, "God's government is infinitely perfect."

As a preacher, Dr. Stillman had few peers and no superiors in New England. His church was frequently visited by President Adams, Gen. Knox, Gov. Hancock, and men of like prominence. While eminently practical, his sermons were sound in doctrine, ever abounding in sketches of character and striking in illustration. "Stirring, eloquent, pathetic, impassioned, graceful," all of these adjectives have been employed by his friends in endeavoring to describe them.

As a pastor, he was untiring in his devotion to his work, declining to enter upon any festivity or social pleasure which in the least interfered with his duties to his church. His own private interests were ever secondary to those of his flock, and even for persons in no way connected with his ministry he had at all times a ready hearing and an open hand.

In his social relations, he was eminently popular, and beloved, affectionate in his manner, of that good-natured temperament which never fails to win the hearts of others. Attentive, even to excessive courtesy, cultured and scholarly, he was a man of whom all spoke well and no one evil. Dignified and discreet, he was yet full of a spiritual joyousness that was exceedingly refreshing to behold, and he was never out of the reach of those who claimed his interest or compassion.

As a public citizen, he had at heart the good of his country, and he was never deaf to the calls that were made upon him to take part in her affairs. Without being a partisan in his politics, he was firm in his convictions. Among his numerous sermons, published at different times from 1766 to 1805, may be mentioned " A Sermon on the Repeal of the Stamp Act," 1766; "A Sermon on the General Election in Massachusetts," 1779; "Thoughts on the French Revolution," 1794; all of which reveal the deep interest which the author felt in national affairs.

It may be said of Dr. Stillman, as it has been

said of few men, he showed himself "approved unto God, a workman that needeth not to be ashamed, rightly dividing the Word of truth."

Stimson, Samuel M., D.D., was born in Winchenden, Worcester Co., Mass., Feb. 6, 1815. He came with his parents into Western New York in 1819. He was baptized in 1831, and became a constituent member of a Free-Will Baptist church in the township in which he resided. In 1834 he joined the Pendleton Baptist church. He was licensed to preach by it in 1840, and at once set about the work of preparation. He studied three years in the best schools he could find in that part of the country. In this preparation his wife was of great service. He was ordained by the Shelby Baptist church in 1843. He has been pastor of six different churches,—Binghamton, Batavia, and Shelby, N. Y., Brighton, Mass., and Terre Haute and Vincennes, Ind. He was in Batavia eleven years, in Terre Haute eight years. At the close of his pastorate in Terre Haute he took an extended tour through Europe. He was appointed district secretary of the American Baptist Missionary Union in 1873, which office he still holds. He was one year president of the Indiana State Convention. He presides with ability, and is attractive in his social qualities.

St. Joseph Female College is located at St. Joseph, Mo. The building cost $100,000. It is on an elevated site near the city, and the location is healthy. The course of instruction is thorough and extensive. The president, Rev. E. S. Dulin, D.D., LL.D., is a man of large experience, and popular as a teacher. The board of trustees is composed of leading men in St. Joseph, and in Missouri.

St. Louis Seminary, for young ladies, is located in St. Louis County, seven miles from St. Louis. Prof. B. T. Blewett, LL.D., is principal. The buildings are spacious and the grounds beautiful, overlooking the city of St. Louis. This school is a Christian home for young ladies, under the management of most experienced teachers.

St. Louis, the Second Baptist Church of, was nearly completed when, on Jan. 3, 1879, it was destroyed by fire. Not discouraged by the disaster, the zealous and generous community for whose worship it was intended immediately commenced to rebuild; and on November 6 of that year their efforts were successful, and the beautiful structure was solemnly dedicated to the worship of Almighty God.

The house and lot cost $218,000. The edifice seats 1300 persons. The building is free from debt. Dr. W. W. Boyd is the able pastor of this influential church.

Stockbridge, John Calvin, D.D., was born in Yarmouth, Me., June 14, 1818. He was the son of Deacon Calvin Stockbridge, of the firm of W. R. & C. Stockbridge, merchants, doing an extensive business in Yarmouth, and warm supporters of the Baptist church in that place. He was fitted

JOHN CALVIN STOCKBRIDGE, D.D.

for college at the academy in his native village. Entered Bowdoin College in 1833, where he remained two years, and was out of college part of a year. He became a member of the Junior class in Brown University in 1836; was hopefully converted in his Senior year, and baptized at Yarmouth in August, 1838, by Rev. Z. Bradford; graduated September, 1838. He took charge of an academy in Cummington, Mass., for six months, and then became principal of the Ladies' Seminary in Warren, R. I., which position he filled for two and a half years. In the autumn of 1841 he entered the Newton Theological Institution, and took the full three years' course. He was called to the pastorate of the First Baptist church in Waterville, Me., in September, 1844, and was ordained Jan. 8, 1845, Prof. J. R. Loomis, now ex-President Loomis, late of Lewisburg University, being ordained at the same time. He remained pastor of the Waterville church three years, when he resigned and accepted a call to the Baptist church in Woburn, Mass. His ministry in this place was greatly blessed, and large accessions were made to the church. At the end of five years he was invited to take charge of the First Baptist church in Providence, R. I., during the absence of its pastor, Rev. Dr. Granger, who, with Rev. Dr. Peck, had been appointed as a deputation to visit the stations of the

SECOND BAPTIST CHURCH, ST. LOUIS, MO.

Missionary Union in the East. He entered upon his work in September, 1852. Before the return of Dr. Granger he received a call from the Charles Street Baptist church, Boston, to take the place made vacant by the death of Rev. Dr. Sharp. He accepted it, and was publicly recognized as pastor Oct. 23, 1853. He remained in this position until the last Sabbath in May, 1861. For a year or two he supplied different churches, and for nearly two years was pastor of the Cary Avenue church in Chelsea, Mass. Impaired health led him to give up all ministerial work and for six months to travel in Europe. Returning home, he accepted a call to the Free Street Baptist church in Portland, Me., and he commenced his labors Nov. 1, 1865. In the autumn of 1867 he removed to Providence, to take charge of a young ladies' private school, of which Prof. J. L. Lincoln had been the principal for eight years, and continued in this position for ten years, preaching nearly the whole of this time, and acting as pastor of the Third Baptist church in Providence between two and three years. The honorary degree of Doctor of Divinity was conferred on Dr. Stockbridge by Harvard College in 1859. He was chosen a member of the corporation of Brown University in 1856. He compiled the memoirs of Rev. Baron Stow, D.D., has written articles for the *Christian Review* and the *Bibliotheca Sacra*, and has been a constant contributor to the religious and secular press. His travels in Europe have afforded him themes for lectures, which he has delivered in various cities and villages in the United States. His residence is in Providence, R. I.

Stockbridge, Joseph, D.D., U.S.N., was born in Yarmouth, Me., in 1811. He pursued his preparatory studies at the academy in his native village, and was a graduate of Bowdoin College in the class of 1830. He studied law at the Harvard Law School, and practised his profession for a few years in his native State, and then took up his residence in New York, where he became a Christian. Having decided to enter the ministry, he spent two years at the Newton Theological Institution. Among his classmates there were Rev. Drs. A. H. Granger, G. W. Samson, H. G. Weston, and President M. B. Anderson, of Rochester University. Having received an appointment as chaplain in the U. S. navy, he was ordained in New York in 1842, the sermon being preached by Rev. Dr. William R. Williams, from the appropriate text, Acts xxvii. 24, "God hath given thee all them that sail with thee." In the discharge of his official duties Dr. Stockbridge has visited many parts of the earth, and occupied several stations as chaplain on land. He has also had intimate connections with the public press, both religious and secular. As a correspondent of *The Watchman*, under the signature of "Mallah," he has furnished a large amount of matter, especially in the form of interesting and instructive letters from foreign lands. He has made himself especially conspicuous in resisting the tendency to appoint so many chaplains from the clergy of the Episcopal Church, claiming that under a government having no state church the leading denominations of Christians may reasonably demand a proper share of representation among the chaplains of the navy. In 1868 he received the degree of D.D. from the University of Western Pennsylvania. He is now (1881) in Europe, having been placed on the retired list.

Stocks, Judge Thomas, a most useful and influential Baptist deacon, was born Feb. 1, 1786, in an Indian fort in Greene Co., Ga. His father died ten years after, and he was brought up by an uncle. In 1807 he married and settled in Greene County. In 1813 he was elected to the Legislature of Georgia, in which he served twenty years, eight as a representative and twelve as a senator, acting as president of the senate for eight years. For thirty-two years he was judge of the Inferior Court of Greene Co. He was converted in 1826, united with the church, and ever after continued an earnest, zealous, liberal, and influential Baptist. He was appointed on the executive committee, in 1829, to raise the money for founding Mercer Institute, and was largely instrumental in its establishment. For ten years, from 1847 to 1856, inclusive, he was president of the Baptist State Convention; for years he was a trustee of Mercer University; and few men in the denomination did more than he to advance education, missions, and the Baptist cause generally in the State. He died at his old home in Greene County, greatly beloved and highly venerated by the whole denomination.

Stockwell, Deacon E. R., is one of the most widely known and influential Baptist laymen in California. He was born of Baptist parents, Dec. 13, 1814, at Jamaica, Vt.; removed to Stockton, Cal., at an early day; united with the church by baptism in 1857; elected deacon in 1858; has been church treasurer and clerk many years, treasurer of San Francisco Association twelve years, superintendent of Sunday-school and deacon of church twenty-one years, member of the Executive Committee of the State Sunday-School Convention eleven years, and is a generous benefactor and helper of every good work. He has been a successful merchant, and endeavors to live as a faithful steward. It is his great delight to engage in revivals and to lead sinners to Christ.

Stoddard, Rev. I. J., D.D., was born in 1820, in Eden, N. Y.; entered the preparatory department of Madison University in 1839; graduated from college in 1845, and from the theological department in 1847. He and his wife sailed for

Assam Nov. 3, 1847. They were assigned to Nowgong, with special reference to the educational institution there, but Mr. Stoddard also preached extensively. Ill health compelled a return to America in 1856. He has rendered important service in the West to foreign missions, and also to the Central University at Pella, Iowa, where Mrs. Stoddard was chosen principal of the ladies' department in 1858. In 1866, leaving their children in America, they sailed again for Assam, expecting to spend the rest of their lives in that land. They were stationed at Gowahati, but when that wonderful work commenced among the Garos, Mr. Stoddard removed to Golvalpara, where he gathered many souls to Christ from that wild people,—a work not excelled up to that time in any of our mission fields. Ill health in 1871 again compelled Mrs. Stoddard's return to America, and for the same reason, a few years later, Mr. Stoddard was obliged to give up his work and return to his native land. Though in feeble health he continued to do good service for the cause of Christ. He resides at Pella, Iowa, and though unable to engage in any continuous labor, he feels the same interest in the foreign mission work which prompted a consecration of his life to it nearly forty years ago.

Stone, George Marvin, D.D., son of Marvin E. and Hannah (West) Stone, was born at Strongsville, O., Dec. 10, 1834; converted in Cleveland, O., in the meetings of the Second Baptist church, Rev. J. Hyatt Smith, pastor, and "Uncle John Vassar, missionary," in 1853; studied at Williston Seminary, Easthampton, Mass., in 1854; entered Madison University, and graduated in 1858; studied for the ministry in Hamilton Theological Seminary; settled in Danbury, Conn., and was ordained in September, 1860; served this church seven years, and in the last year baptized more than ninety persons; in September, 1867, settled with First Baptist church in Winona, Minn.; served it successfully two years; in 1870 became pastor of the Jefferson Street Baptist church in Milwaukee, Wis.; was prospered for three and a half years; September, 1873, settled with First Baptist church in Tarrytown, N. Y.; served seven years with marked honor; made public Bible-reading a specialty and a power; in June, 1879, settled with the Asylum Avenue Baptist church in Hartford, Conn.; received in 1872, from Chicago University, the honorary degree of Doctor of Divinity. He fills most worthily a prominent place in the ministry.

Stone, James R., D.D., was born in Westborough, Mass., in 1818. His father was of Puritan stock. His mother's father, James Hawes, was the first person baptized in Westborough. When he was three or four years old his father removed to Providence, R. I. In a diary kept by his grandmother may be found this entry, made while he was yet a child: "My son Thomas and his wife and children are with us to-night; and after the little ones were asleep I went to their bedside, and kneeling down, with my hands on their heads, prayed for their early conversion to God, and that the Lord would make James a minister of the gospel." Her prayer was answered, for no sooner did he give himself to the Master than he began to wish that he might become a minister. He was baptized in 1833 by the pastor of the First Baptist church, Rev. R. E. Pattison, D.D. His purpose was to complete a course of study in Brown University and Newton Theological Seminary, but, after two years' study at Brown, he was obliged to leave.

He taught a select school in Woonsocket, R. I., and afterwards went to Wickford, R. I., to take charge of Washington Academy. While here he occasionally supplied the church, and at length became the pastor of the Wickford church. He was ordained in 1839, Rev. John Dowling, D.D., preaching the sermon. Years subsequently he was called to the pastorate of the Stewart Street church, Providence, R. I., and spent several years in the work there.

He has had pastorates in Connecticut, New York, Pennsylvania, and Rhode Island, and was also for two years principal of the academy at Worcester, Mass. In 1864 he accepted a district secretaryship from the American Baptist Publication Society for West Virginia, Ohio, Indiana, and Michigan, and proved himself a most earnest worker. In 1869 he became pastor of the Baptist church in Fort Wayne, Ind., where, "having obtained help of God, he continues unto this day."

He has been several times, and is now, president of the Indiana Baptist State Convention. He is also a member of the board of trustees for the Indiana State University.

Stone, Rev. Luther, is a descendant in the sixth generation from Gregory Stone, who came to Massachusetts in 1634. He was born at Oxford, near Worcester, Sept. 26, 1815. At the age of sixteen he was employed as a teacher in the public schools of his own town, acquiring meantime considerable proficiency in such studies as astronomy, natural philosophy, and surveying. About this time he experienced religion, and entering Leicester Academy, began his preparation for college. He entered Brown University in 1835, graduating in 1839. Thence he went to Newton Theological Institution, where he graduated in 1842. Declining the offer of teacher in a Southern university, he determined to become a self-supporting missionary in the great Mississippi Valley. Receiving ordination Oct. 3, 1843, he started for the West, and reached the great river in May, 1844. Making his headquarters at Burlington, Davenport, and Rock Island, he preached in the surrounding country, traveling over 4000 miles to meet his appointments during the first year. The second year he spent on Rock River from its mouth into Wisconsin. There being great need of a Baptist paper for the West, he determined to undertake that enterprise, and Aug. 10, 1847, he began the issue at Chicago of a weekly called *The Watchman of the Prairies*. In 1853 he transferred the proprietorship of the paper to those who have since conducted it, as the oldest religious weekly in the Northwest. In 1863 he was an original trustee and the first secretary of the Baptist Theological Union at Chicago. Subsequently, by purchasing the grounds and buildings of the University of Des Moines, he was enabled to render useful service to that institution at a time of a financial crisis in its affairs. The years 1866–68 he spent in Europe, and since his return devotes himself to the care of his personal estate, and to study in various departments of religious and general culture.

Stone, Marsena, D.D., was born in Homer, N. Y., Jan. 27, 1810; converted under the ministry of Rev. Alfred Bennett in 1830, and, after two years of hesitation and self-examination, was baptized at Manlius, N. Y., by Rev. Charles Morton; he spent some time at Hamilton. In 1837 he entered the ministry, and became pastor of the church in Mendon, N. Y., where he remained until 1840, when he went to Mount Morris, N. Y., and was pastor for five years. After a short interval spent in the service of the New York Baptist Education Society and in supplying the church at Eaton, in October, 1847, he went to Norwich, N. Y., and was pastor there until 1852, when he was called to take charge of the English course in Fairmount Theological Seminary, Cincinnati, O. This position he resigned in 1856, and became pastor of the Baptist church at Lebanon, O., where he remained five years. From 1861 to 1868 he was principal of the Young Ladies' Institute and Professor of Theology at Granville, O. In 1868–69, through the munificence of Hon. J. M. Hoyt and Mr. E. Thresher, he spent a year holding ministers' institutes in Ohio and other States. From 1869 to 1872 he was pastor at Marietta, O. In 1872 he was sent South by the Home Mission Society to hold institutes among the colored preachers. He spent one year at Shaw University, Raleigh, N. C., and two years at Leland University, New Orleans, La. In 1878 retired to Lebanon, O., where he now resides.

Dr. Stone has done much hard and good work, and is worthily regarded as one of the strongest men of his adopted State. He takes an active part in the educational and other work of the denomination in Ohio, and is ever ready, notwithstanding the weight of years, to perform his full share of service for Christ.

Stone, O. B., D.D., was born at Homer, N. Y., Sept. 24, 1823. In the fellowship of that church he was baptized while still but a youth, and by it also he was licensed. He was ordained, in 1852, at Xenia, O. Having served the church there as pastor some two years, he went to California, under appointment of the Home Mission Society. Four years he was pastor at Nevada City and five years at San José. Returning East, he served three years as district secretary of the Home Mission Society in New York. His subsequent pastorates have been three years at Lafayette, Ind., two years at Rockford, Ill., four at Marengo and four at Bloomington, in the same State. His health and that of his wife having failed, he is not now in service, though residing at Bloomington. Dr. Stone was a graduate of Madison University and of the Rochester Theological Seminary. He has held important positions in connection with educational organizations, as a member of the boards of the university and seminary at Chicago and of Shurtleff College. While his health permitted his labors were constant, abundant, and fruitful. As preacher and pastor he ranks with the foremost in the West.

Storrs, Rev. William, now of Belmont. Allegany Co., N. Y., was born in the town of Worcester, Otsego Co., N. Y., Jan. 20, 1810. He obtained hope in the Saviour when he was about eight years old. In his eleventh year he first had a desire to preach the gospel, and this has been a prevailing inclination throughout his life. In April, 1827, his father removed his family to Franklinville, Cattaraugus Co. March 27, 1831, he, with others, was baptized into the fellowship of the Baptist church in Ellicottville, Cattaraugus Co., by Elder Ebenezer Vining. April 18, 1841, he received a license from the East Worcester church to preach. He commenced the work of his life that spring in the meeting-house in East Worcester, where, twenty years before, he first felt a desire to preach. March 8, 1843, he was ordained in the Baptist church in Cherry Valley. During the thirty-eight years of his ministry he has been pastor of the following Baptist churches: Lodi, Bern, Knox, Friendship, Humphrey, Oramel, Belfast, Hermitage, Richburg, West Almond, N. Y., and Ulysses, Pa. He has been engaged in several revivals, in some of which the number reclaimed, with those who professed conversion, amounted to a hundred or more. In 1861 he joined the Union army, and is now a chaplain in the Grand Army of the Republic. He is descended from Puritan ancestors in England. In consequence of religious intolerance, Samuel Storrs came to Barnstable, Mass., about 1663. About 1698 he removed to Mansfield, Conn., and became one of the nine constituent members of the First Congregational church, from whom there has been a line of ministers reaching down to the present time. From him Mr. Storrs is descended. Though sprung from men who showed their loyalty to Christ in times of trial in the Old World and in the New, and who exhibited fidelity to patriotism at Bunker Hill and elsewhere, he glories chiefly in his sonship to God through the blood of Calvary.

Stott, William T., D.D., was born at Vernon, Ind., March 22, 1836. In 1861 he graduated at Franklin College, Ind., having during his college course supported himself by his own exertions, while maintaining a high standing in his studies. In August, 1861, he enlisted in the army, and was gradually promoted, until he became captain of Co. I, 18th Ind. Vols. He took part in fifteen battles, and commanded his regiment in the battle of Cedar Creek. In 1865 he entered Rochester Theological Seminary to prepare himself for the Christian ministry, graduating in 1868. He was for a year pastor of the church in Columbus, Ind. In 1869 he accepted the chair of Natural Science in Franklin College, and in 1872 he became president of this institution. In the several positions which he has held he has exhibited breadth, clearness, fidelity, perseverance, and a high moral purpose. In 1873 he received the degree of D.D. from Kalamazoo College, Mich.

Stott, Rev. William T., Sr., was born in Woodford Co., Ky., in 1789. He was converted at the age of thirteen, and joined the Salt River Baptist church. He came to Indiana in 1815, and was one of the constituent members of the Vernon church. He was pastor of this church about fifty years. He always took a deep interest in the civil government, never allowing an election of importance to occur without depositing his ballot. He was a man of great social power, and a preacher of marked ability in his prime. He was very familiar with the Word of God, and hence was immovable in his religious beliefs. He was a soldier in the war of 1812. He and Rev. John Vauter surveyed the first road laid out from Madison to Indianapolis. About 1000 persons, according to his own estimate, were converted under his preaching and baptized by him. He was unconscious several weeks during his last illness, but he had one hour of consciousness, in which he related his Christian experience, gave cheering words to each one that stood around him, and then suddenly lapsed into unconsciousness again. He died April 14, 1877, and was buried from the church that he had helped to constitute sixty-one years before.

Stough, Rev. A. S., was born in Germany in 1827; was educated for the Catholic priesthood; was baptized in Norfolk, Va., in 1847; read theology for two years with Dr. Geo. W. Purefoy and began to preach; is a successful pastor; has been for some years in charge of the church at Shelby, and moderator of the King's Mountain Association.

Stout, Charles B., was born at Flemington, N. J., in 1824; spent his youth in New Brunswick; became an active member of the Stanton Street Baptist church, New York; has been for years connected with the First or with the Remsen Avenue church in New Brunswick. He is the author of several books, which have had an extensive sale; was one of the first to use the blackboard in Sunday-schools, and is widely known in the Sunday-school work as an able speaker and contributor to the magazines.

Stout, Rev. David Bishop, was born in Hopewell, N. J., in the year 1810; was ordained a minister, and settled in a joint pastorate over the churches at Lambertville and Harborton in the year 1832. After five years' active and successful labor on these fields he was called to take charge of the ancient church at Middletown, where he settled in April, 1837, and where he remained and labored as pastor till his death, a period of thirty-eight years. The forty-three years of his ministerial life and labors were all spent in his native State, and in two pastorates. Few men have ever been more devoted to the Lord's work, and few have received larger measures of success.

Brother Stout was a constituent member of the State Convention, being present at its organization in 1830, and was an active worker and wise counselor in all its operations from the first till the day of his death. As a preacher, he was eminently Scriptural, trusting to the Spirit to make the Word successful. This principle of his ministry made him sound in doctrine, able in counsel, discreet and wise as a minister of Jesus Christ in every sphere of life.

He died May 17, 1874, having baptized during his pastorate of the oldest Baptist church in the State 639 professed believers.

Stout, Rev. John.—From the beginning of Brother Stout's ministry, at Newberry, S. C., in 1870, he took a prominent part in all our religious enterprises, especially State missions. For several years past he has rendered very efficient service in organizing and conducting Woman's Mission Societies. He was born in Mobile, Ala., in 1842, being a son of Rev. Platt Stout. He served in the Confederate army during the war, which much retarded his education. After the close of the war he removed to Darlington Co., S. C., where he learned to know Him whom to know is life eternal, and at once determined to preach the unsearchable riches of Christ. Preparatory to this he entered Furman University, in 1867, and the Southern Baptist Theological Seminary, then at Greenville, S. C., in 1868. He spent three years in the seminary, completing the entire course except one study. He pursued this afterwards, and received a full diploma in 1872. He became pastor of the Newberry church during his seminary course, and settled there on leaving Greenville, in 1871. In 1874 he removed to Darlington, and became pastor of the old Welsh Neck church, and still occupies that position. There has been nothing remarkable in his life except regular, consistent, and successful service in the various departments of the Master's work. A star is better than a meteor.

Stout, Rev. Platt.—For want of facts in his life the writer can only mention the name of Mr. Stout, one of the best and most useful ministers of Alabama. He lived to old age, and died in Wetumpka several years ago. He was famous for distinguished piety, burning zeal, wise judgment, and rare ability. The gifted Rev. John Stout, of South Carolina, is his son.

Stout, Rev. Thomas H., was born at Orange Court-House, Va., July 23, 1835; baptized in Kentucky in 1852; in 1854 he began to preach, and entered Mercer University, Ga., as a student; has spent several years as teacher in Georgia; was a soldier and a chaplain for some time during the late war. From 1862 to 1867 he was the successful pastor at Blakely. In 1867 he became president of the Baptist Female College of North Georgia; at the same time he was pastor of various churches. In 1869 he became pastor at Lumpkin; in 1872 at Thomaston; in 1878 at Talbotton and other neighboring churches. In January, 1879, he accepted the pastorate of the First church in the city of Troy, Ala., and there, as in Georgia, his labors are being honored with success. Six years he was clerk of the Rehoboth Association, and seven years of the Georgia State Convention. He received the degree of A.M. from Mercer University in 1873. He is an active and able minister of Christ.

Stovall, Rev. A. T., a useful minister in Northeast Mississippi, was born in Tennessee in 1809; removed to Alabama, where he began to preach in 1841; during his stay in Alabama he served the following churches near his home in Lawrence County, viz.: Town Creek, Moulton, Macedonia, and Courtland. He removed to Mississippi in 1852, and settled near Tupelo, in the northeastern part of the State, where he spent the remainder of his life preaching to churches in the surrounding country. He aided in the organization of Judson Association, and was its moderator a number of years. He died July 4, 1872, much respected by those among whom he had lived.

Stow, Baron, D.D., one of the most eloquent and successful ministers of the denomination of which he was so distinguished an ornament, was born in Croydon, N. H., June 16, 1801, and spent his early youth on the farm of his father. When but a child he began to show what his tastes were. By the roadside, near the house of his father, was a boulder, which, from its peculiar construction, was called "the pulpit." Taking possession of this pulpit, the boy-preacher would draw around him a crowd of his associates, and, as our fathers

BARON STOW, D.D.

were wont to say, "exercised his gifts" quite to the admiration of his listening friends. He was fitted for college at the academy in Newport, N. H., and became a member of Columbian College, Washington, D. C., in September, 1822, where he had among his instructors Dr. Irah Chace, Dr. Alva Woods, Thomas Sewell, M.D., Dr. R. Babcock, Prof. J. D. Knowles, Prof. T. J. Conant, and Dr. R. E. Pattison. Close attention to his studies enabled him to complete the entire course of the prescribed curriculum in a little more than three years. Mr. Stow acted as editor of the *Columbian Star*, the organ of the Triennial Convention, during the latter part of his college course, and continued to hold that position for more than a year.

He received a call to become the pastor of the Baptist church in Portsmouth, N. H., and was ordained Oct. 24, 1827, his ordination sermon having been preached by Rev. R. Babcock, then pastor of the First Baptist church, Salem, Mass. His ministry in Portsmouth was from the outset eminently successful. The church grew in numbers and strength, and were obliged to make provision for a larger house of worship, and their present edifice in Middle Street was built, and dedicated Sept. 24, 1828. More than one invitation of a most urgent character was extended to him to remove to what were considered more inviting fields of ministerial labor, but he declined all such overtures. For five years, dating from his ordination, he continued at the post which Providence seemed to have assigned to him.

The pulpit of the Baldwin Place church in Boston having become vacant, the thoughts of the church were turned at once to Portsmouth, and Mr. Stow received a hearty invitation to become its pastor. Obeying what seemed to him to be the call of his Master, he decided to remove to Boston. He was installed as pastor Nov. 15, 1832. If his ministry in Portsmouth had been followed with great success, still more prosperous was it at the North End in Boston. At the close of the year 1837 he preached that remarkable sermon from the text, "Boast not thyself of to-morrow, for thou knowest not what a day may bring forth," the traditions of the wonderful results of which lingered for many a year in Boston. More than *one hundred* persons referred to that discourse as the means of their awakening and conversion. A powerful revival commenced with the opening of the year 1838, the influence of which was felt for years. During the next five years 502 persons were added to the church on a profession of their faith in Christ. Meanwhile his interest in every department of Christian work increased, as his zeal for the promotion of the kingdom of Christ grew more intense and intelligent. He threw his soul into the cause of foreign missions, and never was happier than when, by his pen or the living voice, he was pleading for that cause.

At length the labors of the ministry began to tell on his nervous strength, and, exhausted by long-continued work, he was forced to yield, and seek the renewal of his wasted powers by change of scene and the gentle excitements of foreign travel. He left Boston Dec. 1, 1840, and was absent several months abroad, traveling in England, France, Switzerland, and Italy, and returned to his home in the month of June. He took up, with recruited strength, the work which he had laid aside, and again preached and performed his pastoral duties with his accustomed zeal and acceptableness. He shared in the labors and the ingathering of souls into the churches, which made the year 1842 so memorable in the religious history of Boston. At the close of the twelfth year of his ministry at Baldwin Place, during two of which he had been laid aside by sickness, he makes the following record: "I have preached 1237 sermons, made 8532 visits, solemnized 482 marriages, attended 586 funerals, baptized 643, added by letter 261, dismissed 394, and excluded 71." These figures present us a picture of a life of great ministerial activity and success as an ambassador for Christ.

Dr. Stow was the pastor of a church situated in that part of Boston which more than any other section was undergoing constant social changes by the influx of a foreign population. The weakening of his church by the removal of some of his best families proved a source of so great discouragement that, in 1848, he felt it his duty to resign his pastorate of the church of which, for sixteen years, he had been the loving and beloved under-shepherd. After a brief period of relaxation, during which he received invitations to become the pastor of three churches, he decided to accept a call to what was then the Rowe Street church, now the Clarendon Avenue, and began at once to reap the fruits of his labors. It is not possible to sum up what this most indefatigable worker did, as a preacher where the standard for pulpit service was so high, as a pastor of the warmest sympathies and the tenderest love, as a member of the Executive Committee of the Missionary Union, where he performed a vast amount of work, especially with his most graceful and accurate pen, as a writer of books and for the religious press. A second trip to Europe, taken for the same reasons that led him to make the first, proved serviceable to him, and no doubt prolonged his valuable life. His pastorate of the Rowe Street church ended in 1867. Forty years nearly he had been in the ministry, thirty of which had been spent in Boston. The roots had gone down too deep into the soil of the dear old city to be rudely torn up, and although urged to occupy other fields of labor he declined, and spent the remainder of his days in performing such work as his Master gave him to do, and at length came to the end of his days on the 27th of December, 1869.

Dr. Stow takes high rank among the best preachers of his own denomination or any other in this country. Amidst the exhausting labors of his profession he found time to write and give to the world the productions of his pen. He was one of the compilers of the "Psalmist." His "First Things," "Christian Brotherhood," "Daily Manna," and "Whole Family in Heaven" are illustrations of his skill and ability as a writer. His name is hallowed in the memory of many who loved him, and the whole church of God may be thankful that its great Head gave to it so true so faithful, a servant of the Lord Jesus Christ as Baron Stow.

Stowe, Rev. Phineas, was born in Milford, Conn., March 20, 1812. When he was fifteen years of age he was engaged as a clerk in a store in New Haven. He was baptized by Rev. Elisha Cushman, July 2, 1831, and became a member of the First Baptist church in New Haven. Feeling himself called of God to preach the gospel, he spent four years at the New Hampton Literary and Theological Institution in fitting himself for his work. After leaving New Hampton he was pastor for two years of the Baptist church at South Danvers, Mass. But his life-work was to be performed in another sphere. Providence had designed him to be a preacher to seamen, and in Boston he found a field of labor which was suited to him and he to it. "He was adapted to his work," says his friend Dr. Neale, "and his work to him. It fitted exactly all the peculiarities of his mind and heart, as the liquid metal takes the varied features of the mould into which it is cast. It filled his whole soul, and he went into it with all his might." A period of twenty years of constant, unremitting labor produced such results as any man might be thankful to have accomplished. The monuments of his zeal and untiring energy may be found in different sections of the city of Boston, and especially in the better characters and the Christian lives of hundreds and thousands of sailors in all parts of the world. His intense enthusiasm, and his love for the work to which he had given the best years of his life, at last touched the delicate fibres of an over-sensitive brain, and he was forced to spend his last days in one of those retreats which the Christian benevolence of our modern days has provided for sufferers like him. He died at the McLean Hospital for the Insane at Somerville, Mass., Nov. 13, 1868.

Stowell, Rev. Austin H., son of Isaac and Harriet (Hall) Stowell, was born in Starksborough, Vt., Oct. 6, 1818; converted in Bristol in 1830; baptized at Brandon, in 1836, while studying to enter Middlebury College; licensed by the Baptist church in Brandon; ordained, Dec. 11, 1839, in Palmyra, N. Y.; settled in Avon and Moriah; in Saratoga five years, in Providence, R. I., six years, in South Boston, Mass., in Peoria, Ill.; spent twelve years in Chicago in general gospel work; published two sermons to young men in 1852, and a doctrinal sermon on Baptist polity in 1860.

Stradley, Rev. J. A., the son of the venerable minister, Thomas Stradley, was born in Asheville, N. C., March 17, 1832; was baptized by his father; ordained in 1854; took an irregular course at Wake Forest College on account of ill health, and has spent most of his professional life in Granville County. Mr. Stradley is an uncompromising temperance advocate and a strong Baptist.

Stradley, Rev. Thomas, the oldest living Baptist preacher of North Carolina, the missionary of the mountains, was born in Woolwich, England, in 1798; landed in America at Charleston, S. C., and settled in Buncombe Co., N. C., in 1828. He was already a Baptist, and soon began to preach, and was ordained by Revs. Humphrey Posey, Dobbins, and Alfred Webb.

Mr. Stradley attended the third session of the Baptist State Convention, held at Cartledge's Creek church, Richmond County, in 1833, and had the honor to be appointed the first missionary of that body. Mr. Stradley became an excellent and useful preacher. He is what is termed a high-church Baptist, a great temperance apostle, and has the distinguished honor not only of founding the Baptist church in Asheville, but of building, almost unaided, the handsome house in which it worships. Though upwards of eighty, he still preaches with great power.

Straughan, Rev. Samuel Lamkin, was born in Northumberland Co., Va., July 30, 1783. He spent his youth on his father's farm. He was baptized in April, 1803, and united with the Moratico church. He immediately began the congenial work of exhorting the impenitent, and his labors were so successful that in 1806 he was ordained to the work of the ministry. His first pastoral charge was that of the Wicomico church, the membership of which at the beginning was only 24, but which soon increased to nearly 300, so mightily did the Word of the Lord prevail under Mr. Straughan's faithful ministrations. In 1807 he accepted the pastorate of the Moratico church, which also became one of the strongest and most active in that part of the State. In the year 1814 he was chosen by the Missionary Society of Richmond to travel into certain parts of Maryland, where there was great destitution of the means of grace. Here, although at first received with great coldness and some opposition, he secured a strong hold on the affections of the people, and was the means of accomplishing much good. These visits were necessarily only occasional, since he had his own churches in Virginia to supply at regular times. He made his last visit to Maryland in 1820, at which time the pulmonary disease, under which he had long labored, grew rapidly worse, and, resting awhile at Nanjemoy, he finally reached his home in June, from which time he was almost wholly confined to his house until his death, which occurred June 9, 1821. Mr. Straughan was eminent for his deep piety. In every relation of life he was a model man, simple, modest, grave, courteous, and gentle towards all around him. He had a "good report" of all who knew him. As a preacher, he was in many respects more than ordinary. His voice was sonorous, his style always strong and nervous, and sometimes elegant, his address sincere and often animated, and his countenance remarkably prepossessing. His discourses were marked by argument and Scriptural illustrations rather than by eloquence, although occasionally he rose to sublimity of style. Mr. Straughan was only thirty-eight years of age at his death, but in the short time he was permitted to live and labor he accomplished much for the Master, and left behind him, for the admiration of the church, a record such as many whose years are more numerous rarely accomplish.

Stribling, James H., D.D., was born in Alabama in 1822; is a nephew of the distinguished Commodore Stribling of the U. S. navy. With his father's family he removed to Texas, and first located in Washington County; served as a volunteer in the Texan army in the Somerville campaign designed to repel the Mexican invasion of 1842–43; professed conversion in July, 1843, and was baptized by Rev. Wm. M. Tryon in September following; authorized to preach about one year afterwards; pursued studies in Baylor University from May, 1846, to December, 1849; ordained at Independence at last date. In 1850 traveled as a missionary west of the Colorado River, traversing a large scope of country from the sea-coast to the mountains, preaching in a log cabin or private dwelling, under live-oaks or in regular places of worship, facing northers and drenching rains on bleak prairies, swimming streams, crossing the Indian's war-path, but everywhere received kindly, and enjoying many happy seasons, pointing sinners to Christ, and witnessing the triumphs of the gospel. Traveled this year 3000 miles on horseback; served from 1851 to close of 1857 as pastor at Gonzales, and preached to other churches in the country. Many revival seasons were enjoyed, and hundreds brought into the kingdom of Christ. In 1858–59 ministered to old Caney and Wharton churches, enjoying precious seasons of grace. In May, 1860, assumed the pastorate of the First church, Galveston, and continued until the calamities of war broke up this happy relation. In 1863 he began, and in 1873 closed, a successful pastorate at Anderson, preaching at Navisota and other churches during this period; began the pastorate at Tyler, which he now holds, in September, 1873, and ever since one harvest of blessing has been enjoyed by pastor and people; served two years as moderator of Colorado Association, seven years as moderator of Union Association, four years as president of State Sunday-School and Colportage Convention, many times vice-president of State Convention; for three years past has been moderator of Cherokee Association, and at various times has been a prominent member of the Southern Convention. In the course of his ministry he has preached 3000 sermons, and delivered as many lectures; led or assisted in 150 protracted meetings, in which over 2000 professed conversion; solemnized 200 marriages, and attended a larger number of funeral services; baptized over 800 persons; traveled in every mode 20,000 miles from the Sabine to the Nueces, from the Gulf to the mountains; and has preached to gratified audiences in Mobile, Louisville, Baltimore, and other cities; has published, 1. "Sermon on Sunday-Schools;" 2. "In Memory of T. J. Jackson;" 3. "On Future Punishment;" 4. "Sketches of Travels;" 5. "Discussion on Human Depravity;" and miscellaneous articles; received A.M. in 1858 and D.D. in 1871 from Baylor University. Rev. Z. N. Morrell, in "Flowers and Fruits from the Wilderness," says, "He has never turned aside to engage in any secular employment for a year or a month. . . . All love him, none excel him." He esteems it his highest honor, privilege, and blessing to sit at the feet of Jesus and learn of him.

Strickland, Rev. C. H., of Knoxville, Tenn., was born in Lawrenceville, Ga., Dec. 18, 1844. As a boy, he was ambitious to excel, faithful and true to those who trusted him, and passionately fond of reading. He was prepared for college at the Lawrenceville High School.

A few years after his conversion he was called of God to preach the gospel, and was ordained by Bethel church, Walton Co., Ga., Jan. 30, 1870, the Presbytery consisting of Brethren Bedford, Lungford, G. A. Nunnally, Stillwell, and Loring. He was pastor first of this church, afterwards of churches at Farmington, New Hope, Greensborough, and Augusta, Ga., and Knoxville, Tenn., his Master giving him in every place the joy of seeing his work prosper in his hands. As a pastor, he knows his people; their trials, sorrows, and bereavements are his, and so perfectly does he know them all that not one can be absent from the public services that he does not miss. Though still young, he has been a busy worker, and by the blessing of God has accomplished much good.

Strickland, Rev. W. H., was born in Gwinnett Co., Ga. He in early life joined the Presbyterian Church, to which his parents belonged, but four years after he united with the Baptists. After preaching some years in the country, he became pastor of Kallock Street church in Augusta, Ga. In 1871–72 he was chaplain of the house of representatives of the Georgia Legislature. He has since been pastor in Darlington and in Anderson, S. C.

On the 1st of July, 1880, he became corresponding secretary and treasurer of the State Mission Board of South Carolina. In the first five months he collected $6236.90, an unprecedented amount.

His power in the pulpit is very great, and he is much beloved by his people wherever he has been pastor. He was for several years connected with the editorial department of the *Baptist Courier*.

Strong, Augustus H., D.D., was born in Rochester, N. Y., Aug. 3, 1836. His father, Alvah Strong, was a journalist, and for several years published the *Rochester Daily Democrat*. He was graduated from Yale College in 1857. He was converted while in his Junior year in college, and baptized into the fellowship of the First Baptist church of Rochester. After leaving Yale College he entered the Rochester Theological Seminary, where he closed his course of study in 1859. He then went abroad, pursuing his studies in the German universities, and traveling in Europe and the East. For a short time he preached as a supply for the North Baptist church of Chicago. In 1861 he settled as pastor of the First Baptist church of Haver-

AUGUSTUS H. STRONG, D.D.

hill, Mass., where he was ordained. In 1865 he accepted the pastorate of the First Baptist church of Cleveland, O. While there he received the honorary degree of Doctor of Divinity from Brown University. After seven years of successful labor there, his manifest ability as a preacher, and his well-known theological learning, secured for him an election as president and Professor of Theology in the Rochester Theological Seminary, which position he holds at the present time. He is the author of able articles on "Philosophy and Religion" in the *Baptist Quarterly*, also "Miracles as an Attestation of Divine Revelation," and on "The Will in Theology," besides numerous contributions on theology, church polity, and education in the weekly religious journals of the Baptist denomination. He is a man to whom the public have acceded a remarkable fitness for the high position which he fills. The young men who come out from that institution show his training hand and the careful instruction in theology so much needed by the ministry.

Stubbert, Rev. John Roman, son of John and Ann Stubbert, was born on Boulardie, island of Cape Breton, April 8, 1838. His parents were at first devout members of the Church of England, but finally became distinguished pioneer Baptists on the island. His father, at first an opposer of the Baptists, was changed in views and feelings by hearing Rev. John Hull, and among these the once despised became "mighty in the Scriptures and in prayer." John R., after the strictest moral training at home, began his studies in a normal school, and then for three years alternated between teaching and colportage. In 1867 he entered Acadia College, and graduated in 1871, preaching during his vacations; entered Newton Theological Institution, Mass., and graduated in 1874; proposed to be a missionary in China, and was received by the American Baptist Missionary Union, but was finally induced to settle with the Second Baptist church of Suffield, Conn., and was ordained July 2, 1874; in the following winter was blessed with a powerful revival, and baptized 90 persons; was elected a trustee of the Connecticut Literary Institution, and also a trustee of the Connecticut Baptist State Convention and of the Baptist Education Society; was the first secretary of the Baptist Centennial Committee in Connecticut in 1875; has been a leader in temperance societies.

Sturgiss, Rev. C. F., for many years pastor at Carlowville, Ala., and other churches of that part of the State, was distinguished for his learning, extensive culture, eminent piety, and thorough gospel preaching. He occupied a position with the first men of the State. He was author of a prize essay on "The Duties of Masters to their Servants," which had a wide circulation in book form. He died only a few years since.

Sumner, M. T., D.D., was born in Massachusetts, Sept. 6, 1815; graduated at Brown University in the class of 1838; removed to Virginia in February, 1840; ordained, by request of the Second Baptist church in Richmond, in May, 1843. From 1840 to 1850 engaged in teaching in Richmond and preaching to three churches in the country, and in 1850 devoted all his time to the work of the ministry. In January, 1854, accepted the agency of the American Tract Society for Virginia and the District of Columbia, and Jan. 1, 1858, entered upon the duties of corresponding secretary of the Domestic Mission Board of the Southern Baptist Convention, at Marion, Ala. In 1875 resigned this position and entered upon the duties of president of Judson Female Institute, which he held for one year, and, retiring from this position, he occupied the post of agent for the Southern Baptist Theological Seminary about two years, and then about the same length of time he acted as agent of the American Baptist Publication Society. April 1, 1880, he resigned all agency work, and accepted the pastorate of the Baptist church in Athens, Ala., with encouraging prospects. In all these important positions the labors of Dr. Sumner were attended with success. During the seventeen years that he had charge of the home mission interest of Southern Baptists he wielded a commanding influence over the entire South on this subject.

Sunday-School Hymns.—" Let me furnish a nation with its songs and I will govern it" is an aphoristic expression, and history furnishes innumerable instances of the influence upon human thought and feeling of the songs and ballads of the people. From the earliest periods until the present, triumphant hymns or solemn requiems have been used to express the emotions of joy or sorrow. This is especially true of the Christian era, and the Magnificat of Mary, the "Peace on earth" of the angels, and the Te Deum have enjoyed centuries of popularity, and the followers of Christ through all the ages have found expression for their soul exercises in psalms, hymns, and spiritual songs. To the chants of the early Christians have been added the more modern productions so largely used in our churches. None are so susceptible to the influences of music and poetry as children and youth, nor so long retain the first impressions conveyed through their use. The songs of childhood often last for life, and frequently in after-years they are the means of expressing the emotions and experiences of maturity. They thus have an incalculable value in moulding character, and the writers of the best hymns for children have an influence that cannot be overestimated. Leaders of the young have more fully realized this since the development of the Sunday-school movement, and gradually there has been provided a literature especially for this service. At first the "Hymns and Divine Songs for Children" of Dr. Watts, with its quaint little wood-cuts, was extensively used, and, although the collection is now laid aside, such hymns as "How shall the young secure their hearts?" "How doth the little busy bee," will continue their usefulness for years to come. These simple songs have been gradually supplanted by the songs of more recent writers, who have attempted to embody Scriptural truths in a rhythmical form. To this class belong "There is a happy land," by Andrew Young, "I think when I read that sweet story of old," by Mrs. Luke, "Little travelers Zionward," Heber's "From Greenland's icy mountains," and many others equally well known. More recently some of these have been partially obscured by a flood of productions, many of which have no merit either of doctrine or poetry. Their numbers have been legion, but one after another has faded from memory, while the worth of the best hymns of the olden and present time is being more universally recognized and acknowledged. Activity in the production of Sunday-school music has especially manifested itself within the last twenty years, and it is asserted, upon the authority of the publishers, that five books prepared by one editor attained a circulation, up to 1868, of over two million copies. Since that date the sale of this class of books has aggregated 17,000,000. Of the hymns that will remain from this multitude are many admirable productions of P. P. Bliss, Miss Havergal, the Baptist brethren Lowry, Doane, the Rev. J. H. Gilmore, and others. The beautiful hymn "He leadeth me," belonging to this class of authors, was composed by Prof. Gilmore in the parlor of the venerable deacon, Thos. Wattson, after a service in the First Baptist church, Philadelphia.

In the service of song there has been an increasing desire manifested to bring the Sunday-school into closer connection with the worship in the sanctuary. The Gethsemane Baptist church of Philadelphia has recently had organized from their school a choir of several hundred voices, which forms a chorus in the public services of the church. Thus the work of the teachers may be directed by a faithful Christian minister, and young hearts may be led to sing from experience,

> "Tis religion that can give
> Sweetest pleasure while we live."

Sunday-Schools.—*The origin*, in some form, of Sunday-schools may be traced back to an early date. It appears, however, that from the time of the Reformation Christian people have at different periods, though without concerted action or organized system, given attention to Bible instruction for the young on the Lord's day. The schools of Luther were held seven days in the week, and especially provided for religious instruction on Sunday. John Knox introduced into Scotland a system of Sunday-schools, and C. S. Rafinesque asserts that they have existed in Italy for centuries. In America, the early history of New England shows the religious training of the children supplemented by the weekly instruction of the minister, and it is asserted, on credible authority, that in 1740 the German Seventh-Day Baptists established a school at Ephratah, Lancaster Co., Pa., which continued for nearly forty years. A very great impetus was given to the cause by the organized efforts of the philanthropist, Robert Raikes, 1780–1785, who directed the attention of Christians to its importance and formed a systematic plan of teaching, the results of which are apparent to-day. Scarcely less distinguished than Raikes was his contemporary, William Fox, a Baptist of London, who, at the same period, established a Sunday-school at Clapham, and who was greatly encouraged by correspondence with Mr. Raikes. The Sunday-School Society of England, which is still a useful organization, was the result of the labor of Mr. Fox.

The plan of instruction adopted by these men included paid teachers and the use of the Bible as a text-book in reading. The movement extended throughout England until, in 1789, there were

300,000 scholars enrolled by the Sunday-School Society. The influence was felt on this side of the Atlantic, and led to the formation, in January, 1791, of the Philadelphia Society for the Support and Institution of First-Day or Sunday-Schools. In this country, as in England, the Baptists have been abreast with their brethren of other denominations in promoting the cause and in establishing schools. Among the oldest Baptist schools having an unbroken history are the following: the school of the Second Baptist church of Baltimore, organized in 1804; of the First Baptist church of Philadelphia, instituted in 1815; of the Charles Street church, Boston, of the Oliver Street church, New York, and of the Second Baptist church, Philadelphia, founded in 1816. Two Baptist missionaries, Messrs. Peck and Welch, established the first Sunday-school west of the Mississippi River. A Baptist teacher, Miss Harriet E. Bishop, gathered the first school of the kind in the extreme Northwest, in what is now St. Paul, Minn. From these early efforts the Baptist schools of America have grown, until they number, so far as reported, over 13,493, with 116,355 officers and teachers and 1,000,000 scholars. Every State in the Union is represented in this grand total, and who can estimate its steady influence upon society in its inculcation of Christian doctrine, and in training the young in the path of virtue?

The system of instruction in the schools, as well as their increase in numbers, has been the result of a gradual growth and development. From the first these schools were supplied by voluntary teachers, actuated by a desire for the promotion of the religious education of the young. The pupils were boys and girls who understood the rudiments of English, and the text-books were the Old and the New Testament, supplemented in some cases by the Catechism. After a few years an infant class was organized for those of tender years, and still more recently an adult department has been added for men and women. The schools are in most cases attached to churches, though maintaining a voluntary organization, somewhat informal in character, and are generally managed by the officers and teachers as they may best determine, without the formal control and direction of the church. As the first schools were of an isolated character, there was no uniformity in the manner of teaching or in the selection of subjects. In both these particulars a very great change has been gradually effected. The infant department in the best schools is now under the care of a teacher and assistants, who depend largely for the means of impressing truths upon the hearts of the little ones on object teaching. The blackboard and printed sketches are used to depict Bible scenes or illustrate Scripture texts, and these are supplemented by the singing of sacred songs especially intended to teach important truths. In the intermediate department the young of both sexes gather in little groups or classes about teachers who often are familiar with the every-day life of their scholars, and visit them on week-days in their homes, and who endeavor to impress more deeply, if possible, the truth learned on the Lord's day, by the influence of their daily life. The adult department consists of men and women who, either in classes or as a congregation, are led in Bible study by a person of their own selection. A modern Sunday-school represents, and frequently contains, an entire family studying God's Word.

The literature of the school has been created to supply the demands of experience in the service. Since the formation of the American Baptist Publication Society it has been the great Sunday-school society of the Baptist denomination. The adoption, a few years ago, of a system of uniform lessons for the use of all the Protestant denominations rendered it possible and necessary to issue periodical literature containing the best thoughts of Biblical students upon the selected topics. *The Baptist Teacher, Lesson Papers, Our Young People, Our Little Ones*, and other publications of a similar character are very important and valuable assistants to teachers. These papers are not merely sold to schools able to purchase, but are carried by the colporteurs of the society and freely distributed to needy schools in destitute localities. The volumes reported in the libraries of the Baptist schools of America in 1879 amounted to 965,000. This vast aggregate may contain thousands of books whose influence may be of a negative character, and to remedy this as far as possible the Publication Society is continually issuing works especially intended for libraries, and furnishing books by other publishers that have been examined by a careful committee. The Baptist Sunday-school work to-day is well organized, and engages the warm sympathies of thousands of men and women who are looking forward with the hopeful anticipation that the Lord may greatly increase their number and their usefulness, and bless the work to the spiritual advantage of the people.

Sunday-Schools, Infant.—Previous to 1829, so far as can be ascertained, no regular provision was made in Sunday-schools for the care and instruction of children who were too young to study lessons, though frequently such children were present with older brothers or sisters. But in the latter part of that year a beginning was made, which resulted in a very general establishment of infant classes in connection with Sabbath-schools. It happened in this way. A year or two previous two infant week-day schools were opened in Boston, designed for children from two to five years old, whose mothers were employed away from home during the day. One of these was in charge of Miss M. V. Ball, who is still well known in Boston as an active worker for the Baptist Bethel

FIRST INFANT SUNDAY-SCHOOL, FIRST BAPTIST CHURCH, BOSTON.
(Fac-simile of the original engraving.)

and other charities, and the other was in care of Miss Caroline Blood, now wife of Rev. Julius A. Reed, of Columbus, Neb. The exercises consisted of marching, singing, teaching by the use of various objects, including pictures, which were explained by the teachers, and questions were asked which were answered in concert by the little ones.

A printer's apprentice, Henry J. Howland, having occasion to visit one of these schools, became interested in the exercises, and being at the time the teacher of a class of boys in the First Baptist Sabbath-school in Boston, the idea occurred to him that Scriptural teaching and singing would interest young children in the Sabbath-school; and, having borrowed some of the pictures, he explained the matter at a teachers' meeting, and proposed its adoption. It was at once sanctioned, and Mr. Howland was appointed to form and instruct the new class.

In December, 1829, twenty small children were led to the gallery of the First Baptist meeting-house in Boston, and, with the aid of a few pictures representing Bible subjects, the attempt was made to instruct them. As no lesson book adapted to such a class was to be found, the exercises consisted in repeating in concert simple hymns, singing the same, listening to Bible stories, illustrated by the pictures, and answering questions relating to them. The instruction was repeated till each lesson was well understood by the children. Mention was made of the new system in the *Sunday-School Treasury* and other publications, and many similar classes were formed. Inquiry was made for lessons and pictures. In June following the lessons prepared by Mr. Howland, with brief instructions for management, were published in Worcester, in a small volume entitled "Lessons for Infant Sabbath-Schools, with a Plan for Conducting an Infant Class." This is believed to have been the first publication of the kind in existence. A second edition was called for the following winter, which was stereotyped, and bore on its title-page the name of the author. Eight or ten editions were printed and sold before it was superseded by the numerous lesson books since published. The plan of instruction as originally practised by Mr. Howland is still pursued by the best primary Sunday-school instructors, with very little variation, except in the vastly improved helps that are now so numerous.

It is interesting to know that the man who commenced this glorious work among the little ones is a Baptist, and that he is still living in Worcester, Mass.

Sunderland, Rev. James, was born Dec. 16, 1834, near Haworth, Yorkshire, England. His father emigrated to America in 1844, and settled at Busti, Chautauqua Co., N. Y. A few years later he died, leaving his family with exhausted resources. There were five children, of whom James was the oldest. Both father and mother were devout Christians, members of the Wesleyan Methodist Church. One of the sons is now Rev. J. T. Sunderland, of Ann Arbor, Mich., and one of the daughters is Mrs. J. E. Clough, of the Teloogoo Mission. James Sunderland was converted in 1852, and baptized by Rev. David Bernard. He taught school part of the time from 1853 to 1855. In the spring of 1855 he went West, and settled at Strawberry Point, Clayton Co., Iowa. He engaged mainly in teaching and mercantile pursuits till 1860. Among his pupils was J. E. Clough, now of the Teloogoo Mission. In the winter of 1860 he taught in Jamestown, N. Y.

The question of duty in regard to preaching, which had been pressing him for years, was decided while still engaged in teaching. In 1862 he became pastor of the Strawberry Point church. He remained on the field till November, 1866, and organized churches at Volga City and York. He was pastor of the Baptist church at Vinton, Iowa, four years, and at Sioux City three and a half years. While at Vinton he was elected secretary of the Iowa Baptist Sunday-School Union, and served in that position for six years. Impaired health compelled him to leave the active pastorate for a time, during which he served as the chaplain of the Iowa State Penitentiary at Fort Madison for seven months. In the spring of 1875 he became pastor of the Baptist church at Ottumwa, Iowa, and continued to serve the church five years. In October, 1877, was elected secretary of the Iowa Baptist State Convention, and is now giving his entire time to the duties of that position.

Suspension and Excommunication.—The two methods of treating offenders in Baptist churches in the days of our fathers were suspension from the privileges of the church—that is, from the Lord's Supper and from voting at church meetings for a limited time—and excommunication. The former was resorted to for lighter offenses which brought religion into disrepute, and it was regarded as a very proper form of Church Discipline.* It is still in use in some of our churches; the latter is the final resort of a gospel church when all Christian efforts fail. When flagrant dishonesty, or adultery, or murder is the crime proved against a church member, no amount of apparent sorrow should hinder his immediate expulsion. In all ordinary cases, preceding excommunication, the guilty member should be visited by representatives of the church and urged to repentance, and when he still maintains a spirit of wicked indifference to the claims of God, he should be cited to appear at a meeting of the church to show cause why he should not be excluded, and at it he should be solemnly excommunicated.

Sutcliffe, Rev. John, was born near Halifax, England, Aug. 9, 1752. Under the ministry of Dr. Fawcett he was led to the Saviour when he was about seventeen, and he united with the church at Hebden Bridge. By this church he was called to the ministry and sent to Bristol College. In 1775 he became pastor of the church in Olney. It was on his motion that the Northamptonshire Association set apart an hour in the evening of the first Monday of every month for special prayer for the success of the gospel. In 1789 he republished Jonathan Edwards's " Humble Attempt to Promote Explicit Agreement and Visible Union among God's People in Extraordinary Prayer for the Revival of Religion." This work at that time gave great help to the convictions, which resulted in the formation of the English Baptist Missionary Society. In a sermon preached at Clipstone in April, 1791, Mr. Sutcliffe fanned the kindling missionary flame in the hearts of his hearers. From the formation of the society in 1792 no man, except Fuller, rendered it nobler service until his death, June 22, 1814. Fuller, Ryland, Sutcliffe, and Pearce were the chief friends of foreign missions in England at a time when they were regarded with incredulous contempt.

Mr. Sutcliffe gathered a large and valuable library, which he left to Horton College. He was full of gentleness, and of a devotional spirit. He was among the best men that ever lived.

Sutton, Revs. David and John.—David was a native of New Jersey, and received his early education at Hopewell Academy. Five brothers entered the ranks of the Baptist ministry. David and John removed to the Red Stone country, the former settling on the Ten-Mile River and the latter in Fayette County. The church, formerly known as the Big Bethel, now Uniontown, owes its origin and very much of its subsequent prosperity to the labors of John. This church was the mother of many other surrounding churches. David was also signally blessed in his ministry. The revivals under the ministry of both men compare favorably with those of the present day, and in depth of feeling, strength of conviction, clearness in the evidences of a sound conversion, combined with permanent growth, are even more marked. A stalwart class of Baptists to this day dwell in the region once swayed by the teachings of Corbley, Patton, the Suttons, and men of their distinctive type of preaching.

At the time of their settlement the entire region of the Red Stone country was a wilderness in its moral and spiritual, as well as in its natural aspects. Great changes have occurred since that day. The wilderness fairly blossoms, and we trust the fruits of righteousness abound. The time of the decease of these brothers is not known by the writer, but the report is that it was "about the year 1800."

Suydam, Asa, was born near Flemington, N. J., June 3, 1825; baptized by Rev. C. W. Mulford at Flemington, in January, 1848. He is a practical farmer, a Bible-class teacher, a valuable helper in the church, and devoted to public denominational interests. He is treasurer of the New Jersey Baptist State Convention.

Swaim, Samuel Budd, D.D., was born in Pemberton, N. J., June 23, 1809. A part of his preparatory studies he pursued at Washington, D. C., where he entered Columbian College in 1826. He completed his college course at Brown University, graduating in the class of 1830. He went through the Newton Theological Institution, and was ordained in Haverhill, Mass. Five years of his life were spent in different localities, one of them in Granville, O., as an instructor in theology in the

---

* Treatise on Church Discipline in the Philadelphia Confession of Faith of 1743, pp. 96, 97.

college in that place. In 1838 he was called to the First Baptist church in Worcester, Mass. He was in the prime of his life and usefulness, and the sixteen years of his pastorate over that strong church developed and ripened his own powers, while they made his influence largely felt in the community in which he lived. The long strain upon his nervous system compelled him to resign his charge in Worcester. He accepted a call to the Baptist church in West Cambridge, where he labored for eight years, and then, in 1862, he acted as secretary for New England of the American Baptist Home Missionary Society. Brown University, of which he was a trustee for eighteen years, conferred upon him the honorary degree of Doctor of Divinity in 1857. Dr. Swaim died in Cambridge, Mass., Feb. 3, 1865. He was a man of a strong, vigorous mind, one of the ablest of New England Baptist ministers.

Swaim, Judge Thomas, was born Dec. 22, 1783, near Piscataway, N. J. (as is supposed); lost his father in childhood; spent his youth at Connellsville, Pa., where, at eighteen, he was baptized by Rev. Wm. Parkinson, of New York City, then on an evangelizing tour among those new settlements in Western Pennsylvania. At twenty-one he settled at Pemberton, N. J. (then called New Mills), began business for himself, and united with the Baptist church there. Here he resided some fifty-five years, acquired property, became a prominent man in the county of Burlington, and for about thirty years was one of the judges of the County Court,—for a large part of the time its presiding officer. His decisions were seldom reversed. He lived to see the beginning of the civil war, and was deeply concerned for the perpetuity of the Union and the preservation of our institutions. Being a devoted and earnest Christian, he was early chosen deacon, and held that office till his death. Well grounded in the cardinal truths of the gospel under the preaching of Daniel Dodge, John Rodgers, and other prominent ministers of that day, a positive man of strong convictions, he "contended earnestly for the faith once delivered to the saints." Through life his house was a welcome stopping-place for ministers of the gospel. He took a leading part in the support of the gospel at home and in the benevolent enterprises of the denomination. He ardently espoused the cause of faithful versions of the Bible, and was a warm supporter and vice-president of the American Bible Union. After suffering long, he died triumphantly Sept. 15, 1861. He gave two sons to the ministry, Samuel Swaim, D.D., long a pastor in Massachusetts, now deceased, and Thomas Swaim, D.D., formerly pastor at Flemington, N. J., and now (1880) district secretary of the American Baptist Home Mission Society at Philadelphia.

Swaim, Thomas, D.D., was born at Pemberton, N. J., March 30, 1817; entered Brown University, but graduated from Madison University in 1844, and from Hamilton Theological Seminary in 1846; was ordained in November, 1846, and settled with the church at Washington, Pa. After four years of successful labor he accepted the agency of the American Baptist Missionary Union for six months, at the end of which service he became pastor at Flemington, N. J., where he remained for sixteen years. During this pastorate nearly 300 were baptized, and a new and larger meeting-house was built. In 1867 he accepted the financial secretaryship of the New Jersey Classical and Scientific Institute at Hightstown. In 1868 he became district secretary of the American Baptist Home Mission Society, with headquarters at Philadelphia, which position he now holds. The degree of D.D. was conferred, in 1865, by the university at Lewisburg.

Dr. Swaim is an able preacher of the New Testament, and strong in his defense of Bible doctrines as held by the denomination. To the work in which he is now engaged he gives his undivided energies, and zealously labors to secure for the society the largest share of the sympathies and contributions of the churches.

Swan, Rev. Jabez Smith, the distinguished evangelist of Connecticut, son of Joshua and Esther (Smith) Swan, was born in Stonington, Conn., Feb. 23, 1800; had good early advantages; aided as powder-boy in the defense of Stonington, Aug. 9 and 10, 1814; removed with his parents to Lyme, Conn., about 1816; converted at the age of twenty-one,—a deep experience; baptized by Rev. Wm. Palmer; felt called to preach; licensed in May, 1822; studied at Hamilton Literary and Theological Institution, N. Y.; settled with Stonington Borough Baptist church, Conn., and was ordained June 20, 1827; began as an evangelist; settled in Norwich, N. Y., in 1830; greatly blessed in preaching far and near; settled with Baptist church in Preston, N. Y., in 1837; prospered in revivals around; in 1840 settled with church in Oxford, N. Y., and prospered; returned to Connecticut in 1842, and conducted remarkable meetings at Stonington Borough, Mystic Bridge, and New London, also in Albany, N. Y.; in 1843 settled with First Baptist church in New London, Conn.; great blessings followed; preached widely as an evangelist, going even to Charlestown, Mass.; in 1848 settled with High Street church in Albany, N. Y.; in 1849 returned to New London, Conn., and became first pastor of Huntington Street church; another powerful revival; labored in Providence, R. I.; in 1858 settled with Second church in New London; always going out as an evangelist; began in 1860 as a State missionary with Rev. M. E. Shailer; greatly blessed through the State; again labored as evangelist in New York State; settled with Baptist church in Waterford, Conn.; suffered from overwork from 1842 down to his last charge; powerful in his sermons and in addresses; a mighty

REV. JABEZ SMITH SWAN.

man in prayer; strong advocate of education and missions; the most powerful preacher as an evangelist ever known in Connecticut. A sketch of his "Life and Labors," an octavo, was published in 1873, prepared for the press by Rev. F. Denison; more than 10,000 conversions occurred under his ministry.

His son, Rev. Charles Y. Swan, D.D., a very able and successful minister, died in 1880. At the time of his decease he was the honored pastor of South church in Newark, N. J.

Swan, Rev. Thomas, for many years the eminent and successful pastor of the Cannon Street church, Birmingham, England, was born at Manchester, Jan. 5, 1795; baptized by Rev. Christopher Anderson at Edinburgh in 1817; he was called to the ministry, and entered Bristol College in 1821. In 1825 he proceeded to India to take part in the work of Serampore College, but returned to England by way of America in 1828. He settled at Birmingham in the beginning of 1829, and for twenty-eight years held the pastorate of the Cannon Street church. During that period he baptized 966 persons, a yearly average of nearly thirty-five. He died on March 9, 1857, and was buried at Birmingham amidst a large concourse of friends and fellow-citizens. It is recorded of him that he always read his sermons. His pastoral care of the large congregation was a remarkable characteristic of his career.

Swanzey Church is the oldest Baptist church in Massachusetts, and only twenty-four years younger than the First Baptist church in Providence, R. I.,—the one having been formed in 1639 and the other in 1663. The founder of the church was Rev. John Miles, who came with a colony from Swansea, in Wales, and settled in a section of what was then Rehoboth, but subsequently was set off, and received the name of Swanzey, in memory of the home from which many of its settlers came.

The Swansea church of Wales, from which the members of the Swanzey, Mass., church chiefly came, bringing the old church records with them, in 1663, was founded in 1649, and at one time was in a highly prosperous condition, having on the roll of its members the names of 265 persons. The "Act of Uniformity," passed in the reign of Charles II., in 1662, which expelled 2000 ministers from their churches, reached the somewhat secluded Welsh town of Swansea, and Mr. Miles went into exile, many of his flock following him to this country, and settled, as has already been said, in what is now known as Swanzey, Mass., and entered into church relations there in 1663. He took a deep interest in his brethren who were called to suffer persecution for their religious opinions. It is said that "he labored frequently with his brethren in Boston in the time of their trials, and at one period it was proposed that he should become their pastor. Being once brought before the magistrate for preaching, he requested a Bible, and opened to these words in Job: "But ye should say, Why persecute we him? seeing the root of the matter is in me," which, having read, he sat down, and such an effect had the sword of the Spirit that he was afterwards treated with moderation if not with kindness. "What few sketches have been preserved of his life," says Dr. Benedict, "go to show that he bore an excellent character, and was eminently useful in his day." He died Feb. 3, 1683. He was succeeded by Rev. Samuel Luther, who had represented the town of Swanzey in the State Legislature. He was ordained pastor of the church July 22, 1685. "He was much esteemed," says Backus, "both at home and abroad." His ministry continued thirty-two years, his death occurring in 1717. For thirteen years Rev. Ephraim Wheaton had been a colleague with Mr. Luther, and on the decease of his venerable associate he became sole pastor of the church. His ministry was much blessed to the spiritual prosperity of the church. It was ended by his death in 1734. Rev. Samuel Maxwell, who had been colleague with Mr. Wheaton for a few months, took his place on his decease; but becoming a Seventh-Day Baptist, he resigned his pastorate after a few years. The next pastor was Rev. Benjamin Harrington, in office a few years, and left under a cloud of suspicion resting on his character. Rev. Jabez Wood was the next minister, continuing in office about thirty years, and was followed by Rev. Charles Thompson, a sketch of whose life will be found in this volume. The church had a large number of pastors and supplies for quite a term of years, until we come down to 1836, when Dr. Abial Fisher was chosen pastor and held the office for ten years. We thus bring the history of this ancient church down to 1846, where we leave it. Like all the old towns in the eastern section of Massachusetts, Swanzey has suffered from the removal of its inhabitants to other places, but still the old church maintains its visible existence, and preserves the purity of its ancient faith and order.

Swartz, James S., was born in Montgomery Co., Pa., March 21, 1840; was baptized at Falls of Schuylkill, Philadelphia, by Rev. N. J. Clark, March 21, 1858; is still connected with the church at Falls of Schuylkill, and has for a number of years been the efficient superintendent of the Sunday-school. He is also treasurer of the Philadelphia Baptist Association, and prominently connected with the management of city and State mission work. He is a man of marked integrity and intelligence.

Sweden, the Baptists in.—A young Swedish sailor, by the name of W. Schroeder, was one Lord's day morning led to the Baptist Mariners' church in New York, then under the care of Rev. I. R. Steward. He had been converted during his voyage to the United States. On that Sabbath morning two sailors were baptized by Mr. Steward. It was the first time that Mr. Schroeder ever saw the ordinance of baptism. After a few weeks he was baptized himself.

On his return to Sweden he met a Swedish sailor by the name of F. O. Nilson, who was laboring in that country as a missionary among sailors, under the patronage of the Seamen's Friend Society of New York. Through a remark make by Mr. Schroeder Mr. Nilson was led to investigate the subject of baptism. In July, 1847, he also was baptized, by Rev. J. G. Oncken in Hamburg. On the 21st of September, 1848, his wife and four others were baptized in the Kattegat, near Gottenburg, by a Baptist missionary from Denmark, and the same evening the first Baptist church in Sweden was organized. It consisted of six members. Mr. Nilson went around preaching and baptizing until the number of baptized believers was fifty-two.

But this could not be allowed by the Lutheran Romanism of Sweden. Consequently, Mr. Nilson received sentence of banishment in July, 1851, and was obliged to seek refuge in Denmark. In consequence of bitter persecution the majority of the church emigrated to America in the spring of 1853.

The Baptists who remained suffered severe persecution, being often fined and brought before the Consistory, the Inquisition of the Lutheran Church in Sweden, on a charge of not having had their children baptized, and of falling away from the orthodox faith.

While these efforts were made to crush the movement in the south of Sweden, a new interest was springing up in the northern part of the country. A few persons in Stockholm who had been brought to a saving knowledge of Christ had begun to entertain doubts as to the validity of infant baptism. Among these was a furrier named D. Forsell. Just at this time, Andrew Wiberg, whose name is familiar to American Baptists, was, in the providence of God, led to Stockholm, and his name has since then been identified not only with the Baptist movement in Sweden, but with all Christian work. Born in the north of Sweden in 1817, he commenced his career as a clerk in a store, but his love for books soon led him to abandon this occupation and to devote himself to study. As a student, he embraced skeptical ideas. But some one made the remark to him once that the Bible after all might be true, and, if so, it would be a fearful thing to fall into the hands of the living God. This remark left him dissatisfied with his skeptical views, and that awful "if" haunted him night and day. So intense were his feelings that he had no peace until he found peace in Christ; this took place in 1842. In the following year he was ordained as a clergyman of the Lutheran Church, and he remained as a minister in that church until 1849. During this time he preached Christ and him crucified fearlessly and faithfully, not only in the pulpits of the state church, but in obscure villages and farm-houses in the country, and the Lord blessed his labors to the salvation of many. But the relation with the state church troubled him, and in 1849 he resigned his office. In 1850 he traveled from the north of Sweden to Stockholm. There he met with those brethren who were exercised on the subject of baptism. In 1851 he accompanied Mr. Forsell to Hamburg, where he met with the brethren J. G. Oncken and J. Köbner, with whom he entered into earnest discussions on the subject, but continued firm in his belief in infant baptism. On his return to Stockholm he began to study the subject thoroughly. The result was that he became convinced that the immersion of believers was the only Scriptural baptism, and, accordingly, he wrote his first work on baptism, an octavo volume of 320 pages, which was published in Upsala in 1852.

His health having failed, a sea-voyage was recommended by his physician. He left Stockholm for the United States, July 17, 1852. The vessel stopped at the island of Amager, near Copenhagen, and here Mr. Wiberg was baptized in the Baltic, on July 23, by F. O. Nilson. He remained two years in America. During this time the religious movement was making considerable progress in Sweden. There was also an interest awakened among the Christians in America for Sweden. In August, 1855, Mr. Wiberg received an appointment from the American Baptist Publication Society to labor as superintendent of missionary work in Sweden. On the evening of Aug. 23, 1855, a farewell meeting was held at the Fifth church, Sansom Street, Philadelphia, at which he was publicly set apart for the work, and at the same time united in marriage to Miss Caroline Lintemuth, who was a member of that church and a faithful laborer in the Sunday-school. During her twenty-five years of missionary labor in Sweden, Mrs. Wiberg has, under many difficulties and hardships, faithfully and, we may also say, heroically stood by the side of her husband as a true, loyal helper in his missionary work.

During Mr. Wiberg's absence from Sweden the work there had increased year by year. The treatise on baptism, which he wrote in 1852, had been published and extensively circulated, and created a great sensation. By reading it many were convinced of the truth with regard to baptism, and wished to be baptized. As there was no one to administer the ordinance, Brother P. F. Hejdenberg went to Hamburg in the spring of 1854, and was there baptized and ordained. On his return to Sweden he baptized in different parts of the country a number of believers, and, at the close of the year, there were about 200 baptized converts. The following year—1855—was marked by a still greater increase, so that at its close the number had increased to 500.

But the state church could not allow this movement. Brother Hejdenberg was within a short period summoned sixteen times to appear before judicial tribunals to answer the charge of having held religious meetings contrary to law, and he received eight imprisonments, each lasting from two to fourteen days. In the same year persecution was carried on in several provinces of the country. Thus, e.g., Brother D. Forsell was sentenced to a fine of 100 crowns for preaching the gospel, and 5 crowns in addition for violation of the Sabbath in preaching on Sunday.

On their arrival in Stockholm, Mr. and Mrs. Wiberg found a little band of 24 baptized believers. The first Baptist Sunday-school in Sweden was opened with 22 children, which number soon increased to 150.

In 1856, Mr. Wiberg started a semi-monthly religious paper, called the *Evangelist*. In the same year the Missionary Union of Stockholm was formed, and four evangelists sent out into the field. Great good has been done through this and other similar societies afterwards formed in different parts of the country.

At the close of 1856 there were 21 Baptist churches in the country, with 961 members and 24 preachers. As the cause progressed persecution grew fiercer, and fines and imprisonments were reported almost every week. Some persons even died from barbarous punishment. The following year 1292 were baptized, and at the close of the year we had 2105 church members, 45 churches, and 44 preachers.

Even in this year severe persecution continued to rage, especially in the south of Sweden. There the authorities seized upon our Baptist preachers and imprisoned them whenever they found them outside the limits of their own parish. Six of our brethren were at one time imprisoned in solitary confinement at Christianstad, and some were treated most barbarously. One of them, a blind evangelist, was confined in this prison eight days for having circulated religious books and tracts. When he was taken from prison an iron chain was attached to one of his ankles, and he was then taken in a prison-van to another station, where new irons were put upon him. In this condition he was sent back to his home, and compelled to pay a considerable sum of money. As he had no money of his own, they took what he had received from the sale of books, and also a watch which he wore, but which was not his own. Another evangelist and colporteur was seized, severely beaten, stripped of his clothing, thrown into cold water, had his hair cut close to his head, was dressed in a thin prisoner's dress, and then cast into a damp cell in the cold season of the year. There he was seized with an illness, from which he never fully recovered.

In the following year—1858—our membership increased to 3487 in 69 churches.

At this time a young nobleman by the name of A. Drake, who had studied for the ministry at the University of Upsala, joined our denomination. He has since proved to be one of "the excellent of the earth," working most faithfully and efficiently as an editor of our denominational paper, *The Weekly Post*, and as a teacher in our theological seminary, not to mention his work in many other branches of Christian enterprise.

As the meeting-house of the Baptists in Stockholm had for a long time been too small to contain all who attended worship, and as the church in Stockholm had no means for erecting a larger house, Mr. Wiberg undertook, in the year 1861, a journey to England, and succeeded in collecting £1100. But as this sum was entirely too small to justify an attempt to build, he, with Mrs. Wiberg, left again in August, 1863, for America, to collect for the same purpose. There they received a hearty welcome in many places and from many dear Christian friends, who took a lively interest in the Swedish Mission. During their stay in America they met Mr. K. O. Broady, a Swede by birth, who had studied for the ministry at Madison University, and afterwards served in the war. They also met A. E. Edgren, D.D., who had studied at the same place, and served in the war. These brethren were, together with Mr. Wiberg, appointed missionaries to Sweden, and sailed from America the 16th of June, 1866. Mr. Broady has since then been laboring as superintendent of our theological seminary, established the same year, and also as a prominent preacher. Dr. Edgren returned in a few years to America, and has done a good work as principal of the Scandinavian department in the Baptist Theological Seminary in Chicago.

The work from that time till now has wonderfully increased, so that the Baptists in Sweden number to-day about 20,000, united in 300 churches. They have also many missionary societies in different parts of the country. They have been the pioneers of Sunday-school work, and they have about 17,000 scholars in their Sunday-schools, with 2000 teachers. We have also, after many difficulties, recently had a hymn-book prepared for our denomination.

But, though the results of past labors are thus far encouraging, very much remains to be done. The country at large, though nominally Protestant, is still sunk in ignorance, superstition, bigotry, intolerance, and vice. The Baptists in Sweden are poor. Out of 300 churches there are only five or six who can support their own ministers, and the prospect for our young men who go out from our theological seminary is certainly not very bright. We have also, as yet, the same opposition and the same persecution to contend against. Only a few days ago a young, earnest, and good Baptist minister, in the south of Sweden, was sentenced to a fine of 100 crowns for having preached the gospel to the people against the prohibition of the church council. Only three years ago he was imprisoned fifty-one days for the same cause, and, as he has no money to pay the fine, he will be imprisoned the second time. This is the latest addition to the black-list of similar deeds perpetrated by the Lutheran State Church of Sweden.

Sweet, Rev. Joel, was born Feb. 9, 1795, in Burlington, Otsego Co., N. Y. His father was an ordained Baptist minister, who, removing to Illinois about 1820, died near Jacksonville, in that State, in 1837. The son Joel having experienced a change of heart in 1813, was baptized in 1817, uniting with the Baptist church at Virgil Corners, Cortland Co., N. Y. In 1825, removing to Homer, he came under the personal influence of Rev. Alfred Bennett, who now became his pastor, and under that influence found his convictions of duty as to the Christian ministry much strengthened. About two years later he decided to devote himself to that work, and preached his first sermon at Lisle, in Broome County, to which place he had in the mean time removed. An interesting revival occurred at this place, beginning in a Bible-class taught by Mr. Sweet, and in this revival one afterwards well known in the ministry of Illinois, Rev. F. Ketchem, was converted. Mr. Sweet now determined to make the West his future home, and Feb. 23, 1830, arrived at Diamond Grove, near Jacksonville, Ill. He immediately entered with great energy into Western work, becoming especially conspicuous for the vigor with which he assailed the anti-missionary, anti-Sunday-school, and anti-temperance influences in the midst of which he found himself; his first special engagement being as a temperance lecturer under the appointment of the New York State Temperance Society; afterwards agent of the American Sunday-School Union. He was ordained at Diamond Grove in 1833. In his agency work he traveled very extensively through Central Illinois, and was the means of great good in giving right direction to public sentiment, founding Sunday-schools, and encouraging weak churches. He was subsequently engaged in fruitful missionary work in Springfield and Quincy Associations. He also served as pastor the churches of Mount Sterling, Meridian, Barry, Lamarsh, and Treville. He died at the house of his son, E. D. L. Sweet, Esq., in Chicago, May 8, 1857.

Sweet, Rev. John Davis, was born in Kingston, Mass., Oct. 16, 1838. He received his early education in the Lyman School, East Boston, and was fitted for college in the Middleborough Academy and at the Cambridge High School. In these preparatory schools he took the first rank in scholarship, deportment, and attendance. So far advanced was he in his studies that he was able to enter the Sophomore class in Harvard College in 1857. Here he stood very high in his class, and was prosecuting his work with success when failing health compelled him to abandon study for a time and seek restoration by travel in Europe. He had become a hopeful Christian while a student in the Middleborough Academy, and the ministry was his chosen vocation. The failure of his health, however, compelled him to lay aside his plans with reference to preaching. About the commencement of the year 1862 he embarked in business in old Cambridge, Mass., connecting himself with the Baptist church in that place, and becoming one of its most active members. His health improving, his former desire to enter the Christian ministry revived, and he decided to give up his business. He was ordained in October, 1863, as pastor of the Baptist church in Billerica, Mass., where he remained five years. He was then called to the important position of pastor of the First Baptist church in Somerville, Mass., being installed May 4, 1868. In the midst of a career of great usefulness he died at the early age of thirty years. Not long before his death he made arrangements for the payment of $10,000 to the Missionary Union at his decease, subject to the condition that the interest on this sum should be paid to his wife during her life.

Sweet, Rev. Sylvester E., the pastor of the Baptist church at Elkhorn, Wis., was born in Leeds Co., Canada West, in 1839. He passed his early childhood in the place of his birth, but when six years of age he became a resident of Wisconsin. He was almost at the same time thrown upon his own resources, and very early in life developed that independence of character which has signally marked his subsequent career. He obtained a hope in Christ when twenty-three years of age, and a few years later, in 1867, united with the Baptist church at Lone Rock, Wis. Having determined to prepare himself for the Christian ministry, he began a course of studies with a view of fitting himself for that work. Having finished his preparatory studies at Silsby's Academy, he entered Wayland University in 1870, and completed the prescribed course of that institution. He was ordained in 1870 at Marble Ridge, Sauk Co., Wis., Rev. Joel W. Fish being moderator of the council and preaching the sermon. He has been pastor at De Soto two years, Beaver Dam two years, Trempeleau three years, Monticello Prairie and Albany two years, and is at present pastor of the Baptist churches at Elkhorn and Sugar Creek. During his ministry his labors have been largely blessed.

Possessed of great energy and decision, combined with fine business tact and devoted piety, he has shown himself a good preacher, a good pastor, and a successful laborer in the vineyard of the Master.

Swinney, Rev. C. P., M.D., a prominent and useful minister in South Arkansas, was born in 1837. He began his ministry among the Methodists, and came to Arkansas from Mississippi as a Methodist preacher just before the late war. A careful examination of the action and subjects of baptism led to a change of views, and he united with the Baptists at Atlanta, Ark., about 1863, and was soon after ordained as a Baptist minister, and entered upon a successful work in Columbia Co., Ark., and in the adjoining parts of Louisiana. He had many converts, some of whom have become useful ministers. For some years past he has pursued the practice of medicine in connection with the ministry. He died June, 1880.

Sydnor, T. W., D.D., was born in Hanover Co., Va., June 1, 1816. He was brought up a Presbyterian, was awakened under a sermon preached by Dr. W. S. Plumer, and baptized in 1831 into the fellowship of the Second Baptist church, Richmond, Va. In 1835 he entered the Virginia Baptist Seminary (Richmond College), and in 1835 the Columbian College, where he graduated in 1838, afterwards spending two years at Newton Theological Seminary. He was licensed to preach by the Second Baptist church of Richmond in 1836, and ordained at Bruington church, King and Queen Co., in 1841. During 1841 supplied that church; during 1842 was an agent for the Columbian College; during 1843 pastor at Farmville; during 1844–45 was agent of the Baptist General Convention for Foreign Missions; and during 1846 agent of the Southern Baptist Convention. From 1847, through a period of thirty years, Dr. Sydnor preached for several churches in Nottoway Co., Va., where he has been greatly blessed, having baptized more than 3000 persons. In 1870 he was appointed county superintendent of public schools. He has been in the employ of the American Baptist Publication Society in Sunday-school work among the colored population. He is connected with several of the boards of the denomination, and has frequently presided as moderator in Associations, and is a trustee of Richmond College. He has published several excellent sermons, and is a frequent contributor to the *Religious Herald*. Dr. Sydnor's first wife was a daughter of Dr. Chapin, of the Columbian College. A very promising son of his, studying for the ministry, lost his life in the battle of Sharpsburg, Md. The Columbian College conferred the honorary degree of D.D. on Mr. Sydnor in 1873.

T.

Taft, Sylvanus Adon, D.D., was born at Mendon, N. Y., Jan. 6, 1825. In 1830 his parents removed to Washington, Mich., where he confessed the Saviour, and was immersed at Stoney Creek, when he was eleven years old, by Rev. G. D. Simmons. He was educated at Romeo, Rochester, Michigan University, Rochester University, and Rochester Theological Seminary; was ordained at Stoney Creek, Mich., in 1845; graduated at Rochester, N. Y., in 1852. He was pastor at Stoney Creek, Mount Vernon, Ypsilanti, and Holley, Mich.; Webster, N. Y.; Quincy, Ill.; Bethel, Palmyra, and Macon, Mo.; Santa Rosa and Vacaville, Cal.; removing to the Pacific coast in 1875. During his pastorates he has been largely engaged as an instructor. He was principal of Disco Seminary one year; Oxford Institute, three years; Fenton High School, four years; president of the Baptist college at Palmyra three years, and of California College one year. He is the author of the work entitled "An Epitome of the Gospel." Dr. Taft is a clear thinker, ready speaker, warm in his sympathies, and an influential and honored leader in the denomination.

Taggart, Rev. John M., was born near Philadelphia, Pa., Nov. 17, 1817, of Scotch-Irish ancestry. His early years were spent in that city. Driven by the crash of 1837 to seek employment elsewhere, he went to the city of Washington, and remained there about four years. Then he removed to Kentucky, where, under the ministrations of Elder Wm. Vaughan, he was converted, and baptized at Bloomfield, Nelson Co. He was licensed to preach by the Bloomfield church in November, 1843, and ordained Dec. 27, 1845. Removed subsequently to Illinois, and spent several years at Jacksonville. In 1855 removed to Nebraska, just opened for settlement, reaching Omaha about May 1. He was pastor at Nebraska City for four years, during which time the church edifice was built. Since that time he has labored wherever God's providence has called him. Since 1871 he has resided at Palmyra, laboring diligently in the Master's cause, and waiting the signal which shall invite him to rest from his labors. For years he has been the honored president of the State Convention.

Talbird, Henry, D.D., was born Nov. 7, 1811, on Hilton Head Island, Beaufort District, S. C. His family were among the earliest settlers and most prominent citizens of the State. His grandfather, John Talbird, was a commissioned officer in the war of the Revolution, and carried to his grave marks of the wounds he had received in battle.

Henry Talbird was educated at Madison Universith, N. Y., and his studies embraced a full collegiate and theological course. After graduating from the theological department in 1841 he was called to the pastorate of the Baptist church, Tuscaloosa, Ala. At the close of his first year's service the church unanimously invited him to become its permanent pastor, with a considerable increase of salary. But he had received a call to Montgomery, in the same State, and he concluded to remove to that city, where he remained nine years.

In these two pastorates his ministrations were greatly blessed, the churches were built up in faith and zeal, and largely strengthened in numbers. At the time of his resignation of its pastorate the church in Montgomery had become, with one exception, the strongest Baptist church in Alabama.

While in Montgomery he was elected to the professorship of Theology in Howard College, Marion, Ala., and entered upon the duties of his office in January, 1852. At the close of the first year he was elected president of the college, and maintained that relation until the commencement of the civil war, in 1861. In 1854 the honorary degree of Doctor of Divinity was conferred upon him by the University of Alabama. At the beginning of the war he tried to retain his students, but the excited feelings of the people rendered it impossible, and the school became practically empty.

During Dr. Talbird's administration Howard College was prospered as it had never been before. Not only was the number of students largely increased, but the interest of the Baptist denomination throughout the State was aroused, and the brethren came readily and promptly to its assistance. So that in less than six years the endowment fund was increased from $45,000 to $225,000, besides adding to its possessions property to the value of $79,000. At the opening of the war it was one of the most flourishing institutions in the South.

Dr. Talbird embraced the cause of the Confederate States, and lent all his energies to convert their battles into victories. In 1861 he entered the Confederate army with the rank of captain, in the 7th Alabama Regiment. At the close of the first campaign he became a colonel, and organized the 41st Alabama Regiment. While in the army, he was engaged in a number of battles and skirmishes, and enjoyed the full confidence of officers and men. After nearly three years of honorable service he was compelled to resign his commission on account of ill health. At the close of the war his health was still feeble, and he accepted a country pastorate, where his labors would not be so great as in the charges he held before. He spent two and a half years in Carlonville, Dallas Co., Ala., making a faithful and successful pastor, and winning the warm regards of his people. His health remaining feeble, he concluded to spend some time in traveling, and with feelings of profound regret, felt compelled to resign his pastorate and leave his people.

At the close of some six months he received and accepted a call to Henderson, Ky. His ministry here was marked by that deep devotion to the interests of religion which endears the pastor to his people, and the church was greatly strengthened. After laboring in Henderson three years and a half, he received a call to the First Baptist church of Lexington, Mo., and in April, 1872, he entered upon his pastorate there. Over nine years have elapsed since he took charge of this church, and the affectionate regards of his people make his residence in Lexington very happy. He is possessed of much personal magnetism, that attracts men to him. He has been elected a trustee of William Jewell College, and president of its board of education. He is held in high esteem by the faculty of that institution.

He is polished in manners and address. He is devoted to study, and spends a large portion of his time in his well-selected library. He preaches from copious notes, but the greater portion of his discourse is extempore. His preaching is sound and practical, his logic clear and convincing. His sermons exhibit research and careful preparation, and always command the attention of his hearers from the beginning to the end. During his ministry he has baptized over 2000 persons. Dr. Talbird exhibits no evidence of advancing years in his pulpit ministrations.

Talbot, Sansom, D.D., was born near Urbana, O., June 28, 1828; removed with his parents in 1839 to McDonough Co., Ill., where, in 1846, he was converted, and united with the St. Mary's Baptist church. Immediately upon his conversion he decided to study for the ministry, and in the autumn of 1846 entered Granville College, where he graduated with honor in 1851. After spending a year as tutor at Granville, he went to Newton Theological Seminary, where he took a full theological course. While at Newton he was appointed by the Missionary Union as a missionary to Siam, but circumstances causing delay he relinquished his purpose, and accepted a call to the pastorate of the First Baptist church of Dayton, O., a position which he held from 1856 to 1863. In June, 1863, he was elected president of Denison University, then at a very critical period in its history. Assuming at once the duties of this position he gave it all the energies of his nature, and the aspect of things speedily changed. After ten years of most successful but exhausting toil he died at Newton Centre, Mass., where he had gone for rest, June 29, 1873.

Dr. Talbot was a man of boundless energy and courage. He went grandly through his life of study, and attained a scholarship which put him in the front rank of educated men. His presence at Denison was an inspiration. While yet a student at Newton he gave valuable assistance to Dr. Sears in his preparation of Roget's "Thesaurus." His sermons and lectures were models of clearness and conciseness. His early death was an occasion for mourning throughout the entire country.

Taliaferro, Rev. Robert H., was born in Kentucky, Oct. 19, 1824. His mother dying early, he was trained by his sisters; educated at Granville College, O., and the Western Baptist Theological Seminary, Covington, Ky.; professed religion at Granville; ordained to the gospel ministry at Luburgrund church, Montgomery Co., Ky., Sept. 15, 1846; was pastor at Galveston, Texas, several years; spent most of his subsequent life at Austin, except two years, when he was a missionary among the Choctaw Indians. His labors at Austin covered nearly twenty-five years, and were largely without compensation, and at a great sacrifice to himself. The first church in Williamson County was organized by him, when there was not a glass window or plank floor in the county. His labors at Bastrop, Webberville, Round Rock, and Chapel Hill were productive of great good. He was elected and served as chaplain of the senate of the twelfth, thirteenth, and fourteenth Legislatures of Texas, and he was one of the voluntary chaplains of the constitutional convention of 1875.

He was associated with Rev. George W. Baines, Sr., either as editor or special contributor of the *Texas Baptist* for six years. Besides contributions to periodicals, which were numerous and very able, he wrote three works of a religious character,—one on "Infidelity," another entitled "Which is our Saviour, Christ or the Church?" the third is a "Series of Sermons." The first two were published, and are able, exhaustive, and practical works. The third has not been published. He died Nov. 19, 1875, leaving a wife, one son, and four daughters to the care of a devoted father and grandfather. He was remarkable for his indifference to worldly goods, and cared little for secular honors. The number of sermons which he preached, the number of persons he baptized, and the number converted under his ministry must be counted by thousands. No purer, abler, more devoted, self-sacrificing minister of the New Testament has lived or died in Texas. Rev. George W. Baines, Sr., says of him, "that he was the man who did more by his pen to establish Bible truth in the minds of Texas Baptists than any other writer in the State or out of it."

Tallmadge, Judge Matthias B., was born at Stamford, Dutchess Co., N. Y., March 1, 1774; graduated at Yale College 1795; studied law with Chief-Justice Spencer at Hudson, N. Y.; practised at Herkimer; represented his county in the State Legislature and the western district of New York in the State senate. His marked abilities and assiduity in the discharge of public duties brought him to the notice of the President of the United States, who appointed him judge of the U. S. District Court for New York. This resulted in his removal to New York City, where, notwithstanding a feeble constitution and almost constant ailments, he won great distinction for the masterly manner in which he performed the varied and difficult duties of his office. It was during this period of his busy life that he gave profound study to the Word of God, and while spending the summer of 1811 at Poughkeepsie, N. Y., made a profession of faith, and was baptized by Rev. Lewis Leonards, then pastor there.

Although much occupied with his judicial duties and a great sufferer from periodical attacks of fever, he became deeply interested in all the missionary enterprises of the denomination, and occupied positions of high trust in the General Baptist Convention, and on its executive board. His illness in his latter years made it necessary for him to spend his winters in the Southern States, where he improved his opportunities to acquaint himself with the leading men and enterprises of the denomination, and so much did he endear himself to the Southern people that they appointed him to represent their churches in the original and the succeeding meetings of the General Convention. In 1803 he married Miss Elizabeth Clinton, daughter of Hon. George Clinton, then governor of New York, and afterwards Vice-President of the United States. He died Oct. 7, 1819, in the forty-sixth year of his age, at Poughkeepsie, N. Y., greatly lamented by his family, his church, and the nation.

Tanner, Robert Lynn, a prominent layman in Louisiana, was born in South Carolina in 1793; came to Rapides Parish, La., in 1813. He was a man of large means, which he liberally employed for the Master's cause. For many years he supported the pastor of the Cherryville Baptist church, of which he was a deacon; was often elected moderator of the Louisiana Baptist Association and vice-president of the State Convention.

Tappan, Lewis N., a New Englander by birth, was not a professor of religion till actively engaged in business. When he became a Christian he engaged in religious work with all his might. Much of his time was spent in the Rocky Mountains among the miners, but he found opportunities for attending to his religious duties, and shared his means in helping when assistance was needed, whether at home or abroad. He was a natural leader and a good counselor. He died in 1880 at Leadville, Col., where he will be much missed. He was widely known and highly esteemed.

Tatum, S. O.—In 1870 the Baptists of North Carolina were called on to mourn the loss of Mr. S. O. Tatum, a wise and good man, who did much to develop the churches of his part of the State. He was born in Davie Co., N. C., and at the age of twenty-five determined to obtain a liberal education. He graduated at Wake Forest College in 1852. The last years of his life were devoted to teaching and to the improvement of the churches of the Yadkin Association, of which he was moderator.

Taylor, Rev. Alfred, a minister widely known and of great moral worth, was the son of Rev. Joseph Taylor, and was born in Warren Co., Ky., July 19, 1808. When three years of age he was taken by his parents to Butler County, where he grew up to manhood. He attended a school conducted by Rev. D. L. Mansfield, and was afterwards under the tutorship of the distinguished Rev. William Warder. He was for many years the intimate friend and fellow-laborer of Dr. J. M. Pendleton. He united with Sandy Creek Baptist church, in Butler County, in 1829; was licensed to preach in 1831, and ordained in 1834. He soon became "pastor of four country churches." But his labor embraced a much larger field. He introduced into Gasper River Association in 1837 the practice of holding "protracted meetings." "Within less than six months," Rev. Dr. J. S. Coleman states, "he baptized over 800 persons." From this time he labored with indefatigable zeal for more than twenty years, and with a degree of success that few men have attained. Of the multitude baptized by him more than thirty became ministers of the gospel. He was active in all the benevolent enterprises of his denomination in the State. His sons, J. S. Taylor, J. P. Taylor, and W. C. Taylor, are excellent Baptist ministers. He died Oct. 9, 1855.

Taylor, B. F., was born in Lowville, N. Y., in 1822. He was educated at Madison University, Hamilton, N. Y., of which his father was president. He is, and has long been, occupying a prominent position as a racy descriptive writer. For many years he was literary editor of the *Chicago Evening Journal*, and was its principal army correspondent during the civil war, following the headquarters of the Army of the Cumberland. In picturesque description his letters surpassed all contemporaries. Some of them have been gathered into a volume entitled "Pictures in Camp and Field," 1867, of which a new edition has recently appeared. He has published several books, among which are "Attractions of Language," 1845; "January and June," 1853; "Three November Days," "The World on Wheels," 1873; "Old Time-Pictures and Sheaves of Rhyme," 1874. Numerous editions have been issued of all his books.

He is also a popular lecturer on the lyceum platform, especially in the West. He resides at La Porte, Ind.

Taylor, Prof. Charles E.—The Rev. James B. Taylor, D.D., of blessed memory, gave three sons to the ministry. The oldest, Dr. Geo. B., is a missionary at Rome, Italy; the second, James B., is pastor of the First Baptist church of Wilmington, N. C.; and the third, Charles E., has been for ten years the Professor of Latin in Wake Forest College. Prof. Taylor was born in Richmond, Va., Oct. 12, 1842; was baptized by Dr. J. B. Jeter when but ten years of age; went from Richmond College into a regiment of cavalry, and fought through the war; then spent five years at the University of Virginia, graduating in most of the schools of that famous college; made a trip to Europe in 1870, and was ordained in April, 1871, Drs. Wingate, Walters, and J. B. Taylor, Sr., comprising the Presbytery. He is at present agent of the Board of Education, as well as professor in Wake Forest College. He has been pastor of the churches in Lewisburg and Oxford, N. C.

Taylor, Rev. Dan, was born Dec. 21, 1738, near Halifax, England. His mother was his early teacher, and the Bible was his first school-book. When three years old he could read so well that he attracted the attention of all that knew him. He first found the Saviour when about fifteen years of age. He was an Arminian in his doctrinal sentiments, and could not obtain baptism from Particular Baptist ministers; he journeyed on foot in unpleasant weather one hundred and twenty miles to be baptized by Mr. Thompson, in Boston, Lincolnshire. He was pastor at Wadsworth, near Halifax, in Halifax itself, and in London. He founded the General Baptist Academy for the education of young ministers, of which he was president for fifteen years. When *The General Baptist Magazine* was established he became its first editor. He was the author of more than fifty books and pamphlets, the chief of which is an admirable body of divinity, except its Arminianism, entitled "The Christian Religion."

He was fifty-five years in the ministry, and during that period preached nearly twenty thousand sermons; he traveled extensively, attending ordinations, church dedications, and Associations. He was a man of undoubted ability, deep piety, and great usefulness.

Clergymen of all denominations regarded him with confidence and affection; and the Lord of pastors shed abroad much of his love in his heart. He died in London, Nov. 26, 1816, in the seventy-eighth year of his age.

Taylor, Elisha E. L., D.D., was born at Delphi, N. Y., Sept. 25, 1815, and died at Brooklyn, N. Y., Aug. 20, 1874. He graduated at Madison University and at the Theological Seminary at Hamilton, N. Y. He accepted a call to a new interest, now the Pierpont Street Baptist church in Brooklyn, N. Y. After nine years of labor with it, it had grown so large that it was thought best to colonize, and he went out with others and formed the Strong Place Baptist church, which speedily became one of the strongest churches in Brooklyn.

In 1865 he was elected to the secretaryship of the Church Edifice Fund of the American Baptist Home Mission Society. Through his labors a fund of several hundred thousand dollars was accumulated, and many feeble churches on the Western borders were aided in building houses of worship. He has entered the heavenly rest after a life of great usefulness.

Taylor, George B., D.D., eldest son of Rev. James B. Taylor, D.D., and Mary Williams Taylor, who was the daughter of Elisha Williams, a Revolutionary soldier, and aide of Gen. Washington, and afterwards pastor of the Baptist church at Beverly, Mass., was born Dec. 27, 1832, in Richmond, Va. He was educated at Richmond College, and graduated Bachelor of Arts in 1851, after which he was engaged in teaching in Fluvanna Co., Va. Subsequently, he entered the University of Virginia, and after a three years' course graduated in most of the schools of that institution. While a student at the university he was ordained to the ministry at Charlottesville, and during the remainder of his university course served as pastor of two country churches in the vicinity. After leaving the university, he became the first pastor of the Franklin Square Baptist church, Baltimore, and continued in that relation two years. From Baltimore he removed to Staunton, Va., and became pastor of the church in that place, where he remained about twelve years, during which time the church was greatly prospered. After the beginning of the war, he, with the consent of the church, acted as chaplain in Gen. Stonewall Jackson's corps during the entire campaign of 1862, and subsequently officiated both as pastor and chaplain of the post, until the close of hostilities. He also visited the Army of Northern Virginia at the time of the "great revival," and took an active part in that remarkable work of divine grace. In 1869 he became chaplain of the University of Virginia, a position adorned by some of the ablest clergymen in the State, and served during the usual period of two years, at the termination of which he was recalled to the pastorate of the Staunton church. He returned to that place, and remained until 1873, when he was appointed by the Mission Board of the Southern Baptist Convention missionary to Rome, with the special duty of administering the affairs of the Italian mission.

For two years Dr. Taylor was associated with the Rev. F. Wilson, D.D., in editing *The Christian Review*, and during that time contributed to its pages some valuable articles. Since January, 1876, he has, in connection with the evangelist, Sig. Cocorda, conducted *Il Seminatore*, a monthly Baptist magazine in the Italian language, contributing frequent leading articles. He has also added several volumes to our popular literature, having written the "Oakland Stories" (four juvenile volumes), published by Sheldon & Co., New York; "Coster Grew" and "Roger Bernard" (religious stories for youth), "Walter Ennis" (a tale founded on early Virginia Baptist history), and "Life and Times of James B. Taylor," besides several smaller volumes, published by the American Baptist Publication Society. He was one of the recording secretaries of the Southern Baptist Convention from 1856 to 1866. In 1872 he received the degree of D.D., from Richmond College, and also from the University of Chicago. Dr. Taylor was married in 1858 to Susan Spotswood Braxton, great-granddaughter of Carter Braxton, one of the Virginia signers of the Declaration of Independence.

The mission at Rome is one that lies near to the hearts of all Baptists, and especially Southern Baptists. Six years ago serious troubles had embarrassed the work in that city. It was necessary to find a man who should be both gentle and wise, to whom the whole management of the mission must be intrusted if any permanent good was to result from it. Dr. Taylor was thought to be such a man, and accordingly he was urged to accept the position. This he did, and sailed with his family from New York in July, 1873, for Rome, where he soon won the confidence of the evangelists and churches. From the very day of his arrival he made himself felt as a prudent and persevering laborer for the Master. The vexatious troubles vanished, and the mission began at once to thrive, and has been steadily advancing ever since, so much so that the Italian mission is now the most flourishing of all the foreign work of the Southern Baptist Convention. A convenient chapel has been secured at the cost of about $25,000, situated in one of the most eligible positions in the city, being a few steps only from the Pantheon and from the University of Rome. The mission comprises 10 stations, 9 evangelists, and nearly 150 members; and churches have been either established or strengthened at La Tour, Milan, Modena, Naples, Bari, Barletta, Venice, and in the island of Sardinia. In reference to Dr. Taylor, Dr. Prime, editor of the *New York Observer*, wrote: "He is a man of decided character; with a clear and vigorous intellect, a tender and glowing heart, and such a sound judgment as secures for him the respect and confidence of all who represent Protestant missions in Rome. . . . These missions form an important part of the great work now in progress for the spread of evangelical religion in this land of papal darkness. To the eye of unbelief it may seem the day of very small things. But it is enough to plant the seed, and the rains of heaven will descend upon it to the redemption of Italy. Now is the time to sow the seed of the Word. Dr. Taylor is able to extend his missions and multiply the number of laborers just as fast as he has the means to support them. And you may be certain that he is judicious, careful, and wide-awake."

Taylor, Rev. Isaac, son and successor in the pastoral office of Rev. William Taylor, a popular and useful minister of his State, was born in Buffalo, Va., in 1772. He was taken by his parents to Kentucky when he was twelve years old. In his early life he was thoughtless and fond of pleasure. He was baptized by his father, and united with Cox's Creek church in 1801; was licensed to preach in 1810, and ordained in 1813. He became pastor of Cox's Creek and three neighboring churches, and baptized a great number of persons, and was honored by all classes of society. He died suddenly on his way home from preaching, March 13, 1842.

Taylor, James Barnett, D.D., was born in the village of Barton-upon-Humber, England, March 19, 1804. His father having removed to this country in 1805, settled in the city of New York, and in 1817 removed to Virginia. At the age of thirteen young Taylor was baptized, and united with the First Baptist church of New York. At the age of sixteen he began to speak publicly for Christ, and in 1824 he was licensed to preach. Soon after he was appointed by the General Baptist Association of Virginia to labor as a missionary in the lower section of the Meherran district. He was ordained, May 2, 1826, at Sandy Creek. In 1826 he became pastor of the Second Baptist church of Richmond, Va., in which relation he continued sixteen years, during which the church was greatly enlarged and strengthened. While here his labors were indefatigable in developing the graces of the church, in organizing Sunday-schools and Bible societies, and in promoting the cause of education. Six hundred and sixty members were added to the church, three new churches were organized by members mainly from his congregation, and ten or twelve of those whom he baptized entered the ministry. He was a very efficient worker, also, in behalf of foreign missions. Dr. Taylor preached frequently in the surrounding country and in the adjacent cities. As the result of his labors in Baltimore, in connection with the Rev. John Kerr, the Calvert Street Baptist church was formed. In 1838 he traveled West as agent of the Virginia Baptist General Association. In 1839 he was elected chaplain of the University of Virginia, where his labors among the students and in the community resulted in great good. In 1840 he became pastor of the Third Baptist church (Grace church), Richmond, and through his labors their beautiful church edifice was built. In 1844 he traveled South with the missionary Kincaid, stimulating the churches to greater zeal in the cause of missions, and collecting large sums of money for the Northern board. Soon after the organization of the Southern Baptist Convention Dr. Taylor became its corresponding secretary, which responsible position he held until his death, a period of twenty-six years. His labors while secretary were exceedingly onerous. He traveled constantly; preached three times on almost every Sunday; addressed letters of encouragement to missionaries, and of exhortation to churches and individuals; edited several journals, and accomplished an amount of good of which his immediate associates alone were cognizant. For thirteen years during his secretaryship Dr. Taylor was pastor of the Taylorsville church, but at the opening of the war he resigned his pastorate, and labored during the contest in camps and hospitals as colporteur of the Virginia Sunday-School and Publication Board; and for three years as Confederate post-chaplain. At the close of the war the missions of the Southern Baptist Convention were in a disorganized condition, with a debt of $10,000 hanging over them. The secretary immediately undertook the task of liquidating the debt, which he succeeded in doing, at the same time stimulating the churches to new vigor and efforts in behalf of the imperiled missions. He was also greatly interested in the welfare of the freedmen so suddenly removed from all their old relations; and he was appointed to confer with the secretary of the Freedmen's Bureau with regard to the best plans for assisting them. His last sermons were preached in Alexandria to colored congregations, and his interest in the mission in Africa was manifested on his death-bed. This faithful servant of God, having diligently served his generation, fell asleep Dec. 22, 1871. As a preacher, Dr. Taylor was impressive and instructive, simple in style, and solemn in manner. As a pastor, he had but few equals, moving among his people, as well as in the community generally, as a constant messenger for good. As a writer, he has done much for the literature and history of the denomination. He was for a short time editor of the *Religious Herald;* he originated the *Southern Baptist Missionary Journal* and *Home and Foreign Journal.* He wrote a "Life of Lot Cary," a "Life of Luther Rice," and two volumes of the "Lives of Virginia Baptist Ministers," containing more than a thousand pages, a most valuable work, the materials of which were collected only after vast toil and innumerable hindrances. He also began a "History of Virginia Baptists," for which he was specially fitted, but which he did not live to complete. In addition to all these literary, pastoral, and official labors as secretary of the board, he wrote, as editor of the *Foreign Mission Journal,* articles that would fill many volumes. Dr. Poindexter, who was associated with him for some time in the secretaryship of the board, says of him, as illustrating the pressure of his labors, "He was at the same time corresponding secretary, financial manager, general traveling agent, and editor of the board." In the various walks of life, Dr. Taylor quietly and perseveringly accomplished the high and holy purposes which filled his soul. Remembering the fact that he was not physically strong, few have left a more abiding impress on the churches and the great denominational agencies which they employ than the subject of this sketch.

Taylor, Rev. James B., Jr., the second son of Dr. J. B. Taylor, was born in Richmond, Va., Oct. 22, 1837; was baptized by the Rev. Dr. Jeter, Dec. 19, 1852; and was a student at Richmond College, the University of Virginia, and the Southern Baptist Theological Seminary. While pursuing his theological course the war commenced. He joined the army, and was appointed a chaplain in Gen. W. H. F. Lee's command, in which position he was very useful. At the close of the war he was called to the pastorate of the Baptist church in Culpeper, which position he held for ten years, and where a large harvest was reaped for the Master. At the beginning of his labors there the church numbered only 28; at its close 320 had been added to its membership, besides which 500 conversions had taken place in protracted meetings in which he had assisted. The ravages of the war had left the church edifice in Culpeper almost in ruins; but in a little while, through the exertions of Mr. Taylor, it was so repaired as to become one of the most commodious and beautiful buildings in that part of the State. In October, 1875, he accepted an invitation to become pastor of the church in Wilmington, N. C., which position he still holds. He has published an exceedingly popular little pamphlet entitled "Simple Truths," a catechism for infant classes, which has passed to a third edition, and which has been, or is to be, translated into the Yoruban tongue and the Italian language, requests to that effect having been made by the missionaries at those stations. Mr. Taylor has also delivered some very popular addresses at literary commencements.

Taylor, Prof. Jas. M., A.M., was born in Holmdel, N. J., Sept. 19, 1843; graduated at Madison University in 1867, and Hamilton Theological Seminary in 1869; was principal for several years of the grammar-school, now Colgate Academy; at the present time he is Professor of Pure Mathematics in Madison University; a man of great ability and Christian integrity.

Taylor, Rev. John, a distinguished pioneer preacher and writer, was born in Fauquier Co., Va., in 1752. He united with the Baptists in his twentieth year. He began to preach almost immediately after he joined the church, and continued with great success. He located in Kentucky in 1779. The first religious revival in that State commenced under his preaching in Woodford County in 1785. In that year he raised up Clear Creek church, to which he ministered about ten years. In 1795 he removed to Boone County, where he and several others had constituted a small church called Bullittsburg the year before. Here he ministered about seven years, during which time 113 persons were baptized into that church. In 1802 he settled in Trimble County, where, two years before, he had gathered Corn Creek church, to which he ministered about fifteen years. In 1815 he removed to Franklin County, where he aided in constituting a church in Frankfort in 1816, to which he also ministered. In 1818 he formed Buck Run church, and was the pastor for a number of years. He traveled and preached very extensively, and probably performed more labor, and was more successful, than any other pioneer preacher in Kentucky. He was a strong and pointed writer. He published "The History of Ten Churches," "Thoughts on Missions," and several brief biographies, which are of great value to the Baptist historian of Kentucky. He also wrote much that was valuable for the periodical press. He died at his residence near Frankfort in the winter of 1836.

Taylor, Col. Joseph, was born in Oxford township, Philadelphia Co., Pa., March 15, 1791. He was baptized in his fifteenth year into the fellowship of the Second Baptist church, Philadelphia, of which he remained an honored member until his death, in 1869. In early life he was colonel of the 79th Regiment Pa. Militia. He was a member of the General Assembly of Pennsylvania in 1829–30, and of the senate from 1830–34. During his residence in New Jersey he served in the Assembly of that State, and he was its Speaker in the session of 1843–44. He was a member of the common council of Philadelphia, and subsequently of the select council. He was treasurer of the Philadelphia Baptist Association, and president of the Philadelphia Bible Union, and the first layman that ever presided over the Philadelphia Baptist Association, though in 1849, when he was moderator, the Association was in its one hundred and forty-second year.

Col. Taylor was a gentleman of culture and courtesy, an honor to the church with which he was so long connected, and to the denomination whose principles were so dear to him, and which he was so competent to defend and so gratified to commend. In public life his honor was never questioned; as a Christian he was without reproach.

Taylor, Stephen W., LL.D., was born in Adams, Berkshire Co., Mass., Oct. 28, 1791; baptized, in 1810, at Edmeston, Otsego Co., N. Y.; graduated at Hamilton College in 1817, being the valedictorian of his class; entered, in 1818, on his life profession of educator, as principal of Lowville Academy, and under his administration no academy in New York stood higher. In 1834 accepted the principalship of the academic department of Hamilton Literary and Theological Institution. The department being greatly demoralized, Dr. Taylor distinguished himself by effecting a most admirable discipline and by organizing a high grade of instruction. In 1838 he accepted the chair of Mathematics and Natural Philosophy in Madison University, which he resigned in 1845 and went to Lewisburg, Pa., where he founded the university at Lewisburg, and was its president five years. (See LEWISBURG UNIVERSITY.) In 1851 was called to the presidency of Madison University. (See MADISON UNIVERSITY.) His accession was a most happy event in the history of the university, occurring when it did, at the close of the removal controversy. Trusted in the greatest degree by the denomination, the effect was to restore confidence in the fortunes of the university. During the first year of his presidency the number of students increased from 33 to 84, and during the three following years the number reached 216, a number larger than that of the students in attendance at the beginning of the controversy. At the end of the first year the college received an endowment of $60,000. On Jan. 6, 1856, Dr. Taylor died of a long-continued and painful illness. Dr. Taylor was pre-eminently a man of will. By nature and culture a poet, he "suppressed" this rare gift, and made himself one of the best mathematicians of his day. He would have been acknowledged as a master in any department, and his choice of the vocation of teacher was the result of his conscientiousness. For this high calling he trained himself with the greatest care, and gave to it day by day the ripest efforts of his life. He left two sons and a daughter, who inherited much of their father's genius. One of the sons, B. F. Taylor, is widely known by his poems and his other writings.

Taylor, Thomas A., Esq., was born in Jenkintown, Pa., in 1814. His father, who died in 1822, was a man of intelligence, and the year of his death he had every prospect of being elected to the Congress of the United States. The education of Thomas A. Taylor was liberal. In mercantile pursuits in Philadelphia, to which his life was largely devoted, he secured an ample competency, and, finding himself in comfortable circumstances, he retired from business in 1856.

He was forty-six years a member of the Second Baptist church of Philadelphia. For a long period he was the treasurer of the Philadelphia Baptist Association. He was a Christian of large affections, whose gifts bountifully blessed almost every good cause. Never had Bible truth a warmer friend, or the church a more faithful member.

Taylor, Rev. William, a distinguished pioneer preacher, was born in New Jersey in 1737. In his childhood his parents removed to Virginia, where he remained until he was twenty-one, and then returned to his native State. Here he united with the Baptists, and commenced preaching. After a short time spent in New Jersey, he removed to Buffalo (now Bethany), Va., and thence to the southeastern part of Ohio, where he remained eight years. In 1784 he located in Nelson Co., Ky., where he founded Cox's Creek church. In the fall of 1785 he, with others, constituted Salem Association. In addition to his pastorate he was very active in preaching among the new settlements, and was instrumental in raising up churches in Nelson and the adjoining counties. He died, greatly lamented, in September, 1809.

Taylor, Rev. William, a native of New Hampshire, was among the earlier ministers in Michigan. His home was at Schoolcraft, where he devoted his life to the care of the churches and to Christian educational interests. With long persistent labor, and a liberal use of his means, he established an academy called the Cedar Park Female Seminary, the operation of which was very useful for a number of years, and the property avails of which are still serving the education of young women in Kalamazoo College. He also gave liberally to the Baptist Convention for its theological and other work. He peacefully met the end of the righteous June 7, 1852, and is remembered by many with grateful love.

Teague, E. B., D.D., was born in South Carolina in 1820; came with his parents to Alabama, and located in Shelby County when a child; graduated in the University of Alabama in 1840, under Dr. Manly. In his early ministry he was pastor of some strong and wealthy churches in the western part of the State, and professor in the Southern Female College, after which he was called to La Grange, Ga., where he was pastor for ten years, embracing the period of the late war. He next became president of the East Alabama Female College at Tuskegee, and pastor of the church in that place for one year, after which he was pastor of the church in the city of Selma for six or eight years. His principal pastorates were Lagrange and Selma, two of our strongest Southern churches, and his connection with them was a success. For about four years past he has been residing on his beautiful farm—"Red Lawn"—in Shelby County, and preaching for the churches in Columbiana, Montevallo, Fayetteville, and Wilsonville. Superior in scholarship, profound in theological research, eloquent in the presentation of thought, he stands second to no man in the State as an instructive preacher. Gifted beyond measure in conversation, thoroughly read in classic and historical literature, and possessed of a devout Christian spirit, combined with a rich flow of agreeable anecdotes, he is one of the most companionable men. One seldom parts with him without feeling that he has enjoyed a rare social and religious treat. The degree of Doctor of Divinity was conferred on him by Howard College.

Teale, Rev. Josiah Harris, was born Jan. 16, 1846, in Coshocton Co., O.; spent his early years on a farm; was converted, in 1866, while at Wesleyan University, Delaware, O.; baptized and joined the Rock Run church in 1867; dedicated his life to the ministry; graduated at Denison University in 1874; was licensed in 1873 by the Pleasant Hill church, O.; went to California in 1875; was ordained at Santa Cruz in 1876; preached as pastor at Napa, Santa Cruz, and Saint Helena; was pastor at Victoria, British Columbia, from September, 1877, to January, 1879, when he accepted a call to the First Baptist church of Oregon City, Oregon, where he is now laboring with success, and is numbered among the influential preachers of Oregon.

Teasdale, Rev. John, was born in New Jersey, Nov. 12, 1806. He was converted at twenty, and baptized by Rev. Leonard Fletcher. He was soon licensed to preach, and entered Madison University, N. Y. After four years of study he left on account of feeble health. He became pastor of the Baptist church at Newton, N. J. Mr. Teasdale removed to Virginia in 1836, and for four years was pastor at Fredericksburg. In 1842 he returned to New Jersey, and took charge of the Schooley's Mountain church. In 1850 he removed to Alton, Ill., and was an efficient agent of the Alton College. A new building was erected, and funds raised for the endowment. He was called to the pastorate of the Third Baptist church of St. Louis. In a year a good chapel was built and additions to the church were made. While in the midst of this good work his days were ended by the terrible catastrophe at the Gasconade bridge, on the Pacific Railroad, where many prominent citizens of St. Louis lost their lives.

Teasdale, Jos. H., was born in New Jersey in 1817; removed to Virginia when twenty years of age; made a profession of religion at eighteen, and removed to St. Louis in 1847. Mr. Teasdale was one of the constituent members of the Third Baptist church of St. Louis, and for many years has been a deacon, and a generous supporter of the church. His brother, Rev. John Teasdale, was its pastor, and Thomas C. Teasdale, D.D., and Deacon Martin Teasdale, a member of the Second Baptist church, are his brothers. His Christian character and influence are acknowledged in St. Louis and in Missouri.

Teasdale, Thomas Cox, D.D., was born in the township of Wantage, Sussex Co., N. J., Dec. 2, 1808. He is the second son of the late Hon. Thomas Teasdale. His grandfather, Rev. Thos. Teasdale, was an earnest Baptist minister, who emigrated from England to this country when his oldest son, Thomas, the father of Dr. Teasdale, was fourteen years old. Not long after his arrival Elder Teasdale settled in the northern part of Sussex Co., N. J., and took charge of a church which is known as the Hamburg church. In the autumn of 1826 it pleased God to impress young Teasdale most deeply with a sense of his need of salvation. He felt it to be his duty to identify himself with the people of God, and accordingly related the exercises of his mind to the church, and on a bleak November Sabbath in 1826 was baptized by Elder Leonard Fletcher.

For a time after his baptism his mind was greatly exercised in regard to the work of the ministry. He finally decided to obey the call, and in the spring of 1828 he was licensed to preach by his church. May of the same year he entered the theological seminary at Hamilton, N. Y. In the autumn of 1830 he accepted a call to the pastorate of a church in East Bennington, Vt., and was ordained on the 16th day of December, 1830.

In the spring of 1832 he removed to the city of Philadelphia, Pa. He spent four years in Philadelphia and vicinity, devoting most of his time to evangelical labors, which were eminently successful. In the spring of 1836 he was invited to take charge of the high school in Newton, N. J. The First and Second Baptist churches of Newton—one located in the village of Lafayette and the other in the town of Newton—also requested his services as their pastor. He removed to this field, and remained in it four years, and his efforts in awakening a deeper interest in education and religion were highly gratifying.

Mr. Teasdale served as pastor, after this, the First Baptist church of New Haven, Conn. He was next pastor of the Grant Street church, Pittsburgh, Pa., after this, of the First Baptist church of Springfield, Ill., then, of the E Street church, Washington, D. C. It was during his pastorate in Washington, in 1852, that he received the honorary degree of Doctor of Divinity from Union College, Schenectady, N. Y.

In 1858, Dr. Teasdale removed to Columbus, Miss., and took charge of the church at that place. He had held a protracted meeting there six months previous to this removal, which resulted in the conversion of some four hundred persons.

In 1863 he resigned the care of the church in Columbus, and preached to the Confederate soldiers until the close of the war. Dr. Teasdale was for a time corresponding secretary of the Sunday-School Board of the Southern Baptist Convention, which flourished during his term of service.

In 1873, Dr. Teasdale was elected to the chair of Rhetoric and Elocution in the University of Tennessee, at Knoxville, where he now resides. His life has been one of great activity and usefulness.

He has baptized over 3000 persons; witnessed the profession of some 15,000 persons under his ministry; published several pamphlets and books, the principal of the latter of which is a volume of his "Revival Discourses;" contributed materially in building up institutions of learning; assisted in establishing the "Orphans' Home,' in Mississippi. His work on "Baptism and Communion" is of rare merit, and so are his "Revival Discourses."

Teloogoo Theological Seminary, Ramapatam.—This institution is known as Brownson Theological Seminary. While Mr. Clough was in America, in March, 1872, and in January, 1874, he secured an endowment of $50,000 for this school. At the close of 1879 there were five natives and Mr. Williams, a missionary, in the faculty of the seminary, and 152 students were under their care. The course of instruction embraces the purely theological training of similar seminaries in this country, with church history. Sermonizing is not neglected.

The teachers and students take charge of the region for ten miles around the school, conducting worship and Sunday-schools regularly in thirty-five towns and villages. In this way instruction and practice are constantly united in the experience of these candidates for the holiest of offices.

Teloogoos.—The country of the Teloogoos is on the western coast of the Bay of Bengal. It stretches north and south some 600 or 700 miles, and extends inland from the coast from 300 to 400 miles. The latest estimate makes the population of this country not far from 18,000,000. While the territory thus referred to contains the larger portion of Teloogoos, they are found in no small numbers in all the towns and cities of Southern India. The religion of the Teloogoos is Brahmanism, with its accompanying caste system.

The attention of American Baptists was called to this interesting people in 1835 by Rev. Amos Sutton, who urged upon them the desirableness of establishing a mission among them. Influenced by his suggestion, the board sent out in September of that year, in company with missionaries who were to occupy other stations, Rev. S. S. Day and his wife, who, for a time, resided at Vizagapatam, one of the chief cities of the Teloogoo country. Subsequently he removed to a suburban village of Madras, called Wonarapetta. Four years were passed in this locality with but little visible fruit. Mr. Day decided that the interests of the mission would be better promoted by removal to a different locality. Accordingly he selected Nellore as a suitable place for the establishment of a mission station, and removed with his family to that place. At the time of writing this sketch there are seven stations among the Teloogoos, to wit: Nellore, Ongole, Ramapatam, Secunderabad, Kurnool, Madras, and Hanamaconda.

1. The mission at Nellore, as has already been said, was commenced by Mr. and Mrs. Day. Shortly after their arrival at Nellore they were joined by Rev. Stephen Van Husen and wife. The first Teloogoo convert was baptized by Mr. Day in September, 1840. For several years there was but little apparent success in the conversion of the Teloogoos at Nellore. It was emphatically a time for seed-sowing, and faith and patience were tried to their utmost in waiting for results. There was no other baptism until 1843, when a solitary individual submitted to the rite. Mr. Van Husen was obliged to leave the field of his labor in 1845 and go home to America, never to return. Mr. Day followed in 1846. The question of abandoning the Teloogoo Mission was seriously discussed. The Nellore station remained in the hands of native assistants until the return of Mr. Day, who, in company with Mr. and Mrs. Jewett, sailed from the United States Oct. 10, 1848, and, arriving in due time at the place of their destination, began their work with new zeal and courage. But, for five years, the fortunes of the mission were anything but encouraging, and again the question of abandonment was discussed, and decided in the negative. In 1853, Mr. Day having returned to this country, Mr. and Mrs. Jewett were left alone to carry on the mission. Rev. F. A. Douglass and wife joined them in 1855. Amid trials and encouragements the work has been carried on for more than a score of years since this date, and now the Nellore station reports 3 missionaries, 6 native preachers, 3 churches, and 366 members.

2. At the Ongole station work was commenced by Mr. and Mrs. Jewett and one of the native Christians named Jacob, in 1853. Ongole is seventy-seven miles north of Nellore, and is a town made up almost wholly of Teloogoos. Amidst the most discouraging circumstances the mission was carried on for years, and in 1862, Mr. Jewett, broken down in health, was obliged to retire from the field and go home to the United States. Again the question of giving up the Teloogoo Mission was seriously discussed. But Mr. Jewett pleaded earnestly for its continuance and reinforcement, and his pleas were not in vain. Mr. Clough returned with Dr. Jewett to the Teloogoo country, and the station at Ongole came under his special supervision in 1866, and on the 1st of January, 1867, a little church of eight persons was organized. Years of earnest work passed. The seed sown has sprung up into a most bountiful harvest, and tidings of the most thrilling character come to us of the wonderful outpouring of the Spirit of God upon the people, and the hopeful conversion and baptism of thousands of the Teloogoos of Ongole. The report of the executive board, presented in May, 1880, gives the following statistics concerning that station: 5 missionaries, 22 native preachers, 1 church, with 13,106 members.

3. Ramapatam, the third station among the Teloogoos, established in 1869, is also in a prosperous condition. There are here 2 missionaries, 10 native preachers, 3 churches, with 1853 members.

4. The fourth station, Secunderabad, established in 1875, reported in May 2 missionaries, 3 native preachers, 1 church, with 56 members.

5. The Kurnool station, established in 1876, has 3 missionaries, 3 native preachers, 2 churches, with 270 members.

Madras has 4 missionaries, 2 native preachers, and 1 church, with a membership of 9.

Hanamaconda has 2 missionaries.

The Teloogoo Mission has been wonderfully blessed of God, and attracts to itself, in a remarkable degree, the attention of the whole Christian world. On it rests in a large measure the benediction of heaven.

Temperance.—" Wine is a mocker, strong drink is raging, and whosoever is deceived thereby is not wise." This divine testimony is abundantly illustrated in daily life. No habit is so deceptive as that of using alcoholic beverages. Slowly but certainly it rivets its fetters upon its victim, who too frequently only realizes its power when the attempt is made to break it.

With many the struggle is unsuccessful. He only is the victor who trusts not in his own strength but daily seeks divine help.

Careful investigation has proved that the use of alcoholic stimulants is not needful to the enjoyment of the highest health; that it does not secure greater strength for either bodily or mental effort, and that it tends to shorten life. Surely he acts wisely who follows the divine command, "Look not thou upon the wine when it is red, when it giveth his color in the cup, when it moveth itself aright; at the last it biteth like a serpent and stingeth like an adder."

Intemperance brings disgrace, privation, and poverty upon the drunkard and his family, and injures society by the increased burdens imposed by the crime and pauperism resulting from it.

Intemperance deadens the conscience, hardens the heart, and leads men to dishonor God. It is Satan's most successful weapon against the church and the truth, and for the destruction of immortal souls.

Among the obstacles to the temperance reform needing thoughtful consideration by Christians are, *First*. The manufacture of domestic wines, not for sale, but for home use. These are claimed to be unintoxicating, and consequently harmless.

Analysis, however, has shown that they contain from four to twelve per cent., or more, of alcohol, and therefore tend to create the appetite for stronger drink.

Second. The medical use, without the *special* advice of a conscientious physician, of alcoholic liquors.

Ezra M. Hunt, M.D., in a very able paper read before the International Medical Congress, held in connection with the Centennial Exhibition, at Philadelphia, says, "We cannot conceal from ourselves as physicians that thousands with sincerity indulge in the use of alcoholic stimuli because they entertain the idea that health requires it. Some physician had advised a little wine or brandy or ale for a special ailment, and the patient continues the prescription, or renews it repeatedly, because 'his constitution requires it.' We have been saddened to find those pledged to total abstinence thus using the beverage, and really deceiving themselves. So exceptional is the need of alcoholic liquors in any chronic ailment, that no one who claims to be using them as medicines should forget to consult his physician *very frequently* about the necessity for their continuance. If such were the rule, and if physicians were truly conscientious, thousands who now use them medicinally would cease to touch them."

The position of the Baptist denomination on the temperance reform is indicated by the repeated action of leading Associations declaring, in emphatic terms, their approval of total abstinence. No Baptist church in the Northern States would receive or retain in its membership any one engaged in the manufacture or sale of these beverages, neither would it accept as a member the house-owner who rented his property for such purposes.

Let Christians live in the practice of total abstinence from all intoxicating liquors, discountenancing their use on wedding and other private or public occasions, and may God hasten the abolition of their manufacture and use throughout the whole earth!

Ten Brook, Rev. Andrew, was born in Elmira, N. Y., Sept. 21, 1814. He received his education—preparatory, collegiate, and theological—at Hamilton, finishing the course in 1841. In October of that year he was ordained pastor of the First church in Detroit, and remained in this position three years. The University of Michigan was then beginning its work of instruction, and Mr. Ten Brook was placed in the chair of Moral Philosophy. He held this professorship till 1851. For two years he was associated with the late Alexander M. Beebee in the conduct of the *New York Baptist Register*, and had the chief editorial responsibility. In 1856 he was appointed U. S. consul at Munich, Bavaria, and held the office till 1862. Returning to the United States, he became librarian of the University of Michigan, and remained in that position till 1877. In 1875 he published an octavo volume entitled "American State Universities and the University of Michigan." While pastor in Detroit he was also editor of the *Michigan Christian Herald*.

Tennessee, The Baptist of.—This paper, first called *The Baptist*, came into existence at Nashville, Tenn., at some time between the years 1830 and 1835. Rev. R. B. C. Howell, D.D., was its first editor. For some years its circulation was quite limited, and when it came under the editorial supervision of Rev. J. R. Graves, in 1844, its list of subscribers numbered only 1005. For a time the increase was slow but steady. The name was changed to *The Tennessee Baptist*, and in the course of a few years it became the pronounced advocate of what has since been termed "Old-Landmarkism." Its circulation rapidly increased, and its editor became very influential. On May 15, 1858, its editors were announced as follows: J. R. Graves, J. M. Pendleton, and A. C. Dayton. The two brethren last named had been for some years special contributors. The increase in the number of subscribers was constant and rapid, so that at the beginning of the war its circulation was said to have been larger than that of any Baptist paper in the world. The publication of the paper was suspended during the war, but was renewed after the return of peace. The place of publication was changed from Nashville to Memphis. The name of the State was dropped from the title, and it has appeared since as *The Baptist*, a quarto of sixteen pages. Dr. Graves has been since the war its sole editor, and he wields now (1881) as able a pen as at any period of his eventful life, and his paper is a power in a large section of our country.

Tennessee Baptists.—Tennessee is naturally divided into three sections by the Cumberland Mountains and the Tennessee River, both of which cross the State north and south, known as East, Middle, and West Tennessee, and in this order they were originally settled. The people in these divisions have always been as distinct in their pursuits and interests, and in their social and religious intercourse, as if they lived in different and distant States. In sketching the history of the Baptists it will therefore in some measure be necessary to follow this order, though sometimes their proceedings will appear blended.

EAST TENNESSEE.

Some of the northeastern counties of this section began to be occupied previous to 1770, and among the settlers there were some Baptists, emigrants from North Carolina and Virginia. The country at this time was a wilderness infested with wild beasts, and the settlers were subject to murderous incursions from hostile Indians. Though the Baptists do not seem to have been numerous, they were among the first, if not the first, to proclaim the gospel in Tennessee territory. In 1781 they had six organized churches holding associated relations with an Association in North Carolina. These, with one or two others, were formed into the Holston Association in 1786. Among the pioneer ministers at this time in the country, and through whose labors the Baptist denomination was established, may be mentioned James Keel, Thomas Murrell, Matt. Talbot, Isaac Barton, Wm. Murphy, and John Chastine from Virginia, and Tidence Lane, Jonathan Mulky, and Wm. Reno from North Carolina. These ministers brought with them many of their brethren, and in one or more instances regular organized churches. They generally settled on farms and made their support by tilling the soil or teaching school, and preached on Sundays or at night in private houses and in school-houses, or in rude buildings improvised for worship, and sometimes under the shade of trees. They were pious, thoroughly read in the Scriptures, and gave evidence that "they had been with Jesus." They lived among the people who heard their messages gladly, and the pleasure of the Lord prospered in their hands. According to Asplund's "Register" for 1790, the Holston Association had a membership of 889 members, and by the beginning of the next decade they had increased to 37 churches and 2500 members, keeping pace with the increasing population of the country. In 1802 the Tennessee Association was formed in a central territory immediately surrounding Knoxville, the capital of the new State. Some of the ministers connected with this organization were Duke Kimbrough, Elijah Rogers, Joshua Frost, Amos Hardin, Daniel Layman, William Bellew. In 1817 it sent out a colony of twelve churches and as many ministers to form the Powell's Valley Association. And again, in 1822, another colony east of the Tennessee River was organized into the Hiwassee Association, consisting of ten churches, which increased its membership and enlarged its territory until 1830, when it divided and formed the Sweet-Water Association, with 17 churches and 1100 members.

The year 1833 may be regarded as the beginning of a new era in the history and progress of the Baptists of East Tennessee, and the whole State as well. Up to this time they had made commendable progress, having maintained internal harmony, and kept well up with the growth of the population; but the labor of evangelizing had been voluntarily performed by the ministry at their own convenience and expense. An extensive and general revival of religion, which began about this time and continued for two or three years, suggested the importance of a united and organized plan for supplying the destitute with the gospel, and extending the influence of their denominational principles. The initiative of an organization was taken in Middle Tennessee by Elders Garner McConnico, James Whitsitt, and Peter S. Gayle, who called a meeting at Mill Creek, near Nashville, in October, 1833, and organized a Baptist State Convention. Conforming to the peculiar formation of the State, the Convention appointed three boards to conduct its affairs, one in each division of the State. This plan continued for only a year or two, when it was found impracticable to unite the churches on a General Convention, when the East Tennessee brethren withdrew and organized the General Association of East Tennessee. The leading ministers engaged in this enterprise were Samuel Love, James Kennon, Elijah Rogers, Charles and Richard H. Taliaferro, Robert Sneed, and William Bellew. This movement, while it caused the secession of a few thousands of anti-mission Baptists, imparted new life to the great body of the churches, and inspired the ministry with a fresh zeal, which gave increased momentum to denominational progress. In 1847 the Baptists in East Tennessee had increased to 13,390, and 6573 anti-mission, or those who stood aloof from the General Association, making a Baptist population of 19,963. In 1858 they had increased to 19,103 regulars, and, supposing the anti-missionaries to have maintained their strength of 6573, to an aggregate of 25,676. In 1880 their reports give about 45,000 regular white Baptists, 2000 colored, and 5000 anti-mission, or a fraction over 52,000 in East Tennessee. At present the Baptists are numerically much the largest denomination in this section of the State. Although the General Association has contributed much moral, and some pecuniary, support in producing these results, they are due largely to the zeal and voluntary labor of ministers, and to missions supported by Associations.

In 1850 a college was chartered under the patronage of the General Association, known at present as Carson College, located in a beautiful and fertile valley in Jefferson County, near the town of Mossy Creek, on the East Tennessee and Virginia Railroad. It received its name from Hon. James H. Carson, who bequeathed to it $15,000, the interest of which was to be used in the education of young ministers. Mr. Carson was one of the founders of the institution. The college has no endowment, but has maintained its existence for thirty years from the tuition fees, with a regular faculty of four professors. It has trained in whole or in part nearly one hundred young men for the ministry, and has done much in the general cause of education. The Rev. N. B. Goforth, D.D., is its popular president. There is a Female College at Bristol, Rev. D. C. Wester president, which is doing a good work in the education of young ladies. There is also a private institution at Tazewell under the direction of Rev. Mr. Manard, that is accomplishing much in the cause of education among the Baptists. A religious paper, *The Baptist Beacon*, is published at Knoxville, and supported chiefly by the Baptists of this section.

MIDDLE AND WEST TENNESSEE.

The middle division of the State began to be settled in 1780, and, as in the eastern division, among its pioneers there were Baptists and Baptist ministers. The first church known to have been formed was in 1786, on Red River, by Rev. Joseph Grammer, and in 1791 another was founded on the Sulphur Fork of the same river by Rev. Ambrose Dudley and John Taylor, who visited this region as missionaries from Kentucky. The first Association was organized in 1796; but, owing to internal difficulties which sprung up, it was in a few years dissolved, and in 1803 the Cumberland Association was instituted partly of some of its churches. This latter community had for many years considerable prosperity, and had also some of the best churches and ablest ministers in the country; but it is now only a small, declining, anti-mission body, a very different organization from the Cumberland Association, with which are connected three of the Nashville churches and the church in Clarksville, of which Rev. A. D. Sears, D.D., is moderator. In 1810 the Concord Association was formed, its territory embracing Nashville as its centre. In 1812 there was a very general revival within its wide territory, and it had an increase of over 800 by baptism that year. Its prosperity continued until its territory was divided and the Salem formed, in 1822, with twenty-seven churches. Among the ministers who had borne the heat and burden of the day up to this time may be mentioned Joseph Dorris, Daniel Brown, James Whitsitt, Garner McConnico, John Wiseman, Joshua Lester, John Bond, and Jesse Cox.

About the year 1824 the denomination, which had been harmonious and prosperous, began to meet with reverses from internal discord. The doctrine of election and the extent of the atonement became topics of bitter discussion, and resulted in a division of churches and Associations, and two non-affiliating bodies of Baptists; the seceding party were called Separate Baptists, who built up several flourishing Associations. Immediately following this division came Alexander Campbell and his so-called reformation. The church in Nashville, which had grown to be a large and flourishing community, with between three and four hundred members, had for its pastor Rev. Philip Fall, a talented and popular young pastor, who came under the influence of Mr. Campbell, embraced his sentiments, and carried with him the whole church except twelve or fifteen members, who adhered to the Baptist faith. Mr. Campbell's influence was felt more or less throughout the denomination in this State, resulting in the loss of other ministers and members, and from bitter controversies gathering much of its force. This was followed in 1833 by the secession of the anti-mission party and renewed strife. But there was compensation for these last divisions in the new zeal inspired by the organization of the Baptist State Convention, and a reconciliation and reunion with the Separate party, who were quite as numerous and more intelligent and progressive than the anti-mission people. The few brethren who, in the wreck of the church in Nashville, adhered to the Baptist faith reorganized, and had Elder P. S. Gayle for their pastor, and began again to build up. Mr. Gayle resigning in 1833, Rev. R. B. C. Howell, of Virginia, was called to the pastorate, who with enthusiasm and zeal entered into his work, and with such success that within a few years the Baptists had almost regained their lost ground; and from those faithful few, as the germ, the four flourishing churches in the city have grown up. Dr. Howell also entered enthusiastically into the general interests of the denomination at large, and commenced the publication of *The Baptist*, which he edited for many years, by which he did much in diffusing information, promoting harmony, and furthering the benevolent work of the Convention. The paper thus started still exists, and has had a wide circulation for thirty years, with Rev. J. R. Graves as its editor and proprietor. But it has been removed from Nashville to Memphis, on the western border of the State, and *The Baptist Reflector* has taken its place at Nashville, with Revs. J. B. Chevis and R. B. Womack as editors and proprietors.

East and West Tennessee having withdrawn from the Convention and formed independent organizations, the Middle Tennessee brethren discontinued the name, and substituted for it General Association of Middle Tennessee, and afterwards North Alabama was added. In addition to its evangelical work, the General Association, with the co-operation of the other divisions of the State, established at Murfreesborough Union University, an institution of a high order, and, until wrecked by the exigencies of the civil war, one of the most prosperous denominational institutions of learning in the Southwest. Rev. J. H. Eaton, D.D., had been its popular president from its foundation until his death, a few years before the war, and Rev. J. M. Pendleton, D.D., now of Upland, Pa., its excellent theological professor. After the war the institution was reorganized, and it struggled on for existence for several years, with sunshine and clouds alternately, until it was forced to suspend. A Convention of Baptists of the State was called at Murfreesborough in 1873 to consider what should be done. The result which followed the proceedings of that Convention was its final suspension, and the establishment of the Southwestern Baptist University, at Jackson, in the western part of the State, which has now been in successful operation for five years. It has a medical department in Memphis. Middle Tennessee Baptists have the Mary Sharpe Female College, at Winchester, which has had for twenty-five years unparalleled prosperity under the administration of Rev. Z. C. Graves, LL.D.

Though West Tennessee began to be settled in 1820, and Baptist churches and Associations were soon after formed, their progress is not marked with any special interest until about 1833. The West Tennessee Convention was formed in 1835, since which the denomination has made good progress, and has had some of the most liberal and progressive brethren in the State. Some of those who may be regarded as their ablest pioneer ministers, nearly all of whom have passed away, are Jerry Burns, Thomas Owen, P. S. Gayle, C. C. Conner, N. G. Smith, —— Collins, George N. Young, J. M. Hart, and David Haliburton. The West Tennessee Convention established the Brownsville Female College, which has done a good work in female education. In 1876 Middle and West Tennessee dissolved their separate organizations, and with some East Tennessee churches again formed a State Convention, which now gives hope of a successful union of the whole denomination in its missionary and educational interests. The results of the hundred years of labor of the Baptists in the State may be given from official documents, with a few estimates, as follows: East Tennessee, 19 Associations and 45,000 members; Middle Tennessee, 10 Associations and 22,000 members; West Tennessee, 7 Associations and a fraction under 20,000 members; making in the State 87,000 regular Baptists. Besides these, there are estimated to be 8000 anti-mission Baptists and 20,000 colored Baptists.

COLORED BAPTISTS.

It is difficult to get correct statistics of the colored Baptists. There is an increase of intelligence in their preachers as they become educated in the common schools, access to which they now have all over the State. The excellent institution at Nashville, under the direction of Rev. Dr. Phillips, established by the American Baptist Home Mission Society, is doing much to give them an educated ministry, the beneficial results of which are already visible. With their present progress, and their desire for improvement, their future, religiously and as citizens, may be regarded as decidedly hopeful. With judicious and intelligent leaders they will become a liberal and progressive people.

Terrill, Prof. Anderson Wood, was born in Randolph Co., Mo., Dec. 20, 1850. His early life was spent in the country. After a thorough preparatory course, in which he excelled as a scholar, he entered Mount Pleasant College, of which his brother, J. W. Terrill, was president, and graduated before he attained his majority. For four years he was a member of the faculty of that institution. He finally left Mount Pleasant College to accept the presidency of Hardin College, at Mexico, Mo. In character he is positive. His purposes are firm and his plans sure to be executed. In manners he is mild, and he possesses a personal magnetism which attaches his pupils to him strongly. He is a Baptist in religious sentiment, and a member of that church. His wife, a gifted and cultivated lady, is associated with him as a teacher.

Terrill, Rev. Benjamin, was born May 8, 1811, in Boone Co., Ky. He was converted at fourteen, and baptized by Elder Absalom Graves. He settled in Missouri in 1836, and was ordained by Rev. Jesse Terrill. His home was near Moberly. He was a man of good native talent and preached the truth clearly. Ten churches were established in Central Missouri chiefly through his instrumentality. He died at the residence of his son, President A. W. Terrill, of Mexico, June 17, 1877, and was buried at his old home near Moberly, Mo.

Terrill, Edward, the founder of the Baptist college at Bristol, England, was born in 1635. He conducted for several years a flourishing school in that city, and joined the Broadmead church about 1659. He was soon called to the office of preaching elder, and served the church with great acceptance for many years. In common with many other members of the same church, he was cast into prison several times for the crime of nonconformity to the established religion. The Broadmead records show that Mr. Terrill's death took place in 1685–86, for on July 25, 1686, the church met " at sister Terrill's to choose a ruling elder in the place of dear brother Terrill, deceased." Himself a man of learning, and being deeply impressed with the necessity of ministerial education, he left a portion of his estate in trust for the pastor of the Broadmead church, for the time being, under the following conditions: " Provided he be an holy man, well skilled in the Greek and Hebrew tongues, in which the Scriptures were originally written; and devote three afternoons in the week to the instruction of any number of young students, not exceeding twelve, who may be recommended by the churches, in the knowledge of the original languages, and other literature." This bequest became available about 1717, and has been ever since a source of permanent income for the objects contemplated by the testator, under the name of Terrill's Fund.

Terry, Rev. A. J., the efficient pastor at Bayou de Glaise, La., was born in Mississippi in 1846; began to preach in 1866; removed to Louisiana in 1871.

Terry, Rev. Nathaniel G., an eloquent and eminently successful minister in the Green River Valley, was born in Barren Co., Ky., Nov. 17, 1829. He took an academic course at Glasgow, in his native county, and finished his education at Centre College, Danville, Ky., after which he took charge of the Masonic Female College, in Glasgow. He united with Salem Baptist church, near his birthplace, in 1841. He was licensed to preach in August, 1858, and ordained in December of the same year. Soon after his ordination he was called to the Baptist church at Glasgow, where he labored with success for fourteen years. He then removed to his farm near Caverna, Hart Co., Ky., where he has since resided, being pastor of four country and village churches. He has baptized over 1100 persons, and has been moderator of Liberty Association eleven years. He has been engaged in two oral debates, in which he proved himself a skillful polemic, and he is regarded as the ablest defender of Baptist principles in his region of the State.

Test Act.—See CORPORATION AND TEST ACTS.

Texas Baptist.—Before the war a paper by this name was issued from Anderson, Grimes Co., edited by Rev. George W. Baines, Sr. On Jan. 3, 1874, Rev. R. C. Buckner commenced the issue of the *Baptist Messenger* at Paris, Texas. In 1875 he removed to Dallas, thence issuing the *Messenger*. On Jan. 13, 1879, he changed the name to *Texas Baptist*, and he has built up a good publishing house, and secured an encouraging list of subscribers. The paper is exerting a wide influence.

Texas Baptist Educational Society.—Organized in 1845; suspended from 1861 to 1872; reorganized in the latter year. It has aided more than 100 young men in obtaining an education for the ministry. It has a small sum ($500), donated by Rev. J. W. D. Creath, bearing interest, which is annually incorporated with collections, and appropriated to beneficiaries. Rev. J. W. D. Creath is paying an additional $500 in annual installments of $50 per annum. Rev. Henry L. S. Graves is president, Rev. W. Carey Crane is corresponding secretary, and C. R. Breedlove, Esq., is treasurer. The society meets annually with the State Convention.

Texas Baptist Herald.—Under the direction of the Texas Baptist State Convention, on May 31, 1865, one number of the *Texas Christian Herald* was issued, edited by Wm. Carey Crane and Horace Clark. No other number was issued under that name. On Dec. 13, 1865, the books, printing paper, and about $60 in gold were turned over to Rev. J. B. Link, who undertook to issue the *Texas Baptist Herald* on that day, with the understanding that all existing enterprises in Texas should be sustained. Indefatigably laboring, Rev. J. B. Link, aided by strong friends, has won success. The journal thus started has grown in usefulness, until now it has an encouraging list of subscribers, with a strong office, and ranks among the first Baptist newspapers in the Union. Rev. J. B. Link and Rev. O. C. Pope, editors; Rev. Jones Johnston, business manager; published at Houston.

Texas Baptist State Convention was organized Sept. 8, 1848, at Anderson, Grimes Co., Texas. Its objects are home missions, foreign missions, education, and such other measures as will promote the unity and harmony of the whole denomination and extend the gospel in the State. During its existence about $75,000 for the support of missionaries in destitute places in the State have been raised, and thus have laid the foundations of a large number of churches. It has raised and forwarded about $18,000 for foreign missions, and has aided all the general benevolent enterprises of the day. It has fostered Baylor University and Baylor Female College, whose trustees it appoints annually. It comprises over one-half of the State in its present operations, allowing the General Association and the Eastern Convention the remainder of the State. Its presidents have been Henry L. Graves, James Huckins, J. W. D. Creath, R. E. B. Baylor, Rufus C. Burleson, Hosea Garrett, Wm. Carey Crane, and C. C. Chaplin. Hon. O. H. P. Garrett has held the office of recording secretary most of the time since 1848. No other organization has exerted a grander influence on the State than this State Convention. Besides its officers and directors it has a board of trustees, chartered by the Legislature, to which is committed the charge of all bequests and trusts. This board have $1100 loaned out, the bequest of Mrs. Mary Vickers, bearing ten per cent. interest, which interest is annually appropriated to domestic missions in the State.

Texas Baptist Sunday-School Convention, organized at Independence in November, 1866, has sustained a depositary and a general missionary during nearly all its existence. Its missionaries, charged with the work of organizing new Sunday-schools and infusing life into old ones, have been Rev. S. S. Cross, Rev. M. V. Smith, Rev. W. H. Robert, Rev. H. L. Graves, and Rev. W. D. Powell, the present incumbent. In 1877–78 seventy new Sunday-schools were organized. W. R. Howell, Esq., President; Rev. J. M. Carroll, Corresponding Secretary; P. Hawkins, Esq., Recording Secretary, Anderson, Grimes Co., Texas.

Texas Baptists in 1880.—Whole number of communicants, 107,578; churches, 1910; Associations, 81; Sunday-schools, 350; colleges and universities, 4; newspapers, 3; value of college property, $200,000; Anti-Missionary Baptists number 1000 communicants.

Texas, Eastern Baptist Convention of, was organized at Overton, Texas, in 1877. It proposes to sustain missions in that part of Texas chiefly lying between the Trinity and Sabine Rivers. Its managers are men of ability, influence, and piety, and much good will unquestionably result from their efforts.

Texas, Freedmen's College of.—The Baptists of this country are making extraordinary efforts to educate their white and colored ministers. No community in the United States has done more in this department of benevolence, and within the last fifty years no other denomination has done as much.

In October, 1880, a ten-acre lot was purchased in Marshall, Texas, at a cost of $2500, and paid for by the colored Baptists and their friends living on the field. The lot is for Bishop Baptist College. It is on the west side of the city, beautifully ornamented with shade-trees. In the centre of it stands a two-story brick mansion, 40 feet wide and 60 feet long. On the 17th of June, 1881, ground was broken for a new building, to cost $10,000, to be erected by the American Baptist Home Mission Society. The college will open in the autumn for the higher education of colored ministers and teachers in the Southwest, where more than one-tenth of the colored population of the United States resides.

Texas, General Association of, was organized in 1867. It has had the same objects in view as the State Convention, and has sustained missionaries in destitute regions of the State. It has raised nearly $20,000 for various objects since its organization, and has exercised no little influence over all Northern Texas. Its presidents have been Gen. James E. Harrison, Gen. Jos. W. Speight, Rev. A. E. Clemmons, D.D., and Rev. Rufus C. Burleson, D.D.

Texas Union Association was organized at Travis, Austin Co., republic of Texas, Oct. 8, 1840. It was the first in Texas, composed of 3 churches and 45 communicants. First moderator, T. W. Cox; J. W. Collins, Clerk; R. E. B. Baylor, Corresponding Secretary. It has now 51 churches and 3142 communicants. Out of it have sprung all the organizations and institutions in Texas.

Tharp, Benjamin Franklin, D.D., one of the most able and respected ministers of Georgia, and a resident of Perry, Houston Co., was born Sept. 16, 1819, in Twiggs County. His grandfather, Rev. V. A. Tharp, from Virginia, was one of Marion's men towards the close of the Revolutionary war. He removed to Georgia and settled in Warren County after the Revolutionary war. Wm. A. Tharp, Dr. B. F. Tharp's father, sent him to Mercer Institute, in which and in Mercer University he remained six years, graduating in 1841, and then repairing to Newton Theological Seminary to prepare for the ministry. His father dying before his theological course was completed, he returned home and engaged in farming. Nevertheless he entered the ministry immediately, and took charge of some of the most important churches in Southwestern Georgia, including those at Perry, Hayneville, and Jeffersonville. For at least thirty-five years he has been actively engaged in the ministry, having served several churches more than a quarter of a century. He has risen to prominence among the Baptist ministers of Georgia both as a preacher and a scholar, and stands equally high in the estimation of the public and in the affections of his brethren. In the Rehoboth Association his influence is unsurpassed, and he has taken the lead in that benevolent body in promoting its missions in Central Africa and among the Indians of the West. Always wealthy, he has been able to preach much to poor churches without compensation. Among the colored people he has labored largely and with much success, and when, after the war, the colored members of the white churches withdrew and formed churches of their own, with pastors of their own color, Dr. Tharp turned over to the colored pastor of the new colored Perry church 1000 members. To these he had for years preached faithfully, and among them he had established Sunday-schools, which had long been taught by the younger male and female members of the white church at Perry.

Since 1851, Dr. Tharp has been a trustee of Mercer University. During the war he was a voluntary evangelist in the army, and for two years he was an agent, without salary, for Mercer University, and increased its endowment $20,000. He is a strong preacher, a decided Baptist, and a man who, by his intellectual appearance, would attract attention anywhere. His piety is undoubted, and his liberality is great. The degree of Doctor of Divinity was conferred on him by Mercer University in 1873.

Tharp, Rev. Vincent, was born in Virginia in 1760, fought in the Revolutionary war, and removed to Georgia, where he was converted and joined the Brier Creek church, Warren County, by which he was licensed and ordained in 1800. He served several churches in Burke County, afterwards moving to Twiggs County. He was pastor of Stone Creek church. His labors were blessed to the salvation of many. For years he was moderator of the Ebenezer Association, and was very highly esteemed by his brethren. He died in the triumphs of faith in 1825. Many of his descendants are among the most respectable and wealthy citizens of Georgia, among whom may be mentioned Rev. Charnick Tharp, a son, and Dr. B. F. Tharp, a grandson.

Thearle, Rev. F. G., was born in London, England, Oct. 24, 1828. Coming to this country in 1850, he first engaged in mercantile pursuits, but afterwards studied law, and was admitted to practice in the courts of his adopted State,—Wisconsin. His conversion occurred in the year 1858, and he was baptized at Darlington, February 14 of that year. Becoming convinced of his duty to preach the gospel, he entered the ministry, and became pastor of the Baptist church in Tafton, Wis., where he was ordained in October, 1859. In April, 1865, he removed to Decatur, Ill., having accepted the call of the Baptist church in that place, and there continued until forced by failure of health to resign, in 1868. After about one year and a half he was appointed district secretary of the American Baptist Publication Society for the Northwest, his field including Northern Illinois, Wisconsin, Michigan, Minnesota, and Dakota Territory. This immense district was cared for by him in the interest of his society with marked efficiency until his transfer to the business department, as depositary, of the society's branch house at Chicago, March 15, 1879, which place he still holds.

Thickstun, Rev. Thomas F., was born in Crawford Co., Pa., July 3, 1824; was educated in the common schools of his native county and at Kingsville Academy, O. Afterwards for a time studied medicine, and attended a course of lectures in Cleveland, O. After further consideration he devoted himself to teaching, and for twenty-three years he pursued that profession. He taught in Kingsville Academy and the Geauga Seminary, O., Meadville Academy, Pa., and the Baptist Institution, Hastings, Minn. He was ordained in 1861, and in 1865 commenced his first pastorate at Waverly, Iowa, where he remained three years, building a good meeting-house and placing the church in a vigorous condition. In 1868 he became pastor of the newly-organized church at Council Bluffs. A good meeting-house was built, and a position of strength and hope gained. He has served the Iowa Baptist State Convention as secretary two years, one year giving his entire time to the work of the Convention.

Thomas, Rev. Arthur G., was born in New Columbia, Pa., Feb. 23, 1827; ordained to the work of the ministry in Freeport, Ill., March 18, 1858. He has also served as pastor with much acceptance in the following places: Baltimore, Md.; Mount Holly, Camden, and Jacobstown, N. J.; and in Chester, Pa. During the civil war he served as chaplain in the U. S. army hospitals. Mr. Thomas is a diligent student. He has traveled extensively in Europe and in the East. As an author, he has contributed to the Sabbath-school literature of the present day a valuable and interesting volume entitled "The Fields of Boaz."

Thomas, Rev. Benjamin, the father of the Rev. B. D. Thomas, of Philadelphia, Pa., was born near Meidrym, Carmarthensnire, Wales, in the year 1792. Having been found an acceptable preacher by the Baptist church in that vicinity, he was induced to enter Horton, now Rawdon, College, under the presidency of Dr. William Steadman. At the close of his college course he accepted the pastorate of the infant church at Narberth, Pembrokeshire, where he ministered with fidelity and acceptance for a period of forty years. At the commencement of his ministry the English-speaking portion of Pembrokeshire was in great spiritual destitution. By reason of his incessant labors, and the active help of others, the wilderness was made to bloom with a new and spiritual life. Within the period of his ministry churches grew up and flourished in every part of that once neglected region. He was for many years their apostle and quasi-bishop, while at the same time giving the necessary attention to the demands of one of the largest churches in the county as pastor. He died July 6, 1862, but his name and memory are fragrant in all that region of country still.

Thomas, Benjamin, D.D., late president of Judson University, Ark., was born in South Wales in 1823. When quite young he removed to the State of Ohio. He was educated at Denison University, O., and ordained in 1846. Besides teaching in Vermilion College, he has filled the following pastorates in Ohio: Mansfield, Monroeville, First church in Zanesville, Brookfield, and Newark, besides performing much evangelistic labor. Subsequently he removed to Bloomington, Ill., and became Western secretary of the American Bible Union. Having filled other important positions in Illinois, he came to Arkansas in 1864, and became president of Judson University, which position he held until recently. During the war he served as a soldier in the Federal army, and became brevet colonel.

Thomas, Rev. Benjamin D., was born near Narberth, Pembrokeshire, Wales, in January, 1843.

REV. B. D. THOMAS.

His father was pastor of the church in Narberth for forty years. Spent four years in Graig House Academy, Swansea, and graduated at Haverford-West. His first and only pastorate in Wales was at Neath, Glamorganshire, where he labored for six years. He came to the United States in the fall of 1868, and soon afterwards entered upon the pastorate of the church in Pittston, Pa., where he remained nearly three years. He then accepted a call to his present field of labor, the Fifth church, Philadelphia, and entered upon his duties Oct. 1, 1871. He is a man of fine personal appearance, of a modest and retiring disposition, and of unaffected simplicity of manners. As a preacher, he brings forth things new and old from Bible treasures, and presents them to his hearers in "thoughts that breathe and words that burn." He has contributed occasionally to religious journals, and has recently published a little volume of rare merit entitled "Popular Excuses of the Unconverted." He labors earnestly to win souls to the Saviour, and has greatly endeared himself to an appreciative and devoted people.

Thomas, Rev. Cyrus, a native of Sudbury, Rutland Co., Vt., where he was born Aug. 15, 1846; was converted and baptized when eighteen years of age by Rev. C. A. Thomas, D.D., of Brandon, Vt.; educated at Middlebury College, Vt., and at Alton Theological Seminary, Alton, Ill.; ordained at Upper Alton, Ill., in July, 1869; has been pastor of three churches,—Bellville, Ill., East St. Louis, and New Lisbon, Wis., where he has been settled six years, and where he now resides. During the late war Mr. Thomas entered the U. S. service in the 1st Vermont Heavy Artillery, in which he was commissioned a lieutenant. He was twice wounded while in battle, and he is disabled for life. He was twice promoted for gallant conduct. His ministerial record is excellent, and he is highly esteemed for his work's sake.

Thomas, Danford, LL.D., was born in Winthrop, Me., Sept. 20, 1817. After taking a preparatory course at Kent's Hill and Waterville, Me., he entered Colby University, where he graduated in 1838. The next year he was appointed tutor in Colby College. In 1840 he was elected to the chair of Ancient Languages and Literature in Georgetown College, Ky., a position he has now occupied forty years. He united with a Baptist church in his native State in his fourteenth year, and has been a liberal contributor to the benevolent enterprises of his denomination. He takes special interest in literary and theological education, and has for some time been president of the Baptist Sunday-School Board in Kentucky.

Thomas, Rev. David, A.M., of whom Dr. R. B. Semple says, "There were few such men in the world in his day," was born at London Tract, Pa., Aug. 16, 1732. He was educated at Hopewell, N. J., under the famous Isaac Eaton, and received the degree of A.M. from Rhode Island College (now Brown University). He was ordained to the ministry at about the age of eighteen years. In 1751 he went with John Gano and James Miller as a missionary from the Philadelphia Baptist Association to Virginia. During a preaching tour in Fauquier County he formed the Broad Run church, and became its pastor about 1762. Immense crowds were attracted by his ministry, and people traveled from fifty to a hundred miles to hear him. In 1763 he went to Culpeper County to preach, but the mob anticipated and prevented him. He, however, entered Orange County, and was more successful. This was the first time any Baptists had preached in that part of Virginia, and he met with much rude treatment, at one time being dragged from the pulpit and treated in a brutal manner. In spite of opposition he continued his labors with unabated zeal, until many churches were formed in Northern Virginia. During the Revolutionary war he gave his influence and the power of his great eloquence to the cause of the colonies. A poem of his, denouncing the union between the Episcopal church and the state in Virginia, had much to do with the destruction of that unholy relation. Thomas Jefferson held him in high esteem, and Patrick Henry cherished a warm regard for him. In 1788 he removed to Berkeley County, and took charge of Mill Creek church, to which he ministered about eight years. In 1796 he removed to Kentucky, and was settled over Washington church in Mason County. After a short time he located in Jessamine County, and united with East Hickman church. He died about 1801.

Thomas, Rev. D. B., an efficient Louisiana minister, was born in Tennessee in 1804; ordained in 1850, and was some time a missionary of Ouachita Association, La.; died Jan. 22, 1872.

Thomas, Rev. Evan J., was born in South Wales, March 16, 1821. He came with his parents to the United States in 1832, landing in Philadelphia. At the age of thirteen he experienced conversion, and was baptized at Pittsburgh, Pa., by Rev. Peter Lloyd, pastor of the Welsh Baptist church in that city. In 1846 he was ordained as a Baptist minister in Miami Co., O. His pastorates since have been in that State and in Indiana, Michigan, and Illinois; at Atlanta, in the last-named State, he is now living. His name has stood upon the lists of the Illinois Baptist ministry for nearly thirty years, and he retains undiminished the love and confidence of his brethren. Four of Mr. Thomas's brothers have been, or are, Baptist ministers,—John E. Thomas, David E. Thomas, Daniel Thomas, and Benjamin Thomas, D.D. The last named is still in the work, the others have finished their course and gone to their reward. All five of these brothers have been successful in their ministry to a marked degree, having baptized thousands of converts, of whom many are now in the ministry. A son of Mr. Thomas, Rev. J. B. Thomas, graduated at the seminary in Chicago in the class of 1880, and is now pastor at Dubuque, Iowa.

Thomas, John, M.D., was born at Fairford, in England, May 16, 1757. He first practised his profession in London, but subsequently became physician to an East-Indiaman. He was converted through a sermon preached by the celebrated Dr. Samuel Stennett, from John vi. 27. In 1783, when he reached India by the "Oxford," he was very desirous of meeting with serious Christians, Europeans, of course, but he could find none. In 1785 he was baptized in London by the venerable Abraham Booth, and he began to preach in different places soon after. The next year when he reached India he established a prayer-meeting and sometimes preached. From 1787 to 1792 Dr. Thomas remained in India, and labored earnestly to lead its perishing people to Jesus, with the awakening of a few Hindoos.

Dr. Thomas came again to England to take his family to India, that he might devote himself wholly to mission work. To his joyful surprise he learned of the Baptist Missionary Society, just formed, and of the intention of William Carey to labor among the heathen. They both went to India. Dr. Thomas preached with some success, and then for a time became insane. He died of brain fever in Calcutta in September, 1800.

He was imprudent, but full of zeal for souls, and full of faith in the triumph of truth.

Thomas, Rev. J. A. W., is an exception to the general rule that "a prophet is not without honor save in his own country." He has spent his life in Marlborough Co., S. C. He was born Dec. 31, 1822, baptized in his fifteenth year, licensed to preach in 1848, and ordained in 1849. He has been pastor of the Bennettsville church from that time to the present.

He was in the war three years and a half as a captain. He, however, preached almost as regularly as at home, and baptized seventy soldiers. Since his ordination he has baptized about 1000 persons, and preached 5000 times.

Thomas, Jesse B., D.D., was born at Edwardsville, Ill., July 29, 1832. He is the son of the late Hon. Jesse B. Thomas, judge of the Supreme Court of Illinois. He was graduated at Kenyon College, O., in 1850, and commenced preparation for the profession of the law. He was admitted to the bar in Illinois in 1855. In 1852 entered Rochester Theological Seminary to prepare for the ministry, but ill health obliged him to leave after a short period. For a time he was engaged in mercantile pursuits in Chicago. In 1862 he gave himself wholly to the work of the ministry, and became pastor of the Baptist church of Waukegan, Ill. In 1864 he accepted a call to the Pierpont Street Baptist church, Brooklyn, N.Y. He subsequently settled as pastor of the First Baptist church of San Francisco, Cal., of the Michigan Avenue Baptist church, Chicago, and in 1874 he took charge of the First Baptist church of Brooklyn. After the First church edifice was burned its members held united services with the Pierpont Street church, which resulted in the union of the two churches and the erection of the fine edifice which they now occupy.

Dr. Thomas is by nature an orator. His voice, his manner, his wit, and his earnestness captivate

JESSE B. THOMAS, D.D.

and arouse his audiences to an unwonted degree. He is also a scholar in the broadest sense. His lectures on the theories of modern skeptics have been pronounced as equal, if not superior, to those of Dr. Joseph Parker, by their accuracy of statement, faultless rhetoric, and resistless logic. They have been received by learned assemblies with delight. As a lecturer, he uses brief notes, simply indicating the lines of thought. As a preacher, he employs none, yet his ideas are always clothed in appropriate expressions, and the repetition and redundancy of ordinary extemporaneous speakers never mar his discourses. He is genial and unassuming, with great powers of persuasion and a strong intellect. He never discusses the minor differences, but seeks by all means to bring men to Christ, and to strengthen the faith of the church in its divine Teacher. He is sometimes borne away by the strength of his emotions, and indulges in impassioned picturings of the realm of thought he is exploring. His audiences seem to be witnessing a drama where the towers and giants of error and doubt are falling on every side. If his life is spared, for which we devoutly pray, he will be the most influential minister in America, with a reputation as wide as Anglo-Saxondom.

Thomas, Rev. J. D., was born in Lower Providence, Montgomery Co., Pa., Feb. 22, 1836. During student-life in the university at Lewisburg he made a profession of faith, and united with the Baptist Church. Subsequently he entered the ministry, and settled as a missionary pastor over several feeble churches in Huntingdon Co., Pa. For the space of eleven years he faced the winter's storm and endured the summer's heat, and faithfully performed a noble work on a field which few are found to covet. But forbidding as was the toil of travel and the care of three feeble churches, he joyfully accepted his allotted work, and continued in it until, in November, 1878, he was suddenly called to his final rest.

Thomas, Robert S., D.D., was born in Scott Co., Ky., June 20, 1805. He was converted at the age of sixteen, and baptized by Jeremiah Vardeman, in Paris, Ky. He was ordained, in 1830, in Columbia, Mo., and was pastor there for years. He labored as an evangelist; introduced Sabbath-schools into Missouri. In 1835 he aided in organizing the General Association, and was an honored member of it for twenty-five years. His wisdom, ability, scholarship, and successful labors gave him a high place in the denomination in Missouri. He was Professor of Languages and Moral Science in the State University. In 1853, president of William Jewell College. His last days were spent in organizing a church in Kansas City, and in laboring successfully as its pastor until his death, June 12, 1859. In all relations he was a model man. His monument is of a spiritual character, and it will last forever.

Thomas, Rev. Smith, a popular and eloquent pastor and evangelist, was born in Washington Co., Ky., Sept. 4, 1810. He united with Hardin's Creek Baptist church, near his birthplace, in his seventeenth year, and was licensed to preach at the age of twenty-two, and soon afterwards ordained. He was several years pastor of Cox's Creek and other churches in Nelson and Shelby Counties. Upon the death of his wife, in 1854, he gave himself almost wholly to the work of an evangelist in Kentucky and Missouri. During his ministry he baptized about 1300 persons, chiefly into the churches of which he was pastor, and about 2000 others were brought into the churches under his labors, and baptized by pastors, while he was acting as an evangelist. Of those who were converted under his ministry, thirty-four became preachers of the gospel. He made his home in Louisville during the latter years of his life, and was about twelve years moderator of Long Run Association. He died March 27, 1869.

Thomas, Thomas E., Benjamin H., Sr., Benjamin H., Jr.—This group embraces father, son, and grandson, the latter now preparing for the ministry. The father was born in Wales, and possessed more than the usual amount of Welsh fire, and was on this account deservedly popular wherever he labored. He died in November, 1854, aged seventy-six. The son inherits his excellent traits, with the added advantage of culture, and both father and son have for a long succession of years filled the pulpit of Zion church, Clarion Co., Pa. To the son we are indebted for the founding of the Reid Institute in Reidsburg, Clarion Co., Pa.

Thomas, William H., D.D., was born June 6, 1806, in Franklin, Ky. He was converted in 1822. Spent seven sessions at school, under the tuition of Spencer Clark, at Bloomfield. He was ordained in 1832. He has preached ever since, and is now advanced in years. Many have made a profession of faith under his preaching, and have been baptized by him. His talents were more than ordinary; his writings on various subjects are clear and scholarly. He is honored and loved by the people to whom he ministers.

Thompson, Rev. A. D., was converted in Charlotte Co., New Brunswick, where, in 1831, he was baptized by the Rev. Thomas Ainslie; was ordained, in 1834, pastor of the Baptist church in the parish of St. Andrew's, New Brunswick, and continued in that relation until a short time before his death, in 1874. Possessed of a deeply earnest spirit, and gifted with a ready and powerful eloquence, Mr. Thompson's ministry was very useful in these provinces, particularly in New Brunswick.

Thompson, Rev. Charles, was born in Amwell, N. J., April 14, 1748. Having completed his preparatory studies, he repaired to Warren, and was a member of the first class that entered Rhode Island College under the presidency of Dr. Manning, and graduated in 1769 with the highest honors in a class of seven. These seven students "were," in the words of Dr. Guild, "young men of unusual promise. Some of them were destined to fill conspicuous places in the approaching struggle for independence; others were to be leaders in the church and distinguished educators of youth. Probably no class that has gone forth from the university, in her palmiest days of prosperity, has exerted so widely extended and beneficial an influence, the times and circumstances taken into consideration, as this first class that graduated at Warren."

President Manning's removal to Providence with the college dissolved his connection with the church in Warren, and Mr. Thompson was chosen his successor. For three years he acted as chaplain in the American army during the war of the Revolution. As will be seen in the historical sketch of the Warren church, his home and the meeting-house of the church were burned by the British and Hessian troops. At the time he was there with his family.

He was made a prisoner of war, and taken to Newport, where he was placed in confinement on board a guard-ship, where he remained a month, and was then released. He subsequently became the pastor of the church in Swanzey, where he had a successful ministry of twenty-three years. From Swanzey he was called to the Baptist church in Charlton, Mass. Although he accepted the call, he never entered upon the performance of his duties there. He fell a victim to the dreaded disease which carries off so many in New England,—consumption,—and died the 4th of May, 1803.

Mr. Thompson was an honor to his profession, courteous and dignified in his manner, a true Christian gentleman, a ripe scholar, and a most diligent worker as a preacher of the gospel and a teacher of young men who were placed under his tuition. His memory is still revered in the section where he passed so many years of a useful life.

Thompson, Rev. Ivy F., an earnest, eloquent, and effectual preacher in Eastern Louisiana, was born in Mississippi in 1820; distinguished himself as a lawyer; labored ten years in the ministry at Greensburg, La.; four years moderator of the Mississippi River Association. He died in 1860.

Thompson, William, LL.D., was born in Edinburgh, Scotland, Sept. 10, 1821. Came to America with his parents at the age of sixteen, and settled near Washington, D. C. He attended school in the vicinity of the Capitol for several years, and at twenty-one returned to Scotland and entered the University of Edinburgh, where he devoted himself with great energy to his studies, usually spending half and often the entire night with his books.

He graduated with distinction, and returned to America and studied law. He removed to Illinois and began a lucrative practice, and about this time became deeply interested in the subject of religion, and was hopefully converted to God.

He felt it his duty to preach the gospel, but stifled his convictions until meeting with a very dangerous accident. Upon his recovery he determined to enter the ministry. He preached for some time in Illinois with varying success, and came to Missouri about the year 1855, and settled in the central part of the State, where he preached with remarkable power, and baptized hundreds.

His matchless eloquence and scholarly attainments soon attracted the attention of the denomination.

In 1856 he was elected president of Mount Pleasant College at Huntsville, Mo., his name and reputation attracting a large number of students. In 1857 the trustees of William Jewell College called him to its presidency. The institution immediately took on a new life, and made rapid advancement in all the elements of success until the breaking out of the civil war, which caused the closing of the college. He went to Sidney, Iowa, where he had just opened a school with flattering prospects when through disease, aggravated by ills which his sensitive nature could not bear, he sank to rest April 12, 1865, to rise in that coming day with a glory all the more resplendent for the trials and sufferings endured here.

He was eminently successful as an educator. His learning, geniality, and kindness gave him great influence with the students.

The rich, mellow tones of his voice, his masterly command of language, his perfect elocution, his gracefulness of manner, the imagery with which his imagination clothed every thought, his impassioned earnestness, and deep spirituality made him the most attractive and popular preacher in the Southwest. He died "honored for his greatness and loved for his goodness."

Thorp, Elder William, was born in Virginia in 1772. He removed to Kentucky in early manhood with an uncle, Thos. Thorp. He was converted when twenty years of age. He removed to Missouri in 1809, and settled in Boons Lick country. He organized the first Baptist church in Central Missouri, Mount Pleasant, and traveled over much of the State. He was a man of good talents. He aided in organizing the Mount Pleasant Association, the first in Upper Missouri. He died in 1853, eighty-one years of age.

Thresher, Ebenezer, LL.D., was born in Stafford, Conn., Aug. 31, 1798. When eighteen years old he began to seek an education. At this time also, through the prayers of his mother and others, he was led to Christ. In the spring of 1818 he went to New Haven, where, while employed in a store, he was afforded more time for the improvement of his mind. Finding a small Baptist church at New Haven, he cast in his lot with it, and labored earnestly and successfully to secure its growth.

In 1820, having accumulated a few hundred dollars, he gave up business and entered upon a course of study. Going on foot from New Haven to Worcester, Mass., he entered the family of Dr. Jonathan Going, and under the instruction of that noble man began his life-work. From Dr. Going's he went to the school of Rev. Abiel Fisher, at Bellingham, Mass., and subsequently to Amherst Academy, where he prepared for college. The first three years of college-life were spent in Columbian College, Washington, D. C., and the last in Brown University, where he graduated in 1827, a member of the first class under Dr. Wayland.

During his college course Dr. Thresher was unceasingly active in Christian work. One vacation was spent with Baron Stow traveling on horseback among the churches of Northern Virginia. In Providence he was superintendent of the first Baptist Sunday-school, and during a year of post-graduate study taught a Bible class of married women. In 1828 he accepted a call to become the pastor of the Baptist church in Portland, Me., where, on December 8 of the same year, he was or-

EBENEZER THRESHER, LL.D.

dained. This charge he resigned in 1830 on account of sickness in his family and failure of voice. Fearing again to take a pastorate, he accepted the secretaryship of the Northern Baptist Education Society, which position he retained until 1845 with much ability and success. While engaged in this work he associated with it other means of usefulness. He raised $20,000 for founding two temporary professorships for Newton Theological Seminary, and subsequently, in 1843, became the treasurer of that institution. In 1834 he became editor of *The Watchman*, though his name did not appear in connection with the paper until 1836, when he purchased the proprietorship from William Nichols, and held this three or four years.

In 1845, his health having become seriously impaired, Dr. Thresher removed to Dayton, O., where he engaged in business. In 1850, in company with E. E. Barney, he established the Dayton Car-Works, now the largest enterprise of the kind in the country. In 1858 he began the business of manufacturing varnish in Dayton, and this also proved a great success. In 1873 he retired from business, and since that time has been enjoying the leisure to which his years entitle him.

Dr. Thresher has been of great service to the Ohio Baptists. The college at Granville, the State Convention, and the Educational Society have all shared in his bounty. He has contributed many articles to the denominational press, and is profoundly interested in and generous towards Baptist enterprises at home and abroad. He is one of the most valued members of the First Baptist church of Dayton, and his counsel is everywhere sought throughout the State. The honorary degree of LL.D. was conferred upon him by Denison University.

Thurman, Rev. David, a distinguished minister and an able theologian, was born of Baptist parents, in Woodford Co., Ky., Aug. 12, 1792. In his nineteenth year he united with Good Hope Baptist church, in Green County, and was ordained to the ministry in 1814. He spent some time in the study of theology under Rev. Nathan Hall. In 1818 he settled in La Rue Co., Ky., and joined Nolin church. He became pastor of this and several other churches in Salem Association. In this field he labored sixteen years with unflagging zeal and energy, and eminent moral and intellectual power. Besides his almost irresistible appeals to the unconverted, he earnestly urged on the churches the claims of higher education, and home and foreign missions. The whole Association was greatly enlarged by his too brief ministry. He died of typhoid fever, Aug. 25, 1834.

Thurman, Rev. Robert Livingston, son of Rev. David Thurman, was born in Washington Co., Ky., Nov. 19, 1815. He united with Nolin church, being baptized by his father in 1828. He entered Georgetown College in 1839, and graduated in 1842. In 1843 he was ordained pastor of Severn's Valley Baptist church in Elizabethtown, Ky., where he preached seven years, and about half of that period conducted the Elizabethtown Female Seminary. In 1850 he was appointed collecting agent for Indian missions, and the same year became co-editor of *The Baptist Banner*. In 1851 he was appointed financial agent for Georgetown College, and in 1853 was called to the pastorate of the Baptist church in Austin, Texas. He succeeded in collecting money, with which a good house of worship was built for this church. In 1855 he accepted an agency for the Board of Foreign Missions of the Southern Baptist Convention, in Kentucky, and has continued in this work to the present time, except during the late civil war, when he was agent for the General Association of Baptists in Kentucky. He has proved himself a superior agent, and has been of immense service to the cause of missions. His home is at Bardstown, Ky.

Thurston, Rev. Gardiner, was born in Newport, R. I., Nov. 14, 1721. He made a profession of faith in Christ when he was not quite twenty years of age, and soon exhibited such gifts as a speaker that, in due time, he was licensed to preach by the church, and acted as assistant to his pastor, Rev. Nicholas Eyres. The death of Mr. Eyres in 1759 led to his being invited to become his successor in the pastoral office. This position he held, to the great acceptance of his church, until about three years before his death, which occurred May 23, 1802.

Mr. Thurston was regarded as among the ablest ministers of his denomination in the times in which he lived. His colleague, Rev. Joshua Bradley, says of him that "he enjoyed a much more than common degree of popularity as a preacher; he had a great thirst for knowledge, and never lost any opportunity for acquiring it; every one regarded him as a fine example of a tried Christian character." To the testimony of Mr. Bradley may be added that of Rev. Benjamin Pitman, who says that the manners of Mr. Thurston "were in a very high degree amiable and winning. He mingled with great ease and familiarity in the social circle, and had the faculty of making all around him feel perfectly at home. He was undoubtedly a man of much more than ordinary powers of mind. I think few men were his superiors in what is usually called common sense. There was no tendency in his mind to extremes, nothing of what at this day is called *ultraism*. Hence he had the respect and confidence of the whole community."

Tichenor, Isaac Taylor, D.D., was born in Spencer Co., Ky., Nov. 11, 1825. Feeble health while growing up interfered to some extent with his education. He was baptized in 1838 by Rev. Wm. Vaughan, of Bloomfield. Entered the ministry at Taylorsville in 1846. Shortly after that he became pastor at Columbus, Miss., in January, 1849. Returning to Kentucky in 1850, in 1851 he was pastor at Henderson in that State. He accepted the call of the First Baptist church in Montgomery, Ala., in 1852, where he labored until October, 1860, when failing health caused his resignation. He entered the Confederate army as chaplain at the beginning of the war between the States, in which service he continued until called back to his old Montgomery charge, in January, 1863. Became pastor of the First church in Memphis, Tenn., in 1871. Accepted the presidency of the Agricultural and Mechanical College of Alabama at Auburn in 1872, a position which he still holds.

Dr. Tichenor possesses a striking combination of the higher traits of intellectual power. Gov. Watts, his intimate friend, once expressed the opinion that he was endowed with the best intellect with which he ever came in contact. He is thoroughly acquainted with theology, history, and science, and is a clear and independent thinker, a gifted writer, a most eloquent and powerful preacher, and as nearly the perfection of a platform speaker as one will meet in this country.

These qualities have given him a national reputation. He is a fascinating companion, having in social life the pleasant quality of Christian simplicity.

Ticknor, William D., founder of the well-known Boston publishing house of Ticknor & Fields, was born in Lebanon, N. H., in the year 1810. When but a lad he came to Boston and

WILLIAM D. TICKNOR.

began business life in his uncle's brokerage office, being subsequently engaged in the Columbian Bank. But his predisposition was for occupation of a higher caste, and he soon entered upon the business which he so greatly developed, and which he followed as long as he lived. His love of books, his genial manners, his excellent judgment, and his perfect integrity brought him into nearer than merely mercantile relations with many of the great American and English authors whose works were published by his house, and his connection with Nathaniel Hawthorne was especially intimate and tender. From his youth he was a member of the Federal Street (now Clarendon Street) Baptist church. He was superintendent of its Sunday-school for nineteen years, and he rendered the society such eminent services as treasurer during a long and critical period, that in 1854 a service of silver plate was presented to him in recognition. His official position and his personal character bound him in close association with the various pastors of the church during his time, and he was a particular personal friend of Howard Malcom, William Hague, and Baron Stow. He was also for many years treasurer of the Massachusetts Baptist Convention, holding that office at the time of his sudden death, which took place at the Continental Hotel, in Philadelphia, April 10, 1864.

Tillinghast, Rev. John, son of Deacon Pardon and Mary (Sweet) Tillinghast, was born in West Greenwich, R. I., Oct. 3, 1812; a descendant of Rev. Pardon Tillinghast, an early pastor of the First Baptist church in Providence; was converted at the age of fourteen; was studious and industrious; began preaching soon after he was twenty-one; was ordained pastor of the West Greenwich Baptist church Oct. 8, 1840, and remained such till his death; an energetic, practical, powerful preacher in Western Rhode Island; honored by Dr. Wayland and all ministers; represented his town in the General Assembly in 1854 and 1855; after preaching to his church more than forty years he died in the ministry, March 28, 1878, aged sixty-six; one of the best of men. His son, Hon. Pardon E. Tillinghast, resides at Pawtucket, R. I.

Tilly, Rev. James, was a native of Salisbury, in England, but was called and ordained by the church in Charleston, S. C. We next find him laboring acceptably and successfully in the vicinity where Euham church was afterwards organized, in Beaufort District. He afterwards settled on "Edisto Island, where he resided until the time of his death, which happened April 14, 1744, in the forty-sixth year of his age." Rev. Isaac Chanler said of him in his funeral sermon, "As a minister, he was able and faithful to deliver unto you the whole counsel of God." Many whose names have partly or wholly perished from the earth have a glorious and eternal "record on high."

Timmons, Rev. E. B.—Florida has drawn more largely upon South Carolina than any State for her population and ministry in past years, and one of the working and useful ministers furnished the Baptists of Florida by that State is Elijah Benton Timmons, son of Rev. Samuel Timmons, a worthy minister of South Carolina. The subject of this notice was born in Marion District, May 21, 1813. From early childhood he was the subject of religious impressions, but was not baptized until 1832. Elder J. M. Timmons, a cousin, immersed him at Elim church, in Darlington District.

Removing to Florida, he arrived at or near his present location Dec. 26, 1856, since which time he has labored almost without cessation as a minister, his work being mostly in Putnam and Clay Counties, and mainly by his efforts have the churches in that section been raised up. Blessed with a competency, he was able to labor without compensation. He has baptized some 1400 persons, and thinks at least 1000 of them have been in Florida.

He is a decided Baptist, a man of catholic spirit, sound in doctrine, but of a conservative mind.

He preaches with a pathos that gives a minister influence with Southern people, whose feelings are ardent. Elder Timmons is at this time the moderator of the North St. John's River Association, and has been elected moderator several times of the Santa Fé River Association, and was during one or two sessions president of the State Convention. He is a thorough missionary, a devoted friend of Sunday-schools, and a warm advocate of temperance.

Advanced in years now, and at times infirm, yet he attends the Union and Associational meetings, preaches to one church as pastor, and makes missionary tours in his Association. During the year 1879 he traveled almost constantly as a missionary in the North St. John's Association, and labored in the most destitute sections, and nurtured declining and new churches.

Tipton, Hon. John, was born in Tennessee in 1785. He came to Indiana in 1806. He was from the first an active, large-minded citizen. He was often engaged in repelling the encroachments of hostile Indians. He was a soldier of decided courage. He was elected to Congress in 1833, and remained in it until his death, in 1839.

He was made chairman of the Committee of Indian Affairs. He was one of the projectors of the Wabash and Erie Canal. Hon. C. Smith speaks of him as a most faithful Senator,—evading no issue and always in his seat ready for the business of the hour. He died of apoplexy, and was buried in Logansport, Ind. Tipton County, and the town of Tipton, in Indiana, were named in honor of him. Mr. Tipton was a Baptist.

Titcomb, Rev. Benjamin, the founder and first pastor of the First Baptist church in Portland, Me., was born in Falmouth, near Portland, Me., in July, 1761. For some time he and his wife were members of the Congregational Church, but a change in their sentiments led to their joining the Baptists. He was ordained to the work of the Christian ministry in 1801. The few brethren and sisters in Portland now felt strong enough to band together and form a church. Mr. Titcomb was invited to become their pastor. He accepted their call, and for three years ministered to them. He then removed to Brunswick, Me., the seat of Bowdoin College, and was the pastor of the Baptist church in that pleasant village from 1804 to 1827. A remarkable revival, which dated its origin from a sermon preached by Dr. Baldwin, of Boston, July 22, 1816, resulted in adding to Mr. Titcomb's church 152 persons. A new church having been formed in the village, Mr. Titcomb became its pastor, and continued such for seven years. He died, full of years and ripe for heaven, Sept. 30, 1848, at the advanced age of eighty-seven.

Tobey, Rev. Zalmon, was born in 1792; graduated at Brown University in the class of 1817; was ordained as a Baptist minister, and settled first in Bristol, R. I., and subsequently in Providence and Pawtuxet. The latter part of his life was spent in Warren. He died Sept. 17, 1858. "He was a good scholar and a useful and estimable man."

Toby, Thomas W., D.D., was for several years a missionary to China; afterwards pastor in North Carolina; Professor of Theology in Howard College, and professor in Judson Female Institute; professor in Bethel College, Russellville, Ky.; pastor at Union Springs, and then at Camden, Ala.; and now principal of the Collegiate Institute in Eufaula. Dr. Toby is one of the ripest scholars in the South, a graceful writer, a devout Christian, an earnest minister, and an accomplished gentleman.

Todd, Rev. Simpson, was born in Lancashire, England, Aug. 15, 1812; died Dec. 31, 1878, at Brant, Wis. He was ordained to the work of the Christian ministry in 1842; supplied churches in Bacup and Rochdale, in Lancashire, England, with much success. He was pastor of the churches in Sheboygan Falls, Sheboygan City, and Brant, Wis. He was a sound gospel preacher, and entirely consecrated to the work of the ministry.

Todd, Rev. Thomas, was born in Ireland. He was converted and baptized in St. John, New Brunswick, and joined Germain Street Baptist church. He was successively pastor of the following Baptist churches in New Brunswick: Woodstock, Sackville, Moncton, and the church at St. Stephen, where he still preaches. Mr. Todd has also rendered valuable service as a missionary and agent for missions in New Brunswick.

Toleration Act, The. — When William and Mary ascended the throne of England, made vacant by the flight of James II., their warmest friends were the Protestant Dissenters of Great Britain and Ireland. Episcopalians of the thorough loyalty of Bishop Burnet were not numerous, though many of that community rendered a measure of allegiance to William III.

On March 16, 1669, the king, in his speech to the House of Commons, made an appeal to that body for a modification of the oaths taken by men in the service of the government, so that there would be "room for ALL Protestants willing and able to serve" (their sovereigns). To carry out the royal request a bill was introduced into the House of Lords to change the obnoxious oaths. One clause of this bill "took away the necessity of receiving the sacrament (in the Episcopal Church) in order to make a man capable of enjoying any office, employment, or place of trust." This clause was rejected. After this another clause met with the same fate, by which it was provided that all persons should be sufficiently qualified for any office " who within a year before or after their admission did receive the sacrament, either according to the usage of the Church of England, or in any Protestant congregation, and could produce a certificate under the hands of the minister, and two other credible persons, members of such a congregation." The proposition in the same House to remove the necessity "of kneeling at the sacrament," and using the sign of "the cross in baptism," was rejected. The liberality of King William was far in advance of the tyrannical Episcopal Church and Legislature of England. Soon after a bill for the "Toleration of Protestant Dissenters" was passed, and became the law of William's empire. When this act was under discussion it was proposed to limit its duration to a brief period, that "the Dissenters might demean themselves so as to merit the continuance of it when the term of years should end;" but it was passed without this insolent restriction. The full title of this celebrated act is, "An Act for Exempting their Majesties' Protestant Subjects, Dissenting from the Church of England, from the Penalties of Certain Laws." It has eighteen clauses.

By this law, when certain conditions were complied with, Dissenters were freed from the more outrageous persecuting enactments of Queen Elizabeth, James I., and Charles II.

Clause VII. says, "No person dissenting from the Church of England in holy orders, or pretended holy orders, or pretending to holy orders, nor any preacher or teacher of any congregation of dissenting Protestants, that shall make and subscribe the declaration aforesaid, and take the said oaths, at the general or quarter sessions of the peace to be held for the county, town, parts, or division where such person lives, which court is hereby empowered to administer the same; and shall also declare his approbation of, and subscribe the articles of religion mentioned in the statute made in the thirteenth year of the reign of the late Queen Elizabeth, except the 34th, 35th, and 36th, and these words of the 20th article ("The Church hath power to decree rites or ceremonies, and authority in controversies of faith, and yet"), shall be liable to any of the pains or penalties mentioned in an act made in the seventeenth year of the reign of King Charles II.," etc.

Clause IX. says, "Whereas some dissenting Protestants scruple the baptizing of infants, be it enacted by the authority aforesaid, that every person in pretended holy orders, or pretending to holy orders, or preacher or teacher, that shall subscribe the aforesaid articles, except before excepted; and also except part of the 27th article, teaching infant baptism; and shall take the oaths, and make and subscribe the declaration aforesaid, in manner aforesaid, every such person shall enjoy all the privileges, benefits, and advantages which any other dissenting minister, as aforesaid, might have or enjoy by virtue of this act."

Clause XII. exempts Quakers from the penalties of the same persecuting laws, on special conditions.

Clause XVI. declares "that neither this act, nor any clause, article, or thing herein contained, shall extend, or be construed to extend, to give any ease, benefit, or advantage to any Papist or Popish recusant whatever, or any person that shall deny, in his preaching or writing, the doctrine of the blessed Trinity, as it is declared in the aforesaid articles of religion."

Clause XVIII. asserts, "that no congregation, or assembly for religious worship, shall be permitted or allowed by this act, until the place of such meeting shall be certified to the bishop of the diocese, or to the archdeacon of that archdeaconry, or to the justices of the peace at the general or quarter sessions of the peace for the county, city, or place in which such meeting shall be held, and registered in the said bishop's or archdeacon's court respectively, or recorded at the said general or quarter sessions," etc.

Clause IV. affirms that any dissenting assembly, held for religious worship, with "the doors locked, barred, or bolted," shall receive no benefit from this law; "that every person that shall come to, and be at such meeting, shall be liable to all the pains and penalties of all the aforesaid laws recited in this act."*

Such are the chief features of the famous Toleration Act, by which our Baptist fathers in England obtained freedom to worship God, fettered by some restraints and hardships, and by which in Virginia our brethren were frequently shielded from persecution. The Hon. John Blair, deputy governor of Virginia, commenting, in a letter to the king's attorney in Spottsylvania, on the arrest of John Waller, Lewis Craig, and James Childs for preaching Christ, says, "The Act of Toleration has given them a right to apply, in a proper manner, for licensed houses, for the worship of God according to their consciences."† This letter was written in 1768. Dr. R. B. Semple, who has preserved Mr. Blair's letter, says, "Though the Toleration Law (Act) is not believed to have been *strictly* obligatory in Virginia, yet, as was frequently the case at that period, it was acted under in many instances;" that is, it gave protection, when its provisions were complied with, from magisterial and other persecutions.

We abhor the insulting assumption of the word *toleration*. Nevertheless, the Toleration Act pro-

---

* Neal's History of the Puritans, iv. 496, 508-15. Dublin, 1755.
† Semple's History of the Virginia Baptists, pp. 16, 32.

tects our brethren in England now, as it shielded our fathers in Virginia more than a century ago.

Tolman, Rev. C. F., was born at Meridian, N. Y., Oct. 25, 1832. The family having in the mean time removed to Illinois, he was baptized by Rev. Morgan Edwards into the Pavilion Baptist church, in the northern part of that State, in 1844. He was educated at Shurtleff College and Madison University; entering the former as Freshman, in 1850, and graduating at the latter in 1856, and from the seminary there in 1858. In November of the last-named year, with his wife, Mary R. Bronson, a daughter of Dr. M. Bronson, the veteran missionary, he sailed for Assam, under appointment of the Missionary Union. In six months after his arrival at Nowgong he preached his first sermon in Assamese, having acquired the language with remarkable rapidity. In 1859 he commenced the interesting mission among the Mekirs, reducing to writing the language of that tribe, and preparing in it a catechism and vocabulary. The fever of the country, however, made such ravages in his constitution that, under medical direction, he was compelled soon to leave his work and return to this country, arriving in July, 1861. The voyage having in some degree restored his health, he entered the pastorate at Lawrence, Mass., where, however, his health again failed after two years of happy and fruitful service, in which he baptized nearly every month when able to preach. His next settlement was at Fort Madison, Iowa, in 1864; from which he was called to the service of the Missionary Union, as assistant to Dr. S. M. Osgood, the district secretary for the West. Entering this work in 1866, he continued in association with Dr. Osgood until the death of the latter, in 1875, when the entire charge of the district devolved upon himself. During six years he has occupied this laborious post, meeting its demands with the utmost self-devotion, and as a reward of his well-directed service having the satisfaction of seeing the contributions from his field every year increasing.

Tolman, Rev. Frank W., a son of Hon. Philander Tolman, of Harrison, Me., was born in Worcester, Mass., Aug. 13, 1842. He was a graduate of Colby University in the class of 1866. He spent one year at Newton, and two years as a student in the theological department of Shurtleff College. His ordination took place at Farmington, Me., May 18, 1870. For two years and a half he was pastor and supply for this church, and then removed to Campton village, N. H., where he was pastor of the church nearly three years. He subsequently had pastorates in Dexter, Me., and South Hampton, N. H., in which place he died July 14, 1877.

Tolman, Rev. Jeremy F.—During twenty years of his later life this good minister of Jesus Christ, who died at Sandwich, Ill., in 1872, was made nearly helpless by paralysis of his lower limbs, so that he was unable to walk, continuing, however, to the last, useful in various relations as a writer and a counselor among the churches. He was born in Needham, Mass., Dec. 17, 1784. He was of Congregationalist parentage, but upon his conversion became a Baptist through independent and careful study of the New Testament. He was licensed to preach in 1814, at Dana, Mass., and was ordained in 1819, at Junius, N. Y. He labored chiefly at Junius and in Cato, Cayuga Co., until 1834, when he removed to Illinois, under appointment of the Home Mission Society. At Long Grove, in the northern part of the State, at Upper Alton, in the southern, he served as pastor, until the paralysis of which we spoke above closed his pastoral connection with the latter church, April 27, 1850. From this time until his death he was mostly laid aside from active labor. Among the contributions of his pen during that period may be especially named his "History of the Fox River Association," published in 1859. He was to the close of life a student, not only of the Bible and theology, but of science and politics. Though he gave away all his library in his early sickness to young ministers, he afterwards collected another of considerable size. He is well remembered by those who knew him in these last years of his life for his cheerful spirit, and bright, vigorous intellect, and his wide information, embracing whatever related to current questions of every sort. Among the children who survive him are Rev. J. N. Tolman, now of New York, Rev. C. F. Tolman, Chicago, and Mrs. N. M. Bacon, of Dundee, Ill.

Tombes, John, B.D., was born at Bewdley, Worcestershire, England, in 1603. At fifteen years of age he entered Magdalen Hall, Oxford. At college he made such good use of his opportunities, and acquired such a reputation for learning, that upon the decease of his tutor in 1624 he was chosen to succeed him in the catechetical lecture, when he was but twenty-one years of age. This position he held for seven years.

While he was parish clergyman of Leominster he preached a sermon on the reformation of the church, which was published subsequently by the House of Commons. It was a sermon of great power. At the commencement of the Parliamentary war in 1641, he was driven out of his home by the forces of the king, and everything he had was carried away on account of it.

Mr. Tombes in 1637 began to entertain doubts about infant baptism. While in Bristol he was almost persuaded that the practice had no Scriptural authority. When he came to London, in 1643, he determined to consult the most learned Pedobaptists, that the question might be settled forever in his mind. The celebrated Westminster Assembly of Divines being at that time in session, and Mr. Tombes having learned from one of its members that it had a committee on infant baptism, drew up a paper in Latin, containing his chief reasons for doubting the lawfulness of that custom, and he sent it to Mr. Whitaker, the chairman of the committee, that his objections might be removed. But the only notice the Assembly took of his paper was to try and hinder his settlement in London. At Bewdley, three miles from Kidderminster, where Richard Baxter preached, Mr. Tombes became the minister of the parish; and thinking it hopeless to reform the church, he formed a separate community holding Baptist sentiments, and of this church he was pastor, while he still "continued minister of the parish."

Mr. Baxter, the leading Presbyterian minister in England, felt deeply moved by this fountain of heresy almost at his own door, and, like a good soldier, he determined to attack Mr. Tombes. The battle took place on the 1st of January, 1650, in the church at Bewdley; it lasted seven or eight hours. Baxter showed a determination to secure the victory even at the expense of some malice and considerable indecency. And the good man thought that he had succeeded, though all unprejudiced persons were of a different opinion. After this controversy Mr. Tombes was regarded as a champion by the Baptists; and he held public discussions with Mr. Tirer and Mr. Smith at Rosse, with Mr. Cragg and Mr. Vaughn at Abergavenny, and with some one else at Hereford; and many who differed from his views believed that "he had the advantage of his opponents in learning and argument."

After the Restoration, when he was about sixty years of age, he retired from the ministry, the duties of which he could only perform at the risk of his liberty, his property, and his life. Among his friends were Lord Clarendon, the lord chancellor, and Bishops Sanderson, Barlow, and Ward. Mr. Baxter describes him as "the chief of the Anabaptists, the greatest and most learned writer against infant baptism."

The narrow-minded Neal, author of the "History of the Puritans," a Congregationalist, says, "Mr. John Tombes, B.D., was educated in the University of Oxford; he was a person of incomparable parts, well versed in the Greek and Hebrew languages, and a most excellent disputant." He was made a trier in 1653, whose duty it was, with others of a committee, to examine candidates for the ministry in the national church, and investigate the character of "ignorant and scandalous" incumbents, with a view to their removal. After the Act of Uniformity expelled him, in 1662, from his parish, he was offered positions of honor and profit in the National Church, but no persuasions could move him to serve at the altars of the Anglican Establishment as an Episcopalian.

Mr. Tombes was a man of great learning in every department of literature. He had a powerful intellect; he was a ready speaker in public discussions; he was universally known by his writings. He was the author of twenty-eight publications, and in his day he was efficient beyond most men in securing the extension of the Baptist denomination. He died at Salisbury, May 25, 1676.

Tombes, J. B., D.D., was born in Albany, N. Y., in 1821; converted and baptized at the age of sixteen; studied for the ministry, and graduated at Madison University in 1847; became pastor of the Fourth church in Richmond, Va., where he was ordained in 1848; was principal of Meadsville Academy, Va., from 1854 to 1859, when he took charge of Liberty Female College, Mo., and held his position there until 1864, when he removed to Philadelphia, Pa.; was pastor of the North Baptist church of that city for some time, then of the Berean church at Carbondale, Pa., when he removed to Ohio; was pastor at Tiffin, and also at Delaware, and president, in 1870, of the Ohio Baptist Ministers' Conference. In 1871 he became associate editor of *The Baptist Record*, published at Charlestown, W.Va., and in 1873 became president of Carleton College, Meigs Co., O., but was compelled to yield his position on account of ill health. In 1869 he gave a series of articles in the *Journal and Messenger* on "The Writings and Teachings of the Apostolic and Christian Fathers," and in 1873 held a public discussion with the *Central Methodist*, Ky., on "The Mode of Christian Baptism." He is the author of a very useful book on "The Christian Rite of the One Only Baptism." In the pastorate he has had much success in winning souls to Christ. While at Carbondale, Pa., he baptized over 100 converts. In 1875 he removed to Anaheim, Cal., for his health. He occupies a leading position in the Baptist ministry of Central and Southern California.

Tomkies, Rev. J. H., was born in Hanover Co., Va., Nov. 18, 1839. His father has devoted himself to teaching, for which he is well qualified, and is a faithful member of the Ashland Baptist church, Va.

When a boy he consecrated his life to the Lord, and soon gave indications of his future occupation. He was impressed early in life with an earnest desire to preach the gospel, and that it was his duty to fit himself for the work; for this purpose he entered Richmond College when about nineteen, where he remained two sessions, and prosecuted the study of mathematics, French, German, and English. With an intense desire to engage in preaching, he left college, returned to Ashland, and was there ordained. Just before the late war he removed to Florida, and first located at Madison, where he taught school and preached. Remaining there a year, he went to Gainesville, and taught in the East Florida Seminary, and preached to the few Baptists there.

At the breaking out of the war he enlisted as a private in the 7th Florida Regiment. His general deportment was such that in one year he was elected by his comrades chaplain of the regiment. He served in this capacity to the close of the war, and so maintained his character for integrity, faithfulness, and piety that one of his comrades says of him, "Let him but speak, and all were prepared to hear and be influenced by his words."

Returning to his adopted State after the war closed, he settled in Gainesville again, preaching in the town, and to Fort Clark, Wacahoota, and Stafford's Pond churches for two years. From 1868 to 1870 he preached at Fernandina. From 1870 to 1875 he served Elim, Eliam, Providence, and Pleasant Grove churches. While preaching to the First church, Gainesville, in 1875, and others around, his health failed, and his decline was rapid, and Aug. 15, 1878, he died at his house in Gainesville, to which place he had returned.

He was open and generous. He was excessively modest and retiring, except with his intimate friends.

As a preacher, he was doctrinal and practical. The Saviour, in his office, work, and word was his theme, and him he constantly exalted. He was a clear thinker and writer. He was "learned in the Scriptures," and confirmed the faith of saints, and was able to contend with error. He met in public debate the champion of Campbellism in his section, and so completely overpowered him that he left that region.

During its existence he was a warm supporter of the *Florida Baptist*, and its corresponding editor. He was frequently moderator and clerk of the Santa Fé River Association, and he was president and secretary of the State Convention at different times, and at his death was its president. He never sought civil office, and reluctantly accepted the office of county treasurer when unable any longer to preach, which position he held at his death.

Probably no man of his age and short residence in the State held a more prominent position in the denomination. As might be expected, his death was peaceful and triumphant. His family and some friends were assembled at his house, and, as they gathered about him, he repeated the 23d Psalm and the hymns, "How firm a foundation," etc., and "Jesus, lover of my soul," and then asked that they would all pray with him that he might be fully resigned. Repeatedly he said, "I shall soon be at rest."

Tommie, Rev. Joel C., a pioneer preacher in Bradley Co., Ark., was a native of Georgia, where he became a preacher. He settled on L'Aigle Creek, in Bradley Co., Ark., in 1850, and soon after gathered the Bethel church, about four miles south of the present town of Edinburg, in Dorsey Co. Mr. Tommie was very faithful, often walking five or six miles to preach after the labors of the day on his little farm. Wherever he could get a few persons together he always preached. It was remarked not long ago by one who knew him well, "It seems to me that when Brother Tommie was the only preacher in the country we had more preaching than now when we have plenty of preachers." He laid the foundations of a number of churches. He died in 1871.

Topping, Charles Henry, a well-known Baptist layman of Delavan, Wis., a native of Charleston, Montgomery Co., N. Y., where he was born May 22, 1830. He is the oldest son of the late Rev. Henry Topping, one of the first pioneer ministers of Wisconsin. Charles H. spent his early youth in Leesville, Schoharie Co., N. Y., where his father began his labors as a Christian minister. When he was nine years of age his father removed to Wisconsin, reaching Delavan, Walworth Co., in the autumn of 1839. Mr. Topping became the pastor of the Baptist church which had just been organized. His son selected the calling of a merchant as his vocation, and for several years he was in a store perfecting his knowledge of and becoming a first-class business man. In 1851, Mr. Topping began business for himself as a merchant in Delton, Wis. In 1857 he returned to Delavan, and engaged successfully in mercantile pursuits until 1864, when, owing to the total loss of his health, he was obliged to retire for a time. From 1864 to 1874 he resided in Southern Illinois and in Ottawa, Kansas, seeking by change of climate and out-door exercise the restoration of his health. This being secured, he returned, in 1874, to Delavan, and again commenced business. He is now at the head of one of the largest houses in the county, and ranks among its best business men.

But it is as a devoted Christian that Mr. Topping is best known. At the age of eleven he obtained a hope in Christ, and was baptized by his father into the fellowship of the Delavan Baptist church. For nearly forty years he has been one of its most active and useful members. While residing in Illinois, Mr. Topping was a member of the board of the Illinois Industrial University, and he has several times been a member of the board of the Wisconsin Baptist State Convention, and in its earlier history a member of the board of Wayland Academy.

Topping, Rev. Henry, was a native of Charleston, N. Y. He was born in 1804. Both his parents were pious, and took great pains with his early religious education. Converted at nineteen years of age, he made a profession of religion, and united with the Baptist church in his native place. Ordained to the work of the ministry at the age of thirty, he was first settled as pastor of the Baptist church at Leesville, where he remained five years. Extensive revivals of religion attended his ministry. He was eminently fitted for an evangelist. While pastor at Leesville he held special meetings at Charleston, Scotville, and Argusville, where his labors were blessed in turning many to God. In 1839 he removed to Delavan, Wis., and became the first pastor of the Baptist church, which had just been organized, which grew rapidly under his labors. He planted the gospel in all the region around, and was most untiring in his missionary and itinerant labors. Churches at Walworth, Sugar Creek, East Troy, and Turtleville (now Clinton) were founded as the results of his labors. The church at Delavan, organized forty years ago, and of which he was the first pastor, is now the largest church in the State. His two sons, Charles H. and Marshall Topping, and his daughter, Mrs. Hattie La Bar, are active members of the church. Owing to the failure of his health he was obliged to retire from the active work of the ministry about twenty years before his death, but he preached occasionally until he went to receive his crown. He was a man of unblemished character, of gentle and retiring disposition, and highly esteemed in all the region where he labored for his Master.

Toronto, The Jarvis Street Church of, is the most influential Baptist church in Canada. Until within a few months, for a number of years it was under the pastoral care of the distinguished Dr. J. H. Castle, beloved and honored in the United States as well as in Canada. He built a splendid church edifice in Philadelphia, Pa., and during his pastorate the Jarvis Street church was erected. It cost $100,000. It has sittings for 1300 persons, and it was dedicated Dec. 3, 1875. It is one of the finest churches on this side of the Atlantic. (See cut on the following page.)

Torrance, Rev. John, M.A., was born of Presbyterian parents Dec. 6, 1839, in Kilmarnock, Ayrshire, Scotland. He came to Canada in 1849. Until thirteen years of age he enjoyed the best school advantages. At seventeen he entered upon school-teaching, and taught five years, working his way up from the third to the first class in his profession. About the age of twenty he joined the Baptists, and commenced preaching. For four years he preached to the churches of Woodville and West Line of Brock, Ontario, and taught school. During this period he was ordained, but at its close he entered the Canadian Literary Institute as a theological student, and remained two full academical years. For the three years following he was pastor of the church in Mount Elgin, Ontario. At the beginning of 1866 he accepted a call to the Cheltenham and Edmonton churches in the same province. During the last four of the six years' continuance of this relation he took the Arts course in the University of Toronto, at the same time performing his pastoral duties. He graduated B.A. in 1872, and took the M.A. degree in the year following. At his graduation he was Silver Medalist in Metaphysics, and prizeman in Oriental Languages. In the fall of 1872 he settled over the church in Yorkville, a suburb of Toronto. At the New Year of 1875 he accepted the chair of New Testament Exegesis in the theological department of the Canadian Literary Institute at Woodstock. In 1878, on the death of Rev. Dr. Fyfe, he was chosen principal of the same department, and in the beginning of 1881 he became principal of the literary department also. As an expository preacher and as a scholar and educator, Principal Torrance has few equals. Recently he was appointed to a professorship in the new Theological Seminary at Toronto, but before he entered upon its duties he fell asleep in Jesus.

Towle, Francis W., A.M., was born in New London, N. H., Nov. 21, 1835; graduated from Madison University. At present he is the principal of Colgate Academy, in which he is performing a noble work for those who are enjoying the advantages of the institution.

Towner, Rev. Enoch, was born in Newbury, Conn., in 1755; awakened under Joseph Dimock's preaching in Lower Granville, Nova Scotia, in 1790; converted subsequently, and baptized by Rev. Thos. Handley Chipman; ordained, in 1799, pastor of Digby church; was present at the formation of the Baptist Association, June 23, 1800; evangelized in Argyle in 1806, and baptized 120 converts. Mr. Towner's labors were highly useful in Digby County; died in November, 1827, aged seventy-two years.

Toy, Crawford H., D.D., LL.D., Professor of the Semitic Languages in Harvard University, and late Professor of the Interpretation of the Old Testament in the Southern Baptist Theological Seminary, was born in Norfolk, Va., March 23, 1836. From 1847 to 1852 he was at the Norfolk Academy. He entered the University of Virginia in October, 1852, and took the degree of Master of Arts in June, 1856. From October, 1856, to June, 1859, he taught for Mr. John Hart, in the Albemarle Female Institute, Charlottesville, Va. In 1859 he was appointed a missionary to Japan by the Foreign Mission Board of the Southern Baptist Convention, and studied in preparation for that

JARVIS STREET BAPTIST CHURCH, TORONTO, CANADA.

work at the Southern Baptist Theological Seminary in its first session, in 1859-60. He was baptized at Charlottesville, Va., by Rev. John A. Broadus, in April, 1854, and was ordained at the same place in June, 1860. From September to December, 1860, he was engaged in a tour through the Portsmouth Association, which body had agreed to support him in his missionary work in Japan. The breaking out of the war making it impracticable to go to Japan, he went to Richmond College in January, 1861, as Professor of Greek, and thence, the May following, to Norfolk, where he supplied the pulpit of the Cumberland Street Baptist church. In March, 1861, he went into the Army of Virginia as a private, became chaplain in January, 1863, and was made prisoner at Gettysburg, and was in Fort McHenry from July to November, 1863. He was appointed Professor of Physics and Astronomy in the University of Alabama, at Tuscaloosa, in August, 1864. He returned to Virginia, and taught from October, 1865, to May, 1866. He studied at Berlin, Prussia, from August, 1866, to July, 1868, returning to America in September, 1868. In January, 1869, he was appointed Professor of Greek in Furman University, Greenville, S. C. In May, 1869, he was appointed Professor of Old Testament Interpretation in the Southern Baptist Theological Seminary, which position he held until his resignation in May, 1879. His inaugural address delivered Sept. 1, 1869, was published, and is entitled "The Claims of Biblical Interpretation upon Baptists." He has also contributed several articles to the *Baptist Quarterly*.

In June, 1880, he was elected to the chair of Semitic Languages in Harvard University.

He received the degree of D.D. from Wake Forest College in 1870, and that of LL.D. at a later period.

Tozer, Rev. Edward, was born in the city of Bristol, England, Nov. 7, 1815, and died very suddenly Jan. 1, 1878, at Fort Ann, Washington Co., N. Y. Converted at sixteen, he came to this country five years later, and spent four years at Auburn, N. Y., in preparatory study for the work of the ministry. He was ordained, in 1840, at Fayette, Seneca Co., N. Y., where he labored several years as pastor of the Baptist church; also ministered at Geneva and Naples some fourteen years, and spent four years as collecting agent for the American Bible Union. In the spring of 1865 he settled with the Fort Ann Village church, where he continued the remainder of his life. During eight years he also supplied the church at Kingsbury with an afternoon service until 1873. He led this people to renovate their house of worship in 1870, and in 1874 he had the pleasure of seeing a neat and substantial brick sanctuary, costing $17,000, dedicated to the worship of God as the fruit of the joint labors and sacrifices of pastor and people. He was a sound and able preacher and a good pastor. He died very much lamented by the whole community.

Tracy, Rev. Leonard, was born in Tunbridge, Vt., in 1802. As preacher and pastor he served six or seven good churches in three of the New England States, and in the communities in which he labored he was respected as a man who honored his profession by great purity of life, showing earnestness of purpose and conscientious fidelity to every trust. He died at East Bethel, Vt., Nov. 21, 1869.

Train, Arthur Savage, D.D., was born in Framingham, Mass., Sept. 1, 1812. He was the elder son of Rev. Charles Train, who fitted him for Brown University, where he graduated in the class of 1833. He was tutor for two years in his own college, pursuing his theological studies during this time with Dr. Wayland, receiving also such aid in his preparatory work as his father could give him. He was ordained as pastor of the First Baptist church in Haverhill, Mass., in October, 1836, and for twenty-three years was the beloved minister of a people for whom he lived and labored with a zeal and success which are seldom equaled, certainly not surpassed. He resigned his pastorate to accept an appointment in the Newton Theological Institution as Professor of Sacred Rhetoric and Pastoral Duties. Dr. Train brought to his work the results of a long experience, and well-defined conceptions in his own mind of what was needed to make an efficient and useful ministry. He resigned his position at Newton in 1866, after having held it for seven years. The remainder of his life was passed in his native town, officiating for the church of which his father had for so many years been the minister. He was a trustee of Brown University from 1845 to his death, which occurred Jan. 2, 1872.

Train, Rev. Charles, was born in Weston, Mass., Jan. 7, 1783. At the age of eighteen he entered Harvard University, where he graduated in 1805, delivering a Hebrew oration on the occasion. Having decided to enter the ministry, he was licensed by the church in Newton. In 1807 he commenced his labors in Framingham, Mass., which was destined to be his home for the remainder of his life. He was not ordained as the pastor of the Baptist church until Jan. 30, 1811. For several years he supplied two churches,—that of Weston and that of Framingham. For thirteen years he confined his labors to the Framingham church. He resigned his pastorate in 1839. He had seen the little band of disciples grow into a vigorous, active church. The Master had richly blessed his labors. He was honored as few men are in the community in which he had lived for so many years, and when he died, Sept. 17, 1849, he was borne to the grave amidst the sincere lamentations of a generation he had served most faithfully.

Mr. Train was for several years a member of the Legislature of Massachusetts, both in the lower and in the higher branch. "He had the honor of being the first to move in the plan of forming a legislative library, as well as in the yet more important matter of a revision of the laws relating to common schools. He had much to do also in obtaining the charter of Amherst College." He left several published writings in the form of orations and discourses.

Trask, Rev. Enos, was born in Jefferson, Me., April 22, 1794. He was converted at the age of sixteen, but was not baptized till March 10, 1823, Rev. William Burbank administering the ordinance. For most of the thirteen years between his conversion and his baptism his spiritual life was not very encouraging; but at that time a variety of peculiarly trying experiences added weight and force to a conviction he had felt for over five years, that it was his duty to enter the gospel ministry. At the same time he deeply felt his unworthiness for the sacred calling. At last an affliction, deep and sad, which he recognized as from God for the purpose of impressing him forcibly in reference to his duty, mastered his resistance.

He united with the Third Jefferson church, organized in 1824, and was immediately chosen deacon. At this time his brethren, like himself, felt impressed with the thought that God was calling him into the ministry, and in less than a year after the organization of the church, after being closely questioned as to his own impressions, he was unanimously licensed for the work to which he had been called. The First Baptist church, Whitefield (now King's Mills), called a council of churches, and he was ordained as an evangelist May 23, 1827.

The First and Second Palermo, Windsor, First Vassalborough, China Village, South China, Brunswick, Sidney, Alna, Damariscotta, with other churches, enjoyed his labors as an evangelist previous to his call to Nobleborough. He enjoyed revivals, and baptized many into all these churches, and also baptized in New Brunswick, when there as a messenger from the Association to which he belonged to the Association there.

In 1836 he accepted a call to the pastorate of the First Baptist church, Nobleborough, as successor to Rev. Phineas Pillsbury, and for thirteen years faithfully and successfully labored, baptizing, it is said, more than 1000 persons in this locality. During his ministry here the church at Damariscotta Mills was formed, mainly from members of the First church. After he had resigned the pastorate, brethren, in a section of the church called West Neck, invited him to hold a series of meetings there, at a time when the church was pastorless. He consented, and with great power did the work go on; many were converted, and for a short time he supplied the church.

Many other places after this were blessed with his labors, among them the Second Nobleborough, South Thomaston, and one or more of the St. George churches. His labors were continuous for over fifty years, and in that time he had baptized more than 2200 persons.

He was decided in his convictions. His preaching was thoroughly evangelical. He was bold and fearless, while tender and loving in his presentation of the stern doctrines of the inspired volume. The terrible denunciations against unrepented sin, which our Saviour so often uttered, he never shrank from proclaiming. To him all truth in the Word of God was real. He died full of peace, Dec. 19, 1880.

Travis, Rev. Alexander, one of the most widely useful, and one of the most famous of the fathers of fifty years ago. His ministry was devoted mainly to the planting and building up of churches and Associations in Southern Alabama. He was a pioneer for the times, eminently suited to the work. He left a most fragrant memory.

Tremont Temple, Boston, Mass., was purchased early in 1843 by Timothy Gilbert, S. G. Shipley, Thomas Gould, and William S. Danwell for $55,000. It had been the Tremont Theatre. The deed was executed in June, 1843. The object for which the edifice was bought by these gentlemen was to secure a place of worship for the Tremont Street Baptist church, where the seats should be free, that there might be free seats for the poor, and for strangers coming to the city to seek employment, whose means would not allow them to rent pews in other churches.

The purchasers, on their own responsibility, remodeled the interior of the building, and arranged the halls, stores, and other rooms in a manner convenient for the purposes designed. They also furnished the edifice. These changes required an additional outlay of $24,284. The main audience-room of the Temple was 90 by 80 feet, and seated 2000 persons.

It was used as a place of worship until March 31, 1852, when it was destroyed by fire. On the 25th of May, 1853, the foundations of the present building were laid, and on the 25th of December following the church held the first meeting for public worship in the main hall. The new building, with all its furniture, cost $126,814.26. The Evangelical Baptist Benevolent and Missionary Society was formed May 11, 1858, and the property was transferred to it on Nov. 30, 1858. A lease was executed on June 9, 1859, granting the Tremont Street

TREMONT TEMPLE, BOSTON, MASS.   AUDIENCE ROOM OF THE TREMONT STREET BAPTIST CHURCH.

Baptist church and society the use of the great hall, with its organ and furniture, during the daytime on Sundays, as a place of public worship, and basement rooms " for vestry and Sabbath-schools," on condition that the church should always maintain public worship on the Sabbath with free seats, and support a good and efficient pastor.

On the night of Aug. 14, 1879, the Temple was destroyed by fire. The directors, however, took immediate and effective steps to rebuild it, and the denomination now has an edifice worthy to stand beside any of the splendid structures that adorn the city of Boston, where the Word of life is regularly dispensed to listening thousands.

The objects which the Evangelical Baptist Benevolent and Missionary Society aims to accomplish are, the maintenance of evangelical preaching in the Tremont Temple, the employment of colporteur and missionary laborers in Boston and elsewhere, the furnishing of suitable rooms in the Temple for other missionary and benevolent societies, and generally to provide for the spiritual wants of the destitute.

The Tremont property is valued at $230,000. It brings in a large income for the benevolent objects for the promotion of which the society exists. The church worshiping in the Temple has a membership of 1500, and, under the able ministry of F. M. Ellis, D.D., one of the largest congregations in the United States. It is known and designated as the headquarters of New England Baptists. The Missionary Union, the New England departments of the Home Mission Society and the Publication Society, the Woman's Baptist Home and Foreign Missionary Societies, and the *Watchman* have rooms in the Temple. The Baptist Social Union, composed of representatives of the churches in Boston and its vicinity, holds its meetings in the Temple. It is the grand gathering-place of Boston Baptists, and the home of New England Baptist institutions. The conception of the plan which resulted in the Temple enterprise was a magnificent effort of consecrated genius. Its execution was worthy of the capital of New England, and its success deserves the devout gratitude of Baptists everywhere. There should be a Tremont Temple in every large city in the world. Timothy Gilbert, S. G. Shipley, Thomas Gould, and William S. Danwell are worthy of the affectionate remembrance of the friends of truth everywhere. The following are the present officers of the Evangelical Baptist Benevolent and Missionary Society in which is vested the ownership of the Temple estate:

President, James W. Converse; Secretary, Solomon Parsons; Treasurer, Joseph H. Converse; Directors, J. Warren Merrill, J. W. Converse, George W. Chipman, Joseph Story, Cyrus Carpenter, Joseph Sawyer, Lucius B. Marsh, Charles S. Kendall, S. S. Cudworth, George S. Dexter, Joseph Goodnow, Charles S. Butler, Moses C. Warren.

Trestrail, Rev. Frederic, many years one of the secretaries of the English Baptist Missionary Society, was born at Falmouth, England, in 1803, and became a member of the Baptist church there in his youth. The house of his parents was the resort of ministers and missionaries visiting the port, and a zeal for missionary work was enkindled in his heart from very early years. In his twenty-sixth year he entered Bristol College, having been called by the church to ministerial work some years previously. At the end of his course of study he supplied the church at Little Wild Street, London, for six months. Subsequently he became pastor of the church at Clipstone, whence he removed, after three years' service, to Newport, Isle of Wight, where he remained five years. At the request of the Baptist Irish Society he labored in Ireland four years, and when the secretaryship fell vacant he received the appointment. On Dr. Angus's retirement from the secretaryship of the Foreign Missionary Society, Mr. Trestrail was requested to take the office in conjunction with E. B. Underhill, LL.D. After twenty-one years of distinguished service Mr. Trestrail retired, and has since sustained the pastoral relation to the church at Newport, of which he was pastor nearly thirty years ago. He has received significant tokens of the high appreciation of his services, among which was the present, in 1871, of a check for £1350.

Triennial Convention, the common name of the "Baptist General Convention for Missionary Purposes."

Origin.—In 1813 American Baptists, who till then had been chiefly confined to *home* missionary work, without any general organization, were aroused as to their duty in respect to *foreign* missions as by an electric shock. News arrived that Mr. and Mrs. Judson and Mr. Rice, part of the first company of missionaries sent out by the American board, after leaving this country, through the study of God's Word had embraced Baptist sentiments, had been baptized at Serampore, and now appealed for support to their Baptist brethren in the United States. A profound sentiment was awakened. A local society was formed at Boston immediately, which assumed the support of Mr. and Mrs. Judson. Mr. Rice soon returned to America. On the 18th of May, 1814, a convention of thirty-three delegates "from missionary societies (of which many had been formed) and other religious bodies" of American Baptists, most of them eminent men, assembled at the First church in Philadelphia and organized "the General Missionary Convention of the Baptist denomination in the United States of America for Foreign

Missions." Its constitution provided for triennial meetings, for two delegates from each society or other religious body which should contribute annually $100, and for a board of managers to be called the "Baptist Board of Foreign Missions for the United States." The board appointed Mr. Rice as a missionary agent to raise funds in America, and adopted Mr. and Mrs. Judson as its missionaries to Burmah, they having been providentially guided to Rangoon, where they had settled.

History of the Convention.—Triennial meetings of the Convention and annual meetings of the board were regularly held. The presidents were Richard Furman, Robt. B. Semple, Spencer H. Cone, Wm. B. Johnson, and Francis Wayland. The corresponding secretaries, who were the chief executive officers, were Wm. Staughton, Lucius Bolles, Solomon Peck, and Robt. E. Pattison. Dr. Peck was secretary for the foreign department when the Convention was merged in the Missionary Union. The seat of operations was first at Philadelphia, then at Washington, and after 1826 at Boston.

The name and constitution underwent various changes, chiefly as operations were extended beyond, and afterwards restricted to, foreign (including American Indian) missions. The general principle as to membership was one delegate for each annual contribution of $100 continued for three years. Female auxiliaries sent delegates, but these were always men. After 1832 the society was known as "the Baptist General Convention for Foreign Missions." After 1841 the board appointed from its own members an "acting board" of fifteen persons residing in or near Boston.

In early times the annual reports gave the statistics of the denomination. These, in 1816, were, Associations, 126; churches, 2541; ministers, 1558; licentiates, 365; baptized, 4600; members, 158,508. State Conventions then scarcely existed.

In its later history the Convention was much distracted by the anti-slavery agitation. At length the acting board at Boston having declared, in response to queries of the Alabama Baptist Convention, that they would not appoint a slaveholder as a missionary, the brethren in the South, claiming that this decision infringed their equal rights, withdrew and formed the "Southern Baptist Convention." Whereupon, in 1846, the Triennial Convention was merged in a new organization of Northern Baptists, known as the American Baptist Missionary Union, meeting annually, and based solely on $100 life memberships, though this last feature has since been modified. The Union took up the work of the Convention, except in the case of a few missionaries amicably transferred to the Southern Convention.

Foreign Mission Work.—The first mission was the Burman, where Mr. and Mrs. Judson began their work alone, in danger and discomfort, in the midst of a barbarous and pagan nation. The first convert, Moung Nau, was baptized at Rangoon June 27, 1819, by Dr. Judson. Since then the work has spread to the Karens and other tribes, and has assumed magnificent proportions. In 1833 missions were planted in France, now specially hopeful, and in Siam, where a good work has been done. About 1835 great enthusiasm prevailed, and the work was much enlarged. An African Mission (in Liberia) had existed ever since 1823, though nearly every white missionary perished from the climate. In 1835 was begun the mission to China, now prosperous, after a long period of toil with scanty results. Also the mission in Germany, where a wide and wonderful work has been accomplished, spreading into Switzerland, Denmark, Sweden, Russia, and other countries. In 1836 was founded the Teloogoo Mission, so long a "forlorn hope," in which recently there have been such unparalleled displays of divine power. Also the mission in Assam, still prosecuted with much encouragement. In 1837 a mission was begun in Hayti, not long continued. Also in Greece, where no large results have been realized. Great pecuniary embarrassments followed this rapid enlargement, and a heavy debt long impeded the work. The foreign missions of American Baptists have been richly blessed, far beyond those of any other denomination or society. The most fruitful fields have been in Burmah, chiefly among the Karens, in Germany, in Sweden, and recently among the Teloogoos.

Persecution has often been experienced. Dr. Judson and his wife endured terrible sufferings at the hands of the Burman government. Our brethren in Germany, Sweden, Denmark, France, and Russia suffered long from arbitrary laws, fines, and imprisonments. But the results have been the furtherance of the truth and a wonderful advance as to religious liberty.

Indian Missions were projected as early as 1817, and have been carried on with great success, especially among the Cherokees, Creeks, and Choctaws. At the present time these missions (except in cases where they have been abandoned or have become unnecessary) are cared for by the American Baptist Home Mission Society or by the Southern Baptist Convention.

Home Missions were included in the sphere of the Convention in 1817, but were never extensively prosecuted, and were discontinued in 1826. In 1832 was formed the American Baptist Home Mission Society for that work.

Education.—The establishment of a collegiate and theological institution, in furtherance of ministerial education, was undertaken in 1817.

This soon resulted in founding what is now known as the Columbian University, at Washington, with a theological department. Mr. Rice was a general agent. After 1826 the Convention had no other care and control of the college than to select triennially fifty persons from among whom the trustees of the institution were elected. At the formation of the American Baptist Missionary Union this connection wholly ceased.

Bible Translation.—Baptists have always been foremost in the translation and circulation of the Scriptures. Dr. Judson at the earliest possible time began to translate, and to this work consecrated his splendid abilities with untiring devotion. Oct. 24, 1840, he completed the second and final revision of the Burmese Bible, a version declared by competent judges to be almost unequaled. The missionaries of the Convention and of the American Baptist Missionary Union have translated the Bible, in whole or in part, into the various Karen and other dialects used in Burmah, into Teloogoo, Siamese, Chinese, Japanese, and Assamese and other dialects used in Assam; also into various Indian languages in North America. These versions have been freely circulated. Scripture distribution has been extensively carried on in Europe, especially in Germany. This is still vigorously pursued by the American Baptist Missionary Union.

This Bible work, and especially the Burmese version of Dr. Judson, was the occasion of making the Convention the foremost asserter of the principle of absolute fidelity in translating the Word of God. The British and Foreign Bible Society having refused to aid in printing the English Baptist versions in India unless the words relating to baptism were transferred or translated in a manner acceptable to all denominations, the American Baptist Board at Salem in 1833 declared that its missionaries must translate the whole Bible faithfully and intelligibly, transferring no words capable of translation. In 1836 the board of the American Bible Society, following the example of the British and Foreign Bible Society, and with like unfaithfulness to the truth and injustice to its Baptist members and contributors, declared that it would aid only such versions as were conformed in their principles of translation to King James's version, at least so far as that they could be used by all denominations. They sent a check for $5000 to aid in printing Dr. Judson's version, under this restriction. The Baptist board returned the check. The Convention reaffirmed the resolutions of 1833, and called on the denomination for means to carry on a faithful Bible work, which were amply furnished, largely at first through the American and Foreign Bible Society, and later, also, through the American Bible Union. English Baptists, who had refused to mutilate their versions, soon after formed the "Bible Translation Society." In 1879 the American Baptist Missionary Union unanimously and solemnly reaffirmed the position taken by the Convention, and in 1880 the American Baptist Publication Society declared for a "pure translation of the Word of God." Thus the denomination has the high honor of being the champion, at home and abroad, of the great principle of faithful translation, and of steadfastly resisting the monstrous demand that the Word of God shall be translated to suit human opinions and convenience.

Funds.—Contributions received in 1814, $1239.29; in 1816, $12,236.84; 1820, $12,296.21. After that, for nine years, there was a falling off in the annual receipts ranging from $3615.27, the lowest, to $10,639, the highest. In 1830, $21,622. After that there were fluctuations, but on an average view steady growth, till in 1846 the sum reported was $100,150.02. Total contributions to the Convention for thirty-three years, $874,027.92.

Missionaries.—The whole number of missionaries and assistants (including, besides ordained ministers, printers, wives of missionaries, and other female assistants) appointed from 1814 to 1846 was (according to the best information attainable) 257 to foreign fields, including the Indians, and 16 to domestic. A few, not more than 12, did not enter on the service. This does not embrace the great number of native preachers and assistants raised up on the field. Among these missionaries are many names that will never die, as Judson, Wade, Mason, Boardman, Kincaid, Brown, Jones, Goddard, Oncken, Willard, McCoy, and many others.

Conclusion.—The Baptist General Convention has a record of missionary fidelity, self-sacrifice, and achievement for which American Baptists may well thank God. In 1845 its missions were 17, with 109 missionaries and assistant missionaries, of whom 42 were preachers; native preachers and assistants, 123; churches, 79; baptisms in one year, 2593; church members, over 5000,* though the number baptized from the beginning must have been something like double that; schools, 56; scholars, about 1350. This is small when compared with the present aggregate statistics of the American Baptist Missionary Union and Southern Convention, but great in itself and in its promise. The Triennial Convention through years of experiment and faith, of toil and trial, laid the foundations of the foreign mission work, on which its successors are now so prosperously building. (See articles on the MISSIONARY UNION, and on various mission fields, and also on the SOUTHERN BAPTIST CONVENTION.)

Trine Immersion was the baptismal usage of

---

* Probably over 1500 just baptized among the Karens by Myat Kyan were not yet reported as church members.

Christendom from the end of the second to the close of the twelfth century, except among some orthodox Spaniards, who dipped but once, and for their singularity had to enlist the influence of Pope Gregory the Great to protect them from being regarded as religious outlaws; the successors of these men, in the days of Charlemagne, were constrained to accept chastisement from the celebrated Alcuin for their departure from the general custom. In England trine immersion was the usage down to the Reformation. Prince Arthur, the brother of Henry VIII., and Margaret, queen of Scotland, his sister, and his children, Edward VI. and Queen Elizabeth, were baptized in this way. Trine immersion is universal in Russia now, and throughout the Greek and all the churches of the East. Before the end of the second century no Christian writer mentions it. Tertullian is the first author who names it.

If the Scriptures had been read after the third century as they were before it, and if baptism had been translated as it had been previously instead of being transferred, trine immersion could not have been perpetuated. It is one thing for an error to creep into the churches, but with a faithful Bible, widely read and reverenced, errors must perish. Jerome, in his Vulgate, transfers baptism, in Eph. iv. 5, "One Lord, one faith, and one *baptism*." If Jerome had been a faithful reviser, and had rendered baptism *immersion*, how difficult it would have been all over Western Europe, where his Bible was read, to see the words, "One Lord, one faith, *and one immersion*," and at the same time to practise *trine* immersion! Jerome saw the difficulty even with the Greek word baptisma in Roman letters in his Latin text; and in the Commentary which he added to his revised New Testament he gives explanations about the reason why, as he says, "we are immersed three times" (ter mergimur).

It would appear as if "baptize" was transferred into the Latin Vulgate to hide the meaning of the word. The ordinance had been enlarged by two extra dippings, and increased in other foolish ways, but the Greek word baptism covers everything to the masses of readers of the Vulgate.

Tertullian quotes from a Latin New Testament, two hundred years older than Jerome's, and his quotations from it, in his treatise "De Baptismo," always translate the verb "baptize." In the commission, Matt. xxviii., it reads, "Go, teach all nations, *immersing* them," etc. (tinguentes). Here Jerome has "baptizing them." In Matt. iii. 6, Tertullian quotes, "They were immersed (tinguebantur), confessing their sins," cap. 13, 20; Jerome again transfers "baptized." The New Testament quoted by Tertullian translates the word, and in all probability it was one of the versions the revision of which we have in the Vulgate edition. Jerome's translation of the Old Testament is more faithful than his revision of the New.

If Jerome had not transferred the baptismal words, and Christians had continued Bible-reading, trine immersion could not have been permanently sustained among Bible-loving Christians. There is absolutely nothing in the Scriptures to support it, and its historical chain of evidence has no links uniting it to the apostles or their times.

Trinity, The.—The London Baptist Confession of Faith of 1646, in Articles I. and II., says, "The Lord our God is but one God, whose subsistence is in himself, whose essence cannot be comprehended by any but himself; who only hath immortality, dwelling in the light, which no man can approach unto; who is in himself most holy, every way infinite in greatness, wisdom power, love; merciful and gracious, long-suffering, and abundant in goodness and truth, who giveth being, moving, and preservation to all creatures.

"In this divine and infinite being there is the Father, the Word, and the Holy Spirit, each having the whole divine essence, yet the essence undivided; all infinite without any beginning, therefore but one God, who is not to be divided in nature and being, but distinguished by several peculiar relative properties." In these terms our fathers described the great Jehovah,—one God in three persons.

The Trinity rests upon the divinity of the Father, Son, and Spirit. The Deity of the Father admits of no discussion. We shall briefly present the reasons which infallibly show that the Son is God, and that the Spirit is Jehovah.

The Son of God had the Almighty for the father of his human nature, and the word "son" always has reference to the humanity of Christ, either by anticipation or as representing an actual occurrence: "The angel answered and said unto her (Mary), 'The Holy Spirit shall come upon thee, and the power of the Highest shall overshadow thee; *therefore also* that holy thing which shall be born of thee shall be called the Son of God.'"—Luke i. 35. When the Saviour says, "My Father is greater than I," John xiv. 28, the use of the word "father" shows that it is his human nature that is compared to the divinity of the Father, and in that sense the Father is greater than the Son. He does not say that the Father is greater than the Word, the Scriptural name for the divine nature of Jesus. When he compares his divinity and the Father's, he says, "I and my Father are one." —John x. 30. "Philip saith unto him, 'Lord, show us the Father, and it sufficeth us.' Jesus saith unto him, 'Have I been so long time with you, and yet hast thou not known me, Philip?' He that hath seen me hath seen the Father, and how sayest thou then, 'Show us the Father?'" From this it is evident that the divinity of the Son is as like that of the Father as the resemblance between two new gold coins struck in the same mint, and having the same weight and the same stamp,—they are alike but not identical. All references to the subjection of the Son to the Father apply exclusively to his human nature. In his divinity he is a perfect likeness of the Father, "the brightness of his glory, and the *express image* of his person."—Heb. i. 3. The word translated "express image" is χαρακτήρ, and it teaches us that Christ bears the same "*stamp*" of divinity as his Father, that he is his "exact and perfect resemblance or *counterpart*." John says, "In the beginning was the Word, and the Word was with God, and the Word was God, and the Word was made flesh and dwelt among us."—John i. 1, 14. "The beginning" was before the birth of the ages and the worlds, and the Word existed then; and the Word was with God, as an individual member of the Trinity, and he was God; and the Word was made flesh in the person of Jesus. Christ, the Logos, is solemnly pronounced God by the inspired apostle. The word Logos means that Christ is the spokesman of the Trinity, the revealer of God, who manifested Jehovah in creation, in redemption, and in every appearance of the Deity under all dispensations.

Omniscience is ascribed to Christ: "We must all appear before the judgment-seat of Christ, that every one may receive the things done in his body, according to that he hath done, whether it be good or bad." —2 Cor. v. 10. To discharge the duties of this office he must have a perfect knowledge of every human heart, and of every event in the lives of all mankind. Little wonder that Peter said, "Lord, thou knowest all things, thou knowest that I love thee." —John xxi. 17. Everything in the dusty past, in the hazy present, in the misty future, in this earth and in every other world, is completely exposed before him.

Omnipotence belongs to him. Paul says of Christ, "By him were all things created, that are in heaven, and that are in earth, visible and invisible, whether they be thrones, or dominions, or principalities, or powers: all things were created by him and for him."—Col. i. 16. We can conceive no wider stretch of power than the ability needed to create the universe of worlds. And it has no equal unless it be the might needed to sustain his vast creations, and this is attributed to Christ. Paul describes him, "As upholding all things by the word of his power."—Heb. i. 3. The word of Jesus has sufficient weight to support myriads of worlds, and he must be the Almighty.

He is omnipresent: "Where two or three are gathered together in my name, there am I in the midst of them."—Matt. xviii. 20. Thus, on the Lord's day, he must be in a multitude of places at the same time.

He is unchangeable: "Jesus Christ, the same yesterday, to-day, and forever."—Heb. xiii. 5. Men are constantly varying in soul and body, God changes not. Christ is therefore the Lord God.

Jesus could not have *merits* before Jehovah if he were only a creature. God claims from each man the love and service of his whole being; if he gives it, he only renders to the Lord a just debt. He cannot go beyond it. "The blood of Jesus Christ, his Son, cleanses us from all sin" (1 John i. 7), and, as a consequence, he was above creature relations and obligations, and had something to which no being had a claim. He was omnipotent, and could bear the sin and pains which would have crushed the elect in the woes of unending despair; as God he had merits, as a creature he could have none. He is "the first and the last," the eternal Jehovah: "Being in the form of God, he thought it not robbery to be equal with God."—Phil. ii. 6. And as Paul again says, "Whose are the fathers, and of whom as concerning the flesh Christ came, who is over all, God blessed forever."—Rom. ix. 5. Little wonder that Thomas exclaimed, as he saw him after his resurrection, "My Lord and my God." —John xx. 28. The Saviour himself says, "The Father judgeth no man, but hath committed all judgment unto the Son, that all men should honor the Son even as they honor the Father."—John v. 22, 23. Christ has divine honors.

The Holy Spirit is Jehovah. "Except," says Christ, "a man be born of water and of the Spirit he cannot enter into the kingdom of God."—John iii. 5. It follows that all who are truly in Christ's gospel kingdom are born of the Spirit; and as the new birth is blessing men in myriads of places at the same time he must be everywhere present. And, besides, it is expressly said of those who are born again, that they are "born, not of blood, nor of the will of the flesh, nor of the will of men, but *of God*."—John i. 13. The Spirit, according to this statement, is God.

Peter asks Ananias, "Why hath Satan filled thine heart to lie to the Holy Spirit?" And he adds, "Thou hast not lied unto men, but unto God."— Acts v. 3, 4. According to inspired Peter, lying to the Holy Spirit was stating a falsehood to God. Peter on another occasion says, "Holy men of God spake as they were moved by the Holy Spirit."— 1 Peter i. 21. And Paul speaking of the writings of these very men, asserts that "all Scripture is given by inspiration of God."—2 Tim. iii. 16. It follows that he who moved holy men of old to write prophecy was God the Spirit. The Spirit, who regenerated Paul, and all believers, and who carries on the work of grace in many millions of earthly hearts at this hour, and who will continue it until they reach glory, is God, in all his greatness and love.

The three divine persons are one God. This is a great mystery; but not greater than the mysteries presented by some of the material objects around us. We cannot understand the mode by which certain agencies produce the wood of a tree, and its bark, foliage, blossoms, and fruit; or the way by which human food makes bones, and flesh, and skin, and hair, and nails. These are mysteries, but we believe them freely, though we do not understand the process of development. In one sense Father, Son, and Spirit are three persons, and in another they are one. "Webster's Dictionary" defines the Trinity as the union of three persons (the Father, the Son, and the Holy Spirit) in one Godhead, so that all the three are one God as to substance, but three persons as to individuality." This is in the main the doctrine of the trinity, as held by all the great communities of Christendom. St. Patrick is represented as illustrating this triple union by the shamrock. That kind of wild clover has a single stem, and three distinct and equal leaves; it is one at the stem, and three at the leaves. A converted Indian is reported to have compared this wonderful union of three sacred persons to a river in winter, frozen over, with snow lying on the ice; there was the running water, the crystal covering, and the snow, the three forms of one material element, being distinct from each other, and yet united in location and element. But this mystery is incapable of illustration. It is, however, clearly taught in the Scriptures.

The divine command to baptize is, "Go ye therefore and teach all nations, baptizing them in the name of the Father, and of the Son, and of the Holy Spirit."—Matt. xxviii. 19. In this "great commission" the Son and Spirit are placed on an exact equality with the Father. If he is Jehovah so are they. In opposition to all gainsayers, these words, till the death-knell of time shall be reached, will proclaim the Trinity of persons in the Godhead.

In 2 Cor. xiii. 14, we read, "The grace of the Lord Jesus Christ, and the love of God, and the communion of the Holy Ghost be with you all." Here the grace of Christ and the communion of the Spirit are placed on the same grand level with the love of the Father. If the words ran, "The love of God, the grace of Moses, and the communion of Elijah be with you all," they would outrage the whole Christian family, and proclaim an impossible equality of creatures with their Maker. The commission and the benediction show beyond all doubt the equal divinity of Father, Son, and Spirit. We might refer to many other Scripture testimonies, but our space is limited.

As the Bible repeatedly utters the sentiment in Deut. vi. 4, " Hear, O Israel, the Lord our God is one Lord," there must be in the Deity a perfect oneness; and as the same infallible authority places Father, Son, and Spirit as equals in *authority* in all other divine attributes and in *saving power*, that one God must exist in three persons. The writer once saw on a mountain-side three magnificent trees rising up apparently from one set of roots, and close to the roots there was a clear spring of delicious water; the sun was shining warmly and brightly, and the prospect was extensive and even glorious. The Trinity was suggested by the entire scene, and the saving office of each person of it: the grace of the Son, the love of the Father, and the communion of the Spirit making a fountain of life for the perishing, with healing beams from the sun of righteousness, and blessed prospects of the heavenly Canaan.

Tripp, Rev. Henry, from 1831 to his death, in 1863, had his home in Franklin, Lenawee Co., Mich., and his field of ministerial labor in that and in adjoining towns. He was a member of the church in Bristol, England, under Robert Hall's ministry; became a sailor in the English navy, and afterwards in our own under Decatur. He went early as a missionary from England to the West Indies, and was greatly loved by the negroes as their true friend, both there and ever afterwards in this country. He was tireless in his preaching labors, usually with no compensation but that received from the Master alone. His character and labors won the highest confidence of all, and he departed at eighty-two years of age, rich in the esteem of the good. His son, Robert Hall Tripp, has been Professor of Latin in the State University of Minnesota.

Tripp, Rev. John, was born in Dartmouth (now Fairhaven), Mass., March 25, 1761. He developed when very young an ardent passion for study, but the opportunities for gratifying his desire for learning were of the most limited character. Where, however, there is a will there is generally a way. He managed to procure some Greek and Latin books, and did what he could to obtain a knowledge of these languages. Then came the wish to be useful in the Christian ministry, and the desire ripened into a resolution, and the resolution into action. After preaching for a period in different places he was ordained in Carver, Mass., in September, 1791. Here he remained until the inadequacy of the support he received forced him to resign. His next settlement was in Hebron, Me., where he commenced his labors on the 3d of July, 1798. Here he had a most successful pastorate for forty-five years. The Spirit of God was richly poured out on his flock from time to time, and it grew in numbers and in grace. At the ripe old age of eighty-six and a half years he passed on to receive the reward of "a good and faithful servant." His death occurred Sept. 16, 1847.

Trotman, Rev. Quentin H.—The largest Association in North Carolina is the Chowan, which numbers upwards of 10,000 communicants, and for thirty years the most popular and influential man in this large body was Q. H. Trotman. He was born in Perquimans Co., N. C., Jan. 27, 1805. At the age of nineteen he married. He was at this time, and for several years afterwards, notorious for his wickedness, but it was his good fortune to have a praying wife, and the desire of her heart was accomplished when, in April, 1828, she saw him baptized by Rev. Robert T. Daniel. He began to preach in 1830, and having been called to the pastorate of Sandy Cross church, Gates Co., he was ordained by Revs. Jeremiah Ethridge and John Howell in 1831. With the exception of one year, 1833, spent in Raleigh as the pastor of the Baptist church there, he remained the pastor of the Sandy Cross church till just before his death. He lost his sight in 1859, but continued to preach, a friend reading for him. His wife died in February, 1862, and he quickly followed her, dying in the triumphs of faith on the 9th of May of the same year.

Mr. Trotman was a strong Baptist, and fond of controversy. So important a place did he believe baptism to occupy in the gospel system that he once told the writer that if he should remember, after death, that he had ever preached a sermon without mentioning baptism he would turn over in his grave. He was a natural orator of great power, a bold, fearless, generous, noble man, a born ruler of assemblies, a king among men, and he did more to extend Baptist principles in the State than any man of his day.

True, Rev. Benjamin Osgood, son of Reuben and Hannah (Duncan) True, was born in Plainfield, N. H., Dec. 21, 1845; fitted for college at Kimball Union Academy, N. H.; graduated from Dartmouth College in 1866, and from Rochester Theological Seminary in 1870; pastor at Baldwinsville, N. Y., 1870–73; pastor at Meriden, Conn., from 1873–79; traveled eight months in Europe in 1872, and one year in Europe and the East in 1879–80; settled with Central Baptist church in Providence, R. I., Sept. 1, 1880; an able and successful pastor.

Trustees are not officers of a church required by the New Testament, but by the state. Nor are they peculiar to churches; they must be appointed by all benevolent, incorporated societies, owning property. They have no authority over the membership of the church in any of their religious acts or privileges; they simply represent the church in managing its property. Neither have they any control over the minister in electing him, dismissing him, or interfering with his use of the church edifice for any of the regular religious services of his people, or for any of the proper and customary functions of his office. But in all other matters they represent the owners of the church property, and control it in accordance with the authority conferred upon them by law.

As their duties are purely financial, the congregation, as well as the church, is often represented in the board of trustees, and frequently this representation is demanded by the charter. This feature in the composition of boards of trustees works well where it has been tried; of course the majority of every such body will belong to the church.

Tryon, Rev. William Melton, eldest son of William and Jane (Philips) Tryon, was born in the city of New York on the 10th of March, 1809; was converted in his seventeenth year, and baptized by Rev. Chas. G. Sommers, D.D.; united with the church at Augusta, Ga., Dec. 30, 1832; was licensed; pursued studies for the ministry three years at Mercer Institute (now University); served for some time the churches at Washington, Lumpkin, and Columbus. In 1837 accepted the call to the pastoral care of Eufaula church; great success attended his labors. At the close of 1839 he accepted a call from the church at Wetumpka, Ala.; served one year. In 1841 he removed to Texas under the patronage of the American Baptist Home Mission Society, and settled in Washington County; served Independence, Providence, Burleson Co., and Providence, Washington Co., churches. In 1846 he removed to Houston, where he built up a large and prosperous church. For some time previous to his death he had a strong presentiment that he had not much longer time to live. When the yellow fever appeared in Houston, in 1847, he remained at his post discharging his duty until prostrated himself by the fever. After an illness of ten days, he died Nov. 16, 1847, in the thirty-ninth year of his age. Judge Baylor said of him, "He had a rare combination of excellences." "With him originated the project of establishing a Baptist university in Texas. He first suggested the idea, and I immediately fell in with it. Very soon after we sent a memorial to the Congress of the republic. As I was most familiar with such things, I dictated the memorial, and he wrote it."

Tucker, Rev. George, a prominent minister in Louisiana, was born in Tennessee, Dec. 12, 1806; has held many prominent pastorates, as Columbus, Miss., Jackson, Tenn., Marshall and Houston, Texas, and First Baptist church, Shreveport, La.; has presided over the Baptist Conventions of Mississippi and Louisiana; was a major in the Confederate army, and also postmaster at Shreveport, La. During his ministry he has baptized 1400 persons. He still does effective service as an evangelist.

Tucker, Henry Holcombe, D.D., LL.D., editor of the *Christian Index*, and perhaps the most brilliant Baptist Georgia has produced, was born in Warren County, May 10, 1819. His father was the son of a wealthy planter, and was a man of culture and elegant address. His mother was a daughter of Rev. Henry Holcombe, D.D. Both families came

HENRY HOLCOMBE TUCKER, D.D., LL.D.

from Virginia, where the former, especially, is well known and distinguished. When a mere child, young Tucker was taken to Philadelphia, where, with occasional interruptions, he remained until he was eighteen or nineteen years old.

He received his preparatory education at the academic department of the University of Pennsylvania. Having gone through a marvelous amount of most exacting drill in Latin and Greek, he entered the university as Freshman in 1834, and remained until Senior half advanced, when he entered the Senior class of Columbian College, Washington, D. C., where he was graduated A.B. in 1838. Years passed by, and in 1846 he was admitted to the bar in Forsyth, Monroe Co., Ga. He practised his profession until 1848, when he abandoned it to enter the Christian ministry. Selling his law books, he repaired to Mercer University to receive private instruction from its venerable president, Dr. Dagg. His desire was to enter fully and at once into the work of the Christian ministry, but strong pressure was brought to bear upon him, and he was induced reluctantly to give up his plans and become an educator. He taught young ladies for two or three years in the Southern Female College,

La Grange, Ga., and afterwards, for a short time, in the Richmond Female Institute, Richmond, Va. In 1856 he was elected Professor of Belles-Lettres and Metaphysics in Mercer University, which position he held until 1862, when the institution was, in a measure, broken up by the war. In 1866 he was unanimously elected president of Mercer University, and it was during his administration that the university was removed from Penfield to Macon. He has the credit of being one of the chief promoters of that change. Resigning the presidency of Mercer University in 1871, he went to Europe, taking his family with him, and was absent over a year. While there he assisted in the formation of the Baptist church in Rome, and baptized a man in the Tiber, probably the first time such an act was performed there since the days of the early Christians. While in Paris he officiated during a large part of one winter in the American chapel. In 1874 he was elected chancellor of the University of Georgia, a position which he filled four years. He is now the editor-in-chief of the *Christian Index*, Atlanta, Ga., in the zenith of his powers, and wielding a pen of unusual brilliancy.

Dr. Tucker was a regular pastor but once only, in 1854, at Alexandria, Va. Failing health compelled his resignation in less than a year, but he has never ceased to preach, and in many of the cities and towns on the Atlantic coast, from Maine to Georgia, he has proclaimed the truths of the gospel. His sermons always attract and delight large throngs by their originality, great vigor of thought and expression, and intense earnestness. A remarkable sermon of his on "Baptism," preached at Saratoga in 1879, was published by the American Baptist Publication Society, and commanded very general attention because of its originality. About 1855 he published a series of letters on "Religious Liberty," addressed to the Hon. Alexander H. Stephens, which were widely copied all over the United States. He has also published a number of sermons and addresses, one of the best of which is "The Right and the Wrong Way of raising Money for Religious and Benevolent Purposes." In 1868, J. B. Lippincott & Co. published for him a small volume entitled "The Gospel in Enoch," which excited much attention by its originality. Dr. Tucker's style of writing is polished and scholarly, racy, manly, pungent, and strongly Saxon, and, like his thoughts, logical and lucid. It never wearies, but always enchains and sparkles. His manner of speaking is bold, candid, and fearless. He is a logician by nature as well as by culture. His tone of mind is decidedly practical. He opposed secession, and debated the issue publicly; but when the war commenced he took sides with his own people, and, from first to last, co-operated heartily with the Confederates. One of the first to foresee the salt famine, he earnestly advocated the manufacture of salt, and soon became the president of a large salt manufacturing company. When smallpox prevailed in the country, he provided himself with pure vaccine virus and a lancet, and vaccinated all, old and young, black and white, whom he found willing to submit to the operation. He was the author and founder of the "Georgia Relief and Hospital Association," an institution which corresponded largely with the Northern Christian Commission, and which carried aid and comfort to tens of thousands of sick and wounded and dying Confederate soldiers. The institution was very popular with the Southern people, and enormous contributions to its support were made.

He was baptized, in 1834, in the river Delaware, by the elder Brantly, and was ordained at La Grange, Ga., in 1851. The degree of D.D. was conferred on him by the Columbian College, Washington City, in 1860, and the degree of LL.D. was conferred on him by Mercer University in 1876.

A most entertaining companion, he is a profound theologian, a well-informed man on all subjects, with a highly-cultured intellect.

Tucker, Rev. J. H., president of Keachi Female College, La., was born in Alabama in 1829; was educated at Union University, Tenn.; for several years engaged in teaching; in 1855 was Professor of Mathematics in Mount Lebanon University, La.; in 1856 pastor of First Baptist church, Shreveport, La.; elected president of Keachi Female College in 1858, a position which he held until the war. He resumed the position in 1871. While teaching he has preached regularly to churches in the surrounding country. He has served three years as president of Louisiana Baptist Convention, and six years as moderator of Grand Cane Association. He is a man of fine executive abilities, a clear head, sound judgment, and a kind heart.

Tucker, Rev. J. J., was born in Halifax, Vt., Oct. 6, 1827, and was baptized in 1835. He was for some time engaged in teaching and preaching, while he was fitting for college. He graduated at Williams College in the class of 1854. He studied for a while at Newton, and completed his theological education at Rochester, where he graduated in 1860. He was ordained pastor of the Pleasant Street church in Worcester, Mass., Aug. 30, 1860, where he remained a little more than a year. He became pastor of the church in South Dedham, Mass., in the fall of 1862, where he secured a strong hold upon the affections of his church. His health failing, his people gave him leave of absence, and he tried the effect of the climate of Minnesota, hoping that it might arrest the progress of the pulmonary disease from which he was suffering. The experiment proved a failure, and on his return home he was so prostrated that he was obliged to stop at Chicago, where he died Jan. 13, 1864.

Tucker, Rev. W. H., at present engaged as a missionary in New Orleans, was born in 1840. While a soldier in Virginia he was baptized by Dr. Burrows, in Richmond, in 1864, and began to preach at his home at Pontchoutula, La., in 1865; pastor at Magnolia, Miss., in 1868; subsequently pastor at Crawfordsville, Bethesda, and Sharon churches, in Columbus (Miss.) Association; edited the *Orphans' Friend* and preached at Orphan Asylum at Lauderdale, Miss.; pastor at Sardis and Batesville; after the death of the lamented Dr. Wilson, he supplied the Coliseum Place church, New Orleans, for some time, and is at present laboring in the city under appointment of the board of the Mississippi Baptist Convention.

Tuckers, The Five Brothers.—Elisha was born in Rensselaerville, Albany Co., N. Y., Dec. 24, 1794; when twelve years old he was baptized. He was ordained pastor of the church at Coventry, Chenango Co., Aug. 19, 1818; in August, 1822, he took charge of the church in Fredonia. In this as in the first field he labored successfully until the outbreak of that violent epidemic known as the anti-Masonic agitation in 1826. Mr. Tucker was a Mason, and he was a brave man, who would not permit even Baptists to restrain his freedom. He had to defend himself before a council, which acquitted him, and in a community which was prejudiced against an institution which he showed to be purely fraternal, and he survived the excitement and unkind feeling, and his reputation outlived that of the Masonic wrecks around who yielded to the tempest. In September, 1831, he became pastor of the First Baptist church of Buffalo, and in September, 1836, he entered upon the pastorate of the Second church of Rochester, and in 1841 he took charge of the Oliver Street church, N. Y. In 1848 he removed to Chicago; that year Madison University conferred upon him the degree of Doctor of Divinity. In the spring of 1851 he was compelled to suspend regular labor, though his church would not permit him to resign. He died Dec. 29, 1853. Dr. Tucker was an able, independent, courteous, devout, and successful minister of Jesus. His brother Levi was born in Broome, Schoharie Co., N. Y., July 6, 1804. He was converted in his sixteenth year. He graduated in Hamilton in 1829, and soon after he left college he was ordained at Deposit, N. Y. In the two years of his first pastorate he baptized 174 persons. In 1831 he accepted the call of the Blockley church, West Philadelphia, Pa., where he labored five years. From West Philadelphia he removed to Cleveland, O., and bestowed seven years of service upon the church in that city; his next field was Buffalo, to which he gave six years. In December, 1848, he took charge of the Bowdoin Place church, Boston, with which he continued till 1852, when, unable to work for the Master, he resigned. He visited Europe for health, and on his return his disease gained the mastery over him, and he passed away Aug. 20, 1853. In every pastorate he was successful. During his ministry he baptized 784, and he received into his churches 502 otherwise. Charles was born in Broome, Schoharie Co., N. Y., in April, 1809. He was converted in his nineteenth year; after a brief union with the Presbyterian Church he adopted Scriptural teachings about baptism, and was immersed into the fellowship of the church of Deposit. He was educated at Hamilton, N. Y., and Haddington, Pa.; in 1837 he was ordained to the pastorate of the church of Milesburg, Pa.; two and a half years later he took charge of the church at Jersey Shore; after six years' labor he was called to the Tabernacle church, Philadelphia, and in it he toiled for the Master until he was called home, in September, 1850.

Anson Tucker, another of the five brothers who were preachers, was an eloquent and useful minister. He was born at Broome, Schoharie Co., N. Y., June 8, 1811. His father, Charles Tucker, who lived to be eighty-four years of age, was himself in his later life a licensed preacher. At the time of his conversion, Anson Tucker was a teacher in Philadelphia, and attended upon the ministry of his brother, Rev. Levi Tucker. He studied for the ministry at Haddington College, and was ordained in 1835. His pastorates were at Sardinia and Lockport, N. Y., Norwalk, O., Adrian, Mich., Lafayette, Ind., and Dixon and Monmouth, Ill. He died at the last-named place April 23, 1858, aged forty-seven. His health had long been feeble, yet only three days previous to his death he administered the ordinance of baptism.

Silas Tucker, D.D., was born May 16, 1813. He was baptized in Philadelphia by his brother, Rev. Levi Tucker, pastor of the Blockley church, Dec. 22, 1833, and in the following year was licensed to preach by the same church. After studying one year with his brother he entered the Hamilton Literary and Theological Seminary, and studied there in the regular course until 1837. He then accepted a call to the pastorate of the church in Ohio City, now a part of Cleveland. From that time, during a period of thirty-five years, he was a diligent and successful minister and pastor, his death occurring at Aurora, Ill., Nov. 7, 1872. Among the churches which he served were Ohio City and Elyria, O., Laporte and Logansport, Ind., Racine, Wis., Naperville, Galesburg, and Aurora, Ill.

Tuggle, Hon. W. O., a lawyer of La Grange, Ga., a man of distinction in both Church and State. He was born in Henry Co., Ga., Sept. 25, 1841, and settled in La Grange, Troup Co., in 1852. He is a polished and well-educated gentleman. He left college to join the army in 1861, and served until the close of the war. For two years he served under Capt. John Morgan, and was with him in his great raids in Kentucky and Ohio, being captured twice, and escaping both times after one month's imprisonment,—the first time at St. Louis, Mo., and the second time at Indianapolis, Ind. In public life, he was a Presidential elector in 1876. He was a member of the State constitutional convention in 1877, and a delegate to the national convention in 1876 and in 1880, and was elected to the Georgia senate in 1868. As agent for Georgia he collected, in 1879, from the general government, a forgotten claim of $72,000; and he is at present the official agent and attorney of the Creek Nation in the Indian Territory.

He professed conversion and was baptized at the age of fifteen, joining the church at Rome in 1856. He has been a Sunday-school superintendent for sixteen years; for three years he was the secretary of the Southern Baptist Convention; and he is a member of the board of trustees for Mercer University.

Mr. Tuggle is just forty, and in the prime of life; he has a fine intellect and extensive literary acquirements.

Tunkers, that is, Dippers.—See GERMAN BAPTISTS.

Tupper, Charles, D.D., the father of Sir Chas. Tupper, Minister of Public Works, Canada, was born in Cornwallis, Nova Scotia, Aug. 6, 1794; converted Feb. 17, 1815; baptized by Rev. Edward Manning, May 14, 1815; commenced preaching March 24, 1816; ordained at Cornwallis, July 17, 1817; was successively pastor at Amherst, Nova Scotia, St. John, New Brunswick, and Tryon and Bedeque, Prince Edward Island, and Aylesford and Upper Wilmot, till 1870, fifty-three years in all; in his useful ministerial and missionary work he traveled 175,206 miles, preached 8147 sermons, and baptized 565 persons; has taught himself to read the Scriptures in Latin, Greek, Hebrew, Syriac, French, German, etc.; was editor of the *Baptist Magazine*, and secretary to the Foreign Missionary Board; published "Vindication of Baptist Principles," and he has written voluminously for the religious press. Dr. Tupper possesses the highest character for fidelity, piety, and prudence; he is now in the eighty-seventh year of his age.

Tupper, Henry Allen, D.D., was born in Charleston, S. C., Feb. 29, 1828. His early education was directed by Dr. Dyer Ball, for many years a missionary in the East, with whose daughters, afterwards Mrs. French and Mrs. Hopper, distinguished scholars in the Chinese language, he had the pleasure of pursuing his studies. He was baptized by Dr. R. Fuller in 1846; pursued his studies for a while in Charleston College, and then entered Madison University, from which he graduated in 1848, and from the theological seminary in 1850. All Dr. Tupper's previous training and associations led him to desire to labor in the foreign missionary field, but providential circumstances

HENRY ALLEN TUPPER, D.D.

seemed to prevent its fulfillment. For three years he was pastor of the Baptist church in Graniteville, S. C., and he removed thence to assume the pastorate of the church in Washington, Ga., where he was eminently successful in his labors. Repeated offers of professorships, secretaryships, and other pastorates failed to remove him from this field of labor, where he remained for nearly twenty years. Dr. Tupper at one time proposed to become head of a Christian colony to Japan, but the plan proving unsuccessful, he supported, at his own expense, a missionary among our own Indians, and also one in Africa, while at the same time he devoted much of his time to the spiritual welfare of the colored population in his own neighborhood. For many years he preached every Sunday afternoon exclusively to the children, and published many sermons for them. During the war he served as chaplain of the 9th Georgia Regiment of the Confederate army. On the death of Dr. J. B. Taylor, who had been the corresponding secretary of the Foreign Missionary Board of the Southern Baptist Convention from its origin, Dr. Tupper was invited to become his successor, and, being peculiarly fitted for that responsible position, he accepted it. He entered upon his duties in 1872, and his labors have been abundantly blessed. A new interest in missions has been quickened, and the contributions enlarged. Dr. Tupper has been an ardent friend of education. He was a trustee of Mercer University, Ga., and of the Baptist Theological Seminary, Greenville, S. C. He is now a trustee of Richmond College, and also of those two excellent institutions for young ladies, Hollins Institute and Richmond Institute. He has contributed also to the literature of the denomination, having published sundry sermons delivered before education societies, "The First Century of the First Baptist Church of Richmond, Va.," and, at the request of the Southern Baptist Convention, a work entitled "Foreign Missions of the Southern Baptist Convention." In 1852 Madison University conferred on him the degree of A.M. in course, and in 1870 the honorary degree of D.D. In 1855 he visited Europe. Dr. Tupper's wife is a sister of Rev. Dr. Boyce, of the seminary at Louisville, and it may interest his friends to know that the English poet Tupper is a relative of his. One who knew him well has said, "Dr. Tupper is essentially a missionary man, whom circumstances alone prevented from going to the missionary field. Personally, he is one of the most liberal of men, and before the war, when quite wealthy, he contributed thousands annually to the missionary cause."

Tupper, James, Esq., was born in Charleston, S. C., Dec. 9, 1819, and died at Summerville, about twenty miles from Charleston, Aug. 28, 1868. He united with the First Baptist church when about sixteen, and was licensed to preach a few years later, but never was ordained, preferring to be a lay preacher and deacon.

At about twenty-one he was admitted to practise law. He was soon after elected to the Legislature, and was chosen by that body a master in equity. He held this office with great honor to himself and advantage to the public to the time of his death. For several years he also held the important post of State auditor. No public officer ever gave more uniform satisfaction.

Had you seen him in the court-room you would have thought his head and heart were wholly devoted to the law. Had you heard him addressing his brethren in the prayer-meeting, from which he was never absent, or the children in the Sunday-school, of which he was the superintendent, you would have known that he had "determined to know nothing save Jesus Christ and him crucified." His evangelical and cheerful spirit spread as if by contagion and pervaded all present, whether in a social circle or in a large assembly. One of his noblest characteristics was his deep interest in children and young people, and few have had a greater or happier influence over them. Such was James Tupper. "Not slothful in business, fervent in spirit, serving the Lord."

It is true in a far wider sense than that in which the poet used the words, that "The evil that men

JAMES TUPPER, ESQ.

do lives after them." So, too, the good that the departed did will long survive him in his native city, and eternity alone can fully disclose it. "Blessed are the dead who die in the Lord!"

Turnbull, Robert, D.D., was born of Presbyterian parentage, in Whiteburn, Linlithgowshire, Scotland, Sept. 10, 1809; religiously educated; graduated at Glasgow University; attended the theological lectures of Chalmers at Edinburgh; while thus preparing for the ministry, by a study of the Bible he became a Baptist; preached a year and a half in Westmancotte, Worcestershire, England; in 1833, at the age of twenty-four, came to America; settled with the Second Baptist church in Danbury, Conn.; after two years was called to the First Baptist church in Detroit, Mich.; two years later became pastor of the South Baptist church in Hartford, Conn.; always prospered in his work; in 1839 settled with the Harvard Street church, Boston, Mass.; made a tour abroad; a ready writer; in July, 1845, returned to Hartford, Conn., and settled with the First Baptist church, and remained for about twenty-four years; here, as always, greatly blessed with revivals and church progress; on leaving the pastorate, in 1869, labored in various places, and with marked success in New Haven, leading to the formation of the Calvary Baptist church, and also at Ansonia; in 1872 was chosen to the secretaryship of the Connecticut Baptist State Convention, and successfully superintended its work; was a vigorous, eloquent preacher; a broad and thorough scholar; an easy, graceful, prolific writer; among his published works are "The Genius of Scotland," "The Genius of Italy," "Olympia Morenta," "Claims of Jesus," "Theophany, or Manifestation of God in Christ," containing a review of Dr. Bushnell's work, "The Pulpit Orators of France and Switzerland," "The Student Preacher," "The World we Live In," "Christ in History," and "Life-Pictures, or Sketches from a Pastor's Note-Book;" also wrote articles for the *Christian Review*, of which he was the joint editor for a time with Dr. J. N. Murdock; wrote much for the *Christian Secretary*; toiled for missions and for education; gifted, studious, devout, genial, progressive, persevering, benevolent, eloquent, full of love and faith; died in Christian triumph at Hartford, Conn., Nov. 20, 1877, aged sixty-eight; deeply mourned by the State and by all the Baptists of our country.

Turner, Prof. J. A., was born in Greensville Co., Va., Aug. 6, 1839. He entered Richmond College in 1856, and graduated as Bachelor of Arts in 1858, with the highest honors. In 1858 he matriculated at the University of Virginia, and received his diploma as Master of Arts in that institution in 1860. At the opening of the war Prof. Turner was offered the position of major, but declined the honor in order to share with a cherished companion the duties of a private position. Subsequently, however, he served as sergeant-major, and also as an officer of ordnance. He was a very active member of the Masonic fraternity, rising rapidly through its various grades, and it was while attending a meeting of this body in Richmond that he took a severe cold, which resulted in his death. In 1861 he took charge of the Mossy Creek Academy, Augusta Co., Va., which position he left to join the army. During the winter of 1863–64 he was engaged in teaching in the Roanoke Female College, Danville, Va., and subsequently he had charge of a school in Surry Co., Va. In 1867 he was invited to take charge of the chair of Latin and Modern Languages in Hollins Institute, Botetourt Springs, Va., which position he exchanged, in 1869, for that of the English and Modern Languages. Prof. Turner's health continuing gradually to decline, and his voice failing, he decided, at the earnest solicitation of friends, to spend the winter of 1877–78 in Florida. He did so, but found no relief, and, returning to spend his last hours with his family, he died May 5, 1878.

As an instructor, Prof. Turner was active and enthusiastic, interesting in an unusual degree those committed to his care, and so prompt in meeting all his engagements, in official and private life, that the students playfully named him their "timepiece." As an author and writer for prominent literary and religious journals, he was very favorably known. In 1875 he published a valuable little treatise on the principles of punctuation, in which he has based his rules, in every case, upon the laws of grammatical analysis. He had in course of preparation several other small works on versification, on poetry, and on figures of speech, also lectures on general philology, English philology, French grammar, and on English literature. He was also a frequent contributor to *The Nation* and *Appleton's Journal*, New York, and to the *Atlantic Monthly* and the *Literary World*, of Boston.

Prof. Turner was baptized by the Rev. Dr. Jeter while still a student at Richmond College, and he became a most efficient and industrious Christian worker. As deacon, superintendent of the Sunday-school, leader in the prayer-meeting, moderator of Associational meetings, lecturer before the Ministers', Deacons', and Sunday-School Institute, in which he was so often requested to discuss doctrinal questions and present exegeses of obscure Biblical passages, he was recognized as the finished scholar, the learned Bible student, and the devoted Christian. Many of the various papers prepared by him were considered of so much value as to be requested for publication in pamphlet form for general circulation.

Prof. Turner's second wife was the daughter of Prof. Cocke, of Hollins Institute, a lady of culture, who shared his labors as instructor in that excellent institution, and who, with three children, survives him.

Turner, Gov. Thomas, chief magistrate of Rhode Island, was born in Warren, R. I., Oct. 24, 1810. Early in life he engaged in business pursuits, becoming a merchant in his native place, and meeting with deserved success in his vocation. After several years of mercantile life, he retired from business, and accepted the presidency of an extensive insurance company. He retained this position during the remainder of his life. He held various offices of trust in banking and railroad and manufacturing corporations, and was frequently chosen to represent his native town in the General Assembly of the State. From 1857 to 1859 he was lieutenant-governor of the State, and the two years following he was governor. President Lincoln appointed him first collector of the internal revenue of the first district of Rhode Island. The duties of the many offices which he held were discharged with fidelity and without ostentation. Gov. Turner was a subject of the great revival of 1857-58, and united with the Baptist church in Warren, one of the old, historic churches of the State. In all measures tending to promote the prosperity of the denomination he took a deep interest. He was

GOV. THOMAS TURNER.

for some time a member of the board of the Missionary Union. In 1862 he was chosen a trustee of Brown University, and continued in office until his death, which took place at Warren, Jan. 3, 1875.

Turner, Rev. Wm., was born in Davidson Co., N. C., June 23, 1816; baptized by Josiah Wiseman, May 4, 1834; began to preach in 1840; was ordained in 1844. His ministerial labors have been in the counties of Davidson, Davie, Yadkin, Forsythe, and Guilford, and they have been eminently successful. He has been moderator of the Liberty Association for fifteen years, and pastor of Jersey church for thirty years. He is still an active and useful preacher of the gospel.

Turney, Edmund, D.D., was born in Easton, Conn., May 6, 1816; was educated at Hamilton; was pastor of the South church, Hartford, Conn., and in Granville, and of the Broad Street church in Utica, N. Y. In 1850 he was appointed Professor of Biblical Criticism in the seminary, Hamilton. From 1853 he was five years professor in Fairmount Theological Seminary, O. In 1865 he began the first organized effort for the education of colored teachers and preachers in Washington, D. C. No society encouraged him to commence a work upon which the richest blessings rested. How nobly he toiled in that field, with no assured support, and sometimes, we fear, with want threatening him, the writer and a few others know. He seemed inspired with the conviction that God had specially intrusted this great business to him, and nothing could change his impressions of duty. He would have suffered martyrdom while swayed by this holy purpose rather than show recreancy to the will of heaven. Dr. Turney was conscientious to a fault. He had genius of a high order, and his heart was the throne of Jesus. He died Sept. 28, 1872.

Dr. Turney published several works on Christian baptism and three volumes of poetry.

Turpin, Dr. William Henry, a prominent deacon of great moral worth, who was, for many years, a member of the Augusta church, was born in the vicinity of Richmond, Va., in March, 1790. At fifteen years of age he removed to Augusta, Ga., and, entering into mercantile business, succeeded in amassing a large fortune. In 1816 he married Miss Mary Ann D'Antignac, and in 1824 he was converted under the preaching of the elder Brantly, and made a profession of faith in Christ. He united with the Baptist church at Augusta, of which he remained a most useful and conscientious member until his death in 1866, being for nearly forty years a deacon of the church.

It may be said of Dr. Turpin that he rendered the Augusta church more essential service than any other of its members, unconnected with the ministry, since the church was founded. With his ample means he was always ready to make good any deficiency in the salaries of the pastors, and in the other expenses incidental to the maintenance of worship. His business capacity and excellence of judgment were of incalculable benefit to the church; and his wisdom in council, united with his politeness and courtesy of demeanor, and his humility and peace-loving disposition, always exercised a beneficial influence in the church conferences and over the members.

New members were attracted to the church by the simple fact of his connection with it. His character as a Christian and a gentleman of the utmost integrity and honor stood out in such bold relief that the church itself was benefited by it in the eyes of the community.

He was ready to aid every good cause, and no application to him for any such cause ever failed to meet a favorable response. He was one of the earliest and largest contributors towards Mercer University, and it was his habitual custom to send $200 to each of the boards of the Southern Baptist Convention on the first day of every year. His house was the centre of an extensive and generous hospitality, and Luther Rice used to visit him every year, and was accustomed to speak of Dr. Turpin's house as his Georgia home.

With much that was calculated to make a man proud,—wealth, position in society, hosts of friends and admirers,—Dr. Turpin was utterly unassuming; his humility was most unaffected. But the crowning excellence and chief glory of his Christian character was his unwavering trust in God. When grief rent his bosom,—and he had some of the severest kind,—and when the desolations of war threatened his home and his fortune, his comfort was that God was king, and that all things were working together for the good of those who love him.

God allowed this bright light to shine for many years. Rev. James E. Welch said, "I have been traveling all over this country constantly for the past twenty years, and I know multitudes of people, but I have seen but one Wm. H. Turpin." In 1866 an asthmatic affection rendered Dr. Turpin more and more feeble, and it became apparent to himself and family that he could not rally. Calmly, cheerfully, sublimely he accepted the situation, and as the end drew nigh, in full possession of all his mental faculties, he sent farewells and benedictions to the absent, and then resigned himself to the sleep of the Christian, like one

"Who wraps the drapery of his couch about him
And lies down to pleasant dreams."

Tustin, Rev. Francis Wayland, Ph.D., Professor of the Greek Language and Literature in the university at Lewisburg, Pa., was born in Philadelphia in 1834. His early education was received in the public schools of his native city. In 1850 he entered the academy at Lewisburg, and graduated from the university in 1856, with the highest honors of his class.

In 1857 he was made tutor in the college, being the first alumnus of the university in its faculty. In 1860, there being a vacancy in the department of Natural Sciences, caused by the accession of Dr. Loomis to the presidency, Prof. Tustin was elected to fill the chair. This position he held for fourteen years, and in the language of Dr. Loomis, "made the department of Natural Sciences in the university." Although his principal work in these years was in his own department, yet he was known as a fine classical scholar, and frequently assisted Prof. Bliss in the Greek and Latin classes. In 1874, his eyesight becoming seriously affected by the chemical fumes of the laboratory, he was obliged to relinquish the department of Natural Sciences. At that time, Dr. Bliss having accepted the chair of Biblical Interpretation in Crozer Theological Seminary, and the trustees wishing to retain Prof. Tustin's services, he was elected to the chair of the Greek Language and Literature, which position he has since so worthily filled. During the absence of Dr. Loomis in Europe for the greater part of the college year, Prof. Tustin acted as president of the university, and presided at the commencement of 1879. His administration won the praise and gratitude of all connected with the university. In 1879 his fellow-members of the faculty and the curators conferred upon him the degree

PROF. FRANCIS WAYLAND TUSTIN, PH.D.

of Doctor of Philosophy. In 1866, by a council called by the First Baptist church of Lewisburg, he was ordained to the gospel ministry. In addition to his other labors he has, for more than twenty years, managed the finances of the Baptist church, and was largely instrumental in the erection of their handsome church edifice. During these years Prof. Tustin has had several offers to other positions, which he has declined. His life has been given to the building up of the university and the Baptist cause in Lewisburg. Prof. Tustin has great ability and fine scholarship, and he has rendered valuable services to the Baptists of Pennsylvania.

Tutt, Rev. B. G., was born in Cooper Co., Mo., Feb. 11, 1839; professed faith in Christ and united with the church at Liberty, Mo., while at William Jewell College, in 1854, and was baptized by Dr. E. S. Dulin; attended Westminster College, at Fulton, Mo., in 1857; was ordained to the work of the gospel ministry in 1869; was called to the pastorate of the Concord Baptist church in December, 1860, and continued in that relation until January, 1876, in the mean time preaching at intervals to Mount Nebo church, in the same county.

The result of fifteen years' labor at Concord was, first, the gathering of a large and influential membership; second, the building up of a flourishing and effective Sunday-school; third, the erection of a comfortable and commodious house of worship, which was dedicated without a dollar's indebtedness; fourth, bringing the membership into hearty and intelligent co-operation with the benevolent enterprises of the denomination.

In April, 1876, he was called to the pastorate at Marshall, Mo., in which field the labors of four years have developed some very encouraging features.

Twiss, Rev. J. S., settled in Ann Arbor in 1830; was from Sennett, N. Y. He was a preacher of noted strength and vivacity, and a man of the highest moral integrity and Christian probity. He was intelligent and fearless in the performance of duty, he hated oppression and everything which degrades man. His righteous and intense sentiments often took forms of expression which were never forgotten. His powers of debate and his natural delivery made him noted as a speaker, while in conversation few cared to meet the sharpness of his lance. His death occurred in 1857.

Tyler, Rev. Mansfield, is about fifty-five years old; a slave before the war; limited opportunities; a man of strong natural ability, of firm, Christian character, fine sense, well instructed in the Scriptures, gifted in natural eloquence, held in high estimation by whites and blacks; a man of great prudence. He has for several years been president of the Colored Baptist Convention of Alabama, and is a good presiding officer. He resides at Lowndesborough.

Tynes, Rev. W. E., pastor at Canton, Miss., of which State he is a native, was born in 1848. After receiving a good academic education he commenced the practice of law; in 1871 began to preach, and became pastor at Osyka, Miss.; thence at Jackson, La., and Baton Rouge. He returned to Mississippi in 1876. He was an evangelist in Southern Mississippi and in Eastern Louisiana one year; then two years pastor at Summit, Miss. In 1878 he was called to his present field.

Tyree, Cornelius, D.D., was born Sept. 14, 1814, in Amherst Co., Va. He united with the Mount Moriah church in 1832, although strongly persuaded by his family and friends, all ardent Methodists, to join the Methodist Church. After receiving an excellent training in the schools of the neighborhood, he was a teacher for two years near Lynchburg. In the fall of 1837 he was licensed to preach by the Lynchburg church, and sent to William and Mary College. In the fall of 1838 he entered the Columbian College, and pursued the partial course. In 1839 he was appointed by the General Association missionary for the counties of Greenbrier and Monroe, where his labors were greatly blessed. He was ordained in September, 1839, at Amwell church, Fayette Co.

In the latter part of this year he was transferred to Rockbridge County as missionary. In 1840, under his ministry, two new churches were organized, one at Lexington and one at Cow Pasture Bridge, Va., of which churches he remained pastor five years. Here Dr. Tyree baptized Prof. G. E. Dabney and many of the students of the Military Institute of Lexington. In 1845 he succeeded Rev. Jesse Witt as pastor of the churches in Powhatan County, with two of which he remained twenty-seven years. While with these churches he also preached extensively within and without the State as an evangelist, and in the meetings in which he participated not less than 3000 were hopefully converted. Dr. Tyree has been busy with his pen also, although his pastoral and evangelistic labors have been so pressing. In 1858, Sheldon & Blakeman published his "The Living Epistle," with an introduction by Dr. R. Fuller. A number of his sermons have been published in the *Baptist Preacher* and in the *Religious Herald*. A valuable little tract on "Baptism and Restricted Communion" has also been widely circulated. Dr. Tyree has also prepared a small work, "Believe and Live," and a volume of quickening sermons preached at protracted meetings, both which he hopes soon to publish. Some of these sermons have been greatly blessed in the conversion of souls. In the spring of 1872 he removed to Bedford Co., Va., and became pastor of the Liberty church, one of the most thriving bodies in the State. Dr. Tyree has been eminently successful in his labors. In 1869 the Columbian College conferred upon him the degree of D.D.

U.

Underwood, Rev. Enoch Downs, pastor of the Baptist church at Wauwatosa, Wis., and the oldest settled minister in the State, was born in Monongahela Co., Va., in 1817. When a boy of seven years he came with his father's family to Vermilion Co., Ill., and at nineteen he removed again with his father and family to Milwaukee Co., Wis., where he has since resided. Mr. Underwood obtained a hope in Christ after he reached manhood, and united with the Baptist Church. In 1845 he took an active part in forming the Baptist church in Wauwatosa, of which he was a constituent member. This church licensed him to preach, and in 1849 called him to the pastorate and ordained him to the work of the ministry.

Mr. Underwood has never been connected with any other church either as member or minister. His pastorate has been continued for thirty-one years. He is finely balanced intellectually and spiritually, and it would be difficult to determine to which he is most indebted for his power as preacher, his attainments or his natural abilities. He has achieved the rare art of making the most of each. He delivers his messages to his flock in the plain and easily understood language of the people, but with great analytical power and logical force. His hearers are always sure to have the gospel purely, simply, and strongly declared to them. He preaches Jesus. By his gentle and kind spirit, breathing in all his utterances the peace and love of the gospel, he has won the confidence and affection of the ministers and churches of the State. He has frequently been called to preside over the Association of which he is a member, and for many years has been a trusted member of the board of the Convention.

Underwood, Rev. John Levi, as a preacher, is clear, animated, bold, earnest, and tender, showing much independence and freshness of thought. As a pastor, he is faithful, laborious, and sympathetic, making himself beloved by his people. As a man, he is friendly and warm-hearted. He was born in Alabama, March 27, 1836, of Presbyterian parents; graduated at Oglethorpe University, Ga., in 1857, with the highest honors of his class; was converted and joined the church in 1857; studied theology two years at the Columbia, S. C., Theological Seminary; studied one year at Berlin and Heidelberg, Germany; spent eight months at Paris, France, then came home and joined the Confederate army as a private, after being ordained to the ministry. He became a chaplain in 1862, but resigned on account of bad health in 1863. Since the war he has been teaching, preaching, and farming. He has a pleasant home near Camilla, Ga. He has had charge of the churches at Bainbridge and Cuthbert, Ga., but now serves the church at Camilla, and also those at Evergreen and Cairo, in the same neighborhood.

Uniformity, Act of.—When Charles II. was restored to the throne of England the National Church had few Episcopal clergymen worshiping at her altars. More than 7000 of her ministers had taken the Solemn League and Covenant. The forms of worship differed considerably. But after the Restoration the tyrannical men who ruled Church and State were determined to drive from the Anglican Establishment every man who would not conform to extreme Episcopalianism.

The Act of Uniformity, which received the royal assent April 19, 1662, required all clergymen to profess before their congregations " their unfeigned assent and consent to the use of all things in the Book of Common Prayer, and prescribed by it, and to the form or manner of making, ordaining, and consecrating bishops, priests, and deacons."

All persons " holding any office in any way connected with the church," and every teacher of a public or private school, and all tutors in private families were required to make a declaration that " it was not lawful on any pretense whatsoever to take arms against the king," and that they " will conform to the liturgy of the Church of England."

They were also compelled to declare that the oath to maintain the Solemn League and Covenant was a nullity, and that it was " imposed upon the subjects of this realm against the known laws and liberties of this kingdom."

This law was one of the most unrighteous enactments that ever disgraced the statute books of any civilized nation. In it the king and his Parliament wickedly violated the most sacred engagements ever made by man. The principal sufferers under this infamous act were the Presbyterians, who had foolishly placed the king upon the throne. The law was expressly contrived to ruin all Nonconformist clergymen and their families.

On the 24th of August, 1662, the act went into effect. That was a time of fierce trial to thousands of godly ministers and teachers, and to many thousands of their wives and children. The number of ministers who forsook their ecclesiastical residences and church edifices on the day of royal, and of Episcopal vengeance, has been estimated at from 2000 to 2500.

These thousands of pastors going forth from their homes, sacred to them by many precious associations, surrounded by their wives and children, and in not a few instances by their aged parents, with nothing before them but hunger, and rags, and persecution, exhibited to the eye of Jehovah the most pitiable, and at the same time the most glorious scene upon which its lightning glances had ever fallen. They could not be hypocrites, for they loved the God of truth, and they and theirs must become living sacrifices. There were Baptist ministers among these saintly men, though most of our brethren had previously been removed. Henry Jessey, A.M., was ejected from St. George's, Southwark; Francis Bampfield, M.A., from Sherborne, in Dorsetshire; Thomas Jennings, from Brimsfield, in Gloucestershire; Paul Frewen, from Kempley, in the same county; Joshua Head, the place of ejectment uncertain; John Tombes, B.D., from Leominster, in Herefordshire; Daniel Dyke, M.A., from Hadham, in Hertfordshire; Richard Adams, from Humberstone, in Leicestershire; Jeremiah Marsden, from Ardesly, in Yorkshire; Thomas Hardcastle, from Bramham, in Yorkshire; Robert Browne, from Whitelady Aston, in Worcestershire; Gabriel Camelford, from Stavely Chapel in Westmoreland; John Skinner, from Weston, in Herefordshire; —— Baker, from Folkestone, in Kent; John Gosnold, of the Charter House and Pembroke Hall, Cambridge; Thomas Quarrel, from a place in Shropshire; Thomas Ewins, from St. Evens' church, Bristol; Lawrence Wise, from Chatham Dock, Kent; John Donne, from Pertenhall, in Bedfordshire; Paul Dobson, from the chaplaincy of the college, Buckinghamshire; John Gibbs, from Newport Pagnell; John Smith, from Wanlip, Leicestershire; Thomas Ellis, from Lopham, Norfolk; Thomas Paxford, from Clapton, Gloucestershire; Ichabod Chauncy, M.D., chaplain to Sir Edward Harley's regiment; Thomas Horrexe, from Maldon, in Essex; Mr. Woodward, from Southwood; E. Stennett, from Wallingford; B. Cox and about thirteen others were ejected in Wales. These men, with the ardent love which flamed in the hearts of martyrs, gave up their all for Christ. The National Church merely gave them a preaching-house, a place in which they were chaplains. They had churches,—living, godly communities of which they were pastors, entirely distinct from the parish churches in which they preached.

Union, The Baptist, of Canada.—After much preliminary discussion, this society was formed at the twenty-eighth annual meeting of the Baptist Home Missionary Convention of Ontario, by the joint action of that body and the Convention East, the latter being represented by an influential delegation. An act incorporating the Union was passed during the ensuing session of the Dominion Parliament, and, according to the terms of the act, the first annual meeting was held, in October, 1880, in the Jarvis Street church, Toronto. This society seeks to unite within itself, as far as practicable, the whole Baptist body of Canada, for the more successful promotion of all denominational interests and enterprises. At present (1881), however, it only embraces the churches of Ontario and Quebec. Its membership consists of all pastors, all ministers engaged in other departments of denominational work, all persons paying $30 at one time to its funds (life members), and delegates from the churches, appointed according to the numerical standing of the bodies they represent. The Union elects the following boards: Home Missions West,

Home Missions East, Foreign Missions, Manitoba and Northwest Missions, Grande Ligne Mission, trustees of the Canadian Literary Institute, Superannuated Ministers' and Church Edifice Funds. The societies by which these boards were formerly elected having merged their existence into that of the Union, so far as existing legislation will admit, brief sketches of such of the principal ones as are not noted elsewhere will be in place here.

Regular Baptist Home Missionary Convention of Ontario.—This society may be regarded as the parent of most of the others, and for many years it was the only general denominational organization in Western Canada. It was formed, in 1851, in an old Presbyterian meeting-house in the city of Hamilton. There appears to be no published record of its work during the first four years of its existence; but from 1855 to the formation of the Baptist Union it has been ascertained that over 5000 persons were baptized by the missionaries, 120 churches were organized, and more than 100 places of worship erected, many of them in important towns and centres. During this period the amount appropriated by the Convention towards the support of missionary pastors and other laborers on mission fields exceeds $100,000. The great advance made by the denomination in the province of Ontario since 1851 is undoubtedly due in a large measure to the instrumentalities employed by this society. The following Associations are included within its boundaries: Western, Middlesex and Lambton, Elgin, Grand River, Brant, Midland-Counties, Huron, Niagara, Toronto, East Ontario, and Amherstburg, containing in all about 300 churches and 22,000 members.

Canada Baptist Home Missionary Convention, East.—The territorial area of this Convention consists of the province of Quebec and the portion of Ontario lying east of Kingston, thus embracing 3 Associations,—Central Canada, Ottawa, and Danville,—64 churches, and nearly 4800 members. It was formed April 28, 1858, in the St. Helen Street Baptist church, Montreal, at a meeting specially convened for the purpose by a committee of brethren belonging to that church. There were present ten ministers and delegates from fourteen churches, who were entirely unanimous as to the expediency of organizing for home mission work. The subsequent history of the society has demonstrated the wisdom of its founders, and exhibited, in a striking manner, the faith and liberality of its handful of supporters. Up to the time of its affiliation with the Baptist Union $33,000 had been paid out in support of missionaries and in aid of weak churches, and much good accomplished among the small Protestant population of this section of Canada.

Baptist Foreign Missionary Society of Ontario and Quebec.—In the year 1858, at the annual meeting of the Convention West, the question was raised, "Ought Canadian Baptists, as such, to have a Foreign Missionary Society, or ought they to co-operate with existing organizations?" Its fuller consideration was deferred to the following year; but for some reason the discussion was not then resumed, and the subject remained in abeyance. Some years afterwards a strong desire to be employed in the foreign field was expressed by one of the senior theological students of the Canadian Literary Institute. This led to an earnest reconsideration of the whole matter, and in October, 1866, at the fifteenth annual meeting of the Home Missionary Convention, held in Beamsville, Ontario, the Foreign Missionary Society was organized, as an auxiliary to the American Baptist Missionary Union. The first missionary sent out was the Rev. A. V. Timpany, the student to whom reference is made above. He was designated in October, 1867, and appointed to the Teloogoo field in the Madras presidency, British India. Two years afterwards he was followed by Rev. John McLaurin. In 1874 a chain of providential circumstances led to the formation of an independent Canadian Teloogoo mission in the city of Cocanada, 200 miles north of Ongole. A commencement had been already made in Cocanada by the five years' faithful toil of Thomas Gabriel, a well-educated and zealous native, who had gone to this populous heathen city on his own responsibility. Under his labors a church of 150 members had been gathered, several native preachers raised up, and a few native schools established. At his urgent request the Baptists of Canada, with the approbation of the American Baptist Missionary Union, sent Mr. McLaurin to this inviting field, and assumed the entire control of the movement. Subsequently, Mr. Timpany also withdrew from the service of the Union, and went to Cocanada under the direction of the Canadian society. The infant mission was reinforced by Rev. George F. Currie, B.A., in 1876, and by Rev. John Craig, B.A., in 1877. Mr. Currie is stationed at Tuni, and Mr. Craig at Akidu.

United States, The Constitution of; Aid given by the Baptists in its Adoption.—It is a matter of surprise to-day that the wisdom of this instrument was ever doubted, or that it should have been opposed by any number of intelligent and patriotic men. The two great States that supported the Revolution, Virginia and Massachusetts, were equally divided about the Constitution, and some of the best men in these powerful centres of political life regarded it with unmixed alarm, and resisted it with all their influence and eloquence.

In Massachusetts, the convention called to ratify the Constitution assembled on the 9th of January,

1788. It was composed of nearly four hundred members. It possessed much of the intellect and patriotism of the State. The debates lasted for a month, and the contest was carried on with great earnestness. "The prohibition of religious tests in the Constitution made it many enemies in Massachusetts."* The entire United States took the deepest interest in the deliberations. It was universally felt, as Dr. Manning expressed it, that "Massachusetts was the hinge on which the whole must turn," and that if she rejected the Constitution it would be discarded in the other States. The Baptists held the balance of power in the convention, and in Massachusetts they were generally opposed to the Constitution. The Baptist delegates were chiefly ministers, who had the highest regard for Dr. Manning. And he, fully convinced that nothing but the new Constitution could save the country from anarchy, spent two weeks in attendance upon the convention, and he and Dr. Stillman exerted themselves to the utmost to persuade their brethren to support the Constitution. With the Rev. Isaac Backus, the fearless friend of the Baptist cause and of liberty of conscience, they set out, and they met with success in several cases, and the Constitution was adopted by a majority of nineteen votes. There were 187 yeas and 168 nays on the last day of the session, and before "the final question was taken, Gov. Hancock, the president, invited Dr. Manning to close the solemn convocation with thanksgiving and prayer." Dr. Manning addressed the Deity in a spirit glowing with devotion, and with such lofty patriotism that every heart was filled with reverence for God and admiration for his servant. And such an effect was produced by this prayer that, had it not been for the "popularity of Dr. Stillman, the rich men of Boston would have built a church for Dr. Manning."† There is a strong probability that the Baptists of the convention would have turned from Isaac Backus, and changed the insignificant majority into a small minority, if it had not been for Manning and Stillman.

In Virginia the opposition to the Constitution was led by more popular men; but the parties, otherwise, were about equal in strength. The convention met in Richmond, in June, 1788. The most illustrious men in the State were in it. Patrick Henry spoke against the Constitution with a vehemence never surpassed by himself on any occasion in his whole life, and with a power that was sometimes overwhelming. Once, while this matchless orator was addressing the convention, a wild storm broke over Richmond; the heavens were ablaze with lightning, the thunder roared, and the rain came down in torrents; at this moment Henry seemed to see the anger of heaven threatening the State if it should consummate the guilty act of adopting the Constitution, and he invoked celestial witnesses to view and compassionate his distracted country in this grand crisis of her history. And such was the effect of his speech on this occasion that the convention immediately dispersed.‡ The convention, when the final vote on ratification was taken, only gave a majority of ten in favor of the Constitution. Eighty-nine cast their votes for it, and seventy-nine against it.§

James Madison possessed the greatest influence of any man in the convention; had he not been there Patrick Henry would have carried his opposition triumphantly; and Madison was there by the generosity of John Leland, the well-known and eccentric Baptist minister. Madison remained in Philadelphia three months with John Jay and Alexander Hamilton, preparing the articles which now make up *The Federalist;* this permitted Henry and others to secure the public attention in Virginia, and, in a large measure, the public heart. Henry's assertion that the new Constitution "squinted towards monarchy" was eagerly heard and credited by many of the best friends of freedom; and when Madison came home he found Leland a candidate for the county of Orange, the constituency which he wished to represent, with every prospect of success, for Orange was chiefly a Baptist county. Mr. Madison spent half a day with John Leland, and the result of this interview was that Leland withdrew and exerted his whole influence in favor of Madison, who was elected to the convention, and, after sharing in its fierce debates, he was just able to save the Constitution of the United States.

In a eulogy pronounced on James Madison by J. S. Barbour, of Virginia, in 1857, he said "That the credit of adopting the Constitution of the United States properly belonged to a Baptist clergyman, formerly of Virginia, named Leland. If," said he, "Madison had not been in the Virginia convention the Constitution would not have been ratified, and, as the approval of nine States was necessary to give effect to this instrument, and as Virginia was the ninth State, if it had been rejected by her the Constitution would have failed (the remaining States following her example), and it was through Elder Leland's influence that Madison was elected to that convention."‖ It is unquestionable that Mr. Madison was elected through the efforts and resignation of John Leland, and it is all but certain that that act gave our country its famous Constitution.

---

* Backus's Baptist Church History, vol. ii. p. 335. Newton.
† Manning and Brown University, pp. 103, 104. Boston, 1864.
‡ Howison's History of Virginia, ii. 326, 327, 332.
§ Howe's Virginia Historical Collections, p. 124. Charleston, 1846.
‖ Sprague's Annals of the American Baptist Pulpit, p. 179.

United States, The Religious Amendment of the Constitution of.—The first amendment to the United States Constitution was adopted in 1789, the year it went into operation. It reads, "Congress shall make no law respecting an establishment of religion, or prohibiting the free exercise thereof; or abridging the freedom of speech or of the press; or the right of the people peaceably to assemble, and to petition the government for a redress of grievances." The first clause of this amendment occupies properly its prominent place in that addition to the Constitution. Freedom of conscience was in legal bondage in 1789, and its friends had too much cause to be alarmed for its safety.

Had the amendment not been adopted, Massachusetts might have had her State church to-day, and her citizens rotting in prison because they could not conscientiously pay a church-tax; and any State might have established the Episcopal Church and then committed Baptists or other ministers to prison, as Virginia did down to the Revolution. And Congress might have decreed that the Catholic Church was the religious fold of the nation, and might have levied taxes to support her clergy, and made laws to give secular power to her cardinals, archbishops, bishops, and priests over our schools, religious opinions, and personal freedom. With the amendment we have been educated to practise universal religious freedom; without it, sacerdotal tyranny might have destroyed all our liberty. The grandest feature of our Constitution is the first clause of the first amendment. The Baptists have justly claimed that the credit for this amendment belongs chiefly to them. It is in strict accordance with their time-honored maxim, "The major part shall rule in civil things only."

Where else could it have come from? In the Revolution, and for a few years after, there were two great centres of political influence in our country, around which the other States moved with more or less interest,—Massachusetts and Virginia. Freedom of conscience could not come from Massachusetts; she was wedded to a State religion in 1789, which defied any divorcing agency to create a separation. Just ten years before, she adopted her new constitution with an article in it giving legal support to Congregational ministers, as in good old Puritan times. And this tie only perished in 1834.[*] Writing to Benjamin Kent, John Adams says, "I am for the most liberal toleration of all denominations, but I hope Congress will never meddle with religion further than to say their own prayers. . . . *Let every colony have its own religion without molestation.*"[†] That is, from Congress; he wished every colony to have its own *established* church without molestation, if it desired such an institution. He unjustly charged Israel Pemberton, a Quaker, whom, with the Baptists and other Friends, the Massachusetts delegates met during the session of the first Continental Congress, with an effort to destroy the union and labors of Congress, because he pled for the release of Baptists and Quakers imprisoned in Massachusetts for not paying the ministers' tax, and for the repeal of their oppressive laws. And John Adams actually argued that it was against the consciences of the people of his State to make any change in their laws about religion, even though others might have to suffer in their estates or in their personal freedom to satisfy Mr. Adams and his *conscientious* friends. And he declared that they might as well think they could change the movements of the heavenly bodies as alter the religious laws of Massachusetts.[‡] This was the spirit of New England when the first amendment was proposed, except in Rhode Island, and among the Baptists, and the little community of Quakers outside of it. Thomas Jefferson, writing to Dr. Rush, says, "There was a hope confidently cherished about A.D. 1800, that there might be a State church throughout the United States, and this expectation was specially cherished by Episcopalians and Congregationalists."[§] This was the sentiment of not a few New England Pedobaptists, and the hope of the remains of the Episcopal Church in the South. Massachusetts and her allies had no love for the first amendment, and, according to Backus, Massachusetts *did not* adopt it.[∥]

It came from Virginia, and chiefly from Baptists of the Old Dominion. The "mother of Presidents" was the mother of the glorious amendment. In 1776 the first republican Legislature of Virginia convened, and after a violent contest, daily renewed, from the 11th of October to the 5th of December, the *acts of Parliament* were repealed which rendered any form of worship criminal. Dissenters were exempted from all taxes to support the clergy, and the laws were *suspended* which compelled Episcopalians to support their own church. But it was the pressure of Dissenters without that forced this legislation on the Assembly, for a majority of the members were Episcopalians.[¶] While this act relieved Baptists, the unrepealed common law still punished with dismissal from all offices for the first offense, those who denied the Divine existence, or the Trinity, or the truth of Christianity; and for the second, the

---
[*] Backus's Church History, p. 197. Philadelphia.
[†] Life and Works of John Adams, by Charles Francis Adams, vol. ix. p. 402.
[‡] Ibid., vol. ii. p. 399.
[§] Memoirs, Correspondence, etc., vol. iii. p. 341. Charlottesville, 1829.
[∥] Backus's Church History, vol. ii. p. 341. Newton.
[¶] Ibid., vol. i. p. 32.

transgressor should be rendered incapable of suing or of acting as guardian, administrator, or executor, or of receiving a legacy, and, in addition, should be imprisoned for three years.* These persecuting laws were not repealed till 1785. The tithe law, after being agitated frequently in every session, and annually suspended, was repealed in 1779. The Presbyterians and Baptists were the outside powers that swept away the State church of Virginia.

After tithes ceased to be collected, a scheme, known as the "assessment," was extensively discussed in Virginia by Episcopalians and others. The assessment required every citizen to pay tithes to support his minister, no matter what his creed. The Episcopalians warmly advocated the assessment. The united clergy of the Presbyterian Church petitioned for it,† though many of their people disliked and denounced it. Patrick Henry aided it with all the power of his eloquence.‡ Richard Henry Lee, the most polished orator in the country, John Marshall, the future chief justice of the United States, and George Washington himself advocated it.§ The Baptists directed their whole forces against it, and poured petitions into the Legislature for its rejection.

After expending every effort, the friends of the assessment were defeated, and it was finally rejected in 1785, and all the laws punishing opinions repealed. This was a work of great magnitude. The Episcopalians, the Methodists, the Presbyterian clergy, and the eloquence and influence of some of the greatest men the United States ever had, or will have, were overcome by the Baptists, and Jefferson and Madison, their two noble allies, and some Presbyterian and other laymen. Semple truly says, "The inhibition of the general assessment may, in a considerable degree, be ascribed to the opposition made to it by the Baptists. They were the only sect which plainly remonstrated against it. Of some others it is said that the laity and ministry were at variance upon the subject, so as to paralyze their exertions for or against the bill."‖

Nor need any one dream that Jefferson and Madison could have carried this measure by their genius and influence. They were opposed by many men whose transcendent services, or unequaled oratory, or wealth, position, financial interests, or intense prejudices, would have enabled them easily to resist their unsupported assaults. Like a couple of first-class engineers on a "tender," with a train attached, but no locomotive, would Jefferson and Madison have appeared without the Baptists. They furnished the locomotive for these skillful engineers, which drew the train of religious liberty through every persecuting enactment in the penal code of Virginia.

In 1790, just one year after the adoption of the amendment, Dr. Samuel Jones, of Pennsylvania, states that there were 202 Baptist churches in Virginia.¶ Semple, the historian of the Virginia Baptists, says that, in 1792, "The Baptists had members of great weight in civil society; their congregations became more numerous than those of any other Christian sect."** The Baptists outnumbered all the denominations in Virginia, in all probability, in 1789, and they far surpassed them in the burning enthusiasm which persecution engenders, and to them chiefly was Virginia indebted for her complete deliverance from persecuting enactments.

In 1789, a few months after Washington became President, "The Committee of the United Baptist Churches of Virginia" presented him an address, written by John Leland, marked by felicity of expression and great admiration for Washington, in which they informed him that their religious rights were not protected by the new Constitution. The President replied that he would never have signed that instrument had he supposed that it endangered the religious liberty of any denomination, and if he could imagine even now that the government could be so administered as to render freedom of worship insecure for any religious society, he would immediately take steps to erect barriers against the horrors of spiritual tyranny.†† Large numbers were anxious about the new Constitution, and it had many open enemies. The Baptists who presented this address *controlled the government of Virginia, and they were the warmest friends of liberty in America.* They would suffer anything for their principles, and, as they suspect the new Constitution, it must be amended to embrace their soul liberty and secure their hearty support. A few weeks later, James Madison, the special friend of Washington, who aided him five months before in composing his first inaugural address to Congress,‡‡ rises in the House of Representatives and proposes the religious amendment demanded by the Baptists, with other emendations, and declares that "a great number of their constituents were dissatisfied with the Constitution, among whom were many respectable for their talents and their patriotism, and *respectable for the jealousy which*

---

* Jefferson's Notes on the State of Virginia, p. 169. Richmond, 1835.
† Rives's Life and Times of James Madison, vol. i. pp. 601, 602.
‡ Wirt's Life of Patrick Henry, p. 263. Hartford.
§ Rives's Life and Times of James Madison, vol. i. pp. 601, 602.
‖ Semple's History of the Virginia Baptists, pp. 72, 73.

¶ Minutes of Philadelphia Baptist Association, p. 459.
** History of the Virginia Baptists, p. 39.
†† Writings of George Washington, by Sparks, vol. xii. pp. 154, 155. Boston.
‡‡ Rives's Life and Times of James Madison, vol. iii. p. 64.

they feel for their liberty" (religious). This language applies to his Virginia Baptist friends and their co-religionists over the land. He presses his scheme amidst violent opposition, and Congress passes it. Two-thirds of the State Legislatures approve of it, and it becomes a part of the Constitution.*

Denominationally, no community asked for this change in the Constitution but the Baptists. The Quakers would no doubt have petitioned for it if they had thought of it, but they did not. John Adams and the Congregationalists did not desire it; the Episcopalians did not wish for it. It went too far for most Presbyterians in Revolutionary times, or in our own days, when we hear so much especially from them, about putting the divine name in the Constitution. The Baptists asked it through Washington. The request commended itself to his judgment and to the generous soul of Madison, and to the Baptists, beyond a doubt, belongs the glory of engrafting its best enactment on the noblest Constitution ever framed for the government of mankind.

Upham, James, D.D., was born in Salem, Mass., Jan. 23, 1815. He was a graduate of Waterville College in the class of 1835, and studied at the Newton Theological Institution, 1837–39. He was ordained at Thomaston, Me., in August, 1840, and was professor in the theological institute which had a brief existence in that place. On leaving Thomaston he became pastor of the church in Manchester, N. H., and subsequently pastor of the church in Millbury, from which place he was called to a professorship in the New Hampshire Literary Institute. His connection with this institution continued fifteen years, 1846–61, when he was appointed president. In 1866 he retired from this position, and became one of the editors of the *Watchman and Reflector*. He held this office for several years with distinguished ability. Recently he has accepted a position on the editorial staff of the *Richmond Herald*, published in Richmond, Va.

The degree of Doctor of Divinity was conferred on Dr. Upham by Colby University in 1860.

Upham, Rev. William D., was born in Weathersfield, Vt., Feb. 10, 1810. He early indicated the bent of his mind, and showed that if his tastes could be gratified he would devote his life to the pursuit of knowledge. Having reached the age of eighteen, he decided to fit himself to enter the profession of law. His preparatory studies, which he pursued at Chester, Vt., and at Middleborough, Mass., being completed, he entered Brown University in the fall of 1831. He was inclined to adopt infidel sentiments, and with the immaturity and self-conceit of youth, he was disposed to treat very lightly the claims of religion. During the winter of 1831–32, while engaged in teaching in the village of Dedham, Mass., his attention was called by the Spirit of God to his own condition. Before the light of truth his skepticism vanished, and he yielded his heart to the Saviour, in whom heretofore he had seen no charms. When he returned to his college duties he was a changed man. Having connected himself with the First Baptist church in Providence, he received their approbation of his wish in due time to enter upon the work of the Christian ministry. Unable for want of funds to continue his studies at the university, he took charge of a school in the village of Wickford, R. I., where he remained three years. It was in consequence of his efforts and sacrifices that there was formed in that place a Baptist church, which now numbers not far from 150 members. Mr. Upham removed to Ludlow, Vt., in December, 1836, and for two years was principal of the Black River Academy. He was ordained to the work of the ministry in November, 1837, preaching as opportunity presented while carrying on his work as a teacher. In December, 1838, he accepted a call to the pastorate of the Second Baptist church in Townshend, Vt., and served this church between four and five years, when he closed his life, dying June 30, 1843, at the early age of thirty-three years. "His death was much lamented by the ministers and churches in Vermont, among whom his piety, talents, and wisdom had secured him a measure of esteem and confidence possessed by very few at so early an age."

Ustick, Rev. Thomas, was born in New York, Aug. 30, 1753. When about fourteen he was converted. He was baptized by the Rev. John Gano. Soon after he felt called to preach the gospel, and he began to prepare himself for this blessed work. He graduated at Rhode Island College (now Brown University) in 1771. He was ordained to the ministry in Ashford, Conn., in 1777. He became pastor of the First Baptist church of Philadelphia in 1782. In that city his labors were greatly blessed, and his memory is still treasured up as a precious legacy by the children of those whom he led to the Saviour.

Mr. Ustick was an earnest advocate of deep repentance as a prerequisite to the enjoyment of the peace of God, and of a salvation gathering nothing from human feelings or reforms, but coming wholly from the Saviour's merits. The Saviour has had few servants more competent or more faithful. He died in Burlington, N. J., in 1803.

Ustick, Deacon Thomas Watts, was born in Philadelphia, Pa., Aug. 22, 1801. His parents removed to Virginia in 1806, where with an uncle, John Ustick, Thomas learned printing. He afterwards lived in Washington and Chicago, and in

---

* Rives's Life and Times of James Madison, vol. iii. p. 39.

both places was known as a publisher and printer. In 1839 he came to St. Louis, where he died Aug. 13, 1866. He was converted when ten years of age in Virginia, and baptized by Thomas Cally. From a boy Deacon Ustick was intelligent, affectionate, and faithful. He was made a deacon of the Second Baptist church of St. Louis, and of the Third church, of which he was a constituent member. The Third church greatly mourned his death. He, with Deacons John Barnhurst, P. J. Thompson, and R. Campbell, formed a noble band in the Third church. His friends admired and trusted him. Mild but firm, and governed by principle, when suddenly called to die, he said, "I am glad I have no preparation to make." He left a rich legacy to his children in a name untarnished, and an influence which will ever live, like that of his grandfather, Thomas Ustick, who was pastor of the First Baptist church of Philadelphia for twenty-one years.

V.

Vail, Rev. A. L., was born in La Grange, Texas, May 14, 1844. He continued to reside there and in that vicinity till the spring of 1862, when he went to Mexico. In August, 1863, he shipped on the schooner "Matamoras," from the port of the same name, for New York.

Although converted in Texas, he made no public profession of religion until 1864, when he united with the First Baptist church in Plainfield, N. J. Having studied in Connecticut until the close of 1864, he removed to Michigan, where his studies were continued until 1868, partly in Raisin Valley Seminary and partly in Kalamazoo College. He was ordained in Schoolcraft, Mich., in 1868. His Schoolcraft pastorate was ended in about a year by failure of health. After six months' rest, he resumed work limitedly in Brady, a field formerly occupied in connection with Schoolcraft, where he remained till April, 1871, when he became pastor in Sturgis, Mich. In November, 1873, he removed to Chicago, to accept a position on the *Standard*. Two years were spent in editorial work and studying in the university and seminary. About one year of this time he was regular supply of the Winnetka church. Preceding this he furnished the first consecutive Baptist preaching in Hyde Park, which prepared the way for the organization of the church there.

Jan. 1, 1876, he took the pastorate of the Baptist church in Colorado Springs, Col., remaining there three years. He preached the first Baptist sermon in Leadville, two weeks before the church was organized there, and issued the first Baptist paper in that State, of which he was editor and manager. This paper, called *Free Gold*, was a monthly, of which 2000 copies were distributed gratuitously each month in Colorado Springs and in the mountains westward. It was supported by advertisements and free-will offerings. It was a financial success.

Mr. Vail became pastor in Wichita, Kansas, Jan. 1, 1879, a part of the plan being the removal of a debt of nearly $1200, due to the Home Mission Society, during that year. By the generosity of the society and the liberality of the church this was accomplished, the pastor having directly nothing to do with it. Mr. Vail resigned as pastor at Wichita, Jan. 1, 1881, and was immediately secured as pastor at Olathe, Kansas.

Mr. Vail is a clear-headed, able, devoted, and successful minister of the gospel, a close and attentive student of the Bible, and a faithful shepherd to his flock.

Van Horn, Hon. Burt, a respected citizen and influential Christian gentleman, a resident of Lockport, N. Y., was born in Newfane, Niagara Co., N. Y., Oct. 28, 1823. His parents, James and Abigail, both of whom died in 1856, were highly esteemed for their public spirit and excellence of Christian character. Besides filling important positions in the town and county, his father was for many years an honored deacon of the Newfane Baptist church. His mother, a devoted member of the same church, was a woman of rare worth; strong in character, devout in spirit, generous and faithful, her godly life has left its impress on the church and community.

From such parents the son inherited qualities of mind and heart which fitted him for the sphere of usefulness he has occupied. Besides home and common-school training, he spent three years in Yates Academy and one year in Madison University. Converted at the age of fifteen, he became a member of the Newfane Baptist church, and for many years devoted his best energies to its interests. During the years 1858, 1859, and 1860 he served with honor in the State Legislature. In 1860 he was elected to Congress, elected again in 1864, and re-elected in 1866. He identified himself by voice and pen with his party; was an ardent and outspoken advocate of the act of emancipation. During his three years in the State Legislature and his six years in Congress, though on many important committees, and an active participant in the great movements of that most eventful period of the nation's history, there was not raised a breath of suspicion as to the integrity of his conduct. In it all and through it all he maintained the Christian character which he took with him into public life. In August, 1877, he was appointed U. S. collector of internal revenue for nine counties of Central and Western New York, which office he now honorably fills. Though so fully occupied with duties of a political and public character, he is a most active and consistent member of the Lockport Baptist church, whose interests, material and spiritual, he has faithfully served since he became a member, in 1870.

Vanhorn, Rev. William, was born in Bucks Co., Pa., July 8, 1747. After graduating in the academy of Dr. Samuel Jones, at Lower Dublin, he became pastor of the Southampton Baptist church in May, 1772. During the Revolutionary war he was a chaplain in the army, encouraging the heroes who fought against tyranny, hunger, and cold, and sharing with them their greatest dangers and most grievous hardships.

He was pastor of the Southampton church for thirteen years. He was twenty-two years pastor of the Scotch Plains church, N. J. On his way to a new home in Ohio he was seized with a fatal illness in Pittsburgh, where he died Oct. 31, 1807.

Mr. Vanhorn was well known and greatly esteemed by the Baptists of Pennsylvania and New Jersey, and in the armies of the patriots. He lived for the Saviour, and he died in peace.

Van Husan, Hon. Caleb, of Detroit, Mich., was born in Manchester, Ontario Co., N. Y., March 13, 1815. By the death of his mother, when he was thirteen years old, his home was broken up, and he left his native place to seek his fortune. At the age of fourteen he was baptized by Rev. Eleazer Savage, in Knowlesville, N. Y. At twenty he entered upon a business career, and the next year was married to Miss Catherine Jackson. In 1838 he removed to Michigan and established himself in business in Saline, where he was a successful merchant until 1853, when he removed to Detroit. He has been for many years president of the Detroit Fire and Marine Insurance Company.

From his coming to Michigan he has been known as an intelligent and efficient friend of every enterprise contemplating the advancement of the Christian church. One of the original members of the Lafayette Street church in Detroit, he has been one of its deacons from its organization. As a trustee of Kalamazoo College, and for several years its treasurer, as a trustee of Madison University, as a member of the State Convention

HON. CALEB VAN HUSAN.

board, as vice-president of the American Baptist Missionary Union, and as a generous and cheerful contributor to every department of Christian work, he has been for many years an acknowledged leader of the Baptists of Michigan. Mrs. Van Husan, to whom he was married in 1866, is the daughter of Rev. David Corwin, and is a special friend and supporter of all our missionary enterprises.

Van Meter, A. W., was born at Elizabethtown, Hardin Co., Ky., April 1, 1789. He died at the residence of his son, E. A. Van Meter, Esq., of Burlington, Iowa, Nov. 11, 1868, at the age of seventy-nine years. Mr. Van Meter shared with his father the hardships of frontier life in Kentucky, with exposure especially to Indian attack. "Often, when going to their religious meetings, they carried their rifles and large knives for protection." In 1831, at the age of forty-two, he removed with his family to Washington, Tazewell Co., Ill. Here again he found a new country. The Indians had but recently left it, and settlers were few, though rapidly arriving. "For a long time he could hear of no Baptist in that part of the country, the nearest church being at Springfield, seventy miles south." Mr. Van Meter immediately made himself known as a Christian and a Baptist, and in 1833 united with others in forming the Pleasant Grove church, fourteen miles from his home. Of the subsequent growth of the denomination in the central portions of the State he was one of the chief instruments. He made himself conspicuous as a *missionary Baptist* at a time when this was almost a name of reproach, and was among the foremost in the formation of Associations in Central Illinois, and in other forms of organic enterprise. He was much a sufferer in the last years of his life, yet in his suffering, as in his serving, he was still an example of Christian fidelity, patience, and trust. His surviving sons, Rev. W. C. Van Meter, Edward A. Van Meter, and Jacob H. Van Meter, have honored his memory in their lives of useful service. One of his daughters, wife of Rev. H. G. Weston, then of Peoria, now president of Crozer Theological Seminary, was, upon her death in 1857, fitly represented as "a lady of great worth and devoted piety."

Van Meter, Rev. W. C., was born near Elizabethtown, Hardin Co., Ky., Feb. 13, 1820. When he was eleven years of age the family removed to Illinois, where his father, Deacon A. W. Van Meter, became conspicuous as an active Baptist and a friend of missions. The son was converted at the age of thirteen, and united with the Pleasant Grove church, now Tremont. In 1837 he entered Shurtleff College, where he remained a year. It was the time of the great abolition excitement in that quarter, resulting in the death of Rev. E. P. Lovejoy at Alton, at the hands of a mob. Mr. Van Meter was one of fourteen young men who pledged themselves to defend Mr. Lovejoy, and who carried him home after he was killed. After a year at Shurtleff he went to Granville College, O., where he remained until 1843. Upon leaving college he returned to Kentucky, teaching and preaching in that State and in Illinois until 1854, when he removed to New York City and began his important work there, first in connection with the Five Points Mission. In May, 1855, he took, as an experiment, his first company of homeless children to Illinois, eighteen in number. This he continued until 1872, visiting the West within that period about seventy times, and providing homes in this way for between two and three thousand children. They were not indentured, but committed to the honor and tenderness of those who received them. In June, 1861, he founded the Howard Mission, or Home for Little Wanderers, in the Fourth Ward, connecting this with the work before described. In February, 1877, he was appointed by the Publication Society to begin a mission at Rome. In 1878, the society not wishing to continue its appropriations, Mr. Van Meter, under a new organization, the Italian Bible and Sunday-School Mission, resumed it upon a new basis. In Rome the mission has five schools,—for boys, for girls, for infants, a night school for young men, and a school among the Jews. It also sustains a teacher in Naples and one in Milan. Mr. Van Meter has warm supporters in various denominations in this country and in England, and prosecutes his work with an enthusiasm that wins friends to the cause wherever he goes. He has recently retired from the Roman Mission, and resumed his former benevolent labors in New York.

Vann, Rev. R. T., graduated at Wake Forest College in 1874; spent two years at the Southern Baptist Theological Seminary, and is now pastor at Enfield, N. C. He is an accomplished scholar and a popular preacher.

Vardeman, Rev. Jeremiah, was born in Kentucky in 1775; ordained about 1801. In 1810 he preached at Davis' Fork, Sulbegrud, and Grassy Lick churches. He had extensive revivals in these churches. In 1815 he organized a church in Bardstown, Ky., the stronghold of Catholicism, and from a revival which he conducted. In 1816 he held a meeting in Lexington, Ky., and organized a church; also the same year, through a revival meeting in Louisville, Ky., he formed a church. He visited Nashville, Tenn., and had a powerful meeting there, at the close of which he constituted a church, and a house of worship was built. In 1828 he had a gracious revival in Cincinnati, in which over one hundred were converted. In 1830 he removed to Missouri. He and Spencer Black organized the Baptist church in Palmyra, Mo. In 1834 he presided at the first meeting held by Baptists in Missouri for general missionary work, now the General Association. When age was creeping upon him, he visited Sulphur Springs for his health; during his visit he preached, seated in a chair, with pathos and power, and administered baptism for the last time.

It is supposed that he baptized more than 8000 persons. He was a very eloquent preacher. On Saturday morning, May 8, 1842, he called his family to him, bade them farewell, and sank in death like a child falling asleep, in the sixty-seventh year of his age. Labors and successes have made his name immortal.

Vardeman, Rev. William H., was born in Fayette Co., Ky., in 1816; came with his father, Jeremiah Vardeman, to Missouri in 1830. He was baptized, in 1833, by his father. He was ordained in 1845. His labors have been abundantly blessed in the conversion of great numbers in Ralls, Montgomery, and Pike Counties. He has been pastor at Pleasant Hill church for twenty-seven years.

Varden, George, D.D., LL.D., an eminent linguist and classical scholar, was born at East Dereham, County of Norfolk, England, Dec. 9, 1830. He was brought up in the Church of England, but, while attending an academy, experienced a change of heart, and was baptized into the fellowship of a Baptist church. At the age of eighteen he was licensed to preach, and soon afterwards came to the United States. After traveling in this country about two years, he entered Georgetown College, Ky., where he graduated in 1858. He was immediately ordained, and became the pastor of the Baptist church in Paris, Ky., where he still resides. He has been pastor, at different periods, of the churches at Colemansville, Florence, Falmouth, and Maysville. He has also taught a classical school at Paris. He is an enthusiastic student, has written much for the periodical press, both of this country and Europe, and is the author of prize essays on various subjects, and critical reviews of works in English, Latin, German, Dutch, and French. He was for a time an acknowledged contributor to the *Encyclopædia Theologica et Ecclesiastica*. He has attained a reputation for critical scholarship in Europe as well as America.

Varnum, General Joseph Bradley, a brother of Gen. J. M. Varnum, was born in Dracut, Mass., about the year 1750. Like his brother he was distinguished for his patriotism, and the ardor with which he entered into the stirring scenes of the Revolutionary war. He was chosen a member of Congress upon the adoption of the Constitution, and held the office for twelve years, during four of which he was Speaker of the House of Representatives. He was chosen Senator of the United States in 1811. He was a member also of three Massachusetts State conventions. Besides these civil offices he was elected to several high military posts, and at the time of his death he was major-general of the third division of the militia of Massachusetts. "In all the offices he sustained, Gen. Varnum exhibited an assiduity which never tired, and an integrity above suspicion." For reasons, which doubtless seemed valid to himself, he did not make a profession of his faith until July 11, 1819, when he was baptized, with his wife, by Rev. C. O. Kimball, and joined the church in Methuen, Mass. Soon after his baptism a Baptist church was formed in Dracut, of which he was one of the constituent members. He continued an active member of the church to the time of his death, which occurred Sept. 11, 1821. "In the death of this good man," says a writer in noticing the death of Gen. Varnum, "liberty has lost one of its ablest defenders, and the cause of Christianity a firm friend and supporter."

Vass, Rev. J. L., is a native of Monroe Co., Va. He was born April 1, 1840. He was converted when about ten years of age, and baptized some two years later. How many of our really useful men are converted early! Soon after his baptism he began to lead in prayer-meetings. His college course was interrupted by the war, through which he served as a private for two years, and as an officer afterwards to its close. He then resumed study in Richmond College, and subsequently went to the theological seminary.

He located as pastor of the Spartanburg Baptist church, S. C., on leaving the seminary, and repeated efforts to induce him to leave the church of his first love have thus far failed.

The church has grown rapidly in numbers, activity, and piety under his care. He has in a high degree the first quality of success in any sphere of life. He is a persistent and judicious *worker*.

Vassar College, an institution for the liberal education of young women, located in Poughkeepsie, N. Y., was founded and endowed by Matthew Vassar, at an expense to him of more than $700,000. It is the first grand completely endowed college for young women ever projected. Although Mr. Vassar was a Baptist, and although the president and a majority of the board of trustees of the college are Baptists, it is in no sense a sectarian institution. The main edifice is almost 500 feet long and 200 feet wide. The centre buildings and wings are five stories high and the connecting portions four. It has accommodations for 400 students, rooms for recitations, lectures, instruction in music and painting, a chapel, dining-hall, parlors, a library-room, an art-gallery, rooms for philosophical apparatus, laboratories, cabinets of natural history, apartments for the officers of the institution, and for the servants employed in it. It has a completely furnished observatory, a spacious gymnasium, with rooms for a riding-school, bowling-alley, and calisthenics. Its grounds are spacious, handsomely planned, and elegantly adorned. The success of the enterprise has justified the large outlay of money to inaugurate it, and it fully meets the expectations of its friends. (See cut on next page.)

S. L. Caldwell, D.D., is its present president.

Vassar, Rev. D. N., A.M., was born in Bedford Co., Va., Dec. 5, 1847. He was baptized in 1868, and entered the Richmond Institute the same year. After a three years' preliminary course here he entered the grammar-school of Madison University, and was graduated from the college in 1877 as Bachelor of Arts. Immediately after he was elected Professor of Mathematics in Richmond Institute, where he is doing good service in the cause of higher education. He has consecrated his life to the work of elevating the colored race morally and intellectually. Prof. Vassar received from Madison University, in 1880, the degree of Master of Arts.

Vassar, Matthew, was born in East Dereham, in the county of Norfolk, England, April 29, 1792. His ancestors were from France, and the name was spelled Vasseur. One of the Levasseurs accompanied Lafayette to America as his secretary. His parents were Baptists. In 1796 they came to America and settled in Poughkeepsie. Soon they commenced the manufacture of "home-brewed ale," which grew into the great establishment known as Vassar's brewery. The son Matthew was averse to the business, and commenced to learn another, when his father's establishment was burned, his brother was killed in trying to save some of the property, and he resolved to aid his parents to revive the business. Thus he commenced a business which he pursued for more than fifty years. In

was ordained in the city of his birth when at the age of twenty-two. He was called to Amenia in 1857, where he remained eight years. He had one year's leave of absence for service in the field as chaplain of the 150th Regiment of N. Y. Vols. The regiment was attached to the Army of the Potomac, and he was with it in several battles, including Gettysburg. He became pastor of the First church of Lynn, Mass., in 1865; then of Flemington in 1872. Mr. Vassar is a popular preacher, a brilliant lecturer, a good organizer, and

VASSAR COLLEGE.

1845 he, with his wife, visited Europe, and then conceived the plan of devoting his great wealth to the common welfare. After long contemplation he resolved to found a first-class college for young women, complete in all its appointments, and well endowed. Being a Baptist in principle, he put it under Baptist control, but arranged that it should not be denominational in its teaching or management. In his address at the organization of the board he said, "All sectarian influences should be carefully excluded, but the training of our students should never be intrusted to the skeptical, the irreligious, or the immoral." This munificent gift to the cause of higher education amounts to more than $700,000. He died on commencement-day while reading his annual address, June 23, 1868.

Vassar, Rev. Thomas Edwin, was born at Poughkeepsie, N. Y., Dec. 3, 1834. He was early converted, and joined the church there. He pursued theological studies with Dr. Rufus Babcock, and

a genial man. His life of his relative, John Vassar, gathers interest not only from the worth of its subject but from the attractive style of the author. When Dr. Smith resigned the secretaryship of the State Convention, Mr. Vassar was spontaneously chosen as his successor, and he is ably filling the place.

Vaughan, Rev. E. L., was born in Carroll Co., Va., Jan. 26, 1845, and was left an orphan at an early age. Though only sixteen at the opening of our civil war, he enlisted in the army and served until its close. He was converted in the army during the year 1862, and began to preach in 1874. He was ordained at Macon, Ga., in 1876, studied one term in the Southern Baptist Theological Seminary, and then entered upon a useful and laborious career as a missionary of the State Mission Board. He is an exceedingly zealous, faithful, and hard-working minister of the gospel.

Vaughan, Henry, was born at St. Martin's,

New Brunswick, where, in 1828, he was converted and baptized under the ministry of Rev. Mr. Coy. He is now a member of Germain Street Baptist church, St. John, New Brunswick. He is a wealthy ship-owner in that city, and contributes liberally to the support of the church and to denominational enterprises.

Vaughan, Rev. Henry, son of Simon Vaughan, of St. Martin's, New Brunswick, was converted and baptized at Wolfville, Nova Scotia. He was a graduate of Acadia College, and studied theology at Newton. He was ordained pastor of the Baptist church at St. George, New Brunswick, Jan. 8, 1862, and in 1863 took charge of the Germain Street Baptist church, St. John, New Brunswick. He died Aug. 12, 1864, deeply lamented by his brethren in the provinces.

Vaughan, Rev. Howell, was a native of Wales, and a minister of the Baptist denomination. In 1633 a Baptist church was formed at Olchron, in Wales, of which Mr. Vaughan was first a member, and afterwards the pastor. He was among the earliest of our brethren in modern times to preach the gospel to his countrymen. He signed the minutes of the meeting of the Ministerial Association which met at Abergavenny in 1653.

Vaughan, Rev. Thomas M., son of Rev. William Vaughan, D.D., was born in Mason Co., Ky., June 11, 1825. He was educated with much care under several teachers. He finished his literary education at Georgetown College in 1846. He then entered upon the study of law, and was admitted to the bar in 1847. He established himself in the practice of his profession in Versailles, Ky. He soon acquired a good reputation as a lawyer, and for a short time acted in the capacity of circuit judge. But the strong conviction of duty to preach the gospel, which he had felt in his youth, returned with such force that, in 1854, he resolved to abandon the law and give himself to the ministry. He was licensed to preach in February, 1855, and ordained to the pastorate of Burk's Branch church in Shelby Co., Ky., the following September. The next year he accepted the care of Clay Village church, in the same county. He ministered to these churches until 1858, when he was called to the First Baptist church in Bowling Green, where he succeeded Dr. J. M. Pendleton. In 1861 he returned to Shelby County and took charge of Simpsonville church. There he remained nearly ten years, taking rank with the best preachers of the State. While here he supplied at different periods the churches at Buck Creek, Salem, and Lawrenceburg. In December, 1870, he accepted a call to the church at Danville, where he still remains. In 1878 he wrote and published the life of his father, which was favorably received.

Vaughan, William, D.D., an eminent minister of the gospel in Kentucky, was born in Westmoreland Co., Pa., Feb. 22, 1785. His parents removed to Kentucky when he was about three years old, and his youth was spent in the wilderness of the

WILLIAM VAUGHAN, D.D.

great Southwest. Upon arriving at manhood he manifested a strong logical mind and great fondness for study. He adopted a mechanical pursuit, and having married, located in Winchester, Ky. He procured the writings of Paine, Volney, and Voltaire, professed himself a deist, and united with an infidel club. About three years after this, in 1810, he was converted to Christ, and became a member of a Baptist church in Clark Co., Ky. Was licensed to preach in 1811, ordained in 1812, and, applying himself to study with great industry, made rapid advancement, and became not only a good English scholar, but possessed considerable attainments in the Greek language and literature. Soon after his ordination he settled in Mason County, where he preached to several churches, and taught school about fifteen years. In 1827 he removed to Ohio, where he remained one year, and returned to Kentucky. He was now brought into conflict with the disciples of Campbell, who were making many proselytes. Being the only minister in Kentucky at that time who was able to grapple successfully with the adherents of the new doctrine, he was encouraged by the churches to defend their principles against the assaults of Mr. Campbell, and devoted himself with great energy and extraordinary ability to this work. In 1831 he accepted the appointment of general agent for the American Sunday-school Union, and continued in its employment two and a half years, in the face of considerable opposition, establishing about a hundred schools. In 1835 he accepted the position of general agent for Kentucky for the American Bible Society. Six months afterwards the Baptists withdrew from the society, and he resigned. In 1836 he accepted a call to the pastorate of Bloomfield church in Nelson County. Here, as elsewhere, he was held in high esteem. He preached to Bloomfield church thirty-two years. In 1868, in consequence of an injury received by a fall, he resigned his pastoral charge, in his eighty-fourth year, but continued to be a close student, and to preach as his strength would serve him, until he was over ninety-two years of age. It is probable that no minister in Kentucky was ever more universally loved and honored. He died March 31, 1877.

Vaughan, Wm. R., A.M., M.D., principal of the Gordonsville Female Institute, was born in Elizabeth City Co., Va., in 1827. The earlier part of his education was obtained at Hampton Academy and at the Columbian College, after which he was graduated at William and Mary College. After having graduated in medicine also, at the Virginia Medical College, Richmond, he took a course of lectures in the University of Pennsylvania, and soon after entered upon an extensive and lucrative practice. He was baptized, in 1848, by Dr. Jeter, and became a member of the First church, Richmond. Early in the war, Dr. Vaughan was selected as one of Gen. Magruder's personal staff at Yorktown, and served with great bravery and efficiency. In August of 1861 he was appointed full surgeon with the rank of major; resigned, and took a cavalry command, which, owing to ill health, he also resigned in June of 1862. In 1864 he was placed in command of the general hospital at Petersburg, where he did noble service, and was acknowledged to be one of the most skillful surgeons in the Confederate service. After the close of the war, Dr. Vaughan pursued his medical profession with eminent success. He has always been deeply interested in Sunday-school work and educational movements. As a Sunday-school organizer he has but few equals, while as a Sunday-school teacher, superintendent, and lecturer he has been very successful. In 1869 he was invited to take charge of the Bristol Female College, Tenn., where he remained one session, and then accepted the position of principal of the Culpeper Institute, Va., where he built up in a short time one of the most flourishing female seminaries in the State. At the earnest solicitation of many friends and prominent gentlemen, Dr. Vaughan opened a school of high grade for young ladies at Gordonsville, where he is putting on solid foundations one of the best institutions of the kind in Virginia. Had Dr. Vaughan's health permitted him to remain in the practice of his profession, he would easily have acquired distinction and wealth. As a teacher, he is enthusiastic and instructive, winning the attention and love of all who come under his care. His labors as a Christian layman are numerous and successful, being specially interested in efforts to develop a higher education, sanctified by divine truth. As a writer, he is vigorous and instructive, being thoroughly familiar with the many and varied questions that touch upon science and religion. He is a frequent contributor to the press, both secular and religious. His varied stores of information make him a most interesting conversationalist, and his genial social qualities render him a most companionable co-laborer in the different fields of Christian, literary, and scientific activity in which he is so usefully enlisted. Columbian University conferred the honorary degree of A.M. on Dr. Vaughan in 1881.

Vawter, Rev. Jesse, was born in Culpeper Co., Va., Dec. 1, 1755. He was converted in 1774, and joined the Rapidan Baptist church. In 1781 he was drafted as a soldier for a few months. In 1790 he removed to Kentucky, and in 1806 to Indiana. He was ordained in 1800. Among other utterances on "a call to the ministry" we record this, written by his own pen: "But I do believe the best evidence a man can have that it is his duty to preach is the voice of his brethren, for no man is a proper judge of himself; he will judge too high or too low of his own performances." He helped to constitute twelve churches and three Associations. He was regarded as a father in all Southern Indiana; from his judgment in matters of doctrine or polity there was no disposition to dissent. His four sons—John, William, Achilles, and James—were all prominent men in the church. They were all Baptists. He died March 20, 1838.

Vawter, Rev. John, oldest son of Jesse and Elizabeth Vawter, was born Jan. 8, 1782, in Madison Co., Va. His father removed to Kentucky in 1790. Ten years afterwards his son made a public profession of faith in Christ, and joined a Baptist church near Frankfort. In 1807 he removed across the Ohio into Indiana, and built a house in the forest, where North Madison now stands. He here joined the Mount Pleasant church. He was the first magistrate of Madison. He was appointed sheriff of Jefferson and Clarke Counties. President Madison appointed him U. S. marshal for Indiana. In 1815 he removed farther north, and began the building of a town, which he called Vernon. In 1816 he and seven others formed the Vernon Baptist church. In May, 1821, he was ordained to the ministry. In 1831 he was elected to a seat in the lower house of the State Legislature, and in 1836 was sent to the State senate. He was colonel of militia from 1817 to 1821. He was also a vice-president of the convention that nominated President Taylor. He was an acknowledged leader among the Baptists of his State, having been foremost in the organization of many churches and Associations. His heart swelled with the desire of liberty for mankind. He never concealed his sympathy for the enslaved race. In 1848 he removed to Morgantown, where he formed a church, and labored till his death. He was straightforward and positive. He had a kind heart, and was very thoughtful of the happiness of others. He never concealed his hatred of tobacco. He died at his home in Morgantown, Aug. 17, 1872.

REV. JOHN VAWTER.

Veazy, Deacon John, the contemporary and fellow-laborer of Jesse Mercer, was born in North Carolina, March 29, 1769. He came to Georgia in his youth, in company with his parents, and, not long afterwards, was baptized by Silas Mercer, and received into the Powelton church, Hancock Co., of which church he remained a member until his death. He developed into a Christian of rare excellence and usefulness.

He entered into the missionary enterprise with all his heart, and stood side by side with those who formed the first missionary society in the State. The fast friend of all the benevolent operations of his day, he was particularly zealous in the distribution of tracts throughout his neighborhood. While taking a deep interest in the cause of Christ generally, the welfare of the old Powelton church lay especially near his heart, and, during the period of its greatest prosperity, he took the lead in every good word and work. He died Nov. 8, 1847, in the seventy-ninth year of his age. His name is yet a household word in Hancock County.

Venable, Rev. R. A., pastor at Helena, Ark., was born in Georgia, but reared in Arkansas. He was educated at Mississippi College, where he graduated with the first honors of his class in 1876. After his graduation he took charge of the high school at Eldorado, Ark., for two years. He was then called to Okalona, Miss., where he remained two years. He entered his present important field in the beginning of the present year (1880). Mr. Venable is a fine scholar, an eloquent preacher, and a sound theologian, and is fast taking a prominent position among the rising young men in the South.

Vermont Baptists.—In 1768 the first Baptist church in what is now the State of Vermont was formed in the town of Shaftsbury. It arose out of the New-Light movement, and in 1788 it had become the mother of three other churches in the same town. The second church in Vermont was organized in the town of Pownal in 1773. These two towns were the seats (*cathedræ*) of Baptist influence and missionary effort for a considerable period in Vermont. Towards the close of the Revolutionary war the county of Windsor increased rapidly in population, and with the new residents several Baptist ministers found their way to that section of Vermont. A church was formed in Woodstock in 1780, of which Rev. Elisha Ransom became pastor. Between 1780 and 1790 there were thirty-two churches established in Vermont, making with the five previously formed thirty-seven churches, in which there were 28 ordained ministers and 1600 communicants. This was a time of great zeal, prayer, and effort, and the blessing of God descended in great power upon the struggling Baptist communities of the Green Mountain State.

The Baptists suffered severely from the tyranny of the "standing order" at this period in Vermont, and it was only after years of persistent labor that the disabilities under which they groaned were removed, and the complete separation of Church and State was accomplished.

The Shaftsbury, the first Baptist Association, was established in 1780; of the five churches composing it, two belonged to Vermont and three to New York and Massachusetts. The Woodstock Association was organized in 1783 from churches located in Vermont and in New Hampshire. The church of Canaan, of which Dr. Thomas Baldwin, subsequently of Boston, was pastor, was one of the constituent members of this Association. The celebrated Aaron Leland, lieutenant-governor of Vermont, was one of the early ministers of the Woodstock Association. The Vermont Association was formed in 1785 of five churches. There are seven Associations in the State, the largest of which is the Lamoille, and the smallest the Vermont Central. In these seven Associations there are 114 churches, 79 pastors, and 9870 members. There are 101 Baptist Sunday-schools in the State, with 1162 officers and teachers, and 9291 scholars. During the year $6563.73 were given for benevolent objects. While many of the churches are weak, owing to removals to the West, others are enjoying encouraging prosperity.

The Baptist Convention was organized in 1825, and has rendered blessed service in spreading the gospel in Vermont. Its officers in 1880 were, President, Rev. D. Spencer; Vice-Presidents, Rev. M. A. Wilcox, Col. J. J. Estey; Secretary, Rev. W. H. Rugg; Treasurer, Gen. George F. Davis. Vermont has also a Baptist Historical Society and a Baptist Sabbath-School Convention.

Vermont Baptists have been the warm friends of education; they aided Hamilton, and they have sustained academies among themselves with great liberality. They have placed a number of distinguished men in the governor's chair and in other secular positions, as well as in the ministry; and they have given to sister States some of our finest scholars, most distinguished educators, and ablest preachers.

Very, Rev. Edward D., A.M., was born in Salem, Mass.; graduated from Dartmouth College; ordained pastor at Calais, Me.; became pastor at Portland and at St. John, New Brunswick, December, 1846; he was the founder of the *Christian Visitor*, commenced in 1847, and continued its editor until his death, June 7, 1852, which occurred in returning from a geological expedition to Cape Blomedon. Mr. Very, Prof. Chipman, and four students of Acadia College were drowned in the Basin of Mines. The Portland church and the denomination were sadly bereaved. Mr. Very was a sound theologian, an able preacher, a good counselor, and an excellent writer.

Videto, Rev. Nathaniel, was born in Annapolis Co., Nova Scotia; was converted and baptized in 1828; was ordained successor to the Rev. Thomas Ainslie in the pastorate of the Baptist church, Wilmot, Nova Scotia, May 10, 1832, and continued in that office for forty years, during which time large additions were made to the membership of the church. Mr. Videto is a powerful advocate of temperance and prohibition.

Vince, Rev. Charles, was born in the small town of Farnham, in Surrey, England, in 1823. In his youth he diligently improved his mind by study and extensive reading. Reared among the Congregationalists, he became convinced of the Scriptural authority of believers' immersion, and was baptized. When he began to preach in the neighboring villages he leaped at once into popularity. In 1848, at the age of twenty-five, he entered Stepney College, and at the end of his course accepted a call to the pastorate of the Graham Street church, Birmingham. The church met in a large building known as Mount Zion chapel. The congregation

REV. CHARLES VINCE.

was small, and the debt on the building was a heavy burden. But the young pastor showed that he was equal to the situation. The spacious chapel soon became filled with hearers, and every good work was vigorously prosecuted by his people, led and animated by their large-hearted and sagacious pastor. His sterling common sense and practical wisdom were as conspicuous as his oratorical powers, whilst his simple piety and brotherly affection won the hearts of all who came into personal contact with him. In all the midland district of England he was by common consent looked up to as the bishop of the Baptists. His course was one of unbroken harmony with his people, and it was brilliantly successful. He was greatly sought after for extraordinary services, and, so far as he was able, he held himself ready to serve every good cause. The London May meetings' programme was scarcely ever published during the last ten or twelve years of his life without his name in the list for a sermon or a speech. As a preacher, Mr. Vince early attained a standard nearly approaching the general ideal of perfection. The common people heard him gladly, while the cultured and refined always found interest and instruction. His illustrations were generally Biblical, and he was remarkably fond of Bunyan's vivid imagery and quaint humor. For several years the great city of Birmingham regarded Charles Vince as one of her chief champions of civil and religious liberty, and an able leader and counselor in all philanthropic enterprises. On the school board and on the board of guardians of the poor, in the great gatherings of citizens in the town-hall, Mr. Vince was always to be depended on for wisdom not less than eloquence. He was, indeed, a public man of the noblest mould. How well he served the community in the esteem of his fellow-citizens was testified at his funeral by the representatives of all classes and parties and sects. The chief magistrate of Birmingham, and deputations from all the public bodies, the ministers of the various Nonconformist churches, several of the Established clergy, the Jewish rabbi, and one of the dignitaries of the Roman Catholic Church, assembled around the grave to express not only their personal respect, but the universal sense of an irreparable loss. Baptists from all parts of the country were likewise present to mourn with their bereaved brethren of the neighborhood. In the very prime of his powers and reputation, only fifty-one years of age, he died Oct. 22, 1874. His end was peace. The doctrine of the Cross, which had ever been prominent in his preaching, was dear to him in death. Among his last articulate utterances was heard the words,—

"Rock of ages, cleft for me,
Let me hide myself in thee."

Virginia, The Baptist General Association of.—The first General Assemblies of Baptists in this State were called Yearly Meetings. These were mass-meetings for worship and conference, usually held in May and October, and began as early as 1750. When, from denominational growth, they became inconvenient, District Associations were formed composed of delegates from churches. The first District Association composed wholly of Virginia Baptist churches was the Ketockton, organized Aug. 19, 1766. It comprised four churches, three of which had been dismissed from the Philadelphia Association in 1765 for this purpose. May 11, 1771, at Craig's meeting-house, in Orange County, twelve churches formed the General Association of Separate Baptists in Virginia, called also Rapidan Association. At its meeting in 1775 it included sixty churches.

Severe persecutions caused vigorous efforts to secure religious liberty. A general combination of Baptists became necessary, and they organized, Oct. 9, 1784, a General Committee composed of delegates from District Associations. This continued until May, 1800, when the General Meeting of Correspondence was formed, with composition and objects similar to those of the General Committee. When security of conscience, worship, and privileges had become assured by law, the churches turned to missions and other general work. The conception of a General Association for missionary, educational, Bible, Sunday-school, and other enterprises originated in a conversation between the Rev. James Fife and the Rev. Edward Baptist, and on June 7, 1823, the Baptist General Association of Virginia was formed at a meeting held in the Second Baptist church in Richmond, Va. Fifteen delegates and a few visitors were present, none of whom survive. Robert B. Semple was the first moderator. Wm. Todd was clerk. Robert B. Semple preached the introductory sermon. There were then in the State 20 District Associations with about 40,000 members, white and colored. The first missionaries of the General Association were Daniel Witt and Jeremiah Bell Jeter. The General Association gradually secured the co-operation of all the Baptists in the State except a small number opposed to " modern societies," and calling themselves "Old-School Baptists." The growth of the General Association has been regular and rapid; its sessions have been always well attended and harmonious, its supporters zealous and liberal, and its work greatly blessed. At the semi-centennial meeting held with the Second Baptist church in Richmond, Va., it had 137 life-members, of whom 62 were present. There were present over 1000 delegates, and 100 visitors from other States or general organizations.

The General Association is composed of life-members, made such on payment of $200 to its objects, and annual members contributing $25 yearly, or delegates from contributing churches, societies, etc. Each member must be "an orderly member of some regular Baptist church." It has a president, four vice-presidents, a treasurer, a secretary and assistants, a statistical secretary, and five boards, which administer its plans and work, and which report annually. Its boards are State, foreign and home missions, education and Sunday-school and Bible. It has a Ministers' Relief and an Historical Society. All business is transacted in Associational sessions and not by the separate "Society" system. The annual receipts have risen to the aggregate of over $24,000, which includes only what passes through its own treasury. It employs 44 State missionaries. Since 1863 the colored Baptists have formed and maintained separate organizations in Virginia. The General Association includes 22 District Associations, comprising 677 churches, 379 ministers, and 66,715 members. In the whole State there are 32 Associations, 1346 churches, 718 ministers, and 207,559 members. In 1832 the Education Society founded the Virginia Baptist Seminary, which became, in 1843, Richmond College. It has educated for the ministry about 300 young men. A very large part of the Baptist churches in Virginia, and most of those in West Virginia, were organized through the labors of the missionaries of the General Association, the efficient secretary of its State Mission Board, the Hon. Henry K. Ellyson, having for many years zealously performed his labors without pecuniary reward.

Among the officers and members of the General Association have been some of the most pious, prominent, and honored Baptists in the land. The organization has secured unity of energies and given a great impulse to the enterprise of Virginia Baptists. Its meetings are largely attended, devotional, and spirited. Its policy has ever been expansive, aggressive, and prudent. Many thrilling events mark its history. It has occupied destitute sections, aided feeble churches, established Sunday-schools, built "church houses," and participated in all good work for gospel growth. Virginia Baptists love and sustain it, and, best of all, God blesses it.

Virginia, Baptists of.—The earliest account of any Baptists in Virginia is the statement of Rev. Morgan Edwards, that, in 1695, there were some Baptists in North Carolina who had gone over from Virginia to escape the intolerance of the laws of the latter colony. The first organized church of which we find mention is that at Burley, Isle of Wight Co., to which, in 1714, the Rev. Robert Nordain came from England as pastor. From labors in this vicinity several churches were formed, which in part composed the Kehukee Association, organized in 1765. In 1743 some Baptists from Chestnut Ridge, Md., removed to Opeckon Creek, now Occoquan, in Prince William County, and constituted the Occoquan church in 1743, with the Rev. Henry Loveall as pastor. The church was afterwards called Mill Creek. Other churches were organized, and some joined the Philadelphia Association, from which they were regularly dismissed to form, with another church, the Ketockton Association, in Loudon County. This was the first District Association wholly composed of Virginia Baptist churches. Many churches along the southern border of the State belonged to the Sandy Creek Association, mainly in North Carolina, and formed in January, 1758. All the associated Baptist churches of the State belonged to one of these three Associations. The Sandy Creek churches were called "Separate Baptists"; the Kehukee churches, "General Baptists"; and the Ketockton churches, "Strait," or "Calvinistic," or "Regular Baptists." These all coalesced, adopting the doctrinal formulary of the "Regular" Baptists as their "Basis of Union" in 1787. The "Separate Baptist Association," or "General Association of Separate Baptists," or "Rapidan Association," was organized May 11, 1771.

Some of the early laws against "Dissenters" in Virginia bore heavily against Baptists, and they were severely persecuted. The first imprisonment of preachers was that of John Waller, Lewis Craig, James Childs, and others, June 4, 1768, in Spottsylvania County. Many other cases followed elsewhere, accompanied often with fines, whipping, and other penalties. These trials awakened a sturdy determination to sweep away all civil obstacles to religious liberty. To combine efforts, a "General Committee" was formed, Oct. 9, 1784, of two delegates from each Association, the "General Association" having been dissolved in 1783. Four Associations were represented. Instead of this "General Committee," which had nobly and effectively served its purposes, the "General Meeting of Correspondence" was formed of delegates from Associations in May, 1800. This continued as the State board of Baptist co-operation until June 9, 1823, when the present "Baptist General Association of Virginia" was organized for missionary, Sunday-school, and other work. What is now West Virginia was part of the field cultivated by the General Association.

Baptists more than any others, and sometimes against a combined opposition, secured complete religious freedom for Virginia. Many were whipped, imprisoned, fined, or mobbed, and remarkable cases of steadfastness, heroism, and sacrifice are recorded in Virginia Baptist history. They have grown in numbers, intelligence, influence, and enterprise, and now outnumber any other, indeed, almost all other religious denominations in the State. They have one college at Richmond, and many academies for males and females, under Baptist auspices. Since 1863 the colored churches have constituted themselves separately, and have their own Associations.

Virginia Baptists point to their history with gratitude to God and to the memory of their pioneers in the faith. Their ministry is the peer of any other in piety, intelligence, power, and enterprise. Their churches number 1346; ordained ministers, 718; members, 207,559; Associations, 32.

The Baptists of Virginia, in patriotism, in heroic sufferings for Christ, in zeal to spread the gospel in their own and in other States, and in success, have made for themselves a glorious record; Virginia Baptists have given to several other States their divine principles, and preachers who constructed a multitude of Baptist churches.

Vogell, Henry C., D.D., was born in New York, June 1, 1806; graduated at Hamilton in 1827; ordained at Vernon, N. Y., in 1831; pastor in Groton, Seneca Falls, Elmira, and Rome, N. Y.; received the degree of Doctor of Divinity from Union College, Schenectady. Dr. Vogell has intellectual powers of a high order, and has rendered important services to the Saviour's cause in New York.

W.

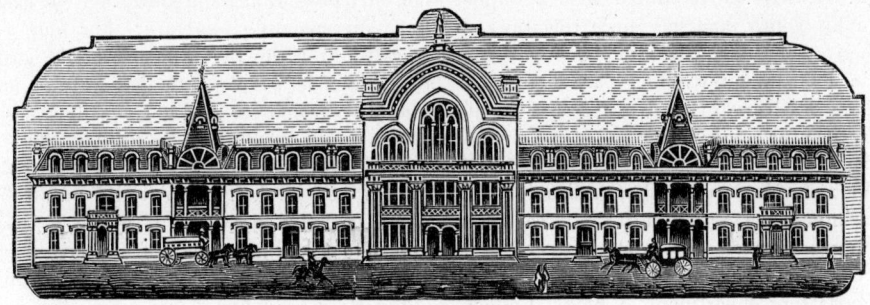

Waco University, Waco, Texas.—In 1845, when there were only 1200 Baptists in the State, they founded Baylor University. But Baylor University was located in Southern Texas. At that time the bloody Comanche and wild Waco Indians covered all the great wheat region of Central and Northern Texas. And it became evident in 1855 that Baylor University could not meet the growing wants of the whole State. Hence the Baptists of Central Texas originated Waco University for "the great wheat and stock region" of a State seven times larger than New York.

The president and professors who had conducted Baylor University for ten years with so much *éclat*, impressed with the great advantages of Waco as the seat of a Baptist university, resigned their positions in Baylor, and accepted similar offices in Waco University.

Waco University became a success at once, and for the last eighteen years it has matriculated more students than any university west of the Mississippi River.

The city of Waco has over 10,000 inhabitants, who for morality, refinement, and intelligence will compare favorably with any city in America. Waco is justly called "the Athens of Texas," and next to Richmond, Va., has the largest percentage of Baptists of any city in the world. It was the first leading institution that adopted the co-education of the sexes.

The property of Waco University is estimated at $53,000 in library, apparatus, telescope, buildings, lands, pledges, and notes. Four brick buildings two stories high have been erected and finished; and a strong effort will be made to erect this year the grand central three-story building, and add $50,000 to the endowment fund.

The president and professors of Waco live in the affection and confidence of the thousands whom they have educated in Texas during the last thirty years, and of many others.

Dr. R. C. Burleson is the honored president of this eminently useful institution.

Wade, Jonathan, D.D., was born in Otsego, N. Y., Dec. 10, 1798. "He was the first Hamilton student." He graduated in 1822. He sailed for Burmah from Boston in June, 1823. His literary activity is remarkable; he has prepared a Karen dictionary; he has aided in the translation of the Scriptures into the language of the Karens; he has published several books and tracts in the tongues of the Burmese and the Karens. He thinks with clearness, he lives near to God, and he preaches with power. He has been a missionary fifty-seven years. He is held in honor by every Christian in Burmah, and by all the friends of missions in America.

Waffle, Prof. Albert E., A.M., was born in Steuben Co., N. Y., Nov. 14, 1846. He graduated at Madison University in 1872, having taken several honors, among them the Senior prize for oratory. After pursuing theological studies in the seminary he was called to Remsen Avenue Baptist church in New Brunswick, N. J., in April, 1873. He was ordained as the first pastor of that church on May 29, and the new church edifice was dedicated on the same day. On the 19th of the following June, Mr. Waffle married Miss Mary R. Harvey, daughter of the Rev. Dr. Harvey, of the Hamilton Theological Seminary. During the next seven years he labored efficiently in New Brunswick, baptizing 271 converts, building up the church in the city, and greatly developing its spirituality and benevolence. A close and tender attachment was created between pastor and people, which was widely shared by all who knew of the pastor's devotion, especially his fellow-ministers, by whom his character and talents were warmly appreciated. In August, 1880, Mr. Waffle was invited to the Crozer professorship of Rhetoric in the university at Lewisburg, and at the same time to the pastorate of the Baptist church of that place. Both positions were accepted, and in both he continues (1881) to render able and valued services. Prof. Waffle is a man of high ideals, especially in all that pertains to spirituality of life and character, a good scholar, a sound theologian, a clear, forcible, and impressive preacher, and a thorough and inspiring teacher. His mind is characterized by clearness and range of intuition, rather than by dialectic subtilty, or by strong and spontaneous feeling. His style is correspondingly lucid and informing, rather than severely argumentative or brilliantly imaginative. He has thus far published nothing but newspaper articles, occasional sermons, and a single tract. The quality of these reveals powers of composition which may yet do great service to literature.

Waggener, Leslie, LL.D., president of Bethel College, Russellville, Ky., was born in Todd Co., Ky., Sept. 11, 1841. He united with a Baptist church in his youth, and has since remained an earnest, active Christian. He graduated at Bethel College in 1860, and the same year entered the Senior class at Harvard University, graduating next year. On his return from college he entered the Southern army as a private; was shot through the lungs at the battle of Shiloh; recovered, and continued in military service until the close of the war, having been promoted to the rank of lieutenant. On his return home he became a teacher in the preparatory department of Bethel College, and, after three years, was elected Professor of English. In 1873 was made chairman of the faculty, and in 1877 he was chosen president of the college.

Wait, Samuel, D.D.—One of the most judicious ministers of the State is accustomed to say that Dr. Wait did more for the development of North Carolina than any man who ever lived in the State. Whether this be true or not, it is certain that his influence upon the Baptists was very great and very good; and as the man to whom more than to any other they are indebted for their State Convention as the first agent of that body, and especially, as the founder of Wake Forest College, he has laid his people under the most sacred obligations ever to cherish his memory with grateful affection.

Dr. Wait was born in Washington Co., N. Y., Dec. 19, 1789; was baptized in Vermont, March 12, 1809; ordained at Sharon, Norfolk Co., Mass., June 3, 1818. Feeling the need of a better education, he went to Columbian College, Washington, D. C. It seems that his diploma bears the seal of Waterville College, Me., though his course of study was pursued at Columbian College, probably because the latter was not then empowered to confer degrees. He was for a time tutor in Columbian College, and first came to North Carolina in February, 1827, with Dr. Staughton, on a collecting tour for the college. Passing through Newbern, Dr. Wait made a favorable impression on the Baptists of the place, and he settled as their pastor in November, 1827. It would seem that in passing through North Carolina his mind was looking to the development of the North Carolina Baptists, for his journal shows that, soon after, in Charleston, S. C., he asked Dr. Manly if he did not think a State Convention might be organized in North Carolina. Dr. Manly feared that the time for such a movement had not yet come, but we no sooner find Dr. Wait settled at Newbern than we see him laboring for the accomplishment of two things,—the organization of a Convention and the establishment of a Baptist organ. The Convention he was permitted to see formed, in March, 1830, in Greenville, Pitt Co., and he was not only present at its organization but became its first corresponding secretary. For four years he traveled over the State, preaching the gospel, enlightening the people as to the cause of missions, removing prejudices, and uniting the disintegrated Baptists into one body. So fully satisfied was he at this time of the necessity of a periodical that, though no one knew who would publish such a paper, or when or where it would be issued, he began to take the names of subscribers at once, and thus prepared the way for the establishment of the *Recorder*, which began a few years later. In August, 1832, the Convention, sitting at Reeves' chapel, Chatham Co., resolved to establish a manual labor school at Wake Forest, and a committee was appointed to secure a man from the North to take charge of it. In December following the board of the Convention met in Raleigh, and the former committee having failed to secure a master for their school, a new committee, consisting of Wm. Hooper, Thos. Meredith, John Armstrong, and Samuel Wait, was appointed, and three of this committee recommended Samuel Wait for this position. Dr. Wait accepted the appointment, but was advised to continue his agency "for the Convention, as the school was not yet ready to go into operation." The year 1833 was spent in circulating information about the school, in securing students, and furniture for the new establishment. From this time till June, 1846, a period of fourteen years, Dr. Wait was the president of this institution. In 1851 he became president of a female school in Oxford, having spent the intervening years as pastor of Yanceyville and Trinity churches, in Caswell County. After five years' service in this position, he retired to the home of his only child, Mrs. J. B. Brewer, at Wake Forest College, and spent the evening of his days amid the scenes of his usefulness, surrounded by loving kindred, and honored and respected by all. He died July 28, 1867. The State Convention, which met in Goldsborough the next autumn, expressed the desire that, as his history would be largely the history of the denomination in North Carolina, a memoir of him should be prepared by some suitable person. It was understood that Judge John Kerr was selected by his family to perform this service, and he expressed his willingness to undertake the grateful task, but for some cause it was never done.

Wake Forest College.—About 1832 much interest was taken in many parts of the United States in manual labor schools. In 1832 the Baptist State Convention, then less than two years old, bought a farm of 615 acres, lying in Wake County, sixteen miles north of Raleigh, for $2000, and began a manual labor school, under the name of Wake Forest Institute.

In 1833 the Baptist State Convention, which held a session of six days at Cartledge's Creek, in Richmond County, appointed a board of forty trustees, all of whom are now dead except the Rev. Thomas Stradley, of Asheville, and Hon. George W. Thompson, of Wake County.

In December, 1833, Dr. Samuel Wait was chosen as principal of the school, and Rev. John Armstrong, one of the teachers, was put into the field to raise money to equip the school properly. There were no adequate buildings on the place, and but little furniture on hand when the school began operations in February, 1834, with twenty-five pupils. By August there were seventy pupils, and within a little more than a year from its origin the institution was blessed with three gracious revivals, a token of the spiritual tone and power which have marked the whole history of the institution.

In 1839 the manual labor system was abandoned, and a college charter was procured with some difficulty. The bill passed the lower branch of the Legislature by a considerable majority, but was a tie in the senate, and was saved by the casting vote of Mr. Mosely, the president. In 1839 the college building was finished. It was of brick, 132 feet long, 60 feet wide, and four stories high, and cost something over $14,000.

Dr. Wait was president till 1846, when Dr. Wm. Hooper was called to that position. Discouraged by the heavy debts of the college, he retired after two years' service, when Rev. J. B. White, a graduate of Brown University, and a native of New Hampshire, became president. In 1853 he removed to Illinois, and Prof. W. H. Owen was chairman of the faculty until June, 1854, when Dr. W. M. Wingate, who had been laboring for two years to endow the college, became president, and continued to hold the position till his death, in February, 1879,—a period of twenty-five years.

WAKE FOREST COLLEGE.

In July, 1879, Rev. Thomas H. Pritchard, D.D., was chosen president, and is working earnestly to build up the college.

At the opening of the war the college had an invested endowment of about $85,000, with bonds worth $30,000; at its close, all was gone except about $14,000 of railroad stock. It now has an invested endowment of $48,000. Three good buildings, one of which, the one mentioned above, is devoted to dormitories; the second, to chapels and lecture-rooms; the third, to society-halls, library, and reading-room. The last-mentioned building was a present three years ago, from Messrs. J. M. Heck and John G. Williams, of Raleigh, and cost, with furniture, about $14,000. The second building was erected in 1879, and cost about $12,000, and is called Wingate Memorial Hall, in honor of the late president. The library contains about 8000 volumes, and is handsomely fitted up.

The college had last year 181 students in attendance, and its income was about $9000. Thirty-two young ministers attended, who paid no tuition fees. The whole college expenses for a year are a little less than $200. The faculty of the college consists of eight members: T. H. Pritchard, D.D., president, and Professor of Moral Philosophy; W. G. Simmons, Professor of Natural Science; W. Royall, D.D., Professor of Modern Languages; W. B. Royall, Professor of Greek; L. R. Mills, Professor of Mathematics; C. E. Taylor, Professor of Latin; W. L. Poteat, Assistant Professor of Natural Science; and C. W. Scarboro, Tutor of Mathematics. The college is nearly out of debt, and the last year (1880) has been the most prosperous of its history.

Besides Wake Forest, the Baptists of North Carolina have excellent female schools in the Chowan Institute; Wilson Seminary, of which Mr. John B. Brewer, a grandson of Dr. Wait, and a graduate of Wake Forest College, is president and proprietor; Thomasville Female College, presided over by Mr. H. W. Rinehart, who is also the proprietor; Oxford Female College, of which Prof. F. P. Hobgood is principal. In Hendersonville there is a mixed school, known as Judson College, and, in addition, there are male academies, such as Reynoldson Institute, in Gates County; Cedar Creek and Carolina Academies, in Anson County; Salem Academy, in Sampson County; Warsaw High School, in Duplin County; Yadkin Institute; Lillington Academy, in Harnett, and others.

Wakeman, Rev. Levi H., of Connecticut origin; studied in New Haven; ordained pastor of the Third Baptist church in Middletown, Conn., in 1843; subsequent settlements, First Baptist church in Woodstock, in Stepney, and in Willington, Conn., Three Rivers and East Longmeadow, Mass.; now residing in Stamford, Conn.

Waldenses, The, are the most interesting people in Europe. Their history reaches back to the period when popes gathered armies without difficulty to desolate prosperous Albigensian regions of what is now the French republic, when the Bible was almost an unknown book, and when the intellect and liberties of Europe were in shackles, except in the case of heretical heroes, who were treated as outlaws by the banded priests and tyrants of the Old World. We speak of this people with reverence, and think of their long records of fidelity and suffering with tender affection.

There is nothing reliable about the Waldenses before the time of Peter Waldo, of Lyons. It is likely that in their celebrated valleys a people who hated Romish errors, and loved the atoning Saviour, lived from the time of Claude, bishop of Turin, in the ninth century. It is possible that such a community may have served God in these secluded retreats from a much earlier period. But we have no clear testimony on this question.

Peter Waldo, a wealthy citizen of Lyons, was converted about 1160, by a sudden death which occurred at a public meeting which he attended. He had an extraordinary desire to see the Word of God in a good translation, and for this purpose he employed Stephen de Ansa and Bernard Ydros to prepare him such a work in the Romance language. He first procured the gospels, and then by degrees the entire Bible. He also had a collection of choice sayings prepared from the early fathers, on faith and practice. Filled with the hope of heaven, he distributed his property among the poor and scattered copies of his Bible around, and converts rewarded his zeal and rejoiced the angels. The archbishop of Lyons denounced Waldo and his efforts, but the seal of Christ was upon the enterprise, and the gospel leaven worked mightily. He was compelled to leave Lyons, and many of his adherents followed him. He entered Dauphiny, where his labors resulted in a great harvest of converts; by persecution he was driven into Picardy, where the gospel as the saving power of God produced the same heart-changing fruits; from France his disciples pressed into Italy, and the Piedmontese mountains, where the Protestant bishop of Turin three centuries before had sowed the seed of the blessed gospel, gave them a comparatively secure refuge from armed superstition; from France the reformer of Lyons proceeded to Germany, where his usual reception awaited him from the common people, and from the priests and rulers. Some fifty years after the death of Waldo there were multitudes of heretics in the districts of the Rhine and elsewhere in the fatherland of Luther. At Triers " there were," says Neander, " three schools of the heretics; there seem to have been various sects, it is true; but the spread of German versions of the Bible, and the doctrine of the universal priesthood (of Christians), are certainly marks which indicate the Waldenses." Waldo finally retired to Bohemia, where he led throngs of men to Jesus, who continued to uphold the banner of the Cross for generations. Altogether the Waldensian movement was a manifest work of God, and its triumphant progress gave the papacy the heaviest blows and the greatest fears.

The Waldenses were not Albigenses, Kathari, or Paterines. They lived frequently in the same regions, and held many things in common with them, but they had a different origin and birthplace, and came into existence hundreds of years later.

The Waldenses were persecuted with atrocious cruelty, and hosts of them were wickedly put to death.

They have no writings older than the end of the twelfth century. " The Treatise on Antichrist" and " The Noble Lesson" are supposed to have been published at the close of the twelfth century.

Their theology in most features is like the Protestant system of the present day, and it is a perfect contrast to the scheme of Rome.

On baptism the Waldenses were divided. There

is reason to believe that some of them practised infant baptism. It is not unlikely that some of them were Quakers about baptism and the Lord's Supper. The inquisitor, Reinerius Saccho, is the chief authority about the Waldenses, to whom he did not belong, and the Albigenses, with whom he was a member for seventeen years; he states about the Waldenses that "they say a man is then first baptized when he is received into their sect. *Some of them hold that baptism is of no use to little children, because they are not yet actually able to believe*" (Quidam eorum baptismum parvulis non valere tradunt, eo quod nondum actualiter credere possunt). (Allix's "Churches of Piedmont," p. 206. Oxford, 1821.) The celebrated Du Pin gives Reinerius the weight of his great learning and truthfulness as he quotes his statement, "And first about baptism they say, that the preliminary admonition is worth nothing; *that the washing of infants is of no avail to them; that the sureties do not understand what they answer to the priest.*" (II. 482. Dublin.) There is no reasonable ground for doubting that for a long period the Baptists were respectably represented among the "Poor of Lyons," the "Leonists," the "Waldenses."

The Waldenses loved the Scriptures, could repeat entire books with ease, sometimes the whole New Testament, and were extremely anxious to circulate Bibles, and to read them to men. Reinerius, the apostate and papal inquisitor, gives the well-known representation of the Waldensian peddler, who, after selling articles to ladies in splendid homes, tells them about a richer jewel, which, if the situation is favorable, he presents; and they see and speedily hear the Scriptures read and expounded. The business of the traveling merchant is undertaken only to make known the teachings of the Bible. According to the testimony of their greatest enemies they were humble, truthful, self-sacrificing Bible Christians.

In 1530, according to Du Pin, the Waldenses united with the Reformers, and were persuaded to renounce certain peculiarities which heretofore they held, and to receive doctrines which till then had been foreign to their creed. This new arrangement harmonized the reformations of the twelfth and sixteenth centuries, and probably removed Baptist doctrines from the valleys of Piedmont. This ancient community is now Presbyterian, and had its delegate in the recent Pan-Presbyterian Council in Philadelphia.

Walker, Deacon Austin Martin, M.D., was born in Putnam Co., Ga., on the 5th of August, 1808. His early education was received from William H. Seward, who at that time taught school in Putnam County. Mr. Walker graduated at the State University, and, whilst residing in Athens, connected himself with the Baptist church of that city when he was seventeen years of age. On leaving college he took a course of medical lectures in Philadelphia, and afterwards practised medicine there for four years. After his return to Georgia he married and settled in Columbus, where he assisted in organizing the first Baptist church in that city. He was a planter. When on his death-bed, in 1846, Deacon James Boykin sent for Dr. Walker, blessed him, prayed that his own mantle might fall on him, and requested that he should be made a deacon by the church. This was done; and Dr. Walker continued an active, zealous, pious, and faithful deacon the rest of his life. He was a wealthy man, and gave freely to the cause of Christ. He was a thoroughly conscientious man, and a strict Bible Baptist. He believed strongly in the maintenance of church discipline, and in orderly Christian conduct. He was a close and earnest student of the Bible, and to his death, at the age of seventy, he was either a superintendent or teacher in the Sunday-school. He regularly employed ministers to preach to the servants on his plantations, and when possible attending the meetings himself. So great was the devotion of his servants to him that, even when emancipated, they desired to sign a paper, contracting to preserve the relation of master and slave for life. Of course this was not done, but it showed how great was their love for him, and their confidence in him. The last years of Dr. Walker's life were spent in Macon, Ga., where he was a deacon, his membership being transferred from Columbus. He died peacefully on the 3d of June, 1878, highly respected by all who knew him.

Walker, Hon. Charles, was one of those earliest and most influentially identified with the growth of Chicago and the West. Born at Plainfield, Otsego Co., N. Y., in 1802, early a Christian, and always a Baptist, he had identified himself with the business and religious interests of Chicago some years before he became a resident there, in 1847. In that year he united with the First Baptist church, and until his death, in June, 1868, he was one of its most active, liberal, and influential members. He was identified from time to time with some of the most important secular enterprises upon a large scale centring at Chicago. "The first shipment of any kind made from that port is believed to have been made by him. The first shipment of wheat certainly was. The first of the railroads running out of the city—the Galena and Chicago—owed its early vigor largely to his enterprise, courage, and faith, while his far-seeing views contributed much to inspire those other great undertakings which made Chicago at length, what he always believed it would become, the commercial centre and metropolis of the West." Mr. Walker, withal, was a devout Christian and an earnest Baptist. He was one of the founders of the University of Chicago, and until his death served upon its board of trustees, while all the various missionary enterprises of the denomination shared in his sympathy, his counsels, and his gifts.

Walker, Rev. C. W., was born in Holden, Worcester Co., Mass., Feb. 13, 1814; attended the Worcester Manual Labor High School, under the principalship of Dr. Silas Bailey, where he was converted; studied at Waterville College, Me. After being principal of several high schools and academies, and rendering eminent service to the cause of education, he was ordained to the ministry Aug. 16, 1860, as pastor of the church of Essex, N. Y. In 1862 he became pastor of the First Baptist church of North Stratford, N. H. In 1864 he was appointed chaplain of the 1st N. H. Heavy Artillery. In 1878 he took charge of the churches in Little Blue Valley and Joy Creek, Kansas. In 1880 he began to preach at Nollenburg. Mr. Walker is possessed of scholarly attainments, and as a teacher and preacher has accomplished much good.

Walker, Rev. Jacob Garrett, A.M., was born at Falls of Schuylkill, Philadelphia, Pa., Dec. 28,

REV. JACOB GARRETT WALKER, A.M.

1840; baptized March 21, 1858, by Rev. N. Judson Clark; graduated from Philadelphia Central High School in 1858, and from the university at Lewisburg, Pa., in 1862, subsequently receiving the degree of A.M. from both institutions. In January, 1863, became principal of public schools at Phœnixville, Pa., and continued in that position three years and a half; during part of this time supplied the neighboring church at Pughtown, Pa., and subsequently became pastor there until May 31, 1868, having been ordained Dec. 5, 1865. In October, 1868, took charge of the church at Balligomingo, Pa., where he remained until November, 1872, when he became pastor of the Mantua church, Philadelphia, Pa., where he still remains.

Mr. Walker, while a most diligent and successful pastor, is also deeply interested in the general work of the denomination. He has done efficient service as president and secretary of the Philadelphia Ministers' Conference. In 1877 he was made moderator of the Philadelphia Baptist Association, and since that time has been its clerk and the secretary of its board of trustees. He is also a member of various boards, and a curator of the university at Lewisburg. He has written considerably for the press, has been twice poet at Lewisburg commencements, and was the poet of the Valley Forge Centenary in 1878. Since 1871 has been editor of the "Baptist Year-Book." He is very popular both as pastor and preacher, has a clear incisive mind, is a thorough-going Baptist, has maintained an unblemished character, and is universally regarded as one of the wisest and best of the Philadelphia Baptist ministers.

Walker, Hon. James Otis, was born in Whiting, Vt., Aug. 6, 1778. His native place was a new settlement, and had a sparse population. Such, however, was his thirst for knowledge that it is said "he used to lie in the corner in the evenings and read, having only pine-knots for a light, occasionally going to school for a few weeks." He held the office of civil magistrate for thirty years. It is referred to "as a proof of the high estimation in which he was held that, while he was a member of the Masonic fraternity, and Whiting was a strongly anti-Masonic town, he held his office through the entire struggle in respect to Masonry, and such was the confidence reposed in his integrity that none of his most bitter opponents questioned the propriety of his retaining his office." For several years he represented the town in the State Legislature. No man was more public-spirited than he. Calls were constantly made upon him for aid to build churches, pay ministers' salaries, support benevolent and educational causes, and the appeals were not made in vain. "His pen was often employed by public request in the preparation of temperance addresses, in which reform he took a deep interest." In his old age he was paralyzed, but amid all the decays of nature he kept a genial spirit, and was busy and active in his habits to the last. He early connected himself with the Baptist Church, and lived and died in its fellowship. His death occurred Nov. 27, 1857.

Walker, Rev. Jeremiah, was born in Bute Co., N. C., about 1747. In early life he was called into the peace of Christ and baptized. He possessed extraordinary talents as a thinker and as a speaker, and he soon became a great preacher. In 1769 he took charge of the Nottoway church, Va., and in a few years, assisted by brethren called to the Saviour and introduced into the ministry through his instrumentality, he established between twenty and thirty churches south of the James River. He was a natural orator, an exemplary Christian, and a magnet to attract the love of men. He was a burning and a shining light. He was incarcerated in Chesterfield jail for preaching without lawful authority, and released with additional popularity. His ministry had enjoyed the divine favor in a remarkable measure, and its fruits were conspicuous all over Virginia. He was tempted and fell into immorality, and after some years of Christian conduct he lapsed from purity again. On repenting of his evil ways he embraced Arminian doctrines, and advocated them even to the extent of schism among his brethren. He was a great, and for many years a good, man, and then a wreck in morals and in doctrines. He died Nov. 20, 1792, a forgiven sinner.

Walker, Col. John B., is a deacon of the Baptist church at Madison, Ga., and a man whose intelligence, liberality, piety, and public spirit made him widely known and highly respected. He was born in Burke County in 1804 or 1805. He had the best academical advantages. He studied law, but never engaged in the practice, his large property demanding all of his time and attention. He has given his thousands to the cause of religion and education. Joining the church at thirty, he has for nearly half a century been a useful church member and Sunday-school worker. He was a member of the first board of trustees of Mercer University, as he was also of Mercer Institute. Mercer University, the Georgia Female College, the Madison Baptist church, and many other good causes have largely enjoyed the benefit of his liberality. During the war his large mansion in Madison was a hospital, opened freely for the benefit of all, and the entire means at his disposal were subject to the demands of charity. In the Madison church he has long been a pillar, and in the community where he has dwelt for seventy years no man stands higher in public estimation.

Walker, Rev. Joseph, was born in Delaware Co., Pa., Feb. 14, 1787. He was baptized into the fellowship of the First Baptist church of Wilmington, Del., in 1806. He was ordained pastor of the church of Marcus Hook in 1824, and for twenty-four years he preached the gospel in that place. In 1848 he became pastor of the Brandywine church, Pa., where he served the Lord with great fidelity and success for twenty years. He then resigned, and went to Pittsburgh, where he rested from his labors in the house of his son-in-law, Dr. Trevor, Feb. 28, 1870. Mr. Walker was beloved by the whole Philadelphia Association, of which, for some years before his death, he was the oldest ministerial member. He was full of brotherly affection and of the grace of God. His Christian life was a precious gospel sermon, and his death was a heavy blow to a multitude of the friends of Jesus. In his two fields of labor he was regarded by Christians and unconverted persons as a tender father, an Israelite indeed.

Walker, Rev. Levi, M.D., was born in 1784 in Massachusetts; removed to Maine; converted in 1804; for a time a Methodist circuit preacher; became a Baptist, and united with the First Baptist church in Fall River, Mass.; still preached; studied medicine and was a physician; became pastor of the Baptist church in Warwick, R. I., in 1816; settled with the Baptist church in Preston, Conn., in 1819; in 1823 removed to a farm in North Stonington, Conn.; preached with success in various places; organized the first Sunday-school in the town; was the first minister of the Third Baptist church in North Stonington; accomplished much in his two professions; a man of talents and toil; his wife, Phebe, a superior woman, died in Andover, Conn., Feb. 11, 1880, aged ninety-two years; had three sons who became Baptist ministers,—Rev. Levi, Rev. William C., and Rev. Orin T.,—last two now living. He died Dec. 12, 1869, aged eighty-five years.

Walker, Rev. Levi, Jr., son of Rev. Levi and Phebe Walker, was born March 22, 1811; converted in 1829; licensed to preach by the Third Baptist church in North Stonington; ordained and settled as pastor in Tolland, Conn.; served churches in Massachusetts and New Hampshire; stricken by disease, died in Griswold, Conn., Feb. 2, 1839, in his twenty-eighth year.

Walker, Rev. O. T., A.M., was born in Preston, Conn., Feb. 1, 1822. He is a son of Rev. Levi Walker, M.D. He studied at Hamilton, N. Y., and at Washington College, Hartford, Conn. He entered the ministry when twenty-four, and was ordained at Orleans, Mass. He was six years pastor of the Second church of New London, Conn., where he baptized about 200. He was six years pastor of the First church of Trenton, N. J., where during his oversight a large and splendid church edifice was built, about 300 persons were baptized, and the church was greatly strengthened. He was six years pastor of Bowdoin Square church, Boston, during which time he baptized nearly 300. The church was almost ready to disband when Mr. Walker began his labors, but the blessing of God attended the efforts of the new pastor, and the faith and hopes of the church were soon wonderfully enlarged.

Mr. Walker has served as pastor in Chicago, Ill., Meriden, Conn., Providence, R. I., and in Orleans, Mass. His present charge is the Harvard Street church, Boston, where he has labored five years. When Mr. Walker entered upon his second pastorate in Boston the meeting-house had been closed for a time, and the congregation was scattered; but under God the church has been blessed with numerous and valuable additions, and a good Sunday-school and an overflowing prayer-meeting have been gathered.

Mr. Walker is an indefatigable worker, ready for any errand of mercy. Very popular among the sick, the mourners weeping for their loved dead, and the happy candidates for the nuptial blessing.

He is one of the most useful ministers in and around Boston, whose labors have been greatly blessed out of it as well as in it.

Walker, Rev. Sanders, was for many years one of the most useful pioneer ministers of Georgia. Born March 17, 1740, in Prince William Co., Va., he was a singular instance of the transforming power of God's grace. Of an unmanageable temper before conversion, his heart and nature were so changed by the Holy Spirit that he was ever afterwards distinguished for the meekness and gravity of his deportment. Among all who knew him the *meek Sanders Walker* was a proverbial expression. He began to preach in North Carolina in 1767, and, about four years afterwards, moved to a place in Bute Co., N. C., notorious for wickedness and ignorance of religion; but his Master was with him, and in a short time a considerable church arose under his ministry. He removed to Georgia in 1772, and joined the Kiokee church, being still unordained; but he must have been ordained prior to May 20, 1775, as his name appears on the Presbytery which ordained Abraham Marshall at that time. In Georgia he labored mostly in Wilkes County, where he resided, and he is thought to have been mainly instrumental in the constitution of Fishing Creek church, the fifth formed in the State. He finished his course with joy, in the sixty-fifth year of his age, in 1805.

Walker, Rev. William Carey, son of Rev. Levi and Phebe (Burroughs) Walker, was born in Warwick, R. I., Dec. 24, 1818; became a teacher; converted at the age of fourteen; united with First Baptist church in Westerly, R. I., in 1837; removed to North Stonington, Conn., in 1838, and to Hartford in 1839; studied for the ministry from 1841 to 1845, preaching two years for South Windsor church; settled with First Baptist church in Groton, Conn., and was ordained in June, 1845; remained five years; settled with the church in Willington in 1850; continued six and a half years; settled in Putnam six and a half years; entered the Union army as chaplain of the 18th Conn. Vol. Regiment of Infantry, serving one year and a half, till close of war; settled with New Britain church, Conn., for about six years; everywhere favored with success and revivals; since 1871 has been a missionary and Sunday-school worker for the Connecticut Baptist State Convention, four of the years with the Sunday-schools; always an evangelist in spirit; earnest and wise worker; active for education, temperance, and anti-slavery; advocate of missions; served on school committees; wrote largely for the *Christian Secretary*, in the interests of the churches and schools; wrote the history of the 18th Conn. Vol. Regiment of Infantry; for last two years has been a representative from Andover, Conn., to the State Legislature; still serving the State as a missionary. Mr. Walker is one of the noble-hearted, laborious, honored, and successful ministers of Connecticut.

Walker, Rev. William P., was born in Jackson Co., W. Va., May 14, 1834. In 1855 he married Miss McClung, in Nicholas County, and soon after united with the Mount Pleasant church, and became at once an active worker. In a short time he was licensed to preach, and entered Alleghany College, where he remained until 1861. He was ordained, and preached in Nicholas and Fayette Counties until 1865, when he became pastor of Williamstown and Pleasant Valley churches, in Wood County. He remained in this locality about twelve years. About 1877 he removed to Huntington, and became pastor of a church of not a score of members, but which, under his faithful labors, has grown to 116. The church has bought a parsonage worth $1000, and is now nearly self-supporting.

Mr. Walker has for many years been president of the General Association of the State, also agent for Shelton College; is one of the very best preachers and pastors in the State, and has always given entire satisfaction to his brethren in every position.

Wallace, Lady Craigie.—Chambers, in his "Domestic Annals of Scotland" (ii. 213), says, "Where there had formerly been no avowed Anabaptists there were now many, so that thrice in the week, namely, on Monday, Wednesday, and Friday, there were some dipped at Bonnington Mill, between Leith and Edinburgh, both men and women of good rank. Some days there would be sundry hundred persons attending that action, and fifteen persons baptized in one day by the Anabaptists. Among the converts was the Lady Craigie Wallace, a lady in the west country. In autumn, at Cupar, Mr. Brown, preacher to Fairfax's regiment, rebaptized several of the soldiers in the Eden, near to Airdrie's lodging, by dipping them over head and ears, many of the inhabitants looking on." This was in 1652. The doctrines of the Baptists were carried to Scotland by the English army, and their form of baptism seemed attractive to the cautious people of that country.

Wallace, Rev. Isaiah, son of Rev. James Wallace, was born in Hillsborough, New Brunswick, Jan. 17, 1826. He was converted early, and baptized by Rev. Samuel Elder in 1848. He graduated from Acadia College in 1855, and was ordained April 3, 1856. He became pastor at Miramichi in 1858, at Carleton, St. John, in 1860. From 1861, Mr. Wallace held successively the pastoral office in Nova Scotia in Lower Granville, Milton, Yarmouth County, and Berwick, and has been agent for the Home Mission Board. As pastor and evangelist, his labors have been very successful in New Brunswick and Nova Scotia.

Wallace, Rev. James, was born Jan. 17, 1797, at Hopewell, New Brunswick. He was converted under the ministry of Rev. Joseph Crandall, and baptized by him in 1826. Mr. Wallace's pastoral and missionary labors in Albert, Westmoreland, and Kings Counties, New Brunswick, proved a great blessing to the churches and people there. He preached successfully, and baptized many converts in these counties. He died March 7, 1871.

Wallace, Hon. Thomas, was born in Petersburg, Va., Sept. 7, 1812; was educated at William and Mary College and at the University of Virginia. He practised law, and was a member of the State Legislature during the sessions of 1850–51. It was mainly through his instrumentality that the elegant house of worship erected by the Baptists of Petersburg was completed. He was a member of the First church of that city for a long time, and one of its deacons, and the efficient superintendent of its Sunday-school. Mr. Wallace was a man of wealth and influence, and he used his influence and money for the cause of Christ. He died May 14, 1868.

Waller, Rev. Edmond, son of Rev. William Edmond Waller, and brother of the distinguished Rev. George Waller, was born in Spottsylvania Co., Va., Jan. 11, 1775. He removed with his parents to Kentucky about 1781, and settled in Fayette County. He united with the Baptist church at Bryant's Station in 1798, and in 1801 he removed to Anderson County, and was ordained to the ministry at Salt River church. He traveled and preached in the new settlements for some years. In 1808 he was called to Hillsborough church in Woodford, and the next year to Mount Pleasant in Jessamine County. With these and some other churches in that region he labored during the remainder of his life. He was one of the most popular and useful ministers of his generation in that part of Kentucky. He died in 1842.

Waller, Rev. George, son of Rev. William Edmond Waller, a well-known Baptist minister in Virginia and Kentucky, and a nephew of the distinguished Rev. John Waller, of Virginia, was born in Spottsylvania Co., Va., in 1777. He removed with his father to Kentucky about 1781, locating for a short time in Lincoln, and then settling in Fayette County. In 1798 he removed to Shelby County, and was baptized by his father into the fellowship of Buck Creek Baptist church, in that county, in 1801. He was ordained in 1802, and succeeded his father (who had returned to Virginia) in the pastorate of Buck Creek church, a position he occupied fifty years. He was pastor of Burk's Branch church about forty years, and of Bethel church a shorter period, and he was a missionary to Louisville before there was a church in that city. He traveled over the State, preaching in the interest of missions. He was editor of a weekly Baptist paper published at Bloomfield, Ky., about 1827, and was moderator of Long Run Association twenty-five years in succession, preaching the introductory sermon before that body seven times. He was a strong, logical preacher, and few men were more widely known, or exercised a greater influence in his State, during his long ministry. He died in July, 1860.

Waller, Rev. John, was born in Spottsylvania Co., Va., on the 23d of December, 1741, and was a descendant of the honorable family of Wallers, in England. His profanity acquired for him the name of "swearing Jack Waller," and his general wickedness that of "the devil's adjutant." He was especially bitter against the Baptists, and was one of the grand jury that persecuted Rev. Lewis Craig for preaching. Mr. Craig's meek address to the jury arrested his attention and touched his heart. For seven or eight months his agony and remorse were intense. At length, having found peace in believing in Jesus, immediately he conferred not with flesh and blood, but began to preach the faith which he had destroyed, serving the Lord with greater zeal, if that was possible, than he had served Satan. Traveling through many counties, he everywhere attracted crowds of hearers and made many converts.

He was soon made to feel the resentment of his former companions in sin. In a letter dated "Urbanna Prison, Middlesex County, Aug. 12, 1771," he gives an account of the arrest and imprisonment of himself and many others, and the cruel scourging of several by "the magistrate and the parson of the parish." "I have also to inform you that six of our brethren are confined in Caroline jail, viz.: Brethren Lewis Craig, John Burrus, John Young, Edward Herndon, James Goodrick, and Bartholomew Cheming." Those days did indeed try men's souls.

In 1775 or 1776 he adopted the Arminian doctrine, declared himself an independent Baptist, and withdrew from his brethren. But in 1787 he returned to his first love. The same year a very great revival began under his preaching, and continued for several years, spreading far and wide.

In 1793 he removed to Abbeville, S. C. Here his success, though considerable, was not equal to that in his native State. His last sermon, at the funeral of a young man, was from Zech. ii. 4: "Run, speak to that young man." He addressed the young in feeble, touching strains, saying that it was his last sermon. He spoke until his strength quite failed, and then tottered to a bed, from which he was carried home, and died July 4, 1802, in his sixty-second year.

He preached thirty-five years, baptized more than 2000 persons, assisted in ordaining twenty-seven ministers, and in constituting eighteen churches, and lay one hundred and thirteen days in four different jails, and he was repeatedly scourged in Virginia. He now rests from his labors, and his works followed him.

Waller, Rev. John Lightfoot, LL.D., an eminent preacher and journalist, was born in Woodford Co., Ky., Nov. 23, 1809. He was educated under private teachers, and became one of the best scholars in the State. At eighteen he wrote "A Church without a Creed," which evinced remarkable genius. After teaching some years in Jessamine County, he became editor of the *Baptist Banner* about 1835. Subsequently he edited the *Baptist Banner and Western Pioneer*, a weekly religious paper published at Louisville, Ky. In this position he speedily established the reputation of being one of the ablest editors of his day. In 1840 he was ordained to the ministry, and the next year was appointed general agent of the General Association of Baptists in Kentucky. In 1843 he succeeded his father as pastor of Glen's Creek church, in Woodford County. In 1845 he commenced the publication of the *Western Baptist Review*, a monthly which took rank with the ablest periodicals of the kind in the country. The title was afterwards changed to the *Christian Repository*. He continued its publication until his death. In 1849 he was elected to a seat in the convention that formed the present constitution of the State of Kentucky, and was said to have been the most talented debater in that very able body. This was the only civil office he ever sought. In 1850 he resumed the editorship of the *Baptist Banner and Western Pioneer*. He was the most prominent mover in originating the Bible Revision Association. In 1842 he held his celebrated debate on baptism with Rev. Nathan L. Rice. He died at his home in Louisville, Ky., Oct. 10, 1854.

Waller, Rev. Jonathan Cox, son of Rev. George Waller, was born in Shelby Co., Ky., March 24, 1812. He united with Buck Creek church, of which his father was pastor, in 1834. He is a powerful writer, and has prepared much for the religious press. In 1863 he published a book on the "Speedy Coming and Personal Reign of Christ," which ran through four editions. For several years he edited the *Western Recorder*. He was ordained to the ministry in 1879, but has not yet taken charge of any church. He resides at Pleasure Ridge Park, Ky.

Waller, Rev. Napoleon Bonaparte, brother of Rev. John Lightfoot Waller, a very brilliant and greatly lamented young minister, was born March 24, 1826. He professed religion at an early age, and united with the Baptist church of which his father was pastor. He graduated at Georgetown College, after which he was ordained to the ministry. On his way to Owensborough, Ky., for the purpose of taking charge of the church at that village, he stopped at Nicholasville, where he died of cholera, Aug. 1, 1855.

Waller, Rev. William Edmond, son of A. D. Waller, and grandson of Rev. George Waller, a young preacher of extraordinary gifts and of distinguished piety and conversation, was born in Shelby Co., Ky., Nov. 17, 1845. He was educated in the city schools of Louisville. He united with Long Run Baptist church in Jefferson Co., Ky., in 1866, and was licensed to preach the same year. In 1868 he was ordained, and soon after he was called to the care of the church at Jeffersontown, in Jefferson County, and afterwards to Harrod's Creek church, in Oldham County, to both of which he preached until his death. He performed much valuable missionary labor, and for several years was clerk of Long Run Association. He died Nov. 10, 1878.

Wallin, Rev. Benjamin, was born in London, England, in 1711. He heard the word of life from his godly father, the Rev. Edward Wallin, from childhood, and in his young manhood he gave himself to the Saviour, and was immersed by his father, and received into the church of which he was pastor.

On Thursday, Oct. 15, 1741, he was ordained pastor of the Maze Pond church, London. Dr. Gill preached the sermon. Six ministers took part in the service, and it lasted from 10.30 A.M. to 2.45 P.M.,—that is, four hours and fifteen minutes. The ministry with which Mr. Wallin was invested he honored for more than forty-one years, and during that lengthened service the Saviour gave him signal marks of his gracious favor. He died Feb. 19, 1782.

He was a man of sagacity, piety, Bible knowledge, and of zeal that burned like a fire. He was a poet, a Scripture expositor, and a great worker.

His writings were numerous and valuable. He was the author of forty-one works, one of which was "Evangelical Hymns on Various Views of the Christian Life." He was a valued correspondent of President Manning, of Brown University, and left it a bequest in his will.

Walsh, Alexander S., D.D., was born in the city of New York, Dec. 14, 1841. His father was for a time an officer in the English army. Coming to America, he was employed by the great merchant A. T. Stewart, for whom Dr. Walsh was named. His father removed to Michigan and engaged in farming. In 1854, under the patronage of an uncle, he entered the Polytechnic Institute of Brooklyn. He soon returned to Michigan, and while a mere lad commenced speaking publicly on the great issues of the day, especially slavery. In 1860 he commenced study at Oberlin College. In 1862 he enlisted in the army, and towards the close of the war was honorably discharged. He returned to Oberlin, and was graduated in 1866. He united with a Congregational church, and commenced preaching in Norwalk, O., organized a church, and was ordained its pastor. In 1868 he settled with a church in Kokomo, Ind. In 1869 he accepted a position in Emerson College, Ala., which he left for a tour in Europe. On his return, in 1870, he joined the Baptists. He settled in Jamaica, L. I., preaching, lecturing, and editing the *Long Island Farmer*. While in the West he edited the *Oberlin Court Record*, the *Student*, and was a contributor to several Western papers. In 1872 he accepted the pastorate of the Gethsemane (now Willowby Avenue) church, Brooklyn, where he met with great success. In 1877 he was called to the South church, New York, where he was equally prosperous. He has baptized since joining the Baptists 500 converts. The degree of D.D. was conferred on him by Hillsdale College, Mich., in 1877.

Walter, Thomas U., LL.D., son of Joseph S. and Deborah Walter, was born in Philadelphia, Pa., Sept. 4, 1804. He was given the name of a former pastor of his parents,—Thomas Ustick.

His taste for architecture and mathematics was very early developed, and gave promise of future distinction.

His education was liberal. After spending some time in the office of William Strickland, Esq., he pursued an elaborate course of mathematics and the study of the physical sciences, and also gave special attention to the art of landscape-painting and the different branches of mechanical construction. He re-entered Mr. Strickland's office in 1828, and devoted two years to the specific study of architecture, the practice of which he began in 1830.

His first important public work was the Philadelphia County prison (Moyamensing). His designs were approved, and he was appointed architect of the work in 1831.

His design for the Girard College for Orphans was adopted by the select and common councils of Philadelphia in 1833; and the corner-stone of

THOMAS U. WALTER, LL.D.

that magnificent building was laid with appropriate ceremonies on the 4th day of July of that year.

This imposing structure constitutes an enduring monument to the liberality of Stephen Girard, as well as to the skill and genius of Mr. Walter, who planned it throughout and carried it on to completion. It was finished in 1847, having been fourteen years in building.

During the progress of this work Mr. Walter spent several months in Great Britain and on the continent of Europe, visiting public institutions and gratifying his taste on classic ground.

Subsequently he submitted to the board of directors an elaborate report, which became their guide in finishing and fitting up the college which now so admirably provides for the comfort, health, and instruction of nearly 1000 boys.

In 1851 the designs of Mr. Walter for the extension of the U. S. Capitol were approved, and he was appointed architect of the work by the President of the United States (Millard Fillmore).

This appointment he held fourteen years, during which time, in addition to his specific work, he planned and executed the iron dome which now crowns the Capitol, the east and west wings of the Patent Office, and the extension of the General Post-office. He also designed the new treasury building, the marine barracks at Brooklyn and Pensacola, and the government hospital for the insane.

As evidencing the estimation in which he is held, because of his literary and scientific attainments, it may be stated that he received the honorary degree of Master of Arts, in 1849, from Madison University, N. Y. In 1855, that of Doctor of Philosophy from the university at Lewisburg, Pa. And in 1857, from Harvard University, that of Doctor of Laws.

Dr. Walter delivered a course of lectures on architecture before the students of Columbian College, Washington, D. C., in 1860. He also delivered many other popular lectures in Philadelphia and vicinity, at one time holding a professorship of Architecture in the Franklin Institute, and lecturing on his art for two successive seasons.

He has been a member of the American Philosophical Society for nearly forty years, and of the Franklin Institute fifty years. He was also one of the original members of the American Institute of Architects, and is now (1879) its honored president.

He made a public profession of religion in 1829, having been baptized July 12 of that year in the river Schuylkill, at Spruce Street, by the Rev. John C. Murphy. On the same day he was publicly received into the membership of the Spruce Street Baptist church, then worshiping temporarily in the court-house at the corner of Sixth and Chestnut Streets, their meeting-house on Spruce Street not being completed. He was many years clerk of this church, and also superintendent of the Sunday-school.

When he removed to Washington, D. C., to take charge of the Capitol extension, he also removed his letter to the E Street Baptist church. His connection there was rich in fruits of well-directed effort, and will long be remembered by many, especially by a Bible-class of more than fifty young men, upon whom he left the impress of his own Bible-loving spirit.

Upon returning to Philadelphia, he became one of the constituent members of the Second Baptist church of Germantown, in which he filled the office of deacon.

More recently he removed to another part of the city, transferring his membership to the Memorial Baptist church. Here again he was called to the deaconship, and among his loved associates he yet lives, enjoying the privileges and activities of a Christian life.

Walters, W. T., D.D., a conspicuous man in his day in the management of Baptist affairs in North Carolina, was born in Pittsylvania Co., Va., in 1825. He was baptized by Rev. J. L. Prichard, and by him influenced to become a student in Wake Forest College, where he graduated in 1848. He soon after became tutor, and in a year or two was made Professor of Mathematics in his *alma mater*. He remained in this position till the exercises of the college were suspended by the war. He was a trustee, and for the last two years of his life treasurer, of the college, but was not again connected with it as instructor. In 1867, Dr. Walters became corresponding secretary of the Baptist State Convention, and did good service for three years in organizing the mission work of the State.

He was three times identified with the press. In 1867 he purchased, in connection with Mr. J. H. Mills, the *Biblical Recorder*, his interest in which he transferred to his partner in a few months. He edited the *Farmer's Journal*, under the management of Gen. Johnston Jones, and for several years he was the valuable agricultural editor of the *Biblical Recorder*. He was one of the best farmers in the State, and was a preacher of much vigor. The churches of Littleton and Wilson owe their existence to him. He died Dec. 31, 1877.

Walton, Rev. W. A., was born the slave of Col. James Mann, March 17, 1836, in Morgan Co., Ga. He was converted in 1856, and was baptized into the fellowship of Antioch church, Morgan Co., Ga., by Rev. J. Stillwell. Having removed to Texas, he became a member of the Washington church, composed both of white and colored persons, under the ministry of Rev. Michael Ross. Under the preaching of Mr. Ross he stored his memory with passages of Scriptures in a wonderful degree, imitative of the mental habit of the preacher, who had been reared in England in the state church. Under the pastorate of Rev. James E. Paxton he was in 1866 licensed to preach the gospel, giving promise of great usefulness. He first went to school one month to Mr. Watt Bonner; second, two weeks to Samuel Carroll; third, to J. H. Washington, two days; fourth, to Dr. W. C. Crane, at Baylor University, Independence, two months. He has had the pastoral care of five churches, and has the pastoral care of four at this time,—Anderson, Grimes Co., with a membership of 275; Navisota, same county, membership, 445; Washington, Washington Co., membership, 363; Hempstead, Waller Co., membership, 385; total membership, 1368. He has baptized 863 persons since he has been ordained to the gospel ministry. No colored minister in Texas draws larger congregations at all times to hear him, and no one exerts a better general influence over his race for time and eternity than W. A. Walton. He bids fair for a long life of usefulness.

Ward, John, LL.D., was born in London, England, in 1679. His father was a Baptist minister, and he belonged to the congregation of Dr. J. Stennett, of his native city. He possessed learning of the highest order, and loved the acquisition of knowledge with an intense affection.

In 1720 he was elected Professor of Rhetoric in

Gresham College, London; some time after, a member of the Royal Society; and in 1752 one of its vice-presidents. The University of Edinburgh conferred on him the degree of LL.D.

He was the author of "The Lives of the Gresham Professors," of "The Westminster Greek Grammar," and of other works. He aided Horsley in his "Britannia Romana," and Ainsworth in his "Dictionary." His information embraced almost every subject, and his character for piety, modesty, and usefulness made him an honor to our denomination.

In 1754, Dr. Ward put £1200 of bank stock in trust for the education of two or more young men for the ministry in a Scotch university, or elsewhere. In 1876 there were four brethren aided by this fund. Some of our most distinguished English ministers have received assistance from "Dr. Ward's Trust." The founder of it died in 1758.

Ward, Prof. Milan L., was born in Meredith, N. Y., in 1829. He graduated at Madison Uni-

PROF. MILAN L. WARD.

versity, after which he taught in Norwich Academy, then in Southampton Co., Va. In 1860 he was called to the chair of Natural Sciences in the Delaware Literary Institute. In 1862 he became principal of Norwich Academy, which position he held until 1869, when he resigned. Under his administration the academy rose from a very low position to one of the highest rank, standing fifth among the two hundred academies in the State of New York. From 1869 to 1873, Prof. Ward had charge of the educational department of Ottawa University, Kansas. In 1873 he was elected Professor of Mathematics and English in the Kansas State Agricultural College, which position he still holds. He is also loan commissioner, librarian, and, in the absence of the president, acting president of the college.

From the commencement of his religious life the predominant desire in Prof. Ward's heart has been to be useful while he lived. To this end he *worked his way* through college. He took a theological course, and was ordained to labor as a missionary preacher among the destitute churches in Southampton Co., Va. But he soon became convinced that teaching, rather than preaching, should be his life-work. His highest ambition is to be recognized as a Christian educator.

Prof. Ward takes an active interest in church and denominational work, and has held for three years the office of secretary of the Kansas Baptist Convention.

Ward, Gov. Samuel, was born in Newport, R. I., May 27, 1725. He was the second son of Gov. Richard Ward, and a lineal descendant of Roger Williams. He removed in early manhood to Westerly, R. I., and met with great pecuniary success in the agricultural and mercantile pursuits in which he engaged. He represented his adopted home for several years in the General Assembly of Rhode Island, and took a prominent part in its deliberations. In 1761 he was appointed chief justice of the colony, and in May, 1762, was chosen its governor. He took a great interest in the founding of Rhode Island College, and was one of its trustees from 1764 to 1776. In 1765 he was re-elected governor. When the Stamp Act, so infamous in the eyes of the colonists, was passed, and the governors of the colonies took an oath to sustain and enforce it, Gov. Ward alone persisted in his refusal to yield compliance. Once more he was chosen governor of the colony. At the end of his third term he retired to comparatively private life, but was a thoughtful observer of what was transpiring in the country, and took a decided stand from the outset against the oppressive acts of the British crown. He, with Stephen Hopkins, represented the State of Rhode Island in the Continental Congress of 1774, and advocated the most vigorous measures against the encroachments of Parliament. When affairs reached a crisis, in consequence of the blood shed at Concord and Lexington, Gov. Ward's counsel and advice in Congress were received with great deference. He was always called to the chair when Congress went into a committee of the whole. He was chairman of several important committees, and among them that which was appointed to nominate a general for the American army, and he reported the name of Col. George Washington. His son, Capt. Samuel Ward, occupied a prominent position in the Revolutionary forces, and enjoyed the intimate friendship of the commander-in-chief. The whole course of Gov. Ward through the early stages of the Revolution showed him to be a true patriot, ready to make any and every sacrifice for his country's welfare. Had his life and health been spared, he would have continued to devote himself to the cause in which he had embarked "his life, his fortune, and his sacred honor." In the midst of arduous duties, which must have taxed his energies to their utmost, he was attacked with the small-pox, and died March 26, 1776. In communicating the sad intelligence to the secretary of the State of Rhode Island, his colleague, Stephen Hopkins, says, among other things, "He will be carried into the great Presbyterian meeting-house in Arch Street, where a funeral discourse will be delivered by the Rev. Samuel Stillman. The corpse will from thence be carried to the Baptist burying-ground in this city, and there interred." John Adams also writes, "Gov. Ward was an amiable and a sensible man, a steadfast friend to his country, upon very pure principles. His funeral was attended with the same solemnities as Mr. Randolph's. Mr. Stillman being the Anabaptist here, of which persuasion was the governor, was desired by Congress to preach a sermon, which he did with great applause."

The body of Gov. Ward was interred in the grounds of the First Baptist church, in Philadelphia, and a monument erected over his remains by order of the Rhode Island General Assembly. In 1860 the body was removed to the cemetery of Newport, R. I.

Ward, Thomas, was the eldest son of John Ward, who had been an officer in one of Cromwell's cavalry regiments, and, emigrating to America from Gloucester, England, after the accession of King Charles II., he settled in Newport, R. I., where he died in April, 1698. His son Thomas preceded his father in taking up his residence in Newport, arriving there not far from 1660. For his second wife he married Amy Smith, granddaughter of Roger Williams. Backus says of him, "That he was a Baptist before he came out of Cromwell's army, and a very useful man in the colony of Rhode Island." For one year—1677-78 —he was general treasurer of the colony under the royal charter of Charles II. His descendants were among the most distinguished citizens of Rhode Island. His son Richard was governor of the colony, 1741-43, having previously been secretary of state for nineteen years, 1714-33. His grandson Samuel filled the highest posts of honor which his fellow-citizens could confer on him. A son of Samuel was secretary of state for thirty-seven years. The widow of Thomas Ward, already referred to as the granddaughter of Roger Williams, married Arnold Collins, and their son, Henry Collins, who was an extensive merchant in Newport, R. I., became so good a patron of letters that he was called by Dr. Benjamin Waterhouse "the Lorenzo de' Medici of Rhode Island."

Ward, Rev. William, the third of the famous Serampore triumvirate, was born at Derby, England, on Oct. 20, 1769. He served an apprenticeship to a printer in his native town, and for a time edited with ability the *Derby Mercury*. He subsequently edited newspapers at Stafford and Hull. In August, 1796, he was converted, and joined the Baptist church in Hull. His great talents could not be hid, and, at the instance of a benevolent friend, who undertook to pay all his expenses, he renounced journalism, and placed himself under the tuition of the Rev. Dr. Fawcett, at Ewood Hall, Yorkshire. Hearing some months afterwards that the Missionary Society wanted a printer to print the Bengalee translations of the Scriptures, he offered himself, and was gladly accepted. In 1811, Mr. Ward published the first edition of his popular and most valuable work on the Hindoos. Experience has fully corroborated his statements, and it remains one of the standard books on the subject. Mr. Ward visited England in 1819, and was incessantly occupied with public engagements. He was the first missionary who had ever returned from the East. His warm and animated addresses were well adapted to move popular assemblies. He also visited Holland, and then proceeded to this country, where he spent three months, and raised $10,000 for Serampore College. He was everywhere greeted with the warmest welcome. Whether in the pulpit or on the platform, he was immensely popular. He returned to India in 1821, and, after a brief illness, died on March 7, 1823, aged fifty-three.

Warder, Joseph W., D.D., was born in Logan Co., Ky., Oct. 13, 1825. He united with the Baptist church at Georgetown, and was licensed to preach while attending college at that place, where he graduated in 1845. He taught one year in the primary department of that institution, and was elected to the chair of Mathematics, but declined the position and entered Newton Theological Seminary, where he graduated in 1849, having meanwhile spent some time at Princeton Theological Seminary. He was ordained to the ministry, and was a short time pastor of the Baptist church at Frankfort, Ky. From 1851 to 1856 he was pastor of the church at Maysville, Ky. He then removed West, and at different periods was pastor at Lexington, Mo., Atchison, Kansas, Kansas City and Clinton, Mo., and Lawrence, Kansas. While at Clinton he was for a time financial agent of William Jewell College. In 1875 he returned to Kentucky and accepted the pastorate of Walnut Street Baptist church, in Louisville. He is now one of the leading ministers of the South, and is distinguished for his learning, piety, and pulpit ability.

Warder, Rev. Walter, son of Joseph Warder, a noted pioneer of Kentucky, was born in Fauquier Co., Va., in 1787. He removed with his father to Barren Co., Ky., about 1807, and the same year united with Dripping Spring Baptist church. He came up out of the baptismal water exhorting sinners to repent, and from that time until his death was one of the most zealous, laborious, and efficient ministers in Kentucky. He was ordained as pastor of Dover church, in Barren County, about 1811. In 1814 he accepted the pastorate of Mayslick church, in Mason Co., Ky., which position he filled until he finished his course. He preached extensively throughout the territory of Bracken Association and the adjacent parts of the State of Ohio. During a pastorate of twenty-two years there were received into Mayslick church 1015 members. In the year 1828 he baptized into that church 485, and in the bounds of Bracken Association more than 1000. He died in Missouri in 1836.

Warder, Rev. William, brother of Walter Warder, and equally brilliant and useful in the gospel ministry, was born in Fauquier Co., Va., Jan. 8, 1786. At the age of nineteen he went with his brother, the late Rev. John Warder, of Missouri, to Barren Co., Ky. He was baptized at the same time and place with his brother Walter, and like him began to preach almost immediately after his baptism. He was licensed in 1809 and was ordained in 1811. For about eight years he gave himself to traveling and preaching over the central part of Kentucky, from the Tennessee line to the border of Ohio, with great success in winning souls to Christ. In 1820 he accepted a call to the church at Russellville, and soon afterwards to the churches of Glasgow and Bowling Green. In 1821 he married Miss Margaret, sister of the late Gov. Charles S. Morehead, of Kentucky, and settled near Russellville, where he spent the remainder of his earthly pilgrimage, except one year passed in Nashville, Tenn. He possessed superior gifts as a preacher, and was a man of enlarged views and active enterprise. He organized an "Educating Society" at Russellville, and thus laid the foundation of Bethel College. He was largely instrumental in organizing Bethel Association, in 1824, out of a small missionary element in old Red River Association, which at its thirtieth anniversary contained an aggregate membership of 7000, and had erected two prosperous colleges. He died Aug. 9, 1836.

Ware, Rev. James Agnew, M.D., an eminent physician and preacher in Pontotoc Co., Miss., was born in South Carolina in 1804. After studying medicine and obtaining his degree he became impressed with the duty of preaching, and during his long life, while actively engaged in the practice of medicine, he was assiduous also in his ministerial labors. He was ordained in 1834. He removed to Pontotoc Co., Miss., in 1836. At this time there were few ministers and churches in North Mississippi. In his own neighborhood there was but one preaching-place,—the Presbyterian mission station among the Indians. Among the foremost and most active of the few ministers then on the ground, he gathered, in 1837, a church called Tokshish, near Red Land, of which he became the first pastor, and almost the only pastor during his life. From this mother-church sprang a number of others, and many ministers went out from it under the fostering care of Dr. Ware. He died in 1865.

Warfield, Rev. William C., a learned and brilliant preacher of Kentucky, was born in Lexington, of that State, in 1796. After a preparatory course he entered Transylvania University, remaining six years. About the end of the term he had an unfortunate altercation, which resulted in the serious injury of a comrade. In the confusion that ensued young Warfield fled from home and went to Bardstown, Ky., where he commenced reading law under the distinguished Judge John Rowan. Soon after this he was converted to Christ, returned to Lexington, and united with the Baptist church, where he was licensed to preach. He then spent two years in Princeton Theological Seminary. Returning home, he was ordained, and, after spending a brief period in preaching around Lexington, he settled within the bounds of Bethel Association, where he spent the remainder of his life. His labors were blessed to the instruction of the young churches, and he was greatly beloved and honored among them. He died Nov. 3, 1835.

Warne, J. A., D.D., was born in the city of London, England, in the year 1795, and at an early age united with the Little Wild Street Baptist church of that great city. After receiving a thorough education at Stepney College, he offered himself as a foreign missionary, but was compelled to relinquish his purpose in that direction owing to feeble health. Determined to do the next best thing, he came with his wife to this country, and settled in North Carolina. While in the South he was pastor at Newbern and principal of Imwan Academy. Compelled again by ill health to make a change, he came North, and was stated supply or pastor of the First church, Providence, R. I., South Reading and Brookline, Mass., and Sansom Street, of Philadelphia. About the year 1845 he went out of the pastorate, and has since lived in retirement. He was not idle, however, in religious things. It was he who edited the Baptist edition of the "Comprehensive Commentary." In his own neighborhood, far out in the suburbs, he has always been engaged in Christian work.

The peculiar feature about his life, and that which gives it special nobility, was his consecration to the cause of foreign missions. Unable to go himself, he was deeply interested in sustaining those who could go. When Dr. Price's children came to this country, and their own relatives refused to receive them because their mother was a Burmese woman, he took them under his roof and gave them an education. Since his retirement from the pastorate he has occupied himself in making and saving money for foreign missions. His little farm becoming valuable on account of the growth of the city, he sold out parts of it to advantage, and reinvested the money in houses. Some time before his death, which occurred early in 1881, feeling that his life was near its close, and wishing to save the expense of an executor and the State tax on willed property, he made over his entire estate to the Missionary Union, accepting in return only a small annuity for himself and wife. The estate will probably amount to $40,000.

All this shows the power of a consecrated purpose. Dr. Warne would have been glad to be a missionary; but when that was denied him, he did not forget that he had given himself to the missionary cause, and determined to do his best to provide the means of sending others. In order to carry out this purpose as fully as possible he subjected himself to the closest economy.

Warren, Gen. Eli, a lawyer of eminence, residing at Perry, Houston Co., Ga., still engaged (1880) in practice, although nearly eighty years of age, was born in Burke County, Feb. 27, 1801. His father was Josiah Warren, whose descendants occupy honorable and useful positions in Georgia. Early left an orphan, Eli Warren was placed under the care of his eldest sister and her husband, Rev. Charles Culpepper, a Baptist minister, who instilled correct principles into his mind, which preserved him from the vices of that age. They gave him the best educational advantages of the day. Choosing the law for his profession, he was admitted to the bar in 1823, and has continued in its successful practice ever since.

Gen. Warren was frequently sent to the State Legislature by his fellow-citizens in his younger days, and was elected brigadier-general of militia in 1828, a position at that time of some prominence. Though urged to do so he has declined all other offices, devoting himself to his profession. In the winter of 1839-40 he settled in Perry, Houston Co., and at present no man in his section stands higher in public estimation. He has long been distinguished for his legal ability; has always been considered a most amiable man, noted for his benevolence and hospitality; and his life has ever been pure, sober, and honorable; he has endeavored invariably to do good to every one, and especially to young men, hundreds of whom he has aided by material assistance and advice, and by impressing on them the importance of honesty, temperance, and truthfulness.

Gen. Warren has always acted on the principle that it is better to give to an unworthy object than fail to help a good one. He has always been a decided Baptist in principle, but never united with the church until October, 1869, since which time he has been a pious, active, and liberal church member. His hospitality knows no bounds.

Warren, E. W., D.D., was born in Conecuh Co., Ala., March 16, 1820. Under the careful in-

E. W. WARREN, D.D.

struction of his father, the Rev. Kittrell Warren, a man of strong natural ability and unusual oratorical powers, he acquired an ordinary English education, while at the same time spending the most of his time in assisting in the cultivation of the farm. For three or four years, and until he was twenty-three, he applied himself with great diligence to study, and then entered on the practice of law, having formed a copartnership with his uncle, the Hon. Lott Warren, a distinguished jurist of Georgia, and at one time a member of Congress. In the prosecution of his profession he met with gratifying success, and continued it for five or six years. In September, 1845, he united with the Baptist church at Starkville, Ga., taking an active part in all the services, and supplying in a measure, during his absence, the place of his pastor, the

Rev. Dr. Winkler. Although quite successful in his occasional preaching, he felt a strong disinclination to give himself wholly to ministerial work, and the afflictive providences of God, only, brought him to complete submission to his will in this matter. He was licensed in 1849; and giving up the practice of his profession he took charge of a school, and for two years, during which time he occasionally preached, he made preparation for his future ministerial work. Having soon become pastor of a country church, his voice failed, and for a short time he edited the *Christian Index*, published at Macon, Ga.

On the removal of the Rev. Dr. Landrum from the church in Macon to Savannah, Dr. Warren became pastor of the church in Macon, and continued in that relation for twelve years. From Macon he removed, in 1871, to Atlanta, Ga., and served the First Baptist church in that place with much success until, in 1876, he accepted the call to the pastorate of the First Baptist church in Richmond, Va., succeeding the Rev. Dr. Burrows. Dr. Warren has always been interested in the educational enterprises of the denomination. For more than twenty years he was an active member of the board of trustees of Mercer University, Ga., and did much for the advancement of liberal education in that State. In 1875 Mercer University conferred on him the degree of D.D. While in Richmond, Dr. Warren preached to one of the largest and most energetic Baptist congregations in the South, and he was highly esteemed by all who knew him. In the fall of 1879 he returned to the First church of Macon, where his labors are highly appreciated.

Warren, Hon. Henry, was born in Nova Scotia in 1817; removed to the United States in 1830, and to Oregon in 1847. He was baptized in 1853; is a member and clerk of the church at McMinnville; has been a trustee of McMinnville College since its organization, in 1857, and is secretary of the college board; was sheriff of Yamhill County seven years; a member of the Oregon Legislature; receiver of U. S. land-office nine years; is now a prosperous business man at McMinnville, a thoroughly active and liberal Baptist of wide influence in Oregon, and one of the strong supporters of the Baptist college in that State.

Warren, Jonah G., D.D., was born in Ward, Mass., Sept. 11, 1812, and graduated at Brown University in 1835. He took the theological course at Newton, graduating in the class of 1838. He was ordained at North Oxford, Mass., in September, 1838, and accepted a call to the church at Chicopee, Mass., where he remained until 1849, when he became pastor of the church at North Troy, N. Y. His relation with this church continued until 1855, when he was elected secretary of the American Baptist Missionary Union, holding the office for seventeen years. He resigned his position in 1872. During this long term of service Dr. Warren rendered most efficient aid in advancing the cause of evangelization among the heathen, and saw the society in whose behalf he labored so zealously take a high position among the missionary organizations of the world.

Dr. Warren received the degree of Doctor of Divinity from the Rochester University in 1856, and was a trustee of Brown University from 1858 to 1873, when he resigned his office on account of ill health.

Warren, Rev. Kittrell, was a son of Josiah Warren, and an elder brother of Hon. Lott Warren and Gen. Eli Warren. His ancestors came from England and settled in Virginia, from which Josiah Warren removed to North Carolina during the Revolutionary war, and from it to Burke Co., Ga., where Kittrell was born Oct. 17, 1786. The family removed to Laurens County in 1804, and settled four miles below Dublin, where Josiah Warren and his wife both died in 1809. Kittrell Warren married Mrs. Floyd, of Jefferson County, a woman of ardent and consistent piety, who afterwards professed conversion and was baptized.

In 1817, Kittrell Warren moved to Alabama and united with a Baptist church in that State, and was ordained about 1827. Returning to Georgia in 1831, he settled in Houston County.

He was a man of a devout spirit and of great benevolence, and to the day of his death diligently preached the gospel. He died in the year 1837.

Warren, Judge Lott, rose to high distinction, and exercised an extended and salutary influence as a member of Congress, as a lawyer, and as a judge of the Superior Court. His ancestors came from England. Lott was born Oct. 30, 1797, in Burke Co., Ga. He was admitted to the bar in 1821. In the year previous he had served as second lieutenant in Capt. Dean's company, under Col. Wright, in the State militia, during the Seminole war, Gen. Gaines being in command of the State troops; and he was present at the burning of the Indian town of Chehaw, in what is now Lee County. He began to practise law in Dublin, but afterwards removed to Marion, Twiggs Co., and from it to Americus in 1836. Half a dozen years later he removed to Albany, where he resided the remainder of his life. He was called by his fellow-citizens to many important positions. For a time he was a member of the State senate. He was, also, solicitor-general and judge of the Southern circuit. Subsequently he was elected twice to serve his State in Congress, and afterwards was elected twice to serve on the bench of the Southwestern circuit. In these various offices he discharged his duties to the entire satisfaction of the people, by whom he was most highly respected. He died on the 17th of June, 1861, but he had not been called away unprepared. For nearly twenty years he had been a decided Christian and a firm Baptist. He had even been set apart to the work of the gospel ministry, but only occasionally officiated in the pulpit. He was a man of earnest piety, decided opinions, and great moral firmness. He was a friend of the poor, a bold and able champion in the cause of temperance, and an unwearied supporter of the Sunday-school cause, laboring for many years with indefatigable zeal as a teacher. He was a lover of gospel truth, and of the gates of Zion. It deserves to be placed on record that the representative, lawyer, statesman, and judge was, on days of public worship, to friends and strangers, rich and poor, the watchful, affectionate, gentlemanly doorkeeper of the sanctuary in providing comfortable seats for those who attended worship.

Warren, R. I., Baptist Church.—In the year 1663, Rev. John Miles came to this country from Wales, and settled in the town of Rehoboth, then in the colony of Plymouth. The town covered a large territory, out of which several others have been formed. Mr. Miles being a heretic of the Roger Williams order was not allowed to remain in Rehoboth. He removed with his church to a grant of land called Wannamoiset, which he had obtained from the Plymouth Colony, and commenced a settlement, to which he gave the name of his home far across the waters, Swanzey. This territory embraced what are now the towns of Somerset, Barrington, Warren, and Swanzey. Until 1746 it was in Massachusetts. In that year a part of the territory was brought within the limits of Rhode Island. On the 15th of November, 1764, twenty brethren and thirty-eight sisters, the majority of the whole number being members of the Swanzey church, were constituted a Baptist church in the village of Warren. The formation of the church at this time was probably hastened by the following circumstance. The Rev. James Manning, of New Jersey, was sent to Rhode Island to found an institution in the "colony of Rhode Island, under the chief direction of the Baptists, in which education might be promoted, and superior learning obtained." Several towns urged their claims to be the home of the new college. It was decided after much discussion to locate it in Warren.

In deciding to lay the foundations of the college in Warren, it was understood that the members of the Swanzey church residing there would carry out a purpose already formed, to withdraw, and with other Baptists form a new church, to the pastorate of which the new president should be called, and thus a salary raised sufficient to meet his pecuniary wants. The call to Mr. Manning is dated Feb. 17, 1764, but the church was not formed, as we have seen, until the following November. The declaration from the religious society which called him to be their minister is worthy of permanent record: "As we are of opinion that they who preach the gospel should live of the gospel, we do here declare our intention to render your life as happy as possible, by our brotherly conduct towards you, and communicating our temporal things to your necessities, so long as God in his providence shall continue us together." A house of worship was built soon after Dr. Manning took up his residence in Warren. Some of the bills which were contracted are a curiosity in their way. The pulpit cost about thirty dollars. The price of meals in those days of rare economy was six cents each. We might suppose that the one-half day's labor of a horse, which was set down at £9, and the one day's work of "Negro Sharpe," which is placed at £4, were indications that very large wages were paid in those primitive times, until we learn that their "pounds" were worth not far from ten cents each. The parsonage erected for the use of the reverend gentleman, who combined in his one person the two offices of president of an infant college and pastor of an infant church, cost $316.

The ministry of Dr. Manning was followed with a rich blessing from the great head of the church. While performing the duties of his presidential office, he watched over the spiritual interests of the people committed to his charge. In 1766, under date of August 28, "it was moved that an association be entered into with sundry churches of the same faith and order, as it was judged a likely method to promote the peace of the churches." Out of that vote sprang the Warren Baptist Association, the venerable mother of all the Associations in New England. Dr. Manning, with all his respect for the rights of conscience, was a man of "law and order." When Brother Samuel Hicks felt moved to preach, whether by a good or a bad spirit we do not venture to say, without a regular license from the church, it was voted "that he is hereby forbidden, as a member of this body, from any further attempts until he is properly called by the church, and that the church see no reason to give him such a call, nor encourage him as a preacher." Brother Hicks, however, was not to be restrained from doing what doubtless he thought was his duty, whereupon it was voted that he be "cut off from the church as a disorderly member, one that causes divisions, contrary to the doctrines of Christ, and must be noted for avoidance."

At length the question of a change of location of the college was decided, and Providence was selected as its future home. The struggle through which Dr. Manning passed in deciding to continue his connection with it and break the tie which bound him to his church was very great, and Mr.

Spalding tells us that "at one time he was about to resign the presidency rather than the pastorate." In light of subsequent events no one can doubt the wisdom of the decision which he finally reached.

The successor of Dr. Manning was Rev. Charles Thompson, of whom there is a sketch in this volume. He was ordained July 3, 1771, and remained as pastor of the church until he was forced to leave in consequence of the destruction by fire of the meeting-house and parsonage, by British and Hessian troops in 1778. The Baptists of Warren worshiped with the old Swanzey church after the loss of their meeting-house, where for seven years they sat under the ministry of Mr. Thompson, who had been called to be the pastor of the mother-church.

In 1784 a new church edifice was erected. The next pastor of the church was Rev. John Pitman, who entered upon his ministry Oct. 26, 1786. His ministry continued three years and a half. The fourth pastor was Rev. Luther Baker, during whose pastorate there were several most fruitful revivals, and large additions were made to the church. The next three pastors were Rev. Messrs. Silas Hall, Daniel Cheesman, and Flavel Shurtleff, whose pastorates were comparatively short. The Rev. John C. Welsh, the next minister, commenced his pastorate June 11, 1823, and continued in his office seventeen years. His ministry was blessed with several revivals. The ninth pastor of the church was Rev. Josiah Phillips Justin, during whose ministry the present elegant and commodious stone edifice was built, and dedicated on the 8th of May, 1845. He resigned Oct. 23, 1849. Rev. Dr. Robert A. Fyfe, Rev. Messrs. Myron Munson Dean, George S. Chase, A. F. Spalding, and S. R. Dexter have ministered to this ancient church during the period which has elapsed between 1849 and the time of writing this sketch.

The Warren church is among the oldest of the New England churches; it gave its name to the first Baptist Association in New England, and it has had in its ministry men of God, "good and true," whose labors have been signally blessed by him whose they were and whom they tried to serve.

Warren, Rev. W. H., was born in Prince Edward Island in 1845, and was converted and baptized in his native place in 1865. He graduated from Acadia College in June, 1871, and was ordained at Cavendish, Prince Edward Island, Feb. 28, 1872. He became pastor in 1874 of the Temple church, Yarmouth, Nova Scotia, leaving there in August, 1878, to take charge of the Baptist church at Bridgetown, Nova Scotia. Mr. Warren also occupied the position of corresponding secretary to the Home Missionary Board at Yarmouth.

Washburn, Hon. Henry Stevenson, was born in Providence, R. I., in 1813. Both of his parents were of Puritan ancestry. At the early age of thirteen he was placed in a store in Boston. His plans for life being changed, he pursued a course of study at the Worcester Academy, and entered Brown University in 1836, where he remained nearly a year, and then was compelled, on account of ill health, to abandon his purpose of obtaining a collegiate education. Soon after leaving college he was appointed depositarian of the New England Sunday-School Union, and held this office seven years. Subsequently he became a manufacturer in Worcester and Boston, and afterwards was appointed president of the Union Mutual Life Insurance Company. He spent three years abroad in behalf of the company. Mr. Washburn has occupied many positions of honor and responsibility. For four years he was president of the Worcester County Manufacturers' and Mechanics' Association, and for nine years was a member of the Boston School Board. He was a representative from Boston two years in the Massachusetts Legislature, and for one year he was in the State senate, where he was chairman of the Committee on Education. He has carefully cultivated his literary tastes, and has published many hymns, lyrics, etc. He originated the *Young Reaper*, of which he was the editor seven years. He has also written and published much on life insurance, as the result of his personal observations in Great Britain, France, and Germany. His present residence is in Boston.

Washington, Mrs. Elizabeth Cobb.—Among those of our Baptist Zion who have adorned the gospel by their works of faith and labors of love the name of this sainted woman merits honorable mention. Her maiden name was Cobb, and she was born in Lenoir Co., N. C., April 27, 1780. In 1800 she married Mr. John Washington, of Kinston, related to Gen. Geo. Washington, and removed to Newbern in 1831.

She was christened in infancy, her family being Episcopalians, but having made a profession of faith in Christ after marriage, she was baptized into the fellowship of Southwest Baptist church, Lenoir Co., where her membership remained as long as she lived. After the death of her husband, in 1837, she made her home with her daughter, Mrs. Gov. W. A. Graham, a Baptist, eminent for her faith and usefulness.

Mrs. Washington's benefactions were many, considering her income, were large, and extended through the whole course of her life. She gave $1000 for the erection of a church at Newbern, $100 each to the churches of Raleigh and Chapel Hill, and $2000 to build the church at Hillsborough. She was an ardent friend of ministerial education, and not only contributed to the Southern Baptist Theological Seminary, but in addition to other gifts to Wake Forest College, bought a scholarship, worth $500, in 1855. She also aided several of our most useful ministers with the means to prosecute their studies at college. She died in Hillsborough, at the house of Gov. Graham, March 8, 1858, and was buried by the side of her husband in Newbern.

Washington Territory is the extreme northwestern portion of the United States possessions, except Alaska. It has splendid harbors, is rich in forests and agricultural resources, and is fast becoming peopled with enterprising men. Colfax, Olympia, Seattle, and Walla Walla are rapidly-growing cities. The Baptists in this State are beginning to show much strength, and are laying foundations for a vigorous future. Several churches have been organized, by its pioneer preachers and others, who have come to their aid, such as Revs. R. Weston, P. H. Harper, W. E. M. James, J. P. Ludlow, Hon. and Rev. Judge Roger S. Greene, and J. L. Blitch, D.D. Two Associations and a Convention are organized, and the foundation-work for a Baptist school of learning has been laid. The Colfax Academy and Business Institute, with Miss L. L. West as principal, gives promise of good service for the denomination in Washington Territory.

Watchman, The, a weekly religious paper, published in Boston, was started, in 1819, by True & Weston, Mr. Weston being its first editor. The original name of the paper was *The Christian Watchman*, and it was intended to be an organ of the Baptist denomination, setting forth and vindicating, in a kind, Christian spirit, the peculiar tenets and practices of the Baptist churches in this country. Messrs. True & Weston did not long retain their connection with the paper, but passed it into the hands of William Nichols, Deacon James Loring acting as its editor. Here it remained for fifteen years, and, as an exponent of Baptist principles and practices, it performed excellent service for the denomination. On the retirement of Deacon Loring from the editorial chair, Rev. B. F. Farnsworth took charge of the paper for a few months, when he was succeeded by Rev. Ebenezer Thresher, who was its editor for three years. During the next ten years—from 1838 to 1848—*The Christian Watchman* was under the editorial management of Rev. William Crowell, whose ability as a writer was everywhere acknowledged. Under his supervision the paper took a high position among the religious periodicals of the day. In consequence of what by many were regarded as too conservative views on the exciting topics which were agitating the community during this period, Mr. Crowell's position was condemned; and there seeming to be a call for the establishment of another paper, the *Christian Reflector* was started in Worcester, Mass., with Cyrus Grosvenor as editor, and W. S. Dannell as publisher. In 1844 the new paper was removed to Boston, and, under the editorial management of Rev. H. A. Graves, it was not long before its circulation exceeded that of *The Christian Watchman*. The health of Mr. Graves led to his resignation, and the paper passed into the hands of Rev. J. W. Olmstead. The two papers were united in 1848, under the editorial management of Messrs. Olmstead and Hague. Mr. D. S. Ford, one of the publishers, soon came upon the editorial staff, his specialty being the arrangement of the outside of the paper, which, by his enterprise and rare tact, was made as attractive as the inside. The general tone and circulation of the paper continued to improve from year to year until 1867, when it was enlarged to an eight-paged sheet, furnishing to its patrons nearly double the amount of reading matter, but with a small increase in its price. Mr. Ford retired from the *Watchman and Reflector* at the close of the year 1867, and the proprietorship and editorial management were in the hands of Dr. Olmstead. The *Christian Era*, which commenced its existence in Lowell, Mass., in 1852, to meet the demand for a more thoroughly outspoken anti-slavery paper, after passing through a successful career, chiefly under the management of its editor, Rev. Dr. Webster, was merged into what, under the present arrangement, is called *The Watchman*, at the close of 1875. The editors of *The Watchman* were Drs. Olmstead, Lorimer, and Johnson during the year 1876. Rev. L. E. Smith, D.D., for a long time connected with the *Examiner*, of New York, took the editorial chair at the beginning of 1877. The circulation of the paper in 1878 was a little under 20,000, and was constantly increasing. Its growth has been extraordinary. *The Christian Watchman*, insignificant in size, has expanded to a sheet 49 inches by 33, nearly eight times as large as at its birth. The expense of a single paper for original matter has been often larger than the former outlay for an entire year. It cannot be doubted that a prosperous future is before it.

Waterhouse, Rev. Charles W., was born in Ridgefield, Conn., Sept. 16, 1811; was graduated at Madison University in 1839, and from the seminary at Hamilton in 1841. In 1852 he was engaged in building up an interest of the city mission in Newark. He has been pastor of several churches, and has taught much, especially the classics. Though in feeble health, he preaches occasionally, and is a prominent member in the church at Lakewood, N. J., where he resides. He has been a close student of the original languages of the Bible; was engaged in translation service for the Bible Union, and has been for years at work upon a critical revision of the New Testament, accompanied with philological notes. He is particularly methodical in his studies, remarkably correct in his translations, an excellent Bible-class teacher, and a frequent contributor to the religious press.

Waters, Rev. James, pastor of the Edgefield Baptist church since June, 1879, was born at Waterstown, Wilson Co., Tenn.,—a son of W. T. Waters, a leading citizen of that part of the State. He was educated at Union University, Murfreesborough, Tenn., where he graduated with the highest honors in 1858. The year previous he united with the Baptist church at Murfreesborough, and at once began the study of theology. After graduating he took charge of the church in his native place, and preached there and in adjacent communities until 1862, when he removed to Pennsylvania, where he spent three years as teacher, principally in Meadville and in the Lewisburg University. In 1866 he resumed the work of the ministry, serving churches in Philadelphia, Pa., Mount Holly, N. J., and Wilmington, Del., until 1873, when he was chosen by the American Baptist Publication Society as district secretary in New York City and vicinity. This position he held successfully until the fall of 1876, when he retired to devote a season to the study of law, in New York City, to which he had given some attention during his secretaryship. He graduated at Columbia College in the law department. Meantime he served the church at Passaic, N. J., as pastor until the spring of 1879, when he settled at Edgefield, Tenn. The average increase in churches he has served has been about twenty-five per annum, and these are distributed over the year. He prepares his sermons with care, and speaks with or without notes with equal ease. He has written considerably for the *Religious Herald* over the *nom de plume* of "Tyro," for the *National Baptist* as "Sajem," and has published occasional sermons. He is a son-in-law of Dr. J. M. Pendleton.

Watkinson, Rev. William E., was born at Pemberton, N. J., June 30, 1821; was baptized by Rev. George B. Ide, and joined the First Baptist church, Philadelphia, in 1841. He was licensed to preach, in 1852, by the First Baptist church of Chicago, Ill., entering the ministry directly from mercantile life. He was ordained at Manayunk, Philadelphia, March 24, 1854; has been pastor at Manayunk, West Chester, Nicetown, Pa., Hamilton Square and Kingwood, N. J. The present pastorate at Kingwood began April 1, 1876. He has baptized a large number, several of whom have entered the ministry, and he has taught a Bible-class for more than thirty-seven years. He is a brother of the Rev. M. R. Watkinson, a minister of unusual talents, who was greatly blessed in his labors both in the North and in the South, who died a few years ago lamented by large numbers who knew his great worth and deep piety.

Watson, James Madison, a deacon of the Central Baptist church, Elizabeth, N. J., was born in Central New York, and is a well-known author and teacher. His series of works on elocution has been widely circulated, and his improved reading books are much used. Mr. Watson is a ready worker in the church as well as in the cause of secular education.

Watson, Rev. Jonathan, was born at Montrose, Scotland, in 1794. He studied medicine and practised his profession in his native place. He began his ministry in early life, his first pastoral charge being at Dundee, whence he removed after a brief residence to Cupar, Fife. In both places he continued the practice of his profession. During his residence at Cupar he was greatly blessed in his ministry, the Baptist church there having been founded by him in 1816. In 1842 he removed to Edinburgh to become the colleague of Dr. Innes, minister of the Elder Street Baptist church. After Dr. Innes's death Mr. Watson became sole pastor. A new edifice was erected in 1858. In 1868 the church associated with him the Rev. Samuel Newman as co-pastor, a relationship which continued until his death, Oct. 19, 1878, at the ripe age of eighty-four. Mr. Watson filled for many years a leading position in evangelical circles in Edinburgh, and associated his name with many important public questions. He was one of the founders of the Medical Missionary Society. In his old age he published a volume entitled "Preparing for Home," which had a wide circulation, and went through several editions. At the time of his death he was supposed to be the oldest of Scottish ministers, having been in the ministry for the long period of sixty-four years. He took a warm interest in the work of the Baptist Missionary Society, and was chosen one of the honorary members of the committee when age disabled him from active service.

Watson, Deacon W. W., who died at Springfield, Ill., in November, 1874, in the eighty-first year of his age, was born at Moorestown, N. J., April 1, 1794. In 1815 he removed to Lexington, Ky., in 1817 to Nashville, Tenn., and in 1836 to Illinois. He was closely identified with denominational movements in the State, especially as connected with missions; having been one of those by whom the General Association was organized.

Watts, Rev. James Molison, was born in Guilford Co., N. C., March 22, 1817. In his early childhood his parents removed to Georgia, and in August, 1834, he professed faith in Christ, and united with the First Baptist church in Columbus. He took an active part in all Christian work, and was clerk of his Association. Subsequently he removed to Alabama, where he was ordained May 26, 1843. During the years 1854 and 1855 he was associated with Dr. Samuel Henderson in the editorship of the *Southwestern Baptist*, at Tuskegee, Ala., in which position he won considerable reputation as a clear and forcible writer. Afterwards he returned to Georgia, and resided in Columbus, where he died of consumption Feb. 2, 1866. His last words were, " All is well."

Watts, Rev. John, was born Nov. 3, 1661, at Lydd, County of Kent, England, and came to America about 1686. He was baptized at Lower Dublin, Nov. 21, 1687, and he succeeded Elias Keach as pastor of the Lower Dublin church in 1691. He held this office until Aug. 27, 1702, when he died of smallpox. Mr. Watts was well acquainted with divinity, and his general learning was respectable; he was also an author of no mean ability.

Watts, Gov. Thomas Hill, was born in Butler Co., Ala., Jan. 3, 1819. Graduated from the University of Virginia in 1840. In 1841 began the practice of law at Greenville in his native county, and soon acquired a profitable business. In 1842 he was elected to the Legislature; was returned in 1844 and in 1845. In 1847 he removed to the city of Montgomery, and has resided there ever since, pursuing mainly the practice of law. In 1849 he was elected to the Legislature from Montgomery County; in 1853 to the State senate. In 1861, with the Hon. William L. Yancey, he represented Montgomery County in the secession convention. The same year, as colonel of the 17th Alabama Regiment, he went to the seat of war, where he remained until April 9, 1862, when he was chosen by President Davis to the position of attorney-general in his cabinet; remained there until elected governor of Alabama, in 1863, a position which he held until the fortunes of war destroyed the Confederate cause. Since that time he has practised law in Montgomery, standing among the most eminent in that profession in Alabama.

GOV. THOMAS HILL WATTS.

In 1846, in Greenville, he was baptized by Rev. David Lee. Since his removal to Montgomery he has occupied a most prominent position in the membership of the First Baptist church. Has often given liberally to the enterprises of the denomination at large as well as in his own city. He is a strict temperance man. Before the war Gov. Watts had acquired a large fortune, but that unhappy struggle stripped him of all. He often expresses it as his chief regret that his changed circumstances deprive him of the ability to give as he once could to religion, education, and the general public weal. With cheerful heart, pleasant face, and kind words he prosecutes the arduous duties of his profession, maintaining his house on a liberal basis, and giving generously to objects of benevolence. Alabama has not a more distinguished citizen.

Waugh, Rev. C. V., is a native of Virginia, and was born at Manchester, in that State, in 1849. His grandfather came from Ireland. His parents are yet living, but advanced in years. They set their hearts upon educating him for a physician, but the late war frustrated their plans, and this was providential, for God designed him for another work.

He was converted in 1865, and was baptized by Dr. W. E. Hatcher at Manchester, in February, 1866. He came up from his baptismal grave asking, " Lord, what wilt thou have me to do?" and was at once impressed that it was his duty to preach, and this conviction grew upon him until he yielded to God's call.

The church at Manchester decided that he should go to Richmond College. He entered it and graduated. During his course he was awarded a gold medal for being the best speaker in his society,—Philologian.

Leaving college with health impaired, he went to Hillsborough, Albemarle Co., taught school, and preached successfully. At this place, March 9, 1873, he was ordained by J. E. Massie, S. P. Huff, P. Cleaveland, and J. C. Long. He resigned his church in 1874, and in October of that year entered the theological seminary, desiring to take a full course, but on account of declining health pursued the pastor's course only, and in 1875 entered the pastorate at Modest Town, Va., to which he had been invited before entering the seminary.

Here he labored until he was providentially directed to Gainesville, Fla., from which a call was extended to him, and at the same time he was advised by his physician to go South. He accepted the invitation to become the pastor of Gainesville church, and came to the State in 1876. During his pastorate the church has been much strengthened, the house of worship enlarged, a baptistery put in, and other improvements have been made. Besides his work in Gainesville, he has visited other important points and assisted successfully in protracted meetings.

Mr. Waugh is industrious and enthusiastic in his undertakings. He is a vigorous thinker and a good sermonizer. He has been clerk of his Association and of the State Convention, and he has been president of the Alachua County Bible Society.

Waukesha, Wis., in its early history was simply Prairieville, a neat rural village, set in the midst of a beautiful farming country. But Prairieville was exchanged for the Indian name which it now bears. It is worthy to be noticed in Baptist history, because here the second Baptist church organized in the State was founded, and here Dr. Robert Boyd, of sainted memory, had his home for many years; here he prepared on his couch of suffering the books which have comforted so many believers and led so many sinners to Christ. Here, too, for more than a quarter of a century has been the home of Dr. A. Kendrick, father of President Kendrick, of Shurtleff College. In recent years it has become famous through its Bethesda Springs as a summer resort, and the place overflows in the summer season with visitors.

Waul, Gen. Thomas N., stands in the front rank among the leading men of Texas, and without a superior as a lawyer at the Galveston bar. He was born in Sumter District, S. C., Jan. 8, 1815. His education was received in South Carolina, from whose State institution, South Carolina College, he graduated. He studied law in Vicksburg, Miss., with Hon. Sergeant S. Prentiss, the distinguished political orator and lawyer. He commenced the practice of law in July, 1835, when twenty years of age. He early distinguished himself in Mississippi, and when chosen judge of the Circuit Court exhibited signal ability. He was a prominent member of the first Confederate Congress from the State of Texas. He was a general in the Confederate army, having raised the command well known as "Waul's Legion." His career as a soldier was marked by eminent skill and gallantry. He received a severe wound in a Louisiana engagement. He professed religion at Grenada, Miss., in 1846, and was baptized by Rev. E. C. Eager. He identified himself with the cause of Christ, taking a deep interest in the promotion of measures for advancing education and home and foreign missions. He served most acceptably as moderator of the Yalobusha Association, Miss., and from May, 1855, to November, 1859, was elected president annually of the Mississippi Baptist State Convention, and served with rare parliamentary tact. The Mississippi Convention then embraced important places in Louisiana, especially New Orleans. He is now a member of the First Baptist church in Galveston, under the care of Rev. Wm. Howard, D.D., and besides discharging his church duties and attending to a large legal practice, gives much attention to the cause of public education.

Wayland Academy.—Early educational movements in Wisconsin resulted in the establishment of Wayland Academy, at Beaver Dam, for young men, and the Baptist Female College, at Fox Lake, for young women; the former in 1854 and the latter in 1855. At Beaver Dam a college building was erected at a cost of $20,000, the corner-stone of which was laid July 4, 1855. At Fox Lake a college building was reared at a cost of $10,000. The preparatory department of the college at Beaver Dam was opened Sept. 19, 1855, with Benjamin Newall, A.B., as principal, and Rev. H. I. Parker, who had recently entered the State from New England, as financial agent. Forty students were entered the first term. The Female College at Fox Lake was opened the second Wednesday in October, and continued through the year with Miss Scriburt as principal, Mrs. Phebe Thompson, associate principal, and fifty-eight students in attendance. In 1858, three years after the opening, the board of instruction at Wayland was Allen S. Hutchens, chairman of the faculty, and Professor of the Greek and Latin Languages; Benjamin Newall, Professor of Mathematics; Charles Hutchens, Tutor; and H. B. Moore, Principal of the Academic Department. Eighty-five students were enrolled. The teachers at the Female College at Fox Lake were the same as at the opening, and 115 pupils were in attendance. About $30,000 had been expended in buildings and college appointments. It is doubtful whether the Baptist denomination in any State ever laid better foundations for Christian education at greater sacrifices than the Baptists of Wisconsin in the founding and establishment of these Christian institutions of learning. Of subsequent sad trials and crushing disappointments it is not necessary here to speak. They were organized and conducted through their early triumphs and defeats by as devoted and self-denying a company of men as ever toiled and prayed in the ranks of the Baptist ministry in America, and carried on through their trials and embarrassments by as brave a band of teachers as ever gathered and taught classes. Many of these noble men are still doing service on earth, but some are now in glory. Fish, De Laney, Underwood, Hutchens, and Newall among the living, and Bright and Whitman among the dead, have left, in the founding of these institutions, their noblest work.

Wayland Academy, in its present position, is doing, and is destined to perform, a splendid work for the Baptists of Wisconsin. It is moving to the front rank of well-endowed academies, where the best preparation is given for the college and the university and all the needs of practical life. It has an able and thoroughly qualified corps of instructors, and generous hearts have made ample provision by will for its future, and though struggling for want of present resources, its prospects are full of promise and hope. The institution has now (1880) a faculty of six instructors:

Rev. N. E. Wood, M.A., Principal; John Sutherland, B.A., Professor of Latin; Mrs. Alice Boise Wood, M.A., Professor of Greek and Modern Languages; Miss M. A. Cuckow, Mathematics; Miss Linnie Aiken, Drawing and Painting; Miss Elizabeth J. Laning, Vocal and Instrumental Music.

It has property valued at $30,000. It has a paying endowment of $12,000. It has no debts. It has a library of 1800 volumes. It never had more intelligent friends. Although it has hitherto confined itself to simple academic work, it is contemplated in the near future to vindicate the purposes and hopes of its founders by taking the position for which it was chartered, and introduce the full college course.

Wayland, Rev. Francis, was born in Frome, Somersetshire, England, in 1772. In 1793 he sailed for New York, where he landed September 30. He immediately established himself in business in New York City, where both he and Mrs. Wayland became members of the Oliver Street Baptist church, then known as Fayette Street, afterwards under the ministry of Rev. John Williams.

By this church Mr. Wayland was licensed to preach the gospel in 1805, and in 1807 he was ordained as pastor of the church in Poughkeepsie. He afterwards was settled at Albany and Troy, N. Y., and in 1819 he became pastor in Saratoga Springs. The church met in a small building, nearly two miles from the village, at what is now known as Geyserville, with occasional services in a school-house in the village. Mr. Wayland soon secured funds for a new church in the village, which was erected in 1821 on the site now occupied by a larger edifice. In 1823, Mr. Wayland resigned, and though afterwards repeatedly invited to other pastorates, he declined any settlement. He continued to reside at Saratoga Springs; was much called upon in councils, where his judgment was highly valued, and to supply feeble and destitute churches, which he did gratuitously and cheerfully. The sick and the sorrowful of all creeds were his charge. He is still held in honored memory. He was early convinced of the dangers of the drinking usages which prevailed, and he was among the first promoters of the temperance movement. He maintained that the church of Christ was the great temperance society, and that all efforts could be permanently successful only as the reform is based on Christian principle. He was a man of strong sense, practical wisdom, unflinching rectitude, and positive ideas. His religious character was consistent and equable. He was pre-eminently a man of prayer and faith. Truth and godly sincerity characterized his intercourse with men. He was English in character and manners, but an honest lover of republican institutions. In social life he was genial and courteous. As a preacher, he was earnest and practical. Having a deep personal experience of divine things, he spoke to the heart and conscience. He died at Saratoga Springs, April 9, 1849, after a short illness. Up to his last sickness he was full of activity, abating nothing of his interest in religious or social duties. It was a wish often expressed by him that he might not "rust out," and the Lord was mindful of this desire of his servant.

Wayland, President Francis, was born in New York City, March 11, 1796. His parents (who

PRESIDENT FRANCIS WAYLAND.

were natives of England) were characterized by great integrity, industry, robust sense, earnest moral convictions, and an almost passionate love of civil and religious liberty. The father, Francis Wayland, Sr., at the age of thirty-five, gave up the business of a currier and devoted himself to the gospel ministry, laboring as pastor of the Baptist churches in Poughkeepsie, Troy, Albany, and Saratoga Springs.

The son, while showing no marks of precocity, was manly, faithful, and industrious. The schools of that day seem to have been nearly worthless. The memory alone was exercised, and the only motive employed was fear of punishment. Of one of his early schools he wrote, late in life, "The only pleasure I have in remembering this school is derived from the belief that boys of the present day are not exposed to such miserable instruction." He adds, "Perhaps my experience was not altogether lost; it has at least served to impress me with the importance of doing everything in my power to bring whatever I attempted to teach within the understanding of the learner." When he was eleven years old he came under the instruction of Mr. Daniel H. Barnes, and for the first time he found himself in the presence of a real teacher.

At the age of seventeen he graduated at Union College, then under the presidency of Dr. Nott, and at once began the study of medicine, which he completed three years later. During the last year of his medical studies he became a Christian and united with the Baptist Church. Feeling that he was called to the ministry, he entered, in the fall of 1816, the Andover Theological Seminary. Here he was chiefly under the instruction of Prof. Moses Stuart, for whom he always cherished a grateful and reverent affection. At the end of a year he left the seminary to become a tutor in Union College. It is probable that nothing could have been a better preparation for the life which Providence had assigned him than this position. The four years which he spent in teaching the various college studies and in learning sermon-making from the wise and eloquent Dr. Nott, he always regarded as of inestimable value.

In 1821 he was called to be the pastor of the First Baptist church in Boston. Here, notwithstanding the drawbacks of a weak church and an unattractive delivery, he became recognized as a man of great moral force, of almost unerring sagacity, of progressive spirit, as a master of thought and expression, and a leader in action. His sermon on "The Moral Dignity of the Missionary Enterprise," in 1823, and that on "The Duties of an American Citizen," in 1825, were but the expression of powers matured by silent study.

In 1826 he accepted a professorship in Union College, though he did not intend permanently to leave the pastorate. A few months later he was called to the presidency of Brown University, and in February, 1827, he entered upon what was to be the great work of his life.

The college was at a very low ebb in funds, in discipline and scholarship, in library, apparatus, and in all of the appliances of education. The new president entered on his work with a high ideal and with a resolute determination to make the college the best possible. The lecture-room became a place of eager inquiry and discussion. He aimed not alone to explain and establish his views of the truth, but above all to lead his pupils to exercise their own powers. An eminent graduate once said, "Six words that he said to the class were worth more to me than all the words I ever heard beside,—'Young gentlemen, cherish your own conceptions.'"

The late Hon. B. F. Thomas, LL.D., one of the judges of the Supreme Court of Massachusetts, expressed the sentiment of many pupils when he said, in 1855, "A quarter of a century has passed since I left these walls with your blessing. I have seen something of men and of the world since. I esteem it to-day the happiest event of my life that brought me here, the best gift of an ever-kind Providence to me that I was permitted for three years to sit at the feet of your instruction." Feeling dissatisfied with the old text-books, he prepared lectures on all the subjects which he taught. It became remarked at the bar and in the pulpit that a graduate of Brown University might be known by his closeness of reasoning and his power of analysis. The enthusiasm created within the college spread through the community, and led to the enlargement of all the means of instruction.

But the impression deepened in the mind of the president that the college was fulfilling but a part of its mission. It was giving a disproportionate amount of attention to the classics and to mathematics; it was confining its blessings almost exclusively to candidates for the professions; it was ignoring the progress of human thought and knowledge and the demands of the productive professions, as well as the boundless diversity of character and aim on the part of students. These views, slowly maturing, led to a reorganization of the university in 1850. Place was given to the more modern studies, larger liberty of election was allowed, and the wants of the industrial and productive classes were especially regarded. The results within the university attested the wisdom of the changes, and the progress made in college education in America during the past thirty years has all been along the path in which he led the way. During all these years the moral and religious good of the students was the object of his untiring solicitude. He preached in the chapel weekly sermons prepared expressly for the students. He often attended the students' prayer-meetings; he counseled and prayed with them in private; he especially welcomed and nourished every revival influence. Not a few of his pupils, rescued from worldliness and unbelief, were led to lives of high devotion and benevolence.

In 1855, after more than twenty-eight years of untiring labor in the presidency, he resigned, feeling imperatively the need of rest, and unwilling to hold a position of which he was not in the fullest sense discharging the duties. A year later, under the most profound sense of duty, he served as pastor of the First Baptist church in Providence, and continued for a year and a half labors which were more taxing to him than his labors in the presidency had been.

The remainder of his life was devoted to such religious and humane labor as his strength permitted. He bestowed much time and care upon the inmates of the State Prison and the Reform School. His only recreation was the care of his garden. Preserving the clearness of his mind, and his sympathy for his fellow-men, he continued until Sept. 30, 1865, when he died from an attack of paralysis.

His labors in authorship were abundant; he published eighteen volumes, among which were the "Moral Science," "Political Economy," "Intellectual Philosophy," two volumes of sermons, "Life of Judson," "Domestic Slavery considered as a Scriptural Institution," etc. He also published about fifty sermons, addresses, etc. The "Moral Science" has had a circulation of 150,000, and has been reprinted in England and Scotland, and translated into Armenian, Modern Greek, Hawaiian, and Nestorian.

As a preacher, he was in his earlier years somewhat elaborate, highly wrought, and rhetorical. With the advance of time, his style became exceedingly simple and direct, sacrificing everything to clearness, pungency, and force. His conception for the moment of religious realities was intense beyond expression. His most marked intellectual characteristics were his love of truth and his clearness of conception and expression. His love of liberty for himself and for others was broad and eager. His hopes for human advancement were unresting. His own words, once uttered in private conversation, "I go for the human race," expressed the spirit of his life. The trait which towered above all else was his profound and unwavering devotion to duty. In the just and striking words of his pupil and successor, President E. G. Robinson, "To him, *ought* and *ought not* were the most potent words that could be spoken."

He held intelligently, firmly, and conscientiously the doctrines of evangelical Christianity and the distinguishing principles of the Baptist denomination. But he rejoiced to labor, wherever it was possible, with his brethren of other Christian bodies, in promotion of the interests of religion and humanity. Dr. Wayland was one of the greatest men to whom our country has given birth.

He was twice married; his second wife survived him seven years. Three sons survived him, one of whom has since died. A memoir of his "Life and Labors" (2 vols.) was prepared by his sons, Francis and H. L. Wayland.

Wayland, Francis, LL.D., son of Francis and Lucy Wayland, was born in Boston, Aug. 23, 1826,

FRANCIS WAYLAND, LL.D.

and graduated at Brown University in 1846. After studying at the Harvard Law-School and in the office of Ashmun & Chapman (Springfield, Mass.), he commenced the practice of law in Worcester, Mass., in 1850. In 1858 he removed to New Haven, Conn., where he now resides. In 1864 he was elected judge of probate for the district of New Haven, and served in that office for two years. In 1869 he was elected lieutenant-governor of Connecticut. In 1872 he was appointed professor in the law-school of Yale College, and in 1873 he was made dean of the law-school. He has written several articles in the *Atlantic Monthly*, and has also prepared papers for the American Social Science Association, especially on "Tramps" and on "Out-Door Relief." He was (with his brother) joint author of "The Life and Labors of Francis Wayland." He was president of the Baptist Educational Convention in Philadelphia, in 1872, and of the Convention of Baptist Social Unions in Brooklyn, in 1874, and for several years he was president of the Connecticut Social Union. He is president of the board of directors of the Connecticut State Prison, of the Connecticut Prison Association, of the board of Organized Charities of the City of New Haven, and of the board of directors of the Connecticut General Hospital at New Haven. In

1874 he was president of the Board of Visitors to the U. S. Military Academy at West Point, and in 1880 vice-president of the Board of Visitors to the U. S. Naval Academy at Annapolis. He has been for several years chairman of the Jurisprudence Department of the American Social Science Association, and in 1880 was chosen president of the Association. In 1879 he received from the University of Rochester the degree of Doctor of Laws.

Wayland, H. L., D.D., son of Francis and Lucy Wayland, was born at Providence, R. I., April 23, 1830; graduated at Brown University in 1849; studied at Newton Theological Institution, 1849–50; taught the academy at Townshend, Vt., 1850–51; resident graduate at Brown University, 1851–52; tutor at University of Rochester, 1852–54; pastor of Third (now Main Street) church in Worcester, Mass., 1854–61; chaplain of 7th Conn. Volunteers, 1861–64; home missionary in Nashville, Tenn., 1864–65; Professor of Rhetoric and Logic in Kalamazoo College, Mich., 1865–70; president of Franklin College, Ind., 1870–72; editor of the *National Baptist*, Philadelphia, since 1872. He has published articles in the *New Englander* and the *Baptist Quarterly*; he has also written very largely for the newspaper press, both at the East and at the West. He was editorially connected with the *Michigan Christian Herald*, the *Standard*, Chicago, and the *Michigan Teacher*. He has published several sermons, beside addresses on education and kindred topics. He was, with his brother, joint author of "The Life and Labors of Francis Wayland." Dr. Wayland possesses great ability, ardent piety, and unusual conscientiousness. In his hands the *National Baptist* has become a decided success. He enjoys the confidence and warm regards of all Pennsylvania Baptists and of a multitude besides.

Wayland Seminary, Washington, D. C.—The history of this institution dates back to 1864. Good and wise men saw the necessity of providing an educated leadership for a race just then emancipated. The leaven of a Christian education seemed to promise the chief safety from evils that threatened the interests of more than 4,000,000 of souls. How should the work commence? How could the material so long neglected be made useful? The most perplexing questions had to be solved; but faith, with its farsightedness, was competent to devise a plan for the introduction of Wayland Seminary.

Wayland Seminary comprises three departments,—a normal, an academic, and a theological. The Bible holds, of course, the first place in the school; but the students must be able to teach in the common schools, and must give attention to other branches of study along with Bible studies.

The school was planted and has been carefully watched over by the American Baptist Home Mission Society. At first there was no building in which pupils could be gathered. To secure land and a building was a task that hung heavily on

WAYLAND SEMINARY.

weary hands, and severely taxed a faith not overstrong. But in God's plans the means are always equal to the demands, and so land was secured for the substantial and handsome building that now stands on Meridian Hill. The property is valued at more than $50,000. The building has accommodations for 100 students; but a history of all the struggles to complete the building can never be written. Donations were always given in small amounts, and the contributions of very many hands were necessary to complete the work. Few gifts exceeded $1000, and many of them were in themselves almost trifling, yet in the aggregate they secured success.

The aim of the school is to furnish an education at the smallest possible expense. To make this effectual, the students have the entire care of the seminary grounds and the building. Each student has his share of the responsibility of keeping the place a model of order and neatness. Thus students are aided in overcoming old objectionable habits, and forming those that will make their own homes models for their race. The seminary has not made the mistake of taking pupils with but little preparation through the higher studies of a college curriculum, and therefore it has wasted but little labor upon poor materials. Nearly 100 students have been connected with the school annually. Of this number more than one-third have entered the seminary to prepare for the ministry. The expenses of the school have been about $7000 annually, which sum is secured by contributions, since only a small endowment fund has been collected. The work of the school appears in the advance made by churches where its influence has extended. In Maryland and Virginia, as well as in the District of Columbia, a large proportion of the colored churches of the Baptist denomination that have made gratifying progress during the past twelve years have been under the care of graduates of this seminary. Mission churches have become self-sustaining, new churches have been planted, and a spirit of enterprise has shown itself in all the church work connected with these congregations. The marked success attending the labors of the graduates of the school has solved a number of the difficult problems that presented themselves at the beginning of the work. Many of the graduates have engaged in teaching, and are filling positions of honor and trust. Already students are coming to the school who have been fitted to enter its classes by those who have been educated there. The seminary constantly aims to supply such wants as appear necessary to the elevation of the colored race. Each year makes larger demands and brings additional proofs that the school is of God. From month to month contributions come to the school from those who love Christ and humanity, and the accomplished principal of the seminary, the Rev. G. M. P. King, with his devoted wife, labor on with the full assurance of faith. Prof. King is worthy of the warmest commendations of the friends of the freedmen, for to his persevering and energetic labors is mainly due the high degree of success which has marked the progress of the Wayland Seminary.

Weaver, Rev. Charles S., son of Silas G. and Dinah (Stone) Weaver, was born in Coventry, R. I., April 10, 1803; studied in common schools; became a teacher; converted in 1822; baptized in 1823; began preaching in 1828; licensed by Coventry and Warwick church; ordained at Arkwright village in 1829; settled with Baptist church in Plainfield, Conn.; in 1836, with church in Voluntown, and remained sixteen years; in 1852, with First Baptist church in Suffield; in 1855, with First Baptist church in Norwich; in 1860, with church in Noank, Groton; in 1870, returned to Voluntown; in 1875, with Second Baptist church in Richmond, R. I., where he is now laboring; has ever been an evangelist; baptized more than 1000 persons; was judge of probate and a member of the Connecticut Legislature; once president of Connecticut Baptist Convention; been moderator of Associations; commissioner of schools among the Narragansett Indians; a man of energy, piety, tact, and power.

Weaver, Rev. Joseph Myrtle, D.D., was born in Shelby Co., Ky., Dec. 18, 1832. In early manhood he professed conversion and united with the Methodists by immersion, but in less than a year afterwards he became dissatisfied with their doctrine and polity and united with the Baptist church at Bloomfield, Ky., "on his Methodist baptism." By this church he was licensed to preach, June 12, 1852, and next year entered Georgetown College, where he finished his education. On leaving college he was ordained, and took charge of the Baptist church at Seymour, Ind. After a short pastorate here he was called to the church at Taylorsville, Ky., where he ministered with much popularity about eight years. In January, 1865, he was called to the Chestnut Street church in Louisville, where he still remains. He has during this pastorate been one of the popular and successful pastors of the city. He has written extensively for the periodical press, and is a clear, forcible, and logical writer. In the winter and spring of 1879 he had an extended discussion in the *Western Recorder* with the editor of that journal, on the subject of the validity of alien immersions. His articles were elegant specimens of composition and logic. But he failed to satisfy his own judgment and conscience, and he submitted to baptism by a qualified administrator, and on the 5th of July, 1879, was immersed by Dr. Boyce, of the Southern Baptist Theological Seminary. Dr. Weaver was for a time co-editor of the *Western Recorder*. He wrote and published "The Myrtle Series" of Sunday-school books, in five volumes, with a question-book added. As a preacher and a pastor he has few superiors in the country.

Webb, Greenleaf S., D.D., son of Moses Webb, who with his six brothers served in the Revolutionary war, was born in Columbia Co., N. Y., May 2, 1789. Most of his youth was spent in Stamford, Conn., his parents having joined the Baptist church there. When a young man he came to New York City, and in his own words, "I first began to hear the Word with interest in 1806, but not till November, 1807, did I see the way clear to unite with God's people." He was then baptized by Rev. William Parkinson, whose ministry he had attended, and united with the First church. He superintended a company in erecting breastworks on Fort Greene in 1812. His mind was drawn to the ministry while attending to his secular duties; receiving encouragement from spiritual advisers, he studied with Dr. Staughton, at Philadelphia, and Dr. Stanford, in New York. In June, 1816, he was ordained, and became co-pastor with Mr. Ferris, at Stamford, and soon became sole pastor. He visited and preached before the Association at Piscataway about 1820. The church at New Brunswick called him, and he settled there in April, 1821. His preaching talent and executive ability soon bore fruit, and when he resigned the pastorate, at the end of more than twenty-two years, the flock that he found small and weak had become large and influential. He went at the call of God to the Third church in Philadelphia. During his pastorate in New Brunswick he had been surrendered by the church for eight months to plead the cause of foreign missions, and while in Philadelphia he was again pressed into that work for three years. Returning at last to his New Brunswick home, he has been very useful in the church there, and in supplying many important churches during vacancies in the pastorate. Tall, straight, healthy, of "sound mind and memory," he still preaches, counsels, and, with the weight of ninety-two years upon him, is venerated, loved, and trusted by his brethren. He is the only survivor of those who formed the State Convention. No man has been more prominent in guiding influence in all missionary directions. For many years he has been a member of the board of the Missionary Union. The university at Lewisburg gave him D.D. in 1856. He was a curator of that institution from 1846 to 1854. He remembers the birth of foreign missions in this country, and has a soul full of the commission which the Master gave to his disciples.

Webb, Jonathan N., D.D., was born in Brownville, N. Y., Jan. 14, 1811; baptized in February, 1825. Dr. Webb studied for some time at Madison University, but was obliged to leave before graduating on account of failing health. He was ordained as pastor of the Smithville and Munnsville Baptist churches at Smithville, N. Y., May, 1835. Here he remained five years. He afterwards was pastor of the following churches in the State of New York: the church at Carthage, six years; Gouverneur, two years; Ogdensburg, four years; Fort Covington, twelve years; Madrid, three years. He was three years with the Baptist church in Titusville, Pa. In 1870 a pressing call came from the Baptist Home Mission Society to superintend the work of that society in Nebraska and Dakota. For nine years he filled with marked fidelity and energy the position of district secretary, closing his labors with the society Feb. 1, 1879. These were years of wonderful toil, in cold and heat, amid difficulties that would have discouraged weaker hearts. His memory and name will be long remembered in the Baptist churches of Nebraska. Since he severed his connection with the Baptist Home Mission Society he has been laboring at his own charges for the interests of five churches in the State.

Webb, W. S., D.D., president of Mississippi College, Clinton, Miss., was born in the State of New York in 1825; prepared for college in Kingsville, O., Academy, presided over by Z. C. Graves, LL.D.; graduated at Madison University, N. Y., in 1849. After graduating he went to Middle Tennessee, and engaged in teaching and preaching near Smyrna, and as pastor at Enon, Rutherford Co.; six years president of Yalobusha Baptist Female Institute, at Grenada, Miss.; pastor six years at West Point, Miss., and fourteen years at Crawfordsville; in 1871 he became Professor of Theology in Mississippi College and pastor of the Clinton church; in 1873, upon the resignation of Dr. Hillman, he was elected president of Mississippi College, and under his administration the institution has greatly prospered.

Webber, Rev. William, was born in Virginia, Aug. 15, 1747. In the early part of 1770 he put his trust in Jesus for a full salvation, and he found it. He was baptized in June, and soon after ordained. He itinerated for several years after his ordination. In 1774 he became pastor of the Dover (Virginia) church, a relation which death only sundered. His labors were greatly favored of God, and churches in various places sprang up as harvests from the seed which he planted. He possessed extensive influence in the denomination, and commonly presided at the meetings of the General Association of Virginia and of the General Convention of Virginia Baptists.

He was several times in jail for preaching, and had much to endure from the "sons of Belial at different places;" but sustained by the love of Christ, nothing troubled him.

Mr. Webber had no one talent of superlative greatness, but he possessed such a combination of wisdom, love, Bible knowledge, grace, and persevering toil in the Master's service that he was a glorious husbandman for God. He was loved by true Christians, hated by the enemies of Jesus, and regarded by his own and subsequent generations as a father in the Baptist Israel of Virginia. He died Feb. 29, 1808, filled with rapturous joy.

Weeks, Hon. F. M., was born in Florida, a few miles south of Lake City, and died in 1879, in the meridian of life, in Alachua County, not very far from his birthplace. He was converted and baptized at Providence church, and at once became an active and useful member. He was universally respected and trusted.

He had acquired considerable reputation; served acceptably his county (Columbia) in the Legislature; was moderator of the Santa Fé River Association at his death, and had been licensed to preach.

Mr. Weeks was a successful Sunday-school worker, and was much loved by the children. He frequently expressed the wish that he might become so situated in life that he could devote himself to Sunday mission work.

Weeks, Rev. Silas.—This venerable and useful minister died at his home in Bradford Co., Fla., Jan. 20, 1880, at the age of sixty-eight. For thirty years he was an acceptable, devoted, and successful minister of the gospel in his denomination. He labored in the counties of Putnam, Nassau, Columbia, Alachua, and Bradford, and well has it been said of him, "Numerous, indeed, would be his spiritual family if all born of God under his ministry could be counted up." His life was without reproach, and his heart was in earnest. He was one of the few of whom it can be truly said, "I never heard anything against him."

Mr. Weeks was several years moderator of the New River Association, of which body he may be called the father.

Welch, Bartholomew T., D.D., was born in Boston, Mass., Sept. 24, 1794. His paternal grandfather was a lieutenant on board the U. S. frigate "Alliance," of Revolutionary fame, and his father was a midshipman in the same vessel. His mother was the daughter of Capt. B. Trow, a leader in the "Tea Party" in Boston Harbor, and a brave soldier at Bunker Hill. He served as an officer throughout the Revolutionary war.

From nine to twelve Bartholomew had many convictions of guilt, and he frequently cried for mercy, but he did not yield to the Saviour until he reached his twenty-first year. Under the ministry of Dr. Staughton, of Philadelphia, where he was then living, he was led to Christ. He united with the Sansom Street church in September, 1815. He soon felt that he must preach Jesus, and, after some missionary service, he became pastor of the Catskill, N. Y., Baptist church, in September, 1825. In 1827 he accepted the pastorate of the First Baptist church of Albany, N. Y.

Here his labors were so successful that in 1834 a new interest, known as the Pearl Street church, was established in a capacious edifice, which was speedily filled to overflowing by all classes of society. "The farmer, the mechanic, merchant, scholar, and the statesman were delighted with his instructive and thrilling discourses." When he entered upon his labors at Albany there was but one Baptist church, and when he left it there were four.

In December, 1848, to the regret of his church and the whole people of Albany, he accepted the call of the Pierpont Street Baptist church, Brooklyn, and entered upon pastoral duties among them. The severity of the climate and the feebleness of his health compelled the change. In Brooklyn his gospel and his eloquence produced the same results as in Albany. He was an eminent servant of the living God, whom his Redeemer greatly honored.

Welch, Rev. James Eley, was born Feb. 28, 1789, in Fayette Co., Ky. During the summer of 1810 he was converted, made a public profession of religion, and was baptized by Rev. Jeremiah Vardeman in October following into the fellowship of the church at Davis' Fork. After many struggles on the subject, he became convinced that God had called him to the great work of preaching the gospel, and in 1815 he was set apart to the ministry. The next year he spent with Rev. Dr. Wm. Staughton at Philadelphia, studying theology, and also acting as pastor of the church in Burlington, N. J., where he was eminently successful. Feeling impressed with the duty of mission work, he tendered his services to the Board of Missions at Philadelphia in May, 1817, and was accepted as a missionary to St. Louis, Mo. On Sunday, May 18, he was set apart to the work, Dr. Furman, Dr. Baldwin, Dr. Mercer, and Dr. Staughton participating in the exercises. He reached his destination after more than two months of travel. The mission work in St. Louis was very difficult. That city was then a small village, the Catholic influence strong, and the people more inclined to wickedness than religion. His diary of this time denotes very great discouragements, as well as a daily consecration of life and work to the Master. The first Baptist church in St. Louis was constituted by Mr. Welch and Dr. J. M. Peck, Feb. 8, 1818. Their first house of worship was opened for service in July, 1819. After three years of laborious struggles and varied

BARTHOLOMEW T. WELCH, D.D.

successes, the board discontinued the mission, and Mr. Welch returned to Burlington, N. J. For more than twenty years he was agent for the American Sunday-School Union, traveling in this capacity over all the States and Territories, forming Sabbath-schools and otherwise actively advancing this work. He removed from Burlington in September, 1848, to Warren Co., Mo. In this vicinity he labored constantly for the Master's cause, preaching and building churches until the year 1875, when he removed to Warrensburg, Mo. In the centennial year he revisited his old home in Burlington, N. J., and on the 18th of July of that year, while with an excursion party of Baptist brethren at the sea-shore, he was seized with apoplexy, and ended a long and useful life. He was a noble man, ever through life discharging faithfully the duties of a Christian gentleman and minister, thereby securing the affection and esteem of those with whom he was associated.

Welch, Rev. Oliver, was born in Madison Co., Va., April 27, 1791; was married to Miss Elizabeth Mallory the 18th of September, 1810; both of them united with the Baptist church at Crooked Run in 1815, and were baptized by the Rev. Daniel James. Not having a single Christian relative, this youthful couple in starting out in the Christian life had many trials to overcome. Mr. Welch began to preach in 1823, and in Virginia was pastor of Good Hope, Gourd Vine, and Cedar Run churches. He removed to Alabama in 1834, united with the Talladega Creek church (now Alpine), which he served as pastor until his death, which occurred at the house of his daughter, Mrs. Reynolds, the 23d of April, 1874, making a pastorate of forty years; he also served several other churches as pastor in Talladega Co. A large family connection came from Virginia to Alabama with Mr. Welch, and settled around him, and under his ministry were brought into his church. They and he, being people of wealth and fine social position, comprised one of the most attractive communities and one of the most influential churches in the State. He lived an unblemished life, and left to his posterity and to his church a precious memory. He had a most amiable, gentle spirit, and a dignified bearing. He was an instructive preacher, and among his large circle of friends—laymen and ministers—he was a safe and wise counselor.

Wellborn, Judge Marshall J., long known in Georgia as "Judge Wellborn," and in the latter years of his life a distinguished Baptist minister, was born in Putnam Co., Ga., May 29, 1808, and died at Columbus, Ga., Oct. 16, 1874. He was the son of Thomas Wellborn, of South Carolina. His mother was a Virginia lady, and both parents were of English extraction. M. J. Wellborn was endowed by nature with rare qualities of head and heart; courage, energy, benevolence, and generosity were always prominent traits in his character. His mind was distinguished for quickness of perception and perseverance in investigation; and it was *the truth* above all things that he sought to learn. This intuitive tendency developed that anxious, humble, prayerful, and unceasing study of God's Word, and caused that prompt surrender of preconceived opinions to the dictates of reason and revelation, for which he was remarkable.

He passed through the Junior class of the State University, at Athens, studied law, and was, by a special act of the Legislature, admitted to the practice of law at nineteen. Early in 1828 he removed to Hamilton, in Harris County, and there the foundation of his fortune and success in after-life was laid. He was a powerful debater and a thrilling orator, and many of his extempore speeches, delivered at the bar, thirty-five or forty years ago, are still remembered as masterpieces of forensic eloquence.

After a few years he removed to the city of Columbus, where he rose rapidly to prominence in his profession, and, without a stain upon his character, accumulated an ample fortune. At twenty-one he was elected to the State Legislature, and in 1842, at thirty-four, he became judge of the Superior Court of the Chattahoochee circuit.

As a judicial officer, his career was eminently distinguished for professional learning, faithfulness, and uprightness. Subsequently, after a prolonged European tour, with characteristic ability and purity, he filled one term in the lower house of Congress. Declining a re-election, he returned to the practice of his profession, which he followed with leading success.

During the celebrated revival of 1858, in Columbus, he professed regeneration, joined the Baptist Church, and was baptized by Dr. J. H. De Votie. His conversion was almost Paul-like in its wonderful transformation; his conviction of sin was peculiarly pungent, and his evidences of regeneration and pardon were most remarkable. Divine grace has seldom made a more signal triumph than in his case, where the exceeding lustre of holy thought, feeling, speech, and conduct profoundly eclipsed the brightest light of human morality. From the moment that he accepted Jesus he became an enthusiastic advocate of the Saviour's cause.

After a long struggle to know his duty, he accepted a license to preach the gospel, and June 29, 1864, he was ordained at Columbus. He accepted the charge of the Hamilton Baptist church and of the Bethesda church, in Harris County, preaching twice a month at each place until his death, and declining to receive any compensation from either; a great mistake, as results show. Ardently desirous of doing all in his power for Jesus, and assured that his period for ministerial service must be short, he abounded in the multitude of his labors. For ten years he preached in the pulpit, by the fireside, on the highways—everywhere, and to everybody, white and black—with a tenderness which nothing could inspire but an overflowing benevolence and a profound conviction of the truths of the gospel. He not only received no compensation for his ministerial services, but with open hands distributed his own private fortune to the poor, to the aid of the churches, to the support of other ministers, and to the various evangelical enterprises of the day.

His work was signally blessed. He baptized an uncommon number of converts under his own ministry. He was greatly beloved by the people among whom he moved, and in hundreds of homes in Western and Southwestern Georgia, and in the adjoining parts of Alabama, his name will abide till this generation is gone, a synonym of all that is good and noble. From youth he was the subject of constant and distressing ill health. The activity of his uncommonly busy life was astonishing. There were times when, sick almost unto death and scarcely able to move a limb, he would be aroused by some call for exertion, and he would go on the Master's business immediately.

As a preacher, he had superior ability, his sermons being well prepared, and delivered earnestly and eloquently. In doctrine he was incorrupt. As a pastor, he was untiringly devoted, and eminently successful in comforting believers and in winning souls to Jesus. He delighted to assist young men, whether it was to give them a start in business or in preparing for the ministry. He manifested great interest in plans for the education and spiritual advancement of our colored population, contributing largely to build houses of worship for them, and constantly preaching to those of them within the bounds of his charges. Worn out by incessant toil, he suddenly fell asleep in Jesus on Saturday, Oct. 16, 1874. By his death a whole community was stirred to its depths, and devout men carried him to his burial and made great lamentation over him.

Welling, James C., LL.D., was born July 1, 1825, at Trenton, N. J. After pursuing his preliminary studies at the Trenton Academy, he entered Princeton College, from which he graduated in 1844. From 1844 to 1846 he was a private tutor in the family of Henry T. Garnett, Esq., of Westmoreland, Va. He afterwards entered upon the study of the law with the Hon. Willoughby Newton, of Virginia, but at the expiration of a year he was recalled to New Jersey by the illness of his father. On the death of his father, in 1848, he became one of the principals of the New York Collegiate School, the oldest grammar-school in that city. In 1853 he resigned this position to accept the associate editorship of *The National Intelligencer*, Washington, D. C., for which celebrated journal he had already, since 1850, written the "Notes on New Books," which were a characteristic feature of the paper. Dr. Welling, as editor of the *Intelligencer* during the trying period of the war, conducted it with signal ability. Being an eminently national journal, circulating extensively both in the North and the South, as well as being read by not a few in Europe, the views of *The National Intelligencer* on all national subjects, and especially at this period, when the contest between the U. S. government and the Confederate States was being so fiercely waged, were eagerly looked for and anxiously scanned. Its opinions were generously indorsed by the most patriotic and discriminating in all sections of the country, and they aided not a little in keeping the judgments of men clear as to the cardinal constitutional features of the contest. Before, during, and after the crisis Dr. Welling stood steadfastly by the Constitution and the Union, though not always approving the policies of the Administration. He resigned his position as editor of the *Intelligencer* Jan. 1, 1865, in consequence of failing health, the result of arduous labors in connection with that journal. In 1863 he was elected by the judges of the U. S. Court of Claims assistant clerk of that tribunal, the duties of which, being at that time very light, did not interfere with his editorial labors. During 1866 he spent six or seven months in Europe in quest of health, and visited England, Scotland, Switzerland, France, and Italy. In 1867 he was elected president of St. John's College, at Annapolis, Md., and during his administration the number of students was enlarged, the course of study made more comprehensive and thorough, and the discipline improved. In 1870 he was called to the chair of Belles-Lettres in Princeton College, which position he resigned in the following year to accept the presidency of the Columbian College (now the Columbian University), on the resignation of the Rev. Dr. Samson. Up to the present period in Dr. Welling's incumbency the course of study has been enlarged and the endowment greatly increased. Mainly through his instrumentality a valuable tract of land on the edge of Washington City was given by Mr. Corcoran for the founding of a scientific school, in addition to which $100,000 were subscribed for the general endowment of the university. Dr. Welling has written a great deal, mainly, however, in the form of editorials and literary addresses, and of contributions to various journals, and to the *North American Review*. He is one of the most accomplished writers in the country. Being so widely and favorably known among journalists, literary and public men, he is frequently called upon to occupy positions of honor and responsibility. He is a corresponding member of the New York Historical Society, of the Connecticut Historical Society; visitor of the Government Hospital for the Insane, Washington, D. C.; vice-president of the Washington Philosophical Society; member of the executive committee of the American Colonization Society; trustee of the Corcoran Art Gallery.

Dr. Welling is one of the most active laymen in the Baptist denomination. He was for many years the efficient superintendent of the Sunday-school of the E Street Baptist church, Washington; is at present a deacon of the North Baptist church, and moderator of the Columbia Baptist Association, comprising the churches of the District of Columbia. He is one of the most thorough of Biblical scholars, and his rich and varied stores of information make him exceedingly interesting in the social meetings of his church. He received the degree of A.M. from Princeton College in 1847, and the honorary degree of LL.D. from the Columbian College in 1868. Dr. Welling married, in 1850, Miss Genevieve H. Garnett, the accomplished daughter of Col. Henry I. Garnett, of Virginia, who, however, survived her marriage less than two years, and since that time he has remained unmarried. He is unwearied in planning and working for the prosperity of the university.

Welsh Baptists, The.—In no country have the principles of our faith as Baptists been more generally understood and more bravely defended than in the little principality of Wales. It is commonly believed that all through the dark reign of popery in the seclusions of her valleys and in the fastnesses of her mountains there were those who preserved the ancient purity of doctrine and worship. The general quickening of religious thought, which was one of the distinguishing features of the Reformation, was, however, the beneficent agency in facilitating their emergence into the clear light of historic recognition. The earnest study of the sacred oracles at this time caused numbers of the most learned and God-fearing of the sons of the Established Church to declare themselves converts to the Baptist faith. Such men as Penry, Wroth, Erbury, and Vavasor Powell became leaders of mighty influence. They suffered much for the principles which they professed and preached. Vavasor Powell was a preacher of extraordinary power. Fluent in both Welsh and English, and withal enriched with a cultivated mind, he reached all classes and commanded all hearts. He was immured in about thirteen prisons, in one of which he died on the 27th of September, 1670.

The ministry of these distinguished Reformers and others of the same type was abundantly fruitful, in spite of the most persistent opposition from every form of worldly power. The seed sprinkled with tears and blood could not fail to grow and flourish. Churches sprang into existence in different parts of the land, and the waters of many a rural stream bore witness to the joyful obedience of hundreds who had been brought to the knowledge of the truth.

The first churches in Wales after the Reformation were missionary centres of wide-reaching activity. In addition to one or more pastors they frequently had numerous assistants. Although separated by immense distances, and that at a time when roads were frequently impassable, there was scarcely a village or neighborhood throughout the length and breadth of the land where the gospel of salvation was not occasionally preached. It is said that Christmas Evans traversed Wales forty times from north to south, preaching the gospel, in the course of his fruitful ministry. Every renowned preacher of the past century gave a large portion of his time to evangelistic work. The religious status of the Welsh people is largely attributable to this liberal diffusion of stimulating and enlightening thought. The rugged heroes of the past century, who with self-sacrificing devotion exposed themselves to every form of indignity and to all the rigors of a variable climate that they might make known the saving truths of the gospel, are worthy of being held in everlasting remembrance.

The influence which the Welsh Baptists have exerted upon the religious thought and life of this country demands special recognition. They have contributed more than any other people who have sought a home in this Western world to the spread of our principles, and to the integrity of our denominational life. Much of the formative work in Rhode Island, New Jersey, Virginia, New York, Delaware, and Pennsylvania was done by them. The first Baptist church in this country was established in Providence, R. I., by a Welshman. The first Baptist church in what is now the State of Massachusetts was founded by a Welshman. The first Baptist church now in Pennsylvania, the mother of the Philadelphia Association and of many churches in Pennsylvania and New Jersey, kept its records in the Welsh language for many years, and its first Bible, which is treasured by the American Baptist Historical Society, was in Welsh. The Welsh Tract church, which was the first holding our faith in Delaware, and for many years a most influential community, was formed in Wales, came out to this country as a body, and, after remaining a short time at Lower Dublin, settled permanently in Delaware. There is not a State in the Union where Welshmen have not had an honored part in furthering Baptist interests. In many instances they have given direction and energy to our denominational life when as yet it could hardly be said to have an organized existence. In not a few neighborhoods, in addition to those already mentioned, where our name is now a power and blessing, they were the fearless pioneers. The superstructure of our Baptist faith owes much of its present strength and grandeur to the solid foundation-work in which they had so large a share.

Roger Williams, the fearless champion of civil and religious liberty, whose teaching and example did so much to introduce into the Constitution of this country its distinguishing excellence; John Miles, who exerted such a powerful influence upon Baptist progress in the early days of our history; Dr. Samuel Jones, of Lower Dublin, and the venerable Isaac Eaton, first master of Hopewell Academy; Abel Morgan and Morgan Edwards, distinguished as writers and preachers; David Thomas, the veteran preacher of Virginia and Kentucky; David Jones, Horatio Gates Jones, and John Williams, of New York, all men of might in their day, were Welshmen or the immediate descendants of Welshmen.

There are in Wales at the present time nearly 500 Baptist churches, with a membership aggregating between 60,000 and 70,000. The practice of restricted communion is universal save in a few English churches in the large centres of population.

Welsh, Rev. John C., was born in Boston, April 11, 1792. He became a hopeful Christian when he was twenty-four years of age, and two or three years later was baptized into the fellowship of the First Baptist church, Boston. Having decided to enter the ministry he studied theology for a time in Waterville, and was ordained pastor of the Baptist church in Warren, R. I., in June, 1823. He remained pastor of the Warren church for eighteen years. From 1840 to 1850 he was pastor of the church in Seekonk, Mass. Having resigned his office here he removed to Providence, where he spent the rest of his life. He was ready to act as a supply for destitute churches, and perform any ministerial service by which he could help on the cause of Christ. He died in Providence, Feb. 13, 1858.

Welsh Tract Church, Del.—Sixteen Baptists in Wales about to emigrate to America formed themselves into a Baptist church in 1701, with Rev. Thomas Griffith, one of their number, as pastor. They came to Pennepek, now in Philadelphia, Pa., where there was a Welsh Baptist church. Leaving in this place some of their number, and receiving accessions in return, they removed, in 1703, to Iron Hill, in the Welsh Tract, New Castle Co., Del. (at that time a part of Pennsylvania). A small meeting-house was then erected upon the site now occupied by the present edifice, built in 1746. Their principles soon spread in Delaware and into Pennsylvania and Maryland, and to Pedee River, S. C. "The community at Welsh Tract in early times held a respectable stand among the American Baptists; it was one of the five churches which formed the Philadelphia Association; its ministers were among the most active in all Baptist operations, and the whole community was not behind any of the members of that quintuple alliance." (Benedict's Baptist History, p. 626.) In 1790, Morgan Edwards wrote: "The Delaware Baptists are Calvinistic in doctrine, and differ little or nothing in discipline from their brethren in neighboring States." (Materials towards a Baptist History, Delaware, p. 224.) This church was the mother of the London Tract, Pa., and Duck Creek, Del., churches, and in some degree of the Wilmington (First), Cowmarsh, and Mispillion churches, Del.; also of the Welsh Neck church, S. C. "The Welsh Tract church was the principal if not the sole means of introducing singing, imposition of hands, church covenants, etc., among the Baptist churches in the Middle States." (Edwards's Materials, p. 232.) Holding to the laying on of hands on baptized believers, they refused to commune for a while with the Philadelphia and Pennepek churches, but the difficulty was settled, in 1706, on the side of peace and unity. Their pastors have been Thomas Griffith, Elisha Thomas, Enoch Morgan, Owen Thomas, David Davis, John Sutton, John Boggs, Gideon Ferrell, S. W. Woolford, Samuel Trott, W. K. Roberson, Thomas Barton, G. W. Staton, and William Grafton. The membership in 1716 was 122; in 1817, 192; and now (1880), 64.

Welton, Rev. Daniel M., Ph.D., was born in Aylesford, Nova Scotia, in 1831; graduated from Acadia College in June, 1855; ordained pastor of the Baptist church, Windsor, Nova Scotia, Sept. 2, 1857; thence became Professor in Acadia College, in 1874; went, in 1876, to Germany, and studied Hebrew and Greek exegesis at Leipsic University for two years. Dr. Welton is now Professor of Hebrew and Systematic Theology in Acadia College.

Wenger, John, D.D., one of the most distinguished oriental scholars and translators of the age, was born in Switzerland, Aug. 31, 1811. Educated for the ministry of the national church, his conscientious convictions of the unscriptural character of infant baptism constrained him to abandon the course which his friends had planned for him. For some years he engaged in teaching in Greece. In 1838 he visited England, and was soon after baptized by Dr. Steane, and received into the church at Camberwell, London. Having offered himself for missionary work in India, he was sent to Calcutta by the Baptist Missionary Society, and joined Dr. Yates in translating the Scriptures. A new Bengali version was then the great work in hand, the translators aiming " to produce an idiomatic version which should be as good Bengali as the English version is good English." Before the close of 1845, a few months after Dr. Yates's death, the entire Bible was printed. In 1852, Dr. Wenger issued from the mission press a revised version, which has continued to be the standard version, and has the support of missionaries of almost every denomination, and of the Christian communities of Bengal. A third edition was begun in 1855, and was finally completed in 1861. In 1862 the committee requested Dr. Wenger to prepare an annotated edition of the Bengali Scriptures. While this important work was in progress he issued several editions of the New Testament, and in 1867 the fourth edition of the entire Bible, printed in small type, and making a handy octavo volume, left the press. His next work was a still more thorough revision of the text of 1861. In some parts, especially in the Psalms and prophets of the Old Testament and the epistles of the New Testament, it may be said to be a new translation. Besides these labors in the Bengali, the language of forty millions of people, Dr. Wenger has devoted himself to the study of the Sanscrit, the ancient and sacred language of India. Dr. Carey and also Dr. Yates had translated the Bible into Sanscrit, but Dr. Wenger's work, consisting of four volumes, is much more valuable. It has received the highest approbation of the learned everywhere, and is much esteemed by those natives of India to whom Sanscrit is familiar. Besides these works, Dr. Wenger has edited a great number of Bengali publications issued by the Calcutta Tract Society. The principles on which he has carried forward these great works are well stated in Dr. Wenger's own words, which apply in America as well as in India: " In carrying on their Biblical translations, especially as regards the New Testament, Baptist missionaries have for nearly forty years past acted independently of the British and Foreign Bible Society and its local auxiliaries. Their severance from that great and noble society originated with an attempt to compel the translators either to leave the terms for baptism untranslated, or to translate them in a way which was contrary to their conscientious convictions. It has often been taken for granted that our differences with the Bible Society concern only this one topic of baptism. But, if I may be allowed to give expression to my own sentiments, I would say that this one point is only a sample of others, and that in all of them a great principle is at stake. The principle is this,—that a Biblical translator should not be compelled merely by a majority of votes given at a committee meeting to translate the Word of God in a way which is not in accordance with his conscientious conviction. In endeavoring to ascertain the grammatical interpretation and the sense of the sacred texts, opinions must be weighed, not counted, and they must be weighed by the man who has to execute the translation. The rules for the guidance of translators which have been laid down by the Bible Society, and which are annually reprinted in the report of the local society, appear to me quite as impertinent as was its attempt to dictate to Baptist translators how they ought to render the terms descriptive of baptism. In short, it is the independence of translators which the Bible Society wants to tamper with, and which, as Baptists, we ought to consider ourselves bound to uphold." Dr. Wenger was once blamed by certain persons for issuing a translation of the third chapter of John's gospel which they said was not correct, simply because it did not teach the doctrine of baptismal regeneration. He replied with characteristic force, " My translation was not intended to teach any doctrine at all. I wish to give God's Word as I find it, and if it runs counter to the errors of any church in Christendom, so much the worse for that church that bases itself on an error which God's Word does not contain." Whilst so much occupied with his special work, Dr. Wenger has constantly engaged in the ministry, and has rendered great services to the cause of missions by his wise counsels, loving spirit, and ripe judgment. In his advanced age, though failing sight interferes with his activity, he is still devoted to his great work, and has a very efficient junior fellow-laborer in the Rev. G. H. Rouse, M.A., upon whom the chief charge of the translation work is now laid.

Wepf, Rev. Lewis, the pastor of the Ebenezer German Baptist church in Milwaukee, is a native of Mülheim, Canton of Thurgovie, Switzerland, where he was born July 11, 1822. He came to America when a young man; was converted and united with the Baptist church in Buffalo, N. Y., in 1848; ordained March 10, 1853, in Buffalo. He came to Wisconsin in 1872, and labored one year as missionary among the Germans in Watertown, one year as missionary among the Germans of Mayville, and for the last six years has been the pastor of the Ebenezer German Baptist church of Milwaukee. He is a man of fine culture, a clear and vigorous thinker, and an evangelical preacher of Christ's gospel. He published, in 1871, a work in the German language entitled "The Church and her Enemies," which had a large sale.

Wescott, Isaac, D.D., was born in Plymouth, Mass., April 10, 1804. In early life he manifested a great fondness for books. When fifteen years of age his father removed to Manchester, N. H., where, with his accustomed avidity, he prosecuted his studies in the common schools, the high school, and the academy. Here he was converted and joined the church, and soon exhibited the same devotion to church work that marked his life while a student. The years 1826 and 1827 he occupied in the study of theology, under the guidance of his pastor, Rev. C. O. Kimball, and before their expiration he was called to preach to a new interest at Dunbarton. From this period until quite recently the ministerial career of Dr. Wescott has been that of a faithful, arduous pastor, whose life has been marked by evangelistic fervor. During his service at Dunbarton a substantial house of worship was erected. In 1831 he became pastor at Whitney, Conn., where he was ordained, and where in two years he baptized 100 converts. In 1833 he removed to Stillwater, N. Y. At this place he remained pastor eighteen years, and during this time the old meeting-house was rebuilt, and an influence created that not only benefited the church at Stillwater, but extended throughout the Saratoga Association. Dr. Wescott has served Laight Street, N. Y., 1851–56; Gloversville, 1856–59 (at this place a large house of worship was built); 1859–61, at Newburgh; 1861–67, at Bloomingdale, New York City; 1867–72, at Plymouth. On account of deafness he has retired as a pastor, but acts as a supply when he has an opportunity. As a preacher, Dr. Wescott is strongly doctrinal. Profound earnestness is probably the most striking characteristic of his sermons and his daily life. His sermons show great ability. Middlebury College, Vt., gave him the honorary degree of A.M. in 1833, and Rochester University, in 1864, made him a Doctor of Divinity.

West, Rev. Samuel, was born in Hopkinton, R. I., Oct. 6, 1766; was converted in 1787; was ordained in 1799; was settled for ten years in New London, Conn.; was a good, deserving, efficient minister; closed his honorable labors and life in North Madison, Conn., in the seventy-first year of his age and the thirty-eighth of his ministry.

West Virginia, Baptists of.—The history of the Baptists in West Virginia is closely related to that of the Baptists of Virginia, and especially to that of the General Association of Virginia. A large number of the churches have been organized by the missionaries of that body. The oldest church in the State is Simpson's Creek, in the Union Association, formed in 1774. The three next in order are Forks of Cheat, 1775; West Fork, 1780; and the Greenbrier, 1781. Rev. John Alderson was the first Baptist minister who visited the southern part of the State. Through his efforts the Greenbrier church was originated, as also the Greenbrier Association in 1800. The Hopewell and Raleigh Associations were formed from the Greenbrier in 1871. The Union Association was organized in 1804, the Teays' Valley in 1812, the Parkersburg in 1818, the Broad Run in 1835, and about 1870–71 the Guyandotte and Kanawha Valley were taken from the Teays' Valley. Before the formation of the General Association of West Virginia there were two mission bodies in its bounds auxiliary to the General Association of Virginia,—the Western and the Northwestern Associations. The General Association was organized Nov. 15, 1865, by delegates from the Parkersburg, Judson, Mount Pisgah, Union, Teays' Valley, and Broad Run Associations. Besides those already named there are two other Associations in the State,—the Goshen and the Harmony,—making thirteen District Associations. In these there were, in 1880, 381 churches, 25,239 members, and 203 ordained ministers. The total reported amount of contributions for State, home, and foreign missions, Sunday-schools, and home expenses was, in 1879, $24,228.63, and while this is the sum reported much more than this was contributed. The thirteen Associations are supporting fourteen native preachers in Burmah, and $943.40 of the amount given to foreign missions passed through the hands of the American Baptist Missionary Union. The General Association had, in 1880, ten missionaries under appointment in the State, some of whom occupy positions of the first importance in towns on the railroads. The Baptists of West Virginia now hold a very favorable position as compared with that of the other denominations in the State. Their Sunday-school and educational work is in advance of all others. The Shelton and Broaddus Colleges are now established, and with proper efforts a brighter day is before them.

Besides the white membership there is one Association of colored Baptists,—the Mount Olivet,—organized in 1874, and which now consists of 24 churches and 974 members. There are colored Baptist churches with 413 members which do not belong to this Association, but to similar bodies in adjacent States, the whole number being 1387, making an aggregate of Regular Baptists in the State of about 26,000. The colored churches have some very acceptable preachers, several of whom are well educated and doing a good work.

Westcott, Rev. Erastus, was born March 27, 1816, in Milford, Otsego Co., N. Y. His parents removed from Cheshire, Mass., where they had enjoyed the ministrations of the celebrated Rev. John Leland. The early years of young Westcott were occupied in farming. At sixteen he made a profession of religion, and united with the Baptist Church. The following year he entered the academic department of Madison University, where he pursued his studies to the close of the Sophomore year. He then pursued his studies privately, preaching when opportunity presented until April, 1837, when he engaged in pastoral labor. For more than forty-three years he has been but one week without a pastorate. He was ordained in Richfield, Otsego Co., N. Y., in 1838, and for twenty-two years served churches in Otsego and Delaware Counties, N. Y. During this period he organized two churches, gathered the funds and superintended the erection of two meeting-houses. At the same time he zealously labored to promote the welfare of neighboring destitute churches. In August, 1857, he removed to Rochester, Minn., and at once organized a church of seventeen members. The same month he attended the first anniversary of the Southern Minnesota Association. In 1858 he gathered the funds for the first meeting-house in Rochester, dedicating it in the month of October. After serving the Rochester church three years he resigned, and located in Concord, Dodge Co., where he still resides. In his present field he has organized four churches, and assisted in forming two others. He has collected the funds on the fields where three meeting-houses have been erected and paid for. His salary has always been inadequate to his support, yet in the erection of these places of worship he gave more than $1000 from his scanty means. He also gave $500 to the Minnesota Academy at Owatonna. He has given liberally for home and foreign missions and other objects of benevolence. At one time he served four churches, and had a covenant meeting every Saturday P.M. in the year. From these meetings he was never absent unless prevented by a severe storm or funeral. He gave attention in part to business for his support, but never allowed worldly engagements to interfere with the duties of the ministry. For four years past he has been largely engaged in building and endowing the Minnesota Academy located at Owatonna. This work is a success.

Weston, Rev. Adolphus, is the pioneer Baptist preacher of Washington Territory. He was born in Willington, Conn., Jan. 29, 1811; converted and baptized in 1829; licensed in 1831; he studied at Madison University six years; was ordained as pastor at Burlington Flats, N. Y., in 1838, and in 1839 was appointed missionary to the Mississippi Valley; preached in many places, became pastor at Carthage, Ill., and had a great revival. He continued as pastor at Carthage twelve years. In 1852 he went overland to Oregon, where he was pastor of the West Union church, and missionary of the Willamette Association until 1863, when he removed to Washington Territory. He gathered the few Baptists who could be found in that wilderness, and preached to them. His labors were greatly blessed. He organized the church in Puyallus Valley in 1867. He was the only Baptist minister in all that region for many years. Nearly every month he had converts to baptize. The churches increased in number until in 1871 the Puget Sound Association was organized with five churches and four ministers. His work has been that of a pioneer missionary without appointment from any society. The churches at Elma, Centreville, Olympia, Seattle, and other places all recognize in "Father Weston" one of the chief founders of the Baptist cause in Washington Territory.

Weston, David, D.D., an American clergyman of the Baptist denomination. He was born in North Middleborough, Mass., Jan. 24, 1836, and died Feb. 22, 1875. He graduated from Brown University and at Newton Theological Seminary. His first pastorate was at Worcester, Mass., but he soon left to take the chair of Ecclesiastical History in the theological seminary at Hamilton, N. Y. By reason of his scholarship and ability as a teacher the University of Rochester bestowed upon him, though a young man, the honorary degree of D.D. Few men had accumulated so much material for ecclesiastical history so early in life as Dr. Weston. The early death of this rising man was lamented by all who knew him. It was a great loss to the whole Baptist denomination.

Weston, Henry G., D.D., was born in Lynn, Mass., Sept. 11, 1820. His father was at that time one of the firm of True & Weston, publishers of the *Christian Watchman*, in Boston. He was baptized

HENRY G. WESTON, D.D.

in Lynn in 1834; graduated from Brown University in 1840, and in the fall of that year entered Newton Theological Institution; was ordained in Frankfort, Ky., in 1843, and immediately proceeded to Illinois, where he preached as a missionary at his own charges for three years, in Tazewell, Woodford, and McLean Counties; settled as pastor of the church in Peoria, Ill., in 1846, and remained thirteen years; removed to Oliver Street church, New York City, where he remained until 1868, when he accepted a call to his present position as president of Crozer Theological Seminary. In connection with the labors incident to these varied and responsible positions, he has been prominently engaged in advancing the general interests of the denomination. He was editor of the *Baptist Quarterly* from the time of its establishment, and has also served as president of the American Baptist Missionary Union. He has published a valuable treatise on the four gospels, and with both pen and voice has rendered other useful and extended service. He received the degree of A.M. in 1846 from Shurtleff College, and that of D.D. in 1859 from the University of Rochester.

Dr. Weston is a man eminently fitted to be an educator of those who are preparing to instruct their fellow-men. As an expositor of the Scriptures, he is clear, thorough, and spiritual. His uninterrupted and zealous pursuit of the truth, his simplicity of speech, his living faith, his invincible courage, and his unbounded confidence in the reliable and unfailing authority of God's Word, render him peculiarly competent to guide the opinions and control the commotions of inquiring and agitated truth-seekers. His mind is richly stored with the results of long-continued Bible study; his heart is an overflowing fountain of manly tenderness, and all his varied and cultured attainments are sanctified by the experiences of successful pastoral ministrations. Knowing the wants of those to whom the gospel must be preached, as well as the necessities of those who are to preach the gospel, he possesses rare qualifications for the position he now holds. The influence of his native genius, sound scholarship, correct taste, and ripe Christian experience reaches far and wide through the able ministry of those who have sat under his instruction. He is one of the ablest men in his position in or out of this country.

Weston, Rev. John E., was born in Amherst, N. H., Oct. 13, 1796. On his mother's side he was of Huguenot descent, and had many of those qualities of character which we associate with those honored French refugees, who suffered so much for the sake of their religion. He established, in connection with Mr. Benjamin True, in 1818, the *Christian Watchman*, now *The Watchman*, of Boston, which has been in existence sixty-three years. His connection with the paper continued not far from three years. While thus engaged his religious impressions ripened into a full hope in Christ, and he was baptized by Rev. James M. Winchell, Feb. 22, 1820, and connected himself with the church under the pastoral care of Rev. Dr. Sharp. Having given up his business as a printer, he now resolved to carry out his early purpose to secure a better intellectual training, with a view to entering the ministry. He repaired to the Andover Phillips' Academy, and subsequently put himself under the tuition of Rev. Dr. Bolles, of Salem, Mass.; then became a student of Columbian College, and completed his theological studies in part at Andover and in part as a member of the first graduating class at Newton. He was ordained at East Cambridge, Mass., Oct. 10, 1827, and was the pastor of the Baptist church in that place for four years. He resigned his charge May 27, 1831. An invitation had been extended to him to become the pastor of the Baptist church in Nashua, N. H., but his work was nearly done. On his way to Nashua to fulfill an engagement he drove into a pond—it being a warm summer's day—to refresh his horse. Unfortunately it was a dangerous place, and Mr. Weston leaped from the carriage, and, being unable to swim, was drowned. The sad event occurred July 2, 1831. Mr. Weston was father of the Rev. H. G. Weston, D.D., president of the Crozer Theological Institution.

Whale, Theophilus, was born in England of an opulent family about 1616; received a university education; served as an officer in Virginia; served through the Parliamentary wars; commanded guards at the execution of Charles I., in 1649; served under the Protectorate; on the restoration of monarchy, in 1660, fled to America; settled, and married Elizabeth Mills, in Virginia, but, being a Baptist, and disliking dominant Episcopacy, removed, and settled in South Kingston, R. I., about 1680; was a writer, teacher, and farmer; read Hebrew, Greek, and Latin; aided Baptist ministers in their education; was reticent, and hence suspected of being connected with the regicide judges; a pure, studious man; became the grandfather of Judge Samuel Hopkins; died about 1719, aged one hundred and three years; was buried with military honors on Hopkins Hill, West Greenwich, R. I.

Wharton, Rev. H. M., was born in Culpeper Co., Va., Sept. 11, 1848. After receiving a good common-school education he attended Roanoke College during the sessions of 1863 and 1864. The latter part of 1864 he entered the Confederate service, and was with the army at its surrender at Appomattox Court-House, in April, 1865. Soon after the war, in 1866, he went to Mexico with his brother, Dr. J. S. Wharton, and remained about twelve months. He then returned to his father's home in Virginia, at Amherst Court-House, to which the latter had removed during the war. Here he soon became interested in religious matters, and united with the Episcopal Church in November, 1867. He was quite prominent in that church, and occasionally acted as lay reader. He chose the law as his profession, being admitted to the bar when only nineteen. He was engaged in the practice of law until 1873, and Judge Sheffey, the distinguished judge of that circuit, pronounced him the most promising young lawyer in the State. On a visit to his brother, Rev. M. B. Wharton, D.D., pastor of the Walnut Street Baptist church in Louisville, Ky., he changed his religious views, and was by him baptized into the fellowship of that church. After some exercise of his ministerial gifts, he attended one session at the Southern Baptist Theological Seminary, then located at Greenville, S. C. He selected the schools of Old and New Testament interpretation, systematic theology, and homiletics, and graduated in them all. Soon after leaving the seminary he accepted a call to the Luray and Front Royal Baptist churches, in the Valley of Virginia, where he remained six years, was eminently successful in advancing the cause, not only in those towns, but in all that region, and was everywhere recognized as a brilliant and eloquent preacher. He traveled much, and did the work of an evangelist, holding protracted meetings in the cities of Alexandria and Richmond, in several smaller places, and with numerous country churches, in all of which his labors were greatly blessed. In December, 1880, a unanimous call was extended to him to become pastor of the Lee Street Baptist church, Baltimore, Md., made vacant by the removal of Dr. John Pollard to Richmond, Va. He has but recently entered upon his work there, and has shown himself to be admirably adapted for the position he occupies in that important field. The church has 400 members, in the midst of a growing population, and presents a fine sphere of usefulness to one possessed of his talents. He is an able preacher. A distinguished lawyer of Richmond says he never heard more eloquent appeals from any public speaker than those that fell from his lips in the revival which he had in that city. As he is quite young, studious, and progressive, the denomination may look for a brilliant future for him.

Wharton, Morton Bryan, D.D., one of the most talented ministers of Georgia, is a Virginian by birth. He was born April 5, 1839, in Orange County. He is a man of varied powers, excelling as a preacher and pastor, and surpassing most men as an agent for the collection of funds for religious or benevolent purposes. A man of wonderful energy, unbounded resources, remarkable business capacity, and with a striking knowledge of men, he has succeeded in whatever he has undertaken.

At the age of eighteen he was converted in Alexandria, Va., and united with the Baptist church of that city. His talents and inclinations soon led him towards the ministry, and in October, 1858, he entered Richmond College, where he

MORTON BRYAN WHARTON, D.D.

graduated in 1861. His first pastorate was at Bristol, Tenn., where he remained two years. He then went to Georgia in 1864, as the agent of the Virginia Army Colportage Board, to collect funds. During the latter part of the war he became the successful agent of "The Domestic and Indian Mission Board" of the Southern Baptist Convention. After the war he became successively the pastor of the Eufaula, Ala., Baptist church, where he was instrumental in erecting a splendid and costly house of worship; of the Walnut Street church in Louisville, Ky., where he was remarkably successful, and where he collected large amounts for benevolent purposes; and of the Greene Street church, Augusta, Ga., where, as in Louisville, he was instrumental in making great improvements in the house of worship, and in adding a large number to the membership of the church. These labors left him, in 1876, so completely broken down in health that he retired to his farm in Southwestern Georgia, where he remained in seclusion, until prevailed upon to accept an agency to collect Georgia's quota for the Southern Baptist Theological Seminary. In that work he has been very successful. At present he is the corresponding secretary of the seminary to raise the $20,000 per annum necessary for the current expenses of the institution, and he is succeeding admirably.

During his pastorate at Augusta the degree of Doctor of Divinity was conferred on him by the Washington and Lee University, of Virginia.

He is a trustee of Mercer University, and of the Baptist Orphans' Home; and he is also a member of the board of trustees for the Southern Baptist Theological Seminary. As a preacher, he is possessed of much oratorical power, and he is highly gifted intellectually. His mental powers are analytical, and he is blessed with an extraordinary memory. He has proved himself equal to any position in which he has been placed, and has never failed, by his striking powers, to draw large congregations wherever he has preached, and to increase greatly the membership of those churches of which he has had charge.

Wheat, Judge Zachariah, was born in Bourbon Co., Ky., July 26, 1806. He chose the law for his profession, and was admitted to the bar at Columbia, Ky., in 1829. He soon established an excellent reputation both for ability and integrity. In 1832 he was appointed Commonwealth's attorney, and held the position, excepting a brief interval, until 1848, when he was appointed circuit judge by Gov. Crittenden. In 1856 he was elected one of the judges of the Court of Appeals, and at the close of his term he resumed the practice of law at Columbia. In 1861 he removed to Shelbyville, Ky., where he practised until his death. He was a man of gentle spirit and great generosity. He became a Baptist in early life, and was a devout Christian. Although never formally licensed to preach, he frequently filled the pulpit acceptably in the absence of his pastor.

Wheeler, Rev. Edwin S., son of Edwin B. and Mary A. Wheeler, was born in Groton, Conn., Aug. 4, 1836; studied at Hamilton Theological Seminary, N. Y.; pastor of Baptist churches at New London and Willimantic, Conn., Rahway, N. J., Valley Falls and East Greenwich, R. I.; now preaching in latter place; was chaplain of 80th U. S. Infantry during the civil war, at Port Hudson, serving two years; has traveled South and written in regard to Florida.

Wheeler, Prof. Nelson, was born in Royalston, Mass., in 1814. He was a graduate of Yale College in the class of 1836. After teaching for a time in Townshend, Vt., he was called to take charge of the Worcester County High School in 1840. Here he performed some of the best work of his life. "Several devoted missionaries now in India, and many persons well known among us for usefulness in professional and other callings, have often testified to his formative influence on their early habits and acquirements." His excessive labors as principal of the Worcester County High School undermined his health, and he resigned his position to take charge of the City Classical and English School, where he remained until 1852, when he was elected Professor of Greek in Brown University. A comparatively brief period was spent in the new position for which he was so well fitted. He was compelled to give up all his professional work and yield to the attacks of the insidious disease which at last removed him from the scene of his earthly labors to his reward in heaven. He died at Royalston, Aug. 25, 1855.

Wheeler, Osgood C., D.D., LL.D., is the pioneer Baptist pastor of California. He was born at Butler, N. Y., March 13, 1816, converted at nine, baptized at fifteen, and worked on his father's farm till he was twenty; taught school two winters; studied at Middleburg Academy; graduated at Madison University in 1845; ordained at East Greenwich, R. I., in November; pastor there two years, and built a church edifice. In 1847 became pastor at Jersey City, and united three discordant bodies into the Union church. In 1848 the American Baptist Home Mission Society, after he had repeatedly refused, gained his consent to become its missionary to California. After a ninety days' voyage, he reached San Francisco Feb. 28, 1849, organized a Sunday-school and church of six members, and built the first Protestant church edifice in California that year. In January, 1852, he removed to Sacramento, as pastor of the first church there. In 1855 he was compelled by throat disease to desist from preaching. But partial recovery has enabled him to resume this work, and for many years he has preached in almost every part of the State, and as regular supply to many of the churches. He has edited and published the *Pacific Banner*, the first Baptist paper on the Pacific coast, and the daily *Times*, and several large volumes on agriculture. For thirty years he has written almost continuously for the press. In 1873, by appointment, he wrote and carried through the press a biographical work of 500 pages, "The First Steamship Pioneers." He was chief clerk of the California Legislative Assembly in 1864; also U. S. internal revenue collector; was secretary and manager of the U. S. Sanitary Commission in California, and general agent of the Freedmen's Commission. In 1871 he was appointed to take charge of a department in the Central Pacific Railroad, and still retains that position. In 1878 California College conferred upon him the degree of D.D., and in July, the same year, the degree of LL.D. was conferred upon him by the Southwest Baptist University of Jackson, Tenn. In the midst of his other important business cares he preaches nearly every Lord's day, is an honored counselor in all Baptist enterprises, and a steadfast laborer for the upbuilding of the Baptist churches in California.

Wheelock, Rev. Edward Willard, was born

in Boston, July 17, 1796. He became a member of the Second Baptist church in Boston when he was fifteen years of age. When eighteen he became a pupil of Rev. Mr. Chaplin, of Danvers, afterwards President Chaplin, of Waterville College. In April, 1817, he made application to the Baptist Board of Foreign Missions to be employed as their missionary. In this application he says, "I would rather be a missionary of the Cross than a king on a throne. To Burmah would I go; in Burmah would I live; in Burmah would I toil; in Burmah would I die; and in Burmah would I be buried." His request was granted, and in company with James Coleman he embarked in November, 1817, for Calcutta, and reached Rangoon in September, 1818, to join Mr. Judson in his missionary labors. He was not destined to see his long-cherished hopes gratified. The seeds of consumption which were in him ripened into a sudden harvest. He lingered for a brief period, oppressed with sadness that his plans were thus blighted. On a passage from Calcutta to Rangoon, which he had taken with the hope of being benefited by a change of air and scene, he passed into a state of delirium, during which he threw himself from his cabin-window into the sea and was drowned. It was a grievous loss to Dr. Judson, who, in a letter, says of him: "Brother Wheelock has a heavenly spirit; from my first acquaintance with him I had special hopes of his great usefulness among the natives. But the Lord has seen fit to disappoint our hopes."

Whidden, Hon. Charles, was born in St. George, New Brunswick, May 22, 1822. The family removed to Calais, Me., in 1831, where he lived until the close of life. He was a graduate of Waterville College in the class of 1843. He studied law, attending lectures at the Cambridge Law-School in 1847, and was admitted to the bar in 1848. He opened an office in Calais, where he continued to practise his profession till his death.

Mr. Whidden occupied a conspicuous place in the business and politics of Eastern Maine. In his own city he was mayor for two years, and in his county, Washington, was district attorney for twelve years. He represented Calais two years in the Maine Legislature. For four years he was collector of customs for Passamaquoddy district. He was also a member of the commission for defining the boundary-line between Maine and New Brunswick, under the Lord Ashburton treaty, and a member of the State commission for the equalization of municipal war debts. The state of his health obliged him to decline an appointment which was tendered to him by Gov. Chamberlain as associate justice of the Supreme Court. For seven years he was a member of the board of trustees of Colby University. His death occurred at Calais, Dec. 3, 1876.

"Mr. Whidden was a man of fine general appearance and bearing, a bold and indefatigable leader, and a warm and generous friend."

Whidden, Rev. John, after his conversion, was baptized and united with the Baptist church in Antigonish, Nova Scotia, where he was ordained Nov. 4, 1832. He labored in that town until his death, which occurred several years ago. His pastoral and missionary labors were of great service to the cause of Christ in the counties of Antigonish and Guysborough.

Whilden, Rev. B. W., was born in Charleston, S. C., on the 29th of May, 1819. He was baptized by the elder Dr. Manly in 1835, and licensed to preach by the First church in 1839, and ordained on his twenty-second birthday. He was pastor of the Baptist church in Camden, S. C., for four years.

In 1849 he was sent by the Southern Baptist Convention as a missionary to Canton, China. About a year after his arrival he lost his wife, and returned home with his children. Having acted for some time as agent for the Foreign Mission Board, he married Miss Mary H. Bonnette, of Orangeburg, S. C., and returned to China, where he remained two years, when Mrs. Whilden's failing sight caused him to return a second time to his native country.

Since that time he has preached and taught in various parts of his native State and Georgia. He was at one time Professor of Belles-Lettres and Adjunct Professor of Ancient Languages in Cherokee College, Ga.

He has been editorially connected with several newspapers, and is now associate editor of the *Illustrated Baptist*, and pastor of several churches in South Carolina. He has two daughters in China, Miss Lulu Whilden and Mrs. Williams.

White, Rev. Daniel, was born in 1784 in Scotland; baptized by Rev. D. McArthur in 1800; came to North Carolina in 1807, and established the Spring Hill church in Richmond County; afterwards served the Welsh Neck church in South Carolina, but returned to Spring Hill, and spent most of his long and useful life in North Carolina. He preached both in Gaelic and English, and was greatly blessed in revivals and in baptizing men who became ministers of the gospel. Rev. Duncan McNeil has written a memoir of this devout Scotchman.

White, Prof. John B., well known in Illinois as an educator, was born at Bow, N. H., March 10, 1810. His mother was descended from the family of Carters, distinguished for patriotism in colonial and Revolutionary times. His father was an officer in the war of 1812, and rose to the rank of colonel. Mr. White's preparation for college was received at Pembroke Academy and New Hampton Institute, in New Hampshire. He graduated at Brown University in 1832, having won especial distinction as a scholar in mathematics. His first service as teacher was at New Hampton, where, in connection with other work of instruction, he organized and conducted a normal class, made up of persons preparing to teach; probably the first, or at least one of the first, examples of a method of instruction which has since been so widely adopted. Resuming the study of law, interrupted by these duties, Mr. White was admitted to the bar, and removed to Illinois in 1836, making his home at Greenville, in Bond County. Here he speedily achieved a distinction which caused his election as judge of probate in 1837.

Mr. White's evident sphere, however, was that of a teacher. Perhaps a consciousness of this fact led him, in 1838, to accept the chair of Mathematics and Natural Philosophy in Wake Forest College, N. C. In 1854, a visit to Greenville, Ill., his former place of residence, led to his return to that place, and to a successful effort, under his inspiration and guidance, to found there a college for young women, of which he was made president. The history of this enterprise is given in another place. (See ALMIRA COLLEGE.) Until a very recent date Mr. White has remained at the head of the college, carrying the institution forward successfully under circumstances of exceptional difficulty.

Mr. White became a Christian while a student of Pembroke Academy. It was while he was a professor in Wake Forest College that special circumstances seemed to lay upon him a ministerial service, resulting in his ordination. In the years 1859 and 1860 he served the church at Greenville as its pastor, and one year as chaplain of an Illinois regiment in the late war.

White, Rev. William, was born in New York, July 26, 1768. Soon after his birth his parents removed to Philadelphia, where, when young, he found the Saviour, and became a member of the First Baptist church. About 1790 he removed to Roxborough township, and by the Roxborough church was licensed to preach in 1793, and in it, the following year, he was ordained. He became pastor of the New Britain church in 1795, and remained with that church for eight years. On Jan. 23, 1804, he became pastor of the Second Baptist church of Philadelphia. The church was not quite a year in existence; their meeting-house had just been dedicated, and their first pastor felt the impulse of their bright hopes, and was encouraged by their zealous and united efforts to spread the gospel. Mr. White was an eloquent preacher, and a thinker of original powers. Except Dr. Staughton, there was no man in Philadelphia or in Pennsylvania the superior of the first pastor of the Second church. His success was almost unexampled in Philadelphia for those times. In thirteen years he baptized over 500 persons, men and women of intelligence, who remained faithful witnesses for Jesus during many subsequent years. The results of Mr. White's labors are felt to this day in the existence and prosperity of some of the largest churches in Philadelphia. Mr. White removed from the Second church in 1817, and for some years gave up preaching. In 1822 he became pastor of the church at Lancaster, O.; subsequently he was pastor of the churches of Muddy Prairie and Chillicothe. He died Feb. 14, 1843, in his seventy-fifth year.

Mr. White was the author of a work on baptism called "Christian Baptism, exhibiting Various Proofs that the Immersion of Believers in Water is the Only Baptism." He had also gathered a large amount of matter for a history of the Baptists of the United States, which was destroyed by the fire which nearly burned down Chillicothe. The Hon. S. S. Cox, a member of Congress from New York City, is a grandson of Mr. White.

White, Rev. W. J. (colored), pastor of the Harmony Baptist church of Augusta, Ga., is one of the most intelligent, useful, and hard-working colored ministers of the State. He was baptized, and united with the Springfield Baptist church of Augusta, Oct. 7, 1855. He was licensed to preach in 1862, and was ordained to the ministry April 1, 1866. In 1859 he organized a Sunday-school, which he superintended until 1868, when, with a few others, he formed the Harmony church, to the pastorate of which he was called in July of that year. The Sunday-school he instituted belongs to the church of which he is pastor. He has taken an active part in the organization of the colored Baptists of Georgia since the war. He was elected treasurer of the State Convention when it was formed in 1870, a post to which he has been annually re-elected since. For years he has been treasurer of the Shiloh Association, and for a year and a half he was missionary agent of the State Convention, resigning on account of ill health. When the Colored Georgia Baptist Sunday-School Convention was established at Macon, in 1872, he was elected its president, and held the position for several years. At present he is the corresponding secretary of both the Missionary Baptist Convention and the State Sunday-School Convention of Georgia, and fills these positions with great ability and success.

Whiteside, James, as the son of one of the earliest settlers of Illinois, from whom the county of Whiteside receives its name, and himself one of the oldest citizens of Madison County, as well as for his personal worth, should have a brief memorial here. He was born near Troy, Ill., and died at that place Jan. 30, 1868, aged sixty-three. He was a useful and influential man.

Whitfield, Theo., D.D., was born in Mississippi; graduated at Chapel Hill, N. C., in 1854; studied theology at Newton, Mass.; was at one time principal of a blind asylum in Mississippi; was Professor of Greek in the University of Missouri; editor of Baptist paper at Meridian, Miss.; came to Charlotte, N. C., as pastor in 1874, where he still remains; was made a D.D. by Wake Forest College in 1878.

Whiting, Charles, D.D., the present pastor of the Baptist church in Canton, Ill., one of the largest and most prosperous in the State, was born in Boston, Mass., Feb. 24, 1830. When he was seven years of age his father removed to Missouri, where he received his education through private tutors. He entered the Baptist ministry in 1860, when he was ordained as pastor of the Dover Baptist church. His subsequent pastorates have been at Boonville and Springfield, Mo., Fort Scott, Kansas, Quincy, Ill. (First church), and his present one at Canton. He has held strongly the regard of his people on these various fields, and has won distinction both as preacher and lecturer.

Whitman, Rev. S. S., a native of Shaftsbury, Vt., was converted and baptized at the age of twelve years. He was a graduate of Hamilton. He also studied theology at Andover, and graduated from Newton Theological Seminary in 1827. He was one of the three students that formed its first class. Dr. Barnas Sears, recently deceased, was another of the three. Immediately upon his graduation from Newton, Mr. Whitman was called to the chair of Biblical Interpretation in Hamilton Theological Institute. He held this position seven years with great ability. He was compelled to retire from this work on account of the almost entire failure of his health. In 1836 he accepted a call to the pastorate of the First Baptist church in Belvidere, Ill., an infant church of fourteen members, located in a field entirely new. Here he remained ten years, building up one of the largest and most efficient churches in the Northwest, a church remaining to this day of great power and usefulness. With health utterly broken down, he resigned the care of the church, and for several years retired from all active labor. In June, 1851, with health somewhat restored, he took charge of the Baptist church in Madison, Wis. His work here was of the briefest character, but awakened the highest hopes of the church and community. He died Jan. 2, 1852, having served the church about eight months.

He was a minister of the highest culture and of entire consecration to his work. His daily life exhibited the loveliest traits of the Christian character. He filled every position with honor. As a professor, he attained the highest rank; as a preacher, he attracted crowds to his faithful presentation of gospel truth, and built up from the foundation a church of great strength. As a pastor, he was gentle, winning, and faithful, and success attended all his work. He has left a memory sacredly cherished by multitudes in Northern Illinois and Southern Wisconsin.

Whitsitt, Rev. James, was born in Amherst Co., Va., Jan. 31, 1771, and educated in the Episcopal Church, then the established church of Virginia.

In the year 1789 he made a profession of religion, and was baptized by Rev. Joseph Anthony, an earnest Baptist minister. He entered at once with great zeal into the revival then prevailing, not only praying and exhorting, but appointing and conducting meetings; and so acceptable were his efforts that, within a few weeks, the church gave him a formal license to preach the gospel.

In the year 1790 he removed to Davidson Co., Tenn., then almost a wilderness. The history of Mr. Whitsitt's labors would be substantially the history of the Baptists in the Cumberland Valley. His co-laborers were Dillahunty, McConnico, and others,—all men of decided power, and eminently fitted to do good service as pioneers in the cause of Christ.

He took the pastoral charge of four churches,— Mill Creek, Concord, Rockspring, and Providence. He continued his labors with these churches from thirty to forty years, up to the time that the infirmities of age compelled him to circumscribe his efforts and remain mostly at home.

Mr. Whitsitt was present at the organization of the Mero District, the first Association formed in the Cumberland Valley. In this, and others of which he was subsequently a member, his influence was paramount. This Association originally included all the churches in Tennessee west of the mountains.

His connection with it continued until the formation of the Cumberland Association, to which his churches were transferred, and he, of course, went with them. Afterwards the Concord Association was formed, which included the churches of Mr. Whitsitt; with it he remained to the day of his death. He always attended the annual meetings of these Associations while his health would permit.

He resigned his charge at Mill Creek and, having obtained a letter of dismission, joined the First church in Nashville, with which he remained till the close of his life. Meanwhile he continued to preach in different churches, as his health would permit.

The summer and autumn previous to his decease he supplied the pulpit of the Second church in Nashville, in the absence of the pastor, most of the time; and, in addition to this, preached funeral sermons, and performed other occasional services at the houses of friends in the neighborhood. He also wrote many articles for the religious press, some of which were decidedly among his best productions. On the second Lord's day in October, 1848, he was with his church in Nashville, at their communion. His address on that occasion was peculiarly affecting. "And now, brethren and sisters, farewell. We shall meet no more upon earth. This is our last interview. I am old and rapidly sinking. The winter is almost upon us, during which I cannot visit you, and before the spring comes I shall die. Farewell." This was, indeed, his last meeting with them. He died in perfect peace on the 12th of April, 1849, in the seventy-ninth year of his age.

As a minister of the gospel, he held a very high rank. His sermons were always able, and had the appearance of being elaborately prepared. Mr. Whitsitt's conceptions were clear and accurate. The reasoning faculty was of unusual strength, and no metaphysical subtleties ever confused him. In the latter part of his life his sermons became less argumentative and more practical. He was also occasionally intensely pathetic, and the effect of his utterances at such times was well-nigh overwhelming. He was the uniform and earnest friend of missions, and had a primary agency in originating and sustaining the missionary operations of our State.

Whitsitt, William Heth, D.D., Professor of Biblical Introduction and Ecclesiastical History in the Southern Baptist Theological Seminary, was born near Nashville, Tenn., Nov. 25, 1841. He entered Union University in 1857, from which he graduated in 1861. The same year he entered the Confederate army as a private, was soon afterwards promoted to the chaplaincy, and served in that capacity until the close of the war. He was twice captured, and was confined in different military prisons about twelve months. In 1866 he entered the University of Virginia, and in 1867 the Southern Baptist Theological Seminary, remaining at the latter two years. In 1869 he went to Europe, where he spent over two years in study at Leipsic and Berlin. On his return to America, he accepted the pastorate of the Baptist church in Albany, Ga., in February, 1872. In September of the same year he entered upon the duties of his present position, when he delivered his inaugural address, entitled "The Relation of Baptists to Culture," which was published in the *Baptist Quarterly*. In 1878 he published a pamphlet on the "History of the Rise of Infant Baptism," and another, on "The History of Communion among Baptists," in 1880.

Wiberg, Rev. Andreas, was born in 1816, near Hudiksvall, in the northeastern part of Sweden. When he was fourteen years of age, his mind was deeply impressed in consequence of his escape from death by drowning, and he felt the importance of being prepared to die. This impression was followed by a desire to do something to prove

REV. ANDREAS WIBERG.

the sincerity of his gratitude to God for his deliverance. He entered the University of Upsala in 1835, and studied four years. Although for a time under the influence of skeptical opinions, he at last emerged from his spiritual darkness, and became a hopeful Christian. He was set apart as a priest in the state church in 1843. Having doubts about the propriety of admitting unconverted persons to the Lord's table, he left his work as a priest for a season, and was occupied for two years in translating and publishing some of Luther's works, and in the editorial charge of a paper called *The Evangelist*. During this time he was brought into connection with some Christians in the north of Sweden who held views similar to his own, and the sympathy which he expressed for these brethren led to his being the subject of persecution.

Mr. Wiberg visited Hamburg in the spring of 1851, and made the acquaintance of Mr. Oncken, and saw the workings of the Baptist church under his pastoral charge. It was not long before his views on the subject and mode of baptism underwent a change, and he was baptized at the island of Amager, near Copenhagen, July 23, 1852, by Rev. Mr. Nilson. He was then on his way to New York. Arriving in this country, he was brought into connection with the Baptists of that city, and for a time labored as colporteur of the American Baptist Pubcliation

Society among seamen. Before leaving Sweden Mr. Wiberg had written a book on baptism. This book had been published and circulated in Sweden, and scores and hundreds of persons were beginning to be shaken in their views of the subject. Those who embraced Baptist sentiments were at once subjected to severe persecutions, but the work went on, and multitudes were brought to accept the "faith once delivered to the saints." The Publication Society decided to establish a system of colportage in Sweden, and to place Mr. Wiberg at its head. Mr. Wiberg sailed from this country the 8th of September, 1855, and on reaching Sweden at once commenced his labors. How earnest and how successful these labors have been may be seen in the history of the mission to Sweden. Twenty-six years have passed since Mr. Wiberg landed at Stockholm. During that time, with the blessing of God on his work, and that of the hundreds of earnest disciples of Christ who have been associated with him, what was the "little one" has literally become "a thousand." The Baptists in Sweden number about 20,000, and still the work goes steadily and hopefully on. To have been a co-worker with God in bringing about such results might well gratify the desires of any large-hearted Christian.

Wier, Deacon Stephen M., was born in Glastonbury, Conn., March 25, 1814; trained on a farm and in rural schools; converted under the preaching of Rev. Rolin H. Neale, D.D., and baptized by him in 1836; always been an active Baptist; at the age of forty became a manufacturer; successful amid all changes and losses; served as one of the selectmen of the town; two years on the board of education; four years a member of the common council; one year as alderman; twice chosen deacon; a number of years superintendent of the Sunday-school; a strong, steady worker.

Wightman, Edward, of Burton-upon-Trent, England, was accused before the bishop of Lichfield and Coventry, and on the 14th of December, 1611, was condemned of numerous heresies. The only charges of supposed false doctrine against Mr. Wightman, about the truth of which there was no doubt, were that he believed "the baptism of infants to be an abominable custom; that the Lord's Supper and baptism should not be celebrated as they are now practised in the Church of England; and that Christianity is not wholly professed and preached in the Church of England, but only in part."

For these shocking doctrines the gentle Richard, Episcopal shepherd of Lichfield and Coventry, delivered Mr. Wightman to the secular power, according to the custom of the Inquisition, to be burned alive. And James I., who could not bear the sight of a naked sword, and who had just issued the present version of the Scriptures, ordered our noble Baptist brother to be committed to the flames. His body was reduced to ashes on the 11th of April, 1612, at Lichfield. And he died so cheerfully that he gathered a harvest of glory from the blazing fagots that consumed his body, and from the same fierce flames James reaped a harvest of infamy, which stopped all future fiery sacrifices during his reign.

Wightman, Rev. Frederick, son of John and Sarah (Greene) Wightman, was born in Warwick, R. I., April 11, 1779; baptized into the fellowship of the Coventry Baptist church by Rev. Charles Stone in May, 1801; had deep experiences; began preaching in 1802–3; settled in Ashford, Conn.; ordained in September, 1807, and labored with large success for eleven years; removed in 1817 to Middletown (now Cromwell), Conn., and preached fifteen years; in 1832 settled with the First Baptist church in East Lyme, Conn., and was eminently successful; returned to Cromwell church for two years; then three years with the church in Haddam; then in Wethersfield; then three years with Second church in East Lyme; everywhere prospered; preached forty years; delivered over 7000 sermons; greatly interested in missions; sound in doctrine; fervent in spirit; foremost among his brethren; died in Cromwell, Conn., Oct. 5, 1856, aged seventy-seven.

Wightman, Rev. John Gano, youngest son of Rev. Timothy and Mary (Stoddard) Wightman, was born in Groton, Conn., Aug. 16, 1766. He was baptized into the First Baptist church in his native town in 1797, and succeeded his father in the pastorate of the church, receiving ordination Aug. 13, 1800. Like his grandfather, Valentine, and his father, Timothy, he was distinguished for solid and practical, rather than glittering, qualities; hence the abiding results of his ministry. Of a susceptible and ingenuous nature, of fervent and consistent piety, of goodly personal appearance and bearing, he won a high rank in the councils and associations of the Baptist denomination. In executive positions he was composed, ready, impartial, dignified. To an attack made on his church by the Rogerine Quakers, in a pamphlet entitled "The Battle-Axe," he simply replied, "The axe will cut farther backward than forward," which proved to be true. His surviving writings are found in "Circular Letters," prepared for the Stonington Union Association, and a sermon on the death of Adams and Jefferson. Like his predecessors, he was a stanch advocate of religious liberty. His influence was felt in securing a change in the constitution of the State indorsing the principles of liberty first introduced into the colony by his grandfather. Not less than ten seasons of revival were experienced under his ministry, some of them powerful and wide-spread, and the parent church sent out its branch—the Third Baptist church in Groton—in 1831. He died July 13, 1841, in the seventy-fifth year of his age, and after a ministry to the church which his father served of forty-one years. His body was laid in the church-yard by the side of his father.

Wightman, Rev. Joseph Colver, was born in Groton, Conn., Jan. 3, 1828. He pursued his preparatory studies at the Suffield Literary Institute, and graduated at Brown University in the class of 1852. He was at Newton three years. His ordination took place April 15, 1857, and he was pastor of the South Abington, Mass., church one year, and of the church in Middleton, Conn., four years. For one year he was chaplain in a regiment of U. S. Volunteers, then pastor of the Baptist church in New London, Conn., where he remained three years. From New London he went to Cambridge, Mass., where he remained two years. He acted as district secretary of the American Bible Union for one year, and then returned to the pastorate, accepting a call to the church in Taunton, Mass., in 1873, where he now continues to preach.

Wightman, Stillman K., A.M., only child of Rev. Frederick Wightman, was born in Rhode Island in 1803; much of his life spent in Middletown, Conn.; graduated from Yale College in 1825; member of the State Legislature from 1835 to 1842, and for three years Speaker of the house; baptized in 1852 by Rev. Spencer H. Cone, D.D., and united with the First Baptist church in New York City, where he yet remains; has attained eminence in the legal profession; has occupied prominent positions upon the board of the American Baptist Home Mission Society; his judgment and counsel are sought and prized; a man wearing and deserving honors.

Wightman, Rev. Timothy, son of Rev. Valentine and Susanna (Holmes) Wightman, was born in Groton, Conn., Nov. 20, 1719. In 1754 he succeeded his father in the pastoral care of the First Baptist church of Groton, though he modestly refused ordination until May 20, 1756. The early part of his ministry was made laborious by the upheaval of affairs in the State by the Separatists from the standing order; but he was equal to the emergency. The Separate movement was especially strong in Eastern Connecticut, and in the whole State about forty Separate churches were formed. Most of these Separatists finally became Baptists. Mr. Wightman was also tried by the erratic ideas and practices of a band of Rogerine Quakers that aimed at times to disturb his meetings; but his serenity and good judgment foiled their designs. His ministry also extended through the stormy period of the Revolution, in which he nobly acted the part of a patriot. He was a plain, fearless, discreet, faithful preacher, and a thoroughly good man, like his honored father before him.

Mr. Wightman's ministry was marked by revivals; in 1764 more than thirty were added to the church, and in the following year was formed the second Baptist church in the town; in 1775 nearly forty were added, and a church was formed in North Groton; in 1784 eighty-four were added; another revival occurred in 1786-87. Like a Jewish priestly family, the Wightmans, in every generation, have had their distinguished preachers. Timothy died Nov. 14, 1796, in his seventy-eighth year, and after a ministry of forty-two years, the exact period of his father's pastorate. He was buried in the church-yard by the side of his father. His epitaph might read, *Modest, solid worth.* Rev. Reuben Palmer preached his funeral discourse.

Wightman, Rev. Valentine, the first Baptist minister in Connecticut, was born in North Kingston, R. I., in 1681. He was a descendant of Edward Wightman, the Baptist, who was burned for heresy at Lichfield, England, in 1612. His father was one of five brothers who came to this country, all of whom were Baptists,—two were preachers, two deacons, and one a private member. Valentine was ordained in Rhode Island; removed to Groton, Conn., in 1705, and planted the First Baptist church,—the first in the town and the first in the State; he afterwards assisted Rev. Nicholas Eyres, from 1712 to 1714, in planting the first Baptist church in the city and State of New York; was a well-educated and scholarly man; was a missionary throughout Eastern Connecticut; aided in planting churches in Stonington, Waterford, and Lyme; wrote a tract in defense of orderly and trained singing; had the famous debate, June 7, 1727, at Lyme, with Rev. John Bulkley, of Colchester, the champion of the standing order, in which it is conceded that Mr. Wightman was the victor; both parties afterwards published their debates in volumes; the heads of discussion were (1) The Subjects of Baptism, (2) The Mode of Baptizing, (3) The Maintenance of Gospel Ministers. Mr. Wightman's writings show that he was a student of the Scriptures and of the patristic writings, with a well-balanced mind, of calm but decided spirit, of sound judgment, clear convictions, warm heart, plain and transparent speech, a wise man in laying foundations. He was married to Susanna Holmes Feb. 10, 1703, and left descendants, who have been honored in the ministry to this day. After the scenes and labors of the Great Awakening, in which he labored and rejoiced, he died June 9, 1747, at the age of sixty-six, and after a ministry of forty-two years. His name will endure on the roll of the fathers that opened the wilderness and, in the name of the Lord, laid the goodly foundations upon which succeeding generations have joyfully built. His grave is in Groton, Conn.

Wilcox, Rev. Asa, of Westerly, R. I., successor of Rev. Isaiah Wilcox, was ordained Feb. 18, 1802; a man of culture in his day, and ready with his pen; labored as an evangelist; removed to Connecticut; successful and honored; died in Colchester, Conn., in 1832; his remains removed to Essex, Conn., one of his fields of labor, and laid by the side of the Baptist church.

Wilcox, Rev. Isaiah, of Westerly, R. I., was baptized in February, 1766; ordained Feb. 14, 1771; was the first pastor of the church organized in 1765, and known as the Wilcox church, a fruit of the Great Awakening; large man, with splendid voice; an able preacher in his day; under his ministry a revival, beginning in 1785, continuing through nearly three years, added more than 200 to the church. He died March 3, 1795, at the age of fifty-five.

Wilder, Rev. William, was born in Buckland, Franklin Co., Mass., March 31, 1819. In his sev-

REV. WILLIAM WILDER.

enteenth year he was converted, and united with the Presbyterian Church, in the faith of which he had been educated by his parents. Three years later his attention was called to the subject of baptism. After an earnest and patient examination, he was surprised to learn that sprinkling was never alluded to as baptism in the Word of God, and that infants were not mentioned as subjects of baptism, but that believers only received the ordinance from apostolic hands. He united with the Baptist Church in September, 1841, and the same year entered the academic department of Madison University, N. Y. He graduated in 1846, and studied a year in the theological seminary. In 1847 he settled as pastor in Baltimore, Md. In 1850 removed to New Britain, Pa., where he remained as pastor until 1854, when he became pastor of the Upland church, and continued with it about eleven years. In 1865 he settled with the Olivet church, Philadelphia, and in 1869 with the First church, Bridgeton, N. J. In 1871 he removed to Minneapolis, Minn., having accepted the pastorate of the First Avenue Baptist church. In 1874 became pastor of the First church at Cedar Rapids, Iowa. In the midst of a prosperous pastorate he was enfeebled by a severe and protracted sickness, and resigned. He was for a year financial secretary of the Iowa Baptist State Convention. In 1877 he became pastor of the church at Hampton, Iowa, where he now resides. He has shared largely in the general work of the denomination. For twelve years he was on the board of the American Baptist Publication Society, and during this entire time was one of the committee on publications. Mr. Wilder possesses scholarly culture, deep piety, great modesty, and every fitness for usefulness.

Wildman, Rev. Daniel, son of Capt. Daniel Wildman, was born in Danbury, Conn., Dec. 10, 1764; subject of convictions when young; deeply wrought upon and converted when about twenty-two years of age; for a time a school-teacher; licensed to preach by the Baptist church in Danbury, in 1791, at the age of twenty-seven; commenced his ministerial labors at Plymouth, Conn., where he continued until 1796, when he removed to Wolcott, where he was ordained, and remained two years; in 1798 removed to Bristol, where his toils resulted in the erection of a meeting-house and in greatly enlarging the church; in 1804 he settled in Middletown, and was favored with a revival; in 1805 gave a part of his time to Suffield (First church), as he was now in the zenith of his strength; in 1806 returned to Bristol, and labored about twelve years; thence to Stratfield, and toiled about three years; thence to Bristol again, and yet again to Stratfield at times; in 1820 preached half the time in Carmel, N. Y., and baptized about 300 persons; spent a few years in Licking Co., O.; in 1826 returned to Connecticut; settled with the church in New London for three years; in one year received seventy members; afterwards served churches in Russell, Mass., Meriden, Conn., First church in Norwich, and church in Andover; died in Lebanon, Conn., Feb. 21, 1849, aged eighty-five; devout, able, beloved man.

Wildman, Rev. Nathan, son of Rev. Daniel Wildman, was born in Bristol, Conn., Feb. 22, 1796; converted at the age of eighteen; commenced his ministry at the age of twenty-five; pastor at Weston, Suffield, New London, Waterford, Lebanon, Plainville, and in other fields; an earnest and impressive preacher; tender and melting in his appeals; often called to labor in revivals; peculiarly gifted in prayer; skilled in pastoral visiting; during his ministry baptized more than 800 persons; married a daughter of Rev. Mr. Darrow, of Waterford; his only daughter is wife of Rev. Jacob Gardner; died at Plainfield, Conn., Feb. 16, 1859, beloved by all who knew him.

Wilhoit, Rev. Fielding, was born April 14, 1799, in Kentucky; removed with his father to Missouri in 1818. He was converted and commenced preaching in 1826. He labored in eleven counties in Central Missouri, and over 4000 were converted under his ministry, most of whom were baptized by himself, and among them S. H. Ford, LL.D., the late T. C. Harris, and Robert, who is still a standard-bearer in the ministry of Missouri. He aided in organizing the General Association, and was several years the moderator. He was the co-laborer of Doyle, Flood, Fristoe, and Thomas. To A. P. Williams he was the Apollos in revival meetings. He died in November, 1872.

Wilhoit, Stephen, was born in Mercer Co., Ky. He removed to Missouri in 1819, and settled in Boone County. He was a successful farmer of energy, integrity, and public spirit. He contributed to the State University and to William Jewell College. He stood high as a citizen, and as a member of his church. He was treasurer of the General Association of Missouri in 1844. He often went on missionary tours with his brother, Fielding Wilhoit. He had an ardent love for the spread of the gospel; was moderator of the Mount Pleasant Association for years, after the death of Rowland Hughes. His son, James M. Wilhoit, of St. Louis, is a valuable and liberal member of the Fourth Baptist church of St. Louis. The subject of this sketch died Oct. 4, 1867.

Wilkes, Rev. Washington, was born in Marlborough District, S. C., March 26, 1822. His parents settled in Barbour Co., Ala., when he was twelve years of age, where he was baptized, in 1845, by the Rev. Peter Eldridge; ordained in 1847; entered Howard College in 1848, where he graduated in 1851. For seventeen years after leaving college his field of ministerial labor was in Autauga County, where he was mainly instrumental in the formation and growth of the Unity Association and its strongest churches. Since that time for more than ten years he has resided in Talladega County, where he has been pastor of several of the best churches. Mr. Wilkes is a preacher of more than average ability, and holds a place in the front ranks of the Alabama pulpit. He is pleasantly located with the church at Sylacauga.

Wilkes, Rev. William Clay, president of the Georgia Baptist Seminary, at Gainesville, a distinguished educator, was born in Spartanburg Co., S. C., Sept. 9, 1819. His father, Deacon Joseph Wilkes, and his mother, Delphia W. Clay, were natives of Virginia. In December, 1829, the family removed from South Carolina to Georgia, and settled in Putnam County. Mr. Wilkes joined the church at Eatonton in 1837, though he had been converted while a school-boy. Having had excellent academical advantages, he entered the Freshman class of Mercer University in 1839, and, while in college, the Penfield church licensed him to preach in 1841. In July, 1843, he graduated with the highest honors of his class; returned home and entered immediately, as an educator, upon that useful and honorable course which he has continued to the present time (1880). Called to become its pastor by the Milledgeville church, he was ordained in Eatonton in 1849, and since that period has preached constantly, serving in the mean while many churches. For sixteen years he taught at Forsythe College; he founded and built up Monroe Female College. He is the father of Spalding Seminary, a flourishing chartered school in Macon County. He organized and built up Crawford High School, at Dalton, which at one time threatened to outstrip Mercer University. He also built and established the Georgia Baptist Seminary, at Gainesville, a flourishing institution under the auspices of the Georgia Baptist Convention. A man of fine intellectual powers, a popular preacher, and at times useful as an editor, Mr. Wilkes has made his life a great success, if success is to be measured by useful results. He has, in a greater or less degree, educated nearly 3000 boys and girls, and he has baptized 1000 persons. Though past his three-score years, he is still a strong and healthy man.

Wilkinson, Wm. Cleaver, D.D., Professor of Homiletics and Pastoral Theology in Rochester Seminary, was born in Westford, Vt., Oct. 19, 1833; graduated at Rochester University in 1857, and the Theological Seminary in 1859. He immediately made a pedestrian tour through Great Britain. Upon his return to America he took pastoral care of the Wooster Place Baptist church, New Haven, Conn., in November, 1859. He resigned because of ill health in 1861, and made a tour of Europe. He returned, in 1863, to become tutor in the University of Rochester. Soon after he became pastor of Mount Auburn church, Cincinnati, O. This charge he resigned in 1866, and opened a private school in Tarrytown, N. Y. In 1872 he was elected to the position he still holds in Rochester Theological Seminary.

Prof. Wilkinson is one of the ablest writers of America, and contributes to the leading newspapers, secular and religious. His chief publications are "The Dance of Modern Society," 1869; "A Free Lance in the Field of Letters," 1874; "Foreshadowing" and "Enticed," poems of much real merit.

Willard, Rev. Benjamin, was born in Lancaster, Mass., in 1783, and joined the Baptist church in Harvard in 1800, by which he was licensed to preach the gospel in 1818. His labors were greatly blessed to the conversion of souls in Littleton, and were attended with much fruit in his missionary tours in Northern New England and Canada, under the direction of the Massachusetts Baptist Missionary Society. He spent the winter of 1822-23 in Northampton, Mass., and under his ministry a church was gathered in that beautiful village, made so memorable as having been the home of the celebrated Jonathan Edwards. Mr. Willard was ordained Nov. 12, 1823. It was not until July 20, 1826, that the church to which he ministered was publicly recognized. By his own personal application, in a large degree, the means for the erection of a meeting-house were procured, and the edifice was dedicated July 8, 1829. He continued to act as pastor of the church until 1838, when he resigned. For several years he labored as an evangelist in Vermont, among the feeble churches of that State. He died at Holyoke, Mass., Dec. 2, 1862.

Willard, Rev. Chas. M., was born at Saxton's River, Vt., Aug. 27, 1815; baptized at Grafton, 1834; ordained, in 1841, at Drewsville, N. H. His preparatory studies at Hamilton Institution, now Madison University, were interrupted by ill health, but he had been a pupil of his brother, Rev. Erastus Willard, and studied theology with Rev. Isaac M. Willmarth, at New Ipswich, N. H. He was an earnest, useful, and successful pastor at Drewsville, N. H., Ogdensburg, N. Y., Fitzwilliam, N. H., Still River, Mass., Eastport, Me., Littleton, Mass., and First Suffield, Conn. He died in 1877.

Willard, Rev. Erastus, of Baptist ancestry, was born in Lancaster, Mass., July 4, 1800; went in boyhood with his parents to Vermont; baptized in 1820, at Saxton's River, by Rev. Joseph Elliott, with whom he fitted for college; was graduated at Waterville College (now Colby University) in 1829; studied at Newton Theological Institution; ordained pastor at Grafton, Vt., Oct. 30, 1833; appointed to the French mission in 1835, where he continued till 1856 (see article MISSION TO FRANCE); served American Baptist Missionary Union as missionary to the Ottawas, in Kansas, 1857-60; after two brief pastorates he settled, in March, 1865, with the First Salem (Shushan) church, N. Y., where he did a good work until his health utterly failed, in 1871. He died December 29, at Newport, R. I.

His great work was in France, as superintendent of the mission and theological instructor. In these he showed much practical wisdom, patience, and energy. His long residence abroad and his retiring disposition prevented him from being widely known; but his influence over his students and others was that of a master-mind, and those who knew him well counted him among our very foremost men. Of commanding ability as a thinker, a linguist, and a theologian, acute, original, self-reliant, he was an indefatigable student of the Word of God in the original languages. Holding tenaciously the faith once delivered, including strict Baptist principles, in interpreting Scripture he called no man master, but he bowed reverently to the supreme authority of inspiration. He was an excellent preacher, delighting especially in Biblical exposition, and an interested student of physical science. A decided and positive man, he was endowed with genial wit and poetic fancy. His religious character was pure, firm, and uniform. He wrote much and carefully, in a style of great force and beauty. It is greatly to be regretted that he published nothing.

Willet, Prof. Joseph Edgerton, of Mercer University, Ga., was born in Macon, Ga., Nov. 17, 1826. His early education was obtained in the schools of Macon and Marshallville, Ga. He entered the Junior class of Mercer University in 1844, and graduated in 1846. In 1847 he was elected Adjunct Professor of Natural Philosophy and Chemistry, and entered at once upon his duties, but soon found it necessary that he should obtain a more thorough preparation elsewhere. He accordingly entered the analytical laboratory of Yale College, and engaged in daily work in analytical chemistry. He returned in 1849, and immediately resumed the care of his classes, and for fifteen or twenty years afterwards was probably the only teacher in Georgia who could perform a chemical analysis. Since that time he has been faithfully and exclusively engaged in teaching natural science in Mercer University, occupying an enviable position among the educators of the whole country in the department of natural science. He was made full Professor of Natural Science in 1848, a position he still holds. Prof. Willet is amiable and benevolent, with a devout spirit. His fine analytical mind has made him unsurpassed as a professor of chemistry and the natural sciences. He possesses generous culture and refined tastes outside of his profession. In 1869 the American Baptist Publication Society offered a prize of $500 for the best small book on science for Sunday-school libraries, and he bore off the prize with a capital little volume entitled "The Wonders of Insect Life." He has also published in the *American Journal of Science* and other papers valuable scientific articles, and when the subject of the "unification of the Georgia colleges" was mooted in the State, some years ago, he published a couple of articles which gave the whole subject a permanent *quietus*. His acquaintance with agricultural science led to his delivery of lectures before the State Agricultural and Horticultural Societies at Macon, Gainesville, and Jonesborough, besides which he, in 1879, delivered a course of six lectures on "Science and Religion" before the Wesleyan Female College, at Macon, Ga. During the war he was employed by the Confederate government to superintend the manufacture of all kinds of ammunition, as superintendent of the laboratory at Atlanta, and since the war he has for three or four years, during vacation, served on the United States Commission to investigate the habits, nature, and ravages of the cotton caterpillar, so injurious to the great Southern staple.

As a professor, he is greatly beloved by the students, over whom he maintains a firm sway as a disciplinarian.

Willett, Rev. Charles, was born in Hanson (then West Pembroke), Mass., Oct. 21, 1809; favored with pious parents (Congregationalists), who sprinkled him in his infancy; was a student throughout life; fell into Universalism; was converted in New Bedford, Mass., and was baptized by Rev. Asa Bronson; united with the Baptist Church; in June, 1838, was licensed by the South Baptist church in Hartford, Conn.; in same year, November 21, was ordained pastor of the Baptist church in Tariffville; after-settlements, in Southwick, Mass.; in 1845 in Central Baptist church, Thompson, Conn.; in 1849 in First Baptist church, New London; in 1854 in Putnam; in 1857, in La Crosse, Wis.; in 1863 in Union church, Minneapolis, Minn.; in 1864 returned to Putnam, Conn.; in 1873 preached in Danielsonville, and organized the Baptist church; in 1875 in First Baptist church in Suffield; served as pastor thirty-nine out of forty-one years; preached above 5000 sermons; baptized about 500 persons; solid preacher and wise counselor.

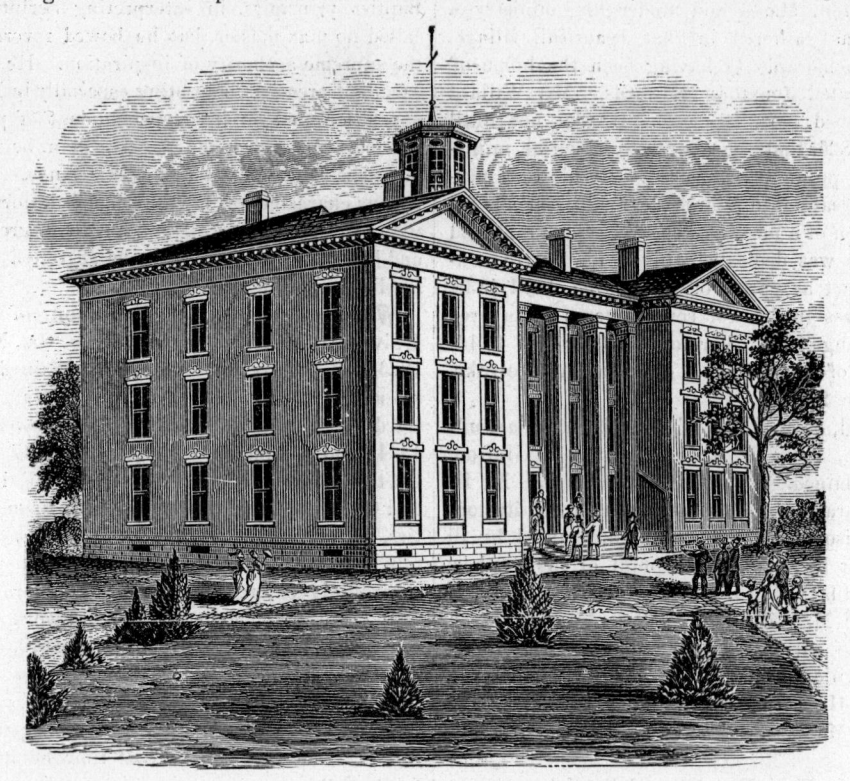

William Jewell College was projected in 1836, and founded in 1849, when a handsome endowment was subscribed, a liberal charter obtained, and the college located at Liberty, Clay Co., Mo. It was named in honor of its principal benefactor, Dr. William Jewell. It was opened in 1852, and took possession of its new building in 1854.

In 1868, through the agency of Thos. Rambaut, LL.D., $40,000 were raised to establish the Jeremiah Vardeman School of Theology. The grounds and buildings of the college are valued at

WILLIAM JEWELL COLLEGE.

$75,000, and the endowment at $100,000. L. B. Ely, the financial agent, has freed the college from debt, and aims to secure $250,000 of an endowment. One hundred and fifty young men, on an average, attended the college during the past ten years, and the School of Theology in the same time matriculated two hundred. The college contemplates seven endowed professorships, besides the School of Theology and any professional schools which may hereafter be added.

Instruction is now given by five professors and three tutors. There is a complete chemical and philosophical apparatus, and 4000 volumes as the beginning of a library. The presidents have been E. S. Dulin, D.D., Rev. R. S. Thomas, A.M., W. Thompson, D.D., Rev. Thomas Rambaut, LL.D., and since 1874, W. R. Rothwell, D.D. The members of the faculty are W. R. Rothwell, D.D., Prof. J. R. Eaton, Ph.D., J. G. Clark, R. B. Semple; A. J. Semple is principal of the preparatory department.

The college is near Kansas City; it is the oldest west of the Mississippi, and its prospects are brighter than ever.

Williams, Rev. Alvin P., D.D., was born in St. Louis Co., Mo., March 13, 1813. His father was a Baptist minister. He was converted at sixteen, and at seventeen was ordained, his father assisting in the service. He gained a knowledge of the languages, and studied the Bible in its original tongues. He labored with great zeal as an evangelist. He was pastor at Lexington, Richmond, St. Joseph, Miami, Bethel, Rehoboth, Good Hope, and Glasgow. He died Nov. 9, 1868, at Glasgow. He had great natural gifts and unusual attainments. As a preacher and expounder of the gospel he occupied a prominent position. His knowledge of the Scriptures was astonishing, and his logic was masterly and convincing. His sermons, expositions, and essays before the Association, and on various occasions, for twenty-five years, mark him as a man of extraordinary ability, a second Andrew Fuller. Dr. Williams was wholly given to study, to preaching, and to pastoral work, and it is estimated that over 3000 persons were converted under his ministry. He possessed a remarkable memory. It has been said that if the New Testament had been blotted out he could have reproduced it. He was unostentatious, cheerful, and kind-hearted. He could express his convictions with boldness. He was a man of faith and sincere piety. His death moved every Baptist heart in Missouri. They mourned the loss of an author whose review of Campbellism is unanswerable, and whose printed works on communion and baptism are clear, instructive, and scholarly. They felt that a father and leader in our Zion had fallen,—a prince in Israel. Though dead, he still lives in the memory of all who knew him, and his name will be honored by coming generations.

Williams, Rev. Granville S., was born Sept. 30, 1847, in Decatur Co., Tenn. He received his academic education in Decaturville, Lexington, and Mifflin. He pursued his collegiate course at Bethel College, Ky., and at Union University, Tenn. He graduated in June, 1873, professed conversion at Lexington, Tenn., in 1866, and was baptized by Rev. D. B. Ray, then the pastor at Lexington. He was licensed to preach by the Hickory Grove church in May, 1867. He was ordained by the church in Murfreesborough, Tenn., in October, 1871, the Presbytery consisting of Rev. Charles Manly, D.D., Rev. Wm. Shelton, D.D., and Rev. T. T. Eaton. He was first called to preside over the Court Street Baptist church, Bowling Green, Ky., in September, 1873, and was there nearly five years. Then he accepted a call to the Central Baptist church, Nashville, Tenn., July 1, 1878, where he is still laboring. Though young, he is greatly beloved by his charge. His talents are of a high order. Mr. Williams is active in all our ecclesiastical gatherings, and a warm supporter of the Tennessee Baptist Convention.

Williams, Rev. John, was born in Hanover Co., Va., in the year 1747. From his parents he received a liberal education. In 1769 he was sheriff of Lunenburg County. At this period the Lord was pleased to call him into the kingdom of his grace. Six months after his conversion he was baptized, and immediately after he began to tell the story of the Cross to the perishing. In 1771 the converts given to him by the Lord were sufficient to form a church in Lunenburg County, called the Meherrin church. This community in a few years grew into six or seven churches. In 1785 he became pastor of Sandy Creek church, Charlotte Co. He never sundered this tie.

Mr. Williams was a great friend of religious liberty and of education. He was much interested in the history of the Virginia Baptists; he had an extensive acquaintance with Christian literature; his manners were polished, and his spirit fraternal; his talents were of a high order. He was very successful in building up the churches, as well as in winning souls to Jesus.

Williams, Rev. John, was born in Wales, March 8, 1767, and died in New York, May 25, 1825. His father's name was William Roberts, this son, according to Welsh custom, taking the first name of his father as his surname. He was educated by his parents for the ministry of the Established Church, but he preferred some other profession, and went to Carnarven to learn a trade. While there, under the preaching of a Calvinistic Methodist he was converted, and joined the Independent church. He then resolved to devote himself to the ministry, and commenced to address Christian assemblies in various places. At that time he entered upon a prayerful investigation of the subject of baptism, and soon after united with the Horeb Baptist church of Garn, and in a little time became its pastor. He formed the acquaintance of Christmas Evans, and traveled and preached with him in many places throughout the principality. In 1795 he came to America, intending to labor among his countrymen, and he preached to them in Rev. John Stanford's church, in Fair (now Fulton) Street, also in the Baptist church in Fayette (now Oliver) Street, New York. He soon mastered the English language, and was settled as pastor of the Oliver Street church. It had but forty members when he took charge of it, and its place of worship was but thirty feet square. The young Welsh preacher soon filled it. It was enlarged, and was still too strait for the crowds who desired to attend. Then a capacious and attractive stone edifice was built, and the successful career of that historic church was commenced. In 1823 his health failed, and Rev. Spencer H. Cone was chosen associate pastor. A son of his, William R. Williams, D.D., the distinguished scholar and author, is pastor of Amity Street church in New York.

Williams, Rev. John G., was born in Colleton Co., S. C., and graduated at Furman University. He was ordained as pastor of Black Swamp church, in Beaufort, now Hampton, County. His early ministry was distinguished by careful preparation and earnest delivery. He was never "a good hater," but a warmer friend never lived. His friendship produces a reciprocity in those on whom it is bestowed. His mere presence brings cheerfulness.

His ministry has been wholly with country and village churches, and when a friend lately proposed to try to get a city church to call him, he positively declined to allow his name to be used.

Mr. Williams is one of the ablest, most popular, and successful preachers in the State. He has for many years preached to the Springtown and Blackville churches. He found the latter quite dilapidated, but under his ministry its growth has fully equaled that of the very flourishing village in which it is situated. He is also preaching at a new church, George's Creek. All three are in Barnwell County. Not one of them would exchange him for Spurgeon.

Williams, Rev. J. P., was born in Virginia, March 19, 1826, and removed to Hannibal, Mo., in 1836, and was there converted and baptized when a youth. He graduated from Georgetown College, Ky., in 1853, and taught in Maysville Seminary one year, and in the Baptist college at Palmyra, Mo., was Professor of Natural Science for a year. In 1858 he conducted the Louisiana Seminary in Louisiana, and was pastor of the church there three years. In 1861 he was president of the Female Seminary in Columbia, and was pastor of the church in that place for three years.

After the war he returned to Louisiana and took charge of the seminary and church there until 1879.

He has been one of the trustees of the Southern Baptist Theological Seminary and of William Jewell College, and for years clerk of the General Association of Missouri. Mr. Williams is a man of ability and attainments, and a zealous Christian worker. He is highly esteemed in the State of Missouri. He is now connected with the *Central Baptist*, of St. Louis.

Williams, J. W. M., D.D., was born in Portsmouth, Va., April 7, 1820, and resided there until

J. W. M. WILLIAMS, D.D.

1838, when, at the age of eighteen, he entered the Virginia Baptist Seminary. In 1840 he joined an advanced class in the Columbian College, Washington, D. C., and graduated in 1843. He at once entered Newton Theological Seminary, Mass., and completed his course in 1845. For several years he was engaged in preaching in the towns of Smithfield and Jerusalem, and also in Lynchburg, Va. In 1850, Dr. Williams was called to the pastorate of the First Baptist church in Baltimore. He preached his first sermon in his new field Jan. 1, 1850, and still remains the useful and honored pastor of the church, which has so remarkable a history. It was founded in 1785; was rebuilt in 1817, and again in 1877, and during the century of its existence has had but five pastors: the Rev. Lewis Richards, from 1785 to 1818; the Rev. Edmund J. Reese, from 1815 to 1818 as associate pastor, and pastor from 1818 to 1821; the Rev. John Finlay, from 1821 to 1834; the Rev. Stephen P. Hill, D.D., from 1834 to 1850; and the Rev. Dr. Williams, from 1850 to the present time. Among its members have been the Wilsons, Spencer H. Cone, Bartholomew T. Welsh, Prof. Hackett, Dr. F. Wilson, Dr. B. Griffith, and numerous others well known to the denomination. Dr. Williams is a popular pastor and a fresh and vigorous preacher. For fifteen years after he became pastor of the First church he was the superintendent of its Sunday-school, and still gives it his valuable counsel and frequent presence. Dr. Williams is also president of the Maryland Tract Society, having succeeded Dr. Johns, a few years since, in that office. He is also an overseer of the Columbian University, from which, in 1866, he received the honorary degree of D.D. Dr. Williams's incessant pastoral labors have prevented him from adding much to the literature of the denomination, but several of his sermons have been published, and he is an occasional contributor to the religious papers.

Williams, Rev. Lewis, was born, in May, 1784, in North Carolina. In 1795 his father came to Missouri. Mr. Williams was converted in 1810, and in two years he became a preacher. His son, Dr. A. P. Williams, said that he knew Fuller's works by heart. Hundreds were brought to Christ through his instrumentality. Men in St. Louis, Franklin, and adjoining counties came twenty miles to hear him preach. Daniel Boone loved to listen to his sermons. He spent many days and nights with him, and baptized some of his family. His son, A. P., was converted under his preaching, and he assisted at his ordination. He formed the Franklin Association, and nearly all its members were baptized by him.

In 1832 the Home Mission Society employed him. In 1837 he removed to Gasconade County, when Home Mission aid failed him. He died in St. Louis, and his body rests in the burial-ground of the old church he first joined, at Fee Fee Creek. A monument marks the spot.

Williams, Rev. Moses C., was for many years identified with Grand Cane Association, La., as one of its most prominent and devoted ministers; born in Georgia; came to Louisiana, and settled near Mansfield, De Soto Parish, about 1852. His influence will long be felt in the part of the State where he labored. He died in 1863.

Williams, Nathaniel M., D.D., was born in Salem, Mass., Nov. 13, 1813. He pursued his college studies partly at Waterville and partly at Washington, D. C. He was a graduate of Columbian College in the class of 1837, and took a two years' course of theological study at Newton. He was ordained Jan. 29, 1840, and was pastor of the church in New Sharon, Me., 1840–42. The next four years of his ministry were spent in Farmington, Me. From this place he removed to Saco, where he remained six years, when he resigned, and became pastor of the church in Somerville, Mass., holding the office nine years. His next pastorate of four years was at Ellsworth, Me., followed by two settlements of three years each in Peabody and Methuen, Mass. In 1871 he accepted a call to Wickford, R. I., which position he held until recently, when he resigned and removed to Lowell, Mass., where at present he resides.

The degree of Doctor of Divinity was conferred on Mr. Williams by the University of Chicago in 1871.

Williams, Rev. Nathaniel W., was born in Salem, Mass., Aug. 24, 1784. His early associations were with the Unitarians. He entered the counting-room of an uncle, and by him was sent to India as a supercargo of one of his ships trading with Calcutta. He made the acquaintance in Calcutta of the eminent English missionaries Carey, Ward, and Marshman. His religious convictions extended on through many years. At last he was brought to submit to an atoning Saviour, and renounced what he ever afterwards regarded as the erroneous system in which, in his early days, he had been educated. He was baptized by Rev. Lucius Bolles, and received as a member of the First Baptist church in Salem, June 5, 1808, of which church he was not long afterwards appointed a deacon. He was licensed to preach July 31, 1812. Abandoning a lucrative business that he might give himself wholly to the work of the ministry, he was ordained at Beverly, Aug. 14, 1816. There he remained nearly nine years. His next pastorate, which was a brief one, was in Windsor, Vt., succeeded by a five years' ministry in Concord, N. H., from which place he removed to Newburyport, Mass., where he spent five years, and then, in 1836, he returned to his former charge in Beverly. His last pastorates, which were only a year or two in each place, were in Malden, Mass., and Augusta, Me. He retired from pastoral work in 1846, and made a home with his son, Rev. N. M. Williams, of Saco, Me. In 1852 he went to Boston, and, with his wife, joined the Rowe Street church, under the ministry of Rev. Dr. Stow. While living in Boston he preached nearly every Sabbath, and to the last continued his habits of study and the preparation of new sermons. He was a diligent student, and such was his reputation in this respect that Brown University conferred on him the degree of Master of Arts in 1824. In 1820 he was a member of the convention chosen to revise the constitution of the State of Massachusetts, "where," says Dr. Stow, "he distinguished himself, and won general favor by his calmness, intelligence, and dignity in debate. It has been conceded that he and Dr. Baldwin contributed largely to those modifications which secured equal rights of conscience in religious matters to all the citizens of this Commonwealth."

Mr. Williams died in Boston, May 27, 1853.

Williams, Rev. O. A., was born in the parish of Dolbenmaen, Carnarvonshire, Wales, March 25, 1837; baptized Nov. 20, 1850; emigrated to America, May 7, 1857; licensed to preach by the Stanton Street Baptist church, New York, Sept. 30, 1859; graduated at Madison University in 1863, and from the Hamilton Theological Seminary in 1865; ordained as the pastor of the Baptist church of Mount Vernon, N. Y., in October, 1865. Failing health compelled him to resign the charge of the church in Mount Vernon, June 1, 1874. Since May 1, 1865, he has been pastor of the First Baptist church in Nebraska City, Neb., and he is deeply interested in the work of laying the proper foundations of the Baptist denomination throughout the State.

Williams, Roger, the founder of Rhode Island, and the great apostle of civil and religious freedom, was born of Welsh parentage in the year 1599. Concerning the place of his birth history is silent. Recent investigations lead to the conclusion that it was in the county of Cornwall, England, where the Cornish tongue, a Celtic dialect now extinct, was then prevalent. It is certain from the records that "Roger Williams," a son of "William Williams, gentleman," was "baptized on the 24th of July, 1600," in the parish church of Guinear. No direct allusion to the parents of Roger has thus far been found in any of his published writings; a brief statement respecting his early years has, however, been placed on record. In the last of his works, "George Fox digg'd out of his Burrowes," dated in the "epistle dedicatory," March 10, 1673, he says, "From my childhood, now about threescore years, the Father of lights and mercies touched my soul with a love to himself, to his only begotten, the true Lord Jesus, and to his holy Scriptures." In a letter to Winthrop, written in 1632, he further states that he had been "persecuted in and out of his father's house these twenty years." His early conversion, his belief in the divinity of Christ, and his attachment to the Word as a sufficient rule and guide in all religious matters, are here clearly and distinctly outlined. His connection with the Puritans accounts for the opposition of his father, and perhaps for his removal to London, where his promising talents, and especially his remarkable skill as a reporter, gained him the favorable notice of Sir Edward Coke, the first lawyer of his age. He, according to the statement of Mrs. Sadleir, his daughter, sent him to Sutton's Hospital, a magnificent school of learning now called the Charter House. It was a propitious circumstance that thus made the author of the "Bill of Rights" and the great "Defender of the Commons" a benefactor of the youth destined to become the advocate of free principles in the New World. Upon the completion of his preparatory studies, young Williams was admitted to Cambridge University, where Coke himself had been educated, and where liberal and Puritan sentiments have always found a more congenial home than at Oxford. He was matriculated a pensioner of Pembroke College, July 7, 1625, and in January, 1627, he took the degree of Bachelor of Arts. The evidence of this, as stated by Arnold, in his elaborate "History of Rhode Island," may be seen in the original records, which the writer has recently been permitted to examine, through the kindness of Mr. Bradshaw, librarian of the university. Under the guidance of his illustrious patron Mr. Williams now commenced the study of law. The providence of God may here be seen, in thus leading his mind to an acquaintance with those principles which were to be so useful to him in after-life as the legislator of an infant colony. He soon, however, relinquished this pursuit and entered upon the study of theology, a study which, to a mind and heart like his, possessed superior attractions. He was admitted to orders in the Established Church, and assumed, it is said, the charge of a parish, probably in the diocese of the excellent Bishop Williams, who, it is well known, winked at the Nonconformists, and spoke with keenness against some of the ceremonies inaugurated by King James and his advisers. It was during this period that the young clergyman became acquainted with many of the leading emigrants to America, including his famous opponent in after-years, John Cotton. He appears, even then, to have been very decided in his opposition to the liturgy and hierarchy of the church, as expounded and enforced by Laud, to escape from whose tyranny he finally fled to the new country. He embarked at Bristol, in the ship "Lyon," and, after a tempestuous passage of nearly ten weeks, arrived off Nantasket, with his wife, Mary, to whom he had been but recently married, on the 5th of February, 1631. He was now in the thirty-second year of his age, and in the full maturity of his mental and physical powers; a devout and zealous Christian, a ripe scholar, and an accomplished linguist,—one who was accustomed to read the Scriptures in their original tongues.

The arrival of this "godly minister" is duly recorded by Winthrop, and in a few weeks he was cordially invited to settle in Boston as a teacher. This flattering invitation he declined, because, as he afterwards wrote to Cotton, he " durst not officiate to an unseparated people." So impure did he regard the Established Church that he would not join with a congregation which, although driven into the wilderness by its persecuting spirit, refused to regard its hierarchy and worldly ceremonies as portions of the abominations of anti-Christ. Not only was he in theory and practice a rigid " Separatist," but he had already become an advocate of the great Baptist doctrine of religious freedom in matters of conscience, as set forth in the " Confession of Faith," published in London in 1611: " The magistrate is not to meddle with religion or matters of conscience, nor compel men to this or that form of religion, because Christ is King and Lawgiver of church and conscience."

"The magistrate," he taught, "might not punish the breach of the Sabbath, nor any other offence, as it was a breach of the first table." Well might the infant "Plantation," which in a single year from the time when its first session for business was held, Aug. 23, 1630, had passed sentences of exclusion from its territory upon fourteen persons of too free carriage and speech, look askance upon one whose opinions were so singularly at variance with their own. Mr. Williams accordingly removed to Salem, and shortly afterwards entered upon his duties as teacher in place of the learned and catholic Higginson, who was in feeble health. The church with which he thus became connected was the oldest in the "Company of the Massachusetts Bay," having been organized on the 6th of August, 1629, " on principles," says its historian, Upham, " of perfect and entire independence of every other ecclesiastical body." It was, for this reason, eminently congenial to the independent and fearless nature of Williams. At once the civil authority interfered to prevent his settlement, on the principle afterwards established, that " if any church, one or more, shall grow schismatical, rending itself from the communion of other churches, or shall walk incorrigibly and obstinately in any corrupt way of their own, contrary to the rule of the Word; in such case the magistrate is to put forth his coercive power, as the matter shall require." The church at Salem notwithstanding, maintained its independence, and on the 12th of April, 1631, received Mr. Williams as its minister. His settlement, however, was of short continuance. Disregarding the wishes and advice of the magistrates in calling him, the church had incurred their disapprobation and raised a storm of persecution, so that, for the sake of peace, Williams withdrew before the close of summer and sought a residence at Plymouth, beyond the jurisdiction of Massachusetts Bay. Here, says Gov. Bradford, he was cordially received and hospitably entertained, having the free exercise of his gifts and the fellowship of the church as a member. He labored in the ministry of the Word faithfully both among the whites and the Indians, the latter of whom he visited in their wigwams, learning their language, and becoming intimate with their chiefs,—Massasoit and Canonicus. In the autumn of 1633 he returned to Salem. Already the principles of separation and religious freedom, which he everywhere proclaimed, had made him an object of jealousy, even among the liberal-minded Pilgrims of the "Mayflower." On requesting a letter of dismission from the church, we find the elder, Mr. Brewster, persuading his people to relinquish communion with him, lest he should " run the same course of rigid separation and anabaptistry which Mr. John Smith, the Se-Baptist at Amsterdam, had done."

Mr. Williams resumed his ministerial duties as an assistant to Mr. Skelton, whose declining health unfitted him for his work. Upon the death of Mr. Skelton, in August, 1634, he was regularly ordained as his successor, notwithstanding the opposition of the magistrates. He was highly popular as a preacher, and the people became strongly attached to him and to his ministry. Among his hearers were not a few of the members of the church at Plymouth, who, after ineffectual attempts to detain him there, had transferred their residence to Salem. A part of the house which he owned and occupied as a dwelling during the years 1635–36 is still standing on the western corner of North and Essex Streets. The original frame-work of the quaint structure in which he preached is carefully preserved as an object of interest to the historian and the antiquary. From the period of his final settlement at Salem may be dated the beginning of the controversy with the clergy and court of Massachusetts Bay, which at length terminated in his banishment from the colony. " He was faithfully and resolutely protected," says Upham, " by the people of Salem, through years of persecution from without, and it was only by the persevering and combined efforts of all the other towns and churches that his separation and banishment were finally effected." . . . " They adhered to him long and faithfully, and sheltered him from all assaults. And when at last he was sentenced by the General Court to banishment from the colony on account of his principles, we cannot but admire the fidelity of that friendship which prompted many of the members of his congregation to accompany him in his exile, and partake of his fortunes, when an outcast upon the earth." Upon the causes of his banishment we cannot here enlarge. It is contended, on the one hand, that it " was a mere question of policy, and not at all of religious liberty;" that his opinions tended to disorder and dissension in a government that was theocratic, and that his offenses were, therefore, purely political in their character. Williams, on the contrary, in his famous controversy with Cotton, contends that he was banished for cause of conscience; in other words, that he was persecuted for his religious opinions. And in this view we fully and heartily concur. He was regarded, indeed, as a disturber of the peace. And so have Baptists in all ages been regarded by the advocates of a state or national church. He was repeatedly summoned to appear before the General Court in Boston to answer for his opinions. These were, in brief, as they were summed up by the presiding magistrate, Gov. Haynes, at his final trial: "First, that we have not our land by patent from the king, but that the natives are the true owners of it, and that we ought to repent of such a receiving of it by patent; secondly, that it is not lawful to call a wicked person to swear, or to pray, as being actions of God's worship; thirdly, that it is not lawful to hear any of the parish assemblies in England; fourthly, that the civil magistrate's power extends only to the bodies and goods and outward state of man," etc. "I acknowledge," says Williams, in his controversy, "the particulars were rightly summed up, and I also hope, as I then maintained the rocky strength of them to my own and other consciences' satisfaction, I shall be ready for the same grounds, not only to be bound and banished, but to die also in New England, as for most holy truths of God in Christ Jesus." The act of banishment, as it stands upon the colonial records, is in these words: "Whereas, Mr. Roger Williams, one of the elders of the church of Salem, hath broached and divulged new and dangerous opinions against the authority of magistrates, as also writ letters of defamation, both of the magistrates and churches here, and that before any conviction, and yet maintaineth the same without any retraction, it is therefore ordered that the said Mr. Williams shall depart out of this jurisdiction within six weeks now next ensuing, which, if he neglect to perform, it shall be lawful for the governor and two of the magistrates to send him to some place out of this jurisdiction, not to return any more without license from the court." This remarkable sentence was passed on the 9th of October, 1635. Three months later the magistrates determined to arrest and send him to England; but when Capt. Underhill, who was commissioned for this purpose, arrived at Salem with his sloop, the illustrious exile had fled.

It was in the middle of January, the coldest month of a New England winter, that Williams, bidding adieu to wife and loved ones at home, betook himself to the wilderness. "For fourteen weeks," as he wrote thirty-five years afterwards to his friend, Maj. Mason, he "was sorely tossed," "not knowing what bread or bed did mean." The effects of this exposure to the severity of the weather he continued to feel to his latest days. The late Hon. Job Durfee, in his "What Cheer?" has, with a poet's license, graphically described some of the scenes relating to this historic event. He first settled at Seekonk, but in the latter part of June, as well as can now be ascertained, he with five companions embarked in a canoe, and after landing on "What Cheer Rock," rowed around India Point and up the Mooshausick River, landing at the foot of a hill, where they commenced a settlement, which, in gratitude to his Supreme deliverer, he gave the name of Providence. Other settlers from Massachusetts joined them, and at an early period they entered into an agreement or compact "only in civil things," and thus became a "town fellowship." Subsequently they became a colony, under the name of "Rhode Island and Providence Plantations," with a liberal charter granted by King Charles II. In their address to the throne, they declared their purpose "to hold forth a lively experiment, that a most flourishing civil state may stand and best be maintained with full liberty in religious concernments." "Thus was founded," says Gervinus, the celebrated German professor, "a small, new society in Rhode Island, upon the principles of entire liberty of conscience, and the uncontrolled power of the majority in secular concerns." . . . "These institutions have not only maintained themselves here, but have spread over the whole Union. They have superseded the aristocratic commencements of Carolina and of New York, the high-church party in Virginia, the theocracy in Massachusetts, and the monarchy throughout America; they have given laws to one quarter of the globe, and, dreaded for their moral influence, they stand in the background of every democratic struggle in Europe."

In the month of March, 1639, Mr. Williams, whose tendency to Baptist views had long been apparent, was publicly immersed. His mode of planting the church, now known as the First Baptist church in Providence, was this. Mr. Ezekiel Holliman, a gifted and pious layman, first baptized Mr. Williams, who in turn baptized Holliman "and some ten more." The names of these twelve original members are given by Benedict in his "History of the Baptists." Thus was founded what is commonly regarded as the oldest Baptist church in America; a church which, for nearly two and a half centuries, has firmly held to the great doctrines of regeneration, believer's baptism, and religious liberty; and which, to-day, is looked upon with veneration and filial pride by the large and flourishing denomination it so worthily represents.

Mr. Williams for some cause did not long retain

his connection with the church, having doubts, it appears, in regard to the validity of this proceeding, in consequence of the absence of a "visible succession" of authorized administrators of the rite of baptism. "In a few months," says Scott, writing thirty-eight years afterwards, "he broke from the society and declared at large the grounds and reason of it,—that their baptism could not be right because it was not administered by an apostle." Perhaps the "society" were lacking in efficiency and zeal. It is certain that for more than sixty years they lived without a meeting-house, worshiping in groves and private dwellings; that they discarded singing and music in public worship; insisted on the imposition of hands, and, until President Manning's time, were content with an untrained, unpaid ministry. Mr. Williams became what in the early history of New England is denominated a *Seeker*; a term, says Gammell, not inaptly applied to those who, in any age of the church, are dissatisfied with its prevailing creeds and institutions, and seek for more congenial views of truth, or a faith better adapted to their spiritual wants. Although he soon terminated his ecclesiastical relations, it must not be inferred that there was ill feeling engendered in consequence, or that he ceased to preach the gospel. He continued on the terms of the closest intimacy and friendship with his successor in the ministry, Chad Brown, and in one of his latest letters, written to Gov. Bradstreet, he expressed a desire to have some of his sermons printed. That he did not undervalue the benefits of Christian fellowship is evident from his writings. In his reply to Geo. Fox, written in 1676, he says, "After all my search, and examinations, and considerations, I said, I do profess to believe that some come nearer to the first primitive churches, and the institutions and appointments of Christ Jesus, than others; as in many respects, so in that gallant, and heavenly, and fundamental principle of the true matter of a Christian congregation, flock, or society, viz., ACTUAL BELIEVERS, TRUE DISCIPLES AND CONVERTS, LIVING STONES, such as can give some account how the grace of God hath appeared unto them." In regard to what is known as the distinguishing sentiments of Baptists at the present day, viz., baptism by immersion, Mr. Williams did not, it appears, change his views. In a letter to Winthrop, dated Sept. 10, 1649, more than ten years after the founding of the church at Providence, he says, "At Seekonk a great many have lately concurred with Mr. John Clarke and our Providence men about the point of a new baptism, and the manner by dipping, and Mr. Clarke hath been there lately, and Mr. Luear, and hath dipped them. I BELIEVE THEIR PRACTICE COMES NEARER THE FIRST PRACTICE OF OUR GREAT FOUNDER, CHRIST JESUS, THAN OTHER PRACTICES OF RELIGION DO."

The limits of a brief sketch like the present compel us to pass rapidly in review the leading events in the further career of this distinguished man, referring our readers to the full and authentic history of Rhode Island by the late Samuel G. Arnold, and to his memoirs by Knowles, Gammell, Underhill, and Elton. His works, in seven large quarto volumes, with a biographical introduction by Guild, recently published under the auspices of the "Narragansett Club," form his most complete and "enduring monument." In 1643 he sailed for England, where, through the influence of his personal friend, Sir Henry Vane, he succeeded in procuring a charter for Rhode Island, bearing date March 14, 1644. In 1645 he was instrumental in making peace between the Narragansetts and the Mohegans, thus preserving the settlements of New England a second time from a general war. In 1651, in company with his "loving friend," Rev. John Clarke, of Newport, he embarked a second time for England to procure from Charles II. a confirmation of the first charter. Returning in the summer of 1654, he succeeded in reorganizing the government upon a permanent basis, and in September following he was chosen president or governor. This position he occupied until May, 1658, when he retired from the office. Concerning the closing years of his life we know but little. He outlived most of his contemporaries, dying at the advanced age of eighty-four, in the full vigor of his mental faculties. He was buried under arms, "with all the solemnity," says Callender, "the colony was able to show."

The name of Roger Williams has been handed down to us by Puritan writers loaded with reproach. He is described by Neal as a rigid Brownist, precise and uncharitable, and of the most turbulent and boisterous passions. But his writings refute the first charge, and his conduct, under circumstances likely to arouse the gentlest spirit, contradicts the second. Gov. Winthrop, in a letter to him, says, "Sir, we have often tried your patience, but could never conquer it." He suffered more than most men from the slanders of those who should have been his friends. Coddington accused him "as a hireling, who, for the sake of money, went to England for the charter." Harris, in the long and angry controversy between them, left no means untried to undermine his influence with those for whom he had supplied a home, when the gates of Massachusetts were closed against them. Palfrey, in his elaborate "History of New England," states that his life, as a whole, "cannot be called, in any common use of the terms, a successful one," while "his official life was mostly passed in a furious turmoil." And even the genial Dexter, in his recently-published monograph, "As to Roger Williams," justifies his banishment from

Massachusetts, and accuses the Baptist denomination of canonizing him without a due regard to facts. His offense, says Marsden, was this,—"He enunciated and lived to carry out the great principle of perfect toleration amongst contending parties by whom it was equally abhorred." But posterity has rendered him justice, and the defender of Baptist principles, as well as the founder of Rhode Island, will be held in grateful and everlasting remembrance. The historian Bancroft pays him a glowing tribute in his immortal work. After seven pages of what Dexter is pleased to term "graceful rhetoric, in which he adroitly manages to evade most of the main points at issue," he closes with these memorable words: "If Copernicus is held in perpetual reverence, because on his death-bed he published to the world that the sun is the centre of our system; if the name of Kepler is preserved in the annals of human excellence for his sagacity in detecting the laws of planetary motion; if the genius of Newton has been almost adored for dissecting a ray of light, and weighing the heavenly bodies in a balance,—let there be for the name of Roger Williams at least some humble place among those who have advanced moral science and made themselves the benefactors of mankind." And Prof. Tyler, in his recent "History of American Literature," gives a masterly analysis of the publications of the "Narragansett Club," to which we have already referred. Williams, he says, in the outset, "never in anything addicted to concealments, has put himself without reserve into his writings. There he still remains. There, if anywhere, we may get well acquainted with him. Searching for him along the two thousand printed pages upon which he has stamped his own portrait, we seem to see a very human and fallible man, with a large head, a warm heart, a healthy body, an eloquent and imprudent tongue; not a symmetrical person, poised, cool, accurate, circumspect; a man very anxious to be genuine and to get at the truth, but impatient of slow methods, trusting gallantly to his own intuitions, easily deluded by his own hopes; an imaginative, sympathetic, affluent, impulsive man; an optimist; his master-passion, benevolence; . . . lovely in his carriage; . . . of a hearty and sociable turn; . . . in truth, a clubable person; a man whose dignity would not have petrified us, nor his saintliness have given us a chill; . . . in New England, a mighty and benignant form, always pleading for some magnanimous idea, some tender charity, the rectification of some wrong, the exercise of some sort of forbearance towards men's bodies or souls."

Williams, Rev. Samuel, was born in Connellsville, Fayette Co., Pa., on the 5th of August, 1802. At the age of twenty, while a student at Zanesville, O., he embraced Christ by faith. Along with light upon his heart came the love of souls, and in two years from his conversion he was ordained in Somerset Co., Pa. In May, 1827, he became pastor of the First Baptist church in Pittsburgh, Pa. This relation continued twenty-eight years, during which period six other churches were organized. Leaving Pittsburgh, he settled in Akron, O. Here he remained eight years, and then became pastor in Springfield. At both these places he, in connection with his wife, conducted a female seminary. Two subsequent years were spent as pastor in New Castle, Pa., and five years more were employed among churches in the vicinity of Pittsburgh. His present residence is Brooklyn, N. Y. Mr. Williams engaged in numerous controversies, both orally and in writing, in defense of Baptist doctrine and practice.

Williams, Rev. William, was born in Hilltown, Pa., in the year 1752. He was fitted for college in the school of Rev. Isaac Eaton, in Hopewell, N. J., and graduated from Brown University, with the first class, in 1769. He was baptized by Rev. Charles Thompson, Sept. 29, 1771, and became a member of the Warren church, then the home of the college. This church gave him a license to preach the gospel, which bears the date of April 18, 1773. Having preached for two years in Wrentham, Mass., the church extended to him a call to become their pastor, and he was ordained July 3, 1776. Soon after removing to Wrentham he opened a school, which became celebrated in all the section of the country in which he lived. As near as can be ascertained he had not far from 200 youths under his charge, 80 of whom were fitted by him to enter Brown University. In after-life not a few of these did honor to him as their early preceptor, in the different professions and callings in which they spent their days. He was about seventy-one years of age when he died. The event occurred Sept. 22, 1823. Dr. Abial Fisher says of him, "His talents and acquirements were highly respectable. His services as a teacher commanded great respect not only in but out of his denomination." Among his pupils were the late Hon. David R. Williams, governor of South Carolina, and the Hon. Tristam Burgess, LL.D., late Professor of Oratory and Belles-Lettres in Brown University.

Williams, William, D.D., LL.D., Professor of Ecclesiastical History, Church Government, and Pastoral Duties in the Southern Baptist Theological Seminary, was born at Eatonton, Putnam Co., Ga., March 15, 1821. He was converted and united with a Baptist church in 1837, and graduated at the University of Georgia in 1840. His attention was first directed to the legal profession, as a preparation for which he attended the law-school of Harvard University, where he graduated in 1847. He entered the ministry in 1851, his first pastoral charge being at Auburn, Ala. In 1856 he became Professor of Theology in Mercer University, then at Penfield, Ga. In 1859 he was elected Professor of Ecclesiastical History, Church Government, and Pastoral Duties in the Southern Baptist Theological Seminary. At various times during the enforced absence of the Professor of Systematic Theology the duties of that chair were filled by Dr. Williams, and in May, 1872, he was formally transferred to that professorship, in which he continued until his death. Dr. Williams was on several occasions elected one of the vice-presidents of the Southern Baptist Convention, and was the appointed preacher of its twenty-fifth annual sermon at St. Louis, Mo., in May, 1871. He received the degree of D.D. from Mercer University in 1859, and of LL.D. from Richmond College in 1876.

He died at Aiken, S. C., Feb. 20, 1877, and was buried at Greenville, S. C., where his former students have erected a monument to his memory.

Williams, William R., D.D., LL.D., was born in New York, Oct. 14, 1804. His father, Rev. John Williams, was pastor of the Oliver Street church twenty-seven years. He was graduated at Columbia College with distinguished honor in 1823, and commenced the study of the law, intending to make that his profession. He was baptized by Dr. S. H. Cone into the fellowship of the Oliver Street

WILLIAM R. WILLIAMS, D.D., LL.D.

church, and took an active part in church work. By his labor a mission Sunday-school was organized in the thirteenth ward, which grew into the East Broome Street Baptist church. Its name was changed to the Cannon Street church, and it is now known as the East Baptist church.

He was then identified with another new interest, and, having been licensed to preach, when the Amity Street church was constituted he was at the same time ordained as its pastor. Dec. 17, 1832.

While in the practice of the law his literary career commenced. He wrote first a biographical notice of his father, and an elaborate address entitled "Conservative Principles in our Literature." His "Miscellanies" and his "Lectures on the Lord's Prayer," with other sermons and addresses, raised him to the first rank among religious authors. The purity of his rhetoric, the clearness of his reasoning, and the brilliance of his style have led literary men to pronounce him the Robert Hall of America. Dr. Williams produces his great works from a well-trained and well-stored mind furnished by the great libraries of New York and his own choice collection of more than 10,000 volumes.

At this present writing Dr. Williams occupies the same pulpit in which he was ordained nearly fifty years ago. He has been invited to chairs in colleges and seminaries, but such is his love for his church and his study that he has declined all such tempting proposals. He is never heard in public debate, nor does he engage in newspaper discussion on any subject.

His late lectures in New York on "Baptist History" and "Bunyan and the Pilgrim's Progress" called out a good attendance of clergymen of all denominations and of literary men, who were delighted by his eloquence and learning.

Dr. Williams is one of the most elegant writers that ever used the English language, and one of the greatest men that ever occupied an American pulpit.

Willis, Rev. C. C., one of the most pious, useful, and laborious of the ministers in the Columbus Association, Ga., was born March 24, 1809, in Baldwin County, and removed to Talbot County at maturity, where, for half a century, he has been faithfully working for Jesus. He has made a most salutary impression on the entire community in his section; has built up and trained to a high degree of excellence several churches; and has exerted a noble influence in behalf of missions and Sunday-schools. He has often been Moderator of the Columbus Association, and is one of the best pastors and revival preachers in the State.

Willis, Rev. Edward J., was born in Culpeper Co., Va., Dec. 19, 1820; was educated in Virginia and in Massachusetts; studied law at the University of Virginia, and graduated in July, 1842. He began the practice of law at once, his home being in Charlottesville. He was baptized in his eighteenth year.

In 1849 he went to California, walking from Independence, Mo., a distance of 2200 miles. He began the practice of the law in Sacramento; in April, 1850, he was elected judge. In 1854 he was licensed to preach; resigned his judgeship, and in October of the same year was ordained a minister of the gospel. The Oakland and Sacramento churches were both organized at his residence. His first pastorate was with the Oakland church, which continued till 1854. He then returned to Virginia, and from 1854 to 1860 was pastor of the Leigh Street church in Richmond.

He was first chaplain, and then captain, of the 15th Virginia Regiment of infantry in the Confederate army, and commanded the regiment in several of the battles of the war.

For two years, 1865–67, he was pastor at Gordonsville and Orange Court-House. From 1867 to 1869 he was pastor of the church in Alexandria; thence he went as missionary pastor to Winchester, and in 1872 took charge of the Winchester Female Institute, now Broaddus Female College, which was removed to Clarksburg, W. Va., in 1876.

Willis, Rev. Joseph, the apostle of the Attakapas (Louisiana), was a mulatto. He first appears in Southwest Mississippi as a licensed preacher in 1798. He was born in 1762. Upon the acquisition of Louisiana he boldly crossed the Mississippi River, and in 1804 preached at Vermilion and at Plaquemine Brulé. For eight years, amid trials and persecutions, he preached the gospel in the Opelousas country, alone and unremunerated, expending a little fortune in the effort, planting the seeds of many churches that afterwards sprang up. In 1812, with the assistance of visiting ministers from Mississippi, he organized a church at Bayou Chicot, the first west of the Mississippi. Father Willis, as he was affectionately called, extended his labors and constituted other churches. Being joined by O'Quin and Nettles in 1816, the churches increased, and in 1818 the Louisiana Association was organized, of which he was moderator many years. He lived to see abundant fruits of his labors. He died in 1854.

Willmarth, Rev. Isaac M., was born at Deerfield, N. Y., Oct. 27, 1804, and was baptized there in 1830; graduated from Hamilton College in 1825, and Newton Theological Institution in 1833; ordained at New York, April 30, 1834, and proceeded to France, where he labored as a missionary until 1837. (See MISSION TO FRANCE.) Compelled by ill health to return to America, his life has been spent in preaching and teaching. He has been pastor at Peterborough, New Ipswich, and Drewsville, N. H., Grafton and Pondville, Vt., and Rowe, Mass. He has been principal of several academies. Is living (1881), and able to preach occasionally. Mr. Willmarth is a devout man, whose life has been full of usefulness.

Willmarth, Rev. James W., was born in Paris, France, of American parents, in 1835. He was baptized in Grafton, Vt., in 1848. His early studies were greatly impeded by an affection of the eyes, but his thirst for knowledge could not be held in check by any difficulty not insurmountable; he gave time and toil to the ancient languages, and his heart to theological acquisitions, and at an early period in life he was a scholarly preacher, well skilled in divinity. His first public service for Christ was performed when he was a missionary colporteur of the American Baptist Publication Society in Chicago. He was ordained, in 1860, in Aurora, Ill. He has been pastor in Metamora, Ill., Amenia, N. Y., Wakefield, Mass., Pemberton, N. J., and he is now the pastor of Roxborough church, Philadelphia. He is a writer of great power, and he uses a prolific pen. His articles on "The Future Life" and "Baptism and Remission," in the *Baptist Quarterly*, showed much originality, and produced a profound impression upon cultured men of God.

No one stands higher in the estimation of his friends, and all that know him may be reckoned among the number. His position on any subject is very decided; he knows nothing of half-heartedness; his thoughts are as transparent as a sunbeam. He shuns no responsibility in defending any truth; he avoids no sacrifice in assisting a friend. He is an able preacher, with a noble intellect, ardent piety, and a bright earthly future, if his slender frame will permit him to stay on earth for a few years.

Wilson, Adam, D.D., was born in Topsham, Me., Feb. 10, 1794. He fitted for college at the Hebron Academy, and entered Bowdoin College, in Brunswick, Me., in 1815. At the close of his Freshman year he was baptized. He graduated in 1819 and studied theology with Rev. Dr. Staughton, then of Philadelphia. In the early part of 1822 he commenced his ministry in Wiscassett, Me., having been previously ordained, Dec. 13, 1820. He remained in Wiscassett two years. For nearly four years he served as pastor of two churches, one in New Gloucester and the other in Turner. While thus engaged, he was invited to take charge of a new paper which was about to be started in Maine, as the organ of the Baptist denomination in that State; the first number of which, *The Zion's Advocate*, appeared Nov. 11, 1828, with the imprint of Adam Wilson as its editor and proprietor. He continued to perform his editorial duties for ten years, when he received and accepted a call to become the pastor of the First Baptist church in Bangor, securing the services of another to take his place as editor of the *Advocate*, although he remained its proprietor. He was pastor of the Bangor church three years and a half, and of the church in Turner, with which he had formerly been connected, two years, at the end of which time, 1843, he resumed the editorial management of his paper. For five years he continued in this

ADAM WILSON, D.D.

position, and then acted as pastor, first of the church in Hebron, and then of the church in Paris, covering a period of nearly ten years. In 1858 he removed to Waterville, which was his home the remainder of his life. He was constantly engaged in supplying the weak churches in the section where he lived, and his usefulness was not abated down to the close of life. He was an able theologian, and worthily won the degree of D.D., conferred on him by Waterville College in 1851. The amount of literary work which he accomplished as the editor of *Zion's Advocate* for sixteen years it is not easy to estimate. He published but little apart from what he prepared for his paper. For more than forty years he was a trustee of Waterville College, now Colby University. "The college records show," says President Champlin, "that his hand framed the greater part of the important reports and resolutions presented during that long period. In all the discussions and difficult questions arising at the sessions of the trustees, Dr. Wilson's uniformly conciliatory spirit had rendered inestimable service." A busy and most useful life terminated Jan. 16, 1871. It is safe to say that probably to no one man is the present prosperity of the Baptist denomination in the State of Maine more due than to the subject of this sketch. The last words which fell from his lips, a few hours before he died, were, "One Lord, one faith, one baptism, one religion, one hope, one Saviour, one heaven, one eternity. Amen, and amen! Amen, and amen!"

Wilson, Daniel M., was born at Morristown, N. J., in 1803. His mother was an excellent Christian woman of marked character. In early life he obtained a hope in Christ, but did not make a profession until mature years. He united with the First Baptist church, Newark. He was at the head of a strong commercial firm, had already acquired a financial competence, and he brought his eminent business capabilities, with a true Christian devotedness, into action for church prosperity. He exerted a powerful influence over the principal commercial corporations with which he was connected; served faithfully as collector of internal revenue for the large eastern district of New Jersey, and filled other public offices involving important trusts. In endeavoring to build up the churches in Newark he was indefatigable. The success of the city mission was largely due to his counsels and efforts. For eighteen successive years he was president of the New Jersey Baptist State Convention, occupying that office at his death in 1873. For most of that time he was treasurer of the Education Society. As president of the New Jersey Classical and Scientific Institute, at Hightstown, he devoted much time and energy to the erection of the fine building and the prosperity of the institution. He was for a time president of the American and Foreign Bible Society, and being a generous contributor to all the societies for the extension of the Saviour's kingdom, his counsels were much prized. When at the age of threescore and ten he departed from earth, his death was regarded as a public loss.

Wilson, Franklin, D.D., was born in Baltimore, Md., Dec. 8, 1822. His father, Thomas Wilson, was a member of the eminent firm of William Wilson & Sons. Franklin's mother died when he was fifteen months old, but her place was largely supplied by the devotion of his father's cousin, Miss P. Stansbury, a very pious and active member of the First Baptist church, who trained the motherless children in "the nurture and admonition of the Lord." He began the study of Latin when only seven years old; at the age of ten was sent to Mount Hope College, near Baltimore, and before he was thirteen he entered the Freshman class. One of his teachers there was the Rev. H. B. Hackett, D.D., who became a Baptist while in Baltimore. Soon after, Dr. Hackett accepted a professorship in Brown University, R. I., and in 1836 Franklin was sent to that college, at first under the special guardianship of Prof. Hackett. At the close of his Junior year, he was obliged to suspend his studies from weakness of the eyes, and

80

he graduated with the succeeding class in 1841, delivering the classical oration at the commencement. He was fortunate in having as classmates or friends while in college such men as Samson, Malcom,

FRANKLIN WILSON, D.D.

Dodge, Lincoln, Brooks, Brantly, Weston, and others since eminent in the denomination. During the revival which followed the day of prayer for colleges, in 1838, he professed conversion, and was baptized in Baltimore, April 22, 1838, by the Rev. Stephen P. Hill, D.D. In 1842 he entered the Newton Theological Institution, but left in 1844, before completing the course, to attend his father in his fatal illness. While at home he began laboring at a mission chapel, erected by his uncle, James Wilson, at Huntington (since Waverly), and finally accepted the pastorship of the church formed there under his ministry. In 1845 he took a trip to Europe, visiting England, Ireland, Scotland, and France. He was ordained in Baltimore, Jan. 18, 1846, at the First Baptist church, where he preached his first sermon in 1842, being then but nineteen years of age, on a theme which always deeply interested him,— "Prayer for Colleges." In 1857 a council of city churches urged him to become the pastor of the High Street church, Baltimore, which was overwhelmed by financial difficulties and about to be sold. He accepted, and held the position till 1850, thus, by his gratuitous services, saving the house of worship, encouraging the church, and adding to its membership eighty-four by baptism. A disease of the vocal organs compelled him at this time to suspend his public labors; but he continued his pastorate until 1852, when he reluctantly resigned. After six years of partial rest his vocal organs were strengthened, and since that he has preached hundreds of sermons.

Dr. Wilson has added much to the literature of the denomination. Early in 1851 he became editor of *The True Union*, a Baptist weekly, then published in Baltimore, which position he held until 1857. He edited it again in 1861, and during these years he not only gave his time and labor gratuitously to the work, but expended, in addition, not less than $200 a year for the privilege of keeping up the paper.

In 1857–58 he edited *The Christian Review* (quarterly), in conjunction with Rev. G. B. Taylor, now missionary in Rome, Italy. In 1865 he edited for one year *The Maryland Baptist*, a monthly paper. In 1853 he gained a prize of $100 for the best essay on "The Duties of Churches to their Pastors." He also published tracts and essays on "Keep the Church Pure," "The Comparative Influence of Baptist and Pedobaptist Principles in the Christian Nurture of Children," "How Far may a Christian indulge in Popular Amusements?" "What Must I Do to be Saved?" (a tract which has proved a blessing to many an inquiring mind) and a very valuable treatise on "Wealth, its Acquisition, Investment, and Use," which has received the warmest commendations of the press.

One of the most important posts he has occupied is that of secretary of the Executive Board of the Maryland Baptist Union Association. Elected in 1847, he has held that office for more than thirty years. The Association was formed in 1836, with only 6 churches and 478 members. In 1877 it numbered 60 churches and 10,716 members, and its annual contributions had increased more than tenfold. In 1854 he was largely instrumental, with Rev. Dr. Williams, in forming the Baltimore Baptist Church Extension Society; was its first secretary for a number of years and a large contributor to its funds. Under its auspices were erected the Lee Street, the Franklin Square, the Leadenhall Street, and the Madison Square meeting-houses. The last was built entirely at the expense of Dr. Wilson, as was also the Rockdale chapel, near Baltimore. He has also given liberally to the erection of nearly every other Baptist meeting-house in Maryland. In 1854 he became one of the constituent members of the Franklin Square church, where he has remained ever since, having been frequently called to act as temporary pastor during the changes in the pastoral relation which the church has experienced. He has preached in that church more than 250 times, and baptized fifty persons. As early as 1860 he became deeply interested in Italy; wrote and published many articles on it as a missionary field for Baptists; and in 1864 induced the Rev. John Berg to write an article for the *London Freeman*, which gave rise to the Italian Mission from the English Baptists. In 1870, Dr. Wilson, by request, delivered an address in Philadelphia, at the anniversary of the American Baptist Publication Society, urging it to engage in distributing religious publications in Italy and Spain; and the Rev. James B. Taylor was confirmed by it in the desire to establish a mission in Italy. Shortly after, the Rev. Dr. Cote was introduced by Dr. Wilson to the Southern Board, and became the first American Baptist missionary in Rome. Since 1847, Dr. Wilson has been one of the trustees of the Columbian College, Washington, D. C., and when the college, in 1872, became the Columbian University, he was made one of its overseers. This institution conferred on him the degree of D.D. in 1865.

Many of the benevolent organizations of Baltimore have his aid and counsel. He originated the Young Men's Christian Association of that city. He has done much towards improving and beautifying the suburbs, and has aided in the erection of more than forty buildings, besides churches. He has done much, also, towards preventing ravages by fire, and is now president of the Fire-Proof Building Company, the first great work of which was rendering fire-proof the noble buildings of the Peabody Institute and the Johns Hopkins Hospital.

Wilson, Rev. J. C., was born in Chatham Co., N. C., July 23, 1820; baptized by Rev. P. W. Doud in 1838; ordained in November, 1849, Revs. P. W. Doud and J. Olin forming the Presbytery; was educated at Wake Forest College, and has served with great acceptance a number of churches in Orange, Chatham, and Wake Counties. Mr. Wilson has been for many years the moderator of the Mount Zion Association.

Wilson, John Butler, M.D., the eldest son of Rev. Dr. A. Wilson, was born in Portland, Me., Feb. 24, 1834. He was a graduate of Waterville College in the class of 1854. For three years he was the principal of an academy in East Corinth and of the high school in Dexter, Me. He received the degree of M.D. at the Jefferson Medical College, in Philadelphia, in 1859, and commenced the practice of his profession at Exeter, Me. Upon the call for troops in the late civil war, Dr. Wilson was commissioned as captain of a company raised by himself, and in the fall of 1861 was stationed at Pensacola as provost-marshal for the District of West Florida and South Alabama. Subsequently he was appointed surgeon of the 7th Regiment, U. S. Infantry, and was medical director of all the forces in Texas. He received other professional appointments as proof of the confidence of the government in his capacity. The state of his health obliged him to resign, and he returned to Maine in 1865. He resumed his profession in Dexter, Me., but did not long survive the hardships which had thoroughly undermined his constitution. He died at Dexter, March 15, 1866.

"Dr. Wilson was a man of fine talents and attainments, qualified for the first rank in his profession, in which he had already won distinction. His ardent love for the study of nature, which he had pursued from early youth, would have earned for him scientific reputation had his life been spared."

Wilson, Rev. John S., was born in Franklin Co., Ky., July 13, 1795. In his infancy his parents settled in Adair County. At the age of eighteen years he was baptized into the fellowship of Mount Gilead Baptist church. Five years afterwards he settled in Todd County. In 1822 he was licensed to preach, and after a few months was ordained and became pastor of Lebanon church. Soon afterwards he became pastoral supply of other churches in his neighborhood. Brilliant success attended his labors wherever he preached. From his ordination until his death he lived in an almost unbroken series of revivals. In 1833 he accepted the Kentucky agency of the American Bible Society, and during the same year was called to the pastorate of the First Baptist church in Louisville. He accepted, and the church prospered under his ministry, but he still continued the work of an evangelist, and multitudes were converted during revivals conducted by him in the counties around Louisville. In the spring of 1835 he preached fifteen days in Shelbyville, and 101 were baptized. The revival spread to the neighboring churches, and it was estimated that 1200 were added to the Lord during its continuance, upwards of 800 of whom were baptized into the churches of Long River Association. His last work was in a great revival at Elizabethtown in August of the same year. He died Aug. 28, 1835.

Wilson, Rev. Joseph Kennard, son of Rev. James E. and Esther B. Wilson, was born at Blackwoodtown, N. J., June 29, 1852; converted December, 1867, and baptized into Blockley Baptist church, Philadelphia, Pa., of which his father was the pastor; removed to Massachusetts in 1868; entered Brown University in 1870; graduated in 1873, and entered Crozer Theological Seminary, at Upland, Pa.; in the summer of 1874 supplied the Baptist church at Broadalbin, N. Y.; called to be pastor of the church, and was ordained Nov. 4, 1874; in the winter of 1875–76 preached at Florence, N. J., and about eighty were converted, and a church afterwards was formed; graduated from Crozer Theological Seminary in 1876; accepted a call from Nyack, N. Y.; in February, 1878, settled with Huntington Street Baptist church in New London, Conn., and is now (1881) laboring there.

Wilson, N. W., D.D., one of the most eloquent ministers in the South, who fell a victim to yellow fever in New Orleans in 1878, while heroically discharging his duties as pastor of Colosseum Place Baptist church, was born in Pendleton Co., Va., Oct. 20, 1834; was ordained in 1858; after filling several country pastorates in Virginia he was called to Chapel Hill, N. C., where his rare talents soon rendered him distinguished; thence to Farmdale, Va., where he labored for two years. But a wider field was awaiting him, and in 1870 he was called to Grace Street church, Richmond, Va., where he ministered with great success until he was called to New Orleans in 1875. In his new field he fully sustained his reputation, and fell a martyr to humanity.

Wilson, William Lyne, was born in Jefferson Co., Va., May 3, 1843. He pursued his early education at the Charlestown Academy, and entering the Columbian College, September, 1858, he graduated with honors in June of 1860. After receiving his degree of A.B. he entered the University of Virginia to prosecute some special studies, and remained there until the war broke out, at which time he left and entered the Confederate service, serving through the contest in the 12th Regular Virginia Cavalry. In 1865 he was elected Assistant Professor of Ancient Languages in the Columbian College, and in 1867 he was chosen Professor of the Latin Language and Literature. While holding this position, Mr. Wilson took the course of law in the Law-School of the Columbian College, and graduated LL.B. in 1867. He was baptized by the Rev. Dr. Cuthbert in November, 1870. In 1871 he resigned his professorship to practise law, which he is still doing, in Winchester, Va. He held for several years the office of county superintendent of schools. Mr. Wilson is greatly interested in educational movements, and on more than one occasion his admirable addresses at Associational meetings have stimulated his hearers to a greater zeal in their behalf.

Wilson, Rev. William V., was born Nov. 18, 1811, in Hunterdon Co., N. J. Early he developed a great inclination and aptitude for study; was converted when about eighteen, and joined the church at Sandy Ridge in 1831. He had a thorough education, covering a number of years, under such men as H. K. Green and Samuel Aaron; entered Princeton Theological Seminary in 1838, the certificate of Mr. Aaron being considered equivalent to a college diploma. After pursuing the full course he became a missionary of the New Jersey Baptist State Convention in Middlesex County. He was for a little time pastor at Keyport and at the Second Middletown Church. In 1854 he became pastor of the Port Monmouth Baptist church, where for more than a quarter of a century he has edified the people of God. Mr. Wilson is treasurer of the Education Society. With preaching talents he combines an unusual aptitude for business, and he has freely and successfully used this for the cause of God. He succeeded in the almost impossible work of extricating Peddie Institute from its financial difficulties, and has frequently by his counsels and labors helped to raise money needed for the carrying on of benevolent operations. His published sermon on giving, and other discourses and writings, have stirred up the people to greater consecration of their means to God and larger efforts to spread the gospel.

Winchell, Rev. James Manning, so well known, especially in New England, as the compiler of "Watts's Psalms and Hymns, with a Supplement," in general use in the Baptist churches before the introduction of the "Psalmist," was born at North East, Dutchess Co., N. Y., Sept. 8, 1791. He became a Christian in early life. For three years he was a student in Union College. The last year of his college course he spent in Providence, and graduated from Brown University in 1812. While pursuing his regular studies in college he turned his attention to theology, and on graduating was licensed to preach by the Baptist church in North East. He supplied the church in Bristol, R. I., for a year, when he was called to Boston to the First Baptist church, where he was installed March 30, 1814, and was its pastor for six years. Dr. Neale says of him, "The favorable impressions made at first were deepened by acquaintance. No remarkable events or stirring scenes occurred during his ministry, and he never sought to create an artificial excitement. No large additions were made at any one time. Neither was there a period of dearth, but a steady and continuous advance in religious knowledge and spiritual life." Mr. Winchell fell a victim to New England's fatal malady, consumption. His death took place Feb. 22, 1820. One who knew him well while he was the pastor of the First church in Boston says of him, "Young Winchell's manner in the pulpit approached more nearly to that of Summerfield, that youthful prodigy of loveliness, than any other that I have ever witnessed. There was the same winning simplicity and naturalness in the one as in the other." Dying at the early age of twenty-nine, he left behind him a memory full of the sweetest fragrance.

Winebrennarians.—See CHURCH OF GOD.

Wingate, W. M., D.D.—This best of men was born in Darlington, S. C., July 28, 1828; was baptized by Dr. J. O. B. Dargan; graduated at Wake Forest College in 1849; studied theology for two years at Furman Institute, S. C.; was agent of Wake Forest College from 1852 to 1854, when he was chosen president, which position he held till his death, a period of twenty-five years. He received the honorary degree of D.D. from Columbian University, Washington, D. C., in 1867. He died of heart disease, Feb. 27, 1879.

He was an admirable college president, the

W. M. WINGATE, D.D.

ablest preacher the Baptists of North Carolina have yet had, and the sweetest saint the writer has ever known. The type of his piety was so exalted that it lifted him above the ordinary infirmities of even good men.

It was meet that such a life should be crowned by a beautiful and glorious death. His last day was the happiest of his life. All that day his face shone as did that of Moses when he came from the presence of God in the mount, and when the supreme hour came the glory of God overshadowed the chamber where the good man met his fate. Just before he breathed his last he seemed to be conversing with the Saviour as though he were personally present. "Oh, how delightful it is! I knew you would be with me when the time came, and I knew it would be sweet, but I did not know it would be so sweet as it is."

A fitting tribute was paid to his virtues in a splendid eulogy pronounced by the Rev. F. H. Ivey, one of his old pupils, at the commencement following his death, and his memory is still further honored in the Wingate Memorial Hall, a large and handsome chapel erected by his friends during the past year.

Winkler, Edwin Theodore, D.D., was born in Savannah, Ga., Nov. 13, 1823; prepared for college in Chatham Academy of his own city; entered Brown University in 1839; graduated in 1843, and the same year entered Newton Theological Seminary; in 1845 was assistant editor of the *Christian Index;* supplied the pulpit of the church in Columbus, Ga., for six months; in 1846 became pastor at Albany, Ga., where he remained until called to Gallisonville, S. C.; in 1852 became corresponding secretary of the Southern Baptist Publication Society, in Charleston, and editor of the *Southern Baptist;* in 1854 called to the First Baptist church in Charleston, and, except during a somewhat lengthy chaplaincy in the Confederate army, he remained pastor in that city until called to Alabama, closing his pastorate there with the Citadel Square church, when he became, in 1872, pastor in the city of Marion. In 1874, when the Baptists of his newly-adopted State inaugurated the *Alabama Baptist*, he became editor-in-chief, a position which he still holds. He has been connected at times with other papers, North and South, as corresponding editor. With a national reputation, he has been frequently invited North and South to deliver sermons and addresses on important occasions. Several of these addresses were called for, and published in permanent form. Of these, we may mention his Centennial address, in 1876, be-

EDWIN THEODORE WINKLER, D.D.

fore the Newton Theological Seminary, and his sermon before the American Baptist Home Mission Society, on the education of the colored ministry, in 1871. He is the author of a catechism for the oral instruction of the colored people, which has been extensively used; of an essay on "The Spirit of Missions, the Spirit of Christ;" of an essay on "The Sphere of the Ministry;" of a preface to the "Sacred Lute," a hymn-book, at the request of the Southern Baptist Publication Society. The degree of Doctor of Divinity was conferred on him in 1858 by Furman University. He twice declined calls to a professorship in the Southern Baptist Theological Seminary.

Dr. Winkler is distinguished for scholarly accuracy, broad culture, clear and forcible style, courtly and dignified personal bearing, and the most elegant language and the finest literary allusions. He is *always ready;* this makes him one of the best and safest speakers in the whole country. His grandfather was a distinguished officer under Gen. Marion in the Revolutionary war.

Winks, Joseph F., was born at Gainsborough, Lincolnshire, England, on Dec. 12, 1792. He was converted in his youth. In his family Bible he made the following record: "Begotten again unto a lively hope through the resurrection of Jesus Christ from the dead about 1812, but not baptized until Sept. 29, 1823." He gave himself with great ardor to the establishment of Sunday-schools in the neighborhood, and was called to the pastorate of the small General Baptist church at Killingholme. Subsequently he labored at Melbourne, Derbyshire, at Loughborough, and finally at Leicester, where he spent the remainder of his life. The establishment and promotion of denominational periodicals and of cheap evangelical literature engrossed his energies for nearly forty years. For several years he edited five monthly magazines, the *Baptist Reporter,* the *Children's Magazine,* the *Christian Pioneer,* the *Baptist Youths' Magazine,* and the *Picture Magazine.* He compiled a number of Sunday-school books, and published many pamphlets and tracts on baptism, which had a wide circulation and a great influence. He was a fearless and unswerving friend of civil and religious freedom, and stood in the front of every local conflict for the cause. His life was full of work. Whilst an attached member of the New Connection of General Baptists, his enthusiastic and enterprising advocacy of Scripture baptism won for him the esteem of all earnest Baptists.

He was ever active and untiring in evangelistic labors of all kinds; he was emphatically "ready to every good work." He died May 28, 1866, aged seventy-three.

Winston, Prof. Charles H., was born in Richmond, Va. His father was Peter Winston, a deacon in the First Baptist church. In 1855 he graduated at Hampden Sidney College, and was at once appointed tutor and assistant professor. In 1858 he took the degree of Master of Arts at the University of Virginia, and was immediately elected Professor of Ancient Languages in Transylvania University. In 1859 he was elected a professor in Richmond Female Institute, and the next year was made president, which position he held until 1873, when he was elected Professor of Physics in Richmond College.

During the war, the exercises in the institute being temporarily suspended, Prof. Winston was in the service of the nitre bureau of the Confederate States, at Charlotte, N. C., making sulphuric acid. By his energy, skill, and fertility of resource he won the approbation of the bureau and of the government.

The war ending, he resumed his life-work, for which he is pre-eminently fitted. As a teacher, he is patient and enthusiastic, with marvelous capacity for simplifying and making clear to the dull or mediocre intellect. Like Procter, Huxley, and other scientists, he has delivered public lectures, illustrated by diagrams and experiments, popularizing abstruse subjects, and awakening much interest and enthusiasm. He has a quick, fertile, and suggestive mind, never satisfied with superficial or first views, but going to the "bottom of things." As a counselor or committee-man, Prof. Winston is invaluable, as preventing hasty and inconsiderate action, and compelling a consideration of the "other side" of a proposition.

Having been president of the City Sunday-School Association, he takes deep interest in the Sunday-school work, and his power to interest and instruct children is often called into requisition. As Professor of Physics, he has given his department prominence and popularity in the college and with the public, and at the South is regarded as one of the leading scientists.

Winston, Rev. Meriwether, was born in Richmond, Va., in 1828; educated at Madison University; ordained pastor of the church in Charlottesville, Va.; subsequently was pastor in New York City, in Norfolk, Va., in Savannah, Ga., and in Philadelphia, Pa. He returned to the South on the breaking out of the war, and entered the heavenly rest in 1866. He was a genial, brotherly minister, an eloquent preacher, and a Christain whose graces secured the love of all that knew him.

Winter, John, M.D., was born in Wellington, England, in July, 1794. After graduating in theology from Bradford Seminary, he emigrated to America in 1822, and settled in Pittsburgh, Pa. Here for some time he taught a school, and served as pastor of the First Baptist church. During sixty years of a very active and successful ministry his labors were chiefly in the western part of the State. For a few years he preached in Illinois, where two sons survive him. He died Nov. 5, 1878, in his eighty-fifth year, after an illness of only three days, in Sharon, Mercer Co., Pa.

His energy was more than ordinary, and his character was of a most positive type, blended with childlike simplicity and tenderness of heart. His clearness of thought was remarkable. These traits made him just the man needed for his day. Hence, in his struggles with the errors of Alexander Campbell, he performed pre-eminent service, and checked materially the spread of error, saving many churches from being overwhelmed and destroyed. His crowning glory was his great success in winning souls to Christ. To the last of an honored and useful life he would not allow his mind to remain inactive, but kept himself well informed in general and theological learning. Hence he was always listened to with marked interest, and continued fresh and green until he closed his earthly labors.

Dr. Winter was twice married. His second wife survives him, and is the mother of two prominent Baptist ministers,—Rev. J. D. Herr, D.D., of New York, and Rev. A. J. Bonsall, of Rochester, Pa. A daughter is also married to Rev. David Williams, of Lewisburg, Pa., while a daughter of Dr. Winter is united in marriage to Judge Justin Miller, of the Supreme Court of the United States.

Winter, Thomas, D.D., son of William and Sarah D. Winter, was born in the ancient borough of Tewkesbury, Gloucestershire, England, Feb. 26, 1798. After attending the best schools which the place afforded, he was put to the business of his father; was baptized May 7, 1815, by Rev. Daniel Trotman; was soon after engaged in labor at the village stations of the church until the summer of 1819, when, with a small company of friends, he came to the United States, landing in New York, October 19. He proceeded at once to Philadelphia, and united with the Sansom Street (Fifth) church. He established a school for young ladies at Burlington, N. J., while Rev. J. H. Kennard was pastor there; was invited to settle with the church at Lyon's Farms, N. J., and was there ordained, Revs. Thomas Brown, of Scotch Plains, and David Jones, then of Newark, and others officiating. In the summer of 1826 he accepted a call to the church at North East, N. Y., where he remained until August, 1839. He then received a call to the neighboring church at Amenia, but declined in favor of a call from the Roxborough church, Philadelphia, where he labored until October, 1863. He then yielded to the earnest request of his former charge, and returned to North East, N. Y., but was unable to remain on account of the climate. He returned to Philadelphia, and in 1865 removed his residence and membership to Roxborough, where he still lives, full of years and honors, amid the homes and hearts of those who cherish his former ministrations in grateful remembrance. He received the degree of D.D. in 1860 from the university at Lewisburg, Pa. He was for many years the secretary of the Board of Trustees of the Philadelphia Baptist Association; was moderator in 1862, and in that year preached the doctrinal sermon on "The Government of God." He is a stanch Baptist, and an able expounder of Bible doctrines. He is quick to detect what he deems heresy, and is vigorous and pungent in his defense of the truth. The years of his life have been many, his labors have been abundant; he has kept the faith, the crown is waiting.

Winters, A. C., A.M., son of Daniel and Mary Winters, was born in Barrington, N. Y., Sept. 20, 1835. He graduated from Rochester University in 1865. The same year was married to Miss Hattie M. Payne, of Hamilton, N. Y. They both obtained positions in the public schools in Nashville, Tenn. Here they remained two years, when they went to Europe, and spent two years attending lectures, and studying language and history in various universities. In 1870 he was elected superintendent of the public schools in Wellsborough, Pa. On the opening of Cook Academy, at Havana, N. Y., in 1873, he became Professor of Mathematics, and in 1875 the principal of the institution, a position which he still holds. Mrs. Winters is teacher of German and French in the academy.

Wisconsin Baptist State Convention was organized at Delavan in July, 1844. Its object was to preach the gospel and plant churches in all the Territory of Wisconsin. The ministers present at the organization were Rev. Henry Topping, Rev. Peter Conrad, Rev. A. B. Winchell, Rev. Benjamin Pierce, Rev. E. M. Underwood, and several others. Peter Conrad and A. B. Winchell were its first itinerant missionaries. For some time previous to this the American Baptist Home Mission Society had sustained missionaries in the Territory and aided the feeble churches. Rev. A. Miner was at this time the general missionary of the American Baptist Home Mission Society. At this early day there seemed to be wide differences among these missionary pioneers in regard to the subject of slavery and missionary societies. The American Baptist Home Mission Society and the American Baptist Missionary Union were supposed to be in affiliation with slavery. Unfortunately, these differences were made prominent at the very first meeting of this body. As the result, it perished in the midst of unhappy strife at its second anniversary.

On the 9th of July, 1846, at East Troy, a new organization was effected. Among the brethren known to be present at this meeting were James Delaney, Lewis Raymond, A. Miner, J. W. Fish, P. Conrad, Silas Tucker, H. W. Reed, N. Clinton, Deacon Wm. H. Byron, and Hon. Charles Burchard. The meeting at which the organization was effected was held in a grove of oaks in the outskirts of the village under the open sky. Deacon William H.

Byron in fervent prayer committed the object of the meeting to the God of missions. Rev. Lewis Raymond was elected moderator, and Rev. Peter Conrad clerk. Wm. H. Byron was chosen president, and H. W. Reed, of Whitewater, secretary. The body thus organized was called "The Wisconsin Baptist General Association," and was auxiliary to the American Baptist Home Mission Society.

The work of the Convention has been to foster the feeble churches of the State, and plant churches in the destitute portions. Its relations with the American Baptist Home Mission Society have been of the most fraternal character, and for many years the two organizations co-operated in the missionary work of the State. The Convention has made in the efforts of thirty-four years, either alone or in co-operation with the American Baptist Home Mission Society, 600 missionary appointments, and through the general and local missionaries has organized more than 100 churches, and extended aid to almost every Baptist church in the State. In this work it has expended about $200,000. Its missionaries have baptized more than 2000 converts. It has fostered the work of the American Baptist Missionary Union and that of the American Baptist Publication Society, and given sympathy to the educational work of the State; and now has its outposts along the lines of new railroads and far out in the newer portions of the State. The Convention is now (1880) better prepared for efficient work than ever before. Rev. D. E. Halteman is the president, M. G. Hodge, D.D., president of the board, and Rev. A. R. Medbury the efficient superintendent and corresponding secretary.

Wisconsin, Baptists of.—The first Baptist minister who preached the gospel in Wisconsin was Rev. James Griffin, who died in Pewaukee in 1876. He organized the first Baptist church in the Territory in Milwaukee in 1837. The city now numbering 150,000 inhabitants was then a small village. Mr. Griffin was its first pastor. Rev. Peter Conrad, then just graduated from Hamilton Theological Institution, was settled as pastor in 1841. Rev. Lewis Raymond was settled in 1843. The church, after passing through some vicissitudes, is now thoroughly established, with Dr. M. G. Hodge as pastor. There are two other American Baptist churches in the city,—the Spring Street and the South,—also two German churches.

The second church in the Territory was organized by Rev. Benjamin Pierce, in 1837, at Rochester, Racine Co., the organization dating a few months later than that of Milwaukee. Rev. Isaac T. Hinton, the first Baptist missionary sent by the American Baptist Home Mission Society to Chicago, was present and assisted in the organization. The church was disbanded several years ago.

The third church organized in the Territory was the church in Delavan. The place was settled by two brothers,—Baptists,—Henry and Samuel Phœnix, of Perry, N. Y. The first sermon preached in the place was by Benjamin Pierce to an audience of eleven persons, in the autumn of 1836. The Baptist church was organized in the autumn of 1839, with seventeen members. Rev. Henry Topping was the first pastor. During his pastorate of five years the church grew from 17 to 139 members. The first meeting-house erected in the Territory was built by this church in 1840.

The fourth church organized was that of Prairieville (now Waukesha), in the autumn of 1839, a little later than that of Delavan. It was gathered and organized by the Rev. Richard Griffin, who was its first pastor. Five years after its organization it reported 158 members. Churches were soon after organized at Southport, Sheboygan, and Lisbon.

The first Association in the Territory was formed at Prairieville in October, 1839, and consisted of seven churches,—Rochester, Southport, Milwaukee, Delavan, Lisbon, Sheboygan, and Jefferson. The name given to the Association was the Wisconsin Central. The number of members is not stated in the minutes. Rev. Benjamin Pierce was moderator, and P. M. Hollister clerk. The only minister present at this meeting besides the moderator was Rev. Richard Griffin. The next session of the Association was held the following year at Southport. At the third meeting of this body, held at Delavan in 1841, and in the first Baptist meeting-house erected in the Territory, thirteen churches were reported and eight ministers. In 1843 the churches had increased to twenty, and there were fourteen ordained ministers, several licentiates, and a membership of between 600 and 700. Among the ministers present were Griffin, Topping, Lake, Conrad, Miner, Carr, and Winchell. So rapid was the growth of this body that at its seventh anniversary it reported more than thirty churches with settled pastors, and 1500 communicants.

Milwaukee Association.—Out of this mother of Associations the Milwaukee Association was organized, Sept. 9, 1846, at Sun Prairie. Rev. T. L. Pillsbury preached the opening sermon. Rev. Peter Conrad was the moderator, and Rev. H. W. Read the clerk. Sixteen churches were represented, of which twelve reported settled pastors, with the regular preaching of the gospel. The total membership of the churches was 620.

Walworth Association.—June 24, 1846, the Walworth Association was organized at Whitewater. Rev. P. W. Lake was the moderator, and Rev. Spencer Carr clerk. Rev. J. H. Dudley preached the opening sermon. Fourteen churches composed the organization. There were ten pastors and a total membership of 889.

Racine Association.—Sept. 24, 1846, the Racine Association was organized at Racine. Rev. Silas Tucker was the moderator, and Charles S. Wright clerk. Eight churches, with eight ministers, entered the Association. A total membership of 414 was reported.

The above Associations having been formed from the churches of the Wisconsin Association, and occupying the field of the mother Association, that body held its last meeting with the Baptist church at Delavan, June 24, 1845. Roswell Cheeney preached the introductory sermon. Lewis Raymond was the moderator, and Henry Topping the clerk.

Thus it appears that in eight years after the organization of the first Baptist church in the Territory there were thirty-six churches organized, with a membership of nearly 2000, and thirty pastors.

Early Educational Movements.—The first meeting for educational purposes in the State was held at Beloit, Nov. 5 and 6, 1851. Of this meeting Nathaniel Crosby, of Janesville, was chairman, and J. W. Fish, of Geneva, was clerk. Among those present were Ichabod Clark, of Rockford, Ill.; Charles Hill Roe, D.D., then just arrived from England, and afterwards the widely-known pastor of the First Baptist church of Belvidere, Ill.; James Schofield, the father of Gen. Schofield, of the U. S. army, and Dr. James V. Schofield, of St. Louis, who was then pastor of the Baptist church in Freeport, Ill.; Lewis Raymond, A. J. Joslyn, Prof. S. S. Whitman, and James Delaney. Profs. Stone and Graves, of Kalamazoo Literary and Theological Institute, Mich., were present, and proposed to these brethren in Wisconsin and Northern Illinois co-operation with the brethren in Michigan in the educational work of the State, by sending students to their school at Kalamazoo, and furnishing their quota of means for its support. The plan of co-operation, after long and mature consideration, was not agreed to. The institution at Kalamazoo was, however, commended to the churches of the State and to young men seeking theological instruction.

The following resolutions were adopted:

I. That this Convention proceed to form an education society, which shall embrace the Baptists of the Northwest, and secure, as far as practicable, the co-operation of brethren in Northern Illinois, Wisconsin, Iowa, and Minnesota.

II. That a committee be appointed to fix upon the location for a literary and theological institution; that that committee be authorized to receive propositions from such places as may desire the institution, and from a survey of the comparative advantages decide, reporting their decision to a future meeting of the Education Society, which shall confirm or annul it.

Articles of constitution were adopted, and officers and a board of directors elected. Elisha Tucker, D.D., was elected president, and Rev. Jirah D. Cole, D.D., corresponding secretary. Among the names of members of the board the following appeared: Rev. L. W. Lawrence, Rev. O. J. Dearborn, George Haskell, D.D., and Rev. H. G. Weston, then pastor of the First Baptist church in Peoria, Ill.

The board at once issued an address to the churches of the Northwest. In giving their reasons for the establishment of a theological seminary in the Northwest, they named among others (1) the great and rapid growth of the Northwest, (2) the hundreds of churches destitute of pastors, (3) the retention, in the East, of the best Western men educated in Eastern colleges and seminaries, (4) the importance of having the pastors of Western churches educated in Western institutions, (5) and the reflex influence upon the churches themselves. It is believed that this was the first Educational Convention of any considerable importance held in the Northwest. The design was to establish a theological school, centrally located, for the States of Illinois, Wisconsin, and Iowa. It originated with Wisconsin Baptists, and Beloit was expected to be the site of the institution; and, although these hopes were not fully realized, the movement inaugurated at this Convention had an important bearing in educating public sentiment and preparing the way for the establishment of the theological seminary at Chicago fifteen years later.

Statistics.—There are in the State 11 English-speaking Associations, containing 165 churches, with a total membership of 10,206. Of this number, 1806 are non-resident members. There are in the State 24 foreign-speaking churches, with a membership of 1200, and adding the membership of unassociated churches, the grand total of Baptists in Wisconsin is 12,000. But 91 of the 165 churches have pastors, and of these 91 some have the pastor but a part of the time. Many of the churches are small and the membership much scattered. In 1875, according to the State census, the population of the State was 1,236,000, giving 23 inhabitants to the square mile. This population is very unequally distributed over the 54,000 square miles of territory. The two northern Associations—the Central and the St. Croix—extend over more than half the area, and yet contain less than one-seventh of the population of the State, they having less than 6 inhabitants to the square mile, while the rest of the State has an average of 44 to the square mile,—the densest population being in the Lake Shore Association, which has 85 inhabitants to the square mile. These two Associations—the Central and the St. Croix—contain respectively 14,000 and 16,000 square miles, while the Walworth Association contains only 700 square miles.

In population the Lake Shore Association, with 330,000 inhabitants, is the largest, and Walworth, with 32,000, the smallest. The total number of members of our associated churches is a little less than one per cent. of the population, there being one Baptist to 108 inhabitants. The smallest proportion of Baptists is in the Dane Association (one to 250 persons), and the largest proportion is in the Walworth Association (one to 26), and in the Janesville Association (one to 43 persons). Next to the Dane the Lake Shore Association has the smallest proportion of Baptists (one to 160 persons). In the city of Milwaukee the Baptists are very few, being in proportion of one Baptist to 190 of population, but the fourteen other cities having a population of over 5000 each will average one Baptist to 64 inhabitants, showing that we are stronger in proportion in the cities than in the country. The churches average 63 members. But one church in the State reports a membership of over 400,—that of Delavan,—and but two churches report a membership of 300 and less than 400. The churches of Janesville and Racine, and the great majority of the 165 churches, have less than 100 members.

Sunday-schools.—There are in the State 149 Sunday-schools, with 1565 officers and teachers, and 10,540 scholars, and an average attendance last year of 8246. Thirty-two churches are without Sunday-schools. There are 22 mission Sunday-schools.

Mission Circles.—There are 61 foreign mission circles and 18 mission bands in the State. These circles raised last year $1500. Of our 165 churches, 104 have no circles. The number of home mission circles cannot be ascertained, as the work of organizing them has but just commenced in the State.

Ministers and Pastors.—There are in the State 197 ordained ministers. Of these, 97 are pastors. One hundred of our ordained ministers are without fields of labor, although 68 of our churches are without pastors, and scores of cities, towns, and villages in the State are without Baptist churches.

Church Property.—The value of the church property is in the aggregate about $500,000. On this property there is an indebtedness of $30,000. The largest and finest Baptist meeting-house in the State is that of the church in Janesville, erected in 1868, at a cost of $45,000. The First church in Milwaukee, First in Oshkosh, Racine, La Crosse, and Beloit have good houses of worship. The church at Delavan is engaged in building a fine house.

Church Expenses and Benevolence.—The churches of the State raised last year for local church expenses $116,727.34, and for Christian benevolence $12,378.67, a grand total of $129,106.01, an average for each resident member of $11.73 for local church expenses and $1.90 for Christian benevolence, a total average of $13.63 per member.

Comparisons.—How Baptists stand in proportion to the population in other States may be ascertained by a glance at the following table, which was prepared by Maj. H. M. Robert, of the U. S. army, and published in the minutes of the Wisconsin State Convention for 1877-78, and I am indebted to his kindness for its use here:

	Population. 1877.	Baptists. 1877.	Population to 1 Baptist.
Wisconsin	1,276,000	12,600	101
Northern States	30,000,000	600,000	50
Southern States	16,700,000	1,400,000	12
United States	46,700,000	2,000,000	23

Foreign Population.—The proportion of foreigners to Americans is greater in Wisconsin than any other State. The proportion of foreigners in the Northern States and in the Southern is very disproportionate, it being nearly five times as great in the Northern States as in the Southern States. Of the Northern States, the greatest proportion of foreigners is in Wisconsin, where it is sixty-four per cent., or two-thirds of the entire population. The following table will give a clear view of the proportion of foreigners to the English-speaking population. For a population of 1,236,000 we should have the following figures:

Americans			446,000
Foreigners	{ English-speaking, 250,000 Foreign-speaking, 540,000 }		790,000
Germans	350,000	Belgians	10,000
Norwegians	87,000	Austrians	10,000
Bohemians	23,000	Swedes	6,000
Hollanders	13,000	French	6,000
Swiss	13,000	All other foreigners	11,000
Danes	11,000		

Wisconsin has three and one-quarter times as many foreigners, or five times as many foreign-speaking foreigners, as the average throughout the Northern States. Omitting the Border States of Maryland and Missouri, Wisconsin has forty times as many foreigners to one thousand Americans as the Southern States. If Wisconsin were to lose 550,000 of her foreign population, she would then have just her share of foreigners compared with the other Northern States.

These facts must be known in order to understand Wisconsin as a mission field. These hundreds of thousands of foreigners are here without evangelical religion, and even without evangelical belief. Every form of unbelief is industriously at work to mould and control these rising communities. Romanism, infidelity, and a subtle liberalism are uniting their forces in almost superhuman effort to shape the foundation of things. There is no more important mission field on the American continent than Wisconsin, and, unless Christians in the older States bestir themselves, these growing centres of population and all sorts of power will crystallize into strongholds of Satan. These facts, too, will explain the feeble condition and slow growth of our churches during the last fifteen years. They are planted right in the centres of this infidelity, and surrounded by an almost impregnable opposition.

Witt, Daniel, D.D., was born in Bedford Co., Va., Nov. 8, 1801. His parents were both exemplary Christians. His health was quite frail all through life, and very few of his friends supposed that he could live any great length of time. His quickening into a new life began in August, 1821, during what was at that time called a "Section meeting," held at Hatcher's meeting-house. Here began that attachment between himself and the Rev. Dr. Jeter which continued unbroken until Mr. Witt's death. For many weeks he continued in deep anguish of spirit; but on the 21st of October, 1821, he was enabled to rejoice in a good hope, through grace; and in December of the same year he was baptized. He immediately began to take part in the neighborhood prayer-meetings and in publicly addressing the impenitent. His first sermon was preached on Feb. 11, 1822, and he was licensed April 13 of the same year. He soon traveled through the counties of Henry, Patrick, Pittsylvania, and Campbell, preaching continually the gospel, and with marked success. In the winter of 1822-23 he visited Richmond, and preached to the congregations there with great acceptance; soon after he made another visit, and formed the acquaintance of some of the most prominent ministers of Lower Virginia, among them Rice, Semple, Broaddus, Baptist, and Kerr. On the formation of the General Association in 1823, Dr. Witt and his friend Dr. Jeter were appointed its first missionaries, and the field assigned them embraced the counties of Henry, Patrick, Montgomery, Grayson, Giles, Wythe, Monroe, Greenbrier, Pocahontas, Alleghany, Bath, Rockbridge, and Botetourt, throughout the whole extent of which there were but a few feeble Baptist churches, while at the same time there was great spiritual darkness, and a bitterly-developing anti-missionary spirit. They preached everywhere and continually, and were the instruments of doing much good. This being rather an exploring trip than a permanent missionary engagement, they passed into and through the southeastern portions of the State, and thence to King and Queen, where they were to make their report to the board of the General Association at its session in the fall. Mr. Witt remained with Dr. Semple for a few months after the meeting of the board, making some preparation with him for wider usefulness in his work. Still acting as missionary, he passed to Williamsburg, which he made his headquarters, and preached with great success both there and in the adjoining counties. After the winter of 1823-24 he returned to his home in Bedford, and, still under the direction of the board, continued his labors in the Valley of Virginia.

Near the close of the year 1824 he removed to Charlotte, to assist the Rev. A. W. Clopton in his interesting field of labor there. The relation thus formed was of great benefit to Mr. Witt, as he enjoyed the instructions of one who had received a collegiate education, and who owned a larger library, perhaps, than any other Baptist minister in the State, and who at the same time was "a diligent student, a sound preacher, an indefatigable laborer, and one of the most devotedly pious men." His preaching here was very attractive, drawing large congregations, and, so far as can be learned, successful. Here also, in 1825, he had a severe attack of sickness, which brought him almost to the grave. After leaving Charlotte he went to Prince Edward County, and having organized the Sharon church at Sandy River, he became its pastor, and continued in that relation, highly honored and loved, for forty-five years, until his death. During this long period his church was blessed with frequent revivals; large numbers were added, not only to his own church, but also to others, and it is said that there were very few persons in the church at any particular time that were not converted. Dr. Witt, while pastor of the Sharon church, was also occasionally pastor of other churches, such as Jamestown, in Cumberland; Union, in Prince Edward; and Lebanon, in Nottoway. It is thought that he baptized during his long career as a minister at least 2500 persons. In all related duties outside the pulpit Dr. Witt was punctual and efficient. In Associational meetings he was genial in manner, dignified in bearing, weighty in counsel, and ready to perform any service assigned him. Sickness and death, at different times, in the household which he so much loved saddened the latter days of this good man's life, though no more submissive spirit ever manifested itself in like circumstances than that which characterized the subject of this sketch. He died Nov. 15, 1871, in his seventy-first year, full of honors, and greatly beloved by all who knew him.

As a man, his most intimate friend has said that he, "of all the active men whom he had known, was the most *faultless.*" He was marked for his genuine humility. He was very disinterested. His piety was beautiful and attractive. As a preacher, he could have no higher encomium than this, "His sermons were full of Christ. He preached him first, him last, him all the time. With Witt the theme never grew old, never lost its interest or its power, and was never exhausted. To the last day of his life he could find something new to preach about Christ."

Witt, Jesse, was born in Virginia. After his conversion he preached with marked success in churches in the region between Petersburg and Lynchburg; removed to Texas about 1851; labored in Eastern Texas with great ability and signal success. In natural force he was in no respect inferior to his brother, Daniel Witt, the early companion and life-long friend of Jeremiah B. Jeter. He rarely failed to produce a profound impression by his perspicuous, earnest, and fervent preaching. He died when about fifty years of age, a short time before the civil war.

Wolfe, Hon. C. S., was born at Lewisburg, Pa., April 6, 1845. He graduated at the university at Lewisburg in 1866, and in Harvard Law-School in July, 1868. He was admitted to Union County bar at the September term of 1868. He was a member of the Lewisburg school board from 1871 to 1873. He has been a member of the Pennsylvania house of representatives since 1873.

Mr. Wolfe is one of the most talented young men in the State. He is a power in the Legislature. His integrity, his indignation against corruption, his fearless courage, his ready use of weighty arguments, have given him a remarkable prominence in a body where there are many men of ability and of mature years. His constituents admire him, and the enemies of corruption in State affairs applaud him. The people of his State regard him as one whose name and influence will not be long confined to Pennsylvania.

Mr. Wolfe is an honored member of the Baptist church of Lewisburg, and since 1875 a member of the board of trustees of the university at that place.

Wolverton, Rev. John, was born about 1775, of New Jersey parentage. But little is known of his earlier life. We find him as a licentiate in the Shamokin Baptist church, Pa., in 1807; he was ordained in 1811. He died May 20, 1822. He served the church with much acceptance and usefulness for fifteen years.

Womack, B. R., D.D., was born Dec. 23, 1846. His parents were Abner C. Womack and Isabella Blackburn Patton. His birthplace was near Bellefonte, Jackson Co., Ala. In early life he was a great reader of all sorts of books, and especially of the New Testament. The Saviour found him and revealed his love in his heart, after which he was baptized, in 1865, at Kyle's Spring, Jackson Co., Ala., where service was sustained by an "arm" of Friendship Baptist church. Soon after he began to pray and speak in public, when a revival descended from the throne of the heavenly grace and scores of his irreligious friends were converted to God, and a church was organized at Kyle's Springs, which he named Bethel.

Determined to secure an education, of which he had a very exalted opinion, and to the acquisition of which he was greatly encouraged by the words in Webster's old spelling-book, "Assiduous study will accomplish anything within human power,"

B. R. WOMACK, D.D.

he entered Union University, Murfreesborough, Tenn., in 1868, where he remained four years, delivering the valedictory in 1872. He declined a professorship in Latin which was offered to him. He entered the Southern Baptist Theological Seminary the same year, and remained in it three sessions, and graduated in all the schools except one. He then entered the theological seminary at Chicago, and graduated as a post-graduate in 1875-76, giving his whole time to ecclesiastical history and philosophy. This last period of study he regarded as the most profitable of his life.

He accepted the pastorate of the Broad Street church of Augusta, Ga., where he labored eighteen months. In October, 1877, he took charge of the First Baptist church of Memphis, Tenn., but, through failing health, resigned in December, 1879, and became editor of the *Baptist Reflector*, of Nashville, Tenn., in connection with the Rev. J. B. Cheves. The paper at the time was in a very low condition, but it speedily received new life, and became a power in Tennessee.

Mr. Womack early in this year yielded to the urgent request of the Baptists of Arkansas to take charge of the *Arkansas Evangel*, with Rev. J. B. Searcy as associate editor, in Southeastern Arkansas. The paper is succeeding admirably. He has recently received the degree of Doctor of Divinity.

Dr. Womack is endowed with a fine intellect, superior attainments, great piety, and enduring perseverance. If his life is spared he will perform effective service for the Saviour and for the Baptist denomination which he instituted, and of which he was the head.

Woman's Baptist (Foreign) Missionary Society.—The formation of women into separate organizations for the promotion of the cause of foreign missions is a thing of comparatively recent date. The leading evangelical denominations in this country have such women's societies in connection with their general missionary societies. Many earnest workers among the women of the Baptist churches felt, as far back as 1869 and 1870, that the time had come for them to organize such societies. In January, 1871, there came from Mrs. Carpenter, of the Bassein Mission, a most touching appeal for the formation of women's societies, which should be auxiliary to the Missionary Union. The first movement towards an answer to this appeal was made in Newton Centre by the meeting together of eleven ladies, members of the church in that place, on the 28th of February, 1871, to consult together about what could be done more effectually to reach heathen women through schools and Christian training. At the meeting a beginning was made by choosing officers, drafting a constitution, and preparing a circular to be presented to the churches, to interest the female members in the work of missions. A meeting of about 200 ladies was held at the Clarendon Street church, Boston, on the 3d of April, 1871, and the Woman's Baptist Missionary Society was formally organized, the purpose being distinctly avowed that it was to be auxiliary to the Union. The compensation of the female missionaries appointed by the society and the distribution of funds raised are left with the parent society. The amount raised during the first seven years of the existence of the society has been $193,448.92. The field of the home operations of the society is the New England and Middle States and the District of Columbia. The following missionaries have been appointed by the Union at the suggestion of the society, and their support has come from its treasury: Miss Kate F. Evans, Miss Cornelia H. Rand. The four following were already on the foreign field: Misses Haswell, Gage, Watson, and Adams. These ladies were the objects of the society's special care the first year of its existence. Miss Sarah B. Barrows was sent out the second year, and the support of Mrs. M. C. Douglass was assumed by the society. Two ladies were sent out the third year,—Miss Lawrence and Mrs. J. J. Longley. Misses Manning, Walling, and Stetson received appointments in the fourth year, and Miss Chace, Mrs. Estabrooks, Miss Sands, and Miss Kidder in the fifth year. Two appointments were made the sixth year,—Miss Sheldon and Miss Payne; and Misses Bromley, McAllister, Rathbun, and Day the last year. Some other female missionaries in the foreign field have also received aid from this society. During the last year Misses Batson and Russell were sent out. It has been felt that it is the special work of the society to look after the education of females. It labors in entire harmony with the Missionary Union, and is its most valuable and reliable helper. The society was incorporated by the Legislature of Massachusetts in October, 1874. Its present officers are Mrs. Gardner Colby, President; Mrs. J. N. Murdoch, Vice-President; Miss S. C. Durfee, Clerk; Mrs. Alvah Hovey, Corresponding Secretary; Miss Mary E. Clarke, Treasurer and Assistant Corresponding Secretary. The receipts for 1880 were $46,178.32.

Woman's Baptist Missionary Society of the West.—The idea of a Baptist woman's organization, to co-operate with the Missionary Union in carrying the gospel, especially to heathen women, seems to have first been discussed in the West, at a farewell service held in Chicago in August, 1870, on the occasion of the departure of one of the missionaries of the Union to the field of his labor in Assam. The idea ripened into the formation of "The Woman's Baptist Missionary Society of the West" on the 9th of May, 1871, with Mrs. Robert Harris as President; Mrs. C. N. Holden, Vice-President; Mrs. C. F. Tolman, Corresponding Secretary; Mrs. A. M. Bacon, Recording Secretary; Mrs. S. M. Osgood, Treasurer; and an executive board of ladies chosen from different churches. The two societies, the one in the East and the other in the West, were formed within a few weeks of each other. They both announced the same object to be accomplished, and both are auxiliary to the Missionary Union, making the eastern boundary of the Ohio the dividing line between the two. The first lady who volunteered to go out under the auspices of the new society was Miss A. L. Stevens, of Wisconsin, who sailed for Burmah in November, 1871, and in a few weeks she was followed by Miss L. Peabody, of Virden, Ill. The first year's report showed that the treasurer had received $4244.69; that 131 auxiliary societies had been formed, and 30 life-members been made. The second year the income had increased to $6390.88. There were 247 auxiliary societies, 81 life-members, 6 missionaries, and 4 Bible women. The work of the Western Woman's Missionary Society has been from the beginning fruitful in the best results. Auxiliary societies have been formed all over the West. The income for last year (1880) was $19,386.11.

Women's Baptist Home Mission Society was organized at Chicago, Feb. 1, 1877, its object being the promotion of Christian evangelism in the homes of the freed people, the Indians, and the foreign population. Its principal officers at the first organization were: President, Mrs. J. N. Crouse, Chicago; Vice-Presidents, Mrs. E. Bacon, Springfield, Ill., Mrs. C. B. Blackall, Chicago; Recording Secretary, Miss Lizzie Goodman, Chicago; Corresponding Secretary, Mrs. C. Swift, Chicago; Treasurer, Miss Olivia Bryant, Chicago; Editor, Mrs. J. A. Smith. The fields at present occupied by the society are New Orleans, La., Newbern, N. C., Beaufort, S. C., Columbia, S. C., Richmond, Va., Raleigh, N. C., Live Oak, Fla., Selma, Ala., the Choctaw, Chickasaw, and Seminole nations in Indian Territory, with missions among the Scandinavians in Illinois and Minnesota. The receipts in money during the first year amounted to $4089.85; in goods, $2618.81. During the year 1879-80 the amounts were, respectively, cash, $9089.16; goods, $2551.81. The present officers are: President, Mrs. Crouse, with eighteen Vice-Presidents, in as many different States: Recording Secretary, Mrs. Wm. Mathews, Chicago; Corresponding Secretary, Mrs. Swift; Treasurer, Mrs. R. R. Donnelly. There is, besides, an executive board of eight ladies residing in Chicago, Mrs. J. S. Dickerson being chairman.

Wood, Rev. Jesse M., was born in Elbert Co., Ga., Oct. 14, 1815. His parents are of English descent, and came to Georgia from Virginia. They removed to Monroe County in 1835, where Jesse M. Wood received in early life the best educational advantages the county afforded. He entered Mercer University at Penfield, where he stood at the head of his classes while in the institution. He did not graduate on account of ill health. He received, however, a certificate of scholarship and moral standing. The degree of A.M. was bestowed on him by the trustees in the year 1842. After leaving Penfield he began to teach at Knoxville, in the academy at that place, but at the end of two and a half years was compelled to cease by failing health.

In 1839 he was hopefully converted, joined the church at Forsyth, and was licensed to preach. In 1843 he was ordained at the same place, and in a short time was actively engaged in ministerial labor, serving various churches in Middle and Southwestern Georgia until 1849, when he took up his residence at Cedar Town, Polk Co., and, besides taking charge of the church there, opened a high school for young ladies. This school was very prosperous, and developed into the Woodland Female College, and was placed first under the care of the Coosa Association, which bought the buildings from Mr. Wood, and then under the care of the Cherokee Baptist Convention.

Under Mr. Wood's pastorate the Cedar Town church was wondrously prosperous, four other churches being formed from it, and yet it still maintained a membership of several hundred.

Under such an accumulation of labors it is not wonderful that his health broke down completely, and that he was forced to suspend all labor and repair to the mountains of Virginia to recuperate in 1856. He continued with the Cedar Town church until 1860. In the mean time he had aided in the formation of the Cherokee Baptist Convention, and had assisted in establishing and building up the Cherokee Baptist College and the *Banner and Baptist*, of which, for several years, he was an editor.

The casualties of war left him with few or no resources when peace was restored, and he was compelled to rely for a support upon his ministerial labors. In 1870 he again entered upon an editorial life by taking an interest in the *Baptist Banner*, published at Cumming, Ga.

Rev. Jesse M. Wood is a man of strong character, with strong likes and dislikes. With great natural courage, he possesses a large amount of caution, which makes him reserved, and sometimes hesitating. He is a pious and faithful Christian; a man of strong convictions on all religious questions, and bold in their avowal. As a preacher, he is logical, eloquent, and effective, sometimes powerful. He has always been a strong advocate of missions and education, and at heart is a regular missionary Baptist, in full accord with the prevailing sentiments of the Georgia Baptists, but with views of his own on some points of mere management. His influence has been considerable in the denomination, and he has sought to use it, to the best of his judgment, for the advancement of Christ's cause.

Wood, Rev. Nathan, pastor of the Baptist church in Wyocena, Wis. A native of Rensselaer Co., N. Y., where he was born Aug. 6, 1807; passed his early childhood on his father's farm, in Augusta, Oneida Co., N. Y. He was converted in 1831, and baptized into the fellowship of the Baptist church in Augusta by Rev. P. P. Brown. Soon after his conversion he felt that God had called him to preach the gospel; but he resisted his convictions for several years, intending to give himself to business pursuits. In 1835 the question of his call to the ministry being so plain that he could not evade the duty without sinning against the clearest light, he entered Madison University, and graduated in 1839. In September of the same year he entered Hamilton Theological Seminary, and graduated in 1841. Before graduating from the seminary he received a call to the pastorate of the Baptist church in Georgetown, Madison Co., N. Y., which he accepted, and was ordained by this church Sept. 2, 1841. Here he remained five years. In 1846 he received and accepted a call to the Baptist church in Versailles, Cattaraugus Co., N. Y. In 1847 he came to Wyocena, Wis., and preached the first sermon ever delivered in the town. In September, 1848, he received and accepted a call to the pastorate of the Baptist church in Forestville, N. Y., and continued in this relation five years. In the autumn of 1853 he returned to Wyocena, Wis., and took charge of the Baptist church which had been formed in his absence. Having received a call from the church in Baraboo, Wis., he removed to that field in 1857, returning to Wyocena three years afterwards to resume his pastorate with that church, which continues to this day.

Mr. Wood's ministry has been attended with powerful revivals of religion. During his pastorate of three years at Baraboo he added over 100 to the church by baptism. Similar results, in a greater or less degree, have attended all his settlements. His aid to pastors in seasons of special religious interest has been invaluable and widely sought. His son, Prof. N. E. Wood, is the able principal of Wayland Academy.

Wood, Nathaniel Milton, D.D., was born in Camden, Me., May 24, 1822. He prepared for college in his native town; entered Waterville College in 1840, and graduated in 1844. He spent a year as tutor in the family of Gen. Browning, of Columbus, Miss. He became a student in the Western Theological Institute, where he had as teachers Rev. Drs. Pattison and E. G. Robinson. He was ordained as pastor of the Baptist church in Skowhegan, Me., and remained there until Jan. 1, 1852, when he removed to Waterville, where he labored for eight years as pastor of the First Baptist church. For the next six years he was pastor at Lewiston, and then, for nearly two years, he was at Thomaston. From Maine he removed, in May, 1868, to Upper Alton, Ill., where he was pastor of the church until March, 1872, at which time he was elected Professor of Systematic Theology in Shurtleff College. He had, for two years, given instruction in this department. At length his health failed him. He resigned his position, returned East, lived for a time in South Boston, preaching as opportunity presented, but growing weaker all the time, until he was forced to lay aside all ministerial work. He went back to his early home, where he was confined but a few weeks, and died Aug. 2, 1876.

Dr. Wood was successful as a minister of the gospel. "He was a strong, clear, and logical thinker and writer, and as a preacher was earnest, pungent, and convincing. Few hearers, intellectually well endowed or trained, failed to appreciate him as a sermonizer of great power." His own college conferred on him the degree of Doctor of Divinity in 1867. He was a member of the board of trustees of Colby University from 1862 to 1869, and of Shurtleff College from 1868 to 1874.

Wood, Prof. N. E., M.A., the principal of Wayland Academy, was born in Forestville, N. Y. His father is Rev. Nathan Wood, pastor of the Baptist church in Wyocena, Wis., one of the early pioneer Baptist ministers of the State. When four years of age, his father removed from the State of New York to Wyocena, Wis., where he passed his boyhood. At an early period in life he obtained a hope in Christ and united with the Baptist church of which his father was pastor. He completed his preparatory course of study at Wayland Academy. He entered the University of Chicago in 1868, and graduated with honor in the class of 1872. He pursued his theological studies at the Baptist Union Theological Seminary of Chicago, completing the full course, and graduating in 1875. He was ordained to the work of the ministry in September of the same year. Having offers to settle in well-established and prominent churches, Mr. Wood declined them, and began his ministry with a small Baptist mission in Chicago which had been under the fostering care of the Second Baptist church. Out of this mission he organized the Centennial Baptist church. During his pastorate of two years he received 200 persons into membership in the church, and the Sunday-school grew to 400. He secured the erection of a house of worship for the church at a cost of $13,000. On the foundation he thus laid in self-denial and prayer has grown one of the most prosperous churches in Chicago. In 1877, Mr. Wood resigned his highly-successful pastorate in Chicago to accept the position of principal of Wayland Academy, which had been tendered him by the board of trustees, and which he now holds. Mr. Wood had long cherished the desire to teach, believing that, next to the work of the ministry, Christian education was of the highest importance. June 27, 1873, Mr. Wood was married to Miss Alice Robinson Boise, daughter of Dr. J. R. Boise, the eminent Greek scholar, now a professor in the Chicago Theological Seminary, a lady of the highest culture, and an accomplished teacher of the Greek and modern languages. All her tastes and acquirements led her to the class-room and the profession of teaching. Doubtless his marriage with Miss Boise, combined with his own admirable qualifications for the work, led Mr. Wood to devote himself to the work of higher Christian education. Prof. Wood, while engaged in teaching, has not abandoned the ministry. He preaches frequently, with constantly-growing power. He is among the ablest preachers in the State, and as an educator has taken a high position. The institution over which he presides is pre-eminently Christian in its character, and the education imparted is most thorough.

Woodburn, B. F., D.D., was born March 23,

1832, in Crescent township, Alleghany Co., Pa. His grandparents emigrated from the north of Ireland, and his father settled fifteen miles below Pittsburgh about the time of Gen. Anthony Wayne's

B. F. WOODBURN, D.D.

expedition. A block-house on the opposite bank was then occupied by sixteen men to guard the settlers from Indian incursions. The son having received an English education, became in early life captain of various steamers plying on the Ohio, Mississippi, Arkansas, and Cumberland Rivers. From his earliest recollections he had occasional serious thoughts. These became more constant in the year 1857, and eventually brought him to a saving knowledge of Christ. On Jan. 10, 1858, he united with the Presbyterian Church, under the shadow of which he had grown up, and which was the home of his kindred. After a mental struggle he determined to prepare for the ministry, and entered Jefferson College in the Freshman year. Among fifty graduates he was awarded the first honor, and delivered the valedictory. Soon after uniting with the Presbyterian Church he had his infant daughter baptized; but while in college, when, according to the rules of the church, duty required the presentation of his second child for baptism, his mind became exercised on this point, and after reading, reflecting, and praying, he was surprised to find that the Word of God shed no light on the relation of baptized infants to the church. His child was not baptized. By degrees the truth of our principles became clear to his mind, and two years before his graduation he was in heart a Baptist; but there being no Baptist church in Canonsburg he did not unite with the Baptists until he was baptized by Rev. A. K. Bell, D.D., May 11, 1862, having then removed to Alleghany City.

After this important event he entered the Western Theological Seminary in Alleghany, receiving nothing but kindness from the Presbyterian professors, notwithstanding his known change of views. In 1865 he graduated, and in September was ordained pastor of the Mount Pleasant Baptist church. In this relation he continued four years, and then accepted the call of the Sandusky Street Baptist church, Alleghany City, made vacant by the resignation of Dr. Bell. This relation still continues, to the edification and comfort of the church and to its general prosperity. Lewisburg at its commencement in 1881 conferred the degree of Doctor of Divinity on Mr. Woodburn. Dr. Woodburn is among the strong men of the Baptists in Pennsylvania.

Woodfin, A. B., D.D., now pastor of the First church of Montgomery, Ala., is one of the most amiable and successful Baptist ministers in the South. He was born in Richmond, Va., and educated at Richmond College. He studied divinity at the Southern Baptist Theological Seminary. In October, 1862, he was ordained to the ministry, and took charge of Muddy Creek church, Powhatan Co., Va., one of the oldest and best country churches in the State. He resigned his charge in 1864, and became a chaplain in Gordon's Georgia Brigade. On the return of peace he settled in the valley of Virginia as pastor of two churches, to both of which large accessions were made during his ministry. In December, 1868, he took charge of the St. Francis Street church, Mobile, where he labored five and a half years, during which 225 were added to the church, and the house was enlarged and improved at a cost of more than $30,000, by which it was rendered one of the most comfortable and beautiful church edifices in the South. Subsequently he was settled in Columbia, S. C., where his ministry was a great blessing. And in Montgomery, Ala., his present pastorate, he is justly esteemed as a man of fine endowments and abilities. He is a superior scholar, a diligent student, a good pastor, one of the best of preachers, and a devoted Christian. His people love him.

Woodland Female College.—This institution was opened as a high school by Rev. J. M. Wood, in 1851, at Cedar Town, Polk Co., Ga., under the name of the "Cedar Town Female High School," and was chartered in 1853, Rev. J. M. Wood being the first president. The property was bought by the Coosa Baptist Association, and afterwards placed under the auspices of the Cherokee Baptist Convention. As professors in the literary department it had J. D. Collins, Dr. W. B. Crawford, and J. A. Arnold. Shortly before the war Rev. J. M. Wood was succeeded in the presidency by Dr. William B. Crawford, who resigned previous to the war. The calamities of war extinguished this institution, which for years was very successful, and educated a large number of young ladies. It maintained a regular corps of instructors, and was beautifully located.

Woodruff, Capt. A. B., was born in Spartanburg District, S. C., in 1825. He was baptized at an early age, and has been clerk, treasurer, and deacon of the only church of which he has ever been a member. He was chiefly instrumental in organizing the Spartanburg Association three or four years ago, and has been clerk ever since, as he long was of the old Tyger River. He has served two terms of two years each in the State Legislature. He is one of the most accurate of business men. He is a natural mechanic, and can make almost anything in wood, iron, silver, or gold. He has been and is a great blessing to his section, being one of the most liberal and progressive of citizens. His hand, voice, pen, and purse are always ready for the public service. As a speaker in political or Sunday-school work, in the latter of which he ever shows a special and practical interest, he is at once graceful and forcible.

Woods, Rev. Abel, was born in Princeton, Mass., Aug. 15, 1765, of parents who were worthy members of the Congregational church in that place. He became a subject of converting grace in 1783, and after prayerful deliberation concluded to enter the Christian ministry. His views having changed on the mode and subjects of Christian baptism, he was baptized and admitted into the Baptist church in Leicester, Mass. He supplied the pulpits of churches in his immediate neighborhood for a few years, and then was ordained pastor of the church in Shoreham, Vt., which had been formed from converts whom he led to the Saviour in that place. The ordination took place in February, 1795.

For fifteen years Mr. Woods remained pastor of the church in Shoreham, and had the satisfaction of witnessing three revivals during this period, and the church greatly strengthened under his ministry. After a year's service for the Vermont Missionary Society, he acted as the pastor of several churches in Vermont, his term of service not being very long with any one of them, but a special blessing following his labors wherever he preached. The home of his declining days was in Hamilton, N. Y., where he died Aug. 11, 1850. Mr. Woods was the father of Rev. Dr. Alva Woods, of Providence, and of the wife of Rev. Dr. R. E. Pattison. He was also the brother of Rev. Dr. Leonard Woods, of Andover.

Woods, Alva, D.D., was born at Shoreham, Vt., Aug. 13, 1794, his father, Rev. Abel Woods, being the pastor of the Baptist church in that place. He was fitted for college at the Phillips Academy in Andover, and graduated at Harvard College in

ALVA WOODS, D.D.

1817. He pursued his theological studies at the seminary in Andover, where he graduated in 1821. On leaving Andover he was chosen Professor of Mathematics and Natural Philosophy in Columbian College, Washington, D. C., and held the office three years, one of which was spent in Europe. In 1824 he was elected Professor of Mathematics and Natural Philosophy in Brown University. He held this chair until 1828, when he was elected president of Transylvania University, Lexington, Ky., and remained in office until 1831, when he removed to Tuscaloosa to take the presidential chair of the University of Alabama. He remained in this position until 1837. Since 1839 he has resided in Providence, R. I. As a trustee and Fellow of Brown University and of the Newton Theological Institution, Dr. Woods has shown his interest in the cause of education, to which he has devoted so many years of his life. Five scholarships in the former and a lectureship on elocution in the latter attest the sincerity of this interest. The honorary degree of Doctor of Divinity was conferred upon Dr. Woods by Brown University in 1828.

Woods, Rev. Byron R., was born in Jersey, Licking Co., O., April 4, 1851; graduated at Madison University, N. Y., in 1873; graduated at Hamilton Theological Seminary, N. Y., in 1875; ordained and settled as pastor of First Baptist church in

New London, Conn., July 1, 1875; has two brothers who are also ministers; he is an able minister of Christ.

Woods, Rev. E. A., A.M., was born in Homer, Licking Co., O. In early life he gave his heart and service to the Saviour, and entered at once upon a course of study preparatory to the Christian ministry.

After suitable academic training he entered Denison University in 1859, and after spending two years there entered the Junior class in Madison University, from which he graduated in 1863.

Eager for the work to which he had solemnly consecrated his life, and resolved to have the best possible mental and spiritual outfit for it, he entered at once upon a course of study in the Hamilton Theological Institution, from which he graduated in 1865.

He was ordained the same year at Little Falls, N. Y., but was soon after called to Flemington, N. J., where he had a prosperous pastorate of about five years. In the mean time a beautiful house of worship was built, and the church enlarged and strengthened. In 1871 he was called to the pastorate of the First Baptist church, Saratoga Springs, where he labored successfully for nearly five years.

In 1876 he received an urgent call to the Stewart Street church, Providence, R. I., where for four years he took rank with the ablest preachers of the city, and was very highly esteemed by a large circle of literary and Christian friends. His decision to leave Providence was received with wide-spread regret, but the order of a Higher Providence seemed imperative, and he must obey. In 1880 he became pastor of the First church, Paterson, N. J., where he now labors with large hopes of future usefulness.

Mr. Woods is a thorough scholar and a sound theologian. As a writer, he is luminous and vigorous; as a preacher, eminently Biblical and evangelical; as a pastor, judicious and sympathetic; as a friend, true-hearted and generous. He is strongly attached to the doctrines and polity of his own denomination, and labors earnestly to promote its interests, but cherishes the most kindly and fraternal feelings towards the followers of Christ of every name. Mr. Woods takes a deep interest in the great missionary and educational movements of the day, and the cause of humanity everywhere finds in him warm sympathy and generous support.

He has two brothers in the Baptist ministry, both of whom have already, though young, distinguished themselves as able ministers of the New Testament,—Rev. H. C. Woods, A.M., pastor of the First church, Minneapolis, Minn., and Rev. B. A. Woods, A.M., pastor of the First Baptist church, New London, Conn.

Woods, Rev. H. C., was born of Baptist parentage in Homer township, Licking Co., O., July 11, 1842; was converted to Christ when about fifteen years of age; was baptized by Rev. David Adams into the fellowship of the Baptist church of Jersey, O.

Very soon after his conversion the duty of preaching the gospel was deeply impressed upon his mind. After preparing for college, he spent the Freshman year at Denison University, Granville, O. The Sophomore year he entered Madison University, N. Y., graduating from college in 1865, and from the theological seminary in 1867.

He was ordained pastor of the Baptist church at Fayetteville, N. Y., Sept. 26, 1867. His labors in his first field were accompanied by the divine blessing in conversions, and in other ways strengthening the church. In consequence of failing health, he resigned the pastorate in the spring of 1872. He spent about one year regaining his health in Colorado. In March, 1873, he accepted the call of the Baptist church of Greeley, Col. He labored in this field one year and a half, and was greatly prospered in his work. In October, 1874, he accepted the call of the First Baptist church of Minneapolis, Minn., and entered upon his labors Nov. 1, 1874. His pastorate with this church still continues (1880), and his labors have been greatly blessed, the church having more than doubled its membership under his ministrations. His excellent wife died Feb. 28, 1876. His second marriage was to Miss Mary A. Eaton, the youngest daughter of the late G. W. Eaton, D.D., of Hamilton, N. Y. He was married July 11, 1878. As a preacher and pastor his position has been an honorable one with the churches he has served. In all the benevolent work of the denomination, at home and abroad, he has borne an active part.

Woodsmall, Rev. Harrison, president of the Alabama Baptist Normal and Theological School for colored people, at Selma, Ala., was born in Owen Co., Ind., June 9, 1841. His parents, Jefferson H. Woodsmall and Malvina Wilhite, were Virginians, and brought him up on a farm, sending him to country schools in the fall and winter months. At sixteen years of age he entered the State University, where he remained a student until the civil war broke out, when he enlisted, in June, 1861, in the 14th Indiana Regiment. He served in Virginia, and was wounded at the battle of Antietam. Afterwards he rose to be first a captain, and then a major, in the 115th Indiana Regiment.

He was converted and baptized in 1863, when at home on a furlough, after being wounded, and joined Little Mount Baptist church. While in the army he managed to study law, and at the return of peace he attended a law-school at Ann Arbor, Mich., afterwards practising the profession in Indiana for about six years. During those years he took an active part in Sunday-school and temperance work, and also in politics. Convictions that it was his duty to enter the ministry were gradually ripening in his mind, and though he removed to St. Paul, Minn., and engaged in the practice of the law, he could not shake off these impressions. They deepened while he was attending the State Convention at Mankato, and, after a week's decisive struggle, on bended knee, with the Bible alone for the man of his counsel, he threw up the law and returned to Indiana, resolved to give himself to such work as the Lord might direct. After spending some months in voluntary labor among the colored people of Indiana, he determined to enter the Southern Baptist Theological Seminary for a course of preparatory study. He went to Greenville in 1872, and remained until the summer of 1873, when he began work among the colored people of Georgia, as an appointee of the Sunday-School Board of the Georgia Baptist Convention. While laboring in this field he was married to Miss Mary E. Howes, of Macon, Dec. 29, 1873. The following year he accepted an appointment under the American Baptist Publication Society, and labored among the colored people in Georgia for six months. He next employed himself as an evangelist for the Home Mission Society, holding ministers' institutes in Georgia, Alabama, Tennessee, and Kentucky until some time in 1877. In such work he is an adept, and fully comprehends the wants of the colored ministers, and knows how to meet those wants. His efforts were very successful while thus engaged.

In January, 1878, he took charge of the Alabama Baptist Normal and Theological School, under the management of the colored Baptists of Alabama. It was opened by Mr. and Mrs. Woodsmall in a Baptist church in Selma. Grounds (36 acres) and temporary buildings were contracted for. Mrs. Woodsmall at once turned to Indiana for a teacher and her support. Miss Emma E. Jordan, of Indianapolis, went as teacher, and the Baptist women of the State guaranteed her salary.

The work has gone on very auspiciously. During the year the colored Baptists of Alabama have raised $9000 for the school. The property is now worth $10,000. The school numbers over 300 pupils.

Mr. Woodsmall, though constitutionally frail of body, has vast energy, clear views, and great faith in God and Christianity. He gave himself and his whole property to the cause, and he is now seeing the fruits of his labor. The Home Mission Society has appropriated $2000 per annum to the work since April 1, 1880.

Woodward, Rev. William, a native of South Carolina, came to Alabama early in his youth, where he enjoyed a long and useful life. He was a citizen of extensive influence. Served several sessions in the senate of the State from West Alabama. But he found his highest honor and happiness in the Christian ministry. Few were better versed in the affairs of state; fewer still were as well acquainted with the Word of God, and he loved it and preached it with great power. He died Sept. 7, 1871, aged seventy-nine. His father was a Baptist minister. His brother, the Hon. J. A. Woodward, now of Talladega, was for many years a distinguished member of Congress from South Carolina.

Woolsey, Rev. J. J., was born in Austerlitz, N. Y., in 1805; converted when quite young; educated at Hamilton, from which he graduated in 1833. Among his classmates were Comstock, Dean, Howard, and Webb, who went as missionaries to the heathen. Before leaving Hamilton, Mr. Woolsey supplied the church at Cassville for about two years, where a goodly shower of converting grace descended and many souls were brought to Jesus. He declined a pressing call to settle in Cassville. In the spring of 1834 he accepted an invitation to become pastor of the church of Pike, in Western New York, where the spirit soon brought souls in numbers to the Saviour. In Pike he received ordination.

Through failing health Mr. Woolsey purposed to visit the South, and on his way he preached in the Central Baptist church of Philadelphia, by whose kind people he was persuaded to try the effect of their climate upon his enfeebled system, and to take charge of their church. He took the oversight of the Central church, and served it with great acceptance for three years. During this period he gained the confidence of the Baptists of Philadelphia and the reputation of a very able and scholarly preacher.

Mr. Woolsey accepted an invitation from the Blockley (Philadelphia) church on his retirement from the pastorate of the Central, and labored among them faithfully for two years, during which signal blessings rested upon his ministry. But his labors were too much for his feeble health, and in March, 1840, he accepted an invitation from the Baptist church of Norwalk, Conn., which he served for seven years, and then was constrained by his old trouble to retire from its pastorate. Afterwards he accepted an agency from the American and Foreign Bible Society, to whose service he gave five years of untiring and fruitful effort, when the Norwalk church gave him a unanimous call to return among them, which brought him back, to their great joy and profit. The Bible Society, highly appreciating his talents and his success, appointed him its financial secretary. In this office he rendered such service as few men had the ability to give.

Mr. Woolsey is the author of several publications, the most remarkable of which is "The Doctrine of Christian Baptism, Examined by the Acknowledged Principles of Biblical Interpretation." Of this work Benedict says, "The title of Mr. Woolsey's book is well sustained throughout his discussions." It is a work of very great merit, a republication of which would be of great service to the cause of truth.

Mr. Woolsey is a man of extensive learning, of decided ability, well versed in general literature, with the manners of one who was naturally fitted for " good society," and who had frequent opportunities for using his special gifts.

His churches and the communities surrounding them had the highest regard for Mr. Woolsey as a minister, a man of learning, and a public benefactor. Church resolutions, newspaper commendations, and the admiration of social circles gave Mr. Woolsey assurances of his great popularity, and of the warm regard which men of all opinions and positions cherished for him.

In a happy old age this blameless and distinguished servant of God, in Germantown, Philadelphia, is awaiting the Master's summons to enter upon his eternal reward.

Worcester Academy was originally chartered as the Worcester County Manual Labor High School. One of the purposes in view in laying the foundations of the institution was to establish a school " where every possible advantage should be afforded for productive manual labor, so that instruction, while it should be good, should not be expensive."

At the first meeting, held in March, 1832, of those who took a special interest in establishing such an institution as was contemplated by the charter, it was resolved to raise a fund of $5000 as a partial endowment of the proposed school, and that it should be located at Worcester, Mass. Nearly all the subscribers to the fund were Baptists. Application was made to the Legislature of Massachusetts for an act of incorporation, which was granted and signed Feb. 28, 1834. Hon. Isaac Davis was chosen president of the board of trustees, and arrangements were made at once for the erection of a suitable building. Sixty acres of land were purchased in the southern part of the city for the purposes of the school.

The new building having been completed, was formally dedicated June 4, 1834, and the school was formally opened with about 30 pupils, under the charge of Silas Bailey, afterwards so well known in the West as Dr. Silas Bailey, who had recently graduated from Brown University. The students continued to increase until, in two years, there were 135. The second principal was Samuel S. Greene, now Prof. S. S. Greene, of Brown University, who remained in office two years, and was succeeded by Mr. Nelson H. Wheeler, whose term of service was ten years. In the number of pupils, and in the value of the instruction imparted, the school was in a condition of decided prosperity. But it became involved in pecuniary embarrassments, which crippled its usefulness, and placed a heavy load of care and responsibility upon its trustees. Gradually, however, through the excellent management of Mr. Davis, the institution emerged from its difficulties, and in 1864 it was reported not only to be free from debt, but in the possession of property worth at least $33,000. Various attempts were made from time to time to merge the institution into another in its immediate neighborhood, or to transfer its funds to the Newton Theological Seminary, to found a professorship for the instruction of students who were not sufficiently advanced to study Hebrew and Greek. All these attempts, although sometimes quite seriously entertained, proved abortive. The friends of the school, convinced that it was needed, rallied once more to its aid. An endowment was raised sufficiently large to settle the question that it was to remain in the city where it had originally been located, and that it should be an academy of a high order, and under the special control of Baptists. In the summer of 1869 the grounds once occupied by the "Ladies' Collegiate Institute," four acres in extent, a pleasant and commanding site within the city limits, were purchased, the buildings erected for the purposes of the institute put in thorough repair, and the Worcester Academy found its new home on one of the most attractive heights of the beautiful city of Worcester. The academy is out of debt, and has a property in real estate estimated to be worth $100,000, and invested funds exceeding $50,000, with pledges to a considerable additional amount. Under its present principal, Mr. N. Leavenworth, it is prospered, and as a feeder of Brown University it is doing a good work in fitting young men to enter our oldest seminary of learning.

The Worcester Academy owes a great debt of gratitude to Hon. Isaac Davis. He was the president of its board of trustees for forty years, and for most of this long period its treasurer. In the darkest days of its adversity he believed that a prosperous future was before it, and it is owing very largely to his wise and judicious management, under the divine blessing, that its present condition of prosperity has been reached. It has had other warm and devoted friends, who have stood by it in all its varying fortunes.

Worden, Rev. Horace, was born at West Stockbridge, Mass., Feb. 9, 1812. At the age of thirteen he was converted, uniting first with the Methodists, but subsequently becoming a Baptist, he was baptized in 1843, uniting with the First Baptist church of Quincy, Ill., to which place he

WORCESTER ACADEMY, WORCESTER, MASS.

had in the mean time removed. He had been a preacher while a Methodist, but was now licensed by the church in Quincy, and shortly after ordained as pastor of the church in Barry. In 1846, under appointment of the Home Mission Society, he became a missionary in Iowa, remaining about six years in that State. His health failing, he returned to Quincy, and has since been engaged in mission labor; a work involving much self-denial, but in which he enjoys many evidences of the divine blessing.

Worden, Rev. Jesse Babcock, the grandson of a brother of Rev. Peter Worden, was born in Washington Co., R. I., July 18, 1787. In 1812 he was drafted, and served his country in several military positions during the war with Great Britain. When hostilities ceased he devoted himself to business, for which he had many qualifications. He was converted and baptized in 1816 in North Woodstock, N. Y., and in 1818 he was ordained. After sixteen years' service elsewhere he became co-pastor with the Rev. Davis Dimock in Montrose, Pa., in 1835 for a short time, and sole pastor of the church from 1838 until 1844. He labored after 1844 in Susquehanna County, where he died Aug. 6, 1855. Mr. Worden was an instructive preacher and a very faithful pastor. He possessed elements of great efficiency as a minister, his labors were attended with more than ordinary success, and his precepts and example made an indelible impression upon many in Northern Pennsylvania.

Worden, Oliver N., was born in New Woodstock, N. Y., in 1817; acquired the art of printing in the office of the Utica *Baptist Register*, and, like many other masters of type-setting, he became a learned historian and a ready writer. For more than forty years he has contributed to various political, moral, religious, and historical periodicals. He has published newspapers in Montrose, Athens, Tunkhannock, and Lewisburg. He was twenty-seven years a member, and eleven years the scribe, of the board of curators of the university at Lewisburg. He was three years a clerk in the senate of Pennsylvania, and fifteen years clerk of the Northumberland Association. He has edited "The Life and Times of Sheardown," "Family Record," "Half-Century History of the Northumberland Association," and "Half-Century History of the Bridgewater Association."

Mr. Worden was an original thinker, a man of patient painstaking in collecting materials, of extreme conscientiousness, of great usefulness in the denomination, and a brother beloved as widely as he is known. He prepared a manuscript Baptist history, the publication of which would be of great advantage to the Baptists of Pennsylvania, and it is hoped that it will soon be given to the printer. He died near New Milford, Pa., April 28, 1881.

Worden, Rev. Peter, was born in 1729, converted among the New-Lights, and ordained at Warwick, R. I., in 1751. He removed to Berkshire Co., Mass., in 1769, and he died in 1805. John Leland, at his death, spoke of him as "the arduous Worden, who had been in the ministry longer than any Baptist preacher left behind in New England." In the minutes of the Shaftsbury Association for 1808 there is the following record about him: "For dignity of nature, soundness of judgment, meekness of temper, and unwearied labors in the ministry but few have equaled him in this age. He was the father, founder, and guardian angel of this Association until his age prevented. He followed the work of the ministry about sixty years."

Work, Rev. Perley, was born in Williamsburg, Vt., Sept. 11, 1813, and died at Oshkosh, Wis., Aug. 11, 1877. He was educated at Oneida Institute, in Whitesborough, N. Y. After his conversion and call to the ministry he pursued a course of theological study at Hamilton, N. Y., and graduated in 1841. He was sent to Wisconsin as a missionary by the American Baptist Home Mission Society in 1847, and began his labors at Sheboygan. Subsequently he served the churches at Omro, Ripon, Waukau, First church, Oshkosh, and Sheboygan Falls. He was a devoted minister of Christ, a faithful preacher, and very successful pastor. He is held in the highest esteem by his brethren in the ministry.

Worrall, A. S., D.D., was born in Georgia in 1831, and graduated from Mercer University with honor in 1855. He studied theology under Dr. J. L. Dagg and Dr. N. M. Crawford. He taught Latin and Greek in the Baptist College in Mississippi, and afterwards Greek and Hebrew in Union University, Tenn. After the war was president of Mount Lebanon University, La., and had unusual success. He was for a time editor of the *Western Recorder*, of Louisville, Ky. For health he removed to California, and there did much to endow the Baptist College. He is now president of Mount Pleasant College, Huntsville, Mo. The college is fortunate in obtaining such a president.

Worrall, Rev. Moses Hoagland, was born at Charlestown, Ind., Aug. 4, 1835. His father, Rev. Isaac Worrall, was an active and influential Baptist minister. The son was converted and baptized into the fellowship of the Charlestown church at the age of fourteen. Receiving his education chiefly at Cincinnati and Covington, his first public service was as principal of the Main School in the latter city. In compliance with the request of citizens, he opened an academy for the preparation of young men for college, and for advanced study in the classics and sciences. The large attendance made the erection of a building at once necessary, and the school became well known as the Covington Classical and Scientific Academy, later as Worrall's Classical and Scientific Academy for Girls and Boys. Notwithstanding his eminent success in this line of work, Mr. Worrall continued to be pressed by convictions of duty as to the ministry. Yielding to these, he was licensed by the First church of Covington, March 31, 1868, and was called as pastor of the Columbia Baptist church, Cincinnati, in February of the following year, receiving ordination in April of the same year. His subsequent pastorates have been at Troy, O., and Springfield and Princeton, Ill., the scene of his present labors. He is an effective preacher and a hard-working pastor. As the result, his work on each of the fields named has been telling and fruitful.

Wright, Rev. David, son of David and Martha (Hubbard) Wright, was born in New London, Conn., July 30, 1788. His father, a graduate of Yale College and a lawyer, died in 1798. David from 1801 to 1810 worked in a printing-office in Boston; converted under Dr. Stillman, and united with First Baptist church in Boston, April 28, 1805; thought to become a missionary printer; studied in Boston, in Norwich, and in Wallingford, Conn., under Rev. Joshua Bradley; assisted Mr. Bradley in teaching, and supplied the pulpit of the North Haven Baptist church; ordained in Southington, Conn., Aug. 9, 1815; in his very long ministry his settlements were at Westfield Farms, Cummington, Westminster, Westfield, and Conway, Mass.; Waterville and Romulus, N. Y.; North Colebrook, North Lyme, and Clinton, Conn.; served as State missionary in Massachusetts and Connecticut, and among Indians of Martha's Vineyard; agent of American and Foreign Bible Society for New Hampshire; member of the Massachusetts Legislature from Westfield Farms; was never physically strong, but strong in heart and intellect; logical and mighty in the Scriptures; an excellent Greek scholar; a wise and prized counselor; preached over 8000 sermons; constituted five churches; now lives in Essex, Conn., at the age of ninety-two; in his prime a preacher of power; wielded withal an efficient pen; honored and beloved by all.

Wright, Rev. J. C., was born in South Carolina, Dec. 10, 1830; came with his parents to Alabama in childhood; graduated in Howard College in 1856. His ministry for many years was with churches in West Alabama; was pastor in Clinton, Greensborough, and Gainesville,—some of the strongest churches in the State, among a wealthy and intelligent people. For some years since the late war he resided on his farm in Calhoun County, and preached in the region around him; now pastor of the Broad Street church in the city of Mobile. Mr. Wright is an eloquent and scholarly preacher; his sermons always have an ornate finish, and are delivered in graceful style.

Wright, Lyman, D.D., son of Deacon Pomeroy and Abigail Wright, was born in Westford, Otsego

LYMAN WRIGHT, D.D.

Co., N. Y., Sept. 28, 1816. He was converted Jan. 5, 1830; baptized Sept. 3, 1831, and joined the Westford Baptist church. He was educated at Hamilton Literary and Theological Institution; ordained as an evangelist Feb. 11, 1838, and supplied the Westford church the succeeding year. He became pastor at Exeter, Otsego Co., N. Y., in 1839; succeeded Rev. A. P. Mason, at Clockville, Madison Co., in 1841; settled at Fayetteville, Onondaga Co., in 1845; served the American Baptist Missionary Union as collecting agent for one year; took charge of the church in Norwich, Chenango Co., in 1854; in Trenton, N. J., in 1858; in Norwich, a second term, in 1859; became financial secretary of the New York Baptist Education Society, and part of the time, in connection with it, agent for Madison University, in 1861. While thus employed he increased the endowment fund of the university $72,000.

He returned to the pastorate after this work was done, settling with the Newburgh church in 1864, and with the Binghamton church in 1869, where he remained until his death, in 1878. He has with his personal supervision assisted the church in erecting a commodious edifice. His ministerial labors extend over a period of more than forty years. In all of his pastorates he has been faithful, and successful in winning souls for the kingdom, having baptized more than 1100 converts into the fellowship of the churches he has served.

Wright, Judge Selden S., is one of the most honored judges in the State of California, and an exemplary member of the First Baptist church, San Francisco. Born March 7, 1822, in Essex Co., Va.; son of Thos. Wright, Jr., and Mary Daley Jones; graduated at William and Mary College in 1842; he removed to Lexington, Miss., in 1843; practised law, in partnership with Hon. Walter Brooke, until 1851, when he removed to Yazoo City, and was the same year elected vice-chancellor of the middle district of Mississippi, and re-elected in 1855. In 1855 he resigned and removed to Carrollton, Miss., and practised law with William B. Helm, as partner, until 1859, when he removed to the Pacific coast, arriving at San Francisco, Cal., Jan. 3, 1860. He practised law until 1868, when he was elected probate judge for the city and county of San Francisco. In 1874 he was appointed judge of the City and County Court, and in 1876 re-elected to the same office, which he held until the office expired, Jan. 1, 1880. He was baptized by Rev. Jas. K. Clinton, at Lexington, Miss., in 1843, where his brother, Rev. Thos. Wright, is an esteemed Baptist minister. While practising his profession he has always identified himself with his brethren in the churches where he has resided, and, on reaching San Francisco, united with the First Baptist church, in whose welfare he has been deeply interested during his twenty years' residence in California.

Wright, Rev. Stephen, was born March 22, 1813, in Cambridge, Washington Co., N. Y., of a New England ancestry, the seventh generation from Lieut. Abel Wright, of Springfield, Mass., in 1655. Converted at eighteen, he was baptized, with 111 other converts, by the venerable Daniel Tinkham, into the White Creek church, in the great revival of 1831. He prepared for college at Union Academy, Bennington, Vt. He was ordained at Stillwater, N. Y., Feb. 23, 1837, and, after preaching two and a half years, entered the seminary at Hamilton in December, 1839, where he spent three years, chiefly in theological study, graduating in 1842; served various churches, mostly in Eastern New York and Western Vermont. His longest pastorate was at old Ticonderoga, from 1854 to 1860, in which time he baptized, with other converts, the father of Rev. Joseph Cook, known as Deacon Wm. H. Cook, of the Baptist Church, a solid farmer. In 1853 he published, by request, "A History of the Old Shaftsbury Association from 1780 to 1853," in a 12mo volume of 464 pages, which interested 100 churches and 6 Associations that now occupy the territory of the original body. He has also published several local church histories, and written for the periodical press, secular and religious. He is located at Glen's Falls, Warren Co., N. Y.

Wright, Rev. Thomas Goddard, son of Rev. David Wright, was born in Westfield, Mass., Jan. 18, 1820; converted and baptized at eleven in Cummington, Mass.; began holding meetings immediately, and soon rejoiced over nearly a score converted through his efforts; graduated at Waterville College (now Colby University), Me., at nineteen, and from Hamilton Theological Seminary, N. Y., at twenty-two; supplied one year at Avon Springs, N. Y., then settled in Lyons, N. Y., and was ordained Aug. 7, 1844. His subsequent ministry was in Claremont, N. H., Sandisfield, Mass., Newark, N. J., Westport and Wappinger's Falls, N. Y., Roadstown, N. J., with First Cohansey church, Philadelphia, Pa., Westerly, R. I., Newfane and Watkins, N. Y., and Media, Pa. In Newark, N. J., he served as missionary, inaugurating its present city mission plan, and organizing the North church; also in Philadelphia, Pa., where, in connection with other labors, he organized the Mantua mission, and left it when ready to be recognized as the present Mantua church. He was always true to New Testament Baptist doctrine. He has been a successful harmonizer of church difficulties, careful in the reception of members into the church, and a promoter of missions and education. He has a son (Wm. R.) who is pastor at Cohoes, N. Y. He was one of the originators of South Jersey Institute, at Bridgeton, N. J., and its first secretary. While at Hamilton he compiled and arranged a music book called the "Chapel Choir," which was published by the institution, and used for many years in the chapel services. He is in good health at sixty, and bids fair to do service for the Master for several years to come.

Wyatt, Rev. Wm. H., a pioneer preacher in Southeastern Arkansas, was born in Alabama in 1805, and removed to Arkansas in 1848. He preached extensively in all the region between the Ouachita and Arkansas Rivers, and gathered many churches. He died in 1853 of malarial fever, contracted during a missionary tour in the Mississippi bottom.

Wyckoff, William H., LL.D., the youngest of the family of Rev. Cornelius P. and Elizabeth Richmond Wyckoff, was born in New York City, Sept. 10, 1807.

He finished his academic studies in Auburn, N. Y.; spent two years at Hamilton College, and was graduated at Union College in 1828.

Having then a high reputation for his wide range of information and accurate scholarship, he was appointed principal of a celebrated collegiate school in New York City.

He studied successively law and medicine; was

regarded as an authority in ancient and modern history; was well versed in general literature, and excelled in mathematics. The late Prof. Charles Anthon, LL.D., said of him, that he believed there was no one in this country superior to him in a knowledge of Greek and Latin. He had also made scholarly attainments in Hebrew and in some of the modern European languages. His study of the Bible was earnest and unremitting.

Having a retentive memory, extensive reading had given him a wealth of intellectual resources, which enhanced his fine conversational gifts, and furnished him with copious illustrations in his preaching.

The Laight Street Baptist church called him to the ministry in 1846. He was the founder and—from 1839 to 1846—the editor of *The Baptist Advocate* (now the *Examiner and Chronicle*).

As a manager of the Sunday-School Union, president of the Young Men's City Bible Society and of the Baptist Domestic Mission Society, and a worker in other benevolent enterprises in his native city, he was active and efficient.

He took part in organizing the American and Foreign Bible Society in 1835, and was its corresponding secretary from 1846 to 1850, when the American Bible Union was founded, of which he was secretary till his death.

To the work of the Bible Union, in its efforts to procure and circulate the most faithful versions of the Scriptures, he gave his best energies and his steadfast support. His voluminous correspondence in the interests of the society attests his devotion to the cause. In the excited controversy occasioned by the movement for the revision of the English Bible his part was prominent, but he was careful not to overstep the bounds of Christian courtesy. The degree of LL.D. was conferred on him by Madison University in 1858.

He was the author of various religious and educational books. His disposition was genial and sympathetic; his nature refined; his life pure and devout.

Of his seven children, five survive him. His sudden death on Nov. 2, 1877, was caused by a rupture of the heart, unaccountable to the eminent physicians who were present at the post-mortem examination. Dr. Wyckoff performed a mighty work for pure versions of the Word of God.

Wyer, Rev. Henry Hartstene, was born in South Carolina, July 26, 1829. He was prepared for college at a classical school in Savannah, Ga.; was graduated from the Columbian College, Washington, D. C., and received his theological education at the Princeton Seminary, N. J. In 1854 he became pastor of the Upperville and Ebenezer churches, Fauquier Co., Va. In 1856 he removed to Lynchburg, where he remained until 1859. From 1859 to 1866 he was pastor of the Oakland and Hopeful churches. From 1866 to 1871, Mr. Wyer was principal of the Fauquier Female Institute, an excellent school, and also pastor of the church in Warrenton, Va. At present he is the pastor of the Carter's Run and Broad Run churches, the former of which was organized by the Rev. John Pickett, who was imprisoned in the county jail for preaching the gospel. The latter was organized by the Rev. David Thomas in 1762, and has had among its pastors such well-known men as Wm. Fristoe, C. George, and John Ogilvie.

Wyer, Rev. Henry Otis, was born in Beverly, Mass., March 19, 1802; educated at Waterville College, Me., and at Columbian College, Washington, D. C. His piety, zeal, and talents attracted attention in Savannah, to which he came in 1824, and, notwithstanding his inexperience, he was elected pastor of the church there, and called to ordination, Dr. Wm. T. Brantly, Sr., then pastor at Augusta, and Rev. James Shannon officiating. He remained pastor of the church about ten years, when excessive labors broke his health down and he had to resign.

Among others whom he was instrumental in bringing to Jesus and baptizing were Dr. Richard Fuller, Dr. J. H. De Votie, and Rev. D. G. Daniel. As a preacher he had few equals, for he was especially fitted for the pulpit by his sonorous voice, comprehensive mind, cultivated intellect, and sanctified heart. His characteristics were clearness, unction, and force. Hundreds were converted under his ministry, the church at Savannah was revived and built up, and the Baptist cause in the city greatly advanced by his labors. He passed away May 8, 1857, at Alexandria, Va., in the fifty-sixth year of his age.

Wynn, Isaac Caldwell, D.D., was born in Cumberland Co., N. J., Feb. 22, 1835; was baptized in the West Branch of the Susquehanna by Rev. I. N. Hayhurst, in March, 1854; was graduated at the University of Lewisburg in 1858; was principal of the academic department of the university at Lewisburg from 1859 to 1864. From 1864 to 1867 he held the principalship of a classical academy at Danville, Pa. Became pastor of the Baptist church at Hatborough, Pa., in November, 1867, where he was ordained Feb. 13, 1868. July 1, 1870, he became pastor of the Tabernacle church of Camden, N. J.

During his pastorate the First and Tabernacle churches of Camden were united in 1872 under the corporate title of the Fourth Street Baptist church of Camden, of which he is still pastor. His spirit is so conciliatory, and his wisdom so practical, that he has been instrumental in bringing into complete harmony two communities formerly worshipping in separate buildings; and the blessing of God has prospered the church in conversions, in the increased piety of the members, and in the favor of the people of Camden. In 1879 the university at Lewisburg gave him the degree of D.D.

ISAAC CALDWELL WYNN, D.D.

Wyoming Institute of Delaware, The, with grounds and building, costing $9000, was established in 1867 by a joint-stock company at Wyoming, Kent Co., Del. Rev. O. F. Flippo, then a missionary in Delaware of the American Baptist Home Mission Society, after consulting prominent Baptists, by assistance from individuals and a loan from the society under which he was acting, purchased it for the denomination for a school and place of worship. For two years he took its general oversight, visiting churches and collecting money to pay for it. In 1872, Rev. M. Heath, A.M., was elected principal, a position which he still holds (1880). He has furnished it with his own apparatus, employed teachers, and conducted its educational interests on his own responsibility. It was rechartered in 1875, providing for a large majority of Baptists in the board of trustees. The courses of study for both sexes require three years beyond common-school branches. Since 1874 there has been a graduating class each year except one. No debts have been incurred since 1873. About $2000 have been paid on the original indebtedness, and $1000 remain unpaid. The institution has usually from four to six teachers. The largest annual attendance was for the year ending June, 1879, when 101 were registered. This institution is of great advantage to that portion of the people of Delaware surrounding it, especially to the citizens of Wyoming.

Y.

Yates, Rev. Aaron, a leading Baptist minister, who resides at Arkadelphia, Ark., was born in Georgia in 1817; removed to Arkansas in 1850; began to preach in 1854. His labors have been chiefly devoted to churches in Dallas and the adjoining counties, and have been eminently successful.

Yates, M. T., D.D., was born in Wake Co., N. C., in 1819; was baptized into the fellowship of the Mount Pisgah church in October, 1836; went to school to George W. Thompson, near Wake Forest College, in 1838; became a beneficiary of the Convention, and was graduated from Wake Forest College in 1846; was ordained in October, 1846, during the session of the Convention in the city of Raleigh. Rev. Thomas Meredith preached the sermon, Rev. William Hill Jordan offered the prayer, Dr. James B. Taylor, of Richmond, delivered the charge, and the venerable Dr. Wait presented the Bible. Immediately after his ordination he and his wife sailed for China, where they have been laboring for *thirty-five* years. Dr. Yates has visited the United States three times during this period, in search of health, and he is now publishing in the *Biblical Recorder* "Reminiscences of a Long Missionary Life," which will be issued in book form after the series has been completed.

Dr. Jeter, *clarum et venerabile nomen*, once said to the writer that "he regarded Dr. Yates as the ablest missionary whom he had ever known." I asked, "Did you know Judson?" "Yes," he replied. "I knew Judson; but Yates has more mind than Judson." During the war between the States, Dr. Yates was enabled, by a judicious investment of some money he had left on interest in New York, to sustain the missionaries of the Southern Baptist Convention in China, who were cut off from all communication with the board that sent them out. Dr. Yates has rendered valuable service

M. T. YATES, D.D.

in the translation of the Scriptures, and in issuing evangelical tracts in Chinese. He was honored with the title of D.D. by Wake Forest College in 1872.

Yeaman, W. Pope, D.D., was born in Hardin Co., Ky., May 28, 1832. He was the third in a family of nine children, eight of whom were sons. His father was a man of culture, and eminent as a lawyer. His mother was Miss Lucretia Helm, sister of ex-Gov. Helm, of Kentucky, a lady of talent. Six of the brothers became lawyers. Dr. Pope Yeaman studied law with his uncle, Gov. John Z. Helm, and was admitted to the bar at the age of nineteen. For nine years Dr. Yeaman devoted himself to the practice of law. He was able as an advocate, and was retained in difficult cases. At the age of twenty-seven he entered the ministry and received ordination. His first pastorate was at Nicholasville, Ky., where he divided his time with East Hickman church, in Fayette County, succeeding Ryland T. Dillard, D.D., who had preached there thirty-seven years. In 1862 he became pastor of the First Baptist church in Covington, Ky. In December, 1867, he was called to the Central Baptist church of New York City. In March, 1870, he accepted a call to the Third Baptist church of St. Louis. In the same year William Jewell College conferred upon him the honorary degree of Doctor of Divinity. Dr. Yeaman has been active in all the denominational interests of the State. He was for a time proprietor and editor of the *Central Baptist*, also chancellor of William Jewell College, and president of the Missouri General Association. He still holds this office, presiding with dignity and giving general satisfaction.

In 1876 he resigned the care of the Third church, and for two years was pastor of the Garrison Avenue church, a new interest. This charge he resigned, and he is now pastor at Glasgow, and secretary of the General Association. His natural eloquence and superior mental endowments give him great power over an audience. He is an independent thinker, bold in his utterances, with

W. POPE YEAMAN, D.D.

throngs of warm friends. His influence and usefulness in Missouri are very great.

Yeiser, Rev. George O., was born in Lancaster, Grand Co., Ky., Dec. 4, 1825. He was brought up in the Presbyterian Church; graduated at Centre College in 1848; followed the profession of the law for eight years; was collector of U. S. internal revenue in the first collection district in Kentucky in 1864 and 1865. On June 5, 1868, he suffered an affliction that was blessed in bringing his soul to God. On searching the Scripture for authority for infant sprinkling he became convinced that immersion alone is baptism. He was baptized in September, 1868; ordained Aug. 5, 1875; became pastor of the Baptist church in Ashland, Neb., Aug. 15, 1875. Since 1878 he has been pastor of the Baptist churches at Red Cloud and Guide Rock, Neb.

Yerkes, David J., D.D., was born in Montgomery Co., Pa., Jan. 27, 1825; was graduated at Columbian College, D. C., in 1848; ordained at Hollidaysburg, Pa., 1849, and, after a pastorate of seven years at that place, took charge of the First church of Pittsburgh for four years, then the First church of Brooklyn, N. Y., for three years, from which he went to the First church of Plainfield, N. J., in the fall of 1863. The degree of D.D. was conferred upon him by Columbian College and the university at Lewisburg in 1870. Since the settlement of Dr. Yerkes in Plainfield a fine new church edifice has been built and paid for, several extensive revivals have been enjoyed, and the membership of the church has increased to 800.

Young, Aaron H., was born in 1780, in Fairfax Co., Va. He was brought to Kentucky by his parents when a child, and was converted at the age of twenty-one years, and baptized by Rev. Peter Dudley. He removed to Missouri in 1819, and lived at Marthaville, where he helped to organize the Friendship Baptist church. Afterwards he removed to St. Louis County and joined the Fee Fee church. His house was the home of Peck, Hurley, Music, and Williams, the pioneer preachers of Missouri. He loved knowledge, art, and the Saviour's gospel. Mr. Young was a useful layman, and a great helper to the church.

Young, Rev. C. B., an aged minister in Marshall Co., Miss., was born in North Carolina in 1815; began to preach in 1837; removed to Mississippi in 1840; ordained in 1845, and during the thirty-five years of his useful ministry he has supplied a number of churches in Marshall and the surrounding counties, where his labors have been greatly blessed. At the age of sixty-six he is waiting beside the river, with a long life of usefulness behind and the prospect of rest beyond.

Young, Hon. Edward, Ph.D., was born in Nova Scotia, Dec. 11, 1814, and was educated at Horton Academy, now Acadia College. He was engaged for a while in commercial pursuits, but, removing to Philadelphia, became a publisher of statistical works. On coming to Washington, he was chosen chief of the U. S. Bureau of Statistics, which position he held for more than eight years, with great honor to himself and usefulness to the commercial interests of the government. While chief of this important bureau, he was appointed by the President of the United States a delegate to the International Statistical Congress held in St. Petersburg, Russia, in 1872, and won for himself in that distinguished assembly a high reputation as a statistician. He served as one of the vice-presidents of that congress. The emperor of Russia was so favorably impressed with the ability of Dr. Young that he sent him a valuable diamond ring, which, by a special act of Congress, he was permitted to accept. It is a fact well worthy of record that Dr. Young, who has always been a zealous advocate of temperance, and an opponent of theatrical representations, in consequence of their corrupting tendencies, while in Russia steadfastly declined to partake of wine, so abundantly furnished at the tables of the emperor and of other members of the royal family; and also to visit the theatre in Moscow, when all the other members of the congress made the visit at the invitation of the authorities of that city. While attending the congress, the fact was brought to Dr. Young's notice that the "Stundists," who are mainly Baptists, were imprisoned in Southern Russia, charged with disseminating heresy and drawing away from the orthodox (Russo-Greek) church some of its members; he used his influence, naturally great under the circumstances of his position, with the high officials of Russia to secure their liberation. In this merciful labor he was greatly aided by his friend, Baron de Rozen, grand master of the court and confidential friend of the emperor, who kindly undertook to interest in behalf of the imprisoned Baptists Prince Dondouroff-Korsakoff, governor-general of Kiev, in which place the "Stundists" were held for trial, the result of which was that a new trial before a higher court was granted, and the decision made that, although the prisoners were culpable, yet they were not guilty of disseminating heresy, and were consequently discharged, with the exception of two, who were sent to the authorities of another jurisdiction. Dr. Young stands deservedly high as a writer in his special field of studies and labors. He edited for many years a temperance paper in Nova Scotia, and subsequently industrial journals in New York and Philadelphia. In addition to numerous regular monthly, quarterly, and annual reports on the commerce and navigation of the United States, he prepared, in 1871, a special report on immigration, in which a vast amount of valuable information with regard to the advantages of the country was furnished for those looking towards a settlement here. Of this work 20,000 copies were published in English, 10,000 in German, and 10,000 in French, for which the author was awarded a medal and diploma by the International Geographical Congress at Paris in 1875. In 1872 he issued a special report on the "Customs-Tariff Legislation of the United States," which is a standard work in this and in other countries. His last work, on "Labor in Europe and America," has received the very highest commendations from economists and statesmen in this country and in Europe. He has also made frequent valuable contributions to the monthly, weekly, and daily journals, chiefly on economical subjects. He is an honorary member of the Statistical Society of London, and owing to his reputation as a statistician the government of Canada has been desirous of securing his services. He is at the present time (1879) at Ottawa, engaged in special service.

Dr. Young has been for many years, and still is, a member of the First Baptist church, Washington; is a deacon of the church, and was for several years the superintendent of the Sunday-school. The Columbian College, in recognition of his valuable services to the government, conferred upon him, in 1867, the honorary degree of A.M. (as did also Acadia College), and in 1871 the degree of Doctor of Philosophy. Dr. Young is interested in the higher education of the youth of the country, and has given to the Columbian College a gold medal, "The Young prize for excellence in metaphysics," annually awarded to the best student in mental philosophy.

Young, Rev. George Whitefield, was born in Amherst Co., Va., Feb. 15, 1807. His father, John

REV. GEORGE WHITEFIELD YOUNG.

Young, was a Baptist minister of whom honorable mention is made in Rev. James B. Taylor's "History of Virginia Baptist Ministers" as "one of those who were imprisoned for Christ's sake."

Rev. George W. Young united with the Prospect Baptist church of Amherst Co., Va., in 1827; in April, 1845, he was ordained in Elim church, Haywood Co., Tenn., having left his native State in October, 1829; he continued serving the best interests of this church until his death, Dec. 3, 1874, in the sixty-eighth year of his age.

He was instrumental in the formation of Hermon church, Lauderdale Co., and he was its pastor for several years. In 1852 he was called to the pastorate of Woodlawn church, and served it until declining health forced him to resign. In 1869 he accepted the pastoral care of Salem church, Lauderdale Co., and in 1873 commenced his labors with Bloomington (now Brighton) church, Tipton Co.

The Big Hatchie Association frequently selected Rev. G. W. Young as its moderator, and he was repeatedly elected president of the West Tennessee Baptist Convention. These offices of dignity and worth were conscientiously and satisfactorily filled. His great influence was always exerted for the good of humanity. His appearance was commanding, his manners were social and easy. He had a kind word for all who came in contact with him; his affection and gentleness won the sympathies of the young, and their welcome made his visits doubly enjoyable.

His piety was of the quiet, practical order, unobtrusive, but not to be mistaken.

A short time previous to his death he reviewed his past life and labors, and in commenting upon them to an intimate friend and associate he remarked that, "so far as the doctrines he had preached were concerned, he believed them all, and in his practice of them had nothing to regret; that with eternity in view, he was more than ever convinced that it was wrong to affiliate with the teachers of error." "I know whom I have believed," were the words uttered by him just before yielding up his spirit, showing that his faith did not forsake him in the hour of death.

He passed away from this life Dec. 3, 1874, but his memory still remains honored by the church and those who knew him.

Young, Rev. Jesse, one of a noble band of pioneers in South Mississippi, was born in South Carolina, and removed to Mississippi in 1811; ordained in 1827; was indefatigable in his labors to plant primitive Christianity in South Mississippi and Eastern Louisiana, and was blessed as the instrument in establishing many churches; died in 1847.

Young, Mrs. M. J., was born in Beaufort, N. C., about 1828. Her father, Nathan Fuller, is a descendant of Samuel Fuller, who came to America in the "Mayflower." His paternal grandmother was a daughter of Michael Pacquenett, a Huguenot, of Bordeaux, who emigrated to this country after the revocation of the Edict of Nantes, and married, in Virginia, a direct descendant of John Rolf and Rebecca, his wife, better known as Pocahontas. Her mother is the daughter of Dr. John Marshall, Essex, England, who was educated at Eton and Trinity College, Oxford. Mrs. Young was educated chiefly under Episcopal influence, at Greensborough, Ala., and never heard a Baptist sermon till sixteen years of age, when she first heard Rev. D. P. Bestor preach. Removing to Houston, Texas, in 1843, she continued to attend the Episcopal church, teach a Sunday-school, read her prayer-book, and felt hurt when it was said, "Oh, never mind, let her read her prayer-book, when she is converted she will join the Baptist Church." Through the influence of Rev. W. M. Tryon she was induced to examine the New Testament as to her duty about baptism, and in 1846 she was baptized by Mr. Tryon into the fellowship of the Houston Baptist church. The administrator, descended from the Welsh Baptists, told her that through him she had received apostolic baptism, through the succession of the ancient Christian church of Wales. In February, 1847, she was married to Dr. S. O. Young, of South Carolina, who died the same year. She has written short poems, stories, and letters of travel; is the author of "Cardena," a serial, showing that Judaism has no consistent, logical development except in Baptist faith, and a work on botany, published by A. S. Barnes & Co., New York, to which is added the most complete flora of Texas yet published. Her attainments as a botanist have been recognized by eminent scientists on both sides of the Atlantic, and she has distinguished correspondents, literary, scientific, historical, poetical, theological, and military. She has been Texas State botanist, and superintendent of public schools at Houston, Texas. She was the Texas member of the Woman's Centennial Committee, and was honored by His Grace the Duke of Richmond and Gordon, K.G. She is connected either actively or honorarily with numerous associations for pomological, horticultural, and scientific purposes in America. She is devoted to the interest of the Houston Baptist church, and all worthy Baptist enterprises. She has fascinating conversational powers, and writes in an attractive style, commanding the high regard of all who are numbered among her friends or acquaintances.

Young, Rev. Robert F., was born near Coatesville, Pa., Sept. 4, 1810. From the time of his great-grandfather, Ninian Young,—who in 1754 resided on and owned a tract of about two hundred acres in East Fallowfield, Chester Co.,—his family were farmers, and Robert himself, until near manhood, led the same hardy life.

Denominationally, the earlier generations of the family were almost exclusively Presbyterian; but, about the close of the year 1774, the grandfather of Mr. Young married Martha, sister of the late and still revered Deacon Thomas Shields, of the First Baptist church of Philadelphia, and to this graft from a more orthodox stock is probably due the large number of Baptists in the Young family. And no doubt, too, it was in part owing to the example and influence of this lady, whom Mr. Young still remembers in her latter days as a constant Bible-reader and a firm Baptist, as well as to his own deep, youthful convictions, that he was led to

REV. ROBERT F. YOUNG.

be baptized in 1824, to unite with the Hephzibah church.

When only seventeen, Mr. Young, feeling called to preach the gospel, began the preparatory study of Latin and Greek at Moscow Academy, above Sadsburyville, Chester Co., Pa.

In 1831 he was licensed by the Bethesda Baptist church, Chester Co., and the same year entered the Literary and Theological Institution at Hamilton, N. Y.

After studying at Hamilton two years, early in the fall of 1833 Mr. Young left, and took charge of religious meetings at Milestown, near Philadelphia, out of which the Union Baptist church was constituted in November, 1833, of which he became the first pastor. He was ordained Feb. 19, 1835. During this year he commenced a course of study in Greek, theology, etc., under the late Rev. Dr. W. T. Brantly, Sr., of Philadelphia, which was perseveringly continued, with other duties, for several years.

In May, 1834, Mr. Young began preaching at Chestnut Hill as an out-station. There was no Baptist church nearer than Roxborough. Assisted by the pastor of that church,—the Rev. D. A. Nichols,—evening meetings were held during the month of August.

After ten evenings thus spent, eleven persons

related their "experience" and were baptized, Miss M. A. Gilbert, now Mrs. Young, her father, the late honored Deacon Israel Gilbert, her mother and brother, the late Dr. Jonathan Gilbert, being among the candidates.

From these meetings the Chestnut Hill Baptist church was summoned into life, and recognized Sept. 17, 1834, of which Mr. Young took charge Jan. 1, 1835. This pastorate was continued for fourteen years. Here he first developed to all that became acquainted with him his now well-known character,—that "of a man above reproach or doubt,"—of pure, humble, prayerful, consistent, and earnest life.

His labors during this period were abundant in his own parish and in several outlying stations. In 1835, by his exertions and by the liberality of his father-in-law, Deacon Gilbert, amid much opposition, the Baptist meeting-house of Chestnut Hill was built. For about eighteen months, while laboring in Chestnut Hill, Mr. Young preached for the church at Mount Pleasant, and during that time its membership was doubled. About this time also he held Sabbath afternoon and week-day evening services in the Mennonite chapel and elsewhere at Germantown, which resulted in the first baptism there, that of a Mrs. Fisher, of School Lane, who afterwards united with the church at "the Hill." For four years he alternated with the Rev. Horatio G. Jones, D.D., in supplying the church at Balligomingo on Sunday afternoons, and in administering the ordinances. Subsequently, Mr. Young began preaching on Lord's day afternoons, and occasionally during the week, in the "school-house" at Cold Point, in Plymouth, Montgomery Co. By subscriptions, which he obtained, he bought a lot, and built the first house of worship there, baptizing about forty converts, who retained their membership at Chestnut Hill until the Plymouth church was organized. In April, 1838, Mr. Young had the privilege of baptizing the first seven persons at the Falls of Schuylkill, the germ of the present church there. On the 20th of May, 1845, Mr. Young baptized Christopher Carr, aged one hundred and one years, a veteran of the Revolution, and, at the same time, his great-granddaughter, aged eleven years, while, on another occasion, he administered the rite to a household, consisting of Capt. John Hunston, his wife, and four daughters.

On the 1st of October, 1849, Mr. Young removed to the First Baptist church of Salem, N. J., where he had a successful pastorate of five years. The church was much strengthened, and 101 persons were added by baptism. Through his efforts most of the debt then remaining on the church edifice was paid, and by his suggestion an attempt was made, by the call of a convention, to establish a school "of higher grade" within the jurisdiction and under the control of the West Jersey Baptist Association.

In April, 1852, an educational committee was appointed, the rear lecture-room of the Salem church was fitted up for school purposes, and, during the first year, sixty pupils were in attendance. Soon, however, this promising enterprise, so dear to the heart of its moving spirit, was for the time abandoned; but it was again renewed in 1865, and became the flourishing South Jersey Institute, located at Bridgeton.

Mr. Young remained at Salem until October, 1854, when he returned to Chestnut Hill, and rebuilt their present neat meeting-house, and gathered the scattered flock.

In March, 1859, at the request of the Baptist Committee on City Missions, he left "the Hill," and went to the nineteenth ward, Philadelphia, and the following May organized the present Frankford Avenue Baptist church, with twenty-six constituent members. Here he remained till December, 1861, when the church numbered 125.

On the 1st of January, 1862, he took charge of the church at Haddonfield, N. J. In this extensive field he has since labored with the most substantial success. The church property has been greatly improved, a debt resting upon it liquidated, and an elegant parsonage provided. To the single Lord's day school, held in the lecture-room of the church, five mission schools, at various points, have been added, and they are all flourishing, while more than 300 converts have been baptized.

Outside of the church, too, here, as in his other parishes, his influence for good has developed itself in various ways, but in none, perhaps, more prominently than as the ever outspoken and uncompromising foe of the demon of intemperance.

As a preacher, Mr. Young is one of a type too fast passing away. His sermons evince careful preparation, abound in Scriptural quotations, and, though intensely Baptistic, are full of generous sentiments to men of different opinions from his own. His voice is pleasantly modulated, his enunciation clear, and his manner in the pulpit is solemn and impressive. He has now spent about forty-eight years in the pastoral office, baptizing more than twenty converts in each year of his ministry. "He is still," in the words of a brother clergyman, "vigilant and earnest in the Master's service, and with little apparent abatement of his early vigor for the work he so much loves."

Young, William McIntosh, D.D., was a native of Edinburgh, Scotland. At a very early age he was brought to this country by an uncle, who resided at Prince Edward Island, and with whom he remained but a short time, as he soon learned that it was the intention of his uncle to have him trained for the Catholic priesthood. Filled with disgust, he left him to dwell among strangers. Finding his way to Providence, R. I., he was soon converted and baptized. He believed that he was called of God to preach Christ, and at the Academical School in Worcester, Mass., he prepared himself to enter Columbian College, from which he graduated with honor, and was chosen class orator. His first charge was near Norfolk, Va. From this place he removed to Williamsburg, Va., and afterwards to Wilmington, N. C. Leaving the South, he came to Pittsburgh, Pa., where he remained several years. Spent one year in Oil City, Pa., two years in Woburn, Mass., and, after a pastorate of nearly four years in Meadville, Pa., he was called to Cheyenne, Wyoming, where, after organizing a church, he was suddenly called to his reward Feb. 20, 1879.

Z.

Zealy, J. T., D.D., late pastor at Jackson, Miss., was born in South Carolina in 1830; educated in the Military School of South Carolina; ordained at Beaufort in 1851; was some time pastor at Talahassee, Fla.; Cheraw, S. C.; five years pastor at Columbia, S. C.; during the war was president of several female colleges; in 1868 became pastor at Houston, Texas, where he continued seven years; was then called to Jackson, Miss., where he continued until recently.

Zion's Advocate, a weekly religious paper, the organ of the Baptist denomination in the State of Maine. The first number of this paper was published Nov. 11, 1828, under the editorial management of Rev. Adam Wilson, who, with great courage and self-denial, conducted its affairs for ten years. It then came into the hands of Rev. Joseph Ricker, whose connection with it continued until Dec. 27, 1842, when Dr. Wilson resumed the editorial chair, having as assistant Rev. Lewis Colby, at the time pastor of the Free Street church in Portland. Mr. Colby held this relation a few months only, and until the paper was sold, in 1848, Dr. Wilson was sole editor. The *Advocate* having been purchased by Mr., now Prof., S. K. Smith, of Colby University, the first number under his management was issued Sept. 1, 1848, and the paper was enlarged to seven columns instead of six, and was called *Zion's Advocate and Eastern Watchman*, the name which it now bears. Mr. Smith held his office until his election to a professorship in Waterville College, when the paper came into the hands of Mr., now Prof., J. B. Foster, who had charge of it for eight years, when *his* election to a professorship in Waterville College led to his resignation and the transfer by purchase to Rev. W. H. Shailer, D.D., then pastor of the First Baptist church in Portland. Mr. J. W. Colard was associate editor with Dr. Shailer during nearly the entire period of the latter gentleman's connection with the paper. The office of the *Advocate* was burned at the time of the great fire in Portland, July 4, 1866. Fortunately, the paper of that week had been sent out, and the next week a small sheet was issued. The paper resumed its old size the week following. Thus there has been no break in the weekly issue of the paper since its commencement in 1828. The present editor and proprietor, Rev. Henry S. Burrage, a graduate of Brown University of the class of 1861, purchased the paper from Rev. Dr. Shailer in September, 1873, and entered upon his editorial duties October 22 of that year. In April, 1877, the paper was enlarged to its present eight-column size, and it has entered upon the second half-century of its existence, taking a place among the best denominational papers in the country. It has had, and now has, a valuable class of contributors to its pages. The influence it has had in the enlargement and elevation of the Baptist churches in Maine has been very great. While kind and courteous in spirit, it has unflinchingly maintained what it has sincerely believed was " the faith once delivered to the saints." Conducted in the same spirit, for the future it will continue to be worthy of the best patronage the Baptists of Maine can give to it.

SUPPLEMENT.

A.

Alderson, Rev. John, was born in Yorkshire, England, in 1699. His father, Rev. John Alderson, was a minister of respectable standing in his denomination. His son, the subject of this notice, was a wayward youth, and, at the age of nineteen or twenty, came to America on board a British man-of-war. Locating in New Jersey, near the old Bethlehem church, he worked in the field for a respectable farmer by the name of Curtis, whose favor he secured, and whose daughter he married.

Having embraced the Saviour in the fullness of his heart, he was baptized, and received into the Bethlehem church. Possessing a clear intellect and a heart deeply imbued by divine grace, he was encouraged to give himself to the ministry of the Word. At length he was sent forth as a herald of the Cross by his church.

Thomas Hollis, of London, who was noted in his day for aiding Baptist ministers with good books, had presented Rev. John Alderson, of Yorkshire, with several volumes, among which were "Keach on the Parables," "Keach on Scripture Metaphors," large folio, and "Cottin's Concordance," quarto, London, 1635. The aged father sent these books to his son as an evidence of his inexpressible pleasure in learning that he had changed his manner of life and was now a preacher of the gospel. Mr. Alderson removed to Germantown, and here continued in the ministry until 1755, when he located in Rockingham Co., Va.

This frontier country had been previously visited by himself, Benjamin Griffith, Samuel Eaton, and John Gano. On the urgent solicitation of the few brethren there Mr. Alderson was induced to settle as their preacher, and on the 6th of August, 1756, he was instrumental in organizing them into a church, called Smith's and Linville Creek church.

A little Baptist church, which became extinct, existed in the Isle of Wight County in 1714. The Opeckon was constituted, in Berkeley County, in 1743, and this church, constituted by Mr. Alderson, was the third that had a name in the State of Virginia. Though twice dispersed by the inroads of the Indians, "after two or three years," says Semple, the historian, "they rallied again, and put their church matters in regular order. On the 12th of October, 1762, Mr. Alderson attended the meeting of the Philadelphia Association, when his church was received as a member of that body." Subsequently, Mr. Alderson removed to Botetourt Co., Va. Like many of the early Baptist ministers of that State, he did not escape persecution. He was imprisoned in the jail at Fincastle. He died in 1781, in the eighty-third year of his age, and was buried in the grave-yard of his neighborhood, afterwards abandoned and overgrown with tall oaks, with neither hillock nor stone to mark his resting-place.

Alexander, Rev. John, was born Jan. 30, 1829, in the city of Quebec. His parents, who were

REV. JOHN ALEXANDER.

Scotch Presbyterians, died when he was yet an infant. Converted in 1845, he at once consecrated himself to God for the ministry, and in 1846 he entered Knox College (Presbyterian), Toronto, where he completed the course of five years then prescribed, with a partial attendance at King's (now University) College. In 1851 he was ordained pastor of the Free Presbyterian church, Niagara, Ontario. From thence, in 1864, he removed to Brantford, where he formed what is now known as Zion Presbyterian church, and secured the erection of the fine edifice owned by that body. While in Brantford, in obedience to Christ and conscience, he left the Presbyterian communion, and was baptized, in December, 1860, by the late Dr. Fyfe, becoming a member and, in a few weeks, pastor of the First Baptist church. In 1863 he was called to the First church, Montreal, where he remained seven years, when he returned to Brantford, and aided in forming the Tabernacle Baptist church. Five years later he took charge of another new interest in the same city, now the East Ward church. He subsequently spent a short time in advocating the cause of the Grand Ligne Mission, three months with the church in Ottawa, Ill., and a year and a half as pastor in Simcoe, Ontario. He entered upon his present pastorate at Brockville, Ontario, in response to a twice-repeated call. Mr. Alexander is one of the most useful and honored men in the Baptist ministry in Canada. His work in Brantford and Montreal was specially fruitful, and laid the foundation of much of the present prosperity of the cause in those cities. For seven years he was secretary of the Eastern Home Missionary Convention and of the Sunday-School Union, and president of the Grande Ligne Mission, in which objects he took a very deep and practical interest.

Allison, Rev. J. V., of Pawnee Rock, Kansas, was born in 1815, in Western Pennsylvania; educated at Philadelphia, and ordained in 1840, and settled as pastor at Willistown. His next charge was that of Vincent Baptist church at Chester Springs, in the same county. From his pastorate at Vincent he was called by the board of the Pennsylvania Baptist Convention to serve as financial agent, and two years later was appointed by the board of trustees of the university at Lewisburg financial agent of that institution. After two years of service on behalf of the university he accepted a call from the Blockley Baptist church, Philadelphia, from which he removed to Mount Carroll, Ill., and labored in the northern part of the State as missionary and pastor for a period of twenty-four years, organizing three churches and building four meeting-houses. In 1874, entirely prostrated physically, and with but faint hope of ever being able to labor in the ministry again, he resigned his charge, and the following year removed to his present location in the Arkansas Valley, Kansas. But the change of climate wonderfully restored his health, and he is now (April, 1881) actively engaged in the work of the ministry under the patronage of the American Baptist Home Mission Society, having four young churches—Raymond, Pawnee Rock, Larned, and Walnut—under his charge, three of which, and one other, having been organized under his labors.

Alward, Rev. Ephraim, was born in New Brunswick, June 2, 1830. His parents removed to Ohio in his infancy, and he was converted at fourteen. At the age of eighteen he removed to St. Joseph, Mo., where he was baptized in January, 1849. Soon after this he entered William Jewell College, Mo., from which he graduated in 1855. About the time of leaving college he was ordained. He removed to Kansas in January, 1858, and was the first Baptist minister that located in Northeast Kansas, and for four consecutive years was the itinerant missionary of the American Baptist Home Mission Society in that region. He has been pastor of the Baptist churches at Springfield, Mo., at Red Oak, Iowa, and in Kansas at Burlingame, Topeka, Hiawatha, and Wathena.

Arnold, Hon. Welcome, was born in Smithfield, R. I., Feb. 5, 1745. He took up his residence in Providence, where he commenced business as a commission merchant. His industry and ability arrested the attention of President Manning, of Brown University, in whose church—the First Baptist—he was a worshiper. As the war of the Revolution came on, Mr. Arnold being now alone in business, began to develop still more strikingly his talents as a merchant. He entered into navigation extensively, and was so largely interested in the ownership of vessels that it is said that, although he accumulated a handsome fortune as the result of his enterprise, thirty vessels were captured by the British or lost in some way during the period of the war of each of which he was a part owner. He represented the town several years in the General Assembly, and four times was elected Speaker of the house. Had he chosen he might, without doubt, have been elected governor of the State. For this position, however, he had no special ambition, his large business requiring so much attention that he could not command the time to attend to the duties of the office. Although not a member of the church, Mr. Arnold was a decided and pronounced Baptist, and liberally contributed, like his fellow-merchants of the Brown family, in sustaining public worship in the new sanctuary, in the erection of which he took a deep interest. He was a personal friend of both President Manning and President Maxcy, and gave generously to the funds of Brown University, of which he was a trustee from 1783 to his death, which occurred Sept. 30, 1798. Among his descendants may be mentioned the name of his grandson, the late Hon. S. G. Arnold, a sketch of whose life may be found in the "Encyclopædia." Among the Baptist laymen of Rhode Island he takes a worthy place, and his memory is respected in his adopted home.

Arthur, William, D.D., was born in County Antrim, of Scotch-Irish stock, a people whose descendants have given the United States several presidents, many valiant soldiers, and hosts of useful citizens. Mr. Arthur was a graduate of Belfast College. He came to the United States in his eighteenth year, and entered the Baptist ministry. From 1855 to 1863 he was pastor of the Calvary church in New York. He served the churches at Bennington, Hinesburg, Fairfield, and Willistown, Vt.; and at York, Perry, Greenwich, Schenectady, Lansingburg, Hoosic, West Troy, and Newtonville, N. Y., where he died in October, 1875. Dr. Arthur was an author of extensive learning, and a minister of great usefulness and piety. His distinguished son, Chester A. Arthur, is now President of the United States.

Asplund, Rev. John, was born in Sweden; came to England in 1775; was in the British navy for some time, from which he deserted, and settled in North Carolina. He joined the Baptist church at Ballard's Bridge, Chowan Co., in 1782; removed to Southampton, Va., and was ordained. In 1791–94 he published his first and second "Baptist Register." In these two productions he treasured up invaluable statistics of the Baptist denomination. Morgan Edwards, Isaac Backus, R. B. Semple, and John Asplund are the greatest literary benefactors of American Baptists. He says "he made a tour of the Baptist churches to obtain the necessary information (for his work). He traveled about 7000 miles in about eighteen months, *chiefly on foot*, and visited about 215 churches and fifteen Associations." (Introduction to his "Register" for 1791.) He was drowned in Fishing Creek, Va., in 1807, while attempting to cross it. The literary work of this Swedish-American is rare and costly.

B.

Balcom, Rev. George, was born at Oxford, Chenango Co., N. Y., and was a brother of the late Hon. Ransom Balcom, of Binghamton, and of Rev. B. F. Balcom, of Steuben Co., N. Y. Converted after he had reached the maturity of early manhood and assumed the responsibilities of life, he gave himself to the ministry with all the ardor of his large heart.

In his native State he labored with marked success, especially as an evangelist. Removing to Kansas in 1870, he devoted himself to the Master's work with his accustomed zeal, aiding pastors in special meetings and laboring with much self-denial among the feeble churches and in the destitute regions on the frontier. During his ministry of twenty-seven years he baptized more than 2000, and several converted under his labors are now preaching the gospel. He died in Cawker City, Kansas, Dec. 21, 1879, in his fifty-seventh year.

Berry, Rev. Philip, was born near Hackensack, N. J., Feb. 16, 1837. His parents were of Huguenotic descent (Berri and Romeyn), and were strict members of the Reformed Dutch Church. He graduated at Rutgers College, N. J., in 1857, and at the Theological Seminary in that place in 1860. During his theological course he paid a visit to Germany, and on his return was shipwrecked by the burning of the steamer "Austria," of the Hamburg line, in which catastrophe 600 persons perished and but 88 were saved. The shock received by this accident was so severe that he never recovered from it. His first settlement after graduation was at Grand Rapids, Mich. In 1863 he was commissioned by the American Board as a missionary to Syria. Here he labored for two years, greatly enjoying the work; besides acquiring the Arabic language, he laid in stores of knowledge of the greatest value in Scriptural interpretation. But owing to the enervating effect of the climate, both upon himself and upon Mrs. Berry, they returned to this country in the autumn of 1865. For six years after this he labored in preaching and teaching among the Pedobaptists. At length his views on baptism, which for twelve or fifteen years had caused him grave doubts and difficulties, were submitted to the test of Scripture alone, and he was baptized into the fellowship of the Second Baptist church, Worcester, Mass., in February, 1872. After laboring in Massachusetts for five years in preaching the gospel, he was chosen assistant editor of the *National Baptist* in the spring of 1878. His special work on the paper is the conducting of the Bible School and the Literary Department.

Mr. Berry is a man of devoted piety, and of great usefulness.

Beugless, Rev. J. D., was born in Delaware Co., Pa., Oct. 18, 1836. In his eighteenth year, his father having removed to Philadelphia, he became acquainted with the Baptists, and he was so thoroughly convinced of the harmony of their principles with divine revelation that the following year, upon a profession of faith, he was baptized into the fellowship of the Eleventh Baptist church, Philadelphia. In 1856 he entered the university at Lewisburg, from which he graduated in 1860.

After leaving the university he was for a time an assistant to the editor of the *Christian Chronicle*, the Baptist paper of Pennsylvania. Subsequently he was ordained as pastor of the Pawtuxet church of Rhode Island. Then he served as chaplain of the 2d R. I. Infantry until wounded in the battle of the Wilderness. He was mustered out of the volunteer service with his regiment in June, 1864, and was commissioned by President Lincoln a chaplain in the navy July 2, 1864, which position he still holds. He has seen active service in peace and war in almost all the lands and waters of the globe. He participated in the two assaults on Fort Fisher.

He is president of the Association of Naval Chaplains of the United States, an organization having for its object the increased efficiency of the corps.

Chaplain Beugless has culture, intellect, and piety; he is fitted by character, genius, and broad education for any position in his profession on sea or on land.

Bevan, Isaac, D.D., was born in South Wales, Jan. 27, 1811. He was converted at seventeen and baptized; commenced preaching at nineteen; was ordained at twenty-one, and immediately left for this country. His parents were worthy members of the Baptist Church.

Very soon after his arrival in this country he went to Cold Spring, N. Y. His first pastorate was in Fishkill Plains, and continued seven years. In connection with his labors on this field he did considerable work that was blessed of God at Red Mills, Carmel, Patterson, Stanford, Pine Plains, Amenia, Pleasant Valley, Matteawan, and Wappinger's Falls. In connection with these labors the following churches were organized: Cold Spring, Putnam Valley, Matteawan, Wappinger's Falls, and Beekman. After this he was pastor at Amenia two years; at Rhinebeck and Tivoli nearly six, and at Hamilton two.

In the State of Pennsylvania his pastorates have been at Reading, eight years; at Scranton, ten years; at Clark's Green and Hyde Park, ten years. For part of two years he was corresponding secretary of the Pennsylvania Baptist State Convention.

Few men have prized more highly the privilege of preaching the gospel. His courteous bearing towards all Christians of whatever name, coupled with an unflinching adherence to truth, endeared him to thousands who listened to his preaching.

Binga, Rev. A., Jr., was born June 1, 1843, at Amherstburg, Ontario, Dominion of Canada. He is the son of a Baptist minister who was one of the fathers of the Baptist churches in that region. After pursuing his studies at King's Institute, Ontario, he spent several years in studying medicine. He was baptized in February, 1867, licensed to preach in the following April, and ordained in September. In 1868 he became principal of the Albany Enterprise Academy in Ohio, in connection with which position he preached regularly every Sunday. In 1872 he accepted the pastorate of the Baptist church in Manchester, Chesterfield Co., Va., and for nine years has been most successful in his labors. During this period he has baptized 544 persons. On three different occasions he had the pleasure of baptizing over 120 candidates, and at one time baptized 128 persons in fifty-five minutes. Mr. Binga has a wide field of usefulness. He has served as principal of the colored school in Manchester, as recording secretary of the Baptist State Convention, as secretary of the Baptist State Sunday-School Convention, and chairman of the Foreign Mission Board. He has written considerably as associate editor of several papers, and as contributor to the columns of the *Religious Herald*. He is a good preacher, a judicious counselor, a warm friend of higher education, earnestly interested in all movements which have for their object the advancement of the interests of the denomination, and is highly esteemed by the colored Baptists of Virginia.

Blackall, Clarence H., was born in New York City in 1856; was graduated after a full course in architecture in the Illinois Industrial University under Dr. John M. Gregory; spent two years in Paris in Ecole des Beaux Arts under the celebrated architect M. André. While in Paris he was an efficient laborer in the American chapel, and corresponded with marked ability for the *Standard*, of Chicago, the *National Baptist*, of Philadelphia, and the *Examiner and Chronicle*, of New York. He gives promise of success in his profession and usefulness in his church.

Broadus, Hon. Edmund, Culpeper Co., Va., long a prominent member of the Virginia Legislature, and a very influential layman in the Shiloh Association; a wise, good, and useful man; elder brother of William F. and Andrew Broaddus, and father of James M. and John A. Broadus. (The name is contracted from Broadhurst, which is now pronounced so in London.)

Buchan, David, was born in Glasgow, Scotland, March 3, 1807. He was descended from a long line of pious ancestors, a line which included Ebenezer Erskine, one of the founders of the United Presbyterian Church of Scotland. His father was an elder in a Scotch Baptist church. He was educated for the legal profession, but relinquished it. When quite a youth he was converted and baptized. In 1834 he emigrated to Canada, and settled near the town of Paris, where he was instrumental in organizing a Baptist church. The beautiful edifice in which this church now worships was erected at his sole cost in 1864. In 1849 he removed to Toronto, and started a weekly Baptist newspaper,—*The Pioneer*. Two years after he was appointed by the government bursar of Toronto University and Colleges, an office which he held until his death. For many years a member of Bond Street Baptist church, Toronto, he at length left it, with others, to form a new church in Yorkville, of which he was the senior deacon and principal supporter. He was also for several years superintendent of the Sunday-school. By his removal the various denominational societies in the province of Ontario lost an earnest advocate, a generous contributor, and a wise counselor. An ardent, loyal Baptist, he was also a friend to the cause of evangelical religion by whomsoever represented. At the time of his death, Oct. 17, 1877, he was president (for the third time) of the Home Mission Convention of Ontario. He was smitten with apoplexy on his own threshold, as he was starting out to attend a meeting of the board.

Buchan, Humphry Ewing, M.A., M.D., son of David Buchan, was born at Braeside, near Paris, Ontario, May 20, 1842. He graduated B.A. in the University of Toronto in 1864, and M.B. in medicine at the same university in 1867, and subsequently spent two years at the leading hospitals of London and Glasgow. While in Scotland he passed the examination and received the license of the Royal College of Physicians, Edinburgh, and the Faculty of Physicians and Surgeons, Glasgow. He is consulting physician to the Hospital for Sick Children, Toronto, and physician to Toronto General Hospital. He is also the representative of Toronto University on the Council of the College of Physicians and Surgeons of Ontario.

Dr. Buchan was baptized by the Rev. Dr. Caldicott in 1863. In 1877 he was elected deacon of the Jarvis Street church, Toronto. He was superintendent of the Sunday-school from 1877 to 1880, when he resigned on account of professional duties. He was president of the Baptist Missionary Convention of Ontario in 1877–78. He is one of the trustees of the Toronto Baptist College, and treasurer of the Baptist Union of Canada. For two years he was managing editor of the *Christian Helper*, which he was mainly instrumental in starting. No layman as young as Dr. Buchan is better known or more deservedly popular in his native province.

Buck, William, was born in Ancaster, Ontario, Aug. 22, 1828. He was trained in the public schools. At the present time (1881) he is one of the largest manufacturers in the Dominion. He is identified with many enterprises of a national, literary, and religious character, and supports everything that seems to promise the welfare of society. He is president of the Brantford Board of Trade, a director of the Royal Loan Society, the Brantford Young Ladies' College, and the Young Men's Christian Association of Brantford. He is one of the trustees of the Tabernacle Baptist church, of which he was one of the earliest members, and also of the Canadian Literary Institute, Woodstock, and of the Toronto Baptist College. In 1869–70 he was president of the Baptist Missionary Convention of Ontario. Mr. Buck is an earnest, practical Christian, a liberal giver, and a wise counselor. He is one of the pillars of the denomination in Canada.

Buckner, Rev. Daniel, was born in Laurens District, S. C., Sept. 30, 1801. His father removed, in 1807, to East Tennessee. In the spring of 1816 the Spirit led him to Christ, and he was baptized into the fellowship of Lick Creek, now Warrensburg, church, Greene Co. He was ordained in 1827. He labored extensively in Tennessee and Kentucky, traveling in all directions and for long distances to tell the story of the Cross. He possessed apostolic zeal, self-denial, and success. In the beginning of the war he removed to Texas, where he still lives, feeble with age and full of hope, and where God has also blessed his labors.

He preached for fifty years, and baptized 2500 persons. Of the 5000 converted under his ministry, twenty-five of those whom he immersed became ministers of the gospel. The distinguished Indian missionary and the able editor of *The Texas Baptist* are his sons.

Buckner, H. F., D.D., resides at Eufaula, Creek Nation. He is a man of consuming zeal, of more than ordinary natural ability, and of great perseverance. He was born Dec. 18, 1818, near Newport, East Tenn. He was converted when a small boy, and united with the Baptist church at Madisonville, Tenn., in 1832, being baptized by his own father. In 1835 he entered the Southwestern Theological Seminary, where he remained three years. He went to Alabama in 1838, and engaged in teaching. From early youth it had been his desire to preach, but it was not until his residence in Alabama that he consented to enter the ministry. Licensed in 1839, he was soon after ordained, and took charge of four churches, at the same time continuing his studies in the University of Alabama. In the mean time his parents had removed to Kentucky, where he rejoined them in 1841. He became a State missionary of the General Association of Kentucky, and labored with great success, chiefly in Greenup and the adjoining counties. In 1848 he became a missionary to the Indians, under the auspices of the American Indian

Mission Association, whose board resided at Louisville, Ky., and when the liabilities and assets of that board were transferred to the Domestic and Indian Mission Board of the Southern Baptist Convention, in 1855, he became the missionary of that Convention, and has continued this relation until the present time. The honorary degree of D.D. was conferred upon him by Baylor University.

Wherever he has been engaged Dr. Buckner has been successful; but it is by his labors as an Indian missionary that he is best known to the denomination. Among the Indians he is exceedingly popular, and he wields a great influence over them. He is the author of a Creek grammar, and has translated the gospel by John into the Creek language, besides which he has compiled a Creek hymn-book. Acting mostly as a superintendent of missions, he has been, and still continues to be, an exceedingly useful missionary among the Indians of the West. (See article on INDIAN MISSIONS.)

Butler, Rev. John, was born in Nottingham West, N. H., April 13, 1789, and hopefully converted at the age of fourteen, under the preaching of Rev. Thomas Paul. On Oct. 6, 1806, he united with the church in Newbury and Newburyport, Mass. He was licensed to preach in April, 1809, and in 1810 ordained pastor of the church in Hanover, Mass., where he remained fourteen years. He then removed to Waterville, Me., where he established a school for young ladies, meanwhile preaching most of the time; during his fourteen months' residence in this place, he baptized sixty persons. His next settlement was in East Winthrop, where he commenced his labors in May, 1825, devoting a part of his time to teaching. Here he remained six years. On the 8th of May, 1831, he began his pastorate in North Yarmouth, where he continued until Oct. 15, 1835, and then accepted an agency from the State Convention, to preach for feeble churches and in destitute sections of Maine. This position he held for nearly two years. The next ten years of his life were spent in doing the work of an evangelist, preaching wherever the providence of God called him. During this period he was engaged in eighteen revivals of religion, in which it is estimated that about 1200 persons were hopefully converted. In the year 1854, several of his children having established homes in Ohio and Kentucky, Mr. Butler removed to that part of the country. The state of his health was such that he was unable to preach much. The last baptismal service which he performed was in Middletown, O., the candidates being his three grandchildren. He died at the home of his son Charles, in Franklin, O., July 1, 1856. During his forty-eight years in the ministry he labored in as many as forty-two revivals, the first and the last being with the church where he was first settled, in Hanover, Mass.

Butler, Nathaniel, D.D., was born in Waterville, Me., Oct. 19, 1824; was fitted for college at the Yarmouth, Me., Academy; spent the first three years of his college course at Georgetown College, and was a graduate of what is now Colby University in the class of 1842. His ordination took place at Turner, Me., Oct. 28, 1845. Here he remained nearly five years,—1845-50,—when he became agent of the Missionary Union for Maine and Eastern Massachusetts, resigning in the fall of 1850 to take the pastorate of the church in Eastport, Me., where he remained till Sept. 3, 1859. From June 14, 1860, to May 10, 1863, he was pastor at Auburn; from 1864 to 1869, at Camden; from 1869 to 1872, at Albion, Ill.; from 1872 to November, 1873, at Leavenworth, Kansas; from November, 1873, to Oct. 1, 1876, at Second church in Bangor, Me.; from November, 1873, to October, 1876, at Dexter; from April, 1877, to April, 1878, at North Vassalborough; and at Hallowell from April, 1880, to April, 1881. He represented Vassalborough and Windsor in the State Legislature of 1880. He was the private secretary of Vice-President Hamlin from 1861 to March 4, 1865. Dr. Butler received the degree of D.D. from his *alma mater*, of which institution he has been a trustee since 1856, in the year 1873. In addition to his labors as a pastor he has, through the whole period of his ministry, performed much labor as an evangelist in Maine, Massachusetts, Illinois, and Kansas.

C.

Cabaniss, Judge E. G., was born in Jasper Co., Ga., in 1805, and died suddenly at Atlanta in 1871. After completing a course at Harvard College, in 1822, he was called to the bar in Georgia, and rose to be one of the most eminent judges in the State. He settled in Forsyth, Monroe Co., and was elected county clerk in 1826, retaining the office twenty-five years. He was also clerk of the Court of Ordinary for the same length of time. He was elected clerk of the house of representatives, in the Legislature, in 1840, and in 1857 was appointed judge of the Flint circuit, which position he held until 1861 with distinguished credit to himself. He was elected State senator in 1862; he was also appointed Confederate States tax collector and commissioner for Georgia, retaining the position honorably until the close of the war. In 1865 he was a member of the State constitutional convention, and in the autumn of the same year was elected to Congress. Early in the year 1871 he was appointed by the governor auditor of the State road, called the "Western and Atlantic Railroad," and removed his family from Forsyth to Atlanta, where he suddenly expired. Judge Cabaniss united with the Baptists in 1836, and was a man of deep piety, and of great faithfulness to Christ. He assisted in organizing the Southern Baptist Convention, in May, 1845, and for many years was a trustee of Mercer University. A strong temperance man, a bright Mason, and a conspicuous example of uprightness, honor, and integrity. In his death Georgia lost one of her noblest citizens and most reliable counselors, in whose heart there was no guile.

Cairns, Rev. James, was born in Scotland, April 9, 1824. At fifteen he was converted and united with the Presbyterian Church. In the summer of 1849 he came to America. After living some time in New York he removed to Zanesville, O. At this period the Baptists were engaged in erecting a house of worship, and the pastor, Rev. D. E. Thomas, came to Mr. Cairns and asked for a contribution; he replied that he could give no assistance to such bigoted people as the Baptists, for although they admitted that others were on the way to heaven, yet they would not admit members of other churches to the Lord's Supper. Mr. Thomas defended his principles, and as the subject turned upon baptism, it was arranged that they should hold a discussion at the home of Mr. Cairns, and that the Bible should be the only authority used. While engaged in preparing for it, Mr. Cairns, much against his will, was convinced that immersion is the only Bible mode of baptism. Mrs. Cairns, who was assisting her husband in his researches, came to the same conclusion. June 12, 1852, they were both baptized. Mr. Cairns removed to Bloomington, Ill., and united with the Baptist church there, where, in October, 1856, he was ordained as pastor of Smith's Grove church. Afterwards he was called to the pastorate of the Fairburg church, and remained five and a half years, during which the church increased from 40 to 288 members. He was afterwards pastor of the churches at Lacon, Rochelle, Polo, and Cambridge, Ill. From the latter place he removed to Winfield, Cowley Co., Kansas, and became the pastor of the First Baptist church of that city.

Mr. Cairns has baptized about 500 persons. He has been instrumental in erecting several church edifices, and he has organized sixteen churches.

Cameron, Rev. A. A., was born in Breadalbane, Perthshire, Scotland, in 1841. He has sprung from a ministerial family; his father, his uncle, grand-uncle, and quite a number of other near relatives have been or are clergymen. He received his early education in the Free Church School of Lawers, and the parish school of Killin. At fifteen years of age he became tutor in a gentleman's family, in Lochs Glenlyon. In 1857 he emigrated to Canada, his father being called to the pastorate of the Breadalbane Baptist church, Ontario. He pursued his further education in the grammar-schools of Vankleek Hill and L'Original. He taught school as a first-class teacher for five years; entered the Baptist College, Woodstock, Ontario, as a theological student in 1864; graduated in April, 1867; was ordained pastor of the Baptist church, Strathroy, the following June; and was called to his present pastorate in Ottawa, the capital of the Dominion, in 1871. In the latter city he has met with much success. He is an eloquent and effective speaker, a great controversialist, and a stanch Baptist.

Cameron, Rev. Robert, was born in 1839, in Oxford Co., Ontario. He became a Christian in 1859. In 1861, under Methodist Episcopal auspices, he began to preach. He was baptized in the autumn of 1862. He graduated B.A. in 1868, and M.A. in 1869, from the University of Toronto. While pursuing his collegiate course he became successively pastor in Lorra, Ontario, and editor of the *Baptist Freeman*. On graduating he settled for a short time over a church in Fairport, N. Y. During this pastorate he went to England in the interests of the Grand Ligne Mission. On his return he was pastor for a time in New York. He was one of the originators of the *Baptist Union*, but in 1875, being dissatisfied with the course of that paper, he withdrew entirely from it, and from further co-operation with the so-called liberal Baptists. On visiting Canada shortly after, he received a unanimous invitation to the Tabernacle Baptist church, Brantford, of which he is still the highly-esteemed and successful pastor.

Cates, Rev. M. D., was born in Orange Co., N. C. In April, 1834, he came to East Tennessee. March 11, 1838, he was baptized into the fellow- of the McMinnville church. In 1843 he went to school in Nashville, after this to Union University, at Murfreesborough. He was ordained by the McMinnville church, Oct. 13, 1844, Elders Bradley, Kimbrough, and Matthew Hillsman constituting the Presbytery. During his missionary work he constituted three churches. In January, 1846, he was elected pastor of the church at Marion, Cannon

Co., and continued as such over nine years. In April, 1846, he returned to the university and remained one session. During this year he published a small hymn-book, the "Companion," of which 3500 were sold. The second edition of 10,000 was sold directly. After this he enlarged the work, and called it "The Baptist Companion;" of it 6000 were published. After the war he made a new selection, "The Sacred Harp," which was published in Philadelphia. Several of the hymns in this collection are his own. He has published some other valuable works, among which is "The Voice of Truth." He is now, and has been for a number of years, editor and publisher of *The Baptist Messenger*, at Woodbury, Tenn., an able Baptist paper.

Cheves, Rev. J. B., was born in Crawford Co., Ga., Jan. 17, 1851, and is a lineal descendant of the once celebrated and distinguished Langdon Cheves. His father died when he was about seven years old. Much, therefore, devolved upon the mother, who nobly met all the demands of a large family, and reared them to occupy useful positions in society. Young Cheves joined the church when about thirteen years of age, and soon after was impressed with the idea of preaching. He was two years at Georgetown College, Ky., and two years at Mercer University, Ga., where he graduated.

When his school duties were over he was called to the pastorate of the Baptist church at Cuthbert, Ga., which he resigned after a year of service to go to Europe to prosecute his studies. He was for a while at the seminary at Greenville, S. C. While in Europe he was at the University of Leipsic nearly two years. He now resides at Nashville, and is the proprietor and one of the editors of the *Baptist Reflector*, which, under the present management, is becoming one of the most popular papers in the Southwest.

Mr. Cheves is a young man of culture, piety, and decided ability.

Cote, Rev. C. H. O., M.D., was born at Quebec, Canada, in the year 1809, of French-Canadian parents. He was educated for the medical profession. In the Canadian rebellion of 1837–38 he joined the "Patriots," after having previously distinguished himself as a leader of the disaffected party in the House of Assembly. For some time he was a resident at Swanton, in the State of New York, with a price set upon his head. Nominally a Roman Catholic, he was secretly an infidel. He was converted in Swanton, under a sermon from the words, "Believe on the Lord Jesus Christ and thou shalt be saved." Shortly afterwards he began to bear public testimony to the gospel. He fixed his residence at Chazy, where he opened his house for worship, and endeavored to guide his French-Canadian neighbors into the way of truth, with encouraging results. In October, 1843, Dr. Cote removed to St. Pie, one of the Grande Ligne Mission stations; but his health gave way shortly after, and he was compelled to seek a warmer climate. He spent some months at Savannah, and returned, in the spring of 1844, completely recovered. In the fall of that year he was ordained at St. Pie. He became the agent of the Grande Ligne Mission in the United States, collecting during the summer and returning to preach in Canada in the winter. St. Marie was the scene of these winter labors, which were greatly blessed. He died in great peace while attending the Lamoille Association at Hinesburgh, in 1850. Dr. Cote's death was a very heavy trial to the mission.

Cresswell, Samuel J., D.D., was born in England in 1802; was for many years a member of the Tabernacle church of Philadelphia. He was a man of much mental activity and power, and possessed the deepest interest in divine truth and religious movements. He united business pursuits with the duties of the ministry, and did much to foster the beginnings of many local interests. He was a lover of good books and good men; and was especially identified with the work of ministerial education. He died Aug. 29, 1877. He received the degree of D.D. from Madison University. His large and valuable library is now in possession of the university at Lewisburg by the gift of his children.

Crowell, William, D.D., was born in Middlefield, Mass., Sept. 22, 1806. He received his literary and theological education at Brown and Newton. While pursuing his studies at the latter he preached in several villages and towns around Boston, especially at Quincy, where he gathered a congregation in a large gambling-room in a house formerly used as a tavern, and such was the blessing attending his ministrations in this room that a church was organized.

Soon after leaving Newton, Mr. Crowell accepted the editorship of the *Christian Watchman*. This position he held for ten years, when the *Watchman* and the *Christian Reflector* were united. During this period the paper prospered, and its reputation was not surpassed by any denominational organ in the country.

While in Boston, in 1845, he preached twice every Sunday, and taught in the Sunday-school. After leaving Boston he accepted the pastorate of the church in Waterville, Me., and continued to serve it for about two years, when he removed to St. Louis, Mo., to take editorial charge of *The Western Watchman*. He held this position for ten years, making the paper a power among the growing hosts of Missouri Baptists. A variety of causes led him, just as the late war was about to convulse the nation, to retire from the editorial chair of *The*

SUFFIELD LITERARY INSTITUTION, CONNECTICUT. (See page 267.)

Western Watchman, after which he served as pastor for a short period at Freeport, Ill., and at the time of his death he was engaged in ministerial and other labors in New Jersey. He died in August, 1871. *The Watchman and Reflector*, of Boston, of August 31, 1871, says of him, "His mind was one of uncommon discrimination and clearness. We mourn the loss of so able and good a man, and that his 'sun should have gone down while it was yet day.'" Dr. Crowell was one of the most talented and cultured men in the Baptist denomination, his piety was all-pervading, and he shed a genial and blessed light over the entire relations of life. Thousands mourned his death as an affliction to the whole Baptist Israel. He was the author of several works, chief among which was "The Church Member's Manual," now used as a text-book in some of our theological seminaries.

D.

Davant, R. J., was born, lived, and died in Beaufort District, S. C. He died in 1872, having probably passed his sixtieth year. A perfect globe presents no salient points to take hold of. Brother Davant's character was so regularly developed and his life so smooth as to present a difficulty somewhat similar. As a lawyer, he had no superior at a bar that ranked second to that of Charleston only. He was for many years commissioner in equity, and all his business, private and professional, was conducted with a regularity approaching mathematical accuracy. Yet no man was ever freer from the stiffness of routine.

But above all, he was a Christian. He was long a deacon of the church where the writer was pastor, and we have never known one to whom the term pillar more properly applied.

He was president of the Augusta and Port Royal Railroad Company for several years, and the completion of the road is largely due to him.

Dawson, John Edmonds, D.D., was born March 7, 1805, in Washington Co., Ga. He enjoyed excellent educational advantages at Madison and at Mount Zion Academy, Hancock Co. In September, 1827, he was converted, and united with the church at Indian Creek. Into all matters of denominational interest he now entered with great zeal and earnestness, and became thoroughly identified with Sherwood, Mallary, Campbell, Hillyer, Crawford, and Mell.

He was ordained Jan. 14, 1835. His first charge was the Eatonton church. From that time until the day of his death, Nov. 18, 1860, he was a zealous preacher of the gospel, laboring mostly in the middle and western part of the State, and rising to the highest rank in the ministry.

Mercer University, of which he had been a trustee for many years, conferred on him the degree of Doctor of Divinity in 1858.

His countenance was cast in a noble mould, whose classic features and swelling brow were indicative of a grand intellect. He possessed an unusual degree of refinement. From his conversion

JOHN EDMONDS DAWSON, D.D.

he was an ardent friend of the State Baptist Convention, the grand promoter of missions, education, temperance, and Sunday-schools among the Baptists of Georgia. Extensive reading, much intercourse with able and well-stored minds, together with an excellent memory and great mental vigor, enabled his bright and rapid intellect to grasp much that was advantageous to him. In any circle where he moved he was the leading spirit.

While discoursing eloquently once at Milledgeville upon the shortness of time and the necessity of instantly accepting Jesus, expressly in view of the uncertainty of life, he accidentally struck one of the pulpit lamps, hurling it to the floor, where it lay broken into a thousand fragments. "See," said he, "that splendid lamp, which but a moment ago stood at my right hand the perfection of beauty and utility! Now it is but a heap of broken glass, —a *ruin!* So frail is *your* life! By what an attenuated thread is it suspended! How small a thing may snap the brittle cord! Let this accident impress upon your minds the solemn truths I have been urging upon your attention, and warn you to flee *now* to the only safe refuge."

He not unfrequently rose to absolute sublimity, completely enthralling and overpowering his hearers. In all the true attributes of oratory and eloquence he probably never had an equal in Georgia, certainly not a superior.

Dr. Dawson was distinguished as an educator and as an able writer. His remains were carried to his native State, and buried at Columbus, Ga., amid the lamentations of thousands.

Dr. John L. Dagg, long president of Mercer University, says, "As a preacher, Dr. Dawson was one of the ablest it has been my privilege to hear."

Deitz, Rev. Charles M., Ridley Park, Pa., was born, Oct. 7, 1830, in Philadelphia; baptized into the fellowship of the Fourth Baptist church, Philadelphia, March 8, 1846; licensed 1854; ordained in March, 1858; graduated from the Central High School, Philadelphia, in 1845, from Lewisburg University in 1854, and from Rochester Theological Seminary in 1856; has been a successful pastor in New Jersey, and for a time financial agent of the South Jersey Institute. He has also been pastor of the Coatesville, Holmesburg, and Ridley Park churches in Pennsylvania; has been moderator of Central Union Association and of Philadelphia Baptist Ministers' Conference. He is a curator of the university at Lewisburg.

Denovan, Rev. Joshua, was born in Glasgow, Scotland, in 1829, and was "born again" in the summer of 1851. His education was obtained in the parish schools and in the University of Glasgow. He was formally ordained to the pastorate of a Presbyterian church, and during a ministry of about eight years was much blessed. In the fall of 1864, when the membership of the church numbered nearly 800, he renounced Pedobaptism and was immersed on a profession of his faith. This act resulted in the severance both of natural and ecclesiastical ties. His health, undermined by years of excessive work, and months of mental anxiety, now utterly broke down. Advised to seek a change of climate, he arrived in Canada in the autumn of 1866, and retired to the quiet and beautiful hill country of Missisquoi, Quebec. Nine months of absolute rest effected a great improvement in his physical condition, and he gradually found his way back into the active ministry. He spent nearly two years in preaching in several needy country places,—St. Armand, Smith's Falls, Carle-

REV. JOSHUA DENOVAN.

ton Place, and Almonte. He was settled as pastor (1869-71) in the town of Stratford, Ontario, and (1871-77) in Montreal. In 1877 he was engaged in a special effort for the evangelization of French Canadian Roman Catholics, and in March, 1878, he entered upon his present pastorate,—Alexander Street, Toronto. He was secretary for five years of the Baptist Home Mission Convention East, and has been secretary of the Baptist Home Mission Convention of Ontario since 1878. A devoted servant of Christ, a great preacher, and a fearless advocate of truth, Mr. Denovan commands the high esteem of the Baptist churches in Canada.

Doubleday, Hon. U. F., was born in Lebanon, N. Y., Dec. 15, 1792, and died in Belvidere, Ill., Nov. 14, 1866. He added to his education in the public schools an extensive knowledge of the higher mathematics and the natural sciences. In early life he settled in Auburn, N. Y., where for about thirty years he edited and published the *Cayuga Patriot*. He was elected to Congress in 1831, and re-elected in 1833, both of which terms he served with marked ability. When the civil war broke out he took strong ground for the Union. His sons, Maj.-Gen. Abner Doubleday, Col. Thomas D. Doubleday, and Brig.-Gen. U. Doubleday, by their devotion and success in arms, showed the power of the father's teaching in respect to the principles of patriotism. He was baptized into the fellowship of the Baptist church of Scipio, N. Y., by Rev. H. J. Eddy, D.D., in 1841. He removed to New York City, and was elected a deacon of the Sixteenth Baptist church. He also served as deacon of the church at Bloomington, Ill. The writer has a manuscript of a work written by him on "The Harmony of Science with the Bible Account of the Six Days of Creation." It is worthy of publication, and may yet be given to the world.

Dryden, John, M.P., was born in 1840, near Brooklin, province of Ontario. Converted in 1858, he united with the Wesleyan Methodist body, to which other members of his family were attached. In 1861 he was led to see the believer's duty regarding baptism, and united with the Baptist church of the township of Whitby, of which he is now the leading supporter. Mr. Dryden received a liberal education, and has attained a high standing for culture and intelligence. In March, 1879, he was unanimously chosen by the Reform convention of South Ontario as their candidate for the representation of the constituency in the Provincial Parliament, and was duly elected in the following June. As a citizen, a legislator, and a follower of Christ, he is abundant in labors for the public good. Mr. Dryden serves the denomination as a director of the Ontario Baptist Missionary Convention, and a member of the board of trustees of the Toronto Theological Seminary.

E.

Eaton, Prof. James R., Ph.D., son of Geo. W. Eaton, D.D., LL.D., was born at Hamilton, N. Y., Dec. 11, 1834. On a profession of faith in Christ he was baptized into the membership of the church at Hamilton, June 14, 1846; graduated from Madison University in 1856, and from Hamilton Theological Seminary in 1858. In 1859 he became Adjunct Professor of Mathematics and Natural Science in Union University, Murfreesborough, Tenn. From 1859 to the spring of 1861 he was Professor of Ancient Languages in Bethel College, Russellville, Ky.; during the war he held a secular position in New York. From 1866 to 1869, Prof. Eaton occupied the chair of Natural Science in the University of Louisville, Ky. In the spring of 1869 he became Professor of Natural Science in William Jewell College, Liberty, Mo., which position he still occupies. In 1876 Madison University conferred on him the degree of Doctor of Philosophy. He has an abiding impression that he was called to teach, and has consecrated himself to the same work in which his distinguished father spent his life,—the education of the Baptist ministry. His motto in the class-room, "What is worth doing at all is worth doing well," is the principle that governs his own life.

Eaton, Leonard Hobart, was born in Groton, Grafton Co., N. H., April 20, 1817. At the age of eleven he removed to Newton, Mass., and at sixteen to Lowell, where he enjoyed the advantages of its excellent public schools. In 1837 he was appointed a teacher in the North Grammar-School. In the same year he was baptized by the Rev. Lemuel Porter, and united with the Worthen Street church. He removed to Pittsburgh, Pa., in 1839, and united with the First Baptist church. He was one of the constituent members of the Grant Street Baptist church. In 1843 he was elected principal of the Third Ward Public School in Alleghany City, and filled that position seventeen years. In 1847 he united with the Sandusky Street Baptist church; and five years later was appointed a deacon. Both these relations have been sustained to the present time. He served as superintendent of the Sunday-school of this church for a period of thirty years, extending from 1848 to 1878. In 1860 he was elected principal of the Forbes Public School of Pittsburgh, the largest in that city. This position he still holds.

He was a member of the board of school controllers in Alleghany City eight years; president of the Baptist Social Union of Pittsburgh, Alleghany, and vicinity five years; and president of the Sunday-School Convention connected with the Pittsburgh Baptist Association thirteen years. He is now (1881) a director of the Baptist Summer Resort at Point Chautauqua, N. Y.; president of the Young Men's Bible Society of Pittsburgh; and president of the Western Pennsylvania Humane Society.

Edwards, Col. B. W., was born in Spartanburg Co., S. C., Jan. 24, 1824. His parents removed to Georgia in his childhood. His health, for many years, was so poor that little hope of his living to manhood was entertained. But his constitution having improved, he entered the South Carolina College in 1847, and graduated in 1850. Having returned to Georgia, he taught school and studied law for one year. He was then admitted to the bar in 1851, and soon after went to the same school at Harvard, Mass., where he graduated in 1853.

He now returned to his native State, locating first at Sumter and afterwards in Darlington County, where he now resides. He was commissioner in equity for five years, beginning in 1861. In the same year he entered the Confederate service, but was soon after discharged on account of ill health.

He has long been a deacon of the Darlington Baptist church and superintendent of the Sunday-school, a member of the board of trustees of Furman University for fifteen years, and for the past two years president of the Baptist State Convention. He is very prompt and efficient as a presiding officer. In quiet, unobtrusive usefulness he has no superior in the State.

Edwards, Gen. O. E., a native of Spartanburg District, S. C., was born Nov. 19, 1819. He took an academic course at Glenn Spring, finishing it in 1843. He was admitted to the bar in 1845, and commenced the practice of law at Spartanburg Court-House. He was repeatedly sent to the Legislature from his native district, and was a member when the war began. He was elected a brigadier-general of militia in 1854. At the beginning of the war he raised a regiment and entered the Confederate army in command of the 13th S. C. Volunteers. He was mortally wounded in the battle of Chancellorsville, while in command of McGowan's brigade, and died a few days after at Goldsborough, N. C., on his way home. He was buried at Spartanburg. He had long been a deacon of the Spartanburg Baptist church and superintendent of the Sabbath-school.

In battle he was brave almost to a fault, as the writer knows personally, and his death was probably due to his entire forgetfulness of his own safety. He left a gap in the church and the community that is scarcely filled even to the present day.

Edwards, Rev. Solomon, was born in Barnwell Co., S. C. He was born in slavery, the property of Rev. Elliott Estess. From his boyhood he was honest and diligent. In early life he was a foreman on the plantation. His education is limited, the writer having taught him most of what he knows. But nature, or rather nature's God, has endowed him with unusual common sense. He has been preaching for many years, and we earnestly hope may long continue to preach, as no man within our knowledge could fill his place. His people receive his words almost as those of an oracle, and it is well that they are words of wisdom and truth.

He is of pure African extraction, nearly six feet high, and strongly built. His countenance is very pleasing, and at a glance shows his superiority to most of his race. Whatever improvement is to be made in the colored race must be made chiefly through such men as Brother Edwards.

Elford, Charles James, was born in Charleston, S. C., May 11, 1820. Left an orphan in early years, he went to Greenville, S. C., when a mere boy. While employed as clerk in a store he used every spare moment for study, and, with the blessing of God on his earnest, patient, and well-directed efforts at self-improvement, he rose from one position to another till he attained to eminent distinction at the bar. An ardent Christian and leader in every good work, he devoted himself especially to the interests of the Sunday-school. In this sphere his influence on the young and on Sunday-school workers throughout the State was productive of results for good far beyond that of many ministers of the gospel. *Kind Words*, a Sunday-school paper, issued first at Greenville, S. C., now at Macon, Ga., owed its origin to him. With his dying breath leaving to the Sunday-school over which he had long presided the message, " Tell them to come to heaven ; that's all," he closed his earthly service in Greenville, May 25, 1867, honored as a public benefactor by the whole community.

Emery, George Freeman, was born at Paris, Oxford Co., Me., Nov. 10, 1817. He fitted for college under private tutors, and at the Farmington Academy, and was a graduate of Bowdoin College, in the class of 1836. On graduating he studied law with his father, Judge Stephen Emery, and was admitted to the bar Nov. 10, 1838, and formed a law partnership with his father, which continued about ten years. In 1846 he removed to Portland. While residing in Paris he was for six years register of probate for Oxford County. After his removal to Portland he was appointed, in 1848, clerk of the U. S. Circuit by Judge Woodbury, and continued under three of his successors. He resigned his office on removal to Boston in 1877, where he became connected with the *Boston Post*, a leading daily paper, of which he was chosen editor-in-chief in 1880, and now (1881) holds this position. Mr. Emery was baptized, with his wife, Sept. 23, 1855, by Rev. G. W. Bosworth, D.D., and united with the Free Street Baptist church in Portland, Me. In all matters pertaining to the prosperity of that church he took a deep interest. He was for a considerable time the superintendent of its Sabbath-school. He took an active part in getting up an organization to provide for poor and devoted ministers, also the corporation to manage the "Greenough Fund" for building churches in Maine. For a time he was a trustee of Colby University, and was a prominent layman among the Baptists of his native State. Mrs. Emery was the daughter of John W.

Appleton, Esq., a leading Baptist of Maine, and sister of Hon. John Appleton, M.C., and minister plenipotentiary to Russia under President Buchanan. The first wife of Vice-President Hamlin was a sister of Mr. Emery, and his second wife a half-sister.

Emery, Hon. James S., was born in Industry, Franklin Co., Me., and was graduated in 1851 at Colby University. He was made president of the Vermont Literary and Scientific Institution at Brandon in that State. He commenced the study of the law in New York City in 1852, where he was admitted to the bar in February, 1854. He was one of a hundred young men who founded Lawrence, Kansas, in September of the same year. This was the first settlement from New England made in the new Territory just entered under the Kansas-Nebraska bill. He took grounds for a free State, and was one of a committee sent to the free States in behalf of free Kansas. He was a member from Lawrence of two of the constitutional conventions which Kansas had before she was received into the Union. He was twice chosen to a seat in the Legislature, and in 1864 was appointed by Mr. Lincoln U. S. district attorney for his State, which post he held about three years. He was one of the seven constituent members of the first Baptist church formed in the Territory, in January, 1855, at Lawrence. It was through his efforts mainly that the State University of Kansas was located at the city of his residence. Being a friend of learning, he is often called before the public in literary, historical, and religious addresses. He is a man of talent and piety.

F.

French, George R. For article, see page 417.

GEORGE R. FRENCH.

Feller, Madame Henrietta, was born April 2, 1800, at Montagny, a village in the Canton de Vaud, Switzerland. In 1803 her father, M. Odin, removed with his family to Lausanne, where Henrietta enjoyed superior educational advantages. In 1822 she married M. Louis Feller, of Lausanne, one of its most respected citizens. Within five years she was left a widow. Her only child, a daughter, had died a short time before. Previous to these sad bereavements she had become a decided and active Christian, and after her husband's death she consecrated herself still more fully to the service of Christ. In 1835, Madame Feller received a letter from a dear friend, the wife of a Swiss missionary in Canada, describing the spiritual destitution of the French Canadians, and exhorting her to give herself to missionary work. This she regarded as a call from God, and on the 17th of August, in the same year, she left Lausanne for the scene of her future toils. She was accompanied by Louis Roussy, a member of the church in Lausanne, and of the Mission Institute in the same city. They reached Montreal on the 31st of October, and shortly after settled in the village of St. Johns. Madame Feller spent her first year in Canada in earnest efforts for the enlightenment and salvation of the French Catholics by domestic visitation, by the instruction of children, and by the distribution of the Scriptures. In September, 1836, she removed to La Grand Ligne, encouraged by the success which had attended Mr. Roussy's ministrations in that place. She commenced her work in the garret of a small log house, where she taught a school of children by day and a class of adults by night. In this garret also she resided, subjecting herself to great privation. She visited the poor and the sick, carrying the Word of life into many a home, when the preacher, Mr. Roussy, would have been repelled. Thus was laid the foundation of the mission of which, for thirty-two years, Madame Feller was the leading spirit, and which, long before she died, had become one of the most useful institutions in Canada. She died at the Grand Ligne Mission-House on the 29th of March, 1868. It has been well said that "Henrietta Feller was raised up for a great work. She has left her mark, by God's grace, on Lower Canada."

Fillmore, Mrs. Millard, widow of ex-President Fillmore, was born at Morristown, N. J., Oct. 27, 1813. Her maiden name was Caroline Carmichael, youngest daughter of Charles Carmichael and Tempe Wickham Blachly. She was baptized by the late Rev. Geo. B. Ide, D.D., and was, with her first husband, the late Ezekiel C. McIntosh, Esq., of Albany, a member of the venerable Dr. Welch's church. She was married to Mr. Fillmore by the Rev. Wm. Hague, D.D. She was a woman of great refinement and culture, and had a richly-stored mind resulting from extensive reading. Her mansion was exquisitely furnished, being adorned with a very large collection of expensive paintings. She was constant in her attendance at her chosen church, the Washington Street Baptist, of Buffalo, of which she was a faithful member. She was a liberal giver to denominational missionary societies and to every good cause. She loved to read the sermons of Spurgeon, and enjoyed direct Christian conversation. She died in Buffalo, Aug. 11, 1881.

G.

Gates, Rev. Granville, was born in Maine, Broome Co., N. Y., April 17, 1829. At the age of eighteen he united with the Baptist Church, having been converted in childhood, through the instrumentality of a mother who did not live to know on earth the result of her faithfulness. For three years subsequent to 1850 he was a member of the board of supervisors of Broome County.

In 1853 he was licensed to preach, and was ordained at West Nanticoke in January of the following year. He continued to labor in the State of New York, and chiefly among the churches of the Broome and Tioga Association, for thirteen years, spending two years at West Nanticoke, six years at Centre Lisle, four years at Mott's Corners, and one year at Ovid.

In the spring of 1867 he accepted an appointment from the Home Mission Society to labor in the West. Locating soon after at Highland, he devoted ten years to missionary work in Northeast Kansas, gathering the churches of Roy's Creek, Hiawatha, Sabetha, Valley Falls, and Blue Rapids. In 1878 he became pastor of the Baptist church of Emporia, which had been in a languishing condition for some years. In June he resigned the care of this church to accept an appointment as general missionary of Kansas.

Gee, Rev. W. Sandford, was born near Bowling Green, Ky., March 19, 1847. His parents removed to Illinois in 1852; was brought up upon a farm; taught school for seven years; was ordained in Illinois; graduated from the theological department of Shurtleff College. His first pastorate, of three years, was at Mount Vernon. At present he is pastor of the First Baptist church of Lincoln, Neb., where he has labored for three years. He was elected chaplain of the house of representatives in the session of 1881.

Grande Ligne, Evangelical Society of, was commenced, at the close of 1835, by Madame Feller and Rev. Louis Roussy, who had recently left Switzerland for the purpose of carrying the gospel to the benighted French Canadians. Numerous Romish churches, colleges, convents, hospitals, and asylums, with their immense wealth, were both the signs and instruments of undisputed papal sway over Lower Canada. It seemed to be absolutely inaccessible to the gospel, and, previous to the arrival of Madame Feller and Mr. Roussy, no sustained effort had been made to enlighten it. There are now several societies engaged in the work of French Canadian evangelization, but the Baptist mission was the pioneer. Very little was done for a year or two; but after the opening had been made many friends of other denominations helped the infant cause. In 1840 an institute was begun at La Grande Ligne, with the primary view of training future laborers,—evangelists, teachers, and pastors. At the same time it furnished the best means of educating the grown-up children of isolated Protestant converts living in the midst of Roman Catholic communities.

In 1851 a school for girls was opened at St. Pie; but in 1855 the mission premises were burned, and the Feller Institute, as it was called, was removed to Longueil. This has since been removed to Grande Ligne, where all the educational work of the mission is now conducted. The new Feller

Institute building was erected at a cost of $8000, and was opened July 1, 1880, free from debt.

"It is estimated," says the Rev. A. Therrien, "that over 4000 French Canadians have been led to embrace the gospel through the direct instrumentality of this mission, 15 churches have been organized, 2000 young people educated, and 22 young men prepared for the ministry, or for evangelists and colporteurs." Several French pastors and missionaries now laboring among their fellow-countrymen in the United States were converted and trained at La Grande Ligne. Of these are Revs. L. Auger, of Stryker, O.; R. B. Desroches, of Detroit, Mich.; F. X. Smith, of Fall River, Mass.; J. N. Williams and E. Lager, who labored among the scattered French Canadians in New England; and A. Chatrand, of Elivon, Kansas. Most of the French churches in the United States also owe their existence, indirectly at least, to the Grande Ligne Mission. There are seven churches directly connected with the mission.

Graves, Rev. Henry L., was born in Yanceyville, N. C., Feb. 22, 1810; graduated from the University of North Carolina and Hamilton Theological Seminary, N. Y.; ordained in November, 1837; was the first president of Baylor University, Texas, from 1846–1851; served acceptably as pastor of the Independence church; during the war was president of the Female College, Fairfield, Texas, and from 1874–75 was president of Baylor Female College. He was the first president of the Texas Baptist State Convention, and ably filled the same office for sixteen years. Morell's "Flowers and Fruits, or Thirty-Six Years in Texas," says of him: "His qualifications entitle him to the position, in the estimation of his brethren, of a refined and educated Christian gentleman." He has been moderator of Union Association, and is now president of the Baptist Education Society of Texas, and has seen much service, and has always been regarded as a wise counselor in Baptist assemblies.

Grier, Prof. William Thompson, A.M., was born near Salem, N. J., May 11, 1850. Having been fitted for college at an academy in his native town, he entered the Freshman class of the university at Lewisburg in September, 1867. In 1871 he was graduated with the highest honors of his class, and was immediately elected Professor of Ancient Languages in Monongahela College, Pa. He remained there four years, during a part of the time acting as president of the college. In this position he was very successful, and his work was highly appreciated. The presidency of the college was offered to him, but he declined to accept it. In 1875 he was elected Professor of the Latin Language and Literature in the university at Lewisburg, and his success has more than justified his choice. He is deservedly popular both in the university and outside of it. The standard of scholarship in his department is high. Prof. Grier promises to become one of the scholars of the denomination. He is a thorough teacher, is an excellent speaker, and everywhere well represents the university.

Groff, Prof. George G., M.D., was born in Chester Co., Pa., in April, 1851. He received his early education in Phœnixville and Norristown and in the State Normal School at West Chester. He subsequently entered the University of Michigan, and afterwards graduated in medicine from the Long Island College Hospital, Brooklyn, N. Y., in 1877. He at once became the teacher of Natural Sciences in the State Normal School at West Chester, which position he held until 1879, when he was elected to the chair of Natural Sciences in the university at Lewisburg. This position he fills with marked ability, and with much acceptance to all who know his daily life.

Grow, Rev. T. D., was born at Hartland, Vt., Jan. 24, 1824. His grandfather was a pioneer Baptist minister in Vermont. His brother, Rev. James Grow, of Connecticut, was one of the first to assist in the foreign work, sending Dr. Judson $50, out of $200 salary, before the mission was thoroughly organized. His cousin was a missionary to Siam, and died there. His widow is now the wife of Dr. Dean. He was educated at New Hampton, N. H., and ordained May 1, 1850, in Kane Co., Ill. Most of his ministerial work has been in Wisconsin, Missouri, and Kansas. Quite a number of churches have been formed under his labors.

Gunn, Rev. David Brainard, was born in Montague, Mass., May 8, 1823; had very early impressions respecting his need of Christ as his Saviour; also that he should become a minister of the gospel. When about ten years of age he was convicted of sin, but he did not at that time indulge a hope in Jesus. In January, 1838, he was specially moved by the Holy Spirit and led into light, and he enlisted as Christ's soldier. Upon the following Thanksgiving-day he was baptized with three brothers and a sister. In 1854, being greatly strengthened by the Holy Spirit, he began in earnest the work of soul-winning. He was licensed by the Shelburne Falls, Mass., Baptist church, of which he was a member. Wishing to devote himself wholly to the ministry, he sold out his business and home, and removing to the West, settled in Warsaw, Ill., organized a church, and was ordained as its pastor in August, 1857. There he toiled nearly four years, and added to it about 150 members. Afterwards he held brief pastorates in Carthage, Ill., and Hannibal, Mo. Early in 1865 he settled in Sandwich, Ill., where in the fourth year of a very pleasant pastorate his health completely failed for two years. Then slowly returning strength enabled him to engage as a supply, which after a year or two led him into evangelistic and missionary labors, which have been continued, mostly in the States of Illinois and Kansas, until the present time. God has signally blessed Mr. Gunn's ministry.

Gunn, Rev. Elihu, was born in Montague, Mass., Jan. 3, 1818. His ancestors were of the Puritan stock, and had been stanch Baptists on both sides for several generations, being the earliest settlers in that part of the State, and among those who suffered persecution from the "standing order" for conscience' sake. He publicly confessed Christ in his twenty-first year. His earliest desire was to secure an education and become a minister of Christ. He entered the Freshman class in Madison University in 1844, and he graduated from the theological seminary in 1849. He was soon after ordained at North Sunderland, Mass., and went as a missionary to the new State of Iowa. Settled first at Keokuk, then a frontier town of 1500 people. He was then president of the Central University, of Iowa, five years. Afterwards he was pastor at Mount Pleasant nearly nine years. He then came to Kansas, and was pastor at Atchison three years, district secretary of the American Baptist Home Mission Society for Kansas and Missouri three and a half years, and since May, 1877, he has been pastor of the Baptist church at Fort Scott, Kansas. Mr. Gunn has baptized 447 persons, including all of his five children.

H.

Hardwicke, Rev. J. F., was born in Virginia in 1837; united with the church when a boy; commenced preaching when but eighteen. After pursuing his studies with his brother, Rev. J. B. Hardwicke, he entered a classical school. In 1869 he matriculated at the Southern Baptist Theological Seminary, at Greenville, S. C. When the war compelled its school to suspend he retired to Virginia, and entered upon the pastorate. He served the church at Milton, N. C., and also that at Ephesus. He then removed to Western Virginia, and succeeded in establishing a church at Huntington. Mr. Hardwicke is now pastor at Bowling Green, Ky. A man of genial disposition, blessed with a mind of decided vigor, and a close student of the Scriptures, he ranks with the best preachers of his State.

Harris, Rev. Elmore, was born in 1854, near the city of Brantford, Ontario, Canada. His father was a manufacturer, and intended his son for the same calling; but God had otherwise designed. He was brought to Christ in April, 1870, and in the following year, when but a lad of seventeen, he preached his first sermon. For nearly two years he studied in the high school in Beamsville, and the Collegiate Institute of the city of St. Catharines. He afterwards attended the University of Toronto, taking two scholarships in classics and the first prizes in Oriental languages. He graduated in 1877, receiving the degree of B.A. In 1876, a year before he finished his university course, he became pastor of the First Baptist church of St. Thomas, where he still labors with great acceptance. During his five years' ministry the First and Zion churches, unfortunately severed, have been united, and a handsome structure erected in the centre of the city, costing $17,000. The membership has more than doubled. Mr. Harris is one of the rising men in the Baptist ministry of the New Dominion.

Harris, John, of Brantford, Ontario, Canada, was born in 1841, in the township of Townsend, in the same province. At the age of twenty-one he entered into partnership with his father, Mr. Alanson Harris. He is a man of considerable means and of distinguished liberality. He is at present the teacher of a large Bible-class, numbering, at times, 150 persons, in the First church, at Brantford. There are continual accessions to the church from this class. He has also an excellent gift in presenting the gospel to the unsaved, and has been greatly blessed in this work in the neighborhood of his own city and at other points. An earnest Bible student, a diligent worker, a generous contributor to all benevolent and denominational objects, and a true friend, he has fairly won the high position he holds among the Baptist laymen of Canada.

Hildreth, William, D.D., was born at South Bend, Ind., Jan. 24, 1838. In 1853 the family removed to Sandyville, Iowa, where Mr. Hildreth was baptized in 1859; licensed to preach in 1860. In 1861 he was called to the church at Lovilia, and the following year was ordained. He entered Central University, preaching once on the Sabbath for the First church of Pella while he remained in the school.

He removed to Chillicothe, Mo., and served the

church there one year, and accepted an appointment from the American Baptist Publication Society as general Sunday-school missionary, in which connection he remained over three years. After a brief pastorate at Pleasant Hill, Mo., he became general missionary of the American Baptist Home Mission Society, in which work he continued three years, and during which he baptized 484 persons.

In 1872 he removed to California, remaining four years, preaching for the Tabernacle church, San Francisco, and the church at San José. He returned East in 1876, and settled with the church at New Albany, Ind., where he remained four years, until called to the Union Baptist church of Pittsburgh, his present field of labor.

Mr. Hildreth has built ten houses of worship, raising for this purpose $107,000. He received into the churches with which he has labored 2017 persons, of whom he has baptized 1530. In 1879 Judson University conferred upon him the degree of D.D.

Hoard, Hon. Samuel, since 1836 has resided at Chicago, one of its earliest and, during the nearly half a century of his residence there, one of its most useful and honored citizens. He was born at Westminster, Mass., May 20, 1800, of English parentage, some of his ancestry having been persons of rank and fortune. Receiving an academical education, he pursued to some extent the study of law, but later embarked in journalism, being connected, in 1828, with the *Republican*, of Franklin, N. Y., in association with Mr. James Long, who, like himself, had married a daughter of John Conant, Esq., of Brandon, Vt. In 1833 we find him associated with Silas Wright, afterwards so prominent in State and national politics, in the editorial management of the St. Lawrence *Republican*. Removing to Chicago in 1836, he was speedily called to various posts of honorable service, among them that of State senator and clerk of the Circuit Court. In 1845 he engaged in mercantile business, and continued in it for many years as one of the successful merchants of the young and growing city. Mr. Lincoln appointed him postmaster of the city in 1865. He has also served for a considerable period as president of the Board of Education. Among the earliest and most efficient members of the First Baptist church, he was one of those who, in 1864, united in constituting the present Second church, and in both these organizations he has been active and efficient to a remarkable degree, for fifteen years conducting with peculiar tact and success a large infant-class in the First church, and for ten years a young men's Bible-class in the Second. During eleven years past he has served in the last-named church as its senior deacon. Mr. Hoard was one of the original corporators of the University of Chicago, and, until advancing age made it seem to himself desirable that he should retire, remained one of the most valued members of the board of trustees.

Homan, Rev. N. B., was born in Spencer Co., Ky., on Sept. 7, 1822. His father removed to Putnam Co., Ind., when he was about five years old. At the age of sixteen he became deeply concerned in regard to his salvation. He removed to Jones Co., Iowa, in 1847. He was "born again" in that place, and baptized in the spring of 1848. In that year he and nine others formed the Baptist church of Fairview, Jones Co. In the year 1855 he was called to the work of the gospel ministry. On the 26th of April, 1856, he was ordained, and he served the Fairview Baptist church as pastor over fifteen years, the Anamosa church four years. On Jan. 1, 1873, he entered upon the pastorate of the church at Vinton, Benton Co. In October, 1875, he went to Kirwin, Phillips Co., where he has remained up to the present time, laboring as pastor of the Baptist churches of Kirwin and Phillipsburg.

Hungate, Rev. James De P., was born in Washington Co., Ind., July 28, 1831. He was received into the Mill Creek Baptist church at fourteen. When eighteen he was impressed that it was his duty to preach. He graduated from Franklin College in 1854, and was ordained in 1856, and became pastor of the church at Salem, Marion Co., Ill., in 1858, where he built a meeting-house and the membership of the church increased from six to seventy-six members. In 1860 he was appointed a missionary by the American Baptist Home Mission Society to Nebraska. In May, 1864, he started across the plains with his wife and children in a wagon, and, after a wearisome journey of 102 days, he arrived safe in the Willamette Valley, Oregon. He was for three years pastor at Salem, the State capital, when the church increased from thirty-six to ninety-eight members. He taught a Bible-class of thirty young people, most of whom he baptized. In December, 1868, he removed to California, where he labored as a supply at Petaluma and other places. In the autumn of 1872 he returned to Nebraska, and in 1879 he became pastor at El Dorado, Kansas, where his labors have been blessed in erecting a meeting-house and in building up the church.

J.

James, Rev. John Sexton, son of Prof. C. S. James, was born in Philadelphia, Pa., July 20, 1848. He was baptized in February, 1864. He was graduated with honor from the university at Lewisburg in 1868, and from Crozer Theological Seminary in 1871. He then spent a year in prosecuting his studies at the Universities of Erlangen and Leipsic, Germany. On his return, he accepted a call to Allentown, Pa., and was ordained in October, 1872. He still serves this important church. Mr. James edited a revision of Kurtz's "Church History," with additions from the seventh German edition. The work is largely used as a text-book in American theological seminaries. He was president of the Pennsylvania Baptist Ministerial Union in 1879, and of the Alumni Association of the University at Lewisburg in 1880. He was moderator of the Reading Association in 1879 and 1880. Mr. James is a successful pastor and a clear and impressive preacher.

Jones, Prof. J. E., A.M., was born in Lynchburg, Va.; baptized in the spring of 1868, and entered the Richmond Institute, Richmond, Va., in October of the same year for the purpose of preparing for the gospel ministry. Having completed the course there in 1871, and having finished his preparatory training in the grammar-school of Madison University, N. Y., he entered Madison University in 1872, and, after a successful course of study, was graduated in 1876. In the same year the American Baptist Home Mission Society appointed him an instructor in the Richmond Institute, and intrusted him with the branches of language and philosophy. In 1877 he was ordained to the ministry. In 1879 his *alma mater* conferred upon him the degree of Master of Arts. Prof. Jones is an efficient teacher, a popular and instructive preacher, and a forcible writer. In 1878 he held a newspaper controversy with the Roman Catholic Bishop Keane, of Richmond, in which the bishop, in the estimation of many most competent to judge, was worsted. Prof. Jones is regarded as one of the most promising of the young colored men of the South.

L.

Lehman, Rev. G. W., the aged and highly revered pastor of the Baptist church in Berlin, Germany, and one of the most prominent Baptist ministers in that land, was born in the city of Hamburg, Oct. 23, 1799. In his youth he was an engraver in Berlin, being at the same time actively engaged in religious labor and in circulating the Bible, which he had early learned to love and cherish. In 1830 he first met with Mr. Oncken and felt himself specially drawn to him. After Mr. Oncken's baptism Mr. Lehman was led prayerfully to consider this question, but it was not until the year 1837 that he became fully settled in his convictions concerning believer's baptism. He was baptized near Berlin by Mr. Oncken, with six others, May 13, 1837, and on the following day the little flock of baptized believers was organized as the Baptist church of Berlin. Mr. Lehman was soon appointed by the church as their pastor, and faithfully preached to the people while still pursuing his daily avocations. He was forced to pursue his work of love under great difficulties and discouragements. In 1838, Mr. Lehman entered the service of the American Baptist Missionary Union, devoting one-half of his time to this work as its missionary. In 1840, Mr. Lehman went to England to receive ordination; he was ordained June 29, 1840, in Salter's Hall chapel, Cannon Street, London, Rev. J. H. Hinton offering the ordaining prayer. Since that time the work in Berlin has been prospering under his faithful labors, and it has extended into the surrounding regions far and wide.

Mr. Lehman is gifted with peculiar talents; he occupies a very influential position among the Baptists in Germany. The cause in that country is indebted to him to a degree which it will not be easy to overestimate. Although partially disabled by the weakness of age, Mr. Lehman still retains the pastorate of the church to which he has devoted his youthful energies and the strength of his manhood.

M.

Mabie, Rev. H. C., was born in Belvidere, Boone Co., Ill., June 20, 1847. He is a descendant of several generations of Baptists. His great-grandfather, Rev. Daniel Mabie, was one of the pioneer ministers of Central New York. His parents removed to Belvidere in 1845. His early life was under the Christian influence of a pious home and of the revered Dr. Roe, pastor of the Belvidere church.

At twelve he was converted and baptized. At sixteen, while in college, his heart was greatly refreshed by divine grace, and from this period, while still studying, his labors were rewarded with conversions among students, in military camps and hospitals, and in neighboring churches.

He graduated from the University of Chicago in 1868, and from the seminary in 1875. He was ordained in Rockford, Ill., in October, 1869, when he spent four prosperous years as the pastor of the State Street church. In 1873 he resigned his charge to complete his theological studies, and in the mean time he organized the church at Oak Park, and served it as pastor for two years. In 1875 he became pastor at Brookline, Mass., and labored there for three and a half years with much success; during this pastorate he was a member for two years of the Executive Committee of the Missionary Union. At the commencement of Brown University in 1878 he preached the annual sermon before the Society of Missionary Inquiry. Early in 1879 he accepted a unanimous call to the First Baptist church of Indianapolis, Ind., where the blessing of God has rested upon his labors abundantly; debts have been paid, union binds the large membership together, liberality distinguishes their gifts, and conversions are frequent. Mr. Mabie is a man of ability and culture, of wisdom and grace, and before him, if the Lord spares his life, there are brilliant prospects of usefulness, while around him there are throngs of loving friends.

Marsh, Rev. W. H. H., was born in Chester Co., Pa., July 14, 1836. He received a liberal education, which he has continually extended until he has become one of the best-informed men in the denomination. He was ordained when twenty-one years of age. After supplying the Bethesda and Caernarvon churches in Chester Co., Pa., he took charge of the Lower Providence church, Montgomery Co., and remained there four years; then settled with the Blockley church, West Philadelphia, where he exercised his ministry until, in 1865, he accepted a pressing call to the Second church of Wilmington, Del. During his six years' pastorate at Wilmington an oppressive debt was paid, the church edifice was greatly improved, an organ purchased, and a lot for a mission secured, upon which the Bethany church now stands. Mr. Marsh removed from Wilmington to take the oversight of the Central church of Salem, Mass., where he labored for eight years. In December, 1880, he settled in New Brunswick, N. J., as pastor of the young and vigorous Remsen Avenue church. In his pastorates Mr. Marsh has always been successful.

He is a diligent student, an extensive reader, and a large-hearted brother. His intellectual powers are of a high order, and his sermons are distinguished by deep thought and gospel truth.

He has written extensively for the *Baptist Quarterly*, the *Bibliotheca Sacra*, and the denominational papers. The Publication Society has issued his "Modern Sunday-School." He has also the manuscript of a work upon which he has been long engaged, and which he expects to publish soon.

Mr. Marsh is regarded with affection wherever he is known, and his labors have been a blessing to the churches and the world.

S.

Staughton, William, D.D. For article, see page 1097.

WILLIAM STAUGHTON, D.D.

T.

Tyler, James E., who for nearly twenty years has been actively identified with Baptist interests in Chicago, was born at Hillsdale, Columbia Co., N. Y., March 11, 1811. During his infancy the family removed to West Stockbridge, Mass. When he was sixteen he became clerk in the village store, and the proprietor removing soon after to Canaan, N. Y., he was persuaded to accompany him. In 1829 he became a resident of Cincinnati, O., connecting himself there with an insurance office. A branch being established in Louisville, Mr. Tyler took charge of it, and that city, in 1834, became his home. Business prospered, and he was in due time ranked with the wealthy and influential citizens of the place. Mr. Tyler undertook, in 1859, a tour of the East, visiting Egypt and the Holy Land; some letters home, descriptive of his journey, finding publication in the *Louisville Journal*, then edited by George D. Prentice. At the outbreak of the war he removed North. In 1862 he established himself in Chicago, and soon took a place beside the successful business men of that city.

Mr. Tyler early interested himself in the University of Chicago, serving as one of its trustees. In the establishment of the Theological Seminary he actively shared, serving also upon the board of this institution. As a member of the First Baptist church, he has contributed generously to the various building and mission enterprises of that body. His gifts to the seminary have also been large.

V.

Vinton, Justus H., D.D., was born in Willington, Conn., Feb. 17, 1806. When ten years of age he was converted, and soon after united with the Baptist church of Ashford. At sixteen he felt the call of God to preach the gospel. In 1826 he entered Hamilton Institution to study for the ministry. In 1830, one year after a day of fasting and prayer, to learn his duty in reference to going West as a missionary, when he was strongly impressed that he should go to Burmah, he finally decided to spend his life in that heathen country. While attending to college duties, and during vacations, he preached wherever he had an opportunity, and he had some great revivals at this early period.

In July, 1834, Mr. and Mrs. Vinton sailed for Burmah in the "Cashmere," and landed in Maulmain in December of that year. During their passage, in answer to fervent prayers and faithful preaching, a number of the officers and men of the vessel were converted. Having learned the language of the Karens from a native at Hamilton, N. Y., the missionary and his wife left for the jungle a week after they landed, and commenced to preach among a people to whom the Saviour had never been presented, and they continued for three months, going from village to village, telling the story of the Cross to hungry multitudes, and converts rewarded these toils wherever they went. For many years Dr. Vinton was engaged in this blessed work, and he was one of the most successful missionaries that ever led souls to Jesus. Throngs were born again, many churches were established, preachers and teachers were sent out, and a mighty work was performed for God and for the races dwelling in Burmah.

In Rangoon his labors for the people at the termination of the last war with England were astonishing; he and his wife cared for a multitude of the sick, they bought rice on credit and distributed it among the famine-stricken, they cared for orphans and widows, and they told the story of the Cross; in any community a preacher of such a spirit would be heard with special interest, and we are not surprised that in twenty months he baptized 441 converts.

He was beloved and almost worshiped throughout the Karen jungles, and the English officials, recognizing his extraordinary worth, sent him money to sustain his schools and gifts to aid him in his work, and cherished him and his wife in their hearts.

Dr. Vinton was mighty in prayer, firm in will to do what was right, untiring in effort, generous to a fault, and wholly consecrated to God. In Connecticut, where he was peculiarly well known, when a difference existed between him and the Missionary Union, the denomination sympathized with the great missionary; they knew his unsurpassed worth, and no society could keep them from contributing liberally to sustain this prince of missionary preachers. He died in Burmah, March 31, 1858.

His noble wife, born in Union, Conn., April 19, 1807, and converted at eighteen, had the same missionary spirit that made her husband ready to sacrifice everything for the salvation of idolaters. She told the women and children of Burmah about the Saviour, and labored in this way for Christ with glorious results, and after Dr. Vinton's death the converts and churches hearkened to her counsels with a reverence almost unparalleled. She died in Burmah, Dec. 18, 1864. Her daughter, Mrs. R. M. Luther, is doing effective service for foreign missions in Pennsylvania, while Justus B. Vinton, D.D., her son, is a worthy successor of his honored father in extending the Redeemer's kingdom in Burmah.

W.

Waldrop, Rev. A. J., was born Feb. 7, 1815, in Christian Co., Ky. Came with his parents to Jefferson Co., Ala., in 1818, and has continued there to this date; was baptized by Rev. Hosea Holcombe in 1832; was ordained in 1842. He has been pastor at Ruhamot thirty-two years, at Springville twenty, and at Cahaba twenty-five years,—three of our best country churches. He is one of the most influential ministers in the State, and a strong and gifted preacher. He held several prominent civil positions. His son, Elisha Waldrop, is also a good minister of Jesus Christ.

APPENDIX.

THE PHILADELPHIA CONFESSION OF FAITH.

I. OF THE HOLY SCRIPTURES.—1. The Holy Scripture is the only sufficient, certain, and infallible rule of all-saving knowledge, faith, and obedience; although the light of nature, and the works of creation and providence do so far manifest the goodness, wisdom, and power of God as to leave men unexcusable; yet are they not sufficient to give that knowledge of God and his will which is necessary unto salvation. Therefore it pleased the Lord at sundry times, and in divers manners, to reveal himself, and to declare that his will unto his church; and afterward, for the better preserving and propagating of the truth, and for the more sure establishment and comfort of the church against the corruption of the flesh, and the malice of Satan and of the world, to commit the same wholly unto writing; which maketh the Holy Scriptures to be most necessary, those former ways of God's revealing his will unto his people being now ceased.

2. Under the name of Holy Scripture, or the Word of God written, are now contained all the books of the Old and New Testament, which are these:

Of the Old Testament,—Genesis, Exodus, Leviticus, Numbers, Deuteronomy, Joshua, Judges, Ruth, 1 Samuel, 2 Samuel, 1 Kings, 2 Kings, 1 Chronicles, 2 Chronicles, Ezra, Nehemiah, Esther, Job, Psalms, Proverbs, Ecclesiastes, The Song of Songs, Isaiah, Jeremiah, Lamentations, Ezekiel, Daniel, Hosea, Joel, Amos, Obadiah, Jonah, Micah, Nahum, Habakkuk, Zephaniah, Haggai, Zechariah, Malachi.

Of the New Testament, Matthew, Mark, Luke, John, The Acts of the Apostles, Paul's Epistle to the Romans, 1 Corinthians, 2 Corinthians, Galatians, Ephesians, Philippians, Colossians, 1 Thessalonians, 2 Thessalonians, 1 Timothy, 2 Timothy, to Titus, to Philemon, the Epistle to the Hebrews, the Epistle of James, the first and second Epistles of Peter, the first, second, and third Epistles of John, the Epistle of Jude, the Revelation. All which are given by the inspiration of God to be the rule of faith and life.

3. The books commonly called Apocrypha, not being of divine inspiration, are no part of the canon (or rule) of the Scripture, and therefore are of no authority to the church of God, nor to be any otherwise approved, or made use of, than other human writings.

4. The authority of the Holy Scriptures, for which it ought to be believed, dependeth not upon the testimony of

---

A CONFESSION OF FAITH, Put forth by the *Elders* and *Brethren* Of many CONGREGATIONS OF CHRISTIANS (Baptized upon Profession of their Faith) In *London* and the *Country*.

Adopted by the Baptist ASSOCIATION met at Philadelphia, Sept. 25. 1742.

The SIXTH EDITION.

To which are added, Two Articles *viz*. Of Imposition of Hands, and Singing of Psalms in Publick Worship. ALSO A Short Treatise of Church Discipline.

With the Heart Man believeth unto Righteousness, and with the Mouth Confession is made unto Salvation, Rom. 10. 20. *Search the Scriptures*, John 5. 39.

PHILADELPHIA: Printed by B. FRANKLIN. M,DCC,XLIII.

FAC-SIMILE OF THE TITLE-PAGE OF THE PHILADELPHIA CONFESSION OF FAITH, ADOPTED BY THE PHILADELPHIA BAPTIST ASSOCIATION, SEPTEMBER 25, 1742, AND PRINTED BY BENJAMIN FRANKLIN IN 1743.

any man or church, but wholly upon God (who is Truth itself), the author thereof; therefore it is to be received, because it is the Word of God.

5. We may be moved and induced by the testimony of the church of God to an high and reverent esteem of the Holy Scriptures; and the heavenliness of the matter, the efficacy of the doctrine, and the majesty of the style, the consent of all the parts, the scope of the whole (which is to give all glory to God), the full discovery it makes of the only way of man's salvation, and many other incomparable excellencies, and entire perfections thereof, are arguments whereby it doth abundantly evidence itself to be the Word of God; yet, notwithstanding our full persuasion, and assurance of the infallible truth, and divine authority thereof, is from the inward work of the Holy Spirit, bearing witness by and with the Word in our hearts.

6. The whole counsel of God concerning all things necessary for his own glory, man's salvation, faith and life, is either expressly set down, or necessarily contained in the Holy Scripture; unto which nothing is at any time to be added, whether by new revelation of the Spirit or traditions of men.

Nevertheless, we acknowledge the inward illumination of the Spirit of God to be necessary for the saving understanding of such things as are revealed in the Word, and that there are some circumstances concerning the worship of God and government of the church common to human actions and societies, which are to be ordered by the light of nature and Christian prudence, according to the general rules of the Word, which are always to be observed.

7. All things in Scripture are not alike plain in themselves, nor alike clear unto all, yet those things which are necessary to be known, believed, and observed for salvation, are so clearly propounded and opened in some place of Scripture or other, that not only the learned, but the unlearned, in a due use of ordinary means, may attain to a sufficient understanding of them.

8. The Old Testament in Hebrew (which was the native language of the people of God of old), and the New Testament in Greek, which (at the time of writing it) was most generally known to the nations, being immediately inspired by God, and, by his singular care and providence, kept pure in all ages, are therefore authentical; so as in all controversies of religion the church is finally to appeal unto them. But because these original tongues are not known to all the people of God who have a right unto, and interest in, the Scriptures, and are commanded, in the fear of God, to read and search them, therefore they are to be translated into the vulgar language of every nation unto which they come, that the Word of God, dwelling plentifully in all, they may worship him in an acceptable manner, and, through patience and comfort of the Scriptures, may hope.

9. The infallible rule of interpretation of Scripture is the Scripture itself: and therefore, when there is a question about the true and full sense of any Scripture (which is not manifold, but one), it must be searched by other places that speak more clearly.

10. The supreme judge by which all controversies of religion are to be determined, and all decrees of councils, opinions of ancient writers, doctrines of men, and private spirits are to be examined, and in whose sentence we are to rest, can be no other but the Holy Scripture delivered by the Spirit, into which Scripture, so delivered, our faith is finally resolved.

II. OF GOD AND OF THE HOLY TRINITY.—1. The Lord our God is but one only living and true God; whose subsistence is in and of himself, infinite in being and perfection, whose essence cannot be comprehended by any but himself; a most pure Spirit, invisible, without body, parts, or passions, who only hath immortality, dwelling in the light which no man can approach unto, who is immutable, immense, eternal, incomprehensible, almighty, every way infinite, most holy, most wise, most free, most absolute, working all things according to the counsel of his own immutable and most righteous will for his own glory, most loving, gracious, merciful, long-suffering, abundant in goodness and truth, forgiving iniquity, transgression, and sin, the rewarder of them that diligently seek him, and withal most just, and terrible in his judgments, hating all sin, and will by no means clear the guilty.

2. God having all life, glory, goodness, blessedness, in and of himself, is alone in, and unto himself all-sufficient, not standing in need of any creature which he hath made, nor deriving any glory from them, but only manifesting his own glory in, by, unto, and upon them, he is the alone fountain of all being, of whom, through whom, and to whom are all things, and he hath most sovereign dominion over all creatures, to do by them, for them, or upon them, whatsoever himself pleaseth; in his sight all things are open and manifest, his knowledge is infinite, infallible, and independent upon the creature, so as nothing is to him contingent or uncertain; he is most holy in all his counsels, in all his works, and in all his commands; to him is due from angels and men whatsoever worship, service, or obedience, as creatures they owe unto the Creator, and whatever he is further pleased to require of them.

3. In this Divine and Infinite Being there are three subsistences, the Father, the Word (or Son), and Holy Spirit, of one substance, power, and eternity, each having the whole divine essence, yet the essence undivided; the Father is of none neither begotten, nor proceeding; the Son is eternally begotten of the Father; the Holy Spirit proceeding from the Father and the Son, all infinite, without beginning, therefore but one God, who is not to be divided in nature and being, but distinguished by several peculiar relative properties and personal relations; which doctrine of the Trinity is the foundation of all our communion with God, and our comfortable dependence on him.

III. OF GOD'S DECREE.—1. God hath decreed in himself from all eternity, by the most wise and holy counsel of his own will, freely and unchangeably, all things whatsoever comes to pass; yet so as thereby is God neither the author of sin, nor hath fellowship with any therein, nor is violence offered to the will of the creature, nor yet is the liberty or contingency of second causes taken away, but rather established, in which appears his wisdom in disposing all things, and power and faithfulness in accomplishing his decree.

2. Although God knoweth whatsoever may or can come to pass upon all supposed conditions, yet hath he not decreed anything because he foresaw it as future, or as that which would come to pass upon such conditions.

3. By the decree of God, for the manifestation of his glory, some men and angels are predestinated or foreordained to eternal life, through Jesus Christ, to the praise of his glorious grace; others being left to act in their sin to their just condemnation, to the praise of his glorious justice.

4. These angels and men thus predestinated and foreor-

dained are particularly and unchangeably designed; and their number so certain and definite, that it cannot be either increased or diminished.

5. Those of mankind that are predestinated to life, God, before the foundation of the world was laid, according to his eternal and immutable purpose, and the secret counsel and good pleasure of his will, hath chosen in Christ unto everlasting glory, out of his mere free grace and love; without any other thing in the creature as a condition or cause moving him thereunto.

6. As God hath appointed the elect unto glory, so he hath by the eternal and most free purpose of his will foreordained all the means thereunto, wherefore they who are elected, being fallen in Adam, are redeemed by Christ, are effectually called unto faith in Christ, by his Spirit working in due season, are justified, adopted, sanctified, and kept by his power through faith unto salvation; neither are any other redeemed by Christ, or effectually called, justified, adopted, sanctified, and saved, but the elect only.

7. The doctrine of this high mystery of predestination is to be handled with special prudence and care; that men attending the will of God revealed in his Word, and yielding obedience thereunto, may, from the certainty of their effectual vocation, be assured of their eternal election; so shall this doctrine afford matter of praise, reverence, and admiration of God, and of humility, diligence, and abundant consolation to all that sincerely obey the gospel.

IV. OF CREATION.—1. In the beginning it pleased God the Father, Son, and Holy Spirit, for the manifestation of the glory of his eternal power, wisdom, and goodness, to create or make the world, and all things therein, whether visible or invisible, in the space of six days, and all very good.

2. After God had made all other creatures he created man, male and female, with reasonable and immortal souls, rendering them fit unto that life to God for which they were created, being made after the image of God, in knowledge, righteousness, and true holiness; having the law of God written in their hearts, and power to fulfill it; and yet under a possibility of transgressing, being left to the liberty of their own will, which was subject to change.

3. Besides the law written in their hearts, they received a command not to eat of the tree of knowledge of good and evil; which, whilst they kept, they were happy in their communion with God, and had dominion over the creatures.

V. OF DIVINE PROVIDENCE.—1. God, the good creator of all things, in his infinite power and wisdom, doth uphold, direct, dispose, and govern all creatures and things, from the greatest even to the least, by his most wise and holy providence, to the end for which they were created, according unto his infallible foreknowledge, and the free and immutable counsel of his own will, to the praise of the glory of his wisdom, power, justice, infinite goodness, and mercy.

2. Although in relation to the foreknowledge and decree of God, the first cause, all things come to pass immutably and infallibly; so that there is not anything befalls any by chance, or without his providence; yet, by the same providence, he ordereth them to fall out according to the nature of second causes, either necessarily, freely, or contingently.

3. God in his ordinary providence maketh use of means; yet is free to work without, above, and against them, at his pleasure.

4. The almighty power, unsearchable wisdom, and infinite goodness of God so far manifest themselves in his providence, that his determinate counsel extendeth itself even to the first fall, and all other sinful actions both of angels and men (and that not by a bare permission), which also he most wisely and powerfully boundeth, and otherwise ordereth and governeth in a manifold dispensation, to his most holy ends; yet so as the sinfulness of their acts proceedeth only from the creatures, and not from God, who, being most holy and righteous, neither is nor can be the author or approver of sin.

5. The most wise, righteous, and gracious God doth oftentimes leave for a season his own children to manifold temptations and the corruptions of their own hearts, to chastise them for their former sins or to discover unto them the hidden strength of corruption and deceitfulness of their hearts, that they may be humbled, and to raise them to a more close and constant dependence for their support upon himself, and to make them more watchful against all future occasions of sin, and for other just and holy ends. So that whatsoever befalls any of his elect is by his appointment, for his glory, and their good.

6. As for those wicked and ungodly men, whom God as a righteous judge, for former sin, doth blind and harden; from them he not only withholdeth his grace, whereby they might have been enlightened in their understanding and wrought upon in their hearts, but sometimes also withdraweth the gifts which they had, and exposeth them to such objects as their corruptions make occasion of sin; and withal gives them over to their own lusts and temptations of the world, and the power of Satan, whereby it comes to pass that they harden themselves, even under those means which God useth for the softening of others.

7. As the providence of God doth in general reach to all creatures, so, after a more special manner, it taketh care of his church, and disposeth of all things to the good thereof.

VI. OF THE FALL OF MAN, SIN, AND THE PUNISHMENT THEREOF.—1. Although God created man upright and perfect, and gave him a righteous law which had been unto life, had he kept it, and threatened death upon the breach thereof; yet he did not long abide in this honor. Satan, using the subtilty of the serpent to seduce Eve, then by her seducing Adam, who, without any compulsion, did willfully transgress the law of their creation and the command given unto them in eating the forbidden fruit; which God was pleased according to his wise and holy counsel to permit, having purposed to order it to his own glory.

2. Our first parents, by this sin, fell from their original righteousness and communion with God, and we in them, whereby death came upon all; all becoming dead in sin and wholly defiled in all the faculties and parts of soul and body.

3. They being the root, and, by God's appointment, standing in the room and stead of all mankind; the guilt of the sin was imputed, and corrupted nature conveyed to all their posterity, descending from them by ordinary generation, being now conceived in sin, and by nature children of wrath, the servants of sin, the subjects of death, and all other miseries, spiritual, temporal, and eternal, unless the Lord Jesus set them free.

4. From this original corruption, whereby we are utterly indisposed, disabled, and made opposite to all good, and wholly inclined to all evil, do proceed all actual transgressions.

5. This corruption of nature, during this life, doth re-

main in those that are regenerated; and, although it be through Christ pardoned and mortified, yet both itself and the first motions thereof are truly and properly sin.

VII. OF GOD'S COVENANT.—1. The distance between God and the creature is so great, that although reasonable creatures do owe obedience unto him as their Creator, yet they could never have attained the reward of life but by some voluntary condescension on God's part, which he hath been pleased to express by way of covenant.

2. Moreover, man having brought himself under the curse of the law by his fall, it pleased the Lord to make a covenant of grace, wherein he freely offereth unto sinners life and salvation by Jesus Christ, requiring of them faith in him, that they might be saved; and promising to give unto all those that are ordained unto eternal life his holy Spirit, to make them willing and able to believe.

3. This covenant is revealed in the gospel, first of all to Adam in the promise of salvation by the seed of the woman, and afterwards by farther steps, until the full discovery thereof was completed in the New Testament; and it is founded in that eternal covenant transaction that was between the Father and the Son about the redemption of the elect; and it is alone by the grace of this covenant that all of the posterity of fallen Adam, that ever were saved, did obtain life and blessed immortality; man being now utterly incapable of acceptance with God upon those terms on which Adam stood in his state of innocency.

VIII. OF CHRIST THE MEDIATOR.—1. It pleased God, in his eternal purpose, to choose and ordain the Lord Jesus, his only and begotten Son, according to the covenant made between them both, to be the Mediator between God and man; the prophet, priest, and king; head and Saviour of his church, the heir of all things, and judge of the world; unto whom he did from all eternity give a people to be his seed, and to be by him in time redeemed, called, justified, sanctified, and glorified.

2. The Son of God, the second person in the Holy Trinity, being very and eternal God, the brightness of the Father's glory, of one substance, and equal with him; who made the world, who upholdeth and governeth all things he hath made; did, when the fullness of time was come, take upon him man's nature, with all the essential properties and common infirmities thereof, yet without sin; being conceived by the Holy Spirit in the womb of the Virgin Mary, the Holy Spirit coming down upon her, and the power of the Most High overshadowing her, and so was made of a woman, of the tribe of Judah, of the seed of Abraham and David, according to the Scriptures: so that two whole, perfect, and distinct natures were inseparably joined together in one person, without conversion, composition, or confusion; which person is very God and very man, yet one Christ, the only Mediator between God and man.

3. The Lord Jesus in his human nature thus united to the divine, in the person of the Son, was sanctified and anointed with the Holy Spirit above measure; having in him all the treasures of wisdom and knowledge; in whom it pleased the Father that all fullness should dwell; to the end that, being holy, harmless, undefiled, and full of grace and truth, he might be thoroughly furnished to execute the office of a Mediator and Surety; which office he took not upon himself, but was thereunto called by his Father; who also put all power and judgment in his hand, and gave him commandment to execute the same.

4. This office the Lord Jesus did most willingly undertake, which that he might discharge, he was made under the law, and did perfectly fulfill it, and underwent the punishment due to us, which we should have borne and suffered, being made sin and a curse for us; enduring most grievous sorrows in his soul and most painful sufferings in his body; was crucified and died, and remained in the state of the dead, yet saw no corruption; on the third day he arose from the dead, with the same body in which he suffered, with which he also ascended into heaven; and there sitteth on the right hand of his Father making intercession; and shall return to judge men and angels at the end of the world.

5. The Lord Jesus, by his perfect obedience and sacrifice of himself, which he through the eternal Spirit once offered up unto God, hath fully satisfied the justice of God, procured reconciliation, and purchased an everlasting inheritance in the kingdom of heaven for all those whom the Father hath given unto him.

6. Although the price of redemption was not actually paid by Christ till after his incarnation, yet the virtue, efficacy, and benefit thereof was communicated to the elect in all ages successively from the beginning of the world, in and by those promises, types, and sacrifices wherein he was revealed and signified to be the seed of the woman which should bruise the serpent's head; and the Lamb slain from the foundation of the world, being the same yesterday, and to-day, and forever.

7. Christ, in the work of mediation, acteth according to both natures, by each nature doing that which is proper to itself; yet, by reason of the unity of the person, that which is proper to one nature is sometimes in Scripture attributed to the person denominated by the other nature.

8. To all those for whom Christ hath obtained eternal redemption he doth certainly and effectually apply and communicate the same; making intercession for them; uniting them to himself by his Spirit; revealing unto them, in and by the Word, the mystery of salvation; persuading them to believe and obey; governing their hearts by his Word and Spirit, and overcoming all their enemies by his Almighty power and wisdom, in such manner and ways as are most consonant to his wonderful and unsearchable dispensation; and all of free and absolute grace, without any condition foreseen in them to procure it.

9. This office of Mediator between God and man is proper only to Christ, who is the prophet, priest, and king of the Church of God; and may not be either in whole, or any part thereof, transferred from him to any other.

10. This number and order of offices is necessary; for, in respect of our ignorance, we stand in need of his prophetical office; and, in respect of our alienation from God and imperfection of the best of our services, we need his priestly office to reconcile us and present us acceptable unto God; and, in respect of our averseness and utter inability to return to God, and for our rescue and security from our spiritual adversaries, we need his kingly office to convince, subdue, draw, uphold, deliver, and preserve us to his heavenly kingdom.

IX. OF FREE WILL.—1. God has indued the will of man with that natural liberty and power of acting upon choice, that it is neither forced nor, by any necessity of nature, determined to do good or evil.

2. Man, in his state of innocency, had freedom and power to will and to do that which was good and well pleasing to God; but yet was mutable, so that he might fall from it.

3. Man, by his fall into a state of sin, hath wholly lost all ability of will to any spiritual good accompanying salva-

tion; so as a natural man, being altogether averse from that good and dead in sin, is not able, by his own strength, to convert himself or to prepare himself thereunto.

4. When God converts a sinner, and translates him into the state of grace, he freeth him from his natural bondage under sin, and, by his grace alone, enables him freely to will and do that which is spiritually good; yet so as that, by reason of his remaining corruptions, he doth not perfectly nor only will that which is good, but doth also will that which is evil.

5. The will of man is made perfectly and immutably free to good alone in the state of glory only.

X. OF EFFECTUAL CALLING.—1. Those whom God had predestinated unto life, he is pleased, in his appointed and accepted time, effectually to call by his Word and Spirit out of that state of sin and death in which they are by nature to grace of salvation by Jesus Christ; enlightening their minds spiritually and savingly to understand the things of God; taking away their heart of stone and giving unto them an heart of flesh; renewing their wills, and, by his almighty power, determining them to that which is good, and effectually drawing them to Jesus Christ; yet so as they come most freely, being made willing by his grace.

2. This effectual call is of God's free and special grace alone, not from anything at all foreseen in man, nor from any power or agency in the creature co-working with his special grace; the creature being wholly passive therein, being dead in sins and trespasses, until, being quickened and renewed by the Holy Spirit, he is thereby enabled to answer this call, and to embrace the grace offered and conveyed in it, and that by no less power than that which raised up Christ from the dead.

3. Elect infants, dying in infancy, are regenerated and saved by Christ through the Spirit, who worketh when, and where, and how he pleaseth; so also are all other elect persons who are incapable of being outwardly called by the ministry of the Word.

4. Others not elected, although they may be called by the ministry of the Word, and may have some common operations of the Spirit, yet, not being effectually drawn by the Father, they neither will nor can truly come to Christ, and therefore cannot be saved; much less can men that receive not the Christian religion be saved, be they never so diligent to frame their lives according to the light of nature and the law of that religion they do profess.

XI. OF JUSTIFICATION.—1. Those whom God effectually calleth he also freely justifieth, not by infusing righteousness into them, but by pardoning their sins, and by accounting and accepting their persons as righteous; not for anything wrought in them or done by them, but for Christ's sake alone; not by imputing faith itself, the act of believing, or any other evangelical obedience to them, as their righteousness, but by imputing Christ's active obedience unto the whole law, and passive obedience in his death, for their whole and sole righteousness; they receiving and resting on him and his righteousness by faith, which they have not of themselves: it is the gift of God.

2. Faith thus receiving and resting on Christ and his righteousness, is the alone instrument of justification; yet it is not alone in the person justified, but is ever accompanied with all other saving graces, and is no dead faith, but worketh by love.

3. Christ, by his obedience and death, did fully discharge the debt of all those that are justified; and did, by the sacrifice of himself, in the blood of his cross, undergoing in their stead the penalty due unto them, make a proper, real, and full satisfaction to God's justice in their behalf; yet, inasmuch as he was given by the Father for them, and his obedience and satisfaction accepted in their stead, and both freely, not for anything in them, their justification is only of free grace, that both the exact justice and rich grace of God might be glorified in the justification of sinners.

4. God did, from all eternity, decree to justify all the elect, and Christ did, in the fullness of time, die for their sins, and rise again for their justification; nevertheless, they are not justified personally until the Holy Spirit doth, in due time, actually apply Christ unto them.

5. God doth continue to forgive the sins of those that are justified; and, although they can never fall from the state of justification, yet they may, by their sins, fall under God's fatherly displeasure; and, in that condition, they have not usually the light of his countenance restored unto them until they humble themselves, confess their sins, beg pardon, and renew their faith and repentance.

6. The justification of believers under the Old Testament was, in all these respects, one and the same with the justification of believers under the New Testament.

XII. OF ADOPTION.—1. All those that are justified, God vouchsafed, in and for the sake of his only Son, Jesus Christ, to make partakers of the grace of adoption, by which they are taken into the number, and enjoy the liberties and privileges, of children of God; have his name put upon them; receive the spirit of adoption; have access to the throne of grace with boldness; are enabled to cry Abba, Father; are pitied, protected, provided for, and chastened by him as a father; yet never cast off, but sealed to the day of redemption, and inherit the promises as heirs of everlasting salvation.

XIII. OF SANCTIFICATION.—1. They who are united to Christ, effectually called, and regenerated, having a new heart and a new spirit created in them, through the virtue of Christ's death and resurrection, are also further sanctified, really and personally, through the same virtue, by his Word and Spirit dwelling in them. The dominion of the whole body of sin is destroyed, and the several lusts thereof are more and more weakened and mortified; and they more and more quickened and strengthened in all saving graces, to the practice of all true holiness, without which no man shall see the Lord.

2. This sanctification is throughout, in the whole man, yet imperfect in this life; there abideth still some remnants of corruption in every part, whence ariseth a continual and irreconcilable war: the flesh lusting against the spirit and the spirit against the flesh.

3. In which war, although the remaining corruption for a time may much prevail, yet, through the continual supply of strength from the sanctifying Spirit of Christ, the regenerate part doth overcome; and so the saints grow in grace, perfecting holiness in the fear of God, pressing after an heavenly life in evangelical obedience to all the commands which Christ, as Head and King, in his Word hath prescribed to them.

XIV. OF SAVING FAITH.—1. The grace of faith, whereby the elect are enabled to believe to the saving of their souls, is the work of the Spirit of Christ in their hearts, and is ordinarily wrought by the ministry of the Word, by which also, and by the administration of Baptism, and the Lord's Supper, prayer, and other means appointed of God it is increased and strengthened.

2. By this faith, a Christian believeth to be true whatsoever is revealed in the Word for the authority of God himself; and also apprehendeth an excellency therein above all other writings and all things in the world, as it bears forth the glory of God in his attributes, the excellency of Christ in his nature and offices, and the power and fullness of the Holy Spirit in his workings and operations; and so is enabled to cast his soul upon the truth thus believed, and also acteth differently upon that which each particular passage thereof containeth; yielding obedience to the commands, trembling at the threatenings, and embracing the promises of God for this life and that which is to come; but the principal acts of saving faith hath immediate relation to Christ, accepting, receiving, and resting upon him alone for justification, sanctification, and eternal life, by virtue of the covenant of grace.

3. This faith, although it be different in degrees, and may be weak or strong, yet it is in the least degree of it different in the kind or nature of it (as is all other saving grace) from the faith and common grace of temporary believers; and therefore, though it may be many times assailed and weakened, yet it gets the victory, growing up in many to the attainment of a full assurance through Christ, who is both the author and finisher of our faith.

XV. OF REPENTANCE UNTO LIFE AND SALVATION.—1. Such of the elect as are converted at riper years, having sometimes lived in the state of nature, and therein served divers lusts and pleasures, God, in their effectual calling, giveth them repentance unto life.

2. Whereas there is none that doeth good and sinneth not, and the best of men may, through the power and deceitfulness of their corruption dwelling in them, with the prevalency of temptation, fall into greater sins and provocations, God hath, in the covenant of grace, mercifully provided that believers so sinning and falling be renewed through repentance unto salvation.

3. This saving repentance is an evangelical grace, whereby a person, being by the Holy Spirit made sensible of the manifold evils of his sin, doth, by faith in Christ, humble himself for it with godly sorrow, detestation of it, and self-abhorrency, praying for pardon and strength of grace, with a purpose and endeavor, by supplies of the Spirit, to walk before God unto all well-pleasing in all things.

4. As repentance is to be continued through the whole course of our lives, upon the account of the body of death and the motions thereof, so it is every man's duty to repent of his particular known sins, particularly.

5. Such is the provision which God hath made, through Christ in the covenant of grace, for the preservation of believers unto salvation, that, although there is no sin so small but it deserves damnation, yet there is no sin so great that it shall bring damnation on them that repent; which makes the constant preaching of repentance necessary.

XVI. OF GOOD WORKS.—1. Good works are only such as God hath commanded in his Holy Word, and not such as, without the warrant thereof, are devised by men out of blind zeal or upon any pretense of good intentions.

2. These good works, done in obedience to God's commandments, are the fruits and evidences of a true and lively faith; and by them believers manifest their thankfulness, strengthen their assurance, edify their brethren, adorn the profession of the gospel, stop the mouths of the adversaries, and glorify God, whose workmanship they are, created in Christ Jesus thereunto, that, having their fruit unto holiness, they may have the end, eternal life.

3. Their ability to do good works is not at all of themselves, but wholly from the Spirit of Christ; and that they may be enabled thereunto, besides the graces they have already received, there is necessary an actual influence of the same Holy Spirit to work in them to will and to do of his good pleasure; yet are they not hereupon to grow negligent, as if they were not bound to perform any duty, unless upon a special motion of the Spirit, but they ought to be diligent in stirring up the grace of God that is in them.

4. They who in their obedience attain to the greatest height which is possible in this life, are so far from being able to supererogate and to do more than God requires, as that they fall short of much which, in duty, they are bound to do.

5. We cannot, by our best works, merit pardon of sin or eternal life at the hand of God, by reason of the great disproportion that is between them and the glory to come, and the infinite distance that is between us and God, whom by them we can never profit nor satisfy for the debt of our former sins; but when we have done all we can, we have done but our duty and are unprofitable servants; and because, as they are good, they proceed from his Spirit, and, as they are wrought by us, they are defiled and mixed with so much weakness and imperfection, that they cannot endure the severity of God's judgment.

6. Yet notwithstanding the persons of believers being accepted through Christ, their good works also are accepted in him, not as though they were in this life wholly unblamable and unreprovable in God's sight, but that he, looking upon them in his Son, is pleased to accept and reward that which is sincere, although accompanied with many weaknesses and imperfections.

7. Works done by unregenerate men, although for the matter of them they may be things which God commands, and of good use both to themselves and others; yet, because they proceed not from a heart purified by faith, nor are done in a right manner according to the Word, nor to a right end, the glory of God, they are sinful and cannot please God, nor make a man meet to receive grace from God; and yet their neglect of them is more sinful and displeasing to God.

XVII. OF THE PERSEVERANCE OF THE SAINTS.—1. Those whom God hath accepted in the Beloved, effectually called and sanctified by his Spirit, and given the precious faith of his elect unto, can neither totally nor finally fall from the state of grace, but shall certainly persevere therein to the end and be eternally saved, seeing the gifts and callings of God are without repentance (whence he still begets and nourisheth in them faith, repentance, love, joy, hope, and all the graces of the Spirit to immortality), and, though many storms and floods arise and beat against them, yet they shall never be able to take them off that foundation and rock which by faith they are fastened upon; notwithstanding, through unbelief and the temptations of Satan, the sensible sight of the light and love of God may, for a time, be clouded and obscured from them, yet it is still the same, and they shall be sure to be kept by the power of God unto salvation, where they shall enjoy their purchased possession, they being engraven upon the palm of his hands, and their names having been written in the book of Life from all eternity.

2. This perseverance of the saints depends not upon their own free will, but upon the immutability of the decree of election, flowing from the free and unchangeable love of God, the Father, upon the efficacy of the merit and in-

tercession of Jesus Christ and union with him, the oath of God, the abiding of his Spirit, and the seed of God within them, and the nature of the covenant of grace; from all which ariseth also the certainty and infallibility thereof.

3. And though they may, through the temptation of Satan and of the world, the prevalency of corruption remaining in them, and the neglect of means of their preservation, fall into grievous sins, and for a time continue therein, whereby they incur God's displeasure and grieve his Holy Spirit, come to have their graces and comforts impaired, have their hearts hardened and their consciences wounded, hurt and scandalize others, and bring temporal judgments upon themselves, yet they shall renew their repentance and be preserved, through faith in Christ Jesus, to the end.

XVIII. OF THE ASSURANCE OF GRACE AND SALVATION.—1. Although temporary believers and other unregenerate men may vainly deceive themselves with false hopes and carnal presumptions of being in the favor of God and state of salvation, which hope of theirs shall perish; yet such as truly believe in the Lord Jesus, and love him in sincerity, endeavoring to walk in all good conscience before him, may, in this life, be certainly assured that they are in the state of grace, and may rejoice in the hope of the glory of God, which hope shall never make them ashamed.

2. This certainly is not a bare conjectural and probable persuasion, grounded upon a fallible hope, but an infallible assurance of faith, founded on the blood and righteousness of Christ, revealed in the gospel; and also upon the inward evidence of those graces of the Spirit unto which promises are made, and on the testimony of the Spirit of adoption, witnessing with our spirits that we are the children of God, and, as a fruit thereof, keeping the heart both humble and holy.

3. This infallible assurance doth not so belong to the essence of faith but that a true believer may wait long, and conflict with many difficulties, before he be partaker of it; yet being enabled by the Spirit to know the things which are freely given him of God, he may, without extraordinary revelation, in the right use of means, attain thereunto; and therefore it is the duty of every one to give all diligence to make their calling and election sure, that thereby his heart may be enlarged in peace and joy in the Holy Spirit, in love and thankfulness to God, and in strength and cheerfulness in the duties of obedience, the proper fruits of this assurance: so far is it from inclining men to looseness.

4. True believers may have the assurance of their salvation divers ways shaken, diminished, and intermitted; as by negligence in preserving of it, by falling into some special sin, which woundeth the conscience and grieveth the Spirit; by some sudden or vehement temptation; by God's withdrawing the light of his countenance and suffering even such as fear him to walk in darkness and to have no light; yet are they never destitute of the seed of God and life of faith, that love of Christ and the brethren, that sincerity of heart, and conscience of duty, out of which, by the operation of the Spirit, this assurance may in due time be revived, and by the which, in the mean time, they are preserved from utter despair.

XIX. OF THE LAW OF GOD.—1. God gave to Adam a law of universal obedience written in his heart, and a particular precept of not eating the fruit of the tree of knowledge of good and evil; by which he bound him and all his posterity to personal, entire, exact, and perpetual obedience, promised life upon the fulfilling, and threatened death upon the breach of it, and indued him with power and ability to keep it.

2. The same law that was first written in the heart of man continued to be a perfect rule of righteousness after the fall, and delivered by God upon Mount Sinai, in ten commandments, and written in two tables, the four first containing our duty towards God, and the other six our duty to man.

3. Besides this law, commonly called moral, God was pleased to give to the people of Israel ceremonial laws, containing several typical ordinances, partly of worship, prefiguring Christ, his graces, actions, sufferings, and benefits, and partly holding forth divers instructions of moral duties, all which ceremonial laws, being appointed only to the time of reformation, are by Jesus Christ, the true Messiah and only Lawgiver, who was furnished with power from the Father for that end, abrogated and taken away.

4. To them also he gave sundry judicial laws, which expired together with the state of that people, not obliging any now by virtue of that institution,—their general equity only being of moral use.

5. The moral law doth forever bind all, as well justified persons as others, to the obedience thereof, and that not only in regard to the matter contained in it, but also in respect of the authority of God, the Creator, who gave it; neither doth Christ in the gospel any way dissolve, but much strengthen this obligation.

6. Although true believers be not under the law, as a covenant of works, to be thereby justified or condemned, yet it is of great use to them, as well as to others, in that, as a rule of life, informing them of the will of God and their duty, it directs and binds them to walk accordingly; discovering also the sinful pollutions of their natures, hearts, and lives, so as, examining themselves thereby, they may come to further conviction of, humiliation for, and hatred against sin, together with a clearer sight of the need they have of Christ and the perfection of his obedience: it is likewise of use to the regenerate to restrain their corruptions, in that it forbids sin, and the threatenings of it serve to show what even their sins deserve, and what afflictions in this life they may expect for them, although freed from the curse and unallayed rigor thereof. These promises of it likewise show that God's approbation of obedience, and what blessings they may expect upon the performance thereof, though not as due to them by the law as a covenant of works; so as man's doing good and refraining from evil, because the law encourageth to the one, and deterreth from the other, is no evidence of his being under the law and not under grace.

7. Neither are the forementioned uses of the law contrary to the grace of the gospel, but do sweetly comply with it, the Spirit of Christ subduing and enabling the will of man to do that freely and cheerfully, which the will of God, revealed in the law, requireth to be done.

XX. OF THE GOSPEL AND THE EXTENT OF THE GRACE THEREOF.—1. The covenant of works being broken by sin, and made unprofitable unto life, God was pleased to give forth the promise of Christ, the seed of the woman, as the means of calling the elect, and begetting in them faith and repentance; in this promise, the gospel, as to the substance of it, was revealed, and therein effectual for the conversion and salvation of sinners.

2. This promise of Christ, and salvation by him, is revealed only by the Word of God; neither do the works of creation or providence, with the light of nature, make dis-

covery of Christ or of grace by him, so much as in a general or obscure way, much less that men, destitute of the revelation of him by the promise or gospel, should be enabled thereby to attain saving faith or repentance.

3. The revelation of the gospel unto sinners, made in divers times and by sundry parts, with the addition of promises and precepts, for the obedience required therein, as to the nations and persons to whom it is granted, is merely of the sovereign will and good pleasure of God, not being annexed by virtue of any promise to the due improvement of men's natural abilities, by virtue of common light received without it, which none ever did make or can so do; and, therefore, in all ages the preaching of the gospel has been granted unto persons and nations, as to the extending or limiting of it, in great variety, according to the counsel of the will of God.

4. Although the gospel be the only outward means of revealing Christ and saving grace, and is, as such, abundantly sufficient thereunto; yet that men, who are dead in trespasses, may be born again, quickened, or regenerated, there is, moreover, necessary an effectual, insuperable work of the Holy Spirit upon the whole soul for the producing in them a new spiritual life, without which no other means will effect their conversion unto God.

XXI. OF CHRISTIAN LIBERTY AND LIBERTY OF CONSCIENCE.—1. The liberty which Christ hath purchased for believers under the gospel consists in their freedom from the guilt of sin, the condemning wrath of God, and rigor and curse of the law, and in their being delivered from this present evil world, bondage to Satan, and dominion of sin, from the evil of afflictions, the fear and sting of death, the victory of the grave, and everlasting damnation; as also in their free access to God, and their yielding obedience unto him, not out of slavish fear, but a childlike love and willing mind.

All which were common also to believers under the law for the substance of them; but, under the New Testament, the liberty of Christians is further enlarged in their freedom from the yoke of the ceremonial law, to which the Jewish church was subjected, and in greater boldness of access to the throne of grace, and in fuller communications of the free Spirit of God, than believers under the law did ordinarily partake of.

2. God alone is Lord of the conscience, and hath left it free from the doctrines and commandments of men, which are in anything contrary to his Word or not contained in it. So that, to believe such doctrines, or to obey such commands, out of conscience, is to betray true liberty of conscience; and the requiring of an implicit faith and absolute and blind obedience is to destroy liberty of conscience and reason also.

3. They who, upon pretense of Christian liberty, do practise any sin, or cherish any sinful lust, as they do thereby pervert the main design of the grace of the gospel to their own destruction, so they wholly destroy the end of Christian liberty; which is, that, being delivered out of the hands of all our enemies, we might serve the Lord without fear, in holiness and righteousness before him all the days of our lives.

XXII. OF RELIGIOUS WORSHIP AND THE SABBATH-DAY.—1. The light of nature shows that there is a God who hath lordship and sovereignty over all; is just, good, and doth good unto all; and is therefore to be feared, loved, praised, called upon, trusted in and served, with all the heart and all the soul, and with all the might. But the acceptable way of worshiping the true God is instituted by himself, and so limited by his own revealed will that he may not be worshiped according to the imaginations and devices of men, or the suggestions of Satan, under any visible representations, or any other way not prescribed in the Holy Scriptures.

2. Religious worship is to be given to God, the Father, Son, and Holy Spirit, and to him alone; not to angels, saints, or any other creatures; and, since the fall, not without a Mediator, nor in the mediation of any other but Christ alone.

3. Prayer and thankfulness being one special part of natural worship, is by God required of all men. But that it may be accepted, it is to be made in the name of the Son, by the help of the Spirit, according to his will; with understanding, reverence, humility, fervency, faith, love, and perseverance, and, with others, in a known tongue.

4. Prayer is to be made for things lawful, and for all sorts of men living, or that shall live hereafter; but not for the dead, nor for those of whom it may be known that they have sinned the sin unto death.

5. The reading of the Scriptures, preaching and hearing the Word of God, teaching and admonishing one another in psalms, hymns, and spiritual songs, singing with grace in our hearts to the Lord, as also the administration of baptism and the Lord's Supper, are all parts of religious worship of God, to be performed in obedience to him with understanding, faith, reverence, and godly fear; moreover, solemn humiliation, with fastings and thanksgiving, upon special occasions, ought to be used in a holy and religious manner.

6. Neither prayer nor any other part of religious worship is now, under the gospel, tied unto or made more acceptable by any place in which it is performed or towards which it is directed; but God is to be worshiped everywhere in spirit and in truth; as in private families daily and in secret, each one by himself, so more solemnly in the public assemblies, which are not carelessly nor willfully to be neglected or forsaken, when God, by his Word or providence, calleth thereunto.

7. As it is the law of nature that in general a proportion of time, by God's appointment, be set apart for the worship of God, so, by his Word, in a positive, moral, and perpetual commandment, binding all men in all ages, he hath particularly appointed one day in seven for a Sabbath to be kept holy unto him, which, from the beginning of the world to the resurrection of Christ, was the last day of the week, and, from the resurrection of Christ, was changed into the first day of the week, which is called the Lord's day; and is to be continued to the end of the world as the Christian Sabbath, the observation of the last day of the week being abolished.

8. The Sabbath is then kept holy unto the Lord when men, after a due preparing of their hearts and ordering their common affairs aforehand, do not only observe a holy rest all the day from their own works, words, and thoughts about their worldly employment and recreations, but also are taken up the whole time in public and private exercises of his worship, and in the duties of necessity and mercy.

XXIII. OF SINGING OF PSALMS.—1. We believe that singing the praises of God is a holy ordinance of Christ, and not a part of natural religion or a moral duty only; but that it is brought under divine institution, it being enjoined on the churches of Christ to sing psalms, hymns, and spiritual songs; and that the whole church, in their public assemblies (as well as private Christians), ought to sing God's praises according to the best light they have received. Moreover, it was practised in the great representative church by our Lord Jesus Christ with his disciples after he had instituted and celebrated the sacred ordinance of his holy supper as a commemorative token of redeeming love.

XXIV. OF LAWFUL OATHS AND VOWS.—1. A lawful oath is a part of religious worship, wherein the person swearing in truth, righteousness, and judgment solemnly calleth God to witness what he sweareth, and to judge him according to the truth or falseness thereof.

2. The name of God only is that by which men ought to swear, and therein it is to be used with all holy fear and reverence; therefore to swear vainly or rashly by that glorious and dreadful name, or to swear at all by any other thing, is sinful and to be abhorred; yet, as in matter of weight and moment, for confirmation of truth and ending all strife, an oath is warranted by the Word of God, so a lawful oath, being imposed by lawful authority, in such matters ought to be taken.

3. Whosoever taketh an oath warranted by the Word of God ought duly to consider the weightiness of so solemn an act, and therein to avouch nothing but what he knoweth to be the truth; for that by rash, false, and vain oaths the Lord is provoked, and for them this land mourns.

4. An oath is to be taken in the plain and common sense of the words, without equivocation or mental reservation.

5. A vow, which is not to be made to any creature, but to God alone, is to be made and performed with all religious care and faithfulness; but popish monastical vows of perpetual single life, professed poverty, and regular obedience are so far from being degrees of higher perfection that they are superstitious and sinful snares in which no Christian may entangle himself.

XXV. OF THE CIVIL MAGISTRATE.—1. God, the supreme Lord and king of all the world, hath ordained civil magistrates to be under him over the people, for his own glory and the public good, and to this end hath armed them with the power of the sword for defense and encouragement of them that do good and for the punishment of evil-doers.

2. It is lawful for Christians to accept and execute the office of a magistrate, when called thereunto; in the management whereof, as they ought especially to maintain justice and peace, according to the wholesome laws of each kingdom and commonwealth, so, for that end, they may lawfully now under the New Testament wage war upon just and necessary occasions.

3. Civil magistrates being set up by God for the ends aforesaid, subjection in all lawful things commanded by them ought to be yielded by us in the Lord, not only for wrath but for conscience' sake; and we ought to make supplications and prayers for kings and all that are in authority, that, under them, we may live a quiet and peaceable life in all godliness and honesty.

XXVI. OF MARRIAGE.—1. Marriage is to be between one man and one woman; neither is it lawful for any man to have more than one wife, nor for any woman to have more than one husband at the same time.

2. Marriage was ordained for the mutual help of husband and wife, for the increase of mankind with a legitimate issue, and for preventing of uncleanness.

3. It is lawful for all sorts of people to marry who are able with judgment to give their consent; yet it is the duty of Christians to marry in the Lord; and therefore such as profess the true religion should not marry with infidels or idolaters, neither should such as are godly be unequally yoked by marrying with such as are wicked in their life or maintain damnable heresy.

4. Marriage ought not to be within the degrees of consanguinity or affinity forbidden in the Word; nor can such incestuous marriage ever be made lawful by any law of man or consent of parties, so as those persons may live together as man and wife.

XXVII. OF THE CHURCH.—1. The catholic or universal church, which, with respect to the internal work of the Spirit and truth of grace, may be called invisible, consists of the whole number of the elect that have been, are, or shall be gathered into one under Christ, the head thereof, and is the spouse, the body, the fullness of him that filleth all in all.

2. All persons, throughout the world, professing the faith of the gospel and obedience unto God by Christ according unto it, not destroying their own profession by any errors, everting the foundation, or unholiness of conversation, are and may be called visible saints; and of such ought all particular congregations to be constituted.

3. The purest churches under heaven are subject to mixture and error, and some have so degenerated as to become no churches of Christ, but synagogues of Satan; nevertheless, Christ always hath had and ever shall have a kingdom in this world, to the end thereof, of such as believe in him and make profession of his name.

4. The Lord Jesus Christ is the head of the church, in whom, by the appointment of the Father, all power for the calling, institution, order, or government of the church is invested in a supreme and sovereign manner; neither can the pope of Rome in any sense be head thereof, but is that Antichrist, that man of sin and son of perdition, that exalteth himself in the church against Christ and all that is called God, whom the Lord shall destroy with the brightness of his coming.

5. In the execution of this power wherewith he is so intrusted, the Lord Jesus calleth out of the world unto himself, through the ministry of his Word by his Spirit, those that are given unto him by his Father, that they may walk before him in all the ways of obedience which he prescribeth to them in his Word. Those thus called he commandeth to walk together in particular societies or churches, for their mutual edification and the due performance of that public worship which he requireth of them in the world.

6. The members of these churches are saints by calling, visibly manifesting and evidencing in and by their profession and walking their obedience unto that call of Christ; and do willingly consent to walk together according to the appointment of Christ, giving up themselves to the Lord and to one another by the will of God, in professed subjection to the ordinances of the gospel.

7. To each of these churches thus gathered according to his mind, declared in his Word, he hath given all that power and authority which is any way needful for their carrying on that order in worship and discipline which he hath instituted for them to observe, with commands and rules for the due and right exerting and executing that power.

8. A particular church, gathered and completely organized according to the mind of Christ, consists of officers and members; and the officers, appointed by Christ to be chosen and set apart by the church so called and gathered, for the peculiar administration of ordinances and execution of

power or duty which he intrusts them with, or calls them to, to be continued to the end of the world, are bishops, or elders, and deacons.

9. The way appointed by Christ for the calling of any person, fitted and gifted by the Holy Spirit, unto the office of bishop, or elder, in a church, is that he be chosen thereunto by the common suffrage of the church itself, and solemnly set apart by fasting and prayer, with imposition of hands of the eldership of the church, if there be any before constituted therein; and of a deacon, that he be chosen by the like suffrage, and set apart by prayer and the like imposition of hands.

10. The work of pastors being constantly to attend the service of Christ in his churches, in the ministry of the Word, and prayer, with watching for their souls as they that must give an account to him, it is incumbent on the churches to whom they minister not only to give them all due respect, but also to communicate to them of all their good things, according to their ability, so as they may have a comfortable supply, without being themselves entangled in secular affairs, and may also be capable of exercising hospitality towards others; and this is required by the law of nature and by the express order of our Lord Jesus, who hath ordained that they that preach the gospel should live of the gospel.

11. Although it be incumbent on the bishops or pastors of the churches to be instant in preaching the Word, by way of office, yet the work of preaching the Word is not so peculiarly confined to them but that others also gifted and fitted by the Holy Spirit for it, and approved and called by the church, may and ought to perform it.

12. As all believers are bound to join themselves to particular churches, when and where they have opportunity so to do, so all that are admitted unto the privileges of a church are also under the censures and government thereof, according to the rule of Christ.

13. No church members, upon any offense taken by them, having performed their duty required of them towards the person they are offended at, ought to disturb church order, or absent themselves from the assemblies of the church, or administration of any ordinance, upon the account of such offense at any of their fellow-members, but to wait upon Christ in further proceeding of the church.

14. As each church and all the members of it are bound to pray continually for the good and prosperity of all the churches of Christ in all places, and upon all occasions to further it, every one within the bounds of their places and callings, in the exercise of their gifts and graces, so the churches, when planted by the providence of God, so as they may enjoy opportunity and advantage for it, ought to hold communion among themselves for their peace, increase of love, and mutual edification.

15. Cases of difficulty or differences, either in point of doctrine or administration, wherein either the churches in general are concerned, or any one church, in their peace, union, and edification; or any member or members of any church are injured in or by any proceedings in censures not agreeable to truth and order; it is according to the mind of Christ that many churches, holding communion together, do, by their messengers, meet to consider and give their advice in or about the matter in difference, to be reported to all the churches concerned; howbeit these messengers assembled are not intrusted with any church power, properly so called; or with any jurisdiction over the churches themselves, to exercise any censures either over any churches or persons; or to impose their determination on the churches or offices.

XXVIII. OF THE COMMUNION OF SAINTS.—1. All saints that are united to Jesus Christ, their head, by his Spirit and faith, although they are not made thereby one person with him, have fellowship in his graces, sufferings, death, resurrection, and glory, and, being united to one another in love, they have communion in each other's gifts and graces, and are obliged to the performance of such duties, public and private, in an orderly way, as to conduce to their mutual good, both in the inward and outward man.

2. Saints by profession are bound to maintain a holy fellowship and communion in the worship of God, and in performing such other spiritual services as tend to their mutual edification; as also in relieving each other in outward things, according to their several abilities and necessities; which communion, according to the rule of the gospel, though especially to be exercised by them in the relations wherein they stand, whether in families or churches, yet as God offereth opportunity, is to be extended to all the household of faith, even all those who in every place call upon the name of the Lord Jesus; nevertheless, their communion one with another as saints doth not take away or infringe the title or property which each man hath in his goods and possessions.

XXIX. OF BAPTISM AND THE LORD'S SUPPER.—1. Baptism and the Lord's Supper are ordinances of positive and sovereign institution, appointed by the Lord Jesus, the only Lawgiver, to be continued in his church to the end of the world.

2. These holy appointments are to be administered by those only who are qualified and thereunto called, according to the commission of Christ.

XXX. OF BAPTISM.—1. Baptism is an ordinance of the New Testament ordained by Jesus Christ, to be unto the party baptized a sign of his fellowship with him in his death and resurrection; of his being engrafted into him; of remission of sins; and of his giving up unto God, through Jesus Christ, to live and walk in newness of life.

2. Those who do actually profess repentance towards God, faith in, and obedience to our Lord Jesus, are the only proper subjects of this ordinance.

3. The outward element to be used in this ordinance is water, wherein the party is to be baptized, in the name of the Father, and of the Son, and of the Holy Spirit.

4. Immersion, or dipping of the person in water, is necessary to the due administration of this ordinance.

XXXI. OF LAYING ON OF HANDS.—1. We believe that laying on of hands, with prayer, upon baptized believers, as such, is an ordinance of Christ, and ought to be submitted unto by all such persons that are admitted to partake of the Lord's Supper, and that the end of this ordinance is not for the extraordinary gifts of the Spirit, but for a farther reception of the Holy Spirit of promise, or for the addition of the graces of the Spirit, and the influences thereof to confirm, strengthen, and comfort them in Christ Jesus; it being ratified and established by the extraordinary gifts of the Spirit in the primitive times, to abide in the church, as meeting together on the first day of the week was, Acts ii. 1, that being the day of worship, or Christian Sabbath, under the gospel; and as preaching the Word was, Acts x. 44, and as baptism was, Matt. iii. 16, and prayer was, Acts iv. 31, and singing psalms, etc., was, Acts xvi. 25, 26, so this of laying on of hands was, Acts viii. and xix.; for, as the whole gospel was confirmed by signs and wonders, and divers miracles and gifts of the Holy Ghost in general, so was every ordinance in like manner confirmed in particular.

XXXII. OF THE LORD'S SUPPER.—1. The Supper of the Lord Jesus was instituted by him the same night wherein he was betrayed, to be observed in his churches unto the end of the world, for the perpetual remembrance and showing forth the sacrifice of himself in his death, confirmation of the faith of believers in all the benefits thereof, their spiritual nourishment and growth in him, their further engagement in and to all duties which they owe unto him, and to be a bond and pledge of their communion with him and with each other.

2. In this ordinance, Christ is not offered up to his Father, nor any real sacrifice made at all for remission of sin, of the quick or dead, but only a memorial of that one offering up of himself by himself upon the cross, once for all; and a spiritual oblation of all possible praise unto God for the same. So that the popish sacrifice of the mass, as they call it, is most abominable, injurious to Christ's own only sacrifice, the alone propitiation for all the sins of the elect.

3. The Lord Jesus hath in this ordinance appointed his ministers to pray, and bless the elements of bread and wine, and thereby to set them apart from a common to a holy use, and to take and break the bread, to take the cup, and, they communicating also themselves, to give both to the communicants.

4. The denial of the cup to the people, worshiping the elements, the lifting them up or carrying them about for adoration, and reserving them for any pretended religious use, are all contrary to the nature of this ordinance and to the institution of Christ.

5. The outward elements of this ordinance, duly set apart to the uses ordained by Christ, have such relation to him crucified as that truly, although in terms used figuratively, they are sometimes called by the name of the things they represent, to wit, the body and blood of Christ, albeit in substance and nature they still remain truly and only bread and wine, as they were before.

6. The doctrine which maintains a change of the substance of bread and wine into the substance of Christ's body and blood, commonly called transubstantiation, by consecration of a priest, or by any other way, is repugnant, not to Scripture alone, but even to common sense and reason, overthroweth the nature of the ordinance, and hath been and is the cause of manifold superstitions, yea, of gross idolatries.

7. Worthy receivers, outwardly partaking of the visible elements in this ordinance, do then also inwardly, by faith really and indeed, yet not carnally and corporeally, but spiritually, receive and feed upon Christ crucified and all the benefits of his death; the body and blood of Christ being then not corporeally or carnally, but spiritually present to the faith of believers in that ordinance, as the elements themselves are to their outward senses.

8. All ignorant and ungodly persons, as they are unfit to enjoy communion with Christ, so are they unworthy of the Lord's table, and cannot, without great sin against him, while they remain such, partake of these holy mysteries, or be admitted thereunto; yea, whosoever shall receive unworthily, are guilty of the body and blood of the Lord, eating and drinking judgment to themselves.

XXXIII. OF THE STATE OF MAN AFTER DEATH AND OF THE RESURRECTION OF THE DEAD.—1. The bodies of men after death return to dust and see corruption; but their souls, which neither die nor sleep, having an immortal subsistence, immediately return to God who gave them; the souls of the righteous, being then made perfect in holiness, are received into paradise, where they are with Christ, and behold the face of God, in light and glory, waiting for the full redemption of their bodies; and the souls of the wicked are cast into hell, where they remain in torment and utter darkness, reserved to the judgment of the great day; besides these two places for souls separated from their bodies, the Scripture acknowledgeth none.

2. At the last day, such of the saints as are found alive shall not sleep but be changed, and all the dead shall be raised up with the self-same bodies, and none other; although with different qualities, which shall be united again to their souls forever.

3. The bodies of the unjust shall, by the power of Christ, be raised to dishonor; the bodies of the just, by his Spirit, unto honor, and be made conformable to his own glorious body.

XXXIV. OF THE LAST JUDGMENT.—1. God hath appointed a day wherein he will judge the world in righteousness by Jesus Christ, to whom all power and judgment is given of the Father; in which day not only the apostate angels shall be judged, but likewise all persons that have lived upon the earth shall appear before the tribunal of Christ to give an account of their thoughts, words, and deeds, and to receive according to what they have done in the body, whether good or evil.

2. The end of God's appointing this day is for the manifestation of the glory of his mercy in the eternal salvation of the elect; and of his justice in the eternal damnation of the reprobate, who are wicked and disobedient; for then shall the righteous go into everlasting life, and receive that fullness of joy and glory with everlasting reward in the presence of the Lord; but the wicked, who know not God, and obey not the gospel of Jesus Christ, shall be cast into eternal torments, and punished with everlasting destruction from the presence of the Lord and from the glory of his power.

3. As Christ would have us to be certainly persuaded that there shall be a day of judgment, both to deter all men from sin and for the greater consolation of the godly in their adversity, so will he have that day unknown to men, that they may shake off all carnal security, and be always watchful, because they know not at what hour the Lord will come, and may ever be prepared to say, Come, Lord Jesus, come quickly. Amen.

THE NEW HAMPSHIRE DECLARATION OF FAITH.*

I. OF THE SCRIPTURES.—We believe that the holy Bible was written by men divinely inspired, and is a perfect treasure of heavenly instruction; that it has God for its author, salvation for its end, and truth without any mixture of error for its matter; that it reveals the principles by which God will judge us, and therefore is, and shall remain to the end of the world, the true centre of Christian union, and the supreme standard by which all human conduct, creeds, and opinions should be tried.

II. OF THE TRUE GOD.—We believe that there is one, and only one, living and true God, an infinite, intelligent Spirit, whose name is Jehovah, the Maker and Supreme Ruler of heaven and earth, inexpressibly glorious in holiness, and worthy of all possible honor, confidence, and love; that in the unity of the Godhead there are three persons,—the Father, the Son, and the Holy Ghost,—equal in every divine perfection, and executing distinct but harmonious offices in the great work of redemption.

III. OF THE FALL OF MAN.—We believe that man was created in holiness, under the law of his Maker; but by voluntary transgression fell from that holy and happy state; in consequence of which all mankind are now sinners, not by constraint but choice; being by nature utterly void of that holiness required by the law of God; positively inclined to evil; and therefore under just condemnation to eternal ruin, without defense or excuse.

IV. OF THE WAY OF SALVATION.—We believe that the salvation of sinners is wholly of grace; through the mediatorial offices of the Son of God; who by the appointment of the Father, freely took upon him our nature, yet without sin; honored the divine law by his personal obedience, and by his death made a full atonement for our sins; that having risen from the dead, he is now enthroned in heaven; and uniting in his wonderful person the tenderest sympathies with divine perfections, he is every way qualified to be a suitable, a compassionate, and an all-sufficient Saviour.

V. OF JUSTIFICATION.—We believe that the great gospel blessing which Christ secures to such as believe in him, is justification; that justification includes the pardon of sin, and the promise of eternal life on principles of righteousness; that it is bestowed, not in consideration of any works of righteousness which we have done, but solely through faith in the Redeemer's blood; by virtue of which faith his perfect righteousness is freely imputed to us of God; that it brings us into a state of most blessed peace and favor with God, and secures every other blessing needful for time and eternity.

VI. OF THE FREENESS OF SALVATION.—We believe that the blessings of salvation are made free to all by the gospel; that it is the immediate duty of all to accept them by a cordial, penitent, and obedient faith; and that nothing prevents the salvation of the greatest sinner on earth but his own determined depravity and voluntary rejection of the gospel; which rejection involves him in an aggravated condemnation.

VII. OF GRACE IN REGENERATION.—We believe that in order to be saved sinners must be regenerated, or born again; that regeneration consists in giving a holy disposition to the mind; that it is effected in a manner above our comprehension by the power of the Holy Spirit, in connection with divine truth, so as to secure our voluntary obedience to the gospel; and that its proper evidence appears in the holy fruits of repentance, and faith, and newness of life.

VIII. OF REPENTANCE AND FAITH.—We believe that repentance and faith are sacred duties, and also inseparable graces, wrought in our souls by the regenerating Spirit of God; whereby, being deeply convinced of our guilt, danger, and helplessness, and of the way of salvation by Christ, we turn to God with unfeigned contrition, confession, and supplication for mercy; at the same time heartily receiving the Lord Jesus Christ as our Prophet, Priest, and King, and relying on him alone as the only and all-sufficient Saviour.

IX. OF GOD'S PURPOSE OF GRACE.—We believe that election is the eternal purpose of God, according to which he graciously regenerates, sanctifies, and saves sinners, that being perfectly consistent with the free agency of man, it comprehends all the means in connection with the end; that it is a most glorious display of God's sovereign goodness, being infinitely free, wise, holy, and unchangeable; that it utterly excludes boasting, and promotes humility, love, prayer, praise, trust in God, and active imitation of his free mercy; that it encourages the use of means in the highest degree; that it may be ascertained by its effects in all who truly believe the gospel; that it is the foundation of Christian assurance; and that to ascertain it with regard to ourselves demands and deserves the utmost diligence.

X. OF SANCTIFICATION.—We believe that sanctification is the process by which, according to the will of God, we are made partakers of his holiness, that it is a progressive work; that it is begun in regeneration; and that it is carried on in the hearts of believers by the presence and power of the Holy Spirit, the Sealer and Comforter, in the continual use of the appointed means—especially, the Word of God, self-examination, self-denial, watchfulness, and prayer.

XI. OF THE PERSEVERANCE OF SAINTS.—We believe that such only are real believers as endure unto the end; that their persevering attachment to Christ is the grand mark

---

* Cutting's Historical Vindications, p. 191.

which distinguishes them from superficial professors; that a special providence watches over their welfare; and they are kept by the power of God through faith unto salvation.

XII. OF THE HARMONY OF THE LAW AND THE GOSPEL.—We believe that the law of God is the eternal and unchangeable rule of his moral government; that it is holy, just, and good; and that the inability which the Scriptures ascribe to fallen men to fulfill its precepts, arises entirely from their love of sin; to deliver them from which, and to restore them through a mediator to unfeigned obedience to the holy law, is one great end of the gospel, and of the means of grace connected with the establishment of the visible church.

XIII. OF A GOSPEL CHURCH.—We believe that a visible church of Christ is a congregation of baptized believers, associated by covenant in the faith and fellowship of the gospel; observing the ordinances of Christ; governed by his laws; and exercising the gifts, rights, and privileges invested in them by his Word; that its only scriptural officers are bishops or pastors, and deacons whose qualifications, claims, and duties are defined in the epistles to Timothy and Titus.

XIV. OF BAPTISM AND THE LORD'S SUPPER.—We believe that Christian baptism is the immersion in water of a believer, into the name of the Father, and Son, and Holy Ghost; to show forth, in a solemn and beautiful emblem, our faith in the crucified, buried, and risen Saviour, with its effect, in our death to sin and resurrection to a new life; that it is prerequisite to the privileges of a church relation; and to the Lord's Supper, in which the members of the church by the sacred use of bread and wine, are to commemorate together the dying love of Christ; preceded always by solemn self-examination.

XV. OF THE CHRISTIAN SABBATH.—We believe that the first day of the week is the Lord's day, or Christian Sabbath; and is to be kept sacred to religious purposes, by abstaining from all secular labor and sinful recreations; by the devout observance of all the means of grace, both private and public; and by preparation for that rest that remaineth for the people of God.

XVI. OF CIVIL GOVERNMENT.—We believe that civil government is of divine appointment, for the interests and good order of human society; and that magistrates are to be prayed for, conscientiously honored, and obeyed; except only in things opposed to the will of our Lord Jesus Christ, who is the only Lord of the conscience, and the Prince of the kings of the earth.

XVII. OF THE RIGHTEOUS AND THE WICKED.—We believe that there is a radical and essential difference between the righteous and the wicked; that such only as through faith are justified in the name of the Lord Jesus, and sanctified by the Spirit of our God, are truly righteous in his esteem; while all such as continue in impenitence and unbelief are in his sight wicked, and under the curse; and this distinction holds among men both in and after death.

XVIII. OF THE WORLD TO COME.—We believe that the end of this world is approaching; that at the last day, Christ will descend from heaven, and raise the dead from the grave to final retribution; that a solemn separation will then take place; that the wicked will be adjudged to endless punishment, and the righteous to endless joy; and that this judgment will fix forever the final state of men in heaven or hell, on principles of righteousness.

[For a form of Church Covenant, see page 283.]

PROGRESS OF THE DENOMINATION SINCE 1770.

State	Churches in 1770	1784 Churches	1784 Ministers	1784 Members	1792 Churches	1792 Ministers	1792 Members	1812 Churches	1812 Ministers	1812 Members	1832 Churches	1832 Ministers	1832 Members	1840 Churches	1840 Ministers	1840 Members	1851 Churches	1851 Ministers	1851 Members	1860 Churches	1860 Ministers	1860 Members	1875 Churches	1875 Ministers	1875 Members	1880 Churches	1880 Ministers	1880 Members
Maine	10	10	5	400	15	21	882	103	83	5,294	222	168	15,000	261	214	20,490	287	226	19,775	277	183	21,380	259	162	19,490	262	176	21,013
New Hampshire	11	24	12	1,000	32	40	1,732	69	48	4,940	90	78	6,705	103	101	9,557	96	85	8,089	93	78	8,359	86	101	8,597	84	90	9,077
Vermont	1	10	5	300	34	36	1,610	76	50	5,135	125	87	10,525	135	98	11,101	105	97	7,999	110	95	8,097	112	87	8,250	114	79	9,870
Massachusetts	12	67	50	4,500	32	105	6,234	81	81	8,104	189	220	20,200	213	193	26,311	249	382	31,652	268	289	36,518	287	317	45,630	289	328	48,764
Connecticut	11	28	18	1,500	55	65	3,214	65	54	5,716	92	90	10,039	103	106	11,725	115	149	16,355	119	117	9,015	111	132	10,631	119	125	21,618
Rhode Island	6	24	26	2,000	38	26	3,502	26	26	3,033	20	57	3,271	39	40	5,962	61	60	7,406	51	61	9,015	60	67	10,031	61	77	10,821
New York	7	11	15	704	62	83	3,987	239	157	18,439	605	545	60,006	775	782	79,155	813	866	85,923	839	784	92,873	846	765	103,859	877	801	114,094
New Jersey	15	22	24	1,875	38	29	2,279	35	26	2,811	60	60	3,981	73	82	9,008	106	121	13,856	120	135	16,911	172	185	29,650	178	200	31,936
Pennsylvania	1	23	20	956	26	33	2,357	63	57	4,365	157	121	11,103	248	152	21,082	332	297	30,053	385	288	37,278	508	406	56,732	547	453	63,585
Delaware	1				7	11	409	7	9	450	9	4	326	9	4	2,390	2	3	337	10	4	426	10	9	956	11	12	2,004
Maryland		7	8	307	13	11	776	14	9	697	34	23	1,341	44	25	4,500	32	26	3,438	34	30	4,143	50	34	6,457	48	42	8,306
Virginia	9	151	136	14,960	218	261	20,443	292	286	35,605	435	261	54,302	512	361	64,500	608	373	89,929	761	412	107,263	1,172	547	169,310	1,346	718	207,559
North Carolina	9	42	47	3,276	94	154	7,503	204	117	12,567	332	211	54,392	511	253	29,330	599	374	42,674	692	374	59,778	1,287	698	113,414	1,905	1,063	172,961
South Carolina	6	27	28	1,620	70	77	4,167	154	95	11,821	273	198	28,496	371	189	34,704	437	284	45,296	469	415	61,965	788	450	95,243	1,126	642	140,442
Georgia			10	428	42	72	3,211	163	109	14,761	509	225	38,382	672	319	48,302	847	613	65,231	996	586	84,022	1,993	1,185	174,543	2,755	1,630	235,381
Tennessee		6	7	370	18	21	889	156	125	11,325	413	243	20,472	653	452	32,000	496	422	37,281	663	386	46,397	1,007	696	100,192	1,317	806	110,847
Kentucky		6	5	300	42	61	3,095	285	183	22,694	484	258	34,124	723	380	61,042	797	498	69,098	845	372	81,262	1,429	708	144,267	1,710	1,006	163,696
Ohio					2	2	62	60	40	2,400	280	166	20,493	484	308	21,850	448	326	24,693	544	376	31,819	678	414	100,192	633	469	49,950
Indiana								29	22	1,376	299	201	11,334	417	260	16,234	451	287	22,119	495	356	28,038	562	333	38,974	557	343	42,029
Illinois								9	7	153	161	123	4,622	348	254	11,018	378	355	19,259	713	401	30,504	943	686	66,354	927	707	69,124
Missouri								7	7	192	146	93	4,972	279	160	10,958	439	297	24,206	496	336	42,080	1,438	842	89,786	1,449	839	95,969
Mississippi								17	11	764	84	39	3,199	119	54	7,837	475	305	30,112	596	305	41,482	1,258	602	93,522	1,537	831	122,369
Alabama											250	145	11,445	308	306	30,182	579	358	41,482	807	415	60,231	1,183	619	74,606	1,080	831	164,784
Louisiana								3	2	130	16	13	728	30	15	930	114	99	4,443	212	109	10,231	611	331	51,513	1,684	428	57,702
Arkansas											17	5	181	34	25	3,209	129	132	10,043	301	145	10,974	949	510	46,460	755	616	52,798
Wisconsin											17	13	667	75	52	445	180	70	4,131	268	159	12,503	311	278	21,726	1,118	307	27,282
Michigan														15	11	300	93	49	1,780	188	123	8,794	185	135	11,718	352	135	11,881
Iowa														12	8		46	31	77	230	159	10,804	377	255	21,345	408	274	24,136
California														5	4	533	3	6	798	53	62	1,822	102	86	4,212	78	78	6,076
District of Columbia																	6	8	2,687	5	8	1,069	29	29	8,551	18	23	8,319
Florida																	73	40	140	112	57	5,216	248	146	12,290	327	207	17,997
Oregon																	9	9	4,259	31	19	833	60	52	2,135	74	50	2,957
Texas																	125	89	2,680	450	240	18,727	1,047	590	59,637	1,910	1,111	107,578
Indian Territory																	29	32		30	15	4,300	62	56	4,262	98	84	5,915
Kansas																				9	5	127	265	174	11,892	441	309	17,648
Nebraska																							119	57	3,427	138	77	4,855
Nevada																							3	3	52	3	1	110
Idaho																							1	1	20	2	1	43
Dakota																							15	11	427	21	18	731
Utah																							1	1	20	1	1	20
New Mexico																							12	9	16	1	1	16
Washington																							2	1	224	17	13	424
Wyoming																									50	2	2	101
Colorado																										24	14	1,239
West Virginia																							339	206	23,638	381	203	25,239
Arizona																										1		14
Minnesota																							168	97	6,917	154	112	7,056
United States	77	471	424	35,101	891	1156	65,345	2164	1605	172,972	5320	3618	384,926	7771	5208	571,291	9552	7393	770,839	12,279	7773	1,014,171	21,423	13,214	1,815,300	26,060	16,596	2,296,327

1324 APPENDIX.

Fac-simile from original Records, of the order for the banishment of Roger Williams.

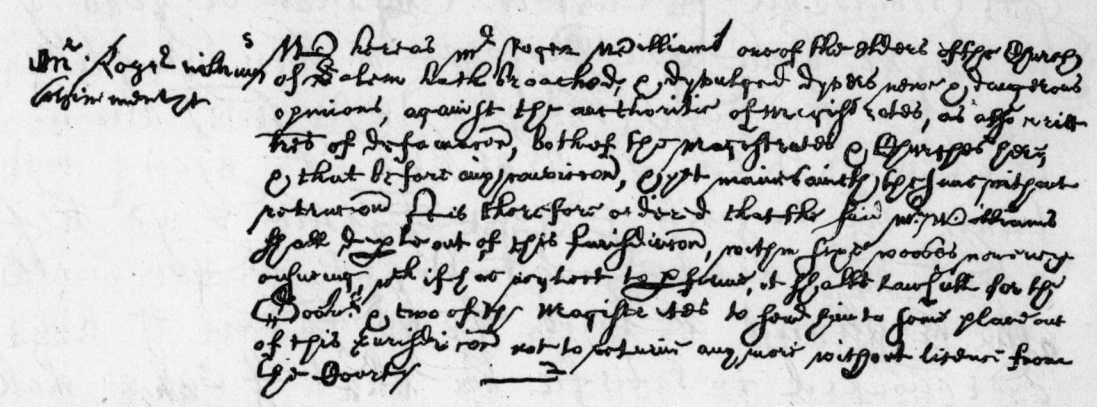

1635. Whereas Mr. Roger Williams, one of the elders of the church of Salem, hath broached and divulged dyvers newe and dangerous opinions against
3rd Sept. the aucthorite of magistrates, as also with others of defamcon, both of the magistrates and churches here, and that before any conviccon, and yet maintaineth the same without retraccon, it is therefore ordered, that the said Mr. Williams shall depte out of this jurisdiccon within sixe weekes nowe nexte ensueing, wch if hee neglect to pforme, it shall be lawfull for the Gouv'r and two of the magistrates to send him to some place out of this jurisdiccon, not to returne any more without licence from the Court.

Order banishing the Founders of the First Baptist Church in Boston.

May. Whereas Thomas Gold (and others) obstinate and turbulent Annabaptists, have some time since combined themselves wh others in a pretended
1668. church estate×× × × to, the great griefe and offence of the godly orthodox. × × × × × × × and about two years since were enjoyned by this Court to desist from said practise and to returne to our allowed Church Assemblies,×× × × × × this Court doe judge it necessary that they be removed to some other part of this country or elsewhere: and accordingly doeth order that (they) doe before the twentieth of July next remove themselves out of this jurisdiccon.

Sr Respective Salutacions to you both & sister Sake ffthis instant (ye first of ye weeke toward Noone) J receaue yrs & shall be glad (if God will) you may gayne a seasonable passage by vs before ye hardest of winter, although J can not aduice you but to stay agst winter flights & Journeyes) yet if ye necessitie of Gods providence so cast it J shall be glad yt we might haue you Prisoner in these parts yet once in a few dayes (though in deepe snow) here is a beaten path &c Sr Wenekunat againe importunes me to write to your Father & yr selfe about his Hunting at Pequt; yt you would also be pleased to write to yr Father J haue endeauoured to satisfie him what J can, & shall, yet J am willing at present to write to you not so much concerning yt you can further gratifie him at this time, but yt J may by this opportunitie salute you with ye tidings from ye Bay the last night

Skipper Isaack & Moline are Come into ye Bay with a Dutch ship & (as it is said) haue brought Letters from ye States to call home this present Dutch Gou't to answer many complaints both from Dutch & English agst him In this ship are come English passengers, & being woord of ye great trialls it pleaseth ye most high & only wise to exercise both ó natiue England & these parts allso

The Prince is said to be strong at Sea & among

these mischiefes hath taken mr Terrice his ship wch went from hence, & sent it for France it seemes their Rendevour:

It is said yt after Cromwell had discomfited ye Welsh, with 6000 he was forced to incoun ter 19 thousand Scots of whome he tooke 9000 prisoners & great store of Scots & Wellsh are Sent & Sold as Slaues into other parts: Cromwell wrote to ye Parliamt yt he hoped to be at Edinburgh in few dayes

A Commission was sent from ye Parliamt to try ye King in ye Ile of Wight, lately preuented from Escape

The Prince of Orenge & ye States are fal ling if not allready fallen into Warres wch makes some of ye States, to tender Munradors as place of Retreat.

Sr to him in whose Fauour is Life I haue You desireing in him to be yr Worsps vnworthy
Roger Williams.

John prayes you to be Earnest with mr Hollet about his howse hoping to be back in a fortnight.

ROGER WILLIAMS TO JOHN WINTHROP, Jr.

FOR THE WORSHIPFULL MR JOHN WINTHROP AT NEMEUG THESE.

SIR,—Respective salutacions to you both and sister Lake: At this instant (the first of the weeke toward noone) I receave yourse and shall be glad (if God will) you may gaine a reasonable passage by us before the hardest of winter, although I cannot advice you (but to pray against winter flights and journeyes) yet if the necessitie of God's providence so cast it I shall be glad that we might have you Prisoner in these parts yet once in a few dayes (though in deepe snow) here is a beaten path &c. Sir Nenékunat againe importunes me to write to youre Father and youreselfe about his and hunting at Pequt, that you would allso be pleased to write to youre Father. I have endeavoured to satisfie him what I can, and shall, yet I am willing at present to write to you, not so much conceaving that you can further gratifie him at this time, but that I may by this opportunitie salute you with the tidings from the Bay the last night. Skipper Isaack and Moline are come into the Bay with a Dutch ship and (as it is said) have brought letters from the States to call home this present Dutch Governoure to answer many complaints both from Dutch and English against him: In this ship are come English passengers and bring word of the great Trialls it pleaseth the Most High and only Wise to exercise both oure native England and these parts allso.

The Prince is said to be strong at sea and among other mischiefes, has taken Mr. Trerice his ship which went from hence, and sent it for France it seemes their Rendevouz.

It is said that after Cromwell had discomfited the Welsh, with 6000 he was forced to incounter 19 thousand Scots of whome he tooke 9000 prisoners &c.—great store of Scots and Wellsh are sent and sold as slaves into other parts: Cromwell wrote to the Parliament, that he hoped to be at Edinburg in few dayes.

A commission was sent from the Parliament to try the King in the Ile of Wight, lately prevented from escape.

The Prince of Orenge and the States are falling, if not already fallen into Warrs which makes some of the States to tender Munnádoes as place of Retreat.

Sir to him in whose favour is Life I leave you, desiring in him to be

Youre Worships unworthy
ROGER WILLIAMS.

John prays you to be earnest with Mr Hollet about his howse hoping to be back in a fortnight.

(Labeled, "rec'd dec^r,—undoubtedly 1648.— J. B.)

Mass. Hist. Collections, Third Series, vol. ix. pp. 276–77.

Ro
286
C36 Cathcart
    Baptist encyclopaedia

2045 7